The Scholarship
Book 13th Edition

The Scholarship Book 13th Edition

The Complete Guide to Private-Sector Scholarships, Fellowships, Grants, and Loans for the Undergraduate

DANIEL J. CASSIDY, FOUNDING EDITOR

Revised by Ellen Schneid Coleman Research Group

PRENTICE HALL PRESS

378.34
SLX

PRENTICE HALL PRESS
Published by the Penguin Group
Penguin Group (USA) Inc.
375 Hudson Street, New York, New York 10014, USA
Penguin Group (Canada), 90 Eglinton Avenue East, Suite 700, Toronto, Ontario M4P 2Y3, Canada
(a division of Pearson Penguin Canada Inc.)
Penguin Books Ltd., 80 Strand, London WC2R 0RL, England
Penguin Group Ireland, 25 St. Stephen's Green, Dublin 2, Ireland (a division of Penguin Books Ltd.)
Penguin Group (Australia), 250 Camberwell Road, Camberwell, Victoria 3124, Australia
(a division of Pearson Australia Group Pty. Ltd.)
Penguin Books India Pvt. Ltd., 11 Community Centre, Panchsheel Park, New Delhi—110 017, India
Penguin Group (NZ), 67 Apollo Drive, Rosedale, North Shore 0632, New Zealand
(a division of Pearson New Zealand Ltd.)
Penguin Books (South Africa) (Pty.) Ltd., 24 Sturdee Avenue, Rosebank, Johannesburg 2196, South
Africa

Penguin Books Ltd., Registered Offices: 80 Strand, London WC2R 0RL, England

While the author has made every effort to provide accurate telephone numbers, e-mail, and Internet addresses at the time of publication, neither the publisher nor the author assumes any responsibility for errors, or for changes that occur after publication. Further, the publisher does not have any control over and does not assume any responsibility for author or third-party websites or their content.

THE SCHOLARSHIP BOOK, 13th EDITION

13th edition: July 2008

ISBN: 978-0-7352-0427-0
ISSN: 1528-9079

PRINTED IN THE UNITED STATES OF AMERICA

10 9 8 7 6 5 4 3 2 1

PUBLISHER'S NOTE: This publication is designed to provide accurate and authoritative information in regard to the subject matter covered. It is sold with the understanding that the publisher is not engaged in rendering legal, accounting or other professional services. If you require legal advice or other expert assistance, you should seek the services of a competent professional.

Most Prentice Hall Press books are available at special quantity discounts for bulk purchases for sales promotions, premiums, fund-raising, or educational use. Special books, or book excerpts, can also be created to fit specific needs. For details, write: Special Markets, Penguin Group (USA) Inc., 375 Hudson Street, New York, New York 10014.

Contents

The Scholarship Book 13th Edition

Introduction

The information in *The Scholarship Book*, Thirteenth Edition, was built upon the database of the largest private-sector financial aid research service in the world—Daniel J. Cassidy's National Scholarship Research Service (NSRS)™. Dan began tracking private-sector scholarships in the late 1970s, using a specialized computer system. Today, the Ellen Schneid Coleman Research Group has taken up the challenge of updating and expanding *The Scholarship Book*'s exhaustive coverage. Once again, the Group has reviewed each of the entries, contacted each scholarship giver either by mail, e-mail, or telephone and combed resources both on- and offline to add new scholarships to the massive database. Prospective college students and present undergraduates will find the information in this book invaluable in directing their applications and broadening their prospects for scholarship selection.

THE FACTS

According to the U.S. Department of Education, in 2003, the average cost of a public 4-year college (including room and board) was $9,828 a year; a private college averaged $23,940. These are the most recent statistics, as with everything else, the costs are no doubt higher in 2008.

As Robert Marqusee, Executive Director of the National Scholarship Providers Association (NSPA), said, "With college prices increasing at more than twice the rate of inflation for more than twenty years, the ability of many students and their families to pay for higher education is becoming a national concern. . . . Student financial assistance is becoming even more critical in the college financing equation, and private aid is a key unexplored component of that equation." In 2005, NSPA members awarded over 358,904 scholarships totaling $953,264,423. It is estimated that over 50 percent of the financing of higher education in the United States comes from private sources.[1]

Despite these rising costs, many scholarships, fellowships, grants, loans, and internships go unclaimed each year—a recent study estimated that private scholarship aid amounted to between $3.1 billion and $3.3 billion in 2003–2004, of which perhaps $100 million annually went unclaimed.[2] All too often the money is not distributed to qualified students, simply because the students don't know that the money is available and therefore don't apply. In addition, some students have misconceptions about how scholarships are awarded and therefore don't apply.

With the Internet, there is more information and misinformation available to students and their families. This, in turn, has created a greater need than ever before to organize this flood of information into a workable resource for today's student. Utilizing the data collected in *The Scholarship Book*, students will have a broad base of information to convert to their advantage. The monies are there. Don't rule yourself out. Apply for them!

- Don't think you can't apply because you earn too much money; 80 percent of the private sector does not require a financial statement or proof of need.

- Don't think that application deadlines occur only in the fall; private-sector deadlines are passing daily because often they are set to coincide with the tax year or organizational meeting dates.

- Don't believe that grades are the only consideration for an award; many application questions deal with personal, occupational, and educational background; organizational affiliation, talent, or ethnic origins; 90 percent are not concerned with grades.

- Don't be concerned with age; many organizations are interested in the returning student and the mid-career development student.

- Don't think you must be an incoming freshman to apply; many scholarships are available beginning at all levels of the college experience.

[1]The Global State of Higher Education and the Rise of Private Finance. *Issue Report* by Ryan Hahn, Institute for Higher Education Policy, August 2007.

[2]Private Scholarships Count: Access to Higher Education and the Critical Role of the Private Sector. A report by Institute for Higher Education Policy in collaboration with Scholarship American and the National Scholarship Providers Association, May 2005.

And don't forget that many scholarships are renewable. You simply sign for them year after year. Most allow you to "piggy-back" several individual scholarships.

PLAN TO COMPETE AND QUALIFY

The plan is simple—use this book and every other resource you can find. Talk to your institution's financial aid office about government assistance and private endowments at the school. If you are a high school student—and don't wait for your junior or senior year—target ten or more schools you might want to attend. Once you've done that, go to the school's website (many schools offer complete listings of available scholarships on their websites) or write to each of them. Select a range of institutions that interest you, large and small, public and private. Request the application materials and school catalogs—many private endowments are available in the forms of scholarships and fellowships bequeathed by alumni and are listed in the school catalog or on the website under financial aid.

The information is available, but the commitment and determination to find it belongs to you. Remind your parents to talk with their employers; many employers offer scholarships to the children of their employees, but some do not publicize them widely. It never hurts to ask. Also, don't forget to check with your church, synagogue, or mosque, local civic groups, clubs, and similar organizations. They may not publicize their awards widely or have a site on the Internet, but many offer grants, awards, and scholarships to members or those who live in their communities. The same is true of local chapters of national organizations. The parent national organization may or may not offer scholarships, but the local organization may offer them or have additional grants available. You may be surprised at the resources you discover!

HOW TO USE *THE SCHOLARSHIP BOOK*

It is easy to locate the scholarships that are right for you. Start with the table of contents. It is divided into broad subject areas. Those of you who are thinking of specializing or have a talent in a particular area of study will want to begin there. Let's say, for example, you plan to study engineering. You can go right to the section entitled "Engineering (All Fields)," and find a complete list of scholarships for students generally interested in some area of engineering. For those of you who really know where you are going, let's say aeronautical engineering, you'll find scholarships designed just for you under that heading, but don't forget to look at the scholarships listed under "Engineering (All Fields)," because you might qualify for two or more scholarships.

Cast your eye down the contents page again, and you'll see "General (Any Field of Study)." Here you will find the scholarships that are open to everyone no matter what they are studying. These scholarships can be used for any and all sorts of pursuit—academic as well as vocational in both two- and four-year programs. Most—but not all—of the scholarships listed in this book are for programs that require some sort of degree or certification or license.

Choose as many as you qualify for, and obtain application forms and any pertinent materials. Some of the donors have specific requirements such as a personal interview, the submission of an essay or related work, or a promise to work for the company on completion of study and/or the earning of a degree. Others may have paid internships or work advancement programs. Some may require that you or your parent or grandparent work for the company or be a member of the organization offering the scholarship. Others are designed for specific groups of people: men, women, African-Americans, Native Americans, Hispanics, Italians, Jews, Catholics, gays and lesbians, and veterans are a few examples. You name a group, and there's probably a scholarship dedicated to it.

Still other scholarships require little more than a completed application form.

Some scholarships are based on grades; some are not. Some require essays; some do not. Some require that you come from a particular state; some that you go to school in that state. Some require that you demonstrate financial need; some do not. The variations may seem endless, but as you review the entries, you'll get the hang of it. Let your imagination guide you. Ask yourself:

- who are you,
- where do you come from,

- where did your parents/grandparents come from,
- where do you live,
- what organizations/clubs/civic groups/sororities/fraternities do you/your parents belong to,
- do you have a special skill or a disability,
- did you or a parent serve in the military,

and so on—the possibilities are limitless.

The next step is to scan the Index at the back of the book. Perhaps the Sons of Norway has something that's just right for you, or the American Association of Blacks in Energy, or, maybe, the International Trumpet Guild will strike the right note.

Students who do not take the time to inquire lose every advantage. The opportunity to advance to a graduate degree will widen many avenues for your future, and the rewards are incalculable. Information is merely a passage waiting to be used. The resources to achieve your goals are available to you; you need only pursue them.

Just for Fun: A Potpourri of Scholarships

To learn more about each of these scholarships, turn to the alphabetical index in the back of the book, and the entry numbers that follow will guide you straight to the detailed entry for details.

- Your tuition troubles could be gone with the wind! If you are a lineal descendant of a worthy Confederate soldier, contact the United Daughters of the Confederacy about their $800 to $1,000 scholarships.
- If you or your parents are actively involved in Harness Racing, you just might hitch yourself to one of the Harness Tracks of America scholarships worth $5,000.
- For students whose ancestors put their John Hancocks on the Declaration of Independence, scholarships worth $3,000 are given by Descendants of the Signers of the Declaration of Independence.
- Do you belong to the NAACP? The NAACP National Office offers the Willems Scholarship for male members studying engineering, chemistry, physics, or mathematics. Undergraduates receive $2,000, and the graduate award is $3,000.
- The America's Junior Miss Program scholarship competition is open to college-bound seniors who are U.S. citizens or permanent residents, but you have to apply in your sophomore or junior years. Winner receives $30,000 for books, fees, and tuition at any college in the world.
- Are you between the ages of 17 and 22 living in the Golden State or the Lone Star State? If you are a Mexican-American resident of California or Texas and in an undergraduate program, you may just strike gold with the Vikki Carr Scholarship of up to $3,000.
- Keep your eye on the target and you may take home the prize; that is, one of Target Stores' up to 600 All Around Scholarships worth anywhere from $1,000 to a whopping $25,000! Volunteering in community activities may be your key to hitting the bull's-eye.
- Love to fly? The International Society of Women Airline Pilots offers an array of scholarships to women throughout the world who are pursuing careers as airline pilots and other aviation-related careers. Some are need-based, some merit-based, some require time in the air, while others are for single moms.
- Starstruck? The Princess Grace Foundation offers scholarships for students under age 25 in acting, directing, film, and design at U.S. schools.

As we said, there are many, many more.

A Note About the Entries

By the time you go through this book and do your own research, you may discover scholarships that were not included or that some scholarships are no longer offered, or that requirements and deadlines have changed. Every effort has been made to ensure that the information provided is as up-to-the-minute and accurate as possible. However, foundations, individuals, colleges and universities, and other organizations do make changes from time to time. Even as this book goes to print—awards are being added and application requirements are being changed by sponsoring organizations. Such circumstances are beyond our control. That's why we can't urge you too strongly to follow up not only on the Internet, but directly with the school or organization offering the award. Use this book only as a guide. Contact the source of the award for the current application information.

You may also find that some organizations are not listed. Some prefer not to be listed in nationally-distributed publications because they are available only to members or are regional in nature. We have respected those requests.

HOW TO APPLY

Most of the entries tell you the essence of the requirements and how to apply. Read that information carefully. If you meet the requirements, your first step is to check with the organization to verify that the requirements have not changed, to verify the deadlines and to obtain an application and any other information the organization may provide. You'll discover that you may be able to apply and get all of the information you need online, or that you can request the information either by e-mail or online, or in some cases you must do it the "old-fashioned way," by writing a letter (in this instance, you'll often be asked to enclose an SASE [self-addressed stamped envelope]). Don't spend time applying for scholarships for which you are not qualified. If you are a freshman, don't apply for a grant intended for seniors. If you are a woman and it's "men only," don't apply; same for you men—don't apply for "women only" scholarships. It wastes your time as well as the sponsor's. It's far more important to concentrate on submitting applications to organizations looking for someone with just your qualifications!

The Search

Just about everything about you comes into play in your search for scholarships—your ancestry, religion, place of birth and residence, parent's union or corporate affiliation, your interest in a particular field—can all be eligibility factors. In other cases, the only requirement is filling out an application.

Using the information in *The Scholarship Book*, students generally find somewhere between 20 and 100 different sources of private-sector scholarships. Next, contact each of them and ask for their scholarship applications and requirements. Write to each source as far in advance of their scholarship deadline as possible (unless specific contact periods are given).

The Calendar

We also find it helpful to keep a calendar with deadlines circled so you can stay organized. You can hang it above your two scholarship boxes (see below) so it is easily visible. Each application should have its own file. On the outside of the file, you might rate your chances of getting the scholarship on a scale of 1 to 10.

If a scholarship application deadline has passed, save it for the next year. If you are turned down for a scholarship, don't worry. Some organizations want to see if you will apply a second time. The important point is to stay motivated and be persistent.

Staying Organized

Once you have written to scholarship sources for complete information, we recommend starting two financial aid boxes in which to organize your information. You might call them "Government Funding" and "Private Sector" (which would include school endowments).

The Government Box

Regardless of your financial status, please, please fill out the Free Application for Federal Student Aid (FAFSA). You can get a FAFSA from any high school, junior college, college, university or to phone FAFSA, call the Federal Student Aid Information Center at 1-800/4-FED-AID (1-800/433-3243) or 1-319/337-5665. If you are hearing-impaired and have questions, contact the TTY line at 1-800/730-8913 or go to http://www.fafsa.ed.gov for web access. Whether you file online or by mail, you will be able to track your information as it is processed and verify that it was sent (as you requested) to the schools you specified and when. These state and federal forms are the beginning of your scholarship profile at the financial aid office at the schools to which you are applying. Most schools now use these forms for their private endowment-based scholarships. Even if you are not eligible for government funding, you will be ready to apply for loans from various outside school sources, such as banks, and the school-based programs, such as school endowments, scholarships, fellowships, grants, loans, college work/study, athletic, military ROTC, etc.

FAFSA is a must, no matter what!

On a quiet Saturday or when you have time, sit down and review the information you have collected. In the "Government" box, you will find that the state and federal forms are very similar, asking a multitude of questions regarding income, assets, and expenses. Don't automatically exclude yourself from state and federal funding thinking that you or your family make too much money. Programs vary tremendously from state to state. We cannot stress enough the importance of filing the FAFSA, so please do it no matter what!

The Private-Sector/School Endowments Box

You will usually find a list of endowments from alumni listed in the financial aid section of the college catalog or website. Although many are listed in *The Scholarship Book*, often endowments to schools are not advertised. Yet, they make up a big segment of the private-sector money that is available. Endowment money is given directly to the school and is administered exclusively by the school's financial aid office or a specific academic department, so you must deal directly with the college. Again, don't exclude yourself because of those old clichés regarding your grades, financial status, deadlines, or age.

In general, you will find that once you have seen one or two private-sector application forms, you have pretty much seen them all. Usually they are one or two pages asking where you are going to school, what you are going to major in, and why you think you deserve the scholarship. Some scholarship sources require that you join their organization. If the organization relates to your field of study, consider joining because it will keep you informed (via newsletters, magazines, etc.) about developments in that field.

The Application

When filling out scholarship application forms, be complete, concise, and creative. People who read these applications want to know the real you, not just your name. Most organizations awarding scholarships require an essay as part of the application process. The essay is the most important part of the private-sector scholarship search. Scholarship applications and essays should clearly emphasize your ambitions, motivations, and what makes you different from everyone else. Be original!

More and more organizations offer (some require) online filing, but if they don't, make certain that your application is easy-to-read, correctly completed (some organizations will disqualify you if something is omitted or a required document is missing), and don't forget, neatness counts.

Once your essay is finished, make a master file of it and other supporting documents. Photocopy your essay and attach it to each application. If requested, also include: a résumé or curriculum vitae, extracurricular activities sheet (usually one page), transcripts, GPA (we use a 4.0 scale throughout this book), SAT and/or ACT scores, letters of recommendation (usually one each from a teacher, employer, and friend) outlining your moral character, and if there are any newspaper articles, etc., about you, it is a good idea to include them, as well.

Application Checklist

The following supporting documents may be requested with your application. We suggest you make a master file for these documents and photocopy or print a quantity so you will have them handy. You can then just pull a copy from your file and attach it to the application upon request.

1. Essay.
2. Extracurricular activities sheet, or
3. Curriculum vitae if in college, or résumé if you are in the job market.
4. Transcripts.
5. SAT and/or ACT scores.
6. Letters of recommendation.
7. Newspaper articles, etc., about yourself (if you have any).

You might also include your photograph, whether it's a high school picture or a snapshot of you working at your favorite hobby. This helps the selection committee feel a little closer to you. Instead of just seeing a name, they will have a face to match it. Sometimes a photo is requested for publicity purposes. Unless otherwise specified, send what's called a "head shot," a photo from the shoulders up.

Mail your applications early, at least a month before the deadline.

Now, take a deep breath, relax—you can do it!—and begin your journey into the next exciting part of your life.

Scholarships, Awards and Grants

ART (ALL FIELDS)

1—ALLIANCE FOR YOUNG ARTISTS AND WRITERS, INC. (The Scholastic Art & Writing Awards)

555 Broadway
New York NY 10012-3999
212/343-6493
Internet: http://www.artand
writing.org
AMOUNT: Varies; Up to $10,000
DEADLINE(S): Varies (upon location)
FIELD(S): Art; Writing
ELIGIBILITY/REQUIREMENTS: For all students in grades 7-12 currently enrolled in a public or nonpublic school in the U.S., Canada, U.S. territories, or U.S.-sponsored schools abroad. Awards are available in 10 writing categories and 16 art categories. Publishing opportunities may be available for winning students in both art and writing categories.
HOW TO APPLY: See website or write.
NUMBER OF AWARDS: 1,000+ awards annually, including 11 $10,000 scholarships.

2—DAUGHTERS OF THE AMERICAN REVOLUTION/NATIONAL SOCIETY (Occupational/Physical Therapy Scholarship)

Committee Services Office
Attn: Scholarships
1776 D Street NW
Washington DC 20006-5392
202/628-1776
Internet: http://www.dar.org
AMOUNT: $500
DEADLINE(S): FEB 15 or AUG 15
FIELD(S): Occupational/Physical
  Therapy
ELIGIBILITY/REQUIREMENTS: Awarded to students who are in financial need and are accepted and enrolled into an accredited school of occupational therapy (including art, music, or physical therapy). Affiliation with DAR not required.
HOW TO APPLY: Must submit application with a letter of sponsorship from local DAR chapter (send SASE to address above to obtain name and application); statement of 1,000 words or less stating career objectives, how college major (if required) or college plans relate to future professional goals and reasons for these choices; transcripts; list of extracurricular activities, honors received, scholastic achievements, or other significant accomplishments; 2-4 letters of recommendation from the high school or college you now attend who are familiar with your work, and proof of acceptance and enrollment (letter of acceptance or transcript), citizenship and financial need. See website for additional information.
NUMBER OF AWARDS: Varies
RENEWABLE: No

3—FIVE WINGS ARTS COUNCIL (Artist Mentor Scholarships for Students)

200 First Street NE
Staples MN 56479
218/894-5485
FAX: 218/894-3045
E-mail: mturner@ncscmn.org
Internet: http://www.fwac.org
AMOUNT: Up to $500
DEADLINE(S): OCT 15
FIELD(S): Literary Arts; Visual Arts;
  Music; Theater; Media Arts; Dance
ELIGIBILITY/REQUIREMENTS: Open to rural high school students in grades 9 through 12 enrolled in an independent school district within the counties of Cass, Crow Wing, Morrison, Todd, and Wadena, Minnesota. Each recipient is matched with a qualified mentor who will establish a study schedule with student. Award is based on creative potential, accomplishments in art, maturity, and personal motivation.
HOW TO APPLY: Contact Director for details.
NUMBER OF AWARDS: 10
CONTACT: Mark Turner, Director

4—HAWAII COMMUNITY FOUNDATION (Community Scholarship Fund)

1164 Bishop St., Suite 800
Honolulu HI 96813
808/537-6333 or toll free:
888/731-3863
FAX: 808/521-6286
E-mail: info@hcf-hawaii.org
Internet: http://www.hcf-hawaii.org
DEADLINE(S): MAR 1
FIELD(S): Arts; Architecture; Education;
  Humanities; Social Science
ELIGIBILITY/REQUIREMENTS: Applicants must be Hawaii residents; be junior or senior undergraduate or graduate students enrolled full time in an accredited 2- or 4-year college or university; demonstrate financial need, good moral character, and academic achievement with a minimum GPA of 3.0; show potential for filling a community need; and demonstrate accomplishment, motivation, initiative, vision, and intention of returning to or staying in Hawaii to work. Students who have received this scholarship in the past but are not majoring in any of the above fields of study are also eligible.
HOW TO APPLY: Send application with 2 letters of recommendation.

5—HAWAII COMMUNITY FOUNDATION (Laheenae Rebecca Hart Gay Scholarship)

1164 Bishop St., Suite 800
Honolulu HI 96813
808/537-6333 or toll free:
888/731-3863
FAX: 808/521-6286
E-mail: info@hcf-hawaii.org
Internet: http://www.hcf-hawaii.org
DEADLINE(S): MAR 1
FIELD(S): Art
ELIGIBILITY/REQUIREMENTS: Applicants must be residents of the state of Hawaii; plan to attend full time an accredited 2- or 4-year college or university; and demonstrate financial need, good moral character, and strong academic achievement, with a minimum GPA of 2.7. Students studying film, video, performing arts, or the culinary arts are not eligible.
HOW TO APPLY: Send application with 2 letters of recommendation.

6—HAWAII COMMUNITY FOUNDATION (PHG Foundation Scholarship)

1164 Bishop St., Suite 800
Honolulu HI 96813
808/537-6333 or toll free:
888/731-3863
FAX: 808/521-6286
E-mail: info@hcf-hawaii.org
Internet: http://www.hcf-hawaii.org
DEADLINE(S): MAR 1
FIELD(S): Art
ELIGIBILITY/REQUIREMENTS: Applicants must be residents of the state of Hawaii; plan to attend an accredited 2- or 4-year college or university, either full- or part-time; and demonstrate financial need, good moral character, and strong academic achievement, with a minimum GPA of 2.7. Students studying film, video, performing arts, or the culinary arts are not eligible.
HOW TO APPLY: Send application with 2 letters of recommendation.

7—IRISH ARTS COUNCIL (Awards and Opportunities)

70 Merrion Square
Dublin 2 IRELAND
+353 1 618 0200
FAX: +353 1 661 0349/676 1302
E-mail: info@artscouncil.ie
Internet: http://www.artscouncil.ie
AMOUNT: Varies (with program)
DEADLINE(S): Varies (with program)
FIELD(S): Creative Arts; Visual Arts; Performing Arts
ELIGIBILITY/REQUIREMENTS: Numerous programs open to young and established artists who are Irish citizens or legal residents. Purpose is to assist in pursuit of talents and recognize achievements.
HOW TO APPLY: See website or contact above address for an application.

8—JACKSONVILLE STATE UNIVERSITY (Art Scholarship)

Jacksonville AL 36265
256/782-5677 or 800/231-5291
Internet: http://www.jsu.edu
AMOUNT: Varies
DEADLINE(S): FEB 1
FIELD(S): Art
ELIGIBILITY/REQUIREMENTS: Open to students majoring in art.
HOW TO APPLY: Contact Art Department for application and additional information.
CONTACT: Art Department, 256/782-5626

9—JACKSONVILLE STATE UNIVERSITY (Ed Hill Memorial Leadership Scholarship)

Financial Aid Office
Jacksonville AL 36265
256/782-5677 or 1-800/231-5291
Internet: www.jsu.edu
AMOUNT: Full tuition
DEADLINE(S): FEB 1
FIELD(S): Communications; Art
ELIGIBILITY/REQUIREMENTS: Open to students majoring in communications or art with an interest in photography as a profession.
HOW TO APPLY: An official high school transcript and ACT/SAT scores must be submitted with scholarship applications. See website for application. Supporting documentation should be mailed.
RENEWABLE: Yes
CONTACT: Scholarship Committee

10—JACKSONVILLE STATE UNIVERSITY (Lee and Jetta Manners Scholarship)

Jacksonville AL 36265
256/782-5677 or 1-800/231-5291
Internet: www.jsu.edu
AMOUNT: Varies
DEADLINE(S): FEB 1
FIELD(S): Art
ELIGIBILITY/REQUIREMENTS: Open to students majoring in art.
HOW TO APPLY: Contact Art Department for application and additional information.
CONTACT: Art Department, 256/782-5626

11—JACKSONVILLE STATE UNIVERSITY (Opal R. & Opal A. Lovett Scholarship)

Financial Aid Office
Jacksonville AL 36265
256/782-5677 or 1-800/231-5291
Internet: www.jsu.edu
AMOUNT: Varies
DEADLINE(S): FEB 1
FIELD(S): History; Art; English
ELIGIBILITY/REQUIREMENTS: Open to sophomore or above with a minimum 2.5 GPA.
HOW TO APPLY: An official transcript and ACT/SAT scores must be submitted with scholarship applications. See website for application. Supporting documentation should be mailed.
NUMBER OF AWARDS: 1
RENEWABLE: No
CONTACT: Scholarship Committee

12—JACKSONVILLE STATE UNIVERSITY (Shirley Kirkland Scholarship)

Jacksonville AL 36265
256/782-5677 or 1-800/231-5291
Internet: www.jsu.edu
AMOUNT: Varies
DEADLINE(S): FEB 1
FIELD(S): Art
ELIGIBILITY/REQUIREMENTS: Open to students majoring in art.
HOW TO APPLY: Contact Art Department for application and additional information.
CONTACT: Art Department, 256/782-5626

13—KOSCIUSZKO FOUNDATION (Summer Sessions in Poland and Rome)

15 East 65th Street
New York NY 10021-6595
212/734-2130
FAX: 212/628-4552
E-mail: addy@thekf.org
Internet: http://www.kosciuszko foundation.org
AMOUNT: Varies
DEADLINE(S): Varies
FIELD(S): Polish Studies; History; Literature; Art; Economics; Social Studies; Language; Culture
ELIGIBILITY/REQUIREMENTS: Open to undergraduate and graduate students, graduating high school students who are 18 or older, and persons of any age who are not enrolled in a college or university program. Study programs are offered in Poland and Rome from mid-June through the end of August in above fields. Must be U.S. citizen/permanent resident.
HOW TO APPLY: See website or send a SASE for an application.
CONTACT: Addy Tymczyszyn, Summer Studies Abroad Coordinator, ext. 210

14—LINCOLN COMMUNITY FOUNDATION (Jane T. Anderson Scholarship)

215 Centennial Mall South
Suite 100
Lincoln NE 68508
402/474-2354
FAX: 402/474-2345
E-mail: lcf@lcf.org
Internet: http://www.lcf.org
AMOUNT: Varies
DEADLINE(S): APR 15
FIELD(S): Art; Art History; Museum Studies
ELIGIBILITY/REQUIREMENTS: Current graduating senior of a public high school in Lancaster County, Nebraska, who demonstrates scholastic performance and artistic talent, and intends to continue his/her education pursuing a degree in the above fields.
HOW TO APPLY: Submit application form; transcript; copy of ACT/SAT or similar test scores if not already included on transcript; and current letter of recommendation (no more than 1 year old) from applicant's high school art teacher.
NUMBER OF AWARDS: Varies
ADDITIONAL INFORMATION: Scholarship shall not be awarded to any immediate or distant member of the Jane T. Anderson family.

15—MENSA EDUCATION AND RESEARCH FOUNDATION (Harper Fowley—Isolated M Award)

Internet: http://www.mensa foundation.org/AM/Template.cfm? Section=Scholarships1
AMOUNT: $600
DEADLINE(S): JAN 15
FIELD(S): Liberal Arts
ELIGIBILITY/REQUIREMENTS: Awards based on essays written by the applicant. No requirement for Mensa membership nor is consideration given for

grades, academic program, or financial need. Applicants must currently be a resident of a participating American Mensa local group's area and enrolled in a degree program in an accredited U.S. institution of higher learning during the academic year following the application date.
HOW TO APPLY: Each year the list of participating groups may change, see website for up-to-date information. Send application, available (if eligible) from the website or, by request with SASE, from local scholarship chairs. Submit with essay of not more than 550 words explaining your academic and/or vocational goals and plans to achieve those goals to the scholarship chair in your area.

16—MENSA EDUCATION AND RESEARCH FOUNDATION (Rosemary Greathouse Scholarship)

Internet: http://www.mensa foundation.org/AM/Template.cfm? Section=Scholarships1
AMOUNT: $600
DEADLINE(S): JAN 15
FIELD(S): Arts (including creative writing and journalism)
ELIGIBILITY/REQUIREMENTS: Awards based on essays written by the applicant. No requirement for Mensa membership nor is consideration given for grades, academic program or financial need. Applicants must currently be a resident of a participating American Mensa local group's area and enrolled in a degree program in an accredited U.S. institution of higher learning during the academic year following the application date.
HOW TO APPLY: Each year the list of participating groups may change, see website for up-to-date information. Send application, available (if eligible) from the website or, by request with SASE, from local scholarship chairs. Submit with essay of not more than 550 words explaining your academic and/or vocational goals and plans to achieve those goals to the scholarship chair in your area.

17—NATIONAL ART MATERIALS TRADE ASSOCIATION (NAMTA Art/Art Education Major Scholarship)

15806 Brookway Drive, Suite 300
Huntersville NC 28078
704/892-6244
FAX: 704/892-6247
E-mail: scholarships@namta.org
Internet: www.namta.org
AMOUNT: $2,500
DEADLINE(S): APR 1
FIELD(S): Art; Art Education

ELIGIBILITY/REQUIREMENTS: Students majoring or planning to major in the field of art, whether as an art major or an art educator. Candidates do not have to be an employee or family member of an employee of a NAMTA member firm to apply. Candidates must graduate from high school or its equivalent before July 1 of the year in which they receive the scholarship; and must attend an accredited university, college or technical institute. Candidates are judged on extracurricular activities, GPA and financial need.
HOW TO APPLY: See website. Contact NAMTA for application. Submit with transcripts.
NUMBER OF AWARDS: 2
RENEWABLE: No

18—NATIONAL FOUNDATION FOR ADVANCEMENT IN THE ARTS (Arts Recognition and Talent Search)

800 Brickell Avenue
Miami FL 33131
800/970-ARTS or 305/377-1140
FAX: 305/377-1149
E-mail: info@nfaa.org
Internet: http://www.ARTSawards.org
AMOUNT: $100-$3,000
DEADLINE(S): OCT 1
FIELD(S): Creative and Performing Arts; Writing
ELIGIBILITY/REQUIREMENTS: Talent contest for high school seniors and 17- to 18-year-olds in dance, film, jazz, music, photography, theater, visual arts, voice, and writing. Except for those applying in music and jazz, applicants must be U.S. citizens or permanent residents.
HOW TO APPLY: Applications available online or write. May apply in more than one category, but only one financial award will be given to any individual. A fee is required for each category in which student applies.
NUMBER OF AWARDS: 400
RENEWABLE: No

19—RIPON COLLEGE (Performance/Recognition Tuition Scholarships)

Admissions Office
300 Seward Street
P.O. Box 248
Ripon WI 54971
920/748-8101
E-mail: adminfo@ripon.edu
Internet: http://www.ripon.edu
AMOUNT: $5,000-$10,000/year
DEADLINE(S): MAR 1
FIELD(S): Music; Art; Theater
ELIGIBILITY/REQUIREMENTS: Open to undergraduate and graduate students

attending or planning to attend Ripon College.
HOW TO APPLY: Contact Office of Admission for an application. Interview, audition, or nomination may be required.
RENEWABLE: Yes
CONTACT: Office of Admission

20—SONOMA CHAMBOLLE-MUSIGNY SISTER CITIES, INC. (Henri Cardinaux Memorial Scholarship)

Chamson Scholarship Committee
P.O. Box 1633
Sonoma CA 95476-1633
707/938-9081
E-mail: icardin@aol.com
AMOUNT: Up to $1,500 (travel + expenses)
DEADLINE(S): JUL 15
FIELD(S): Culinary Arts; Wine Industry; Art; Architecture; Music; History; Fashion
ELIGIBILITY/REQUIREMENTS: Hands-on experience working in above or similar fields and living with a family in small French village in Burgundy or other French city. Must be Sonoma County, California, resident at least 18 years of age and be able to communicate in French.
HOW TO APPLY: Transcripts, employer recommendation, photograph, and essay (stating why, where, and when) required.
NUMBER OF AWARDS: 1
RENEWABLE: No
CONTACT: Ivy Cardinaux

21—WESTERN MICHIGAN UNIVERSITY (Kathryn and Grant Leaske Memorial Endowed Scholarship)

1903 W. Michigan
Kalamazoo MI 49008-5337
269/387-8777
FAX: 269/387-6989
E-mail: finaid-info@mich.edu
Internet: http://www.wmich.edu/finaid
AMOUNT: Varies
DEADLINE(S): MAR 1
FIELD(S): Arts; Sciences; Humanities; Social Sciences
ELIGIBILITY/REQUIREMENTS: Applicant must be a full-time undergraduate student whose major is in the College of Arts & Sciences; demonstrate financial need; have a 3.0 GPA; be able to document history of community/university service and volunteerism.
HOW TO APPLY: Contact the College of Arts and Sciences for an application or apply online or print application from website.

RENEWABLE: Yes. Up to 2 years depending on academic status.
CONTACT: Financial Aid

22—WHITTIER COLLEGE (Talent Scholarship)

13406 E. Philadelphia Street
Whittier CA 90608
562/907-4285
FAX: 562/464-4560
E-mail: admission@whittier.edu
Internet: http://www.whittier.edu
AMOUNT: $5,000-$10,000
DEADLINE(S): FEB 1
FIELD(S): Art, Music, Theater
ELIGIBILITY/REQUIREMENTS: Eligibility based on portfolio or audition submissions judged by music, art, or theater department. Recipients are not required to major in their talent discipline.
HOW TO APPLY: Write or see website for complete information.

ART HISTORY

23—EAA AVIATION FOUNDATION (EAA AirVenture Museum—Wittman Aviation Studies Internship)

EAA Scholarship Department
P.O. 3086
Oshkosh WI 54903-3065
920/426-6823
E-mail: scholarships@eaa.org
Internet: http://www.young eagles.org
AMOUNT: Approximately $2,500
DEADLINE(S): MAR 1
FIELD(S): Aviation and Related Areas
ELIGIBILITY/REQUIREMENTS: Open to applicant (must be at least 18 years of age by the start of the internship) wishing to work with the collections department of the EAA AirVenture Museum. The work will be in support of the museum's artifact management program and is suitable for a person with curatorial work. Duties may include cataloging, moving, and researching artifacts in the museum collection. Must be able to deal effectively, tactfully and pleasantly with volunteers, staff, program participants and Museum visitors. Strong verbal and written skills and the ability to work independently. Must also be a current member of EAA (Experimental Aircraft Association) or recommended by a current EAA member to apply for these internships. Learn more about joining EAA (www.eaa.org) or call 800/843-3612. Individual and student memberships are available.

HOW TO APPLY: Apply online.
NUMBER OF AWARDS: 2

24—FOUNDATION FOR THE ADVANCEMENT OF MESOAMERICAN STUDIES, INC. (FAMSI) (Research Grants)

268 S. Suncoast Boulevard
Crystal River FL 34429-5498
352/795-5990
FAX: 352/795-1970
E-mail: famsi@famsi.org
Internet: http://www.famsi.org/grants/apply.html
AMOUNT: $500-$10,000 (max.)
DEADLINE(S): SEP 15
FIELD(S): Ancient Mesoamerican Cultures, Anthropology, Archaeology, Art History, Ethnohistory, Linguistics
ELIGIBILITY/REQUIREMENTS: Grants are awarded to the most qualified scholars regardless of degree level. FAMSI favors the most qualified scholars regardless of degree level. FAMSI favors degree candidates, graduates, and researchers in Mesoamerican Studies whose projects have not had extensive financial support.
HOW TO APPLY: Visit website to download a brochure or e-mail (see below).
NUMBER OF AWARDS: 30-35 awards annually.
RENEWABLE: Yes. Previous grantees can reapply, but new applicants may be given greater priority.
CONTACT: jessica@famsi.org

25—LEMMERMANN FOUNDATION, THE (Fondazione Lemmermann Scholarship Awards)

c/o Studio Associato Romanelli
via Cosseria, 5
00192 Roma ITALY
(06) 324.30.23
FAX: (06) 322.17.88
E-mail: lemmermann@mail.nexus.it
Internet: http://www.lemmermann.nexus.it/lemmermann/
AMOUNT: 750 euro/month
DEADLINE(S): MAR 15; SEP 30
FIELD(S): Italian/Roman studies in the subject areas of literature, archaeology, history of art
ELIGIBILITY/REQUIREMENTS: For university students who need to study in Rome to carry out research and prepare their theses concerning Rome and the Roman culture from the period Pre-Roman to present-day time in the subject areas above.

HOW TO APPLY: Contact above organization for details. Access website for application form.

26—LINCOLN COMMUNITY FOUNDATION (Jane T. Anderson Scholarship)

215 Centennial Mall South, Suite 100
Lincoln NE 68508
402/474-2354
FAX: 402/474-2345
E-mail: lcf@lcf.org
Internet: http://www.lcf.org
AMOUNT: Varies
DEADLINE(S): APR 15
FIELD(S): Art; Art History; Museum Studies
ELIGIBILITY/REQUIREMENTS: Current graduating senior of a public high school in Lancaster County, Nebraska who demonstrates scholastic performance and artistic talent, and intends to continue his/her education pursuing a degree in the above fields.
HOW TO APPLY: Submit application form; transcript; copy of ACT/SAT or similar test scores if not already included on transcript; and current letter of recommendation (no more than 1 year old) from applicant's high school art teacher.
NUMBER OF AWARDS: Varies
ADDITIONAL INFORMATION: Scholarship shall not be awarded to any immediate or distant member of the Jane T. Anderson family.

27—METROPOLITAN MUSEUM OF ART (Internships)

1000 Fifth Avenue
New York NY 10028-0198
212/570-3710
E-mail: mmainterns@metmuseum.org
Internet: http://www.metmuseum.org/education/erinternship.asp
AMOUNT: $2,500-$20,000
DEADLINE(S): JAN; FEB
FIELD(S): Art History
ELIGIBILITY/REQUIREMENTS: Internships for undergraduates and graduates who intend to pursue careers in art museums. Programs vary in length and requirements. Interns work in curatorial, education, conservation, administration, or library department of museum. Some require demonstration of economic need. Duration ranges from 9 weeks to 10 months. Volunteer positions also available.
HOW TO APPLY: See website or contact Museum for information.

28—SMITHSONIAN INSTITUTION-COOPER-HEWITT, NATIONAL DESIGN MUSEUM (Peter Krueger Summer Internships)

2 East 91st Street
New York NY 10128
212/849-8380
FAX: 212/860-6909
E-mail: edu@si.edu
Internet: http://www.si.edu/ndm
AMOUNT: $2,500 stipend
DEADLINE(S): FEB 1
FIELD(S): Art History; Architectural History; Museum Studies; Museum Education; Design
ELIGIBILITY/REQUIREMENTS: This 10-week (June-August) internship is open to college students considering a career in one of the above fields as well as graduate students who have not yet completed their M.A. degree. Interns are assigned to specific curatorial, education, or administrative departments where they will assist on special research or exhibition projects, as well as participate in daily museum activities. Housing NOT provided.
HOW TO APPLY: See website for details and application. Submit with cover letter stating area of interest, résumé, official transcript, 2 letters of recommendation, and 1- to 2-page essay on interest.
RENEWABLE: No
CONTACT: Internship Coordinator

29—SMITHSONIAN INSTITUTION-FREER/SACKLER GALLERIES (Dick Louie Memorial Internship for Americans of Asian Descent)

Education Department
Washington DC 20560-0707
202/357-4880
TTY: 202/786-2374
Internet: http://www.asia.si.edu
AMOUNT: Stipend
DEADLINE(S): Varies
FIELD(S): Asian Art; Art History; Museum Studies
ELIGIBILITY/REQUIREMENTS: This summer internship is an opportunity for high school students of Asian descent to gain practical experience in a museum setting. Must be entering or completing senior year of high school, and must live and attend high school in the Washington metropolitan area.
HOW TO APPLY: Contact the Internship Coordinator for an application.
CONTACT: Internship Coordinator

30—SOLOMON R. GUGGENHEIM MUSEUM (Internship Programs)

1071 Fifth Avenue
New York NY 10128-0173
212/423-3526
E-mail: education@guggenheim.org
Internet: http://www.guggenheim.org/new york index
AMOUNT: Varies (some positions unpaid)
DEADLINE(S): FEB 15 (Summer); MAY 15 (Fall); NOV 1 (Spring)
FIELD(S): Art Administration; Art History
ELIGIBILITY/REQUIREMENTS: Various internships, which offer practical museum training experience, are available for undergraduates, recent graduates, and graduate students in art history, administration, conservation, education, and related fields. Location varies, including New York, Italy, and Spain. Housing NOT included. Cover letter, résumé, transcripts, letters of recommendation, list of foreign languages/relevant coursework, and essay (less than 500 words, describing interest) required.
HOW TO APPLY: Contact the Internship Coordinator, Education Department for details of each internship and application procedures.
CONTACT: Internship Coordinator, Education Department

31—VIRGINIA MUSEUM OF FINE ARTS (Fellowships)

200 North Boulevard
Richmond VA 23220-4007
804/204-2661
Internet: http://vmfa.state.va.us
AMOUNT: $4,000 (undergraduate-maximum); $6,000 (graduates); $8,000 (professionals)
DEADLINE(S): MAR 1
FIELD(S): Crafts; Drawing; Filmmaking; Mixed Media Painting; Photography; Printmaking; Sculpture; Video; Art History (graduate only)
ELIGIBILITY/REQUIREMENTS: Open to Virginia residents of at least one year who are U.S. citizens or legal residents. Fellowships are available to undergraduates, graduates, and professional artists. Financial need is considered.
HOW TO APPLY: Application and guidelines on website.

32—WESTERN MICHIGAN UNIVERSITY (College of Fine Arts/Charles E. Meyer Award in Art History)

1903 W. Michigan
Kalamazoo MI 49008-5337
269/387-6000
FAX: 269/387-6989
E-mail: finaid-info@wmich.edu
Internet: http://www.wmich.edu/finaid
AMOUNT: Varies
FIELD(S): Art History
ELIGIBILITY/REQUIREMENTS: Must be an undergraduate majoring in art history.
HOW TO APPLY: Student is nominated by faculty. Contact the Art Advising office for an application.
NUMBER OF AWARDS: Multiple awards
CONTACT: Art Department

CRAFT

33—AMERICAN SHEEP INDUSTRY WOMEN (National Make It with Wool Competition)

P.O. Box 175
Lavina MT 59046
406/636-2731
FAX: 406/636-2731
E-mail: levi@midrivers.com
Internet: http://www.sheepusa.org
AMOUNT: $1,000
DEADLINE(S): Varies (with state)
FIELD(S): Sewing; Knitting; Crocheting
ELIGIBILITY/REQUIREMENTS: State/National Contests: Open to students who make a wool garment from a current pattern. Fabric must contain at least 60% wool. Awards tenable at any recognized college or university. To be eligible for Fashion/Apparel/Design Scholarship: must also major in the field.
HOW TO APPLY: Entry fee $10. See website for additional information and application or contact national office or participating states (include SASE for application). State winners advance to national competition.
NUMBER OF AWARDS: 3; $1,000 scholarship for Fashion/Apparel/Design major (1), $1,000 award (2)
RENEWABLE: No
CONTACT: Marie Lehfeldt, National Coordinator

34—CLAYFOLK (Ellice T. Johnston Scholarship)

P.O. Box 274
Talent OR 97540
Internet: http://www.clayfolk.org
AMOUNT: $1,500
DEADLINE(S): JUN 15
FIELD(S): Ceramics

ELIGIBILITY/REQUIREMENTS: Two years of college or equivalent level of art education–this may include sculpture, drawing, design, etc., and the study of aesthetics or technical ceramics. Must be a resident or student in Oregon or northern California. Financial need is a consideration but will not restrict the selection of the applicant. Clayfolk members as sponsors of this scholarship are not eligible to apply.
HOW TO APPLY: Contact Clayfolk for application and submit along with portfolio of work—8-12 slides and/or photographs. A brief statement about your work and how you plan to use the award. 2 letters of recommendation from persons in the academic or work field. A recent academic transcript. College Scholarship Service Financial Aid Form (FAF) or a 1040 tax form from the previous year. Self-addressed envelope of appropriate size to return portfolio and with sufficient postage.
NUMBER OF AWARDS: 1
RENEWABLE: Yes. Must reapply.

35—HAYSTACK MOUNTAIN SCHOOL OF CRAFTS

Admissions Office
P.O. Box 518
Deer Isle ME 04627
207/348-2306
FAX: 207/348-2307
E-mail: haystack@haystack-mtn.org
Internet: http://www.haystack-mtn.org
AMOUNT: Varies
DEADLINE(S): MAR 25
FIELD(S): Crafts (metals, clay, wood); Graphics (painting, drawing and related fields); Weaving; Glass; Blacksmithing
ELIGIBILITY/REQUIREMENTS: 18 years old with dedicated interest in crafts.
HOW TO APPLY: Write or e-mail for application.
NUMBER OF AWARDS: 90+
RENEWABLE: No

36—VIRGINIA MUSEUM OF FINE ARTS (Fellowships)

200 North Boulevard
Richmond VA 23220-4007
804/204-2661
Internet: http://vmfa.state.va.us
AMOUNT: $4,000 (undergraduate-maximum); $6,000 (graduates); $8,000 (professionals)
DEADLINE(S): MAR 1
FIELD(S): Crafts; Drawing; Filmmaking; Mixed Media Painting; Photography; Printmaking; Sculpture; Video; Art History (graduate only)

ELIGIBILITY/REQUIREMENTS: Open to Virginia residents of at least one year who are U.S. citizens or legal residents. Fellowships are available to undergraduates, graduates, and professional artists. Financial need is considered.
HOW TO APPLY: Application and guidelines on website.

37—WOMEN'S STUDIO WORKSHOP (Fellowship Grants)

P.O. Box 489
Rosendale NY 12472
845/658-9133
FAX: 845/658-9031
E-mail: info@wsworkshop.org
Internet: http://www.wsworkshop.org/
AMOUNT: Tuition
DEADLINE(S): MAR 15; NOV 1
FIELD(S): Visual Arts
ELIGIBILITY/REQUIREMENTS: Designed to provide concentrated work time for artists to explore new ideas in a dynamic and supportive community of women artists. WSW welcomes applications from emerging artists.
HOW TO APPLY: Application form plus a résumé, 6-10 slides, a letter of interest that addresses the purpose of the residency, explaining areas of proficiency and studio skills, and a SASE for return of materials. Applications available on website.

38—WOMEN'S STUDIO WORKSHOP (Chili Bowl Internship)

P.O. Box 489
Rosendale NY 12472
845/658-9133
FAX: 845/658-9031
E-mail: info@wsworkshop.org
Internet: http://www.wsworkshop.org/
AMOUNT: $150/month + housing
DEADLINE(S): OCT 15
FIELD(S): Ceramics
ELIGIBILITY/REQUIREMENTS: Must have wheel throwing experience, be motivated, and hard working.
HOW TO APPLY: Send a letter of interest, résumé, up to 20 slides with slide list, 3 reference letters, and a SASE.
NUMBER OF AWARDS: 1
RENEWABLE: No
CONTACT: Ayumi Horie

39—WOMEN'S STUDIO WORKSHOP (Internship)

P.O. Box 489
Rosendale NY 12472

845/658-9133
FAX: 845/658-9031
E-mail: info@wsworkshop.org
Internet: http://www.wsworkshop.org/
AMOUNT: $150/month + housing
DEADLINE(S): APR 1 and OCT 15
FIELD(S): Visual Arts including Printmaking, Papermaking, Book Arts, Photography, Ceramics
ELIGIBILITY/REQUIREMENTS: Must have experience in one or more of fields.
HOW TO APPLY: Send a letter of interest, résumé, up to 20 slides with slide list, 3 reference letters, and a SASE.
NUMBER OF AWARDS: 6
RENEWABLE: No
CONTACT: Ellen Kucera

40—WOMEN'S STUDIO WORKSHOP (Summer Arts Institute Internship)

P.O. Box 489
Rosendale NY 12472
845/658-9133
FAX: 845/658-9031
E-mail: info@wsworkshop.org
Internet: http://www.wsworkshop.org/
AMOUNT: $150/month + housing
DEADLINE(S): APR 1 and OCT 15
FIELD(S): Visual Arts; Papermaking; Book Arts
ELIGIBILITY/REQUIREMENTS: Must have experience in one or more of fields.
HOW TO APPLY: Send a letter of interest, résumé, up to 20 slides with slide list, 3 reference letters, and a SASE.
NUMBER OF AWARDS: 1
RENEWABLE: No
CONTACT: Ellen Kucera

41—WORLDSTUDIO FOUNDATION

200 Varick Street, Suite 507
New York NY 10014
212/366-1317
FAX: 212/807-0024
E-mail: info@worldstudio.org
Internet: http://www.worldstudio.org or http://www.aiga.org
AMOUNT: $1,500-$5,000
DEADLINE(S): APR 14
FIELD(S): Advertising; Animation; Architecture; Cartooning; Crafts; Environmental graphics; Film/video; Film/theater design; Fine arts; Furniture design; Industrial/product design; Interior architecture and design; Landscape architecture; New media; Photography; Surface/textile design; Urban planning
ELIGIBILITY/REQUIREMENTS: Applicants must be pursuing a degree in

the fine or commercial arts, design or architecture, and plan to enter a career in the creative professions. Undergraduates and graduates are eligible. Minority status and/or social agenda are significant factors. Financial need a prerequisite. Minimum 2.0 GPA.
HOW TO APPLY: See websites for application. The application is a 2-part process. Applications must include personal and school information, including transcripts and copies of letters of acceptance; financial information; portfolio; written statement of purpose; examples of a commitment to a social agenda; 2 letters of recommendation from college instructors, high school teachers, or employers; head shot of applicant.
NUMBER OF AWARDS: 20-30
RENEWABLE: Yes. Must reapply.
CONTACT: Mark Randall

DANCE

42—ADELPHI UNIVERSITY (Talent Awards)

South Avenue
Garden City NY 11530
516/877-3000
FAX: 516/877-3380
Internet: http://www.ecampus. adelphi.edu/sfs/au_scholarships_ grants.php#art
AMOUNT: $4,000-$10,000
DEADLINE(S): FEB 15
FIELD(S): Theater; Dance; Art; Music
ELIGIBILITY/REQUIREMENTS: Various scholarships for full-time students at Adelphi University in the above fields.
HOW TO APPLY: See website for further information; contact school to apply. Audition required.
RENEWABLE: Yes. Must maintain 3.0 GPA in major and 2.5 overall to maintain scholarship.

43—AMERICAN ALLIANCE FOR HEALTH, PHYSICAL EDUCATION, RECREATION & DANCE

1900 Association Drive
Reston VA 20191
703/476-3400 or 800/213-7193
Internet: http://www.aahperd.org
AMOUNT: Varies
DEADLINE(S): Varies
FIELD(S): Health Education, Leisure and Recreation, Girls and Women in Sports, Sport and Physical Education, Dance

ELIGIBILITY/REQUIREMENTS: This organization has six national suborganizations specializing in the above fields. Some have grants and fellowships for both individuals and group projects. The website has the details for each group.
HOW TO APPLY: Visit website for details or write to above address for details.

44—GOLDEN KEY INTERNATIONAL HONOUR SOCIETY—PERFORMING ARTS SHOWCASE

1189 Ponce de Leon Avenue
Atlanta GA 30306
404/377-2400 or 800/377-2401
FAX: 404/373-7033
E-mail: scholarships@goldenkey.org
Internet: http://www.goldenkey.org
AMOUNT: $1,000
DEADLINE(S): MAR 1
FIELD(S): Dance, Drama, Instrumental Performance, Filmmaking, Musical Composition, Vocal Performance
ELIGIBILITY/REQUIREMENTS: This award recognizes performing arts talents of Golden Key members in six categories: dance, drama, instrumental performance, filmmaking, musical composition, and vocal performance. Undergraduate, graduate, and post-graduate members who are currently enrolled in classes at a degree-granting program may apply. Award is based on the quality of work submitted.
HOW TO APPLY: Applications must be posted online with Golden Key member number. Entries must be submitted on VHS videotape. (Compact discs and audiocassettes are accepted for original musical composition ONLY.) Performances may not exceed 10 minutes (except for filmmaking entries). All submissions become the property of Golden Key. Only one entry per member per category will be accepted.
NUMBER OF AWARDS/YEAR: Six (one/category)/year.
RENEWABLE: No

45—GUSTAVUS ADOLPHUS COLLEGE (Anderson Theatre and Dance Scholarships)

Office of Admission
800 West College Avenue
St. Peter MN 56082
507/933-7676 or 800/GUSTAVUS
E-mail: admission@gustavus.edu
Internet: http://www.gustavus.edu
AMOUNT: $500-$2,000
DEADLINE(S): JAN 1
FIELD(S): Theater; Dance

ELIGIBILITY/REQUIREMENTS: Scholarships tenable at Gustavus Adolphus College, St. Peter, Minnesota, for students pursuing studies in theatre and/or dance. Students may be enrolled in any major.
HOW TO APPLY: Contact college for details.
RENEWABLE: Yes. Must participate in a departmental project and maintain a 3.0 GPA.

46—HAWAII COMMUNITY FOUNDATION (Jean Erdman Scholarship)

1164 Bishop St., Suite 800
Honolulu HI 96813
808/537-6333 or toll free: 888/731-3863
FAX: 808/521-6286
E-mail: info@hcf-hawaii.org
Internet: http://www.hcf-hawaii.org
DEADLINE(S): MAR 1
FIELD(S): Dance
ELIGIBILITY/REQUIREMENTS: Applicants must be planning to attend or attending the University of Hawaii at Manoa; be residents of the state of Hawaii; and demonstrate financial need, good moral character, and academic achievement, with a minimum GPA of 2.7.
HOW TO APPLY: Send application with 2 letters of recommendation.
CONTACT: UH Manoa Dance Department

47—IRISH ARTS COUNCIL (Awards and Opportunities)

70 Merrion Square
Dublin 2 IRELAND
+353 1 618 0200
FAX: +353 1 661 0349/676 1302
E-mail: info@artscouncil.ie
Internet: http://www.artscouncil.ie
AMOUNT: Varies (with program)
DEADLINE(S): Varies (with program)
FIELD(S): Creative Arts; Visual Arts; Performing Arts
ELIGIBILITY/REQUIREMENTS: Numerous programs open to young and established artists who are Irish citizens or legal residents. Purpose is to assist in pursuit of talents and recognize achievements.
HOW TO APPLY: See website or contact above address for an application.

48—JUNIATA COLLEGE (Ron & Ann Wertz Arts Scholarship)

Office of Financial Planning
1700 Moore Street
Huntingdon PA 16652

814/641-3142
FAX: 814/641-5311
E-mail: frankv@juniata.edu
Internet: http://www.juniata.edu/
admission/finplan/index.html
AMOUNT: Full tuition, room & board
DEADLINE(S): JAN 4
FIELD(S): Ceative and/or performing
arts, Fine Arts, Graphic Design,
Writing, Choral and Instrumental
Music, Theater, Dance
ELIGIBILITY/REQUIREMENTS: Open
to incoming freshmen (upperclassmen and
transfer students are ineligible). Must be
nominated by a Juniata alumnus/a, parent
of a Juniata student, guidance counselor,
pastor, teacher, or someone familiar with
the student's involvement in school and
community activities, who have excelled in
the creative and/or performing arts, including drawing, painting, sculpting, graphic
design, writing, choral and instrumental
music, theatre and dance.
HOW TO APPLY: Submit a Nomination
Essay (in addition to the essay required for
admission) of no more than 2 pages discussing
why you should be considered for a scholarship, including supporting activities and
involvement. You may also attach up to 3
extra pages of supporting information of any
kind. Must submit a portfolio. See website for
additional information or contact College.
NUMBER OF AWARDS: 1
RENEWABLE: No
CONTACT: Vincent Frank, Director of
Student Financial Planning, 814/641-3140;
e-mail: frankv@juniata.edu

49—LIBERACE FOUNDATION FOR THE PERFORMING AND CREATIVE ARTS

1775 East Tropicana Avenue
Las Vegas NV 89119-6529
702/798-5595
FAX: 702/798-7386
E-mail: foundation@liberace.org
Internet: http://www.liberace.org
AMOUNT: Varies
DEADLINE(S): MAR 15
FIELD(S): Music (Instrumental and Vocal);
Theater; Dance; Visual Arts; Fine Art
ELIGIBILITY/REQUIREMENTS:
Provides grants to accredited institutions
that offer training in above fields. Grants
are to be used exclusively for scholarship
assistance to talented and deserving stu-
dents. Recipients should be promising and
deserving upperclassmen (junior, senior,
graduate) enrolled in a course of study
leading up to a career in the arts.
HOW TO APPLY: See website or write to
above address for details.
RENEWABLE: Yes
CONTACT: Joel Strote

50—NATIONAL PTA (Reflections Program)

541 N. Fairbanks Ct., Suite 1300
Chicago IL 60611
800/307-4PTA or 312/670-6782
FAX: 312/670-6783
E-mail: info@pta.org
Internet: http://www.pta.org
AMOUNT: Varies
DEADLINE(S): Varies
FIELD(S): Literature; Musical
Composition; Photography; Visual
Arts; Dance/Choreography
ELIGIBILITY/REQUIREMENTS: Open
to students in preschool through grade
twelve to express themselves and to
receive positive recognition for their artis-
tic efforts. Young artists can get involved
in the Reflections Program of their local
PTA or PTSA.
HOW TO APPLY: Contact your state
PTA office for information about the
Reflections Program in your area.

51—UNIVERSITY OF ILLINOIS AT URBANA-CHAMPAIGN (Lydia E. Parker Bates Scholarship)

620 East John Street
Champaign IL 61820
217/333-0100
Internet: http://www.uiuc.edu/
AMOUNT: Up to $1,000
DEADLINE(S): MAR 15
FIELD(S): Art, Architecture, Landscape
Architecture, Urban Planning, Dance,
Theater, and all related subjects except
Music
ELIGIBILITY/REQUIREMENTS: Open
to undergraduate students in the College
of Fine and Applied Arts who are attend-
ing the University of Illinois at Urbana-
Champaign. Must demonstrate financial
need and have 2.85 GPA. Recipients must
carry at least 12 credit hours per semester.
HOW TO APPLY: Contact office of stu-
dent financial aid for application.
Complete the Free Application for Federal
Student Aid with UIUC admission appli-
cation.
NUMBER OF AWARDS: 175

FILM, THEATER, RADIO, TELEVISION

52—ACADEMY OF CANADIAN CINEMA AND TELEVISION (National Apprenticeship Training Program)

172 King Street East
Toronto Ontario M5A 1J3 CANADA

800/644-5194
FAX: 416/366/8454
E-mail: info@academy.ca
Internet: http://www.academy.ca/
dev/natp.htm/Academy/About/
GeneralACCTInfo.html
AMOUNT: $300 per week for 12 weeks
DEADLINE(S): MARCH
FIELD(S): Film and Television
Production and Management
ELIGIBILITY/REQUIREMENTS:
Program designed to provide hands-on
professional training to students in their
graduating year from film and/or television
diploma/degree programs. Must be
Canadian citizen or landed immigrant
studying full-time in Canada.
HOW TO APPLY: See website or contact
Academy for application for complete
information.
NUMBER OF AWARDS: 5
CONTACT: Jennifer Clapp

53—ACADEMY OF MOTION PICTURE ARTS AND SCIENCES (Student Academy Awards)

8949 Wilshire Boulevard
Beverly Hills CA 90211-1972
310/247-3000 ext. 130
FAX: 310/859-9351
E-mail: rmiller@oscars.org
Internet: http://www.oscars.org/
saa/index.html
AMOUNT: $1,000, $1,500, and $2,000
DEADLINE(S): APR 1
FIELD(S): Film Production: Alternative,
Animation, Documentary, or Dramatic
ELIGIBILITY/REQUIREMENTS:
Student Academy Awards competition is
open to students enrolled at a U.S. college,
university, film school, or art school. The
film must have been made in a teacher-
student relationship. No professional may
be involved in the production.
HOW TO APPLY: Contact Academy or
access website for complete information.
NUMBER OF AWARDS: Up to 5
CONTACT: Richard Miller

54—ACADEMY OF TELEVISION ARTS & SCIENCES COLLEGE TELEVISION AWARD

5220 Lankershim Boulevard
North Hollywood CA 91601-3109
818/754-2820
FAX: 818/761-2827
E-mail: /foundation
alavkin@emmys.org
Internet: http://www.emmys
foundation.org/foundation
AMOUNT: $500-$2,000

DEADLINE(S): JAN 15
FIELD(S): Television
ELIGIBILITY/REQUIREMENTS: Awards achievement in each of the following categories: Animation (all forms), Children's, Comedy, Comedy Series, Commercial, Documentary, Drama, Drama Series, Magazine, Music (best composition), Music (best use of music), and Newscast.
HOW TO APPLY: See website for application information and guidelines
NUMBER OF AWARDS: Up to 27 (at least 1 in each category)
CONTACT: Debbie Slavkin, Program Manager/Development Associate
ADDITIONAL INFORMATION: May apply in more than 1 category; 1st entry is free; each subsequent entry is $25.00. (See complete guidelines and rules for more details.)

55—ADELPHI UNIVERSITY (Talent Awards)

1 South Avenue
Garden City NY 11530
516/877-3080
FAX: 516/877-3380
Internet: http://www.ecampus. adelphi.edu/sfs/au scholarships grants.php#art
AMOUNT: $4,000-$10,000
DEADLINE(S): FEB 15
FIELD(S): Theater; Dance; Art; Music
ELIGIBILITY/REQUIREMENTS: Various scholarships for full-time students at Adelphi University in the above fields.
HOW TO APPLY: See website for further information; contact school to apply. Portfolio or audition required.
RENEWABLE: Yes. Must maintain 3.0 GPA in major and 2.5 overall to maintain scholarship.

56—AMERICAN HISTORICAL ASSOCIATION (John E. O'Connor Film Award)

400 A Street SE
Washington DC 20003
E-mail: aha@theaha.org
Internet: http://www.theaha.org
AMOUNT: Varies
DEADLINE(S): Varies
FIELD(S): Filmmaking; History
ELIGIBILITY/REQUIREMENTS: This honorific award seeks to recognize outstanding interpretations of history through the medium of film or video. Films and videos may provide unique perspectives on the past using techniques that are different from those employed by the author of a

book. The production should reflect such imaginative use of the medium.
HOW TO APPLY: Contact Association or see website for additional information.

57—AMERICAN INTERCONTINENTAL UNIVERSITY (Emilio Pucci Scholarships)

Admissions Committee
3330 Peachtree Road NE
Atlanta GA 30326
404/812-8192 or 888/248-7392
AMOUNT: $1,800 (applied toward tuition over 6 quarters)
DEADLINE(S): None
FIELD(S): Fashion Design; Fashion Marketing; Interior Design; Commercial Art; Business Administration; Video Production
ELIGIBILITY/REQUIREMENTS: Scholarships are for high school seniors who are interested in either a 2-year or 4-year program at one of the campuses of the American Intercontinental University: Atlanta, GA; Los Angeles, CA; London, UK; or Dubai, United Arab Emirates.
HOW TO APPLY: Write for applications and complete information.

58—ART INSTITUTE OF CHICAGO (Student Academy Awards)

Columbus Drive at
Jackson Boulevard
Chicago IL 60603
312/443-3735
Internet: http://www.oscars.org/saa
AMOUNT: Up to $2,000
DEADLINE(S): APR
FIELD(S): Filmmaking
ELIGIBILITY/REQUIREMENTS: The purpose of the Student Academy Awards competition is to support and encourage filmmakers with no previous professional experience who are enrolled in accredited colleges and universities. While professional advice may be requested and given during the making of student films, as a full-time student, the Academy believes that professional camerapersons, directors, editors, and writers should not play any major role in the production of such films.
HOW TO APPLY: See website or contact Institute for additional information.

59—ART INSTITUTES INTERNATIONAL, THE (Evelyn Keedy Memorial Scholarship)

300 Sixth Avenue, Suite 800
Pittsburgh PA 15222-2598
412/562-9800
FAX: 412/562-9802

E-mail: webadmin@aii.edu
Internet: http://www.aii.edu
AMOUNT: 2 years full tuition
DEADLINE(S): MAY 1
FIELD(S): Creative and applied: video production, broadcasting, culinary arts, fashion design, website administration, etc.
ELIGIBILITY/REQUIREMENTS: Scholarships at 12 different locations nationwide in various fields described above. For graduating high school seniors admitted to an Art Institutes International School, the New York Restaurant School, or NCPT.
HOW TO APPLY: See website or contact AII for more information. Transcripts, letters of recommendation, and résumé must be submitted with application.
NUMBER OF AWARDS: Multiple

60—ASIFA (Helen Victoria Haynes World Peace Storyboard and Animation Contest)

School of Communications
Lake Superior Hall
Grand Valley State University
Allendale MI 49401
E-mail: HaynesWorldPeace@aol.com
Internet: http://www.swcp.com/ animate/contest.htm
AMOUNT: $500 + software
DEADLINE(S): APR
FIELD(S): Animation; Cartooning
ELIGIBILITY/REQUIREMENTS: For high school and college students to design, draw, and mount a storyboard for an animated short for the Annual ASIFA/Central Conference and Retreat. The storyboard should depict your vision of how to achieve World Peace.
HOW TO APPLY: See website for official rules or contact ASIFA for more information.
NUMBER OF AWARDS: 2 (1 for high school students and 1 for college students)
CONTACT: Donna Morse or Mary Lou Haynes

61—BROADCAST EDUCATION ASSOCIATION (Abe Voron Scholarship)

1771 N Street NW
Washington DC 20036
202/429-3935 or 888/380-7222
FAX: 202/775-2981
Internet: http://www.bea.org
AMOUNT: $5,000
DEADLINE(S): SEP 15
FIELD(S): Radio
ELIGIBILITY/REQUIREMENTS: Applicants must be freshmen or sophomores studying at 2-year community col-

lege BEA schools studying toward a career in radio. Applicant must demonstrate superior academic performance and potential to be an outstanding electronic media professional. Should be compelling evidence that the applicant possesses high integrity and a well-articulated sense of personal and professional responsibility. Must attend full time.
HOW TO APPLY: See website for application or from your campus facility. Submit application along with personal and academic data and transcripts, broadcast and other experiences, a written statement of goals, and 3 references.
NUMBER OF AWARDS: 2
RENEWABLE: No
CONTACT: Louisa A. Nielsen

62—BROADCAST EDUCATION ASSOCIATION (Alexander M. Tanger Scholarship)

1771 N Street NW
Washington DC 20036
202/429-3935 or 888/380-7222
FAX: 202/775-2981
Internet: http://www.bea.org
AMOUNT: $5,000
DEADLINE(S): SEP 15
FIELD(S): Radio; Television; Electronic Media
ELIGIBILITY/REQUIREMENTS:
Applicants must be juniors, seniors, or graduate students at BEA member universities studying toward a career in any area of broadcasting. Applicant must demonstrate superior academic performance and potential to be an outstanding electronic media professional. Should be compelling evidence that the applicant possesses high integrity and a well-articulated sense of personal and professional responsibility. Must attend full time.
HOW TO APPLY: See website for application or from your campus facility. Submit application along with personal and academic data and transcripts, broadcast and other experiences, a written statement of goals, and 3 references.
NUMBER OF AWARDS: 1
RENEWABLE: No
CONTACT: Louisa A. Nielsen

63—BROADCAST EDUCATION ASSOCIATION (Broadcasters' Foundation/ Helen J. Sioussat/Fay Wells Scholarship)

1771 N Street NW
Washington DC 20036
202/429-3935 or 888/380-7222
FAX: 202/775-2981
Internet: http://www.bea.org
AMOUNT: $1,250
DEADLINE(S): SEP 15
FIELD(S): Radio; Television; Electronic Media

ELIGIBILITY/REQUIREMENTS:
Applicants must be juniors, seniors, or graduate students at BEA member universities studying any area of broadcasting. Applicant must demonstrate superior academic performance and potential to be an outstanding electronic media professional. Should be compelling evidence that the applicant possesses high integrity and a well-articulated sense of personal and professional responsibility. Must attend full time.
HOW TO APPLY: See website for application or from your campus facility. Submit application along with personal and academic data and transcripts, broadcast and other experiences, a written statement of goals, and 3 references.
NUMBER OF AWARDS: 2
RENEWABLE: No
CONTACT: Louisa A. Nielsen

64—BROADCAST EDUCATION ASSOCIATION (Harold E. Fellows Scholarship)

1771 N Street NW
Washington DC 20036
202/429-3935 or 888/380-7222
FAX: 202/775-2981
Internet: http://www.bea.org
AMOUNT: $1,250
DEADLINE(S): SEP 15
FIELD(S): Radio; Television; Electronic Media
ELIGIBILITY/REQUIREMENTS:
Applicants must be juniors, seniors, or graduate students at BEA member universities studying toward a career in any area of broadcasting. Applicant must demonstrate superior academic performance and potential to be an outstanding electronic media professional. Should be compelling evidence that the applicant possesses high integrity and a well-articulated sense of personal and professional responsibility. Must attend full time.
HOW TO APPLY: See website for application or from your campus facility. Submit application along with personal and academic data and transcripts, broadcast and other experiences, a written statement of goals, and 3 references.
NUMBER OF AWARDS: 4
RENEWABLE: No
CONTACT: Louisa A. Nielsen

65—BROADCAST EDUCATION ASSOCIATION (National Association of Broadcasters/ Walter S. Patterson Scholarship)

1771 N Street NW
Washington DC 20036
202/429-3935 or 888/380-7222
FAX: 202/775-2981
Internet: http://www.bea.org
AMOUNT: $1,250

DEADLINE(S): SEP 15
FIELD(S): Radio
ELIGIBILITY/REQUIREMENTS:
Applicants must be juniors, seniors, or graduate students at BEA member universities studying toward a career in radio. Applicant must demonstrate superior academic performance and potential to be an outstanding electronic media professional. Should be compelling evidence that the applicant possesses high integrity and a well-articulated sense of personal and professional responsibility. Must attend full time.
HOW TO APPLY: See website for application or from your campus facility. Submit application along with personal and academic data and transcripts, broadcast and other experiences, a written statement of goals, and 3 references.
NUMBER OF AWARDS: 2
RENEWABLE: No
CONTACT: Louisa A. Nielsen

66—BROADCAST EDUCATION ASSOCIATION (Philo T. Farnsworth Scholarship)

1771 N Street NW
Washington DC 20036
202/429-3935 or 888/380-7222
FAX: 202/775-2981
Internet: http://www.bea.org
AMOUNT: $1,500
DEADLINE(S): SEP 15
FIELD(S): Radio; Television; Electronic Media
ELIGIBILITY/REQUIREMENTS:
Applicants must be juniors, seniors, or graduate students at BEA member universities studying toward a career in any area of broadcasting. Applicant must demonstrate superior academic performance and potential to be an outstanding electronic media professional. Should be compelling evidence that the applicant possesses high integrity and a well-articulated sense of personal and professional responsibility. Must attend full time.
HOW TO APPLY: See website for application or from your campus facility. Submit application along with personal and academic data and transcripts, broadcast and other experiences, a written statement of goals, and 3 references.
NUMBER OF AWARDS: 1
RENEWABLE: No
CONTACT: Louisa A. Nielsen

67—BROADCAST EDUCATION ASSOCIATION (RCS Charitable Foundation/Andrew M. Economos Scholarship)

1771 N Street NW
Washington DC 20036
202/429-3935 or 888/380-7222

FAX: 202/775-2981
Internet: http://www.bea.org
AMOUNT: $3,500
DEADLINE(S): SEP 15
FIELD(S): Radio
ELIGIBILITY/REQUIREMENTS: Applicants must be juniors, seniors, or graduate students at BEA member universities studying toward a career in radio. Applicant must demonstrate superior academic performance and potential to be an outstanding electronic media professional. Should be compelling evidence that the applicant possesses high integrity and a well-articulated sense of personal and professional responsibility. Must attend full time.
HOW TO APPLY: See website for application or from your campus facility. Submit application along with personal and academic data and transcripts, broadcast and other experiences, a written statement of goals, and 3 references.
NUMBER OF AWARDS: 1
RENEWABLE: No
CONTACT: Louisa A. Nielsen

68—BROADCAST EDUCATION ASSOCIATION (Two Year/Community College BEA Scholarship)

1771 N Street NW
Washington DC 20036
202/429-3935 or 888/380-7222
FAX: 202/775-2981
Internet: http://www.bea.org
AMOUNT: $1,500
DEADLINE(S): SEP 15
FIELD(S): Radio; Television; Electronic Media
ELIGIBILITY/REQUIREMENTS: Applicants must be freshmen or sophomores studying at 2-year community college BEA schools studying toward a career in any area of broadcasting. Applicant must demonstrate superior academic performance and potential to be an outstanding electronic media professional. Should be compelling evidence that the applicant possesses high integrity and a well-articulated sense of personal and professional responsibility. Must attend full time.
HOW TO APPLY: See website for application or from your campus facility. Submit application along with personal and academic data and transcripts, broadcast and other experiences, a written statement of goals, and 3 references.
NUMBER OF AWARDS: 2
RENEWABLE: No
CONTACT: Louisa A. Nielsen

69—CHARLES AND LUCILLE KING FAMILY FOUNDATION

366 Madison Avenue, 10th Floor
New York NY 10017
212/682-2913
E-mail: info@kingfoundation.org
Internet: http://www.king foundation.org
AMOUNT: $2,500 (max.)
DEADLINE(S): APR 15
FIELD(S): Film; Television
ELIGIBILITY/REQUIREMENTS: Open to juniors, seniors, and graduate students who are majoring in television or film at 4-year universities. Must demonstrate academic ability, financial need, and professional potential.
HOW TO APPLY: See your financial aid office or contact Foundation for an application. Must submit transcripts, 3 letters of recommendation, and a typed personal statement.
RENEWABLE: Yes

70—DONNA REED FOUNDATION (Performing Arts Scholarships for High School Seniors)

1305 Broadway
Denison IA 51442
712/263-3334
FAX: 712/263-8026
E-mail: info@donnareed.org
Internet: http://www.donnareed.org
AMOUNT: $200-$1,000
DEADLINE(S): JUN 1
FIELD(S) Acting, Musical Theater
ELIGIBILITY/REQUIREMENTS: Must demonstrate excellence and a high level of interest in the performing arts; be a current high school senior, a U.S. citizen or permanent resident of U.S. or U.S. territory, and enrolled in the Donna Reed Performing Arts Workshop Program and perform in the final competition.
HOW TO APPLY: Must submit a video or DVD for consideration in each category. Students may audition in both Acting and Musical Theater, but each category entry has different length requirements and must be made with a separate video or DVD. See website or contact Foundation for application and additional information.
NUMBER OF AWARDS: 6 (3 in each category, 1st, 2nd and 3rd place)

71—DONNA REED FOUNDATION (Performing Arts Scholarships for Iowa Students)

1305 Broadway
Denison IA 51442
712/263-3334
FAX: 712/263-8026

E-mail: info@donnareed.org
Internet: http://www.donnareed.org
AMOUNT: $500
DEADLINE(S): JUN 17 (on-site)
FIELD(S) Acting, Musical Theater
ELIGIBILITY/REQUIREMENTS: Must reside in and attend school in the state for the academic year and must register as a full-time student for the Festival.
HOW TO APPLY: Auditions held during the Festival. May perform a monologue, song, or original piece. This award has no categories. Audition time is limited to 3 minutes.
NUMBER OF AWARDS: 2

72—GOLDEN KEY INTERNATIONAL HONOUR SOCIETY—PERFORMING ARTS SHOWCASE

1189 Ponce de Leon Avenue
Atlanta GA 30306
404/377-2400 or 800/377-2401
FAX: 404/373-7033
E-mail: scholarships@goldenkey.org
Internet: http://www.goldenkey.org
AMOUNT: $1,000
DEADLINE(S): MAR 1
FIELD(S): Dance, Drama, Instrumental Performance, Filmmaking, Musical Composition, Vocal Performance
ELIGIBILITY/REQUIREMENTS: This award recognizes performing arts talents of Golden Key members in categories: dance, drama, instrumental performance, filmmaking, musical composition, and vocal performance. Undergraduate, graduate, and post-graduate members who are currently enrolled in classes at a degree-granting program may apply. Award is based on the quality of work submitted.
HOW TO APPLY: Applications must be posted online with Golden Key member number. Entries must be submitted on VHS videotape. (Compact discs and audio-cassettes are accepted for original musical composition ONLY.) Performances may not exceed 10 minutes (except for film-making entries). All submissions become the property of Golden Key. Only one entry per member per category will be accepted. The only way to apply for these scholarships is to do so via the Internet followed by submitting required documentation. See website for further information.
NUMBER OF AWARDS/YEAR: One/category/year
RENEWABLE: No

73—GUSTAVUS ADOLPHUS COLLEGE (Anderson Theatre and Dance Scholarships)

Office of Admission
800 West College Avenue

St. Peter MN 56082
507/933-7676 or 800/GUSTAVUS
E-mail: admission@gustavus.edu
Internet: http://www.gustavus.edu
AMOUNT: $500-$2,000
DEADLINE(S): JAN 1
FIELD(S): Theater; Dance
ELIGIBILITY/REQUIREMENTS:
Scholarships tenable at Gustavus
Adolphus College, St. Peter, Minnesota for
students pursuing studies in theatre and/or
dance. Students may be enrolled in any
major.
HOW TO APPLY: Contact college for
details.
RENEWABLE: Yes. Must participate in a
departmental project and maintain a 3.0
GPA.

74—INSTITUTE FOR HUMANE STUDIES
(Summer Seminars Program)

3401 N. Fairfax Drive, Suite 440
Arlington VA 22201-4432
703/993-4880 or 800/697-8799
FAX: 703/993-4890
Internet: http://www.TheIHS.org
AMOUNT: Free summer seminars,
including room/board, lectures, semi-
nar materials, and books
DEADLINE(S): MAR
FIELD(S): Social Sciences; Humanities;
Law; Journalism; Public Policy;
Education; Film; Writing; Economics;
Philosophy
ELIGIBILITY/REQUIREMENTS: Open
to college students, recent graduates, and
graduate students who share an interest in
learning and exchanging ideas about the
scope of individual rights, free markets, the
rule of law, peace, and tolerance.
HOW TO APPLY: See website for seminar information and to apply online, or
contact IHS for an application.

75—JACKSONVILLE STATE UNIVERSITY
(Drama Scholarship)

Jacksonville AL 36265
256/782-5677 or 1-800/231-5291
Internet: www.jsu.edu
AMOUNT: Varies
DEADLINE(S): FEB 1
FIELD(S): Drama
ELIGIBILITY/REQUIREMENTS: Open
to students with interest in drama.
HOW TO APPLY: Contact Drama Depart-
ment for application and details.
RENEWABLE: Yes
CONTACT: Drama Department, 256/782-
5623

76—JOURNALISM EDUCATION
ASSOCIATION (Ryan White Excellence in
Journalism Award, The)

Kansas State University
103 Kedzie Hall
Manhattan KS 66506-1505
785/532-5532
FAX: 785/532-5563
E-mail: jea@spub.ksu.edu
Internet: http://www.jea.org
AMOUNT: $50-$500
DEADLINE(S): OCT 30
FIELD(S): Journalism on Health issues
ELIGIBILITY/REQUIREMENTS:
Applicants (or team of students who
worked on the same entry) must be high
school students who are members of the
staff of their high school newspaper, news
magazine, yearbook, literary art magazine,
Web page, radio station, or TV station.
The entry must be a feature, an editorial,
or a commentary; original student work;
and must publish or broadcast within a
year of the contest deadline.
HOW TO APPLY: Send completed application with (if print medium) a copy of the
published feature, editorial, or commentary, or (if broadcast medium) a taped
copy/URL, with a typed transcript of the
Web, radio, or television entries. Also send
a statement in the sources used for background information; a list of individuals
interviewed (include job title or why
selected); and whether there was response
to this work from the applicant's community (i.e., high school, city, county, or a targeted segment of the population).
NUMBER OF AWARDS: 6
RENEWABLE: No
CONTACT: Carol Lange at langejour
@aol.com

77—JOURNALISM EDUCATION
ASSOCIATION (Sister Rita Jeanne High
School Journalist of the Year Scholarships)

Kansas State University
103 Kedzie Hall
Manhattan KS 66506-1505
785/532-5532
FAX: 785/532-5563
E-mail: jea@spub.ksu.edu
Internet: http://www.jea.org
AMOUNT: $2,000-$5,000
DEADLINE(S): FEB 15
FIELD(S): Journalism
ELIGIBILITY/REQUIREMENTS:
Applicant must be a graduating high
school senior; be planning to study journal-
ism or mass communications in college and
to pursue a journalism or mass communi-

cations career; have at least a 3.0 GPA;
have participated in high school journalism
for at least 2 years; submit a portfolio; be a
state winner; and be a student of a JEA
member advisor.
HOW TO APPLY: Send completed application with a portfolio that includes: a self-
analytical evaluation of your "journalistic
life," using your most creative form; an
action photo of you doing something journalistic (e.g., interviewing someone, taking
a photograph, designing a page, doing a
broadcast standup), copy of your transcript; 3-4 letters of recommendation from
your advisor, other teachers who know
your leadership and journalistic abilities,
and practitioners with whom you have
worked (a letter from the principal is desirable); samples of your work, demonstrating its quality and diversity. Photocopies of
letters, clippings and art are acceptable,
but original prints of photographs should
accompany entries based on published pictures. Send 1 issue of your newspaper or
magazine or photocopies of relevant
spreads from your yearbook (not the
entire book). Send entire portfolio package to your state contest coordinator; do
NOT mail your entry to JEA
Headquarters. Entry material should not
exceed 36 one-sided or 18 two-sided pages.
NUMBER OF AWARDS: 7
RENEWABLE: No
CONTACT: State Contest Coordinator.
For a list see www.jea.org/contact/state-
directors.html.

78—KATU THOMAS R. DARGAN
MINORITY SCHOLARSHIP

Human Resources
P.O. Box 2
Portland OR 97207-0002
Internet: http://www.katu.com/
about/scholarship
AMOUNT: $4,000
DEADLINE(S): APR 30
FIELD(S): Broadcast Communications
ELIGIBILITY/REQUIREMENTS:
Applicant must be a minority citizen of the
United States (i.e., Native American,
African American, Hispanic, or Asian); be
enrolled in the 1st, 2nd, or 3rd year of a
broadcast communications curriculum at a
4-year college or university or an accredit-
ed community college in Oregon or
Washington, or as a permanent resident of
Oregon or Washington attending an out-
of-state institution; and have a minimum
GPA of 3.0. Community college students
must be enrolled in a broadcast curriculum
that is transferable to a 4-year accredited
university.

HOW TO APPLY: Send completed application; statement of need that includes an estimate of the cost of one year at your institution and a list of other resources of financial assistance, such as grants, scholarships, funding from parents, etc.; official transcripts; 3 letters of recommendation (2 from academic sources, 1 personal); and an essay describing your personal and professional goals, i.e., what you perceive will be your contribution as a minority in the field of broadcasting.
NUMBER OF AWARDS: 1
RENEWABLE: Yes. Annually

79—LIBERACE FOUNDATION FOR THE PERFORMING AND CREATIVE ARTS

1775 East Tropicana Avenue
Las Vegas NV 89119-6529
702/798-5595
FAX: 702/798-7386
E-mail: foundation@liberace.org
Internet: http://www.liberace.org
AMOUNT: Varies
DEADLINE(S): MAR 15
FIELD(S): Music (Instrumental and Vocal); Theater; Dance; Visual Arts; Fine Art
ELIGIBILITY/REQUIREMENTS: Provides grants to accredited institutions that offer training in above fields. Grants are to be used exclusively for scholarship assistance to talented and deserving students. Recipients should be promising and deserving upperclassmen (junior, senior, graduate) enrolled in a course of study leading up to a career in the arts.
HOW TO APPLY: See website or write to above address for details.
RENEWABLE: Yes
CONTACT: Joel Strote

80—MANA, A National Latina Organization (Rita DiMartino Scholarship)

1725 K Street NW, Suite 105
Washington DC 20006
202/833-0060
FAX: 202/496-0588
E-mail: Hermana2@aol.com
Internet: http://www.hermana.org
AMOUNT: Varies
DEADLINE(S): FEB 28
FIELD(S): Communications; Journalism
ELIGIBILITY/REQUIREMENTS: For Hispanic female students enrolled in undergraduate programs in communication at accredited colleges or universities. Must demonstrate financial need and academic achievement. Must be MANA member.

HOW TO APPLY: Download application from website or call national office. There is a $10 application fee.
NUMBER OF AWARDS: Varies
RENEWABLE: No
CONTACT: Alma Morales Riojas

81—MINNESOTA GAY/LESBIAN/ BISEXUAL/TRANSGENDER EDUCATIONAL FUND ("Green and Yellow TV" Award)

Philanthrofund Foundation
1409 Willow Street, Suite 305
Minneapolis MN 55403-3251
612/220-4888
FAX: 612/871-6587
E-mail: philanth@scc.net
Internet: http://www.scc.net/~t-bonham/EDFUND.HTM
AMOUNT: $500
DEADLINE(S): FEB 1
FIELD(S): All (emphasis on journalism/media)
ELIGIBILITY/REQUIREMENTS: Open to GLBT students who will be enrolled in a post-secondary program or planning to attend a post-secondary program during the next academic year; must be a Minnesota resident. Special consideration will be given to youth considering a career in the field of journalism or media (including newspaper, radio, TV, film, or video). Criteria include applicant's affirmation of their GLBT identity; demonstrated integrity and honesty, participation and leadership in community activities, and service as role model, mentor, colleague or advisor for the GLBT community. Purpose is to recognize outstanding GLBT students and activities, to support the continuing education for self-identified GLBT persons, and to foster a positive public image of GLBT people in society.
HOW TO APPLY: See website for application or contact Minnesota GLBT Educational Fund for an application. Submit application by mail. E-mail or faxed materials will not be accepted.
RENEWABLE: No

82—NATIONAL ASSOCIATION OF HISPANIC JOURNALISTS (Cristina Saralegui Scholarship Program)

1000 National Press Building
529 14th Street NW
Washington DC 20045-2001
202/662-7145
E-mail: nahj@nahj.org
Internet: http://www.nahj.org
AMOUNT: $5,000
FIELD(S): Journalism

ELIGIBILITY/REQUIREMENTS: Applicants must be current college students fluent in Spanish, planning to pursue a career in broadcast journalism.
CONTACT: Nancy Tita

83—NATIONAL ASSOCIATION OF HISPANIC JOURNALISTS (NAHJ ABC News Joanna Bistany Memorial Scholarship Program)

1000 National Press Building
529 14th Street NW
Washington DC 20045-2001
202/662-7145
FAX: 202/662-7144
E-mail: kolivas@nahj.org
Internet: http://www.nahj.org
AMOUNT: $5,000
DEADLINE(S): JAN (last Friday)
FIELD(S): Broadcast Journalism; Producers
ELIGIBILITY/REQUIREMENTS: College undergraduates and first-year graduate students who are pursuing careers as English-language television journalists or producers.
HOW TO APPLY: See website for an application. Do NOT write or call for application.
RENEWABLE: No

84—NATIONAL ASSOCIATION OF HISPANIC JOURNALISTS (NAHJ Maria Elena Salinas Scholarship Program)

1000 National Press Building
529 14th Street NW
Washington DC 20045-2001
202/662-7145
FAX: 202/662-7144
E-mail: kolivas@nahj.org
Internet: http://www.nahj.org
AMOUNT: $5,000
DEADLINE(S): JAN (last Friday)
FIELD(S): Print/Broadcast Journalism; Producers
ELIGIBILITY/REQUIREMENTS: Bilingual high school seniors, college undergraduates, and first-year graduate students who are pursuing careers as Spanish-language television or radio journalists or producers. Applicants MUST be fluent in Spanish. Recipient is required to intern at a Newhouse newspaper following their junior year.
HOW TO APPLY: See website for an application. Do NOT write or call for application. Applicants must also write an essay IN SPANISH that explains why they seek a career as a Spanish-language broad-

cast journalist. They must also submit work samples that are written in Spanish.
RENEWABLE: No

85—NATIONAL ASSOCIATION OF HISPANIC JOURNALISTS (NAHJ Newhouse Scholarship Program)

1000 National Press Building
529 14th Street NW
Washington DC 20045-2001
202/662-7145
FAX: 202/662-7144
E-mail: kolivas@nahj.org
Internet: http://www.nahj.org
AMOUNT: $5,000/year (2-year scholarship)
DEADLINE(S): FEB 25
FIELD(S): Journalism; Photojournalism
ELIGIBILITY/REQUIREMENTS: Applicants MUST be sophomores who are committed to pursuing a career in English-language (NOT Spanish-language) newspaper journalism as reporters, editors, photographers, or graphic artists. Award will be for junior and senior years. Recipient is required to intern at a Newhouse newspaper following their junior year.
HOW TO APPLY: See website for an application. Do NOT write or call for application.
RENEWABLE: No

86—NATIONAL ASSOCIATION OF HISPANIC JOURNALISTS (NAHJ Newsroom Bound Program)

1000 National Press Building
529 14th Street NW
Washington DC 20045-2001
202/662-7145
FAX: 202/662-7144
E-mail: kolivas@nahj.org
Internet: http://www.nahj.org
AMOUNT: $1,000
DEADLINE(S): JAN (last Friday)
FIELD(S): Journalism; Photojournalism
ELIGIBILITY/REQUIREMENTS: For college freshmen and sophomores who are pursuing careers in English-language print, photo, broadcast, or online journalism; NAHJ will select students from among its scholarship recipients.
HOW TO APPLY: See website for an application. Do NOT write or call for application.
RENEWABLE: No

87—NATIONAL ASSOCIATION OF HISPANIC JOURNALISTS (NAHJ Rubén Salazar Scholarships)

1000 National Press Building
529 14th Street NW

Washington DC 20045-2001
202/662-7145
FAX: 202/662-7144
E-mail: kolivas@nahj.org
Internet: http://www.nahj.org
AMOUNT: $1,000-$2,000
DEADLINE(S): JAN (last Friday)
FIELD(S): Print/Broadcast Journalism; Photojournalism
ELIGIBILITY/REQUIREMENTS: Open to high school seniors, undergraduates, and first-year graduate students who are committed to a career in print or broadcast journalism or photojournalism. Tenable at 2- or 4-year schools in the U.S. and its territories. Hispanic ancestry NOT required.
HOW TO APPLY: See website for an application. Do NOT write or call for application.
RENEWABLE: No

88—NATIONAL PRESS CLUB (Ellen Masin Persina Scholarship for Minorities in Journalism)

529 14th Street NW, 13th Floor
Washington DC 20045-2001
Internet: http://press.org/activities/scholarships.cfm
AMOUNT: $5,000/year for 4 years
DEADLINE(S): MAR 1
FIELD(S): Journalism (newspaper, radio, TV, magazine, trade paper)
ELIGIBILITY/REQUIREMENTS: Scholarships for talented high school senior minorities planning to pursue a career in journalism (see above fields). Must provide work samples, an essay, letters of recommendation, etc. Minimum 2.75 GPA required.
HOW TO APPLY: Access application from website or address above.
RENEWABLE: 4-year scholarship

89—NATIVE AMERICAN JOURNALISTS ASSOCIATION (NAJA Scholarships and Internships)

University of South Dakota
414 E. Clark Street
Vermillion SD 57069
605/677-5282
FAX: 605/694-4264
E-mail: info@naja.com
Internet: http://www.naja.com
AMOUNT: $1,000-$3,000
DEADLINE(S): APR 15
FIELD(S): Journalism (print, broadcast, photojournalism, new media, journalism education)
ELIGIBILITY/REQUIREMENTS: Must be Native American pursuing journalism

degree at institution of higher learning and a current member of NAJA.
HOW TO APPLY: Cover letter stating financial need, area of interest (see above), and reasons for pursuing a career in journalism. Include 3 letters of recommendation from academic advisor, counselor, or a professional individual familiar with applicant's background and skills; 2 copies of transcript, work samples (if available), proof of enrollment in a federal or state-recognized tribe (if not enrolled, briefly explain). Application fee $20.

90—NEW YORK STATE THEATRE INSTITUTE (Internships in Theatrical Production)

37 First Street
Troy NY 12180
518/274-3200
E-mail: nysti@capital.net
Internet: http://www.nysti.org/not-for-profit/nysti/int.htm
AMOUNT: None
DEADLINE(S): None
FIELD(S): Theatrical Production and related fields
ELIGIBILITY/REQUIREMENTS: Internships for college and graduate students, high school seniors, and educators-in-residence interested in developing skills in above fields. Unpaid academic credit is earned. Gain experience in box office, costumes, education, electrics, music, stage management, scenery, properties, performance, and public relations. Interns come from all over the world.
HOW TO APPLY: Must be associated with an accredited institution. See website for more information, call or write. Include your postal mailing address.
CONTACT: Arlene Leff, Intern Program Director, 518/274-3573

91—OUTDOOR WRITERS ASSOCIATION OF AMERICA (OWAA Scholarship Awards)

121 Hickory Street
Missoula MT 59801
406/728-7434
FAX: 406/728-7445
E-mail: owaaa@montana.com
Internet: http://www.owaa.org
AMOUNT: $2,500-$3,500
DEADLINE(S): MAR 1
FIELD(S): Communications; Journalism; Film; Broadcasting; Photography
ELIGIBILITY/REQUIREMENTS: Open to junior and senior undergraduates and graduate students. Must attend an accredited school of journalism or mass communications that has registered with OWAA as a scholarship program participant.

Selection based on career goals in outdoor communications, examples of work, letters of recommendation, and academic achievement. Must be U.S. or Canadian citizen or permanent resident.
HOW TO APPLY: See website for application or contact your school or send a SASE to Executive Director for guidelines.
NUMBER OF AWARDS: At least 3
CONTACT: Steve Wagner, Executive Director

92—RADIO AND TELEVISION NEWS DIRECTORS ASSOCIATION & FOUNDATION (Carole Simpson Scholarship)

1600 K Street NW, Suite 700
Washington DC 20006
202/467-5218
FAX: 202/223-4007
E-mail: melaniel@rtndf.org
Internet: http://www.rtndf.org
AMOUNT: $2,000
DEADLINE(S): MAY 3
FIELD(S): All (emphasis on Electronic Journalism)
ELIGIBILITY/REQUIREMENTS: College sophomore or higher with at least one full year of college remaining may apply. May be enrolled in any major so long as applicant intends a career in television or radio news. Preference given to an undergraduate student of color.
HOW TO APPLY: Submit application along with a résumé, 1-3 examples of work demonstrating journalistic skills (15 minutes or less on audio or video cassette accompanied by script); brief statement describing your role (writing, editing, producing, reporting, videography) in each story and a list of colleagues, if any, who worked on each story and what they did; a 1-page statement explaining interest in career in broadcast or cable journalism, with reference to your specific career preferences (radio or television, reporting, producing or newsroom management), and letter of reference from dean or faculty sponsor. See website for application or contact Project Coordinator.
NUMBER OF AWARDS: 1
CONTACT: Melanie Lo, Program Coordinator
ADDITIONAL INFORMATION: All winners receive travel, hotel accommodation and registration to annual convention.

93—RADIO AND TELEVISION NEWS DIRECTORS ASSOCIATION & FOUNDATION (Ed Bradley Scholarship)

1600 K Street NW, Suite 700
Washington DC 20006
202/467-5218

FAX: 202/223-4007
E-mail: melaniel@rtndf.org
Internet: http://www.rtndf.org
AMOUNT: $10,000
DEADLINE(S): MAY 3
FIELD(S): All (emphasis on Electronic Journalism)
ELIGIBILITY/REQUIREMENTS: College sophomore or higher with at least one full year of college remaining may apply. May be enrolled in any major so long as applicant intends a career in television or radio news. Preference given to an undergraduate student of color.
HOW TO APPLY: Submit application along with a résumé, 1-3 examples of work demonstrating journalistic skills (15 minutes or less on audio or video cassette accompanied by script); brief statement describing your role (writing, editing, producing, reporting, videography) in each story and a list of colleagues, if any, who worked on each story and what they did; a 1-page statement explaining interest in career in broadcast or cable journalism, with reference to your specific career preferences (radio or television, reporting, producing or newsroom management), and letter of reference from dean or faculty sponsor. See website for application or contact Project Coordinator.
NUMBER OF AWARDS: 1
CONTACT: Melanie Lo
ADDITIONAL INFORMATION: All winners receive travel, hotel accommodation and registration to annual convention.

94—RADIO AND TELEVISION NEWS DIRECTORS ASSOCIATION & FOUNDATION (George Foreman Tribute to Lyndon B. Johnson Scholarship)

1600 K Street NW, Suite 700
Washington DC 20006
202/467-5218
FAX: 202/223-4007
E-mail: melaniel@rtndf.org
Internet: http://www.rtndf.org
AMOUNT: $6,000
DEADLINE(S): MAY 3
FIELD(S): Broadcast/Cable Journalism
ELIGIBILITY/REQUIREMENTS: Any full-time graduate or undergraduate with at least one full year of college remaining may apply. Must be officially enrolled in University of Texas in Austin, in good standing, and a U.S. citizen. Entry must include 1-3 examples (less than 15 minutes) showing skills on audio/VHS tape, accompanied by scripts and brief statement describing applicant's role in stories, who worked on each one, and what each person did. Letter of endorsement and statement explaining career goals required.

HOW TO APPLY: See website or contact Project Coordinator.
NUMBER OF AWARDS: 1
CONTACT: Melanie Lo, Program Coordinator
ADDITIONAL INFORMATION: All winners receive travel, hotel accommodation and registration to annual convention.

95—RADIO AND TELEVISION NEWS DIRECTORS ASSOCIATION & FOUNDATION (Ken Kashiwahara Scholarship)

1600 K Street NW, Suite 700
Washington DC 20006
202/467-5218
FAX: 202/223-4007
E-mail: melaniel@rtndf.org
Internet: http://www.rtndf.org
AMOUNT: $2,500
DEADLINE(S): MAY 3
FIELD(S): All
ELIGIBILITY/REQUIREMENTS: Open to sophomores, juniors, and seniors currently enrolled in college (must have at least one full year remaining). Preference is given to student of color. May be enrolled in any major, but must intend a career in television or radio news.
HOW TO APPLY: See website or contact Project Coordinator.
NUMBER OF AWARDS: 1
CONTACT: Melanie Lo, Program Coordinator
ADDITIONAL INFORMATION: All winners receive travel, hotel accommodation and registration to annual convention.

96—RADIO AND TELEVISION NEWS DIRECTORS ASSOCIATION & FOUNDATION (Lou and Carole Prato Sports Reporting Scholarship)

1600 K Street NW, Suite 700
Washington DC 20006
202/467-5218
FAX: 202/223-4007
E-mail: melaniel@rtndf.org
Internet: http://www.rtndf.org
AMOUNT: $1,000
DEADLINE(S): MAY 5
FIELD(S): All (emphasis on Broadcast/Cable Journalism)
ELIGIBILITY/REQUIREMENTS: College sophomore or higher with at least one full year of college remaining may apply. May be enrolled in any major so long as applicant intends a career as a sports reporter in television or radio.
HOW TO APPLY: Submit application along with a résumé, 1-3 examples of work demonstrating journalistic skills (15 minutes or less on audio or video cassette

accompanied by script); brief statement describing your role (writing, editing, producing, reporting, videography) in each story and a list of colleagues, if any, who worked on each story and what they did; a 1-page statement explaining interest in career in broadcast or cable journalism, with reference to your specific career preferences (radio or television, reporting, producing or newsroom management), and letter of reference from dean or faculty sponsor. See website for application or contact Project Coordinator.
NUMBER OF AWARDS: 1
CONTACT: Melanie Lo, Program Coordinator
ADDITIONAL INFORMATION: All winners receive travel, hotel accommodation and registration to annual convention.

97—RADIO AND TELEVISION NEWS DIRECTORS ASSOCIATION & FOUNDATION (Mike Reynolds Scholarship)

1600 K Street NW, Suite 700
Washington DC 20006
202/467-5218
FAX: 202/223-4007
E-mail: melaniel@rtndf.org
Internet: http://www.rtndf.org
AMOUNT: $1,000
DEADLINE(S): MAY 3
FIELD(S): All (emphasis on Broadcast/Cable Journalism)
ELIGIBILITY/REQUIREMENTS: College sophomore or higher with at least one full year of college remaining may apply. May be enrolled in any major so long as applicant intends a career in television or radio news. Preference given to an undergraduate student demonstrating need for financial assistance by indicating media-related jobs held and contribution made to funding his or her own education.
HOW TO APPLY: Submit application along with a résumé, 1-3 examples of work demonstrating journalistic skills (15 minutes or less on audio or video cassette accompanied by script); brief statement describing your role (writing, editing, producing, reporting, videography) in each story and a list of colleagues, if any, who worked on each story and what they did; a 1-page statement explaining interest in career in broadcast or cable journalism, with reference to your specific career preferences (radio or television, reporting, producing or newsroom management), and letter of reference from dean or faculty sponsor. Must submit FAFSA. See website for application or contact Project Coordinator.
NUMBER OF AWARDS: 1

CONTACT: Melanie Lo, Program Coordinator
ADDITIONAL INFORMATION: All winners receive travel, hotel accommodation and registration to annual convention.

98—RADIO AND TELEVISION NEWS DIRECTORS ASSOCIATION & FOUNDATION (Pete Wilson Journalism Scholarship)

1600 K Street NW, Suite 700
Washington DC 20006
202/467-5218
FAX: 202/223-4007
E-mail: melaniel@rtndf.org
Internet: http://www.rtndf.org
AMOUNT: $4,000
DEADLINE(S): MAY 3
FIELD(S): All (emphasis on Broadcast/Cable Journalism)
ELIGIBILITY/REQUIREMENTS: College sophomore or higher with at least one full year of college remaining may apply. May be enrolled in any major so long as applicant intends a career in television or radio news. Open to students from the Bay Area pursuing a journalism undergraduate or graduate degree.
HOW TO APPLY: Submit application along with a résumé, 1-3 examples of work demonstrating journalistic skills (15 minutes or less on audio or video cassette accompanied by script); brief statement describing your role (writing, editing, producing, reporting, videography) in each story and a list of colleagues, if any, who worked on each story and what they did; a 1-page statement explaining interest in career in broadcast or cable journalism, with reference to your specific career preferences (radio or television, reporting, producing or newsroom management), and letter of reference from dean or faculty sponsor. See website for application or contact Project Coordinator.
NUMBER OF AWARDS: 1
CONTACT: Melanie Lo, Program Coordinator
ADDITIONAL INFORMATION: All winners receive travel, hotel accommodation and registration to annual convention.

99—RADIO AND TELEVISION NEWS DIRECTORS ASSOCIATION & FOUNDATION (Presidents' Scholarships)

1600 K Street NW, Suite 700
Washington DC 20006
202/467-5218
FAX: 202/223-4007
E-mail: melaniel@rtnda.org
Internet: http://www.rtndf.org
AMOUNT: $2,500

DEADLINE(S): MAY 3
FIELD(S): All
ELIGIBILITY/REQUIREMENTS: Open to sophomores, juniors, and seniors currently enrolled in college (must have at least one full year remaining). May be enrolled in any major, but must intend a career in television or radio news.
HOW TO APPLY: See website or contact Project Coordinator.
NUMBER OF AWARDS: 2
CONTACT: Melanie Lo, Program Coordinator
ADDITIONAL INFORMATION: All winners receive travel, hotel accommodation and registration to annual convention.

100—RHYTHM AND HUES STUDIOS (Computer Graphics Scholarship)

5404 Jandy Place
Los Angeles CA 90066
310/448-7500
E-mail: scholarship@rhythm.com
Internet: http://www.rhythm.com/recruiting/scholarship/index.html
AMOUNT: $1,000-$4,000
DEADLINE(S): Mid MAY
FIELD(S): Computer Modeling; Computer Character Animation; Digital Cinematography
ELIGIBILITY/REQUIREMENTS: Open to all students enrolled full time in an accredited undergraduate or graduate degree program within 6 months of the deadline.
HOW TO APPLY: Entries should include cover sheet stating name, address, phone, SSN, school, major, faculty advisor name/address/phone, and category under which entry is being submitted. Also include photocopy of current student ID and typewritten description of entry, including hardware/software used. Contact Rhythm and Hues Studios for more information.
NUMBER OF AWARDS: 5 (1 award in modeling, 1 in animation, and 3 in cinematography)

101—SOUTHERN ILLINOIS UNIVERSITY (Music Scholarships)

School of Music, Mailcode 4302
Carbondale IL 62901-4302
618/536-8742
FAX: 618/453-5808
Internet:http://www.siu.edu/music/resources/scholarships.html
AMOUNT: Varies
DEADLINE(S): MAR 15
FIELD(S): Music Performance, Composition, Theater, Music Business, Music Education
ELIGIBILITY/REQUIREMENTS: Must be music major or minor.

HOW TO APPLY: An audition is required, usually held in February. A personal audition or taped audition can be arranged. See website or Undergraduate Office, School of Music.
RENEWABLE: Yes. Recommendation of music faculty required.
CONTACT: Dr. Jeanine Wagner

102—TEXAS BROADCAST EDUCATION FOUNDATION (Belo Corporation Scholarship)

502 East 11th Street, Suite 200
Austin TX 78701
512/322-9944
FAX: 512/322-0522
E-mail: craig@tab.org
Internet: http://www.tab.org
AMOUNT: $2,000
DEADLINE(S): MAY 7
FIELD(S): Broadcasting; Communications
ELIGIBILITY/REQUIREMENTS: Junior or senior student enrolled in a fully accredited program that emphasizes radio or television broadcasting or communications at a 4-year Texas college or university.
HOW TO APPLY: Download application from website.
NUMBER OF AWARDS: 1
CONTACT: Craig Bean

103—TEXAS BROADCAST EDUCATION FOUNDATION (Bonner McLane Scholarship)

502 East 11th Street, Suite 200
Austin TX 78701
512/322-9944
FAX: 512/322-0522
E-mail: craig@tab.org
Internet: http://www.tab.org
AMOUNT: $2,000
DEADLINE(S): MAY 7
FIELD(S): Broadcasting; Communications
ELIGIBILITY/REQUIREMENTS: Junior or senior student enrolled in a fully accredited program that emphasizes radio or television broadcasting or communications at a 4-year Texas college or university.
HOW TO APPLY: Download application from website.
NUMBER OF AWARDS: 1
CONTACT: Craig Bean

104—TEXAS BROADCAST EDUCATION FOUNDATION (Lady Bird Johnson Internship)

502 East 11th Street, Suite 200
Austin TX 78701
512/322-9944

FAX: 512/322-0522
E-mail: craig@tab.org
Internet: http://www.tab.org
AMOUNT: $2,000
DEADLINE(S): MAY 7
FIELD(S): Broadcasting; Communications
ELIGIBILITY/REQUIREMENTS: University of Texas at Austin student in a program with an emphasis on communications. This award will be made in the name of Lady Bird Johnson and the recipient will intern at the Lady Bird Johnson Wildflower Center.
HOW TO APPLY: Download application from website.
NUMBER OF AWARDS: 1
CONTACT: Craig Bean

105—TEXAS BROADCAST EDUCATION FOUNDATION (Tom Reiff Scholarship)

502 East 11th Street, Suite 200
Austin TX 78701
512/322-9944
FAX: 512/322-0522
E-mail: craig@tab.org
Internet: http://www.tab.org
AMOUNT: $2,000
DEADLINE(S): MAY 7
FIELD(S): Broadcasting; Communications
ELIGIBILITY/REQUIREMENTS: Upcoming junior or senior student enrolled in a fully accredited program that emphasizes radio or television broadcasting or communications at a 4-year Texas college or university.
HOW TO APPLY: Download application from website.
NUMBER OF AWARDS: 1
CONTACT: Craig Bean

106—TEXAS BROADCAST EDUCATION FOUNDATION (Two- and Four-Year Scholarship Programs)

502 East 11th Street, Suite 200
Austin TX 78701
512/322-9944
FAX: 512/322-0522
E-mail: craig@tab.org
Internet: http://www.tab.org
AMOUNT: $2,000
DEADLINE(S): MAY 7
FIELD(S): Broadcasting; Communications
ELIGIBILITY/REQUIREMENTS: Must attend Texas school, and program of study must emphasize communications or broadcasting. 4-year program: Must be a freshman or sophomore enrolled in a fully accredited program of instruction at a 4-

year college; 2-year program: Must be enrolled in a program of instruction at a 2-year or technical school.
HOW TO APPLY: Download application from website.
NUMBER OF AWARDS: 2
CONTACT: Craig Bean

107—TEXAS BROADCAST EDUCATION FOUNDATION (Vann Kennedy Scholarship)

502 East 11th Street, Suite 200
Austin TX 78701
512/322-9944
FAX: 512/322-0522
E-mail: craig@tab.org
Internet: http://www.tab.org
AMOUNT: $2,000
DEADLINE(S): MAY 7
FIELD(S): Broadcasting; Communications
ELIGIBILITY/REQUIREMENTS: Student enrolled in a fully accredited program that emphasizes radio or television broadcasting or communications at a Texas college or university.
HOW TO APPLY: Download application from website.
NUMBER OF AWARDS: 1
CONTACT: Craig Bean

108—TEXAS BROADCAST EDUCATION FOUNDATION (Wendell Mayes, Jr. Scholarship)

502 East 11th Street, Suite 200
Austin TX 78701
512/322-9944
FAX: 512/322-0522
E-mail: craig@tab.org
Internet: http://www.tab.org
AMOUNT: $2,000
DEADLINE(S): MAY 7
FIELD(S): Broadcasting; Communications
ELIGIBILITY/REQUIREMENTS: Student enrolled in a fully accredited program that emphasizes radio or television broadcasting or communications at a Texas college or university.
HOW TO APPLY: Download application from website.
NUMBER OF AWARDS: 1
CONTACT: Craig Bean

109—UNITED METHODIST COMMUNICATIONS (Leonard Perryman Communications Scholarships)

Communications Resourcing Team
P.O. Box 320
Nashville TN 37202-0320
888/278-4862
FAX: 615/742-5485

E-mail: scholarships@umcom.org
Internet: http://www.umcom.org/
scholarships
AMOUNT: $2,500
DEADLINE(S): MAR 15
FIELD(S): Journalism/Communications
ELIGIBILITY/REQUIREMENTS: Open
to United Methodist students who are ethnic
minority undergraduate juniors and seniors
enrolled in accredited U.S. schools of com-
munication or journalism (print, electronic,
or audiovisual). Candidates should be pur-
suing career in communication.
HOW TO APPLY: See website or contact
at UMC for an application.
NUMBER OF AWARDS: 1
RENEWABLE: No
CONTACT: Amelia Tucker-Shaw

110—UNIVERSITY FILM AND VIDEO ASSOCIATION (Carole Fielding Student Grants)

Framington State College
100 State Street
Framington MA 01701
Internet: http://www.ufva.org/
publication.php
AMOUNT: $1,000-$4,000
DEADLINE(S): DEC 15
FIELD(S): Film, video, multimedia produc-
tion, research, animation, new media
ELIGIBILITY/REQUIREMENTS: Open
to undergraduate and graduate students.
Categories are narrative, experimental,
animation, documentary, multimedia.
Applicant must be sponsored by a faculty
member who is an active member of the
University Film and Video Association.
HOW TO APPLY: Write or see website
for application and complete details.
NUMBER OF AWARDS: 5 (1 in each
category)
CONTACT: Professor Robert Johnson,
UFVA Carole Fielding Grants Chair

111—UNIVERSITY FILM AND VIDEO FOUNDATION (Kodak Scholarship Endowment Fund)

SMPTE
595 West Hartsdale Avenue
White Plains NY 10607
Internet: http://www.kodak.com
AMOUNT: $5,000 (max.)
DEADLINE(S): Varies (spring)
FIELD(S): Cinematography
ELIGIBILITY/REQUIREMENTS: Open
to junior, senior, and graduate-level stu-
dents of cinematography at U.S. colleges
and universities offering degree programs
(BA, BFA, MA, or MFA) in motion pic-
ture filmmaking.

HOW TO APPLY: Nomination requires
endorsement of the applicant's school's fac-
ulty/administration as to the outstanding
potential and cinematographic ability of the
student. School must conduct portfolio
review to nominate up to two candidates.

112—UNIVERSITY OF ILLINOIS AT URBANA-CHAMPAIGN (Lydia E. Parker Bates Scholarship)

620 East John Street
Champaign IL 61820
217/333-0100
Internet: http://www.uiuc.edu/
AMOUNT: Up to $1,000
DEADLINE(S): MAR 15
FIELD(S): Art, Architecture, Landscape
Architecture, Urban Planning, Dance,
Theater, and all related subjects except
Music
ELIGIBILITY/REQUIREMENTS: Open
to undergraduate students in the College
of Fine and Applied Arts who are attend-
ing the University of Illinois at Urbana-
Champaign. Must demonstrate financial
need and have 2.85 GPA. Recipients must
carry at least 12 credit hours per semester.
HOW TO APPLY: Contact office of stu-
dent financial aid for application. Complete
the Free Application for Federal Student
Aid with UIUC admission application.
NUMBER OF AWARDS: 175

113—VIRGINIA MUSEUM OF FINE ARTS (Fellowships)

200 North Boulevard
Richmond VA 23220-4007
804/204-2661
Internet: http://vmfa.state.va.us
AMOUNT: $4,000 (undergraduate-maxi-
mum); $6,000 (graduates); $8,000 (pro-
fessionals)
DEADLINE(S): MAR 1
FIELD(S): Crafts; Drawing; Filmmaking;
Mixed Media Painting; Photography;
Printmaking; Sculpture; Video; Art
History (graduate only)
ELIGIBILITY/REQUIREMENTS: Open
to Virginia residents of at least one year
who are U.S. citizens or legal residents.
Fellowships are available to undergradu-
ates, graduates, and professional artists.
Financial need is considered.
HOW TO APPLY: Application and guide-
lines on website.

114—WESTERN MICHIGAN UNIVERSITY (College of Arts and Sciences/Undergraduate Research and Creative Activities Award)

1903 W. Michigan
Kalamazoo MI 49008-5337

269/387-8777
FAX: 269/387-6989
E-mail: finaid-info@wmich.edu
Internet: http://www.wmich.edu/cas
AMOUNT: $500/semester
DEADLINE(S): MAR 1
FIELD(S): Sciences; Humanities; Social
Sciences; Radio & Television
ELIGIBILITY/REQUIREMENTS:
Applicant must have declared a major in a
department or program in the College of
Arts and Sciences of at least 30 credit
hours; be in good academic standing; and
have a faculty mentor for the project and a
project plan.
HOW TO APPLY: Contact the College of
Arts and Sciences for an application or apply
online or print application from website.
RENEWABLE: Yes. May request renew-
al for 1 additional term.
CONTACT: College of Arts and Sciences

115—WESTERN MICHIGAN UNIVERSITY (College of Arts and Sciences/WWMT Communications Scholarship)

1903 W. Michigan
Kalamazoo MI 49008-5337
269/387-8777
FAX: 269/387-6989
E-mail: finaid-info@wmich.edu
Internet: http://www.wmich.edu/cas
AMOUNT: $1,000
FIELD(S): Television; Communications
ELIGIBILITY/REQUIREMENTS: Full-
time, undergraduate student at WMU in
junior or senior year; Television Broadcast
major with 3.5 GPA.
HOW TO APPLY: Contact the Office of
Communications for further details.
RENEWABLE: No

116—WESTERN MICHIGAN UNIVERSITY (College of Fine Arts/Anna L. Tobin—An Actress—Memorial Scholarship)

1903 W. Michigan
Kalamazoo MI 49008-5337
269/387-8777
E-mail: finaid-info@wmich.edu
Internet: http://www.wmich.edu/
finaid
AMOUNT: Varies
DEADLINE(S): MAR (for current
Theater majors); on acceptance into
program for freshmen and transfer stu-
dents
FIELD(S): Theater Education; Theater
Design; Technical Theater; Arts
Management; Music Theater
Performance

ELIGIBILITY/REQUIREMENTS: Scholarships are ONLY for Theater Majors and Minors. Must have a 3.0 GPA.
HOW TO APPLY: Freshmen or transfer students—by audition/interview and acceptance into major or minor in Theater program. Current Theater majors—by application form from the department.
RENEWABLE: No
CONTACT: Theater Department

117—WESTERN MICHIGAN UNIVERSITY (College of Fine Arts/Beth Louise Critchett Sebaly and Avis Leo "Mike" Sebaly Scholarship)

1903 W. Michigan
Kalamazoo MI 49008-5337
269/387-8777
FAX: 269/387-6989
E-mail: finaid-info@wmich.edu
Internet: http://www.wmich.edu/finaid
AMOUNT: Varies
DEADLINE(S): MAR
FIELD(S): Theater Education; Theater Design; Technical Theater; Arts Management; Music Theater Performance
ELIGIBILITY/REQUIREMENTS: Recipient must be full-time undergraduate student majoring in theater with a concentration in the area of theater production; must demonstrate financial need; have a minimum 2.5 GPA, and maintain satisfactory academic progress as specified by the Office of Student Financial Aid.
HOW TO APPLY: Contact Theater Department for more information.
RENEWABLE: Yes. Up to 4 consecutive academic years.
CONTACT: Theater Department

118—WESTERN MICHIGAN UNIVERSITY (College of Fine Arts/Beulah and Harold McKee Theatre Scholarship)

1903 W. Michigan
Kalamazoo MI 49008-5337
269/387-8777
FAX: 269/387-6989
E-mail: finaid-info@wmich.edu
Internet: http://www.wmich.edu/finaid
AMOUNT: Varies
DEADLINE(S): On acceptance into program
FIELD(S): Theater Education; Theater Design; Technical Theater; Arts Management; Music Theater Performance

ELIGIBILITY/REQUIREMENTS: Freshmen or transfer students accepted into a major or minor in Theater program.
HOW TO APPLY: By application form from the Department and by audition and interview.
RENEWABLE: No
CONTACT: Theater Department

119—WESTERN MICHIGAN UNIVERSITY (College of Fine Arts/Beverly Belson Scholarship Fund for Music Theatre)

1903 W. Michigan
Kalamazoo MI 49008-5337
269/387-8777
FAX: 269/387-6989
E-mail: finaid-info@wmich.edu
Internet: http://www.wmich.edu/finaid
AMOUNT: Varies
DEADLINE(S): MAR (for current Theater majors); on acceptance into program for freshmen and transfer students
FIELD(S): Theater Education; Theater Design; Technical Theater; Arts Management; Music Theater Performance
ELIGIBILITY/REQUIREMENTS: Scholarships are ONLY for Theater majors and minors. Must have a 3.0 GPA.
HOW TO APPLY: Freshmen or transfer students—by audition/interview and acceptance into major or minor in Theater program. Current Theater majors—by application form from the department.
RENEWABLE: No
CONTACT: Theater Department

120—WESTERN MICHIGAN UNIVERSITY (College of Fine Arts/Carol Haenicke University Theater Guild Scholarship)

1903 W. Michigan
Kalamazoo MI 49008-5337
269/387-8777
FAX: 269/387-6989
E-mail: finaid-info@wmich.edu
Internet: http://www.wmich.edu/finaid
AMOUNT: Varies
DEADLINE(S): MAR (for current Theater majors); on acceptance into program for freshmen and transfer students
FIELD(S): Theater Education; Theater Design; Technical Theater; Arts Management; Music Theater Performance
ELIGIBILITY/REQUIREMENTS: Scholarships are ONLY for Theater majors and minors. Must have a 3.0 GPA.

HOW TO APPLY: Freshmen or transfer students—by audition/interview and acceptance into major or minor in Theater program. Current Theater majors—by application form from the department.
RENEWABLE: No
CONTACT: Theater Department

121—WESTERN MICHIGAN UNIVERSITY (College of Fine Arts/David P. Karsten Theater Scholarship)

1903 W. Michigan
Kalamazoo MI 49008-5337
269/387-8777
FAX: 269/387-6989
E-mail: finaid-info@wmich.edu
Internet: http://www.wmich.edu/finaid
AMOUNT: Varies
DEADLINE(S): MAR
FIELD(S): Theater Education; Theater Design; Technical Theater; Arts Management; Music Theater Performance
ELIGIBILITY/REQUIREMENTS: Recipient must be a junior or senior and a full-time student with a GPA of 3.25. Must demonstrate diversity in their curriculum and/or their production/performance experiences on or off campus. Applicants shall provide supporting documentation (if applicable) and demonstrate financial need. Must be U.S. citizen.
HOW TO APPLY: Contact Theater Department for more information.
RENEWABLE: No
CONTACT: Theater Department

122—WESTERN MICHIGAN UNIVERSITY (College of Fine Arts/David Wayne Quasi Endowment Scholarship Fund)

1903 W. Michigan
Kalamazoo MI 49008-5337
269/387-8777
FAX: 269/387-6989
E-mail: finaid-info@wmich.edu
Internet: http://www.wmich.edu/finaid
AMOUNT: Varies
DEADLINE(S): MAR (for current Theater majors); on acceptance into program for freshmen and transfer students
FIELD(S): Theater Education; Theater Design; Technical Theater; Arts Management; Music Theater Performance
ELIGIBILITY/REQUIREMENTS: Scholarships are ONLY for Theater majors and minors. Must have a 3.0 GPA.

HOW TO APPLY: Freshmen or transfer students—by audition/interview and acceptance into major or minor in Theater program. Current Theater majors—by application form from the department.
RENEWABLE: No
CONTACT: Theater Department

123—WESTERN MICHIGAN UNIVERSITY (College of Fine Arts/Diether H. Haenicke British Isles Theater Scholarship Award)

1903 W. Michigan
Kalamazoo MI 49008-5337
269/387-8777
FAX: 269/387-6989
E-mail: finaid-info@wmich.edu
Internet: http://www.wmich.edu/finaid
AMOUNT: $6,000
DEADLINE(S): NOV
FIELD(S): Theater Education; Theater Design; Technical Theater; Arts Management; Music Theater Performance
ELIGIBILITY/REQUIREMENTS: Scholarships are ONLY for Theater majors. Must have a 3.0 GPA.
HOW TO APPLY: By application form from the Department and by audition and interview.
RENEWABLE: No
CONTACT: Theater Department

124—WESTERN MICHIGAN UNIVERSITY (College of Fine Arts/Evelyn Burke Scholarship)

1903 W. Michigan
Kalamazoo MI 49008-5337
269/387-8777
FAX: 269/387-6989
E-mail: finaid-info@wmich.edu
Internet: http://www.wmich.edu/finaid
AMOUNT: Varies
DEADLINE(S): MAR (for current Theater majors); on acceptance into program for freshmen and transfer students
FIELD(S): Theater Education; Theater Design; Technical Theater; Arts Management; Music Theater Performance
ELIGIBILITY/REQUIREMENTS: Scholarships are ONLY for Theater majors and minors. Must have a 3.0 GPA.
HOW TO APPLY: Freshmen or transfer students—by audition/interview and acceptance into major or minor in Theater program. Current Theater majors—by application form from the department.

RENEWABLE: No
CONTACT: Theater Department

125—WESTERN MICHIGAN UNIVERSITY (College of Fine Arts/Hearron-Sommerfeld Music Theater Scholarship)

1903 W. Michigan
Kalamazoo MI 49008-5337
269/387-8777
FAX: 269/387-6989
E-mail: finaid-info@wmich.edu
Internet: http://www.wmich.edu/finaid
AMOUNT: $2,500
DEADLINE(S): MAR
FIELD(S): Theater Education; Theater Design; Technical Theater; Arts Management; Music Theater Performance
ELIGIBILITY/REQUIREMENTS: Recipient must be a junior or senior seeking a BFA degree in Music Theater. Must have a minimum 3.0 GPA.
HOW TO APPLY: Music Theater Faculty Steering Committee evaluates junior and senior candidates to determine an appropriate recipient.
RENEWABLE: No
CONTACT: Theater Department

126—WESTERN MICHIGAN UNIVERSITY (College of Fine Arts/Janet E. Stillwell Music Theater Scholarship)

1903 W. Michigan
Kalamazoo MI 49008-5337
269/387-8777
FAX: 269/387-6989
E-mail: finaid-info@wmich.edu
Internet: http://www.wmich.edu/finaid
AMOUNT: $1,000/semester
DEADLINE(S): MAR (for current Theater majors); on acceptance into program for freshmen and transfer students
FIELD(S): Theater Education; Theater Design; Technical Theater; Arts Management; Music Theater Performance
ELIGIBILITY/REQUIREMENTS: Scholarships are ONLY for Theater majors and minors. Must have a 3.0 GPA.
HOW TO APPLY: Freshmen or transfer students—by audition/interview and acceptance into major or minor in Theater program. Current Theater majors—by application form from the department.
RENEWABLE: No
CONTACT: Theater Department

127—WESTERN MICHIGAN UNIVERSITY (College of Fine Arts/John and Susanna Gemela Memorial Scholarship for Design and Technical Theater)

1903 W. Michigan
Kalamazoo MI 49008-5337
269/387-8777
FAX: 269/387-6989
E-mail: finaid-info@wmich.edu
Internet: http://www.wmich.edu/finaid
AMOUNT: Varies
DEADLINE(S): MAR (for current Theater majors); on acceptance into program for freshmen and transfer students
FIELD(S): Theater Education; Theater Design; Technical Theater; Arts Management; Music Theater Performance
ELIGIBILITY/REQUIREMENTS: Scholarships are ONLY for Theater majors and minors. Must have a 3.0 GPA.
HOW TO APPLY: Freshmen or transfer students—by audition/interview and acceptance into major or minor in Theater program. Current Theater majors—by application form from the department.
RENEWABLE: No
CONTACT: Theater Department

128—WESTERN MICHIGAN UNIVERSITY (College of Fine Arts/Katherine Larsen Scholarship Fund for Theater Education Award)

1903 W. Michigan
Kalamazoo MI 49008-5337
269/387-8777
FAX: 269/387-6989
E-mail: finaid-info@wmich.edu
Internet: http://www.wmich.edu/finaid
AMOUNT: Varies
DEADLINE(S): MAR (for current Theater majors); on acceptance into program for freshmen and transfer students
FIELD(S): Theater Education
ELIGIBILITY/REQUIREMENTS: Scholarships are ONLY for Theater majors and minors. Must have a 3.0 GPA.
HOW TO APPLY: Freshmen or transfer students—by audition/interview and acceptance into major or minor in Theater program. Current Theater majors—by application form from the department.
RENEWABLE: No
CONTACT: Theater Department

129—WESTERN MICHIGAN UNIVERSITY (College of Fine Arts/Laura V. Shaw Quasi Endowment Scholarship Fund)

1903 W. Michigan
Kalamazoo MI 49008-5337
269/387-8777
FAX: 269/387-6989
E-mail: finaid-info@wmich.edu
Internet: http://www.wmich.edu/finaid
AMOUNT: Varies
DEADLINE(S): MAR (for current Theater majors); on acceptance into program for freshmen and transfer students
FIELD(S): Theater Education; Theater Design; Technical Theater; Arts Management; Music Theater Performance
ELIGIBILITY/REQUIREMENTS: Scholarships are ONLY for Theater majors and minors. Must have a 3.0 GPA.
HOW TO APPLY: Freshmen or transfer students—by audition/interview and acceptance into major or minor in Theater program. Current Theater majors—by application form from the department.
RENEWABLE: No
CONTACT: Theater Department

130—WESTERN MICHIGAN UNIVERSITY (College of Fine Arts/Marcella S. and Philip F. Faustman Music Theater Scholarship)

1903 W. Michigan
Kalamazoo MI 49008-5337
269/387-8777
FAX: 269/387-6989
E-mail: finaid-info@wmich.edu
Internet: http://www.wmich.edu/finaid
AMOUNT: Varies
FIELD(S): Theater Education; Theater Design; Technical Theater; Arts Management; Music Theater Performance
ELIGIBILITY/REQUIREMENTS: Recipient must be a full-time junior or senior in the area of music theater in the Department of Theater. Must have a minimum 3.0 GPA.
HOW TO APPLY: By application form from the Department and by audition and interview.
RENEWABLE: No
CONTACT: Theater Department

131—WESTERN MICHIGAN UNIVERSITY (College of Fine Arts/Mary and R. E. Jackson Scholarship Fund Award)

1903 W. Michigan
Kalamazoo MI 49008-5337

269/387-8777
FAX: 269/387-6989
E-mail: finaid-info@wmich.edu
Internet: http://www.wmich.edu/finaid
AMOUNT: Varies
DEADLINE(S): MAR (for current Theater majors); on acceptance into program for freshmen and transfer students
FIELD(S): Theater Education; Theater Design; Technical Theater; Arts Management; Music Theater Performance
ELIGIBILITY/REQUIREMENTS: Scholarships are ONLY for Theater majors and minors. Must have a 3.0 GPA.
HOW TO APPLY: Freshmen or transfer students—by audition/interview and acceptance into major or minor in Theater program. Current Theater majors—by application form from the department.
RENEWABLE: No
CONTACT: Theater Department

132—WESTERN MICHIGAN UNIVERSITY (College of Fine Arts/Mary Thorne University Theater Guild Scholarship)

1903 W. Michigan
Kalamazoo MI 49008-5337
269/387-8777
FAX: 269/387-6989
E-mail: finaid-info@wmich.edu
Internet: http://www.wmich.edu/finaid
AMOUNT: Varies
DEADLINE(S): MAR (for current Theater majors); on acceptance into program for freshmen and transfer students
FIELD(S): Theater Education; Theater Design; Technical Theater; Arts Management; Music Theater Performance
ELIGIBILITY/REQUIREMENTS: Scholarships are ONLY for Theater majors and minors. Must have a 3.0 GPA.
HOW TO APPLY: Freshmen or transfer students—by audition/interview and acceptance into major or minor in Theater program. Current Theater majors—by application form from the department.
RENEWABLE: No
CONTACT: Theater Department

133—WESTERN MICHIGAN UNIVERSITY (College of Fine Arts/Music Theater Performance Scholarships)

1903 W. Michigan
Kalamazoo MI 49008-5337
269/387-8777
FAX: 269/387-6989

E-mail: finaid-info@wmich.edu
Internet: http://www.wmich.edu/finaid
AMOUNT: $400/semester
DEADLINE(S): MAR (for current Theater majors); on acceptance into program for freshmen and transfer students
FIELD(S): Theater Education; Theater Design; Technical Theater; Arts Management; Music Theater Performance
ELIGIBILITY/REQUIREMENTS: Scholarships are ONLY for Theater majors and minors. Must have a 3.0 GPA.
HOW TO APPLY: Freshmen or transfer students—by audition/interview and acceptance into major or minor in Theater program. Current Theater majors—by application form from the department.
RENEWABLE: No
CONTACT: Theater Department

134—WESTERN MICHIGAN UNIVERSITY (College of Fine Arts/Patricia Chisholm Scholarship for Theater Education)

1903 W. Michigan
Kalamazoo MI 49008-5337
269/387-8777
FAX: 269/387-6989
E-mail: finaid-info@wmich.edu
Internet: http://www.wmich.edu/finaid
AMOUNT: Varies
DEADLINE(S): MAR (for current Theater majors); on acceptance into program for freshmen and transfer students
FIELD(S): Theater Education
ELIGIBILITY/REQUIREMENTS: Scholarships are ONLY for Theater majors and minors. Must have a 3.0 GPA.
HOW TO APPLY: Freshmen or transfer students—by audition/interview and acceptance into major or minor in Theater program. Current Theater majors—by application form from the department.
RENEWABLE: No
CONTACT: Theater Department

135—WESTERN MICHIGAN UNIVERSITY (College of Fine Arts/Robert and Marion Denison Scholarship for Theater Education)

1903 W. Michigan
Kalamazoo MI 49008-5337
269/387-8777
FAX: 269/387-6989
E-mail: finaid-info@wmich.edu
Internet: http://www.wmich.edu/finaid

AMOUNT: Varies
DEADLINE(S): MAR (for current Theater majors); on acceptance into program for freshmen and transfer students
FIELD(S): Theater Education
ELIGIBILITY/REQUIREMENTS: Scholarships are ONLY for Theater majors and minors. Must have a 3.0 GPA.
HOW TO APPLY: Freshmen or transfer students—by audition/interview and acceptance into major or minor in Theater program. Current Theater majors—by application form from the department.
RENEWABLE: No
CONTACT: Theater Department

136—WESTERN MICHIGAN UNIVERSITY (College of Fine Arts/Robert Girard Memorial Award)

1903 W. Michigan
Kalamazoo MI 49008-5337
269/387-6000
FAX: 269/387-6989
E-mail: finaid-info@wmich.edu
Internet: http://www.wmich.edu/finaid
AMOUNT: $200 /spring semester
FIELD(S): Photography or related medium
ELIGIBILITY/REQUIREMENTS: Art major selected from annual student exhibit.
HOW TO APPLY: Student is nominated by faculty. Contact the Art Advising office for an application.
NUMBER OF AWARDS: Multiple awards, number varies
RENEWABLE: No

137—WESTERN MICHIGAN UNIVERSITY (College of Fine Arts/University Theater Guild Scholarship)

1903 W. Michigan
Kalamazoo MI 49008-5337
269/387-8777
FAX: 269/387-6989
E-mail: finaid-info@wmich.edu
Internet: http://www.wmich.edu/finaid
AMOUNT: Varies
DEADLINE(S): MAR (for current Theater majors); on acceptance into program for freshmen and transfer students
FIELD(S): Theater Education; Theater Design; Technical Theater; Arts Management; Music Theater Performance
ELIGIBILITY/REQUIREMENTS: Scholarships are ONLY for Theater majors and minors. Must have a 3.0 GPA.

HOW TO APPLY: Freshmen or transfer students—by audition/interview and acceptance into major or minor in Theater program. Current Theater majors—by application form from the department.
RENEWABLE: No
CONTACT: Theater Department

138—WESTERN MICHIGAN UNIVERSITY (Lawrence, Clara & Evelyn E. Burke Scholarship)

1903 W. Michigan
Kalamazoo MI 49008-5337
269/387-8777
FAX: 269/387-6989
E-mail: alumni@wmich.edu
E-mail: finaid-info@wmich.edu
Internet: http://www.www.wmich.edu/alumni
AMOUNT: Varies
DEADLINE(S): APR 1
FIELD(S): Theater; Journalism
ELIGIBILITY/REQUIREMENTS: Full- or part-time graduate or undergraduate students enrolled in Theater or Journalism. GPA of 3.0 or higher; selected on the basis of scholastic achievement. Theater students: Have participated in a theater production either at the high school or college level; must be deemed to have outstanding potential for a career in theater. Journalism students: Shall have had journalism experience, such as involvement with a school paper or yearbook, either at the high school or college level; must be deemed to have outstanding potential in the field of journalism.
HOW TO APPLY: Contact the Office of Financial Aid for more details.
RENEWABLE: Yes. Up to a maximum of 4 consecutive academic years as long as the recipient maintains a 3.0 GPA at WMU.

139—WESTERN MICHIGAN UNIVERSITY (Lynne C. McCauley Memorial Scholarship)

1903 West Michigan
Kalamazoo MI 49008-5337
269/387-8777
FAX: 269/387-6989
E-mail: alumni@wmich.edu
Internet: http://www.wmich.edu/ENDOWED
AMOUNT: Varies
DEADLINE(S): APR 1
FIELD(S): English, Music, Theater
ELIGIBILITY/REQUIREMENTS: Full-time students majoring in the Humanities, such as English, Music or Theater at WMU. Must have a minimum GPA of 3.0 to apply. Preference given to women.
HOW TO APPLY: See website for application and submit with FAFSA.

RENEWABLE: No
NUMBER OF AWARDS: Varies
CONTACT: Office of Student Financial Aid

140—WORLDSTUDIO FOUNDATION

200 Varick Street, Suite 507
New York NY 10014
212/366-1317
FAX: 212/807-0024
E-mail: info@worldstudio.org
Internet: http://www.worldstudio.org or http://www.aiga.org
AMOUNT: $1,500-$5,000
DEADLINE(S): APR 14
FIELD(S): Advertising, Animation, Architecture, Cartooning, Crafts, Environmental graphics, Film/video, Film/theater design, Fine arts, Furniture design, Industrial/product design, Interior architecture and design, Landscape architecture, New media, Photography, Surface/textile design, Urban planning
ELIGIBILITY/REQUIREMENTS: Applicants must be pursuing a degree in the fine or commercial arts, design or architecture, and plan to enter a career in the creative professions. Undergraduates and graduates are eligible. Minority status and/or social agenda are significant factors. Financial need a prerequisite. Minimum 2.0 GPA.
HOW TO APPLY: See websites for application. The application is a 2-part process. Applications must include personal and school information, including transcripts and copies of letters of acceptance; financial information; portfolio; written statement of purpose; examples of a commitment to a social agenda, 2 letters of recommendation from college instructors, high school teachers, or employers; head shot of applicant.
NUMBER OF AWARDS: 20-30
RENEWABLE: Yes. Must reapply.
CONTACT: Mark Randall

FINE ARTS

141—ADELPHI UNIVERSITY (Talent Awards)

1 South Avenue
Garden City NY 11530
516/877-3080
FAX: 516/877-3380
Internet: http://www.ecampus.adelphi.edu/sfs/au scholarships grants.php#art
AMOUNT: $4,000-$10,000

DEADLINE(S): FEB 15
FIELD(S): Theater, Dance, Art, Music
ELIGIBILITY/REQUIREMENTS: Various scholarships for full-time students at Adelphi University in the above fields.
HOW TO APPLY: See website for further information; contact school to apply. Portfolio required.
RENEWABLE: Yes. Must maintain 3.0 GPA in major and 2.5 overall to maintain scholarship.

142—AMERICAN INDIAN ARTS COUNCIL, INC.

Scholarship Committee
725 Preston Forest Shopping Center, Suite B
Dallas TX 75230
214/891-9640
Internet: http://www.American IndianArtFestival.org
AMOUNT: $250-$1,000
DEADLINE(S): MAR 1 and OCT 1
FIELD(S): Fine Arts
ELIGIBILITY/REQUIREMENTS: The Academic Scholarship Fund was created to encourage excellence in the study of fine arts, traditional/tribal arts, performing arts, visual arts, creative writing, communications arts, and arts administration by Native American students enrolled in institutions of higher learning. Need official tribal documentation, a 2.5 GPA, and a major in one of the Fine Arts.
HOW TO APPLY: Contact prior to submitting application packet to determine if funds are available. See website to download application.
NUMBER OF AWARDS: Varies; 1992-2005: $28,000

143—AMERICAN MOTHERS, INC. (Gertrude Fogelson Cultural and Creative Arts Awards)

1296 E. 21st Street
Brooklyn NY 11201
718/253-5676
AMOUNT: Up to $1,000
DEADLINE(S): JAN 1
FIELD(S): Visual Arts; Creative Writing; Vocal Music
ELIGIBILITY/REQUIREMENTS: An award to encourage and honor mothers in artistic pursuits.
HOW TO APPLY: Write for details.

144—ELIZABETH GREENSHIELDS FOUNDATION (Grants)

1814 Sherbrooke Street West, Suite 1
Montreal Quebec H3H 1E4
CANADA
514/937-9225
FAX: 514/937-0141
E-mail: greenshields@bellnet.ca
AMOUNT: $12,500 (Canadian)
DEADLINE(S): None
FIELD(S): Painting; Drawing; Printmaking; Sculpture
ELIGIBILITY/REQUIREMENTS: Grants are to aid artists in the early stages of their careers. Work must be representational or figurative. Applicants must have started or completed art school training and/or must demonstrate, through past work and future plans, a commitment to making art a lifetime career. Funds may be used for any art-related purpose: study, travel, studio rental, purchase of materials, etc.
HOW TO APPLY: Write for application.
NUMBER OF AWARDS: 45-55/year
CONTACT: Micheline Leduc, Administrator

145—GENERAL FEDERATION OF WOMEN'S CLUBS OF MASSACHUSETTS (Pennies For Art Scholarship)

P.O. Box 679
Sudbury MA 01776-0679
978/443-4569
FAX: 978/443-1617
E-mail: GFWCMA@aol.com
Internet: http://www.gfwcma.org/id39.html
AMOUNT: Up to $800
DEADLINE(S): FEB 1
FIELD(S): Art
ELIGIBILITY/REQUIREMENTS: Competitive scholarships for seniors in Massachusetts high schools.
HOW TO APPLY: For more information or an application, see website or send a SASE to Coordinator, Arts Department at above address. Submit application with letter of recommendation from high school art instructor; portfolio of 3 examples of original artwork, matted, not framed, not larger than 12″ × 18″.
NUMBER OF AWARDS: 1
RENEWABLE: No

146—GOLDEN KEY INTERNATIONAL HONOUR SOCIETY (Art International)

1189 Ponce de Leon Avenue
Atlanta GA 30306
404/377-2400 or 800/377-2401
FAX: 404/373-7033
E-mail: scholarships@goldenkey.org
Internet: http//www.goldenkey.org
AMOUNT: $1,000
DEADLINE(S): APR
FIELD(S): All
ELIGIBILITY/REQUIREMENTS: This award recognizes the visual art talent categories—applied art, computer-generated art/graphic design/illustration, drawing, mixed media, painting, photography, printmaking, and sculpture. Undergraduate, graduate, and post-graduate members who are currently enrolled in classes at a degree-granting program are eligible. Awards based on quality of work submitted, as determined by the selection committee.
HOW TO APPLY: Apply online with your Golden Key member number; follow up with a single slide or slides with multiple view of your original work. Do NOT submit the artwork itself. It will not be considered or returned. Only 1 entry per member per category will be accepted.
NUMBER OF AWARDS/YEAR: 8
RENEWABLE: No

147—HAWAII COMMUNITY FOUNDATION (Esther Kanagawa Memorial Art Scholarship)

1164 Bishop Street, Suite 800
Honolulu HI 96813
808/537-6333 or toll free: 888/731-3863
FAX: 808/521-6286
E-mail: info@hcf-hawaii.org
Internet: http://www.hcf-hawaii.org
DEADLINE(S): MAR 1
FIELD(S): Fine Art
ELIGIBILITY/REQUIREMENTS: Applicants must be residents of the state of Hawaii; be junior or senior undergraduate or graduate students attending full time an accredited 2- or 4-year college or university; and demonstrate financial need, good moral character, and academic achievement with a minimum GPA of 2.7. This scholarship is not for students studying video, film, or the performing arts.
HOW TO APPLY: Send application with 2 letters of recommendation.

148—HAYSTACK MOUNTAIN SCHOOL OF CRAFTS

Admissions Office
P.O. Box 518
Deer Isle ME 04627
207/348-2306
FAX: 207/348-2307
E-mail: haystack@haystack-mtn.org
Internet: http://www.haystack-mtn.org
AMOUNT: Varies
DEADLINE(S): MAR 25

FIELD(S): Crafts (metals, clay, wood); Graphics (painting, drawing, and related fields); Weaving; Glass; Blacksmithing

ELIGIBILITY/REQUIREMENTS: 18 years old with dedicated interest in crafts.

HOW TO APPLY: Write or e-mail for application.

NUMBER OF AWARDS: 90+

RENEWABLE: No

149—INSTITUTE OF INTERNATIONAL EDUCATION (Cintas Fellowship)

809 United Nations Plaza
New York NY 10017-3580
E-mail: cintas@iie.org
Internet: http://www.iie.org/cintas

AMOUNT: $10,000

DEADLINE(S): APR

FIELD(S): Fine Arts; Architecture; Literature; Music Composition; Visual Arts; Photography

ELIGIBILITY/REQUIREMENTS: Acknowledges outstanding creative accomplishments and encourages the further development of creative talents in the fields of architecture, literature, music composition, and the visual arts and photography. For artists of Cuban citizenship or direct descent who do not live in Cuba.

HOW TO APPLY: Contact Institute or see website for additional information.

150—JUNIATA COLLEGE (Ron & Ann Wertz Arts Scholarship)

Office of Financial Planning
1700 Moore Street
Huntingdon PA 16652
814/641-3142
FAX: 814/641-5311
E-mail: frankv@juniata.edu
Internet: http://www.juniata.edu/admission/finplan/index.html

AMOUNT: Full tuition, room & board

DEADLINE(S): JAN 4

FIELD(S): Ceative and/or performing arts, Fine Arts, Graphic Design, Writing, Choral and Instrumental Music, Theater, Dance

ELIGIBILITY/REQUIREMENTS: Open to incoming freshmen. (upperclassmen and transfer students are ineligible). Must be nominated by a Juniata alumnus/a, parent of a Juniata student, guidance counselor, pastor, teacher, or someone familiar with the student's involvement in school and community activities. who have excelled in the creative and/or performing arts, including drawing, painting, sculpting, graphic design, writing, choral and instrumental music, theatre and dance.

HOW TO APPLY: Submit a Nomination Essay (in addition to the essay required for admission) of no more than 2 pages discussing why you should be considered for a scholarship, including supporting activities and involvement. You may also attach up to 3 extra pages of supporting information of any kind. Must submit a portfolio. See website for additional information or contact College.

NUMBER OF AWARDS: 1

RENEWABLE: No

CONTACT: Vincent Frank, Director of Student Financial Planning, 814/641-3140; e-mail: frankv@juniata.edu

151—JUNIOR ACHIEVEMENT INC. (The Walt Disney Company Foundation Scholarship)

One Education Way
719/540-8000
FAX: 719/540-6299
E-mail: newmedia@ja.org
Internet: http://www.ja.org

AMOUNT: Full tuition

DEADLINE(S): FEB 1

FIELD(S): Business Administration; Fine Arts

ELIGIBILITY/REQUIREMENTS: Graduating high school seniors with excellent academic and extracurricular credentials who have participated in JA Company Program or JA Economics.

HOW TO APPLY: Send completed application and 3 letters of recommendation: 1 from a JA Company Program or JA Economics consultant, and 2 others.

NUMBER OF AWARDS: 1

RENEWABLE: Yes. Annually up to 4 years

CONTACT: To obtain application, contact Scholarship/Education Team, Junior Achievement Inc. at 954/566-8623; submit complete application to Walt Disney Scholarship, Junior Achievement Inc., P.O. Box 5186, Fort Lauderdale FL 33310.

152—LIBERACE FOUNDATION FOR THE PERFORMING AND CREATIVE ARTS

1775 East Tropicana Avenue
Las Vegas NV 89119-6529
702/798-5595
FAX: 702/798-7386
E-mail: foundation@liberace.org
Internet: http://www.liberace.org

AMOUNT: Varies

DEADLINE(S): MAR 15

FIELD(S): Music (Instrumental and Vocal); Theater; Dance; Visual Arts; Fine Art

ELIGIBILITY/REQUIREMENTS: Provides grants to accredited institutions

that offer training in above fields. Grants are to be used exclusively for scholarship assistance to talented and deserving students. Recipients should be promising and deserving upperclassmen (junior, senior, graduate) enrolled in a course of study leading up to a career in the arts.

HOW TO APPLY: See website or write to above address for details.

RENEWABLE: Yes

CONTACT: Joel Strote

153—MEMPHIS COLLEGE OF ART (Portfolio Awards)

Overton Park
1930 Poplar Avenue
Memphis TN 38104-2764
800/727-1088
E-mail: admissions@mca.edu
Internet: http://www.mca.edu/index.cfm

AMOUNT: Half tuition

DEADLINE(S): Varies (NOV 15 through JUL 31)

FIELD(S): Visual Arts

ELIGIBILITY/REQUIREMENTS: Awards are given to excellent visual art portfolios submitted by either high school students or transfer students and are to be used for full-time enrollment at Memphis College of Art. International students are welcome to apply. Financial need is not a consideration.

HOW TO APPLY: Contact MCA for application and submission details or see website.

NUMBER OF AWARDS: 2

154—NATIONAL PTA (Reflections Program)

541 N. Fairbanks Ct., Suite 1300
Chicago IL 60611
800/307-4PTA or 312/670-6782
FAX: 312/670-6783
E-mail: info@pta.org
Internet: http://www.pta.org

AMOUNT: Varies

DEADLINE(S): Varies

FIELD(S): Literature; Musical Composition; Photography; Visual Arts; Dance/Choreography

ELIGIBILITY/REQUIREMENTS: Open to students in preschool through grade twelve to express themselves and to receive positive recognition for their artistic efforts. Young artists can get involved in the Reflections Program of their local PTA or PTSA.

HOW TO APPLY: Contact your state PTA office for information about the Reflections Program in your area.

155—NATIONAL SCULPTURE SOCIETY (Educational Scholarships)

237 Park Avenue
New York NY 10017
212/764-5645
Internet: http://www.national
sculpture.org/
AMOUNT: $1,000 each
DEADLINE(S): APR 30
FIELD(S): Sculpture
ELIGIBILITY/REQUIREMENTS: For students of figurative or representational sculpture. Young artists are also eligible for the National Sculpture competition through this Society, including prizes given for a figure modeling competition and other Young Sculptor Awards given based on jurying of slides.
HOW TO APPLY: See website for other scholarship opportunities.

156—NOVA SCOTIA COLLEGE OF ART AND DESIGN

5163 Duke Street
Halifax, Nova Scotia B3J 3J6
CANADA
902/494-8129
FAX: 902/425-2987
E-mail: bkehoe@nscad.ns.ca
Internet: http://www.nscad.ca
AMOUNT: $500-$13,500 (Canadian)
DEADLINE(S): Varies
FIELD(S): Art; Fine Arts
ELIGIBILITY/REQUIREMENTS: The Nova Scotia College of Art and Design administers a number of scholarships and bursary awards that acknowledge high achievement and special promise. Awards restricted to students accepted to or officially registered at the university.
HOW TO APPLY: Write for details on specific scholarships.
CONTACT: Bernadette Kehoe, Student Services

157—POLISH ARTS CLUB OF BUFFALO SCHOLARSHIP FOUNDATION

3210 Main Street, Suite A
Buffalo NY 14214
AMOUNT: $1,000
DEADLINE(S): MAR 1
FIELD(S): Fine Arts
ELIGIBILITY/REQUIREMENTS: Open to students of Polish background who are studying the fine arts and are enrolled in an accredited college or university. Must be junior or senior or graduate student.
HOW TO APPLY: To receive an application, write to Selection Chairman, P.O. Box 1362, Williamsville, NY 14231-1362.

NUMBER OF AWARDS: Varies
RENEWABLE: Yes
CONTACT: Leonard S. Sikora, Trustee, at 716/655-1823 or kingregis@prodigy.net

158—SCHOLASTIC ART & WRITING AWARDS, THE (Alliance for Young Artists and Writers, Inc.)

557 Broadway
New York NY 10012
212/343-6493
E-mail: A&Wgeneralinfo@scholastic.com
Internet: http://www.artandwriting.org
AMOUNT: Varies; up to $10,000
DEADLINE(S): Varies (upon location)
FIELD(S): Art; Writing; Photography
ELIGIBILITY/REQUIREMENTS: For students in grades 7-12 enrolled in schools in the U.S., Canada, U.S. territories, or U.S.-sponsored schools abroad. 10 writing and 16 art categories. Publishing opportunities may be available for winners in both art and writing categories. Scholarship consideration for seniors submitting portfolios of art, photography or writing.
HOW TO APPLY: See website or write.
NUMBER OF AWARDS: 1,000+ awards annually, including 11 $10,000 scholarships.

159—SMITHSONIAN INSTITUTION-FREER/SACKLER GALLERIES (Dick Louie Memorial Internship for Americans of Asian Descent)

Education Department
Washington DC 20560-0707
202/357-4880
TTY: 202/786-2374
Internet: http://www.asia.si.edu
AMOUNT: Stipend
DEADLINE(S): Varies
FIELD(S): Asian Art; Art History; Museum Studies
ELIGIBILITY/REQUIREMENTS: This summer internship is an opportunity for high school students of Asian descent to gain practical experience in a museum setting. Must be entering or completing senior year of high school, and must live and attend high school in the Washington metropolitan area.
HOW TO APPLY: Contact the Internship Coordinator for an application.
CONTACT: Internship Coordinator

160—TRUST COMPANY LIMITED (Portia Geach Memorial Award)

Level 3, 35 Clarence Street
Sydney NSW 2000 AUSTRALIA
(02)8295 8316

FAX: (02)8295 8496
E-mail: trustawards@cauzgroup.com
Internet: http://www.trust.com.au/
philanthropy/awards/
AMOUNT: Aus. $18,000
DEADLINE(S): AUG 28
FIELD(S): Portrait painting
ELIGIBILITY/REQUIREMENTS: Award for a female painter who is an Australia resident, either Australian or British-born. Portrait is to be of a person distinguished in arts, letters, or sciences; self-portraits are accepted.
HOW TO APPLY: $30 entry fee per painting. Contact Trust Administrator for more information and entry form.
CONTACT: Petrea Salter

161—UNIVERSITY OF ILLINOIS AT URBANA-CHAMPAIGN (Lydia E. Parker Bates Scholarship)

620 East John Street
Champaign IL 61820
217/333-0100
Internet: http://www.uiuc.edu/
AMOUNT: Up to $1,000
DEADLINE(S): MAR 15
FIELD(S): Art, Architecture, Landscape Architecture, Urban Planning, Dance, Theater, and all related subjects except Music
ELIGIBILITY/REQUIREMENTS: Open to undergraduate students in the College of Fine and Applied Arts who are attending the University of Illinois at Urbana-Champaign. Must demonstrate financial need and have 2.85 GPA. Recipients must carry at least 12 credit hours per semester.
HOW TO APPLY: Contact office of student financial aid for application. Complete the Free Application for Federal Student Aid with UIUC admission application.
NUMBER OF AWARDS: 175

162—VIRGINIA MUSEUM OF FINE ARTS (Fellowships)

2800 Grove Avenue
Richmond VA 23221-2466
804/204-2661
Internet: http://vmfa.state.va.us
AMOUNT: $4,000 (undergraduate-maximum); $6,000 (graduates); $8,000 (professionals)
DEADLINE(S): MAR 1
FIELD(S): Crafts; Drawing; Filmmaking; Painting; Photography; Printmaking; Sculpture; Video
ELIGIBILITY/REQUIREMENTS: Open to Virginia residents of at least one year who are U.S. citizens or legal residents. Fellowships are available to undergradu-

ates, graduates, and professional artists. Financial need is considered.

HOW TO APPLY: Application and guidelines on website.

163—WESTERN MICHIGAN UNIVERSITY (College of Fine Arts/Angie Gayman Carmer Art Scholarship)

1903 W. Michigan
Kalamazoo MI 49008-5337
269/387-6000
FAX: 269/387-6989
E-mail: finaid-info@wmich.edu
Internet: http://www.wmich.edu/finaid

AMOUNT: Varies
DEADLINE(S): FEB (first Friday)
FIELD(S): Art
ELIGIBILITY/REQUIREMENTS: Art major, enrolled full-time with a minimum 3.5 GPA.
HOW TO APPLY: Typed statement of goals and slide portfolio review required. See website for application or contact the Art Advising office for an application.
NUMBER OF AWARDS: Multiple awards

164—WESTERN MICHIGAN UNIVERSITY (College of Fine Arts/Art Department Enrichment Grants)

1903 W. Michigan
Kalamazoo MI 49008-5337
269/387-6000
FAX: 269/387-6989
E-mail: finaid-info@wmich.edu
Internet: http://www.wmich.edu/finaid

AMOUNT: Varies
DEADLINE(S): OCT (first Friday)
FIELD(S): Art
ELIGIBILITY/REQUIREMENTS: Full-time art majors pursuing a BFA or MFA degree.
HOW TO APPLY: Submit project proposals with specific goals. Contact the Art Department or see website for an application.
NUMBER OF AWARDS: Multiple, number varies.
RENEWABLE: Yes, for 1 year if recipient is a junior

165—WESTERN MICHIGAN UNIVERSITY (College of Fine Arts/Art Department Freshman Scholarships)

1903 W. Michigan
Kalamazoo MI 49008-5337
269/387-6000
FAX: 269/387-6989
E-mail: finaid-info@wmich.edu

Internet: http://www.wmich.edu/finaid

AMOUNT: $500
DEADLINE(S): FEB (first Friday)
FIELD(S): Art
ELIGIBILITY/REQUIREMENTS: Open to entering freshmen, Art majors, enrolled full time; based on portfolio.
HOW TO APPLY: Awards selected from Department.
NUMBER OF AWARDS: Multiple, number varies
RENEWABLE: No

166—WESTERN MICHIGAN UNIVERSITY (College of Fine Arts/Art Department Student Exhibit Awards)

1903 W. Michigan
Kalamazoo MI 49008-5337
269/387-6000
FAX: 269/387-6989
E-mail: finaid-info@wmich.edu
Internet: http://www.wmich.edu/finaid

AMOUNT: $250/spring semester
DEADLINE(S): FEB (first Friday)
FIELD(S): Art
ELIGIBILITY/REQUIREMENTS: Open to Art majors (graduate or undergraduate); selected from annual student exhibit.
HOW TO APPLY: Contact the Exhibitions Office for information.
NUMBER OF AWARDS: 4
RENEWABLE: No

167—WESTERN MICHIGAN UNIVERSITY (College of Fine Arts/Art Star Award)

1903 W. Michigan
Kalamazoo MI 49008-5337
269/387-6000
FAX: 269/387-6989
E-mail: finaid-info@wmich.edu
Internet: http://www.wmich.edu/finaid

AMOUNT: $200 /spring semester
DEADLINE(S): FEB (first Friday)
FIELD(S): Art
ELIGIBILITY/REQUIREMENTS: Open to Art majors in their junior and senior years.
HOW TO APPLY: Student is nominated by faculty.
RENEWABLE: No

168—WESTERN MICHIGAN UNIVERSITY (College of Fine Arts/Elizabeth Smutz Award)

1903 W. Michigan
Kalamazoo MI 49008-5337
269/387-6000
FAX: 269/387-6989

E-mail: finaid-info@wmich.edu
Internet: http://www.wmich.edu/finaid

AMOUNT: Varies
FIELD(S): Art Education
ELIGIBILITY/REQUIREMENTS: Must be a major in art education.
HOW TO APPLY: Student is nominated by faculty.
NUMBER OF AWARDS: 1
RENEWABLE: No

169—WESTERN MICHIGAN UNIVERSITY (College of Fine Arts/Foundation Scholarships)

1903 W. Michigan
Kalamazoo MI 49008-5337
269/387-6000
FAX: 269/387-6989
E-mail: finaid-info@wmich.edu
Internet: http://www.wmich.edu/finaid

AMOUNT: $200/spring semester
FIELD(S): Art
ELIGIBILITY/REQUIREMENTS: Art majors in freshman or sophomore years who are enrolled full time in foundation classes (introductory level).
HOW TO APPLY: Student is nominated by faculty.
NUMBER OF AWARDS: Multiple awards, number varies
RENEWABLE: No

170—WESTERN MICHIGAN UNIVERSITY (College of Fine Arts/Haig and Janette Tashjian Scholarship)

1903 W. Michigan
Kalamazoo MI 49008-5337
269/387-6000
FAX: 269/387-6989
E-mail: finaid-info@wmich.edu
Internet: http://www.wmich.edu/finaid

AMOUNT: Varies
FIELD(S): Art Education
ELIGIBILITY/REQUIREMENTS: Open to Art Education major in junior or senior year, who is enrolled full time, has a 3.5 or higher GPA.
HOW TO APPLY: Student is nominated by faculty.
NUMBER OF AWARDS: 1
RENEWABLE: No

171—WESTERN MICHIGAN UNIVERSITY (College of Fine Arts/Lydia Siedschlag Scholarship)

1903 W. Michigan
Kalamazoo MI 49008-5337
269/387-6000

FAX: 269/387-6989
E-mail: finaid-info@wmich.edu
Internet: http://www.wmich.edu/
finaid
AMOUNT: Varies
FIELD(S): Art
ELIGIBILITY/REQUIREMENTS: Must
be an Art major, resident of Siedschlag
Hall with a 3.3 or higher GPA.
HOW TO APPLY: Contact the Art Advising office for an application.
NUMBER OF AWARDS: Multiple awards

172—WESTERN MICHIGAN UNIVERSITY (College of Fine Arts/Margaret H. Ward Art Scholarship)

1903 W. Michigan
Kalamazoo MI 49008-5337
269/387-6000
FAX: 269/387-6989
E-mail: finaid-info@wmich.edu
Internet: http://www.wmich.edu/
finaid
AMOUNT: Varies
FIELD(S): Art Education
ELIGIBILITY/REQUIREMENTS: Open
to Art major in junior or senior year, who
is enrolled full time, has a 3.25 or higher
GPA. Recipient must exhibit above-average artistic and creative ability and demonstrate financial need. Must be U.S. citizen.
HOW TO APPLY: Contact the Art Department for more information.
NUMBER OF AWARDS: 1
RENEWABLE: No

173—WESTERN MICHIGAN UNIVERSITY (College of Fine Arts/Robert and Eleanor DeVries Student Art Award)

1903 W. Michigan
Kalamazoo MI 49008-5337
269/387-6000
FAX: 269/387-6989
E-mail: finaid-info@wmich.edu
Internet: http://www.wmich.edu/
finaid
AMOUNT: Varies
FIELD(S): Art
ELIGIBILITY/REQUIREMENTS:
Selected from annual student exhibit.
HOW TO APPLY: Contact for an application.
NUMBER OF AWARDS: Multiple awards
RENEWABLE: No

174—WESTERN MICHIGAN UNIVERSITY (College of Fine Arts/Walter F. Enz Memorial Award)

1903 W. Michigan
Kalamazoo MI 49008-5337

269/387-6000
FAX: 269/387-6989
E-mail: finaid-info@wmich.edu
Internet: http://www.wmich.edu/
finaid
AMOUNT: Varies
FIELD(S): Art
ELIGIBILITY/REQUIREMENTS: Open
to Art major (graduate or undergraduate)
who is enrolled full time.
HOW TO APPLY: Student is nominated
by faculty.
NUMBER OF AWARDS: 1-2
RENEWABLE: No

175—WOMEN'S STUDIO WORKSHOP (Chili Bowl Internship)

P.O. Box 489
Rosendale NY 12472
845/658-9133
FAX: 845/658-9031
E-mail: info@wsworkshop.org
Internet: http://www.wsworkshop.
org/
AMOUNT: $150/month + housing
DEADLINE(S): OCT 15
FIELD(S): Ceramics
ELIGIBILITY/REQUIREMENTS: Must
have wheel throwing experience, be motivated, and hard working.
HOW TO APPLY: Send a letter of interest, résumé, up to 20 slides with slide list, 3
reference letters, and a SASE.
NUMBER OF AWARDS: 1
RENEWABLE: No
CONTACT: Ayumi Horie

176—WOMEN'S STUDIO WORKSHOP (Fellowship Grants)

P.O. Box 489
Rosendale NY 12472
845/658-9133
FAX: 845/658-9031
E-mail: info@wsworkshop.org
Internet: http://www.wsworkshop.
org/
AMOUNT: Tuition
DEADLINE(S): MAR 15; NOV 1
FIELD(S): Visual Arts
ELIGIBILITY/REQUIREMENTS:
Designed to provide concentrated work
time for artists to explore new ideas in a
dynamic and supportive community of
women artists. WSW welcomes applications from emerging artists.
HOW TO APPLY: Application form plus
a résumé, 6-10 slides, a letter of interest
with purpose of residency, explaining areas
of proficiency and studio skills, and a
SASE for return of materials. Applications
available on website.

177—WORLDSTUDIO FOUNDATION

200 Varick Street, Suite 507
New York NY 10014
212/366-1317
FAX: 212/807-0024
E-mail: info@worldstudio.org
Internet: http://www.worldstudio.
org or http://www.aiga.org
AMOUNT: $1,500-$5,000
DEADLINE(S): APR 14
FIELD(S): Advertising, Animation,
Architecture, Cartooning, Crafts,
Environmental graphics, Film/video,
Film/theater design, Fine arts,
Furniture design, Industrial/product
design, Interior architecture and
design, Landscape architecture, New
media, Photography, Surface/textile
design, Urban planning
ELIGIBILITY/REQUIREMENTS:
Applicants must be pursuing a degree in
the fine or commercial arts, design or
architecture, and plan to enter a career in
the creative professions. Undergraduates
and graduates are eligible. Minority status
and/or social agenda are significant factors.
Financial need a prerequisite. Minimum
2.0 GPA.
HOW TO APPLY: See websites for application. The application is a 2-part process.
Applications must include personal and
school information, including transcripts
and copies of letters of acceptance; financial information; portfolio; written statement of purpose; examples of a commitment to a social agenda, 2 letters of recommendation from college instructors, high
school teachers, or employers; head shot of
applicant.
NUMBER OF AWARDS: 20-30
RENEWABLE: Yes. Must reapply.
CONTACT: Mark Randall

GRAPHIC ART, COMPUTER GRAPHICS/DESIGN

178—ACADEMY OF TELEVISION ARTS & SCIENCES COLLEGE TELEVISION AWARD

5220 Lankershim Boulevard
North Hollywood CA 91601-3109
818/754-2820
FAX: 818/761-2827
E-mail: alavkin@emmys.org
Internet:
http://www.emmysfoundation.org
AMOUNT: $500-$2,000
DEADLINE(S): JAN 15
FIELD(S): Television
ELIGIBILITY/REQUIREMENTS:
Awards achievement in each of the follow-

ing categories: Animation (all forms), Children's, Comedy, Comedy Series, Commercial, Documentary, Drama, Drama Series, Magazine, Music (best composition), Music (best use of music), and Newscast.
HOW TO APPLY: See website for application information and guidelines
NUMBER OF AWARDS: Up to 27 (at least 1 in each category)
CONTACT: Debbie Slavkin, Program Manager/Development Associate
ADDITIONAL INFORMATION: May apply in more than 1 category; 1st entry is free; each subsequent entry is $25.00. (See complete guidelines and rules for more details.)

179—AMERICAN INTERCONTINENTAL UNIVERSITY (Emilio Pucci Scholarships)

Admissions Committee
3330 Peachtree Road NE
Atlanta GA 30326
404/812-8192 or 888/248-7392
AMOUNT: $1,800 (applied toward tuition over 6 quarters)
DEADLINE(S): None
FIELD(S): Fashion Design; Fashion Marketing; Interior Design; Commercial Art; Business Administration; Video Production
ELIGIBILITY/REQUIREMENTS: Scholarships are for high school seniors who are interested in either a 2-year or 4-year program at one of the campuses of the American Intercontinental University: Atlanta, GA; Los Angeles, CA; London, UK; or Dubai, United Arab Emirates.
HOW TO APPLY: Write for applications and complete information.

180—AMERICAN MOTHERS, INC. (Gertrude Fogelson Cultural and Creative Arts Awards)

1296 E. 21st Street
Brooklyn NY 11201
718/253-5676
AMOUNT: Up to $1,000
DEADLINE(S): JAN 1
FIELD(S): Visual Arts; Creative Writing; Vocal Music
ELIGIBILITY/REQUIREMENTS: An award to encourage and honor mothers in artistic pursuits.
HOW TO APPLY: Write for details.

181—ASIFA (Helen Victoria Haynes World Peace Storyboard and Animation Contest)

School of Communications
Lake Superior Hall
Grand Valley State University
Allendale MI 49401
E-mail: HaynesWorldPeace@aol.com
Internet: http://www.swcp.com/animate/contest.htm
AMOUNT: $500 + software and ASIFA conference registration
DEADLINE(S): APR
FIELD(S): Animation; Cartooning
ELIGIBILITY/REQUIREMENTS: For high school and college students to design, draw, and mount a storyboard for an animated short for the Annual ASIFA/Central Conference and Retreat. The storyboard should depict your vision of how to achieve World Peace.
HOW TO APPLY: See website for official rules or contact ASIFA for more information.
NUMBER OF AWARDS: 2 (1 for high school students and 1 for college students)
CONTACT: Donna Morse or Mary Lou Haynes

182—ASSOCIATION FOR WOMEN IN COMMUNICATIONS, THE

c/o USA Weekend
Attention: Frappa Stout
7950 Jones Branch Drive
McLean VA 22107
703/854-5631
FAX: 703/854-2122
AMOUNT: $1,000
DEADLINE(S): MAR 19
FIELD(S): Journalism; Public Relations
ELIGIBILITY/REQUIREMENTS: Current sophomore or junior female student attending a Washington, DC-area university or college studying communications, advertising, journalism, public relations, marketing, graphic arts, or a related field with an overall GPA of 3.0 or higher.
HOW TO APPLY: Send résumé, cover letter, application, and transcripts to address above.
NUMBER OF AWARDS: 1
CONTACT: Frappa Stout, Vice President of Student Affairs, AWC DC Chapter

183—CANADIAN PRINTING INDUSTRIES ASSOCIATION (Scholarship Trust Fund)

75 Albert Street, Suite 906
Ottawa Ontario K1P 5E7 CANADA
613/236-7208 or 800/267-7280
FAX: 613/236-8169
E-mail: kerri@cpia-aci.ca
Internet: http://www.cpia-aci.ca/b-schol.html
AMOUNT: $1,250 (Canadian) per year
DEADLINE(S): JUN 30
FIELD(S): Printing; Graphic Arts
ELIGIBILITY/REQUIREMENTS: Open to undergraduates enrolled in their first year as a full-time student in recognized Canadian 2-year, 3-year, or 4-year colleges or universities who are interested in a career in printing or graphic arts. Must maintain at least a B average. Part-time students and design or art majors are not eligible.
HOW TO APPLY: Write for complete information.
NUMBER OF AWARDS: 50/year
CONTACT: Kerri MacKenzie, Administrative Assistant

184—DESIGN FOUNDATION (IDSA Undergraduate Scholarships)

45195 Business Court, Suite 250
Dulles VA 20166
703/707-6000
FAX: 703/787-8501
E-mail: idsa@idsa.org
Internet: http://www.idsa.org
AMOUNT: $1,500 to $2,000
DEADLINE(S): MAY 3
FIELD(S): Industrial Design
ELIGIBILITY/REQUIREMENTS: Must be enrolled as a full-time student in an IDSA-listed program. Must be in your next-to-final year ("Juniors" 3rd year in a 4-year program or 4th year in a 5-year program) AND must be earning a B or better cumulative GPA since entering the Industrial Design program. Must be a member of an IDSA student chapter and a U.S. citizen or U.S. resident. Awards will be based solely on the excellence of the work that the students have submitted.
HOW TO APPLY: Along with application form, send a letter of intent including your goals; 3 letters of recommendation; 20 visual examples of your work showing your various projects—the images should be in JPG format saved at 300 dpi on a PC CD or disk (different views preferred); a 1-page research summary is optional; current transcript. There MUST NOT be any identification of the school or your name on the images.
NUMBER OF AWARDS: 2
RENEWABLE: No

185—ELIZABETH GREENSHIELDS FOUNDATION (Grants)

1814 Sherbrooke Street W., Suite 1
Montreal Quebec H3H 1E4
CANADA
514/937-9225
FAX: 514/937-0141
E-mail: greenshields@bellnet.ca
AMOUNT: $12,500 (Canadian)
DEADLINE(S): None
FIELD(S): Painting; Drawing; Printmaking; Sculpture

ELIGIBILITY/REQUIREMENTS: Grants are to aid artists in the early stages of their careers. Work must be representational or figurative. Applicants must have started or completed art school training and/or must demonstrate, through past work and future plans, a commitment to making art a lifetime career. Funds may be used for any art-related purpose: study, travel, studio rental, purchase of materials, etc.
HOW TO APPLY: Write for application.
NUMBER OF AWARDS: 45-55/year
RENEWABLE: Yes. 1 year after grant was awarded.
CONTACT: Micheline Leduc, Administrator

186—FOUNDATION OF LEXOGRAPHIC TECHNICAL ASSOCIATION (Flexographic Scholarship)

900 Marconi Avenue
Ronkonkoma NY 11779
516/737-6020
FAX: 516/737-6813
E-mail: education@flexography.org
Internet: http://www.fta-ffta.org
AMOUNT: $2,000
DEADLINE(S): Varies
FIELD(S): Graphic Communication-Flexography
ELIGIBILITY/REQUIREMENTS: Must have a GPA of at least 3.0 and be going to a school offering flexography as a course of study. Must be a high school senior going to college (proof of enrollment is required), or a college sophomore, junior, or senior.
HOW TO APPLY: See website or contact Foundation for application.
NUMBER OF AWARDS: 19
RENEWABLE: Yes

187—GOLDEN KEY INTERNATIONAL HONOUR SOCIETY (Art International)

1189 Ponce de Leon Avenue
Atlanta GA 30306
404/377-2400 or 800/377-2401
FAX: 404/373-7033
E-mail: scholarships@goldenkey.org
Internet: http//www.goldenkey.org
AMOUNT: $1,000.
DEADLINE(S): APR
FIELD(S): All
ELIGIBILITY/REQUIREMENTS: This award recognizes the visual art talents of Golden Key members in eight categories—applied art, computer-generated art/graphic design/illustration, drawing, mixed media, painting, photography, printmaking, and sculpture. Undergraduate, graduate, and post-graduate members who are currently enrolled in classes at a degree-

granting program are eligible. Awards based on quality of work submitted, as determined by the selection committee.
HOW TO APPLY: Apply online with your Golden Key member number; follow up with a single slide or slides with multiple view of your original work. Do NOT submit the artwork itself. It will not be considered or returned. Only one entry per member per category will be accepted.
NUMBER OF AWARDS/YEAR: 8
RENEWABLE: No

188—HAYSTACK MOUNTAIN SCHOOL OF CRAFTS

Admissions Office
P.O. Box 518
Deer Isle ME 04627
207/348-2306
FAX: 207/348-2307
E-mail: haystack@haystack-mtn.org
Internet: http://www.haystack-mtn.org
AMOUNT: Varies
DEADLINE(S): MAR 25
FIELD(S): Crafts (metals, clay, wood); Graphics (painting, drawing, and related fields); Weaving; Glass; Blacksmithing
ELIGIBILITY/REQUIREMENTS: 18 years old with dedicated interest in crafts.
HOW TO APPLY: Write or e-mail for application.
NUMBER OF AWARDS: 90+
RENEWABLE: No

189—IMATION COMPUTER ARTS SCHOLARSHIP

1 Imation Place
Oakdale MN 55128-3414
FAX: 651/704-3892
E-mail: CAS@imation.com
Internet: http://www.imation.com/computerarts
AMOUNT: $1,000
DEADLINE(S): DEC 12
FIELD(S): All
ELIGIBILITY/REQUIREMENTS: Open to high school students in the U.S. (U.S. students in U.S. military base schools are also eligible.) Need not be enrolled in art classes. Must be nominated to the national competition by their school through a school competition (home-schooled students in recognized home-school programs are eligible to participate; must be sponsored by an instructor; school competition rules do not apply).
HOW TO APPLY: Entries must be submitted by the student and school representative (together). Art must be less than 1MB, saved in JPEG format and submitted via Imation's website. NO paper applica-

tions. Art must be accompanied by the completed online application. All work must be the original, unique creation of the student. No work that has been directly copied from any published source, or which includes such material, unless the student has creatively modified and reinterpreted the original work using the student's own vision and style. Entries become property of Imation and may be used in promotion, advertising, or other publicity. Full recognition and credit will be given the student artist. For additional information about entry, types of artwork accepted, and contest rules, read FAQ on website.
RENEWABLE: No
CONTACT: CAS@imation.com

190—JACOB'S PILLOW DANCE FESTIVAL

The Intern Program at Jacob's Pillow
P.O. Box 287
Lee MA 01238
413/637-1322
Fax: 413/243-4744
E-mail: info@jacobspillow.org
Internet: http://www.jacobspillow.org
AMOUNT: Varies (full and partial tuition)
DEADLINE(S): APR 5
FIELD(S): Dance
ELIGIBILITY/REQUIREMENTS: Awards based on demonstrated financial need and talent. In exchange for scholarship support, all recipients assist with Festival tasks when not in class and agree to be exemplary Pillow community members.
HOW TO APPLY: See website for application and detailed information. In addition to application, provide summary of work experience including name, address, phone number, and earnings for current and past 2 employers; previous aid, prizes, grants, scholarship awards, including name of granting institution or agency, name of aid or award, amount, and year received. Describe other funds to which you are applying that would assist with Pillow program fees, amount requested, and notification date of award status.
NUMBER OF AWARDS: Multiple

191—JUNIATA COLLEGE (Ron & Ann Wertz Arts Scholarship)

Office of Financial Planning
1700 Moore Street
Huntingdon PA 16652
814/641-3142
FAX: 814/641-5311
E-mail: frankv@juniata.edu

Internet: http://www.juniata.edu/
admission/finplan/index.html
AMOUNT: Full tuition, room & board
DEADLINE(S): JAN 4
FIELD(S): Creative and/or performing
arts, Fine Arts, Graphic Design, Writing,
Choral and Instrumental Music, Theater,
Dance
ELIGIBILITY/REQUIREMENTS: Open
to incoming freshmen (upperclassmen and
transfer students are ineligible). Must be
nominated by a Juniata alumnus/a, parent
of a Juniata student, guidance counselor,
pastor, teacher, or someone familiar with
the student's involvement in school and
community activities. who have excelled in
the creative and/or performing arts, including drawing, painting, sculpting, graphic
design, writing, choral and instrumental
music, theatre and dance.
HOW TO APPLY: Submit a Nomination
Essay (in addition to the essay required for
admission) of no more than 2 pages discussing why you should be considered for a
scholarship, including supporting activities
and involvement. You may also attach up
to 3 extra pages of supporting information
of any kind. Must submit a portfolio. See
website for additional information or contact College.
NUMBER OF AWARDS: 1
RENEWABLE: No
CONTACT: Vincent Frank, Director of
Student Financial Planning, 814/641-3140;
e-mail: frankv@juniata.edu

192—LANDMARK COMMUNICATIONS, INC.

150 W Branbleton Avenue
Norfolk VA 23510
757/446-2913
FAX: 757/222-5850
E-mail: jlamkin@lcimedia.com
Internet: http://www.landmark
communications.com
AMOUNT: Newsroom internship
DEADLINE(S): NOV 30
FIELD(S): Reporters; Photographers;
Graphic Artists; Sports Writers; Copy
Editors; Page Designers
ELIGIBILITY/REQUIREMENTS: Be a
U.S. citizen or registered permanent resi-
dent. Have a goal of becoming a print jour-
nalism professional. Have ties to the Mid-
Atlantic/Southern region. Be a member of
a minority group—Asian, Hispanic,
African American, Native American. Be a
college sophomore enrolled full time (at
least 12 credit hours per semester) in a 4-
year degree program. GPA of 2.5 or better.
Have a personal vehicle for necessary on-
the-job transportation during the workday.
Compete on the basis of grades, work samples, financial needs, recommendations,

and interview skills. Your internship will
be during the summer between your
sophomore and junior years and junior and
senior years. At the end of each summer,
you'll be awarded a $5,000 scholarship.
Eligible for a 1-year internship with full
benefits and the possibility of continuing
employment.
HOW TO APPLY: Download application
from website and submit with 500-word
autobiography; résumé (include expected
graduation date); college transcript; and 3
letters of recommendation from professional colleagues or professors. Provide
work samples, a minimum of 3 college or
professional newspaper/magazine or other
work samples (include 3 copies of your
sample, Xeroxes or disks as well as e-mail
attachments if applying online).
NUMBER OF AWARDS: Up to 3
RENEWABLE: Yes: 2 years—maintain a
2.5 GPA throughout college; adhere to
standards and ethics of professional journalism; uphold a positive public image as a
Landmark Scholar; be punctual and have
good attendance; comply with Landmark's
general employment policies during
internship; and participate in available
training, workshops, and seminars.
CONTACT: Jean Lamkin

193—LIBERACE FOUNDATION FOR THE PERFORMING AND CREATIVE ARTS

1775 East Tropicana Avenue
Las Vegas NV 89119-6529
702/798-5595
FAX: 702/798-7386
E-mail: foundation@liberace.org
Internet: http://www.liberace.org
AMOUNT: Varies
DEADLINE(S): MAR 15
FIELD(S): Music (Instrumental and
Vocal); Theater; Dance; Visual Arts;
Fine Art
ELIGIBILITY/REQUIREMENTS:
Provides grants to accredited institutions
that offer training in above fields. Grants
are to be used exclusively for scholarship
assistance to talented and deserving stu-
dents. Recipients should be promising and
deserving upperclassmen (junior, senior,
graduate) enrolled in a course of study
leading up to a career in the arts.
HOW TO APPLY: See website or write to
above address for details.
RENEWABLE: Yes
CONTACT: Joel Strote

194—LIGHT WORK (Artist-in-Residence Program)

316 Waverly Avenue
Syracuse NY 13244
315/443-1300

FAX: 315/443-9516
E-mail: cdlight@syr.edu
Internet: http://www.lightwork.org/
AMOUNT: $2,000 stipend
DEADLINE(S): None
FIELD(S): Photography; Computer
Graphics
ELIGIBILITY/REQUIREMENTS:
Career support for artists from around the
world working with photography or digital
imaging. Residency is for one month, and
financial need is NOT considered.
HOW TO APPLY: There is no application
form. Send a letter of intent, current
résumé, 15-20 slides, artist's statement, and
return postage for work.
NUMBER OF AWARDS: 12-15 awards
annually
RENEWABLE: No

195—MEMPHIS COLLEGE OF ART (Portfolio Awards)

Overton Park
1930 Poplar Avenue
Memphis TN 38104-2764
800/727-1088
E-mail: admissions@mca.edu
Internet: http://www.mca.edu/
index.cfm
AMOUNT: Half tuition
DEADLINE(S): Varies (NOV 15 through
JUL 31)
FIELD(S): Visual Arts
ELIGIBILITY/REQUIREMENTS:
Awards are given to excellent visual art
portfolios submitted by either high school
students or transfer students and are to be
used for full-time enrollment at Memphis
College of Art. International students are
welcome to apply. Financial need is not a
consideration.
HOW TO APPLY: Contact MCA for
application and submission details or see
website.
NUMBER OF AWARDS: 2

196—NATIONAL PTA (Reflections Program)

541 N. Fairbanks Ct., Suite 1300
Chicago IL 60611
800/307-4PTA or 312/670-6782
FAX: 312/670-6783
E-mail: info@pta.org
Internet: http://www.pta.org
AMOUNT: Varies
DEADLINE(S): Varies
FIELD(S): Literature; Musical
Composition; Photography; Visual
Arts; Dance/Choreography
ELIGIBILITY/REQUIREMENTS: Open
to students in preschool through grade

twelve to express themselves and to receive positive recognition for their artistic efforts. Young artists can get involved in the Reflections Program of their local PTA or PTSA.

HOW TO APPLY: Contact your state PTA office for information about the Reflections Program in your area.

197—NAVAL HISTORICAL CENTER (Internship Program)

Washington Navy Yard
805 Kidder Breese Street SE
Washington DC 20374-5060
202/433-6901
FAX: 202/433-8200
E-mail: edward.furgol@navy.mil
Internet: http://www.history.navy.mil
AMOUNT: $400 possible honoraria; otherwise, unpaid
DEADLINE(S): none
FIELD(S): Education; History; Public Relations; Design
ELIGIBILITY/REQUIREMENTS: Registered students of colleges/universities and graduates thereof are eligible for this program, which must be a minimum of 3 weeks, full- or part-time. Four specialties are available: Curator, Education, Public Relations, and Design. Interns receive orientation and assist in their department, and they must complete an individual project that contributes to the Center.
HOW TO APPLY: Submit completed application, available from the website, before the desired initiation of an internship. Also send one letter of recommendation, an unofficial transcript, and (except for graphic design applicants) a writing sample of not less than 1,000 words.
NUMBER OF AWARDS: 60
RENEWABLE: Yes; must reapply.
CONTACT: Dr. Edward Furgol

198—NOVA SCOTIA COLLEGE OF ART AND DESIGN

5163 Duke Street
Halifax Nova Scotia B3J 3J6
CANADA
902/494-8129
FAX: 902/425-2987
E-mail: bkehoe@nscad.ns.ca
Internet: http://www.nscad.ca
AMOUNT: $500-$13,500 (Canadian)
DEADLINE(S): Varies
FIELD(S): Art; Fine Arts
ELIGIBILITY/REQUIREMENTS: The Nova Scotia College of Art and Design administers a number of scholarships and bursary awards that acknowledge high achievement and special promise. Awards restricted to students accepted to or officially registered at the university.

HOW TO APPLY: Write for details on specific scholarships.
CONTACT: Bernadette Kehoe, Student Services

199—PIXAR ANIMATION STUDIOS (Summer Internships)

1200 Park Avenue
Emeryville CA 94608
510/752-3000
FAX: 510/725-3151
E-mail: hr@pixar.com
Internet: http://www.pixar.com/companyinfo/jobs
AMOUNT: Varies
DEADLINE(S): MAR
FIELD(S): Animation
ELIGIBILITY/REQUIREMENTS: Summer internships offer "hands-on" experience for currently enrolled college or university students, based on departmental needs.
HOW TO APPLY: Send a résumé with name/address/phone, position, work experience/education, internships, and hardware/software experience. Must also submit reels: VHS (NTSC or PAL) or 3/4″ (NTSC), 5 minutes in length starting with most recent work, music optional—visual skills nicer, and credit list explaining your reel and software used. See website for details/available positions.

200—PRINT AND GRAPHICS SCHOLARSHIP FOUNDATION, THE (PGSF)

200 Deer Run Road
Sewickley PA 15143-2600
412/259-1740 or 800/910-4283
FAX: 412/741-2311
E-mail: pgsf@piagatf.org
Internet: http://www. pgsf.org
AMOUNT: $500-$5,000
DEADLINE(S): MAR 1 (high school seniors), APR 1 (college undergraduates)
FIELD(S): Graphic Communications; Printing Technology; Printing Management; Publishing
ELIGIBILITY/REQUIREMENTS: For students pursuing careers in above fields, who are enrolled in a 2- or 4-year accredited program at a technical school, college or university in the U.S..
HOW TO APPLY: For more information and application, see website or call, fax or e-mail. Submit with SAT, ACT or SAT/NMSQT (high school students only), official transcript, 2 recommendation forms from a school representative, such as an instructor, counselor, or advisor (1 may be from an employer), a photocopy of course of study,

NUMBER OF AWARDS: 200-300
RENEWABLE: Yes; must meet basic criteria
CONTACT: Bernie Eckert

201—RHYTHM AND HUES STUDIOS (Computer Graphics Scholarship)

5404 Jandy Place
Los Angeles CA 90066
310/448-7500
E-mail: scholarship@rhythm.com
Internet: http://www.rhythm.com/recruiting/scholarship/index.html
AMOUNT: $1,000-$4,000
DEADLINE(S): Mid MAY
FIELD(S): Computer Modeling; Computer Character Animation; Digital Cinematography
ELIGIBILITY/REQUIREMENTS: Open to all students enrolled full time in an accredited undergraduate or graduate degree program within 6 months of the deadline.
HOW TO APPLY: Entries should include cover sheet stating name, address, phone, SSN, school, major, faculty advisor name/address/phone, and category under which entry is being submitted. Also include photocopy of current student ID and typewritten description of entry, including hardware/software used. Contact Rhythm and Hues Studios for more information.
NUMBER OF AWARDS: 5 (1 award in modeling, 1 in animation, and 3 in cinematography)

202—SOCIETY FOR TECHNICAL COMMUNICATION

901 N. Stuart Street, Suite 904
Arlington VA 22203
703/522-4114
FAX: 703/522-2075
E-mail: stc@stc.org
Internet: http://www.stcva.org/scholarships.html
AMOUNT: $1,500
DEADLINE(S): FEB 15
FIELD(S): Communications including Technical Writing, Editing, Graphic Design, Multimedia Art and related fields
ELIGIBILITY/REQUIREMENTS: Open to full-time students who have completed at least one year of post-secondary education working toward a Bachelor's degree and are enrolled in an accredited 2- or 4-year degree program for career in any area of technical communication: technical writing, editing, graphic design, multimedia art, etc.
HOW TO APPLY: See website and/or write for complete information.
NUMBER OF AWARDS: 2

203—SOCIETY OF ILLUSTRATORS (Student Scholarship Competition)

128 E. 63rd Street
New York NY 10021-7303
212/838-2560
FAX: 212/838-2561
E-mail: info@societyillustrators.org
Internet: http://www.society
illustrators.org
AMOUNT: Varies
DEADLINE(S): FEB 1
FIELD(S): Illustration; Cartooning;
Animation; Graphic Design
ELIGIBILITY/REQUIREMENTS: Cash
awards are given to selected college-level
art students who enter an annual juried
exhibition.
HOW TO APPLY: Contact the Chair of
your college's art program, who should
request, on school letterhead, the "Call for
Entries" for the Student Scholarship
Competition. Individual student inquiries
will NOT be honored.

204—SUPREME LODGE KNIGHTS OF PYTHIAS (Poster Contest)

59 Coddington Street
Quincy MA 02169
617/472-8800
FAX: 617/376-0363
E-mail: kop@earthlink.net
Internet: http://www.pythias.org
AMOUNT: First Prize: $1,000; Second
Prize: $500; Third Prize: $250; Fourth
to Eighth Prizes: $100 each
DEADLINE(S): Varies by local lodge
FIELD(S): All
ELIGIBILITY/REQUIREMENTS:
Poster contest for high school students in
the United States and Canada.
HOW TO APPLY: Contact local lodge for
detailed guidelines on subject matter, for-
mat, etc. Submit posters to local lodge.
NUMBER OF AWARDS: 8
RENEWABLE: Yes
CONTACT: Alfred A. Saltzman

205—TAPPI COATING & GRAPHIC ARTS DIVISION (Best Paper Award Scholarship)

P.O. Box 105113
Atlanta GA 30092
770/446-1400
FAX: 770/446-6947
E-mail: vedmondson@tappi.org
Internet: http://www.tappi.org
AMOUNT: $1,000
DEADLINE(S): JAN 31
FIELD(S): Paper Industry; Graphic Arts
ELIGIBILITY/REQUIREMENTS:
Annual scholarship presented to 1 school

each year (announced in May). Students
from that school may then apply.
HOW TO APPLY: Contact TAPPI
Project Event Manager to determine
which school has received the award; then
contact school directly for more information on how to apply.
NUMBER OF AWARDS: 1
RENEWABLE: No
CONTACT: Veranda Edmondson, 770/
208-7536

206—TAPPI COATING & GRAPHIC ARTS DIVISION SCHOLARSHIP PROGRAM

P.O. Box 105113
Atlanta GA 30092
770/446-1400
FAX: 770/446-6947
E-mail: vedmondson@tappi.org
Internet: http://www.tappi.org
AMOUNT: $1,000
DEADLINE(S): JAN 31
FIELD(S): Paper Industry; Graphic Arts
ELIGIBILITY/REQUIREMENTS: Must
be enrolled as a full-time student in an
accredited college or university in a program related to the coated paper and
paperboard or the graphic arts industries;
be a TAPPI Student Chapter member (if
available), be at least a junior with a minimum GPA of 3.0, and have demonstrated
interest in a career in coating and graphic
arts industry.
HOW TO APPLY: Contact TCDA or see
website for an application and additional
information.
NUMBER OF AWARDS: 4
RENEWABLE: No
CONTACT: Veranda Edmondson, 770/
208-7536

207—VIRGINIA MUSEUM OF FINE ARTS (Fellowships)

2800 Grove Avenue
Richmond VA 23221-2466
804/204-2661
Internet: http://vmfa.state.va.us
AMOUNT: $4,000 (undergraduate-maxi-
mum); $6,000 (graduates); $8,000 (pro-
fessionals)
DEADLINE(S): MAR 1
FIELD(S): Crafts; Drawing; Filmmaking;
Painting; Photography; Printmaking;
Sculpture; Video; Art History (gradu-
ate only)
ELIGIBILITY/REQUIREMENTS: Open
to Virginia residents of at least one year
who are U.S. citizens or legal residents.
Fellowships are available to undergradu-
ates, graduates, and professional artists.
Financial need is considered.
HOW TO APPLY: Application and guide-
lines on website.

208—WESTERN MICHIGAN UNIVERSITY (College of Fine Arts/Art Department Enrichment Grants)

1903 W. Michigan
Kalamazoo MI 49008-5337
269/387-6000
FAX: 269/387-6989
E-mail: finaid-info@wmich.edu
Internet: http://www.wmich.edu/
finaid
AMOUNT: Varies
DEADLINE(S): OCT (first Friday)
FIELD(S): Art
ELIGIBILITY/REQUIREMENTS: Full-
time Art majors pursuing a BFA or MFA
degree.
HOW TO APPLY: Submit project propos-
als with specific goals. Contact the Art
Department or see website for an applica-
tion.
NUMBER OF AWARDS: Multiple, num-
ber varies
RENEWABLE: Yes, for 1 year if recipient
is a junior
CONTACT: Art Department

209—WESTERN MICHIGAN UNIVERSITY (College of Fine Arts/Art Department Freshman Scholarships)

1903 W. Michigan
Kalamazoo MI 49008-5337
269/387-6000
FAX: 269/387-6989
E-mail: finaid-info@wmich.edu
Internet: http://www.wmich.edu/
finaid
AMOUNT: $500
DEADLINE(S): With application
FIELD(S): Art
ELIGIBILITY/REQUIREMENTS: Open
to entering freshmen, Art majors, enrolled
full time; based on portfolio.
HOW TO APPLY: Awards selected from
Department Application Portfolios.
NUMBER OF AWARDS: Multiple, num-
ber varies
RENEWABLE: No
CONTACT: Art Department

210—WESTERN MICHIGAN UNIVERSITY (College of Fine Arts/Art Department Student Exhibit Awards)

1903 W. Michigan
Kalamazoo MI 49008-5337
269/387-6000
FAX: 269/387-6989
E-mail: finaid-info@wmich.edu
Internet: http://www.wmich.edu/
finaid

AMOUNT: $250/spring semester
FIELD(S): Art
ELIGIBILITY/REQUIREMENTS: Open to Art majors (graduate or undergraduate); selected from annual student exhibit.
HOW TO APPLY: Contact the Exhibitions Office for information.
NUMBER OF AWARDS: 4
RENEWABLE: No
CONTACT: Exhibitions Office, Art Department

211—WESTERN MICHIGAN UNIVERSITY (College of Fine Arts/Angie Gayman Carmer Art Scholarship)

1903 W. Michigan
Kalamazoo MI 49008-5337
269/387-6000
FAX: 269/387-6989
E-mail: finaid-info@wmich.edu
Internet: http://www.wmich.edu/finaid
AMOUNT: Varies
DEADLINE(S): FEB (first Friday)
FIELD(S): Art
ELIGIBILITY/REQUIREMENTS: Art major (graduate or undergraduate), enrolled full time with a minimum 3.5 GPA for undergraduates and 3.6 GPA for graduates.
HOW TO APPLY: Typed statement of goals and slide portfolio review required. See website for application or contact the Art Advising office for an application.
NUMBER OF AWARDS: Multiple awards
CONTACT: Art Department

212—WESTERN MICHIGAN UNIVERSITY (College of Fine Arts/Art Star Award)

1903 W. Michigan
Kalamazoo MI 49008-5337
269/387-6000
FAX: 269/387-6989
E-mail: finaid-info@wmich.edu
Internet: http://www.wmich.edu/finaid
AMOUNT: $200/spring semester
FIELD(S): Art
ELIGIBILITY/REQUIREMENTS: Open to Art majors in their junior and senior years.
HOW TO APPLY: Student is nominated by faculty.
RENEWABLE: No
CONTACT: Art Department

213—WESTERN MICHIGAN UNIVERSITY (College of Fine Arts/Elizabeth Smutz Award)

1903 W. Michigan
Kalamazoo MI 49008-5337
269/387-6000

FAX: 269/387-6989
E-mail: finaid-info@wmich.edu
Internet: http://www.wmich.edu/finaid
AMOUNT: Varies
FIELD(S): Art Education
ELIGIBILITY/REQUIREMENTS: Must be a major in art education.
HOW TO APPLY: Student is nominated by faculty.
NUMBER OF AWARDS: 1
RENEWABLE: No
CONTACT: Art Department

214—WESTERN MICHIGAN UNIVERSITY (College of Fine Arts/Foundation Scholarships)

1903 W. Michigan
Kalamazoo MI 49008-5337
269/387-6000
FAX: 269/387-6989
E-mail: finaid-info@wmich.edu
Internet: http://www.wmich.edu/finaid
AMOUNT: $200/spring semester
FIELD(S): Art
ELIGIBILITY/REQUIREMENTS: Art majors in freshman or sophomore years who are enrolled full time in foundation classes (introductory level).
HOW TO APPLY: Student is nominated by faculty.
NUMBER OF AWARDS: Multiple awards, number varies
RENEWABLE: No
CONTACT: Art Department

215—WESTERN MICHIGAN UNIVERSITY (College of Fine Arts/Haig and Janette Tashjian Scholarship)

1903 W. Michigan
Kalamazoo MI 49008-5337
269/387-6000
FAX: 269/387-6989
E-mail: finaid-info@wmich.edu
Internet: http://www.wmich.edu/finaid
AMOUNT: Varies
FIELD(S): Art Education
ELIGIBILITY/REQUIREMENTS: Open to Art Education major in junior or senior year, who is enrolled full time, has a 3.5 or higher GPA.
HOW TO APPLY: Student is nominated by faculty.
NUMBER OF AWARDS: 1
RENEWABLE: No
CONTACT: Art Department

216—WESTERN MICHIGAN UNIVERSITY (College of Fine Arts/Lydia Siedschlag Scholarship)

1903 W. Michigan
Kalamazoo MI 49008-5337
269/387-6000
FAX: 269/387-6989
E-mail: finaid-info@wmich.edu
Internet: http://www.wmich.edu/finaid
AMOUNT: Varies
FIELD(S): Art
ELIGIBILITY/REQUIREMENTS: Must be an Art major, resident of Siedschlag Hall with a 3.3 or higher GPA.
HOW TO APPLY: Contact the Art Advising office for an application.
NUMBER OF AWARDS: Multiple awards
CONTACT: Art Department

217—WESTERN MICHIGAN UNIVERSITY (College of Fine Arts/Margaret H. Ward Art Scholarship)

1903 W. Michigan
Kalamazoo MI 49008-5337
269/387-6000
FAX: 269/387-6989
E-mail: finaid-info@wmich.edu
Internet: http://www.wmich.edu/finaid
AMOUNT: Varies
FIELD(S): Art Education
ELIGIBILITY/REQUIREMENTS: Open to Art major in junior or senior year, who is enrolled full time, has a 3.25 or higher GPA. Recipient must exhibit above-average artistic and creative ability and demonstrate financial need. Must be U.S. citizen.
HOW TO APPLY: Contact the Art Department for more information.
NUMBER OF AWARDS: 1
RENEWABLE: No
CONTACT: Art Department

218—WESTERN MICHIGAN UNIVERSITY (College of Fine Arts/Robert and Eleanor DeVries Student Art Award)

1903 W. Michigan
Kalamazoo MI 49008-5337
269/387-6000
FAX: 269/387-6989
E-mail: finaid-info@wmich.edu
Internet: http://www.wmich.edu/finaid
AMOUNT: Varies
FIELD(S): Art
ELIGIBILITY/REQUIREMENTS: Selected from annual student exhibit.

HOW TO APPLY: Contact the Art Advising office for an application.
NUMBER OF AWARDS: Multiple awards
RENEWABLE: No
CONTACT: Art Advisor, Art Department

219—WESTERN MICHIGAN UNIVERSITY (College of Fine Arts/Rose Netzorg Kerr and James W. Kerr Award)

1903 W. Michigan
Kalamazoo MI 49008-5337
269/387-6000
FAX: 269/387-6989
E-mail: finaid-info@wmich.edu
Internet: http://www.wmich.edu/finaid
AMOUNT: Varies
FIELD(S): Graphic Design
ELIGIBILITY/REQUIREMENTS: Must be an undergraduate majoring in graphic design.
HOW TO APPLY: Student is nominated by faculty. Contact the Art Advising office for an application.
NUMBER OF AWARDS: Multiple awards
CONTACT: Art Department

220—WESTERN MICHIGAN UNIVERSITY (College of Fine Arts/Walter F. Enz Memorial Award)

1903 W. Michigan
Kalamazoo MI 49008-5337
269/387-6000
FAX: 269/387-6989
E-mail: finaid-info@wmich.edu
Internet: http://www.wmich.edu/finaid
AMOUNT: Varies
FIELD(S): Art
ELIGIBILITY/REQUIREMENTS: Open to art major (graduate or undergraduate) who is enrolled full time.
HOW TO APPLY: Student is nominated by faculty.
NUMBER OF AWARDS: 1-2
RENEWABLE: No
CONTACT: Art Department

221—WESTERN MICHIGAN UNIVERSITY (Pete Repins Memorial Scholarship)

1903 West Michigan
Kalamazoo MI 49008-5337
269/387-8777
FAX: 269/387-6989
E-mail: alumni@wmich.edu
Internet: http://www.wmich.edu/
ENDOWED

AMOUNT: Tuition, fees, and book expenses
DEADLINE(S): APR 1
FIELD(S): All
ELIGIBILITY/REQUIREMENTS: Must be a junior or senior undergraduate student majoring in advertising, printing production, or graphics; must have a 3.0 GPA or higher. Preference given to a student who demonstrates a strong commitment to the academic programs and professions of advertising, printing production, or graphics as well as related extracurricular activities such as work-related experience, organization membership, etc.
HOW TO APPLY: See website for application and submit with FAFSA.
NUMBER OF AWARDS: Varies
RENEWABLE: Yes. Up to 2 consecutive years
CONTACT: Office of Financial Aid

222—WOMEN'S STUDIO WORKSHOP (Fellowship Grants)

P.O. Box 489
Rosendale NY 12472
845/658-9133
FAX: 845/658-9031
E-mail: info@wsworkshop.org
Internet: http://www.wsworkshop.org/
AMOUNT: Tuition
DEADLINE(S): MAR 15; NOV 1
FIELD(S): Visual Arts
ELIGIBILITY/REQUIREMENTS: Designed to provide concentrated work time for artists to explore new ideas in a dynamic and supportive community of women artists. WSW welcomes applications from emerging artists.
HOW TO APPLY: Application form plus a résumé, 6-10 slides, a letter of interest that addresses the purpose of the residency, explaining areas of proficiency and studio skills, and a SASE for return of materials. Applications available on website.

223—WOMEN'S STUDIO WORKSHOP (Internship)

P.O. Box 489
Rosendale NY 12472
845/658-9133
FAX: 845/658-9031
E-mail: info@wsworkshop.org
Internet: http://www.wsworkshop.org/
AMOUNT: $150/month + housing
DEADLINE(S): APR 1 and OCT 15
FIELD(S): Visual Arts including Printmaking, Papermaking, Book Arts, Photography, Ceramics

ELIGIBILITY/REQUIREMENTS: Must have experience in one or more of fields.
HOW TO APPLY: Send a letter of interest, résumé, up to 20 slides with slide list, 3 reference letters, and a SASE.
NUMBER OF AWARDS: 6
RENEWABLE: No
CONTACT: Ellen Kucera

224—WORLDSTUDIO FOUNDATION

200 Varick Street, Suite 507
New York NY 10014
212/366-1317
FAX: 212/807-0024
E-mail: info@worldstudio.org
Internet: http://www.worldstudio.org or http://www.aiga.org
AMOUNT: $1,500-$5,000
DEADLINE(S): APR 14
FIELD(S): Advertising, Animation, Architecture, Cartooning, Crafts, Environmental graphics, Film/video, Film/theater design, Fine arts, Furniture design, Industrial/product design, Interior architecture and design, Landscape architecture, New media, Photography, Surface/textile design, Urban planning
ELIGIBILITY/REQUIREMENTS: Applicants must be pursuing a degree in the fine or commercial arts, design or architecture, and plan to enter a career in the creative professions. Undergraduates and graduates are eligible. Minority status and/or social agenda are significant factors. Financial need a prerequisite. Minimum 2.0 GPA.
HOW TO APPLY: See websites for application. The application is a 2-part process. Applications must include personal and school information, including transcripts and copies of letters of acceptance; financial information; portfolio; written statement of purpose; examples of a commitment to a social agenda, 2 letters of recommendation from college instructors, high school teachers, or employers; head shot of applicant.
NUMBER OF AWARDS: 20-30
RENEWABLE: Yes. Must reapply.
CONTACT: Mark Randall

MUSIC

225—ACADEMY OF VOCAL ARTS

1920 Spruce Street
Philadelphia PA 19103-6685
215/735-1685
FAX: 215/732-2189
E-mail: info@avaopera.org
Internet: http://www.avaopera.com

AMOUNT: Tuition free, based on competitive audition
DEADLINE(S): Late JAN
FIELD(S): Vocal Music; Operatic Acting
ELIGIBILITY/REQUIREMENTS: Tenable only at the Academy of Vocal Arts. Open to unusually gifted singers with at least four years' college vocal training or equivalent. College degree recommended. Award includes full-tuition scholarships and complete training in voice, operatic acting, and repertoire. Merit-based fellowships for additional expenses are also available. Total student enrollment limited to 30.
HOW TO APPLY: Contact the Academy of Vocal Arts for an application. Winners are selected in Spring competitive auditions.
NUMBER OF AWARDS: 8-12
RENEWABLE: Yes
CONTACT: Val Starr, Audition Coordinator

226—ADELPHI UNIVERSITY (Talent Awards)

1 South Avenue
Garden City NY 11530
516/877-3080
FAX: 516/877-3380
Internet: http://www.ecampus.
adelphi.edu/sfs/au scholarships
grants.php#art
AMOUNT: $4,000-$10,000
DEADLINE(S): FEB 15
FIELD(S): Theater; Dance; Art; Music
ELIGIBILITY/REQUIREMENTS: Various scholarships for full-time students at Adelphi University in the above fields. Audition required.
HOW TO APPLY: See website for further information; contact school to apply.
RENEWABLE: Yes. Must maintain 3.0 GPA in major and 2.5 overall to maintain scholarship.

227—AMERICAN ACCORDION MUSICOLOGICAL SOCIETY

506 S Broadway
Pitman NJ 08071
856/854-6628
AMOUNT: $500 and $300
DEADLINE(S): MAR
FIELD(S): Music Composition for Accordion
ELIGIBILITY/REQUIREMENTS: Annual competition open to amateur or professional music composers who write a serious piece music (of six minutes or more) for the accordion.
HOW TO APPLY: Write for complete information.
NUMBER OF AWARDS: 3

228—AMERICAN FOUNDATION FOR THE BLIND (Gladys C. Anderson Memorial Scholarship)

11 Penn Plaza, Suite 300
New York NY 10001
212/502-7661
FAX: 212/502-7771
E-mail: afbinfo@afb.net
Internet: http://www.afb.org/
scholar/scholarships.asp
AMOUNT: $1,000
DEADLINE(S): Varies
FIELD(S): Religious/Classical Music
ELIGIBILITY/REQUIREMENTS: Open to legally blind women studying religious or classical music at the college level. Must be U.S. citizen. Must submit evidence of legal blindness; official transcripts; proof of college/university acceptance; 3 letters of recommendation; performance tape of voice/instrumental selection (30 minutes max.); and typewritten statement (no more than 3 double-spaced pages) describing the field of study you are pursuing, educational and personal goals, work experience, extracurricular activities, and how scholarship monies will be used.
HOW TO APPLY: See website or contact the AFB for an application.
NUMBER OF AWARDS: 1

229—AMERICAN FOUNDATION FOR THE BLIND (R. L. Gillette Scholarships)

11 Penn Plaza, Suite 300
New York NY 10001
212/502-7661
FAX: 212/502-7771
E-mail: afbinfo@afb.net
Internet: http://www.afb.org/
scholar/scholarships.asp
AMOUNT: $1,000
DEADLINE(S): MAR 31
FIELD(S): Literature; Music
ELIGIBILITY/REQUIREMENTS: Open to legally blind women enrolled in a 4-year undergraduate degree program in literature or music. Must be U.S. citizen. Must submit evidence of legal blindness; official transcripts; proof of college/university acceptance; 3 letters of recommendation; performance tape (30 minutes max.) or creative writing sample; and typewritten statement describing the field of study you are pursuing, educational and personal goals, work experience, extracurricular activities, and how monies will be used.
HOW TO APPLY: See website or contact AFB for an application.
NUMBER OF AWARDS: 2
CONTACT: Alina Vayntrub

230—AMERICAN GUILD OF ORGANISTS (National Competition in Organ Improvisation)

475 Riverside Drive, Suite 1260
New York NY 10115
212/870-2310
FAX: 212/870-2163
Internet: http://www.agohq.org
AMOUNT: $2,000 (first prize); $1,000 (second); $500 (third)
DEADLINE(S): Varies
FIELD(S): Organ Performance
ELIGIBILITY/REQUIREMENTS: Biannual competition seeks to further the art of improvisation in organ performance by recognizing and rewarding superior performers in the field. Membership in AGO required. Open to all members, including student members.
HOW TO APPLY: Contact AGO for membership information or an application. $35 registration fee.

231—AMERICAN GUILD OF ORGANISTS (National Young Artists Competition)

475 Riverside Drive, Suite 1260
New York NY 10115
212/870-2310
FAX: 212/870-2163
Internet: http://www.agohq.org
AMOUNT: $2,000 (first prize); $1,500 (second); $750 (third)
DEADLINE(S): Varies
FIELD(S): Organ Performance
ELIGIBILITY/REQUIREMENTS: Competition for organists between the ages of 22 and 32. Must be members of AGO.
HOW TO APPLY: Contact AGO for membership information or an application.

232—AMERICAN GUILD OF ORGANISTS (Regional Competitions for Young Organists)

475 Riverside Drive, Suite 1260
New York NY 10115
212/870-2310
FAX: 212/870-2163
Internet: http://www.agohq.org
AMOUNT: $1,000 (first prize); $500 (second)
DEADLINE(S): Varies
FIELD(S): Organ Performance
ELIGIBILITY/REQUIREMENTS: Biannual competition for young people up to age 23 in nine different regions of the U.S. Membership NOT required.
HOW TO APPLY: Contact AGO for an application. $25 registration fee.

233—AMERICAN MOTHERS, INC. (Gertrude Fogelson Cultural and Creative Arts Awards)

1296 E. 21st Street
Brooklyn NY 11201
718/253-5676
AMOUNT: Up to $1,000
DEADLINE(S): JAN 1
FIELD(S): Visual Arts; Creative Writing; Vocal Music
ELIGIBILITY/REQUIREMENTS: An award to encourage and honor mothers in artistic pursuits.
HOW TO APPLY: Write for details.

234—AMERICAN STRING TEACHERS ASSOCIATION (ASTA) (Merle J. Isaac Composition Competition)

4153 Chain Bridge Road
Fairfax VA 22030
703/279-2113
FAX: 703/279-2114
E-mail: asta@astaweb.com
Internet: http://www.astaweb.com
AMOUNT: Up to $1,000
DEADLINE(S): MAY 1
FIELD(S): Music Composition
ELIGIBILITY/REQUIREMENTS: Applicant must submit an original composition that is unpublished and has never been submitted for publication, suitable for String Orchestra. Entries for middle school/junior high and high school level full orchestra will be accepted. Manuscripts will be judged on score analysis and a live performance.
HOW TO APPLY: See website for details of rules.

235—AMERICAN STRING TEACHERS ASSOCIATION (ASTA) (Solo Competitions)

4153 Chain Bridge Road
Fairfax VA 22030
703/279-2113
FAX: 703/279-2114
E-mail: asta@astaweb.com
Internet: http://www.astaweb.com
AMOUNT: Up to $4,500
DEADLINE(S): Varies
FIELD(S): Music (Strings): Violin, Viola, Cello, Double Bass, Classical Guitar, and Harp
ELIGIBILITY/REQUIREMENTS: Participants must be ASTA members or current students of ASTA members. Involves state competitions that lead to national competition. Two age groups: Junior Division—under 19; and Senior Division—19-25. Application fees required. For U.S. and Canadian citizens/legal residents.

HOW TO APPLY: Details of rules and deadlines are on website above. List of state solo competition chairpersons is on website.

236—ASSOCIATED BOARD OF THE ROYAL SCHOOLS OF MUSIC

24 Portland Place
London W1B 1LU
UNITED KINGDOM
+44 20 7636 5400
FAX: +44 20 7637 0234
E-mail: international@abrsm.ac.uk
Internet: http://www.abrsm.ac.uk
AMOUNT: £4,500
FIELD(S): Music Performance
ELIGIBILITY/REQUIREMENTS: Open to undergraduates. Must be at least 17 by January 31; must be nationals of a country that is not a member of the European Union. (Candidates who have been living or studying in the UK for more than a year immediately preceding January 31 in the year of entry to the course and those with home status are not eligible.) Must demonstrate outstanding musical promise and proficiency in principal field of study. Elected scholars will normally be required to begin their courses at the Royal Academy of Music, the Royal College of Music, the Royal Northern College of Music, or the Royal Scottish Academy of Music and Drama within one year of the date of their election.
HOW TO APPLY: See website.
NUMBER OF AWARDS: 8 (2 annually at each of 4 colleges listed above).

237—ASSOCIATED MALE CHORUSES OF AMERICA (Music Scholarships)

E-mail: scholarship@amcofa.net
Internet: http://amcofa.net/scholar.shtml
AMOUNT: $1,000 (3)-$1,200 (1)
DEADLINE(S): MAR 1
FIELD(S): Music: Voice/Choral or Instrumental
ELIGIBILITY/REQUIREMENTS: Scholarships for music majors, both male and female, enrolled as full-time college students in Bachelor's Degree programs. Student must be sponsored by a member chorus of the AMCA (list of member choruses available online).
HOW TO APPLY: Contact your closest AMCA Chorus for forms describing requirements, instructions, and applications or see website. Audition tape or CD required.
NUMBER OF AWARDS: Varies
RENEWABLE: Yes
CONTACT: Robert H. Torborg

238—BAGBY FOUNDATION FOR THE MUSICAL ARTS, INC., THE (Study Grants)

501 Fifth Avenue, Suite 1401
New York NY 10017
212/986-6094
AMOUNT: $2,000-$6,000
DEADLINE(S): Ongoing
FIELD(S): Music
ELIGIBILITY/REQUIREMENTS: Musical study grants based on talent and need.
HOW TO APPLY: Send a letter to above location outlining financial need as well as credentials.
NUMBER OF AWARDS: Multiple

239—BEEBE FUND (Frank Huntington Beebe Fund for Musicians)

290 Huntington Avenue
Boston MA 02115
617/585-1267
AMOUNT: $16,000 (transportation, room and board, and tuition)
DEADLINE(S): DEC
FIELD(S): Music
ELIGIBILITY/REQUIREMENTS: For gifted young musicians (generally no older than mid-20s), generally performers in classical disciplines, who wish to pursue advanced music study and performance abroad, usually in Europe. Fellowships are awarded to musicians at the outset of their professional lives, for whom this would be the first extended period of study abroad.
HOW TO APPLY: Applicants must demonstrate a solid base of accomplishment.
CONTACT: Secretary

240—BLUES HEAVEN FOUNDATION, INC. (Muddy Waters Scholarship)

2120 S. Michigan Avenue
Chicago IL 60616
312/808-1286
AMOUNT: $2,000
DEADLINE(S): APR 30
FIELD(S): Music; Music Education; African-American Studies; Folklore; Performing Arts; Arts Management; Journalism; Radio/TV/Film
ELIGIBILITY/REQUIREMENTS: Scholarship awarded on a competitive basis with consideration given to scholastic achievement, concentration of studies, and financial need. Applicant must be full-time graduate or undergraduate in a Chicago area college or university. Scholastic aptitude, extracurricular involvement, GPA, and financial need are all considered.

HOW TO APPLY: Contact Foundation between February and April to request an application.

241—CHOPIN FOUNDATION OF THE UNITED STATES, INC. (Scholarship Program for Young Pianists)

1440 79th St. Causeway, Suite 117
Miami FL 33141
305/868-0624
FAX: 305/865-5150
E-mail: info@chopin.org
Internet: http://www.chopin.org
AMOUNT: $1,000/year up to 4 years
DEADLINE(S): FEB 15
FIELD(S): Music: Piano
ELIGIBILITY/REQUIREMENTS: Scholarship program for pianists 14 to 17 years old who demonstrate an affinity for the interpretation of Chopin's music. The pianist is supported and encouraged for 4 years of preparation to qualify for the American National Chopin Piano Competition held in Miami, Florida, every 5 years. The winners of this competition compete in the International Chopin Piano Competition in Warsaw, Poland. For U.S. citizens or legal residents whose field of study is music and whose major is piano. Must be a full-time student.
HOW TO APPLY: Submit references, audiotape, and formal application, which is available at the above website or write for details. $25 registration fee.
NUMBER OF AWARDS: 10
RENEWABLE: Yes

242—COLBURN-PLEDGE MUSIC SCHOLARSHIP FOUNDATION (Scholarships for Texas String Instrument Students)

101 Cardinal Avenue
San Antonio TX 78209
AMOUNT: Varies
DEADLINE(S): APR
FIELD(S): Music: String instruments
ELIGIBILITY/REQUIREMENTS: Awards for Texas residents studying a string instrument (violin, viola, cello, bass) in classical music with the intention of becoming a professional musician and in need of financial aid. Applicants can be in junior high, high school, or college. Texas residents may attend out-of-state music schools and/or music camps.
HOW TO APPLY: Auditions of selected applicants are held in San Antonio around June 1. Write for detailed information.

243—COLUMBIA UNIVERSITY (Joseph H. Bearns Prize in Music)

Columbia University
Department of Music
2960 Broadway
621 Dodge Hall MC #1813
New York NY 10027
AMOUNT: Up to $6,000
DEADLINE(S): MAR 15
FIELD(S): Music Composition
ELIGIBILITY/REQUIREMENTS: Contest open to composers between the ages of 18 and 25 (as of JAN 1 of award year). Submissions must be original compositions.
HOW TO APPLY: Send entry with information about self, prior studies, title of work and note of public performance, if any, and a list of compositions to date. No more than 1 entry per person.
NUMBER OF AWARDS: 2 (1 larger works, such as orchestral and choral works; 1 smaller works, such as solo, quartet, and sextet)
RENEWABLE: Yes. May compete a second time, but not in 2 successive competitions.
CONTACT: Bearns Prize Committee

244—COMMUNITY FOUNDATION FOR GREATER ATLANTA, INC., THE (James M. & Virginia M. Smyth Scholarship Fund)

50 Hurt Plaza, Suite 449
Atlanta GA 30303
404/688-5525
FAX: 404/688-3060
E-mail: scholarships@atlcf.org
Internet: http://www.atlcf.org/GrantsScholarships/Scholarships.aspx
AMOUNT $500-$1,000
DEADLINE(S): Varies
FIELD(S): Humanities, Science, Human Services, Music Ministry
ELIGIBILITY/REQUIREMENTS: Open to students enrolled at an accredited college pursuing an undergraduate degree and adults returning to school in order to increase employability. Must have a cumulative 3.0 GPA; be accepted for enrollment or enrolled at an accredited college, university or technical school; demonstrate financial need, and commitment to community service through school, community or religious organizations. Preference will be given to applicants from Missouri, Mississippi, Georgia, Illinois, Oklahoma, Texas and Tennessee.
HOW TO APPLY: See website for additional information and application. Submit with a personal essay (2-3 pages) that explains why you feel a college education is important, your statement of educational and career goals, post college career interests, highlights of your high school extracurricular/community service activities, special

strengths, skills, and qualifications, any unusual family or personal circumstances that have affected your achievement in school, work experience, or your participation in school and community activities, and present financial need; official transcript; and SAT and ACT scores, if a recent high school graduate. Send to The Community Foundation for Greater Atlanta, James M. & Virginia M. Smyth Scholarship Fund, Scholarship Management Services, Scholarship America, One Scholarship Way, P.O. Box 297, Saint Peter, MN 56082. If you have questions, call 507/931-1682 or e-mail communityfoundation@scholarship-america.org.
NUMBER OF AWARDS: 12-15
RENEWABLE: Yes; previous recipients are renewed if they continue to meet the scholarship's criteria and submit the current year's renewal application
CONTACT: Lisa Glanville, 404/308-0055

245—COMMUNITY FOUNDATION OF WESTERN MASSACHUSETTS (Kevin Bresnahan Memorial Scholarship)

1500 Main Street
P.O. Box 15769
Springfield MA 01115
413/732-2858
FAX: 413/733/8565
E-mail: scholar@communityfoundation.org
Internet: http://www.communityfoundation.org
AMOUNT: $1,000
DEADLINE(S): MAR 31
FIELD(S): Music
ELIGIBILITY/REQUIREMENTS: For graduates of Holyoke High School or Holyoke Catholic High School, both in Massachusetts, who plan to further their education at the post-secondary level, or at any trade or professional school beyond high school, and plan to pursue a career in music.
HOW TO APPLY: See website for application.
NUMBER OF AWARDS: 1
RENEWABLE: No

246—COMMUNITY FOUNDATION OF WESTERN MASSACHUSETTS (Liliana Marie Cordes Scholarships)

1500 Main Street
P.O. Box 15769
Springfield MA 01115
413/732-2858
FAX: 413/733/8565
E-mail: scholar@communityfoundation.org
Internet: http://www.communityfoundation.org

AMOUNT: $2,000
DEADLINE(S): MAR 31
FIELD(S): All
ELIGIBILITY/REQUIREMENTS: Open to graduating senior from South Hadley High School in Massachusetts who has chosen to study music.
HOW TO APPLY: See website for application.
NUMBER OF AWARDS: 1
RENEWABLE: No

247—CONCLAVE, THE (McNally-Smith Scholarship)

4517 Minnetonka Boulevard, #104
Minneapolis MN 55416
952/927-4487
FAX: 952/927-6427
Internet: http://www.theconclave. com or radioscholarships. com
AMOUNT: Tuition ($25,000+)
DEADLINE(S): APR 1
FIELD(S): Music industry
ELIGIBILITY/REQUIREMENTS: Granted to the applicant who best demonstrates his or her ambition to pursue a career in the music industry, who has maintained a good academic record, and demonstrates financial need. Open to any student who has applied for admission to McNally Smith College's Associate of Applied Science Degree in Music Business Program.
HOW TO APPLY: Apply online at either website or contact The Conclave for an application. Submit with an audio cassette or CD recording of supplied script.
NUMBER OF AWARDS: 1
RENEWABLE: Yes. Renewal is automatic as long as the student achieves a GPA of 3.0 for each semester's work and enrolls full time. Books, course materials, room and board are not included.
CONTACT: Tom Kay

248—CONCORSO INTERNAZIONALE DI VIOLINO (Premio N. Paganini Competition)

Comune di Genova
Via Sottoripa 5
1 16124 Genova ITALY
39/010-5574215/9
FAX: 39/010-5574326
E-mail: violinopaganini@comune. genova.it
Internet: http://www.paganini. comune.genova.it
AMOUNT: 25,000 euros (1st prize); 10,000 euros (2nd prize); 5,000 euros (3rd prize); 1,500 euros (other finalists)
DEADLINE(S): APR 30
FIELD(S): Violin

ELIGIBILITY/REQUIREMENTS: Contest for violinists of all nationalities between the ages of 16 and 33. See website or contact address below for official rules.
HOW TO APPLY: Mail application form together with the required documents and 100-euro entrance fee to Secretariat of International Violin Competition Premio Paganini Comune di Genova–Archivo Generale; Via XX Settembre, 15=2° piano; I–1`6121 GENOVA
NUMBER OF AWARDS: 3 plus 4 special prizes
CONTACT: Anna Rita Certo, Secretary General
ADDITIONAL INFORMATION: Special prizes from other donors: 3,000 euros in memory of Enrico Costa to the youngest participant admitted to the Final; 3,000 euros in memory of Renato De Barbieri to one of the finalists for the best interpretation of Paganini's Capricci; 2,000 euros Friends of Paganini Association for the finest performance of the Paganini Concerto; 1,600 euros in memory of Mario Ruminelli to the first prize winner; 1,000 euros Friends of the Nuovo Carlo Felice Association for the finest performance of the commissioned piece.

249—CONCORSO INTERNAZIONALE PER QUARTETTO D'ARCHI (Premio Paolo Borciani Competition)

c/o Teatro Municipale Valli
Piazza Martiri del 7 luglio
42100 Reggio Emilia ITALY
++ (39) 0522 458 811 or 458 908
FAX: ++ (39) 0522 458 822
E-mail: premioborciani@iteatri.re.it
Internet: http://premioborciani. iteatri.re.it/
AMOUNT: 19,000 + international tour of Europe, U.S., and Japan (first prize); 13,800 (second prize); 6,600 (third prize) + special prize; 2,500 for the best performance of the commissioned quartet
DEADLINE(S): JAN 31
FIELD(S): String Quartets
ELIGIBILITY/REQUIREMENTS: This competition, which takes place in June, is open to string quartets of all nationalities; the total age of the ensemble shall not exceed 128 years in June of contest year.
HOW TO APPLY: Submit application with biography of the quartet; 2 recent black/white photos; letter of reference from the School of Music attended by the quartet during the final three years of study and/or by their teacher for the same period and/or references from 2 musicians written specifically for the purposes of the competition; a tape recording (analog sys-

tem, speed 4.75 cm/s) or CD of a few recent recordings of the quartet's own choice (total length not less than 30'). Also submit for each member: birth certificate, or copy of other official document bearing the date of birth; biography indicating studies and teachers. Contact above address for competition guidelines and application procedures.
NUMBER OF AWARDS: 4
ADDITIONAL INFORMATION: If chosen, there is an enrollment fee of 80.00. I Teatri di Reggio Emilia shall pay board and lodging expenses of participating quartets for as long as they are actively competing.

250—CONCORSO PIANISTICO INTERNAZIONALE (International Piano Competition)

Via Paradiso 6
20038 Seregno Milan ITALY
Phone/FAX: +39/0362/222914
E-mail: pozzoli@concorsopozzoli.it
Internet: http://www.concorso pozzoli.it
AMOUNT: Varies
DEADLINE(S): MAY 31
FIELD(S): Piano
ELIGIBILITY/REQUIREMENTS: International piano competition for persons age 32 and older held every two years. Open to persons of all nationalities.
HOW TO APPLY: For details access website and/or send for booklet which explains in detail the prizes and requirements.
CONTACT: Lia Dotti, Secretary

251—CONCOURS CLARA HASKIL (International Piano Competition)

Rue de Conseil 31
Case postale 234
CH-1800 Vevey 1
SWITZERLAND
41-21-922 67 04
FAX: 41-21-922 67 34
Internet: http://www.regart.ch/ clara-haskil
AMOUNT: CHF 20,000
DEADLINE(S): middle of even numbered years
FIELD(S): Piano
ELIGIBILITY/REQUIREMENTS: Competition offered in odd numbered years is open to pianists of all nationalities who are not more than 27 years of age. Traveling expenses and accommodations are the responsibility of the candidate; however, competition office can supply addresses of welcoming families (generally free of charge). Must submit 3 good-quality, black

and white, 9x15cm photographs for brochure along with completed application form.
HOW TO APPLY: Contact Clara Haskil for brochure detailing timetable, program, and regulations. CHF 250 entry fee.
CONTACT: Clara Haskil

252—CONCOURS GEZA ANDA
(International Piano Competition)

Bleicherweg 18
CH-8002 Zurich SWITZERLAND
0041/1/205 14 23
FAX: 0041/1/205 14 29
E-mail: info@gezaanda.ch
Internet: http://www.gezaanda.ch
AMOUNT: CHF 60,000
DEADLINE(S): MAR 1
FIELD(S): Piano
ELIGIBILITY/REQUIREMENTS: Pianists under 31 years of age from any nation may participate in the triennial June competition. Competition is divided into four rounds: Audition, Recital, Mozart Piano Concerto with orchestra, and Piano Concerto with orchestra.
HOW TO APPLY: Contact Concours Geza Anda for an application packet. Applications must be accompanied by curriculum vitae, certificate of birth (photocopy), and two photographs (suitable for publication). The Jury will select candidates for audition on the basis of written applications. Application fee of CH 300 required.

253—CURTIS INSTITUTE OF MUSIC
(Tuition Scholarships)

1726 Locust Street
Philadelphia PA 19103-6187
215/893-5262
FAX: 215/893-7900
E-mail: admissions@curtis.edu
Internet: http://www.curtis.edu
AMOUNT: Full tuition
DEADLINE(S): DEC 16
FIELD(S): Music; Voice; Opera
ELIGIBILITY/REQUIREMENTS: Full-tuition scholarships open to students in the above areas who are accepted for full-time study at the Curtis Institute of Music. (Opera is for master of music only.)
HOW TO APPLY: Write or see website for complete information.
RENEWABLE: Yes
CONTACT: Admissions Office

254—DAUGHTERS OF THE AMERICAN REVOLUTION/NATIONAL SOCIETY (Nellie Love Butcher Music Scholarship)

Committee Services Office
Attn: Scholarships
1776 D Street NW
Washington DC 20006-5392
202/628-1776
Internet: http://www.dar.org
AMOUNT: Varies
DEADLINE(S): APR 15
FIELD(S): Piano; Voice
ELIGIBILITY/REQUIREMENTS: Awarded to music student who is pursuing an education in piano or voice.
HOW TO APPLY: Must submit application with a letter of sponsorship from local DAR chapter (send SASE to address above to obtain name and application); statement of 1,000 words or less stating career objectives, how college major (if required) or college plans relate to future professional goals and reasons for these choices; transcripts; list of extracurricular activities, honors received, scholastic achievements, or other significant accomplishments; 2-4 letters of recommendation from the high school or college you now attend who are familiar with your work, and proof of citizenship. DAR Member Number of mother must be on the application.
RENEWABLE: Yes. Up to 4 years. Must maintain a 3.0 GPA.
ADDITIONAL INFORMATION: Special consideration given to students currently attending the Duke Ellington School of the Performing Arts, Washington, DC.

255—DAUGHTERS OF THE AMERICAN REVOLUTION/NATIONAL SOCIETY (Occupational Therapy Scholarship)

Committee Services Office
Attn: Scholarships
1776 D Street NW
Washington DC 20006-5392
202/628-1776
Internet: http://www.dar.org
AMOUNT: $500
DEADLINE(S): FEB 15 or AUG 15
FIELD(S): Occupational Therapy (including music, art, and physical therapy)
ELIGIBILITY/REQUIREMENTS: Awarded to students who are in financial need and are accepted and enrolled into an accredited school of occupational therapy (including art, music, or physical therapy). Affiliation with DAR not required.
HOW TO APPLY: Must submit application with a letter of sponsorship from local DAR chapter (send SASE to address above to obtain name and application); statement of 1,000 words or less stating career objectives, how college major (if required) or college plans relate to future professional goals and reasons for these choices; transcripts; list of extracurricular activities, honors received, scholastic achievements, or other significant accomplishments; 2-4 letters of recommendation from the high school or college you now attend who are familiar with your work, and proof of acceptance, enrollment (letter of acceptance or transcript) and citizenship and financial need. See website for additional information.
NUMBER OF AWARDS: Varies
RENEWABLE: No

256—DAVIDSON INSTITUTE FOR TALENT DEVELOPMENT

9665 Gateway
Reno NV 89521
775/852-3483 Ext. 423
FAX: 775/852-2184
E-mail: tmoessner@ditd.org
Internet: http://www.davidson fellows.org
AMOUNT: $10,000; $20,000; $50,000
DEADLINE(S): MAR (last Friday)
FIELD(S): Science; Technology; Mathematics; Philosophy; Music; Literature and Outside the Box
ELIGIBILITY/REQUIREMENTS: Must be a U.S. citizen residing in the U.S., or a permanent resident of the U.S. residing in the U.S.; under the age of 18 as of October 1 (there is no minimum age for eligibility); completed a significant piece of work in one of the designated application categories; and available to attend, with at least 1 parent or guardian, the awards reception and other recognition events in September (travel expenses and lodging will be paid by the Institute).
HOW TO APPLY: See website including FAQ section and application booklet; download and complete all components.
NUMBER OF AWARDS: 15-20
RENEWABLE: No
CONTACT: Tacie Moessner, Davidson Fellows Program Manager
ADDITIONAL INFORMATION: Group and team projects are not eligible. Scholarships must be used at an accredited institute of learning within 10 years of the award date.

257—DELTA OMICRON INTERNATIONAL MUSIC FRATERNITY (Triennial Composition Competition for Sacred Choral Anthem for Three- or Four-Part Voices)

12297 W. Tennessee Place
Lakewood CO 80228-3325
256/782-5623
E-mail: DOExecSec@aol.com
Internet: http://deltaomicron. people.virginia.edu
AMOUNT: $500 and premiere
DEADLINE(S): MAR

FIELD(S): Music Composition
ELIGIBILITY/REQUIREMENTS: Sacred choral anthem for 3- or 4-part voices; SSA, SAB, or SATB with keyboard accompaniment or a capella with optional obligato. Competition open to composers of college age or over. No music fraternity affiliation required.
HOW TO APPLY: Prior publication or public performance of entry is NOT allowed. Entry fee of $10 is required. Contact Judith Eidson at above address for complete information.
CONTACT: Judith Eidson, Drama Department

258—DELTA OMICRON INTERNATIONAL MUSIC FRATERNITY (Triennial Composition Competition for Solo Piano)

12297 W. Tennessee Place
Lakewood CO 80228-3325
256/782-5623
E-mail: DOExecSec@aol.com
Internet: http://deltaomicron.
people.virginia.edu
AMOUNT: $500 + premiere performance at Conference
DEADLINE(S): MAR
FIELD(S): Music composition competition
ELIGIBILITY/REQUIREMENTS: Award for solo piano composition. Length of piece between 7 and 10 minutes. No music fraternity affiliation required.
HOW TO APPLY: Write for details. Note: Prior publication or performance NOT allowed.
CONTACT: Judith Eidson

259—DIXIE COLLEGE (Music Scholarships)

225 South 700 East
St. George UT 84770
435/652-7802 (vocal) or
435/652-7996 (strings) or
435/652-7997 (brass, woodwinds, percussion)
E-mail: caldwell@ dixie.edu
Internet: http://dsc.dixie.edu/music
AMOUNT: Varies
DEADLINE(S): MAR 1
FIELD(S): Music
ELIGIBILITY/REQUIREMENTS: Scholarships at Dixie College in St. George, Utah, for music students. Available for ensemble participants, whether music majors or not. Available for both vocal and instrumental. Auditions required.
HOW TO APPLY: See website for audition details. Request scholarship forms from your high school counselor or from the Dixie College Financial Aid Office at 435/652-7575.

CONTACT: Gary Caldwell, Director of Bands

260—DONNA REED FOUNDATION (Performing Arts Scholarships)

1305 Broadway
Denison IA 51442
712/263-3334
FAX: 712/263-8026
E-mail: info@donnareed.org
Internet: http://www.donnareed.org
AMOUNT: $200-$1,000
DEADLINE(S): JUN 1
FIELD(S) Acting, Musical Theater
ELIGIBILITY/REQUIREMENTS: Must demonstrate excellence and a high level of interest in the performing arts; be a current high school senior, a U.S. citizen or permanent resident of U.S. or U.S. territory, and enrolled in the Donna Reed Performing Arts Workshop Program and perform in the final competition.
HOW TO APPLY: Must submit a video or DVD for consideration in each category. Students may audition in both Acting and Musical Theater, but each category entry has different length requirements and must be made with a separate video or DVD. See website or contact Foundation for application and additional information.
NUMBER OF AWARDS: 6 (3 in each category, 1st, 2nd and 3rd place)

261—DONNA REED FOUNDATION (Performing Arts Scholarships for Iowa Students)

1305 Broadway
Denison IA 51442
712/263-3334
FAX: 712/263-8026
E-mail: info@donnareed.org
Internet: http://www.donnareed.org
AMOUNT: $500
DEADLINE(S): JUN 17 (on-site)
FIELD(S) Acting, Musical Theater
ELIGIBILITY/REQUIREMENTS: Must reside in and attend school in the state for the academic year and must register as a full-time student for the Festival.
HOW TO APPLY: Auditions held during the Festival. May perform a monologue, song, or original piece. This award has no categories. Audition time is limited to 3 minutes.
NUMBER OF AWARDS: 2

262—EASTERN KENTUCKY UNIVERSITY (Music Scholarships)

Department of Music
521 Lancaster Avenue

Richmond KY 40475-3102
859/622-1341
FAX: 859/622-3266
E-mail: rob.james@eku.edu
Internet: http://www.music.eku.edu
AMOUNT: Varies
DEADLINE(S): Varies
FIELD(S): Music Education
ELIGIBILITY/REQUIREMENTS: Scholarships for talented young instrument or voice musicians preparing themselves for careers in music or music education.
HOW TO APPLY: Must audition for scholarship. Application (on website) is due at least two weeks prior to the desired audition date.
RENEWABLE: Yes. Scholarship recipients are required to participate in performing ensembles and maintain a GPA of 2.5 to retain scholarship.
CONTACT: Dr. Robert James, Chair, Department of Music

263—ESA FOUNDATION (Frances Kilgore Endowment)

P.O. Box 270517
Fort Collins CO 80527
970/223-2824
FAX: 970/223-4456
E-mail: kloyd@iland.net
Internet: http://www.esaintl.com/esaf
AMOUNT: $500
DEADLINE(S): FEB 1
FIELD(S): Music; Teaching
ELIGIBILITY/REQUIREMENTS: Applicant must be a college student currently enrolled in an accredited college or university who has maintained a "B" average (i.e., at least a 3.0 GPA); or be a high school senior in the top 25% of his/her high school class, or have a score of at least ACT 20 or SAT 950, or have a minimum GPA of 3.0; or be enrolled for training in a technical school or be returning to school after an absence to retrain job skills or obtain a degree. Criteria for selection are character, leadership, service, financial need, scholastic ability, and special criteria set by the donor. Preference is given to music majors.
HOW TO APPLY: Submit completed application; 1-page (maximum) original letter from the applicant stating reasons for applying; 2 (only; no more or less) letters of recommendation; an official, most recent transcript; and a $5 processing fee. Applicants must apply for only one scholarship from the ESA Foundation.
NUMBER OF AWARDS: 1
RENEWABLE: Yes. Recipients must re-apply annually, and no special consideration will be given to previous winners.
CONTACT: Kathy Loyd

264—FELLOWSHIP OF UNITED METHODISTS IN MUSIC AND WORSHIP ARTS (Fellowship Scholarships)

P.O. Box 24787
Nashville TN 37202-4787
800/952-8977
FAX: 615/749-6874
Internet: http://www.fummwa.org
AMOUNT: $1,500 (maximum)
DEADLINE(S): MAR 1
FIELD(S): Music; Theology
ELIGIBILITY/REQUIREMENTS: Open to college-bound high school seniors and undergraduates who are active members of the United Methodist church. Based on talent, leadership ability, and potential for success.
HOW TO APPLY: Contact Fellowship for an application.
NUMBER OF AWARDS: 5 or 6
RENEWABLE: Yes

265—FIVE WINGS ARTS COUNCIL (Artist Mentor Scholarships for Students)

200 First Street NE
Staples MN 56479
218/894-5485
FAX: 218/894-3045
E-mail: mturner@ncscmn.org
Internet: http://www.fwac.org
AMOUNT: Up to $500
DEADLINE(S): OCT 15
FIELD(S): Literary Arts; Visual Arts; Music; Theater; Media Arts; Dance
ELIGIBILITY/REQUIREMENTS: Open to rural high school students in grades 9 through 12 enrolled in an independent school district within the counties of Cass, Crow Wing, Morrison, Todd, and Wadena, Minnesota. Each recipient is matched with a qualified mentor who will establish a study schedule with student. Award is based on creative potential, accomplishments in art, maturity, and personal motivation.
HOW TO APPLY: Contact Director for details.
NUMBER OF AWARDS: 10
CONTACT: Mark Turner, Director

266—FRANCIS CHAGRIN FUND (Grants)

Francis House; Francis Street
London SWIP 1DE ENGLAND
0207 828 9696
FAX: 0207 931 9928
E-mail: spnm@spnm.org.uk
Internet: http://www.spnm.org.uk
AMOUNT: 250 pounds sterling (max.)
DEADLINE(S): None
FIELD(S): Music Composition

ELIGIBILITY/REQUIREMENTS: For British composers or composers resident in the UK. The fund considers applications for: 1) reproduction of scores and parts by photocopying or other reprographic means; 2) covering and binding of scores and parts; and 3) reproduction of tapes for use in performance. Financial need is NOT considered. Applications are considered monthly.
HOW TO APPLY: Contact Fund for additional information and application.
RENEWABLE: No
CONTACT: Gwen Tietze

267—GENERAL FEDERATION OF WOMEN'S CLUBS OF MASSACHUSETTS (Dorchester Women's Club Scholarship)

P.O. Box 679
Sudbury MA 01776-0679
978/443-4569
FAX: 978/443-1617
E-mail: GFWCMA@aol.com
Internet: http://www.gfwcma.org/id39.html
AMOUNT: $600
DEADLINE(S): FEB 1
FIELD(S): Voice
ELIGIBILITY/REQUIREMENTS: For undergraduates enrolled in a 4-year accredited college, university, or school of music. Must be Massachusetts resident.
HOW TO APPLY: For more information see website or contact Federation. Submit application along with personal statement of no more than 500 words addressing professional goals, experience, repertoire, and financial need; letter of reference from department head of your major or voice instructor; and transcript. Personal audition required.
NUMBER OF AWARDS: At least 1
RENEWABLE: No

268—GENERAL FEDERATION OF WOMEN'S CLUBS OF MASSACHUSETTS (Music Scholarship)

P.O. Box 679
Sudbury MA 01776-0679
978/443-4569
FAX: 978/443-1617
E-mail: GFWCMA@aol.com
Internet: http://www.gfwcma.org/id39.html
AMOUNT: Up to $800
DEADLINE(S): FEB 1
FIELD(S): Piano; Instrument; Music Education; Music Therapy; Voice
ELIGIBILITY/REQUIREMENTS: Competitive scholarships for seniors in Massachusetts high schools.

HOW TO APPLY: For more information or an application, see website or send a SASE to Coordinator, Arts Department at above address. Submit application with letter of recommendation from either high school principal or music instructor and transcript. Audition required.
NUMBER OF AWARDS: 1
RENEWABLE: No

269—GLENN MILLER BIRTHPLACE SOCIETY (Scholarship Program)

107 E. Main
P. O. Box 61
Clarinda IA 51632
Phone/Fax: 712/542-2461
E-mail: gmbs@heartland.net
Internet: http://www.glennmiller.org
AMOUNT: $1,000-$3,000
DEADLINE(S): MAR 15
FIELD(S): All (especially) Music Performance (Instrumental and Vocal)
ELIGIBILITY/REQUIREMENTS: Competitions open to high school seniors and undergraduate freshmen who intend to make music a central part of their future life (music major NOT required). Must submit a clear high-quality audio CD or cassette tape containing your competition pieces or pieces similar to them in style and difficulty. A good length of tape performance would be about 10 minutes total. Not more than 10 finalists will be accepted in each category. Finalists will come to Clarinda's Glenn Miller Festival at their own expense for live auditions to be held in June.
HOW TO APPLY: Send SASE for an application or see website for additional information about each category and specific requirements.
NUMBER OF AWARDS: 6
RENEWABLE: Yes. Those who have entered as high school seniors are eligible to compete again as college freshmen, unless they have been previous first-place winners.

270—GOLDEN KEY INTERNATIONAL HONOUR SOCIETY PERFORMING ARTS SHOWCASE

1189 Ponce de Leon Avenue
Atlanta GA 30306
404/377-2400 or 800/377-2401
FAX: 404/373-7033
E-mail: scholarships@goldenkey.org
Internet: http//www.goldenkey.org
AMOUNT: $1,000
DEADLINE(S): MAR 1
FIELD(S): Dance; Drama; Instrumental Performance; Filmmaking; Musical Composition; Vocal Performance

ELIGIBILITY/REQUIREMENTS: This award recognizes performing arts talents of Golden Key members in six categories: dance, drama, instrumental performance, filmmaking, musical composition, and vocal performance. Undergraduate, graduate, and post-graduate members who are currently enrolled in classes at a degree-granting program may apply. Award is based on the quality of work submitted.

HOW TO APPLY: Applications must be posted online with Golden Key member number. Entries must be submitted on VHS videotape. (Compact discs and audio-cassettes are accepted for original musical composition ONLY.) Performances may not exceed 10 minutes (except for film-making entries). All submissions become the property of Golden Key. Only one entry per member per category will be accepted. The only way to apply for these scholarships is to do so via the Internet followed by submitting required documentation. See website http://www.goldenkey.org/GKweb/scholar/scholarshipsandawards/ for further information.

NUMBER OF AWARDS: 6 (one/category)/year

RENEWABLE: No

271—GUSTAVUS ADOLPHUS COLLEGE (Anderson Theater and Dance Scholarships)

800 West College Avenue
St. Peter MN 56082
507/933-7676 or 800/GUSTAVUS
E-mail: admission@gustavus.edu
Internet: http://www.gustavus.edu

AMOUNT: $500-$2,000

DEADLINE(S): JAN 1

FIELD(S): Theater and/or Dance

ELIGIBILITY/REQUIREMENTS: Scholarships tenable at Gustavus Adolphus College, St. Peter, Minnesota, for students pursuing studies in theater and/or dance. Students may be enrolled in any major.

HOW TO APPLY: See website for application or contact Office of Admission.

RENEWABLE: Yes. Must participate in a departmental project and maintain a 3.0 GPA.

CONTACT: Office of Admission

272—GUSTAVUS ADOLPHUS COLLEGE (The Jussi Bjorling Music Scholarships)

800 West College Avenue
St. Peter MN 56082
507/933-7676 or 800/GUSTAVUS
E-mail: admission@gustavus.edu
Internet: http://www.gustavus.edu/

AMOUNT: Up to $2,000

DEADLINE(S): JAN 15

FIELD(S): Music

ELIGIBILITY/REQUIREMENTS: Scholarships tenable at Gustavus Adolphus College, St. Peter, Minnesota, for students pursuing studies and participation in music. Recipients may be of any major, but are required to participate in a performing ensemble and take private lessons.

HOW TO APPLY: See website for application or contact Office of Admission.

NUMBER OF AWARDS: 25-30

RENEWABLE: Yes

CONTACT: Office of Admission

273—HATTORI FOUNDATION FOR YOUNG MUSICIANS (Awards for Young Soloists)

7 Exton Street
London SE1 8UE ENGLAND
020 7620 3054
FAX: 020 8946 6970
E-mail: admin@hattorifoundation.org.uk
Internet: http://www.hattorifoundation.org.uk

DEADLINE(S): None; applicants may apply at any time of the year

FIELD(S): Instrumental Music Performance

ELIGIBILITY/REQUIREMENTS: Applicants must be instrumental soloists between the ages of 15 and 20 who are resident of the UK and have demonstrated both exceptional talent and achievement. Financial assistance is provided only for traveling expenses to attend national or international competitions, master classes within the UK or abroad, and specific assistance in the case of hardship. Funding is not given for full-time study or instrument purchase.

HOW TO APPLY: Submit a biography or C.V.; full details of the project you are applying for assistance with and an indication of all costs involved; a cassette, CD, or video recording (minimum 30 minutes) that has been recorded within the last 6 months and which includes at least 3 contrasting works from different periods, including classical and contemporary; and 2 references under sealed cover (on the forms provided): 1 from your current teacher and 1 from a prominent musician. Your biography or C.V. should include information on the age at which your studies commenced; a list of teachers and dates of study with each; a list of examinations taken (if any) with dates and results; name, date, and result of any national or international competition in which you have competed; and details of solo concert experience within the last 2 years and of future solo engagements both confirmed and unconfirmed.

CONTACT: The Administrator, Hattori Foundation

RENEWABLE: Yes

274—HAWAII COMMUNITY FOUNDATION (Doris and Clarence Glick Classical Music Scholarship)

1164 Bishop St., Suite 800
Honolulu HI 96813
808/537-6333 or toll free:
888/731-3863
FAX: 808/521-6286
E-mail: info@hcf-hawaii.org
Internet: http://www.hcf-hawaii.org

DEADLINE(S): MAR 1

FIELD(S): Music

ELIGIBILITY/REQUIREMENTS: Applicants must be Hawaii residents; be junior or senior undergraduate or graduate students enrolled full time in an accredited 2- or 4-year college or university; major in music, with an emphasis on classical music; and demonstrate financial need, good moral character, and academic achievement with a minimum GPA of 2.7.

HOW TO APPLY: Send application with 2 letters of recommendation and a personal statement describing your course of study as it relates to classical music.

275—HISPANIC COLLEGE FUND (HSF/Club Musica Latina Scholarship Program)

55 Second Street, Suite 1500
San Francisco CA 94105
877/HSF-INFO (877/473-4636)
FAX: 415/808-2302
E-mail: pip@hsf.net
Internet: http://hispanicfund.org

AMOUNT: At least $2,500

DEADLINE(S): Fall

FIELD(S): Music

ELIGIBILITY/REQUIREMENTS: Open on a competitive basis to students of Hispanic background who are Club members and will be entering freshman or sophomore years at a 4-year college. Must be U.S. citizens or legal permanent residents of Hispanic heritage (one parent fully Hispanic or both parents half Hispanic).

HOW TO APPLY: Contact Fund for details or visit website for application.

276—INDIANA UNIVERSITY SCHOOL OF MUSIC (Music Scholarships)

School of Music
Admissions MU101

1201 E. 3rd Street
Bloomington IN 47405-2200
812/855-1352
FAX: 812/856-6086
E-mail: MUSICADM@indiana.edu
Internet: http://www.music.
indiana.edu
AMOUNT: Varies
DEADLINE(S): Varies
FIELD(S): Music
ELIGIBILITY/REQUIREMENTS:
Several scholarships are available in the
Indiana University Department of Music.
All undergraduate music majors must
audition prior to admission and study a
classical instrument. Music minors need
not audition.
HOW TO APPLY: A listing of the schol-
arships and deadline and audition dates is
on the website. Deadlines begin as early as
Nov. 11 for applying to the department,
and auditions occur as early as December.
CONTACT: Dr. Todd Sullivan, Depart-
ment of Music

277—INTERNATIONAL TRUMPET GUILD (Conference Scholarships)

241 East Main Street, #247
Westfield MA 01086-1633
413/564-0337
FAX: 413/568-1913
E-mail: competitions@trumpetguild.org
Internet: http://www.trumpetguild.org
AMOUNT: $200 + waive Conference reg-
istration fee
DEADLINE(S): FEB 15
FIELD(S): Trumpet
ELIGIBILITY/REQUIREMENTS:
Performance competitions in three categories: solo, jazz, and mock orchestra. For
trumpet players under age 25 to enable
them to attend ITG's annual conference.
Must be a student member of ITG by the
deadline. Must submit the appropriate
taped audition to the scholarship competition chair. Generally, the student's trumpet
playing must be at a relatively advanced
level in order to play the repertoire.
HOW TO APPLY: See website for membership information and audition requirements.

278—INTERNATIONALER MUSIKWETTBEWERB (International Music Competition of the ARD Munich)

ARD Internationaler
Musikwettbewerb
c/o Bayerischer Rundfunk
Rundfunkplatz 1
D-80335 M nchen GERMANY

(+49-89) 5900-2471
FAX: (+49-89) 5900-3573
E-mail: ard.musikwettbewerb@
brnet.de
Internet: http://www.br-online.de/
kultur-szene/klassik e/pages/ard/
ard teilnahme.html
DEADLINE(S): APR 30
FIELD(S): Viola; Flute; Harp; String
Quartet
ELIGIBILITY/REQUIREMENTS: The
competition is open to musicians of all
nations, born between 1976 and 1987;
string quartet between 1974 and 1987
(average age not above 30, total age not
above 120, one member may be older than
30).
HOW TO APPLY: Candidates should
send a completed application, available
from website, to above address; a recording of their own performance for the preliminary selection process (a CD is preferable, though a DAT or cassette tape is
acceptable); recommendations by two
leading musicians; confirmation by current
teacher granting permission to participate;
a curriculum vitae; and a passport photo.
Participants must confirm that they will be
free from any professional engagements or
concerts for the duration of the competition.

279—IRISH ARTS COUNCIL (Awards and Opportunities)

70 Merrion Square
Dublin 2 IRELAND
+353 1 618 0200
FAX: +353 1 661 0349/676 1302
E-mail: info@artscouncil.ie
Internet: http://www.artscouncil.ie
AMOUNT: Varies (with program)
DEADLINE(S): Varies (with program)
FIELD(S): Creative Arts; Visual Arts;
Performing Arts
ELIGIBILITY/REQUIREMENTS:
Numerous programs open to young and
established artists who are Irish citizens or
legal residents. Purpose is to assist in pur-
suit of talents and recognize achievements.
HOW TO APPLY: See website or contact
above address for an application.

280—JACKSONVILLE STATE UNIVERSITY (Dr. Dave Walters-Gray Echelon Scholarship)

Jacksonville AL 36265
256/782-5677 or 800/231-5291
Internet: www.jsu.edu
AMOUNT: Varies
FIELD(S): Music

ELIGIBILITY/REQUIREMENTS:
Interest in music; particularly playing in
band.
HOW TO APPLY: Contact Department
for application and additional information.
RENEWABLE: No
CONTACT: Director of Bands, 256/782-
5562

281—JACKSONVILLE STATE UNIVERSITY (Gadsden Music Company Scholarship)

Jacksonville AL 36265
256/782-5677 or 800/231-5291
Internet: www.jsu.edu
AMOUNT: Varies
FIELD(S): Music
ELIGIBILITY/REQUIREMENTS:
Interest in music; particularly playing in
band.
HOW TO APPLY: Contact Department
for application and additional information.
RENEWABLE: No
CONTACT: Director of Bands, 256/782-
5562

282—JACKSONVILLE STATE UNIVERSITY (Miles T. Sparrowhawk Scholarship)

Jacksonville AL 36265
256/782-5677 or
1-800/231-5291
Internet: www.jsu.edu
AMOUNT: Varies
FIELD(S): Music
ELIGIBILITY/REQUIREMENTS:
Interest in music; particularly playing in
band.
HOW TO APPLY: Contact Department
for application and additional information.
RENEWABLE: No
CONTACT: Director of Bands, 256/782-
5562

283—JUNIATA COLLEGE (Ron & Ann Wertz Arts Scholarship)

Office of Financial Planning
1700 Moore Street
Huntingdon PA 16652
814/641-3142
FAX: 814/641-5311
E-mail: frankv@juniata.edu
Internet: http://www.juniata.edu/
admission/finplan/index.html
AMOUNT: Full tuition, room & board
DEADLINE(S): JAN 4
FIELD(S): Ceative and/or performing
arts, Fine Arts, Graphic Design,
Writing, Choral and Instrumental
Music, Theater, Dance
ELIGIBILITY/REQUIREMENTS: Open
to incoming freshmen (upperclassmen and
transfer students are ineligible). Must be

nominated by a Juniata alumnus/a, parent of a Juniata student, guidance counselor, pastor, teacher, or someone familiar with the student's involvement in school and community activities. who have excelled in the creative and/or performing arts, including drawing, painting, sculpting, graphic design, writing, choral and instrumental music, theatre and dance.

HOW TO APPLY: Submit a Nomination Essay (in addition to the essay required for admission) of no more than 2 pages discussing why you should be considered for a scholarship, including supporting activities and involvement. You may also attach up to 3 extra pages of supporting information of any kind. Must submit a portfolio. See website for additional information or contact College.

NUMBER OF AWARDS: 1
RTENEWABLE: No
CONTACT: Vincent Frank, Director of Student Financial Planning, 814/641-3140; e-mail: frankv@juniata.edu

284—JUNIOR ACHIEVEMENT INC. (DePauw University Holton Memorial Scholarship)

One Education Way
Colorado Springs CO 80906
719/540-8000
FAX: 719/540-6299
E-mail: newmedia@ja.org
Internet: http://www.ja.org
AMOUNT: $1,000 to full tuition
DEADLINE(S): FEB 1
FIELD(S): Liberal Arts; Music
ELIGIBILITY/REQUIREMENTS: Applicants must be excellent students who have demonstrated outstanding leadership and/or exceptional service to their schools, family, church, or community.
HOW TO APPLY: Send completed application; SAT or ACT scores (or TOEFL if English is 2nd language); and a 250-word essay describing applicant's commitment to service and/or leadership, with a résumé of applicant's involvement.
NUMBER OF AWARDS: 50
RENEWABLE: Yes
CONTACT: Office of Admission, DePauw University, 101 East Seminary Street, Greencastle IN 46135-1611; 800/447-2495 or 765/658-4006; or admissions@depauw.edu or at www.depauw.edu.

285—KATHLEEN FERRIER MEMORIAL SCHOLARSHIP FUND

Courtyard House
Neopardy, Crediton
Devon EX17 SEP
UNITED KINGDOM
01363 777844
FAX: 01363 777845
E-mail: info@ferrierawards.org.uk
Internet: http://www.ferrierawards.org.uk
AMOUNT: £10,000 (first prize); £5,000 (second prize); £2,500 (recital prize for best performance of a song in the semi-final or final rounds); £2,000 (pianist's prize provided by the MBF)
DEADLINE(S): Varies
FIELD(S): Singing Competition
ELIGIBILITY/REQUIREMENTS: Open to singers of any nationality who have completed at least 1 year of a continuous recognized course in music in higher education in the UK or who are resident in the UK having completed such a course. Must be under 29 years old at time of competition.
HOW TO APPLY: Write for application form or download from website.
NUMBER OF AWARDS: 4
RENEWABLE: No
CONTACT: The Administrator

286—KOSCIUSZKO FOUNDATION (Chopin Piano Competition)

15 East 65 Street
New York NY 10021-6595
212/734-2130
FAX: 212/628-4552
E-mail: tompkf@aol.com
Internet: http://www.kosciuszkofoundation.org
AMOUNT: $5,000 (first place)
DEADLINE(S): MAR
FIELD(S): Piano
ELIGIBILITY/REQUIREMENTS: Open to U.S. citizens/permanent residents and international full-time students with valid student visas. Must be between the ages of 16 and 22 as of April in contest year. Preliminaries are held in the spring in Chicago, Houston, and New York City, with finals in New York City. Must have ready a program of 60-75 minutes, including Chopin and other required composers. Must also submit biography/curriculum vitae, letters of recommendation, proof of age, and photo.
HOW TO APPLY: See website or send a SASE to the Cultural Department for an application after December 1. $35 application fee.
CONTACT: Cultural Department

287—KOSCIUSZKO FOUNDATION (Marcella Sembrich Voice Competition)

15 East 65 Street
New York NY 10021-6595
212/734-2130
FAX: 212/628-4552
E-mail: tompkf@aol.com
Internet: http://www.kosciuszkofoundation.org
AMOUNT: $1,000 (max.) + travel to various domestic and international recitals
DEADLINE(S): DEC
FIELD(S): Voice
ELIGIBILITY/REQUIREMENTS: This voice competition is held every third year and is open to students between the ages of 18 and 35 who are U.S. citizens or full-time international students in the U.S. with valid visas who wish to pursue a career in voice.
HOW TO APPLY: See website or send a SASE to the Cultural Department for an application.

288—KUN SHOULDER REST, INC., THE (Listing of Music Competitions)

200 MacLaren Street
Ottawa Ontario K2P 0L6 CANADA
+1 (613) 232-1861
FAX: +1 (613) 232-9771
E-mail: kun@kunrest.com
Internet: http://www.kunrest.com
AMOUNT: Varies
DEADLINE(S): Varies
FIELD(S): Music: Various instruments and voice
ELIGIBILITY/REQUIREMENTS: This manufacturer of shoulder rests for violinists offers a listing of international competitions in various types of music, primarily for (but not limited to) players of stringed instruments.
HOW TO APPLY: The information is available on the website or may be requested of the company.

289—LIBERACE FOUNDATION FOR THE PERFORMING AND CREATIVE ARTS

1775 East Tropicana Avenue
Las Vegas NV 89119-6529
702/798-5595
FAX: 702/798-7386
E-mail: foundation@liberace.org
Internet: http://www.liberace.org
AMOUNT: Varies
DEADLINE(S): MAR 15
FIELD(S): Music (Instrumental and Vocal); Theater; Dance; Visual Arts; Fine Art
ELIGIBILITY/REQUIREMENTS: Provides grants to accredited institutions that offer training in above fields. Grants are to be used exclusively for scholarship assistance to talented and deserving students. Recipients should be promising and deserving upperclassmen (junior, senior, graduate) enrolled in a course of study leading up to a career in the arts.

HOW TO APPLY: See website or write to above address for details.
RENEWABLE: Yes
CONTACT: Joel Strote

290—LIEDERKRANZ FOUNDATION, INC.

6 East 87th Street
New York NY 10128
212/534-0880
Internet: http://www.liederkranz
nycity.org/home.asp
AMOUNT: $1,000-$5,000
DEADLINE(S): NOV 15
FIELD(S): Vocal Music
ELIGIBILITY/REQUIREMENTS: Awards can be used anywhere. Age limit for General Voice 20-35 years old, and limit for Wagnerian Voice is 25-45 years. There is a $50 application fee.
HOW TO APPLY: Send a SASE to the address above for application regulations, audition schedules, and other details.
NUMBER OF AWARDS: 14-18
RENEWABLE: No

291—MENDELSSOHN SCHOLARSHIP FOUNDATION (Composers Scholarships)

Royal Academy of Music
Marylebone Road
London NW1 5HT ENGLAND
+44(0)1413324101
FAX: +44(0)1413328901
E-mail: e.kemp-luck@ram.ac.uk
AMOUNT: £5,000
DEADLINE(S): FEB 1
FIELD(S): Musical Composition
ELIGIBILITY/REQUIREMENTS: Open to composers of any nationality under the age of 30 who are residents (for at least 3 years) in the UK or Ireland. For further studies in composition.
HOW TO APPLY: Write to the Foundation for complete information.
CONTACT: Edward Kemp-Luck, Admissions Officer

292—MERCYHURST COLLEGE (D'Angelo Young Artists Competition)

501 East 38th Street
Erie PA 16546
814/824-2394
Internet: http://music.mercyhurst.
edu/resident.html
AMOUNT: Up to $10,000
DEADLINE(S): JAN
FIELD(S): Music: voice, strings, piano
ELIGIBILITY/REQUIREMENTS: For international musicians who demonstrate the ability to embark on a performance career in voice, strings, or piano. Undergraduates must be between the ages of 18

and 30 and wish to attend the D'Angelo School of Music at Mercyhurst College in Erie, Pennsylvania. Audition required.
HOW TO APPLY: Contact Executive Director for an application.
RENEWABLE: Yes. Up to 4 years.
CONTACT: Rebecca Ryan, Executive Director

293—MR. HOLLAND'S OPUS FOUNDATION, THE (The Melody Program)

15125 Ventura Boulevard,
Suite 204
Sherman Oaks CA 91403
818/787-6787
FAX: 818/784-6788
E-mail: info@mhopus.org
Internet: http://www.mhopus.org
AMOUNT: A musical instrument
DEADLINE(S): None
FIELD(S): Instrumental Music
ELIGIBILITY/REQUIREMENTS: Founded by actor Richard Dreyfuss, composer Michael Kamen, and director Stephen Herek, all of whom were involved in the film with the same name, the program provides used and/or new instruments to schools and individuals who are financially limited. Targets qualified K-12 school music programs in need of assistance. The students must have completed at least 3 years of continuous group or private study and must have performed with school and/or community ensembles or provided accompaniment for same.
HOW TO APPLY: Send SASE (with 60 cents postage) for application or access website, which has an application as well as more details. Recommendations and cassette performance tape required.

294—MR. HOLLAND'S OPUS FOUNDATION, THE (The Special Projects Program)

15125 Ventura Boulevard, Suite 204
Sherman Oaks CA 91403
818/787-6787
FAX: 818/784-6788
E-mail: info@mhopus.org
Internet: http://www.mhopus.org
AMOUNT: A musical instrument
DEADLINE(S): None
FIELD(S): Instrumental Music
ELIGIBILITY/REQUIREMENTS: Founded by actor Richard Dreyfuss, composer Michael Kamen, and director Stephen Herek, all of whom were involved in the film with the same name as this group, the program provides used and/or new instruments to schools and individuals

who are financially limited. Targets community schools of the arts, hospitals, music therapy programs, after-school music programs, and youth symphonies in need of assistance. The students must have completed at least three years of continuous group or private study and must have performed with school and/or community ensembles or provided accompaniment for same.
HOW TO APPLY: Send SASE (with 60 cents postage) for application, or access website, which has an application as well as more details. Recommendations and cassette performance tape required.

295—MUSIC ACADEMY OF THE WEST

1070 Fairway Road
Santa Barbara CA 93108-2899
805/969-4726
FAX: 805/969-0686
E-mail: admissions@musicacademy.org
Internet:
http://www.musicacademy. org
AMOUNT: Tuition, room and board
DEADLINE(S): Varies from JAN 3 through FEB 28 and OCT 1 through JAN 15 (depending on program/instrument)
FIELD(S): Pre-professional Classical Music Training
ELIGIBILITY/REQUIREMENTS: Admission to the Music Academy of the West's Summer School and Festival 8-week summer session is competitive for musicians age 16 and up. Maximum age for vocalists is 34. Student must pay transportation and limited fees. Audition dates are set up throughout the U.S..
HOW TO APPLY: Access website for details and application, or write for information.

296—NATIONAL ASSOCIATION OF NEGRO MUSICIANS, THE (Brantley Choral Arranging Competition)

P.O. Box 2024
Gardena CA 90247
773/779-1325 or 213/756-5354
Internet: http://www.nanm.org/
Scholarship_competition.htm
AMOUNT: $500
DEADLINE(S): APR 30
FIELD(S): Music: Choral Arrangement
ELIGIBILITY/REQUIREMENTS: An annual competition for African Americans talented in music arrangement. The work must be a choral arrangement of a Negro spiritual. Should be between 3-5 minutes in length. Arranger's name must not appear on the score—use a nom de plume. See more information on website.

HOW TO APPLY: For specific details, contact organization. Send scores, fees ($25 entrance fee), and information to Coordinator at above address.
CONTACT: Byron J. Smith, Coordinator

297—NATIONAL ASSOCIATION OF NEGRO MUSICIANS, THE (Scholarship Competitions)

8120-B Prairie Park Place
Chicago IL 60619-4808
773/779-1325
Internet: http://www.nanm.org/Scholarship_competition.htm
AMOUNT: $1,500 (first); $1,000 (second); $750 (third); $500 (fourth); $250 (fifth)
DEADLINE(S): Varies
FIELD(S): Music: organ, winds, piano, voice, or strings
ELIGIBILITY/REQUIREMENTS: An annual competition for African Americans talented in music performance in the above areas. For ages 18-30. Contestants must be sponsored by a local branch in good standing. Competition involves local, regional, and national events. Winners proceed to next level.
HOW TO APPLY: Contact organization for location of your nearest branch. Specialty rotates yearly. See website for further information. There is a $5 fee for the local competitions. Professional musicians are NOT eligible.
NUMBER OF AWARDS: 5

298—NATIONAL FEDERATION OF MUSIC CLUBS (Competitions and Awards)

1336 North Delaware Street
Indianapolis IN 46202-2481
317/638-4003
Internet: http://www.nfmc-music.org/
AMOUNT: Varies
DEADLINE(S): Varies
FIELD(S): Music Performance
ELIGIBILITY/REQUIREMENTS: Several monetary awards available for students' voice, piano, composition, accompanying instruments, and music education.
HOW TO APPLY: Apply through website.

299—NATIONAL FOUNDATION FOR ADVANCEMENT IN THE ARTS (Arts Recognition and Talent Search)

800 Brickell Avenue
Miami FL 33131
800/970-ARTS or 305/377-1140
FAX: 305/377-1149
E-mail: info@nfaa.org
Internet: http://www.ARTSawards.org
AMOUNT: $100-$3,000
DEADLINE(S): OCT 1
FIELD(S): Creative and Performing Arts; Writing
ELIGIBILITY/REQUIREMENTS: Talent contest for high school seniors and 17- to 18-year-olds in dance, film, jazz, music, photography, theater, visual arts, voice, and writing. Except for those applying in Music/Jazz, applicants must be U.S. citizens or permanent residents.
HOW TO APPLY: Applications available online or write. May apply in more than one category, but only one financial award will be given to any individual. A fee is required for each category in which student applies: $35 application fee ($25 if apply by June 1); $5 discount for online applications; fee may be waived if you are unable to meet this requirement.
NUMBER OF AWARDS: 400 awards annually
RENEWABLE: No

300—NATIONAL PTA (Reflections Program)

541 N. Fairbanks Ct., Suite 1300
Chicago IL 60611
800/307-4PTA or 312/670-6782
FAX: 312/670-6783
E-mail: info@pta.org
Internet: http://www.pta.org
AMOUNT: Varies
DEADLINE(S): Varies
FIELD(S): Literature; Musical Composition; Photography; Visual Arts; Dance/Choreography
ELIGIBILITY/REQUIREMENTS: Open to students in preschool through grade twelve to express themselves and to receive positive recognition for their artistic efforts. Young artists can get involved in the Reflections Program of their local PTA or PTSA.
HOW TO APPLY: Contact your state PTA office for information about the Reflections Program in your area.

301—NATIONAL SYMPHONY ORCHESTRA EDUCATION PROGRAM AT THE KENNEDY CENTER (Instrumental and Piano Competition)

115 Gresham Place
Falls Church VA 22046
202/416-8827
Internet: http://www.kennedy-center.org/nso/nsoed
DEADLINE(S): FEB 20
FIELD(S): Instrumental; Piano; Voice
ELIGIBILITY/REQUIREMENTS: Students grades 10-12, who are residents of, or studying with, an instrumental teacher in the area of the metropolitan Washington Council of Governments, District of Columbia; in Maryland counties of Frederick, Montgomery, Prince George's; in Virginia counties of Arlington, Fairfax, Loudoun, and Prince William; or Virginia cities of Alexandria and Falls Church. Preliminary audition, followed by final audition at the Kennedy Center, Washington, DC. Performers under professional management are not eligible.
HOW TO APPLY: See website for additional information and application. Submit with non-refundable entry fee of $15 and SASE. Students whose résumé does not reflect sufficient musical experience in solo performance may not be accepted for competition.
NUMBER OF AWARDS: 1
RENEWABLE: No
CONTACT: Merithew Benington, 202/416-8827, e-mail: mhbenington@kennedy-center.org

302—NATIONAL SYMPHONY ORCHESTRA EDUCATION PROGRAM AT THE KENNEDY CENTER (Instrumental, Piano, Voice Competition)

115 Gresham Place
Falls Church VA 22046
202/416-8820
Internet: http://www.kennedy-center.org/nso/nsoed
DEADLINE(S): FEB 6
FIELD(S): Instrumental; Piano; Voice
ELIGIBILITY/REQUIREMENTS: Open to high school graduates currently studying music in the District of Columbia, Maryland, Virginia, West Virginia, and Delaware OR Washington area residents from District of Columbia; Maryland counties of Frederick, Montgomery, Prince George's; Virginia counties of Arlington, Fairfax, Loudoun, and Prince William; or Virginia cities of Alexandria and Falls Church currently studying elsewhere. Pianists and instrumentalist must be no older than 23; singers must be no older than 26 as of last day of February. Preliminary audition followed by final audition at the Kennedy Center, Washington, DC. Pianists and instrumentalists who have completed undergraduate degree and singers who have completed a doctorate are not eligible; neither are performers under professional management or previous college winners. Send application to Sharyn L. Beyer, Competition Administrator, at above address.
HOW TO APPLY: See website for additional information and application. Submit with non-refundable entry fee of $15 and SASE. Students whose résumé does not reflect sufficient musical experience in solo

performance may not be accepted for competition.
NUMBER OF AWARDS: 1
RENEWABLE: No
CONTACT: Merithew Benington, 202/416-8827, e-mail: mhbenington@kennedy-center.org

303—NATIONAL TRUMPET COMPETITION, THE (Ensemble Division)

3500 North Third Street
Arlington VA 22201
703/524-6260
E-mail: edlbrk@aol.com
Internet: http://www.national
trumpetcomp.org
AMOUNT: Varies
DEADLINE(S): DEC 15
FIELD(S): Trumpet
ELIGIBILITY/REQUIREMENTS:
Ensembles will play a chosen work plus a required work.
HOW TO APPLY: Submit application, a cassette or CD of audition material, personnel and repertoire. A registration fee ($35/player) is required. See website for application and additional information.
NUMBER OF AWARDS: 6 (1 in each category)
CONTACT: Dr. Dennis Edelbrock

304—NATIONAL TRUMPET COMPETITION, THE (Solo Division)

3500 North Third Street
Arlington VA 22201
703/524-6260
E-mail: edlbrk@aol.com
Internet: http://www.national
trumpetcomp.org
AMOUNT: Varies
DEADLINE(S): DEC 15
FIELD(S): Trumpet
ELIGIBILITY/REQUIREMENTS:
Guidelines vary among groups. Except for Masters, students may only compete within their own age category. Contact Competition for details.
HOW TO APPLY: Submit application, a cassette or CD of audition material (with piano accompaniment). A registration fee (amount varies) is required. See website for application and additional information.
NUMBER OF AWARDS: 6 (1 in each category)
CONTACT: Dr. Dennis Edelbrock

305—"NEGRO SPIRITUAL" SCHOLARSHIP FOUNDATION, THE (The GRADY-RAYAM PRIZE in Sacred Music)

1111 North Orange Avenue
Orlando FL 32804
407/426-1717 ext. 105
FAX: 407/426-1705
Internet: http://www.negro
spiritual.org
AMOUNT: 2 first-place (male/female), $3,000 each; 2 runners-up (male/female), $2,000 each
DEADLINE(S): DEC 1
ELIGIBILITY/REQUIREMENTS:
Academically qualified senior high students (grades 11-12) of Afro-ethnic heritage who are U.S. citizens or permanent residents currently attending school in any district of the states of Florida and Tennessee. Individuals who are currently contracted with musical or theatrical professional management are not eligible. Each entrant will be required to perform 2 songs, 1 assigned and 1 selected to be performed with the accompaniment of a single keyboard instrument (acoustic piano). Entrants must secure their own accompanist or their selected piece. Entrants must provide a copy (music and words) of this selection for the judges.
HOW TO APPLY: Request application by mail or fax or apply online at website. Entrants will be required to perform by memory. Will be open to 100 vocalists, 50 male and 50 female, with an equitable number of slots assigned to each regional site. Male and female finalists will be selected from each regional site's competition to enter the final round of competition. Entrants must submit a clear photograph (head and shoulders) along with biographical information on the day of preliminary competition.
NUMBER OF AWARDS: 4
RENEWABLE: No
CONTACT: Sherina Johnson, Administration Manager; or Rudolph Cleare, Managing Director

306—NEW JERSEY STATE OPERA (International Vocal Competition)

Robert Treat Center
50 Park Pl., 10th Floor
Newark NJ 07102
973/623-5757
FAX: 973/623-5761
AMOUNT: Varies
DEADLINE(S): Varies
FIELD(S): Opera singing
ELIGIBILITY/REQUIREMENTS:
Professional opera singers between the ages of 22 and 34 can apply for this international competition.
HOW TO APPLY: Contact State Opera at above address for information.
RENEWABLE: Yes
CONTACT: Judy Marrasce

307—NEW YORK STATE THEATRE INSTITUTE (Internships in Theatrical Production)

37 First Street
Troy NY 12180
518/274-3200
FAX: 518/274-3815
E-mail: nysti@capital.net
Internet: http://www.nysti.org/not-for-profit/nysti/int.htm
AMOUNT: None
DEADLINE(S): None
FIELD(S): Theatrical Production and related fields
ELIGIBILITY/REQUIREMENTS:
Internships for college and graduate students, high school seniors, and educators-in-residence interested in developing skills in above fields. Unpaid academic credit is earned. Gain experience in box office, costumes, education, electrics, music, stage management, scenery, properties, performance, and public relations. Interns come from all over the world.
HOW TO APPLY: Must be associated with an accredited institution. See website for more information, call or write. Include your postal mailing address.
CONTACT: Arlene Leff, Intern Program Director, 518/274-3573

308—ORCHESTRA SONOMA GUILD

6040 Della Court
Rohnert Park CA 49428
E-mail: RubyCh@ap.net
AMOUNT: $350 (first); $100 (second)
DEADLINE(S): MAY
FIELD(S): Music
ELIGIBILITY/REQUIREMENTS:
Scholarships for youth in grades 5 to 12 who excel in music. Applicants not selected may reapply until they win first place.
HOW TO APPLY: Send SASE to Secretary, at above address for application and details. Recommendations from private or school music teacher and audition tape with 2 contrasting pieces required.
CONTACT: Ruby Chroninger, Secretary

309—ORGAN HISTORICAL SOCIETY (E. Power Biggs Fellowship)

P.O. Box 26811
Richmond VA 23261
804/353-9226
AMOUNT: Funding of attendance at Annual Convention
DEADLINE(S): DEC 31
FIELD(S): Historic Pipe Organs
ELIGIBILITY/REQUIREMENTS:
Fellowships are to encourage students and

others to become involved in the appreciation of historic pipe organs by funding their attendance at the OHS Annual Convention.

HOW TO APPLY: Contact Biggs Committee Chair for an application.

NUMBER OF AWARDS: 3-4

CONTACT: Robert Zanca, Biggs Committee Chair

309A—PHILADELPHIA BIBLICAL UNIVERSITY (Scholarships, Grants, and Loans)

Financial Aid Department
200 Manor Avenue
Langhorne PA 19047
800/366-0049
FAX: 215/702-4248
E-mail: financialaid@pbu.edu
Internet: http://www.pbu.edu

AMOUNT: Varies

DEADLINE(S): Varies

FIELD(S): Bible, Business, Teacher Education, Music, Social Work, Missions, Church Ministries

ELIGIBILITY/REQUIREMENTS: Academic and needs-based grants are available to students attending full time. Academic awards are based on GPA and SAT/ACT scores. Need-based grants are based on FAFSA results. Grants are also available to needy dependents of full-time Christian workers and scholarships presented to those exhibiting excellence in the field of music.

HOW TO APPLY: Apply to university and complete an application for student aid.

CONTACT: David Haggard

310—PHILHARMONIA ORCHESTRA (The John E. Mortimer Foundation Awards)

"Beeches"
Well Hill
Chelsfield Kent BR6 7PR
UNITED KINGDOM
+ 44 01959 532299

AMOUNT: Varies

DEADLINE(S): FEB 1

FIELD(S): Instrumental Music

ELIGIBILITY/REQUIREMENTS: Recipient must be 25 or under; UK citizens may use the award for study in the United Kingdom or abroad; non-UK citizens must use it for study in the United Kingdom. Must be studying for a performing career as a soloist, chamber musician or orchestral player (organists, singers, guitarists and academic studies are NOT supported by the Fund).

HOW TO APPLY: See website for application; submit with 2 references (1 from teacher and 1 from another musician), let-

ter of acceptance from teacher or coach, and £15 registration fee. Auditions take place during the Easter Holiday period.

NUMBER OF AWARDS: Varies

RENEWABLE: Awards are valid for 2 years.

CONTACT: Martyn Jones

311—PHILHARMONIA ORCHESTRA (The June Allison Award)

"Beeches"
Well Hill
Chelsfield Kent BR6 7PR
UNITED KINGDOM
+ 44 01959 532299

AMOUNT: £500

DEADLINE(S): FEB 1

FIELD(S): Viola

ELIGIBILITY/REQUIREMENTS: Recipient must be 25 or under; UK citizens may use the award for study in the United Kingdom or abroad; non-UK citizens must use it for study in the United Kingdom. Must be studying for a performing career as a soloist, chamber musician or orchestral player (organists, singers, guitarists and academic studies are NOT supported by the Fund).

HOW TO APPLY: See website for application; submit with 2 references (1 from teacher and 1 from another musician), letter of acceptance from teacher or coach, and £15 registration fee. Auditions take place during the Easter Holiday period.

NUMBER OF AWARDS: 1

RENEWABLE: Awards are valid for 2 years.

312—PHILHARMONIA ORCHESTRA (The Lady Marga Alexander Awards)

"Beeches"
Well Hill
Chelsfield Kent BR6 7PR
UNITED KINGDOM
+ 44 01959 532299

AMOUNT: £1,000

DEADLINE(S): FEB 1

FIELD(S): Cello

ELIGIBILITY/REQUIREMENTS: Recipient must be 25 or under; UK citizens may use the award for study in the United Kingdom or abroad; non-UK citizens must use it for study in the United Kingdom. Must be studying for a performing career as a soloist, chamber musician or orchestral player (organists, singers, guitarists and academic studies are NOT supported by the Fund).

HOW TO APPLY: See website for application; submit with 2 references (1 from teacher and 1 from another musician), let-

ter of acceptance from teacher or coach, and £15 registration fee. Auditions take place during the Easter Holiday period.

NUMBER OF AWARDS: 1

RENEWABLE: Awards are valid for 2 years.

313—PHILHARMONIA ORCHESTRA (Martin Musical Scholarship Fund)

"Beeches"
Well Hill
Chelsfield Kent BR6 7PR
UNITED KINGDOM
+ 44 01959 532299

AMOUNT: Varies

DEADLINE(S): FEB 1

FIELD(S): Instrumental Music

ELIGIBILITY/REQUIREMENTS: Recipient must be 25 or under; UK citizens may use the award for study in the United Kingdom or abroad; non-UK citizens must use it for study in the United Kingdom. Must be studying for a performing career as a soloist, chamber musician or orchestral player (organists, singers, guitarists and academic studies are NOT supported by the Fund).

HOW TO APPLY: See website for application; submit with 2 references (1 from teacher and 1 from another musician), letter of acceptance from teacher or coach, and £15 registration fee. Auditions take place during the Easter Holiday period.

NUMBER OF AWARDS: Varies

RENEWABLE: Awards are valid for 2 years.

CONTACT: Martyn Jones

314—PHILHARMONIA ORCHESTRA (The Reginald Conway Memorial Award)

"Beeches"
Well Hill
Chelsfield Kent BR6 7PR
UNITED KINGDOM
+ 44 01959 532299

AMOUNT: £500

DEADLINE(S): FEB 1

FIELD(S): String Instruments

ELIGIBILITY/REQUIREMENTS: Recipient must be 25 or under; UK citizens may use the award for study in the United Kingdom or abroad; non-UK citizens must use it for study in the United Kingdom. Must be studying for a performing career as a soloist, chamber musician or orchestral player (organists, singers, guitarists and academic studies are NOT supported by the Fund).

HOW TO APPLY: See website for application; submit with 2 references (1 from teacher and 1 from another musician), letter of acceptance from teacher or coach,

and £15 registration fee. Auditions take place during the Easter Holiday period.
NUMBER OF AWARDS: 1
RENEWABLE: Awards are valid for 2 years.

315—PHILHARMONIA ORCHESTRA (Trevor Snoad Memorial Award)

"Beeches"
Well Hill
Chelsfield Kent BR6 7PR
UNITED KINGDOM
+ 44 01959 532299
AMOUNT: £500
DEADLINE(S): FEB 1
FIELD(S): Viola
ELIGIBILITY/REQUIREMENTS: Recipient must be 25 or under; UK citizens may use the award for study in the United Kingdom or abroad; non-UK citizens must use it for study in the United Kingdom. Must be studying for a performing career as a soloist, chamber musician or orchestral player (organists, singers, guitarists and academic studies are NOT supported by the Fund).
HOW TO APPLY: See website for application; submit with 2 references (1 from teacher and 1 from another musician), letter of acceptance from teacher or coach, and £15 registration fee. Auditions take place during the Easter Holiday period.
NUMBER OF AWARDS: 1
RENEWABLE: Awards are valid for 2 years.

316—PRINCESS GRACE FOUNDATION-USA (Drama Scholarships and Fellowships, Film Scholarships)

150 East 58th Street, 25th Floor
New York NY 10155
212/317-1470
FAX: 212/317-1473
E-mail: grants@pgfusa.org
Internet: http://www.pgfusa.org
AMOUNT: Varies
DEADLINE(S): MAR 31
FIELD(S): Theater; Drama; Dance; Film
ELIGIBILITY/REQUIREMENTS: For students in acting, directing, and design (scenic, lighting, and costume design) in their last year of professional training at a nonprofit school or organization in the U.S. Fellowships for salary assistance for an apprentice or new member in a theater company. New members must have been with the company for less than 5 years. U.S. citizenship or legal residency required.
HOW TO APPLY: Must be nominated by the artistic director of a theater company

or by the dean or department chair of a professional school in theater. Write or access website for further information.
NUMBER OF AWARDS: Varies
CONTACT: Kathleen Richards, Program Manager

317—QUEEN ELISABETH INTERNATIONAL MUSIC COMPETITION OF BELGIUM

20 Rue Au Laines
B-1000 Brussels BELGIUM
00 32 2 213 40 50
FAX: 00 32 2 514 32 97
E-mail: info@qeimc.be
Internet: http://www.qeimc.be
AMOUNT: 1.250-12.400 euros
DEADLINE(S): JAN 15
FIELD(S): Piano; Singing; Violin, Composition
ELIGIBILITY/REQUIREMENTS: Open to all nationalities. Age limit for piano and violin sessions: 27; singers: 30; and composers: 40.
HOW TO APPLY: Contact Competition for information and application. Applications must include certified copy of birth certificate, proof of nationality, curriculum vitae, a list with main repertoire, and 3 photographs, including 1 black and white glossy.
CONTACT: Michel-Etienne Van Neste
ADDITIONAL INFORMATION: During participation in the competition, host family may accommodate candidates free of charge. Semi-finalists not from Belgium are entitled to 50% reimbursement of traveling expenses.

318—QUEEN MARIE JOSE (International Musical Prize Contest)

Box 19, CH-1252 Meinier
Geneva SWITZERLAND
Internet: http://musnov1.unige.ch/prixrmj/
AMOUNT: 10,000 Swiss francs
DEADLINE(S): MAY 31
FIELD(S): Music Composition
ELIGIBILITY/REQUIREMENTS: This competition is open to composers of all nationalities without age limit. It is designed to award a new work never performed before and is given every other year.
HOW TO APPLY: See website or write for yearly subject and official rules.
RENEWABLE: No

319—RIPON COLLEGE (Performance/Recognition Tuition Scholarships)

Admissions Office
300 Seward Street
P.O. Box 248

Ripon WI 54971
920/748-8101
E-mail: adminfo@ripon.edu
Internet: http://www.ripon.edu
AMOUNT: $5,000-$10,000/year
DEADLINE(S): MAR 1
FIELD(S): Music; Art; Theater
ELIGIBILITY/REQUIREMENTS: Open to undergraduate and graduate students attending or planning to attend Ripon College.
HOW TO APPLY: Contact Office of Admission for an application. Interview, audition, or nomination may be required.
RENEWABLE: Yes
CONTACT: Office of Admission

320—ROYAL ACADEMY OF MUSIC (Raffy Manoukian Scholarships)

Royal Academy of Music
Marylebone Road
London NW1 5HT ENGLAND
+44 (0)141 332 4101
FAX: +44 (0)141 332 8901
E-mail: e.kemp-luck@ram.ac.uk
DEADLINE(S): March
FIELD(S): Musical Composition
ELIGIBILITY/REQUIREMENTS: Awarded on a competitive basis to students of Armenian nationality or descent who successfully audition for an Academy place.
HOW TO APPLY: Write to the Foundation for complete information.
CONTACT: Edward Kemp-Luck

321—SAN ANGELO SYMPHONY SOCIETY (Sorantin Young Artist Award Competition)

P.O. Box 5922
San Angelo TX 76902
325/658-5877
FAX: 325/658-1045
Internet: http://www.sanangelo symphony.org
AMOUNT: $5,000 + solo performance (winner); $2,000 (3 others); $1,000 (runners-up)
DEADLINE(S): OCT 2
FIELD(S): Piano and Strings
ELIGIBILITY/REQUIREMENTS: Open to instrumentalists who have not reached their 28th birthdays by competition date. All candidates will be judged according to technical proficiency, musicianship, rhythm, selection of repertoire, stage presence, and communication. All contestants will perform all repertoire from memory. Required Repertoire: 1 standard 3-movement concerto (minimum duration 15 minutes); 1 contrasting unaccompanied solo concert piece written for the instrument.

HOW TO APPLY: Download an application from website or contact the Society at 325/658-5877. There is a $60 fee.

322—SAN FRANCISCO CONSERVATORY OF MUSIC

50 Oak Street
San Francisco CA 94102
800/899-SFCM
E-mail: admit@sfcm.edu
Internet: http://www.sfcm.edu

AMOUNT: $1,000 to full tuition
DEADLINE(S): Priority given to students who complete scholarship/financial aid process by MAR 1
FIELD(S): Music (voice and instrumental)
ELIGIBILITY/REQUIREMENTS: Scholarships awarded on the basis of musical ability, financial need, and the musical needs of the school. Available to full-time students in the Music Diploma program, the Bachelor of Music, Master of Music, and the Artist Certificate program.
HOW TO APPLY: See website under Admissions/Financial Aid tab.
NUMBER OF AWARDS: 283
RENEWABLE: Yes. Undergraduates must maintain a 2.0 GPA to be eligible for renewal of their scholarships; graduate students must maintain a 2.75 GPA. Renewal also depends on the successful fulfillment of all obligations to the Conservatory, including orchestra and ensemble assignments.
CONTACT: Doris Howard

323—SKIDMORE COLLEGE (Filene Music Scholarships)

Music Department
815 North Broadway
Saratoga Springs NY 12866-1632
Internet: www.skidmore.edu/
academics/music/scholarships/
Schlrshp.htm

AMOUNT: $6,000/year
DEADLINE(S): FEB 1
FIELD(S): Music: instrumental, voice
ELIGIBILITY/REQUIREMENTS: Scholarships for talented young musicians. Awards are based on musical excellence as revealed by a competition. Filene scholars need not major in music; however, recipients are expected to continue to develop their skills through private instruction in the Music Department each semester and to participate in department ensembles.
HOW TO APPLY: Must submit a cassette performance tape by Feb. 1. Final round of competitions occurs in April and is performed in person.

NUMBER OF AWARDS: 4
RENEWABLE: Yes, if student continues in good academic standing and receives the recommendation of the Department of Music.

324—SOUTHERN ILLINOIS UNIVERSITY (Music Scholarships)

School of Music
Mailcode 4302
Carbondale IL 62901-4302
618/536-8742
FAX: 618/453-5808
Internet: http://www.siu.edu/
~music/resources/scholarships.html

AMOUNT: Varies
DEADLINE(S): MAR 15
FIELD(S): Music Performance, Composition, Theater, Music Business, Music Education
ELIGIBILITY/REQUIREMENTS: Must be music major or minor.
HOW TO APPLY: An audition is required, usually held in February. A personal audition or taped audition can be arranged. See website or Undergraduate Office, School of Music.
RENEWABLE: Yes. Recommendation of music faculty required.
CONTACT: Dr. Jeanine Wagner

325—STEPHEN ARLEN MEMORIAL FUND (Grant Award)

English National Opera
London Coliseum
St. Martin's Lane
London WC2N 4ES ENGLAND
020 7845 9355
FAX: 020 7845 9274
E-mail: SAMFund@eno.org

AMOUNT: £3,000
DEADLINE(S): FEB 28
FIELD(S): Opera; Ballet; Drama; Music
ELIGIBILITY/REQUIREMENTS: Annual grant to an artist less than 30 years of age who has completed formal training and now wishes to pursue a career in the arts. Awarded to artist proposing an independent project rather than funding further training. Must be UK resident.
HOW TO APPLY: Contact the Fund's Secretary at above address for an application.
CONTACT: Secretary

326—SUZUKI ASSOCIATION OF THE AMERICAS (Music Teacher Scholarships)

P.O. Box 17310
Boulder CO 80308
303/444-0948
FAX: 303/444-0984

E-mail: info@suzukiassociation.org
Internet: http://www.suzuki
association.org

AMOUNT: $225-$600
DEADLINE(S): FEB 1
FIELD(S): Teaching: Music
ELIGIBILITY/REQUIREMENTS: Open to music teachers and prospective music teachers who are full-time college students. Membership in above organization for a minimum of 6 months prior to application required.
HOW TO APPLY: Visit website for details or contact Association to request membership information or application.

327—TEXAS CHORAL DIRECTORS ASSOCIATION SCHOLARSHIP FUND

7900 Centre Park Drive
Austin TX 78754
514/474-2801
FAX: 514/474-7873
E-mail: tcda@ensemble.org
Internet: http://www.ensemble.org/
tcda

AMOUNT: $500-$1,000
DEADLINE(S): JUN 1
FIELD(S): Choral Direction; Music Education
ELIGIBILITY/REQUIREMENTS: Must have completed 60 hours in music education degree program.
HOW TO APPLY: Contact TCDA for an application
NUMBER OF AWARDS: 4
RENEWABLE: No
CONTACT: Dan L. Wood

328—THELONIOUS MONK INSTITUTE OF JAZZ (International Jazz Composers Competition)

5225 Wisconsin Avenue NW
Washington DC 20015
202/364-7272
FAX: 202/364-0176
E-mail: info@monkinst.org
Internet: http://www.monkinstitute.
org

AMOUNT: $10,000 grand prize
DEADLINE(S): AUG 5
FIELD(S): Music: Composition for Jazz Instrument
ELIGIBILITY/REQUIREMENTS: Competition presented by the Thelonious Monk Institute of Jazz and BMI to reward excellence in jazz composition. Composition to be written for trumpet. Can be written for up to five instruments with trumpet being the featured instrument. Solos for trumpet okay. Composers

must not have had their jazz compositions recorded on a major label or recorded by a major jazz artist.
HOW TO APPLY: Application is on website or contact above organization for current information regarding application. Instructions for audiotape selections are very specific.

329—THELONIOUS MONK INSTITUTE OF JAZZ (International Jazz Instrument Competition)

5225 Wisconsin Avenue NW
Washington DC 20015
202/364-7272
FAX: 202/364-0176
E-mail: info@monkinst.org
Internet: http://www.monkinstitute.org
AMOUNT: $20,000 (first); $10,000 (second); $5,000 (third); $1,000 (additional finalists)
DEADLINE(S): AUG 5
FIELD(S): Music: Jazz instrument
ELIGIBILITY/REQUIREMENTS: Competition for the world's most promising young musicians to receive college-level training by America's jazz masters, worldwide recognition, and performance opportunities. Musicians under contract with a major label are not eligible. Decisions based on audiotape presentation and application.
HOW TO APPLY: Application is on website or contact above organization for current information regarding application. Instructions for audiotape selections are very specific.

330—UNIVERSITY OF NORTH TEXAS (Music Scholarships)

College of Music
P.O. Box 311367
Denton TX 76203-1367
940/565-2791
FAX: 940/565-2002
E-mail: undergrad@music.unt.edu
Internet: http://www.music.unt.edu/admissions/ugprocedure.sthml
AMOUNT: Varies
DEADLINE(S): MAY 1
FIELD(S): Music
ELIGIBILITY/REQUIREMENTS: Several scholarships for music students are offered at the University of North Texas. Specialties and eligibility requirements vary.
HOW TO APPLY: See website for more information. Contact school for details.
NUMBER OF AWARDS: See website for more information. Contact school for details.

RENEWABLE: See website for more information. Contact school for details.

331—UNIVERSITY OF TEXAS AT EL PASO (Music Scholarships)

Department of Music
Fox Fine Arts Center, Room 301
500 West University Avenue
El Paso TX 79968-0552
915/747-5606
FAX: 915/747-5023
E-mail: music@utep.edu
Internet: http://www.utep.edu
AMOUNT: Varies
DEADLINE(S): MAR 1
FIELD(S): Music
ELIGIBILITY/REQUIREMENTS: Several music scholarships are available at the University of Texas at El Paso. Virtually all members of large ensembles receive a service award of some type, while more serious students may audition for a music scholarship. Auditions are usually held in March or April.
HOW TO APPLY: See website or contact Chair, Department of Music, for more information.
CONTACT: Dr. Ron Hufstader, Chair, Department of Music

332—UNIVERSITY OF WINDSOR (Outstanding Scholars Award)

401 Sunset Avenue
Windsor Ontario N9B 3P4
CANADA
519/253-3000
FAX: 519/973-7081
E-mail: awards1@uwindsor.ca
Internet: http://www.uwindsor.ca
AMOUNT: $1,000-$2500/year (Canadian); maximum 4 years
DEADLINE(S): MAY 31
FIELD(S): Classics, Modern Languages, French, Philosophy, Music, Physics, Earth Sciences (not Environmental Studies), Economics (not Business and Economics), Chemistry (not Biochemistry), Mathematics and Statistics, Industrial, Mechanical (Materials Option) or Environmental Engineering or Bachelor of Arts and Science
ELIGIBILITY/REQUIREMENTS: Open to undergraduate students registering in year 1 at the University of Windsor. Must have superior grades. Amount of award based on secondary school accomplishments.
HOW TO APPLY: Automatic. No application required.
RENEWABLE: Yes. Up to 4 years.

CONTACT: Aase Houser
ADDITIONAL INFORMATION: Students in this program will also be mentored in their first year in preparation for guaranteed Outstanding Scholars Appointments in their Department/School (valued at $2,000 Canadian in earnings for each of the 2nd, 3rd, and 4th years) provided all conditions are met.

333—UTA ALUMNI ASSOCIATION (Sue and Art Mosby Scholarship Endowment in Music)

University of Texas at Arlington
Box 19457
Arlington TX 76019
817/272-2594
FAX: 817/272-2597
E-mail: alumni@uta.edu
Internet: http://www.uta.edu/alumni/scholar.htm
AMOUNT: $500
DEADLINE(S): Varies
FIELD(S): Music
ELIGIBILITY/REQUIREMENTS: Must be a full-time student in good standing at the University of Texas at Arlington. Must demonstrate financial need and musical ability with potential to complete UTA degree.
HOW TO APPLY: Contact UTA Alumni Association for an application. Audition required.
NUMBER OF AWARDS: 1

334—WAMSO (Elaine Louise Lagerstrom Memorial Award)

1111 Nicollet Mall
Minneapolis MN 55403
612/371-5654
Fax: 612/371-7176
E-mail: wamso@mnorch.org
Internet: http://www.wamso.org
AMOUNT: $1,000
DEADLINE(S): SEPT
FIELD(S): Violin
ELIGIBILITY/REQUIREMENTS: Contestants must be performers of instruments which have permanent chairs in the Minnesota Orchestra, and be legal residents or students in Illinois, Indiana, Iowa, Kansas, Michigan, Minnesota, Missouri, Nebraska, North Dakota, South Dakota, Wisconsin, and the Canadian provinces of Manitoba and Ontario. Entrants may not have passed their 26th birthday on date of competition (which is usually held in January).
HOW TO APPLY: See website for more information and application. Submit application form together with a $75 non-

refundable fee followed by CD/tape of performance (concerto or significant concert piece from the standard repertoire plus 2 additional solo works chosen by applicant) required for preliminary round of judging.
NUMBER OF AWARDS: 1 + performance and summer study opportunities
RENEWABLE: No

335—WAMSO (Mary Winston Smail Memorial Award)

1111 Nicollet Mall
Minneapolis MN 55403
612/371-5654
Fax: 612/371-7176
E-mail: wamso@mnorch.org
Internet: http://www.wamso.org
AMOUNT: $500
DEADLINE(S): SEPT
FIELD(S): Piano
ELIGIBILITY/REQUIREMENTS:
Contestants must be performers of instruments which have permanent chairs in the Minnesota Orchestra, and be legal residents or students in Illinois, Indiana, Iowa, Kansas, Michigan, Minnesota, Missouri, Nebraska, North Dakota, South Dakota, Wisconsin, and the Canadian provinces of Manitoba and Ontario. Entrants may not have passed their 26th birthday on date of competition (which is usually held in January).
HOW TO APPLY: See website for more information and application. Submit application form together with a $75 nonrefundable fee followed by CD/tape of performance (concerto or significant concert piece from the standard repertoire plus 2 additional solo works chosen by applicant) required for preliminary round of judging.
NUMBER OF AWARDS: 1 + performance and summer study opportunities
RENEWABLE: No

336—WAMSO (Mathilda Heck Award)

1111 Nicollet Mall
Minneapolis MN 55403
612/371-5654
Fax: 612/371-7176
E-mail: wamso@mnorch.org
Internet: http://www.wamso.org
AMOUNT: $1,000
DEADLINE(S): SEPT
FIELD(S): Woodwiind
ELIGIBILITY/REQUIREMENTS:
Contestants must be performers of instruments which have permanent chairs in the Minnesota Orchestra, and be legal residents or students in Illinois, Indiana, Iowa, Kansas, Michigan, Minnesota, Missouri,

Nebraska, North Dakota, South Dakota, Wisconsin, and the Canadian provinces of Manitoba and Ontario. Entrants may not have passed their 26th birthday on date of competition (which is usually held in January).
HOW TO APPLY: See website for more information and application. Submit application form together with a $75 nonrefundable fee followed by CD/tape of performance (concerto or significant concert piece from the standard repertoire plus 2 additional solo works chosen by applicant) required for preliminary round of judging.
NUMBER OF AWARDS: 1 + performance and summer study opportunities
RENEWABLE: No

337—WAMSO (Twin Cities Musicians Union AFM Award)

1111 Nicollet Mall
Minneapolis MN 55403
612/371-5654
Fax: 612/371-7176
E-mail: wamso@mnorch.org
Internet: http://www.wamso.org
AMOUNT: $1,000
DEADLINE(S): SEPT
FIELD(S): Woodwiind
ELIGIBILITY/REQUIREMENTS:
Contestants must be performers of instruments which have permanent chairs in the Minnesota Orchestra, and be legal residents or students in Illinois, Indiana, Iowa, Kansas, Michigan, Minnesota, Missouri, Nebraska, North Dakota, South Dakota, Wisconsin, and the Canadian provinces of Manitoba and Ontario. Entrants may not have passed their 26th birthday on date of competition (which is usually held in January).
HOW TO APPLY: See website for more information and application. Submit application form together with a $75 nonrefundable fee followed by CD/tape of performance (concerto or significant concert piece from the standard repertoire plus 2 additional solo works chosen by applicant) required for preliminary round of judging.
NUMBER OF AWARDS: 1 + performance and summer study opportunities
RENEWABLE: No

338—WAMSO (Vincent R. Bastien Memorial Award)

1111 Nicollet Mall
Minneapolis MN 55403
612/371-5654
Fax: 612/371-7176
E-mail: wamso@mnorch.org

Internet: http://www.wamso.org
AMOUNT: $500
DEADLINE(S): SEPT
FIELD(S): Cello
ELIGIBILITY/REQUIREMENTS:
Contestants must be performers of instruments which have permanent chairs in the Minnesota Orchestra, and be legal residents or students in Illinois, Indiana, Iowa, Kansas, Michigan, Minnesota, Missouri, Nebraska, North Dakota, South Dakota, Wisconsin, and the Canadian provinces of Manitoba and Ontario. Entrants may not have passed their 26th birthday on date of competition (which is usually held in January).
HOW TO APPLY: See website for more information and application. Submit application form together with a $75 nonrefundable fee followed by CD/tape of performance (concerto or significant concert piece from the standard repertoire plus 2 additional solo works chosen by applicant) required for preliminary round of judging.
NUMBER OF AWARDS: 1 + performance and summer study opportunities
RENEWABLE: No

339—WAMSO (Young Artist Competition)

1111 Nicollet Mall
Minneapolis MN 55403
612/371-5654
Fax: 612/371-7176
E-mail: wamso@mnorch.org
Internet: http://www.wamso.org
AMOUNT: $5,000 + $2,500 WAMSO Achievement Award and performance with Minneapolis Orchestra (first prize), $2,500 (second prize), $1,000 (third prize)
DEADLINE(S): SEPT
FIELD(S): Piano and Orchestral Instruments
ELIGIBILITY/REQUIREMENTS:
Contestants must be performers of instruments which have permanent chairs in the Minnesota Orchestra, and be legal residents or students in Illinois, Indiana, Iowa, Kansas, Michigan, Minnesota, Missouri, Nebraska, North Dakota, South Dakota, Wisconsin, and the Canadian provinces of Manitoba and Ontario. Entrants may not have passed their 26th birthday on date of competition (which is usually held in January).
HOW TO APPLY: See website for more information and application. Submit application form together with a $75 nonrefundable fee followed by CD/tape of performance (concerto or significant concert piece from the standard repertoire

plus 2 additional solo works chosen by applicant) required for preliminary round of judging.
NUMBER OF AWARDS: 4 + performance and summer study opportunities
RENEWABLE: No

340—WESTERN MICHIGAN UNIVERSITY (College of Fine Arts/Anna L. Tobin—An Actress—Memorial Scholarship)

1903 W. Michigan
Kalamazoo MI 49008-5337
269/387-8777
FAX: 269/387-6989
E-mail: finaid-info@wmich.edu
Internet: http://www.wmich.edu/finaid
AMOUNT: Varies
DEADLINE(S): MAR (for current Theater majors); on acceptance into program for freshmen and transfer students
FIELD(S): Theater Education; Theater Design; Technical Theater; Arts Management; Music Theater Performance
ELIGIBILITY/REQUIREMENTS: Scholarships are ONLY for Theater majors and minors. Must have a 3.0 GPA.
HOW TO APPLY: Freshmen or transfer students—by audition/interview and acceptance into major or minor in Theater program. Current Theater majors—by application form from the department.
RENEWABLE: No
CONTACT: Theater Department

341—WESTERN MICHIGAN UNIVERSITY (College of Fine Arts/Audrey Ekdahl Davidson Early Music Scholarship)

School of Music
Kalamazoo MI 49008-3831
269/387-8777
FAX: 269/387-6989
E-mail: finaid-info@wmich.edu
Internet: http://www.wmich.edu/finaid
AMOUNT: $500-$2,000+
DEADLINE(S): MAR
FIELD(S): Music (voice)
ELIGIBILITY/REQUIREMENTS: This scholarship recognizes an outstanding vocalist who will perform with the Collegium Musicum. Recipients must carry an overall GPA of 3.0. Certain conditions for holding a music scholarship will be stipulated at the time of award. These conditions include such requirements as maintaining a certain GPA, being a full-time music major, studying with appropriate faculty member, performing in School of Music ensembles, providing library assis-

tance, accompanying, or other professional services. All special conditions relating to a scholarship are stated in writing prior to the student's accepting the award.
HOW TO APPLY: Undergraduate students may receive consideration for a scholarship award at the same time they audition for admission to the music curriculum; no separate application form is required.
RENEWABLE: Yes. Recipients qualify to hold award until graduation, 4-year maximum, providing musical and academic excellence are maintained.
CONTACT: Music Student Advisor, School of Music

342—WESTERN MICHIGAN UNIVERSITY (College of Fine Arts/Beth Louise Critchett Sebaly and Avis Leo 'Mike' Sebaly Scholarship)

1903 W. Michigan
Kalamazoo MI 49008-5337
269/387-8777
FAX: 269/387-6989
E-mail: finaid-info@wmich.edu
Internet: http://www.wmich.edu/finaid
AMOUNT: Varies
DEADLINE(S): MAR
FIELD(S): Theater Education; Theater Design; Technical Theater; Arts Management; Music Theater Performance
ELIGIBILITY/REQUIREMENTS: Recipient must be full-time undergraduate student majoring in theater with a concentration in the area of theater production; must demonstrate financial need; have a minimum 2.5 GPA, and maintain satisfactory academic progress as specified by the Office of Student Financial Aid.
HOW TO APPLY: Contact Theater Department for more information.
RENEWABLE: Yes. Up to 4 consecutive academic years.
CONTACT: Theater Department

343—WESTERN MICHIGAN UNIVERSITY (College of Fine Arts/Beulah and Harold McKee Scholarship)

School of Music
Kalamazoo MI 49008-3831
269/387-8777
FAX: 269/387-6989
E-mail: finaid-info@wmich.edu
Internet: http://www.wmich.edu/finaid
AMOUNT: $500-$2,000+
DEADLINE(S): MAR
FIELD(S): Music

ELIGIBILITY/REQUIREMENTS: This scholarship recognizes a senior music major who demonstrates major accomplishment in his/her chosen field of music concentration. Certain conditions for holding a music scholarship will be stipulated at the time of award. These conditions include such requirements as maintaining a certain GPA, being a full-time music major, studying with appropriate faculty member, performing in School of Music ensembles, providing library assistance, accompanying, or other professional services. All special conditions relating to a scholarship are stated in writing prior to the student's accepting the award.
HOW TO APPLY: Undergraduate students may receive consideration for a scholarship award at the same time they audition for admission to the music curriculum; no separate application form is required.
NUMBER OF AWARDS: 1
RENEWABLE: Yes. Recipients qualify to hold award until graduation, 4-year maximum, providing musical and academic excellence are maintained.
CONTACT: Music Student Advisor, School of Music

344—WESTERN MICHIGAN UNIVERSITY (College of Fine Arts/Beulah and Harold McKee Theater Scholarship)

1903 W. Michigan
Kalamazoo MI 49008-5337
269/387-8777
FAX: 269/387-6989
E-mail: finaid-info@wmich.edu
Internet: http://www.wmich.edu/finaid
AMOUNT: Varies
DEADLINE(S): On acceptance into program
FIELD(S): Theater Education; Theater Design; Technical Theater; Arts Management; Music Theater Performance
ELIGIBILITY/REQUIREMENTS: Freshmen or transfer students accepted into a major or minor in Theater program.
HOW TO APPLY: By application form from the Department and by audition and interview.
RENEWABLE: No
CONTACT: Theater Department

345—WESTERN MICHIGAN UNIVERSITY (College of Fine Arts/Carol Haenicke University Theater Guild Scholarship)

1903 W. Michigan
Kalamazoo MI 49008-5337
269/387-8777
FAX: 269/387-6989

E-mail: finaid-info@wmich.edu
Internet: http://www.wmich.edu/
finaid
AMOUNT: Varies
DEADLINE(S): MAR (for current
Theater majors); on acceptance into
program for freshmen and transfer stu-
dents
FIELD(S): Theater Education; Theater
Design; Technical Theater; Arts
Management; Music Theater
Performance
ELIGIBILITY/REQUIREMENTS:
Scholarships are ONLY for Theater
majors and minors. Must have a 3.0 GPA.
HOW TO APPLY: Freshmen or transfer
students—by audition/interview and accep-
tance into major or minor in Theater pro-
gram. Current Theater majors—by applica-
tion form from the department.
RENEWABLE: No
CONTACT: Theater Department

346—WESTERN MICHIGAN UNIVERSITY (College of Fine Arts/Carroll J. Haas Sr. Violoncello Scholarship)

School of Music
Kalamazoo MI 49008-3831
269/387-8777
FAX: 269/387-6989
E-mail: finaid-info@wmich.edu
Internet: http://www.wmich.edu/
finaid
AMOUNT: Varies
DEADLINE(S): MAR
FIELD(S): Music (violoncello)
ELIGIBILITY/REQUIREMENTS: Full-
time Music major pursuing studies on the
violoncello. Minimum GPA of 3.0 (in case
of first-year student, this would be the high
school GPA). Certain conditions for holding a music scholarship will be stipulated at
the time of award. These conditions
include such requirements as maintaining a
certain GPA, being a full-time music
major, studying with appropriate faculty
member, performing in School of Music
ensembles, providing library assistance,
accompanying, or other professional services. All special conditions relating to a
scholarship are stated in writing prior to
the student's accepting the award.
HOW TO APPLY: The selection of the
scholarship recipient shall be based upon
talent as determined through the audition/
interview process conducted by appropriate personnel of the School of Music.
Contact Music Student Advisor.
RENEWABLE: Yes. Maximum of 3 consecutive academic years provided recipient
remains full-time undergraduate pursuing
studies on violoncello and demonstrates
satisfactory academic progress.

CONTACT: Music Student Advisor,
School of Music

347—WESTERN MICHIGAN UNIVERSITY (College of Fine Arts/Dalton Dancers with Musicians Scholarship)

1903 W. Michigan
Kalamazoo MI 49008-5337
269/387-6000
FAX: 269/387-6989
E-mail: finaid-info@wmich.edu
Internet: http://www.wmich.edu/
finaid
AMOUNT: $500/project
DEADLINE(S): NOV and FEB
FIELD(S): Dance; Music
ELIGIBILITY/REQUIREMENTS: To
acknowledge the dance major who has
exhibited exceptional choreographic ability and musicality; to provide an educational opportunity for such students to collabo-
rate in rehearsal and/or performance in a
music/dance project; to enhance the quality of music involved in dance productions
at WMU. Award will be given to students
whose proposals are accepted in one of the
following categories: Choreographers with
Composers: student choreographers who
wish to work with a composer in creating a
dance to an original score; Choreographers
with Musicians: student choreographers
who wish to work with one or more musicians in presenting a dance to an existing
score which is to be performed "live."
HOW TO APPLY: Contact the Department of Dance or download this PDF
application.
RENEWABLE: No

348—WESTERN MICHIGAN UNIVERSITY (College of Fine Arts/David P. Karsten Theater Scholarship)

1903 W. Michigan
Kalamazoo MI 49008-5337
269/387-8777
FAX: 269/387-6989
E-mail: finaid-info@wmich.edu
Internet: http://www.wmich.edu/
finaid
AMOUNT: Varies
DEADLINE(S): MAR
FIELD(S): Theater Education; Theater
Design; Technical Theater; Arts
Management; Music Theater
Performance
ELIGIBILITY/REQUIREMENTS:
Recipient must be a junior or senior and a
full-time student with a GPA of 3.25. Must
demonstrate diversity in their curriculum
and/or their production/performance expe-
rience on or off campus. Applicants shall

provide supporting documentation (if
applicable) and demonstrate financial
need. Must be U.S. citizen.
HOW TO APPLY: Contact Theater
Department for more information.
RENEWABLE: No
CONTACT: Theater Department

349—WESTERN MICHIGAN UNIVERSITY (College of Fine Arts/David Wayne Quasi Endowment Scholarship Fund)

1903 W. Michigan
Kalamazoo MI 49008-5337
269/387-8777
FAX: 269/387-6989
E-mail: finaid-info@wmich.edu
Internet: http://www.wmich.edu/
finaid
AMOUNT: Varies
DEADLINE(S): MAR (for current
Theater majors); on acceptance into
program for freshmen and transfer stu-
dents
FIELD(S): Theater Education; Theater
Design; Technical Theater; Arts
Management; Music Theater
Performance
ELIGIBILITY/REQUIREMENTS:
Scholarships are ONLY for Theater
majors and minors. Must have a 3.0 GPA.
HOW TO APPLY: Freshmen or transfer
students—by audition/interview and
acceptance into major or minor in Theater
program. Current Theater majors—by
application form from the department.
RENEWABLE: No
CONTACT: Theater Department

350—WESTERN MICHIGAN UNIVERSITY (College of Fine Arts/Diether H. Haenicke British Isles Theater Scholarship Award)

1903 W. Michigan
Kalamazoo MI 49008-5337
269/387-8777
FAX: 269/387-6989
E-mail: finaid-info@wmich.edu
Internet: http://www.wmich.edu/
finaid
AMOUNT: $6,000
DEADLINE(S): NOV
FIELD(S): Theater Education; Theater
Design; Technical Theater; Arts
Management; Music Theater
Performance
ELIGIBILITY/REQUIREMENTS:
Scholarships are ONLY for Theater
Majors. Must have a 3.0 GPA.
HOW TO APPLY: By application form
from the Department and by audition and
interview.
RENEWABLE: No
CONTACT: Theater Department

351—WESTERN MICHIGAN UNIVERSITY (College of Fine Arts/Dorothy U. Dalton Scholarship)

School of Music
Kalamazoo MI 49008-3831
269/387-8777
FAX: 269/387-6989
E-mail: finaid-info@wmich.edu
Internet: http://www.wmich.edu/finaid
AMOUNT: $500-$2,000+
DEADLINE(S): MAR
FIELD(S): Music
ELIGIBILITY/REQUIREMENTS: Dalton Scholarships recognize incoming students (freshmen and transfer) who demonstrate accomplishment and promise in their music auditions. Certain conditions for holding a music scholarship will be stipulated at the time of award. These conditions include such requirements as maintaining a certain GPA, being a full-time music major, studying with appropriate faculty member, performing in School of Music ensembles, providing library assistance, accompanying, or other professional services. All special conditions relating to a scholarship are stated in writing prior to the student's accepting the award.
HOW TO APPLY: Undergraduate students may receive consideration for a scholarship award at the same time they audition for admission to the music curriculum; no separate application form is required. Contact Music Student Advisor for more information.
RENEWABLE: Yes. Recipients qualify to hold award until graduation, 4-year maximum, providing musical and academic excellence are maintained.
CONTACT: Music Student Advisor, School of Music

352—WESTERN MICHIGAN UNIVERSITY (College of Fine Arts/Evelyn Rosen Hart Endowed Scholarship for Elementary Education/Music Majors)

School of Music
Kalamazoo MI 49008-3831
269/387-8777
FAX: 269/387-6989
E-mail: finaid-info@wmich.edu
Internet: http://www.wmich.edu/finaid
AMOUNT: $500-$2,000+
DEADLINE(S): MAR
FIELD(S): Elementary Education/Music
ELIGIBILITY/REQUIREMENTS: This scholarship recognizes outstanding Elementary Education/Music (EEM) majors and Music Education Majors (secondary).

Certain conditions for holding a music scholarship will be stipulated at the time of award. These conditions include such requirements as maintaining a certain GPA, being a full-time music major, studying with appropriate faculty member, performing in School of Music ensembles, providing library assistance, accompanying, or other professional services. All special conditions relating to a scholarship are stated in writing prior to the student's accepting the award.
HOW TO APPLY: Contact Music Student Advisor for more information.
RENEWABLE: Yes. Recipients qualify to hold award until graduation, 4-year maximum, providing musical and academic excellence are maintained.
CONTACT: Music Student Advisor, School of Music

353—WESTERN MICHIGAN UNIVERSITY (College of Fine Arts/Excellence in Accompanying Scholarship)

School of Music
Kalamazoo MI 49008-3831
269/387-8777
FAX: 269/387-6989
E-mail: finaid-info@wmich.edu
Internet: http://www.wmich.edu/finaid
AMOUNT: Varies
DEADLINE(S): MAR
FIELD(S): Music (piano)
ELIGIBILITY/REQUIREMENTS: Sophomore, junior, or senior enrolled full time in the Department of Music and demonstrating excellence in piano accompaniment; minimum GPA of 3.2. Financial need a secondary consideration. Certain conditions for holding a music scholarship will be stipulated at the time of award. These conditions include such requirements as maintaining a certain GPA, being a full-time music major, studying with appropriate faculty member, performing in School of Music ensembles, providing library assistance, accompanying, or other professional services. All special conditions relating to a scholarship are stated in writing prior to the student's accepting the award.
HOW TO APPLY: Contact Music Student Advisor.
RENEWABLE: Yes. Recipients must have 3.2 GPA to renew.
CONTACT: Music Student Advisor, School of Music

354—WESTERN MICHIGAN UNIVERSITY (College of Fine Arts/Gene Whitfield Jazz Scholarship)

School of Music
Kalamazoo MI 49008-3831

269/387-8777
FAX: 269/387-6989
E-mail: finaid-info@wmich.edu
Internet: http://www.wmich.edu/finaid
AMOUNT: $500-$2,000+
DEADLINE(S): MAR
FIELD(S): Music (jazz)
ELIGIBILITY/REQUIREMENTS: The scholarship recognizes the music student who demonstrates outstanding accomplishment as a jazz major. Certain conditions for holding a music scholarship will be stipulated at the time of award. These conditions include such requirements as maintaining a certain GPA, being a full-time music major, studying with appropriate faculty member, performing in School of Music ensembles, providing library assistance, accompanying, or other professional services. All special conditions relating to a scholarship are stated in writing prior to the student's accepting the award.
HOW TO APPLY: Undergraduate students may receive consideration for a scholarship award at the same time they audition for admission to the music curriculum; no separate application form is required. Contact Music Student Advisor for more information.
RENEWABLE: Yes. Recipients qualify to hold award until graduation, 4-year maximum, providing musical and academic excellence are maintained.
CONTACT: Music Student Advisor, School of Music

355—WESTERN MICHIGAN UNIVERSITY (College of Fine Arts/Haenicke Scholarships for International Music Study)

School of Music
Kalamazoo MI 49008-3831
269/387-8777
FAX: 269/387-6989
E-mail: finaid-info@wmich.edu
Internet: http://www.wmich.edu/finaid
AMOUNT: $500-$2,000+
DEADLINE(S): MAR
FIELD(S): Music (voice, piano)
ELIGIBILITY/REQUIREMENTS: These scholarships for singers and pianists are designated for summer study at the American Institute for Musical Studies (AIMS) in Graz, Austria. Certain conditions for holding a music scholarship will be stipulated at the time of award. These conditions include such requirements as maintaining a certain GPA, being a full-time music major, studying with appropriate faculty member, performing in School of Music ensembles, providing library

assistance, accompanying, or other professional services. All special conditions relating to a scholarship are stated in writing prior to the student's accepting the award.
HOW TO APPLY: Chosen by audition. Contact Music Student Advisor for more information.
RENEWABLE: Yes. Recipients qualify to hold award until graduation, 4-year maximum, providing musical and academic excellence are maintained.
CONTACT: Music Student Advisor, School of Music

356—WESTERN MICHIGAN UNIVERSITY (College of Fine Arts/Harper C. Maybee Scholarship)

School of Music
Kalamazoo MI 49008-3831
269/387-6000
FAX: 269/387-6989
E-mail: finaid-info@wmich.edu
Internet: http://www.wmich.edu/finaid
AMOUNT: $500-$2,000+
DEADLINE(S): MAR
FIELD(S): Music
ELIGIBILITY/REQUIREMENTS: This award recognizes an outstanding senior who demonstrates major evidence of accomplishment in the chosen field of music concentration. Certain conditions for holding a music scholarship will be stipulated at the time of award. These conditions include such requirements as maintaining a certain GPA, being a full-time music major, studying with appropriate faculty member, performing in School of Music ensembles, providing library assistance, accompanying, or other professional services. All special conditions relating to a scholarship are stated in writing prior to the student's accepting the award.
HOW TO APPLY: Contact Music Student Advisor for more information.
RENEWABLE: No
CONTACT: Music Student Advisor, School of Music

357—WESTERN MICHIGAN UNIVERSITY (College of Fine Arts/Hearron-Sommerfeld Music Theater Scholarship)

1903 W. Michigan
Kalamazoo MI 49008-5337
269/387-8777
FAX: 269/387-6989
E-mail: finaid-info@wmich.edu
Internet: http://www.wmich.edu/finaid
AMOUNT: $2,500
DEADLINE(S): MAR

FIELD(S): Theater Education; Theater Design; Technical Theater; Arts Management; Music Theater Performance
ELIGIBILITY/REQUIREMENTS: Recipient must be a junior or senior seeking a BFA degree in Music Theater. Must have a minimum 3.0 GPA.
HOW TO APPLY: Music Theater Faculty Steering Committee evaluates junior and senior candidates to determine an appropriate recipient.
RENEWABLE: No
CONTACT: Theater Department

358—WESTERN MICHIGAN UNIVERSITY (College of Fine Arts/Herbert Butler Chair)

School of Music
Kalamazoo MI 49008-3831
269/387-8777
FAX: 269/387-6989
E-mail: finaid-info@wmich.edu
Internet: http://www.wmich.edu/finaid
AMOUNT: $500-$2,000+
DEADLINE(S): MAR
FIELD(S): Music (cello)
ELIGIBILITY/REQUIREMENTS: This scholarship recognizes a cellist of outstanding ability and/or potential. Certain conditions for holding a music scholarship will be stipulated at the time of award. These conditions include such requirements as maintaining a certain GPA, being a full-time music major, studying with appropriate faculty member, performing in School of Music ensembles, providing library assistance, accompanying, or other professional services. All special conditions relating to a scholarship are stated in writing prior to the student's accepting the award.
HOW TO APPLY: Undergraduate students may receive consideration for a scholarship award at the same time they audition for admission to the music curriculum; no separate application form is required. Contact Music Student Advisor for more information.
NUMBER OF AWARDS: 1
RENEWABLE: Yes. Recipients qualify to hold award until graduation, 4-year maximum, providing musical and academic excellence are maintained.
CONTACT: Music Student Advisor, School of Music

359—WESTERN MICHIGAN UNIVERSITY (College of Fine Arts/H. Glenn Henderson Scholarship)

School of Music
Kalamazoo MI 49008-3831

269/387-8777
FAX: 269/387-6989
E-mail: finaid-info@wmich.edu
Internet: http://www.wmich.edu/finaid
AMOUNT: $500-$2,000+
DEADLINE(S): MAR
FIELD(S): Music (keyboard)
ELIGIBILITY/REQUIREMENTS: The scholarship recognizes a keyboard major who demonstrates major evidence of accomplishment in his or her chosen field of music concentration. Certain conditions for holding a music scholarship will be stipulated at the time of award. These conditions include such requirements as maintaining a certain GPA, being a full-time music major, studying with appropriate faculty member, performing in School of Music ensembles, providing library assistance, accompanying, or other professional services. All special conditions relating to a scholarship are stated in writing prior to the student's accepting the award.
HOW TO APPLY: Undergraduate students may receive consideration for a scholarship award at the same time they audition for admission to the music curriculum; no separate application form is required.
RENEWABLE: Yes. Recipients qualify to hold award until graduation, 4-year maximum, providing musical and academic excellence are maintained.
CONTACT: Music Student Advisor, School of Music

360—WESTERN MICHIGAN UNIVERSITY (College of Fine Arts/Irving S. Gilmore Piano Scholarships)

School of Music
Kalamazoo MI 49008-3831
269/387-8777
FAX: 269/387-6989
E-mail: finaid-info@wmich.edu
Internet: http://www.wmich.edu/finaid
AMOUNT: $500-$2,000+
DEADLINE(S): MAR
FIELD(S): Music (piano)
ELIGIBILITY/REQUIREMENTS: Scholarship recognizes outstanding pianists. Certain conditions for holding a music scholarship will be stipulated at the time of award. These conditions include such requirements as maintaining a certain GPA, being a full-time music major, studying with appropriate faculty member, performing in School of Music ensembles, providing library assistance, accompanying, or other professional services. All special conditions relating to are

stated in writing prior to the student's accepting the award.

HOW TO APPLY: Undergraduate students may receive consideration for a scholarship award at the same time they audition for admission to the music curriculum; no separate application form is required.

RENEWABLE: Yes. Recipients qualify to hold award until graduation, 4-year maximum, providing musical and academic excellence are maintained.

CONTACT: Music Student Advisor, School of Music

361—WESTERN MICHIGAN UNIVERSITY (College of Fine Arts/Janet E. Stillwell Music Theater Scholarship)

1903 W. Michigan
Kalamazoo MI 49008-5337
269/387-8777
FAX: 269/387-6989
E-mail: finaid-info@wmich.edu
Internet: http://www.wmich.edu/finaid
AMOUNT: $1,000/semester
DEADLINE(S): MAR (for current Theater majors); on acceptance into program for freshmen and transfer students
FIELD(S): Theater Education; Theater Design; Technical Theater; Arts Management; Music Theater Performance
ELIGIBILITY/REQUIREMENTS: Scholarships are ONLY for Theater majors and minors. Must have a 3.0 GPA.
HOW TO APPLY: Freshmen or transfer students—by audition/interview and acceptance into major or minor in Theater program. Current Theater majors—by application form from the department.
RENEWABLE: No
CONTACT: Theater Department

362—WESTERN MICHIGAN UNIVERSITY (College of Fine Arts/Joyce R. Zastrow Music Scholarship for Vocal Students)

School of Music
Kalamazoo MI 49008-3831
269/387-8777
FAX: 269/387-6989
E-mail: finaid-info@wmich.edu
Internet: http://www.wmich.edu/finaid
AMOUNT: Varies
DEADLINE(S): MAR
FIELD(S): Music (voice)
ELIGIBILITY/REQUIREMENTS: Full-time student who is a voice major in the College of Fine Arts, School of Music;

preference given to soprano voice major; award is merit-based, minimum 3.25 GPA, must demonstrate outstanding vocal talent as determined through audition, must maintain satisfactory academic progress.

HOW TO APPLY: The selection of the scholarship recipient shall be based upon talent as determined through the audition/interview process conducted by appropriate personnel of the School of Music.

RENEWABLE: Yes. Maximum of 3 consecutive academic years provided recipient remains full-time undergraduate pursuing studies in voice and demonstrates satisfactory academic progress.

CONTACT: Music Student Advisor, School of Music

363—WESTERN MICHIGAN UNIVERSITY (College of Fine Arts/Julius Stulberg Chair)

School of Music
Kalamazoo MI 49008-3831
269/387-8777
FAX: 269/387-6989
E-mail: finaid-info@wmich.edu
Internet: http://www.wmich.edu/finaid
AMOUNT: $500-$2,000+
DEADLINE(S): MAR
FIELD(S): Music (violin)
ELIGIBILITY/REQUIREMENTS: This scholarship recognizes a violinist of outstanding ability and/or potential. Certain conditions for holding a music scholarship will be stipulated at the time of award. These conditions include such requirements as maintaining a certain GPA, being a full-time music major, studying with appropriate faculty member, performing in School of Music ensembles, providing library assistance, accompanying, or other professional services. All special conditions relating to a scholarship are stated in writing prior to the student's accepting the award.

HOW TO APPLY: Undergraduate students may receive consideration for a scholarship award at the same time they audition for admission to the music curriculum; no separate application form is required.

NUMBER OF AWARDS: 1
RENEWABLE: Yes. Recipients qualify to hold award until graduation, 4-year maximum, providing musical and academic excellence are maintained.

CONTACT: Music Student Advisor, School of Music

364—WESTERN MICHIGAN UNIVERSITY (College of Fine Arts/Laura V. Shaw Quasi Endowment Scholarship Fund)

1903 W. Michigan
Kalamazoo MI 49008-5337

269/387-8777
FAX: 269/387-6989
E-mail: finaid-info@wmich.edu
Internet: http://www.wmich.edu/finaid
AMOUNT: Varies
DEADLINE(S): MAR (for current Theater majors); on acceptance into program for freshmen and transfer students
FIELD(S): Theater Education; Theater Design; Technical Theater; Arts Management; Music Theater Performance
ELIGIBILITY/REQUIREMENTS: Scholarships are ONLY for Theater majors and minors. Must have a 3.0 GPA.
HOW TO APPLY: Freshmen or transfer students—by audition/interview and acceptance into major or minor in Theater program. Current Theater majors—by application form from the department.
RENEWABLE: No
CONTACT: Theater Department

365—WESTERN MICHIGAN UNIVERSITY (College of Fine Arts/Leonard Meretta Band Scholarship)

School of Music
Kalamazoo MI 49008-3831
269/387-8777
FAX: 269/387-6989
E-mail: finaid-info@wmich.edu
Internet: http://www.wmich.edu/finaid
AMOUNT: $500-$2,000+
DEADLINE(S): MAR
FIELD(S): Music (band)
ELIGIBILITY/REQUIREMENTS: The scholarship recognizes an outstanding woodwind, brass, or percussion student. Certain conditions for holding a music scholarship will be stipulated at the time of award. These conditions include such requirements as maintaining a certain GPA, being a full-time music major, studying with appropriate faculty member, performing in School of Music ensembles, providing library assistance, accompanying, or other professional services. All special conditions relating to a scholarship are stated in writing prior to the student's accepting the award.

HOW TO APPLY: Undergraduate students may receive consideration for a scholarship award at the same time they audition for admission to the music curriculum; no separate application form is required. Winner is selected by the Director of Bands.

NUMBER OF AWARDS: 1

RENEWABLE: Yes. Recipients qualify to hold award until graduation, 4-year maximum, providing musical and academic excellence are maintained.
CONTACT: Music Student Advisor, School of Music

366—WESTERN MICHIGAN UNIVERSITY (College of Fine Arts/Mae Arnold Thacker Scholarships)

School of Music
Kalamazoo MI 49008-3831
269/387-8777
FAX: 269/387-6989
E-mail: finaid-info@wmich.edu
Internet: http://www.wmich.edu/finaid
AMOUNT: $500-$2,000+
DEADLINE(S): MAR
FIELD(S): Music (voice)
ELIGIBILITY/REQUIREMENTS: Recognizing voice students at the sophomore and junior level, these awards are made to outstanding music majors who demonstrate major evidence of accomplishment in their music study. Certain conditions for holding a music scholarship will be stipulated at the time of award. These conditions include such requirements as maintaining a certain GPA, being a full-time music major, studying with appropriate faculty member, performing in School of Music ensembles, providing library assistance, accompanying, or other professional services. All special conditions relating to a scholarship are stated in writing prior to the student's accepting the award.
HOW TO APPLY: Contact Music Student Advisor for more information.
RENEWABLE: No
CONTACT: Music Student Advisor, School of Music

367—WESTERN MICHIGAN UNIVERSITY (College of Fine Arts/Mary and R. E. Jackson Scholarship Fund Award)

1903 W. Michigan
Kalamazoo MI 49008-5337
269/387-8777
FAX: 269/387-6989
E-mail: finaid-info@wmich.edu
Internet: http://www.wmich.edu/finaid
AMOUNT: Varies
DEADLINE(S): MAR (for current Theater majors); on acceptance into program for freshmen and transfer students
FIELD(S): Theater Education; Theater Design; Technical Theater; Arts Management; Music Theater Performance
ELIGIBILITY/REQUIREMENTS: Scholarships are ONLY for Theater majors and minors. Must have a 3.0 GPA.
HOW TO APPLY: Freshmen or transfer students—by audition/interview and acceptance into major or minor in Theater program. Current Theater majors—by application form from the department.
RENEWABLE: No
CONTACT: Theater Department

368—WESTERN MICHIGAN UNIVERSITY (College of Fine Arts/Mary Thorne University Theater Guild Scholarship)

1903 W. Michigan
Kalamazoo MI 49008-5337
269/387-8777
FAX: 269/387-6989
E-mail: finaid-info@wmich.edu
Internet: http://www.wmich.edu/finaid
AMOUNT: Varies
DEADLINE(S): MAR (for current Theater majors); on acceptance into program for freshmen and transfer students
FIELD(S): Theater Education; Theater Design; Technical Theater; Arts Management; Music Theater Performance
ELIGIBILITY/REQUIREMENTS: Scholarships are ONLY for Theater majors and minors. Must have a 3.0 GPA.
HOW TO APPLY: Freshmen or transfer students—by audition/interview and acceptance into major or minor in Theater program. Current Theater majors—by application form from the department.
RENEWABLE: No
CONTACT: Theater Department

369—WESTERN MICHIGAN UNIVERSITY (College of Fine Arts/Michael Listiak Scholarships)

School of Music
Kalamazoo MI 49008-3831
269/387-8777
FAX: 269/387-6989
E-mail: finaid-info@wmich.edu
Internet: http://www.wmich.edu/finaid
AMOUNT: $500-$2,000+
DEADLINE(S): MAR
FIELD(S): Education/Music
ELIGIBILITY/REQUIREMENTS: These scholarships are awarded to music majors from southwestern Michigan who plan to pursue a teaching career. Certain conditions for holding a music scholarship will be stipulated at the time of award.

These conditions include such requirements as maintaining a certain GPA, being a full-time music major, studying with appropriate faculty member, performing in School of Music ensembles, providing library assistance, accompanying, or other professional services. All special conditions relating to a scholarship are stated in writing prior to the student's accepting the award.
HOW TO APPLY: Contact Music Student Advisor, School of Music, for more information.
RENEWABLE: Yes. Recipients qualify to hold award until graduation, 4-year maximum, providing musical and academic excellence are maintained.
CONTACT: Music Student Advisor, School of Music

370—WESTERN MICHIGAN UNIVERSITY (College of Fine Arts/Music Theater Performance Scholarship Scholarships)

1903 W. Michigan
Kalamazoo MI 49008-5337
269/387-8777
FAX: 269/387-6989
E-mail: finaid-info@wmich.edu
Internet: http://www.wmich.edu/finaid
AMOUNT: $400/semester
DEADLINE(S): MAR (for current Theater majors); on acceptance into program for freshmen and transfer students
FIELD(S): Theater Education; Theater Design; Technical Theater; Arts Management; Music Theater Performance
ELIGIBILITY/REQUIREMENTS: Scholarships are ONLY for Theater majors and minors. Must have a 3.0 GPA.
HOW TO APPLY: Freshmen or transfer students—by audition/interview and acceptance into major or minor in Theater program. Current Theater majors—by application form from the department.
RENEWABLE: No
CONTACT: Theater Department

371—WESTERN MICHIGAN UNIVERSITY (College of Fine Arts/Rhea Yeager Fetzer Music Scholarship)

School of Music
Kalamazoo MI 49008-3831
269/387-8777
FAX: 269/387-6989
E-mail: finaid-info@wmich.edu
Internet: http://www.wmich.edu/finaid
AMOUNT: $500-$2,000+

DEADLINE(S): MAR
FIELD(S): Music (strings)
ELIGIBILITY/REQUIREMENTS: These scholarships are awarded to music majors from southwestern Michigan who are pursuing study on a string instrument. It shall be open within the strings section for students studying violin, viola, violoncello, and double bass. Certain conditions for holding a music scholarship will be stipulated at the time of award. These conditions include such requirements as maintaining a certain GPA, being a full-time music major, studying with appropriate faculty member, performing in School of Music ensembles, providing library assistance, accompanying, or other professional services. All special conditions relating to a scholarship are stated in writing prior to the student's accepting the award.
HOW TO APPLY: Undergraduate students may receive consideration for a scholarship award at the same time they audition for admission to the music curriculum; no separate application form is required.
RENEWABLE: Yes. Recipients qualify to hold award until graduation, 4-year maximum, providing musical and academic excellence are maintained.
CONTACT: Music Student Advisor, School of Music

372—WESTERN MICHIGAN UNIVERSITY (College of Fine Arts/Russell Brown Honors Brass Quintet Scholarships)

School of Music
Kalamazoo MI 49008-3831
269/387-8777
FAX: 269/387-6989
E-mail: finaid-info@wmich.edu
Internet: http://www.wmich.edu/finaid
AMOUNT: $500-$2,000+
DEADLINE(S): MAR
FIELD(S): Music (trumpet, tuba, trombone, horn)
ELIGIBILITY/REQUIREMENTS: Awards are available to trumpet, tuba, trombone, and horn students who perform in an Honors Brass Quintet. Certain conditions for holding a music scholarship will be stipulated at the time of award. These conditions include such requirements as maintaining a certain GPA, being a full-time music major, studying with appropriate faculty member, performing in School of Music ensembles, providing library assistance, accompanying, or other professional services. All special conditions relating to a scholarship are stated in writing prior to the student's accepting the award.

HOW TO APPLY: Undergraduate students may receive consideration for a scholarship award at the same time they audition for admission to the music curriculum; no separate application form is required.
RENEWABLE: Yes. Recipients qualify to hold award until graduation, 4-year maximum, providing musical and academic excellence are maintained.
CONTACT: Music Student Advisor, School of Music

373—WESTERN MICHIGAN UNIVERSITY (College of Fine Arts/Sam B. Adams Memorial Vocal Endowed Scholarship)

School of Music
Kalamazoo MI 49008-3831
269/387-8777
FAX: 269/387-6989
E-mail: finaid-info@wmich.edu
Internet: http://www.wmich.edu/finaid
AMOUNT: $500-$2,000+
DEADLINE(S): MAR
FIELD(S): Music (voice)
ELIGIBILITY/REQUIREMENTS: The scholarship is awarded to an outstanding vocal music major. A minimum GPA of 3.0 is necessary. Certain conditions for holding a music scholarship will be stipulated at the time of award. These conditions include such requirements as maintaining a certain GPA, being a full-time music major, studying with appropriate faculty member, performing in School of Music ensembles, providing library assistance, accompanying, or other professional services. All special conditions relating to a scholarship are stated in writing prior to the student's accepting the award.
HOW TO APPLY: Undergraduate students may receive consideration for a scholarship award at the same time they audition for admission to the music curriculum; no separate application form is required. Selected by the vocal music faculty.
RENEWABLE: Yes. Recipients qualify to hold award until graduation, 4-year maximum, providing musical and academic excellence are maintained.
CONTACT: Music Student Advisor, School of Music

374—WESTERN MICHIGAN UNIVERSITY (College of Education/Stuart and Norma Hall Scholarship)

1903 W. Michigan
Kalamazoo MI 49008-5337
269/387-6000
FAX: 269/387-6989
E-mail: finaid-info@wmich.edu
Internet: http://www.wmich.edu/finaid
AMOUNT: Varies
DEADLINE(S): MAR 1
FIELD(S): Music Education
ELIGIBILITY/REQUIREMENTS: Must be a full-time undergraduate in the College of Education majoring in music education; minimum of a 2.5 GPA. Preference given to students who demonstrate financial need.
HOW TO APPLY: See website or contact College of Education for application.
RENEWABLE: Yes. Up to 3 years.
CONTACT: College of Education

375—WESTERN MICHIGAN UNIVERSITY (College of Fine Arts/The Carol and Donald Coggan Music Education Scholarship)

School of Music
Kalamazoo MI 49008-3831
269/387-8777
FAX: 269/387-6989
E-mail: finaid-info@wmich.edu
Internet: http://www.wmich.edu/finaid
AMOUNT: Varies
DEADLINE(S): MAR
FIELD(S): Music Education
ELIGIBILITY/REQUIREMENTS: Must be full-time undergraduate in music education. Certain conditions for holding a music scholarship will be stipulated at the time of award. These conditions include such requirements as maintaining a certain GPA, being a full-time music major, studying with appropriate faculty member, performing in School of Music ensembles, providing library assistance, accompanying, or other professional services. All special conditions relating to a scholarship are stated in writing prior to the student's accepting the award. Maintain satisfactory academic progress as specified by the Office of Student Financial Aid.
HOW TO APPLY: The selection of the scholarship recipient shall be based upon talent as determined through the audition/interview process conducted by appropriate personnel of the School of Music.
RENEWABLE: Yes. Up to 3 consecutive years.
CONTACT: Music Student Advisor, School of Music

376—WESTERN MICHIGAN UNIVERSITY (College of Fine Arts/The Marcella S. and Philip F. Faustman Music Theater Scholarship)

1903 W. Michigan
Kalamazoo MI 49008-5337
269/387-8777

FAX: 269/387-6989
E-mail: finaid-info@wmich.edu
Internet: http://www.wmich.edu/finaid
AMOUNT: Varies
FIELD(S): Theater Education; Theater Design; Technical Theater; Arts Management; Music Theater Performance
ELIGIBILITY/REQUIREMENTS: Recipient must be a full-time junior or senior in the area of music theater in the Department of Theater. Must have a minimum 3.0 GPA.
HOW TO APPLY: By application form from the Department and by audition and interview.
RENEWABLE: No
CONTACT: Theater Department

377—WESTERN MICHIGAN UNIVERSITY (College of Fine Arts/Theodore Presser Foundation Scholarship)

School of Music
Kalamazoo MI 49008-3831
269/387-8777
FAX: 269/387-6989
E-mail: finaid-info@wmich.edu
Internet: http://www.wmich.edu/finaid
AMOUNT: $500-$2,000+
DEADLINE(S): MAR
FIELD(S): Music
ELIGIBILITY/REQUIREMENTS: This award is presented to a senior who is majoring in music. In addition to showing outstanding promise, the recipient must carry an overall grade-point-average of 3.5. Certain conditions for holding a music scholarship will be stipulated at the time of award. These conditions include such requirements as maintaining a certain GPA, being a full-time music major, studying with appropriate faculty member, performing in School of Music ensembles, providing library assistance, accompanying, or other professional services. All special conditions relating to a scholarship are stated in writing prior to the student's accepting the award.
HOW TO APPLY: The recipient is selected from a list of students who are nominated by the School of Music faculty members.
RENEWABLE: No
CONTACT: Music Student Advisor, School of Music

378—WESTERN MICHIGAN UNIVERSITY (College of Fine Arts/The Tucky M. and Charles W. Elliot Endowed Clarinet Scholarship)

School of Music
Kalamazoo MI 49008-3831

269/387-8777
FAX: 269/387-6989
E-mail: finaid-info@wmich.edu
Internet: http://www.wmich.edu/finaid
AMOUNT: Varies
DEADLINE(S): MAR
FIELD(S): Music (clarinet)
ELIGIBILITY/REQUIREMENTS: Must be a full-time music major pursuing studies on the clarinet. Must have a minimum 3.0 GPA. Certain conditions for holding a music scholarship will be stipulated at the time of award. These conditions include such requirements as maintaining a certain GPA, being a full-time music major, studying with appropriate faculty member, performing in School of Music ensembles, providing library assistance, accompanying, or other professional services. All special conditions relating to a scholarship are stated in writing prior to the student's accepting the award.
HOW TO APPLY: Based upon talent as determined through audition process conducted by the appropriate personnel of the School of Music.
RENEWABLE: Yes. Recipients qualify to hold award for 3 consecutive years.
CONTACT: Music Student Advisor, School of Music

379—WESTERN MICHIGAN UNIVERSITY (College of Fine Arts/University Theater Guild Scholarship)

1903 W. Michigan
Kalamazoo MI 49008-5337
269/387-8777
FAX: 269/387-6989
E-mail: finaid-info@wmich.edu
Internet: http://www.wmich.edu/finaid
AMOUNT: Varies
DEADLINE(S): MAR (for current Theater majors); on acceptance into program for freshmen and transfer students
FIELD(S): Theater Education; Theater Design; Technical Theater; Arts Management; Music Theater Performance
ELIGIBILITY/REQUIREMENTS: Scholarships are ONLY for Theater majors and minors. Must have a 3.0 GPA.
HOW TO APPLY: Freshmen or transfer students—by audition/interview and acceptance into major or minor in Theater program. Current Theater majors—by application form from the department.
RENEWABLE: No
CONTACT: Theater Department

380—WESTERN MICHIGAN UNIVERSITY (Lynne C. McCauley Memorial Scholarship)

1903 West Michigan
Kalamazoo MI 49008-5337
269/387-8777
FAX: 269/387-6989
E-mail: alumni@wmich.edu
Internet: http://www.wmich.edu/
ENDOWED
AMOUNT: Varies
DEADLINE(S): APR 1
FIELD(S): English, Music, Theater
ELIGIBILITY/REQUIREMENTS: Full-time students majoring in the Humanities, such as English, Music or Theater at WMU. Must have a minimum GPA of 3.0 to apply. Preference given to women.
HOW TO APPLY: See website for application and submit with FAFSA.
NUMBER OF AWARDS: Varies
RENEWABLE: No
CONTACT: Office of Student Financial Aid

381—WITTENBERG UNIVERSITY (Music Scholarship Funds)

Krieg Hall
P.O. Box 720
Springfield OH 45501-0720
937/327-7341 or 800/677-7347
FAX: 937/327-7558
E-mail: Music@wittenberg.edu
Internet: http://www.wittenberg.edu/academics/music/scholaid.shtml
AMOUNT: $600-$5,000
DEADLINE(S): MAR 15
FIELD(S): All, Music
ELIGIBILITY/REQUIREMENTS: Scholarships are available not only to music majors and minors but also for students who continue to study and participate in music ensembles while pursuing non-music degrees. Interested students must complete application to the University and be accepted and participate in an audition by mid-March.
HOW TO APPLY: See website for more information or write to Music Department Assistant, Melanie Gillaugh (see below). Request a Music Audition Packet for instructions.
NUMBER OF AWARDS: Varies
RENEWABLE: Yes. Must maintain a B average in music lessons and continue to participate in an approved music ensemble.
CONTACT: Melanie Gillaugh, Department Assistant, mgillaugh@wittenberg.edu or 937/327-7341
ADDITIONAL INFORMATION: All music scholarships are talent-based.

382—YVAR MIKHASHOFF TRUST FOR NEW MUSIC

P.O. Box 8
Forestville NY 14062
716/965-2128
FAX: 716/965-9726
E-mail: info@mikhashofftrust.org
Internet: http://www.mikhashofftrust.org
AMOUNT: Varies, typically $1,000 to $3,000
DEADLINE(S): Postmarked between OCT 15 and NOV 15
FIELD(S): New Music
ELIGIBILITY/REQUIREMENTS: Applicants must demonstrate interest and expertise in new music (performance or composition), i.e., 20th/21st-century classical music.
HOW TO APPLY: See website for required documents.
NUMBER OF AWARDS: Open
RENEWABLE: No
CONTACT: Mr. Jan Williams

PHOTOGRAPHY

383—AMERICAN MOTHERS, INC. (Gertrude Fogelson Cultural and Creative Arts Awards)

1296 E. 21st Street
Brooklyn NY 11201
718/253-5676
AMOUNT: Up to $1,000
DEADLINE(S): JAN 1
FIELD(S): Visual Arts; Creative Writing; Vocal Music
ELIGIBILITY/REQUIREMENTS: An award to encourage and honor mothers in artistic pursuits.
HOW TO APPLY: Write for details.

384—ASPRS: THE IMAGING & GEOSPATIAL INFORMATION SOCIETY (Kenneth J. Osborn Memorial Scholarship)

ASPRS Awards Program
5410 Grosvenor Lane, Suite 210
Bethesda MD 20814-2160
301/493-0290, ext. 101
FAX: 301/493-0208
E-mail: scholarships@asprs.org
Internet: http://www.asprs.org
AMOUNT: $1,000
DEADLINE(S): DEC 1
FIELD(S): Surveying, Mapping, Photogrammetry, Geospatial Information and Technology
ELIGIBILITY/REQUIREMENTS: Open to undergraduates who display exceptional interest, desire, ability, and aptitude to enter the profession of surveying, mapping, photogrammetry, or geospatial information and technology. In addition, the Scholarship recognizes students who excel at communications and collaboration.
HOW TO APPLY: Submit 6 copies of the completed application and the following supporting materials: academic transcripts, including a separate list of relevant courses taken; 2 completed reference forms from faculty members who have knowledge of your abilities; samples of your work; description of your research goals; statement of work experience that may include internships, other forms of work experience, or special projects that demonstrate excellence in these fields and in communications and collaboration (including the nature, location and date(s) of the experience); a 2-page statement regarding your plans for continuing studies in theoretical photogrammetry; and papers, research reports, or other items that indicate capability in these fields. Note: Electronic submissions encouraged.
NUMBER OF AWARDS: 1
RENEWABLE: No
CONTACT: Scholarship Administrator at above address or see website.
ADDITIONAL INFORMATION: The recipient is obligated to provide a final report to ASPRS of his/her scholastic accomplishments during the period for which the award is granted.

385—ASPRS: THE IMAGING & GEOSPATIAL INFORMATION SOCIETY (Robert E. Altenhofen Memorial Scholarship)

ASPRS Awards Program
5410 Grosvenor Lane, Suite 210
Bethesda MD 20814-2160
301/493-0290, ext. 101
FAX: 301/493-0208
E-mail: scholarships@asprs.org
Internet: http://www.asprs.org
AMOUNT: $2,000
DEADLINE(S): DEC 1
FIELD(S): Photogrammetry
ELIGIBILITY/REQUIREMENTS: Undergraduates or graduates who display exceptional interest and ability in the theoretical aspects of photogrammetry; must be enrolled in an accredited college or university and be active or student members of ASPRS.
HOW TO APPLY: Submit 6 copies of the completed application and the following supporting materials: academic transcripts, including a separate list of relevant courses taken; 2 completed reference forms from faculty members who have knowledge of your abilities; samples of your work; description of your research goals; a 2-page statement regarding your plans for continuing studies in theoretical photogrammetry; and papers, research reports, or other items that indicate capability in these fields. Note: Electronic submissions encouraged.
NUMBER OF AWARDS: 1
RENEWABLE: No
CONTACT: Scholarship Administrator at above address or see website.
ADDITIONAL INFORMATION: The recipient is obligated to provide a final report to ASPRS of his/her scholastic accomplishments during the period for which the award is granted.

386—ASPRS: THE IMAGING & GEOSPATIAL INFORMATION SOCIETY (Student Travel Grants)

ASPRS Awards Program
5410 Grosvenor Lane, Suite 210
Bethesda MD 20814-2160
301/493-0290, ext. 101
FAX: 301/493-0208
E-mail: scholarships@asprs.org
Internet: http://www.asprs.org
AMOUNT: $500
DEADLINE(S): DEC 1
FIELD(S): Photogrammetry
ELIGIBILITY/REQUIREMENTS: ASPRS selects qualified students to attend the ASPRS Annual Conference with financial support from the ASPRS Foundation.
HOW TO APPLY: Submit written statement of no more than 1 page outlining the importance of attending this conference in relation to the applicant's course of study and career development plans. Supplemental materials are also permitted (transcripts, publications, etc.) and at least one letter of recommendation from a faculty advisor. Note: Electronic submissions encouraged.
NUMBER OF AWARDS: 2
RENEWABLE: No
CONTACT: Scholarship Administrator at above address or see website.
ADDITIONAL INFORMATION: The grants also include a 1-year student membership in ASPRS and a complimentary conference registration for the selected student(s) provided they volunteer to help at the conference.

387—JACKSONVILLE STATE UNIVERSITY (Ed Hill Memorial Leadership)

Financial Aid Office
Jacksonville AL 36265
256/782-5677 or
800/231-5291

Internet: www.jsu.edu
AMOUNT: Full tuition
DEADLINE(S): FEB 1
FIELD(S): Communications; Art
ELIGIBILITY/REQUIREMENTS: Open to students majoring in communications or art with an interest in photography as a profession.
HOW TO APPLY: An official high school transcript and ACT/SAT scores must be submitted with scholarship applications. See website for application. Supporting documentation should be mailed.
RENEWABLE: Yes
CONTACT: Scholarship Committee

388—LANDMARK COMMUNICATIONS, INC.

150 W Branbleton Ave
Norfolk VA 23510
757/446-2913
FAX: 757/222-5850
E-mail: jlamkin@lcimedia.com
Internet: http://www.landmark communications.com
AMOUNT: $10,000 and newsroom internship
DEADLINE(S): NOV 30
FIELD(S): Reporters; Photographers; Graphic Artists; Sports Writers; Copy Editors; Page Designers
ELIGIBILITY/REQUIREMENTS: Be a U.S. citizen or registered permanent resident. Have a goal of becoming a print journalism professional. Have ties to the Mid-Atlantic/Southern region. Be a member of a minority group—Asian, Hispanic, African American, Native American. Be a college sophomore enrolled full time (at least 12 credit hours per semester) in a 4-year degree program. Provide copy of college transcript showing a GPA of 2.5 or better. Have a personal vehicle for necessary on-the-job transportation during the workday. Compete on the basis of grades, work samples, financial needs, recommendations and targeted selection interview skills. Be able to pass a pre-employment drug screening. Your internship will be during the summer between your sophomore and junior years and again between your junior and senior years. At the end of each summer, you'll be awarded a $5,000 scholarship. And when you graduate, you're eligible for a 1-year internship with full benefits and the possibility of continuing employment.
HOW TO APPLY: Download application from website and submit with 500-word autobiography; résumé (include expected graduation date); college transcript; and 3 letters of recommendation from professional colleagues or professors. Provide

work samples, a minimum of 3 college or professional newspaper/magazine or other work samples (include 3 copies of your sample, Xeroxes or disks as well as e-mail attachments if applying online).
NUMBER OF AWARDS: Up to 3
RENEWABLE: Yes. 2 years—maintain a 2.5 GPA throughout college; adhere to standards and ethics of professional journalism; uphold a positive public image as a Landmark Scholar; be punctual and have good attendance; comply with Landmark's general employment policies during internship; and participate in available training, workshops and seminars.
CONTACT: Jean Lamkin

389—LIGHT WORK (Artist-in-Residence Program)

316 Waverly Avenue
Syracuse NY 13244
315/443-1300
FAX: 315/443-9516
E-mail: cdlight@syr.edu
Internet: http://www.lightwork.org/
AMOUNT: $2,000 stipend
DEADLINE(S): None
FIELD(S): Photography; Computer Graphics
ELIGIBILITY/REQUIREMENTS: Career support for artists from around the world working with photography or digital imaging. Residency is for one month, and financial need is NOT considered.
HOW TO APPLY: There is no application form. Send a letter of intent, current résumé, 15-20 slides, artist's statement, and return postage for work.
NUMBER OF AWARDS: 12-15 awards annually
RENEWABLE: No

390—MEMPHIS COLLEGE OF ART (Portfolio Awards)

Overton Park
1930 Poplar Avenue
Memphis TN 38104-2764
800/727-1088
E-mail: admissions@mca.edu
Internet: http://www.mca.edu/index.cfm
AMOUNT: Half tuition
DEADLINE(S): Varies (NOV 15 through JUL 31)
FIELD(S): Visual Arts
ELIGIBILITY/REQUIREMENTS: Awards are given to excellent visual art portfolios submitted by either high school students or transfer students and are to be used for full-time enrollment at Memphis College of Art. International students are

welcome to apply. Financial need is not a consideration.
HOW TO APPLY: Contact MCA for application and submission details or see website.
NUMBER OF AWARDS: 2

391—NATIONAL ASSOCIATION OF HISPANIC JOURNALISTS

1000 National Press Building
Washington DC 20045-2001
202/662-7145
E-mail: nahj@nahj.org
Internet: http://www.nahj.org
AMOUNT: $1,000-$2,000
DEADLINE(S): JAN 31
FIELD(S): Journalism
ELIGIBILITY/REQUIREMENTS: Applicants must be Hispanic students (graduating high school seniors or undergraduate or graduate students) pursuing a degree in broadcast, print, or photojournalism.
CONTACT: Nancy Tita

392—NATIONAL ASSOCIATION OF HISPANIC JOURNALISTS (Cristina Saralegui Scholarship Program)

1000 National Press Building
Washington DC 20045-2001
202/662-7145
E-mail: nahj@nahj.org
Internet: http://www.nahj.org
AMOUNT: $5,000
FIELD(S): Journalism
ELIGIBILITY/REQUIREMENTS: Applicants must be current college students fluent in Spanish, planning to pursue a career in broadcast journalism.
CONTACT: Nancy Tita

393—NATIONAL ASSOCIATION OF HISPANIC JOURNALISTS (NAHJ Newhouse Scholarship Program)

1000 National Press Building
529 14th Street NW
Washington DC 20045-2001
202/662-7145
FAX: 202/662-7144
E-mail: kolivas@nahj.org
Internet: http://www.nahj.org
AMOUNT: $5,000/year (2-year scholarship)
DEADLINE(S): FEB 25
FIELD(S): Journalism; Photojournalism
ELIGIBILITY/REQUIREMENTS: Applicants MUST be sophomores who are committed to pursuing a career in English-language (NOT Spanish-language) news-

paper journalism as reporters, editors, photographers, or graphic artists. Award will be for junior and senior years. Recipient is required to intern at a Newhouse newspaper following their junior year.

HOW TO APPLY: See website for an application. Do NOT write or call for application.

RENEWABLE: No

394—NATIONAL ASSOCIATION OF HISPANIC JOURNALISTS (NAHJ Newsroom Bound Program)

1000 National Press Building
529 14th Street NW
Washington DC 20045-2001
202/662-7145
FAX: 202/662-7144
E-mail: kolivas@nahj.org
Internet: http://www.nahj.org
AMOUNT: $1,000
DEADLINE(S): JAN (last Friday)
FIELD(S): Journalism; Photojournalism
ELIGIBILITY/REQUIREMENTS: For college freshmen and sophomores who are pursuing careers in English-language print, photo, broadcast, or online journalism; NAHJ will select students from among its scholarship recipients.
HOW TO APPLY: See website for an application. Do NOT write or call for application.
RENEWABLE: No

395—NATIONAL ASSOCIATION OF HISPANIC JOURNALISTS (NAHJ Rubén Salazar Scholarships)

1000 National Press Building
529 14th Street NW
Washington DC 20045-2001
202/662-7145
FAX: 202/662-7144
E-mail: kolivas@nahj.org
Internet: http://www.nahj.org
AMOUNT: $1,000-$2,000
DEADLINE(S): JAN (last Friday)
FIELD(S): Print/Broadcast Journalism; Photojournalism
ELIGIBILITY/REQUIREMENTS: Open to high school seniors, undergraduates, and first-year graduate students who are committed to a career in print or broadcast journalism or photojournalism. Tenable at 2- or 4-year schools in the U.S. and its territories. Hispanic ancestry NOT required.
HOW TO APPLY: See website for an application. Do NOT write or call for application.
RENEWABLE: No. This is a 1-year scholarship.

396—NATIONAL PTA (Reflections Program)

541 N. Fairbanks Ct., Suite 1300
Chicago IL 60611
800/307-4PTA or 312/670-6782
FAX: 312/670-6783
E-mail: info@pta.org
Internet: http://www.pta.org
AMOUNT: Varies
DEADLINE(S): Varies
FIELD(S): Literature; Musical Composition; Photography; Visual Arts; Dance/Choreography
ELIGIBILITY/REQUIREMENTS: Open to students in preschool through grade twelve to express themselves and to receive positive recognition for their artistic efforts. Young artists can get involved in the Reflections Program of their local PTA or PTSA.
HOW TO APPLY: Contact your state PTA office for information about the Reflections Program in your area.

397—NATIVE AMERICAN JOURNALISTS ASSOCIATION (NAJA Scholarships and Internships)

University of South Dakota
414 E. Clark Street
Vermillion SD 57069
605/677-5282
FAX: 605/694-4264
E-mail: info@naja.com
Internet: http://www.naja.com
AMOUNT: $1,000-$3,000
DEADLINE(S): APR 15
FIELD(S): Journalism (Print, Broadcast, Photojournalism, New Media, Journalism Education)
ELIGIBILITY/REQUIREMENTS: Must be Native American pursuing journalism degree at institution of higher learning and a current member of NAJA.
HOW TO APPLY: Cover letter stating financial need, area of interest (see above), and reasons for pursuing a career in journalism. Include 3 letters of recommendation from academic advisor, counselor, or a professional individual familiar with applicant's background and skills; 2 copies of transcript, work samples (if available), proof of enrollment in a federal or state-recognized tribe (if not enrolled, briefly explain). Application fee $20.

398—OUTDOOR WRITERS ASSOCIATION OF AMERICA (OWAA Scholarship Awards)

121 Hickory Street
Missoula MT 59801
406/728-7434
FAX: 406/728-7445
E-mail: owaaa@montana.com
Internet: http://www.owaa.org
AMOUNT: $2,500-$3,500
DEADLINE(S): MAR 1
FIELD(S): Communications; Journalism; Film; Broadcasting; Photography
ELIGIBILITY/REQUIREMENTS: Open to junior and senior undergraduates and graduate students. Must attend an accredited school of journalism or mass communications that has registered with OWAA as a scholarship program participant. Selection based on career goals in outdoor communications, examples of work, letters of recommendation, and academic achievement. Must be U.S. or Canadian citizen or permanent resident.
HOW TO APPLY: See website for application or contact your school or send a SASE to Executive Director for guidelines.
NUMBER OF AWARDS: At least 3
CONTACT: Steve Wagner, Executive Director

399—NOVA SCOTIA COLLEGE OF ART AND DESIGN (Scholarships)

5163 Duke Street
Halifax Nova Scotia B3J 3J6
CANADA
902/494-8129
FAX: 902/425-2987
E-mail: bkehoe@nscad.ca
Internet: http://www.nscad.ca
AMOUNT: $500-$13,500 (Canadian)
DEADLINE(S): Varies
FIELD(S): Art; Fine Arts
ELIGIBILITY/REQUIREMENTS: The Nova Scotia College of Art and Design administers a number of scholarships and bursary awards that acknowledge high achievement and special promise. Awards restricted to students accepted to or officially registered at the university.
HOW TO APPLY: Write for details on specific scholarships.
CONTACT: Bernadette Kehoe, Student Services

400—SCHOLASTIC ART & WRITING AWARDS, THE (Alliance for Young Artists and Writers, Inc.)

557 Broadway
New York NY 10012
212/343-6493
E-mail: A&Wgeneralinfo@scholastic.com
Internet: http://www.artandwriting.org
AMOUNT: Varies; Up to $10,000
DEADLINE(S): Varies (upon location)

FIELD(S): Art; Writing; Photography
ELIGIBILITY/REQUIREMENTS: For students in grades 7-12 enrolled in schools in the U.S., Canada, U.S. territories, or U.S.-sponsored schools abroad. 10 writing and 16 art categories. Publishing opportunities may be available for winners in both art and writing categories. Scholarship consideration for seniors submitting portfolios of art, photography or writing.
HOW TO APPLY: See website or write.
NUMBER OF AWARDS: 1,000+ awards annually, including 11 $10,000 scholarships.

401—VIRGINIA MUSEUM OF FINE ARTS (Fellowships)

2800 Grove Avenue
Richmond VA 23221-2466
804/204-2661
Internet: http://vmfa.state.va.us
AMOUNT: $4,000 (undergraduate-maximum); $6,000 (graduates); $8,000 (professionals)
DEADLINE(S): MAR 1
FIELD(S): Crafts; Drawing; Filmmaking; Painting; Photography; Printmaking; Sculpture; Video; Art History (graduate only)
ELIGIBILITY/REQUIREMENTS: Open to Virginia residents of at least one year who are U.S. citizens or legal residents. Fellowships are available to undergraduates, graduates, and professional artists. Financial need is considered.
HOW TO APPLY: Application and guidelines on website.

402—WESTERN MICHIGAN UNIVERSITY (College of Fine Arts/James W. Kerr and Rose Netzorg Kerr Awards)

1903 W. Michigan
Kalamazoo MI 49008-5337
269/387-6000
FAX: 269/387-6989
Internet: http://www.wmich.edu/finaid
AMOUNT: $200/spring semester
DEADLINE(S): FEB (first Friday)
FIELD(S): Photography or related medium
ELIGIBILITY/REQUIREMENTS: Art major (graduate or undergraduate), enrolled full time; slide portfolio review.
HOW TO APPLY: Student is nominated by faculty. Contact the Art Advising office for an application.
NUMBER OF AWARDS: 1-2
RENEWABLE: No
CONTACT: Art Department

403—WESTERN MICHIGAN UNIVERSITY (College of Fine Arts/Robert Girard Memorial Award)

1903 W. Michigan
Kalamazoo MI 49008-5337
269/387-6000
FAX: 269/387-6989
Internet: http://www.wmich.edu/finaid
AMOUNT: $200/spring semester
FIELD(S): Photography or related medium
ELIGIBILITY/REQUIREMENTS: Art major selected from annual student exhibit.
HOW TO APPLY: Student is nominated by faculty. Contact the Art Advising office for an application.
NUMBER OF AWARDS: Multiple awards, number varies
RENEWABLE: No
CONTACT: Art Department

404—W. EUGENE SMITH MEMORIAL FUND, INC. (Howard Chapnick Grant for the Advancement of Photojournalism)

c/o International Center for Creative Photography
1133 Avenue of the Americas
New York NY 10036
212/857-0038
Internet: http://www.smithfund.org/fund.html
AMOUNT: $5,000
DEADLINE(S): JUL 15
FIELD(S): Photojournalism
ELIGIBILITY/REQUIREMENTS: May be used to finance a range of qualified undertakings such as further education, research, a special long-term sabbatical project, or an internship to work with a noteworthy group or individual. Special consideration will be given to projects that promote social change and/or serve significant concerns of photojournalism.
HOW TO APPLY: See website or write for application.
NUMBER OF AWARDS: 1
RENEWABLE: No
CONTACT: Anna Winand

405—W. EUGENE SMITH MEMORIAL FUND, INC. (W. Eugene Smith Grant in Humanistic Photography)

c/o International Center for Creative Photography
1133 Avenue of the Americas
New York NY 10036
212/857-0038
Internet: http://www.smithfund.org/fund.html
AMOUNT: $20,000
DEADLINE(S): JUL 15
FIELD(S): Photojournalism
ELIGIBILITY/REQUIREMENTS: Career support for photojournalists of any nationality.
HOW TO APPLY: Must submit a photographic project with a written proposal, illustrated in the humanistic manner of W. Eugene Smith. Financial need NOT a factor. Write or phone for application.
NUMBER OF AWARDS: 2
RENEWABLE: No
CONTACT: Anna Winand

406—WOMEN'S STUDIO WORKSHOP (Fellowship Grants)

P.O. Box 489
Rosendale NY 12472
845/658-9133
FAX: 845/658-9031
E-mail: info@wsworkshop.org
Internet: http://www.wsworkshop.org/
AMOUNT: Tuition
DEADLINE(S): MAR 15; NOV 1
FIELD(S): Visual Arts
ELIGIBILITY/REQUIREMENTS: Designed to provide concentrated work time for artists to explore new ideas in a dynamic and supportive community of women artists. WSW welcomes applications from emerging artists.
HOW TO APPLY: Application form plus a résumé, 6-10 slides, a letter of interest that addresses the purpose of the residency, explaining areas of proficiency and studio skills, and a SASE for return of materials. Applications available on website.

407—WOMEN'S STUDIO WORKSHOP (Internship)

P.O. Box 489
Rosendale NY 12472
845/658-9133
FAX: 845/658-9031
E-mail: info@wsworkshop.org
Internet: http://www.wsworkshop.org/
AMOUNT: $150/month + housing
DEADLINE(S): APR 1 and OCT 15
FIELD(S): Visual Arts including Printmaking, Papermaking, Book Arts, Photography, Ceramics
ELIGIBILITY/REQUIREMENTS: Must have experience in one or more of fields.
HOW TO APPLY: Send a letter of interest, résumé, up to 20 slides with slide list, 3 reference letters, and a SASE.

NUMBER OF AWARDS: 6
RENEWABLE: No
CONTACT: Ellen Kucera

408—WORLDSTUDIO FOUNDATION

200 Varick Street, Suite 507
New York NY 10014
212/366-1317
FAX: 212/807-0024
E-mail: info@worldstudio.org
Internet: http://www.worldstudio.
org or http://www.www.aiga.org
AMOUNT: $1,500-$5,000
DEADLINE(S): APR 14
FIELD(S): Advertising, Animation,
Architecture, Cartooning, Crafts,
Environmental graphics, Film/video,
Film/theater design, Fine arts,
Furniture design, Industrial/product
design, Interior architecture and
design, Landscape architecture, New
media, Photography, Surface/textile
design, Urban planning
ELIGIBILITY/REQUIREMENTS:
Applicants must be pursuing a degree in
the fine or commercial arts, design or
architecture, and plan to enter a career in
the creative professions. Undergraduates
and graduates are eligible. Minority status
and/or social agenda are significant factors.
Financial need a prerequisite. Minimum
2.0 GPA.
HOW TO APPLY: See websites for application. The application is a 2-part process.
Applications must include personal and
school information, including transcripts
and copies of letters of acceptance; financial information; portfolio; written statement of purpose; examples of a commitment to a social agenda, 2 letters of recommendation from college instructors, high
school teachers, or employers; head shot of
applicant.
NUMBER OF AWARDS: 20-30
RENEWABLE: Yes. Must reapply.
CONTACT: Mark Randall

BUSINESS
(ALL FIELDS)

409—AMERICAN HEALTH AND BEAUTY AIDS INSTITUTE (Fred Luster, Sr. Education Foundation Scholarships for College-Bound High School Seniors)

P.O. Box 19510
Chicago IL 60619
708/333-8740
FAX: 708/333-8741

Internet: http://www.proudlady.org
AMOUNT: $250-$500
DEADLINE(S): APR 15
FIELD(S): Chemistry; Business;
Engineering
ELIGIBILITY/REQUIREMENTS: Open
to college-bound high school seniors who
will be enrolled as a college freshman in a
4-year college majoring in chemistry, busi-
ness, or engineering. 3.0 GPA required.
Scholastic record, school activities, and
extracurricular activities considered.
HOW TO APPLY: Send two letters of rec-
ommendation (one from a school official)
and high school transcript.
NUMBER OF AWARDS: 2

410—AMERICAN INDIAN SCIENCE AND ENGINEERING SOCIETY (Burlington Northern Santa Fe Pacific Foundation Scholarships)

P.O. Box 9828
Albuquerque NM 87119-9828
505/765-1052
FAX: 505/765-5608
E-mail: scholarships@aises.org
Internet: http://www.aises.org/
scholar/scholarships
AMOUNT: $2,500
DEADLINE(S): APR 15
FIELD(S): Business; Education; Science;
Engineering; Health Administration
ELIGIBILITY/REQUIREMENTS: Open
to high school seniors who are at least one
quarter American Indian. Must reside in
Kansas, Oklahoma, Colorado, Arizona,
New Mexico, Minnesota, North Dakota,
Oregon, South Dakota, Washington,
Montana, or San Bernardino County,
California (Burlington Northern and Santa
Fe Pacific service areas). Must demon-
strate financial need; minimum GPA 2.0.
HOW TO APPLY: See website or contact
Society for an application.
NUMBER OF AWARDS: 5
RENEWABLE: Yes. Up to 4 years.
CONTACT: Patricia Browne

411—AMERICAN RADIO RELAY LEAGUE FOUNDATION (William R. Goldfarb Memorial Scholarship)

225 Main Street
Newington CT 06111
860/594-0397
860/594-0200
FAX: 860/594-0259
E-mail: foundation@arrl.org
Internet: http://www.arrl.org/
AMOUNT: $10,000 or more
DEADLINE(S): FEB 1

FIELD(S): Business, Computer Science,
Medicine (including Nursing),
Engineering, Sciences
ELIGIBILITY/REQUIREMENTS: For
student with any class of license pursuing
baccalaureate or higher degree at a regionally accredited institution. Must demonstrate financial need.
HOW TO APPLY: See website or contact
Foundation for information and application. Submit with FAFSA and a 1-page
essay on the role amateur radio has played
in your life. A recent high school (or equivalent) or college transcript required; submit with application or mail separately.
NUMBER OF AWARDS: 1
CONTACT: Mary M. Hobart, K1MMH,
Secretary

412—ASSOCIATION OF SCHOOL BUSINESS OFFICIALS OF MARYLAND AND THE DISTRICT OF COLUMBIA (Dwight P. Jacobus Scholarships)

ASBO-MD & DC
Scholarship Committee
200 E. North Avenue
Baltimore MD 21202
Internet: http://www.asbo.org
AMOUNT: $1,000
DEADLINE(S): MAR 1
FIELD(S): Business; Education
ELIGIBILITY/REQUIREMENTS:
Applicants must be residents of Maryland
or the District of Columbia for at least one
year preceding the date of application; be
pursuing a career in business or education
at an accredited institution of higher education within Maryland or the District of
Columbia; be accepted for admission as a
full-time student; demonstrate financial
need; and have a minimum overall GPA of
3.0. Awards are based on scholastic
achievement, financial need, SAT or ACT
scores, and the quality of extracurricular
activities.
HOW TO APPLY: Submit completed
application; copy of most current high
school or college transcript; copies of parents' and applicant's current income tax
returns; copy of acceptance letter from an
accredited institution of higher education
in Maryland or the District of Columbia; a
500-word typed essay, written by the applicant explaining why he/she is uniquely
qualified to receive this scholarship and
including academic achievements and
activities, community and civic activities,
and personal aims and goals; and a copy of
SAT or ACT test results.
NUMBER OF AWARDS: 6
RENEWABLE: Yes. For up to 4 years:
recipients must reapply annually; continue

to be accepted for admission to the undergraduate program in education; be enrolled full time; and submit proof of continued academic good standing (i.e., a minimum 3.0 GPA).
CONTACT: Kathy Jackson, Chair

413—CELANESE CANADA, INC. (AUCC)

350 Albert Street, Suite 600
Ottawa Ontario K1R 1B1
CANADA
613/563-1236
FAX: 613/563-9745
E-mail: awards@aucc.ca
Internet: http://www.aucc.ca
AMOUNT: $1,500
DEADLINE(S): JUL 2
FIELD(S): Mechanical and Chemical Engineering; Chemistry; Business Administration and Commerce
ELIGIBILITY/REQUIREMENTS: Open to Canadian citizens/permanent residents for their final year of an undergraduate program in one of above fields. Must attend a college or university that is a member, or affiliated to a member, of the Association of Universities and Colleges of Canada. Candidates are expected to have achieved a high level of academic excellence as well as to have exhibited superior intellectual ability and judgment. In some cases, study in certain province/school is required.
HOW TO APPLY: Applications are by nomination only. See website or contact AUCC for nomination procedures.
RENEWABLE: No

414—CHICAGO ROOFING CONTRACTORS ASSOCIATION

4415 W. Harrison Street, #322
Hillside IL 60162
708/449-3340
FAX: 708/449-0837
E-mail: info@crca.org
Internet: http://www.crca.org
AMOUNT: $3,000
DEADLINE(S): MAR (1st Friday)
FIELD(S): Business; Engineering; Architecture; Liberal Arts; Sciences
ELIGIBILITY/REQUIREMENTS: Open to high school seniors who reside in one of the eight counties in Northern Illinois: Cook, DuPage, Lake, Kane, Kendall, DeKalb, McHenry, or Will. Must be accepted as a full-time student in a 4-year college or university to pursue a degree in one of the above fields. Must be U.S. citizen. Based on academic achievements, extracurricular activities, and community involvement.

HOW TO APPLY: See website for an application. Submit with 2 completed Personal Reference Forms (1 from high school guidance counselor or faculty member, an optional letter of recommendation may also be included; the other from an adult not related to the student); an official transcript of all high school records, and official ACT and/or SAT results or official high school transcript.
NUMBER OF AWARDS: 1 (In the event of a tie, financial need considered.)
RENEWABLE: Yes (up to 3 times). Must maintain a 2.75 grade point average.

415—CONCLAVE, THE (McNally-Smith Scholarship)

4517 Minnetonka Boulevard, #104
Minneapolis MN 55416
952/927-4487
FAX: 952/927-6427
Internet: http://www.theconclave.com and www.radioscholarships.com
AMOUNT: Tuition ($25,000+)
DEADLINE(S): APR 1
FIELD(S): Music industry
ELIGIBILITY/REQUIREMENTS: Granted to the applicant who best demonstrates his or her ambition to pursue a career in the music industry, who has maintained a good academic record, and demonstrates financial need. Open to any student who has applied for admission to McNally Smith College's Associate of Applied Science Degree in Music Business Program
HOW TO APPLY: Apply online at either website or contact The Conclave for an application. Submit with an audio cassette or CD recording of supplied script.
NUMBER OF AWARDS: 1
RENEWABLE: Yes. Renewal is automatic as long as the student achieves a GPA of 3.0 for each semester's work and enrolls full time. Books, course materials, room and board are not included.
CONTACT: Tom Kay

416—COUNCIL OF ENERGY RESOURCE TRIBES (CERT)

CERT Education Program
Attention: Scholars Program
695 S. Colorado Blvd, Suite 10
Denver CO 80246
303/282-7576
FAX: 303/282-7584
E-mail: info@CERTRedEarth.com
Internet: http://www.certredearth.com/
AMOUNT: $1,000

DEADLINE(S): SEP 14 (Fall), FEB 15 (Spring)
FIELD(S): Science; Engineering; Business, Mathematics, Computer Technology, or related fields.
ELIGIBILITY/REQUIREMENTS: Applicants must meet the criteria to become a TRIBES Institute candidate and a full-time undergraduate (12 hrs/semester) student enrolled in an accredited 2- or 4-year tribal, private, or public university/college, and must maintain at least a 2.5 GPA, although academic excellence far above this GPA is preferred. (Should scholarship funds be limited, GPA will be weighed in decision.)
HOW TO APPLY: See website or contact CERT. Submit application along with official Tribal affiliation documentation (with enrollment number or other statement of Tribal acknowledgment of membership), an official transcript of most recent coursework with the cumulative GPA, as well as the GPA for current hours detailed on the transcript, and a class schedule for the next term demonstrating that you will be attending school full time and/or verification of full-time enrollment for the next semester.
RENEWABLE: Yes. Must reapply.
CONTACT: Tom Talache, ttalache@CERTRedEarth.com or 303/282-7576 ext. 12

417—GOLDEN KEY INTERNATIONAL HONOUR SOCIETY (Business Achievement Awards)

1189 Ponce de Leon Avenue
Atlanta GA 30306
404/377-2400 or 800/377-2401
FAX: 404/373-7033
E-mail: scholarships@goldenkey.org
Internet: http//www.goldenkey.org
AMOUNT: $1,000 first place; $750 second place; $500 third place
DEADLINE(S): MAR
FIELD(S): All; emphasis on Business
ELIGIBILITY REQUIREMENTS: This award recognizes members who excel in the study of business. Those eligible are undergraduate, graduate, and post-graduate members who are currently enrolled in classes at a degree-granting program. Awards based on academic achievement, quality of paper submitted.
HOW TO APPLY: Apply online with Golden Key number. Attach a business related paper/report (must not exceed 10 pages) you have prepared. Attach an essay (no more than 2 pages) describing the assignment for writing the paper, what the greatest challenge was in writing the paper,

what lessons were learned from completing the assignment, and if you were to redo the report, what would be changed. Attach a letter of recommendation from a professor in the discipline and an official academic transcript.
NUMBER OF AWARDS/YEAR: 3
RENEWABLE: No
CONTACT: Fabian J. De Rozario, Associate Vice President of North American Operations

418—HAWAII COMMUNITY FOUNDATION (Financial Women International Scholarship)

1164 Bishop Street, Suite 800
Honolulu HI 96813
808/537-6333 or toll free:
888/731-3863
FAX: 808/521-6286
E-mail: info@hcf-hawaii.org
Internet: http://www.hcf-hawaii.org
DEADLINE(S): MAR 1
FIELD(S): Business or business-related field
ELIGIBILITY/REQUIREMENTS: Applicants must be female residents of the state of Hawaii; be junior or senior undergraduate or graduate students attending full time an accredited 4-year college or university; and demonstrate financial need, good moral character, strong academic potential, motivation, and accomplishment, with a minimum GPA of 3.5.
HOW TO APPLY: Send application with 2 letters of recommendation.

419—HAWAII COMMUNITY FOUNDATION (Oscar & Rosetta Fish Fund)

1164 Bishop Street, Suite 800
Honolulu HI 96813
808/537-6333 or toll free:
888/731-3863
FAX: 808/521-6286
E-mail: info@hcf-hawaii.org
Internet: http://www.hcf-hawaii.org
DEADLINE(S): MAR 1
FIELD(S): Business
ELIGIBILITY/REQUIREMENTS: Applicants must attend, full time, any University of Hawaii campus excluding Manoa and must demonstrate financial need, good moral character, and academic achievement with a minimum GPA of 2.7.
HOW TO APPLY: Send application with 2 letters of recommendation.

420—HILLSDALE COLLEGE (Freedom as Vocation Scholarship)

33 E. College Street
Hillsdale MI 49242-1298
517/437-7341
Internet: http://www.hillsdale.edu
AMOUNT: Varies
DEADLINE(S): None
FIELD(S): Business; History; Political Science; Economics
ELIGIBILITY/REQUIREMENTS: Open to Hillsdale College undergraduates who maintain a minimum 3.0 GPA and commit to a series of courses in the above fields. Student must rank in top 20% of class and top 10% of test scores. Must possess excellent communications, public speaking, and leadership skills and demonstrate outstanding character and citizenship. Financial need NOT a factor.
HOW TO APPLY: No application process; students are selected. See website for details.
RENEWABLE: Yes

421—HISPANIC COLLEGE FUND (HSF/General Motors Scholarship)

55 Second Street, Suite 1500
San Francisco CA 94105
1-877/HSF-INFO
(1-877/473-4636)
FAX: 415/808-2302
E-mail: pip@hsf.net
Internet: http://hispanicfund.org
AMOUNT: At least $2,500
DEADLINE(S): JUN 16
FIELD(S): Engineering; Business
ELIGIBILITY/REQUIREMENTS: Must be U.S. citizen or legal permanent residents of Hispanic heritage (one parent fully Hispanic or both parents half Hispanic). Applicant should have earned at least 12 undergraduate college credits in the U.S. or Puerto Rico and have a minimum GPA of 3.0. Must carry at least 12 credits each term. Selection is based on academic achievement, personal strengths, leadership and financial need.
HOW TO APPLY: Contact Fund for details or visit website for application.
NUMBER OF AWARDS: 83

422—HISPANIC COLLEGE FUND (HSF/JP Morgan Chase Scholarship Program)

55 Second Street, Suite 1500
San Francisco CA 94105
1-877/HSF-INFO
(1-877/473-4636)
FAX: 415/808-2302
E-mail: pip@hsf.net
Internet: http://hispanicfund.org
AMOUNT: $2,500
DEADLINE(S): NOV 26
FIELD(S): Business; Finance; Economics
ELIGIBILITY/REQUIREMENTS: Open to students in their sophomore and junior years. Must be U.S. citizens or legal permanent residents of Hispanic heritage (one parent fully Hispanic or both parents half Hispanic). Minimum GPA of 3.0. Must carry at least 12 credits each term. Selection is based on academic achievement, personal strengths, leadership and financial need.
HOW TO APPLY: Contact Fund for details or visit website for application.

423—HISPANIC COLLEGE FUND (HSF/Little Village Chamber of Commerce Ambassador's Scholarship Program)

55 Second Street, Suite 1500
San Francisco CA 94105
1-877/HSF-INFO
(1-877/473-4636)
FAX: 415/808-2302
E-mail: pip@hsf.net
Internet: http://hispanicfund.org
AMOUNT: At least $2,000
DEADLINE(S): JUN 23
FIELD(S): Business; Finance; Marketing and related fields
ELIGIBILITY/REQUIREMENTS: Open to entering and continuing full-time undergraduate and graduate students from the Little Village Community. Must be U.S. citizens or legal permanent residents of Hispanic heritage (one parent fully Hispanic or both parents half Hispanic). Minimum GPA of 3.0. Must carry at least 12 credits each term. Selection is based on academic achievement, personal strengths, leadership and financial need.
HOW TO APPLY: Contact Fund for details or visit website for application.

424—JACKSONVILLE STATE UNIVERSITY (Alabama Power Scholarship)

Financial Aid Office
Jacksonville AL 36265
256/782-5677 or 800/231-5291
Internet: http://www.jsu.edu
AMOUNT: Varies
DEADLINE(S): FEB 1
FIELD(S): Commerce; Business
ELIGIBILITY/REQUIREMENTS: Must be Alabama resident and demonstrate academic aptitude.
HOW TO APPLY: An official high school transcript and ACT/SAT scores must be submitted with scholarship applications. See website for application. Supporting documentation should be mailed.
RENEWABLE: No
CONTACT: Scholarship Committee

425—JACKSONVILLE STATE UNIVERSITY (Bob and Lou Kennamer Scholarship)

Financial Aid Office
Jacksonville AL 36265
256/782-5677 or 800/231-5291
Internet: http://www.jsu.edu
AMOUNT: Varies
DEADLINE(S): FEB 1
FIELD(S): Commerce; Business
ELIGIBILITY/REQUIREMENTS:
Open to juniors or seniors; minimum 3.0
GPA; leadership and need considered.
HOW TO APPLY: An official high school
transcript and ACT/SAT scores must be
submitted with scholarship applications.
See website for application. Supporting
documentation should be mailed.
RENEWABLE: No
CONTACT: Scholarship Committee

426—JACKSONVILLE STATE UNIVERSITY (Jeffrey Parker Scholarship)

Jacksonville AL 36265
256/782-5677 or 800/231-5291
Internet: http://www.jsu.edu
AMOUNT: Varies
DEADLINE(S): FEB 1
FIELD(S): Commerce; Business
ELIGIBILITY/REQUIREMENTS:
Open to upperclass students.
HOW TO APPLY: Contact College of
Commerce & Business Administration for
application and additional information.
RENEWABLE: No
CONTACT: College of Commerce &
Business Administration, 256/782-5780

427—JACKSONVILLE STATE UNIVERSITY (South Trust Bank Scholarship)

Financial Aid Office
Jacksonville AL 36265
256/782-5677 or 800/231-5291
Internet: http://www.jsu.edu
AMOUNT: Varies
DEADLINE(S): FEB 1
FIELD(S): Commerce; Business
ELIGIBILITY/REQUIREMENTS:
Open to all students.
HOW TO APPLY: An official high school
transcript and ACT/SAT scores must be
submitted with scholarship applications.
See website for application. Supporting
documentation should be mailed.
RENEWABLE: No
CONTACT: Scholarship Committee

428—JACKSONVILLE STATE UNIVERSITY (Sunny King Toyota Scholarship)

Financial Aid Office
Jacksonville AL 36265
256/782-5677 or 800/231-5291
Internet: http://www.jsu.edu
AMOUNT: Varies
DEADLINE(S): FEB 1
FIELD(S): Commerce; Business
ELIGIBILITY/REQUIREMENTS:
Open to senior who demonstrates entre-
preneurial spirit.
HOW TO APPLY: An official transcript
and ACT/SAT scores must be submitted
with scholarship applications. See website
for application. Supporting documentation
should be mailed.
NUMBER OF AWARDS: 1
RENEWABLE: No
CONTACT: Scholarship Committee

429—JACOB'S PILLOW DANCE FESTIVAL (Internships)

The Intern Program at Jacob's Pillow
P.O. Box 287
Lee MA 01238
413/637-1322
Fax: 413/243-4744
E-mail: info@jacobspillow.org
Internet: http://www.jacobspillow.
org
AMOUNT: Varies
DEADLINE(S): APR 5
FIELD(S): Archives/Preservation;
Business; Development; Education;
Marketing/Press;
Operations/Production
ELIGIBILITY/REQUIREMENTS: Full-
and part-time internships for the fall, win-
ter, and spring can be tailored to meet col-
lege credit needs and individual interests.
HOW TO APPLY: Send 2 copies of each:
a cover letter, résumé, and writing/design
samples as applicable.

430—JOHNSON AND WALES UNIVERSITY (Annual Johnson and Wales University National High School Recipe Contest)

8 Abbott Place
Providence RI 02903
401/598-2345
Internet: http://www.jwu.edu/
admiss/scholarships/
AMOUNT: $1,000-$5,000
DEADLINE(S): JAN 31
FIELD(S): Business, Hospitality,
Technology, Culinary Arts
ELIGIBILITY/REQUIREMENTS: For
students planning to attend Johnson &
Wales University, Providence, Rhode
Island.
HOW TO APPLY: Write for detailed de-
scription.

431—JOHNSON AND WALES UNIVERSITY (Gilbane Building Company Eagle Scout Scholarship)

8 Abbott Place
Providence RI 02903
401/598-2345
Internet: http://www.jwu.edu/
admiss/scholarships/
AMOUNT: $1,200
DEADLINE(S): None
FIELD(S): Business, Hospitality,
Technology, Culinary Arts
ELIGIBILITY/REQUIREMENTS: For
students attending Johnson & Wales
University, Providence, Rhode Island.
Must be Eagle Scouts.
HOW TO APPLY: Send letter of recom-
mendation and transcript to above
address.

432—JOHNSON AND WALES UNIVERSITY (National High School Entrepreneur of the Year Contest)

8 Abbott Place
Providence RI 02903
401/598-2345
Internet: http://www.jwu.edu/
admiss/scholarships/
AMOUNT: $1,000-$10,000
DEADLINE(S): DEC 27
FIELD(S): Business, Hospitality,
Technology, Culinary Arts
ELIGIBILITY/REQUIREMENTS: For
students attending Johnson & Wales
University, Providence, Rhode Island.
HOW TO APPLY: Send for detailed
description.

433—JORGE MAS CANOSA FREEDOM FOUNDATION (Mas Family Scholarships)

P.O. Box 14-1898
Miami FL 33114
305/529-0075, ext. 35
E-mail: mmartinez@jmcffmasfamily
scholarships.org
Internet: http://www.jmcffmas
scholarships.org
AMOUNT: Up to $10,000
DEADLINE(S): MAR 31
FIELD(S): Engineering, Business,
International Relations, Economics,
Communications, Journalism
ELIGIBILITY/REQUIREMENTS: For
Cuban-American students, graduates and
undergraduates, born in Cuba or direct
descendants (1 parent or 2 grandparents)
of those who left Cuba. Must be in top
10% of high school class or maintain a 3.5
GPA in college. Financial need considered

along with academic success, SAT and GRE scores, and leadership potential.
HOW TO APPLY: Contact Foundation for application. 2 short essays and 2 character evaluations along with proof of Cuban descent required.
NUMBER OF AWARDS: 10
RENEWABLE: Yes. Maximum $40,000; must reapply.

434—JUNIATA COLLEGE (Anna Groninger Smith Memorial Scholarship)

Office of Financial Planning
1700 Moore Street
Huntingdon PA 16652
814/641-3142
FAX: 814/641-5311
E-mail: frankv@juniata.edu
Internet: http://www.juniata.edu/admission/finplan/index.html
AMOUNT: Up to $4,000
DEADLINE(S): MAR 1
FIELD(S): Business
ELIGIBILITY/REQUIREMENTS: Open to females in business studies applying to Juniata College. Must demonstrate financial need and fill out government FAFSA form.
HOW TO APPLY: Contact College for an application or enrollment information. See your financial aid office for FAFSA.
CONTACT: Vincent Frank, Director of Student Financial Planning, 814/641-3140; e-mail: frankv@juniata.edu

435—JUNIATA COLLEGE (Metz Scholarship)

Office of Financial Planning
1700 Moore Street
Huntingdon PA 16652
814/641-3142
FAX: 814/641-5311
E-mail: frankv@juniata.edu
Internet: http://www.juniata.edu/admission/finplan/index.html
AMOUNT: Up to $5,000
DEADLINE(S): MAR 1
FIELD(S): Business; Economics
ELIGIBILITY/REQUIREMENTS: Open to Business or Economics majors. Must demonstrate financial need and fill out government FAFSA form.
HOW TO APPLY: Contact College for an application or enrollment information. See Financial Aid Office for FAFSA.
CONTACT: Vincent Frank, Director of Student Financial Planning, 814/641-3140; e-mail: frankv@juniata.edu

436—JUNIATA COLLEGE (W & M Donham Scholarships)

Office of Financial Planning
1700 Moore Street

Huntingdon PA 16652
814/641-3142
FAX: 814/641-5311
E-mail: frankv@juniata.edu
Internet: http://www.juniata.edu/admission/finplan/index.html
AMOUNT: Up to $2,000
DEADLINE(S): MAR 1
FIELD(S): Business; Economics
ELIGIBILITY/REQUIREMENTS: Open to Business or Economics majors. Must demonstrate financial need and fill out government FAFSA form.
HOW TO APPLY: Contact College for an application or enrollment information. See Financial Aid Office for FAFSA.
CONTACT: Vincent Frank, Director of Student Financial Planning, 814/641-3140; e-mail: frankv@juniata.edu

437—JUNIOR ACHIEVEMENT INC. (Johnson and Wales University Scholarship)

One Education Way
Colorado Springs CO 80906-4477
719/540-8000
FAX: 719/540-6299
E-mail: newmedia@ja.org
Internet: http://www.ja.org
AMOUNT: $10,000 (4 years)
DEADLINE(S): FEB 1
FIELD(S): Business; Culinary Arts; Hospitality; Technology
ELIGIBILITY/REQUIREMENTS: Applicants must be high school seniors who have been accepted by and will be attending Johnson and Wales University and be majoring in one of the above fields.
HOW TO APPLY: Send completed application with 1 letter of recommendation from a JA High School Programs consultant.
NUMBER OF AWARDS: 2 4-year $10,000 scholarships; unlimited partial scholarships
RENEWABLE: No
CONTACT: To obtain application, contact Tom Gauthier, Coordinator of Specialty Recruitment, Johnson and Wales University, 8 Abbott Place, Providence RI 02903; 800/DIAL-JWU, ext. 2345 or at www.jwu.edu; submit completed application to Johnson and Wales University.

438—JUNIOR ACHIEVEMENT INC. (NFIB Free Enterprise Scholarship Award)

One Education Way
Colorado Springs CO 80906-4477
719/540-8000
FAX: 719/540-6299

E-mail: newmedia@ja.org
Internet: http://www.ja.org
AMOUNT: $1,000
DEADLINE(S): JAN 1-MAR 31
FIELD(S): Business; Entrepreneurship
ELIGIBILITY/REQUIREMENTS: Applicants must be high school seniors or entering freshman year at an accredited, nonprofit 2- or 4-year university, college, or vocational/technical institute. Must be nominated by a dues-paying member of the National Federation of Independent Business (NFIB); have shown an interest in business and entrepreneurship and have demonstrated entrepreneurial spirit and initiative (e.g., have started his/her own business; or participated in organizations such as DECA, Junior Achievement, The National Foundation for Teaching Entrepreneurship, or others; or through other initiatives).
HOW TO APPLY: Send completed application, including the NFIB member's nomination and signature; completed essay and activity sheet; high school record with a copy of SAT and/or ACT scores.
NUMBER OF AWARDS: 100
RENEWABLE: No
CONTACT: Submit completed application to NFIB Free Enterprise Scholars Award, c/o Scholarship Program Administrators, Inc., P.O. Box 22492, Nashville TN 37202.

439—JUNIOR ACHIEVEMENT INC. (Northwood University Scholarships)

One Education Way
Colorado Springs CO 80906-4477
719/540-8000
FAX: 719/540-6299
E-mail: newmedia@ja.org
Internet: http://www.ja.org
AMOUNT: $500-$2,000 annually for Business Club Scholarships; up to $8,000 annually for Merit Scholarships
DEADLINE(S): MAY 1
FIELD(S): Business
ELIGIBILITY/REQUIREMENTS: Applicants must be high school seniors who will be majoring in any business curriculum at Northwood University; Business Club Scholarship requires a minimum 2.5 GPA; Merit Scholarships require a 2.7 GPA/20 ACT for the $4,000 award, a 3.0 GPA/25 ACT for the $5,000 award, and a 4.0 GPA/30 ACT for the $8,000 award.
HOW TO APPLY: Send completed application, a one-page typed essay entitled "What Free Enterprise Means to Me"; also a letter of recommendation from a JA staff person or a JA High School Programs consultant.

NUMBER OF AWARDS: Varies
RENEWABLE: Yes. Annually.
CONTACT: To obtain application, contact the Office of Admission at each campus: Cedar Hill (Dallas) TX: 800/927-9663; Midland MI: 800/457-7878; West Palm Beach FL: 800/458-8325; e-mail info@ northwood.edu or at www.northwood.edu; submit completed application to Northwood University, Office of Admission.

440—JUNIOR ACHIEVEMENT INC. (Office Depot Scholarships)

One Education Way
Colorado Springs CO 80906-4477
719/540-8000
FAX: 719/540-6299
E-mail: newmedia@ja.org
Internet: http://www.ja.org
AMOUNT: $10,000
DEADLINE(S): FEB 27
FIELD(S): Business
ELIGIBILITY/REQUIREMENTS: Applicants must be graduating high school seniors who have demonstrated academic achievement and leadership skills; have a minimum GPA of 3.0; have participated in a Junior Achievement program during high school; demonstrate financial need.
HOW TO APPLY: Send completed application; copy of parents' prior-year federal income tax return; official transcript, including SAT/ACT scores; a one-page typed essay answering this question: "How important is diversity in today's corporate environment? Why?"; and 3 letters of recommendation supporting academic achievement, leadership skills, and college potential.
NUMBER OF AWARDS: 6
RENEWABLE: No
CONTACT: To obtain application, contact Scholarship/Education Team, Junior Achievement Inc. at 954/566-8623; submit completed application to Junior Achievement Inc., P.O. Box 5186, Fort Lauderdale FL 33310.

441—LEAGUE OF UNITED LATIN AMERICAN CITIZENS/LULAC NATIONAL EDUCATIONAL SERVICE CENTERS (General Electric/LULAC Scholarship Program)

2000 L Street NW, #610
Washington DC 20036
202/835-9646 or 202/833-6130
FAX: 202/835-9685
Internet: http://www.lulac.org/
programs/scholar.html
AMOUNT: $5,000

FIELD(S): Business; Engineering
ELIGIBILITY/REQUIREMENTS: Applicants must be college sophomores or higher, plan to major in business or engineering and exhibit leadership involvement.
HOW TO APPLY: Contact LULAC for additional information and application.
NUMBER OF AWARDS: 2
CONTACT: Lorena Maymi

442—MEXICAN AMERICAN GROCERS ASSOCIATION (Scholarships)

405 N. San Fernando Road
Los Angeles CA 90031
213/227-1565
FAX: 213/227-6935
Internet: http://www.maga.org/
new_page_3.htm
AMOUNT: Varies
DEADLINE(S): JUL 31
FIELD(S): Business
ELIGIBILITY/REQUIREMENTS: Scholarships for Hispanic college students who are at least college sophomores. Must have 2.5 GPA or above, be U.S. citizen or permanent resident, and demonstrate financial need.
HOW TO APPLY: Send SASE for further information.
CONTACT: Jackie Solis

443—NATIONAL BLACK MBA ASSOCIATION

Member and Partner Services/
Education and Programs
180 North Michigan Avenue,
Suite 1400
Chicago IL 60601
312/236-2622, ext. 8086
FAX: 312/236-0390
E-mail: scholarship@nbmbaa.org.
Internet: http://www.nbmbaa.org
AMOUNT: $1,000
DEADLINE(S): Varies by chapter
FIELD(S): Business
ELIGIBILITY/REQUIREMENTS: Must be qualified minority undergraduate students.
HOW TO APPLY: Send completed application; high school or undergraduate transcripts; and an essay on a topic determined by the NBMBAA National Office.
NUMBER OF AWARDS: 39 (1 for each member chapter)
CONTACT: Lori Johnson
ADDITIONAL INFORMATION: This program is implemented at the local chapter level only. Interested candidates must directly contact the nearest chapter.

444—NATIVE AMERICAN SCHOLARSHIP FUND, INC.

8200 Mountain Road NE, Suite 203
Albuquerque NM 87110
505/262-2351
FAX: 505/262-0543
E-mail: NScholarsh@aol.com
AMOUNT: Varies
DEADLINE(S): MAR 15; APR 15; SEP 15
FIELD(S): Mathematics; Engineering;
  Science; Business; Education;
  Computer Science
ELIGIBILITY/REQUIREMENTS: Open to American Indians or Alaskan Natives (one-quarter degree or more) enrolled as members of a federally recognized, state recognized, or terminated tribe. For graduate or undergraduate study at an accredited 4-year college or university.
HOW TO APPLY: Contact Director of Recruitment for an application.
NUMBER OF AWARDS: 208
CONTACT: Lucille Kelley, Director of Recruitment

445—PHILADELPHIA BIBLICAL UNIVERSITY (Scholarships, Grants, and Loans)

200 Manor Avenue
Langhorne PA 19047
800/366-0049
FAX: 215/702-4248
E-mail: financialaid@pbu.edu
Internet: http://www.pbu.edu
AMOUNT: Varies
DEADLINE(S): Varies
FIELD(S): Bible; Business; Teacher
  Education; Music; Social Work;
  Missions; Church Ministries
ELIGIBILITY/REQUIREMENTS: Academic and needs-based grants are available to students attending full time. Academic awards are based on GPA and SAT/ACT scores. Need-based grants are based on FAFSA results. Grants are also available to needy dependents of full-time Christian workers and scholarships presented to those exhibiting excellence in the field of music.
HOW TO APPLY: Apply to university and complete an application for student aid.
CONTACT: David Haggard

446—SOCIETY OF SATELLITE PROFESSIONALS INTERNATIONAL (SSPI Scholarship Program)

SSPI International Headquarters
The New York Information
Technology Center
55 Broad Street, 14th floor

New York NY 10004
212/809-5199
FAX: 212/825-0075
E-mail: neworbit@aol.com
Internet: http://www.sspi.org
AMOUNT: $1,500-$4,000
DEADLINE(S): DEC 1
FIELD(S): Satellites as related to communications, domestic and international telecommunications policy, remote sensing, journalism, law, meteorology, energy, navigation, business, government, and broadcasting services
ELIGIBILITY/REQUIREMENTS: Applicants must be current high school seniors, college or university undergraduate students or graduate students who are studying or intend to study satellite-related technologies, policies or applications. Must demonstrate commitment to pursue education and career opportunities in the satellite industry or a field making direct use of satellite technology; academic and leadership achievement; potential for significant contribution to the satellite communications industry; and a scientific, engineering, research, business or creative submission meeting high standards.
HOW TO APPLY: Before applying, all applicants must complete a Scholarship Qualification Form that will help determine whether your interests and career plans are a good fit for the program. This will ensure that you have a reasonable chance of winning before you spend the time and money to apply. See website for Qualification form and additional details or send SASE.

447—SOUTHERN ILLINOIS UNIVERSITY (Music Scholarships)

School of Music, Mailcode 4302
Carbondale IL 62901-4302
618/536-8742
FAX: 618/453-5808
Internet: http://www.siu.edu/
~music/resources/Scholarships.html
AMOUNT: Varies
DEADLINE(S): MAR 15
FIELD(S): Music Performance, Composition, Theater, Music Business, Music Education
ELIGIBILITY/REQUIREMENTS: Must be music major or minor.
HOW TO APPLY: An audition is required, usually held in February. A personal audition or taped audition can be arranged. See website or Undergraduate Office, School of Music.
RENEWABLE: Yes. Recommendation of music faculty required.
CONTACT: Dr. Jeanine Wagner

448—WASHINGTON APPLE EDUCATION FOUNDATION (Wenatchee Traffic Club Scholarship)

P.O. Box 3720
Wenatchee WA 98807
509/663-7713
FAX: 509/663-7713
E-mail: waef@waef.org
Internet: http://www.ussui.org
AMOUNT: Varies
DEADLINE(S): APR 1
FIELD(S): Agriculture; Horticulture; Business
ELIGIBILITY/REQUIREMENTS: Applicants must be Washington state high school seniors or current college undergraduate students from Washington state pursuing a commodity-related career. Applicants must be residents of Chelan, Douglas, Grant, or Okanogan counties. Parents or guardians or applicant should be involved in Washington's tree fruit industry.
HOW TO APPLY: See website for application.
NUMBER OF AWARDS: Varies
RENEWABLE: No
CONTACT: Jennifer Whitney

449—WASHINGTON APPLE EDUCATION FOUNDATION (Yakima Valley Grower-Shippers Association Scholarship)

P.O. Box 3720
Wenatchee WA 98807
509/663-7713
FAX: 509/663-7713
E-mail: waef@waef.org
Internet: http://www.ussui.org
AMOUNT: $750
DEADLINE(S): APR 1
FIELD(S): Agriculture; Horticulture; Business; Mechanical Engineering
ELIGIBILITY/REQUIREMENTS: Applicant must be employee or child of a general member of the YVGSA or the child of an employee or grower of a general member of the YVGSA. Applicant must be pursuing a degree compatible with service to the tree fruit industry.
HOW TO APPLY: See website for application.
NUMBER OF AWARDS: 2
RENEWABLE: No
CONTACT: Jennifer Whitney

450—WESTERN MICHIGAN UNIVERSITY (College of Education/Merze Tate Undergraduate Scholarship)

1903 W. Michigan
Kalamazoo MI 49008-5337
269/387-6000

FAX: 269/387-6989
Internet: http://www.wmich.edu/finaid
AMOUNT: $250-$2,000
DEADLINE(S): MAR 1
FIELD(S): Business; Education
ELIGIBILITY/REQUIREMENTS: May be enrolled full or part time. Preference is given to students in need of financial aid (including, but not limited to, deserving foreign students in need of financial assistance).
HOW TO APPLY: See website for application or contact College of Education.
NUMBER OF AWARDS: 1 (minimum)
RENEWABLE: No
CONTACT: College of Education

451—WESTERN MICHIGAN UNIVERSITY (College of Engineering and Applied Sciences/Robert A. Welborn Scholarship)

1903 W. Michigan
Kalamazoo MI 49008-5337
269/387-6000
FAX: 269/387-6989
Internet: http://www.wmich.edu/finaid
AMOUNT: Varies
FIELD(S): Business; Paper Science
ELIGIBILITY/REQUIREMENTS: Open to students pursuing degree in Business or Paper Science in good academic standing and within 3 semesters of graduation. Must demonstrate financial need and reside in the 13th senatorial district as it was when Welborn was senator.
HOW TO APPLY: Recipient is selected by faculty. Contact the Paper and Printing Science and Engineering Department for an application.
NUMBER OF AWARDS: 1
RENEWABLE: No
CONTACT: Paper and Printing Science and Engineering Department, 1104 Welborn Hall

452—WESTERN MICHIGAN UNIVERSITY (Haworth College of Business/G & R Felpausch Company Endowed Scholarship)

1903 W. Michigan
Kalamazoo MI 49008-5337
269/387-6000
FAX: 269/387-6989
Internet: http://www.wmich.edu/finaid
AMOUNT: Varies
DEADLINE(S): FEB 15
FIELD(S): Food Marketing; Business
ELIGIBILITY/REQUIREMENTS: Student majoring in food marketing; mini-

mum GPA of 2.5. Preference given to Felpausch Food Centers employees, or family of employees, majoring in food marketing or business-related major. Consideration given to financial need, interest in food marketing, work experience, and participation in university and community activities.

HOW TO APPLY: Application forms must be obtained from and returned to the Marketing Department.

NUMBER OF AWARDS: 2

RENEWABLE: Yes

CONTACT: Marketing Department

453—WESTERN MICHIGAN UNIVERSITY (Haworth College of Business/Magellan Scholarship)

1903 W. Michigan
Kalamazoo MI 49008-5337
269/387-6000
FAX: 269/387-6989
Internet: http://www.wmich.edu/finaid

AMOUNT: $500 (fall semester)

DEADLINE(S): FEB 15

FIELD(S): Finance; Business; International Business

ELIGIBILITY/REQUIREMENTS: Undergraduate BBA with minimum GPA of 3.0. Recipient will be a business student participating in a study-abroad program or participating in an international business seminar. Need-based award.

HOW TO APPLY: Contact the Department of Finance & Commercial Law, 3290 Schneider Hall, Haworth College of Business, e–mail: edEdwards@wmich.edu (269/387-5722).

NUMBER OF AWARDS: 2

RENEWABLE: No

CONTACT: Department of Finance & Commercial Law

454—WESTERN MICHIGAN UNIVERSITY (Pfizer Cultural Diversity Scholarship)

1903 W. Michigan
Kalamazoo MI 49008-5337
269/387-8777
FAX: 269/387-6989
Internet: http://www.wmich.edu/finaid

AMOUNT: $2,000 for senior year

DEADLINE(S): APR 1

FIELD(S): Biomedical Science; Biology; Business

ELIGIBILITY/REQUIREMENTS: Applicant must be U.S. citizen; in junior year, majoring in one of the above fields. Must be a full-time student, with a 3.0 cumulative GPA in program of study. Business majors must complete pre-business classes before applying.

HOW TO APPLY: Contact the Division of Minority Affairs for an application. Must complete a FAFSA and indicate WMU as a school choice.

RENEWABLE: No

CONTACT: Division of Minority affairs

455—WOMEN IN DEFENSE (HORIZONS Scholarship Foundation)

2111 Wilson Boulevard, Suite 400
Arlington VA 22201-3061
703/247-2552
FAX: 703/522-1885
E-mail: wid@ndia.org
Internet: http://www.ndia.org

AMOUNT: $500+

DEADLINE(S): NOV 1; JUL 1

FIELD(S): Security Studies; Engineering; Computer Science; Physics; Mathematics; International Relations; Political Science; Operations Research; Economics; National Security/Defense; Business and Law (as they relate to national security or defense); other fields considered if relevance to national security or defense can be demonstrated

ELIGIBILITY/REQUIREMENTS: Open to women employed/planning careers in defense/national security areas (NOT law enforcement or criminal justice). Must be currently enrolled full- or part-time at an accredited college or university at the graduate or undergraduate junior/senior level. Must have a minimum 3.25 GPA, demonstrate financial need, and be U.S. citizen. Based on academic achievement, work experience, objectives, and recommendations.

HOW TO APPLY: See website or send SASE for application.

RENEWABLE: Yes

456—WOODROW WILSON NATIONAL FELLOWSHIP FOUNDATION/U.S. DEPARTMENTS OF COMMERCE AND AGRICULTURE (Fellowships)

CN 5329
Princeton NJ 08543-5329
609/452-7007
FAX: 609/452-0066
E-mail: richard@woodrow.org
Internet: http://www.woodrow.org

AMOUNT: Varies

DEADLINE(S): Varies

FIELD(S): Commerce; Agriculture

ELIGIBILITY/REQUIREMENTS: Open to minority students in the U.S. who are interested in careers in commerce or agriculture.

HOW TO APPLY: See website or contact WWNFF for an application.

457—ZONTA INTERNATIONAL FOUNDATION (Jane M. Klausman Women in Business Scholarships)

557 West Randolph Street
Chicago IL 60661-2206
312/930-5848
FAX: 312/930-0951
E-mail: zontafdtn@zonta.org
Internet: http://www.zonta.org

AMOUNT: $4,000

DEADLINE(S): Varies

FIELD(S): Business

ELIGIBILITY/REQUIREMENTS: Women of any nationality pursuing undergraduate business degrees who demonstrate outstanding potential in the field are eligible. To apply, you must meet the following minimum requirements: Be eligible to enter the third or fourth year of an undergraduate degree program at an accredited university/college/institute program at the time the funds are received; have achieved an outstanding academic record during the first 2 to 3 years of academic studies; demonstrate intent to complete a program in business and show outstanding achievement in business-related subjects, as recorded on the official university/college/institute transcript.

HOW TO APPLY: Contact the Zonta Club nearest you or e-mail your name and contact information to Zonta International Headquarters. Applicants must be nominated by their local Zonta Club. In addition to application, nominees must supply 1 confidential letter of recommendation from a faculty member in the major field of study; 1 confidential letter of recommendation from an employer, volunteer supervisor, or academic advisor; an essay that clearly describes immediate and future academic and career goals; and verification of enrollment from the university/college/institute registrar. See website or contact Foundation for application.

458—ZONTA INTERNATIONAL FOUNDATION (Young Women in Public Affairs Award)

557 West Randolph Street
Chicago IL 60661-2206
312/930-5848
FAX: 312/930-0951
E-mail: zontafdtn@zonta.org
Internet: http://www.zonta.org

AMOUNT: $500, district awards; $1,000 international awards

DEADLINE(S): Varies

FIELD(S): Public Affairs

ELIGIBILITY/REQUIREMENTS: Pre-university or pre-college women students (ages 16-20) at the time of the International recipients selection (June 30) are eligible to apply.

HOW TO APPLY: The YWPA Awards Program operates at the Club, District, and International levels. To apply, contact the Zonta Club nearest you or e-mail your name and contact information to Zonta International Headquarters. See website for application and additional information.

NUMBER OF AWARDS: 35 (30 district awards; 5 international awards)

ACCOUNTING

459—ACTUARIAL FOUNDATION, THE (Actuary of Tomorrow—Stuart A. Robertson Memorial Scholarship)

475 North Martingale Road, Suite 600
Schaumburg IL 60173
847/706-3535
FAX: 847/706-3599
E-mail: scholarships@actfnd.org
Internet: http://www.actuarial foundation.org
AMOUNT: $7,500
DEADLINE(S): JUN 1
FIELD(S): Actuary
ELIGIBILITY/REQUIREMENTS: Open to undergraduates demonstrating an interest in pursuing an actuarial career. Must be sophomore or higher, minimum cumulative GPA 3.0; have successfully completed 2 actuarial exams (Spring exams meet 2-exam requirement).

HOW TO APPLY: See website for application, and submit with a personal essay of approximately 500 words focusing on why you want to be an actuary; a current transcript, a letter of recommendation supporting academic achievement and leadership and communication skills from professor or advisor.

NUMBER OF AWARDS: 1 or more (depending on funds)
RENEWABLE: No
CONTACT: Susan Gehm, Foundation Coordinator

460—ACTUARIAL FOUNDATION, THE (John Culver Wooddy Scholarship)

475 North Martingale Road, Suite 600
Schaumburg, IL 60173
847/706-3535
FAX: 847/706-3599
E-mail: scholarships@actfnd.org
Internet: http://www.actuarial foundation.org

AMOUNT: $2,000
DEADLINE(S): JUN (last Friday)
FIELD(S): Actuary
ELIGIBILITY/REQUIREMENTS: Open to student entering senior year in college, who is eligible to graduate within 1 year of date of award; must have passed at least 1 actuarial exam by application due date (international students need to major in Actuarial Science but exam is not required); must be recommended by a professor (limit 1 application/school); applicant must rank in top quartile of class. Preference will be given to candidates who have demonstrated leadership potential through extracurricular activities.

HOW TO APPLY: See website for application, and submit with a personal essay to professor, who must then provide verification of student's class ranking and senior status within their letter of recommendation.

NUMBER OF AWARDS: Multiple
RENEWABLE: No
CONTACT: Susan Gehm, Foundation Coordinator

461—AMERICAN ASSOCIATION OF ATTORNEY-CERTIFIED PUBLIC ACCOUNTANTS FOUNDATION, THE (Student Writing Competition)

3921 Old Lee Highway, Suite 71A
Fairfax VA 22030
800/CPA-ATTY or 888/288-9272
FAX: 703/352-8073
E-mail: info@attorney-cpa.com
Internet: http://www.atorney-cpa.com
AMOUNT: $250-$1,500
DEADLINE(S): MAY 1
FIELD(S): Accounting; Law
ELIGIBILITY/REQUIREMENTS: Essay contest for accounting and/or law students. Open to undergraduate or graduate students in related field/major/program.

HOW TO APPLY: Check out topics and info on website. Complete necessary forms and essay and mail to AAA-CPA office in Fairfax VA.

NUMBER OF AWARDS: 8 per division (graduate and undergraduate)
CONTACT: AAA-CPA office by phone.

462—AMERICAN INSTITUTE OF CERTIFIED PUBLIC ACCOUNTANTS (AICPA) (Accountemps Scholarships)

Palladian One
220 Leigh Farm Road
Durham NC 27707

919/401-4014
FAX: 919/419-4705
E-mail: educat@aicpa.org
Internet: http://www.aicpa.org
AMOUNT: $2,500
DEADLINE(S): Spring
FIELD(S): Accounting; Finance; Information Systems
ELIGIBILITY/REQUIREMENTS: Open to full-time students (minimum 12 semester hours or equivalent) at regionally accredited institutions in the U.S.; must be U.S. citizen. Must be a student affiliate member of AICPA; a declared accounting, finance, or information systems major with an overall GPA of at least 3.0; must have satisfactorily completed at least 30 semester hours or 45 quarter hours, or equivalent college work, including at least 6 semester hours (or equivalent) in accounting.

HOW TO APPLY: Submit application along with official transcripts, tests (if applicable), and 2 letters of recommendation. See website for additional information.

NUMBER OF AWARDS: 5
RENEWABLE: No

463—AMERICAN WOMAN'S SOCIETY OF CPA'S—GEORGIA AFFILIATE (AWSCPA—GA)

222 Piedmont Avenue NE, 6th floor
Atlanta GA 30308
404/653-1242
FAX: 404/653-1575
E-mail: aknowles-jones @oxfordinc.com
Internet: http://www.awscpa.org
AMOUNT: Varies
DEADLINE(S): MAR 31
FIELD(S): Accounting
ELIGIBILITY/REQUIREMENTS: Student (male or female) enrolled in a Georgia University or college who has successfully completed intermediate accounting II.

HOW TO APPLY: Write for application (attention contact below).
RENEWABLE: Yes. Renewals $3,000.
CONTACT: Amy Knowles-Jones

464—AMERICAN SOCIETY OF WOMEN ACCOUNTANTS FOUNDATION SCHOLARSHIP PROGRAM (2-Year College Scholarships)

ASWA National Headquarters
8405 Greensboro Drive, Suite 800
McLean VA 22102
800/326-2163 or 703/506-3265
FAX: 703/506-3266
E-mail: aswa@aswa.org
Internet: http://www.aswa.org/ scholarship.html

AMOUNT: $4,000 (1); $3,000 (2); $2,000 (4)

DEADLINE(S): Varies

FIELD(S): Accounting, Finance

ELIGIBILITY/REQUIREMENTS: Open to community college students entering their 2nd year of an Associates Degree Program who have completed 15 semester hours or the equivalent by time of application deadline. Candidates must have a minimum cumulative college grade point average (GPA) of 3.0 on a 4.0 scale (or the equivalent), and be majoring in accounting or finance. Scholarship candidates will be reviewed on leadership, character, communication skills, scholastic average and financial need.

HOW TO APPLY: Apply through the local chapter. See website or call ASWA for the name of a local chapter. Submit application with 75-word essay describing career goals and objectives, what impact the candidate wants to have on the accounting world and what the candidate most likes about accounting, 1 personal and 2 references from accounting faculty, and transcript from school, showing academic performance and credit hours obtained.

465—AMERICAN SOCIETY OF WOMEN ACCOUNTANTS FOUNDATION SCHOLARSHIP PROGRAM (Undergraduate Scholarships)

ASWA National Headquarters
8405 Greensboro Drive, Suite 800
McLean VA 22102
800/326-2163 or 703/506-3265
FAX: 703/506-3266
E-mail: aswa@aswa.org
Internet: http://www.aswa.org/scholarship.html

AMOUNT: $4,000 (1); $3,000 (2); $2,000 (4)

DEADLINE(S): Varies

FIELD(S): Accounting, Finance

ELIGIBILITY/REQUIREMENTS: Scholarships for female accounting or finance majors who are either full- or part-time students. Must have completed a minimum of 60 semester hours or 90 quarter hours and be enrolled in an accredited college, university, or professional school of accounting (which is designated to award a post-baccalaureate Certificate of Accounting). Scholarship candidates will be reviewed on leadership, character, communication skills, scholastic average and financial need.

HOW TO APPLY: Apply through the local chapter. See website or call ASWA for the name of a local chapter. Submit application with 75-word essay describing career goals and objectives, what impact the candidate wants to have on the accounting world and what the candidate most likes about accounting, 1 personal and 2 references from accounting faculty, and transcript from school, showing academic performance and credit hours obtained. (For certification candidates only: a copy of the letter indicating passing and the receipt indicating proof of payment for the certification exam fees must accompany the application form.)

466—ASSOCIATION OF CERTIFIED FRAUD EXAMINERS (Scholarships)

The Gregor Building
716 West Avenue
Austin TX 78701
800/245-3321 or 512/478-9070
FAX: 512/478-9297
Internet: http://www.cfenet.com

AMOUNT: $1,000

DEADLINE(S): APR 30

FIELD(S): Accounting; Criminal Justice

ELIGIBILITY/REQUIREMENTS: Scholarships for full-time graduate or undergraduate students majoring in accounting or criminal justice degree programs.

HOW TO APPLY: Awards are based on overall academic achievement, 3 letters of recommendation plus a letter of recommendation from a Certified Fraud Examiner or a local CFE Chapter, and an original 250-word essay explaining why the applicant deserves the award and how fraud awareness will affect his or her professional career development. Download application from website.

NUMBER OF AWARDS: 15

467—COLORADO SOCIETY OF CPAs EDUCATIONAL FOUNDATION (Gordon Scheer Scholarship)

7979 East Tufts Avenue, Suite 500
Denver CO 80237-2843
303/773-2877
FAX: 303/773-6344
E-mail: grantz@cocpa.org
Internet: http://www.cocpa.org

AMOUNT: $2,500

DEADLINE(S): JUN 30

FIELD(S): Accounting

ELIGIBILITY/REQUIREMENTS: For undergraduates who have completed intermediate accounting, have a 3.5 or better GPA, and are majoring in accounting at a Colorado college or university offering accredited accounting majors.

HOW TO APPLY: See website or write for an application. Submit with a copy of official high school transcript verifying your GPA, class ranking, and SAT and ACT scores. Accounting faculty reference required.

NUMBER OF AWARDS: 1

RENEWABLE: Yes, must reapply.

CONTACT: Gena Mantz

468—COLORADO SOCIETY OF CPAs EDUCATIONAL FOUNDATION (Scholarships for Ethnically Diverse High School Seniors)

7979 East Tufts Avenue, Suite 500
Denver CO 80237-2843
303/773-2877
FAX: 303/773-6344
E-mail: grantz@cocpa.org
Internet: http://www.cocpa.org

AMOUNT: $1,000

DEADLINE(S): MAR 1

FIELD(S): Accounting

ELIGIBILITY/REQUIREMENTS: Open to African-American, Hispanic, Asian-American, American Indian, or Pacific Islander. Colorado high school students who will major in accounting at Colorado community colleges or Colorado colleges or universities with accredited accounting programs; mimimum GPA 3.0. Must enroll in courses equal to not less than 6 semester/quarter hours for the semester/quarter for which they are applying.

HOW TO APPLY: See website or write for an application. Submit with a copy of official high school transcript verifying your GPA, class ranking, and SAT and ACT scores.

RENEWABLE: Yes, must reapply.

CONTACT: Gena Mantz

469—COLORADO SOCIETY OF CPAs EDUCATIONAL FOUNDATION (Scholarships for Ethnically Diverse Undergraduates and Graduates)

7979 East Tufts Avenue, Suite 500
Denver CO 80237-2843
303/773-2877
FAX: 303/773-6344
E-mail: grantz@cocpa.org
Internet: http://www.cocpa.org

AMOUNT: $2,500

DEADLINE(S): JUN 30

FIELD(S): Accounting

ELIGIBILITY/REQUIREMENTS: For African-American, Hispanic, Asian-American, American Indian, or Pacific Islander undergraduates and graduates who have a declared accounting major and have completed at least 8 semester hours of accounting courses, including one intermediate accounting course. Must attend a Colorado college or university with an accredited accounting program. Students must enroll in courses equal to not less than 6 semester/quarter hours for the semester/quarter for which they are applying. Graduate students must be enrolled in an accounting-related graduate program. Minimum GPA 3.0.

HOW TO APPLY: See website or write for an application. Submit with transcript from the school in which you are currently enrolled.

NUMBER OF AWARDS: 2
RENEWABLE: Yes, must reapply.
CONTACT: Gena Mantz

470—COLORADO SOCIETY OF CPAs EDUCATIONAL FOUNDATION (Scholarships for High School Seniors)

7979 East Tufts Avenue, Suite 500
Denver CO 80237-2843
303/773-2877
FAX: 303/773-6344
E-mail: grantz@cocpa.org
Internet: http://www.cocpa.org
AMOUNT: $1,000
DEADLINE(S): MAR 1
FIELD(S): Accounting
ELIGIBILITY/REQUIREMENTS: Open to all Colorado high school seniors who will major in accounting at Colorado community colleges or Colorado colleges or universities with accredited accounting programs; minimum GPA 3.0. Must enroll in courses equal to not less than 6 semester/quarter hours for the semester/quarter for which they are applying.
HOW TO APPLY: See website or write for an application. Submit with a copy of official high school transcript verifying your GPA, class ranking, and SAT and ACT scores.
RENEWABLE: Yes, must reapply.
CONTACT: Gena Mantz

471—COLORADO SOCIETY OF CPAs EDUCATIONAL FOUNDATION (Scholarships for Undergraduates and Graduates)

7979 East Tufts Avenue, Suite 500
Denver CO 80237-2843
303/773-2877
FAX: 303/773-6344
E-mail: grantz@cocpa.org
Internet: http://www.cocpa.org
AMOUNT: $2,500
DEADLINE(S): JUN 30; NOV 30
FIELD(S): Accounting
ELIGIBILITY/REQUIREMENTS: Open to any declared accounting major who has completed at least 8 semester hours of accounting courses, including one intermediate accounting course. Must attend a

Colorado college or university with an accredited accounting program. Students must enroll in courses equal to not less than 6 semester/quarter hours for the semester/quarter for which they are applying. Graduate students must be enrolled in an accounting-related graduate program. Minimum GPA 3.0.

HOW TO APPLY: See website or write for an application. Submit with transcript from the school in which you are currently enrolled.

NUMBER OF AWARDS: 15-20
RENEWABLE: Yes, must reapply.
CONTACT: Gena Mantz

472—EDUCATIONAL FOUNDATION FOR WOMEN IN ACCOUNTING (Women in Transition and Women at Risk Scholarships)

P.O. Box 1925
Southeastern PA 19399-1925
610/407-9229
Internet: http://www.efwa.org/laurels.htm
AMOUNT: $4,000 (transition); $2,000 (at risk)
DEADLINE(S): APR 15
FIELD(S): Accounting
ELIGIBILITY/REQUIREMENTS: Open to women who, either through divorce or death of a spouse, have become the sole source of support for themselves and their families and wish to pursue a bachelor's degree in accounting. Based on commitment and need. Must submit transcripts, letters of reference, evidence of leadership potential, statement of employment history, statement of need, and statement of both professional and personal goals/objectives.
HOW TO APPLY: See website for an application. Selection made by June 15.
RENEWABLE: Yes
CONTACT: Cynthia Hires

473—EMPIRE COLLEGE (Dean's Scholarship)

3035 Cleveland Avenue
Santa Rosa CA 95403
707/546-4000
FAX: 707/546-4058
Internet: http://www.wmpcol.edu
AMOUNT: $250-$1,500
DEADLINE(S): APR 15
FIELD(S): Accounting; Office Administration; Paralegal; Medical (Clinical and Administrative); Tourism; Hospitality; General Business; Computer Assembly; Network Assembly/Administration; Security

ELIGIBILITY/REQUIREMENTS: Open to high school seniors who plan to attend Empire College. Must be U.S. citizen.
HOW TO APPLY: Contact College for an application.
NUMBER OF AWARDS: 10
RENEWABLE: No
CONTACT: Mary Farha

474—GOVERNMENT FINANCE OFFICERS ASSOCIATION (Frank L. Greathouse Government Accounting Scholarship)

Scholarship Committee
203 N. LaSalle Street, Suite 2700
Chicago IL 60601-1210
312/977-9700
Internet: http://www.gfoa.org
AMOUNT: $3,500
DEADLINE(S): FEB 15
FIELD(S): Accounting
ELIGIBILITY/REQUIREMENTS: Applicant must be a full-time student in the senior year of an undergraduate program who is preparing for a career in state and local government finance; must be a citizen or permanent resident of the U.S. or Canada; and must be recommended by the student's academic advisor or the chair of the accounting program.
HOW TO APPLY: Submit application.
NUMBER OF AWARDS: 1 or more

475—GOVERNMENT FINANCE OFFICERS ASSOCIATION (Minorities in Government Finance Scholarship)

Scholarship Committee
203 N. LaSalle Street, Suite 2700
Chicago IL 60601-1210
312/977-9700
Internet: http://www.gfoa.org
AMOUNT: $5,000
DEADLINE(S): FEB 15
FIELD(S): Public Administration; Accounting; Finance; Political Science; Economics; Business Administration (with a specific focus on government or nonprofit management)
ELIGIBILITY/REQUIREMENTS: Applicants must belong to one of the following groups: Black, Indian, Eskimo or Aleut, Asian or Pacific Islander, Hispanic; must be a citizen or permanent resident of the U.S. or Canada; and must be recommended by the student's academic advisor or department chair.
HOW TO APPLY: Send completed application.
CONTACT: www.gfoa.org/services/scholarships.shtml

476—HISPANIC COLLEGE FUND (HSF/Association of Latino Professionals in Finance and Accounting)

55 Second Street, Suite 1500
San Francisco CA 94105
1-877/HSF-INFO
(1-877/473-4636)
FAX: 415/808-2302
E-mail: pip@hsf.net
Internet: http://hispanicfund.org
AMOUNT: $1,250-$2,500
DEADLINE(S): APR 15
FIELD(S): Accounting; Finance-related
fields
ELIGIBILITY/REQUIREMENTS: Must
be U.S. citizens or legal permanent residents of Hispanic heritage (one parent fully Hispanic or both parents half Hispanic). Applicant should have earned at least 12 undergraduate college credits in the U.S. or Puerto Rico and have a minimum GPA of 3.0. Must carry at least 12 credits each term. Selection is based on academic achievement, personal strengths, leaderships and financial need.
HOW TO APPLY: Contact Fund for details or visit website for application.

477—HOSPITALITY FINANCIAL AND TECHNOLOGY PROFESSIONALS

11709 Boulder Lane, Suite 110
Austin TX 78726
512/249-5333 or 800/646-4387
FAX: 512/249-1533
Internet: http://www.hftp.org
AMOUNT: $1,000-$1,500
DEADLINE(S): JUL 15
FIELD(S): Accounting; Hospitality
Management
ELIGIBILITY/REQUIREMENTS: For
students majoring in either accounting or hospitality management at an accredited college or university.
HOW TO APPLY: Applications must come through an IAHA local chapter president. Send SASE for details.

478—INDEPENDENT POOL AND SPA SERVICE ASSOCIATION, INC. (IPSSA) SCHOLARSHIP FUND

P.O. Box 15828
Long Beach CA 90815-0828
1-888/360-9505
E-mail: ipssamail@aol.com
Internet: http://www.ipssa.com
AMOUNT: No specific limit
DEADLINE(S): Enrollment is between
MAY 1-JUL 15 and NOV 1-JAN 15;
applications must be postmarked during these periods.

FIELD(S): Any class or program that is related to the business of being a self-employed pool or spa service technician (bookkeeping, accounting, computers, chemistry, plumbing, electrical, mechanical)
ELIGIBILITY/REQUIREMENTS: Any
self-employed pool service professional whose business is in California, Arizona, Texas, or Nevada and who earns more than 50% of income from the business, and/or his/her immediate family members (i.e., spouses, children) are eligible to apply. Applicant should explain on application how the course or class is related to the business.
HOW TO APPLY: Download application from website.

479—INSTITUTE FOR HUMANE STUDIES (Koch Summer Fellow Program)

3401 N. Fairfax Drive, Suite 440
Arlington VA 22201-4432
703/993-4880 or 800/697-8799
FAX: 703/993-4890
Internet: http://www.TheIHS.org
AMOUNT: $1,500 + airfare and housing
DEADLINE(S): FEB 15
FIELD(S): Economics; Public Policy;
Law; Government; Politics
ELIGIBILITY/REQUIREMENTS:
Open to undergraduates and graduates to build skills and gain experience by participating in an 8-week summer internship program. Includes two week-long seminars, the internship, and research and writing projects with professionals. Must submit college transcripts, essays, and application. Financial need NOT a factor.
HOW TO APPLY: Apply online or contact IHS for an application.
NUMBER OF AWARDS: 32
RENEWABLE: No

480—JACKSONVILLE STATE UNIVERSITY (John H. Collins Memorial Scholarship)

Jacksonville AL 36265
256/782-5677 or 800/231-5291
Internet: www.jsu.edu
AMOUNT: Varies
FIELD(S): Accounting
ELIGIBILITY/REQUIREMENTS:
Open to students majoring in accounting.
HOW TO APPLY: Contact Accounting Department for application and details.
RENEWABLE: Yes
CONTACT: Accounting Department;
256/782-5776

481—JACKSONVILLE STATE UNIVERSITY (Robert Trathen Memorial Scholarship)

Jacksonville AL 36265
256/782-5677 or 800/231-5291
Internet: www.jsu.edu
AMOUNT: Varies
FIELD(S): Accounting
ELIGIBILITY/REQUIREMENTS:
Open to students majoring in accounting.
HOW TO APPLY: Contact Accounting Department for application and details.
RENEWABLE: Yes
CONTACT: Accounting Department;
256/782-5776

482—KENTUCKY SOCIETY OF CERTIFIED PUBLIC ACCOUNTANTS

1735 Alliant Avenue
Louisville KY 40299
502/266-5272 or 800/292-1754
FAX: 502/292-1754
E-mail: backerman@kycpa.org
Internet: http://www.cpa2b.org
AMOUNT: $1,000-$2,500
DEADLINE(S): MAR 31
FIELD(S): Accounting
ELIGIBILITY/REQUIREMENTS: Must
be enrolled in a Kentucky college or university and be a sophomore at the time of application; have an overall GPA of at least 2.75 and an Accounting GPA of 3.0; completed Principles of Accounting and be currently enrolled in or have completed intermediate Accounting.
HOW TO APPLY: Download official application form from website; submit with college transcript; essay of 500 words or less stating career goals, reasons for choosing accounting and any other relevant information; and 2 recommendations, 1 of which must be from an accounting faculty member.
NUMBER OF AWARDS: 30-35
RENEWABLE: Yes; one of the named scholarships is renewable.
CONTACT: Betty Ackerman

483—LONDON SCHOOL OF ECONOMICS AND POLITICAL SCIENCE

Financial Support Office
Houghton Street
London WC2A 2AE ENGLAND
+44 020 7955
FAX: +44 020 7216
E-mail: financialsupport@lse.ac.uk
Internet: http://www.lse.ac.uk
AMOUNT: Varies with award
DEADLINE(S): Varies
FIELD(S): Economics; Accounting;
Finance; Political Science;
International Relations

ELIGIBILITY/REQUIREMENTS: Various scholarships, awards, and prizes are available to international students. Several are for students from specific countries, and some are limited to certain fields of study. Some include all expenses, and others pay partial expenses. For undergraduates and graduate students.
HOW TO APPLY: Access LSE's website and using their "search" option, enter "scholarships," and a vast array of programs will appear.
RENEWABLE: Varies

484—NATIONAL CONFERENCE OF CPA PRACTITIONERS (NCCPAP)/AMERICAN INSTITUTE OF CERTIFIED PUBLIC ACCOUNTANTS (AICPA)

NCCPAP
23 Jericho Turnpike, Suite 110
Mineola NY 11501
516/333-8282
FAX: 516/333-4099
E-mail: lanak.ncCPAp@verizon.net
Internet: http://www.nccpap.org
AMOUNT: $1,000
DEADLINE(S): TBA (Spring)
FIELD(S): Accounting
ELIGIBILITY/REQUIREMENTS: Merit-based scholarships for graduating high school seniors planning to pursue a career as a certified public accountant; must have 3,3 minimum GPA, applied or been accepted at a 2- or 4-year college as a full-time student.
HOW TO APPLY: See website for application; submit with most recent copy of your high school transcript.
NUMBER OF AWARDS: Varies
RENEWABLE: No
CONTACT: For additional information, call 732/649-1024.

485—NATIONAL SOCIETY OF ACCOUNTANTS/NSA SCHOLARSHIP FOUNDATION (NSA Annual Awards)

1010 North Fairfax Street
Alexandria VA 22314-1574
703/549-6400 or 800-966-6679, ext. 1307
FAX: 703/549-2984
E-mail: sbrasse@nsacct.org
Internet: http://www.nsacct.org
AMOUNT: $500-$1,000
DEADLINE(S): MAR 10
FIELD(S): Accounting
ELIGIBILITY/REQUIREMENTS: Open to undergraduate accounting students in an accredited 2- or 4-year college in the U.S. who are U.S. or Canadian citizens. Must

maintain an overall GPA of 3.0. Selection based on academic attainment, leadership ability, and financial need. Payment by Foundation is made directly to your college or university.
HOW TO APPLY: See website or contact Foundation Director for an application.
RENEWABLE: 30
CONTACT: Sally Brassé

486—NATIONAL SOCIETY OF ACCOUNTANTS/NSA SCHOLARSHIP FOUNDATION (Stanley H. Stearman Scholarship Award)

1010 North Fairfax Street
Alexandria VA 22314-1574
703/549-6400 or 800-966-6679, ext. 1307
FAX: 703/549-2984
E-mail: sbrasse@nsacct.org
Internet: http://www.nsacct.org
AMOUNT: $2,000/year
DEADLINE(S): MAR 10
FIELD(S): Accounting
ELIGIBILITY/REQUIREMENTS: For U.S. or Canadian citizens in undergraduate or graduate programs in the U.S. who have a minimum 3.0 GPA. Must be the spouse, child, grandchild, niece, nephew, or son-/daughter-in-law of an active or deceased NSA member who has held membership for at least one year. Must include letter of intent, outlining reasons for seeking award, intended career objective, and how this award would be used to accomplish that objective.
HOW TO APPLY: See website or contact Foundation Director for an application.
NUMBER OF AWARDS: 1
RENEWABLE: Yes. Up to 3 years.
CONTACT: Sally Brassé

487—NEW ENGLAND EMPLOYEE BENEFITS COUNCIL

440 Totten Pond Road
Waltham MA 02145
781/684-8700
FAX: 781/684-9200
E-mail: linda@neebc.org
Internet: http://www.neebc.org
AMOUNT: Up to $5,000
DEADLINE(S): APR 1
FIELD(S): Health Care Program Design; Pension Plan Design, Implementation or Administration; Retirement Strategies; ERISA and Legal Aspects of Employee Benefits; Work/Life Programs; Health Risk Management; Institutional Investing of Retirement Savings; Multiemployer Plans;

Workers Compensation; Actuarial and Underwriting Analysis; Employee Benefits Communications
ELIGIBILITY/REQUIREMENTS: Full-time student (undergraduate or graduate) studying in an accredited academic program leading to a degree who demonstrates an interest through either course study or work experience in a career in the benefits field. Must be a New England resident or enrolled at a college in New England. Current NEEBC Board members, their spouses and children are not eligible to participate.
HOW TO APPLY: Completed application; all college transcripts; two or more references from college professors, NEEBC members, or other benefits professionals.
NUMBER OF AWARDS: 1 or 2
RENEWABLE: Yes
CONTACT: Linda Viens, Manager of Operations and Member Services

488—NEW JERSEY UTILITIES ASSOCIATION

50 West State Street, Suite 1006
Trenton NJ 08608
609/392-1000
FAX: 609/396-4231
Internet: http://www.njua.org
AMOUNT: $1,500
FIELD(S): Engineering; Environmental Science; Chemistry; Biology; Business Administration; Accounting.
ELIGIBILITY/REQUIREMENTS: Applicants must be minority (i.e., Black, Hispanic, American Indian/Alaskan Native, or Asian American/Pacific Islander), female, and/or disabled students; be a New Jersey resident; be enrolled on a full-time basis at an institute of higher education; have overall academic excellence; and demonstrate financial need. Children of employees of any NJUA member company are not eligible.
HOW TO APPLY: Contact Association.
NUMBER OF AWARDS: 2

489—NEW YORK STATE HIGHER EDUCATION SERVICES CORPORATION (N.Y. State Regents Professional/Health Care Opportunity Scholarships)

Cultural Education Center, Room 5C64
Albany NY 12230
518/486-1319
Internet: http://www.hesc.com
AMOUNT: $1,000-$10,000/year
DEADLINE(S): Varies
FIELD(S): Medicine, Dentistry and related fields; Architecture, Nursing,

Psychology, Audiology, Landscape Architecture, Social Work, Chiropractic, Law, Pharmacy, Accounting, Speech Language Pathology

ELIGIBILITY/REQUIREMENTS: Open to U.S. citizens or qualifying non-citizens who are New York State residents, economically disadvantaged, and members of a minority group underrepresented in the chosen profession and attending school in New York State.

HOW TO APPLY: See website or contact NYS HESC.

RENEWABLE: Yes

ADDITIONAL INFORMATION: Some programs carry a service obligation in New York for each year of support. Medical/dental scholarships require 1 year of professional work in New York.

490—WESTERN MICHIGAN UNIVERSITY (Haworth College of Business/Arthur Andersen Scholarship)

1903 West Michigan
Kalamazoo MI 49008-5337
269/387-6000
FAX: 269/387-6989
Internet: http://www.wmich.edu/finaid

AMOUNT: $1,000

DEADLINE(S): FEB 15

FIELD(S): Accounting

ELIGIBILITY/REQUIREMENTS: Senior undergraduate majoring in accountancy. Award based on academic accomplishment and commitment.

HOW TO APPLY: Contact Haworth College of Business Advising Office for an application.

491—WESTERN MICHIGAN UNIVERSITY (Haworth College of Business/BDO Seidman Accounting Scholarship)

1903 West Michigan
Kalamazoo MI 49008-5337
269/387-6000
FAX: 269/387-6989
Internet: http://www.wmich.edu/finaid

AMOUNT: $1,000

DEADLINE(S): FEB 15

FIELD(S): Accounting

ELIGIBILITY/REQUIREMENTS: Must be senior majoring in accountancy. Must demonstrate academic accomplishment and commitment.

HOW TO APPLY: Contact Haworth College of Business Advising Office for an application.

492—WESTERN MICHIGAN UNIVERSITY (Haworth College of Business/Crowe Chizek and Company Scholarship)

1903 West Michigan
Kalamazoo MI 49008-5337
269/387-6000
FAX: 269/387-6989
Internet: http://www.wmich.edu/finaid

AMOUNT: $1,000

DEADLINE(S): FEB 15

FIELD(S): Accounting

ELIGIBILITY/REQUIREMENTS: Must be senior majoring in accountancy. Must demonstrate academic accomplishment and commitment.

HOW TO APPLY: Contact Haworth College of Business Advising Office for an application.

493—WESTERN MICHIGAN UNIVERSITY (Haworth College of Business/David and Sandy Rozelle Accountancy Scholarship)

1903 West Michigan
Kalamazoo MI 49008-5337
269/387-6000
FAX: 269/387-6989
Internet: http://www.wmich.edu/finaid

AMOUNT: $500

DEADLINE(S): FEB 15

FIELD(S): Accounting

ELIGIBILITY/REQUIREMENTS: Must be junior majoring in accountancy. Must demonstrate academic accomplishment and commitment.

HOW TO APPLY: Contact Haworth College of Business Advising Office for an application.

NUMBER OF AWARDS: 2

494—WESTERN MICHIGAN UNIVERSITY (Haworth College of Business/Deloitte and Touche Accounting Scholarship)

1903 West Michigan
Kalamazoo MI 49008-5337
269/387-6000
FAX: 269/387-6989
Internet: http://www.wmich.edu/finaid

AMOUNT: $1,000

DEADLINE(S): FEB 15

FIELD(S): Accounting

ELIGIBILITY/REQUIREMENTS: Must be senior majoring in accountancy. Must demonstrate academic accomplishment and commitment.

HOW TO APPLY: Contact Haworth College of Business Advising Office for an application.

495—WESTERN MICHIGAN UNIVERSITY (Haworth College of Business/Ernst and Young Scholarship)

1903 West Michigan
Kalamazoo MI 49008-5337
269/387-6000
FAX: 269/387-6989
Internet: http://www.wmich.edu/finaid

AMOUNT: $500

DEADLINE(S): FEB 15

FIELD(S): Accounting

ELIGIBILITY/REQUIREMENTS: Must be senior majoring in accountancy. Must demonstrate academic accomplishment and commitment.

HOW TO APPLY: Contact Haworth College of Business Advising Office for an application.

496—WESTERN MICHIGAN UNIVERSITY (Haworth College of Business/Marshall and Poe Scholarship)

1903 West Michigan
Kalamazoo MI 49008-5337
269/387-6000
FAX: 269/387-6989
Internet: http://www.wmich.edu/finaid

AMOUNT: $1,000

DEADLINE(S): FEB 15

FIELD(S): Accounting

ELIGIBILITY/REQUIREMENTS: Must be senior majoring in accountancy. Must demonstrate academic accomplishment and commitment.

HOW TO APPLY: Contact Haworth College of Business Advising Office for an application.

497—WESTERN MICHIGAN UNIVERSITY (Haworth College of Business/Plante and Moran Accountancy Scholarship)

1903 West Michigan
Kalamazoo MI 49008-5337
269/387-6000
FAX: 269/387-6989
Internet: http://www.wmich.edu/finaid

AMOUNT: $1,000

DEADLINE(S): FEB 15

FIELD(S): Accounting

ELIGIBILITY/REQUIREMENTS: Must be senior majoring in accountancy. Must demonstrate academic accomplishment and commitment.

HOW TO APPLY: Contact Haworth College of Business Advising Office for an application.

498—WESTERN MICHIGAN UNIVERSITY (Haworth College of Business/ Pricewaterhouse Coopers Scholarship)

1903 West Michigan
Kalamazoo MI 49008-5337
269/387-6000
FAX: 269/387-6989
Internet: http://www.wmich.edu/finaid
AMOUNT: $1,000
DEADLINE(S): FEB 15
FIELD(S): Accounting
ELIGIBILITY/REQUIREMENTS: Must be senior majoring in accountancy. Must demonstrate academic accomplishment and commitment.
HOW TO APPLY: Contact Haworth College of Business Advising Office for an application.

499—WESTERN MICHIGAN UNIVERSITY (Haworth College of Business/Seigfried, Crandall, Vos, & Lewis Scholarship)

1903 West Michigan
Kalamazoo MI 49008-5337
269/387-6000
FAX: 269/387-6989
Internet: http://www.wmich.edu/finaid
AMOUNT: $1,000
DEADLINE(S): FEB 15
FIELD(S): Accounting
ELIGIBILITY/REQUIREMENTS: Must be senior majoring in accountancy. Must demonstrate academic accomplishment and commitment.
HOW TO APPLY: Contact Haworth College of Business Advising Office for an application.

500—WYOMING TRUCKING ASSOCIATION

P.O. Box 1909
Casper WY 82602
AMOUNT: $500-$1,000
DEADLINE(S): MAR 1
FIELD(S): Transportation Industry including safety, diesel mechanics, truck driving, business management, computer skills, accounting, office procedures, management and related fields
ELIGIBILITY/REQUIREMENTS: For Wyoming high school graduates enrolled in a Wyoming college, approved trade school, or the University of Wyoming. Must be pursuing a course of study that will result in a career in the transportation industry in Wyoming, including but not limited to: safety, diesel mechanics, truck driving, business management, computer skills, accounting, office procedures, and management.
HOW TO APPLY: Write to WYTA for an application.
NUMBER OF AWARDS: 1-10

BUSINESS ADMINISTRATION

501—ACADEMY OF CANADIAN CINEMA AND TELEVISION (Internship; National Apprenticeship Training Program)

172 King Street East
Toronto Ontario M5A 1J3
CANADA
800/644-5194
FAX: 416/366/8454
E-mail: info@academy.ca
Internet: http://www.academy.ca/dev/natp.htm/Academy/About/GeneralACCTInfo.html
AMOUNT: $300 (Canadian) per week for 12 weeks
DEADLINE(S): MARCH
FIELD(S): Film and Television Production and Management
ELIGIBILITY/REQUIREMENTS: Program designed to provide hands-on professional training to students in their graduating year from film and/or television diploma/degree programs. Must be Canadian citizen or landed immigrant studying full time in Canada.
HOW TO APPLY: See website or contact Academy for application for complete information.
NUMBER OF AWARDS: 6
CONTACT: Jennifer Clapp

502—AIRCRAFT ELECTRONICS ASSOCIATION EDUCATIONAL FOUNDATION (Chuck Peacock Memorial Scholarship)

4217 South Hocker
Independence MO 64055
816/373-6565
FAX: 816/478-3100
E-mail: info@aea.net
Internet: http://aeaavnews.org
AMOUNT: $1,000
DEADLINE(S): FEB 1
FIELD(S): Aviation Management
ELIGIBILITY/REQUIREMENTS: This scholarship recognizes the importance of management skills and is available to high school seniors and/or college students who plan to or are attending an accredited school in an aviation management program.
HOW TO APPLY: See website for application and detailed instructions. An essay and transcript will be required with application.
NUMBER OF AWARDS: 1
CONTACT: Attn: Scholarship Application

503—AIR FORCE RESERVE OFFICER TRAINING CORPS (AFROTC Scholarships)

551 E. Maxwell Boulevard
Maxwell AFB AL 36112-6106
866/4AFROTC
E-mail: info@afrotc.com
Internet: http://www.afrotc.com
AMOUNT: Varies, but up to full tuition and fees plus $600/year for books
DEADLINE(S): DEC 1
FIELD(S): Science; Engineering; Business; Political Science; Psychology; Geography; Foreign Studies; Foreign Language
ELIGIBILITY/REQUIREMENTS: 4- and 3-year competitive scholarships based on individual merit to high school seniors and graduates who have not enrolled full time at a college or university. Academic performance is measured using an academic composite, which combines SAT (Math and Verbal only)/ACT scores, class rank, GPA and the number of advanced placement or honors courses completed through grade 11. To be eligible for consideration, students should achieve a 1100 SAT (Math and Verbal only) or 24 ACT, minimum 3.0 GPA and class ranking in the top 40%. Must be a U.S. citizen between the ages of 17-27. Must also have GPA of 2.5 or above, be in top 40% of class, and complete Applicant Fitness Test. Cannot be a single parent. Your college or university must offer AFROTC.
HOW TO APPLY: Visit www.afrotc.com to apply.
NUMBER OF AWARDS: N/A
RENEWABLE: No

504—AMERICAN ASSOCIATION OF AIRPORT EXECUTIVES

601 Madison Street, Suite 400
Alexandria VA 22314
703-824-0500
FAX: 703-820-1395
Internet: http://www.aaae.org/
AMOUNT: $1,000
DEADLINE(S): MAY 15
FIELD(S): Airport Management; Airport Administration
ELIGIBILITY/REQUIREMENTS: Scholarships for undergraduates who have reached junior standing or higher through graduate school. Selection based on scholastic achievement, financial need, and

extracurricular/community activities. Must be focusing on a career in airport management and have at least a 3.0 GPA.
HOW TO APPLY: Must be nominated by university; contact your university for additional information. Each university may submit only 1 student's application.
NUMBER OF AWARDS: 10

505—AMERICAN HEALTH AND BEAUTY AIDS INSTITUTE (Fred Luster Sr. Education Foundation Scholarships for College-Bound High School Seniors)

PO Box 19510
Chicago IL 60619
708/333-8740
FAX: 708/333-8741
AMOUNT: $250-$500
DEADLINE(S): APR 15
FIELD(S): Chemistry, Business, Engineering
ELIGIBILITY/REQUIREMENTS: Open to college-bound high school seniors who will be enrolled as a college freshman in a 4-year college majoring in chemistry, business, or engineering. 3.0 GPA required. Scholastic record, financial need, school activities, and extracurricular activities considered.
HOW TO APPLY: Send two letters of recommendation (one from a school official) and high school transcript.
NUMBER OF AWARDS: 2

506—AMERICAN HOTEL & LODGING EDUCATIONAL FOUNDATION (AAA Five Diamond Hospitality Scholarship, The)

1201 New York Avenue NW, Suite 600
Washington DC 20005-3931
202/289-3188
FAX: 202/289-3199
E-mail: ahlef@ahlef.org
Internet: http://www. ahlef.org
AMOUNT: $5,000
DEADLINE(S): MAY 1
FIELD(S): Hospitality/Hotel Management; Travel & Tourism; Culinary Arts
ELIGIBILITY/REQUIREMENTS: Each year, AAA selects one of the 4-year programs participating in AH&LEF's Annual Scholarship Grant Program to receive the award.
HOW TO APPLY: The chosen school selects the scholarship recipient based upon a set of minimum eligibility criteria. See website for additional information and name of school chosen each year.

507—AMERICAN HOTEL & LODGING EDUCATIONAL FOUNDATION (American Express Academic Scholarships)

1201 New York Avenue NW, Suite 600
Washington DC 20005-3931
202/289-3188
FAX: 202/289-3199
E-mail: ahlef@ahlef.org
Internet: http://www.ei-ahlef.org
AMOUNT: $500-$2,000
DEADLINE(S): MAY 1
FIELD(S): Hospitality/Hotel Management; Travel & Tourism; Culinary Arts
ELIGIBILITY/REQUIREMENTS: For full-time (minimum 20 hours/week) AH&LA-member property employees and their dependents enrolled in accredited, undergraduate academic programs leading to a degree in hospitality management. The applicant does not have to attend an AH& LEF-affiliated school.
HOW TO APPLY: Applications available on website.

508—AMERICAN HOTEL & LODGING EDUCATION FOUNDATION (Annual Scholarship Grant Program)

1201 New York Avenue NW, Suite 600
Washington DC 20005-3931
202/289-3188
FAX: 202/289-3199
E-mail: ahlef@ahlef.org
Internet: http://www.ahlef.org
AMOUNT: Varies
DEADLINE(S): MAY 1
FIELD(S): Hospitality/Hotel Management
ELIGIBILITY/REQUIREMENTS: Co-administered with 79 2- and 4-year universities and colleges in the United States offering hospitality management programs (see website for complete list) that are affiliated with AH&LEF. Criteria include full-time enrollment status, minimum GPA of 3.0, U.S. citizenship or permanent U.S. resident status, and completion of at least 1 or 2 years of school. Note: A few scholarships have slightly different criteria, depending on the program. Interested students should inquire at their school's dean's office.
HOW TO APPLY: Schools must submit their student nominations to the Foundation for upcoming academic year.

509—AMERICAN HOTEL & LODGING EDUCATION FOUNDATION (Arthur J. Packard Memorial Scholarship Competition, The)

1201 New York Avenue NW, Suite 600
Washington DC 20005-3931
202/289-3188
FAX: 202/289-3199
E-mail: ahlef@ahlef.org
Internet: http://www.ahlef.org
AMOUNT: $5,000 (1st place); $3,000 (2nd place); $2,000 (3rd place)
DEADLINE(S): MAY 1
FIELD(S): Hospitality/Hotel Management
ELIGIBILITY/REQUIREMENTS: Provides scholarships to the most outstanding students of lodging management and 2 runner-ups through an annual competition among the AH&LEF-affiliated 4-year programs.
HOW TO APPLY: Each university nominates the one student most qualified according to the criteria to compete in the national competition. Students should inquire in their dean's office for consideration of the nomination and application.
NUMBER OF AWARDS: 3

510—AMERICAN HOTEL & LODGING EDUCATION FOUNDATION (Ecolab Certification Scholarships) (Lodging Management Program [LMP])

1201 New York Avenue NW, Suite 600
Washington DC 20005-3931
202/289-3188
FAX: 202/289-3199
E-mail: ahlef@ahlef.org
Internet: http://www.ahlef.org
AMOUNT: Varies (cost of certification)
DEADLINE(S): APR 1
FIELD(S): Hospitality/Hotel Management
ELIGIBILITY/REQUIREMENTS: Applicants must be hospitality professionals working at an AH&EF member property a minimum of 35 hours per week and qualify for the certification program. The scholarship includes the cost of the certification for the following professional designations: Certified Hotel Administrator, Certified Engineering Operations Executive, Certified Lodging Manager, and Certified Hospitality Housekeeping Executive.

HOW TO APPLY: Call EI at 800/349-0299 or visit www.ei-ahla.org for certification information.

511—AMERICAN HOTEL & LODGING EDUCATION FOUNDATION (Hyatt Hotel Fund for Minority Lodging Management Students)

1201 New York Avenue NW,
Suite 600
Washington DC 20005-3931
202/289-3188
FAX: 202/289-3199
E-mail: ahf@ahlef.org
Internet: http://www.ahlef.org
AMOUNT: $2,000
DEADLINE(S): APR 1
FIELD(S): Hospitality/Hotel
   Management
ELIGIBILITY/REQUIREMENTS: For minority students pursuing a 4-year undergraduate degree in hospitality or hotel management on a full-time basis (minimum 12 hours/week). Recipients are nominated by their colleges. Criteria are academic performance, hospitality work experience, extracurricular involvement, career goals, and financial need.
HOW TO APPLY: Inquire at your dean's office; applications are sent directly to the schools between January and March each year.
NUMBER OF AWARDS: Approximately 18

512—AMERICAN HOTEL & LODGING EDUCATION FOUNDATION (Lodging Management Program [LMP])

1201 New York Avenue NW,
Suite 600
Washington DC 20005-3931
202/289-3188
FAX: 202/289-3199
E-mail: ahlef@ahlef.org
Internet: http://www.ahlef.org
AMOUNT: Varies (cost of certification)
DEADLINE(S): APR 1
FIELD(S): Hospitality/Hotel
   Management
ELIGIBILITY/REQUIREMENTS: Open to high school students who have successfully completed both years of the LMP high school curriculum for accredited undergraduate hospitality management degree-granting program or in an Educational Institute distance learning course or professional certification.
HOW TO APPLY: See website or consult instructor for additional information and

application; submit with essay of no more than 500 words describing your personal background, including how you learned about and why you took the LMP class; what you learned most from your LMP class; what the most important and most interesting part of this class was; why you think the hospitality industry is the right career choice for you; and how this scholarship will help you achieve your career objectives and future goals. Also required are your most recent high school transcript including GPA; a copy of your college curriculum; and a copy of acceptance letter.

513—AMERICAN INTERCONTINENTAL UNIVERSITY (Emilio Pucci Scholarships)

Admissions Committee
3330 Peachtree Road NE
Atlanta GA 30326
404/812-8192 or 888/248-7392
AMOUNT: $1,800 (applied toward tuition over 6 quarters)
DEADLINE(S): None
FIELD(S): Fashion Design; Fashion
   Marketing; Interior Design;
   Commercial Art; Business
   Administration; Video Production
ELIGIBILITY/REQUIREMENTS: Scholarships are for high school seniors who are interested in either a 2-year or 4-year program at one of the campuses of the American Intercontinental University: Atlanta, GA; Los Angeles, CA; London, UK; or Dubai, United Arab Emirates.
HOW TO APPLY: Write for application and complete information.

514—AMERICAN SOCIETY OF TRANSPORTATION & LOGISTICS, THE (The L. L. Waters Scholarship Program)

1400 Eye Street, NW, Suite 1050
Washington DC 20005
202/580-7270
FAX: 202/962-3939
E-mail: info@astl.org
Internet: http://www.astl.org
AMOUNT: $2,000
FIELD(S): Transportation; Logistics;
   Physical Distribution
ELIGIBILITY/REQUIREMENTS: Applicants must be undergraduate students in their junior year at a fully accredited 4-year U.S. college or university. Awards are based on scholastic performance and potential as well as evidence of the degree of commitment to the pursuit of a professional career in transportation/logistics/physical distribution.

HOW TO APPLY: Send completed application to the Scholarship Judging Panel; official transcript; 2 letters of recommendation (sent separately) from faculty members of the applicant's school who have major teaching and research commitments in transportation/logistics/physical distribution.
CONTACT: Laurie Denham, Executive Director

515—APICS EDUCATION AND RESEARCH FOUNDATION (Donald W. Fogarty International Student Paper Competition)

5301 Shawnee Road
Alexandria VA 22312
800/444-2742
Internet: http://www.apics.org
AMOUNT: $100-$1,700+
DEADLINE(S): MAY 15
FIELD(S): Production/Operations
   Management; Resource Management
ELIGIBILITY/REQUIREMENTS: Awards offered for winning papers on the subject of production and operations management or resource management, including inventory issues. Open to full-time or part-time undergraduate or graduate students; NOT for high school students. Financial need is NOT a factor.
HOW TO APPLY: Participants must submit papers to their local APICS chapter. Use the APICS Chapter Locator to find the APICS chapter nearest you. For complete information, visit website (http://www.apics.org/Education/ERFoundation/Competitions/dwf.htm) or call APICS.
NUMBER OF AWARDS: Up to 90

516—ART INSTITUTES INTERNATIONAL, THE (Evelyn Keedy Memorial Scholarship)

300 Sixth Avenue, Suite 800
Pittsburgh PA 15222-2598
412/562-9800
FAX: 412/562-9802
E-mail: webadmin@aii.edu
Internet: http://www.aii.edu
AMOUNT: 2 years' full tuition
DEADLINE(S): MAY 1
FIELD(S): Various fields in the creative and applied arts: video production, broadcasting, culinary arts, fashion design, website administration, and related fields
ELIGIBILITY/REQUIREMENTS: Scholarships at 12 different locations nationwide in various fields described above. For graduating high school seniors

admitted to an Art Institutes International School, the New York Restaurant School, or NCPT.
HOW TO APPLY: See website or contact AII for more information. Transcripts, letters of recommendation, and résumé must be submitted with application.
NUMBER OF AWARDS: Multiple

517—AVIATION DISTRIBUTORS AND MANUFACTURERS ASSOCIATION INTERNATIONAL (ADMA International Scholarship Fund)

1900 Arch Street
Philadelphia PA 19103-1498
215/564-3484
FAX: 215/564-2175
E-mail: assnhqt@netaxs.com
AMOUNT: Varies
DEADLINE(S): MAR 15
FIELD(S): Aviation Management; Professional Pilot; Aviation Maintenance; Aeronautics
ELIGIBILITY/REQUIREMENTS: Open to students seeking a career in aviation management or as a professional pilot. Emphasis may be in general aviation, airway science management, aviation maintenance, flight engineering, or airway air-conditioning systems management. Applicants must be studying in the aviation field in a 4-year school having an aviation program.
HOW TO APPLY: Write for complete information.

518—AYN RAND INSTITUTE (Atlas Shrugged Essay Competition)

Atlas Shrugged Essay Contest
Department W
2121 Alton Parkway, Suite 250
Irvine CA 92606
E-mail: essay@aynrand.org
Internet: http://www.aynrand.org/contests/
AMOUNT: First prize: $5,000; second prizes: $1,000; third prizes: $400; finalist prizes: $100; semifinalist prizes: $50 cash awards
DEADLINE(S): FEB 15
FIELD(S): Business; Philosophy
ELIGIBILITY/REQUIREMENTS: Open to students enrolled in a graduate or undergraduate business-degree program who write a 1,000–1,200-word essay on Ayn Rand's *Atlas Shrugged*. Essays judged on style and content and must demonstrate an outstanding grasp of the philosophical meaning of *Atlas Shrugged*.
HOW TO APPLY: See website or contact your Business Ethics professor for guide-

lines. Do NOT write to above address. Essays will be judged on both style and content. Judges will look for writing that is clear, articulate, and logically organized. Winning essays must demonstrate an outstanding grasp of the philosophic meaning of *Atlas Shrugged*. Essays may be submitted online.
NUMBER OF AWARDS: 48 (1 first, 3 second, 5 third, 20 finalist, 20 semifinalist)

519—BLUES HEAVEN FOUNDATION, INC. (Muddy Waters Scholarship)

2120 S. Michigan Avenue
Chicago IL 60616
312/808-1286
AMOUNT: $2,000
DEADLINE(S): APR 30
FIELD(S): Music; Music Education; African American Studies; Folklore; Performing Arts; Arts Management; Journalism; Radio/TV/Film
ELIGIBILITY/REQUIREMENTS: Scholarship awarded on a competitive basis with consideration given to scholastic achievement, concentration of studies, and financial need. Applicant must be full-time graduate or undergraduate in a Chicago area college or university. Scholastic aptitude, extracurricular involvement, GPA, and financial need are all considered.
HOW TO APPLY: Contact Foundation between February and April to request an application.

520—CELANESE CANADA, INC. (AUCC)

350 Albert Street, Suite 600
Ottawa Ontario K1R 1B1
CANADA
613/563-1236
FAX: 613/563-9745
E-mail: awards@aucc.ca
Internet: http://www.aucc.ca
AMOUNT: $1,500 (Canadian)
DEADLINE(S): JUL 2
FIELD(S): Mechanical and Chemical Engineering; Chemistry; Business Administration and Commerce
ELIGIBILITY/REQUIREMENTS: Open to Canadian citizens/permanent residents for their final year of an undergraduate program in one of above fields. Must attend a college or university that is a member, or affiliated to a member, of the Association of Universities and Colleges of Canada. Candidates are expected to have achieved a high level of academic excellence as well as to have exhibited superior intellectual ability and judgment. In some cases, study in certain province/school is required.

HOW TO APPLY: Applications are by nomination only. See website or contact AUCC for nomination procedures.
RENEWABLE: No

521—CLUB FOUNDATION, THE

1733 King Street
Alexandria VA 22314
703/739-9500
FAX: 703/739-0124
E-mail: ashleigh.hill@clubfoundation.org
Internet: http://www.clubfoundation.org
AMOUNT: $2,500
DEADLINE(S): APR 15
FIELD(S): Business Administration; Hospitality
ELIGIBILITY/REQUIREMENTS: Candidates must provide strong evidence that they are pursuing managerial careers in the private club industry. A candidate must have completed his/her freshman year of college and be enrolled for the full academic year in an accredited 4-year institution. In addition, the candidate must have achieved and continue to maintain a GPA of at least 2.5 on a 4.0 scale, or 4.5 on a 6.0 scale. Additional points are awarded for CMMA chapter members.
HOW TO APPLY: Application available on website; write an essay addressing the questions; attach an official, current transcript; include recommendation letter from an advisor/professor and a private club industry professional; include a copy of current résumé.
NUMBER OF AWARDS: 2
RENEWABLE: No
CONTACT: Ashleigh Hill, Program Specialist

522—COLORADO RESTAURANT ASSOCIATION (Scholarship Education Fund)

430 E. 7th Avenue
Denver CO 80203
800/522-2972 or 303/830-2972
FAX: 303/830-2973
E-mail: info@coloradorestaurant.com
Internet: http://www.coloradorestaurant.com
AMOUNT: $500-$2,500
DEADLINE(S): MAR 20
FIELD(S): Food service; Hospitality
ELIGIBILITY/REQUIREMENTS: Open to junior- and senior-level college students enrolled in a 2- or 4-year degree program in food service and hospitality-related fields at a Colorado college or university.
HOW TO APPLY: Contact CRA for an application.

523—EMPIRE COLLEGE (Dean's Scholarship)

3035 Cleveland Avenue
Santa Rosa CA 95403
707/546-4000
FAX: 707/546-4058
Internet: http://www.wmpcol.edu
AMOUNT: $250-$1,500
DEADLINE(S): APR 15
FIELD(S): Accounting; Office Administration; Paralegal; Medical (Clinical and Administrative); Tourism; Hospitality; General Business; Computer Assembly; Network Assembly/Administration; Security
ELIGIBILITY/REQUIREMENTS: Open to high school seniors who plan to attend Empire College. Must be U.S. citizen.
HOW TO APPLY: Contact College for an application.
NUMBER OF AWARDS: 10
RENEWABLE: No
CONTACT: Mary Farha

524—GOVERNMENT FINANCE OFFICERS ASSOCIATION (Minorities in Government Finance Scholarship)

Scholarship Committee
203 N. LaSalle Street, Suite 2700
Chicago IL 60601-1210
312/977-9700
Internet: http://www.gfoa.org
AMOUNT: $5,000
DEADLINE(S): FEB 15
FIELD(S): Public Administration; Accounting; Finance; Political Science; Economics; Business Administration (with a specific focus on government or nonprofit management)
ELIGIBILITY/REQUIREMENTS: Applicants must belong to one of the following groups: Black, Indian, Eskimo or Aleut, Asian or Pacific Islander, Hispanic; must be a citizen or permanent resident of the U.S. or Canada; and must be recommended by the student's academic advisor or department chair.
HOW TO APPLY: Send completed application.
CONTACT: www.gfoa.org/services/scholarships.shtml

525—HAWAII COMMUNITY FOUNDATION (George Mason Business Scholarship Fund)

1164 Bishop Street, Suite 800
Honolulu HI 96813
808/537-6333 or toll free:
888/731-3863
FAX: 808/521-6286
E-mail: info@hcf-hawaii.org
Internet: http://www.hcf-hawaii.org
DEADLINE(S): MAR 1
FIELD(S): Business Administration
ELIGIBILITY/REQUIREMENTS: Applicants must be residents of Hawaii; be seniors enrolled full time in an accredited 4-year college or university in Hawaii; and demonstrate financial need, good moral character, and academic achievement with a minimum GPA of 3.0.
HOW TO APPLY: Send application with 2 letters of recommendation and a personal statement describing why you chose business as an intended career and how you expect to make a difference in the business world.

526—HOSPITALITY FINANCIAL AND TECHNOLOGY PROFESSIONALS

11709 Boulder Lane, Suite 110
Austin TX 78726
512/249-5333 or 800/646-4387
FAX: 512/249-1533
Internet: http://www.hftp.org
AMOUNT: $1,000-$1,500
DEADLINE(S): JUL 15
FIELD(S): Accounting; Hospitality Management
ELIGIBILITY/REQUIREMENTS: For students majoring in either accounting or hospitality management at an accredited college or university.
HOW TO APPLY: Applications must come through an IAHA local chapter president. Send SASE for details.

526A—INDEPENDENT POOL AND SPA SERVICE ASSOCIATION, INC. (IPSSA) SCHOLARSHIP FUND

P.O. Box 15828
Long Beach CA 90815-0828
1-888/360-9505
E-mail: ipssamail@aol.com
Internet: http://www.ipssa.com
AMOUNT: No specific limit
DEADLINE(S): Enrollment is between MAY 1-JUL 15 and NOV 1-JAN 15; applications must be postmarked during these periods
FIELD(S): Any class or program related to self-employment as pool or spa service technician (bookkeeping, accounting, computers, chemistry, plumbing, electrical, mechanical)
ELIGIBILITY/REQUIREMENTS: Any self-employed pool service professional whose business is in California, Arizona, Texas, or Nevada and who earns more than 50% of income from the business, and/or his/her immediate family members (i.e., spouses, children) are eligible to apply. Applicant should explain on application how the course or class is related to the business.
HOW TO APPLY: Download application from website.

527—INSTITUTE FOR HUMANE STUDIES (Summer Seminars Program)

3401 N. Fairfax Drive, Suite 440
Arlington VA 22201-4432
703/993-4880 or 800/697-8799
FAX: 703/993-4890
Internet: http://www.TheIHS.org
AMOUNT: Free summer seminars, including room/board, lectures, seminar materials, and books
DEADLINE(S): MAR
FIELD(S): Social Sciences; Humanities; Law; Journalism; Public Policy; Education; Film; Writing; Economics; Philosophy
ELIGIBILITY/REQUIREMENTS: Open to college students, recent graduates, and graduate students who share an interest in learning and exchanging ideas about the scope of individual rights, free markets, the rule of law, peace, and tolerance.
HOW TO APPLY: See website for seminar information and to apply online, or contact IHS for an application.

528—INSTITUTE FOR OPERATIONS RESEARCH AND THE MANAGEMENT SCIENCES (George Nicholson Student Paper Competition)

7240 Parkway Drive, Suite 310
Hanover MD 21076-1310
443/757-3500 or 800/446-3676
FAX: 443/757-3515
E-mail: informs@informs.org
Internet: http://www.informs.org/INTERN/
AMOUNT: $600 (first place), $300 (second place), $100 (honorable mention)
DEADLINE(S): JUN 30
FIELD(S): Fields related to information management: business management, engineering, mathematics
ELIGIBILITY/REQUIREMENTS: Entrant must have been a student on or after January 1 of the year; the paper must present original research results and must have been conducted while entrant was a student; must be written with only minor editorial assistance (advisors may appear as co-authors, but the student must be "first author").
HOW TO APPLY: Paper must not exceed 25 pages with 35 lines of text (excluding references). Electronic submissions (PDF)

and hard copy are required. Entry must be accompanied by a letter signed by both a faculty advisor and the entrant attesting that the eligibility conditions have been satisfied. For additional information, see website.
NUMBER OF AWARDS: Up to 6
RENEWABLE: No
CONTACT: Committee Chair (see website for current year's chairperson and contact information)
ADDITIONAL INFORMATION: First- and second-place awards will be announced at the Awards Ceremony.

529—INSTITUTE FOR OPERATIONS RESEARCH AND THE MANAGEMENT SCIENCES (INFORMS Summer Internship Directory)

7240 Parkway Drive, Suite 310
Hanover MD 21076-1310
443/757-3500 or 800/446-3676
FAX: 443/757-3515
E-mail: informs@informs.org
Internet: http://www.informs.org/ INTERN/
AMOUNT: Varies
DEADLINE(S): Varies
FIELD(S): Fields related to information management: business management, engineering, mathematics
ELIGIBILITY/REQUIREMENTS: See website listing of summer internships in the field of operations research and management sciences. Both applicants and employers can register online.
HOW TO APPLY: See website for list.
NUMBER OF AWARDS: Varies

530—INTERNATIONAL FACILITY MANAGEMENT ASSOCIATION (Student Scholarships)

1 East Greenway Plaza, Suite 1100
Houston TX 77046-0194
Internet: http://www.ifma.org
AMOUNT: $1,000-$5,000
DEADLINE(S): MAY 31
FIELD(S): Facility Management
ELIGIBILITY/REQUIREMENTS: Open to full-time graduate and junior- or senior-level undergraduate students who are enrolled in a facility management or related program. Graduates must have a minimum 3.0 GPA; undergrads must have a minimum 2.75 GPA. Students may not be employed full time as a facility management professional.
HOW TO APPLY: See website or contact IFMA Foundation for an application. Must submit official transcripts, letter of professional intent, and 2 appraisals.

531—JORGE MAS CANOSA FREEDOM FOUNDATION (Mas Family Scholarships)

P.O. Box 14-1898
Miami FL 33114
305/529-0075, ext.35
E-mail: mmartinez@jmcffmas familyscholarships.org
Internet: http://www.jmcffmas scholarships.org
AMOUNT: Up to $10,000
DEADLINE(S): MAR 31
FIELD(S): Engineering, Business, International Relations, Economics, Communications, Journalism
ELIGIBILITY/REQUIREMENTS: For Cuban-American students, graduates and undergraduates, born in Cuba or direct descendants (1 parent or 2 grandparents) of those who left Cuba. Must be in top 10% of high school class or maintain a 3.5 GPA in college. Financial need considered along with academic success, SAT and GRE scores, and leadership potential.
HOW TO APPLY: Contact Foundation for application. 2 short essays and 2 character evaluations along with proof of Cuban descent required.
NUMBER OF AWARDS: 10
RENEWABLE: Yes. Maximum $40,000; must reapply.

532—JUNIOR ACHIEVEMENT INC. (The Walt Disney Company Foundation Scholarship)

One Education Way
Colorado Springs CO 80906-4477
719/540-8000
FAX: 719/540-6299
E-mail: newmedia@ja.org
Internet: http://www.ja.org
AMOUNT: Full tuition
DEADLINE(S): FEB 1
FIELD(S): Business Administration; Fine Arts
ELIGIBILITY/REQUIREMENTS: Applicants must be graduating high school seniors with excellent academic and extracurricular credentials who have participated in JA Company Program or JA Economics.
HOW TO APPLY: Send completed application and 3 letters of recommendation: 1 from a JA Company Program or JA Economics consultant, and 2 others.
NUMBER OF AWARDS: 1
RENEWABLE: Yes, annually up to 4 years.
CONTACT: To obtain application, contact Scholarship/Education Team, Junior Achievement Inc. at 954/566-8623; submit complete application to Walt Disney

Scholarship, Junior Achievement Inc., P.O. Box 5186, Fort Lauderdale FL 33310.

533—LOUISIANA STATE UNIVERSITY AT SHREVEPORT (College of Business Administration Scholarships)

One University Place
Shreveport LA 71115-2399
318/797-5363
FAX: 318/797-5366
E-mail: finaid@pilot.lsus.edu
Internet: http://www.lsus.edu
AMOUNT: Varies
DEADLINE(S): Varies
FIELD(S): Business Administration
ELIGIBILITY/REQUIREMENTS: A number of scholarships are funded for business students enrolled at various levels at LSUS.
HOW TO APPLY: Contact the Dean's Office in the College of Business Administration at LSUS for details on specific scholarships.
CONTACT: Dean's Office

534—MIDWAY COLLEGE

512 East Stephens Street
Midway KY 40347
800/755-0031
E-mail: admissions@midway.edu
Internet: http://www.midway.edu
AMOUNT: Up to full tuition
DEADLINE(S): Varies
FIELD(S): Nursing; Education; Psychology; Biology; Equine Studies; Computer Information Systems; Business Administration; English; Pre-Med; Pre-Vet
ELIGIBILITY/REQUIREMENTS: Merit scholarships for admitted students who are considered full time in Midway's women's college. Depending on scholarship, minimum GPA ranges from 2.5 to 3.2, minimum ACT ranges 18 to 29, minimum SAT from 860 to 1290. In some cases, students must live on campus.
HOW TO APPLY: Contact Admissions Office or high school guidance counselor for application. Complete FAFSA online.
NUMBER OF AWARDS: Varies (up to 100)
RENEWABLE: Yes. Must meet GPA requirements which vary based on the scholarship.
CONTACT: Admissions Office or high school guidance counselor
ADDITIONAL INFORMATION: Athletes may be eligible for an athletic scholarship in conjunction with a merit grant; contact coach for eligibility and award information.

535—NATIONAL ASSOCIATION OF WATER COMPANIES-NEW JERSEY CHAPTER

Elizabethtown Water Co.
600 South Avenue
Westfield NJ 07091
908/654-1234
FAX: 908/232-2719
E-mail: gbradygbconsult
@comcast.net
AMOUNT: $2,500
DEADLINE(S): APR 1
FIELD(S): Business Administration;
Biology; Chemistry; Engineering
Communications
ELIGIBILITY/REQUIREMENTS: For
U.S. citizens who have lived in NJ at least 5
years and plan a career in the investor-
owned water utility industry in disciplines
such as those above. Must be undergradu-
ate or graduate student in a 2- or 4-year NJ
college or university. GPA of 3.0 or better
required.
HOW TO APPLY: Contact Association
for complete information.
CONTACT: Gail P. Brady

536—NATIONAL DEFENSE TRANS-PORTATION ASSOCIATION—NDTA (Academic Scholarship Program A)

50 S Pickett Street, Suite 220
Alexandria VA 22304-7296
703/751-5011
FAX: 703/823-8761
E-mail: mark@ndtahq.com
Internet: http://www.ndtahq.com
AMOUNT: Varies, approximately $500-
$2,000
DEADLINE(S): APR 16
FIELD(S): Transportation; Physical
Distribution; Logistics; Information
Technology
ELIGIBILITY/REQUIREMENTS: Must
be an NDTA member or financial depen-
dent of a member; must have completed 45
semester hours satisfactorily at an accredit-
ed college; college must offer at least 15
semester hours in the above fields; must
take at least 15 semester hours of these
types of courses; scholarships are limited to
undergraduate degrees.
HOW TO APPLY: Applications available
from national headquarters or download
from website.
NUMBER OF AWARDS: Varies,
approximately 15
RENEWABLE: Yes. Must reapply and
submit updated transcripts.
CONTACT: Mark Victorson, Executive
Assistant

537—NATIONAL POULTRY AND FOOD DISTRIBUTORS ASSOCIATION SCHOLARSHIP FOUNDATION

958 McEver Road Extension,
Unit B8
Gainesville GA 30504
770/535-9901
FAX: 770/535-7385
E-mail: kkm@npfda.org
Internet: http://www.npfda.org
AMOUNT: $1,500 to $2,000 each/annual
DEADLINE(S): MAY 31
FIELD(S): Poultry, Food, or related agri-
cultural degree; Food Science;
Dietetics; Poultry Science; Agricultural
Economics; International Business, etc.
ELIGIBILITY/REQUIREMENTS: Must
be enrolled full time as a college junior or
senior the upcoming (award) year at a U.S.
institution pursuing one of the above
fields.
HOW TO APPLY: Complete application
and provide your current official tran-
script, letter of recommendation from your
dean, along with a 1-page letter describing
your goals and aspirations.
NUMBER OF AWARDS: 4
RENEWABLE: No
CONTACT: Kristin McWhorter

538—NATIONAL TOURISM FOUNDATION (NTF Scholarships)

P.O. Box 3071
Lexington KY 40596-3071
800/682-8886
FAX: 606/226-4414
Internet: http://www.ntfonline.com
AMOUNT: $3,000 personal stipend to
offset travel and lodging expenses
while in Lexington, Kentucky
DEADLINE(S): APR 15
FIELD(S): Travel and Tourism;
Hospitality; Restaurant Management
ELIGIBILITY/REQUIREMENTS:
Various scholarships for full-time students
at 2- or 4-year colleges or universities in
North America who are entering their
junior or senior year of study. Must be a
strong academic performer and have at
least a 3.0 GPA. Degree emphasis must be
in a travel- and tourism-related field, such
as hotel management, restaurant management, or tourism.
HOW TO APPLY: Send a completed copy of
the National Tourism Foundation Internship
Application, which is available from website;
a typed résumé; information on any work or
internship experience in travel and tourism;
and information on any extracurricular or volunteer experience. See website for additional
requirements of each individual scholarship.

Students may apply for more than one award
but may only receive one.
NUMBER OF AWARDS: 2

539—NEW ENGLAND WATER WORKS ASSOCIATION

125 Hopping Brook Road
Holliston MA 01746
508/893-7979
FAX: 508/93-9898
E-mail: mruozzi@newwa.org
Internet: http://www.newwa.org
AMOUNT: Varies
DEADLINE(S): JUL 1
FIELD(S): Water Industry; Civil or
Environmental Engineering; Business
Management; Science
ELIGIBILITY/REQUIREMENTS: Based
on merit, character, and need, with prefer-
ence given to those students whose programs
are considered beneficial to water works
practice in New England. Each scholarship
applicant must be a member or student
member of either the New England Water
Works Association, or the American Water
Works Association, with a New England sec-
tion, before their application will be consid-
ered. The membership fee is $25 for a
NEWWA student membership or $36 for a
NEWWA/AWWA student membership.
HOW TO APPLY: Mail application to:
Thomas MacElhaney, Scholarship Com-
mittee Chair, 631/231-8100 or tmacel-
haney@preloadinc.com.
NUMBER OF AWARDS: 6
RENEWABLE: No
CONTACT: Marina Mukandala

540—NEW JERSEY UTILITIES ASSOCIATION

50 West State Street, Suite 1006
Trenton NJ 08608
609/392-1000
FAX: 609/396-4231
Internet: http://www.njua.org
AMOUNT: $1,500
FIELD(S): Engineering; Environmental
Science; Chemistry; Biology; Business
Administration; Accounting.
ELIGIBILITY/REQUIREMENTS: Must
be minority (i.e., Black, Hispanic, American
Indian/Alaskan Native, or Asian American/
Pacific Islander), female, and/or disabled
students; be a New Jersey resident; be
enrolled on a full-time basis at an institute
of higher education; have overall academic
excellence; and demonstrate financial need.
Children of employees of any NJUA mem-
ber company are NOT eligible.
HOW TO APPLY: Contact Association.
NUMBER OF AWARDS: 2

541—PRINT AND GRAPHICS SCHOLARSHIP FOUNDATION, THE (PGSF)

200 Deer Run Road
Sewickley PA 15143-2600
412/259-1740 or 800/910-4283
FAX: 412/741-2311
E-mail: pgsf@piagatf.org.
Internet: http://www. pgsf.org
AMOUNT: $500-$5,000
DEADLINE(S): MAR 1 (high school seniors), APR 1 (college undergraduates)
FIELD(S): Graphic Communications; Printing Technology; Printing Management; Publishing
ELIGIBILITY/REQUIREMENTS: For students pursuing careers in above fields, who are enrolled in a 2- or 4-year accredited program at a technical school, college or university in the U.S.
HOW TO APPLY: For more information and application, see website or call, fax or e-mail. Submit with SAT, ACT or SAT/NMSQT (high school students only), official transcript, 2 recommendation forms from a school representative, such as an instructor, counselor, or advisor (1 may be from an employer), a photocopy of course of study,
NUMBER OF AWARDS: 200-300
RENEWABLE: Yes; must meet basic criteria
CONTACT: Bernie Eckert

542—ROYAL THAI EMBASSY, OFFICE OF EDUCATIONAL AFFAIRS (Revenue Department Scholarships for Thai Students)

1906 23rd Street NW
Washington DC 20008
202/667-9111 or 202/667-8010
FAX: 202/265-7239
AMOUNT: Varies
DEADLINE(S): APR
FIELD(S): Computer Science (Telecommunications); Law; Economics; Finance; Business Administration
ELIGIBILITY/REQUIREMENTS: Scholarships for students under age 35 from Thailand who have been accepted to study in the U.S. or U.K. pursuing any level degree in one of the above fields.
HOW TO APPLY: Selections based on academic records, employment history, and advisor recommendations.

543—SCRIPPS HOWARD FOUNDATION (Robert P. Scripps Graphic Arts Scholarships)

312 Walnut Street
P.O. Box 5380
Cincinnati OH 45201-5380
513/977-3847
FAX: 513/977-3800
E-mail: cottingham@scripps.com
Internet: http://www.scripps.com/foundation
AMOUNT: Varies
DEADLINE(S): Varies
FIELD(S): Newspaper Operations Management
ELIGIBILITY/REQUIREMENTS: Students must be attending the University of Rochester (New York) and majoring in newspaper operations management.
HOW TO APPLY: Applications are available at the university.
NUMBER OF AWARDS: 5

544—SOLOMON R. GUGGENHEIM MUSEUM (Internship Programs)

New York NY 10128-0173
212/423-3526
E-mail: education@guggenheim.org
Internet: http://www.guggenheim.org/new york index
AMOUNT: Varies (some positions unpaid)
DEADLINE(S): FEB 15 (Summer); MAY 15 (Fall); NOV 1 (Spring)
FIELD(S): Art Administration; Art History
ELIGIBILITY/REQUIREMENTS: Various internships, which offer practical museum training experience, are available for undergraduates, recent graduates, and graduate students in art history, administration, conservation, education, and related fields. Location varies, including New York, Italy, and Spain. Housing NOT included.
HOW TO APPLY: Contact the Internship Coordinator, Education Department, for details of each internship and application procedures. Cover letter, résumé, transcripts, letters of recommendation, list of foreign languages/relevant coursework, and essay (less than 500 words, describing interest) required.
CONTACT: Internship Coordinator, Education Department

545—STATE FARM COMPANIES FOUNDATION (Exceptional Student Fellowship)

One State Farm Plaza, SC-3
Bloomington IL 61710-0001
309/766-2039/2161
E-mail: Nancy.Lynn.gr3o@statefarm.com
Internet: http://www.statefarm.com
AMOUNT: $3,000 (nominating institution receives $250)
DEADLINE(S): FEB 15
FIELD(S): Accounting; Business Administration; Actuarial Science; Computer Science; Economics; Finance; Insurance/Risk Management; Investments; Management; Marketing; Mathematics; Statistics
ELIGIBILITY/REQUIREMENTS: For U.S. citizens who are full-time juniors or seniors when they apply. Must demonstrate significant leadership in extracurricular activities, have minimum 3.6 GPA, and attend accredited U.S. college or university. Must be nominated by dean, department head, professor, or academic advisor.
HOW TO APPLY: See website, visit your financial aid office, or write to above address for an application.
NUMBER OF AWARDS: 50
RENEWABLE: No

546—UNIVERSITY AVIATION ASSOCIATION (Airports Council International–North America/Commissioners' Committee Scholarship)

3410 Skyway Drive
Auburn AL 36830-6444
334/844-2434
FAX 334/844-2432
Internet: http://www.uaa.aero
AMOUNT: $2,500-$5,000
DEADLINE(S): APR 15
FIELD(S): Aviation Management, Airport Management
ELIGIBILITY/REQUIREMENTS: Scholarships for undergraduates enrolled in an accredited college or university focusing on a career in airport management. Must have at least a 3.0 GPA. Must reside and attend school in U.S. or Canada.
HOW TO APPLY: See website for application and submit with official transcript, 2 recent letters of recommendation (1 from a professor and 1 from someone other than a professor), a 250-300 word personal statement focusing on interest in airports, and résumé.
NUMBER OF AWARDS: 3
RENEWABLE: No
CONTACT: Dr. Gregory Schwab, Indiana State University, TC 26, Terre Haute IN 47890; 812/237-2641. Send all requests for information and applications to the attention of Dr. Schwab.

547—UNIVERSITY OF WAIKATO (International Management Programme Scholarship)

Scholarships Office
Private Bag 3105
Hamilton NEW ZEALAND

+64 7 856 2889 ext. 7883, 6682, or 6723
FAX: +64 7 858 3795
E-mail: scholarships@waikato.ac.nz
AMOUNT: Varies
DEADLINE(S): MAY
FIELD(S): International Management Studies
ELIGIBILITY/REQUIREMENTS: For overseas travel in connection with studies in the International Management Programme within the degree of Bachelor of Management Studies. For students who have completed at least 2 years of study.
HOW TO APPLY: Contact Scholarships Administrator or see website for application and details.
CONTACT: Scholarships Administrator

548—UNIVERSITY OF TEXAS AT ARLINGTON ALUMNI ASSOCIATION (Daniel Kauth Scholarship)

505 W. Nedderman Drive, Suite 109
Arlington TX 76019
817/272-2594 or 800/687-8855
FAX: 817/272-2597
E-mail: alumni@uta.edu
Internet: http://www.uta.edu/alumni/ scholarships.php
AMOUNT: $250
DEADLINE(S): Varies
FIELD(S): Marketing
ELIGIBILITY/REQUIREMENTS: For full-time students at the University of Texas at Arlington who are majoring in marketing.
HOW TO APPLY: See website for application or contact UTA Alumni Association for an application. Must submit transcript and letter stating career goals, future commitment to UTA, and financial need.
NUMBER OF AWARDS: 1
CONTACT: UTA Alumni Association

549—WESTERN MICHIGAN UNIVERSITY (College of Engineering and Applied Sciences/Ann Arbor Graphic Arts Memorial Foundation Scholarship)

1903 West Michigan
Kalamazoo MI 49008-5337
269/387-6000
FAX: 269/387-6989
Internet: http://www.wmich.edu/finaid
AMOUNT: Varies
FIELD(S): Printing Management/Marketing

ELIGIBILITY/REQUIREMENTS: Recipient must be enrolled in printing management/marketing curriculum.
HOW TO APPLY: Contact the Paper and Printing Science and Engineering Department for an application.
NUMBER OF AWARDS: 1
CONTACT: Paper and Printing Science and Engineering Department, 1104 Welborn Hall

550—WESTERN MICHIGAN UNIVERSITY (College of Engineering and Applied Sciences/Brian Scott Lacombe Humanitarian Scholarship)

1903 West Michigan
Kalamazoo MI 49008-5337
269/387-6000
FAX: 269/387-6989
Internet: http://www.wmich.edu/finaid
AMOUNT: $1,000
FIELD(S): Printing Management/Marketing
ELIGIBILITY/REQUIREMENTS: Open to full-time transfer student with 30 credit hours or more toward a printing program enrolled in printing management/marketing curriculum. Award is based on financial need.
HOW TO APPLY: Contact the Paper and Printing Science and Engineering Department for an application.
NUMBER OF AWARDS: 1
CONTACT: Paper and Printing Science and Engineering Department, 1104 Welborn Hall

551—WESTERN MICHIGAN UNIVERSITY (College of Engineering and Applied Sciences/Charles W. Thomasma Printing Scholarship)

1903 West Michigan
Kalamazoo MI 49008-5337
269/387-6000
FAX: 269/387-6989
Internet: http://www.wmich.edu/finaid
AMOUNT: $1,000
FIELD(S): Printing Management/Marketing
ELIGIBILITY/REQUIREMENTS: Open to freshmen enrolled in printing management/marketing curriculum.
HOW TO APPLY: Contact the Paper and Printing Science and Engineering Department for an application.
NUMBER OF AWARDS: 1
CONTACT: Paper and Printing Science and Engineering Department, 1104 Welborn Hall

552—WESTERN MICHIGAN UNIVERSITY (College of Engineering and Applied Sciences/E. J. Kelly Endowment Memorial Scholarship in Printing)

1903 West Michigan
Kalamazoo MI 49008-5337
269/387-6000
FAX: 269/387-6989
Internet: http://www.wmich.edu/finaid
AMOUNT: $500-$1,000
FIELD(S): Printing Management/Marketing
ELIGIBILITY/REQUIREMENTS: Open to full-time sophomores or juniors enrolled in printing management/marketing curriculum. Award is based on financial need.
HOW TO APPLY: Contact the Paper and Printing Science and Engineering Department for an application.
NUMBER OF AWARDS: 1
CONTACT: Paper and Printing Science and Engineering Department, 1104 Welborn Hall

553—WESTERN MICHIGAN UNIVERSITY (College of Engineering and Applied Sciences/Gravure Education Foundation Scholarship)

1903 West Michigan
Kalamazoo MI 49008-5337
269/387-6000
FAX: 269/387-6989
Internet: http://www.wmich.edu/finaid
AMOUNT: $1,500
FIELD(S): Printing Management/Marketing
ELIGIBILITY/REQUIREMENTS: Open to students enrolled full time in printing management/marketing curriculum. Extracurricular activities required. Coordination of "Gravure Day" at WMU a requirement.
HOW TO APPLY: Contact the Paper and Printing Science and Engineering Department for an application.
NUMBER OF AWARDS: 1
CONTACT: Paper and Printing Science and Engineering Department, 1104 Welborn Hall

554—WESTERN MICHIGAN UNIVERSITY (College of Engineering and Applied Sciences/Herbert F. Ramage Jr. Memorial Scholarship)

1903 West Michigan
Kalamazoo MI 49008-5337
269/387-6000
FAX: 269/387-6989

Internet: http://www.wmich.edu/
finaid
AMOUNT: $750
FIELD(S): Printing Management/
Marketing
ELIGIBILITY/REQUIREMENTS: Open
to full-time sophomore students enrolled
in printing management/marketing cur-
riculum. Award is based on financial need.
HOW TO APPLY: Contact the Paper and
Printing Science and Engineering Depart-
ment for an application.
NUMBER OF AWARDS: 1
CONTACT: Paper and Printing Science
and Engineering Department, 1104
Welborn Hall

555—WESTERN MICHIGAN UNIVERSITY (College of Engineering and Applied Sciences/Print and Graphics Foundation Scholarship)

1903 West Michigan
Kalamazoo MI 49008-5337
269/387-6000
FAX: 269/387-6989
Internet: http://www.wmich.edu/
finaid
AMOUNT: Varies
FIELD(S): Printing Management/
Marketing
ELIGIBILITY/REQUIREMENTS: Open
to full-time student, enrolled in printing
management/marketing curriculum, and
having an overall GPA of at least 3.0.
HOW TO APPLY: Contact the Paper and
Printing Science and Engineering Depart-
ment for an application.
NUMBER OF AWARDS: 1
CONTACT: Paper and Printing Science
and Engineering Department, 1104
Welborn Hall

556—WESTERN MICHIGAN UNIVERSITY (College of Engineering and Applied Sciences/Robert Caine Outstanding Student Award)

1903 West Michigan
Kalamazoo MI 49008-5337
269/387-6000
FAX: 269/387-6989
Internet: http://www.wmich.edu/
finaid
AMOUNT: Varies
FIELD(S): Printing Management/
Marketing
ELIGIBILITY/REQUIREMENTS: Open
to graduating seniors; extracurricular activ-
ities required.
HOW TO APPLY: Recipient is selected
by faculty. Contact the Paper and Printing
Science and Engineering Department for
an application.

NUMBER OF AWARDS: 1
RENEWABLE: No
CONTACT: Paper and Printing Science
and Engineering Department, 1104
Welborn Hall

557—WESTERN MICHIGAN UNIVERSITY (College of Engineering and Applied Sciences/The Lawrence J. Brink Scholarship)

1903 West Michigan
Kalamazoo MI 49008-5337
269/387-6000
FAX: 269/387-6989
Internet: http://www.wmich.edu/
finaid
AMOUNT: $1,000
FIELD(S): Printing Management/
Marketing
ELIGIBILITY/REQUIREMENTS: Open
to full-time students (freshman to senior)
enrolled in printing management/marketing
curriculum. Award is based on financial need.
HOW TO APPLY: Contact the Paper and
Printing Science and Engineering Depart-
ment for an application.
NUMBER OF AWARDS: 1
CONTACT: Paper and Printing Science
and Engineering Department, 1104
Welborn Hall

558—WESTERN MICHIGAN UNIVERSITY (College of Engineering and Applied Sciences/Web Offset Scholarship)

1903 West Michigan
Kalamazoo MI 49008-5337
269/387-6000
FAX: 269/387-6989
Internet: http://www.wmich.edu/
finaid
AMOUNT: Varies
FIELD(S): Printing Management/
Marketing
ELIGIBILITY/REQUIREMENTS:
Recipient must be enrolled in printing
management/marketing curriculum.
HOW TO APPLY: Contact the Paper and
Printing Science and Engineering Depart-
ment for an application.
NUMBER OF AWARDS: 1
RENEWABLE: No
CONTACT: Paper and Printing Science
and Engineering Department, 1104 Wel-
born Hall

559—WESTERN MICHIGAN UNIVERSITY (Haworth College of Business/Brant Rubin Endowed Integrated Supply Management Scholarship)

1903 West Michigan
Kalamazoo MI 49008-5337

269/387-6000
FAX: 269/387-6989
Internet: http://www.wmich.edu/
finaid
AMOUNT: Varies
DEADLINE(S): FEB 15
FIELD(S): Management
ELIGIBILITY/REQUIREMENTS: Must
be junior or senior. Minimum 3.0 GPA.
HOW TO APPLY: Contact the Depart-
ment of Management.
RENEWABLE: Yes
CONTACT: Department of Management

560—WESTERN MICHIGAN UNIVERSITY (Haworth College of Business/Enterprise Rent-A-Car Scholarship)

1903 West Michigan
Kalamazoo MI 49008-5337
269/387-6000
FAX: 269/387-6989
Internet: http://www.wmich.edu/
finaid
AMOUNT: Varies
DEADLINE(S): FEB 15
FIELD(S): Sales; Marketing;
Management
ELIGIBILITY/REQUIREMENTS:
Junior or senior; must be full-time student
majoring in or intending to major in sales
and marketing or management; minimum
3.0 GPA for this merit-based scholarship.
Must be available to participate in a paid
internship during summer months if open-
ing exists.
HOW TO APPLY: Application forms
must be obtained from and returned to the
Marketing Department.
NUMBER OF AWARDS: 2
CONTACT: Marketing Department

561—WESTERN MICHIGAN UNIVERSITY (Haworth College of Business/The Dean Arnold E. Schneider Management Achievement Award)

1903 West Michigan
Kalamazoo MI 49008-5337
269/387-6000
FAX: 269/387-6989
Internet: http://www.wmich.edu/
finaid
AMOUNT: Varies
DEADLINE(S): FEB 15
FIELD(S): Management
ELIGIBILITY/REQUIREMENTS: Must
be junior or senior. Management majors
preferred, although consideration will be
given to others who have excelled in management as a minor or through involvement in student clubs. Based solely on aca-

demic performance. Recipients must have distinguished themselves in scholarship, service to the department, or other worthy endeavors.
HOW TO APPLY: Students are nominated by the Department of Management faculty members.
RENEWABLE: No
CONTACT: Department of Management

562—WESTERN MICHIGAN UNIVERSITY (Haworth College of Business/The Distinguished Service Award for the Department of Management)

1903 West Michigan
Kalamazoo MI 49008-5337
269/387-6000
FAX: 269/387-6989
Internet: http://www.wmich.edu/finaid
AMOUNT: Varies
DEADLINE(S): FEB 15
FIELD(S): Management
ELIGIBILITY/REQUIREMENTS: Must be junior or senior; management major or minor. Awarded for distinguished service to the Department of Management and based solely on academic performance.
HOW TO APPLY: Contact the Department of Management.
CONTACT: Department of Management

563—WESTERN MICHIGAN UNIVERSITY (Haworth College of Business/The Dr. Kimon Bournazos Award for Study and Practice of HRM)

1903 West Michigan
Kalamazoo MI 49008-5337
269/387-6000
FAX: 269/387-6989
Internet: http://www.wmich.edu/finaid
AMOUNT: $250/semester
DEADLINE(S): FEB 15
FIELD(S): Human Resource Management
ELIGIBILITY/REQUIREMENTS: Must be junior or senior HRM student. Award is based solely on academic performance. Recipient must demonstrate scholarship, leadership, interpersonal and communication skills, and be planning a career as human resources manager.
HOW TO APPLY: Contact the Department of Management.
NUMBER OF AWARDS: 2 (1 male and 1 female)
RENEWABLE: No
CONTACT: Department of Management

564—WESTERN MICHIGAN UNIVERSITY (Haworth College of Business/The Jeff Robideau Award for Meritorious Scholarship)

1903 West Michigan
Kalamazoo MI 49008-5337
269/387-6000
FAX: 269/387-6989
Internet: http://www.wmich.edu/finaid
AMOUNT: Varies
DEADLINE(S): FEB 15
FIELD(S): Management
ELIGIBILITY/REQUIREMENTS: Must be junior or senior in the Management Department. Based solely on academic performance. Awarded to student with the highest GPA.
HOW TO APPLY: Contact the Department of Management.
NUMBER OF AWARDS: 2 (1 male, 1 female)

565—WOMEN GROCERS OF AMERICA (Mary Macey Scholarships)

1005 North Glebe Road, Suite 250
Arlington VA 22201-5758
703/516-0700
FAX: 703/516-0115
E-mail: wga@nationalgrocers.org
Internet: http://www.national grocers.org
AMOUNT: $1,000 (minimum)
DEADLINE(S): JUN 1
FIELD(S): Food Marketing/Management; Food Service Technology; Business Administration (as related to the Grocery Industry)
ELIGIBILITY/REQUIREMENTS: For students with a minimum 2.0 GPA attending a U.S. college or university. Must be entering sophomores or continuing students in good standing in a 2-year associate degree or 4-year degree-granting institution or a graduate program, planning a career in the independent sector grocery industry. Financial need NOT considered.
HOW TO APPLY: See website for downloadable PDF application form or write to the address above for an application.
NUMBER OF AWARDS: 2+
RENEWABLE: Yes, must reapply.

566—WOMEN'S SPORTS FOUNDATION (Jackie Joyner-Kersee and Zina Garrison Minority Internships)

Eisenhower Park
East Meadow NY 11554

800/227-3988 (U.S. only) or
516/542-4700
FAX: 516/542-4716
E-mail: WoSport@aol.com
Internet: http://www.womenssports foundation.org
AMOUNT: $4,000-$5,000
DEADLINE(S): Ongoing
FIELD(S): Sports-related careers
ELIGIBILITY/REQUIREMENTS: Women of color who are undergraduate students, college graduates, graduate students, or women in career change. Internships are located at the Women's Sports Foundation in East Meadow, New York.
HOW TO APPLY: See website or write to above address for details.
NUMBER OF AWARDS: 4-6

567—WYOMING TRUCKING ASSOCIATION

P.O. Box 1909
Casper WY 82602
AMOUNT: $250-$960
DEADLINE(S): MAR 1
FIELD(S): Transportation Industry
ELIGIBILITY/REQUIREMENTS: For Wyoming high school graduates enrolled in a Wyoming college, approved trade school, or the University of Wyoming. Must be pursuing a course of study that will result in a career in the transportation industry in Wyoming, including but not limited to: safety, diesel mechanics, truck driving, business management, computer skills, accounting, office procedures, and management.
HOW TO APPLY: Write to WYTA for an application.
NUMBER OF AWARDS: 1-10

568—Y'S MEN INTERNATIONAL—U.S. AREA (Alexander Scholarship Loan Fund)

629 Lantana Lane
Imperial CA 92251
Internet: http://www.ysmenusa.com/ aslf1.htm
AMOUNT: $1,000-$1,500/year
DEADLINE(S): MAY 30; OCT 30
FIELD(S): Business Administration; Youth Leadership
ELIGIBILITY/REQUIREMENTS: Open to U.S. citizens/permanent residents with a strong desire to pursue professional YMCA service. Must be YMCA staff pursuing undergraduate or graduate study and demonstrate financial need. Repayment of loan is waived if recipient enters YMCA employment after graduation.
HOW TO APPLY: See website for application.

FINANCE

569—ACTUARIAL FOUNDATION, THE (Actuary of Tomorrow—Stuart A. Robertson Memorial Scholarship)

475 North Martingale Road,
Suite 600
Schaumburg IL 60173
847/706-3535
FAX: 847/706-3599
E-mail: scholarships@actfnd.org
Internet: http://www.actuarial
foundation.org
AMOUNT: $7,500
DEADLINE(S): JUN 1
FIELD(S): Actuary
ELIGIBILITY/REQUIREMENTS: Open to undergraduates demonstrating an interest in pursuing an actuarial career. Must be sophomore or higher, minimum cumulative GPA 3.0; have successfully completed 2 actuarial exams (Spring exams meet 2-exam requirement).
HOW TO APPLY: See website for application, and submit with a personal essay of approximately 500 words focusing on why you want to be an actuary; a current transcript, a letter of recommendation supporting academic achievement and leadership and communication skills from professor or advisor.
NUMBER OF AWARDS: 1 or more (depending on funds)
RENEWABLE: No
CONTACT: Susan Gehm, Foundation Coordinator

570—ACTUARIAL FOUNDATION, THE (John Culver Wooddy Scholarship)

475 North Martingale Road,
Suite 600
Schaumburg IL 60173
847/706-3535
FAX: 847/706-3599
E-mail: scholarships@actfnd.org
Internet: http://www.actuarial
foundation.org
AMOUNT: $2,000
DEADLINE(S): JUN (last Friday)
FIELD(S): Actuary
ELIGIBILITY/REQUIREMENTS: Open to student entering senior year in college, who is eligible to graduate within 1 year of date of award; must have passed at least 1 actuarial exam by application due date (international students need to major in Actuarial Science but exam is not required); must be recommended by a professor (limit 1 application/school); applicant must rank in top quartile of class.

Preference will be given to candidates who have demonstrated leadership potential through extracurricular activities.
HOW TO APPLY: See website for application, and submit with a personal essay to professor, who must then provide verification of student's class ranking and senior status within their letter of recommendation.
NUMBER OF AWARDS: Multiple
RENEWABLE: No
CONTACT: Susan Gehm, Foundation Coordinator

571—AMERICAN INSTITUTE OF CERTIFIED PUBLIC ACCOUNTANTS (AICPA) (Accountemps Scholarships)

Palladian One
220 Leigh Farm Road
Durham NC 27707
919/401-4014
FAX: 919/419-4705
E-mail: educat@aicpa.org
Internet: http://www.aicpa.org
AMOUNT: $2,500
DEADLINE(S): Spring
FIELD(S): Accounting; Finance; Information Systems
ELIGIBILITY/REQUIREMENTS: Open to full-time students (minimum 12 semester hours or equivalent) at regionally accredited institutions in the U.S.; must be U.S. citizen. Must be a student affiliate member of AICPA; a declared accounting, finance, or information systems major with an overall GPA of at least 3.0; must have satisfactorily completed at least 30 semester hours or 45 quarter hours, or equivalent college work, including at least 6 semester hours (or equivalent) in accounting.
HOW TO APPLY: Submit application along with official transcripts, tests (if applicable), and 2 letters of recommendation. See website for additional information.
NUMBER OF AWARDS: 5
RENEWABLE: No

572—AMERICAN SOCIETY OF WOMEN ACCOUNTANTS FOUNDATION SCHOLARSHIP PROGRAM (2-Year College Scholarships)

ASWA National Headquarters
8405 Greensboro Drive, Suite 800
McLean VA 22102
800/326-2163 or 703/506-3265
FAX: 703/506-3266
E-mail: aswa@aswa.org
Internet: http://www.aswa.org/
scholarship.html

AMOUNT: $4,000 (1); $3,000 (2); $2,000 (4)
DEADLINE(S): Varies
FIELD(S): Accounting, Finance
ELIGIBILITY/REQUIREMENTS: Open to community college students entering their 2nd year of an Associates Degree Program who have completed 15 semester hours or the equivalent by time of application deadline. Candidates must have a minimum cumulative college grade point average (GPA) of 3.0 on a 4.0 scale (or the equivalent), and be majoring in accounting or finance. Scholarship candidates will be reviewed on leadership, character, communication skills, scholastic average and financial need.
HOW TO APPLY: Apply through the local chapter. See website or call ASWA for the name of a local chapter. Submit application with 75-word essay describing career goals and objectives, what impact the candidate wants to have on the accounting world and what the candidate most likes about accounting, 1 personal and 2 references from accounting faculty, and transcript from school, showing academic performance and credit hours obtained.

573—AMERICAN SOCIETY OF WOMEN ACCOUNTANTS FOUNDATION SCHOLARSHIP PROGRAM (Undergraduate Scholarships)

ASWA National Headquarters
8405 Greensboro Drive, Suite 800
McLean VA 22102
800/326-2163 or 703/506-3265
FAX: 703/506-3266
E-mail: aswa@aswa.org
Internet: http://www.aswa.org/
scholarship.html
AMOUNT: $4,000 (1); $3,000 (2); $2,000 (4)
DEADLINE(S): Varies
FIELD(S): Accounting, Finance
ELIGIBILITY/REQUIREMENTS: Scholarships for female accounting or finance majors who are either full- or part-time students. Must have completed a minimum of 60 semester hours or 90 quarter hours and be enrolled in an accredited college, university, or professional school of accounting (which is designated to award a post-baccalaureate Certificate of Accounting). Membership in ASWA not required. Scholarship candidates will be reviewed on leadership, character, communication skills, scholastic average and financial need.
HOW TO APPLY: Apply through the local chapter. See website or call ASWA

for the name of a local chapter. Submit application with 75-word essay describing career goals and objectives, what impact the candidate wants to have on the accounting world and what the candidate most likes about accounting, 1 personal and 2 references from accounting faculty, and transcript from school, showing academic performance and credit hours obtained. Please provide one [1] original. (For certification candidates only: a copy of the letter indicating passing and the receipt indicating proof of payment for the certification exam fees must accompany the application form.)

574—HISPANIC COLLEGE FUND (HSF/Association of Latino Professionals in Finance and Accounting)

55 Second Street, Suite 1500
San Francisco CA 94105
877/HSF-INFO
(877/473-4636)
FAX: 415/808-2302
E-mail: pip@hsf.net
Internet: http://hispanicfund.org
AMOUNT: $1,250-$2,500
DEADLINE(S): APR 15
FIELD(S): Accounting; Finance-related fields
ELIGIBILITY/REQUIREMENTS: Must be U.S. citizens or legal permanent residents of Hispanic heritage (one parent fully Hispanic or both parents half Hispanic). Applicant should have earned at least 12 undergraduate college credits in the U.S. or Puerto Rico and have a minimum GPA of 3.0. Must carry at least 12 credits each term. Selection is based on academic achievement, personal strengths, leadership, and financial need.
HOW TO APPLY: Contact Fund for details or visit website for application.

575—HISPANIC COLLEGE FUND (HSF/JP Morgan Chase Scholarship Program)

55 Second Street, Suite 1500
San Francisco CA 94105
877/HSF-INFO
(877/473-4636)
FAX: 415/808-2302
E-mail: pip@hsf.net
Internet: http://hispanicfund.org
AMOUNT: $2,500
DEADLINE(S): NOV 16
FIELD(S): Business; Finance; Economics
ELIGIBILITY/REQUIREMENTS: Open to students in their sophomore and junior years. Must be U.S. citizens or legal permanent residents of Hispanic heritage (one parent fully Hispanic or both parents half

Hispanic). Minimum GPA of 3.0. Must carry at least 12 credits each term. Selection is based on academic achievement, personal strengths, leadership, and financial need.
HOW TO APPLY: Contact Fund for details or visit website for application.

576—HISPANIC COLLEGE FUND (HSF/Little Village Chamber of Commerce Ambassador's Scholarship Program)

55 Second Street, Suite 1500
San Francisco CA 94105
877/HSF-INFO
(877/473-4636)
FAX: 415/808-2302
E-mail: pip@hsf.net
Internet: http://hispanicfund.org
AMOUNT: At least $2,000
DEADLINE(S): JUN 23
FIELD(S): Business; Finance; Marketing and related fields
ELIGIBILITY/REQUIREMENTS: Open to entering and continuing full-time undergraduate and graduate students from the Little Village Community. Must be U.S. citizens or legal permanent residents of Hispanic heritage (one parent fully Hispanic or both parents half Hispanic). Minimum GPA of 3.0. Must carry at least 12 credits each term. Selection is based on academic achievement, personal strengths, leadership, and financial need.
HOW TO APPLY: Contact Fund for details or visit website for application.

577—INSTITUT D'ETUDES POLITIQUES DE PARIS (U.S. Sciences Po Alumni Association Scholarships)

27 rue Saint Guillaume
75337 Paris Cedex 07 FRANCE
331/4549-5047
FAX: 331/4544-1252
E-mail: contact@sciencespo.org
Internet: http://sciencespo.org
AMOUNT: Up to $5,000
DEADLINE(S): Varies
FIELD(S): European Studies; Political Science; Economics; Finance
ELIGIBILITY/REQUIREMENTS: Open to U.S. citizens who will pursue undergraduate, graduate, or post-graduate studies at IEP Paris, either through admission to the school or through an exchange program with an accredited U.S. school. Must have sufficient fluency in French to meet instructional requirements. Must submit cover letter, résumé, and brief essay. Award may be used to cover educational costs and related expenses, including fees,

round-trip airfare to Paris, textbooks, and school supplies.
HOW TO APPLY: See website or contact Director of International Student Services for an application.
CONTACT: Mr. P. Cauchy, Director of International Student Services

578—INSTITUTE FOR HUMANE STUDIES (Koch Summer Fellow Program)

3401 N. Fairfax Drive, Suite 440
Arlington VA 22201-4432
703/993-4880 or 800/697-8799
FAX: 703/993-4890
Internet: http://www.TheIHS.org
AMOUNT: $1,500 + airfare and housing
DEADLINE(S): FEB 15
FIELD(S): Economics; Public Policy; Law; Government; Politics
ELIGIBILITY/REQUIREMENTS: Open to undergraduates and graduates to build skills and gain experience by participating in an 8-week summer internship program. Includes two week-long seminars, the internship, and research and writing projects with professionals. Must submit college transcripts, essays, and application. Financial need NOT a factor.
HOW TO APPLY: Apply online or contact IHS for an application.
NUMBER OF AWARDS: 32
RENEWABLE: No

579—JACKSONVILLE STATE UNIVERSITY (Dr. and Mrs. Robert Moersch Scholarship)

Jacksonville AL 36265
256/782-5677 or 800/231-5291
Internet: www.jsu.edu
AMOUNT: Varies
DEADLINE(S): FEB 1
FIELD(S): Finance; Economics
ELIGIBILITY/REQUIREMENTS: Open to juniors or seniors majoring in economics or finance; 2.5 overall GPA, 3.0 in major.
HOW TO APPLY: Contact Finance Department for application and additional information.
RENEWABLE: No
CONTACT: Finance Department; 256/782-5773

580—LONDON SCHOOL OF ECONOMICS AND POLITICAL SCIENCE

Financial Support Office
Houghton Street
London WC2A 2AE ENGLAND
+44 020 7955
FAX: +44 020 7216
E-mail: financial support@lse.ac.uk
Internet: http://www.lse.ac.uk

AMOUNT: Varies with award
DEADLINE(S): Varies
FIELD(S): Economics; Accounting; Finance; Political Science; International Relations
ELIGIBILITY/REQUIREMENTS: Various scholarships, awards, and prizes are available to international students. Several are for students from specific countries, and some are limited to certain fields of study. Some include all expenses, and others pay partial expenses. For undergraduates and graduate students.
HOW TO APPLY: Access LSE's website and using their "search" option, enter "scholarships," and programs will appear.
RENEWABLE: Varies

581—NATIONAL POULTRY AND FOOD DISTRIBUTORS ASSOCIATION SCHOLARSHIP FOUNDATION

958 McEver Road Extension,
Unit B8
Gainesville GA 30504
770/535-9901
FAX: 770/535-7385
E-mail: kkm@npfda.org
Internet: http://www.npfda.org
AMOUNT: $1,500-$2,000 each/annual
DEADLINE(S): MAY 31
FIELD(S): Poultry, Food or related agricultural degree; Food Science; Dietetics; Poultry Science; Agricultural Economics; International Business, etc.
ELIGIBILITY/REQUIREMENTS: Must be enrolled full time as a college junior or senior the upcoming (award) year at a U.S. institution.
HOW TO APPLY: Complete application and provide your current official transcript, letter of recommendation from your dean along with a 1-page letter describing your goals and aspirations.
NUMBER OF AWARDS: 4
RENEWABLE: No
CONTACT: Kristin McWhorter

582—NEW ENGLAND EMPLOYEE BENEFITS COUNCIL

440 Totten Pond Road
Waltham MA 02145
781/684-8700
FAX: 781/684-9200
E-mail: linda@neebc.org
Internet: http://www.neebc.org
AMOUNT: Up to $5,000
DEADLINE(S): APR 1
FIELD(S): Health Care Program Design; Pension Plan Design, Implementation or Administration; Retirement Strategies; ERISA and Legal Aspects

of Employee Benefits; Work/Life Programs; Health Risk Management; Institutional Investing of Retirement Savings; Multiemployer Plans; Workers Compensation; Actuarial and Underwriting Analysis; Employee Benefits Communications
ELIGIBILITY/REQUIREMENTS: Full-time student (undergraduate or graduate) studying in an accredited academic program leading to a degree who demonstrates an interest through either course study or work experience in a career in the benefits field. Must be a New England resident or enrolled at a college in New England. Current NEEBC Board members, their spouses and children are not eligible to participate.
HOW TO APPLY: Completed application; all college transcripts; two or more references from college professors, NEEBC members, or other benefits professionals.
NUMBER OF AWARDS: 1 or 2
RENEWABLE: Yes
CONTACT: Linda Viens, Manager of Operations and Member Services

583—REAL ESTATE EDUCATION FOUNDATION (The Foundation Scholarship)

3180 Adloff Lane, Suite 400
Springfield IL 62703
217/529-2600
FAX: 217/529-3904
Internet: http://www.illinoisrealtor. org
AMOUNT: $1,000-$2,000
DEADLINE(S): APR 1
FIELD(S): Real Estate and allied fields (Construction; Land Use Planning; Mortgage Banking; Property Management; Real Estate Appraising; Real Estate Assessing; Real Estate Brokerage; Real Estate Development; Real Estate Investment Counseling; Real Estate Law; Real Estate Syndication)
ELIGIBILITY/REQUIREMENTS: Recipients will be selected based on: the applicant's interest in pursuing a career in real estate or an allied field; record of scholastic achievement, including GPA; economic need or situation; and references and recommendations by instructors, employers, Realtors and others.
HOW TO APPLY: Along with the application, submit a signed statement of your general activities and intellectual interests, employment (if any), your contemplated line of study and the career you expect to follow (no more than 1,000 words); a record of military service, or details of

civilian war work, if any; proposed program of study, including a brief description of each course you plan to take, signed by the Dean or appropriate official; a recommendation from the real estate instructor, or, if none, the Dean of your college; official copies of transcripts; and 2 letters of recommendation (it is preferred, but not required, that 1 of these letters be from a Realtor). Finalists will be asked to appear for a personal interview in June or July.
NUMBER OF AWARDS: 8
CONTACT: Larranne Wells

584—ROYAL THAI EMBASSY—OFFICE OF EDUCATIONAL AFFAIRS (Revenue Department Scholarships for Thai Students)

1906 23rd Street NW
Washington DC 20008
202/667-9111 or 202/667-8010
FAX: 202/265-7239
AMOUNT: Varies
DEADLINE(S): APR
FIELD(S): Computer Science (Telecommunications), Law, Economics, Finance, Business Administration
ELIGIBILITY/REQUIREMENTS: Scholarships for students under age 35 from Thailand who have been accepted to study in the U.S. or U.K. pursuing any level degree in one of the above fields.
HOW TO APPLY: Selections based on academic records, employment history, and advisor recommendations.

585—RHODE ISLAND FOUNDATION (Raymond H. Trott Scholarship for Banking)

One Union Station
Providence RI 02903
402/274-4564
Internet: http://www.rifoundation. org
AMOUNT: $1,000
DEADLINE: JUN 14
FIELDS: Banking
ELIGIBILITY/REQUIREMENTS: Open to minority students entering their senior year in college who wish to pursue a career in banking. Must be attending an accredited college, a Rhode Island resident, and able to demonstrate financial need.
HOW TO APPLY: See website for additional information and application or send SASE to the Foundation. Submit with an essay, copy of your financial aid award letter, a copy of your final Student Aid Report, your official college transcript, and a letter of recommendation.

NUMBER OF AWARDS: 1
RENEWABLE: No
CONTACT: Libby Monahan

586—WESTERN MICHIGAN UNIVERSITY (Haworth College of Business/Charles C. and Lynn Zhang and Associates Scholarships)

1903 West Michigan
Kalamazoo MI 49008-5337
269/387-6000
FAX: 269/387-6989
Internet: http://www.wmich.edu/finaid
AMOUNT: $500
DEADLINE(S): FEB 15
FIELD(S): Finance
ELIGIBILITY/REQUIREMENTS: Undergraduate BBA with Finance major. Academic-based award awarded to student with highest cumulative GPA for their respective classes.
HOW TO APPLY: Contact the Department of Finance & Commercial Law, 3290 Schneider Hall, Haworth College of Business, e–mail: edEdwards@wmich.edu (269/387-5722).
NUMBER OF AWARDS: 2 (1 junior, 1 senior)
CONTACT: Department of Finance & Commercial Law

587—WESTERN MICHIGAN UNIVERSITY (Haworth College of Business/Chubb Group of Insurance Companies Scholarship)

1903 West Michigan
Kalamazoo MI 49008-5337
269/387-6000
FAX: 269/387-6989
Internet: http://www.wmich.edu/finaid
AMOUNT: $1,000/semester
DEADLINE(S): FEB 15
FIELD(S): Finance
ELIGIBILITY/REQUIREMENTS: Must be a Junior or Senior BBA student with Finance major; minimum GPA of 3.0. Must maintain a minimum course load of 12 credit hours while receiving scholarship. Extracurricular activities considered. Need-based award with preference given to students from under-represented ethnic groups. Must have solid history of prior work experience, especially during previous semesters enrolled at WMU.
HOW TO APPLY: Contact the Department of Finance & Commercial Law, 3290 Schneider Hall, Haworth College of Business, e-mail: edEdwards@wmich.edu (269/387-5722).

NUMBER OF AWARDS: 2 (1 junior, 1 senior)

588—WESTERN MICHIGAN UNIVERSITY (Haworth College of Business/Cinq-Mars Jarvis Scholarship)

1903 West Michigan
Kalamazoo MI 49008-5337
269/387-6000
FAX: 269/387-6989
Internet: http://www.wmich.edu/finaid
AMOUNT: $10,000 ($2,500/semester for 4 semesters)
DEADLINE(S): FEB 15
FIELD(S): Finance
ELIGIBILITY/REQUIREMENTS: Must be entering Junior BBA student with Finance major; minimum GPA of 3.0. Must maintain a minimum course load of 12 credit hours while receiving scholarship. Extracurricular activities at WMU considered. Need-based award. Must have solid history of prior work experience, especially during previous semesters enrolled at WMU.
HOW TO APPLY: Contact the Department of Finance & Commercial Law, 3290 Schneider Hall, Haworth College of Business, e-mail: edEdwards@wmich.edu (269/387-5722).
RENEWABLE: No

589—WESTERN MICHIGAN UNIVERSITY (Haworth College of Business/Cinq-Mars Scholarship)

1903 West Michigan
Kalamazoo MI 49008-5337
269/387-6000
FAX: 269/387-6989
E-mail: finaid-info@Wmich.edu
Internet: http://www.wmich.edu/finaid
AMOUNT: $10,000 ($2,500/ per semester for 4 semesters)
DEADLINE(S): FEB 15
FIELD(S): Finance
ELIGIBILITY/REQUIREMENTS: Must be entering Junior BBA student with Finance major; minimum GPA of 3.0. Must maintain a minimum course load of 12 credit hours while receiving scholarship. Extra-curricular activities at WMU considered. Need-based award. Must have solid history of prior work experience, especially during previous semesters enrolled at WMU.
HOW TO APPLY: Contact the Department of Finance & Commercial Law, 3290 Schneider Hall, Haworth College of Business, e-mail: edEdwards@wmich.edu (269/387-5722).

590—WESTERN MICHIGAN UNIVERSITY (Haworth College of Business/Edwin Grossnickle Scholarship)

1903 West Michigan
Kalamazoo MI 49008-5337
269/387-6000
FAX: 269/387-6989
E-mail: finaid-info@wmich.edu
Internet: http://www.wmich.edu/finaid
AMOUNT: $1,000 (fall semester tuition)
DEADLINE(S): FEB 15
FIELD(S): Finance
ELIGIBILITY/REQUIREMENTS: Must be full-time entering Junior BBA student with Finance major; minimum GPA of 3.0. Not a need-based award.
HOW TO APPLY: Contact the Department of Finance & Commercial Law, 3290 Schneider Hall, Haworth College of Business, e-mail: edEdwards@wmich.edu (269/387-5722).
RENEWABLE: No

591—WESTERN MICHIGAN UNIVERSITY (Haworth College of Business/Greenleaf Asset Management Scholarships in Finance)

1903 West Michigan
Kalamazoo MI 49008-5337
269/387-6000
FAX: 269/387-6989
E-mail: finaid-info@wmich.edu
Internet: http://www.wmich.edu/finaid
AMOUNT: $8,000
DEADLINE(S): FEB 15
FIELD(S): Finance
ELIGIBILITY/REQUIREMENTS: Awarded to first-year full-time undergraduate student in pre-business who intends to major in Finance, 2.5 minimum GPA. Must have declared finance major by junior year to retain the scholarship. Preference shall be given to students from under-represented ethnic groups.
HOW TO APPLY: Contact the Department of Finance & Commercial Law, 3290 Schneider Hall, Haworth College of Business, e-mail: edEdwards@wmich.edu (269/387-5722).
NUMBER OF AWARDS: 2
RENEWABLE: Yes. Up to 4 years.

592—WESTERN MICHIGAN UNIVERSITY (Haworth College of Business/Magellan Scholarship)

1903 West Michigan
Kalamazoo MI 49008-5337
269/387-6000

FAX: 269/387-6989
E-mail: finaid-info@wmich.edu
Internet: http://www.wmich.edu/finaid
AMOUNT: $500 (fall semester)
DEADLINE(S): FEB 15
FIELD(S): Finance; Business;
International Business
ELIGIBILITY/REQUIREMENTS:
Undergraduate BBA with minimum GPA
of 3.0. Recipient will be a business student
participating in a study abroad program or
participating in an international business
seminar. Need-based award.
HOW TO APPLY: Contact the Department of Finance & Commercial Law, 3290
Schneider Hall, Haworth College of
Business, e-mail: edEdwards@ wmich.edu
(269/387-5722).
NUMBER OF AWARDS: 2
RENEWABLE: No

PUBLIC ADMINISTRATION

593—AMERICAN PUBLIC TRANSIT ASSOCIATION (Transit Hall of Fame Scholarships)

1666 K Street NW
Washington DC 20006
202/496-4800
FAX: 202/898-4029
Internet: http://www.apta.com/services/human resources/ program guidelines.cfm
AMOUNT: $2,500 or more
DEADLINE(S): None
FIELD(S): Transit-related fields of study
ELIGIBILITY/REQUIREMENTS: For
college juniors, seniors, or graduate students enrolled in a degree program in a
fully accredited institution who demonstrate an interest in entering the transit
industry. Criteria include interest in the
transit field, financial need, leadership
characteristics, scholastic achievement, citizenship, and extracurricular activities.
HOW TO APPLY: Must be nominated by
an APTF representative who can oversee
an internship program. Write to above
address to inquire about how to be nominated and other information. An essay and
a brief in-person or telephone interview.
NUMBER OF AWARDS: At least 6

594—ASSOCIATION OF CALIFORNIA WATER AGENCIES (ACWA)

910 K Street, Suite 100
Sacramento CA 95814
916/441-4545
FAX: 916/325-4849

E-mail: acwabox@acwanet.com
Internet: http://www.acwanet.com
AMOUNT: $1,500
DEADLINE(S): APR 1
FIELD(S): Water resources-related fields
including engineering, agriculture,
environmental studies, public administration
ELIGIBILITY/REQUIREMENTS:
ACWA's awards are based not only on
scholastic achievement but also on the
individual's commitment and motivation
to their chosen field. Financial need will
also be considered.
HOW TO APPLY: Download applications and guidelines for the ACWA scholarship program from website, or call or e-mail ACWA or contact your school's
financial aid department.
NUMBER OF AWARDS: At least 6

595—ASSOCIATION OF SCHOOL BUSINESS OFFICIALS OF MARYLAND AND THE DISTRICT OF COLUMBIA (Dwight P. Jacobus Scholarships)

Scholarship Committee
200 East North Avenue
Baltimore MD 21202
Internet: http://www.asbo.org
AMOUNT: $1,000
DEADLINE(S): MAR 1
FIELD(S): Business; Education
ELIGIBILITY/REQUIREMENTS: Must
be residents of Maryland or the District of
Columbia for at least 1 year preceding the
date of application; be pursuing a career in
business or education at an accredited
institution of higher education within
Maryland or the District of Columbia; be
accepted for admission as a full-time student; demonstrate financial need; and have
a minimum overall GPA of 3.0. Awards
are based on scholastic achievement, financial need, SAT or ACT scores, and the
quality of extracurricular activities.
HOW TO APPLY: Submit completed
application; copy of most current high
school or college transcript; copies of parents' and applicant's current income tax
returns; copy of acceptance letter from an
accredited institution of higher education
in Maryland or the District of Columbia; a
500-word typed essay, written by the applicant explaining why he/she is uniquely
qualified to receive this scholarship and
including academic achievements and
activities, community and civic activities,
and personal aims and goals; and a copy of
SAT or ACT results.
NUMBER OF AWARDS: 6
RENEWABLE: Yes. Up to 4 years; recipients must reapply annually; continue to be
accepted for admission to the undergraduate

program in education; be enrolled full-time;
and submit proof of continued academic
good standing (i.e., a minimum 3.0 GPA).
CONTACT: Kathy Jackson, Chair

596—CONFERENCE OF MINORITY PUBLIC ADMINISTRATORS (Ronald H. Brown Memorial Scholarship)

COMPA Awards Committee
9717 Summit Circle, Suite 3E
Largo MD 20774
301/333-5282
E-mail: hwilliamjhunter@aol.com
Internet: http://www.natcompa.org
AMOUNT: $1,000
DEADLINE(S): Varies
FIELD(S): Public Administration; Public
Affairs
ELIGIBILITY/REQUIREMENTS: Must
be a public high school senior residing in
the city where the Conference of Minority
Public Administrators holds its annual
conference. Must be legal residents of the
host city.
HOW TO APPLY: Submit application and
acceptance letter to a 4-year institution of
higher learning; a minimum GPA of 3.25
on a 4.0 scale (official high school transcript required); a minimum ACT/SAT
score of 22 or 1000; a 2-page typewritten
essay describing how your future goals
align with Ronald H. Brown's philosophy
of fighting to create opportunities for people of every race, social class, and nationality.
NUMBER OF AWARDS: 1
RENEWABLE: No
CONTACT: William J. Hunter, Chair,
COMPA Awards Committee

597—CONNECTICUT BUILDING CONGRESS SCHOLARSHIP FUND

2600 Dixwell Avenue, Suite 7
Hamden CT 06514
203/281-3183
FAX: 203/248-8932
E-mail: bdavidson@ctengineers.org
Internet: http://www.cbc-ct.org
AMOUNT: $500-$2,000 per year for 4
years depending on grades
DEADLINE(S): MAR 31
FIELD(S): Construction Industry-related
subjects (Architecture; Engineering;
Construction Management; Planning;
Drafting, etc.)
ELIGIBILITY/REQUIREMENTS:
Connecticut resident. Must submit an
essay of not more than 500 words that
explains how your planned studies will
relate to a career in the construction industry; transcript of high school grades; class

standing and SAT/ACT scores; copy of Student Aid Report of FAFSA and custodial parent's statement (from College Board) if applicable.
HOW TO APPLY: Call, write or e-mail for application.
NUMBER OF AWARDS: 2 to 4
RENEWABLE: Yes. Must maintain grades.
CONTACT: Beverly Davidson at CBCSF

598—GARDEN CLUB FEDERATION OF MAINE, THE—ST. CROIX DISTRICT (Nell Goff Memorial Scholarship Foundation)

46 Birch Bay Drive
Bar Harbor ME 04609
207/288-8003
E-mail: creevey@adelphia.net
Internet: http://www.mainegarden clubs.com
AMOUNT: $1,000
DEADLINE(S): MAR 1
FIELD(S): Horticulture; Floriculture; Landscape Design; Conservation; Forestry; Botany; Agronomy; Plant Pathology; Environmental Control; City Planning and/or other gardening-related fields
ELIGIBILITY/REQUIREMENTS: Open to all college juniors, seniors or graduate students who are legal residents of the state of Maine, priority is given to a resident of St. Croix District (Hancock County and the southern part of Washington County). Must major in some aspect of horticulture. College sophomores are eligible as they will be entering their junior year the following fall.
HOW TO APPLY: Application is available on the website, click on Scholarship Information; submit along with personal letter by applicant, not to exceed 2 pages, discussing goals, background, financial need and personal commitment; 3 letters of recommendation, 1 typed page each to include scholarship ability, personal reference and work-related experience; transcript of all college credits to date and list of activities.
NUMBER OF AWARDS: 1
RENEWABLE: Yes. Must reapply.
CONTACT: Lucy Creevey

599—GOVERNMENT FINANCE OFFICERS ASSOCIATION (Minorities in Government Finance Scholarship)

Scholarship Committee
203 N. LaSalle Street, Suite 2700
Chicago IL 60601-1210
312/977-9700
Internet: http://www.gfoa.org
AMOUNT: $5,000
DEADLINE(S): FEB 15
FIELD(S): Public Administration; (Governmental) Accounting; Finance; Political Science; Economics; Business Administration (with a specific focus on government or nonprofit management)
ELIGIBILITY/REQUIREMENTS: Applicants must belong to one of the following groups: Black, Indian, Eskimo or Aleut, Asian or Pacific Islander, Hispanic; must be a citizen or permanent resident of the U.S. or Canada; and must be recommended by the student's academic advisor or department chair.
HOW TO APPLY: Send completed application.

600—INSTITUTE FOR HUMANE STUDIES (Koch Summer Fellow Program)

3401 N. Fairfax Drive, Suite 440
Arlington VA 22201-4432
703/993-4880 or 800/697-8799
FAX: 703/993-4890
Internet: http://www.TheIHS.org
AMOUNT: $1,500 + airfare and housing
DEADLINE(S): FEB 15
FIELD(S): Economics; Public Policy; Law; Government; Politics
ELIGIBILITY/REQUIREMENTS: Open to undergraduates and graduates to build skills and gain experience by participating in an 8-week summer internship program. Includes two week-long seminars, the internship, and research and writing projects with professionals. Must submit college transcripts, essays, and application. Financial need NOT a factor.
HOW TO APPLY: Apply online or contact IHS for an application.
NUMBER OF AWARDS: 32
RENEWABLE: No

601—INTERNATIONAL ASSOCIATION OF FIRE CHIEFS (IAFC) FOUNDATION

4025 Fair Ridge Drive
Fairfax VA 22033-2868
703/273-0911
E-mail: foundation@iafc.org
Internet: http://www.iafcf.org
AMOUNT: $250-$4,000
DEADLINE(S): AUG 1
FIELD(S): Fire sciences and related academic programs
ELIGIBILITY/REQUIREMENTS: Any person who is an active member with a minimum of 3 years' volunteer work, or 2 years' paid work, or a combination of paid and volunteer work, or 3 years with a state, county, provincial, municipal, community,

industrial, or federal fire department, and who has demonstrated proficiency as a member, is eligible to apply for a scholarship to a recognized institution of higher education. Dependents of members are not eligible.
HOW TO APPLY: Send completed application form, including a 250-word statement outlining your reasons for applying for assistance and explaining why you think your course of study will be useful to you in your chosen field. Also list credits previously attained in college-level courses and provide a transcript. Preference will be given to those demonstrating need, desire, and initiative.

602—NATIONAL GARDEN CLUBS, INC.

4401 Magnolia Avenue
St. Louis MO 63110-3492
314/776-7574
FAX: 314/776-5108
E-mail: glaustin2@bellsouth.net or headquarters@gardenclub.org
Internet: http://www.gardenclub.org
AMOUNT: $3,500
DEADLINE(S): MAR 1
FIELD(S): Horticulture, Floriculture, Landscape Design, City Planning, Land Management, and allied subjects
ELIGIBILITY/REQUIREMENTS: Open to juniors, seniors, and graduate students who are U.S. citizens and are studying any of the above or related subjects. Student must have the endorsement of the state in which he/she resides permanently. Applications will be forwarded to the National State Chairman and judged on a national level.
HOW TO APPLY: Write for complete information.
NUMBER OF AWARDS: 30-35

603—NEW ENGLAND EMPLOYEE BENEFITS COUNCIL

440 Totten Pond Road
Waltham MA 02145
781/684-8700
FAX: 781/684-9200
E-mail: linda@neebc.org
Internet: http://www.neebc.org
AMOUNT: Up to $5,000
DEADLINE(S): APR 1
FIELD(S): Health Care Program Design; Pension Plan Design, Implementation or Administration; Retirement Strategies; ERISA and Legal Aspects of Employee Benefits; Work/Life Programs; Health Risk Management; Institutional Investing of Retirement Savings; Multiemployer Plans;

Workers Compensation; Actuarial and Underwriting Analysis; Employee Benefits Communications
ELIGIBILITY/REQUIREMENTS: Full-time student (undergraduate or graduate) studying in an accredited academic program leading to a degree who demonstrates an interest through either course study or work experience in a career in the benefits field. Must be a New England resident or enrolled at a college in New England. Current NEEBC Board members, their spouses and children are not eligible to participate.
HOW TO APPLY: Completed application; all college transcripts; two or more references from college professors, NEEBC members, or other benefits professionals.
NUMBER OF AWARDS: 1 or 2
RENEWABLE: Yes
CONTACT: Linda Viens, Manager of Operations and Member Services

604—NEW YORK CITY DEPARTMENT OF CITYWIDE ADMINISTRATIVE SERVICES (Government Scholars Internship Program)

1 Centre Street, 24th Floor
New York NY 10007
212/487-5600
FAX: 212/487-5720
AMOUNT: $3,000
DEADLINE(S): JAN 13
FIELD(S): Public Administration; Urban Planning; Government; Public Service; Urban Affairs
ELIGIBILITY/REQUIREMENTS: 10-week summer intern program open to undergraduate sophomores, juniors, and seniors. Program provides students with unique opportunity to learn about NY City government. Internships available in virtually every city agency and mayoral office.
HOW TO APPLY: Write to New York City Fellowship Programs at above address for complete information.

605—SOCIETY OF DESIGN ADMINISTRATION, THE (ProNet Scholarship)

The Spector Group
311 New Hyde Park Road
North Hills NY 11040
516/365-4240
FAX: 516/365-3604
AMOUNT: $800 and $1,500
DEADLINE(S): MAR 1
FIELD(S): Architecture; Engineering; Practice Management
ELIGIBILITY/REQUIREMENTS: Applicants must demonstrate an interest in practice management studies in their edu-

cation programs, as this scholarship is intended to promote the education and training of design firm administrators.
HOW TO APPLY: Send completed application.
CONTACT: Patricia A. Manfre-Staab

606—TRANSPORTATION CLUBS INTERNATIONAL (Charlotte Woods Memorial Scholarship)

P. O. Box 2223
Ocean Shores WA 98569
AMOUNT: $1,000
DEADLINE(S): MAY 31
FIELD(S): Transportation Logistics; Traffic Management
ELIGIBILITY/REQUIREMENTS: Open to TCI members or their dependents enrolled at an accredited college or university in a program in transportation, traffic management, or related area and considering a career in transportation.
HOW TO APPLY: Type an essay of not more than 200 words on why you have chosen transportation or an allied field as a career path. Include your objectives. Financial need is also considered. Send SASE (business size) for complete information and application.
CONTACT: Katie DeJonge, Executive Director

607—TRANSPORTATION CLUBS INTERNATIONAL (Ginger and Fred Deines Canada Scholarships)

P. O. Box 2223
Ocean Shores WA 98569
AMOUNT: $500 and/or $1,000
DEADLINE(S): MAY 31
FIELD(S): Transportation Logistics; Traffic Management
ELIGIBILITY/REQUIREMENTS: For a student of Canadian nationality and enrolled in a school in Canada or U.S. in a degree or vocational program in the above or related areas.
HOW TO APPLY: Type an essay of not more than 200 words on why you have chosen transportation or an allied field as a career path. Include your objectives. Send an SASE for further details.
CONTACT: Katie DeJonge, Executive Director

608—TRANSPORTATION CLUBS INTERNATIONAL (Ginger and Fred Deines Mexico Scholarship)

P. O. Box 2223
Ocean Shores WA 98569
AMOUNT: $500-$1,000

FIELD(S): Logistics; Civil Engineering; Transportation
ELIGIBILITY/REQUIREMENTS: Applicants must have completed at least one year of undergraduate study at a 4-year institution in Mexico or the U.S. and be pursuing a career in logistics, civil engineering, or transportation.
HOW TO APPLY: Send SASE.
CONTACT: Katie DeJonge, Executive Director

609—TRANSPORTATION CLUBS INTERNATIONAL (Hooper Memorial Scholarships)

P. O. Box 2223
Ocean Shores WA 98569
AMOUNT: $1,500
DEADLINE(S): MAY 31
FIELD(S): Transportation Logistics; Traffic Management
ELIGIBILITY/REQUIREMENTS: For students enrolled in an accredited college or university in a degree or vocational program in transportation logistics, traffic management, or related fields and preparing for a career in transportation.
HOW TO APPLY: Type an essay of not more than 200 words on why you have chosen transportation or an allied field as a career. Include your objectives. Financial need is considered. Send SASE (business size) for complete information.
CONTACT: Katie DeJonge, Executive Director

610—UNIVERSITY OF ILLINOIS AT URBANA-CHAMPAIGN (Lydia E. Parker Bates Scholarship)

620 East John Street
Champaign IL 61820
217/333-0100
Internet: http://www.uiuc.edu/
AMOUNT: Up to $1,000
DEADLINE(S): MAR 15
FIELD(S): Art, Architecture, Landscape Architecture, Urban Planning, Dance, Theater, and all related subjects except Music
ELIGIBILITY/REQUIREMENTS: Open to undergraduate students in the College of Fine and Applied Arts who are attending the University of Illinois at Urbana-Champaign. Must demonstrate financial need and have 2.85 GPA. Recipients must carry at least 12 credit hours per semester.
HOW TO APPLY: Contact office of student financial aid for application. Complete the Free Application for Federal Student Aid with UIUC admission application.
NUMBER OF AWARDS: 175

611—WESTERN MICHIGAN UNIVERSITY (Mayor Dennis Archer Endowed Scholarship)

1903 West Michigan
Kalamazoo MI 49008-5337
269/387-8777
FAX: 269/387-6989
E-mail: alumni@wmich.edu
Internet: http://www.wmich.edu/alumni
AMOUNT: $2,000
DEADLINE(S): APR 1
FIELD(S): Education; Public Administration; Pre-Law
ELIGIBILITY/REQUIREMENTS: Undergraduate student; Detroit resident, or resident of Wayne, Oakland or Macomb counties; major in Education, Public Administration or Pre-Law programs; minimum 3.0 high school GPA. Preference given to those with financial need. Recipient must demonstrate evidence of public service/volunteer activities.
HOW TO APPLY: Contact the Office of Financial Aid for more details.
RENEWABLE: Yes. Up to a maximum of 4 consecutive academic years as long as the recipient maintains a 3.0 GPA at WMU.
CONTACT: Office of Financial Aid

612—WORLDSTUDIO FOUNDATION

200 Varick Street, Suite 507
New York NY 10014
212/366-1317
FAX: 212/807-0024
E-mail: info@worldstudio.org
Internet: http://www.worldstudio.org or http://www.www.aiga.org
AMOUNT: $1,500-$5,000
DEADLINE(S): APR 14
FIELD(S): Advertising, Animation, Architecture, Cartooning, Crafts, Environmental graphics, Film/video, Film/theater design, Fine arts, Furniture design, Industrial/product design, Interior architecture and design, Landscape architecture, New media, Photography, Surface/textile design, Urban planning
ELIGIBILITY/REQUIREMENTS: Applicants must be pursuing a degree in the fine or commercial arts, design or architecture, and plan to enter a career in the creative professions. Undergraduates and graduates are eligible. Minority status and/or social agenda are significant factors. Financial need a prerequisite. Minimum 2.0 GPA.
HOW TO APPLY: See websites for application. The application is a 2-part process.

Applications must include personal and school information, including transcripts and copies of letters of acceptance; financial information; portfolio; written statement of purpose; examples of a commitment to a social agenda, 2 letters of recommendation from college instructors, high school teachers, or employers; head shot of applicant.
NUMBER OF AWARDS: 20-30
RENEWABLE: Yes. Must reapply.
CONTACT: Mark Randall

SALES, MARKETING, PUBLIC RELATIONS

613—AD CLUB SEATTLE (Kerin Keller Memorial Scholarship)

1006 Industry Drive
Seattle WA 98188
206/448-4481
E-mail: adclubdirector@verizon.net
Internet: http://www.collegeplan.org/cpnow/pnwguide/onlineaps/safonap.htm
AMOUNT: $500
DEADLINE(S): MAR 31
FIELD(S): Business (especially marketing, advertising, and public relations), Communications
ELIGIBILITY/REQUIREMENTS: Open to residents of Washington state attending or about to attend an in-state 2- or 4-year public, private, accredited college or university at the undergraduate level. Must demonstrate financial need (not necessarily the determining factor) and major in business or communications. Focus on marketing, advertising and public relations is strongly encouraged. Because Keller was victim of breast cancer, applicant must be related to a victim of breast cancer.
HOW TO APPLY: See website for application; submit with a 1-page personal essay explaining your relationship to a victim of breast cancer and how this award will help you achieve your educational goals, a 1-page list of significant activities and honors, 2 letters of recommendation, an official transcript from the high school or college the student is currently attending or if not currently in school, an official transcript from the last school they attended, and FAFSA or FAFSA Student Aid Report (SAR).
NUMBER OF AWARDS: 1
RENEWABLE: No
CONTACT: Cindy Pennington, Executive Director

614—AMERICAN ASSOCIATION OF ADVERTISING AGENCIES, INC. (Multicultural Advertising Internship Program)

405 Lexington Avenue, 18th Floor
New York NY 10174-1801
212/682-2500 or 800/676-9333
FAX: 212/682-2028
Internet: http://www.aaaa.org
AMOUNT: $350/week + partial expenses and travel
DEADLINE(S): JAN 22
FIELD(S): Advertising; Marketing; Public Relations
ELIGIBILITY/REQUIREMENTS: 10-week summer internship at advertising agency in the U.S. is open to African Americans, Native Americans, Hispanics, or Asians interested in a career in advertising. Must be U.S. citizen/permanent resident, have a minimum 3.0 GPA, and be a college junior, senior, or graduate student.
HOW TO APPLY: See website or contact AAAA for an application.
NUMBER OF AWARDS: 75-100

615—AMERICAN INSTITUTE OF POLISH CULTURE

1440 79th Street Causeway, Suite 117
Miami FL 33141
305/864-2349
FAX: 305/865-5150
E-mail: info@ampolinstitute.org
Internet: http://www.ampolinstitute.org
AMOUNT: $1,000
DEADLINE(S): FEB 15
FIELD(S): Journalism; Public Relations; Communications
ELIGIBILITY/REQUIREMENTS: Awards are to encourage young Americans of Polish descent to pursue the above professions. Can be used for full-time study at any accredited American college. Criteria for selection include achievement, talent, and involvement in public life.
HOW TO APPLY: Send SASE for an application. $25 processing fee.
RENEWABLE: Yes
CONTACT: Harriet Irsay

616—AMERICAN INTERCONTINENTAL UNIVERSITY (Emilio Pucci Scholarships)

Admissions Committee
3330 Peachtree Road NE
Atlanta GA 30326
404/812-8192 or 888/248-7392

AMOUNT: $1,800 (applied toward tuition over 6 quarters)
DEADLINE(S): None
FIELD(S): Fashion Design; Fashion Marketing; Interior Design; Commercial Art; Business Administration; Video Production
ELIGIBILITY/REQUIREMENTS: Scholarships are for high school seniors who are interested in either a 2-year or 4-year program at one of the campuses of the American Intercontinental University: Atlanta, GA; Los Angeles, CA; London, UK; or Dubai, United Arab Emirates.
HOW TO APPLY: Write for applications and complete information.

617—ASSOCIATION FOR WOMEN IN COMMUNICATIONS, THE

c/o USA Weekend
7950 Jones Branch Drive
McLean VA 22107
703/854-5631
FAX: 703/854-2122
Internet: http://www.womcom.org
AMOUNT: $1,000
DEADLINE(S): MAR 19
FIELD(S): Journalism; Public Relations
ELIGIBILITY/REQUIREMENTS: Current sophomore or junior female student attending a Washington, DC-area university or college studying communications, advertising, journalism, public relations, marketing, graphic arts, or a related field with an overall GPA of 3.0 or higher.
HOW TO APPLY: Send résumé, cover letter, application, and transcripts.
NUMBER OF AWARDS: 1
CONTACT: Frappa Stout, Vice President of Student Affairs, AWC DC Chapter

618—CONNECTICUT BROADCASTERS ASSOCIATION

90 South Park Street
Willimantic CT 06226
860/633-5031
FAX: 860/456-5688
Internet: http://www.ctba.org
AMOUNT: Varies
DEADLINE(S): JAN 31
FIELD(S): Broadcasting, Marketing, Engineering, Electronics
ELIGIBILITY/REQUIREMENTS: Open to Connecticut residents pursuing a broadcasting career or a career in related fields.
HOW TO APPLY: Applications are available from Connecticut broadcast stations and on website.
NUMBER OF AWARDS: Varies

RENEWABLE: Yes. Some are 4-year, subject to performance; others must reapply.
CONTACT: M.C. Rice, CBA President

619—EAA AVIATION FOUNDATION (EAA Air Academy-EADS Socata Internship)

EAA Scholarship Department
P.O. 3086
Oshkosh WI 54903-3065
920/426-6823
E-mail: scholarships@eaa.org
Internet: http://www.young eagles.org
AMOUNT: Travel and accommodations in France and Oshkosh WI
DEADLINE(S): MAR 1
FIELD(S): Aviation and Related Areas, Engineering, Marketing, Manufacturing
ELIGIBILITY/REQUIREMENTS: Open to college junior or seniors, intending to pursue a career in aviation. Applicants must be in full-time education and able to demonstrate an interest in aeronautical career—engineering, marketing, manufacturing, or other areas focused on aviation. Applicants must be U.S. or Canadian citizens and able to obtain their own passport. Knowledge of French would enhance the experience but is not an absolute requirement. Must also be a current member of EAA (Experimental Aircraft Association) or recommended by a current EAA member to apply for these internships. Learn more about joining EAA (www.eaa.org) or call 800/843-3612.
HOW TO APPLY: Apply online.
NUMBER OF AWARDS: 2 (1 male, 1 female)
ADDITIONAL INFORMATION: The internship will provide an opportunity for each young person to visit France for an internship of five weeks' duration in June and July. They will work at an EADS Socata facility and be exposed to a variety of aviation disciplines. Recipients will conclude their summer by attending a week-long session of the EAA Advanced Air Academy in Oshkosh, providing mentorship opportunities to young people aged 16-18 who are participating in the camp. This will include an opportunity to experience the EAA AirVenture Oshkosh.

620—HAWAII COMMUNITY FOUNDATION (Bick Bickson Scholarship)

1164 Bishop Street, Suite 800
Honolulu HI 96813
808/537-6333 or toll free:
888/731-3863

FAX: 808/521-6286
E-mail: info@hcf-hawaii.org
Internet: http://www.hcf-hawaii.org
DEADLINE(S): MAR 1
FIELD(S): Marketing; Law; Travel Industry Management
ELIGIBILITY/REQUIREMENTS: Applicant must be resident of the state of Hawaii; plan to attend full time an accredited 2- or 4-year college or university; and demonstrate financial need, good moral character, and academic achievement with a minimum GPA of 2.7.
HOW TO APPLY: See website. Send application with 2 letters of recommendation.

621—HAWAII COMMUNITY FOUNDATION (PRSA-Hawaii/Roy Leffingwell Public Relations Scholarship)

1164 Bishop Street, Suite 800
Honolulu HI 96813
808/537-6333 or toll free:
888/731-3863
FAX: 808/521-6286
E-mail: info@hcf-hawaii.org
Internet: http://www.hcf-hawaii.org
DEADLINE(S): MAR 1
FIELD(S): Public Relations; Journalism; Communications
ELIGIBILITY/REQUIREMENTS: Applicants must intend to pursue a career in public relations; be residents of Hawaii; be junior or senior undergraduate or graduate students enrolled full time in an accredited 2- or 4-year college or university; and demonstrate financial need, good moral character, and academic achievement with a minimum GPA of 2.7.
HOW TO APPLY: See website. Send application with 2 letters of recommendation.

622—HISPANIC COLLEGE FUND (HSF/Little Village Chamber of Commerce Ambassador's Scholarship Program)

55 Second Street, Suite 1500
San Francisco CA 94105
1-877/HSF-INFO
(1-877/473-4636)
FAX: 415/808-2302
E-mail: pip@hsf.net
Internet: http://hispanicfund.org
AMOUNT: At least $2,000
DEADLINE(S): JUN 23
FIELD(S): Business; Finance; Marketing and related fields

ELIGIBILITY/REQUIREMENTS: Open to entering and continuing full-time undergraduate and graduate students from the Little Village Community. Must be U.S. citizens or legal permanent residents of Hispanic heritage (one parent fully Hispanic or both parents half Hispanic). Minimum GPA of 3.0. Must carry at least 12 credits each term. Selection is based on academic achievement, personal strengths, leadership and financial need.
HOW TO APPLY: Contact Fund for details or visit website for application.

623—INTERNATIONAL RADIO AND TELEVISION SOCIETY FOUNDATION (Summer Fellowship Program)

420 Lexington Avenue, Suite 1714
New York NY 10170
212/867-6650
FAX: 212/867-6653
Internet: http://www.irts.org
AMOUNT: Housing, stipend, and travel
DEADLINE(S): NOV 12
FIELD(S): Broadcasting; Communications; Sales; Marketing
ELIGIBILITY/REQUIREMENTS: 9-week summer fellowship program in New York City is open to outstanding full-time undergraduate juniors and seniors with a demonstrated interest in a career in communications. Financial need NOT a factor.
HOW TO APPLY: See website or contact IRTS for an application.
NUMBER OF AWARDS: 20-25
RENEWABLE: No
CONTACT: Maria DeLeon-Fisher

624—JACOB'S PILLOW DANCE FESTIVAL (Internships)

The Intern Program at Jacob's Pillow
P.O. Box 287
Lee MA 01238
413/637-1322
FAX: 413/243-4744
E-mail: info@jacobspillow.org
Internet: http://www.jacobs pillow.org
AMOUNT: Varies
DEADLINE(S): APR 5
FIELD(S): Archives/Preservation; Business; Development; Education; Marketing/Press; Operations/Production
ELIGIBILITY/REQUIREMENTS: Full- and part-time internships for the fall, winter, and spring can be tailored to meet college credit needs and individual interests.
HOW TO APPLY: Apply by sending 2 copies of each: a cover letter, résumé, and writing/design samples as applicable.

CONTACT: Intern Program at Jacob's Pillow

625—JUNIOR ACHIEVEMENT INC. (N. Donald Edwards Scholarship to the University of Bridgeport)

One Education Way
Colorado Springs CO 80906-4477
719/540-8000
FAX: 719/540-6299
E-mail: newmedia@ja.org
Internet: http://www.ja.org
AMOUNT: $1,000
DEADLINE(S): APR 1
FIELD(S): Marketing
ELIGIBILITY/REQUIREMENTS: Applicants must enroll in the School of Business at the University of Bridgeport, with a major in marketing and must have financial need.
HOW TO APPLY: Send completed application, with a letter of recommendation from local Junior Achievement area verifying participation in either JA Economics or JA Company Program.
NUMBER OF AWARDS: Varies
RENEWABLE: No
CONTACT: To obtain application, contact Ms. Suzanne Dale Wilcox, Director of Financial Aid, University of Bridgeport, 126 Park Avenue, Wahlstrom Library, Bridgeport CT 06601; 203/576-4568; or www.bridgeport.edu. Submit completed application to the University of Bridgeport.

626—NATIONAL DAIRY SHRINE (NDS/DMT Milk Marketing Scholarship)

1224 Alton Darby Creek Rd.
Columbus OH 43228-9792
614/878-5333
FAX: 614/870-2622
E-mail: shrine@cobaselect.com
Internet: http://www.dairyshrine.org
AMOUNT: $1,000 and $2,500
DEADLINE(S): MAR 15
FIELD(S): Dairy Industry; Marketing; Business Administration; Journalism; Home Economics
ELIGIBILITY/REQUIREMENTS: College sophomores, juniors or seniors majoring in dairy marketing, dairy manufacturing, dairy science, home economics or journalism at a college or university approved by the appropriate National Dairy Shrine committee. Awards are based on ability, interests and need.
HOW TO APPLY: Download application from website.
NUMBER OF AWARDS: 5 to 9 depending on number and quality of applicants
RENEWABLE: No

CONTACT: Maurice E. Core, Executive Director

627—NAVAL HISTORICAL CENTER (Internship Program)

Washington Navy Yard
805 Kidder Breese Street SE
Washington DC 20374-5060
202/433-6901
FAX: 202/433-8200
E-mail: edward.furgol@navy.mil
Internet: http://www.history.navy.mil
AMOUNT: $400 possible honoraria; otherwise, unpaid
DEADLINE(S): None
FIELD(S): Education; History; Public Relations; Design
ELIGIBILITY/REQUIREMENTS: Registered students of colleges/universities and graduates thereof are eligible for this program, which must be a minimum of 3 weeks, full- or part-time. Four specialties are available: Curator, Education, Public Relations, and Design. Interns receive orientation and assist in their department, and they must complete an individual project that contributes to the Center.
HOW TO APPLY: Submit completed application, available from the website, before the desired initiation of an internship. Also send one letter of recommendation, an unofficial transcript, and (except for graphic design applicants) a writing sample of not less than 1,000 words.
NUMBER OF AWARDS: 60
RENEWABLE: Yes; must reapply.
CONTACT: Dr. Edward Furgol

628—NEW YORK STATE THEATRE INSTITUTE (Internships in Theatrical Production)

37 First Street
Troy NY 12180
518/274-3200
FAX: 518/274-3815
E-mail: nysti@capital.net
Internet: http://www.nysti.org/not-for-profit/nysti/int.htm
AMOUNT: None
DEADLINE(S): None
FIELD(S): Theatrical Production and related fields
ELIGIBILITY/REQUIREMENTS: Internships for college and graduate students, high school seniors, and educators-in-residence interested in developing skills in above fields. Unpaid academic credit is earned. Gain experience in box office, costumes, education, electrics, music, stage management, scenery, properties, perfor-

mance, and public relations. Interns come from all over the world.

HOW TO APPLY: Must be associated with an accredited institution. See website for more information, call or write. Include your postal mailing address.

CONTACT: Arlene Leff, Intern Program Director, 518/274-3573

629—PRESS CLUB OF DALLAS FOUNDATION

400 N. Olive
Dallas TX 75201
214/740-9988
AMOUNT: $1,000-$3,000
DEADLINE(S): APR 15
FIELD(S): Journalism; Public Relations
ELIGIBILITY/REQUIREMENTS: Open to students who are at least sophomore level in undergraduate studies or working toward a master's degree in the above fields in a Texas college or university. This scholarship is renewable by reapplication.

HOW TO APPLY: Write to the above address for complete information.
CONTACT: Carol Wortham

630—SEARS CRAFTSMAN SCHOLARSHIP

NHRA Youth & Education Services
2035 Financial Way
Glendora CA 91741-4602
626/250-2296
FAX: 212/204-3972/73
E-mail: rkaizoji@nhra.com
Internet: http://www.nhra.org
AMOUNT: $250
DEADLINE(S): MAY 1
FIELD(S): Automotive Technology; Industrial/Technical Manufacturing; Marketing
ELIGIBILITY/REQUIREMENTS: Applicants must be seniors graduating from a public, private, or parochial school or education center between January and June. Applicants must be of good character, possess minimum 2.5 GPA, show evidence of leadership ability, involvement in extracurricular school and community activities, and plan to attend an accredited 2- or 4-year college, university or technical/vocational program. Students with a failing grade during their high school career will not be considered. Preference will be given to those applicants planning a career in above fields. Awards will be based on scholastic record, school activities and community involvement, personal essay, recommendations, and financial need.

HOW TO APPLY: Submit application; personal essay; 2 recommendations, 1 of which must be from a teacher, counselor, or administrator; and transcript.
NUMBER OF AWARDS: 21 (3 in each of the 7 National Hot Rod Association Divisions)
CONTACT: Rachel Kaizoji

631—STATE NEWS

Michigan State University
343 Student Services
East Lansing MI 48824-1113
E-mail: recruiter@statenews.com
Internet: http://statenews.com/scholar/scholarship/
AMOUNT: $2,000/year for 4 years + job
DEADLINE(S): FEB 5
FIELD(S): All; Journalism; Advertising
ELIGIBILITY/REQUIREMENTS: Open to high school seniors who will start at MSU in the fall. Must have an above-average GPA and have demonstrated a strong interest in high school journalism or advertising through their newspapers and yearbooks. Recipients work in paying positions at *The State News* after the first semester of their freshman year, either in the newsroom or in the advertising department. *State News* pay is in addition to the scholarship. May major in any academic program.

HOW TO APPLY: See website or contact *State News* General Manager for an application.
NUMBER OF AWARDS: 2
CONTACT: Ben Schwartz, *State News* General Manager

632—UNIVERSITY OF NORTH TEXAS (Merchandising and Hospitality Scholarships)

Dean, School of Merchandising/Hospitality Management
P.O. Box 311100
Denton TX 76203-1100
817/565-2436
Internet: http://www.unt./scholar/scholarshipedu/scholarships/smhm.htm
AMOUNT: Varies
DEADLINE(S): Varies
FIELD(S): Merchandising and Hospitality Management
ELIGIBILITY/REQUIREMENTS: Several scholarships for students in the above fields are offered at the University of North Texas. Specialties and eligibility requirements vary.

HOW TO APPLY: See website for more information. Contact school for details.

633—UNIVERSITY OF OKLAHOMA-H. H. HERBERT SCHOOL OF JOURNALISM AND MASS COMMUNICATION (Undergraduate Scholarships)

860 Van Vleet Oval, Room 101
Norman OK 73019
405/325-2721
AMOUNT: $5,000/year
DEADLINE(S): FEB
FIELD(S): Journalism: Print or Broadcast, Advertising, Electronic Media, News Communication, Professional Writing, Public Relations
ELIGIBILITY/REQUIREMENTS: For undergraduate students studying in the above fields who plan to attend the University of Oklahoma.

HOW TO APPLY: Contact Herbert School for additional information and application. Interview is part of acceptance process.
CONTACT: David Dary

634—WESTERN MICHIGAN UNIVERSITY (College of Engineering and Applied Sciences/Ann Arbor Graphic Arts Memorial Foundation Scholarship)

1903 West Michigan
Kalamazoo MI 49008-5337
269/387-6000
FAX: 269/387-6989
Internet: http://www.wmich.edu/finaid
AMOUNT: Varies
FIELD(S): Printing Management/Marketing
ELIGIBILITY/REQUIREMENTS: Recipient must be enrolled in printing management/marketing curriculum.

HOW TO APPLY: Contact the Paper and Printing Science and Engineering Department, 1104 Welborn Hall for an application.
NUMBER OF AWARDS: 1

635—WESTERN MICHIGAN UNIVERSITY (College of Engineering and Applied Sciences/Brian Scott Lacombe Humanitarian Scholarship)

1903 West Michigan
Kalamazoo MI 49008-5337
269/387-6000
FAX: 269/387-6989
Internet: http://www.wmich.edu/finaid

AMOUNT: $1,000
FIELD(S): Printing Management/
   Marketing
ELIGIBILITY/REQUIREMENTS: Open to full-time transfer student with 30 credit hours or more toward a printing program enrolled in printing management/ marketing curriculum. Award is based on financial need.
HOW TO APPLY: Contact the Paper and Printing Science and Engineering Department, 1104 Welborn Hall for an application.
NUMBER OF AWARDS: 1

636—WESTERN MICHIGAN UNIVERSITY (College of Engineering and Applied Sciences/Charles W. Thomasma Printing Scholarship)

1903 West Michigan
Kalamazoo MI 49008-5337
269/387-6000
FAX: 269/387-6989
Internet: http://www.wmich.edu/finaid
AMOUNT: $1,000
FIELD(S): Printing Management/
   Marketing
ELIGIBILITY/REQUIREMENTS: Open to freshman enrolled in printing management/marketing curriculum.
HOW TO APPLY: Contact the Paper and Printing Science and Engineering Department, 1104 Welborn Hall for an application.
NUMBER OF AWARDS: 1

637—WESTERN MICHIGAN UNIVERSITY (College of Engineering and Applied Sciences/E. J. Kelly Endowment Memorial Scholarship in Printing)

1903 West Michigan
Kalamazoo MI 49008-5337
269/387-6000
FAX: 269/387-6989
Internet: http://www.wmich.edu/finaid
AMOUNT: $500-$1,000
FIELD(S): Printing Management/
   Marketing
ELIGIBILITY/REQUIREMENTS: Open to full-time sophomores or juniors enrolled in printing management/marketing curriculum. Award is based on financial need.
HOW TO APPLY: Contact the Paper and Printing Science and Engineering Department, 1104 Welborn Hall for an application.
NUMBER OF AWARDS: 1

638—WESTERN MICHIGAN UNIVERSITY (College of Engineering and Applied Sciences/Gravure Education Foundation Scholarship)

1903 West Michigan
Kalamazoo MI 49008-5337
269/387-6000
FAX: 269/387-6989
Internet: http://www.wmich.edu/finaid
AMOUNT: $1,500
FIELD(S): Printing
   Management/Marketing
ELIGIBILITY/REQUIREMENTS: Open to students enrolled full time in printing management/marketing curriculum. Extracurricular activities required. Coordination of "Gravure Day" at WMU a requirement.
HOW TO APPLY: Contact the Paper and Printing Science and Engineering Department, 1104 Welborn Hall for an application.
NUMBER OF AWARDS: 1

639—WESTERN MICHIGAN UNIVERSITY (College of Engineering and Applied Sciences/Herbert F. Ramage Jr. Memorial Scholarship)

1903 West Michigan
Kalamazoo MI 49008-5337
269/387-6000
FAX: 269/387-6989
Internet: http://www.wmich.edu/finaid
AMOUNT: $750
FIELD(S): Printing Management/
   Marketing
ELIGIBILITY/REQUIREMENTS: Open to full-time sophomores enrolled in printing management/marketing curriculum. Award is based on financial need.
HOW TO APPLY: Contact the Paper and Printing Science and Engineering Department, 1104 Welborn Hall for an application.
NUMBER OF AWARDS: 1

640—WESTERN MICHIGAN UNIVERSITY (College of Engineering and Applied Sciences/Jane L. Ulmer Memorial Scholarship)

1903 West Michigan
Kalamazoo MI 49008-5337
269/387-6000
FAX: 269/387-6989
Internet: http://www.wmich.edu/finaid

AMOUNT: $1,000
FIELD(S): Printing Management/
   Marketing
ELIGIBILITY/REQUIREMENTS: Open to students enrolled full time in printing management/marketing curriculum. Based on financial need and department involvement.
HOW TO APPLY: Contact the Paper and Printing Science and Engineering Department, 1104 Welborn Hall for an application.
NUMBER OF AWARDS: 1
RENEWABLE: No

641—WESTERN MICHIGAN UNIVERSITY (College of Engineering and Applied Sciences/Print and Graphics Foundation Scholarship)

1903 West Michigan
Kalamazoo MI 49008-5337
269/387-6000
FAX: 269/387-6989
E-mail: finaid-info@wmich.edu
Internet: http://www.wmich.edu/finaid
AMOUNT: Varies
FIELD(S): Printing Management/
   Marketing
ELIGIBILITY/REQUIREMENTS: Open to full-time student, enrolled in printing management/marketing curriculum, and having an overall GPA of at least 3.0.
HOW TO APPLY: Contact the Paper and Printing Science and Engineering Department, 1104 Welborn Hall for an application.
NUMBER OF AWARDS: 1

642—WESTERN MICHIGAN UNIVERSITY (College of Engineering and Applied Sciences/Robert Caine Outstanding Student Award)

1903 West Michigan
Kalamazoo MI 49008-5337
269/387-6000
FAX: 269/387-6989
E-mail: finaid-info@wmich.edu
Internet: http://www.wmich.edu/finaid
AMOUNT: Varies
FIELD(S): Printing Management/
   Marketing
ELIGIBILITY/REQUIREMENTS: Open to graduating seniors; extracurricular activities required.
HOW TO APPLY: Recipient is selected by faculty. Contact the Paper and Printing

Science and Engineering Department, 1104 Welborn Hall for an application.
NUMBER OF AWARDS: 1
RENEWABLE: No

643—WESTERN MICHIGAN UNIVERSITY (College of Engineering and Applied Sciences/The Lawrence J. Brink Scholarship)

1903 West Michigan
Kalamazoo MI 49008-5337
269/387-6000
FAX: 269/387-6989
E-mail: finaid-info@wmich.edu
Internet:
http://www.wmich.edu/finaid
AMOUNT: $1,000
FIELD(S): Printing Management/ Marketing
ELIGIBILITY/REQUIREMENTS: Open to full-time students (freshman to senior) enrolled in printing management/marketing curriculum. Award is based on financial need.
HOW TO APPLY: Contact the Paper and Printing Science and Engineering Department, 1104 Welborn Hall for an application.
NUMBER OF AWARDS: 1

644—WESTERN MICHIGAN UNIVERSITY (College of Engineering and Applied Sciences/Web Offset Scholarship)

1903 West Michigan
Kalamazoo MI 49008-5337
269/387-6000
FAX: 269/387-6989
E-mail: finaid-info@wmich.edu
Internet: http://www.wmich.edu/finaid
AMOUNT: Varies
FIELD(S): Printing Management/ Marketing
ELIGIBILITY/REQUIREMENTS: Recipient must be enrolled in printing management/marketing curriculum.
HOW TO APPLY: Contact the Paper and Printing Science and Engineering Department, 1104 Welborn Hall for an application.
NUMBER OF AWARDS: 1
RENEWABLE: No

645—WESTERN MICHIGAN UNIVERSITY (Haworth College of Business/Associated Food Dealers of Michigan Scholarship)

1903 West Michigan
Kalamazoo MI 49008-5337

269/387-6000
FAX: 269/387-6989
E-mail: finaid-info@wmich.edu
Internet: http://www.wmich.edu/finaid
AMOUNT: $1,000
DEADLINE(S): FEB 15
FIELD(S): Food Marketing
ELIGIBILITY/REQUIREMENTS: Food Marketing majors; cumulative GPA of at least 2.5; unless otherwise specified, students must have a signed major slip on file and must be at least at the sophomore level; consideration given to a demonstrated career in food marketing, work experience, participation in University and community activities, financial need, and faculty recommendations.
HOW TO APPLY: Applications available December 1 through March 1. Contact the Marketing Department for more details.
NUMBER OF AWARDS: 2
RENEWABLE: Yes

646—WESTERN MICHIGAN UNIVERSITY (Haworth College of Business/Biggs/ Gilmore Advertising Scholarship)

1903 West Michigan
Kalamazoo MI 49008-5337
269/387-6000
FAX: 269/387-6989
E-mail: finaid-info@wmich.edu
Internet: http://www.wmich.edu/finaid
AMOUNT: $500
DEADLINE(S): FEB 15
FIELD(S): Advertising; Promotion; Marketing
ELIGIBILITY/REQUIREMENTS: Advertising and Promotion majors who have completed 55 to 95 credit hours with a cumulative GPA of at least 2.5; must be enrolled for a minimum of 12 credit hours; consideration given to student with a demonstrated career interest in advertising/marketing, work experience, participation in University and community activities, and faculty recommendations.
HOW TO APPLY: Contact the Marketing Department for more information.

647—WESTERN MICHIGAN UNIVERSITY (Haworth College of Business/Chicago Food Brokers Association Scholarships)

1903 West Michigan
Kalamazoo MI 49008-5337
269/387-6000
FAX: 269/387-6989
E-mail: finaid-info@wmich.edu

Internet: http://www.wmich.edu/finaid
AMOUNT: At least $1,000
DEADLINE(S): FEB 15
FIELD(S): Food Marketing
ELIGIBILITY/REQUIREMENTS: Food Marketing majors affiliated with Chicago-based food companies and retailers; cumulative GPA of at least 2.5; unless otherwise specified, students must have a signed major slip on file and must be at least at the sophomore level; consideration given to a demonstrated career in food marketing, work experience, participation in University and community activities, financial need, and faculty recommendations.
HOW TO APPLY: Contact the Marketing Department for more details.
NUMBER OF AWARDS: Multiple
RENEWABLE: Yes

648—WESTERN MICHIGAN UNIVERSITY (Haworth College of Business/Coca-Cola Food Marketing Fellowships)

1903 West Michigan
Kalamazoo MI 49008-5337
269/387-6000
FAX: 269/387-6989
E-mail: finaid-info@wmich.edu
Internet: http://www.wmich.edu/finaid
AMOUNT: At least $2,000
DEADLINE(S): FEB 15
FIELD(S): Food Marketing
ELIGIBILITY/REQUIREMENTS: Food Marketing majors with cumulative GPA of at least 2.5. Unless otherwise specified, students must have a signed major slip on file and must be at least at the sophomore level. Consideration given to a demonstrated career in food marketing, work experience, participation in University and community activities, financial need, and faculty recommendations.
HOW TO APPLY: Contact the Marketing Department for more details.
NUMBER OF AWARDS: 3

649—WESTERN MICHIGAN UNIVERSITY (Haworth College of Business/Cynthia Wrazien-Hirt Endowed Memorial Advertising Scholarship)

1903 West Michigan
Kalamazoo MI 49008-5337
269/387-6000
FAX: 269/387-6989
Internet: http://www.wmich.edu/finaid
AMOUNT: Varies

DEADLINE(S): FEB 15
FIELD(S): Advertising; Promotion; Marketing; English (writing)
ELIGIBILITY/REQUIREMENTS: Open to full-time juniors and seniors who are Advertising and Promotion majors who have completed 55 to 95 credit hours with a cumulative GPA of at least 3.0. Preference given to students who, in addition to majoring in Advertising and Promotion, are pursuing either a major or minor in English with a creative or practical writing emphasis. Extracurricular activities considered, including work experience.
HOW TO APPLY: Contact the Marketing Department for more information.
RENEWABLE: Yes. Up to a maximum of two consecutive academic years.

650—WESTERN MICHIGAN UNIVERSITY (Haworth College of Business/Dorothy J. and Clinton J. Christoff Endowed Scholarship)

1903 West Michigan
Kalamazoo MI 49008-5337
269/387-6000
FAX: 269/387-6989
E-mail: finaid-info@wmich.edu
Internet: http://www.wmich.edu/finaid
AMOUNT: At least $2,000
DEADLINE(S): FEB 15
FIELD(S): Food Marketing
ELIGIBILITY/REQUIREMENTS: Entering freshman or transfer student admitted to the Food Marketing Program. Preference given to students from the Lowell Public School system, or to family members of employees or customers of Chadalee Farms/Litehouse, Inc.
HOW TO APPLY: Contact the Marketing Department for more details.
NUMBER OF AWARDS: 1
RENEWABLE: Yes

651—WESTERN MICHIGAN UNIVERSITY (Haworth College of Business/Enterprise Rent-A-Car Scholarship)

1903 West Michigan
Kalamazoo MI 49008-5337
269/387-6000
FAX: 269/387-6989
E-mail: finaid-info@wmich.edu
Internet: http://www.wmich.edu/finaid
AMOUNT: Varies
DEADLINE(S): FEB 15

FIELD(S): Sales; Marketing; Management
ELIGIBILITY/REQUIREMENTS: Junior or senior; must be full-time student majoring in or intending to major in, sales and marketing or management; minimum 3.0 GPA for this merit-based scholarship. Must be available to participate in a paid internship during summer months if opening exists.
HOW TO APPLY: Application forms must be obtained from and returned to the Marketing Department.
NUMBER OF AWARDS: 2

652—WESTERN MICHIGAN UNIVERSITY (Haworth College of Business/Farmer Jack Supermarkets Scholarships)

1903 West Michigan
Kalamazoo MI 49008-5337
269/387-6000
FAX: 269/387-6989
E-mail: finaid-info@wmich.edu
Internet: http://www.wmich.edu/finaid
AMOUNT: $5,000
DEADLINE(S): FEB 15
FIELD(S): Food Marketing
ELIGIBILITY/REQUIREMENTS: One scholarship is designated for a current employee of Farmer Jack who is enrolled in, or plans to enroll in the Food Marketing Program. The other is awarded to a current food marketing major with a career interest in retail store operations.
HOW TO APPLY: Contact the Marketing Department for more details.
NUMBER OF AWARDS: 2
RENEWABLE: Yes

653—WESTERN MICHIGAN UNIVERSITY (Haworth College of Business/G & R Felpausch Company Endowed Scholarship)

1903 West Michigan
Kalamazoo MI 49008-5337
269/387-6000
FAX: 269/387-6989
E-mail: finaid-info@wmich.edu
Internet: http://www.wmich.edu/finaid
AMOUNT: Varies
DEADLINE(S): FEB 15
FIELD(S): Food Marketing; Business
ELIGIBILITY/REQUIREMENTS: Student majoring in food marketing; minimum GPA of 2.5. Preference given to Felpausch Food Centers employees, or family of employees, majoring in food mar-

keting or business related major. Consideration given to financial need, interest in food marketing, work experience, and participation in University and community activities.
HOW TO APPLY: Application forms must be obtained from and returned to the Marketing Department.
NUMBER OF AWARDS: 2
RENEWABLE: Yes

654—WESTERN MICHIGAN UNIVERSITY (Haworth College of Business/Georgia-Pacific Corporation Food Marketing Scholarships)

1903 West Michigan
Kalamazoo MI 49008-5337
269/387-6000
FAX: 269/387-6989
E-mail: finaid-info@wmich.edu
Internet: http://www.wmich.edu/finaid
AMOUNT: $5,000
DEADLINE(S): FEB 15
FIELD(S): Food Marketing
ELIGIBILITY/REQUIREMENTS: Awarded on the basis of outstanding academic achievement.
HOW TO APPLY: Contact the Marketing Department for more details.
NUMBER OF AWARDS: 2
RENEWABLE: No

655—WESTERN MICHIGAN UNIVERSITY (Haworth College of Business/James W. Richmond Sales and Business Marketing Scholarship)

1903 West Michigan
Kalamazoo MI 49008-5337
269/387-6000
FAX: 269/387-6989
E-mail: finaid-info@wmich.edu
Internet: http://www.wmich.edu/finaid
AMOUNT: Varies
DEADLINE(S): FEB 15
FIELD(S): Food Marketing; Manufacturing Technology
ELIGIBILITY/REQUIREMENTS: Preference shall be given to sophomore, junior, or senior Sales and Business Marketing majors who are pursuing a minor in Manufacturing Technology. Must have GPA of 3.0 and be a full-time student.
HOW TO APPLY: Contact the Marketing Department for more details.
NUMBER OF AWARDS: 1 or more
RENEWABLE: Yes

656—WESTERN MICHIGAN UNIVERSITY (Haworth College of Business/Jules W. Englander Memorial Endowed Scholarship)

1903 West Michigan
Kalamazoo MI 49008-5337
269/387-6000
FAX: 269/387-6989
E-mail: finaid-info@wmich.edu
Internet: http://www.wmich.edu/finaid
AMOUNT: At least $1,000
DEADLINE(S): FEB 15
FIELD(S): Food Marketing
ELIGIBILITY/REQUIREMENTS: Junior or senior food marketing student. Selected on the basis of need and potential for career success within the food industry.
HOW TO APPLY: Contact the Marketing Department for more details.
NUMBER OF AWARDS: 1
RENEWABLE: Yes

657—WESTERN MICHIGAN UNIVERSITY (Haworth College of Business/Julie Kravitz Endowed Memorial Scholarship)

1903 West Michigan
Kalamazoo MI 49008-5337
269/387-6000
FAX: 269/387-6989
E-mail: finaid-info@wmich.edu
Internet: http://www.wmich.edu/finaid
AMOUNT: At least $1,000
DEADLINE(S): FEB 15
FIELD(S): Food Marketing
ELIGIBILITY/REQUIREMENTS: Recipient must be a full-time student with a minimum GPA of 3.0. Preference given to students from the Cleveland, Ohio area.
HOW TO APPLY: Contact the Marketing Department for more details.
NUMBER OF AWARDS: 1
RENEWABLE: Yes

658—WESTERN MICHIGAN UNIVERSITY (Haworth College of Business/Kellogg's Food Marketing Scholarship)

1903 West Michigan
Kalamazoo MI 49008-5337
269/387-6000
FAX: 269/387-6989
E-mail: finaid-info@wmich.edu
Internet: http://www.wmich.edu/finaid
AMOUNT: At least $1,000
DEADLINE(S): FEB 15
FIELD(S): Food Marketing
ELIGIBILITY/REQUIREMENTS: Awarded on the basis of scholarship and need. Preference given to members of Sigma Phi Omega.
HOW TO APPLY: Contact the Marketing Department for more details.
NUMBER OF AWARDS: 1 or more

659—WESTERN MICHIGAN UNIVERSITY (Haworth College of Business/Louis P. Johnston Advertising Scholarship)

1903 West Michigan
Kalamazoo MI 49008-5337
269/387-6000
FAX: 269/387-6989
E-mail: finaid-info@wmich.edu
Internet: http://www.wmich.edu/finaid
AMOUNT: $500
DEADLINE(S): FEB 15
FIELD(S): Advertising; Promotion; Marketing
ELIGIBILITY/REQUIREMENTS: Advertising and Promotion majors who have completed 55 to 95 credit hours with a cumulative GPA of at least 2.5; must be enrolled for a minimum of 12 credit hours; consideration given to student with a demonstrated career interest in advertising/marketing, work experience, participation in University and community activities, and faculty recommendations.
HOW TO APPLY: Contact the Marketing Department for more information.

660—WESTERN MICHIGAN UNIVERSITY (Haworth College of Business/Michigan Food & Beverage Association Scholarships)

1903 West Michigan
Kalamazoo MI 49008-5337
269/387-6000
FAX: 269/387-6989
E-mail: finaid-info@wmich.edu
Internet: http://www.wmich.edu/finaid
AMOUNT: $1,000
DEADLINE(S): FEB 15
FIELD(S): Food Marketing
ELIGIBILITY/REQUIREMENTS: Recipient must be a food marketing major.
HOW TO APPLY: Contact the Marketing Department for more details.
NUMBER OF AWARDS: 2
RENEWABLE: Yes

661—WESTERN MICHIGAN UNIVERSITY (Haworth College of Business/MSM Solutions Scholarship)

1903 West Michigan
Kalamazoo MI 49008-5337
269/387-6000
FAX: 269/387-6989
E-mail: finaid-info@wmich.edu
Internet: http://www.wmich.edu/finaid
AMOUNT: $4,000
DEADLINE(S): FEB 15
FIELD(S): Food Marketing
ELIGIBILITY/REQUIREMENTS: Awarded to a food marketing major.
HOW TO APPLY: Contact the Marketing Department for more details.
NUMBER OF AWARDS: 1
RENEWABLE: No

662—WESTERN MICHIGAN UNIVERSITY (Haworth College of Business/Nabisco Foods Group Endowed Scholarships)

1903 West Michigan
Kalamazoo MI 49008-5337
269/387-6000
FAX: 269/387-6989
E-mail: finaid-info@wmich.edu
Internet: http://www.wmich.edu/finaid
AMOUNT: $2,000
DEADLINE(S): FEB 15
FIELD(S): Food Marketing
ELIGIBILITY/REQUIREMENTS: Awarded to a food marketing major.
HOW TO APPLY: Contact the Marketing Department for more details.
NUMBER OF AWARDS: 2
RENEWABLE: No

663—WESTERN MICHIGAN UNIVERSITY (Haworth College of Business/Pat Mitchell CFBA Award)

1903 West Michigan
Kalamazoo MI 49008-5337
269/387-6000
FAX: 269/387-6989
E-mail: finaid-info@wmich.edu
Internet: http://www.wmich.edu/finaid
AMOUNT: $2,000
DEADLINE(S): FEB 15
FIELD(S): Food Marketing
ELIGIBILITY/REQUIREMENTS: Presented to the outstanding food marketing student affiliated with a Chicago-based food company or retailer.
HOW TO APPLY: Contact the Marketing Department for more details.
NUMBER OF AWARDS: 2

664—WESTERN MICHIGAN UNIVERSITY (Haworth College of Business/Patrick M. Quinn Endowed Food Marketing Scholarship)

1903 West Michigan
Kalamazoo MI 49008-5337

269/387-6000
FAX: 269/387-6989
E-mail: finaid-info@wmich.edu
Internet: http://www.wmich.edu/
finaid
AMOUNT: $1,000
DEADLINE(S): FEB 15
FIELD(S): Food Marketing
ELIGIBILITY/REQUIREMENTS:
Preference given to employees of Spartan
Stores or its affiliated retailers, or family of
employees.
HOW TO APPLY: Contact the Marketing
Department for more details.
NUMBER OF AWARDS: 1 or more
RENEWABLE: Yes

**665—WESTERN MICHIGAN UNIVERSITY
(Haworth College of Business/Pioneer
Group Tony Walker Memorial Scholarship)**

1903 West Michigan
Kalamazoo MI 49008-5337
269/387-6000
FAX: 269/387-6989
E-mail: finaid-info@wmich.edu
Internet:
http://www.wmich.edu/finaid
AMOUNT: Varies
DEADLINE(S): FEB 15
FIELD(S): Advertising; Promotion;
Marketing; English (writing)
ELIGIBILITY/REQUIREMENTS: Open
to full-time undergraduate or graduate stu-
dent who works at least 15 hours per week
at the *Western Herald* in Circulation,
Business (Secretary, Classifieds), Display
Advertising, or a Student Manager of a
Department. Preference shall be given to
applicants who have a 3.0 GPA or higher
at time of application.
HOW TO APPLY: Contact the Marketing
Department for more information.
RENEWABLE: Yes

**666—WESTERN MICHIGAN UNIVERSITY
(Haworth College of Business/Richard
Neschich Endowed Food Marketing
Scholarship)**

1903 West Michigan
Kalamazoo MI 49008-5337
269/387-6000
FAX: 269/387-6989
E-mail: finaid-info@wmich.edu
Internet: http://www.wmich.edu/
finaid
AMOUNT: At least $1,000
DEADLINE(S): FEB 15
FIELD(S): Food Marketing

ELIGIBILITY/REQUIREMENTS:
Awarded on the basis of scholarship and
need. Preference given to members of
Sigma Phi Omega.
HOW TO APPLY: Contact the Marketing
Department for more details.
NUMBER OF AWARDS: 2
RENEWABLE: Yes

**667—WESTERN MICHIGAN UNIVERSITY
(Haworth College of Business/Robert B.
Trader Marketing Scholarship)**

1903 West Michigan
Kalamazoo MI 49008-5337
269/387-6000
FAX: 269/387-6989
E-mail: finaid-info@wmich.edu
Internet: http://www.wmich.edu/
finaid
AMOUNT: $750
DEADLINE(S): FEB 15
FIELD(S): Marketing; Sales; Business
ELIGIBILITY/REQUIREMENTS:
Major in Marketing or Sales and Business
Marketing; completion of 55 to 95 credit
hours; minimum course load of 12 semes-
ter hours; cumulative GPA of 3.0, related
work experience; and participation in
University and community activities.
HOW TO APPLY: Application forms
must be obtained from and returned to the
Marketing Department.
NUMBER OF AWARDS: 1 or more

**668—WESTERN MICHIGAN UNIVERSITY
(Haworth College of Business/Sid Brooks
Endowed Memorial Scholarship)**

1903 West Michigan
Kalamazoo MI 49008-5337
269/387-6000
FAX: 269/387-6989
E-mail: finaid-info@wmich.edu
Internet: http://www.wmich.edu/
finaid
AMOUNT: At least $1,000
DEADLINE(S): FEB 15
FIELD(S): Food Marketing
ELIGIBILITY/REQUIREMENTS: Food
Marketing majors; cumulative GPA of at
least 2.5; unless otherwise specified, stu-
dents must have a signed major slip on file
and must be at least at the sophomore
level; consideration given to a demonstrat-
ed career in food marketing, work experi-
ence, participation in University and community activities, financial need, and faculty recommendations.
HOW TO APPLY: Contact the Marketing
Department for more details.

NUMBER OF AWARDS: 1
RENEWABLE: Yes

**669—WESTERN MICHIGAN UNIVERSITY
(Haworth College of Business/Stap and
Co.)**

1903 West Michigan
Kalamazoo MI 49008-5337
269/387-6000
FAX: 269/387-6989
E-mail: finaid-info@wmich.edu
Internet: http://www.wmich.edu/
finaid
AMOUNT: $500
DEADLINE(S): FEB 15
FIELD(S): Advertising; Promotion;
Marketing
ELIGIBILITY/REQUIREMENTS:
Advertising and Promotion majors who
have completed 55 to 95 credit hours with
a cumulative GPA of at least 2.5; must be
enrolled for a minimum of 12 credit hours;
consideration given to student with a
demonstrated career interest in advertis-
ing/marketing, work experience, participa-
tion in University and community activi-
ties, and faculty recommendations.
HOW TO APPLY: Contact the Marketing
Department for more information.
RENEWABLE: Not available

**670—WESTERN MICHIGAN UNIVERSITY
(Haworth College of Business/Wal-Mart
Stores Food Marketing Scholarships)**

1903 West Michigan
Kalamazoo MI 49008-5337
269/387-6000
FAX: 269/387-6989
E-mail: finaid-info@wmich.edu
Internet: http://www.wmich.edu/
finaid
AMOUNT: $1,000
DEADLINE(S): FEB 15
FIELD(S): Food Marketing
ELIGIBILITY/REQUIREMENTS:
Preference for food marketing majors with
a career interest in retail management.
HOW TO APPLY: Contact the Marketing
Department for more details.
NUMBER OF AWARDS: Multiple
RENEWABLE: Yes

**671—WESTERN MICHIGAN UNIVERSITY
(Haworth College of Business/William O.
Haynes Food Distribution Endowed
Scholarship)**

1903 West Michigan
Kalamazoo MI 49008-5337

269/387-6000
FAX: 269/387-6989
E-mail: finaid-info@wmich.edu
Internet: http://www.wmich.edu/
finaid
AMOUNT: At least $1,000
DEADLINE(S): FEB 15
FIELD(S): Food Marketing
ELIGIBILITY/REQUIREMENTS:
Awarded on the basis of scholarship and
need. Preference given to members of
Sigma Phi Omega.
HOW TO APPLY: Contact the Marketing
Department for more details.
NUMBER OF AWARDS: 1 or more

672—WESTERN MICHIGAN UNIVERSITY (Haworth College of Business/Zane Cannon Memorial Scholarship)

1903 West Michigan
Kalamazoo MI 49008-5337
269/387-6000
FAX: 269/387-6989
E-mail: finaid-info@wmich.edu
Internet: http://www.wmich.edu/
finaid
AMOUNT: $500
DEADLINE(S): FEB 15
FIELD(S): Advertising; Promotion;
Marketing
ELIGIBILITY/REQUIREMENTS:
Advertising and Promotion majors who
have completed 55 to 95 credit hours with
a cumulative GPA of at least 2.5; must be
enrolled for a minimum of 12 credit hours;
consideration given to student with a
demonstrated career interest in advertis-
ing/marketing, work experience, participa-
tion in University and community activi-
ties, and faculty recommendations.
HOW TO APPLY: Contact the Marketing
Department for more information.

673—WESTERN MICHIGAN UNIVERSITY (Pete Repins Memorial Scholarship)

1903 West Michigan
Kalamazoo MI 49008-5337
269/387-8777
FAX: 269/387-6989
E-mail: alumni@wmich.edu
Internet: http://www.wmich.edu/
ENDOWED
AMOUNT: Tuition, fees, and book
expenses
DEADLINE(S): APR 1
FIELD(S): All
ELIGIBILITY/REQUIREMENTS: Must
be a junior or senior undergraduate stu-
dent majoring in advertising, printing pro-
duction, or graphics; must have a 3.0 GPA

or higher. Preference given to a student
who demonstrates a strong commitment to
the academic programs and professions of
advertising, printing production, or graphics as well as related extracurricular activities such as work-related experience, organization membership, etc.
HOW TO APPLY: See website for application and submit with FAFSA.
NUMBER OF AWARDS: Varies
RENEWABLE: Yes. Up to 2 consecutive
years
CONTACT: Office of Financial Aid

674—WOMEN GROCERS OF AMERICA (Mary Macey Scholarships)

1005 North Glebe Road, Suite 250
Arlington VA 22201-5758
703/516-0700
FAX: 703/516-0115
E-mail: wga@nationalgrocers.org
Internet: http://www.national
grocers.org
AMOUNT: $1,000 (minimum)
DEADLINE(S): JUN 1
FIELD(S): Food Marketing/Management;
Food Service Technology; Business
Administration (as related to the
Grocery Industry)
ELIGIBILITY/REQUIREMENTS: For
students with a minimum 2.0 GPA attend-
ing a U.S. college or university. Must be
entering sophomores or continuing stu-
dents in good standing in a 2-year associate
degree or 4-year degree-granting institu-
tion or a graduate program, planning a
career in the independent sector grocery
industry. Financial need NOT considered.
HOW TO APPLY: See website for downloadable PDF application form or write to
the address above for an application.
NUMBER OF AWARDS: 2+
RENEWABLE: Yes, must reapply.

675—WOMEN'S JEWELRY ASSOCIATION (WJA Scholarship Fund)

373 Route 46 West
Building E, Suite 215
Fairfield NJ 07004-2442
973/575-7130
FAX: 973/575-1445
E-mail: info@womensjewelry.org
Internet: http://www.unusa.org
AMOUNT: $500-$2,500
DEADLINE(S): MAY
FIELD(S): Jewelry Design and
Manufacture; Marketing; Retailing
ELIGIBILITY/REQUIREMENTS:
Based on drawings or slides of jewelry
designs.

HOW TO APPLY: See website or call for
an application. Submit with 2 written references, short essay, and slides or drawings
of work. Winners will be selected by a
panel of judges from the jewelry industry.
NUMBER OF AWARDS: 5-15
RENEWABLE: No
CONTACT: Gillian Schultz

EDUCATION/ TEACHING (ALL FIELDS)

676—ALASKA COMMISSION ON POSTSECONDARY EDUCATION (Alaska Teacher Scholarship Loan Program)

3030 Vintage Boulevard
Juneau AK 99801
907/465-6741
FAX: 907/465-5316
AMOUNT: Up to $7,500
DEADLINE(S): MAY 1 (nominations
from school superintendents)
FIELD(S): Elementary or Secondary
Education
ELIGIBILITY/REQUIREMENTS:
Loans for Alaska high school graduates
from rural areas who intend to teach in
rural areas. Students are nominated by
their rural schools. Employment as a
teacher in a rural area in Alaska can result
in up to 100% forgiveness of the loan.
Awards may be used in Alaska and else-
where.
HOW TO APPLY: Contact ACPE for
details and the qualifications of a "rural"
resident.
NUMBER OF AWARDS: 75-100
RENEWABLE: Yes. $37,500 lifetime
maximum.

677—ALPHA DELTA KAPPA (International Teacher Education Scholarship)

1615 West 92 Street
Kansas City MO 64113
816/363-5525
FAX: 816/363-4010
E-mail: headquarters@alphadelta
kappa.org
Internet: http://www.alpha delta
kappa.org
AMOUNT: $10,000
DEADLINE(S): JAN 1
FIELD(S): Education; Teaching
ELIGIBILITY/REQUIREMENTS: Open
to young women ages 20 to 35, single and

without dependents, to study in U.S. colleges or universities. Must be a non-U.S. citizen residing outside the U.S. and maintain that residency status from the time of application to the awarding of the scholarship. Must plan to enter the teaching profession or be engaged in the teaching profession. Must have completed at least 1 year of college. Doctoral studies not eligible.
HOW TO APPLY: Contact Scholarships and Grants Coordinator for an application.
NUMBER OF AWARDS: 7
RENEWABLE: Yes, must reapply.
CONTACT: Dee Frost, Scholarships and Grants Coordinator

678—AMERICAN ALLIANCE FOR HEALTH, PHYSICAL EDUCATION, RECREATION & DANCE

1900 Association Drive
Reston VA 20191
703/476-3400 or 800/213-7193
Internet: http://www.aahperd.org
AMOUNT: Varies
DEADLINE(S): Varies
FIELD(S): Health Education, Leisure and Recreation, Girls and Women in Sports, Sport and Physical Education, Dance
ELIGIBILITY/REQUIREMENTS: This organization has six national suborganizations specializing in the above fields. Some have grants and fellowships for both individuals and group projects. The website has the details for each group.
HOW TO APPLY: Visit website for details or write to above address for details.

679—AMERICAN CLASSICAL LEAGUE, THE

Miami University
Oxford OH 45056
513/529-7741
FAX: 513/529-7742
E-mail: info@aclclassics.org
Internet: http://www.aclclassics.org
AMOUNT: $500-$1,500
DEADLINE(S): MAY 1
FIELD(S): Education; Teaching of Classics; Latin; Greek
ELIGIBILITY/REQUIREMENTS: Current member of the ACL including teachers of Classics at the elementary through secondary level, undergraduate or graduate classics major planning to teach at the elementary through college level. Additional criteria pertain to the various scholarships.

HOW TO APPLY: See website for application and additional information.
RENEWABLE: Yes. Previous winners may compete again for the same award in the fourth year after the original award.

680—AMERICAN CLASSICAL LEAGUE, THE (Ed Phinney Commemorative Scholarship)

Miami University
Oxford OH 45056
513/529-7741
FAX: 513/529-7742
E-mail: info@aclclassics.org
Internet: http://www.aclclassics.org
AMOUNT: Up to $750
DEADLINE(S): JAN 15
FIELD(S): Teaching (Latin and/or Greek)
ELIGIBILITY/REQUIREMENTS: Scholarships for first-time attendance at the League's institute or up to $500 to cover cost of other activities that serve to enhance a teacher's skills in the classroom in the classics or up to $150 for purchase of materials from the ACL Teaching and Materials Resource Center. Memberships required except for first-time attendance at institute.
HOW TO APPLY: See website for application and additional information.
RENEWABLE: No

681—AMERICAN FOUNDATION FOR THE BLIND (Delta Gamma Foundation Memorial Scholarship)

11 Penn Plaza, Suite 300
New York NY 10001
212/502-7661
FAX: 212/502-7771
E-mail: afbinfo@afb.org
Internet: http://www.afb.org
AMOUNT: $1,000
DEADLINE(S): MAR 31
FIELD(S): Rehabilitation/Education of Visually Impaired/Blind
ELIGIBILITY/REQUIREMENTS: Open to legally blind undergraduate and graduate students of good character who have exhibited academic excellence and are studying in field of rehabilitation/education of persons who are blind or visually impaired. Must be U.S. citizen.
HOW TO APPLY: Submit evidence of legal blindness; official transcripts; proof of college or university acceptance; 3 letters of recommendation; and typewritten statement describing field of study you are pursuing, goals, work experience, activities,

and how money will be used. See website or contact AFB for an application.
NUMBER OF AWARDS: 2
CONTACT: Alina Vayntrub

682—AMERICAN FOUNDATION FOR THE BLIND (Rudolph Dillman Scholarship)

11 Penn Plaza, Suite 300
New York NY 10001
212/502-7661
FAX: 212/502-7771
E-mail: afbinfo@afb.net
Internet: http://www.afb.org/scholar/scholarships.asp
AMOUNT: $2,500
DEADLINE(S): MAR 31
FIELD(S): Rehabilitation/Education of Blind or Visually Impaired
ELIGIBILITY/REQUIREMENTS: Undergraduate or graduate students who are studying in the field of rehabilitation and/or education of persons who are blind or visually impaired. One of these grants is specifically for a student who meets all requirements and submits evidence of economic need.
HOW TO APPLY: Must submit official transcripts, proof of acceptance, evidence of economic need (if applicable), 3 letters of recommendation, proof of legal blindness, proof of U.S. citizenship, and a typewritten statement of no more than 3 double-spaced pages describing the field of study you are pursuing, educational or personal goals, work experience, extracurricular activities and how the scholarship award will be used. See website or contact AFB for an application.
NUMBER OF AWARDS: 4
RENEWABLE: No
CONTACT: Alina Vayntrub

683—AMERICAN INDIAN SCIENCE AND ENGINEERING SOCIETY (Burlington Northern Santa Fe Pacific Foundation Scholarships)

P.O. Box 9828
Albuquerque NM 87119-9828
505/765-1052
FAX: 505/765-5608
E-mail: scholarships@aises.org
Internet: http://www.aises.org/scholar/scholarships
AMOUNT: $2,500
DEADLINE(S): MAR 31
FIELD(S): Business; Education; Science; Engineering; Health Administration
ELIGIBILITY/REQUIREMENTS: Open to high school seniors who are at least one quarter American Indian. Must reside in

Kansas, Oklahoma, Colorado, Arizona, New Mexico, Minnesota, North Dakota, Oregon, South Dakota, Washington, Montana, or San Bernardino County, California (Burlington Northern and Santa Fe Pacific service areas). Must demonstrate financial need.
HOW TO APPLY: See website or contact Society for an application.
NUMBER OF AWARDS: 5
RENEWABLE: Yes. Up to 4 years.
CONTACT: Patricia Browne

684—ARCTIC INSTITUTE OF NORTH AMERICA (Jim Bourque Scholarship)

University of Calgary
2500 University Drive NW
Calgary Alberta T2N 1N4
CANADA
403/220-7515
FAX: 403/282-4609
Internet: http://www.ucalgary.ca/aina
AMOUNT: $1,000 (Canadian)
DEADLINE(S): JUL 15
FIELD(S): Education; Environmental Studies; Traditional Knowledge; Telecommunications
ELIGIBILITY/REQUIREMENTS: Open to Canadian Aboriginal students enrolled in postsecondary training in above fields.
HOW TO APPLY: See website or contact Executive Director for details. Applicants must submit description of program of study and reason for choice, transcript, 2 signed letters of recommendation from community leader, statement of financial need, and proof of enrollment in, or application to, a postsecondary institution. Award announced on August 1.
NUMBER OF AWARDS: 1
CONTACT: Executive Director

685—ARMED FORCES COMMUNICATIONS AND ELECTRONICS ASSOCIATION (AFCEA ROTC Scholarships)

4400 Fair Lakes Court
Fairfax VA 22033-3899
800/336-4583, ext. 6147 or
703/631-6149
FAX: 703/631-4693
E-mail: scholarships@afcea.org
Internet: http://www.afcea.org
AMOUNT: $2,000
DEADLINE(S): APR 1
FIELD(S): Electrical Engineering, Electronics, Computer Science, Computer Systems, or Aerospace Engineering, Physics, Mathematics, Science or Mathematics Education; Technology Management or other technical fields, or fields related to U.S. intelligence or national security
ELIGIBILITY/REQUIREMENTS: Scholarships for ROTC students working toward a degree in an accredited degree-granting 4-year college or university in the U.S.
HOW TO APPLY: MUST be nominated by Professors of Military Science, Naval Science, or Aerospace Studies. Contact the commander of each ROTC unit at your school or see website for application.

686—ARMED FORCES COMMUNICATIONS AND ELECTRONICS ASSOCIATION (AFCEA Scholarship for Online or Distance-Learning Programs)

4400 Fair Lakes Court
Fairfax VA 22033-3899
800/336-4583, ext. 6147 or
703/631-6149
FAX: 703/631-4693
E-mail: scholarships@afcea.org
Internet: http://www.afcea.org
AMOUNT: $1,500
DEADLINE(S): JUN 1
FIELD(S): Electrical, Chemical or Aerospace Engineering: Computer Science; Mathematics; Physics; Science or Math Education; Technology Management or fields related to U.S. intelligence or national security
ELIGIBILITY/REQUIREMENTS: Full-time students; undergraduates must have completed 2 semesters of calculus (30-semester hour equivalent). Must be a U.S. citizen and be currently enrolled in a 4-year college or university in the U.S. at time of application.
HOW TO APPLY: Applications and further information on website.
RENEWABLE: No

687—ARMED FORCES COMMUNICATIONS AND ELECTRONICS ASSOCIATION (General Emmett Paige Scholarships for Military Personnel, Veterans, and Their Dependents)

4400 Fair Lakes Court
Fairfax VA 22033-3899
800/336-4583, ext. 6147 or
703/631-6149
FAX: 703/631-4693
E-mail: scholarships@afcea.org
Internet: http://www.afcea.org
AMOUNT: $2,000
DEADLINE(S): MAR 1
FIELD(S): Electrical Engineering, Electronics, Computer Science, Computer or Aerospace Engineering, Physics, Mathematics, Science or Mathematics Education; Technology Management or other technical fields, or fields related to U.S. intelligence or national security
ELIGIBILITY/REQUIREMENTS: Scholarships in the above fields for persons on active duty in a military service or veterans and to their spouses or dependents who are working toward a degree in an accredited 4-year college or university in the U.S. Must have GPA of 3.4 or more.
HOW TO APPLY: Applications and further information on website.

688—ARMED FORCES COMMUNICATIONS AND ELECTRONICS ASSOCIATION (General John A. Wickham Scholarships)

4400 Fair Lakes Court
Fairfax VA 22033-3899
800/336-4583, ext. 6147 or
703/631-6149
FAX: 703/631-4693
E-mail: scholarships@afcea.org
Internet: http://www.afcea.org
AMOUNT: $2,000
DEADLINE(S): MAY 1
FIELD(S): Electrical Engineering, Electronics, Computer Science, Computer or Aerospace Engineering, Physics, Mathematics, Science or Mathematics Education; Technology Management or other technical fields, or fields related to U.S. intelligence or national security
ELIGIBILITY/REQUIREMENTS: Scholarships in the above fields for persons working toward degrees in accredited 4-year colleges or universities in the U.S. Must have GPA of 3.5 or more.
HOW TO APPLY: Applications and further information on website.

689—ASSOCIATION FOR EDUCATION AND REHABILITATION OF THE BLIND AND VISUALLY IMPAIRED (Telesensory Scholarship)

4600 Duke Street, Suite 430
P.O. Box 22397
Alexandria VA 22304
703/823-9690
FAX: 703/823-9695
E-mail: aer@aerbvi.org
Internet: http://www.aerbvi.org

AMOUNT: $1,000

DEADLINE(S): APR 15 (of even-numbered years)

FIELD(S): Fields of study related to the blind/visually impaired

ELIGIBILITY/REQUIREMENTS: Scholarships for students who are members of AER pursuing postsecondary education in a field related to services for the blind or visually impaired. Must become an AER member before applying. Financial need NOT a factor.

HOW TO APPLY: For membership information or an application, see website or contact the Association.

NUMBER OF AWARDS: 1

CONTACT: Carolyn Sharp

690—ASSOCIATION FOR EDUCATION AND REHABILITATION OF THE BLIND AND VISUALLY IMPAIRED (William and Dorothy Ferrell Scholarship)

4600 Duke Street, Suite 430
P.O. Box 22397
Alexandria VA 22304
703/823-9690
FAX: 703/823-9695
E-mail: aer@aerbvi.org
Internet: http://www.aerbvi.org

AMOUNT: $500

DEADLINE(S): APR 15 (of even-numbered years)

FIELD(S): Fields of study related to the blind/visually impaired

ELIGIBILITY/REQUIREMENTS: Open to students who are legally blind, pursuing postsecondary education in a field related to services for the blind or visually impaired. Financial need NOT a factor.

HOW TO APPLY: See website or contact Association for details.

NUMBER OF AWARDS: 2

CONTACT: Carolyn Sharp

691—ASSOCIATION OF SCHOOL BUSINESS OFFICIALS OF MARYLAND AND THE DISTRICT OF COLUMBIA (Dwight P. Jacobus Scholarships)

ASBO-MD & DC
Scholarship Committee
200 E. North Avenue
Baltimore MD 21202
Internet: http://www.asbo.org

AMOUNT: $1,000

DEADLINE(S): MAR 1

FIELD(S): Business; Education

ELIGIBILITY/REQUIREMENTS: Must be residents of Maryland or the District of Columbia for at least 1 year preceding the date of application; be pursuing a career in business or education at an accredited institution of higher education within Maryland or the District of Columbia; be accepted for admission as a full-time student; demonstrate financial need; and have a minimum overall GPA of 3.0. Awards are based on scholastic achievement, financial need, SAT or ACT scores, and the quality of extracurricular activities.

HOW TO APPLY: Submit completed application; copy of most current high school or college transcript; copies of parents' and applicant's current income tax returns; copy of acceptance letter from an accredited institution of higher education in Maryland or the District of Columbia; a 500-word typed essay, written by the applicant explaining why he/she is uniquely qualified to receive this scholarship and including academic achievements and activities, community and civic activities, and personal aims and goals; and a copy of SAT or ACT results.

NUMBER OF AWARDS: 6

RENEWABLE: Yes, for up to 4 years: recipients must reapply annually; continue to be accepted for admission to the undergraduate program in education; be enrolled full time; and submit proof of continued academic good standing (minimum 3.0 GPA).

CONTACT: Kathy Jackson, Chair

692—ASSOCIATION ON AMERICAN INDIAN AFFAIRS (Emilie Hesemeyer Memorial Scholarships)

Executive Office
966 Hungerford Drive, Suite 12-B
Rockville, MD 20850
240/314-7155
FAX: 240/314-7159
E-mail: general.aaia@verizon.net
Internet: http://www.indian-affairs.org

AMOUNT: $1,500

DEADLINE(S): Fall and Spring semesters only

FIELD(S): All; Education

ELIGIBILITY/REQUIREMENTS: Open to full-time undergraduate students who are minimally 1/4 degree Indian blood from a federally recognized tribe. Open to students pursuing any field of study, but preference is given to education majors. Award is based on financial need and is limited to North America/Alaska.

HOW TO APPLY: See website for application. Please send only the information requested; additional information will not be considered. Must submit essay on need, certificate of enrollment and quantum from your tribe or BIA, transcript, schedule of classes, and current financial aid award letter.

RENEWABLE: Yes Must reapply. Note: Disbursements of $750 made each semester pending satisfactory progress. No funding for summer semester.

CONTACT: Lisa Wyzlic at lw.aaia@verizon.net or 240/314-7155.

ADDITIONAL INFORMATION: If applying for more than 1 AAIA scholarship, send 1 application package only. Students will be considered for all scholarships they are qualified for.

693—BETHESDA LUTHERAN HOMES AND SERVICES (Development Disabilities Scholastic Excellence Award for Lutheran College Students)

600 Hoffmann Drive
Watertown WI 53094
920/206-4449
FAX: 920/262-6513
E-mail: ncrc@blhs.org
Internet: http://www.blhs.org

AMOUNT: $1,500

DEADLINE(S): MAR 15

FIELD(S): Special Education or any field that supports people with developmental disabilities

ELIGIBILITY/REQUIREMENTS: Must be Lutheran and have GPA 3.0 or higher; sophomore or higher when applying; career in field of developmental disabilities.

HOW TO APPLY: Write to above address or download from website.

NUMBER OF AWARDS: 3

RENEWABLE: No

CONTACT: Thomas Heuer

694—BLUES HEAVEN FOUNDATION, INC. (Muddy Waters Scholarship)

2120 S. Michigan Avenue
Chicago IL 60616
312/808-1286

AMOUNT: $2,000

DEADLINE(S): APR 30

FIELD(S): Music; Music Education; African American Studies; Folklore; Performing Arts; Arts Management; Journalism; Radio/TV/Film

ELIGIBILITY/REQUIREMENTS: Scholarship awarded on a competitive basis with consideration given to scholastic achievement, concentration of studies, and financial need. Applicant must be full-time graduate or undergraduate in a Chicago area college or university. Scholastic aptitude, extracurricular involvement, GPA, and financial need are all considered.

HOW TO APPLY: Contact Foundation between February and April to request an application.

695—B. M. WOLTMAN FOUNDATION (Lutheran Scholarships for Students of the Ministry and Teaching)

7900 U.S. 290 East
Austin TX 78724
512/926-4272
AMOUNT: $500-$2,500
DEADLINE(S): Varies
FIELD(S): Theology (Lutheran Ministry); Teacher Education (Lutheran Schools)
ELIGIBILITY/REQUIREMENTS: Scholarships for undergrads and graduate students studying for careers in the Lutheran ministry or for teaching in a Lutheran school. For Texas residents attending, or planning to attend, any college in Texas.
HOW TO APPLY: Write for details.
NUMBER OF AWARDS: 45
RENEWABLE: Yes

696—CALCOT SEITZ FOUNDATION

P.O. Box 259
Bakersfield CA 93302
661/327-5961
E-mail: staff@calcot.com
Internet: http://www.calcot.com
AMOUNT: Varies, usually $1,000
DEADLINE(S): MAR 31
FIELD(S): Agriculture; Agriculture Education
ELIGIBILITY/REQUIREMENTS: Must be enrolled in a 4-year college or university with a major in Agriculture and be from a cotton-growing area of California or Arizona.
HOW TO APPLY: Download application from website, complete and submit as directed on application.
NUMBER OF AWARDS: Varies
RENEWABLE: Yes. Up to 3 years.

697—-CALIFORNIA SCHOOL LIBRARY ASSOCIATION (John Blanchard Memorial Scholarship)

1001 26th Street
Sacramento CA 95816
916-447-2684
FAX: 916-447-2695
E-mail: csla@pacbell.net
Internet: http://www.schoollibrary. org/awa/scholarships.htm
AMOUNT: $1,000
DEADLINE(S): APR 30

FIELD(S): School Librarian; Media Teacher
ELIGIBILITY/REQUIREMENTS: Open to school library paraprofessionals who wish to obtain the preparation needed to qualify and serve as a school library media teacher. Must be working or have worked within the last 3 years in a classified position in the library media field either in a school, district or county office; member of CSLA; enrolled in a college or university working towards a BA, BS or advanced degree in preparation to become a library media teacher in California.
HOW TO APPLY: See website for application; 3 letters of recommendation (1 each from a CSLA member, a professor in the department in which the applicant is enrolled, and a former or current supervisor should be mailed to Scholarship Chair), and transcript or verification.
NUMBER OF AWARDS: 1

698—CALIFORNIA SCHOOL LIBRARY ASSOCIATION (Leadership for Diversity Scholarship)

1001 26th Street
Sacramento CA 95816
916-447-2684
FAX: 916-447-2695
E-mail: csla@pacbell.net
Internet: http://www.schoollibrary. org/awa/scholarships.htm
AMOUNT: $1,500
DEADLINE(S): APR 30
FIELD(S): School Librarian; Media Teacher
ELIGIBILITY/REQUIREMENTS: Scholarship for a member of a traditionally underrepresented group enrolled in a California accredited library media teacher credential program. Must intend to work as a library media teacher in a California school library media center for a minimum of 3 years. Must show ability to complete program through college transcript or other verification. Financial need considered.
HOW TO APPLY: See website for application and submit with a personal statement, 2 letters of recommendation, and transcript or verification.
NUMBER OF AWARDS: 1+ (based on money available)

699—CALIFORNIA MATHEMATICS COUNCIL

Glendale Community College
Math Department
1500 North Verdugo Road
Glendale CA 91208-2894

E-mail: sjkolpas@glendale.edu
Internet: http://www.cmc-math.org/SouthGrant
AMOUNT: $100-$1,000
DEADLINE(S): JAN 31
FIELD(S): Education; Teaching Mathematics
ELIGIBILITY/REQUIREMENTS: Scholarships for students enrolled in an elementary or secondary education credential program. Only applicants who teach, reside, or go to school in Southern California will be considered.
HOW TO APPLY: See website or contact CMC c/o Glendale Community College for additional information.
CONTACT: Dr. Sid Kolpas, CMC-S Scholarships

700—CIVIL AIR PATROL (CAP Undergraduate Scholarships)

National Headquarters
Maxwell AFB AL 36112-6332
334/953-5315
AMOUNT: $750
DEADLINE(S): JAN 31
FIELD(S): Humanities; Science; Engineering; Education
ELIGIBILITY/REQUIREMENTS: Open to CAP members who have received the Billy Mitchell Award or the senior rating in Level II of the senior training program. For undergraduate study in the above areas.
HOW TO APPLY: Write for complete information.

701—COLORADO YOUNG FARMERS EDUCATIONAL ASSOCIATION

Northwestern Junior College
100 College Avenue
Sterling CO 80751
970/521-6690
FAX: 970/521-6636
E-mail: jack.annan@njc.edu
Internet: http://www.colorado youngfarmer.com
AMOUNT: $500 (freshman & sophomore); $750 (junior); $1250 (senior)
DEADLINE(S): MAR 15
FIELD(S): Agriculture (Freshman & Sophomore); Agriculture Education (Junior & Senior)
ELIGIBILITY/REQUIREMENTS: Must be enrolled as a full-time student at a Colorado junior/community college, college or university, a Colorado resident working toward degrees specified above. Award based upon scholarship, activities and interest in field.

HOW TO APPLY: See website for application.
NUMBER OF AWARDS: 5
RENEWABLE: No
CONTACT: Jack Annan

702—COMMUNITY FOUNDATION FOR GREATER ATLANTA, INC., THE (William Lucas Memorial Scholarship)

50 Hurt Plaza, Suite 449
Atlanta GA 30303
404/688-5525
FAX: 404/688-3060
E-mail: scholarships@atlcf.org
Internet: http://www.atlcf.org/Grants
Scholarships/Scholarships.aspx
AMOUNT: $1,250
DEADLINE(S): APR 11
FIELD(S): Social Work, Education, Allied Health
ELIGIBILITY/REQUIREMENTS: Open to graduating high school seniors beginning college in Fall. Must be a resident of Atlanta or Gainesville, Georgia, have a minimum 2.5 GPA, and be accepted to an accredited institution of higher learning and pursuing an undergraduate degree. Must demonstrate a history of commitment to community service.
HOW TO APPLY: See website for additional information and application. Submit with essay (1-2 pages) describing your educational plans and your commitment to community service; 1-page résumé listing school and community activities, awards, offices held and other relevant experiences; official transcript; SAT/ACT scores if you are a recent high school graduate; and 2 letters of recommendation from a teacher, school personnel, volunteer advisor, or other influential adult who can attest to your merits and commitment to community service.
NUMBER OF AWARDS: 1
RENEWABLE: Yes; must reapply.
CONTACT: Brenda Jackson, William Lucas Memorial Scholarship, c/o Georgia Campaign for Adolescent Pregnancy Prevention, 100 Auburn Avenue, Suite 200, Atlanta, GA 30303, 404/524-2277.

703—COMMUNITY FOUNDATION OF WESTERN MASSACHUSETTS (Margaret E. O'Donnell and Agnes K. O'Donnell Scholarship)

1500 Main Street
P.O. Box 15769
Springfield MA 01115
413/732-2858
FAX: 413/733-8565
E-mail: scholar@community
foundation.org
Internet: http://www.community
foundation.org
AMOUNT: $700
DEADLINE(S): MAR 31
FIELD(S): All
ELIGIBILITY/REQUIREMENTS: Open to graduating seniors of Northampton High School and Smith Vocational High School, and to students of the College of Our Lady of the Elms and Fitchburg State College majoring in education.
HOW TO APPLY: See website for application.
NUMBER OF AWARDS: 12
RENEWABLE: No

704—COUNCIL FOR EXCEPTIONAL CHILDREN, THE (Black Caucus Ethnic Diversity Scholarship)

1110 North Glebe Road, Suite 300
Arlington VA 22201-5704
888/CEC-SPED or 703/620-3660
TTY: 866/915-5000
FAX: 703/264-9494
Internet: http://www.cec.sped.org
AMOUNT: $500
DEADLINE(S): DEC 2
FIELD(S): Special Education
ELIGIBILITY/REQUIREMENTS: Scholarship for a student pursuing a degree in Special Education and who is of African American background. Must be U.S. or Canadian citizen. Must be a student member of the Council for Exceptional Children. Minimum GPA of 2.5 required.
HOW TO APPLY: Write to Coordinator of Student Activities at above address or visit website for further information. Application is on website.
CONTACT: Coordinator of Student Activities

705—EASTERN KENTUCKY UNIVERSITY (Music Scholarships)

Department of Music
521 Lancaster Avenue
Richmond KY 40475-3102
859/622-1341
FAX: 859/622-3266
E-mail: rob.james@eku.edu
Internet: http://www.music.eku.edu
AMOUNT: Varies
DEADLINE(S): Varies
FIELD(S): Music Education
ELIGIBILITY/REQUIREMENTS: Scholarships for talented young instrument or voice musicians preparing themselves for careers in music or music education.
HOW TO APPLY: Must audition for scholarship. Application (on website) is due at least two weeks prior to the desired audition date.
RENEWABLE: Yes. Scholarship recipients are required to participate in performing ensembles and maintain a GPA of 2.5 to retain scholarship.
CONTACT: Dr. Robert James, Chair, Department of Music

706—ESA FOUNDATION (Frances Kilgore Endowment)

P.O. Box 270517
Fort Collins CO 80527
970/223-2824
FAX: 970/223-4456
E-mail: kloyd@iland.net
Internet: http://www.esaintl.com/esaf
AMOUNT: $500
DEADLINE(S): FEB 1
FIELD(S): Music; Teaching
ELIGIBILITY/REQUIREMENTS: Must be a college student currently enrolled in an accredited college or university who has maintained a "B" average (i.e., at least a 3.0 GPA); or be a high school senior in the top 25% of high school class, or have a score of at least ACT 20 or SAT 950, or have a minimum GPA of 3.0; or be enrolled in a technical school or returning to school after an absence to retrain or obtain a degree. Criteria for selection are character, leadership, service, financial need, scholastic ability, and special criteria set by the donor. Preference is given to music majors.
HOW TO APPLY: Submit application; 1-page (maximum) original letter from the applicant stating reasons for applying; 2 (no more or fewer) letters of recommendation; most recent transcript; and a $5 processing fee. Applicants must apply for only one scholarship from the ESA Foundation.
NUMBER OF AWARDS: 1
RENEWABLE: Yes. Recipients must reapply annually. NO special consideration will be given to previous winners.
CONTACT: Kathy Loyd

707—FLORIDA EDUCATION ASSOCIATION TRUST SCHOLARSHIP AWARD

213 South Adams Street
Tallahassee FL 32301
850/201-2800
FAX: 850/224-6406

E-mail: FloridaEA.org
Internet: http://www.FloridaEA.org
or FEA.org
AMOUNT: $2,000 (winner); $1,000 (runner-up)
DEADLINE(S): FEB 28
FIELD(S): Education or related field
ELIGIBILITY/REQUIREMENTS: Public high school seniors whose parent or guardians are FEA members or retired members. Minimum 3.0 GPA; outstanding achievement in extra- curricular activities also considered.
HOW TO APPLY: See website for application or contact the local office or FEA headquarters. Submit with proof of GPA and participation in extracurricular activities; 2 letters of recommendation (1 must be from a faculty member), original essay no longer than 5 pages; proof of acceptance at college, university or vo-tech school.
NUMBER OF AWARDS: 3 winners; 1 runner-up
RENEWABLE: No
CONTACT: Michael Gilliard

708—INTERNATIONAL TECHNOLOGY EDUCATION ASSOCIATION (ITEA) (Litherland/FTE Scholarship)

Foundation for Technology Education 1914 Association Drive, Suite 201
Reston VA 20191-1539
703/860-2100
FAX: 703/860-0353
E-mail: itea@iteaconnect.org
Internet: http://www.iteaconnect.
org/Awards/scholarshiplitherland.
htm
AMOUNT: $1,000
DEADLINE(S): DEC 1
FIELD(S): Technology Education
ELIGIBILITY/REQUIREMENTS: Scholarship for an undergraduate student majoring in technology education teacher preparation. Based upon interest in teaching, academic ability, need, and faculty recommendation. Must not be a senior by application deadline and must be a current, full-time undergraduate. Minimum GPA of 2.5 required. Applicant must be member of the ITEA. (Membership may be enclosed with scholarship application.)
HOW TO APPLY: See website for details. Submit letter of application that includes statement about personal interest in teaching technology and résumé (material not to exceed 3 pages) and should identify career goals, current professional and college activities and achievements along with col-

lege transcript and 3 faculty recommendations.

709—FREEDOM FROM RELIGION FOUNDATION (Student Essay Contests)

P.O. Box 750
Madison WI 53701
608/256-5800
Internet: http://www.ffrf.org
AMOUNT: $1,000; $500; $250
DEADLINE(S): College essays due JUL 1; High school essays due JUN 1
FIELD(S): Humanities; English; Education; Philosophy; Science
ELIGIBILITY/REQUIREMENTS: Topics change yearly, but all are on general theme of maintaining separation of church and state. New topics available on February 1. Open to high school seniors and students currently enrolled in college or technical schools. Must be U.S. citizen.
HOW TO APPLY: See website for details. Send SASE to address above for complete information. Indicate whether you will be competing in the college or high school competition. Information will be sent when new topics are announced each February 1.

710—GENERAL FEDERATION OF WOMEN'S CLUBS OF MASSACHUSETTS (Music Scholarship)

P.O. Box 679
Sudbury MA 01776-0679
978/443-4569
FAX: 978/443-1617
E-mail: GFWCMA@aol.com
Internet: http://www.gfwcma.
org/id39.html
AMOUNT: Up to $800
DEADLINE(S): FEB 1
FIELD(S): Piano; Instrument; Music Education; Music Therapy; Voice
ELIGIBILITY/REQUIREMENTS: Competitive scholarships for seniors in Massachusetts high schools. Letter of endorsement from sponsoring GFWC of MA club, letter of recommendation from either a high school principal or music teacher, transcripts, and personal audition (two short pieces contrasting in nature) required with application.
HOW TO APPLY: For more information or an application, see website or send a SASE to Coordinator, Arts Department at above address. Submit application with letter of recommendation from either high school principal or music instructor and transcript. Audition required.
NUMBER OF AWARDS: 1

711—GENERAL FEDERATION OF WOMEN'S CLUBS OF MASSACHUSETTS (Newtonville Woman's Club Scholarship)

P.O. Box 679
Sudbury MA 01776-0679
978/443-4569
FAX: 978/443-1617
E-mail: GFWCMA@aol.com
Internet: http://www.gfwcma.
org/id39.html
AMOUNT: $600
DEADLINE(S): MAR 1
FIELD(S): Teaching
ELIGIBILITY/REQUIREMENTS: For high school seniors in Massachusetts who will enroll in a 4-year accredited college or university in a teacher training program that leads to certification to teach.
HOW TO APPLY: For more information or an application, send SASE to Scholarship Chairman. Letter of endorsement from sponsoring GFWC of MA club, personal letter of no more than 500 words addressing professional goals and financial need; letter of recommendation from a high school principal or counselor relevant to this award, and transcript.
NUMBER OF AWARDS: At least 1
RENEWABLE: No

712—GOLDEN KEY INTERNATIONAL HONOUR SOCIETY (Education Achievement Awards)

1189 Ponce de Leon Avenue
Atlanta GA 30306
404/377-2400 or 800/377-2401
FAX: 404/373-7033
E-mail: scholarships@goldenkey.org
Internet: http://www.goldenkey.org
AMOUNT: $1,000 first place; $750 second place; $500 third place
DEADLINE(S): MAR
FIELD(S): Education
ELIGIBILITY/REQUIREMENTS: This award recognizes members who excel in the study of education. Undergraduate, graduate, and postgraduate members who are currently enrolled in classes at a degree-granting program are eligible. Awards based on academic achievement, quality of paper submitted, as determined by the selection committee.
HOW TO APPLY: Apply online with Golden Key member number. Attach an education-related paper/report (not to exceed 10 pages) you have prepared. Attach an essay (no more than 2 pages) describing the assignment for writing the paper, what the greatest challenge was in writing the paper, what lessons were

learned from completing the assignment, and if you were to redo the report, what would be changed? Include a letter of recommendation from a professor in the discipline and an official academic transcript.
NUMBER OF AWARDS/YEAR: 3
RENEWABLE: No
CONTACT: Fabian J. De Rozario, Associate Vice President of North American Operations

713—HAWAII COMMUNITY FOUNDATION (Alma White Delta Kappa Gamma Scholarship)

1164 Bishop Street, Suite 800
Honolulu HI 96813
808/537-6333 or toll free:
888/731-3863
FAX: 808/521-6286
E-mail: info@hcf-hawaii.org
Internet: http://www.hcf-hawaii.org
DEADLINE(S): MAR 1
FIELD(S): Education
ELIGIBILITY/REQUIREMENTS: Applicants must be Hawaii residents; be full-time junior or senior undergraduate or graduate students enrolled in an accredited 4-year college or university; and demonstrate financial need, good moral character, and academic achievement with a minimum GPA of 2.7.
HOW TO APPLY: Send application with 2 letters of recommendation.

714—HAWAII COMMUNITY FOUNDATION (Billie Beamer Educational Fund)

1164 Bishop Street, Suite 800
Honolulu HI 96813
808/537-6333 or toll free:
888/731-3863
FAX: 808/521-6286
E-mail: info@hcf-hawaii.org
Internet: http://www.hcf-hawaii.org
DEADLINE(S): MAR 1
FIELD(S): Education
ELIGIBILITY/REQUIREMENTS: Applicants must be of Hawaiian ancestry and be residents of the state of Hawaii; be a junior or senior undergraduate or graduate student majoring in education (or a graduate student attending law school); attend full time an accredited 4-year college or university; and demonstrate financial need, good moral character, and academic achievement with a minimum GPA of 2.7. Applicants returning to school to obtain a degree or certification in education also qualify.

HOW TO APPLY: Send application, 2 letters of recommendation, copy of birth certificate verifying Hawaiian ancestry, and an essay (typed double-spaced) describing how your educational and exposure opportunities (past, present, or future) will assist you in preparing the Hawaiian community to survive and flourish harmoniously in the world.

715—HAWAII COMMUNITY FOUNDATION (Dr. Hans and Clara Zimmerman Foundation Education Scholarship)

1164 Bishop Street, Suite 800
Honolulu HI 96813
808/537-6333 or toll free:
888/731-3863
FAX: 808/521-6286
E-mail: info@hcf-hawaii.org
Internet: http://www.hcf-hawaii.org
DEADLINE(S): MAR 1
FIELD(S): Education
ELIGIBILITY/REQUIREMENTS: Applicants must be nontraditional students who have worked for at least 2 years and are returning to school in the U.S.; be Hawaii residents; major in education with an emphasis on teaching; demonstrate leadership potential; be full-time undergraduate or graduate students enrolled in an accredited 2- or 4-year college or university; and demonstrate financial need, good moral character, and academic achievement with a minimum GPA of 2.7.
HOW TO APPLY: Send application with 2 letters of recommendation and a personal statement describing your participation in community service projects or activities.
CONTACT: See website.

716—HAWAII COMMUNITY FOUNDATION (Henry and Dorothy Castle Memorial Fund Scholarship)

1164 Bishop Street, Suite 800
Honolulu HI 96813
808/537-6333 or toll free:
888/731-3863
FAX: 808/521-6286
E-mail: info@hcf-hawaii.org
Internet: http://www.hcf-hawaii.org
DEADLINE(S): MAR 1
FIELD(S): Early Childhood Education
ELIGIBILITY/REQUIREMENTS: Applicants must be Hawaii residents; major in education and pursue studies in early childhood education (birth through 3rd grade), including childcare and preschool; be full-time undergraduate or grad-

uate students enrolled in an accredited 2- or 4-year college or university; and demonstrate financial need, good moral character, and academic achievement with a minimum GPA of 2.7.
HOW TO APPLY: Send application with 2 letters of recommendation, a personal statement, and an essay stating your interests and goals in studying Early Childhood Education and how you plan to contribute to the field.

717—HAWAII COMMUNITY FOUNDATION (Nick Van Pernis Scholarship Fund)

1164 Bishop Street, Suite 800
Honolulu HI 96813
808/537-6333 or toll free:
888/731-3863
FAX: 808/521-6286
E-mail: info@hcf-hawaii.org
Internet: http://www.hcf-hawaii.org
DEADLINE(S): MAR 1
FIELD(S): Marine Sciences; Health Sciences; Biotechnology; Early Childhood Education
ELIGIBILITY/REQUIREMENTS: Applicants must be graduates of one of the public or private high schools in the Districts of North Kona, South Kona, North Kohala, or Ka'u; plan to attend full time an accredited 2- or 4-year college or university; and demonstrate financial need, good moral character, and academic achievement with a minimum GPA of 2.7.
HOW TO APPLY: Send application; 2 letters of recommendation; a short essay explaining how your career can benefit the lives of Hawaii residents upon completing your education; and a record of community service.

718—HAWAII COMMUNITY FOUNDATION (Ron Bright Scholarship)

1164 Bishop Street, Suite 800
Honolulu HI 96813
808/537-6333 or toll free:
888/731-3863
FAX: 808/521-6286
E-mail: info@hcf-hawaii.org
Internet: http://www.hcf-hawaii.org
DEADLINE(S): MAR 1
FIELD(S): Education
ELIGIBILITY/REQUIREMENTS: Must be Hawaii residents; be graduating seniors from one of the following public Windward Oahu high schools: Castle, Kahuku, Kailua, Kaleheo, or Olomana; plan to enroll full time in an accredited 2- or 4-year college or university; and demonstrate

financial need, good moral character, and academic achievement with a minimum GPA of 2.7. Preference given to students with extracurricular activities in the performing arts.

HOW TO APPLY: Send application with 2 letters of recommendation and grades from the 1st semester of the 12th grade.

719—INSTITUTE FOR HUMANE STUDIES (Summer Seminars Program)

3401 N. Fairfax Drive, Suite 440
Arlington VA 22201-4432
703/993-4880 or 800/697-8799
FAX: 703/993-4890
Internet: http://www.TheIHS.org
AMOUNT: Free summer seminars, including room/board, lectures, seminar materials, and books
DEADLINE(S): MAR
FIELD(S): Social Sciences; Humanities; Law; Journalism; Public Policy; Education; Film; Writing; Economics; Philosophy
ELIGIBILITY/REQUIREMENTS: Open to college students, recent graduates, and graduate students who share an interest in learning and exchanging ideas about the scope of individual rights, free markets, the rule of law, peace, and tolerance.
HOW TO APPLY: See website for seminar information and to apply online, or contact IHS for an application.

720—INSTITUTE OF MINING AND METALLURGY (G. Vernon Hobson Bequest)

Danum House, South Parade
Doncaster DN1 2DY
UNITED KINGDOM
+44 (0)1302 320486
FAX: +44(0)1302 380900
E-mail: graham.woodrow@iom3.org
Internet: http://www.iom3.org/
awards/scholarships.htm
AMOUNT: Up to £1,300
DEADLINE(S): APR 8
FIELD(S): Mining; Metallurgy, Education
ELIGIBILITY/REQUIREMENTS: 'Advancement of teaching and practice of geology as applied to mining.' One or more awards may therefore be made for travel, research or other objects in accordance with these terms. Preference given to IMM members.
HOW TO APPLY: Contact Dr. Woodrow at above address or see website for an application or membership information.
NUMBER OF AWARDS: 1
CONTACT: Dr G.J.M. Woodrow, Deputy Chief Executive

721—INTERNATIONAL ORDER OF ALHAMBRA (Scholarship Grants)

4200 Leeds Avenue
Baltimore MD 21229-5496
410/242-0660
FAX: 410/536-5729
AMOUNT: $400 (max.)
DEADLINE(S): JAN 1; JUL 1
FIELD(S): Special Education
ELIGIBILITY/REQUIREMENTS: Open to students entering at least their junior or senior year of college in preparation for placement in special education, including teacher training for work with the mentally and physically disabled. Tenable at any accredited public/private college or university where student will earn a minimum of 3 credit hours during semester. With completed application, student must submit letter from school confirming enrollment/major.
HOW TO APPLY: Contact the Supreme Office for an application.
CONTACT: Supreme Office

722—JACK J. ISGUR FOUNDATION

Stinson Morrison Hecker LLP
1201 Walnut Street, 26th Floor
Kansas City MO 64106
816/691-2760
FAX: 816/691-3495
E-mail: cjensen@stinson.com
AMOUNT: Varies
DEADLINE(S): APR 15
FIELD(S): Humanities Education
ELIGIBILITY/REQUIREMENTS: Funds for students desiring to teach humanities at the elementary and middle school levels. Preference is awards to students (1) entering junior or subsequent years of college; (2) interested in teaching within the state of Missouri in nonmetropolitan school districts.
HOW TO APPLY: Applications can be obtained at address above.
NUMBER OF AWARDS: Varies
RENEWABLE: Yes, must reapply.
CONTACT: Charles F. Jensen

723—JACKSONVILLE STATE UNIVERSITY (Andrew Curley Memorial Scholarship)

Financial Aid Office
Jacksonville AL 36265
256/782-5677 or 800/231-5291
Internet: www.jsu.edu
AMOUNT: Varies
DEADLINE(S): FEB 1
FIELD(S): Education

ELIGIBILITY/REQUIREMENTS: Open to junior level and above; based on academics and character.
HOW TO APPLY: An official transcript and ACT/SAT scores must be submitted with scholarship applications. See website for application. Supporting documentation should be mailed.
RENEWABLE: No
CONTACT: Scholarship Committee

724—JACKSONVILLE STATE UNIVERSITY (Athena Arrington Scholarship)

Financial Aid Office
Jacksonville AL 36265
256/782-5677 or 800/231-5291
Internet: www.jsu.edu
AMOUNT: Varies
DEADLINE(S): FEB 1
FIELD(S): Elementary Education
ELIGIBILITY/REQUIREMENTS: Open to seniors.
HOW TO APPLY: An official high school transcript and ACT/SAT scores must be submitted with scholarship applications. See website for application. Supporting documentation should be mailed.
RENEWABLE: No
CONTACT: Scholarship Committee

725—JACKSONVILLE STATE UNIVERSITY (Doris Ledbetter Memorial Scholarship)

Financial Aid Office
Jacksonville AL 36265
256/782-5677 or 800/231-5291
Internet: www.jsu.edu
AMOUNT: Varies
DEADLINE(S): FEB 1
FIELD(S): Education (Nursing)
ELIGIBILITY/REQUIREMENTS: Financial need considered.
HOW TO APPLY: Contact Nursing Department for application and additional information.
RENEWABLE: No
CONTACT: Nursing Department; 256/782-5425

726—JACKSONVILLE STATE UNIVERSITY (Drs. Wayne & Sara Finley Scholarship)

Financial Aid Office
Jacksonville AL 36265
256/782-5677 or 800/231-5291
Internet: www.jsu.edu
AMOUNT: Varies
DEADLINE(S): FEB 1
FIELD(S): Math; Science; Pre-Prof Secondary Education

ELIGIBILITY/REQUIREMENTS: Open to junior or senior; 3.0 GPA; Clay, Coosa, or Randolph Counties, Alabama.
HOW TO APPLY: An official transcript and ACT/SAT scores must be submitted with scholarship applications. See website for application. Supporting documentation should be mailed.
RENEWABLE: No
CONTACT: Scholarship Committee

727—JACKSONVILLE STATE UNIVERSITY (Harold Shamblin Scholarship)

Financial Aid Office
Jacksonville AL 36265
256/782-5677 or 800/231-5291
Internet: www.jsu.edu
AMOUNT: Full tuition
DEADLINE(S): FEB 1
FIELD(S): Education
ELIGIBILITY/REQUIREMENTS: Applicant must be accepted to College of Education.
HOW TO APPLY: An official transcript and ACT/SAT scores must be submitted with scholarship applications. See website for application. Supporting documentation should be mailed.
RENEWABLE: No
CONTACT: Scholarship Committee

728—JACKSONVILLE STATE UNIVERSITY (J.C.U. Johnson Memorial Scholarship)

Financial Aid Office
Jacksonville AL 36265
256/782-5677 or 800/231-5291
Internet: www.jsu.edu
AMOUNT: Varies
DEADLINE(S): FEB 1
FIELD(S): Education
ELIGIBILITY/REQUIREMENTS: Open to junior, senior, or graduate students from Calhoun County, Alabama.
HOW TO APPLY: An official transcript and ACT/SAT scores must be submitted with scholarship applications. See website for application. Supporting documentation should be mailed.
RENEWABLE: No
CONTACT: Scholarship Committee

729—JACKSONVILLE STATE UNIVERSITY (Mildred Sheppard Scholarship)

Financial Aid Office
Jacksonville AL 36265
256/782-5677 or 800/231-5291
Internet: www.jsu.edu
AMOUNT: Varies

DEADLINE(S): FEB 1
FIELD(S): Education
ELIGIBILITY/REQUIREMENTS: Open to student with commitment in writing to teach K-12 for at least 2 years.
HOW TO APPLY: An official transcript and ACT/SAT scores must be submitted with scholarship applications. See website for application. Supporting documentation should be mailed.
RENEWABLE: No
CONTACT: Scholarship Committee

730—JACKSONVILLE STATE UNIVERSITY (Sharon Dempsey Memorial Scholarship)

Financial Aid Office
Jacksonville AL 36265
256/782-5677 or 800/231-5291
Internet: www.jsu.edu
AMOUNT: Varies
DEADLINE(S): FEB 1
FIELD(S): Math; Math Education
ELIGIBILITY/REQUIREMENTS: Open to junior or senior; at least 30 hours at JSU.
HOW TO APPLY: An official transcript and ACT/SAT scores must be submitted with scholarship applications. See website for application. Supporting documentation should be mailed.
RENEWABLE: No
CONTACT: Scholarship Committee

731—JACKSONVILLE STATE UNIVERSITY (Wanda White Memorial Scholarship)

Financial Aid Office
Jacksonville AL 36265
256/782-5677 or 800/231-5291
Internet: www.jsu.edu
AMOUNT: Varies
DEADLINE(S): FEB 1
FIELD(S): Early Childhood Education
ELIGIBILITY/REQUIREMENTS: Award based on character, academics, and extracurricular activities.
HOW TO APPLY: An official high school transcript and ACT/SAT scores must be submitted with scholarship applications. See website for application. Supporting documentation should be mailed.
RENEWABLE: No
CONTACT: Scholarship Committee

732—JACOB'S PILLOW DANCE FESTIVAL (Internships)

The Intern Program at Jacob's Pillow
P.O. Box 287
Lee MA 01238

413/637-1322
FAX: 413/243-4744
E-mail: info@jacobspillow.org
Internet: http://www.jacobs pillow.org
AMOUNT: Varies
DEADLINE(S): APR 5
FIELD(S): Archives/Preservation; Business; Development; Education; Marketing/Press; Operations/Production
ELIGIBILITY/REQUIREMENTS: Full- and part-time internships for the fall, winter, and spring can be tailored to meet college credit needs and individual interests.
HOW TO APPLY: Apply by sending 2 copies of each: a cover letter, résumé, and writing/design samples as applicable.
CONTACT: Intern Program at Jacob's Pillow

733—JEWISH FEDERATION OF METROPOLITAN CHICAGO (Academic Scholarship Program)

Jewish Vocational Service
216 West Jackson Blvd., Suite 700
Chicago IL 60606-6921
312/673-3400
FAX: 312/553-5544
TTY: 312/444-2877
E-mail: jvsscholarship@jvs chicago.org
Internet: www.jvs/chicago.org
AMOUNT: Varies
DEADLINE(S): FEB 15
FIELD(S): Mathematics, Engineering, Science, Medicine, Social Work, Education, Psychology, Rabbinate, Law (except corporate), Communications
ELIGIBILITY/REQUIREMENTS: Open to Jewish men and women legally domiciled in the greater Chicago metropolitan area, who are identified as having promise for significant contributions in their chosen careers, and are in need of financial assistance for full-time academic programs in above areas. Must have entered undergraduate junior year in career programs requiring no postgraduate education, or be in a vo-tech training program.
HOW TO APPLY: Phone JVS Scholarship Secretary (312/673-3457), fax, or visit website (click on Scholarship Services) for an application in the Fall. Interview required.
RENEWABLE: Yes
CONTACT: JVS Scholarship Secretary, 312/673-3457

734—JOURNALISM EDUCATION ASSOCIATION (Future Teacher Scholarship)

Kansas State University
103 Kedzie Hall
Manhattan KS 66506-1505
785/532-5532
FAX: 785/532-5563
E-mail: jea@spub.ksu.edu
Internet: http://www.jea.org
AMOUNT: $1,000
DEADLINE(S): OCT 30
FIELD(S): Education; Journalism
ELIGIBILITY/REQUIREMENTS: Must be an upper-division (or master's degree) student in a college program designed to prepare applicant for teaching journalism at the secondary school level.
HOW TO APPLY: Send completed application; a 250-word essay explaining applicant's desire to teach high school journalism; 2 recommendation letters (preferably from those who have firsthand knowledge of applicant's work with student journalists); college transcript(s) showing academic standing; list of journalism courses completed and grade in each; description of any high school journalism experience; and description of any specific experience applicant has had working with high school journalists since attending high school.
NUMBER OF AWARDS: Up to 3
RENEWABLE: No
CONTACT: Candace Perkins Bowen at cbowen@kent.edu or at 303/672-8297

735—J. W. SAXE MEMORIAL PRIZE

1524 31st Street NW
Washington DC 20007-3074
E-mail: ruthsaxe@aol.com or sachsedc@verizon.net
Internet: http://www.jwsaxefund.org
DEADLINE(S): MAR 15
AMOUNT: $1,500
FIELD(S): All (Emphasis on Public
   Service; Community Service)
ELIGIBILITY/REQUIREMENTS: Must be a college or university student. Award enables student to gain practical experience in public service by taking a no-pay or low-pay job or internship during the summer or other term.
HOW TO APPLY: Send résumé together with an essay stating short- and long-term goals. Also include statements from 4 references including at least 1 from a faculty member.
NUMBER OF AWARDS: 1-12
RENEWABLE: No
CONTACT: Ruth Saxe, President; or Elinor Sachse, VP and Secretary

736—KOSCIUSZKO FOUNDATION (UNESCO Teaching in Poland Program)

15 East 65 Street
New York NY 10021-6595
212/734-2130
FAX: 212/628-4552
E-mail: cbkuskowski@thekf.org
Internet: http://www.kosciuszko foundation.org
AMOUNT: $1,000-$5,000
DEADLINE(S): JAN 29
FIELD(S): Education
ELIGIBILITY/REQUIREMENTS: Open to American teachers, university faculty, university, college, and high school students over the age of 18 who wish to apply for teaching and teaching assistant positions. This is an educational and cultural summer exchange program that takes place at 6 locations in Poland during the month of July.
HOW TO APPLY: See website or send SASE to the Cultural Department for an application.
CONTACT: Christine B. Kuskowski, ext. 209

737—LINCOLN COMMUNITY FOUNDATION (Dale E. Siefkes Memorial Scholarship)

215 Centennial Mall South,
Suite 100
Lincoln NE 68508
402/474-2354
FAX: 402/476-8532
E-mail: lcf@lcf.org
Internet: http://www.lcf.org
AMOUNT: Varies
DEADLINE(S): MAR 15
FIELD(S): All
ELIGIBILITY/REQUIREMENTS: Must be at the junior or senior level attending a Nebraska college or university and pursuing a career in education; must have a 3.8 GPA or equivalent; demonstrate financial need.
HOW TO APPLY: Submit LCF application form, with first page of the applicant's and parents' most recent federal income tax form, and, if available, the first page of the applicant's Student Aid Report and Financial Aid Notification letter from the college applicant is attending. An essay based on a roadside sign describing how the sign symbolizes or explains your life.
NUMBER OF AWARDS/YEAR: Varies
RENEWABLE: Yes; must reapply.
ADDITIONAL INFORMATION: Scholarship may be used only for college credit

courses; may not be used for workshops, seminars or other learning experiences.

738—LINCOLN COMMUNITY FOUNDATION (Florence Turner Karlin Scholarship)

215 Centennial Mall South,
Suite 100
Lincoln NE 68508
402/474-2354
FAX: 402/476-8532
E-mail: lcf@lcf.org
Internet: http://www.lcf.org
AMOUNT: Varies
DEADLINE(S): MAR 15
FIELD(S): All
ELIGIBILITY/REQUIREMENTS: Must be a former graduate of any high school in Nebraska pursuing a degree in education at a qualified college or university in Nebraska. Must have completed at least sophomore year in college, and have achieved a minimum GPA of 3.0. Also open to teachers seeking graduate degree.
HOW TO APPLY: Submit LCF application form, with grade transcripts, essay addressing what your plans for teaching after graduation are and where you plan to teach and why, and letters of recommendation from college instructors/professors to the Foundation.
NUMBER OF AWARDS/YEAR: Varies.
RENEWABLE: Yes; must reapply.
ADDITIONAL INFORMATION: Scholarship may be used only for college credit courses; may not be used for workshops, seminars or other learning experiences.

739—LINCOLN COMMUNITY FOUNDATION (Nebraska Rural Community Schools Association [NRSCA] Scholarship)

215 Centennial Mall South,
Suite 100
Lincoln NE 68508
402/474-2345
FAX: 402/476-8532
E-mail: lcf@lcf.org
Internet: http://www.lcf.org
AMOUNT: Varies
DEADLINE(S): FEB 11
FIELD(S): Education
ELIGIBILITY/REQUIREMENTS: Open to graduating seniors. Applicant must have a minimum 3.5 GPA and ACT composite of 22 or SAT of 1020. Selection will be based equally on academic achievement, level of involvement in activities, student goals, financial need, leadership, character, initiative, and school/community involvement.

HOW TO APPLY: Application sent to each high school holding NRCSA membership; 1 female and 1 male application accepted from each school. Submit with letters of recommendation from a counselor, teacher and a personal choice. Letters should address applicant's leadership abilities, character, initiative, and school/community involvement.
NUMBER OF AWARDS: 6 (3 men, 3 women)

740—MEMORIAL FOUNDATION FOR JEWISH CULTURE (International Scholarship Program for Community Service)

50 Broadway, 34th floor
New York NY 10004
212/425-6606
E-mail: office@mfjc.org
Internet: http://www.mfjc.org/index.htm
AMOUNT: Varies
DEADLINE(S): NOV 30
FIELD(S): Jewish Education; Theology; Social Work
ELIGIBILITY/REQUIREMENTS: Open to any individual regardless of country of origin for undergraduate study that leads to careers in the Rabbinate, Jewish education, social work, or as religious functionaries in Diaspora Jewish communities outside the U.S., Israel, and Canada. Must commit to serve in a community of need for 3 years. Those planning to serve in the U.S., Canada, or Israel are excluded from this program.
HOW TO APPLY: Write for complete information.
RENEWABLE: Yes
CONTACT: Jerry Hechbaum, Executive Vice-President; or Dr. Marc Brandriss, Associate Director

741—MEMORIAL FOUNDATION FOR JEWISH CULTURE (Soviet Jewry Community Service Scholarship Program)

50 Broadway, 34th floor
New York NY 10004
212/425-6606
E-mail: office@mfjc.org
Internet: http://www.mfjc.org/index.htm
AMOUNT: Varies
DEADLINE(S): NOV 30
FIELD(S): Theology; Education; Social Work
ELIGIBILITY/REQUIREMENTS: Open to Jews from the former Soviet Union enrolled or planning to enroll in recog-

nized institutions of higher Jewish learning. Must agree to serve a community of Soviet Jews anywhere in the world for a minimum of 3 years. Grants are to help prepare well-qualified Soviet Jews to serve in the former Soviet Union.
HOW TO APPLY: Write for complete information.
RENEWABLE: Yes
CONTACT: Jerry Hechbaum, Executive Vice-President; or Dr. Marc Brandriss, Associate Director

742—MIDWAY COLLEGE

512 East Stephens Street
Midway KY 40347
800/755-0031
E-mail: admissions@midway.edu
Internet: http://www.midway.edu
AMOUNT: Up to full tuition
DEADLINE(S): Varies
FIELD(S): Nursing; Education; Psychology; Biology; Equine Studies; Computer Information Systems; Business Administration; English; Pre-Med; Pre-Vet
ELIGIBILITY/REQUIREMENTS: Merit scholarships for admitted students who are considered full time in Midway's women's college. Depending on scholarship, minimum GPA ranges from 2.5 to 3.2, minimum ACT ranges 18 to 29, minimum SAT from 860 to 1290. In some cases, students must live on campus.
HOW TO APPLY: Contact Admissions Office or high school guidance counselor for application. Complete FAFSA online.
NUMBER OF AWARDS: Varies; up to 100
RENEWABLE: Yes. Must meet GPA requirements which vary based on the scholarship.
CONTACT: Admissions Office or high school guidance counselor
ADDITIONAL INFORMATION: Athletes may be eligible for an athletic scholarship in conjunction with a merit grant; contact coach for eligibility and award information.

743—NAACP NATIONAL OFFICE (Sutton Education Scholarship)

4805 Mount Hope Drive
Baltimore MD 21215
410/620-5372 or 877/NAACP-98
E-mail: education@naacp.org
Internet: http://www.naacp.org/work/education/eduscholarship.shtml
AMOUNT: $1,000 undergraduates; $2,000 graduates

DEADLINE(S): APR 30
FIELD(S): Education
ELIGIBILITY/REQUIREMENTS: Open to NAACP members majoring in education. Undergraduates must have GPA of 2.5+; graduates' GPAs must be 3.0+. Financial need must be established.
HOW TO APPLY: Write for complete information. Include a legal size SASE.
RENEWABLE: Yes, provided 3.0 GPA is maintained

744—NATIONAL ART MATERIALS TRADE ASSOCIATION (NAMTA Art/Art Education Major Scholarship)

15806 Brookway Drive, Suite 300
Huntersville NC 28078
704/892-6244
FAX: 704/892-6247
E-mail: scholarships@namta.org
Internet: http://www.namta.org
AMOUNT: $2,500
DEADLINE(S): APR 1
FIELD(S): Art; Art Education
ELIGIBILITY/REQUIREMENTS: Students majoring or planning to major in the field of art, whether as an art major or an art educator. Candidates do not have to be an employee or family member of an employee of a NAMTA member firm to apply. Candidates must graduate from high school or its equivalent before July 1 of the year in which they receive the scholarship; and must attend an accredited university, college or technical institute. Candidates will be judged on extracurricular activities, grade point average and financial need.
HOW TO APPLY: See website. Contact NAMTA for application. Submit with transcripts.
NUMBER OF AWARDS: 2
RENEWABLE: No

745—NATIONAL ASSOCIATION OF AMERICAN BUSINESS CLUBS (AMBUCS Scholarships for Therapists)

P.O. Box 5127
High Point NC 27262
800/838-1845, ext. 10
FAX:336/852-6830
E-mail: janiceb@ambucs.org
Internet: http://www.ambucs.ORG
AMOUNT: $500-$1,500, $6,000
DEADLINE(S): APR 15
FIELD(S): Physical Therapy, Music Therapy, Occupational Therapy, Speech-Language Pathology, Audiology,
ELIGIBILITY/REQUIREMENTS: Open to undergraduate juniors and seniors or

graduate students who have good scholastic standing and plan to enter the fields listed above. The institution to which you are accepted must present a curriculum accredited by the appropriate health/therapy profession authority. GPA of 3.0 or better (4.0 scale) and U.S. citizenship required. Must demonstrate financial need.

HOW TO APPLY: See website for additional information and application. MUST apply online. Semi-finalists must provide proof of enrollment, IRS Form 1040s, and a personal statement of not more than 1 page describing the development of your chosen field of therapy; your plan of study; career plans after graduation; and why financial assistance is needed. It is recommended, but not mandatory, that applicants seek sponsorship of an AMBUCS chapter, provided a chapter is located within a reasonable distance of your home or school.

RENEWABLE: Yes
CONTACT: Janice Blankenship, Membership/Scholarship Coordinator

746—NATIONAL FEDERATION OF THE BLIND (Educator of Tomorrow Award)

805 Fifth Avenue
Grinnell IA 50112
515/236-3366
Internet: http://www.nfb.org/nfb/
scholarship_program.asp
AMOUNT: $3,000
DEADLINE(S): MAR 31
FIELD(S): Education: Elementary, Secondary, and Postsecondary
ELIGIBILITY/REQUIREMENTS: For legally blind students pursuing or planning to pursue a full-time postsecondary course of study in the U.S. Based on academic excellence, service to the community, and financial need. Membership NOT required.
HOW TO APPLY: Contact Scholarship Committee Chairman for an application.
NUMBER OF AWARDS: 1
RENEWABLE: Yes
CONTACT: Peggy Elliot, Scholarship Committee Chairman

747—NATIONAL INSTITUTE FOR LABOR RELATIONS RESEARCH [NILRR] (Applegate/Jackson/Parks Future Teacher Scholarship)

5211 Port Royal Road
Springfield VA 22151
703/321-9606
FAX: 703/321-7342

E-mail: research@nilrr.org
Internet: http://www.nilrr.org
AMOUNT: $1,000
DEADLINE(S): DEC 31
FIELD(S): Education
ELIGIBILITY/REQUIREMENTS: Applicant will demonstrate potential for the completion of the educational requirements in a college or university Department of Education program, the potential to achieve a teaching license, and an understanding of the principles of voluntary unionism and the problems of compulsory unionism in relation to education.
HOW TO APPLY: Download application and information from website or request application by e-mail. Requests must specify "Teacher," "Education" or "Applegate/Jackson/Parks" scholarships and e-mail requests must include complete accurate mailing address. Submit application and required essay (500 words clearly demonstrating an interest in and knowledge of the Right to Work principle as it applies to educators) along with official copy of the most up-to-date transcript of grades.
NUMBER OF AWARDS: 1
RENEWABLE: No
CONTACT: Cathy Jones

748—NATIVE AMERICAN JOURNALISTS ASSOCIATION (NAJA Scholarships and Internships)

University of South Dakota
414 East Clark Street
Vermillion SD 57069
605/677-5282
FAX: 605/694-4264
E-mail: info@naja.com
Internet: http://www.naja.com
AMOUNT: $1,000-$3,000
DEADLINE(S): APR 15
FIELD(S): Journalism (Print, Broadcast, Photojournalism, New Media, Journalism Education)
ELIGIBILITY/REQUIREMENTS: Must be Native American pursuing journalism degree at institution of higher learning and a current member of NAJA.
HOW TO APPLY: Cover letter stating financial need, area of interest (see above), and reasons for pursuing a career in journalism. Include 3 letters of recommendation from academic advisor, counselor, or a professional individual familiar with applicant's background and skills; 2 copies of transcript, work samples (if available), proof of enrollment in a federal or state-recognized tribe (if not enrolled, briefly explain). Application fee $20.

749—NATIVE AMERICAN SCHOLARSHIP FUND, INC.

8200 Mountain Road NE, Suite 203
Albuquerque NM 87110
505/262-2351
FAX: 505/262-0543
E-mail: NScholarsh@aol.com
AMOUNT: Varies
DEADLINE(S): MAR 15; APR 15; SEP 15
FIELD(S): Mathematics; Engineering; Science; Business; Education; Computer Science
ELIGIBILITY/REQUIREMENTS: Open to American Indians or Alaskan Natives (one-quarter degree or more) enrolled as members of a federally recognized, state recognized, or terminated tribe. For graduate or undergraduate study at an accredited 4-year college or university.
HOW TO APPLY: Contact Director of Recruitment for an application.
NUMBER OF AWARDS: 208
CONTACT: Lucille Kelley, Director of Recruitment

750—NAVAL HISTORICAL CENTER (Internship Program)

Washington Navy Yard
805 Kidder Breese Street SE
Washington DC 20374-5060
202/433-6901
FAX: 202/433-8200
E-mail: edward.furgol@navy.mil
Internet: http://www.history.navy.mil
AMOUNT: $400 possible honoraria; otherwise, unpaid
DEADLINE(S): None
FIELD(S): Education; History; Public Relations; Design
ELIGIBILITY/REQUIREMENTS: Registered students of colleges/universities and graduates thereof are eligible for this program, which must be a minimum of 3 weeks, full- or part-time. Four specialties are available: Curator, Education, Public Relations, and Design. Interns receive orientation and assist in their department, and they must complete an individual project that contributes to the Center.
HOW TO APPLY: Submit completed application, available from the website, before the desired start date of an internship. Submit with 1 letter of recommendation, an unofficial transcript, and (except for graphic design applicants) a writing sample of not less than 1,000 words.
NUMBER OF AWARDS: 60
RENEWABLE: Yes; must reapply.
CONTACT: Dr. Edward Furgol

751—PHI DELTA KAPPA (Scholarship Grants for Prospective Educators)

408 North Union Street
P.O. Box 789
Bloomington IN 47402-0789
812/339-1156
FAX: 812/339-0018
E-mail: information@PDKintl.org
Internet: http://www.PDKintl.org
AMOUNT: $500 to renewable awards of $5,000 over 4 years
DEADLINE(S): FEB 1
FIELD(S): Education/Teaching Career
ELIGIBILITY/REQUIREMENTS: Open to high school seniors who plan to pursue careers as teachers or educators. Student teachers who are undergraduate members of PDK may also apply. Based on scholastic achievement, leadership activities, recommendations, and an essay.
HOW TO APPLY: See website or contact PDK for information and application. Send SASE for printed application.
NUMBER OF AWARDS: 30
CONTACT: Sandra Weith, Associative Executive Director; or Pat Robertson, Program Director

752—PHILADELPHIA BIBLICAL UNIVERSITY (Scholarships, Grants, and Loans)

Financial Aid Department
200 Manor Avenue
Langhorne PA 19047
800/366-0049
FAX: 215/702-4248
E-mail: financialaid@pbu.edu
Internet: http://www.pbu.edu
AMOUNT: Varies
DEADLINE(S): Varies
FIELD(S): Bible, Business, Teacher Education, Music, Social Work, Missions, Church Ministries
ELIGIBILITY/REQUIREMENTS: Academic and need-based grants, based on FAFSA results, are available to students attending full time. Academic awards based on GPA and SAT/ACT scores. Need-based grants are also available to needy dependents of full-time Christian workers and scholarships presented to those exhibiting excellence in the field of music.
HOW TO APPLY: Apply to university and complete student aid application.
CONTACT: David Haggard

753—PI LAMBDA THETA (Distinguished Student Scholar Award for Education Majors)

P.O. Box 6626
Bloomington IN 47401-5599
812/339-3411
FAX: 812/339-3462
E-mail: pam@pilambda.org
Internet: http://www.pilambda.org
AMOUNT: $500
DEADLINE(S): NOV 1
FIELD(S): Education
ELIGIBILITY/REQUIREMENTS: Award for an outstanding undergraduate student who is an education major and is a second-semester sophomore or higher. GPA of 3.5 required. Must demonstrate leadership potential and a strong dedication to the field of education. Membership in Pi Lambda Theta NOT required.
HOW TO APPLY: Nomination must be made by a college or university instructor, professor, or supervisor. See website for application and details.

754—PILOT INTERNATIONAL FOUNDATION (PIF/Lifeline Scholarship)

P.O. Box 5600
Macon GA 31208-5600
478/743-7403
FAX: 478/743-2173
E-mail: pifinfo@pilothq.org
Internet: http://www.pilot-international.org
AMOUNT: Varies
DEADLINE(S): FEB 15
FIELD(S): Disabilities/Brain-related disorders
ELIGIBILITY/REQUIREMENTS: This program assists ADULT students reentering the job market, preparing for a second career, or improving their professional skills for an established career. Applicants must be preparing for, or already involved in, careers working with people with disabilities/brain-related disorders. GPA of 3.5 or more is required. MUST be a Pilot Club member.
HOW TO APPLY: Must be sponsored by your local Pilot Club or in the city in which your college or university is located. See website for application.

755—PILOT INTERNATIONAL FOUNDATION (The Pilot International Scholarship Program)

P.O. Box 5600
Macon GA 31208-5600
478/743-7403
FAX: 478/743-2173
E-mail: pifinfo@pilothq.org
Internet: http://www.pilot international.org
AMOUNT: Varies
DEADLINE(S): FEB 15
FIELD(S): Disabilities/Brain-related disorders
ELIGIBILITY/REQUIREMENTS: This program provides assistance to undergraduate students preparing for careers working directly with people with disabilities or training those who will. GPA of 3.25 or greater required. MUST be a Pilot Club member.
HOW TO APPLY: Must be sponsored by your local Pilot Club or in the city in which your college or university is located. See website for application.

756—SCOTTISH RITE CHARITABLE FOUNDATION (Bursaries for College Students)

Roeher Institute, Kinsmen Building
4700 Keele Street
North York Ontario M3J 1P3
CANADA
416/661-9611
TDD: 416/661-2023
FAX: 416/661-5701
E-mail: mail@aacl.org
Internet: http://www.aacl.org
AMOUNT: Up to $2,000 (Canadian)
DEADLINE(S): JUL 1
FIELD(S): Human Services; Intellectual Disability; Special Education; Social Work
ELIGIBILITY/REQUIREMENTS: Open to Canadian citizens/landed immigrants accepted into a full-time undergraduate college program in a Canadian college or university. Financial need NOT a factor.
HOW TO APPLY: Must be recommended by a Provincial Association of the Canadian Association for Community Living. Must submit outline of intended study, transcripts, community involvement, and letters of reference from supervisors. Contact your provincial association for details.
NUMBER OF AWARDS: 3

757—SOUTH CAROLINA SPACE GRANT CONSORTIUM (Undergraduate Research Program)

66 George Street
College of Charleston
Charleston SC 29424
843/953-5463
FAX: 843/953-5446
E-mail: scozzarot@cofc.edu
Internet: http://www.cofu.edu/ ~scs.grant
AMOUNT: $3,000

DEADLINE(S): End of JAN; check application for SPECIFIC deadline date

FIELD(S): Aerospace or Space-related Studies (Areas of interest include, but are not limited to, the Basic Sciences; Science Education; Astronomy; Planetary Science; Environmental Studies; Engineering; Fine Arts; Journalism)

ELIGIBILITY/REQUIREMENTS: Must be a citizen of the U.S.; attend a consortium member institution; have sponsorship from a faculty advisor; be a rising junior or senior; have an interest in aerospace and space-related studies. Selection of awards is based on academic qualifications of the applicant; 2 letters of recommendation; description of past activities, current interests and future plans concerning a space science or aerospace related field; faculty sponsorship and a research proposal including its relevance to a NASA mission.

HOW TO APPLY: Attend a SC Space Grant Consortium member school; apply to your institution's campus director.

NUMBER OF AWARDS: 1

RENEWABLE: No

CONTACT: Tara B. Scozzaro

758—SOUTHERN ILLINOIS UNIVERSITY (Music Scholarships)

School of Music, Mailcode 4302
Carbondale IL 62901-4302
618/536-8742
FAX: 618/453-5808
Internet: http://www.siu.edu/
~music/resources/scholarships.html

AMOUNT: Varies

DEADLINE(S): MAR 15

FIELD(S): Music Performance, Composition, Theater, Music Business, Music Education

ELIGIBILITY/REQUIREMENTS: Must be music major or minor.

HOW TO APPLY: An audition is required, usually held in February. A personal audition or taped audition can be arranged. See website or Undergraduate Office, School of Music.

RENEWABLE: Yes. Recommendation of music faculty required.

CONTACT: Dr. Jeanine Wagner

759—TENNESSEE STUDENT ASSISTANCE CORPORATION (TSAC Minority Teaching Fellows Program)

404 James Robertson Parkway
Nashville TN 37243-0820
615/532-3499 or 800/447-1523
FAX: 615/741-5555

AMOUNT: $5,000/year (up to $20,000)

DEADLINE(S): APR 15

FIELD(S): Education; Teaching

ELIGIBILITY/REQUIREMENTS: For minority Tennessee residents who are attending Tennessee institutions and studying to be teachers. Entering freshmen must have at least a 2.75 high school GPA, and continuing college students must have a minimum 2.5 college GPA. Must also be in top 25% of class or have at least 18 ACT or 850 SAT.

HOW TO APPLY: Apply at your high school guidance office, college Financial Aid Office, or contact Michael C. Roberts, Student Aid Compliance Administrator, at above address.

ADDITIONAL INFORMATION: Recipients must agree to teach at a K-12 level Tennessee public school one year for each year the award is received.

760—TEXAS CHORAL DIRECTORS ASSOCIATION SCHOLARSHIP FUND

7900 Centre Park Drive
Austin TX 78754
514/474-2801
FAX: 514/474-7873
E-mail: tcda@ensemble.org
Internet: http://www.ensemble.org/tcda

AMOUNT: $500-$1,000

DEADLINE(S): JUN 1

FIELD(S): Choral Direction; Music Education

ELIGIBILITY/REQUIREMENTS: Must have completed 60 hours in music education degree program.

HOW TO APPLY: Contact TCDA for an application.

NUMBER OF AWARDS: 4

RENEWABLE: No

CONTACT: Dan L. Wood

761—TRAVELERS PROTECTIVE ASSOCIATION OF AMERICA (TPA) SCHOLARSHIP TRUST FOR THE DEAF AND NEAR DEAF

3755 Lindell Blvd
St Louis MO 63108
314/371-0533
FAX: 314/371-0537
E-mail: ghartman@tpahq.org
Internet: http://www.ttahq.org

AMOUNT: Varies

DEADLINE(S): MAR 1

FIELD(S): Education: Mechanical Devices; Medical Treatment of Deafness

ELIGIBILITY/REQUIREMENTS: Children and adults who suffer deafness or hearing impairment and who need assistance in obtaining mechanical devices, medical or specialized treatment or specialized education, as well as speech classes, note takers, interpreters, etc., and in other areas of need that are directly related to hearing impairment. Selection of recipients and amount of scholarship awarded shall be decided upon by the majority of the Trustees meeting in April to review all applications. Applicants demonstrating the greatest financial need are given preference regardless of race, creed, age or sex. Distributions are made from the interest earned by Trust investments.

HOW TO APPLY: Request application from The Travelers Protective Association of America at above address.

RENEWABLE: Yes. Recipients may receive additional aid and must complete a new application for aid each time they seek additional aid.

762—UNITED METHODIST CHURCH SCHOLARSHIP PROGRAM (Edith M. Allen Scholarship)

P.O. Box 34007
Nashville TN 37203-0007
615/340-7344
FAX: 615/340-7367
E-mail: umscholar@gbhem.org
Internet: http://www.gbhem.org

AMOUNT: Up to $1,000

DEADLINE(S): MAY 1

FIELD(S): Education; Social Work; Medicine and related professions

ELIGIBILITY/REQUIREMENTS: Open to African-American students enrolled full-time at a UM college or university, have a B+ average or higher, a full and active member of the UMC for at least 3 years, citizen or permanent resident of the U.S., and demonstrate financial need.

HOW TO APPLY: See website for application or contact the director of financial aid at the United Methodist college or university of your choice, the chairperson of your annual conference Board of Higher Education and Campus Ministry or the United Methodist Scholarship Office at the address listed for information and/or application form.

CONTACT: Scholarship Department

763—UNIVERSITY OF NORTH TEXAS (Scholarships for Elementary and Secondary Education Majors)

P.O. Box 311337
Denton TX 76203-1337

940/565-2992 (Elementary) or 940/565-2826 (Secondary)
Internet: http://www.unt./scholar/scholarshipedu/scholarships/gelem.htm and http://www.unt.edu/scholarships/teacher.htm
AMOUNT: Varies
DEADLINE(S): Varies
FIELD(S): Education: Elementary and Secondary Teaching
ELIGIBILITY/REQUIREMENTS: Open to students in the teacher education departments at the University of North Texas. Requirements vary by scholarship.
HOW TO APPLY: See website for more information. Write to either Department of Elementary, Early Childhood, and Reading Education or Department of Teacher Education and Administration/Secondary Education for details.
NUMBER OF AWARDS: Multiple

764—UNIVERSITY OF WINDSOR (U.S./Mexico Entrance Scholarship)

401 Sunset Avenue
Windsor Ontario N9B 3P4
CANADA
519/253-3000
FAX: 519/973-7081
E-mail: awards1@uwindsor.ca
Internet: http://www.uwindsor.ca
AMOUNT: $3,000/term (Canadian) Engineering, Education, Law, Nursing; all other fields $1,500/term (Canadian)
DEADLINE(S): MAY 31
FIELD(S): All
ELIGIBILITY/REQUIREMENTS: Open to undergraduate students with U.S./Mexican citizenship or permanent resident status registering in year 1 at the University of Windsor. Must have superior grades.
HOW TO APPLY: Automatic. No application required.
RENEWABLE: Yes. Up to 4 years, contingent upon successful completion of the previous term and a cumulative A- GPA.
CONTACT: Aase Houser

765—UNIVERSITY OF WYOMING (Superior Students in Education Scholarship)

College of Education
Office of Teacher Education
McWhinnie Hall, Room 100
Dept. 3374 - 100 E University Ave
Laramie WY 82071-3374
307/766-2230
Internet: http://www.uwyo.edu/ted/superior.asp
AMOUNT: Varies
DEADLINE(S): Last Friday in JAN
FIELD(S): Education
ELIGIBILITY/REQUIREMENTS: For Wyoming high school graduates who have demonstrated high scholastic achievement and qualities of leadership and who plan to teach in Wyoming public schools. May attend the University of Wyoming or any community college in the state and major in education. Based on residency, ACT scores, grades, courses taken, school activities, letters of recommendation, and student responses to prepared questions. Must maintain a 2.5 GPA to remain in program.
HOW TO APPLY: Download application from website or contact the College of Education, Office of Teacher Education.
NUMBER OF AWARDS: 16
RENEWABLE: Yes. Up to ten semesters (no more than five may be at a community college).

766—WASHINGTON ASSOCIATION OF SCHOOL ADMINISTRATORS (21st Century Education Scholarships)

825 Fifth Avenue SE
Olympia WA 98501
360/943-5717
FAX: 360/352-2043
E-mail: ejohnson@wasa-oly.org
Internet: http://www.wasa-oly.org
AMOUNT: $1,000
DEADLINE(S): MAR 7
FIELD(S): Education
ELIGIBILITY/REQUIREMENTS: High school senior who is enrolled in a Washington public or accredited private school; has at least a 3.0 cumulative GPA on a 4.0 scale; intends to major in and pursue a career in K-12 education. Preference is given to students who have accomplishments in the following areas: leadership, community service, honors and awards, student activities and educational goals.
HOW TO APPLY: You are required to write 2 essays, 1 describing your educational goals (no longer than 1 single-spaced page) and one describing your accomplishments in the following criteria categories: leadership, community service, honors and awards, student activities and educational goals. Also required are an application form (no longer than 2 single-spaced pages).
NUMBER OF AWARDS: 3
RENEWABLE: Yes. Up to 4 years. Must maintain a 3.0 GPA and continue to major in education.
CONTACT: Evelyn Johnson

767—WESTERN MICHIGAN UNIVERSITY (College of Arts and Sciences/Elizabeth M. Garrett Endowed Scholarship for Women in Science)

1903 West Michigan
Kalamazoo MI 49008-5337
269/387-8777
FAX: 269/387-6989
E-mail: finaid-info@wmich.edu
Internet: http://www.wmich.edu/finaid
AMOUNT: Varies
DEADLINE(S): MAR 1
FIELD(S): Science; Science Education
ELIGIBILITY/REQUIREMENTS: Junior, senior, or graduate student preparing for career in science or teaching of science with minimum GPA of 3.0. Preference given to nontraditional student.
HOW TO APPLY: Contact Science Department for an application.
RENEWABLE: Yes

768—WESTERN MICHIGAN UNIVERSITY (College of Arts and Sciences/Erik A. Schreiner Endowed Memorial Scholarship)

1903 West Michigan
Kalamazoo MI 49008-5337
269/387-8777
FAX: 269/387-6989
E-mail: finaid-info@wmich.edu
Internet: http://www.wmich.edu/finaid
AMOUNT: $1,000/semester
DEADLINE(S): MAR 1
FIELD(S): Mathematics; Mathematics Education; Statistics
ELIGIBILITY/REQUIREMENTS: Junior, mathematics or statistics major.
HOW TO APPLY: Winners are selected by a committee composed of members from the Department of Mathematics and the Department of Statistics.
NUMBER OF AWARDS: 2 (1 of the awards is normally designated for a student in the Mathematics Education area).

769—WESTERN MICHIGAN UNIVERSITY (College of Arts and Sciences/Fred A. Beeler Memorial Scholarship)

1903 West Michigan
Kalamazoo MI 49008-5337
269/387-8777
FAX: 269/387-6989
E-mail: finaid-info@wmich.edu
Internet: http://www.wmich.edu/finaid
AMOUNT: Varies

DEADLINE(S): MAR 1
FIELD(S): Mathematics; Mathematics Education; Statistics
ELIGIBILITY/REQUIREMENTS: Undergraduate freshman or sophomore with a GPA of 3.0 majoring in Mathematics, Statistics, or Mathematics Education. Must demonstrate financial need.
HOW TO APPLY: Winners are selected by a committee composed of members from the Department of Mathematics and the Department of Statistics.
NUMBER OF AWARDS: 2 (1 of the awards is normally designated for a student in the Mathematics Education area).
RENEWABLE: Yes. Up to maximum of 4 consecutive academic years.

770—WESTERN MICHIGAN UNIVERSITY (College of Arts and Sciences/Gwenivere Rabe Endowed Scholarship)

1903 West Michigan
Kalamazoo MI 49008-5337
269/387-8777
FAX: 269/387-6989
E-mail: finaid-info@wmich.edu
Internet: http://www.wmich.edu/finaid
AMOUNT: Varies
DEADLINE(S): MAR 1
FIELD(S): Science; Science Education
ELIGIBILITY/REQUIREMENTS: Undergraduate students majoring in natural or physical science with 3.0 minimum GPA. Financial need-based. Michigan resident preparing for career in science or teaching of science with minimum GPA of 3.0. Preference given to nontraditional student.
HOW TO APPLY: Contact Science Department for an application.
RENEWABLE: Yes

771—WESTERN MICHIGAN UNIVERSITY (College of Arts and Sciences/James Knauss/Smith Burnham Senior History Award)

1903 West Michigan
Kalamazoo MI 49008-5337
269/387-8777
FAX: 269/387-6989
E-mail: finaid-info@wmich.edu
Internet: http://www.wmich.edu/finaid
AMOUNT: Varies
FIELD(S): Liberal Education; Public History; Secondary Education
ELIGIBILITY/REQUIREMENTS: Awarded to the top seniors in above fields.

HOW TO APPLY: History Department faculty selects recipient.
RENEWABLE: No

772—WESTERN MICHIGAN UNIVERSITY (College of Arts and Sciences/Margaret Thomas DuMond Scholarship)

1903 West Michigan
Kalamazoo MI 49008-5337
269/387-8777
FAX: 269/387-6989
E-mail: finaid-info@wmich.edu
Internet: http://www.wmich.edu/finaid
AMOUNT: $500 (spring semester)
DEADLINE(S): MAR 1
FIELD(S): Education; Biology
ELIGIBILITY/REQUIREMENTS: Junior or senior (minimum of 62 credit hours); Secondary Education Biology major with 3.0 GPA.
HOW TO APPLY: Contact the Biological Sciences Department for an application.
RENEWABLE: No

773—WESTERN MICHIGAN UNIVERSITY (College of Arts and Sciences/The George Sprau Award in English)

1903 West Michigan
Kalamazoo MI 49008-5337
269/387-8777
FAX: 269/387-6989
E-mail: finaid-info@wmich.edu
Internet: http://www.wmich.edu/finaid
AMOUNT: $25-$175 (fall semester)
DEADLINE(S): Not applicable
FIELD(S): English Language; English Education
ELIGIBILITY/REQUIREMENTS: Seniors (occasionally juniors) with superior academic record.
HOW TO APPLY: Nominated by Department of English faculty.
RENEWABLE: No

774—WESTERN MICHIGAN UNIVERSITY (College of Arts and Sciences/The Jean and Vincent Malmstrom Scholarship)

1903 West Michigan
Kalamazoo MI 49008-5337
269/387-8777
FAX: 269/387-6989
Internet: http://www.wmich.edu/finaid
AMOUNT: $500 (fall semester)
DEADLINE(S): Fall semester

FIELD(S): English Language; English Education
ELIGIBILITY/REQUIREMENTS: Second-semester junior or first-semester senior with a major or minor in English Education and courses in English Language (grammar, structure, history, dialects). Minimum GPA 3.5.
HOW TO APPLY: Contact the English Department for application.
RENEWABLE: No

775—WESTERN MICHIGAN UNIVERSITY (College of Arts and Sciences/The Ralph N. Miller Memorial Award)

1903 West Michigan
Kalamazoo MI 49008-5337
269/387-8777
FAX: 269/387-6989
E-mail: finaid-info@wmich.edu
Internet: http://www.wmich.edu/finaid
AMOUNT: $300 (fall semester)
FIELD(S): English Language; English Education
ELIGIBILITY/REQUIREMENTS: English major or minor in junior year; GPA considered, but no minimum requirements; criteria include intellectual curiosity, daring, forcefulness, and enthusiasm.
HOW TO APPLY: Students nominated (or self-nominated); submit writing samples.
RENEWABLE: No
CONTACT: Department of English

776—WESTERN MICHIGAN UNIVERSITY (College of Education/Agnes Robb Bouyoucos International Internship Fund)

1903 West Michigan
Kalamazoo MI 49008-5337
269/387-6000
FAX: 269/387-6989
E-mail: finaid-info@wmich.edu
Internet: http://www.wmich.edu/finaid
AMOUNT: Varies
FIELD(S): Education; Teaching
ELIGIBILITY/REQUIREMENTS: Must be a full-time undergraduate student in College of Education; must use scholarship for the purpose of study-abroad internships. Preference given to students pursuing a teacher prep curriculum. Must demonstrate financial need.
HOW TO APPLY: See website for application or contact College of Education.
RENEWABLE: No

777—WESTERN MICHIGAN UNIVERSITY (College of Education/Alfred Griffin Scholarship Fund)

1903 West Michigan
Kalamazoo MI 49008-5337
269/387-6000
FAX: 269/387-6989
E-mail: finaid-info@wmich.edu
Internet: http://www.wmich.edu/finaid
AMOUNT: Tuition costs
FIELD(S): Elementary Education
ELIGIBILITY/REQUIREMENTS: Must be senior in Elementary Education and enrolled full time; African American or Native American preferred. Must maintain a minimum 2.5 GPA and be a resident of the state of Michigan.
HOW TO APPLY: See website for application or contact College of Education.
RENEWABLE: No

778—WESTERN MICHIGAN UNIVERSITY (College of Education/Beulah and Harold McKee Scholarship in Early Childhood Education)

1903 West Michigan
Kalamazoo MI 49008-5337
269/387-6000
FAX: 269/387-6989
E-mail: finaid-info@wmich.edu
Internet: http://www.wmich.edu/finaid
AMOUNT: $1,500/semester
FIELD(S): Early Childhood Education
ELIGIBILITY/REQUIREMENTS: Enrolled full time in Early Childhood Education curriculum and maintain a 3.0 GPA.
HOW TO APPLY: See website for application or contact College of Education.
RENEWABLE: Yes. Until the current recipient graduates.

779—WESTERN MICHIGAN UNIVERSITY (College of Education/Chrystal I. Grady Family and Consumer Sciences Scholarship)

1903 West Michigan
Kalamazoo MI 49008-5337
269/387-6000
FAX: 269/387-6989
E-mail: finaid-info@wmich.edu
Internet: http://www.wmich.edu/finaid
AMOUNT: Varies
DEADLINE(S): MAR 1
FIELD(S): Home Economics
ELIGIBILITY/REQUIREMENTS: Declared major in Home Economics related curriculum; must be junior or senior at time of award with a 3.0 GPA or better. Must have completed substantial course work at WMU in FCS Department.
HOW TO APPLY: Applications are available February 1.
RENEWABLE: No
CONTACT: Dr. Linda Dannison, 3018 Kohrman Hall, 269/387-3704, or e-mail: linda.dannison@wmich.edu

780—WESTERN MICHIGAN UNIVERSITY (College of Education/Chrystal Grady Home Economics Scholarship)

1903 West Michigan
Kalamazoo MI 49008-5337
269/387-6000
FAX: 269/387-6989
E-mail: finaid-info@wmich.edu
Internet: http://www.wmich.edu/finaid
AMOUNT: $100-$500
FIELD(S): Home Economics
ELIGIBILITY/REQUIREMENTS: Enrolled in Home Economics program; must be junior or senior at time of award with a 3.0 GPA or better.
HOW TO APPLY: See website for application.
RENEWABLE: No
CONTACT: Dr. Linda Dannison, 3018 Kohrman Hall, 269/387-3704, or e-mail: linda.dannison@wmich.edu

781—WESTERN MICHIGAN UNIVERSITY (College of Education/D. B. "Tim" and Gloria Shaw, Jr. Tutorial Support Endowment Fund)

1903 West Michigan
Kalamazoo MI 49008-5337
269/387-6000
FAX: 269/387-6989
E-mail: finaid-info@wmich.edu
Internet: http://www.wmich.edu/finaid
AMOUNT: Varies
DEADLINE(S): MAR 1
FIELD(S): Special Education
ELIGIBILITY/REQUIREMENTS: Provides funding for tutoring by special education majors in the Department of Educational Studies for special education. Funding available to school-age students from throughout the community who have a demonstrated learning disability and are entitled to receive public school service under current and future Michigan law. Funds available to assist with the cost of the tutor. This tutorial program is only intended to make available limited short-term assistance to the participants and at the same time provide the special education major student with hands-on practical field experience in special education.
HOW TO APPLY: Applications are available February 1.
RENEWABLE: No
CONTACT: Dr. Elizabeth Whitten, Chair, Department of Educational Studies, 3506 Sangren Hall, 269/387-5935, or e-mail: elizabeth.whitten@wmich.edu

782—WESTERN MICHIGAN UNIVERSITY (College of Education/Doris A. Lance Fund)

1903 West Michigan
Kalamazoo MI 49008-5337
269/387-6000
FAX: 269/387-6989
E-mail: finaid-info@wmich.edu
Internet: http://www.wmich.edu/finaid
AMOUNT: $500/semester
DEADLINE(S): MAR 1
FIELD(S): Business Education
ELIGIBILITY/REQUIREMENTS: Full- or part-time student enrolled in Secondary Education in Business (Business Education); maintain a minimum 3.0 GPA. Recipients selected on the basis of academic achievement and/or financial need, and must not have been censured for a major violation of University regulations.
HOW TO APPLY: See website for application or contact College of Education.
RENEWABLE: Yes. Upon recommendation of the selection committee and student need, this award may be renewed from year to year.
CONTACT: College of Education

783—WESTERN MICHIGAN UNIVERSITY (College of Education/Dorothy H. and Cora Hurd Charles Scholarship)

1903 West Michigan
Kalamazoo MI 49008-5337
269/387-6000
FAX: 269/387-6989
E-mail: finaid-info@wmich.edu
Internet: http://www.wmich.edu/finaid
AMOUNT: $500/semester
DEADLINE(S): MAR 1
FIELD(S): Teaching
ELIGIBILITY/REQUIREMENTS: Must be junior or senior enrolled full time in program leading to teacher certification. Maintain a minimum 3.0 GPA.

HOW TO APPLY: See website for application or contact College of Education.
RENEWABLE: No

784—WESTERN MICHIGAN UNIVERSITY (College of Education/E. Fern Hudson Scholarship)

1903 West Michigan
Kalamazoo MI 49008-5337
269/387-6000
FAX: 269/387-6989
E-mail: finaid-info@wmich.edu
Internet: http://www.wmich.edu/finaid
AMOUNT: $500-$1,000/semester
DEADLINE(S): MAR 1
FIELD(S): Teaching
ELIGIBILITY/REQUIREMENTS: Must be junior or senior enrolled full time in program leading to teacher certification. Maintain a minimum 3.0 GPA. Demonstrate financial need.
HOW TO APPLY: See website for application or contact College of Education.
RENEWABLE: No

785—WESTERN MICHIGAN UNIVERSITY (College of Education/Florence E. and Vernon A. Martin Prestigious Education Scholarship)

1903 West Michigan
Kalamazoo MI 49008-5337
269/387-6000
FAX: 269/387-6989
E-mail: finaid-info@wmich.edu
Internet: http://www.wmich.edu/finaid
AMOUNT: $500-$1,000/semester
DEADLINE(S): MAR 1FIELD(S): Teaching
ELIGIBILITY/REQUIREMENTS: Must be enrolled full time in program leading to teacher certification. Maintain a minimum 3.0 GPA.
HOW TO APPLY: See website for application or contact College of Education.
RENEWABLE: No

786—WESTERN MICHIGAN UNIVERSITY (College of Education/Fund for the Advancement of Minorities in Education [FAME])

1903 West Michigan
Kalamazoo MI 49008-5337
269/387-6000
FAX: 269/387-6989
E-mail: finaid-info@wmich.edu
Internet: http://www.wmich.edu/finaid

AMOUNT: Full tuition and fees
DEADLINE(S): MAR 1
FIELD(S): Education
ELIGIBILITY/REQUIREMENTS: May be incoming first-year student, community college transfer student, or current WMU student. Special consideration given to students of under-represented populations.
HOW TO APPLY: See website for application or contact College of Education.
RENEWABLE: Yes. May be awarded for up to 4 years.

787—WESTERN MICHIGAN UNIVERSITY (College of Education/Harriett Kiser Creed Endowment Fund)

1903 West Michigan
Kalamazoo MI 49008-5337
269/387-6000
FAX: 269/387-6989
E-mail: finaid-info@wmich.edu
Internet: http://www.wmich.edu/finaid
AMOUNT: $500/semester
DEADLINE(S): MAR 1
FIELD(S): Health, Physical Education and Recreation
ELIGIBILITY/REQUIREMENTS: Full-time junior or senior enrolled in HPER Curriculum, preference to HPER majors, with 3.0 or higher GPA. Must be involved in HPER-related activities and show financial need.
HOW TO APPLY: Contact the HPER Department, 4024 Student Recreation Center, or College of Education, 2304 Sangren Hall.
CONTACT: HPER Department or College of Education

788—WESTERN MICHIGAN UNIVERSITY (College of Education/Harriett Kiser Creed HPER Scholarship)

1903 West Michigan
Kalamazoo MI 49008-5337
269/387-6000
FAX: 269/387-6989
E-mail: debra.berkey@wmich.edu
Internet: http://www.wmich.edu/finaid
AMOUNT: $500/semester
DEADLINE(S): MAR 1
FIELD(S): Health, Physical Education and Recreation
ELIGIBILITY/REQUIREMENTS: Full-time junior or senior enrolled in HPER Curriculum, with 3.0 or higher GPA.
HOW TO APPLY: Contact Dr. Debra Berkey for more information, 269/387-2710; 4021 Student Recreation Center.

NUMBER OF AWARDS: 1
RENEWABLE: No

789—WESTERN MICHIGAN UNIVERSITY (College of Education/Howard E. Thompson Endowed Scholarship Fund for Physical Education)

1903 West Michigan
Kalamazoo MI 49008-5337
269/387-6000
FAX: 269/387-6989
E-mail: debra.berkey@wmich.edu
Internet: http://www.wmich.edu/finaid
AMOUNT: $1,000/semester
DEADLINE(S): MAR 1
FIELD(S): Physical Education
ELIGIBILITY/REQUIREMENTS: Major in physical education preparing for a professional career in teaching in the public schools.
HOW TO APPLY: Contact Dr. Debra Berkey for more information, 269/387-2710; 4021 Student Recreation Center.
NUMBER OF AWARDS: 1

790—WESTERN MICHIGAN UNIVERSITY (College of Education/Isadore Turansky Memorial Special Education Scholarship)

1903 West Michigan
Kalamazoo MI 49008-5337
269/387-6000
FAX: 269/387-6989
E-mail: elizabeth.whitten@wmich.edu
Internet: http://www.wmich.edu/finaid
AMOUNT: $500/semester
DEADLINE(S): MAR 1
FIELD(S): Special Education
ELIGIBILITY/REQUIREMENTS: Major in special education; preparing for a career teaching in the public schools.
HOW TO APPLY: Contact Dr. Elizabeth Whitten, Chair, Department of Educational Studies, 3506 Sangren Hall, 269/387-5935 for more information.
NUMBER OF AWARDS: 1

791—WESTERN MICHIGAN UNIVERSITY (College of Education/Jane Blackburn Memorial Scholarship for Undergraduates in Elementary Education)

1903 West Michigan
Kalamazoo MI 49008-5337
269/387-6000
FAX: 269/387-6989
E-mail: finaid-info@wmich.edu
Internet: http://www.wmich.edu/finaid

AMOUNT: $500/semester
DEADLINE(S): MAR 1
FIELD(S): Elementary Education
ELIGIBILITY/REQUIREMENTS: Junior or senior enrolled full time in Elementary Education; must maintain a minimum 3.0 GPA.
HOW TO APPLY: See website for application or contact College of Education.
RENEWABLE: No
CONTACT: College of Education

792—WESTERN MICHIGAN UNIVERSITY (College of Education/Katherine Pratt Burrell Endowed Education Scholarship)

1903 West Michigan
Kalamazoo MI 49008-5337
269/387-6000
FAX: 269/387-6989
E-mail: finaid-info@wmich.edu
Internet: http://www.wmich.edu/finaid
AMOUNT: $500/semester
DEADLINE(S): MAR 1
FIELD(S): Teaching
ELIGIBILITY/REQUIREMENTS: Junior or senior enrolled full time in program leading to teacher certification; must maintain a minimum 3.0 GPA and demonstrate financial need. Females preferred.
HOW TO APPLY: See website for application or contact College of Education.
RENEWABLE: No
CONTACT: College of Education

793—WESTERN MICHIGAN UNIVERSITY (College of Education/Lloyd F. Hutt Memorial Scholarship)

1903 West Michigan
Kalamazoo MI 49008-5337
269/387-6000
FAX: 269/387-6989
E-mail: finaid-info@wmich.edu
Internet: http://www.wmich.edu/finaid
AMOUNT: $500-$1,000
DEADLINE(S): MAR 1
FIELD(S): Industrial Education and Technology
ELIGIBILITY/REQUIREMENTS: Recipient must be enrolled full time in the Industrial Education and Technology (Industrial Arts) program. Must have demonstrated ability in the field of Industrial Arts and come from the Grand Rapids area. Awarded to an undergraduate or graduate.
HOW TO APPLY: Application available from Dr. Linda Dannison, Chair, Department of Family and Consumer Sciences, 3018 Kohrman Hall, 269/387-3705, linda.dannison@wmich.edu

RENEWABLE: Yes. May be renewed based upon achievement and recommendation.

794—WESTERN MICHIGAN UNIVERSITY (College of Education/Lloyd F. Hutt Memorial Scholarship Endowment in Industrial Education and Technology)

1903 West Michigan
Kalamazoo MI 49008-5337
269/387-6000
FAX: 269/387-6989
E-mail: finaid-info@wmich.edu
Internet: http://www.wmich.edu/finaid
AMOUNT: Varies
DEADLINE(S): MAR 1
FIELD(S): Industrial Education and Technology
ELIGIBILITY/REQUIREMENTS: Preference given to students pursuing or intending to pursue an organized program of study in the Department of Industrial Education and Technology (Industrial Arts) from the Grand Rapids (Michigan) area. Must be full-time student demonstrating ability in the field of industrial arts.
HOW TO APPLY: Contact the Department of Industrial Education for more information.
RENEWABLE: No

795—WESTERN MICHIGAN UNIVERSITY (College of Education/Lofton & Georgiann Burge Scholarship for Undergraduates in Elementary Education)

1903 West Michigan
Kalamazoo MI 49008-5337
269/387-6000
FAX: 269/387-6989
E-mail: finaid-info@wmich.edu
Internet: http://www.wmich.edu/finaid
AMOUNT: $500-$2,000
DEADLINE(S): MAR 1
FIELD(S): Early Elementary Education
ELIGIBILITY/REQUIREMENTS: Junior or senior enrolled full time in Early Elementary Education; must maintain a 3.0 GPA.
HOW TO APPLY: See website for application.
RENEWABLE: No
CONTACT: College of Education

796—WESTERN MICHIGAN UNIVERSITY (College of Education/Lofton Burge Educational Scholarship)

1903 West Michigan
Kalamazoo MI 49008-5337

269/387-6000
FAX: 269/387-6989
E-mail: finaid-info@wmich.edu
Internet: http://www.wmich.edu/finaid
AMOUNT: $500-$2,000
DEADLINE(S): MAR 1
FIELD(S): Elementary Education
ELIGIBILITY/REQUIREMENTS: Junior or senior enrolled full time in Elementary Education; must maintain a 3.0 GPA.
HOW TO APPLY: See website for application or contact College of Education.
RENEWABLE: No

797—WESTERN MICHIGAN UNIVERSITY (College of Education/Lucille Abbott Nobbs Endowed Scholarship)

1903 West Michigan
Kalamazoo MI 49008-5337
269/387-6000
FAX: 269/387-6989
E-mail: finaid-info@wmich.edu
Internet: http://www.wmich.edu/finaid
AMOUNT: $2,000
DEADLINE(S): MAR 1
FIELD(S): Education; Teaching
ELIGIBILITY/REQUIREMENTS: Must be a member, or direct descendent of a member, of Alpha Beta Epsilon WMU sorority; full-time junior, senior or graduate student enrolled in the College of Education. Preference given to student enrolled in a teacher education program. 3.0 or higher GPA. Must be available to attend the spring Alpha Beta Epsilon meeting.
HOW TO APPLY: Contact Mrs. Kathryn B. Walker, ABE Chapter President, 21522 Robinson Road, Jackson, MI 49203, 517/750-2059 for additional information.
CONTACT: Kathryn B. Walker

798—WESTERN MICHIGAN UNIVERSITY (College of Education/Lucille J. Haines Education Scholarship)

1903 West Michigan
Kalamazoo MI 49008-5337
269/387-6000
FAX: 269/387-6989
E-mail: finaid-info@wmich.edu
Internet: http://www.wmich.edu/finaid
AMOUNT: $500/semester
DEADLINE(S): MAR 1
FIELD(S): Early Childhood Education
ELIGIBILITY/REQUIREMENTS: Junior or senior enrolled full time in Early

Childhood Education curriculum. Maintain a 3.0 GPA.

HOW TO APPLY: See website for application or contact College of Education.

799—WESTERN MICHIGAN UNIVERSITY (College of Education/Margaret Isobel Black Endowed Scholarship)

1903 West Michigan
Kalamazoo MI 49008-5337
269/387-6000
FAX: 269/387-6989
E-mail: finaid-info@wmich.edu
Internet: http://www.wmich.edu/finaid

AMOUNT: Full tuition, fees and books
DEADLINE(S): MAR 1
FIELD(S): Education
ELIGIBILITY/REQUIREMENTS: Limited to incoming first-year students, community college transfer students, or current WMU students who are graduates of Warren Consolidated School District and possess a minimum 3.0 GPA.
HOW TO APPLY: See website for application or contact College of Education.
RENEWABLE: Yes. Must reapply each year.

800—WESTERN MICHIGAN UNIVERSITY (College of Education/Marion I. Hall Undergraduate Scholarship)

1903 West Michigan
Kalamazoo MI 49008-5337
269/387-6000
FAX: 269/387-6989
E-mail: finaid-info@wmich.edu
Internet: http://www.wmich.edu/finaid

AMOUNT: $500-$1,000/semester
DEADLINE(S): MAR 1
FIELD(S): Teaching
ELIGIBILITY/REQUIREMENTS: Enrolled full time in program leading to teacher certification; must maintain a minimum 3.0. GPA.
HOW TO APPLY: See website for application or contact College of Education.
RENEWABLE: No

801—WESTERN MICHIGAN UNIVERSITY (College of Education/McKinley Financial Foundation Endowed Scholarship)

1903 West Michigan
Kalamazoo MI 49008-5337
269/387-6000
FAX: 269/387-6989
E-mail: finaid-info@wmich.edu

Internet: http://www.wmich.edu/finaid
AMOUNT: Varies
DEADLINE(S): MAR 1
FIELD(S): Business; Education
ELIGIBILITY/REQUIREMENTS: Must be full-time incoming freshman in the Haworth College of Business (awarded even years) and the College of Education (awarded odd years). Preference given to African American students. Must have a minimum of 2.5 GPA.
HOW TO APPLY: See website for application or contact College of Education.
NUMBER OF AWARDS: 1 (minimum)
RENEWABLE: Yes. Up to three years, provided recipient maintains a 2.5 GPA.

802—WESTERN MICHIGAN UNIVERSITY (College of Education/Merze Tate Undergraduate Scholarship)

1903 West Michigan
Kalamazoo MI 49008-5337
269/387-6000
FAX: 269/387-6989
E-mail: finaid-info@wmich.edu
Internet: http://www.wmich.edu/finaid

AMOUNT: $250-$2,000
DEADLINE(S): MAR 1
FIELD(S): Business; Education
ELIGIBILITY/REQUIREMENTS: May be enrolled full- or part-time. Preference is given to students in need of financial aid (including, but not limited to, deserving foreign students in need of financial assistance).
HOW TO APPLY: See website for application or contact College of Education.
NUMBER OF AWARDS: 1 (minimum)
RENEWABLE: No

803—WESTERN MICHIGAN UNIVERSITY (College of Education/Neil L. and Leta C. Schoenhals Undergraduate Memorial Scholarship)

1903 West Michigan
Kalamazoo MI 49008-5337
269/387-6000
FAX: 269/387-6989
E-mail: finaid-info@wmich.edu
Internet: http://www.wmich.edu/finaid

AMOUNT: Varies
DEADLINE(S): MAR 1
FIELD(S): Industrial Technology
ELIGIBILITY/REQUIREMENTS: Graduating senior; must be Industrial Technology major.

HOW TO APPLY: Selection is made by scholarship benefactor and select FCS faculty.
NUMBER OF AWARDS: 1
RENEWABLE: No
CONTACT: College of Education

804—WESTERN MICHIGAN UNIVERSITY (College of Education/Robert and Irene [Smith] Davies Education Scholarship)

1903 West Michigan
Kalamazoo MI 49008-5337
269/387-6000
FAX: 269/387-6989
E-mail: finaid-info@wmich.edu
Internet: http://www.wmich.edu/finaid

AMOUNT: $500/semester
DEADLINE(S): MAR 1
FIELD(S): Elementary Education
ELIGIBILITY/REQUIREMENTS: Single women, either junior or senior at time of award, enrolled full time in Elementary Education. Must maintain minimum 3.0 GPA.
HOW TO APPLY: See website or contact College of Education for application.
RENEWABLE: No

805—WESTERN MICHIGAN UNIVERSITY (College of Education/Robert J. and Evelyn S. Armstrong Scholarship)

1903 West Michigan
Kalamazoo MI 49008-5337
269/387-6000
FAX: 269/387-6989
E-mail: finaid-info@wmich.edu
Internet: http://www.wmich.edu/finaid

AMOUNT: $500/semester
DEADLINE(S): MAR 1
FIELD(S): Education (especially Early Childhood Education)
ELIGIBILITY/REQUIREMENTS: Full-time undergraduate students, majoring in College of Education, preference given to students with an emphasis on Early Childhood Education. 3.0 or higher GPA.
HOW TO APPLY: See website or contact College of Education for application.

806—WESTERN MICHIGAN UNIVERSITY (College of Education/Rose M. Iciek Memorial Scholarship for Elementary and Secondary Education)

1903 West Michigan
Kalamazoo MI 49008-5337
269/387-6000
FAX: 269/387-6989

E-mail: finaid-info@wmich.edu
Internet: http://www.wmich.edu/finaid
AMOUNT: $500/semester
DEADLINE(S): MAR 1
FIELD(S): Pre-Education
ELIGIBILITY/REQUIREMENTS: Awarded to a first-year, full-time undergraduate student majoring in Pre-Education, who plans to teach either at the elementary or secondary level. 3.0 or higher GPA. Must demonstrate financial need.
HOW TO APPLY: See website or contact College of Education for application.
NUMBER OF AWARDS: 1

807—WESTERN MICHIGAN UNIVERSITY (College of Education/Samuel K. Smart Jr. Fund Eligibility Criteria)

1903 West Michigan
Kalamazoo MI 49008-5337
269/387-6000
FAX: 269/387-6989
E-mail: finaid-info@wmich.edu
Internet: http://www.wmich.edu/finaid
AMOUNT: $500-$1,000/semester
DEADLINE(S): MAR 1
FIELD(S): Teaching (Science or Mathematics)
ELIGIBILITY/REQUIREMENTS: Full-time status, in need of financial aid. Must maintain a minimum 3.0 GPA and pursue a curriculum that will prepare them to become an instructor in Science or Mathematics.
HOW TO APPLY: See website or contact College of Education for application.
RENEWABLE: No

808—WESTERN MICHIGAN UNIVERSITY (College of Education/Stuart and Norma Hall Scholarship)

1903 West Michigan
Kalamazoo MI 49008-5337
269/387-6000
FAX: 269/387-6989
E-mail: finaid-info@wmich.edu
Internet: http://www.wmich.edu/finaid
AMOUNT: Varies
DEADLINE(S): MAR 1
FIELD(S): Music Education
ELIGIBILITY/REQUIREMENTS: Must be a full-time undergraduate in the College of Education majoring in music education; minimum 2.5 GPA. Preference given to students who demonstrate financial need.

HOW TO APPLY: See website or contact College of Education for application.
RENEWABLE: Yes. Up to 3 years

809—WESTERN MICHIGAN UNIVERSITY (College of Education/Teacher Education Assistance for Minorities [TEAM]/Morris Hood Jr. Educator Development Scholarship)

1903 West Michigan
Kalamazoo MI 49008-5337
269/387-6000
FAX: 269/387-6989
E-mail: finaid-info@wmich.edu
Internet: http://www.wmich.edu/finaid
AMOUNT: Varies
DEADLINE(S): MAR 1
FIELD(S): Teaching
ELIGIBILITY/REQUIREMENTS: Junior, senior or post-baccalaureate status; must be accepted into a professional education program leading to teacher certification. Must demonstrate financial need. Available only to members of the TEAM program and active participation in the TEAM mentoring program is required. Preference given to male students and to Michigan residents.
HOW TO APPLY: See website or contact College of Education for application.
RENEWABLE: Yes. Up to 3 years.

810—WESTERN MICHIGAN UNIVERSITY (College of Education/The Ronald and Kathleen Wagner Scholarship)

1903 West Michigan
Kalamazoo MI 49008-5337
269/387-6000
FAX: 269/387-6989
E-mail: finaid-info@wmich.edu
Internet: http://www.wmich.edu/finaid
AMOUNT: Varies
DEADLINE(S): MAR 1
FIELD(S): Teaching
ELIGIBILITY/REQUIREMENTS: Awarded to a first-year full-time undergraduate student enrolled in College of Education. 3.0 GPA required. Preference given to minority high school graduates of Wayne County public schools. Financial need considered and recipient must maintain satisfactory academic performance as specified by the Office of Student Financial Need.
HOW TO APPLY: See website or contact College of Education for application.

811—WESTERN MICHIGAN UNIVERSITY (College of Education Undergraduate Scholarship)

1903 West Michigan
Kalamazoo MI 49008-5337
269/387-6000
FAX: 269/387-6989
E-mail: finaid-info@wmich.edu
Internet: http://www.wmich.edu/finaid
AMOUNT: $250-$1,000
FIELD(S): Education
ELIGIBILITY/REQUIREMENTS: Incoming freshmen, community college transfer students, and current WMU students are eligible.
HOW TO APPLY: See website for application or contact College of Education.
RENEWABLE: No

812—WESTERN MICHIGAN UNIVERSITY (College of Education/Zora and Frank Ellsworth Scholarship Fund)

1903 West Michigan
Kalamazoo MI 49008-5337
269/387-6000
FAX: 269/387-6989
E-mail: finaid-info@wmich.edu
Internet: http://www.wmich.edu/finaid
AMOUNT: $1,000-$2,000/semester
DEADLINE(S): MAR 1
FIELD(S): Education (Latin preferred)
ELIGIBILITY/REQUIREMENTS: Full-time student in junior or senior year; be enrolled in Elementary Education (Latin majors preferred); must maintain 3.0 GPA; demonstrate a career purpose in education and financial need.
HOW TO APPLY: See website or contact College of Education for application.

813—WESTERN MICHIGAN UNIVERSITY (College of Fine Arts/Beverly Belson Scholarship Fund for Music Theater)

1903 West Michigan
Kalamazoo MI 49008-5337
269/387-8777
FAX: 269/387-6989
E-mail: finaid-info@wmich.edu
Internet: http://www.wmich.edu/finaid
AMOUNT: Varies
DEADLINE(S): MAR (for current Theater majors); on acceptance into program for freshmen and transfer students

FIELD(S): Theater Education; Theater Design; Technical Theater; Arts Management; Music Theater Performance

ELIGIBILITY/REQUIREMENTS: Scholarships are ONLY for Theater majors and minors. Must have a 3.0 GPA.

HOW TO APPLY: Freshmen or transfer students—by audition/interview and acceptance into major or minor in Theater program. Current Theater majors—by application form from the department.

RENEWABLE: No

CONTACT: Theater Department

814—WESTERN MICHIGAN UNIVERSITY (College of Fine Arts/Evelyn Burke Scholarship)

1903 West Michigan
Kalamazoo MI 49008-5337
269/387-8777
FAX: 269/387-6989
E-mail: finaid-info@wmich.edu
Internet: http://www.wmich.edu/finaid

AMOUNT: Varies

DEADLINE(S): MAR (for current Theater majors); on acceptance into program for freshmen and transfer students.

FIELD(S): Theater Education; Theater Design; Technical Theater; Arts Management; Music Theater Performance

ELIGIBILITY/REQUIREMENTS: Scholarships are ONLY for Theater majors and minors. Must have a 3.0 GPA.

HOW TO APPLY: Freshmen or transfer students—by audition/interview and acceptance into major or minor in Theater program. Current Theater majors—by application form from the department.

RENEWABLE: No

CONTACT: Theater Department

815—WESTERN MICHIGAN UNIVERSITY (College of Fine Arts/John and Susanna Gemela Memorial Scholarship for Design and Technical Theater)

1903 West Michigan
Kalamazoo MI 49008-5337
269/387-8777
FAX: 269/387-6989
E-mail: finaid-info@wmich.edu
Internet: http://www.wmich.edu/finaid

AMOUNT: Varies

DEADLINE(S): MAR (for current Theater majors); on acceptance into program for freshmen and transfer students

FIELD(S): Theater Education; Theater Design; Technical Theater; Arts Management; Music Theater Performance

ELIGIBILITY/REQUIREMENTS: Scholarships are ONLY for Theater majors and minors. Must have a 3.0 GPA.

HOW TO APPLY: Freshmen or transfer students—by audition/interview and acceptance into major or minor in Theater program. Current Theater majors—by application form from the department.

RENEWABLE: No

CONTACT: Theater Department

816—WESTERN MICHIGAN UNIVERSITY (College of Fine Arts/Patricia Chisholm Scholarship for Theater Education)

1903 West Michigan
Kalamazoo MI 49008-5337
269/387-8777
FAX: 269/387-6989
E-mail: finaid-info@wmich.edu
Internet: http://www.wmich.edu/finaid

AMOUNT: Varies

DEADLINE(S): MAR (for current Theater majors); on acceptance into program for freshmen and transfer students

FIELD(S): Theater Education

ELIGIBILITY/REQUIREMENTS: Scholarships are ONLY for Theater majors and minors. Must have a 3.0 GPA.

HOW TO APPLY: Freshmen or transfer students—by audition/interview and acceptance into major or minor in Theater program. Current Theater majors—by application form from the department.

RENEWABLE: No

CONTACT: Theater Department

817—WESTERN MICHIGAN UNIVERSITY (College of Fine Arts/Robert and Marion Denison Scholarship for Theater Education)

1903 West Michigan
Kalamazoo MI 49008-5337
269/387-8777
FAX: 269/387-6989
E-mail: finaid-info@wmich.edu
Internet: http://www.wmich.edu/finaid

AMOUNT: Varies

DEADLINE(S): MAR (for current Theater majors); on acceptance into program for freshmen and transfer students

FIELD(S): Theater Education

ELIGIBILITY/REQUIREMENTS: Scholarships are ONLY for Theater majors and minors. Must have a 3.0 GPA.

HOW TO APPLY: Freshmen or transfer students—by audition/interview and acceptance into major or minor in Theater program. Current Theater majors—by application form from the department.

RENEWABLE: No

CONTACT: Theater Department

818—WESTERN MICHIGAN UNIVERSITY (Mayor Dennis Archer Endowed Scholarship)

1903 West Michigan
Kalamazoo MI 49008-5337
269/387-8777
FAX: 269/387-6989
E-mail: alumni@wmich.edu
Internet: http://www.wmich.edu/alumni

AMOUNT: $2000

DEADLINE(S): APR 1

FIELD(S): Education; Public Administration; Pre-Law

ELIGIBILITY/REQUIREMENTS: Undergraduate student; Detroit resident, or resident of Wayne, Oakland or Macomb counties; major in Education, Public Administration or Pre-Law programs; minimum 3.0 high school GPA. Preference given to those with financial need. Recipient must demonstrate evidence of public service/volunteer activities.

HOW TO APPLY: Contact the Office of Financial Aid for more details.

RENEWABLE: Yes. Up to a maximum of 4 consecutive academic years as long as the recipient maintains a 3.0 GPA at WMU.

CONTACT: Office of Financial Aid

819—Y'S MEN INTERNATIONAL-U.S. AREA (Alexander Scholarship Loan Fund)

629 Lantana Lane
Imperial CA 92251
Internet: http://www.ysmenusa.com/aslf1.htm

AMOUNT: $1,000-$1,500/year

DEADLINE(S): MAY 30; OCT 30

FIELD(S): Business Administration; Youth Leadership

ELIGIBILITY/REQUIREMENTS: Open to U.S. citizens/permanent residents with a strong desire to pursue professional YMCA service. Must be YMCA staff pursuing undergraduate or graduate study and demonstrate financial need. Repayment of loan is waived if recipient enters YMCA employment after graduation.

HOW TO APPLY: See website for application.

820—ZETA PHI BETA SORORITY, INC./NATIONAL EDUCATIONAL FOUNDATION (Isabel M. Herson Scholarship in Education)

1734 New Hampshire Avenue NW
Washington DC 20009
Internet: http://www.ZphiB1920.org
AMOUNT: $500-$1,000
DEADLINE(S): FEB 1
FIELD(S): Elementary and Secondary Education
ELIGIBILITY/REQUIREMENTS: Open to graduate- and undergraduate-level students enrolled in a degree program in either elementary or secondary education. Award is for full-time study for one academic year (Fall-Spring). Must submit proof of enrollment.
HOW TO APPLY: See website for additional information and application or send SASE to Foundation. Must submit documented proof of academic study and plan of program to Scholarship Chairperson with signature of school administrator or Program Director; 3 letters of recommendation (professor or high school teacher, minister or community leader, other—for Zeta members 3rd reference must be from the graduate Zeta chapter and signed by the Basileus or Advisor); transcript; essay (minimum 150 words) with information about yourself, your educational goals and professional aspirations and how this award will help you achieve them, and why you should receive this award.
RENEWABLE: No

ENGINEERING (ALL FIELDS)

821—A.C.E.C. RESEARCH AND MANAGEMENT FOUNDATION (A.C.E.C./ProNet Scholarship)

1015 15th Street NW, Suite 802
Washington DC 20005
202/347-7474
FAX: 202/898-0868
AMOUNT: $2,500
FIELD(S): Engineering; Business Administration
ELIGIBILITY/REQUIREMENTS: Applicants must be 3rd- or 4th-year undergraduate (or graduate) students of an accredited engineering school, who express interest in practice management studies in addition to their engineering curriculum, and whose career interests will lead them into private engineering practice.
HOW TO APPLY: Send completed application.
CONTACT: Francis George, Scholarship Program Administrator

822—AIR FORCE RESERVE OFFICER TRAINING CORPS (AFROTC Scholarships)

551 East Maxwell Boulevard
Maxwell AFB AL 36112-6106
866/4AFROTC
E-mail: info@afrotc.com
Internet: http://www.afrotc.com
AMOUNT: Varies, but up to full tuition and fees plus $600/year for books
DEADLINE(S): DEC 1
FIELD(S): Science; Engineering; Business; Political Science; Psychology; Geography; Foreign Studies; Foreign Language
ELIGIBILITY/REQUIREMENTS: 4- and 3-year competitive scholarships based on individual merit to high school seniors and graduates who have not enrolled full time at a college or university. Academic performance is measured using an academic composite, which combines SAT (Math and Verbal only)/ACT scores, class rank, GPA and the number of advanced placement or honors courses completed through grade 11. To be eligible for consideration, students should achieve a 1100 SAT (Math and Verbal only) or 24 ACT, minimum 3.0 GPA and class ranking in top 40%. Must be a U.S. citizen between the ages of 17-27. Must also have GPA of 2.5 or above, be in top 40% of class, and complete Applicant Fitness Test. Cannot be a single parent. Your college or university must offer AFROTC.
HOW TO APPLY: Visit www.afrotc.com to apply.
NUMBER OF AWARDS: Not applicable
RENEWABLE; No

823—AMERICAN ASSOCIATION OF BLACKS IN ENERGY (AABE)

Western Michigan University
1903 West Michigan
Kalamazoo MI 49008-5337
269/387-8777
FAX: 269/387-6989
E-mail: alumni@wmich.edu
Internet: http://www.wmich.edu/cas/research.html
AMOUNT: Varies
DEADLINE(S): MAR 1
FIELD(S): Mathematics; Computer Science; Engineering; Physical Sciences
ELIGIBILITY/REQUIREMENTS: Freshman with 2.5 GPA overall and a 3.0 GPA in mathematics and the sciences planning to major in engineering, mathematics, computer or the physical sciences. Applicant must demonstrate financial need and be a member of one of the underrepresented minority groups in the sciences and technology.
HOW TO APPLY: Contact the Office for Student Financial Aid.
NUMBER OF AWARDS: Varies
RENEWABLE: Yes

824—AMERICAN COUNCIL OF ENGINEERING COMPANIES/PA

2040 Linglestown Road,
Suite 200
Harrisburg PA 1710
717/540-6811
FAX: 717/540-6815
E-mail: jvannatta@acecpa.org
Internet: http://www.acecpa.org
AMOUNT: $2,000
DEADLINE(S): DEC 1
FIELD(S): Engineering
ELIGIBILITY/REQUIREMENTS: Must be a full-time student working to earn a B.S in Engineering and a U.S. citizen. Essay requirement.
HOW TO APPLY: Write for more information or download application from website.
NUMBER OF AWARDS: At least 1
RENEWABLE: No
CONTACT: John G. VanNatta II

825—AMERICAN FOUNDATION FOR THE BLIND (Paul W. Ruckes Scholarship)

11 Penn Plaza, Suite 300
New York NY 10001
212/502-7661
FAX: 212/502-7771
E-mail: afbino@afb.net
Internet: http://www.afb.org/scholar/scholarships.asp
AMOUNT: $1,000
DEADLINE(S): APR 30
FIELD(S): Engineering; Computer/Physical/Life Sciences
ELIGIBILITY/REQUIREMENTS: Open to legally blind and visually impaired undergraduate and graduate students pursuing a degree in one of above fields. Must be U.S. citizen.
HOW TO APPLY: See website or contact AFB for an application. Must submit evidence of legal blindness; official transcripts; proof of college or university acceptance; 3 letters of recommendation; and typewritten statement describing

goals, work experience, extracurricular activities, and how monies will be used.
NUMBER OF AWARDS: 1
CONTACT: Alina Vayntrub

826—AMERICAN HEALTH AND BEAUTY AIDS INSTITUTE (Fred Luster, Sr. Education Foundation Scholarships for College-Bound High School Seniors)

P.O. Box 19510
Chicago IL 60619
708/333-8740
FAX: 708/333-8741
Internet: http://www.proudlady.org
AMOUNT: $250-$500
DEADLINE(S): APR 15
FIELD(S): Chemistry, Business, Engineering
ELIGIBILITY/REQUIREMENTS: Open to college-bound high school seniors who will be enrolled as a college freshman in a 4-year college majoring in chemistry, business, or engineering. 3.0 GPA required. Scholastic record, school activities, and extracurricular activities considered.
HOW TO APPLY: Send two letters of recommendation (one from a school official) and high school transcript.
NUMBER OF AWARDS: 2

827—AMERICAN INDIAN SCIENCE AND ENGINEERING SOCIETY (A. T. Anderson Memorial Scholarship)

P.O. Box 9828
Albuquerque NM 87119-9828
505/765-1052
FAX: 505/765-5608
E-mail: scholarships@aises.org
Internet: http://www.aises.org/scholarships
AMOUNT: $1,000-$2,000
DEADLINE(S): JUN 15
FIELD(S): Medicine; Natural Resources; Science; Engineering
ELIGIBILITY/REQUIREMENTS: Open to undergraduate and graduate students who are at least 1/4 American Indian or recognized as member of a tribe. Must be member of AISES ($10 fee), enrolled full time at an accredited institution, and demonstrate financial need.
HOW TO APPLY: See website or contact Society for an application and/or membership information.
RENEWABLE: Yes
CONTACT: Patricia Browne

828—AMERICAN INDIAN SCIENCE AND ENGINEERING SOCIETY (Burlington Northern Santa Fe Pacific Foundation Scholarships)

P.O. Box 9828
Albuquerque NM 87119-9828
505/765-1052
FAX: 505/765-5608
E-mail: scholarships@aises.org
Internet: http://www.aises.org/scholar/scholarships
AMOUNT: $2,500
DEADLINE(S): MAR 31
FIELD(S): Business; Education; Science; Engineering; Health Administration
ELIGIBILITY/REQUIREMENTS: Open to high school seniors who are at least one quarter American Indian. Must reside in Kansas, Oklahoma, Colorado, Arizona, New Mexico, Minnesota, North Dakota, Oregon, South Dakota, Washington, Montana, or San Bernardino County, California (Burlington Northern and Santa Fe Pacific service areas). Must demonstrate financial need.
HOW TO APPLY: See website or contact Society for an application.
NUMBER OF AWARDS: 5
RENEWABLE: Yes. Up to 4 years.
CONTACT: Patricia Browne

829—AMERICAN INSTITUTE OF AERONAUTICS AND ASTRONAUTICS (Undergraduate Scholarships)

1801 Alexander Bell Drive, Suite 500
Reston VA 20191-4344
800/639-AIAA or 703/264-7500
FAX: 703/264-7551
E-mail: custserv@aiaa.org
Internet: http://www.aiaa.org
AMOUNT: $2,000
DEADLINE(S): JAN 31
FIELD(S): Science, Engineering, Aeronautics, Astronautics
ELIGIBILITY/REQUIREMENTS: For students who have completed at least one academic semester or quarter of full-time college work in the area of science or engineering encompassed by the technical activities of the AIAA. Must have GPA of at least 3.0, be enrolled in accredited college or university. Membership in AIAA not required to apply but must become one before receiving a scholarship award.
HOW TO APPLY: See website, students and educators page; submit with career essay, transcripts and 2 letters of recommendation from college professor.

RENEWABLE: Yes. Eligible for yearly continuation through senior year.
CONTACT: Customer Service

830—AMERICAN RADIO RELAY LEAGUE FOUNDATION (Gary Wagner, K3OMI) Scholarship)

225 Main Street
Newington CT 06111
860/594-0397
FAX: 860/594-0259
E-mail: foundation@arrl.org
Internet: http://www.arrlf.org/
AMOUNT: $1,000
DEADLINE(S): FEB 1
FIELD(S): Engineering
ELIGIBILITY/REQUIREMENTS: For radio amateurs, general class or higher, who are residents of North Carolina, Virginia, West Virginia, Maryland or Tennessee for study in 1 of those states leading to a bachelor of science degree in engineering at an accredited 4-year college or university. Must demonstrate financial need.
HOW TO APPLY: See website or contact Foundation for information and application. Submit with a 1-page essay on the role amateur radio has played in your life. A recent high school (or equivalent) or college transcript required; submit with application or mail separately.
NUMBER OF AWARDS: 1
RENEWABLE: Yes. 2 of the rewards are renewable for up to 3 years. Based on academic performance and annual transcript review.
CONTACT: Mary M. Hobart, K1MMH, Secretary

831—AMERICAN RADIO RELAY LEAGUE FOUNDATION (Perry F. Hadlock Memorial Scholarship)

225 Main Street
Newington CT 06111
860/594-0397
FAX: 860/594-0259
E-mail: foundation@arrl.org
Internet: http://www.arrlf.org/
AMOUNT: $2,000
DEADLINE(S): FEB 1
FIELD(S): Technology-related studies (Electrical and Electronics Engineering)
ELIGIBILITY/REQUIREMENTS: For student with technician's license or higher pursuing baccalaureate or higher degree at a regionally accredited institution. Regional preference ARRL Atlantic and

Hudson divisions; institutional preference Clarkson University, Potsdam, NY.
HOW TO APPLY: See website or contact Foundation for information and application. Submit with a 1-page essay on the role amateur radio has played in your life. A recent high school (or equivalent) or college transcript required; submit with application or mail separately.
NUMBER OF AWARDS: 1
RENEWABLE: No
CONTACT: Mary M. Hobart, K1MMH, Secretary

832—AMERICAN RADIO RELAY LEAGUE FOUNDATION (Henry Broughton, K2AE Memorial Scholarship)

225 Main Street
Newington CT 06111
860/594-0397
FAX: 860/594-0259
E-mail: foundation@arrl.org
Internet: http://www.arrlf.org/
AMOUNT: $1,000
DEADLINE(S): FEB 1
FIELD(S): Engineering; Science
ELIGIBILITY/REQUIREMENTS: For radio amateurs with a general class license whose home residence is within 70 miles of Schenectady, New York. For study leading to a bachelor's degree at an accredited 4-year college or university.
HOW TO APPLY: See website or contact Foundation for information and application. Submit with a 1-page essay on the role amateur radio has played in your life. A recent high school (or equivalent) or college transcript required; submit with application or mail separately.
NUMBER OF AWARDS: At least 1
RENEWABLE: No
CONTACT: Mary M. Hobart, K1MMH, Secretary

833—AMERICAN RADIO RELAY LEAGUE FOUNDATION (William R. Goldfarb Memorial Scholarship)

225 Main Street
Newington CT 06111
860/594-0397
FAX: 860/594-0259
E-mail: foundation@arrl.org
Internet: http://www.arrlf.org/
AMOUNT: $10,000 or more
DEADLINE(S): FEB 1
FIELD(S): Business, Computer Science, Medicine (including Nursing), Engineering, Sciences
ELIGIBILITY/REQUIREMENTS: For high school senior with any class of license

pursuing baccalaureate or higher degree at a regionally accredited institution. Must demonstrate financial need.
HOW TO APPLY: See website or contact Foundation for information and application. Submit with a 1-page essay on the role amateur radio has played in your life. A recent high school (or equivalent) or college transcript required; submit with application or mail separately.
NUMBER OF AWARDS: 1
RENEWABLE: No
CONTACT: Mary M. Hobart, K1MMH, Secretary

834—AMERICAN RADIO RELAY LEAGUE FOUNDATION (Yasme Foundation Scholarship, The)

225 Main Street
Newington CT 06111
860/594-0397
FAX: 860/594-0259
E-mail: foundation@arrl.org
Internet: http://www.arrlf.org/
AMOUNT: $2,000
DEADLINE(S): FEB 1
FIELD(S): Engineering; Science
ELIGIBILITY/REQUIREMENTS: For radio amateurs for study leading to a bachelor's degree at an accredited 4-year college or university. Preference given to high school applicants ranked in the top 5 to 10% of their class or to college students in the top 10% of their class. Participation in local amateur radio club and community service is important to selection.
HOW TO APPLY: See website or contact Foundation for information and application. Submit with a 1-page essay on the role amateur radio has played in your life. A recent high school (or equivalent) or college transcript required; submit with application or mail separately.
NUMBER OF AWARDS: Varies (approximately 5)
RENEWABLE: Yes. 2 of the rewards are renewable for up to 3 years. Based on academic performance and annual transcript review.
CONTACT: Mary M. Hobart, K1MMH, Secretary

835—AMERICAN RAILWAY ENGINEERING AND MAINTENANCE-OF-WAY ASSOCIATION (AREMA)

10003 Derekwood Lane,
Suite 210
Lanham MD 20706
301/459-3200
FAX: 301/459-8077

E-mail: selder@arema.org
Internet: http//www.arema.org
AMOUNT: $1,000 or more
DEADLINE(S): MAR 15
FIELD(S): Engineering; Engineering Technology
ELIGIBILITY/REQUIREMENTS: Applicants must be enrolled as full-time students in a 4- or 5-year program leading to a bachelor's degree in a curriculum which has been accredited by the Accreditation Board of Engineering and Technology (or comparable accreditation in Canada and Mexico). Must have completed at least 1 quarter or semester in college prior to submitting an application, and have at least a 2.00 GPA.
HOW TO APPLY: See website for application. Submit with a cover letter, not exceeding 350 words, explaining why the applicant believes he/she deserves scholarship (should indicate areas of railroading that might be of particular interest, and describe how his/her attributes relate to these areas); a résumé; 2 letters of recommendation (1 from a faculty member, and 1 from another faculty member, present or former employer, AREMA member, or other responsible person); and transcript from the school(s) attended. Send all material to AREMA Educational Foundation Scholarship Committee, American Railway Engineering and Maintenance of Way Association, 10003 Derekwood Lane, Suite 210, Lanham, MD 20706.
NUMBER OF AWARDS: 15 or more
RENEWABLE: No
CONTACT: Stacy Elder

836—AMERICAN SOCIETY OF HEATING, REFRIGERATING, AND AIR-CONDITIONING ENGINEERS (Alwin B. Newton Scholarship)

1791 Tullie Circle NE
Atlanta GA 30329
404/636-8400
FAX: 404/321-5478
E-mail: benedict@ashrae.org
Internet: http://www.ashrae.org
AMOUNT: $3,000
DEADLINE(S): DEC 1
FIELD(S): Engineering
ELIGIBILITY/REQUIREMENTS: Open to engineering undergraduate students enrolled full time in an ABET-accredited program leading to a Bachelor of Science or Bachelor of Engineering degree. Must have a minimum college GPA of 3.0; be enrolled full time in a college or university with at least 1 full year of studies remaining in the year for which the scholarship will be awarded; demonstrate potential service to

the HVAC&R profession, need for financial assistance, leadership ability, and character.

HOW TO APPLY: See website or contact Society for information and application. Submit with letters of recommendation, transcripts, and demonstration of financial need.

NUMBER OF AWARDS: 1

RENEWABLE: No

CONTACT: Lois Benedict, Scholarship Administrator

837—AMERICAN SOCIETY OF HEATING, REFRIGERATING, AND AIR-CONDITIONING ENGINEERS (ASHRAE Donald E. Nichols Scholarship)

1791 Tullie Circle NE
Atlanta GA 30329
404/636-8400
FAX: 404/321-5478
E-mail: benedict@ashrae.org
Internet: http://www.ashrae.org

AMOUNT: $3,000

DEADLINE(S): DEC 1

FIELD(S): Engineering

ELIGIBILITY/REQUIREMENTS: Available to a qualified undergraduate engineering student pursuing a bachelor's degree enrolled full time in an ABET-accredited program at Tennessee Technological University. Must have a minimum college GPA of 3.0; be enrolled full time in a college or university with at least 1 full year of studies remaining in the year for which the scholarship will be awarded; demonstrate potential service to the HVAC&R profession, need for financial assistance, leadership ability, and character.

HOW TO APPLY: See website or contact Society for information and application. Submit with letters of recommendation, transcripts, and demonstration of financial need.

NUMBER OF AWARDS: 1

RENEWABLE: No

CONTACT: Lois Benedict, Scholarship Administrator

838—AMERICAN SOCIETY OF HEATING, REFRIGERATING, AND AIR-CONDITIONING ENGINEERS (ASHRAE Memorial Scholarship)

1791 Tullie Circle NE
Atlanta GA 30329
404/636-8400
FAX: 404/321-5478
E-mail: benedict@ashrae.org
Internet: http://www.ashrae.org

AMOUNT: $3,000

DEADLINE(S): DEC 1

FIELD(S): Engineering

ELIGIBILITY/REQUIREMENTS: Open to engineering undergraduate students enrolled full time in an ABET-accredited program leading to a Bachelor of Science or Bachelor of Engineering Degree. Must have a minimum college GPA of 3.0; be enrolled full time in a college or university with at least 1 full year of studies remaining in the year for which the scholarship will be awarded; demonstrate potential service to the HVAC&R profession, need for financial assistance, leadership ability, and character.

HOW TO APPLY: See website or contact Society for information and application. Submit with letters of recommendation, transcripts, and demonstration of financial need.

NUMBER OF AWARDS: 1

RENEWABLE: No

CONTACT: Lois Benedict, Scholarship Administrator

839—AMERICAN SOCIETY OF HEATING, REFRIGERATING, AND AIR-CONDITIONING ENGINEERS (ASHRAE Region IV Benny Bootle Scholarship)

1791 Tullie Circle NE
Atlanta GA 30329
404/636-8400
FAX: 404/321-5478
E-mail: benedict@ashrae.org
Internet: http://www.ashrae.org

AMOUNT: $3,000

DEADLINE(S): DEC 1

FIELD(S): Engineering; Architecture

ELIGIBILITY/REQUIREMENTS: Available to a qualified undergraduate engineering or architecture student pursuing a bachelor's degree enrolled full time in an ABET- or NAAB-accredited program at a school located within the geographic boundaries of ASHRAE's Region IV (currently NC, SC, and GA). Must have a minimum college GPA of 3.0; be enrolled full time in a college or university with at least 1 full year of studies remaining in the year for which the scholarship will be awarded; demonstrate potential service to the HVAC&R profession, need for financial assistance, leadership ability, and character.

HOW TO APPLY: See website or contact Society for information and application. Submit with letters of recommendation, transcripts, and demonstration of financial need.

NUMBER OF AWARDS: 1

RENEWABLE: No

CONTACT: Lois Benedict, Scholarship Administrator

840—AMERICAN SOCIETY OF HEATING, REFRIGERATING, AND AIR-CONDITIONING ENGINEERS (ASHRAE Region VIII Scholarship)

1791 Tullie Circle NE
Atlanta GA 30329
404/636-8400
FAX: 404/321-5478
E-mail: benedict@ashrae.org
Internet: http://www.ashrae.org

AMOUNT: $3,000

DEADLINE(S): DEC 1

FIELD(S): Engineering, Architecture

ELIGIBILITY/REQUIREMENTS: Available to a qualified undergraduate engineering student pursuing a bachelor's degree enrolled full time in an ABET-accredited program at a school located within the geographic boundaries of ASHRAE's Region VIII (currently parts of AK, LA, TX and OK and Mexico). Must have a minimum college GPA of 3.0; be enrolled full time in a college or university with at least 1 full year of studies remaining in the year for which the scholarship will be awarded; demonstrate potential service to the HVAC&R profession, need for financial assistance, leadership ability, and character.

HOW TO APPLY: See website or contact Society for information and application. Submit with letters of recommendation, transcripts, and demonstration of financial need.

NUMBER OF AWARDS: 1

RENEWABLE: No

CONTACT: Lois Benedict, Scholarship Administrator

841—AMERICAN SOCIETY OF HEATING, REFRIGERATING, AND AIR-CONDITIONING ENGINEERS (ASHRAE Scholarships)

1791 Tullie Circle NE
Atlanta GA 30329
404/636-8400
FAX: 404/321-5478
E-mail: benedict@ashrae.org
Internet: http://www.ashrae.org

AMOUNT: $3,000

DEADLINE(S): DEC 1

FIELD(S): Engineering

ELIGIBILITY/REQUIREMENTS: Open to engineering undergraduate students enrolled full time in an ABET-accredited program leading to a Bachelor of Science or Bachelor of Engineering Degree. Must have a minimum college GPA of 3.0; be enrolled full time in a college or university with at least 1 full year of studies remaining in the year for which the scholarship will be

awarded; demonstrate potential service to the HVAC&R profession, need for financial assistance, leadership ability, and character.
HOW TO APPLY: See website or contact Society for information and application. Submit with letters of recommendation, transcripts, and demonstration of financial need.
NUMBER OF AWARDS: 2
RENEWABLE: No
CONTACT: Lois Benedict

842—AMERICAN SOCIETY OF HEATING, REFRIGERATING, AND AIR-CONDITIONING ENGINEERS (Duane Hanson Scholarship)

1791 Tullie Circle NE
Atlanta GA 30329
404/636-8400
FAX: 404/321-5478
E-mail: benedict@ashrae.org
Internet: http://www.ashrae.org
AMOUNT: $3,000
DEADLINE(S): DEC 1
FIELD(S): Engineering; Science
ELIGIBILITY/REQUIREMENTS: Open to engineering undergraduate students enrolled full time in an ABET-accredited program leading to a Bachelor of Science or Bachelor of Engineering Degree. Minimum 3.0 GPA. Must have a minimum college GPA of 3.0; be enrolled full time in a college or university with at least 1 full year of studies remaining in the year for which the scholarship will be awarded; demonstrate potential service to the HVAC&R profession, need for financial assistance, leadership ability, and character.
HOW TO APPLY: See website or contact Society for information and application. Submit with letters of recommendation, transcripts, and demonstration of financial need.
NUMBER OF AWARDS: 1
RENEWABLE: No
CONTACT: Lois Benedict, Scholarship Administrator

843—AMERICAN SOCIETY OF HEATING, REFRIGERATING, AND AIR-CONDITIONING ENGINEERS (Frank M. Coda Scholarship)

1791 Tullie Circle NE
Atlanta GA 30329
404/636-8400
FAX: 404/321-5478
E-mail: benedict@ashrae.org
Internet: http://www.ashrae.org
AMOUNT: $5,000
DEADLINE(S): DEC 1
FIELD(S): Engineering; Science

ELIGIBILITY/REQUIREMENTS: Open to engineering undergraduate students enrolled full time in an ABET-accredited program leading to a Bachelor of Science or Bachelor of Engineering Degree. Must have a minimum college GPA of 3.0; be enrolled full time in a college or university with at least 1 full year of studies remaining in the year for which the scholarship will be awarded; demonstrate potential service to the HVAC&R profession, need for financial assistance, leadership ability, and character.
HOW TO APPLY: See website or contact Society for information and application. Submit with letters of recommendation, transcripts, and demonstration of financial need.
NUMBER OF AWARDS: 1
RENEWABLE: No
CONTACT: Lois Benedict, Scholarship Administrator

844—AMERICAN SOCIETY OF HEATING, REFRIGERATING, AND AIR-CONDITIONING ENGINEERS (Henry Adams Scholarship)

1791 Tullie Circle NE
Atlanta GA 30329
404/636-8400
FAX: 404/321-5478
E-mail: benedict@ashrae.org
Internet: http://www.ashrae.org
AMOUNT: $3,000
DEADLINE(S): DEC 1
FIELD(S): Engineering; Science
ELIGIBILITY/REQUIREMENTS: Open to engineering undergraduate students enrolled full time in an ABET-accredited program leading to a Bachelor of Science or Bachelor of Engineering Degree. Must have a minimum college GPA of 3.0; be enrolled full time in a college or university with at least 1 full year of studies remaining in the year for which the scholarship will be awarded; demonstrate potential service to the HVAC&R profession, need for financial assistance, leadership ability, and character.
HOW TO APPLY: See website or contact Society for information and application. Submit with letters of recommendation, transcripts, and demonstration of financial need.
NUMBER OF AWARDS: 1
RENEWABLE: No
CONTACT: Lois Benedict, Scholarship Administrator

845—AMERICAN SOCIETY OF HEATING, REFRIGERATING, AND AIR-CONDITIONING ENGINEERS (Reuben Trane Scholarships)

1791 Tullie Circle NE

Atlanta GA 30329-2305
404/636-8400
FAX: 404/321-5478
E-mail: benedict@ashrae.org
Internet: http://www.ashrae.org
AMOUNT: $5,000/year (2 years)
DEADLINE(S): DEC 1
FIELD(S): Heating, Ventilation, Air-Conditioning & Refrigeration
ELIGIBILITY/REQUIREMENTS: Available to qualified undergraduate engineering students with at least 2 full years of studies remaining in an ABET-accredited program. Must have a minimum college GPA of 3.0; be enrolled full time in a college or university with at least 1 full year of studies remaining in the year for which the scholarship will be awarded; demonstrate potential service to the HVAC&R profession, need for financial assistance, leadership ability, and character. To remain eligible for the 2nd year, recipients must continue to meet all ASHRAE basic criteria.
HOW TO APPLY: See website or contact Society for information and application. Submit with letters of recommendation, transcripts, and demonstration of financial need.
NUMBER OF AWARDS: 4 2-year awards
CONTACT: Lois Benedict, Scholarship Administrator

846—AMERICAN SOCIETY OF NAVAL ENGINEERS (ASNE)

1452 Duke Street
Alexandria VA 22314-3458
703/836-6727
Internet: http://www.naval engineers.org
AMOUNT: Up to $3,500
DEADLINE(S): FEB
FIELD(S): Engineering, Physical Sciences, Mathematics
ELIGIBILITY/REQUIREMENTS: Application must be for support for the last year of a full-time or co-op undergraduate program or for one year of full-time graduate study leading to a designated engineering or physical science degree in an accredited college or university. A scholarship will not be awarded to a doctoral candidate or to a person already having an advanced degree. All applicants must be U.S. citizens.
HOW TO APPLY: Contact Society for additional information and application.

847—ASSOCIATED WESTERN UNIVERSITIES, INC. (AWU Undergraduate Student Fellowships)

4190 South Highland Drive,

Suite 211
Salt Lake City UT 84124-2600
801/273-8900
FAX: 801/277-5632
Internet: http://www.awu.org
AMOUNT: $300/week stipend + possible travel allowance
DEADLINE(S): FEB 1
FIELD(S): Science; Mathematics; Engineering; Technology
ELIGIBILITY/REQUIREMENTS: Students who have been or will be enrolled in any accredited institution within six months of the start of their award. Academic performance and class standing, career goals, recommendations, and compatibility of interests and abilities with the needs and resources of the host facility.
HOW TO APPLY: See website for application and list of participating laboratories. Must also submit résumé, at least 1 (2 preferred) recommendations from a faculty member who is familiar with your academic achievements, and transcript. Applicants who received an AWU award within the last year and have approval for reappointment with their previous mentor, need only to complete the application form and submit a copy of their current transcripts.
NUMBER OF AWARDS: 500

848—ASSOCIATION FOR WOMEN IN SCIENCE (AWIS Education Foundation College Scholarship)

7008 Richard Drive
Bethesda MD 20817-4838
E-mail: awisedfd@awis.org
Internet: http://www.awis.org/careers/edfoundation.html
AMOUNT: $100-$1,000
DEADLINE(S): Mid JAN
FIELD(S): Science; Mathematics; Engineering
ELIGIBILITY/REQUIREMENTS: High school seniors may apply. Must have GPA of at least 3.75 and math plus verbal SAT of at least 1200 (or ACT of 2.5), be a U.S. citizen, plan a career in research or teaching, and plan to attend a college in the U.S.
HOW TO APPLY: See website for application and instructions.
NUMBER OF AWARDS: 10
RENEWABLE: No
CONTACT: Dr. Barbara Filner at e-mail above

849—ASTRONAUT SCHOLARSHIP FOUNDATION

6225 Vectorspace Boulevard
Titusville FL 32780
321/269/6119
FAX: 321/267-3970
E-mail: MercurySvn@aol.com
Internet: http://www.astronauts cholarship.org/ guidelines.html
AMOUNT: $10,000
DEADLINE(S): APR 15
FIELD(S): Engineering and Physical Sciences (Medical Research ok, but NOT Professional Medicine)
ELIGIBILITY/REQUIREMENTS: Open to juniors, seniors, and graduate students at a select group of schools. Must be U.S. citizen with the intention to pursue research or advance field of study upon completion of final degree. Special consideration given to students who have shown initiative, creativity, excellence, and/or resourcefulness in their field. Must be NOMINATED by faculty or staff.
HOW TO APPLY: See website for list of eligible schools. Contact Executive Director for details.
CONTACT: Howard Benedict, Executive Director

850—AT&T BELL LABORATORIES (Summer Research Program for Minorities and Women)

101 Crawfords Corner Road
Holmdel NJ 07733-3030
AMOUNT: Salary + travel and living expenses for summer
DEADLINE(S): DEC 1
FIELD(S): Engineering; Mathematics; Sciences; Computer Science
ELIGIBILITY/REQUIREMENTS: Program offers minority students and women students technical employment experience at Bell Laboratories. Students should have completed their third year of study at an accredited college or university. U.S. citizen or permanent resident.
HOW TO APPLY: Selection is based partially on academic achievement and personal motivation. Write special programs manager-SRP for complete information.

851—BARRY GOLDWATER SCHOLARSHIP AND EXCELLENCE IN EDUCATION FOUNDATION

6225 Brandon Avenue, Suite 315
Springfield VA 22150-2519
703/756-6012
FAX: 703/756-6015
Internet: http://www.act.org/goldwater
AMOUNT: Up to $7,500/year
DEADLINE(S): FEB 1
FIELD(S): Mathematics; Natural Sciences; Engineering
ELIGIBILITY/REQUIREMENTS: Open to college sophomores and juniors with a minimum 3.0 GPA. Must be U.S. citizen, resident alien, or American national pursuing a degree in math, natural sciences, or engineering at an accredited institution that contributes to technological advances.
HOW TO APPLY: See website or contact your Goldwater Faculty Representative on campus. Students must be nominated by their institution and cannot apply on their own.
NUMBER OF AWARDS: 300
CONTACT: Goldwater Faculty Representative

852—BOYS AND GIRLS CLUBS OF GREATER SAN DIEGO (Spence Reese Scholarship Fund)

4635 Clairemont Mesa Boulevard
San Diego CA 92117
619/298-3520
AMOUNT: $2,000
DEADLINE(S): APR 15
FIELD(S): Medicine; Law; Engineering; Political Science
ELIGIBILITY/REQUIREMENTS: Open to male high school seniors planning a career in one of the above fields. Boys and Girls Club affiliation NOT required.
HOW TO APPLY: Send SASE to Boys and Girls Club for an application after January 1.
RENEWABLE: Yes. Up to 4 years.

853—BRITISH COLUMBIA PARAPLEGIC FOUNDATION (C. W. Deans Memorial Scholarship)

780 SW Marine Drive
Vancouver BC V6P 5Y7
CANADA
604/324-3611
FAX: 604/324-3671
AMOUNT: Varies
DEADLINE(S): JUL 31
FIELD(S): Engineering
ELIGIBILITY/REQUIREMENTS: Open to spinal cord-injured engineering students for beginning or continuing study at a university in British Columbia. Considerations include academic standing and financial need. Must be member of the British Columbia Paraplegic Association and a Canadian citizen, legal resident, or resident of British Columbia.
HOW TO APPLY: Write for complete information.

854—CANADIAN BUREAU OF INTERNATIONAL EDUCATION (Lucent Global Science Scholars)

220 Laurier Avenue, West,
Suite 1100
Ottawa Ontario K1P 5Z9
CANADA
613/237-4820, ext. 243
FAX: 613/237-1073
E-mail: info@cbie.ca
Internet: http://www.cbie.ca
AMOUNT: $5,000 U.S. + internship
DEADLINE: MAR 15
FIELD(S): Engineering, Computer Science
ELIGIBILITY/REQUIREMENTS: Open to full-time students who are in their first year at a Canadian university and majoring in a computer-related field. Students will attend a week-long summit with other winners at the Lucent/Bell Labs headquarters in New Jersey and complete a paid summer internship, probably at Lucent Canada. Applicants must be in high academic standing, eligible to work in Canada, and competent in English.
HOW TO APPLY: See website or contact CBIE for more details and an application form.
NUMBER OF AWARDS: 2
RENEWABLE: No

855—CHICAGO ENGINEERS' FOUNDATION (Engineering Incentive Awards)

Union League Club of Chicago
65 West Jackson Boulevard
Chicago IL 60604-3598
312/435-5961 or 312/427-7800
FAX: 312/427-9177
E-mail: commdept@ulcc.org
Internet: http://www.ulcc.org/chicago.htm
AMOUNT: Varies
DEADLINE(S): Varies
FIELD(S): Engineering
ELIGIBILITY/REQUIREMENTS: Open to Chicago-area high school seniors who have been admitted to an accredited college or university engineering program. Selections are made on the basis of academic excellence.
HOW TO APPLY: Contact ULCC for an application.
NUMBER OF AWARDS: 26

856—CHICAGO ROOFING CONTRACTORS ASSOCIATION

4415 W. Harrison Street, #322
Hillside IL 60162
708/449-3340
FAX: 708/449-0837
E-mail: info@crca.org
Internet: http://www.crca.org
AMOUNT: $3,000
DEADLINE(S): MAR (1st Friday)
FIELD(S): Business; Engineering; Architecture; Liberal Arts; Sciences
ELIGIBILITY/REQUIREMENTS: Open to high school seniors who reside in one of the eight counties in Northern Illinois: Cook, DuPage, Lake, Kane, Kendall, DeKalb, McHenry, or Will. Must be accepted as a full-time student in a 4-year college or university to pursue a degree in one of the above fields. Must be U.S. citizen. Based on academic achievements, extracurricular activities, and community involvement.
HOW TO APPLY: See website for an application. Submit with 2 completed Personal Reference Forms (1 from high school guidance counselor or faculty member, an optional letter of recommendation may also be included; the other from an adult not related to the student); an official transcript of all high school records, and official ACT and/or SAT Test results or official high school transcript.
NUMBER OF AWARDS: 1 (In the event of a tie, financial need considered.)
RENEWABLE: Yes (up to 3 times). Must maintain a 2.75 grade point average.

857—CIVIL AIR PATROL (CAP Undergraduate Scholarships)

National Headquarters
Maxwell AFB AL 36112-6332
334/953-5315
AMOUNT: $750
DEADLINE(S): JAN 31
FIELD(S): Humanities; Science; Engineering; Education
ELIGIBILITY/REQUIREMENTS: Open to CAP members who have received the Billy Mitchell Award or the senior rating in Level II of the senior training program. For undergraduate study in the above areas.
HOW TO APPLY: Write for complete information.

858—COMMUNITY FOUNDATION FOR GREATER ATLANTA, INC., THE (Tech High/W.O. Cheney Scholarship)

50 Hurt Plaza, Suite 449
Atlanta GA 30303
404/688-5525
FAX: 404/688-3060
E-mail: scholarships@atlcf.org
Internet: http://www.atlcf.org/GrantsScholarships/Scholarships.aspx
AMOUNT: $5,000
DEADLINE(S): MAR 26
FIELD(S): Mathematics, Engineering, Physical Sciences
ELIGIBILITY/REQUIREMENTS: Open to graduating high school seniors. Must be a citizen of the U.S. and a legal resident of Georgia for at least 3 years prior to application, have a cumulative high school GPA of 3.7 or higher or be in the upper 10% of graduating class, SAT composite (math and critical reading) of at least 1300, be accepted as a full-time student to a 4-year accredited college or university, and demonstrate a commitment to community service.
HOW TO APPLY: See website for additional information and application. Submit with a personal essay (2-3 pages) that includes why you feel a college education is important; your statement of educational and career goals; post college career interests; highlights of your high school extracurricular/community service activities, special strengths, skills, and qualifications; any unusual family or personal circumstances have affected your achievement in school, work experience, or your participation in school and community activities; present financial need. Send to The Community Foundation for Greater Atlanta, Tech High/W.O. Cheney Scholarship, Scholarship Management Services, Scholarship America, One Scholarship Way, P.O. Box 297, Saint Peter, MN 56082. If you have questions, call 507/931-1682 or e-mail communityfoundation@scholarshipamerica.org.
NUMBER OF AWARDS: 4
RENEWABLE: Yes; must reapply.
CONTACT: Lisa Glanville, 404/308-0055

859—COMMUNITY FOUNDATION OF WESTERN MASSACHUSETTS (James L. Shriver Scholarship)

1500 Main Street
P.O. Box 15769
Springfield MA 01115
413/732-2858
FAX: 413/733/8565
E-mail: scholar@communityfoundation.org
Internet: http://www.communityfoundation.org
AMOUNT: $600
DEADLINE(S): MAR 31
FIELD(S): Technical Fields
ELIGIBILITY/REQUIREMENTS: Open to residents of Western Massachusetts to

pursue technical careers through college, trade, or technical school. Based on financial need, academic merit, and extracurricular activities.
HOW TO APPLY: See website for application.
NUMBER OF AWARDS: 1
RENEWABLE: No

860—CONNECTICUT BUILDING CONGRESS SCHOLARSHIP FUND

2600 Dixwell Avenue, Suite 7
Hamden CT 06514
203/281-3183
FAX: 203/248-8932
E-mail: bdavidson@ctengineers.org
Internet: http://www.cbc-ct.org
AMOUNT: $500-$2,000
DEADLINE(S): MAR 31
FIELD(S): Construction Industry related subjects (Architecture; Engineering; Construction Management; Planning; Drafting; etc.)
ELIGIBILITY/REQUIREMENTS: Connecticut resident. Must submit an essay of not more than 500 words that explains how your planned studies will relate to a career in the construction industry; transcript of high school grades; class standing and SAT/ACT scores; copy of Student Aid Report of FAFSA and custodial parent's statement (from College Board) if applicable.
HOW TO APPLY: Call, write or e-mail for application.
NUMBER OF AWARDS: 2 to 4
RENEWABLE: Yes. Per year for 4 years; must maintain grades.
CONTACT: Beverly Davidson at CBCSF

861—AMERICAN COUNCIL OF ENGINEERING COMPANIES OF NEW JERSEY (Louis Goldberg Scholarship Fund)

66 Morris Avenue, Suite 1A
Springfield NJ 07081
973/564-5848
FAX: 973/564-7480
E-mail: Barbara@acecnj.org
Internet: http://www.acecnj.org
AMOUNT: $1,000
DEADLINE(S): JAN 1
FIELD(S): Engineering; Land Surveying
ELIGIBILITY/REQUIREMENTS: Must be a U.S. citizen; enrolled in an ABET-accredited engineering or land surveying program, in a New Jersey college or university; seeking a bachelor of science in engineering; and be entering their 3rd or 4th year (5th year in a 5-year program) in the fall. Scholarships will be awarded in March and will be based on scholastic

merit and achievements. Students graduating in December are not eligible.
HOW TO APPLY: Write or download application from website.
NUMBER OF AWARDS: 5

862—CONSULTING ENGINEERS COUNCIL OF PENNSYLVANIA

2040 Linglestown Road, Suite 200
Harrisburg PA 17110
717/540-6811
Internet: http://www.cecpa.org
AMOUNT: $2,000
DEADLINE(S): DEC
FIELD(S): Engineering
ELIGIBILITY/REQUIREMENTS: For engineering students entering their senior or fifth year (in a five-year program). Must be enrolled in an accredited engineering school in Pennsylvania. Winners will go on to compete at the national level.
HOW TO APPLY: Write for complete information.

863—COUNCIL OF ENERGY RESOURCE TRIBES (CERT)

CERT Education Program
Attention: Scholars Program
695 S. Colorado Blvd, Suite 10
Denver CO 80246
303/282-7576
FAX: 303/282-7584
E-mail: info@CERTRedEarth.com
Internet: http://www.certredearth.com/
AMOUNT: $1,000
DEADLINE(S): SEP 14 (Fall), FEB 15 (Spring)
FIELD(S): Science; Engineering; Business, Mathematics, Computer Technology, or related fields
ELIGIBILITY/REQUIREMENTS: Applicants must meet the criteria to become a TRIBES Institute candidate and a full-time undergraduate (12 hrs/semester) student enrolled in an accredited 2- or 4-year tribal, private, or public university/college, and must maintain at least a 2.5 GPA, although academic excellence far above this GPA is preferred. (Should scholarship funds be limited, GPA will be weighed in decision.)
HOW TO APPLY: See website or contact CERT. Submit application along with official Tribal affiliation documentation (with enrollment number or other statement of Tribal acknowledgment of membership), an official transcript of most recent coursework with the cumulative GPA, as well as the GPA for current hours detailed on the transcript, and a class schedule for the next

term demonstrating that you will be attending school full time and/or verification of full-time enrollment for the next semester.
RENEWABLE: Yes. Must reapply.
CONTACT: Tom Talache, ttalache @CERTRedEarth.com or 303/282-7576 ext. 12

864—EAA AVIATION FOUNDATION (Payzer Scholarship)

EAA Scholarship Department
P.O. 3086
Oshkosh WI 54903-3065
920/426-6823
E-mail: scholarships@eaa.org
Internet: http://www.young eagles.org
AMOUNT: $5,000
DEADLINE(S): MAR 1
FIELD(S): Engineering, Mathematics, Physical or Biological Science
ELIGIBILITY/REQUIREMENTS: Open to well-rounded individuals involved in school and community activities as well as aviation accepted at or attending 4-year accredited college, university or postsecondary school with am emphasis on technical information who is majoring one of above fields. Applicant's academic records should verify his/her ability to complete educational activity for which scholarship is requested. Financial need considered in some programs. Must also be a current member of EAA (Experimental Aircraft Association) or recommended by a current EAA member.
HOW TO APPLY: Apply online. A personal statement (500 words or less) addressing career aspirations, educational plan, why you want to receive this scholarship, what you learned from work/volunteer experiences, and explaining how your education will be financed, including loans, family assistance, your own savings, scholarships, etc., and any unusual financial circumstances affecting your college financial plan required.

865—GEORGIA ENGINEERING FOUNDATION

Harris Tower, Suite 700
233 Peachtree Street
Atlanta GA 30303
404/521-2324
FAX: 404/521-0283
E-mail: kbdye@mindspring.com
Internet: http://www.gefinc.org
AMOUNT: $500-$5,000
DEADLINE(S): AUG 31

FIELD(S): Engineering; Engineering
Technology
ELIGIBILITY/REQUIREMENTS:
Applicants must be U.S. citizens, legal resident in Georgia, attending or planning to attend an ABET-accredited engineering or engineering technology program.
HOW TO APPLY: Applicants who are incoming freshmen should send completed application with transcript of final grades and SAT scores, 2 letters of recommendation, and a small photograph. Applicants who are college students should send completed application, a transcript of all college grades, and a small photograph.
NUMBER OF AWARDS: 45
CONTACT: Jan Hunt, Resource Director; Roger Austin, Scholarship Chairman; or the Georgia Engineering Center at above phone number.

866—GERBER SCIENTIFIC, INC. (The David J. Logan Scholarship Endowment at Trinity College, Hartford, Connecticut)

83 Gerber Road West
South Windsor CT 06074
860/648-8027
Internet: http://www.gerber
scientific.com/community/
scholarships.htm
AMOUNT: Varies
DEADLINE(S): MAR 15
FIELD(S): Engineering
ELIGIBILITY/REQUIREMENTS:
Available to high school seniors in the Greater Hartford area who plan to obtain a 4-year degree in engineering from Trinity.
HOW TO APPLY: Applications are available from the Rensselaer Office of Financial Aid.

867—GERBER SCIENTIFIC, INC. (H. Joseph Gerber 1947 Scholars Fund Endowment at Rensselaer Polytechnic Institute)

83 Gerber Road West
South Windsor CT 06074
860/648-8027
Internet: http://www.gerber
scientific.com/community/
scholarships.htm
AMOUNT: Varies
DEADLINE(S): MAR 15
FIELD(S): Engineering, Mathematics, Computer Science, Natural Sciences
ELIGIBILITY/REQUIREMENTS:
Available to full-time students pursuing a baccalaureate degree at Rensselaer Polytechnic Institute's Troy, New York, campus. Awards are determined by the

Rensselaer Office of Financial Aid. Preference is given to residents of the state of Connecticut.
HOW TO APPLY: Applications are available from the Rensselaer Office of Financial Aid.

868—GERBER SCIENTIFIC, INC. (H. Joseph Gerber Vision Scholarship Program)

83 Gerber Road West
South Windsor CT 06074
860/648-8027
Internet: http://www.gerber
scientific.com/community/
scholarships.htm
AMOUNT: Varies
DEADLINE(S): MAR 15
FIELD(S): Engineering, Mathematics, Computer Science, Natural Sciences
ELIGIBILITY/REQUIREMENTS:
Available to high school seniors attending South Windsor, Manchester or Tolland High, or Gerber employees' children who meet the requirements. Selection of recipients is made solely by Citizens' Scholarship Foundation of America.
HOW TO APPLY: Applications are available in the high school guidance office.
NUMBER OF AWARDS: 50

869—GOLDEN KEY INTERNATIONAL HONOUR SOCIETY (Engineering Achievement Awards)

1189 Ponce de Leon Avenue
Atlanta GA 30306
404/377-2400 or 800/377-2401
FAX: 404/373-7033
E-mail: scholarships@goldenkey.org
Internet: http//www.goldenkey.org
AMOUNT: One winner will receive $1,000, a second-place winner will receive $750, and a third-place winner will receive $500
DEADLINE(S): MAR
FIELD(S): Engineering
ELIGIBILITY/REQUIREMENTS:
Award recognizes members who excel in the study of engineering. Undergraduate, graduate, and postgraduate members who are currently enrolled in classes at a degree-granting program are eligible. Award based on academic achievement, quality of paper submitted.
HOW TO APPLY: Apply online with your Golden Key member number. Attach an engineering-related paper/report (not to exceed 10 pages). Attach an essay (no more than 2 pages) describing the assignment for writing the paper, what the greatest challenge was in writing the paper, what lessons

were learned from completing the assignment, and if you were to re-do the report, what would be changed. Attach a letter of recommendation from a professor in the discipline and an official academic transcript.
NUMBER OF AWARDS/YEAR: 3
RENEWABLE: No
CONTACT: Fabian J. De Rozario, Associate Vice President of North American Operations

870—HAWAII COMMUNITY FOUNDATION (Earl Bakken Engineering Scholarship)

1164 Bishop Street, Suite 800
Honolulu HI 96813
808/537-6333 or toll free:
888/731-3863
FAX: 808/521-6286
E-mail: info@hcf-hawaii.org
Internet: http://www.hcf-hawaii.org
DEADLINE(S): MAR 1
FIELD(S): Engineering
ELIGIBILITY/REQUIREMENTS: Must be residents of the island of Hawaii; be junior or senior undergraduate or graduate students enrolled full time in an accredited 2- or 4-year college or university; and demonstrate financial need, good moral character, and academic achievement with a minimum GPA of 2.7. Preference is given to students of Hawaiian ethnicity.
HOW TO APPLY: Send application with 2 letters of recommendation.

871—H. FLETCHER BROWN FUND

c/o Donald W. Davis
PNC Bank Delaware
Trust Department
222 Delaware Avenue, 16th floor
Wilmington DE 19899
302/429-2827 or 302/429-5658
E-mail: Robbie.testa@pncadvisors.com
AMOUNT: Varies
DEADLINE(S): MAR 22
FIELD(S): Medicine; Dentistry; Law; Engineering; Chemistry
ELIGIBILITY/REQUIREMENTS: Open to U.S. citizens born in Delaware and still residing in Delaware. For 4 years of study (undergrad or grad) leading to a degree that enables applicant to practice in chosen field. Must have minimum 1000 SAT score and rank in upper 20 percent of class. Interview required. Scholarships are based on need, scholastic achievement, and good moral character.
HOW TO APPLY: Write to Account Administrator for application.
CONTACT: Robbie Testa in February

872—HISPANIC COLLEGE FUND
(HSF/General Motors Scholarship)

55 Second Street, Suite 1500
San Francisco CA 94105
877/HSF-INFO (877/473-4636)
FAX: 415/808/2302
E-mail: pip@hsf.net
Internet: http://hispanicfund.org
AMOUNT: At least $2,500
DEADLINE(S): JUN 16
FIELD(S): Engineering; Business
ELIGIBILITY/REQUIREMENTS: Must
be U.S. citizens or legal permanent residents of Hispanic heritage (one parent fully Hispanic or both parents half Hispanic). Applicant should have earned at least 12 undergraduate college credits in the U.S. or Puerto Rico and have a minimum GPA of 3.0. Must carry at least 12 credits each term. Selection is based on academic achievement, personal strengths, leadership and financial need.
HOW TO APPLY: Contact Fund for details or visit website for application.
NUMBER OF AWARDS: 83

873—HISPANIC COLLEGE FUND
(HSF/SHPE Inc. Scholarship Program)

55 Second Street, Suite 1500
San Francisco CA 94105
877/HSF-INFO (877/473-4636)
FAX: 415/808/2302
E-mail: pip@hsf.net
Internet: http://hispanicfund.org
AMOUNT: At least $2,500
DEADLINE(S): JUN 2
FIELD(S): Engineering; Mathematics;
Science; Computer Science
ELIGIBILITY/REQUIREMENTS: Must
be U.S. citizens or legal permanent residents of Hispanic heritage (one parent fully Hispanic or both parents half Hispanic). Open to high school graduates, community college transfer students, 4-year university undergraduates, and graduate students. All students must be enrolled full time in a degree-seeking program in the U.S. or Puerto Rico.
HOW TO APPLY: Contact Fund for details or visit website for application.

874—ILLINOIS SOCIETY OF
PROFESSIONAL ENGINEERS FOUNDATION
(ISPE Advantage Award/Foundation Scholarship)

600 South Second Street, Suite 403
Springfield IL 62704
217/544-7424
FAX: 217/528-6545
Internet: http://illinoisengineer.
com/studentsandyouth.asp
AMOUNT: $1,200
DEADLINE(S): JAN 31
FIELD(S): Engineering
ELIGIBILITY/REQUIREMENTS:
Applicants must be the son or daughter of an ISPE member in good standing and should be among the top 5 candidates for the IPSE/M.E. Amstutz Memorial Award Scholarship; attend an Illinois university; be enrolled in an Accreditation Board of Engineering and Technology program; be at least a junior; have a 'B' average or better in those courses that are accredited toward the engineering degree; and show evidence of financial need.
HOW TO APPLY: Send completed application and financial need analysis; official transcripts of all college and university work; 2 letters of reference (1 from the department chair or department faculty member and 1 from a past employer or character reference); and a typewritten essay of 200 words or less on "Why I would like to become a professional engineer."
NUMBER OF AWARDS: 1

875—ILLINOIS SOCIETY OF
PROFESSIONAL ENGINEERS FOUNDATION
(ISPE/M.E. Amstutz Memorial Award)

600 South Second Street, Suite 403
Springfield IL 62704
217/544-7424
FAX: 217/528-6545
Internet: http://illinoisengineer.
com/studentsandyouth.asp
AMOUNT: $1,500
DEADLINE(S): JAN 31
FIELD(S): Engineering
ELIGIBILITY/REQUIREMENTS:
Applicants must attend an Illinois university; be enrolled in an Accreditation Board of Engineering and Technology program; be at least a junior; have a 'B' average or better in those courses that are accredited toward the engineering degree; and show evidence of financial need.
HOW TO APPLY: Send completed application and financial need analysis; official transcripts of all college and university work; 2 letters of reference (1 from the department chair or department faculty member and 1 from a past employer or character reference); and a typewritten essay of 200 words or less on "Why I would like to become a professional engineer."
NUMBER OF AWARDS: 1

876—ILLINOIS SOCIETY OF
PROFESSIONAL ENGINEERS FOUNDATION
(ISPE/Peppy Moldovan Memorial Award)

600 South Second Street, Suite 403
Springfield IL 62704
217/544-7424
FAX: 217/528-6545
Internet: http://illinoisengineer.
com/studentsandyouth.asp
AMOUNT: $1,000
DEADLINE(S): MAR 31
FIELD(S): Engineering
ELIGIBILITY/REQUIREMENTS:
Applicants must be female engineering students currently enrolled at the sophomore level at one of the following colleges or universities who intend to continue their engineering studies in an ABET-accredited curriculum: Illinois Central College, Kaskaskia Community College, Rend Lake Community College, Bradley University, Southern Illinois University at Carbondale, Southern Illinois University at Edwardsville, University of Illinois at Urbana/Champaign.
HOW TO APPLY: Send completed application; official transcripts of all college and university work; record of your work experience, including any co-op programs, listing employer, dates of employment, and duties; list of memberships in organizations, societies, and clubs; and activities, both technical and nontechnical, including years active and offices held since you entered college; list of any special honors and scholarships received, either in or out of school since you entered college; 2 letters of reference (1 from the department chair or department faculty member and 1 from a past employer or character reference); a double-spaced typewritten or computer-printed essay of no more than 500 words addressing your interest in engineering, your major areas of study and area of specialization, and the occupation you propose to pursue after graduation, your long-term goals and how you hope to achieve them; and a description of any family/financial responsibilities or special circumstances the ISPE should consider.
NUMBER OF AWARDS: 1

877—INSTITUTE FOR OPERATIONS
RESEARCH AND THE MANAGEMENT
SCIENCES (George Nicholson Student
Paper Competition)

7240 Parkway Drive, Suite 310
Hanover MD 21076-1310 USA
443/757-3500 or 800/446-3676)
FAX: 443/757-3515

E-mail: informs@informs.org
Internet: http://www.informs.org/
INTERN/
AMOUNT: $600 (first place), $300 (second place), $100 (honorable mention)
DEADLINE(S): JUN 30
FIELD(S): Fields related to Information Management: Business Management, Engineering, Mathematics
ELIGIBILITY/REQUIREMENTS: Entrant must have been a student on or after January 1 of the year; the paper must present original research results and must have been conducted while entrant was a student; must be written with only minor editorial assistance (advisors may appear as co-authors, but the student must be "first author").
HOW TO APPLY: Paper must not exceed 25 pages with 35 lines of text (excluding references). Electronic submissions (PDF) and hard copy are required. Entry must be accompanied by a letter signed by both a faculty advisor and the entrant attesting that the eligibility conditions have been satisfied. For additional information, see website.
NUMBER OF AWARDS: Up to 6
RENEWABLE: No
CONTACT: Committee Chair (see website for current year's chairperson and contact information)
ADDITIONAL INFORMATION: First- and second-place awards will be announced at the Awards Ceremony.

878—INSTITUTE FOR OPERATIONS RESEARCH AND THE MANAGEMENT SCIENCES (INFORMS Summer Internship Directory)

7240 Parkway Drive, Suite 310
Hanover, MD 21076-1310 USA
443/757-3500 or 800/446-3676)
FAX: 443/757-3515
E-mail: informs@informs.org
Internet: http://www.informs.org/
INTERN/
AMOUNT: Varies
DEADLINE(S): Varies
FIELD(S): Information Management: Business Management, Engineering, Mathematics and related fields
ELIGIBILITY/REQUIREMENTS: A website listing of summer internships in the field of operations research and management sciences. Both applicants and employers can register online.
HOW TO APPLY: Access website for list.
NUMBER OF AWARDS: Varies

879—IET, THE (IET Engineering Degree Scholarships for Women)

Michael Faraday House
Six Hills Way, Stevenage
Hertfordshire SG1 2AY
UNITED KINGDOM
E-mail: awards@theiet.org
Internet: http://www.theiet.org/ambition
AMOUNT: £1,000 per annum
DEADLINE(S): JUNE 30
FIELD(S): Engineering
ELIGIBILITY/REQUIREMENTS: For women pursuing IET-accredited degrees. Candidates must be undertaking mathematics and physics "A" level or Scottish Higher examinations.
HOW TO APPLY: Check website.
RENEWABLE: Yes. For entire period of an IET-accredited course.

880—IET, THE (IET Undergraduate Scholarships)

Michael Faraday House
Six Hills Way, Stevenage
Hertfordshire SG1 2AY
UNITED KINGDOM
E-mail: awards@theiet.org
Internet: http://www.theiet.org/ambition
AMOUNT: £1,000
DEADLINE(S): JUN 30
FIELD(S): Engineering
ELIGIBILITY/REQUIREMENTS: Scholarships for students pursuing IET-accredited degrees in various engineering specialties in the UK. Criteria vary, including academic excellence and financial need.
HOW TO APPLY: Check website or contact organization for application details.

881—IEEE COMPUTER SOCIETY (Richard E. Merwin Student Scholarship)

1730 Massachusetts Avenue NW
Washington DC 20036-1992
202/371-1013
FAX: 202/728-0884
AMOUNT: $3,000
DEADLINE(S): MAY 31
FIELD(S): Computers; Engineering
ELIGIBILITY/REQUIREMENTS: Full-time graduate students, juniors and seniors in electrical engineering, computer engineering, computer science, or well-defined computer related field who are active members of the IEEE Computer Society

student branch chapter at their institution. Minimum overall GPA 2.5.
HOW TO APPLY: Contact IEEE for application and details.
NUMBER OF AWARDS: Up to 4

882—JEWISH FEDERATION OF METROPOLITAN CHICAGO (Academic Scholarship Program)

Jewish Vocational Service
216 West Jackson Blvd., Suite 700
Chicago IL 60606-6921
312/673-3400
FAX: 312/553-5544
TTY: 312/444-2877
E-mail: jvsscholarship@jvs chicago.org
Internet: http://www.jvs./chicago.org
AMOUNT: Varies
DEADLINE(S): FEB 15
FIELD(S): Mathematics, Engineering, Science, Medicine, Social Work, Education, Psychology, Rabbinate, Law (except corporate), Communications
ELIGIBILITY/REQUIREMENTS: Open to Jewish men and women legally domiciled in the greater Chicago metropolitan area, who are identified as having promise for significant contributions in their chosen careers, and are in need of financial assistance for full-time academic programs in above areas. Must have entered undergraduate junior year in career programs requiring no postgraduate education, be in graduate/professional school, or be in a vo-tech training program.
HOW TO APPLY: Phone JVS Scholarship Secretary (312/673-3457), fax, or visit website (click on Scholarship Services) for an application in the Fall. Interview required.
RENEWABLE: Yes
CONTACT: JVS Scholarship Secretary at 312/673-3457

883—JORGE MAS CANOSA FREEDOM FOUNDATION (Mas Family Scholarships)

P.O. Box 14-1898
Miami FL 33114
305/529-0075 Ext. 35
E-mail: mmartinez@jmcffmas familyscholarships.org
Internet: http://www.jmcffmas scholarships.org
AMOUNT: Up to $10,000
DEADLINE(S): MAR 31

FIELD(S): Engineering, Business, International Relations, Economics, Communications, Journalism
ELIGIBILITY/REQUIREMENTS: For Cuban-American students, graduates and undergraduates, born in Cuba or direct descendants (1 parent or 2 grandparents) of those who left Cuba. Must be in top 10% of high school class or maintain a 3.5 GPA in college. Financial need considered along with academic success, SAT and GRE scores, and leadership potential.
HOW TO APPLY: Contact Foundation for application. 2 short essays and 2 character evaluations along with proof of Cuban descent required.
NUMBER OF AWARDS: 10
RENEWABLE: Yes, maximum $40,000; must reapply.

884—KALAMAZOO TECHNOLOGY & SCIENCE FELLOWS PROGRAM

Southwest Michigan First
The Chamber Building
356 West Michigan Avenue
Kalamazoo MI 49007-3737
269/553-9588
FAX: 269/553-6897
E-mail: alumni@wmich.edu
Internet: http://www.wmich.edu/cas/research.html
AMOUNT: Full scholarship plus internship
DEADLINE(S): MAR 1
FIELD(S): Science; Technology
ELIGIBILITY/REQUIREMENTS: High school graduating senior who is a Kalamazoo County resident or enrolled at school within the Kalamazoo Regional Education Service Agency district. Maintain satisfactory academic progress. Be able to intern with a mentoring corporation in Kalamazoo County. Willing to make a 2-year pledge to work in Kalamazoo County following graduation from college.
HOW TO APPLY: Contact the KTS Fellows Program for an application or apply online or print application from website.
RENEWABLE: Yes. May request renewal for 1 additional term.
CONTACT: College of Arts and Sciences

885—KOREAN-AMERICAN SCIENTISTS AND ENGINEERS ASSOCIATION (KSEA Scholarships)

1952 Gallows Road, Suite 300
Vienna VA 22182
703/748-1221
FAX: 703/748-1331
E-mail: admin@ksea.org
Internet: http://www.ksea.org
AMOUNT: $1,000
DEADLINE(S): FEB 28
FIELD(S): Science; Engineering; Medicine
ELIGIBILITY/REQUIREMENTS: Must have graduated from a high school in the U.S. and must be a student member of KSEA or a child of a member. Evaluation criteria are academic performance-30%; recommendation letters-30%; work experience and extracurricular activities-20%; and essay-20%.
HOW TO APPLY: See website for application. Submit Curriculum Vitae (including work experiences and extracurricular activities); official transcript from high school and college attended; an essay on one of the following topics (approximately 500 words, typed): your career goals and their contributions to the society or the meaning of Korean heritage in your life; and 3 recommendation letters (1 from a current or previous KSEA officer or chapter president).
NUMBER OF AWARDS: 5-8 (2 are specifically designated for women)

886—LEAGUE OF UNITED LATIN AMERICAN CITIZENS/LULAC NATIONAL EDUCATIONAL SERVICE CENTERS (General Electric/LULAC Scholarship Program)

2000 L Street NW, Suite 610
Washington DC 20036
202/835-9646 or 202/833-6130
FAX: 202/835-9685
Internet: http://www.lulac.org/programs/scholar.html
AMOUNT: $5,000
FIELD(S): Business; Engineering
ELIGIBILITY/REQUIREMENTS: Must be college sophomores or higher planning on studying business or engineering and exhibit leadership involvement.
NUMBER OF AWARDS: 2
CONTACT: Lorena Maymi

887—LEAGUE OF UNITED LATIN AMERICAN CITIZENS/LULAC NATIONAL EDUCATIONAL SERVICE CENTERS (General Motors Corporation/LULAC Scholarship Program)

2000 L Street NW, Suite 610
Washington DC 20036
202/835-9646
FAX: 202/835-9685
Internet: http://www.lulac.org/programs/scholar.html
AMOUNT: $2,000
DEADLINE(S): JUL 15
FIELD(S): Engineering
ELIGIBILITY/REQUIREMENTS: Open to minority students with career interests in engineering. Must be enrolled or planning to enroll as an engineering major leading to a bachelor's degree at a college or university approved by LULAC and GM. Program is intended to assist and encourage outstanding minority students in completing their college education.
HOW TO APPLY: See website for application.
NUMBER OF AWARDS: 20

888—LOS ANGELES COUNCIL OF BLACK PROFESSIONAL ENGINEERS (Al-Ben Scholarship)

P.O. Box 881029
Los Angeles CA 90009
310/635-7734
E-mail: secy1@lablackengineers.org
Internet: http://www.lablackengineers.org/scholarships.html
AMOUNT: Varies
DEADLINE(S): Varies
FIELD(S): Engineering; Mathematics; Computer Studies; Applied Scientific Studies
ELIGIBILITY/REQUIREMENTS: Open to technically inclined precollege and undergraduate students enrolled in one of the above fields. Must be of African American, Native American, or Hispanic ancestry. Preference given to students attending college in Southern California or who are Southern California residents.
HOW TO APPLY: See website to download an application.

889—MICHIGAN SOCIETY OF PROFESSIONAL ENGINEERS, THE (MSPE 1980 NSPE Annual Meeting Committee Grant)

P.O. Box 15276
Lansing MI 48901-5276
517/487-9388
FAX: 517/487-0635
E-mail: mspe@voyager.net
Internet: http://www.michiganspe.org
AMOUNT: $2,000
DEADLINE(S): 2nd Monday in JAN
FIELD(S): Engineering
ELIGIBILITY/REQUIREMENTS: Applicant must be a high school senior; be a U.S. citizen and a resident of Michigan; be currently accepted at a Michigan ABET-accredited college or university and enrolled in an engineering program;

have at least a 3.0 average on a 4.0 scale for the 10th and 11th grades; and attain a minimum composite test score of 26 on the ACT.
HOW TO APPLY: Send completed application; a list of senior classes being taken; documented high school transcript and ACT score; copy of official ACT Test Report; and a double-spaced typed essay of 250 words on "How I was influenced to pursue an engineering career."
NUMBER OF AWARDS: 1
CONTACT: Submit application to MSPE Chapter Representative; contact the MSPE headquarters at address above to find out rep; do NOT send applications to MSPE headquarters.

890—MICHIGAN SOCIETY OF PROFESSIONAL ENGINEERS, THE (MSPE Auxiliary Grant)

P.O. Box 15276
Lansing MI 48901-5276
517/487-9388
FAX: 517/487-0635
E-mail: mspe@voyager.net
Internet: http://www.michiganspe.org
AMOUNT: $1,000
DEADLINE(S): 2nd Monday in JAN
FIELD(S): Engineering
ELIGIBILITY/REQUIREMENTS: Applicant must be a high school senior; be a U.S. citizen and a resident of Michigan; be currently accepted at a Michigan ABET-accredited college or university and enrolled in an engineering program; have at least a 3.0 average on a 4.0 scale for the 10th and 11th grades; and attain a minimum composite test score of 26 on the ACT. Preference is given to a son/daughter of an MSPE member.
HOW TO APPLY: Send completed application; a list of senior classes being taken; documented high school transcript and ACT score; copy of official ACT Test Report; and a double-spaced typed essay of 250 words on "How I was influenced to pursue an engineering career."
NUMBER OF AWARDS: 1
CONTACT: Submit application to MSPE Chapter Representative; contact the MSPE headquarters at address above to find out rep; do NOT send applications to MSPE headquarters.

891—MICHIGAN SOCIETY OF PROFESSIONAL ENGINEERS, THE (MSPE Grand Valley State University Padnos Engineering Grants)

P.O. Box 15276

Lansing MI 48901-5276
517/487-9388
FAX: 517/487-0635
E-mail: mspe@voyager.net
Internet: http://www.michiganspe.org
AMOUNT: $1,500
DEADLINE(S): 2nd Monday in JAN
FIELD(S): Engineering
ELIGIBILITY/REQUIREMENTS: Applicant must be a high school senior intending to pursue a degree in engineering on a full-time basis; have been admitted to Grand Valley State University; be a U.S. citizen and a resident of Michigan; have at least a 3.0 average on a 4.0 scale for the 10th and 11th grades; and attain a minimum composite test score of 26 on the ACT.
HOW TO APPLY: Send completed application; a list of senior classes being taken; documented high school transcript and ACT test score; copy of official ACT Test Report; and a double-spaced typed essay of 250 words on "How I was influenced to pursue an engineering career."
NUMBER OF AWARDS: 2
CONTACT: Submit application to MSPE Chapter Representative; contact the MSPE headquarters at address above to find out rep; do NOT send applications to MSPE headquarters.

892—MICHIGAN SOCIETY OF PROFESSIONAL ENGINEERS, THE (MSPE Grant)

P.O. Box 15276
Lansing MI 48901-5276
517/487-9388
FAX: 517/487-0635
E-mail: mspe@voyager.net
Internet: http://www.michiganspe.org
AMOUNT: $2,000
DEADLINE(S): 2nd Monday in JAN
FIELD(S): Engineering
ELIGIBILITY/REQUIREMENTS: Applicant must be a high school senior; be a U.S. citizen and a resident of Michigan; be currently accepted at a Michigan ABET-accredited college or university and enrolled in an engineering program; have at least a 3.0 average on a 4.0 scale for the 10th and 11th grades; and attain a minimum composite test score of 26 on the ACT.
HOW TO APPLY: Send completed application; a list of senior classes being taken; documented high school transcript and ACT score; copy of official ACT Test Report; and a double-spaced typed essay

of 250 words on "How I was influenced to pursue an engineering career."
NUMBER OF AWARDS: 1
RENEWABLE: Yes. For the sophomore year, upon application submitted to the MSPE Scholarship Chair for approval; a 3.0 GPA must be maintained.
CONTACT: Submit application to MSPE Chapter Representative; contact the MSPE headquarters at address above to find out rep; do NOT send applications to MSPE headquarters.

893—MICHIGAN SOCIETY OF PROFESSIONAL ENGINEERS, THE (MSPE Harry R. Ball, P.E. Grant)

P.O. Box 15276
Lansing MI 48901-5276
517/487-9388
FAX: 517/487-0635
E-mail: mspe@voyager.net
Internet: http://www.michiganspe.org
AMOUNT: $2,000
DEADLINE(S): 2nd Monday in JAN
FIELD(S): Engineering
ELIGIBILITY/REQUIREMENTS: Applicant must be a high school senior; be a U.S. citizen and a resident of Michigan; be currently accepted at a Michigan ABET-accredited college or university and enrolled in an engineering program; have at least a 3.0 average on a 4.0 scale for the 10th and 11th grades; and attain a minimum composite test score of 26 on the ACT.
HOW TO APPLY: Send completed application; a list of senior classes being taken; documented high school transcript and ACT score; copy of official ACT Test Report; and a double-spaced typed essay of 250 words on "How I was influenced to pursue an engineering career."
NUMBER OF AWARDS: 1
CONTACT: Submit application to MSPE Chapter Representative; contact the MSPE headquarters at address above to find out rep; do NOT send applications to MSPE headquarters.

894—MICHIGAN SOCIETY OF PROFESSIONAL ENGINEERS, THE (MSPE Kenneth B. Fishbeck, P.E. Memorial Grant)

P.O. Box 15276
Lansing MI 48901-5276
517/487-9388
FAX: 517/487-0635
E-mail: mspe@voyager.net
Internet: http://www.michiganspe.org

AMOUNT: $1,000
DEADLINE(S): 2nd Monday in JAN
FIELD(S): Engineering
ELIGIBILITY/REQUIREMENTS:
Applicant must be a high school senior; be a U.S. citizen and a resident of Michigan; be currently accepted at a Michigan ABET-accredited college or university and enrolled in an engineering program; have at least a 3.0 average on a 4.0 scale for the 10th and 11th grades; attain a minimum composite test score of 26 on the ACT; and demonstrate qualifications of high merit and professional ethics.
HOW TO APPLY: Send completed application; a list of senior classes being taken; documented high school transcript and ACT score; copy of official ACT Test Report; and a double-spaced typed essay of 250 words on "How I was influenced to pursue an engineering career."
NUMBER OF AWARDS: 1
CONTACT: Submit application to MSPE Chapter Representative; contact the MSPE headquarters at address above to find out rep; do NOT send applications to MSPE headquarters.

895—MICHIGAN SOCIETY OF PROFESSIONAL ENGINEERS, THE (MSPE Kettering University Grant)

P.O. Box 15276
Lansing MI 48901-5276
517/487-9388
FAX: 517/487-0635
E-mail: mspe@voyager.net
Internet: http://www.michiganspe.org
AMOUNT: $2,000
DEADLINE(S): 2nd Monday in JAN
FIELD(S): Engineering
ELIGIBILITY/REQUIREMENTS:
Applicant must be a high school senior; be a U.S. citizen and a resident of Michigan; be currently accepted at a Michigan ABET-accredited college or university and enrolled in an engineering program; have at least a 3.0 average on a 4.0 scale for the 10th and 11th grades; and attain a minimum composite test score of 26 on the ACT. Selection is based on scholastic achievement, especially in mathematics and science courses.
HOW TO APPLY: Send completed application; a list of senior classes being taken; documented high school transcript and ACT score; copy of official ACT Test Report; and a double-spaced typed essay of 250 words on "How I was influenced to pursue an engineering career."
NUMBER OF AWARDS: 1

CONTACT: Submit application to MSPE Chapter Representative; contact the MSPE headquarters at address above to find out rep; do NOT send applications to MSPE headquarters.

896—MICHIGAN SOCIETY OF PROFESSIONAL ENGINEERS, THE (MSPE Lawrence Technological University Grants)

P.O. Box 15276
Lansing MI 48901-5276
517/487-9388
FAX: 517/487-0635
E-mail: mspe@voyager.net
Internet: http://www.michiganspe.org
AMOUNT: $2,000
DEADLINE(S): 2nd Monday in JAN
FIELD(S): Engineering
ELIGIBILITY/REQUIREMENTS:
Applicant must be a high school senior; be a U.S. citizen and a resident of Michigan; be currently accepted at a Michigan ABET-accredited college or university and enrolled in an engineering program; have at least a 3.0 average on a 4.0 scale for the 10th and 11th grades; and attain a minimum composite test score of 26 on the ACT.
HOW TO APPLY: Send completed application; a list of senior classes being taken; documented high school transcript and ACT score; copy of official ACT Test Report; and a double-spaced typed essay of 250 words on "How I was influenced to pursue an engineering career."
NUMBER OF AWARDS: 2
CONTACT: Submit application to MSPE Chapter Representative; contact the MSPE headquarters at address above to find out rep; do NOT send applications to MSPE headquarters.

897—MICHIGAN SOCIETY OF PROFESSIONAL ENGINEERS, THE (MSPE Michigan Bell Telephone Company, University of Michigan, Hazel Quick, P.E. Memorial Grant)

P.O. Box 15276
Lansing MI 48901-5276
517/487-9388
FAX: 517/487-0635
E-mail: mspe@voyager.net
Internet: http://www.michiganspe.org
AMOUNT: $2,000
DEADLINE(S): 2nd Monday in JAN
FIELD(S): Engineering

ELIGIBILITY/REQUIREMENTS:
Applicant must be a female high school senior; be a U.S. citizen and a resident of Michigan; be currently accepted at a Michigan ABET-accredited college or university and enrolled in an engineering program; have at least a 3.0 average on a 4.0 scale for the 10th and 11th grades; and attain a minimum composite test score of 26 on the ACT.
HOW TO APPLY: Send completed application; a list of senior classes being taken; documented high school transcript and ACT score; copy of official ACT Test Report; and a double-spaced typed essay of 250 words on "How I was influenced to pursue an engineering career."
NUMBER OF AWARDS: 1
CONTACT: Submit application to MSPE Chapter Representative; contact the MSPE headquarters at address above to find out rep; do NOT send applications to MSPE headquarters.

898—MICHIGAN SOCIETY OF PROFESSIONAL ENGINEERS, THE (MSPE Michigan State University, B. Charles Tiney Memorial Grant)

P.O. Box 15276
Lansing MI 48901-5276
517/487-9388
FAX: 517/487-0635
E-mail: mspe@voyager.net
Internet: http://www.michiganspe.org
AMOUNT: $2,000
DEADLINE(S): 2nd Monday in JAN
FIELD(S): Engineering
ELIGIBILITY/REQUIREMENTS:
Applicant must be a high school senior; be a U.S. citizen and a resident of Michigan; be currently accepted at a Michigan ABET-accredited college or university and enrolled in an engineering program; have at least a 3.0 average on a 4.0 scale for the 10th and 11th grades; and attain a minimum composite test score of 26 on the ACT.
HOW TO APPLY: Send completed application; a list of senior classes being taken; documented high school transcript and ACT score; copy of official ACT Test Report; and a double-spaced typed essay of 250 words on "How I was influenced to pursue an engineering career."
NUMBER OF AWARDS: 1
CONTACT: Submit application to MSPE Chapter Representative; contact the MSPE headquarters at address above to find out rep; do NOT send applications to MSPE headquarters.

899—MICHIGAN SOCIETY OF PROFESSIONAL ENGINEERS, THE (MSPE Michigan State University Biosystems Engineering Alumni Scholarship Grant)

P.O. Box 15276
Lansing MI 48901-5276
517/487-9388
FAX: 517/487-0635
E-mail: mspe@voyager.net
Internet: http://www.michiganspe.
org
AMOUNT: $2,000
DEADLINE(S): 2nd Monday in JAN
FIELD(S): Engineering
ELIGIBILITY/REQUIREMENTS: Must be a high school senior; be a U.S. citizen and a resident of Michigan; be accepted at a Michigan ABET-accredited college or university and enrolled in an engineering program; be interested in the biosystem engineering profession; have at least a 3.0 average for the 10th and 11th grades; and a minimum composite test score of 26 on the ACT. Selection is based on scholastic achievement, especially in mathematics and science courses.
HOW TO APPLY: Send completed application; a list of senior classes being taken; documented high school transcript and ACT score; copy of official ACT Test Report; and a double-spaced typed essay of 250 words on "How I was influenced to pursue an engineering career."
NUMBER OF AWARDS: 1
CONTACT: Submit application to MSPE Chapter Representative; contact the MSPE headquarters at address above to find out rep; do NOT send applications to MSPE headquarters.

900—MICHIGAN SOCIETY OF PROFESSIONAL ENGINEERS, THE (MSPE Michigan State University Grants)

P.O. Box 15276
Lansing MI 48901-5276
517/487-9388
FAX: 517/487-0635
E-mail: mspe@voyager.net
Internet: http://www.michiganspe.
org
AMOUNT: $1,500
DEADLINE(S): 2nd Monday in JAN
FIELD(S): Engineering
ELIGIBILITY/REQUIREMENTS: Applicant must be a high school senior; be a U.S. citizen and a resident of Michigan; be currently accepted at a Michigan ABET-accredited college or university and enrolled in an engineering program; have at least a 3.0 average on a 4.0 scale for the

10th and 11th grades; and attain a minimum composite test score of 26 on the ACT.
HOW TO APPLY: Send completed application; a list of senior classes being taken; documented high school transcript and ACT score; copy of official ACT Test Report; and a double-spaced typed essay of 250 words on "How I was influenced to pursue an engineering career."
NUMBER OF AWARDS: 2
CONTACT: Submit application to MSPE Chapter Representative; contact the MSPE headquarters at address above to find out rep; do NOT send applications to MSPE headquarters.

901—MICHIGAN SOCIETY OF PROFESSIONAL ENGINEERS, THE (MSPE Michigan Technological University Grant)

P.O. Box 15276
Lansing MI 48901-5276
517/487-9388
FAX: 517/487-0635
E-mail: mspe@voyager.net
Internet: http://www.michiganspe.
org
AMOUNT: $1,500
DEADLINE(S): 2nd Monday in JAN
FIELD(S): Engineering
ELIGIBILITY/REQUIREMENTS: Must be a high school senior; be a U.S. citizen and a resident of Michigan; be currently accepted at a Michigan ABET-accredited college or university and enrolled in an engineering program; have at least a 3.0 average for the 10th and 11th grades; and attain a minimum composite test score of 26 on the ACT.
HOW TO APPLY: Send completed application; a list of senior classes being taken; documented high school transcript and ACT score; copy of official ACT Test Report; and a double-spaced typed essay of 250 words on "How I was influenced to pursue an engineering career."
NUMBER OF AWARDS: 1
CONTACT: Submit application to MSPE Chapter Representative; contact the MSPE headquarters at address above to find out rep; do NOT send applications to MSPE headquarters.

902—MICHIGAN SOCIETY OF PROFESSIONAL ENGINEERS, THE (MSPE Oakland University Grant)

P.O. Box 15276
Lansing MI 48901-5276
517/487-9388
FAX: 517/487-0635
E-mail: mspe@voyager.net

Internet: http://www.michiganspe.
org
AMOUNT: $2,000
DEADLINE(S): 2nd Monday in JAN
FIELD(S): Engineering
ELIGIBILITY/REQUIREMENTS: Must be a high school senior; be a U.S. citizen and a resident of Michigan; be currently accepted at a Michigan ABET-accredited college or university and enrolled in an engineering program; have at least a 3.0 average on a 4.0 scale for the 10th and 11th grades; and attain a minimum composite test score of 26 on the ACT.
HOW TO APPLY: Send completed application; a list of senior classes being taken; documented high school transcript and ACT score; copy of official ACT Test Report; and a double-spaced typed essay of 250 words on "How I was influenced to pursue an engineering career."
NUMBER OF AWARDS: 2
CONTACT: Submit application to MSPE Chapter Representative; contact the MSPE headquarters at address above to find out rep; do NOT send applications to MSPE headquarters.

903—MICHIGAN SOCIETY OF PROFESSIONAL ENGINEERS, THE (MSPE Raymond P. Elliott, P.E. U of M Memorial Grant)

P.O. Box 15276
Lansing MI 48901-5276
517/487-9388
FAX: 517/487-0635
E-mail: mspe@voyager.net
Internet: http://www.michiganspe.
org
AMOUNT: $2,000
DEADLINE(S): 2nd Monday in JAN
FIELD(S): Engineering
ELIGIBILITY/REQUIREMENTS: Applicant must be a high school senior; be a U.S. citizen and a resident of Michigan; be currently accepted at a Michigan ABET-accredited college or university and enrolled in an engineering program; have at least a 3.0 average on a 4.0 scale for the 10th and 11th grades; and attain a minimum composite test score of 26 on the ACT.
HOW TO APPLY: Send completed application; a list of senior classes being taken; documented high school transcript and ACT score; copy of official ACT Test Report; and a double-spaced typed essay of 250 words on "How I was influenced to pursue an engineering career."
NUMBER OF AWARDS: 1
CONTACT: Submit application to MSPE Chapter Representative; contact the

MSPE headquarters at address above to find out rep; do NOT send applications to MSPE headquarters.

904—MICHIGAN SOCIETY OF PROFESSIONAL ENGINEERS, THE (MSPE Scholarship Trust)

P.O. Box 15276
Lansing MI 48901-5276
517/487-9388
FAX: 517/487-0635
E-mail: mspe@voyager.net
Internet: http://www.michiganspe.org
AMOUNT: $2,000
DEADLINE(S): 2nd Monday in JAN
FIELD(S): Engineering
ELIGIBILITY/REQUIREMENTS: Applicant must be a high school senior; be a U.S. citizen and a resident of Michigan; be currently accepted at a Michigan ABET-accredited college or university and enrolled in an engineering program; have at least a 3.0 average on a 4.0 scale for the 10th and 11th grades; and attain a minimum composite test score of 26 on the ACT.
HOW TO APPLY: Send completed application; a list of senior classes being taken; documented high school transcript and ACT score; copy of official ACT Test Report; and a double-spaced typed essay of 250 words on "How I was influenced to pursue an engineering career."
NUMBER OF AWARDS: 1
CONTACT: Submit application to MSPE Chapter Representative; contact the MSPE headquarters at address above to find out rep; do NOT send applications to MSPE headquarters.

905—MICHIGAN SOCIETY OF PROFESSIONAL ENGINEERS, THE (MSPE Undesignated Grant)

P.O. Box 15276
Lansing MI 48901-5276
517/487-9388
FAX: 517/487-0635
E-mail: mspe@voyager.net
Internet: http://www.michiganspe.org
AMOUNT: $2,000
DEADLINE(S): 2nd Monday in APR
FIELD(S): Engineering
ELIGIBILITY/REQUIREMENTS: Applicant must be an MSPE member; be a U.S. citizen and a resident of Michigan; be in an ABET-accredited engineering program at a Michigan college or university; have a minimum GPA of 3.0 on a 4.0 scale;

demonstrate leadership and an interest in the engineering profession through involvement in school and/or outside activities.
HOW TO APPLY: Send completed application; official grade transcript(s); recommendations from at least 2 professors in the applicant's field of engineering study or appropriate math/science professor, specifying academic and personal traits and extracurricular activities; proof of acceptance in an ABET-accredited engineering program; information on co-op programs (i.e., information relating to or comprising a program of combined studies in which applicant might be involved); and a typed, 2-page essay of approximately 500 words, discussing applicant's interest in engineering, specific field of engineering that is being pursued, and occupation applicant proposes to pursue after graduation.
NUMBER OF AWARDS: 1
RENEWABLE: Yes. For a second year, with the approval of the MSPE Scholarship Trust; based on academic performance and approval of the Dean.

906—MICHIGAN SOCIETY OF PROFESSIONAL ENGINEERS, THE (MSPE University of Detroit-Mercy Grant)

P.O. Box 15276
Lansing MI 48901-5276
517/487-9388
FAX: 517/487-0635
E-mail: mspe@voyager.net
Internet: http://www.michiganspe.org
AMOUNT: $1,000
DEADLINE(S): 2nd Monday in JAN
FIELD(S): Engineering
ELIGIBILITY/REQUIREMENTS: Must be a high school senior; be a U.S. citizen and a resident of Michigan; be currently accepted at a Michigan ABET-accredited college or university and enrolled in an engineering program; have at least a 3.0 average on a 4.0 scale for the 10th and 11th grades; and attain a minimum composite test score of 26 on the ACT; and be willing to enroll in this 4-year program that includes a year in industry (co-op).
HOW TO APPLY: Send completed application; a list of senior classes being taken; documented high school transcript and ACT score; copy of official ACT Test Report; and a double-spaced typed essay of 250 words on "How I was influenced to pursue an engineering career."
NUMBER OF AWARDS: 1
CONTACT: Submit application to MSPE Chapter Representative; contact the MSPE headquarters at address above to

find out rep; do NOT send applications to MSPE headquarters.

907—MICHIGAN SOCIETY OF PROFESSIONAL ENGINEERS, THE (MSPE University of Michigan-Ann Arbor Grants)

P.O. Box 15276
Lansing MI 48901-5276
517/487-9388
FAX: 517/487-0635
E-mail: mspe@voyager.net
Internet: http://www.michigan spe.org
AMOUNT: $1,000
DEADLINE(S): 2nd Monday in JAN
FIELD(S): Engineering
ELIGIBILITY/REQUIREMENTS: Must be a high school senior; be a U.S. citizen and a resident of Michigan; be currently accepted at a Michigan ABET-accredited college or university and enrolled in an engineering program; have at least a 3.0 average on a 4.0 scale for the 10th and 11th grades; and attain a minimum composite test score of 26 on the ACT.
HOW TO APPLY: Send completed application; a list of senior classes being taken; documented high school transcript and ACT score; copy of official ACT Test Report; and a double-spaced typed essay of 250 words on "How I was influenced to pursue an engineering career."
NUMBER OF AWARDS: 4
CONTACT: Submit application to MSPE Chapter Representative; contact the MSPE headquarters at address above to find out rep; do NOT send applications to MSPE headquarters.

908—MICHIGAN SOCIETY OF PROFESSIONAL ENGINEERS, THE (MSPE University of Michigan-Dearborn Grants)

P.O. Box 15276
Lansing MI 48901-5276
517/487-9388
FAX: 517/487-0635
E-mail: mspe@voyager.net
Internet: http://www.michiganspe.org
AMOUNT: $1,000
DEADLINE(S): 2nd Monday in JAN
FIELD(S): Engineering
ELIGIBILITY/REQUIREMENTS: Applicant must be a high school senior; be a U.S. citizen and a resident of Michigan; be currently accepted at a Michigan ABET-accredited college or university and enrolled in an engineering program; have at least a 3.0 average on a 4.0 scale for the 10th and 11th grades; and attain a min-

imum composite test score of 26 on the ACT.

HOW TO APPLY: Send completed application; a list of senior classes being taken; documented high school transcript and ACT score; copy of official ACT Test Report; and a double-spaced typed essay of 250 words on "How I was influenced to pursue an engineering career."

NUMBER OF AWARDS: 2

CONTACT: Submit application to MSPE Chapter Representative; contact the MSPE headquarters at address above to find out rep; do NOT send applications to MSPE headquarters.

909—MICHIGAN SOCIETY OF PROFESSIONAL ENGINEERS, THE (MSPE Wayne State University Grants)

P.O. Box 15276
Lansing MI 48901-5276
517/487-9388
FAX: 517/487-0635
E-mail: mspe@voyager.net
Internet: http://www.michiganspe.
org

AMOUNT: $1,500

DEADLINE(S): 2nd Monday in JAN

FIELD(S): Engineering

ELIGIBILITY/REQUIREMENTS: Must be a high school senior; be a U.S. citizen and a resident of Michigan; be currently accepted at a Michigan ABET-accredited college or university and enrolled in an engineering program; have at least a 3.0 average on a 4.0 scale for the 10th and 11th grades; and attain a minimum composite test score of 26 on the ACT.

HOW TO APPLY: Send completed application; a list of senior classes being taken; documented high school transcript and ACT score; copy of official ACT Test Report; and a double-spaced typed essay of 250 words on "How I was influenced to pursue an engineering career."

NUMBER OF AWARDS: 2

RENEWABLE: Yes. Annually upon application submitted to the MSPE Scholarship Chair for approval; a 3.5 GPA must be maintained.

CONTACT: Submit application to MSPE Chapter Representative; contact the MSPE headquarters at address above to find out rep; do NOT send applications to MSPE headquarters.

910—MICHIGAN SOCIETY OF PROFESSIONAL ENGINEERS, THE (MSPE Western Michigan University Grant)

P.O. Box 15276
Lansing MI 48901-5276

517/487-9388
FAX: 517/487-0635
E-mail: mspe@voyager.net
Internet: http://www.michiganspe.
org

AMOUNT: $3,000

DEADLINE(S): 2nd Monday in JAN

FIELD(S): Engineering

ELIGIBILITY/REQUIREMENTS: Must be a high school senior; be a U.S. citizen and a resident of Michigan; be currently accepted at a Michigan ABET-accredited college or university and enrolled in an engineering program; have at least a 3.0 average on a 4.0 scale for the 10th and 11th grades; and attain a minimum composite test score of 26 on the ACT.

HOW TO APPLY: Send completed application; a list of senior classes being taken; documented high school transcript and ACT score; copy of official ACT Test Report; and a double-spaced typed essay of 250 words on "How I was influenced to pursue an engineering career."

NUMBER OF AWARDS: 1

CONTACT: Submit application to MSPE Chapter Representative; contact the MSPE headquarters at address above to find out rep; do NOT send applications to MSPE headquarters.

911—NAACP NATIONAL OFFICE (NAACP Willems Scholarship)

4805 Mount Hope Drive
Baltimore MD 21215
401/358-8900
Internet: http:www.naacp.org/work/
education/eduscholarship.shtm

AMOUNT: $2,000 undergraduate; $3,000 graduate

DEADLINE(S): APR 30

FIELD(S): Engineering; Chemistry; Physics; Mathematics

ELIGIBILITY/REQUIREMENTS: Open to NAACP male members majoring in one of the above areas. Must have GPA of 2.5+; graduates' GPAs must be 3.0+.

HOW TO APPLY: See Website for application or write for complete information (include a legal size SASE) to the United Negro College Fund, Scholarships & Grants Administration, 8260 Willow Oaks Corporate Drive, Fairfax, VA 22032, Attn: Kimberly Hall.

RENEWABLE: Yes. If the required GPA is maintained.

912—NATIONAL ASSOCIATION OF WATER COMPANIES-NEW JERSEY CHAPTER

Elizabethtown Water Co.
600 South Avenue

Westfield NJ 07091
908/654-1234
FAX: 908/232-2719
E-mail: gbradygbconsult@
comcast.net

AMOUNT: $2,500

DEADLINE(S): APR 1

FIELD(S): Business Administration; Biology; Chemistry; Engineering; Communications

ELIGIBILITY/REQUIREMENTS: For U.S. citizens who have lived in New Jersey at least 5 years and plan a career in the investor-owned water utility industry in disciplines such as those above. Must be undergraduate or graduate student in a 2- or 4-year New Jersey college or university. GPA of 3.0 or better required.

HOW TO APPLY: Contact Association for complete information.

CONTACT: Gail P. Brady

913—NATIONAL FEDERATION OF THE BLIND (Frank Walton Horn Memorial Scholarship)

805 Fifth Avenue
Grinnell IA 50112
515/236-3366
Internet: http://www.nfb.org/nfb/
scholarship_program.asp

AMOUNT: $3,000

DEADLINE(S): MAR 31

FIELD(S): Architecture; Engineering

ELIGIBILITY/REQUIREMENTS: Open to legally blind students pursuing or planning to pursue a full-time postsecondary course of study in the U.S. Based on academic excellence, service to the community, and financial need. Membership NOT required.

HOW TO APPLY: Contact Scholarship Committee Chairman for an application.

NUMBER OF AWARDS: 1

RENEWABLE: Yes

CONTACT: Peggy Elliot, Scholarship Committee Chairman

914—NATIONAL FEDERATION OF THE BLIND (Howard Brown Rickard Scholarship)

805 Fifth Avenue
Grinnell IA 50112
515/236-3366
Internet: http://www.nfb.org/nfb/
scholarship_program.asp

AMOUNT: $3,000

DEADLINE(S): MAR 31

FIELD(S): Law; Medicine; Engineering; Architecture; Natural Sciences

ELIGIBILITY/REQUIREMENTS: For legally blind students pursuing or planning to pursue a full-time postsecondary course of study in the U.S. Based on academic excellence, service to the community, and financial need. Membership NOT required.
HOW TO APPLY: Contact Scholarship Committee Chairman for an application.
NUMBER OF AWARDS: 1
RENEWABLE: Yes
CONTACT: Peggy Elliot, Scholarship Committee Chairman

915—NATIONAL INVENTORS HALL OF FAME, THE (Collegiate Inventors Competition)

221 South Broadway Street
Akron Ohio 44308-1505
330/849-6887
E-mail: rdepuy@invent.org.
Internet: http://www.invent.org/ bfg/ bfghome.html
AMOUNT: $25,000 (graduate); $15,000 (undergraduate)
DEADLINE(S): JUN 1
FIELD(S): Mathematics, Engineering, Biology, Chemistry, Physics, Information Technology, Medicine
ELIGIBILITY/REQUIREMENTS: Students must be enrolled (or have been enrolled) full time (in any college or university) at least part of the 12-month period prior to the date the entry is submitted. In the case of a team (maximum 4 students) at least 1 member of the team must meet the full-time eligibility criteria. The other team members must have been enrolled on a part-time basis (at a minimum) some time during the 24-month period prior to the date the entry is submitted. There are no limits on the number of entries a student or team may submit in a given year; however, only 1 prize per student or team will be awarded. There are no specific age requirements; however, if an entrant is under 18, a parent or guardian must sign the Student/Advisor Release Form. Entries are judged on the originality and inventiveness of the new idea, process, or technology. The entry must be complete, workable, and well articulated. Entries are also judged on their potential value to society (socially, environmentally, and economically), and on the scope of use. The judges' decisions are final.
HOW TO APPLY: Applicants should submit an original invention or idea that has not been made public. See website for application and detailed information. The application must include: Student and Advisor Information; Student Essay and Advisor Letter following the outlined format; diagrams, illustrations, photos, slides, or videos of the invention (clearly labeled); the signed Student/Advisor Release Form.
CONTACT: Ray DePuy

916—NATIONAL SOCIETY OF BLACK ENGINEERS (NSBE Fellows Scholarship Program)

1454 Duke Street
Alexandria VA 22314
703/549-2207
FAX: 703/683-5312
E-mail: nsbehq@nsbe.org
Internet: http://www.nsbe.org
AMOUNT: $1,000-$3,000
DEADLINE(S): Varies
FIELD(S): Engineering; Engineering Technologies
ELIGIBILITY/REQUIREMENTS: All paid NSBE undergraduate and graduate student members are eligible to apply. (Non-engineering/technical majors are not eligible.) All applicants must attend a college/university in the United States. Award GPA Minimum Requirements (4.0 scale): Mike Shinn (3.5), BCA (3.0), Major Sponsors (3.0), NSBE (2.7). Recipients will be selected based on a combination of the following criteria: University academic achievement (GPA, Honors, etc.); service to NSBE (Chapter, Regional, and/or National); other professional, campus, and community activities; essay response.
HOW TO APPLY: See website for application and details. The application must be submitted online and must include an official university/college transcript and a current résumé.
NUMBER OF AWARDS: 4

917—NATIONAL SPACE CLUB (Dr. Robert H. Goddard Scholarship)

2025 M Street NW, Suite 800
Washington DC 20036-4907
202/973/8661
Internet: http://www.spaceclub.org
AMOUNT: $10,000 + plaque
DEADLINE(S): JAN 6
FIELD(S): Science, Engineering
ELIGIBILITY/REQUIREMENTS: Essay competition open to any U.S. citizen, in at least junior year of an accredited university, and having the intention of pursuing undergraduate or graduate studies in science or engineering. Transcript of college record, letters of recommendation from faculty, accomplishments demonstrating personal qualities of creativity and leadership; scholastic plans leading to participation in some phase of the aerospace sciences and technology; proven past research and participation in space-related science and engineering. Personal need considered, but not controlling.
HOW TO APPLY: Apply by letter accompanied by documentation listed above.
RENEWABLE: Yes. For second year if circumstance and accomplishments warrant.

918—NATIONAL STONE, SAND & GRAVEL ASSOCIATION (NSSGA Barry K. Wendt Memorial Scholarship)

1605 King Street
Alexandria VA 22314
703/525-8788
FAX: 703/525-7782
E-mail: info@nssga.org
Internet: http://www.nssga.org
AMOUNT: $2,500
DEADLINE(S): APR 30
FIELD(S): Engineering; Mining; Minerals; Construction Management
ELIGIBILITY/REQUIREMENTS: Open to graduating seniors or college students who plan to pursue a career in the crushed stone, sand and gravel production industry.
HOW TO APPLY: See website or write for information and application.
NUMBER OF AWARDS: 1
RENEWABLE: No

919—NATIONAL TECHNICAL ASSOCIATION, INC. (Scholarship Competitions for Minorities and Women in Science and Engineering)

5810 Kingstowne Center, Suite 120221
Alexandria VA 22315-5711
E-mail: ntamfj1@aol.com
Internet: http://www.huenet.com/ nta
AMOUNT: $500-$5,000
DEADLINE(S): Varies
FIELD(S): Science; Mathematics; Engineering; Applied Technology
ELIGIBILITY/REQUIREMENTS: Scholarship competitions for minorities and women pursuing degrees in the above fields. Additional scholarships are available through local chapters of NTA.
HOW TO APPLY: See website or write to above address for details and for locations of local chapters.

920—NATIVE AMERICAN SCHOLARSHIP FUND, INC.

8200 Mountain Road NE, Suite 203
Albuquerque NM 87110
505/262-2351

FAX: 505/262-0543
E-mail: NScholarsh@aol.com
AMOUNT: Varies
DEADLINE(S): MAR 15; APR 15;
SEP 15
FIELD(S): Mathematics; Engineering;
Science; Business; Education;
Computer Science
ELIGIBILITY/REQUIREMENTS: Open
to American Indians or Alaskan Natives
(one-quarter degree or more) enrolled as
members of a federally recognized, state
recognized, or terminated tribe. For gradu-
ate or undergraduate study at an accredit-
ed 4-year college or university.
HOW TO APPLY: Contact Director of
Recruitment for an application.
NUMBER OF AWARDS: 208
CONTACT: Lucille Kelley, Director of
Recruitment

921—NATURAL SCIENCES AND ENGINEERING RESEARCH COUNCIL OF CANADA (Undergraduate Student Research Awards in Industry)

350 Albert Street
Ottawa Ontario K1A 1H5
CANADA
613/995-5992 or 613/995-4273
FAX: 613/992-5337
E-mail: schol@nserc.ca
Internet: http://www.nserc.ca
AMOUNT: $3,600 (Canadian; max.)
DEADLINE(S): Varies
FIELD(S): Natural Sciences (except
health sciences); Engineering
ELIGIBILITY/REQUIREMENTS:
Tenable in approved Canadian industrial
organizations. For Canadian citizens or
permanent residents, who have no more
than 4 academic terms remaining to complete bachelor's degree. Cumulative GPA
of at least second class (B). Recipients
must be employed full time in research and
development activities during award
tenure. Travel allowance may be granted.
Those already holding a bachelor's and
studying for a second may apply, but those
holding higher degrees in the natural sciences or engineering may not.
HOW TO APPLY: See website or contact
NSERC for more information and application.

922—NATURAL SCIENCES AND ENGINEERING RESEARCH COUNCIL OF CANADA (Undergraduate Student Research Awards in Small Universities)

350 Albert Street
Ottawa Ontario K1A 1H5
CANADA

613/995-5992
FAX: 613/992-5337
E-mail: schol@nserc.ca
Internet: http://www.nserc.ca/
programs/usrasmen.htm
AMOUNT: $3,600 (Canadian; max.)
DEADLINE(S): Varies
FIELD(S): Natural Sciences; Engineering
ELIGIBILITY/REQUIREMENTS:
Research awards for Canadian citizens/
permanent residents attending eligible
institutions, who have no more than 6 and
no fewer than 2 academic terms remaining
to complete bachelor's degree. Cumulative
GPA of at least second class (B). Must be
doing full time in research and develop-
ment activities during award tenure.
HOW TO APPLY: Students in health sciences not eligible. Students with BAs and
who are studying for a second may apply.

923—NEW JERSEY UTILITIES ASSOCIATION

50 West State Street, Suite 1006
Trenton NJ 08608
609/392-1000
FAX: 609/396-4231
Internet: http://www.njua.org
AMOUNT: $1,500
FIELD(S): Engineering; Environmental
Science; Chemistry; Biology; Business
Administration; Accounting
ELIGIBILITY/REQUIREMENTS: Must
be minority (i.e., Black, Hispanic,
American Indian/Alaskan Native, or Asian
Islander), female, and/or disabled students;
be a New Jersey resident; be enrolled on a
full-time basis at an institute of higher edu-
cation; have overall academic excellence;
and demonstrate financial need. Children
of employees of any NJUA member com-
pany are NOT eligible.
HOW TO APPLY: Contact Association.
NUMBER OF AWARDS: 2

924—OFFICE OF NAVAL RESEARCH (NSAP-Naval Science Awards Program)

ONR 353
800 North Quincy Street
Arlington VA 22217/5660
800/422-6727 or 703/696-5787
Internet: http://www.jshs.org
AMOUNT: $2,000-$20,000
DEADLINE(S): Varies (established by
individual regional, state, and district
science fairs)
FIELD(S): Science; Engineering
ELIGIBILITY/REQUIREMENTS: For
high school students (grades 9-12) who
participate in a regional/district/state science fair. Winners can participate in Junior

Science and Humanities Symposia (JSHS)
Program. Awards also offered in each of 14
categories at International Science and
Engineering Fair (ISEF), sponsored by
Science Service, Inc. Must be U.S. citizen
or permanent resident.
HOW TO APPLY: See website or contact
Project Officer for complete information
on NSAP, ISEF, and JSHS.
NUMBER OF AWARDS: 24
RENEWABLE: Yes
CONTACT: Barbara M. Thurman

925—OKLAHOMA ENGINEERING FOUNDATION (OEF), INC.

201 NE 27th Street, Room 125
Oklahoma City OK 73105
405/528-1435
FAX: 405/557-1820
E-mail: OSPEInfo@ospe.org
Internet: http://www.ospe.org
AMOUNT: $500-$1,000
DEADLINE(S): Pre-application form by
DEC 15; application form by JAN 30
FIELD(S): Engineering
ELIGIBILITY/REQUIREMENTS: High
school senior entering an engineering cur-
riculum at an ABET-accredited university
in Oklahoma; minimum 3.0 GPA and max-
imum 32 ACT composite score.
HOW TO APPLY: Applications can be
completed online between SEPT 11 and
DEC 15, click on OEF button and then go
to Scholarships on the side bar.
NUMBER OF AWARDS: 10 Freshmen
RENEWABLE: Yes. Students who win an
OEF freshman scholarship are eligible to
apply for a sophomore, junior and senior
scholarship in the following years. Only 3
undergraduate scholarships are offered
each year—1 each to a sophomore, a junior
and a senior.
CONTACT: Kathy Dunn, General
Manager

926—RAYMOND J. HARRIS EDUCATION TRUST

c/o Mellon Bank, N.A.
P.O. Box 7899
Philadelphia PA 19101-7899
AMOUNT: Varies
DEADLINE(S): FEB 1
FIELD(S): Medicine, Law, Engineering,
Dentistry, Agriculture
ELIGIBILITY/REQUIREMENTS:
Scholarships for Christian men to obtain a
professional education in medicine, law,
engineering, dentistry, or agriculture at 9
Philadelphia area colleges.
HOW TO APPLY: Contact Bank for
details and the names of the 9 colleges.

927—ROBERT SCHRECK MEMORIAL FUND (Grants)

c/o Texas Commerce Bank
Trust Department
P.O. Drawer 140
El Paso TX 79980
915/546-6515
AMOUNT: $500-$1,500
DEADLINE(S): JUL 15; NOV 15
FIELD(S): Medicine; Veterinary
Medicine; Physics; Chemistry;
Architecture; Engineering; Episcopal
Clergy
ELIGIBILITY/REQUIREMENTS:
Grants to undergraduate juniors or seniors
or graduate students who have been residents of El Paso County for at least 2
years. Must be U.S. citizen or legal resident
and have a high grade point average.
Financial need is a consideration.
HOW TO APPLY: Write for complete
information.
NUMBER OF AWARDS: 3
RENEWABLE: No

928—SAN DIEGO AIR &SPACE MUSEUM (Bill Gibbs Endowment Fund)

Education Office
2001 Pan American Plaza
San Diego CA 92101
619/234-8291, ext. 119
FAX: 619/233-4526
Internet: http://aerospace
museum.org
AMOUNT: $1,500-$2,500
DEADLINE(S): APR 1
FIELD(S): Aerospace, Mathematics,
Physics, Science, Engineering
ELIGIBILITY/REQUIREMENTS:
Graduating seniors of San Diego County
high schools who have been accepted to a
4-year college or university. Academic
achievement, strong aviation/aerospace
career interests.
HOW TO APPLY: See website or write
museum for application.

929—SCIENCE SERVICE (Intel International Science and Engineering Fair)

1719 N Street NW
Washington DC 20036
202/785-2255
FAX: 202/785-1243
E-mail: jcole@sciserv.org
Internet: http://www.sciserv.org
AMOUNT: Varies (totaling $3 million)
DEADLINE(S): Varies (consult local,
regional or state ISEF affiliated Fair)
FIELD(S): Science; Mathematics;
Engineering; Medicine
ELIGIBILITY/REQUIREMENTS: Open
to high school students (grades 9-12) who
participate in this worldwide science competition. Scholarships, tuition grants, and
travel and equipment grants are awarded.
HOW TO APPLY: Contact Science
Service for official ISEF entry book.
CONTACT: Jill Cole

930—SCIENCE SERVICE (Intel Science Talent Search)

1719 N Street NW
Washington DC 20036
202/785-2255
FAX: 202/785-1243
E-mail: jkee@sciserv.org
Internet: http://www.sciserv.org
AMOUNT: $100,000 (1st place); $75,000
(2nd); $50,000 (3rd); $25,000 (4th-6th);
$20,000 (7th-10th); 30 at $5,000; 300 at
$1,000; 40 laptops
DEADLINE(S): Mid to late NOV
FIELD(S): Science; Mathematics;
Engineering; Medicine
ELIGIBILITY/REQUIREMENTS: Open
to high school seniors in the United States
and territories and American students
attending school abroad. Each student
must submit a research report, a completed
entry form, an official high school transcript, and available standardized test
scores.
HOW TO APPLY: Contact Science
Service for official STS entry book.
NUMBER OF AWARDS: 40
CONTACT: June Kee

931—SIEMENS WESTINGHOUSE (Science and Technology Competition)

186 Wood Avenue South
Iselin NJ 08830
877/822-5233
E-mail: foundation.us@siemens.com
Internet: http://www.siemens-
foundation.org
AMOUNT: $120,000 (maximum)
DEADLINE(S): Varies
FIELD(S): Biology; Physical Sciences;
Mathematics; Physics; Chemistry;
Computer Science; Environmental
Science
ELIGIBILITY/REQUIREMENTS: Open
to U.S. high school seniors to pursue independent science research projects, working
individually or in teams of 2 or 3 to develop and test their own ideas. May work with
one of the universities/laboratories that
serve as Siemens' partners. Students from
the 50 states, DC, and territories may compete in one of six geographic areas.
Individual and team national prize winners
receive a second scholarship award to be
applied to undergraduate or graduate education.
HOW TO APPLY: See website or contact
Siemens Foundation for details.

932—SOCIETY FOR THE ADVANCEMENT OF MATERIAL & PROCESS ENGINEERING

5300 Forge Road
Whitemarsh MD 21162
Internet: http://www.sampe.org
AMOUNT: $750-$3,000
DEADLINE(S): FEB 1
FIELD(S): Engineering
ELIGIBILITY/REQUIREMENTS:
Engineering students with a minimum 3.3
GPA who are freshman, sophomore, and
junior members of SAMPE Student
Chapters are eligible.
HOW TO APPLY: Include letter of recommendation from SAMPE advisor and
transcripts.

933—SOCIETY OF AUTOMOTIVE ENGINEERS (BMW/SAE Engineering Scholarship)

SAE Customer Service
400 Commonwealth Drive
Warrendale PA 15096-0001
724/776-4970
FAX: 724/776-1615
E-mail: customerservice@sae.org
Internet:
http://www.sae.org/students/schol
arships/
AMOUNT: $1,500
DEADLINE(S): DEC 1
FIELD(S): Automotive Industry;
Engineering
ELIGIBILITY/REQUIREMENTS:
Applicants must have 3.75 GPA, rank in
the 90th percentile in both math and verbal
on SAT or the composite ACT scores, and
pursue an engineering-degree program
accredited by ABET.
HOW TO APPLY: See website for application. Submit application, including personal essay; 2 recommendations, 1 of
which must be from a teacher, counselor,
or administrator; and transcript.
NUMBER OF AWARDS: 1
RENEWABLE: Yes. A total of $6,000
(over 4-year period) will be awarded if student maintains a 3.0 GPA and continued
enrollment in an engineering program.

934—SOCIETY OF AUTOMOTIVE ENGINEERS (Bradley University/SAE Engineering Scholarships)

SAE Customer Service
400 Commonwealth Drive
Warrendale PA 15096-0001
724/776-4970
FAX: 724/776-1615
E-mail: customerservice@sae.org
Internet: http://www.sae.org/
students/scholarships
AMOUNT: $1,000
DEADLINE(S): DEC 1
FIELD(S): Engineering; Automotive Industry
ELIGIBILITY/REQUIREMENTS: Applicants must be an incoming freshman accepted into the College of Engineering and Technology at Bradley. Selection is based on high school GPA, rank in class, curriculum and SAT/ACT scores: a minimum 980 SAT or 21 ACT composite score, and 3.25 GPA.
HOW TO APPLY: See website for application. Submit application; a personal essay that demonstrates hands-on experience or activity (such as rebuilding engines, working on cars/trucks, etc.); 2 recommendations, 1 of which must be from a teacher, counselor, or administrator; and transcript.
NUMBER OF AWARDS: Varies
RENEWABLE: Yes. A total of $4,000 (4-year period) will be awarded if student remains enrolled in one of the specified majors in the College of Engineering and Technology and maintains a 3.0 GPA.

935—SOCIETY OF AUTOMOTIVE ENGINEERS (Calvin College/The James Bosscher/SAE Engineering Scholarship)

SAE Customer Service
400 Commonwealth Drive
Warrendale PA 15096-0001
724/776-4970
FAX: 724/776-1615
E-mail: customerservice@sae.org
Internet: http://www.sae.org/
students/scholarships
AMOUNT: $2,000
DEADLINE(S): DEC 1
FIELD(S): Engineering; Automotive Industry
ELIGIBILITY/REQUIREMENTS: High school seniors entering as freshmen enrolled in the engineering program who have demonstrated outstanding academic achievement and potential.
HOW TO APPLY: See website for application. Submit application; a personal

essay that demonstrates hands-on experience or activity (such as rebuilding engines, working on cars/trucks, etc.); 2 recommendations, 1 of which must be from a teacher, counselor, or administrator; and transcript.
NUMBER OF AWARDS: 1
RENEWABLE: Yes. For sophomore year contingent on continued enrollment in engineering and satisfactory performance in first year.

936—SOCIETY OF AUTOMOTIVE ENGINEERS (Cedarville University/SAE Engineering Scholarship)

SAE Customer Service
400 Commonwealth Drive
Warrendale PA 15096-0001
724/776-4970
FAX: 724/776-1615
E-mail: customerservice@sae.org
Internet: http://www.sae.org/
students/scholar/scholarships
AMOUNT: $1,000
DEADLINE(S): DEC 1
FIELD(S): Engineering; Automotive Industry
ELIGIBILITY/REQUIREMENTS: High school seniors entering as freshmen enrolled in the engineering program are awarded based on academic achievement. Criteria include ACT/SAT scores and high school GPA. Financial need is considered.
HOW TO APPLY: See website for application. Submit application; a personal essay that demonstrates hands-on experience or activity (such as rebuilding engines, working on cars/trucks, etc.); 2 recommendations, 1 of which must be from a teacher, counselor, or administrator; and transcript.
NUMBER OF AWARDS: 2
RENEWABLE: No

937—SOCIETY OF AUTOMOTIVE ENGINEERS (Central Missouri State University/SAE Engineering Scholarship)

SAE Customer Service
400 Commonwealth Drive
Warrendale PA 15096-0001
724/776-4970
FAX: 724/776-1615
E-mail: customerservice@sae.org
Internet: http://www.sae.org/
students/scholar/scholarships
AMOUNT: $500
DEADLINE(S): DEC 1
FIELD(S): Engineering; Automotive Industry

ELIGIBILITY/REQUIREMENTS: Incoming freshman pursuing a Bachelor of Science degree in Automotive/Power Technology; applicants must have 25 ACT Composite, a 3.2 GPA, and be in upper 15% of graduating class.
HOW TO APPLY: See website for application. Submit application; a personal essay that demonstrates hands-on experience or activity (such as rebuilding engines, working on cars/trucks, etc.); 2 recommendations, 1 of which must be from a teacher, counselor, or administrator; and transcript.
NUMBER OF AWARDS: 1
RENEWABLE: Yes. For 1 year if a 3.5 GPA is maintained.

938—SOCIETY OF AUTOMOTIVE ENGINEERS (Clarkson University/SAE Engineering Scholarship)

SAE Customer Service
400 Commonwealth Drive
Warrendale PA 15096-0001
724/776-4970
FAX: 724/776-1615
E-mail: customerservice@sae.org
Internet: http://www.sae.org/
students/scholar/scholarships
AMOUNT: $6,000
DEADLINE(S): DEC 1
FIELD(S): Engineering; Automotive Industry
ELIGIBILITY/REQUIREMENTS: Applicant must be an incoming freshman. Selection criteria include ACT/SAT scores, high school GPA (90 or 3.5 minimum), and extracurricular activities.
HOW TO APPLY: See website for application. Submit application; a personal essay that demonstrates hands-on experience or activity (such as rebuilding engines, working on cars/trucks, etc.); 2 recommendations, 1 of which must be from a teacher, counselor, or administrator; and transcript. Students must complete an interview (either on- or off-campus) by March 1 of senior year of high school.
NUMBER OF AWARDS: 8
RENEWABLE: Yes. For up to 4 years if provided the student remains in good academic standing and is enrolled full time at the university.

939—SOCIETY OF AUTOMOTIVE ENGINEERS (Detroit Section SAE Technical Scholarship)

SAE Customer Service
400 Commonwealth Drive
Warrendale PA 15096-0001
724/776-4970

FAX: 724/776-1615
E-mail: customerservice@sae.org
Internet: http://www.sae.org/
students/scholarships
AMOUNT: $2,500
DEADLINE(S): DEC 1
FIELD(S): Automotive Industry;
Engineering; Science
ELIGIBILITY/REQUIREMENTS:
Applicants must be child or grandchild of a current SAE Detroit Section member and intend to enroll in a 2- or 4-year engineering or science program at an accredited college or university. A minimum 3.0 GPA and 1200 SAT or 28 ACT composite score and demonstrated financial need is required. Must be entering freshman or transfer student who has completed a 2-year program.
HOW TO APPLY: See website for application. Submit application, including copies of FAFSA forms; a personal essay that demonstrates hands-on experience or activity (such as rebuilding engines, working on cars/trucks, etc.); 2 recommendations, 1 of which must be from a teacher, counselor, or administrator; and transcript.
NUMBER OF AWARDS: 1
RENEWABLE: Yes. A total of $10,000 (over 4-year period) will be awarded if student maintains a 2.5 GPA and remains in good standing at the college or university.

940—SOCIETY OF AUTOMOTIVE ENGINEERS (Edward D. Hendrickson/SAE Engineering Scholarship)

SAE Customer Service
400 Commonwealth Drive
Warrendale PA 15096-0001
724/776-4970
FAX: 724/776-1615
E-mail: customerservice@sae.org
Internet: http://www.sae.org/
students/scholarships
AMOUNT: $1,000
DEADLINE(S): DEC 1
FIELD(S): Automotive Industry,
Engineering
ELIGIBILITY/REQUIREMENTS: Must have 3.75 GPA, rank in the 90th percentile in both math and verbal on SAT or the composite ACT scores, and pursue an engineering degree program accredited by ABET.
HOW TO APPLY: See website for application. Submit application; personal essay; 2 recommendations, 1 of which must be from a teacher, counselor, or administrator; and transcript.
NUMBER OF AWARDS: 1
RENEWABLE: Yes. A total of $4,000 (over 4-year period) will be awarded if stu-

dent maintains a 3.0 GPA and continued enrollment in an engineering program.

941—SOCIETY OF AUTOMOTIVE ENGINEERS (Embry-Riddle Aeronautical University Scholarship [Daytona Beach])

SAE Customer Service
400 Commonwealth Drive
Warrendale PA 15096-0001
724/776-4970
FAX: 724/776-1615
E-mail: customerservice@sae.org
Internet: http://www.sae.org/
students/scholarships
AMOUNT: $5,000
DEADLINE(S): DEC 1
FIELD(S): Engineering; Automotive
Industry; Aviation Industry
ELIGIBILITY/REQUIREMENTS: Must be an incoming freshman pursuing a degree in the College of Engineering. Must have a minimum 1300 SAT or 30 ACT score and a 3.5 GPA and involvement in high school activities.
HOW TO APPLY: See website for application. Submit application; a personal essay that demonstrates hands-on experience or activity (such as rebuilding engines, working on cars/trucks, etc.); 2 recommendations, 1 of which must be from a teacher, counselor, or administrator; and transcript.
NUMBER OF AWARDS: 1
RENEWABLE: Yes. For 1 additional year if a 3.0 GPA is maintained and student remains in the engineering program.

942—SOCIETY OF AUTOMOTIVE ENGINEERS (Fred M. Young Sr./SAE Engineering Scholarship)

SAE Customer Service
400 Commonwealth Drive
Warrendale PA 15096-0001
724/776-4970
FAX: 724/776-1615
E-mail: customerservice@sae.org
Internet: http://www.sae.org/
students/scholarships
AMOUNT: $1,000
DEADLINE(S): DEC 1
FIELD(S): Automotive Industry,
Engineering
ELIGIBILITY/REQUIREMENTS: Must have 3.75 GPA, rank in the 90th percentile in both math and verbal on SAT or the composite ACT scores, and pursue an engineering degree program accredited by ABET.
HOW TO APPLY: See website for application. Submit application; personal essay that demonstrates hands-on experience or

activity (such as rebuilding engines, working on cars/trucks, etc.); 2 recommendations, 1 of which must be from a teacher, counselor, or administrator; and transcript.
NUMBER OF AWARDS: 1
RENEWABLE: Yes. A total of $4,000 (over 4-year period) will be awarded if student maintains a 3.0 GPA and continued enrollment in an engineering program.

943—SOCIETY OF AUTOMOTIVE ENGINEERS (Gannon University/SAE Engineering Scholarship)

SAE Customer Service
400 Commonwealth Drive
Warrendale PA 15096-0001
724/776-4970
FAX: 724/776-1615
E-mail: customerservice@sae.org
Internet: http://www.sae.org/
students/scholarships
AMOUNT: $1,000
DEADLINE(S): DEC 1
FIELD(S): Engineering; Automotive
Industry
ELIGIBILITY/REQUIREMENTS: Must be accepted to one of Gannon University's engineering programs. Award based on SAT/ACT, rank in class, and GPA.
HOW TO APPLY: See website for application. Submit application; a personal essay that demonstrates hands-on experience or activity (such as rebuilding engines, working on cars/trucks, etc.); 2 recommendations, 1 of which must be from a teacher, counselor, or administrator; and transcript.
NUMBER OF AWARDS: 1
RENEWABLE: Yes. Up to 3 years if 3.0 GPA is maintained.

944—SOCIETY OF AUTOMOTIVE ENGINEERS (Geneva College/SAE Engineering Scholarship)

SAE Customer Service
400 Commonwealth Drive
Warrendale PA 15096-0001
724/776-4970
FAX: 724/776-1615
E-mail: customerservice@sae.org
Internet: http://www.sae.org/
students/scholarships
AMOUNT: $2,000
DEADLINE(S): DEC 1
FIELD(S): Engineering; Automotive
Industry
ELIGIBILITY/REQUIREMENTS: Must be incoming freshman who will major in engineering. Based on merit and financial need.

HOW TO APPLY: See website for application. Submit application; a personal essay that demonstrates hands-on experience or activity (such as rebuilding engines, working on cars/trucks, etc.); 2 recommendations, 1 of which must be from a teacher, counselor, or administrator; and transcript. File FAFSA if application based on financial need.
NUMBER OF AWARDS: 1
RENEWABLE: Yes. Up to 3 years if 3.0 GPA is maintained.

945—SOCIETY OF AUTOMOTIVE ENGINEERS (Grand Valley State University/Padnos/SAE Engineering Scholarship)

SAE Customer Service
400 Commonwealth Drive
Warrendale PA 15096-0001
724/776-4970
FAX: 724/776-1615
E-mail: customerservice@sae.org
Internet: http://www.sae.org/students/scholarships
AMOUNT: $1,000
DEADLINE(S): DEC 1
FIELD(S): Engineering; Automotive Industry
ELIGIBILITY/REQUIREMENTS: Must be incoming full-time freshman who will major in engineering.
HOW TO APPLY: See website for application. Submit application; a personal essay that demonstrates hands-on experience or activity (such as rebuilding engines, working on cars/trucks, etc.); 2 recommendations, 1 of which must be from a teacher, counselor, or administrator; and transcript.
NUMBER OF AWARDS: 1
RENEWABLE: No

946—SOCIETY OF AUTOMOTIVE ENGINEERS (Illinois Institute of Technology/SAE Engineering Scholarship)

SAE Customer Service
400 Commonwealth Drive
Warrendale PA 15096-0001
724/776-4970
FAX: 724/776-1615
E-mail: customerservice@sae.org
Internet: http://www.sae.org/students/scholarships
AMOUNT: Half tuition
DEADLINE(S): DEC 1

FIELD(S): Engineering; Automotive Industry
ELIGIBILITY/REQUIREMENTS: Applicant must be incoming full-time freshman who will major in engineering. Selection will be based on test scores, GPA, activities, community service, and work experience.
HOW TO APPLY: See website for application. Submit application; a personal essay that demonstrates hands-on experience or activity (such as rebuilding engines, working on cars/trucks, etc.); 2 recommendations, 1 of which must be from a teacher, counselor, or administrator; and transcript.
NUMBER OF AWARDS: 5
RENEWABLE: Yes. Up to 4 years upon satisfactory academic performance.

947—SOCIETY OF AUTOMOTIVE ENGINEERS (Iowa State University/SAE Engineering Scholarship)

SAE Customer Service
400 Commonwealth Drive
Warrendale PA 15096-0001
724/776-4970
FAX: 724/776-1615
E-mail: customerservice@sae.org
Internet: http://www.sae.org/students/scholarships
AMOUNT: $1,000
DEADLINE(S): DEC 1
FIELD(S): Engineering; Automotive Industry
ELIGIBILITY/REQUIREMENTS: Applicant must be incoming freshman who will be pursuing a degree in the College of Engineering with an interest in the automotive engineering applications. Applicants should have ACT math scores of 26 or above or equivalent SAT scores, and rank in top 20% of high school class.
HOW TO APPLY: See website for application. Submit application; a personal essay that demonstrates hands-on experience or activity (such as rebuilding engines, working on cars/trucks, etc.); 2 recommendations, 1 of which must be from a teacher, counselor, or administrator; and transcript.
NUMBER OF AWARDS: 1
RENEWABLE: No

948—SOCIETY OF AUTOMOTIVE ENGINEERS (Kansas State University-Manhattan/SAE Engineering Scholarship)

SAE Customer Service
400 Commonwealth Drive
Warrendale PA 15096-0001

724/776-4970
FAX: 724/776-1615
E-mail: customerservice@sae.org
Internet: http://www.sae.org/students/scholarships
AMOUNT: $1,000
DEADLINE(S): DEC 1
FIELD(S): Engineering; Automotive Industry
ELIGIBILITY/REQUIREMENTS: Applicant must be incoming freshman who will be pursuing a degree in the College of Engineering. Applicants must have ACT scores of 30 composite, 3.5 GPA, and rank in top 10% of high school class.
HOW TO APPLY: See website for application. Submit application; a personal essay that demonstrates hands-on experience or activity (such as rebuilding engines, working on cars/trucks, etc.); 2 recommendations, 1 of which must be from a teacher, counselor, or administrator; and transcript.
NUMBER OF AWARDS: 1
RENEWABLE: Yes. Up to 4 years; a 3.5 GPA must be maintained.

949—SOCIETY OF AUTOMOTIVE ENGINEERS (Kansas State University-Salina/SAE Engineering Scholarship)

SAE Customer Service
400 Commonwealth Drive
Warrendale PA 15096-0001
724/776-4970
FAX: 724/776-1615
E-mail: customerservice@sae.org
Internet: http://www.sae.org/students/scholarships
AMOUNT: $1,000
DEADLINE(S): DEC 1
FIELD(S): Engineering; Automotive Industry; Aviation Industry
ELIGIBILITY/REQUIREMENTS: Applicant must be incoming freshman who will be pursuing a degree in the College of Technology & Aviation. Applicants must have ACT scores of 21 composite or 950 SAT, or 3.2 GPA.
HOW TO APPLY: See website for application. Submit application; a personal essay that demonstrates hands-on experience or activity (such as rebuilding engines, working on cars/trucks, etc.); 2 recommendations, 1 of which must be from a teacher, counselor, or administrator; and transcript.
NUMBER OF AWARDS: 5
RENEWABLE: Yes. Up to 4 years; a 3.5 GPA must be maintained along with continued enrollment in College of Technology and Aviation.

950—SOCIETY OF AUTOMOTIVE ENGINEERS (Kettering University/SAE Engineering Scholarship)

SAE Customer Service
400 Commonwealth Drive
Warrendale PA 15096-0001
724/776-4970
FAX: 724/776-1615
E-mail: customerservice@sae.org
Internet: http://www.sae.org/students/scholarships
AMOUNT: $5,000
DEADLINE(S): DEC 1
FIELD(S): Engineering; Automotive Industry
ELIGIBILITY/REQUIREMENTS: High school juniors and seniors as well as high school graduates entering college for the first time are eligible.
HOW TO APPLY: See website for application. Submit application; a personal essay that demonstrates hands-on experience or activity (such as rebuilding engines, working on cars/trucks, etc.); 2 recommendations, 1 of which must be from a teacher, counselor, or administrator; and transcript.
NUMBER OF AWARDS: 5
RENEWABLE: Yes. Up to 4 years.

951—SOCIETY OF AUTOMOTIVE ENGINEERS (Lawrence Technological University/SAE Engineering Scholarship)

SAE Customer Service
400 Commonwealth Drive
Warrendale PA 15096-0001
724/776-4970
FAX: 724/776-1615
E-mail: customerservice@sae.org
Internet: http://www.sae.org/students/scholarships
AMOUNT: $2,000
DEADLINE(S): DEC 1
FIELD(S): Engineering; Automotive Industry
ELIGIBILITY/REQUIREMENTS: Applicants must be incoming freshmen who intend to major in engineering. Selection will be based on high school grades and ACT or SAT scores.
HOW TO APPLY: See website for application. Submit application; a personal essay that demonstrates hands-on experience or activity (such as rebuilding engines, working on cars/trucks, etc.); 2 recommendations, 1 of which must be from a teacher, counselor, or administrator; and transcript.
NUMBER OF AWARDS: 5

RENEWABLE: Yes. Up to 4 years with GPA of 3.0.

952—SOCIETY OF AUTOMOTIVE ENGINEERS (Mary Baldwin College/SAE Engineering Scholarship)

SAE Customer Service
400 Commonwealth Drive
Warrendale PA 15096-0001
724/776-4970
FAX: 724/776-1615
E-mail: customerservice@sae.org
Internet: http://www.sae.org/students/scholarships
AMOUNT: $6,100-$9,000
DEADLINE(S): DEC 1
FIELD(S): Engineering; Automotive Industry
ELIGIBILITY/REQUIREMENTS: Must be pursuing admission to the Mary Baldwin College or University of Virginia Cooperative Program in Engineering, and should have a minimum 1050 SAT or 23 ACT score, and at least a 3.0 GPA. Amount awarded will be based on the combination of SAT/ACT scores and GPA.
HOW TO APPLY: See website for application. Submit application; a personal essay that demonstrates hands-on experience or activity (such as rebuilding engines, working on cars/trucks, etc.); 2 recommendations, 1 of which must be from a teacher, counselor, or administrator; and transcript.
NUMBER OF AWARDS: Unlimited
RENEWABLE: Yes. Up to 2 additional years with GPA of 3.0.

953—SOCIETY OF AUTOMOTIVE ENGINEERS (Mercer University/SAE Engineering Scholarship)

SAE Customer Service
400 Commonwealth Drive
Warrendale PA 15096-0001
724/776-4970
FAX: 724/776-1615
E-mail: customerservice@sae.org
Internet: http://www.sae.org/students/scholarships
AMOUNT: $2,500
DEADLINE(S): DEC 1
FIELD(S): Engineering; Automotive Industry
ELIGIBILITY/REQUIREMENTS: Incoming freshman majoring in engineering with an SAT score of 1400 or better or an ACT score of 31 or greater in both English

and Math, and a high school academic GPA of 3.7 or greater.
HOW TO APPLY: See website for application. Submit application; a personal essay that demonstrates hands-on experience or activity (such as rebuilding engines, working on cars/trucks, etc.); 2 recommendations, 1 of which must be from a teacher, counselor, or administrator; and transcript.
NUMBER OF AWARDS: 1
RENEWABLE: Yes. Up to 3 additional years.

954—SOCIETY OF AUTOMOTIVE ENGINEERS (Miami University-Ohio/The Ken Shinn/SAE Engineering Scholarship)

SAE Customer Service
400 Commonwealth Drive
Warrendale PA 15096-0001
724/776-4970
FAX: 724/776-1615
E-mail: customerservice@sae.org
Internet: http://www.sae.org/students/scholarships
AMOUNT: $1,000
DEADLINE(S): DEC 1
FIELD(S): Engineering; Automotive Industry
ELIGIBILITY/REQUIREMENTS: Applicants must be high school seniors, intending to pursue studies in Manufacturing Engineering or Mechanical Engineering. Scholarships will be granted on the basis of SAT and/or ACT scores, high school GPA, and extracurricular activities.
HOW TO APPLY: See website for application. Submit application; a personal essay that demonstrates hands-on experience or activity (such as rebuilding engines, working on cars/trucks, etc.); 2 recommendations, 1 of which must be from a teacher, counselor, or administrator; and transcript.
NUMBER OF AWARDS: 1
RENEWABLE: No

955—SOCIETY OF AUTOMOTIVE ENGINEERS (Michigan State University/SAE Engineering Scholarship)

SAE Customer Service
400 Commonwealth Drive
Warrendale PA 15096-0001
724/776-4970
FAX: 724/776-1615
E-mail: customerservice@sae.org
Internet: http://www.sae.org/students/scholarships
AMOUNT: $1,500

DEADLINE(S): DEC 1
FIELD(S): Engineering; Automotive Industry
ELIGIBILITY/REQUIREMENTS: Applicants must be incoming freshmen who will be pursuing a degree in the College of Engineering and must have a strong interest in the automotive industry. Selection will be based on high school grades, ACT or SAT scores, and quality of essay in relation to student's goals.
HOW TO APPLY: See website for application. Submit application; a personal essay that demonstrates hands-on experience or activity (such as rebuilding engines, working on cars/trucks, etc.); 2 recommendations, 1 of which must be from a teacher, counselor, or administrator; and transcript.
NUMBER OF AWARDS: 1
RENEWABLE: No

956—SOCIETY OF AUTOMOTIVE ENGINEERS (Oakland University/SAE Engineering Scholarship)

SAE Customer Service
400 Commonwealth Drive
Warrendale PA 15096-0001
724/776-4970
FAX: 724/776-1615
E-mail: customerservice@sae.org
Internet: http://www.sae.org/students/scholarships
AMOUNT: $1,000
DEADLINE(S): DEC 1
FIELD(S): Engineering; Computer Science; Automotive Industry
ELIGIBILITY/REQUIREMENTS: Applicants must be incoming freshmen who will be pursuing a degree in the School of Engineering and Computer Science.
HOW TO APPLY: See website for application. Submit application; a personal essay that demonstrates hands-on experience or activity (such as rebuilding engines, working on cars/trucks, etc.); 2 recommendations, 1 of which must be from a teacher, counselor, or administrator; and transcript.
NUMBER OF AWARDS: 1
RENEWABLE: No

957—SOCIETY OF AUTOMOTIVE ENGINEERS (Ohio State University/Motorsports Team/SAE Engineering Scholarship)

SAE Customer Service
400 Commonwealth Drive
Warrendale PA 15096-0001
724/776-4970
FAX: 724/776-1615
E-mail: customerservice@sae.org
Internet: http://www.sae.org/students/scholarships
AMOUNT: $500
DEADLINE(S): DEC 1
FIELD(S): Engineering; Automotive Industry
ELIGIBILITY/REQUIREMENTS: Incoming (first-year or transfer) students. Undergraduate scholarship winners will be selected on the basis of demonstrated potential to contribute to the success of OSU's motorsports teams. Prior participation in successful team efforts, technical aptitude, leadership potential, and a solid record are elements of the selection process.
HOW TO APPLY: See website for application. Submit application; a personal essay that demonstrates hands-on experience or activity (such as rebuilding engines, working on cars/trucks, etc.); 2 recommendations, 1 of which must be from a teacher, counselor, or administrator; and transcript.
NUMBER OF AWARDS: Up to 3
RENEWABLE: No

958—SOCIETY OF AUTOMOTIVE ENGINEERS (Penn State-Erie/The Behrend College/SAE Scholarship)

SAE Customer Service
400 Commonwealth Drive
Warrendale PA 15096-0001
724/776-4970
FAX: 724/776-1615
E-mail: customerservice@sae.org
Internet: http://www.sae.org/students/scholarships
AMOUNT: $1,000
DEADLINE(S): DEC 1
FIELD(S): Engineering; Engineering Technology
ELIGIBILITY/REQUIREMENTS: Applicants must be incoming freshmen accepted into a Penn State Behrend engineering or engineering technology program.
HOW TO APPLY: See website for application. Submit application; a personal essay that demonstrates hands-on experience or activity (such as rebuilding engines, working on cars/trucks, etc.); 2 recommendations, 1 of which must be from a teacher, counselor, or administrator; and transcript.
NUMBER OF AWARDS: 1
RENEWABLE: No

959—SOCIETY OF AUTOMOTIVE ENGINEERS (Penn State University [PSES]/SAE Scholarship)

SAE Customer Service
400 Commonwealth Drive
Warrendale PA 15096-0001
724/776-4970
FAX: 724/776-1615
E-mail: customerservice@sae.org
Internet: http://www.sae.org/students/scholarships
AMOUNT: $2,500
DEADLINE(S): DEC 1
FIELD(S): Engineering
ELIGIBILITY/REQUIREMENTS: Applicants must be accepted at the University Park Campus and pursue a major in the College of Engineering.
HOW TO APPLY: See website for application. Submit application; a personal essay that demonstrates hands-on experience or activity (such as rebuilding engines, working on cars/trucks, etc.); 2 recommendations, 1 of which must be from a teacher, counselor, or administrator; and transcript.
NUMBER OF AWARDS: 1
RENEWABLE: Yes. Up to 3 additional years if conditions are met.

960—SOCIETY OF AUTOMOTIVE ENGINEERS (Pittsburgh State University-Kansas/SAE Automotive Technology Scholarship)

SAE Customer Service
400 Commonwealth Drive
Warrendale PA 15096-0001
724/776-4970
FAX: 724/776-1615
E-mail: customerservice@sae.org
Internet: http://www.sae.org/students/scholarships
AMOUNT: $1,500
DEADLINE(S): DEC 1
FIELD(S): Engineering; Automotive Industry
ELIGIBILITY/REQUIREMENTS: Zero-hour freshmen must be in upper 20% of high school graduating class. College transfers must have a 3.5 GPA.
HOW TO APPLY: See website for application. Submit application; a personal essay that demonstrates hands-on experience or activity (such as rebuilding engines, working on cars/trucks, etc.); 2 recommendations, 1 of which must be from a teacher, counselor, or administrator; and transcript.
NUMBER OF AWARDS: 1

RENEWABLE: Yes. Up to 4 years if a 3.5 GPA is maintained and a minimum of 30 hours completed each year.

961—SOCIETY OF AUTOMOTIVE ENGINEERS (Portland State University/SAE Engineering Scholarship)

SAE Customer Service
400 Commonwealth Drive
Warrendale PA 15096-0001
724/776-4970
FAX: 724/776-1615
E-mail: customerservice@sae.org
Internet: http://www.sae.org/ students/scholarships
AMOUNT: $2,000
DEADLINE(S): DEC 1
FIELD(S): Engineering; Automotive Industry
ELIGIBILITY/REQUIREMENTS: Applicant must be incoming freshman majoring in engineering. Must have minimum 3.5 GPA and 1000 SAT.
HOW TO APPLY: See website for application. Submit application; a personal essay that demonstrates hands-on experience or activity (such as rebuilding engines, working on cars/trucks, etc.); 2 recommendations, 1 of which must be from a teacher, counselor, or administrator; and transcript.
NUMBER OF AWARDS: 1
RENEWABLE: Yes. Up to 4 years if a 3.0 GPA and full-time enrollment in an engineering major is maintained.

962—SOCIETY OF AUTOMOTIVE ENGINEERS (Robert Morris University/SAE Engineering Scholarship)

SAE Customer Service
400 Commonwealth Drive
Warrendale PA 15096-0001
724/776-4970
FAX: 724/776-1615
E-mail: customerservice@sae.org
Internet: http://www.sae.org/ students/scholarships
AMOUNT: $4,000
DEADLINE(S): DEC 1
FIELD(S): Engineering; Automotive Industry
ELIGIBILITY/REQUIREMENTS: Incoming freshmen pursuing a degree in the School of Engineering are eligible. Students with a minimum 1100 SAT or 24 ACT and 3.2 GPA scores are eligible. Based on merit and financial need.
HOW TO APPLY: See website for application. Submit application; a personal essay that demonstrates hands-on experience or activity (such as rebuilding

engines, working on cars/trucks, etc.); 2 recommendations, 1 of which must be from a teacher, counselor, or administrator; and transcript. Must also apply to the school and be accepted by March 1.
NUMBER OF AWARDS: 1
RENEWABLE: Yes. A 3.0 or better GPA required.

963—SOCIETY OF AUTOMOTIVE ENGINEERS (Rochester Institute of Technology/SAE Scholarship)

SAE Customer Service
400 Commonwealth Drive
Warrendale PA 15096-0001
724/776-4970
FAX: 724/776-1615
E-mail: customerservice@sae.org
Internet: http://www.sae.org/ students/scholarships
AMOUNT: $5,000
DEADLINE(S): DEC 1
FIELD(S): Engineering; Engineering Technology
ELIGIBILITY/REQUIREMENTS: Applicants must be incoming freshmen and enrolled in one of RIT's engineering or engineering technology programs. Awards based on academic credentials and leadership potential.
HOW TO APPLY: See website for application. Submit application; a personal essay that demonstrates hands-on experience or activity (such as rebuilding engines, working on cars/trucks, etc.); 2 recommendations, 1 of which must be from a teacher, counselor, or administrator; and transcript. A personal interview is recommended.
NUMBER OF AWARDS: Up to 25
RENEWABLE: Yes. Up to 3 additional years; must maintain 3.0 GPA.

964—SOCIETY OF AUTOMOTIVE ENGINEERS (SAE Long-Term Member Sponsored Scholarships)

SAE Customer Service
400 Commonwealth Drive
Warrendale PA 15096-0001
724/776-4970
FAX: 724/776-1615
E-mail: customerservice@sae.org
Internet: http://www.sae.org/ students/scholarships
AMOUNT: $1,000
DEADLINE(S): APR 1
FIELD(S): Engineering
ELIGIBILITY/REQUIREMENTS: Applicants must be in their junior year of undergraduate engineering, and a student member of SAE. Application must be sup-

ported by the SAE Faculty Advisory, Section Chair, or Vice Chair for Student Activities. Must show leadership and support of SAE, the SAE collegiate chapter on campus, and the local SAE section. GPA is not a determining factor.
HOW TO APPLY: See website for application. Applications may be submitted by the student or by the SAE Faculty Advisor, an SAE Section Chair, or a community leader.
NUMBER OF AWARDS: 2-3
RENEWABLE: No
CONTACT: LTM Scholarships

965—SOCIETY OF AUTOMOTIVE ENGINEERS (SAE Women Engineers Committee Scholarship)

SAE Customer Service
400 Commonwealth Drive
Warrendale PA 15096-0001
724/776-4970
FAX: 724/776-1615
E-mail: customerservice@sae.org
Internet: http://www.sae.org/ students/scholarships
AMOUNT: $1,500
DEADLINE(S): DEC 1
FIELD(S): Automotive Industry, Engineering
ELIGIBILITY/REQUIREMENTS: Must be female, entering freshman year, have 3.0 GPA, and pursue an engineering degree program accredited by ABET.
HOW TO APPLY: See website for application. Submit application; personal essay; 2 recommendations, 1 of which must be from a teacher, counselor, or administrator; and transcript.
NUMBER OF AWARDS: 1
RENEWABLE: No

966—SOCIETY OF AUTOMOTIVE ENGINEERS (Saginaw Valley State University/Cardinal Racing/SAE Engineering Scholarship)

SAE Customer Service
400 Commonwealth Drive
Warrendale PA 15096-0001
724/776-4970
FAX: 724/776-1615
E-mail: customerservice@sae.org
Internet: http://www.sae.org/ students/scholarships
AMOUNT: $1,000
DEADLINE(S): DEC 1
FIELD(S): Engineering; Automotive Industry
ELIGIBILITY/REQUIREMENTS: Incoming (first-year or transfer) engineer-

ing students are eligible. Selection based on potential to contribute to SVSU Cardinal racing teams. Prior participation in successful team efforts, technical aptitude, leadership potential, and a solid academic record.
HOW TO APPLY: See website for application. Submit application; a personal essay that demonstrates hands-on experience or activity (such as rebuilding engines, working on cars/trucks, etc.); 2 recommendations, 1 of which must be from a teacher, counselor, or administrator; and transcript.
NUMBER OF AWARDS: 1
RENEWABLE: No

967—SOCIETY OF AUTOMOTIVE ENGINEERS (Southern Illinois University-Carbondale/SAE Engineering Scholarship)

SAE Customer Service
400 Commonwealth Drive
Warrendale PA 15096-0001
724/776-4970
FAX: 724/776-1615
E-mail: customerservice@sae.org
Internet: http://www.sae.org/students/scholarships
AMOUNT: $1,000
DEADLINE(S): DEC 1
FIELD(S): Engineering; Automotive Industry
ELIGIBILITY/REQUIREMENTS: Incoming freshmen admitted to any of the undergraduate degree programs in the College of Engineering. Selection based on a minimum 25 ACT or 1140 SAT scores, minimum 25 math ACT or 600 SAT math scores, and top 25% class rank or a minimum GPA of 3.4.
HOW TO APPLY: See website for application. Submit application; a personal essay that demonstrates hands-on experience or activity (such as rebuilding engines, working on cars/trucks, etc.); 2 recommendations, 1 of which must be from a teacher, counselor, or administrator; and transcript.
NUMBER OF AWARDS: 3
RENEWABLE: No

968—SOCIETY OF AUTOMOTIVE ENGINEERS (Southern Illinois University-Carbondale/Women Engineer/SAE Engineering Scholarship)

SAE Customer Service
400 Commonwealth Drive
Warrendale PA 15096-0001
724/776-4970
FAX: 724/776-1615
E-mail: customerservice@sae.org
Internet: http://www.sae.org/students/scholarships
AMOUNT: $1,000
DEADLINE(S): DEC 1
FIELD(S): Engineering; Automotive Industry
ELIGIBILITY/REQUIREMENTS: Incoming female freshmen admitted to any of the undergraduate degree programs in the College of Engineering. Selection based on a minimum 25 ACT or 1140 SAT scores, minimum 25 math ACT or 600 SAT math scores, and top 25% class rank or a minimum GPA of 3.4.
HOW TO APPLY: See website for application. Submit application; a personal essay that demonstrates hands-on experience or activity (such as rebuilding engines, working on cars/trucks, etc.); 2 recommendations, 1 of which must be from a teacher, counselor, or administrator; and transcript.
NUMBER OF AWARDS: 3
RENEWABLE: No

969—SOCIETY OF AUTOMOTIVE ENGINEERS (Stevens Institute of Technology/SAE Scholarship)

SAE Customer Service
400 Commonwealth Drive
Warrendale PA 15096-0001
724/776-4970
FAX: 724/776-1615
E-mail: customerservice@sae.org
Internet: http://www.sae.org/students/scholarships
AMOUNT: $6,000+/year
DEADLINE(S): DEC 1
FIELD(S): Engineering; Automotive Industry
ELIGIBILITY/REQUIREMENTS: For incoming freshmen studying engineering.
HOW TO APPLY: See website for application. Complete application; submit 3 recommendation letters (2 from a teacher or school official and 1 from an employer or non-relative); high school and/or college transcript for last 2 years; a 1- to 2-page statement telling why you are applying for the scholarship and educational and career goals in the plastics industry.
NUMBER OF AWARDS: 2
RENEWABLE: Yes. Up to 3 additional years; must maintain a "B" average.
CONTACT: Dean of Undergraduate Admissions at Stevens (201/216-5194)

970—SOCIETY OF AUTOMOTIVE ENGINEERS (SUNY-Buffalo/James & Nancy McLemon/SAE Engineering Scholarship)

SAE Customer Service
400 Commonwealth Drive
Warrendale PA 15096-0001
724/776-4970
FAX: 724/776-1615
E-mail: customerservice@sae.org
Internet: http://www.sae.org/students/scholarships
AMOUNT: $1,000
DEADLINE(S): DEC 1
FIELD(S): Engineering; Automotive Industry
ELIGIBILITY/REQUIREMENTS: Eligible applicants must have a minimum 30 ACT or 1300 SAT score; GPA of 3.5 or higher, and be enrolled in an engineering program. School and civic honors and activities and employment record considered.
HOW TO APPLY: See website for application. Submit application; a personal essay that demonstrates hands-on experience or activity (such as rebuilding engines, working on cars/trucks, etc.); 2 recommendations, 1 of which must be from a teacher, counselor, or administrator; and transcript.
NUMBER OF AWARDS: 3
RENEWABLE: Yes. For 4 years provided student maintains a record of academic excellence and demonstrates leadership.

971—SOCIETY OF AUTOMOTIVE ENGINEERS (SUNY-Stony Brook/SAE Scholarship)

SAE Customer Service
400 Commonwealth Drive
Warrendale PA 15096-0001
724/776-4970
FAX: 724/776-1615
E-mail: customerservice@sae.org
Internet: http://www.sae.org/students/scholarships
AMOUNT: $2,000
DEADLINE(S): DEC 1
FIELD(S): Engineering; Computer Science
ELIGIBILITY/REQUIREMENTS: Incoming freshmen admitted directly to 1 of 5 Bachelor of Engineering degree programs are eligible. Based on academic achievement and demonstrated motivation for a career as a professional engineer.

HOW TO APPLY: See website for application. Submit application; a personal essay that demonstrates hands-on experience or activity (such as rebuilding engines, working on cars/trucks, etc.); 2 recommendations, 1 of which must be from a teacher, counselor, or administrator; and transcript.
NUMBER OF AWARDS: 4
RENEWABLE: Yes. For 3 additional years; must maintain a 3.0 GPA in a Bachelor of Engineering degree program and make contribution to SAE campus chapter.

972—SOCIETY OF AUTOMOTIVE ENGINEERS (SUNY-Alfred/Vernon Gleasman/SAE Scholarship)

SAE Customer Service
400 Commonwealth Drive
Warrendale PA 15096-0001
724/776-4970
FAX: 724/776-1615
E-mail: customerservice@sae.org
Internet: http://www.sae.org/students/scholarships
AMOUNT: $500
DEADLINE(S): DEC 1
FIELD(S): Engineering (especially Mechanical Engineering Technology)
ELIGIBILITY/REQUIREMENTS: For incoming freshmen and transfer students pursuing an associate or baccalaureate degree in engineering technology. Preference given to students enrolling in Mechanical Engineering Technology.
HOW TO APPLY: See website for application. Submit application; a personal essay that demonstrates hands-on experience or activity (such as rebuilding engines, working on cars/trucks, etc.); 2 recommendations, 1 of which must be from a teacher, counselor, or administrator; and transcript.
NUMBER OF AWARDS: 1
RENEWABLE: No
CONTACT: Admissions Office

973—SOCIETY OF AUTOMOTIVE ENGINEERS (SUNY-New Paltz/SAE Scholarship)

SAE Customer Service
400 Commonwealth Drive
Warrendale PA 15096-0001
724/776-4970
FAX: 724/776-1615
E-mail: customerservice@sae.org
Internet: http://www.sae.org/students/scholarships
AMOUNT: $1,000
DEADLINE(S): DEC 1

FIELD(S): Engineering; Computer Science
ELIGIBILITY/REQUIREMENTS: Applicants must be incoming freshmen accepted for study at SUNY-New Paltz School of Engineering. Minimum high school average of 90 (100-point scale) in a college preparatory program and a 1250 SAT combined score (28 ACT composite) are required.
HOW TO APPLY: See website for application. Submit application; a personal essay that demonstrates hands-on experience or activity (such as rebuilding engines, working on cars/trucks, etc.); 2 recommendations, 1 of which must be from a teacher, counselor, or administrator; and transcript.
NUMBER OF AWARDS: 2
RENEWABLE: Yes. Up to 4 years; must maintain 3.0 GPA for renewal.

974—SOCIETY OF AUTOMOTIVE ENGINEERS (Tau Beta Pi/SAE Engineering Scholarship)

SAE Customer Service
400 Commonwealth Drive
Warrendale PA 15096-0001
724/776-4970
FAX: 724/776-1615
E-mail: customerservice@sae.org
Internet: http://www.sae.org/students/scholarships
AMOUNT: $1,000
DEADLINE(S): DEC 1
FIELD(S): Automotive Industry, Engineering
ELIGIBILITY/REQUIREMENTS: Applicants must be entering freshman, have 3.75 GPA, rank in the 90th percentile in both math and verbal on SAT or the composite ACT scores, and pursue an engineering degree program accredited by ABET.
HOW TO APPLY: See website for application. Submit application; personal essay; 2 recommendations, 1 of which must be from a teacher, counselor, or administrator; and transcript.
NUMBER OF AWARDS: 6
RENEWABLE: No

975—SOCIETY OF AUTOMOTIVE ENGINEERS (TMC/SAE Donald D. Dawson Technical Scholarship)

SAE Customer Service
400 Commonwealth Drive
Warrendale PA 15096-0001
724/776-4970
FAX: 724/776-1615
E-mail: customerservice@sae.org

Internet: http://www.sae.org/students/scholarships
AMOUNT: $1,500
DEADLINE(S): DEC 1
FIELD(S): Automotive Industry, Engineering
ELIGIBILITY/REQUIREMENTS: Applicants must have 3.25 GPA or higher, SAT math 600 or above and verbal 550 or above, composite ACT score 27 or above. Transfer students from accredited 4-year colleges or universities must have a 3.0 or higher GPA. Students or graduates from postsecondary technical/vocational schools must have a 3.5 or higher GPA and must meet all other requirements of the engineering program to which they apply. Students must pursue an engineering degree program accredited by ABET.
HOW TO APPLY: See website for application. Submit application; personal essay that demonstrates hands-on experience or activity (such as rebuilding engines, working on cars/trucks, etc.); 2 recommendations, 1 of which must be from a teacher, counselor, or administrator; and transcript.
NUMBER OF AWARDS: 1
RENEWABLE: Yes. A total of $6,000 (over 4-year period) will be awarded if student maintains a 3.0 GPA and continued enrollment in an engineering program.

976—SOCIETY OF AUTOMOTIVE ENGINEERS (Universidad del Turabo-Puerto Rico/SAE Engineering Scholarship)

SAE Customer Service
400 Commonwealth Drive
Warrendale PA 15096-0001
724/776-4970
FAX: 724/776-1615
E-mail: customerservice@sae.org
Internet: http://www.sae.org/students/scholarships
AMOUNT: $5,000
DEADLINE(S): DEC 1
FIELD(S): Engineering; Automotive Industry
ELIGIBILITY/REQUIREMENTS: Open to incoming freshmen who have been accepted into Electrical, Mechanical, or Industrial program; minimum 1300 SAT score and 3.0 GPA and activities.
HOW TO APPLY: See website for application. Submit application; a personal essay that demonstrates hands-on experience or activity (such as rebuilding engines, working on cars/trucks, etc.); 2 recommendations, 1 of which must be from a teacher, counselor, or administrator; and transcript.
NUMBER OF AWARDS: 2
RENEWABLE: Yes. For 4 or 5 years provided student is enrolled full time in the

Mechanical, Electrical, or Industrial Engineering program and maintains a 3.0 GPA.

977—SOCIETY OF AUTOMOTIVE ENGINEERS (University of Detroit-Mercy/SAE Engineering Scholarship)

SAE Customer Service
400 Commonwealth Drive
Warrendale PA 15096-0001
724/776-4970
FAX: 724/776-1615
E-mail: customerservice@sae.org
Internet: http://www.sae.org/
students/scholarships
AMOUNT: $500
DEADLINE(S): DEC 1
FIELD(S): Engineering; Automotive Industry
ELIGIBILITY/REQUIREMENTS: Must be an incoming freshman or transfer student admitted directly into an engineering program at UDM. Selection based on academic and leadership achievement.
HOW TO APPLY: See website for application. Submit application; a personal essay that demonstrates hands-on experience or activity (such as rebuilding engines, working on cars/trucks, etc.); 2 recommendations, 1 of which must be from a teacher, counselor, or administrator; and transcript.
NUMBER OF AWARDS: 2
RENEWABLE: Yes. For 1 additional year if a 3.0 GPA is maintained and student remains in the engineering program.

978—SOCIETY OF AUTOMOTIVE ENGINEERS (University of Evansville/John R. Tooley/Scholarship)

SAE Customer Service
400 Commonwealth Drive
Warrendale PA 15096-0001
724/776-4970
FAX: 724/776-1615
E-mail: customerservice@sae.org
Internet: http://www.sae.org/
students/scholarships
AMOUNT: $1,000
DEADLINE(S): DEC 1
FIELD(S): Engineering; Automotive Industry
ELIGIBILITY/REQUIREMENTS: Must be an incoming freshman pursuing a degree in the School of Engineering. Scholarships awarded on the basis of academic achievement and involvement in extracurricular

activities. A minimum 1200 SAT or 27 ACT, and 3.5 high school GPA required.
HOW TO APPLY: See website for application. Submit application; a personal essay that demonstrates hands-on experience or activity (such as rebuilding engines, working on cars/trucks, etc.); 2 recommendations, 1 of which must be from a teacher, counselor, or administrator; and transcript.
NUMBER OF AWARDS: 3
RENEWABLE: Yes. For 3 additional years if a cumulative 3.0 GPA is maintained and student remains in the engineering program.

979—SOCIETY OF AUTOMOTIVE ENGINEERS (University of Florida/Dean's Engineering Scholar/SAE Engineering Scholarship)

SAE Customer Service
400 Commonwealth Drive
Warrendale PA 15096-0001
724/776-4970
FAX: 724/776-1615
E-mail: customerservice@sae.org
Internet: http://www.sae.org/
students/scholarships
AMOUNT: $1,000
DEADLINE(S): DEC 1
FIELD(S): Engineering; Automotive Industry
ELIGIBILITY/REQUIREMENTS: Applicant must be an incoming freshman pursuing a degree in the School of Engineering.
HOW TO APPLY: See website for application. Submit application; a personal essay that demonstrates hands-on experience or activity (such as rebuilding engines, working on cars/trucks, etc.); 2 recommendations, 1 of which must be from a teacher, counselor, or administrator; and transcript.
NUMBER OF AWARDS: 1
RENEWABLE: No

980—SOCIETY OF AUTOMOTIVE ENGINEERS (University of Houston/SAE Engineering Scholarship)

SAE Customer Service
400 Commonwealth Drive
Warrendale PA 15096-0001
724/776-4970
FAX: 724/776-1615
E-mail: customerservice@sae.org
Internet: http://www.sae.org/
students/scholarships
AMOUNT: $2,500

DEADLINE(S): DEC 1
FIELD(S): Engineering; Automotive Industry
ELIGIBILITY/REQUIREMENTS: Applicant must be incoming full-time freshman who will major in engineering. Eligible applicants must have a minimum 1300 SAT or 30 ACT, a GPA of 3.25, and be in the top 10% of high school graduating class.
HOW TO APPLY: See website for application. Submit application; a personal essay that demonstrates hands-on experience or activity (such as rebuilding engines, working on cars/trucks, etc.); 2 recommendations, 1 of which must be from a teacher, counselor, or administrator; and transcript.
NUMBER OF AWARDS: 2
RENEWABLE: Yes. Up to 4 years provided a 3.0 GPA and engineering enrollment in 12 credit hours each semester is maintained.

981—SOCIETY OF AUTOMOTIVE ENGINEERS (University of Illinois at Chicago/SAE Engineering Scholarship)

SAE Customer Service
400 Commonwealth Drive
Warrendale PA 15096-0001
724/776-4970
FAX: 724/776-1615
E-mail: customerservice@sae.org
Internet: http://www.sae.org/
students/scholarships
AMOUNT: $1,000
DEADLINE(S): DEC 1
FIELD(S): Engineering; Automotive Industry
ELIGIBILITY/REQUIREMENTS: Applicant must be incoming freshman who will be pursuing a degree in the UIC College of Engineering with an interest in the automotive engineering applications. Selection will be based on ACT scores, high school rank, application essay, outside activities and experiences. A minimum ACT composite score of 29 (SAT 1240) is required to apply.
HOW TO APPLY: See website for application. Submit application; a personal essay that demonstrates hands-on experience or activity (such as rebuilding engines, working on cars/trucks, etc.); 2 recommendations, 1 of which must be from a teacher, counselor, or administrator; and transcript.
NUMBER OF AWARDS: 2 maximum
RENEWABLE: Yes. Up to 4 years and a GPA of 4.0 (out of 5.0) must be maintained.

982—SOCIETY OF AUTOMOTIVE ENGINEERS (University of Pittsburgh/SAE Scholarship)

SAE Customer Service
400 Commonwealth Drive
Warrendale PA 15096-0001
724/776-4970
FAX: 724/776-1615
E-mail: customerservice@sae.org
Internet: http://www.sae.org/
students/scholarships
AMOUNT: $1,000/year
DEADLINE(S): DEC 1
FIELD(S): Engineering
ELIGIBILITY/REQUIREMENTS: Must be a freshman engineering applicant with a 1300 SAT and high class rank in top 10%. Applicant must be a U.S. citizen or permanent resident and must be accepted and matriculate at the Pittsburgh campus.
HOW TO APPLY: See website for application. Complete application; submit 3 recommendation letters (2 from a teacher or school official and 1 from an employer or non-relative); high school and/or college transcript for last 2 years; a 1- to 2-page statement telling why you are applying for the scholarship and educational and career goals in the plastics industry.
NUMBER OF AWARDS: 1
RENEWABLE: Yes. Up to 4 years/8 semesters; 3.0 cumulative GPA required.

983—SOCIETY OF AUTOMOTIVE ENGINEERS (University of South Carolina/ Frank B. Herty/SAE Engineering Scholarship)

SAE Customer Service
400 Commonwealth Drive
Warrendale PA 15096-0001
724/776-4970
FAX: 724/776-1615
E-mail: customerservice@sae.org
Internet: http://www.sae.org/
students/scholarships
AMOUNT: $2,000
DEADLINE(S): DEC 1
FIELD(S): Engineering; Automotive Industry
ELIGIBILITY/REQUIREMENTS: Incoming freshmen who have been accepted into the mechanical engineering program. Selection based on a minimum 1300 SAT score and 3.0 GPA and activities.
HOW TO APPLY: See website for application. Submit application; a personal essay that demonstrates hands-on experience or activity (such as rebuilding engines, working on cars/trucks, etc.); 2 recommendations, 1 of which must be from

a teacher, counselor, or administrator; and transcript.
NUMBER OF AWARDS: 1
RENEWABLE: Yes. For 3 additional years provided student is enrolled full time in the mechanical engineering program and maintains a minimum 3.0 GPA.

984—SOCIETY OF AUTOMOTIVE ENGINEERS (University of Tennessee at Chattanooga/Chancellor's Scholarship/ SAE Engineering Scholarship)

SAE Customer Service
400 Commonwealth Drive
Warrendale PA 15096-0001
724/776-4970
FAX: 724/776-1615
E-mail: customerservice@sae.org
Internet: http://www.sae.org/
students/scholarships
AMOUNT: $6,000
DEADLINE(S): DEC 1
FIELD(S): Engineering; Automotive Industry
ELIGIBILITY/REQUIREMENTS: Eligible to incoming freshmen with a minimum 30 ACT or 1320 SAT score; GPA of 3.75. Must be fully admitted to the university by February 1 of the student's senior year in high school and pursue an engineering major.
HOW TO APPLY: See website for application. Submit application; a personal essay that demonstrates hands-on experience or activity (such as rebuilding engines, working on cars/trucks, etc.); 2 recommendations, 1 of which must be from a teacher, counselor, or administrator; and transcript.
NUMBER OF AWARDS: Up to 10
RENEWABLE: Yes. For total of 4 years provided student maintains a minimum 3.5 GPA.

985—SOCIETY OF AUTOMOTIVE ENGINEERS (University of Tennessee at Chattanooga/Provost Scholarship/SAE Engineering Scholarship)

SAE Customer Service
400 Commonwealth Drive
Warrendale PA 15096-0001
724/776-4970
FAX: 724/776-1615
E-mail: customerservice@sae.org
Internet: http://www.sae.org/
students/scholarships
AMOUNT: $4,500
DEADLINE(S): DEC 1
FIELD(S): Engineering; Automotive Industry

ELIGIBILITY/REQUIREMENTS: Eligible to incoming freshmen with a minimum 26 ACT or 1170 SAT score; GPA of 3.5. Must be fully admitted to the university by February 1 of the student's senior year in high school and pursue an engineering major.
HOW TO APPLY: See website for application. Submit application; a personal essay that demonstrates hands-on experience or activity (such as rebuilding engines, working on cars/trucks, etc.); 2 recommendations, 1 of which must be from a teacher, counselor, or administrator; and transcript.
NUMBER OF AWARDS: Up to 25
RENEWABLE: Yes. For total of 4 years provided student maintains a minimum 3.5 GPA.

986—SOCIETY OF AUTOMOTIVE ENGINEERS (University of Texas-Austin/ SAE Scholarship)

SAE Customer Service
400 Commonwealth Drive
Warrendale PA 15096-0001
724/776-4970
FAX: 724/776-1615
E-mail: customerservice@sae.org
Internet: http://www.sae.org/
students/scholarships
AMOUNT: $3,000
DEADLINE(S): DEC 1
FIELD(S): Engineering
ELIGIBILITY/REQUIREMENTS: Selection is based on high school grades and SAT (1350 minimum) or ACT (31 minimum) scores. Recipients must be admitted to School of Engineering. Must maintain GPA of 3.25 for renewal.
HOW TO APPLY: See website for application. Submit application; a personal essay that demonstrates hands-on experience or activity (such as rebuilding engines, working on cars/trucks, etc.); 2 recommendations, 1 of which must be from a teacher, counselor, or administrator; and transcript. In addition, SAT/ACT scores must be sent to University of Texas by February 1.
NUMBER OF AWARDS: 2
RENEWABLE: Yes. Up to 3 years; must maintain a minimum GPA of 3.5.

987—SOCIETY OF AUTOMOTIVE ENGINEERS (University of Toledo/SAE Scholarship)

SAE Customer Service
400 Commonwealth Drive
Warrendale PA 15096-0001
724/776-4970

FAX: 724/776-1615
E-mail: customerservice@sae.org
Internet: http://www.sae.org/
students/scholarships
AMOUNT: $1,000
DEADLINE(S): DEC 1
FIELD(S): Engineering
ELIGIBILITY/REQUIREMENTS:
Applicants must be incoming freshmen who have been accepted into College of Engineering. Must be U.S. citizen.
HOW TO APPLY: See website for application. Submit application; a personal essay that demonstrates hands-on experience or activity (such as rebuilding engines, working on cars/trucks, etc.); 2 recommendations, 1 of which must be from a teacher, counselor, or administrator; and transcript.
NUMBER OF AWARDS: 1
RENEWABLE: Yes. For up to 3 additional years contingent upon maintaining 3.0 cumulative GPA.
CONTACT: University of Toledo, Office of Admissions, 2802 West Bancroft, Toledo, OH 43606 or call 800/5TOLEDO.

988—SOCIETY OF AUTOMOTIVE ENGINEERS (Wayne State University/College of Engineering/Dean's/SAE Scholarship)

SAE Customer Service
400 Commonwealth Drive
Warrendale PA 15096-0001
724/776-4970
FAX: 724/776-1615
E-mail: customerservice@sae.org
Internet: http://www.sae.org/
students/scholarships
AMOUNT: $1,500
DEADLINE(S): DEC 1
FIELD(S): Engineering; Computer Science
ELIGIBILITY/REQUIREMENTS: For high school seniors and/or transfer students, must have 3.5 GPA, must be pursuing a degree in the College of Engineering, and maintain full-time enrollment status. Must be a U.S. citizen. Selection also based on ACT/SAT scores. Award is based solely on merit, NOT financial need.
HOW TO APPLY: See website for application. Submit application; a personal essay that demonstrates hands-on experience or activity (such as rebuilding engines, working on cars/trucks, etc.); 2 recommendations, 1 of which must be from a teacher, counselor, or administrator; and transcript. Students must also apply to the university by February 28.
NUMBER OF AWARDS: 1

RENEWABLE: Yes. Up to 4 years; must reapply. Student must be enrolled as a full-time student each of the academic year terms (minimum of 12 credit hours each semester) completing a minimum of 24 credits each year that count toward degree requirements of the engineering program, must maintain a grade of "C" or better in each course, and all courses toward engineering degree must be taken at WSU. Minimum cumulative GPA of 3.0.
CONTACT: Dr. Gerald Thompkins, assistant Dean of Student Affairs, Wayne State University, College of Engineering, 5050 Anthony Wayne Drive, Detroit, MI 48202 or call 313/577-3780.

989—SOCIETY OF AUTOMOTIVE ENGINEERS (Washington University/SAE Scholarship)

SAE Customer Service
400 Commonwealth Drive
Warrendale PA 15096-0001
724/776-4970
FAX: 724/776-1615
E-mail: customerservice@sae.org
Internet: http://www.sae.org/
students/scholarships
AMOUNT: $3,000
DEADLINE(S): DEC 1
FIELD(S): Engineering
ELIGIBILITY/REQUIREMENTS: Must be incoming freshmen to the School of Engineering and Applied Science. Selection will be based on demonstrated academic achievement and leadership ability, contribution to school and community, and potential for professional achievement.
HOW TO APPLY: See website for application. Submit application; a personal essay that demonstrates hands-on experience or activity (such as rebuilding engines, working on cars/trucks, etc.); 2 recommendations, 1 of which must be from a teacher, counselor, or administrator; and transcript.
NUMBER OF AWARDS: 3
RENEWABLE: Yes. Up to 4 years of undergraduate study; if later admitted to a 5-year BS/MS program, scholarship will be extended for additional year.

990—SOCIETY OF AUTOMOTIVE ENGINEERS (Western Michigan University/SAE Scholarship)

SAE Customer Service
400 Commonwealth Drive
Warrendale PA 15096-0001
724/776-4970

FAX: 724/776-1615
E-mail: customerservice@sae.org
Internet: http://www.sae.org/
students/scholarships
AMOUNT: $1,000
DEADLINE(S): DEC 1
FIELD(S): Engineering; Engineering Technology
ELIGIBILITY/REQUIREMENTS:
Applicants must be residents of Michigan. The top 2 candidates from the pool will be awarded a scholarship based on appropriateness of high school courses to preparation for engineering technology education, admission GPA and ACT scores.
HOW TO APPLY: See website for application. Submit application; a personal essay that demonstrates hands-on experience or activity (such as rebuilding engines, working on cars/trucks, etc.); 2 recommendations, 1 of which must be from a teacher, counselor, or administrator; and transcript.
NUMBER OF AWARDS: 2
RENEWABLE: Yes. For 3 additional years; recipient must maintain 2.5 GPA.

991—SOCIETY OF AUTOMOTIVE ENGINEERS (Whitworth College/SAE Engineering Scholarship)

SAE Customer Service
400 Commonwealth Drive
Warrendale PA 15096-0001
724/776-4970
FAX: 724/776-1615
E-mail: customerservice@sae.org
Internet: http://www.sae.org/
students/scholarships
AMOUNT: $500/semester
DEADLINE(S): DEC 1
FIELD(S): Engineering; Science; Automotive Industry
ELIGIBILITY/REQUIREMENTS: Open to incoming freshmen or transfer students who plan to major in science or engineering and have a minimum 1200 SAT or 2.7 ACT score and 3.6 GPA.
HOW TO APPLY: See website for application. Submit application; a personal essay that demonstrates hands-on experience or activity (such as rebuilding engines, working on cars/trucks, etc.); 2 recommendations, 1 of which must be from a teacher, counselor, or administrator; and transcript.
NUMBER OF AWARDS: 1
RENEWABLE: Yes. Up to 8 semesters provided student is enrolled full time in a science or pre-engineering major program and maintains a 3.0 GPA.

992—SOCIETY OF AUTOMOTIVE ENGINEERS (Wichita State University/SAE Scholarship)

SAE Customer Service
400 Commonwealth Drive
Warrendale PA 15096-0001
724/776-4970
FAX: 724/776-1615
E-mail: customerservice@sae.org
Internet: http://www.sae.org/students/scholarships
AMOUNT: $2,000
DEADLINE(S): DEC 1
FIELD(S): Engineering; Automotive Industry
ELIGIBILITY/REQUIREMENTS: Applicants must be incoming freshmen majoring in engineering. Selection based on academic and leadership achievement.
HOW TO APPLY: Submit application; a personal essay that demonstrates hands-on experience or activity (such as rebuilding engines, working on cars/trucks, etc.); 2 recommendations, 1 of which must be from a teacher, counselor, or administrator; and transcript.
NUMBER OF AWARDS: 1
RENEWABLE: Yes. Up to 3 additional years; must maintain 3.0 GPA and demonstrate continued progress toward an engineering degree with a minimum 12-hour enrollment.

993—SOCIETY OF AUTOMOTIVE ENGINEERS (Wright State University/SAE Scholarship)

SAE Customer Service
400 Commonwealth Drive
Warrendale PA 15096-0001
724/776-4970
FAX: 724/776-1615
E-mail: customerservice@sae.org
Internet: http://www.sae.org/students/scholarships
AMOUNT: $1,000
DEADLINE(S): DEC 1
FIELD(S): Engineering; Computer Science
ELIGIBILITY/REQUIREMENTS: Applicants must be freshmen in any engineering program. Award based on scholarship and achievement.
HOW TO APPLY: See website for application. Submit application; a personal essay that demonstrates hands-on experience or activity (such as rebuilding engines, working on cars/trucks, etc.); 2 recommendations, 1 of which must be from a teacher, counselor, or administrator; and transcript.

NUMBER OF AWARDS: 1
RENEWABLE: No

994—SOCIETY OF DESIGN ADMINISTRATION, THE (ProNet Scholarship)

The Spector Group
311 New Hyde Park Road
North Hills NY 11040
516/365-4240
FAX: 516/365-3604
AMOUNT: $800-$1,500
DEADLINE(S): MAR 1
FIELD(S): Architecture; Engineering
ELIGIBILITY/REQUIREMENTS: Applicants must demonstrate an interest in practice management studies in their education programs, as this scholarship is intended to promote the education and training of design firm administrators.
HOW TO APPLY: Send completed application.
CONTACT: Patricia A. Manfre-Staab

995—SOCIETY OF PETROLEUM ENGINEERS (Gus Archie Memorial Scholarship)

P.O. Box 833836
Richardson TX 75083-3836
972/952-9315
FAX: 972/952-9393
Internet: http://www.spe.org
AMOUNT: $6,000/year (4 years)
DEADLINE(S): MAY
FIELD(S): Petroleum Engineering
ELIGIBILITY/REQUIREMENTS: Open to students pursuing petroleum engineering degree with 3.0 GPA; 1800 minimum SAT (or 27 ACT) score for US residents; other academic evidence for non-US applicants. (Non-U.S. applicants should provide exit examination or placement scores with documentation explaining how to interpret the score.
HOW TO APPLY: Submit application to any section of the SPE or apply directly to the Student Activities Manager at address above along with statement by student that it is his/her intent to enroll in petroleum engineering in an accredited school, appraisal of student from principal, adviser or counselor.
NUMBER OF AWARDS: 1-2
RENEWABLE: Yes

996—SOCIETY OF HISPANIC PROFESSIONAL ENGINEERS (SHPE)

University of Texas at Arlington
Box 19019

SHPE AHETEMS, Inc.
Arlington TX 76019
817/272-1116
FAX: 817/272-2548
Internet: http://www.shpe.org
AMOUNT: $1,000-$3,000
DEADLINE(S): APR 1
FIELD(S): Engineering; Science
ELIGIBILITY/REQUIREMENTS: Applicants must be Hispanic undergraduate or graduate students or graduating high school seniors interested in studying engineering or science with 3.0 GPA for undergraduates and 3.2 GPA for graduate students.
HOW TO APPLY: See website for application or contact Rafaela Schwan
RENEWABLE: Yes. Must reapply.
CONTACT: Rafaela Schwan

997—SOCIETY OF WOMEN ENGINEERS (3M Company Scholarships)

120 Wall Street, 11th Floor
New York NY 10005-3902
800/666-ISWE or 212/509-9577
FAX: 212/509-0224
E-mail: hq@swe.org
Internet: http://www.swe.org
AMOUNT: $1,050
DEADLINE(S): MAY 15
FIELD(S): Engineering
ELIGIBILITY/REQUIREMENTS: Open to women who are entering freshmen in a college or university with an ABET-accredited program or in a SWE-approved school. Must be U.S. citizen. Preference is given to chemical, electrical, industrial, and mechanical engineering majors.
HOW TO APPLY: Send SASE to SWE for an application.
NUMBER OF AWARDS: 3

998—SOCIETY OF WOMEN ENGINEERS (Anne Maureen Whitney Barrow Memorial Scholarship)

120 Wall Street, 11th Floor
New York NY 10005-3902
800/666-ISWE or 212/509-9577
FAX: 212/509-0224
E-mail: hq@swe.org
Internet: http://www.swe.org
AMOUNT: $5,000
DEADLINE(S): MAY 15
FIELD(S): Engineering
ELIGIBILITY/REQUIREMENTS: Open to incoming freshmen women in a college or university with an ABET-accredited program or in a SWE-approved school.
HOW TO APPLY: Send SASE to SWE for an application.

NUMBER OF AWARDS: 1
RENEWABLE: Yes. Up to 3 years.

999—SOCIETY OF WOMEN ENGINEERS (B. K. Krenzer Memorial Re-entry Scholarship)

120 Wall Street, 11th Floor
New York NY 10005-3902
800/666-ISWE or 212/509-9577
FAX: 212/509-0224
E-mail: hq@swe.org
Internet: http://www.swe.org
AMOUNT: $1,000
DEADLINE(S): MAY 15
FIELD(S): Engineering; Computer Science

ELIGIBILITY/REQUIREMENTS: For women who have been out of the engineering job market as well as out of school for a minimum of 2 years. For any year undergraduate or graduate study, full- or part-time, at a college or university with an ABET-accredited program or in a SWE-approved school. Must have a minimum 3.5 GPA. Preference is given to degreed engineers desiring to return to the workforce following a period of temporary retirement.
HOW TO APPLY: Send SASE to SWE for an application.
NUMBER OF AWARDS: 1

1000—SOCIETY OF WOMEN ENGINEERS (Central Intelligence Agency Scholarship)

120 Wall Street, 11th Floor
New York NY 10005-3902
800/666-ISWE or 212/509-9577
FAX: 212/509-0224
E-mail: hq@swe.org
Internet: http://www.swe.org
AMOUNT: $1,000
DEADLINE(S): FEB 1
FIELD(S): Electrical Engineering; Computer Science

ELIGIBILITY/REQUIREMENTS: Open to entering sophomores at a college or university with an ABET-accredited program or in a SWE-approved school. Must have a minimum 3.5 GPA and be a U.S. citizen.
HOW TO APPLY: Send SASE to SWE for an application.
NUMBER OF AWARDS: 1

1001—SOCIETY OF WOMEN ENGINEERS (Chrysler Corporation Re-entry Scholarship)

120 Wall Street, 11th Floor
New York NY 10005-3902
800/666-ISWE or 212/509-9577

FAX: 212/509-0224
E-mail: hq@swe.org
Internet: http://www.swe.org
AMOUNT: $2,000
DEADLINE(S): MAY 15
FIELD(S): Engineering; Computer Science

ELIGIBILITY/REQUIREMENTS: For women who have been out of the engineering job market as well as out of school for a minimum of 2 years. For any level of study at a college or university with an ABET-accredited program or in a SWE-approved school. Must have a minimum 3.5 GPA.
HOW TO APPLY: Send SASE to SWE for an application.
NUMBER OF AWARDS: 1

1002—SOCIETY OF WOMEN ENGINEERS (Chrysler Corporation Scholarships)

120 Wall Street, 11th Floor
New York NY 10005-3902
800/666-ISWE or 212/509-9577
FAX: 212/509-0224
E-mail: hq@swe.org
Internet: http://www.swe.org
AMOUNT: $1,500
DEADLINE(S): MAY 15
FIELD(S): Engineering; Computer Science

ELIGIBILITY/REQUIREMENTS: Open to entering female freshmen in a college or university with an ABET-accredited program or in a SWE-approved school.
HOW TO APPLY: Send SASE to SWE for an application.
NUMBER OF AWARDS: 2

1003—SOCIETY OF WOMEN ENGINEERS (Chrysler Corporation Scholarship)

120 Wall Street, 11th Floor
New York NY 10005-3902
800/666-ISWE or 212/509-9577
FAX: 212/509-0224
E-mail: hq@swe.org
Internet: http://www.swe.org
AMOUNT: $1,750
DEADLINE(S): FEB 1
FIELD(S): Engineering; Computer Science

ELIGIBILITY/REQUIREMENTS: Open to women who are entering sophomores, juniors, or seniors in a college or university with an ABET-accredited program or in a SWE-approved school. Must be a member of an underrepresented group in the engineering or computer science field. Must have a minimum 3.5 GPA.

HOW TO APPLY: Send SASE to SWE for an application.
NUMBER OF AWARDS: 1

1004—SOCIETY OF WOMEN ENGINEERS (Chevron Scholarships)

120 Wall Street, 11th Floor
New York NY 10005-3902
800/666-ISWE or 212/509-9577
FAX: 212/509-0224
E-mail: hq@swe.org
Internet: http://www.swe.org
AMOUNT: $2,000
DEADLINE(S): FEB 1
FIELD(S): Chemical, Civil, and Petroleum Engineering

ELIGIBILITY/REQUIREMENTS: Open to entering sophomores and juniors at a college or university with an ABET-accredited program or in a SWE-approved school. Must have a minimum 3.5 GPA and be majoring in one of the above fields.
HOW TO APPLY: Send SASE to SWE for an application.
NUMBER OF AWARDS: 2

1005—SOCIETY OF WOMEN ENGINEERS (David Sarnoff Research Center Scholarship)

120 Wall Street, 11th Floor
New York NY 10005-3902
800/666-ISWE or 212/509-9577
FAX: 212/509-0224
E-mail: hq@swe.org
Internet: http://www.swe.org
AMOUNT: $1,500
DEADLINE(S): FEB 1
FIELD(S): Engineering; Computer Science

ELIGIBILITY/REQUIREMENTS: Open to women who are entering juniors at a college or university with an ABET-accredited program or in a SWE-approved school. Must have a minimum 3.5 GPA and be a U.S. citizen.
HOW TO APPLY: Send SASE to SWE for an application.
NUMBER OF AWARDS: 1

1006—SOCIETY OF WOMEN ENGINEERS (GTE Foundation Scholarships)

120 Wall Street, 11th Floor
New York NY 10005-3902
800/666-ISWE or 212/509-9577
FAX: 212/509-0224
E-mail: hq@swe.org
Internet: http://www.swe.org
AMOUNT: $1,000
DEADLINE(S): FEB 1

FIELD(S): Electrical Engineering;
Computer Science

ELIGIBILITY/REQUIREMENTS: Open to entering sophomore or junior women at a college or university with an ABET-accredited program or in a SWE-approved school. Must have a minimum 3.5 GPA.

HOW TO APPLY: Send SASE to SWE for an application.

NUMBER OF AWARDS: 9

1007—SOCIETY OF WOMEN ENGINEERS (General Motors Foundation Scholarships)

120 Wall Street, 11th Floor
New York NY 10005-3902
800/666-ISWE or 212/509-9577
FAX: 212/509-0224
E-mail: hq@swe.org
Internet: http://www.swe.org

AMOUNT: $1,500 + $500 travel grant

DEADLINE(S): FEB 1

FIELD(S): Engineering: Mechanical, Electrical, Chemical, Industrial, Materials, Automotive, Manufacturing, Technology

ELIGIBILITY/REQUIREMENTS: For women entering as juniors at a college or university with ABET-accredited program or in SWE-approved school. Must exhibit career interest in automotive industry or manufacturing environment. Must have minimum 3.5 GPA and demonstrate leadership by holding position of responsibility in student organization. Travel grant available to recipients to attend SWE National Convention and Student Conference.

HOW TO APPLY: Send SASE to SWE for application.

NUMBER OF AWARDS: 2

RENEWABLE: Yes, Senior year

1008—SOCIETY OF WOMEN ENGINEERS (Ivy Parker Memorial Scholarship)

120 Wall Street, 11th Floor
New York NY 10005-3902
800/666-ISWE or 212/509-9577
FAX: 212/509-0224
E-mail: hq@swe.org
Internet: http://www.swe.org

AMOUNT: $2,000

DEADLINE(S): FEB 1

FIELD(S): Engineering; Computer Science

ELIGIBILITY/REQUIREMENTS: Open to women who are entering sophomores or juniors at a college or university with an ABET-accredited program or in a SWE-approved school. Must have a minimum 3.5 GPA and demonstrate financial need.

HOW TO APPLY: Send SASE to SWE for an application.

NUMBER OF AWARDS: 1

1009—SOCIETY OF WOMEN ENGINEERS (Judith Resnick Memorial Scholarship)

120 Wall Street, 11th Floor
New York NY 10005-3902
800/666-ISWE or 212/509-9577
FAX: 212/509-0224
E-mail: hq@swe.org
Internet: http://www.swe.org

AMOUNT: $2,000

DEADLINE(S): FEB 1

FIELD(S): Aerospace; Aeronautical/Astronautical Engineering

ELIGIBILITY/REQUIREMENTS: Open to women who are entering seniors at a college or university with an ABET-accredited program or in a SWE-approved school. Must have a minimum 3.5 GPA and be an active SWE Student Member. This award is in memory of astronaut Judith Resnik, who lost her life aboard the space shuttle Challenger.

HOW TO APPLY: Send SASE to SWE for an application.

NUMBER OF AWARDS: 1

1010—SOCIETY OF WOMEN ENGINEERS (Lillian Moller Gilbreth Scholarship)

120 Wall Street, 11th Floor
New York NY 10005-3902
800/666-ISWE or 212/509-9577
FAX: 212/509-0224
E-mail: hq@swe.org
Internet: http://www.swe.org

AMOUNT: $5,000

DEADLINE(S): FEB 1

FIELD(S): Engineering; Computer Science

ELIGIBILITY/REQUIREMENTS: Open to women who are entering juniors or seniors at a college or university with an ABET-accredited program or in a SWE-approved school. Must have a minimum 3.5 GPA and demonstrate outstanding achievement and potential.

HOW TO APPLY: Send SASE to SWE for an application.

NUMBER OF AWARDS: 1

1011—SOCIETY OF WOMEN ENGINEERS (Lockheed-Martin Fort Worth Scholarships)

120 Wall Street, 11th Floor
New York NY 10005-3902
800/666-ISWE or 212/509-9577
FAX: 212/509-0224
E-mail: hq@swe.org
Internet: http://www.swe.org

AMOUNT: $3,000

DEADLINE(S): MAY 15

FIELD(S): Engineering

ELIGIBILITY/REQUIREMENTS: Open to entering freshmen women in a college or university with an ABET-accredited program or in a SWE-approved school.

HOW TO APPLY: Send SASE to SWE for an application.

NUMBER OF AWARDS: 2

1012—SOCIETY OF WOMEN ENGINEERS (Lockheed-Martin Fort Worth Scholarships)

120 Wall Street, 11th Floor
New York NY 10005-3902
800/666-ISWE or 212/509-9577
FAX: 212/509-0224
E-mail: hq@swe.org
Internet: http://www.swe.org

AMOUNT: $1,000

DEADLINE(S): FEB 1

FIELD(S): Electrical and Mechanical Engineering

ELIGIBILITY/REQUIREMENTS: Open to women who are entering juniors at a college or university with an ABET-accredited program or in a SWE-approved school. Must have a minimum 3.5 GPA.

HOW TO APPLY: Send SASE to SWE for an application.

NUMBER OF AWARDS: 2

1013—SOCIETY OF WOMEN ENGINEERS (MASWE Memorial Scholarships)

120 Wall Street, 11th Floor
New York NY 10005-3902
800/666-ISWE or 212/509-9577
FAX: 212/509-0224
E-mail: hq@swe.org
Internet: http://www.swe.org

AMOUNT: $1,000-$2,000

DEADLINE(S): FEB 1

FIELD(S): Engineering; Computer Science

ELIGIBILITY/REQUIREMENTS: Open to women who are entering sophomores, juniors, or seniors at a college or university with an ABET-accredited program or in a SWE-approved school. Must have a minimum 3.5 GPA, show outstanding scholarship, and demonstrate financial need.

HOW TO APPLY: Send SASE to SWE for an application. Recipients are notified in May.

NUMBER OF AWARDS: 3

1014—SOCIETY OF WOMEN ENGINEERS (Northrop Corporation Founders Scholarship)

120 Wall Street, 11th Floor
New York NY 10005-3902
800/666-ISWE or 212/509-9577
FAX: 212/509-0224
E-mail: hq@swe.org
Internet: http://www.swe.org
AMOUNT: $1,000
DEADLINE(S): FEB 1
FIELD(S): Engineering
ELIGIBILITY/REQUIREMENTS: Open to entering sophomore women at a college or university with an ABET-accredited program or in a SWE-approved school. Must have a minimum 3.5 GPA, be a U.S. citizen, and a current SWE Student Member.
HOW TO APPLY: Send SASE to SWE for an application.
NUMBER OF AWARDS: 1

1015—SOCIETY OF WOMEN ENGINEERS (Northrop Grumman Scholarships)

120 Wall Street, 11th Floor
New York NY 10005-3902
800/666-ISWE or 212/509-9577
FAX: 212/509-0224
E-mail: hq@swe.org
Internet: http://www.swe.org
AMOUNT: $1,000-$1,500
DEADLINE(S): MAY 15
FIELD(S): Engineering; Computer Science
ELIGIBILITY/REQUIREMENTS: Open to women who are entering freshmen in a college or university with an ABET-accredited program or in a SWE-approved school.
HOW TO APPLY: Send SASE to SWE for an application. Recipients are notified in September.
NUMBER OF AWARDS: 3

1016—SOCIETY OF WOMEN ENGINEERS (Olive Lynn Salembier Scholarship)

120 Wall Street, 11th Floor
New York NY 10005-3902
800/666-ISWE or 212/509-9577
FAX: 212/509-0224
E-mail: hq@swe.org
Internet: http://www.swe.org
AMOUNT: $2,000
DEADLINE(S): MAY 15
FIELD(S): Engineering; Computer Science
ELIGIBILITY/REQUIREMENTS: For women who have been out of the engineering job market as well as out of school for a minimum of 2 years. For any year undergraduate or graduate study, full- or part-time, at a college or university with an ABET-accredited program or in a SWE-approved school. Must have a minimum 3.5 GPA.
HOW TO APPLY: Send SASE to SWE for an application.
NUMBER OF AWARDS: 1

1017—SOCIETY OF WOMEN ENGINEERS (Rockwell Corporation Scholarships)

120 Wall Street, 11th Floor
New York NY 10005-3902
800/666-ISWE or 212/509-9577
FAX: 212/509-0224
E-mail: hq@swe.org
Internet: http://www.swe.org
AMOUNT: $3,000
DEADLINE(S): FEB 1
FIELD(S): Engineering; Computer Science
ELIGIBILITY/REQUIREMENTS: Open to minority women who are entering juniors at a college or university with an ABET-accredited program or in a SWE-approved school. Must demonstrate leadership ability and have a minimum 3.5 GPA.
HOW TO APPLY: Send SASE to SWE for an application.
NUMBER OF AWARDS: 2

1018—SOCIETY OF WOMEN ENGINEERS (Stone and Webster Scholarships)

120 Wall Street, 11th Floor
New York NY 10005-3902
800/666-ISWE or 212/509-9577
FAX: 212/509-0224
E-mail: hq@swe.org
Internet: http://www.swe.org
AMOUNT: $1,000-$1,500
DEADLINE(S): FEB 1
FIELD(S): Engineering; Computer Science
ELIGIBILITY/REQUIREMENTS: Open to women who are entering sophomores, juniors, or seniors at a college or university with an ABET-accredited program or in a SWE-approved school. Must have a minimum 3.5 GPA.
HOW TO APPLY: Send SASE to SWE for an application.
NUMBER OF AWARDS: 4

1019—SOUTH CAROLINA SPACE GRANT CONSORTIUM/SOUTH CAROLINA SEA GRANT CONSORTIUM (Kathryn D. Sullivan Science and Engineering Fellowship)

66 George Street
College of Charleston
Charleston SC 29424
843/953-5463
FAX: 843/953-5446
E-mail: scozzarot@cofc.edu
Internet: http://www.cofu.edu/ ~scs.grant
AMOUNT: $7,000 (maximum)
DEADLINE(S): End of JAN; check application for actual deadline date
FIELD(S): Science; Engineering
ELIGIBILITY/REQUIREMENTS: Must be entering senior year at 4-year college or university and a citizen of the U.S. Must be sponsored by a faculty advisor. Selection will be based on academic qualifications; 2 letters of recommendation; description of past activities, current interests, and future plans concerning natural science-related and engineering-related studies.
HOW TO APPLY: See website for additional information.
NUMBER OF AWARDS: 1
RENEWABLE: No
CONTACT: Tara B. Scozzaro

1020—TAU BETA PI ASSOCIATION, INC. (Undergraduate Scholarships)

P.O. Box 2697
Knoxville TN 37901-2697
423/546-4578
AMOUNT: $2,000
DEADLINE(S): JAN 15
FIELD(S): Engineering
ELIGIBILITY/REQUIREMENTS: For members of Tau Beta Pi to use for their senior year of full-time undergraduate study. Membership is not by application; only by collegiate chapter invitation and initiation. Reference letters are required to apply for scholarship.
HOW TO APPLY: Write for complete information.
NUMBER OF AWARDS: 9
RENEWABLE: No

1021—TEXAS SOCIETY OF PROFESSIONAL ENGINEERS

Austin TX 78768
512/472-9286 or 800/580-8973
Internet: http://www.tspe.org
AMOUNT: Varies
DEADLINE(S): JAN 30

FIELD(S): Engineering, Mathematics, Sciences

ELIGIBILITY/REQUIREMENTS: Scholarships for graduating high school seniors who are Texas residents planning to attend Texas engineering colleges.

HOW TO APPLY: Contact organization for details. Application is on website.

1022—TAPPI CORRUGATED CONTAINERS DIVISION SCHOLARSHIP

P.O. Box 105113
Atlanta GA 30092
770/446-1400
FAX: 770/446-6947
E-mail: vedmondson@tappi.org
Internet: http://www.tappi.org
AMOUNT: $1,000-$2,000
DEADLINE(S): JAN 31
FIELD(S): Engineering; Science; Paper Industry

ELIGIBILITY/REQUIREMENTS: Candidates must be an undergraduate or currently employed in the corrugated container, pulp, and paper industry. Must be able to demonstrate significant interest in the corrugated container segment of paper industry, and must be attending college full time or working in the box business and attending night school, be a junior or senior in the upcoming school year, maintain a GPA of 3.0 or higher, and be recommended and endorsed by an instructor or faculty member.

HOW TO APPLY: Contact TAPPI or see website for an application and additional information. Submit application along with transcript, letter of recommendation from faculty member, and at least 2 additional letters of recommendation from persons familiar with the applicant's character, educational accomplishments, school activities, and leadership roles, and likelihood of success in the pulp and paper industry.

NUMBER OF AWARDS: Multiple (4, $2,000; several, $1,000)

CONTACT: Veranda Edmondson, 770/208-7536

1023—TAPPI ENGINEERING DIVISION SCHOLARSHIP

P.O. Box 105113
Atlanta GA 30092
770/446-1400
FAX: 770/446-6947
E-mail: vedmondson@tappi.org
Internet: http://www.tappi.org
AMOUNT: $2,500
DEADLINE(S): JAN 31

FIELD(S): Engineering; Science; Paper Industry

ELIGIBILITY/REQUIREMENTS: Candidates must be an undergraduate member of a TAPPI Student Chapter, or submit comparable evidence of professional development and participation relative to the paper industry, and must meet the following criteria: enrolled in an engineering or science program, attending college full time; be an upcoming junior or senior, maintaining a GPA of 3.0 or higher, and able to demonstrate a significant interest in the pulp and paper industry.

HOW TO APPLY: Contact TAPPI or see website for an application and additional information. Submit application along with transcript, letter of recommendation from the TAPPI Student Chapter's Faculty Advisor or equivalent (faculty instructor), and 2 additional letters of recommendation from persons familiar with the applicant's character, accomplishments, and likelihood of success in the pulp and paper industry.

NUMBER OF AWARDS: Up to 2 (1 to junior, 1 to senior).

RENEWABLE: Yes, must reapply.

CONTACT: Veranda Edmondson, 770/208-7536

1024—TAPPI FINISHING AND CONVERTING DIVISION (Paul Smith Scholarship Award)

P.O. Box 105113
Atlanta GA 30092
770/446-1400
FAX: 770/446-6947
E-mail: vedmondson@tappi.org
Internet: http://www.tappi.org
AMOUNT: $1,000
DEADLINE(S): JAN 31
FIELD(S): Science; Engineering; Technology; Paper Industry

ELIGIBILITY/REQUIREMENTS: Applicant must be enrolled as a full-time student in a state-accredited undergraduate college program; must have a GPA of 3.0 or its equivalent, must be in a program preparatory to a career in the nonwovens industry or demonstrate an interest in the areas covered by TAPPI's Nonwovens Division. Must be recommended and endorsed by an instructor or faculty member.

HOW TO APPLY: See website or contact TAPPI for applications. Submit application along with transcript, 3 letters of recommendation from persons familiar with the applicant's character, academic and extracurricular accomplishments, etc. Interview may be requested.

NUMBER OF AWARDS: Multiple

RENEWABLE: Yes. Must reapply but not in consecutive years.

CONTACT: Veranda Edmondson, 770/208-7536

1025—TAPPI NONWOVENS DIVISION SCHOLARSHIP AWARD

P.O. Box 105113
Atlanta GA 30092
770/446-1400
FAX: 770/446-6947
E-mail: vedmondson@tappi.org
Internet: http://www.tappi.org
AMOUNT: $1,000
DEADLINE(S): JAN 31
FIELD(S): Science; Engineering; Paper Industry

ELIGIBILITY/REQUIREMENTS: Applicant must be enrolled as a full-time student in a state-accredited undergraduate college program; must have a GPA of 3.0 or its equivalent, must be in a program preparatory to a career in the nonwovens industry or demonstrate an interest in the areas covered by TAPPI's Nonwovens Division. Must be recommended and endorsed by an instructor or faculty member.

HOW TO APPLY: See website or contact TAPPI for applications. Submit application along with transcript, 3 letters of recommendation from persons familiar with the applicant's character, academic and extracurricular accomplishments, etc. Interview may be requested.

NUMBER OF AWARDS: Multiple

RENEWABLE: Yes. Must reapply but not in consecutive years.

CONTACT: Veranda Edmondson, 770/208-7536

1026—TAPPI PAPER AND BOARD DIVISION SCHOLARSHIP PROGRAM

P.O. Box 105113
Atlanta GA 30092
770/446-1400
FAX: 770/446-6947
E-mail: vedmondson@tappi.org
Internet: http://www.tappi.org
AMOUNT: $1,000
DEADLINE(S): JAN 31
FIELD(S): Science; Engineering; Paper Industry

ELIGIBILITY/REQUIREMENTS: Applicant must be a TAPPI student member or an undergraduate member of a TAPPI chapter; enrolled as a college or university undergraduate in an engineering or science program; a full-time student or a full-time participant in a cooperative work-study program recognized and supported by the educational institution; a sophomore, junior or senior in the fall semester, and able to show a significant interest in the paper industry.

HOW TO APPLY: See website or contact TAPPI for applications. Submit application along with transcript, a personal statement regarding career goals and personal objectives, letter of recommendation from faculty member, and 2 letters of recommendation from persons familiar with the applicant's character, academic and extracurricular accomplishments, etc. Interview may be requested.

NUMBER OF AWARDS: Multiple

RENEWABLE: Yes. Must reapply but not in consecutive years.

CONTACT: Veranda Edmondson, 770/208-7536

1027—TAPPI PULP MANUFACTURE DIVISION (High Impact Award Scholarship)

P.O. Box 105113
Atlanta GA 30092
770/446-1400
FAX: 770/446-6947
E-mail: vedmondson@tappi.org
Internet: http://www.tappi.org
AMOUNT: $1,000
DEADLINE(S): JAN 31
FIELD(S): Chemistry; Environmental Studies; Engineering; Paper Industry
ELIGIBILITY/REQUIREMENTS: Annual scholarship presented to 1 school each year (announced in fall). Students from that school may then apply.

HOW TO APPLY: Contact TAPPI Project Event Manager to determine which school has received the award; then contact school directly for more information on how to apply.

NUMBER OF AWARDS: 1

RENEWABLE: Yes, must reapply.

CONTACT: Veranda Edmondson, 770/208-7536

1028—TAPPI PULP MANUFACTURE DIVISION (Johan C.F.C. Richter Scholarship Prize)

P.O. Box 105113
Atlanta GA 30092
770/446-1400
FAX: 770/446-6947
E-mail: vedmondson@tappi.org
Internet: http://www.tappi.org
AMOUNT: $1,000
DEADLINE(S): JAN 31
FIELD(S): Chemistry; Environmental Studies; Engineering; Paper Industry
ELIGIBILITY/REQUIREMENTS: Biannual scholarship presented to 1 school

each year (announced in fall). Students from that school may then apply. School selected by winner of the High Impact Paper Award.

HOW TO APPLY: Contact TAPPI Project Event Manager to determine which school has received the award; then contact school directly for more information on how to apply.

NUMBER OF AWARDS: 1

RENEWABLE: Yes, must reapply.

CONTACT: Veranda Edmondson, 770/208-7536

1029—TAPPI PULP MANUFACTURE DIVISION (Joseph K. Perkins Scholarship Prize)

P.O. Box 105113
Atlanta GA 30092
770/446-1400
FAX: 770/446-6947
E-mail: vedmondson@tappi.org
Internet: http://www.tappi.org
AMOUNT: $1,000
DEADLINE(S): JAN 31
FIELD(S): Chemistry; Environmental Studies; Engineering; Paper Industry
ELIGIBILITY/REQUIREMENTS: Biannual scholarship presented to 1 school each year (announced in fall). Students from that school may then apply. School is selected by recipient of the Division's Technical Award.

HOW TO APPLY: Contact TAPPI Project Event Manager to determine which school has received the award; then contact school directly for more information on how to apply.

NUMBER OF AWARDS: 1

RENEWABLE: Yes, must reapply.

CONTACT: Veranda Edmondson, 770/208-7536

1030—UNIVERSITY OF MARYLAND (John B. and Ida Slaughter Endowed Scholarship in Science, Technology, and the Black Community)

2169 Lefrak Hall
College Park MD 20742-7225
301/405/1158
FAX: 301/314-986
Internet: http://www.bsos.umd.edu/aasp/scholarship.html
AMOUNT: Varies (in-state tuition costs)
DEADLINE(S): MAR
FIELD(S): Science; Technology
ELIGIBILITY/REQUIREMENTS: Open to African Americans who are U.S. residents with a minimum 2.8 GPA. Must be accepted to or enrolled at UMCP for freshman year. Should have an interest in applying science and technology to the problems of the Black community.

HOW TO APPLY: Contact the Center for Minorities in Science and Engineering at UMCP for an application. Must submit letter of recommendation from high school counselor or UMCP faculty member. Essay required.

RENEWABLE: Yes

1031—UNIVERSITY OF WALES-BANGOR-SCHOOL OF INFORMATICS AND COMPUTER SYSTEMS (Undergraduate Scholarships)

Dean Street
Bangor, Gwynedd
LL57 1UT
WALES UK
+44 (0)1248 382686
FAX: +44(0)1248 361429
E-mail: admissions@informatics.bangor.ac.uk
Internet: http://www.informatics.bangor.ac.uk
AMOUNT: £1,500
DEADLINE(S): NOV
FIELD(S): Electronic Engineering; Computer Science
ELIGIBILITY/REQUIREMENTS: Undergraduate scholarships in the above fields in Bangor, North Wales.

HOW TO APPLY: E-mail a.smith@bangor.ac.uk and mention School of Informatics Scholarships.

1032—UNIVERSITY OF WINDSOR (President's National Alumni Incentive Scholarships)

401 Sunset Avenue
Windsor Ontario N9B 3P4
CANADA
519/253-3000
FAX: 519/973-7081
E-mail: awards1@uwindsor.ca
Internet: http://www.uwindsor.ca
AMOUNT: $1,000 (Canadian)
DEADLINE(S): MAY 31
FIELD(S): Engineering
ELIGIBILITY/REQUIREMENTS: Open to women undergraduate students registering in year 1 at the University of Windsor. Must have superior grades.

HOW TO APPLY: Automatic. No application required.

RENEWABLE: Yes. Up to 4 years.

CONTACT: Aase Houser

1033—UNIVERSITY OF WINDSOR (U.S./Mexico Entrance Scholarship)

401 Sunset Avenue

165

Windsor Ontario N9B 3P4
CANADA
519/253-3000
FAX: 519/973-7081
E-mail: awards1@uwindsor.ca
Internet: http://www.uwindsor.ca
AMOUNT: $3,000/term (Canadian)
Engineering, Education, Law, Nursing;
all other fields $1,500/term (Canadian)
DEADLINE(S): MAY 31
FIELD(S): All
ELIGIBILITY/REQUIREMENTS: Open
to undergraduate students with U.S./
Mexican citizenship or permanent resident
status registering in year 1 at the
University of Windsor. Must have superior
grades.
HOW TO APPLY: Automatic. No application required.
RENEWABLE: Yes. Up to 4 years, contingent upon successful completion of the
previous term and a cumulative A- GPA.
CONTACT: Aase Houser

1034—WASHINGTON APPLE EDUCATION FOUNDATION (Howard Hauff Memorial Scholarship)

P.O. Box 3720
Wenatchee WA 98807
509/663-7713
FAX: 509/663-7713
E-mail: waef@waef.org
Internet: http://www.ussui.org
AMOUNT: $500
DEADLINE(S): APR 1
FIELD(S): Agriculture; Horticulture;
Engineering
ELIGIBILITY/REQUIREMENTS: Open
to Washington state high school seniors or
current college students from Washington
state. Applicants should be studying for a
degree in engineering; pursuing a career in
the tree fruit industry, or been raised in a
family involved in the tree fruit industry.
HOW TO APPLY: See website for application.
NUMBER OF AWARDS: 1
CONTACT: Jennifer Whitney

1035—WESTERN MICHIGAN UNIVERSITY (College of Engineering and Applied Sciences/Arthur H. Hupp Endowed Memorial Scholarship)

1903 West Michigan
Kalamazoo MI 49008-5337
269/387-6000
FAX: 269/387-6989

E-mail: finaid-info@wmich.edu
Internet: http://www.wmich.edu/
finaid
AMOUNT: Varies
FIELD(S): Engineering
ELIGIBILITY/REQUIREMENTS: Fulltime undergraduate student majoring in
engineering; preference given to
Watervliet High School graduates; recipient should have displayed consistent parttime work experience during school years.
Financial need a consideration. Minimum
2.5 GPA and must maintain satisfactory
academic progress as specified by the
Office of Student Financial Aid.
HOW TO APPLY: Contact the College of
Engineering Applied Science Advising
Office, Room E-102 Parkview Campus
(269/276-3270) for an application.
RENEWABLE: Yes. Depending on academic level.

1036—WESTERN MICHIGAN UNIVERSITY (College of Engineering and Applied Sciences/George E. Kohrman Scholarship)

1903 West Michigan
Kalamazoo MI 49008-5337
269/387-6000
FAX: 269/387-6989
E-mail: finaid-info@wmich.edu
Internet: http://www.wmich.edu/
finaid
AMOUNT: $1,500
FIELD(S): Engineering
ELIGIBILITY/REQUIREMENTS:
Recipient must have been admitted to
WMU as a degree-seeking student; now
completing the final year of his or her
bachelor's degree in one of the curricula
within the College of Engineering and
Applied Sciences. Must be a senior at the
time the award is granted with a cumulative GPA of at least 3.25 in all course work
approved in meeting the requirement of
senior status, and a citizen of the United
States. Other factors that may be considered are demonstrated leadership ability,
participation in community and school
activities, financial need, and special aptitudes in the technological area of the college.
HOW TO APPLY: Seniors are selected by
the College of Engineering and Applied
Science Scholarship Committee based primarily on scholarship. Contact the College
of Engineering Applied Science Advising
Office, Room E-102 Parkview Campus
(269/276-3270) for more information.
RENEWABLE: No

1037—WESTERN MICHIGAN UNIVERSITY (College of Engineering and Applied Sciences/Joseph and Anna Seidel Educational Opportunity Scholarship)

1903 West Michigan
Kalamazoo MI 49008-5337
269/387-6000
FAX: 269/387-6989
E-mail: finaid-info@wmich.edu
Internet: http://www.wmich.edu/
finaid
AMOUNT: $1,000
FIELD(S): Engineering; Engineering
Technology
ELIGIBILITY/REQUIREMENTS:
Recipient must be graduate of Cass
Technical High School, Detroit and a fulltime undergraduate student majoring in
engineering or engineering technology
with a minimum 3.0 GPA.
HOW TO APPLY: Contact the College of
Engineering and Applied Science Advising
Office, Room E-102 Parkview Campus
(269/276-3270) for an application.
NUMBER OF AWARDS: 2
RENEWABLE: No

1038—WESTERN MICHIGAN UNIVERSITY (College of Engineering and Applied Sciences/Kenneth W. Knight Scholarship)

1903 West Michigan
Kalamazoo MI 49008-5337
269/387-6000
FAX: 269/387-6989
E-mail: finaid-info@wmich.edu
Internet: http://www.wmich.edu/
finaid
AMOUNT: Up to $5,000
FIELD(S): Engineering; Engineering
Technology
ELIGIBILITY/REQUIREMENTS: Fullor part-time graduate or undergraduate
student enrolled in the engineering curriculums of the CEAS. Undergraduate
applicants must have a minimum 3.25 GPA
in all enrolled courses including repeated
courses, demonstrated leadership within
the college, and a commitment to their
profession. Undergraduate applicants
must meet requirements for advancement
to upper division course. Graduate candidates will be selected by individual departments.
HOW TO APPLY: Contact the College of
Engineering and Applied Science Advising
Office, Room E-102 Parkview Campus
(269/276-3270) for an application.

RENEWABLE: Yes. One time if enrolled in an engineering curriculum in the CEAS. Undergraduates must maintain a minimum 3.25 GPA in all enrolled courses included repeated courses. Graduates must maintain a minimum 3.25 GPA and provide a letter of support from their research advisor documenting satisfactory research progress.

1039—WOMEN IN DEFENSE (HORIZONS Scholarship Foundation)

2111 Wilson Boulevard, Suite 400
Arlington VA 22201-3061
703/247-2552
FAX: 703/522-1885
E-mail: wid@ndia.org
Internet: http://www.ndia.org
AMOUNT: $500+
DEADLINE(S): NOV 1; JUL 1
FIELD(S): Security Studies; Engineering; Computer Science; Physics; Mathematics; International Relations; Political Science; Operations Research; Economics; National Security/Defense; Business and Law (as they relate to national security or defense); other fields relevant to national security or defense
ELIGIBILITY/REQUIREMENTS: Open to women employed/planning careers in defense/national security areas (NOT law enforcement or criminal justice). Must be currently enrolled full- or part-time at an accredited college or university at the graduate or undergraduate junior/senior level. Must have a minimum 3.25 GPA, demonstrate financial need, and be U.S. citizen. Based on academic achievement, work experience, objectives, and recommendations.
HOW TO APPLY: See website or send SASE for application.
RENEWABLE: Yes

1040—WOODS HOLE OCEANOGRAPHIC INSTITUTION (Summer Student Fellowship)

Clark Laboratory 223, MS #31
Woods Hole MA 02543-1541
508/289-2219
FAX: 508/457-2188
E-mail: education@whoi.edu
Internet: http://www.whoi.edu
AMOUNT: $380/week for 10-12 weeks; possible travel allowance
DEADLINE(S): FEB 15
FIELD(S): Science; Engineering; Mathematics; Marine Sciences/Engineering; Policy
ELIGIBILITY/REQUIREMENTS: Open to undergraduates who have completed their junior or senior year, with backgrounds in science, math, and engineering interested in the marine sciences and oceanography. Selection based on academic and scientific achievements and promise as future ocean scientists and engineers.
HOW TO APPLY: For an application and additional information, contact the Academic Programs Office, Clark Laboratory. Submit with résumé demonstrating educational background and work experience; an official transcript and/or other official documentation of undergraduate record; at least 3 letters of recommendation from professors, employers, others; a statement of research interests, future education and career plans; and reasons for applying for fellowship.

1041—WOODS HOLE OCEANOGRAPHIC INSTITUTION (Traineeships in Oceanography for Minority Group Undergraduates)

Clark Laboratory 223, MS #31
Woods Hole MA 02543-1541
508/289-2219
FAX: 508/457-2188
E-mail: education@whoi.edu
Internet: http://www.whoi.edu
AMOUNT: Varies
DEADLINE(S): FEB 15
FIELD(S): Physical/Natural Sciences, Mathematics, Engineering
ELIGIBILITY/REQUIREMENTS: For minority undergraduates (African-American or Black, Asian-American, Chicano, Mexican-American, Puerto Rican or other Hispanic, and Native American) who are enrolled in U.S. colleges/universities and have completed at least 2 semesters. Traineeships may be awarded for a 10- to 12-week period in the summer or for a semester during the academic year.
HOW TO APPLY: For an application and additional information, contact the Academic Programs Office, Clark Laboratory. Submit with current résumé demonstrating educational background and work experience; an official transcript and/or other official documentation of undergraduate record; at least 3 letters of recommendation from professors, employers, others; a statement of research interests, future education and career plans; and reasons for applying for fellowship.

1042—XEROX EXPERIENTIAL LEARNING (XCEL) PROGRAMS

150 State Street
Rochester NY 14614
585/256-4647
FAX: 585/482-3095
E-mail: xtmsp@rballiance.com
Internet: www.xerox.com
AMOUNT: Varies
DEADLINE(S): SEP 15
FIELD(S): Engineering; Science
ELIGIBILITY/REQUIREMENTS: Scholarships for minorities enrolled in a technical degree program at the bachelor level or above. Must be full-time matriculated student enrolled in a college-level program. Xerox will match your skills with a sponsoring organization that will offer a meaningful summer work experience complementing your academic learning.
HOW TO APPLY: Send résumé and a cover letter to Xerox Corporation, Corporate Employment and College Relations. Reference XHXSTUDENT.

1043—XEROX TECHNICAL MINORITY SCHOLARSHIP

150 State Street
Rochester NY 14614
585/256-4647
FAX: 585/482-3095
E-mail: xtmsp@rballiance.com
Internet: www.xerox.com
AMOUNT: Up to $10,000
DEADLINE(S): SEP 15
FIELD(S): Engineering, Computer Science, Science
ELIGIBILITY/REQUIREMENTS: Scholarships for minorities enrolled full time in a technical degree program at the bachelor level or above. Must be African American, Native American, Hispanic, or Asian. Recipient may not have tuition or related expenses covered by other scholarships or grants.
HOW TO APPLY: Obtain application from website or address above. Your Financial Aid Office must fill out the bottom half of the form. Send completed application, résumé and a cover letter to Xerox Technical Minority Scholarship Program.
RENEWABLE: Yes, must reapply.

AERONAUTICAL ENGINEERING

1044—AIRCRAFT ELECTRONICS ASSOCIATION EDUCATIONAL FOUNDATION (Bendix/King Avionics Scholarship)

4217 South Hocker
Independence MO 64055
816/373-6565
FAX: 816/478-3100

E-mail: info@aea.net
Internet: http://www.aea.net
AMOUNT: $1,000
DEADLINE(S): FEB 17
FIELD(S): Avionics; Aviation
ELIGIBILITY/REQUIREMENTS:
Available to high school, college, or voca-
tional/technical school students who plan
to or are attending an accredited school in
an avionics or aircraft-repair program.
HOW TO APPLY: Mail completed application form, with an official transcript
(transcripts sent separately will not be
accepted); answers to application questions; and one 300-word typewritten essay
(see website for topics, which are related to
avionics, aviation maintenance, and aircraft electronics).
CONTACT: Scholarship Application

1045—AIRCRAFT ELECTRONICS ASSOCIATION EDUCATIONAL FOUNDATION (Bud Glover Memorial Scholarship)

4217 South Hocker
Independence MO 64055
816/373-6565
FAX: 816/478-3100
E-mail: info@aea.net
Internet: http://www.aea.net
AMOUNT: $1,000
DEADLINE(S): FEB 17
FIELD(S): Avionics; Aviation
ELIGIBILITY/REQUIREMENTS: For
high school seniors and/or college students
who plan to or are attending an accredited
school in an avionics or aircraft-repair program.
HOW TO APPLY: Mail completed application form (see website), with an official
transcript (transcripts sent separately will
not be accepted); answers to application
questions; and one 300-word typewritten
essay (see website for topics, which are
related to avionics, aviation maintenance,
and aircraft electronics).
CONTACT: Scholarship Application

1046—AIRCRAFT ELECTRONICS ASSOCIATION EDUCATIONAL FOUNDATION (Chuck Peacock Memorial Scholarship)

4217 South Hocker
Independence MO 64055
816/373-6565
FAX: 816/478-3100
E-mail: info@aea.net
Internet: http://www.aea.net
AMOUNT: $1,000
DEADLINE(S): FEB 17
FIELD(S): Avionics; Aviation

ELIGIBILITY/REQUIREMENTS:
Available to high school seniors and/or
college students who plan to or are attending an accredited school in an aviation
management program; this scholarship is
offered to recognize the importance of
management skills.
HOW TO APPLY: Mail completed application form (see website), with an official
transcript (transcripts sent separately will
not be accepted); answers to application
questions; and one 300-word typewritten
essay (see website for topics, which are
related to avionics, aviation maintenance,
and aircraft electronics).
CONTACT: Scholarship Application

1047—AIRCRAFT ELECTRONICS ASSOCIATION EDUCATIONAL FOUNDATION (College of Aeronautics Scholarship)

4217 South Hocker
Independence MO 64055
816/373-6565
FAX: 816/478-3100
E-mail: info@aea.net
Internet: http://www.aea.net
AMOUNT: $3,000 ($750 per semester;
$3,000 maximum for four semesters)
DEADLINE(S): FEB 17
FIELD(S): Avionics; Aviation
ELIGIBILITY/REQUIREMENTS:
Available to students in the 2-year avionics
technology program (Associate in Applied
Sciences) at the College of Aeronautics in
Flushing, NY.
HOW TO APPLY: Mail completed appli-
cation form (see website), with an official
transcript (transcripts sent separately will
not be accepted); answers to application
questions (see website); and one 300-word
typewritten essay (see website for topics,
which are related to avionics, aviation
maintenance, and aircraft electronics).
CONTACT: Scholarship Application

1048—AIRCRAFT ELECTRONICS ASSOCIATION EDUCATIONAL FOUNDATION (David Arver Memorial Scholarship)

4217 South Hocker
Independence MO 64055
816/373-6565
FAX: 816/478-3100
E-mail: info@aea.net
Internet: http://www.aea.net
AMOUNT: $1,000
DEADLINE(S): FEB 17
FIELD(S): Avionics; Aviation
ELIGIBILITY/REQUIREMENTS: For a
high school senior and/or college student
who plans to attend an accredited voca-
tional/technical school located in Illinois,

Indiana, Iowa, Kansas, Michigan,
Minnesota, Missouri, Nebraska, North
Dakota, South Dakota, or Wisconsin; student must enroll in an avionics or aircraft-
repair program.
HOW TO APPLY: Mail completed application form (see website), with an official
transcript (transcripts sent separately will
not be accepted); answers to application
questions; and one 300-word typewritten
essay (see website for topics, which are
related to avionics, aviation maintenance,
and aircraft electronics).
NUMBER OF AWARDS: 1
CONTACT: Scholarship Application

1049—AIRCRAFT ELECTRONICS ASSOCIATION EDUCATIONAL FOUNDATION (Dutch and Ginger Arver Scholarship)

4217 South Hocker
Independence MO 64055
816/373-6565
FAX: 816/478-3100
E-mail: info@aea.net
Internet: http://www.aea.net
AMOUNT: $1,000
DEADLINE(S): FEB 17
FIELD(S): Avionics; Aviation
ELIGIBILITY/REQUIREMENTS:
Available to high school seniors and/or
college students who plan to or are attending an accredited school in an avionics or
aircraft-repair program.
HOW TO APPLY: Mail completed application form (see website), with an official
transcript (transcripts sent separately will
not be accepted); answers to application
questions; and one 300-word typewritten
essay (see website for topics, which are
related to avionics, aviation maintenance,
and aircraft electronics).
CONTACT: Scholarship Application

1050—AIRCRAFT ELECTRONICS ASSOCIATION EDUCATIONAL FOUNDATION (Field Aviation Co., Inc. Scholarship)

4217 South Hocker
Independence MO 64055
816/373-6565
FAX: 816/478-3100
E-mail: info@aea.net
Internet: http://www.aea.net
AMOUNT: $1,000
DEADLINE(S): FEB 17
FIELD(S): Avionics; Aviation
ELIGIBILITY/REQUIREMENTS:
Available to high school seniors and/or
college students who plan to or are attend-
ing an accredited college or university in
Canada, in an avionics or aircraft-repair
program.

HOW TO APPLY: Mail completed application form (see website), with an official transcript (transcripts sent separately will not be accepted); answers to application questions; and one 300-word typewritten essay (see website for topics, which are related to avionics, aviation maintenance, and aircraft electronics).
CONTACT: Scholarship Application

1051—AIRCRAFT ELECTRONICS ASSOCIATION EDUCATIONAL FOUNDATION (Garmin Scholarship)

4217 South Hocker
Independence MO 64055
816/373-6565
FAX: 816/478-3100
E-mail: info@aea.net
Internet: http://www.aea.net
AMOUNT: $2,000
DEADLINE(S): FEB 17
FIELD(S): Avionics; Aviation
ELIGIBILITY/REQUIREMENTS: Available to high school, college, or vocational/technical school students who plan to or are attending an accredited school in an avionics or aircraft-repair program.
HOW TO APPLY: Mail completed application form (see website), with an official transcript (transcripts sent separately will not be accepted); answers to application questions; and one 300-word typewritten essay (see website for topics, which are related to avionics, aviation maintenance, and aircraft electronics).
CONTACT: Scholarship Application

1052—AIRCRAFT ELECTRONICS ASSOCIATION EDUCATIONAL FOUNDATION (L-3 Avionics Systems Scholarship)

4217 South Hocker
Independence MO 64055
816/373-6565
FAX: 816/478-3100
E-mail: info@aea.net
Internet: http://www.aea.net
AMOUNT: $2,500
DEADLINE(S): FEB 17
FIELD(S): Avionics; Aviation
ELIGIBILITY/REQUIREMENTS: Available to high school seniors and/or college students who plan to or are attending an accredited school in an avionics or aircraft-repair program.
HOW TO APPLY: Mail completed application form (see website), with an official transcript (transcripts sent separately will not be accepted); answers to application

questions; and one 300-word typewritten essay (see website for topics, which are related to avionics, aviation maintenance, and aircraft electronics).
CONTACT: Scholarship Application

1053—AIRCRAFT ELECTRONICS ASSOCIATION EDUCATIONAL FOUNDATION (Lee Tarbox Memorial Scholarship)

4217 South Hocker
Independence MO 64055
816/373-6565
FAX: 816/478-3100
E-mail: info@aea.net
Internet: http://www.aea.net
AMOUNT: $2,500
DEADLINE(S): FEB 17
FIELD(S): Avionics; Aviation
ELIGIBILITY/REQUIREMENTS: Available to high school seniors or college students who plan to or are attending an accredited school in an avionics or aircraft-repair program.
HOW TO APPLY: Mail completed application form (see website), with an official transcript (transcripts sent separately will not be accepted); answers to application questions; and one 300-word typewritten essay (see website for topics, which are related to avionics, aviation maintenance, and aircraft electronics).
CONTACT: Scholarship Application

1054—AIRCRAFT ELECTRONICS ASSOCIATION EDUCATIONAL FOUNDATION (Leon Harris/Les Nichols Memorial Scholarship to Spartan School of Aeronautics)

4217 South Hocker
Independence MO 64055
816/373-6565
FAX: 816/478-3100
E-mail: info@aea.net
Internet: http://www.aea.net
AMOUNT: Over $22,000
DEADLINE(S): FEB 17
FIELD(S): Avionics; Aviation
ELIGIBILITY/REQUIREMENTS: For students who plan to pursue an Associate's Degree in Applied Science in Aviation Electronics (avionics) at NEC Spartan School of Aeronautics campus in Tulsa, OK; the applicant may not be currently enrolled in the avionics program at Spartan.
HOW TO APPLY: Mail completed application form (see website), with an official transcript (transcripts sent separately will

not be accepted); answers to application questions; and one 300-word typewritten essay (see website for topics, which are related to avionics, aviation maintenance, and aircraft electronics).
CONTACT: Scholarship Application

1055—AIRCRAFT ELECTRONICS ASSOCIATION EDUCATIONAL FOUNDATION (Lowell Gaylor Memorial Scholarship)

4217 South Hocker
Independence MO 64055
816/373-6565
FAX: 816/478-3100
E-mail: info@aea.net
Internet: http://www.aea.net
AMOUNT: $1,000
DEADLINE(S): FEB 17
FIELD(S): Avionics; Aviation
ELIGIBILITY/REQUIREMENTS: For high school seniors and/or college students who plan to or are attending an accredited school in an avionics or aircraft-repair program.
HOW TO APPLY: Mail completed application form (see website), with an official transcript (transcripts sent separately will not be accepted); answers to application questions; and one 300-word typewritten essay (see website for topics, which are related to avionics, aviation maintenance, and aircraft electronics).
CONTACT: Scholarship Application

1056—AIRCRAFT ELECTRONICS ASSOCIATION EDUCATIONAL FOUNDATION (Mid-Continent Instrument Scholarship)

4217 South Hocker
Independence MO 64055
816/373-6565
FAX: 816/478-3100
E-mail: info@aea.net
Internet: http://www.aea.net
AMOUNT: $1,000
DEADLINE(S): FEB 17
FIELD(S): Avionics; Aviation
ELIGIBILITY/REQUIREMENTS: Available to high school seniors and/or college students who plan to or are attending an accredited school in an avionics or aircraft-repair program.
HOW TO APPLY: Mail completed application form (see website), with an official transcript (transcripts sent separately will not be accepted); answers to application questions; and one 300-word typewritten essay (see website for topics, which are

related to avionics, aviation maintenance, and aircraft electronics).
CONTACT: Scholarship Application

1057—AIRCRAFT ELECTRONICS ASSOCIATION EDUCATIONAL FOUNDATION (Monte R. Mitchell Global Scholarship)

4217 South Hocker
Independence MO 64055
816/373-6565
FAX: 816/478-3100
E-mail: info@aea.net
Internet: http://www.aea.net
AMOUNT: $1,000
DEADLINE(S): FEB 17
FIELD(S): Avionics; Aviation
ELIGIBILITY/REQUIREMENTS: Available to a European student pursuing a degree in aviation maintenance technology, avionics, or aircraft repair at an accredited school located in Europe or the United States.
HOW TO APPLY: Mail completed application form (see website), with an official transcript (transcripts sent separately will not be accepted); answers to application questions; and one 300-word typewritten essay (see website for topics, which are related to avionics, aviation maintenance, and aircraft electronics).
CONTACT: Scholarship Application

1058—AIRCRAFT ELECTRONICS ASSOCIATION EDUCATIONAL FOUNDATION (Plane & Pilot Magazine/Garmin Scholarship)

4217 South Hocker
Independence MO 64055
816/373-6565
FAX: 816/478-3100
E-mail: info@aea.net
Internet: http://www.aea.net
AMOUNT: $2,000
DEADLINE(S): FEB 17
FIELD(S): Avionics; Aviation
ELIGIBILITY/REQUIREMENTS: Available to high school, college, or vocational/technical school students who plan to or are attending an accredited school in an avionics or aircraft-repair program.
HOW TO APPLY: Mail completed application form (see website), with an official transcript (transcripts sent separately will not be accepted); answers to application questions; and one 300-word typewritten essay (see website for topics, which are

related to avionics, aviation maintenance, and aircraft electronics).
CONTACT: Scholarship Application

1059—AIRCRAFT ELECTRONICS ASSOCIATION EDUCATIONAL FOUNDATION (Russell Leroy Jones Memorial Scholarship to Westwood College of Aviation Technology)

4217 South Hocker
Independence MO 64055
816/373-6565
FAX: 816/478-3100
E-mail: info@aea.net
Internet: http://www.aea.net
AMOUNT: $6,000
DEADLINE(S): FEB 17
FIELD(S): Avionics; Aviation
ELIGIBILITY/REQUIREMENTS: Students must plan to attend Westwood College of Aviation Technology in Broomfield, CO, in the electronics/avionics program; applicants may not be currently enrolled at Westwood College of Aviation Technology.
HOW TO APPLY: Mail completed application form (see website), with an official transcript (transcripts sent separately will not be accepted); answers to application questions; and one 300-word typewritten essay (see website for topics, which are related to avionics, aviation maintenance, and aircraft electronics).
NUMBER OF AWARDS: 3
CONTACT: Scholarship Application

1060—AIRCRAFT ELECTRONICS ASSOCIATION EDUCATIONAL FOUNDATION (Sporty's Pilot Shop/Cincinnati Avionics)

4217 South Hocker
Independence MO 64055
816/373-6565
FAX: 816/478-3100
E-mail: info@aea.net
Internet: http://www.aea.net
AMOUNT: $2,000
DEADLINE(S): FEB 17
FIELD(S): Avionics; Aviation
ELIGIBILITY/REQUIREMENTS: Available to high school seniors and/or college students who plan to or are attending an accredited college or university in an avionics or aircraft-repair program.
HOW TO APPLY: Mail completed application form (see website), with an official transcript (transcripts sent separately will not be accepted); answers to application questions; and one 300-word typewritten

essay (see website for topics, which are related to avionics, aviation maintenance, and aircraft electronics).
CONTACT: Scholarship Application

1061—AIRCRAFT ELECTRONICS ASSOCIATION EDUCATIONAL FOUNDATION (Thomas J. Slocum Memorial Scholarship to Westwood College of Aviation)

4217 South Hocker
Independence MO 64055
816/373-6565
FAX: 816/478-3100
E-mail: info@aea.net
Internet: http://www.aea.net
AMOUNT: $6,000
DEADLINE(S): FEB 17
FIELD(S): Avionics; Aviation
ELIGIBILITY/REQUIREMENTS: For students applying to and enrolling in the avionics program at Westwood College in Broomfield, CO.
HOW TO APPLY: Mail completed application form (see website), with an official transcript (transcripts sent separately will not be accepted); answers to application questions; and one 300-word typewritten essay (see website for topics, which are related to avionics, aviation maintenance, and aircraft electronics).
NUMBER OF AWARDS: 3
CONTACT: Scholarship Application

1062—AIRCRAFT ELECTRONICS ASSOCIATION EDUCATIONAL FOUNDATION (Tom Taylor Memorial Scholarship to Spartan School of Aeronautics)

4217 South Hocker
Independence MO 64055
816/373-6565
FAX: 816/478-3100
E-mail: info@aea.net
Internet: http://www.aea.net
AMOUNT: Over $22,000
DEADLINE(S): FEB 17
FIELD(S): Avionics; Aviation
ELIGIBILITY/REQUIREMENTS: Available to students who plan to pursue an Associate's Degree in Applied Science or a diploma in Aviation Maintenance Technology (AMT) at Spartan School of Aeronautics campus in Tulsa, OK; the applicant may not be currently enrolled in the AMT program at Spartan.
HOW TO APPLY: Mail completed application form (see website), with an official transcript (transcripts sent separately will not be accepted); answers to application

questions; and one 300-word typewritten essay (see website for topics, which are related to avionics, aviation maintenance, and aircraft electronics).
CONTACT: Scholarship Application

1063—AMERICAN HELICOPTER SOCIETY (AHS) VERTICAL FLIGHT FOUNDATION, THE (Engineering Scholarships)

217 North Washington Street
Alexandria VA 22314-2538
703/684-6777
AMOUNT: $2,000-$4,000 (depending upon endowment earnings)
DEADLINE(S): FEB 1
FIELD(S): Rotorcraft and Vertical-Takeoff-and-Landing (VTOL) Engineering
ELIGIBILITY/REQUIREMENTS: Applicant must be a full-time student at an accredited school of engineering; demonstrate an interest in pursuing an engineering career in the vertical flight industry. Applicants need NOT be a member of the AHS (American Helicopter Society).
HOW TO APPLY: Send completed application, which includes a narrative of the following items: 1) past and future academic interests (including reasons for selecting the school at which the scholarship will be used, as well as reasons for the specific curriculum), 2) future career interest in the rotorcraft or VTOL engineering field, 3) past work/research experience related to rotorcraft or VTOL aircraft, and 4) other reasons for consideration; also official grade transcript (including the most recent set of grades issued); and an academic endorsement from a professor or dean at applicant's school.
NUMBER OF AWARDS: Several
RENEWABLE: No

1064—AMERICAN INSTITUTE OF AERONAUTICS AND ASTRONAUTICS (Undergraduate Scholarships)

1801 Alexander Bell Drive,
Suite 500
Reston VA 20191-4344
800/639-AIAA or 703/264-7500
FAX: 703/264-7551
E-mail: custserv@aiaa.org
Internet: http://www.aiaa.org
AMOUNT: $2,000
DEADLINE(S): JAN 31
FIELD(S): Science; Engineering; Aeronautics; Astronautics
ELIGIBILITY/REQUIREMENTS: For students who have completed at least one academic semester or quarter of full-time

college work in the area of science or engineering encompassed by the technical activities of the AIAA. Must have GPA of at least 3.0, be currently enrolled in accredited college or university. Membership in AIAA not required to apply but must become one before receiving a scholarship award.
HOW TO APPLY: See website for application; submit with career essay, transcripts and 2 letters of recommendation from college professor.
RENEWABLE: Yes. Eligible for yearly continuation until completion of senior year.
CONTACT: Customer Service

1065—ARMED FORCES COMMUNICATIONS AND ELECTRONICS ASSOCIATION (AFCEA/ORINCON IT Scholarship)

4400 Fair Lakes Court
Fairfax VA 22033-3899
800/336-4583, ext. 6147 or
703/631-6149
FAX: 703/631-4693
E-mail: scholarships@afcea.org
Internet: http://www.afcea.org
AMOUNT: $2,750
DEADLINE(S): Varies according to eligibility
FIELD(S): Electrical or Aerospace Engineering, Computer Science, Physics, Mathematics
ELIGIBILITY/REQUIREMENTS: Scholarships in the above fields for persons on active duty in a military service or veterans, their spouses or dependents, or civilians who meet the general criteria for the General Wickham Scholarship, provided the school they are attending is an accredited 4-year college or university in the Greater San Diego, CA, area, and they are working toward a degree in an accredited 4-year college or university in the U.S. Must have GPA of 3.4 or more.
HOW TO APPLY: Check website or contact AFCEA for information and application.

1066—ARMED FORCES COMMUNICATIONS AND ELECTRONICS ASSOCIATION (AFCEA ROTC Scholarships)

4400 Fair Lakes Court
Fairfax VA 22033-3899
800/336-4583, ext. 6147 or
703/631-6149
FAX: 703/631-4693
E-mail: scholarships@afcea.org
Internet: http://www.afcea.org

AMOUNT: $2,000
DEADLINE(S): APR 1
FIELD(S): Electrical Engineering, Electronics, Computer Science, Computer Systems, or Aerospace Engineering, Physics, Mathematics, science or mathematics education; technology management or other technical fields, or fields related to U.S. intelligence or national security
ELIGIBILITY/REQUIREMENTS: Scholarships for ROTC students working toward a degree in an accredited degree-granting 4-year college or university in the U.S.
HOW TO APPLY: MUST be nominated by Professors of Military Science, Naval Science, or Aerospace Studies. Contact the commander of each ROTC unit at your school or see website for application.

1067—ARMED FORCES COMMUNICATIONS AND ELECTRONICS ASSOCIATION (AFCEA Scholarship for Online or Distance-Learning Programs)

4400 Fair Lakes Court
Fairfax VA 22033-3899
800/336-4583, ext. 6147 or
703/631-6149
FAX: 703/631-4693
E-mail: scholarships@afcea.org
Internet: http://www.afcea.org
AMOUNT: $1,500
DEADLINE(S): JUN 1
FIELD(S): Electrical, Chemical or Aerospace Engineering: Computer Science; Mathematics; Physics; Science or Math Education; Technology Management or fields related to U.S. intelligence or national security
ELIGIBILITY/REQUIREMENTS: Full-time students; undergraduates must have completed 2 semesters of calculus (30-semester hour equivalent). Must be a U.S. citizen and be currently enrolled in a 4-year college or university in the U.S. at time of application.
HOW TO APPLY: Applications and further information on website.
RENEWABLE: No

1068—ARMED FORCES COMMUNICATIONS AND ELECTRONICS ASSOCIATION (AFCEA Scholarship for Working Professionals)

4400 Fair Lakes Court
Fairfax VA 22033-3899
800/336-4583, ext. 6147 or
703/631-6149
FAX: 703/631-4693

E-mail: scholarships@afcea.org
Internet: http://www.afcea.org
AMOUNT: $1,500
DEADLINE(S): AUG 15-SEP 15
FIELD(S): Electrical, Aerospace, or
   Computer Engineering, Computer
   Science, Computer Information
   Systems, Mathematics
ELIGIBILITY/REQUIREMENTS: Part-
time students (at least 2 classes per semester) working toward an undergraduate
degree at any accredited 2-year community college or 4-year institution in the U.S.
while currently employed in government
or industry. Distance learning programs do
not qualify. Must be a U.S. citizen and be
currently enrolled as a sophomore, junior,
or senior at time of application.
HOW TO APPLY: Applications and further information on website.

1069—ARMED FORCES COMMUNICATIONS AND ELECTRONICS ASSOCIATION (General Emmett Paige Scholarships for Military Personnel, Veterans, and Their Dependents)

4400 Fair Lakes Court
Fairfax VA 22033-3899
800/336-4583, ext. 6147 or
703/631-6149
FAX: 703/631-4693
E-mail: scholarships@afcea.org
Internet: http://www.afcea.org
AMOUNT: $2,000
DEADLINE(S): MAR 1
FIELD(S): Electrical Engineering,
   Electronics, Computer Science,
   Computer or Aerospace Engineering,
   Physics, Mathematics, Science or
   Mathematics Education; Technology
   Management or other technical fields,
   or fields related to U.S. intelligence or
   national security
ELIGIBILITY/REQUIREMENTS:
Scholarships in the above fields for persons
on active duty in a military service or vet-
erans and to their spouses or dependents
who are working toward a degree in an
accredited 4-year college or university in
the U.S. Must have GPA of 3.4 or more.
HOW TO APPLY: Applications and further information on website.

1070—ARMED FORCES COMMUNICATIONS AND ELECTRONICS ASSOCIATION (General John A. Wickham Scholarships)

4400 Fair Lakes Court
Fairfax VA 22033-3899

800/336-4583, ext. 6147 or
703/631-6149
FAX: 703/631-4693
E-mail: scholarships@afcea.org
Internet: http://www.afcea.org
AMOUNT: $2,000
DEADLINE(S): MAY 1
FIELD(S): Electrical Engineering,
   Electronics, Computer Science,
   Computer or Aerospace Engineering,
   Physics, Mathematics, Science or
   Mathematics Education; Technology
   Management or other technical fields,
   or fields related to U.S. intelligence or
   national security
ELIGIBILITY/REQUIREMENTS:
Scholarships in the above fields for persons
working toward degrees in accredited 4-
year colleges or universities in the U.S.
Must have GPA of 3.5 or more.
HOW TO APPLY: Applications and fur-
ther information on website.

1071—ASTRONAUT SCHOLARSHIP FOUNDATION

6225 Vectorspace Boulevard
Titusville FL 32780
321/269/6119
FAX: 321/267-3970
E-mail: MercurySvn@aol.com
Internet: http://www.astronaut
scholarship.org/guidelines.html
AMOUNT: $10,000
DEADLINE(S): APR 15
FIELD(S): Engineering and Physical
   Sciences (Medical Research ok, but
   NOT Professional Medicine)
ELIGIBILITY/REQUIREMENTS: Open
to juniors, seniors, and graduate students
at a select group of schools. Must be U.S.
citizen with the intention to pursue
research or advanced field of study upon
completion of final degree. Special consid-
eration given to students who have shown
initiative, creativity, excellence, and/or
resourcefulness in their field. Must be
NOMINATED by faculty or staff.
HOW TO APPLY: See website for list of
eligible schools. Contact Executive
Director for details.
CONTACT: Howard Benedict, Executive
Director

1072—AVIATION DISTRIBUTORS AND MANUFACTURERS ASSOCIATION INTERNATIONAL (ADMA International Scholarship Fund)

1900 Arch Street
Philadelphia PA 19103-1498
215/564-3484

FAX: 215/564-2175
E-mail: assnhqt@netaxs.com
AMOUNT: Varies
DEADLINE(S): MAR 15
FIELD(S): Aviation Management;
   Professional Pilot; Aviation
   Maintenance; Aeronautics
ELIGIBILITY/REQUIREMENTS: Open
to students seeking a career in aviation
management or as a professional pilot.
Emphasis may be in general aviation, air-
way science management, aviation mainte-
nance, flight engineering, or airway air
conditioning systems management. Must
be studying in the aviation field in a 4-year
school having an aviation program.
HOW TO APPLY: Write for information.

1073—AVIATION INSURANCE ASSOCIATION

Aviation Technology Department
1 Purdue Airport
West Lafayette IN 47906-3398
765/494-5782
AMOUNT: $1,000
DEADLINE(S): FEB 28
FIELD(S): Aviation
ELIGIBILITY/REQUIREMENTS:
Scholarships for aviation students who
have completed at least 30 college credits,
15 of which are in aviation. Must have
GPA of at least 2.5 and be a U.S. citizen.
HOW TO APPLY: Write to Professor
Bernard Wulle at Purdue University at
above address for application and details.
CONTACT: Professor Bernard Wulle

1074—EAA AVIATION FOUNDATION (David Alan Quick Scholarship)

EAA Scholarship Department
P.O. 3086
Oshkosh WI 54903-3065
920/426-6823
E-mail: scholarships@eaa.org
Internet: http://www.young
eagles.org
AMOUNT: $1,000
DEADLINE(S): MAR 1
FIELD(S): Aerospace or Aeronautical
   Engineering
ELIGIBILITY/REQUIREMENTS: Open
to well-rounded individuals involved in
school and community activities as well as
aviation accepted at or attending 4-year
accredited college or university. Applicant's academic records should verify
his/her ability to complete educational
activity for which scholarship is requested.
Awarded to a junior or senior in good
standing, enrolled in an accredited college

or university, pursuing a degree in. Must also be a current member of EAA (Experimental Aircraft Association) or recommended by a current EAA member. HOW TO APPLY: Apply online. A personal statement (500 words or less.) addressing career aspirations. educational plan, why you want to receive this scholarship, what you learned from work/volunteer experiences, and explaining how your education will be financed, including loans, family assistance, your own savings, scholarships, etc., and any unusual financial circumstances affecting your college financial plan required.
NUMBER OF AWARDS: 1

1075—EAA AVIATION FOUNDATION
(EAA Air Academy-EADS Socata Internship)

EAA Scholarship Department
P.O. 3086
Oshkosh WI 54903-3065
920/426-6823
E-mail: scholarships@eaa.org
Internet: http://www.young eagles.org
AMOUNT: Travel and accommodations in France and Oshkosh, WI
DEADLINE(S): MAR 1
FIELD(S): Aviation and Related Areas, Engineering, Marketing, Manufacturing
ELIGIBILITY/REQUIREMENTS: Open to college junior or seniors, intending to pursue a career in aviation. Applicants must be in full-time education and able to demonstrate an interest in aeronautical career—engineering, marketing, manufacturing, or other areas focused on aviation. Applicants must be U.S. or Canadian citizens and able to obtain their own passport. Knowledge of French would enhance the experience but is not an absolute requirement.
HOW TO APPLY: Apply online.
NUMBER OF AWARDS: 2 (1 male, 1 female)
ADDITIONAL INFORMATION: The internship will provide an opportunity for each young person to visit France for an internship of five weeks' duration in June and July. They will work at an EADS Socata facility and be exposed to a variety of aviation disciplines. Recipients will conclude their summer by attending a week-long session of the EAA Advanced Air Academy in Oshkosh, providing mentorship opportunities to young people aged 16-18 who are participating in the camp. This will include an opportunity to experience the EAA AirVenture Oshkosh.

1076—EAA AVIATION FOUNDATION
(Hansen Scholarship)

EAA Scholarship Department
P.O. 3086
Oshkosh WI 54903-3065
920/426-6823
E-mail: scholarships@eaa.org
Internet: http://www.young eagles.org
AMOUNT: $1,000
DEADLINE(S): MAR 1
FIELD(S): Aerospace/Aeronautical Engineering.
ELIGIBILITY/REQUIREMENTS: Open to well-rounded individuals involved in school and community activities as well as aviation accepted at or attending 4-year accredited college, university or technical college. Applicant's academic records should verify his/her ability to complete educational activity for which scholarship is requested. Must also be a current member of EAA (Experimental Aircraft Association) or recommended by a current EAA member.
HOW TO APPLY: Apply online. A personal statement (500 words or less) addressing career aspirations. educational plan, why you want to receive this scholarship, what you learned from work/volunteer experiences, and explaining how your education will be financed, including loans, family assistance, your own savings, scholarships, etc., and any unusual financial circumstances affecting your college financial plan required.
NUMBER OF AWARDS: 1

1077—EAA AVIATION FOUNDATION
(Herbert L. Cox Memorial Scholarship)

EAA Scholarship Department
P.O. 3086
Oshkosh WI 54903-3065
920/426-6823
E-mail: scholarships@eaa.org
Internet: http://www.young eagles.org
AMOUNT: $500
DEADLINE(S): MAR 1
FIELD(S): Aviation or related field
ELIGIBILITY/REQUIREMENTS: Open to well-rounded individuals involved in school and community activities as well as aviation accepted at or attending 4-year accredited college or university. Applicant's academic records should verify his/her ability to complete educational activity for which scholarship is requested. Must also be a current member of EAA

(Experimental Aircraft Association) or recommended by a current EAA member.
HOW TO APPLY: Apply online. A personal statement (500 words or less) addressing career aspirations, educational plan, why you want to receive this scholarship, what you learned from work/volunteer experiences, and explaining how your education will be financed, including loans, family assistance, your own savings, scholarships, etc., and any unusual financial circumstances affecting your college financial plan required.
NUMBER OF AWARDS: 1

1078—EAA AVIATION FOUNDATION
(H.P. "Bud" Milligan Aviation Scholarship)

EAA Scholarship Department
P.O. 3086
Oshkosh WI 54903-3065
920/426-6823
E-mail: scholarships@eaa.org
Internet: http://www.young eagles.org
AMOUNT: $1,000
DEADLINE(S): MAR 1
FIELD(S): Aviation or related field
ELIGIBILITY/REQUIREMENTS: Open to well-rounded individuals involved in school and community activities as well as aviation accepted at or attending a student an accredited aviation program at a college, technical school, or aviation academy. Financial need is not a requirement. Applicant's academic records should verify his/her ability to complete educational activity for which scholarship is requested. Must also be a current member of EAA (Experimental Aircraft Association) or recommended by a current EAA member.
HOW TO APPLY: Apply online. A personal statement (500 words or less) addressing career aspirations. educational plan, why you want to receive this scholarship, what you learned from work/volunteer experiences, and explaining how your education will be financed, including loans, family assistance, your own savings, scholarships, etc., and any unusual financial circumstances affecting your college financial plan required.
NUMBER OF AWARDS: 1

1079—EAA AVIATION FOUNDATION
(Richard Lee Vernon Aviation Scholarship)

EAA Scholarship Department
P.O. 3086
Oshkosh WI 54903-3065
920/426-6823
E-mail: scholarships@eaa.org

Internet: http://www.young
eagles.org
AMOUNT: $500
DEADLINE(S): MAR 1
FIELD(S): Aviation or related field
ELIGIBILITY/REQUIREMENTS: Open
to well-rounded individuals involved in
school and community activities as well as
aviation accepted at or attending a student
an accredited aviation program at a college, technical school, or aviation academy.
Financial need is a requirement. Applicant's academic records should verify
his/her ability to complete educational
activity for which scholarship is requested.
Must also be a current member of EAA
(Experimental Aircraft Association) or
recommended by a current EAA member.
HOW TO APPLY: Apply online. A personal statement (500 words or less)
addressing career aspirations. educational
plan, why you want to receive this scholarship, what you learned from work/volun-
teer experiences, and explaining how your
education will be financed, including loans,
family assistance, your own savings, scholarships, etc., and any unusual financial circumstances affecting your college financial
plan required.
NUMBER OF AWARDS: 1

1080—ILLINOIS PILOTS ASSOCIATION (IPA Memorial Scholarship)

40 W 297 Apache Lane
Huntley IL 60142
Internet: http://www.illinois
pilots.com/
AMOUNT: $500
DEADLINE(S): APR 1
FIELD(S): Aviation
ELIGIBILITY/REQUIREMENTS:
Applicant must be a resident of Illinois; be
majoring in an aviation-oriented curricu-
lum; and be a full-time student at an
Illinois college or university.
HOW TO APPLY: Submit a completed
application form (or equivalent informa-
tion) and evidence of strong academic per-
formance, including a transcript of grades
and 3 recommendations, at least 1 of which
must be academic.
RENEWABLE: Yes, the recipient may
reapply for the following year.
CONTACT: Ruth Frantz

1081—ILLUMINATING ENGINEERING SOCIETY OF NORTH AMERICA (Robert W. Thunen Memorial Scholarships)

Golden Gate Section
P.O. Box 77527
San Francisco CA 94107-1527

E-mail: riverfield@juno.com
AMOUNT: $2,500
DEADLINE(S): APR 1
FIELD(S): Illumination (Architectural,
Commercial, Residential, Airport,
Navigational, Theatrical, TV,
Agricultural, Vision, etc.)
ELIGIBILITY/REQUIREMENTS: Open
to full-time undergraduate juniors and
seniors and graduate students in an accred-
ited 4-year college or university located in
Northern California, Nevada, Oregon, or
Washington.
HOW TO APPLY: Contact Chair for an
application. Must submit statement of pur-
pose (with respect to lighting education)
and 3 letters of recommendation. Awards
announced by May 3.
NUMBER OF AWARDS: At least 2
CONTACT: Heide M. Kawahata, Chair

1082—INTERNATIONAL SOCIETY OF WOMEN AIRLINE PILOTS (ISA Airline Scholarship)

2250 East Tropicana Avenue,
Suite 19-395
Las Vegas NV 89119-6594
E-mail: isa21scholarbev@aol.com
Internet: http://www.iswap.org
AMOUNT: Varies
DEADLINE(S): APR 15
FIELD(S): Flight Engineering and Type
Ratings
ELIGIBILITY/REQUIREMENTS: For
women seeking careers in aviation who
need Flight Engineer Certificates and
Type Ratings on 727, 737, 747, 757, and
DC-10 aircraft. For Flight Engineers, 1,000
hours flight time and a current FE written
required. For Type Rating scholarship, an
ATP Certificate and a current FE written.
HOW TO APPLY: Check website or write
for more information and application.
CONTACT: Beverly Sinclair at e-mail
above.

1083—MENSA EDUCATION AND RESEARCH FOUNDATION (David Mann Scholarship)

Internet: http://www.mensa
foundation.org/AM/
Template.cfm?Section=Scholarships1
AMOUNT: $1,000
DEADLINE(S): JAN 15
FIELD(S): Aeronautical Engineering;
Aerospace
ELIGIBILITY/REQUIREMENTS: May
be enrolled at time of application. Awards
based on essays written by the applicant.
No requirement for Mensa membership
nor is consideration given for grades, aca-

demic program or financial need. Applicants must currently be a resident of a participating American Mensa local group's
area and enrolled in a degree program in
an accredited U.S. institution of higher
learning during the academic year following the application date.
HOW TO APPLY: Each year the list of
participating groups may change, see website for up-to-date information. Send application, available (if eligible) from the website or, by request with SASE, from local
scholarship chairs. Submit with essay of
not more than 550 words explaining your
academic and/or vocational goals and
plans to achieve those goals to the scholarship chair in your area.

1084—NATIONAL AGRICULTURAL AVIATION ASSOCIATION

1005 E Street SE
Washington DC 20003
202/546-5722
FAX: 202/546-5726
E-mail: information@agaviation.org
Internet: http://www.agaviation.org
AMOUNT: Varies
DEADLINE(S): AUG 15
FIELD(S): Agriculture, Aviation,
Aeronautics
ELIGIBILITY/REQUIREMENTS:
Spouse, child, son-/daughter-in-law, grand-
child of an operator, pilot, or allied indus-
try member of NAAA. Sponsor must be a
currently active dues-paying member.
Financial need considered.
HOW TO APPLY: See website and click
on WNAAA after MAR 1.
NUMBER OF AWARDS: 2
CONTACT: Lindsay Barber

1085—NATIONAL AIR AND SPACE MUSEUM (Ramsey Fellowship in Naval Aviation History)

Smithsonian Institution
Independence Avenue
at Sixth Street SW
Room 3313, MRC 312
P.O. Box 37012
Washington DC 20013-7012
202/633-2648
FAX: 202/786-2447
E-mail: NASM-Fellowships@si.edu
Internet: http://www.nasm.si.edu
AMOUNT: $45,000
DEADLINE(S): JAN 15
FIELD(S): Aeronautics; History of
Aviation
ELIGIBILITY/REQUIREMENTS: 9- to
12-month in-residence fellowship candi-

dates who provide a critical approach to trends and accomplishments in aviation or space history. Good writing skills required. Advanced degree is NOT required. Scholarships are open to undergraduates enrolled in accredited institutions, who have completed at least 1 year of college by start of fellowship. Based on academic performance/class standing, career goals, recommendations, and compatibility of scientific interests/abilities with needs/resources of host facility. Citizenship restrictions may apply for some facilities.

HOW TO APPLY: See website for application.

CONTACT: Colette Williams, Fellowship Program Coordinator, Collections and Research Department, 202/633-2648.

1086—NATIONAL AIR AND SPACE MUSEUM (Verville Fellowship)

Smithsonian Institution
Independence Avenue
at Sixth Street SW
Room 3313, MRC 312
P.O. Box 37012
Washington DC 20013-7012
202/633-2648
FAX: 202/786-2447
E-mail: NASM-Fellowships@si.edu
Internet: http://www.nasm.si.edu
AMOUNT: $45,000
DEADLINE(S): JAN 15
FIELD(S): Aeronautics; History of Aviation or Space Studies
ELIGIBILITY/REQUIREMENTS: 9- to 12-month in-residence fellowship candidates who provide a critical approach to trends and accomplishments in aviation or space history. Good writing skills required. Advanced degree is NOT required. Scholarships are open to undergraduates enrolled in accredited institutions, who have completed at least 1 year of college by start of fellowship. Based on academic performance/class standing, career goals, recommendations, and compatibility of scientific interests/abilities with needs/resources of host facility. Citizenship restrictions may apply for some facilities.
HOW TO APPLY: See website for application.
CONTACT: Colette Williams, Fellowship Program Coordinator, Collections and Research Department, 202/633-2648.

1087—NATIONAL BUSINESS AVIATION ASSOCIATION (Indiana Business Aviation Association PDP Scholarships)

1200 Eighteenth Street NW,
Suite 400

Washington DC 20036-2527
202/783-9353
FAX: 202/331-8364
E-mail: jevans@nbaa.org
Internet: http://www.nbaa.org/
scholar/scholarships/
AMOUNT: $1,150
DEADLINE(S): AUG 31
FIELD(S): Aviation-related curricula
ELIGIBILITY/REQUIREMENTS: Valid only for students enrolled at institutions that are NBAA and University Aviation Association (UAA) members. Open to college sophomores, juniors, or seniors who will be continuing in school the following academic year in an aviation-related baccalaureate or graduate program at these specific member institutions. Must be U.S. citizen and have 3.0 or better GPA.
HOW TO APPLY: Check website or contact NBAA for information and application.
NUMBER OF AWARDS: 4

1088—NATIONAL BUSINESS AVIATION ASSOCIATION (Lawrence Ginocchio Aviation Scholarship)

1200 Eighteenth Street NW,
Suite 400
Washington DC 20036-2527
202/783-9353
FAX: 202/331-8364
E-mail: jevans@nbaa.org
Internet: http://www.nbaa.org/
scholar/scholarships/
AMOUNT: $5,000
DEADLINE(S): AUG 22
FIELD(S): Aviation-related curricula
ELIGIBILITY/REQUIREMENTS: Valid only for students enrolled at institutions that are NBAA and University Aviation Association (UAA) members. Open to college sophomores, juniors, or seniors who will be continuing in school the following academic year in an aviation-related baccalaureate or graduate program at these specific member institutions. Must be U.S. citizen and have 3.0 or better GPA.
HOW TO APPLY: Check website or contact NBAA for information and application.
NUMBER OF AWARDS: 5

1089—NATIONAL GAY PILOTS ASSOCIATION (Pilot Scholarships)

13140 Coit Road, Suite 320,
LB 120
Dallas TX 75240
972/233-9107, ext. 203
FAX: 972/490-4219

E-mail: ngpa@ngpa.org
Internet: http://www.ngpa.org
AMOUNT: $2,000
DEADLINE(S): APR 30
FIELD(S): Pilot Training and Related Fields in Aerospace, Aerodynamics, Engineering, Airport Management, etc.
ELIGIBILITY/REQUIREMENTS: Scholarships for tuition or flight training costs for student pilots enrolled at a college or university offering an accredited aviation curriculum in the above fields. Also for flight training costs in a professional pilot training program at any training facility certified by the FAA. Not for training for a Private Pilot license. Send SASE for application or visit website for further instructions. Sexual orientation not considered; contribution to Gay and Lesbian community is a factor.
HOW TO APPLY: Submit application documenting prior academic record and work experience, financial need, extracurricular activities and/or community activities, honors, awards, etc., along with supporting references and a letter of recommendation. Must also submit 2 essays: one outlining career objectives, and the other documenting service in contributing to the Gay and Lesbian community in some positive way.

1090—NATIONAL SPACE CLUB (Dr. Robert H. Goddard Historical Essay Award)

2025 M Street NW, Suite 800
Washington DC 20036-4907
202/973/8661
AMOUNT: $1,000 + plaque
DEADLINE(S): DEC 4
FIELD(S): Aerospace History
ELIGIBILITY/REQUIREMENTS: Essay competition open to any U.S. citizen on a topic dealing with any significant aspect of the historical development of rocketry and astronautics. Essays should not exceed 5,000 words and should be fully documented. Will be judged on originality and scholarship.
HOW TO APPLY: Send SASE for information. Previous winners not eligible.

1091—NATIONAL SPACE CLUB (Dr. Robert H. Goddard Scholarship)

2025 M Street NW, Suite 800
Washington DC 20036-4907
202/973/8661
AMOUNT: $10,000 + plaque
DEADLINE(S): JAN 6
FIELD(S): Science, Engineering

ELIGIBILITY/REQUIREMENTS: Essay competition open to any U.S. citizen, in at least junior year of an accredited university, and intend to pursue undergraduate or graduate studies in science or engineering. Transcript of college record, letters of recommendation from faculty, accomplishments demonstrating personal qualities of creativity and leadership; scholastic plans leading to participation in some phase of the aerospace sciences and technology; proven past research and participation in space-related science and engineering. Personal need considered, but not controlling.

HOW TO APPLY: Apply by letter accompanied by documentation listed above.

RENEWABLE: Yes. For second year if circumstance and accomplishments warrant.

1092—SAN DIEGO AIR &SPACE MUSEUM (Bill Gibbs Endowment Fund)

Education Office
2001 Pan American Plaza
San Diego CA 92101
619/234-8291, ext. 119
FAX: 619/233-4526
Internet: http://aerospace
museum.org
AMOUNT: $1,500-$2,500
DEADLINE(S): APR 1
FIELD(S): Aerospace, Mathematics, Physics, Science, Engineering
ELIGIBILITY/REQUIREMENTS: Graduating seniors of San Diego County high schools who have been accepted to a 4-year college or university. Academic achievement, strong aviation/aerospace career interests.
HOW TO APPLY: See website or write museum for application. Eligible applications will be interviewed.

1093—SAN DIEGO AIR & SPACE MUSEUM (R. A. Rearwin Scholarship Fund)

Education Office
2001 Pan American Plaza
San Diego CA 92101
619/234-8291, ext. 19
FAX: 619/233-4526
Internet: http://aerospace
museum.org
AMOUNT: $3,000-$4,000
DEADLINE(S): APR 1
FIELD(S): Aviation, Aerospace
ELIGIBILITY/REQUIREMENTS: For graduating seniors of San Diego County high schools, who will be attending a 4-year college. Unweighted GPA of 3.0 or

higher, strong aviation/aerospace career interests, pursuing a baccalaureate in an aerospace-related field.
HOW TO APPLY: Call or write museum for application. Eligible applications will be interviewed.

1094—SOCIETY OF AUTOMOTIVE ENGINEERS (Parks College of Saint Louis University/SAE Engineering Scholarship)

SAE Customer Service
400 Commonwealth Drive
Warrendale PA 15096-0001
724/776-4970
FAX: 724/776-1615
E-mail: customerservice@sae.org
Internet: http://www.sae.org/
students/scholarships/
students/scholar/scholarships
AMOUNT: $1,000
DEADLINE(S): DEC 1
FIELD(S): Aerospace Engineering; Mechanical Engineering; Electrical Engineering; Biomedical Engineering; Aircraft Maintenance Engineering; Avionics Engineering; Applied Computer Science; Computer Software Systems; Physics
ELIGIBILITY/REQUIREMENTS: Entering freshman majoring in any of the above areas, enrolled in a baccalaureate program. Award based on academic achievement and financial need.
HOW TO APPLY: See website for application. Submit application; a personal essay that demonstrates hands-on experience or activity (such as rebuilding engines, working on cars/trucks, etc.); 2 recommendations, 1 of which must be from a teacher, counselor, or administrator; and transcript.
NUMBER OF AWARDS: 1
RENEWABLE: No

1095—SOUTH CAROLINA SPACE GRANT CONSORTIUM (Undergraduate Research Program)

Department of Geology and
Environmental Geosciences
College of Charleston
66 George Street
Charleston SC 29424
843/953-5463
FAX: 843/953-5446
E-mail: scozzarot@cofc.edu
Internet: http://www.cofc.edu/
~scs.grant
AMOUNT: $3,000

DEADLINE(S): End of JAN; check application for SPECIFIC deadline date
FIELD(S): Aerospace or Space-related Studies (including, but not limited to, the Basic Sciences; Science Education; Astronomy; Planetary Science; Environmental Studies; Engineering; Fine Arts; Journalism)
ELIGIBILITY/REQUIREMENTS: Must be a citizen of the U.S.; attend a consortium member institution; have sponsorship from a faculty advisor; be a rising junior or senior; have an interest in aerospace and space-related studies. Selection of awards is based on academic qualifications of the applicant; 2 letters of recommendation; description of past activities, current interests and future plans concerning a space science or aerospace related field; faculty sponsorship and a research proposal including its relevance to a NASA mission.
HOW TO APPLY: Submit application to your institution's campus director.
NUMBER OF AWARDS: 1
RENEWABLE: No
CONTACT: Tara B. Scozzaro

1096—SPIE: THE INTERNATIONAL SOCIETY FOR OPTICAL ENGINEERING (SPIE Educational Scholarships & Grants in Optical Science and Engineering)

P.O. Box 10
Bellingham WA 98227-0010
360/676-3290
FAX: 360/647-1445
E-mail: scholarships@spie.org
Internet: http://www.spie.org
AMOUNT: $1,000-$10,000
DEADLINE(S): JAN 6
FIELD(S): Optics, Photonics, Imaging, Optoelectronics or related discipline
ELIGIBILITY/REQUIREMENTS: Undergraduate and graduate students must be enrolled full time in one of the fields as mentioned above at an educational institution for the academic year in which the award is used. This requirement does not apply to high school students.
HOW TO APPLY: See website. Must submit application, 2 letters of reference, a 450-word essay and the annual scholarship award report (if applicable) by deadline.
RENEWABLE: Yes. Must submit an annual scholarship award report if reapplying. Your application must show new activities beyond those upon which a previous award was based.
ADDITIONAL INFORMATION: Must be an SPIE student member or submit an application for student membership including dues payment with the scholar-

ship application to SPIE by the deadline. NOTE: High school students may receive a complimentary (free) student membership after submitting a membership application.

1097—VERTICAL FLIGHT FOUNDATION (AHS Vertical Flight Foundation Engineering Scholarships)

217 North Washington Street
Alexandria VA 22314-2538
703/684-6777
FAX: 703/739-9279
E-mail: staff@vtol.org
Internet: http://www.vtol.org/vff.html
AMOUNT: $2,000-$4,000
DEADLINE(S): FEB 1
FIELD(S): Engineering related to vertical flight
ELIGIBILITY/REQUIREMENTS: These merit-based awards, from the American Helicopter Society, are open to undergraduate juniors and seniors and graduate students pursuing full-time studies in vertical flight at accredited schools of engineering. Must submit transcripts and references. Financial need NOT a factor.
HOW TO APPLY: See website or contact VFF for an application.
NUMBER OF AWARDS: 3 to 8
RENEWABLE: Yes. Scholarships awarded to student once as an undergraduate senior, once as a master's student, and once as a Ph.D. student.

1098—VIRGINIA AIRPORT OPERATORS COUNCIL (John R. Lillard VAOC Scholarship Program)

Virginia Aviation and Space Education Forum
5702 Gulfstream Road
Richmond VA 23250-2422
202/546-5722
FAX: 202/546-5726
E-mail: information@agaviation.org
Internet: http://www.agaviation.org
AMOUNT: $1,500
DEADLINE(S): FEB 20
FIELD(S): Aviation; Aeronautics
ELIGIBILITY/REQUIREMENTS: Spouse, child, son-/daughter-in-law, grandchild of an operator, pilot, or allied industry member of NAAA. Sponsor must be a currently active dues-paying member. Financial need considered.
HOW TO APPLY: See website or call for an application. Submit with official copy of high school transcript and a copy of acceptance letters or other verification of enroll-

ment. Include a 350-500-word essay on "Why I Wish a Career in Aviation"; up to 3 letters of recommendation and a list of both school-related and extracurricular activities demonstrating accomplishments and leadership capabilities. Applications evaluated as follows: 35% Scholarship (GPA), 30% Essay, 20% Accomplishments and Leadership, and 15% financial need.
CONTACT: Betty Wilson

APPLIED ENGINEERING/ ENGINEERING TECHNOLOGY

1099—AMERICAN RADIO RELAY LEAGUE FOUNDATION (Charles N. Fisher Memorial Scholarship)

225 Main Street
Newington CT 06111
860/594-0397
FAX: 860/594-0259
E-mail: foundation@arrl.org
Internet: http://www.arrlf.org/
AMOUNT: $1,000
DEADLINE(S): FEB 1
FIELD(S): Electronics, Communications or related fields
ELIGIBILITY/REQUIREMENTS: For student with any class license pursuing baccalaureate or higher degree at a regionally accredited institution. Must be a resident of Southwestern Division (AZ and Los Angeles, Orange, San Diego, Santa Barbara, CA) attending a regionally accredited school.
HOW TO APPLY: See website or contact Foundation for information and application. Submit with a 1-page essay on the role amateur radio has played in your life. A recent high school (or equivalent) or college transcript required; submit with application or mail separately.
NUMBER OF AWARDS: 1
RENEWABLE: No
CONTACT: Mary M. Hobart, K1MMH, Secretary

1100—AMERICAN RADIO RELAY LEAGUE FOUNDATION (Dr. James L. Lawson Memorial Scholarship)

225 Main Street
Newington CT 06111
860/594-0397
FAX: 860/594-0259
E-mail: foundation@arrl.org
Internet: http://www.arrlf.org/
AMOUNT: $500

DEADLINE(S): FEB 1
FIELD(S): Electronics, Communications or related fields
ELIGIBILITY/REQUIREMENTS: For student with general license or higher pursuing baccalaureate or higher degree who is resident of New England states (ME, NH, VT, MA, CT, RI) or New York State and attending college in one of those states.
HOW TO APPLY: See website or contact Foundation for information and application. Submit with a 1-page essay on the role amateur radio has played in your life. A recent high school (or equivalent) or college transcript required; submit with application or mail separately.
NUMBER OF AWARDS: 1
RENEWABLE: No
CONTACT: Mary M. Hobart, K1MMH, Secretary

1101—AMERICAN RADIO RELAY LEAGUE FOUNDATION (Earl I. Anderson Scholarship)

225 Main Street
Newington CT 06111
860/594-0397
FAX: 860/594-0259
E-mail: foundation@arrl.org
Internet: http://www.arrlf.org/
AMOUNT: $1,250
DEADLINE(S): FEB 1
FIELD(S): Electronic Engineering or related technical field
ELIGIBILITY/REQUIREMENTS: For student with general or higher license attending an accredited 1- or 4-year college or university. Must be an ARR member and a resident attending classes in IL, IN, MI, or FL.
HOW TO APPLY: See website or contact Foundation for information and application. Submit with a 1-page essay on the role amateur radio has played in your life. A recent high school (or equivalent) or college transcript required; submit with application or mail separately.
NUMBER OF AWARDS: 3
RENEWABLE: No
CONTACT: Mary M. Hobart, K1MMH, Secretary

1102—AMERICAN RADIO RELAY LEAGUE FOUNDATION (Fred R. McDaniel Memorial Scholarship)

225 Main Street
Newington CT 06111
860/594-0397
FAX: 860/594-0259

E-mail: foundation@arrl.org
Internet: http://www.arrlf.org/
AMOUNT: $500
DEADLINE(S): FEB 1
FIELD(S): Electronics, Communications or related fields
ELIGIBILITY/REQUIREMENTS: Open to radio amateurs holding a general license or higher who are FCC Fifth Call District (TX, OK, AR, LA, MS, NM) residents attending 4-year college or university in the District and enrolled in baccalaureate or higher program. Minimum 3.0 GPA required.
HOW TO APPLY: See website or contact Foundation for information and application. Submit with a 1-page essay on the role amateur radio has played in your life. A recent high school (or equivalent) or college transcript required; submit with application or mail separately.
NUMBER OF AWARDS: 1
RENEWABLE: No
CONTACT: Mary M. Hobart, K1MMH, Secretary

1103—AMERICAN RADIO RELAY LEAGUE FOUNDATION (Irving W. Cook, WAOCGS Scholarship)

225 Main Street
Newington CT 06111
860/594-0397
FAX: 860/594-0259
E-mail: foundation@arrl.org
Internet: http://www.arrlf.org/
AMOUNT: $1,000
DEADLINE(S): FEB 1
FIELD(S): Electronics, Communications or related fields
ELIGIBILITY/REQUIREMENTS: For student or child of deceased radio amateur with any class license pursuing baccalaureate or higher degree at an accredited institution. Must be a resident of Kansas.
HOW TO APPLY: See website or contact Foundation for information and application. Submit with a 1-page essay on the role amateur radio has played in your life. A recent high school (or equivalent) or college transcript required; submit with application or mail separately.
NUMBER OF AWARDS: 1
RENEWABLE: No
CONTACT: Mary M. Hobart, K1MMH, Secretary

1104—AMERICAN RADIO RELAY LEAGUE FOUNDATION (L. Phil Wicker Scholarship)

225 Main Street
Newington CT 06111

860/594-0397
FAX: 860/594-0259
E-mail: foundation@arrl.org
Internet: http://www.arrl.org/
AMOUNT: $1,000
DEADLINE(S): FEB 1
FIELD(S): Electronics, Communications or related fields
ELIGIBILITY/REQUIREMENTS: For student with general license or higher pursuing baccalaureate or higher degree at a regionally accredited institution. Must be a resident of Roanoke Division (NC, SC, VA, WV) attending school in that area.
HOW TO APPLY: See website or contact Foundation for information and application. Submit with a 1-page essay on the role amateur radio has played in your life. A recent high school (or equivalent) or college transcript required; submit with application or mail separately.
NUMBER OF AWARDS: 1
RENEWABLE: No
CONTACT: Mary M. Hobart, K1MMH, Secretary

1105—AMERICAN RADIO RELAY LEAGUE FOUNDATION (Mississippi Scholarship)

225 Main Street
Newington CT 06111
860/594-0397
FAX: 860/594-0259
E-mail: foundation@arrl.org
Internet: http://www.arrlf.org/
AMOUNT: $500
DEADLINE(S): FEB 1
FIELD(S): Electronics, Communications or related fields
ELIGIBILITY/REQUIREMENTS: For student under 30 with any class license pursuing baccalaureate or higher degree. Must be a resident of Mississippi attending school at a Mississippi institution.
HOW TO APPLY: See website or contact Foundation for information and application. Submit with a 1-page essay on the role amateur radio has played in your life. A recent high school (or equivalent) or college transcript required; submit with application or mail separately.
NUMBER OF AWARDS: 1
RENEWABLE: No
CONTACT: Mary M. Hobart, K1MMH, Secretary

1106—AMERICAN RADIO RELAY LEAGUE FOUNDATION (NEMAL Electronics Scholarship)

225 Main Street
Newington CT 06111

860/594-0397
FAX: 860/594-0259
E-mail: foundation@arrl.org
Internet: http://www.arrlf.org/
AMOUNT: $1,000
DEADLINE(S): FEB 1
FIELD(S): Electronics, Communications or related fields
ELIGIBILITY/REQUIREMENTS: For student with any general or higher license pursuing baccalaureate or higher degree at an accredited 2- or 4-year college or university. Preference given to applicants residing in the southeastern U.S. Must demonstrate financial need and have a minimum 3.0 GPA. Participation in community service or civic volunteer organizations preferred.
HOW TO APPLY: See website or contact Foundation for information and application. Submit with a 1-page essay on the role amateur radio has played in your life. A recent high school (or equivalent) or college transcript required; submit with application or mail separately.
NUMBER OF AWARDS: 1
RENEWABLE: No
CONTACT: Mary M. Hobart, K1MMH, Secretary

1107—AMERICAN RADIO RELAY LEAGUE FOUNDATION (Paul and Helen L. Grauer Scholarship)

225 Main Street
Newington CT 06111
860/594-0397
FAX: 860/594-0259
E-mail: foundation@arrl.org
Internet: http://www.arrlf.org/
AMOUNT: $1,000
DEADLINE(S): FEB 1
FIELD(S): Electronics, Communications or related fields
ELIGIBILITY/REQUIREMENTS: For student with novice license or higher pursuing baccalaureate or higher degree at a regionally accredited institution. Must be a resident of Midwest Division (IA, KS, MO, NE) attending school in that area.
HOW TO APPLY: See website or contact Foundation for information and application. Submit with a 1-page essay on the role amateur radio has played in your life. A recent high school (or equivalent) or college transcript required; submit with application or mail separately.
NUMBER OF AWARDS: 1
RENEWABLE: No
CONTACT: Mary M. Hobart, K1MMH, Secretary

1108—AMERICAN RAILWAY ENGINEERING AND MAINTENANCE-OF-WAY ASSOCIATION (AREMA)

10003 Derekwood Lane,
Suite 210
Lanham MD 20706
301/459-3200
FAX: 301/459-8077
E-mail: selder@arema.org
Internet: http//www.arema.org
AMOUNT: $1,000 or more
DEADLINE(S): MAR 15
FIELD(S): Engineering; Engineering
Technology
ELIGIBILITY/REQUIREMENTS:
Applicants must be enrolled as full-time students in a 4- or 5-year program leading to a bachelor's degree in a curriculum which has been accredited by the Accreditation Board of Engineering and Technology (or comparable accreditation in Canada and Mexico). Must have completed at least 1 quarter or semester in college prior to submitting an application, and have at least a 2.00 GPA.
HOW TO APPLY: See website for application. Submit with a cover letter, not exceeding 350 words, explaining why the applicant believes he/she deserves scholarship (should indicate areas of railroading that might be of particular interest, and describe how his/her attributes relate to these areas); a résumé; 2 letters of recommendation (1 from a faculty member, and 1 from another faculty member, present or former employer, AREMA member, or other responsible person); and transcript from the school(s) attended. Send all material to AREMA Educational Foundation Scholarship Committee, American Railway Engineering and Maintenance of Way Association, 10003 Derekwood Lane, Suite 210, Lanham, MD 20706.
NUMBER OF AWARDS: 15 or more
RENEWABLE: No
CONTACT: Stacy Elder

1109—AMERICAN SOCIETY OF AGRICULTURAL ENGINEERS (ASAE Foundation Scholarship)

2950 Niles Road
St. Joseph MI 49085-9659
269/429-0300
FAX: 269/429-3852
E-mail: hq@asae.org
Internet: http://www.asae.org
AMOUNT: $1,000
DEADLINE(S): APR 15
FIELD(S): Agricultural Engineering;
Biological Engineering
ELIGIBILITY/REQUIREMENTS:
Applicants must verify that graduation from their agricultural or biological degree program assures eligibility for the Professional Engineer licensing examination; be sophomore or junior undergraduate in the U.S. or Canada; major in an agricultural or biological engineering curriculum that is accredited by ABET or CEAB; be a student member of ASAE; have a GPA of at least 2.5; and demonstrate financial need.
HOW TO APPLY: Send completed application; personal letter (of no more than 2 pages) formally requesting the ASAE Foundation Scholarship and stating how the money will be used; and letter from college dean or department chair on corroborating applicant's information.
NUMBER OF AWARDS: 1

1110—AMERICAN SOCIETY OF AGRICULTURAL ENGINEERS (John L. & Sarah G. Merriam Scholarship)

2950 Niles Road
St. Joseph MI 49085-9659
269/429-0300
FAX: 269/429-3852
E-mail: hq@asae.org
Internet: http://www.asae.org
AMOUNT: $1,000
DEADLINE(S): APR 15
FIELD(S): Agricultural Engineering;
Biological Engineering
ELIGIBILITY/REQUIREMENTS:
Applicants must have a special interest in the soil and water field of study; be sophomore or junior undergraduate students in the U.S. or Canada; major in an agricultural or biological engineering curriculum, with an emphasis of study in soil & water, that is accredited by ABET or CEAB; be a student member of ASAE; have a GPA of at least 2.5 on a 4.0 scale; and demonstrate need for financial aid.
HOW TO APPLY: Send completed application; personal letter (of no more than 2 pages) formally requesting the Merriam Scholarship grant and stating why applicant has selected the soil & water discipline as the focus of applicant's degree; and letter from college dean or department chair on official college stationery corroborating applicant's information.
NUMBER OF AWARDS: 1

1111—AMERICAN SOCIETY OF AGRICULTURAL ENGINEERS (Student Engineer of the Year Scholarship)

2950 Niles Road
St. Joseph MI 49085-9659

269/429-0300
FAX: 269/429-3852
E-mail: hq@asae.org
Internet: http://www.asae.org
AMOUNT: $1,000
DEADLINE(S): FEB 15
FIELD(S): Agricultural Engineering;
Biological Engineering
ELIGIBILITY/REQUIREMENTS:
Applicants must be sophomore or junior undergraduate students in the U.S. or Canada; major in an agricultural/biological engineering curriculum that is accredited by ABET or CEAB; be a student member of ASAE; and have a GPA of at least 3.0 on a 4.0 scale. Award criteria include scholarship excellence; outstanding character and personal development; student membership in ASAE and active participation in a student branch organization; participation in overall school activities; leadership qualities, creativity, initiative, and responsibility; and some financial self-support.
HOW TO APPLY: Send completed application, signed by the department head or representative, and an essay not exceeding 500 words on "My Goals in the Engineering Profession."

1112—AMERICAN SOCIETY OF AGRICULTURAL ENGINEERS (William J. and Marijane E. Adams Jr. Scholarship)

2950 Niles Road
St. Joseph MI 49085-9659
269/429-0300
FAX: 269/429-3852
E-mail: hq@asae.org
Internet: http://www.asae.org
AMOUNT: $1,000
DEADLINE(S): APR 15
FIELD(S): Agricultural Engineering;
Biological Engineering
ELIGIBILITY/REQUIREMENTS:
Applicants must have a special interest in agricultural machinery product design and development; be sophomore or junior undergraduate students in the U.S. or Canada; major in an agricultural or biological engineering curriculum that is accredited by ABET or CEAB; be a student member of ASAE; have a GPA of at least 2.5 on a 4.0 scale; and demonstrate need for financial aid.
HOW TO APPLY: Send completed application; personal letter (of no more than 2 pages) formally requesting the Adams Scholarship grant and stating the extent of financial need, how the money will be used, and why applicant has selected the design and development of new agricultural machinery products as the focus of applicant's degree; and letter from college dean

or department chair on official college stationery corroborating applicant's information.
NUMBER OF AWARDS: 1

1113—AMERICAN SOCIETY OF ENGINEERS OF INDIAN ORIGIN

47790 Pavillon Road
Canton MI 48188
248/354-6895
FAX: 248/354-6818
E-mail: awards@asei-ncc.org
Internet: http://www.asei-ncc.org/Awards.htm
AMOUNT: $1,000
DEADLINE(S): AUG 15
FIELD(S): Engineering: Architecture, Computer or allied science, Geotechnical or Geo-environmental Engineering, and allied sciences
ELIGIBILITY/REQUIREMENTS: Open to students who are Indian by birth, ancestry, or relation. Based on demonstrated ability, academic achievement, including GPA (minimum 3.0)/honors/awards, career objectives, faculty recommendations, student involvement in science fair, campus activities, and industrial exposure including part-time work and internship; must attend an accredited college or university anywhere in the U.S.
HOW TO APPLY: See website for application and details or contact Society for applications. Submit with résumé; an essay (maximum 1 page) stating qualifications, career goals, reasons for seeking the scholarship; 1 letter of recommendation in the current or intended field of study.
CONTACT: Dr. Ramu Ramamurthy, ASEI Scholarship Committee Chairman

1114—AMERICAN SOCIETY OF HEATING, REFRIGERATING, AND AIR-CONDITIONING ENGINEERS (Associate Degree Engineering Technology Scholarships)

1791 Tullie Circle NE
Atlanta GA 30329
404/636-8400
FAX: 404/321-5478
E-mail: benedict@ashrae.org
Internet: http://www.ashrae.org
AMOUNT: $3,000
DEADLINE(S): MAY 1
FIELD(S): Engineering Technology
ELIGIBILITY/REQUIREMENTS: For full-time students in a 2-year associates degree engineering technology program. Must have a minimum college GPA of 3.0; be enrolled full time in a college or university with at least 1 full year of studies remaining in the year for which the schol-

arship will be awarded; demonstrate potential service to the HVAC&R profession, need for financial assistance, leadership ability, and character.
HOW TO APPLY: See website or contact Society for information and application.
NUMBER OF AWARDS: 2
RENEWABLE: No
CONTACT: Lois Benedict, Scholarship Administrator

1115—AMERICAN SOCIETY OF HEATING, REFRIGERATING, AND AIR-CONDITIONING ENGINEERS (Associate Degree Engineering Technology Scholarships)

1791 Tullie Circle NE
Atlanta GA 30329
404/636-8400
FAX: 404/321-5478
E-mail: benedict@ashrae.org
Internet: http://www.ashrae.org
AMOUNT: $3,000
DEADLINE(S): MAY 1
FIELD(S): Engineering Technology
ELIGIBILITY/REQUIREMENTS: For full-time students in a 5-year bachelor degree engineering technology program. Must have a minimum college GPA of 3.0; be enrolled full time in a college or university with at least 1 full year of studies remaining in the year for which the scholarship will be awarded; demonstrate potential service to the HVAC&R profession, need for financial assistance, leadership ability, and character.
HOW TO APPLY: See website or contact Society for information and application. Submit with letters of recommendation, transcripts, and demonstration of financial need.
NUMBER OF AWARDS: 1
RENEWABLE: No
CONTACT: Lois Benedict, Scholarship Administrator

1116—AMERICAN WATER RESOURCES ASSOCIATION (Richard A. Herbert Memorial Scholarships)

4 West Federal Street
P.O. Box 1626
Middleburg VA 20118-1626
540/687-8390
FAX: 540/687-8395
E-mail: info@awra.org
Internet: http://www.awra.org
AMOUNT: $2,000
DEADLINE(S): APR 30
FIELD(S): Water Resources and related fields (Hydrology, Hydrogeology, G.I.S., Earth Science, Watershed Studies, and others)

ELIGIBILITY/REQUIREMENTS: Applicant must be a national AWRA member, either a full-time undergraduate working towards first degree or graduate student. Must be enrolled in a program relating to water resources for the academic year. Awards are based on academic performance, including cumulative GPA, relevance of curriculum to water resources, and leadership in extracurricular activities related to water resources. Quality and relevance of research is also considered from graduate students. Transcripts, 3 letters of reference (preferably from professors or advisors), and 2-page summary of academic interests/achievements, extracurricular interests, and career goals required.
HOW TO APPLY: Contact AWRA Student Activities Committee for an application. Recipients announced in the summer.
NUMBER OF AWARDS: 2 (1 undergrad and 1 graduate)

1117—AMERICAN WELDING SOCIETY

550 NW LeJeune Road
Miami FL 33126
800/443-9353, ext. 250
305/445-6628
FAX: 305/443-7559
Internet: http://www.aws.org
AMOUNT: $2,500-$3,000
DEADLINE(S): JAN 15
FIELD(S): Welding Engineering and Technology
ELIGIBILITY/REQUIREMENTS: AWS has 9 different scholarship programs for U.S. citizens pursuing undergraduate study at an accredited U.S. institution. Two programs are also for Canadian citizens studying at Canadian institutions. Must be at least 18 years of age with a high school diploma or equivalent and a minimum 2.0 GPA. Some programs require financial need.
HOW TO APPLY: Contact AWS for details on specific scholarships. Must submit 2 letters of reference, brief biography, transcript, proposed curriculum, and verification of enrollment/employment. Awards announced in February.
RENEWABLE: Yes. Up to 4 years.

1118—ASPRS: THE IMAGING & GEOSPATIAL INFORMATION SOCIETY (Kenneth J. Osborn Memorial Scholarship)

ASPRS Awards Program
5410 Grosvenor Lane, Suite 210
Bethesda MD 20814-2160
301/493-0290, ext. 101
FAX: 301/493-0208
E-mail: scholarships@asprs.org

Internet: http://www.asprs.org
AMOUNT: $1,000
DEADLINE(S): DEC 1
FIELD(S): Surveying, Mapping, Photogrammetry, Geospatial Information and Technology
ELIGIBILITY/REQUIREMENTS: Open to undergraduates who display exceptional interest, desire, ability, and aptitude to enter the profession of surveying, mapping, photogrammetry, or geospatial information and technology. In addition, the Scholarship recognizes students who excel at communications and collaboration.
HOW TO APPLY: Submit 6 copies of the completed application and the following supporting materials: academic transcripts, including a separate list of relevant courses taken; 2 completed reference forms from faculty members who have knowledge of your abilities; samples of your work; description of your research goals; statement of work experience that may include internships, other forms of work experience, or special projects that demonstrate excellence in these fields and in communications and collaboration (including the nature, location and date(s) of the experience); a 2-page statement regarding your plans for continuing studies in theoretical photogrammetry; and papers, research reports, or other items that indicate capability in these fields. Note: Electronic submissions encouraged.
NUMBER OF AWARDS: 1
RENEWABLE: No
CONTACT: Scholarship Administrator at above address or see website.
ADDITIONAL INFORMATION: The recipient is obligated to provide a final report to ASPRS of his/her scholastic accomplishments during the period for which the award is granted.

1119—ASPRS: THE IMAGING & GEOSPATIAL INFORMATION SOCIETY (Robert E. Altenhofen Memorial Scholarship)

ASPRS Awards Program
5410 Grosvenor Lane, Suite 210
Bethesda MD 20814-2160
301/493-0290, ext. 101
FAX: 301/493-0208
E-mail: scholarships@asprs.org
Internet: http://www.asprs.org
AMOUNT: $2,000
DEADLINE(S): DEC 1
FIELD(S): Photogrammetry
ELIGIBILITY/REQUIREMENTS: Graduates who display exceptional interest and ability in the theoretical aspects of photogrammetry; must be enrolled in an accredited college or university and be active student members of ASPRS.
HOW TO APPLY: Submit 6 copies of the completed application and the following supporting materials: academic transcripts, including a separate list of relevant courses taken; 2 completed reference forms from faculty members who have knowledge of your abilities; samples of your work; description of your research goals; a 2-page statement regarding your plans for continuing studies in theoretical photogrammetry; and papers, research reports, or other items that indicate capability in these fields. Note: Electronic submissions encouraged.
NUMBER OF AWARDS: 1
RENEWABLE: No
CONTACT: Scholarship Administrator
ADDITIONAL INFORMATION: The recipient is obligated to provide a final report to ASPRS of his/her scholastic accomplishments during the period for which the award is granted.

1120—ASPRS: THE IMAGING & GEOSPATIAL INFORMATION SOCIETY (Space Imaging Award for Application of High Resolution Digital Satellite Imagery)

ASPRS Awards Program
5410 Grosvenor Lane, Suite 210
Bethesda MD 20814-2160
301/493-0290, ext. 101
FAX: 301/493-0208
E-mail: scholarships@asprs.org
Internet: http://www.asprs.org
AMOUNT: Grant of data valued up to $4,000
DEADLINE(S): DEC 1
FIELD(S): Remote Sensing; Digital Satellite Imagery
ELIGIBILITY/REQUIREMENTS: Full-time undergraduate or graduate students at an accredited college or university with image processing facilities appropriate for conducting the proposed work.
HOW TO APPLY: Submit 6 copies of the application and the following supporting materials: 2 completed reference forms from faculty members; samples of your work; description of your research goals; and a brief proposal describing the proposed research, the purpose of the research, the application it might address, the physical features of the study area, the analysis procedure, your anticipated results, an itemized budget, and a list of all courses, workshops, and other training/experience that demonstrate your ability to conduct the proposed research. Note: Electronic submissions encouraged.
NUMBER OF AWARDS: 1
RENEWABLE: No
CONTACT: Scholarship Administrator
ADDITIONAL INFORMATION: The recipient (or his/her representative) must attend presentation ceremony during the annual meeting to receive the award certificate and plaque. Must prepare a written report of the project and submit it to ASPRS and Space Imaging for possible company use within 1 year of receipt of data.

1121—ASPRS: THE IMAGING & GEOSPATIAL INFORMATION SOCIETY (Student Travel Grants)

ASPRS Awards Program
5410 Grosvenor Lane, Suite 210
Bethesda MD 20814-2160
301/493-0290, ext. 101
FAX: 301/493-0208
E-mail: scholarships@asprs.org
Internet: http://www.asprs.org
AMOUNT: $500
DEADLINE(S): DEC 1
FIELD(S): Photogrammetry
ELIGIBILITY/REQUIREMENTS: ASPRS selects qualified students to attend the ASPRS Annual Conference with financial support from the ASPRS Foundation.
HOW TO APPLY: Submit written statement of no more than 1 page outlining the importance of attending this conference in relation to the applicant's course of study and career development plans. Supplemental materials are also permitted (transcripts, publications, etc.) and at least one letter of recommendation from a faculty advisor. Note: Electronic submissions encouraged.
NUMBER OF AWARDS: 2
RENEWABLE: No
CONTACT: Scholarship Administrator at above address or see website.
ADDITIONAL INFORMATION: The grants also include a 1-year student membership in ASPRS and a complimentary conference registration for the selected student(s) provided they volunteer to help at the conference.

1122—ASPRS: THE IMAGING & GEOSPATIAL INFORMATION SOCIETY (William A. Fischer Memorial Scholarship)

5410 Grosvenor Lane, Suite 210
Bethesda MD 20814-2160
301/493-0290
FAX: 301/493-0208
E-mail: asprs@asprs.org
Internet: http://www.asprs.org
AMOUNT: $2,000 + certificate
DEADLINE(S): DEC 2

FIELD(S): Remote Sensing
ELIGIBILITY/REQUIREMENTS: Open to current or prospective graduate students enrolled full time at an accredited college or university with image processing facilities appropriate for conducting proposed work. Must be ASPRS member.
HOW TO APPLY: See website or contact ASPRS for an application or membership information. May need to submit samples of technical papers or research reports to demonstrate research capability. Upon completion of award period, must submit written report of project. Note: Electronic submissions encouraged.

1123—CONNECTICUT BROADCASTERS ASSOCIATION

90 South Park Street
Willimantic CT 06226
860/633-5031
FAX: 860/456-5688
Internet: http://www.ctba.org
AMOUNT: Varies
DEADLINE(S): JAN 31
FIELD(S): Broadcasting, Marketing, Engineering, Electronics
ELIGIBILITY/REQUIREMENTS: Open to Connecticut residents pursuing a broadcasting career or a career in related fields.
HOW TO APPLY: Applications are available from Connecticut broadcast stations and on website.
NUMBER OF AWARDS: Varies
RENEWABLE: Yes. Some are 4-year, subject to performance; others must reapply.
CONTACT: M. C. Rice, CBA President

1124—GEORGIA ENGINEERING FOUNDATION

Harris Tower, Suite 700
233 Peachtree Street
Atlanta GA 30303
404/521-2324
FAX: 404/521-0283
E-mail: kbdye@mindspring.net
Internet: http://www.gefinc.org
AMOUNT: $500-$5,000
DEADLINE(S): AUG 31
FIELD(S): Engineering; Engineering Technology
ELIGIBILITY/REQUIREMENTS: Must be U.S. citizens, legally resident in Georgia, attending or planning to attend an ABET-accredited engineering or engineering technology program.
HOW TO APPLY: Applicants who are incoming freshmen should send application with transcript of final grades and SAT scores, 2 letters of recommendation, and a

small photograph. Applicants who are college students should send application, a transcript of all college grades, and a small photograph.
NUMBER OF AWARDS: 45
CONTACT: Jan Hunt, Resource Director; Roger Austin, Scholarship Chairman; or the Georgia Engineering Center at above phone number

1125—INSTITUTE OF MINING AND METALLURGY (Centenary Scholarship)

Danum House, South Parade
Doncaster DN1 2DY ENGLAND
+44 (0)1302 320486
FAX: +44(0)1302 380900
E-mail: graham.woodrow@iom3.org
Internet: http://www.iom3.org/awards/scholarships.htm
AMOUNT: £500 pounds
DEADLINE(S): APR 8
FIELD(S): Mining; Metallurgy
ELIGIBILITY/REQUIREMENTS: Open to first- or second-year undergraduates who are student members of the institution. To be used for projects, visits, etc., in furtherance of applicants' career development. Based on academic excellence and scholarship, NOT financial need. Preference will be given to Institute members. Student Membership of the Institute is a requirement.
HOW TO APPLY: Contact Dr. Woodrow at above address or see website for an application or membership information.
CONTACT: Dr. G.J.M. Woodrow, Deputy Chief Executive

1126—INSTITUTE OF MINING AND METALLURGY (G. Vernon Hobson Bequest)

Danum House, South Parade
Doncaster DN1 2DY ENGLAND
+44 (0)1302 320486
FAX: +44(0)1302 380900
E-mail: graham.woodrow@iom3.org
Internet: http://www.iom3.org/awards/scholarships.htm
AMOUNT: Up to £1,300
DEADLINE(S): APR 8
FIELD(S): Mining; Metallurgy, Education
ELIGIBILITY/REQUIREMENTS: 'Advancement of teaching and practice of geology as applied to mining.' One or more awards may therefore be made for travel, research or other objects in accordance with these terms. Preference given to IMM members.
HOW TO APPLY: Contact Dr. Woodrow at above address or see website for an application or membership information.

NUMBER OF AWARDS: 1
CONTACT: Dr. G.J.M. Woodrow, Deputy Chief Executive

1127—INSTITUTE OF MINING AND METALLURGY (Stanley Elmore Fellowship Fund)

Danum House, South Parade
Doncaster DN1 2DY ENGLAND
+44 (0)1302 320486
FAX: +44(0)1302 380900
E-mail: graham.woodrow@iom3.org
Internet: http://www.iom3.org/awards/scholarships.htm
AMOUNT: Up to £14,000
DEADLINE(S): APR 8
FIELD(S): Mining; Metallurgy
ELIGIBILITY/REQUIREMENTS: Fellowships tenable at a United Kingdom university for research into all branches of extractive metallurgy and mineral processing, and in special cases, for expenditure related to such research. Based on academic excellence and scholarship, NOT financial need. Preference given to IMM members.
HOW TO APPLY: Contact Dr. Woodrow at above address or see website for an application or membership information.
NUMBER OF AWARDS: 2
RENEWABLE: Normally funded for any 1 year
CONTACT: Dr. G.J.M. Woodrow, Deputy Chief Executive

1128—INTERNATIONAL SOCIETY OF EXPLOSIVES ENGINEERS (McDowell/Nelson/Bob Hermiah/Paul Muehl Combined Scholarship Program)

30325 Bainbridge Road
Cleveland OH 44139
440/349-4400
FAX: 440/349-3788
Internet: http://www.isee.org
AMOUNT: Varies
DEADLINE(S): MAY 31
FIELD(S): Explosives
ELIGIBILITY/REQUIREMENTS: Open to students pursuing their first associate, undergraduate, or graduate degree as full-time students at an accredited college or university. Must be in the process of applying or be already accepted for college admission. Must have a minimum 2.9 GPA and demonstrate financial need.
HOW TO APPLY: See website or contact ISEE for an application. Funds will be sent directly to the educational institution.
RENEWABLE: Yes

1129—JAMES F. LINCOLN ARC WELDING FOUNDATION (Award Program)

P.O. Box 17188
Cleveland OH 44117
216/481-4300
Internet: http://www.jflf.org
AMOUNT: Varies
DEADLINE(S): MAY 1
FIELD(S): Arc Welding and Engineering
Design
ELIGIBILITY/REQUIREMENTS: Open
to high school students, college undergraduates, and graduate students, and to professionals working in the fields of arc welding and engineering design. Various programs are available.
HOW TO APPLY: See website or send
SASE to Roy Morrow, President, at above
address.

1130—LOS ANGELES COUNCIL OF BLACK PROFESSIONAL ENGINEERS (Al-Ben Scholarship)

P.O. Box 881029
Los Angeles CA 90009
310/635-7734
E-mail: secy1@lablackengineers.org
Internet: http://www.lablack
engineers. org/scholarships.html
AMOUNT: Varies
DEADLINE(S): Varies
FIELD(S): Engineering; Mathematics;
Computer Studies; Applied Science
ELIGIBILITY/REQUIREMENTS: Open
to technically inclined high school and
undergraduate students enrolled in one of
the above fields. Must be of African
American, Native American, or Hispanic
ancestry. Preference given to students
attending college in Southern California or
who are Southern California residents.
HOW TO APPLY: See website to download an application.

1131—NATIONAL ASSOCIATION OF WATER COMPANIES-NEW JERSEY CHAPTER

Elizabethtown Water Company
600 South Avenue
Westfield NJ 07091
908/654-1234
FAX: 908/232-2719
E-mail: gbradygbconsult@
comcast.net
AMOUNT: $2,500
DEADLINE(S): APR 1
FIELD(S): Business Administration;
Biology; Chemistry; Engineering
Communications

ELIGIBILITY/REQUIREMENTS: For
U.S. citizens who have lived in NJ at least 5
years and plan a career in the investor-
owned water utility industry. Must be
undergraduate or graduate student in a 2-
or 4-year NJ college or university. GPA of
3.0 or better required.
HOW TO APPLY: Contact Association
for complete information.
CONTACT: Gail P. Brady

1132—NATIONAL SOCIETY OF BLACK ENGINEERS (NSBE Fellows Scholarship Program)

1454 Duke Street
Alexandria VA 22314
703/549-2207
FAX: 703/683-5312
E-mail: nsbehq@nsbe.org
Internet: http://www.nsbe.org
AMOUNT: $1,000-$3,000
DEADLINE(S): Varies
FIELD(S): Engineering; Engineering
Technologies
ELIGIBILITY/REQUIREMENTS: All
paid NSBE undergraduate and graduate
student members are eligible to apply.
(Non-engineering/technical majors are not
eligible.) All applicants must attend a
College/University in the United States.
Award GPA Minimum Requirements (4.0
scale): Mike Shinn (3.5), BCA (3.0), Major
Sponsors (3.0), NSBE (2.7). Recipients will
be selected based on a combination of the
following criteria: university academic
achievement (GPA, honors, etc.); service
to NSBE (Chapter, Regional, and/or
National); other professional, campus, and
community activities; essay response.
HOW TO APPLY: See website for application and details. The application must be
submitted online and must include an official university/college transcript and a current résumé.
NUMBER OF AWARDS: 4

1133—NEW ENGLAND WATER WORKS ASSOCIATION

125 Hopping Brook Road
Holliston MA 01746
508/893-7979
FAX: 508/93-9898
E-mail: mruozzi@newwa.org
Internet: http://www.newwa.org
AMOUNT: Varies
DEADLINE(S): JUL 1
FIELD(S): Water Industry; Civil or
Environmental Engineering; Business
Management; Science
ELIGIBILITY/REQUIREMENTS:
Based on merit, character, and need, with

preference given to those students whose
programs are considered beneficial to
water works practice in New England.
Each scholarship applicant must be a member or student member of either the New
England Water Works Association, or the
American Water Works Association, with
a New England section, before their application will be considered. The membership
fee is $25 for a NEWWA student membership or $36 for a NEWWA/AWWA student membership.
HOW TO APPLY: Mail application to:
Thomas MacElhaney, Scholarship Committee Chair, 631/231-8100 or tmacelhaney@preloadinc.com.
NUMBER OF AWARDS: 6
RENEWABLE: No
CONTACT: Marina Mukandala

1134—PLUMBING-HEATING-COOLING CONTRACTORS/NATIONAL ASSOCIATION EDUCATIONAL FOUNDATION (Delta Faucet Company Scholarship Program)

P.O. Box 6808
Falls Church VA 22040
703/237-8100 or 800/533-7694
FAX: 703/237-7442
Internet: http://www.foundation.
phccweb.org/scholarships/
AMOUNT: $2,500
DEADLINE(S): JUN 1
FIELD(S): Plumbing; Heating; Cooling or
related areas
ELIGIBILITY/REQUIREMENTS: Open
to undergraduates enrolled in an accredited 4-year college or university. Must be
sponsored by an active member of the
PHCC National Association who has
maintained that status for at least the 2-
year period prior to date of application.
HOW TO APPLY: See website or contact
NAPHCC for an application or to search
for PHCC members in your area for sponsorship.
NUMBER OF AWARDS: 6
RENEWABLE: No

1135—PLUMBING-HEATING-COOLING CONTRACTORS/NATIONAL ASSOCIATION EDUCATIONAL FOUNDATION (Educational Foundation Scholarship Program)

P.O. Box 6808
Falls Church VA 22040
703/237-8100 or 800/533-7694
FAX: 703/237-7442
Internet: http://www.foundation.
phccweb.org/scholarships/
AMOUNT: $3,000/year
DEADLINE(S): MAY 1

FIELD(S): Plumbing; Heating; Cooling and related fields

ELIGIBILITY/REQUIREMENTS: Open to undergraduates enrolled at an accredited 4-year college or university. Must be sponsored by an active member of the PHCC National Association who has maintained that status for at least the 2-year period prior to date of application.

HOW TO APPLY: See website or contact NAPHCC for an application or to search for PHCC members in your area for sponsorship. Must submit academic information, letters of recommendation, and maintain a "C" average or better throughout period for which scholarship is awarded.

NUMBER OF AWARDS: 4

RENEWABLE: Yes. Up to 4 years.

1136—SEARS CRAFTSMAN SCHOLARSHIP

NHRA Youth & Education Services
2035 Financial Way
Glendora CA 91741-4602
626/250-2208
FAX: 626/914-9109
E-mail: excel@nhra.org
Internet: http://www.nhra.com

AMOUNT: $250

DEADLINE(S): MAY 1

FIELD(S): Automotive Technology; Industrial/Technical Manufacturing; Marketing

ELIGIBILITY/REQUIREMENTS: Applicants must be seniors graduating from a public, private, or parochial school or education center between January and June. Applicants must be of good character, possess a minimum 2.5 GPA, show evidence of leadership ability, involvement in extracurricular school and community activities, and plan to attend an accredited 2- or 4-year college, university, or technical/vocational program. Students with a failing grade during their high school career will not be considered. Awards will be based on scholastic record, school activities and community involvement, personal essay, recommendations, and financial need.

HOW TO APPLY: Submit application; personal essay; 2 recommendations, 1 of which must be from a teacher, counselor, or administrator; and transcript.

NUMBER OF AWARDS: 21 (3 in each of the 7 National Hot Rod Association Divisions).

CONTACT: Rachel Kaizoji

1137—SOCIETY FOR IMAGING SCIENCE AND TECHNOLOGY (Raymond Davis Scholarship)

7003 Kilworth Lane

Springfield VA 22151
703/642-9090
FAX: 703/642-9094
E-mail: info@imaging.org
Internet: http://www.imaging.org

AMOUNT: $1,000

DEADLINE(S): DEC 15

FIELD(S): Photographic/Imaging Science; Engineering

ELIGIBILITY/REQUIREMENTS: Scholarships for undergraduate juniors or seniors or graduate students for full-time continuing studies in the theory or practice of photographic or imaging science or engineering, including research in the theory or practice of image formation by radiant energy.

HOW TO APPLY: Check the website or write for information and application.

1138—SOCIETY OF AUTOMOTIVE ENGINEERS (Milwaukee School of Engineering/SAE Engineering Scholarship)

SAE Customer Service
400 Commonwealth Drive
Warrendale PA 15096-0001
724/776-4970
FAX: 724/776-1615
E-mail: customerservice@sae.org
Internet: http://www.sae.org/students/scholarships

AMOUNT: $1,000

DEADLINE(S): DEC 1

FIELD(S): Mechanical Engineering; Mechanical Engineering Technology

ELIGIBILITY/REQUIREMENTS: Applicants must be incoming freshmen accepted into either the Mechanical Engineering or Mechanical Engineering Technology program.

HOW TO APPLY: See website for application. Submit application; a personal essay that demonstrates hands-on experience or activity (such as rebuilding engines, working on cars/trucks, etc.); 2 recommendations, 1 of which must be from a teacher, counselor, or administrator; and transcript.

NUMBER OF AWARDS: 1

RENEWABLE: Yes. For up to 3 additional years if the student maintains a 2.5 GPA.

1139—SOCIETY OF AUTOMOTIVE ENGINEERS (Minnesota State University-Mankato/SAE Automotive Technology Scholarship)

SAE Customer Service
400 Commonwealth Drive
Warrendale PA 15096-0001
724/776-4970

FAX: 724/776-1615
E-mail: customerservice@sae.org
Internet: http://www.sae.org/students/scholarships/

AMOUNT: $750

DEADLINE(S): DEC 1

FIELD(S): Automotive Engineering Technology

ELIGIBILITY/REQUIREMENTS: Applicants must be incoming freshmen planning on a major in Automotive Engineering Technology. Scholarship based on merit.

HOW TO APPLY: See website for application. Submit application; a personal essay that demonstrates hands-on experience or activity (such as rebuilding engines, working on cars/trucks, etc.); 2 recommendations, 1 of which must be from a teacher, counselor, or administrator; and transcript.

NUMBER OF AWARDS: 2

RENEWABLE: Yes, must reapply.

1140—SOCIETY OF SATELLITE PROFESSIONALS INTERNATIONAL (SSPI Scholarship Program)

SSPI International Headquarters
The New York Information
Technology Center
55 Broad Street, 14th floor
New York NY 10004
212/809-5199
FAX: 212/825-0075
E-mail: neworbit@aol.com
Internet: http://www.sspi.org

AMOUNT: $1,500-$4,000

DEADLINE(S): DEC 1

FIELD(S): Satellites as related to communications, domestic and international telecommunications policy, remote sensing, journalism, law, meteorology, energy, navigation, business, government, and broadcasting services

ELIGIBILITY/REQUIREMENTS: Applicants must be studying or intend to study satellite-related technologies, policies or applications. Must demonstrate commitment to pursue education and career opportunities in the satellite industry or a field making direct use of satellite technology; academic and leadership achievement; potential for significant contribution to the satellite communications industry.

HOW TO APPLY: Before applying, all applicants must complete a Scholarship Qualification Form that will help determine whether your interests and career plans are a good fit for the program. This will ensure that you have a reasonable chance of winning before you spend the time and money to apply. See website for form and details or send SASE.

1141—SPIE: THE INTERNATIONAL SOCIETY FOR OPTICAL ENGINEERING (SPIE Educational Scholarships & Grants in Optical Science and Engineering)

P.O. Box 10
Bellingham WA 98227-0010
360/676-3290
FAX: 360/647-1445
E-mail: scholarships@spie.org
Internet: http://www.spie.org
AMOUNT: $1,000-$10,000
DEADLINE(S): JAN 6
FIELD(S): Optics, Photonics, Imaging, Optoelectronics or related discipline
ELIGIBILITY/REQUIREMENTS: Undergraduate and graduate students must be enrolled full time in one of the fields as mentioned above at an educational institution for the academic year in which the award is used. This requirement does not apply to high school students.
HOW TO APPLY: See website. Must submit application, 2 letters of reference, a 450-word essay and the annual scholarship award report (if applicable) by deadline.
RENEWABLE: Yes. Must submit an annual scholarship award report if reapplying. Your application must show new activities beyond those upon which a previous award was based.
ADDITIONAL INFORMATION: Must be an SPIE student member or submit an application for student membership including dues payment with the scholarship application to SPIE by the deadline. NOTE: High school students may receive a complimentary (free) student membership after submitting a membership application.

1142—SPIE: THE INTERNATIONAL SOCIETY FOR OPTICAL ENGINEERING (Michael Kidger Memorial Scholarship)

P.O. Box 10
Bellingham WA 98227-0010
E-mail: scholarships@spie.org
Internet: http://www.kidger.com
AMOUNT: $5,000
DEADLINE(S): FEB 6
FIELD(S): Optical Design
ELIGIBILITY/REQUIREMENTS: Must be a student of optical design who meets the entry criteria for the chosen course of study or research. Must have at least 1 year after the award to completion of their chosen course of study.
HOW TO APPLY: See website. With application must submit a summary (5 pages maximum) of your academic background and interest in pursuing training or research in optical design (limited supporting material may be attached) and 2 letters of recommendation.
NUMBER OF AWARDS: 1
RENEWABLE: No
CONTACT: davidwilliamson@msn.com or tina@kidger.com

1143—STUDENT CONSERVATION ASSOCIATION (SCA Resource Assistant Program)

P.O. Box 550
Charlestown NH 03603
603/543-1700
FAX: 603/543-1828
E-mail: internships@sca-inc.org
Internet: http://www.sca-inc.org
AMOUNT: $1,180-$4,725
DEADLINE(S): Varies
FIELD(S): Environment and related fields (agriculture, archaeology, anthropology, botany, caves, civil engineering, environmental design, engineering and education, fisheries, forests, herpetology, history, landscape architecture, paleontology, recreation/resource/range management, wildlife management, geology, hydrology, library/museums, surveying)
ELIGIBILITY/REQUIREMENTS: Must be 18 and U.S. citizen; need not be student.
HOW TO APPLY: Send $1 for postage for application; outside U.S./Canada, send $20.
NUMBER OF AWARDS: 900 positions

1144—UNIVERSITY OF MARYLAND (John B. and Ida Slaughter Endowed Scholarship in Science, Technology, and the Black Community)

Afro-American Studies Program
2169 Lefrak Hall
University of Maryland
College Park MD 20742-7225
301/405-1158
or to:
Center for Minorities in Science
Science and Engineering
1134 Engineering Classroom
University of Maryland
College Park MD 20742-7225
301/405-3878
Internet: http://www.bsos.umd.edu/aasp/scholarship.html
AMOUNT: Varies
DEADLINE(S): MAR
FIELD(S): Science; Technology
ELIGIBILITY/REQUIREMENTS: Open to African Americans who are U.S. residents with a minimum 2.8 GPA. Must be accepted to or enrolled at UMCP for freshman year. Should have an interest in applying science and technology to the problems of the Black community.
HOW TO APPLY: Contact the Center for Minorities in Science and Engineering at UMCP for an application. Must submit letter of recommendation from high school counselor or UMCP faculty member. Essay required.
RENEWABLE: Yes

1145—WESTERN MICHIGAN UNIVERSITY (Haworth College of Business/James W. Richmond Sales and Business Marketing Scholarship)

1903 West Michigan
Kalamazoo MI 49008-5337
269/387-6000
FAX: 269/387-6989
E-mail: finaid-info@wmich.edu
Internet: http://www.wmich.edu/finaid
AMOUNT: Varies
DEADLINE(S): FEB 15
FIELD(S): Food Marketing; Manufacturing Technology
ELIGIBILITY/REQUIREMENTS: Preference shall be given to sophomore, junior, or senior Sales and Business Marketing majors who are pursuing a minor in Manufacturing Technology. Must have GPA of 3.0 and be a full-time student.
HOW TO APPLY: Contact the Marketing Department for more details.
NUMBER OF AWARDS: 1 or more
RENEWABLE: Yes

1146—WORLDSTUDIO FOUNDATION

200 Varick Street, Suite 507
New York NY 10014
212/366-1317
FAX: 212/807-0024
E-mail: info@worldstudio.org
Internet: http://www.worldstudio.org or http://www.aiga.org
AMOUNT: $1,500-$5,000
DEADLINE(S): APR 14
FIELD(S): Advertising, Animation, Architecture, Cartooning, Crafts, Environmental graphics, Film/video, Film/theater design, Fine arts, Furniture design, Industrial/product design, Interior architecture and design, Landscape architecture, New media, Photography, Surface/textile design, Urban planning

ELIGIBILITY/REQUIREMENTS: Applicants must be pursuing a degree in the fine or commercial arts, design or architecture, and plan to enter a career in the creative professions. Undergraduates and graduates are eligible. Minority status and/or social agenda are significant factors. Financial need a prerequisite. Minimum 2.0 GPA.

HOW TO APPLY: See websites for application. The application is a 2-part process. Applications must include personal and school information, including transcripts and copies of letters of acceptance; financial information; portfolio; written statement of purpose; examples of a commitment to a social agenda, 2 letters of recommendation from college instructors, high school teachers, or employers; head shot of applicant.

NUMBER OF AWARDS: 20-30
RENEWABLE: Yes. Must reapply.
CONTACT: Mark Randall

ARCHITECTURE

1147—AMERICAN INSTITUTE OF ARCHITECTS/NEW YORK CHAPTER (Douglas Haskell Award)

200 Lexington Avenue, 6th Floor
New York NY 10016
212/683-0023, ext. 14
FAX: 212/696-5022
E-mail: info@aiany.org
Internet: http://www.aiany.org/nyfoundation/scholarships.html
AMOUNT: $2,000 (minimum)
DEADLINE(S): MAR 21
FIELD(S): Architectural Writing
ELIGIBILITY/REQUIREMENTS: Awards to encourage fine writing on architecture and related design subjects and to foster regard for intelligent criticism among future professionals. For students enrolled in a professional architecture or related program, such as art history, interior design, urban studies, and landscape architecture. Submit a news story, an essay or feature article, book review, or journal accompanied by a 100-word statement describing the purpose of the piece.
HOW TO APPLY: See website or contact AIANY for complete information.

1148—AMERICAN SOCIETY OF ENGINEERS OF INDIAN ORIGIN

47790 Pavillon Road
Canton MI 48188
248/354-6895
FAX: 248/354-6818

E-mail: awards@asei-ncc.org
Internet: http://www.asei-ncc.org/Awards.htm
AMOUNT: $1,000
DEADLINE(S): AUG 15
FIELD(S): Engineering: Architecture, Computer or allied science, Geotechnical or Geo-environmental Engineering, and allied sciences
ELIGIBILITY/REQUIREMENTS: Open to students who are Indian by birth, ancestry, or relation. Based on demonstrated ability, academic achievement, including GPA (minimum 3.0)/honors/awards, career objectives, faculty recommendations, student involvement in science fair, campus activities, and industrial exposure including part-time work and internships; must attend an accredited college or university anywhere in the U.S.
HOW TO APPLY: See website for application and details or contact Society for applications. Submit with résumé; an essay (maximum 1 page) stating qualifications, career goals, reasons for seeking the scholarship; 1 letter of recommendation in the current or intended field of study.
CONTACT: Dr. Ramu Ramamurthy, ASEI Scholarship Committee Chairman

1149—AMERICAN SOCIETY OF HEATING, REFRIGERATING, AND AIR-CONDITIONING ENGINEERS (ASHRAE Region IV Benny Bootle Scholarship)

1791 Tullie Circle NE
Atlanta GA 30329
404/636-8400
FAX: 404/321-5478
E-mail: benedict@ashrae.org
Internet: http://www.ashrae.org
AMOUNT: $3,000
DEADLINE(S): DEC 1
FIELD(S): Engineering; Architecture
ELIGIBILITY/REQUIREMENTS: Available to a qualified undergraduate engineering or architecture student pursuing a bachelor's degree enrolled full time in an ABET- or NAAB-accredited program at a school located within the geographic boundaries of ASHRAE's Region IV (currently NC, SC, and GA). Must have a minimum college GPA of 3.0; be enrolled full time in a college or university with at least 1 full year of studies remaining in the year for which the scholarship will be awarded; demonstrate potential service to the HVAC&R profession, need for financial assistance, leadership ability, and character.
HOW TO APPLY: See website or contact Society for information and application. Submit with letters of recommendation,

transcripts, and demonstration of financial need.
NUMBER OF AWARDS: 1
RENEWABLE: No
CONTACT: Lois Benedict, Scholarship Administrator

1150—CHICAGO ROOFING CONTRACTORS ASSOCIATION

4415 W. Harrison Street, #322
Hillside IL 60162
708/449-3340
FAX: 708/449-0837
E-mail: info@crca.org
Internet: http://www.crca.org
AMOUNT: $3,000
DEADLINE(S): MAR (1st Friday)
FIELD(S): Business; Engineering; Architecture; Liberal Arts; Sciences
ELIGIBILITY/REQUIREMENTS: Open to high school seniors who reside in one of the eight counties in Northern Illinois: Cook, DuPage, Lake, Kane, Kendall, DeKalb, McHenry, or Will. Must be accepted as a full-time student in a 4-year college or university to pursue a degree in one of the above fields. Must be U.S. citizen. Based on academic achievements, extracurricular activities, and community involvement.
HOW TO APPLY: See website for an application. Submit with 2 completed Personal Reference Forms (1 from high school guidance counselor or faculty member, an optional letter of recommendation may also be included; the other from an adult not related to the student); an official transcript of all high school records, and official ACT and/or SAT Test results or official high school transcript.
NUMBER OF AWARDS: 1 (In the event of a tie, financial need considered.)
RENEWABLE: Yes (up to 3 times). Must maintain a 2.75 grade point average.

1151—CONNECTICUT BUILDING CONGRESS SCHOLARSHIP FUND

2600 Dixwell Avenue, Suite 7
Hamden CT 06514
203/281-3183
FAX: 203/248-8932
E-mail: bdavidson@ctengineers.org
Internet: http://www.cbc-ct.org
AMOUNT: $500-$2,000
DEADLINE(S): MAR 31
FIELD(S): Construction Industry related subjects (Architecture; Engineering; Construction Management; Planning; Drafting, etc.)
ELIGIBILITY/REQUIREMENTS: Connecticut resident. Must submit an essay

of not more than 500 words that explains how your planned studies will relate to a career in the construction industry; transcript of high school grades; class standing, and SAT/ACT scores; copy of Student Aid Report of FAFSA.
HOW TO APPLY: Call, write or e-mail for application.
NUMBER OF AWARDS: 2 to 4
RENEWABLE: Yes. Up to 4 years; must maintain grades.
CONTACT: Beverly Davidson at CBCSF

1152—FLORIDA FEDERATION OF GARDEN CLUBS, INC. (FFGC Scholarships for College Students)

706 Glen Eagle Drive
Winter Springs FL 32708
561/778-1023
Internet: http://www.ffgc.org
AMOUNT: $1,500-$3,500
DEADLINE(S): MAY 1
FIELD(S): Ecology; Environmental Issues; Land Management; City Planning; Environmental Control; Horticulture; Landscape Design; Conservation; Botany; Forestry; Marine Biology; Floriculture; Agriculture
ELIGIBILITY/REQUIREMENTS: Various scholarships for Florida residents with a "B" average or better enrolled full time as a junior, senior, or graduate student at a Florida college or university.
HOW TO APPLY: See website or contact FFGC for an application.
CONTACT: Jane Meherg, Scholarship Chairman

1153—FLORIDA FEDERATION OF GARDEN CLUBS, INC. (FFGC Scholarships for High School Students)

706 Glen Eagle Drive
Winter Springs FL 32708
Internet: http://www.ffgc.org
AMOUNT: $1,500
DEADLINE(S): MAY 1
FIELD(S): Ecology; Environmental Issues; Land Management; City Planning; Environmental Control; Horticulture; Landscape Design; Conservation; Botany; Forestry; Marine Biology; Floriculture; Agriculture
ELIGIBILITY/REQUIREMENTS: Scholarships for Florida residents, who have a "B" or better average who will be incoming freshmen at a Florida college or university.
HOW TO APPLY: See website or contact FFGC for an application.

CONTACT: Jane Meherg, Scholarship Chairman

1154—GARDEN CLUB FEDERATION OF MAINE, THE-ST. CROIX DISTRICT (Nell Goff Memorial Scholarship Foundation)

46 Birch Bay Drive
Bar Harbor ME 04609
207/288-8003
E-mail: creevey@adelphia.net
Internet: http://www.mainegarden clubs.com
AMOUNT: $1,000
DEADLINE(S): MAR 1
FIELD(S): Horticulture; Floriculture; Landscape Design; Conservation; Forestry; Botany; Agronomy; Plant Pathology; Environmental Control; City Planning and/or other gardening-related fields
ELIGIBILITY/REQUIREMENTS: Open to all college incoming juniors, seniors or graduate students who are legal residents of the state of Maine; priority is given to a resident of St. Croix District (Hancock County and the southern part of Washington County). Must major in some aspect of horticulture.
HOW TO APPLY: Application is available on our website, click on Scholarship Information; submit along with personal letter by applicant, not to exceed 2 pages, discussing goals, background, financial need and personal commitment; 3 letters of recommendation, 1 typed page each to include scholarship ability, personal reference and work-related experience; transcript of all college credits to date and list of activities.
NUMBER OF AWARDS: 1
RENEWABLE: Yes. Must reapply.
CONTACT: Lucy Creevey

1155—ILLUMINATING ENGINEERING SOCIETY OF NORTH AMERICA (Robert W. Thunen Memorial Scholarships)

Golden Gate Section
P.O. Box 77527
San Francisco CA 94107-1527
E-mail: riverfield@juno.com
AMOUNT: $2,500
DEADLINE(S): APR 1
FIELD(S): Illumination (Architectural, Commercial, Residential, Airport, Navigational, Theatrical, TV, Agricultural, Vision, etc.)
ELIGIBILITY/REQUIREMENTS: Open to full-time undergraduate juniors and seniors and graduate students in an accredited 4-year college or university located in

Northern California or Nevada, Oregon, or Washington.
HOW TO APPLY: Contact Chair for an application. Must submit statement of purpose (with respect to lighting education) and 3 letters of recommendation. Awards announced by May 3.
NUMBER OF AWARDS: At least 2
CONTACT: Heide M. Kawahata, Chair

1156—INSTITUTE OF INTERNATIONAL EDUCATION (Cintas Fellowship)

809 United Nations Plaza
New York NY 10017-3580
E-mail: cintas@iie.org
Internet: http://www.iie.org/cintas
AMOUNT: $10,000
DEADLINE(S): APR
FIELD(S): Fine Arts; Architecture; Literature; Music Composition; Visual Arts; Photography
ELIGIBILITY/REQUIREMENTS: Acknowledges outstanding creative accomplishments and encourages the further development of creative talents in the fields of architecture, literature, music composition, and the visual arts and photography. For artists of Cuban citizenship or direct descent who do not live in Cuba.
HOW TO APPLY: Contact Institute or see website for additional information.

1157—LANDSCAPE ARCHITECTURE FOUNDATION (Courtland Paul Scholarship)

818 18th Street NW, Suite 810
Washington, DC 20006
202/331-7070
FAX: 202/331-7079
E-mail: scholarships@ lafoundation.org.
Internet: http://www.scholarships@ lafoundation.org.
AMOUNT: $3,000
DEADLINE(S): FEB 15
FIELD(S): Landscape Architecture
ELIGIBILITY/REQUIREMENTS: Open to U.S. citizens who are undergraduate students in the final 2 years of study in LAAB-accredited schools. Applicants must demonstrate financial need and a minimum GPA of "C."
HOW TO APPLY: See website for application and additional information. Must apply online. Submit with personal profile (2-page maximum) including financial information and extracurricular activities; a 500-word maximum essay describing the applicant's aspirations; ability to surmount obstacles, high level of drive, and need for financial assistance; 2 letters of recommendation from current professors familiar

with the applicant's character and goals in pursuing an education in landscape architecture.
NUMBER OF AWARDS: 1

1158—LANDSCAPE ARCHITECTURE FOUNDATION (Landscape Forms Design for People Scholarship)

818 18th Street NW, Suite 810
Washington, DC 20006
202/331-7070
FAX: 202/331-7079
E-mail: scholarships@ lafoundation.org.
Internet: http://www.scholarships@ lafoundation.org.
AMOUNT: $3,000
DEADLINE(S): FEB 15
FIELD(S): Landscape Architecture
ELIGIBILITY/REQUIREMENTS: Open to landscape architecture students who will be starting their final year of full-time undergraduate study in an LAAB-accredited program and who demonstrate passion, commitment, and competence in creating great spaces for people. Applicants must show a proven contribution to the design of public spaces that integrates landscape design and the use of amenities to promote social interaction. The scholarship will be awarded on the basis of academic accomplishment and creative ability.
HOW TO APPLY: See website for application and additional information. Must apply online. Submit with personal profile (2-page maximum) including financial information and extracurricular activities; a 300-word statement describing the qualities essential to the creation of great and successful public spaces; 3 8^1/$_2$" x 11" academic or internship work samples in either jpg or PDF format, and 2 letters of recommendation from current professors and/or internship employers.
NUMBER OF AWARDS: 1
RENEWABLE: No

1159—LANDSCAPE ARCHITECTURE FOUNDATION (Steven G. King Play Environments Scholarship)

818 18th Street NW, Suite 810
Washington, DC 20006
202/331-7070
FAX: 202/331-7079
E-mail: scholarships@lafoundation.org.
Internet: http://www.scholarships@ lafoundation.org.
AMOUNT: $5,000
DEADLINE(S): FEB 15

FIELD(S): Landscape Architecture
ELIGIBILITY/REQUIREMENTS: Open to landscape architecture students with a demonstrated interest and aptitude in the design of play environments who are enrolled in graduate or the final 2 years of undergraduate study in LAAB-accredited schools. Based on creativity, openness to innovation, and a demonstrated interest in park and playground planning.

1160—NATIONAL FEDERATION OF THE BLIND (Frank Walton Horn Memorial Scholarship)

805 Fifth Avenue
Grinnell IA 50112
515/236-3366
Internet: http://www.nfb.org/ nfb/scholarship_program.asp
AMOUNT: $3,000
DEADLINE(S): MAR 31
FIELD(S): Architecture; Engineering
ELIGIBILITY/REQUIREMENTS: Open to legally blind students pursuing or planning to pursue a full-time postsecondary course of study in the U.S. Based on academic excellence, service to the community, and financial need. Membership NOT required.
HOW TO APPLY: Contact Scholarship Committee Chairman for an application.
NUMBER OF AWARDS: 1
RENEWABLE: Yes
CONTACT: Peggy Elliot, Scholarship Committee Chairman

1161—NATIONAL FEDERATION OF THE BLIND (Howard Brown Rickard Scholarship)

805 Fifth Avenue
Grinnell IA 50112
515/236-3366
Internet: http://www.nfb.org/ nfb/scholarship_program.asp
AMOUNT: $3,000
DEADLINE(S): MAR 31
FIELD(S): Law; Medicine; Engineering; Architecture; Natural Sciences
ELIGIBILITY/REQUIREMENTS: For legally blind students pursuing or planning to pursue a full-time postsecondary course of study in the U.S. Based on academic excellence, service to the community, and financial need. Membership NOT required.
HOW TO APPLY: Contact Scholarship Committee Chairman for an application.
NUMBER OF AWARDS: 1
RENEWABLE: Yes
CONTACT: Peggy Elliot, Scholarship Committee Chairman

1162—NATIONAL GARDEN CLUBS, INC.

4401 Magnolia Avenue
St. Louis MO 63110-3492
314/776-7574
FAX: 314/776-5108
E-mail: glaustin2@bellsouth.net or headquarters@gardenclub.org
Internet: http://www.gardenclub.org
AMOUNT: $3,500
DEADLINE(S): MAR 1
FIELD(S): Horticulture, Floriculture, Landscape Design, City Planning, Land Management, and allied subjects
ELIGIBILITY/REQUIREMENTS: Open to juniors, seniors, and graduate students who are U.S. citizens and are studying any of the above or related subjects. Student must have the endorsement of the state in which he/she resides permanently. Applications will be forwarded to the National State Chairman and judged on a national level.
HOW TO APPLY: Write for complete information.
NUMBER OF AWARDS: 30-35

1163—NATIONAL STONE, SAND & GRAVEL ASSOCIATION (NSSGA Quarry Engineering Scholarships)

1605 King Street
Alexandria VA 22314
800/342-1415 or 703/525-8788
FAX: 703/525-7782
E-mail: info@nssga.org
Internet: http://www.nssga.org
AMOUNT: $2,000; $1,000; $600
DEADLINE(S): APR 15
FIELD(S): Landscape Architecture
ELIGIBILITY/REQUIREMENTS: Undergraduate landscape architecture students work with a local rock quarry to produce a reclamation proposal.
HOW TO APPLY: See website or write for information and application.

1164—NEW YORK CITY DEPARTMENT OF CITYWIDE ADMINISTRATIVE SERVICES (Government Scholars Internship Program)

1 Centre Street, 24th Floor
New York NY 10007
212/487-5600
FAX: 212/487-5720
AMOUNT: $3,000
DEADLINE(S): JAN 13
FIELD(S): Public Administration; Urban Planning; Government; Public Service; Urban Affairs

ELIGIBILITY/REQUIREMENTS: 10-week summer intern program open to undergraduate sophomores, juniors, and seniors. Program provides students with unique opportunity to learn about NY City government. Internships available in virtually every city agency and mayoral office.
HOW TO APPLY: Write to New York City Fellowship Programs at above address for complete information.

1165—NEW YORK STATE HIGHER EDUCATION SERVICES CORPORATION (N.Y. State Regents Professional/Health Care Opportunity Scholarships)

Cultural Education Center,
Room 5C64
Albany NY 12230
518/486-1319
Internet: http://www.hesc.com
AMOUNT: $1,000-$10,000/year
DEADLINE(S): Varies
FIELD(S): Medicine, Dentistry and related fields; Architecture, Nursing, Psychology, Audiology, Landscape Architecture, Social Work, Chiropractic, Law, Pharmacy, Accounting, Speech Language Pathology
ELIGIBILITY/REQUIREMENTS: For New York State residents who are economically disadvantaged and members of a minority group underrepresented in the chosen profession and attending school in New York State. For U.S. citizens or qualifying noncitizens.
HOW TO APPLY: See website or contact NYS HESC.
RENEWABLE: Yes
ADDITIONAL INFORMATION: Some programs carry a service obligation in New York for each year of support. Medical/dental scholarships require one year of professional work in New York.

1166—SMITHSONIAN INSTITUTION—COOPER-HEWITT, NATIONAL DESIGN MUSEUM (Peter Krueger Summer Internships)

2 East 91st Street
New York NY 10128
212/849-8380
FAX: 212/860-6909
E-mail: edu@si.edu.
Internet: http://www.si.edu/ndm
AMOUNT: $2,500 stipend
DEADLINE(S): FEB 1
FIELD(S): Art History; Architectural History; Museum Studies; Museum Education; Design

ELIGIBILITY/REQUIREMENTS: This 10-week (June-August) internship is open to college students considering a career in one of the above fields as well as graduate students who have not yet completed their M.A. degree. Interns are assigned to specific curatorial, education, or administrative departments where they will assist on special research or exhibition projects, as well as participate in daily museum activities. Housing NOT provided.
HOW TO APPLY: See website for details and application. Submit with cover letter stating area of interest, résumé, official transcript, 2 letters of recommendation, and 1- to 2-page essay on interest.
RENEWABLE: No
CONTACT: Internship Coordinator

1167—SOCIETY OF DESIGN ADMINISTRATION, THE (ProNet Scholarship)

The Spector Group
311 New Hyde Park Road
North Hills NY 11040
516/365-4240
FAX: 516/365-3604
AMOUNT: $800/$1,500
DEADLINE(S): MAR 1
FIELD(S): Architecture; Engineering
ELIGIBILITY/REQUIREMENTS: Applicants must demonstrate an interest in practice management studies in their education programs, as this scholarship is intended to promote the education and training of design firm administrators.
HOW TO APPLY: Send application.
CONTACT: Patricia A. Manfre-Staab

1168—SOCIETY OF NAVAL ARCHITECTS AND MARINE ENGINEERS, THE (Undergraduate Scholarship)

601 Pavonia Avenue
Jersey City NJ 07306
800/798-2188 or 201/798-4800
FAX: 201/798-4975
Internet: http://www.sname.org
AMOUNT: $2,000
DEADLINE(S): MAY 1
FIELD(S): Naval Architecture; Marine Engineering, Ocean Engineering, or marine industry-related field
ELIGIBILITY/REQUIREMENTS: Open to citizens of the U.S. and Canada; study toward a degree in one of the above fields at participating schools; must be entering junior or senior year; membership in the society at the time of the award.
HOW TO APPLY: Submit application through your school with 3 letters of recommendation and transcript, and state-

ment indicating your career goals and why you are interested in marine science.
RENEWABLE: Yes. Repeat as an undergraduate and reapply for graduate scholarship.

1169—SONOMA CHAMBOLLE-MUSIGNY SISTER CITIES, INC. (Henri Cardinaux Memorial Scholarship)

Chamson Scholarship Committee
P.O. Box 1633
Sonoma CA 95476-1633
707/938-9081
E-mail: icardin@aol.com
AMOUNT: Up to $1,500 (travel + expenses)
DEADLINE(S): JUL 15
FIELD(S): Culinary Arts; Wine Industry; Art; Architecture; Music; History; Fashion
ELIGIBILITY/REQUIREMENTS: Hands-on experience working in above or similar fields and living with a family in small French village in Burgundy or other French city. Must be Sonoma County, California, resident at least 18 years of age, and be able to communicate in French.
HOW TO APPLY: Transcripts, employer recommendation, photograph, and essay (stating why, where, and when) required.
NUMBER OF AWARDS: 1
RENEWABLE: No
CONTACT: Ivy Cardinaux

1170—STUDENT CONSERVATION ASSOCIATION (SCA Resource Assistant Program)

P.O. Box 550
Charlestown NH 03603
603/543-1700
FAX: 603/543-1828
E-mail: internships@sca-inc.org
Internet: http://www.sca-inc.org
AMOUNT: $1,180-$4,725
DEADLINE(S): Varies
FIELD(S): Environment and related fields (agriculture, archaeology, anthropology, botany, caves, civil engineering, environmental engineering and education, fisheries, forests, herpetology, history, landscape architecture, environmental design, paleontology, recreation/resource/range management, wildlife management, geology, hydrology, library/museums, surveying)
ELIGIBILITY/REQUIREMENTS: Must be 18 and U.S. citizen; need not be student.
HOW TO APPLY: Send $1 for postage for application; outside U.S./Canada, send $20.

NUMBER OF AWARDS: 900 positions in U.S. and Canada.

1171—TRUST COMPANY LIMITED (Marten Bequest Travelling Scholarships)

35 Clarence Street
Sydney NSW 2000 AUSTRALIA
+61 (02) 8295-8191
FAX: +61 (02) 8295-8695
E-mail: trustawards@cauzgroup.com
Internet: http://www.trust.com. au/philanthropy/awards/
AMOUNT: Aus. $18,000
DEADLINE(S): OCT 25
FIELD(S): Art; Performing Arts; Creative Writing; Architecture
ELIGIBILITY/REQUIREMENTS: Open to native-born Australians aged 21-35 (17-35 ballet) who are of outstanding ability and promise in one or more categories of the Arts. The scholarships are intended to augment a scholar's own resources toward a cultural education and may be used for study, maintenance, and travel either in Australia or overseas. Categories are: instrumental music, painting, singing, sculpture, architecture, ballet, prose, poetry, and acting.
HOW TO APPLY: Contact Group for more information and entry form.
NUMBER OF AWARDS: 54: 6 in each of 9 categories, which rotate in 2 groups on an annual basis
CONTACT: Petrea Salter

1172—UNIVERSITY OF ILLINOIS AT URBANA-CHAMPAIGN (Lydia E. Parker Bates Scholarship)

620 East John Street
Champaign IL 61820
217/333-0100
Internet: http://www.uiuc.edu/
AMOUNT: Up to $1,000
DEADLINE(S): MAR 15
FIELD(S): Art, Architecture, Landscape Architecture, Urban Planning, Dance, Theater, and all related subjects except Music
ELIGIBILITY/REQUIREMENTS: Open to undergraduate students in the College of Fine and Applied Arts who are attending the University of Illinois at Urbana-Champaign. Must demonstrate financial need and have 2.85 GPA. Recipients must carry at least 12 credit hours per semester.
HOW TO APPLY: Contact office of student financial aid for application. Complete the Free Application for Federal Student Aid with UIUC admission application.
NUMBER OF AWARDS: 175

1173—WAVERLY COMMUNITY HOUSE INC. (F. Lammot Belin Arts Scholarships)

P.O. Box 142
Waverly PA 18471
570/586-8191
FAX: 570/586-0185
Internet: http://www.waverly comm.org/arts.htm
AMOUNT: $10,000
DEADLINE(S): DEC 15
FIELD(S): Painting; Sculpture; Music; Drama; Dance; Literature; Architecture; Photography
ELIGIBILITY/REQUIREMENTS: Applicants must have resided in the Abington or Pocono regions of Northeastern Pennsylvania. They must furnish proof of exceptional ability in their chosen field but no formal training in any academic or professional program. U.S. citizenship required.
HOW TO APPLY:. Submit application with detailed proposal for the use of the grant including a projected budget and letters of recommendation from recognized experts in related field required. Finalists must appear in person before the selection committee. See website or write for complete information
CONTACT: Scholarships Selection Committee

1174—WEBB INSTITUTE (Naval Architecture Scholarships)

298 Crescent Beach Road
Glen Cove NY 11542-1398
516/671-2213
FAX: 516/674-9838
E-mail: admissions@webb-institute.edu
Internet: http://www.webb-institute.edu
AMOUNT: Full tuition for 4 years
DEADLINE(S): FEB 15
FIELD(S): Naval Architecture; Marine Engineering
ELIGIBILITY/REQUIREMENTS: Open to high school students aged 16-24 who are in the top 10% of their class and have a minimum 3.2 GPA. Based on college boards, SAT scores, and demonstrated interest in above areas. Must be U.S. citizen.
HOW TO APPLY: Contact Webb Institute for an application. Interview required.
NUMBER OF AWARDS: 20-25

1175—WESTERN EUROPEAN ARCHITECTURE FOUNDATION (Gabriel Prize for Architecture)

306 West Sunset, Suite 119
San Antonio TX 78209
210/829-4040
FAX: 210/829-4049
E-mail: contact@gabrielprize.org
Internet: http://www.gabriel prize.org/ about.php
AMOUNT: $15,000
DEADLINE(S): DEC
FIELD(S): Architecture
ELIGIBILITY/REQUIREMENTS: Supports all travel and study costs in France for a period of 3 months, during which time the student will study architectural environments in France or its immediate spheres of influence, between 1630 and 1930.
HOW TO APPLY: The selection process has 3 phases: candidates register their interest by submitting pertinent illustrations of personal work and an outline of the studies contemplated. A first jury selects 3 candidates, who then meet a second jury which names the final winner and a runner up. The winner is required to begin studies in France by May 1, keep a traveling sketchbook, and prepare 3 large colored drawings within a period of 3 months under the supervision of the European representative.
NUMBER OF AWARDS: 1
RENEWABLE: No
CONTACT: Patrick J. Fleming, President

1176—WORLDSTUDIO FOUNDATION

200 Varick Street, Suite 507
New York NY 10014
212/366-1317
FAX: 212/807-0024
E-mail: info@worldstudio.org
Internet: http://www.worldstudio. org or http://www.aiga.org
AMOUNT: $1,500-$5,000
DEADLINE(S): APR 14
FIELD(S): Advertising, Animation, Architecture, Cartooning, Crafts, Environmental graphics, Film/video, Film/theater design, Fine arts, Furniture design, Industrial/product design, Interior architecture and design, Landscape architecture, New

media, Photography, Surface/textile design, Urban planning

ELIGIBILITY/REQUIREMENTS: Applicants must be pursuing a degree in the fine or commercial arts, design or architecture, and plan to enter a career in the creative professions. Undergraduates and graduates are eligible. Minority status and/or social agenda are significant factors. Financial need a prerequisite. Minimum 2.0 GPA.

HOW TO APPLY: See websites for application. The application is a 2-part process. Applications must include personal and school information, including transcripts and copies of letters of acceptance; financial information; portfolio; written statement of purpose; examples of a commitment to a social agenda, 2 letters of recommendation from college instructors, high school teachers, or employers; head shot of applicant.

NUMBER OF AWARDS: 20-30
RENEWABLE: Yes. Must reapply.
CONTACT: Mark Randall

CHEMICAL ENGINEERING

1177—AMERICAN CHEMICAL SOCIETY-RUBBER DIVISION

P.O. Box 499
Akron OH 44309-0499
330/972-7814
FAX: 330/972-5269
E-mail: crobinson@rubber.org
Internet: http://www.rubber.org/awards/scholarships.htm
AMOUNT: $5,000
DEADLINE(S): MAR 15
FIELD(S): Chemistry, Physics, Chemical Engineering, Mechanical Engineering, Polymer Science, or other rubber-related discipline

ELIGIBILITY/REQUIREMENTS: Incoming junior or senior enrolled in an accredited college or university in the United States, Canada, Mexico, Brazil or India (countries may change) majoring in a rubber industry-related field. Must have "B" or better overall academic average, and a minimum of 3 semesters or 6 terms completed, and intend to pursue full-time professional employment in the industry.

HOW TO APPLY: Download application from website and fax or mail application along with 2 or more nomination letters from professor/nominator. Official transcripts may follow.

NUMBER OF AWARDS: 3
RENEWABLE: Yes. Must reapply for 2nd and final year.

CONTACT: Christie Robinson, Education & Publications Manager

1178—ARMED FORCES COMMUNICATIONS AND ELECTRONICS ASSOCIATION (AFCEA Scholarship for Online or Distance-Learning Programs)

4400 Fair Lakes Court
Fairfax VA 22033-3899
800/336-4583, ext. 6147
703/631-6149
FAX: 703/631-4693
E-mail: scholarships@afcea.org
Internet: http://www.afcea.org
AMOUNT: $1,500
DEADLINE(S): JUN 1
FIELD(S): Electrical, Chemical or Aerospace Engineering: Computer Science; Mathematics; Physics; Science or Math Education; Technology Management or fields related to U.S. intelligence or national security

ELIGIBILITY/REQUIREMENTS: Full-time students; undergraduates must have completed 2 semesters of calculus (30-semester hour equivalent). Must be a U.S. citizen and be currently enrolled in a 4-year college or university in the U.S. at time of application.

HOW TO APPLY: Applications and further information on website.
RENEWABLE: No

1179—CANADIAN SOCIETY FOR CHEMICAL ENGINEERING (Edmonton Chemical Engineering Scholarship)

130 Slater Street, Suite 550
Ottawa Ontario K1P 6E2
CANADA
613/232-6252 or 888/542-2242
FAX: 613/232-5862
E-mail: lhuskins@cheminst.ca
Internet: http://www.chemeng.ca/
AMOUNT: $1,000 (Canadian)
DEADLINE(S): APR 30
FIELD(S): Chemical Engineering

ELIGIBILITY/REQUIREMENTS: For undergraduates in chemical engineering entering the 2nd, 3rd, 4th, or 5th year of studies at a Canadian university. Offered to a student who has demonstrated leadership and contributed to the CSChE through participation in student chapters, and above-average academic performance.

HOW TO APPLY: Contact the Program Manager, Awards, for an application. Letter of application should document contributions to the Society and be accom-

panied by a transcript and 2 letters of support.
NUMBER OF AWARDS: 1

1180—CANADIAN SOCIETY FOR CHEMICAL ENGINEERING (Sarnia Chemical Engineering Scholarship)

130 Slater Street, Suite 550
Ottawa Ontario K1P 6E2
CANADA
613/232-6252 or 888/542-2242
FAX: 613/232-5862
E-mail: lhuskins@cheminst.ca
Internet: http://www.chemeng.ca/
AMOUNT: $1,000 (Canadian)
DEADLINE(S): APR 30
FIELD(S): Chemical Engineering

ELIGIBILITY/REQUIREMENTS: For undergraduate students about to enter their final year of studies at a Canadian university. Offered to student who has achieved academic excellence and has contributed to CSChE through participation in student chapters.

HOW TO APPLY: Contact the Program Manager, Awards, for an application. Letter of application (6 copies) should include evidence of contributions to the Society as well as academic transcript (1 original and 5 copies), and 2 letters of reference.

NUMBER OF AWARDS: 1
RENEWABLE: No

1181—CANADIAN SOCIETY FOR CHEMICAL ENGINEERING (SNC/LAVALIN Plant Competition)

130 Slater Street, Suite 550
Ottawa Ontario K1P 6E2
CANADA
613/232-6252 or 888/542-2242
FAX: 613/232-5862
E-mail: lhuskins@cheminst.ca
Internet: http://www.chemeng.ca/
AMOUNT: $1,000 (Canadian)
DEADLINE(S): MAY 15
FIELD(S): Chemical Engineering

ELIGIBILITY/REQUIREMENTS: Competition for individuals and groups of 6 or less undergraduate students registered in chemical engineering programs in Canadian universities.

HOW TO APPLY: Contact the Program Manager, Awards, for an application. Entries should include summary/flow sheet of process, copy of final report submitted to university, list of students who performed work with their addresses and phone numbers, name of collaborating

organization and engineers who assisted students, and a brief description of the assistance provided.
NUMBER OF AWARDS: 1

1182—CELANESE CANADA, INC.

AUCC
350 Albert Street, Suite 600
Ottawa Ontario K1R 1B1
CANADA
613/563-1236
FAX: 613/563-9745
E-mail: awards@aucc.ca
Internet: http://www.aucc.ca
AMOUNT: $1,500 (Canadian)
DEADLINE(S): JUL 2
FIELD(S): Mechanical and Chemical Engineering; Chemistry; Business Administration and Commerce
ELIGIBILITY/REQUIREMENTS: Open to Canadian citizens/permanent residents for their final year of an undergraduate program in one of above fields. Must attend a college or university that is a member, or affiliated to a member, of the Association of Universities and Colleges of Canada. Candidates are expected to have achieved a high level of academic excellence as well as to have exhibited superior intellectual ability and judgment. In some cases, study in certain province/school is required.
HOW TO APPLY: Applications are by nomination only. See website or contact AUCC for nomination procedures.
RENEWABLE: No

1183—MICRON TECHNOLOGY FOUNDATION

8000 South Federal Way
Mailstop 1-407
Boise ID 83706
208/368-2658
FAX: 208/368-4435
Internet: http://www.micron.com/about/foundation/edgrants.aspx
AMOUNT: $55,000 and up to 12 @ $16,500
DEADLINE(S): JAN 20
FIELD(S): Electrical, Chemical, Computer, & Mechanical Engineering; Chemistry; Physics; Computer & Material Science
ELIGIBILITY/REQUIREMENTS: High school senior; resident of Idaho, Colorado, Texas or Virginia; combined SAT score of at least 1350 or a composite. ACT score of at least 30; unweighted GPA of at least 3.5; demonstrated leadership in school, work and/or extracurricular activities. An essay and possible interview are also required.

Scholarships can be used at any U.S. 4-year accredited school.
HOW TO APPLY: Download an application from www.micron.scholarshipamerica.org or see your high school counselor.
NUMBER OF AWARDS: Up to 13
RENEWABLE: Yes. Remain eligible, the money is spread over 4 years.
CONTACT: Scholarship America at 800/537-4180

1184—NASF/AESF Foundation Headquarters

Scholarship Committee
1155 Fifteenth Street, NW, Suite 500
Washington, DC 20005
NASF Headquarters Phone: 202/457-8404
AESF Foundation Phone: 202/457-8401
FAX: 202/530-0659
E-mail: attkoehler@nasf.org or mwalker@nasf.org.
Internet: http://www.nasf.org
AMOUNT: $1,500
DEADLINE(S): APR 15
FIELD(S): Metallurgy; Chemistry; Materials Science; Metallurgical, Chemical, & Environmental Engineering
ELIGIBILITY/REQUIREMENTS: Must be full-time junior or senior undergraduate. Selection based on achievement, scholarship potential, motivation, and career interest in surface finishing technologies, not necessarily financial need.
HOW TO APPLY: See website for application or contact AESF for application and additional information. Submit with statement (maximum of 2 pages) describing career objectives, plans for study in plating and surface finishing technologies, and long-range goals; list or résumé (maximum 2 pages) detailing educational achievements; 3 letters of recommendation from teachers, professors, or employers (1 of which must be from academic major advisor); and transcript of recent academic records.
NUMBER OF AWARDS: Varies
RENEWABLE: Yes. Must reapply; maximum 2 years undergraduate; may reapply as a graduate student.
CONTACT: Tracey Koehler, Membership Director, or Melissa Walker

1185—PROFESSIONAL GROUNDS MANAGEMENT SOCIETY (Anne Seaman Memorial Scholarship)

720 Light Street

Baltimore MD 21230
410/223-2861
FAX: 410/752-8295
E-mail: pgms@assnhqtrs.com
Internet: http://www.pgms.org
AMOUNT: $2,000
DEADLINE(S): SEP 14
FIELD(S): Landscape and Grounds Management; Turf Management; Irrigation Technology or a closely related field
ELIGIBILITY/REQUIREMENTS: U.S. citizen; full-time student.
HOW TO APPLY: Completed application with cover letter; current résumé; college or school transcripts; 2 letters of recommendation; and a letter from the PGMS member who is sponsoring the applicant.
NUMBER OF AWARDS: 3
RENEWABLE: No

1186—SOCIETY OF MANUFACTURING ENGINEERS EDUCATION FOUNDATION

Scholarship Review Committee
One SME Drive
P.O. Box 930
Dearborn MI 48121-0930
313/452-3300
FAX: 313/425-3411
E-mail: foundation@sme.org
Internet: http://www.sme.org/foundation
AMOUNT: $1,000 (minimum)
DEADLINE(S): DEC 5
FIELD(S): Manufacturing Engineering/Technology; Industrial Engineering
ELIGIBILITY/REQUIREMENTS: Available to graduating high school seniors, undergraduate students, and graduate or doctorate degree students. Some of the scholarships have a residency requirement or geographic restriction. All scholarships have a GPA requirement. Applicant must reside in and be enrolled in or accepted at an accredited institution in the U.S. or Canada, and meet the individual criteria needed for the desired scholarship.
HOW TO APPLY: See website for application and additional requirements.
NUMBER OF AWARDS: 100
RENEWABLE: No

1187—SOCIETY OF SATELLITE PROFESSIONALS INTERNATIONAL (SSPI Scholarship Program)

SSPI International Headquarters
The New York Information Technology Center
55 Broad Street, 14th floor

New York NY 10004
212/809-5199
FAX: 212/825-0075
E-mail: neworbit@aol.com
Internet: http://www.sspi.org
AMOUNT: $1,500 to $4,000
DEADLINE(S): DEC 1
FIELD(S): Satellites as related to communications, domestic and international telecommunications policy, remote sensing, journalism, law, meteorology, energy, navigation, business, government, and broadcasting services
ELIGIBILITY/REQUIREMENTS: Open to high school seniors, college or university undergraduate or graduate students who are studying or intend to study satellite-related technologies, policies or applications. Must demonstrate commitment to pursue education and career opportunities in the satellite industry or a field making direct use of satellite technology; academic and leadership achievement; potential for significant contribution to the satellite communications industry; and a scientific, engineering, research, business or creative submission meeting high standards.
HOW TO APPLY: Before applying, all applicants must complete a Scholarship Qualification Form that will help determine whether their interests and career plans are a good fit for the program. See website for form and additional details or send SASE.

1188—SOCIETY OF WOMEN ENGINEERS (Dupont Company Scholarship)

120 Wall Street, 11th Floor
New York NY 10005-3902
800/666-ISWE or 212/509-9577
FAX: 212/509-0224
E-mail: hq@swe.org
Internet: http://www.swe.org
AMOUNT: $2,000
DEADLINE(S): MAY 15
FIELD(S): Chemical Engineering; Mechanical Engineering
ELIGIBILITY/REQUIREMENTS: Open to women who are entering freshmen in a college or university in the eastern U.S. who have an ABET-accredited program or in an eastern SWE-approved school. Must have a 3.0 GPA on 4.0 scale.
HOW TO APPLY: See website or send SASE to SWE for an application. Recipient is notified in September.
NUMBER OF AWARDS: 2

1189—SPE FOUNDATION, THE (Blow Molding Division Memorial Scholarship)

14 Fairfield Drive
Brookfield CT 06804
203/740-5447
FAX: 203/775-1157
E-mail: foundation@4spe.org
Internet: http://www.4spe.org/ foundation/scholarships.php
AMOUNT: $8,000 (payable over 2 years)
DEADLINE(S): JAN 15
FIELD(S): Polymer Science; Chemistry; Physics; Plastics, Chemical, Mechanical, & Industrial Engineering
ELIGIBILITY/REQUIREMENTS: Must be in good standing with their colleges and have demonstrated an interest in the plastics industry; majoring in or taking courses that would be beneficial to a career in the plastics/polymer industry. Financial need is considered for most scholarships. Applicants must be completing the 2nd year of a 4-year undergraduate plastics engineering program and be a member of a Society of Plastics Engineers (SPE) student chapter.
HOW TO APPLY: Complete application; submit 3 recommendation letters (2 from a teacher or school official and 1 from an employer or non-relative); high school and/or college transcript for last 2 years; a 1- to 2-page brief essay on the importance of blow molding to the technical parts and packaging industries. Submit brief essay that describes the importance of blow molding to the technical parts and packaging industries, and why the applicant desires a career in the plastics industry.
NUMBER OF AWARDS: 1

1190—SPE FOUNDATION, THE (Composites Division/Harold Giles Scholarship)

14 Fairfield Drive
Brookfield CT 06804
203/740-5447
FAX: 203/775-1157
E-mail: foundation@4spe.org
Internet: http://www.4spe.org/ foundation/scholarships.php
AMOUNT: $1,000
DEADLINE(S): JAN 15
FIELD(S): Polymer Science; Chemistry; Physics; Chemical, Plastics, Mechanical & Industrial Engineering
ELIGIBILITY/REQUIREMENTS: Applicants must have experience in the composites industry (such as courses taken, research conducted, or jobs held); must be in good standing with their colleges and have demonstrated an interest in the plastics industry; majoring in or taking courses that would be beneficial to a career in the plastics/polymer industry. Financial need is considered.

HOW TO APPLY: Complete application; submit 3 recommendation letters (2 from a teacher or school official and 1 from an employer or non-relative); high school and/or college transcript for last 2 years; a 1- to 2-page statement telling why you are applying for the scholarship and educational and career goals in the plastics industry. Include a statement detailing exposure to the composites industry.
NUMBER OF AWARDS: 1
RENEWABLE: Yes. Must reapply for 3 additional years.

1191—SPE FOUNDATION, THE (Extrusion Division/Lew Erwin Memorial Scholarship)

14 Fairfield Drive
Brookfield CT 06804
203/740-5447
FAX: 203/775-1157
E-mail: foundation@4spe.org
Internet: http://www.4spe.org/ foundation/scholarships.php
AMOUNT: $2,500
DEADLINE(S): JAN 15
FIELD(S): Polymer Science; Chemistry; Physics; Chemical, Plastics, Mechanical & Industrial Engineering
ELIGIBILITY/REQUIREMENTS: Supports undergraduate or graduate research in the field of polymer extrusion. Applicants must be working in a senior or MS project. Financial need is considered for most scholarships.
HOW TO APPLY: The project must be described in writing, including background, objective and proposed experiments. The recipient will be expected to furnish a final research summary report. Complete application; submit 3 recommendation letters (2 from a teacher or school official and 1 from an employer or non-relative); high school and/or college transcript for last 2 years; a 1- to 2-page statement telling why you are applying for the scholarship and educational and career goals in the plastics industry.
NUMBER OF AWARDS: 1
RENEWABLE: Yes. Must reapply for 3 additional years.

1192—SPE FOUNDATION, THE (Fleming/Biaszcek Scholarship)

14 Fairfield Drive
Brookfield CT 06804
203/740-5447
FAX: 203/775-1157
E-mail: foundation@4spe.org
Internet: http://www.4spe.org/ foundation/scholarships.php

AMOUNT: $2,000
DEADLINE(S): JAN 15
FIELD(S): Polymer Science; Chemistry; Physics; Chemical, Plastics, Mechanical & Industrial Engineering
ELIGIBILITY/REQUIREMENTS: Available to full-time undergraduate students at a 4-year college. Must be of Mexican descent and citizens or legal residents of the U.S. Applicants must be in good standing with their colleges and have demonstrated an interest in the plastics industry; majoring in or taking courses that would be beneficial to a career in the plastics/polymer industry. Financial need is considered.
HOW TO APPLY: Complete application; submit 3 recommendation letters (2 from a teacher or school official and 1 from an employer or non-relative); high school and/or college transcript for last 2 years; a 1- to 2-page statement telling why you are applying for the scholarship and educational and career goals in the plastics industry. Detail Mexican lineage in essay or on a separate sheet of paper.
NUMBER OF AWARDS: 1
RENEWABLE: Yes. Must reapply for 3 additional years.

1193—SPE FOUNDATION, THE (Foundation Scholarships)

14 Fairfield Drive
Brookfield CT 06804
203/740-5447
FAX: 203/775-1157
E-mail: foundation@4spe.org
Internet: http://www.4spe.org/foundation/scholarships.php
AMOUNT: $4,000
DEADLINE(S): JAN 15
FIELD(S): Polymer Science; Chemistry; Physics; Chemical, Plastics, Mechanical & Industrial Engineering
ELIGIBILITY/REQUIREMENTS: Must be in good standing with their colleges and have demonstrated an interest in the plastics industry; majoring in or taking courses that would be beneficial to a career in the plastics/polymer industry. Financial need is considered.
HOW TO APPLY: Complete application; submit 3 recommendation letters (2 from a teacher or school official and 1 from an employer or non-relative); high school and/or college transcript for last 2 years; a 1- to 2-page statement telling why you are applying for the scholarship and educational and career goals in the plastics industry.
NUMBER OF AWARDS: Multiple
RENEWABLE: Yes. Must reapply for 3 additional years.

1194—SPE FOUNDATION, THE (Gulf Coast Hurricane Scholarships)

14 Fairfield Drive
Brookfield CT 06804
203/740-5447
FAX: 203/775-1157
E-mail: foundation@4spe.org
Internet: http://www.4spe.org/foundation/scholarships.php
AMOUNT: $6,000 (college or university), $2,000 (junior or technical)
DEADLINE(S): JAN 15
FIELD(S): Polymer Science; Chemistry; Physics; Chemical, Plastics, Mechanical & Industrial Engineering
ELIGIBILITY/REQUIREMENTS: Must have been a resident of a Gulf Coast County declared a national disaster area as a result of Hurricanes Katrina, Rita or Wilma, and must be attending a university, college or technical institute in a Gulf Coast State (Florida, Alabama, Mississippi, Louisiana, Texas). Must be in good standing with their colleges (minimum GPA 2.0) and enrolled 6 hours/semester. Must have demonstrated an interest in the plastics industry; majoring in or taking courses that would be beneficial to a career in the plastics/polymer industry. Financial need is considered for most scholarships.
HOW TO APPLY: Complete application; submit 3 recommendation letters (2 from a teacher or school official and 1 from an employer or non-relative); high school and/or college transcript for last 2 years; a 1- to 2-page statement telling why you are applying for the scholarship and educational and career goals in the plastics industry. Must provide proof of residence.
NUMBER OF AWARDS: 3; 1 college or university, 2 junior college or technical school
RENEWABLE: Yes. Must reapply for 3 additional years.

1195—SPE FOUNDATION, THE (Injection Molding Division Scholarship)

14 Fairfield Drive
Brookfield CT 06804
203/740-5447
FAX: 203/775-1157
E-mail: foundation@4spe.org
Internet: http://www.4spe.org/foundation/scholarships.php
AMOUNT: $3,000
DEADLINE(S): JAN 15
FIELD(S): Polymer Science; Chemistry; Physics; Chemical, Plastics, Mechanical & Industrial Engineering
ELIGIBILITY/REQUIREMENTS: Available to undergraduates at a 4-year. Applicants must have experience in the injection molding industry (such as courses taken, research conducted, or jobs held), be in good standing with their colleges and have demonstrated an interest in the plastics industry; majoring in or taking courses that would be beneficial to a career in the plastics/polymer industry. Financial need is considered.
HOW TO APPLY: Complete application; submit 3 recommendation letters (2 from a teacher or school official and 1 from an employer or non-relative); high school and/or college transcript for last 2 years; a 1- to 2-page statement telling why you are applying for the scholarship and educational and career goals in the plastics industry.
NUMBER OF AWARDS: 1
RENEWABLE: Yes. Must reapply for 3 additional years.

1196—SPE FOUNDATION, THE (Pittsburgh Section Scholarships)

14 Fairfield Drive
Brookfield CT 06804
203/740-5447
FAX: 203/775-1157
E-mail: foundation@4spe.org
Internet: http://www.4spe.org/foundation/scholarships.php
AMOUNT: $2,000
DEADLINE(S): JAN 15
FIELD(S): Polymer Science; Chemistry; Physics; Chemical, Plastics, Mechanical & Industrial Engineering
ELIGIBILITY/REQUIREMENTS: Must have graduated from a high school in one of the following PA counties: Allegheny, Armstrong, Beaver, Bedford, Blair, Brooke, Butler, Cambria, Clarion, Clearfield, Fayette, Greene, Hancock, Indiana, Jefferson, Lawrence, Mercer, Somerset, Venango, Washington, Westmoreland. Must be in good standing with their colleges and have demonstrated an interest in the plastics industry; majoring in or taking courses that would be beneficial to a career in the plastics/polymer industry. Financial need is considered for most scholarships.
HOW TO APPLY: Complete application; submit 3 recommendation letters (2 from a teacher or school official and 1 from an employer or non-relative); high school and/or college transcript for last 2 years; a 1- to 2-page statement telling why you are applying for the scholarship and educational and career goals in the plastics industry. Must provide proof of graduation from school in one of above counties.
NUMBER OF AWARDS: Up to 2

RENEWABLE: Yes. Must reapply for 3 additional years.

1197—SPE FOUNDATION, THE (Plastics Pioneers Association Scholarships)

14 Fairfield Drive
Brookfield CT 06804
203/740-5447
FAX: 203/775-1157
E-mail: foundation@4spe.org
Internet: http://www.4spe.org/
foundation/scholarships.php
AMOUNT: $3,000
DEADLINE(S): JAN 15
FIELD(S): Polymer Science; Chemistry; Physics; Chemical, Plastics, Mechanical & Industrial Engineering
ELIGIBILITY/REQUIREMENTS: Open to undergraduate students, including those enrolled in associate or technical degree programs, who are committed to becoming "hands on" workers in the plastics industry as plastics technicians or engineers. Must be in good standing with their colleges and have demonstrated an interest in the plastics industry; majoring in or taking courses that would be beneficial to a career in the plastics/polymer industry. Financial need is considered for most scholarships.
HOW TO APPLY: Complete application; submit 3 recommendation letters (2 from a teacher or school official and 1 from an employer or non-relative); high school and/or college transcript for last 2 years; a 1- to 2-page statement telling why you are applying for the scholarship and educational and career goals in the plastics industry.
NUMBER OF AWARDS: Multiple
RENEWABLE: Yes. Must reapply for 3 additional years.

1198—SPE FOUNDATION, THE (Polymer Modifiers & Additives Division Scholarships)

14 Fairfield Drive
Brookfield CT 06804
203/740-5447
FAX: 203/775-1157
E-mail: foundation@4spe.org
Internet: http://www.4spe.org/
foundation/scholarships.php
AMOUNT: $4,000
DEADLINE(S): JAN 15
FIELD(S): Polymer Science; Chemistry; Physics; Chemical, Plastics, Mechanical & Industrial Engineering
ELIGIBILITY/REQUIREMENTS: Must be in good standing with their colleges and have demonstrated an interest in the plastics industry; majoring in or taking courses that would be beneficial to a career in the plastics/polymer industry. Financial need is considered for most scholarships.
HOW TO APPLY: Complete application; submit 3 recommendation letters (2 from a teacher or school official and 1 from an employer or non-relative); high school and/or college transcript for last 2 years; a 1- to 2-page statement telling why you are applying for the scholarship and educational and career goals in the plastics industry.
NUMBER OF AWARDS: 3
RENEWABLE: Yes. Must reapply for 3 additional years.

1199—SPE FOUNDATION, THE (Robert E. Cramer/Product Design & Development Division Scholarship)

14 Fairfield Drive
Brookfield CT 06804
203/740-5447
FAX: 203/775-1157
E-mail: foundation@4spe.org
Internet: http://www.4spe.org/
foundation/scholarships.php
AMOUNT: $1,000
DEADLINE(S): JAN 15
FIELD(S): Polymer Science; Chemistry; Physics; Chemical, Plastics, Mechanical & Industrial Engineering
ELIGIBILITY/REQUIREMENTS: Must be in good standing with their colleges and have demonstrated an interest in the plastics industry; majoring in or taking courses that would be beneficial to a career in the plastics/polymer industry. Financial need is considered for most scholarships.
HOW TO APPLY: Complete application; submit 3 recommendation letters (2 from a teacher or school official and 1 from an employer or non-relative); high school and/or college transcript for last 2 years; a 1- to 2-page statement telling why you are applying for the scholarship and educational and career goals in the plastics industry.
NUMBER OF AWARDS: 1
RENEWABLE: Yes. Must reapply for 3 additional years.

1200—SPE FOUNDATION, THE (Robert G. Dailey/Detroit Section Scholarship)

14 Fairfield Drive
Brookfield CT 06804
203/740-5447
FAX: 203/775-1157
E-mail: foundation@4spe.org
Internet: http://www.4spe.org/
foundation/scholarships.php
AMOUNT: $4,000
DEADLINE(S): JAN 15
FIELD(S): Polymer Science; Chemistry; Physics; Chemical, Plastics, Mechanical & Industrial Engineering
ELIGIBILITY/REQUIREMENTS: Must be in good standing with their colleges and have demonstrated an interest in the plastics industry; majoring in or taking courses that would be beneficial to a career in the plastics/polymer industry. Financial need is considered for most scholarships.
HOW TO APPLY: Complete application; submit 3 recommendation letters (2 from a teacher or school official and 1 from an employer or non-relative); high school and/or college transcript for last 2 years; a 1- to 2-page statement telling why you are applying for the scholarship and educational and career goals in the plastics industry.
NUMBER OF AWARDS: 1
RENEWABLE: Yes. Must reapply for 3 additional years.

1201—SPE FOUNDATION, THE (Ted and Ruth Neward Scholarships)

14 Fairfield Drive
Brookfield CT 06804
203/740-5447
FAX: 203/775-1157
E-mail: foundation@4spe.org
Internet: http://www.4spe.org/
foundation/scholarships.php
AMOUNT: $3,000
DEADLINE(S): JAN 15
FIELD(S): Polymer Science; Chemistry; Physics; Chemical, Plastics, Mechanical & Industrial Engineering
ELIGIBILITY/REQUIREMENTS: Must be U.S. citizens in good standing with their colleges and have demonstrated an interest in the plastics industry; majoring in or taking courses that would be beneficial to a career in the plastics/polymer industry. Financial need is considered for most scholarships.
HOW TO APPLY: Complete application; submit 3 recommendation letters (2 from a teacher or school official and 1 from an employer or non-relative); high school and/or college transcript for last 2 years; a 1- to 2-page statement telling why you are applying for the scholarship and educational and career goals in the plastics industry.
NUMBER OF AWARDS: 3
RENEWABLE: Yes. Must reapply for 3 additional years.

1202—SPE FOUNDATION, THE (Thermoforming Division Memorial Scholarships)

14 Fairfield Drive
Brookfield CT 06804

203/740-5447
FAX: 203/775-1157
E-mail: foundation@4spe.org
Internet: http://www.4spe.org/
foundation/scholarships.php
AMOUNT: $7,500
DEADLINE(S): JAN 15
FIELD(S): Polymer Science; Chemistry;
Physics; Chemical, Plastics, Mechanical
& Industrial Engineering
ELIGIBILITY/REQUIREMENTS:
Available to graduate or undergraduate
students at a 4-year college. Undergraduates must have completed at least 2
years of credits. Applicants must have
experience in the thermoforming industry
(such as courses taken, research conducted, or jobs held), be in good standing with
their colleges and have demonstrated an
interest in the plastics industry; majoring in
or taking courses that would be beneficial
to a career in the plastics/polymer industry.
Financial need is considered.
HOW TO APPLY: Complete application;
submit 3 recommendation letters (2 from a
teacher or school official and 1 from an
employer or non-relative); high school
and/or college transcript for last 2 years; a
1- to 2-page statement telling why you are
applying for the scholarship and educational and career goals in the plastics
industry. Include a statement detailing
exposure to the thermoforming industry.
NUMBER OF AWARDS: Varies (multiple awards)
RENEWABLE: Yes. Must reapply for 3
additional years.

1203—SPE FOUNDATION, THE (Thermoplastic Elastomers Special Interest Group Scholarship)

14 Fairfield Drive
Brookfield CT 06804
203/740-5447
FAX: 203/775-1157
E-mail: foundation@4spe.org
Internet: http://www.4spe.org/
foundation/scholarships.php
AMOUNT: $1,000
DEADLINE(S): JAN 15
FIELD(S): Polymer Science; Chemistry;
Physics; Chemical, Plastics, Mechanical
& Industrial Engineering
ELIGIBILITY/REQUIREMENTS:
Available to graduate or undergraduate
students at a 4-year college. Applicants
must have experience in the thermoplastic
elastometers industry (such as courses
taken, research conducted, or jobs held);
must be in good standing with their col-
leges and have demonstrated an interest in
the plastics industry; majoring in or taking

courses that would be beneficial to a career
in the plastics/polymer industry. Financial
need is considered.
HOW TO APPLY: Complete application;
submit 3 recommendation letters (2 from a
teacher or school official and 1 from an
employer or non-relative); high school
and/or college transcript for last 2 years; a
1- to 2-page statement telling why you are
applying for the scholarship and educational and career goals in the plastics
industry. Include a statement detailing
exposure to the thermoplastic elastometers
industry.
NUMBER OF AWARDS: 1

1204—SPE FOUNDATION, THE (Thermoplastic Materials & Foams Division Scholarship)

14 Fairfield Drive
Brookfield CT 06804
203/740-5447
FAX: 203/775-1157
E-mail: foundation@4spe.org
Internet: http://www.4spe.org/
foundation/scholarships.php
AMOUNT: $1,000
DEADLINE(S): JAN 15
FIELD(S): Polymer Science; Chemistry;
Physics; Chemical, Plastics, Mechanical
& Industrial Engineering
ELIGIBILITY/REQUIREMENTS: Must
be in good standing with their colleges and
have demonstrated an interest in the plastics industry; majoring in or taking courses
that would be beneficial to a career in the
plastics/polymer industry. Financial need is
considered for most scholarships.
HOW TO APPLY: Complete application;
submit 3 recommendation letters (2 from a
teacher or school official and 1 from an
employer or non-relative); high school
and/or college transcript for last 2 years; a
1- to 2-page statement telling why you are
applying for the scholarship and educational and career goals in the plastics
industry.
NUMBER OF AWARDS: 1
RENEWABLE: Yes. Must reapply for 3
additional years.

1205—SPE FOUNDATION, THE (Thermoset Division/James I. MacKenzie Memorial Scholarship)

14 Fairfield Drive
Brookfield CT 06804
203/740-5447
FAX: 203/775-1157
E-mail: foundation@4spe.org
Internet: http://www.4spe.org/
foundation/scholarships.php

AMOUNT: $2,500
DEADLINE(S): JAN 15
FIELD(S): Polymer Science; Chemistry;
Physics; Chemical, Plastics, Mechanical
& Industrial Engineering
ELIGIBILITY/REQUIREMENTS:
Available to undergraduates at a 4-year.
Applicants must have experience in the
thermoset industry (such as courses taken,
research conducted, or jobs held), be in
good standing with their colleges and have
demonstrated an interest in the plastics
industry; majoring in or taking courses that
would be beneficial to a career in the plas-
tics/polymer industry. Financial need is
considered.
HOW TO APPLY: Complete application;
submit 3 recommendation letters (2 from a
teacher or school official and 1 from an
employer or non-relative); high school
and/or college transcript for last 2 years; a
1- to 2-page statement telling why you are
applying for the scholarship and educational and career goals in the plastics
industry.
NUMBER OF AWARDS: 1
RENEWABLE: Yes. Must reapply for 3
additional years.
ADDITIONAL INFORMATION: Also
includes all-expense-paid trip to, and
speaking opportunity at, annual Madison
Thermoset Molding Conference.

1206—SPE FOUNDATION, THE (Vinyl Plastics Division Scholarship)

14 Fairfield Drive
Brookfield CT 06804
203/740-5447
FAX: 203/775-1157
E-mail: foundation@4spe.org
Internet: http://www.4spe.org/
foundation/scholarships.php
AMOUNT: $3,000
DEADLINE(S): JAN 15
FIELD(S): Polymer Science; Chemistry;
Physics; Chemical, Plastics, Mechanical
& Industrial Engineering
ELIGIBILITY/REQUIREMENTS: Must
be in good standing with their colleges and
have demonstrated an interest in the plastics industry; majoring in or taking courses
that would be beneficial to a career in the
plastics/polymer industry. Preference
given to applicants with experience in the
vinyl industry (such as courses taken,
research conducted, or jobs held).
Financial need is considered for most
scholarships.
HOW TO APPLY: Complete application;
submit 3 recommendation letters (2 from a
teacher or school official and 1 from an
employer or non-relative); high school
and/or college transcript for last 2 years; a

1- to 2-page statement telling why you are applying for the scholarship and educational and career goals in the plastics industry.
NUMBER OF AWARDS: 1
RENEWABLE: Yes. Must reapply for 3 additional years.

1207—WESTERN MICHIGAN UNIVERSITY (College of Engineering and Applied Sciences Endowed Scholarship)

1903 West Michigan
Kalamazoo MI 49008-5337
269/387-6000
FAX: 269/387-6989
E-mail: finaid-info@wmich.edu
Internet: http://www.wmich.edu/finaid
AMOUNT: $1,000 per academic year for each of 4 years
FIELD(S): Chemical Engineering; Energy Management
ELIGIBILITY/REQUIREMENTS: Open to degree-seeking freshman (entering in the fall semester) who is admitted to an ABET-accredited, undergraduate degree program at WMU. Must be a resident of Michigan and a U.S. citizen. Awards are competitive. The top candidate from the pool will receive a scholarship based on appropriateness of high school courses in preparation for engineering education, admission GPA, and ACT scores.
HOW TO APPLY: Contact the College of Engineering and Applied Science Advising Office, Room E-102 Parkview Campus (269/276-3270) for an application.
NUMBER OF AWARDS: 2-3
RENEWABLE: Yes. If enrolled as a full-time student (minimum of 12 semester hours fall and spring semesters) in an ABET-accredited, undergraduate degree program, maintaining a 2.5 overall GPA on a 4.0 scale.

1208—WESTERN MICHIGAN UNIVERSITY (College of Engineering and Applied Sciences Scholarship)

1903 West Michigan
Kalamazoo, MI 49008-5337
269/387-6000
FAX: 269/387-6989
E-mail: finaid-info@wmich.edu
Internet: http://www.wmich.edu/finaid
AMOUNT: $250-$500
FIELD(S): Chemical Engineering; Energy Management
ELIGIBILITY/REQUIREMENTS: Open to full-time student (minimum of 12 credit hours) who has completed enough semes-

ter hours of coursework to be classified at the sophomore level or higher (at least 26 semester hours), is enrolled in a 4-year degree program in the College of Engineering and Applied Sciences, who has accumulated a minimum of 12 semester hours at WMU.
HOW TO APPLY: Contact the College of Engineering and Applied Science Advising Office, Room E-102 Parkview Campus (269/276-3270) for an application.
RENEWABLE: No

CIVIL ENGINEERING & CONSTRUCTION

1209—AGC SCHOLARSHIP FUND

10 Airline Drive, Suite 203
Albany NY 12205
518-456-1134
FAX: 518-456-1198
E-mail: cnewell@agcnys.org
Internet: http://www.agcnys.org
AMOUNT: $2,500 (construction and, civil engineering), $1,500 (diesel technology)
DEADLINE(S): MAY 15
FIELD(S): Construction, Civil Engineering, Diesel Technology
ELIGIBILITY/REQUIREMENTS: Applicant must be entering the 2nd, 3rd or 4th year of a 2- or 4-year college. Must intend to pursue a career in the highway construction industry, and pursuing a Bachelor or Associate degree in construction or civil engineering and have at least a 2.5 GPA.
HOW TO APPLY: See website for additional information and application. Submit with grades and 3 evaluation forms.
NUMBER OF AWARDS: 16-25, includes 2 diesel technology scholarships
RENEWABLE: Yes. Up to 3 years; must reapply.
CONTACT: Cathy Newell

1210—AMERICAN SOCIETY OF CIVIL ENGINEERS (B. Charles Tiney Memorial Student Chapter Scholarship)

Student Services
1801 Alexander Bell Drive
Reston VA 20191-4400
800/548-2723 or 703/295-6000
FAX: 703/295-6222
E-mail: student@asce.org
Internet: http://www.asce.org/inside/stud scholar.cfm
AMOUNT: $2,000

DEADLINE(S): FEB 7
FIELD(S): Civil Engineering
ELIGIBILITY/REQUIREMENTS: Open to undergraduate freshmen, sophomores, and juniors who are ASCE National Student Members (NSM applications may be submitted along with scholarship applications). To be used toward tuition.
HOW TO APPLY: See website or contact ASCE for an application between October and February.
NUMBER OF AWARDS: 12

1211—AMERICAN SOCIETY OF CIVIL ENGINEERS (O. H. Ammann Research Fellowship in Structural Engineering)

Student Services
1801 Alexander Bell Drive
Reston VA 20191-4400
800/548-2723 or 703/295-6000
FAX: 703/295-6222
E-mail: student@asce.org
Internet: http://www.asce.org inside/stud scholar.cfm
AMOUNT: $5,000
DEADLINE(S): FEB 24
FIELD(S): Structural Engineering
ELIGIBILITY/REQUIREMENTS: For ASCE members at any level to create new knowledge in the field of structural design and construction. Membership application may be submitted along with fellowship application.
HOW TO APPLY: See website or contact ASCE for an application between October and February.
NUMBER OF AWARDS: 1

1212—AMERICAN SOCIETY OF CIVIL ENGINEERS (Samuel Fletcher Tapman Student Chapter/Club Scholarships)

Student Services
1801 Alexander Bell Drive
Reston VA 20191-4400
800/548-2723 or 703/295-6000
FAX: 703/295-6222
E-mail: student@asce.org
Internet: http://www.asce.org/inside/stud scholar.cfm
AMOUNT: $2,000
DEADLINE(S): FEB 7
FIELD(S): Civil Engineering
ELIGIBILITY/REQUIREMENTS: Open to undergraduate freshmen, sophomores, and juniors who are ASCE National Student Members (NSM applications may be submitted along with scholarship applications).

HOW TO APPLY: See website or contact ASCE for an application between October and February.
NUMBER OF AWARDS: 12

1213—ASSOCIATED BUILDERS AND CONTRACTORS SCHOLARSHIP PROGRAM

4250 North Fairfax Drive, 9th Floor
Arlington VA 22203
703/812-2008
FAX: 703/812-8234
E-mail: hess@abc.org or
studentchapters@abc.org
Internet: http://www.abc.org
AMOUNT: $1,000
DEADLINE(S): MAY 28
FIELD(S): Construction
ELIGIBILITY/REQUIREMENTS: Open to undergraduates enrolled in 2- or 4-year construction-related degree program. Applicants must have completed at least 1 year of study and must have at least 1 full semester remaining subsequent to application deadline. Must be a member of an ABC student chapter or work for an ABC member.
HOW TO APPLY: See website or contact ABC for information and application.
NUMBER OF AWARDS: About 45

1214—ASSOCIATION OF CALIFORNIA WATER AGENCIES (ACWA)

910 K Street, Suite 100
Sacramento CA 95814
916/441-4545
FAX: 916/325-4849
E-mail: acwabox@acwanet.com
Internet: http://www.acwanet.com
AMOUNT: $1,500
DEADLINE(S): APR 1
FIELD(S): Water Resources-related fields including Engineering, Agriculture, Environmental Studies, Public Administration
ELIGIBILITY/REQUIREMENTS: ACWA's awards are based not only on scholastic achievement but also on the individual's commitment and motivation to their chosen field. Financial need will also be considered.
HOW TO APPLY: Download applications and guidelines for the ACWA scholarship program from website, or call or e-mail ACWA or contact your school's financial aid department.
NUMBER OF AWARDS: At least 6

1215—ASSOCIATION OF STATE DAM SAFETY OFFICIALS

450 Old Vine Street, 2nd Floor

Lexington KY 40507
859/257-5140
Internet: http://www.damsafety.org
AMOUNT: Up to $5,000
DEADLINE(S): Mid-FEB
FIELD(S): Civil Engineering and related fields
ELIGIBILITY/REQUIREMENTS: Must be U.S. citizen and enrolled at the senior level in an accredited civil engineering program, or in a related field as determined by ASDSO, and must demonstrate an interest in pursuing a career in hydraulics, hydrology or geotechnical disciplines, or in another discipline related to the design, construction, and operation of dams. Minimum GPA for previous 3 years is 2.5. Financial need and work experience also considered.
HOW TO APPLY: See website for application. Recommendation from academic advisor and an essay are required. Winners are announced in May.

1216—COMMUNITY FOUNDATION OF WESTERN MASSACHUSETTS (Edward J. Bayon Memorial Scholarship)

1500 Main Street
P.O. Box 15769
Springfield MA 01115
413/732-2858
FAX: 413/733-8565
E-mail: scholar@community foundation.org
Internet: http://www.community foundation.org
AMOUNT: $2,200
DEADLINE(S): MAR 31
FIELD(S): Civil Engineering
ELIGIBILITY/REQUIREMENTS: Open to residents of Holyoke, Massachusetts, who are graduating seniors at Holyoke high schools planning to attend a 4-year college to pursue a career in civil engineering or related fields.
HOW TO APPLY: See website for application.
NUMBER OF AWARDS: 1
RENEWABLE: No

1217—COMMUNITY FOUNDATION OF WESTERN MASSACHUSETTS (George H. McDonnell Scholarship)

1500 Main Street
P.O. Box 15769
Springfield MA 01115
413/732-2858
FAX: 413/733-8565
E-mail: scholar@community foundation.org

Internet: http://www.community foundation.org
AMOUNT: $2,200
DEADLINE(S): MAR 31
FIELD(S): Civil Engineering
ELIGIBILITY/REQUIREMENTS: For a graduating senior of South Hadley High School and town resident of South Hadley, Massachusetts, who will attend a 4-year college with a major in civil engineering or a related field.
HOW TO APPLY: See website for application.
NUMBER OF AWARDS: 1
RENEWABLE: No

1218—CONNECTICUT BUILDING CONGRESS SCHOLARSHIP FUND

2600 Dixwell Avenue, Suite 7
Hamden CT 06514
203/281-3183
FAX: 203/248-8932
E-mail: bdavidson@ctengineers.org
Internet: http://www.cbc-ct.org
AMOUNT: $500-$2,000
DEADLINE(S): MAR 31
FIELD(S): Construction Industry-related subjects (Architecture; Engineering; Construction Management; Planning; Drafting, etc.)
ELIGIBILITY/REQUIREMENTS: Connecticut resident. Must submit an essay of not more than 500 words that explains how your planned studies will relate to a career in the construction industry; transcript of high school grades; class standing and SAT/ACT tests; copy of Student Aid Report of FAFSA and custodial parent's statement (from College Board) if applicable.
HOW TO APPLY: Call, write or e-mail for application.
NUMBER OF AWARDS: 2 to 4
RENEWABLE: Yes. Per year for 4 years; must maintain grades.
CONTACT: Beverly Davidson at CBCSF

1219—ILLUMINATING ENGINEERING SOCIETY OF NORTH AMERICA (Robert W. Thunen Memorial Scholarships)

Golden Gate Section
P.O. Box 77527
San Francisco CA 94107-1527
E-mail: riverfield@juno.com
AMOUNT: $2,500
DEADLINE(S): APR 1
FIELD(S): Illumination (Architectural, Commercial, Residential, Airport, Navigational, Theatrical, TV, Agricultural, Vision, etc.)

ELIGIBILITY/REQUIREMENTS: Open to full-time juniors, seniors and graduate students in an accredited 4-year college or university located in Northern California, Nevada, Oregon, or Washington.

HOW TO APPLY: Contact Chair for an application. Must submit statement of purpose (with respect to lighting education) and 3 letters of recommendation. Awards announced by May 3.

NUMBER OF AWARDS: At least 2

RENEWABLE: Yes. Automatically for up to 3 years if minimum 3.0 annual GPA is maintained and student remains enrolled full time in an eligible program.

CONTACT: Heide M. Kawahata, Chair

1220—MICHIGAN SOCIETY OF PROFESSIONAL ENGINEERS, THE (McNamee, Porter & Seeley/University of Michigan/ John C. Seeley, P.E. Memorial Scholarship)

215 North Walnut
P.O. Box 15276
Lansing MI 48901-5276
517/487-9388
FAX: 517/487-0635
E-mail: mspe@voyager.net
Internet: http://www.michiganspe.org

AMOUNT: $1,500

DEADLINE(S): 2nd Monday in APR

FIELD(S): Civil Engineering

ELIGIBILITY/REQUIREMENTS: Applicant must be an MSPE member; be a U.S. citizen and a resident of Michigan; be in an ABET-accredited engineering program at a Michigan college or university; have a minimum GPA of 3.0 on a 4.0 scale; demonstrate leadership and an interest in the engineering profession through involvement in school and/or outside activities. Preference is given to a student in sanitary engineering, although any civil engineering student may qualify.

HOW TO APPLY: Send completed application; official grade transcript(s); recommendations from at least 2 professors in the applicant's field of engineering study or appropriate math/science professor, specifying academic and personal traits and extracurricular activities; proof of acceptance in an ABET-accredited engineering program; information on co-op programs (i.e., information relating to or comprising a program of combined studies in which applicant might be involved); and a typed, 2-page essay of approximately 500 words, discussing applicant's interest in engineering, specific field of engineering that is being pursued, and occupation applicant proposes to pursue after graduation.

NUMBER OF AWARDS: 1

1221—MICHIGAN SOCIETY OF PROFESSIONAL ENGINEERS, THE (MSPE/Abrams Foundation Grant)

215 North Walnut
P.O. Box 15276
Lansing MI 48901-5276
517/487-9388
FAX: 517/487-0635
E-mail: mspe@voyager.net
Internet: http://www.michiganspe.org

AMOUNT: $3,000

DEADLINE(S): 2nd Monday in APR

FIELD(S): Civil Engineering; Surveying Engineering

ELIGIBILITY/REQUIREMENTS: Applicant must be an MSPE member; be a U.S. citizen and a resident of Michigan; be in an ABET-accredited engineering program at a Michigan college or university; have a minimum GPA of 3.0 on a 4.0 scale; demonstrate leadership and an interest in the engineering profession through involvement in school and/or outside activities.

HOW TO APPLY: Send completed application; official grade transcript(s); recommendations from at least 2 professors in the applicant's field of engineering study or appropriate math/science professor, specifying academic and personal traits and extracurricular activities; proof of acceptance in an ABET-accredited engineering program; information on co-op programs (i.e., information relating to or comprising a program of combined studies in which applicant might be involved); and a typed, 2-page essay of approximately 500 words, discussing applicant's interest in engineering, specific field of engineering that is being pursued, and occupation applicant proposes to pursue after graduation.

NUMBER OF AWARDS: 1

CONTACT: Address above.

1222—MICHIGAN SOCIETY OF PROFESSIONAL ENGINEERS, THE (Robert E. Folmsbee, P.E. Memorial Grant)

215 North Walnut
P.O. Box 15276
Lansing MI 48901-5276
517/487-9388
FAX: 517/487-0635
E-mail: mspe@voyager.net
Internet: http://www.michiganspe.org

AMOUNT: $2,000

DEADLINE(S): 2nd Monday in APR

FIELD(S): Construction Engineering

ELIGIBILITY/REQUIREMENTS: Applicant must be an MSPE member; be a

U.S. citizen and a resident of Michigan; be in an ABET-accredited engineering program at a Michigan college or university; have a minimum GPA of 3.0 on a 4.0 scale; demonstrate leadership and an interest in the engineering profession through involvement in school and/or outside activities.

HOW TO APPLY: Send completed application; official grade transcript(s); recommendations from at least 2 professors in the applicant's field of engineering study or appropriate math/science professor, specifying academic and personal traits and extracurricular activities; proof of acceptance in an ABET-accredited engineering program; information on co-op programs (i.e., information relating to or comprising a program of combined studies in which applicant might be involved); and a typed, 2-page essay of approximately 500 words, discussing applicant's interest in engineering, specific field of engineering that is being pursued, and occupation applicant proposes to pursue after graduation.

NUMBER OF AWARDS: 1

1223—MIDWEST ROOFING CONTRACTORS ASSOCIATION (Construction Industry Scholarships)

4840 Bob Billings Parkway, Suite 1000
Lawrence KS 66049-3876
800/497-6722
FAX: 785/843-7555
E-mail: mrca@mrca.org
Internet: http://www.mrca.org

AMOUNT: Varies

DEADLINE(S): JUN 20

FIELD(S): Construction

ELIGIBILITY/REQUIREMENTS: Applicants must be pursuing or planning to pursue a curriculum at an accredited university, college, community college, vocational, or trade school that will lead to a career in the construction industry. Three letters of recommendation required.

HOW TO APPLY: Contact MRCA for an application.

1224—NEW ENGLAND WATER WORKS ASSOCIATION

125 Hopping Brook Road
Holliston MA 01746
508/893-7979
FAX: 508/893-9898
E-mail: marina@newwa.org
Internet: http://www.newwa.org

AMOUNT: Varies

DEADLINE(S): JUL 1

FIELD(S): Water Industry; Civil or Environmental Engineering; Business Management; Science

ELIGIBILITY/REQUIREMENTS: Based on merit, character, and need, with preference given to those students whose programs are considered beneficial to water works practice in New England. Each scholarship applicant must be a member or student member of either the New England Water Works Association, or the American Water Works Association, with a New England section, before their application will be considered. The membership fee is $25 for a NEWWA student membership or $36 for a NEWWA/ AWWA student membership.

HOW TO APPLY: Mail application to: Thomas MacElhaney, Scholarship Committee Chair, 631/231-8100 or tmacelhaney@preloadinc.com.

NUMBER OF AWARDS: 6

RENEWABLE: No

CONTACT: Marina Mukandala

1225—SOCIETY OF AUTOMOTIVE ENGINEERS (Yanmar/SAE Scholarship)

SAE Customer Service
400 Commonwealth Drive
Warrendale PA 15096-0001
724/776-4970
FAX: 724/776-1615
E-mail: customerservice@sae.org
Internet: http://www.sae.org/students/scholarships

AMOUNT: $2,000 ($1,000/year for 2 years)

DEADLINE(S): APR 1

FIELD(S): Engineering, related to Conservation of Energy in Transportation, Agriculture, Construction, & Power Generation

ELIGIBILITY/REQUIREMENTS: For graduate students and undergraduates in their senior year who are citizens of North America (U.S./Canada/Mexico). Based on previous scholastic performance with additional consideration given for special study or honors in the field of award, and for leadership achievement related to engineering or science. Applicants must be pursuing a course of study or research related to the conservation of energy in transportation, agriculture and construction, and power generation. Emphasis will be placed on research or study related to the internal combustion engine.

HOW TO APPLY: Submit application; an essay that demonstrates hands-on experience or activity (such as rebuilding engines, working on cars/trucks, etc.); 2 recommen-

dations, 1 of which must be from a teacher, counselor, or administrator; and transcript.

NUMBER OF AWARDS: 1

RENEWABLE: No

CONTACT: Yanmar/SAE Scholarship

1226—STUDENT CONSERVATION ASSOCIATION (SCA Resource Assistant Program)

P.O. Box 550
Charlestown NH 03603
603/543-1700
FAX: 603/543-1828
E-mail: internships@sca-inc.org
Internet: http://www.sca-inc.org

AMOUNT: $1,180-$4,725

DEADLINE(S): Varies

FIELD(S): Environment and related fields (agriculture, archaeology, anthropology, botany, caves, civil engineering, environmental design engineering and education, fisheries, forests, herpetology, history, landscape architecture, environmental design, paleontology, recreation/resource/range management, wildlife management, geology, hydrology, library/museums, surveying)

ELIGIBILITY/REQUIREMENTS: Must be 18 and U.S. citizen; need not be student.

HOW TO APPLY: Send $1 for postage for application; outside U.S./Canada, send $20.

NUMBER OF AWARDS: 900 positions in U.S. and Canada

1227—TRANSPORTATION CLUBS INTERNATIONAL (Ginger and Fred Deines Mexico Scholarship)

1275 Kamus Drive, Suite 101
Fox Island WA 98333-9605

AMOUNT: $500-$1,000

FIELD(S): Logistics; Civil Engineering; Transportation

ELIGIBILITY/REQUIREMENTS: Applicants must have completed at least one year of undergraduate study at a 4-year institution in Mexico or the U.S. and be pursuing a career in logistics, civil engineering, or transportation.

HOW TO APPLY: Send SASE.

1228—WESTERN MICHIGAN UNIVERSITY (College of Engineering and Applied Sciences/Kalamazoo Builders Exchange Scholarship)

1903 West Michigan
Kalamazoo, MI 49008-5337
269/387-6000
FAX: 269/387-6989

E-mail: finaid-info@wmich.edu
Internet: http://www.wmich.edu/finaid

AMOUNT: $1,000 ($500 fall/$500 spring)

FIELD(S): Construction Engineering; Materials Engineering; Industrial Engineering

ELIGIBILITY/REQUIREMENTS: Awarded to a full-time undergraduate student majoring in construction, materials, or industrial design. Preference given to juniors and seniors who have experience in the construction industry through an internship or part-time work with special preference for association with the Kalamazoo Builders Exchange, and to those living within the greater Southwest Michigan area. Coursework supported through this program must be applicable toward a degree program relevant to the construction industry.

HOW TO APPLY: Applicants may be recommended by a member of the Builders Exchange. Contact the Construction Engineering undergraduate advisor for more information.

NUMBER OF AWARDS: 1

RENEWABLE: Yes. Must reapply and maintain a minimum 3.3 GPA at WMU enrolled as an undergraduate student in construction engineering.

CONTACT: Construction Engineering undergraduate advisor

COMPUTER SCIENCE & ENGINEERING/INFORMATION TECHNOLOGY

1229—AMERICAN ASSOCIATION OF BLACKS IN ENERGY (AABE)

Western Michigan University
1903 West Michigan
Kalamazoo MI 49008-5337
269/387-8777
FAX: 269/387-6989
E-mail: alumni@wmich.edu
Internet: http://www.wmich.edu/cas/research.html

AMOUNT: Varies

DEADLINE(S): MAR 1

FIELD(S): Mathematics; Computer Science; Engineering; Physical Sciences

ELIGIBILITY/REQUIREMENTS: Freshman with 2.5 GPA overall and a 3.0 GPA in mathematics and the sciences. Planning to major in engineering, mathematics, computer or the physical sciences. Applicant must demonstrate financial need and be a member of one of the underrepresented minority groups in the sciences and technology.

HOW TO APPLY: Contact the Office for Student Financial Aid.

NUMBER OF AWARDS: Varies

RENEWABLE: Yes

CONTACT: Office for Student Financial Aid

1230—AMERICAN FOUNDATION FOR THE BLIND (Paul W. Ruckes Scholarship)

11 Penn Plaza, Suite 300
New York NY 10001
212/502-7661
FAX: 212/502-7771
E-mail: fbinfo@afb.org
Internet: http://www.afb.org/
scholar/scholarships.asp

AMOUNT: $1,000

DEADLINE(S): MAR 31

FIELD(S): Engineering; Computer Science; Physical/Life Sciences

ELIGIBILITY/REQUIREMENTS: Open to legally blind and visually impaired undergraduate and graduate students pursuing a degree in one of above fields. Must be U.S. citizen.

HOW TO APPLY: See website or contact AFB for an application. Submit documentation of evidence of legal blindness; official transcripts; proof of college or university acceptance; 3 letters of recommendation; and statement describing goals, work experience, extracurricular activities, and how monies will be used.

NUMBER OF AWARDS: 1

CONTACT: Alina Vayntrub

1231—AMERICAN RADIO RELAY LEAGUE FOUNDATION (The PHD ARA Scholarship)

225 Main Street
Newington CT 06111
860/594-0397
FAX: 860/594-0259
E-mail: foundation@arrl.org
Internet: http://www.arrlf.org/

AMOUNT: $1,000

DEADLINE(S): FEB 1

FIELD(S): Journalism; Computer Science; Electronic Engineering

ELIGIBILITY/REQUIREMENTS: For undergraduate or graduate students who are residents of the ARRL Midwest Division (IA, KS, MO, NE) who hold any class of radio amateur license—or student may be the child of a deceased radio amateur.

HOW TO APPLY: See website or contact Foundation for information and application. Submit with a 1-page essay on the role amateur radio has played in your life. A

recent high school (or equivalent) or college transcript required; submit with application or mail separately.

NUMBER OF AWARDS: 1

RENEWABLE: No

CONTACT: Mary M. Hobart, K1MMH, Secretary

1232—AMERICAN RADIO RELAY LEAGUE FOUNDATION (William R. Goldfarb Memorial Scholarship)

225 Main Street
Newington CT 06111
860/594-0397
FAX: 860/594-0259
E-mail: foundation@arrl.org
Internet: http://www.arrlf.org/

AMOUNT: $1,000

DEADLINE(S): FEB 1

FIELD(S): Business, Computer Science, Medicine (including Nursing), Engineering, Sciences

ELIGIBILITY/REQUIREMENTS: For student with any class of license pursuing baccalaureate or higher degree at a regionally accredited institution. Must demonstrate financial need.

HOW TO APPLY: See website or contact Foundation for information and application. Submit with FAFSA and a 1-page essay on the role amateur radio has played in your life. A recent high school (or equivalent) or college transcript required; submit with application or mail separately.

NUMBER OF AWARDS: 1

RENEWABLE: No

CONTACT: Mary M. Hobart, K1MMH, Secretary

1233—AMERICAN SOCIETY OF ENGINEERS OF INDIAN ORIGIN (Undergraduate Scholarship Programs)

47790 Pavillon Road
Canton MI 48188
248/354-6895
FAX: 248/354-6818
E-mail: awards@asei-ncc.org
Internet: http://www.asei-ncc.org/Awards.htm

AMOUNT: $1,000

DEADLINE(S): AUG 15

FIELD(S): Engineering: Architecture, Computer or allied science, Geotechnical or Geo-environmental Engineering, and allied sciences

ELIGIBILITY/REQUIREMENTS: Open to students who are Indian by birth, ancestry, or relation. Based on demonstrated ability, academic achievement, including GPA (minimum 3.0)/honors/awards, ca-

reer objectives, faculty recommendations, student involvement in science fair, campus activities, and industrial exposure including part-time work and internships; must attend an accredited college or university anywhere in the U.S.

HOW TO APPLY: See website for application and details or contact Society for applications. Submit with résumé; an essay (maximum 1 page) stating qualifications, career goals, reasons for seeking the scholarship; 1 letter of recommendation in the current or intended field of study.

CONTACT: Dr. Ramu Ramamurthy, ASEI Scholarship Committee Chairman

1234—ARMED FORCES COMMUNICATIONS AND ELECTRONICS ASSOCIATION (AFCEA/ORINCON IT Scholarship)

4400 Fair Lakes Court
Fairfax VA 22033-3899
800/336-4583, ext. 6147 or
703/631-6100
E-mail: scholarships@afcea.org
Internet: http://www.afcea.org

AMOUNT: $2,750

DEADLINE(S): Varies according to eligibility

FIELD(S): Electrical or Aerospace Engineering, Computer Science, Physics, Mathematics

ELIGIBILITY/REQUIREMENTS: Scholarships for persons on active duty in a military service or veterans, their spouses or dependents or civilians, provided the school they are attending is an accredited 4-year college or university in the Greater San Diego, California, area. Must have GPA of 3.4 or more.

HOW TO APPLY: See website or contact AFCEA for information and application.

1235—ARMED FORCES COMMUNICATIONS AND ELECTRONICS ASSOCIATION (AFCEA ROTC Scholarships)

4400 Fair Lakes Court
Fairfax VA 22033-3899
800/336-4583, ext. 6147 or
703/631-6149
FAX: 703/631-4693
E-mail: scholarships@afcea.org
Internet: http://www.afcea.org

AMOUNT: $2,000

DEADLINE(S): APR 1

FIELD(S): Electrical Engineering, Electronics, Computer Science, Computer Systems, or Aerospace Engineering, Physics, Mathematics, science or mathematics education; technology management or other technical fields, or fields related to U.S. intelligence or national security

ELIGIBILITY/REQUIREMENTS: Scholarships for ROTC students working toward a degree in an accredited degree-granting 4-year college or university in the U.S.

HOW TO APPLY: MUST be nominated by Professors of Military Science, Naval Science, or Aerospace Studies. Contact the commander of each ROTC unit at your school or see website for application.

1235A—ARMED FORCES COMMUNICATIONS AND ELECTRONICS ASSOCIATION (AFCEA Scholarship for Online or Distance-Learning Programs)

4400 Fair Lakes Court
Fairfax VA 22033-3899
800/336-4583, ext. 6147 or
703/631-6149
FAX: 703/631-4693
E-mail: scholarships@afcea.org
Internet: http://www.afcea.org
AMOUNT: $1,500
DEADLINE(S): JUN 1
FIELD(S): Electrical, Chemical or Aerospace Engineering: Computer Science; Mathematics; Physics; Science or Math Education; Technology Management or fields related to U.S. intelligence or national security
ELIGIBILITY/REQUIREMENTS: Full-time students; undergraduates must have completed 2 semesters of calculus (30-semester hour equivalent). Must be a U.S. citizen and be currently enrolled in a 4-year college or university in the U.S. at time of application.
HOW TO APPLY: Applications and further information on website.
RENEWABLE: No

1236—ARMED FORCES COMMUNICATIONS AND ELECTRONICS ASSOCIATION (AFCEA Scholarship for Working Professionals)

4400 Fair Lakes Court
Fairfax VA 22033-3899
800/336-4583, ext. 6147 or
703/631-6100
E-mail: scholarships@afcea.org
Internet: http://www.afcea.org
AMOUNT: $1,500
DEADLINE(S): AUG 15-SEP 15 (NOT before)
FIELD(S): Electrical, Aerospace, or Computer Engineering; Computer

Science; Computer Information Systems; Mathematics
ELIGIBILITY/REQUIREMENTS: Part-time students (at least 2 classes/semester) working toward an undergraduate degree at any accredited 2-year community college or 4-year institution in the U.S. while currently employed in government or industry. Distance learning programs do not qualify. Must be a U.S. citizen and be currently enrolled as a sophomore, junior, or senior at time of application.
HOW TO APPLY: Applications and further information on website.

1237—ARMED FORCES COMMUNICATIONS AND ELECTRONICS ASSOCIATION (General Emmett Paige Scholarships for Military Personnel, Veterans, and Their Dependents)

4400 Fair Lakes Court
Fairfax VA 22033-3899
800/336-4583, ext. 6147 or
703/631-6149
FAX: 703/631-4693
E-mail: scholarships@afcea.org
Internet: http://www.afcea.org
AMOUNT: $2,000
DEADLINE(S): MAR 1
FIELD(S): Electrical Engineering, Electronics, Computer Science, Computer or Aerospace Engineering, Physics, Mathematics, science or mathematics education; technology management or other technical fields, or fields related to U.S. intelligence or national security
ELIGIBILITY/REQUIREMENTS: Scholarships in the above fields for persons on active duty in a military service or veterans and to their spouses or dependents who are working toward a degree in an accredited 4-year college or university in the U.S. Must have GPA of 3.4 or more.
HOW TO APPLY: Applications and further information on website.

1238—ARMED FORCES COMMUNICATIONS AND ELECTRONICS ASSOCIATION (General John A. Wickham Scholarships)

4400 Fair Lakes Court
Fairfax VA 22033-3899
800/336-4583, ext. 6147 or
703/631-6100
E-mail: scholarships@afcea.org
Internet: http://www.afcea.org
AMOUNT: $2,000
DEADLINE(S): MAY 1

FIELD(S): Electrical Engineering, Electronics, Computer Science, Computer or Aerospace Engineering, Physics, Mathematics, Science or Mathematics Education; Technology Management or other technical fields, or fields related to U.S. intelligence or national security
ELIGIBILITY/REQUIREMENTS: Scholarships in the above fields for persons working toward degrees in accredited 4-year colleges or universities in the U.S. Must have GPA of 3.5 or more.
HOW TO APPLY: Applications and further information on website.

1239—ARMED FORCES COMMUNICATIONS AND ELECTRONICS ASSOCIATION (Vice Adm. Jerry O. Tuttle [Ret.] and Mrs. Barbara A. Tuttle Science and Technology Scholarships)

4400 Fair Lakes Court
Fairfax VA 22033-3899
800/336-4583, ext. 6147 or
703/631-6100
E-mail: scholarships@afcea.org
Internet: http://www.afcea.org
AMOUNT: $2,000
DEADLINE(S): OCT 1-NOV 1 (NOT before)
FIELD(S): Computer Engineering Technology, Computer Information Systems, Electronics Engineering
ELIGIBILITY/REQUIREMENTS: Current students working full time toward an undergraduate technology degree at any accredited technological institute or a technology program at an accredited 4-year college or university in the U.S. Must be a U.S. citizen and be a sophomore or junior at time of application. Primary consideration will be given to military enlisted candidates.
HOW TO APPLY: Applications and further information on website.

1240—ASPRS: THE IMAGING & GEOSPATIAL INFORMATION SOCIETY (Kenneth J. Osborn Memorial Scholarship)

ASPRS Awards Program
5410 Grosvenor Lane, Suite 210
Bethesda MD 20814-2160
301/493-0290, ext. 101
FAX: 301/493-0208
E-mail: scholarships@asprs.org
Internet: http://www.asprs.org
AMOUNT: $1.000
DEADLINE(S): DEC 1
FIELD(S): Surveying, Mapping, Photogrammetry, Geospatial Information and Technology

ELIGIBILITY/REQUIREMENTS: Open to undergraduates who display exceptional interest, desire, ability, and aptitude to enter the profession of surveying, mapping, photogrammetry, or geospatial information and technology. In addition, the Scholarship recognizes students who excel at communications and collaboration.

HOW TO APPLY: Submit 6 copies of the completed application and the following supporting materials: academic transcripts, including a separate list of relevant courses taken; 2 completed reference forms from faculty members who have knowledge of your abilities; samples of your work; description of your research goals; statement of work experience that may include internships, other forms of work experience, or special projects that demonstrate excellence in these fields and in communications and collaboration (including the nature, location and date(s) of the experience); a 2-page statement regarding your plans for continuing studies in theoretical photogrammetry; and papers, research reports, or other items that indicate capability in these fields. Note: Electronic submissions encouraged.

NUMBER OF AWARDS: 1

RENEWABLE: No

CONTACT: Scholarship Administrator at above address or see website

ADDITIONAL INFORMATION: The recipient is obligated to provide a final report to ASPRS of his/her scholastic accomplishments during the period for which the award is granted.

1241—ASPRS: THE IMAGING & GEOSPATIAL INFORMATION SOCIETY (Space Imaging Award for Application of High Resolution Digital Satellite Imagery)

ASPRS Awards Program
5410 Grosvenor Lane, Suite 210
Bethesda MD 20814-2160
301/493-0290, ext. 101
FAX: 301/493-0208
E-mail: scholarships@asprs.org
Internet: http://www.asprs.org
AMOUNT: $2,000
DEADLINE(S): DEC 1
FIELD(S): Remote Sensing; Digital Satellite Imagery

ELIGIBILITY/REQUIREMENTS: Full-time undergraduate or graduate students at an accredited college or university with image processing facilities appropriate for conducting the proposed work. Must be active or student members of ASPRS.

HOW TO APPLY: Submit 6 copies of the application and the following supporting materials: 2 completed reference forms from faculty members; samples of your

work; description of your research goals; and a brief proposal describing the proposed research, the purpose of the research, the application it might address, the physical features of the study area, the analysis procedure, your anticipated results, an itemized budget, and a list of all courses, workshops, and other training/ experience that demonstrate your ability to conduct the proposed research. Note: Electronic submissions encouraged.

NUMBER OF AWARDS: 1

RENEWABLE: No

CONTACT: Scholarship Administrator

ADDITIONAL INFORMATION: The recipient (or his/her representative) must attend presentation ceremony during the annual meeting to receive the award certificate and plaque. Must prepare a written report of the project and submit it to ASPRS and Space Imaging for possible company use within 1 year of receipt of data.

1242—AT&T BELL LABORATORIES (Summer Research Program for Minorities and Women)

101 Crawfords Corner Road
Holmdel NJ 07733-3030
AMOUNT: Salary + travel and living expenses for summer
DEADLINE(S): DEC 1
FIELD(S): Engineering; Mathematics; Sciences; Computer Science

ELIGIBILITY/REQUIREMENTS: Program offers minority students and women students technical employment experience at Bell Laboratories. Students should have completed their third year of study at an accredited college or university. U.S. citizen or permanent resident.

HOW TO APPLY: Selection is based partially on academic achievement and personal motivation. Write special programs manager-SRP for complete information.

1243—CANADIAN BUREAU OF INTERNATIONAL EDUCATION (Lucent Global Science Scholars)

220 Laurier Avenue, West, Suite 1100
Ottawa Ontario K1P 5Z9
CANADA
613/237-4820, ext. 243
FAX: 613/237-1073
E-mail: info@cbie.ca
Internet: http://www.cbie.ca
AMOUNT: $5,000 (U.S.) + internship
DEADLINE(S): MAR 15
FIELD(S): Engineering, Computer Science

ELIGIBILITY/REQUIREMENTS: Open to full-time students who are in their first year at a Canadian university and majoring in a computer-related field. Students will attend a week-long summit with other winners at the Lucent/Bell Labs headquarters in New Jersey and complete a paid summer internship, probably at Lucent Canada. Applicants must be in high academic standing, eligible to work in Canada, and competent in English.

HOW TO APPLY: See website or contact CBIE for more details and an application form.

NUMBER OF AWARDS: 2

RENEWABLE: No

1244—GERBER SCIENTIFIC, INC. (H. Joseph Gerber 1947 Scholars Fund Endowment at Rensselaer Polytechnic Institute)

83 Gerber Road West
South Windsor CT 06074
860/648-8027
Internet: http://www.gerber scientific.com/community/ scholarships.htm
AMOUNT: Varies
DEADLINE(S): MAR 15
FIELD(S): Engineering, Mathematics, Computer Science, Natural Sciences

ELIGIBILITY/REQUIREMENTS: Available to full-time students pursuing a baccalaureate degree at Rensselaer Polytechnic Institute's Troy, New York, campus. Awards are determined by the Rensselaer Office of Financial Aid. Preference is given to residents of the state of Connecticut.

HOW TO APPLY: Applications are available from the Office of Financial Aid.

1245—GERBER SCIENTIFIC, INC. (H. Joseph Gerber Vision Scholarship Program)

83 Gerber Road West
South Windsor CT 06074
860/648-8027
Internet: http://www.gerber scientific.com/community/ scholarships.htm
AMOUNT: Varies
DEADLINE(S): MAR 15
FIELD(S): Engineering, Mathematics, Computer Science, Natural Sciences

ELIGIBILITY/REQUIREMENTS: Available to high school seniors attending South Windsor, Manchester, or Tolland High, or Gerber employees' children who meet the requirements. Selection of recipi-

ents is made solely by Citizens' Scholarship Foundation of America.
HOW TO APPLY: Applications are available in the high school guidance office.
NUMBER OF AWARDS: 50

1246—GREAT LAKES COMMISSION (Carol A. Ratza Memorial Scholarship)

2805 South Industrial Hwy,
Suite 100
Ann Arbor MI 48104-6791
E-mail: manninen@glc.org
Internet: http://www.glc.org
AMOUNT: $500
DEADLINE(S): MAR 28
FIELD(S): Electronic Communications Technology (Environmental/Economic Applications)
ELIGIBILITY/REQUIREMENTS: Open to high school seniors and returning students enrolled full time at a Great Lakes college or university (Illinois, Indiana, Michigan, New York, Ohio, Pennsylvania, Wisconsin, Ontario, Quebec). Must have a demonstrated interest in the environmental or economic applications of electronic communications technology, exhibit academic excellence, and have a sincere appreciation for the Great Lakes and their protection.
HOW TO APPLY: See website or contact Commission for an application. Must submit résumé, transcripts, recommendations, and essay or Web page on Great Lakes issue. Recipient announced by May 1.
CONTACT: Christine Manninen

1247—HAWAII COMMUNITY FOUNDATION (Kawasaki-McGaha Scholarship Fund)

1164 Bishop Street, Suite 800
Honolulu HI 96813
808/537-6333 or toll free:
888/731-3863
FAX: 808/521-6286
E-mail: info@hcf-hawaii.org
Internet: http://www.hcf-hawaii.org
DEADLINE(S): MAR 1
FIELD(S): Computer Studies; International Studies
ELIGIBILITY/REQUIREMENTS: Applicants must be pursuing an undergraduate degree at Hawaii Pacific University and demonstrate financial need, good moral character, and academic achievement with a minimum GPA of 2.7.
HOW TO APPLY: Send application with 2 letters of recommendation.

1248—HISPANIC COLLEGE FUND (HSF/SHPE Inc. Scholarship Program)

55 Second Street, Suite 1500

San Francisco CA 94105
877/HSF-INFO (877/473-4636)
FAX: 415/808/2302
E-mail: pip@hsf.net
Internet: http://hispanicfund.org
AMOUNT: At least $2,500
DEADLINE(S): JUN 2
FIELD(S): Engineering; Mathematics; Science; Computer Science
ELIGIBILITY/REQUIREMENTS: Must be U.S. citizens or legal permanent residents of Hispanic heritage (one parent fully Hispanic or both parents half Hispanic). Open to high school graduates, community college transfer students, 4-year university undergraduates, and graduate students. They must be enrolled full time in a degree-seeking program in the U.S. or Puerto Rico.
HOW TO APPLY: Contact Fund for details or visit website for application.

1249—INSTITUTE FOR OPERATIONS RESEARCH AND THE MANAGEMENT SCIENCES (INFORMS Summer Internship Directory)

7240 Parkway Drive, Suite 310
Hanover, MD 21076-1310 USA
443/757-3500 or 800/446-3676)
FAX: 443/757-3515
E-mail: informs@informs.org
Internet: http://www.informs.org/INTERN/
AMOUNT: Varies
DEADLINE(S): Varies
FIELD(S): Information Management: Business Management, Engineering, Mathematics and related fields
ELIGIBILITY/REQUIREMENTS: See website listing of summer internships in the field of operations research and management sciences. Both applicants and employers can register online.
HOW TO APPLY: See website for list.
NUMBER OF AWARDS: Varies

1250—ISA EDUCATIONAL FOUNDATION SCHOLARSHIP FUND

67 Alexander Drive
Research Triangle Park NC 27709
919/549-8411
E-mail: info@isa.org
Internet: http://www.isa.org
AMOUNT: Varies
DEADLINE(S): FEB 25
FIELD(S): Instrumentation; Systems; Automation or related field
ELIGIBILITY/REQUIREMENTS: Currently enrolled in a graduate or undergraduate program in an instrumentation,

systems, or automation discipline (2-year or 4-year baccalaureate program or its equivalent) at an educational institute in their country of residence. 2-year program applicants must have completed at least 1 academic semester or 12 semester hours or its equivalent. 4-year degree program applicants must be in their sophomore year or higher and have at least an overall GPA of 3.0 on a 4.0 scale.
HOW TO APPLY: Download application from website, click on Educators and Students. Submit 1 original of all application documentation and 6 copies with each copy stapled (please do not paperclip). All materials must be submitted in English.
NUMBER OF AWARDS: Varies
RENEWABLE: Yes, must reapply.
CONTACT: Kristy Becker, CMP; 919/990-9426; kbecker@isa.org

1251—JUNIATA COLLEGE (John & Irene Dale Information Technology Scholarships)

Office of Student Financial Aid Planning
1700 Moore Street
Huntingdon PA 16652
814/641-3140
FAX: 814/641-5311
E-mail: frankv@juniata.edu
Internet: http://www.juniata.edu/admission/finplan/index.html
AMOUNT: $3,000
DEADLINE(S): MAR 1
FIELD(S): Information Technology
ELIGIBILITY/REQUIREMENTS: Open to students applying to Juniata College with a major of information technology.
HOW TO APPLY: See website or contact Director of Student Financial Planning for additional information and application.
CONTACT: Vincent Frank, Director of Student Financial Planning, 814/641-3140; e-mail: frankv@juniata.edu
RENEWABLE: Up to 3 years if minimum 3.0 annual GPA is maintained and student remains enrolled full time in an eligible program.

1252—MICRON TECHNOLOGY FOUNDATION

8000 S Federal Way
Mailstop 1-407
Boise ID 83706
208/368-2658
FAX: 208/368-4435
Internet: http://www.micron.com/about/foundation/edgrants.aspx
AMOUNT: $55,000 and up to 12 @ $16,500
DEADLINE(S): JAN 20

FIELD(S): Electrical, Chemical, Computer & Mechanical Engineering; Chemistry; Physics; Computer & Material Science

ELIGIBILITY/REQUIREMENTS: High school senior; resident of Idaho, Colorado, Texas or Virginia; combined SAT score of at least 1350 or a composite ACT score of at least 30; unweighted GPA of at least 3.5; demonstrated leadership in school, work and/or extracurricular activities. An essay and possible interview are also required. Scholarships can be used at any U.S. 4-year accredited school.

HOW TO APPLY: Download an application from www.micron.scholarshipamerica.org or see your high school counselor.

NUMBER OF AWARDS: Up to 13

RENEWABLE: Yes. Remain eligible, the money is spread over 4 years.

CONTACT: Scholarship America at 800/537-4180

1253—MICROSOFT CORPORATION (National Minority and/or Women's Scholarships)

Microsoft Scholarship Program
One Microsoft Way
Redmond WA 98052-8303
425/882-8080
E-mail: scholars@microsoft.com
Internet: http://www.microsoft.com/college/scholarships/

AMOUNT: Tuition for 1 year

DEADLINE(S): JAN 31

FIELD(S): Computer Science; Computer Engineering; or a related technical discipline, such as Electrical Engineering, Math, Physics

ELIGIBILITY/REQUIREMENTS: May apply only after beginning classes on full-time basis. Full tuition scholarships awarded for 1 academic year to women, minorities (African Americans, Hispanics, or Native Americans), and people with disabilities enrolled full time in the above fields, or related technical discipline with a demonstrated interest in computer science, and making satisfactory progress towards a degree. Awards are made through designated schools and are not transferable to other institutions. Students must be enrolled full time in a bachelor's degree program at a college or university in the U.S., Canada, or Mexico at the time the application is submitted and be making satisfactory progress toward an undergraduate degree in computer science or computer engineering. All recipients of scholarships will be required to complete a salaried summer internship of 12 weeks or more at Microsoft in Redmond, WA (unless waived by Microsoft).

HOW TO APPLY: Application available online only. Submit résumé, transcript, answers to essay questions, and letter of referral from faculty member or academic advisor. No separate application form required. Note your gender, ethnicity, or disability on the page with your essay questions if you would like that information to be considered with your application. See website for detailed information and essay questions.

RENEWABLE: Yes: Must maintain a 3.0 cumulative GPA out of a possible 4.0, or a 4.0 cumulative GPA out of a possible 5.0.

1254—MICROSOFT CORPORATION (Summer Internships)

Microsoft Scholarship Program
One Microsoft Way
Redmond WA 98052-8303
425/882-8080
E-mail: scholars@microsoft.com
Internet: http://www.microsoft.com/college/scholarships/

AMOUNT: Varies

DEADLINE(S): None

FIELD(S): Computer Science and Engineering, or related technical discipline, such as Mathematics or Physics

ELIGIBILITY/REQUIREMENTS: Summer internships for individuals with a deep passion for technological advancement. Must commit to a 12-week minimum. Includes transportation, shipping costs, and shared cost of housing. Competitive compensation offered.

HOW TO APPLY: See website for application and additional information. Interview required.

1255—NAACP NATIONAL OFFICE (Louis Stokes Science & Technology Award)

4805 Mount Hope Drive
Baltimore MD 21215
410/620-5372 or 877/NAACP-98
E-mail: education@naacp.org
Internet: http://www.naacp.org/departments/education/scholarship.index.html

AMOUNT: $2,000

DEADLINE(S): APR 30

FIELD(S): Engineering, Science, Computer Science, or Mathematics

ELIGIBILITY/REQUIREMENTS: Open to incoming freshmen who are members of NAACP majoring in one of the above areas. Financial need must be established.

HOW TO APPLY: See website for application or write for complete information (include a legal size SASE) to The United Negro College Fund, Scholarships & Grants Administration, 8260 Willow Oaks Corporate Drive, Fairfax, VA 22031, Attention: Kimberly Hall.

1256—NATIONAL FEDERATION OF THE BLIND (Computer Science Scholarship)

805 Fifth Avenue
Grinnell IA 50112
641/236-3366
Internet: http://www.nfb.org/

AMOUNT: $3,000

DEADLINE(S): MAR 31

FIELD(S): Computer Science

ELIGIBILITY/REQUIREMENTS: For legally blind students pursuing or planning to pursue a full-time postsecondary course of study in the U.S. Based on academic excellence, service to the community, and financial need. Membership NOT required.

HOW TO APPLY: Contact Scholarship Committee Chairman for information and application.

NUMBER OF AWARDS: 1

RENEWABLE: Yes

CONTACT: Peggy Elliot, Scholarship Committee Chairman

1257—NATIONAL INVENTORS HALL OF FAME, THE (Collegiate Inventors Competition)

221 South Broadway Street
Akron OH 44308-1505
330/849-6887
E-mail: rdepuy@invent.org
Internet: http://www.invent.org/bfg/bfghome.html

AMOUNT: $15,000 (undergraduate)

DEADLINE(S): JUN 1

FIELD(S): Mathematics, Engineering, Biology, Chemistry, Physics, Information Technology, Medicine

ELIGIBILITY/REQUIREMENTS: Students must be enrolled (or have been enrolled) full-time (in any college or university) at least part of the 12-month period prior to the date the entry is submitted. In the case of a team (maximum 4 students), at least 1 member of the team must meet the full-time eligibility criteria; the others must have been enrolled on a part-time basis (at a minimum) sometime during the 24-month period prior to the date the entry is submitted. There are no limits on the number of entries a student or team may submit; however, only 1 prize per student or team will be awarded. Entries are judged on the originality and inventiveness of the new idea, process, or technology, their potential value to society (socially, environmentally, and economically), and

on the scope of use. The entry must be complete, workable, and well articulated.
HOW TO APPLY: See website for application and detailed information. Submit an original invention or idea that has not been made public. Also include: Student and Advisor Information; Student Essay and Advisor Letter following the outlined format; diagrams, illustrations, photos, slides, or videos of the invention (clearly labeled); the signed Student/Advisor Release Form.
CONTACT: Ray DePuy

1258—ROYAL THAI EMBASSY, OFFICE OF EDUCATIONAL AFFAIRS (Revenue Department Scholarships for Thai Students)

1906 23rd Street NW
Washington DC 20008
202/667-9111 or 202/667-8010
FAX: 202/265-7239
AMOUNT: Varies
DEADLINE(S): APR
FIELD(S): Computer Science (Telecommunications), Law, Economics, Finance, Business Administration
ELIGIBILITY/REQUIREMENTS: Scholarships for students under age 35 from Thailand who have been accepted to study in the U.S or UK pursuing any level degree.
HOW TO APPLY: Selections based on academic records, employment history, and advisor recommendations.

1259—SIEMENS WESTINGHOUSE (Science and Technology Competition)

186 Wood Avenue South
Iselin NJ 08830
877/822-5233
E-mail: foundation.us@siemens.com
Internet: http://www.siemens-foundation.org
AMOUNT: $120,000 (maximum)
DEADLINE(S): Varies
FIELD(S): Biology; Physical Sciences; Mathematics; Physics; Chemistry; Computer Science; Environmental Science
ELIGIBILITY/REQUIREMENTS: Open to U.S. high school seniors to pursue independent science research projects, working individually or in teams of 2 or 3 to develop and test their own ideas. May work with one of the universities/laboratories that serve as Siemens' partners. Students from the 50 states, DC, and Territories may compete in 1 of 6 geographic areas. Individual and team national prize winners receive a second scholarship award.

HOW TO APPLY: See website or contact Siemens Foundation for details.

1260—SOCIETY OF AUTOMOTIVE ENGINEERS (Oakland University/SAE Engineering Scholarship)

SAE Customer Service
400 Commonwealth Drive
Warrendale PA 15096-0001
724/776-4970
FAX: 724/776-1615
E-mail: customerservice@sae.org
Internet: http://www.sae.org/students/scholarships
AMOUNT: $1,000
DEADLINE(S): DEC 1
FIELD(S): Engineering; Computer Science; Automotive Industry
ELIGIBILITY/REQUIREMENTS: Open to incoming freshman who will be pursuing a degree in the School of Engineering and Computer Science.
HOW TO APPLY: See website for application. Submit application; a personal essay that demonstrates hands-on experience or activity (such as rebuilding engines, working on cars/trucks, etc.); 2 recommendations, 1 of which must be from a teacher, counselor, or administrator; and transcript.
NUMBER OF AWARDS: 1
RENEWABLE: No

1261—SOCIETY OF AUTOMOTIVE ENGINEERS (University of Bridgeport/SAE Engineering Scholarships)

SAE Customer Service
400 Commonwealth Drive
Warrendale PA 15096-0001
724/776-4970
FAX: 724/776-1615
E-mail: customerservice@sae.org
Internet: http://www.sae.org/students/scholarships
AMOUNT: $9,000
DEADLINE(S): DEC 1
FIELD(S): Computer Science & Engineering; Mathematics; Automotive Industry
ELIGIBILITY/REQUIREMENTS: High school seniors entering as freshmen pursuing a bachelor's degree are eligible. Requirements include a minimum 3.0 GPA and 1100 SAT or 24 ACT composite.
HOW TO APPLY: See website for application. Submit application; a personal essay that demonstrates hands-on experience or activity (such as rebuilding engines, working on cars/trucks, etc.); 2 recommendations, 1 of which must be from

a teacher, counselor, or administrator; and transcript. Eligible students must also apply to the University of Bridgeport and submit the appropriate attachments, in addition to SAE submission.
NUMBER OF AWARDS: 3
RENEWABLE: Yes. A total of $36,000 (4-year period) if student remains enrolled in good standing and maintains a 3.0 GPA.

1262—SOCIETY OF AUTOMOTIVE ENGINEERS (Wayne State University/College of Engineering/Dean's/SAE Scholarship)

SAE Customer Service
400 Commonwealth Drive
Warrendale PA 15096-0001
724/776-4970
FAX: 724/776-1615
E-mail: customerservice@sae.org
Internet: http://www.sae.org/students/scholarships
AMOUNT: $1,500
DEADLINE(S): DEC 1
FIELD(S): Engineering; Computer Science
ELIGIBILITY/REQUIREMENTS: For high school seniors and/or transfer students, must have 3.5 GPA, must be pursuing a degree in the College of Engineering, and maintain full-time enrollment status. Must be a U.S. citizen. Selection based on ACT/SAT scores. Awarded on merit, NOT financial need.
HOW TO APPLY: See website for application. Submit application; a personal essay that demonstrates hands-on experience or activity (such as rebuilding engines, working on cars/trucks, etc.); 2 recommendations, 1 of which must be from a teacher, counselor, or administrator; and transcript. Students must also apply to the university by February 28.
NUMBER OF AWARDS: 1
RENEWABLE: Yes. Up to 4 years; must reapply. Student must be enrolled as a full-time student each of the academic year terms (minimum of 12 credit hours each semester) completing a minimum of 24 credits each year that count toward degree requirements of the engineering program, must maintain a grade of "C" or better in each course and all courses toward engineering degree must be taken at WSU. Minimum cumulative GPA of 3.0.
CONTACT: Dr. Gerald Thompkins, Assistant Dean of Student Affairs, Wayne State University, College of Engineering, 5050 Anthony Wayne Drive, Detroit, MI 48202 or call 313/577-3780.

1263—SOCIETY OF AUTOMOTIVE ENGINEERS (Wright State University/SAE Scholarship)

SAE Customer Service
400 Commonwealth Drive
Warrendale PA 15096-0001
724/776-4970
FAX: 724/776-1615
E-mail: customerservice@sae.org
Internet: http://www.sae.org/
students/scholarships
AMOUNT: $1,000
DEADLINE(S): DEC 1
FIELD(S): Engineering; Computer
Science
ELIGIBILITY/REQUIREMENTS: Applicants must be freshmen in any engineering program. Award based on scholarship and achievement.
HOW TO APPLY: See website for application. Submit application; a personal essay that demonstrates hands-on experience or activity (such as rebuilding engines, working on cars/trucks, etc.); 2 recommendations, 1 of which must be from a teacher, counselor, or administrator; and transcript.
NUMBER OF AWARDS: 1
RENEWABLE: No

1264—SOCIETY OF WOMEN ENGINEERS (Admiral Grace Murray Hopper Scholarships)

230 East Ohio Street, Suite 400
Chicago IL 60611-3265
312/596-5223
FAX: 312/644-8557
E-mail: hq@swe.org
Internet: http://www.swe.org
AMOUNT: $1,000
DEADLINE(S): MAY 15
FIELD(S): Engineering; Computer
Science; Computer Engineering
ELIGIBILITY/REQUIREMENTS: Open to women who are entering freshmen at a college or university with an ABET-accredited program or in a SWE-approved school. Must be studying computer engineering or computer science in any form of a 4-year program.
HOW TO APPLY: See website or send SASE to SWE for an application.
NUMBER OF AWARDS: 5

1265—SOCIETY OF WOMEN ENGINEERS (B. K. Krenzer Memorial Re-entry Scholarship)

230 East Ohio Street, Suite 400
Chicago IL 60611-3265
312/596-5223

FAX: 312/644-8557
E-mail: hq@swe.org
Internet: http://www.swe.org
AMOUNT: $1,000
DEADLINE(S): MAY 15
FIELD(S): Engineering; Computer
Science
ELIGIBILITY/REQUIREMENTS: For women who have been out of the engineering job market as well as out of school for a minimum of 2 years. May be used for full- or part-time study at a college or university with an ABET-accredited program or in a SWE-approved school. Must have a minimum 3.5 GPA. Open to undergraduates, but preference is given to degreed engineers desiring to return to the workforce following a period of temporary retirement.
HOW TO APPLY: Send SASE to SWE for an application.
NUMBER OF AWARDS: 1

1266—SOCIETY OF WOMEN ENGINEERS (Microsoft Corporation Scholarships)

230 East Ohio Street, Suite 400
Chicago IL 60611-3265
312/596-5223
FAX: 312/644-8557
E-mail: hq@swe.org
Internet: http://www.swe.org
AMOUNT: $2,500
DEADLINE(S): FEB 1
FIELD(S): Computer Science; Computer
Engineering
ELIGIBILITY/REQUIREMENTS: Open to women who are entering sophomores, juniors, or seniors or graduate students at a college or university with an ABET-accredited program or in a SWE-approved school. Must have a minimum 3.5 GPA.
HOW TO APPLY: See website or send SASE to SWE for an application.
NUMBER OF AWARDS: 2

1267—STATE FARM COMPANIES FOUNDATION (Exceptional Student Fellowship)

One State Farm Plaza, SC-3
Bloomington IL 61710-0001
309/766-2039/2161
E-mail: Nancy.Lynn.gr3o@
statefarm.com
Internet: http://www.statefarm.com
AMOUNT: $3,000 (nominating institution
receives $250)
DEADLINE(S): FEB 15
FIELD(S): Accounting; Business
Administration; Actuarial Science;
Computer Science; Economics;

Finance; Insurance/Risk Management;
Investments; Management; Marketing;
Mathematics; Statistics
ELIGIBILITY/REQUIREMENTS: For U.S. citizens who are full-time juniors or seniors when they apply. Must demonstrate significant leadership in extracurricular activities, have minimum 3.6 GPA, and attend accredited U.S. college or university. Must be nominated by dean, department head, professor, or academic advisor.
HOW TO APPLY: See website, visit your financial aid office, or write for application.
NUMBER OF AWARDS: 50
RENEWABLE: No

1268—UNIVERSITY OF WALES-BANGOR-SCHOOL OF INFORMATICS AND COMPUTER SYSTEMS (Undergraduate Scholarships)

Dean Street
Bangor, Gwynedd
LL57 1UT WALES UK
+44 (0)1248 382686
FAX: +44(0)1248 361429
E-mail: admissions@informatics.
bangor.ac.uk
Internet: http://www.informatics.
bangor.ac.uk
AMOUNT: £1,500
DEADLINE(S): NOV
FIELD(S): Electronic Engineering;
Computer Science
ELIGIBILITY/REQUIREMENTS: Undergraduate scholarships in the above fields in Bangor, North Wales.
HOW TO APPLY: E-mail a.smith@bangor.ac.uk and mention School of Informatics Scholarships.

1269—WESTERN MICHIGAN UNIVERSITY (College of Arts and Sciences/Jim Sleep Memorial Award)

1903 West Michigan
Kalamazoo MI 49008-5337
269/387-8777
FAX: 269/387-6989
E-mail: finaid-info@wmich.edu
Internet: http://www.wmich.edu/
finaid
AMOUNT: Varies (spring session)
DEADLINE(S): Not applicable
FIELD(S): Computer Science
ELIGIBILITY/REQUIREMENTS: Computer science major (individual or group).
HOW TO APPLY: Must complete a worthy project that has application within the department, the university, or the commu-

nity. Contact the Director of the Computer Science Undergraduate Programs for more information.
RENEWABLE: No

1270—WESTERN MICHIGAN UNIVERSITY (CS Faculty Undergraduate Scholarship)

1903 West Michigan
Kalamazoo MI 49008-5337
269/387-8777
FAX: 269/387-6989
E-mail: finaid-info@wmich.edu
Internet: http://www.wmich.edu/finaid
AMOUNT: $500/semester
DEADLINE(S): Not applicable
FIELD(S): Computer Science
ELIGIBILITY/REQUIREMENTS: Computer Science major in junior year; GPA of at least 3.0.
HOW TO APPLY: Department faculty selects recipient.
RENEWABLE: No
CONTACT: Director of Computer Science

1271—WOMEN IN DEFENSE (HORIZONS Scholarship Foundation)

2111 Wilson Boulevard, Suite 400
Arlington VA 22201/3061
703/247-2552
FAX: 703/522-1885
E-mail: wid@ndia.org
Internet: http://www.ndia.org
AMOUNT: $500+
DEADLINE(S): NOV 1; JUL 1
FIELD(S): Security Studies; Engineering; Computer Science; Physics; Mathematics; International Relations; Political Science; Operations Research; Economics; National Security/Defense; Business and Law (as they relate to national security or defense); other fields considered if relevant to national security or defense
ELIGIBILITY/REQUIREMENTS: Open to women employed/planning careers in defense/national security areas (NOT law enforcement or criminal justice). Must be enrolled full- or part-time at an accredited college or university at the graduate or undergraduate junior/senior level, have a minimum 3.25 GPA, demonstrate financial need, and be U.S. citizen. Based on academic achievement, work experience, objectives, and recommendations.
HOW TO APPLY: See website or send SASE for application.
RENEWABLE: Yes

1272—XEROX TECHNICAL MINORITY SCHOLARSHIP

150 State Street
Rochester NY 14614
585/244-1800
E-mail: xtmsp@rballiance.com
Internet: www.xerox.com
AMOUNT: Up to $5,000 (varies according to tuition and academic excellence)
DEADLINE(S): SEP 15
FIELD(S): Engineering; Computer Science; Science
ELIGIBILITY/REQUIREMENTS: Scholarships for minorities (African-American, Native American, Hispanic, or Asian) enrolled full time in a technical degree program at the bachelor level or above. Recipient may not have tuition or related expenses covered by other scholarships or grants.
HOW TO APPLY: Obtain application from website or address above. Send completed application, résumé and a cover letter to Xerox Technical Minority Scholarship Program.
RENEWABLE: Yes, must reapply.

ELECTRICAL/ELECTRONIC/ NUCLEAR ENGINEERING

1273—AMERICAN NUCLEAR SOCIETY (Angelo S. Bisesti Scholarship)

555 North Kensington Avenue
La Grange Park IL 60526
708/352-6611
FAX: 708/352-0499
E-mail: outreach@ans.org
Internet: http://www.ans.org
AMOUNT: $2,000
DEADLINE(S): FEB 1
FIELD(S): Nuclear Science & Engineering
ELIGIBILITY/REQUIREMENTS: Must be juniors or seniors enrolled in a U.S. institution; be U.S. citizens or permanent residents; and be pursuing a career in the field of commercial nuclear power.
HOW TO APPLY: See website for application.
NUMBER OF AWARDS: 1
RENEWABLE: No
CONTACT: Scholarship Coordinator

1274—AMERICAN NUCLEAR SOCIETY (Charles "Tommy" Thomas Memorial Scholarship)

555 North Kensington Avenue
La Grange Park IL 60526
708/352-6611
FAX: 708/352-0499
E-mail: outreach@ans.org
Internet: http://www.ans.org
AMOUNT: $2,000
DEADLINE(S): FEB 1
FIELD(S): Nuclear Science & Engineering, Environmental Studies
ELIGIBILITY/REQUIREMENTS: Must be juniors or seniors enrolled in a U.S. institution; be U.S. citizens or permanent residents; and be pursuing a career dealing with the environmental aspects of nuclear science or nuclear engineering..
HOW TO APPLY: See website for application. Submit with brief essay describing how your perception of environmental science and engineering related topics fit into the nuclear field and how you plan to contribute to the field during the course of your professional career.
NUMBER OF AWARDS: 1
RENEWABLE: No
CONTACT: Scholarship Coordinator

1275—AMERICAN NUCLEAR SOCIETY (Decommissioning, Decontamination & Reutilization Division Scholarship)

555 North Kensington Avenue
La Grange Park IL 60526
708/352-6611
FAX: 708/352-0499
E-mail: outreach@ans.org
Internet: http://www.ans.org
AMOUNT: $2,000
DEADLINE(S): FEB 1
FIELD(S): Nuclear Science & Engineering
ELIGIBILITY/REQUIREMENTS: Must be junior or senior enrolled in a U.S. institution; U.S. citizen or permanent residents; a curriculum of engineering or science that is associated either with decommissioning/decontamination of nuclear facilities, management/characterization of nuclear waste, or restoration of the environment; join the ANS; and designate the DD&R Division as one of their professional divisions. Must commit to participating in the DD&R Division Activities by attending the annual and winter meetings of the ANS and serving as a student representative at the DD&R Executive Committee meetings at both ANS meetings.
HOW TO APPLY: See website for application; submit with brief essay discussing the importance of some aspect of DD&R to the future of the nuclear field.
NUMBER OF AWARDS: 1
RENEWABLE: No
CONTACT: Scholarship Coordinator
ADDITIONAL INFORMATION: Funding for travel to annual and winter meetings of the ANS, including student registration, reasonable transportation, food, and lodging also provided.

1276—AMERICAN NUCLEAR SOCIETY (Delayed Education Scholarship for Women)

555 North Kensington Avenue
La Grange Park IL 60526
708/352-6611
FAX: 708/352-0499
E-mail: outreach@ans.org
Internet: http://www.ans.org
AMOUNT: $4,000
DEADLINE(S): FEB 1
FIELD(S): Nuclear Science & Engineering
ELIGIBILITY/REQUIREMENTS: Applicant must be a mature female undergraduate whose studies in nuclear science, nuclear engineering, or a nuclear-related field have been delayed; be enrolled in a U.S. institution; and be a U.S. citizen or permanent resident.
HOW TO APPLY: See website for application.
NUMBER OF AWARDS: 1
RENEWABLE: No
CONTACT: Scholarship Coordinator

1277—AMERICAN NUCLEAR SOCIETY (James R. Vogt Radiochemistry Scholarship)

555 North Kensington Avenue
La Grange Park IL 60526
708/352-6611
FAX: 708/352-0499
E-mail: outreach@ans.org
Internet: http://www.ans.org
AMOUNT: $2,000
DEADLINE(S): FEB 1
FIELD(S): Nuclear Science & Engineering
ELIGIBILITY/REQUIREMENTS: Applicants must be juniors or seniors (or graduate students) enrolled in a U.S. institution; be U.S. citizens or permanent residents; and be enrolled in or proposing to undertake research in radioanalytical chemistry, analytical chemistry, or analytical applications of nuclear science.
HOW TO APPLY: See website for application.
NUMBER OF AWARDS: 1
RENEWABLE: No
CONTACT: Scholarship Coordinator

1278—AMERICAN NUCLEAR SOCIETY (John & Muriel Landis Scholarship)

555 North Kensington Avenue
La Grange Park IL 60526
708/352-6611
FAX: 708/352-0499
E-mail: outreach@ans.org
Internet: http://www.ans.org
AMOUNT: $4,000
DEADLINE(S): FEB 1
FIELD(S): Nuclear Science & Engineering
ELIGIBILITY/REQUIREMENTS: Must be undergraduates enrolled in a U.S. institution; be U.S. citizens or permanent residents; and have greater than average financial need.
HOW TO APPLY: See website for application.
NUMBER OF AWARDS: Up to 8
RENEWABLE: No
CONTACT: Scholarship Coordinator

1279—AMERICAN NUCLEAR SOCIETY (John R. Lamarsh Scholarship)

555 North Kensington Avenue
La Grange Park IL 60526
708/352-6611
FAX: 708/352-0499
E-mail: outreach@ans.org
Internet: http://www.ans.org
AMOUNT: $2,000
DEADLINE(S): FEB 1
FIELD(S): Nuclear Science & Engineering
ELIGIBILITY/REQUIREMENTS: Applicants must be juniors or seniors enrolled in a U.S. institution and be U.S. citizens or permanent residents.
HOW TO APPLY: See website for application.
NUMBER OF AWARDS: 1
RENEWABLE: No
CONTACT: Scholarship Coordinator

1280—AMERICAN NUCLEAR SOCIETY (Joseph R. Dietrich Scholarship)

555 North Kensington Avenue
La Grange Park IL 60526
708/352-6611
FAX: 708//352-0499
E-mail: outreach@ans.org
Internet: http://www.ans.org
AMOUNT: $2,000
DEADLINE(S): FEB 1
FIELD(S): Nuclear Science & Engineering
ELIGIBILITY/REQUIREMENTS: Applicants must be juniors or seniors enrolled in a U.S. institution and be U.S. citizens or permanent residents.
HOW TO APPLY: See website for application.
NUMBER OF AWARDS: 1
RENEWABLE: No
CONTACT: Scholarship Coordinator

1281—AMERICAN NUCLEAR SOCIETY (Operations & Power Division Scholarship)

555 North Kensington Avenue
La Grange Park IL 60526
708/352-6611
FAX: 708/352-0499
E-mail: outreach@ans.org
Internet: http://www.ans.org
AMOUNT: $2,500
DEADLINE(S): FEB 1
FIELD(S): Nuclear Science & Engineering
ELIGIBILITY/REQUIREMENTS: Applicants must be juniors or seniors enrolled in a U.S. institution and be U.S. citizens or permanent residents.
HOW TO APPLY: Send application.
NUMBER OF AWARDS: 1
RENEWABLE: No
CONTACT: Scholarship Coordinator

1282—AMERICAN NUCLEAR SOCIETY (Pittsburgh Local Section Scholarship)

555 North Kensington Avenue
La Grange Park IL 60526
708/352-6611
FAX: 708/352-0499
E-mail: outreach@ans.org
Internet: http://www.ans.org
AMOUNT: $2,000
DEADLINE(S): FEB 1
FIELD(S): Nuclear Science & Engineering
ELIGIBILITY/REQUIREMENTS: Must be juniors or seniors enrolled in a U.S. institution; U.S. citizen or permanent residents; and have some affiliation with Western Pennsylvania or attend school at a nearby university in the region.
HOW TO APPLY: See website for application.
NUMBER OF AWARDS: 1
RENEWABLE: No
CONTACT: Scholarship Coordinator

1283—AMERICAN NUCLEAR SOCIETY (Raymond DiSalvo Scholarship)

555 North Kensington Avenue
La Grange Park IL 60526
708/352-6611
FAX: 708/352-0499
E-mail: outreach@ans.org
Internet: http://www.ans.org
AMOUNT: $2,000
DEADLINE(S): FEB 1
FIELD(S): Nuclear Science & Engineering
ELIGIBILITY/REQUIREMENTS: Applicants must be juniors or seniors

enrolled in a U.S. institution and be U.S. citizens or permanent residents.
HOW TO APPLY: See website for application.
NUMBER OF AWARDS: 1
RENEWABLE: No
CONTACT: Scholarship Coordinator

1284—AMERICAN NUCLEAR SOCIETY (Robert G. Lacy Scholarship)

555 North Kensington Avenue
La Grange Park IL 60526
708/352-6611
FAX: 708/352-0499
E-mail: outreach@ans.org
Internet: http://www.ans.org
AMOUNT: $2,000
DEADLINE(S): FEB 1
FIELD(S): Nuclear Science & Engineering
ELIGIBILITY/REQUIREMENTS: Applicants must be juniors or seniors enrolled in a U.S. institution and be U.S. citizens or permanent residents.
HOW TO APPLY: See website for application.
NUMBER OF AWARDS: 1
RENEWABLE: No
CONTACT: Scholarship Coordinator

1285—AMERICAN NUCLEAR SOCIETY (Robert T. Liner Scholarship)

555 North Kensington Avenue
La Grange Park IL 60526
708/352-6611
FAX: 708/352-0499
E-mail: outreach@ans.org
Internet: http://www.ans.org
AMOUNT: $2,000
DEADLINE(S): FEB 1
FIELD(S): Nuclear Science & Engineering
ELIGIBILITY/REQUIREMENTS: Applicants must be juniors or seniors enrolled in a U.S. institution and be U.S. citizens or permanent residents.
HOW TO APPLY: See website for application.
NUMBER OF AWARDS: 1
RENEWABLE: No
CONTACT: Scholarship Coordinator

1286—AMERICAN NUCLEAR SOCIETY (William R. and Mila Kimmel Scholarship)

555 North Kensington Avenue
La Grange Park IL 60526
708/352-6611
FAX: 708/352-0499
E-mail: outreach@ans.org

Internet: http://www.ans.org
AMOUNT: $2,000
DEADLINE(S): FEB 1
FIELD(S): Nuclear Science & Engineering
ELIGIBILITY/REQUIREMENTS: Applicants must be nuclear engineering students enrolled in a U.S. institution and be U.S. citizens or permanent residents.
HOW TO APPLY: See website for application.
NUMBER OF AWARDS: 1
RENEWABLE: No
CONTACT: Scholarship Coordinator

1287—AMERICAN PUBLIC POWER ASSOCIATION (DEED Student Research Grants and Internships)

2301 M Street, NW
Washington DC 20037-1427
202//467-2900
FAX: 202/467-2910
E-mail: DEED@APPAnet.org
Internet: http://www.appanet.org/
AMOUNT: $4,,000
DEADLINE(S): FEB 15 and OCT 1
FIELD(S): Electric, Energy
ELIGIBILITY/REQUIREMENTS: Open to students studying in energy-related disciplines at accredited colleges or universities in the U.S. or Canada. DEED member to sponsor their research grant or internship (find a DEED member utility, and e-mail request for specific contact information to DEED).
HOW TO APPLY: See website for information and application. Applications and transcript must be sent from a DEED member utility and must be dated and signed on the last page by an authorized individual at that utility. A copy must also be sent to the DEED regional board director.
NUMBER OF AWARDS: up to10
RENEWABLE: No
ADDITIONAL INFORMATION: Student research grants/internships may be split among students collaborating on a single project. $1,500 will be withheld until satisfactory completion of the project.

1288—AMERICAN PUBLIC POWER ASSOCIATION (DEED Technical Design Project)

2301 M Street, NW
Washington DC 20037-1427
202//467-2900
FAX: 202/467-2910
E-mail: DEED@APPAnet.org
Internet: http://www.appanet.org/
AMOUNT: $5,000

DEADLINE(S): FEB 15 and OCT 1
FIELD(S): Electric, Energy
ELIGIBILITY/REQUIREMENTS: Open to students studying in energy-related disciplines at accredited colleges or universities in the U.S. or Canada.
HOW TO APPLY: See website for information and application. Submit with required signatures and transcript to the DEED regional board director.
NUMBER OF AWARDS: 1
RENEWABLE: No
ADDITIONAL INFORMATION: Student research grants/internships may be split among students collaborating on a single project. $1,500 will be withheld until satisfactory completion of the project.

1289—AMERICAN RADIO RELAY LEAGUE FOUNDATION (Charles N. Fisher Memorial Scholarship)

225 Main Street
Newington CT 06111
860/594-0397
FAX: 860/594-0259
E-mail: foundation@arrl.org
Internet: http://www.arrlf.org/
AMOUNT: $1,000
DEADLINE(S): FEB 1
FIELD(S): Electronics, Communications or related fields
ELIGIBILITY/REQUIREMENTS: For student with any class license pursuing baccalaureate or higher degree at a regionally accredited institution. Must be a resident of Southwestern Division (AZ and Los Angeles, Orange, San Diego, Santa Barbara, CA) attending a regionally accredited school.
HOW TO APPLY: See website or contact Foundation for information and application. Submit with a 1-page essay on the role amateur radio has played in your life. A recent high school (or equivalent) or college transcript required; submit with application or mail separately. Transcripts need not accompany the application form and may be mailed separately.
NUMBER OF AWARDS: 1
RENEWABLE: No
CONTACT: Mary M. Hobart, K1MMH, Secretary

1290—AMERICAN RADIO RELAY LEAGUE FOUNDATION (Earl I. Anderson Scholarship)

225 Main Street
Newington CT 06111
860/594-0397
FAX: 860/594-0259
E-mail: foundation@arrl.org

Internet: http://www.arrlf.org/
AMOUNT: $1,250
DEADLINE(S): FEB 1
FIELD(S): Electronic Engineering or
related technical field
ELIGIBILITY/REQUIREMENTS: Open
to radio amateurs holding any class of
license who are residents of Illinois,
Indiana, Michigan or Florida working on
an undergraduate degree in above field.
HOW TO APPLY: See website or contact
Foundation for information and applica-
tion. Submit with a 1-page essay on the role
amateur radio has played in your life. A
recent high school (or equivalent) or col-
lege transcript required; submit with application or mail separately.
NUMBER OF AWARDS: 3
RENEWABLE: No
CONTACT: Mary M. Hobart, K1MMH,
Secretary

1291—AMERICAN RADIO RELAY LEAGUE FOUNDATION (Dr. James L. Lawson Memorial Scholarship)

225 Main Street
Newington CT 06111
860/594-0397
FAX: 860/594-0259
E-mail: foundation@arrl.org
Internet: http://www.arrlf.org/
AMOUNT: $500
DEADLINE(S): FEB 1
FIELD(S): Electronics, Communications
or related fields
ELIGIBILITY/REQUIREMENTS: For
student with general license or higher pursuing baccalaureate or higher degree who
is resident of New England states (ME,
NH, VT, MA, CT, RI) or New York State
and attending college in one of those states
and pursuing degree in electronics, com-
munications or related field.
HOW TO APPLY See website or contact
Foundation for information and application. Submit with a 1-page essay on the role
amateur radio has played in your life. A
recent high school (or equivalent) or college transcript required; submit with application or mail separately.
NUMBER OF AWARDS: 1
RENEWABLE: No
CONTACT: Mary M. Hobart, K1MMH,
Secretary

1292—AMERICAN RADIO RELAY LEAGUE FOUNDATION (Edmond A. Metzger Scholarship)

225 Main Street
Newington CT 06111
860/594-0397

FAX: 860/594-0259
E-mail: foundation@arrl.org
Internet: http://www.arrlf.org/
AMOUNT: $500
DEADLINE(S): FEB 1
FIELD(S): Electrical Engineering
ELIGIBILITY/REQUIREMENTS: For
member with novice license or higher pur-
suing baccalaureate or higher degree resid-
ing and attending college or university in
ARRL Central Division (IL, IN, WI).
HOW TO APPLY: See website or contact
Foundation for information and applica-
tion. Submit with a 1-page essay on the role
amateur radio has played in your life. A
recent high school (or equivalent) or col-
lege transcript required; submit with appli-
cation or mail separately.
NUMBER OF AWARDS: 1
RENEWABLE: No
CONTACT: Mary M. Hobart, K1MMH,
Secretary

1293—AMERICAN RADIO RELAY LEAGUE FOUNDATION (Fred R. McDaniel Memorial Scholarship)

225 Main Street
Newington CT 06111
860/594-0397
FAX: 860/594-0259
E-mail: foundation@arrl.org
Internet: http://www.arrlf.org/
AMOUNT: $500
DEADLINE(S): FEB 1
FIELD(S): Electronics, Communications
or related fields
ELIGIBILITY/REQUIREMENTS: Open
to radio amateurs holding a general license
or higher who are FCC Fifth Call District
(TX, OK, AR, LA, MS, NM) residents
attending 4-year college or university in
the District and enrolled in baccalaureate
or higher program. Minimum 3.0 GPA
required.
HOW TO APPLY: See website or contact
Foundation for information and application. Submit with a 1-page essay on the role
amateur radio has played in your life. A
recent high school (or equivalent) or college transcript required; submit with application or mail separately.
NUMBER OF AWARDS: 1
RENEWABLE: No
CONTACT: Mary M. Hobart, K1MMH,
Secretary

1294—AMERICAN RADIO RELAY LEAGUE FOUNDATION (Irving W. Cook, WAOCGS Scholarship)

225 Main Street
Newington CT 06111

860/594-0397
FAX: 860/594-0259
E-mail: foundation@arrl.org
Internet: http://www.arrlf.org/
AMOUNT: $1,000
DEADLINE(S): FEB 1
FIELD(S): Electronics, Communications
or related fields
ELIGIBILITY/REQUIREMENTS: For
student or child of deceased radio amateur
with any class license pursuing baccalaure-
ate or higher degree at an accredited insti-
tution. Must be a resident of Kansas.
HOW TO APPLY: See website or contact
Foundation for information and applica-
tion. Submit with a 1-page essay on the role
amateur radio has played in your life. A
recent high school (or equivalent) or college transcript required; submit with application or mail separately.
NUMBER OF AWARDS: 1
RENEWABLE: No
CONTACT: Mary M. Hobart, K1MMH,
Secretary

1295—AMERICAN RADIO RELAY LEAGUE FOUNDATION (L. Phil Wicker Scholarship)

225 Main Street
Newington CT 06111
860/594-0397
FAX: 860/594-0259
E-mail: foundation@arrl.org
Internet: http://www.arrlf.org/
AMOUNT: $1,000
DEADLINE(S): FEB 1
FIELD(S): Electronics, communications
or related fields
ELIGIBILITY/REQUIREMENTS: For
student with general license or higher pur-
suing baccalaureate or higher degree at a
regionally accredited institution. Must be a
resident of Roanoke Division (NC, SC,
VA, WV) attending school in that area.
HOW TO APPLY: See website or contact
Foundation for information and applica-
tion. Submit with a 1-page essay on the role
amateur radio has played in your life. A
recent high school (or equivalent) or college transcript required; submit with application or mail separately.
NUMBER OF AWARDS: 1
RENEWABLE: No
CONTACT: Mary M. Hobart, K1MMH,
Secretary

1296—AMERICAN RADIO RELAY LEAGUE FOUNDATION (Mississippi Scholarship)

225 Main Street
Newington CT 06111
860/594-0397
FAX: 860/594-0259

E-mail: foundation@arrl.org
Internet: http://www.arrlf.org/
AMOUNT: $500
DEADLINE(S): FEB 1
FIELD(S): Electronics, Communications
or related fields
ELIGIBILITY/REQUIREMENTS: For
student under 30 with any class license pursuing baccalaureate or higher degree. Must be a resident of Mississippi attending school at a Mississippi institution.
HOW TO APPLY: See website or contact Foundation for information and application. Submit with a 1-page essay on the role amateur radio has played in your life. A recent high school (or equivalent) or college transcript required; submit with application or mail separately.
NUMBER OF AWARDS: 1
RENEWABLE: No
CONTACT: Mary M. Hobart, K1MMH, Secretary

1297—AMERICAN RADIO RELAY LEAGUE FOUNDATION (NEMAL Electronics Scholarship)

225 Main Street
Newington CT 06111
860/594-0397
FAX: 860/594-0259
E-mail: foundation@arrl.org
Internet: http://www.arrlf.org/
AMOUNT: $1,000
DEADLINE(S): FEB 1
FIELD(S): Electronics, Communications
or related fields
ELIGIBILITY/REQUIREMENTS: For
student with any general or higher license pursuing baccalaureate or higher degree at an accredited 2- or 4-year college or university. Preference given to applicants residing in the southeastern U.S. Must demonstrate financial need and have a minimum 3.0 GPA. Participation in community service or civic volunteer organizations preferred.
HOW TO APPLY: See website or contact Foundation for information and application. Submit with a 1-page essay on the role amateur radio has played in your life. A recent high school (or equivalent) or college transcript required; submit with application or mail separately.
NUMBER OF AWARDS: 1
RENEWABLE: No
CONTACT: Mary M. Hobart, K1MMH, Secretary

1298—AMERICAN RADIO RELAY LEAGUE FOUNDATION (Paul and Helen L. Grauer Scholarship)

225 Main Street

Newington CT 06111
860/594-0397
FAX: 860/594-0259
E-mail: foundation@arrl.org
Internet: http://www.arrlf.org/
AMOUNT: $1,000
DEADLINE(S): FEB 1
FIELD(S): Electronics, Communications
or related fields
ELIGIBILITY/REQUIREMENTS: For
student with novice license or higher pursuing baccalaureate or higher degree at a regionally accredited institution. Must be a resident of Midwest Division (IA, KS, MO, NE) attending school in that area.
HOW TO APPLY: See website or contact Foundation for information and application. Submit with a 1-page essay on the role amateur radio has played in your life. A recent high school (or equivalent) or college transcript required; submit with application or mail separately.
NUMBER OF AWARDS: 1
RENEWABLE: No
CONTACT: Mary M. Hobart, K1MMH, Secretary

1299—AMERICAN RADIO RELAY LEAGUE FOUNDATION (Perry F. Hadlock Memorial Scholarship)

225 Main Street
Newington CT 06111
860/594-0397
FAX: 860/594-0259
E-mail: foundation@arrl.org
Internet: http://www.arrlf.org/
AMOUNT: $2,000
DEADLINE(S): FEB 1
FIELD(S): Technology-related studies
(Electrical and Electronics
Engineering)
ELIGIBILITY/REQUIREMENTS: For
student with technician's license or higher pursuing baccalaureate or higher degree at a regionally accredited institution. Regional preference ARRL Atlantic and Hudson divisions; institutional preference Clarkson University, Potsdam, NY.
HOW TO APPLY: See website or contact Foundation for information and application. Submit with a 1-page essay on the role amateur radio has played in your life. A recent high school (or equivalent) or college transcript required; submit with application or mail separately.
NUMBER OF AWARDS: 1
RENEWABLE: No
CONTACT: Mary M. Hobart, K1MMH, Secretary

1300—AMERICAN RADIO RELAY LEAGUE FOUNDATION (PHD ARA Scholarship)

225 Main Street

Newington CT 06111
860/594-0397
FAX: 860/594-0259
E-mail: foundation@arrl.org
Internet: http://www.arrlf.org/
AMOUNT: $1,000
DEADLINE(S): FEB 1
FIELD(S): Journalism; Computer
Science; Electronic Engineering
ELIGIBILITY/REQUIREMENTS: For
undergraduate or graduate students who are residents of the ARRL Midwest Division (IA, KS, MO, NE) who hold any class of radio amateur license—or student may be the child of a deceased radio amateur.
HOW TO APPLY: See website or contact Foundation for information and application. Submit with a 1-page essay on the role amateur radio has played in your life. A recent high school (or equivalent) or college transcript required; submit with application or mail separately.
NUMBER OF AWARDS: 1
RENEWABLE: No
CONTACT: Mary M. Hobart, K1MMH, Secretary

1301—ARMED FORCES COMMUNICATIONS AND ELECTRONICS ASSOCIATION (AFCEA/ORINCON IT Scholarship)

4400 Fair Lakes Court
Fairfax VA 22033-3899
800/336-4583, ext. 6147 or
703/631-6149
FAX: 703/631-4693
E-mail: scholarships@afcea.org
Internet: http://www.afcea.org
AMOUNT: $2,750
DEADLINE(S): Varies
FIELD(S): Electrical/Aerospace
Engineering, Computer Science,
Physics, Mathematics
ELIGIBILITY/REQUIREMENTS:
Scholarships for persons on active duty in a military service or veterans, their spouses or dependents or civilians, provided the school they are attending is an accredited 4-year college or university in the Greater San Diego, California, area. Must have GPA of 3.4 or more.
HOW TO APPLY: Check website or contact AFCEA for information and application.

1302—ARMED FORCES COMMUNICATIONS AND ELECTRONICS ASSOCIATION (AFCEA ROTC Scholarships)

4400 Fair Lakes Court
Fairfax VA 22033-3899

800/336-4583, ext. 6147 or
703/631-6149
FAX: 703/631-4693
E-mail: scholarships@afcea.org
Internet: http://www.afcea.org
AMOUNT: $2,000
DEADLINE(S): APR 1
FIELD(S): Electrical Engineering,
Electronics, Computer Science,
Computer Systems, or Aerospace
Engineering, Physics, Mathematics, sci-
ence or mathematics education; tech-
nology management or other technical
fields, or fields related to U.S. intelli-
gence or national security
ELIGIBILITY/REQUIREMENTS:
Scholarships for ROTC students working
toward a degree in an accredited degree-
granting 4-year college or university in the
U.S.
HOW TO APPLY: MUST be nominated
by Professors of Military Science, Naval
Science, or Aerospace Studies. Contact the
commander of each ROTC unit at your
school or see website for application.

1303—ARMED FORCES COMMUNICATIONS AND ELECTRONICS ASSOCIATION (AFCEA Scholarship for Online or Distance-Learning Programs)

4400 Fair Lakes Court
Fairfax VA 22033-3899
800/336-4583, ext. 6147 or
703/631-6149
FAX: 703/631-4693
E-mail: scholarships@afcea.org
Internet: http://www.afcea.org
AMOUNT: $1,500
DEADLINE(S): JUN 1
FIELD(S): Electrical, Chemical or
Aerospace Engineering: Computer
Science; Mathematics; Physics; Science
or Math Education; Technology
Management or fields related to U.S.
intelligence or national security
ELIGIBILITY/REQUIREMENTS: Full-
time students; undergraduates must have
completed 2 semesters of calculus (30-
semester hour equivalent). Must be a U.S.
citizen and be currently enrolled in a 4-
year college or university in the U.S. at
time of application.
HOW TO APPLY: Applications and further information on website.
RENEWABLE: No

1304—ARMED FORCES COMMUNICATIONS AND ELECTRONICS ASSOCIATION (AFCEA Scholarship for Working Professionals)

4400 Fair Lakes Court
Fairfax VA 22033-3899

800/336-4583, ext. 6147 or
703/631-6149
FAX: 703/631-4693
E-mail: scholarships@afcea.org
Internet: http://www.afcea.org
AMOUNT: $1,500
DEADLINE(S): AUG 15-SEP 15 (NOT
before)
FIELD(S): Electrical, Aerospace, or
Computer Engineering; Computer
Science; Computer Information
Systems; Mathematics
ELIGIBILITY/REQUIREMENTS: Part-
time students (at least 2 classes per semester) working toward an undergraduate
degree at any accredited 2-year community college or 4-year institution in the U.S.
while currently employed in government
or industry. Distance learning programs do
not qualify. Must be a U.S. citizen and be
currently enrolled as a sophomore, junior,
or senior at time of application.
HOW TO APPLY: Applications and further information on website.

1305—ARMED FORCES COMMUNICATIONS AND ELECTRONICS ASSOCIATION (General Emmett Paige Scholarships for Military Personnel, Veterans, and Their Dependents)

4400 Fair Lakes Court
Fairfax VA 22033-3899
800/336-4583, ext. 6147 or
703/631-6149
FAX: 703/631-4693
E-mail: scholarships@afcea.org
Internet: http://www.afcea.org
AMOUNT: $2,000
DEADLINE(S): MAR 1
FIELD(S): Electrical Engineering,
Electronics, Computer Science,
Computer or Aerospace Engineering,
Physics, Mathematics, science or math-
ematics education; technology manage-
ment or other technical fields, or fields
related to U.S. intelligence or national
security
ELIGIBILITY/REQUIREMENTS:
Scholarships in the above fields for persons
on active duty in a military service or vet-
erans and to their spouses or dependents
who are working toward a degree in an
accredited 4-year college or university in
the U.S. Must have GPA of 3.4 or more.
HOW TO APPLY: Applications and further information on website.

1306—ARMED FORCES COMMUNICATIONS AND ELECTRONICS ASSOCIATION (General John A. Wickham Scholarships)

4400 Fair Lakes Court

Fairfax VA 22033-3899
800/336-4583, ext. 6147 or
703/631-6149
FAX: 703/631-4693
E-mail: scholarships@afcea.org
Internet: http://www.afcea.org
AMOUNT: $2,000
DEADLINE(S): MAY 1
FIELD(S): Electrical Engineering,
Electronics, Computer Science,
Computer/Aerospace Engineering,
Physics, Mathematics, Science or
Mathematics Education; Technology
Management or other technical fields,
or fields related to U.S. intelligence or
national security
ELIGIBILITY/REQUIREMENTS:
Scholarships in the above fields for persons
working toward degrees in accredited 4-
year colleges or universities in the U.S.
Must have GPA of 3.5 or more.
HOW TO APPLY: Applications and fur-
ther information on website.

1307—ARMED FORCES COMMUNICATIONS AND ELECTRONICS ASSOCIATION (Vice Adm. Jerry O. Tuttle [Ret.] and Mrs. Barbara A. Tuttle Science and Technology Scholarships)

4400 Fair Lakes Court
Fairfax VA 22033-3899
800/336-4583, ext. 6147 or
703/631-6149
FAX: 703/631-4693
E-mail: scholarships@afcea.org
Internet: http://www.afcea.org
AMOUNT: $2,000
DEADLINE(S): OCT 1-NOV 1 (NOT
before)
FIELD(S): Computer Engineering
Technology, Computer Information
Systems, Electronics Engineering
ELIGIBILITY/REQUIREMENTS:
Current students working full time toward
an undergraduate technology degree at
any accredited technological institute or a
technology program at an accredited 4-
year college or university in the U.S. Must
be a U.S. citizen and be a sophomore or
junior at time of application. Primary consideration will be given to military enlisted
candidates.
HOW TO APPLY: Applications and further information on website.

1308—ASSOCIATED WESTERN UNIVERSITIES, INC. (AWU Undergraduate Student Fellowships)

4190 South Highland Drive,
Suite 211

Salt Lake City UT 84124-2600
801/273-8900
FAX: 801/277-5632
Internet: http://www.awu.org
AMOUNT: $300/week stipend + possible travel allowance
DEADLINE(S): FEB 1
FIELD(S): Science; Mathematics; Engineering; Technology
ELIGIBILITY/REQUIREMENTS: Students who have been or will be enrolled in any accredited institution within six months of the start of their award. Academic performance and class standing, career goals, recommendations, and compatibility of interests and abilities with the needs and resources of the host facility.
HOW TO APPLY: See website for application and list of participating laboratories. Must also submit résumé, at least 1 (2 preferred) recommendation from a faculty member who is familiar with your academic achievements, and transcript. Applicants who received an AWU award within the last year and have approval for reappointment with their previous mentor, need only to complete the application form and submit a copy of their current transcripts.
NUMBER OF AWARDS: 500
RENEWABLE: Yes, must reapply.
CONTACT: Kathy Hecker, Director of Finance and Property Management

1309—ASSOCIATION OF CALIFORNIA WATER AGENCIES (ACWA)

910 K Street, Suite 100
Sacramento CA 95814
916/441-4545
FAX: 916/325-4849
E-mail: acwabox@acwanet.com
Internet: http://www.acwanet.com
AMOUNT: $1,500
DEADLINE(S): APR 1
FIELD(S): Water resources-related fields including engineering, agriculture, environmental studies, public administration
ELIGIBILITY/REQUIREMENTS: ACWA's awards are based not only on scholastic achievement but also on the individual's commitment and motivation to their chosen field. Financial need will also be considered.
HOW TO APPLY: Download applications and guidelines for the ACWA scholarship program from website, or call or e-mail ACWA or contact your school's financial aid department.
NUMBER OF AWARDS: At least 6
HOW TO APPLY: Selection is based partially on academic achievement and personal motivation. Write special programs manager-SRP for complete information.

1310—CONNECTICUT BROADCASTERS ASSOCIATION

90 South Park Street
Willimantic CT 06226
860/633-5031
FAX: 860/456-5688
Internet: http://www.ctba.org
AMOUNT: Varues
DEADLINE(S): JAN 31
FIELD(S): Broadcasting, Marketing, Engineering, Electronics
ELIGIBILITY/REQUIREMENTS: Open to Connecticut residents pursuing a broadcasting career or a career in related fields.
HOW TO APPLY: Applications are available from Connecticut broadcast stations and on website.
NUMBER OF AWARDS: Varies
RENEWABLE: Yes. Some are 4-year, subject to performance; others must reapply.
CONTACT: M.C. Rice, CBA President

1311—GREAT LAKES COMMISSION (Carol A. Ratza Memorial Scholarship)

2805 South Industrial Highway, Suite 100
Ann Arbor MI 48104-6791
E-mail: manninen@glc.org
Internet: http://www.glc.org
AMOUNT: $500
DEADLINE(S): MAR 28
FIELD(S): Electronic Communications Technology (Environmental/Economic Applications)
ELIGIBILITY/REQUIREMENTS: Open to high school seniors and returning students enrolled full time at a Great Lakes college or university (Illinois, Indiana, Michigan, New York, Ohio, Pennsylvania, Wisconsin, Ontario, Quebec). Must have a demonstrated interest in the environmental or economic applications of electronic communications technology, exhibit academic excellence, and have a sincere appreciation for the Great Lakes and their protection.
HOW TO APPLY: See website or contact Commission for an application. Must submit résumé, transcripts, recommendations, and essay or Web page on Great Lakes issue. Recipient announced by May 1.
CONTACT: Christine Manninen

1312— THE IET (IET Jubilee Scholarships & BP/IET Faraday Scholarship)

Michael Faraday House
Six Hills Way, Stevenage
Hertfordshire SG1 2AY

UNITED KINGDOM
E-mail: awards@theiet.org
Internet: http://www.theiet.org/ambition
AMOUNT: £1,000
DEADLINE(S): JUN 30
FIELD(S): Electrical, Electronic, IT, Manufacturing Engineering and related fields
ELIGIBILITY/REQUIREMENTS: Scholarships for students on IET-accredited degree courses in the UK.
HOW TO APPLY: See website.
NUMBER OF AWARDS: 12
RENEWABLE: Yes. For the entire period of an IET-accredited course.

1313—MICHIGAN SOCIETY OF PROFESSIONAL ENGINEERS, THE (MSPE Saginaw Valley State GM Endowed Scholarship Grant)

P.O. Box 15276
Lansing MI 48901-5276
517/487-9388
FAX: 517/487-0635
E-mail: mspe@voyager.net
Internet: http://www.michiganspe.org
AMOUNT: $2,000
DEADLINE(S): 2nd Monday in JAN
FIELD(S): Electrical Engineering; Mechanical Engineering
ELIGIBILITY/REQUIREMENTS: Applicants must be students who are attending college for the first time or are first-time transfer students; be U.S. citizen and resident of Michigan; be currently accepted at a Michigan ABET-accredited college or university and enrolled in an engineering program; have at least a 3.0 average on a 4.0 scale for the 10th and 11th grades; attain a minimum composite test score of 26 on the ACT; and demonstrate academic achievement, character, and leadership potential.
HOW TO APPLY: Send completed application; a list of senior classes being taken; documented high school transcript and ACT score; and an essay of 250 words on "How I was influenced to pursue an engineering career."
NUMBER OF AWARDS: 1
CONTACT: Submit application to MSPE Chapter Representative; contact the MSPE headquarters at address above to obtain name; do NOT send applications to MSPE headquarters.

1314—MICRON TECHNOLOGY FOUNDATION

8000 South Federal Way

Mailstop 1-407
Boise ID 83706
208/368-2658
FAX: 208/368-4435
Internet: http://www.micron.com about/foundation/edgrants.aspx
AMOUNT: $55,000 and up to 12 @ $16,500
DEADLINE(S): JAN 20
FIELD(S): Electrical, Chemical, Computer & Mechanical Engineering; Chemistry; Physics; Computer & Material Science
ELIGIBILITY/REQUIREMENTS: High school senior residing in Idaho, Colorado, Texas or Virginia; with a combined SAT score of at least 1350 or a composite ACT score of at least 30; an unweighted GPA of at least 3.5; demonstrated leadership in school, work and/or extracurricular activities. An essay and possible interview are also required. Scholarships can be used at any U.S. 4-year accredited school.
HOW TO APPLY: Download an application from www.micron.scholarshipamerica.org or see your high school counselor.
NUMBER OF AWARDS: Up to 13
RENEWABLE: Yes. Remain eligible, the money is spread over 4 years.
CONTACT: Scholarship America at 800/537-4180

1315—ROCKY MOUNTAIN COAL MINING INSTITUTE, THE (Engineering-Geology Scholarship)

8057 South Yukon Way
Littleton CO 80128-5510
303/948-3300
FAX: 303/948-1132
E-mail: mail@rmcmi.org
Internet: http://www.rmcmi.org
AMOUNT: $4,000 ($2,000 per year)
DEADLINE(S): FEB 3
FIELD(S): Mining; Geology, Mineral Processing; Metallurgy, Electrical, Mechanical, Environmental Engineering
ELIGIBILITY/REQUIREMENTS: Applicant must be a full-time college sophomore or junior in good standing at the time of selection; be both a U.S. citizen and a legal resident of 1 of the RMCMI member states (Arizona, Colorado, Montana, New Mexico, North Dakota, Texas, Utah, Wyoming); be pursuing a degree in a mining-related field; and have an expressed interest in Western coal as a career path.
HOW TO APPLY: See website for application. Send completed application; list of academic and athletic honors received; list of miscellaneous extracurricular activities

and work experience; 3 references; answers of 100 words or less to each of the following questions: "Why are you pursuing your present degree? What do you envision doing after graduation? What do you do to make learning exciting and productive?" Personal statement (why you are applying for this scholarship, special skills or trainings, etc.) optional.
RENEWABLE: Yes. Upon recommendation from the dean of the college university. Must remain a full-time student in good academic standing.

1316—SOCIETY OF AUTOMOTIVE ENGINEERS (Arkansas Tech University/SAE Engineering Scholarship)

SAE Customer Service
400 Commonwealth Drive
Warrendale PA 15096-0001
724/776-4970
FAX: 724/776-1615
E-mail: customerservice@sae.org
Internet: http://www.sae.org/students/scholarships
AMOUNT: $1,000-$4,000
DEADLINE(S): DEC 1
FIELD(S): Mechanical & Electrical Engineering; Automotive Industry
ELIGIBILITY/REQUIREMENTS: Incoming freshman or transfer student. Selection is based on academic and leadership activities. Eligible students will have a minimum 980 SAT or 21 ACT composite score, and 3.25 GPA.
HOW TO APPLY: See website for application. Submit application; a personal essay that demonstrates hands-on experience or activity (such as rebuilding engines, working on cars/trucks, etc.); 2 recommendations, 1 of which must be from a teacher, counselor, or administrator; and transcript.
NUMBER OF AWARDS: At least 2
RENEWABLE: Yes. A total of $4,000-$16,000 (over 4-year period) will be awarded if student remains an engineering student in good standing and enrolls in and completes 15 or more hours with a 3.25 GPA each semester.

1317—SOCIETY OF AUTOMOTIVE ENGINEERS (John Deere and Bradley University/SAE Engineering Scholarships)

SAE Customer Service
400 Commonwealth Drive
Warrendale PA 15096-0001
724/776-4970
FAX: 724/776-1615
E-mail: customerservice@sae.org

Internet: http://www.sae.org/students/scholarships
AMOUNT: $1,250
DEADLINE(S): DEC 1
FIELD(S): Mechanical, Electrical, Computer, Industrial, or Manufacturing Engineering; Automotive Industry
ELIGIBILITY/REQUIREMENTS: Must be an incoming freshman accepted into the College of Engineering and Technology at Bradley. Selection is based on high school GPA, rank in class, curriculum and SAT/ACT scores. A minimum 980 SAT or 21 ACT composite score, and 3.25 GPA.
HOW TO APPLY: See website for application. Submit application; a personal essay that demonstrates hands-on experience or activity (such as rebuilding engines, working on cars/trucks, etc.); 2 recommendations, 1 of which must be from a teacher, counselor, or administrator; and transcript.
NUMBER OF AWARDS: Varies
RENEWABLE: Yes. A total of $5,000 (4-year period) will be awarded if student remains enrolled in one of the specified majors in the College of Engineering and Technology and maintains a 3.0 GPA.

1318—SOCIETY OF AUTOMOTIVE ENGINEERS (Oklahoma State University [CEAT]/SAE Engineering Scholarship)

SAE Customer Service
400 Commonwealth Drive
Warrendale PA 15096-0001
724/776-4970
FAX: 724/776-1615
E-mail: customerservice@sae.org
Internet: http://www.sae.org/students/scholarships
AMOUNT: $1,000
DEADLINE(S): DEC 1
FIELD(S): Mechanical, Electrical, Industrial Engineering; Automotive Industry
ELIGIBILITY/REQUIREMENTS: High school graduates with a 3.8 or greater GPA and an ACT of 30 (SAT 1350) or above who plan to major in mechanical, electrical, or industrial engineering.
HOW TO APPLY: See website for application. Submit application; a personal essay that demonstrates hands-on experience or activity (such as rebuilding engines, working on cars/trucks, etc.); 2 recommendations, 1 of which must be from a teacher, counselor, or administrator; and transcript.
NUMBER OF AWARDS: 1
RENEWABLE: Yes. For 3 additional years.

1319—SOCIETY OF AUTOMOTIVE ENGINEERS (Parks College of Saint Louis University/SAE Engineering Scholarship)

SAE Customer Service
400 Commonwealth Drive
Warrendale PA 15096-0001
724/776-4970
FAX: 724/776-1615
E-mail: customerservice@sae.org
Internet: http://www.sae.org/
students/scholarships
AMOUNT: $1,000
DEADLINE(S): DEC 1
FIELD(S): Aerospace, Mechanical, Electrical, Biomedical or Aircraft Maintenance Engineering; Avionics Engineering; Applied Computer Science; Computer Software Systems; Physics
ELIGIBILITY/REQUIREMENTS: Entering freshman majoring in any of the above areas, enrolled in a baccalaureate program. Award based on academic achievement and financial need.
HOW TO APPLY: See website for application. Submit application; a personal essay that demonstrates hands-on experience or activity (such as rebuilding engines, working on cars/trucks, etc.); 2 recommendations, 1 of which must be from a teacher, counselor, or administrator; and transcript.
NUMBER OF AWARDS: 1
RENEWABLE: No

1320—SOCIETY OF AUTOMOTIVE ENGINEERS (Yanmar/SAE Scholarship)

SAE Customer Service
400 Commonwealth Drive
Warrendale PA 15096-0001
724/776-4970
FAX: 724/776-1615
E-mail: customerservice@sae.org
Internet: http://www.sae.org/
students/scholarships
AMOUNT: $2,000 ($1,000/year for 2 years)
DEADLINE(S): APR 1
FIELD(S): Engineering, relating to Conservation of Energy in Transportation, Agriculture, Construction, & Power Generation
ELIGIBILITY/REQUIREMENTS: For graduate students and undergraduates in their senior year who are citizens of North America (U.S./Canada/Mexico). Based on previous scholastic performance with additional consideration given for special study or honors in the field of award, and for leadership achievement related to engineering or science. Applicants must be pursuing a course of study or research related to the conservation of energy in transportation, agriculture and construction, and power generation. Emphasis will be placed on research or study related to the internal combustion engine.
HOW TO APPLY: Submit application; a personal essay that demonstrates hands-on experience or activity (such as rebuilding engines, working on cars/trucks, etc.); 2 recommendations, 1 must be from a teacher, counselor, or administrator; and transcript.
NUMBER OF AWARDS: 1
RENEWABLE: No
CONTACT: Yanmar/SAE Scholarship

1321—SOCIETY OF NAVAL ARCHITECTS AND MARINE ENGINEERS, THE (Undergraduate Scholarship)

601 Pavonia Avenue
Jersey City NJ 07306
800/798-2188 or 201/798-4800
FAX: 201/798-4975
Internet: http://www.sname.org
AMOUNT: Up to $2,000
DEADLINE(S): MAY 1
FIELD(S): Naval Architecture; Marine Engineering, Ocean Engineering, or marine industry-related field
ELIGIBILITY/REQUIREMENTS: Open to citizens of the U.S. and Canada; study toward a degree in one of the above fields at participating schools; must be entering junior or senior year; membership in the society at the time of the award.
HOW TO APPLY: Submit application through your school with 3 letters of recommendation, transcript, and statement indicating your career goals and why you are interested in marine science.
RENEWABLE: Yes, may repeat as an undergraduate and reapply for graduate scholarship

INDUSTRIAL ENGINEERING/ MANUFACTURING TECHNOLOGY

1322—AMERICAN SOCIETY OF SAFETY ENGINEERS (ASSE) FOUNDATION (America Responds Memorial Scholarship)

1800 East Oakton Street
Des Plaines IL 60018-2187
847/699-2929
FAX: 847/296-3769
Internet: http://www.asse.org/
foundation
AMOUNT: $1,000
DEADLINE(S): DEC 1
FIELD(S): Occupational Safety & Health or closely related fields
ELIGIBILITY/REQUIREMENTS: Applicant must be an ASSE student member; a United States citizen, in good academic standing; have completed at least 60 semester hours; and have an overall GPA of at least 3.0.
HOW TO APPLY: See website or contact Customer Service Department for application. Submit with reference letter by safety faculty member; and essay of 300 words or less that explains why you are seeking a degree in occupational safety & health or closely related field, briefly describes current activities and how they relate to career goal and objective, and states why you believe you should receive this scholarship (e.g., career goals, financial need, etc.).
NUMBER OF AWARDS: 1
RENEWABLE: No
CONTACT: Adele Gabanski
ADDITIONAL INFORMATION: To obtain an application for membership ($15/year), contact ASSE's Customer Service department at or download the application at http://www.asse.org/membership/becomeamember.php.

1323—AMERICAN SOCIETY OF SAFETY ENGINEERS (ASSE) FOUNDATION (ASSE Construction Safety Scholarship)

1800 East Oakton Street
Des Plaines IL 60018-2187
847/699-2929
FAX: 847/296-3769
Internet: http://www.asse.org/
foundation
AMOUNT: $1,000
DEADLINE(S): DEC 1
FIELD(S): Occupational Safety & Health, with an emphasis on Construction Safety
ELIGIBILITY/REQUIREMENTS: Must be an ASSE student member; a U.S. citizen, in good academic standing; have completed at least 60 semester hours; and have an overall GPA of at least 3.0.
HOW TO APPLY: See website or contact Customer Service for an application. Submit with reference letter by safety faculty member; and essay of 300 words or less that explains why you are seeking a degree in occupational safety & health or closely related field, briefly describes current activities and how they relate to career goal and objective, and states why you believe you should receive this scholarship (e.g., career goals, financial need, etc.).
NUMBER OF AWARDS: 1
RENEWABLE: No
CONTACT: Adele Gabanski

ADDITIONAL INFORMATION: To obtain an application for membership ($15/year), contact ASSE's Customer Service department at or download the application at http://www.asse.org/membership/becomeamember.php.

1324—AMERICAN SOCIETY OF SAFETY ENGINEERS (ASSE) FOUNDATION (ASSE Diversity Committee Scholarship)

1800 East Oakton Street
Des Plaines IL 60018-2187
847/699-2929
FAX: 847/296-3769
Internet: http://www.asse.org/foundation
AMOUNT: $1,000
DEADLINE(S): DEC 1
FIELD(S): Occupational Safety & Health, with an emphasis on Construction Safety
ELIGIBILITY/REQUIREMENTS: Open to any individual regardless of race, ethnicity, gender, religion, personal beliefs, age, sexual orientation, physical challenges, geographic location, university or specific area of study. Must be an ASSE student member; a U.S. citizen, in good academic standing; have completed at least 60 semester hours; and have an overall GPA of at least 3.0.
HOW TO APPLY: See website or contact Customer Service for an application. Submit with reference letter by safety faculty member; and essay of 300 words or less that explains why you are seeking a degree in occupational safety & health or closely related field, briefly describes current activities and how they relate to career goal and objective, and states why you believe you should receive this scholarship (e.g., career goals, financial need, etc.).
NUMBER OF AWARDS: 1
RENEWABLE: No
CONTACT: Adele Gabanski
ADDITIONAL INFORMATION: To obtain an application for membership ($15/year), contact ASSE's Customer Service department at or download the application at http://www.asse.org/membership/becomeamember.php.

1325—AMERICAN SOCIETY OF SAFETY ENGINEERS (ASSE) FOUNDATION (Bechtel Group Foundation Scholarship Program for Safety & Health, The)

1800 East Oakton Street
Des Plaines IL 60018-2187
847/699-2929
FAX: 847/296-3769

Internet: http://www.asse.org/foundation
AMOUNT: $8,000
DEADLINE(S): DEC 1
FIELD(S): Occupational Safety & Health, with an emphasis on Construction Safety
ELIGIBILITY/REQUIREMENTS: Must be an ASSE student member; a U.S. citizen, in good academic standing; have completed at least 60 semester hours; and have an overall GPA of at least 3.0.
HOW TO APPLY: See website or contact Customer Service for an application. Submit with reference letter by safety faculty member; and essay of 300 words or less that explains why you are seeking a degree in occupational safety & health or closely related field, briefly describes current activities and how they relate to career goal and objective, and states why you believe you should receive this scholarship (e.g., career goals, financial need, etc.).
NUMBER OF AWARDS: 1
RENEWABLE: No
CONTACT: Adele Gabanski
ADDITIONAL INFORMATION: To obtain an application for membership ($15/year), contact ASSE's Customer Service department at or download the application at http://www.asse.org/membership/becomeamember.php.

1326—AMERICAN SOCIETY OF SAFETY ENGINEERS (ASSE) FOUNDATION (Central Indiana ASSE Scholarship)

1800 East Oakton Street
Des Plaines IL 60018-2187
847/699-2929
FAX: 847/296-3769
Internet: http://www.asse.org/foundation
AMOUNT: $1,000
DEADLINE(S): DEC 1
FIELD(S): Occupational Safety & Health, with an emphasis on Construction Safety
ELIGIBILITY/REQUIREMENTS: Must be an ASSE student member; a U.S. citizen, in good academic standing; have completed at least 60 semester hours; and have an overall GPA of at least 3.0. Priority will be given to Indiana residents attending school in Indiana or anywhere in the U.S. or to non-residents attending an Indiana university.
HOW TO APPLY: See website or contact Customer Service for an application. Submit with reference letter by safety faculty member; and essay of 300 words or less that explains why you are seeking a degree in occupational safety & health or closely related field, briefly describes cur-

rent activities and how they relate to career goal and objective, and states why you believe you should receive this scholarship (e.g., career goals, financial need, etc.).
NUMBER OF AWARDS: 1
RENEWABLE: No
CONTACT: Adele Gabanski
ADDITIONAL INFORMATION: To obtain an application for membership ($15/year), contact ASSE's Customer Service department at or download the application at http://www.asse.org/membership/becomeamember.php.

1327—AMERICAN SOCIETY OF SAFETY ENGINEERS (ASSE) FOUNDATION (C N A Foundation Scholarship)

1800 East Oakton Street
Des Plaines IL 60018-2187
847/699-2929
FAX: 847/296-3769
Internet: http://www.asse.org/foundation
AMOUNT: $4,000
DEADLINE(S): DEC 1
FIELD(S): Occupational Safety & Health, with an emphasis on Construction Safety
ELIGIBILITY/REQUIREMENTS: Must be an ASSE student member; a U.S. citizen, in good academic standing; have completed at least 60 semester hours; and have an overall GPA of at least 3.0.
HOW TO APPLY: See website or contact Customer Service for an application. Submit with reference letter by safety faculty member; and essay of 300 words or less that explains why you are seeking a degree in occupational safety & health or closely related field, briefly describes current activities and how they relate to career goal and objective, and states why you believe you should receive this scholarship (e.g., career goals, financial need, etc.).
NUMBER OF AWARDS: 2
RENEWABLE: No
CONTACT: Adele Gabanski
ADDITIONAL INFORMATION: To obtain an application for membership ($15/year), contact ASSE's Customer Service department at or download the application at http://www.asse.org/membership/becomeamember.php.

1328—AMERICAN SOCIETY OF SAFETY ENGINEERS (ASSE) FOUNDATION (David Iden Memorial Safety Scholarship sponsored by UPS)

1800 East Oakton Street
Des Plaines IL 60018-2187
847/699-2929

FAX: 847/296-3769
Internet: http://www.asse.org/
foundation
AMOUNT: $5,250
DEADLINE(S): DEC 1
FIELD(S): Occupational Safety & Health
or a closely related field
ELIGIBILITY/REQUIREMENTS: Must
be an ASSE student member; in good academic standing; have completed at least 60 semester hours; and have an overall GPA of at least 3.0.
HOW TO APPLY: Send application; reference letter by safety faculty member; and essay of 300 words or less that explains why you are seeking a degree in occupational safety & health or closely related field, briefly describes current activities and how they relate to career goal and objective, and states why you believe you should receive this scholarship (e.g., career goals, financial need, etc.).
NUMBER OF AWARDS: 4
RENEWABLE: No
CONTACT: Adele Gabanski
ADDITIONAL INFORMATION: (1) To obtain an application for membership ($15/year), contact ASSE's Customer Service department at or download the application at http://www.asse.org/membership/becomeamember.php. (2) Students will also be provided with the opportunity to attend annual conference.

1329—AMERICAN SOCIETY OF SAFETY ENGINEERS (ASSE) FOUNDATION (George Gustafson HSE Memorial Scholarship sponsored by the Texas Safety Foundation)

1800 East Oakton Street
Des Plaines IL 60018-2187
847/699-2929
FAX: 847/296-3769
Internet: http://www.asse.org/
foundation
AMOUNT: $4,000
DEADLINE(S): DEC 1
FIELD(S): Occupational Safety & Health,
with an emphasis on Construction
Safety
ELIGIBILITY/REQUIREMENTS: Must be an ASSE student member; a U.S. citizen, in good academic standing; have completed at least 60 semester hours; and have an overall GPA of at least 3.0. Priority will be given to students from Texas attending a Texas university.
HOW TO APPLY: See website or contact Customer Service for an application. Submit with reference letter by safety faculty member; and essay of 300 words or less that explains why you are seeking a

degree in occupational safety & health or closely related field, briefly describes current activities and how they relate to career goal and objective, and states why you believe you should receive this scholarship (e.g., career goals, financial need, etc.).
NUMBER OF AWARDS: 1
RENEWABLE: No
CONTACT: Adele Gabanski
ADDITIONAL INFORMATION: To obtain an application for membership ($15/year), contact ASSE's Customer Service department at or download the application at http://www.asse.org/membership/becomeamember.php.

1330—AMERICAN SOCIETY OF SAFETY ENGINEERS (ASSE) FOUNDATION (Georgia Chapter of ASSE Annual Scholarship, The)

1800 East Oakton Street
Des Plaines IL 60018-2187
847/699-2929
FAX: 847/296-3769
Internet: http://www.asse.org/
foundation
AMOUNT: $1,000
DEADLINE(S): DEC 1
FIELD(S): Occupational Safety & Health
or a closely related field
ELIGIBILITY/REQUIREMENTS: Must reside in a county within the ASSE Georgia Chapter; enrolled at a college or university in Georgia; an ASSE student member; in good academic standing; have completed at least 60 semester hours; and have an overall GPA of at least 3.0.
HOW TO APPLY: See website or contact Customer Service for an application. Submit with reference letter by safety faculty member; and essay of 300 words or less that explains why you are seeking a degree in occupational safety & health or closely related field, briefly describes current activities and how they relate to career goal and objective, and states why you believe you should receive this scholarship (e.g., career goals, financial need, etc.).
NUMBER OF AWARDS: 1
RENEWABLE: No
CONTACT: Adele Gabanski
ADDITIONAL INFORMATION: To obtain an application for membership ($15/year), contact ASSE's Customer Service department at or download the application at http://www.asse.org/membership/becomeamember.php.

1331—AMERICAN SOCIETY OF SAFETY ENGINEERS (ASSE) FOUNDATION (Gold Country Section & Region II Scholarship)

1800 East Oakton Street

Des Plaines IL 60018-2187
847/699-2929
FAX: 847/296-3769
Internet: http://www.asse.org/
foundation
AMOUNT: $1,000
DEADLINE(S): DEC 1
FIELD(S): Occupational Safety & Health
or a closely related field
ELIGIBILITY/REQUIREMENTS: Must be an ASSE student member; be in good academic standing; have completed at least 60 semester hours; and have an overall GPA of at least 3.0. Priority will be given to students who reside in the Region II area (i.e., Montana, Idaho, Wyoming, Colorado, Utah, Nevada, Arizona, New Mexico).
HOW TO APPLY: See website or contact Customer Service Department for application. Submit with reference letter by safety faculty member; and essay of 300 words or less that explains why you are seeking a degree in occupational safety & health or closely related field, briefly describes current activities and how they relate to career goal and objective, and states why you believe you should receive this scholarship (e.g., career goals, financial need, etc.).
NUMBER OF AWARDS: 1
RENEWABLE: No
CONTACT: Adele Gabanski
ADDITIONAL INFORMATION: To obtain an application for membership ($15/year), contact ASSE's Customer Service department at or download the application at http://www.asse.org/membership/becomeamember.php.

1332—AMERICAN SOCIETY OF SAFETY ENGINEERS (ASSE) FOUNDATION (Greater Baton Rouge Chapter-Don Jones Excellence in Safety Scholarship)

1800 East Oakton Street
Des Plaines IL 60018-2187
847/699-2929
FAX: 847/296-3769
Internet: http://www.asse.org/
foundation
AMOUNT: $1,000
DEADLINE(S): DEC 1
FIELD(S): Occupational Safety & Health
or a closely related field
ELIGIBILITY/REQUIREMENTS: Open to part-time or full-time students; priority given to students attending Southeastern Louisiana University in Hammond then to those attending any college or university within Louisiana or within the southeast U.S. region (in that order); part-time students must be an ASSE general or professional, all others must be student members;

be in good academic standing; have completed at least 60 semester hours; and have an overall GPA of at least 3.0.

HOW TO APPLY: See website or contact Customer Service Department for application. Submit with reference letter by safety faculty member; and essay of 300 words or less that explains why you are seeking a degree in occupational safety & health or closely related field, briefly describes current activities and how they relate to career goal and objective, and states why you believe you should receive this scholarship (e.g., career goals, financial need, etc.).

NUMBER OF AWARDS: 1

RENEWABLE: No

CONTACT: Adele Gabanski

ADDITIONAL INFORMATION: To obtain an application for membership ($15/year), contact ASSE's Customer Service department at or download the application at http://www.asse.org/membership/becomeamember.php.

1333—AMERICAN SOCIETY OF SAFETY ENGINEERS (ASSE) FOUNDATION (Greater Boston Chapter Leadership Award)

1800 East Oakton Street
Des Plaines IL 60018-2187
847/699-2929
FAX: 847/296-3769
Internet: http://www.asse.org/foundation

AMOUNT: $1,000 and $2,000

DEADLINE(S): DEC 1

FIELD(S): Occupational Safety & Health, with an emphasis on Construction Safety

ELIGIBILITY/REQUIREMENTS: Must be a member of any ASSE chapter in New England including Greater Boston, Connecticut Valley, Granite State, Maine, Nutmeg or Worcester County, or an immediate family member (spouse or child) of any ASSE chapter member in New England or a member of any ASSE student section in New England. Must be a U.S. citizen, in good academic standing; have completed at least 60 semester hours; and have an overall GPA of at least 3.0.

HOW TO APPLY: See website or contact Customer Service for an application. Submit with reference letter by safety faculty member; and essay of 300 words or less that explains why you are seeking a degree in occupational safety & health or closely related field, briefly describes current activities and how they relate to career goal and objective, and states why you believe you should receive this scholarship (e.g., career goals, financial need, etc.).

NUMBER OF AWARDS: 2 (1 each)

RENEWABLE: Yes

CONTACT: Adele Gabanski

ADDITIONAL INFORMATION: To obtain an application for membership ($15/year), contact ASSE's Customer Service department at or download the application at http://www.asse.org/membership/becomeamember.php.

1334—AMERICAN SOCIETY OF SAFETY ENGINEERS (ASSE) FOUNDATION (Gulf Coast Past President's Scholarship)

1800 East Oakton Street
Des Plaines IL 60018-2187
847/699-2929
FAX: 847/296-3769
Internet: http://www.asse.org/foundation

AMOUNT: $1,000

DEADLINE(S): DEC 1

FIELD(S): Occupational Safety & Health or a closely related field

ELIGIBILITY/REQUIREMENTS: Must be a part- or full-time student; an ASSE student member (if part-time student); in good academic standing; have completed at least 60 semester hours; and have an overall GPA of at least 3.0.

HOW TO APPLY: See website or contact Customer Service Department for application. Submit with reference letter from safety faculty member; and essay of 300 words or less that explains why you are seeking a degree in occupational safety & health or closely related field, briefly describes current activities and how they relate to career goal and objective, and states why you believe you should receive this scholarship (e.g., career goals, financial need, etc.).

NUMBER OF AWARDS: 2

RENEWABLE: No

CONTACT: Adele Gabanski

ADDITIONAL INFORMATION: To obtain an application for membership ($15/year), contact ASSE's Customer Service department at or download the application at http://www.asse.org/membership/becomeamember.php.

1335—AMERICAN SOCIETY OF SAFETY ENGINEERS (ASSE) FOUNDATION (Harold F. Polston Scholarship sponsored by the Middle Tennessee Chapter)

1800 East Oakton Street
Des Plaines IL 60018-2187
847/699-2929
FAX: 847/296-3769
Internet: http://www.asse.org/foundation

AMOUNT: $2,000

DEADLINE(S): DEC 1

FIELD(S): Occupational Safety & Health, with an emphasis on Construction Safety

ELIGIBILITY/REQUIREMENTS:. Priority will be given to students that belong to the Middle Tennessee Chapter, attending Middle Tennessee State University in Murfreesboro, TN, Murray State University in Murray, KY and those that live in the Region VII (in that order). Must be a U.S. citizen, in good academic standing; have completed at least 60 semester hours; and have an overall GPA of at least 3.0.

HOW TO APPLY: See website or contact Customer Service for an application. Submit with reference letter by safety faculty member; and essay of 300 words or less that explains why you are seeking a degree in occupational safety & health or closely related field, briefly describes current activities and how they relate to career goal and objective, and states why you believe you should receive this scholarship (e.g., career goals, financial need, etc.).

NUMBER OF AWARDS: 1

RENEWABLE: No

CONTACT: Adele Gabanski

ADDITIONAL INFORMATION: To obtain an application for membership ($15/year), contact ASSE's Customer Service department at or download the application at http://www.asse.org/membership/becomeamember.php.

1336—AMERICAN SOCIETY OF SAFETY ENGINEERS (ASSE) FOUNDATION (Harry Taback 9/11 Memorial Scholarship)

1800 East Oakton Street
Des Plaines IL 60018-2187
847/699-2929
FAX: 847/296-3769
Internet: http://www.asse.org/foundation

AMOUNT: $1,000

DEADLINE(S): DEC 1

FIELD(S): Occupational Safety & Health, with an emphasis on Construction Safety

ELIGIBILITY/REQUIREMENTS: Must be a U.S. citizen, in good academic standing; have completed at least 60 semester hours; and have an overall GPA of at least 3.0.

HOW TO APPLY: See website or contact Customer Service for an application. Submit with reference letter by safety faculty member; and essay of 300 words or less that explains why you are seeking a degree in occupational safety & health or

closely related field, briefly describes current activities and how they relate to career goal and objective, and states why you believe you should receive this scholarship (e.g., career goals, financial need, etc.).
NUMBER OF AWARDS: 1
RENEWABLE: No
CONTACT: Adele Gabanski
ADDITIONAL INFORMATION: To obtain an application for membership ($15/year), contact ASSE's Customer Service department at or download the application at http://www.asse.org/membership/becomeamember.php.

1337—AMERICAN SOCIETY OF SAFETY ENGINEERS (ASSE) FOUNDATION (Karl A. Jacobson, CSP Distinguished Service Award Scholarship)

1800 East Oakton Street
Des Plaines IL 60018-2187
847/699-2929
FAX: 847/296-3769
Internet: http://www.asse.org/foundation
AMOUNT: $2,000
DEADLINE(S): DEC 1
FIELD(S): Occupational Safety & Health, with an emphasis on Construction Safety
ELIGIBILITY/REQUIREMENTS: Must be a U.S. citizen, in good academic standing; have completed at least 60 semester hours; and have an overall GPA of at least 3.0.
HOW TO APPLY: See website or contact Customer Service for an application. Submit with reference letter by safety faculty member; and essay of 300 words or less that explains why you are seeking a degree in occupational safety & health or closely related field, briefly describes current activities and how they relate to career goal and objective, and states why you believe you should receive this scholarship (e.g., career goals, financial need, etc.).
NUMBER OF AWARDS: 2 (1 each)
RENEWABLE: No
CONTACT: Adele Gabanski
ADDITIONAL INFORMATION: To obtain an application for membership ($15/year), contact ASSE's Customer Service department at or download the application at http://www.asse.org/membership/becomeamember.php.

1338—AMERICAN SOCIETY OF SAFETY ENGINEERS (ASSE) FOUNDATION (Liberty Mutual Scholarship)

1800 East Oakton Street
Des Plaines IL 60018-2187

847/699-2929
FAX: 847/296-3769
Internet: http://www.asse.org/foundation
AMOUNT: $3,000
DEADLINE(S): DEC 1
FIELD(S): Occupational Safety & Health or a closely related field
ELIGIBILITY/REQUIREMENTS: Must be an ASSE student member; be in good academic standing; have completed at least 60 semester hours; and have an overall GPA of at least 3.0.
HOW TO APPLY: See website or contact Customer Service Department for application. Submit with reference letter by safety faculty member; and essay of 300 words or less that explains why you are seeking a degree in occupational safety & health or closely related field, briefly describes current activities and how they relate to career goal and objective, and states why you believe you should receive this scholarship (e.g., career goals, financial need, etc.).
NUMBER OF AWARDS: 2
RENEWABLE: No
CONTACT: Adele Gabanski
ADDITIONAL INFORMATION: (1) To obtain an application for membership ($15/year), contact ASSE's Customer Service department at or download the application at http://www.asse.org/membership/becomeamember.php. (2) Students will also be provided with the opportunity to attend annual conference.

1339—AMERICAN SOCIETY OF SAFETY ENGINEERS (ASSE) FOUNDATION (Marsh Risk-Consulting Scholarship)

1800 East Oakton Street
Des Plaines IL 60018-2187
847/699-2929
FAX: 847/296-3769
Internet: http://www.asse.org/foundation
AMOUNT: $1,000
DEADLINE(S): DEC 1
FIELD(S): Occupational Safety & Health or a closely related field
ELIGIBILITY/REQUIREMENTS: Must be an ASSE student member; be in good academic standing; have completed at least 60 semester hours; and have an overall GPA of at least 3.0.
HOW TO APPLY: See website or contact Customer Service Department for application. Submit with reference letter by safety faculty member; and essay of 300 words or less that explains why you are seeking a degree in occupational safety & health or closely related field, briefly describes current activities and how they relate to career goal and objective, and states why you

believe you should receive this scholarship (e.g., career goals, financial need, etc.).
NUMBER OF AWARDS: 1
RENEWABLE: No
CONTACT: Adele Gabanski
ADDITIONAL INFORMATION: To obtain an application for membership ($15/year), contact ASSE's Customer Service department at or download the application at http://www.asse.org/membership/becomeamember.php.

1340—AMERICAN SOCIETY OF SAFETY ENGINEERS (ASSE) FOUNDATION (Medina Scholarship for Hispanics in Safety)

1800 East Oakton Street
Des Plaines IL 60018-2187
847/699-2929
FAX: 847/296-3769
Internet: http://www.asse.org/foundation
AMOUNT: $2,000
DEADLINE(S): DEC 1
FIELD(S): Occupational Safety & Health, with an emphasis on Construction Safety
ELIGIBILITY/REQUIREMENTS: Open to bilingual student (Spanish-English); Hispanic ethnicity preferred. Must be a U.S. citizen, in good academic standing; have completed at least 60 semester hours; and have an overall GPA of at least 3.0. Attendance at an ASAC/ABET-accredited program preferred.
HOW TO APPLY: See website or contact Customer Service for an application. Submit with reference letter by safety faculty member; and essay of 300 words or less that explains why you are seeking a degree in occupational safety & health or closely related field, briefly describes current activities and how they relate to career goal and objective, and states why you believe you should receive this scholarship (e.g., career goals, financial need, etc.).
NUMBER OF AWARDS: 2
RENEWABLE: Yes
CONTACT: Adele Gabanski
ADDITIONAL INFORMATION: To obtain an application for membership ($15/year), contact ASSE's Customer Service department at or download the application at http://www.asse.org/membership/becomeamember.php.

1341—AMERICAN SOCIETY OF SAFETY ENGINEERS ENGINEERS (ASSE) FOUNDATION (Northeastern Illinois Chapter Scholarship)

1800 East Oakton Street
Des Plaines IL 60018-2187

847/699-2929
FAX: 847/296-3769
Internet: http://www.asse.org/
foundation
AMOUNT: $2,000
DEADLINE(S): DEC 1
FIELD(S): Occupational Safety & Health
or a closely related field
ELIGIBILITY/REQUIREMENTS: Must
be an ASSE student member; be in good
academic standing; have completed at least
60 semester hours; and have an overall
GPA of at least 3.0. Priority will be given
to applicants attending school in the northeastern Illinois region, including Illinois
and Wisconsin.
HOW TO APPLY: See website or contact
Customer Service Department for application. Submit with reference letter from
safety faculty member; and essay of 300
words or less that explains why you are
seeking a degree in occupational safety &
health or closely related field, briefly
describes current activities and how they
relate to career goal and objective, and
states why you believe you should receive
this scholarship (e.g., career goals, financial
need, etc.).
NUMBER OF AWARDS: 2
RENEWABLE: No
CONTACT: Adele Gabanski
ADDITIONAL INFORMATION: To
obtain an application for membership
($15/year), contact ASSE's Customer
Service department at or download the
application at http://www.asse.org/mem-
bership/becomeamember.php.

1342—AMERICAN SOCIETY OF SAFETY ENGINEERS (ASSE) FOUNDATION (North Florida Chapter Safety Education Scholarship)

1800 East Oakton Street
Des Plaines IL 60018-2187
847/699-2929
FAX: 847/296-3769
Internet: http://www.asse.org/
foundation
AMOUNT: $1,000
DEADLINE(S): DEC 1
FIELD(S): Occupational Safety & Health,
with an emphasis on Construction
Safety
ELIGIBILITY/REQUIREMENTS: Must
be a U.S. citizen, in good academic stand-
ing; have completed at least 60 semester
hours; and have an overall GPA of at least
3.0. Priority given to part-time or full-time
students that belong to the North Florida
Chapter, full-time students that attend any
Florida college or university or to full-time

students that attend an ASAC/ABET
accredited program nationwide (in that
order). Part-time students must be ASSE
general or professional member; full-time
members must be student members.
HOW TO APPLY: See website or contact
Customer Service for an application.
Submit with reference letter by safety faculty member; and essay of 300 words or
less that explains why you are seeking a
degree in occupational safety & health or
closely related field, briefly describes current activities and how they relate to career
goal and objective, and states why you
believe you should receive this scholarship
(e.g., career goals, financial need, etc.).
NUMBER OF AWARDS: 1
RENEWABLE: No
CONTACT: Adele Gabanski
ADDITIONAL INFORMATION: To
obtain an application for membership
($15/year), contact ASSE's Customer
Service department at or download the
application at http://www.asse.org/mem-
bership/becomeamember.php.

1343—AMERICAN SOCIETY OF SAFETY ENGINEERS (ASSE) FOUNDATION (PDC Scholarship sponsored by the Practice Specialty Groups)

1800 East Oakton Street
Des Plaines IL 60018-2187
847/699-2929
FAX: 847/296-3769
Internet: http://www.asse.org/
foundation
AMOUNT: $1,200
DEADLINE(S): DEC 1
FIELD(S): Occupational Safety & Health,
with an emphasis on Construction
Safety
ELIGIBILITY/REQUIREMENTS: Must
be a U.S. citizen, in good academic standing; have completed at least 60 semester
hours; and have an overall GPA of at least
3.0.
HOW TO APPLY: See website or contact
Customer Service for an application.
Submit with reference letter by safety faculty member; and essay of 300 words or
less that explains why you are seeking a
degree in occupational safety & health or
closely related field, briefly describes current activities and how they relate to career
goal and objective, and states why you
believe you should receive this scholarship
(e.g., career goals, financial need, etc.).
NUMBER OF AWARDS: 2
RENEWABLE: No
CONTACT: Adele Gabanski
ADDITIONAL INFORMATION: (1) To
obtain an application for membership

($15/year), contact ASSE's Customer
Service department at or download the
application at http://www.asse.org/mem-
bership/becomeamember.php. (2) Full
ASSE Professional Development Conference experience including airfare, hotel,
meals and registration also provided.

1344—AMERICAN SOCIETY OF SAFETY ENGINEERS (ASSE) FOUNDATION (Scott Dominguez-Craters of the Moon Chapter Scholarship)

1800 East Oakton Street
Des Plaines IL 60018-2187
847/699-2929
FAX: 847/296-3769
Internet: http://www.asse.org/
foundation
AMOUNT: $1,000
DEADLINE(S): DEC 1
FIELD(S): Occupational Safety & Health
or a closely related field
ELIGIBILITY/REQUIREMENTS: Must
be an ASSE student member; a part- or
full-time student in good academic standing; have completed at least 60 semester
hours; and have an overall GPA of at least
3.0. Priority is given to applicants who
reside in the Craters of the Moon, Idaho,
and Region II (i.e., Montana, Idaho,
Wyoming, Colorado, Utah, Nevada,
Arizona, New Mexico). Priority is also
given to applicants who are employees or
dependents of employees of a sponsoring
organization, serving the country through
active duty in the armed forces or honorably discharged, members of the Boy or
Girl Scouts, FFA, 4H, etc., and recipients
of awards from service organizations, those
who have served an ASSE chapter in a
leadership role. Part-time students must be
ASSE general or professional members;
others must be student members.
HOW TO APPLY: See website or contact
Customer Service Department for application. Submit with reference letter by safety
faculty member; and essay of 300 words or
less that explains why you are seeking a
degree in occupational safety & health or
closely related field, briefly describes current activities and how they relate to career
goal and objective, and states why you
believe you should receive this scholarship
(e.g., career goals, financial need, etc.).
NUMBER OF AWARDS: 1
RENEWABLE: No
CONTACT: Adele Gabanski
ADDITIONAL INFORMATION: To
obtain an application for membership
($15/year), contact ASSE's Customer
Service department at or download the

application at http://www.asse.org/membership/becomeamember.php.

1345—AMERICAN SOCIETY OF SAFETY ENGINEERS (ASSE) FOUNDATION (Southwest Chapter Roy Kinslow Scholarship)

1800 East Oakton Street
Des Plaines IL 60018-2187
847/699-2929
FAX: 847/296-3769
Internet: http://www.asse.org/foundation
AMOUNT: $1,000
DEADLINE(S): DEC 1
FIELD(S): Occupational Safety & Health, with an emphasis on Construction Safety
ELIGIBILITY/REQUIREMENTS: Must be a U.S. citizen, in good academic standing; have completed at least 60 semester hours; and have an overall GPA of at least 3.0. Open to members attending Southeastern Oklahoma State University in Durant, OK or be a member of the Southwest Chapter area attending a school within the Region III boundaries.
HOW TO APPLY: See website or contact Customer Service for an application. Submit with reference letter by safety faculty member; and essay of 300 words or less that explains why you are seeking a degree in occupational safety & health or closely related field, briefly describes current activities and how they relate to career goal and objective, and states why you believe you should receive this scholarship (e.g., career goals, financial need, etc.).
NUMBER OF AWARDS: 1
RENEWABLE: No
CONTACT: Adele Gabanski
ADDITIONAL INFORMATION: (1) To obtain an application for membership ($15/year), contact ASSE's Customer Service department at or download the application at http://www.asse.org/membership/becomeamember.php. (2) Full ASSE Professional Development Conference experience including airfare, hotel, meals and registration also provided.

1346—AMERICAN SOCIETY OF SAFETY ENGINEERS (ASSE) FOUNDATION (UPS Diversity Scholarship)

1800 East Oakton Street
Des Plaines IL 60018-2187
847/699-2929
FAX: 847/296-3769
Internet: http://www.asse.org/foundation
AMOUNT: $5,250
DEADLINE(S): DEC 1
FIELD(S): Occupational Safety & Health or a closely related field
ELIGIBILITY/REQUIREMENTS: Must be of a minority ethnic or racial group; a U.S. citizen; an ASSE student member; in good academic standing; have completed at least 60 semester hours; and have an overall GPA of at least 3.0.
HOW TO APPLY: See website or contact Customer Service Department for application. Submit with reference letter by safety faculty member; and essay of 300 words or less that explains why you are seeking a degree in occupational safety & health or closely related field, briefly describes current activities and how they relate to career goal and objective, and states why you believe you should receive this scholarship (e.g., career goals, financial need, etc.).
NUMBER OF AWARDS: 2
RENEWABLE: No
CONTACT: Adele Gabanski
ADDITIONAL INFORMATION: (1) To obtain an application for membership ($15/year), contact ASSE's Customer Service department at or download the application at http://www.asse.org/membership/becomeamember.php. (2) Students will also be provided with the opportunity to attend annual conference.

1347—AMERICAN SOCIETY OF SAFETY ENGINEERS (ASSE) FOUNDATION (Warren K. Brown Scholarship)

1800 East Oakton Street
Des Plaines IL 60018-2187
847/699-2929
FAX: 847/296-3769
Internet: http://www.asse.org/foundation
AMOUNT: $1,000
DEADLINE(S): DEC 1
FIELD(S): Occupational Safety & Health, with an emphasis on Construction Safety
ELIGIBILITY/REQUIREMENTS: Must be a U.S. citizen, in good academic standing; have completed at least 60 semester hours; and have an overall GPA of at least 3.0. and attend Murray State University in Murray, KY or Indiana State University in Terre Haute, IN.
HOW TO APPLY: See website or contact Customer Service for an application. Submit with reference letter by safety faculty member; and essay of 300 words or less that explains why you are seeking a degree in occupational safety & health or closely related field, briefly describes cur-

rent activities and how they relate to career goal and objective, and states why you believe you should receive this scholarship (e.g., career goals, financial need, etc.).
NUMBER OF AWARDS: 1
RENEWABLE: No
CONTACT: Adele Gabanski
ADDITIONAL INFORMATION: To obtain an application for membership ($15/year), contact ASSE's Customer Service department at or download the application at http://www.asse.org/membership/becomeamember.php.

1348—AMERICAN SOCIETY OF SAFETY ENGINEERS (ASSE) FOUNDATION (Washington Group International Safety Scholarship)

1800 East Oakton Street
Des Plaines IL 60018-2187
847/699-2929
FAX: 847/296-3769
Internet: http://www.asse.org/foundation
AMOUNT: $5,000
DEADLINE(S): DEC 1
FIELD(S): Occupational Safety & Health, with an emphasis on Construction Safety
ELIGIBILITY/REQUIREMENTS: Must be a U.S. citizen, in good academic standing; have completed at least 60 semester hours; and have an overall GPA of at least 3.0.
HOW TO APPLY: See website or contact Customer Service for an application. Submit with reference letter by safety faculty member; and essay of 300 words or less that explains why you are seeking a degree in occupational safety & health or closely related field, briefly describes current activities and how they relate to career goal and objective, and states why you believe you should receive this scholarship (e.g., career goals, financial need, etc.).
NUMBER OF AWARDS: 1
RENEWABLE: No
CONTACT: Adele Gabanski
ADDITIONAL INFORMATION: (1) To obtain an application for membership ($15/year), contact ASSE's Customer Service department at or download the application at http://www.asse.org/membership/becomeamember.php. (2) Opportunity to attend Conference and an internship that includes salary and living expenses.

1349—AMERICAN SOCIETY OF SAFETY ENGINEERS (ASSE) FOUNDATION (William C. Ray, CIH, CSP Arizona Scholarship)

1800 East Oakton Street

Des Plaines IL 60018-2187
847/699-2929
FAX: 847/296-3769
Internet: http://www.asse.org/foundation
AMOUNT: $1,000
DEADLINE(S): DEC 1
FIELD(S): Occupational Safety & Health, with an emphasis on Construction Safety
ELIGIBILITY/REQUIREMENTS: Must be a U.S. citizen, in good academic standing; have completed at least 60 semester hours; and have an overall GPA of at least 3.0 Students residing in Arizona, then the Region II area (MT, ID, WY, CO, UT, NV, NM) will have priority.
HOW TO APPLY: See website or contact Customer Service for an application. Submit with reference letter by safety faculty member; and essay of 300 words or less that explains why you are seeking a degree in occupational safety & health or closely related field, briefly describes current activities and how they relate to career goal and objective, and states why you believe you should receive this scholarship (e.g., career goals, financial need, etc.).
NUMBER OF AWARDS: 1
RENEWABLE: No
CONTACT: Adele Gabanski
ADDITIONAL INFORMATION: To obtain an application for membership ($15/year), contact ASSE's Customer Service department at or download the application at http://www.asse.org/membership/becomeamember.php.

1350— THE IET (IET Jubilee Scholarships & BP/IET Faraday Scholarship)

Michael Faraday House
Six Hills Way, Stevenage
Hertfordshire SG1 2AY
UNITED KINGDOM
E-mail: awards@theiet.org
Internet: http://www.theiet.org/ambition
AMOUNT: £1,000
DEADLINE(S): JUN 30
FIELD(S): Electrical, Electronic, IT, Manufacturing Engineering and related fields
ELIGIBILITY/REQUIREMENTS: Scholarships for students on IET-accredited degree courses in the UK.
HOW TO APPLY: See website.
NUMBER OF AWARDS: 12
RENEWABLE: Yes. For the entire period of an IET-accredited course.

1351—ILLUMINATING ENGINEERING SOCIETY OF NORTH AMERICA (Robert W. Thunen Memorial Scholarships)

Golden Gate Section
P.O. Box 77527
San Francisco CA 94107-1527
E-mail: riverfield@juno.com
AMOUNT: $2,500
DEADLINE(S): APR 1
FIELD(S): Illumination (Architectural, Commercial, Residential, Airport, Navigational, Theatrical, TV, Agricultural, Vision, etc.)
ELIGIBILITY/REQUIREMENTS: Open to full-time undergraduate juniors and seniors and graduate students in an accredited 4-year college or university located in Northern California or Nevada, Oregon, or Washington.
HOW TO APPLY: Contact Chair for an application. Must submit statement of purpose (with respect to lighting education) and 3 letters of recommendation. Awards announced by May 3.
NUMBER OF AWARDS: At least 2
CONTACT: Heide M. Kawahata, Chair

1352—INSTITUTE OF INDUSTRIAL ENGINEERS (A. O. Putnam Scholarship)

Royal Peachtree Corners
3577 Parkway Lane
Building 5, Suite 200
Norcross GA 30092
770/449-0461, ext. 105 or
800/494-0460
FAX: 770/441-3295
E-mail: bcameron@iienet.org
Internet: http://www.iienet.org
AMOUNT: Varies
DEADLINE(S): NOV 15
FIELD(S): Industrial Engineering; Management Consulting
ELIGIBILITY/REQUIREMENTS: Undergraduate scholarships for active IIE members with at least 3 semesters (5 quarters) remaining at an accredited college or university in the U.S. and its territories, Canada, or Mexico, provided the school's engineering program is accredited by an agency recognized by IIE and the student is pursuing a course of study in industrial engineering. Priority is given to, but not limited to, students who have demonstrated an interest in management consulting. Must be full-time student (co-op is not considered full-time). GPA of 3.4 or better is required.
HOW TO APPLY: Must be nominated by department head or faculty advisor. Call for nominations is sent out in the fall.

CONTACT: Bonnie Cameron, headquarters operations administrator, 770/449-0461, ext. 105

1353—INSTITUTE OF INDUSTRIAL ENGINEERS (Benjamin Willard Niebel Scholarship)

Royal Peachtree Corners
3577 Parkway Lane
Building 5, Suite 200
Norcross GA 30092
770/449-0461, ext. 105 or
800/494-0460
FAX: 770/441-3295
E-mail: bcameron@iienet.org
Internet: http://www.iienet.org
AMOUNT: Varies
DEADLINE(S): NOV 15
FIELD(S): Industrial Engineering
ELIGIBILITY/REQUIREMENTS: Undergraduate scholarships for active IIE members with at least 3 semesters (5 quarters) remaining at an accredited college or university in the U.S. and its territories, Canada, or Mexico, provided the school's engineering program is accredited by an agency recognized by IIE and the student is pursuing a course of study in industrial engineering. with interest in methods, standards, and work design. Must be full-time student (co-op is not considered full-time). GPA of 3.4 or better is required.
HOW TO APPLY: Must be nominated by department head or faculty advisor. Call for nominations is sent out in the fall.
CONTACT: Bonnie Cameron, headquarters operations administrator, 770/449-0461, ext. 105

1354—INSTITUTE OF INDUSTRIAL ENGINEERS (C. B. Gambrell Undergraduate Scholarship)

Royal Peachtree Corners
3577 Parkway Lane
Building 5, Suite 200
Norcross GA 30092
770/449-0461, ext. 105 or
800/494-0460
FAX: 770/441-3295
E-mail: bcameron@iienet.org
Internet: http://www.iienet.org
AMOUNT: Varies
DEADLINE(S): NOV 15
FIELD(S): Industrial Engineering
ELIGIBILITY/REQUIREMENTS: Undergraduate scholarships for active IIE members with at least 3 semesters (5 quarters) remaining at an accredited college or university in the U.S. and its territories,

Canada, or Mexico, provided the school's engineering program is accredited by an agency recognized by IIE and the student is pursuing a course of study in industrial engineering. Priority is given to, but not limited to, students who have demonstrated an interest in management consulting. Must be full-time student (co-op is not considered full time). GPA of 3.4 or better is required.

HOW TO APPLY: Must be nominated by department head or faculty advisor. Call for nominations is sent out in the fall.

CONTACT: Bonnie Cameron, headquarters operations administrator, 770/449-0461, ext. 105

1355—INSTITUTE OF INDUSTRIAL ENGINEERS (Dwight D. Gardner Scholarship)

Royal Peachtree Corners
3577 Parkway Lane
Building 5, Suite 200
Norcross GA 30092
770/449-0461, ext. 105 or
800/494-0460
FAX: 770/441-3295
E-mail: bcameron@iienet.org
Internet: http://www.iienet.org
AMOUNT: Varies
DEADLINE(S): NOV 15
FIELD(S): Industrial Engineering
ELIGIBILITY/REQUIREMENTS: Undergraduate scholarships for active IIE members with at least 3 semesters (5 quarters) remaining at an accredited college or university in the U.S. and its territories, Canada, or Mexico, provided the school's engineering program is accredited by an agency recognized by IIE and the student is pursuing a course of study in industrial engineering. Priority is given to, but not limited to, students who have demonstrated an interest in management consulting. Must be full-time student (co-op is not considered full-time). GPA of 3.4 or better is required.
HOW TO APPLY: Must be nominated by department head or faculty advisor. Call for nominations is sent out in the fall.
NUMBER OF AWARDS: Varies
CONTACT: Bonnie Cameron, headquarters operations administrator, 770/449-0461, ext. 105

1356—INSTITUTE OF INDUSTRIAL ENGINEERS (IIE Council of Fellows Undergraduate Scholarships)

Royal Peachtree Corners
3577 Parkway Lane
Building 5, Suite 200

Norcross GA 30092
770/449-0461, ext. 105 or
800/494-0460
FAX: 770/441-3295
E-mail: bcameron@iienet.org
Internet: http://www.iienet.org
AMOUNT: Varies
DEADLINE(S): NOV 15
FIELD(S): Industrial Engineering
ELIGIBILITY/REQUIREMENTS: Undergraduate scholarships for active IIE members with at least 3 semesters (5 quarters) remaining at an accredited college or university in the U.S. and its territories, Canada, or Mexico, provided the school's engineering program is accredited by an agency recognized by IIE and the student is pursuing a course of study in industrial engineering. Priority is given to, but not limited to, students who have demonstrated an interest in management consulting. Must be full-time student (co-op is not considered full-time). GPA of 3.4 or better is required.
HOW TO APPLY: Write IIE to request application.
NUMBER OF AWARDS: Varies
CONTACT: Bonnie Cameron, headquarters operations administrator, 770/449-0461, ext. 105

1357—INSTITUTE OF INDUSTRIAL ENGINEERS (Harold and Inge Marcus Scholarship)

Royal Peachtree Corners
3577 Parkway Lane
Building 5, Suite 200
Norcross GA 30092
770/449-0461, ext. 105 or
800/494-0460
FAX: 770/441-3295
E-mail: bcameron@iienet.org
Internet: http://www.iienet.org
AMOUNT: Varies
DEADLINE(S): NOV 15
FIELD(S): Industrial Engineering
ELIGIBILITY/REQUIREMENTS: Undergraduate scholarships for active IIE members with at least 3 semesters (5 quarters) remaining at an accredited college or university in the U.S. provided the school's engineering provided the program is accredited by an agency recognized by IIE and the student is pursuing a course of study in industrial engineering. Must be full-time student (co-op is not considered full-time). GPA of 3.4 or better is required.
HOW TO APPLY: Must be nominated by department head or faculty advisor. Call for nominations is sent out in the fall.

CONTACT: Bonnie Cameron, headquarters operations administrator, 770/449-0461, ext. 105

1358—INSTITUTE OF INDUSTRIAL ENGINEERS (Marvin Mundel Memorial Scholarship)

Royal Peachtree Corners
3577 Parkway Lane
Building 5, Suite 200
Norcross GA 30092
770/449-0461, ext. 105 or
800/494-0460
FAX: 770/441-3295
E-mail: bcameron@iienet.org
Internet: http://www.iienet.org
AMOUNT: Varies
DEADLINE(S): NOV 15
FIELD(S): Industrial Engineering
ELIGIBILITY/REQUIREMENTS: Undergraduate scholarships for active IIE members with at least 3 semesters (5 quarters) remaining at an accredited college or university in the U.S. and its territories, Canada, or Mexico, provided the school's engineering program is accredited by an agency recognized by IIE and the student is pursuing a course of study in industrial engineering. Priority is given to, but not limited to, students who have demonstrated an interest in management consulting. Must be full-time student (co-op is not considered full-time). GPA of 3.4 or better is required.
HOW TO APPLY: Must be nominated by department head or faculty advisor. Call for nominations is sent out in the fall.
CONTACT: Bonnie Cameron, headquarters operations administrator, 770/449-0461, ext. 105

1359—INSTITUTE OF INDUSTRIAL ENGINEERS (Presidents Scholarship)

Royal Peachtree Corners
3577 Parkway Lane
Building 5, Suite 200
Norcross GA 30092
770/449-0461, ext. 105 or
800/494-0460
FAX: 770/441-3295
E-mail: bcameron@iienet.org
Internet: http://www.iienet.org
AMOUNT: Varies
DEADLINE(S): NOV 15
FIELD(S): Industrial Engineering
ELIGIBILITY/REQUIREMENTS: Undergraduate scholarships for active IIE members with at least 3 semesters (5 quarters) remaining at an accredited college or university in the U.S. and its territories,

Canada, or Mexico, provided the school's engineering program is accredited by an agency recognized by IIE and the student is pursuing a course of study in industrial engineering. Recipient must demonstrate leadership and promote IEE involvement on campus.. Must be full-time student (co-op is not considered full-time). GPA of 3.4 or better is required.

HOW TO APPLY: Must be nominated by department head or faculty advisor. Call for nominations is sent out in the fall.

CONTACT: Bonnie Cameron, headquarters operations administrator, 770/449-0461, ext. 105

1360—INSTITUTE OF INDUSTRIAL ENGINEERS (United Parcel Service Scholarships for Female and Minority Students)

Royal Peachtree Corners
3577 Parkway Lane
Building 5, Suite 200
Norcross GA 30092
770/449-0461, ext. 105 or
800/494-0460
FAX: 770/441-3295
E-mail: bcameron@iienet.org
Internet: http://www.iienet.org
AMOUNT: $4,000 (each)
DEADLINE(S): NOV 15
FIELD(S): Industrial Engineering
ELIGIBILITY/REQUIREMENTS: Undergraduate scholarships for active IIE members with at least 3 semesters (5 quarters) remaining at an accredited college or university in the U.S. and its territories, Canada, or Mexico, provided the school's engineering program is accredited by an agency recognized by IIE and the student is pursuing a course of study in industrial engineering. Priority is given to, but not limited to, students who have demonstrated an interest in management consulting. Must be full-time student (co-op is not considered full-time). GPA of 3.4 or better is required.

HOW TO APPLY: Write IIE to request application.

CONTACT: Bonnie Cameron, headquarters operations administrator, 770/449-0461, ext. 105

1361—MICHIGAN SOCIETY OF PROFESSIONAL ENGINEERS, THE (Anthony C. Fortunski, P.E. Memorial Grant)

215 North Walnut
P.O. Box 15276
Lansing MI 48901-5276
517/487-9388
FAX: 517/487-0635
E-mail: mspe@voyager.net
Internet: http://www.michigan spe.org
AMOUNT: $2,000
DEADLINE(S): Second Monday in APR
FIELD(S): Manufacturing Engineering
ELIGIBILITY/REQUIREMENTS: Must be an MSPE member; a U.S. citizen and a resident of Michigan; in an ABET-accredited engineering program at a Michigan college or university; have a minimum GPA of 3.0; demonstrate leadership and an interest in the engineering profession (especially manufacturing and industry) through involvement in school and/or outside activities. Preference is given to students attending Lawrence Technological University.

HOW TO APPLY: Send application; official grade transcript(s); recommendations from at least 2 professors in the applicant's field of engineering study or appropriate math/science professor, specifying academic and personal traits and extracurricular activities; proof of acceptance in an ABET-accredited engineering program; information on co-op programs; and an essay of approximately 500 words, discussing applicant's interest in engineering, specific field of engineering that is being pursued, and occupation applicant proposes to pursue after graduation.

NUMBER OF AWARDS: 1

1362—SEARS CRAFTSMAN SCHOLARSHIP

NHRA Youth & Education Services
2035 Financial Way
Glendora CA 91741-4602
626/250-2208
FAX: 626/914-9109
E-mail: rkaizojil@nhra.com
Internet: http://www.nhra.com
AMOUNT: $250
DEADLINE(S): MAY 1
FIELD(S): Automotive Technology; Industrial/Technical Manufacturing; Marketing
ELIGIBILITY/REQUIREMENTS: Must be seniors graduating from a public, private, or parochial school or education center between January and June; must be of good character, possess minimum 2.5 GPA, show evidence of leadership ability, involvement in extracurricular school and community activities, and plan to attend an accredited 2- or 4-year college, university or technical/vocational program. Students with a failing grade during their high school career will not be considered. Preference given to applicants planning a career in automotive technology, industrial/technical manufacturing or marketing. Awards will be based on scholastic record, school activities and community involvement, personal essay, recommendations, and financial need.

HOW TO APPLY: Submit application, including personal essay; 2 recommendations, 1 of which must be from a teacher, counselor, or administrator; and transcript.

NUMBER OF AWARDS: 21 (3 in each of the 7 National Hot Rod Association Divisions)

CONTACT: Rachel Kaizoji

1363—SOCIETY OF AUTOMOTIVE ENGINEERS (Central State University/SAE Engineering Scholarship)

SAE Customer Service
400 Commonwealth Drive
Warrendale PA 15096-0001
724/776-4970
FAX: 724/776-1615
E-mail: customerservice@sae.org
Internet: http://www.sae.org/ students/scholarships
AMOUNT: $1,000
DEADLINE(S): DEC 1
FIELD(S): Manufacturing Engineering; Industrial Technology; Automotive Industry
ELIGIBILITY/REQUIREMENTS: Must be an incoming freshman, enrolled full time. Selection criteria include ACT/SAT scores and a minimum 3.0 GPA. Financial need is also considered.

HOW TO APPLY: See website for application. Submit application; a personal essay that demonstrates hands-on experience or activity (such as rebuilding engines, working on cars/trucks, etc.); 2 recommendations, 1 of which must be from a teacher, counselor, or administrator; and transcript.

NUMBER OF AWARDS: 3

RENEWABLE: Yes. For 1 year if criteria are met.

1364—SOCIETY OF AUTOMOTIVE ENGINEERS (John Deere and Bradley University/SAE Engineering Scholarships)

SAE Customer Service
400 Commonwealth Drive
Warrendale PA 15096-0001
724/776-4970
FAX: 724/776-1615
E-mail: customerservice@sae.org

Internet: http://www.sae.org/
students/scholarships
AMOUNT: $1,250
DEADLINE(S): DEC 1
FIELD(S): Mechanical, Electrical,
Computer, Industrial, or
Manufacturing Engineering;
Automotive Industry
ELIGIBILITY/REQUIREMENTS: Must
be an incoming freshman accepted into the
College of Engineering and Technology at
Bradley. Selection is based on high school
GPA, rank in class, curriculum and
SAT/ACT scores. A minimum 980 SAT or
21 ACT composite score, and 3.25 GPA.
HOW TO APPLY: See website for appli-
cation. Submit application; a personal
essay that demonstrates hands-on experience or activity (such as rebuilding
engines, working on cars/trucks, etc.); 2
recommendations, 1 of which must be from
a teacher, counselor, or administrator; and
transcript.
NUMBER OF AWARDS: Varies
RENEWABLE: Yes. A total of $5,000 (4-
year period) will be awarded if student
remains enrolled in one of the specified
majors and maintains a 3.0 GPA.

1365—SOCIETY OF AUTOMOTIVE ENGINEERS (Oklahoma State University [CEAT]/SAE Engineering Scholarship)

SAE Customer Service
400 Commonwealth Drive
Warrendale PA 15096-0001
724/776-4970
FAX: 724/776-1615
E-mail: customerservice@sae.org
Internet: http://www.sae.org/
students/scholarships
AMOUNT: $1,000
DEADLINE(S): DEC 1
FIELD(S): Mechanical, Electrical,
Industrial Engineering; Automotive
Industry
ELIGIBILITY/REQUIREMENTS: High
school graduates with a 3.8 or greater GPA
and an ACT of 30 (SAT 1350) or above
who plan to major in mechanical, electrical, or industrial engineering.
HOW TO APPLY: See website for application. Submit application; a personal
essay that demonstrates hands-on experience or activity (such as rebuilding
engines, working on cars/trucks, etc.); 2
recommendations, 1 of which must be from
a teacher, counselor, or administrator; and
transcript.
NUMBER OF AWARDS: 1
RENEWABLE: Yes. For 3 additional
years.

1366—SOCIETY OF AUTOMOTIVE ENGINEERS (University of Bridgeport/SAE Engineering Scholarships)

SAE Customer Service
400 Commonwealth Drive
Warrendale PA 15096-0001
724/776-4970
FAX: 724/776-1615
E-mail: customerservice@sae.org
Internet: http://www.sae.org/
students/scholarships
AMOUNT: $9,000
DEADLINE(S): DEC 1
FIELD(S): Computer Science &
Engineering; Mathematics;
Automotive Industry
ELIGIBILITY/REQUIREMENTS:
Entering freshmen pursuing a bachelor's
degree in above fields are eligible.
Requirements include a minimum 3.0
GPA and 1100 SAT or 24 ACT composite.
HOW TO APPLY: See website for application. Submit application; a personal
essay that demonstrates hands-on experi-
ence or activity (such as rebuilding
engines, working on cars/trucks, etc.); 2
recommendations, 1 of which must be from
a teacher, counselor, or administrator; and
transcript. Eligible students must also
apply to the University of Bridgeport and
submit the appropriate attachments, in
addition to SAE submission.
NUMBER OF AWARDS: 3
RENEWABLE: Yes. A total of $36,000
(4-year period) will be awarded if student
remains enrolled in good standing at the
University and maintains a 3.0 GPA.

1367—SOCIETY OF AUTOMOTIVE ENGINEERS (University of Cincinnati/College of Applied Science Alumni/SAE Engineering Scholarship)

SAE Customer Service
400 Commonwealth Drive
Warrendale PA 15096-0001
724/776-4970
FAX: 724/776-1615
E-mail: customerservice@sae.org
Internet: http://www.sae.org/
students/scholarships
AMOUNT: $1,000
DEADLINE(S): DEC 1
FIELD(S): Manufacturing Engineering;
Industrial Technology; Automotive
Industry
ELIGIBILITY/REQUIREMENTS:
Applicant must be an incoming freshman,
accepted to either the Mechanical or
Manufacturing Engineering Technology
degree program. Selection criteria include

ACT/SAT scores, GPA, and academic and
leadership achievements.
HOW TO APPLY: See website for application. Submit application; a personal
essay that demonstrates hands-on experience or activity (such as rebuilding
engines, working on cars/trucks, etc.); 2
recommendations, 1 of which must be from
a teacher, counselor, or administrator; and
transcript.
NUMBER OF AWARDS: 2
RENEWABLE: Yes. For up to 4 years if
3.2 GPA is maintained.

1368—SOCIETY OF MANUFACTURING ENGINEERS EDUCATION FOUNDATION (Scholarships and Fellowship)

Scholarship Review Committee
One SME Drive
P.O. Box 930
Dearborn MI 48121-0930
313/452-3300
FAX: 313/425-3411
E-mail: foundation@sme.org
Internet: http://www.sme.org/
foundation
AMOUNT: $1,000 (minimum)
DEADLINE(S): DEC 5
FIELD(S): Manufacturing
Engineering/Technology; Industrial
Engineering
ELIGIBILITY/REQUIREMENTS:
Available to graduating high school
seniors, undergraduate students, and grad-
uate or doctorate degree students. Some of
the scholarships have a residency require-
ment or geographic restriction. All scholar-
ships have a GPA requirement. Applicant
must reside in and be enrolled in or accepted at an accredited institution in the U.S.
or Canada, and meet the individual criteria
needed for the desired scholarship.
HOW TO APPLY: See website for application and additional requirements.
NUMBER OF AWARDS: 100
RENEWABLE: No

1369—SPE FOUNDATION, THE (Blow Molding Division Memorial Scholarships)

14 Fairfield Drive
Brookfield CT 06804
203/740-5447
FAX: 203/775-1157
E-mail: foundation@4spe.org
Internet: http://www.4spe.org/
foundation/scholarships.php
AMOUNT: $8,000 (payable over 2 years)
DEADLINE(S): JAN 15
FIELD(S): Polymer Science; Chemistry;
Physics; Plastics, Chemical,
Mechanical, & Industrial Engineering

ELIGIBILITY/REQUIREMENTS: Applicants must be completing the 2nd year of a 4-year undergraduate plastics engineering program and be a member of a Society of Plastics Engineers (SPE) student chapter.

HOW TO APPLY: Complete application; submit 3 recommendation letters (2 from a teacher or school official and 1 from an employer or non-relative); high school and/or college transcript for last 2 years; a 1- to 2-page brief essay on the importance of blow molding to the technical parts and packaging industries. Submit brief essay that describes the importance of blow molding to the technical parts and packaging industries, and why the applicant desires a career in the plastics industry.

NUMBER OF AWARDS: Up to 2

1370—SPE FOUNDATION, THE (Composites Division/Harold Giles Scholarship)

14 Fairfield Drive
Brookfield CT 06804
203/740-5447
FAX: 203/775-1157
E-mail: foundation@4spe.org
Internet: http://www.4spe.org/
foundation/scholarships.php
AMOUNT: $1,000
DEADLINE(S): JAN 15
FIELD(S): Polymer Science; Chemistry; Physics; Chemical, Plastics, Mechanical & Industrial Engineering
ELIGIBILITY/REQUIREMENTS: Applicants must have experience in the composites industry (such as courses taken, research conducted, or jobs held); must be in good standing with their colleges and have demonstrated an interest in the plastics industry; majoring in or taking courses that would be beneficial to a career in the plastics/polymer industry. Financial need is considered.

HOW TO APPLY: Complete application; submit 3 recommendation letters (2 from a teacher or school official and 1 from an employer or non-relative); high school and/or college transcript for last 2 years; a 1- to 2-page statement telling why you are applying for the scholarship and educational and career goals in the plastics industry. Include a statement detailing exposure to the composites industry.

NUMBER OF AWARDS: 1

1371—SPE FOUNDATION, THE (Extrusion Division/Lew Erwin Memorial Scholarship)

14 Fairfield Drive

Brookfield CT 06804
203/740-5447
FAX: 203/775-1157
E-mail: foundation@4spe.org
Internet: http://www.4spe.org/
foundation/scholarships.php
AMOUNT: $2,500
DEADLINE(S): JAN 15
FIELD(S): Polymer Science; Chemistry; Physics; Chemical, Plastics, Mechanical & Industrial Engineering
ELIGIBILITY/REQUIREMENTS: Supports undergraduate or graduate research in the field of polymer extrusion. Must be working in a senior or MS project that the scholarship will help support.

HOW TO APPLY: The project must be described in writing, including background, objective and proposed experiments. The recipient will be expected to furnish a final research summary report. Complete application; submit 3 recommendation letters (2 from a teacher or school official and 1 from an employer or non-relative); high school and/or college transcript for last 2 years; a 1- to 2-page statement telling why you are applying for the scholarship and educational and career goals in the plastics industry.

NUMBER OF AWARDS: 1
RENEWABLE: Yes. Must reapply for 3 additional years.

1372—SPE FOUNDATION, THE (Fleming/Biaszcek Scholarship)

14 Fairfield Drive
Brookfield CT 06804
203/740-5447
FAX: 203/775-1157
E-mail: foundation@4spe.org
Internet: http://www.4spe.org/
foundation/scholarships.php
AMOUNT: $2,000
DEADLINE(S): JAN 15
FIELD(S): Polymer Science; Chemistry; Physics; Chemical, Plastics, Mechanical & Industrial Engineering
ELIGIBILITY/REQUIREMENTS: Available to full-time undergraduate students at a 4-year college, or students enrolled in a graduate program. Applicants for this award must be of Mexican descent and citizens or legal residents of the U.S. Applicants must be in good standing with their colleges and have demonstrated an interest in the plastics industry; majoring in or taking courses that would be beneficial to a career in the plastics/polymer industry. Financial need is considered for most scholarships.

HOW TO APPLY: Complete application; submit 3 recommendation letters (2 from a

teacher or school official and 1 from an employer or non-relative); high school and/or college transcript for last 2 years; a 1- to 2-page statement telling why you are applying for the scholarship and educational and career goals in the plastics industry. Detail Mexican lineage in essay or on a separate sheet of paper.

NUMBER OF AWARDS: 1
RENEWABLE: Yes. Must reapply for 3 additional years.

1373—SPE FOUNDATION, THE (Foundation Scholarships)

14 Fairfield Drive
Brookfield CT 06804
203/740-5447
FAX: 203/775-1157
E-mail: foundation@4spe.org
Internet: http://www.4spe.org/
foundation/scholarships.php
AMOUNT: $4,000
DEADLINE(S): JAN 15
FIELD(S): Polymer Science; Chemistry; Physics; Chemical, Plastics, Mechanical & Industrial Engineering
ELIGIBILITY/REQUIREMENTS: Must be in good standing with their colleges and have demonstrated an interest in the plastics industry; majoring in or taking courses that would be beneficial to a career in the plastics/polymer industry. Financial need is considered for most scholarships.

HOW TO APPLY: Complete application; submit 3 recommendation letters (2 from a teacher or school official and 1 from an employer or non-relative); high school and/or college transcript for last 2 years; a 1- to 2-page statement telling why you are applying for the scholarship and educational and career goals in the plastics industry.

NUMBER OF AWARDS: Multiple
RENEWABLE: Yes. Must reapply for 3 additional years.

1374—SPE FOUNDATION, THE (Gulf Coast Hurricane Scholarships)

14 Fairfield Drive
Brookfield CT 06804
203/740-5447
FAX: 203/775-1157
E-mail: foundation@4spe.org
Internet: http://www.4spe.org/
foundation/scholarships.php
AMOUNT: $6,000 (college or university), $2,000 (junior or technical)
DEADLINE(S): JAN 15
FIELD(S): Polymer Science; Chemistry; Physics; Chemical, Plastics, Mechanical & Industrial Engineering

ELIGIBILITY/REQUIREMENTS: Must have been a resident of a Gulf Coast County declared a national disaster area as a result of Hurricanes Katrina, Rita or Wilma, and must be attending a university, college or technical institute in a Gulf Coast State (Florida, Alabama, Mississippi, Louisiana, Texas). Must be in good standing with their colleges (minimum GPA 2.0) and enrolled 6 hours/semester. Must have demonstrated an interest in the plastics industry; majoring in or taking courses that would be beneficial to a career in the plastics/polymer industry. Financial need is considered for most scholarships.

HOW TO APPLY: Complete application; submit 3 recommendation letters (2 from a teacher or school official and 1 from an employer or non-relative); high school and/or college transcript for last 2 years; a 1- to 2-page statement telling why you are applying for the scholarship and educational and career goals in the plastics industry. Must provide proof of residence.

NUMBER OF AWARDS: 3; 1 college or university, 2 junior college or technical school

RENEWABLE: Yes. Must reapply for 3 additional years.

1375—SPE FOUNDATION, THE (Injection Molding Division Scholarship)

14 Fairfield Drive
Brookfield CT 06804
203/740-5447
FAX: 203/775-1157
E-mail: foundation@4spe.org
Internet: http://www.4spe.org/
foundation/scholarships.php
AMOUNT: $3,000
DEADLINE(S): JAN 15
FIELD(S): Polymer Science; Chemistry;
Physics; Chemical, Plastics, Mechanical
& Industrial Engineering

ELIGIBILITY/REQUIREMENTS: Available to undergraduates at a 4-year. Applicants must have experience in the injection molding industry (such as courses taken, research conducted, or jobs held), be in good standing with their colleges and have demonstrated an interest in the plastics industry; majoring in or taking courses that would be beneficial to a career in the plastics/polymer industry. Financial need is considered.

HOW TO APPLY: Complete application; submit 3 recommendation letters (2 from a teacher or school official and 1 from an employer or non-relative); high school and/or college transcript for last 2 years; a 1- to 2-page statement telling why you are

applying for the scholarship and educational and career goals in the plastics industry.
NUMBER OF AWARDS: 1
RENEWABLE: Yes. Must reapply for 3 additional years.

1376—SPE FOUNDATION, THE (Pittsburgh Section Scholarships)

14 Fairfield Drive
Brookfield CT 06804
203/740-5447
FAX: 203/775-1157
E-mail: foundation@4spe.org
Internet: http://www.4spe.org/
foundation/scholarships.php
AMOUNT: $2,000
DEADLINE(S): JAN 15
FIELD(S): Polymer Science; Chemistry;
Physics; Chemical, Plastics, Mechanical
& Industrial Engineering

ELIGIBILITY/REQUIREMENTS: Must have graduated from a high school in one of the following PA counties: Allegheny, Armstrong, Beaver, Bedford, Blair, Brooke, Butler, Cambria, Clarion, Clearfield, Fayette, Greene, Hancock, Indiana, Jefferson, Lawrence, Mercer, Somerset, Venango, Washington, Westmoreland. Must be in good standing with their colleges and have demonstrated an interest in the plastics industry; majoring in or taking courses that would be beneficial to a career in the plastics/polymer industry. Financial need is considered for most scholarships.

HOW TO APPLY: Complete application; submit 3 recommendation letters (2 from a teacher or school official and 1 from an employer or non-relative); high school and/or college transcript for last 2 years; a 1- to 2-page statement telling why you are applying for the scholarship and educational and career goals in the plastics industry. Must provide proof of graduation from school in one of above counties.

NUMBER OF AWARDS: Up to 2
RENEWABLE: Yes. Must reapply for 3 additional years.

1377—SPE FOUNDATION, THE (Plastics Pioneers Association Scholarships)

14 Fairfield Drive
Brookfield CT 06804
203/740-5447
FAX: 203/775-1157
E-mail: foundation@4spe.org
Internet: http://www.4spe.org/
foundation/scholarships.php
AMOUNT: $3,000
DEADLINE(S): JAN 15

FIELD(S): Polymer Science; Chemistry;
Physics; Chemical, Plastics, Mechanical
& Industrial Engineering

ELIGIBILITY/REQUIREMENTS: Open to undergraduate students, including those enrolled in associate or technical degree programs, who are committed to becoming "hands on" workers in the plastics industry as plastics technicians or engineers. Must be in good standing with their colleges and have demonstrated an interest in the plastics industry; majoring in or taking courses that would be beneficial to a career in the plastics/polymer industry. Financial need is considered for most scholarships.

HOW TO APPLY: Complete application; submit 3 recommendation letters (2 from a teacher or school official and 1 from an employer or non-relative); high school and/or college transcript for last 2 years; a 1- to 2-page statement telling why you are applying for the scholarship and educational and career goals in the plastics industry.

NUMBER OF AWARDS: Multiple
RENEWABLE: Yes. Must reapply for 3 additional years.

1378—SPE FOUNDATION, THE (Polymer Modifiers & Additives Division Scholarships)

14 Fairfield Drive
Brookfield CT 06804
203/740-5447
FAX: 203/775-1157
E-mail: foundation@4spe.org
Internet: http://www.4spe.org/
foundation/scholarships.php
AMOUNT: $4,000
DEADLINE(S): JAN 15
FIELD(S): Polymer Science; Chemistry;
Physics; Chemical, Plastics, Mechanical
& Industrial Engineering

ELIGIBILITY/REQUIREMENTS: Must be in good standing with their colleges and have demonstrated an interest in the plastics industry; majoring in or taking courses that would be beneficial to a career in the plastics/polymer industry. Financial need is considered for most scholarships.

HOW TO APPLY: Complete application; submit 3 recommendation letters (2 from a teacher or school official and 1 from an employer or non-relative); high school and/or college transcript for last 2 years; a 1- to 2-page statement telling why you are applying for the scholarship and educational and career goals in the plastics industry.

NUMBER OF AWARDS: 3
RENEWABLE: Yes. Must reapply for 3 additional years.

1379—SPE FOUNDATION, THE (Robert E. Cramer/Product Design & Development Division Scholarship)

14 Fairfield Drive
Brookfield CT 06804
203/740-5447
FAX: 203/775-1157
E-mail: foundation@4spe.org
Internet: http://www.4spe.org/
foundation/scholarships.php
AMOUNT: $1,000
DEADLINE(S): JAN 15
FIELD(S): Polymer Science; Chemistry; Physics; Chemical, Plastics, Mechanical & Industrial Engineering
ELIGIBILITY/REQUIREMENTS: Must be in good standing with their colleges and have demonstrated an interest in the plastics industry; majoring in or taking courses that would be beneficial to a career in the plastics/polymer industry. Financial need is considered for most scholarships.
HOW TO APPLY: Complete application; submit 3 recommendation letters (2 from a teacher or school official and 1 from an employer or non-relative); high school and/or college transcript for last 2 years; a 1- to 2-page statement telling why you are applying for the scholarship and educational and career goals in the plastics industry.
NUMBER OF AWARDS: 1
RENEWABLE: Yes. Must reapply for 3 additional years.

1380—SPE FOUNDATION, THE (Robert G. Dailey/Detroit Section Scholarship)

14 Fairfield Drive
Brookfield CT 06804
203/740-5447
FAX: 203/775-1157
E-mail: foundation@4spe.org
Internet: http://www.4spe.org/
foundation/scholarships.php
AMOUNT: $4,000
DEADLINE(S): JAN 15
FIELD(S): Polymer Science; Chemistry; Physics; Chemical, Plastics, Mechanical & Industrial Engineering
ELIGIBILITY/REQUIREMENTS: Must be in good standing with their colleges and have demonstrated an interest in the plastics industry; majoring in or taking courses that would be beneficial to a career in the plastics/polymer industry. Financial need is considered for most scholarships.
HOW TO APPLY: Complete application; submit 3 recommendation letters (2 from a teacher or school official and 1 from an employer or non-relative); high school and/or college transcript for last 2 years; a 1- to 2-page statement telling why you are applying for the scholarship and educational and career goals in the plastics industry.
NUMBER OF AWARDS: 1
RENEWABLE: Yes. Must reapply for 3 additional years.

1381—SPE FOUNDATION, THE (Ted and Ruth Neward Scholarships)

14 Fairfield Drive
Brookfield CT 06804
203/740-5447
FAX: 203/775-1157
E-mail: foundation@4spe.org
Internet: http://www.4spe.org/
foundation/scholarships.php
AMOUNT: $3,000
DEADLINE(S): JAN 15
FIELD(S): Polymer Science; Chemistry; Physics; Chemical, Plastics, Mechanical & Industrial Engineering
ELIGIBILITY/REQUIREMENTS: Must be U.S. citizens in good standing with their colleges and have demonstrated an interest in the plastics industry; majoring in or taking courses that would be beneficial to a career in the plastics/polymer industry. Financial need is considered for most scholarships.
HOW TO APPLY: Complete application; submit 3 recommendation letters (2 from a teacher or school official and 1 from an employer or non-relative); high school and/or college transcript for last 2 years; a 1- to 2-page statement telling why you are applying for the scholarship and educational and career goals in the plastics industry.
NUMBER OF AWARDS: 3
RENEWABLE: Yes. Must reapply for 3 additional years.

1382—SPE FOUNDATION, THE (Thermoforming Division Memorial Scholarships)

14 Fairfield Drive
Brookfield CT 06804
203/740-5447
FAX: 203/775-1157
E-mail: foundation@4spe.org
Internet: http://www.4spe.org/
foundation/scholarships.php
AMOUNT: $7,500
DEADLINE(S): JAN 15
FIELD(S): Polymer Science; Chemistry; Physics; Chemical, Plastics, Mechanical & Industrial Engineering
ELIGIBILITY/REQUIREMENTS: Available to graduate or undergraduate students at a 4-year college with GPA of 3.0 or better. Undergraduates must have completed at least 2 years of credits. Applicants must have experience in the thermoforming industry (such as courses taken, research conducted, or jobs held), be in good standing with their colleges and have demonstrated an interest in the plastics industry; majoring in or taking courses that would be beneficial to a career in the plastics/polymer industry. Financial need is considered for most scholarships.
HOW TO APPLY: Complete application; submit 3 recommendation letters (2 from a teacher or school official and 1 from an employer or non-relative); high school and/or college transcript for last 2 years; a 1- to 2-page statement telling why you are applying for the scholarship and educational and career goals in the plastics industry. Include a statement detailing exposure to the thermoforming industry.
NUMBER OF AWARDS: Varies (multiple awards)
RENEWABLE: Yes. Must reapply for 3 additional years.

1383—SPE FOUNDATION, THE (Thermoplastic Elastomers Special Interest Group Scholarship)

14 Fairfield Drive
Brookfield CT 06804
203/740-5447
FAX: 203/775-1157
E-mail: foundation@4spe.org
Internet: http://www.4spe.org/
foundation/scholarships.php
AMOUNT: $1,000
DEADLINE(S): JAN 15
FIELD(S): Polymer Science; Chemistry; Physics; Chemical, Plastics, Mechanical & Industrial Engineering
ELIGIBILITY/REQUIREMENTS: Available to graduate or undergraduate students at a 4-year college. Applicants must have experience in the thermoplastic elastometers industry (such as courses taken, research conducted, or jobs held); must be in good standing with their colleges and have demonstrated an interest in the plastics industry; majoring in or taking courses that would be beneficial to a career in the plastics/polymer industry. Financial need is considered.
HOW TO APPLY: Complete application; submit 3 recommendation letters (2 from a teacher or school official and 1 from an employer or non-relative); high school and/or college transcript for last 2 years; a 1- to 2-page statement telling why you are applying for the scholarship and educational and career goals in the plastics industry. Include a statement detailing exposure to the thermoplastic elastometers industry.
NUMBER OF AWARDS: 1

1384—SPE FOUNDATION, THE (Thermoplastic Materials & Foams Division Scholarship)

14 Fairfield Drive
Brookfield CT 06804
203/740-5447
FAX: 203/775-1157
E-mail: foundation@4spe.org
Internet: http://www.4spe.org/
foundation/scholarships.php
AMOUNT: $1,000
DEADLINE(S): JAN 15
FIELD(S): Polymer Science; Chemistry; Physics; Chemical, Plastics, Mechanical & Industrial Engineering

ELIGIBILITY/REQUIREMENTS: Must be in good standing with their colleges and have demonstrated an interest in the plastics industry; majoring in or taking courses that would be beneficial to a career in the plastics/polymer industry. Financial need is considered for most scholarships.
HOW TO APPLY: Complete application; submit 3 recommendation letters (2 from a teacher or school official and 1 from an employer or non-relative); high school and/or college transcript for last 2 years; a 1- to 2-page statement telling why you are applying for the scholarship and educational and career goals in the plastics industry.
NUMBER OF AWARDS: 1
RENEWABLE: Yes. Must reapply for 3 additional years.

1385—SPE FOUNDATION, THE (Thermoset Division/James I. MacKenzie Memorial Scholarship)

14 Fairfield Drive
Brookfield CT 06804
203/740-5447
FAX: 203/775-1157
E-mail: foundation@4spe.org
Internet: http://www.4spe.org/
foundation/scholarships.php
AMOUNT: $2,500
DEADLINE(S): JAN 15
FIELD(S): Polymer Science; Chemistry; Physics; Chemical, Plastics, Mechanical & Industrial Engineering

ELIGIBILITY/REQUIREMENTS: Available to undergraduates at a 4-year college with GPA of 3.0 or better. Applicants must have experience in the thermoset industry (such as courses taken, research conducted, or jobs held), be in good standing with their colleges and have demonstrated an interest in the plastics industry; majoring in or taking courses that would be beneficial to a career in the plas-

tics/polymer industry. Financial need is considered for most scholarships.
HOW TO APPLY: Complete application; submit 3 recommendation letters (2 from a teacher or school official and 1 from an employer or non-relative); high school and/or college transcript for last 2 years; a 1- to 2-page statement telling why you are applying for the scholarship and educational and career goals in the plastics industry.
NUMBER OF AWARDS: 1
RENEWABLE: Yes. Must reapply for 3 additional years.
ADDITIONAL INFORMATION: Also includes all-expense-paid trip to, and speaking opportunity at, annual Madison Thermoset Molding Conference.

1386—SPE FOUNDATION, THE (Vinyl Plastics Division Scholarship)

14 Fairfield Drive
Brookfield CT 06804
203/740-5447
FAX: 203/775-1157
E-mail: foundation@4spe.org
Internet: http://www.4spe.org/
foundation/scholarships.php
AMOUNT: $3,000
DEADLINE(S): JAN 15
FIELD(S): Polymer Science; Chemistry; Physics; Chemical, Plastics, Mechanical & Industrial Engineering

ELIGIBILITY/REQUIREMENTS: Must be in good standing with their colleges and have demonstrated an interest in the plastics industry; majoring in or taking courses that would be beneficial to a career in the plastics/polymer industry. Preference given to applicants with experience in the vinyl industry (such as courses taken, research conducted, or jobs held). Financial need is considered for most scholarships.
HOW TO APPLY: Complete application; submit 3 recommendation letters (2 from a teacher or school official and 1 from an employer or non-relative); high school and/or college transcript for last 2 years; a 1- to 2-page statement telling why you are applying for the scholarship and educational and career goals in the plastics industry.
NUMBER OF AWARDS: 1
RENEWABLE: Yes. Must reapply for 3 additional years.

1387—UNIVERSITY OF WINDSOR (Outstanding Scholars Award)

401 Sunset Avenue
Windsor Ontario N9B 3P4
CANADA

519/253-3000
FAX: 519/973-7081
E-mail: awards1@uwindsor.ca
Internet: http://www.uwindsor.ca
AMOUNT: $1,000-$2,500/year (Canadian); maximum 4 years
DEADLINE(S): MAY 31
FIELD(S): Classics, Modern Languages, French, Philosophy, Music, Physics, Earth Sciences (not Environmental Studies), Economics (not Business and Economics), Chemistry (not Biochemistry), Mathematics and Statistics, Industrial, Mechanical (Materials Option) or Environmental Engineering or Bachelor of Arts and Science

ELIGIBILITY/REQUIREMENTS: Open to undergraduate students registering in year 1 at the University of Windsor. Must have superior grades. Amount of award based on secondary school accomplishments.
HOW TO APPLY: Automatic. No application required.
RENEWABLE: Yes. Up to 4 years.
CONTACT: Aase Houser
ADDITIONAL INFORMATION: Students in this program will also be mentored in their first year in preparation for guaranteed Outstanding Scholars Appointments in their Department/School (valued at $2,000 Canadian in earnings for each of the 2nd, 3rd, and 4th years) provided all conditions are met.

1388—WESTERN MICHIGAN UNIVERSITY (College of Engineering and Applied Sciences/Kalamazoo Builders Exchange Scholarship)

1903 West Michigan
Kalamazoo MI 49008-5337
269/387-6000
FAX: 269/387-6989
E-mail: finaid-info@wmich.edu
Internet: http://www.wmich.
edu/finaid
AMOUNT: $1,000 ($500 fall/$500 spring)
FIELD(S): Construction Engineering; Materials Engineering; Industrial Engineering

ELIGIBILITY/REQUIREMENTS: Shall be awarded to a full-time undergraduate student majoring in construction engineering, materials engineering and industrial design. Preference shall be given to juniors and seniors who have experience in the construction industry through an internship or part-time work with special preference for association with the Kalamazoo Builders Exchange. Preference given to individuals living within the greater

Southwest Michigan area. Coursework elected by students supported through this program must be applicable toward a degree program relevant to the construction industry.

HOW TO APPLY: Applicants may be recommended by a member of the Builders Exchange. Contact the Construction Engineering undergraduate advisor for more information.

NUMBER OF AWARDS: 1

RENEWABLE: No. However to continue receiving award, student must maintain a minimum 3.3 GPA at WMU. Enrolled as an undergraduate student in construction engineering.

CONTACT: Construction Engineering undergraduate advisor

1389—WORLDSTUDIO FOUNDATION

200 Varick Street, Suite 507
New York NY 10014
212/366-1317
FAX: 212/807-0024
E-mail: info@worldstudio.org
Internet: http://www.worldstudio.
org or http://www.aiga.org

AMOUNT: $1,500-$5,000

DEADLINE(S): APR 14

FIELD(S): Advertising, Animation, Architecture, Cartooning, Crafts, Environmental graphics, Film/video, Film/theater design, Fine arts, Furniture design, Industrial/product design, Interior architecture and design, Landscape architecture, New media, Photography, Surface/textile design, Urban planning

ELIGIBILITY/REQUIREMENTS: Applicants must be pursuing a degree in the fine or commercial arts, design or architecture, and plan to enter a career in the creative professions. Undergraduates and graduates are eligible. Minority status and/or social agenda are significant factors. Financial need a prerequisite. Minimum 2.0 GPA.

HOW TO APPLY: See websites for application. The application is a 2-part process. Applications must include personal and school information, including transcripts and copies of letters of acceptance; financial information; portfolio; written statement of purpose; examples of a commitment to a social agenda, 2 letters of recommendation from college instructors, high school teachers, or employers; head shot of applicant.

NUMBER OF AWARDS: 20-30

RENEWABLE: Yes. Must reapply.

CONTACT: Mark Randall

MECHANICAL ENGINEERING

1390—AMERICAN CHEMICAL SOCIETY-RUBBER DIVISION

P.O. Box 499
Akron OH 44309-0499
330/972-7814
FAX: 330/972-5269
E-mail: crobinson@rubber.org
Internet: http://www.rubber.org/
awards/scholarships.htm

AMOUNT: $5,000

DEADLINE(S): MAR 15

FIELD(S): Chemistry, Physics, Chemical Engineering, Mechanical Engineering, Polymer Science, or other rubber-related discipline

ELIGIBILITY/REQUIREMENTS: Incoming junior or senior enrolled in an accredited college or university in the United States, Canada, Mexico, Brazil or India (countries may change) majoring in a rubber industry-related field. Must have "B" or better overall academic average, and a minimum of 3 semesters or 6 terms completed, and intend to pursue full-time professional employment in the industry.

HOW TO APPLY: Download application from website and fax or mail application along with 2 or more nomination letters from professor/nominator. Official transcripts may follow.

NUMBER OF AWARDS: 3

RENEWABLE: Yes. Must reapply for 2nd and final year.

CONTACT: Christie Robinson, Education & Publications Manager

1391—AMERICAN SOCIETY OF HEATING, REFRIGERATING, AND AIR-CONDITIONING ENGINEERS (ASHRAE J. Richard Mehalick Scholarship)

1791 Tullie Circle NE
Atlanta GA 30329
404/636-8400
FAX: 404/321-5478
E-mail: benedict@ashrae.org
Internet: http://www.ashrae.org

AMOUNT: $3,000

DEADLINE(S): DEC 1

FIELD(S): Engineering

ELIGIBILITY/REQUIREMENTS: Available to a qualified undergraduate mechanical engineering student pursuing a bachelor's degree and enrolled full time in the mechanical engineering program (ABET-accredited) at the University of Pittsburgh. Must have a minimum college GPA of 3.0; be enrolled full time in a col-

lege or university with at least 1 full year of studies remaining in the year for which the scholarship will be awarded; demonstrate potential service to the HVAC&R profession, need for financial assistance, leadership ability, and character.

HOW TO APPLY: See website or contact Society for information and application. Submit with letters of recommendation, transcripts, and demonstration of financial need.

NUMBER OF AWARDS: 1

RENEWABLE: No

CONTACT: Lois Benedict, Scholarship Administrator

1392—AMERICAN SOCIETY OF MECHANICAL ENGINEERS (ASME Student Loans)

3 Park Avenue
New York NY 10016-5990
212/591-8131
FAX: 212/591-7143
E-mail: oluwanifiset@asme.org
Internet: http://www.asme.org/
education/enged/aid/index.htm

AMOUNT: $3,000

DEADLINE(S): APR 15; OCT 15

FIELD(S): Mechanical Engineering

ELIGIBILITY/REQUIREMENTS: Loans for ASME student members in a mechanical engineering or related program. Must be citizens or residents of the U.S., Canada, or Mexico. Loans are 1% below the Stafford loan rate. Financial need is considered.

HOW TO APPLY: See website for an application or membership information. Must apply online.

1393—AMERICAN SOCIETY OF MECHANICAL ENGINEERS (Frank William and Dorothy Given Miller ASME Auxiliary Scholarship)

3 Park Avenue, 22nd floor
New York NY 10016-5990
212/591-7397
FAX: 212/591-7856
E-mail: soukupDt@asme.org
Internet: http://www.asme.org

AMOUNT: $1,500

DEADLINE(S): MAR 15

FIELD(S): Mechanical Engineering

ELIGIBILITY/REQUIREMENTS: For ASME student members in their junior or senior undergraduate year in mechanical engineering or related program. Must be U.S. citizen or North American resident. Financial need NOT considered.

HOW TO APPLY: Contact Society for an application or membership information.
NUMBER OF AWARDS: 2
RENEWABLE: No
CONTACT: David Soukup
ADDITIONAL INFORMATION: The student membership fee is $25.00/year.

1394—AMERICAN SOCIETY OF MECHANICAL ENGINEERS (Garland Duncan Scholarship)

3 Park Avenue, 22nd floor
New York NY 10016-5990
212/591-7397
FAX: 212/591-7856
E-mail: soukupDt@asme.org
Internet: http://www.asme.org
AMOUNT: $3,500
DEADLINE(S): MAR 15
FIELD(S): Mechanical Engineering
ELIGIBILITY/REQUIREMENTS: For ASME student members in their junior or senior undergraduate years studying mechanical engineering or a related program. Must demonstrate financial need.
HOW TO APPLY: Contact ASME or see website for an application or membership information.
NUMBER OF AWARDS: 3
CONTACT: David Soukup
ADDITIONAL INFORMATION: The student membership fee is $25.00/year.

1395—AMERICAN SOCIETY OF MECHANICAL ENGINEERS (Kenneth Andrew Roe Scholarship)

3 Park Avenue, 22nd floor
New York NY 10016-5990
212/591-7397
FAX: 212/591-7856
E-mail: soukupDt@asme.org
Internet: http://www.asme.org
AMOUNT: $10,000
DEADLINE(S): MAR 15
FIELD(S): Mechanical Engineering
ELIGIBILITY/REQUIREMENTS: Open to student members in their junior or senior years studying mechanical engineering or related program. Must be U.S. citizen or North American resident. Financial need considered.
HOW TO APPLY: Contact ASME or see website for an application or membership information.
NUMBER OF AWARDS: 1
CONTACT: David Soukup
ADDITIONAL INFORMATION: The student membership fee is $25.00/year.

1396—AMERICAN SOCIETY OF MECHANICAL ENGINEERS (Melvin R. Green Scholarship)

3 Park Avenue, 22nd floor
New York NY 10016-5990
212/591-7397
FAX: 212/591-7856
E-mail: soukupDt@asme.org
Internet: http://www.asme.org
AMOUNT: $3,500
DEADLINE(S): MAR 15
FIELD(S): Mechanical Engineering
ELIGIBILITY/REQUIREMENTS: For ASME student members who are in their junior or senior years studying mechanical engineering or a related program. Financial need NOT considered.
HOW TO APPLY: Contact ASME or see website for an application or membership information.
NUMBER OF AWARDS: 2
CONTACT: David Soukup
ADDITIONAL INFORMATION: The student membership fee is $25.00/year.

1397—AMERICAN SOCIETY OF MECHANICAL ENGINEERS AUXILIARY INC. (F. W. Beichley Scholarship)

3 Park Avenue, 22nd floor
New York NY 10016-5990
212/591-7397
FAX: 212/591-7856
E-mail: soukupDt@asme.org
Internet: http://www.asme.org
AMOUNT: $2,000
DEADLINE(S): MAR 15
FIELD(S): Mechanical Engineering
ELIGIBILITY/REQUIREMENTS: For junior and senior undergraduate students who are student members of ASME, studying mechanical engineering or a related program. Must demonstrate financial need.
HOW TO APPLY: Contact ASME or see website for an application or membership information.
NUMBER OF AWARDS: 1
CONTACT: David Soukup
ADDITIONAL INFORMATION: The student membership fee is $25.00/year.

1398—CELANESE CANADA, INC.

Association of Universities and Colleges in Canada
350 Albert Street, Suite 600
Ottawa Ontario K1R 1B1 CANADA
613/563-1236
FAX: 613/563-9745
E-mail: awards@aucc.ca
Internet: http://www.aucc.ca
AMOUNT: $1,500 (Canadian)
DEADLINE(S): JUL 2
FIELD(S): Mechanical and Chemical Engineering; Chemistry; Business Administration and Commerce
ELIGIBILITY/REQUIREMENTS: Open to Canadian citizens and permanent residents for their final year of an undergraduate program. Must attend a college or university, which is a member or affiliated to a member of the AUCC. Candidates are expected to have achieved a high level of academic excellence as well as to have exhibited superior intellectual ability and judgment. In some cases, study in certain province or school is required.
HOW TO APPLY: Applications are by nomination only. See website or contact AUCC for nomination procedures.
RENEWABLE: No
CONTACT: AUCC

1399—INSTITUTION OF MECHANICAL ENGINEERS (James Clayton Undergraduate Scholarships)

Educational Services
Northgate Avenue Bury St. Edmunds
Suffolk IP32 6BN ENGLAND
+44(01284) 718617
FAX: +44(01284) 724471
E-mail: k frost@imeche.org.uk
Internet: http://www.imeche.org.uk
AMOUNT: £500
DEADLINE(S): JUN 30
FIELD(S): Mechanical Engineering
ELIGIBILITY/REQUIREMENTS: For UK residents undertaking full-time secondary education, planning to begin their degree in the next academic session. Must be accepted into an accredited course and expect to obtain "A" level grades. Recipients must become members of the IME and maintain membership throughout course.
HOW TO APPLY: Check website or contact IME for an application.
NUMBER OF AWARDS: 20
RENEWABLE: Yes. Up to 4 years.

1400—INSTITUTION OF MECHANICAL ENGINEERS (Grants and Scholarships)

1 Birdcage Walk
Westminster London SW1H 9JJ ENGLAND
+44 (0)20 7222 7899
FAX: +44 (0)20 7222 4557
Internet: http://www.imeche.org.uk
AMOUNT: Varies
DEADLINE(S): JUN 30 (scholarships); varies (grants)

FIELD(S): Mechanical Engineering
ELIGIBILITY/REQUIREMENTS: Grants for study or research in mechanical engineering or a related science. Some require membership or student membership in the IME. Some require UK residency.
HOW TO APPLY: See website or contact IME for details.
RENEWABLE: Grants are normally for less than 1 year.

1401—INSTITUTION OF MECHANICAL ENGINEERS (James Clayton Undergraduate Scholarships)

1 Birdcage Walk
Westminster London SW1H 9JJ
ENGLAND
+44 (0)20 7222 7899
FAX: +44 (0)20 7222 4557
Internet: http://www.imeche.org.uk
AMOUNT: £500
DEADLINE(S): JUN 30
FIELD(S): Mechanical Engineering
ELIGIBILITY/REQUIREMENTS: For UK residents undertaking full-time secondary education, planning to begin their degree in the next academic session. Must be accepted into an accredited course and expect to obtain "A" level grades. Recipients must become members of the IME and maintain membership throughout course.
HOW TO APPLY: Check website or contact IME for an application.
NUMBER OF AWARDS: 20
RENEWABLE: Yes. Up to 4 years.

1402—MAINE METAL PRODUCTS ASSOCIATION

28 Stroudwater Street, Suite #4
Westbrook ME 04092
207/854-2153
FAX: 207/854-3865
E-mail: info@maine-metals.org
Internet: http://www.maine-metals.org
AMOUNT: Varies
DEADLINE(S): MAY 1
FIELD(S): Mechanical Engineering; Machine Tool Technician; Sheet Metal Fabrication; Welding; CAD/CAM for Metals Industry
ELIGIBILITY/REQUIREMENTS: Applicant must have applied to and been accepted in a metal trades program at a Maine college. Must be a Maine resident.
HOW TO APPLY: Send application; copy of high school diploma or equivalent or expected graduation date; copy of high-school and postsecondary transcripts; let-

ter of recommendation from current employer (if applicable), teachers, community leaders, business people, etc.; and a description in applicant's own words of applicant's goals, aspirations, and accomplishments that also answers the questions "Why and how did you decide on a career in metal working? Why do you think you should receive this scholarship?"
RENEWABLE: Yes. Must reapply.
CONTACT: Lisa Martin, Executive Director, at lisa@maine-metals.org or at 207/329-9923

1403—MICRON TECHNOLOGY FOUNDATION

8000 S Federal Way
Mailstop 1-407
Boise ID 83706
208/368-2658
FAX: 208/368-4435
Internet: http://www.micron.com/ab out/foundation/scholarships
AMOUNT: $55,000 and up to 12 @ $16,500
DEADLINE(S): JAN 20
FIELD(S): Electrical, Chemical, Computer & Mechanical Engineering; Chemistry; Physics; Computer & Material Science
ELIGIBILITY/REQUIREMENTS: High school senior; resident of Idaho, Colorado, Texas or Virginia; combined SAT score of at least 1350 or a composite ACT score of at least 30; unweighted GPA of at least 3.5; demonstrated leadership in school, work and/or extracurricular activities. An essay and possible interview are also required. Scholarships can be used at any U.S. 4-year accredited school.
HOW TO APPLY: Download an application from www.micron.scholarshipamerica.org or see your high school counselor.
NUMBER OF AWARDS: Up to 13
RENEWABLE: Yes. Remain eligible, the money is spread over 4 years.
CONTACT: Scholarship America at 800/537-4180

1404—NASF/AESF FOUNDATION HEADQUARTERS

Scholarship Committee
1155 Fifteenth Street, NW, Suite 500
Washington, DC 20005
NASF Headquarters Phone: 202/457-8404
AESF Foundation Phone: 202/457-8401
FAX: 202-530-0659

E-mail: tkoehler@nasf.org or mwalker@nasf.org.
Internet: http://www.nasf.org
AMOUNT: $1,500
DEADLINE(S): APR 15
FIELD(S): Metallurgy; Chemistry; Materials Science; Metallurgical, Chemical, & Environmental Engineering
ELIGIBILITY/REQUIREMENTS: Must be full-time junior or senior undergraduate. Selection based on achievement, scholarship potential, motivation, and career interest in surface finishing technologies, not necessarily financial need.
HOW TO APPLY: See website for application or contact AESF for application and additional information. Submit with statement (maximum of 2 pages) describing career objectives, plans for study in plating and surface finishing technologies, and long-range goals; list or résumé (maximum 2 pages) detailing educational achievements; 3 letters of recommendation from teachers, professors, or employers (1 of which must be from academic major advisor); and transcript of recent academic records.
NUMBER OF AWARDS: Varies
RENEWABLE: Yes. Must reapply; maximum 2 years undergraduate; may reapply as a graduate student.
CONTACT: Tracey Koehler, Membership Director, or Melissa Walker

1405—THE ROCKY MOUNTAIN COAL MINING INSTITUTE (Engineering-Geology Scholarship)

8057 South Yukon Way
Littleton CO 80128-5510
303/948-3300
FAX: 303/948-1132
E-mail: mail@rmcmi.org
Internet: http://www.rmcmi.org
AMOUNT: $4,000 ($2,000 per year)
DEADLINE(S): FEB 3
FIELD(S): Mining; Geology, Mineral Processing; Metallurgy, Electrical, Mechanical, & Environmental Engineering
ELIGIBILITY/REQUIREMENTS: Must be a full-time college sophomore or junior in good standing at the time of selection; a U.S. citizen and a legal resident of one of the RMCMI member states (Arizona, Colorado, Montana, New Mexico, North Dakota, Texas, Utah, and Wyoming); pursuing a degree in a mining-related field; and have an expressed interest in Western coal as a career path.
HOW TO APPLY: See website for application. Send completed application; list of academic and athletic honors received; list of miscellaneous extracurricular activities;

list of work experience; 3 references; answers of 100 words or less to each of the following questions: "Why are you pursuing your present degree? What do you envision doing after graduation? What do you do to make learning exciting and productive?" Personal statement (why you are applying for this scholarship, special skills or trainings, etc.) optional.
RENEWABLE: Yes. Upon recommendation from the dean of college/university. Must remain a full-time student in good standing.

1406—SOCIETY OF AUTOMOTIVE ENGINEERS (Arkansas Tech University/ SAE Engineering Scholarship)

SAE Customer Service
400 Commonwealth Drive
Warrendale PA 15096-0001
724/776-4970
FAX: 724/776-1615
E-mail: customerservice@sae.org
Internet: http://www.sae.org/ students/scholarships
AMOUNT: $1,000-$4,000
DEADLINE(S): DEC 1
FIELD(S): Mechanical Engineering; Electrical Engineering; Automotive Industry
ELIGIBILITY/REQUIREMENTS: Must be an incoming freshman or transfer student. Selection will be based on academic and leadership activities. Eligible students will have a minimum 980 SAT or 21 ACT composite score, and 3.25 GPA.
HOW TO APPLY: See website for application. Submit application; a personal essay that demonstrates hands-on experience or activity (such as rebuilding engines, working on cars/trucks, etc.); 2 recommendations, 1 of which must be from a teacher, counselor, or administrator; and transcript.
NUMBER OF AWARDS: At least 2
RENEWABLE: Yes. A total of $4,000-$16,000 (over 4-year period) will be awarded if student remains an engineering student in good standing and enrolls in and completes 15 or more hours with a 3.25 GPA each semester.

1407—SOCIETY OF AUTOMOTIVE ENGINEERS (Drexel University/SAE Engineering Scholarship)

400 Commonwealth Drive
Warrendale PA 15096-0001
724/776-4970
FAX: 724/776-1615
E-mail: customerservice@sae.org

Internet: http://www.sae.org/ students/scholarships
AMOUNT: $5,000
DEADLINE(S): DEC 1
FIELD(S): Mechanical Engineering; Automotive Industry
ELIGIBILITY/REQUIREMENTS: Applicant must be an incoming freshman. Must have a minimum 1200 SAT or 27 ACT score and a 3.0 GPA.
HOW TO APPLY: See website for application. Submit application; a personal essay that demonstrates hands-on experience or activity (such as rebuilding engines, working on cars/trucks, etc.); 2 recommendations, 1 of which must be from a teacher, counselor, or administrator; and transcript.
NUMBER OF AWARDS: 1
RENEWABLE: Yes. For 1 additional year if a 3.0 GPA is maintained and student remains in the engineering program.

1408—SOCIETY OF AUTOMOTIVE ENGINEERS (John Deere and Bradley University/SAE Engineering Scholarships)

SAE Customer Service
400 Commonwealth Drive
Warrendale PA 15096-0001
724/776-4970
FAX: 724/776-1615
E-mail: customerservice@sae.org
Internet: http://www.sae.org/ students/scholarships
AMOUNT: $1,250
DEADLINE(S): DEC 1
FIELD(S): Mechanical, Electrical, Computer, Industrial, or Manufacturing Engineering; Automotive Industry
ELIGIBILITY/REQUIREMENTS: Applicants must be incoming freshmen accepted into the College of Engineering and Technology at Bradley. Selection is based on high school GPA, rank in class, curriculum and SAT/ACT scores. A minimum 980 SAT or 21 ACT composite score, and 3.25 GPA.
HOW TO APPLY: See website for application. Submit application; a personal essay that demonstrates hands-on experience or activity (such as rebuilding engines, working on cars/trucks, etc.); 2 recommendations, 1 of which must be from a teacher, counselor, or administrator; and transcript.
NUMBER OF AWARDS: Varies
RENEWABLE: Yes. A total of $5,000 (4-year period) if student remains enrolled in one of the specified majors and maintains a 3.0 GPA.

1409—SOCIETY OF AUTOMOTIVE ENGINEERS (Milwaukee School of Engineering/SAE Engineering Scholarship)

SAE Customer Service
400 Commonwealth Drive
Warrendale PA 15096-0001
724/776-4970
FAX: 724/776-1615
E-mail: customerservice@sae.org
Internet: http://www.sae.org/ students/scholarships
AMOUNT: $1,000
DEADLINE(S): DEC 1
FIELD(S): Mechanical Engineering; Mechanical Engineering Technology
ELIGIBILITY/REQUIREMENTS: Must be incoming freshman accepted into either the Mechanical Engineering or Mechanical Engineering Technology program.
HOW TO APPLY: See website for application. Submit application; a personal essay that demonstrates hands-on experience or activity (such as rebuilding engines, working on cars/trucks, etc.); 2 recommendations, 1 of which must be from a teacher, counselor, or administrator; and transcript.
NUMBER OF AWARDS: 1
RENEWABLE: Yes. For up to 3 additional years if the student maintains a 2.5 GPA.

1410—SOCIETY OF AUTOMOTIVE ENGINEERS (Ohio Northern University/ SAE Engineering Scholarship)

SAE Customer Service
400 Commonwealth Drive
Warrendale PA 15096-0001
724/776-4970
FAX: 724/776-1615
E-mail: customerservice@sae.org
Internet: http://www.sae.org/ students/scholarships
AMOUNT: $1,000
DEADLINE(S): DEC 1
FIELD(S): Mechanical Engineering; Automotive Industry
ELIGIBILITY/REQUIREMENTS: Students must be high school seniors intending to pursue a degree in mechanical engineering on a full-time basis, who have been admitted to the College of Engineering. Eligible applicants will have a minimum 1230 SAT or 27 ACT composite score, and a 3.5 GPA. Recipient will be expected to participate and assume a leadership role with the student branch of SAE at ONU.
HOW TO APPLY: See website for application. Submit application; a personal

essay that demonstrates hands-on experience or activity (such as rebuilding engines, working on cars/trucks, etc.); 2 recommendations, 1 of which must be from a teacher, counselor, or administrator; and transcript.
NUMBER OF AWARDS: 1
RENEWABLE: Yes. Providing the student maintains a cumulative GPA of 3.0 and remains enrolled full time in the mechanical engineering program.

1411—SOCIETY OF AUTOMOTIVE ENGINEERS (Oklahoma State University [CEAT]/SAE Engineering Scholarship)

SAE Customer Service
400 Commonwealth Drive
Warrendale PA 15096-0001
724/776-4970
FAX: 724/776-1615
E-mail: customerservice@sae.org
Internet: http://www.sae.org/students/scholarships
AMOUNT: $1,000
DEADLINE(S): DEC 1
FIELD(S): Mechanical, Electrical, & Industrial Engineering
ELIGIBILITY/REQUIREMENTS: High school graduates with a 3.8 or greater GPA and an ACT of 30 (SAT 1350) or above who plan to major in mechanical, electrical, or industrial engineering.
HOW TO APPLY: See website for application. Submit application; a personal essay that demonstrates hands-on experience or activity (such as rebuilding engines, working on cars/trucks, etc.); 2 recommendations, 1 of which must be from a teacher, counselor, or administrator; and transcript.
NUMBER OF AWARDS: 1
RENEWABLE: Yes. For 3 additional years.

1412—SOCIETY OF AUTOMOTIVE ENGINEERS (Parks College of Saint Louis University/SAE Engineering Scholarship)

SAE Customer Service
400 Commonwealth Drive
Warrendale PA 15096-0001
724/776-4970
FAX: 724/776-1615
E-mail: customerservice@sae.org
Internet: http://www.sae.org/students/scholarships
AMOUNT: $1,000
DEADLINE(S): DEC 1
FIELD(S): Aerospace, Mechanical, Electrical, Biomedical, Aircraft Maintenance, Avionics Engineering;

Applied Computer Science & Software Systems; Physics
ELIGIBILITY/REQUIREMENTS: Entering freshman majoring and enrolled in a baccalaureate program. Award based on academic achievement and financial need.
HOW TO APPLY: See website for application. Submit application; a personal essay that demonstrates hands-on experience or activity (such as rebuilding engines, working on cars/trucks, etc.); 2 recommendations, 1 of which must be from a teacher, counselor, or administrator; and transcript.
NUMBER OF AWARDS: 1
RENEWABLE: No

1413—SOCIETY OF AUTOMOTIVE ENGINEERS (Ralph K. Hillquist Honorary SAE Scholarship)

SAE Customer Service
400 Commonwealth Drive
Warrendale PA 15096-0001
724/776-4970
FAX: 724/776-1615
E-mail: customerservice@sae.org
Internet: http://www.sae.org/students/scholarships
AMOUNT: $1,000
DEADLINE(S): FEB 1
FIELD(S): Mechanical Engineering; Physics
ELIGIBILITY/REQUIREMENTS: U.S. citizen enrolled full time as a junior in a U.S. university. A minimum 3.0 GPA with significant academic and leadership achievements is required. Must also have a declared major in mechanical engineering or an automotive-related engineering discipline, with preference given to those with studies/courses in the areas of experience/expertise related to noise and vibrations (for example: statistics, dynamics, physics, vibration).
HOW TO APPLY: See website for application. Submit application; personal essay; 2 recommendations, 1 of which must be from a teacher, counselor, or administrator; and transcript.
NUMBER OF AWARDS: 1
RENEWABLE: No

1414—SOCIETY OF AUTOMOTIVE ENGINEERS (University of Alabama/James C. Lewis/SAE Engineering Scholarship)

SAE Customer Service
400 Commonwealth Drive
Warrendale PA 15096-0001
724/776-4970
FAX: 724/776-1615

E-mail: customerservice@sae.org
Internet: http://www.sae.org/students/scholarships
AMOUNT: $1,000
DEADLINE(S): DEC 1
FIELD(S): Mechanical Engineering; Automotive Industry
ELIGIBILITY/REQUIREMENTS: Must be admitted to the College of Engineering with a major in mechanical engineering. Applicants with a minimum ACT of 27 and minimum academic GPA of 3.5 will be considered based on academic performance, extracurricular activities, and essay.
HOW TO APPLY: See website for application. Submit application, including copies of FAFSA forms, a personal essay that demonstrates hands-on experience or activity (such as rebuilding engines, working on cars/trucks, etc.); 2 recommendations, 1 of which must be from a teacher, counselor, or administrator; and transcript.
NUMBER OF AWARDS: 1
RENEWABLE: Yes. A total of $4,000 (over 4-year period) will be awarded if student maintains a minimum 3.0 GPA and continued enrollment in Mechanical Engineering at the University of Alabama.

1415—SOCIETY OF AUTOMOTIVE ENGINEERS (University of Arkansas/SAE Engineering Scholarship)

400 Commonwealth Drive
Warrendale PA 15096-0001
724/776-4970
FAX: 724/776-1615
E-mail: customerservice@sae.org
Internet: http://www.sae.org/students/scholarships
AMOUNT: $500
DEADLINE(S): DEC 1
FIELD(S): Mechanical Engineering; Automotive Industry
ELIGIBILITY/REQUIREMENTS: Must be high school seniors seeking a degree in mechanical engineering. Applicants will be awarded based on the merits of SAT or ACT scores, high school GPA, and extracurricular activities.
HOW TO APPLY: See website for application. Submit application; a personal essay that demonstrates hands-on experience or activity (such as rebuilding engines, working on cars/trucks, etc.); 2 recommendations, 1 of which must be from a teacher, counselor, or administrator; and transcript.
NUMBER OF AWARDS: 1
RENEWABLE: Yes. A total of $2,000 (over 4-year period) will be awarded if student maintains reasonable progress toward degree.

1416—SOCIETY OF AUTOMOTIVE ENGINEERS (University of Wisconsin/Sundstrand/SAE Engineering Scholarship)

SAE Customer Service
400 Commonwealth Drive
Warrendale PA 15096-0001
724/776-4970
FAX: 724/776-1615
E-mail: customerservice@sae.org
Internet: http://www.sae.org/students/scholarships
AMOUNT: $500
DEADLINE(S): DEC 1
FIELD(S): Mechanical Engineering; Automotive Industry
ELIGIBILITY/REQUIREMENTS: Must be high school seniors planning to enter the Mechanical Engineering Program. Based on the following minimum requirements: 1100 SAT or 26 ACT and a 3.3 high school GPA.
HOW TO APPLY: See website for application. Submit application; a personal essay that demonstrates hands-on experience or activity (such as rebuilding engines, working on cars/trucks, etc.); 2 recommendations, 1 of which must be from a teacher, counselor, or administrator; and transcript. Recipient must be accepted into the College of Engineering and Applied Science by April 1.
NUMBER OF AWARDS: 1
RENEWABLE: No
CONTACT: UWM Office of Admissions, P.O. Box 749, Milwaukee, WI 53201

1417—SOCIETY OF AUTOMOTIVE ENGINEERS (University of Wyoming/Mechanical Engineering/SAE Engineering Scholarship)

SAE Customer Service
400 Commonwealth Drive
Warrendale PA 15096-0001
724/776-4970
FAX: 724/776-1615
E-mail: customerservice@sae.org
Internet: http://www.sae.org/students/scholarships
AMOUNT: $1,000
DEADLINE(S): DEC 1
FIELD(S): Mechanical Engineering; Automotive Industry
ELIGIBILITY/REQUIREMENTS: Open to incoming freshmen pursuing a degree in Mechanical Engineering Program. Based on merit and the following minimum requirements: 1350 SAT or 28 ACT, a 3.5 high school GPA, and school and civic honors and activities participation.

HOW TO APPLY: See website for application. Submit application; a personal essay that demonstrates hands-on experience or activity (such as rebuilding engines, working on cars/trucks, etc.); 2 recommendations, 1 of which must be from a teacher, counselor, or administrator; and transcript. Recipient must be accepted into the College of Engineering and Applied Science by April 1.
NUMBER OF AWARDS: 1
RENEWABLE: Yes. Up to 4 years if student maintains a 3.4 or better GPA, with a minimum of 24 credit hours applicable to degree.

1418—SOCIETY OF AUTOMOTIVE ENGINEERS (York College/IAC Scholar/SAE Engineering Scholarship)

SAE Customer Service
400 Commonwealth Drive
Warrendale PA 15096-0001
724/776-4970
FAX: 724/776-1615
E-mail: customerservice@sae.org
Internet: http://www.sae.org/students/scholarships
AMOUNT: 1/3 tuition
DEADLINE(S): DEC 1
FIELD(S): Mechanical Engineering; Automotive Industry
ELIGIBILITY/REQUIREMENTS: Open to incoming freshmen pursuing a degree in Mechanical Engineering Program. Based on merit and the following minimum requirements: 1200 SAT, top 1/5 of high school graduating class, and full admission into engineering program.
HOW TO APPLY: See website for application. Submit application; a personal essay that demonstrates hands-on experience or activity (such as rebuilding engines, working on cars/trucks, etc.); 2 recommendations, 1 of which must be from a teacher, counselor, or administrator; and transcript. Prospective recipient must be accepted to York College by February 1.
NUMBER OF AWARDS: 1
RENEWABLE: Yes. Up to 4 years if student maintains a 3.25 or better GPA (for students with GPA between 3.0 and 3.24, 1/2 of the scholarship will be awarded).

1419—SPE FOUNDATION, THE (Blow Molding Division Memorial Scholarships)

14 Fairfield Drive
Brookfield CT 06804
203/740-5447
FAX: 203/775-1157
E-mail: foundation@4spe.org

Internet: http://www.4spe.org/foundation/scholarships.php
AMOUNT: $8,000 (payable over 2 years)
DEADLINE(S): JAN 15
FIELD(S): Polymer Science; Chemistry; Physics; Plastics, Chemical, Mechanical, & Industrial Engineering
ELIGIBILITY/REQUIREMENTS: Applicants must be completing the 2nd year of a 4-year undergraduate plastics engineering program and be a member of a Society of Plastics Engineers (SPE student chapter.
HOW TO APPLY: Complete application; submit 3 recommendation letters (2 from a teacher or school official and 1 from an employer or non-relative); high school and/or college transcript for last 2 years; a 1- to 2-page brief essay on the importance of blow molding to the technical parts and packaging industries. Submit brief essay that describes the importance of blow molding to the technical parts and packaging industries, and why the applicant desires a career in the plastics industry.
NUMBER OF AWARDS: Up to 2

1420—SPE FOUNDATION, THE (Composites Division/Harold Giles Scholarship)

14 Fairfield Drive
Brookfield CT 06804
203/740-5447
FAX: 203/775-1157
E-mail: foundation@4spe.org
Internet: http://www.4spe.org/foundation/scholarships.php
AMOUNT: $1,000
DEADLINE(S): JAN 15
FIELD(S): Polymer Science; Chemistry; Physics; Chemical, Plastics, Mechanical & Industrial Engineering
ELIGIBILITY/REQUIREMENTS: Applicants must have experience in the composites industry (such as courses taken, research conducted, or jobs held); must be in good standing with their colleges and have demonstrated an interest in the plastics industry; majoring in or taking courses that would be beneficial to a career in the plastics/polymer industry. Financial need is considered.
HOW TO APPLY: Complete application; submit 3 recommendation letters (2 from a teacher or school official and 1 from an employer or non-relative); high school and/or college transcript for last 2 years; a 1- to 2-page statement telling why you are applying for the scholarship and educational and career goals in the plastics industry. Include a statement detailing exposure to the composites industry.
NUMBER OF AWARDS: 1

1421—SPE FOUNDATION, THE (Extrusion Division/Lew Erwin Memorial Scholarship)

14 Fairfield Drive
Brookfield CT 06804
203/740-5447
FAX: 203/775-1157
E-mail: foundation@4spe.org
Internet: http://www.4spe.org/foundation/scholarships.php
AMOUNT: $2,500
DEADLINE(S): JAN 15
FIELD(S): Polymer Science; Chemistry; Physics; Chemical, Plastics, Mechanical & Industrial Engineering
ELIGIBILITY/REQUIREMENTS: Supports undergraduate or graduate research in the field of polymer extrusion. Must be working in a senior or MS project that the scholarship will help support.
HOW TO APPLY: The project must be described in writing, including background, objective and proposed experiments. The recipient will be expected to furnish a final research summary report. Complete application; submit 3 recommendation letters (2 from a teacher or school official and 1 from an employer or non-relative); high school and/or college transcript for last 2 years; a 1- to 2-page statement telling why you are applying for the scholarship and educational and career goals in the plastics industry.
NUMBER OF AWARDS: 1
RENEWABLE: Yes. Must reapply for 3 additional years.

1422—SPE FOUNDATION, THE (Fleming/Biaszcek Scholarship)

14 Fairfield Drive
Brookfield CT 06804
203/740-5447
FAX: 203/775-1157
E-mail: foundation@4spe.org
Internet: http://www.4spe.org/foundation/scholarships.php
AMOUNT: $2,000
DEADLINE(S): JAN 15
FIELD(S): Polymer Science; Chemistry; Physics; Chemical, Plastics, Mechanical & Industrial Engineering
ELIGIBILITY/REQUIREMENTS: Available to full-time undergraduate students at a 4-year college, or students enrolled in a graduate program. Applicants for this award must be of Mexican descent and citizens or legal residents of the U.S. Applicants must be in good standing with their colleges and have demonstrated an interest in the plastics industry; majoring in or taking courses that would be beneficial to a career in the plastics/polymer industry. Financial need is considered for most scholarships.
HOW TO APPLY: Complete application; submit 3 recommendation letters (2 from a teacher or school official and 1 from an employer or non-relative); high school and/or college transcript for last 2 years; a 1- to 2-page statement telling why you are applying for the scholarship and educational and career goals in the plastics industry. Detail Mexican lineage in essay or on a separate sheet of paper.
NUMBER OF AWARDS: 1
RENEWABLE: Yes. Must reapply for 3 additional years.

1423—SPE FOUNDATION, THE (Foundation Scholarships)

14 Fairfield Drive
Brookfield CT 06804
203/740-5447
FAX: 203/775-1157
E-mail: foundation@4spe.org
Internet: http://www.4spe.org/foundation/scholarships.php
AMOUNT: $4,000
DEADLINE(S): JAN 15
FIELD(S): Polymer Science; Chemistry; Physics; Chemical, Plastics, Mechanical & Industrial Engineering
ELIGIBILITY/REQUIREMENTS: Must be in good standing with their colleges and have demonstrated an interest in the plastics industry; majoring in or taking courses that would be beneficial to a career in the plastics/polymer industry. Financial need is considered for most scholarships.
HOW TO APPLY: Complete application; submit 3 recommendation letters (2 from a teacher or school official and 1 from an employer or non-relative); high school and/or college transcript for last 2 years; a 1- to 2-page statement telling why you are applying for the scholarship and educational and career goals in the plastics industry.
NUMBER OF AWARDS: Multiple
RENEWABLE: Yes. Must reapply for 3 additional years.

1424—SPE FOUNDATION, THE (Gulf Coast Hurricane Scholarships)

14 Fairfield Drive
Brookfield CT 06804
203/740-5447
FAX: 203/775-1157
E-mail: foundation@4spe.org
Internet: http://www.4spe.org/foundation/scholarships.php
AMOUNT: $6,000 (college or university), $2,000 (junior or technical)
DEADLINE(S): JAN 15
FIELD(S): Polymer Science; Chemistry; Physics; Chemical, Plastics, Mechanical & Industrial Engineering
ELIGIBILITY/REQUIREMENTS: Must have been a resident of a Gulf Coast County declared a national disaster area as a result of Hurricanes Katrina, Rita or Wilma, and must be attending a university, college or technical institute in a Gulf Coast State (Florida, Alabama, Mississippi, Louisiana, Texas). Must be in good standing with their colleges (minimum GPA 2.0) and enrolled 6 hours/semester. Must have demonstrated an interest in the plastics industry; majoring in or taking courses that would be beneficial to a career in the plastics/polymer industry. Financial need is considered for most scholarships.
HOW TO APPLY: Complete application; submit 3 recommendation letters (2 from a teacher or school official and 1 from an employer or non-relative); high school and/or college transcript for last 2 years; a 1- to 2-page statement telling why you are applying for the scholarship and educational and career goals in the plastics industry. Must provide proof of residence.
NUMBER OF AWARDS: 3; 1 college or university, 2 junior college or technical school
RENEWABLE: Yes. Must reapply for 3 additional years.

1425—SPE FOUNDATION, THE (Injection Molding Division Scholarship)

14 Fairfield Drive
Brookfield CT 06804
203/740-5447
FAX: 203/775-1157
E-mail: foundation@4spe.org
Internet: http://www.4spe.org/foundation/scholarships.php
AMOUNT: $3,000
DEADLINE(S): JAN 15
FIELD(S): Polymer Science; Chemistry; Physics; Chemical, Plastics, Mechanical & Industrial Engineering
ELIGIBILITY/REQUIREMENTS: Available to undergraduates at a 4-year. Applicants must have experience in the injection molding industry (such as courses taken, research conducted, or jobs held), be in good standing with their colleges and have demonstrated an interest in the plastics industry; majoring in or taking courses that would be beneficial to a career in the plastics/polymer industry. Financial need is considered.
HOW TO APPLY: Complete application; submit 3 recommendation letters (2 from a

teacher or school official and 1 from an employer or non-relative); high school and/or college transcript for last 2 years; a 1- to 2-page statement telling why you are applying for the scholarship and educational and career goals in the plastics industry.
NUMBER OF AWARDS: 1
RENEWABLE: Yes. Must reapply for 3 additional years.

1426—SPE FOUNDATION, THE (Pittsburgh Section Scholarships)

14 Fairfield Drive
Brookfield CT 06804
203/740-5447
FAX: 203/775-1157
E-mail: foundation@4spe.org
Internet: http://www.4spe.org/ foundation/scholarships.php
AMOUNT: $2,000
DEADLINE(S): JAN 15
FIELD(S): Polymer Science; Chemistry; Physics; Chemical, Plastics, Mechanical & Industrial Engineering
ELIGIBILITY/REQUIREMENTS: Must have graduated from a high school in one of the following PA counties: Allegheny, Armstrong, Beaver, Bedford, Blair, Brooke, Butler, Cambria, Clarion, Clearfield, Fayette, Greene, Hancock, Indiana, Jefferson, Lawrence, Mercer, Somerset, Venango, Washington, Westmoreland. Must be in good standing with their colleges and have demonstrated an interest in the plastics industry; majoring in or taking courses that would be beneficial to a career in the plastics/polymer industry. Financial need is considered for most scholarships.
HOW TO APPLY: Complete application; submit 3 recommendation letters (2 from a teacher or school official and 1 from an employer or non-relative); high school and/or college transcript for last 2 years; a 1- to 2-page statement telling why you are applying for the scholarship and educational and career goals in the plastics industry. Must provide proof of graduation from school in one of above counties.
NUMBER OF AWARDS: Up to 2
RENEWABLE: Yes. Must reapply for 3 additional years.

1427—SPE FOUNDATION, THE (Plastics Pioneers Association Scholarships)

14 Fairfield Drive
Brookfield CT 06804
203/740-5447
FAX: 203/775-1157
E-mail: foundation@4spe.org

Internet: http://www.4spe.org/ foundation/scholarships.php
AMOUNT: $3,000
DEADLINE(S): JAN 15
FIELD(S): Polymer Science; Chemistry; Physics; Chemical, Plastics, Mechanical & Industrial Engineering
ELIGIBILITY/REQUIREMENTS: Open to undergraduate students, including those enrolled in associate or technical degree programs, who are committed to becoming "hands on" workers in the plastics industry as plastics technicians or engineers. Must be in good standing with their colleges and have demonstrated an interest in the plastics industry; majoring in or taking courses that would be beneficial to a career in the plastics/polymer industry. Financial need is considered for most scholarships.
HOW TO APPLY: Complete application; submit 3 recommendation letters (2 from a teacher or school official and 1 from an employer or non-relative); high school and/or college transcript for last 2 years; a 1- to 2-page statement telling why you are applying for the scholarship and educational and career goals in the plastics industry.
NUMBER OF AWARDS: Multiple
RENEWABLE: Yes. Must reapply for 3 additional years.

1428—SPE FOUNDATION, THE (Polymer Modifiers & Additives Division Scholarships)

14 Fairfield Drive
Brookfield CT 06804
203/740-5447
FAX: 203/775-1157
E-mail: foundation@4spe.org
Internet: http://www.4spe.org/ foundation/scholarships.php
AMOUNT: $4,000
DEADLINE(S): JAN 15
FIELD(S): Polymer Science; Chemistry; Physics; Chemical, Plastics, Mechanical & Industrial Engineering
ELIGIBILITY/REQUIREMENTS: Must be in good standing with their colleges and have demonstrated an interest in the plastics industry; majoring in or taking courses that would be beneficial to a career in the plastics/polymer industry. Financial need is considered for most scholarships.
HOW TO APPLY: Complete application; submit 3 recommendation letters (2 from a teacher or school official and 1 from an employer or non-relative); high school and/or college transcript for last 2 years; a 1- to 2-page statement telling why you are applying for the scholarship and educational and career goals in the plastics industry.

NUMBER OF AWARDS: 3
RENEWABLE: Yes. Must reapply for 3 additional years.

1429—SPE FOUNDATION, THE (Robert E. Cramer/Product Design & Development Division Scholarship)

14 Fairfield Drive
Brookfield CT 06804
203/740-5447
FAX: 203/775-1157
E-mail: foundation@4spe.org
Internet: http://www.4spe.org/ foundation/scholarships.php
AMOUNT: $1,000
DEADLINE(S): JAN 15
FIELD(S): Polymer Science; Chemistry; Physics; Chemical, Plastics, Mechanical & Industrial Engineering
ELIGIBILITY/REQUIREMENTS: Must be in good standing with their colleges and have demonstrated an interest in the plastics industry; majoring in or taking courses that would be beneficial to a career in the plastics/polymer industry. Financial need is considered for most scholarships.
HOW TO APPLY: Complete application; submit 3 recommendation letters (2 from a teacher or school official and 1 from an employer or non-relative); high school and/or college transcript for last 2 years; a 1- to 2-page statement telling why you are applying for the scholarship and educational and career goals in the plastics industry.
NUMBER OF AWARDS: 1
RENEWABLE: Yes. Must reapply for 3 additional years.

1430—SPE FOUNDATION, THE (Robert G. Dailey/Detroit Section Scholarship)

14 Fairfield Drive
Brookfield CT 06804
203/740-5447
FAX: 203/775-1157
E-mail: foundation@4spe.org
Internet: http://www.4spe.org/ foundation/scholarships.php
AMOUNT: $4,000
DEADLINE(S): JAN 15
FIELD(S): Polymer Science; Chemistry; Physics; Chemical, Plastics, Mechanical & Industrial Engineering
ELIGIBILITY/REQUIREMENTS: Must be in good standing with their colleges and have demonstrated an interest in the plastics industry; majoring in or taking courses that would be beneficial to a career in the plastics/polymer industry. Financial need is considered for most scholarships.

HOW TO APPLY: Complete application; submit 3 recommendation letters (2 from a teacher or school official and 1 from an employer or non-relative); high school and/or college transcript for last 2 years; a 1- to 2-page statement telling why you are applying for the scholarship and educational and career goals in the plastics industry.
NUMBER OF AWARDS: 1
RENEWABLE: Yes. Must reapply for 3 additional years.

1431—SPE FOUNDATION, THE (Ted and Ruth Neward Scholarships)

14 Fairfield Drive
Brookfield CT 06804
203/740-5447
FAX: 203/775-1157
E-mail: foundation@4spe.org
Internet: http://www.4spe.org/foundation/scholarships.php
AMOUNT: $3,000
DEADLINE(S): JAN 15
FIELD(S): Polymer Science; Chemistry; Physics; Chemical, Plastics, Mechanical & Industrial Engineering
ELIGIBILITY/REQUIREMENTS: Must be U.S. citizens in good standing with their colleges and have demonstrated an interest in the plastics industry; majoring in or taking courses that would be beneficial to a career in the plastics/polymer industry. Financial need is considered for most scholarships.
HOW TO APPLY: Complete application; submit 3 recommendation letters (2 from a teacher or school official and 1 from an employer or non-relative); high school and/or college transcript for last 2 years; a 1- to 2-page statement telling why you are applying for the scholarship and educational and career goals in the plastics industry.
NUMBER OF AWARDS: 3
RENEWABLE: Yes. Must reapply for 3 additional years.

1432—SPE FOUNDATION, THE (Thermoforming Division Memorial Scholarships)

14 Fairfield Drive
Brookfield CT 06804
203/740-5447
FAX: 203/775-1157
E-mail: foundation@4spe.org
Internet: http://www.4spe.org/foundation/scholarships.php
AMOUNT: $7,500
DEADLINE(S): JAN 15
FIELD(S): Polymer Science; Chemistry; Physics; Chemical, Plastics, Mechanical & Industrial Engineering

ELIGIBILITY/REQUIREMENTS: Available to graduate or undergraduate students at a 4-year college. Undergraduates must have completed at least 2 years of credits. Applicants must have experience in the thermoforming industry (such as courses taken, research conducted, or jobs held), be in good standing with their colleges and have demonstrated an interest in the plastics industry; majoring in or taking courses that would be beneficial to a career in the plastics/polymer industry. Financial need is considered for most scholarships.
HOW TO APPLY: Complete application; submit 3 recommendation letters (2 from a teacher or school official and 1 from an employer or non-relative); high school and/or college transcript for last 2 years; a 1- to 2-page statement telling why you are applying for the scholarship and educational and career goals in the plastics industry. Include a statement detailing exposure to the thermoforming industry.
NUMBER OF AWARDS: Varies (multiple awards)
RENEWABLE: Yes. Must reapply for 3 additional years.

1433—SPE FOUNDATION, THE (Thermoplastic Elastomers Special Interest Group Scholarship)

14 Fairfield Drive
Brookfield CT 06804
203/740-5447
FAX: 203/775-1157
E-mail: foundation@4spe.org
Internet: http://www.4spe.org/foundation/scholarships.php
AMOUNT: $1,000
DEADLINE(S): JAN 15
FIELD(S): Polymer Science; Chemistry; Physics; Chemical, Plastics, Mechanical & Industrial Engineering
ELIGIBILITY/REQUIREMENTS: Available to graduate or undergraduate students at a 4-year college. Applicants must have experience in the thermoplastic elastometers industry (such as courses taken, research conducted, or jobs held); must be in good standing with their colleges and have demonstrated an interest in the plastics industry; majoring in or taking courses that would be beneficial to a career in the plastics/polymer industry. Financial need is considered.
HOW TO APPLY: Complete application; submit 3 recommendation letters (2 from a teacher or school official and 1 from an employer or non-relative); high school and/or college transcript for last 2 years; a 1- to 2-page statement telling why you are applying for the scholarship and education-

al and career goals in the plastics industry. Include a statement detailing exposure to the thermoplastic elastometers industry.
NUMBER OF AWARDS: 1

1434—SPE FOUNDATION, THE (Thermoplastic Materials & Foams Division Scholarship)

14 Fairfield Drive
Brookfield CT 06804
203/740-5447
FAX: 203/775-1157
E-mail: foundation@4spe.org
Internet: http://www.4spe.org/foundation/scholarships.php
AMOUNT: $1,000
DEADLINE(S): JAN 15
FIELD(S): Polymer Science; Chemistry; Physics; Chemical, Plastics, Mechanical & Industrial Engineering
ELIGIBILITY/REQUIREMENTS: Must be in good standing with their colleges and have demonstrated an interest in the plastics industry; majoring in or taking courses that would be beneficial to a career in the plastics/polymer industry. Financial need is considered for most scholarships.
HOW TO APPLY: Complete application; submit 3 recommendation letters (2 from a teacher or school official and 1 from an employer or non-relative); high school and/or college transcript for last 2 years; a 1- to 2-page statement telling why you are applying for the scholarship and educational and career goals in the plastics industry.
NUMBER OF AWARDS: 1
RENEWABLE: Yes. Must reapply for 3 additional years.

1435—SPE FOUNDATION, THE (Thermoset Division/James I. MacKenzie Memorial Scholarship)

14 Fairfield Drive
Brookfield CT 06804
203/740-5447
FAX: 203/775-1157
E-mail: foundation@4spe.org
Internet: http://www.4spe.org/foundation/scholarships.php
AMOUNT: $2,500
DEADLINE(S): JAN 15
FIELD(S): Polymer Science; Chemistry; Physics; Chemical, Plastics, Mechanical & Industrial Engineering
ELIGIBILITY/REQUIREMENTS: Available to undergraduates at a 4-year college with GPA of 3.0 or better. Applicants must have experience in the thermoset industry (such as courses taken, research conducted, or jobs held), be in good standing with their colleges and have

demonstrated an interest in the plastics industry; majoring in or taking courses that would be beneficial to a career in the plastics/polymer industry. Financial need is considered for most scholarships.

HOW TO APPLY: Complete application; submit 3 recommendation letters (2 from a teacher or school official and 1 from an employer or non-relative); high school and/or college transcript for last 2 years; a 1- to 2-page statement telling why you are applying for the scholarship and educational and career goals in the plastics industry. Include a statement detailing exposure to the thermoset industry.

NUMBER OF AWARDS: 1

RENEWABLE: Yes. Must reapply for 3 additional years.

ADDITIONAL INFORMATION: Also includes all-expense-paid trip to, and speaking opportunity at, annual Madison Thermoset Molding Conference.

1436—SPE FOUNDATION, THE (Vinyl Plastics Division Scholarship)

14 Fairfield Drive
Brookfield CT 06804
203/740-5447
FAX: 203/775-1157
E-mail: foundation@4spe.org
Internet: http://www.4spe.org/
foundation/scholarships.php
AMOUNT: $3,000
DEADLINE(S): JAN 15
FIELD(S): Polymer Science; Chemistry; Physics; Chemical, Plastics, Mechanical & Industrial Engineering

ELIGIBILITY/REQUIREMENTS: Must be in good standing with their colleges and have demonstrated an interest in the plastics industry; majoring in or taking courses that would be beneficial to a career in the plastics/polymer industry. Preference given to applicants with experience in the vinyl industry (such as courses taken, research conducted, or jobs held). Financial need is considered for most scholarships.

HOW TO APPLY: Complete application; submit 3 recommendation letters (2 from a teacher or school official and 1 from an employer or non-relative); high school and/or college transcript for last 2 years; a 1- to 2-page statement telling why you are applying for the scholarship and educational and career goals in the plastics industry.

NUMBER OF AWARDS: 1

RENEWABLE: Yes. Must reapply for 3 additional years.

1436A—UNIVERSITY OF WINDSOR (Outstanding Scholars Award)

401 Sunset Avenue
Windsor Ontario N9B 3P4
CANADA
519/253-3000
FAX: 519/973-7081
E-mail: awards1@uwindsor.ca
Internet: http://www.uwindsor.ca
AMOUNT: $1,000-$2,500/year (Canadian); maximum 4 years
DEADLINE(S): MAY 31
FIELD(S): Classics, Modern Languages, French, Philosophy, Music, Physics, Earth Sciences (not Environmental Studies), Economics (not Business and Economics), Chemistry (not Biochemistry), Mathematics and Statistics, Industrial, Mechanical (Materials Option) or Environmental Engineering or Bachelor of Arts and Science program.

ELIGIBILITY/REQUIREMENTS: Open to undergraduate students registering in year 1 at the University of Windsor. Must have superior grades. Amount of award based on secondary school accomplishments.

HOW TO APPLY: Automatic. No application required.

RENEWABLE: Yes. Up to 4 years.

CONTACT: Aase Houser

ADDITIONAL INFORMATION: Students in this program will also be mentored in their first year in preparation for guaranteed Outstanding Scholars Appointments in their Department/School (valued at $2,000 Canadian in earnings for each of the 2nd, 3rd, and 4th years) provided all conditions are met.

1437—WASHINGTON APPLE EDUCATION FOUNDATION (Yakima Valley Grower-Shippers Association Scholarship)

P.O. Box 3720
Wenatchee WA 98807
509/663-7713
FAX: 509/663-7713
E-mail: waef@waef.org
Internet: http://www.ussui.org
AMOUNT: $750
DEADLINE(S): APR 1
FIELD(S): Agriculture; Horticulture; Business; Mechanical Engineering

ELIGIBILITY/REQUIREMENTS: Applicant must be employee or child of a general member of the YVGSA or the child of an employee or grower of a general member of the YVGSA. Applicant must be pursuing a degree compatible with service to the tree fruit industry.

HOW TO APPLY: See website for application.

NUMBER OF AWARDS: 2

RENEWABLE: No

CONTACT: Jennifer Whitney

1438—WEBB INSTITUTE (Naval Architecture Scholarships)

298 Crescent Beach Road
Glen Cove NY 11542-1398
516/671-2213
FAX: 516/674-9838
E-mail: admissions@webb-institute.edu
Internet: http://www.webb-institute.edu
AMOUNT: Full tuition for 4 years
DEADLINE(S): FEB 15
FIELD(S): Naval Architecture; Marine Engineering

ELIGIBILITY/REQUIREMENTS: Open to high school students aged 16-24 who are in the top 10% of their class, with a minimum 3.2 GPA. Based on college boards, SAT scores, and demonstrated interest in above areas. Must be U.S. citizen.

HOW TO APPLY: Contact Webb Institute for an application. Interview required.

NUMBER OF AWARDS: 20-25

1439—WESTERN MICHIGAN UNIVERSITY (College of Engineering and Applied Sciences/Edward Ravitz Memorial Scholarship in Construction Engineering)

1903 West Michigan
Kalamazoo MI 49008-5337
269/387-6000
FAX: 269/387-6989
E-mail: finaid-info@wmich.edu
Internet: http://www.wmich.edu/finaid
AMOUNT: $4,000/academic year for each of 4 years
FIELD(S): Mechanical Engineering (especially automotive)

ELIGIBILITY/REQUIREMENTS: Awarded to 1 new freshman admitted as an incoming, full-time (at least 12 credit hours) majoring in pre-engineering construction. Minimum 3.3 high school GPA. Award may be applied to tuition, fees, books, and educational expenses related to the general well-being of the student.

HOW TO APPLY: Contact the College of Engineering and Applied Science, Advising Office, Room E-102 Parkview Campus (269/276-3270) for an application.

NUMBER OF AWARDS: 1

RENEWABLE: No. However to continue receiving award, student must maintain a minimum 3.3 GPA at WMU. Enrolled as an undergraduate student in construction engineering.

1440—WESTERN MICHIGAN UNIVERSITY (College of Engineering and Applied Sciences/Kalamazoo Antique Auto Restorers Club Scholarship)

1903 West Michigan
Kalamazoo MI 49008-5337
269/387-6000
FAX: 269/387-6989
E-mail: finaid-info@wmich.edu
Internet: http://www.wmich.edu/finaid
AMOUNT: $500/semester
FIELD(S): Mechanical Engineering (especially automotive)
ELIGIBILITY/REQUIREMENTS: Open to Mechanical Engineering major with emphasis on automotive and an interest in restored vintage automobiles, GPA 2.5 or higher, Michigan resident. Must have completed 30 hours towards mechanical engineering major.
HOW TO APPLY: Advisor reviews records of potential candidates. Contact Mechanical Engineering Department for further information.
NUMBER OF AWARDS: 1
RENEWABLE: No

HUMANITIES
(ALL FIELDS)

1441—AMERICAN BAR FOUNDATION (Summer Research Diversity Fellowships in Law & Social Science)

750 North Lake Shore Drive
Chicago IL 60611
312/988-6560
FAX: 312/988-6579
E-mail: fellowships@abfn.org
Internet: http://www.americanbarfoundation.org
AMOUNT: $3,600
DEADLINE(S): Varies FEB/MAR 1
FIELD(S): Social Sciences; Humanities; Law
ELIGIBILITY/REQUIREMENTS: Open to sophomore and junior undergraduates including, but not limited to, Native American, African-American, Mexican, Puerto Rican, as well as other individuals who will add diversity to the field of law and social science. Must be U.S. citizen or permanent resident with 3.0 GPA. Students assigned a research mentor, participate in seminars, and work at the Foundation's office in Chicago for 35 hours/week for 8 weeks.

HOW TO APPLY: See website or contact ABF for application. Essay, transcripts, and letter of recommendation required.
NUMBER OF AWARDS: 4

1442—CALIFORNIA NURSES ASSOCIATION (Shirley Titus Scholarship Scholarship)

2000 Franklin Street
Oakland CA 94612
510/622-8310
FAX: 510/663-1625
E-mail: scholarship@calnurses.org
Internet: http://www.calnurses.org
AMOUNT: Varies
DEADLINE(S): JUL 1
FIELD(S): Nursing; Humanities, The Cultural, Political, Economic, Legal and Social Sciences
ELIGIBILITY/REQUIREMENTS: Open to California nurses for academic preparation and continuing education in above fields appropriate for developing effective nursing leadership.
HOW TO APPLY: See website for application or write or call for application. Submit with a 1 page typed essay, describing educational goals and how they relate to personal and professional vision for healthcare; 2 letters of recommendation, from non-relatives which must relate to this scholarship and address at least one of the following: CNA activities, competence in work setting, and academic ability; a curriculum vitae; and a copy of current RN license.
NUMBER OF AWARDS: Varies
CONTACT: Shaun Copeland

1442A—CHICAGO ROOFING CONTRACTORS ASSOCIATION

4415 W. Harrison Street, #322
Hillside IL 60162
708/449-3340
FAX: 708/449-0837
E-mail: info@crca.org
Internet: http://www.crca.org
AMOUNT: $3,000
DEADLINE(S): MAR (1st Friday)
FIELD(S): Business; Engineering; Architecture; Liberal Arts; Sciences
ELIGIBILITY/REQUIREMENTS: Open to high school seniors who reside in one of the eight counties in Northern Illinois: Cook, DuPage, Lake, Kane, Kendall, DeKalb, McHenry, or Will. Must be accepted as a full-time student in a 4-year college or university to pursue a degree in one of the above fields. Must be U.S. citizen. Based on academic achievements,

extracurricular activities, and community involvement.
HOW TO APPLY: See website for an application. Submit with 2 completed Personal Reference Forms (1 from high school guidance counselor or faculty member, an optional letter of recommendation may also be included; the other from an adult not related to the student); an official transcript of all high school records, and official ACT and/or SAT Test results or official high school transcript.
NUMBER OF AWARDS: 1 (In the event of a tie, financial need considered).
RENEWABLE: Yes (up to 3 times). Must maintain a 2.75 grade point average.

1443—CHINESE HISTORICAL SOCIETY OF SOUTHERN CALIFORNIA/DAVID AND PEARL LOUIE FOUNDATION

415 Bernard Street
Los Angeles CA 90012-1703
323/222-0856
FAX: 323/221-4812
E-mail: chssc@earthlink.net
Internet: http://www.chssc.org
AMOUNT: $1,000
DEADLINE(S): MAR 21, 1 PM
FIELD(S): Humanities; Social Sciences (emphasis on Chinese-American studies)
ELIGIBILITY/REQUIREMENTS: Must be enrolled undergraduate in an accredited college or university in Southern California. Preference given to those who will continue enrollment for full academic year. Minimum cumulative GPA of 3.0 required. Academic emphasis related to Chinese-American studies in the humanities or social sciences.
HOW TO APPLY: See website for application. Submit with research paper, preferably on Chinese-American theme (1,000-3,000 words), biographical essay discussing importance of Chinese studies to applicant as well as information about financial need, employment history, campus/community activities, and future plans (300-500 words), transcripts since high school (4 copies of each). Letters of recommendation optional. Finalists will be contacted for an oral interview.
NUMBER OF AWARDS: 1
CONTACT: Susie Ling, Scholarship Chair, shling@pasadena.edu

1444—CIVIL AIR PATROL (CAP Undergraduate Scholarships)

National Headquarters
Maxwell AFB AL 36112-6332
334/953-5315

AMOUNT: $750
DEADLINE(S): JAN 31
FIELD(S): Humanities; Science; Engineering; Education
ELIGIBILITY/REQUIREMENTS: Open to CAP members who have received the Billy Mitchell Award or the senior rating in Level II of the senior training program.
HOW TO APPLY: Write for information.

1445—COLLEGE MISERICORDIA (Presidential Scholarships)

301 Lake Street
Dallas PA 18612-1098
800/852-7675
E-mail: admiss@misericordia.edu
Internet: http://www.miseri.edu
AMOUNT: Full or part tuition
DEADLINE(S): MAR 1
FIELD(S): Pre-Law; Humanities
ELIGIBILITY/REQUIREMENTS: Open to high school seniors ranking in the upper 20% of their class, who have achieved SAT or ACT scores in the 8th percentile or better.
HOW TO APPLY: Obtain application from the Admissions Office.

1446—COMMUNITY FOUNDATION FOR GREATER ATLANTA, INC., THE (James M. & Virginia M. Smyth Scholarship Fund)

50 Hurt Plaza, Suite 449
Atlanta GA 30303
404/688-5525
FAX: 404/688-3060
E-mail: scholarships@atlcf.org
Internet: http://www.atlcf.org/GrantsScholarships/Scholarships.aspx
AMOUNT: $500-$1,000
DEADLINE(S): Varies
FIELD(S): Humanities, Science, Human Services, Music. Ministry
ELIGIBILITY/REQUIREMENTS: Open to students enrolled at an accredited college pursuing an undergraduate degree and adults returning to school in order to increase employability. Must have a cumulative 3.0 GPA; be accepted for enrollment or enrolled at an accredited college, university or technical school, demonstrate financial need; and commitment to community service through school; community or religious organizations. Preference will be given to applicants from Missouri, Mississippi, Georgia, Illinois, Oklahoma, Texas and Tennessee.
HOW TO APPLY: See website for additional information and application. Submit with a personal essay (2-3 pages) that explains why you feel a college education is important, your statement of educational and career goals, post college career interests, highlights of your high school extracurricular/community service activities, special strengths, skills, and qualifications, any unusual family or personal circumstances have affected your achievement in school, work experience, or your participation in school and community activities, and present financial need; official transcript; and SAT and ACT scores, if a recent high school graduate. Send to The Community Foundation for Greater Atlanta, James M. & Virginia M. Smyth Scholarship Fund, Scholarship Management Services, Scholarship America, One Scholarship Way, P.O. Box 297, Saint Peter, MN 56082. If you have questions, call 507/931-1682 or e-mail community-foundation@scholarshipamerica.org.
NUMBER OF AWARDS: 12-15
RENEWABLE: Yes; Previous recipients are renewed if they continue to meet the scholarship's criteria and submit the current year's renewal application
CONTACT: Lisa Glanville, 404/308-0055

1447—FREEDOM FROM RELIGION FOUNDATION (Student Essay Contests)

P.O. Box 750
Madison WI 53701
608/256-5800
Internet: http://www.ffrf.org
AMOUNT: $1,000; $500; $250
DEADLINE(S): College essays due JUL 1; High school essays due JUN 1
FIELD(S): Humanities; English; Education; Philosophy; Science
ELIGIBILITY/REQUIREMENTS: Topics change yearly, but all are on general theme of maintaining separation of church and state. Open to high school seniors and students currently enrolled in college or technical schools. Must be U.S. citizen.
HOW TO APPLY: See website for details. Send SASE to address above for complete information. Indicate whether you will be competing in the college or high school competition. Information will be sent when new topics are announced each February.

1448—INSTITUTE FOR HUMANE STUDIES (Humane Studies Fellowship)

3301 North Fairfax Drive, Suite 440
Arlington VA 22201-4432
703/993-4880 or 800/697-8799
FAX: 703/993-4890
E-mail: ihs@gmu.edu
Internet: http://www.TheIHS.org
AMOUNT: $12,000 (maximum)
DEADLINE(S): DEC
FIELD(S): Social Sciences; Liberal Arts; Law; Humanities; Jurisprudence; Journalism
ELIGIBILITY/REQUIREMENTS: Open to graduate and advanced undergraduate or law students pursuing degrees at any accredited domestic or foreign college or university. Based on academic performance, demonstrated interest in the classical liberal tradition, and potential to contribute to the advancement of a free society.
HOW TO APPLY: Apply online or contact IHS for an application.
NUMBER OF AWARDS: 90

1449—INSTITUTE FOR HUMANE STUDIES (Summer Seminars Program)

3401 North Fairfax Drive, Suite 440
Arlington VA 22201-4432
703/993-4880 or 800/697-8799
FAX: 703/993-4890
E-mail: ihs@gmu.edu
Internet: http://www.TheIHS.org
AMOUNT: Free summer seminars, including room/board, lectures, seminar materials, and books
DEADLINE(S): MAR
FIELD(S): Social Sciences; Humanities; Law; Journalism; Public Policy; Education; Film; Writing; Economics; Philosophy
ELIGIBILITY/REQUIREMENTS: Open to college students, recent graduates, and graduate students who share an interest in learning and exchanging ideas about the scope of individual rights, free markets, the rule of law, peace, and tolerance.
HOW TO APPLY: See website for information and to apply online, or contact IHS for an application.

1450—JACK J. ISGUR FOUNDATION

Stinson Morrison Hecker LLP
1201 Walnut Street, 26th Floor
Kansas City MO 64106
816/691-2760
FAX: 816/691-3495
E-mail: cjensen@stinson.com
AMOUNT: Varies
DEADLINE(S): APR 15
FIELD(S): Humanities Education
ELIGIBILITY/REQUIREMENTS: Funds for students desiring to teach humanities at the elementary and middle school levels. Preference given to students entering junior or subsequent years of college, and interested in teaching in the state

of Missouri in non-metropolitan school districts.

HOW TO APPLY: Contact Foundation for application.

NUMBER OF AWARDS: Varies

RENEWABLE: Yes, must reapply.

CONTACT: Charles F. Jensen

1451—JUNIOR ACHIEVEMENT INC. (DePauw University Holton Memorial Scholarship)

One Education Way
Colorado Springs CO 80906
719/540-8000
FAX: 719/540-6299
E-mail: newmedia@ja.org
Internet: http://www.ja.org
AMOUNT: $1,000-full tuition
DEADLINE(S): FEB 1
FIELD(S): Liberal Arts; Music

ELIGIBILITY/REQUIREMENTS: Applicants must be excellent students who have demonstrated outstanding leadership and/or exceptional service to their schools, family, church, or community.

HOW TO APPLY: Send application; SAT or ACT scores (TOEFL if English is second language); and a 250-word essay describing your commitment to service and/or leadership, with a résumé of your involvement.

NUMBER OF AWARDS: 50

RENEWABLE: Yes

CONTACT: Office of Admission, DePauw University, 101 East Seminary Street, Greencastle IN 46135-1611; 800/447-2495 or 765/658-4006; or admissions@depauw.edu; or at www.depauw.edu.

1452—MENSA EDUCATION AND RESEARCH FOUNDATION (Harper Fowley-Isolated M Award)

Internet: http://www.mensa foundation.org/AM/Template.cfm? Section=Scholarships1
AMOUNT: $600
DEADLINE(S): JAN 15
FIELD(S): Liberal Arts

ELIGIBILITY/REQUIREMENTS: Awards based on essays written by the applicant. No requirement for Mensa membership nor is consideration given for grades, academic program or financial need. Applicants must currently be a resident of a participating American Mensa local group's area and enrolled in a degree program in an accredited U.S. institution of higher learning during the academic year following the application date.

HOW TO APPLY: Each year the list of participating groups may change, see website for up-to-date information. Send application, available (if eligible) from the website or, by request with SASE, from local scholarship chairs. Submit with essay of not more than 550 words explaining your academic and/or vocational goals and plans to achieve those goals to the scholarship chair in your area.

1453—MIDWAY COLLEGE

512 East Stephens Street
Midway KY 40347
800/755-0031
E-mail: admissions@midway.edu
Internet: http://www.midway.edu
AMOUNT: Up to full tuition
DEADLINE(S): Varies
FIELD(S): Nursing; Education; Psychology; Biology; Equine Studies; Computer Information Systems; Business Administration; English; Pre-Med; Pre-Vet

ELIGIBILITY/REQUIREMENTS: Merit scholarships for admitted students who are considered full-time in Midway's women's college. Depending on scholarship, minimum GPA ranges from 2.5 to 3.2, minimum ACT ranges 18 to 29, minimum SAT from 860 to 1290. In some cases, students must live on campus.

HOW TO APPLY: Contact Admissions Office or high school guidance counselor for application. Complete FAFSA online.

NUMBER OF AWARDS: Varies, up to 100

RENEWABLE: Yes. Must meet GPA requirements which vary based on the scholarship.

CONTACT: Admissions Office or high school guidance counselor

ADDITIONAL INFORMATION: Athletes may be eligible for an athletic scholarship in conjunction with a merit grant; contact coach for eligibility and award information.

1454—NATIONAL FEDERATION OF THE BLIND (Humanities Scholarship)

805 5th Avenue
Grinnell IA 50112
641/236-3369
Internet: http://www.nfb.org/nfb/scholarship_program.asp
Internet: http://www.nfb.org
AMOUNT: $3,000
DEADLINE(S): MAR 31
FIELD(S): Humanities (Art, English, Foreign Languages, History, Philosophy, Religion)

ELIGIBILITY/REQUIREMENTS: Open to legally blind students pursuing or planning to pursue a full-time postsecondary education in the U.S. Awarded on basis of academic excellence, service to the community, and financial need. Membership NOT required.

HOW TO APPLY: Contact Scholarship Committee Chair for an application. Submit with transcripts and 2 letters of recommendation.

NUMBER OF AWARDS: 1

RENEWABLE: Yes

CONTACT: Peggy Elliot, Scholarship Committee Chair

1455—NORTH CAROLINA STATE UNIVERSITY (Thomas Jefferson Scholarship in Agriculture and Humanities)

Jefferson Scholars
College of Agriculture and Life Sciences
Box 7642
Raleigh NC 27695-7642
Internet: http://www.cals.ncsu.edu/student orgs/jeffer/apply.html
AMOUNT: $1,000
DEADLINE(S): FEB 6
FIELD(S): Agriculture AND Humanities

ELIGIBILITY/REQUIREMENTS: Open to first-year undergraduate students with a double major in agriculture and humanities.

HOW TO APPLY: See website or write for application and additional information. Submit with an essay, evaluation from a teacher or school official, and transcript.

NUMBER OF AWARDS: 15

RENEWABLE: Yes

1456—WESTERN MICHIGAN UNIVERSITY (College of Arts and Sciences Undergraduate Research and Creative Activities Award)

1903 West Michigan
Kalamazoo MI 49008-5337
269/387-8777
FAX: 269/387-6989
E-mail: finaid-info@wmich.edu
Internet: http://www.wmich.edu/finaid
AMOUNT: $500/semester
FIELD(S): Art; Science; History; Humanities; Law; Social Sciences

ELIGIBILITY/REQUIREMENTS: Must have declared a major in a department or program within the College; completed at least 30 credit hours; be in good academic standing; have a faculty mentor for the project and a project plan.

HOW TO APPLY: Contact the College of Arts and Sciences or www.wmich.edu/cas/research.html for an application.
RENEWABLE: Yes. May request renewal for 1 additional term.

1457—WESTERN MICHIGAN UNIVERSITY (Kathryn and Grant Leaske Memorial Endowed Scholarship)

1903 W. Michigan
Kalamazoo MI 49008-5337
269/387-8777
FAX: 269/387-6989
E-mail: finaid-info@wmich.edu
Internet: http://www.wmich.edu/finaid
AMOUNT: Varies
DEADLINE(S): MAR 1
FIELD(S): Arts; Sciences; Humanities; Social Sciences
ELIGIBILITY/REQUIREMENTS: Applicant must be a full-time undergraduate student whose major is in the College of Arts & Sciences; demonstrate financial need; have a 3.0 GPA; be able to document history of community/university service and volunteerism.
HOW TO APPLY: Contact the College of Arts and Sciences for an application or apply online or print application from website.
RENEWABLE: Yes. Up to 2 years depending on academic status.
CONTACT: Financial Aid

1458—WESTERN MICHIGAN UNIVERSITY (College of Arts and Sciences/Undergraduate Research and Creative Activities Award)

1903 W. Michigan
Kalamazoo MI 49008-5337
269/387-8777
FAX: 269/387-6989
E-mail: finaid-info@wmich.edu
Internet: http://www.wmich.edu/cas
AMOUNT: $500/semester
DEADLINE(S): MAR 1
FIELD(S): Sciences; Humanities; Social Sciences, Radio & Television
ELIGIBILITY/REQUIREMENTS: Applicant must have declared a major in a department or program in the College of Arts and Sciences; completed at least 30 credit hours; be in good academic standing; and have a faculty mentor for the project and a project plan.
HOW TO APPLY: Contact the College of Arts and Sciences for an application or apply online or print application from website.

RENEWABLE: Yes. May request renewal for 1 additional term.
CONTACT: College of Arts and Sciences

COMMUNICATIONS/ JOURNALISM

1459— ACADEMY OF TELEVISION ARTS & SCIENCES COLLEGE TELEVISION AWARD

5220 Lankershim Boulevard
North Hollywood CA 91601-3109
818/754-2820
FAX: 818/761-2827
E-mail: alavkin@emmys.org
Internet: http://www.emmys foundation.org
AMOUNT: $500-$2,000
DEADLINE(S): JAN 15
FIELD(S): Television
ELIGIBILITY/REQUIREMENTS: Awards achievement in each of the following categories: Animation (all forms), Children's, Comedy, Comedy Series, Commercial, Documentary, Drama, Drama Series, Magazine, Music (best composition), Music (best use of music), and Newscast.
HOW TO APPLY: See website for application information and guidelines
NUMBER OF AWARDS: Up to 27 (at least 1 in each category)
CONTACT: Debbie Slavkin, Program Manager/Development Associate
ADDITIONAL INFORMATION: May apply in more than 1 category; 1st entry is free; each subsequent entry is $25.00. (See complete guidelines and rules for more details.)

1460—AD CLUB SEATTLE (Kerin Keller Memorial Scholarship)

1006 Industry Drive
Seattle WA 98188
206/448-4481
E-mail: adclubdirector@verizon.net
Internet: http://www.collegeplan.org/cpnow/pnwguide/onlineaps/safonap.htm
AMOUNT: $500
DEADLINE(S): MAR 31
FIELD(S): Business (especially marketing, advertising, and public relations), Communications
ELIGIBILITY/REQUIREMENTS: Open to residents of Washington state attending or about to attend an in-state 2- or 4-year public, private, accredited college or university at the undergraduate level. Must demonstrate financial need (not necessarily the determining factor) and major in

business or communications. Focus on marketing, advertising and public relations is strongly encouraged. Because Keller was victim of breast cancer, applicant must be related to a victim of breast cancer.
HOW TO APPLY: See website for application; submit with a 1-page personal essay explaining your relationship to a victim of breast cancer and how this award will help you achieve your educational goals, a 1-page list of significant activities and honors, 2 letters of recommendation, an official transcript from the high school or college the student is currently attending or if not currently in school, an official transcript from the last school they attended, and FAFSA or FAFSA Student Aid Report (SAR).
NUMBER OF AWARDS: 1
RENEWABLE: No
CONTACT: Cindy Pennington, Executive Director

1461—ALASKA PROFESSIONAL COMMUNICATORS (Memorial Scholarship)

P.O. Box 104056
Anchorage, AK 99510
E-mail: chuff@kska.org
Internet: http://www.akprocom.org
AMOUNT: $2,500 (Gaston), $1,500 (Nolle)
DEADLINE(S): FEB 22
FIELD(S): Communications
ELIGIBILITY/REQUIREMENTS: Open to members of Alpha Chi; must be planning to enroll full time in the senior year of an undergraduate program in the fall of the award year.
HOW TO APPLY: See website for application. Submit with statement written by you, presenting your career goals and explaining why you desire the scholarship, at least 1 letter of reference, your transcripts and, if you choose, three samples of your work (recommended but optional).
NUMBER OF AWARDS: 2 (may vary)
CONTACT: Connie Huff, 907/273-9414 or e-mail

1462—AMERICAN INSTITUTE OF POLISH CULTURE

1440 79th Street Causeway,
Suite 117
Miami FL 33141
305/864-2349
FAX: 305/865-5150
E-mail: info@ampolinstitute.org
Internet: http://www.ampol institute.org
AMOUNT: $1,000
DEADLINE(S): FEB 15

FIELD(S): Journalism; Public Relations; Communications

ELIGIBILITY/REQUIREMENTS: Awards are to encourage young Americans of Polish descent to pursue the above professions. Can be used for full-time study at any accredited American college. Criteria include achievement, talent, and involvement in public life.

HOW TO APPLY: Send SASE to Institute for an application. $25 processing fee.

RENEWABLE: Yes

CONTACT: Harriet Irsay

1463—AMERICAN RADIO RELAY LEAGUE FOUNDATION (Charles N. Fisher Memorial Scholarship)

225 Main Street
Newington CT 06111
860/594-0397
FAX: 860/594-0259
E-mail: foundation@arrl.org
Internet: http://www.arrlf.org/

AMOUNT: $1,000

DEADLINE(S): FEB 1

FIELD(S): Electronics, Communications or related fields

ELIGIBILITY/REQUIREMENTS: For student with any class license pursuing baccalaureate or higher degree at a regionally accredited institution. Must be a resident of Southwestern Division (AZ and Los Angeles, Orange, San Diego, Santa Barbara, CA) attending a regionally accredited school.

HOW TO APPLY: See website or contact Foundation for information and application. Submit with a 1-page essay on the role amateur radio has played in your life. A recent high school (or equivalent) or college transcript required; submit with application or mail separately.

NUMBER OF AWARDS: 1

RENEWABLE: No

CONTACT: Mary M. Hobart, K1MMH, Secretary

1464—AMERICAN RADIO RELAY LEAGUE FOUNDATION (Dr. James L. Lawson Memorial Scholarship)

225 Main Street
Newington CT 06111
860/594-0397
FAX: 860/594-0259
E-mail: foundation@arrl.org
Internet: http://www.arrlf.org/

AMOUNT: $500

DEADLINE(S): FEB 1

FIELD(S): Electronics, Communications or related fields

ELIGIBILITY/REQUIREMENTS: For student with general license or higher pursuing baccalaureate or higher degree who is resident of New England states (ME, NH, VT, MA, CT, RI) or New York State and attending college in one of those states and pursuing degree in electronics, communications or related field.

HOW TO APPLY: See website or contact Foundation for information and application. Submit with a 1-page essay on the role amateur radio has played in your life. A recent high school (or equivalent) or college transcript required; submit with application or mail separately.

NUMBER OF AWARDS: 1

RENEWABLE: No

CONTACT: Mary M. Hobart, K1MMH, Secretary

1465—AMERICAN RADIO RELAY LEAGUE FOUNDATION (Fred R. McDaniel Memorial Scholarship)

225 Main Street
Newington CT 06111
860/594-0397
FAX: 860/594-0259
E-mail: foundation@arrl.org
Internet: http://www.arrlf.org/

AMOUNT: $500

DEADLINE(S): FEB 1

FIELD(S): Electronics, Communications or related fields

ELIGIBILITY/REQUIREMENTS: Open to radio amateurs holding a general license or higher who are FCC Fifth Call District (TX, OK, AR, LAS, MS, NM) residents attending 4-year college or university in the District and enrolled in baccalaureate or higher program. Minimum 3.0 GPA required.

HOW TO APPLY: See website or contact Foundation for information and application. Submit with a 1-page essay on the role amateur radio has played in your life. A recent high school (or equivalent) or college transcript required; submit with application or mail separately.

NUMBER OF AWARDS: 1

RENEWABLE: No

CONTACT: Mary M. Hobart, K1MMH, Secretary

1466—AMERICAN RADIO RELAY LEAGUE FOUNDATION (Irving W. Cook, WAOCGS Scholarship)

225 Main Street
Newington CT 06111
860/594-0397
FAX: 860/594-0259
E-mail: foundation@arrl.org
Internet: http://www.arrlf.org/

AMOUNT: $1,000

DEADLINE(S): FEB 1

FIELD(S): Electronics, Communications or related fields

ELIGIBILITY/REQUIREMENTS: For student or child of deceased radio amateur with any class license pursuing baccalaureate or higher degree at an accredited institution. Must be a resident of Kansas.

HOW TO APPLY: See website or contact Foundation for information and application. Submit with a 1-page essay on the role amateur radio has played in your life. A recent high school (or equivalent) or college transcript required; submit with application or mail separately.

NUMBER OF AWARDS: 1

RENEWABLE: No

CONTACT: Mary M. Hobart, K1MMH, Secretary

1467—AMERICAN RADIO RELAY LEAGUE FOUNDATION (L. Phil Wicker Scholarship)

225 Main Street
Newington CT 06111
860/594-0397
FAX: 860/594-0259
E-mail: foundation@arrl.org
Internet: http://www.arrlf.org/

AMOUNT: $1,000

DEADLINE(S): FEB 1

FIELD(S): Electronics, Communications or related fields

ELIGIBILITY/REQUIREMENTS: For student with general license or higher pursuing baccalaureate or higher degree at a regionally accredited institution. Must be a resident of Roanoke Division (NC, SC, VA, WV) attending school in that area.

HOW TO APPLY: See website or contact Foundation for information and application. Submit with a 1-page essay on the role amateur radio has played in your life. A recent high school (or equivalent) or college transcript required; submit with application or mail separately.

NUMBER OF AWARDS: 1

RENEWABLE: No

CONTACT: Mary M. Hobart, K1MMH, Secretary

1468—AMERICAN RADIO RELAY LEAGUE FOUNDATION (NEMAL Electronics Scholarship)

225 Main Street
Newington CT 06111
860/594-0397
FAX: 860/594-0259
E-mail: foundation@arrl.org
Internet: http://www.arrlf.org/

AMOUNT: $1,000

DEADLINE(S): FEB 1
FIELD(S): Electronics, Communications or related fields
ELIGIBILITY/REQUIREMENTS: For student with any general or higher license pursuing baccalaureate or higher degree at an accredited 2- or 4-year college or university. Preference given to applicants residing in the southeastern U.S. Must demonstrate financial need and have a minimum 3.0 GPA. Participation in community service or civic volunteer organizations preferred.
HOW TO APPLY: See website or contact Foundation for information and application. Submit with a 1-page essay on the role amateur radio has played in your life. A recent high school (or equivalent) or college transcript required; submit with application or mail separately.
NUMBER OF AWARDS: 1
RENEWABLE: No
CONTACT: Mary M. Hobart, K1MMH, Secretary

1469—AMERICAN RADIO RELAY LEAGUE FOUNDATION (Paul and Helen L. Grauer Scholarship)

225 Main Street
Newington CT 06111
860/594-0397
FAX: 860/594-0259
E-mail: foundation@arrl.org
Internet: http://www.arrlf.org/
AMOUNT: $1,000
DEADLINE(S): FEB 1
FIELD(S): Electronics, Communications or related fields
ELIGIBILITY/REQUIREMENTS: For student with novice license or higher pursuing baccalaureate or higher degree at a regionally accredited institution. Must be a resident of Midwest Division (IA, KS, MO, NE) attending school in that area.
HOW TO APPLY: See website or contact Foundation for information and application. Submit with a 1-page essay on the role amateur radio has played in your life. A recent high school (or equivalent) or college transcript required; submit with application or mail separately.
NUMBER OF AWARDS: 1
RENEWABLE: No
CONTACT: Mary M. Hobart, K1MMH, Secretary

1470—AMERICAN RADIO RELAY LEAGUE FOUNDATION (The Mississippi Scholarship)

225 Main Street
Newington CT 06111
860/594-0397
FAX: 860/594-0259
E-mail: foundation@arrl.org
Internet: http://www.arrl.org/
AMOUNT: $500
DEADLINE(S): FEB 1
FIELD(S): Electronics, Communications or related fields
ELIGIBILITY/REQUIREMENTS: For student under 30 with any class license pursuing baccalaureate or higher degree. Must be a resident of Mississippi attending school at a Mississippi institution.
HOW TO APPLY: See website or contact Foundation for information and application. Submit with a 1-page essay on the role amateur radio has played in your life. A recent high school (or equivalent) or college transcript required; submit with application or mail separately.
NUMBER OF AWARDS: 1
RENEWABLE: No
CONTACT: Mary M. Hobart, K1MMH, Secretary

1471—AMERICAN RADIO RELAY LEAGUE FOUNDATION (The PHD ARA Scholarship)

225 Main Street
Newington CT 06111
860/594-0397
FAX: 860/594-0259
E-mail: foundation@arrl.org
Internet: http://www.arrlf.org/
AMOUNT: $1,000
DEADLINE(S): FEB 1
FIELD(S): Journalism; Computer Science; Electronic Engineering
ELIGIBILITY/REQUIREMENTS: For students who are residents of the ARRL Midwest Division (Iowa, Kansas, Missouri, Nebraska), who hold any class of radio amateur license or are children of a deceased radio amateur.
HOW TO APPLY: See website or contact Foundation for information and application. Submit with a 1-page essay on the role amateur radio has played in your life. A recent high school (or equivalent) or college transcript required; submit with application or mail separately.
NUMBER OF AWARDS: 1
RENEWABLE: No
CONTACT: Mary M. Hobart, K1MMH, Secretary

1472—AMERICAN WOMEN IN RADIO AND TELEVISION-HOUSTON CHAPTER (Scholarship Program)

c/o Susan Miller
KHOU
1945 Allen Parkway
Houston TX 77019
713/521-4345
FAX: 713/284-8808
Internet: http://www.awrthouston. org/cgi-bin/natlfoundation.pl
AMOUNT: $1,000
DEADLINE(S): MAR
FIELD(S): Broadcasting and allied fields
ELIGIBILITY/REQUIREMENTS: Open to Houston area college juniors and seniors.
HOW TO APPLY: Contact AWRT Houston Chapter President for an application.
RENEWABLE: Yes
CONTACT: Susan Miller, AWRT Houston Chapter President

1473—ANDRE SOBEL RIVER OF LIFE FOUNDATION (Essay Contest)

8899 Beverly Boulevard, Suite 111
Los Angeles CA 90048
310//276-7111
FAX: 310/276-0244
E-mail: info@andreriveroflife.org
Internet: http//www.andreriver oflife.org
AMOUNT: $5,,000 (1st prize); 5 additional prizes at various amounts
DEADLINE(S): JUN 15
FIELD(S): Essay Contest
ELIGIBILITY/REQUIREMENTS: Award honors cancer survivors under the age of 21; must submit an essay on a topic selected each year (see website), for example on a topic like "The Letter I Would Like to Have Received From a Friend or Relative During My Illness."
HOW TO APPLY: See website for complete rules, submission guidelines, and application.
NUMBER OF AWARDS: 6 (1 top prize, 5 additional prizes)
RENEWABLE: No

1474—ARCTIC INSTITUTE OF NORTH AMERICA (Jim Bourque Scholarship)

University of Calgary
2500 University Drive NW
Calgary Alberta T2N 1N4
CANADA
403/220-7515
FAX: 403/282-4609
Internet: http://www.ucalgary. ca/aina
AMOUNT: $1,000 (Canadian)
DEADLINE(S): JUL 15
FIELD(S): Education; Environmental Studies; Traditional Knowledge; Telecommunications
ELIGIBILITY/REQUIREMENTS: Open to Canadian Aboriginal students who

intend to take, or are enrolled in, postsecondary training.

HOW TO APPLY: No application; submit description of program and reasons for choice, transcript, letter of recommendation, statement of financial need, and proof of enrollment or application to a postsecondary institution. See website or contact AINA for details.

1475—ASSOCIATED PRESS TELEVISION-RADIO ASSOCIATION OF CALIFORNIA/NEVADA (APTRA-Clete Roberts & Kathryn Dettman Memorial Journalism Scholarship Awards)

1600 Holloway Avenue
San Francisco CA 94132-4011
Internet: http://www.aptra.org
AMOUNT: $1,500
DEADLINE(S): DEC 15
FIELD(S): Broadcast Journalism
ELIGIBILITY/REQUIREMENTS: Open to students pursuing a career in broadcast journalism. MUST be enrolled in a California, Nevada or Hawaii college or university.
HOW TO APPLY: Download application from website. May also submit examples of broadcast-related work. Mail application to Roberta Gonzales, CBS 5TV, 855 Battery Street, San Francisco CA 94111

1476—ASSOCIATION FOR EDUCATION IN JOURNALISM & MASS COMMUNICATION (Mary A. Gardner Scholarship)

234 Outlet Pointe Boulevard
Columbia SC 29210
803/798-0271
FAX: 803/772-3509
E-mail: aejmcassistant@aol.com
Internet: http:www.aejmc.org
AMOUNT: $300
DEADLINE(S): APR 1
FIELD(S): News Reporting and/or Editing
ELIGIBILITY/REQUIREMENTS: Must be enrolled in an undergraduate news-editorial program; have minimum GPA of 3.0; and show demonstrable interest in pursuing a career in news reporting and/or editing.
HOW TO APPLY: Statement of qualifications/career objectives, biographical narrative (including school/home address/phone), letter of support from professor, official transcript, 2 letters of recommendation, and copies of clippings/other evidence of journalistic accomplishments required with application.
NUMBER OF AWARDS: 1
RENEWABLE: No

CONTACT: Janet Harley, AEJMC Office Assistant

1477—ASSOCIATION FOR WOMEN IN COMMUNICATIONS, THE

USA Weekend
7950 Jones Branch Drive
McLean VA 22107
703/854-5631
FAX: 703/854-2122
Internet: http://www.womcom.org
AMOUNT: $1,000
DEADLINE(S): MAR 19
FIELD(S): Journalism; Public Relations
ELIGIBILITY/REQUIREMENTS: Current sophomore or junior female student attending a Washington, DC-area university or college studying communications, advertising, journalism, public relations, marketing, graphic arts, or a related field with an overall GPA of 3.0 or higher.
HOW TO APPLY: Send résumé, cover letter, application, and transcripts.
NUMBER OF AWARDS: 1
CONTACT: Frappa Stout, Vice President of Student Affairs, AWC DC Chapter

1478—ATLANTA ASSOCIATION OF BLACK JOURNALISTS (Xernona Clayton Scholarship Fund)

Scholarship Committee
P.O. Box 54128
Atlanta GA 30308
404/508-4612
Internet: http://www.aabj.org/
AMOUNT: $2,000-$5,000
DEADLINE(S): MAY 1
FIELD(S): Journalism, Mass Communications
ELIGIBILITY/REQUIREMENTS: For African-American students enrolled full time in an accredited college or university in Georgia. Must be pursuing a degree in journalism or mass communications, have GPA of 3.0 or better, and be a U.S. citizen or legal alien.
HOW TO APPLY: See website for application and additional information. Submit with essay, official transcript, 2 letters of recommendation (non-AABJ related), samples of published work, and disclaimer for Scholarship Funds Disbursement.
CONTACT: Carletta S. Hurt, AABJ Scholarship Chair

1479—BLUES HEAVEN FOUNDATION, INC. (Muddy Waters Scholarship)

2120 South Michigan Avenue
Chicago IL 60616
312/808-1286

AMOUNT: $2,000
DEADLINE(S): APR 30
FIELD(S): Music; Music Education; African-American Studies; Folklore; Performing Arts; Arts Management; Journalism; Radio/TV/Film
ELIGIBILITY/REQUIREMENTS: Applicant must be full-time graduate or undergraduate in a Chicago area college or university. Scholastic aptitude, extracurricular involvement, GPA, and financial need are considered.
HOW TO APPLY: Contact Foundation between February and April to request an application.

1480—BROADCAST EDUCATION ASSOCIATION (Scholarships in Broadcasting)

1771 N Street NW
Washington DC 20036-2891
202/429-5354
E-mail: fweaver@nab.org
Internet: http://www.beaweb.org
AMOUNT: $1,250-$5,000
DEADLINE(S): JAN 14
FIELD(S): Broadcasting; Radio
ELIGIBILITY/REQUIREMENTS: For full-time juniors, seniors, and graduate students at BEA member universities. Must demonstrate superior academic performance and potential to become an outstanding electronic media professional and compelling evidence of high integrity and a well-articulated sense of personal and professional responsibility.
HOW TO APPLY: Contact BEA or your campus faculty for an application no later than December 17. See website for list of BEA member institutions.
NUMBER OF AWARDS: 15
RENEWABLE: No

1481—BUCKS COUNTY COURIER TIMES (Summer Internship Program)

8400 Route 13
Levittown PA 19057
215/949-4160
FAX: 215/949-4177
E-mail: pwalker@phillyburbs.com
Internet: http://www.philly burbs.com
AMOUNT: $4,380 ($365/wk.)
DEADLINE(S): FEB 1
FIELD(S): News; Business; Feature Reporting
ELIGIBILITY/REQUIREMENTS: 10-week internship for minority students at the Bucks County *Courier Times*. Must be U.S. resident and have car. Financial need NOT a factor.

HOW TO APPLY: Send résumé; NO calls.
NUMBER OF AWARDS: 3
RENEWABLE: No
CONTACT: Patricia S. Walker

1482—CCNMA: LATINO JOURNALISTS OF CALIFORNIA (Joel Garcia Memorial Scholarship & Frank del Olmo Memorial Scholarships)

300 S. Grand Avenue, Suite 3950
Los Angeles CA 90071-3175
213//437-4408
FAX: 213/447-4423
E-mail: educat@aicpa.org
Internet: http://www.ccnma.org
AMOUNT: $500-$1,000
DEADLINE(S): APR 4
FIELD(S): Journalism
ELIGIBILITY/REQUIREMENTS:
Based on commitment to the field of journalism, scholastic achievement, awareness of Latino issues, and financial need. Must be enrolled full-time and must be a California resident or attend an accredited college or university in California.
HOW TO APPLY: See website or write to Association for application after mid-January. Submit application along with autobiographical essay (300-500 words) explaining family background and what you believe the role of a Latino journalist is, transcripts, 2 letters of recommendation and samples of journalism-related work.
NUMBER OF AWARDS: approximately 10
RENEWABLE: Yes. Must reapply.
CONTACT: Julio Moron, Executive Director
ADDITIONAL INFORMATION: All winners will be invited and recognized at annual CCNMA Scholarship Banquet.

1483—CENTRAL NEWSPAPERS, INC. (The Pulliam Journalism Fellowships)

Indianapolis Star
P.O. Box 145
Indianapolis IN 46206-0145
317/444-6001
Internet: www.indystar.com/pjf
AMOUNT: $6,500 stipend
DEADLINE(S): NOV 15 FIELD(S): Journalism
ELIGIBILITY/REQUIREMENTS: Open to undergraduate sophomores, juniors, and seniors enrolled in a related degree program. Award is for a 10-week work and study internship at either *The Indianapolis Star* or *The Arizona Republic*. Previous newspaper internships and/or experience on a college newspaper preferred.

HOW TO APPLY: See website for application. Submit application along with recent photo (for publicity purposes); from 5-15 writing samples, 3 letters of recommendation, and college transcripts.
NUMBER OF AWARDS: 20
RENEWABLE: Yes
CONTACT: Russell B. Pulliam, Director, at russell.pulliam@indystar.com, or Bill Hill@indystar.com/pjf
ADDITIONAL INFORMATION: Recipients will need reliable transportation and will be expected to make their own housing arrangements.

1484—CONCLAVE, THE (The Brown College-Specs Howard School of Broadcasting)

4517 Minnetonka Boulevard, #104
Minneapolis MN 55416
952/927-4487
FAX: 952/927-6427
E-mail: info@theconclave.com
Internet: http://www.theconclave.comand www.radioscholarships.com
AMOUNT: Tuition
DEADLINE(S): APR 1
FIELD(S): Broadcasting
ELIGIBILITY/REQUIREMENTS: This 9-month program at either the Brown College in Minneapolis or Specs-Howard in Detroit, Michigan, open to high school graduates, must be U.S. citizens or permanent residents. Financial need NOT a factor. Applicant must be a high school senior, a high school graduate or have a general education diploma (GED) and must meet each school's entrance requirements, who has NO professional paid music business/broadcast experience either full or part-time (high school radio, college radio or unpaid internship experience is OK).
HOW TO APPLY: Apply online at either website or contact The Conclave for an application. Submit with an audio cassette or CD recording of supplied script
NUMBER OF AWARDS: 2
RENEWABLE: No
CONTACT: Tom Kay

1485—CONCORDIA UNIVERSITY (Susan Carson Memorial Bursary and Gordon Fisher Bursaries)

Journalism Department
455 de Maisonneuve Boulevard,
W Loyola BR 305
Montreal Quebec H3G 1M8
CANADA
514/848-3809
FAX: 514/848-2812

E-mail: awardsgs@vax2.concordia.ca
AMOUNT: $1,800; $2,000 (Canadian)
DEADLINE(S): SEP 20
FIELD(S): Journalism
ELIGIBILITY/REQUIREMENTS: Based on academic achievement/performance and financial need. Must demonstrate the highest ideals, concern for humankind, and qualities of citizenship. Selection will be made by the Chair of the Journalism Department in consultation with colleagues and/or relatives of the late Ms. Susan Carson. Preference will be given to students who have custody of 1 or more dependent children (does not apply to Gordon Fisher awards).
HOW TO APPLY: Contact the Chair of the Journalism Department at Concordia University for applications.
NUMBER OF AWARDS: 3
RENEWABLE: No

1486—CONNECTICUT BROADCASTERS ASSOCIATION

90 South Park Street
Willimantic CT 06226
860/633-5031
FAX: 860/456-5688
Internet: http://www.ctba.org
AMOUNT: Varies
DEADLINE(S): JAN 31
FIELD(S): Broadcasting, Marketing, Engineering, Electronics
ELIGIBILITY/REQUIREMENTS: Open to Connecticut residents pursuing a broadcasting career or a career in related fields.
HOW TO APPLY: Applications are available from Connecticut broadcast stations and on website.
NUMBER OF AWARDS: Varies
RENEWABLE: Yes. Some are 4-year, subject to performance; others must reapply.
CONTACT: M. C. Rice, CBA President

1487—DOW JONES NEWSPAPER FUND, INC. (Business Reporting Intern Program for Sophomores, Juniors and Seniors)

P.O. Box 300
Princeton NJ 08543-0300
609/452-2820
E-mail: newsfund@wsj.dowjones.com
Internet: http://www.NewspaperFund.org
AMOUNT: Paid summer internship + $1,000
DEADLINE(S): NOV 1
FIELD(S): Journalism; Business Reporting; Editing

ELIGIBILITY/REQUIREMENTS: Summer internships for college sophomores, juniors and seniors to work at daily newspapers as business reporters. Must demonstrate interest in similar career, though journalism major not required. Interns will attend a 1-week training program.
HOW TO APPLY: Applications available from August 15 to September 25. Applications available on website.
NUMBER OF AWARDS: 12

1488—DOW JONES NEWSPAPER FUND, INC. (Summer Workshops in Journalism, Writing, and Photography Competition)

P.O. Box 300
Princeton NJ 08543-0300
609/452-2820
E-mail: newsfund@wsj.dowjone.com
Internet: http://www.Newspaper Fund.org
AMOUNT: $1,000 + paid summer internship
DEADLINE(S): SEP 1
FIELD(S): Journalism
ELIGIBILITY/REQUIREMENTS: Workshops are offered at 26 colleges around the U.S. Open to high school seniors and college freshmen interested in journalism. 10 days of learning to write, report, design, and lay out a newspaper.
HOW TO APPLY: Contact Dow Jones or see website for list of participating colleges/states. Prizewinners are nominated by the director; must submit an essay and a published story, which will be judged by 3 professional journalists.
NUMBER OF AWARDS: 8
RENEWABLE: No.

1489—GEORGIA PRESS EDUCATIONAL FOUNDATION

3066 Mercer University Drive, Suite 200
Atlanta GA 30341
770/454-6776
FAX: 770/454-6778
E-mail: jfarmer@gapress.org
Internet: http://www.gapress.org
AMOUNT: $1,000
DEADLINE(S): FEB 1
FIELD(S): Print Journalism
ELIGIBILITY/REQUIREMENTS: Georgia resident attending Georgia college or university pursuing a career in print journalism.
HOW TO APPLY: Send application.
NUMBER OF AWARDS: 15
RENEWABLE: Yes, must reapply.
CONTACT: Jennifer Farmer

1490—GOLDEN KEY INTERNATIONAL HONOUR SOCIETY (Speech and Debate Awards)

1189 Ponce de Leon Avenue
Atlanta GA 30306
404/377-2400 or 800/377-2401
FAX: 404/373-7033
E-mail: scholarships@goldenkey.org
Internet: http://www.goldenkey.org
AMOUNT: $1,000 (winner); $500 (runner-up)
DEADLINE(S): APR 1
FIELD(S): All
ELIGIBILITY REQUIREMENTS: This award recognizes talented members for their oratory skills. Undergraduate, graduate, and postgraduate members are eligible. Must be able to attend the Golden Key International Conference.
HOW TO APPLY: Apply online with your Golden Key member number. Submit a videotaped monologue no more than 5 minutes long on topic posted on website.
NUMBER OF AWARDS: 2
RENEWABLE: No
CONTACT: Fabian J. De Rozario, Associate Vice President of North American Operations

1491—HAWAII COMMUNITY FOUNDATION (Edward Payson and Bernice Piilani Irwin Scholarship)

1164 Bishop Street, Suite 800
Honolulu HI 96813
808/537-6333 or toll free:
888/731-3863
FAX: 808/521-6286
E-mail: info@hcf-hawaii.org
Internet: http://www.hcf-hawaii.org
DEADLINE(S): MAR 1
FIELD(S): Journalism; Communications
ELIGIBILITY/REQUIREMENTS: Hawaii residents; be junior or senior undergraduate or graduate students enrolled full time in an accredited 2- or 4-year college or university; and demonstrate financial need, good moral character, and academic achievement (minimum GPA of 2.7).
HOW TO APPLY: Send application with 2 letters of recommendation.

1492—HAWAII COMMUNITY FOUNDATION (PRSA-Hawaii/Roy Leffingwell Public Relations Scholarship)

1164 Bishop Street, Suite 800
Honolulu HI 96813
808/537-6333 or toll free:
888/731-3863
FAX: 808/521-6286
E-mail: info@hcf-hawaii.org
Internet: http://www.hcf-hawaii.org
DEADLINE(S): MAR 1
FIELD(S): Public Relations; Journalism; Communications
ELIGIBILITY/REQUIREMENTS: Applicants must intend to pursue a career in public relations; Hawaii residents; be junior or senior undergraduate or graduate students enrolled full time in an accredited 2- or 4-year college or university; and demonstrate financial need, good moral character, and academic achievement (minimum GPA of 2.7).
HOW TO APPLY: Send application with 2 letters of recommendation.

1493—HILLEL: THE FOUNDATION FOR JEWISH CAMPUS LIFE (Steinhardt Jewish Campus Service Corps)

1640 Rhode Island Avenue NW
Washington DC 20036
202/857-6559
FAX: 202/857-6626
E-mail: mgruenwald@hillel.org
Internet: http://www.hillel.org
AMOUNT: One-year fellowship
DEADLINE(S): MAR
FIELD(S): All (student leadership)
ELIGIBILITY/REQUIREMENTS: Open to college seniors and recent college graduates with leadership skills and ability to create dynamic and innovative engagement strategies designed to reach Jewish college students. Must possess commitment to service; willingness to use time, abilities, and talents to enhance lives of others; and dedication to strengthening Jewish identity among students with whom they work. Corps fellows get to know interests and concerns of students and build programs and activities to match.
HOW TO APPLY: See website or contact Foundation for an application.
CONTACT: Melanie Sasson Gruenwald or Rachel Gurshman

1494—INSTITUTE FOR HUMANE STUDIES (Felix Morley Journalism Competition)

3401 North Fairfax Drive, Suite 440
Arlington VA 22201-4432
703/993-4880 or 800/697-8799
FAX: 703/993-4890
Internet: http://www.TheIHS.org
AMOUNT: $2,500 (1st prize)
DEADLINE(S): DEC 1
FIELD(S): Journalism

ELIGIBILITY/REQUIREMENTS: Open to young writers whose work demonstrates an appreciation of classical liberal principles (i.e., individual rights; their protection through private property, contract, and law; voluntarism in human relations; and the self-ordering market, free trade, free migration, and peace). Must be a full-time student aged 25 or younger.

HOW TO APPLY: Must submit 3-5 articles, editorials, opinion pieces, essays, and reviews published in student newspapers or other periodicals between July 1 and December 1. See website for rules or contact IHS for an entry form.

1495—INSTITUTE FOR HUMANE STUDIES (Summer Seminars Program)

3401 North Fairfax Drive, Suite 440
Arlington VA 22201-4432
703/993-4880 or 800/697-8799
FAX: 703/993-4890
E-mail: ihs@gmu.edu
Internet: http://www.TheIHS.org
AMOUNT: Free summer seminars, including room/board, lectures, seminar materials, and books
DEADLINE(S): MAR
FIELD(S): Social Sciences; Humanities; Law; Journalism; Public Policy; Education; Film; Writing; Economics; Philosophy

ELIGIBILITY/REQUIREMENTS: Open to college students, recent graduates, and graduate students who share an interest in learning and exchanging ideas about the scope of individual rights, free markets, the rule of law, peace, and tolerance.

HOW TO APPLY: See website for information and to apply online or contact IHS for an application.

1496—INTERNATIONAL RADIO AND TELEVISION SOCIETY FOUNDATION (Summer Fellowship Program)

420 Lexington Avenue, Suite 1714
New York NY 10170
212/867-6650
FAX: 212/867-6653
Internet: http://www.irts.org
AMOUNT: Housing, stipend, and travel
DEADLINE(S): NOV 12
FIELD(S): Broadcasting; Communications; Sales; Marketing
ELIGIBILITY/REQUIREMENTS: 9-week summer fellowship program in New York City is open to outstanding full-time undergraduate juniors and seniors with a demonstrated interest in a career in communications. Financial need NOT a factor.

HOW TO APPLY: See website or contact IRTS for an application.
NUMBER OF AWARDS: 20-25
RENEWABLE: No
CONTACT: Maria DeLeon-Fisher

1497—JACKSONVILLE STATE UNIVERSITY (Communication Scholarship)

Financial Aid Office
Jacksonville AL 36265
256/782-5677 or 800/231-5291
Internet: www.jsu.edu
AMOUNT: Varies
DEADLINE(S): FEB 1
FIELD(S): Communications
ELIGIBILITY/REQUIREMENTS: Open to students majoring in communications.
HOW TO APPLY: Contact Communication Department for application and details.
RENEWABLE: Yes
CONTACT: Communication Department; 256/782-5300

1498—JACKSONVILLE STATE UNIVERSITY (Ed Hill Memorial Leadership)

Financial Aid Office
Jacksonville AL 36265
256/782-5677 or 800/231-5291
Internet: www.jsu.edu
AMOUNT: Full tuition
DEADLINE(S): FEB 1
FIELD(S): Communications; Art
ELIGIBILITY/REQUIREMENTS: Open to students majoring in communications or art with an interest in photography as a profession.
HOW TO APPLY: Submit application, high school transcript, and ACT/SAT scores. See website for application.
RENEWABLE: Yes
CONTACT: Scholarship Committee

1499—JAPANESE AMERICAN CITIZENS LEAGUE

1765 Sutter Street
San Francisco CA 94115
415/921-5225
FAX: 415/931-4671
E-mail: jacl@jacl.org
Internet: http://www.jacl.org
AMOUNT: $1,000-$5,000
DEADLINE(S): APR 1
FIELD(S): Agriculture; Journalism
ELIGIBILITY/REQUIREMENTS: Open to JACL members only. For undergraduate students interested in either journalism or agriculture, who are planning to attend a college, university, trade school, business school, or any other institution of higher learning. Financial need NOT a factor.
HOW TO APPLY: For membership information or application, see website or send SASE stating your level of study. Submit with personal statement, letters of recommendation, and transcripts.

1500—JEWISH FEDERATION OF METROPOLITAN CHICAGO (Academic Scholarship Program)

Jewish Vocational Service
216 West Jackson Blvd., Suite 700
Chicago IL 60606-6921
312/673-3400
TTY: 312/444-2877
FAX: 312/553-5544
E-mail: http://www.jvs/chicago.org
AMOUNT: Varies
DEADLINE(S): FEB 15
FIELD(S): Mathematics, Engineering, Science, Medicine, Social Work, Education, Psychology, Rabbinate, Law (except corporate), Communications
ELIGIBILITY/REQUIREMENTS: Open to Jewish men and women legally domiciled in the greater Chicago metropolitan area, who demonstrate promise for significant contributions in their chosen careers, and are in need of financial assistance for full-time academic study. Must have entered undergraduate junior year in career programs requiring no postgraduate education, be in graduate/professional school or a vo-tech training program.
HOW TO APPLY: Phone JVS Scholarship Secretary (312/673-3457), fax, or visit website (click on Scholarship Services) for an application in the Fall. Interview required.
RENEWABLE: Yes
CONTACT: JVS Scholarship Secretary at 312/673-3457
ADDITIONAL INFORMATION: Recipients must attend the College of Communications, University of Illinois at Urbana-Champaign.

1501—JOHN F. KENNEDY LIBRARY FOUNDATION (John F. Kennedy Profile in Courage Essay Contest)

Columbia Point
Boston MA 02125
617/514-1649
FAX: 617/514-1641
E-mail: profiles@nara.gov
Internet: http://www.jfklibrary.org
AMOUNT: $500-$3,000
DEADLINE(S): Early JAN

FIELD(S): All, especially Political Science, History, English Language and Literature, and Communications and Journalism

ELIGIBILITY REQUIREMENTS: Open to U.S. high school students in grades 9-12, or home-schools; or enrolled in a high school correspondence/GED program in any of the 50 states, D.C., or U.S. territories; or U.S. citizens attending schools overseas.

HOW TO APPLY: Write an essay on an elected official in the U.S. who is acting or has acted courageously to address a political issue at the local, state, national, or international level; also send completed contest registration form.

NUMBER OF AWARDS: 7 (1 first place, 1 second place, 5 finalists)

RENEWABLE: No

1502—JORGE MAS CANOSA FREEDOM FOUNDATION (Mas Family Scholarships)

P.O. Box 14-1898
Miami FL 33114
305/529-0075, ext. 35
E-mail: mmartinez@jmcffmas
familyscholarships.org
Internet: http://www.jmcffmas
scholarships.org

AMOUNT: Up to $10,000

DEADLINE(S): MAR 31

FIELD(S): Engineering, Business, International Relations, Economics, Communications, Journalism

ELIGIBILITY/REQUIREMENTS: For Cuban-American students, graduates and undergraduates, born in Cuba or direct descendants (1 parent or 2 grandparents) of those who left Cuba. Must be in top 10% of high school class or maintain a 3.5 GPA in college. Financial need considered along with academic success, SAT and GRE scores, and leadership potential.

HOW TO APPLY: Contact Foundation for application. Two short essays and 2 character evaluations along with proof of Cuban descent required.

NUMBER OF AWARDS: 10

RENEWABLE: Yes, maximum $40,000; must reapply

1503—JOURNALISM EDUCATION ASSOCIATION (Ryan White Excellence in Journalism Award, The)

Kansas State University
103 Kedzie Hall
Manhattan KS 66506-1505
785/532-5532
FAX: 785/532-5563
E-mail: jea@spub.ksu.edu
Internet: http://www.jea.org

AMOUNT: $50-$500

DEADLINE(S): JUL 1

FIELD(S): Journalism (health-related topics)

ELIGIBILITY/REQUIREMENTS: Applicants (or team of students who worked on the same entry) must be high school students who are members of the staff of their high school newspaper, news magazine, yearbook, literary art magazine, Web page, radio station, or TV station. The entry must be a feature, an editorial, or a commentary; must be original student work; and must have been published or broadcast within 1 year of the contest deadline.

HOW TO APPLY: Submit with (if print medium) a copy of the published feature, editorial, or commentary, or (if broadcast medium) a taped copy/URL and a typed transcript of the Web, radio, or television entries; a statement indicating background sources; list of individuals interviewed (include job title or why selected), and response to this work from the community (high school, city, county, or a targeted segment of the population). For additional information, see www.jea.org/awards/ryan-white.html.

NUMBER OF AWARDS: 30

RENEWABLE: No

CONTACT: Carol Lange at langejour@aol.com

1504—JOURNALISM EDUCATION ASSOCIATION (Sister Rita Jeanne High School Journalist of the Year Scholarships)

Kansas State University
103 Kedzie Hall
Manhattan KS 66506-1505
785/532-5532
FAX: 785/532-5563
E-mail: jea@spub.ksu.edu
Internet: http://www.jea.org

AMOUNT: $2,000-$5,000

DEADLINE(S): FEB 15

FIELD(S): Journalism

ELIGIBILITY/REQUIREMENTS: Must be a graduating high school senior; planning to study journalism or mass communications and pursue a career in journalism or mass communications, and have at least a 3.0 GPA; 2-year participation in high school journalism; a state winner; and a student of a JEA member advisor.

HOW TO APPLY: Send application with a portfolio that includes a self-analytical evaluation of your "journalistic life," a photo of you interviewing someone, taking a photograph, designing a page, broadcasting, an official transcript; 3-4 letters of recommendation from advisor, other teachers, and practitioners with whom you have

worked (letter from principal is desirable, but not necessary); samples of your work, including 1 issue of your newspaper, magazine, or photocopies of relevant spreads from your yearbook. Original prints of photographs should accompany entries based on published pictures. Send to your state contest coordinator; do NOT mail your entry to JEA Headquarters.

NUMBER OF AWARDS: 7

RENEWABLE: No

CONTACT: State Contest Coordinator; for a list, see www.jea.org/contact/state-directors.html

1505—JOURNALISM EDUCATION ASSOCIATION (Student Journalist Impact Award)

Kansas State University
103 Kedzie Hall
Manhattan KS 66506-1505
785/532-5532
FAX: 785/532-5563
E-mail: jea@spub.ksu.edu
Internet: http://www.jea.org

AMOUNT: $1,000

DEADLINE(S): MAR 1

FIELD(S): Journalism

ELIGIBILITY/REQUIREMENTS: Secondary school student who, through journalism, has made a significant difference on the lives of others. Applicant's teacher/advisor must be a JEA member at the time the applicant's work was published, broadcast, or created.

HOW TO APPLY: Send application with the article/series of articles (as it/they appeared in print) or with mass communication media (radio, broadcast, video, etc.) that made the impact, and a narrative of at least 250 words explaining why the piece was produced and how it had an impact on the individual, the school and/or community. Include any media coverage that the entry generated, 3 letters attesting to the impact of the work, NOT the author's (from the advisor, school administrator, professional journalist, and/or member of the community-parent, student, resident).

NUMBER OF AWARDS: 1

RENEWABLE: No

1506—KATU THOMAS R. DARGAN MINORITY SCHOLARSHIP

Human Resources
P.O. Box 2
Portland OR 97207/0002
Internet: http://www.katu.com/about/scholarship

AMOUNT: $4,000

DEADLINE(S): APR 30

FIELD(S): Broadcast Communications
ELIGIBILITY/REQUIREMENTS: Applicant must be a minority (Native American, African-American, Hispanic, or Asian), U.S. citizen; enrolled in the 1st, 2nd, or 3rd year of a broadcast communications curriculum at a 4-year college or university or an accredited community college in Oregon or Washington, or a permanent resident of Oregon or Washington attending an out-of-state institution. Minimum GPA 3.0. Community college students must be enrolled in a broadcast curriculum that is transferable to a 4-year accredited university.
HOW TO APPLY: Send application; statement of need, including estimated cost for 1 year and a list of other sources of financial assistance (grants, scholarships, funding from parents, etc.); official transcripts; 3 letters of recommendation (2 from academic sources, 1 personal); and an essay describing your personal and professional goals (include your contribution as a minority in the field of broadcasting).
NUMBER OF AWARDS: 1
RENEWABLE: Yes, must reapply.

1507—LANDMARK COMMUNICATIONS, INC.

150 West Brambleton Avenue
Norfolk VA 23510
757/446-2913
FAX: 757/222-5850
E-mail: jlamkin@lcimedia.com
Internet: http://www.landmark
communications.com
AMOUNT: $5,000 + newsroom internship
DEADLINE(S): NOV 30
FIELD(S): Reporters; photographers; graphic artists; sports writers; copy editors; page designers
ELIGIBILITY/REQUIREMENTS: Must be a U.S. citizen or registered permanent resident with GPA of 2.5 or better and goal of becoming a print journalism professional. Must have ties to the Mid-Atlantic/Southern region; be a member of a minority group (Asian, Hispanic, African-American, Native American); be a college sophomore enrolled full time (at least 12 credit hours/semester) in a 4-year degree program; and have a personal vehicle for on-the-job transportation. Award based on grades, work samples, financial needs, recommendations, and targeted selection/interview skills. Summer internship between sophomore and junior years and junior and senior years. At the end of each summer, scholarship awarded. On graduation, eligible for a 1-year internship with full benefits and the possibility of continued employment.

HOW TO APPLY: Download application from website and submit with 500-word autobiography; résumé (include expected graduation date); college transcript; and 3 letters of recommendation from professional colleagues or professors. Provide work samples, a minimum of 3 college or professional newspaper/magazine or other work samples (include 3 copies of your sample, photocopies, or disks as well as e-mail attachments if applying online).
NUMBER OF AWARDS: Up to 3
RENEWABLE: Yes, 2 years; maintain a 2.5 GPA; adhere to standards and ethics of professional journalism; uphold a positive public image as a Landmark Scholar; be punctual and have good attendance; comply with Landmark's general employment policies during internship; and participate in available training, workshops and seminars.
CONTACT: Jean Lamkin

1508—MANA: A National Latina Organization (Rita DiMartino Scholarship)

1725 K Street NW, Suite 105
Washington DC 20006
202/833-0060
FAX: 202/496-0588
E-mail: Hermana2@aol.com
Internet: http://www.hermana.org
AMOUNT: Varies
DEADLINE(S): FEB 28
FIELD(S): Communications; Journalism
ELIGIBILITY/REQUIREMENTS: For Hispanic female students enrolled in undergraduate programs in communication at accredited colleges or universities. Must demonstrate financial need and academic achievement. Must be MANA member.
HOW TO APPLY: Download application from website or call national office. $10 application fee.
NUMBER OF AWARDS: Varies
RENEWABLE: No
CONTACT: Alma Morales Riojas

1509—MEDILL (Eric Lund Global Reporting and Research Grant)

Medill School of Journalism
Northwestern University
1845 Sheridan Road
Evanston IL 60208-2101
847/467-1882
E-mail: ug-admission@
northwestern.edu
Internet: http://www.medill.
northwestern.edu/journalism/under
grad/page.aspx?id=60867
AMOUNT: $2,000-$3,000

DEADLINE(S): JAN 14
FIELD(S): Journalism
ELIGIBILITY/REQUIREMENTS: Open to students with financial need to pursue research and reporting experiences abroad, particularly in underreported parts of the world.
HOW TO APPLY: Submit proposal by e-mail and hard copy to Donna Kwiatkowski, grant coordinator, in Fisk 109, d-kwiatkowski@northwestern.edu.
NUMBER OF AWARDS: 6—1 winner, 5 runnerups
RENEWABLE: No
CONTACT: For more information m-bitoun@northwestern.edu; to submit proposal.

1510—MENSA EDUCATION AND RESEARCH FOUNDATION (Grace Harrington Wilson Scholarship)

Internet: http://www.mensa
foundation.org/AM/Template.cfm?
Section=Scholarships1
AMOUNT: $600
DEADLINE(S): JAN 15
FIELD(S): Journalism
ELIGIBILITY/REQUIREMENTS: Female student with a focus in journalism. May be enrolled at time of application. Awards based on essays written by the applicant. No requirement for Mensa membership nor is consideration given for grades, academic program or financial need. Applicants must currently be a resident of a participating American Mensa local group's area and enrolled in a degree program in an accredited U.S. institution of higher learning during the academic year following the application date.
HOW TO APPLY: Each year the list of participating groups may change, see website for up-to-date information. Send application, available (if eligible) from the website or, by request with SASE, from local scholarship chairs. Submit with essay of not more than 550 words explaining your academic and/or vocational goals and plans to achieve those goals to the scholarship chair in your area.

1511—MENSA EDUCATION AND RESEARCH FOUNDATION (Margie Mandelblatt Award)

Internet: http://www.mensa
foundation.org/AM/Template.cfm?
Section=Scholarships1
AMOUNT: $600
DEADLINE(S): JAN 15
FIELD(S): Journalism

ELIGIBILITY/REQUIREMENTS: Awards based on essays written by the applicant. No requirement for Mensa membership nor is consideration given for grades, academic program or financial need. Applicants must currently be a resident of a participating American Mensa local group's area and enrolled in a degree program in an accredited U.S. institution of higher learning during the academic year following the application date.

HOW TO APPLY: Each year the list of participating groups may change, see website for up-to-date information. Send application, available (if eligible) from the website or, by request with SASE, from local scholarship chairs. Submit with essay of not more than 550 words explaining your academic and/or vocational goals and plans to achieve those goals to the scholarship chair in your area.

1512—MENSA EDUCATION AND RESEARCH FOUNDATION (Rosemary Greathouse Scholarship)

Internet: http://www.mensa foundation.org/AM/Template.cfm? Section=Scholarships1
AMOUNT: $600
DEADLINE(S): JAN 15
FIELD(S): Arts (including creative writing and journalism)
ELIGIBILITY/REQUIREMENTS: Awards based on essays written by the applicant. No requirement for Mensa membership nor is consideration given for grades, academic program or financial need. Applicants must currently be a resident of a participating American Mensa local group's area and enrolled in a degree program in an accredited U.S. institution of higher learning during the academic year following the application date.

HOW TO APPLY: Each year the list of participating groups may change, see website for up-to-date information. Send application, available (if eligible) from the website or, by request with SASE, from local scholarship chairs. Submit with essay of not more than 550 words explaining your academic and/or vocational goals and plans to achieve those goals to the scholarship chair in your area.

1513—MICHIGAN OUTDOOR WRITERS ASSOCIATION, THE (Marc Wesley Scholarship)

MOWA Scholarship Committee
3601 Avery
St. Johns MI 48879
989/224-3465

E-mail: scholarship@mi outdoorwriters.org
AMOUNT: $1,000
DEADLINE(S): JAN 25
FIELD(S): Journalism/writing
ELIGIBILITY/REQUIREMENTS: Senior at a Michigan college or university interested in and qualified for a career in outdoor writing. Must be Michigan resident for at least 5 years.
HOW TO APPLY: Write for application. Submit letters of support and proof of performance (VCR samples of outdoor communications and class assignments) with application.
CONTACT: Bob Holzhei

1514—NATION INSTITUTE, THE (I. F. Stone Award for Student Journalism)

33 Irving Place, 8th Floor
New York NY 10003
212/209-5400
E-mail: rkim@nationinstitute.org
Internet: http://www.thenation. com/institute/masur.htm
AMOUNT: $1,000
DEADLINE(S): SEP 30
FIELD(S): Journalism
ELIGIBILITY/REQUIREMENTS: Open to undergraduate students enrolled in a U.S. college. Entries published in student publications preferred, others considered (may NOT be part of regular coursework). Winning article will represent the most outstanding example of student journalism in the tradition of I. F. Stone.
HOW TO APPLY: This award is NOT given each year. See website or contact the Institute for additional information. Articles (up to 3 entries) may be submitted by writers themselves or nominated by editors of student publications or faculty members.
CONTACT: Richard Kim

1515—NATION INSTITUTE, THE (Nation Internship Program)

33 Irving Place, 8th Floor
New York NY 10003
212/209-5400
E-mail: rkim@nationinstitute.org
Internet: http://www.nation institute.org/internships/
AMOUNT: $150/week
DEADLINE(S): NOV 7; MAR 26; JUL 9
FIELD(S): Journalism; Publishing
ELIGIBILITY/REQUIREMENTS: Full-time internships for college students and recent graduates interested in magazine journalism and publishing. Each applicant evaluated on basis of résumé, recommen-

dations, and writing samples. Possible housing and travel grants based on financial need. Internships available in New York and Washington, DC.
HOW TO APPLY: In addition to a cover letter indicating your interest in The Nation and describing your prospective career goals, send a résumé, 2 letters of recommendation (from professors or former employers), and 2 writing samples. Published clips are preferred, though academic papers and creative writing samples are acceptable (maximum 8 pages). All application materials become the property of The Nation Institute. Faxes and e-mails are NOT acceptable. See website or contact The Nation for additional information.
NUMBER OF AWARDS: 16
CONTACT: Richard Kim

1516—NATIONAL ASSOCIATION OF BLACK JOURNALISTS (NABJ Scholarship Program)

University of Maryland
3100 Taliaferro Hall
College Park MD 20742-7717
301/405/8500
FAX: 301/405/8555
E-mail: nabj@jmail.umd.edu or nabj@nabj.org
Internet: http://www.nabj.org
AMOUNT: $2,500
DEADLINE(S): MAR 20
FIELD(S): Journalism: print, photography, radio, television
ELIGIBILITY/REQUIREMENTS: For African-American high school seniors planning to pursue education for a journalism career, undergraduate or graduate students who are accepted to, or enrolled in an accredited, 4-year journalism program majoring in print, photo, radio, or television journalism or planning a career in 1 of those fields. GPA of 2.5 or better is required.
HOW TO APPLY: See website for application forms or write for information.
NUMBER OF AWARDS: At least 10 undergraduate and graduate; 2-4 high school seniors

1517—NATIONAL ASSOCIATION OF BLACK JOURNALISTS (NABJ Summer Internships)

University of Maryland
3100 Taliaferro Hall
College Park MD 20742-7717
301/405/8500
FAX: 301/405/8555
E-mail: nabj@jmail.umd.edu or nabj@nabj.org
Internet: http://www.nabj.org

AMOUNT: Varies
DEADLINE(S): DEC 15
FIELD(S): Journalism: print, photography, radio, television
ELIGIBILITY/REQUIREMENTS: Internships for African-American sophomores, juniors, seniors, and graduate students committed to careers in journalism. Programs offered throughout the U.S. Minimum 2.5 GPA required.
HOW TO APPLY: See website for application forms or contact NABJ for further information.

1518—NATIONAL ASSOCIATION OF HISPANIC JOURNALISTS (Cristina Saralegui Scholarship Program)

1000 National Press Building
Washington DC 20045-2001
202/662-7145
E-mail: nahj@nahj.org
Internet: http://www.nahj.org/
student/scholarshipinformation.html
AMOUNT: $5,000
FIELD(S): Journalism
ELIGIBILITY/REQUIREMENTS: Must be college student, fluent in Spanish, planning to pursue a career in broadcast journalism.
HOW TO APPLY: See website for application and additional information. Send to NAHJ Scholarship Committee.
CONTACT: Nancy Tita

1519—NATIONAL ASSOCIATION OF HISPANIC JOURNALISTS (NAHJ ABC News Joanna Bistany Memorial Scholarship Program)

1000 National Press Building
529 14th Street NW
Washington DC 20045-2001
202/662-7145
FAX: 202/662-7144
E-mail: kolivas@nahj.org
Internet: http://www.nahj.org
AMOUNT: $5,000
DEADLINE(S): JAN (last Friday)
FIELD(S): Broadcast Journalism; Producers
ELIGIBILITY/REQUIREMENTS: College undergraduates and first-year graduate students who are pursuing careers as English-language television journalists or producers.
HOW TO APPLY: See website for an application. Do NOT write or call for application.
RENEWABLE: No

1520—NATIONAL ASSOCIATION OF HISPANIC JOURNALISTS (NAHJ Maria Elena Salinas Scholarship Program)

1000 National Press Building
529 14th Street NW
Washington DC 20045-2001
202/662-7145
FAX: 202/662-7144
E-mail: kolivas@nahj.org
Internet: http://www.nahj.org
AMOUNT: $5,000
DEADLINE(S):): JAN (last Friday)
FIELD(S): Print/Broadcast Journalism; Producers
ELIGIBILITY/REQUIREMENTS: Bilingual high school seniors, college undergraduates and first-year graduate students pursuing careers as Spanish-language television or radio journalists or producers. Applicants MUST be fluent in Spanish. Recipient is required to intern at a Newhouse newspaper following their junior year.
HOW TO APPLY: See website for an application. Do NOT write or call for application. Applicants must also write an essay IN SPANISH that explains why they seek this career as a Spanish-language broadcast journalist. Must submit samples written in Spanish.
RENEWABLE: No

1521—NATIONAL ASSOCIATION OF HISPANIC JOURNALISTS (NAHJ Newhouse Scholarship Program)

1000 National Press Building
529 14th Street NW
Washington DC 20045-2001
202/662-7145
FAX: 202/662-7144
E-mail: kolivas@nahj.org
Internet: http://www.nahj.org
AMOUNT: $5,000/year for 2 years
DEADLINE(S): JAN (last Friday)
FIELD(S): Journalism; Photojournalism
ELIGIBILITY/REQUIREMENTS: Applicants MUST be sophomores who are committed to pursuing a career in English-language (NOT Spanish-language) newspaper journalism as reporters, editors, photographers, or graphic artists. Award will be for junior and senior years. Recipient is required to intern at a Newhouse newspaper following their junior year.
HOW TO APPLY: See website for an application. Do NOT write or call for application. Submit to NAHJ Scholarship Committee.
RENEWABLE: No

1522—NATIONAL ASSOCIATION OF HISPANIC JOURNALISTS (NAHJ Newsroom Bound Program)

1000 National Press Building
529 14th Street NW
Washington DC 20045-2001
202/662-7145
FAX: 202/662-7144
E-mail: kolivas@nahj.org
Internet: http://www.nahj.org
AMOUNT: $1,000
DEADLINE(S): JAN (last Friday)
FIELD(S): Journalism; Photojournalism
ELIGIBILITY/REQUIREMENTS: For college freshmen and sophomores who are pursuing careers in English-language print, photo, broadcast or online journalism; NAHJ will select students from among its scholarship recipients.
HOW TO APPLY: See website for an application. Do NOT write or call for application. Submit to NAHJ Scholarship Committee.
RENEWABLE: No

1523—NATIONAL ASSOCIATION OF HISPANIC JOURNALISTS (NAHJ Rubén Salazar Scholarships)

1000 National Press Building
529 14th Street NW
Washington DC 20045-2001
202/662-7145
FAX: 202/662-7144
E-mail: kolivas@nahj.org
Internet: http://www.nahj.org
AMOUNT: $1,000-$2,000
DEADLINE(S): JAN (last Friday)
FIELD(S): Print/Broadcast Journalism; Photojournalism
ELIGIBILITY/REQUIREMENTS: Open to high school seniors, undergraduates, and first-year graduate students committed to a career in print or broadcast journalism or photojournalism. Tenable at 2- or 4-year schools in the U.S. and its territories. Hispanic ancestry NOT required.
HOW TO APPLY: See website for an application. Do NOT write or call for application. Submit to NAHJ Scholarship Committee.
RENEWABLE: No

1524—NATIONAL ASSOCIATION OF WATER COMPANIES-NEW JERSEY CHAPTER

Elizabethtown Water Company
600 South Avenue
Westfield NJ 07091
908/654-1234
FAX: 908/232-2719

E-mail:
gbradygbconsult@comcast.net
AMOUNT: $2,500
DEADLINE(S): APR 1
FIELD(S): Business Administration; Biology; Chemistry; Engineering; Communications
ELIGIBILITY/REQUIREMENTS: For U.S. citizens who have lived in New Jersey at least 5 years and plan a career in the investor-owned water utility industry. Must be undergraduate or graduate student in a 2- or 4-year New Jersey college or university. GPA of 3.0 or better required.
HOW TO APPLY: Contact Association for complete information.
CONTACT: Gail P. Brady

1525—NATIONAL DAIRY SHRINE (McCullough Scholarships)

1224 Alton Darby Creek Road
Columbus OH 43228-9792
614/878-5333
FAX: 614/870-2622
E-mail: shrine@cobaselect.com
Internet: http://www.dairyshrine.org
AMOUNT: $1,000 and $2,500
DEADLINE(S): MAR 15
FIELD(S): Dairy Science; Agriculture; Journalism
ELIGIBILITY/REQUIREMENTS: Must be high school senior planning to enter 4-year college or university to major in Dairy/Animal Science with a communications emphasis or Agriculture Journalism.
HOW TO APPLY: Download application from website.
NUMBER OF AWARDS: 2
RENEWABLE: No
CONTACT: Maurice E. Core, Executive Director

1526—NATIONAL DAIRY SHRINE (NDS/DMT Milk Marketing Scholarship)

1224 Alton Darby Creek Road
Columbus OH 43228-9792
614/878-5333
FAX: 614/870-2622
E-mail: shrine@cobaselect.com
Internet: http://www.dairyshrine.org
AMOUNT: $1,000 and $2,500
DEADLINE(S): MAR 15
FIELD(S): Dairy Industry; Marketing; Business Administration; Journalism; Home Economics
ELIGIBILITY/REQUIREMENTS: College sophomores, juniors or seniors majoring in dairy marketing, dairy manufacturing, dairy science, home economics, or journalism at a college or university approved by the appropriate National

Dairy Shrine committee. Awards are based on ability, interests and need.
HOW TO APPLY: Download application from website.
NUMBER OF AWARDS: 5-9
RENEWABLE: No
CONTACT: Maurice E. Core, Executive Director

1527—NATIONAL INSTITUTE FOR LABOR RELATIONS RESEARCH (William B. Ruggles Scholarship)

5211 Port Royal Road
Springfield VA 22151
703/321-9606
FAX: 703/321-7342
E-mail: research@nilrr.org
Internet: http://www.nilrr.org
AMOUNT: $2,000
DEADLINE(S): DEC 31
FIELD(S): Journalism; English; Communications or related majors
ELIGIBILITY/REQUIREMENTS: Open to students majoring in journalism or related area.
HOW TO APPLY: Download application and information from website or request application by e-mail (specify "Ruggles" or "Journalism" scholarships); e-mail requests must include accurate mailing address. Submit with a most up-to-date transcript and an essay of approximately 500 words demonstrating an interest in, and knowledge of, the Right to Work principle.
NUMBER OF AWARDS: 1
RENEWABLE: No
CONTACT: Cathy Jones

1528—NATIONAL PRESS CLUB (Ellen Masin Persina Scholarship for Minorities in Journalism)

529 14th Street NW, 13th Floor
Washington DC 20045-2001
Internet: http://press.org/activities/scholarships.cfm
AMOUNT: $5,000/year for 4 years
DEADLINE(S): MAR 1
FIELD(S): Journalism (newspaper, radio, TV, magazine, trade paper)
ELIGIBILITY/REQUIREMENTS: Scholarships for talented high school senior minorities planning to pursue a career in journalism (see above fields). Must provide work samples, an essay, letters of recommendation, etc. Minimum 2.75 GPA required.
HOW TO APPLY: Access application from website or address above.
RENEWABLE: 4-year scholarship

1529—NATIONAL PRESS PHOTOGRAPHERS FOUNDATION (Bob East Scholarship)

3200 Croasdaile Drive, Suite 306
Durham NC 27705
919/383-7246 or 800/289-6772
FAX: 919/383-7261
E-mail: info@nppa.org
Internet: http://www.nppa.org/professionaldevelopment/students/scholar/scholarships/
AMOUNT: $1,000
DEADLINE(S): MAR 1
FIELD(S): Photojournalism
ELIGIBILITY/REQUIREMENTS: Must be undergraduate in the first 31/2 years of college or planning to pursue graduate work (with proof of acceptance). Primary consideration is portfolio; academic ability and financial need considered. Applicant's school must be in the U.S. or Canada.
HOW TO APPLY: See website or contact NPPF for an application and specific details. Submit with 6+ photos (photo-story counts as 1); video journalists should submit a tape with 3 stories.
NUMBER OF AWARDS: 1
CONTACT: Submit to Chuck Fadely, The Miami Herald, One Herald Plaza, Miami, FL 33132, 305/376-2015.

1530—NATIONAL PRESS PHOTOGRAPHERS FOUNDATION (Joseph Ehrenreich Scholarships)

3200 Croasdaile Drive, Suite 306
Durham NC 27705
919/383-7246 or 800/289-6772
FAX: 919/383-7261
E-mail: info@nppa.org
Internet: http://www.nppa.org/professionaldevelopment/students/scholar/scholarships/
AMOUNT: $1,000
DEADLINE(S): MAR 1
FIELD(S): Photojournalism
ELIGIBILITY/REQUIREMENTS: Must have completed at least 1 year at a 4-year college or university (with at least 1/2 year of undergraduate schooling remaining at time of award) offering courses in photojournalism leading to a bachelor's degree. Financial need major consideration.
HOW TO APPLY: Must include portfolio (6+ photos, photo-story counts as 1; video journalists must submit tape with 3 stories). Applicant's school must be in U.S. or Canada. See website or contact NPPF for an application and specific details.
NUMBER OF AWARDS: 5
CONTACT: Send to Mike Smith, Picture Desk, The New York Times, 229 West

43rd Street, New York, NY 10036, 212/556-7742, smithmi@nytimes.com.

1531—NATIONAL PRESS PHOTOGRAPHERS FOUNDATION (NPPF Still Scholarship)

3200 Croasdaile Drive, Suite 306
Durham NC 27705
919/383-7246 or 800/289-6772
FAX: 919/383-7261
E-mail: info@nppa.org
Internet: http://www.nppa.org/
professionaldevelopment/students/
scholar/scholarships/
AMOUNT: $1,000
DEADLINE(S): MAR 1
FIELD(S): Photojournalism
ELIGIBILITY/REQUIREMENTS: Must have completed 1 year at a recognized 4-year college or university having courses in photojournalism leading to a bachelor's degree. Must have at least 1/2 year of undergraduate schooling remaining at time of award. Aimed at those with journalism potential but with little opportunity and great need. Applicant's school must be in U.S. or Canada.
HOW TO APPLY: Must submit portfolio of 6+ photos (picture-story counts as 1) or for video journalists, tape with 3 stories. See website or contact NPPF for an application and specific details.
CONTACT: Send to Bill Sanders, 640 NW 100 Way, Coral Springs, FL 33071, 954/341-9718, bsand@worldnet.att.net.

1532—NATIONAL PRESS PHOTOGRAPHERS FOUNDATION (NPPF Television News Scholarship)

3200 Croasdaile Drive, Suite 306
Durham NC 27705
919/383-7246 or 800/289-6772
FAX: 919/383-7261
E-mail: info@nppa.org
Internet: http://www.nppa.org/
professionaldevelopment/students/
scholar/scholarships/
AMOUNT: $1,000
DEADLINE(S): MAR 1
FIELD(S): TV News Photojournalism
ELIGIBILITY/REQUIREMENTS: Must be enrolled in recognized 4-year college or university in U.S. or Canada with courses in TV news photojournalism leading to bachelor's degree. Must be junior or senior at time award is given. Financial need major consideration.
HOW TO APPLY: Entry should include videotape with examples of work (no more than 3 complete stories, 6 minutes total) with voice narration and natural sound.

Letter from professor/advisor and biographical sketch with goals required. See website or contact NPPF for an application and additional information.
NUMBER OF AWARDS: 1
CONTACT: Submit entry to Dave Hamer, 3702 North 53rd Street, Omaha, NE 68104, 75271.1707@compuserve.com.

1533—NATIONAL PRESS PHOTOGRAPHERS FOUNDATION (Reid Blackburn Scholarship)

3200 Croasdaile Drive, Suite 306
Durham NC 27705
919/383-7246 or 800/289-6772
FAX: 919/383-7261
E-mail: info@nppa.org
Internet: http://www.nppa.org/
professionaldevelopment/students/
scholar/scholarships/
AMOUNT: $1,000
DEADLINE(S): MAR 1
FIELD(S): Photojournalism
ELIGIBILITY/REQUIREMENTS: Must have completed 1 year at a recognized 4-year college or university in the U.S. or Canada having courses in photojournalism leading towards a bachelor's degree; at least 1/2 year of undergraduate schooling remaining at time of award. Academic ability, aptitude, and financial need are considered.
HOW TO APPLY: Portfolio required with entry (6+ photos, picture-story counts as 1; video journalists should send a tape of 3 stories). See website or contact NPPF for an application and details.
NUMBER OF AWARDS: 1
CONTACT: Submit entries to Jeremiah Coughlan, The Columbian, 701 West 8th Street, Vancouver, WA 98660, 360/694-3391, coughlan@attbi.com.

1534—NATIONAL PRESS PHOTOGRAPHERS FOUNDATION, KAPPA ALPHA MU (College Photographer of the Year Competition)

University of Missouri
School of Journalism
105 Lee Hills Hall
Columbia MO 65211
573/882-4442
E-mail: info@cpoy.org
Internet: http://www.cpoy.org
AMOUNT: $250-$1,000 + plaque/ certificate and film
DEADLINE(S): MAR 31
FIELD(S): Photojournalism
ELIGIBILITY/REQUIREMENTS: Undergraduate or graduate students who

have NOT worked 2 years or more as full-time professional photographers may enter. All entries must have been taken or published for the first time between Mar 1 and Feb 28 of the current year.
HOW TO APPLY: See website or contact CPOY Director for rules and entry form. No limit on number of pictures; no entry fee.
CONTACT: David Rees, CPOY Director, jourdlr@showme.missouri.edu

1535—NATIONAL SPEAKERS ASSOCIATION

1500 South Drive
Tempe AZ 85281
480/968-2552
FAX: 480/968-0911
E-mail: Information@nsaspeaker.org
Internet: http://www.nsaspeaker.org
AMOUNT: $4,000
DEADLINE(S): JUN 1
FIELD(S): Speech
ELIGIBILITY/REQUIREMENTS: For college juniors, seniors, and graduate students who major or minor in speech. Must be full-time student with above-average academic record. Must be well rounded, capable of leadership, with the potential to make an impact using oral communication skills.
HOW TO APPLY: Must submit official transcript, 500-word essay on career objectives, and letter of recommendation from speech teacher/department head along with application (7 copies each).

1536—NATIONAL STONE, SAND & GRAVEL ASSOCIATION (NSSGA Jennifer Curtis Byler Scholarship in Public Affairs)

1605 King Street
Alexandria VA 22314
703/525-8788
FAX: 703/525-7782
E-mail: info@nssga.org
Internet: http://www.nssga.org
AMOUNT: $2,500
DEADLINE(S): MAY 31
FIELD(S): Public Affairs, Political
    Science, Journalism, International
    Affairs, Public Relations, International
    Studies
ELIGIBILITY/REQUIREMENTS: Open to graduating seniors, or college students already enrolled as a public affairs major, who are children of an aggregate employee. Applicants must demonstrate their commitment to a career in public affairs.
HOW TO APPLY: See website or write for information and application.
NUMBER OF AWARDS: 1
RENEWABLE: No

1537—NATIVE AMERICAN JOURNALISTS ASSOCIATION (NAJA Scholarships and Internships)

University of South Dakota
414 East Clark Street
Vermillion SD 57069
605/677-5282
FAX: 605/694-4264
E-mail: info@naja.com
Internet: http://www.naja.com
AMOUNT: $1,000-$3,000
DEADLINE(S): APR 15
FIELD(S): Journalism (Print, Broadcast, Photojournalism, New Media, Journalism Education)
ELIGIBILITY/REQUIREMENTS: Must be Native American pursuing journalism degree at institution of higher learning and a current member of NAJA.
HOW TO APPLY: Cover letter stating financial need, area of interest, and reasons for pursuing a career in journalism. Include 3 letters of recommendation from academic advisor, counselor, or a professional familiar with your background and skills; 2 copies of transcript, work samples (if available), proof of enrollment in a federal or state-recognized tribe (if not enrolled, briefly explain). Application fee $20.

1538—NEW YORK FINANCIAL WRITERS' ASSOCIATION

Scholarship Program
P.O. Box 338
Ridgewood NJ 07450
201/612-0100
FAX: 201/612-9915
E-mail: nyfwa@aol.com
Internet: http://www.nyfwa.org
AMOUNT: $2,000-$3,000
DEADLINE(S): APR 15
FIELD(S): Financial Journalism
ELIGIBILITY/REQUIREMENTS: Open to undergraduate and graduate students enrolled in an accredited college or university in metropolitan New York City who are pursuing careers in business or financial journalism.
HOW TO APPLY: See website for application.
NUMBER OF AWARDS: 8-12
RENEWABLE: No
CONTACT: Jane Reilly

1539—ORGANIZATION OF CHINESE AMERICANS (Journalist Award)

1001 Connecticut Avenue NW, Suite 601
Washington DC 20036
202/223-5500
FAX: 202/296-0540
E-mail: oca@ocanatl.org
Internet: http://www.ocanatl.org
AMOUNT: $500 (1st prize); $300 (2nd); $200 (3rd)
DEADLINE(S): MAY 1
FIELD(S): Journalism
ELIGIBILITY/REQUIREMENTS: Open to Chinese-American journalists who submit an article relating to social, political, economic, or cultural issues facing Chinese-Americans and/or Asian Americans printed since January of current year from a publication with national circulation. May be in English or Chinese. Based on completeness, accuracy, readability, and importance to understanding issues.
HOW TO APPLY: See website or send SASE to OCA for details.

1540—OUTDOOR WRITERS ASSOCIATION OF AMERICA (Bodie McDowell Scholarship Program)

121 Hickory Street
Missoula MT 59801
406/728-7434
FAX: 406/728-7445
E-mail: owaaa@montana.com
Internet: http://www.owaa.org
AMOUNT: $2,000-$3,000
DEADLINE(S): FEB
FIELD(S): Outdoor Communications; Journalism
ELIGIBILITY/REQUIREMENTS: Open to undergraduate and graduate students interested in writing about outdoor activities, not including organized sports. Acceptable topics include hiking, backpacking, climbing, etc.
HOW TO APPLY: Send SASE to OWAA for an application.
NUMBER OF AWARDS: Availability varies with school participation.
CONTACT: Steve Wagner, Executive Director

1541—OUTDOOR WRITERS ASSOCIATION OF AMERICA (OWAA Scholarship Awards)

121 Hickory Street
Missoula MT 59801
406/728-7434
FAX: 406/728-7445
E-mail: owaaa@montana.com
Internet: http://www.owaa.org
AMOUNT: $2,500-$3,500
DEADLINE(S): MAR 1
FIELD(S): Communications; Journalism; Film; Broadcasting; Photography
ELIGIBILITY/REQUIREMENTS: Open to junior and senior undergraduates and graduate students. Must attend an accredited school of journalism or mass communications that has registered with OWAA as a scholarship program participant. Selection based on career goals in outdoor communications, examples of work, letters of recommendation, and academic achievement. Must be U.S. or Canadian citizen or permanent resident.
HOW TO APPLY: See website or contact your school for application, or send SASE to Executive Director for guidelines.
NUMBER OF AWARDS: At least 3
CONTACT: Steve Wagner, Executive Director

1542—OVERSEAS PRESS CLUB FOUNDATION

40 West 45th Street
New York NY 10036
212/493-9087
FAX: 212/612-9915
E-mail: foundation@opcof america.org
Internet: http://www.opcofamerica. org
AMOUNT: $2,000
DEADLINE(S): DEC 1
FIELD(S): Journalism
ELIGIBILITY/REQUIREMENTS: Undergraduate or graduate students currently enrolled at an American college or university who aspire to become foreign correspondents at some point in their careers.
HOW TO APPLY: Send cover letter, résumé and essay. Cover letter should be biographical in nature and address applicant's interest in international journalism. Essay should be about 500 words and concentrate on a foreign country or international issue.
NUMBER OF AWARDS: 12
RENEWABLE: No
CONTACT: Jane Reilly

1543—PENNSYLVANIA WOMEN'S PRESS ASSOCIATION

PWPA Scholarship Committee
P.O. Box 152
Sharpsville PA 16150
724/962-0990
Internet: http://www.pnpa.com/ pwpa/newscholarship.htm
AMOUNT: At least $1,000
DEADLINE(S): APR 20
FIELD(S): Print Journalism
ELIGIBILITY/REQUIREMENTS: Scholarship for Pennsylvania residents

(male or female) majoring in print journalism in a 4-year or graduate-level program in a Pennsylvania college or university. Must be a junior, senior, or graduate. Selection based on proven ability, dedication to journalism, and general merit.
HOW TO APPLY: Submit with 500-word essay summarizing your interest in journalism, career plans, and related information. Include a copy of college transcript; clippings of published work from school newspapers and other publications (photocopies are acceptable; cite name of publication); a list of your brothers and sisters, their ages, and educational status; and statement of financial need (if applicable).
NUMBER OF AWARDS: 1
CONTACT: Teresa Spatara

1544—PHILLIPS FOUNDATION (Journalism Fellowship Program)

7811 Montrose Road, Suite 100
Potomac MD 20854
301/340-2100
FAX: 301/424-0245
Internet: http://www.thephillips foundation.org
AMOUNT: $50,000 (full-time); $25,000 (part-time)
DEADLINE(S): MAR 1
FIELD(S): Journalism
ELIGIBILITY/REQUIREMENTS: For working print journalists with less than 5 years' professional experience to complete 1-year writing project supportive of American culture and a free society.
HOW TO APPLY: See website for application and complete information about the program.
NUMBER OF AWARDS: 1 full-time and 2 part-time awards annually
RENEWABLE: No
CONTACT: John Farley

1545—PRESS CLUB OF DALLAS FOUNDATION

400 North Olive
Dallas TX 75201
214/740-9988
AMOUNT: $1,000-$3,000
DEADLINE(S): APR 15
FIELD(S): Journalism; Public Relations
ELIGIBILITY/REQUIREMENTS: Open to students who are at least sophomores in undergraduate studies or working toward a master's degree in a Texas college or university.
HOW TO APPLY: Write to Foundation address for complete information.
RENEWABLE: Yes, must reapply.
CONTACT: Carol Wortham

1546—PRINT AND GRAPHICS SCHOLARSHIP FOUNDATION, THE (PGSF)

200 Deer Run Road
Sewickley PA 15143-2600
412/259-1740 or 800/ 910-4283
FAX: 412/741-2311
E-mail: pgsf@piagatf.org.
Internet: http://www. pgsf.org
AMOUNT: $500-$5,000
DEADLINE(S): MAR 1 (high school seniors), APR 1 (college undergraduates)
FIELD(S): Graphic Communications; Printing Technology; Printing Management; Publishing
ELIGIBILITY/REQUIREMENTS: For students pursuing careers in above fields, who are enrolled in a 2- or 4-year accredited program at a technical school, college or university in the U.S..
HOW TO APPLY: For more information and application, see website or call, fax or e-mail. Submit with SAT, ACT or SAT/NMSQT (high school students only), official transcript, 2 recommendation forms from a school representative, such as an instructor, counselor, or advisor (1 may be from an employer), a photocopy of course of study,
NUMBER OF AWARDS: 200-300
RENEWABLE: Yes; must meet basic criteria.
CONTACT: Bernie Eckert

1547—PUBLIC RELATIONS STUDENT SOCIETY OF AMERICA (Gary Yoshimura Scholarship)

33 Maiden Lane, 11th Floor
New York NY 10038-5150
212/460-1474
FAX: 212/995-0757
E-mail: prssa@prsa.org
Internet: http://www.prssa.org
AMOUNT: $2,400
DEADLINE(S): JAN 15
FIELD(S): Public Relations
ELIGIBILITY/REQUIREMENTS: Must be a PRSSA member with a minimum 3.0 GPA.
HOW TO APPLY: Submit n transcript and letter of recommendation from an internship supervisor/employer or faculty advisor. In a 1,000-word essay, describe a personal or professional challenge you faced, and how you overcame it (no more than 2 pages).
CONTACT: Director

1548—PUBLIC RELATIONS STUDENT SOCIETY OF AMERICA, THE (Multicultural Affairs Scholarship)

33 Maiden Lane, 11th Floor
New York NY 10038-5150
212/460-1474
FAX: 212/995-0757
E-mail: prssa@prsa.org
Internet: http://www.prssa.org
AMOUNT: $1,500
DEADLINE(S): APR 11
FIELD(S): Communications Studies; Public Relations
ELIGIBILITY/REQUIREMENTS: For African-American, Hispanic, Asian, Native American, Alaskan Native, or Pacific Islander students interested in pursuing a career in public relations. Must be a full-time undergraduate student at an accredited 4-year college or university, at least a junior, and have a GPA of 3.0 or better.
HOW TO APPLY: Contact PSA for details and application.
NUMBER OF AWARDS: 2

1549—QUILL & SCROLL (Edward J. Nell Memorial Scholarship)

School of Journalism E3346AJB
100 Adler Journalism Bldg.
Iowa City IA 52242-2004
319/335-3457
E-mail: quill-scroll@uiowa.edu
Internet: http://www.uiowa. edu/~quill-sc
AMOUNT: $500-$2,000
DEADLINE(S): MAY 10
FIELD(S): Journalism
ELIGIBILITY/REQUIREMENTS: Open to high school seniors who are winners in the National Writing/Photo Contest (deadline FEB 5) or Yearbook Excellence Contest (deadline NOV 1) sponsored by Quill & Scroll, who plan to enroll in an accredited journalism program. Must be U.S. citizen or legal resident.
HOW TO APPLY: Contact your journalism teacher or Quill & Scroll for information.

1550—RADIO AND TELEVISION NEWS DIRECTORS ASSOCIATION & FOUNDATION (Carole Simpson Scholarship)

1600 K Street NW, Suite 700
Washington DC 20006
202/467-5218
FAX: 202/223-4007
E-mail: melaniel@rtndf.org
Internet: http://www.rtndf.org
AMOUNT: $2,000

DEADLINE(S): MAY 3
FIELD(S): All (emphasis on
Broadcast/Cable Journalism)
ELIGIBILITY/REQUIREMENTS:
College sophomore or higher with at least
1 full year of college remaining may apply.
May be enrolled in any major, but must
intend a career in television or radio news.
Preference given to an undergraduate stu-
dent of color.
HOW TO APPLY: Submit application
along with a résumé, 1-3 examples (less
than 15 minutes) showing skills on
audio/VHS tape, accompanied by scripts
and brief statement describing applicant's
role in stories, who worked on each, and
what each person did. Letter of endorsement from dean or project advisor, and
statement explaining career goals required.
See website for application or contact
Project Coordinator.
NUMBER OF AWARDS: 1
CONTACT: Melanie Lo, Program
Coordinator

1551—RADIO AND TELEVISION NEWS DIRECTORS ASSOCIATION & FOUNDATION (Ed Bradley Scholarship)

1600 K Street NW, Suite 700
Washington DC 20006
202/467-5218
FAX: 202/223-4007
E-mail: melaniel@rtnda.org
Internet: http://www.rtndf.org
AMOUNT: $10,000
DEADLINE(S): MAY 3
FIELD(S): All (emphasis on
Broadcast/Cable Journalism)
ELIGIBILITY/REQUIREMENTS:
College sophomore or higher with at least
1 full year of college remaining may apply.
May be enrolled in any major, but must
intend a career in television or radio news.
Preference given to an undergraduate stu-
dent of color.
HOW TO APPLY: Submit application
along with a résumé and 1-3 examples (less
than 15 minutes) showing skills on
audio/VHS tape, accompanied by scripts
and brief statement describing applicant's
role in stories, who worked on each, and
what each person did. Letter of endorsement from dean or project advisor, and
statement explaining career goals required.
See website for application or contact
Project Coordinator.
NUMBER OF AWARDS: 1
CONTACT: Melanie Lo, Program
Coordinator

1552—RADIO AND TELEVISION NEWS DIRECTORS ASSOCIATION & FOUNDATION (George Foreman Tribute to Lyndon B. Johnson Scholarship)

1600 K Street NW, Suite 700
Washington DC 20006
202/467-5218
FAX: 202/223-4007
E-mail: melaniel@rtnda.org
Internet: http://www.rtndf.org
AMOUNT: $6,000
DEADLINE(S): MAY 3
FIELD(S): Broadcast/Cable Journalism
ELIGIBILITY/REQUIREMENTS: Any
full-time graduate or undergraduate in
good standing enrolled in University of
Texas in Austin, with at least 1 full year of
college remaining may apply. Must be U.S.
citizen.
HOW TO APPLY: Entry must include 1-3
examples (less than 15 minutes) showing
skills on audio/VHS tape, accompanied by
scripts and brief statement describing
applicant's role in stories, who worked on
each, and what each person did. Letter of
endorsement and statement explaining
career goals required. See website or contact Project Coordinator.
NUMBER OF AWARDS: 1
CONTACT: Melanie Lo, Program
Coordinator

1553—RADIO AND TELEVISION NEWS DIRECTORS ASSOCIATION & FOUNDATION (Ken Kashiwahara Scholarship)

1600 K Street NW, Suite 700
Washington DC 20006
202/467-5218
FAX: 202/223-4007
E-mail: melaniel@rtnda.org
Internet: http://www.rtndf.org
AMOUNT: $2,500
DEADLINE(S): MAY 3
FIELD(S): All
ELIGIBILITY/REQUIREMENTS: Open
to sophomores, juniors and seniors cur-
rently enrolled in college (must have at
least 1 full year remaining). Preference is
given to student of color. May be enrolled
in any major, but must intend a career in
television or radio news.
HOW TO APPLY: See website or contact
Project Coordinator.
NUMBER OF AWARDS: 1
CONTACT: Melanie Lo, Program
Coordinator

1554—RADIO AND TELEVISION NEWS DIRECTORS ASSOCIATION & FOUNDATION (Lou and Carole Prato Sports Reporting Scholarship)

1600 K Street NW, Suite 700
Washington DC 20006
202/467-5218
FAX: 202/223-4007
E-mail: melaniel@rtnda.org
Internet: http://www.rtndf.org
AMOUNT: $1,000
DEADLINE(S): MAY 5
FIELD(S): All (emphasis on
Broadcast/Cable Journalism)
ELIGIBILITY/REQUIREMENTS:
College sophomore or higher with at least
1 full year of college remaining may apply.
May be enrolled in any major so long as
applicant intends a career as a sports
reporter in television or radio.
HOW TO APPLY: Submit application
along with a résumé and 1-3 examples (less
than 15 minutes) showing skills on audio/
VHS tape, accompanied by scripts and
brief statement describing applicant's role
in stories, who worked on each, and what
each person did. Letter of endorsement
from dean or project advisor, and statement explaining career goals required. See
website for application or contact Project
Coordinator.
NUMBER OF AWARDS: 1
CONTACT: Melanie Lo, Program
Coordinator

1555—RADIO AND TELEVISION NEWS DIRECTORS ASSOCIATION & FOUNDATION (Mike Reynolds Scholarship)

1600 K Street NW, Suite 700
Washington DC 20006
202/467-5218
FAX: 202/223-4007
E-mail: melaniel@rtnda.org
Internet: http://www.rtndf.org
AMOUNT: $1,000
DEADLINE(S): MAY 3
FIELD(S): All (emphasis on
Broadcast/Cable Journalism)
ELIGIBILITY/REQUIREMENTS:
College sophomore or higher with at least
1 full year of college remaining may apply.
May be enrolled in any major, but must
intend a career in television or radio news.
Preference given to student demonstrating
financial need.
HOW TO APPLY: Submit application
along with a résumé and 1-3 examples (less
than 15 minutes) showing skills on

audio/VHS tape, accompanied by scripts and brief statement describing applicant's role in stories, who worked on each, and what each person did. Letter of endorsement from dean or project advisor, and statement explaining career goals required. Indicate media-related jobs held and contribution made to funding education. Must submit FAFSA. See website for application or contact Project Coordinator.
NUMBER OF AWARDS: 1
CONTACT: Melanie Lo, Program Coordinator

1556—RADIO AND TELEVISION NEWS DIRECTORS ASSOCIATION & FOUNDATION (Pete Wilson Journalism Scholarship)

1600 K Street NW, Suite 700
Washington DC 20006
202/467-5218
FAX: 202/223-4007
E-mail: melaniel@rtndf.org
Internet: http://www.rtndf.org
AMOUNT: $4,000
DEADLINE(S): MAY 3
FIELD(S): All (emphasis on Broadcast/Cable Journalism)
ELIGIBILITY/REQUIREMENTS: College sophomore or higher with at least one full year of college remaining may apply. May be enrolled in any major so long as applicant intends a career in television or radio news. Open to students from the Bay Area pursuing a journalism undergraduate or graduate degree.
HOW TO APPLY: Submit application along with a résumé, 1-3 examples of work demonstrating journalistic skills (15 minutes or less on audio or video cassette accompanied by script); brief statement describing your role (writing, editing, producing, reporting, videography) in each story and a list of colleagues, if any, who worked on each story and what they did; a 1-page statement explaining interest in career in broadcast or cable journalism, with reference to your specific career preferences (radio or television, reporting, producing or newsroom management), and letter of reference from dean or faculty sponsor. See website for application or contact Project Coordinator.
NUMBER OF AWARDS: 1
CONTACT: Melanie Lo, Program Coordinator
ADDITIONAL INFORMATION: All winners receive travel, hotel accommodation and registration to annual convention.

1557—RADIO AND TELEVISION NEWS DIRECTORS ASSOCIATION & FOUNDATION (Presidents' Scholarships)

1600 K Street NW, Suite 700

Washington DC 20006
202/467-5218
FAX: 202/223-4007
E-mail: melaniel@rtndf.org
Internet: http://www.rtndf.org
AMOUNT: $2,500
DEADLINE(S): MAY 3
FIELD(S): All
ELIGIBILITY/REQUIREMENTS: Open to sophomores, juniors, and seniors currently enrolled in college (must have at least one full year remaining). May be enrolled in any major, but must intend a career in television or radio news.
HOW TO APPLY: See website or contact Project Coordinator.
NUMBER OF AWARDS: 2
CONTACT: Melanie Lo, Program Coordinator
ADDITIONAL INFORMATION: All winners receive travel, hotel accommodation and registration to annual convention.

1558—SACRAMENTO SCOTTISH RITE BODIES (Edson L. Bryson Memorial Scholarship)

Sacramento Scottish Rite of Freemasonry
P.O. Box 19497
Sacramento CA 95819
AMOUNT: Varies
DEADLINE(S): JUN 10
FIELD(S): Communications; Speech Therapy
ELIGIBILITY/REQUIREMENTS: Open to students studying for the ministry.
HOW TO APPLY: Write to General Secretary for application and additional information. Submit application with transcripts of all high school and college work, photograph and brief biographical sketch. Finalists may be required to meet with a screening committee.
NUMBER OF AWARDS: At least 1
CONTACT: Michael L. Sellick, General Secretary

1559—SAN DIEGO PRESS CLUB FOUNDATION (Joe Lipper Memorial Scholarship)

2454 Heritage Park Row
San Diego CA 92110
619/299-5747
E-mail: sdpressc@cts.com
Internet: http://www.sddt.com/~pressclub
AMOUNT: $1,500-$2,500
DEADLINE(S): JUL 1
FIELD(S): Journalism; English

ELIGIBILITY/REQUIREMENTS: Open to university and community college students, who are San Diego County residents, pursuing a career in journalism or a related field. Selection based on GPA, participation in community service, and media-related internships. Writing and producing news for college newspapers, radio, or television is considered.
HOW TO APPLY: Submit an essay expressing interest in a journalism career.
NUMBER OF AWARDS: 2
CONTACT: Denise Vedder, 619/531-3536, thevedders@sbcglobal.net

1560—SCRIPPS HOWARD FOUNDATION (Ted Scripps Scholarships & Lecture)

312 Walnut Street
P.O. Box 5380
Cincinnati OH 45201/5380
513/977-3847
FAX: 513/977-3800
E-mail: cottingham@scripps.com
Internet: http://www.scripps.com/foundation
AMOUNT: $3,000 + medal
DEADLINE(S): Varies
FIELD(S): Journalism
ELIGIBILITY/REQUIREMENTS: Students must be majoring in journalism at the University of Nevada at Reno.
HOW TO APPLY: Applications are available from UN-Reno.
NUMBER OF AWARDS: 4

1561—SOCIETY FOR TECHNICAL COMMUNICATION

901 North Stuart Street, Suite 904
Arlington VA 22203
703/522-4114
FAX: 703/522-2075
E-mail: stc@stc.org
Internet: http://www.stcva.org/scholar/scholarships.html
AMOUNT: $1,000
DEADLINE(S): FEB 15
FIELD(S): Communications (including technical writing, editing, graphic design, multimedia art, and related fields)
ELIGIBILITY/REQUIREMENTS: Open to full-time students who have completed at least 1 year of postsecondary education working toward a Bachelor's degree and enrolled in an accredited 2- or 4-year degree program for career in any area of technical communications.
HOW TO APPLY: See website or write for information.
NUMBER OF AWARDS: 7

1562—SOCIETY OF PROFESSIONAL JOURNALISTS-LOS ANGELES CHAPTER (Bill Farr Scholarship)

Department of Journalism
California State University-LB
1250 Bellflower Boulevard
Long Beach CA 90840
562/985-5779
FAX: 562/985-5300
E-mail: cburnett@csulb.edu
Internet: http://www.spj.org/losangeles
AMOUNT: Up to $1,000
DEADLINE(S): APR 15
FIELD(S): Journalism
ELIGIBILITY/REQUIREMENTS: Open to college juniors, seniors, or graduate students who attend school in Los Angeles, Orange, or Ventura counties in California and are preparing for a career in journalism.
HOW TO APPLY: See website for application; submit by mail.
NUMBER OF AWARDS: 1
RENEWABLE: No
CONTACT: Christopher Burnett

1563—SOCIETY OF PROFESSIONAL JOURNALISTS-LOS ANGELES CHAPTER (Carl Greenberg Prize)

Department of Journalism
California State University-LB
1250 Bellflower Boulevard
Long Beach CA 90840
562/985-5779
FAX: 562/985-5300
E-mail: cburnett@csulb.edu
Internet: http://www.spj.org/losangeles
AMOUNT: Up to $1,000
DEADLINE(S): APR 15
FIELD(S): Journalism: Political or Investigative Reporting
ELIGIBILITY/REQUIREMENTS: Open to college juniors, seniors, or graduate students who reside or attend school in Los Angeles, Orange, or Ventura counties in California and are preparing for a career in journalism.
HOW TO APPLY: See website for application; submit by mail with published political or investigative report. Mail application to address above.
NUMBER OF AWARDS: 1
RENEWABLE: No
CONTACT: Christopher Burnett

1564—SOCIETY OF PROFESSIONAL JOURNALISTS-LOS ANGELES CHAPTER (Helen Johnson Scholarship)

Department of Journalism

California State University-LB
1250 Bellflower Boulevard
Long Beach CA 90840
562/985-5779
FAX: 562/985-5300
E-mail: cburnett@csulb.edu
Internet: http://www.spj.org/losangeles
DEADLINE(S): APR 15
FIELD(S): Broadcast Journalism
ELIGIBILITY/REQUIREMENTS: Open to college juniors, seniors, or graduate students who reside or attend school in Los Angeles, Ventura, or Orange counties in California and are preparing for a career in broadcast journalism.
HOW TO APPLY: See website for application; mail application to address above.
NUMBER OF AWARDS: 1
RENEWABLE: No
CONTACT: Christopher Burnett

1565—SOCIETY OF PROFESSIONAL JOURNALISTS-LOS ANGELES CHAPTER (Ken Inouye Scholarship)

Department of Journalism
California State University-LB
1250 Bellflower Boulevard
Long Beach CA 90840
562/985-5779
FAX: 562/985-5300
E-mail: cburnett@csulb.edu
Internet: http://www.spj.org/losangeles
DEADLINE(S): APR 15
FIELD(S): Journalism
ELIGIBILITY/REQUIREMENTS: Open to ethnic minority students who will be juniors, seniors, or graduate students the following year. Must reside or attend school in Los Angeles, Orange, or Ventura counties in California and be preparing for a career in journalism.
HOW TO APPLY: See website for application; mail application to address above.
NUMBER OF AWARDS: 1
RENEWABLE: No
CONTACT: Christopher Burnett

1566—SOCIETY OF PROFESSIONAL JOURNALISTS (Mark of Excellence Awards Competition)

Eugene South Pulliam
National Journalism Center
3909 North Meridian Street
Indianapolis IN 46208
317/927-8000
FAX: 317/920-4789
E-mail: questions@spj.org

Internet: http://www.spj.org/
AMOUNT: Varies
DEADLINE(S): FEB 2
FIELD(S): All (print, radio, television, and online collegiate journalism)
ELIGIBILITY/REQUIREMENTS: Open to students enrolled in a college or university and studying for an academic degree. Entries must have been published or broadcast during calendar year in which the award is presented, and entrant must have been a student at the time of publication or broadcast. Work published, broadcast or produced while working as a student intern is acceptable. Unpublished manuscripts, classroom exercises, and unaired news broadcasts do not qualify. Entries are judged on the regional level. First-place winning entries will go on to the national competition.
HOW TO APPLY: See website for detailed entry requirements for each category and entry form. Contestants may enter as many categories as desired, up to 2 entries/category. Fee/entry is $9 for members; $18 for nonmembers.
NUMBER OF AWARDS: 45 categories (print, radio, television, and online journalism).

1567—SOCIETY OF SATELLITE PROFESSIONALS INTERNATIONAL (SSPI Scholarship Program)

The New York Information
Technology Center
55 Broad Street, 14th Floor
New York NY 10004
212/809-5199
FAX: 212/825-0075
E-mail: neworbit@aol.com
Internet: http://www.sspi.org
AMOUNT: $1,500-$4,000
DEADLINE(S): DEC 1
FIELD(S): Satellites (relating to communications, domestic and international telecommunications policy, remote sensing, journalism, law, meteorology, energy, navigation, business, government, and broadcasting services)
ELIGIBILITY/REQUIREMENTS: Open to current high school seniors, college or university undergraduate or graduate students studying or intending to study satellite-related technologies, policies or applications. Must demonstrate commitment to pursue education and career opportunities in the satellite industry or a field making direct use of satellite technology; academic and leadership achievement; and potential for significant contribution to the industry.
HOW TO APPLY: Before applying, all applicants must complete a Scholarship

Qualification Form to determine whether your interests and career plans are a good fit for the program. See website for form and details or send SASE.

1568—SOUTHERN CALIFORNIA CHAPTER OF WOMEN IN CABLE AND TELECOMMUNICATIONS, THE (The Jeanne Cardinal Grant)

Avenue TV Cable Service
P.O. Box 1458
Ventura CA 93002
AMOUNT: $1,000
DEADLINE(S): JAN 31
FIELD(S): Telecommunications
ELIGIBILITY/REQUIREMENTS: Available to junior and senior class women pursuing a degree in telecommunications. Minimum GPA of 3.0. Must be involved in at least 1 school-related organization or participate in community service.
HOW TO APPLY: Contact Scholarship Committee Chair for application and details.
CONTACT: Pamela Drake, Scholarship Committee Chair

1569—SPORTS JOURNALISM INSTITUTE (Internships)

Gregory Lee
The Boston Globe
135 Morrissey Blvd.
Boston MA 02125
Internet: http://www.sports journalisminstitute.org/
AMOUNT: $500 for 9-week internship
DEADLINE(S): DEC 5
FIELD(S): All (emphasis on print journalism, especially sports reporting and editing)
ELIGIBILITY/REQUIREMENTS: 9-week training and internship program for college students interested in sports journalism careers. Preference given to ethnic and racial minority groups, with a mix of male and female students. Applicants should be college sophomores or juniors. Selection based on academic achievement, demonstrated interest in sports journalism as a career, and required essay. NOT limited to journalism majors.
HOW TO APPLY: See website for application and details. Submit with transcript, 2 letters of recommendation, a head shot, up to 7 writing samples or clips, and an essay of no more than 500 words stating why you should be selected.
NUMBER OF AWARDS: 10
CONTACT: Gregory Lee

1570—STATE NEWS

Michigan State University
343 Student Services
East Lansing MI 48824-1113
E-mail: recruiter@statenews.com
Internet: http://statenews.com/scholar/scholarship/
AMOUNT: $2,000 + job
DEADLINE(S): FEB 5
FIELD(S): All (emphasis on journalism and advertising)
ELIGIBILITY/REQUIREMENTS: Open to high school seniors entering MSU in the fall. Must have an above-average GPA and have demonstrated a strong interest in journalism or advertising through high school. Recipients work in paying positions at *The State News* after the first semester of their freshman year, either in the newsroom or in the advertising department. *State News* salary is in addition to scholarship. May major in any academic program.
HOW TO APPLY: See website or contact Ben Schwartz, State News General Manager, for an application.
NUMBER OF AWARDS: 2
RENEWABLE: Yes. Up to 4 years

1571—STUDENT CONSERVATION ASSOCIATION (SCA Resource Assistant Program)

P.O. Box 550
Charlestown NH 03603
603/543-1700
FAX: 603/543-1828
E-mail: internships@sca-inc.org
Internet: http://www.sca-inc.org
AMOUNT: $1,180-$4,725
DEADLINE(S): Varies
FIELD(S): Environment and related fields (agriculture, archaeology, anthropology, botany, caves, civil engineering, environmental design, engineering & education, fisheries, forestry, herpetology, history, landscape architecture, paleontology, recreation/resource/range management, wildlife management, geology, hydrology, library/museums, surveying)
ELIGIBILITY/REQUIREMENTS: Must be 18 and U.S. citizen; need not be student.
HOW TO APPLY: Send $1 postage for application; outside U.S./Canada, $20.
NUMBER OF AWARDS: 900 positions

1572—TEXAS BROADCAST EDUCATION FOUNDATION (Belo Corporation Scholarship)

502 East 11th Street, Suite 200

Austin TX 78701
512/322-9944
FAX: 512/322-0522
E-mail: craig@tab.org
Internet: http://www.tab.org
AMOUNT: $2,000
DEADLINE(S): MAY 7
FIELD(S): Broadcasting; Communications
ELIGIBILITY/REQUIREMENTS: Junior or senior student enrolled in a fully accredited program emphasizing radio or television broadcasting or communications at a 4-year Texas college or university.
HOW TO APPLY: Download application from website.
NUMBER OF AWARDS: 1
CONTACT: Craig Bean

1573—TEXAS BROADCAST EDUCATION FOUNDATION (Bonner McLane Scholarship)

502 East 11th Street, Suite 200
Austin TX 78701
512/322-9944
FAX: 512/322-0522
E-mail: craig@tab.org
Internet: http://www.tab.org
AMOUNT: $2,000
DEADLINE(S): MAY 7
FIELD(S): Broadcasting; Communications
ELIGIBILITY/REQUIREMENTS: Junior or senior student enrolled in a fully accredited program emphasizing radio or television broadcasting or communications at a 4-year Texas college or university.
HOW TO APPLY: Download application from website.
NUMBER OF AWARDS: 1
CONTACT: Craig Bean

1574—TEXAS BROADCAST EDUCATION FOUNDATION (Lady Bird Johnson Internship)

502 East 11th Street, Suite 200
Austin TX 78701
512/322-9944
FAX: 512/322-0522
E-mail: craig@tab.org
Internet: http://www.tab.org
AMOUNT: $2,000
DEADLINE(S): MAY 7
FIELD(S): Broadcasting; Communications
ELIGIBILITY/REQUIREMENTS: Student enrolled at University of Texas-Austin in a program emphasizing communications. Recipient will intern at the Lady Bird Johnson Wildflower Center.

HOW TO APPLY: Download application from website.
NUMBER OF AWARDS: 1
CONTACT: Craig Bean

1575—TEXAS BROADCAST EDUCATION FOUNDATION (Tom Reiff Scholarship)

502 East 11th Street, Suite 200
Austin TX 78701
512/322-9944
FAX: 512/322-0522
E-mail: craig@tab.org
Internet: http://www.tab.org
AMOUNT: $2,000
DEADLINE(S): MAY 7
FIELD(S): Broadcasting;
    Communications
ELIGIBILITY/REQUIREMENTS: Upcoming junior or senior student enrolled in a fully accredited program emphasizing radio or television broadcasting or communications at a 4-year Texas college or university.
HOW TO APPLY: Download application from website.
NUMBER OF AWARDS: 1
CONTACT: Craig Bean

1576—TEXAS BROADCAST EDUCATION FOUNDATION (Two- and Four-Year Scholarship Programs)

502 East 11th Street, Suite 200
Austin TX 78701
512/322-9944
FAX: 512/322-0522
E-mail: craig@tab.org
Internet: http://www.tab.org
AMOUNT: $2,000
DEADLINE(S): MAY 7
FIELD(S): Broadcasting;
    Communications
ELIGIBILITY/REQUIREMENTS: Must attend fully accredited Texas school in a program emphasizing communications or broadcasting. Open to freshman or sophomore enrolled in a 4-year program and students enrolled in a 2-year or technical school.
HOW TO APPLY: Download application from website.
NUMBER OF AWARDS: 2
CONTACT: Craig Bean

1577—TEXAS BROADCAST EDUCATION FOUNDATION (Vann Kennedy Scholarship)

502 East 11th Street, Suite 200
Austin TX 78701
512/322-9944
FAX: 512/322-0522

E-mail: craig@tab.org
Internet: http://www.tab.org
AMOUNT: $2,000
DEADLINE(S): MAY 7
FIELD(S): Broadcasting;
    Communications
ELIGIBILITY/REQUIREMENTS: Student enrolled in a fully accredited program emphasizing radio or television broadcasting or communications at a Texas college or university.
HOW TO APPLY: Download application from website.
NUMBER OF AWARDS: 1
CONTACT: Craig Bean

1578—TEXAS BROADCAST EDUCATION FOUNDATION (Wendell Mayes, Jr. Scholarship)

502 East 11th Street, Suite 200
Austin TX 78701
512/322-9944
FAX: 512/322-0522
E-mail: craig@tab.org
Internet: http://www.tab.org
AMOUNT: $2,000
DEADLINE(S): MAY 7
FIELD(S): Broadcasting;
    Communications
ELIGIBILITY/REQUIREMENTS: Student enrolled in a fully accredited program emphasizing radio or television broadcasting or communications at a Texas college or university.
HOW TO APPLY: Download application from website.
NUMBER OF AWARDS: 1
CONTACT: Craig Bean

1579—TURF AND ORNAMENTAL COMMUNICATORS ASSOCIATION

120 West Main Street
P.O. Box 156
New Prague MN 56071
952/758-6340
FAX: 952/758-5813
E-mail: tocaassociation@aol.com
Internet: http://www.toca.org
AMOUNT: $1,000
DEADLINE(S): MAR 1
FIELD(S): Technical Communications; or
    Green industry-related fields:
    Horticulture; Plant Science, Botany;
    Agronomy, Plant Pathology
ELIGIBILITY/REQUIREMENTS: Must be enrolled in college or university as undergraduate in a 2- or 4-year program. Overall GPA of 2.5; major subject GPA 3.0+.

HOW TO APPLY: Contact TOCA for application forms, include your mailing address.
NUMBER OF AWARDS: 2
RENEWABLE: No, must reapply.

1580—UNITED METHODIST COMMUNICATIONS (Leonard Perryman Communications Scholarships)

Communications Resourcing Team
P.O. Box 320
Nashville TN 37202-0320
888/278-4862
FAX: 615/742-5485
E-mail: scholarships@umcom.org
Internet: http://www.umcom.org/
    scholar/scholarships
AMOUNT: $2,500
DEADLINE(S): MAR 15
FIELD(S): Journalism; Communications
ELIGIBILITY/REQUIREMENTS: Open to United Methodist undergraduate juniors and seniors, enrolled in accredited U.S. schools of communication or journalism (print, electronic, or audiovisual). Must be members of an ethnic minority pursuing career in communication.
HOW TO APPLY: See website or contact UMC for an application.
NUMBER OF AWARDS: 2
RENEWABLE: No
CONTACT: Jackie Vaughan

1581—UNIVERSITY OF MARYLAND (College of Journalism Scholarships)

Journalism Building,
Room 1117
College Park MD 20742-7111
301/405-2399
Internet: http://www.inform.
umd.edu/jour
AMOUNT: $250-$1,500
DEADLINE(S): FEB 15
FIELD(S): Journalism
ELIGIBILITY/REQUIREMENTS: Variety of journalism scholarships, prizes, and awards tenable at the University of Maryland.
HOW TO APPLY: See website or write for complete information.

1582—UNIVERSITY OF OKLAHOMA– H.H. HERBERT SCHOOL OF JOURNALISM AND MASS COMMUNICATION (Undergraduate Scholarships)

860 Van Vleet Oval, Room 101
Norman OK 73019
405/325-2721
AMOUNT: $5,000/year

DEADLINE(S): FEB

FIELD(S): Journalism: Print or Broadcast, Advertising, Electronic Media, News Communication, Professional Writing, Public Relations

ELIGIBILITY/REQUIREMENTS: For undergraduate students who plan to attend the University of Oklahoma.

HOW TO APPLY: Contact Herbert School for additional information and application. Interview is part of acceptance process.

CONTACT: David Dary

1583—UTA ALUMNI ASSOCIATION (Karin McCallum Scholarship)

University of Texas-Arlington
Box 19457
Arlington TX 76019
Internet: http://www.uta.edu/alumni/scholar.htm

AMOUNT: $250

DEADLINE(S): Varies

FIELD(S): Speech; Communications

ELIGIBILITY/REQUIREMENTS: Must be a full-time junior or senior at the University of Texas-Arlington.

HOW TO APPLY: Contact UTA Alumni Association for an application. Must submit transcript, professional résumé, and letter of recommendation from a Communications professor.

NUMBER OF AWARDS: 1

1584—UTA ALUMNI ASSOCIATION (Lloyd Clark Scholarship Journalism)

University of Texas-Arlington
Box 19457
Arlington TX 76019
Internet: http://www.uta.edu/alumni/scholar.htm

AMOUNT: $250

DEADLINE(S): Varies

FIELD(S): Journalism

ELIGIBILITY/REQUIREMENTS: Must be a full-time junior or higher with at least 15 hours completed at the University of Texas-Arlington and have a commitment to a career in journalism. Must demonstrate academic achievement and evidence of success in journalism. Financial need may be considered.

HOW TO APPLY: Contact UTA Alumni Association for an application. Writing sample required.

NUMBER OF AWARDS: 1

1585—WESTERN MICHIGAN UNIVERSITY (College of Arts and Sciences/The Lawrence, Clara, and Evelyn E. Burke Scholarship)

1903 West Michigan
Kalamazoo MI 49008-5337
269/387-8777
FAX: 269/387-6989
E-mail: finaid-info@wmich.edu
Internet: http://www.wmich.edu/finaid

AMOUNT: $300 for fall semester

DEADLINE(S): Not applicable

FIELD(S): Journalism; Communications

ELIGIBILITY/REQUIREMENTS: Must be enrolled in the journalism curriculum; minimum GPA 3.0; extracurricular activities, such as involvement with a school paper, yearbook, or other high school or college journalism experience required. Award based on scholastic achievement.

HOW TO APPLY: Nominated by faculty, selected by journalism staff. Contact the Undergraduate Program, Office of Communications for details.

RENEWABLE: No

1586—WESTERN MICHIGAN UNIVERSITY (College of Arts and Sciences/WWMT Communications Scholarship)

1903 West Michigan
Kalamazoo MI 49008-5337
269/387-8777
FAX: 269/387-6989
E-mail: finaid-info@wmich.edu
Internet: http://www.wmich.edu/finaid

AMOUNT: $1,000

DEADLINE(S): Not applicable

FIELD(S): Television; Communications

ELIGIBILITY/REQUIREMENTS: Full-time, undergraduate student at WMU in junior or senior year; television broadcast major with 3.5 GPA.

HOW TO APPLY: Contact the Office of Communications for details.

RENEWABLE: No

1587—WESTERN MICHIGAN UNIVERSITY (Haworth College of Business/Piler Group Tony Walker Memorial Scholarship)

1903 West Michigan
Kalamazoo MI 49008-5337
269/387-6000
FAX: 269/387-6989
E-mail: finaid-info@wmich.edu
Internet: http://www.wmich.edu/finaid

AMOUNT: Varies

DEADLINE(S): FEB 15

FIELD(S): Advertising; Promotion; Marketing; Writing, Journalism

ELIGIBILITY/REQUIREMENTS: Open to full-time undergraduate or graduate student who works at least 15 hours per week at the *Western Herald* in Circulation, Business (Secretary, Classifieds), Display Advertising, or as Student Manager of a Department. Preference given to applicants with a 3.0 GPA or higher.

HOW TO APPLY: Contact the Marketing Department for more information.

RENEWABLE: Yes

1588—WESTERN MICHIGAN UNIVERSITY (Lawrence, Clara & Evelyn E. Burke Scholarship)

1903 West Michigan
Kalamazoo MI 49008-5337
269/387-8777
FAX: 269/387-6989
E-mail: alumni@wmich.edu
Internet: http://www.www.wmich.edu/alumni

AMOUNT: Varies

DEADLINE(S): APR 1

FIELD(S): Theater; Journalism

ELIGIBILITY/REQUIREMENTS: Full- or part-time graduate or undergraduate students enrolled in Theater or Journalism. GPA 3.0 or higher; selection based on scholastic achievement. Theater students: participation in a theater production at the high school or college level; potential for a career in theater. Journalism students: involvement with a school paper or yearbook at the high school or college level; potential for a career in journalism.

HOW TO APPLY: Contact the Office of Financial Aid for more details.

RENEWABLE: Yes. Up to a maximum of 4 consecutive academic years, must maintain a 3.0 GPA.

1589—W. EUGENE SMITH MEMORIAL FUND, INC. (Howard Chapnick Grant for the Advancement of Photojournalism)

c/o International Center for Creative Photography
1133 Avenue of the Americas
New York NY 10036
212/857-0038
Internet: http://www.smithfund.org/fund.html

AMOUNT: $5,000

DEADLINE(S): JUL 15

FIELD(S): Photojournalism

ELIGIBILITY/REQUIREMENTS: May be used to finance a range of qualified undertakings such as education, research, long-term sabbatical project, or internship to work with a noteworthy group of individuals. Special consideration will be given to projects that promote social change

and/or serve significant concerns of photojournalism.
HOW TO APPLY: See website or write for application.
NUMBER OF AWARDS: 2
RENEWABLE: No
CONTACT: Anna Winand

1590—W. EUGENE SMITH MEMORIAL FUND, INC. (W. Eugene Smith Grant in Humanistic Photography)

c/o International Center for Creative Photography
1133 Avenue of the Americas
New York NY 10036
212/857-0038
Internet: http://www.smithfund.org/fund.html
AMOUNT: $20,000; $5,000
DEADLINE(S): JUL 15
FIELD(S): Photojournalism
ELIGIBILITY/REQUIREMENTS: Career support for photojournalists of any nationality.
HOW TO APPLY: Must submit a photographic project with a written proposal, illustrated in the humanistic manner of W. Eugene Smith. Financial need NOT a factor. Write or phone for application.
NUMBER OF AWARDS: 2
RENEWABLE: No
CONTACT: Anna Winand

1591—WILLIAM RANDOLPH HEARST FOUNDATION (Journalism Awards Program)

90 New Montgomery Street, Suite 1212
San Francisco CA 94105
415/543-6033
FAX: 415/243-0760
AMOUNT: $500-$3,000
DEADLINE(S): Varies (OCT-APR)
FIELD(S): Print Journalism; Photo-journalism; Broadcast News
ELIGIBILITY/REQUIREMENTS: Monthly competitions open to undergraduate college journalism majors who are enrolled in 1 of 107 participating journalism schools.
HOW TO APPLY: Entry forms and details available ONLY through the journalism department of participating schools.
NUMBER OF AWARDS: 13 (6 print journalism, 3 photojournalism, 4 broadcast news competitions).

1592—WOMEN'S SPORTS FOUNDATION (Jackie Joyner-Kersee and Zina Garrison Minority Internships)

Eisenhower Park
East Meadow NY 11554
800/227-3988 (U.S. only) or
516/542-4700
FAX: 516/542-4716
E-mail: WoSport@aol.com
Internet: http://www.womenssports foundation.org
AMOUNT: $4,000-$5,000
DEADLINE(S): Ongoing
FIELD(S): Sports-related careers
ELIGIBILITY/REQUIREMENTS: Women of color who are undergraduate students, college graduates, graduate students, or women in career change. Internships are located at the Women's Sports Foundation in East Meadow, New York.
HOW TO APPLY: See website or write to above address for details.
NUMBER OF AWARDS: 4-6

ENGLISH LANGUAGE AND LITERATURE

1593—AMERICAN FOUNDATION FOR THE BLIND (R. L. Gillette Scholarships)

11 Penn Plaza, Suite 300
New York NY 10001
212/502-7661
FAX: 212/502-7771
E-mail: afbinfo@afb.net
Internet: http://www.afb.org/scholar/scholarships.asp
AMOUNT: $1,000
DEADLINE(S): MAR 31
FIELD(S): Literature; Music
ELIGIBILITY/REQUIREMENTS: Open to legally blind women, U.S. citizens, enrolled in a 4-year undergraduate degree program in literature or music.
HOW TO APPLY: See website or contact AFB for an application. Submit with evidence of legal blindness; official transcripts; proof of college/university acceptance; 3 letters of recommendation; performance tape (30 minutes maximum) or creative writing sample; and description of educational and personal goals, work experience, extracurricular activities, and how monies will be used.
NUMBER OF AWARDS: 2
CONTACT: Alina Vayntrub

1594—AMERICAN INSTITUTE OF ARCHITECTS-NEW YORK CHAPTER (Douglas Haskell Award)

200 Lexington Avenue, 6th Floor
New York NY 10016
212/683-0023, ext. 14
FAX: 212/696-5022
E-mail: info@aiany.org
Internet: http://www.aiany.org/nyfoundation/scholarships.html
AMOUNT: $2,000 (minimum)
DEADLINE(S): MAR 21
FIELD(S): Architectural Writing
ELIGIBILITY/REQUIREMENTS: For students enrolled in a professional architecture or related program, such as art history, interior design, urban studies, and landscape architecture.
HOW TO APPLY: See website or contact AIANY for details. Submit a news story, an essay or feature article, book review, or journal and 100-word statement describing the purpose of the piece.

1595—AMERICAN LEGION (National High School Oratorical Contest)

P.O. Box 1055
Indianapolis IN 46206
317/630-1249
E-mail: mbuss@legion.org
Internet: http://www.legion.org
AMOUNT: $14,000-$18,000 (national); $1,500 (quarter finalist); $1,500 (each state winner)
DEADLINE(S): Varies
FIELD(S): English Language/Literature
ELIGIBILITY/REQUIREMENTS: Must be U.S. citizen or permanent resident, aged 20 or less on the date of the contest and enrolled in a high school or junior high school (public, parochial, military, private, or state-accredited home school) at the time of participation at any level of the contest.
HOW TO APPLY: See website and contact local Post for details.

1596—AMY LOWELL POETRY TRAVELLING SCHOLARSHIP TRUST

Choate, Hall, and Stewart, LLC
Two International Place
Boston MA 02110
617/248-5000
FAX: 617/248-4000
AMOUNT: $40,000
DEADLINE(S): OCT. 15
FIELD(S): Literature; Poetry; Writing
ELIGIBILITY/REQUIREMENTS: Open to American-born poets of good standing. Preference given to those of progressive literary tendencies. Recipient agrees to spend 1 year outside the continent of North America in a place chosen by the recipient. At the end of the year, the recipient shall submit at least 3 poems for consideration by the Trust's committee.

HOW TO APPLY: Contact Trust for details.

NUMBER OF AWARDS: 1

1597—ANDRE SOBEL RIVER OF LIFE FOUNDATION (Essay Contest)

8899 Beverly Boulevard, Suite 111
Los Angeles CA 90048
310//276-7111
FAX: 310/276-0244
E-mail: info@andreriveroflife.org
Internet: http//www.andreriver
oflife.org

AMOUNT: $5,,000 (1st prize); 5 additional prizes at various amounts

DEADLINE(S): JUN 15

FIELD(S): Essay Contest

ELIGIBILITY/REQUIREMENTS: Award honors cancer survivors under the age of 21; must submit an essay on a topic selected each year (see website), for example on a topic like "The Letter I Would Like to Have Received From a Friend or Relative During My Illness."

HOW TO APPLY: See website for complete rules, submission guidelines, and application.

NUMBER OF AWARDS: 6 (1 top prize, 5 additional prizes)

RENEWABLE: No

1598—ASSOCIATION FOR THE STUDY OF AFRO-AMERICAN LIFE & HISTORY, INC. (Afro-American Life and History Essay Contest)

C.B. Powell Building
525 Bryant Street, Suite C142
Washington, DC 20059
202/865-0053
FAX: 202/265-7920
Email: info@asalh.netInternet:
http://asalh.org/EssayContests.html

AMOUNT: $500

DEADLINE(S): JUN 30

FIELD(S): Afro American Studies

ELIGIBILITY/REQUIREMENTS: Any full-time student in a 2- or 4-year college may enter the competition. Essays may be submitted on any topic that explores the life, history and culture of Africans throughout the Americas and the Caribbean. Papers that are only polemical and offer only personal opinions are not acceptable; a research approach is required. Essays should cite the appropriate primary and secondary sources related to the topic under examination (see website for further details). Criteria include clarity, organization, orginality, and documentation.

HOW TO APPLY: Via e-mail (essaycontest@asalh.net), submit a copy of your paper (see website or e-mail contact below for details) and an endorsement letter from ASALH faculty advisor/sponsor, who must be a current member of ASALH. (An original signed copy of this letter is to be mailed to Felix Armfield, ASALH ESSAY CONTEST at the above address.)

NUMBER OF AWARDS: 1 undergraduate; 1 graduate

CONTACT: Questions MUST be directed to Felix Armfield at armfiefl@buffalostate.edu

ADDITIONAL INFORMATION: Winning writers will be invited to present their essays at the ASALH Annual Meeting.

1599—ASSOCIATION OF ATTORNEY-CERTIFIED PUBLIC ACCOUNTANTS FOUNDATION, THE (Student Writing Competition)

3921 Old Lee Highway,
Suite 71A
Fairfax VA 22030
703/352-8064
FAX: 703/352-8073
E-mail: info@attorney-cpa.com
Internet: http://www.attorney-cpa.com

AMOUNT: $250-$1,500

DEADLINE(S): APR 1

FIELD(S): Accounting; Law

ELIGIBILITY/REQUIREMENTS: Essay contest for accounting and/or law students.

HOW TO APPLY: See website to download form.

NUMBER OF AWARDS: 10

RENEWABLE: No

1600—AYN RAND INSTITUTE (Anthem Essay Contest)

Department W
P.O. Box 57044
Irvine CA 92619-7044
E-mail: anthemessay@aynrand.org
Internet: http://www.aynrand.org/contests/

AMOUNT: $2,000 (1st prize); $500 (2nd); $200 (3rd); $50 (finalists); $30 (semifinalists)

DEADLINE(S): March 18

FIELD(S): All (emphasis on philosophy)

ELIGIBILITY/REQUIREMENTS: Open to 9th and 10th graders who write a 600- to 1,200-word essay on Ayn Rand's novelette *Anthem*. Essays will be judged on both style and content. Judges will look for writing that is clear, articulate and logically organized. Winning essays must demonstrate an outstanding grasp of the philosophic meaning of *Anthem*.

HOW TO APPLY: See website or contact your English teacher or guidance counselor for guidelines. Do NOT write to above address. Submit online, e-mail, or by mail.

NUMBER OF AWARDS: 236 (1 first, 5 second, 10 third, 45 finalist, 175 semifinalists)

1601—AYN RAND INSTITUTE (Atlas Shrugged Essay Competition)

Department W
2121 Alton Parkway, Suite 250
Irvine CA 92606
E-mail: essay@aynrand.org
Internet: http://www.aynrand.org/contests/

AMOUNT: $5,000 (1st prize); $1,000 (2nd); $400 (3rd); $100 (finalist); $50 (semifinalist)

DEADLINE(S): FEB 15

FIELD(S): Business; Philosophy

ELIGIBILITY/REQUIREMENTS: Open to students enrolled in a graduate or undergraduate business-degree program, who write a 1,000- to 1,200-word essay on Ayn Rand's *Atlas Shrugged*. Essays judged on both style and content. Judges will look for writing that is clear, articulate and logically organized. Winning essays must demonstrate an outstanding grasp of the philosophic meaning of *Atlas Shrugged*.

HOW TO APPLY: See website or contact your Business Ethics professor for guidelines. Do NOT write to above address. Submit online, e-mail, or by mail.

NUMBER OF AWARDS: 224 (1 first, 3 second, 5 third, 20 finalist, 200 semifinalist)

1602—AYN RAND INSTITUTE (Fountainhead Essay Contest)

Department W
P.O. Box 57044
Irvine CA 92619-7044
E-mail: tf-essay@aynrand.org
Internet: http://www.aynrand.org/contests/

AMOUNT: $10,000 (1st prize); $2,000 (2nd); $1,000 (3rd); $100 (finalist); $50 (semifinalist)

DEADLINE(S): APR 15

FIELD(S): All

ELIGIBILITY/REQUIREMENTS: Open to 11th and 12th graders who write an 800- to 1,600-word essay on Ayn Rand's *The Fountainhead*. Essays judged on both style and content. Judges will look for writing that is clear, articulate and logically organized. Winning essays must demonstrate

an outstanding grasp of the philosophic and psychological meaning of *The Fountainhead*.
HOW TO APPLY: See website for guidelines. Do NOT write to above address. Submit online, e-mail, or by mail.
NUMBER OF AWARDS: 251 (1 first, 5 second, 10 third, 35 finalist, 200 semifinalist)

1603—BEVERLY HILLS THEATRE GUILD (Julie Harris Playwright Award Competition)

P.O. Box 39729
Los Angeles CA 90039-0729
AMOUNT: $3,5000 (1st award); $2,500 (2nd); $1,500 (3rd)
DEADLINE(S): NOV 1
FIELD(S): Playwriting
ELIGIBILITY/REQUIREMENTS: Must be U.S. citizen or legal resident. Entries (1/entrant) must be in English, original, full-length (minimum 90 minutes playing time), unpublished, unproduced, unoptioned.
HOW TO APPLY: Submit entry with application. To maintain anonymity, all entries identified by number. DO NOT show any identifying information anywhere on your entry. Separate sheet containing the title, your name, address, phone number, etc.
NUMBER OF AWARDS: 1
RENEWABLE: No
CONTACT: Playwright Award Competition

1604—BLUES HEAVEN FOUNDATION, INC. (Muddy Waters Scholarship)

2120 South Michigan Avenue
Chicago IL 60616
312/808/1286
AMOUNT: $2,000
DEADLINE(S): APR 30
FIELD(S): Music; Music Education; African-American Studies; Folklore; Performing Arts; Arts Management; Journalism; Radio/TV/Film
ELIGIBILITY/REQUIREMENTS: Applicant must be full-time graduate or undergraduate in a Chicago area college or university. Scholastic aptitude, extracurricular involvement, GPA, and financial need are considered.
HOW TO APPLY: Contact Foundation between February and April to request an application.

1605—DAVIDSON INSTITUTE FOR TALENT DEVELOPMENT

9665 Gateway

Reno NV 89521
775/852-3483, ext. 423
FAX: 775/852-2184
E-mail: tmoessner@ditd.org
Internet: http://www.davidson fellows.org
AMOUNT: $10,000, $20,000, $50,000
DEADLINE(S): Last Friday of MAR
FIELD(S): Science, Technology, Mathematics, Philosophy, Music, Literature and Outside the Box
ELIGIBILITY/REQUIREMENTS: Must be a U.S. citizen residing in the U.S., or a permanent resident of the U.S. residing in the U.S.; under the age of 18 as of October 1 (there is no minimum age for eligibility); completed a significant piece of work in one of the designated application categories; and available to attend, with at least 1 parent or guardian, the awards reception and other recognition events in September (travel expenses and lodging will be paid by the Institute).
HOW TO APPLY: See website including FAQ section and application booklet; download and complete all components.
NUMBER OF AWARDS: 15-20
RENEWABLE: No
CONTACT: Tacie Moessner, Davidson Fellows Program Manager
ADDITIONAL INFORMATION: Group and team projects are not eligible. Scholarships must be used at an accredited institute of learning within 10 years of the award date.

1606—DOW JONES NEWSPAPER FUND, INC. (Summer Workshops in Journalism & Writing Competition for Minority Students)

P.O. Box 300
Princeton NJ 08543-0300
609/452-2820
E-mail: newsfund@wsj.dowj1s.com
Internet: http://djnewspaperfund. dowj1s.com/fund/default.asp
AMOUNT: $1,000 + paid summer internship
DEADLINE(S): NOV 15
FIELD(S): Journalism
ELIGIBILITY/REQUIREMENTS: Workshops offered at 26 colleges around the U.S. Open to high school seniors and college freshmen interested in journalism, whose ethnic backgrounds are African-American, Pacific Islander, American Indian/Eskimo, Asian, or Hispanic. 10 days of learning to write, report, design, and lay out a newspaper.
HOW TO APPLY: Contact Dow Jones or see website for list of participating colleges/states. Prizewinners are nominated by the director; must submit an essay and a

published story, which will be judged by 3 professional journalists.
NUMBER OF AWARDS: 8
RENEWABLE: Yes. High school students may receive the award for their freshman and sophomore years, provided they maintain a 2.5 GPA and an interest in journalism. Incoming college freshmen receive the award only in their sophomore year.

1607—FIVE WINGS ARTS COUNCIL (Artist Mentor Scholarships for Students)

200 First Street NE
Staples MN 56479
218/894-5485
FAX: 218/894-3045
E-mail: mturner@ncscmn.org
Internet: http://www.fwac.org
AMOUNT: Up to $500
DEADLINE(S): OCT 15
FIELD(S): Literary Arts; Visual Arts; Music; Theater; Media Arts; Dance
ELIGIBILITY/REQUIREMENTS: Open to rural high school students in grades 9 through 12 enrolled in an independent school district within the counties of Cass, Crow Wing, Morrison, Todd, and Wadena, Minnesota. Each recipient is matched with a qualified mentor who will establish a study schedule with student. Award is based on creative potential, accomplishments in art, maturity, and personal motivation.
HOW TO APPLY: Contact Director for details.
NUMBER OF AWARDS: 10
CONTACT: Mark Turner, Director

1608—FOREST ROBERTS THEATRE (Mildred and Albert Panowski Playwriting Award)

Northern Michigan University
1401 Presque Isle Avenue
Marquette MI 49855-5364
906/227-2553
Internet: http://www.nmu.edu/ theater
AMOUNT: $2,000
DEADLINE(S): NOV 21
FIELD(S): Playwriting
ELIGIBILITY/REQUIREMENTS: Open to any playwright. Entries must be original, full-length plays not previously produced or published. May be co-authored, based upon factual material, or an adaptation. Scripts must be typewritten or word processed and securely bound within a cover or folder and clearly identified.
HOW TO APPLY: Only 1 play/playwright may be entered. Include bound script in folder, entry form, or postcard that

includes contact information, 1-page synopsis. SASE must be included. Optional: Additional SASE if you would like the play returned.
NUMBER OF AWARDS: 1
RENEWABLE: No

1609—FREEDOM FROM RELIGION FOUNDATION (Student Essay Contests)

P.O. Box 750
Madison WI 53701
608/256-5800
Internet: http://www.ffrf.org
AMOUNT: $1,000; $500; $250
DEADLINE(S): JUN 1
FIELD(S): Humanities; English; Education; Philosophy; Science
ELIGIBILITY/REQUIREMENTS: Topics change yearly, but all are on general theme of maintaining separation of church and state. Open to high school seniors and students currently enrolled in college or technical schools. Must be U.S. citizen.
HOW TO APPLY: See website for details. Send SASE to address above for complete information. Indicate whether you will be competing in the college or high school competition. Information will be sent when new topics are announced each February.

1610—GOLDEN KEY INTERNATIONAL HONOUR SOCIETY (Literary Achievement Awards)

1189 Ponce de Leon Avenue
Atlanta GA 30306
404/377-2400 or 800/377-2401
FAX: 404/373-7033
E-mail: scholarships@goldenkey.org
Internet: http//www.goldenkey.org
AMOUNT: $1,000
DEADLINE(S): MAR
FIELD(S): All (fiction, nonfiction, poetry, and news writing)
ELIGIBILITY REQUIREMENTS: Undergraduate, graduate, and postgraduate members who are currently enrolled in classes at a degree-granting program may apply. Award based on quality of writing submitted. Previously published works will NOT be accepted.
HOW TO APPLY: Must apply online with your Golden Key member number. Attach an original composition. Only 1 composition/member/category will be accepted. Entries must not exceed 1,000 words. See website for additional information.
NUMBER OF AWARDS/YEAR: 4
RENEWABLE: No
CONTACT: Fabian J. De Rozario, Associate Vice President of North American Operations

1611—ILLINOIS ARTS COUNCIL (Artists Fellowship Awards)

James R. Thompson Center
100 West Randolph, Suite 10-500
Chicago IL 60601-3298
312/814-6750
E-mail: rose@arts.state.il.us
Internet: http://www.state.il.us/agency/iac/Guidelines/guidelines.htm
AMOUNT: $7,000
DEADLINE(S): SEP 1
FIELD(S): Choreography, Crafts, Ethnic and Folk Arts, Interdisciplinary/Performance Art, Media Arts, Music Composition, Photography, Playwriting/ Screenwriting, Poetry, Prose, and Visual Arts
ELIGIBILITY/REQUIREMENTS: Annual award to Illinois artists of exceptional talent is based on the quality of the works submitted and the professional accomplishments of the applicant.
HOW TO APPLY: See website for application.

1612—INSTITUTE FOR HUMANE STUDIES (Felix Morley Journalism Competition)

3401 North Fairfax Drive, Suite 440
Arlington VA 22201-4432
703/993-4880 or 800/697-8799
FAX: 703/993-4890
Internet: http://www.TheIHS.org
AMOUNT: $2,500 (1st prize)
DEADLINE(S): DEC 1
FIELD(S): Journalism
ELIGIBILITY/REQUIREMENTS: Open to young writers whose work demonstrates an appreciation of classical liberal principles (i.e., individual rights; their protection through private property, contract, and law; voluntarism in human relations; and the self-ordering market, free trade, free migration, and peace). Must be a full-time student aged 25 or younger.
HOW TO APPLY: Must submit 3-5 articles, editorials, opinion pieces, essays, and reviews published in student newspapers or other periodicals between July 1 and December 1. See website for rules or contact IHS for an entry form.

1613—INSTITUTE FOR HUMANE STUDIES (Humane Studies Fellowship)

3301 North Fairfax Drive, Suite 440
Arlington VA 22201-4432
703/993-4880 or 800/697-8799
FAX: 703/993-4890
Internet: http://www.TheIHS.org
AMOUNT: $12,000 (maximum)
DEADLINE(S): DEC
FIELD(S): Social Sciences; Liberal Arts; Law; Humanities; Jurisprudence; Journalism
ELIGIBILITY/REQUIREMENTS: Open to graduate and advanced undergraduate or law students pursuing degrees at any accredited domestic or foreign college or university. Based on academic performance, demonstrated interest in the classical liberal tradition, and potential to contribute to the advancement of a free society.
HOW TO APPLY: Apply online or contact IHS for an application.
NUMBER OF AWARDS: 90

1614—INSTITUTE FOR HUMANE STUDIES (Summer Seminars Program)

3401 North Fairfax Drive, Suite 440
Arlington VA 22201-4432
703/993-4880 or 800/697-8799
FAX: 703/993-4890
E-mail: ihs@gmu.edu
Internet: http://www.TheIHS.org
AMOUNT: Free summer seminars, including room/board, lectures, seminar materials, and books
DEADLINE(S): MAR
FIELD(S): Social Sciences; Humanities; Law; Journalism; Public Policy; Education; Film; Writing; Economics; Philosophy
ELIGIBILITY/REQUIREMENTS: Open to college students, recent graduates, and graduate students who share an interest in learning and exchanging ideas about the scope of individual rights, free markets, the rule of law, peace, and tolerance.
HOW TO APPLY: See website for information and to apply online, or contact IHS for an application.

1615—INSTITUTE OF INTERNATIONAL EDUCATION (Cintas Fellowship)

809 United Nations Plaza
New York NY 10017-3580
E-mail: cintas@iie.org
Internet: http://www.iie.org/cintas
AMOUNT: $10,000
DEADLINE(S): APR
FIELD(S): Fine Arts; Architecture; Literature; Music Composition; Visual Arts; Photography
ELIGIBILITY/REQUIREMENTS: Acknowledges outstanding creative accomplishments of artists of Cuban citizenship or direct descent who do not live in Cuba.

HOW TO APPLY: Contact Institute or see website for additional information.

1616—IOWA SCHOOL OF LETTERS (The Iowa Short Fiction Award and John Simmons Short Fiction Award)

102 Dey House
507 North Clinton Street
Iowa City IA 52242-1000
319/335-2000
AMOUNT: University of Iowa publication contract
DEADLINE(S): SEP 30
FIELD(S): Creative Writing: Fiction
ELIGIBILITY/REQUIREMENTS: Any writer, who has not previously published a volume fiction, may submit a collection of short stories (stories previously published in periodicals are eligible for inclusion).
HOW TO APPLY: Send SASE to Iowa Short Fiction for guidelines. Manuscript must be at least 150 double-spaced pages. Revised manuscripts may be re-entered.
NUMBER OF AWARDS: 1

1617—JACKSONVILLE STATE UNIVERSITY (Dr. William Calvert Scholarship)

Financial Aid Office
Jacksonville AL 36265
256/782-5677 or 800/231-5291
Internet: http://www.jsu.edu
AMOUNT: Full tuition
DEADLINE(S): FEB 1
FIELD(S): English
ELIGIBILITY/REQUIREMENTS: Open to junior or senior.
HOW TO APPLY: Contact English Department for application and details.
NUMBER OF AWARDS: 1
RENEWABLE: No
CONTACT: English Department, 256/782-5411 or 782-5412

1618—JACKSONVILLE STATE UNIVERSITY (Opal R. & Opal A. Lovett Scholarship)

Financial Aid Office
Jacksonville AL 36265
256/782-5677 or 800/231-5291
Internet: http://www.jsu.edu
AMOUNT: Varies
DEADLINE(S): FEB 1
FIELD(S): History; Art; English
ELIGIBILITY/REQUIREMENTS: Open to sophomore or above with a minimum 2.5 GPA.
HOW TO APPLY: An official transcript and ACT/SAT scores must be submitted with scholarship applications. See website

for application. Supporting documentation should be mailed.
NUMBER OF AWARDS: 1
RENEWABLE: No
CONTACT: Scholarship Committee

1619—JACKSONVILLE STATE UNIVERSITY (Randy Owen Scholarship)

Financial Aid Office
Jacksonville AL 36265
256/782-5677 or 800/231-5291
Internet: http://www.jsu.edu
AMOUNT: Varies
DEADLINE(S): FEB 1
FIELD(S): English
ELIGIBILITY/REQUIREMENTS: Open to Alabama residents; minimum 3.5 overall GPA and 3.5 in English.
HOW TO APPLY: See website to apply online. Submit an official transcript and ACT/SAT scores and supporting documentation by mail.
NUMBER OF AWARDS: 1
RENEWABLE: No
CONTACT: Scholarship Committee

1620—JACKSONVILLE STATE UNIVERSITY (Writing Scholarships)

Jacksonville AL 36265
256/782-5677 or 800/231-5291
Internet: http://www.jsu.edu
AMOUNT: Full tuition
DEADLINE(S): FEB 1
FIELD(S): All (emphasis on writing)
ELIGIBILITY/REQUIREMENTS: Open to students with demonstrated ability in writing.
HOW TO APPLY: Contact English Department for application and details.
NUMBER OF AWARDS: 1
RENEWABLE: No
CONTACT: English Department, 256/782-5411 or 782-5412

1621—JOHN F. KENNEDY CENTER FOR THE PERFORMING ARTS, THE (Awards, Fellowships, and Scholarships)

The Kennedy Center
2700 F Street NW
Washington DC 20566-0001
202/416-8857
FAX: 202/416-8802
E-mail: skshaffer@kennedy-center.org
Internet: http://www.kennedy-center.org/actf
AMOUNT: Varies
DEADLINE(S): Varies
FIELD(S): Playwriting; Stage Design; Acting

ELIGIBILITY/REQUIREMENTS: Various scholarships and awards.
HOW TO APPLY: See website or contact The Kennedy Center, American College Theater Festival, for details.

1622—JOHN F. KENNEDY LIBRARY FOUNDATION (John F. Kennedy Profile in Courage Essay Contest)

Columbia Point
Boston MA 02125
617/514-1649
FAX: 617/514-1641
E-mail: profiles@nara.gov
Internet: http://www.jfklibrary.org
AMOUNT: $500-$3,000
DEADLINE(S): Early JAN
FIELD(S): All, especially Political Science, History, English Language and Literature, and Communications and Journalism
ELIGIBILITY REQUIREMENTS: Open to U.S. high school students in grades 9-12, or home schools; or enrolled in a high school correspondence/GED program in any of the 50 states, D.C., or U.S. territories; or U.S. citizens attending schools overseas.
HOW TO APPLY: Write an essay on an elected official in the U.S. who is acting or has acted courageously to address a political issue at the local, state, national, or international level; also send completed contest registration form.
NUMBER OF AWARDS: 7 (1 first place, 1 second place, 5 finalists)
RENEWABLE: No

1623—KAPLAN/NEWSWEEK ("My Turn" Essay Contest)

Pre-College
1440 Broadway
New York NY 10018
800/527-8378
Internet: http://www.kaptest.com/essay
AMOUNT: $5,000 (1st place); $2,000 (2nd place); $1,000
DEADLINE(S): FEB 1
FIELD(S): Writing
ELIGIBILITY/REQUIREMENTS: Essay (500-1,000 words) on topic chosen by student should be based on personal opinion or experience; must be factually accurate. Must be U.S. citizen or resident of U.S. (and its territories and possessions), who as of January 1 is a high school student intending to attend college following graduation. All other entries will be disqualified. Essays are judged on effectiveness, creativity, insight, organization

and development, consistent use of language, variety in sentence structure and vocabulary, use of proper grammar, spelling and punctuation.
HOW TO APPLY: See official rules and instructions and download entry form from website or see guidance counselor. Submit with 2 copies of essay.
NUMBER OF AWARDS: 10
RENEWABLE: No

1624—KOSCIUSZKO FOUNDATION (Summer Sessions in Poland and Rome)

15 East 65th Street
New York NY 10021-6595
212/734-2130
FAX: 212/628-4552
E-mail: addy@thekf.orgthekf
Internet: http://www.kosciuszko foundation.org
AMOUNT: Varies
DEADLINE(S): Varies
FIELD(S): Polish Studies; History; Literature; Art; Economics; Social Studies; Language; Culture
ELIGIBILITY/REQUIREMENTS: Open to U.S. citizens and permanent residents who are undergraduate or graduate students, high school seniors 18 or older, and persons of any age not enrolled in a college or university program.
HOW TO APPLY: See website or send SASE for an application.
CONTACT: Addy Tymczyszyn, Summer Studies Abroad Coordinator, ext. 210

1625—LAMBDA IOTA TAU (LIT) HONOR SOCIETY FOR LITERATURE OF ALL LANGUAGES

Department of English
Ball State University
2000 West University Avenue
Muncie IN 47306-0460
765/285-8456/765-285-8370
FAX: 765/285-3965
E-mail: bhozeski@bsu.edu
Internet: http://www.bsu.edu/ csh/english/undergraduate/lit/
AMOUNT: $1,000
DEADLINE(S): JUN 30
FIELD(S): Literature (all languages)
ELIGIBILITY/REQUIREMENTS: Must be a member of LIT; demonstrate superior leadership and academic accomplishments.
HOW TO APPLY: Must be nominated by letter from chapter sponsor; candidate must submit 1,000 words or less on career goals and objectives.
NUMBER OF AWARDS: 3 or more
RENEWABLE: No

CONTACT: Bruce W. Hozeski, Executive Secretary

1626—LOUISIANA STATE UNIVERSITY AT SHREVEPORT (H.J. Sachs English Scholarship)

Bronson Hall
Shreveport LA 71115-2399
318/797-5371
Internet: http://www.lsus.edu
AMOUNT: $600
DEADLINE(S): Varies
FIELD(S): English
ELIGIBILITY/REQUIREMENTS: Awarded for 1 academic year to either an English or an English education major. Selection based on academic merit, character, and need.
HOW TO APPLY: Contact the Dean's Office, College of Liberal Arts, for an application.

1627—LOUISIANA STATE UNIVERSITY AT SHREVEPORT (Walter O. Bigby Scholarship)

Bronson Hall
Shreveport LA 71115-2399
318/797-5371
Internet: http://www.lsus.edu
AMOUNT: Up to $500/semester
DEADLINE(S): Varies
FIELD(S): Political Science; English; History; Law
ELIGIBILITY/REQUIREMENTS: Must be entering junior or senior year; majoring in one of above subjects; other Liberal Arts major acceptable, if preparing for law school.
HOW TO APPLY: Contact the Dean's Office, College of Liberal Arts, for an application.

1628—MENSA EDUCATION AND RESEARCH FOUNDATION (Rosemary Greathouse Scholarship)

Internet: http://www.mensa foundation.org/AM/Template.cfm ?Section=Scholarships1
AMOUNT: $600
DEADLINE(S): JAN 15
FIELD(S): Arts (including creative writing and journalism)
ELIGIBILITY/REQUIREMENTS: Awards based on essays written by the applicant. No requirement for Mensa membership nor is consideration given for grades, academic program or financial need. Applicants must currently be a resident of a participating American Mensa

local group's area and enrolled in a degree program in an accredited U.S. institution of higher learning during the academic year following the application date.
HOW TO APPLY: Each year the list of participating groups may change, see website for up-to-date information. Send application, available (if eligible) from the website or, by request with SASE, from local scholarship chairs. Submit with essay of not more than 550 words explaining your academic and/or vocational goals and plans to achieve those goals to the scholarship chair in your area.

1629—MICHAEL KANIN PLAYWRITING AWARDS PROGRAM KC/ACTF

The John F. Kennedy Center for the Performing Arts
2700 F Street NW
Washington DC 20566
202/416-8000
Internet: http://www.kennedy-center.org/education
AMOUNT: $2,500
DEADLINE(S): DEC
FIELD(S): Playwriting
ELIGIBILITY/REQUIREMENTS: Open to undergraduate and continuing part-time student playwrights; must be matriculating, degree-seeking students carrying a minimum of 6 semester hours (or equivalent quarter hours). Work on the new play will have begun during the period the student is so enrolled, and the production must be presented during that period or within 2 years after enrollment ends. Plays are produced as part of the Kennedy Center American College Theater Festival (KC/ACTF).
HOW TO APPLY: See website for rules and regulations. Enrollment must be verified in writing to the regional Playwriting Awards Committee chair by school's theater department head.

1630—MICHIGAN OUTDOOR WRITERS ASSOCIATION, THE (Marc Wesley Scholarship)

MOWA Scholarship Committee
3601 Avery
St. Johns MI 48879
989/224-3465
E-mail: scholarship@mioutdoor writers.org
AMOUNT: $1,000
DEADLINE(S): JAN 25
FIELD(S): Journalism/writing
ELIGIBILITY/REQUIREMENTS: Senior at a Michigan college or university interested in and qualified for a career in

outdoor writing. Must be Michigan resident for at least 5 years.
HOW TO APPLY: Write for application. Submit letters of support and proof of performance (VCR samples of outdoor communications and class assignments) with application.
CONTACT: Bob Holzhei

1631—MILL MOUNTAIN THEATRE (NEW PLAY COMPETITION)

Center in the Square
Roanoke VA 24011-1437
540/342-5749
FAX: 540/342-5745
E-mail: outreach@millmountain.org
Internet: http://www.millmountain.org
AMOUNT: $500-$1,000
DEADLINE(S): JAN 1
FIELD(S): Playwriting
ELIGIBILITY/REQUIREMENTS: Open to any playwright living in the U.S.
HOW TO APPLY: Must be agent-submitted or recommended by a director, literary manager, or dramaturgy. Include 1 unproduced, unpublished theatrical script in English with author's biography, history of play, and brief synopsis of scenes.

1632—NATIONAL FEDERATION OF STATE POETRY SOCIETIES (Edna Meudt Memorial Scholarship Fund)

Madelyn Eastlund
310 S. Adams Street
Beverly Hills FL 34465
Internet: http://www.nfsps.com/scholarship.htm
AMOUNT: $500
DEADLINE(S): FEB 1
FIELD(S): Poetry
ELIGIBILITY/REQUIREMENTS: Any junior or senior of an accredited university or college is eligible. Financial need NOT a factor. Winning manuscripts are published by NFSPS, each recipient will receive 75 copies and can read at annual convention.
HOW TO APPLY: Send a SASE (business-sized) to NFSPS for an application. Submit application; with 10 original poems, single-spaced, 1-page limit, 50-character-per-line limit, 40-line-per-poem limit; manuscript must be titled.
NUMBER OF AWARDS: 2

1633—NATIONAL FEDERATION OF THE BLIND (Humanities Scholarship)

805 5th Avenue
Grinnell IA 50112

641/236-3369
Internet: http://www.nfb.org/nfb/scholarship_program.asp
AMOUNT: $3,000
DEADLINE(S): MAR 31
FIELD(S): Humanities (Art, English, Foreign Languages, History, Philosophy, Religion)
ELIGIBILITY/REQUIREMENTS: Open to legally blind students pursuing or planning to pursue a full-time postsecondary education in the U.S. Awarded on basis of academic excellence, service to the community, and financial need. Membership NOT required.
HOW TO APPLY: Contact Scholarship Committee Chair for an application. Submit with transcripts and 2 letters of recommendation.
NUMBER OF AWARDS: 1
RENEWABLE: Yes
CONTACT: Peggy Elliot, Scholarship Committee Chair

1634—NATIONAL FOUNDATION FOR ADVANCEMENT IN THE ARTS (Arts Recognition and Talent Search)

800 Brickell Avenue
Miami FL 33131
800/970-ARTS or 305/377-1140
FAX: 305/377-1149
E-mail: info@nfaa.org
Internet: http://www.ARTSawards.org
AMOUNT: $100-$3,000
DEADLINE(S): OCT 1
FIELD(S): Creative and Performing Arts; Writing
ELIGIBILITY/REQUIREMENTS: Open to high school seniors and 17- to 18-year-olds in dance, film, jazz, music, photography, theater, visual arts, voice, and writing. Except for Music/Jazz, applicants must be U.S. citizens or permanent residents.
HOW TO APPLY: Applications available online or write. May apply in more than 1 category, but only 1 financial award will be given to any individual. A fee is required for each category in which student applies.
NUMBER OF AWARDS: 400
RENEWABLE: No

1635—NATIONAL INSTITUTE FOR LABOR RELATIONS RESEARCH (William B. Ruggles Scholarship)

5211 Port Royal Road
Springfield VA 22151
703/321-9606
FAX: 703/321-7342
E-mail: research@tnilrr.org

Internet: http://www.nilrr.org
AMOUNT: $2,000
DEADLINE(S): DEC 31
FIELD(S): Journalism; English; Communications or related majors
ELIGIBILITY/REQUIREMENTS: Open to students majoring in journalism or related area.
HOW TO APPLY: Download application and information from website or request application by e-mail (specify "Ruggles" or "Journalism" scholarships); e-mail requests must include accurate mailing address. Submit with a most up-to-date transcript and an essay of approximately 500 words demonstrating an interest in, and knowledge of, the Right to Work principle.
NUMBER OF AWARDS: 1
RENEWABLE: No
CONTACT: Cathy Jones

1636—OPTIMIST INTERNATIONAL FOUNDATION (Essay Contest)

Programs Department
4494 Lindell Boulevard
St. Louis MO 63108
314/371-6000, ext. 235
FAX: 314/371-6006
E-mail: programs@optimist.org
Internet: http://www.optimist.org
AMOUNT: $5,000 (1st prize); $3,000 (2nd), $2,000 (3rd/international), $650 (district level)
DEADLINE(S): Varies by district
FIELD(S): All
ELIGIBILITY/REQUIREMENTS: Eligible students are under age 19 as of December 31 of the current school year. Open to residents of the U.S., Canada, and the Caribbean.
HOW TO APPLY: Send SASE to Programs Coordinator for informational letter and list of district chairpersons; contact local chairperson for contest dates and where to submit essay.
NUMBER OF AWARDS: 3 international awards plus district winners
CONTACT: Danielle Baugher, Programs Coordinator

1637—PHILLIPS EXETER ACADEMY (George Bennett Fellowship)

20 Main Street
Exeter NH 03833-2460
Internet: http://www.exeter.edu/english/bennett.html
AMOUNT: $10,000 plus housing
DEADLINE(S): DEC 1
FIELD(S): Writing

ELIGIBILITY/REQUIREMENTS: Must intend to be a professional writer, and have a manuscript in progress.
HOW TO APPLY: Send SASE or visit website for information and application. Submit with 2 professional references, information about work-in-progress, about 50 pages or representative samples of longer work, or 20-30 pages of poetry.
NUMBER OF AWARDS: 1
RENEWABLE: No

1638—POETRY SOCIETY OF AMERICA (George Bogin Memorial Award)

15 Gramercy Park
New York NY 10003
212/254-9628
FAX: 212/673-2352
Internet: http://www.poetry society.org
AMOUNT: $500
DEADLINE(S): DEC
FIELD(S): Poetry
ELIGIBILITY/REQUIREMENTS: Prizes for the best selections of 4 or 5 poems that reflect the encounter of the ordinary and the extraordinary, use language in an original way, and take a stand against oppression in any of its forms.
HOW TO APPLY: $15 entry fee for non-members. Contact PSA for guidelines.

1639—POETRY SOCIETY OF AMERICA (Robert H. Winner Memorial Award)

15 Gramercy Park
New York NY 10003
212/254-9628
FAX: 212/673-2352
Internet: http://www.poetry society.org
AMOUNT: $2,500
DEADLINE(S): DEC 21
FIELD(S): Poetry
ELIGIBILITY/REQUIREMENTS: For poets over 40 years of age who have not published or who have no more than 1 book. This award acknowledges original work done in midlife by someone who has not had substantial recognition. Send a brief but cohesive manuscript of up to 10 poems or 20 pages. Poems entered here may be submitted to other contests as well. Please include date of birth on cover page.
HOW TO APPLY: $15 entry fee for non-members.
CONTACT: PSA for submission guidelines.

1640—POETRY SOCIETY OF AMERICA (Shelley Memorial Award)

15 Gramercy Park

New York NY 10003
212/254-9628
FAX: 212/673-2352
Internet: http://www.poetry society.org
AMOUNT: $6,000-$9,000
DEADLINE(S): DEC
FIELD(S): Poetry
ELIGIBILITY/REQUIREMENTS: All submissions must be unpublished on the date of entry and not scheduled for publication by the date of the PSA awards ceremony held in the spring.
HOW TO APPLY: $15 entry fee for non-members. Contact PSA for submission guidelines.

1641—PRINCESS GRACE FOUNDATION-USA (Grants for Young Playwrights)

150 East 58th Street, 25th Floor
New York NY 10155
212/317-1470
FAX: 212/317-1473
E-mail: grants@pgfusa.org
Internet: http://www.pgfusa.org
AMOUNT: $7,500
DEADLINE(S): MAR 31
FIELD(S): Playwriting
ELIGIBILITY/REQUIREMENTS: Offers 10-week residency at New Dramatists, Inc., New York. Must be U.S. citizen or permanent resident. Based primarily on artistic quality of submitted play, appropriateness of activities to individual's artistic growth, and potential future excellence. Script will be included in New Dramatists' lending library, be distributed to catalog subscribers for 1 year. Complete representation and publication by Samuel French, Inc.
HOW TO APPLY: See website or contact Grants Coordinator for an application.
NUMBER OF AWARDS: 1
CONTACT: Kathleen Richards, Program

1642—RAGDALE FOUNDATION (Frances Shaw Writing Fellowship)

1260 North Green Bay Road
Lake Forest IL 60045-1106
847/234-1063
FAX: 847/234-1075
E-mail: eventsragdale@aol.com
Internet: http://www.ragdale.org
AMOUNT: 4-week residency plus travel expense
DEADLINE(S): FEB 1
FIELD(S): Creative Writing
ELIGIBILITY/REQUIREMENTS: Writing residency for women who have begun to write seriously after the age of 55.

U.S. citizenship required, and financial need must be demonstrated.
HOW TO APPLY: Write or e-mail for further details.
NUMBER OF AWARDS: 1
RENEWABLE: No
CONTACT: Sylvia Brown, 847/234-1063, ext. 205

1643—RIPON COLLEGE (Performance/Recognition Tuition Scholarships)

300 Seward Street
P.O. Box 248
Ripon WI 54971
920/748-8101
E-mail: adminfo@ripon.edu
Internet: http://www.ripon.edu
AMOUNT: $5,000-$10,000/year
DEADLINE(S): MAR 1
FIELD(S): Music; Art; Theater
ELIGIBILITY/REQUIREMENTS: Open to students attending or planning to attend Ripon College.
HOW TO APPLY: Contact Office of Admission for an application. Interview, audition, or nomination may be required.
RENEWABLE: Yes
CONTACT: Office of Admission

1644—SAN DIEGO PRESS CLUB FOUNDATION (Joe Lipper Memorial Scholarship)

2454 Heritage Park Row
San Diego CA 92110
619/299-5747
E-mail: sdpressc@cts.com
Internet: http://www.sddt.com/~pressclub
AMOUNT: $1,500-$2,500
DEADLINE(S): JUL 1
FIELD(S): Journalism; English
ELIGIBILITY/REQUIREMENTS: Open to university and community college students, who are San Diego County residents, pursuing a career in journalism or a related field. Selection based on GPA, participation in community service, and media-related internships. Writing and producing news for college newspapers, radio, or television is considered.
HOW TO APPLY: Submit an essay expressing interest in a journalism career.
NUMBER OF AWARDS: 2
CONTACT: Denise Vedder, 619/531-3536, thevedders@sbcglobal.net

1645—SCHOLASTIC ART & WRITING AWARDS (Alliance for Young Artists and Writers, Inc.)

557 Broadway

New York NY 10012
212/343-6493
E-mail: A&Wgeneralinfo@
scholastic.com
Internet: http://www.artand
writing.org
AMOUNT: Varies; up to $10,000
DEADLINE(S): Varies with location
FIELD(S): Art; Writing
ELIGIBILITY/REQUIREMENTS: For students in grades 7-12 enrolled in schools in the U.S., Canada, U.S. territories, or U.S-sponsored schools abroad. 10 writing and 16 art categories. Publishing opportunities may be available for winners in both art and writing categories.
HOW TO APPLY: See website or write.
NUMBER OF AWARDS: 1,000+ awards annually, including 11 $10,000 scholarships.

1646—SEVENTEEN (Fiction Contest)

1440 Broadway, 13th floor
New York NY 10018
212/2034-4300
FAX: 212/204-3972/73
E-mail: excel@ieha.org
Internet: http://www.ieha.org
AMOUNT: $250
DEADLINE(S): APR 30
FIELD(S): All; Creative Writing
ELIGIBILITY/REQUIREMENTS: Must be between 13 and 21 as of April 30. Fiction must not have been previously published in any form except school publications. Stories may not exceed 3,500 words (about 14 pages); may submit unlimited number.
HOW TO APPLY: Winners or legal guardians must sign an affidavit of compliance with rules and a publicity release. Acceptance of prize constitutes winner's permission to use their names, likeness, cities and states of residence, and to be photographed for advertising and publicity purposes without additional compensation, except where prohibited by law.
NUMBER OF AWARDS: 1

1647—SOCIETY FOR TECHNICAL COMMUNICATION

901 North Stuart Street, Suite 904
Arlington VA 22203
703/522-4114
FAX: 703/522-2075
E-mail: stc@stc.org
Internet: http://www.stcva.org/
scholar/scholarships.html
AMOUNT: $1,500
DEADLINE(S): FEB 15

FIELD(S): Communications (technical writing, editing, graphic design, multimedia art, and related fields)
ELIGIBILITY/REQUIREMENTS: Open to full-time students who have completed at least 1 year of postsecondary education working toward a Bachelor's degree and are enrolled in an accredited 2- or 4-year degree program for career in any area of technical communication.
HOW TO APPLY: See website or write for complete information.
NUMBER OF AWARDS: 2

1648—STANFORD UNIVERSITY (Creative Writing Fellowships)

Stanford University
Stanford CA 94305-2087
Internet: http://www.stanford.
edu/dept/english/cw/
AMOUNT: $57,000 (2 years, includes living stipend, workshop tuition)
DEADLINE(S): DEC 1 (do not apply before SEP 1)
FIELD(S): Creative Writing
ELIGIBILITY/REQUIREMENTS: For poets and creative writers (fiction) to spend 2 years at Stanford in the Creative Writing Program. Fellowships are awarded based on creative work, potential for growth, and ability to contribute to and profit from workshops.
HOW TO APPLY: Contact Program Coordinator for application. Submit with a manuscript, a brief statement of writing plans, mailing labels, and SASE.
NUMBER OF AWARDS: 10 (5 poetry, 5 fiction)
CONTACT: Mary Popek, Program Coordinator, Creative Writing Office

1649—TET '68, Inc. (Essay Contest)

P.O. Box 31885
Richmond VA 23294
804/550-3692
FAX: 804/550-1406
E-mail: billyktet@aol.com
Internet: http://www.tet68.org
AMOUNT: $1,000
DEADLINE(S): MAR 31
FIELD(S): All
ELIGIBILITY/REQUIREMENTS: Open to high school seniors who are children or stepchildren of a Vietnam veteran.
HOW TO APPLY: See website or write for application, contest rules, and essay topic. Submit with proof of status-parent or stepparent's DD-214.
NUMBER OF AWARDS: 4-6
RENEWABLE: Yes
CONTACT: William E. Kirkland

1650—TRUST COMPANY LIMITED (Miles Franklin Literary Award)

Level 3, 35 Clarence Street
Sydney NSW 2000 AUSTRALIA
(02)9332 1559
FAX: (02)9332 1298
E-mail: trustawards@cauz
group.com.au
Internet: http://www.trust.com.
au/philanthropy/awards/
AMOUNT: Aus. $28,000
DEADLINE(S): JAN 31
FIELD(S): Novel/Playwriting
ELIGIBILITY/REQUIREMENTS: Annual award for the best book on some aspect of Australian life published in the 12-month period prior to the award deadline. If no novel is worthy, a play is chosen. More than 1 entry and/or a novel/play written by 2 or more authors are eligible.
HOW TO APPLY: See website.
CONTACT: Petrea Salter, Cavz Group, psalter@cauzgroup.com.au

1651—UCLA CENTER FOR 17TH- AND 18TH-CENTURY STUDIES (Fellowships)

310 Royce Hall
Los Angeles CA 90095-1404
310/206-8552
FAX: 310/206-8577
E-mail: c1718cs@humnet.ucla.edu
Internet: http://www.humnet.ucla.
edu/ humnet/C1718CS/Postd.
htm#undergrad
AMOUNT: $1,000-$18,400
DEADLINE(S): FEB 1
FIELD(S): British Literature; History (17th and 18th Centuries)
ELIGIBILITY/REQUIREMENTS: Undergraduate stipends for advanced study and research.
HOW TO APPLY: Contact the Center for current year's theme and an application.
NUMBER OF AWARDS: Up to 10

1652—UNIVERSITY OF ILLINOIS AT URBANA-CHAMPAIGN (Lydia E. Parker Bates Scholarship)

620 East John Street
Champaign IL 61820
217/333-0100
Internet: http://www.uiuc.edu/
AMOUNT: Up to $1,000
DEADLINE(S): MAR 15
FIELD(S): Art, Architecture, Landscape Architecture, Urban Planning, Dance,

Theater, and all related subjects except Music

ELIGIBILITY/REQUIREMENTS: Open to undergraduate students in the College of Fine and Applied Arts. Must demonstrate financial need; have 2.85 GPA and carry at least 12 credit hours/semester.

HOW TO APPLY: Contact Office of Student Financial Aid for application. Complete the FAFSA with UIUC admission application.

NUMBER OF AWARDS: 175

1653—UNIVERSITY OF OKLAHOMA—H. H. HERBERT SCHOOL OF JOURNALISM AND MASS COMMUNICATION (Undergraduate Scholarships)

860 Van Vleet Oval, Room 101
Norman OK 73019
405/325-2721
AMOUNT: $5,000/year
DEADLINE(S): FEB
FIELD(S): Journalism: Print or Broadcast, Advertising, Electronic Media, News Communication, Professional Writing, Public Relations
ELIGIBILITY/REQUIREMENTS: For undergraduate students who plan to attend the University of Oklahoma.
HOW TO APPLY: Contact Herbert School for additional information and application. Interview is part of acceptance process.
CONTACT: David Dary

1654—UNIVERSITY OF WINDSOR (Outstanding Scholars Award)

401 Sunset Avenue
Windsor Ontario N9B 3P4
CANADA
519/253-3000
FAX: 519/973-7081
E-mail: awards1@uwindsor.ca
Internet: http://www.uwindsor.ca
AMOUNT: $1,000-$2,500/year (Canadian); maximum 4 years
DEADLINE(S): MAY 31
FIELD(S): Classics, Modern Languages, French, Philosophy, Music, Physics, Earth Sciences (not Environmental Studies), Economics (not Business and Economics), Chemistry (not Biochemistry), Mathematics and Statistics, Industrial, Mechanical (Materials Option) or Environmental Engineering or Bachelor of Arts and Science
ELIGIBILITY/REQUIREMENTS: Open to undergraduate students registering in year 1 at the University of Windsor. Must

have superior grades. Amount of award based on secondary school accomplishments.

HOW TO APPLY: Automatic. No application required.

RENEWABLE: Yes. Up to 4 years.

CONTACT: Aase Houser

ADDITIONAL INFORMATION: Students in this program will also be mentored in their first year in preparation for guaranteed Outstanding Scholars Appointments in their Department/School (valued at $2,000 Canadian in earnings for each of the 2nd, 3rd, and 4th years) provided all conditions are met.

1655—U.S. INSTITUTE OF PEACE (National Peace Essay Contest)

1200 17th Street NW, Suite 200
Washington DC 20036
202/457-1700
FAX: 202/429-6063
E-mail: essaycontest@usip.org
Internet: http://www.usip.org
AMOUNT: $1,000-$10,000
DEADLINE(S): JAN
FIELD(S): All (emphasis on Political Science; U.S. History)
ELIGIBILITY/REQUIREMENTS: 1,500-word essay contest for high school students on the U.S. response to international conflict. No restrictions as to citizenship or residency.
HOW TO APPLY: See website or contact USIP for specific guidelines.
RENEWABLE: No

1656—VINCENT L. HAWKINSON FOUNDATION FOR PEACE AND JUSTICE, THE

324 Harvard Street SE
Minneapolis MN 55414
612/331-8125
Internet: http://www.grace attheu.org
AMOUNT: Up to $1,500
DEADLINE(S): APR 1
FIELD(S): All
ELIGIBILITY/REQUIREMENTS: Open to residents or students attending school in Minnesota, Iowa, Wisconsin, North Dakota or South Dakota. Demonstrate commitment to peace and justice in a short essay. No religious affiliation requirement.
HOW TO APPLY: Write or call for application form or download from website. Submit essay with 3 references, nomination by 1 of the 3 references, and academic transcript. Finalists receive personal interview in Minneapolis.

NUMBER OF AWARDS: 1 (3-5 runners-up receive lower amounts)
RENEWABLE: No

1657—WESTERN MICHIGAN UNIVERSITY (College of Arts and Sciences/The Frederick J. and Katherine Rogers Memorial Shakespeare Award)

1903 West Michigan
Kalamazoo MI 49008-5337
269/387-8777
FAX: 269/387-6989
Internet: http://www.wmich.edu/finaid
AMOUNT: $250
FIELD(S): English Literature
ELIGIBILITY/REQUIREMENTS: Anyone enrolled in an English course in which he or she wrote a paper on Shakespeare within the last year.
HOW TO APPLY: Submit essay with instructor's name, course name, and the semester it was completed to Department of English.
RENEWABLE: No

1658—WESTERN MICHIGAN UNIVERSITY (College of Arts and Sciences/The George Sprau Award in English)

1903 West Michigan
Kalamazoo MI 49008-5337
269/387-8777
FAX: 269/387-6989
E-mail: finaid-info@wmich.edu
Internet: http://www.wmich.edu/finaid
AMOUNT: $25-$175 (fall semester)
DEADLINE(S): Not applicable
FIELD(S): English Language; English Education
ELIGIBILITY/REQUIREMENTS: Seniors (occasionally juniors) with superior academic record.
HOW TO APPLY: Students nominated by Department of English faculty.
RENEWABLE: No

1659—WESTERN MICHIGAN UNIVERSITY (College of Arts and Sciences/The Jean and Vincent Malmstrom Scholarship)

1903 West Michigan
Kalamazoo MI 49008-5337
269/387-8777
FAX: 269/387-6989
E-mail: finaid-info@wmich.edu
Internet: http://www.wmich.edu/finaid
AMOUNT: $500 (fall semester)

DEADLINE(S): Fall semester
FIELD(S): English Language; English Education
ELIGIBILITY/REQUIREMENTS: Second-semester junior or first-semester senior with a major or minor in English Education and courses in grammar, structure, history, dialects. Minimum GPA 3.5.
HOW TO APPLY: Contact the English Department for application.
RENEWABLE: No

1660—WESTERN MICHIGAN UNIVERSITY (College of Arts and Sciences/The Patrick D. Hagerty Promising Scholarship in English Award)

1903 West Michigan
Kalamazoo MI 49008-5337
269/387-8777
FAX: 269/387-6989
E-mail: finaid-info@wmich.edu
Internet: http://www.wmich.edu/finaid
AMOUNT: $250 (fall semester)
FIELD(S): English
ELIGIBILITY/REQUIREMENTS: Second-semester sophomore or first-semester junior, majoring in English, with outstanding promise; no minimum GPA, but strongly considered.
HOW TO APPLY: Nominated by Department of English faculty, selected by awards committee.
NUMBER OF AWARDS: 1
RENEWABLE: No

1661—WESTERN MICHIGAN UNIVERSITY (College of Arts and Sciences/The Ralph N. Miller Memorial Award)

1903 West Michigan
Kalamazoo MI 49008-5337
269/387-8777
FAX: 269/387-6989
E-mail: finaid-info@wmich.edu
Internet: http://www.wmich.edu/finaid
AMOUNT: $300 (fall semester)
FIELD(S): English Language; English Education
ELIGIBILITY/REQUIREMENTS: English major or minor in junior year; GPA considered, but no minimum requirements; criteria include intellectual curiosity, daring, forcefulness, and enthusiasm.
HOW TO APPLY: Students nominated (or self-nominated); must submit writing samples to Department of English.
RENEWABLE: No

1662—WESTERN MICHIGAN UNIVERSITY (College of Arts and Sciences/WMU Creative Writing Awards)

1903 West Michigan
Kalamazoo MI 49008-5337
269/387-8777
FAX: 269/387-6989
E-mail: finaid-info@wmich.edu
Internet: http://www.wmich.edu/finaid
AMOUNT: $50-$100 (fall semester)
DEADLINE(S): FEB
FIELD(S): Playwriting; Poetry; Fiction; Creative Nonfiction
ELIGIBILITY/REQUIREMENTS: Awards in each category. Winners selected by judges from outside WMU.
HOW TO APPLY: Submit work, not exceeding 20 pages, or up to 5 poems, to the English Department.
NUMBER OF AWARDS: 8, $50; 4, $100
RENEWABLE: No

1663—WESTERN MICHIGAN UNIVERSITY (Haworth College of Business/Cynthia Wrazien-Hirt Endowed Memorial Advertising Scholarship)

1903 West Michigan
Kalamazoo MI 49008-5337
269/387-6000
FAX: 269/387-6989
E-mail: finaid-info@wmich.edu
Internet: http://www.wmich.edu/finaid
AMOUNT: Varies
DEADLINE(S): FEB 15
FIELD(S): Advertising; Promotion; Marketing; English (writing)
ELIGIBILITY/REQUIREMENTS: Open to full-time juniors and seniors who are Advertising and Promotion majors who have completed 55 to 95 credit hours with a cumulative GPA of at least 3.0. Preference given to students who are also pursuing either a major or minor in English with a creative or practical writing emphasis. Extracurricular activities considered, including work experience.
HOW TO APPLY: Contact the Marketing Department for more information.
RENEWABLE: Yes: Maximum of 2 consecutive academic years.

1664—WESTERN MICHIGAN UNIVERSITY (Haworth College of Business/Piler Group Tony Walker Memorial Scholarship)

1903 West Michigan
Kalamazoo MI 49008-5337
269/387-6000
FAX: 269/387-6989
E-mail: finaid-info@wmich.edu
Internet: http://www.wmich.edu/finaid
AMOUNT: Varies
DEADLINE(S): FEB 15
FIELD(S): Advertising; Promotion; Marketing; Writing, Journalism
ELIGIBILITY/REQUIREMENTS: Open to full-time undergraduate or graduate student who works at least 15 hours per week at the *Western Herald* in Circulation, Business (Secretary, Classifieds), Display Advertising, or as Student Manager of a Department. Preference given to applicants with a 3.0 GPA or higher.
HOW TO APPLY: Contact the Marketing Department for more information.
RENEWABLE: Yes

1665—WESTERN MICHIGAN UNIVERSITY (Lynne C. McCauley Memorial Scholarship)

1903 West Michigan
Kalamazoo MI 49008-5337
269/387-8777
FAX: 269/387-6989
E-mail: alumni@wmich.edu
Internet: http://www.wmich.edu/ENDOWED
AMOUNT: Varies
DEADLINE(S): APR 1
FIELD(S): English, Music, Theater
ELIGIBILITY/REQUIREMENTS: Full-time students majoring in the Humanities, such as English, Music or Theater at WMU. Must have a minimum GPA of 3.0 to apply. Preference given to women.
HOW TO APPLY: See website for application and submit with FAFSA.
RENEWABLE: No
NUMBER OF AWARDS: Varies
CONTACT: Office of Student Financial Aid

1666—WILLA CATHER PIONEER MEMORIAL AND EDUCATIONAL FOUNDATION

413 North Webster
Red Cloud NE 68970
402/746-2653
FAX: 402/746-2652
E-mail: wcpm@gpcom.net
Internet: http://www.willacather.org
AMOUNT: $1,000
DEADLINE(S): JAN 31
FIELD(S): English
ELIGIBILITY/REQUIREMENTS: Female graduate of a Nebraska high school.

HOW TO APPLY: Applications are sent to each high school or call for application.
NUMBER OF AWARDS: 1
RENEWABLE: No
CONTACT: Betty Kort, Executive Director

FOREIGN LANGUAGE AND LITERATURE

1667—AIR FORCE RESERVE OFFICER TRAINING CORPS (AFROTC SCHOLARSHIPS)

551 East Maxwell Boulevard
Maxwell AFB AL 36112-6106
866/4AFROTC
E-mail: info@afrotc.com
Internet: http://www.afrotc.com
AMOUNT: Varies, but up to full tuition and fees plus $600/year for books
DEADLINE(S): DEC 1
FIELD(S): Science; Engineering; Business; Political Science; Psychology; Geography; Foreign Studies; Foreign Language
ELIGIBILITY/REQUIREMENTS: 4- and 3-year competitive scholarships based on individual merit to high school seniors and graduates who have not enrolled full time at a college or university. Academic performance is measured using an academic composite, which combines SAT (Math and Verbal only)/ACT scores, class rank, GPA and the number of advanced placement or honors courses completed through Grade 11. To be eligible for consideration, students should achieve a 1100 SAT (Math and Verbal only) or 24 ACT, minimum 3.0 GPA and class ranking in top 40%. Must be a U.S. citizen between the ages of 17-27. Must also have GPA of 2.5 or above, be in top 40% of class, and complete Applicant Fitness Test. Cannot be a single parent. Your college or university must offer AFROTC.
HOW TO APPLY: Visit www.afrotc.com to apply.
NUMBER OF AWARDS: N/A
RENEWABLE; No

1668—AMERICAN ASSOCIATION OF TEACHERS OF ITALIAN (College Essay Contest)

Cal State University-Chico
Foreign Language Department
Chico CA 95929
AMOUNT: $100-$300
DEADLINE(S): JUN 15
FIELD(S): Italian Language; Italian Studies

ELIGIBILITY/REQUIREMENTS: Contest open to undergraduate students at accredited colleges and universities in North America. Essay in Italian language on topic pertaining to literature or culture.
HOW TO APPLY: Write to Association care of Cal State for complete information.
CONTACT: Prof. Eugenio Frongia

1669—AMERICAN CLASSICAL LEAGUE, THE (Ed Phinney Commemorative Scholarship)

Miami University
Oxford OH 45056
513/529-7741
FAX: 513/529-7742
E-mail: info@aclclassics.org
Internet: http://www.aclclassics.org
AMOUNT: Up to $750
DEADLINE(S): JAN 15
FIELD(S): Teachers or teacher candidates in the classics (Latin and/or Greek)
ELIGIBILITY/REQUIREMENTS: Scholarships for first-time attendance at the League's institute or to cover cost of other activities that enhance a teacher's skills in the classroom in the classics or for purchase of materials from the ACL Teaching and Materials Resource Center. Memberships required except for first-time attendance at institute.
HOW TO APPLY: See website for application and additional information.
RENEWABLE: No

1670—AMERICAN INSTITUTE OF INDIAN STUDIES (Language Program)

1130 East 59th Street
Chicago IL 60637
773/702-8638
E-mail: aiis@uchicago.edu
Internet: http://www.india studies.org/ aiislang/AIIS.html
AMOUNT: Varies
DEADLINE(S): JAN 31
FIELD(S): Languages of India
ELIGIBILITY/REQUIREMENTS: Students at U.S. universities with at least 2 years of study in the language are eligible. Must be U.S. citizens.
HOW TO APPLY: See website for application, instructions, related forms, and to determine which languages are eligible each year.
NUMBER OF AWARDS: 10
CONTACT: Suren Gambhir, Chair, AIIS Language Committee, sgambhir@mail.sas.upenn.edu

1671—BNAI ZION FOUNDATION, INC.

Bnai Zion/Brith Abraham
136 East 39th Street
New York NY 10016
212/725-1211
FAX: 212/679-1109
Internet: http://www.bnaizion.com/
AMOUNT: $100
DEADLINE(S): APR 15
FIELD(S): Hebrew
ELIGIBILITY/REQUIREMENTS: Available for students pursuing the study of Hebrew in American institutions. Must demonstrate excellence in Hebrew study.
HOW TO APPLY: Contact local office. See website for list.
CONTACT: Scholarship Director

1672—CENTER FOR ARABIC STUDY ABROAD (CASA)

Emory University
Woodruff Library, 4th Floor
540 Asbury Circle
Atlanta GA 30322
404/727-2575
E-mail: casa@emory.edu
Internet: http://www.casa.emory.edu
AMOUNT: Tuition, stipend, airfare
DEADLINE(S): First week of JAN
FIELD(S): Arabic
ELIGIBILITY/REQUIREMENTS: A minimum of 2 to 3 years prior formal instruction in Arabic. Must be a U.S. citizen or permanent resident. Written exam and oral interview required.
HOW TO APPLY: Download application from website. Submit completed form and supporting documents as required.
NUMBER OF AWARDS: 30
RENEWABLE: No
CONTACT: Program Coordinator
ADDITIONAL INFORMATION: Advanced level Arabic language instruction at the American University in Cairo.

1673—CENTER FOR CROSS-CULTURAL STUDY, THE (Tuition Awards)

446 Main Street
Amherst MA 01002-2314
413/256-0011 or 800/377-2621
FAX: 413/256-1968
E-mail: admin@cccs.com
Internet: http://www.cccs.com
AMOUNT: $500-$2,500
DEADLINE(S): Fall semester/MAY 15; Spring semester/NOV 15
FIELD(S): Spanish and Spanish Culture

ELIGIBILITY/REQUIREMENTS: Partial tuition assistance to study at Center in Seville, Spain. Must submit an original 2- to 3-page essay in Spanish.

HOW TO APPLY: Contact organization for specific details regarding the essays. Submit with a short description in English of your experience with the Spanish language and culture and a faculty recommendation.

RENEWABLE: Awards are for 1 semester or academic year.

1674—CENTRO DE IDIOMAS DEL SURESTE A.C. (Intensive Spanish Scholarship)

Calle 14 #106 X 25 Colonia
Mérida Yucatan 97128 MEXICO
(011)52-999-926-11-55
FAX: (011)52-999-926-90-20
E-mail: admin@cccs.com
Internet: http://www.cisyucatan.com.mx
AMOUNT: Varies
DEADLINE(S): Varies (45 days before enrollment)
FIELD(S): Spanish

ELIGIBILITY/REQUIREMENTS: For study at CIS, open to students currently enrolled in an undergraduate or graduate program. No citizenship requirements. Preference given to students with financial need.

HOW TO APPLY: Write or e-mail for an application.
RENEWABLE: Yes
CONTACT: Chloe C. Pacheco

1675—COMMUNITY FOUNDATION OF WESTERN MASSACHUSETTS (Lucille and William Lucey Scholarship Fund)

1500 Main Street
P.O. Box 15769
Springfield MA 01115
413/732-2858
FAX: 413/733/8565
E-mail: scholar@community foundation.org
Internet: http://www.community foundation.org
AMOUNT: $400
DEADLINE(S): MAR 31
FIELD(S): French

ELIGIBILITY/REQUIREMENTS: For graduating high school students from high schools in Holyoke, Massachusetts, who have demonstrated excellence in French language study.

HOW TO APPLY: See website for application.

NUMBER OF AWARDS: 1
RENEWABLE: No

1676—DONALD KEENE CENTER OF JAPANESE CULTURE (Japan-U.S. Friendship Commission Prizes for the Translation of Japanese Literature)

Columbia University
507 Kent Hall, MC 3920
New York NY 10027
212/854-5036
FAX: 212/854-4019
E-mail: donald-keene-center@ columbia.edu
Internet: http://www.columbia.edu/ cu/ealac/dkc
AMOUNT: $2,500
DEADLINE(S): FEB 15
FIELD(S): Japanese

ELIGIBILITY/REQUIREMENTS: Prizes for best translation of a work of modern literature and work of classical literature. Must be book-length; may be novel, collection of short stories, literary essays, memoir, drama, or poetry; unpublished manuscripts, works in press, or books published in the 2 years prior to the prize year considered. Judged on the literary merit and the accuracy with which it reflects the spirit of the Japanese original. Translators of any nationality may apply.

HOW TO APPLY: Applications accepted from translators or their publishers. See website for application and information.

NUMBER OF AWARDS: 2 (1 in each category)
RENEWABLE: No
CONTACT: Donald Keene Center

1677—GERMAN ACADEMIC EXCHANGE SERVICE (DAAD Programs)

871 United Nations Plaza
New York NY 10017
212/758-3223
FAX: 212/755-5780
E-mail: daadny@daad.org
Internet: http://www.daad.org
AMOUNT: All (varies with program)
ELIGIBILITY/REQUIREMENTS: For study, research and other academic activities in Germany to students, citizens and permanent residents of the U.S. and Canada. Support for visiting professorships for highly qualified faculty.

HOW TO APPLY: See website for application instructions.

NUMBER OF AWARDS: 100+
RENEWABLE: Yes, for those interested in completing a degree in Germany
CONTACT: E-mail or phone

1678—HAWAII COMMUNITY FOUNDATION (Blossom Kalama Evans Memorial Scholarship Fund)

1164 Bishop Street, Suite 800
Honolulu HI 96813
808/537-6333 or toll free:
888/731-3863
FAX: 808/521-6286
E-mail: info@hcf-hawaii.org
Internet: http://www.hcf-hawaii.org
DEADLINE(S): MAR 1
FIELD(S): Hawaiian Studies; Hawaiian Language

ELIGIBILITY/REQUIREMENTS: Applicants must be Hawaii residents; junior, senior, or graduate students enrolled full time in an accredited 2- or 4-year college or university; demonstrate financial need, good moral character, and minimum GPA of 2.7. Preference given to students of Hawaiian ancestry. Members of the Hawaiian Girls Golf Association are not eligible.

HOW TO APPLY: Send application with 2 letters of recommendation.

1679—INSTITUTE OF INTERNATIONAL EDUCATION NATIONAL SECURITY EDUCATION PROGRAM (NSEP David L. Boren Undergraduate Scholarships)

1400 K Street NW, 6th floor
Washington DC 20005
800/618-6737
FAX: 202/326-7672
E-mail: nsep@iie.org
Internet: http://www.iie.org/nsep
AMOUNT: Up to $20,000
DEADLINE(S): Mid FEB
FIELD(S): All, emphasis on geographic areas, languages, and fields of study deemed critical to U.S. national security

ELIGIBILITY/REQUIREMENTS: Intended to provide support to U.S. undergraduates who will pursue the study of languages and cultures currently underrepresented in study abroad and critical to U.S. national security. Must be U.S. citizen matriculated at a U.S. university or college. Provides a unique funding opportunity for U.S. students to study world regions critical to U.S. interests (including Africa, Asia, Central & Eastern Europe, Latin American and the Caribbean, and the Middle East). Must be matriculated in an undergraduate degree program in a U.S. university, college or community college accredited by an accrediting body recognized by the U.S. Department of Education, and applying to engage in a study-abroad experience in a country outside of Western Europe, Canada,

Australia, or New Zealand that meets home institution standards.

HOW TO APPLY: See website for additional information and application. Apply online. Submit to your NSEP campus representative with 2 reference forms, language self-assessment form, language proficiency form (optional), official transcripts, 1-page study abroad program description, and letters of support for direct enrollment (if applicable).

RENEWABLE: No

CONTACT: Susan Sharp, Program Officer

ADDITIONAL INFORMATION: The NSEP service requirement stipulates that award recipients work in the federal government in positions with national security responsibilities. The Departments of Defense, Homeland Security, State, or any element of the Intelligence Community are priority agencies.

1680—JAPANESE AMERICAN CITIZENS LEAGUE (Yoshiko Tanaka Memorial Scholarship)

1765 Sutter Street
San Francisco CA 94115
415/921-5225
FAX: 415/931-4671
E-mail: jacl@jacl.org
Internet: http://www.jacl.org
AMOUNT: $1,000-$5,000
DEADLINE(S): APR 1
FIELD(S): Japanese Language/Culture; U.S.-Japan Relations
ELIGIBILITY/REQUIREMENTS: Only open to JACL members and their children. For undergraduate students who are planning to attend a college, university, trade, business, or any other institution of higher learning. Financial need NOT a factor.
HOW TO APPLY: For membership information or an application, send SASE to above address, stating your level of study. Submit personal statement, letters of recommendation, and transcripts.

1681—JUNIATA COLLEGE (Eagles Abroad Scholarship)

Office of Financial Planning
1700 Moore Street
Huntingdon PA 16652
814/641-3142
FAX: 814/641-5311
E-mail: frankv@juniata.edu
Internet: http://www.juniata.edu/admission/finplan/index.html
AMOUNT: Expense paid international experience + $3,000
DEADLINE(S): JAN 4

FIELD(S): All (Study Abroad), World Languages
ELIGIBILITY/REQUIREMENTS: Students will first be required to complete an international experience at no cost after their freshman year, an additional $3,000 will then be awarded during the junior year for 2 semesters of study abroad. Students must be committed to an international experience in France, Germany, Mexico, Spain or Russia and may study any academic program at the college. High school students applying for this award should have demonstrated interest in world languages by having at least 3 years of language in high school and a strong academic curriculum.
HOW TO APPLY: Contact College for an application or enrollment information. An application and interview are required.
NUMBER OF AWARDS: 1
CONTACT: Vincent Frank, Director of Student Financial Planning, 814/641-3140; e-mail: frankv@juniata.edu

1682—KOSCIUSZKO FOUNDATION (Summer Sessions in Poland and Rome)

15 East 65th Street
New York NY 10021-6595
212/734-2130
FAX: 212/628-4552
E-mail: addy@thekf.orgthekf
Internet: http://www.kosciuszko foundation.org
AMOUNT: Varies
DEADLINE(S): Varies
FIELD(S): Polish Studies; History; Literature; Art; Economics; Social Studies; Language; Culture
ELIGIBILITY/REQUIREMENTS: Open to U.S. citizens and permanent residents who are undergraduate or graduate students, high school seniors 18 or older, and persons of any age not enrolled in a college or university program.
HOW TO APPLY: See website or send SASE for an application.
CONTACT: Addy Tymczyszyn, Summer Studies Abroad Coordinator, ext. 210

1683—LAMBDA IOTA TAU (LIT) HONOR SOCIETY FOR LITERATURE OF ALL LANGUAGES

Department of English
Ball State University
2000 West University Avenue
Muncie IN 47306-0460
765/285-8456 or 765/285-8370
FAX: 765/285-3965
E-mail: bhozeski@bsu.edu

Internet: http://www.bsu.edu/csh/english/undergraduate/lit/
AMOUNT: $1,000
DEADLINE(S): JUN 30
FIELD(S): Literature (all languages)
ELIGIBILITY/REQUIREMENTS: Must be a member of LIT; demonstrate superior leadership and academic accomplishments.
HOW TO APPLY: Must be nominated by letter from chapter sponsor; candidate must submit 1,000 words or less on career goals and objectives.
NUMBER OF AWARDS: 3 or more
RENEWABLE: No
CONTACT: Bruce W. Hozeski, Executive Secretary

1684—MINISTRY OF EDUCATION OF THE REPUBLIC OF CHINA (Scholarships for Foreign Students)

5 South Chung-Shan Road
Taipei, Taiwan
REPUBLIC OF CHINA
(86) (02) 356-5696
FAX: (86) (02) 397-6778
E-mail: emic@moe.edu.cn
Internet: http://www.moe.edu.cn
AMOUNT: NT$25,000 (per month)
DEADLINE(S): Varies (inquire of school)
FIELD(S): Chinese Studies or Language
ELIGIBILITY/REQUIREMENTS: Open to full-time students wishing to study in Taiwan. Must have studied in R.O.C. for at least 1 term prior to scholarship.
HOW TO APPLY: Write for complete information or contact colleges directly.
NUMBER OF AWARDS: 300

1685—NATIONAL FEDERATION OF THE BLIND (Humanities Scholarship)

805 5th Avenue
Grinnell IA 50112
641/236-3369
Internet: http://www.nfb.org/nfb/scholarship_program.asp
AMOUNT: $3,000
DEADLINE(S): MAR 31
FIELD(S): Humanities (Art, English, Foreign Languages, History, Philosophy, Religion)
ELIGIBILITY/REQUIREMENTS: Open to legally blind students pursuing or planning to pursue a full-time postsecondary education in the U.S. Awarded on basis of academic excellence, service to the community, and financial need. Membership NOT required.
HOW TO APPLY: Contact Scholarship Committee Chair for an application.

278

Submit with transcripts and 2 letters of recommendation.
NUMBER OF AWARDS: 1
RENEWABLE: Yes
CONTACT: Peggy Elliot, Scholarship Committee Chair

1686—NATIONAL ITALIAN AMERICAN FOUNDATION

1860 19th Street NW
Washington DC 20009
202/387-0600
FAX: 202/387-0800
E-mail: scholarships@niaf.org
Internet: http://www.niaf@org/scholar/scholarships/about.asp
AMOUNT: $2,500-$10,000
DEADLINE(S): MAR 1
FIELD(S): All (category I), Area Studies, Italian (category II)
ELIGIBILITY/REQUIREMENTS: Open to U.S. citizens or permanent resident aliens enrolled in an accredited institution of higher education; have a GPA of at 3.5 (or equivalent); demonstrate outstanding potential and high academic achievements; and fit into 1 of 2 NIAF scholarship categories: Category I—Italian-American students (must have 1 ancestor who has emigrated from any region in Italy) area of study open; Category II—students from any ethnic background majoring or minoring in Italian language, Italian studies, Italian American studies or a related field, Scholarships are awarded on the basis of academic performance, field of study, career objectives, and potential commitment and ability to make significant contributions to their chosen field of study. Some scholarships awarded on basis of financial need.
HOW TO APPLY: Application available on website and can ONLY be submitted online. Official transcript must be mailed and postmarked. FAFSA optional; if submitted must be postmarked by March 1. Teacher evaluation required; submit using online Teacher Evaluation form no later than March 15.
RENEWABLE: Yes
ADDITIONAL INFORMATION: If awarded, recipient must sign a written statement pledging that upon completion of the scholarship academic year, student will submit a typed narrative of approximately 500 words for publication describing the benefits of the NIAF Scholarship. May not be used as a substitute for or diminish any other award, grant or scholarship. The combined benefits from all sources may not exceed the cost of tuition, fees and university-provided room and board.

1687—SONS OF NORWAY FOUNDATION (King Olav V Norwegian American Heritage Fund)

c/o Sons of Norway
1455 West Lake Street
Minneapolis MN 55408
612/821-4632
E-mail: colson@sofn.com
Internet: http://www.sofn.com/foundation/foundation scholarships.html
AMOUNT: $250-$3,000
DEADLINE(S): MAR 1
FIELD(S): Norwegian Studies/American Studies: Arts; Crafts; Literature; History; Music; Folklore and related fields
ELIGIBILITY/REQUIREMENTS: Must be U.S. citizens, 18 or older, enrolled in a recognized educational institution, who has demonstrated interest in Norwegian heritage or any Norwegian. Award based on GPA, participation in school and community activities, work experience, education and career goals, and personal and school references. Financial need also considered. Same opportunity available to Norwegian students interested in pursuing American studies at U.S. university.
HOW TO APPLY: Submit application along with an essay (500 words or less) giving reasons for applying, course of study to be pursued, the length of course, name of the institution to be attended, tuition and costs, and amount of financial assistance needed. Include 3 letters of recommendation and copy of high school or college transcript. See website for an application and additional details.
NUMBER OF AWARDS: 12
RENEWABLE: Yes. Maximum of 2 awards in 5 years.
CONTACT: Cindy Olson, Director

1688—SOUTHEAST MISSOURI STATE UNIVERSITY (Constance Rowe French Scholarship)

One University Plaza
Cape Girardeau MO 63701
573/651/2476
E-mail: dmacleay@semovm.semo.edu
Internet: http://www2.semo.edu/foreignlang/sch-fr.html
AMOUNT: Up to full tuition and fees
DEADLINE(S): Varies
FIELD(S): French or Education with a French minor
ELIGIBILITY/REQUIREMENTS: For study in a French-speaking country in the summer before or after junior year, or either semester of junior year. Applicants must have 45 credit hours completed and be enrolled in at least 12 semester hours. Financial need may be considered. Students not currently holding other scholarships and students from other countries, states, or provinces where French is not the predominant language receive preference.
HOW TO APPLY: Contact the University for more information.
CONTACT: Dr. Daniel A. MacLeay

1689—SOUTHEAST MISSOURI STATE UNIVERSITY (Frances and Cornelius Crowley Scholarship)

One University Plaza
Cape Girardeau MO 63701
573/651/2000
E-mail: djedan@semo.edu
Internet: http://www2.semo.edu/foreignlang/sch-sn.html
AMOUNT: Varies
DEADLINE(S): Varies
FIELD(S): Spanish
ELIGIBILITY/REQUIREMENTS: Scholarships for full-time students who are members of the Spanish club at SMSU. Must have a 2.8 or higher overall GPA, 3.0 Spanish GPA. Applicants must compose an assigned essay.
HOW TO APPLY: For information contact Department Chair.
CONTACT: Dr. Dieter Jedan, Department Chair

1690—SOUTHEAST MISSOURI STATE UNIVERSITY (German Scholarship)

One University Plaza
Cape Girardeau MO 63701
573/651/2000
E-mail: djedan@semo.edu
Internet: http://www2.semo.edu/foreignlang/sch-sn.html
AMOUNT: Varies
DEADLINE(S): Varies
FIELD(S): German
ELIGIBILITY/REQUIREMENTS: Must be a full-time student majoring in German with a 2.5 GPA. Funds must be used for overseas study purposes.
HOW TO APPLY: For information contact Department Chair.
CONTACT: Dr. Dieter Jedan, Department Chair

1691—UNIVERSITY OF ROCHESTER (The Mildred R. Burton Summer Study Grants)

Box 270251

Rochester NY 14627-0251
585/275-4251
Internet: http://www.rochester.edu/
College/MLC/burton.html
AMOUNT: Varies
DEADLINE(S): FEB 26
FIELD(S): Foreign Language
ELIGIBILITY/REQUIREMENTS: For undergraduate students to complete an approved course of summer language study in a country where that language is spoken. Preference given to students who intend to study in a program run by the UR, if program is available in that language. Must have completed at least 1 year of foreign language study at UR. Based on merit and need.
HOW TO APPLY: Applications are available from the Department of Modern Languages and Cultures (408 Lattimore). Submit with statement of project, anticipated expenses, faculty letter of recommendation, academic transcript (or first-semester grade report for freshmen).

1692—UNIVERSITY OF WINDSOR (Outstanding Scholars Award)

401 Sunset Avenue
Windsor Ontario N9B 3P4
CANADA
519/253-3000
FAX: 519/973-7081
E-mail: awards1@uwindsor.ca
Internet: http://www.uwindsor.ca
AMOUNT: $1,000-$2500/year (Canadian); maximum 4 years
DEADLINE(S): MAY 31
FIELD(S): Classics, Modern Languages, French, Philosophy, Music, Physics, Earth Sciences (not Environmental Studies), Economics (not Business and Economics), Chemistry (not Biochemistry), Mathematics and Statistics, Industrial, Mechanical (Materials Option) or Environmental Engineering or Bachelor of Arts and Science
ELIGIBILITY/REQUIREMENTS: Open to undergraduate students registering in year 1 at the University of Windsor. Must have superior grades. Amount of award based on secondary school accomplishments.
HOW TO APPLY: Automatic. No application required.
RENEWABLE: Yes. Up to 4 years.
CONTACT: Aase Houser
ADDITIONAL INFORMATION: Students in this program will also be mentored in their first year in preparation for guaranteed Outstanding Scholars Appoint-

ments in their Department/School (valued at $2,000 Canadian in earnings for each of the 2nd, 3rd, and 4th years) provided all conditions are met.

1693—WESTERN MICHIGAN UNIVERSITY (College of Arts and Sciences/Ruth Y. Kirby Awards for Travel and Study Abroad)

1903 West Michigan
Kalamazoo MI 49008-5337
269/387-8777
FAX: 269/387-6989
E-mail: finaid-info!wmich.edu
Internet: http://www.wmich.edu/finaid
AMOUNT: Varies
DEADLINE(S): Fall semester
FIELD(S): Spanish
ELIGIBILITY/REQUIREMENTS: Must be an undergraduate student, have declared major in Spanish; completed at WMU a 300-level course in Spanish; minimum cumulative GPA of 3.0 and a minimum 3.25 GPA in Spanish, and be enrolled in a study-abroad program in a Spanish-speaking country.
HOW TO APPLY: Applications available in Department of Spanish, 410 Sprau Tower (Phone: 269/387-3001, Fax: 269/387-3103). Application includes 300- to 500-word essay detailing interests and goals as they relate to the study and/or use of Spanish, recommendations and interview.
NUMBER OF AWARDS: Varies

1694—WESTERN MICHIGAN UNIVERSITY (College of Arts and Sciences/Ruth Y. Kirby Scholarship Awards)

1903 West Michigan
Kalamazoo MI 49008-5337
269/387-8777
FAX: 269/387-6989
E-mail: finaid-info!wmich.edu
Internet: http://www.wmich.edu/finaid
AMOUNT: Varies
DEADLINE(S): Fall semester
FIELD(S): Spanish
ELIGIBILITY/REQUIREMENTS: Must be an undergraduate student, have declared major in Spanish; completed at WMU a 300-level course in Spanish and must complete at least 2 additional 300-level Spanish courses by the end of the semester of application, and at least 1 500-level Spanish course after receiving award. Minimum cumulative GPA of 3.0 and a minimum 3.25 GPA in Spanish.

HOW TO APPLY: Applications available in Department of Spanish, 410 Sprau Tower (Phone: 269/387-3001, Fax: 269/387-3103). Application includes short essay, recommendations and interview.
NUMBER OF AWARDS: Varies

1695—WESTERN MICHIGAN UNIVERSITY (College of Arts and Sciences/Spanish Department Travel/Study Abroad Awards)

1903 West Michigan
Kalamazoo MI 49008-5337
269/387-8777
FAX: 269/387-6989
E-mail: finaid-info!wmich.edu
Internet: http://www.wmich.edu/finaid
AMOUNT: Varies
DEADLINE(S): Fall semester
FIELD(S): Spanish
ELIGIBILITY/REQUIREMENTS: Must be undergraduate student with declared major in Spanish, have completed a minimum of 2 Spanish courses (at least 1 of which must be a 300-level or higher) at WMU by the end of the semester of application, have a minimum overall GPA of 3.25 and a minimum GPA of 3.50 in Spanish major. Must enroll in departmentally-approved study-abroad program (applicable to summer, 1-semester or 1-year approved programs) whose credits are transferable to WMU.
HOW TO APPLY: Applications available in Department of Spanish, 410 Sprau Tower (Phone: 269/387-3001, Fax: 269/387-3103). Application includes short essay, recommendations and interview.
NUMBER OF AWARDS: Varies

1696—WESTERN MICHIGAN UNIVERSITY (College of Arts and Sciences/Sue C. Mardis Foreign Language Scholarship)

1903 West Michigan
Kalamazoo MI 49008-5337
269/387-8777
FAX: 269/387-6989
E-mail: finaid-info!wmich.edu
Internet: http://www.wmich.edu/finaid
AMOUNT: $2,500
DEADLINE(S): Fall semester
FIELD(S): Spanish
ELIGIBILITY/REQUIREMENTS: Must be female student enrolled full time. Minority candidates are encouraged to apply. Must have a declared Spanish major, have completed at WMU a 300-level Spanish course prior to the semester of application and must complete at least 1

more 300-level Spanish course by the end of the semester of application, have minimum 3.0 GPA overall. Must enroll in department-approved study-abroad program to begin within 1 year of award for at least 1 full semester.
HOW TO APPLY: Applications available in Department of Spanish, 410 Sprau Tower (Phone: 269/387-3001, Fax: 269/387-3103). Application includes short essay, recommendations and interview.
NUMBER OF AWARDS: Varies

1697—WESTERN MICHIGAN UNIVERSITY (College of Arts and Sciences/The President's Award/Scholarships for Study Abroad in Spanish)

1903 West Michigan
Kalamazoo MI 49008-5337
269/387-8777
FAX: 269/387-6989
E-mail: finaid-info!wmich.edu
Internet: http://www.wmich.edu/finaid
AMOUNT: $2,000-$2,500
DEADLINE(S): Fall and Spring semesters
FIELD(S): Spanish
ELIGIBILITY/REQUIREMENTS: Must be undergraduate with declared major in Spanish, have completed at WMU at least 1 300-level Spanish course prior to the semester of application and must complete at least 1 more 300-level Spanish course at WMU by the end of the semester of application. Minimum overall GPA of 3.00 and a minimum GPA of 3.75 for $2,500 award or 3.5 for $2,000 award in Spanish major. Must enroll in a department-approved study-abroad program (applicable to programs with duration of 1 semester or longer) whose credits are transferable to WMU.
HOW TO APPLY: Applications available in Department of Spanish, 410 Sprau Tower (Phone: 269/387-3001, Fax: 269/387-3103). Application includes short essay, recommendations and interview.
NUMBER OF AWARDS: 1, $2,500; 6, $2,000

1698—WESTERN MICHIGAN UNIVERSITY (College of Education/Zora and Frank Ellsworth Scholarship Fund)

1903 West Michigan
Kalamazoo MI 49008-5337
269/387-6000
FAX: 269/387-6989
E-mail: finaid-info!wmich.edu
Internet: http://www.wmich.edu/finaid
AMOUNT: $1,000-$2,000/semester
DEADLINE(S): MAR 1
FIELD(S): Education (Latin preferred)
ELIGIBILITY/REQUIREMENTS: Full-time student in junior or senior year; enrolled in Elementary Education (Latin majors preferred); must maintain 3.0 GPA; demonstrate a career purpose in education and financial need.
HOW TO APPLY: See website or contact College of Education for application.
CONTACT: College of Education

1699—WESTERN MICHIGAN UNIVERSITY (Keio University Exchange Scholarship)

Office of Study Abroad
B200 Ellsworth Hall
Battle Creek MI 49017
269/387-5890
E-mail: study-abroad@wmich.edu
Internet: http://www.wmich.edu/studyabroad
AMOUNT: Tuition, housing, and living stipend
DEADLINE(S): MAY 30
FIELD(S): Japanese
ELIGIBILITY/REQUIREMENTS: Must be selected to study Japanese language for an academic year by the Japan Exchange Program Selection Committee.
HOW TO APPLY: Contact Office of Study Abroad for an application and details.

PHILOSOPHY

1700—AYN RAND INSTITUTE (Anthem Essay Contest)

Department W
P.O. Box 57044
Irvine CA 92619-7044
E-mail: anthemessay@aynrand.org
Internet: http://www.aynrand.org/contests/
AMOUNT: $2,000 (1st prize); $500 (2nd); $200 (3rd); $50 (finalists); $30 (semifinalists)
DEADLINE(S): March 18
FIELD(S): All (emphasis on philosophy)
ELIGIBILITY/REQUIREMENTS: Open to 9th and 10th graders who write a 600- to 1,200-word essay on Ayn Rand's novelette *Anthem*. Essays will be judged on both style and content. Judges will look for writing that is clear, articulate and logically organized. Winning essays must demonstrate an outstanding grasp of the philosophic meaning of *Anthem*.
HOW TO APPLY: See website or contact your English teacher or guidance counselor for guidelines. Do NOT write to above address. Submit online, e-mail, or by mail.
NUMBER OF AWARDS: 236 (1 first, 5 second, 10 third, 45 finalist, 175 semifinalists)

1701—AYN RAND INSTITUTE (Atlas Shrugged Essay Competition)

Department W
2121 Alton Parkway, Suite 250
Irvine CA 92606
E-mail: essay@aynrand.org
Internet: http://www.aynrand.org/contests/
AMOUNT: $5,000 (1st prize); $1,000 (2nd); $400 (3rd); $100 (finalist); $50 (semifinalist)
DEADLINE(S): FEB 15
FIELD(S): Business; Philosophy
ELIGIBILITY/REQUIREMENTS: Open to students enrolled in a graduate or undergraduate business degree program, who write a 1,000- to 1,200-word essay on Ayn Rand's *Atlas Shrugged*. Essays judged on both style and content. Judges will look for writing that is clear, articulate and logically organized. Winning essays must demonstrate an outstanding grasp of the philosophic meaning of *Atlas Shrugged*.
HOW TO APPLY: See website or contact your Business Ethics professor for guidelines. Do NOT write to above address. Submit online, e-mail, or by mail.
NUMBER OF AWARDS: 224 (1 first, 3, second, 5 third, 20 finalist, 200 semifinalist)

1702—AYN RAND INSTITUTE (Fountainhead Essay Contest)

Department W
P.O. Box 57044
Irvine CA 92619-7044
E-mail: tf-essay@aynrand.org
Internet: http://www.aynrand.org/contests/
AMOUNT: $10,000 (1st prize); $2,000 (2nd); $1,000 (3rd); $100 (finalist); $50 (semifinalist)
DEADLINE(S): APR 15
FIELD(S): All
ELIGIBILITY/REQUIREMENTS: Open to 11th and 12th graders who write an 800-1,600-word essay on Ayn Rand's *The Fountainhead*. Essays judged on both style and content. Judges will look for writing that is clear, articulate and logically organized. Winning essays must demonstrate an outstanding grasp of the philosophic and psychological meaning of *The Fountainhead*.

HOW TO APPLY: See website for guidelines. Do NOT write to above address. Submit online, e-mail, or by mail.
NUMBER OF AWARDS: 251 (1 first, 5 second, 10 third, 35 finalist, 200 semifinalist)

1703—DAVIDSON INSTITUTE FOR TALENT DEVELOPMENT

9665 Gateway
Reno NV 89521
775/852-3483, ext. 423
FAX: 775/852-2184
E-mail: tmoessner@ditd.org
Internet: http://www.davidson fellows.org
AMOUNT: $10,000, $20,000, $50,000
DEADLINE(S): Last Friday of MAR
FIELD(S): Science, Technology, Mathematics, Philosophy, Music, Literature and Outside the Box
ELIGIBILITY/REQUIREMENTS: Must be a U.S. citizen residing in the U.S., or a permanent resident of the U.S. residing in the U.S.; under the age of 18 as of October 1 (there is no minimum age for eligibility); completed a significant piece of work in one of the designated application categories; and available to attend, with at least 1 parent or guardian, the awards reception and other recognition events in September (travel expenses and lodging will be paid by the Institute).
HOW TO APPLY: See website including FAQ section and application booklet; download and complete all components.
NUMBER OF AWARDS: 15-20
RENEWABLE: No
CONTACT: Tacie Moessner, Davidson Fellows Program Manager
ADDITIONAL INFORMATION: Group and team projects are not eligible. Scholarships must be used at an accredited institute of learning within 10 years of the award date.

1704—FREEDOM FROM RELIGION FOUNDATION (Student Essay Contests)

P.O. Box 750
Madison WI 53701
608/256-5800
Internet: http://www.ffrf.org
AMOUNT: $1,000; $500; $250
DEADLINE(S): JUL 15
FIELD(S): Humanities; English; Education; Philosophy; Science
ELIGIBILITY/REQUIREMENTS: Topics change yearly, but all are on general theme of maintaining separation of church and state. Open to high school

seniors and students currently enrolled in college or technical schools. Must be U.S. citizen.
HOW TO APPLY: See website for details. Send SASE to address above for complete information. Indicate whether you will be competing in the college or high school competition. Information will be sent when new topics are announced each February.

1705—INSTITUTE FOR HUMANE STUDIES (Summer Seminars Program)

3401 North Fairfax Drive, Suite 440
Arlington VA 22201-4432
703/993-4880 or 800/697-8799
FAX: 703/993-4890
Internet: http://www.TheIHS.org
AMOUNT: Free summer seminars, including room/board, lectures, seminar materials, and books
DEADLINE(S): MAR
FIELD(S): Social Sciences; Humanities; Law; Journalism; Public Policy; Education; Film; Writing; Economics; Philosophy
ELIGIBILITY/REQUIREMENTS: Open to college students, recent graduates, and graduate students who share an interest in learning and exchanging ideas about the scope of individual rights, free markets, the rule of law, peace, and tolerance.
HOW TO APPLY: See website for information and to apply online, or contact IHS for an application.

1706—NATIONAL FEDERATION OF THE BLIND (Humanities Scholarship)

805 5th Avenue
Grinnell IA 50112
641/236-3369
Internet: http://www.nfb.org/ nfb/scholarship_program.asp
AMOUNT: $3,000
DEADLINE(S): MAR 31
FIELD(S): Humanities (Art, English, Foreign Languages, History, Philosophy, Religion)
ELIGIBILITY/REQUIREMENTS: Open to legally blind students pursuing or planning to pursue a full-time postsecondary education in the U.S. Awarded on basis of academic excellence, service to the community, and financial need. Membership NOT required.
HOW TO APPLY: Contact Scholarship Committee Chair for an application. Submit with transcripts and 2 letters of recommendation.
NUMBER OF AWARDS: 1
RENEWABLE: Yes

CONTACT: Peggy Elliot, Scholarship Committee Chair

1707—UNIVERSITY OF WINDSOR (Outstanding Scholars Award)

401 Sunset Avenue
Windsor Ontario N9B 3P4
CANADA
519/253-3000
FAX: 519/973-7081
E-mail: awards1@uwindsor.ca
Internet: http://www.uwindsor.ca
AMOUNT: $1,000-$2,500/year (Canadian); maximum 4 years
DEADLINE(S): MAY 31
FIELD(S): Classics, Modern Languages, French, Philosophy, Music, Physics, Earth Sciences (not Environmental Studies), Economics (not Business and Economics), Chemistry (not Biochemistry), Mathematics and Statistics, Industrial, Mechanical (Materials Option) or Environmental Engineering or Bachelor of Arts and Science
ELIGIBILITY/REQUIREMENTS: Open to undergraduate students registering in year 1 at the University of Windsor. Must have superior grades. Amount of award based on secondary school accomplishments.
HOW TO APPLY: Automatic. No application required.
RENEWABLE: Yes. Up to 4 years.
CONTACT: Aase Houser
ADDITIONAL INFORMATION: Students in this program will also be mentored in their first year in preparation for guaranteed Outstanding Scholars Appointments in their Department/School (valued at $2,000 Canadian in earnings for each of the 2nd, 3rd, and 4th years) provided all conditions are met.

RELIGION/THEOLOGY

1708—AMERICAN BAPTIST FINANCIAL AID PROGRAM (Asian American Summer Intern Grants)

P.O. Box 851
Valley Forge PA 19482-0851
800/ABC-3USA, ext. 2067 or 610/768-2000
FAX: 610/768-2056
Internet: http://www.abc-em.org/ dm/fa.cfm
AMOUNT: $500
DEADLINE(S): MAY 31

FIELD(S): Religion/Theology
ELIGIBILITY/REQUIREMENTS: Must be Asian-American member of an American Baptist church for at least 1 year. Employing church is expected to contribute matching funds and supervision during the internship.
HOW TO APPLY: Church pastors nominate a seminarian.
RENEWABLE: Yes
CONTACT: Lynne Eckman, Director of Financial Aid

1709—AMERICAN BAPTIST FINANCIAL AID PROGRAM (Daniel E. Weiss Fund for Excellence)

P.O. Box 851
Valley Forge PA 19482-0851
800/ABC-3USA, ext. 2067 or
610/768-2000
FAX: 610/768-2056
Internet: http://www.abc-em.org/dm/fa.cfm
DEADLINE(S): NOV 1
FIELD(S): Theology
ELIGIBILITY/REQUIREMENTS: Program designed to identify gifted American Baptists who might not otherwise undertake theological study and to provide them with "substantial financial assistance" for their first year of seminary studies.
HOW TO APPLY: Church pastors may nominate a seminarian.
RENEWABLE: Yes
CONTACT: Lynne Eckman, Director of Financial Aid

1710—AMERICAN BAPTIST FINANCIAL AID PROGRAM (Hispanic Scholarship Funds)

P.O. Box 851
Valley Forge PA 19482-0851
800/ABC-3USA, ext. 2067 or
610/768-2000
FAX: 610/768-2056
Internet: http://www.abc-em.org/dm/fa.cfm
AMOUNT: $500
DEADLINE(S): MAY 31
FIELD(S): Theology
ELIGIBILITY/REQUIREMENTS: Must be Hispanic member of an American Baptist church for at least 1 year before applying; must be pursuing an undergraduate or graduate degree in a seminary in the U.S. or Puerto Rico; U.S. citizen. Must demonstrate financial need and plan to serve in a church-related ministry.
HOW TO APPLY: Write for information.
RENEWABLE: Yes

CONTACT: Lynne Eckman, Director of Financial Aid

1711—AMERICAN JEWISH LEAGUE FOR ISRAEL

450 Seventh Avenue,
Suite 808
New York NY 10123
212/371-1583
FAX: 212/279-1456
E-mail: ajlijms@aol.com
Internet: http://www.american jewishleague.org
AMOUNT: Varies
DEADLINE(S): MAY 1
FIELD(S): Religion
ELIGIBILITY/REQUIREMENTS: Merit-based scholarship; open to U.S. undergraduate or graduate students to study at a participating university in Israel. Acceptance at university is prerequisite.
HOW TO APPLY: Visit website or contact AJLI to receive an application.
NUMBER OF AWARDS: About 10
RENEWABLE: No
CONTACT: Jeff Scheckner

1712—B. M. WOLTMAN FOUNDATION (Lutheran Scholarships for Students of the Ministry and Teaching)

7900 U.S. 290 East
Austin TX 78724
512/926-4272
AMOUNT: $500-$2,500
DEADLINE(S): JUL 1
FIELD(S): Theology (LCMS Ministry); Teacher Education (LCMS Schools)
ELIGIBILITY/REQUIREMENTS: Open to undergraduate and graduate students. Must be Texas residents attending, or planning to attend, Concordia University in Austin, TX, or an LCSM seminary.
HOW TO APPLY: Write for details.
NUMBER OF AWARDS: 45
RENEWABLE: Yes, must reapply.

1713—CHRISTIAN CHURCH-DISCIPLES OF CHRIST (Katherine J. Schutze Memorial and Edwin G. and Lauretta M. Michael Scholarship)

P.O. Box 1986
Indianapolis IN 46206-1986
317/635-3100
FAX: 317/635-4426
E-mail: cwebb@dhm.disciples.org
AMOUNT: Varies
DEADLINE(S): MAR 15
FIELD(S): Theology

ELIGIBILITY/REQUIREMENTS: Open to Christian Church (Disciples of Christ) members who are female seminary students preparing for the ordained ministry. Must be enrolled as a full-time student in an accredited school or seminary, have an above-average GPA (minimum C+), and demonstrate financial need. Schutze scholarship is open to all women who meet above criteria; Michael Scholarship is for ministers' wives only.
HOW TO APPLY: Contact Division of Homeland Ministries for an application. Submit with transcripts and references.
RENEWABLE: Yes

1714—CHRISTIAN CHURCH-DISCIPLES OF CHRIST (Rowley/Ministerial Education Scholarship)

P.O. Box 1986
Indianapolis IN 46206-1986
317/635-3100
FAX: 317/635-4426
E-mail: cwebb@dhm.disciples.org
AMOUNT: Varies
DEADLINE(S): MAR 15
FIELD(S): Theology
ELIGIBILITY/REQUIREMENTS: Open to Christian Church (Disciples of Christ) members who are seminary students preparing for the ordained ministry. Must be enrolled as a full-time student in an accredited school or seminary, have an above-average GPA (minimum C+), and demonstrate financial need.
HOW TO APPLY: Contact Church, Division of Homeland Ministries, for an application. Submit with transcripts and references.
RENEWABLE: Yes

1715—CHRISTIAN CHURCH-DISCIPLES OF CHRIST (Star Supporter Scholarship/Loan)

P.O. Box 1986
Indianapolis IN 46206-1986
317/635-3100
FAX: 317/635-4426
E-mail: cwebb@dhm.disciples.org
AMOUNT: $2,000
DEADLINE(S): MAR 15
FIELD(S): Theology
ELIGIBILITY/REQUIREMENTS: Open to Christian Church (Disciples of Christ) members who are Black/Afro-American students preparing for the ordained ministry. Must be enrolled as a full-time student at an accredited school or seminary, have an above-average GPA (minimum C+), and demonstrate financial need.

HOW TO APPLY: Contact Division of Homeland Ministries for an application. Submit with transcripts and references. 3 years of service in a full-time professional ministry will repay the scholarship/loan.
NUMBER OF AWARDS: 100
RENEWABLE: Yes

1716—COMMUNITY FOUNDATION FOR GREATER ATLANTA, INC., THE (James M. & Virginia M. Smyth Scholarship Fund)

50 Hurt Plaza, Suite 449
Atlanta GA 30303
404/688-5525
FAX: 404/688-3060
E-mail: scholarships@atlcf.org
Internet:
http://www.atlcf.org/GrantsScholarships/Scholarships.aspx
AMOUNT: $500-$1,000
DEADLINE(S): Varies
FIELD(S): Humanities, Science, Human Services, Music, Ministry
ELIGIBILITY/REQUIREMENTS: Open to students enrolled at an accredited college pursuing an undergraduate degree and adults returning to school in order to increase employability. Must have a cumulative 3.0 GPA, be accepted for enrollment or enrolled at an accredited college, university or technical school, demonstrate financial need, and commitment to community service through school, community or religious organizations. Preference will be given to applicants from Missouri, Mississippi, Georgia, Illinois, Oklahoma, Texas and Tennessee.
HOW TO APPLY: See website for additional information and application. Submit with a personal essay (2-3 pages) that explains why you feel a college education is important, your statement of educational and career goals, post college career interests, highlights of your high school extracurricular/community service activities, special strengths, skills, and qualifications, any unusual family or personal circumstances have affected your achievement in school, work experience, or your participation in school and community activities, and present financial need; official transcript; and SAT and ACT scores, if a recent high school graduate. Send to The Community Foundation for Greater Atlanta, James M. & Virginia M. Smyth Scholarship Fund, Scholarship Management Services, Scholarship America, One Scholarship Way, P.O. Box 297, Saint Peter, MN 56082. If you have questions, call 507/931-1682 or e-mail communityfoundation@scholarshipamerica.org.
NUMBER OF AWARDS: 12-15

RENEWABLE: Yes; Previous recipients are renewed if they continue to meet the scholarship's criteria and submit the current year's renewal application
CONTACT: Lisa Glanville, 404/308-0055

1717—FELLOWSHIP OF UNITED METHODISTS IN MUSIC & WORSHIP ARTS (Fellowship Scholarships)

4702 Graceland Avenue
Indianapolis IN 46208-3504
AMOUNT: $1,500 (maximum)
DEADLINE(S): MAR 1
FIELD(S): Church Music; Worship Arts
ELIGIBILITY/REQUIREMENTS: Must be full-time music degree candidate, either entering freshman or undergraduate attending an accredited university, college, or school of theology or pursuing special education in worship or the arts related to worship. Must be a member of the United Methodist Church for at least 1 year prior to applying; demonstrate participation in activities of the church and/or campus and exceptional musical or other artistic talent, effective leadership ability, and outstanding promise of future usefulness to the Church in the areas of music and/or worship.
HOW TO APPLY: Submit application along with transcript; a 1-page statement describing intention to pursue church music or other music or arts related to worship as vocation; 3 letters of recommendation from major professor or teacher, the pastor of your church, someone who can vouch for abilities as musician, artist, or performer and can attest to your vocational potential.
NUMBER OF AWARDS: 5 or 6 1
CONTACT: Michael L. Sellick, General Secretary

1718—FUND FOR THEOLOGICAL EDUCATION, INC., THE (Undergraduate Fellows Program)

825 Houston Mill Road, Suite 250
Atlanta GA 30329-4211
404/727-1450
FAX: 404/727-1490
E-mail: fte@thefund.org
Internet: http://www.thefund.org
AMOUNT: $1,500
DEADLINE(S): MAR 1
FIELD(S): Religion; Ministry
ELIGIBILITY/REQUIREMENTS: Must be enrolled as a sophomore or junior in an undergraduate program at a North American college or university. Should be considering Christian ministry as a career.

Must demonstrate high academic performance, a cumulative GPA of 3.0 or above, and potential gifts for ministry. Must be under 30 years, and U.S. citizen.
HOW TO APPLY: Applications available on website.
NUMBER OF AWARDS: 70
RENEWABLE: No
CONTACT: Melissa Winginton
ADDITIONAL INFORMATION: Students who are open to the possibility of ministry and may not have made a decision are encouraged to apply. Recipients attend a 4-day summer conference to explore theology, theological education, and the possibilities of congregational ministry.

1719—JEWISH FEDERATION OF METROPOLITAN CHICAGO (Academic Scholarship Program)

Jewish Vocational Service
216 West Jackson Boulevard, Suite 700
Chicago IL 60606-6921
312/673-3400
TTY: 312/444-2877
FAX: 312/553-5544
Internet: http://www.jvs/chicago.org
AMOUNT: Varies
DEADLINE(S): FEB 15
FIELD(S): Mathematics; Engineering; Science, Medicine; Social Work; Education; Psychology; Rabbinate; Law (except corporate); Communications
ELIGIBILITY/REQUIREMENTS: Open to Jewish men and women legally domiciled in the greater Chicago metropolitan area, who demonstrate promise for significant contributions in their chosen careers, and are in need of financial assistance for full-time academic study. Must have entered undergraduate junior year in career programs requiring no postgraduate education, be in graduate/professional school or a vo-tech training program.
HOW TO APPLY: Phone JVS Scholarship Secretary (312/673-3457), fax, or visit website (click on Scholarship Services) for an application in the Fall. Interview required.
RENEWABLE: Yes
CONTACT: JVS Scholarship Secretary at 312/673-3457

1720—LINCOLN COMMUNITY FOUNDATION (George & Lynna Cook Scholarship)

215 Centennial Mall South,

Suite 100
Lincoln NE 68508
402/474-2345
FAX: 402/476-8532
E-mail: lcf@lcf.org
Internet: http://www.lcf.org
AMOUNT: Varies
DEADLINE(S): MAR 15
FIELD(S): Ministry; Education
ELIGIBILITY/REQUIREMENTS: Open to graduating senior or former graduate of any Nebraska high school, who is pursuing a degree in ministry at, and is a member of, any First Church of God college or university affiliated with the church body located in Anderson, Indiana. Must demonstrate scholastic achievement in high school and/or college studies. Financial need a priority.
HOW TO APPLY: Submit application form; transcripts from all high schools, college and universities; copy of ACT/SAT or similar test scores; and financial aid form.
NUMBER OF AWARDS: Varies
RENEWABLE: Yes: Must demonstrate satisfactory academic progress.

1721—LINCOLN COMMUNITY FOUNDATION (Henry J. and Pauline M. Armstrong Scholarship)

215 Centennial Mall South,
Suite 100
Lincoln NE 68508
402/474-2345
FAX: 402/476-8532
E-mail: lcf@lcf.org
Internet: http://www.lcf.org
AMOUNT: Varies
DEADLINE(S): APR 1
FIELD(S): Agriculture; Home Economics; Veterinary Medicine; Ministry
ELIGIBILITY/REQUIREMENTS: Open to all graduating seniors or former graduates of Waverly High School in Waverly, Nebraska, who demonstrate scholastic achievement in high school and/or college studies and financial need. Applicants planning to attend a Lutheran seminary school to become a minister must be male.
HOW TO APPLY: Mail or deliver application form, transcripts, copy of ACT/SAT or similar test scores, and financial aid form to Waverly High School, 15621 Heywood, Waverly, NE 68462. Mail or deliver financial aid form to the Foundation.
NUMBER OF AWARDS: Varies
RENEWABLE: Yes: Must demonstrate satisfactory academic progress.

CONTACT: Mark Clymer, Nebraska Chapter, Charter Property Casualty Under-writers

1722—MEMORIAL FOUNDATION FOR JEWISH CULTURE (International Scholarship Program for Community Service)

50 Broadway, 34th Floor
New York NY 10004
212/425-6606
E-mail: office@mfjc.com
Internet: http://www.mfjc.org/index.htm
AMOUNT: Varies
DEADLINE(S): NOV 30
FIELD(S): Jewish Education; Theology; Social Work
ELIGIBILITY/REQUIREMENTS: Open to any individual regardless of country of origin for undergraduate study that leads to careers in the Rabbinate, Jewish education, social work, or as religious functionaries in Diaspora Jewish communities outside the U.S., Israel, and Canada. Must commit to serve in a community of need for 3 years.
HOW TO APPLY: Write for information.
CONTACT: Jerry Hechbaum, Executive Vice-President; or Dr. Marc Brandriss, Associate Director

1723—MEMORIAL FOUNDATION FOR JEWISH CULTURE (Soviet Jewry Community Service Scholarship Program)

50 Broadway, 34th Floor
New York NY 10004
212/425-6606
E-mail: office@mfjc.com
Internet: http://www.mfjc.org/index.htm
AMOUNT: Varies
DEADLINE(S): NOV 30
FIELD(S): Theology; Education; Social Work
ELIGIBILITY/REQUIREMENTS: Open to Jews from the former Soviet Union enrolled or planning to enroll in recognized institutions of higher Jewish learning. Must agree to serve a community of Soviet Jews anywhere in the world for a minimum of 3 years. Grants are to help prepare well-qualified Soviet Jews to serve in the former Soviet Union.
HOW TO APPLY: Write for information.

1724—NATIONAL FEDERATION OF THE BLIND (Humanities Scholarship)

805 5th Avenue

Grinnell IA 50112
641/236-3369
Internet: http://www.nfb.org/nfb/scholarship_program.asp
AMOUNT: $3,000
DEADLINE(S): MAR 31
FIELD(S): Humanities (Art, English, Foreign Languages, History, Philosophy, Religion)
ELIGIBILITY/REQUIREMENTS: Open to legally blind students pursuing or planning to pursue a full-time postsecondary education in the U.S. Awarded on basis of academic excellence, service to the community, and financial need. Membership NOT required.
HOW TO APPLY: Contact Scholarship Committee Chair for an application. Submit with transcripts and 2 letters of recommendation.
NUMBER OF AWARDS: 1
RENEWABLE: Yes
CONTACT: Peggy Elliot, Scholarship Committee Chair

1725—PHILADELPHIA BIBLICAL UNIVERSITY (Scholarships, Grants, and Loans)

Financial Aid Department
200 Manor Avenue
Langhorne PA 19047
800/366-0049
FAX: 215/702-4248
E-mail: financialaid@pbu.edu
Internet: http://www.pbu.edu
AMOUNT: Varies
DEADLINE(S): Varies
FIELD(S): Bible, Business, Teacher Education, Music, Social Work, Missions, Church Ministries
ELIGIBILITY/REQUIREMENTS: Academic and need-based grants, based on FAFSA, for full-time students, needy dependents of full-time Christian workers, and scholarships and grants to those exhibiting excellence in the field of music. Academic awards based on GPA and SAT/ACT scores.
HOW TO APPLY: Apply to university and complete an application for student aid.
CONTACT: David Haggard

1726—ROBERT SCHRECK MEMORIAL FUND (Grants)

Texas Commerce Bank
Trust Department
P.O. Drawer 140
El Paso TX 79980
915/546-6515

AMOUNT: $500-$1,500
DEADLINE(S): JUL 15; NOV 15
FIELD(S): Medicine; Veterinary Medicine; Physics; Chemistry; Architecture; Engineering; Episcopal Clergy
ELIGIBILITY/REQUIREMENTS: Grants to undergraduate juniors, seniors, or graduate students who have been residents of El Paso County for at least 2 years. Must be U.S. citizen or legal resident and have a high grade point average. Financial need is a consideration.
HOW TO APPLY: Write for information.
NUMBER OF AWARDS: 3
RENEWABLE: No

1727—UNIVERSITY OF OXFORD (Squire and Marriott Bursaries)

University Offices
Wellington Square
Oxford OX1 2JD ENGLAND
+44 (0)1865 270000
Internet: http://www.ox.ac.uk/
AMOUNT: Varies
DEADLINE(S): MAR; SEP
FIELD(S): Theology
ELIGIBILITY/REQUIREMENTS: Applicants must intend to offer themselves for ordination in the Church of England or any church in communion with the Church of England, and need financial assistance. Tenable at the University of Oxford.
HOW TO APPLY: Contact Assistant to the Secretary, Board of the Faculty of Theology for an application and enrollment information.
NUMBER OF AWARDS: 6
RENEWABLE: Yes
CONTACT: E.A. MacAllister, Assistant to the Secretary, Board of the Faculty of Theology

1728—WOMEN OF THE EVANGELICAL LUTHERAN CHURCH IN AMERICA (Opportunity Scholarships for Lutheran Laywomen)

8765 West Higgins Road
Chicago IL 6063-4189
800/638-3522, ext. 2736
FAX: 773/380-2419
E-mail: emilyhansen@elca.org
Internet: http://www.women oftheelca.org/whatwedo/scholar/ scholarships.html
AMOUNT: $2,000 maximum
DEADLINE(S): FEB 15
FIELD(S): All (emphasis on health professions; vocational education; religion)

ELIGIBILITY/REQUIREMENTS: Open to women enrolled in undergraduate, graduate, professional, or vocational courses preparing for a career other than the ordained ministry. Must be at least 21 years old, a citizen of the U.S., a member of the ELCA, and have experienced an interruption in education of 2 or more years since completion of high school. Additional considerations include clearly stated and attainable goals, impact of Women of the ELCA dollars on total cost of program, and applicant's involvement in Women of the ELCA.
HOW TO APPLY: Contact Program Director for an application and additional information. Submit with transcript and 3 references (from pastor, academic, personal).
RENEWABLE: Yes, maximum of 2 years
CONTACT: Emily Hansen

MATHEMATICS (ALL FIELDS)

1729—ACTUARIAL FOUNDATION, THE (Actuary of Tomorrow-Stuart A. Robertson Memorial Scholarship)

475 North Martingale Road,
Suite 600
Schaumburg IL 60173
847/706-3535
FAX: 847/706-3599
E-mail: scholarships@actfnd.org
Internet: http://www.actuarial foundation.org
AMOUNT: $7,500
DEADLINE(S): JUN 1
FIELD(S): Actuary
ELIGIBILITY/REQUIREMENTS: Open to undergraduates demonstrating an interest in pursuing an actuarial career. Must be sophomore or higher, minimum cumulative GPA 3.0; have successfully completed 2 actuarial exams (Spring exams meet 2 exam requirement).
HOW TO APPLY: See website for application, and submit with a personal essay of approximately 500 words focusing on why you want to be an actuary; a current transcript, a letter of recommendation supporting academic achievement and leadership and communication skills from professor or advisor.
NUMBER OF AWARDS: 1 or more (depending on funds)
RENEWABLE: No.
CONTACT: Susan Gehm, Foundation Coordinator

1730—ACTUARIAL FOUNDATION, THE (John Culver Wooddy Scholarship)

475 North Martingale Road,
Suite 600
Schaumburg IL 60173
847/706-3535
FAX: 847/706-3599
E-mail: scholarships@actfnd.org
Internet: http://www.actuarial foundation.org
AMOUNT: $2,000
DEADLINE(S): JUN (last Friday)
FIELD(S): Actuary
ELIGIBILITY/REQUIREMENTS: Open to students entering senior year in college, who is eligible to graduate within 1 year of date of award; must have passed at least 1 actuarial exam by application due date (international students need to major in Actuarial Science but exam is not required); must be recommended by a professor (limit 1 application/school; applicant must rank in top quartile of class. Preference will be given to candidates who have demonstrated leadership potential through extracurricular activities
HOW TO APPLY: See website for application, and submit with a personal essay to professor, who must then provide verification of student's class ranking and senior status within their letter of recommendation.
NUMBER OF AWARDS: Multiple
RENEWABLE: No.
CONTACT: Susan Gehm, Foundation Coordinator

1731—ALICE T. SCHAFER MATHEMATICS PRIZE

11240 Waples Mill Road,
Suite 200
Fairfax VA 22030
703/934-0163
FAX: 703/359-7562
E-mail: awm@awm-math.org
Internet: http://www.awm-math.org
AMOUNT: $1,000
DEADLINE(S): OCT
FIELD(S): Mathematics
ELIGIBILITY/REQUIREMENTS: For female students in any year of undergraduate study. Performance in mathematics competitions considered for prize.
HOW TO APPLY: See website for application and information.
NUMBER OF AWARDS: 1
RENEWABLE: No
CONTACT: Jennifer Lewis

1732—ALPHA KAPPA ALPHA SORORITY INC. (AKA/PIMS Summer Youth Mathematics and Science Camp)

5656 South Stony Island Avenue
Chicago IL 60637
800/653-6528
Internet: http://www.akaeaf.org
AMOUNT: $1,000 value
DEADLINE(S): MAY 1
FIELD(S): Mathematics; Science
ELIGIBILITY/REQUIREMENTS: Open to high school students grades 9-11 who have at least a 'B' average. Essay required for entry. This 2-week camp includes a.m. classes, p.m. activities and a minimum of 4 field trips.
HOW TO APPLY: Write for information.
NUMBER OF AWARDS: 30

1733—AMERICAN ASSOCIATION OF BLACKS IN ENERGY (AABE)

Western Michigan University
1903 West Michigan
Kalamazoo MI 49008-5337
269/387-8777
FAX: 269/387-6989
E-mail: alumni@wmich.edu
Internet: http://www.wmich.edu/cas/research.html
AMOUNT: Varies
DEADLINE(S): MAR 1
FIELD(S): Mathematics; Computer Science; Engineering; Physical Sciences
ELIGIBILITY/REQUIREMENTS: Freshman with 2.5 GPA overall and a 3.0 GPA in mathematics and the sciences. Planning to major in engineering, mathematics, computer or the physical sciences. Must demonstrate financial need and be a member of one of the underrepresented minority groups in the sciences and technology.
HOW TO APPLY: Contact the Office for Student Financial Aid.
NUMBER OF AWARDS: Varies
RENEWABLE: Yes

1734—AMERICAN SOCIETY OF NAVAL ENGINEERS (ASNE)

1452 Duke Street
Alexandria VA 22314-3458
703/836-6727
Internet: http://www.naval engineers.org
AMOUNT: Up to $3,500
DEADLINE(S): FEB
FIELD(S): Engineering; Physical Sciences; Mathematics

ELIGIBILITY/REQUIREMENTS: Application must be for support for the last year of a full-time or co-op undergraduate program or for one year of full-time graduate study leading to a designated engineering or physical science degree in an accredited college or university. A scholarship will not be awarded to a doctoral candidate or to a person already having an advanced degree. Applicants must be U.S. citizens.
HOW TO APPLY: Contact Society for additional information and application.

1735—ARMED FORCES COMMUNICATIONS AND ELECTRONICS ASSOCIATION (AFCEA/ORINCON IT Scholarship)

4400 Fair Lakes Court
Fairfax VA 22033-3899
800/336-4583, ext. 6147 or 703/631-6100
E-mail: scholarships@afcea.org
Internet: http://www.afcea.org/awards/scholarships.htm
AMOUNT: $2,750
DEADLINE(S): Varies according to eligibility
FIELD(S): Electrical or Aerospace Engineering, Computer Science, Physics, Mathematics
ELIGIBILITY/REQUIREMENTS: Scholarships in the above fields for persons on active duty in a military service or veterans, their spouses or dependents or civilians who meet the general criteria for the General Wickham Scholarship, if the school they are attending is an accredited 4-year college or university in the Greater San Diego, CA area, and working toward a degree in an accredited 4-year college or university in the U.S. Must have GPA of 3.4 or more.
HOW TO APPLY: Check website or contact AFCEA for information and application.

1736—ARMED FORCES COMMUNICATIONS AND ELECTRONICS ASSOCIATION (AFCEA ROTC Scholarships)

4400 Fair Lakes Court
Fairfax VA 22033-3899
800/336-4583, ext. 6147 or 703/631-6149
FAX: 703/631-4693
E-mail: scholarships@afcea.org
Internet: http://www.afcea.org
AMOUNT: $2,000
DEADLINE(S): APR 1
FIELD(S): Electrical Engineering, Electronics, Computer Science,

Computer Systems, or Aerospace Engineering, Physics, Mathematics, science or mathematics education; technology management or other technical fields, or fields related to U.S. intelligence or national security
ELIGIBILITY/REQUIREMENTS: Scholarships for ROTC students working toward a degree in an accredited degree-granting 4-year college or university in the U.S.
HOW TO APPLY: MUST be nominated by Professors of Military Science, Naval Science, or Aerospace Studies. Contact the commander of each ROTC unit at your school or see website for application.

1737—ARMED FORCES COMMUNICATIONS AND ELECTRONICS ASSOCIATION (AFCEA Scholarship for Online or Distance-Learning Programs)

4400 Fair Lakes Court
Fairfax VA 22033-3899
800/336-4583, ext. 6147 or 703/631-6149
FAX: 703/631-4693
E-mail: scholarships@afcea.org
Internet: http://www.afcea.org
AMOUNT: $1,500
DEADLINE(S): JUN 1
FIELD(S): Electrical, Chemical or Aerospace Engineering: Computer Science; Mathematics; Physics; Science or Math Education; Technology Management or fields related to U.S. intelligence or national security
ELIGIBILITY/REQUIREMENTS: Full-time students; undergraduates must have completed 2 semesters of calculus (30-semester hour equivalent). Must be a U.S. citizen and be currently enrolled in a 4-year college or university in the U.S. at time of application.
HOW TO APPLY: Applications and further information on website.
RENEWABLE: No

1738—ARMED FORCES COMMUNICATIONS AND ELECTRONICS ASSOCIATION (AFCEA Scholarship for Working Professionals)

4400 Fair Lakes Court
Fairfax VA 22033-3899
800/336-4583, ext. 6147 or 703/631-6100
E-mail: scholarships@afcea.org
Internet: http://www.afcea.org/awards/scholarships.htm
AMOUNT: $1,500
DEADLINE(S): AUG 15-SEP 15

FIELD(S): Electrical, Aerospace, or Computer Engineering, Computer Science, Computer Information Systems, Mathematics

ELIGIBILITY/REQUIREMENTS: Part-time students (at least 2 classes per semester) working toward an undergraduate degree at any accredited 2-year community college or 4-year institution in the U.S. while currently employed in government or industry. Distance learning programs do not qualify. Must be a U.S. citizen and be currently enrolled as a sophomore, junior, or senior at time of application.

HOW TO APPLY: Applications and further information on website.

1739—ARMED FORCES COMMUNICATIONS AND ELECTRONICS ASSOCIATION (General Emmett Paige Scholarships for Military Personnel, Veterans, and Their Dependents)

4400 Fair Lakes Court
Fairfax VA 22033-3899
800/336-4583, ext. 6147 or
703/631-6149
FAX: 703/631-4693
E-mail: scholarships@afcea.org
Internet: http://www.afcea.org

AMOUNT: $2,000

DEADLINE(S): MAR 1

FIELD(S): Electrical Engineering, Electronics, Computer Science, Computer or Aerospace Engineering, Physics, Mathematics, science or mathematics education; technology management or other technical fields, or fields related to U.S. intelligence or national security

ELIGIBILITY/REQUIREMENTS: Scholarships in the above fields for persons on active duty in a military service or veterans and to their spouses or dependents who are working toward a degree in an accredited 4-year college or university in the U.S. Must have GPA of 3.4 or more.

HOW TO APPLY: Applications and further information on website.

1740—ARMED FORCES COMMUNICATIONS AND ELECTRONICS ASSOCIATION (General John A. Wickham Scholarships)

4400 Fair Lakes Court
Fairfax VA 22033-3899
800/336-4583, ext. 6147 or
703/631-6100
E-mail: scholarships@afcea.org
Internet: http://www.afcea.org/
awards/scholarships.htm

AMOUNT: $2,000

DEADLINE(S): MAY 1

FIELD(S): Electrical Engineering, Electronics, Computer Science, Computer or Aerospace Engineering, Physics, Mathematics, Science or Mathematics Education; Technology Management or other technical fields, or fields related to U.S. intelligence or national security

ELIGIBILITY/REQUIREMENTS: Scholarships in the above fields for persons working toward degrees in accredited 4-year colleges or universities in the U.S. Must have GPA of 3.5 or more.

HOW TO APPLY: Applications and further information on website.

1741—ASSOCIATED WESTERN UNIVERSITIES, INC. (AWU Undergraduate Student Fellowships)

4190 South Highland Drive,
Suite 211
Salt Lake City UT 84124-2600
801/273-8900
FAX: 801/277-5632
E-mail: info@awu.org
Internet: http://www.awu.org

AMOUNT: $300/week stipend + possible travel allowance

DEADLINE(S): FEB 1

FIELD(S): Science; Mathematics; Engineering; Technology

ELIGIBILITY/REQUIREMENTS: Students who have been or will be enrolled in any accredited institution within six months of the start of their award. Academic performance and class standing, career goals, recommendations, and compatibility of interests and abilities with the needs and resources of the host facility.

HOW TO APPLY: See website for application and list of participating laboratories. Must also submit résumé, at least 1 (2 preferred) recommendations from a faculty member who is familiar with your academic achievements, and transcript. Applicants who received an AWU award within the last year and have approval for reappointment with their previous mentor, need only to complete the application form and submit a copy of their current transcripts.

NUMBER OF AWARDS: 500

1742—ASSOCIATION FOR WOMEN IN SCIENCE (AWIS Education Foundation College Scholarship)

7008 Richard Drive
Bethesda MD 20817-4838
E-mail: awisedfd@
awisedfd@awis.org

Internet: http://www.awis.org/
careers/edfoundation.html

AMOUNT: $100-$1,000

DEADLINE(S): Mid JAN

FIELD(S): Science; Mathematics; Engineering

ELIGIBILITY/REQUIREMENTS: High school seniors may apply. Must have GPA of at least 3.75 and math plus verbal SAT of at least 1200 (or ACT of 2.5), be a U.S. citizen, plan a career in research or teaching, and plan to attend a college in the U.S.

HOW TO APPLY: See website for application and instructions.

NUMBER OF AWARDS: 10

RENEWABLE: No

CONTACT: Dr. Barbara Filner at e-mail above

1743—AT&T BELL LABORATORIES (Summer Research Program for Minorities and Women)

101 Crawfords Corner Road
Holmdel NJ 07733-3030

AMOUNT: Salary + travel and living expenses for summer

DEADLINE(S): DEC 1

FIELD(S): Engineering; Mathematics; Sciences; Computer Science

ELIGIBILITY/REQUIREMENTS: Program offers minority students and women students technical employment experience at Bell Laboratories. Students should have completed their third year of study at an accredited college or university. U.S. citizen or permanent resident.

HOW TO APPLY: Selection is based partially on academic achievement and personal motivation. Write special programs manager-SRP for complete information.

1744—BARRY GOLDWATER SCHOLARSHIP AND EXCELLENCE IN EDUCATION FOUNDATION

6225 Brandon Avenue, Suite 315
Springfield VA 22150-2519
703/756-6012
FAX: 703/756-6015
Internet: http://www.act.org/
goldwater

AMOUNT: Up to $7,500/year

DEADLINE(S): FEB 1

FIELD(S): Mathematics; Natural Sciences; Engineering

ELIGIBILITY/REQUIREMENTS: Open to college sophomores and juniors with a minimum 3.0 GPA. Must be U.S. citizen, resident alien, or American national pursuing a degree in mathematics, natural sciences, or engineering at an accredited institution that contributes to technological advances.

HOW TO APPLY: See website or contact your Goldwater Faculty Representative on campus. Students must be nominated by their institution and cannot apply on their own.

NUMBER OF AWARDS: 300

CONTACT: Goldwater Faculty Representative

1745—BROOKHAVEN WOMEN IN SCIENCE (Renate W. Chasman Scholarship)

Chasman Scholarship Fund
P. O. Box 183
Upton NY 11973-5000
Internet: http://www.bnl.gov/bnlweb/pubaf/pr/PR_display.asp?prID=05-06
AMOUNT: $2,000
DEADLINE(S): APR 1
FIELD(S): Natural Sciences; Engineering; Mathematics

ELIGIBILITY/REQUIREMENTS: Open ONLY to women who are residents of the boroughs of Brooklyn or Queens or the counties of Nassau or Suffolk in New York who are reentering school after a period of study. Must be junior, senior, or first-year graduate student.

HOW TO APPLY: Phone calls are NOT accepted. See website or write for application.

NUMBER OF AWARDS: 1

RENEWABLE: No

1746—CALIFORNIA MATHEMATICS COUNCIL

Glendale Community College
Mathematics Department
1500 North Verdugo Road
Glendale CA 91208-2894
E-mail: sjkolpas@glendale.edu
Internet: http://www.cmc-math.org/SouthGrant
AMOUNT: $100-$1,000
DEADLINE(S): JAN 31
FIELD(S): Education; Teaching Mathematics

ELIGIBILITY/REQUIREMENTS: Scholarships for students enrolled in an elementary or secondary education credential program. Only applicants who teach, reside, or go to school in Southern California will be considered.

HOW TO APPLY: See website ir contact CMC c/o Glendale Community College for information.

CONTACT: Dr. Sid Kolpas, CMC Scholarships

1747—COUNCIL OF ENERGY RESOURCE TRIBES (CERT)

CERT Education Program
Attention: Scholars Program
695 S. Colorado Blvd, Suite 10
Denver CO 80246
303/282-7576
FAX: 303/282-7584
E-mail: info@CERTRedEarth.com
Internet: http://www.certredearth.com/
AMOUNT: $1,000
DEADLINE(S): SEP 14 (Fall), FEB 15 (Spring)
FIELD(S): Science; Engineering; Business, Mathematics, Computer Technology, or related fields

ELIGIBILITY/REQUIREMENTS: Applicants must meet the criteria to become a TRIBES Institute candidate and a full-time undergraduate (12 hrs/semester) student enrolled in an accredited 2- or 4-year tribal, private, or public university/college, and must maintain at least a 2.5 GPA, although academic excellence far above this GPA is preferred. (Should scholarship funds be limited, GPA will be weighed in decision.)

HOW TO APPLY: See website or contact CERT. Submit application along with official Tribal affiliation documentation (with enrollment number or other statement of Tribal acknowledgment of membership), an official transcript of most recent coursework with the cumulative GPA, as well as the GPA for current hours detailed on the transcript, and a class schedule for the next term demonstrating that you will be attending school full-time and/or verification of full-time enrollment for the next semester.

RENEWABLE: Yes. Must reapply.

CONTACT: Tom Talache, ttalache@CERTRedEarth.com or 303/282-7576 ext. 12.

1748—DAVIDSON INSTITUTE FOR TALENT DEVELOPMENT

9665 Gateway
Reno NV 89521
775/852-3483, ext. 423
FAX: 775/852-2184
E-mail: tmoessner@ditd.org
Internet: http://www.davidson fellows.org
AMOUNT: $10,000, $20,000, $50,000

DEADLINE(S): Last Friday of MAR
FIELD(S): Science, Technology, Mathematics, Philosophy, Music, Literature and Outside the Box

ELIGIBILITY/REQUIREMENTS: Must be a U.S. citizen residing in the U.S., or a permanent resident of the U.S. residing in the U.S.; under the age of 18 as of October 1 (there is no minimum age for eligibility); completed a significant piece of work in one of the designated application categories; and available to attend, with at least 1 parent or guardian, the awards reception and other recognition events in September (travel expenses and lodging will be paid by the Institute).

HOW TO APPLY: See website including FAQ section and application booklet; download and complete all components.

NUMBER OF AWARDS: 15-20

RENEWABLE: No

CONTACT: Tacie Moessner, Davidson Fellows Program Manager

ADDITIONAL INFORMATION: Group and team projects are not eligible. Scholarships must be used at an accredited institute of learning within 10 years of the award date.

1749—EAA AVIATION FOUNDATION (Payzer Scholarship)

EAA Scholarship Department
P.O. 3086
Oshkosh WI 54903-3065
920/426-6823
E-mail: scholarships@eaa.org
Internet: http://www.young eagles.org
AMOUNT: $5,000
DEADLINE(S): MAR 1
FIELD(S): Engineering, Mathematics, Physical or Biological Science

ELIGIBILITY/REQUIREMENTS: Open to well-rounded individuals involved in school and community activities as well as aviation accepted at or attending 4-year accredited college, university or postsecondary school with am emphasis on technical information who is majoring one of above fields. Applicant's academic records should verify his/her ability to complete educational activity for which scholarship is requested. Must also be a current member of EAA (Experimental Aircraft Association) or recommended by a current EAA member.

HOW TO APPLY: Apply online. A personal statement (500 words or less.) addressing career aspirations. educational plan, why you want to receive this scholarship. what you learned from work/volunteer experiences, and explaining how your

education will be financed, including loans, family assistance, your own savings, scholarships, etc., and any unusual financial circumstances affecting your college financial plan required.
NUMBER OF AWARDS: 1

1750—GERBER SCIENTIFIC, INC. (H. Joseph Gerber 1947 Scholars Fund Endowment at Rensselaer Polytechnic Institute)

83 Gerber Road West
South Windsor CT 06074
860/648-8027
Internet: http://www.gerber scientific.com/community/ scholarships.htm
AMOUNT: Varies
DEADLINE(S): MAR 15
FIELD(S): Engineering, Mathematics, Computer Science, Natural Sciences
ELIGIBILITY/REQUIREMENTS: Available to full-time students pursuing a baccalaureate degree at Rensselaer Polytechnic Institute's Troy, New York, campus. Awards are determined by the Rensselaer Office of Financial Aid. Preference is given to residents of the state of Connecticut.
HOW TO APPLY: Applications are available from the Rensselaer Office of Financial Aid.

1751—GERBER SCIENTIFIC, INC. (H. Joseph Gerber Vision Scholarship Program)

83 Gerber Road West
South Windsor CT 06074
860/648-8027
Internet: http://www.gerber scientific.com/community/ scholarships.htm
AMOUNT: Varies
DEADLINE(S): MAR 15
FIELD(S): Engineering; Mathematics; Computer Science; Natural Sciences
ELIGIBILITY/REQUIREMENTS: Available to high school seniors attending South Windsor, Manchester or Tolland High, or Gerber employees' children who meet the requirements.
HOW TO APPLY: Applications are available in the high school guidance office.
NUMBER OF AWARDS: 50

1752—HAWAII COMMUNITY FOUNDATION (Shuichi, Katsu & Itsuyo Suga Scholarship)

1164 Bishop Street, Suite 800

Honolulu HI 96813
808/537-6333 or toll free: 888/731-3863
FAX: 808/521-6286
E-mail: info@hcf-hawaii.org
Internet: http://www.hcf-hawaii.org
DEADLINE(S): MAR 1
FIELD(S): Mathematics; Physics; Science; Technology
ELIGIBILITY/REQUIREMENTS: Applicants must be residents of the state of Hawaii; plan to attend full time an accredited 2- or 4-year college or university; and demonstrate financial need, good moral character, and strong academic achievement, with a minimum GPA of 3.0.
HOW TO APPLY: Send application with 2 letters of recommendation.
CONTACT: See website.

1753—HISPANIC COLLEGE FUND (HSF/SHPE Inc. Scholarship Program)

55 Second Street, Suite 1500
San Francisco CA 94105
877/HSF-INFO (877/473-4636)
FAX: 415/808/2302
E-mail: pip@hsf.net
Internet: http://hispanicfund.org
AMOUNT: At least $2,500
DEADLINE(S): JUN 2
FIELD(S): Engineering; Mathematics; Science; Computer Science
ELIGIBILITY/REQUIREMENTS: Must be U.S. citizens or legal permanent residents of Hispanic heritage (one parent fully Hispanic or both parents half Hispanic). Open to high school graduates, community college transfer students, 4-year university undergraduates, and graduate students. All students must be enrolled full time in a degree-seeking program in the U.S. or Puerto Rico.
HOW TO APPLY: Contact Fund for details or visit website for application.

1754—INSTITUTE FOR OPERATIONS RESEARCH AND THE MANAGEMENT SCIENCES (George Nicholson Student Paper Competition)

7240 Parkway Drive, Suite 310
Hanover MD 21076-1310
443/757-3500 or 800/446-3676
FAX: 443/757-3515
E-mail: informs@informs.org
Internet: http://www.informs.org/ INTERN/
AMOUNT: $600 (first place); $300 (second place); $100 (honorable mention)
DEADLINE(S): JUN 30

FIELD(S): Information Management: Business Management, Engineering, Mathematics and related fields
ELIGIBILITY/REQUIREMENTS: Entrant must have been a student on or after January 1 or the year; the paper must present original research results and must have been conducted while entrant was a student; must be written with only minor editorial assistance (advisors may appear as co-authors, but the student must be "first author").
HOW TO APPLY: Paper must not exceed 25 pages with 35 lines of text (excluding references). Electronic submissions (PDF) and hard copy are required. Entry must be accompanied by a letter signed by both a faculty advisor and the entrant attesting that the eligibility conditions have been satisfied. For additional information, see website.
NUMBER OF AWARDS: Up to 6
RENEWABLE: No
CONTACT: Committee Chair (see website for current year's chairperson and contact information)
ADDITIONAL INFORMATION: First- and second-place awards will be announced at the Awards Ceremony.

1755—INSTITUTE FOR OPERATIONS RESEARCH AND THE MANAGEMENT SCIENCES (INFORMS Summer Internship Directory)

7240 Parkway Drive, Suite 310
Hanover MD 21076-1310
443/757-3500 or 800/446-3676
FAX: 443/757-3515
E-mail: informs@informs.org
Internet: http://www.informs.org/ INTERN/
AMOUNT: Varies
DEADLINE(S): Varies
FIELD(S): Information Management: Business Management, Engineering, Mathematics and related fields
ELIGIBILITY/REQUIREMENTS: See website listing of summer internships in the field of operations research and management sciences. Both applicants and employers can register online.
HOW TO APPLY: See website for list.
NUMBER OF AWARDS: Varies

1756—IET, THE (IET Engineering Degree Scholarships for Women)

Michael Faraday House
Six Hills Way, Stevenage
Hertfordshire SG1 2AY
UNITED KINGDOM
E-mail: awards@theiet.org

Internet: http://www.theiet.org/
ambitionscholarships
AMOUNT: £750
DEADLINE(S): JUN 30
FIELD(S): Engineering; Mathematics;
Physics
ELIGIBILITY/REQUIREMENTS: For
women residing in the United Kingdom
and pursuing IET-accredited degrees.
Candidates must be undertaking mathe-
matics and physics "A" level or Scottish
Higher examinations.
HOW TO APPLY: Check website or con-
tact organization for an application.
NUMBER OF AWARDS: 10
RENEWABLE: Yes. For entire period of
an IET-accredited course

1757—JACKSONVILLE STATE UNIVERSITY (Drs. Wayne & Sara Finley Scholarship)

Financial Aid Office
Jacksonville AL 36265
256/782-5677 or 800/231-5291
Internet: www.jsu.edu
AMOUNT: Varies
DEADLINE(S): FEB 1
FIELD(S): Mathematics; Science; Pre-
Prof Secondary Education
ELIGIBILITY/REQUIREMENTS: Open
to junior or senior; 3.0 GPA; Clay, Coosa,
or Randolph Counties, Alabama.
HOW TO APPLY: See website for appli-
cation. Mail official transcript and
ACT/SAT scores.
RENEWABLE: No
CONTACT: Scholarship Committee

1758—JACKSONVILLE STATE UNIVERSITY (Newbern Bush Scholarship)

Financial Aid Office
Jacksonville AL 36265
256/782-5677 or 800/231-5291
Internet: www.jsu.edu
AMOUNT: Varies
DEADLINE(S): FEB 1
FIELD(S): Mathematics
ELIGIBILITY/REQUIREMENTS: Open
to native-born Alabamians in junior year
of high school.
HOW TO APPLY: See website for appli-
cation. Mail transcript and ACT/SAT
scores.
RENEWABLE: No
CONTACT: Scholarship Committee

1759—JACKSONVILLE STATE UNIVERSITY (Sharon Dempsey Memorial Scholarship)

Financial Aid Office
Jacksonville AL 36265

256/782-5677 or 800/231-5291
Internet: www.jsu.edu
AMOUNT: Varies
DEADLINE(S): FEB 1
FIELD(S): Mathematics; Mathematics
Education
ELIGIBILITY/REQUIREMENTS: Open
to junior or senior; at least 30 hours at JSU.
HOW TO APPLY: See website for appli-
cation. Mail official transcript and ACT/
SAT scores.
RENEWABLE: No
CONTACT: Scholarship Committee

1760—JEWISH FEDERATION OF METRO-POLITAN CHICAGO (Academic Scholarship Program)

Jewish Vocational Service
216 West Jackson Blvd., Suite 700
Chicago IL 60606-6921
312/673-3400
FAX: 312/553-5544
TTY: 312/444-2877
E-mail: jvsscholarship@jvs
chicago.org
Internet: http://www.jvs/
chicago.org
AMOUNT: Varies
DEADLINE(S): FEB 15
FIELD(S): Mathematics, Engineering,
Science, Medicine, Social Work,
Education, Psychology, Rabbinate,
Law (except corporate),
Communications
ELIGIBILITY/REQUIREMENTS: Open
to Jewish men and women legally domiciled in the greater Chicago metropolitan
area, who are identified as having promise
for significant contributions in their chosen
careers, and are in need of financial assistance for full-time academic programs in
above areas. Must have entered undergraduate junior year in career programs
requiring no postgraduate education, be in
graduate/professional school, or be in a vo-
tech training program.
HOW TO APPLY: Phone JVS Scholar-
ship Secretary (312/673-3457), fax, or visit
website (click on Scholarship Services) for
an application in the Fall. Interview
required.
RENEWABLE: Yes
CONTACT: JVS Scholarship Secretary at
312/673-3457

1761—LOS ANGELES COUNCIL OF BLACK PROFESSIONAL ENGINEERS (Al-Ben Scholarship)

P.O. Box 881029
Los Angeles CA 90009

310/635-7734
E-mail: secy1@lablackengineers.org
Internet: http://www.lablack
engineers.org/scholarships.html
AMOUNT: Varies
DEADLINE(S): Varies
FIELD(S): Engineering; Mathematics;
Computer Studies; Applied Science
ELIGIBILITY/REQUIREMENTS: Open
to technically inclined high school and
undergraduate students enrolled in one of
the above fields. Must be of African-
American, Native American, or Hispanic
ancestry. Preference given to students
attending college in Southern California or
who are Southern California residents.
HOW TO APPLY: See website to download an application.

1762—MICROSOFT CORPORATION (National Minority and/or Women's Scholarships)

Microsoft Scholarship Program
One Microsoft Way
Redmond WA 98052-8303
425/882-8080
E-mail: scholars@microsoft.com
Internet: http://www.microsoft.
com/college/scholarships/
AMOUNT: Tuition for 1 year
DEADLINE(S): JAN 15
FIELD(S): Computer Science, Computer
Engineering, or a related technical
discipline, such as Electrical
Engineering, Math, Physics
ELIGIBILITY/REQUIREMENTS: May
apply only after beginning classes on full-
time basis. Full tuition scholarships awarded for 1 academic year to women, minorities (African-Americans, Hispanics, or
Native Americans), and people with disabilities enrolled full time in the above
fields, or related technical discipline with a
demonstrated interest in computer science,
and making satisfactory progress towards a
degree. Awards are made through designated schools and are not transferable to
other institutions. Students must be
enrolled full time in a bachelor's degree
program at a college or university in the
U.S., Canada, or Mexico at the time the
application is submitted and be making satisfactory progress toward an undergraduate degree in computer science or computer engineering. All recipients of scholarships will be required to complete a
salaried summer internship of 12 weeks or
more at Microsoft in Redmond, WA
(unless waived by Microsoft).
HOW TO APPLY: Application available
online only. Submit résumé, transcript,
answers to essay questions, and letter of

referral from faculty member or academic advisor. No separate application form required. Note your gender, ethnicity, or disability on the page with your essay questions if you would like that information to be considered with your application. See website for detailed information and essay questions.

RENEWABLE: Yes. Must maintain a 3.0 cumulative GPA out of a possible 4.0, or a 4.0 cumulative GPA out of a possible 5.0

1763—MICROSOFT CORPORATION (Summer Internships)

Microsoft Scholarship Program
One Microsoft Way
Redmond WA 98052-8303
425/882-8080
E-mail: scholars@microsoft.com
Internet: http://www.microsoft.com/college/scholarships/

AMOUNT: Competitive compensation
DEADLINE(S): None
FIELD(S): Computer Science, Computer Engineering, or a related technical discipline, such as Mathematics or Physics

ELIGIBILITY/REQUIREMENTS: Must commit to 12-week minimum. Includes transportation, shipping costs, and shared cost of housing.

HOW TO APPLY: See website for application and details. Interview required.

1764—MINNESOTA GAY/LESBIAN/ BISEXUAL/TRANSGENDER EDUCATIONAL FUND (Pat McCart Memorial Award)

Philanthrofund Foundation
1409 Willow Street, Suite 305
Minneapolis MN 55403-3251
612/220-4888
FAX: 612/871-6587
E-mail: philanth@scc.net
Internet: http://www.scc.net/~t-bonham/EDFUND.HTM

AMOUNT: $500-$1,000
DEADLINE(S): FEB 1
FIELD(S): Mathematics; Science

ELIGIBILITY/REQUIREMENTS: Open to GLBT graduating high school senior woman who will be attending a 4-year college or university and is planning to major in mathematics or one of the sciences; must be a Minnesota resident. Criteria include applicant's affirmation of her GLBT identity; demonstrated integrity and honesty, participation and leadership in community activities; and service as role model, mentor, colleague or advisor for the GLBT community.

HOW TO APPLY: See website for application or contact Minnesota GLBT Educational Fund for an application. Submit application by mail. E-mail or faxed materials will NOT be accepted.

RENEWABLE: No

1765—NAACP NATIONAL OFFICE (NAACP Willems Scholarship)

4805 Mount Hope Drive
Baltimore MD 21215
401/358-8900

AMOUNT: $2,000
DEADLINE(S): APR 30
FIELD(S): Engineering; Chemistry; Physics; Mathematics

ELIGIBILITY/REQUIREMENTS: Open to male NAACP members majoring in one of the above areas. Must have GPA of 2.5+. Financial need must be established.

HOW TO APPLY: Write for complete information. Include a legal-sized SASE. Submit with 2 letters of recommendation from teachers or professors in major field of specialization.

RENEWABLE: Yes. If the required GPA is maintained.

1766—NATIONAL INVENTORS HALL OF FAME, THE (Collegiate Inventors Competition)

221 South Broadway Street
Akron OH 44308-1505
330/849-6887
E-mail: rdepuy@invent.org.
Internet: http://www.invent.org/bfg/ bfghome.html

AMOUNT: $15,000
DEADLINE(S): JUN 1
FIELD(S): Mathematics, Engineering, Biology, Chemistry, Physics, Information Technology, Medicine

ELIGIBILITY/REQUIREMENTS: Must be enrolled (or have been enrolled) full time (in any college or university) at least part of the 12-month period prior to the date the entry is submitted. In the case of a team (maximum 4 students), at least 1 member of the team must meet the full-time eligibility criteria. The other team members must have been enrolled on a part-time basis (at a minimum) sometime during the 24-month period prior to the date the entry is submitted. There are no limits on the number of entries a student or team may submit in a given year; however, only 1 prize/student or team will be awarded. No specific age requirements; however, if an entrant is under 18, a parent or guardian must sign the Student/Advisor Release Form. Entries judged on the origi-

nality and inventiveness of the new idea, process, or technology, on their potential value to society (socially, environmentally, and economically), and on the scope of use. Entries must be complete, workable, and well articulated.

HOW TO APPLY: Submit an original invention or idea that has not been made public. See website for application and details. The application must include: Student and Advisor Information; Student Essay and Advisor Letter following the outlined format; diagrams, illustrations, photos, slides, or videos of the invention (clearly labeled); the signed Student/Advisor Release Form.

CONTACT: Ray DePuy

1767—NATIONAL TECHNICAL ASSOCIATION, INC. (Scholarship Competitions for Minorities and Women in Science and Engineering)

5810 Kingstowne Center,
Suite 120221
Alexandria VA 22315-5711
E-mail: ntamfj1@aol.com
Internet: http://www.huenet.com/nta

AMOUNT: $500-$5,000
DEADLINE(S): Varies
FIELD(S): Science; Mathematics; Engineering; Applied Technology

ELIGIBILITY/REQUIREMENTS: Scholarship competitions for minorities and women pursuing degrees in the above fields. Additional scholarships are available through local chapters of NTA.

HOW TO APPLY: See website or write to above address for details and for locations of local chapters.

1768—NATIVE AMERICAN SCHOLARSHIP FUND, INC.

8200 Mountain Road NE, Suite 203
Albuquerque NM 87110
505/262-2351
FAX: 505/262-0543
E-mail: NScholarsh@aol.com

AMOUNT: Varies
DEADLINE(S): MAR 15; APR 15; SEP 15
FIELD(S): Mathematics; Engineering; Science; Business; Education; Computer Science

ELIGIBILITY/REQUIREMENTS: Open to American Indians or Alaskan Natives (one-quarter degree or more) enrolled as members of a federally recognized, state recognized, or terminated tribe. For graduate or undergraduate study at an accredited 4-year college or university.

HOW TO APPLY: Contact Director of Recruitment for an application.
NUMBER OF AWARDS: 208
CONTACT: Lucille Kelley, Director of Recruitment

1769—RIPON COLLEGE (Math/Science Scholarship)

300 Seward Street
P.O. Box 248
Ripon, WI 54971
800/947-4766
FAX: 920/746-8335
E-mail: adminfo@ripon.edu
Internet: http://www.ripon.edu
AMOUNT: Full tuition
DEADLINE(S): JAN 1
FIELD(S): Natural Science; Mathematics
ELIGIBILITY/REQUIREMENTS: Minimum high school GPA 3.8, rank in top 5% of class; academic credentials and community service activities considered. Must major in natural science or mathematics.
HOW TO APPLY: Contact Office of Admission for an application; submit with a letter of recommendation from high school teacher. An on-campus interview required.
NUMBER OF AWARDS: 1
RENEWABLE: Yes. Must maintain enrollment as a full-time student majoring in math or science, minimum GPA of 3.0 and evidence satisfactory progress toward a 4-year degree.
CONTACT: Office of Admission

1770—SAN DIEGO AIR &SPACE MUSEUM (Bill Gibbs Endowment Fund)

Education Office
2001 Pan American Plaza
San Diego CA 92101
619/234-8291, ext. 119
FAX: 619/233-4526
Internet: http://aerospace museum.org
AMOUNT: $1,500-$2,500
DEADLINE(S): APR 1
FIELD(S): Aerospace, Mathematics, Physics, Science, Engineering
ELIGIBILITY/REQUIREMENTS: Graduating seniors of San Diego County high schools who have been accepted to a 4-year college or university. Academic achievement, strong aviation/aerospace career interests.
HOW TO APPLY: See website or write museum for application.

1771—SCIENCE SERVICE (Intel International Science and Engineering Fair)

1719 N Street NW

Washington DC 20036
202/785-2255
FAX: 202/785-1243
E-mail: jcole@sciserv.org
Internet: http://www.sciserv.org
AMOUNT: Varies
DEADLINE(S): Varies (consult local, regional or state ISEF)
FIELD(S): Science; Mathematics; Engineering; Medicine
ELIGIBILITY/REQUIREMENTS: High school students (grades 9-12) may participate in this worldwide competition.
HOW TO APPLY: Contact Science Service for official ISEF entry book.

1772—SCIENCE SERVICE (Intel Science Talent Search)

1719 N Street NW
Washington DC 20036
202/785-2255
FAX: 202/785-1243
E-mail: jkee@sciserv.org
Internet: http://www.sciserv.org
AMOUNT: $100,000 (1st place); $75,000 (2nd); $50,000 (3rd); $25,000 (4th-6th); $20,000 (7th-10th); 30 at $5,000; 300 at $1,000; 40 laptops
DEADLINE(S): Mid to late NOV
FIELD(S): Science; Mathematics; Engineering; Medicine
ELIGIBILITY/REQUIREMENTS: Open to high school seniors in the U.S. and territories and American students attending school abroad.
HOW TO APPLY: Contact Science Service for official STS entry book. Submit completed entry form, with research report, high school transcript, and standardized test scores.
NUMBER OF AWARDS: 40
CONTACT: June Kee

1773—SIEMENS WESTINGHOUSE (Science and Technology Competition)

186 Wood Avenue South
Iselin NJ 08830
877/822-5233
E-mail: foundation.us@siemens.com
Internet: http://www.siemens-foundation.org
AMOUNT: $120,000 (maximum)
DEADLINE(S): Varies
FIELD(S): Biology; Physical Sciences; Mathematics; Physics; Chemistry; Computer Science; Environmental Science
ELIGIBILITY/REQUIREMENTS: Open to U.S. high school seniors to pursue independent science research projects, working

individually or in teams of 2 or 3 to develop and test their own ideas. May work with 1 of the universities/laboratories that serve as Siemens' partners. Students from the U.S. and its territories may compete in 1 of 6 geographic areas. Individual and team national prizewinners receive a second scholarship to be applied to undergraduate or graduate education.
HOW TO APPLY: See website or contact Siemens Foundation for details.

1774—SKIDMORE COLLEGE (Porter Presidential Scholarships in Science and Mathematics)

Office of Admissions
815 North Broadway
Saratoga Springs NY 12866-1632
800/867-6007
E-mail: admissions@skidmore.edu
Internet: http://www.skidmore.edu/administration/financial aid/porter scholarship.htm
AMOUNT: $10,000
DEADLINE(S): JAN 15
FIELD(S): Mathematics,;Science; Computer Science
ELIGIBILITY/REQUIREMENTS: Scholarships for students excelling in the above fields. Awards are based on talent, not financial need. Recipients are not required to major in a scientific or mathematical discipline, but they will be expected to demonstrate serious research in one or more of these areas.
HOW TO APPLY: For more information, see website.
NUMBER OF AWARDS: 5
RENEWABLE: Yes

1775—SOCIETY OF AUTOMOTIVE ENGINEERS (University of Bridgeport/SAE Engineering Scholarships)

SAE Customer Service
400 Commonwealth Drive
Warrendale PA 15096-0001
724/776-4970
FAX: 724/776-1615
E-mail: customerservice@sae.org
Internet: http://www.sae.org/students/scholarships
AMOUNT: $9,000
DEADLINE(S): DEC 1
FIELD(S): Computer Science & Engineering; Mathematics; Automotive Industry
ELIGIBILITY/REQUIREMENTS: Open to high school seniors entering as freshmen pursuing a bachelor's degree in above

fields; must have a minimum 3.0 GPA and 1100 SAT or 24 ACT composite.

HOW TO APPLY: See website for application. Submit application; a personal essay that demonstrates hands-on experience or activity (such as rebuilding engines, working on cars/trucks, etc.); 2 recommendations, 1 of which must be from a teacher, counselor, or administrator; and transcript. Must also apply to the University of Bridgeport and submit the appropriate attachments, in addition to SAE submission.

NUMBER OF AWARDS: 3

RENEWABLE: Yes. Up to $36,000 (4-year period); be in good standing and maintain a 3.0 GPA.

1776—STATE FARM COMPANIES FOUNDATION (Exceptional Student Fellowship)

One State Farm Plaza, SC-3
Bloomington IL 61710-0001
309/766-2039/2161
E-mail: Nancy.Lynn.gr3o@
statefarm.com
Internet: http://www.statefarm.com

AMOUNT: $3,000 (nominating institution receives $250)

DEADLINE(S): FEB 15

FIELD(S): Accounting; Business Administration; Actuarial Science; Computer Science; Economics; Finance; Insurance/Risk Management; Investments; Management; Marketing; Mathematics; Statistics

ELIGIBILITY/REQUIREMENTS: For U.S. citizens who are full-time juniors or seniors when they apply. Must demonstrate significant leadership in extracurricular activities, have minimum 3.6 GPA, and attend accredited U.S. college or university. Must be nominated by dean, department head, professor, or academic advisor.

HOW TO APPLY: See website, visit your financial aid office, or write to above address for an application.

NUMBER OF AWARDS: 50

RENEWABLE: No

1777—TEXAS SOCIETY OF PROFESSIONAL ENGINEERS

Austin TX 78768
512/472-9286 or 800/580-8973
Internet: http://www.tspe.org

AMOUNT: Varies

DEADLINE(S): JAN 30

FIELD(S): Engineering, Mathematics, Sciences

ELIGIBILITY/REQUIREMENTS: Scholarships for graduating high school seniors who are Texas residents planning to attend Texas engineering colleges.

HOW TO APPLY: Contact organization for details. Application is on website.

1778—UNIVERSITY OF WINDSOR (Outstanding Scholars Award)

401 Sunset Avenue
Windsor Ontario N9B 3P4
CANADA
519/253-3000
FAX: 519/973-7081
E-mail: awards1@uwindsor.ca
Internet: http://www.uwindsor.ca

AMOUNT: $1,000-$2500/year (Canadian); maximum 4 years

DEADLINE(S): MAY 31

FIELD(S): Classics, Modern Languages, French, Philosophy, Music, Physics, Earth Sciences (not Environmental Studies), Economics (not Business and Economics), Chemistry (not Biochemistry), Mathematics and Statistics, Industrial, Mechanical (Materials Option) or Environmental Engineering or Bachelor of Arts and Science

ELIGIBILITY/REQUIREMENTS: Open to undergraduate students registering in year 1 at the University of Windsor. Must have superior grades. Amount of award based on secondary school accomplishments.

HOW TO APPLY: Automatic. No application required.

RENEWABLE: Yes. Up to 4 years.

CONTACT: Aase Houser

ADDITIONAL INFORMATION: Students in this program will also be mentored in their first year in preparation for guaranteed Outstanding Scholars Appointments in their Department/School (valued at $2,000 Canadian in earnings for each of the 2nd, 3rd, and 4th years) provided all conditions are met.

1779—WESTERN MICHIGAN UNIVERSITY (College of Arts and Sciences/A. Bruce Clarke Senior Award)

1903 West Michigan
Kalamazoo MI 49008-5337
269/387-8777
FAX: 269/387-6989
E-mail: finaid-info@wmich.edu
Internet: http://www.wmich.edu/finaid

AMOUNT: $100 (spring semester)

DEADLINE(S): MAR 1

FIELD(S): Mathematics; Statistics

ELIGIBILITY/REQUIREMENTS: Open to seniors majoring in mathematics or statistics.

HOW TO APPLY: Winners are selected by a committee composed of members from the Mathematics and Statistics Departments.

NUMBER OF AWARDS: 2 (1 award usually designated for student in Mathematics Education)

RENEWABLE: No

CONTACT: Department of Mathematics or Statistics

1780—WESTERN MICHIGAN UNIVERSITY (College of Arts and Sciences/Colonel Charles E. Bayliss Scholarship)

1903 West Michigan
Kalamazoo MI 49008-5337
269/387-8777
FAX: 269/387-6989
E-mail: finaid-info@wmich.edu
Internet: http://www.wmich.edu/finaid

AMOUNT: Varies

DEADLINE(S): MAR 1

FIELD(S): Mathematics; Statistics

ELIGIBILITY/REQUIREMENTS: Mathematics or statistics major; outstanding academic merit.

HOW TO APPLY: Winners are selected by a committee composed of members from the Mathematics and Statistics Departments.

RENEWABLE: Yes

CONTACT: Department of Mathematics or Statistics

1781—WESTERN MICHIGAN UNIVERSITY (College of Arts and Sciences/Erik A. Schreiner Endowed Memorial Scholarship)

1903 West Michigan
Kalamazoo MI 49008-5337
269/387-8777
FAX: 269/387-6989
E-mail: finaid-info@wmich.edu
Internet: http://www.wmich.edu/finaid

AMOUNT: $1,000/semester

DEADLINE(S): MAR 1

FIELD(S): Mathematics; Mathematics Education; Statistics

ELIGIBILITY/REQUIREMENTS: Junior; mathematics or statistics major.

HOW TO APPLY: Winners are selected by a committee composed of members from the Mathematics and Statistics Departments.

NUMBER OF AWARDS: 2 (1 award normally designated for student in Mathematics Education)

RENEWABLE: No

1782—WESTERN MICHIGAN UNIVERSITY (College of Arts and Sciences/Fred A. Beeler Memorial Scholarship)

1903 West Michigan
Kalamazoo MI 49008-5337
269/387-8777
FAX: 269/387-6989
E-mail: finaid-info@wmich.edu
Internet: http://www.wmich.edu/finaid
AMOUNT: Varies
DEADLINE(S): MAR 1
FIELD(S): Mathematics; Mathematics Education; Statistics
ELIGIBILITY/REQUIREMENTS: Undergraduate freshman or sophomore with a GPA of 3.0 majoring in Mathematics, Statistics, or Mathematics Education. Must demonstrate financial need.
HOW TO APPLY: Winners are selected by a committee composed of members from the Mathematics and Statistics Departments.
NUMBER OF AWARDS: 2 (1 of the awards is normally designated for a student in the Mathematics Education area).
RENEWABLE: Yes. Up to maximum of 4 consecutive academic years.

1783—WESTERN MICHIGAN UNIVERSITY (College of Arts and Sciences/Grover Bartoo Scholarship)

1903 West Michigan
Kalamazoo MI 49008-5337
269/387-8777
FAX: 269/387-6989
E-mail: finaid-info@wmich.edu
Internet: http://www.wmich.edu/finaid
AMOUNT: Varies
DEADLINE(S): MAR 1
FIELD(S): Mathematics; Statistics
ELIGIBILITY/REQUIREMENTS: Junior; 3.75 GPA or above; mathematics or statistics major.
HOW TO APPLY: Winners are selected by a committee composed of members from the Mathematics and Statistics Departments.
CONTACT: Department of Mathematics or Statistics

1784—WESTERN MICHIGAN UNIVERSITY (College of Arts and Sciences/James H. Powell Award in Statistics)

1903 West Michigan
Kalamazoo MI 49008-5337
269/387-8777
FAX: 269/387-6989
E-mail: finaid-info@wmich.edu
Internet: http://www.wmich.edu/finaid
AMOUNT: $100 (spring semester)
DEADLINE(S): MAR 1
FIELD(S): Statistics
ELIGIBILITY/REQUIREMENTS: Senior, statistics major, high academic achievement in statistics.
HOW TO APPLY: Winners are selected by a committee composed of members of the Department of Statistics.
NUMBER OF AWARDS: 2 (1 of the awards is normally designated for a student in the Mathematics Education area).
RENEWABLE: No
CONTACT: Department of Statistics

1785—WESTERN MICHIGAN UNIVERSITY (College of Arts and Sciences/Robert Meagher Memorial Scholarship)

1903 West Michigan
Kalamazoo MI 49008-5337
269/387-8777
FAX: 269/387-6989
E-mail: finaid-info@wmich.edu
Internet: http://www.wmich.edu/finaid
AMOUNT: $500/semester
DEADLINE(S): MAR 1
FIELD(S): Mathematics; Statistics
ELIGIBILITY/REQUIREMENTS: Junior; mathematics or statistics major; high academic achievement.
HOW TO APPLY: Winners are selected by a committee composed of members from the Mathematics and Statistics Departments.
RENEWABLE: No
CONTACT: Department of Mathematics or Statistics

1786—WOMEN IN DEFENSE (HORIZONS Scholarship Foundation)

2111 Wilson Boulevard, Suite 400
Arlington VA 22201-3061
703/247-2552
FAX: 703/522-1885
E-mail: wid@ndia.org
Internet: http://www.ndia.org
AMOUNT: $500+
DEADLINE(S): NOV 1; JUL 1
FIELD(S): Security Studies; Engineering; Computer Science; Physics; Mathematics; International Relations; Political Science; Operations Research; Economics; National Security/Defense; Business and Law (as they relate to national security or defense); other fields considered if relevance to national security or defense can be demonstrated
ELIGIBILITY/REQUIREMENTS: Open to women employed/planning careers in defense/national security areas (NOT law enforcement or criminal justice). Must be currently enrolled full- or part-time at an accredited college or university at the graduate or undergraduate junior/senior level. Must have a minimum 3.25 GPA, demonstrate financial need, and be U.S. citizen. Based on academic achievement, work experience, objectives, and recommendations.
HOW TO APPLY: See website or send SASE for application.
RENEWABLE: Yes

1787—WOODS HOLE OCEANOGRAPHIC INSTITUTION (Summer Student Fellowship)

Clark Laboratory 223, MS #31
Woods Hole MA 02543-1541
508/289-2219
FAX: 508/457-2188
E-mail: education@whoi.edu
Internet: http://www.whoi.edu
AMOUNT: $380/week for 10-12 weeks; possible travel allowance
DEADLINE(S): FEB 15
FIELD(S): Science; Engineering; Mathematics; Marine Sciences/Engineering; Policy
ELIGIBILITY/REQUIREMENTS: Open to undergraduates who have completed their junior or senior year, with backgrounds in science, mathematics, and engineering interested in the marine sciences and oceanography. Selection based on academic and scientific achievements and promise as future ocean scientists and engineers.
HOW TO APPLY: For an application and additional information, contact the Academic Programs Office, Clark Laboratory. Submit with résumé demonstrating educational background and work experience; an official transcript and/or other official documentation of undergraduate record; at least 3 letters of recommendation from professors, employers, others; a statement of research interests, future education and career plans, and reasons for applying for fellowship.

1788—WOODS HOLE OCEANOGRAPHIC INSTITUTION (Traineeships in Oceanography for Minority Group Undergraduates)

Clark Laboratory 223, MS #31
Woods Hole MA 02543-1541
508/289-2219

FAX: 508/457-2188
E-mail: education@whoi.edu
Internet: http://www.whoi.edu
AMOUNT: Varies
DEADLINE(S): FEB 15
FIELD(S): Physical/Natural Sciences, Mathematics, Engineering
ELIGIBILITY/REQUIREMENTS: For minority undergraduates (African-American or Black, Asian-American, Chicano, Mexican-American, Puerto Rican or other Hispanic, and Native American) who are enrolled in U.S. colleges/universities and have completed at least 2 semesters. Traineeships may be awarded for a 10- to 12-week period in the summer or for a semester during the academic year.
HOW TO APPLY: For an application and additional information, contact the Academic Programs Office, Clark Laboratory. Submit with current résumé demonstrating educational background and work experience; an official transcript and/or other official documentation of undergraduate record; at least 3 letters of recommendation from professors, employers and others; a statement of research interests, future education and career plans, and reasons for applying for fellowship.

MEDICINE/ HEALTHCARE (ALL FIELDS)

1789—AMERICAN FOUNDATION FOR THE BLIND (Rudolph Dillman Scholarship)

11 Penn Plaza, Suite 300
New York NY 10001
212/502-7661
FAX: 212/502-7771
E-mail: afbinfo@afb.net
Internet: http://www.afb.org/ scholar/scholarships.asp
AMOUNT: $2,500
DEADLINE(S): MAR 31
FIELD(S): Rehabilitation/Education of Blind or Visually Impaired
ELIGIBILITY/REQUIREMENTS: Undergraduate or graduate students who are studying in the field of rehabilitation and/or education of persons who are blind or visually impaired. One of these grants is specifically for a student who meets all requirements and submits evidence of economic need.

HOW TO APPLY: Must submit official transcripts, proof of acceptance, evidence of economic need (if applicable), 3 letters of recommendation, proof of legal blindness, proof of U.S. citizenship, and a typewritten statement of no more than 3 double-spaced pages describing the field of study you are pursuing, educational or personal goals, work experience, extracurricular activities and how the scholarship award will be used. See website or contact AFB for an application.
NUMBER OF AWARDS: 4
RENEWABLE: No
CONTACT: Alina Vayntrub

1790—AMERICAN INDIAN SCIENCE AND ENGINEERING SOCIETY (A. T. Anderson Memorial Scholarship)

P.O. Box 9828
Albuquerque NM 87119-9828
505/765-1052
FAX: 505/765-5608
E-mail: scholarships@aises.org
Internet: http://www.aises.org/ scholar/scholarships
AMOUNT: $1,000
DEADLINE(S): JUN 15
FIELD(S): Medicine; Natural Resources; Science; Engineering
ELIGIBILITY/REQUIREMENTS: Open to students who are at least 1/4 American Indian or recognized as member of a tribe. Must be member of AISES ($10 fee), enrolled full time at an accredited institution, and demonstrate financial need. Minimum GPA 2.7.
HOW TO APPLY: See website or contact Society for an application.
RENEWABLE: Yes
CONTACT: Tina Pino

1791—AMERICAN RADIO RELAY LEAGUE FOUNDATION (Carole J. Streeter [KB9JBR] Scholarship)

225 Main Street
Newington CT 06111
860/594-0397
FAX: 860/594-0259
E-mail: foundation@arrl.org
Internet: http://www.arrlf.org/
AMOUNT: $750 (based on annual earnings)
DEADLINE(S): FEB 1
FIELD(S): Health and Healing Arts
ELIGIBILITY/REQUIREMENTS: Open to students with any class amateur radio license with a preference for an applicant who is capable of basic communication using the Morse code, pursuing a baccalau-

reate or higher degree attending any accredited college or university without regard to the required length of study, including study related to the healing arts including the courses at teaching hospitals and local colleges.
HOW TO APPLY: See website or contact Foundation for information and application. Submit with a 1-page essay on the role amateur radio has played in your life. A recent high school (or equivalent) or college transcript required; submit with application or mail separately.
NUMBER OF AWARDS: 1
RENEWABLE: No
CONTACT: Mary M. Hobart, K1MMH, Secretary

1792—AMERICAN RADIO RELAY LEAGUE FOUNDATION (William R. Goldfarb Memorial Scholarship)

225 Main Street
Newington CT 06111
860/594-0397
FAX: 860/594-0259
E-mail: foundation@arrl.org
Internet: http://www.arrlf.org/
AMOUNT: $1,000
DEADLINE(S): FEB 1
FIELD(S): Business; Computer Science; Medicine (including Nursing); Engineering; Sciences
ELIGIBILITY/REQUIREMENTS: For student with any class of license pursuing baccalaureate or higher degree at a regionally accredited institution. Must demonstrate financial need.
HOW TO APPLY: See website or contact Foundation for information and application. Submit with a 1-page essay on the role amateur radio has played in your life. A recent high school (or equivalent) or college transcript required; submit with application or mail separately.
NUMBER OF AWARDS: 1
RENEWABLE: No
CONTACT: Mary M. Hobart, K1MMH, Secretary

1793—ARTHUR M. MILLER FUND

Bank of America
TX1-945-07-04
P.O. Box 830259
Dallas TX 75283-0259
800/257-0332
FAX: 800/658-6507
AMOUNT: Varies
DEADLINE(S): MAR 31
FIELD(S): Medicine or related field

ELIGIBILITY/REQUIREMENTS: Open to Kansas residents studying at educational institutions in Kansas.

HOW TO APPLY: Send application to above address.

1794—BECA FOUNDATION (Alice Newell Joslyn Medical Fund)

830 East Grand Avenue, Suite B
Escondido CA 92025
760/471-8246
FAX: 760/471-8176
E-mail: sdbeca@sbcglobal.net
Internet: http://www.beca foundation.org
AMOUNT: $1,000-$2,000
DEADLINE(S): MAR 3
FIELD(S): Medicine; Healthcare; Nursing; Dental/Medical Assisting; Physical Therapy

ELIGIBILITY/REQUIREMENTS: Open to Latino students entering the medical/healthcare profession; must be living or attending a high school or college in San Diego County at time of application. Based on financial need, scholastic determination, and community/cultural awareness.

HOW TO APPLY: See website for application. Submit with official copy of high school transcript; 2 letters of recommendation from a high school official, high school teacher/college professor/advisor, or anyone other than family member, who has known you for at least 2 years addressing your leadership abilities, your future potential, and other factors that contribute to your community involvement; and Financial Profile, either a copy of your FAFSA/SAR or questions on application.
RENEWABLE: Yes. Must reapply.

1795—COLUMBIANA COUNTY PUBLIC HEALTH LEAGUE TRUST FUND (Grants)

Bank One P.O. Box 511
Wheeling WV 26003
304/234-4128
FAX: 304/234-4142
AMOUNT: Varies
DEADLINE(S): FEB 28
FIELD(S): Medicine (emphasis on medical research; pharmacology; medical technology; physical therapy; nursing; dental hygiene; occupational therapy; respiratory illness)

ELIGIBILITY/REQUIREMENTS: Open ONLY to undergraduate and graduate residents of Columbiana County, Ohio, who are pursuing medical education or research. Preference is given to the study of respiratory illness.

HOW TO APPLY: Write for application.
CONTACT: Mary Kay Withum, c/o Bank One

1796—COMMUNITY FOUNDATION FOR GREATER ATLANTA, INC., THE (Pattillo Scholarship Fund)

50 Hurt Plaza, Suite 449
Atlanta GA 30303
404/688-5525
FAX: 404/688-3060
E-mail: scholarships@atlcf.org
Internet: http://www.atlcf.org/ GrantsScholarships/Scholarships. aspx
AMOUNT: $3,500
DEADLINE(S): MAR 26
FIELD(S): Medicine; Social Work

ELIGIBILITY/REQUIREMENTS: Open to graduating high school seniors or undergraduate students. Must have GPA 2.0 or higher through the 2 previous quarters or the previous semester. Eligible applicants include but are not limited to full-time employees (working a minimum of 40 hours/week) of Pattillo Construction Corporation or its affiliates, for a minimum of 3 years, and their dependents (spouse, children, and step-children).

HOW TO APPLY: See website for additional information and application. Submit with current complete official transcript(s), 2 scholarship recommendation forms and optional recommendation letters, letter of acceptance from the school you plan to attend next fall (if a recent high school graduate). Send to The Community Foundation for Greater Atlanta, Pattillo Scholarship Fund, Scholarship Management Services, Scholarship America, One Scholarship Way, P.O. Box 297, Saint Peter, MN 56082. If you have questions, call 507/931-1682 or e-mail communityfoundation@scholarshipamerica.org.
NUMBER OF AWARDS: 15-25
RENEWABLE: Yes; up to 4 years. Must maintain a 2.0 minimum GPA, be enrolled as a full-time student or as a part-time student who is working full-time (preference given to Patillo employees) and submit the current year's renewal application.
CONTACT: Lisa Glanville, 404/308-0055

1797—COMMUNITY FOUNDATION FOR GREATER ATLANTA, INC., THE (Russell Corporation Scholarship Fund)

50 Hurt Plaza, Suite 449
Atlanta GA 30303
404/688-5525
FAX: 404/688-3060

E-mail: scholarships@atlcf.org
Internet: http://www.atlcf.org/ GrantsScholarships/Scholarships. aspx
AMOUNT: $5,000
DEADLINE(S): MAR 26
FIELD(S): Medicine; Social Work

ELIGIBILITY/REQUIREMENTS: Open to high school students graduating in the Spring and attending college in the Fall. Must be enrolled as a full-time at an accredited college or university; have a minimum cumulative 3.0 GPA through the two previous quarters or the previous semester; demonstrate financial need. Parents of applicants must be full-time employees of Russell Corporation for a minimum of 2 years.

HOW TO APPLY: See website for additional information and application. Submit with current complete official transcript(s), 2 scholarship recommendation forms, letter of acceptance from the school you plan to attend next fall (if a recent high school graduate). Send to The Community Foundation for Greater Atlanta, Russell Corporation Scholarship Fund, Scholarship Management Services, Scholarship America, One Scholarship Way, P.O. Box 297, Saint Peter, MN 56082. If you have questions, call 507/931-1682 or e-mail communityfoundation@scholarshipamerica.org.
NUMBER OF AWARDS: 2
RENEWABLE: Yes; up to 4 years. Must maintain a 3.0 GPA, remain enrolled as full-time students, and submit the current year's renewal application form.
CONTACT: Lisa Glanville, 404/308-0055

1798—COMMUNITY FOUNDATION FOR GREATER ATLANTA, INC., THE (Steve Deardurff Scholarship Fund)

50 Hurt Plaza, Suite 449
Atlanta GA 30303
404/688-5525
FAX: 404/688-3060
E-mail: scholarships@atlcf.org
Internet: http://www.atlcf.org/ GrantsScholarships/Scholarships. aspx
AMOUNT: $500-$1,000
DEADLINE(S): MAR 26
FIELD(S): Medicine; Social Work

ELIGIBILITY/REQUIREMENTS: Must be a legal resident of Georgia, enrolled in or accepted to an accredited institution of higher learning and pursuing an undergraduate or graduate degree in medicine or social work, and have a demonstrated history of commitment to community service, potential for success in chosen field, minimum 2.0 GPA, and demonstrates financial need.

HOW TO APPLY: Must be nominated (call for nomination sent early each year). See website for additional information; submit documentation of status as an individual with autism, secondary school transcripts, documentation of acceptance into an accredited, postsecondary educational or vocational program of study, 2 letters of recommendation, a personal statement of no more than 500 words, outlining applicant's qualifications and proposed plan of study. Send to The Community Foundation for Greater Atlanta, Steve Dearduff Scholarship Fund, Scholarship Management Services, Scholarship America, One Scholarship Way, P.O. Box 297, Saint Peter, MN 56082. If you have questions, call 507/931-1682 or e-mail community-foundation@scholarshipamerica.org.
NUMBER OF AWARDS: 3
RENEWABLE: Yes; must reapply.
CONTACT: Lisa Glanville, 404/308-0055

1799—COMMUNITY FOUNDATION FOR GREATER ATLANTA, INC., THE (Tech High/W.O. Cheney Scholarship)

50 Hurt Plaza, Suite 449
Atlanta GA 30303
404/688-5525
FAX: 404/688-3060
E-mail: scholarships@atlcf.org
Internet: http://www.atlcf.org/GrantsScholarships/Scholarships.aspx
AMOUNT: $5,000
DEADLINE(S): MAR 26
FIELD(S): Mathematics, Engineering, Physical Sciences
ELIGIBILITY/REQUIREMENTS: Open to graduating high school seniors. Must be a citizen of the U.S. and a legal resident of Georgia for at least 3 years prior to application, have a cumulative high school GPA of 3.7 or higher or be in the upper 10% of graduating class, SAT composite (math and critical reading) of at least 1300, be accepted as a full-time student to a 4-year accredited college or university, and demonstrate a commitment to community service.

HOW TO APPLY: See website for additional information and application. Submit with a personal essay (2-3 pages) that includes why you feel a college education is important; your statement of educational and career goals; post college career interests; highlights of your high school extracurricular/community service activities, special strengths, skills, and qualifications; any unusual family or personal circumstances have affected your achieve-

ment in school, work experience, or your participation in school and community activities; present financial need. Send to The Community Foundation for Greater Atlanta, Tech High/W.O. Cheney Scholarship, Scholarship Management Services, Scholarship America, One Scholarship Way, P.O. Box 297, Saint Peter, MN 56082. If you have questions, call 507/931-1682 or e-mail community-foundation@scholarshipamerica.org.
NUMBER OF AWARDS: 4
RENEWABLE: Yes; must reapply.
CONTACT: Lisa Glanville, 404/308-0055

1800—EDWARD BANGS KELLEY AND ELZA KELLEY FOUNDATION, INC.

P.O. Drawer M
Hyannis MA 02601-1412
508/775-3117
AMOUNT: $500-$4,000
DEADLINE(S): APR 30
FIELD(S): Medicine; Health; Nursing; Education; Social Sciences
ELIGIBILITY/REQUIREMENTS: Open to residents of Barnstable County, Massachusetts. Awards support study at recognized undergraduate, graduate, and professional institutions. Financial need is considered.
HOW TO APPLY: Contact Foundation for an application.

1801—FIRST UNITED METHODIST CHURCH (Robert Stevenson and Doreene E. Cater Scholarships)

302 5th Avenue South
St. Cloud MN 56301
FAX: 320/251-0878
E-mail: fumc@fumc-stcloud.org
AMOUNT: $200-1,500
DEADLINE(S): JUN 1
FIELD(S): Humanitarian and Christian Service: Teaching, Medicine, Social Work, Environmental Studies, and related fields
ELIGIBILITY/REQUIREMENTS: Stevenson Scholarship is open to undergraduate members of the First United Methodist Church of St. Cloud. Cater Scholarship is open to members of the Minnesota United Methodist Conference who are entering the sophomore year or higher of college work. Both require two letters of reference, transcripts, and financial need.
HOW TO APPLY: Contact Scholarship Committee for an application.
NUMBER OF AWARDS: 5-6

1802—FOUNDATION FOR SEACOAST HEALTH

100 Campus Drive, Suite 1
Portsmouth NH 03801
603/422-8200
FAX: 603/422-8207
E-mail: ffsh@communitycampus.org
Internet: http://www.ffsh.org
AMOUNT: $5,000
DEADLINE(S): FEB 1
FIELD(S): Health-related fields
ELIGIBILITY/REQUIREMENTS: Open to students pursuing health-related fields. Must be legal residents of the following cities in New Hampshire: Portsmouth, Newington, New Castle, Rye, Greenland, N. Hampton, or these cities in Maine: Kittery, Eliot, or York. Must have resided in the area for at least 2 years.
HOW TO APPLY: Write or see website for details.
NUMBER OF AWARDS: 2

1803—HAWAII COMMUNITY FOUNDATION (Aiea General Hospital Association Scholarship)

1164 Bishop Street, Suite 800
Honolulu HI 96813
808/537-6333 or toll free: 888/731-3863
FAX: 808/521-6286
E-mail: info@hcf-hawaii.org
Internet: http://www.hcf-hawaii.org
DEADLINE(S): MAR 1
FIELD(S): Health-related
ELIGIBILITY/REQUIREMENTS: Must be full-time undergraduates attending an accredited 2- or 4-year college or university; major in a health-related field; demonstrate financial need, good moral character, and academic achievement (minimum GPA of 2.7); and reside in one of these ZIP codes: 96701, 96706, 96707, 96782, 96792, or 96797.
HOW TO APPLY: See website. Send application with 2 letters of recommendation.

1804—HAWAII COMMUNITY FOUNDATION (Cora Aguda Manayan Fund)

1164 Bishop Street, Suite 800
Honolulu HI 96813
808/537-6333 or toll free: 888/731-3863
FAX: 808/521-6286
E-mail: info@hcf-hawaii.org
Internet: http://www.hcf-hawaii.org
DEADLINE(S): MAR 1
FIELD(S): Health-related

ELIGIBILITY/REQUIREMENTS: Must be Hawaii residents of Filipino ancestry; full-time undergraduate students attending an accredited 2- or 4-year college or university; major in a health-related field; and demonstrate financial need, good moral character, and academic achievement (minimum GPA of 2.7). Preference may be given to applicants studying in Hawaii.

HOW TO APPLY: See website. Send application with 2 letters of recommendation.

1805—HAWAII COMMUNITY FOUNDA-TION (Dr. Hans and Clara Zimmerman Foundation Health Scholarships)

1164 Bishop Street, Suite 800
Honolulu HI 96813
808/537-6333 or toll free:
888/731-3863
FAX: 808/521-6286
E-mail: info@hcf-hawaii.org
Internet: http://www.hcf-hawaii.org
DEADLINE(S): MAR 1
FIELD(S): Health-related
ELIGIBILITY/REQUIREMENTS: Must be Hawaii residents; full-time students (juniors or seniors), or attending an accredited 4-year college or university in the U.S.; major in a health-related field (not including sports medicine, psychology unless clinical, or social work); and demonstrate financial need, good moral character, and academic achievement (minimum GPA of 3.0).

HOW TO APPLY: See website. Send application with 2 letters of recommendation and a personal statement describing participation in community service projects or activities.

1806—HAWAII COMMUNITY FOUNDA-TION (Edward Doty Scholarship)

1164 Bishop Street, Suite 800
Honolulu HI 96813
808/537-6333 or toll free:
888/731-3863
FAX: 808/521-6286
E-mail: info@hcf-hawaii.org
Internet: http://www.hcf-hawaii.org
DEADLINE(S): MAR 1
FIELD(S): Gerontology
ELIGIBILITY/REQUIREMENTS: Must be resident of the state of Hawaii; be a junior or senior undergraduate attending full time an accredited 2- or 4-year college or university; and demonstrate financial need, good moral character, and academic achievement (minimum GPA of 2.7).

HOW TO APPLY: See website. Send application with 2 letters of recommendation.

1807—HAWAII COMMUNITY FOUNDA-TION (Nick Van Pernis Scholarship Fund)

1164 Bishop Street, Suite 800
Honolulu HI 96813
808/537-6333 or
toll free: 888/731-3863
FAX: 808/521-6286
E-mail: info@hcf-hawaii.org
Internet: http://www.hcf-hawaii.org
DEADLINE(S): MAR 1
FIELD(S): Marine Sciences; Health Sciences; Biotechnology; Early Childhood Education
ELIGIBILITY/REQUIREMENTS: Must be graduates of a public or private high school in the Districts of North Kona, South Kona, North Kohala, or Ka'u; plan to attend full time an accredited 2- or 4-year college or university; demonstrate financial need, good moral character, and academic achievement (minimum GPA of 2.7).

HOW TO APPLY: See website. Send application; 2 letters of recommendation; a short essay explaining how your career can benefit the lives of Hawaiians; and a record of community service.

1808—HAWAII COMMUNITY FOUNDA-TION (Thz Fo Farm Scholarship)

1164 Bishop Street, Suite 800
Honolulu HI 96813
808/537-6333 or toll free:
888/731-3863
FAX: 808/521-6286
E-mail: info@hcf-hawaii.org
Internet: http://www.hcf-hawaii.org
DEADLINE(S): MAR 1
FIELD(S): Gerontology
ELIGIBILITY/REQUIREMENTS: Applicants must be of Chinese ancestry; residents of the state of Hawaii; plan to attend full time an accredited 2- or 4-year college or university; and demonstrate financial need, good moral character, and strong academic achievement (minimum GPA of 3.0).

HOW TO APPLY: See website. Send application with 2 letters of recommendation.

1809—HAWAII COMMUNITY FOUNDA-TION (William James & Dorothy Bading Lanquist Fund)

1164 Bishop Street, Suite 800

Honolulu HI 96813
808/537-6333 or toll free:
888/731-3863
FAX: 808/521-6286
E-mail: info@hcf-hawaii.org
Internet: http://www.hcf-hawaii.org
DEADLINE(S): MAR 1
FIELD(S): Physical Sciences and related fields (excluding Biology and Social Sciences)
ELIGIBILITY/REQUIREMENTS: Must be residents of Hawaii; junior or senior undergraduate students enrolled full time in an accredited 2- or 4-year college or university; and demonstrate financial need, good moral character, and academic achievement (minimum GPA of 2.7).

HOW TO APPLY: See website. Send application with 2 letters of recommendation.

1810—JEWISH FEDERATION OF METRO-POLITAN CHICAGO (Academic Scholarship Program)

Jewish Vocational Service
216 West Jackson Blvd, Suite 700
Chicago IL 60606-6921
312/673-3400
TTY: 312/444-2877
FAX: 312/553-5544
E-mail: jvsscholarship@
jvschicago.org
Internet: www.jvs/chicago.org
(click on Scholarship Services)
AMOUNT: Varies
DEADLINE(S): FEB 15
FIELD(S): Mathematics, Engineering, Science, Medicine, Social Work, Education, Psychology, Rabbinate, Law (except corporate), Communications
ELIGIBILITY/REQUIREMENTS: Open to Jewish men and women legally domiciled in the greater Chicago metropolitan area, who are identified as having promise for significant contributions in their chosen careers, and are in need of financial assistance for full-time academic programs in above areas. Must have entered undergraduate junior year in career programs requiring no postgraduate education, be in graduate/professional school, or be in a vo-tech training program.

HOW TO APPLY: Phone JVS Scholarship Secretary (312/673-3457), fax, or visit website (click on Scholarship Services) for an application in the Fall. Interview required.

RENEWABLE: Yes
CONTACT: JVS Scholarship Secretary at 312/673-3457

1811—JUNIATA COLLEGE (Robert Steele Memorial Scholarship)

Office of Financial Planning
1700 Moore Street
Huntingdon PA 16652
814/641-3142
FAX: 814/641-5311
E-mail: frankv@juniata.edu
Internet: http://www.juniata.edu/
admission/finplan/index.html
AMOUNT: Up to $4,000
DEADLINE(S): MAR 1
FIELD(S): Medicine, Science
ELIGIBILITY/REQUIREMENTS: Open to science/medical students applying to Juniata College. Must demonstrate financial need and fill out FAFSA form.
HOW TO APPLY: Contact College for an application or enrollment information. See Financial Aid Office for FAFSA.
CONTACT: Vincent Frank, Director of Student Financial Planning, 814/641-3140; e-mail: frankv@juniata.edu

1812—KOREAN-AMERICAN SCIENTISTS AND ENGINEERS ASSOCIATION (KSEA Scholarships)

1952 Gallows Road, Suite 300
Vienna VA 22182
703/748-1221
FAX: 703/748-1331
E-mail: admin@ksea.org
Internet: http://www.ksea.org
AMOUNT: $1,000
DEADLINE(S): FEB 28
FIELD(S): Science; Engineering; Medicine
ELIGIBILITY/REQUIREMENTS: Must have graduated from a high school in the U.S. and must be a student member of KSEA or a child of a member. Evaluation criteria are academic performance-30%; recommendation letters-30%; work experience and extracurricular activities-20%; and essay-20%.
HOW TO APPLY: See website for application. Submit Curriculum Vitae (including work experience and extracurricular activities); transcript from high school and college attended; an essay on 1 of the following topics (approximately 500 words): your career goals and their contributions to the society or meaning of Korean heritage in your life; and 3 recommendation letters (1 from a current or previous KSEA officer or chapter president).
NUMBER OF AWARDS: 5-8 (2 are ONLY for women).

1813—NATIONAL FEDERATION OF THE BLIND (Howard Brown Rickard Scholarship)

805 Fifth Avenue
Grinnell IA 50112
515/236-3366
Internet: http://www.nfb.org/
nfb/scholarship_program.asp
AMOUNT: $3,000
DEADLINE(S): MAR 31
FIELD(S): Law; Medicine; Engineering; Architecture; Natural Sciences
ELIGIBILITY/REQUIREMENTS: For legally blind students pursuing or planning to pursue a full-time postsecondary course of study in the U.S. Based on academic excellence, service to the community, and financial need. Membership NOT required.
HOW TO APPLY: Contact Scholarship Committee Chair for an application.
NUMBER OF AWARDS: 1
RENEWABLE: Yes
CONTACT: Peggy Elliot, Scholarship Committee Chair

1814—NATIONAL INVENTORS HALL OF FAME, THE (Collegiate Inventors Competition)

221 South Broadway Street
Akron OH 44308-1505
330/849-6887
E-mail: rdepuy@invent.org.
Internet: http://www.invent.
org/bfg/bfghome.html
AMOUNT: $15,000
DEADLINE(S): JUN 1
FIELD(S): Mathematics, Engineering, Biology, Chemistry, Physics, Information Technology, Medicine
ELIGIBILITY/REQUIREMENTS: Must be enrolled (or have been enrolled) full time (in any college or university) at least part of the 12-month period prior to the date the entry is submitted. In the case of a team (maximum 4 students), at least 1 member of the team must meet the full-time eligibility criteria. The other team members must have been enrolled on a part-time basis (at a minimum) sometime during the 24-month period prior to the date the entry is submitted. There are no limits on the number of entries a student or team may submit in a given year; however, only 1 prize/student or team will be awarded. No specific age requirements; however, if an entrant is under 18, a parent or guardian must sign the Student/Advisor Release Form. Entries judged on the originality and inventiveness of the new idea, process, or technology, on their potential value to society (socially, environmentally, and economically), and on the scope of use. Entries must be complete, workable, and well articulated.
HOW TO APPLY: Submit an original invention or idea that has not been made public. See website for application and details. The application must include: Student and Advisor Information; Student Essay and Advisor Letter following the outlined format; diagrams, illustrations, photos, slides, or videos of the invention (clearly labeled); the signed Student/Advisor Release Form.
CONTACT: Ray DePuy

1815—NEW YORK STATE HIGHER EDUCATION SERVICES CORPORATION (N.Y. State Regents Professional/Health Care Opportunity Scholarships)

Cultural Education Center
Room 5C64
Albany NY 12230
518/486-1319
Internet: http://www.hesc.com
AMOUNT: $1,000-$10,000/year
DEADLINE(S): Varies
FIELD(S): Medicine, Dentistry & related fields; Architecture, Nursing, Psychology, Audiology, Landscape Architecture, Social Work, Chiropractic, Law, Pharmacy, Accounting, Speech Language Pathology
ELIGIBILITY/REQUIREMENTS: For New York State residents who are economically disadvantaged and members of a minority group underrepresented in the chosen profession and attending school in New York State. For U.S. citizens or qualifying non-citizens.
HOW TO APPLY: See website or contact NYS HESC.
RENEWABLE: Yes

1816—PILOT INTERNATIONAL FOUNDATION (Ruby Newhall Memorial Scholarship)

P.O. Box 5600
Macon GA 31208-5600
478/743-7403
FAX: 478/743-2173
E-mail: pifinfo@pilothq.org
Internet: http://www.pilot
international.org
AMOUNT: Varies
DEADLINE(S): FEB 15
FIELD(S): Medicine; Healthcare

ELIGIBILITY/REQUIREMENTS: For international students who have studied in the U.S. for at least 1 year, and who intend to return to their home country 6 months after graduation. Must be full-time students majoring in a field related to human health and welfare, GPA of 3.0 or more.
HOW TO APPLY: Must be sponsored by home, college, or university town Pilot Club. See website or send SASE for information and application.

1817—SCIENCE SERVICE (Intel International Science and Engineering Fair)

1719 N Street NW
Washington DC 20036
202/785-2255
FAX: 202/785-1243
E-mail: jcole@sciserv.org
Internet: http://www.sciserv.org
AMOUNT: Varies
DEADLINE(S): Varies (consult local, regional or state ISEF)
FIELD(S): Science; Mathematics; Engineering; Medicine
ELIGIBILITY/REQUIREMENTS: High school students (grades 9-12) may participate in this worldwide competition.
HOW TO APPLY: Contact Science Service for official ISEF entry book.

1818—SCIENCE SERVICE (Intel Science Talent Search)

1719 N Street NW
Washington DC 20036
202/785-2255
FAX: 202/785-1243
E-mail: jkee@sciserv.org
Internet: http://www.sciserv.org
AMOUNT: $100,000 (1st place); $75,000 (2nd); $50,000 (3rd); $25,000 (4th-6th); $20,000 (7th-10th); 30 at $5,000; 300 at $1,000; 40 laptops
DEADLINE(S): Mid to late NOV
FIELD(S): Science; Mathematics; Engineering; Medicine
ELIGIBILITY/REQUIREMENTS: Open to high school seniors in the U.S. and territories and American students attending school abroad.
HOW TO APPLY: Contact Science Service for official STS entry book. Submit completed entry form, with research report, high school transcript, and standardized test scores.
NUMBER OF AWARDS: 40
CONTACT: June Kee

1819—UNITED METHODIST CHURCH SCHOLARSHIP PROGRAM (Edith M. Allen Scholarship)

P.O. Box 34007
Nashville TN 37203-0007
615/340-7344
FAX: 615/340-7367
E-mail: umscholar@gbhem.org
Internet: http://www.gbhem.org
AMOUNT: Up to $1,000
DEADLINE(S): MAY 1
FIELD(S): Education; Social Work; Medicine and related professions
ELIGIBILITY/REQUIREMENTS: Open to African-American students enrolled full time at a UM college or university, have a B+ average or higher, a full and active member of the UMC for at least 3 years, citizen or permanent resident of the U.S., and demonstrate financial need.
HOW TO APPLY: See website for application or contact the director of financial aid at the United Methodist college or university of your choice, the chairperson of your annual conference Board of Higher Education and Campus Ministry or the United Methodist Scholarship Office at the address listed for information and/or application form.
CONTACT: Scholarship Department

1820—WESTERN MICHIGAN UNIVERSITY (College of Health and Human Services/The Leonard Gernant and Frances A. Gernant Gerontology Scholarship)

1903 West Michigan
Kalamazoo MI 49008-5337
269/387-8777
FAX: 269/387-6989
E-mail: finaid-info@wmich.edu
Internet: http://www.wmich.edu/finaid
AMOUNT: $500/semester
DEADLINE(S): MAR 1
FIELD(S): Gerontology
ELIGIBILITY/REQUIREMENTS: Undergraduates pursuing a major or minor in the Gerontology Program; must be enrolled full time (a minimum of 12 semester hours). Preference given to students demonstrating high academic achievement and dedication to a career in Health and Human Service areas with an emphasis on serving the aging. Financial need a secondary consideration.
HOW TO APPLY: Contact Gerontology Program, B302 Ellsworth Hall, for an application.
RENEWABLE: Yes. Maximum 2 years.

1821—WOMEN OF THE EVANGELICAL LUTHERAN CHURCH IN AMERICA (Opportunity Scholarships for Lutheran Laywomen)

8765 West Higgins Road
Chicago IL 6063-4189
800/638-3522, ext. 2736
FAX: 773/380-2419
E-mail: emilyhansen@elca.org
Internet: http://www.womenof theelca.org/whatwedo/scholar/scholarships.html
AMOUNT: Up to $2,000
DEADLINE(S): FEB 15
FIELD(S): All (emphasis on health professions; vocational education; religion)
ELIGIBILITY/REQUIREMENTS: Open to women enrolled in undergraduate, graduate, professional, or vocational courses of study preparing for a career other than the ordained ministry. Must be at least 21 years old, a citizen of the U.S., a member of the ELCA, and have experienced an interruption in education of 2 or more years. Additional considerations include clearly stated and attainable goals, impact of Women of the ELCA dollars on total cost of program, and applicant's involvement in Women of the ELCA.
HOW TO APPLY: Contact Program Director for an application and information. Submit with transcript and 3 references (from pastor, academic, personal).
RENEWABLE: Yes. Maximum of 2 years.
CONTACT: Emily Hansen

1822—ZETA PHI BETA SORORITY/NATIONAL EDUCATIONAL FOUNDATION (S. Evelyn Lewis Memorial Scholarship in Medical Health Sciences)

1734 New Hampshire Avenue NW
Washington DC 20009
Internet: http://www.zpb1920.org
AMOUNT: $500-$1,000
DEADLINE(S): JAN 1
FIELD(S): Medicine; Health Sciences
ELIGIBILITY/REQUIREMENTS: Open to graduate and undergraduate young women enrolled in a program leading to a degree in medicine or health sciences. Award is for full-time study for one academic year (Fall-Spring) and is paid directly to college or university. Must submit proof of enrollment.
HOW TO APPLY: See website for additional information and application or send SASE to Foundation. Must submit documented proof of academic study and plan of program to Scholarship Chairperson

with signature of school administrator or Program Director; 3 letters of recommendation (professor or high school teacher, minister or community leader, other—for Zeta members 3rd reference must be from the graduate Zeta chapter and signed by the Basileus or Advisor); transcript; essay (minimum 150 words) with information about yourself, your educational goals and professional aspirations and how this award will help you achieve them, and why you should receive this award.
RENEWABLE: No

ALLIED HEALTH PROFESSIONS

1823—AABB (Suzanne Ledin Travel Award)

8101 Glenbrook Road
Bethesda MD 20814-2749
301/907-6977
FAX: 301/907-6895
E-mail: tzein@abba.org
Internet: http://www.alphachi honor.org
AMOUNT: $1,500 travel grant
DEADLINE(S): JUL 1
FIELD(S): Blood Banking
ELIGIBILITY/REQUIREMENTS: Must be enrolled in or recently graduated from (past 12 months) an accredited specialist in blood banking (SBB) program.
HOW TO APPLY: See website for information and application. Submit by mail along with an essay focusing on the vision of being an SBB certified professional, incorporating how you became interest in the profession, how to increase awareness of the profession, ideas regarding recruitment of future SBBs, and vision for the profession in the next 10 years. along with a current résumé, SBB Coordinator/Director letter of support and assessment questionnaire.
NUMBER OF AWARDS: 2 SBBs, 2 transfusion medicine
RENEWABLE: No
CONTACT: Tamara Zein, 240/333-6604
ADDITIONAL INFORMATION: Must attend the current year's AABB Annual meeting to receive the award.

1824—AMERICAN DENTAL ASSISTANT ASSOCIATION (Juliette A. Southard/Oral-B Lab Scholarship)

35 East Wacker Drive, Suite 1730
Chicago IL 60601-2211
312/541-1550
FAX: 312/541-1496
E-mail: dmarrell@adaa1.com
Internet: http://www.dental assistant.org
AMOUNT: $500
DEADLINE(S): JAN 31
FIELD(S): Dental Assisting
ELIGIBILITY/REQUIREMENTS: Must be high school grad/GED enrolled in dental assisting program/furthering career in dental assisting. Based on academic achievement, ability, and commitment to career.
HOW TO APPLY: Request application from Central Office and submit with transcripts, proof of acceptance, 2 letters of reference, and letter of intent to pursue career in Dental Assisting.
NUMBER OF AWARDS: 5-15
RENEWABLE: No
CONTACT: Dennis Marrell, Membership Development Manager

1825—AMERICAN DENTAL ASSOCIATION FOUNDATION (Allied Health Scholarship Program)

211 East Chicago Avenue
Chicago IL 60611
312/440-4639
AMOUNT: $1,000
DEADLINE(S): AUG 15 (dental hygiene and dental lab tech); SEP 15 (dental assisting)
FIELD(S): Dental Hygiene; Dental Assisting; Dental Laboratory Technician
ELIGIBILITY/REQUIREMENTS: Demonstrate financial need and academic achievement (3.0 GPA). Hygiene students must be entering the final year of an accredited program; dental assisting students must be entering into an accredited program; and dental lab tech students must be entering final year in an accredited program.
HOW TO APPLY: Submit biographical sketch, questionnaire and 2 references along with applications and financial documentation.
CONTACT: Marsha L. Mountz, Director, Charitable Assistance Programs

1826—ADHA Institute for Oral Health Scholarship Fund

444 North Michigan Avenue, Suite 3400
Chicago IL 60611
800/735-4916
E-mail: institute@adha.net
Internet: http://www.adha. org/institute
AMOUNT: $1,000-$2,000
DEADLINE(S): MAY 1
FIELD(S): Dental Hygiene
ELIGIBILITY/REQUIREMENTS: SADHA member. Must be enrolled in first year or later of dental hygiene school.
HOW TO APPLY: Visit website to download application packet.
NUMBER OF AWARDS: 40-70
RENEWABLE: No

1827—ASSOCIATION ON AMERICAN INDIAN AFFAIRS (Elizabeth and Sherman Asche Memorial Scholarship Fund)

Executive Office
966 Hungerford Drive, Suite 12-B
Rockville, MD 20850
240/314-7155
FAX: 240/314-7159
E-mail: general.aaia@verizon.net
Internet: http://www.indian-affairs.org
AMOUNT: $1,500
DEADLINE(S): Fall and Spring semesters only
FIELD(S): Public Health; Science
ELIGIBILITY/REQUIREMENTS: Open to full-time undergraduate students who are minimally 1/4 degree Indian blood from a federally recognized tribe. Must be pursuing a degree in 1 of above fields. Award is based on financial need and is limited to North America/Alaska.
HOW TO APPLY: See website for application; Please send only the information requested; additional information will not be considered. Must submit essay on need, certificate of enrollment and quantum from your tribe or BIA, transcript, schedule of classes, and current financial aid award letter.
RENEWABLE: Yes. Must reapply. Note: Disbursements of $750 made each semester pending satisfactory progress. No funding for summer semester.
CONTACT: Lisa Wyzlic at lw.aaia@verizon.net or 240/314-7155.
ADDITIONAL INFORMATION: If applying for more than 1 AAIA scholarship, send 1 application package only. Students will be considered for all scholarships they are qualified for.

1828—BECA FOUNDATION (Alice Newell Joslyn Medical Fund)

830 East Grand Avenue, Suite B
Escondido CA 92025
760/471-8246
FAX: 760/471-8176
E-mail: sdbeca@sbcglobal.net
Internet: http://www.beca foundation.org
AMOUNT: $1,000-$2,000

DEADLINE(S): MAR 3
FIELD(S): Medicine; Healthcare; Nursing; Dental/Medical Assisting; Physical Therapy
ELIGIBILITY/REQUIREMENTS: Open to Latino students entering the medical/healthcare profession; must be living or attending a high school or college in San Diego County at time of application, Based on financial need, scholastic determination, and community/cultural awareness.
HOW TO APPLY: See website for application. Submit with official copy of high school transcript; 2 letters of recommendation from a high school official, high school teacher/college professor/advisor, or anyone other than family member, who has known you for at least 2 years addressing your leadership abilities, your future potential, and other factors that contribute to your community involvement; and Financial Profile, either a copy of your FAFSA/SAR or questions on application.
RENEWABLE: Yes. Must reapply.

1829—CHIROPRACTIC ASSOCIATION OF LOUISIANA (William S. Boyd Scholarship)

3070 Teddy Drive, Suite A
Baton Rouge LA 20809
225/924-6978
FAX: 225/925-3139
E-mail: lachiro@premier.net
Internet: http://www.cal-online.org
AMOUNT: $1,000
DEADLINE(S): AUG 15
FIELD(S): Chiropractic
ELIGIBILITY/REQUIREMENTS: Louisiana resident intending to practice in Louisiana upon graduation. Must be a junior or senior, in a CCE-accredited chiropractic college with a current GPA of 2.75 or better.
HOW TO APPLY: Call or write for application. Submit with transcript; recommendation from an active, dues-paying member of CAL; 3 letters of recommendation (family excluded), 1 of which must be from a faculty member of the college.
NUMBER OF AWARDS: 1-2
RENEWABLE: Yes, must reapply

1830—COMMUNITY FOUNDATION FOR GREATER ATLANTA, INC., THE (William Lucas Memorial Scholarship)

50 Hurt Plaza, Suite 449
Atlanta GA 30303
404/688-5525
FAX: 404/688-3060
E-mail: scholarships@atlcf.org
Internet: http://www.atlcf.org/
GrantsScholarships/Scholarships.aspx
AMOUNT: $1,250
DEADLINE(S): APR 11
FIELD(S): Social Work, Education, Allied Health
ELIGIBILITY/REQUIREMENTS: Open to graduating high school seniors beginning college in Fall. Must be a resident of Atlanta or Gainesville, Georgia, have a minimum 2.5 GPA, and be accepted to an accredited institution of higher learning and pursuing an undergraduate degree. Must demonstrate a history of commitment to community service.
HOW TO APPLY: See website for additional information and application. Submit with essay (1-2 pages) describing your educational plans and your commitment to community service; 1-page résumé listing school and community activities, awards, offices held and other relevant experiences, official transcript, SAT/ACT scores if you are a recent high school graduate, and 2 letters of recommendation from a teacher, school personnel, volunteer advisor, or other influential adult who can attest to your merits and commitment to community service. Send to William Lucas Memorial Scholarship, c/o Georgia Campaign for Adolescent Pregnancy Prevention, 100 Auburn Avenue, Suite 200, Atlanta, GA 30303.
NUMBER OF AWARDS: 1
RENEWABLE: Yes; must reapply.
CONTACT: Brenda Jackson, William Lucas Memorial Scholarship. c/o Georgia Campaign for Adolescent Pregnancy Prevention, 100 Auburn Avenue, Suite 200, Atlanta, GA 30303, 404/524-2277.

1831—DAUGHTERS OF THE AMERICAN REVOLUTION, NATIONAL SOCIETY (Occupational Therapy Scholarship)

Committee Services Office
Attn: Scholarships
1776 D Street NW
Washington DC 20006-5392
202/628-1776
Internet: http://www.dar.org
AMOUNT: $500
DEADLINE(S): FEB 15 or AUG 15
FIELD(S): Occupational Therapy (including music, art, and physical therapy)
ELIGIBILITY/REQUIREMENTS: Awarded to students who are in financial need and are accepted and enrolled into an accredited school of occupational therapy (including art, music, or physical therapy). Affiliation with DAR not required.

HOW TO APPLY: Must submit application with a letter of sponsorship from local DAR chapter (send SASE to address above to obtain name and application); statement of 1,000 words or less stating career objectives, how college major (if required) or college plans relate to future professional goals and reasons for these choices; transcripts list of extracurricular activities, honors received, scholastic achievements, or other significant accomplishments; 2-4 letters of recommendation from the high school or college you now attend who are familiar with your work; and proof of acceptance and enrollment, citizenship and financial need. See website for additional information.
NUMBER OF AWARDS: Varies
RENEWABLE: No

1832—EMPIRE COLLEGE (Dean's Scholarship)

3035 Cleveland Avenue
Santa Rosa CA 95403
707/546-4000
FAX: 707/546-4058
Internet: http://www.wmpcol.edu
AMOUNT: $250-$1,500
DEADLINE(S): APR 15
FIELD(S): Accounting; Office Administration; Paralegal; Medical (Clinical and Administrative); Tourism; Hospitality; General Business; Computer Assembly; Network Assembly/Administration; Security
ELIGIBILITY/REQUIREMENTS: Open to high school seniors who plan to attend Empire College. Must be U.S. citizen.
HOW TO APPLY: Contact College for an application.
NUMBER OF AWARDS: 10
RENEWABLE: No
CONTACT: Mary Farha

1833—HAWAII COMMUNITY FOUNDATION (John Dawe Dental Education Fund)

1164 Bishop Street, Suite 800
Honolulu HI 96813
808/537-6333 or toll free:
888/731-3863
FAX: 808/521-6286
E-mail: scholarships@hcf-hawaii.org
Internet: http://www.hcf-hawaii.org
DEADLINE(S): MAR 1
FIELD(S): Dentistry (including Dental Hygiene and Dental Assisting)
ELIGIBILITY/REQUIREMENTS: Must be Hawaii residents; full-time students enrolled in an accredited school of dentistry, dental hygiene, or dental assisting;

and demonstrate financial need, good moral character, and academic achievement with a minimum GPA of 2.7.

HOW TO APPLY: See website. Send application with 2 letters of recommendation and Dawe Supplemental Financial Form; dental hygiene students must also send a letter confirming enrollment in program.

1834—HAWAII COMMUNITY FOUNDATION (Paulina L. Sorg Scholarship)

1164 Bishop Street, Suite 800
Honolulu HI 96813
808/537-6333 or toll free:
888/731-3863
FAX: 808/521-6286
E-mail: info@hcf-hawaii.org
Internet: http://www.hcf-hawaii.org

DEADLINE(S): MAR 1

FIELD(S): Physical Therapy

ELIGIBILITY/REQUIREMENTS: Applicants must be Hawaii residents; be full-time junior or senior undergraduate or graduate students enrolled in an accredited 4-year college or university; and demonstrate financial need, good moral character, and academic achievement with a minimum GPA of 3.0.

HOW TO APPLY: See website. Send application with 2 letters of recommendation and a personal statement describing your participation in community service projects or activities.

1835—HISPANIC DENTAL ASSOCIATION FOUNDATION (Dr. Genaro Romo Jr. & HDA Foundation Scholarship)

3085 Stevenson Drive, Suite 200
Springfield IL 62703
217/529-6517
FAX: 217/529-9120
E-mail: rjeppesen@hdassoc.org
Internet: http://www.hdassoc.org

AMOUNT: $500 and $1,000

DEADLINE(S): JUL 20

FIELD(S): Dental; Dental Hygiene

ELIGIBILITY/REQUIREMENTS: Must be accepted or currently enrolled in a dental or dental hygiene program at University of Illinois Chicago, be of Hispanic descent; and be a full-time student during the academic year for which you are applying, and a member of HDA. Show evidence of commitment and dedication to serve the Hispanic community.

HOW TO APPLY: See website for application and submit in English to address below.

CONTACT: Rebecca Jeppesen, Executive Director

ADDITIONAL INFORMATION: HDAF/Dr. Genaro Romo Jr. Scholarship Program, 3085 Stevenson Drive, Suite 200, Springfield, IL 62703; for additional information call: 800/852-7921 or fax: 217/529-9120)

1836—HISPANIC DENTAL ASSOCIATION FOUNDATION (Dr. Juan Villarreal Scholarship & HDA Foundation)

3085 Stevenson Drive, Suite 200
Springfield IL 62703
217/529-6517
FAX: 217/529-9120
E-mail: rjeppesen@hdassoc.org
Internet: http://www.hdassoc.org

AMOUNT: $500 and $1,000

DEADLINE(S): JUL 1 (dental); JUL 15 (dental hygiene)

FIELD(S): Dental; Dental Hygiene

ELIGIBILITY/REQUIREMENTS: Must be accepted or enrolled as a student in a dental or dental hygiene program in the state of Texas; be of Hispanic descent; be a full-time student during the academic year for which you are applying; and demonstrate commitment and dedication to serve the Hispanic community.

HOW TO APPLY: See website for application and submit in English to address below.

CONTACT: Rebecca Jeppesen, Executive Director

ADDITIONAL INFORMATION: Dr. Juan D. Villarreal/HDAF Scholarship Program, 3085 Stevenson Drive, Suite 200 Springfield, IL 62703 or FAX to 217/529-9120.

1837—HISPANIC DENTAL ASSOCIATION FOUNDATION (GlaxoSmithKline

3085 Stevenson Drive, Suite 200
Springfield IL 62703
217/529-6517
FAX: 217/529-9120
E-mail: rjeppesen@hdassoc.org
Internet: http://www.hdassoc.org

AMOUNT: $2,000

DEADLINE(S): JUL 1 (dental students); JUL 15 (hygiene assistant & lab technician)

FIELD(S): Dental, Dental Hygiene

ELIGIBILITY/REQUIREMENTS: Open to Hispanic U.S. students who have finished one year of dental school or a dental hygiene program. The student may be at any stage of the undergraduate program, second through fourth years, as long as one full year has been completed. Must have a minimum GPA of 3.0; have at least 1 parent of Hispanic descent; and show evi-

dence of community service, leadership and/or extracurricular activities. Winners may be asked to report on their activities and progress six months after receiving the scholarship.

HOW TO APPLY: Call to request application; e-mail lvaldivia@hdASSOCIATION.
org; or visit website.

NUMBER OF AWARDS: 4 (2 dental, 2 dental hygiene)

RENEWABLE: No

CONTACT: Rebecca Jeppesen, Executive Director

ADDITIONAL INFORMATION: Phone 800/852-7921; Fax 217/529-9120; E-Mail: hispanicdental@hdassoc.org.

1838—HISPANIC DENTAL ASSOCIATION FOUNDATION (Procter & Gamble Oral Care & HDA Foundation)

3085 Stevenson Drive, Suite 200
Springfield IL 62703
217/529-6517
FAX: 217/529-9120
E-mail: rjeppesen@hdassoc.org
Internet: http://www.hdassoc.org

AMOUNT: $500 and $1,000

DEADLINE(S): JUL 20

FIELD(S): All Dental Professions

ELIGIBILITY/REQUIREMENTS: Entry-level program; applicants must be accepted into a dental, dental hygiene program, dental assisting program, or dental technician program nationwide, during the academic year for which you are applying; have a minimum GPA of 3.0; have at least 1 parent of Hispanic descent; and show evidence of community service, leadership and/or extracurricular activities.

HOW TO APPLY: Call to request application; e-mail lvaldivia@hdASSOCIATION.
org; or visit website.

NUMBER OF AWARDS: Numerous

RENEWABLE: No

CONTACT: Rebecca Jeppesen, Executive Director

ADDITIONAL INFORMATION: Phone 800/852-7921; Fax 217/529-9120; E-Mail: hispanicdental@hdassoc.org

1839—INTERNATIONAL ORDER OF THE KING'S DAUGHTERS AND SONS (Health Careers Scholarships)

Health Careers Department
736 Ardmore Lane
Shelbyville KY 40065

AMOUNT: $1,000 (maximum)

DEADLINE(S): APR 1

FIELD(S): Medicine; Dentistry; Nursing; Physical Therapy; Occupational Therapy; Medical Technologies; Pharmacy

ELIGIBILITY/REQUIREMENTS: Must be U.S. or Canadian citizen, enrolled full time in a school accredited in the field involved and located in the U.S. or Canada. For all students, except those preparing for an RN degree, application must be for at least the third year of college. RN students must have completed the first year of schooling. Pre-med students are not eligible to apply. For those students seeking degrees of MD or DDS, application must be for at least the second year of medical or dental school. Each applicant must supply proof of acceptance in the school involved. There is no age limit.

HOW TO APPLY: Send SASE for an application between January 1 and March 15 with a letter stating the field of study and present level. Submit application with résumé, including personal statement as to the reason for selection of the chosen field and intentions for a career following graduation; letters of recommendation from at least 2 informed persons, with their identification and relationship to applicant made clear; up-to-date official transcripts from current school which MUST be mailed directly from the registrar office (if graduating on a pass/fail system, a statement is required from the Dean of Students or a professor in regard to academic progress); and an itemized budget, endorsed by the school Financial Aid officer, including: school and living expenses, income, loans, awards, family contributions, etc., for the current year and projected estimate for the next year.

RENEWABLE: Yes, for 2 additional years if qualified.

CONTACT: Ida Lyons, Director

1840—JEWISH FEDERATION OF METRO-POLITAN CHICAGO (Academic Scholarship Program/The Marcus and Theresa Levie Educational Fund)

One South Franklin Street
Chicago IL 60606
312/357-4521
FAX: 312/855-3282
E-mail: jvsscholarship@jvs
chicago.org
Internet: http://www.jvs/
chicago.org

AMOUNT: Varies
DEADLINE(S): FEB 15
FIELD(S): Medicine, Dentistry, Dental Hygiene, Nursing or Physicians' Assistant, Occupational Therapy,

Optometry, Clinical Psychology/Counseling, Education

ELIGIBILITY/REQUIREMENTS: Open to college juniors, seniors, and graduate students, or students in vocational training programs, who are Jewish and residents of Chicago or Cook County, Illinois. Academic achievement and financial need are considered.

HOW TO APPLY: Phone JVS Scholarship Secretary (312/673-3457), fax, or visit website (click on Scholarship Services) for an application in the Fall.

1841—JEWISH FEDERATION OF METRO-POLITAN CHICAGO (Academic Scholarship Program)

Jewish Vocational Service
216 West Jackson Blvd., Suite 700
Chicago IL 60606-6921
312/673-3400
FAX: 312/553-5544
TTY: 312/444-2877
E-mail: jvsscholarship@jvs
chicago.org
Internet: http://www.jvs/
chicago.org

AMOUNT: Varies
DEADLINE(S): FEB 15
FIELD(S): Mathematics, Engineering, Science, Medicine, Social Work, Education, Psychology, Rabbinate, Law (except corporate), Communications

ELIGIBILITY/REQUIREMENTS: Open to Jewish men and women legally domiciled in the greater Chicago metropolitan area, who are identified as having promise for significant contributions in their chosen careers, and are in need of financial assistance for full-time academic programs in above areas. Must have entered undergraduate junior year in career programs requiring no postgraduate education, be in graduate/professional school, or be in a vo-tech training program.

HOW TO APPLY: Phone JVS Scholarship Secretary (312/673-3457), fax, or visit website (click on Scholarship Services) for an application in the Fall. Interview required.

RENEWABLE: Yes

CONTACT: JVS Scholarship Secretary at 312/673-3457

1842—MASSAGE MAGAZINE

1636 West First Avenue, Suite 100
Spokane WA 99205
509/324-8117
FAX: 509/324-8606
E-mail: schools@massagemag.com

Internet: http://www.massage
mag.com

AMOUNT: $1,000
DEADLINE(S): Early DEC
FIELD(S): Massage Therapy

ELIGIBILITY/REQUIREMENTS: Be enrolled in school on deadline date; have completed 90 hours of training; attend a Massage Magazine Schools Program member (see website); maintain a B grade average; attendance record of 90% or better.

HOW TO APPLY: Applications available in September; call or download from website or request from member school.

NUMBER OF AWARDS: 5
RENEWABLE: No
CONTACT: Adrianna Webber

1843—NATIONAL ASSOCIATION OF AMERICAN BUSINESS CLUBS (AMBUCS Scholarships for Therapists)

P.O. Box 5127
High Point NC 27262
800/838-1845, ext. 10
FAX: 336/852-6830
E-mail: janiceb@ambucs.org
Internet: http://www.ambucs.org

AMOUNT: $500-$1,500, $6,000
DEADLINE(S): APR 15
FIELD(S): Physical Therapy, Music Therapy, Occupational Therapy, Speech-Language Pathology, Audiology

ELIGIBILITY/REQUIREMENTS: Open to undergraduate juniors and seniors or graduate students who have good scholastic standing and plan to enter the fields listed above. The institution to which you are accepted must present a curriculum accredited by the appropriate health/therapy profession authority. GPA of 3.0 or better (4.0 scale) and U.S. citizenship required. Must demonstrate financial need.

HOW TO APPLY: See website for additional information and application. MUST apply online. Semi-finalists must provide proof of enrollment, IRS Form 1040s, and a personal statement of not more than 1 page describing the development of your chosen field of therapy; your plan of study; career plans after graduation; and why financial assistance is needed. It is recommended, but not mandatory, that applicants seek sponsorship of an AMBUCS chapter, provided a chapter is located within a reasonable distance of your home or school.

RENEWABLE: Yes
NUMBER OF AWARDS: Multiple
CONTACT: Janice Blankenship, Membership/Scholarship Coordinator, 336/852-0052, ext. 10.

1844—PHYSICIAN ASSISTANT FOUNDATION

950 North Washington Street
Alexandria VA 22314
703/519-5686
FAX: 703/684-1924
E-mail: aapa@aapa.org
Internet: http://www.aapa.org
AMOUNT: $2,000
DEADLINE(S): JAN 15
FIELD(S): Physician Assistant
ELIGIBILITY/REQUIREMENTS: Must attend an accredited PA Program and be enrolled in the professional phase of their program and a student member of the AAPA. Based on financial need, academic record, community and professional activities, and future goals as a physician assistant.
HOW TO APPLY: Visit our website for application and submit with the PA Program Verification letter and other documentation.
NUMBER OF AWARDS: Varies
RENEWABLE: No
CONTACT: Francesca Rusk

1845—WESTERN MICHIGAN UNIVERSITY (College of Health and Human Services/Alma S. Boughey Occupational Therapy Scholarship)

1903 West Michigan
Kalamazoo MI 49008-5337
269/387-8777
FAX: 269/387-6989
E-mail: finaid-info@wmich.edu
Internet: http://www.wmich.edu/finaid
AMOUNT: Varies
DEADLINE(S): MAR 1
FIELD(S): Occupational Therapy
ELIGIBILITY/REQUIREMENTS: Given to junior and senior status students with 3.0 GPA majoring in occupational therapy. Must demonstrate financial need.
HOW TO APPLY: Contact the Occupational Therapy Department for application.

1846—WESTERN MICHIGAN UNIVERSITY (College of Health and Human Services/Don F. Thomas and Jane E. Thomas Scholarship)

1903 West Michigan
Kalamazoo MI 49008-5337
269/387-8777
FAX: 269/387-6989

E-mail: finaid-info@wmich.edu
Internet: http://www.wmich.edu/finaid
AMOUNT: Varies
DEADLINE(S): MAR 1
FIELD(S): Occupational Therapy
ELIGIBILITY/REQUIREMENTS Full- or part-time graduate or undergraduate student in the Occupational Therapy curriculum. Must show financial need and have progressed in OT training far enough to exhibit excellent potential for success.
HOW TO APPLY: Contact the Occupational Therapy Department for application.

1847—WESTERN MICHIGAN UNIVERSITY (College of Health and Human Services/Elissa Gatlin Scholarship)

1903 West Michigan
Kalamazoo MI 49008-5337
269/387-8777
FAX: 269/387-6989
E-mail: finaid-info@wmich.edu
Internet: http://www.wmich.edu/finaid
AMOUNT: $500/semester
DEADLINE(S): MAR 1
FIELD(S): Occupational Therapy; Nursing; Speech Pathology; Blind Rehabilitation; Social Work; Physician Assistant
ELIGIBILITY/REQUIREMENTS: Intended for minority students (African-Americans, Native American, or Hispanic American); 2.75 GPA for undergraduates, 3.00 GPA for graduates; must be enrolled in professional program, U.S. citizen, and demonstrate financial need.
HOW TO APPLY: Contact the College of Health and Human Services for an application.
NUMBER OF AWARDS: 2 (1 undergraduate; 1 graduate)
RENEWABLE: Yes. Maximum 2 years.

1848—WESTERN MICHIGAN UNIVERSITY (College of Health and Human Services/Helen Elizabeth Gibbens Physician Assistant Scholarship Fund)

1903 West Michigan
Kalamazoo MI 49008-5337
269/387-8777
FAX: 269/387-6989
E-mail: finaid-info@wmich.edu
Internet: http://www.wmich.edu/finaid
DEADLINE(S): MAR 1
FIELD(S): Physician Assistant

ELIGIBILITY/REQUIREMENTS: Given to a student enrolled in the physician assistant program who demonstrates financial need.
HOW TO APPLY: Contact the Physician Assistant Department for application.

1849—WESTERN MICHIGAN UNIVERSITY (College of Health and Human Services/Jeffrey and Barbara Vortman Scholarship

1903 West Michigan
Kalamazoo MI 49008-5337
269/387-8777
FAX: 269/387-6989
E-mail: finaid-info@wmich.edu
Internet: http://www.wmich.edu/finaid
AMOUNT: $500
DEADLINE(S): MAR 1
FIELD(S): Occupational Therapy; Nursing; Speech Pathology; Blind Rehabilitation; Social Work; Physician Assistant
ELIGIBILITY/REQUIREMENTS: Each year one of the departments/schools is responsible for awarding the scholarship to a student admitted to one of the professional programs in the College.
HOW TO APPLY: Contact the College of Health and Human Services for an application.
NUMBER OF AWARDS: 2 (1 undergraduate; 1 graduate)
RENEWABLE: Yes. Maximum 2 years.

1850—WESTERN MICHIGAN UNIVERSITY (College of Health and Human Services/John Josten Alumni Scholarships)

1903 West Michigan
Kalamazoo MI 49008-5337
269/387-8777
FAX: 269/387-6989
E-mail: finaid-info@wmich.edu
Internet: http://www.wmich.edu/finaid
DEADLINE(S): MAR 1
FIELD(S): Physician Assistant
ELIGIBILITY/REQUIREMENTS: Given to outstanding students who have demonstrated academic excellence (through 2 semesters of the Physician Assistant Programs) who demonstrate need.
HOW TO APPLY: Contact the Physician Assistant Department for application.

MEDICAL ADMINISTRATION

1851—AMERICAN COLLEGE OF MEDICAL PRACTICE EXECUTIVES

104 Inverness Terrace East
Englewood CO 80112-5306
303/799-1111
E-mail: acmpe@mgma.com
Internet: http:www.mgma.com
AMOUNT: $1,000-$3,000
DEADLINE(S): MAY 1
FIELD(S): Health Care
 Administration/Medical Practice
 Management
ELIGIBILITY/REQUIREMENTS: Open to undergraduate or graduate students pursuing a degree relevant to medical practice management at an accredited university or college.
HOW TO APPLY: See website for application (available in January of each year).
NUMBER OF AWARDS: Varies

1852—AMERICAN HEALTH INFORMATION MANAGEMENT ASSOCIATION (FORE Undergraduate Merit Scholarships)

Attn: Undergraduate Scholarships
233 North Michigan Ave.,
21st Floor
Chicago IL 60601-5800
312/233-1100
E-mail: fore@ahima.org
Internet: http://www.ahima.org
AMOUNT: $1,000-$5,000
DEADLINE(S): APR 25
FIELD(S): Health Information, Health
 Technology
ELIGIBILITY/REQUIREMENTS: Must be enrolled in CAHIIM accredited program and a member of AHIMA. Must have minimum GPA 3.0, taking a minimum of 6 credit hours or 8 quarter hours per semester, and have at least 1 full semester remaining after August 31. Volunteer and work experience, commitment to and suitability for the profession will be considered.
HOW TO APPLY: See website for additional information and application. Submit by mail with verification of enrollment form, 3 letters of references (educators and/or employers-at least 1 educator), official transcripts from the 3 most recent postsecondary institutions attended with past 10 years, and official checklist.
NUMBER OF AWARDS: Approximately 100
ADDITIONAL INFORMATION: Most scholarships are available to all eligible applicants. But a few have specific qualifications, see website for details.

1853—AMERICAN INDIAN SCIENCE AND ENGINEERING SOCIETY (Burlington Northern Santa Fe Pacific Foundation Scholarships)

P.O. Box 9828
Albuquerque NM 87119-9828
505/765-1052
FAX: 505/765-5608
E-mail: scholarships@aises.org
Internet: http://www.aises.org/
 highered
AMOUNT: $2,500
DEADLINE(S): MAR 31
FIELD(S): Business; Education; Science;
 Engineering; Health Administration
ELIGIBILITY/REQUIREMENTS: Open to high school seniors who are at least one quarter American Indian. Must reside in Kansas, Oklahoma, Colorado, Arizona, New Mexico, Minnesota, North Dakota, Oregon, South Dakota, Washington, Montana, or San Bernardino County, California (Burlington Northern and Santa Fe Pacific service areas). Must demonstrate financial need. Minimum GPA 2.0.
HOW TO APPLY: See website or contact Society for an application.
NUMBER OF AWARDS: 5
RENEWABLE: Yes. Up to 4 years.
CONTACT: Tina Pino

1854—AMERICAN MEDICAL TECHNOLOGISTS

10700 W. Higgins Road, Suite 150
Rosemont IL 60018
847/823-5169
FAX: 847/823-0458
E-mail: mail@amt1.com
Internet: www.amt1.com
AMOUNT: $500
DEADLINE(S): APR 1
FIELD(S): Medical Technologist; Medical
 Laboratory Technician; Medical
 Assistant; Medical Administrative
 Specialist; Dental Assisting; Office
 Laboratory Technician
ELIGIBILITY/REQUIREMENTS: Must be a graduate of, or a senior in, an accredited high school (GED acceptable). Must be enrolled in a school accredited by agency recognized by U.S. Department of Education, or enrolled in regionally accredited college or university in the U.S. Must pursue one of above careers.
HOW TO APPLY: See website for an application. Submit evidence of career goals, as well as financial need, transcripts, 2 letters of personal reference, and statement of why career chosen.
NUMBER OF AWARDS: 5
CONTACT: Linda Halblander, AMT Scholarship Program Coordinator

1855—AMERICAN SOCIETY FOR HEALTH-CARE FOOD SERVICE ADMINISTRATORS (Bonnie Miller Continuing Education Fund)

304 West Liberty Street,
Suite 201
Louisville KY 40202
800/620-6422
Internet: http://www.ashfsa.org
AMOUNT: $500 (part-time); $1,000 (full-time)
DEADLINE(S): MAR 1
FIELD(S): Healthcare Food Service
 Management
ELIGIBILITY/REQUIREMENTS: Open to undergraduate students at 2- or 4-year colleges.
HOW TO APPLY: Contact Society for an application.
CONTACT: Keith Howard

1856—EMPIRE COLLEGE (Dean's Scholarship)

3035 Cleveland Avenue
Santa Rosa CA 95403
707/546-4000
FAX: 707/546-4058
Internet: http://www.wmpcol.edu
AMOUNT: $250-$1,500
DEADLINE(S): APR 15
FIELD(S): Accounting; Office
 Administration; Paralegal; Medical
 (Clinical and Administrative);
 Tourism; Hospitality; General
 Business; Computer Assembly;
 Network Assembly/Administration;
 Security
ELIGIBILITY/REQUIREMENTS: Open to high school seniors who plan to attend Empire College. Must be U.S. citizen.
HOW TO APPLY: Contact College for an application.
NUMBER OF AWARDS: 10
RENEWABLE: No
CONTACT: Mary Farha

1857—INTERNATIONAL EXECUTIVE HOUSEKEEPERS ASSOCIATION EDUCATIONAL FOUNDATION, INC.

1001 Eastwind Drive, Suite 301
Westerville OH 43081-3361
800/200-6342
FAX: 614/895-1248
E-mail: excel@ieha.org

Internet: http://www.ieha.org
AMOUNT: $800
DEADLINE(S): JAN 10
FIELD(S): Healthcare, Hotels, Education Facilities, Rehabilitation Centers and related facilities
ELIGIBILITY/REQUIREMENTS: Open to members enrolled in a program of study leading to IEHA certification.
HOW TO APPLY: Submit original manuscript (no more than 1,000 words) regarding housekeeping within any industry segment as noted.
NUMBER OF AWARDS: Multiple
RENEWABLE: No

MEDICAL-RELATED DISCIPLINES

1858—AABB (Suzanne Ledin Travel Award)

8101 Glenbrook Road
Bethesda MD 20814-2749
301/907-6977
FAX: 301/907-6895
E-mail: tzein@abba.org
Internet: http://www.alphachi honor.org
AMOUNT: $1,500 travel grant
DEADLINE(S): JUL 1
FIELD(S): Blood Banking
ELIGIBILITY/REQUIREMENTS: Must be enrolled in or recently graduated from (past 12 months) an accredited specialist in blood banking (SBB) program.
HOW TO APPLY: See website for information and application. Submit by mail along with an essay focusing on the vision of being an SBB certified professional, incorporating how you became interest in the profession, how to increase awareness of the profession, ideas regarding recruitment of future SBBs, and vision for the profession in the next 10 years. along with a current résumé, SBB Coordinator/Director letter of support and assessment questionnaire.
NUMBER OF AWARDS: 2 SBBs, 2 transfusion medicine
RENEWABLE: No
CONTACT: Tamara Zein, 240/333-6604
ADDITIONAL INFORMATION: Must attend the current year's AABB Annual meeting to receive the award.

1859—AMERICAN FOUNDATION FOR THE BLIND (Rudolph Dillman Society)

11 Penn Plaza, Suite 300
New York NY 10001

212/502-7661
FAX: 212/502-7771
E-mail: afbinfo@afb.net
Internet: http://www.afb.org/ scholar/scholarships.asp
AMOUNT: $2,500
DEADLINE(S): MAR 31
FIELD(S): Rehabilitation/Education of Blind or Visually Impaired
ELIGIBILITY/REQUIREMENTS: Undergraduate or graduate students who are studying in the field of rehabilitation and/or education of persons who are blind or visually impaired. One of these grants is specifically for a student who meets all requirements and submits evidence of economic need.
HOW TO APPLY: Must submit official transcripts, proof of acceptance, evidence of economic need (if applicable), 3 letters of recommendation, proof of legal blindness, proof of U.S. citizenship, and a typewritten statement of no more than 3 double-spaced pages describing the field of study you are pursuing, educational or personal goals, work experience, extracurricular activities and how the scholarship award will be used. See website or contact AFB for an application.
NUMBER OF AWARDS: 4
RENEWABLE: No
CONTACT: Alina Vayntrub

1860—AMERICAN SOCIETY OF SAFETY ENGINEERS (ASSE) FOUNDATION (America Responds Memorial Scholarship)

1800 East Oakton Street
Des Plaines IL 60018-2187
847/699-2929
FAX: 847/296-3769
Internet: http://www.asse.org/ foundation
AMOUNT: $1,000
DEADLINE(S): DEC 1
FIELD(S): Occupational Safety & Health or closely related fields
ELIGIBILITY/REQUIREMENTS: Must be an ASSE student member; a U.S. citizen, in good academic standing; have completed at least 60 semester hours; and have an overall GPA of at least 3.0.
HOW TO APPLY: See website or contact Customer Service Department for application. Submit with letter from safety faculty member; and essay of 300 words or less that explains why you are seeking a degree in occupational safety & health or closely related field, briefly describes current activities and how they relate to career goal and objective, and states why you believe you should receive this scholarship (e.g., career goals, financial need, etc.).

NUMBER OF AWARDS: 1
RENEWABLE: No
CONTACT: Adele Gabanski
ADDITIONAL INFORMATION: To obtain an application for membership ($15/year), contact ASSE's Customer Service department at or download the application at http://www.asse.org/membership/become a member.php.

1861—AMERICAN SOCIETY OF SAFETY ENGINEERS (ASSE) FOUNDATION (ASSE Construction Safety Scholarship)

1800 East Oakton Street
Des Plaines IL 60018-2187
847/699-2929
FAX: 847/296-3769
Internet: http://www.asse.org/ foundation
AMOUNT: $1,000
DEADLINE(S): DEC 1
FIELD(S): Occupational Safety & Health, with an emphasis on Construction Safety
ELIGIBILITY/REQUIREMENTS: Must be an ASSE student member; a U.S. citizen, in good academic standing; have completed at least 60 semester hours; and have an overall GPA of at least 3.0.
HOW TO APPLY: See website or contact Customer Service for an application. Submit with reference letter by safety faculty member; and essay of 300 words or less that explains why you are seeking a degree in occupational safety & health or closely related field, briefly describes current activities and how they relate to career goal and objective, and states why you believe you should receive this scholarship (e.g., career goals, financial need, etc.).
NUMBER OF AWARDS: 1
RENEWABLE: No
CONTACT: Adele Gabanski
ADDITIONAL INFORMATION: To obtain an application for membership ($15/year), contact ASSE's Customer Service department at or download the application at http://www.asse.org/membership/become a member.php.

1862—AMERICAN SOCIETY OF SAFETY ENGINEERS (ASSE) FOUNDATION (ASSE Diversity Committee Scholarship)

1800 East Oakton Street
Des Plaines IL 60018-2187
847/699-2929
FAX: 847/296-3769
Internet: http://www.asse.org/ foundation
AMOUNT: $1,000
DEADLINE(S): DEC 1

FIELD(S): Occupational Safety & Health, with an emphasis on Construction Safety

ELIGIBILITY/REQUIREMENTS: Open to any individual regardless of race, ethnicity, gender, religion, personal beliefs, age, sexual orientation, physical challenges, geographic location, university or specific area of study. Must be an ASSE student member; a U.S. citizen, in good academic standing; have completed at least 60 semester hours; and have an overall GPA of at least 3.0.

HOW TO APPLY: See website or contaact Customer Service for an application. Submit with reference letter by safety faculty member; and essay of 300 words or less that explains why you are seeking a degree in occupational safety & health or closely related field, briefly describes current activities and how they relate to career goal and objective, and states why you believe you should receive this scholarship (e.g., career goals, financial need, etc.).

NUMBER OF AWARDS: 1

RENEWABLE: No

CONTACT: Adele Gabanski

ADDITIONAL INFORMATION: To obtain an application for membership ($15/year), contact ASSE's Customer Service department at or download the application at http://www.asse.org/membership/become a member.php.

1863—AMERICAN SOCIETY OF SAFETY ENGINEERS (ASSE) FOUNDATION (Bechtel Group Foundation Scholarship Program for Safety & Health, The)

1800 East Oakton Street
Des Plaines IL 60018-2187
847/699-2929
FAX: 847/296-3769
Internet: http://www.asse.org/foundation

AMOUNT: $8,000

DEADLINE(S): DEC 1

FIELD(S): Occupational Safety & Health, with an emphasis on Construction Safety

ELIGIBILITY/REQUIREMENTS: Must be an ASSE student member; a U.S. citizen, in good academic standing; have completed at least 60 semester hours; and have an overall GPA of at least 3.0.

HOW TO APPLY: See website or contaact Customer Service for an application. Submit with reference letter by safety faculty member; and essay of 300 words or less that explains why you are seeking a degree in occupational safety & health or closely related field, briefly describes current activities and how they relate to career goal and objective, and states why you

believe you should receive this scholarship (e.g., career goals, financial need, etc.).

NUMBER OF AWARDS: 1

RENEWABLE: No

CONTACT: Maria Rosario
Adele Gabanski

ADDITIONAL INFORMATION: To obtain an application for membership ($15/year), contact ASSE's Customer Service department at or download the application at http://www.asse.org/membership/become a member.php

1864—AMERICAN SOCIETY OF SAFETY ENGINEERS (ASSE) FOUNDATION (Central Indiana ASSE Scholarship)

1800 East Oakton Street
Des Plaines IL 60018-2187
847/699-2929
FAX: 847/296-3769
Internet: http://www.asse.org/foundation

AMOUNT: $1,000

DEADLINE(S): DEC 1

FIELD(S): Occupational Safety & Health, with an emphasis on Construction Safety

ELIGIBILITY/REQUIREMENTS: Must be an ASSE student member; a U.S. citizen, in good academic standing; have completed at least 60 semester hours; and have an overall GPA of at least 3.0. Priority will be given to Indiana residents attending school in Indiana or anywhere in the U.S. or to non-residents attending an Indiana university.

HOW TO APPLY: See website or contaact Customer Service for an application. Submit with reference letter by safety faculty member; and essay of 300 words or less that explains why you are seeking a degree in occupational safety & health or closely related field, briefly describes current activities and how they relate to career goal and objective, and states why you believe you should receive this scholarship (e.g., career goals, financial need, etc.).

NUMBER OF AWARDS: 1

RENEWABLE: No

CONTACT: Adele Gabanski

ADDITIONAL INFORMATION: To obtain an application for membership ($15/year), contact ASSE's Customer Service department at or download the application at http://www.asse.org/membership/become a member.php.

1865—AMERICAN SOCIETY OF SAFETY ENGINEERS (ASSE) FOUNDATION (C N A Foundation Scholarship)

1800 East Oakton Street

Des Plaines IL 60018-2187
847/699-2929
FAX: 847/296-3769
Internet: http://www.asse.org/foundation

AMOUNT: $4,000

DEADLINE(S): DEC 1

FIELD(S): Occupational Safety & Health, with an emphasis on Construction Safety

ELIGIBILITY/REQUIREMENTS: Must be an ASSE student member; a U.S. citizen, in good academic standing; have completed at least 60 semester hours; and have an overall GPA of at least 3.0.

HOW TO APPLY: See website or contaact Customer Service for an application. Submit with reference letter by safety faculty member; and essay of 300 words or less that explains why you are seeking a degree in occupational safety & health or closely related field, briefly describes current activities and how they relate to career goal and objective, and states why you believe you should receive this scholarship (e.g., career goals, financial need, etc.).

NUMBER OF AWARDS: 2

RENEWABLE: No

CONTACT: Adele Gabanski

ADDITIONAL INFORMATION: To obtain an application for membership ($15/year), contact ASSE's Customer Service department at or download the application at http://www.asse.org/membership/become a member.php.

1866—AMERICAN SOCIETY OF SAFETY ENGINEERS (ASSE) FOUNDATION (David Iden Memorial Safety Scholarship sponsored by UPS)

1800 East Oakton Street
Des Plaines IL 60018-2187
847/699-2929
FAX: 847/296-3769
Internet: http://www.asse.org/foundation

AMOUNT: $5,250

DEADLINE(S): DEC 1

FIELD(S): Occupational Safety & Health or a closely related field

ELIGIBILITY/REQUIREMENTS: Must be an ASSE student member; in good academic standing; have completed at least 60 semester hours; and have an overall GPA of at least 3.0.

HOW TO APPLY: Send application; reference letter by safety faculty member; and essay of 300 words or less that explains why you are seeking a degree in occupational safety & health or closely related field, briefly describes current activities and how they relate to career goal and objective, and states why you believe you should receive this scholarship (e.g., career goals, financial need, etc.).

NUMBER OF AWARDS: 4
RENEWABLE: No
CONTACT: Adele Gabanski
ADDITIONAL INFORMATION: (1) To obtain an application for membership ($15/year), contact ASSE's Customer Service department at or download the application at http://www.asse.org/membership/become a member.php. (2) Students will also be provided with the opportunity to attend annual conference.

1867—AMERICAN SOCIETY OF SAFETY ENGINEERS (ASSE) FOUNDATION (George Gustafson HSE Memorial Scholarship sponsored by the Texas Safety Foundation)

1800 East Oakton Street
Des Plaines IL 60018-2187
847/699-2929
FAX: 847/296-3769
Internet: http://www.asse.org/foundation
AMOUNT: $4,000
DEADLINE(S): DEC 1
FIELD(S): Occupational Safety & Health, with an emphasis on Construction Safety

ELIGIBILITY/REQUIREMENTS: Must be an ASSE student member; a U.S. citizen, in good academic standing; have completed at least 60 semester hours; and have an overall GPA of at least 3.0. Priority will be given to students from Texas attending a Texas university.

HOW TO APPLY: See website or contaact Customer Service for an application. Submit with reference letter by safety faculty member; and essay of 300 words or less that explains why you are seeking a degree in occupational safety & health or closely related field, briefly describes current activities and how they relate to career goal and objective, and states why you believe you should receive this scholarship (e.g., career goals, financial need, etc.).

NUMBER OF AWARDS: 1
RENEWABLE: No
CONTACT: Adele Gabanski
ADDITIONAL INFORMATION: To obtain an application for membership ($15/year), contact ASSE's Customer Service department at or download the application at http://www.asse.org/membership/become a member.php.

1868—AMERICAN SOCIETY OF SAFETY ENGINEERS (ASSE) FOUNDATION (Georgia Chapter of ASSE Annual Scholarship, The)

1800 East Oakton Street

Des Plaines IL 60018-2187
847/699-2929
FAX: 847/296-3769
Internet: http://www.asse.org/foundation
AMOUNT: $1,000
DEADLINE(S): DEC 1
FIELD(S): Occupational Safety & Health or a closely related field

ELIGIBILITY/REQUIREMENTS: Must reside in a county within the ASSE Georgia Chapter; enrolled at a college or university in Georgia; an ASSE student member; in good academic standing; have completed at least 60 semester hours; and have an overall GPA of at least 3.0.

HOW TO APPLY: See website or contaact Customer Service for an application. Submit with reference letter by safety faculty member; and essay of 300 words or less that explains why you are seeking a degree in occupational safety & health or closely related field, briefly describes current activities and how they relate to career goal and objective, and states why you believe you should receive this scholarship (e.g., career goals, financial need, etc.).

NUMBER OF AWARDS: 1
RENEWABLE: No
CONTACT: Adele Gabanski
ADDITIONAL INFORMATION: To obtain an application for membership ($15/year), contact ASSE's Customer Service department at or download the application at http://www.asse.org/membership/become a member.php.

1869—AMERICAN SOCIETY OF SAFETY ENGINEERS (ASSE) FOUNDATION (Gold Country Section & Region II Scholarship)

1800 East Oakton Street
Des Plaines IL 60018-2187
847/699-2929
FAX: 847/296-3769
Internet: http://www.asse.org/foundation
AMOUNT: $1,000
DEADLINE(S): DEC 1
FIELD(S): Occupational Safety & Health or a closely related field

ELIGIBILITY/REQUIREMENTS: Must be an ASSE student member; be in good academic standing; have completed at least 60 semester hours; and have an overall GPA of at least 3.0. Priority will be given to students who reside in the Region II area (i.e., Montana, Idaho, Wyoming, Colorado, Utah, Nevada, Arizona, New Mexico).

HOW TO APPLY: See website or contact Customer Service Department for applica-

tion. Submit with reference letter by safety faculty member; and essay of 300 words or less that explains why you are seeking a degree in occupational safety & health or closely related field, briefly describes current activities and how they relate to career goal and objective, and states why you believe you should receive this scholarship (e.g., career goals, financial need, etc.).

NUMBER OF AWARDS: 1
RENEWABLE: No
CONTACT: Adele Gabanski
ADDITIONAL INFORMATION: To obtain an application for membership ($15/year), contact ASSE's Customer Service department at or download the application at http://www.asse.org/membership/become a member.php.

1870—AMERICAN SOCIETY OF SAFETY ENGINEERS (ASSE) FOUNDATION (Greater Baton Rouge Chapter-Don Jones Excellence in Safety Scholarship)

1800 East Oakton Street
Des Plaines IL 60018-2187
847/699-2929
FAX: 847/296-3769
Internet: http://www.asse.org/foundation
AMOUNT: $1,000
DEADLINE(S): DEC 1
FIELD(S): Occupational Safety & Health or a closely related field

ELIGIBILITY/REQUIREMENTS: Open to part-time or full-time students; priority given to students attending Southeastern Louisiana University in Hammond then to those attending any college or university within Louisiana or within the southeast U.S. region (in that order); part-time students must be an ASSE general or professional, all others must be student members; be in good academic standing; have completed at least 60 semester hours; and have an overall GPA of at least 3.0.

HOW TO APPLY: See website or contact Customer Service Department for application. Submit with reference letter by safety faculty member; and essay of 300 words or less that explains why you are seeking a degree in occupational safety & health or closely related field, briefly describes current activities and how they relate to career goal and objective, and states why you believe you should receive this scholarship (e.g., career goals, financial need, etc.).

NUMBER OF AWARDS: 1
RENEWABLE: No
CONTACT: Adele Gabanski
ADDITIONAL INFORMATION: To obtain an application for membership ($15/year), contact ASSE's Customer

Service department at or download the application at http://www.asse.org/membership/become a member.php.

1871—AMERICAN SOCIETY OF SAFETY ENGINEERS (ASSE) FOUNDATION (Greater Boston Chapter Leadership Award)

1800 East Oakton Street
Des Plaines IL 60018-2187
847/699-2929
FAX: 847/296-3769
Internet: http://www.asse.org/foundation
AMOUNT: $1,000 and $2,000
DEADLINE(S): DEC 1
FIELD(S): Occupational Safety & Health, with an emphasis on Construction Safety
ELIGIBILITY/REQUIREMENTS: Must be a member of any ASSE chapter in New England including Greater Boston, Connecticut Valley, Granite State, Maine, Nutmeg or Worcester County, or an immediate family member (spouse or child) of any ASSE chapter member in New England or, a member of any ASSE student section in New England. Must be a U.S. citizen, in good academic standing; have completed at least 60 semester hours; and have an overall GPA of at least 3.0.
HOW TO APPLY: See website or contaact Customer Service for an application. Submit with reference letter by safety faculty member; and essay of 300 words or less that explains why you are seeking a degree in occupational safety & health or closely related field, briefly describes current activities and how they relate to career goal and objective, and states why you believe you should receive this scholarship (e.g., career goals, financial need, etc.).
NUMBER OF AWARDS: 2 (1 each)
RENEWABLE: Yes
CONTACT: Adele Gabanski
ADDITIONAL INFORMATION: To obtain an application for membership ($15/year), contact ASSE's Customer Service department at or download the application at http://www.asse.org/membership/become a member.php.

1872—AMERICAN SOCIETY OF SAFETY ENGINEERS (ASSE) FOUNDATION (Gulf Coast Past President's Scholarship)

1800 East Oakton Street
Des Plaines IL 60018-2187
847/699-2929
FAX: 847/296-3769
Internet: http://www.asse.org/foundation
AMOUNT: $1,000

DEADLINE(S): DEC 1
FIELD(S): Occupational Safety & Health or a closely related field
ELIGIBILITY/REQUIREMENTS: Must be a part- or full-time student; an ASSE student member (if part-time student); in good academic standing; have completed at least 60 semester hours; and have an overall GPA of at least 3.0.
HOW TO APPLY: See website or contact Customer Service Department for application. Submit with reference letter from safety faculty member; and essay of 300 words or less that explains why you are seeking a degree in occupational safety & health or closely related field, briefly describes current activities and how they relate to career goal and objective, and states why you believe you should receive this scholarship (e.g., career goals, financial need, etc.).
NUMBER OF AWARDS: 2
RENEWABLE: No
CONTACT: Adele Gabanski
ADDITIONAL INFORMATION: To obtain an application for membership ($15/year), contact ASSE's Customer Service department at or download the application at http://www.asse.org/membership/become a member.php.

1873—AMERICAN SOCIETY OF SAFETY ENGINEERS (ASSE) FOUNDATION (Harold F. Polston Scholarship sponsored by the Middle Tennessee Chapter)

1800 East Oakton Street
Des Plaines IL 60018-2187
847/699-2929
FAX: 847/296-3769
Internet: http://www.asse.org/foundation
AMOUNT: $2,000
DEADLINE(S): DEC 1
FIELD(S): Occupational Safety & Health, with an emphasis on Construction Safety
ELIGIBILITY/REQUIREMENTS: Priority will be given to students that belong to the Middle Tennessee Chapter, attending Middle Tennessee State University in Murfreesboro, TN, Murray State University in Murray, KY and those that live in the Region VII (in that order). Must be a U.S. citizen, in good academic standing; have completed at least 60 semester hours; and have an overall GPA of at least 3.0.
HOW TO APPLY: See website or contaact Customer Service for an application. Submit with reference letter by safety faculty member; and essay of 300 words or less that explains why you are seeking a degree

in occupational safety & health or closely related field, briefly describes current activities and how they relate to career goal and objective, and states why you believe you should receive this scholarship (e.g., career goals, financial need, etc.).
NUMBER OF AWARDS: 1
RENEWABLE: No
CONTACT: Adele Gabanski
ADDITIONAL INFORMATION: To obtain an application for membership ($15/year), contact ASSE's Customer Service department at or download the application at http://www.asse.org/membership/become a member.php.

1874—AMERICAN SOCIETY OF SAFETY ENGINEERS (ASSE) FOUNDATION (Harry Taback 9/11 Memorial Scholarship)

1800 East Oakton Street
Des Plaines IL 60018-2187
847/699-2929
FAX: 847/296-3769
Internet: http://www.asse.org/foundation
AMOUNT: $1,000
DEADLINE(S): DEC 1
FIELD(S): Occupational Safety & Health, with an emphasis on Construction Safety
ELIGIBILITY/REQUIREMENTS: Must be a U.S. citizen, in good academic standing; have completed at least 60 semester hours; and have an overall GPA of at least 3.0.
HOW TO APPLY: See website or contaact Customer Service for an application. Submit with reference letter by safety faculty member; and essay of 300 words or less that explains why you are seeking a degree in occupational safety & health or closely related field, briefly describes current activities and how they relate to career goal and objective, and states why you believe you should receive this scholarship (e.g., career goals, financial need, etc.).
NUMBER OF AWARDS: 1
RENEWABLE: No
CONTACT: Adele Gabanski
ADDITIONAL INFORMATION: To obtain an application for membership ($15/year), contact ASSE's Customer Service department at or download the application at http://www.asse.org/membership/become a member.php.

1875—AMERICAN SOCIETY OF SAFETY ENGINEERS (ASSE) FOUNDATION (Karl A. Jacobson, CSP Distinguished Service Award Scholarship)

1800 East Oakton Street

Des Plaines IL 60018-2187
847/699-2929
FAX: 847/296-3769
Internet: http://www.asse.org/
foundation
AMOUNT: $2,000
DEADLINE(S): DEC 1
FIELD(S): Occupational Safety & Health,
with an emphasis on Construction
Safety
ELIGIBILITY/REQUIREMENTS: Must
be a U.S. citizen, in good academic standing; have completed at least 60 semester
hours; and have an overall GPA of at least
3.0.
HOW TO APPLY: See website or contaact Customer Service for an application.
Submit with reference letter by safety faculty member; and essay of 300 words or
less that explains why you are seeking a
degree in occupational safety & health or
closely related field, briefly describes current activities and how they relate to career
goal and objective, and states why you
believe you should receive this scholarship
(e.g., career goals, financial need, etc.).
NUMBER OF AWARDS: 2 (1 each)
RENEWABLE: No
CONTACT: Adele Gabanski
ADDITIONAL INFORMATION: To
obtain an application for membership
($15/year), contact ASSE's Customer
Service department at or download the
application at http://www.asse.org/mem-
bership/become a member.php.

1876—AMERICAN SOCIETY OF SAFETY ENGINEERS (ASSE) FOUNDATION (Liberty Mutual Scholarship)

1800 East Oakton Street
Des Plaines IL 60018-2187
847/699-2929
FAX: 847/296-3769
Internet: http://www.asse.org/
foundation
AMOUNT: $3,000
DEADLINE(S): DEC 1
FIELD(S): Occupational Safety & Health
or a closely related field
ELIGIBILITY/REQUIREMENTS: Must
be an ASSE student member; be in good
academic standing; have completed at least
60 semester hours; and have an overall
GPA of at least 3.0.
HOW TO APPLY: See website or contact
Customer Service Department for application. Submit with reference letter by safety
faculty member; and essay of 300 words or
less that explains why you are seeking a
degree in occupational safety & health or
closely related field, briefly describes current activities and how they relate to career

goal and objective, and states why you
believe you should receive this scholarship
(e.g., career goals, financial need, etc.).
NUMBER OF AWARDS: 2
RENEWABLE: No
CONTACT: Adele Gabanski
ADDITIONAL INFORMATION: (1) To
obtain an application for membership
($15/year), contact ASSE's Customer
Service department at or download the
application at http://www.asse.org/mem-
bership/become a member.php. (2)
Students will also be provided with the
opportunity to attend annual conference.

1877—AMERICAN SOCIETY OF SAFETY ENGINEERS (ASSE) FOUNDATION (Marsh Risk-Consulting Scholarship)

1800 East Oakton Street
Des Plaines IL 60018-2187
847/699-2929
FAX: 847/296-3769
Internet: http://www.asse.org
foundation
AMOUNT: $1,000
DEADLINE(S): DEC 1
FIELD(S): Occupational Safety & Health
or a closely related field
ELIGIBILITY/REQUIREMENTS: Must
be an ASSE student member; be in good
academic standing; have completed at least
60 semester hours; and have an overall
GPA of at least 3.0.
HOW TO APPLY: See website or contact
Customer Service Department for application. Submit with reference letter by safety
faculty member; and essay of 300 words or
less that explains why you are seeking a
degree in occupational safety & health or
closely related field, briefly describes current activities and how they relate to career
goal and objective, and states why you
believe you should receive this scholarship
(e.g., career goals, financial need, etc.).
NUMBER OF AWARDS: 1
RENEWABLE: No
CONTACT: Adele Gabanski
ADDITIONAL INFORMATION: To
obtain an application for membership
($15/year), contact ASSE's Customer
Service department at or download the
application at http://www.asse.org/mem-
bership/become a member.php.

1878—AMERICAN SOCIETY OF SAFETY ENGINEERS (ASSE) FOUNDATION (Medina Scholarship for Hispanics in Safety)

1800 East Oakton Street
Des Plaines IL 60018-2187
847/699-2929
FAX: 847/296-3769

Internet: http://www.asse.org/
foundation
AMOUNT: $2,000
DEADLINE(S): DEC 1
FIELD(S): Occupational Safety & Health,
with an emphasis on Construction
Safety
ELIGIBILITY/REQUIREMENTS: Open
to bilingual student (Spanish-English);
Hispanic ethnicity preferred. Must be a
U.S. citizen, in good academic standing;
have completed at least 60 semester hours;
and have an overall GPA of at least 3.0.
Attendance at an ASAC/ABET-accredit-
ed program preferred.
HOW TO APPLY: See website or contaact Customer Service for an application.
Submit with reference letter by safety faculty member; and essay of 300 words or
less that explains why you are seeking a
degree in occupational safety & health or
closely related field, briefly describes current activities and how they relate to career
goal and objective, and states why you
believe you should receive this scholarship
(e.g., career goals, financial need, etc.).
NUMBER OF AWARDS: 2
RENEWABLE: Yes
CONTACT: Adele Gabanski
ADDITIONAL INFORMATION: To
obtain an application for membership
($15/year), contact ASSE's Customer
Service department at or download the
application at http://www.asse.org/mem-
bership/become a member.php.

1879—AMERICAN SOCIETY OF SAFETY ENGINEERS (ASSE) FOUNDATION (Northeastern Illinois Chapter Scholarship)

1800 East Oakton Street
Des Plaines IL 60018-2187
847/699-2929
FAX: 847/296-3769
Internet: http://www.asse.org
foundation
AMOUNT: $2,000
DEADLINE(S): DEC 1
FIELD(S): Occupational Safety & Health
or a closely related field
ELIGIBILITY/REQUIREMENTS: Must
be an ASSE student member; be in good
academic standing; have completed at least
60 semester hours; and have an overall
GPA of at least 3.0. Priority will be given
to applicants attending school in the northeastern Illinois region, including Illinois
and Wisconsin.
HOW TO APPLY: See website or contact
Customer Service Department for application. Submit with reference letter from
safety faculty member; and essay of 300
words or less that explains why you are

seeking a degree in occupational safety & health or closely related field, briefly describes current activities and how they relate to career goal and objective, and states why you believe you should receive this scholarship (e.g., career goals, financial need, etc.).
NUMBER OF AWARDS: 2
RENEWABLE: No
CONTACT: Adele Gabanski
ADDITIONAL INFORMATION: To obtain an application for membership ($15/year), contact ASSE's Customer Service department at or download the application at http://www.asse.org/membership/become a member.php.

1880—AMERICAN SOCIETY OF SAFETY ENGINEERS (ASSE) FOUNDATION (North Florida Chapter Safety Education Scholarship)

1800 East Oakton Street
Des Plaines IL 60018-2187
847/699-2929
FAX: 847/296-3769
Internet: http://www.asse.org foundation
AMOUNT: $1,000
DEADLINE(S): DEC 1
FIELD(S): Occupational Safety & Health, with an emphasis on Construction Safety
ELIGIBILITY/REQUIREMENTS: Must be a U.S. citizen, in good academic standing; have completed at least 60 semester hours; and have an overall GPA of at least 3.0. Priority given to part-time or full-time students that belong to the North Florida Chapter, full-time students that attend any Florida college or university or to full-time students that attend an ASAC/ABET accredited program nationwide (in that order). Part-time students must be ASSE general or professional member; full-time members must be student members.
HOW TO APPLY: See website or contact Customer Service for an application. Submit with reference letter by safety faculty member; and essay of 300 words or less that explains why you are seeking a degree in occupational safety & health or closely related field, briefly describes current activities and how they relate to career goal and objective, and states why you believe you should receive this scholarship (e.g., career goals, financial need, etc.).
NUMBER OF AWARDS: 1
RENEWABLE: No
CONTACT: Adele Gabanski
ADDITIONAL INFORMATION: To obtain an application for membership ($15/year), contact ASSE's Customer

Service department at or download the application at http://www.asse.org/membership/become a member.php.

1881—AMERICAN SOCIETY OF SAFETY ENGINEERS (ASSE) FOUNDATION (PDC Scholarship sponsored by the Practice Specialty Groups)

1800 East Oakton Street
Des Plaines IL 60018-2187
847/699-2929
FAX: 847/296-3769
Internet: http://www.asse.org foundation
AMOUNT: $1,200
DEADLINE(S): DEC 1
FIELD(S): Occupational Safety & Health, with an emphasis on Construction Safety
ELIGIBILITY/REQUIREMENTS: Must be a U.S. citizen, in good academic standing; have completed at least 60 semester hours; and have an overall GPA of at least 3.0.
HOW TO APPLY: See website or contaact Customer Service for an application. Submit with reference letter by safety faculty member; and essay of 300 words or less that explains why you are seeking a degree in occupational safety & health or closely related field, briefly describes current activities and how they relate to career goal and objective, and states why you believe you should receive this scholarship (e.g., career goals, financial need, etc.).
NUMBER OF AWARDS: 2
RENEWABLE: Yes
CONTACT: Adele Gabanski
ADDITIONAL INFORMATION: (1) To obtain an application for membership ($15/year), contact ASSE's Customer Service department at or download the application at http://www.asse.org/membership/become a member.php. (2) Full ASSE Professional Development Conference experience including airfare, hotel, meals and registration also provided.

1882—AMERICAN SOCIETY OF SAFETY ENGINEERS (ASSE) FOUNDATION (Scott Dominguez-Craters of the Moon Chapter Scholarship)

1800 East Oakton Street
Des Plaines IL 60018-2187
847/699-2929
FAX: 847/296-3769
Internet: http://www.asse.org foundation
AMOUNT: $1,000
DEADLINE(S): DEC 1

FIELD(S): Occupational Safety & Health or a closely related field
ELIGIBILITY/REQUIREMENTS: Must be an ASSE student member; a part- or full-time student in good academic standing; have completed at least 60 semester hours; and have an overall GPA of at least 3.0. Priority is given to applicants who reside in the Craters of the Moon, Idaho, and Region II (i.e., Montana, Idaho, Wyoming, Colorado, Utah, Nevada, Arizona, New Mexico). Priority is also given to applicants who are employees or dependents of employees of a sponsoring organization, serving the country through active duty in the armed forces or honorably discharged, members of the Boy or Girl Scouts, FFA, 4H, etc., and recipients of awards from service organizations, those who have served an ASSE chapter in a leadership role. Part-time students must be ASSE general or professional members; others must be student members.
HOW TO APPLY: See website or contact Customer Service Department for application. Submit with reference letter by safety faculty member; and essay of 300 words or less that explains why you are seeking a degree in occupational safety & health or closely related field, briefly describes current activities and how they relate to career goal and objective, and states why you believe you should receive this scholarship (e.g., career goals, financial need, etc.).
NUMBER OF AWARDS: 1
RENEWABLE: No
CONTACT: Adele Gabanski
ADDITIONAL INFORMATION: To obtain an application for membership ($15/year), contact ASSE's Customer Service department at or download the application at http://www.asse.org/membership/become a member.php.

1883—AMERICAN SOCIETY OF SAFETY ENGINEERS (ASSE) FOUNDATION (Southwest Chapter Roy Kinslow Scholarship)

1800 East Oakton Street
Des Plaines IL 60018-2187
847/699-2929
FAX: 847/296-3769
Internet: http://www.asse.org foundation
AMOUNT: $1,000
DEADLINE(S): DEC 1
FIELD(S): Occupational Safety & Health, with an emphasis on Construction Safety
ELIGIBILITY/REQUIREMENTS: Must be a U.S. citizen, in good academic standing; have completed at least 60 semester

hours; and have an overall GPA of at least 3.0. Open to members attending Southeastern Oklahoma State University in Durant, OK or be a member of the Southwest Chapter area attending a school within the Region III boundaries.

HOW TO APPLY: See website or contaact Customer Service for an application. Submit with reference letter by safety faculty member; and essay of 300 words or less that explains why you are seeking a degree in occupational safety & health or closely related field, briefly describes current activities and how they relate to career goal and objective, and states why you believe you should receive this scholarship (e.g., career goals, financial need, etc.).

NUMBER OF AWARDS: 1

RENEWABLE: No

CONTACT: Adele Gabanski

ADDITIONAL INFORMATION: (1) To obtain an application for membership ($15/year), contact ASSE's Customer Service department at or download the application at http://www.asse.org/membership/become a member.php. (2) Full ASSE Professional Development Conference experience including airfare, hotel, meals and registration also provided.

1884—AMERICAN SOCIETY OF SAFETY ENGINEERS (ASSE) FOUNDATION (UPS Diversity Scholarship)

1800 East Oakton Street
Des Plaines IL 60018-2187
847/699-2929
FAX: 847/296-3769
Internet: http://www.asse.org foundation

AMOUNT: $5,250

DEADLINE(S): DEC 1

FIELD(S): Occupational Safety & Health or a closely related field

ELIGIBILITY/REQUIREMENTS: Must be of a minority ethnic or racial group; a U.S. citizen; an ASSE student member; in good academic standing; have completed at least 60 semester hours; and have an overall GPA of at least 3.0.

HOW TO APPLY: See website or contact Customer Service Department for application. Submit with reference letter by safety faculty member; and essay of 300 words or less that explains why you are seeking a degree in occupational safety & health or closely related field, briefly describes current activities and how they relate to career goal and objective, and states why you believe you should receive this scholarship (e.g., career goals, financial need, etc.).

NUMBER OF AWARDS: 2

RENEWABLE: No

CONTACT: Adele Gabanski

ADDITIONAL INFORMATION: (1) To obtain an application for membership ($15/year), contact ASSE's Customer Service department at or download the application at http://www.asse.org/membership/become a member.php. (2) Students will also be provided with the opportunity to attend annual conference.

1885—AMERICAN SOCIETY OF SAFETY ENGINEERS (ASSE) FOUNDATION (Warren K. Brown Scholarship)

1800 East Oakton Street
Des Plaines IL 60018-2187
847/699-2929
FAX: 847/296-3769
Internet: http://www.asse.org foundation

AMOUNT: $1,000

DEADLINE(S): DEC 1

FIELD(S): Occupational Safety & Health, with an emphasis on Construction Safety

ELIGIBILITY/REQUIREMENTS: Must be a U.S. citizen, in good academic standing; have completed at least 60 semester hours; and have an overall GPA of at least 3.0. and attend Murray State University in Murray, KY or Indiana State University in Terre Haute, IN.

HOW TO APPLY: See website or contaact Customer Service for an application. Submit with reference letter by safety faculty member; and essay of 300 words or less that explains why you are seeking a degree in occupational safety & health or closely related field, briefly describes current activities and how they relate to career goal and objective, and states why you believe you should receive this scholarship (e.g., career goals, financial need, etc.).

NUMBER OF AWARDS: 1

RENEWABLE: No

CONTACT: Adele Gabanski

ADDITIONAL INFORMATION: To obtain an application for membership ($15/year), contact ASSE's Customer Service department at or download the application at http://www.asse.org/membership/become a member.php.

1886—AMERICAN SOCIETY OF SAFETY ENGINEERS (ASSE) FOUNDATION (Washington Group International Safety Scholarship)

1800 East Oakton Street
Des Plaines IL 60018-2187
847/699-2929
FAX: 847/296-3769
Internet: http://www.asse.org foundation

AMOUNT: $5,000

DEADLINE(S): DEC 1

FIELD(S): Occupational Safety & Health, with an emphasis on Construction Safety

ELIGIBILITY/REQUIREMENTS: Must be a U.S. citizen, in good academic standing; have completed at least 60 semester hours; and have an overall GPA of at least 3.0.

HOW TO APPLY: See website or contaact Customer Service for an application. Submit with reference letter by safety faculty member; and essay of 300 words or less that explains why you are seeking a degree in occupational safety & health or closely related field, briefly describes current activities and how they relate to career goal and objective, and states why you believe you should receive this scholarship (e.g., career goals, financial need, etc.).

NUMBER OF AWARDS: 1

RENEWABLE: No

CONTACT: Adele Gabanski

ADDITIONAL INFORMATION: To obtain an application for membership ($15/year), contact ASSE's Customer Service department at or download the application at http://www.asse.org/membership/become a member.php.

1887—AMERICAN SOCIETY OF SAFETY ENGINEERS (ASSE) FOUNDATION (William C. Ray, CIH, CSP Arizona Scholarship)

1800 East Oakton Street
Des Plaines IL 60018-2187
847/699-2929
FAX: 847/296-3769
Internet: http://www.asse.org foundation

AMOUNT: $1,000

DEADLINE(S): DEC 1

FIELD(S): Occupational Safety & Health, with an emphasis on Construction Safety

ELIGIBILITY/REQUIREMENTS: Must be a U.S. citizen, in good academic standing; have completed at least 60 semester hours; and have an overall GPA of at least 3.0 Students residing in Arizona, then the Region II area (MT, ID, WY, CO, UT, NV, NM) will have priority.

HOW TO APPLY: See website or contaact Customer Service for an application. Submit with reference letter by safety faculty member; and essay of 300 words or less that explains why you are seeking a degree in occupational safety & health or closely related field, briefly describes current activities and how they relate to career goal and objective, and states why you

believe you should receive this scholarship (e.g., career goals, financial need, etc.).
NUMBER OF AWARDS: 1
RENEWABLE: No
CONTACT: Adele Gabanski
ADDITIONAL INFORMATION: To obtain an application for membership ($15/year), contact ASSE's Customer Service department at or download the application at http://www.asse.org/membership/become a member.php.

1888—ASSOCIATION FOR EDUCATION AND REHABILITATION OF THE BLIND AND VISUALLY IMPAIRED (Telesensory Scholarship)

4600 Duke Street, Suite 430
P.O. Box 22397
Alexandria VA 22304
703/823-9690
FAX: 703/823-9695
E-mail: aer@aerbvi.org
Internet: http://www.aerbvi.org
AMOUNT: $1,000
DEADLINE(S): APR 15 (even-numbered years)
FIELD(S): Services for the Blind/Visually Impaired
ELIGIBILITY/REQUIREMENTS: Scholarships for students who are members of AER pursuing postsecondary education in a field related to services for the blind or visually impaired. Must be an AER member. Financial need NOT a factor.
HOW TO APPLY: For membership information or an application, see website or contact the Association.
NUMBER OF AWARDS: 1
CONTACT: Carolyn Sharp

1889—ASSOCIATION FOR EDUCATION AND REHABILITATION OF THE BLIND AND VISUALLY IMPAIRED (William and Dorothy Ferrell Scholarship)

4600 Duke Street, Suite 430
P.O. Box 22397
Alexandria VA 22304
703/823-9690
FAX: 703/823-9695
E-mail: aer@aerbvi.org
Internet: http://www.aerbvi.org
AMOUNT: $500
DEADLINE(S): APR 15 (of even-numbered years)
FIELD(S): Services for the Blind/Visually Impaired
ELIGIBILITY/REQUIREMENTS: Scholarships for students who are legally blind, pursuing postsecondary education in

a field related to services for the blind or visually impaired. Financial need NOT a factor.
HOW TO APPLY: See website or contact Association for details.
NUMBER OF AWARDS: 2
CONTACT: Carolyn Sharp

1890—FORD FOUNDATION/NATIONAL RESEARCH COUNCIL (Howard Hughes Medical Institute Predoctoral Fellowships in Biological Sciences)

2101 Constitution Avenue NW
Washington DC 20418
202/334-2872
FAX: 202/334-3419
Internet: http://www7.national academies.org/FORDfellowships/fordpredoc.html
AMOUNT: $16,000 stipend + tuition at U.S. institution
DEADLINE(S): NOV 9
FIELD(S): Biochemistry; Biophysics; Epidemiology; Genetics; Immunology; Microbiology; Neuroscience; Pharmacology; Physiology; Virology
ELIGIBILITY/REQUIREMENTS: 5-year award open to college seniors and first-year graduate students pursuing a Ph.D. or Sc.D. U.S. citizens/nationals may choose any institution in the U.S. or abroad; foreign students must choose U.S. institution. Based on ability, academic records, proposed study/research, previous experience, reference reports, and GRE scores.
HOW TO APPLY: See website or contact NRC for an application.
NUMBER OF AWARDS: 80

1891—GENERAL FEDERATION OF WOMEN'S CLUBS OF MASSACHUSETTS (Public Health Scholarship)

P.O. Box 679
Sudbury MA 01776-0679
978/443-4569
FAX: 978/443-1617
E-mail: GFWCMA@aol.com
AMOUNT: $600
DEADLINE(S): MAR 1
FIELD(S): Public Health
ELIGIBILITY/REQUIREMENTS: Undergraduate or graduate student maintaining legal residence in Massachusetts studying public-health-related discipline.
HOW TO APPLY: Submit application along with personal statement of no more than 500 words addressing professional goals and financial need; letter of reference from department head of your major; transcript.
CONTACT: Jane Howard, Scholarship Chairman

1892—GENERAL FEDERATION OF WOMEN'S CLUBS OF MASSACHUSETTS (Speech Therapy/Speech Disorders Scholarship)

P.O. Box 679
Sudbury MA 01776-0679
978/443-4569
FAX: 978/443-1617
E-mail: GFWCMA@aol.com
Internet: http://www.gfwcma. org/id39.html
AMOUNT: $800
DEADLINE(S): MAR 1
FIELD(S): Communication disorders; Speech therapy
ELIGIBILITY/REQUIREMENTS: Undergraduate or graduate student maintaining legal residence in Massachusetts studying communication disorders or speech therapy.
HOW TO APPLY: Submit application along with personal statement of no more than 500 words addressing professional goals and financial need; letter of reference from department head of your major; transcript.
NUMBER OF AWARDS: 1
RENEWABLE: No

1893—INTERNATIONAL ORDER OF THE KING'S DAUGHTERS AND SONS (Health Careers Scholarships)

Health Careers Department
736 Ardmore Lane
Shelbyville KY 40065
AMOUNT: $1,000 (maximum)
DEADLINE(S): APR 1
FIELD(S): Medicine; Dentistry; Nursing; Physical Therapy; Occupational Therapy; Medical Technologies; Pharmacy
ELIGIBILITY/REQUIREMENTS: Must be U.S. or Canadian citizen, enrolled full time in a school accredited in the field involved and located in the U.S. or Canada. For all students, except those preparing for an RN degree, application must be for at least the third year of college. RN students must have completed the first year of schooling. Pre-med students are not eligible to apply. For those students seeking degrees of MD or DDS, application must be for at least the second year of medical or dental school. Each applicant must supply proof of acceptance in the school involved. There is no age limit.
HOW TO APPLY: Send SASE for an application between January 1 and March 15 with a letter stating the field of study and present level. Submit application with résumé, including personal statement as to

the reason for selection of the chosen field and intentions for a career following graduation; letters of recommendation from at least 2 informed persons, with their identification and relationship to applicant made clear; up-to-date official transcripts from current school which MUST be mailed directly from the registrar office (if graduating on a pass/fail system, a statement is required from the Dean of Students or a professor in regard to academic progress); and an itemized budget, endorsed by the school Financial Aid officer, including: school and living expenses, income, loans, awards, family contributions, etc., for the current year and projected estimate for the next year.

RENEWABLE: Yes, for 2 additional years if qualified

CONTACT: Ida Lyons, Director

1894—JEWISH FEDERATION OF METROPOLITAN CHICAGO (Academic Scholarship Program)

Jewish Vocational Service
216 West Jackson Blvd., Suite 700
Chicago IL 60606-6921
312/673-3400
TTY: 312/444-2877
FAX: 312/553-5544
E-mail: jvsscholarship@jvs chicago.org
Internet: http://www.jvs/ chicago.org

AMOUNT: Varies

DEADLINE(S): FEB 15

FIELD(S): Mathematics, Engineering, Science, Medicine, Social Work, Education, Psychology, Rabbinate, Law (except corporate), Communications

ELIGIBILITY/REQUIREMENTS: Open to Jewish men and women legally domiciled in the greater Chicago metropolitan area, who are identified as having promise for significant contributions in their chosen careers, and are in need of financial assistance for full-time academic programs in above areas. Must have entered undergraduate junior year in career programs requiring no postgraduate education, be in graduate/professional school, or be in a vo-tech training program.

HOW TO APPLY: Phone JVS Scholarship Secretary (312/673-3457), fax, or visit website (click on Scholarship Services) for an application in the Fall. Interview required.

RENEWABLE: Yes

CONTACT: JVS Scholarship Secretary at 312/673-3457

1895—JEWISH FEDERATION OF METROPOLITAN CHICAGO (Academic Scholarship Program/The Marcus and Theresa Levie Educational Fund)

One South Franklin Street
Chicago IL 60606
312/357-4521
FAX: 312/855-3282
E-mail: jvsscholarship@jvs chicago.org
Internet: http://www.jvs chicago.org

AMOUNT: Varies

DEADLINE(S): FEB 1

FIELD(S): Medicine, Dentistry, Dental Hygiene, Emergency Medical Technology, Health Technology, Nursing or Physicians' Assistant, Occupational Therapy, Optometry, Clinical Psychology/Counseling, Education

ELIGIBILITY/REQUIREMENTS: Open to college juniors, seniors, and graduate students, or students in vocational training programs, who are Jewish and residents of Chicago or Cook County, Illinois. Academic achievement and financial need are considered.

HOW TO APPLY: Phone JVS Scholarship Secretary (312/673-3457), fax, or visit website (click on Scholarship Services) for an application in the Fall.

1896—MIDWAY COLLEGE

512 East Stephens Street
Midway KY 40347
800/755-0031
E-mail: admissions@midway.edu
Internet: http://www.midway.edu

AMOUNT: Merit Scholarships

ELIGIBILITY/REQUIREMENTS: Merit scholarships for admitted students who are considered full time in Midway's women's college. Depending on scholarship, minimum GPA ranges from 2.5 to 3.2, minimum ACT ranges 18 to 29, minimum SAT from 860 to 1290. In some cases, students must live on campus.

HOW TO APPLY: Contact Admissions Office or high school guidance counselor for application. Complete FAFSA online.

NUMBER OF AWARDS: Varies, up to 100

RENEWABLE: Yes. Must meet GPA requirements which vary based on the scholarship.

CONTACT: Admissions Office or high school guidance counselor

ADDITIONAL INFORMATION: Athletes may be eligible for an athletic scholarship in conjunction with a merit grant;

contact coach for eligibility and award information.

1897—NATIONAL ATHLETIC TRAINERS' ASSOCIATION

2952 Stemmons Freeway
Dallas TX 75247
214/637-6282, ext. 121
FAX: 214/637-2206
E-mail: barbara@nata.org
Internet: http://natafoundation.org

AMOUNT: $2,000

DEADLINE(S): FEB 1

FIELD(S): Athletic Training

ELIGIBILITY/REQUIREMENTS: Open to student members of NATA who have excellent academic records and excelled as student athletic trainers. Undergraduates may apply after completion of junior year, and graduates after completion of fall semester of their undergraduate senior year. Must have a minimum 3.2 GPA.

HOW TO APPLY: Send SASE to NATA for membership information or an application.

CONTACT: Barbara Niland

1898—NATIONAL ENVIRONMENTAL HEALTH ASSOCIATION (NEHA/AAS Scholarship)

720 S. Colorado Boulevard, Suite 970, South Tower
Denver CO 80246-1925
303/756-9090
E-mail: cdimmitt@neha.org
Internet: http://www.neha.org

AMOUNT: Varies

DEADLINE(S): FEB 1

FIELD(S): Environmental Health/Science; Public Health

ELIGIBILITY/REQUIREMENTS: Open to juniors or seniors at an Environmental Health Accreditation Council-accredited school or NEHA school.

HOW TO APPLY: Transcript, letters of recommendation, and financial need considered.

RENEWABLE: Yes

1899—NATIONAL STRENGTH AND CONDITIONING ASSOCIATION (Challenge Scholarship)

1885 Bob Johnson Drive
Colorado Springs CO 80932-0908
719/632-6722 or 800/815-6826
FAX: 719/632-6367
E-mail: nsca@nsca-lift.org
Internet: http://www.colosoft. com/nsca

AMOUNT: $1,000
DEADLINE(S): MAR 15
FIELD(S): Body Strength and
Conditioning
ELIGIBILITY/REQUIREMENTS: Open to members pursuing undergraduate or graduate study in fields related to body strength and conditioning. Also considered are grades/GPA, courses completed, overall academic achievement, strength and conditioning experience, NSCA involvement (must be an NSCA member for at least 1 year prior to application deadline; high school students may sign up for membership at time of application), essay (clarity, expression, goals, lucidity, grammar, and articulateness), and recommendations.
HOW TO APPLY: Contact NSCA for an application or membership information. With application include current résumé, school transcript from each school attended or attending; 3 letters of recommendation; and 500-word essay describing course of study, career goals, and financial need.

1900—NATIONAL STRENGTH AND CONDITIONING ASSOCIATION (High School Scholarship)

1885 Bob Johnson Drive
Colorado Springs CO 80932-0908
719/632-6722 or 800/815-6826
FAX: 719/632-6367
E-mail: nsca@nsca-lift.org
Internet: http://www.colosoft.
com/nsca
AMOUNT: $1,000
DEADLINE(S): MAR 15
FIELD(S): Body Strength and
Conditioning
ELIGIBILITY/REQUIREMENTS: Must be a current senior and demonstrate acceptance into an accredited institution, intention to graduate with a degree in the strength and conditioning field, their goals beyond college, and their record of community service. Minimum GPA of 3.0. Also considered are courses completed, overall academic achievement, strength and conditioning experience, and essay (clarity, expression, goals, lucidity, grammar, and articulateness), and recommendations. Must be a member or join NSCA.
HOW TO APPLY: Contact NSCA for an application or membership information. With application include current transcript; acceptance letter; 2 letters of recommendation; and 500-word essay describing life ambitions, future in strength and conditioning arena, information about sanctioned extracurricular activities and community involvement, and financial need.
NUMBER OF AWARDS: 2

1901—NATIONAL STRENGTH AND CONDITIONING ASSOCIATION (Power Systems Professional Scholarship)

1885 Bob Johnson Drive
Colorado Springs CO 80932-0908
719/632-6722 or 800/815-6826
FAX: 719/632-6367
E-mail: nsca@nsca-lift.org
Internet: http://www.colosoft.
com/nsca
AMOUNT: $1,000
DEADLINE(S): MAR 15
FIELD(S): Body Strength and
Conditioning
ELIGIBILITY/REQUIREMENTS: Open to members, who are working under a strength and conditioning coach in the school's athletic department as a student assistant or volunteer or graduate student, and pursuing undergraduate or graduate study. Also considered are grades/GPA, courses completed, overall academic achievement, strength and conditioning experience, NSCA involvement (must be an NSCA member for at least 1 year prior to application deadline; high school students may sign up for membership at time of application), essay (clarity, expression, goals, lucidity, grammar, and articulateness), and recommendations.
HOW TO APPLY: Contact NSCA for an application or membership information. Application must be submitted by the head strength and conditioning coach from the applicant's school (1 candidate/school). With application include current résumé, school transcript from each school attended or attending; letter of recommendation from head strength coach; and 500-word essay describing course of study, career goals, and financial need.
NUMBER OF AWARDS: 1

1902—NATIONAL STRENGTH AND CONDITIONING ASSOCIATION (Undergraduate Research Grant)

1885 Bob Johnson Drive
Colorado Springs CO 80932-0908
719/632-6722 or 800/815-6826
FAX: 719/632-6367
E-mail: nsca@nsca-lift.org
Internet: http://www.colosoft.
com/nsca
AMOUNT: Up to $1,500
DEADLINE(S): MAR 15
FIELD(S): Body Strength and
Conditioning
ELIGIBILITY/REQUIREMENTS: Open to undergraduate members to fund research in strength and conditioning that falls within the mission of the NSCA. A faculty member is required to serve as co-investigator in the study. Also considered are grades/GPA, courses completed, overall academic achievement, strength and conditioning experience, NSCA involvement (must be an NSCA member for at least 1 year prior to application deadline; high school students may sign up for membership at time of application), essay (clarity, expression, goals, lucidity, grammar, and articulateness), and recommendations.
HOW TO APPLY: Contact NSCA for an application or membership information. With application include current résumé, school transcript from each school attended or attending, abstract, 2 copies of proposal-up to 10 single-spaced pages: rationale (2), study purpose (1), methods (7); references; itemized budget; time schedule; "Human Subject Consent Form" and proof of review board approval; and abbreviated vitae of the faculty co-investigator.

1903—NEW YORK STATE HIGHER EDUCATION SERVICES CORPORATION (N.Y. State Regents Professional/Health Care Opportunity Scholarships)

Cultural Education Center
Room 5C64
Albany NY 12230
518/486-1319
Internet: http://www.hesc.com
AMOUNT: $1,000-$10,000/year
DEADLINE(S): Varies
FIELD(S): Medicine, Dentistry & related fields; Architecture, Nursing, Psychology, Audiology, Landscape Architecture, Social Work, Chiropractic, Law, Pharmacy, Accounting, Speech Language Pathology
ELIGIBILITY/REQUIREMENTS: For New York State residents who are economically disadvantaged and members of a minority group underrepresented in the chosen profession and attending school in New York State. For U.S. citizens or qualifying non-citizens.
HOW TO APPLY: See website or contact NYS HESC.
RENEWABLE: Yes

1904—PILOT INTERNATIONAL FOUNDATION (PIF/Lifeline Scholarship)

P.O. Box 5600
Macon GA 31208-5600
478/743-7403
FAX: 478/743-2173
E-mail: pifinfo@pilothq.org

Internet: http://www.pilot international.org
AMOUNT: Varies
DEADLINE(S): FEB 15
FIELD(S): Disabilities/Brain-related disorders
ELIGIBILITY/REQUIREMENTS: Assists ADULT students re-entering the job market, preparing for a second career, or improving their professional skills in an established career. Must be preparing for, or already involved in, careers working with people with disabilities/brain-related disorders. GPA of 3.5 or more is required. Must be a Pilot Club member.
HOW TO APPLY: Must be sponsored by home, college, or university town Pilot Club. See website or send SASE for information and application.

1905—PILOT INTERNATIONAL FOUNDATION (The Pilot International Scholarship Program)

P.O. Box 5600
Macon GA 31208-5600
478/743-7403
FAX: 478/743-2173
E-mail: pifinfo@pilothq.org
Internet: http://www.pilot international.org
AMOUNT: Varies
DEADLINE(S): FEB 15
FIELD(S): Disabilities/Brain-related disorders
ELIGIBILITY/REQUIREMENTS: Open to undergraduate students preparing for careers working directly with people with disabilities or training those who will. GPA of 3.25 or greater required. MUST be a Pilot Club member.
HOW TO APPLY: Must be sponsored by home, college, or university town Pilot Club. See website or send SASE for information and application.

1906—RIPON COLLEGE (Forensic Scholarship)

300 Seward Street
P.O. Box 248
Ripon, WI 54971
800/947-4766
FAX: 920/746-8335
E-mail: adminfo@ripon.edu
Internet: http://www.ripon.edu
AMOUNT: $5,000
DEADLINE(S):MAR 1
FIELD(S): Forensics
ELIGIBILITY/REQUIREMENTS: Recognizes a student's commitment to academic excellence and service to their school and community. Must demonstrate proven success and talent in the area of forensics. Candidate's academic credentials, community service activities and references considered.
HOW TO APPLY: Contact Office of Admission for an application; submit with a letter of recommendation from high school teacher. An on-campus interview required.
NUMBER OF AWARDS: 1
RENEWABLE: Yes. Must participate in 3 invitationals, the Wisconsin state tournament and, if qualified, the nationals.
CONTACT: Office of Admission

1907—ROBERT SCHRECK MEMORIAL FUND (Grants)

c/o Texas Commerce Bank
Trust Department
P.O. Drawer 140
El Paso TX 79980
915/546-6515
AMOUNT: $500-$1,500
DEADLINE(S): JUL 15; NOV 15
FIELD(S): Medicine; Veterinary Medicine; Physics; Chemistry; Architecture; Engineering; Episcopal Clergy
ELIGIBILITY/REQUIREMENTS: Grants to undergraduate juniors or seniors or graduate students who have been residents of El Paso County for at least 2 years. Must be U.S. citizen or legal resident and have a high grade point average. Financial need is a consideration.
HOW TO APPLY: Write for information.
NUMBER OF AWARDS: 3
RENEWABLE: No

1908—SOCIETY OF AUTOMOTIVE ENGINEERS (Parks College of Saint Louis University/SAE Engineering Scholarship)

SAE Customer Service
400 Commonwealth Drive
Warrendale PA 15096-0001
724/776-4970
FAX: 724/776-1615
E-mail: customerservice@sae.org
Internet: http://www.sae.org/ students/scholar/scholarships
AMOUNT: $1,000
DEADLINE(S): DEC 1
FIELD(S): Aerospace Engineering; Mechanical Engineering; Electrical Engineering; Biomedical Engineering; Aircraft Maintenance Engineering; Avionics Engineering; Applied Computer Science; Computer Software Systems; Physics

ELIGIBILITY/REQUIREMENTS: Entering freshman majoring in any of the above areas, enrolled in a baccalaureate program. Award based on academic achievement and financial need.
HOW TO APPLY: See website for application. Submit application; a personal essay that demonstrates hands-on experience or activity (such as rebuilding engines, working on cars/trucks, etc.); 2 recommendations, 1 of which must be from a teacher, counselor, or administrator; and transcript.
NUMBER OF AWARDS: 1
RENEWABLE: No

1909—WESTERN MICHIGAN UNIVERSITY (College of Arts and Sciences/Distinguished Senior in Biomedical Sciences)

1903 West Michigan
Kalamazoo MI 49008-5337
269/387-8777
FAX: 269/387-6989
E-mail: finaid-info@wmich.edu
Internet: http://www.wmich.edu/ finaid
AMOUNT: $150 (spring semester)
FIELD(S): Biomedical Sciences
ELIGIBILITY/REQUIREMENTS: Senior, Biological Sciences major.
HOW TO APPLY: Nominated by Faculty.
RENEWABLE: No
CONTACT: Biological Sciences Department

1910—WESTERN MICHIGAN UNIVERSITY (College of Education/Harriett Kiser Creed Endowment Fund)

1903 West Michigan
Kalamazoo MI 49008-5337
269/387-6000
FAX: 269/387-6989
E-mail: finaid-info@wmich.edu
Internet: http://www.wmich.edu/ finaid
AMOUNT: $500/semester
DEADLINE(S): MAR 1
FIELD(S): Health, Physical Education and Recreation
ELIGIBILITY/REQUIREMENTS: Full-time junior or senior enrolled in HPER Curriculum, preference to HPER majors, with 3.0 or higher GPA. Must be involved in HPER-related activities and show financial need.
HOW TO APPLY: Contact the HPER Department, 4024 Student Recreation Center, or College of Education, 2304 Sangren Hall.

CONTACT: HPER Department or College of Education

1911—WESTERN MICHIGAN UNIVERSITY (College of Education/Harriett Kiser Creed HPER Scholarship)

1903 West Michigan
Kalamazoo MI 49008-5337
269/387-6000
FAX: 269/387-6989
E-mail: finaid-info@wmich.edu
Internet: http://www.wmich.edu/finaid
AMOUNT: $500/semester
DEADLINE(S): MAR 1
FIELD(S): Health, Physical Education and Recreation
ELIGIBILITY/REQUIREMENTS: Full-time junior or senior enrolled in HPER Curriculum, with 3.0 or higher GPA.
HOW TO APPLY: Contact Dr. Debra Berkey, 269/387-2710, 4021 Student Recreation Center, or e-mail: debra.berkey@wmich.edu for more information.
NUMBER OF AWARDS: 1
RENEWABLE: No

1912—WESTERN MICHIGAN UNIVERSITY (College of Education/Howard E. Thompson Endowed Scholarship Fund for Physical Education)

1903 West Michigan
Kalamazoo MI 49008-5337
269/387-6000
FAX: 269/387-6989
E-mail: finaid-info@wmich.edu
Internet: http://www.wmich.edu/finaid
AMOUNT: $1,000/semester
DEADLINE(S): MAR 1
FIELD(S): Physical Education
ELIGIBILITY/REQUIREMENTS: Major in physical education preparing for a professional career in teaching in the public schools.
HOW TO APPLY: Contact Dr. Debra Berkey, 4021 Student Recreation Center, 269/387-2710, or e-mail: debra.berkey@wmich.edu for more information.
NUMBER OF AWARDS: 1

1913—WESTERN MICHIGAN UNIVERSITY (College of Health and Human Services/Elissa Gatlin Scholarship)

1903 West Michigan
Kalamazoo MI 49008-5337
269/387-8777
FAX: 269/387-6989
Internet: http://www.wmich.edu/finaid
AMOUNT: $500/semester
DEADLINE(S): MAR 1
FIELD(S): Occupational Therapy; Nursing; Speech Pathology; Blind Rehabilitation; Social Work; Physician Assistant
ELIGIBILITY/REQUIREMENTS: Intended for minority students (African-Americans, Native American, or Hispanic American); 2.75 GPA for undergraduates, 3.00 GPA for graduates; must be enrolled in professional program, U.S. citizen, and demonstrate financial need.
HOW TO APPLY: Contact the College of Health and Human Services for application.
NUMBER OF AWARDS: 2 (1 undergraduate; 1 graduate)
RENEWABLE: Yes. Maximum 2 years.

1914—WESTERN MICHIGAN UNIVERSITY (College of Health and Human Services/Jeffrey and Barbara Vortman Scholarship

1903 West Michigan
Kalamazoo MI 49008-5337
269/387-8777
FAX: 269/387-6989
E-mail: finaid-info@wmich.edu
Internet: http://www.wmich.edu/finaid
AMOUNT: $500
DEADLINE(S): MAR 1
FIELD(S): Occupational Therapy; Nursing; Speech Pathology; Blind Rehabilitation; Social Work; Physician Assistant
ELIGIBILITY/REQUIREMENTS: Each year one of the departments/schools is responsible for awarding the scholarship to a student admitted to one of the professional programs in the College.
HOW TO APPLY: Contact the College of Health and Human Services for application.
NUMBER OF AWARDS: 2 (1 undergraduate; 1 graduate)
RENEWABLE: Yes. Maximum 2 years.

1915—WESTERN MICHIGAN UNIVERSITY (College of Health and Human Services/Malamazian Memorial Endowed Blind Rehabilitation Scholarship)

1903 West Michigan
Kalamazoo MI 49008-5337
269/387-8777
FAX: 269/387-6989
E-mail: finaid-info@wmich.edu
Internet: http://www.wmich.edu/finaid
AMOUNT: Varies
DEADLINE(S): JUN 1
FIELD(S): Blind Rehabilitation
ELIGIBILITY/REQUIREMENTS: Must be enrolled in the Orientation and Mobility Program of the Blind Rehabilitation Department, meet the basic program requirements, and demonstrate financial need.
HOW TO APPLY: Contact the Blind Rehabilitation Department for application.

1916—WESTERN MICHIGAN UNIVERSITY (Pfizer Cultural Diversity Scholarship)

1903 W. Michigan
Kalamazoo MI 49008-5337
269/387-8777
FAX: 269/387-6989
E-mail: finaid-info@wmich.edu
Internet: http://www.wmich.edu/finaid
AMOUNT: $2,000 for senior year
DEADLINE(S): APR 1
FIELD(S): Biomedical Science; Biology; Business
ELIGIBILITY/REQUIREMENTS: Must be U.S. citizen; in junior year, majoring in one of the above fields. Must be a full-time student, with a 3.0 cumulative GPA in program of study. Business majors must complete pre-business classes before applying.
HOW TO APPLY: Contact the Division of Minority Affairs for an application. Must complete a FAFSA and indicate WMU as a school choice.
RENEWABLE: No
CONTACT: Division of Minority Affairs

1917—WOMEN'S SPORTS FOUNDATION (Jackie Joyner-Kersee and Zina Garrison Minority Internships)

Eisenhower Park
East Meadow NY 11554
800/227-3988 (U.S. only) or 516/542-4700
FAX: 516/542-4716
E-mail: WoSport@aol.com
Internet: http://www.womenssportsfoundation.org
AMOUNT: $4,000-$5,000
DEADLINE(S): Ongoing
FIELD(S): Sports-related careers
ELIGIBILITY/REQUIREMENTS: Women of color who are undergraduate students, college graduates, graduate students or women in career change. Internships are located at the Women's

Sports Foundation in East Meadow, New York.
HOW TO APPLY: See website or write for details.
NUMBER OF AWARDS: 4-6

MEDICAL RESEARCH

1918—AMERICAN INDIAN SCIENCE AND ENGINEERING SOCIETY (A. T. Anderson Memorial Scholarship)

P.O. Box 9828
Albuquerque NM 87119-9828
505/765-1052
FAX: 505/765-5608
E-mail: scholarships@aises.org
Internet: http://www.aises.org/higthered
AMOUNT: $1,000
DEADLINE(S): JUN 15
FIELD(S): Medicine; Natural Resources; Science; Engineering
ELIGIBILITY/REQUIREMENTS: Open to undergraduate and graduate students who are at least 1/4 American Indian or recognized as member of a tribe. Must be member of AISES ($10 fee), enrolled full time at an accredited institution, and demonstrate financial need. Minimum GPA 2.7.
HOW TO APPLY: See website or contact Society for an application and membership information.
RENEWABLE: Yes
CONTACT: Tina Pino

1919—AMERICAN SOCIETY FOR CLINICAL LABORATORY SCIENCE (Alpha Mu Tau and Education and Research Fund/AMTF Undergraduate Scholarship)

6701 Democracy Boulevard,
Suite 300
Bethesda MD 20817
301/657-2768
FAX: 301/657-2909
E-mail: alphamutaujoe@yahoo.com
Internet: http://www.ascls.org/leadership/awards/amt.asp
AMOUNT: Up to $1,500
DEADLINE(S): APR 1
FIELD(S): Clinical Laboratory Science/Medical Technology, Clinical Laboratory Technician/Medical Laboratory Technician, Cytotechnology or Histotechnology
ELIGIBILITY/REQUIREMENTS: Open to seniors and graduate students enrolled in an approved undergraduate or graduate

program; must be U.S. citizen or permanent resident.
HOW TO APPLY: See website or e-mail or send #10 SASE to address below for application, available after Nov. 1.
NUMBER OF AWARDS: Varies
CONTACT: Joe Briden, AMTF Scholarship Coordinator, 7809 S. 21st Drive, Phoenix, AZ 95041-7736.

1920—AMERICAN SOCIETY FOR CLINICAL LABORATORY SCIENCE (Alpha Mu Tau and Education and Research Fund/Dorothy Morrison Undergraduate Scholarship)

6701 Democracy Boulevard,
Suite 300
Bethesda MD 20817
301/657-2768
FAX: 301/657-2909
E-mail: alphamutaujoe@yahoo.com
Internet: http://www.ascls.org/leadership/awards/amt.asp
AMOUNT: Up to $2,000
DEADLINE(S): APR 1
FIELD(S): Clinical Laboratory Science/Medical Technology, Clinical Laboratory Technician/Medical Laboratory Technician, Cytotechnology or Histotechnology
ELIGIBILITY/REQUIREMENTS: For undergraduate students entering or in their last year of study enrolled in an approved NAACLS accredited program. U.S. citizenship or permanent resident.
HOW TO APPLY: See website or e-mail or send #10 SASE to address below for application, available after Nov. 1.
CONTACT: Joe Briden, AMTF Scholarship Coordinator, 7809 S. 21st Drive, Phoenix, AZ 95041-7736.

1921—AMERICAN SOCIETY FOR CLINICAL LABORATORY SCIENCE (Alpha Mu Tau and Education and Research Fund/Ida and May Reilly Graduate or Undergraduate Scholarships)

6701 Democracy Boulevard,
Suite 300
Bethesda MD 20817
301/657-2768
FAX: 301/657-2909
E-mail: alphamutaujoe@yahoo.com
Internet: http://www.ascls.org/leadership/awards/amt.asp
AMOUNT: Up to $2,500
DEADLINE(S): APR 1
FIELD(S): Clinical Laboratory Science/Medical Technology, Clinical Laboratory Technician/Medical

Laboratory Technician, Cytotechnology or Histotechnology
ELIGIBILITY/REQUIREMENTS: Open to seniors and graduate students enrolled in an approved undergraduate or graduate program; must be U.S. citizen or permanent resident.
HOW TO APPLY: See website or e-mail or send #10 SASE to address below for application, available after Nov. 1.
CONTACT: Joe Briden, AMTF Scholarship Coordinator, 7809 S. 21st Drive, Phoenix, AZ 95041-7736.

1922—AMERICAN SOCIETY FOR CLINICAL LABORATORY SCIENCE (Alpha Mu Tau and Education and Research Fund/Martha Winstead Undergraduate Scholarship)

6701 Democracy Boulevard,
Suite 300
Bethesda MD 20817
301/657-2768
FAX: 301/657-2909
E-mail: alphamutaujoe@yahoo.com
Internet: http://www.ascls.org/leadership/awards/amt.asp
AMOUNT: Up to $1,500
DEADLINE(S): APR 1
FIELD(S): Clinical Laboratory Science/Medical Technology, Clinical Laboratory Technician/Medical Laboratory Technician, Cytotechnology or Histotechnology
ELIGIBILITY/REQUIREMENTS: Open to seniors and graduate students enrolled in an approved undergraduate or graduate program; must be U.S. citizen or permanent resident.
HOW TO APPLY: See website or e-mail or send #10 SASE to address below for application, available after Nov. 1.
CONTACT: Joe Briden, AMTF Scholarship Coordinator, 7809 S. 21st Drive, Phoenix, AZ 95041-7736.
ADDITIONAL INFORMATION: May not be offered every year.

1923—AMERICAN SOCIETY FOR CLINICAL LABORATORY SCIENCE (Alpha Mu Tau and Education and Research Fund/Ruth M. French Graduate or Undergraduate Scholarship)

6701 Democracy Boulevard,
Suite 300
Bethesda MD 20817
301/657-2768
FAX: 301/657-2909
E-mail: alphamutaujoe@yahoo.com
Internet: http://www.ascls.org/leadership/awards/amt.asp

AMOUNT: Up to $3,000
DEADLINE(S): APR 1
FIELD(S): Clinical Laboratory Science; Medical Technology
ELIGIBILITY/REQUIREMENTS: Open to seniors and graduate students enrolled in an approved undergraduate or graduate program; must be U.S. citizen or permanent resident.
HOW TO APPLY: See website or e-mail or send #10 SASE to address below for application, available after Nov. 1.
CONTACT: Joe Briden, AMTF Scholarship Coordinator, 7809 S. 21st Drive, Phoenix, AZ 95041-7736.

1924—AMERICAN SOCIETY FOR CLINICAL LABORATORY SCIENCE (ASCLS Education and Research Fund, Inc. Scholarships)

6701 Democracy Boulevard, Suite 300
Bethesda MD 20817
301/657-2768
FAX: 301/657-2909
E-mail: alphamutaujoe@yahoo.com
Internet: http://www.ascls.org/leadership/awards/amt.asp
AMOUNT: Up to $1,500
DEADLINE(S): APR 1
FIELD(S): Clinical Laboratory Science/Medical Technology, Clinical Laboratory Technician/Medical Laboratory Technician, Cytotechnology or Histotechnology
ELIGIBILITY/REQUIREMENTS: Open to seniors and graduate students enrolled in an approved undergraduate or graduate program; must be U.S. citizen or permanent resident.
HOW TO APPLY: See website or e-mail or send #10 SASE to address below for application, available after Nov. 1.
NUMBER OF AWARDS: Varies
CONTACT: Joe Briden, AMTF Scholarship Coordinator, 7809 S. 21st Drive, Phoenix, AZ 95041-7736.

1925—ASTRONAUT SCHOLARSHIP FOUNDATION

6225 Vectorspace Boulevard
Titusville FL 32780
321/269/6119
FAX: 321/267-3970
E-mail: MercurySvn@aol.com
Internet: http://www.astronaut scholarship.org/guidelines.html
AMOUNT: $10,000
DEADLINE(S): APR 15

FIELD(S): Engineering; Physical Sciences (Medical Research; NOT Professional Medicine)
ELIGIBILITY/REQUIREMENTS: Open to juniors, seniors, and graduate students at a select group of schools (see website for list). Must be U.S. citizen planning to pursue research or advance field of study.
HOW TO APPLY: Must be nominated by faculty or staff. Contact Executive Director for details.
CONTACT: Howard Benedict, Executive Director

1926—EPILEPSY FOUNDATION OF AMERICA (Behavioral Sciences Student Fellowships)

4351 Garden City Drive
Landover MD 20785-2267
301/459-3700 or 800/EFA-1000
TDD: 800/332-2070
FAX: 301/577-2684
Internet: http://www.epilepsy foundation.org
AMOUNT: $3,000
DEADLINE(S): MAR 1
FIELD(S): Epilepsy Research/Practice; Sociology; Social Work; Psychology; Anthropology; Nursing; Economics; Vocational Rehabilitation; Counseling; Political Science
ELIGIBILITY/REQUIREMENTS: 3-month fellowships awarded to undergraduate and graduate students for work on a project during the summer or other free period. Students propose an epilepsy-related study or training project to be carried out at a U.S. institution. A preceptor must supervise the student and the project.
HOW TO APPLY: Contact EFA for an application.

1927—FIRST UNITED METHODIST CHURCH (Robert Stevenson and Doreene E. Cater Scholarships)

302 5th Avenue South
St. Cloud MN 56301
FAX: 320/251-0878
E-mail: fumc@fumc-stcloud.org
AMOUNT: $200-1,500
DEADLINE(S): JUN 1
FIELD(S): Humanitarian and Christian Service: Teaching, Medicine, Social Work, Environmental Studies, and related fields
ELIGIBILITY/REQUIREMENTS: Stevenson Scholarship is open to undergraduate members of the First United Methodist Church of St. Cloud. Cater Scholarship is open to members of the Minnesota United Methodist Conference

who are entering the sophomore year or higher of college work. Both require two letters of reference, transcripts, and financial need.
HOW TO APPLY: Contact Scholarship Committee for an application.
NUMBER OF AWARDS: 5-6

1928—FORD FOUNDATION/NATIONAL RESEARCH COUNCIL (Howard Hughes Medical Institute Predoctoral Fellowships in Biological Sciences)

2101 Constitution Avenue NW
Washington DC 20418
202/334-2872
FAX: 202/334-3419
Internet: http://www7.national academies.org/FORDfellowships/fordpredoc.html
AMOUNT: $16,000 stipend + tuition at U.S. institution
DEADLINE(S): NOV 9
FIELD(S): Biochemistry; Biophysics; Epidemiology; Genetics; Immunology; Microbiology; Neuroscience; Pharmacology; Physiology; Virology
ELIGIBILITY/REQUIREMENTS: 5-year award open to college seniors and first-year graduate students pursuing a Ph.D. or Sc.D. U.S. citizens/nationals may choose any institution in the U.S. or abroad; foreign students must choose U.S. institution. Based on ability, academic records, proposed study/research, previous experience, reference reports, and GRE scores.
HOW TO APPLY: See website or contact NRC for an application.
NUMBER OF AWARDS: 80

1929—JEWISH FEDERATION OF METROPOLITAN CHICAGO (Academic Scholarship Program)

Jewish Vocational Service
216 West Jackson Blvd, Suite 700
Chicago IL 60606-6921
312/673-3400
TTY: 312/444-2877
FAX: 312/553-5544
Internet: http://www.jvs/chicago.org
AMOUNT: Varies
DEADLINE(S): FEB 15
FIELD(S): Mathematics, Engineering, Science, Medicine, Social Work, Education, Psychology, Rabbinate, Law (except corporate), Communications
ELIGIBILITY/REQUIREMENTS: Open to Jewish men and women legally domiciled in the greater Chicago metropolitan

area, who are identified as having promise for significant contributions in their chosen careers, and are in need of financial assistance for full-time academic programs in above areas. Must have entered undergraduate junior year in career programs requiring no postgraduate education, be in graduate/professional school, or be in a vo-tech training program.
HOW TO APPLY: Phone JVS Scholarship Secretary (312/673-3457), fax, or visit website (click on Scholarship Services) for an application in the Fall. Interview required.
RENEWABLE: Yes

1930—LUPUS FOUNDATION OF AMERICA, INC. (Finzi Student Summer Fellowship)

National Office
2000 L Street, NW, Suite 710
Washington DC 20036
202/349-1155
800/558-0121 (information request line-English)
800/558-0231 (information request line-Spanish)
FAX: 202/349-1156
E-mail: info@lupus.org
Internet: http://www.lupus.org
AMOUNT: $2,000
DEADLINE(S): JUN 1
FIELD(S): Lupus Erythematosus Research

ELIGIBILITY/REQUIREMENTS: Open to undergraduates, graduates, and postgraduates (college graduate preferred) for basic, clinical, or psychosocial research related to the causes, treatments, prevention, or cure of lupus. Student is responsible for locating supervisor and lab (must be in U.S.) to supervise research.
HOW TO APPLY: See website or contact LFA for an application.; submit with SAT/ACT score and other supporting documents

1931—MICROSCOPY SOCIETY OF AMERICA SCHOLARSHIPS (Undergraduate Research Scholarships)

230 East Ohio Street, Suite 400
Chicago IL 60611-3265
800/538-3672
Internet: http://www.msa.microscopy.org/
AMOUNT: Up to $3,000
DEADLINE(S): DEC
FIELD(S): Science (microscopy)
ELIGIBILITY/REQUIREMENTS: Scholarship provides funds to junior or

senior undergraduates conducting research involving any area of microscopy.
HOW TO APPLY: Contact Society for application and information.
RENEWABLE: No

1932—OHIO ENVIRONMENTAL HEALTH ASSOCIATION (OEA) (George Eagle Memorial Scholarship)

P.O. Box 234
Columbus OH 43216-0234
740/349-6535
FAX: 740/349-6510
E-mail: jebel@lickingcohealth.org
Internet: http://www.oeha.org
AMOUNT: $2,000
DEADLINE(S): FEB 28
FIELD(S): Environmental Health, Environmental Studies, Biology
ELIGIBILITY/REQUIREMENTS: Must be Ohio resident enrolled as sophomore, junior or senior in a program leading to a baccalaureate degree in environmental health, environmental management or related field and express intent to become employed in environmental health in Ohio following graduation.
HOW TO APPLY: See website or write for application or further information.
NUMBER OF AWARDS: 1
RENEWABLE: No
CONTACT: Joe Ebel

1933—OKLAHOMA MEDICAL RESEARCH FOUNDATION (Sir Alexander Fleming Summer Scholar Program)

825 NE 13th Street
Oklahoma City OK 73104-5046
405/271-8537 or 800/522-0211
Internet: http://www.omrf.org/fleming
AMOUNT: $2,500 salary + housing
DEADLINE(S): FEB 15
FIELD(S): Science
ELIGIBILITY/REQUIREMENTS: Open ONLY to Oklahoma students who have completed their junior year of high school through those in their junior year of college at time of application. Excellent academic standing and aptitude in science and math are essential. Students will work in Foundation's laboratories in June and July.
HOW TO APPLY: See website for further information and application forms.

1934—PILOT INTERNATIONAL FOUNDATION (PIF/Lifeline Scholarship)

P.O. Box 5600
Macon GA 31208-5600

478/743-7403
FAX: 478/743-2173
E-mail: pifinfo@pilothq.org
Internet: http://www.pilot international.org
AMOUNT: Varies
DEADLINE(S): FEB 15
FIELD(S): Disabilities/Brain-related disorders
ELIGIBILITY/REQUIREMENTS: Assists ADULT students re-entering the job market, preparing for a second career, or improving their professional skills in an established career. Must be preparing for, or already involved in, careers working with people with disabilities/brain-related disorders. GPA of 3.5 or more is required. Must be a Pilot Club member.
HOW TO APPLY: Must be sponsored by home, college, or university town Pilot Club. See website or send SASE for information and application.

1935—PILOT INTERNATIONAL FOUNDATION (The Pilot International Scholarship Program)

P.O. Box 5600
Macon GA 31208-5600
478/743-7403
FAX: 478/743-2173
E-mail: pifinfo@pilothq.org
Internet: http://www.pilot international.org
AMOUNT: Varies
DEADLINE(S): FEB 15
FIELD(S): Disabilities/Brain-related disorders
ELIGIBILITY/REQUIREMENTS: Open to undergraduate students preparing for careers working directly with people with disabilities or training those who will. GPA of 3.25 or greater required. MUST be a Pilot Club member.
HOW TO APPLY: Must be sponsored by home, college, or university town Pilot Club. See website or send SASE for information and application.

1936—RIPON COLLEGE (Math/Science Scholarship)

300 Seward Street
P.O. Box 248
Ripon, WI 54971
800/947-4766
FAX: 920/746-8335
E-mail: adminfo@ripon.edu
Internet: http://www.ripon.edu
AMOUNT: $1,000-$5,000
DEADLINE(S): MAR 1
FIELD(S): Forensics

ELIGIBILITY/REQUIREMENTS: Open to undergraduate students planning to pursue forensic studies.
HOW TO APPLY: Contact Office of Admission for an application. An on-campus interview required.
NUMBER OF AWARDS: 1
RENEWABLE: Yes. Must maintain enrollment as a full-time student majoring in math or science, minimum GPA of 3.0 and evidence satisfactory progress toward a 4-year degree.
CONTACT: Office of Admission

MEDICAL TECHNOLOGIES

1937—AMERICAN FOUNDATION FOR THE BLIND (Paul and Ellen Ruckes Scholarship)

11 Penn Plaza, Suite 300
New York NY 10001
212/502-7661
FAX: 212/502-7771
E-mail: afbinfo@afb.net
Internet: http://www.afb.org/scholar/scholarships.asp
AMOUNT: $1,000
DEADLINE(S): MAR 31
FIELD(S): Engineering; Computer/Physical/Life Sciences
ELIGIBILITY/REQUIREMENTS: Open to legally blind and visually impaired undergraduate and graduate students pursuing a degree in one of above fields. Must be U.S. citizen.
HOW TO APPLY: See website or contact AFB for an application. Must submit written documentation of evidence of legal blindness; official transcripts; proof of college or university acceptance; 3 letters of recommendation; and typewritten statement describing field of study you are pursuing, goals, work experience, extracurricular activities, and how monies will be used.
NUMBER OF AWARDS: 1
CONTACT: Alina Vaynbrub

1938—AMERICAN HEALTH INFORMATION MANAGEMENT ASSOCIATION (For Undergraduate Merit Scholarships)

Attn: Undergraduate Scholarships
233 North Michigan Ave.,
21st Floor
Chicago IL 60601-5800
312/233-1100
E-mail: fore@ahima.orgInternet:
Internet: http://www.ahima.org
AMOUNT: $1,000-$5,000
DEADLINE(S): APR 25

FIELD(S): Health Information, Health Technology
ELIGIBILITY/REQUIREMENTS: Must be enrolled in CAHIIM accredited program and a member of AHIMA. Must have minimum GPA 3.0, taking a minimum of 6 credit hours or 8 quarter hours per semester, and have at least 1 full semester remaining after August 31. Volunteer and work experience, commitment to and suitability for the profession will be considered.
HOW TO APPLY: See website for additional information and application. Submit by mail with verification of enrollment form, 3 letters of references (educators and/or employers-at least 1 educator), official transcripts from the 3 most recent post-secondary institutions attended with past 10 years, and official checklist.
NUMBER OF AWARDS: Approximately 100
ADDITIONAL INFORMATION: Most scholarships are available to all eligible applicants. But a few have specific qualifications, see website for details.

1939—AMERICAN INDIAN SCIENCE AND ENGINEERING SOCIETY (A. T. Anderson Memorial Scholarship)

P.O. Box 9828
Albuquerque NM 87119-9828
505/765-1052
FAX: 505/765-5608
E-mail: scholarships@aises.org
Internet: http://www.aises.org/highered
AMOUNT: $1,000
DEADLINE(S): JUN 15
FIELD(S): Medicine; Natural Resources; Science; Engineering
ELIGIBILITY/REQUIREMENTS: Open to students who are at least 1/4 American Indian or recognized as member of a tribe. Must be member of AISES ($10 fee), enrolled full time at an accredited institution, and demonstrate financial need. Minimum GPA 2.7.
HOW TO APPLY: See website or contact Society for an application and/or membership information.
RENEWABLE: Yes
CONTACT: Tina Pino

1940—AMERICAN MEDICAL TECHNOLOGISTS

10700 W. Higgins Road, Suite 150
Rosemont IL 60018
847/823-5169
FAX: 847/823-0458
E-mail: mail@amt1.com

Internet: www.amt1.com
AMOUNT: $500
DEADLINE(S): APR 1
FIELD(S): Medical Technologist; Medical Laboratory Technician; Medical Assistant; Medical Administrative Specialist; Dental Assisting; Office Laboratory Technician
ELIGIBILITY/REQUIREMENTS: Must be a graduate of, or a senior in, an accredited high school (GED acceptable). Must be enrolled in a school accredited by agency recognized by U.S. Department of Education, or enrolled in regionally accredited college or university in the U.S. Must pursue one of above careers.
HOW TO APPLY: See website for an application. Submit evidence of career goals, as well as financial need, transcripts, 2 letters of personal reference, and statement of why career chosen.
NUMBER OF AWARDS: 5
CONTACT: Linda Halbander, AMT Scholarship Program Coordinator

1941—AMERICAN SOCIETY FOR CLINICAL LABORATORY SCIENCE (Alpha Mu Tau and Education and Research Fund/AMTF Undergraduate Scholarship)

6701 Democracy Boulevard,
Suite 300
Bethesda MD 20817
301/657-2768
FAX: 301/657-2909
E-mail: alphamutaujoe@yahoo.com
Internet: http://www.ascls.org/leadership/awards/amt.asp
AMOUNT: Up to $1,500
DEADLINE(S): APR 1
FIELD(S): Clinical Laboratory Science/Medical Technology, Clinical Laboratory Technician/Medical Laboratory Technician, Cytotechnology or Histotechnology
ELIGIBILITY/REQUIREMENTS: Open to seniors and graduate students enrolled in an approved undergraduate or graduate program; must be U.S. citizen or permanent resident.
HOW TO APPLY: See website or e-mail or send #10 SASE to address below for application, available after Nov. 1.
NUMBER OF AWARDS: Varies
CONTACT: Joe Briden, AMTF Scholarship Coordinator, 7809 S. 21st Drive, Phoenix, AZ 95041-7736.

1942—AMERICAN SOCIETY FOR CLINICAL LABORATORY SCIENCE (ASCLS Education and Research Fund, Inc. Scholarships)

6701 Democracy Boulevard,

Suite 300
Bethesda MD 20817
301/657-2768
FAX: 301/657-2909
E-mail: alphamutaujoe@yahoo.com
Internet: http://www.ascls.org/
leadership/awards/amt.asp
AMOUNT: Up to $1,500
DEADLINE(S): APR 1
FIELD(S): Clinical Laboratory
Science/Medical Technology, Clinical
Laboratory Technician/Medical
Laboratory Technician,
Cytotechnology or Histotechnology
ELIGIBILITY/REQUIREMENTS: Open
to seniors and graduate students enrolled
in an approved undergraduate or graduate
program; must be U.S. citizen or perma-
nent resident.
HOW TO APPLY: See website or e-mail
or send #10 SASE to address below for
application, available after Nov. 1.
NUMBER OF AWARDS: Varies
CONTACT: Joe Briden, AMTF
Scholarship Coordinator, 7809 S. 21st
Drive, Phoenix, AZ 95041-7736.

1943—AMERICAN SOCIETY FOR CLINI-CAL LABORATORY SCIENCE (Alpha Mu Tau and Education and Research Fund/Dorothy Morrison Undergraduate Scholarship)

6701 Democracy Boulevard,
Suite 300
Bethesda MD 20817
301/657-2768
FAX: 301/657-2909
E-mail: alphamutaujoe@yahoo.com
Internet: http://www.ascls.org/
leadership/awards/amt.asp
AMOUNT: Up to $2,000
DEADLINE(S): APR 1
FIELD(S): Clinical Laboratory
Science/Medical Technology, Clinical
Laboratory Technician/Medical
Laboratory Technician,
Cytotechnology or Histotechnology
ELIGIBILITY/REQUIREMENTS: For
undergraduate students entering or in their
last year of study enrolled in an approved
NAACLS accredited program. U.S. cit-
izenship or permanent resident.
HOW TO APPLY: See website or e-mail
or send #10 SASE to address below for
application, available after Nov. 1.
CONTACT: Joe Briden, AMTF Scholar-
ship Coordinator, 7809 S. 21st Drive,
Phoenix, AZ 95041-7736.

1944—AMERICAN SOCIETY FOR CLINI-CAL LABORATORY SCIENCE (Alpha Mu Tau and Education and Research Fund/Ida and May Reilly Graduate or Undergraduate Scholarships)

6701 Democracy Boulevard,
Suite 300
Bethesda MD 20817
301/657-2768
FAX: 301/657-2909
E-mail: alphamutaujoe@yahoo.com
Internet: http://www.ascls.org/
leadership/awards/amt.asp
AMOUNT: Up to $2,500
DEADLINE(S): APR 1
FIELD(S): Clinical Laboratory
Science/Medical Technology, Clinical
Laboratory Technician/Medical
Laboratory Technician,
Cytotechnology or Histotechnology
ELIGIBILITY/REQUIREMENTS: Open
to seniors and graduate students enrolled
in an approved undergraduate or graduate
program; must be U.S. citizen or perma-
nent resident.
HOW TO APPLY: See website or e-mail
or send #10 SASE to address below for
application, available after Nov. 1.
CONTACT: Joe Briden, AMTF
Scholarship Coordinator, 7809 S. 21st
Drive, Phoenix, AZ 95041-7736.

1945—AMERICAN SOCIETY FOR CLINI-CAL LABORATORY SCIENCE (Alpha Mu Tau and Education and Research Fund/Martha Winstead Undergraduate Scholarship)

6701 Democracy Boulevard,
Suite 300
Bethesda MD 20817
301/657-2768
FAX: 301/657-2909
E-mail: alphamutaujoe@yahoo.com
Internet: http://www.ascls.org/
leadership/awards/amt.asp
AMOUNT: Up to $1,500
DEADLINE(S): APR 1
FIELD(S): Clinical Laboratory
Science/Medical Technology, Clinical
Laboratory Technician/Medical
Laboratory Technician,
Cytotechnology or Histotechnology
ELIGIBILITY/REQUIREMENTS: Open
to seniors and graduate students enrolled
in an approved undergraduate or graduate
program; must be U.S. citizen or perma-
nent resident.
HOW TO APPLY: See website or e-mail
or send #10 SASE to address below for
application, available after Nov. 1.

CONTACT: Joe Briden, AMTF
Scholarship Coordinator, 7809 S. 21st
Drive, Phoenix, AZ 95041-7736.
ADDITIONAL INFORMATION: May
not be offered every year.

1946—AMERICAN SOCIETY FOR CLINI-CAL LABORATORY SCIENCE (Alpha Mu Tau and Education and Research Fund/Ruth M. French Graduate or Undergraduate Scholarship)

6701 Democracy Boulevard,
Suite 300
Bethesda MD 20817
301/657-2768
FAX: 301/657-2909
E-mail: alphamutaujoe@yahoo.com
Internet: http://www.ascls.org/
leadership/awards/amt.asp
AMOUNT: Up to $3,000
DEADLINE(S): APR 1
FIELD(S): Clinical Laboratory
Science/Medical Technology, Clinical
Laboratory Technician/Medical
Laboratory Technician,
Cytotechnology or Histotechnology
ELIGIBILITY/REQUIREMENTS: Open
to seniors and graduate students enrolled
in an approved undergraduate or graduate
program; must be U.S. citizen or perma-
nent resident.
HOW TO APPLY: See website or e-mail
or send #10 SASE to address below for
application, available after Nov. 1.
CONTACT: Joe Briden, AMTF
Scholarship Coordinator, 7809 S. 21st
Drive, Phoenix, AZ 95041-7736.

1947—AMERICAN SOCIETY OF RADIO-LOGIC TECHNOLOGISTS EDUCATION AND RESEARCH FOUNDATION (Elekta Radiation Therapy Educators Scholarship)

15000 Central Avenue SE
Albuquerque NM 87123-3917
505/298-4500
FAX: 505/298-5063
E-mail: foundation@asrt.org
Internet: http://www.asrt.org
AMOUNT: $5,000
DEADLINE: FEB 1
FIELD(S): Radiologic Sciences
ELIGIBILITY/REQUIREMENTS: Open
ONLY to ASRT members who are radia-
tion therapy educators and pursuing their
baccalaureate, master's or doctoral degree
to enhance their position as a program
director, faculty member, clinical coordi-
nator or clinical instructor. Must have an
ARRT registered/unrestricted state license
and have worked in the radiologic sciences

profession for at least 1 of the past 5 years. Financial need is a factor.
HOW TO APPLY: Contact the ASRT Foundation for an application.
NUMBER OF AWARDS: 4
RENEWABLE: No
CONTACT: Phelosha Collaros

1948—AMERICAN SOCIETY OF RADIO-LOGIC TECHNOLOGISTS EDUCATION AND RESEARCH FOUNDATION (GE Healthcare Management Scholarship)

15000 Central Avenue SE
Albuquerque NM 87123-3917
505/298-4500
FAX: 505/298-5063
E-mail: foundation@asrt.org
Internet: http://www.asrt.org
AMOUNT: $5,000
DEADLINE: FEB 1
FIELD(S): Radiologic Sciences
ELIGIBILITY/REQUIREMENTS: Open ONLY to ASRT members who have applied to an accredited advanced degree program (masters or above) related to management and intended to further his/her career in the radiologic sciences. Must have an ARRT registered/unrestricted state license and have worked in the radiologic sciences profession for at least 1 of the past 5 years. Financial need is a factor.
HOW TO APPLY: Contact the ASRT Foundation for an application.
NUMBER OF AWARDS: 2
RENEWABLE: No
CONTACT: Phelosha Collaros

1949—AMERICAN SOCIETY OF RADIO-LOGIC TECHNOLOGISTS EDUCATION AND RESEARCH FOUNDATION (Howard S. Stern Scholarship)

15000 Central Avenue SE
Albuquerque NM 87123-3917
505/298-4500
FAX: 505/298-5063
E-mail: foundation@asrt.org
Internet: http://www.asrt.org
AMOUNT: $1,000
DEADLINE(S): FEB 1
FIELD(S): Radiologic Sciences
ELIGIBILITY/REQUIREMENTS: Open ONLY to ASRT members who are certificate, associate, baccalaureate, or graduate students. Must have 1-year membership with ASRT, ARRT registered/unrestricted state license, and have worked in the radiologic sciences profession for at least 1 of the past 5 years. Financial need is a factor.

HOW TO APPLY: Contact the ASRT Foundation for an application.
NUMBER OF AWARDS: 9
RENEWABLE: No
CONTACT: Phelosha Collaros

1950—AMERICAN SOCIETY OF RADIO-LOGIC TECHNOLOGISTS EDUCATION AND RESEARCH FOUNDATION (Jerman-Cahoon Student Scholarship)

15000 Central Avenue SE
Albuquerque NM 87123-3917
505/298-4500
FAX: 505/298-5063
E-mail: foundation@asrt.org
Internet: http://www.asrt.org
AMOUNT: $2,500
DEADLINE(S): FEB 1
FIELD(S): Radiologic Sciences
ELIGIBILITY/REQUIREMENTS: Open to outstanding students attending an entry-level radiologic sciences program with a minimum 3.0 GPA. Financial need is a factor.
HOW TO APPLY: Contact the ASRT Foundation for an application. Submit with a transcript, evaluation form and a 450- to 500-word essay.
NUMBER OF AWARDS: 7
RENEWABLE: No
CONTACT: Phelosha Collaros

1951—AMERICAN SOCIETY OF RADIO-LOGIC TECHNOLOGISTS EDUCATION AND RESEARCH FOUNDATION (Monster Medical Imaging Educators Scholarship)

15000 Central Avenue SE
Albuquerque NM 87123-3917
505/298-4500
FAX: 505/298-5063
E-mail: foundation@asrt.org
Internet: http://www.asrt.org
AMOUNT: $5,000
DEADLINE: FEB 1
FIELD(S): Radiologic Sciences
ELIGIBILITY/REQUIREMENTS: Open ONLY to ASRT members who are medical imaging educators and pursuing their baccalaureate, master's or doctoral degree to enhance their position as a program director, faculty member, clinical coordinator or clinical instructor. Must have an ARRT registered/unrestricted state license and have worked in the radiologic sciences profession for at least 1 of the past 5 years. Financial need is a factor.
HOW TO APPLY: Contact the ASRT Foundation for an application.
NUMBER OF AWARDS: 4
RENEWABLE: No
CONTACT: Phelosha Collaros

1952—AMERICAN SOCIETY OF RADIO-LOGIC TECHNOLOGISTS EDUCATION AND RESEARCH FOUNDATION (Royce Osborn Minority Student Scholarship)

15000 Central Avenue SE
Albuquerque NM 87123-3917
505/298-4500
FAX: 505/298-5063
E-mail: foundation@asrt.org
Internet: http://www.asrt.org
AMOUNT: $4,000
DEADLINE(S): FEB 1
FIELD(S): Radiologic Sciences
ELIGIBILITY/REQUIREMENTS: Open to outstanding students attending an entry-level radiologic sciences program with a minimum 3.0 GPA. Requirements include a transcript, evaluation form and a 450- to 500-word essay. Financial need is a factor.
HOW TO APPLY: Contact the ASRT Foundation for an application.
NUMBER OF AWARDS: 7
RENEWABLE: No
CONTACT: Phelosha Collaros

1953—AMERICAN SOCIETY OF RADIO-LOGIC TECHNOLOGISTS EDUCATION AND RESEARCH FOUNDATION (Siemens Clinical Advancement Scholarship)

15000 Central Avenue SE
Albuquerque NM 87123-3917
505/298-4500
FAX: 505/298-5063
E-mail: foundation.us@siemens.com
AMOUNT: $3,000
DEADLINE(S): FEB 1
FIELD(S): Radiologic Sciences
ELIGIBILITY/REQUIREMENTS: Open ONLY to ASRT members who are seeking to enhance their clinical practice skills and ability to provide excellent patient care. Must have an ARRT registered/unrestricted state license, and must have worked in the radiologic sciences profession for at least 1 year of the past 5 years. Financial need is a factor.
HOW TO APPLY: Contact the ASRT Foundation for an application.
NUMBER OF AWARDS: 6
RENEWABLE: No
CONTACT: Phelosha Collaros

1954—AMERICAN SOCIETY OF RADIO-LOGIC TECHNOLOGISTS EDUCATION AND RESEARCH FOUNDATION (Varian Radiation Therapy Student Scholarship)

15000 Central Avenue SE
Albuquerque NM 87123-3917
505/298-4500

FAX: 505/298-5063
E-mail: foundation@asrt.org
Internet: http://www.asrt.org
AMOUNT: $5,000
DEADLINE(S): FEB 1
FIELD(S): Radiologic Sciences
ELIGIBILITY/REQUIREMENTS: Open to outstanding students accepted or enrolled in an entry-level radiation therapy program with a minimum 3.0 GPA. Financial need is a factor. Requirements include a transcript, evaluation form and a 450- to 500-word essay.
HOW TO APPLY: Contact the ASRT Foundation for an application.
NUMBER OF AWARDS: 2
RENEWABLE: No
CONTACT: Phelosha Collaros

1955—ASSOCIATED WESTERN UNIVERSITIES,INC. (AWU Undergraduate Student Fellowships)

4190 South Highland Drive,
Suite 211
Salt Lake City UT 84124-2600
801/273-8900
FAX: 801/277-5632
Internet: http://www.awu.org
AMOUNT: $300/week stipend
DEADLINE(S): FEB 1
FIELD(S): Science; Mathematics; Engineering; Technology
ELIGIBILITY/REQUIREMENTS: Students who have been, or will be, enrolled in any accredited institution within 6 months of the start of their award. Academic performance, class standing, career goals, recommendations, and compatibility of interests and abilities with the needs and resources of the host facility.
HOW TO APPLY: See website for application and list of participating laboratories. Must also submit résumé, at least 1 (2 preferred) recommendations from a faculty member who is familiar with your academic achievements, and transcript. Applicants who received an AWU award within the last year and have approval for reappointment with their previous mentor, need only to complete the application form and submit a copy of their current transcripts.
NUMBER OF AWARDS: 500
CONTACT: Kathy Hecker, Director of Finance and Property Management

1956—AUSTIN PEAY STATE UNIVERSITY (Dr. Robert T. Crews Medical Technology Scholarship)

Medical Technology
Department of Biological Sciences
Box 7148

Clarksville TN 37044
931/221-7781
FAX: 931/221-5996
E-mail: robison@apsu.edu
DEADLINE(S): MAR 15
FIELD(S): Medical Technology and related fields
ELIGIBILITY/REQUIREMENTS: Open to senior with financial need who has demonstrated high academic achievement. Selection is based upon criteria established by the members of the Alpha Pi Chapter (APSU) of Lambda Tau National Medical Technology Honor Society.
HOW TO APPLY: See website for application; mail to Dr. Sarah Lundin-Schilller. Department of Biology, P.O. Box 4718, Clarksville, TN 37044.
NUMBER OF AWARDS: 1
CONTACT: Department of Biology, APSU Box 4718, telephone 931/221-7781
RENEWABLE: No

1957—COMMUNITY FOUNDATION OF WESTERN MASSACHUSETTS (James L. Shriver Scholarship)

1500 Main Street
P.O. Box 15769
Springfield MA 01115
413/732-2858
FAX: 413/733/8565
E-mail: scholar@community foundation.org
Internet: http://www.community foundation.org
AMOUNT: $600
DEADLINE(S): MAR 31
FIELD(S): Technical Fields
ELIGIBILITY/REQUIREMENTS: Open to residents of Western Massachusetts to pursue technical careers through college, trade, or technical school. Based on financial need, academic merit, and extracurricular activities.
HOW TO APPLY: See website for application.
NUMBER OF AWARDS: 1
RENEWABLE: No

1958—ILLUMINATING ENGINEERING SOCIETY OF NORTH AMERICA (Robert W. Thunen Memorial Scholarships)

Golden Gate Section
P.O. Box 77527
San Francisco CA 94107-1527
E-mail: riverfield@juno.com
AMOUNT: $2,500
DEADLINE(S): APR 1
FIELD(S): Illumination (Architectural, Commercial, Residential, Airport,

Navigational, Theatrical, TV, Agricultural, Vision, etc.)
ELIGIBILITY/REQUIREMENTS: Open to full-time undergraduate juniors and seniors and graduate students in an accredited 4-year college or university located in Northern California or Nevada, Oregon, or Washington.
HOW TO APPLY: Contact Chair for an application. Must submit statement of purpose (with respect to lighting education) and 3 letters of recommendation. Awards announced by May 3.
NUMBER OF AWARDS: At least 2
CONTACT: Heide M. Kawahata, Chair

1959—INTERNATIONAL ORDER OF THE KING'S DAUGHTERS AND SONS (Health Careers Scholarships)

Health Careers Department
736 Ardmore Lane
Shelbyville KY 40065
AMOUNT: $1,000 (maximum)
DEADLINE(S): APR 1
FIELD(S): Medicine; Dentistry; Nursing; Physical Therapy; Occupational Therapy; Medical Technologies; Pharmacy
ELIGIBILITY/REQUIREMENTS: Must be U.S. or Canadian citizen, enrolled full time in a school accredited in the field involved and located in the U.S. or Canada. For all students, except those preparing for an RN degree, application must be for at least the third year of college. RN students must have completed the first year of schooling. Pre-med students are not eligible to apply. For those students seeking degrees of MD or DDS, application must be for at least the second year of medical or dental school. Each applicant must supply proof of acceptance in the school involved. There is no age limit.
HOW TO APPLY: Send SASE for an application between January 1 and March 15 with a letter stating the field of study and present level. Submit application with résumé, including personal statement as to the reason for selection of the chosen field and intentions for a career following graduation; letters of recommendation from at least 2 informed persons, with their identification and relationship to applicant made clear; up-to-date official transcripts from current school which MUST be mailed directly from the registrar office (if graduating on a pass/fail system, a statement is required from the Dean of Students or a professor in regard to academic progress); and an itemized budget, endorsed by the school Financial Aid officer, including: school and living expenses, income, loans,

awards, family contributions, etc., for the current year and projected estimate for the next year.

RENEWABLE: Yes, for 2 additional years if qualified

CONTACT: Ida Lyons, Director

1960—JEWISH FEDERATION OF METROPOLITAN CHICAGO (Academic Scholarship Program)

Jewish Vocational Service
216 West Jackson Blvd., Suite 700
Chicago IL 60606-6921
312/673-3400
TTY: 312/444-2877
FAX: 312/553-5544
E-mail: jvsscholarship@jvs
chicago.org
Internet: http://www.jvs/
chicago.org

AMOUNT: Varies

DEADLINE(S): FEB 15

FIELD(S): Mathematics, Engineering, Science, Medicine, Social Work, Education, Psychology, Rabbinate, Law (except corporate), Communications

ELIGIBILITY/REQUIREMENTS: Open to Jewish men and women legally domiciled in the greater Chicago metropolitan area, who are identified as having promise for significant contributions in their chosen careers, and are in need of financial assistance for full-time academic programs in above areas. Must have entered undergraduate junior year in career programs requiring no postgraduate education, be in graduate/professional school, or be in a vo-tech training program.

HOW TO APPLY: Contact JVS Scholarship Secretary (312/673-3457) or fax or visit website (click on Scholarship Services) for an application in the Fall. Interview required.

RENEWABLE: Yes

1961—JEWISH FEDERATION OF METROPOLITAN CHICAGO (Academic Scholarship Program/The Marcus and Theresa Levie Educational Fund)

One South Franklin Street
Chicago IL 60606
312/357-4521
FAX: 312/855-3282
E-mail: jvsscholarship@jvs
chicago.org
Internet: http://www.jvs/
chicago.org

AMOUNT: Varies

DEADLINE(S): FEB 15

FIELD(S): Medicine, Dentistry, Dental Hygiene, Emergency Medical Technology, Health Technology, Nursing or Physicians' Assistant, Occupational Therapy, Optometry, Clinical Psychology/Counseling, Education

ELIGIBILITY/REQUIREMENTS: Open to college juniors, seniors, and graduate students, or students in vocational training programs, who are Jewish and residents of Chicago or Cook County, Illinois. Academic achievement and financial need are considered.

HOW TO APPLY: Phone JVS Scholarship Secretary (312/673-3457), fax, or visit website (click on Scholarship Services) for an application in the Fall.

1962—J. HUGH AND EARLE W. FELLOWS MEMORIAL FUND (Scholarship Loans)

Pensacola Junior College
1000 College Boulevard
Pensacola FL 32504-8998
904/484-1700
Internet: http://www.pjc.cc.fl.us/

AMOUNT: Varies

DEADLINE(S): MAY 1

FIELD(S): Medicine; Nursing; Medical Technology; Theology (Episcopal)

ELIGIBILITY/REQUIREMENTS: For undergraduate study only. Open to bona fide residents of the Florida counties of Escambia, Santa Rosa, Okaloosa, or Walton; U.S. citizenship required.

HOW TO APPLY: Write for information.

CONTACT: Dr. Charles A. Atwell

1963—NATIONAL ASSOCIATION OF AMERICAN BUSINESS CLUBS (AMBUCS Scholarships for Therapists)

P.O. Box 5127
High Point NC 27262
800/838-1845, ext. 10
FAX:336/852-6830
E-mail: janiceb@ambucs.org
Internet: http://www.ambucs.ORG

AMOUNT: $500-$1,500, $6,000 (2-year award)

DEADLINE(S): APR 15

FIELD(S): Physical Therapy, Music Therapy, Occupational Therapy, Speech-Language Pathology, Audiology

ELIGIBILITY/REQUIREMENTS: Open to undergraduate juniors and seniors or graduate students who have good scholastic standing and plan to enter the fields listed above. The institution to which you are accepted must present a curriculum accredited by the appropriate health/therapy profession authority. GPA of 3.0 or better (4.0 scale) and U.S. citizenship required. Must demonstrate financial need.

HOW TO APPLY: See website for additional information and application. MUST apply online. Semi-finalists must provide proof of enrollment, IRS Form 1040s, and a personal statement of not more than 1 page describing the development of your chosen field of therapy; your plan of study; career plans after graduation; and why financial assistance is needed. It is recommended, but not mandatory, that applicants seek sponsorship of an AMBUCS chapter, provided a chapter is located within a reasonable distance of your home or school.

RENEWABLE: Yes

NUMBER OF AWARDS: Multiple

CONTACT: Janice Blankenship, Membership/Scholarship Coordinator, 336/852-0052, ext. 10.

1964—NEW YORK STATE HIGHER EDUCATION SERVICES CORPORATION (N.Y. State Regents Professional/Health Care Opportunity Scholarships)

Cultural Education Center
Room 5C64
Albany NY 12230
518/486-1319
Internet: http://www.hesc.com

AMOUNT: $1,000-$10,000/year

DEADLINE(S): Varies

FIELD(S): Medicine, Dentistry & related fields; Architecture, Nursing, Psychology, Audiology, Landscape Architecture, Social Work, Chiropractic, Law, Pharmacy, Accounting, Speech Language Pathology

ELIGIBILITY/REQUIREMENTS: For New York State residents who are economically disadvantaged and members of a minority group underrepresented in the chosen profession and attending school in New York State. For U.S. citizens or qualifying noncitizens.

HOW TO APPLY: See website or contact NYS HESC.

RENEWABLE: Yes

1965—SPIE: THE INTERNATIONAL SOCIETY FOR OPTICAL ENGINEERING (Michael Kidger Memorial Scholarship)

P.O. Box 10
Bellingham WA 98227-0010

E-mail: scholarships@spie.org
Internet: http://www.kidger.com
DEADLINE(S): FEB 6
FIELD(S): Optical Design
ELIGIBILITY/REQUIREMENTS: Must be a student of optical design who meets the entry criteria for the chosen course of study or research. Must have at least 1 year after the award to completion of their chosen course of study.
HOW TO APPLY: See website. With application must submit a summary (5 pages maximum) of your academic background and interest in pursuing training or research in optical design (limited supporting material may be attached) and 2 letters of recommendation.
NUMBER OF AWARDS: 1
RENEWABLE: No
CONTACT: davidwilliamson@msn.com or tina@kidger.com

1966—SPIE: THE INTERNATIONAL SOCIETY FOR OPTICAL ENGINEERING (SPIE Educational Scholarships & Grants in Optical Science and Engineering)

P.O. Box 10
Bellingham WA 98227-0010
360/676-3290
FAX: 360/647-1445
E-mail: scholarships@spie.org
Internet: http://www.spie.org
AMOUNT: $1,000-$10,000
DEADLINE(S): JAN 6
FIELD(S): Optics, Photonics, Imaging, Optoelectronics or related discipline
ELIGIBILITY/REQUIREMENTS: Undergraduate and graduate students must be enrolled full time in one of the fields as mentioned above at an educational institution for the academic year in which the award is used. This requirement does not apply to high school students.
HOW TO APPLY: See website. Must submit application, 2 letters of reference, a 450-word essay and the annual scholarship award report (if applicable) by deadline.
RENEWABLE: Yes. Must submit an annual scholarship award report if reapplying. Your application must show new activities beyond those upon which a previous award was based.
ADDITIONAL INFORMATION: Must be an SPIE student member or submit an application for student membership including dues payment with the scholarship application to SPIE by the deadline.
NOTE: High school students may receive a complimentary (free) student membership after submitting a membership application.

NURSING

1967—AAOHN FOUNDATION (Professional Development Scholarships)

2920 Brandywine Road, Suite 100
Atlanta GA 30341-4146
770/455-7757, ext. 107
FAX: 770/455-7271
E-mail: don@aaohn.org
Internet: http://www.aaohn.org/foundation/scholarships/academic_study.cfm
AMOUNT: $2,500-$3,000
DEADLINE(S): DEC 1
FIELD(S): Occupational and Environmental Health
ELIGIBILITY/REQUIREMENTS: Must be a registered nurse enrolled full- or part-time in a nationally accredited school of nursing baccalaureate program and demonstrate an interest in, and commitment to, occupational and environmental health. Awards based on professional goals (50%), impact of education on career (20%), and letters of recommendation (30%).
HOW TO APPLY: See website for application; Submit with a 500-word narrative of professional goals as they pertain to the academic activity and the field of occupational and environmental health. Address impact of education on applicant's career in occupational and environmental health nursing. 2 letters of recommendation, (1 from an occupational/environmental health professional) and proof of enrollment status.
NUMBER OF AWARDS: 5 (3, $3,000; 2, $2,500)
RENEWABLE: Yes. Contingent upon successful completion of the year's coursework and availability of funds, Must reapply; up to maximum of 2 additional years
ADDITIONAL INFORMATION: At the end of each year of scholarship participation, recipient must submit a copy of the transcripts reflecting completion of educational courses.

1968—ALBERT BAKER FUND EDUCATION GRANTS, THE (Christian Science Nurses' Training Grant Fund)

P.O. Box 179
Amador City CA 95601-0179
209/267-5701 or 800/269-0388
FAX: 209/267-0569
E-mail: abf@albertbakerfund.org
Internet: http://www.albertbakerfund.org
AMOUNT: Up to $1,500

DEADLINE(S): JUL 1
FIELD(S): Christian Science Journal-listed Nursing
ELIGIBILITY/REQUIREMENTS: Open to students who are members of the First Church of Christ Scientist in Boston, Massachusetts, or one of its branch churches. When applying, must have all financing in place except ABF loan. Must be enrolled in an accredited college, university, or trade school.
HOW TO APPLY: See website and complete online application or contact Fund for information.
NUMBER OF AWARDS: Varies

1969—AMERICAN ASSOCIATION OF COLLEGES OF NURSING (CampusRN/AACN Nursing Scholarship FundMedical Technology)

Department of Biological Sciences
Box 7148
Clarksville TN 37044
931/221-7781
FAX: 931/221-5996
E-mail: info@campuscareercenter.com
Internet: http://aacn.campusrn.com/scholar/scholarships rn.asp
AMOUNT: $2,500
DEADLINE(S): JAN 1, MAR 1, MAY 1, JUL 1, SEP 1, NOV 1
FIELD(S): Nursing
ELIGIBILITY/REQUIREMENTS: Must be enrolled in a BSN, master's, or doctoral degree program in nursing at an AACN member school and a CampusRN member with a minimum 3.25 GPA. Special consideration will be given to students who are enrolled in a master's or doctoral program with the goal of pursuing a nursing faculty career, or who are completing an RN-to-BSN program or are enrolled in an accelerated baccalaureate or master's degree nursing program.
HOW TO APPLY: See website for application; must be submitted by e-mail to scholarships@campuscareercenter.com along with a complete profile on CampusRN.
NUMBER OF AWARDS: 6
CONTACT: E-mail to above address; put AACN Scholarship Question in subject line.

1970—AMERICAN COLLEGE OF NURSE-MIDWIVES FOUNDATION (Basic Midwifery Scholarship)

8404 Colesville Road, Suite 1550
Silver Spring MD 20910

240/485-1800
FAX: 240/485-1818
Internet: http://www.midwife.org
AMOUNT: Varies
DEADLINE(S): MAR 15
FIELD(S): Nurse-Midwifery
ELIGIBILITY/REQUIREMENTS: Open to students enrolled in ACNM DOA-accredited certificate or graduate nurse-midwifery programs in the U.S. Must be student member of ACNM and complete one clinical module or semester. Based on academic criteria and financial need.
HOW TO APPLY: Download application and other forms from website. Submit by mail.
NUMBER OF AWARDS: Varies

1971—AMERICAN LEGION AUXILIARY (Department of Colorado/Past President's Parley Nurse's Training Scholarship)

179 South Ogden Street
Denver CO 80209
720/253-6681
E-mail: uniquarters@aol.com
AMOUNT: TBD (based on contributions received)
DEADLINE(S): APR 15
FIELD(S): Nursing
ELIGIBILITY/REQUIREMENTS: Must be the child or spouse of a veteran who has served in the Armed Forces during any war since WWI; resident of Colorado.
HOW TO APPLY: Submit application along with 5 letters of character recommendation (2 classroom teachers, and school counselor or dean, family doctor, minister or employer) and essay of no more than 500 words "Americanism," and a certified transcript to Chris Harvey at above address,
NUMBER OF AWARDS: TBD (based on contributions received)
RENEWABLE: No

1972—AMERICAN LEGION AUXILIARY (Department of Oregon/Department Nurses Scholarship)

401 Van Ness Avenue, Room 113
San Francisco CA 94102-4586
415/861-5092
FAX: 415/861-8365
E-mail: calegionaux@calegion
aux.org
Internet: http://www.calegion
aux.org
AMOUNT: $1,500
DEADLINE(S): MAY 15 (to Local Unit Sponsor), JUN 1 (to Department Chairperson)

FIELD(S): Nursing
ELIGIBILITY/REQUIREMENTS: Must be the child or widow of a veteran or the wife of a disabled veteran and a resident of Oregon attending an accredited Hospital of Nursing anywhere.
HOW TO APPLY: Apply on Department forms, available from the Department Secretary or the Department of Education Chairperson, signed by the Unit President and the Education Chairman of the sponsoring unit to Local American Legion Auxiliary Unit along with 5 letters of character recommendation (2 classroom teachers, and school counselor or dean, family doctor, minister or employer) and essay "Look to the Future." For information and applications, Department Education Chairperson, 2525NE 39th Avenue, Portland, OR 97212 or The Department Office, American Legion Auxiliary, P.O. Box #1730, Wilsonville, OR 97070.
NUMBER OF AWARDS: 1
RENEWABLE: No
CONTACT: Angie McKinney, Department Education Chairman
ADDITIONAL INFORMATION: For further information, see "Need a Lift" which is available in the office of your Counselor or Library or write the Education and Scholarship Chairperson.

1973—AMERICAN RADIO RELAY LEAGUE FOUNDATION (William R. Goldfarb Memorial Scholarship)

225 Main Street
Newington CT 06111
860/594-0397
FAX: 860/594-0259
E-mail: foundation@arrl.org
Internet: http://www.arrlf.org/
AMOUNT: $10,000 or more
DEADLINE(S): FEB 1
FIELD(S): Business, Computer Science, Medicine (including Nursing), Engineering, Sciences
ELIGIBILITY/REQUIREMENTS: For student with any class of license pursuing baccalaureate or higher degree at a regionally accredited institution. Must demonstrate financial need.
HOW TO APPLY: See website or contact Foundation for information and application. Submit with a 1-page essay on the role amateur radio has played in your life. A recent high school (or equivalent) or college transcript required; submit with application or mail separately.
NUMBER OF AWARDS: 1
RENEWABLE: No
CONTACT: Mary M. Hobart, K1MMH, Secretary

1974—ANNA: AMERICAN NEPHROLOGY NURSES' ASSOCIATION (Abbott/Pamela Balzer Career Mobility Scholarship)

East Holly Avenue
P.O. Box 56
Pitman NJ 08071-0056
856/256-2320
FAX: 888/600-2662
E-mail: anna@ajj.com
Internet: http://www.annanurse.org
AMOUNT: $2,500
DEADLINE(S): OCT 15
FIELD(S): Nephrology Nursing
ELIGIBILITY/REQUIREMENTS: Open to a full member of ANNA for at least 2 years; must be accepted or enrolled in a baccalaureate or higher degree program in nursing; and currently employed in nephrology nursing.
HOW TO APPLY: Send application; transcript(s); letter from college confirming your acceptance into a course of full- or part-time study; 3 letters of reference from persons who can comment on your ability; and an essay of 250 words or less describing career and educational goals, including how the degree will apply to a nephrology nursing practice, time frame for completion of program, and how acquired funds will be applied to meet educational needs.
NUMBER OF AWARDS: 1

1975—ANNA: AMERICAN NEPHROLOGY NURSES' ASSOCIATION (Alcavis International, Inc.)

East Holly Avenue
P.O. Box 56
Pitman NJ 08071-0056
856/256-2320
FAX: 888/600-2662
E-mail: anna@ajj.com
Internet: http://www.annanurse.org
AMOUNT: $2,000
DEADLINE(S): OCT 15
FIELD(S): Nephrology Nursing
ELIGIBILITY/REQUIREMENTS: Open to a full member of ANNA for at least 2 years; must be accepted or enrolled in a baccalaureate or higher degree program in nursing; and currently employed in nephrology nursing.
HOW TO APPLY: Send application; transcript(s); letter from college confirming your acceptance into a course of full- or part-time study; 3 letters of reference from persons who can comment on your ability; and an essay of 250 words or less describing career and educational goals, including how the degree will apply to a nephrology nursing practice, time frame for comple-

tion of program, and how acquired funds will be applied to meet educational needs. NUMBER OF AWARDS: 1

1976—ANNA: AMERICAN NEPHROLOGY NURSES' ASSOCIATION (Amgen Career Mobility Scholarship)

East Holly Avenue
P.O. Box 56
Pitman NJ 08071-0056
856/256-2320
FAX: 888/600-2662
E-mail: anna@ajj.com
Internet: http://www.annanurse.org
AMOUNT: $2,000
DEADLINE(S): OCT 15
FIELD(S): Nephrology Nursing
ELIGIBILITY/REQUIREMENTS: Open to a full member of ANNA for at least 2 years; must be accepted or enrolled in a baccalaureate or higher degree program in nursing; and currently employed in nephrology nursing.
HOW TO APPLY: Send application; transcript(s); letter from college confirming your acceptance into a course of full- or part-time study; 3 letters of reference from persons who can comment on your ability; and an essay of 250 words or less describing career and educational goals, including how the degree will apply to a nephrology nursing practice, time frame for completion of program, and how acquired funds will be applied to meet educational needs. NUMBER OF AWARDS: 1

1977—ANNA: AMERICAN NEPHROLOGY NURSES' ASSOCIATION (ANNA Career Mobility Scholarship)

East Holly Avenue
P.O. Box 56
Pitman NJ 08071-0056
856/256-2320
FAX: 888/600-2662
E-mail: anna@ajj.com
Internet: http://www.annanurse.org
AMOUNT: $2,500
DEADLINE(S): OCT 15
FIELD(S): Nephrology Nursing
ELIGIBILITY/REQUIREMENTS: Open to a full member of ANNA for at least 2 years; must be accepted or enrolled in a baccalaureate or higher degree program in nursing; and currently employed in nephrology nursing.
HOW TO APPLY: Send application; transcript(s); letter from college confirming your acceptance into a course of full- or part-time study; 3 letters of reference from persons who can comment on your ability; and an essay of 250 words or less describ-

ing career and educational goals, including how the degree will apply to a nephrology nursing practice, time frame for completion of program, and how acquired funds will be applied to meet educational needs. NUMBER OF AWARDS: 1

1978—ANNA: AMERICAN NEPHROLOGY NURSES' ASSOCIATION (GE Osmonics Career Mobility Scholarships)

East Holly Avenue
P.O. Box 56
Pitman NJ 08071-0056
856/256-2320
FAX: 888/600-2662
E-mail: anna@ajj.com
Internet: http://www.annanurse.org
AMOUNT: $2,500
DEADLINE(S): OCT 15
FIELD(S): Nephrology Nursing
ELIGIBILITY/REQUIREMENTS: Open to a full member of ANNA for at least 2 years; must be accepted or enrolled in a baccalaureate or higher degree program in nursing; and currently employed in nephrology nursing.
HOW TO APPLY: Send application; transcript(s); letter from college confirming your acceptance into a course of full- or part-time study; 3 letters of reference from persons who can comment on your ability; and an essay of 250 words or less describing career and educational goals, including how the degree will apply to a nephrology nursing practice, time frame for completion of program, and how acquired funds will be applied to meet educational needs. NUMBER OF AWARDS: 2

1979—ANNA: AMERICAN NEPHROLOGY NURSES' ASSOCIATION (Janel Parker Career Mobility Scholarship)

East Holly Avenue
P.O. Box 56
Pitman NJ 08071-0056
856/256-2320
FAX: 888/600-2662
E-mail: anna@ajj.com
Internet: http://www.annanurse.org
AMOUNT: $2,000
DEADLINE(S): OCT 15
FIELD(S): Nephrology Nursing
ELIGIBILITY/REQUIREMENTS: Open to a full member of ANNA for at least 2 years; must be accepted or enrolled in a baccalaureate or higher degree program in nursing; and currently employed in nephrology nursing.
HOW TO APPLY: Send application; transcript(s); letter from college confirming

your acceptance into a course of full- or part-time study; 3 letters of reference from persons who can comment on your ability; and an essay of 250 words or less describing career and educational goals, including how the degree will apply to a nephrology nursing practice, time frame for completion of program, and how acquired funds will be applied to meet educational needs. NUMBER OF AWARDS: 1

1980—ANNA: AMERICAN NEPHROLOGY NURSES' ASSOCIATION (Nephrology Nursing Certification Commission Career Mobility Scholarships)

East Holly Avenue
P.O. Box 56
Pitman NJ 08071-0056
856/256-2320
FAX: 888/600-2662
E-mail: anna@ajj.com
Internet: http://www.annanurse.org
AMOUNT: $2,000
DEADLINE(S): OCT 15
FIELD(S): Nephrology Nursing
ELIGIBILITY/REQUIREMENTS: Open to a full member of ANNA for at least 2 years; must be accepted or enrolled in a baccalaureate or higher degree program in nursing; and currently employed in nephrology nursing.
HOW TO APPLY: Send application; transcript(s); letter from college confirming your acceptance into a course of full- or part-time study; 3 letters of reference from persons who can comment on your ability; and an essay of 250 words or less describing career and educational goals, including how the degree will apply to a nephrology nursing practice, time frame for completion of program, and how acquired funds will be applied to meet educational needs. NUMBER OF AWARDS: 3

1981—ASSOCIATION OF OPERATING ROOM NURSES (AORN Scholarship Program)

2170 South Parker Road,
Suite 300
Denver CO 80231-5711
800/755-2676,
Internet: http://www.aorn.org/
foundation
AMOUNT: $500-$5,000
DEADLINE(S): JUN 15
FIELD(S): Perioperative Nursing
ELIGIBILITY/REQUIREMENTS: Open to full- or part-time students of nursing or complementary fields in the U.S. Must have a minimum 3.0 GPA and have been

AORN members for at least 1 year prior to deadline. Program must be accredited by the NLN or other acceptable accrediting body.
HOW TO APPLY: Apply online.
NUMBER OF AWARDS: 90-110
RENEWABLE: No
CONTACT: Heidi Arsenault, ext 295

1982—BECA FOUNDATION (Alice Newell Joslyn Medical Fund)

830 East Grand Avenue, Suite B
Escondido CA 92025
760/471-8246
FAX: 760/471-8176
E-mail: sdbeca@sbcglobal.net
Internet: http://www.beca foundation.org
AMOUNT: $1,000-$2,000
DEADLINE(S): MAR 3
FIELD(S): Medicine; Healthcare; Nursing; Dental/Medical Assisting; Physical Therapy
ELIGIBILITY/REQUIREMENTS: Open to Latino students entering the medical/healthcare profession; must be living or attending a high school or college in San Diego County at time of application, Based on financial need, scholastic determination, and community/cultural awareness.
HOW TO APPLY: See website for application. Submit with official copy of high school transcript; 2 letters of recommendation from a high school official, high school teacher/college professor/advisor, or anyone other than family member, who has known you for at least 2 years addressing your leadership abilities, your future potential, and other factors that contribute to your community involvement; and Financial Profile, either a copy of your FAFSA/SAR or questions on application.
RENEWABLE: Yes. Must reapply.

1983—BETHESDA LUTHERAN HOMES AND SERVICES (Development Disabilities Scholastic Excellence Award for Lutheran Nursing Students)

600 Hoffmann Drive
Watertown WI 53094
920/206-4449
FAX: 920/262-6513
E-mail: ncrc@blhs.org
Internet: http://www.blhs.org
AMOUNT: $1,500
DEADLINE(S): MAR 15 for following school year
FIELD(S): Nursing

ELIGIBILITY/REQUIREMENTS: Must be Lutheran; sophomore or higher when applying, minimum GPA 3.0.
HOW TO APPLY: See website or write for application.
NUMBER OF AWARDS: 2
RENEWABLE: No
CONTACT: Thomas Heuer

1984—CALIFORNIA NURSES ASSOCIATION (Sandra R. Spaulding Memorial Scholarship Fund)

2000 Franklin Street
Oakland CA 94612
510/622-8310
FAX: 510/663-1625
E-mail: scholarship@calnurses.org
Internet: http://www.calnurses.org
AMOUNT: Varies
DEADLINE(S): JUL 1
FIELD(S): Nursing
ELIGIBILITY/REQUIREMENTS: Open to students accepted for admission to a 2nd year accredited ADN degree program, who are enrolled in at least half-time study, as defined by the student's institution, and planning to complete the degree program within 2 years.
HOW TO APPLY: See website for application or write or call for application. Submit with a 1 page typed essay, describing educational goals and how they relate to personal and professional vision for healthcare; 2 letters of recommendation, from non-relatives which must relate to this scholarship and address at least one of the following: CNA activities, competence in work setting, and academic ability; a curriculum vitae; and a copy of current RN license.
NUMBER OF AWARDS: Varies
CONTACT: Shaun Copeland

1985—CALIFORNIA NURSES ASSOCIATION (Shirley Titus Scholarship)

2000 Franklin Street
Oakland CA 94612
510/622-8310
FAX: 510/663-1625
E-mail: scholarship@calnurses.org
Internet: http://www.calnurses.org
AMOUNT: Varies
DEADLINE(S): JUL 1
FIELD(S): Nursing; Humanities, Cultural, Political, Economic, Legal and Social Sciences
ELIGIBILITY/REQUIREMENTS: Open to California nurses for academic preparation and continuing education in above fields appropriate for developing effective nursing leadership.

HOW TO APPLY: See website for application or write or call for application. Submit with 2 letters of recommendation which cover academic ability and personal commitment to the field of study; verification of acceptance into 2nd year accredited ADN degree program; a 1 page typed essay describing personal and professional goals; copy of current year's tax return or verification of income (if no tax return was filed) or copy of parent/guardian's tax return (if applicant is claimed as dependent.); and copy of transcript from 1st completed year of nursing program.
NUMBER OF AWARDS: Varies
CONTACT: Shaun Copeland

1986—COMMUNITY FOUNDATION OF WESTERN MASSACHUSETTS (Deborah Brodeur Foley Memorial Scholarship)

1500 Main Street
P.O. Box 15769
Springfield MA 01115
413/732-2858
FAX: 413/733/8565
E-mail: scholar@community foundation.org
Internet: http://www.community foundation.org
AMOUNT: $1,000
DEADLINE(S): MAR 31
FIELD(S): Nursing
ELIGIBILITY/REQUIREMENTS: For a graduating senior from Minnechaug Regional High School pursuing a career in nursing or an allied field.
HOW TO APPLY: See website for application.
NUMBER OF AWARDS: 1
RENEWABLE: No

1987—COMMUNITY FOUNDATION OF WESTERN MASSACHUSETTS (Edward C. and Mary Marth Scholarship)

1500 Main Street
P.O. Box 15769
Springfield MA 01115
413/732-2858
FAX: 413/733/8565
E-mail: scholar@community foundation.org
Internet: http://www.community foundation.org
AMOUNT: $500
DEADLINE(S): MAR 31
FIELD(S): Nursing
ELIGIBILITY/REQUIREMENTS: Open to graduating seniors of St. Mary's High School in Westfield, Massachusetts who will be attending college or a technical

school for a career in nursing or allied health field.

HOW TO APPLY: See website for application.

NUMBER OF AWARDS: 1

RENEWABLE: No

1988—COMMUNITY FOUNDATION OF WESTERN MASSACHUSETTS (Eleanor M. Morrissey Scholarship)

1500 Main Street
P.O. Box 15769
Springfield MA 01115
413/732-2858
FAX: 413/733/8565
E-mail: scholar@community foundation.org
Internet: http://www.community foundation.org

AMOUNT: $700

DEADLINE(S): MAR 31

FIELD(S): All (4-year programs); Nursing

ELIGIBILITY/REQUIREMENTS: Open to graduating seniors from Holyoke high schools in Holyoke, Massachusetts who will be attending a 4-year college or to study nursing. GPA of 3.0 or higher required. Must demonstrate financial need and have participated in extracurricular activities.

HOW TO APPLY: See website for application.

NUMBER OF AWARDS: 1

RENEWABLE: No

1989—CONNECTICUT LEAGUE FOR NURSING (CLN Nursing Scholarship Information)

P.O. Box 365
Wallingford CT 06492
312/233-1100
E-mail: fore@ahima.org
Internet: http://www.ahima.org

AMOUNT: Varies

DEADLINE(S): APR 25

FIELD(S): Health Information, Health Technology

ELIGIBILITY/REQUIREMENTS: Open to Connecticut residents enrolled in a Connecticut accredited nursing program (NLN or AACN). is eligible to apply. The nursing program must be a that is a CLN Supporting Member. Applicants must demonstrate scholastic ability, professional potential, and financial need. Baccalaureate degree applicants must have completed the 3rd year of a 4-year program. Associate degree applicants must have completed the 1st year of a 2-year pro-

gram. Diploma applicants must have completed the 1st year of a 2-year program. Registered nurse applicants in an upper division nursing program must be entering the senior year of the nursing curriculum.

HOW TO APPLY: See website for additional information and application; submit with official a transcript, reference from the Dean/Director or Nursing Faculty from your current school, and those enrolled in BSN program must provide a verification of status form.

NUMBER OF AWARDS: Varies

1990—DAUGHTERS OF THE AMERICAN REVOLUTION, NATIONAL SOCIETY (Caroline E. Holt Nursing Scholarship)

Committee Services Office
Attn: Scholarships
1776 D Street NW
Washington DC 20006-5392
202/628-1776
Internet: http://www.dar.org

AMOUNT: $500

DEADLINE(S): FEB 15 or AUG 15

FIELD(S): Nursing

ELIGIBILITY/REQUIREMENTS: Awarded to students who are in financial need and are accepted and enrolled into an accredited school of nursing. Affiliation with DAR not required.

HOW TO APPLY: Must submit application with a letter of sponsorship from local DAR chapter (send SASE to address above to obtain name and application); statement of 1,000 words or less stating career objectives, how college major (if required) or college plans relate to future professional goals and reasons for these choices; transcripts list of extracurricular activities, honors received, scholastic achievements, or other significant accomplishments; 2-4 letters of recommendation from the high school or college you now attend who are familiar with your work, and proof of acceptance and enrollment (letter of acceptance or transcript), citizenship and financial need. See website for additional information. DAR Member Number must be on the application.

NUMBER OF AWARDS: Varies

RENEWABLE: No

1991—DAUGHTERS OF THE AMERICAN REVOLUTION, NATIONAL SOCIETY (Madeline Pickett Halbert Cogswell Nursing Scholarship)

Committee Services Office
Attn: Scholarships
1776 D Street NW
Washington DC 20006-5392

202/628-1776
Internet: http://www.dar.org

AMOUNT: $500

DEADLINE(S): FEB 15 or AUG 15

FIELD(S): Nursing

ELIGIBILITY/REQUIREMENTS: Awarded to students who are accepted or enrolled in an accredited school of nursing. Applicants must be members, descendents of members or eligible for membership in NSDAR.

HOW TO APPLY: Must submit application with a letter of sponsorship from local DAR chapter (send SASE to address above to obtain name and application); statement of 1,000 words or less stating career objectives, how college major (if required) or college plans relate to future professional goals and reasons for these choices; transcripts list of extracurricular activities, honors received, scholastic achievements, or other significant accomplishments; 2-4 letters of recommendation from the high school or college you now attend who are familiar with your work, and proof of acceptance and enrollment (letter of acceptance or transcript) and citizenship DAR Member Number must be on application. See website for additional information.

NUMBER OF AWARDS: Varies

RENEWABLE: No

1992—DAUGHTERS OF THE AMERICAN REVOLUTION, NATIONAL SOCIETY (Mildred Nutting Scholarship)

Committee Services Office
Attn: Scholarships
1776 D Street NW
Washington DC 20006-5392
202/628-1776
Internet: http://www.dar.org

AMOUNT: $500

DEADLINE(S): FEB 15 or AUG 15

FIELD(S): Nursing

ELIGIBILITY/REQUIREMENTS: Awarded to students who are in financial need and are accepted and enrolled into an accredited school of nursing. Affiliation with DAR not required.

HOW TO APPLY: Must submit application with a letter of sponsorship from local DAR chapter (send SASE to address above to obtain name and application); statement of 1,000 words or less stating career objectives, how college major (if required) or college plans relate to future professional goals and reasons for these choices; transcripts list of extracurricular activities, honors received, scholastic achievements, or other significant accomplishments; 2-4 letters of recommendation from the high school or college you now attend who are familiar with your work, and proof of acceptance and enrollment (letter of acceptance or transcript), citizenship and financial need. See website for additional information.

NUMBER OF AWARDS: Varies
RENEWABLE: No

1993—EDWARD BANGS KELLEY AND ELZA KELLEY FOUNDATION, INC.

P.O. Drawer M
Hyannis MA 02601-1412
508/775-3117
AMOUNT: $500-$4,000
DEADLINE(S): APR 30
FIELD(S): Medicine; Nursing; Education; Health; Social Sciences

ELIGIBILITY/REQUIREMENTS: Open to residents of Barnstable County, Massachusetts. Awards support study at recognized undergraduate, graduate, and professional institutions. Financial need is considered.

HOW TO APPLY: Contact Foundation for an application.

1994—EPILEPSY FOUNDATION OF AMERICA (Behavioral Sciences Student Fellowships)

4351 Garden City Drive
Landover MD 20785-2267
301/459-3700 or 800/EFA-1000
TDD: 800/332-2070
FAX: 301/577-2684
Internet: http://www.epilepsy foundation.org
AMOUNT: $2,000
DEADLINE(S): MAR 1
FIELD(S): Epilepsy Research/Practice; Sociology; Social Work; Psychology; Anthropology; Nursing; Economics; Vocational Rehabilitation; Counseling; Political Science

ELIGIBILITY/REQUIREMENTS: 3-month fellowships awarded to undergraduate and graduate students for work on a project during the summer or other free period. Students propose an epilepsy-related study or training project to be carried out at a U.S. institution. A preceptor must supervise the student and the project.

HOW TO APPLY: Contact EFA for an application.

1995—HAWAII COMMUNITY FOUNDATION (Dan & Pauline Lutkenhouse Tropical Garden Scholarship)

1164 Bishop Street, Suite 800

Honolulu HI 96813
808/537-6333 or toll free:
888/731-3863
FAX: 808/521-6286
E-mail: info@hcf-hawaii.org
Internet: http://www.hcf-hawaii.org
DEADLINE(S): MAR 1
FIELD(S): Agriculture; Science; Medicine; Nursing

ELIGIBILITY/REQUIREMENTS: Must be resident of the Hilo coast and the Hamakua coast, north of the Wailuku River; plan to attend full time an accredited 2- or 4-year college or university; and demonstrate financial need, good moral character, and academic achievement (minimum GPA of 2.7).

HOW TO APPLY: See website for additional information. Send application with 2 letters of recommendation.

1996—HAWAII COMMUNITY FOUNDATION (Filipino Nurses' Organization of Hawaii Scholarship)

1164 Bishop Street, Suite 800
Honolulu HI 96813
808/537-6333 or toll free:
888/731-3863
FAX: 808/521-6286
E-mail: info@hcf-hawaii.org
Internet: http://www.hcf-hawaii.org
DEADLINE(S): MAR 1
FIELD(S): Nursing

ELIGIBILITY/REQUIREMENTS: Must be of Filipino ancestry; be resident of the state of Hawaii; plan to attend full time an accredited 2- or 4-year college or university; and demonstrate financial need, good moral character, and academic achievement with a minimum GPA of 2.7.

HOW TO APPLY: See website for additional information. Send application with 2 letters of recommendation.

1997—HAWAII COMMUNITY FOUNDATION (Hawaii Student Nurses' Association Fund)

1164 Bishop Street, Suite 800
Honolulu HI 96813
808/537-6333 or toll free:
888/731-3863
FAX: 808/521-6286
E-mail: info@hcf-hawaii.org
Internet: http://www.hcf-hawaii.org
DEADLINE(S): MAR 1
FIELD(S): Nursing

ELIGIBILITY/REQUIREMENTS: Must be current undergraduate students in a school of nursing in Hawaii and demonstrate financial need, good moral charac-

ter, and academic achievement with a minimum GPA of 3.0. Current and past HSNA and NSNA officers are not eligible.

HOW TO APPLY: See website for additional information. Send application with 2 letters of recommendation.

1998—HAWAII COMMUNITY FOUNDATION (Margaret Jones Memorial Nursing Fund)

1164 Bishop Street, Suite 800
Honolulu HI 96813
808/537-6333 or toll free:
888/731-3863
FAX: 808/521-6286
E-mail: info@hcf-hawaii.org
Internet: http://www.hcf-hawaii.org
DEADLINE(S): MAR 1
FIELD(S): Nursing

ELIGIBILITY/REQUIREMENTS: Must be Hawaii residents; be full-time junior or senior undergraduate or graduate students enrolled in an accredited BSN, MSN, or doctoral nursing program in Hawaii; and demonstrate financial need, good moral character, and academic achievement with a minimum GPA of 3.0. Preference may be given to members of the Hawaii Nurses Association.

HOW TO APPLY: See website for additional information. Send application with 2 letters of recommendation.

1999—ILLINOIS AMVETS (Sad Sacks Nursing Scholarship)

2200 South Sixth Street
Springfield IL 62703-3496
217/528-4713 or 800/638-8387
FAX: 217/528-9896
E-mail: sara@ilamvets.org
Internet: http://www.ilamvets.org
AMOUNT: $500
DEADLINE(S): MAR 1
FIELD(S): All

ELIGIBILITY/REQUIREMENTS: Recipient must be Illinois high school senior, who has been accepted into or is already enrolled in a pre-approved nursing program in approved school of nursing in Illinois; must demonstrate satisfactory academic record, character, interest, and activity record, as well as financial need. Priority will be given to the dependant of a deceased or disabled veteran, child or grandchild of a veteran. Must have taken ACT or SAT at time of application.

HOW TO APPLY: See website for additional information and application or contact Foundation. Submit with transcript and ACT or SAT scores. Copy of acceptance letter must accompany application.

RENEWABLE: No
CONTACT: Sara Garcia, Program Director
ADDITIONAL INFORMATION: The scholarship will be given to a student nurse-in-training in the following order: 3rd-, 2nd-, 1st-year student.

2000—INTERNATIONAL ORDER OF THE KING'S DAUGHTERS AND SONS (Health Careers Scholarships)

Health Careers Department
736 Ardmore Lane
Shelbyville KY 40065
AMOUNT: $1,000 (maximum)
DEADLINE(S): APR 1
FIELD(S): Medicine; Dentistry; Nursing; Physical Therapy; Occupational Therapy; Medical Technologies; Pharmacy
ELIGIBILITY/REQUIREMENTS: Must be U.S. or Canadian citizen, enrolled full time in a school accredited in the field involved and located in the U.S. or Canada. For all students, except those preparing for an RN degree, application must be for at least the third year of college. RN students must have completed the first year of schooling. Pre-med students are not eligible to apply. For those students seeking degrees of MD or DDS, application must be for at least the second year of medical or dental school. Each applicant must supply proof of acceptance in the school involved. There is no age limit.
HOW TO APPLY: Send SASE for an application between January 1 and March 15 with a letter stating the field of study and present level. Submit application with résumé, including personal statement as to the reason for selection of the chosen field and intentions for a career following graduation; letters of recommendation from at least 2 informed persons, with their identification and relationship to applicant made clear; up-to-date official transcripts from current school which MUST be mailed directly from the registrar office (if graduating on a pass/fail system, a statement is required from the Dean of Students or a professor in regard to academic progress); and an itemized budget, endorsed by the school Financial Aid officer, including: school and living expenses, income, loans, awards, family contributions, etc., for the current year and projected estimate for the next year.
RENEWABLE: Yes, for 2 additional years if qualified
CONTACT: Ida Lyons, Director

2001—JACKSONVILLE STATE UNIVERSITY (Doris Ledbetter Memorial Scholarship)

Jacksonville AL 36265
256/782-5677 or 800/231-5291
Internet: www.jsu.edu
AMOUNT: Varies
DEADLINE(S): FEB 1
FIELD(S): Education (Nursing)
ELIGIBILITY/REQUIREMENTS: Financial need considered.
HOW TO APPLY: Contact Nursing Department for application and information.
RENEWABLE: No
CONTACT: Nursing Department; 256/782-5425

2002—J. HUGH AND EARLE W. FELLOWS MEMORIAL FUND (Scholarship Loans)

Pensacola Junior College
1000 College Boulevard
Pensacola FL 32504-8998
904/484-1700
Internet: http://www.pjc.cc.fl.us/
AMOUNT: Varies
DEADLINE(S): MAY 1
FIELD(S): Medicine; Nursing; Medical Technology; Theology (Episcopal)
ELIGIBILITY/REQUIREMENTS: For undergraduate study only. Open to bona fide residents of the Florida counties of Escambia, Santa Rosa, Okaloosa, or Walton; U.S. citizenship required.
HOW TO APPLY: Write for information.
CONTACT: Dr. Charles A. Atwell

2003—JEWISH FEDERATION OF METROPOLITAN CHICAGO (Academic Scholarship Program/The Marcus and Theresa Levie Educational Fund)

One South Franklin Street
Chicago IL 60606
312/357-4521
FAX: 312/855-3282
E-mail: jvsscholarship@jvs chicago.org
Internet: http://www.jvs/chicago.org/
AMOUNT: Varies
DEADLINE(S): FEB 15
FIELD(S): Medicine, Dentistry, Dental Hygiene, Emergency Medical Technology, Health Technology, Nursing, Physicians' Assistant, Occupational Therapy, Optometry, Clinical Psychology/Counseling, Education
ELIGIBILITY/REQUIREMENTS: Open to college juniors, seniors, graduate students, or students in vocational training programs, who are Jewish and residents of Chicago or Cook County, Illinois. Academic achievement and financial need are considered.
HOW TO APPLY: Phone JVS Scholarship Secretary (312/673-3457), fax, or visit website (click on Scholarship Services) for an application in the Fall.

2004—MIDWAY COLLEGE

512 East Stephens Street
Midway KY 40347
800/755-0031
E-mail: admissions@midway.edu
Internet: http://www.midway.edu
AMOUNT: Merit Scholarships
ELIGIBILITY/REQUIREMENTS: Merit scholarships for admitted students who are considered full time in Midway's women's college. Depending on scholarship, minimum GPA ranges from 2.5 to 3.2, minimum ACT ranges 18 to 29, minimum SAT from 860 to 1290. In some cases, students must live on campus.
HOW TO APPLY: Contact Admissions Office or high school guidance counselor for application. Complete FAFSA online.
NUMBER OF AWARDS: Varies, up to 100
RENEWABLE: Yes. Must meet GPA requirements which vary based on the scholarship.
CONTACT: Admissions Office or high school guidance counselor
ADDITIONAL INFORMATION: Athletes may be eligible for an athletic scholarship in conjunction with a merit grant; contact coach for eligibility and award information.

2005—MINORITY NURSE MAGAZINE

211 W. Wacker Drive, Suite 900
Chicago IL 60606
312/525-3095
FAX: 312/429-3336
E-mail: pchwedyk@alloy marketing.com
Internet: http://www.minority nurse.com
AMOUNT: $500-$1,000
DEADLINE(S): JUN 15
FIELD(S): Nursing
ELIGIBILITY/REQUIREMENTS: Open to racial and ethnic minority students entering 3rd or 4th year of an accredited 4-year BSN degree program or an accelerated program leading to a BSN degree (such as RN to BSN or BA to BSN) or an accelerated Master's entry program in nursing that bypasses the traditional BSN degree

(e.g., BA to MSN). Must be a U.S. citizen or permanent resident and have a minimum GPA of 3.0.

HOW TO APPLY: Submit application and transcript or other proof of GPA; letter of recommendation from a faculty member outlining academic achievement; letter from Financial Aid Officer outlining financial need; letter of recommendation outlining volunteer work or community service performed by applicant; and 250-word written statement summarizing applicant's academic and personal accomplishments and goals for his/her future nursing career. Nursing faculty members may nominate students and submit application forms provided that all required documentation is included with application.

NUMBER OF AWARDS: 4
RENEWABLE: No
CONTACT: Pam Chwedyk, Editorial Manager

2006—NATIONAL GERONTOLOGICAL NURSING ASSOCIATION

7794 Grow Drive
Pensacola FL 32514
800/723-0560
FAX: 850/484-9987
E-mail: ngna@puetzamc.com
Internet: http://www.ngna.org

AMOUNT: $1,500
DEADLINE(S): JUN 1
FIELD(S): Nursing (Gerontological, Geriatric)

ELIGIBILITY/REQUIREMENTS: U.S. citizen; member of the National Gerontological Nursing Association (may join with application for scholarship).

HOW TO APPLY: Download application from website or contact national office.
NUMBER OF AWARDS: 2
RENEWABLE: No
CONTACT: Harriet McClung

2007—NATIONAL STUDENT NURSES' ASSOCIATION FOUNDATION

555 West 57th Street, Suite 1327
New York NY 10019
212/581-2211
FAX: 212/581-2368
E-mail: nsna@nsna.org
Internet: http://www.nsna.org

AMOUNT: $1,000-$2,000
DEADLINE(S): FEB 1
FIELD(S): Nursing

ELIGIBILITY/REQUIREMENTS: Open to students enrolled in state-approved nursing schools or pre-nursing in associate degree, baccalaureate, diploma, doctorate, or master's programs. Based on academic achievement, financial need, and involvement in nursing student organizations and community activities related to health care. Transcripts required.

HOW TO APPLY: See website, or beginning in August, send SASE (business size) to NSNA for an application. $10 application fee. Graduating high school seniors NOT eligible.

2008—NEUROSCIENCE NURSING FOUNDATION

4700 West Lake Avenue
Glenview IL 60025
888/557-2266
FAX: 877/734-8677
E-mail: info@aann.org
Internet: http://www.aann.org/nnf

AMOUNT: $1,500
DEADLINE(S): JAN 15
FIELD(S): Neuroscience Nursing

ELIGIBILITY/REQUIREMENTS: Must be licensed nurse; seeking BSN or higher degree; GPA of 3.0 at an accredited school.

HOW TO APPLY: Print application from website or call to request application.
NUMBER OF AWARDS: Varies
RENEWABLE: No

2008A—NEW YORK STATE GRANGE SCHOLARSHIPS (June Gill Nursing Scholarship)

100 Grange Place
Cortland NY 13045
607/756-7553
FAX: 607/756-7757
E-mail: nysgrange@nysgrange.com
Internet: http://www.nysgrange.com

AMOUNT: Varies
FIELD(S): Nursing

ELIGIBILITY/REQUIREMENTS: Must be a Grange member in good standing.

HOW TO APPLY: Send application; verification of enrollment in a nursing program and of Grange membership; career statement; academic records; and description of financial need.
NUMBER OF AWARDS: 1
RENEWABLE: No

2009—NEW YORK STATE HIGHER EDUCATION SERVICES CORPORATION (N.Y. State Regents Professional/Health Care Opportunity Scholarships)

Cultural Education Center
Room 5C64
Albany NY 12230
518/486-1319
Internet: http://www.hesc.com

AMOUNT: $1,000-$10,000/year
DEADLINE(S): Varies
FIELD(S): Medicine, Dentistry & related fields; Architecture, Nursing, Psychology, Audiology, Landscape Architecture, Social Work, Chiropractic, Law, Pharmacy, Accounting, Speech Language Pathology

ELIGIBILITY/REQUIREMENTS: For New York State residents who are economically disadvantaged and members of a minority group underrepresented in the chosen profession and attending school in New York State. For U.S. citizens or qualifying non-citizens.

HOW TO APPLY: See website or contact NYS HESC.
RENEWABLE: Yes

2010—NORTH CAROLINA DEPARTMENT OF PUBLIC INSTRUCTION (Scholarship Loan Program for Prospective Teachers)

301 North Wilmington Street
Raleigh NC 27601-2825
919/715-1120

AMOUNT: Up to $2,500
DEADLINE(S): FEB
FIELD(S): Education: Teaching, School Psychology and Counseling, Speech/Language Impaired, Audiology, Library/Media Services

ELIGIBILITY/REQUIREMENTS: For North Carolina residents planning to teach in North Carolina public schools. At least 3.0 high school GPA required; must maintain 2.5 GPA during freshman year and 3.0 cumulative thereafter. Must be full-time students.

HOW TO APPLY: Applications available in December from high school counselors and college and university departments of education.
NUMBER OF AWARDS: 200
RENEWABLE: Yes

2011—ODD FELLOWS AND REBEKAHS (The Ellen F. Washburn Nursing Training Awards)

131 Queens Street Extension
Gorham ME 04038
207/839-4723

AMOUNT: $150-$300
DEADLINE(S): APR 15
FIELD(S): Nursing

ELIGIBILITY/REQUIREMENTS: For undergraduate students in an RN program enrolled in an accredited Maine school of nursing. Must demonstrate financial need.

HOW TO APPLY: Contact Chairperson for more information.

NUMBER OF AWARDS: 20
RENEWABLE: Yes
CONTACT: Joyce B. Young, Chairperson

2012—ONCOLOGY NURSING FOUNDATION (Scholarships, Grants, Awards, and Honors)

125 Enterprise Drive
Pittsburgh PA 15275-1214
412/859-6100
FAX: 412/859-6160
E-mail: foundation@ons.org
AMOUNT: Varies (with program)
DEADLINE(S): Varies (with program)
FIELD(S): Oncology Nursing
ELIGIBILITY/REQUIREMENTS: For registered nurses seeking further training or to engage in research. Various programs range from bachelor's degree level through postmaster's and career development. Also honors and awards for oncology nurses who have contributed to professional literature and excellence in their field. Some require ONF membership.
HOW TO APPLY: Contact Oncology Nursing Society Foundation for application.

2013—PILOT INTERNATIONAL FOUNDATION (Ruby Newhall Memorial Scholarship)

P.O. Box 5600
Macon GA 31208-5600
478/743-7403
FAX: 478/743-2173
E-mail: pifinfo@pilothq.org
Internet: http://www.pilot
international.org
AMOUNT: Varies
DEADLINE(S): FEB 15
FIELD(S): Human Health & Welfare
ELIGIBILITY/REQUIREMENTS: For international students who have studied in the U.S. for at least 1 year, and who intend to return to their home country 6 months after graduation. Must be full-time students majoring in a field related to human health and welfare, and have a GPA of 3.0 or more.
HOW TO APPLY: Must be sponsored by a Pilot Club in their home, college, or university town or city. Send SASE for complete information. See website for application.

2014—RHODE ISLAND FOUNDATION, THE (Albert E. and Florence W. Newton Nurse Scholarship)

One Union Station

Providence RI 03908
401/274-4564
Internet: http://www.ri
foundation.org
AMOUNT: $500-$2,500
DEADLINE(S): APR 1(fall semester); OCT 1 (spring semester)
FIELD(S): Nursing
ELIGIBILITY/REQUIREMENTS: Open to RN-seeking baccalaureate; junior or senior in baccalaureate program, 2nd- or 3rd-year nursing student in a 3-year nursing program, or student in a 2-year associate degree nursing program.
HOW TO APPLY: Submit application form, transcripts from all high schools, college and universities attended; copy of ACT/SAT or similar test scores; and financial aid form.
NUMBER OF AWARDS: Multiple
RENEWABLE: Yes
CONTACT: Libby Monahan

2015—UNIVERSITY OF WINDSOR (U.S./Mexico Entrance Scholarship)

401 Sunset Avenue
Windsor Ontario N9B 3P4
CANADA
519/253-3000
FAX: 519/973-7081
E-mail: awards1@uwindsor.ca
Internet: http://www.uwindsor.ca
AMOUNT: $3,000/term (Canadian) Engineering, Education, Law, Nursing; all other fields $1,500/term (Canadian)
DEADLINE(S): MAY 31
FIELD(S): All
ELIGIBILITY/REQUIREMENTS: Open to undergraduate students with U.S./Mexican citizenship or permanent resident status registering in year 1 at the University of Windsor. Must have superior grades.
HOW TO APPLY: Automatic. No application required.
RENEWABLE: Yes. Up to 4 years, contingent upon successful completion of the previous term and a cumulative A- GPA.
CONTACT: Aase Houser

2016—WESTERN MICHIGAN UNIVERSITY (College of Health and Human Services/Borgess Excellence in Nursing Scholarship)

1903 West Michigan
Kalamazoo MI 49008-5337
269/387-8777
FAX: 269/387-6989
E-mail: finaid-info@wmich.edu
Internet: http://www.wmich.edu/

finaid
AMOUNT: Varies
DEADLINE(S): JUN 1
FIELD(S): Nursing
ELIGIBILITY/REQUIREMENTS: Must show financial need, and have a 3.0 minimum GPA. Recipients shall participate in the Borgess Nurse Extern Program.
HOW TO APPLY: Contact the Bronson School of Nursing for more information.
CONTACT: Bronson School of Nursing

2017—WESTERN MICHIGAN UNIVERSITY (College of Health and Human Services/Bronson Health Foundation Scholarship)

1903 West Michigan
Kalamazoo MI 49008-5337
269/387-8777
FAX: 269/387-6989
E-mail: finaid-info@wmich.edu
Internet: http://www.wmich.edu/
finaid
AMOUNT: $500-$2,000
DEADLINE(S): JUN 1
FIELD(S): Nursing
ELIGIBILITY/REQUIREMENTS: Preference shall be given to a full-time WMU Bronson School of Nursing undergraduate student who is a resident of Kalamazoo County with a minimum GPA of 3.0; must demonstrate a financial need.
HOW TO APPLY: See website for application and financial aid authorization form.
RENEWABLE: Yes. Up to 3 academic years.
CONTACT: Bronson School of Nursing

2018—WESTERN MICHIGAN UNIVERSITY (College of Health and Human Services/Elissa Gatlin Scholarship)

1903 West Michigan
Kalamazoo MI 49008-5337
269/387-8777
FAX: 269/387-6989
E-mail: finaid-info@wmich.edu
Internet: http://www.wmich.edu/
finaid
AMOUNT: $500/semester
DEADLINE(S): MAR 1
FIELD(S): Occupational Therapy; Nursing; Speech Pathology; Blind Rehabilitation; Social Work; Physician Assistant
ELIGIBILITY/REQUIREMENTS: Intended for minority students (African-American, Native American, or Hispanic American); 2.75 GPA for undergraduates, 3.00 GPA for graduates; must be enrolled

in professional program, U.S. citizen, and demonstrate financial need.

HOW TO APPLY: Contact the College of Health and Human Services for an application.

NUMBER OF AWARDS: 2 (1 undergraduate; 1 graduate).

RENEWABLE: Yes. Maximum 2 years.

2019—WESTERN MICHIGAN UNIVERSITY (College of Health and Human Services/F. W. and Elsie L. Heyl Scholarship)

1903 West Michigan
Kalamazoo MI 49008-5337
269/387-8777
FAX: 269/387-6989
E-mail: finaid-info@wmich.edu
Internet: http://www.wmich.edu/finaid

AMOUNT: Varies (tuition, fees, housing, and a book allowance)

DEADLINE(S): JUN 1

FIELD(S): Nursing

ELIGIBILITY/REQUIREMENTS: Available to selected graduates of Kalamazoo Central and Loy Norrix high schools who wish to enter the Bronson School of Nursing Program.

HOW TO APPLY: Contact the Bronson School of Nursing for more information.

CONTACT: Marsha Mahan or Marie Gates at the Bronson School of Nursing at 269/387-8150.

2020—WESTERN MICHIGAN UNIVERSITY (College of Health and Human Services/Jeffrey and Barbara Vortman Scholarship

1903 West Michigan
Kalamazoo MI 49008-5337
269/387-8777
FAX: 269/387-6989
E-mail: finaid-info@wmich.edu
Internet: http://www.wmich.edu/finaid

AMOUNT: $500

DEADLINE(S): MAR 1

FIELD(S): Occupational Therapy; Nursing; Speech Pathology; Blind Rehabilitation; Social Work; Physician Assistant

ELIGIBILITY/REQUIREMENTS: Each year one of the departments/schools is responsible for awarding the scholarship to a student admitted to one of the professional programs in the College.

HOW TO APPLY: Contact the College of Health and Human Services for an application.

NUMBER OF AWARDS: 2 (1 undergraduate; 1 graduate).

RENEWABLE: Yes. Maximum 2 years.

2021—WESTERN MICHIGAN UNIVERSITY (College of Health and Human Services/June M. Sherman NOLA Scholarship)

1903 West Michigan
Kalamazoo MI 49008-5337
269/387-8777
FAX: 269/387-6989
E-mail: finaid-info@wmich.edu
Internet: http://www.wmich.edu/finaid

AMOUNT: Varies (dependent upon fund accumulation)

DEADLINE(S): JUN 1

FIELD(S): Nursing

ELIGIBILITY/REQUIREMENTS: Available to nontraditional nursing students, defined as either students who are single parents or from working single parent families, who have a career interest in mental health, pediatrics, oncology, or nursing administration. Must be third- or fourth-level students with a 3.0 minimum GPA.

HOW TO APPLY: Contact the Bronson School of Nursing for more information.

CONTACT: Bronson School of Nursing

2022—WESTERN MICHIGAN UNIVERSITY (College of Health and Human Services/Lois L. Richmond Nursing Scholarship)

1903 West Michigan
Kalamazoo MI 49008-5337
269/387-8777
FAX: 269/387-6989
E-mail: finaid-info@wmich.edu
Internet: http://www.wmich.edu/finaid

AMOUNT: Varies

DEADLINE(S): JUN 1

FIELD(S): Nursing

ELIGIBILITY/REQUIREMENTS: Applicants must be accepted into Bronson School of Nursing at the undergraduate level, attend full time, show financial need, and have a GPA of 3.0.

HOW TO APPLY: Contact the Bronson School of Nursing for more information.

CONTACT: Bronson School of Nursing

2023—WESTERN MICHIGAN UNIVERSITY (College of Health and Human Services/Loren E. and Nellie M. Clark Nursing Scholarship)

1903 West Michigan

Kalamazoo MI 49008-5337
269/387-8777
FAX: 269/387-6989
E-mail: finaid-info@wmich.edu
Internet: http://www.wmich.edu/finaid

AMOUNT: Varies

DEADLINE(S): JUN 1

FIELD(S): Nursing

ELIGIBILITY/REQUIREMENTS: Undergraduate or graduate student accepted into Bronson School of Nursing on a full- or part-time basis; must have a 2.25 GPA. Preference given to eligible students representing a nondominant underrepresented culture. If a graduate student is selected, preference shall be given to a nursing student concentrating in the field of Family Nursing or Community Health Nursing.

HOW TO APPLY: See website for application and financial aid authorization form.

CONTACT: Bronson School of Nursing

2024—WESTERN MICHIGAN UNIVERSITY (College of Health and Human Services/Rosalie Clauwaert Lloyd Memorial Scholarship)

1903 West Michigan
Kalamazoo MI 49008-5337
269/387-8777
FAX: 269/387-6989
E-mail: finaid-info@wmich.edu
Internet: http://www.wmich.edu/finaid

AMOUNT: Varies

DEADLINE(S): JUN 1

FIELD(S): Nursing

ELIGIBILITY/REQUIREMENTS: Must be admitted to the professional nursing curriculum at WMU Bronson School of Nursing and a graduate of a Kalamazoo County high school. Award is based on financial need, demonstrated compassion, sensitivity and commitment to the ideals of the profession.

HOW TO APPLY: Contact the Bronson School of Nursing for more information.

CONTACT: Bronson School of Nursing

2025—WESTERN MICHIGAN UNIVERSITY (College of Health and Human Services/Sheila D. Ware Nursing Scholarship)

1903 West Michigan
Kalamazoo MI 49008-5337
269/387-8777
FAX: 269/387-6989
E-mail: finaid-info@wmich.edu

Internet: http://www.wmich.edu/finaid
AMOUNT: Varies
DEADLINE(S): JUN 1
FIELD(S): Nursing
ELIGIBILITY/REQUIREMENTS: Need-based scholarship for full-time junior or senior undergraduate.
HOW TO APPLY: See website for application and financial aid authorization form.
RENEWABLE: Yes. Up to 4 consecutive academic years.
CONTACT: Bronson School of Nursing

2026—WESTERN MICHIGAN UNIVERSITY (College of Health and Human Services/The Theodore and Hazel Perg Scholarship)

1903 West Michigan
Kalamazoo MI 49008-5337
269/387-8777
FAX: 269/387-6989
E-mail: finaid-info@wmich.edu
Internet: http://www.wmich.edu/finaid
AMOUNT: Up to a maximum amount of $1,000 per semester; $500 per session
DEADLINE(S): JUN 1
FIELD(S): Nursing
ELIGIBILITY/REQUIREMENTS: Must be admitted to the Professional Nursing Curriculum at WMU Bronson School of Nursing and enrolled or will be enrolled in required nursing courses during the semesters/sessions for which scholarship funds are requested. A graduate of a high school from one of the following counties in southwest Michigan: Allegan, Barry, Berrien, Branch, Calhoun, Cass, Kalamazoo, St. Joseph, or Van Buren. Financial need a consideration.
HOW TO APPLY: File FASFA showing financial need, and indicate WMU as your school choice, four weeks prior to the application deadline. See website for application form and financial aid authorization form.
NUMBER OF AWARDS: 2 (1 undergraduate; 1 graduate)
RENEWABLE: Yes. Maximum 2 years.
CONTACT: Bronson School of Nursing

2027—WOCN FOUNDATION (Accredited Nursing Education Scholarship)

4700 West Lake Avenue
Glenview IL 60025
888/224-WOCN (9626)
FAX: 866/615-8560
Internet: http://www.wocn.org
AMOUNT: Varies
DEADLINE(S): MAY 1; NOV 1
FIELD(S): Nursing
ELIGIBILITY/REQUIREMENTS: Must be accepted into a Wound, Ostomy, and Continence Nurses Society (WOCN) accredited nursing education program.
HOW TO APPLY: See website for application.
NUMBER OF AWARDS: Depends on funds available.
RENEWABLE: No

2028—WOCN FOUNDATION (Advanced Education Scholarship)

4700 West Lake Avenue
Glenview IL 60025
888/224-WOCN (9626)
FAX: 866/615-8560
Internet: http://www.wocn.org
AMOUNT: Varies
DEADLINE(S): MAY 1; NOV 1
FIELD(S): Nursing
ELIGIBILITY/REQUIREMENTS: Applicant must be accepted into a Wound, Ostomy, and Continence Nurses Society (WOCN) accredited nursing education program. Financial aid to offset costs of a baccalaureate, masters, doctoral degree or NP certification for people committed to working within the WOCN specialty.
HOW TO APPLY: See website for application.
NUMBER OF AWARDS: Depends on funds available.
RENEWABLE: No

NUTRITION

2029—AMERICAN SOCIETY FOR HEALTH-CARE FOOD SERVICE ADMINISTRATORS (Bonnie Miller Continuing Education Fund)

304 West Liberty Street,
Suite 201
Louisville KY 40202
800/620-6422
Internet: http://www.ashfsa.org
AMOUNT: $500 (part-time); $1,000 (full-time)
DEADLINE(S): MAR 15
FIELD(S): Healthcare Food Service Management
ELIGIBILITY/REQUIREMENTS: Open to undergraduate students at 2- or 4-year colleges.
HOW TO APPLY: Contact Society for an application.
CONTACT: Keith Howard

2030—CHILD NUTRITION FOUNDATION

700 S. Washington Street,
Suite 300
Alexandria VA 22314
703/739-3900
FAX: 703/739-3915
E-mail: cnf@asfsa.org
Internet: http://www.asfsa.org/cnfoundation
AMOUNT: $300-$1,200
DEADLINE(S): APR 15
FIELD(S): Child Nutrition; Food Service Management; Business Administration
ELIGIBILITY/REQUIREMENTS: Must be an American School Food Service Association (ASFSA) member and/or the dependent of an ASFSA member. Must study a field designed to improve school food service (such as those above) at a vocational/technical school, community college, college or university.
HOW TO APPLY: Applications available at www.asfsa.org/continuinged/assistance/scholar/scholarships.
NUMBER OF AWARDS: 70
RENEWABLE: Yes, must reapply.
CONTACT: Child Nutrition Foundation Financial Aid Manager

2031—HAWAII COMMUNITY FOUNDATION (Dan & Pauline Lutkenhouse Tropical Garden Scholarship)

1164 Bishop Street, Suite 800
Honolulu HI 96813
808/537-6333 or toll free: 888/731-3863
FAX: 808/521-6286
E-mail: info@hcf-hawaii.org
Internet: http://www.hcf-hawaii.org
DEADLINE(S): MAR 1
FIELD(S): Agriculture; Science; Medicine; Nursing
ELIGIBILITY/REQUIREMENTS: Must be resident of the Hilo coast and the Hamakua coast, north of the Wailuku River; plan to attend full time an accredited 2- or 4-year college or university; and demonstrate financial need, good moral character, and academic achievement (minimum GPA of 2.7).
HOW TO APPLY: See website. Send application with 2 letters of recommendation.

2032—HAWAII COMMUNITY FOUNDATION (John Dawe Dental Education Fund)

1164 Bishop Street, Suite 800
Honolulu HI 96813

808/537-6333 or toll free:
888/731-3863
FAX: 808/521-6286
E-mail: scholarships@hcf-hawaii.org
Internet: http://www.hcf-hawaii.org
DEADLINE(S): MAR 1
FIELD(S): Dentistry (including Dental Hygiene and Dental Assisting)
ELIGIBILITY/REQUIREMENTS: Must be Hawaii residents; full-time students enrolled in an accredited school of dentistry, dental hygiene, or dental assisting; and demonstrate financial need, good moral character, and academic achievement with a minimum GPA of 2.7.
HOW TO APPLY: See website. Send application with 2 letters of recommendation and Dawe Supplemental Financial Form; dental hygiene students must also send a letter confirming enrollment in program.

2033—INSTITUTE OF FOOD TECHNOLOGISTS (Freshman Scholarships)

525 West Van Buren, Suite 1000
Chicago IL 60607
312/782-8424
FAX: 313/782-8348
E-mail: info@ift.org
AMOUNT: $1,000-$1,500
DEADLINE(S): FEB 15
FIELD(S): Food Science; Food Technology
ELIGIBILITY/REQUIREMENTS: Open to scholastically outstanding high school graduates and seniors expecting to graduate from high school. Must be entering college for the first time in an approved program in food science/technology.
HOW TO APPLY: Contact IFT for application.
NUMBER OF AWARDS: 25

2034—INSTITUTE OF FOOD TECHNOLOGISTS (Junior/Senior Scholarships)

525 West Van Buren, Suite 1000
Chicago IL 60607
312/782-8424
FAX: 312/782-8348
E-mail: info@ift.org
AMOUNT: $1,000-$2,250
DEADLINE(S): FEB 1
FIELD(S): Food Science; Food Technology
ELIGIBILITY/REQUIREMENTS: Open to scholastically outstanding sophomores and juniors enrolled in an approved food science/technology program.
HOW TO APPLY: Contact IFT for application.
NUMBER OF AWARDS: 64

2035—INSTITUTE OF FOOD TECHNOLOGISTS (Sophomore Scholarships)

525 West Van Buren, Suite 1000
Chicago IL 60607
312/782-8424
FAX: 312/782-8348
E-mail: info@ift.org
AMOUNT: $1,000
DEADLINE(S): MAR 1
FIELD(S): Food Science; Food Technology
ELIGIBILITY/REQUIREMENTS: Open to scholastically outstanding freshmen with a minimum 2.5 GPA and either pursuing or transferring to an approved program in food science/technology.
HOW TO APPLY: Contact IFT for application.
NUMBER OF AWARDS: 23

2036—INTERNATIONAL ORDER OF THE KING'S DAUGHTERS AND SONS (Health Careers Scholarships)

Health Careers Department
736 Ardmore Lane
Shelbyville KY 40065
AMOUNT: $1,000 (maximum)
DEADLINE(S): APR 1
FIELD(S): Medicine; Dentistry; Nursing; Physical Therapy; Occupational Therapy; Medical Technologies; Pharmacy
ELIGIBILITY/REQUIREMENTS: Must be U.S. or Canadian citizen, enrolled full time in a school accredited in the field involved and located in the U.S. or Canada. For all students, except those preparing for an RN degree, application must be for at least the third year of college. RN students must have completed the first year of schooling. Pre-med students are not eligible to apply. For those students seeking degrees of MD or DDS, application must be for at least the second year of medical or dental school. Each applicant must supply proof of acceptance in the school involved. There is no age limit.
HOW TO APPLY: Send SASE for an application between January 1 and March 15 with a letter stating the field of study and present level. Submit application with résumé, including personal statement as to the reason for selection of the chosen field and intentions for a career following graduation; letters of recommendation from at least 2 informed persons, with their identification and relationship to applicant made clear; up-to-date official transcripts from current school which MUST be mailed directly from the registrar office (if gradu-

ating on a pass/fail system, a statement is required from the Dean of Students or a professor in regard to academic progress); and an itemized budget, endorsed by the school Financial Aid officer, including: school and living expenses, income, loans, awards, family contributions, etc., for the current year and projected estimate for the next year.
RENEWABLE: Yes, for 2 additional years if qualified
CONTACT: Ida Lyons, Director

2037—JACKSONVILLE STATE UNIVERSITY (Elizabeth Sowell Scholarship)

Jacksonville AL 36265
256/782-5677 or 800/231-5291
Internet: http://www.jsu.edu
AMOUNT: Varies
FIELD(S): Nutrition; Food
ELIGIBILITY/REQUIREMENTS: Major in Family & Consumer Science or related area.
HOW TO APPLY: Contact Department for application and additional information.
RENEWABLE: No
CONTACT: Family & Consumer Science Department; 256/782-5054

2038—J. HUGH AND EARLE W. FELLOWS MEMORIAL FUND (Scholarship Loans)

Pensacola Junior College
1000 College Boulevard
Pensacola FL 32504-8998
904/484-1700
Internet: http://www.pjc.cc.fl.us/
AMOUNT: Varies
DEADLINE(S): MAY 1
FIELD(S): Medicine; Nursing; Medical Technology; Theology (Episcopal)
ELIGIBILITY/REQUIREMENTS: For undergraduate study only. Open to bona fide residents of the Florida counties of Escambia, Santa Rosa, Okaloosa, or Walton; U.S. citizenship required.
HOW TO APPLY: Write for information.
CONTACT: Dr. Charles A. Atwell

2039—LINCOLN COMMUNITY FOUNDATION (Lucile E. Wright Scholarship))

215 Centennial Mall South, Suite 100
Lincoln NE 68508
402/474-2354
FAX: 402/476-8532
E-mail: lcf@lcf.org
Internet: http://www.lcf.org
AMOUNT: Varies

DEADLINE(S): APR 8
FIELD(S): Nutrition, Dietetics, Food
  Service Management
ELIGIBILITY/REQUIREMENTS:
Applicant must be seeking a degree in one
of the above fields and enrolled in the
College of Education and Human Sciences
at the University of Nebraska-Lincoln.
HOW TO APPLY: Complete application
provided by the College of Education and
Human Sciences and submit it along with
any required attachments to Diane
Sealock, College of Education and Human
Sciences, University of Nebraska-Lincoln,
104 Henzlik, Lincoln, NE 68588-0371.
NUMBER OF AWARDS/YEAR: Varies
RENEWABLE: Yes; must reapply.
ADDITIONAL INFORMATION: The
College of Education and Human Sciences
shall make recipient recommendations of
the Foundation for final selection.

2040—NATIONAL POULTRY AND FOOD DISTRIBUTORS ASSOCIATION SCHOLARSHIP FOUNDATION

958 McEver Road Extension,
Unit B8
Gainesville GA 30504
770/535-9901
FAX: 770/535-7385
E-mail: kkm@npfda.org
Internet: http://www.npfda.org
AMOUNT: $1,500-$2,000 each/annual
DEADLINE(S): MAY 31
FIELD(S): Poultry, Food or related
  agricultural degree (food science;
  dietetics; poultry science; agricultural
  economics; international business, etc.)
ELIGIBILITY/REQUIREMENTS: Must
be full-time college junior or senior in the
award year at a U.S. institution.
HOW TO APPLY: Submit application
with transcript, letter of recommendation
from your dean along with a 1-page letter
describing your goals and aspirations.
NUMBER OF AWARDS: 4
RENEWABLE: No
CONTACT: Kristin McWhorter

2041—UNIVERSITY OF ILLINOIS COLLEGE OF ACES (Jonathan Baldwin Turner Agricultural Scholarship Program)

115 ACES Library
1101 South Goodwin Street
Urbana IL 61801
217/244-4540
Internet: http://w3.aces.uiuc.edu/
  Acad-Prog/
AMOUNT: $1,000

DEADLINE(S): Varies (start of high
  school senior year)
FIELD(S): Agriculture; Nutritional
  Science; Natural Resources;
  Environmental; Social Sciences
  (agricultural economics,
  communications, or education)
ELIGIBILITY/REQUIREMENTS:
Scholarships in agricultural, food, and
human nutritional sciences for outstanding
incoming freshmen at the University of
Illinois. Must have minimum ACT com-
posite score of 27, equivalent SAT com-
bined scores, or be in the 10th percentile of
high school class rank at the end of junior
year. Interview required.
HOW TO APPLY: Contact Assistant
Dean of Academic Programs, College of
Agricultural, Consumer and Environ-
mental Sci-ences, for an application.
NUMBER OF AWARDS: 55
RENEWABLE: Yes. 4-year award; up to
$4,000.
CONTACT: Charles Olson

PRE-MED (PHYSICIANS, DENTISTS, VETERINARIANS)

2042—ABBIE SARGENT MEMORIAL SCHOLARSHIP INC.

295 Sheep Davis Road
Concord NH 03301
603/224-1934
FAX: 603/228-8432
AMOUNT: $200-$400
DEADLINE(S): MAR 15
FIELD(S): Agriculture; Veterinary
  Medicine; Home Economics
ELIGIBILITY/REQUIREMENTS: Open
to New Hampshire residents who are high
school graduates with good grades and
character. For undergraduate or graduate
study. Must be legal resident of U.S. and
demonstrate financial need.
HOW TO APPLY: Write for application.
RENEWABLE: Yes, must reapply.

2043—ALBUQUERQUE VETERINARY ASSOCIATION

1921 Carlisle Blvd., NE
Albuquerque NM 87110
FAX: 505/155-4654
E-mail: twheeler@cybermesa.net
AMOUNT: $500 (pre-vet), $1,000 (vet)
DEADLINE(S): APR 15
FIELD(S): Veterinary & Pre-Veterinary
  Medicine
ELIGIBILITY/REQUIREMENTS: Must
be a permanent resident of New Mexico

enrolled in a pre-vet or veterinary program.
HOW TO APPLY: Write or e-mail for
application if you are a permanent resident
of New Mexico and in a veterinary or pre-
veterinary program.
NUMBER OF AWARDS: 2 (1 of each)
RENEWABLE: No
CONTACT: Dr. Teri Wheeler

2044—AMERICAN HEART ASSOCIATION (Helen N. and Harold B. Shapira Scholarship)

4701 West 77th Street
Minneapolis MN 55435
952/835-3300
AMOUNT: $1,000
DEADLINE(S): APR 1
FIELD(S): Pre-Med
ELIGIBILITY/REQUIREMENTS: For
pre-med undergraduate students and medical students who are accepted to or
enrolled in an accredited Minnesota college or university. Must be U.S. citizen or
legal resident.
HOW TO APPLY: Contact AHA for an
application.
RENEWABLE: Yes. 1 additional year.

2045—AMERICAN INDIAN SCIENCE AND ENGINEERING SOCIETY (A. T. Anderson Memorial Scholarship)

P.O. Box 9828
Albuquerque NM 87119-9828
505/765-1052
FAX: 505/765-5608
E-mail: scholarships@aises.org
Internet: http://www.aises.org/
  highered
AMOUNT: $1,000
DEADLINE(S): JUN 15
FIELD(S): Medicine; Natural Resources;
  Science; Engineering
ELIGIBILITY/REQUIREMENTS: Open
to undergraduate and graduate students
who are at least 1/4 American Indian or
recognized as member of a tribe. Must be
member of AISES ($10 fee), enrolled full
time at an accredited institution, and
demonstrate financial need. Minimum
GPA 2.7.
HOW TO APPLY: See website or contact
Society for an application and/or member-
ship information.
RENEWABLE: Yes
CONTACT: Tina Pino

2046—DEMOLAY FOUNDATION, INC. & GROTTO HUMANITARIAN FOUNDATION

10200 NW Ambassador Drive

Kansas City MO 64153
816/891-8333
FAX: 816/891-9062
E-mail: demolay@demolay.org
Internet: http://www.demolay.org
AMOUNT: $1,500
DEADLINE(S): APR 1
FIELD(S): Dentistry; Medicine
ELIGIBILITY/REQUIREMENTS: Open to all active and/or senior DeMolays. Considerations are leadership, academic achievement, and goals.
HOW TO APPLY: Request application.
NUMBER OF AWARDS: 4
RENEWABLE: Yes
CONTACT: Carol Newman

2047—ESA FOUNDATION (McConnell Family Scholarship)

P.O. Box 270517
Fort Collins CO 80527
970/223-2824
FAX: 970/223-4456
E-mail: kloyd@iland.net
Internet: http://www.esaintl. com/esaf
AMOUNT: $1,000
DEADLINE(S): FEB 1
FIELD(S): Veterinary Medicine
ELIGIBILITY/REQUIREMENTS: Must be a female college student enrolled in an accredited college or university who has maintained at least a 3.0 GPA; or a high school senior in the top 25% of her high school class, or have a score of at least ACT 20 or SAT 950, or have a minimum GPA of 3.0; or enrolled for training in a technical school or returning to school after an absence to retrain job skills or obtain a degree. Criteria for selection are character, leadership, service, financial need, scholastic ability, and special criteria set by the donor.
HOW TO APPLY: Send application to the ESA Foundation State Counselor in your area (see website); do not send applications to the ESA Foundation Office. Submit with 1-page (maximum) original letter stating reasons for applying; 2 letters of recommendation; a transcript. $5 processing fee.
NUMBER OF AWARDS: 1
RENEWABLE: Yes, must reapply.
CONTACT: Kathy Loyd

2048—HAWAII COMMUNITY FOUNDATION (Dan & Pauline Lutkenhouse Tropical Garden Scholarship)

1164 Bishop Street, Suite 800
Honolulu HI 96813

808/537-6333 or toll free:
888/731-3863
FAX: 808/521-6286
E-mail: info@hcf-hawaii.org
Internet: http://www.hcf-hawaii.org
DEADLINE(S): MAR 1
FIELD(S): Agriculture; Science; Medicine; Nursing
ELIGIBILITY/REQUIREMENTS: Must be resident of the Hilo coast and the Hamakua coast, north of the Wailuku River; plan to attend full time an accredited 2- or 4-year college or university; and demonstrate financial need, good moral character, and academic achievement (minimum GPA of 2.7).
HOW TO APPLY: See website. Send application with 2 letters of recommendation.

2049—HAWAII COMMUNITY FOUNDATION (John Dawe Dental Education Fund)

1164 Bishop Street, Suite 800
Honolulu HI 96813
808/537-6333 or toll free:
888/731-3863
FAX: 808/521-6286
E-mail: scholarships@hcf-hawaii.org
Internet: http://www.hcf-hawaii.org
DEADLINE(S): MAR 1
FIELD(S): Dentistry (including Dental Hygiene and Dental Assisting)
ELIGIBILITY/REQUIREMENTS: Must be Hawaii residents; full-time students enrolled in an accredited school of dentistry, dental hygiene, or dental assisting; and demonstrate financial need, good moral character, and academic achievement with a minimum GPA of 2.7.
HOW TO APPLY: See website. Send application with 2 letters of recommendation and Dawe Supplemental Financial Form; dental hygiene students must also send a letter confirming enrollment in program.

2050—H. FLETCHER BROWN FUND

c/o Donald W. Davis
PNC Bank Delaware
Trust Department
222 Delaware Avenue, 16th floor
Wilmington DE 19899
302/429- 2827 or 302/429-5658
E-mail: Robbie.testa@pnc advisors.com
AMOUNT: Varies
DEADLINE(S): MAR 22
FIELD(S): Medicine; Dentistry; Law; Engineering; Chemistry

ELIGIBILITY/REQUIREMENTS: Open to U.S. citizens born in Delaware and still residing in Delaware. For 4 years of study (undergraduate or graduate) leading to a degree that enables applicant to practice in chosen field. Must have minimum 1000 SAT score and rank in upper 20 percent of class. Interview required. Scholarships are based on need, scholastic achievement, and good moral character.
HOW TO APPLY: Applications available in February. Write to Account Administrator for application.
CONTACT: Robbie Testa

2051—HISPANIC DENTAL ASSOCIATION FOUNDATION (Dr. Genaro Romo Jr. & HDA Foundation Scholarship)

3085 Stevenson Drive, Suite 200
Springfield IL 62703
217/529-6517
FAX: 217/529-9120
E-mail: rjeppesen@hdassoc.org
Internet: http://www.hdassoc.org
AMOUNT: $500 and $1,000
DEADLINE(S): JUL 20
FIELD(S): Dental; Dental Hygiene
ELIGIBILITY/REQUIREMENTS: Must be accepted or currently enrolled in a dental or dental hygiene program at University of Illinois Chicago, be of Hispanic descent; and be a full-time student during the academic year for which you are applying, and a member of HDA. Show evidence of commitment and dedication to serve the Hispanic community.
HOW TO APPLY: See website for application and submit in English to address below.
CONTACT: Rebecca Jeppesen, Executive Director
ADDITIONAL INFORMATION: HDAF/Dr. Genaro Romo Jr. Scholarship Program, 3085 Stevenson Drive, Suite 200, Springfield, IL 62703; for additional information call: 800/852-7921 or FAX to 217/529-9120

2052—HISPANIC DENTAL ASSOCIATION FOUNDATION (Dr. Juan Villarreal Scholarship & HDA Foundation)

3085 Stevenson Drive, Suite 200
Springfield IL 62703
217/529-6517
FAX: 217/529-9120
E-mail: rjeppesen@hdassoc.org
Internet: http://www.hdassoc.org
AMOUNT: $500 and $1,000
DEADLINE(S): JUL 1 (dental); JUL 15 (dental hygiene)
FIELD(S): Dental; Dental Hygiene

ELIGIBILITY/REQUIREMENTS: Must be accepted or enrolled as a student in a dental or dental hygiene program in the state of Texas; be of Hispanic descent; be a full-time student during the academic year for which you are applying; and demonstrate commitment and dedication to serve the Hispanic community.
HOW TO APPLY: See website for application and submit in English to address below.
CONTACT: Rebecca Jeppesen, Executive Director
ADDITIONAL INFORMATION: Dr. Juan D. Villarreal/HDAF Scholarship Program, 3085 Stevenson Drive, Suite 200 Springfield, IL 62703 or FAX to 217/529-9120.

2053—HISPANIC DENTAL ASSOCIATION FOUNDATION (GlaxoSmithKline)

3085 Stevenson Drive, Suite 200
Springfield IL 62703
217/529-6517
FAX: 217/529-9120
E-mail: rjeppesen@hdassoc.org
Internet: http://www.hdassoc.org
AMOUNT: $2,000
DEADLINE(S): JUL 1 (dental students); JUL 15 (hygiene assistant & lab technician)
FIELD(S): Dental, Dental Hygiene
ELIGIBILITY/REQUIREMENTS: Open to Hispanic U.S. students who have finished one year of dental school or a dental hygiene program. The student may be at any stage of the undergraduate program, second through fourth years, as long as one full year has been completed. Must have a minimum GPA of 3.0; have at least 1 parent of Hispanic descent; and show evidence of community service, leadership and/or extracurricular activities. Winners may be asked to report on their activities and progress six months after receiving the scholarship.
HOW TO APPLY: Call to request application; e-mail lvaldivia@hdASSOCIATION.org; or visit website.
NUMBER OF AWARDS: 4 (2 dental, 2 dental hygiene)
RENEWABLE: No
CONTACT: Rebecca Jeppesen, Executive Director
ADDITIONAL INFORMATION: Phone 800/852-7921; Fax 217/529-9120; E-Mail: hispanicdental@hdassoc.org.

2054—HISPANIC DENTAL ASSOCIATION FOUNDATION (Procter & Gamble Oral Care & HDA Foundation)

3085 Stevenson Drive, Suite 200

Springfield IL 62703
217/529-6517
FAX: 217/529-9120
E-mail: rjeppesen@hdassoc.org
Internet: http://www.hdassoc.org
AMOUNT: $500 and $1,000
DEADLINE(S): JUL 1 (dental students); JUL 15 (hygiene assistant & lab technician)
FIELD(S): All Dental Professions
ELIGIBILITY/REQUIREMENTS: Entry level program; applicants must be accepted into a dental, dental hygiene program, dental assisting program, or dental technician program nationwide, during the academic year for which you are applying; have a minimum GPA of 3.0; have at least 1 parent of Hispanic descent; and show evidence of community service, leadership and/or extracurricular activities.
HOW TO APPLY: Call to request application; e-mail lvaldivia@hdASSOCIATION.org; or visit website.
NUMBER OF AWARDS: Numerous
RENEWABLE: No
CONTACT: Rebecca Jeppesen, Executive Director
ADDITIONAL INFORMATION: Phone 800/852-7921; Fax 217/529-9120; E-Mail: hispanicdental@hdassoc.org

2055—INTERNATIONAL ORDER OF THE KING'S DAUGHTERS AND SONS (Health Careers Scholarships)

Health Careers Department
736 Ardmore Lane
Shelbyville KY 40065
AMOUNT: $1,000 (maximum)
DEADLINE(S): APR 1
FIELD(S): Medicine; Dentistry; Nursing; Physical Therapy; Occupational Therapy; Medical Technologies; Pharmacy
ELIGIBILITY/REQUIREMENTS: Must be U.S. or Canadian citizen, enrolled full time in a school accredited in the field involved and located in the U.S. or Canada. For all students, except those preparing for an RN degree, application must be for at least the third year of college. RN students must have completed the first year of schooling. Pre-med students are not eligible to apply. For those students seeking degrees of MD or DDS, application must be for at least the second year of medical or dental school. Each applicant must supply proof of acceptance in the school involved. There is no age limit.
HOW TO APPLY: Send SASE for an application between January 1 and March 15 with a letter stating the field of study and present level. Submit application with

résumé, including personal statement as to the reason for selection of the chosen field and intentions for a career following graduation; letters of recommendation from at least 2 informed persons, with their identification and relationship to applicant made clear; up-to-date official transcripts from current school which MUST be mailed directly from the registrar office (if graduating on a pass/fail system, a statement is required from the Dean of Students or a professor in regard to academic progress); and an itemized budget, endorsed by the school Financial Aid officer, including: school and living expenses, income, loans, awards, family contributions, etc., for the current year and projected estimate for the next year.
RENEWABLE: Yes, for 2 additional years if qualified
CONTACT: Ida Lyons, Director

2056—JACKSONVILLE STATE UNIVERSITY (Drs. Wayne & Sara Finley Scholarship)

Financial Aid Office
Jacksonville AL 36265
256/782-5677 or 800/231-5291
Internet: www.jsu.edu
AMOUNT: Varies
DEADLINE(S): FEB 1
FIELD(S): Mathematics; Science; Pre-Prof Secondary Education
ELIGIBILITY/REQUIREMENTS: Open to junior or senior; 3.0 GPA; Clay, Coosa, or Randolph Counties, Alabama.
HOW TO APPLY: See website for application. Mail transcript and ACT/SAT scores.
RENEWABLE: No
CONTACT: Scholarship Committee

2057—J. HUGH AND EARLE W. FELLOWS MEMORIAL FUND (Scholarship Loans)

Pensacola Junior College
1000 College Boulevard
Pensacola FL 32504-8998
904/484-1700
Internet: http://www.pjc.cc.fl.us/
AMOUNT: Varies
DEADLINE(S): MAY 1
FIELD(S): Medicine; Nursing; Medical Technology; Theology (Episcopal)
ELIGIBILITY/REQUIREMENTS: For undergraduate study only. Open to bona fide residents of the Florida counties of Escambia, Santa Rosa, Okaloosa, or Walton; U.S. citizenship required.
HOW TO APPLY: Write for information.
CONTACT: Dr. Charles A. Atwell

2058—JUNIATA COLLEGE (Robert Steele Memorial Scholarship)

Office of Financial Planning
1700 Moore Street
Huntingdon PA 16652
814/641-3142
FAX: 814/641-5311
E-mail: frankv@juniata.edu
Internet: http://www.juniata.edu/admission/finplan/index.html
AMOUNT: Up to $4,000
DEADLINE(S): APR 1
FIELD(S): Science; Medical Studies
ELIGIBILITY/REQUIREMENTS: Open to science/medical students applying to Juniata College. Must demonstrate financial need and fill out government FAFSA form.
HOW TO APPLY: Vincent Frank, Director of Student Financial Planning, 814/641-3140; e-mail: frankv@juniata.edu. See your financial aid office for FAFSA.

2059—MIDWAY COLLEGE

512 East Stephens Street
Midway KY 40347
800/755-0031
E-mail: admissions@midway.edu
Internet: http://www.midway.edu
AMOUNT: Up to full tuition
DEADLINE(S): Varies
FIELD(S): Nursing; Education; Psychology; Biology; Equine Studies; Computer Information Systems; Business Administration; English; Pre-Med; Pre-Vet
ELIGIBILITY/REQUIREMENTS: Merit scholarships for admitted students who are considered full time in Midway's women's college. Depending on scholarship, minimum GPA ranges from 2.5 to 3.2, minimum ACT ranges 18 to 29, minimum SAT from 860 to 1290. In some cases, students must live on campus.
HOW TO APPLY: Contact Admissions Office or high school guidance counselor for application Complete FAFSA online.
NUMBER OF AWARDS: Varies, up to 100
RENEWABLE: Yes. Must meet GPA requirements which vary based on the scholarship.
CONTACT: Admissions Office or high school guidance counselor
ADDITIONAL INFORMATION: Athletes may be eligible for an athletic scholarship in conjunction with a merit grant; contact coach for eligibility and award information.

2060—PILOT INTERNATIONAL FOUNDATION (PIF/Lifeline Scholarship)

P.O. Box 5600
Macon GA 31208-5600
478/743-7403
FAX: 478/743-2173
E-mail: pifinfo@pilothq.org
Internet: http://www.pilot international.org
AMOUNT: Varies
DEADLINE(S): FEB 15
FIELD(S): Disabilities/Brain-related disorders
ELIGIBILITY/REQUIREMENTS: Assists ADULT students re-entering the job market, preparing for a second career, or improving their professional skills in an established career. Must be preparing for, or already involved in, careers working with people with disabilities/brain-related disorders. GPA of 3.5 or more is required. Must be a Pilot Club member.
HOW TO APPLY: Must be sponsored by home, college, or university town Pilot Club. See website or send SASE for information and application.

2061—PILOT INTERNATIONAL FOUNDATION (The Pilot International Scholarship Program)

P.O. Box 5600
Macon GA 31208-5600
478/743-7403
FAX: 478/743-2173
E-mail: pifinfo@pilothq.org
Internet: http://www.pilot international.org
AMOUNT: Varies
DEADLINE(S): FEB 15
FIELD(S): Disabilities/Brain-related disorders
ELIGIBILITY/REQUIREMENTS: Open to undergraduate students preparing for careers working directly with people with disabilities or training those who will. GPA of 3.25 or greater required. MUST be a Pilot Club member.
HOW TO APPLY: Must be sponsored by home, college, or university town Pilot Club. See website or send SASE for information and application.

2062—RAYMOND J. HARRIS EDUCATION TRUST

Mellon Bank, N.A.
P.O. Box 7899
Philadelphia PA 19101-7899
AMOUNT: Varies

DEADLINE(S): FEB 1
FIELD(S): Medicine, Law, Engineering, Dentistry, or Agriculture
ELIGIBILITY/REQUIREMENTS: Scholarships for Christian men to obtain a professional education in medicine, law, engineering, dentistry, or agriculture at nine Philadelphia area colleges.
HOW TO APPLY: Contact Bank for details and the names of the nine colleges.

2063—ROBERT SCHRECK MEMORIAL FUND (Grants)

Texas Commerce Bank
Trust Department
P.O. Drawer 140
El Paso TX 79980
915/546-6515
AMOUNT: $500-$1500
DEADLINE(S): JUL 15; NOV 15
FIELD(S): Medicine; Veterinary Medicine; Physics; Chemistry; Architecture; Engineering; Episcopal Clergy
ELIGIBILITY/REQUIREMENTS: Grants to undergraduate juniors or seniors or graduate students who have been residents of El Paso County for at least 2 years. Must be U.S. citizen and have a high GPA. Financial need considered.
HOW TO APPLY: Write for information.
NUMBER OF AWARDS: 3
RENEWABLE: No

SCIENCE (ALL FIELDS)

2064—AIR FORCE RESERVE OFFICER TRAINING CORPS (AFROTC Scholarships)

551 East Maxwell Boulevard
Maxwell AFB AL 36112-6106
334/953-7783
AMOUNT: Full tuition, books, and fees for all 4 years of college
DEADLINE(S): DEC 1
FIELD(S): Science; Engineering; Business; Political Science; Psychology; Geography; Foreign Studies; Foreign Language
ELIGIBILITY/REQUIREMENTS: Competitive scholarships based on individual merit to high school seniors and graduates who have not completed any full-time college work, and have GPA of 2.5 or above, are in top 40% of class, and complete Applicant Fitness Test. Must be U.S. citizen between the ages of 17-27. Cannot

be a single parent. Your college or university must offer AFROTC.
HOW TO APPLY: Contact AFROTC for application packet.
NUMBER OF AWARDS: 2,300

2065—ALPHA KAPPA ALPHA SORORITY INC. (AKA/PIMS Summer Youth Mathematics and Science Camp)

5656 South Stony Island Avenue
Chicago IL 60637
800/653-6528
Internet: http://www.akaeaf.org
AMOUNT: $1,000 value
DEADLINE(S): MAY 1
FIELD(S): Mathematics; Science
ELIGIBILITY/REQUIREMENTS: Open to high school students grades 9-11 who have at least a 'B' average. Essay required for entry. 2-week camp includes a.m. classes; p.m. activities and a minimum of 4 field trips.
HOW TO APPLY: Write for complete information.
NUMBER OF AWARDS: 30

2066—AMERICAN FOUNDATION FOR THE BLIND (Paul W. Ruckes Scholarship)

11 Penn Plaza, Suite 300
New York NY 10001
212/502-7661
FAX: 212/502-7771
E-mail: juliet@afb.org
Internet: http://www.afb.org
AMOUNT: $1,000
DEADLINE(S): APR 30
FIELD(S): Engineering; Computer, Physical, & Life Sciences
ELIGIBILITY/REQUIREMENTS: Open to legally blind and visually impaired undergraduate and graduate students pursuing a degree in one of above fields. Must be U.S. citizen.
HOW TO APPLY: See website or contact AFB for an application Must submit written documentation of visual impairment from ophthalmologist or optometrist (need not be legally blind); official transcripts; proof of college or university acceptance; 3 letters of recommendation; and typewritten statement describing goals, work experience, extracurricular activities, and how monies will be used.
NUMBER OF AWARDS: 1
CONTACT: Julie Tucker

2067—AMERICAN INDIAN FUND (Al Qoyawayma Award)

P.O. Box 59033
Potomac MD 20859

301/424-2440
FAX: 301/424-8281
AMOUNT: Up to $1,000
DEADLINE(S): JUN 1
FIELD(S): Science; Engineering
ELIGIBILITY/REQUIREMENTS: Open to Native American students majoring in science or engineering who have demonstrated an outstanding interest and skill in any one of the arts. Must be American Indian/Alaska Native (documented with Certified Degree of Indian Blood), enrolled in college or university, able to demonstrate commitment to serving community or other tribal nations, and able to document financial need.
HOW TO APPLY: Contact Fund's President for an application after January 1.
CONTACT: Dr. Paula M. Mintzies

2068—AMERICAN INDIAN SCIENCE AND ENGINEERING SOCIETY (A. T. Anderson Memorial Scholarship)

P.O. Box 9828
Albuquerque NM 87119-9828
505/765-1052
FAX: 505/765-5608
E-mail: scholarships@aises.org
Internet: http://www.aises.org/highered
AMOUNT: $1,000
DEADLINE(S): JUN 15
FIELD(S): Medicine; Natural Resources; Science; Engineering
ELIGIBILITY/REQUIREMENTS: Open to undergraduate and graduate students who are at least one quarter American Indian or recognized as member of a tribe. Must be member of AISES ($10 fee), enrolled full time at an accredited institution, and demonstrate financial need. Minimum GPA 2.7.
HOW TO APPLY: See website or contact Society for an application and/or membership information.
RENEWABLE: Yes
CONTACT: Tina Pino

2069—AMERICAN INDIAN SCIENCE AND ENGINEERING SOCIETY (Burlington Northern Santa Fe Pacific Foundation Scholarships)

P.O. Box 9828
Albuquerque NM 87119-9828
505/765-1052
FAX: 505/765-5608
E-mail: scholarships@aises.org
Internet: http://www.aises.org/highered
AMOUNT: $2,500

DEADLINE(S): MAR 31
FIELD(S): Business; Education; Science; Engineering; Health Administration
ELIGIBILITY/REQUIREMENTS: Open to high school seniors who are at least one quarter American Indian. Must reside in Kansas, Oklahoma, Colorado, Arizona, New Mexico, Minnesota, North Dakota, Oregon, South Dakota, Washington, Montana, or San Bernardino County, California (Burlington Northern and Santa Fe Pacific service areas). Must demonstrate financial need. Minimum GPA 2.0.
HOW TO APPLY: See website or contact Society for an application.
NUMBER OF AWARDS: 5
RENEWABLE: Yes. Up to 4 years.
CONTACT: Tina Pino

2070—AMERICAN MUSEUM OF NATURAL HISTORY (Research Experiences for Undergraduates)

Central Park West at 79th Street
New York NY 10024-5192
FAX: 212/769-5495
E-mail: grants@amnh.org
Internet: http://research.amnh.org/grants
AMOUNT: Stipend, research expenses, intracity travel, housing
DEADLINE(S): APR
FIELD(S): Evolutionary Biology, Physical Sciences
ELIGIBILITY/REQUIREMENTS: 10-week summer internships to pursue scientific projects in conjunction with Museum scientists. Must be enrolled in a degree program at a college or university, have a high GPA, and a strong science background.
HOW TO APPLY: See website or contact Office of Grants and Fellowships for an application. Submit with list of courses, statement of interest, and recommendations.

2071—AMERICAN RADIO RELAY LEAGUE FOUNDATION (Henry Broughton, K2AE Memorial Scholarship)

225 Main Street
Newington CT 06111
860/594-0397
FAX: 860/594-0259
E-mail: foundation@arrl.org
Internet: http://www.arrlf.org/
AMOUNT: $1,000
DEADLINE(S): FEB 1
FIELD(S): Engineering; Science
ELIGIBILITY/REQUIREMENTS: For radio amateurs with a general class license whose home residence is within 70 miles of

Schenectady, New York. For study leading to a bachelor's degree at an accredited 4-year college or university.
HOW TO APPLY: See website or contact Foundation for information and application. Submit with a 1-page essay on the role amateur radio has played in your life. A recent high school (or equivalent) or college transcript required; submit with application or mail separately.
NUMBER OF AWARDS: At least 1
RENEWABLE: No
CONTACT: Mary M. Hobart, K1MMH, Secretary

2072—AMERICAN RADIO RELAY LEAGUE FOUNDATION (William R. Goldfarb Memorial Scholarship)

225 Main Street
Newington CT 06111
860/594-0397
FAX: 860/594-0259
E-mail: foundation@arrl.org
Internet: http://www.arrlf.org/
AMOUNT: $10,000 or more
DEADLINE(S): FEB 1
FIELD(S): Business, Computer Science, Medicine (including Nursing), Engineering, Sciences
ELIGIBILITY/REQUIREMENTS: For student with any class of license pursuing baccalaureate or higher degree at a regionally accredited institution. Must demonstrate financial need.
HOW TO APPLY: See website or contact Foundation for information and application. Submit with a 1-page essay on the role amateur radio has played in your life. A recent high school (or equivalent) or college transcript required; submit with application or mail separately.
NUMBER OF AWARDS: 1
RENEWABLE: No
CONTACT: Mary M. Hobart, K1MMH, Secretary

2073—ASSOCIATED WESTERN UNIVERSITIES, INC. (AWU Undergraduate Student Fellowships)

4190 South Highland Drive, Suite 211
Salt Lake City UT 84124-2600
801/273-8900
FAX: 801/277-5632
Internet: http://www.awu.org
AMOUNT: $300/week stipend + possible travel allowance
DEADLINE(S): FEB 1
FIELD(S): Science; Mathematics; Engineering; Technology

ELIGIBILITY/REQUIREMENTS: Students who have been or will be enrolled in any accredited institution within six months of the start of their award. Academic performance and class standing, career goals, recommendations, and compatibility of interests and abilities with the needs and resources of the host facility.
HOW TO APPLY: See website for application and list of participating laboratories. Must also submit résumé, at least 1 (2 preferred) recommendation from a faculty member who is familiar with your academic achievements, and transcript. Applicants who received an AWU award within the last year and have approval for reappointment with their previous mentor, need only to complete the application form and submit a copy of their current transcripts.
NUMBER OF AWARDS: 500
RENEWABLE: Yes, must reapply.
CONTACT: Kathy Hecker, Director of Finance and Property Management

2074—ASSOCIATION FOR WOMEN IN SCIENCE (AWIS Education Foundation College Scholarship)

7008 Richard Drive
Bethesda MD 20817-4838
E-mail: awisedfd@awisedfd@awis.org
Internet: http://www.awis.org/careers/edfoundation.html
AMOUNT: $100-$1,000
DEADLINE(S): Mid JAN
FIELD(S): Science; Mathematics; Engineering
ELIGIBILITY/REQUIREMENTS: High school seniors may apply. Must have GPA of at least 3.75 and math plus verbal SAT of at least 1200 (or ACT of 2.5), be a U.S. citizen, plan a career in research or teaching, and plan to attend a college in the U.S.
HOW TO APPLY: See website for application and instructions.
NUMBER OF AWARDS: 10
RENEWABLE: No
CONTACT: Dr. Barbara Filner

2075—ASSOCIATION ON AMERICAN INDIAN AFFAIRS (Elizabeth and Sherman Asche Memorial Scholarship Fund)

Executive Office
966 Hungerford Drive, Suite 12-B
Rockville MD 20850
240/314-7155
FAX: 240/314-7159
E-mail: general.aaia@verizon.net
Internet: http://www.indian-affairs.org

AMOUNT: $1,500
DEADLINE(S): Fall and Spring semesters only
FIELD(S): Public Health; Science
ELIGIBILITY/REQUIREMENTS: Open to full-time undergraduate students who are minimally 1/4 degree Indian blood from a federally recognized tribe. Must be pursuing a degree in 1 of above fields. Award is based on financial need and is limited to North America/Alaska.
HOW TO APPLY: See website for application; Please send only the information requested; additional information will not be considered. Must submit essay on need, certificate of enrollment and quantum from your tribe or BIA, transcript, schedule of classes, and current financial aid award letter.
RENEWABLE: Yes Must reapply. Note: Disbursements of $750 made each semester pending satisfactory progress. No funding for summer semester.
CONTACT: Lisa Wyzlic at lw.aaia@verizon.net or 240/314-7155.
ADDITIONAL INFORMATION: If applying for more than 1 AAIA scholarship, send 1 application package only. Students will be considered for all scholarships they are qualified for.

2076—CHICAGO ROOFING CONTRACTORS ASSOCIATION

4415 W. Harrison Street, #322
Hillside IL 60162
708/449-3340
FAX: 708/449-0837
E-mail: info@crca.org
Internet: http://www.crca.org
AMOUNT: $3,000
DEADLINE(S): MAR (1st Friday)
FIELD(S): Business; Engineering; Architecture; Liberal Arts; Sciences
ELIGIBILITY/REQUIREMENTS: Open to high school seniors who reside in one of the eight counties in Northern Illinois: Cook, DuPage, Lake, Kane, Kendall, DeKalb, McHenry, or Will. Must be accepted as a full time student in a 4-year college or university to pursue a degree in one of the above fields. Must be U.S. citizen. Based on academic achievements, extracurricular activities, and community involvement.
HOW TO APPLY: See website for an application. Submit with 2 completed Personal Reference Forms (1 from high school guidance counselor or faculty member, an optional letter of recommendation may also be included; the other from an adult not related to the student); an official transcript of all high school records, and

official ACT and/or SAT Test results or official high school transcript.

NUMBER OF AWARDS: 1 (In the event of a tie, financial need considered).

RENEWABLE: Yes (up to 3 times). Must maintain a 2.75 grade point average.

2077—CIVIL AIR PATROL (CAP Undergraduate Scholarships)

National Headquarters
Maxwell AFB AL 36112-6332
334/953-5315
AMOUNT: $750
DEADLINE(S): JAN 31
FIELD(S): Humanities; Science; Engineering; Education

ELIGIBILITY/REQUIREMENTS: Open to CAP members who have received the Billy Mitchell Award or the senior rating in Level II of the senior training program.

HOW TO APPLY: Write for information.

2078—COMMUNITY FOUNDATION FOR GREATER ATLANTA, INC., THE (James M. & Virginia M. Smyth Scholarship Fund)

50 Hurt Plaza, Suite 449
Atlanta GA 30303
404/688-5525
FAX: 404/688-3060
E-mail: scholarships@atlcf.org
Internet: http://www.atlcf.org/GrantsScholarships/Scholarships.aspx
AMOUNT: $500-$1,000
DEADLINE(S): Varies
FIELD(S): Humanities, Science, Human Services, Music Ministry

ELIGIBILITY/REQUIREMENTS: Open to students enrolled at an accredited college pursuing an undergraduate degree and adults returning to school in order to increase employability. Must have a cumulative 3.0 GPA, be accepted for enrollment or enrolled at an accredited college, university or technical school, demonstrate financial need, and commitment to community service through school, community or religious organizations. Preference will be given to applicants from Missouri, Mississippi, Georgia, Illinois, Oklahoma, Texas and Tennessee.

HOW TO APPLY: See website for additional information and application. Submit with a personal essay (2-3 pages) that explains why you feel a college education is important, your statement of educational and career goals, post college career interests, highlights of your high school extracurricular/community service activities, special strengths, skills, and qualifications, any unusual family or personal cir-

cumstances have affected your achievement in school, work experience, or your participation in school and community activities, and present financial need; official transcript; and SAT and ACT scores, if a recent high school graduate. Send to The Community Foundation for Greater Atlanta, James M. & Virginia M. Smyth Scholarship Fund, Scholarship Management Services, Scholarship America, One Scholarship Way, P.O. Box 297, Saint Peter, MN 56082. If you have questions, call 507/931-1682 or e-mail community-foundation@scholarshipamerica.org.

NUMBER OF AWARDS: 12-15

RENEWABLE: Yes; Previous recipients are renewed if they continue to meet the scholarship's criteria and submit the current year's renewal application

CONTACT: Lisa Glanville, 404/308-0055

2078A—COMMUNITY FOUNDATION OF WESTERN MASSACHUSETTS (Mary Alby Markel Memorial Scholarship Fund)

1500 Main Street
P.O. Box 15769
Springfield MA 01115
413/732-2858
FAX: 413/733/8565
E-mail: scholar@community foundation.org
Internet: http://www.community foundation.org
AMOUNT: $500
DEADLINE(S): MAR 31
FIELD(S): Science

ELIGIBILITY/REQUIREMENTS: For graduating seniors at Central High School in Springfield, Massachusetts, pursuing postsecondary education in science.

HOW TO APPLY: See website for application.

NUMBER OF AWARDS: 1

RENEWABLE: No

2079—COUNCIL OF ENERGY RESOURCE TRIBES (CERT)

CERT Education Program
Attention: Scholars Program
695 S. Colorado Blvd, Suite 10
Denver CO 80246
303/282-7576
FAX: 303/282-7584
E-mail: info@CERTRedEarth.com
Internet: http://www.certred earth.com/
AMOUNT: $1,000
DEADLINE(S): SEP 14 (Fall), FEB 15 (Spring)

FIELD(S): Science; Engineering; Business, Mathematics, Computer Technology, or related fields

ELIGIBILITY/REQUIREMENTS: Applicants must meet the criteria to become a TRIBES Institute candidate and a full-time undergraduate (12hrs/semester) student enrolled in an accredited 2- or 4-year tribal, private, or public university/college, and must maintain at least a 2.5 GPA, although academic excellence far above this GPA is preferred. (Should scholarship funds be limited, GPA will be weighed in decision.)

HOW TO APPLY: Submit application along with official Tribal affiliation documentation (with enrollment number or other statement of Tribal acknowledgment of membership), an official transcript of most recent coursework with the cumulative GPA, as well as the GPA for current hours detailed on the transcript, and a class schedule for the next term demonstrating that you will be attending school full-time and/or verification of full-time enrollment for the next semester.

RENEWABLE: Yes. Must reapply.

CONTACT: Tom Talache, ttalache@CERTRedEarth.com or 303/282-7576, ext. 12

HOW TO APPLY: Indian students who wish to attend TRIBES may contact CERT for information and an application.

2080—DAVIDSON INSTITUTE FOR TALENT DEVELOPMENT

9665 Gateway
Reno NV 89521
775/852-3483, ext. 423
FAX: 775/852-2184
E-mail: tmoessner@ditd.org
Internet: http://www.davidson fellows.org
AMOUNT: $10,000; $20,000; $50,000
DEADLINE(S): Last Friday of MAR
FIELD(S): Science, Technology, Mathematics, Philosophy, Music, Literature and Outside the Box

ELIGIBILITY/REQUIREMENTS: Must be a U.S. citizen residing in the U.S., or a permanent resident of the U.S. residing in the U.S.; under the age of 18 as of October 1 (there is no minimum age for eligibility); completed a significant piece of work in one of the designated application categories; and available to attend, with at least 1 parent or guardian, the awards reception and other recognition events in September (travel expenses and lodging will be paid by the Institute).

HOW TO APPLY: See website including FAQ section and application booklet; download and complete all components.

NUMBER OF AWARDS: 15-20
RENEWABLE: No
CONTACT: Tacie Moessner, Davidson Fellows Program Manager
ADDITIONAL INFORMATION: Group and team projects are not eligible. Scholarships must be used at an accredited institute of learning within 10 years of the award date.

2081—DUPONT CHALLENGE (Science Essay Competition)

Department GLC
900 Skokie Boulevard, Suite 200
Northbrook IL 60062-4028
847/205-3000
FAX: 847/564-8197
Internet: http://www.glcomm.com/dupont
AMOUNT: $5,000 (first place); $1,000 (finalists); Award Certificate (honorable mention)
DEADLINE(S): JAN 20
FIELD(S): Science
ELIGIBILITY/REQUIREMENTS: Open to students in grades 7 to 12 enrolled in a public or non-public school in the United States and its territories and Canada.
HOW TO APPLY: Submit an essay of 700 to 1,000 words discussing a scientific or technological development, event, or theory. For a more detailed description including rules, guidelines and entry form, see website.
NUMBER OF AWARDS: 1 first place; 4 finalists, 30 honorable mentions in each of 2 divisions (junior: grades 7, 8 and 9; senior: grades 10, 11, and 12). The first-place winner in each division will be flown to Space Center Houston, along with a parent and sponsoring science teacher, as special guests. Airfare and hotel expenses will be provided by DuPont.

2082—EAA AVIATION FOUNDATION (Payzer Scholarship)

EAA Scholarship Department
P.O. 3086
Oshkosh WI 54903-3065
920/426-6823
E-mail: scholarships@eaa.org
Internet: http://www.youngeagles.org
AMOUNT: $5,000
DEADLINE(S): MAR 1
FIELD(S): Engineering, Mathematics, Physical or Biological Science
ELIGIBILITY/REQUIREMENTS: Open to well-rounded individuals involved in school and community activities as well as aviation accepted at or attending 4-year accredited colledge, university or postsecondary school with am emphasis on technical information who is majoring one of above fields. Applicant's academic records should verify his/her ability to complete educational activity for which scholarship is requested. Must also be a current member of EAA (Experimental Aircraft Association) or recommended by a current EAA member.
HOW TO APPLY: Apply online. A personal statement (500 words or less) addressing career aspirations. educational plan, why you want to receive this scholarship. what you learned from work/volunteer experiences, and explaining how your education will be financed, including loans, family assistance, your own savings, scholarships, etc. and any unusual financial circumstances affecting your college financial plan required.
NUMBER OF AWARDS: 1

2083—FREEDOM FROM RELIGION FOUNDATION (Student Essay Contests)

P.O. Box 750
Madison WI 53701
608/256-5800
Internet: http://www.ffrf.org
AMOUNT: $1,000; $500; $250
DEADLINE(S): JUL 15
FIELD(S): Humanities; English; Education; Philosophy; Science
ELIGIBILITY/REQUIREMENTS: Topics change yearly, but are on general theme of maintaining separation of church and state. Open to high school seniors and students enrolled in college or technical school; must be U.S. citizen.
HOW TO APPLY: See website or send SASE for complete information. Indicate whether you will be competing in the college or high school competition. Information sent when new topics announced each February.

2084—GERBER SCIENTIFIC, INC. (H. Joseph Gerber 1947 Scholars Fund Endowment at Rensselaer Polytechnic Institute)

83 Gerber Road West
South Windsor CT 06074
860/648-8027
Internet: http://www.gerberscientific.com/community/scholarships.htm
AMOUNT: Varies
DEADLINE(S): MAR 15
FIELD(S): Engineering, Mathematics, Computer Science, Natural Sciences
ELIGIBILITY/REQUIREMENTS: Available to full-time students pursuing a baccalaureate degree at Rensselaer Polytechnic Institute's Troy, New York, campus. Awards are determined by the Rensselaer Office of Financial Aid. Preference is given to residents of the state of Connecticut.
HOW TO APPLY: Applications are available from the Rensselaer Office of Financial Aid.

2085—GERBER SCIENTIFIC, INC. (H. Joseph Gerber Vision Scholarship Program)

83 Gerber Road West
South Windsor CT 06074
860/648-8027
Internet: http://www.gerberscientific.com/community/scholarships.htm
AMOUNT: Varies
DEADLINE(S): MAR 15
FIELD(S): Engineering, Mathematics, Computer Science, Natural Sciences
ELIGIBILITY/REQUIREMENTS: Available to high school seniors attending South Windsor, Manchester or Tolland High, or Gerber employees' children who meet the requirements.
HOW TO APPLY: Applications are available in the high school guidance office.
NUMBER OF AWARDS: 50

2086—HAWAII COMMUNITY FOUNDATION (Dan & Pauline Lutkenhouse Tropical Garden Scholarship)

1164 Bishop Street, Suite 800
Honolulu HI 96813
808/537-6333 or toll free: 888/731-3863
FAX: 808/521-6286
E-mail: info@hcf-hawaii.org
Internet: http://www.hcf-hawaii.org
DEADLINE(S): MAR 1
FIELD(S): Agriculture; Science; Medicine; Nursing
ELIGIBILITY/REQUIREMENTS: Must be resident of the Hilo coast and the Hamakua coast, north of the Wailuku River; plan to attend full time an accredited 2- or 4-year college or university; and demonstrate financial need, good moral character, and academic achievement (minimum GPA of 2.7).
HOW TO APPLY: See website. Send application with 2 letters of recommendation.

2087—HAWAII COMMUNITY FOUNDATION (Shuichi, Katsu & Itsuyo Suga Scholarship)

1164 Bishop Street, Suite 800
Honolulu HI 96813
808/537-6333 or toll free:
888/731-3863
FAX: 808/521-6286
E-mail: info@hcf-hawaii.org
Internet: http://www.hcf-hawaii.org
DEADLINE(S): MAR 1
FIELD(S): Mathematics; Physics; Science; Technology
ELIGIBILITY/REQUIREMENTS: Applicants must be residents of the state of Hawaii; plan to attend full time an accredited 2- or 4-year college or university; and demonstrate financial need, good moral character, and strong academic achievement, with a minimum GPA of 3.0.
HOW TO APPLY: Send application with 2 letters of recommendation.
CONTACT: See website

2088—HISPANIC COLLEGE FUND (HSF/SHPE Inc. Scholarship Program)

55 Second Street, Suite 1500
San Francisco CA 94105
877/HSF-INFO (877/473-4636)
FAX: 415/808-2302
E-mail: pip@hsf.net
Internet: http://hispanicfund.org
AMOUNT: At least $2,500
DEADLINE(S): JUN 2
FIELD(S): Engineering; Mathematics; Science; Computer Science
ELIGIBILITY/REQUIREMENTS: Must be U.S. citizens or legal permanent residents of Hispanic heritage (one parent fully Hispanic or both parents half Hispanic). Open to high school graduates, community college transfer students, 4-year university undergraduates, and graduate students. All students must be enrolled full time in a degree-seeking program in the U.S. or Puerto Rico.
HOW TO APPLY: Contact Fund for details or visit website for application.

2089—JACKSONVILLE STATE UNIVERSITY (Drs. Wayne & Sara Finley Scholarship)

Financial Aid Office
Jacksonville AL 36265
256/782-5677 or 800/231-5291
Internet: www.jsu.edu
AMOUNT: Varies
DEADLINE(S): FEB 1

FIELD(S): Mathematics; Science; Pre-Prof Secondary Education
ELIGIBILITY/REQUIREMENTS: Open to junior or senior; 3.0 GPA; Clay, Coosa, or Randolph Counties, Alabama.
HOW TO APPLY: See website for application. Mail transcript and ACT/SAT scores.
RENEWABLE: No
CONTACT: Scholarship Committee

2090—JEWISH FEDERATION OF METROPOLITAN CHICAGO (Academic Scholarship Program)

Jewish Vocational Service
216 West Jackson Blvd., Suite 700
Chicago IL 60606-6921
312/673-3400
TTY: 312/444-2877
FAX: 312/553-5544
E-mail: jvsscholarship@
jvschicago.orgship
Internet: http://www.jvs/
chicago.org
AMOUNT: Varies
DEADLINE(S): FEB 15
FIELD(S): Mathematics, Engineering, Science, Medicine, Social Work, Education, Psychology, Rabbinate, Law (except corporate), Communications
ELIGIBILITY/REQUIREMENTS: Open to Jewish men and women legally domiciled in the greater Chicago metropolitan area, who are identified as having promise for significant contributions in their chosen careers, and are in need of financial assistance for full-time academic programs in above areas. Must have entered undergraduate junior year in career programs requiring no postgraduate education, be in graduate/professional school, or be in a vo-tech training program.
HOW TO APPLY: Phone JVS Scholarship Secretary (312/673-3457), fax, or visit website (click on Scholarship Services) for an application in the Fall. Interview required.
RENEWABLE: Yes

2091—JUNIATA COLLEGE (Robert Steele Memorial Scholarship)

Office of Financial Planning
1700 Moore Street
Huntingdon PA 16652
814/641-3142
FAX: 814/641-5311
E-mail: frankv@juniata.edu
Internet: http://www.juniata.

edu/admission/finplan/index.html
AMOUNT: Up to $4,000
DEADLINE(S): MAR 1
FIELD(S): Science; Medical Studies
ELIGIBILITY/REQUIREMENTS: Open to science/medical students applying to Juniata College. Must demonstrate financial need and fill out government FAFSA form.
HOW TO APPLY: Vincent Frank, Director of Student Financial Planning, 814/641-3140; e-mail: frankv@juniata.edu. See your financial aid office for FAFSA.

2092—KALAMAZOO TECHNOLOGY & SCIENCE FELLOWS PROGRAM

Southwest Michigan First
The Chamber Building
356 West Michigan Avenue
Kalamazoo MI 49007-3737
269/553-9588
FAX: 269/553-6897
E-mail: alumni@wmich.edu
Internet: http://www.wmich.
edu/cas/ research.html
AMOUNT: Full scholarship plus internship
DEADLINE(S): MAR 1
FIELD(S): Science; Technology
ELIGIBILITY/REQUIREMENTS: Open to high school graduating senior, Kalamazoo County resident or enrolled at school within the Kalamazoo Regional Education Service Agency district. Must maintain satisfactory academic progress; be able to intern with a mentoring corporation in Kalamazoo County; be willing to make a 2-year pledge to work in Kalamazoo County following graduation from college.
HOW TO APPLY: Contact the KTS Fellows Program for an application or see website for application.
RENEWABLE: Yes. May request renewal for 1 additional term.
CONTACT: College of Arts and Sciences

2093—KOREAN-AMERICAN SCIENTISTS AND ENGINEERS ASSOCIATION (KSEA Scholarships)

1952 Gallows Road, Suite 300
Vienna VA 22182
703/748-1221
FAX: 703/748-1331
E-mail: admin@ksea.org
Internet: http://www.ksea.org
AMOUNT: $1,000
DEADLINE(S): FEB 28

FIELD(S): Science, Engineering, Medicine

ELIGIBILITY/REQUIREMENTS: Must have graduated from a high school in the U.S. and must be a student member of KSEA or a child of a member. Evaluation criteria are academic performance-30%; recommendation letters-30%; work experience and extracurricular activities-20%; and essay-20%.

HOW TO APPLY: See website for application. Submit Curriculum Vitae (including work experience and extracurricular activities); transcript from high school and college attended; an essay on one of the following topics (approximately 500 words): your career goals and their contributions to the society or meaning of Korean heritage in your life; and 3 recommendation letters (1 from a current or previous KSEA officer or chapter president).

NUMBER OF AWARDS: 5-8 (2 are ONLY for women)

2094—MICROSCOPY SOCIETY OF AMERICA SCHOLARSHIPS (Undergraduate Research Scholarships)

230 East Ohio Street, Suite 400
Chicago IL 60611-3265
800/538-3672
Internet: http://www.msa.
microscopy.org

AMOUNT: Up to $3,000

DEADLINE(S): DEC

FIELD(S): Science (microscopy)

ELIGIBILITY/REQUIREMENTS: Scholarship provides funds to junior or senior undergraduates conducting research involving any area of microscopy.

HOW TO APPLY: Contact Society for application and information.

RENEWABLE: No

2095—MINNESOTA GAY/LESBIAN/ BISEXUAL/TRANSGENDER EDUCATIONAL FUND (Pat McCart Memorial Award)

Philanthrofund Foundation
1409 Willow Street, Suite 305
Minneapolis MN 55403-3251
612/220-4888
FAX: 612/871-6587
E-mail: philanth@scc.net
Internet: http://www.scc.net/~t-
bonham/EDFUND.HTM

AMOUNT: $500-$1,000

DEADLINE(S): FEB 1

FIELD(S): Mathematics; Science

ELIGIBILITY/REQUIREMENTS: Open to GLBT graduating high school senior woman who will be attending a 4-year college or university and is planning to major in mathematics or one of the sciences; must be a Minnesota resident. Criteria include applicant's affirmation of her GLBT identity; demonstrated integrity and honesty, participation and leadership in community activities, and service as role model, mentor, colleague or advisor for the GLBT community.

HOW TO APPLY: See website for application or contact Fund for application. Submit by mail. E-mail or faxed materials will NOT be accepted.

RENEWABLE: No.

2096—NATIONAL SPACE CLUB (Dr. Robert H. Goddard Historical Essay Award)

2025 M Street NW, Suite 800
Washington DC 20036-4907
202/973/8661

AMOUNT: $1,000

DEADLINE(S): DEC 4

FIELD(S): Science & Engineering (emphasis on aerospace) History

ELIGIBILITY/REQUIREMENTS: Essay competition open to any U.S. citizen on a topic dealing with any significant aspect of the historical development of rocketry and astronautics. Essays should not exceed 5,000 words and be fully documented. Judged on originality and scholarship.

HOW TO APPLY: Send SASE for complete information. Previous winners not eligible.

2097—NATIONAL SPACE CLUB (Dr. Robert H. Goddard Scholarship)

2025 M Street NW, Suite 800
Washington DC 20036-4907
202/973/8661

AMOUNT: $10,000

DEADLINE(S): JAN 6

FIELD(S): Science, Engineering (emphasis on aerospace science & technology)

ELIGIBILITY/REQUIREMENTS: Essay competition open to any U.S. citizen, in at least junior year of an accredited university, intending to pursue undergraduate or graduate studies in science or engineering. Financial need considered, but not controlling.

HOW TO APPLY: Submit letter and transcript of college record, letters of recommendation from faculty, demonstrating personal qualities of creativity and leadership; scholastic plans relating to participation in aerospace science and technology; proven past research and participation in space-related science and engineering.

RENEWABLE: Yes. Up to 1 additional year if warranted.

2098—NATIONAL TECHNICAL ASSOCIATION, INC. (Scholarship Competitions for Minorities and Women in Science and Engineering)

5810 Kingstowne Center,
Suite 120221
Alexandria VA 22315-5711
E-mail: ntamfj1@aol.com
Internet: http://www.huenet.
com/nta

AMOUNT: $500-$5,000

DEADLINE(S): Varies

FIELD(S): Science; Mathematics; Engineering; Applied Technology

ELIGIBILITY/REQUIREMENTS: Open to minorities and women pursuing degrees in the above fields. Additional scholarships are available through local chapters of NTA.

HOW TO APPLY: See website or write for details and for locations of local chapters.

2099—NATIVE AMERICAN SCHOLARSHIP FUND, INC.

8200 Mountain Road NE, Suite 203
Albuquerque NM 87110
505/262-2351
FAX: 505/262-0543
E-mail: NScholarsh@aol.com

AMOUNT: Varies

DEADLINE(S): MAR 15; APR 15; SEP 15

FIELD(S): Mathematics; Engineering; Science; Business; Education; Computer Science

ELIGIBILITY/REQUIREMENTS: Open to American Indians or Alaskan Natives (1/4 degree or more) enrolled as members of a federally recognized, state recognized, or terminated tribe. For graduate or undergraduate study at an accredited 4-year college or university.

HOW TO APPLY: Contact Director of Recruitment for an application.

NUMBER OF AWARDS: 208

CONTACT: Lucille Kelley, Director of Recruitment

2100—NEW ENGLAND WATER WORKS ASSOCIATION

125 Hopping Brook Road
Holliston MA 01746
508/893-7979
FAX: 508/93-9898
E-mail: mruozzi@newwa.org
Internet: http://www.newwa.org

AMOUNT: Varies

DEADLINE(S): JUL 1

FIELD(S): Water Industry; Civil or Environmental Engineering; Business Management; Science

ELIGIBILITY/REQUIREMENTS: Based on merit, character, and need, with preference given to those students whose programs are considered beneficial to water works practice in New England. Each scholarship applicant must be a member or student member of either the New England Water Works Association, or the American Water Works Association, with a New England section, before their application will be considered. The membership fee is $25 for a NEWWA student membership or $36 for a NEWWA/AWWA student membership.

HOW TO APPLY: Mail application to: Thomas MacElhaney, Scholarship Committee Chair, 631/231-8100 or tmacelhaney@preloadinc.com.

NUMBER OF AWARDS: 6

RENEWABLE: No

CONTACT: Marina Mukandala

2101—OFFICE OF NAVAL RESEARCH (Naval Science Awards Program)

ONR 353
800 North Quincy Street
Arlington VA 22217/5660
800/422-6727 or 703/696-5787
Internet: http://www.jshs.org

AMOUNT: $2,000-$20,000

DEADLINE(S): Varies (established by individual regional, state, and district science fairs)

FIELD(S): Science; Engineering

ELIGIBILITY/REQUIREMENTS: For high school students (grades 9-12) who participate in regional/district/state science fairs; must be U.S. citizen or permanent resident. Winners may participate in Junior Science and Humanities Symposia (JSHS) Program. Awards also offered in each of 14 categories at International Science and Engineering Fair (ISEF), sponsored by Science Service, Inc.

HOW TO APPLY: See website or contact Project Officer at address above for complete information on NSAP, ISEF, and JSHS.

NUMBER OF AWARDS: 24

RENEWABLE: Yes

CONTACT: Barbara M. Thurman

2102—OKLAHOMA MEDICAL RESEARCH FOUNDATION (Sir Alexander Fleming Summer Scholar Program)

825 NE 13th Street
Oklahoma City OK 73104-5046
405/271-8537 or 800/522-0211
Internet: http://www.omrf.org/fleming

AMOUNT: $2,500 salary + housing

DEADLINE(S): FEB 15

FIELD(S): Science (all fields)

ELIGIBILITY/REQUIREMENTS: Open ONLY to Oklahoma students who have completed their junior year of high school through those in their junior year of college at time of application. Excellent academic standing and aptitude in science and math are essential. Students will work in Foundation's laboratories in June and July.

HOW TO APPLY: See website for further information and application forms.

2103—RIPON COLLEGE (Math/Science Scholarship)

300 Seward Street
P.O. Box 248
Ripon WI 54971
800/947-4766
FAX: 920/746-8335
E-mail: adminfo@ripon.edu
Internet: http://www.ripon.edu

AMOUNT: Full tuition

DEADLINE(S): JAN 1

FIELD(S): Natural Science; Mathematics

ELIGIBILITY/REQUIREMENTS: Minimum high school GPA 3.8, rank in top 5% of class; academic credentials and community service activities considered. Must major in natural science or mathematics.

HOW TO APPLY: Contact Office of Admission for an application; submit with a letter of recommendation from high school teacher. An on-campus interview required.

NUMBER OF AWARDS: 1

RENEWABLE: Yes. Must maintain enrollment as a full-time student majoring in math or science, minimum GPA of 3.0 and evidence satisfactory progress toward a 4-year degree.

CONTACT: Office of Admission

2104—SAN DIEGO AIR &SPACE MUSEUM (Bill Gibbs Endowment Fund)

Education Office
2001 Pan American Plaza
San Diego CA 92101
619/234-8291, ext. 119
FAX: 619/233-4526
Internet: http://aerospacemuseum.org

AMOUNT: $1,500-$2,500

DEADLINE(S): APR 1

FIELD(S): Aerospace, Mathematics, Physics, Science, Engineering

ELIGIBILITY/REQUIREMENTS: Graduating seniors of San Diego County high schools who have been accepted to a 4-year college or university. Academic achievement, strong aviation/aerospace career interests.

HOW TO APPLY: See website or write museum for application.

2105—SCIENCE SERVICE (Intel International Science and Engineering Fair)

1719 N Street NW
Washington DC 20036
202/785-2255
FAX: 202/785-1243
E-mail: jcole@sciserv.org
Internet: http://www.sciserv.org

AMOUNT: Varies

DEADLINE(S): Varies (consult local, regional or state ISEF)

FIELD(S): Science; Mathematics; Engineering; Medicine

ELIGIBILITY/REQUIREMENTS: High school students (grades 9-12) may participate in this worldwide competition.

HOW TO APPLY: Contact Science Service for official ISEF entry book.

2106—SCIENCE SERVICE (Intel Science Talent Search)

1719 N Street NW
Washington DC 20036
202/785-2255
FAX: 202/785-1243
E-mail: jkee@sciserv.org
Internet: http://www.sciserv.org

AMOUNT: $100,000 (1st place); $75,000 (2nd); $50,000 (3rd); $25,000 (4th-6th); $20,000 (7th-10th); 30 at $5,000; 300 at $1,000; 40 laptops

DEADLINE(S): Mid to late NOV

FIELD(S): Science; Mathematics; Engineering; Medicine

ELIGIBILITY/REQUIREMENTS: Open to high school seniors in the U.S. and territories and American students attending school abroad.

HOW TO APPLY: Contact Science Service for official STS entry book. Submit completed entry form, with research report, high school transcript, and standardized test scores.

NUMBER OF AWARDS: 40

CONTACT: June Kee

2107—SIEMENS WESTINGHOUSE (Science and Technology Competition)

186 Wood Avenue South

Iselin NJ 08830
877/822-5233
E-mail: foundation.us@siemens.com
Internet: http://www.siemens-foundation.org
AMOUNT: $120,000 (maximum)
DEADLINE(S): Varies
FIELD(S): Biology; Physical Sciences; Mathematics; Physics; Chemistry; Computer Science; Environmental Science
ELIGIBILITY/REQUIREMENTS: Open to U.S. high school seniors to pursue independent science research projects, working individually or in teams of 2 or 3 to develop and test their own ideas. May work with one of the universities/laboratories that serve as Siemens' partners. Students from the U.S. and its territories may compete in 1 of 6 geographic areas. Individual and team national prizewinners receive a second scholarship to be applied to undergraduate or graduate education.
HOW TO APPLY: See website or contact Siemens Foundation for details.

2108—SKIDMORE COLLEGE (Porter Presidential Scholarships in Science and Mathematics)

Office of Admissions
815 North Broadway
Saratoga Springs NY 12866-1632
800/867-6007
E-mail: admissions@skidmore.edu
Internet: http://www.skidmore.edu/administration/financial aid/porter scholarship.htm
AMOUNT: $10,000
DEADLINE(S): JAN 15
FIELD(S): Mathematics, Science, or Computer Science
ELIGIBILITY/REQUIREMENTS: Scholarships for students excelling in the above fields. Awards are based on talent, not financial need. Recipients are not required to major in a scientific or mathematical discipline, but they will be expected to demonstrate serious research in one or more of these areas.
HOW TO APPLY: For more information, see website.
NUMBER OF AWARDS: 5
RENEWABLE: Yes

2109—SOCIETY OF AUTOMOTIVE ENGINEERS (Detroit Section SAE Technical Scholarship)

SAE Customer Service
400 Commonwealth Drive
Warrendale PA 15096-0001
724/776-4970
FAX: 724/776-1615
E-mail: customerservice@sae.org
Internet: http://www.sae.org/students/scholarships
AMOUNT: $2,500
DEADLINE(S): DEC 1
FIELD(S): Automotive Industry; Engineering; Science
ELIGIBILITY/REQUIREMENTS: Must be child or grandchild of a current SAE Detroit Section member and intend to enroll in a 2- or 4-year engineering or science program at an accredited college or university. A minimum 3.0 GPA and 1200 SAT or 28 ACT composite score and demonstrated financial need is required. Must be entering freshman or transfer student who has completed a 2-year program.
HOW TO APPLY: See website for application. Submit with copies of FAFSA forms; a personal essay that demonstrates hands-on experience or activity (such as rebuilding engines, working on cars/trucks, etc.); 2 recommendations, 1 of which must be from a teacher, counselor, or administrator; and transcript.
NUMBER OF AWARDS: 1
RENEWABLE: Yes. Up to $10,000 (over 4-year period) if student maintains a 2.5 GPA and remains in good standing.

2110—SOCIETY OF AUTOMOTIVE ENGINEERS (Whitworth College/SAE Engineering Scholarship)

SAE Customer Service
400 Commonwealth Drive
Warrendale PA 15096-0001
724/776-4970
FAX: 724/776-1615
E-mail: customerservice@sae.org
Internet: http://www.sae.org/students/scholarships
AMOUNT: $500/semester
DEADLINE(S): DEC 1
FIELD(S): Engineering; Science; Automotive Industry
ELIGIBILITY/REQUIREMENTS: Open to incoming freshmen or transfer students who plan to major in science or engineering and have a minimum 1200 SAT or 2.7 ACT score and 3.6 GPA.
HOW TO APPLY: See website for application. Submit application; a personal essay that demonstrates hands-on experience or activity (such as rebuilding engines, working on cars/trucks, etc.); 2 recommendations, 1 of which must be from a teacher, counselor, or administrator; and transcript.
NUMBER OF AWARDS: 1

RENEWABLE: Yes. Up to 8 semesters provided student is enrolled full time in a science or pre-engineering major program and maintains a 3.0 GPA.

2111—SOCIETY OF HISPANIC PROFESSIONAL ENGINEERS (SHPE)

University of Texas at Arlington
Box 19019
SHPE AHETEMS, Inc.
Arlington TX 76019
817/272-1116
FAX: 817/272-2548
Internet: http://www.shpe.org
AMOUNT: $1,000-$3,000
DEADLINE(S): APR 1
FIELD(S): Engineering; Science
ELIGIBILITY/REQUIREMENTS: Applicants must be Hispanic undergraduate or graduate students or graduating high school seniors interested in studying engineering or science with 3.0 GPA for undergraduates and 3.2 GPA for graduate students.
HOW TO APPLY: See website for application or contact Rafaela Schwan.
RENEWABLE: Yes
CONTACT: Rafaela Schwan

2112—SOUTH CAROLINA SPACE GRANT CONSORTIUM (Undergraduate Research Program)

Department of Geology and Environmental Geosciences
College of Charleston
66 George Street
Charleston SC 29424
843/953-5463
FAX: 843/953-5446
E-mail: scozzarot@cofc.edu
Internet: http://www.cofc.edu/~scs.grant
AMOUNT: $3,000
DEADLINE(S): End of JAN; check application for SPECIFIC deadline date
FIELD(S): Aerospace or Space-related Studies (including, but not limited to, the basic sciences; science education; astronomy; planetary science; environmental studies; engineering; fine arts; journalism)
ELIGIBILITY/REQUIREMENTS: Must be U.S citizen; attend a consortium member institution; be sponsored by a faculty advisor; entering junior or senior year; have an interest in aerospace and space-related studies. Selection is based on academic qualifications.

HOW TO APPLY: Send application to your institution's campus director with 2 letters of recommendation; description of past activities, current interests and future plans concerning a space science or aerospace related field; faculty sponsorship and a research proposal including its relevance to a NASA mission.
NUMBER OF AWARDS: 1
RENEWABLE: No
CONTACT: Tara B. Scozzaro

2113—SOUTH CAROLINA SPACE GRANT CONSORTIUM/SOUTH CAROLINA SEA GRANT CONSORTIUM (Kathryn D. Sullivan Science and Engineering Fellowship)

66 George Street
College of Charleston
Charleston SC 29424
843/953-5463
FAX: 843/953-5446
E-mail: scozzarot@cofc.edu
Internet: http://www.cofu.edu/
~scs.grant
AMOUNT: $7,000 (maximum)
DEADLINE(S): End of JAN; check application for actual deadline date
FIELD(S): Science; Engineering
ELIGIBILITY/REQUIREMENTS: Must be entering senior year at 4-year college or university and a citizen of the U.S. Must be sponsored by a faculty advisor. Selection will be based on academic qualifications; 2 letters of recommendation; description of past activities, current interests, and future plans concerning natural science-related and engineering-related studies.
HOW TO APPLY: See website for additional information.
NUMBER OF AWARDS: 1
RENEWABLE: No
CONTACT: Tara B. Scozzaro

2114—TAPPI CORRUGATED CONTAINERS DIVISION SCHOLARSHIP

P.O. Box 105113
Atlanta GA 30092
770/446-1400
FAX: 770/446-6947
E-mail: vedmondson@tappi.org
Internet: http://www.tappi.org
AMOUNT: $1,000-$2,000
DEADLINE(S): JAN 31
FIELD(S): Engineering; Science; Paper Industry
ELIGIBILITY/REQUIREMENTS: Must be an undergraduate or currently employed in the corrugated container, pulp, and paper industry; be able to demonstrate

significant interest in the corrugated container segment of industry; be attending college full time or working in the box business and attending night school; be a junior or senior in the upcoming school year, and maintain a GPA of 3.0 or higher.
HOW TO APPLY: Contact TAPPI or see website for an application and additional information. Submit along with transcript, letter of recommendation from the TAPPI Student Chapter's Faculty Advisor or equivalent (faculty instructor), and 2 additional letters of recommendation from persons familiar with your character, accomplishments, and likelihood of success.
NUMBER OF AWARDS: Multiple (4, $2,000; several, $1,000).
CONTACT: Veranda Edmondson, 770/208-7536

2115—TAPPI ENGINEERING DIVISION SCHOLARSHIP

P.O. Box 105113
Atlanta GA 30092
770/446-1400
FAX: 770/446-6947
E-mail: vedmondson@tappi.org
Internet: http://www.tappi.org
AMOUNT: $2,500
DEADLINE(S): JAN 31
FIELD(S): Engineering; Science; Paper Industry
ELIGIBILITY/REQUIREMENTS: Must be an undergraduate member of a TAPPI Student Chapter, or submit comparable evidence of professional development and participation in the paper industry. Must be an upcoming junior or senior enrolled in an engineering or science program, attending college full time; maintaining a GPA of 3.0 or higher.
HOW TO APPLY: Contact TAPPI or see website for an application and additional information. Submit along with transcript, letter of recommendation from the TAPPI Student Chapter's Faculty Advisor or equivalent (faculty instructor), and 2 additional letters of recommendation from persons familiar with your character, accomplishments, and likelihood of success.
NUMBER OF AWARDS: Up to 2 (1 to junior, 1 to senior)
RENEWABLE: Yes, must reapply.
CONTACT: Veranda Edmondson, 770/208-7536

2116—TAPPI FINISHING AND CONVERTING DIVISION (Paul Smith Scholarship Award)

P.O. Box 105113

Atlanta GA 30092
770/446-1400
FAX: 770/446-6947
E-mail: vedmondson@tappi.org
Internet: http://www.tappi.org
AMOUNT: $1,000
DEADLINE(S): JAN 31
FIELD(S): Science; Engineering; Technology; Paper Industry
ELIGIBILITY/REQUIREMENTS: Applicant must be enrolled as a full-time student in a state-accredited undergraduate college program; must have a GPA of 3.0 or its equivalent, must be in a program preparatory to a career in the nonwovens industry or demonstrate an interest in the areas covered by the Nonwovens Division.
HOW TO APPLY: See website or contact TAPPI for applications. Submit application along with transcript, 3 letters of recommendation from persons familiar with the applicant's character, including an instructor or faculty member; academic and extracurricular accomplishments, etc. Interview may be requested.
NUMBER OF AWARDS: Multiple
RENEWABLE: Yes. Must reapply; same person may not receive award in consecutive years.
CONTACT: Veranda Edmondson, 770/208-7536

2117—TAPPI NONWOVENS DIVISION SCHOLARSHIP AWARD

P.O. Box 105113
Atlanta GA 30092
770/446-1400
FAX: 770/446-6947
E-mail: vedmondson@tappi.org
Internet: http://www.tappi.org
AMOUNT: $1,000
DEADLINE(S): JAN 31
FIELD(S): Science; Engineering; Paper Industry
ELIGIBILITY/REQUIREMENTS: Must be enrolled as a full-time student in a state-accredited undergraduate college program; have a GPA of 3.0 or equivalent, be in a program preparatory to a career in the nonwovens industry or demonstrate an interest in the areas covered by the Nonwovens Division.
HOW TO APPLY: See website or contact TAPPI for applications. Submit application along with transcript, 3 letters of recommendation from persons familiar with the applicant's character, including an instructor or faculty member; academic and extracurricular accomplishments, etc. Inter-view may be requested.
NUMBER OF AWARDS: Multiple

RENEWABLE: Yes, must reapply; same person may not receive award in consecutive years.
CONTACT: Veranda Edmondson, 770/208-7536

2118—TAPPI PAPER AND BOARD DIVISION SCHOLARSHIP PROGRAM

P.O. Box 105113
Atlanta GA 30092
770/446-1400
FAX: 770/446-6947
E-mail: vedmondson@tappi.org
Internet: http://www.tappi.org
AMOUNT: $1,000
DEADLINE(S): JAN 31
FIELD(S): Science; Engineering; Paper Industry
ELIGIBILITY/REQUIREMENTS: Open to TAPPI student member or an undergraduate member of a TAPPI chapter. Must be a college or university sophomore, junior, or senior enrolled in an engineering or science program; a full-time student or a full-time participant in a cooperative work-study program recognized and supported by the educational institution; and able to show a significant interest in the paper industry.
HOW TO APPLY: See website or contact TAPPI for applications. Submit application along with transcript, a personal statement from the applicant regarding his or her career goals and personal objectives, letter of recommendation from faculty member, and 2 letters of recommendation from persons familiar with your character, academic and extracurricular accomplishments, etc. Interview may be requested.
NUMBER OF AWARDS: Multiple
RENEWABLE: Yes. Must reapply; same person may not receive award in consecutive years.
CONTACT: Veranda Edmondson, 770/208-7536

2119—UNCF/MERCK SCIENCE INITIATIVE (Undergraduate Science Research Scholarship Awards)

8260 Willow Oaks Corporate Drive
P.O. Box 10444
Fairfax VA 22031-4511
703/205-3503
FAX: 703/205-3574
E-mail: uncfmerck@uncf.org
Internet: http://www.uncf.org/merck
AMOUNT: $25,000/year (maximum)
DEADLINE(S): DEC 15
FIELD(S): Life & Physical Sciences
ELIGIBILITY/REQUIREMENTS: Open to African-Americans in their junior year of college who will receive a bachelor's degree in the following academic year. Must be enrolled full time in any 4-year college or university in the U.S. and have a minimum 3.3 GPA. Must be U.S. citizen or permanent resident. Financial need NOT a factor.
HOW TO APPLY: Contact UNCF/Merck for an application.
NUMBER OF AWARDS: 15
RENEWABLE: No
CONTACT: Jerry Bryant, Ph.D.

2120—UNIVERSITY OF MARYLAND (John B. and Ida Slaughter Endowed Scholarship in Science, Technology, and the Black Community)

Afro-American Studies Program
2169 Lefrak Hall
College Park MD 20742-7225
301/405-1158 or
Center for Minorities in Science and Engineering
1134 Engineering Classroom
College Park MD 20742-7225
301/405-3878
Internet: http://www.bsos.umd.edu/aasp/scholarship.html
AMOUNT: Varies (in-state tuition costs)
DEADLINE(S): MAR
FIELD(S): Science; Technology
ELIGIBILITY/REQUIREMENTS: Open to African-Americans who are U.S. residents; minimum 2.8 GPA. Must be accepted to or enrolled at UMCP for freshman year. Should have an interest in applying science and technology to the problems of the Black community.
HOW TO APPLY: Contact the Center for Minorities in Science and Engineering at UMCP for an application. Must submit letter of recommendation from high school counselor or UMCP faculty member. Essay required.
RENEWABLE: Yes

2121—WESTERN MICHIGAN UNIVERSITY (College of Arts and Sciences/Elizabeth M. Garrett Endowed Scholarship for Women in Science)

1903 West Michigan
Kalamazoo MI 49008-5337
269/387-8777
FAX: 269/387-6989
E-mail: finaid-info@wmich.edu
Internet: http://www.wmich.edu/finaid
AMOUNT: Varies
DEADLINE(S): MAR 1
FIELD(S): Science; Science Education
ELIGIBILITY/REQUIREMENTS: Junior, senior, or graduate student preparing for career in science or teaching of science with minimum GPA of 3.0. Preference given to nontraditional student.
HOW TO APPLY: Contact Science Department for an application.
RENEWABLE: Yes

2122—WESTERN MICHIGAN UNIVERSITY (College of Arts and Sciences/Gwenivere Rabe Endowed Scholarship)

1903 West Michigan
Kalamazoo MI 49008-5337
269/387-8777
FAX: 269/387-6989
E-mail: finaid-info@wmich.edu
Internet: http://www.wmich.edu/finaid
AMOUNT: Varies
DEADLINE(S): MAR 1
FIELD(S): Science; Science Education
ELIGIBILITY/REQUIREMENTS: Undergraduate students majoring in natural or physical science; 3.0 minimum GPA. Financial need-based.
HOW TO APPLY: Contact Science Department for an application.
RENEWABLE: Yes

2123—WESTERN MICHIGAN UNIVERSITY (College of Arts and Sciences/Kathryn and Grant Leaske Memorial Endowed Scholarship)

1903 West Michigan
Kalamazoo MI 49008-5337
269/387-8777
FAX: 269/387-6989
E-mail: finaid-info@wmich.edu
Internet: http://www.wmich.edu/finaid
AMOUNT: Varies
DEADLINE(S): Not available until fall 2006
FIELD(S): Art; Science; History; Humanities; Law; Social Sciences
ELIGIBILITY/REQUIREMENTS: Must be full-time undergraduate student whose major is in the College of Arts & Sciences. Must demonstrate financial need; 3.0 GPA; and provide documentation of community/university service and volunteerism.
HOW TO APPLY: Contact the College of Arts and Sciences or www.wmich.edu/cas/research.html for an application.

RENEWABLE: Yes. Up to 2 years depending on academic status.

2124—WESTERN MICHIGAN UNIVERSITY (College of Arts and Sciences/ Undergraduate Research and Creative Activities Award)

1903 W. Michigan
Kalamazoo MI 49008-5337
269/387-8777
FAX: 269/387-6989
Internet: http://www.wmich.edu/cas
AMOUNT: $500/semester
DEADLINE(S): MAR 1
FIELD(S): Sciences; Humanities; Social Sciences, Radio & Television
ELIGIBILITY/REQUIREMENTS: Applicant must have declared a major in a department or program in the College of Arts and Sciences at least 30 credit hours; be in good academic standing; and have a faculty mentor for the project and a project plan.
HOW TO APPLY: Contact the College of Arts and Sciences for an application or apply online or print application from website.
RENEWABLE: Yes. May request renewal for 1 additional term.
CONTACT: College of Arts and Sciences

2125—WESTERN MICHIGAN UNIVERSITY (Kathryn and Grant Leaske Memorial Endowed Scholarship)

1903 W. Michigan
Kalamazoo MI 49008-5337
269/387-8777
FAX: 269/387-6989
Internet: http://www.wmich.edu/finaid
AMOUNT: Varies
DEADLINE(S): MAR 1
FIELD(S): Arts; Sciences; Humanities; Social Sciences
ELIGIBILITY/REQUIREMENTS: Applicant must be a full-time undergraduate student whose major is in the College of Arts & Sciences; demonstrate financial need; have a 3.0 GPA; be able to document history of community/university service and volunteerism.
HOW TO APPLY: Contact the College of Arts and Sciences for an application or apply online or print application from website.
RENEWABLE: Yes. Up to 2 years depending on academic status.
CONTACT: Financial Aid

2126—WOODS HOLE OCEANOGRAPHIC INSTITUTION (Summer Student Fellowship)

Clark Laboratory 223, MS #31
Woods Hole MA 02543-1541
508/289-2219
FAX: 508/457-2188
E-mail: education@whoi.edu
Internet: http://www.whoi.edu
AMOUNT: $380/week for 10-12 weeks; possible travel allowance
DEADLINE(S): FEB 15
FIELD(S): Science; Engineering; Mathematics; Marine Sciences/ Engineering; Policy
ELIGIBILITY/REQUIREMENTS: Open to undergraduates who have completed their junior or senior year, with backgrounds in science, mathematics, and engineering interested in the marine sciences and oceanography. Selection based on academic and scientific achievements and promise as future ocean scientists and engineers.
HOW TO APPLY: For an application and additional information, contact the Academic Programs Office, Clark Laboratory. Submit with résumé demonstrating educational background and work experience; a transcript and/or other official documentation of undergraduate record; at least 3 letters of recommendation from professors, employers, others; a statement of research interests, future education and career plans, and reasons for applying for fellowship.

2127—WOODS HOLE OCEANOGRAPHIC INSTITUTION (Traineeships in Oceanography for Minority Group Undergraduates)

Clark Laboratory 223, MS #31
Woods Hole MA 02543-1541
508/289-2219
FAX: 508/457-2188
E-mail: education@whoi.edu
Internet: http://www.whoi.edu
AMOUNT: Varies
DEADLINE(S): FEB 15
FIELD(S): Physical/Natural Sciences, Mathematics, Engineering
ELIGIBILITY/REQUIREMENTS: For minority undergraduates (African-American or Black, Asian-American, Chicano, Mexican-American, Puerto Rican or other Hispanic, and Native American) who are enrolled in U.S. colleges/universities and have completed at least 2 semesters. Traineeships may be awarded for a 10- to 12-week period in the summer or for a semester during the academic year.
HOW TO APPLY: For an application and additional information, contact the Academic Programs Office, Clark Laboratory. Submit with current résumé demonstrating educational background and work experience; an official transcript and/or other official documentation of undergraduate record; at least 3 letters of recommendation from professors, employers, others; a statement of research interests, future education and career plans, and reasons for applying for fellowship.

AGRICULTURE/BOTANY

2128—ABBIE SARGENT MEMORIAL SCHOLARSHIP INC.

295 Sheep Davis Road
Concord NH 03301
603/224-1934
FAX: 603/228-8432
AMOUNT: $200-$400
DEADLINE(S): MAR 15
FIELD(S): Agriculture; Veterinary Medicine; Home Economics
ELIGIBILITY/REQUIREMENTS: Open to New Hampshire residents who are high school graduates with good grades and character. For undergraduate or graduate study. Must be legal resident of U.S. and demonstrate financial need.
HOW TO APPLY: Write for application.
RENEWABLE: Yes, must reapply.

2129—AACC INTERNATIONAL

3340 Pilot Knob Road
St. Paul MN 55121-2097
651/454-7250
FAX: 651/454-0766
E-mail: aacc@scisoc.org
Internet: http://www.aaccnet. org/foundation/default.asp aacc/ABOUT/foundation/top.html
AMOUNT: $1,000-$2,000
DEADLINE(S): MAR 1
FIELD(S): Grain-Based Food Science and Technology (culinary arts or dietetics NOT eligible)
ELIGIBILITY/REQUIREMENTS: Applicants must be a current AACC International Student Division member. Open to undergraduate and graduate students majoring or interested in a career in grain-based food science or technology (including baking or related areas) as evidenced by coursework or employment.

Only advanced undergraduate applicants (those entering their junior or senior year) will be considered. Undergrads must have completed at least one quarter or semester of college or university work. Strong academic record and career interest important; AACC membership helpful but not necessary. Department head endorsement required. Financial need NOT a factor.
HOW TO APPLY: Applications are available online or by contacting the Scholarship Coordinator.
NUMBER OF AWARDS: Up to 30

2130—AMERICAN JUNIOR BRAHMAN ASSOCIATION (AJBA Scholarships)

3003 South Loop West, Suite 140
Houston TX 77054
713/349-0854
FAX: 713/349-9795
E-mail: cshivers@brahman.org
Internet: http://www.brahman.org
AMOUNT: $1,000
DEADLINE(S): MAY 1
FIELD(S): Agriculture
ELIGIBILITY/REQUIREMENTS: Open to graduating high school seniors who are members of the Junior Brahman Association. For full-time undergraduate study. U.S. citizenship required.
HOW TO APPLY: Contact the AJBA for complete information.
NUMBER OF AWARDS: Up to 3

2131—AMERICAN JUNIOR BRAHMAN ASSOCIATION (Ladies of the ABBA Scholarship)

3003 South Loop West, Suite 140
Houston TX 77054
713/349-0854
FAX: 713/349-9795
E-mail: cshivers@brahman.org
Internet: http://www.brahman.org
AMOUNT: $500
DEADLINE(S): MAY 1
FIELD(S): Agriculture
ELIGIBILITY/REQUIREMENTS: Open to graduating high school seniors who are members of the Junior Brahman Association. For full-time undergraduate study. U.S. citizenship required.
HOW TO APPLY: Contact the AJBA for complete information.
NUMBER OF AWARDS: Up to 4

2132—AMERICAN NATIONAL CATTLE-WOMEN FOUNDATION

9110 East Nichols Avenue
Centennial CO 80112
303/694-0313

FAX: 303/694-2390
Internet: http://www.ancw.org or http://www.nationalbeef ambassador.org
AMOUNT: $1,000, $750, $500
DEADLINE(S): Varies
FIELD(S): Beef Industry
ELIGIBILITY/REQUIREMENTS: Must qualify at a state-level speaking competition, then compete at national competition.
HOW TO APPLY: See website; click on National Beef Ambassador Program.
NUMBER OF AWARDS: 3
RENEWABLE: No
CONTACT: Project Manager Carol Abrahamzon at 507/724-3905 or cabrahamzon@beef.org

2133—AMERICAN RADIO RELAY LEAGUE FOUNDATION (Yasme Foundation Scholarship)

225 Main Street
Newington CT 06111
860/594-0397
FAX: 860/594-0259
E-mail: foundation@arrl.org
Internet: http://www.arrlf.org/
AMOUNT: $2,000
DEADLINE(S): FEB 1
FIELD(S): Engineering; Science
ELIGIBILITY/REQUIREMENTS: For radio amateurs for study leading to a bachelor's degree at an accredited 4-year college or university. Preference given to high school applicants ranked in the top 5 to 10% of their class or to college students in the top 10% of their class. Participation in local amateur radio club and community service is important to selection.
HOW TO APPLY: See website or contact Foundation for information and application. Submit with a 1-page essay on the role amateur radio has played in your life. A recent high school (or equivalent) or college transcript required; submit with application or mail separately.
NUMBER OF AWARDS: Varies (approximately 5)
RENEWABLE: Yes. 2 of the rewards are renewable for up to 3 years. Based on academic performance and annual transcript review.
CONTACT: Mary M. Hobart, K1MMH, Secretary

2134—AMERICAN SOCIETY OF AGRICULTURAL ENGINEERS (ASAE Foundation Scholarship)

2950 Niles Road
St. Joseph MI 49085-9659
269/429-0300

FAX: 269/429-3852
E-mail: hq@asae.org
Internet: http://www.asae.org
AMOUNT: $1,000
DEADLINE(S): APR 15
FIELD(S): Agricultural Engineering; Biological Engineering
ELIGIBILITY/REQUIREMENTS: Must verify that graduation from their agricultural or biological degree program assures eligibility for the Professional Engineer (PE) licensing examination; be sophomore or junior undergraduate in the U.S. or Canada; major in an agricultural or biological engineering curriculum that is accredited by ABET or CEAB; be a student member of ASAE; have a GPA of at least 2.5; and demonstrate financial need.
HOW TO APPLY: Send application; personal letter (no more than 2 pages) formally requesting the ASAE Foundation Scholarship grant and stating how the money will be used; and letter from dean or department chair corroborating information.
NUMBER OF AWARDS: 1

2135—AMERICAN SOCIETY OF AGRICULTURAL ENGINEERS (John L. & Sarah G. Merriam Scholarship)

2950 Niles Road
St. Joseph MI 49085-9659
269/429-0300
FAX: 269/429-3852
E-mail: hq@asae.org
Internet: http://www.asae.org
AMOUNT: $1,000
DEADLINE(S): APR 15
FIELD(S): Agricultural Engineering; Biological Engineering
ELIGIBILITY/REQUIREMENTS: Must be sophomore or junior undergraduate in the U.S. or Canada; major in an agricultural or biological engineering curriculum, with an emphasis of study in soil and water, that is accredited by ABET or CEAB; be a student member of ASAE; have a GPA of at least 2.5; and demonstrate need for financial aid.
HOW TO APPLY: Send application; personal letter (no more than 2 pages) formally requesting the grant and stating why you have selected soil and water as the focus of your degree; and letter from dean or department chair corroborating information.
NUMBER OF AWARDS: 1

2136—AMERICAN SOCIETY OF AGRICULTURAL ENGINEERS (Student Engineer of the Year Scholarship)

2950 Niles Road

St. Joseph MI 49085-9659
269/429-0300
FAX: 269/429-3852
E-mail: hq@asae.org
Internet: http://www.asae.org
AMOUNT: $1,000
DEADLINE(S): FEB 15
FIELD(S): Agricultural Engineering;
    Biological Engineering
ELIGIBILITY/REQUIREMENTS: Must
be sophomore or junior undergraduate
students in the U.S. or Canada; major in an
agricultural/biological engineering curriculum accredited by ABET or CEAB; and
have a GPA of at least 3.0. Based on scholarship excellence; character and personal
development; student membership in
ASAE and active participation in a student
branch; participation in school activities;
leadership qualities, creativity, initiative,
and responsibility; and some financial self-
support.
HOW TO APPLY: Send application,
signed by the department head or representative, and an essay not exceeding 500
words on "My Goals in the Engineering
Profession."

2137—AMERICAN SOCIETY OF AGRICUL-TURAL ENGINEERS (William J. and Marijane E. Adams, Jr. Scholarship)

2950 Niles Road
St. Joseph MI 49085-9659
269/429-0300
FAX: 269/429-3852
E-mail: hq@asae.org
Internet: http://www.asae.org
AMOUNT: $1,000
DEADLINE(S): APR 15
FIELD(S): Agricultural Engineering;
    Biological Engineering
ELIGIBILITY/REQUIREMENTS: Must
have a special interest in agricultural
machinery product design and development; be sophomore or junior undergraduate in the U.S. or Canada; major in an agricultural or biological engineering curriculum that is accredited by ABET or CEAB;
be a student member of ASAE; have a
GPA of at least 2.5; and demonstrate
financial need.
HOW TO APPLY: Send application; personal letter (no more than 2 pages) formally requesting the grant, stating the extent
of financial need, how the money will be
used, why you have selected the design and
development of agricultural machinery
products as the focus of your degree; and
letter from dean or department chair corroborating information.
NUMBER OF AWARDS: 1

2138—AMERICAN SOCIETY FOR ENOLO-GY AND VITICULTURE

P.O. Box 1855
Davis CA 95617-1855
530/753-3142
Email: society@asev.org
Internet: http://www.asev.com
AMOUNT: Varies (no predetermined
    amounts)
DEADLINE(S): MAR 1
FIELD(S): Enology (Wine Making);
    Viticulture (Grape Growing)
ELIGIBILITY/REQUIREMENTS: For
college juniors, seniors, or graduate stu-
dents enrolled in an accredited North
American college or university in a science
curriculum basic to the wine and grape
industry. Must be resident of North
America, have a minimum 3.0 GPA
(undergrad) or 3.2 GPA (grad), and
demonstrate financial need.
HOW TO APPLY: Contact ASEV for an
application.
RENEWABLE: Yes

2139—ASSOCIATION OF CALIFORNIA WATER AGENCIES (ACWA)

910 K Street, Suite 100
Sacramento CA 95814
916/441-4545
FAX: 916/325-4849
E-mail: acwabox@acwanet.com
Internet: http://www.acwanet.com
AMOUNT: $1,500
DEADLINE(S): APR 1
FIELD(S): Water Resources-related
    fields (including engineering,
    agriculture, environmental studies,
    public administration)
ELIGIBILITY/REQUIREMENTS:
Based on scholastic achievement, commit-
ment and motivation as well as financial
need.
HOW TO APPLY: Download applica-
tions and guidelines from website, or call
or e-mail ACWA, or contact your school's
financial aid department.
NUMBER OF AWARDS: At least 6

2140—CALCOT SEITZ FOUNDATION

P.O. Box 259
Bakersfield CA 93302
661/327-5961
E-mail: staff@calcot.com
Internet: http://www.calcot.com
AMOUNT: Varies, usually $1,000
DEADLINE(S): MAR 31
FIELD(S): Agriculture; Agriculture
    Education

ELIGIBILITY/REQUIREMENTS: Must
be enrolled in a 4-year college or university with a major in Agriculture and from a
cotton-growing area of California or
Arizona.
HOW TO APPLY: Download application
from website.
NUMBER OF AWARDS: Varies
RENEWABLE: Yes. Up to 3 years.

2141—CALIFORNIA ASSOCIATION OF WINEGRAPE GROWERS (Robert Miller Scholarship for Viticulture and Enology for Viticulture & Enology Students on the Central Coast)

1325 J Street Suite 1560
Sacramento CA 95814
800/241-1800 or 916/379-8995
FAX: 916/379-8999
E-mail: info@cawg.org
Internet: http://www.cawg.
    org/cwggf
AMOUNT: $500 or $1,000
DEADLINE(S): Late MAR (see website)
FIELD(S): Viticulture, Enology
ELIGIBILITY/REQUIREMENTS:
Applicant's parent or guardian must be
employed by a California winegrape grow-
er; scholarships are based on financial need
and academic achievement. May be used at
Alan Hanconck Community College or
Cal Poly, San Luis Obispo. Must major in
above fields.
HOW TO APPLY: Must be a graduating
high school senioror a student enrolled at
Alan Hancock Community College or
CalPoly, San Luis Obispo. See website for
application; submit with high school transcript, a copy of your SAT or ACT results
if you are applying for a 4-year scholarship,
a letter of recommendation from an
instructor, the school principal or counselor, and a 2-page essay (approximately
500 words) focusing on you and your
career goals.
NUMBER OF AWARDS: 2, up to 4 years
($1,000/year); 4, up to 2 years ($500/year)
RENEWABLE: Yes. Studies must continue to be completed satisfactorily.
CONTACT: Carolee Williams
ADDITIONAL INFORMATION: Children of winegrape growers may request a
waiver from the eligibility requirement
based upon financial need.

2142—CHICAGO MERCANTILE EXCHANGE ADMINISTERED BY THE NATIONAL PORK PRODUCERS COUNCIL

P.O. Box 10383
Des Moines IA 50306-9960
515/278-8012

FAX: 515/278-8011
E-mail: wrigley@nppc.org
Internet: http://www.nppc.org
AMOUNT: $2,500
DEADLINE(S): JAN 15
FIELD(S): Agriculture
ELIGIBILITY/REQUIREMENTS: Must be an undergraduate student in a 2-year swine program or 4-year college of agriculture.
HOW TO APPLY: Prepare a cover sheet and submit with a brief letter indicating what role you see yourself playing in the pork industry after graduation; an essay of 750 words or less describing an issue confronting the industry today or in the future, and offer solutions; and 2 letters of reference from current or former professors or industry professionals.
NUMBER OF AWARDS: 4
CONTACT: John Wrigley

2143—CHS COOPERATIVES FOUNDATION SCHOLARSHIP PROGRAM (Agricultural Studies)

5500 Cenex Drive
Inver Grove Heights MN 55077
651/355-5129
E-mail: william.nelson@chsinc.com
Internet: http://www.chs
foundation.org
AMOUNT: $600
DEADLINE(S): FEB 15
FIELD(S): Agriculture
ELIGIBILITY/REQUIREMENTS: For students attending a participating vo-tech or community college in the first or second year of a 2-year program. Participating schools are located in the CHS market area: Colorado, Idaho, Iowa, Kansas, Minnesota, Montana, Nebraska, North Dakota, Oregon, South Dakota, Utah, Washington, Wisconsin, and Wyoming. Selection based on scholastic achievement.
HOW TO APPLY: Contact CHS Foundation or your participating school for an application (schools must submit applications).
NUMBER OF AWARDS: 81

2144—CHS COOPERATIVES FOUNDATION SCHOLARSHIP PROGRAM (Cooperative Studies)

5500 Cenex Drive
Inver Grove Heights MN 55077
651/355-5129
E-mail: william.nelson@chsinc.com
Internet: http://www.chs
foundation.org
AMOUNT: $750

DEADLINE(S): Varies
FIELD(S): Agriculture
ELIGIBILITY/REQUIREMENTS: For juniors or seniors attending agricultural college of participating university enrolled in courses on cooperative principles and business practices. Selection based on scholastic achievement. Participating universities: Colorado State, University of Idaho, Iowa State, Kansas State, Minnesota State, University of Minnesota, Montana State, University of Nebraska, North Dakota State, Oregon State, South Dakota State, Utah State, Washington State, University of Wisconsin, and University of Wyoming.
HOW TO APPLY: Contact CHS Cooperatives Foundation or your participating school for an application.
NUMBER OF AWARDS: 82
RENEWABLE: Yes. Up to 2 years.

2145—COLORADO YOUNG FARMERS EDUCATIONAL ASSOCIATION

Northwestern Junior College
100 College Avenue
Sterling CO 80751
970/521-6690
FAX: 970/521-6636
E-mail: jack.annan@njc.edu
Internet: http://www.colorado
youngfarmer.com
AMOUNT: $500 (freshman & sophomore); $750 (junior); $1250 (senior)
DEADLINE(S): MAR 15
FIELD(S): Agriculture (Freshman & Sophomore); Agriculture Education (Junior & Senior)
ELIGIBILITY/REQUIREMENTS: Must be enrolled as a full-time student at a Colorado junior/community college, college or university, and a Colorado resident working toward degrees specified above. Award based upon scholarship, activities and interest in field.
HOW TO APPLY: See website for application.
NUMBER OF AWARDS: 5
RENEWABLE: No
CONTACT: Jack Annan

2146—FLORIDA FEDERATION OF GARDEN CLUBS, INC. (FFGC Scholarships for College Students)

706 Glen Eagle Drive
Winter Springs FL 32708
407/971 6979
Internet: http://www.ffgc.org
AMOUNT: $1,500-$3,500
DEADLINE(S): MAY 1

FIELD(S): Ecology; Environmental Issues; Land Management; City Planning; Environmental Control; Horticulture; Landscape Design; Conservation; Botany; Forestry; Marine Biology; Floriculture; Agriculture
ELIGIBILITY/REQUIREMENTS: Scholarships for Florida residents with a "B" or better average enrolled full time as a junior, senior, or graduate student at a Florida college or university.
HOW TO APPLY: See website or contact FFGC for an application.
CONTACT: Jane Meherg, Scholarship Chairman

2147—FLORIDA FEDERATION OF GARDEN CLUBS, INC. (FFGC Scholarships for High School Students)

706 Glen Eagle Drive
Winter Springs FL 32708
407/971 6979
Internet: http://www.ffgc.org
AMOUNT: $1,500
DEADLINE(S): MAY 1
FIELD(S): Ecology; Environmental Issues; Land Management; City Planning; Environmental Control; Horticulture; Landscape Design; Conservation; Botany; Forestry; Marine Biology; Floriculture; Agriculture
ELIGIBILITY/REQUIREMENTS: Scholarships for Florida residents with a "B" or better average who will be incoming freshmen at a Florida college or university.
HOW TO APPLY: See website or contact FFGC for an application.
CONTACT: Jane Meherg, Scholarship Chairman

2148—GARDEN CLUB FEDERATION OF MAINE, THE-ST. CROIX DISTRICT, THE (Nell Goff Memorial Scholarship Foundation)

46 Birch Bay Drive
Bar Harbor ME 04609
207/288-8003
E-mail: creevey@adelphia.net
Internet: http://www.maine-gardenclubs.com
AMOUNT: $1,000
DEADLINE(S): MAR 1
FIELD(S): Horticulture; Floriculture; Landscape Design; Conservation; Forestry; Botany, Agronomy; Plant Pathology; Environmental Control; City Planning and/or other gardening-related fields

ELIGIBILITY/REQUIREMENTS: Open to college juniors, seniors or graduate students (sophomores are eligible if they will enter their junior year in the fall) who are legal residents of the state of Maine, priority given to a resident of St. Croix District (Hancock County, and the southern part of Washington County), and major in some aspect of horticulture.

HOW TO APPLY: See website for application and information. Submit along with personal letter (up to 2 pages), discussing goals, background, financial need and personal commitment; 3 letters of recommendation (1 page each) to include scholarship ability, personal reference, and work-related experience; transcript and list of activities.

NUMBER OF AWARDS: 1

RENEWABLE: Yes, must reapply.

CONTACT: Lucy Creeveyu

2149—HAWAII COMMUNITY FOUNDATION (Dan & Pauline Lutkenhouse Tropical Garden Scholarship)

1164 Bishop Street, Suite 800
Honolulu HI 96813
808/537-6333 or toll free:
888/731-3863
FAX: 808/521-6286
E-mail: info@hcf-hawaii.org
Internet: http://www.hcf-hawaii.org

DEADLINE(S): MAR 1

FIELD(S): Agriculture; Science; Medicine; Nursing

ELIGIBILITY/REQUIREMENTS: Must be resident of the Hilo coast and the Hamakua coast, north of the Wailuku River; plan to attend full time an accredited 2- or 4-year college or university; and demonstrate financial need, good moral character, and academic achievement (minimum GPA of 2.7).

HOW TO APPLY: See website. Send application with 2 letters of recommendation.

2150—HAWAII COMMUNITY FOUNDATION (William James & Dorothy Bading Lanquist Fund)

1164 Bishop Street, Suite 800
Honolulu HI 96813
808/537-6333 or toll free:
888/731-3863
FAX: 808/521-6286
E-mail: info@hcf-hawaii.org
Internet: http://www.hcf-hawaii.org

DEADLINE(S): MAR 1

FIELD(S): Physical Sciences and related fields (excluding Biology)

ELIGIBILITY/REQUIREMENTS: Must be residents of Hawaii; junior or senior undergraduate students enrolled full time in an accredited 2- or 4-year college or university; and demonstrate financial need, good moral character, and academic achievement (minimum GPA of 2.7).

HOW TO APPLY: See website. Send application with 2 letters of recommendation.

2151—HOUSTON LIVESTOCK SHOW AND RODEO (4H and FFA Scholarships)

2000 South Loop West
Houston TX 77054
713/791-9000
FAX: 713/794-9528
E-mail: info@rodeohouston.com
Internet: http://www.hlsr.com/education/

AMOUNT: $10,000

DEADLINE(S): Varies

FIELD(S): Agriculture; Life Sciences

ELIGIBILITY/REQUIREMENTS: Open to undergraduate students who are actively involved in the 4-H or FFA programs. Must major in an agriculture or life sciences-related field at a Texas college or university and demonstrate academic potential, citizenship/leadership, and financial need.

HOW TO APPLY: Contact HLSR for an application.

NUMBER OF AWARDS: 140

2152—JAPANESE AMERICAN CITIZENS LEAGUE

1765 Sutter Street
San Francisco CA 94115
415/921-5225
FAX: 415/931-4671
E-mail: jacl@jacl.org
Internet: http://www.jacl.org

AMOUNT: $1,000-$5,000

DEADLINE(S): APR 1

FIELD(S): Agriculture; Journalism

ELIGIBILITY/REQUIREMENTS: For undergraduate JACL members interested in either journalism or agriculture, who are planning to attend a college, university, trade school, business school, or any other institution of higher learning. Financial need NOT a factor.

HOW TO APPLY: For membership information or application, see website or send SASE stating your level of study. Submit with personal statement, letters of recommendation, and transcripts.

2153—LINCOLN COMMUNITY FOUNDATION (James M. and Martha J. Perry Agricultural Scholarship)

215 Centennial Mall South,
Suite 100
Lincoln NE 68508
402/474-2354
FAX: 402/476-8532
E-mail: lcf@lcf.org
Internet: http://www.lcf.org

AMOUNT: Varies

DEADLINE(S): APR 15

FIELD(S): All

ELIGIBILITY/REQUIREMENTS: Applicant must be a current graduating senior of Elgin Public High School, Elgin, NE. Must plan to attend a qualified college or technical seeking a degree in the field of agriculture. Must demonstrate ability to do postsecondary work in a satisfactory manner.

HOW TO APPLY: Submit Foundation application and submit it with grade transcripts from all high schools, colleges or universities; copy of ACT/SAT or similar test scores; essay explaining why you are interested in pursuing education in agriculture, how this education has a direct relationship to your permanent career objective, and why you deserve the award; and 2 current letters of recommendation to Elgin Public Schools, P.O. Box 399, Elgin, NE 68636.

NUMBER OF AWARDS/YEAR: 1

RENEWABLE: Yes; must reapply.

ADDITIONAL INFORMATION: Scholarship will not be awarded to any student who receives another scholarship which sufficiently finances all tuition, fees, and books during the student's first year.

2154—NATIONAL AGRICULTURAL AVIATION ASSOCIATION

1005 E Street SE
Washington DC 20003
202/546-5722
FAX: 202/546-5726
E-mail: information@agaviation.org
Internet: http://www.agaviation.org

AMOUNT: Varies

DEADLINE(S): AUG 15

FIELD(S): Agriculture, Aviation, Aeronautics

ELIGIBILITY/REQUIREMENTS: Spouse, child, son-/daughter-in-law, grandchild of an operator, pilot, or allied industry member of NAAA. Sponsor must be a currently active dues-paying member. Financial need considered.

HOW TO APPLY: See website and click on WNAAA after MAR 1.
NUMBER OF AWARDS: 2
CONTACT: Lindsay Barber

2155—NATIONAL DAIRY SHRINE (Dairy Student Recognition Program)

1224 Alton Darby Creek Road
Columbus OH 43228-9792
614/878-5333
FAX: 614/870-2622
E-mail: shrine@cobaselect.com
Internet: http://www.dairyshrine.org
AMOUNT: 1st $1,500; 2nd $1,000; 3rd-9th $500
DEADLINE(S): MAR 15
FIELD(S): Dairy Industry
ELIGIBILITY/REQUIREMENTS: For students enrolled in dairy courses who demonstrate leadership ability, activities, interest in and experience with dairy cattle; academic standing and future plans are considered.
HOW TO APPLY: Download application from website. Local committees select school winners who compete nationally.
NUMBER OF AWARDS: 9
RENEWABLE: No
CONTACT: Maurice E. Core, Executive Director

2156—NATIONAL DAIRY SHRINE (Kildee Scholarship-Undergraduate)

1224 Alton Darby Creek Road
Columbus OH 43228-9792
614/878-5333
FAX: 614/870-2622
E-mail: shrine@cobaselect.com
Internet: http://www.dairyshrine.org
AMOUNT: $2,000
DEADLINE(S): MAR 15
FIELD(S): Dairy Industry
ELIGIBILITY/REQUIREMENTS: Must rank in top 25 at National 4-H or FFA Dairy Judging Contest.
HOW TO APPLY: Download application from website.
NUMBER OF AWARDS: 1
RENEWABLE: No
CONTACT: Maurice E. Core, Executive Director

2157—NATIONAL DAIRY SHRINE (McCullough Scholarships)

1224 Alton Darby Creek Road
Columbus OH 43228-9792
614/878-5333
FAX: 614/870-2622
E-mail: shrine@cobaselect.com

Internet: http://www.dairyshrine.org
AMOUNT: $1,000 and $2,500
DEADLINE(S): MAR 15
FIELD(S): Dairy Science; Agriculture; Journalism
ELIGIBILITY/REQUIREMENTS: Must be high school senior planning to enter 4-year college or university to major in dairy/animal science with a communications emphasis or agriculture journalism.
HOW TO APPLY: Download application from website.
NUMBER OF AWARDS: 2
RENEWABLE: No
CONTACT: Maurice E. Core, Executive Director

2158—NATIONAL DAIRY SHRINE (NDS/DMT Milk Marketing Scholarship)

1224 Alton Darby Creek Road
Columbus OH 43228-9792
614/878-5333
FAX: 614/870-2622
E-mail: shrine@cobaselect.com
Internet: www.dairyshrine.org
AMOUNT: $1,000 and $2,500
DEADLINE(S): MAR 15
FIELD(S): Dairy Industry; Marketing; Business Administration; Journalism; Home Economics
ELIGIBILITY/REQUIREMENTS: College sophomores, juniors or seniors majoring in dairy marketing, dairy manufacturing, dairy science, home economics, or journalism at a college or university approved by the appropriate National Dairy Shrine committee. Awards based on ability, interests and need.
HOW TO APPLY: Download application from website.
NUMBER OF AWARDS: 5-9
RENEWABLE: No
CONTACT: Maurice E. Core, Executive Director

2159—NATIONAL POULTRY AND FOOD DISTRIBUTORS ASSOCIATION SCHOLARSHIP FOUNDATION

958 McEver Road Extension, Unit B8
Gainesville GA 30504
770/535-9901
FAX: 770/535-7385
E-mail: kkm@npfda.org
Internet: http://www.npfda.org
AMOUNT: $1,500-$2,000 each/annual
DEADLINE(S): MAY 31
FIELD(S): Poultry, Food or related agricultural degree; Food Science; Dietetics; Poultry Science; Agricultural

Economics.; International Business, etc.
ELIGIBILITY/REQUIREMENTS: Must be enrolled full time as a college junior or senior the upcoming (award) year at a U.S. institution pursuing one of the above fields.
HOW TO APPLY: Complete application and provide your current official transcript, letter of recommendation from your dean along with a 1-page letter describing your goals and aspirations.
NUMBER OF AWARDS: 4
RENEWABLE: No
CONTACT: Kristin McWhorter

2160—NEW YORK STATE GRANGE (Susan W. Freestone Education Award)

100 Grange Place
Cortland NY 13045
607/756-7553
FAX: 607/756-7757
E-mail: nysgrange@nysgrange.com
Internet: http://www.nysgrange.com
AMOUNT: $500-$1,000
DEADLINE(S): APR 15
FIELD(S): Agriculture
ELIGIBILITY/REQUIREMENTS: $1,000 Award: Must have been a member of Junior Grange and must be member in good standing of a Subordinate Grange (both in New York State); $500 Award: Must be member in good standing in Subordinate Grange (not Junior Grange member). All applicants must graduate from high school and enroll in an approved 2- or 4-year college in New York State.
HOW TO APPLY: Send application with high school transcript of activities and scholarship.
NUMBER OF AWARDS: 1
RENEWABLE: Yes, must reapply, with satisfactory transcript.

2161—NEW YORK STATE GRANGE (The DeNise Scholarship Fund)

100 Grange Place
Cortland NY 13045
607/756-7553
FAX: 607/756-7757
E-mail: nysgrange@nysgrange.com
Internet: http://www.nysgrange.com
AMOUNT: Varies
DEADLINE(S): APR 15
FIELD(S): Agriculture
ELIGIBILITY/REQUIREMENTS: Must be a Grange member in good standing; an undergraduate student pursuing either a 2-year associate degree or a 4-year baccalaureate degree; and a resident of New York State.

HOW TO APPLY: Send application with transcript of activities and scholarship.
NUMBER OF AWARDS: 1

2162—NEW YORK STATE GRANGE (Cornell Fund Scholarships)

100 Grange Place
Cortland NY 13045
607/756-7553
FAX: 607/756-7757
E-mail: nysgrange@nysgrange.com
Internet: http://www.nysgrange.com
FIELD(S): Agriculture; Life Sciences
ELIGIBILITY/REQUIREMENTS: Must be enrolled in the College of Agriculture and Life Sciences at Cornell University. Selection is based on character, scholastic record, and need for financial assistance (reference given to farm-reared students whose families are Grange members and to students who transfer from an Agricultural and Technical College of the State University of New York).
HOW TO APPLY: Contact College of Agriculture and Life Sciences for details.

2163—NJAA/CAB

3201 Fredrick Avenue
St. Joseph MO 64506
816/383-5100
FAX: 816/233-9703
E-mail: angus@angus.org
Internet: http://www.angus foundation.org or www.njaa.info
AMOUNT: $1,000
DEADLINE(S): MAY 15
FIELD(S): Agriculture-related
ELIGIBILITY/REQUIREMENTS: Must be junior; regular or life member of the American Angus Association; 25 years old or younger; sophomore, junior or senior in college.
HOW TO APPLY: Print application from website.
NUMBER OF AWARDS: 1
RENEWABLE: No
CONTACT: James Fisher

2164—NORTH CAROLINA STATE UNIVERSITY (Thomas Jefferson Scholarship in Agriculture and Humanities)

Jefferson Scholars
College of Agriculture and Life Sciences
Box 7642
Raleigh NC 27695-7642
Internet: http://www.cals.ncsu.edu/student orgs/jeffer/apply.html
AMOUNT: $1,000

DEADLINE(S): FEB 6
FIELD(S): Agriculture/Life Sciences AND Humanities
ELIGIBILITY/REQUIREMENTS: Open to first-year undergraduate students with a double major in agriculture/life sciences and humanities.
HOW TO APPLY: See website or write for application and additional information. Submit with an essay, evaluation from a teacher or school official, the other from another teacher or school official, and transcript.
NUMBER OF AWARDS: 15
RENEWABLE: Yes

2165—NORTHERN NEW JERSEY UNIT-HERB SOCIETY OF AMERICA

2068 Dogwood Drive
Scotch Plains NJ 07076
908/233-2348
AMOUNT: $2,000
DEADLINE(S): FEB 15
FIELD(S): Horticulture; Botany
ELIGIBILITY/REQUIREMENTS: For New Jersey residents, undergraduate through postgraduate, who will attend colleges/universities east of the Mississippi River. Financial need is considered.
HOW TO APPLY: Write for application.
NUMBER OF AWARDS: 1
RENEWABLE: Yes
CONTACT: Charlotte R. Baker

2166—RAYMOND J. HARRIS EDUCATION TRUST

Mellon Bank, N.A.
P.O. Box 7899
Philadelphia PA 19101-7899
AMOUNT: Varies
DEADLINE(S): FEB 1
FIELD(S): Medicine, Law, Engineering, Dentistry, or Agriculture
ELIGIBILITY/REQUIREMENTS: Scholarships for Christian men to obtain a professional education in medicine, law, engineering, dentistry, or agriculture at 9 Philadelphia area colleges.
HOW TO APPLY: Contact Bank for details and the names of the colleges.

2167—SOUTH CAROLINA FARM BUREAU FOUNDATION

P.O. Box 754
Columbia SC 29202-0754
803/936-4212
FAX: 800/421-6515
Internet: http://www.scfb.org
AMOUNT: $500-$1,000

DEADLINE(S): APR 30
FIELD(S): Agriculture
ELIGIBILITY/REQUIREMENTS: Open to family members of valid South Carolina Farm Bureau members who are rising college sophomores, juniors or seniors pursuing a degree in agriculture or an agriculture-related major. Based on character, demonstrated leadership abilities, and dedication to agriculture or related fields. Must have minimum 2.3 GPA. Financial need NOT a factor.
HOW TO APPLY: Write for information.

2168—STUDENT CONSERVATION ASSOCIATION (SCA Resource Assistant Program)

P.O. Box 550
Charlestown NH 03603
603/543-1700
FAX: 603/543-1828
E-mail: internships@sca-inc.org
Internet: http://www.sca-inc.org
AMOUNT: $1,180-$4,725
DEADLINE(S): Varies
FIELD(S): Environment and related fields (agriculture, archaeology, anthropology, botany, caves, civil engineering, environmental design, engineering & education, fisheries, forests, herpetology, history, landscape architecture, environmental design, paleontology, wildlife management, geology, hydrology, library/museums, surveying)
ELIGIBILITY/REQUIREMENTS: Must be 18 and U.S. citizen; need not be student.
HOW TO APPLY: Send $1 for postage for application; outside U.S./Canada, send $20.
NUMBER OF AWARDS: 900 positions in U.S. and Canada

2169—TEXAS FFA FOUNDATION

614 East 12th Street
Austin TX 78701
512/480-8047
FAX: 512/472-0555
E-mail: kellie@texasffa.org
Internet: http://www.texasffa.org
AMOUNT: $1,000-$15,000
DEADLINE(S): Spring
FIELD(S): Agriculture or related field
ELIGIBILITY/REQUIREMENTS: Must be a member of Texas FFA.
HOW TO APPLY: Submit application form (1 for all Texas FFA Foundation scholarships).
NUMBER OF AWARDS: Varies
RENEWABLE: Yes. Automatic.
CONTACT: Kellie Griffin

2170—TURF AND ORNAMENTAL COM-MUNICATORS ASSOCIATION (TOCA)

120 West Main Street
P.O. Box 156
New Prague MN 56071
952/758-6340
FAX: 952/758-5813
E-mail: tocaassociation@aol.com
Internet: http://www.toca.org
AMOUNT: $1,000
DEADLINE(S): MAR 1
FIELD(S): Technical Communications or Green Industry fields: Horticulture; Plant Science, Botany; Agronomy, Plant Pathology
ELIGIBILITY/REQUIREMENTS: Overall GPA of 2.5; major subject GPA 3.0+. Must be enrolled in college or university as undergraduate in a 2- or 4-year program.
HOW TO APPLY: Contact TOCA at above address or by e-mail for application forms, include your mailing address.
NUMBER OF AWARDS: 2
RENEWABLE: Yes, must reapply.

2171—UNITED AGRIBUSINESS LEAGUE (UAL Scholarship Program)

54 Corporate Park
Irvine CA 92606-5105
800/223-4590 or 949/975-1424
FAX: 949/975-1671
E-mail: info@ual.org
Internet: http://www.ual.org
AMOUNT: Varies
DEADLINE(S): MAR 28
FIELD(S): Agriculture; Agribusiness
ELIGIBILITY/REQUIREMENTS: Open to students enrolled, or who will be enrolled, during the year of application in an accredited college or university offering a degree in agriculture; minimum GPA of 2.5 is required. Financial need will not be considered unless you specifically request it and provide documentation.
HOW TO APPLY: With application, must submit an essay; résumé of education, work, community activities, etc.; and 3 letters of recommendation.
RENEWABLE: Yes, must reapply.
CONTACT: Christine M. Steele

2172—UNIVERSITY OF ILLINOIS COLLEGE OF ACES (Jonathan Baldwin Turner Agricultural Scholarship Program)

115 ACES Library
1101 South Goodwin Street
Urbana IL 61801
217/244-4540
Internet: http://w3.aces.uiuc.edu/Acad-Prog/
AMOUNT: $1,000
DEADLINE(S): Varies (start of high school senior year)
FIELD(S): Agriculture; Nutritional Science; Natural Resources; Environmental; Social Sciences (agricultural economics, communications, or education)
ELIGIBILITY/REQUIREMENTS: Scholarships in agricultural, food, and human nutritional sciences for outstanding incoming freshmen at the University of Illinois. Must have minimum ACT composite score of 27, equivalent SAT combined scores, or be in the 10th percentile of high school class rank at the end of junior year. Interview required.
HOW TO APPLY: Contact Assistant Dean of Academic Programs, College of Agricultural, Consumer and Environmental Sciences, for an application.
NUMBER OF AWARDS: 55
RENEWABLE: Yes. 4-year award; up to $4,000.
CONTACT: Charles Olson

2173—UNIVERSITY OF CALIFORNIA-DAVIS (Brad Webb Scholarship Fund)

Enology and Viticulture Department
One Shields Avenue
Davis CA 95616-8749
530/752-0380
FAX: 530/752-0382
Internet: http://wineserver@ucdavis.edu
AMOUNT: Varies
DEADLINE(S): Varies
FIELD(S): Enology/Viticulture
ELIGIBILITY/REQUIREMENTS: Open to students attending or planning to attend UC Davis.
HOW TO APPLY: Contact the Department of Enology and Viticulture for an application.

2174—WASHINGTON APPLE EDUCATION FOUNDATION (Brian Kershaw Memorial Scholarship)

P.O. Box 3720
Wenatchee WA 98807
509/663-7713
FAX: 509/663-7713
E-mail: waef@waef.org
Internet: http://www.waef.org
AMOUNT: $1,500
DEADLINE(S): APR 1
FIELD(S): Agriculture; Horticulture

ELIGIBILITY/REQUIREMENTS: Open to graduating high school seniors and students currently enrolled in a 2- or 4-year college or university in Washington State. Applicants must be studying in a tree fruit-related field and be the children of parents who are employed within Washington's tree fruit industry.
HOW TO APPLY: See website for application.
NUMBER OF AWARDS: 40+
RENEWABLE: Yes, must reapply; maximum 2 years.
CONTACT: Jennifer Whitney

2175—WASHINGTON APPLE EDUCATION FOUNDATION (Fruit Packers Supply Scholarship)

P.O. Box 3720
Wenatchee WA 98807
509/663-7713
FAX: 509/663-7713
E-mail: waef@waef.org
Internet: http://www.ussui.org
AMOUNT: $1,000
DEADLINE(S): APR 1
FIELD(S): Agriculture; Horticulture
ELIGIBILITY/REQUIREMENTS: Open to juniors and seniors enrolled full time in the agriculture department at Washington State University studying for a career in Washington's tree fruit industry.
HOW TO APPLY: See website for application.
NUMBER OF AWARDS: 1
CONTACT: Jennifer Whitney

2176—WASHINGTON APPLE EDUCATION FOUNDATION (Howard Hauff Memorial Scholarship)

P.O. Box 3720
Wenatchee WA 98807
509/663-7713
FAX: 509/663-7713
E-mail: waef@waef.org
Internet: http://www.ussui.org
AMOUNT: $500
DEADLINE(S): APR 1
FIELD(S): Agriculture; Horticulture; Engineering
ELIGIBILITY/REQUIREMENTS: Open to Washington State high school seniors or current college students from Washington State. Applicants should be studying for a degree in engineering; pursuing a career in the tree fruit industry, or been raised in a family involved in the tree fruit industry.
HOW TO APPLY: See website for application.
NUMBER OF AWARDS: 1
CONTACT: Jennifer Whitney

2177—WASHINGTON APPLE EDUCATION FOUNDATION (Phil Jenkins Scholarship)

P.O. Box 3720
Wenatchee WA 98807
509/663-7713
FAX: 509/663-7713
E-mail: waef@waef.org
Internet: http://www.ussui.org
AMOUNT: Varies
DEADLINE(S): APR 1
FIELD(S): Agriculture; Horticulture
ELIGIBILITY/REQUIREMENTS: Open to students currently enrolled or entering a college or university who plan to live and work in the tree fruit industry in the Yakima Valley following the completion of their degree.
HOW TO APPLY: See website for application.
NUMBER OF AWARDS: 1
CONTACT: Jennifer Whitney

2178—WASHINGTON APPLE EDUCATION FOUNDATION (Valent USA Scholarship)

P.O. Box 3720
Wenatchee WA 98807
509/663-7713
FAX: 509/663-7713
E-mail: waef@waef.org
Internet: http://www.ussui.org
AMOUNT: $1,000
DEADLINE(S): APR 1
FIELD(S): Agriculture; Horticulture
ELIGIBILITY/REQUIREMENTS: Open to students enrolled in the tree fruit program at Yakima Valley Community College, Wenatchee Valley College, or Washington State University.
HOW TO APPLY: See website for application.
NUMBER OF AWARDS: 3
CONTACT: Jennifer Whitney

2179—WASHINGTON APPLE EDUCATION FOUNDATION (Valley Fruit Company Scholarship)

P.O. Box 3720
Wenatchee WA 98807
509/663-7713
FAX: 509/663-7713
E-mail: waef@waef.org
Internet: http://www.ussui.org
AMOUNT: Tuition fees
DEADLINE(S): APR 1
FIELD(S): Agriculture; Horticulture
ELIGIBILITY/REQUIREMENTS: Open to Wapato High School (Wapato, Washington) seniors, who plan to attend Yakima Valley Community College.

HOW TO APPLY: See website for application.
NUMBER OF AWARDS: 1
CONTACT: Jennifer Whitney

2180—WASHINGTON APPLE EDUCATION FOUNDATION (Wenatchee Traffic Club Scholarship)

P.O. Box 3720
Wenatchee WA 98807
509/663-7713
FAX: 509/663-7713
E-mail: waef@waef.org
Internet: http://www.ussui.org
AMOUNT: Varies
DEADLINE(S): APR 1
FIELD(S): Agriculture; Horticulture; Business
ELIGIBILITY/REQUIREMENTS: Applicants must be Washington State high school seniors or current college undergraduate students from Washington State pursuing a commodity-related career. Applicants must be residents of Chelan, Douglas, Grant, or Okanogan counties. Parents or guardians of applicant should be involved in Washington's tree fruit industry.
HOW TO APPLY: See website for application.
NUMBER OF AWARDS: Varies
RENEWABLE: No
CONTACT: Jennifer Whitney

2181—WASHINGTON APPLE EDUCATION FOUNDATION (Yakima Valley Grower-Shippers Association Scholarship)

P.O. Box 3720
Wenatchee WA 98807
509/663-7713
FAX: 509/663-7713
E-mail: waef@waef.org
Internet: http://www.ussui.org
AMOUNT: $750
DEADLINE(S): APR 1
FIELD(S): Agriculture; Horticulture; Business; Mechanical Engineering
ELIGIBILITY/REQUIREMENTS: Applicant must be employee or child of a general member of the YVGSA or the child of an employee or grower of a general member of the YVGSA. Applicant must be pursuing a degree compatible with service to the tree fruit industry.
HOW TO APPLY: See website for application.
NUMBER OF AWARDS: 2
RENEWABLE: No
CONTACT: Jennifer Whitney

2182—WESTERN MICHIGAN UNIVERSITY (College of Arts and Sciences/Leo C. VanderBeek Award in Botany)

1903 West Michigan
Kalamazoo MI 49008-5337
269/387-8777
FAX: 269/387-6989
E-mail: finaid-info@wmich.edu
Internet: http://www.wmich.edu/finaid
AMOUNT: $150 (spring semester)
FIELD(S): Botany
ELIGIBILITY/REQUIREMENTS: Junior or senior, botany major.
HOW TO APPLY: Nominated by Faculty Biological Sciences Department.
RENEWABLE: No

BIOLOGY

2183—AMERICAN CHEMICAL SOCIETY (Minority Scholars Program)

1155 Sixteenth Street NW
Washington DC 20036
202/872-6250 or 800/227-5558
FAX: 202/776-8003
Internet: http://www.acs.org
AMOUNT: Up to $3,000
DEADLINE(S): FEB 15
FIELD(S): Chemistry; Biochemistry; Chemical Engineering; Chemical Technology
ELIGIBILITY/REQUIREMENTS: Open to high school seniors entering college in the coming year, college and community college students planning to pursue full-time study, and community college transfer students pursuing a bachelor's degree. Awarded based on merit and financial need to African-American, Hispanic, and American Indian students with outstanding academic records combined with strong interest in chemistry. Must be U.S. citizen or permanent resident.
HOW TO APPLY: See website or contact ACS for an application.
CONTACT: Patricia Browne

2184—AMERICAN FOUNDATION FOR THE BLIND (Paul and Ellen Ruckes Scholarship)

11 Penn Plaza, Suite 300
New York NY 10001
212/502-7661
FAX: 212/502-7771
E-mail: afbinfo@afb.net
Internet: http://www.afb.org/scholar/scholarships.asp

AMOUNT: $1,000
DEADLINE(S): APR 30
FIELD(S): Engineering; Computer, Physical, & Life Sciences
ELIGIBILITY/REQUIREMENTS: Open to legally blind and visually impaired undergraduate and graduate students pursuing a degree in one of above fields. Must be U.S. citizen.
HOW TO APPLY: See website or contact AFB for an application. Must submit written documentation of evidence of legal blindness; official transcripts; proof of college or university acceptance; 3 letters of recommendation; and typewritten statement describing field of study you are pursuing, goals, work experience, extracurricular activities, and how monies will be used.
NUMBER OF AWARDS: 1
CONTACT: Alina Vayntrub

2185—AMERICAN INDIAN SCIENCE AND ENGINEERING SOCIETY (EPA Tribal Lands Environmental Science Scholarship)

P.O. Box 9828
Albuquerque NM 87119-9828
505/765-1052
FAX: 505/765-5608
E-mail: scholarships@aises.org
Internet: http://www.aises.org/highered
AMOUNT: $4,000
DEADLINE(S): JUN 15
FIELD(S): Biochemistry; Biology; Chemical Engineering; Chemistry; Entomology; Environmental Economics/Science; Hydrology; Environmental Studies
ELIGIBILITY/REQUIREMENTS: Open to American Indian college juniors, seniors, and graduate students enrolled full time at an accredited institution. Must demonstrate financial need and be a member of AISES ($10 fee). Certificate of Indian blood NOT required.
HOW TO APPLY: See website for more information and/or an application.
RENEWABLE: No

2186—AMERICAN MUSEUM OF NATURAL HISTORY (Research Experiences for Undergraduates)

Central Park West at 79th Street
New York NY 10024-5192
FAX: 212/769-5495
E-mail: grants@amnh.org
Internet: http://research.amnh.org/grants
AMOUNT: Stipend, research expenses, intracity travel, housing

DEADLINE(S): APR
FIELD(S): Evolutionary Biology, Physical Sciences
ELIGIBILITY/REQUIREMENTS: 10-week summer internships to pursue scientific projects in conjunction with Museum scientists. Must be enrolled in a degree program at a college or university, have a high GPA, and a strong science background.
HOW TO APPLY: See website or contact Office of Grants and Fellowships for an application. Submit with list of courses, statement of interest, and recommendations.

2187—AMERICAN ORNITHOLOGISTS' UNION (Research Awards)

Department of Biological Sciences
Eastern Kentucky University
521 Lancaster Avenue
Richmond KY 40475
859/622-1541
E-mail: Gary.Ritchison@eku.edu
Internet: http://www.biology.eku.edu
AMOUNT: $1,800
DEADLINE(S): JAN 30
FIELD(S): Ornithology
ELIGIBILITY/REQUIREMENTS: Applicants must be a member of the AOU.
HOW TO APPLY: Send 10 copies of proposed research project and letter of recommendation from major professor. Project evaluated on the significance and originality of the scientific question; clarity of the objectives; feasibility of the plan of research; appropriateness of the budget (which cannot exceed $1,800); and on the letter of recommendation. Include background information; alternative hypotheses (if appropriate); relevant citations and figures; and clear, concise writing. Mail application; do NOT fax or e-mail.
NUMBER OF AWARDS: 28-30 grants
CONTACT: Gary Ritchison, Chair, AOU Research Awards Committee

2188—AMERICAN PHYSIOLOGICAL SOCIETY, THE (David S. Bruce Awards for Excellence in Undergraduate Research)

Education Office
9650 Rockville Pike
Bethesda MD 20814-3991
301/634-7098
FAX: 301/634-7242
E-mail: awards@the-aps.org
Internet: http://www.the-aps.org/education/undergrad/stuaward.html
AMOUNT: $500

DEADLINE: JAN (1st week, date varies)
FIELDS: Microbiology
ELIGIBILITY/REQUIREMENTS: Open to undergraduate students who are presenting their research at the Experimental Biology meeting. Candidate must be enrolled as an undergraduate student at the time of the application and EB meeting; be the first author on a submitted abstract for the EB meeting; and be working with an APS member. Selection of awardees is based both on the abstract and letter of application, as well as an oral presentation to Selection Committee.
HOW TO APPLY: See website for detailed information and application. Must apply online at http://www.theaps.org/awardapps. Upload a 1-page letter that discusses your role in the research, the significance of the research, and your career plans. Request a recommendation letter from your research advisor to be uploaded that includes a statement that you were deserving of first authorship.
NUMBER OF AWARDS: Varies
RENEWABLE: No

2189—AMERICAN PHYSIOLOGICAL SOCIETY, THE (Undergraduate Summer Research Fellowship)

Education Office
9650 Rockville Pike
Bethesda MD 20814-3991
301/634-7098
FAX: 301/634-7242
E-mail: awards@the-aps.org
Internet: http://www.the-aps.org/education/undergrad/stuaward.html
AMOUNT: $3,000
DEADLINE: FEB (first week, date varies)
FIELDS: Physiology
ELIGIBILITY/REQUIREMENTS: These fellowships are to support full-time undergraduate students to work in the laboratory of an established investigator. The intent of this program is to excite and encourage students to pursue a career as a basic research scientist. Faculty sponsors/advisors must be active members of the APS.
HOW TO APPLY: See website for detailed information and application. Must apply online at http://www.theaps.org/awardapps. Submit with transcript, 1-page personal statement, research advisor's document, letter of recommendation from research advisor and additional letter of recommendation from another faculty member.
NUMBER OF AWARDS: Up to 24
CONTACT: Melinda Lowy at mlowy@thate-aps.org or 302/634-7787

ADDITIONAL INFORMATION: Up to $1,000 travel award/reimbursement to attend and present data at annual meeting or fall conference. Also $3,200 grant to faculty sponsor/advisor.

2190—AMERICAN SOCIETY FOR MICRO-BIOLOGY

ASM Undergraduate Research
Fellowship Program
Education Board
1752 N Street, NW
Washington DC 20036
202/942-9283
E-mail: fellowships-
careerinformation@asmusa.org
Internet: http://www.asm.org/
education/index.asp?bid+4319
AMOUNT: Up to $4,000
DEADLINE: FEB 1
FIELDS: Microbiology
ELIGIBILITY/REQUIREMENTS: Must be a U.S. citizen or permanent U.S. resident; be enrolled as a full-time matriculating undergraduate student during the academic year at an accredited U.S. institution; be either a freshman with college level research experience, sophomore, junior, or senior who will not graduate before the completion date of the summer program; be a member of an underrepresented group in microbiology; have taken introductory courses in biology, chemistry, and preferably microbiology prior to submission of the application; have a strong interest in obtaining a Ph.D. or a M.D./Ph.D. in the microbiological sciences; and have lab research experience.
HOW TO APPLY: Must submit a joint application from both the student and a faculty mentor. The faculty mentor must be an ASM member and willing to serve as the applicant's mentor for the duration of the research experience. It is student's responsibility to submit a completed application. See website for additional information and application.
RENEWABLE: No

2191—AMERICAN SOCIETY OF AGRICULTURAL ENGINEERS (ASAE Foundation Scholarship)

2950 Niles Road
St. Joseph MI 49085-9659
269/429-0300
FAX: 269/429-3852
E-mail: hq@asae.org
Internet: http://www.asae.org
AMOUNT: $1,000
DEADLINE(S): APR 15

FIELD(S): Agricultural Engineering;
Biological Engineering
ELIGIBILITY/REQUIREMENTS: Must verify that graduation from their agricultural or biological degree program assures eligibility for the Professional Engineer (PE) licensing examination; be sophomore or junior undergraduate in the U.S. or Canada; major in an agricultural or biological engineering curriculum that is accredited by ABET or CEAB; be a student member of ASAE; have a GPA of at least 2.5; and demonstrate financial need.
HOW TO APPLY: Send application; personal letter (no more than 2 pages) formally requesting the ASAE Foundation Scholarship grant and stating how the money will be used; and letter from dean or department chair corroborating information.
NUMBER OF AWARDS: 1

2192—AMERICAN SOCIETY OF AGRICULTURAL ENGINEERS (John L. & Sarah G. Merriam Scholarship)

2950 Niles Road
St. Joseph MI 49085-9659
269/429-0300
FAX: 269/429-3852
E-mail: hq@asae.org
Internet: http://www.asae.org
AMOUNT: $1,000
DEADLINE(S): APR 15
FIELD(S): Agricultural Engineering;
Biological Engineering
ELIGIBILITY/REQUIREMENTS: Must be sophomore or junior undergraduate in the U.S. or Canada; major in an agricultural or biological engineering curriculum, with an emphasis of study in soil and water, that is accredited by ABET or CEAB; be a student member of ASAE; have a GPA of at least 2.5; and have need for financial aid.
HOW TO APPLY: Send application; personal letter (no more than 2 pages) formally requesting the grant and stating why you have selected soil and water as the focus of your degree; and letter from dean or department chair corroborating information.
NUMBER OF AWARDS: 1

2193—AMERICAN SOCIETY OF AGRICULTURAL ENGINEERS (Student Engineer of the Year Scholarship)

2950 Niles Road
St. Joseph MI 49085-9659
269/429-0300
FAX: 269/429-3852
E-mail: hq@asae.org
Internet: http://www.asae.org

AMOUNT: $1,000
DEADLINE(S): FEB 15
FIELD(S): Agricultural Engineering;
Biological Engineering
ELIGIBILITY/REQUIREMENTS: Must be sophomore or junior undergraduate students in the U.S. or Canada; major in an agricultural/biological engineering curriculum accredited by ABET or CEAB; and have a GPA of at least 3.0. Based on scholarship excellence; character and personal development; student membership in ASAE and active participation in a student branch; participation in school activities; leadership qualities, creativity, initiative, and responsibility; and some financial self-support.
HOW TO APPLY: Send application, signed by the department head or representative, and an essay not exceeding 500 words on "My Goals in the Engineering Profession."

2194—AMERICAN SOCIETY OF AGRICULTURAL ENGINEERS (William J. and Marijane E. Adams Jr. Scholarship)

2950 Niles Road
St. Joseph MI 49085-9659
269/429-0300
FAX: 269/429-3852
E-mail: hq@asae.org
Internet: http://www.asae.org
AMOUNT: $1,000
DEADLINE(S): APR 15
FIELD(S): Agricultural Engineering;
Biological Engineering
ELIGIBILITY/REQUIREMENTS: Must have a special interest in agricultural machinery product design and development; be sophomore or junior undergraduate students in the U.S. or Canada; major in an agricultural or biological engineering curriculum that is accredited by ABET or CEAB; be a student member of ASAE; have a GPA of at least 2.5; and have financial need.
HOW TO APPLY: Send application; personal letter (no more than 2 pages) requesting the grant, stating the extent of financial need, how the money will be used, why you have selected the design and development of agricultural machinery products as the focus of your degree; and letter from dean or department chair corroborating information.
NUMBER OF AWARDS: 1

2195—EARTHWATCH STUDENT CHALLENGE AWARDS (High School Student Research Expeditions)

3 Clock Tower Place, Suite 100

P.O. Box 75
Maynard MA 01754
800/776-0188 or
978/461-0081, ext. 116
FAX: 978/450-1288
E-mail: scap@earthwatch.org
Internet: http://www.earthwatch.org
AMOUNT: Travel/Living expenses (1- to
3-week field expedition)
DEADLINE(S): Late Fall-call for details
FIELD(S): Biology, Field Studies,
Physics, Natural Resources,
Environmental Science
ELIGIBILITY/REQUIREMENTS:
Awards for high school sophomores,
juniors, and seniors, especially those with
limited exposure to the sciences. Must
attend high school in the U.S., be at least
age 16 by June 15 during year of program.
Teams of 6 to 8 students spend 1 to 3 weeks
at sites in North or Central America.
HOW TO APPLY: Students must be nominated by a teacher. Write or visit website
for further information.
NUMBER OF AWARDS: Approximately 85

2196—ENTOMOLOGICAL FOUNDATION (Bioquip Scholarship)

9332 Annapolis Road, Suite 210
Lanham MD 20706
301/459-9082
FAX: 301/459-9084
E-mail: melodie@entfdn.org
Internet: http://www.entfdn.org
AMOUNT: Varies
DEADLINE(S): JUN 1
FIELD(S): Entomology
ELIGIBILITY/REQUIREMENTS: Must
be an entomology major, have been
enrolled in the previous fall as an under-
graduate student at a college or university
in the U.S., Mexico or Canada, have accu-
mulated a minimum of 30 college credit
hours at the time the award is presented in
August, have completed at least 1 course,
or a project, in entomology. Preference
given to students with demonstrated finan-
cial need.
HOW TO APPLY: See website. MUST
apply online.
NUMBER OF AWARDS: 1
RENEWABLE: Yes, must reapply.
CONTACT: Melodie Dziduch, Awards
Coordinator

2197—ENTOMOLOGICAL FOUNDATION (Stan Beck Fellowship)

9332 Annapolis Road, Suite 210
Lanham MD 20706
301/459-9082

FAX: 301/459-9084
E-mail: melodie@entfdn.org
Internet: http://www.entfdn.org
AMOUNT: Varies
DEADLINE(S): JUL 1
FIELD(S): Entomology; Zoology;
Biology; or related science
ELIGIBILITY/REQUIREMENTS: Open
to students with physical or economic,
minority, or environmental limitations.
Must be attending a college or university in
the U.S., Canada, or Mexico studying ento-
mology or related disciplines.
HOW TO APPLY: See website. MUST
apply online.
NUMBER OF AWARDS: 3
RENEWABLE: Yes, must reapply.
CONTACT: Melodie Dziduch, Awards
Coordinator

2198—FLORIDA FEDERATION OF GAR-DEN CLUBS, INC. (FFGC Scholarships for College Students)

706 Glen Eagle Drive
Winter Springs FL 32708
407/971-6979
Internet: http://www.ffgc.org
AMOUNT: $650-$3,000
DEADLINE(S): MAY 1
FIELD(S): Agriculture; Environmental &
Conservation issues; Botany; Biology;
Forestry; Horticulture; Ecology;
Marine Biology; Wildflowers;
Butterflies; Landscaping
ELIGIBILITY/REQUIREMENTS: Must
be U.S. citizen and Florida resident for at
least 1 year, with 3.0 GPA, attending a col-
lege or university in Florida. Financial
need considered.
HOW TO APPLY: See website or contact
FFGC Chair for an application.
RENEWABLE: Yes, must reapply.
CONTACT: Jane Meherg, Scholarship
Chairman

2199—FORD FOUNDATION/NATIONAL RESEARCH COUNCIL (Howard Hughes Medical Institute Predoctoral Fellowships in Biological Sciences)

2101 Constitution Avenue NW
Washington DC 20418
202/334-2872
FAX: 202/334-3419
Internet: http://www7.national
academies.org/FORDfellowships/
fordpredoc.html
AMOUNT: $16,000 stipend + tuition at
U.S. institution
DEADLINE(S): NOV 9
FIELD(S): Biochemistry; Biophysics;
Epidemiology; Genetics; Immunology;

Microbiology; Neuroscience;
Pharmacology; Physiology; Virology
ELIGIBILITY/REQUIREMENTS: 5-
year award open to college seniors and
first-year graduate students pursuing a
Ph.D. or Sc.D. U.S. citizens/nationals may
choose any institution in the U.S. or
abroad; foreign students must choose U.S.
institution. Based on ability, academic
records, proposed study/research, previous
experience, reference reports, and GRE
scores.
HOW TO APPLY: See website or contact
NRC for an application.
NUMBER OF AWARDS: 80

2200—GARDEN CLUB FEDERATION OF MAINE, THE-ST. CROIX DISTRICT, THE (Nell Goff Memorial Scholarship Foundation)

46 Birch Bay Drive
Bar Harbor ME 04609
207/288-8003
E-mail: creevey@adelphia.net
Internet: http://www.maine
gardenclubs.com
AMOUNT: $1,000
DEADLINE(S): MAR 1
FIELD(S): Horticulture; Floriculture;
Landscape Design; Conservation;
Forestry; Botany; Agronomy; Plant
Pathology; Environmental Control;
City Planning and/or other gardening-
related fields
ELIGIBILITY/REQUIREMENTS: Open
to college juniors, seniors or graduate students (sophomores are eligible if they will
enter their junior year in the fall) who are
legal residents of the state of Maine, priority given to a resident of St. Croix District
(Hancock County, and the southern part of
Washington County), and major in some
aspect of horticulture.
HOW TO APPLY: See website for application and information. Submit along with
personal letter (up to 2 pages), discussing
goals, background, financial need and personal commitment; 3 letters of recommendation (1 page each) to include scholarship
ability, personal reference, and work-related experience; transcript and list of activities.
NUMBER OF AWARDS: 1
RENEWABLE: Yes, must reapply.
CONTACT: Lucy Creevey

2201—GARDEN CLUB OF AMERICA (GCA Awards for Summer Environmental Studies)

14 East 60th Street
New York NY 10022-1002
212/753-8287

FAX: 212/753-0134
E-mail: scholarships@gcamerica.org
Internet: http://www.gcamerica.org
AMOUNT: $1,500
DEADLINE(S): FEB 10
FIELD(S): Environmental Studies
(including endangered plant species,
conservation biology, ecological
restoration, plant resources of the
tropics, historical vegetation, wetland/
marine ecology, journalism &
legislation)
ELIGIBILITY/REQUIREMENTS:
Financial aid toward a SUMMER studies
doing fieldwork or research in above field
for college students following their freshman, sophomore, or junior year. Purpose
of award is to encourage studies and
careers in the environmental field.
HOW TO APPLY: Application available
on website or contact GCA.
CONTACT: Connie Sutton, Scholarship
Committee

2202—HOUSTON LIVESTOCK SHOW AND RODEO (4H and FFA Scholarships)

2000 South Loop West
Houston TX 77054
713/791-9000
FAX: 713/794-9528
E-mail: info@rodeohouston.com
Internet: http://www.hlsr.com/
education/
AMOUNT: $10,000
DEADLINE(S): Varies
FIELD(S): Agriculture; Life Sciences
ELIGIBILITY/REQUIREMENTS: Open
to undergraduate students who are active-
ly involved in the 4-H or FFA programs.
Must major in an agriculture or life sci-
ences-related field at a Texas college or
university and demonstrate academic
potential, citizenship/leadership, and
financial need.
HOW TO APPLY: Contact HLSR for an
application.
NUMBER OF AWARDS: 140

2203—MIDWAY COLLEGE

512 East Stephens Street
Midway KY 40347
800/755-0031
E-mail: admissions@midway.edu
Internet: http://www.midway.edu
AMOUNT: Up to full tuition
DEADLINE(S): Varies
FIELD(S): Nursing; Education;
Psychology; Biology; Equine Studies;
Computer Information Systems;

Business Administration; English; Pre-
Med; Pre-Vet
ELIGIBILITY/REQUIREMENTS: Merit
scholarships for admitted students who are
considered full time in Midway's women's
college. Depending on scholarship, minimum GPA ranges from 2.5 to 3.2, minimum ACT ranges 18 to 29, minimum SAT
from 860 to 1290. In some cases, students
must live on campus.
HOW TO APPLY: Contact Admissions
Office or high school guidance counselor
for application. Complete FAFSA online.
NUMBER OF AWARDS: Varies, up to
100
RENEWABLE: Yes. Must meet GPA
requirements which vary based on the
scholarship.
CONTACT: Admissions Office or high
school guidance counselor
ADDITIONAL INFORMATION: Ath-
letes may be eligible for an athletic scholarship in conjunction with a merit grant;
contact coach for eligibility and award
information.

2204—NATIONAL ASSOCIATION OF WATER COMPANIES-NEW JERSEY CHAPTER

Elizabethtown Water Company 600
South Avenue
Westfield NJ 07091
908/654-1234
FAX: 908/232-2719
E-mail: gbradygbconsult@
comcast.net
AMOUNT: $2,500
DEADLINE(S): APR 1
FIELD(S): Business Administration;
Biology; Chemistry; Engineering;
Communications
ELIGIBILITY/REQUIREMENTS: For
U.S. citizens who have lived in New Jersey
for at least 5 years and plan a career in the
investor-owned water utility industry.
Must be undergraduate in a 2- or 4-year
New Jersey college or university. GPA of
3.0 or better required.
HOW TO APPLY: Contact Association
for complete information.
CONTACT: Gail P. Brady

2205—NATIONAL DAIRY SHRINE (Dairy Student Recognition Program)

1224 Alton Darby Creek Road
Columbus OH 43228-9792
614/878-5333
FAX: 614/870-2622
E-mail: shrine@cobaselect.com
Internet: http://www.dairyshrine.org
AMOUNT: 1st $1,500; 2nd $1,000; 3rd—
9th $500

DEADLINE(S): MAR 15
FIELD(S): Dairy Industry
ELIGIBILITY/REQUIREMENTS: For
students enrolled in dairy courses who
demonstrate leadership ability. Activities,
interest in and experience with dairy cattle;
academic standing and plans are considered.
HOW TO APPLY: Download application
from website. Local committees select
school winners who compete nationally.
NUMBER OF AWARDS: 9
RENEWABLE: No
CONTACT: Maurice E. Core, Executive
Director

2206—NATIONAL DAIRY SHRINE (Kildee Scholarship-Undergraduate)

1224 Alton Darby Creek Road
Columbus OH 43228-9792
614/878-5333
FAX: 614/870-2622
E-mail: shrine@cobaselect.com
Internet: http://www.dairyshrine.org
AMOUNT: $2,000
DEADLINE(S): MAR 15
FIELD(S): Dairy Industry
ELIGIBILITY/REQUIREMENTS: Must
rank in top 25 at National 4-H or FFA
Dairy Judging Contest.
HOW TO APPLY: Download application
from website.
NUMBER OF AWARDS: 1
RENEWABLE: No
CONTACT: Maurice E. Core, Executive
Director

2207—NATIONAL DAIRY SHRINE (McCullough Scholarships)

1224 Alton Darby Creek Road
Columbus OH 43228-9792
614/878-5333
FAX: 614/870-2622
E-mail: shrine@cobaselect.com
Internet: http://www.dairyshrine.org
AMOUNT: $1,000 and $2,500
DEADLINE(S): MAR 15
FIELD(S): Dairy Science; Agriculture;
Journalism
ELIGIBILITY/REQUIREMENTS: Must
be high school senior planning to enter 4-
year college or university to major in
dairy/animal science with a communica-
tions emphasis or agriculture journalism.
HOW TO APPLY: Download application
from website.
NUMBER OF AWARDS: 2
RENEWABLE: No
CONTACT: Maurice E. Core, Executive
Director

2208—NATIONAL DAIRY SHRINE (NDS/DMT Milk Marketing Scholarship)

1224 Alton Darby Creek Road
Columbus OH 43228-9792
614/878-5333
FAX: 614/870-2622
E-mail: shrine@cobaselect.com
Internet: http://www.dairyshrine.org
AMOUNT: $1,000 and $2,500
DEADLINE(S): MAR 15
FIELD(S): Dairy Industry; Marketing; Business Administration; Journalism; Home Economics
ELIGIBILITY/REQUIREMENTS: College sophomores, juniors or seniors majoring in dairy marketing, dairy manufacturing, dairy science, home economics, or journalism at a college or university approved by the appropriate National Dairy Shrine committee. Awards based on ability, interests and need.
HOW TO APPLY: Download application from website.
NUMBER OF AWARDS: 5-9
RENEWABLE: No
CONTACT: Maurice E. Core, Executive Director

2209—NATIONAL INVENTORS HALL OF FAME, THE (Collegiate Inventors Competition)

221 South Broadway Street
Akron OH 44308-1505
330/849-6887
E-mail: rdepuy@invent.org
Internet: http://www.invent.org/bfg/bfghome.html
AMOUNT: $15,000
DEADLINE(S): JUN 1
FIELD(S): Mathematics, Engineering, Biology, Chemistry, Physics, Information Technology, Medicine
ELIGIBILITY/REQUIREMENTS: Must be enrolled (or have been enrolled) full time (in any college or university) at least part of the 12-month period prior to the date the entry is submitted. For teams (maximum 4 students), at least 1 member of the team must meet the full-time eligibility criteria. The other team members must have been enrolled on a part-time basis (at minimum) sometime during the 24-month period prior to the date entry is submitted. There are no limits on the number of entries a student or team may submit; however, only 1 prize/student or team will be awarded. No specific age requirements. Entries judged on the originality and inventiveness of the new idea, process, or technology; on their potential value to society (socially, environmentally, and economically); and on the scope of use. Entries must be complete, workable, and well articulated.
HOW TO APPLY: Submit an original invention or idea that has not been made public. See website for application and details. The application must include: Student and Advisor Information; Student Essay and Advisor Letter following the outlined format; diagrams, illustrations, photos, slides, or videos of the invention (clearly labeled); the signed Student/Advisor Release Form.
CONTACT: Ray DePuy

2210—NATURAL SCIENCES AND ENGINEERING RESEARCH COUNCIL OF CANADA (Undergraduate Student Research Awards in Industry)

350 Albert Street
Ottawa Ontario K1A 1H5 CANADA
613/995-5992 or 613/995-4273
FAX: 613/992-5337
E-mail: schol@nserc.ca or webapp@nserc.ca
Internet: http://www.nserc.ca
AMOUNT: Up to $3,600 (Canadian)
DEADLINE(S): Varies
FIELD(S): Natural Sciences (except health sciences); Engineering
ELIGIBILITY/REQUIREMENTS: Tenable in approved Canadian industrial organizations. For Canadian citizens or permanent residents, who have no more than 4 academic terms remaining to complete bachelor's degree; cumulative GPA of at least second class (B); must be employed full time in research and development activities during award tenure. Travel allowance may be granted.
HOW TO APPLY: See website or contact NSERC for more information and application.

2211—NATURAL SCIENCES AND ENGINEERING RESEARCH COUNCIL OF CANADA (Undergraduate Student Research Awards in Small Universities)

350 Albert Street
Ottawa Ontario K1A 1H5 CANADA
613/995-5992
FAX: 613/992-5337
E-mail: schol@nserc.ca
Internet: http://www.nserc.ca/programs/usrasmen.htm
AMOUNT: $3,600 (Canadian) max.
DEADLINE(S): Varies
FIELD(S): Natural Sciences (except health sciences); Engineering
ELIGIBILITY/REQUIREMENTS: Research awards for Canadian citizens/permanent residents attending eligible institutions, who have no more than 6 and no fewer than 2 academic terms remaining to complete bachelor's degree; cumulative GPA of at least second class (B); must be doing full-time research and development activities during award tenure.
HOW TO APPLY: See website or contact NSERC for more information and application.

2212—NEW JERSEY UTILITIES ASSOCIATION

50 West State Street, Suite 1006
Trenton NJ 08608
609/392-1000
FAX: 609/396-4231
Internet: http://www.njua.org
AMOUNT: $1,500
FIELD(S): Engineering; Environmental Science; Chemistry; Biology; Business Administration; Accounting
ELIGIBILITY/REQUIREMENTS: Applicants must be minority (Black, Hispanic, American Indian/Alaskan Native, or Asian American/Pacific Islander), female, and/or disabled students; a New Jersey resident; enrolled full time at an institute of higher education; have overall academic excellence; and demonstrate financial need.
HOW TO APPLY: Contact Association.
NUMBER OF AWARDS: 2

2213—NEW YORK STATE GRANGE (Cornell Fund Scholarships)

100 Grange Place
Cortland NY 13045
607/756-7553
FAX: 607/756-7757
E-mail: nysgrange@nysgrange.com
Internet: http://www.nysgrange.com
FIELD(S): Agriculture; Life Sciences
ELIGIBILITY/REQUIREMENTS: Must be enrolled in the College of Agriculture and Life Sciences at Cornell University. Selection is based on character, scholastic record, and need for financial assistance (reference given to farm-reared students whose families are Grange members and to students who transfer from an Agricultural and Technical College of the State University of New York).
HOW TO APPLY: Contact College of Agriculture and Life Sciences for details.

2214—NORTH CAROLINA STATE UNIVERSITY (Thomas Jefferson Scholarship in Agriculture/Life Sciences and Humanities)

Jefferson Scholars
College of Agriculture and Life Sciences
Box 7642
Raleigh NC 27695-7642
Internet: http://www.cals.ncsu.edu/student orgs/jeffer/apply.html
AMOUNT: $1,000
DEADLINE(S): FEB
FIELD(S): Agriculture/Life Sciences AND Humanities
ELIGIBILITY/REQUIREMENTS: Open to first-year undergraduate students with a double major in agriculture/life sciences and humanities.
HOW TO APPLY: See website or write for application and additional information. Submit with an essay, evaluation from a teacher or school official, and transcript.
NUMBER OF AWARDS: 15
RENEWABLE: Yes

2215—OHIO ENVIRONMENTAL HEALTH ASSOCIATION (OEHA) (George Eagle Memorial Scholarship)

P.O. Box 234
Columbus OH 43216-0234
740/349-6535
FAX: 740/349-6510
E-mail: jebel@lickingcohealth.org
Internet: http://www.oeha.org
AMOUNT: $2,000
DEADLINE(S): FEB 28
FIELD(S): Environmental Health, Environmental Studies, Biology
ELIGIBILITY/REQUIREMENTS: Must be Ohio resident enrolled as sophomore, junior or senior in a program leading to a baccalaureate degree in environmental health, environmental management or related field and express intent to become employed in environmental health in Ohio following graduation.
HOW TO APPLY: See website or write for application or further information.
NUMBER OF AWARDS: 1
RENEWABLE: No
CONTACT: Joe Ebel

2216—OUR WORLD-UNDERWATER SCHOLARSHIP SOCIETY (Scholarship and Internships)

P.O. Box 4428
Chicago IL 60680
630/969-6990
FAX: 630/969-6690
E-mail: execadmin@owu scholarship.org
Internet: http://www.owu scholarship.org
AMOUNT: $20,000 (experience-based scholarship reimbursable funds)
DEADLINE(S): DEC 31
FIELD(S): Marine Biology and Aqua-marine related disciplines
ELIGIBILITY/REQUIREMENTS: Must be certified SCUBA diver between 21 AND 24 on March 1 of the scholarship year. Cannot have received a postgraduate degree. Funds for transportation and living expenses for active participation in field studies, underwater research, scientific expeditions, laboratory assignments, equipment testing and design, and photographic instruction. Financial need NOT a factor.
HOW TO APPLY: Check the website for more information or contact the OWU for an application.
NUMBER OF AWARDS: 2 scholarships (1 for North American and 1 for European) and several internships.
RENEWABLE: No
CONTACT: Roberta Flanders, Executive Administrator

2217—SIEMENS WESTINGHOUSE (Science and Technology Competition)

186 Wood Avenue South
Iselin NJ 08830
877/822-5233
E-mail: foundation.us@siemens.com
Internet: http://www.siemens-foundation.org
AMOUNT: $120,000 (maximum)
DEADLINE(S): Varies
FIELD(S): Biology; Physical Sciences; Mathematics; Physics; Chemistry; Computer Science; Environmental Science
ELIGIBILITY/REQUIREMENTS: Open to U.S. high school seniors to pursue independent science research projects, working individually or in teams of 2 or 3 to develop and test their own ideas. May work with one of the universities/laboratories that serve as Siemens' partners. Students from the U.S. and its territories may compete in 1 of 6 geographic areas. Individual and team national prizewinners receive a second scholarship to be applied to undergraduate or graduate education.
HOW TO APPLY: See website or contact Siemens Foundation for details.

2218—SMITHSONIAN INSTITUTION (Minority Student Internship Program)

Office of Research Training and Services
470 L'Enfant SW, Suite 7102
MRC 902 P.O. Box 37012
Washington DC 20013-7012
202/633-7070
FAX: 202/633-7069
E-mail: siofg@si.edu
Internet: http://www.si.edu/research+study
AMOUNT: $500/week + possible travel expenses
DEADLINE(S): FEB 1 (for Summer or for Fall); OCT 1 (for Spring)
FIELD(S): Humanities; Environmental Studies; Cultural Studies; Natural History; Earth Science; Art History; Biology
ELIGIBILITY/REQUIREMENTS: 10-week, full-time internships in residence at the Smithsonian are open to U.S. minority students who wish to participate in research or museum-related activities in above and related fields. Must be undergraduates or beginning graduate students with a minimum 3.0 GPA. Must submit essay, résumé, and official transcript.
HOW TO APPLY: Contact the Office of Research Training and Services or see website for an application. Submit with the required essay or research proposal, résumé, and transcripts.

2219—STUDENT CONSERVATION ASSOCIATION (SCA Resource Assistant Program)

P.O. Box 550
Charlestown NH 03603
603/543-1700
FAX: 603/543-1828
E-mail: internships@sca-inc.org
Internet: http://www.sca-inc.org
AMOUNT: $1,180-$4,725
DEADLINE(S): Varies
FIELD(S): Environment and related fields (agriculture, archaeology, anthropology, botany, caves, civil engineering, environmental design, engineering & education, fisheries, forests, herpetology, history, landscape architecture, environmental design, paleontology, wildlife management, geology, hydrology, library/museums, surveying)
ELIGIBILITY/REQUIREMENTS: Must be 18 and U.S. citizen; need not be student.
HOW TO APPLY: Send $1 for postage for application; outside U.S./Canada, send $20.
NUMBER OF AWARDS: 900 positions in U.S. and Canada

2220—TURF AND ORNAMENTAL COMMUNICATORS ASSOCIATION (TOCA)

120 West Main Street

P.O. Box 156
New Prague MN 56071
952/758-6340
FAX: 952/758-5813
E-mail: tocaassociation@aol.com
Internet: http://www.toca.org
AMOUNT: $1,000
DEADLINE(S): MAR 1
FIELD(S): Technical Communications or
Green Industry fields: Horticulture;
Plant Science, Botany; Agronomy,
Plant Pathology
ELIGIBILITY/REQUIREMENTS:
Overall GPA of 2.5; major subject GPA
3.0+. Must be enrolled in college or university as undergraduate in a 2- or 4-year program.
HOW TO APPLY: Contact TOCA at
above address or by e-mail for application
forms, include your mailing address.
NUMBER OF AWARDS: 2
RENEWABLE: Yes, must reapply.

2221—UNCF/MERCK SCIENCE INITIATIVE (Undergraduate Science Research Scholarship Awards)

8260 Willow Oaks Corporate Drive
P.O. Box 10444
Fairfax VA 22031-4511
703/205-3503
FAX: 703/205-3574
E-mail: uncfmerck@uncf.org
Internet: http://www.uncf.org/merck
AMOUNT: $25,000/year (maximum)
DEADLINE(S): DEC 15
FIELD(S): Life and Physical Sciences
ELIGIBILITY/REQUIREMENTS: Open
to African-Americans in their junior year
of college who will receive a bachelor's
degree in the following academic year.
Must be enrolled full time in any 4-year
college or university in the U.S. and have a
minimum 3.3 GPA. Must be U.S.
citizen/permanent resident. Financial need
NOT a factor.
HOW TO APPLY: Contact UNCF/Merck
for an application.
NUMBER OF AWARDS: 15
RENEWABLE: No
CONTACT: Jerry Bryant, Ph.D.

2222—WESTERN MICHIGAN UNIVERSITY (College of Arts and Sciences/Colin J. Gould Memorial Scholarship)

1903 West Michigan
Kalamazoo MI 49008-5337
269/387-8777
FAX: 269/387-6989
E-mail: finaid-info@wmich.edu
Internet: http://www.wmich.edu/

finaid
AMOUNT: Varies
FIELD(S): Biology
ELIGIBILITY/REQUIREMENTS: Full-
time undergraduate in junior or senior year
at WMU, who is enrolled in Lee Honors
College majoring in biological sciences.
HOW TO APPLY: Contact Biological
Sciences Department for an application.
RENEWABLE: Yes. Must demonstrate
satisfactory academic progress and remain
in program.

2223—WESTERN MICHIGAN UNIVERSITY (College of Arts and Sciences/Distinguished Senior in Biomedical Sciences)

1903 West Michigan
Kalamazoo MI 49008-5337
269/387-8777
FAX: 269/387-6989
E-mail: finaid-info@wmich.edu
Internet: http://www.wmich.edu/
finaid
AMOUNT: $150 (spring semester)
FIELD(S): Biomedical Sciences
ELIGIBILITY/REQUIREMENTS:
Senior, biological sciences major.
HOW TO APPLY: Nominated by faculty
of Biological Sciences Department.
RENEWABLE: No

2224—WESTERN MICHIGAN UNIVERSITY (College of Arts and Sciences/Hazel Wirick Scholarship)

1903 West Michigan
Kalamazoo MI 49008-5337
269/387-8777
FAX: 269/387-6989
E-mail: finaid-info@wmich.edu
Internet: http://www.wmich.edu/
finaid
AMOUNT: $1,000
DEADLINE(S): MAR 1
FIELD(S): Plant Biology; Ecology
ELIGIBILITY/REQUIREMENTS:
Upperclassmen or graduate students
majoring in plant biology or ecology; high
GPA.
HOW TO APPLY: Contact the Biological
Sciences Department for an application.
RENEWABLE: No

2225—WESTERN MICHIGAN UNIVERSITY (College of Arts and Sciences/Margaret Thomas DuMond Scholarship)

1903 West Michigan
Kalamazoo MI 49008-5337
269/387-8777

FAX: 269/387-6989
E-mail: finaid-info@wmich.edu
Internet: http://www.wmich.edu/
finaid
AMOUNT: $500 (spring semester)
DEADLINE(S): MAR 1
FIELD(S): Education; Biology
ELIGIBILITY/REQUIREMENTS:
Junior or senior (minimum of 62 credit
hours); secondary education biology major
with 3.0 GPA.
HOW TO APPLY: Contact the Biological
Sciences Department for an application.
RENEWABLE: No

2226—WESTERN MICHIGAN UNIVERSITY (College of Arts and Sciences/Merrill Wiseman Microbiology Award Seniors or Grad Students)

1903 West Michigan
Kalamazoo MI 49008-5337
269/387-8777
FAX: 269/387-6989
E-mail: finaid-info@wmich.edu
Internet: http://www.wmich.edu/
finaid
AMOUNT: $150 (spring semester)
FIELD(S): Biology
ELIGIBILITY/REQUIREMENTS:
Upperclassmen or graduate students, biological sciences major, 3.0 GPA.
HOW TO APPLY: Nominated by faculty
of Biological Sciences Department.
RENEWABLE: No

2227—WESTERN MICHIGAN UNIVERSITY (Pfizer Cultural Diversity Scholarship)

1903 West Michigan
Kalamazoo MI 49008-5337
269/387-8777
FAX: 269/387-6989
E-mail: finaid-info@wmich.edu
Internet: http://www.wmich.edu/
finaid
AMOUNT: $2,000
DEADLINE(S): APR 1
FIELD(S): Biomedical Science; Biology;
Business
ELIGIBILITY/REQUIREMENTS: Must
be U.S. citizen; in junior year, majoring in
one of the above fields. Must be a full-time
student, with a 3.0 cumulative GPA in program of study. Business majors must complete pre-business classes before applying.
HOW TO APPLY: Contact the Division
of Minority Affairs for an application.
Must complete a FAFSA and indicate
WMU as a school choice.
RENEWABLE: No

2228—WILSON ORNITHOLOGICAL SOCIETY (Fuertes, Hall/Mayfield and Stewart Grants)

Midcontinent Ecological Science Center
4512 McMurray Avenue
Ft. Collins CO 80525-3400
970/226-9466
E-mail: jim sedgwick@usgs.gov
Internet: http://www.ummz.lsa.umich.edu/birds/wos.html
AMOUNT: $2,500 (Fuertes); $1,000 (Hall/Mayfield); $500 (Stewart)
DEADLINE(S): JAN 15
FIELD(S): Ornithology
ELIGIBILITY/REQUIREMENTS: Grants to support research on birds; NOT for college funding. Open to anyone presenting a suitable research proposal.
HOW TO APPLY: See website for an application.
NUMBER OF AWARDS: 5-6
RENEWABLE: No

CHEMISTRY

2229—AMERICAN ASSOCIATION OF BLACKS IN ENERGY (AABE)

1903 West Michigan
Kalamazoo MI 49008-5337
269/387-8777
FAX: 269/387-6989
E-mail: alumni@wmich.edu
Internet: http://www.wmich.edu/cas/research.html
AMOUNT: Varies
DEADLINE(S): MAR 1
FIELD(S): Mathematics; Computer Science; Engineering; Physical Sciences
ELIGIBILITY/REQUIREMENTS: Freshman with 2.5 GPA overall and a 3.0 GPA in mathematics and the sciences. Planning to major in engineering, mathematics, computer or the physical sciences. Applicant must demonstrate financial need and be a member of one of the underrepresented minority groups in the sciences and technology.
HOW TO APPLY: Contact the Office for Student Financial Aid.
NUMBER OF AWARDS: Varies
RENEWABLE: Yes

2230—AMERICAN CHEMICAL SOCIETY (Minority Scholars Program)

1155 Sixteenth Street NW
Washington DC 20036
202/872-6250 or 800/227-5558
FAX: 202/776-8003
Internet: http://www.acs.org
AMOUNT: Up to $3,000
DEADLINE(S): FEB 15
FIELD(S): Chemistry; Biochemistry; Chemical Engineering; Chemical Technology
ELIGIBILITY/REQUIREMENTS: Open to high school seniors entering college in the coming year, college and community college students planning to pursue full-time study, and community college transfer students pursuing a bachelor's degree. Awarded based on merit and financial need to African-American, Hispanic, and American Indian students with outstanding academic records combined with strong interest in chemistry. Must be U.S. citizen or permanent resident.
HOW TO APPLY: See website or contact ACS for an application.

2231—AMERICAN CHEMICAL SOCIETY-RUBBER DIVISION

P.O. Box 499
Akron OH 44309-0499
330/972-7814
FAX: 330/972-5269
E-mail: crobinson@rubber.org
Internet: http://www.rubber.org/awards/scholarships.htm
AMOUNT: $5,000
DEADLINE(S): MAR 15
FIELD(S): Chemistry, Physics, Chemical Engineering, Mechanical Engineering, Polymer Science, or other rubber-related discipline
ELIGIBILITY/REQUIREMENTS: Incoming junior or senior enrolled in an accredited college or university in the United States, Canada, Mexico, Brazil or India (countries may change) majoring in a rubber industry-related field. Must have "B" or better overall academic average, and a minimum of 3 semesters or 6 terms completed, and intend to pursue full-time professional employment in the industry.
HOW TO APPLY: Download application from website and fax or mail application along with 2 or more nomination letters from professor/nominator. Official transcripts may follow. NUMBER OF AWARDS: 3
RENEWABLE: Yes. Must reapply for 2nd and final year.
CONTACT: Christie Robinson, Education & Publications Manager

2232—AMERICAN FOUNDATION FOR THE BLIND (Paul W. Ruckes Scholarship)

11 Penn Plaza, Suite 300
New York NY 10001
212/502-7661
FAX: 212/502-7771
E-mail: afbinfo@afb.net
Internet: http://www.afb.org/scholar/scholarships.asp
AMOUNT: $1,000
DEADLINE(S): MAR 31
FIELD(S): Engineering; Computer, Physical, & Life Sciences
ELIGIBILITY/REQUIREMENTS: Open to legally blind and visually impaired undergraduate and graduate students pursuing a degree in one of above fields. Must be U.S. citizen.
HOW TO APPLY: See website or contact AFB for an application. Must submit written documentation of evidence of legal blindness; official transcripts; proof of college or university acceptance; 3 letters of recommendation; and typewritten statement describing goals, work experience, extracurricular activities, and how monies will be used.
NUMBER OF AWARDS: 1
CONTACT: Alina Vayntrub

2233—AMERICAN HEALTH AND BEAUTY AIDS INSTITUTE (Fred Luster Sr. Education Foundation Scholarships for College-Bound High School Seniors)

PO Box 19510
Chicago IL 60619
708/333-8740
FAX: 708/333-8741
Internet: http://www.proudlady.org
AMOUNT: $250-$500
DEADLINE(S): APR 15
FIELD(S): Chemistry, Business, Engineering
ELIGIBILITY/REQUIREMENTS: Open to students who will be enrolled as a college freshman in a 4-year college majoring in chemistry, business, or engineering. 3.0 GPA required. Scholastic record, school activities, and extracurricular activities considered.
HOW TO APPLY: Send 2 letters of recommendation (1 from a school official) and high school transcript.
NUMBER OF AWARDS: 2

2234—AMERICAN INDIAN SCIENCE AND ENGINEERING SOCIETY (EPA Tribal Lands Environmental Science Scholarship)

P.O. Box 9828
Albuquerque NM 87119-9828
505/765-1052
FAX: 505/765-5608
E-mail: scholarships@aises.org
Internet: http://www.aises.org/highered

AMOUNT: $4,000
DEADLINE(S): JUN 15
FIELD(S): Biochemistry; Biology; Chemical Engineering; Chemistry; Entomology; Environmental Economics/Science; Hydrology; Environmental Studies
ELIGIBILITY/REQUIREMENTS: Open to American Indian college juniors, seniors, and graduate students enrolled full time at an accredited institution. Must demonstrate financial need and be a member of AISES ($10 fee). Certificate of Indian blood NOT required.
HOW TO APPLY: See website for more information and/or an application.
RENEWABLE: No
CONTACT: Tina Pino

2235—ASTRONAUT SCHOLARSHIP FOUNDATION

6225 Vectorspace Boulevard
Titusville FL 32780
321/269/6119
FAX: 321/267-3970
E-mail: MercurySvn@aol.com
Internet: http://www.astronaut
scholarship.org/guidelines.html
AMOUNT: $10,000
DEADLINE(S): APR 15
FIELD(S): Engineering; Physical Sciences (Medical Research; NOT Professional Medicine)
ELIGIBILITY/REQUIREMENTS: Open to juniors, seniors, and graduate students at a select group of schools (see website for list). Must be U.S. citizen planning to pursue research or advance field of study.
HOW TO APPLY: Must be nominated by faculty or staff. Contact Executive Director for details.

2236—COMMUNITY FOUNDATION FOR GREATER ATLANTA, INC., THE (Tech High/W.O. Cheney Scholarship)

50 Hurt Plaza, Suite 449
Atlanta GA 30303
404/688-5525
FAX: 404/688-3060
E-mail: scholarships@atlcf.org
Internet: http://www.atlcf.org/
GrantsScholarships/Scholarships.
aspx
AMOUNT: $5,000
DEADLINE(S): MAR 26
FIELD(S): Mathematics, Engineering, Physical Sciences
ELIGIBILITY/REQUIREMENTS: Open to graduating high school seniors. Must be a citizen of the U.S. and a legal resident of Georgia for at least 3 years prior to appli-

cation, have a cumulative high school GPA of 3.7 or higher or be in the upper 10% of graduating class, SAT composite (math and critical reading) of at least 1300, be accepted as a full-time student to a 4-year accredited college or university, and demonstrate a commitment to community service.
HOW TO APPLY: See website for additional information and application. Submit with a personal essay (2-3 pages) that includes why you feel a college education is important; your statement of educational and career goals; post college career interests; highlights of your high school extracurricular/community service activities, special strengths, skills, and qualifications; any unusual family or personal circumstances have affected your achievement in school, work experience, or your participation in school and community activities; present financial need. Send to The Community Foundation for Greater Atlanta, Tech High/W.O. Cheney Scholarship, Scholarship Management Services, Scholarship America, One Scholarship Way, P.O. Box 297, Saint Peter, MN 56082. If you have questions, call 507/931-1682 or e-mail communityfoundation@scholarshipamerica.org.
NUMBER OF AWARDS: 4
RENEWABLE: Yes; must reapply.
CONTACT: Lisa Glanville, 404/308-0055

2237—FORD FOUNDATION/NATIONAL RESEARCH COUNCIL (Howard Hughes Medical Institute Predoctoral Fellowships in Biological Sciences)

2101 Constitution Avenue NW
Washington DC 20418
202/334-2872
FAX: 202/334-3419
Internet: http://www7.national
academies.org/FORDfellowships/
fordpredoc.html
AMOUNT: $16,000 stipend + tuition at U.S. institution
DEADLINE(S): NOV 9
FIELD(S): Biochemistry; Biophysics; Epidemiology; Genetics; Immunology; Microbiology; Neuroscience; Pharmacology; Physiology; Virology
ELIGIBILITY/REQUIREMENTS: 5-year award open to college seniors and first-year graduate students pursuing a Ph.D. or Sc.D. U.S. citizens/nationals may choose any institution in the U.S. or abroad; foreign students must choose U.S. institution. Based on ability, academic records, proposed study/research, previous experience, reference reports, and GRE scores.
HOW TO APPLY: See website or contact NRC for an application.
NUMBER OF AWARDS: 80

2238—H. FLETCHER BROWN FUND

c/o Donald W. Davis
PNC Bank Delaware
Trust Department
222 Delaware Avenue, 16th floor
Wilmington DE 19899
302/429- 2827 or 302/429-5658
E-mail: Robbie.testa@
pncadvisors.com
AMOUNT: Varies
DEADLINE(S): MAR 22
FIELD(S): Medicine; Dentistry; Law; Engineering; Chemistry
ELIGIBILITY/REQUIREMENTS: Open to U.S. citizens born in Delaware and still residing in Delaware. For 4 years of study (undergrad or graduate) leading to a degree that enables applicant to practice in chosen field. Must have minimum 1000 SAT score and rank in upper 20 percent of class. Interview required. Scholarships are based on need, scholastic achievement, and good moral character.
HOW TO APPLY: Applications available in February. Write to Account Administrator for application.
CONTACT: Robbie Testa

2239—HAWAII COMMUNITY FOUNDATION (William James & Dorothy Bading Lanquist Fund)

1164 Bishop Street, Suite 800
Honolulu HI 96813
808/537-6333 or toll free:
888/731-3863
FAX: 808/521-6286
E-mail: info@hcf-hawaii.org
Internet: http://www.hcf-hawaii.org
DEADLINE(S): MAR 1
FIELD(S): Physical Sciences and related fields (excluding Biology and Social Sciences)
ELIGIBILITY/REQUIREMENTS: Must be residents of Hawaii; junior or senior undergraduate students enrolled full time in an accredited 2- or 4-year college or university; and demonstrate financial need, good moral character, and academic achievement (minimum GPA of 2.7).
HOW TO APPLY: See website. Send application with 2 letters of recommendation.

2240—MENSA EDUCATION AND RESEARCH FOUNDATION (McGrew-Fruecht Scholarship)

Northern NJ MERF Scholarships
(Group 01-071)
Internet: http://www.mensa

foundation.org/AM/Template.cfm?
Section=Scholarships1
AMOUNT: $500
DEADLINE(S): JAN 15
FIELD(S): All; Physics; Chemistry
ELIGIBILITY/REQUIREMENTS: Must be studying physics or chemistry or someone who has been out of formal education for a period of 5 or more years and enrolled, for the academic year following the award, in a degree program in an accredited U.S. institution of postsecondary education. Must be a U.S. citizen or legal resident residing in Mensa Region 5 (portions of Alabama, Georgia, North Carolina, South Carolina, Mississippi, and Tennessee).
HOW TO APPLY: Submit application to the local scholarship chair (available from the website or by sending a request with SASE to the local scholarship chair), and an essay of not more than 550 words explaining your academic and/or vocational goals and how you plan to achieve those goals.
CONTACT: Denley Chew

2241—MICRON TECHNOLOGY FOUNDATION

8000 South Federal Way
Mailstop 1-407
Boise ID 83706
208/368-2658
FAX: 208/368-4435
Internet: http://www.micron.com/about/foundation/edgrants.aspx
AMOUNT: $55,000 and up to 12 @ $16,500
DEADLINE(S): JAN 20
FIELD(S): Electrical, Chemical, Computer & Mechanical Engineering; Chemistry; Physics; Computer & Material Science
ELIGIBILITY/REQUIREMENTS: High school senior; resident of Idaho, Colorado, Texas or Virginia; with a combined SAT score of at least 1350 or a composite ACT score of at least 30; must have an unweighted GPA of at least 3.5; demonstrated leadership in school, work and/or extracurricular activities.
HOW TO APPLY: Download an application from www.micron.scholarshipamerica. org or see your high school counselor. An essay and possible interview are also required.
NUMBER OF AWARDS: Up to 13
RENEWABLE: Yes. Up to 4 years; must remain eligible.

CONTACT: Scholarship America at 800/537-4180

2242—NAACP NATIONAL OFFICE (NAACP Willems Scholarship)

4805 Mount Hope Drive
Baltimore MD 21215
401/358-8900
Internet: http://www.naacp.org/work/education/eduscholarship.shtml
AMOUNT: $2,000 undergraduate; $3,000 graduate
DEADLINE(S): APR 30
FIELD(S): Engineering; Chemistry; Physics; Mathematics
ELIGIBILITY/REQUIREMENTS: Open to NAACP male members majoring in one of the above areas. Undergraduates must have GPA of 2.5+; graduates' GPAs must be 3.0+. Financial need must be established.
HOW TO APPLY: 2 letters of recommendation from teachers or professors in major field of specialization.
HOW TO APPLY: See website for application or write for complete information (include a legal size SASE) to The United Negro College Fund, Scholarships & Grants Administration, 8260 Willow Oaks Corporate Drive, Fairfax, VA 22031, attention: Kimberly Hall
RENEWABLE: Yes. If the required GPA is maintained.

2243—NASF/AESF Foundation Headquarters

Scholarship Committee
1155 Fifteenth Street, NW, Suite 500
Washington DC 20005
NASF Headquarters Phone: 202/457-8404
AESF Foundation Phone: 202/457-8401
FAX: 202/530-0659
E-mail: at tkoehler@nasf.org or mwalker@nasf.org.
Internet: http://www.nasf.org
AMOUNT: $1,500
DEADLINE(S): APR 15
FIELD(S): Metallurgy; Chemistry; Materials Science; Metallurgical, Chemical, & Environmental Engineering
ELIGIBILITY/REQUIREMENTS: Must be full-time junior or senior undergraduate. Selection based on achievement, scholarship potential, motivation, and

career interest in surface finishing technologies, not necessarily financial need.
HOW TO APPLY: See website for application or contact AESF for application and additional information. Submit with statement (maximum of 2 pages) describing career objectives, plans for study in plating and surface finishing technologies, and long-range goals; list or résumé (maximum 2 pages) detailing educational achievements; 3 letters of recommendation from teachers, professors, or employers (1 of which must be from academic major advisor); and transcript of recent academic records.
NUMBER OF AWARDS: Varies
RENEWABLE: Yes. Must reapply; maximum 2 years undergraduate; may reapply as a graduate student.
CONTACT: Tracey Koehler, Membership Director or Melissa Walker

2244—NATIONAL ASSOCIATION OF WATER COMPANIES-NEW JERSEY CHAPTER

Elizabethtown Water Company
600 South Avenue
Westfield NJ 07091
908/654-1234
FAX: 908/232-2719
E-mail: gbradygbconsult@comcast.net
AMOUNT: $2,500
DEADLINE(S): APR 1
FIELD(S): Business Administration; Biology; Chemistry; Engineering; Communications
ELIGIBILITY/REQUIREMENTS: For U.S. citizens who have lived in New Jersey for at least 5 years and plan a career in the investor-owned water utility industry. Must be undergraduate in a 2- or 4-year New Jersey college or university. GPA of 3.0 or better required.
HOW TO APPLY: Contact Association for complete information.
CONTACT: Gail P. Brady

2245—NATIONAL INVENTORS HALL OF FAME, THE (Collegiate Inventors Competition)

221 South Broadway Street
Akron OH 44308-1505
330/849-6887
E-mail: rdepuy@invent.org
Internet: http://www.invent.org/bfg/bfghome.html
AMOUNT: $15,000
DEADLINE(S): JUN 1

FIELD(S): Mathematics, Engineering, Biology, Chemistry, Physics, Information Technology, Medicine
ELIGIBILITY/REQUIREMENTS: Must be enrolled (or have been enrolled) full time (in any college or university) at least part of the 12-month period prior to the date the entry is submitted. For teams (maximum 4 students), at least 1 member of the team must meet the full-time eligibility criteria. The other team members must have been enrolled on a part-time basis (at minimum) sometime during the 24-month period prior to the date entry is submitted. There are no limits on the number of entries a student or team may submit; however, only 1 prize/student or team will be awarded. No specific age requirements. Entries judged on the originality and inventiveness of the new idea, process, or technology, on their potential value to society (socially; environmentally, and economically); and on the scope of use. Entries must be complete, workable, and well articulated.
HOW TO APPLY: Submit an original invention or idea that has not been made public. See website for application and details. The application must include: Student and Advisor Information; Student Essay and Advisor Letter following the outlined format; diagrams, illustrations, photos, slides, or videos of the invention (clearly labeled); the signed Student/Advisor Release Form.
CONTACT: Ray DePuy

2246—NATURAL SCIENCES AND ENGINEERING RESEARCH COUNCIL OF CANADA (Undergraduate Student Research Awards in Industry)

350 Albert Street
Ottawa Ontario K1A 1H5 CANADA
613/995-5992 or 613/995-4273
FAX: 613/992-5337
E-mail: schol@nserc.ca or webapp@nserc.ca
Internet: http://www.nserc.ca
AMOUNT: Up to $3,600 (Canadian)
DEADLINE(S): Varies
FIELD(S): Natural Sciences (except health sciences); Engineering
ELIGIBILITY/REQUIREMENTS: Tenable in approved Canadian industrial organizations. For Canadian citizens or permanent residents, who have no more than 4 academic terms remaining to complete bachelor's degree; cumulative GPA of at least second class (B); must be employed full time in research and development activities during award tenure. Travel allowance may be granted.

HOW TO APPLY: See website or contact NSERC for more information and application.

2247—NATURAL SCIENCES AND ENGINEERING RESEARCH COUNCIL OF CANADA (Undergraduate Student Research Awards in Small Universities)

350 Albert Street
Ottawa Ontario K1A 1H5 CANADA
613/995-5992
FAX: 613/992-5337
E-mail: schol@nserc.ca
Internet: http://www.nserc.ca/programs/usrasmen.htm
AMOUNT: $3,600 (Canadian) max.
DEADLINE(S): Varies
FIELD(S): Natural Sciences (except health sciences); Engineering
ELIGIBILITY/REQUIREMENTS: Research awards for Canadian citizens/permanent residents attending eligible institutions, who have no more than 6 and no fewer than 2 academic terms remaining to complete bachelor's degree; cumulative GPA of at least second class (B); must be doing full-time research and development activities during award tenure.
HOW TO APPLY: See website or contact NSERC for more information and application.

2248—NEW JERSEY UTILITIES ASSOCIATION

50 West State Street, Suite 1006
Trenton NJ 08608
609/392-1000
FAX: 609/396-4231
Internet: http://www.njua.org
AMOUNT: $1,500
FIELD(S): Engineering; Environmental Science; Chemistry; Biology; Business Administration; Accounting
ELIGIBILITY/REQUIREMENTS: Applicants must be minority (Black, Hispanic, American Indian/Alaskan Native, or Asian American/Pacific Islander), female, and/or disabled students; a New Jersey resident; enrolled full time at an institute of higher education; have overall academic excellence; and demonstrate financial need.
HOW TO APPLY: Contact Association.
NUMBER OF AWARDS: 2

2249—NORTH CAROLINA STATE UNIVERSITY (Thomas Jefferson Scholarship in Agriculture/Life Sciences and Humanities)

Jefferson Scholars

College of Agriculture and Life Sciences
Box 7642
Raleigh NC 27695-7642
Internet: http://www.cals.ncsu.edu/student orgs/jeffer/apply.html
AMOUNT: $1,000
DEADLINE(S): FEB
FIELD(S): Agriculture/Life Sciences AND Humanities
ELIGIBILITY/REQUIREMENTS: Open to first-year undergraduate students with a double major in agriculture/life sciences and humanities.
HOW TO APPLY: See website or write for application and additional information. Submit with an essay, evaluation from a teacher or school official, and transcript.
NUMBER OF AWARDS: 15
RENEWABLE: Yes

2250—ROBERT SCHRECK MEMORIAL FUND (Grants)

c/o Texas Commerce Bank
Trust Department
P.O. Drawer 140
El Paso TX 79980
915/546-6515
AMOUNT: $500-$1,500
DEADLINE(S): JUL 15; NOV 15
FIELD(S): Medicine; Veterinary Medicine; Physics; Chemistry; Architecture; Engineering; Episcopal Clergy
ELIGIBILITY/REQUIREMENTS: Grants to undergraduate juniors or seniors or graduate students who have been residents of El Paso County for at least 2 years. Must be U.S. citizen or legal resident and have a high GPA. Financial need considered.
HOW TO APPLY: Write for information.
NUMBER OF AWARDS: 3
RENEWABLE: No

2251—SIEMENS WESTINGHOUSE (Science and Technology Competition)

186 Wood Avenue South
Iselin NJ 08830
877/822-5233
E-mail: foundation.us@siemens.com
Internet: http://www.siemens-foundation.org
AMOUNT: $120,000 (maximum)
DEADLINE(S): Varies
FIELD(S): Biology; Physical Sciences; Mathematics; Physics; Chemistry; Computer Science; Environmental Science

ELIGIBILITY/REQUIREMENTS: Open to U.S. high school seniors to pursue independent science research projects, working individually or in teams of 2 or 3 to develop and test their own ideas. May work with one of the universities/laboratories that serve as Siemens' partners. Students from the U.S. and its territories may compete in 1 of 6 geographic areas. Individual and team national prizewinners receive a second scholarship to be applied to undergraduate or graduate education.

HOW TO APPLY: See website or contact Siemens Foundation for details.

2252—SONS OF NORWAY FOUNDATION (Nancy Lorraine Jensen Memorial Scholarship Fund)

c/o Sons of Norway
1455 West Lake Street
Minneapolis MN 55408
612/821-4632
E-mail: colson@sofn.com
Internet: http://www.sofn.com/ foundation/foundation scholarships.html

AMOUNT: 50%-100% of tuition
DEADLINE(S): MAR 1
FIELD(S): Chemistry; Physics; Chemical, Electrical & Mechanical Engineering

ELIGIBILITY/REQUIREMENTS: Must be U.S. citizen, female, aged 17-35, a member or daughter or granddaughter of a current member of for at least 3 years, or a daughter or granddaughter of current employee. Must be full-time undergraduate who has completed at least 1 term, majoring in one of above subjects. SAT of at least 1200 or ACT of at least 26.

HOW TO APPLY: Submit application along with an essay (500 words or less) giving proof of accomplishments and stating how you will pursue your career and involvement in SON, youth, community or research activities, and 3 letters of recommendation. Transcript should be sent directly from school. See website for an application and additional details.

NUMBER OF AWARDS: Varies
RENEWABLE: Yes. Up to 3 undergraduate awards.
CONTACT: Cindy Olson, Director

2253—SPE FOUNDATION, THE (Blow Molding Division Memorial Scholarships)

14 Fairfield Drive
Brookfield CT 06804
203/740-5447
FAX: 203/775-1157
E-mail: foundation@4spe.org
Internet: http://www.4spe.org/ foundation/scholarships.php

AMOUNT: $8,000 (payable over 2 years)
DEADLINE(S): JAN 15
FIELD(S): Polymer Science; Chemistry; Physics; Plastics, Chemical, Mechanical, & Industrial Engineering

ELIGIBILITY/REQUIREMENTS: Applicants must be completing the 2nd year of a 4-year undergraduate plastics engineering program and be a member of a Society of Plastics Engineers (SPE) student chapter.

HOW TO APPLY: Complete application; submit 3 recommendation letters (2 from a teacher or school official and 1 from an employer or non-relative); high school and/or college transcript for last 2 years; a 1- to 2 page brief essay on the importance of blow molding to the technical parts and packaging industries. Submit brief essay that describes the importance of blow molding to the techical parts and packaging industries, and why the applicant desires a career in the plastics industry.

NUMBER OF AWARDS: Up to 2

2254—SPE FOUNDATION, THE (Composites Division/Harold Giles Scholarship)

14 Fairfield Drive
Brookfield CT 06804
203/740-5447
FAX: 203/775-1157
E-mail: foundation@4spe.org
Internet: http://www.4spe.org/ foundation/scholarships.php

AMOUNT: $1,000
DEADLINE(S): JAN 15
FIELD(S): Polymer Science; Chemistry; Physics; Chemical, Plastics, Mechanical & Industrial Engineering

ELIGIBILITY/REQUIREMENTS: Applicants must have experience in the composites industry (such as courses taken, research conducted, or jobs held; must be in good standing with their colleges and have demonstrated an interest in the plastics industry; majoring in or taking courses that would be beneficial to a career in the plastics/polymer industry. Financial need is considered.

HOW TO APPLY: Complete application; submit 3 recommendation letters (2 from a teacher or school official and 1 from an employer or non-relative); high school and/or college transcript for last 2 years; a 1- to 2-page statement telling why you are applying for the scholarship and educational and career goals in the plastics industry. Include a statement detailing exposure to the composites industry.

NUMBER OF AWARDS: 1

2255—SPE FOUNDATION, THE (Extrusion Division/Lew Erwin Memorial Scholarship)

14 Fairfield Drive
Brookfield CT 06804
203/740-5447
FAX: 203/775-1157
E-mail: foundation@4spe.org
Internet: http://www.4spe.org/ foundation/scholarships.php

AMOUNT: $2,500
DEADLINE(S): JAN 15
FIELD(S): Polymer Science; Chemistry; Physics; Plastics, Chemical, Mechanical, & Industrial Engineering

ELIGIBILITY/REQUIREMENTS: Supports undergraduate or graduate research in the field of polymer extrusion. Must be working on a senior or MS project, which must be described in writing, including background, objective and proposed experiments. Final research summary report required.

HOW TO APPLY: Complete application; submit 3 recommendation letters (2 from a teacher or school official and 1 from an employer or non-relative); high school and/or college transcript for last 2 years; a 1- to 2-page statement giving reasons for applying and educational and career goals in the plastics industry.

NUMBER OF AWARDS: 1
RENEWABLE: Yes, must reapply.

2256—SPE FOUNDATION, THE (Fleming/Biaszcek Scholarship)

14 Fairfield Drive
Brookfield CT 06804
203/740-5447
FAX: 203/775-1157
E-mail: foundation@4spe.org
Internet: http://www.4spe.org/ foundation/scholarships.php

AMOUNT: $2,000
DEADLINE(S): JAN 15
FIELD(S): Polymer Science; Chemistry; Physics; Plastics, Chemical, Mechanical, & Industrial Engineering

ELIGIBILITY/REQUIREMENTS: Open to full-time undergraduate and graduate students, in good standing who have demonstrated an interest in the plastics industry; majoring in or taking courses that would be beneficial to a career in the plastics/polymer industry. Must be of Mexican descent and citizens or legal residents of the U.S. Financial need is considered.

HOW TO APPLY: Complete application; submit 3 recommendation letters (2 from a teacher or school official and 1 from an employer or non-relative); high school and/or college transcript for last 2 years; a 1- to 2-page statement giving reasons for applying and educational and career goals in the plastics industry. Detail Mexican lineage in essay or on a separate sheet of paper.

NUMBER OF AWARDS: 1
RENEWABLE: Yes. Must reapply for 3 additional years.

2257—SPE FOUNDATION, THE (Foundation Scholarships)

14 Fairfield Drive
Brookfield CT 06804
203/740-5447
FAX: 203/775-1157
E-mail: foundation@4spe.org
Internet: http://www.4spe.org/foundation/scholarships.php
AMOUNT: $4,000
DEADLINE(S): JAN 15
FIELD(S): Polymer Science; Chemistry; Physics; Plastics, Chemical, Mechanical, & Industrial Engineering
ELIGIBILITY/REQUIREMENTS: Open to students in good standing who have demonstrated an interest in the plastics industry; majoring in or taking courses that would be beneficial to a career in the plastics/polymer industry. Financial need is considered for most scholarships.
HOW TO APPLY: Submit application with 3 recommendation letters (2 from a teacher or school official and 1 from an employer or non-relative); high school and/or college transcript for last 2 years; a 1- to 2-page statement giving reasons for applying, and educational and career goals in the plastics industry.
NUMBER OF AWARDS: Multiple
RENEWABLE: Yes, must reapply; up to 3 additional years.

2258—SPE FOUNDATION, THE (Gulf Coast Hurricane Scholarships)

14 Fairfield Drive
Brookfield CT 06804
203/740-5447
FAX: 203/775-1157
E-mail: foundation@4spe.org
Internet: http://www.4spe.org/foundation/scholarships.php
AMOUNT: $6,000 (college or university); $2,000 (junior or technical)
DEADLINE(S): JAN 15
FIELD(S): Polymer Science; Chemistry; Physics; Chemical, Plastics, Mechanical & Industrial Engineering
ELIGIBILITY/REQUIREMENTS: Must have been a resident of a Gulf Coast County declared a national disaster area as

a result of Hurricanes Katrina, Rita or Wilma, and must be attending a university, college or technical institute in a Gulf Coast State (Florida, Alabama, Mississippi, Louisiana, Texas). Must be in good standing with their colleges (minimum GPA 2.0) and enrolled 6 hours/semester. Must have demonstrated an interest in the plastics industry; majoring in or taking courses that would be beneficial to a career in the plastics/polymer industry. Financial need is considered for most scholarships.
HOW TO APPLY: Complete application; submit 3 recommendation letters (2 from a teacher or school official and 1 from an employer or non-relative); high school and/or college transcript for last 2 years; a 1- to 2-page statement telling why you are applying for the scholarship and educational and career goals in the plastics industry. Must provide proof of residence.
NUMBER OF AWARDS: 3; 1 college or university, 2 junior college or technical school
RENEWABLE: Yes. Must reapply for 3 additional years.

2259—SPE FOUNDATION, THE (Injection Molding Division Scholarship)

14 Fairfield Drive
Brookfield CT 06804
203/740-5447
FAX: 203/775-1157
E-mail: foundation@4spe.org
Internet: http://www.4spe.org/foundation/scholarships.php
AMOUNT: $3,000
DEADLINE(S): JAN 15
FIELD(S): Polymer Science; Chemistry; Physics; Chemical, Plastics, Mechanical & Industrial Engineering
ELIGIBILITY/REQUIREMENTS: Available to undergraduates at a 4-year. Applicants must have experience in the injection molding industry (such as courses taken, research conducted, or jobs held), be in good standing with their colleges and have demonstrated an interest in the plastics industry; majoring in or taking courses that would be beneficial to a career in the plastics/polymer industry. Financial need is considered.
HOW TO APPLY: Complete application; submit 3 recommendation letters (2 from a teacher or school official and 1 from an employer or non-relative); high school and/or college transcript for last 2 years; a 1- to 2-page statement telling why you are applying for the scholarship and educational and career goals in the plastics industry.
NUMBER OF AWARDS: 1
RENEWABLE: Yes. Must reapply for 3 additional years.

2260—SPE FOUNDATION, THE (Pittsburgh Section Scholarships)

14 Fairfield Drive
Brookfield CT 06804
203/740-5447
FAX: 203/775-1157
E-mail: foundation@4spe.org
Internet: http://www.4spe.org/foundation/scholarships.php
AMOUNT: $2,000
DEADLINE(S): JAN 15
FIELD(S): Polymer Science; Chemistry; Physics; Chemical, Plastics, Mechanical & Industrial Engineering
ELIGIBILITY/REQUIREMENTS: Must have graduated from a high school in one of the following PA counties: Allegheny, Armstrong, Beaver, Bedford, Blair, Brooke, Butler, Cambria, Clarion, Clearfield, Fayette, Greene, Hancock, Indiana, Jefferson, Lawrence, Mercer, Somerset, Venango, Washington, Westmoreland. Must be in good standing with their colleges and have demonstrated an interest in the plastics industry; majoring in or taking courses that would be beneficial to a career in the plastics/polymer industry. Financial need is considered for most scholarships.
HOW TO APPLY: Complete application; submit 3 recommendation letters (2 from a teacher or school official and 1 from an employer or non-relative); high school and/or college transcript for last 2 years; a 1- to 2-page statement telling why you are applying for the scholarship and educational and career goals in the plastics industry. Must provide proof of graduation from school in one of above counties.
NUMBER OF AWARDS: Up to 2
RENEWABLE: Yes. Must reapply for 3 additional years.

2261—SPE FOUNDATION, THE (Plastics Pioneers Association Scholarships)

14 Fairfield Drive
Brookfield CT 06804
203/740-5447
FAX: 203/775-1157
E-mail: foundation@4spe.org
Internet: http://www.4spe.org/foundation/scholarships.php
AMOUNT: $3,000
DEADLINE(S): JAN 15
FIELD(S): Polymer Science; Chemistry; Physics; Chemical, Plastics, Mechanical & Industrial Engineering
ELIGIBILITY/REQUIREMENTS: Open to undergraduate students, including those enrolled in associate or technical degree programs, who are committed to becoming

"hands on" workers in the plastics industry as plastics technicians or engineers. Must be in good standing with their colleges and have demonstrated an interest in the plastics industry; majoring in or taking courses that would be beneficial to a career in the plastics/polymer industry. Financial need is considered for most scholarships.

HOW TO APPLY: Complete application; submit 3 recommendation letters (2 from a teacher or school official and 1 from an employer or non-relative); high school and/or college transcript for last 2 years; a 1- to 2-page statement telling why you are applying for the scholarship and educational and career goals in the plastics industry.

NUMBER OF AWARDS: Multiple
RENEWABLE: Yes. Must reapply for 3 additional years.

2262—SPE FOUNDATION, THE (Polymer Modifiers & Additives Division Scholarships)

14 Fairfield Drive
Brookfield CT 06804
203/740-5447
FAX: 203/775-1157
E-mail: foundation@4spe.org
Internet: http://www.4spe.org/foundation/scholarships.php
AMOUNT: $4,000
DEADLINE(S): JAN 15
FIELD(S): Polymer Science; Chemistry; Physics; Chemical, Plastics, Mechanical & Industrial Engineering
ELIGIBILITY/REQUIREMENTS: Must be in good standing with their colleges and have demonstrated an interest in the plastics industry; majoring in or taking courses that would be beneficial to a career in the plastics/polymer industry. Financial need is considered for most scholarships.
HOW TO APPLY: Complete application; submit 3 recommendation letters (2 from a teacher or school official and 1 from an employer or non-relative); high school and/or college transcript for last 2 years; a 1- to 2-page statement telling why you are applying for the scholarship and educational and career goals in the plastics industry.
NUMBER OF AWARDS: 3
RENEWABLE: Yes. Must reapply for 3 additional years.

2263—SPE FOUNDATION, THE (Robert E. Cramer/Product Design & Development Division Scholarship)

14 Fairfield Drive
Brookfield CT 06804

203/740-5447
FAX: 203/775-1157
E-mail: foundation@4spe.org
Internet: http://www.4spe.org/foundation/scholarships.php
AMOUNT: $1,000
DEADLINE(S): JAN 15
FIELD(S): Polymer Science; Chemistry; Physics; Chemical, Plastics, Mechanical & Industrial Engineering
ELIGIBILITY/REQUIREMENTS: Must be in good standing with their colleges and have demonstrated an interest in the plastics industry; majoring in or taking courses that would be beneficial to a career in the plastics/polymer industry. Financial need is considered for most scholarships.
HOW TO APPLY: Complete application; submit 3 recommendation letters (2 from a teacher or school official and 1 from an employer or non-relative); high school and/or college transcript for last 2 years; a 1- to 2-page statement telling why you are applying for the scholarship and educational and career goals in the plastics industry.
NUMBER OF AWARDS: 1
RENEWABLE: Yes. Must reapply for 3 additional years.

2264—SPE FOUNDATION, THE (Robert G. Dailey/Detroit Section Scholarship)

14 Fairfield Drive
Brookfield CT 06804
203/740-5447
FAX: 203/775-1157
E-mail: foundation@4spe.org
Internet: http://www.4spe.org/foundation/scholarships.php
AMOUNT: $4,000
DEADLINE(S): JAN 15
FIELD(S): Polymer Science; Chemistry; Physics; Chemical, Plastics, Mechanical & Industrial Engineering
ELIGIBILITY/REQUIREMENTS: Must be in good standing with their colleges and have demonstrated an interest in the plastics industry; majoring in or taking courses that would be beneficial to a career in the plastics/polymer industry. Financial need is considered for most scholarships.
HOW TO APPLY: Complete application; submit 3 recommendation letters (2 from a teacher or school official and 1 from an employer or non-relative); high school and/or college transcript for last 2 years; a 1- to 2-page statement telling why you are applying for the scholarship and educational and career goals in the plastics industry.
NUMBER OF AWARDS: 1

RENEWABLE: Yes. Must reapply for 3 additional years.

2265—SPE FOUNDATION, THE (Ted and Ruth Neward Scholarships)

14 Fairfield Drive
Brookfield CT 06804
203/740-5447
FAX: 203/775-1157
E-mail: foundation@4spe.org
Internet: http://www.4spe.org/foundation/scholarships.php
AMOUNT: $3,000
DEADLINE(S): JAN 15
FIELD(S): Polymer Science; Chemistry; Physics; Chemical, Plastics, Mechanical & Industrial Engineering
ELIGIBILITY/REQUIREMENTS: Must be U.S. citizens in good standing with their colleges and have demonstrated an interest in the plastics industry; majoring in or taking courses that would be beneficial to a career in the plastics/polymer industry. Financial need is considered for most scholarships.
HOW TO APPLY: Complete application; submit 3 recommendation letters (2 from a teacher or school official and 1 from an employer or non-relative); high school and/or college transcript for last 2 years; a 1- to 2-page statement telling why you are applying for the scholarship and educational and career goals in the plastics industry.
NUMBER OF AWARDS: 3
RENEWABLE: Yes. Must reapply for 3 additional years.

2266—SPE FOUNDATION, THE (Thermoforming Scholarships)

14 Fairfield Drive
Brookfield CT 06804
203/740-5447
FAX: 203/775-1157
E-mail: foundation@4spe.org
Internet: http://www.4spe.org/foundation/scholarships.php
AMOUNT: $7,500
DEADLINE(S): JAN 15
FIELD(S): Polymer Science; Chemistry; Physics; Plastics, Chemical, Mechanical, & Industrial Engineering
ELIGIBILITY/REQUIREMENTS: Available to graduate or undergraduate students. Undergraduates must have completed at least 2 years of credits. Must have experience in the thermoforming industry (courses taken, research conducted, or jobs held), be in good standing and have demonstrated an interest in the plastics industry; majoring in or taking courses that

would be beneficial to a career in the plastics/polymer industry.

HOW TO APPLY: Complete application; submit 3 recommendation letters (2 from a teacher or school official and 1 from an employer or non-relative); high school and/or college transcript for last 2 years; a 1- to 2-page statement giving reasons for applying and educational and career goals in the plastics industry. Include a statement detailing exposure to the thermoforming industry.

NUMBER OF AWARDS: Varies (multiple awards)

RENEWABLE: Yes, must reapply for 3 additional years.

2267—SPE FOUNDATION, THE (Thermoplastic Materials & Foams Division Scholarship)

14 Fairfield Drive
Brookfield CT 06804
203/740-5447
FAX: 203/775-1157
E-mail: foundation@4spe.org
Internet: http://www.4spe.org/foundation/scholarships.php
AMOUNT: $1,000
DEADLINE(S): JAN 15
FIELD(S): Polymer Science; Chemistry; Physics; Chemical, Plastics, Mechanical & Industrial Engineering

ELIGIBILITY/REQUIREMENTS: Must be in good standing with their colleges and have demonstrated an interest in the plastics industry; majoring in or taking courses that would be beneficial to a career in the plastics/polymer industry. Financial need is considered for most scholarships.

HOW TO APPLY: Complete application; submit 3 recommendation letters (2 from a teacher or school official and 1 from an employer or non-relative); high school and/or college transcript for last 2 years; a 1- to 2-page statement telling why you are applying for the scholarship and educational and career goals in the plastics industry.

NUMBER OF AWARDS: 1
RENEWABLE: Yes. Must reapply for 3 additional years.

2268—SPE FOUNDATION, THE (Thermoplastic Elastomers Special Interest Group Scholarship)

14 Fairfield Drive
Brookfield CT 06804
203/740-5447
FAX: 203/775-1157
E-mail: foundation@4spe.org
Internet: http://www.4spe.org/foundation/scholarships.php

AMOUNT: $1,000
DEADLINE(S): JAN 15
FIELD(S): Polymer Science; Chemistry; Physics; Chemical, Plastics, Mechanical & Industrial Engineering

ELIGIBILITY/REQUIREMENTS: Available to graduate or undergraduate students at a 4-year college. Applicants must have experience in the thermoplastic elastometers industry (such as courses taken, research conducted, or jobs held); must be in good standing with their colleges and have demonstrated an interest in the plastics industry; majoring in or taking courses that would be beneficial to a career in the plastics/polymer industry. Financial need is considered.

HOW TO APPLY: Complete application; submit 3 recommendation letters (2 from a teacher or school official and 1 from an employer or non-relative); high school and/or college transcript for last 2 years; a 1- to 2-page statement telling why you are applying for the scholarship and educational and career goals in the plastics industry. Include a statement detailing exposure to the thermoplastic elastometers industry.

NUMBER OF AWARDS: 1

2269—SPE FOUNDATION, THE (Thermoset Division/James I. MacKenzie Memorial Scholarship)

14 Fairfield Drive
Brookfield CT 06804
203/740-5447
FAX: 203/775-1157
E-mail: foundation@4spe.org
Internet: http://www.4spe.org/foundation/scholarships.php

AMOUNT: $2,500
DEADLINE(S): JAN 15
FIELD(S): Polymer Science; Chemistry; Physics; Plastics, Chemical, Mechanical, & Industrial Engineering

ELIGIBILITY/REQUIREMENTS: Available to undergraduates at a 4-year college. Must have experience in the thermoset industry (courses taken, research conducted, or jobs held), be in good standing and have demonstrated an interest in the plastics industry; majoring in or taking courses that would be beneficial to a career in the plastics/polymer industry. Financial need is considered for most scholarships.

HOW TO APPLY: Complete application; submit 3 recommendation letters (2 from a teacher or school official and 1 from an employer or non-relative); high school and/or college transcript for last 2 years; a 1- to 2-page statement giving reasons for applying and educational and career goals in the plastics industry.

NUMBER OF AWARDS: 1
RENEWABLE: Yes. Must reapply for 3 additional years.

ADDITIONAL INFORMATION: Also includes all-expense-paid trip to, and speaking opportunity at, annual Madison Thermoset Molding Conference.

2270—SPE FOUNDATION, THE (Vinyl Plastics Division Scholarship)

14 Fairfield Drive
Brookfield CT 06804
203/740-5447
FAX: 203/775-1157
E-mail: foundation@4spe.org
Internet: http://www.4spe.org/foundation/scholarships.php
AMOUNT: $3,000
DEADLINE(S): JAN 15
FIELD(S): Polymer Science; Chemistry; Physics; Chemical, Plastics, Mechanical & Industrial Engineering

ELIGIBILITY/REQUIREMENTS: Must be in good standing with their colleges and have demonstrated an interest in the plastics industry; majoring in or taking courses that would be beneficial to a career in the plastics/polymer industry. Preference given to applicants with experience in the vinyl industry (such as courses taken, research conducted, or jobs held). Financial need is considered for most scholarships.

HOW TO APPLY: Complete application; submit 3 recommendation letters (2 from a teacher or school official and 1 from an employer or non-relative); high school and/or college transcript for last 2 years; a 1- to 2-page statement telling why you are applying for the scholarship and educational and career goals in the plastics industry.

NUMBER OF AWARDS: 1
RENEWABLE: Yes. Must reapply for 3 additional years.

2271—TAPPI PULP MANUFACTURE DIVISION (High Impact Award Scholarship)

P.O. Box 105113
Atlanta GA 30092
770/446-1400
FAX: 770/446-6947
E-mail: vedmondson@tappi.org
Internet: http://www.tappi.org
AMOUNT: $1,000
DEADLINE(S): JAN 31
FIELD(S): Chemistry; Environmental Studies; Engineering; Paper Industry

ELIGIBILITY/REQUIREMENTS: Presented to 1 school each year (announced in fall), whose students may then apply.

HOW TO APPLY: Contact Project Event Manager to determine which school has received the award; then contact school directly for information on how to apply.
NUMBER OF AWARDS: 1
RENEWABLE: Yes, must reapply.
CONTACT: Veranda Edmondson, 770/208-7536

2272—TAPPI PULP MANUFACTURE DIVISION (Johan C.F.C. Richter Scholarship Prize)

P.O. Box 105113
Atlanta GA 30092
770/446-1400
FAX: 770/446-6947
E-mail: vedmondson@tappi.org
Internet: http://www.tappi.org
AMOUNT: $1,000
DEADLINE(S): JAN 31
FIELD(S): Chemistry; Environmental Studies; Engineering; Paper Industry
ELIGIBILITY/REQUIREMENTS: Biannual scholarship presented to 1 school each year (announced in fall), whose students may then apply.
HOW TO APPLY: Contact TAPPI Project Event Manager to determine which school has received the award; then contact school directly for information on how to apply.
NUMBER OF AWARDS: 1
RENEWABLE: Yes, must reapply.
CONTACT: Veranda Edmondson, 770/208-7536

2273—TAPPI PULP MANUFACTURE DIVISION (Joseph K. Perkins Scholarship Prize)

P.O. Box 105113
Atlanta GA 30092
770/446-1400
FAX: 770/446-6947
E-mail: vedmondson@tappi.org
Internet: http://www.tappi.org
AMOUNT: $1,000
DEADLINE(S): JAN 31
FIELD(S): Chemistry; Environmental Studies; Engineering; Paper Industry
ELIGIBILITY/REQUIREMENTS: Biannual scholarship presented to 1 school each year (announced in fall), whose students may then apply.
HOW TO APPLY: Contact TAPPI Project Event Manager to determine which school has received the award; then contact school directly for information on how to apply.
NUMBER OF AWARDS: 1
RENEWABLE: Yes, must reapply.

CONTACT: Veranda Edmondson, 770/208-7536

2274—TAPPI PULP MANUFACTURE DIVISION/THE PLACE DIVISION (The Ralph A. Klucken Scholarship Award)

P.O. Box 105113
Atlanta GA 30092
770/446-1400
FAX: 770/446-6947
E-mail: vedmondson@tappi.org
Internet: http://www.tappi.org
AMOUNT: $1,000
DEADLINE(S): MAY 15
FIELD(S): Chemistry; Paper Industry
ELIGIBILITY/REQUIREMENTS: Must be a college undergraduate or graduate student as of the date of the application and attending college full time on the date of the award in September; maintain a GPA of 3.0, and demonstrate responsibility and maturity throughout a history of part-time and summer employment; and demonstrate an interest in the technological areas covered by the polymers, laminations and coating division.
HOW TO APPLY: See website or contact TAPPI for applications. Submit application along with transcript, letter of recommendation from part-time/summer employer, letter of recommendation from faculty member and any individual familiar with the applicant's character, academic and extracurricular accomplishments, etc.
NUMBER OF AWARDS: 1
RENEWABLE: Yes, must reapply; same person may not receive award in consecutive years.
CONTACT: Veranda Edmondson, 770/208-7536

2275—UNIVERSITY OF WINDSOR (Outstanding Scholars Award)

401 Sunset Avenue
Windsor Ontario N9B 3P4
CANADA
519/253-3000
FAX: 519/973-7081
E-mail: awards1@uwindsor.ca
Internet: http://www.uwindsor.ca
AMOUNT: $1,000-$2500/year (Canadian); maximum 4 years
DEADLINE(S): MAY 31
FIELD(S): Classics, Modern Languages, French, Philosophy, Music, Physics, Earth Sciences (not Environmental Studies), Economics (not Business and Economics), Chemistry (not Biochemistry), Mathematics and Statistics, Industrial, Mechanical (Materials Option) or Environmental

Engineering or Bachelor of Arts and Science
ELIGIBILITY/REQUIREMENTS: Open to undergraduate students registering in year 1 at the University of Windsor. Must have superior grades. Amount of award based on secondary school accomplishments.
HOW TO APPLY: Automatic. No application required.
RENEWABLE: Yes. Up to 4 years.
CONTACT: Aase Houser
ADDITIONAL INFORMATION: Students in this program will also be mentored in their first year in preparation for guaranteed Outstanding Scholars Appointments in their Department/School (valued at $2,000 Canadian in earnings for each of the 2nd, 3rd, and 4th years) provided all conditions are met.

2276—WESTERN MICHIGAN UNIVERSITY (College of Arts and Sciences/Adli Kara'an Award)

1903 West Michigan
Kalamazoo MI 49008-5337
269/387-8777
FAX: 269/387-6989
E-mail: finaid-info@wmich.edu
Internet: http://www.wmich.edu/finaid
AMOUNT: $75 (spring semester)
FIELD(S): Physical Chemistry
ELIGIBILITY/REQUIREMENTS: Presented to junior who has completed physical chemistry and demonstrated outstanding achievement.
HOW TO APPLY: Chemistry Department faculty selects recipient.

2277—WESTERN MICHIGAN UNIVERSITY (College of Arts and Sciences/Craig B. Peot Memorial Endowed Scholarship)

1903 West Michigan
Kalamazoo MI 49008-5337
269/387-8777
FAX: 269/387-6989
E-mail: finaid-info@wmich.edu
Internet: http://www.wmich.edu/finaid
AMOUNT: Varies
FIELD(S): Chemistry
ELIGIBILITY/REQUIREMENTS: Must be a full-time undergraduate with junior or senior status; must major in Chemistry; minimum 3.0 GPA; demonstrate community service and/or volunteerism.
HOW TO APPLY: Chemistry Department faculty selects recipient.
RENEWABLE: Yes. Up to 2 years.

2278—WESTERN MICHIGAN UNIVERSITY (College of Arts and Sciences/Dr. Susan E. Burns Memorial Scholarship)

1903 West Michigan
Kalamazoo MI 49008-5337
269/387-8777
FAX: 269/387-6989
E-mail: finaid-info@wmich.edu
Internet: http://www.wmich.edu/finaid
AMOUNT: $1,000
DEADLINE(S): MAR 1
FIELD(S): Chemistry
ELIGIBILITY/REQUIREMENTS: Recipient must show financial need. Preference given to women majoring in chemistry. GPA 3.0 for undergraduate and 3.5 for graduate students.
HOW TO APPLY: Contact the Office of Financial Aid for more details.
RENEWABLE: Yes. Up to 2 years.

2279—WESTERN MICHIGAN UNIVERSITY (College of Arts and Sciences/Frederick W. Stanley Jr. Memorial Chemistry Award)

1903 West Michigan
Kalamazoo MI 49008-5337
269/387-8777
FAX: 269/387-6989
E-mail: finaid-info@wmich.edu
Internet: http://www.wmich.edu/finaid
AMOUNT: Varies
DEADLINE(S): MAR 1
FIELD(S): Chemistry
ELIGIBILITY/REQUIREMENTS: Full-time junior, senior, or graduate student majoring in chemistry. Minimum GPA of 2.5; maximum 3.5.
HOW TO APPLY: Contact the Office of Financial Aid for more details.
RENEWABLE: Yes. Must reapply; up to 3 consecutive academic years.

2280—WESTERN MICHIGAN UNIVERSITY (College of Arts and Sciences/Jensen Award)

1903 West Michigan
Kalamazoo MI 49008-5337
269/387-8777
FAX: 269/387-6989
E-mail: finaid-info@wmich.edu
Internet: http://www.wmich.edu/finaid
AMOUNT: $100 (spring semester)
FIELD(S): Organic Chemistry

ELIGIBILITY/REQUIREMENTS: Must have completed 2 semesters of organic chemistry within 1 year and demonstrated outstanding achievement.
HOW TO APPLY: Chemistry Department faculty selects recipient.

2281—WESTERN MICHIGAN UNIVERSITY (College of Arts and Sciences/Kalamazoo Section of the American Chemical Society's Outstanding College Chemistry Student)

1903 West Michigan
Kalamazoo MI 49008-5337
269/387-8777
FAX: 269/387-6989
E-mail: finaid-info@wmich.edu
Internet: http://www.wmich.edu/finaid
AMOUNT: $500 (spring semester)
DEADLINE(S): MAR 1
FIELD(S): Chemistry; Physical Chemistry
ELIGIBILITY/REQUIREMENTS: Open to undergraduates who have completed first-semester Physical Chemistry, who is not a previous award recipient. Must demonstrate excellence both inside and outside the classroom.
HOW TO APPLY: Recommendations from Department. KSACS selects student.
RENEWABLE: No

2282—WESTERN MICHIGAN UNIVERSITY (College of Arts and Sciences/William McCracken Award)

1903 West Michigan
Kalamazoo MI 49008-5337
269/387-8777
FAX: 269/387-6989
E-mail: finaid-info@wmich.edu
Internet: http://www.wmich.edu/finaid
AMOUNT: $50 (spring semester)
DEADLINE(S): MAR 1
FIELD(S): Chemistry
ELIGIBILITY/REQUIREMENTS: Chemistry major who has demonstrated great aptitude in basic chemistry.
HOW TO APPLY: Department faculty selects recipient.
RENEWABLE: No

EARTH SCIENCE/NATURAL RESOURCES

2283—AMERICAN ASSOCIATION OF BLACKS IN ENERGY (AABE)

Western Michigan University

1903 West Michigan
Kalamazoo MI 49008-5337
269/387-8777
FAX: 269/387-6989
E-mail: alumni@wmich.edu
Internet: http://www.wmich.edu/casresearch.html
AMOUNT: Varies
DEADLINE(S): MAR 1
FIELD(S): Mathematics; Computer Science; Engineering; Physical Sciences
ELIGIBILITY/REQUIREMENTS: Freshmen with 2.5 GPA overall and a 3.0 GPA in mathematics and the sciences. Planning to major in engineering, mathematics, computer or physical sciences. Must demonstrate financial need and be a member of one of the underrepresented minority groups in the sciences and technology.
HOW TO APPLY: Contact the Office for Student Financial Aid.
NUMBER OF AWARDS: Varies
RENEWABLE: Yes

2284—AMERICAN CHEMICAL SOCIETY-RUBBER DIVISION

P.O. Box 499
Akron OH 44309-0499
330/972-7814
FAX: 330/972-5269
E-mail: crobinson@rubber.org
Internet: http://www.rubber.org/awards/scholarships.htm
AMOUNT: $5,000
DEADLINE(S): MAR 1
FIELD(S): Chemistry, Physics, Chemical Engineering, Mechanical Engineering, Polymer Science, or other rubber-related discipline
ELIGIBILITY/REQUIREMENTS: Incoming junior or senior enrolled in an accredited college or university in the United States, Canada, Mexico, Brazil or India (countries may change) majoring in a rubber industry-related field. Must have "B" or better overall academic average, and a minimum of 3 semesters or 6 terms completed, and intend to pursue full-time professional employment in the industry.
HOW TO APPLY: Download application from website and fax or mail application , 2 or more nomination letters from professor/nominator. Official transcripts may follow.
NUMBER OF AWARDS: 3
RENEWABLE: Yes. Must reapply for 2nd and final year.
CONTACT: Christie Robinson, Education & Publications Manager

2285—AMERICAN CONGRESS ON SUR-VEYING AND MAPPING (AAGS Joseph F. Dracup Scholarship Award and Nettie Dracup Memorial Scholarships)

6 Montgomery Village Avenue, Suite 403
Gaithersburg MD 20879
240/632-9716, ext. 105
FAX: 240/632-1321
E-mail: pat.canfield@acsm.net
Internet: http://www.acsm.net/scholar.html
AMOUNT: $2,000
DEADLINE(S): DEC 1
FIELD(S): Geodetic Surveying
ELIGIBILITY/REQUIREMENTS: Open to students enrolled in 4-year degree programs in surveying or closely related degree programs, such as geomatics or surveying engineering; must be U.S. citizen. Must join ACSM.
HOW TO APPLY: Contact ACSM for membership information and applications. Must submit personal statement (including goals and financial need), letters of recommendation, and transcripts.
NUMBER OF AWARDS: 3

2286—AMERICAN CONGRESS ON SUR-VEYING AND MAPPING (Allen Chelf Scholarship)

6 Montgomery Village Avenue, Suite 403
Gaithersburg MD 20879
240/632-9716, ext. 105
FAX: 240/632-1321
E-mail: pat.canfield@acsm.net
Internet: http://www.acsm.net/scholar.html
AMOUNT: $500
DEADLINE(S): DEC 1
FIELD(S): Surveying
ELIGIBILITY/REQUIREMENTS: Open to students enrolled in a 2-year or 4-year surveying (or closely related fields) degree program, either full or part time, in the U.S.; must join ACSM.
HOW TO APPLY: Contact ACSM for membership information and applications. Submit personal statement (including goals and financial need), letters of recommendation, and transcripts.
NUMBER OF AWARDS: 1

2287—AMERICAN CONGRESS ON SUR-VEYING AND MAPPING (Bernsten International Scholarship in Surveying Technology)

6 Montgomery Village Avenue,
Suite 403
Gaithersburg MD 20879
240/632-9716, ext. 105
FAX: 240/632-1321
E-mail: pat.canfield@acsm.net
Internet: http://www.acsm.net/scholar.html
AMOUNT: $500
DEADLINE(S): DEC 31
FIELD(S): Surveying Technology
ELIGIBILITY/REQUIREMENTS: Open to students enrolled in 2-year degree programs in surveying technology; must join ACSM.
HOW TO APPLY: Contact ACSM for membership information and applications. Submit personal statement (including goals and financial need), letters of recommendation, and transcripts.
NUMBER OF AWARDS: 1

2288—AMERICAN CONGRESS ON SUR-VEYING AND MAPPING (Cady McDonnell Memorial Scholarship)

6 Montgomery Village Avenue, Suite 403
Gaithersburg MD 20879
240/632-9716, ext. 105
FAX: 240/632-1321
E-mail: pat.canfield@acsm.net
Internet: http://www.acsm.net/scholar.html
AMOUNT: $1,000
DEADLINE(S): DEC 31
FIELD(S): Surveying
ELIGIBILITY/REQUIREMENTS: Open to women enrolled in a 2-year or 4-year surveying (or closely related) degree program, either full or part time. Must be residents of Montana, Idaho, Washington, Oregon, Wyoming, Colorado, Utah, Nevada, California, Arizona, New Mexico, Arkansas or Hawaii; must join ACSM.
HOW TO APPLY: Contact ACSM for membership information and applications. Submit personal statement (including goals and financial need), letters of recommendation, and transcripts.
NUMBER OF AWARDS: 1

2289—AMERICAN CONGRESS ON SUR-VEYING AND MAPPING (Cartography and Geographic Information Society Scholarship)

6 Montgomery Village Avenue, Suite 403
Gaithersburg MD 20879
240/632-9716, ext. 105
FAX: 240/632-1321
E-mail: pat.canfield@acsm.net
Internet: http://www.acsm.net/scholar.html
AMOUNT: $1,000
DEADLINE(S): DEC 31
FIELD(S): Cartography; Geographic Information Science
ELIGIBILITY/REQUIREMENTS: Open to outstanding students enrolled full time in a 4-year or graduate-degree program. Preference given to undergraduates with junior or senior standing; must join ACSM.
HOW TO APPLY: Contact ACSM for membership information and applications. Submit personal statement (including goals and financial need), letters of recommendation, and transcripts.
NUMBER OF AWARDS: 1

2290—AMERICAN CONGRESS ON SUR-VEYING AND MAPPING (National Society of Professional Surveyors Board of Governor's Scholarship)

6 Montgomery Village Avenue, Suite 403
Gaithersburg MD 20879
240/632-9716, ext. 105
FAX: 240/632-1321
E-mail: pat.canfield@acsm.net
Internet: http://www.acsm.net/scholar.html
AMOUNT: $1,000
DEADLINE(S): DEC 31
FIELD(S): Surveying
ELIGIBILITY/REQUIREMENTS: Open to students enrolled in studies in surveying, entering their junior year in a 4-year degree program, who have maintained a minimum 3.0 GPA; must join ACSM.
HOW TO APPLY: Contact ACSM for membership information and applications. Submit personal statement (including goals and financial need), letters of recommendation, and transcripts.
NUMBER OF AWARDS: 1

2291—AMERICAN CONGRESS ON SUR-VEYING AND MAPPING (National Society of Professional Surveyors Forum for Equal Opportunity/Mary Feindt Scholarship)

6 Montgomery Village Avenue, Suite 403
Gaithersburg MD 20879
240/632-9716, ext. 105
FAX: 240/632-1321
pat.canfield@acsm.net
Internet: http://www.acsm.net/scholar.html
AMOUNT: $1,000

DEADLINE(S): DEC 31
FIELD(S): Surveying
ELIGIBILITY/REQUIREMENTS: Open to women enrolled in a 4-year degree program in a surveying and mapping curriculum within the U.S. Must submit personal statement (including goals and financial need), letters of recommendation, and transcripts. Must join ACSM.
HOW TO APPLY: Contact ACSM for membership information and applications. Submit personal statement (including goals and financial need), letters of recommendation, and transcripts.
NUMBER OF AWARDS: 1

2292—AMERICAN CONGRESS ON SURVEYING AND MAPPING (National Society of Professional Surveyors Scholarships)

6 Montgomery Village Avenue, Suite 403
Gaithersburg MD 20879
240/632-9716, ext. 105
FAX: 240/632-1321
E-mail: pat.canfield@acsm.net
Internet: http://www.acsm.net/scholar.html
AMOUNT: $1,000
DEADLINE(S): DEC 31
FIELD(S): Surveying
ELIGIBILITY/REQUIREMENTS: Open to students enrolled in 4-year degree programs in surveying or closely related degree programs, such as geomatics or surveying engineering. Awards recognize outstanding students enrolled full time. Must submit personal statement (including goals and financial need), letters of recommendation, and transcripts. Must join ACSM.
HOW TO APPLY: Contact ACSM for membership information and applications. Submit personal statement (including goals and financial need), letters of recommendation, and transcripts.
NUMBER OF AWARDS: 2

2293—AMERICAN CONGRESS ON SURVEYING AND MAPPING (Schonstedt Scholarships in Surveying)

6 Montgomery Village Avenue, Suite 403
Gaithersburg MD 20879
240/632-9716, ext. 105
FAX: 240/632-1321
E-mail: pat.canfield@acsm.net
Internet: http://www.acsm.net/scholar.html
AMOUNT: $1,500
DEADLINE(S): DEC 31
FIELD(S): Surveying

ELIGIBILITY/REQUIREMENTS: Open to students enrolled in 4-year degree programs in surveying or closely related degree programs, such as geomatics or surveying engineering. Preference given to applicants with junior or senior standing; must join ACSM.
HOW TO APPLY: Contact ACSM for membership information and applications. Submit personal statement (including goals and financial need), letters of recommendation, and transcripts.
NUMBER OF AWARDS: 2 (Schonstedt also donates a magnetic locator to the surveying program at each recipient's school.)

2294—AMERICAN COUNCIL OF ENGINEERING COMPANIES OF NEW JERSEY (Louis Goldberg Scholarship Fund)

66 Morris Avenue, Suite 1A
Springfield NJ 07081
973/564-5848
FAX: 973/564-7480
E-mail: Barbara@acecnj.org
Internet: http://www.acecnj.org
AMOUNT: $1,000
DEADLINE(S): DEC 5
FIELD(S): Engineering; Land Surveying
ELIGIBILITY/REQUIREMENTS: Must be a U.S. citizen; enrolled in an ABET-accredited engineering or land surveying program, in a New Jersey college or university; seeking a bachelor of science in engineering; and be entering their 3rd or 4th year (5th year in a 5-year program) in the fall. Scholarships will be awarded in March and will be based on scholastic merit and achievements. Students graduating in December are not eligible.
HOW TO APPLY: Write or download application from website.

2295—AMERICAN GROUND WATER TRUST (Amtrol, Inc. Scholarship)

16 Centre Street
Concord NH 03301
603/228-5444
FAX: 603/228-6557
E-mail: trustinfo@agwt.org
Internet: http://www.amtrol.com/scholarships.htm
AMOUNT: $1,000
DEADLINE(S): JUN 1
FIELD(S): Environmental Science; Environmental Engineering; Marine Science; Natural Resources
ELIGIBILITY/REQUIREMENTS: Must be high school seniors; intend to pursue a career in a ground water-related field; be entering their freshmen year at a 4-year accredited college or university; have a

minimum 3.0 GPA in high school; have completed a science/environmental project in high school that directly involved ground water resources or have had vacation/out-of-school work experience related to the environment and natural resources; be U.S. citizens or legal residents of the U.S.
HOW TO APPLY: Send application that has been signed by a teacher at the applicant's high school; a 500-word essay (on "Ground Water: An Important Environmental and Economic Resource for America") and a 300-word description of the applicant's high school ground water project and/or practical work experience; and 2 letters of recommendation. Also, documentary evidence of scholastic achievements and references will be requested in mid-June from finalists.

2296—AMERICAN GROUND WATER TRUST (Baroid Award)

16 Centre Street
Concord NH 03301
603/228-5444
FAX: 603/228-6557
E-mail: trustinfo@agwt.org
Internet: http://www.agwt.org/scholarships.htm
AMOUNT: $1,000
DEADLINE(S): JUN 1
FIELD(S): Environmental Science; Earth Science
ELIGIBILITY/REQUIREMENTS: Open to high school seniors entering their freshman year at a 4-year accredited college or university intending to pursue a career in ground water-related fields. Minimum 3.0 GPA. Must either have completed a science/environmental project in high school that directly involved ground water resources or have had vacation/out-of-schoolwork experience related to the environment and natural resources; and be a U.S. citizen or legal resident of the U.S.
HOW TO APPLY: See website for application, countersigned by high school teacher. Submit with a 500-word essay and a 300-word description of your ground water project and/or practical environmental work experience, along with 2 letters of recommendation, transcripts, and confirmation of acceptance from the college or university.
NUMBER OF AWARDS: 1
RENEWABLE: No

2297—AMERICAN GROUND WATER TRUST (Ben Everson Award)

16 Centre Street
Concord NH 03301

603/228-5444
FAX: 603/228-6557
E-mail: trustinfo@agwt.org
Internet: http://www.agwt.org/
scholarships.htm
AMOUNT: $2,500
DEADLINE(S): JUN 1
FIELD(S): Environmental Science; Earth
Science
ELIGIBILITY/REQUIREMENTS: Open
to high school seniors entering their freshman year at a 4-year accredited college or
university, who intend to pursue a career in
ground water-related fields. Minimum 3.0
GPA. Must either have completed a sci-
ence/environmental project in high school
directly involving ground water resources
or have had vacation/out-of-schoolwork
experience related to the environment and
natural resources; be a U.S. citizen or legal
resident; and attest that 1 parent is
employed in the ground water industry.
HOW TO APPLY: See website for application, countersigned by high school
teacher. Submit with a 500-word essay and
a 300-word description of your ground
water project and/or practical environmental work experience, along with 2 letters of
recommendation, transcripts, and confirmation of acceptance from the college or
university, and letter establishing parent's
employment.
NUMBER OF AWARDS: 1
RENEWABLE: No

2298—AMERICAN INDIAN SCIENCE AND ENGINEERING SOCIETY (A. T. Anderson Memorial Scholarship)

P.O. Box 9828
Albuquerque NM 87119-9828
505/765-1052
FAX: 505/765-5608
E-mail: scholarships@aises.org
Internet: http://www.aises.org/
highered
AMOUNT: $1,000
DEADLINE(S): JUN 15
FIELD(S): Medicine; Natural Resources;
Science; Engineering
ELIGIBILITY/REQUIREMENTS: Open
to undergraduate and graduate students
who are at least 1/4 American Indian or
recognized as member of a tribe. Must be
member of AISES ($10 fee), enrolled full
time at an accredited institution, and
demonstrate financial need. Minimum
GPA 2.7.
HOW TO APPLY: See website or contact
Society for an application and/or member-
ship information.
RENEWABLE: Yes
CONTACT: Tina Pino

2299—AMERICAN METEOROLOGY SOCIETY (AMS/Crow Scholarship)

Fellowship/Scholarship Program
45 Beacon Street
Boston MA 02108-3693
617/227-2426
FAX: 617/742-8718
E-mail: dfernand@ametsoc.org or
armstrong@ametsoc.org
Internet: http://www.ametsoc.org
AMOUNT: Varies
DEADLINE(S): FEB 21
FIELD(S): Atmospheric Sciences;
Oceanography; Hydrology
ELIGIBILITY/REQUIREMENTS: Open
to juniors entering senior year, who are
U.S. citizens or permanent residents and
has evidenced an interest in applied meteorology. MUST be majoring in atmospheric or related oceanic or hydrologic sciences
and/or must show clear intent to make the
atmospheric or related sciences their
career.
HOW TO APPLY: See website for additional information and application or e-
mail or write to contact below at AMS
headquarters (include SASE).
NUMBER OF AWARDS: Varies
CONTACT: Donna Sampson, Development & Student Programs Manager, ext.
246 or Stephanie Armstrong, Director of
Development, ext 235

2300—AMERICAN METEOROLOGY SOCIETY (AMS/Freshman Undergraduate Scholarship Program)

Fellowship/Scholarship Program
45 Beacon Street
Boston MA 02108-3693
617/227-2426
FAX: 617/742-8718
E-mail: dfernand@ametsoc.org or
armstrong@ametsoc.org
Internet: http://www.ametsoc.org
AMOUNT: $2,500
DEADLINE(S): FEB 21
FIELD(S): Atmospheric Sciences;
Oceanography; Hydrology
ELIGIBILITY/REQUIREMENTS: Open
to high school seniors entering freshman
year, who are U.S. citizens or permanent
residents; based on academic excellence.
HOW TO APPLY: See website for addi-
tional information and application or e-
mail or write to contact below at AMS
headquarters (include SASE).
NUMBER OF AWARDS: Varies
RENEWABLE: Yes. For sophomore year
only. Must demonstrate a successful 1st

year and plans to continue studies in the
AMS-related sciences.
CONTACT: Donna Sampson, Develop-
ment & Student Programs Manager, ext.
246 or Stephanie Armstrong, Director of
Development, ext 235

2301—AMERICAN METEOROLOGY SOCIETY (AMS/Glahn Scholarship)

Fellowship/Scholarship Program
45 Beacon Street
Boston MA 02108-3693
617/227-2426
FAX: 617/742-8718
E-mail: dfernand@ametsoc.org or
armstrong@ametsoc.org
Internet: http://www.ametsoc.org
AMOUNT: Varies
DEADLINE(S): FEB 21
FIELD(S): Atmospheric Sciences;
Oceanography; Hydrology
ELIGIBILITY/REQUIREMENTS: Open
to juniors entering senior year, who are
U.S. citizens or permanent residents and
has evidenced an interest in statistical
meteorology. MUST be majoring in atmospheric or related oceanic or hydrologic sciences and/or must show clear intent to
make the atmospheric or related sciences
their career.
HOW TO APPLY: See website for additional information and application or e-
mail or write to contact below at AMS
headquarters (include SASE).
NUMBER OF AWARDS: Varies
CONTACT: Donna Sampson, Development & Student Programs Manager, ext.
246 or Stephanie Armstrong, Director of
Development, ext 235

2302—AMERICAN METEOROLOGY SOCIETY (AMS/Industry Minority Scholarships)

Fellowship/Scholarship Program
45 Beacon Street
Boston MA 02108-3693
617/227-2426
FAX: 617/742-8718
E-mail: dfernand@ametsoc.org or
armstrong@ametsoc.org
Internet: http://www.ametsoc.org
AMOUNT: $3,000
DEADLINE(S): FEB 21
FIELD(S): Atmospheric Sciences;
Oceanography; Hydrology
ELIGIBILITY/REQUIREMENTS: Open
to minority—especially Hispanic, Native
American, and Black/African American—
high school seniors entering freshman year
at a 4-year U.S. accredited institution.
Must be U.S. citizens or permanent resi-

dents and mustplan to pursue a career in the atmospheric or related oceanic or hydrologic sciences.

HOW TO APPLY: See website for additional information and application or e-mail or write to contact below at AMS headquarters (include SASE).

NUMBER OF AWARDS: Varies

RENEWABLE: Yes. For sophomore year only. Must demonstrate a successful 1st year and plans to continue studies in the AMS-related sciences.

CONTACT: Donna Sampson, Development & Student Programs Manager, ext. 246 or Stephanie Armstrong, Director of Development, ext 235

2303—AMERICAN METEOROLOGY SOCIETY (AMS/Murphy Scholarship)

Fellowship/Scholarship Program
45 Beacon Street
Boston MA 02108-3693
617/227-2426
FAX: 617/742-8718
E-mail: dfernand@ametsoc.org or armstrong@ametsoc.org
Internet: http://www.ametsoc.org
AMOUNT: Varies
DEADLINE(S): FEB 21
FIELD(S): Atmospheric Sciences; Oceanography; Hydrology

ELIGIBILITY/REQUIREMENTS: Open to juniors entering senior year, who are U.S. citizens or permanent residents, and who, through curricular or extracurricular activities, has evidenced an interest in weather forecasting or in the value and utilization of forecasts. MUST be majoring in atmospheric or related oceanic or hydrologic sciences and/or must show clear intent to make the atmospheric or related sciences their career.

HOW TO APPLY: See website for additional information and application or e-mail or write to contact below at AMS headquarters (include SASE).

NUMBER OF AWARDS: Varies

CONTACT: Donna Sampson, Development & Student Programs Manager, ext. 246 or Stephanie Armstrong, Director of Development, ext 235

2304—AMERICAN METEOROLOGY SOCIETY (AMS/Schroeder Scholarship)

Fellowship/Scholarship Program
45 Beacon Street
Boston MA 02108-3693
617/227-2426
FAX: 617/742-8718
E-mail: dfernand@ametsoc.org or armstrong@ametsoc.org

Internet: http://www.ametsoc.org
AMOUNT: Varies
DEADLINE(S): FEB 21
FIELD(S): Atmospheric Sciences; Oceanography; Hydrology

ELIGIBILITY/REQUIREMENTS: Open to juniors entering senior year, who are U.S. citizens or permanent residents. MUST be majoring in atmospheric or related oceanic or hydrologic sciences and/or must show clear intent to make the atmospheric or related sciences their career. Must demonstrate financial need.

HOW TO APPLY: See website for additional information and application or e-mail or write to contact below at AMS headquarters (include SASE).

NUMBER OF AWARDS: Varies

CONTACT: Donna Sampson, Development & Student Programs Manager, ext. 246 or Stephanie Armstrong, Director of Development, ext 235

2305—AMERICAN MUSEUM OF NATURAL HISTORY (Young Naturalist Awards)

Scholastic, Inc.
555 Broadway
New York NY 10012-3999
212/343-6582 or
800/SCHOLASTIC
FAX: 212/343-4885
E-mail: A&WGeneralinfo@scholastic.com
Internet: http://www.amnh.org/youngnaturalistawards
AMOUNT: Up to $2,500
DEADLINE(S): JAN
FIELD(S): Earth Science, Astronomy, & Cultural Studies

ELIGIBILITY/REQUIREMENTS: For students in grades 7-12 in a school in the U.S., Canada, U.S. territories, or U.S.-sponsored school abroad. Program focuses on finding and rewarding excellence in biology. Students are encouraged to perform observation-based projects that require creativity, inquiry, and critical analysis. Specific topics vary annually.

HOW TO APPLY: See website for application.

NUMBER OF AWARDS: 48

2306—AMERICAN PUBLIC POWER ASSOCIATION (DEED Student Research Grants and Internships)

2301 M Street, NW
Washington DC 20036-1484
202/467-2900
FAX: 202/467-2910
E-mail: DEED@APPAnet.org

Internet: http://www.appanet.org/
AMOUNT: $4,000
DEADLINE(S): FEB 15 and OCT 1
FIELD(S): Electric, Energy

ELIGIBILITY/REQUIREMENTS: Open to students studying in energy-related disciplines at accredited colleges or universities in the U.S. or Canada. DEED member to sponsor their research grant or internship (find a DEED member utility, and email request for specific contact information to DEED).

HOW TO APPLY: See website for information and application. Applications and transcript must be sent from a DEED member utility and must be dated and signed on the last page by an authorized individual at that utility. A copy must also be sent to the DEED regional board director.

NUMBER OF AWARDS: Up to 10

RENEWABLE: No

ADDITIONAL INFORMATION: Student research grants/internships may be split among students collaborating on a single project. $1,500 will be withheld until satisfactory completion of the project.

2307—AMERICAN PUBLIC POWER ASSOCIATION (DEED Technical Design Project)

2301 M Street, NW
Washington DC 20036-1484
202/467-2900
FAX: 202/467-2910
E-mail: DEED@APPAnet.org
Internet: http://www.appanet.org/
AMOUNT: $5,000
DEADLINE(S): FEB 15 and OCT 1
FIELD(S): Electric, Energy

ELIGIBILITY/REQUIREMENTS: Open to students studying in energy-related disciplines at accredited colleges or universites in the U.S. or Canada.

HOW TO APPLY: See website for information and application. Submit with required signatures and transcript with a to the DEED regional board director.

NUMBER OF AWARDS: 1

RENEWABLE: No

ADDITIONAL INFORMATION: Student research grants/internships may be split among students collaborating on a single project. $1,500 will be withheld until satisfactory completion of the project.

2308—ASM MATERIALS EDUCATION FOUNDATION (Undergraduate Scholarships)

9639 Kinsman Road
Materials Park OH 44073-0002
440/338-5151

FAX: 440/338-4634
Internet: http://www.asm
international.org/foundation
AMOUNT: $500 to full tuition
DEADLINE(S): MAY 1
FIELD(S): Metallurgy; Materials Science
ELIGIBILITY/REQUIREMENTS: For undergraduate students majoring in metallurgy or materials. For citizens of the U.S, Canada, or Mexico who are enrolled in a recognized college or university in one of those countries. Must be a student member of ASM International. Some awards have more specific requirements.
HOW TO APPLY: See website or write to ASM for membership information or more details and application.
NUMBER OF AWARDS: 10-37

2309—ASPRS: THE IMAGING & GEOSPATIAL INFORMATION SOCIETY (Robert E. Altenhofen Memorial Scholarship)

ASPRS Awards Program
5410 Grosvenor Lane, Suite 210
Bethesda MD 20814-2160
301/493-0290
FAX: 301/493-0208
E-mail: scholarships@asprs.org
Internet: http://www.asprs.org
AMOUNT: $2,000
DEADLINE(S): DEC 1
FIELD(S): Photogrammetry
ELIGIBILITY/REQUIREMENTS: Undergraduates or graduates who display exceptional interest and ability in the theoretical aspects of photogrammetry; must be enrolled in an accredited college or university and be active or student members of ASPRS.
HOW TO APPLY: Submit 6 copies of the completed application and the following supporting materials: academic transcripts, including a separate list of relevant courses taken; 2 completed reference forms from faculty members who have knowledge of your abilities; samples of your work; description of your research goals; a 2-page statement regarding your plans for continuing studies in theoretical photogrammetry; and papers, research reports, or other items that indicate capability in these fields. Note: Electronic submissions encouraged.
NUMBER OF AWARDS: 1
RENEWABLE: No
CONTACT: Scholarship Administrator
ADDITIONAL INFORMATION: The recipient is obligated to provide a final report to ASPRS of his/her scholastic accomplishments during the period for which the award is granted.

2310—ASSOCIATION FOR WOMEN IN SCIENCE (Kirsten R. Lorentzen Award in Physics)

7008 Richard Drive
Bethesda MD 20817-4838
E-mail: awisedfd@awisedfd@awis.org
Internet: http://www.awis.org/careers/edfoundation.html
AMOUNT: $1,000
DEADLINE(S): Late JAN
FIELD(S): Physics; Geoscience
ELIGIBILITY/REQUIREMENTS: College sophomore or junior may apply. Must be a U.S. citizen attending a college in the U.S.
HOW TO APPLY: See website for application and instructions.
NUMBER OF AWARDS: 1
RENEWABLE: No
CONTACT: Dr. Barbara Filner at e-mail above

2311—ASSOCIATION OF CALIFORNIA WATER AGENCIES (ACWA)

910 K Street, Suite 100
Sacramento CA 95814
916/441-4545
FAX: 916/325-4849
E-mail: acwabox@acwanet.com
Internet: http://www.acwanet.com
AMOUNT: $1,500
DEADLINE(S): APR 1
FIELD(S): Water Resources-related fields (including engineering, agriculture, environmental studies, public administration)
ELIGIBILITY/REQUIREMENTS: Based on scholastic achievement, commitment and motivation as well as financial need.
HOW TO APPLY: Download applications and guidelines from website, or call or e-mail ACWA, or contact your school's financial aid department.
NUMBER OF AWARDS: At least 6

2312—BARRY GOLDWATER SCHOLARSHIP AND EXCELLENCE IN EDUCATION FOUNDATION

6225 Brandon Avenue, Suite 315
Springfield VA 22150-2519
703/756-6012
FAX: 703/756-6015
Internet: http://www.act.org/goldwater
AMOUNT: Up to $7,500/year
DEADLINE(S): FEB 1

FIELD(S): Mathematics; Natural Sciences; Engineering
ELIGIBILITY/REQUIREMENTS: Open to college sophomores and juniors with a minimum 3.0 GPA. Must be U.S. citizen, resident alien, or American national pursuing a degree in math, natural sciences, or engineering at an accredited institution that contributes to technological advances.
HOW TO APPLY: See website or contact your Goldwater Faculty Representative on campus. Students must be nominated by their institution.
NUMBER OF AWARDS: 300
CONTACT: Goldwater Faculty Representative

2313—CALIFORNIA LAND SURVEYORS EDUCATION FOUNDATION

P.O. Box 9098
Santa Rosa CA 95404
707/578-6016
FAX: 707/578-4406
E-mail: clsa@californiasurveyors.org
Internet: http://www.california
surveyors.org
AMOUNT: $375-$2,000
DEADLINE(S): DEC 7
FIELD(S): Land Surveying
ELIGIBILITY/REQUIREMENTS: Criteria vary with scholarship; see website for details.
HOW TO APPLY: See website to apply online.
CONTACT: Dorothy Calegari, Executive Director

2314—CANADIAN SOCIETY OF EXPLORATION GEOPHYSICISTS (CSEG Trust Fund)

905, 510-5th Street, SW
Calgary Alberta T2P 3S2 CANADA
403/262-0015
FAX: 403/262-7383
E-mail: cseg.office@shaw.ca
Internet: http://www.cseg.ca
AMOUNT: $2,000 Canadian
DEADLINE(S): JUL 15
FIELD(S): Exploration Geophysics
ELIGIBILITY/REQUIREMENTS: For undergraduate students whose grades are above-average and graduate students. Must be pursuing a course of studies in Canada directed toward a career in exploration geophysics in industry, teaching, or research. Certain awards impose additional qualifications. Financial need is considered.
HOW TO APPLY: Contact CSEG or check the website for an application. Complete questionnaire to determine eli-

gibility. Submit application with letters of recommendation.

2315—CONNECTICUT FOREST AND PARK ASSOCIATION (James L. Goodwin Memorial Scholarship)

16 Meriden Road
Rockfall CT 06481
860/346-2372
FAX: 860/347-7463
E-mail: info@ctwoodlands.org
Internet: http://www.ctwood
lands.org
AMOUNT: $1,000-$5,000
DEADLINE(S): APR 1
FIELD(S): Forestry; Forest Resource Management; Silviculture
ELIGIBILITY/REQUIREMENTS: Must be a Connecticut resident enrolled in or about to enroll in an undergraduate or graduate curriculum of silviculture or forest resource management. Financial need considered.
HOW TO APPLY: Call for application.
NUMBER OF AWARDS: Multiple
RENEWABLE: Yes
CONTACT: Adam R. Moore, Executive Director

2316—EARTHWATCH STUDENT CHALLENGE AWARDS (High School Student Research Expeditions)

3 Clock Tower Place, Suite 100
P.O. Box 75
Maynard MA 01754
800/776-0188
978/461-0081, ext. 116
FAX: 978/450-1288
E-mail: scap@earthwatch.org
Internet: www.earthwatch.org
AMOUNT: Travel/Living expenses (1-3 week field expedition)
DEADLINE(S): Late Fall—call for details
FIELD(S): Biology, Field Studies, Physics, Natural Resources, Environmental Science
ELIGIBILITY/REQUIREMENTS: Awards for high school sophomores, juniors, and seniors, especially those with limited exposure to the sciences. Must attend high school in the U.S., be at least age 16 by June 15 during year of program. Teams of 6 to 8 students spend 1 to 3 weeks at sites in North or Central America.
HOW TO APPLY: Students must be nominated by a teacher. Write or visit website for further information.
NUMBER OF AWARDS: About 85

2317—EDWARD AND ANNA RANGE SCHMIDT CHARITABLE TRUST (Grants and Emergency Financial Assistance)

P.O. Box 770982
Eagle River AK 99577
AMOUNT: Varies
DEADLINE(S): Immediate consideration
FIELD(S): Earth and Environmental Sciences
ELIGIBILITY/REQUIREMENTS: Open to Alaska residents or students in Alaska programs for a variety of expenses incurred by students, such as internship support, travel, expenses related to workshops and science fairs, support needed to secure employment in earth science-related fields, or emergency needs. Alaska Natives and other minorities are urged to apply.
HOW TO APPLY: Apply by letter from self and a sponsor (teacher, advisor, or other adult familiar with applicant's situation) describing applicant, nature of financial need, and amount requested.
RENEWABLE: No

2318—EXPLORERS CLUB, THE (Youth Activity Fund)

46 East 70th Street
New York NY 10021
212/628-8383
FAX: 212/639-9391
E-mail: office@explorers.org
Internet: http://www.explorers.org
AMOUNT: $500-$1,500
DEADLINE(S): JAN 31
FIELD(S): Natural Sciences
ELIGIBILITY/REQUIREMENTS: Open to high school and undergraduate college student for field research anywhere in the world under the supervision of a trained scientist. Must be U.S. citizen or permanent resident.
HOW TO APPLY: Write or see website for details. Provide a brief explanation of proposed project, as well as 2 letters of recommendation. Joint funding is encouraged.

2319—FLORIDA FEDERATION OF GARDEN CLUBS, INC. (FFGC Scholarships for College Students)

706 Glen Eagle Drive
Winter Springs FL 32708
407/971-6979
Internet: http://www.ffgc.org
AMOUNT: $650-$3,000
DEADLINE(S): MAY 1

FIELD(S): Agriculture; Environmental & Conservation issues; Botany; Biology; Forestry; Horticulture; Ecology; Marine Biology; Wildflowers; Butterflies; Landscaping
ELIGIBILITY/REQUIREMENTS: Must be U.S. citizen and Florida resident for at least 1 year, with 3.0 GPA, attending a college or university in Florida. Financial need considered.
HOW TO APPLY: See website or contact FFGC Chair for an application.
RENEWABLE: Yes, must reapply.
CONTACT: Jane Meherg, Scholarship Chairman

2320—GERBER SCIENTIFIC, INC. (H. Joseph Gerber 1947 Scholars Fund Endowment at Rensselaer Polytechnic Institute)

83 Gerber Road West
South Windsor CT 06074
860/648-8027
Internet: http://www.gerber
scientific.com/community/
scholarships.htm
AMOUNT: Varies
DEADLINE(S): MAR 15
FIELD(S): Engineering, Mathematics, Computer Science, Natural Sciences
ELIGIBILITY/REQUIREMENTS: Available to full-time students pursuing a baccalaureate degree at Rensselaer Polytechnic Institute's Troy, New York, campus. Awards are determined by the Rensselaer Office of Financial Aid. Preference is given to residents of the state of Connecticut.
HOW TO APPLY: Applications are available from the Rensselaer Office of Financial Aid.

2321—GERBER SCIENTIFIC, INC. (H. Joseph Gerber Vision Scholarship Program)

83 Gerber Road West
South Windsor CT 06074
860/648-8027
Internet: http://www.gerber
scientific.com/community/
scholarships.htm
AMOUNT: Varies
DEADLINE(S): MAR 15
FIELD(S): Engineering, Mathematics, Computer Science, Natural Sciences
ELIGIBILITY/REQUIREMENTS: Available to high school seniors attending South Windsor, Manchester or Tolland

High, or Gerber employees' children who meet the requirements.

HOW TO APPLY: Applications are available in the high school guidance office.

NUMBER OF AWARDS: 50

2322—HAWAII COMMUNITY FOUNDATION (William James & Dorothy Bading Lanquist Fund)

1164 Bishop Street, Suite 800
Honolulu HI 96813
808/537-6333 or toll free:
888/731-3863
FAX: 808/521-6286
E-mail: info@hcf-hawaii.org
Internet: http://www.hcf-hawaii.org

DEADLINE(S): MAR 1

FIELD(S): Physical Sciences and related fields (excluding Biology and Social Sciences)

ELIGIBILITY/REQUIREMENTS: Must be residents of Hawaii; junior or senior undergraduate students enrolled full time in an accredited 2- or 4-year college or university; and demonstrate financial need, good moral character, and academic achievement (minimum GPA of 2.7).

HOW TO APPLY: See website. Send application with 2 letters of recommendation.

2323—INSTITUTE OF MINING AND METALLURGY (G. Vernon Hobson Bequest)

Danum House, South Parade
Doncaster DN1 2DY ENGLAND
+44 (0)1302 320486
FAX: +44(0)1302 380900
E-mail: graham.woodrow@iom3.org
Internet: http://www.iom3.org/
awards/scholarships.htm

AMOUNT: Up to £1,300

DEADLINE(S): APR 8

FIELD(S): Mining; Metallurgy

ELIGIBILITY/REQUIREMENTS: Fellowships tenable at a United Kingdom university for research into all branches of extractive metallurgy and mineral processing, and in special cases, for expenditure related to such research. Based on academic excellence and scholarship, NOT financial need. Preference given to IMM members.

HOW TO APPLY: Contact Dr. Woodrow at above address or see website for an application or membership information.

NUMBER OF AWARDS: 1

CONTACT: Dr. G. J. M. Woodrow, Deputy Chief Executive

2324—INTERTRIBAL TIMBER COUNCIL (Truman D. Picard Scholarship)

Education Committee

1112 NE 21st Avenue, Suite 4
Portland OR 97232
503/282-4296
FAX: 503/282-1274
E-mail: itc1@teleport.com
Internet: http://www.itcnet.org

AMOUNT: $1,500-$2,000

DEADLINE(S): Varies

FIELD(S): Natural Resources (such as forestry; range management; environmental science)

ELIGIBILITY/REQUIREMENTS: Applicant must be an enrolled member of a federally recognized tribe in the U.S.

HOW TO APPLY: Send letter of application (maximum 2 pages) demonstrating interest in natural resources; commitment to education, community/culture; academic merit; and financial need. Also send résumé; 3 letters of reference (1 from school advisor); and validated enrollment in a federally recognized tribe or Native Alaska Corporation. High school students must also provide documented proof of acceptance to an institution of higher education to study in the area of natural resources, along with high school transcripts; college students must submit documented proof of study in the area of natural resources, along with college transcripts.

NUMBER OF AWARDS: 6-8 for college students and 1-2 for graduating high school seniors.

RENEWABLE: Yes, must reapply.

2325—MINERALOGICAL SOCIETY OF AMERICA (MSA Grant for Research in Crystallography)

1015 18th Street NW, Suite 601
Washington DC 20036-5212
202/775-4344
FAX: 202/775-0018
E-mail: j_a_speer@minsocam.org
Internet: http://www.minsocam.org

AMOUNT: $5,000

DEADLINE(S): JUN 1

FIELD(S): Crystallography

ELIGIBILITY/REQUIREMENTS: Research grant based on qualifications of applicant; quality, innovativeness, and scientific significance of proposed research; and the likelihood of success of the project. Applicant must have reached his or her 25th birthday but not have reached his or her 36th birthday on the date the grant is awarded. There are no restrictions on how funds are spent, as long as they are used in support of research.

HOW TO APPLY: See website or contact MSA Business Office for application.

CONTACT: Dr. J. Alex Speer at the MSA Business Office

2326—MINERALOGICAL SOCIETY OF AMERICA (MSA Grant for Student Research in Mineralogy and Petrology)

1015 18th Street NW, Suite 601
Washington DC 20036-5212
202/775-4344
FAX: 202/775-0018
E-mail: j_a_speer@minsocam.org
Internet: http://www.minsocam.org

AMOUNT: $5,000

DEADLINE(S): JUN 1

FIELD(S): Mineralogy; Petrology

ELIGIBILITY/REQUIREMENTS: Research grant for undergraduate or graduate students based on qualifications of applicant; the quality, innovativeness, and scientific significance of the proposed research; and the likelihood of success of the project. There are no restrictions on how funds are spent, as long as they are used in support of research.

HOW TO APPLY: See website or contact MSA Business Office for application.

NUMBER OF AWARDS: 2

CONTACT: Dr. J. Alex Speer

2327—MONTANA FEDERATION OF GARDEN CLUBS LIFE MEMBERS

214 Wayne Lane
Hamilton MT 59340
406/363-5693
E-mail: elizabethhammt@aol.com

AMOUNT: $1,000

DEADLINE(S): MAY 1

FIELD(S): Conservation; Horticulture; Park Forestry; Floriculture; Greenhouse Management

ELIGIBILITY/REQUIREMENTS: Must be a sophomore in a Montana college; demonstrate financial need; and GPA of 2.7.

HOW TO APPLY: No formal application form. Submit college transcript; letter of application detailing future plans, short autobiography; color photo; letters of reference from instructors.

NUMBER OF AWARDS: 1

RENEWABLE: Yes, must reapply.

CONTACT: Elizabeth Kehmeier, Life Member Chair

2328—NASF/AESF Foundation Headquarters

Scholarship Committee
1155 Fifteenth Street, NW,
Suite 500
Washington DC 20005
NASF Headquarters Phone:
202/457-8404

AESF Foundation Phone:
202/457-8401
FAX: 202-530-0659
E-mail: at tkoehler@nasf.org or
mwalker@nasf.org.
Internet: http://www.nasf.org
AMOUNT: $1,500
DEADLINE(S): APR 15
FIELD(S): Metallurgy; Chemistry;
Materials Science; Metallurgical,
Chemical, & Environmental
Engineering
ELIGIBILITY/REQUIREMENTS: Must
be full-time junior or senior undergraduate. Selection based on achievement, scholarship potential, motivation, and career
interest in surface finishing technologies,
not necessarily financial need.
HOW TO APPLY: See website for application or contact AESF for application and
additional information. Submit with statement (maximum of 2 pages) describing
career objectives, plans for study in plating
and surface finishing technologies, and
long-range goals; list or résumé (maximum
2 pages) detailing educational achievements; 3 letters of recommendation from
teachers, professors, or employers (1 of
which must be from academic major advisor); and transcript of recent academic
records.
NUMBER OF AWARDS: Varies
RENEWABLE: Yes. Must reapply; maximum 2 years undergraduate; may reapply
as a graduate student.
CONTACT: Tracey Koehler, Membership
Director or Melissa Walker

2329—NATIONAL FEDERATION OF THE BLIND (Howard Brown Rickard Scholarship)

805 Fifth Avenue
Grinnell IA 50112
515/236-3366
Internet: http://www.nfb.org/
nfb/scholarship_program.asp
AMOUNT: $3,000
DEADLINE(S): MAR 31
FIELD(S): Law; Medicine; Engineering;
Architecture; Natural Sciences
ELIGIBILITY/REQUIREMENTS: For
legally blind students pursuing or planning
to pursue a full-time postsecondary course
of study in the U.S. Based on academic
excellence, service to the community, and
financial need. Membership NOT
required.
HOW TO APPLY: Contact Scholarship
Committee Chair for an application.
NUMBER OF AWARDS: 1
RENEWABLE: Yes

CONTACT: Peggy Elliot, Scholarship
Committee Chairman

2330—NATIONAL GARDEN CLUBS, INC.

4401 Magnolia Avenue
St. Louis MO 63110-3492
314/776-7574
FAX: 314/776-5108
E-mail: glaustin2@bellsouth.net or
headquarters@gardenclub.org
Internet: http://www.gardenclub.org
AMOUNT: $3,500
DEADLINE(S): MAR 1
FIELD(S): Horticulture, Floriculture,
Landscape Design, City Planning,
Land Management, and allied subjects
ELIGIBILITY/REQUIREMENTS: Open
to juniors, seniors, and graduate students
who are U.S. citizens. Must have the
endorsement of the state in which he/she
resides permanently.
HOW TO APPLY: Write for information.
Submit to local chapter; judged nationally.
NUMBER OF AWARDS: 30-35

2331—NATIONAL STONE, SAND & GRAVEL ASSOCIATION (NSSGA Barry K. Wendt Memorial Scholarship)

1605 King Street
Alexandria VA 22314
703/525-8788
FAX: 703/525-7782
E-mail: info@nssga.org
Internet: http://www.nssga.org
AMOUNT: $2,500
DEADLINE(S): APR 30
FIELD(S): Engineering; Mining;
Minerals; Construction Management
ELIGIBILITY/REQUIREMENTS: Open
to graduating seniors or college students
who plan to pursue a career in the crushed
stone, sand and gravel production industry.
HOW TO APPLY: See website or write
for information and application.
NUMBER OF AWARDS: 1
RENEWABLE: No

2332—NATURAL SCIENCES AND ENGINEERING RESEARCH COUNCIL OF CANADA (Undergraduate Student Research Awards in Industry)

350 Albert Street
Ottawa Ontario K1A 1H5 CANADA
613/995-5992 or 613/995-4273
FAX: 613/992-5337
E-mail: schol@nserc.ca or
webapp@nserc.ca
Internet: http://www.nserc.ca
AMOUNT: Up to $3,600 (Canadian)

DEADLINE(S): Varies
FIELD(S): Natural Sciences (except
health sciences); Engineering
ELIGIBILITY/REQUIREMENTS:
Tenable in approved Canadian industrial
organizations. For Canadian citizens or
permanent residents, who have no more
than 4 academic terms remaining to complete bachelor's degree; cumulative GPA
of at least second class (B); must be
employed full time in research and development activities during award tenure.
Travel allowance may be granted.
HOW TO APPLY: See website or contact
NSERC for information and application.

2333—NATURAL SCIENCES AND ENGINEERING RESEARCH COUNCIL OF CANADA (Undergraduate Student Research Awards in Small Universities)

350 Albert Street
Ottawa Ontario K1A 1H5 CANADA
613/995-5992
FAX: 613/992-5337
E-mail: schol@nserc.ca
Internet: http://www.nserc.ca/
programs/usrasmen.htm
AMOUNT: $3,600 (Canadian) max.
DEADLINE(S): Varies
FIELD(S): Natural Sciences (except
health sciences); Engineering
ELIGIBILITY/REQUIREMENTS:
Research awards for Canadian citi-
zens/permanent residents attending eligi-
ble institutions, who have no more than 6
and no fewer than 2 academic terms
remaining to complete bachelor's degree;
cumulative GPA of at least second class
(B); must be doing full-time research and
development activities during award
tenure.
HOW TO APPLY: See website or contact
NSERC for more information and application.

2334—PENN STATE UNIVERSITY-COLLEGE OF EARTH and MINERAL SCIENCES

Committee on Scholarships and
Awards
116 Deike Building
University Park PA 16802
814/865-7482
FAX: 814/863-7708
Internet: http://www.ems.psu.edu/
prospective/financial.html
AMOUNT: $500-$3,500
DEADLINE(S): None
FIELD(S): Geosciences; Meteorology;
Energy, Environmental, and Mineral
Economics; Materials Science and

Engineering; Mineral Engineering; Geography

ELIGIBILITY/REQUIREMENTS: Scholarship program open to outstanding undergraduate students accepted to or enrolled in Penn State's College of Earth and Mineral Sciences. Minimum GPA of 3.3 or 3.7 (entering student) on 4.0 scale.

HOW TO APPLY: Contact Dean's office for complete information.

NUMBER OF AWARDS: About 275

RENEWABLE: Yes

2335—RAILWAY TIE ASSOCIATION, THE (John Mabry Forestry Scholarship)

115 Commerce Drive, Suite C
Fayetteville GA 30214
770/460-5553
FAX: 770/460-5573
E-mail: ties@rta.org
Internet: http://rta.org/Programs andServices/ScholarshipInfo.aspx

AMOUNT: $1,250

DEADLINE(S): JUN 30

FIELD(S): Forestry

ELIGIBILITY/REQUIREMENTS: College juniors and seniors as well as college students in 2-year institutions who will be enrolled in accredited forestry schools are eligible. Selection is based on leadership qualities, career objectives, scholastic achievement, and financial need.

HOW TO APPLY: See website for additional information and application (posted in early March). Requirements vary.

2336—RESOURCES FOR THE FUTURE (RFF Summer Internship Program)

1616 P Street NW
Washington DC 20036-1400
202/328-5000
FAX: 202/939-3460
E-mail: mankin@rff.org or voigt@rff.org
Internet: http://www.rff.org/about rff/fellowships internships.htm

AMOUNT: $350-$375/week

DEADLINE(S): MAR 14 (5 p.m., Eastern time)

FIELD(S): Social Sciences, Natural Resources, Energy, Environment

ELIGIBILITY/REQUIREMENTS: Open to U.S. and non-U.S. citizens, undergraduate and graduate students for research in the areas of risk, resource and environmental management, energy and natural resources, and quality of the environment. Candidates should have outstanding policy analysis and writing skills.

HOW TO APPLY: See website for application and additional information.

Address inquiries and applications to John Mankin (Energy and Natural Resources and Quality of the Environment) or Marilyn Voigt (Risk, Resource and Environmental Management). These scholarships are not available to immediate family members of anyone involved in the selection of winners or the administration of the scholarship. For any given year, no educational institution may have more than 1 winner.

NUMBER OF AWARDS: Multiple: 1/institution

2336A—ROCKY MOUNTAIN COAL MINING INSTITUTE, THE (Engineering-Geology Scholarship)

8057 South Yukon Way
Littleton CO 80128-5510
303/948-3300
FAX: 303/948-1132
E-mail: mail@rmcmi.org
Internet: http://www.rmcmi.org

AMOUNT: $4,000 ($2,000 per year)

DEADLINE(S): FEB 3

FIELD(S): Mining; Geology; Mineral Processing; Metallurgy; Electrical Engineering; Mechanical Engineering; Environmental Engineering

ELIGIBILITY/REQUIREMENTS: Must be a full-time college sophomore or junior in good standing; be both a U.S. citizen and a legal resident of one of Arizona, Colorado, Montana, New Mexico, North Dakota, Texas, Utah, or Wyoming; pursuing a degree in a mining-related field; and have an expressed interest in western coal as a career path.

HOW TO APPLY: See website for application. Send application; list of academic and athletic honors received; list of extracurricular activities; work experience; 3 references; answers of 100 words or less to each of the following questions: "Why are you pursuing your present degree? What do you envision doing after graduation? What do you do to make learning exciting and productive?" Personal statement (why are you applying for this scholarship, special skills or training, etc.) optional.

RENEWABLE: Yes. Recommendation from dean; good academic standing.

2337—SIEMENS WESTINGHOUSE (Science and Technology Competition)

186 Wood Avenue South
Iselin NJ 08830
877/822-5233
E-mail: foundation.us@siemens.com

Internet: http://www.siemens-foundation.org

AMOUNT: $120,000 (maximum)

DEADLINE(S): Varies

FIELD(S): Biology; Physical Sciences; Mathematics; Physics; Chemistry; Computer Science; Environmental Science

ELIGIBILITY/REQUIREMENTS: Open to U.S. high school seniors to pursue independent science research projects, working individually or in teams of 2 or 3 to develop and test their own ideas. May work with one of the universities/laboratories that serve as Siemens' partners. Students from the U.S. and its territories may compete in 1 of 6 geographic areas. Individual and team national prizewinners receive a second scholarship to be applied to undergraduate or graduate education.

HOW TO APPLY: See website or contact Siemens Foundation for details.

2338—SKIDMORE COLLEGE (Porter Presidential Scholarships in Science and Mathematics)

Office of Admissions
815 North Broadway
Saratoga Springs NY 12866-1632
800/867-6007
E-mail: admissions@skidmore.edu
Internet: http://www.skidmore.edu/ administration/financial aid/porter scholarship.htm

AMOUNT: $10,000

DEADLINE(S): JAN 15

FIELD(S): Mathematics, Science, or Computer Science

ELIGIBILITY/REQUIREMENTS: Scholarships for students excelling in the above fields. Awards are based on talent, not financial need. Recipients are not required to major in a scientific or mathematical discipline, but they will be expected to demonstrate serious research in one or more of these areas.

HOW TO APPLY: For more information, see website.

NUMBER OF AWARDS: 5

RENEWABLE: Yes

2339—SMITHSONIAN INSTITUTION (Minority Student Internship Program)

Office of Research Training and Services
470 L'Enfant SW, Suite 7102
MRC 902 P.O. Box 37012
Washington DC 20013-7012
202/633-7070
FAX: 202/633-7069

E-mail: siofg@si.edu
Internet: http://www.si.edu/
research+study
AMOUNT: $500/week + possible travel
expenses
DEADLINE(S): FEB 1 (for Summer or
for Fall); OCT 1 (for Spring)
FIELD(S): Humanities; Environmental
Studies; Cultural Studies; Natural
History; Earth Science; Art History;
Biology
ELIGIBILITY/REQUIREMENTS: 10-
week, full-time internships in residence at
the Smithsonian are open to U.S. minority
students who wish to participate in
research or museum-related activities in
above and related fields. Must be undergraduates or beginning graduate students
with a minimum 3.0 GPA. Must submit
essay, résumé, and official transcript.
HOW TO APPLY: Contact the Office of
Research Training and Services or see
website for an application. Submit with the
required essay or research proposal,
résumé, and transcripts.

2340—SOCIETY FOR RANGE MANAGE-MENT (Masonic-Range Science Scholarship)

10030 W 27th Avenue
Wheat Ridge CO 80215-6601
303/986-3309
FAX: 303/986-3892
Email: vskiff@rangelands.org
Internet: http://www.rangelands.org
AMOUNT: Varies
DEADLINE(S): DEC 31 (subject to
change)
FIELD(S): Range Science/Management
or closely related field
ELIGIBILITY/REQUIREMENTS: Open
to high school seniors or college freshmen
or sophomores planning to major or currently majoring in range science/manage-
ment or a closely related field. Must be
planning or currently attending a college or
university with a range science program.
Must be sponsored by a member of SRM,
the National Association of Conservation
Districts (NACD), or the Soil and Water
Conservation Society (SWCS).
HOW TO APPLY: See website or contact
Society for an application and more information. Submit with high school transcript
and if applicable a copy of college transcripts; SAT or ACT scores (even if college
student); and 2 letters of reference from
teachers, county agents, employers, etc.,
who might have insight as to your qualifications. Mail to Paul Loeffler, Texas
General Land Office, 500 West Avenue H,
Box 2, Alpine, TX 79830-6008
NUMBER OF AWARDS: 1

RENEWABLE: Yes, maximum 8 semesters. Must maintain a 2.5 GPA during the
first 2 semesters (freshman year only) and
a 3.0 GPA in any subsequent semester
(GPA is per semester not cumulative) to
continue to receive the scholarship for the
remaining years of eligibility.

2341—SOCIETY OF EXPLORATION GEO-PHYSICISTS (SEG) FOUNDATION

P.O. Box 702740
Tulsa OK 74170-2740
918/497-5500
FAX: 918/497-5557
Internet: http://www.seg.org/
business/foundation/
AMOUNT: $500-$12,000
DEADLINE(S): MAR 1
FIELD(S): Geophysics
ELIGIBILITY/REQUIREMENTS: Open
to a high school student with above-average grades planning to enter college the
next fall term or an undergraduate college
student whose grades are above average,
or a graduate college student whose studies
are directed toward a career in exploration
geophysics in operations, teaching, or
research.
HOW TO APPLY: Check the website or
write for complete information.

2342—SOCIETY OF SATELLITE PROFES-SIONALS INTERNATIONAL (SSPI Scholarship Program)

The New York Information
Technology Center
55 Broad Street, 14th Floor
New York NY 10004
212/809-5199
FAX: 212/825-0075
E-mail: neworbit@aol.com
Internet: http://www.sspi.org
AMOUNT: $1,500-$4,000
DEADLINE(S): DEC 1
FIELD(S): Satellites (relating to
communications, domestic and
international telecommunications
policy, remote sensing, journalism, law,
meteorology, energy, navigation,
business, government, and broadcasting services)
ELIGIBILITY/REQUIREMENTS: Open
to current high school seniors, college or
university undergraduate or graduate students studying or intending to study satellite-related technologies, policies or applications. Must demonstrate commitment to
pursue education and career opportunities
in the satellite industry or a field making
direct use of satellite technology; academic

and leadership achievement; and potential
for significant contribution to the industry.
HOW TO APPLY: Before applying, all
applicants must complete a Scholarship
Qualification Form to determine whether
your interests and career plans are a good
fit for the program. See website for form
and details or send SASE.

2343—SOIL AND WATER CONSERVATION SOCIETY (Donald A. Williams Soil Conservation Scholarship)

945 SW Ankeny Road
Ankeny IA 50021-9764
515/289-2331 or 800/THE-SOIL
FAX: 515/289-1227
E-mail: swcs@swcs.org
Internet: http://www.swcs.org/
AMOUNT: $1,500
DEADLINE(S): FEB 12
FIELD(S): Conservation-related fields
(technical or administrative course
work)
ELIGIBILITY/REQUIREMENTS: For
SWCS members currently employed in a
related field who have completed at least 1
year of natural resource conservation work
with a governmental agency or private
organization. Need not be working toward
a degree, but must be undergraduate. Must
demonstrate financial need.
HOW TO APPLY: Write or see website
(click on About SWCS and then on
Chapters) for information.
NUMBER OF AWARDS: Up to 3

2344—STUDENT CONSERVATION ASSO-CIATION (SCA Resource Assistant Program)

P.O. Box 550
Charlestown NH 03603
603/543-1700
FAX: 603/543-1828
E-mail: internships@sca-inc.org
Internet: http://www.sca-inc.org
AMOUNT: $1,180-$4,725
DEADLINE(S): Varies
FIELD(S): Environment and related
fields (agriculture, archaeology,
anthropology, botany, caves, civil
engineering, environmental design,
engineering & education, fisheries,
forests, herpetology, history, landscape
architecture, environmental design,
paleontology, wildlife management,
geology, hydrology, library/museums,
surveying)
ELIGIBILITY/REQUIREMENTS: Must
be 18 and U.S. citizen; need not be student.
HOW TO APPLY: Send $1 for postage for
application; outside U.S./Canada, send
$20.

NUMBER OF AWARDS: 900 positions in U.S. and Canada

2345—TAPPI COATING & GRAPHIC ARTS DIVISION (Best Paper Award Scholarship)

P.O. Box 105113
Atlanta GA 30092
770/446-1400
FAX: 770/446-6947
E-mail: vedmondson@tappi.org
Internet: http://www.tappi.org
AMOUNT: $1,000
DEADLINE(S): JAN 31
FIELD(S): Paper Industry; Graphic Arts
ELIGIBILITY/REQUIREMENTS: Annual scholarship presented to one school each year. Students from that school may then apply.
HOW TO APPLY: Contact TAPPI Project Event Manager to determine which school has received the award; then contact school directly for more information on how to apply.
NUMBER OF AWARDS: 1
RENEWABLE: No
CONTACT: Veranda Edmondson, 770/208-7536

2346—TAPPI COATING & GRAPHIC ARTS DIVISION SCHOLARSHIP PROGRAM

P.O. Box 105113
Atlanta GA 30092
770/446-1400
FAX: 770/446-6947
E-mail: vedmondson@tappi.org
Internet: http://www.tappi.org
AMOUNT: $1,000
DEADLINE(S): JAN 31
FIELD(S): Paper Industry; Graphic Arts
ELIGIBILITY/REQUIREMENTS: Must be enrolled full-time student in an accredited college or university in a program related to the coated paper and paperboard or the graphic arts industries; be a TAPPI Student Chapter member (if available), be at least a junior with a minimum GPA of 3.0, and have demonstrated interest in a career in coating and graphic arts industry.
HOW TO APPLY: Contact TCDA or see website for an application and information.
NUMBER OF AWARDS: 4
RENEWABLE: No
CONTACT: Veranda Edmondson, 770/208-7536

2347—TAPPI CORRUGATED CONTAINERS DIVISION SCHOLARSHIP

P.O. Box 105113
Atlanta GA 30092
770/446-1400
FAX: 770/446-6947
E-mail: vedmondson@tappi.org
Internet: http://www.tappi.org
AMOUNT: $1,000-$2,000
DEADLINE(S): JAN 31
FIELD(S): Engineering; Science; Paper Industry
ELIGIBILITY/REQUIREMENTS: Must be an undergraduate or currently employed in the corrugated container, pulp, and paper industry; be able to demonstrate significant interest in the corrugated container segment of paper industry, be attending college full time or working in the box business and attending night school, be a junior or senior in the upcoming school year, and maintain a GPA of 3.0 or higher.
HOW TO APPLY: Contact TCDA or see website for an application and additional information. Submit application along with transcript, letter of recommendation from faculty member, and at least 2 additional letters of recommendation from persons familiar with the applicant's character, educational accomplishments, school activities, and leadership roles, and likelihood of success in the pulp and paper industry.
NUMBER OF AWARDS: Multiple (4, $2,000; several, $1,000)
CONTACT: Veranda Edmondson, 770/208-7536

2348—TAPPI ENGINEERING DIVISION SCHOLARSHIP

P.O. Box 105113
Atlanta GA 30092
770/446-1400
FAX: 770/446-6947
E-mail: vedmondson@tappi.org
Internet: http://www.tappi.org
AMOUNT: $2,500
DEADLINE(S): JAN 31
FIELD(S): Engineering; Science; Paper Industry
ELIGIBILITY/REQUIREMENTS: Must be an undergraduate member of a TAPPI Student Chapter, or submit comparable evidence of professional development and participation relative to the paper industry; must be enrolled in an engineering or science program, attending college full time; be an upcoming junior or senior, maintain a GPA of 3.0 or higher, and able to demonstrate a significant interest in the pulp and paper industry.
HOW TO APPLY: Contact TCDA or see website for an application and additional information. Submit with transcript, letter

of recommendation from the TAPPI Student Chapter's Faculty Advisor or equivalent (faculty instructor), and 2 additional letters of recommendation from persons familiar with your character, accomplishments, and likelihood of success.
NUMBER OF AWARDS: Up to 2 (1 to junior, 1 to senior)
RENEWABLE: Yes, must reapply.
CONTACT: Veranda Edmondson, 770/208-7536

2349—TAPPI ENVIRONMENTAL DIVISION SCHOLARSHIP

P.O. Box 105113
Atlanta GA 30092
770/446-1400
FAX: 770/446-6947
E-mail: vedmondson@tappi.org
Internet: http://www.tappi.org
AMOUNT: $2,500
DEADLINE(S): JAN 31
FIELD(S): Environmental Science; Paper Industry
ELIGIBILITY/REQUIREMENTS: Must be a full-time student (sophomore or higher) attending an ABET-accredited or equivalent college; cumulative minimum GPA of 3.0, and have demonstrated interest in a career in environmental control as it relates to pulp, paper, and allied industries.
HOW TO APPLY: Contact TCDA or see website for an application and additional information. Submit application along with transcript, 3 letters of recommendation addressing professional and personal aspects of candidate; submit current résumé, and a brief description of how the applicant will advance the state of the environment as it relates to the pulp, paper, and allied industries. An interview may also be required.
NUMBER OF AWARDS: At least 1
RENEWABLE: No
CONTACT: Veranda Edmondson, 770/208-7536

2350—TAPPI FINISHING AND CONVERTING DIVISION (Paul Smith Scholarship Award)

P.O. Box 105113
Atlanta GA 30092
770/446-1400
FAX: 770/446-6947
E-mail: vedmondson@tappi.org
Internet: http://www.tappi.org
AMOUNT: $1,000
DEADLINE(S): JAN 31
FIELD(S): Science; Engineering; Technology; Paper Industry

ELIGIBILITY/REQUIREMENTS: Applicant must be enrolled as a full-time student in a state-accredited undergraduate college program; must have a GPA of 3.0 or its equivalent, must be in a program preparatory to a career in the nonwovens industry or demonstrate an interest in the areas covered by the Nonwovens Division.
HOW TO APPLY: See website or contact TAPPI for applications. Submit application along with transcript, 3 letters of recommendation from persons familiar with the applicant's character, including an instructor or faculty member; academic and extracurricular accomplishments, etc. Interview may be requested.
NUMBER OF AWARDS: Multiple
RENEWABLE: Yes. Must reapply; same person may not receive award in consecutive years.
CONTACT: Veranda Edmondson, 770/208-7536

2351—TAPPI NONWOVENS DIVISION SCHOLARSHIP AWARD

P.O. Box 105113
Atlanta GA 30092
770/446-1400
FAX: 770/446-6947
E-mail: vedmondson@tappi.org
Internet: http://www.tappi.org
AMOUNT: $1,000
DEADLINE(S): JAN 31
FIELD(S): Science; Engineering; Paper Industry
ELIGIBILITY/REQUIREMENTS: Must be enrolled as a full-time student in a state-accredited undergraduate college program; have a GPA of 3.0 or its equivalent; be in a program preparatory to a career in the nonwovens industry or demonstrate an interest in the areas covered by TAPPI's Nonwovens Division; and be recommended and endorsed by an instructor or faculty member.
HOW TO APPLY: See website or contact TAPPI for applications. Submit application along with transcript, 3 letters of recommendation from persons familiar with the applicant's character, academic and extracurricular accomplishments, etc. Interview may be requested.
NUMBER OF AWARDS: Multiple
RENEWABLE: Yes. Must reapply; same person may not receive award in consecutive years.
CONTACT: Veranda Edmondson, 770/208-7536

2352—TAPPI PAPER AND BOARD DIVISION SCHOLARSHIP PROGRAM

P.O. Box 105113

Atlanta GA 30092
770/446-1400
FAX: 770/446-6947
E-mail: vedmondson@tappi.org
Internet: http://www.tappi.org
AMOUNT: $1,000
DEADLINE(S): JAN 31
FIELD(S): Science; Engineering; Paper Industry
ELIGIBILITY/REQUIREMENTS: Open to TAPPI student member or an undergraduate member of a TAPPI chapter. Must be a college or university sophomore, junior, or senior enrolled in an engineering or science program; a full-time student or a full-time participant in a cooperative work-study program recognized and supported by the educational institution; and able to show a significant interest in the paper industry.
HOW TO APPLY: See website or contact TAPPI for applications. Submit application along with transcript, a personal statement from the applicant regarding your career goals and personal objectives, letter of recommendation from faculty member, and 2 letters of recommendation from persons familiar with your character, academic and extracurricular accomplishments, etc. Interview may be requested.
NUMBER OF AWARDS: Multiple
RENEWABLE: Yes. Must reapply; same person may not receive award in consecutive years.
CONTACT: Veranda Edmondson, 770/208-7536

2353—TAPPI PULP MANUFACTURE DIVISION (High Impact Award Scholarship)

P.O. Box 105113
Atlanta GA 30092
770/446-1400
FAX: 770/446-6947
E-mail: vedmondson@tappi.org
Internet: http://www.tappi.org
AMOUNT: $1,000
DEADLINE(S): JAN 31
FIELD(S): Chemistry; Environmental Studies; Engineering; Paper Industry
ELIGIBILITY/REQUIREMENTS: Presented to one school each year (announced in fall), whose students may then apply.
HOW TO APPLY: Contact Project Event Manager to determine which school has received the award; then contact school directly for information on how to apply.
NUMBER OF AWARDS: 1
RENEWABLE: Yes, must reapply.
CONTACT: Veranda Edmondson, 770/208-7536

2354—TAPPI PULP MANUFACTURE DIVISION (Johan C.F.C. Richter Scholarship Prize)

P.O. Box 105113
Atlanta GA 30092
770/446-1400
FAX: 770/446-6947
E-mail: vedmondson@tappi.org
Internet: http://www.tappi.org
AMOUNT: $1,000
DEADLINE(S): JAN 31
FIELD(S): Chemistry; Environmental Studies; Engineering; Paper Industry
ELIGIBILITY/REQUIREMENTS: Biannual scholarship presented to one school each year (announced in fall), whose students may then apply.
HOW TO APPLY: Contact TAPPI Project Event Manager to determine which school has received the award; then contact school directly for information on how to apply.
NUMBER OF AWARDS: 1
RENEWABLE: Yes, must reapply.
CONTACT: Veranda Edmondson, 770/208-7536

2355—TAPPI PULP MANUFACTURE DIVISION (Joseph K. Perkins Scholarship Prize)

P.O. Box 105113
Atlanta GA 30092
770/446-1400
FAX: 770/446-6947
E-mail: vedmondson@tappi.org
Internet: http://www.tappi.org
AMOUNT: $1,000
DEADLINE(S): JAN 31
FIELD(S): Chemistry; Environmental Studies; Engineering; Paper Industry
ELIGIBILITY/REQUIREMENTS: Biannual scholarship presented to one school each year (announced in fall), whose students may then apply.
HOW TO APPLY: Contact TAPPI Project Event Manager to determine which school has received the award; then contact school directly for information on how to apply.
NUMBER OF AWARDS: 1
RENEWABLE: Yes, must reapply.
CONTACT: Veranda Edmondson, 770/208-7536

2356—TAPPI PULP MANUFACTURE DIVISION/MOTAG-SOUTH (James A. Hoclkamp Memorial Scholarship in Forest Resources)

P.O. Box 105113
Atlanta GA 30092
770/446-1400

FAX: 770/446-6947
E-mail: vedmondson@tappi.org
Internet: http://www.tappi.org
AMOUNT: $2,000
DEADLINE(S): MAY 15
FIELD(S): Forestry
ELIGIBILITY/REQUIREMENTS: Must be a sophomore in a southern school of forest resources.
HOW TO APPLY: Contact MOTAG-South through TAPPI or participating school for application and additional information. Submit with transcript, letter of recommendation from faculty member, and at least 2 additional letters of recommendation from persons familiar with your character, educational accomplishments, school activities, and leadership roles, and likelihood of success in the pulp and paper industry.
NUMBER OF AWARDS: 1
RENEWABLE: Yes, must reapply.
CONTACT: Veranda Edmondson, 770/208-7536

2357—TAPPI PULP MANUFACTURE DIVISION/THE PLACE DIVISION (The Ralph A. Klucken Scholarship Award)

P.O. Box 105113
Atlanta GA 30092
770/446-1400
FAX: 770/446-6947
E-mail: vedmondson@tappi.org
Internet: http://www.tappi.org
AMOUNT: $1,000
DEADLINE(S): MAY 15
FIELD(S): Chemistry; Paper Industry
ELIGIBILITY/REQUIREMENTS: Must be a college undergraduate or graduate student as of the date of the application and attending college full time on the date of the award in September; maintain a GPA of 3.0, and demonstrate responsibility and maturity throughout a history of part-time and summer employment; and demonstrate an interest in the technological areas covered by the polymers, laminations and coating division.
HOW TO APPLY: See website or contact TAPPI for applications. Submit application along with transcript, letter of recommendation from part-time/summer employer, letter of recommendation from faculty member and any individual familiar with the applicant's character, academic and extracurricular accomplishments, etc.
NUMBER OF AWARDS: 1
RENEWABLE: Yes. Must reapply; same person may not receive award in consecutive years.
CONTACT: Veranda Edmondson, 770/208-7536

2358—UNCF/MERCK SCIENCE INITIATIVE (Undergraduate Science Research Scholarship Awards)

8260 Willow Oaks Corporate Dr.
P.O. Box 10444
Fairfax VA 22031-4511
703/205-3503
FAX: 703/205-3574
E-mail: uncfmerck@uncf.org
Internet: http://www.uncf.org/merck
AMOUNT: $25,000/year (maximum)
DEADLINE(S): DEC 15
FIELD(S): Life and Physical Sciences
ELIGIBILITY/REQUIREMENTS: Open to African-Americans in their junior year of college who will receive a bachelor's degree in the following academic year. Must be enrolled full time in any 4-year college or university in the U.S. and have a minimum 3.3 GPA. Must be U.S. citizen/permanent resident. Financial need NOT a factor.
HOW TO APPLY: Contact UNCF/Merck for an application.
NUMBER OF AWARDS: 15
RENEWABLE: No
CONTACT: Jerry Bryant, Ph.D.

2359—UNIVERSITY OF WINDSOR (Outstanding Scholars Award)

401 Sunset Avenue
Windsor Ontario N9B 3P4
CANADA
519/253-3000
FAX: 519/973-7081
E-mail: awards1@uwindsor.ca
Internet: http://www.uwindsor.ca
AMOUNT: $1,000-$2,500/year (Canadian); maximum 4 years
DEADLINE(S): MAY 31
FIELD(S): Classics, Modern Languages, French, Philosophy, Music, Physics, Earth Sciences (not Environmental Studies), Economics (not Business and Economics), Chemistry (not Biochemistry), Mathematics and Statistics, Industrial, Mechanical (Materials Option) or Environmental Engineering or Bachelor of Arts and Science
ELIGIBILITY/REQUIREMENTS: Open to undergraduate students registering in year 1 at the University of Windsor. Must have superior grades. Amount of award based on secondary school accomplishments.
HOW TO APPLY: Automatic. No application required.
RENEWABLE: Yes. Up to 4 years.
CONTACT: Aase Houser

ADDITIONAL INFORMATION: Students in this program will also be mentored in their first year in preparation for guaranteed Outstanding Scholars Appointments in their Department/School (valued at $2,000 Canadian in earnings for each of the 2nd, 3rd, and 4th years) provided all conditions are met.

2360—WESTERN MICHIGAN UNIVERSITY (College of Arts and Sciences/Advisory Council Field Camp Scholarship)

1903 West Michigan
Kalamazoo MI 49008-5337
269/387-8777
FAX: 269/387-6989
E-mail: finaid-info@wmich.edu
Internet: http://www.wmich.edu/finaid
AMOUNT: $250 (spring semester)
FIELD(S): Geosciences
ELIGIBILITY/REQUIREMENTS: Recipient must be enrolled in Geosciences Department and show financial need.
HOW TO APPLY: Contact the Geosciences Department for an application.
RENEWABLE: No

2361—WESTERN MICHIGAN UNIVERSITY (College of Arts and Sciences/Kalamazoo Geological and Mineral Society Scholarship)

1903 West Michigan
Kalamazoo MI 49008-5337
269/387-8777
FAX: 269/387-6989
E-mail: finaid-info@wmich.edu
Internet: http://www.wmich.edu/finaid
AMOUNT: Varies (spring semester)
FIELD(S): Geosciences
ELIGIBILITY/REQUIREMENTS: Recipient must be enrolled in Geosciences Department with a minimum of 12 hours and a 3.0 GPA.
HOW TO APPLY: Contact the Geosciences Department for an application.
RENEWABLE: No

2362—WESTERN MICHIGAN UNIVERSITY (College of Arts and Sciences/Kuenzi Memorial Scholarship)

1903 West Michigan
Kalamazoo MI 49008-5337
269/387-8777
FAX: 269/387-6989
E-mail: finaid-info@wmich.edu
Internet: http://www.wmich.edu/finaid

AMOUNT: Approximately $600 (spring semester)
FIELD(S): Geosciences
ELIGIBILITY/REQUIREMENTS: Recipient must be enrolled in Geosciences Department.
HOW TO APPLY: Contact the Geosciences Department for an application.
RENEWABLE: No

2363—WESTERN MICHIGAN UNIVERSITY (College of Arts and Sciences/Lloyd and Marilyn Schmaltz Award)

1903 West Michigan
Kalamazoo MI 49008-5337
269/387-8777
FAX: 269/387-6989
E-mail: finaid-info@wmich.edu
Internet: http://www.wmich.edu/finaid
AMOUNT: Approximately $600 (spring semester)
FIELD(S): Geosciences
ELIGIBILITY/REQUIREMENTS: Recipient must currently be enrolled in Geosciences Department.
HOW TO APPLY: Contact the Geosciences Department for an application.
RENEWABLE: No

2364—WESTERN MICHIGAN UNIVERSITY (College of Arts and Sciences/W. Richard Laton Field Camp Scholarship)

1903 West Michigan
Kalamazoo MI 49008-5337
269/387-8777
FAX: 269/387-6989
E-mail: finaid-info@wmich.edu
Internet: http://www.wmich.edu/finaid
AMOUNT: Approximately $300 (spring semester)
FIELD(S): Geosciences
ELIGIBILITY/REQUIREMENTS: Recipient must be enrolled in Geosciences Department.
HOW TO APPLY: Contact the Geosciences Department for an application.
RENEWABLE: No

2365—WESTERN MICHIGAN UNIVERSITY (College of Engineering and Applied Sciences Endowed Scholarship)

1903 West Michigan
Kalamazoo MI 49008-5337
269/387-6000
FAX: 269/387-6989
E-mail: finaid-info@wmich.edu

Internet: http://www.wmich.edu/finaid
AMOUNT: $1,000
FIELD(S): Chemical Engineering; Energy Management
ELIGIBILITY/REQUIREMENTS: Open to degree-seeking freshman (entering in the fall semester) who is admitted to an ABET-accredited, undergraduate-degree program at WMU. Must be a resident of Michigan and a U.S. citizen. Based on appropriateness of high school courses in preparation for engineering education, admission GPA, and ACT scores.
HOW TO APPLY: Contact the Advising Office, Room E-102, Parkview Campus (269/276-3270) for an application.
NUMBER OF AWARDS: 2-3
RENEWABLE: Yes. Up to 4 years, must reapply.

2366—WESTERN MICHIGAN UNIVERSITY (College of Engineering and Applied Sciences/Robert A. Welborn Scholarship)

1903 West Michigan
Kalamazoo MI 49008-5337
269/387-6000
FAX: 269/387-6989
E-mail: finaid-info@wmich.edu
Internet: http://www.wmich.edu/finaid
AMOUNT: Varies
FIELD(S): Business; Paper Science
ELIGIBILITY/REQUIREMENTS: Open to students pursuing degree in business or paper science in good academic standing and within 3 semesters of graduation. Must demonstrate financial need and reside in the 13th senatorial district as it was when Welborn was senator.
HOW TO APPLY: Selected by faculty. Contact the Paper and Printing Science and Engineering Department, 1104 Welborn Hall, for an application.
NUMBER OF AWARDS: 1
RENEWABLE: No

2367—WESTERN MICHIGAN UNIVERSITY (College of Engineering and Applied Sciences Scholarship)

1903 West Michigan
Kalamazoo MI 49008-5337
269/387-6000
FAX: 269/387-6989
E-mail: finaid-info@wmich.edu
Internet: http://www.wmich.edu/finaid
AMOUNT: $250-$500
FIELD(S): Chemical Engineering; Energy Management

ELIGIBILITY/REQUIREMENTS: Open to full-time student (minimum of 12 credit hours) who has completed enough semester hours to be classified at the sophomore level or higher (at least 26 semester hours), is enrolled in a 4-year degree program in the College, and has accumulated a minimum of 12 semester hours at WMU.
HOW TO APPLY: Contact the College of Engineering Applied Science Advising Office, Room E-102, Parkview Campus (269/276-3270) for an application.
RENEWABLE: No

2368—WOODS HOLE OCEANOGRAPHIC INSTITUTION (Traineeships in Oceanography for Minority Group Undergraduates)

Clark Laboratory 223, MS #31
Woods Hole MA 02543-1541
508/289-2219
FAX: 508/457-2188
E-mail: education@whoi.edu
Internet: http://www.whoi.edu
AMOUNT: Varies
DEADLINE(S): FEB 15
FIELD(S): Physical/Natural Sciences, Mathematics, Engineering
ELIGIBILITY/REQUIREMENTS: For minority undergraduates (African-American or Black, Asian-American, Chicano, Mexican-American, Puerto Rican or other Hispanic, and Native American) who are enrolled in U.S. colleges/universities and have completed at least 2 semesters. Trainee-ships may be awarded for a 10- to 12-week period in the summer or for a semester during the academic year.
HOW TO APPLY: For an application and additional information, contact the Academic Programs Office, Clark Laboratory. Submit with current résumé demonstrating educational background and work experience; an official transcript and/or other official documentation of undergraduate record; at least 3 letters of recommendation from professors, employers, others; a statement of research interests, future education and career plans, and reasons for applying for fellowship.

ENVIRONMENTAL STUDIES

2369—AMERICAN ASSOCIATION OF BLACKS IN ENERGY (AABE)

Western Michigan University
1903 West Michigan
Kalamazoo MI 49008-5337
269/387-8777

FAX: 269/387-6989

E-mail: alumni@wmich.edu

Internet: http://www.wmich.edu/cas/research.html

AMOUNT: Varies

DEADLINE(S): MAR 1

FIELD(S): Mathematics; Computer Science; Engineering; Physical Sciences

ELIGIBILITY/REQUIREMENTS: Freshman with 2.5 GPA overall and a 3.0 GPA in mathematics and the sciences. Planning to major in engineering, mathematics, computer or the physical sciences. Applicant must demonstrate financial need and be a member of one of the underrepresented minority groups in the sciences and technology.

HOW TO APPLY: Contact the Office for Student Financial Aid.

NUMBER OF AWARDS: Varies

RENEWABLE: Yes

2370—AMERICAN GROUND WATER TRUST (Amtrol, Inc. Scholarship)

16 Centre Street

Concord NH 03301

603/228-5444

FAX: 603/228-6557

E-mail: trustinfo@agwt.org

Internet: http://www.agwt.org/scholarships.htm

AMOUNT: $1,000-$2,000

DEADLINE(S): JUN 1

FIELD(S): Environmental Science; Environmental Engineering; Marine Science; Natural Resources

ELIGIBILITY/REQUIREMENTS: Must be high school seniors; intend to pursue a career in a ground water-related field; be entering their freshmen year at a 4-year accredited college or university; have a minimum 3.0 GPA in high school; have completed a science/environmental project in high school that directly involved ground water resources or have had vacation/out-of-school work experience related to the environment and natural resources; be U.S. citizens or legal residents of the U.S.

HOW TO APPLY: Send application that has been signed by a teacher at the applicant's high school; a 500-word essay (on "Ground Water: An Important Environmental and Economic Resource for America") and a 300-word description of the applicant's high school ground water project and/or practical work experience; and 2 letters of recommendation. Also, documentary evidence of scholastic achievements and references will be requested in mid-June from finalists.

2371—AMERICAN GROUND WATER TRUST (Baroid Award)

16 Centre Street

Concord NH 03301

603/228-5444

FAX: 603/228-6557

E-mail: trustinfo@agwt.org

Internet: http://www.agwt.org/scholarships.htm

AMOUNT: $1,000

DEADLINE(S): JUN 1

FIELD(S): Environmental Science; Earth Science

ELIGIBILITY/REQUIREMENTS: Open to high school seniors entering their freshman year at a 4-year accredited college or university intending to pursue a career in ground water-related fields. Minimum 3.0 GPA. Must either have completed a science/environmental project in high school that directly involved ground water resources or have had vacation/out-of-school work experience related to the environment and natural resources; and be a U.S. citizen or legal resident of the U.S.

HOW TO APPLY: See website for application, countersigned by high school teacher. Submit with a 500-word essay and a 300-word description of your ground water project and/or practical environmental work experience, along with 2 letters of recommendation, transcripts, and confirmation of acceptance from the college or university.

NUMBER OF AWARDS: 1

RENEWABLE: No

2372—AMERICAN GROUND WATER TRUST (Ben Everson Award)

16 Centre Street

Concord NH 03301

603/228-5444

FAX: 603/228-6557

E-mail: trustinfo@agwt.org

Internet: http://www.agwt.org/scholarships.htm

AMOUNT: $2,500

DEADLINE(S): JUN 1

FIELD(S): Environmental Science; Earth Science

ELIGIBILITY/REQUIREMENTS: Open to high school seniors entering their freshman year at a 4-year accredited college or university, who intend to pursue a career in ground water-related fields. Minimum 3.0 GPA. Must either have completed a science/environmental project in high school directly involving ground water resources or have had vacation/out-of-school work experience that is related to the environment and natural resources; be a U.S. citi-

zen or legal resident; and attest that 1 parent is employed in the ground water industry.

HOW TO APPLY: See website for application, countersigned by high school teacher. Submit with a 500-word essay and a 300-word description of your ground water project and/or practical environmental work experience, along with 2 letters of recommendation, transcripts, and confirmation of acceptance from the college or university, and letter establishing parent's employment.

NUMBER OF AWARDS: 1

RENEWABLE: No

2373—AMERICAN INDIAN SCIENCE AND ENGINEERING SOCIETY (EPA Tribal Lands Environmental Science Scholarship)

P.O. Box 9828

Albuquerque NM 87119-9828

505/765-1052

FAX: 505/765-5608

E-mail: scholarships@aises.org

Internet: http://www.aises.org/scholar/highered

AMOUNT: $4,000

DEADLINE(S): JUN 15

FIELD(S): Biochemistry; Biology; Chemical Engineering; Chemistry; Entomology; Environmental Economics/Science; Hydrology; Environmental Studies

ELIGIBILITY/REQUIREMENTS: Open to American Indian college juniors, seniors, and graduate students enrolled full time at an accredited institution. Must demonstrate financial need and be a member of AISES ($10 fee). Certificate of Indian blood NOT required.

HOW TO APPLY: See website for more information and/or an application.

RENEWABLE: No

CONTACT: Tina Pino

2374—AMERICAN METEOROLOGY SOCIETY (AMS/Crow Scholarship)

Fellowship/Scholarship Program

45 Beacon Street

Boston MA 02108-3693

617/227-2426

FAX: 617/742-8718

E-mail: dfernand@ametsoc.org or armstrong@ametsoc.org

Internet: http://www.ametsoc.org

AMOUNT: Varies

DEADLINE(S): FEB 21

FIELD(S): Atmospheric Sciences; Oceanography; Hydrology

ELIGIBILITY/REQUIREMENTS: Open to juniors entering senior year, who are U.S. citizens or permanent residents and has evidenced an interest in applied meteorology. MUST be majoring in atmospheric or related oceanic or hydrologic sciences and/or must show clear intent to make the atmospheric or related sciences their career.

HOW TO APPLY: See website for additional information and application or e-mail or write to contact below at AMS headquarters (include SASE).

NUMBER OF AWARDS: Varies

CONTACT: Donna Sampson, Development & Student Programs Manager, ext. 246 or Stephanie Armstrong, Director of Development, ext 235

2375—AMERICAN METEOROLOGY SOCIETY (AMS/Freshman Undergraduate Scholarship Program)

Fellowship/Scholarship Program
45 Beacon Street
Boston MA 02108-3693
617/227-2426
FAX: 617/742-8718
E-mail: dfernand@ametsoc.org or armstrong@ametsoc.org
Internet: http://www.ametsoc.org
AMOUNT: $2,500
DEADLINE(S): FEB 21
FIELD(S): Atmospheric Sciences; Oceanography; Hydrology

ELIGIBILITY/REQUIREMENTS: Open to high school seniors entering freshman year, who are U.S. citizens or permanent residents. Awards based on academic excellence.

HOW TO APPLY: See website for additional information and application or e-mail or write to contact below at AMS headquarters (include SASE).

NUMBER OF AWARDS: Varies

RENEWABLE: Yes. For sophomore year only. Must demonstrate a successful 1st year and plans to continue studies in the AMS-related sciences.

CONTACT: Donna Sampson, Development & Student Programs Manager, ext. 246 or Stephanie Armstrong, Director of Development, ext 235

2376—AMERICAN METEOROLOGY SOCIETY (AMS/Glahn Scholarship)

Fellowship/Scholarship Program
45 Beacon Street
Boston MA 02108-3693
617/227-2426
FAX: 617/742-8718

E-mail: dfernand@ametsoc.org or armstrong@ametsoc.org
Internet: http://www.ametsoc.org
AMOUNT: Varies
DEADLINE(S): FEB 21
FIELD(S): Atmospheric Sciences; Oceanography; Hydrology

ELIGIBILITY/REQUIREMENTS: Open to juniors entering senior year, who are U.S. citizens or permanent residents and has evidenced an interest in statistical meteorology. MUST be majoring in atmospheric or related oceanic or hydrologic sciences and/or must show clear intent to make the atmospheric or related sciences their career.

HOW TO APPLY: See website for additional information and application or e-mail or write to contact below at AMS headquarters (include SASE).

NUMBER OF AWARDS: Varies

CONTACT: Donna Sampson, Development & Student Programs Manager, ext. 246 or Stephanie Armstrong, Director of Development, ext 235

2377—AMERICAN METEOROLOGY SOCIETY (AMS/Industry Minority Scholarships)

Fellowship/Scholarship Program
45 Beacon Street
Boston MA 02108-3693
617/227-2426
FAX: 617/742-8718
E-mail: dfernand@ametsoc.org or armstrong@ametsoc.org
Internet: http://www.ametsoc.org
AMOUNT: $3,000
DEADLINE(S): FEB 21
FIELD(S): Atmospheric Sciences; Oceanography; Hydrology

ELIGIBILITY/REQUIREMENTS: Open to minority—especially Hispanic, Native American, and Black/African American—high school seniors entering freshman year at a 4-year U.S. accredited institution. Must be U.S. citizens or permanent residents and must plan to pursue a career in the atmospheric or related oceanic or hydrologic sciences.

HOW TO APPLY: See website for additional information and application or e-mail or write to contact below at AMS headquarters (include SASE).

NUMBER OF AWARDS: Varies

RENEWABLE: Yes. For sophomore year only. Must demonstrate a successful 1st year and plans to continue studies in the AMS-related sciences.

2378—AMERICAN METEOROLOGY SOCIETY (AMS/Murphy Scholarship)

Fellowship/Scholarship Program

45 Beacon Street
Boston MA 02108-3693
617/227-2426
FAX: 617/742-8718
E-mail: dfernand@ametsoc.org or armstrong@ametsoc.org
Internet: http://www.ametsoc.org
AMOUNT: Varies
DEADLINE(S): FEB 21
FIELD(S): Atmospheric Sciences; Oceanography; Hydrology

ELIGIBILITY/REQUIREMENTS: Open to juniors entering senior year, who are U.S. citizens or permanent residents, and who, through curricular or extracurricular activities, has evidenced an interest in weather forecasting or in the value and utilization of forecasts. MUST be majoring in atmospheric or related oceanic or hydrologic sciences and/or must show clear intent to make the atmospheric or related sciences their career.

HOW TO APPLY: See website for additional information and application or e-mail or write to contact below at AMS headquarters (include SASE).

NUMBER OF AWARDS: Varies

CONTACT: Donna Sampson, Development & Student Programs Manager, ext. 246 or Stephanie Armstrong, Director of Development, ext 235

2379—AMERICAN METEOROLOGY SOCIETY (AMS/Schroeder Scholarship)

Fellowship/Scholarship Program
45 Beacon Street
Boston MA 02108-3693
617/227-2426
FAX: 617/742-8718
E-mail: dfernand@ametsoc.org or armstrong@ametsoc.org
Internet: http://www.ametsoc.org
AMOUNT: Varies
DEADLINE(S): FEB 21
FIELD(S): Atmospheric Sciences; Oceanography; Hydrology

ELIGIBILITY/REQUIREMENTS: Open to juniors entering senior year, who are U.S. citizens or permanent residents. MUST be majoring in atmospheric or related oceanic or hydrologic sciences and/or must show clear intent to make the atmospheric or related sciences their career. Must demonstrate financial need.

HOW TO APPLY: See website for additional information and application or e-mail or write to contact below at AMS headquarters (include SASE).

NUMBER OF AWARDS: Varies

CONTACT: Donna Sampson, Development & Student Programs Manager, ext.

246 or Stephanie Armstrong, Director of Development, ext 235

2380—AMERICAN NUCLEAR SOCIETY (Decommissioning, Decontamination & Reutilization Division Scholarship)

555 North Kensington Avenue
La Grange Park IL 60526
708/352-6611
FAX: 708/352-0499
E-mail: outreach@ans.org
Internet: http://www.ans.org
AMOUNT: $2,000
DEADLINE(S): FEB 1
FIELD(S): Nuclear Science; Nuclear Engineering
ELIGIBILITY/REQUIREMENTS: Must be junior or senior enrolled in a U.S. institution and U.S. citizen or permanent resident; enrolled in an engineering or science curriculum associated either with decommissioning/decontamination of nuclear facilities, management/characterization of nuclear waste, or restoration of the environment; join the ANS; and designate the DD&R Division as professional division. Must commit to participating in the DD&R Division Activities by attending the annual and winter meetings of the ANS and serving as a student representative at the DD&R Executive Committee meetings at both ANS meetings.
HOW TO APPLY: See website for application; submit to Scholarship Coordinator, with brief essay discussing the importance of some aspect of DD&R to the future of the nuclear field.
NUMBER OF AWARDS: 1
RENEWABLE: No
ADDITIONAL INFORMATION: Funding for travel, including student registration, reasonable transportation, food, and lodging also provided.

2381—AMERICAN NUCLEAR SOCIETY (Charles "Tommy" Thomas Memorial Scholarship)

555 North Kensington Avenue
La Grange Park IL 60526
708/352-6611
FAX: 708/352-0499
E-mail: outreach@ans.org
Internet: http://www.ans.org
AMOUNT: $2,000
DEADLINE(S): FEB 1
FIELD(S): Nuclear Science & Engineering, Environmental Studies
ELIGIBILITY/REQUIREMENTS: Must be juniors or seniors enrolled in a U.S. institution; be U.S. citizens or permanent residents; and be pursuing a career dealing with the environmental aspects of nuclear science or nuclear engineering.
HOW TO APPLY: See website for application Submit with brief essay describing how your perception of environmental science and engineering related topics fitting into the nuclear field and how you plan to contribute to the field during the course of your professional career.
NUMBER OF AWARDS: 1
RENEWABLE: No
CONTACT: Scholarship Coordinator

2382—ASSOCIATION OF CALIFORNIA WATER AGENCIES (ACWA)

910 K Street, Suite 100
Sacramento CA 95814
916/441-4545
FAX: 916/325-4849
E-mail: acwabox@acwanet.com
Internet: http://www.acwanet.com
AMOUNT: $1,500
DEADLINE(S): APR 1
FIELD(S): Water Resources-related fields (including engineering, agriculture, environmental studies, public administration)
ELIGIBILITY/REQUIREMENTS: Based on scholastic achievement, commitment and motivation as well as financial need.
HOW TO APPLY: Download applications and guidelines from website, or call or e-mail ACWA, or contact your school's financial aid department.
NUMBER OF AWARDS: At least 6

2383—EARTHWATCH STUDENT CHALLENGE AWARDS (High School Student Research Expeditions)

3 Clock Tower Place, Suite 100
P.O. Box 75
Maynard MA 01754
800/776-0188 or
978/461-0081, ext. 116
FAX: 978/450-1288
E-mail: scap@earthwatch.org
Internet: http://www.earthwatch.org
AMOUNT: Travel/Living expenses (1- to 3-week field expedition)
DEADLINE(S): Late Fall—call for details
FIELD(S): Biology, Field Studies, Physics, Natural Resources, Environmental Science
ELIGIBILITY/REQUIREMENTS: Awards for high school sophomores, juniors, and seniors, especially those with limited exposure to the sciences. Must attend high school in the U.S., attend high school in the U.S. Must be at least age 16 by June 15 during year of program. Teams of 6 to 8 students spend 1 to 3 weeks at sites in North or Central America.
HOW TO APPLY: Students must be nominated by a teacher. Write or visit website for further information.
NUMBER OF AWARDS: Approximately 85

2384—EDWARD AND ANNA RANGE SCHMIDT CHARITABLE TRUST (Grants and Emergency Financial Assistance)

P.O. Box 770982
Eagle River AK 99577
AMOUNT: Varies
DEADLINE(S): Immediate consideration
FIELD(S): Earth and Environmental Sciences
ELIGIBILITY/REQUIREMENTS: Open to Alaska residents or students in Alaska programs for a variety of expenses incurred by students, such as internship support, travel, expenses related to workshops and science fairs, support needed to secure employment in earth science-related fields, or emergency needs. Alaska Natives and other minorities are urged to apply.
HOW TO APPLY: Apply by letter from self and a sponsor (teacher, advisor, or other adult familiar with applicant's situation) describing applicant, nature of financial need, and amount requested.
RENEWABLE: No

2385—FIRST UNITED METHODIST CHURCH (Robert Stevenson and Doreene E. Cater Scholarships)

302 5th Avenue South
St. Cloud MN 56301
FAX: 320/251-0878
E-mail: fumc@fumc-stcloud.org
AMOUNT: $200-$1,500
DEADLINE(S): JUN 1
FIELD(S): Humanitarian and Christian Service: Teaching, Medicine, Social Work, Environmental Studies, and related fields
ELIGIBILITY/REQUIREMENTS: Stevenson Scholarship is open to undergraduate members of the First United Methodist Church of St. Cloud. Cater Scholarship is open to members of the Minnesota United Methodist Conference who are entering the sophomore year or higher of college work. Both require two letters of reference, transcripts, and financial need.
HOW TO APPLY: Contact Scholarship Committee for an application.
NUMBER OF AWARDS: 5-6

2386—FLORIDA FEDERATION OF GARDEN CLUBS, INC. (FFGC Scholarships for College Students)

706 Glen Eagle Drive
Winter Springs FL 32708
407/971-6979
Internet: http://www.ffgc.org
AMOUNT: $650-$3,000
DEADLINE(S): MAY 1
FIELD(S): Agriculture; Environmental & Conservation issues; Botany; Biology; Forestry; Horticulture; Ecology; Marine Biology; Wildflowers; Butterflies; Landscaping
ELIGIBILITY/REQUIREMENTS: Must be U.S. citizen and Florida resident for at least 1 year, with 3.0 GPA, attending a college or university in Florida. Financial need considered.
HOW TO APPLY: See website or contact FFGC Chair for an application.
RENEWABLE: Yes, must reapply.
CONTACT: Jane Meherg, Scholarship Chairman

2387—GARDEN CLUB FEDERATION OF MAINE, THE-ST. CROIX DISTRICT, THE (Nell Goff Memorial Scholarship Foundation)

P.O. Box 56
Salisbury Cove ME 04672
207/288-3709
E-mail: janetlmeryweather@juno.com
Internet: http://www.maine
gardenclubs.com
AMOUNT: $1,000
DEADLINE(S): MAR 1
FIELD(S): Horticulture; Floriculture; Landscape Design; Conservation; Forestry; Botany, Agronomy; Plant Pathology; Environmental Control; City Planning and/or other gardening-related fields
ELIGIBILITY/REQUIREMENTS: Open to college juniors, seniors or graduate students (sophomores are eligible if they will enter their junior year in the fall) who are legal residents of the state of Maine, priority given to a resident of St. Croix District (Hancock County, and the southern part of Washington County), and major in some aspect of horticulture.
HOW TO APPLY: See website for application and information. Submit along with personal letter (up to 2 pages) discussing goals, background, financial need and personal commitment, 3 letters of recommendation (1 page each) to include scholarship ability, personal reference, and work-related experience, and transcript and list of activities.
NUMBER OF AWARDS: 1

RENEWABLE: Yes, must reapply.
CONTACT: Janet Meryweather (above). January through April, contact May Opdyke at P.O. Box 44, Salisbury Cove, ME 04672 207/288-9689 or by e-mail at mbo810@aol.com

2388—GARDEN CLUB OF AMERICA (Frances M. Peacock Scholarship for Native Bird Habitat)

Cornell Lab of Ornithology
Ithaca NY 14850
No Phone Calls
FAX: 607/254/2435
E-mail: cornellbirds@cornell.edu
Internet: www.birds.cornell.edu/about/jobs.html
AMOUNT: $4,000
DEADLINE(S): JAN 15
FIELD(S): Habitats of Threatened/Endangered Native Birds
ELIGIBILITY/REQUIREMENTS: Open to college senior (2nd semester juniors may submit application for senior year) or graduate student to study habitat-related issues that will benefit threatened or endangered bird species and lend useful information for land management decisions.
HOW TO APPLY: See website for details; no formal application; submit a brief proposal of no more than 5 pages (1st page should include: summary, title, abstract, schedule, university affiliation, name of major advisor, name/address of applicant, and Social Security Number) and personal information form.
NUMBER OF AWARDS: 1
RENEWABLE: Yes
CONTACT: Scott Sutcliffe, Associate Director

2389—GARDEN CLUB OF AMERICA (GCA Awards for Summer Environmental Studies)

14 East 60th Street
New York NY 10022-1002
212/753-8287
FAX: 212/753-0134
E-mail: scholarships@gcamerica.org
Internet: http://www.gcamerica.org
AMOUNT: $1,500
DEADLINE(S): FEB 10
FIELD(S): Environmental Studies (including endangered plant species, conservation biology, ecological restoration, plant resources of the tropics, historical vegetation, wetland/marine ecology, journalism & legislation)
ELIGIBILITY/REQUIREMENTS: Financial aid toward a SUMMER studies

doing fieldwork or research in above fields for college students following their freshman, sophomore, or junior year. Purpose of award is to encourage studies and careers in the environmental field.
HOW TO APPLY: Application available on website or contact GCA.
CONTACT: Connie Sutton, Scholarship Committee

2390—GREAT LAKES COMMISSION (Carol A. Ratza Memorial Scholarship)

2805 South Industrial Highway, Suite 100
Ann Arbor MI 48104-6791
E-mail: manninen@glc.org
Internet: http://www.glc.org
AMOUNT: $500
DEADLINE(S): MAR 28
FIELD(S): Electronic Communications Technology (Environmental/Economic Applications)
ELIGIBILITY/REQUIREMENTS: Open to high school seniors and returning students enrolled full time at a Great Lakes college or university (Illinois, Indiana, Michigan, New York, Ohio, Pennsylvania, Wisconsin, Ontario, Quebec). Must have a demonstrated interest in the environmental or economic applications of electronic communications technology, exhibit academic excellence, and have a sincere appreciation for the Great Lakes and their protection.
HOW TO APPLY: See website or contact Commission for an application. Must submit résumé, transcripts, recommendations, and essay or Web page on Great Lakes issue. Recipient announced by May 1.
CONTACT: Christine Manninen

2391—HAWAII COMMUNITY FOUNDATION (William James & Dorothy Bading Lanquist Fund)

1164 Bishop Street, Suite 800
Honolulu HI 96813
808/537-6333 or toll free:
888/731-3863
FAX: 808/521-6286
E-mail: info@hcf-hawaii.org
Internet: http://www.hcf-hawaii.org
DEADLINE(S): MAR 1
FIELD(S): Physical Sciences and related fields (excluding Biology)
ELIGIBILITY/REQUIREMENTS: Must be residents of Hawaii; junior or senior undergraduate students enrolled full time in an accredited 2- or 4-year college or university; and demonstrate financial need, good moral character, and academic achievement (minimum GPA of 2.7).

HOW TO APPLY: See website. Send application with 2 letters of recommendation.

2392—INTERTRIBAL TIMBER COUNCIL (Truman D. Picard Scholarship)

Education Committee
1112 NE 21st Avenue, Suite 4
Portland OR 97232
503/282-4296
FAX: 503/282-1274
E-mail: itc1@teleport.com
Internet: http://www.itcnet.org
AMOUNT: $1,500-$2,000
DEADLINE(S): Varies
FIELD(S): Natural Resources (such as forestry; range management; environmental science)
ELIGIBILITY/REQUIREMENTS: Applicant must be an enrolled member of a federally recognized tribe in the U.S.
HOW TO APPLY: Send letter of application (maximum 2 pages) demonstrating interest in natural resources; commitment to education, community/culture; academic merit; and financial need. Also send résumé; 3 letters of reference (1 from school advisor); and validated enrollment in a federally recognized tribe or Native Alaska Corporation. High school students must also provide documented proof of acceptance to an institution of higher education to study in the area of natural resources, along with high school transcripts; college students must submit documented proof of study in the area of natural resources, along with college transcripts.
NUMBER OF AWARDS: 6-8 for college students and 1-2 for graduating high school seniors.
RENEWABLE: Yes, must reapply.

2393—JUNIATA COLLEGE (Environmental Responsibility Scholarship)

Office of Financial Planning
1700 Moore Street
Huntingdon PA 16652
814/641-3142
FAX: 814/641-5311
E-mail: frankv@juniata.edu
Internet: http://www.juniata.edu/admission/finplan/index.html
AMOUNT: Full tuition
DEADLINE(S): JAN 9
FIELD(S): Environment
ELIGIBILITY/REQUIREMENTS: Must demonstrate personal interest and involvement in environmental issues.
HOW TO APPLY: Contact College for an application or enrollment information.

NUMBER OF AWARDS: 1 full tuition, room & board; 2 full tuition.
CONTACT: Vincent Frank, Director of Student Financial Planning, 814/641-3140; e-mail: frankv@juniata.edu

2394—MONTANA FEDERATION OF GARDEN CLUBS LIFE MEMBERS

214 Wayne Lane
Hamilton MT 59340
406/363-5693
E-mail: elizabethhammt@aol.com
AMOUNT: $1,000
DEADLINE(S): MAY 1
FIELD(S): Conservation; Horticulture; Park Forestry; Floriculture; Greenhouse Management
ELIGIBILITY/REQUIREMENTS: Must be a sophomore in a Montana college; demonstrate financial need; GPA of 2.7.
HOW TO APPLY: No formal application form. Submit college transcript; letter of application detailing future plans; short autobiography; color photo; letters of reference from instructors.
NUMBER OF AWARDS: 1
RENEWABLE: Yes, must reapply.
CONTACT: Elizabeth Kehmeier, Life Member Chair

2395—NASF/AESF Foundation Headquarters

Scholarship Committee
1155 Fifteenth Street, NW, Suite 500
Washington DC 20005
NASF Headquarters Phone: 202/457-8404
AESF Foundation Phone: 202/457-8401
FAX: 202/530-0659
E-mail: at tkoehler@nasf.org or mwalker@nasf.org.
Internet: http://www.nasf.org
AMOUNT: $1,500
DEADLINE(S): APR 15
FIELD(S): Metallurgy; Chemistry; Materials Science; Metallurgical, Chemical, & Environmental Engineering
ELIGIBILITY/REQUIREMENTS: Must be full-time junior or senior undergraduate. Selection based on achievement, scholarship potential, motivation, and career interest in surface finishing technologies, not necessarily financial need.
HOW TO APPLY: See website for application or contact AESF for application and additional information. Submit with statement (maximum of 2 pages) describing

career objectives, plans for study in plating and surface finishing technologies, and long-range goals; list or résumé (maximum 2 pages) detailing educational achievements; 3 letters of recommendation from teachers, professors, or employers (1 of which must be from academic major advisor); and transcript of recent academic records.
NUMBER OF AWARDS: Varies
RENEWABLE: Yes. Must reapply; maximum 2 years undergraduate; may reapply as a graduate student.
CONTACT: Tracey Koehler, Membership Director or Melissa Walker

2396—NATIONAL ENVIRONMENTAL HEALTH ASSOCIATION (NEHA/AAS Scholarship)

720 South Colorado Boulevard, Suite 970, South Tower
Denver CO 80246-1925
303/756-9090
E-mail: cdimmitt@neha.org
Internet: http://www.neha.org
AMOUNT: Varies
DEADLINE(S): FEB 1
FIELD(S): Environmental Health/Science; Public Health
ELIGIBILITY/REQUIREMENTS: Open to juniors or seniors at an Environmental Health Accreditation Council accredited school or NEHA school.
HOW TO APPLY: Transcript, letters of recommendation, and financial need considered.
RENEWABLE: Yes

2397—NATURAL SCIENCES AND ENGINEERING RESEARCH COUNCIL OF CANADA (Undergraduate Student Research Awards in Industry)

350 Albert Street
Ottawa Ontario K1A 1H5 CANADA
613/995-5992 or 613/995-4273
FAX: 613/992-5337
E-mail: schol@nserc.ca or webapp@nserc.ca
Internet: http://www.nserc.ca
AMOUNT: Up to $3,600 (Canadian)
DEADLINE(S): Varies
FIELD(S): Natural Sciences (except health sciences); Engineering
ELIGIBILITY/REQUIREMENTS: Tenable in approved Canadian industrial organizations. For Canadian citizens or permanent residents, who have no more than 4 academic terms remaining to complete bachelor's degree; cumulative GPA

of at least second class (B); must be employed full time in research and development activities during award tenure. Travel allowance may be granted.

HOW TO APPLY: See website or contact NSERC for more information and application.

2398—NATURAL SCIENCES AND ENGINEERING RESEARCH COUNCIL OF CANADA (Undergraduate Student Research Awards in Small Universities)

350 Albert Street
Ottawa Ontario K1A 1H5 CANADA
613/995-5992
FAX: 613/992-5337
E-mail: schol@nserc.ca
Internet: http://www.nserc.ca/programs/usrasmen.htm
AMOUNT: $3,600 (Canadian) max.
DEADLINE(S): Varies
FIELD(S): Natural Sciences (except health sciences); Engineering
ELIGIBILITY/REQUIREMENTS: Research awards for Canadian citizens/permanent residents attending eligible institutions, who have no more than 6 and no fewer than 2 academic terms remaining to complete bachelor's degree; cumulative GPA of at least second class (B); must be doing full-time research and development activities during award tenure.

HOW TO APPLY: See website or contact NSERC for more information and application.

2399—NEW JERSEY UTILITIES ASSOCIATION

50 West State Street, Suite 1006
Trenton NJ 08608
609/392-1000
FAX: 609/396-4231
Internet: http://www.njua.org
AMOUNT: $1,500
FIELD(S): Engineering; Environmental Science; Chemistry; Biology; Business Administration; Accounting
ELIGIBILITY/REQUIREMENTS: Must be minority (Black, Hispanic, American Indian/Alaskan Native, or Asian American/Pacific Islander), female, and/or disabled students; a New Jersey resident; enrolled full time at an institute of higher education; have overall academic excellence; and demonstrate financial need.
HOW TO APPLY: Contact Association.
NUMBER OF AWARDS: 2

2400—NEW YORK STATE GRANGE (Cornell Fund Scholarships)

100 Grange Place

Cortland NY 13045
607/756-7553
FAX: 607/756-7757
E-mail: nysgrange@nysgrange.com
Internet: http://www.nysgrange.com
FIELD(S): Agriculture; Life Sciences
ELIGIBILITY/REQUIREMENTS: Must be enrolled in the College of Agriculture and Life Sciences at Cornell University. Selection is based on character, scholastic record, and need for financial assistance (reference given to farm-reared students whose families are Grange members and to students who transfer from an Agricultural and Technical College of the State University of New York).
HOW TO APPLY: Contact College of Agriculture and Life Sciences for details.

2401—OHIO ENVIRONMENTAL HEALTH ASSOCIATION (OEHA) (George Eagle Memorial Scholarship)

P.O. Box 234
Columbus OH 43216-0234
740/349-6535
FAX: 740/349-6510
E-mail: jebel@lickingcohealth.org
Internet: http://www.oeha.org
AMOUNT: $2,000
DEADLINE(S): FEB 28
FIELD(S): Environmental Health, Environmental Studies, Biology
ELIGIBILITY/REQUIREMENTS: Must be Ohio resident enrolled as sophomore, junior or senior in a program leading to a baccalaureate degree in environmental health, environmental management or related field and express intent to become employed in environmental health in Ohio following graduation.
HOW TO APPLY: See website or write for application or further information.
NUMBER OF AWARDS: 1
RENEWABLE: No
CONTACT: Joe Ebel

2402—PENN STATE UNIVERSITY-COLLEGE OF EARTH AND MINERAL SCIENCES

Committee on Scholarships and Awards
116 Deike Building
University Park PA 16802
814/865-7482
FAX: 814/863-7708
Internet: http://www.ems.psu.edu/prospective/financial.html
AMOUNT: $500-$3,500
DEADLINE(S): None
FIELD(S): Geosciences; Meteorology; Energy, Environmental, and Mineral

Economics; Materials Science and Engineering; Mineral Engineering; Geography
ELIGIBILITY/REQUIREMENTS: Scholarship program open to outstanding undergraduate students accepted to or enrolled in Penn State's College of Earth and Mineral Sciences. Minimum GPA of 3.3 or 3.7 (entering student) on 4.0 scale.
HOW TO APPLY: Contact Dean's office for complete information.
NUMBER OF AWARDS: About 275
RENEWABLE: Yes

2403—RAILWAY TIE ASSOCIATION, THE (John Mabry Forestry Scholarship)

115 Commerce Drive, Suite C
Fayetteville GA 30214
770/460-5553
FAX: 770/460-5573
E-mail: ties@rta.org
Internet: http://rta.org/Programs andServices/ScholarshipInfo.aspx
AMOUNT: $1,250
DEADLINE(S): JUN 30
FIELD(S): Forestry
ELIGIBILITY/REQUIREMENTS: College juniors and seniors as well as college students in 2-year institutions who will be enrolled in accredited forestry schools are eligible. Selection is based on leadership qualities, career objectives, scholastic achievement, and financial need.
HOW TO APPLY: See website for additional information and application (posted in early March). Requirements vary.

2404—RESOURCES FOR THE FUTURE (RFF Summer Internship Program)

1616 P Street NW
Washington DC 20036-1400
202/328-5000
FAX: 202/939-3460
E-mail: mankin@rff.org or voigt@rff.org
Internet: http://www.rff.org/about rff/fellowships internships.htm
AMOUNT: $350-$375/week
DEADLINE(S): MAR 14 (5 p.m., Eastern time)
FIELD(S): Social Sciences, Natural Resources, Energy, Environment
ELIGIBILITY/REQUIREMENTS: Open to U.S. and non-U.S. citizens, undergraduate and graduate students for research in the areas of risk, resource and environmental management, energy and natural resources, and quality of the environment. Candidates should have outstanding policy analysis and writing skills.

HOW TO APPLY: See website for application and additional information. Address inquiries and applications to John Mankin (Energy and Natural Resources and Quality of the Environment) or Marilyn Voigt (Risk, Resource and Environmental Management). These scholarships are not available to immediate family members of anyone involved in the selection of winners or the administration of the scholarship. For any given year, no educational institution may have more than 1 winner.
NUMBER OF AWARDS: Multiple: 1/institution

2405—SAN DIEGO AIR &SPACE MUSEUM (Bill Gibbs Endowment Fund)

Education Office
2001 Pan American Plaza
San Diego CA 92101
619/234-8291, ext. 119
FAX: 619/233-4526
Internet: http://aerospace
museum.org
AMOUNT: $1,500-$2,500
DEADLINE(S): APR 1
FIELD(S): Aerospace, Mathematics, Physics, Science, Engineering
ELIGIBILITY/REQUIREMENTS: Graduating seniors of San Diego County high schools who have been accepted to a 4-year college or university. Academic achievement, strong aviation/aerospace career interests.
HOW TO APPLY: See website or write museum for application.

2406—SIEMENS WESTINGHOUSE (Science and Technology Competition)

186 Wood Avenue South
Iselin NJ 08830
877/822-5233
E-mail: foundation.us@siemens.com
Internet: http://www.siemens-foundation.org
AMOUNT: $120,000 (max.)
DEADLINE(S): Varies
FIELD(S): Biology; Physical Sciences; Mathematics; Physics; Chemistry; Computer Science; Environmental Science
ELIGIBILITY/REQUIREMENTS: Open to U.S. high school seniors to pursue independent science research projects, working individually or in teams of 2 or 3 to develop and test their own ideas. May work with one of the universities/laboratories that serve as Siemens' partners. Students from the U.S. and its territories may compete in 1 of 6 geographic areas. Individual and team national prizewinners receive a second scholarship to be applied to undergraduate or graduate education.
HOW TO APPLY: See website or contact Siemens Foundation for details.

2407—SMITHSONIAN INSTITUTION-ENVIRONMENTAL RESEARCH CENTER (Internship Program)

647 Contees Wharf Road
P.O. Box 28
Edgewater MD 21037-0028
443/482-2217
E-mail: gustafsond@si.edu
Internet: http://www.serc.si.edu/pro_training/internships/internships.jsp
AMOUNT: $400/week (stipend)
DEADLINE(S): NOV 15 (spring interns); FEB 1 (summer interns); JUN 1 (fall interns)
FIELD(S): Environmental Studies
ELIGIBILITY/REQUIREMENTS: 10- to 16-week (40 hours per week) internships for enrolled, or about to be enrolled, undergraduates and beginning graduate students who wish to conduct individual projects in environmental studies under the supervision of professional staff members at the Center. Projects include terrestrial or estuarine environmental research, resource planning and decision-making, and environmental education research and development. U.S. citizenship is not a requirement to participate in this program. Selection is based upon the student's academic credentials, extent of relevant training or experience, letters of recommendation, and the congruence of the student's expressed goals with those of the internship program.
HOW TO APPLY: Contact the Office of Fellowships or see website for application. Submit with essay outlining your past and present academic and nonacademic experience and their relation to the goals you are pursuing at the Smithsonian Environmental Research Center's Internship Program in Environmental Studies, 2 letters of reference, and transcripts. Send attention Internship Coordinator (see below).
CONTACT: Dan Gustafson, Internship Coordinator

2408—SMITHSONIAN INSTITUTION (Minority Student Internship Program)

Office of Research Training and Services
470 L'Enfant SW, Suite 7102
MRC 902, P.O. Box 37012
Washington DC 20013-7012
202/633-7070
FAX: 202/633-7069
E-mail: siofg@si.edu
Internet: http://www.si.edu/research+study
AMOUNT: $500/week + possible travel expenses
DEADLINE(S): FEB 1 (for Summer or for Fall); OCT 1 (for Spring)
FIELD(S): Humanities; Environmental Studies; Cultural Studies; Natural History; Earth Science; Art History; Biology
ELIGIBILITY/REQUIREMENTS: 10-week, full-time internships in residence at the Smithsonian are open to U.S. minority students who wish to participate in research or museum-related activities in above and related fields. Must be undergraduates or beginning graduate students with a minimum 3.0 GPA. Must submit essay, résumé, and official transcript.
HOW TO APPLY: Contact the Office of Research Training and Services or see website for an application. Submit with the required essay or research proposal, résumé, and transcripts.

2409—SOCIETY FOR RANGE MANAGEMENT (Masonic-Range Science Scholarship)

10030 W 27th Avenue
Wheat Ridge CO 80215-6601
303/986-3309
FAX: 303/986-3892
Email: vskiff@rangelands.orgInternet: http://www.rangelands.org
AMOUNT: Varies
DEADLINE(S): JAN 15 (subject to change)
FIELD(S): Range Science/Management or closely related field
ELIGIBILITY/REQUIREMENTS: Open to high school seniors or college freshmen or sophomores planning to major or currently majoring in range science/management or a closely related field. Must be planning or currently attending a college or university with a range science program. Must be sponsored by a member of SRM, the National Association of Conservation Districts (NACD), or the Soil and Water Conservation Society (SWCS).
HOW TO APPLY: See website or contact Society for an application and more information. Submit with high school transcript and if applicable a copy of college transcripts; SAT or ACT scores (even if college

student); and 2 letters of reference from teachers, county agents, employers, etc., who might have insight as to your qualifications. Mail to Paul Loeffler, Texas General Land Office, 500 West Avenue H, Box 2, Alpine, TX 79830-6008.
NUMBER OF AWARDS: 1
RENEWABLE: Yes, maximum 8 semesters. Must maintain a 2.5 GPA during the first 2 semesters (freshman year only) and a 3.0 GPA in any subsequent semester (GPA is per semester not cumulative) to continue to receive the scholarship for the remaining years of eligibility.

2410—SOIL AND WATER CONSERVATION SOCIETY (Donald A. Williams Soil Conservation Scholarship)

7515 Southwest Ankeny Road
Ankeny IA 50021-9764
515/289-2331 or 800/THE-SOIL
FAX: 515/289-1227
E-mail: swcs@swcs.org
Internet: http://www.swcs.org/
AMOUNT: $1,500
DEADLINE(S): FEB 12
FIELD(S): Conservation-related fields (technical or administrative course work)
ELIGIBILITY/REQUIREMENTS: For SWCS members currently employed in a related field who have completed at least 1 year of natural resource conservation work with a governmental agency or private organization. Need not be working toward a degree, but must be undergraduate. Must demonstrate financial need.
HOW TO APPLY: Write or see website (click on About SWCS and then on Chapters) for information.
NUMBER OF AWARDS: Up to 3

2411—STUDENT CONSERVATION ASSOCIATION (SCA Resource Assistant Program)

P.O. Box 550
Charlestown NH 03603
603/543-1700
FAX: 603/543-1828
E-mail: internships@sca-inc.org
Internet: http://www.sca-inc.org
AMOUNT: $1,180-$4,725
DEADLINE(S): Varies
FIELD(S): Environment and related fields (agriculture, archaeology, anthropology, botany, caves, civil engineering, environmental design, engineering & education, fisheries, forests, herpetology, history, landscape architecture, environmental design, paleontology, wildlife management,

geology, hydrology, library/museums, surveying)
ELIGIBILITY/REQUIREMENTS: Must be 18 and U.S. citizen; need not be student.
HOW TO APPLY: Send $1 for postage for application; outside U.S./Canada, send $20.
NUMBER OF AWARDS: 900 positions in U.S. and Canada

2412—UNCF/MERCK SCIENCE INITIATIVE (Undergraduate Science Research Scholarship Awards)

8260 Willow Oaks Corporate Dr.
P.O. Box 10444
Fairfax VA 22031-4511
703/205-3503
FAX: 703/205-3574
E-mail: uncfmerck@uncf.org
Internet: http://www.uncf.org/merck
AMOUNT: $25,000/year (maximum)
DEADLINE(S): DEC 15
FIELD(S): Life and Physical Sciences
ELIGIBILITY/REQUIREMENTS: Open to African-Americans in their junior year of college who will receive a bachelor's degree in the following academic year. Must be enrolled full time in any 4-year college or university in the U.S. and have a minimum 3.3 GPA. Must be U.S. citizen/permanent resident. Financial need NOT a factor.
HOW TO APPLY: Contact UNCF/Merck for an application.
NUMBER OF AWARDS: 15
RENEWABLE: No
CONTACT: Jerry Bryant, Ph.D.

2413—WESTERN MICHIGAN UNIVERSITY (College of Arts and Sciences/Hazel Wirick Scholarship)

1903 West Michigan
Kalamazoo MI 49008-5337
269/387-8777
FAX: 269/387-6989
E-mail: finaid-info@wmich.edu
Internet: http://www.wmich.edu/finaid
AMOUNT: $1,000
DEADLINE(S): MAR 1
FIELD(S): Plant Biology; Ecology
ELIGIBILITY/REQUIREMENTS: Upper classmen or graduate students majoring in plant biology or ecology; high GPA.
HOW TO APPLY: Contact the Biological Sciences Department for an application.
RENEWABLE: No

MARINE SCIENCE

2414—AMERICAN GROUND WATER TRUST (Amtrol, Inc. Scholarship)

16 Centre Street
Concord NH 03301
603/228-5444
FAX: 603/228-6557
E-mail: trustinfo@agwt.org
Internet: http://www.amtrol.com/scholarships.htm
AMOUNT: $1,000
DEADLINE(S): JUN 1
FIELD(S): Environmental Science; Environmental Engineering; Marine Science; Natural Resources
ELIGIBILITY/REQUIREMENTS: Must be high school seniors; intend to pursue a career in a ground water-related field; be entering their freshmen year at a 4-year accredited college or university; have a minimum 3.0 GPA in high school; have completed a science/environmental project in high school that directly involved ground water resources or have had vacation/out-of-school work experience related to the environment and natural resources; be U.S. citizens or legal residents of the U.S.
HOW TO APPLY: Send application that has been signed by a teacher at the applicant's high school; a 500-word essay (on "Ground Water: An Important Environmental and Economic Resource for America") and a 300-word description of the applicant's high school ground water project and/or practical work experience; and 2 letters of recommendation. Also, documentary evidence of scholastic achievements and references will be requested in mid-June from finalists.

2415—AMERICAN METEOROLOGY SOCIETY (AMS/Crow Scholarship)

Fellowship/Scholarship Program
45 Beacon Street
Boston MA 02108-3693
617/227-2426
FAX: 617/742-8718
E-mail: dfernand@ametsoc.org or armstrong@ametsoc.org
Internet: http://www.ametsoc.org
AMOUNT: Varies
DEADLINE(S): FEB 21
FIELD(S): Atmospheric Sciences; Oceanography; Hydrology
ELIGIBILITY/REQUIREMENTS: Open to juniors entering senior year, who are U.S. citizens or permanent residents and

has evidenced an interest in applied meteorology. MUST be majoring in atmospheric or related oceanic or hydrologic sciences and/or must show clear intent to make the atmospheric or related sciences their career.

HOW TO APPLY: See website for additional information and application or e-mail or write to contact below at AMS headquarters (include SASE).

NUMBER OF AWARDS: Varies

CONTACT: Donna Sampson, Development & Student Programs Manager, ext. 246 or Stephanie Armstrong, Director of Development, ext 235

2416—AMERICAN METEOROLOGY SOCIETY (AMS/Freshman Undergraduate Scholarship Program)

Fellowship/Scholarship Program
45 Beacon Street
Boston MA 02108-3693
617/227-2426
FAX: 617/742-8718
E-mail: dfernand@ametsoc.org or armstrong@ametsoc.org
Internet: http://www.ametsoc.org
AMOUNT: $2,500
DEADLINE(S): FEB 21
FIELD(S): Atmospheric Sciences; Oceanography; Hydrology
ELIGIBILITY/REQUIREMENTS: Open to high school seniors entering freshman year, who are U.S. citizens or permanent residents. Awards based on academic excellence.

HOW TO APPLY: See website for additional information and application or e-mail or write to contact below at AMS headquarters (include SASE).

NUMBER OF AWARDS: Varies

RENEWABLE: Yes. For sophomore year only. Must demonstrate a successful 1st year and plans to continue studies in the AMS-related sciences.

CONTACT: Donna Sampson, Development & Student Programs Manager, ext. 246 or Stephanie Armstrong, Director of Development, ext. 235

2417—AMERICAN METEOROLOGY SOCIETY (AMS/Glahn Scholarship)

Fellowship/Scholarship Program
45 Beacon Street
Boston MA 02108-3693
617/227-2426
FAX: 617/742-8718
E-mail: dfernand@ametsoc.org or armstrong@ametsoc.org
Internet: http://www.ametsoc.org

AMOUNT: Varies
DEADLINE(S): FEB 21
FIELD(S): Atmospheric Sciences; Oceanography; Hydrology
ELIGIBILITY/REQUIREMENTS: Open to juniors entering senior year, who are U.S. citizens or permanent residents and has evidenced an interest in statistical meteorology. MUST be majoring in atmospheric or related oceanic or hydrologic sciences and/or must show clear intent to make the atmospheric or related sciences their career.

HOW TO APPLY: See website for additional information and application or e-mail or write to contact below at AMS headquarters (include SASE).

NUMBER OF AWARDS: Varies

CONTACT: Donna Sampson, Development & Student Programs Manager, ext. 246 or Stephanie Armstrong, Director of Development, ext. 235

2418—AMERICAN METEOROLOGY SOCIETY (AMS/Industry Minority Scholarships)

Fellowship/Scholarship Program
45 Beacon Street
Boston MA 02108-3693
617/227-2426
FAX: 617/742-8718
E-mail: dfernand@ametsoc.org or armstrong@ametsoc.org
Internet: http://www.ametsoc.org
AMOUNT: $3,000
DEADLINE(S): FEB 21
FIELD(S): Atmospheric Sciences; Oceanography; Hydrology
ELIGIBILITY/REQUIREMENTS: Open to minority—especially Hispanic, Native American, and Black/African American—high school seniors entering freshman year at a 4-year U.S. accredited institution. Must be U.S. citizens or permanent residents and mustplan to pursue a career in the atmospheric or related oceanic or hydrologic sciences.

HOW TO APPLY: See website for additional information and application or e-mail or write to contact below at AMS headquarters (include SASE).

NUMBER OF AWARDS: Varies

RENEWABLE: Yes. For sophomore year only. Must demonstrate a successful 1st year and plans to continue studies in the AMS-related sciences.

2419—AMERICAN METEOROLOGY SOCIETY (AMS/Murphy Scholarship)

Fellowship/Scholarship Program
45 Beacon Street

Boston MA 02108-3693
617/227-2426
FAX: 617/742-8718
E-mail: dfernand@ametsoc.org or armstrong@ametsoc.org
Internet: http://www.ametsoc.org
AMOUNT: Varies
DEADLINE(S): FEB 21
FIELD(S): Atmospheric Sciences; Oceanography; Hydrology
ELIGIBILITY/REQUIREMENTS: Open to juniors entering senior year, who are U.S. citizens or permanent residents, and who, through curricular or extracurricular activities, has evidenced an interest in weather forecasting or in the value and utilization of forecasts. MUST be majoring in atmospheric or related oceanic or hydrologic sciences and/or must show clear intent to make the atmospheric or related sciences their career.

HOW TO APPLY: See website for additional information and application or e-mail or write to contact below at AMS headquarters (include SASE).

NUMBER OF AWARDS: Varies

CONTACT: Donna Sampson, Development & Student Programs Manager, ext. 246 or Stephanie Armstrong, Director of Development, ext. 235

2420—AMERICAN METEOROLOGY SOCIETY (AMS/Schroeder Scholarship)

Fellowship/Scholarship Program
45 Beacon Street
Boston MA 02108-3693
617/227-2426
FAX: 617/742-8718
E-mail: dfernand@ametsoc.org or armstrong@ametsoc.org
Internet: http://www.ametsoc.org
AMOUNT: Varies
DEADLINE(S): FEB 21
FIELD(S): Atmospheric Sciences; Oceanography; Hydrology
ELIGIBILITY/REQUIREMENTS: Open to juniors entering senior year, who are U.S. citizens or permanent residents. MUST be majoring in atmospheric or related oceanic or hydrologic sciences and/or must show clear intent to make the atmospheric or related sciences their career. Must demonstrate financial need.

HOW TO APPLY: See website for additional information and application or e-mail or write to contact below at AMS headquarters (include SASE).

NUMBER OF AWARDS: Varies

CONTACT: Donna Sampson, Development & Student Programs Manager, ext.

246 or Stephanie Armstrong, Director of Development, ext. 235

2421—AMERICAN WATER RESOURCES ASSOCIATION (Richard A. Herbert Memorial Scholarships)

4 West Federal Street
P.O. Box 1626
Middleburg VA 20118-1626
540/687-8390
FAX: 540/687-8395
E-mail: info@awra.org
Internet: http://www.awra.org
AMOUNT: $2,000
DEADLINE(S): APR 30
FIELD(S): Water Resources and related fields (hydrology, hydrogeology, G.I.S., earth science, watershed studies and others)
ELIGIBILITY/REQUIREMENTS: Must be a national AWRA member, either a full-time undergraduate working towards first degree or graduate student. Must be enrolled in a program relating to water resources for the academic year. Based on academic performance, including cumulative GPA, relevance of curriculum to water resources, and leadership in extracurricular activities related to water resources. Quality and relevance of research is also considered from graduate students.
HOW TO APPLY: Contact AWRA Student Activities Committee for an application. Transcripts, 3 letters of reference (preferably from professors or advisors), and 2-page summary of academic interests/achievements, extracurricular interests, and career goals required.
NUMBER OF AWARDS: 2 (1 undergrad and 1 graduate)

2422—FLORIDA FEDERATION OF GARDEN CLUBS, INC. (FFGC Scholarships for College Students)

706 Glen Eagle Drive
Winter Springs FL 32708
407/971-6979
Internet: http://www.ffgc.org
AMOUNT: $650-$3,000
DEADLINE(S): MAY 1
FIELD(S): Agriculture; Environmental & Conservation issues; Botany; Biology; Forestry; Horticulture; Ecology; Marine Biology; Wildflowers; Butterflies; Landscaping
ELIGIBILITY/REQUIREMENTS: Must be U.S. citizen and Florida resident for at least 1 year, with 3.0 GPA, attending a college or university in Florida. Financial need considered.

HOW TO APPLY: See website or contact FFGC Chair for an application.
RENEWABLE: Yes, must reapply.
CONTACT: Jane Meherg, Scholarship Chairman

2423—HAWAII COMMUNITY FOUNDATION (Nick Van Pernis Scholarship Fund)

1164 Bishop Street, Suite 800
Honolulu HI 96813
808/537-6333 or 888/731-3863
FAX: 808/521-6286
E-mail: info@hcf-hawaii.org
Internet: http://www.hcf-hawaii.org
DEADLINE(S): MAR 1
FIELD(S): Marine Sciences; Health Sciences; Biotechnology; Early Childhood Education
ELIGIBILITY/REQUIREMENTS: Must be graduates of a public or private high school in the Districts of North Kona, South Kona, North Kohala, or Ka'u; plan to attend full time an accredited 2- or 4-year college or university; demonstrate financial need, good moral character, and academic achievement (minimum GPA of 2.7).
HOW TO APPLY: See website. Send application; 2 letters of recommendation; a short essay explaining how your career can benefit Hawaii; and a record of community service.

2424—NORTH CAROLINA STATE UNIVERSITY (Thomas Jefferson Scholarship in Agriculture/Life Sciences and Humanities)

Jefferson Scholars
College of Agriculture and Life Sciences
Box 7642
Raleigh NC 27695-7642
Internet: http://www.cals.ncsu.edu/student orgs/jeffer/apply.html
AMOUNT: $1,000
DEADLINE(S): FEB
FIELD(S): Agriculture/Life Sciences AND Humanities
ELIGIBILITY/REQUIREMENTS: Open to first-year undergraduate students with a double major in agriculture/life sciences and humanities.
HOW TO APPLY: See website or write for application and additional information. Submit with an essay, evaluation from a teacher or school official, and transcript.
NUMBER OF AWARDS: 15
RENEWABLE: Yes

2425—OUR WORLD-UNDERWATER SCHOLARSHIP SOCIETY (Scholarship and Internships)

P.O. Box 4428
Chicago IL 60680
630/969-6990
FAX: 630/958-6690
E-mail: execadmin@owu scholarship.org
Internet: http://www.owu scholarship.org
AMOUNT: $20,000 (experience-based scholarship reimbursable funds)
DEADLINE(S): NOV 30
FIELD(S): Marine Biology and Aquamarine related disciplines
ELIGIBILITY/REQUIREMENTS: Must be certified SCUBA diver between 21 AND 24 on March 1 of the scholarship year. Cannot have received a postgraduate degree. Funds for transportation and living expenses for active participation in field studies, underwater research, scientific expeditions, laboratory assignments, equipment testing and design, and photographic instruction. Financial need NOT a factor.
HOW TO APPLY: Check the website for more information or contact the OWU for an application.
NUMBER OF AWARDS: 2 scholarships (1 for North American and 1 for European) and several internships
RENEWABLE: No
CONTACT: Roberta Flanders, Executive Administrator

2426—SAN DIEGO AIR &SPACE MUSEUM (Bill Gibbs Endowment Fund)

Education Office
2001 Pan American Plaza
San Diego CA 92101
619/234-8291, ext. 119
FAX: 619/233-4526
Internet: http://aerospace museum.org
AMOUNT: $1,500-$2,500
DEADLINE(S): APR 1
FIELD(S): Aerospace, Mathematics, Physics, Science, Engineering
ELIGIBILITY/REQUIREMENTS: Graduating seniors of San Diego County high schools who have been accepted to a 4-year college or university. Academic achievement, strong aviation/aerospace career interests. Eligible applications will be interviewed.
HOW TO APPLY: See website or write museum for application.

2427—SEASPACE

P.O. Box 3753
Houston TX 77253-3753
E-mail: captx@piovere.com
Internet: http://www.seaspace.org/
schship.htm
AMOUNT: $500-$3,000
DEADLINE(S): FEB 1
FIELD(S): Marine/Aquatic Sciences
ELIGIBILITY/REQUIREMENTS: Open
to college juniors, seniors, and graduate
students attending school in the U.S. Must
have a 3.3/4.0 GPA and demonstrate finan-
cial need.
HOW TO APPLY: See website or contact
SEASPACE for an application.
NUMBER OF AWARDS: 10-15

2428—SIEMENS WESTINGHOUSE (Science and Technology Competition)

186 Wood Avenue South
Iselin NJ 08830
877/822-5233
E-mail: foundation.us@siemens.com
Internet: http://www.siemens-
foundation.org
AMOUNT: $120,000 (maximum)
DEADLINE(S): Varies
FIELD(S): Biology; Physical Sciences;
Mathematics; Physics; Chemistry;
Computer Science; Environmental
Science
ELIGIBILITY/REQUIREMENTS: Open
to U.S. high school seniors to pursue independent science research projects, working
individually or in teams of 2 or 3 to develop and test their own ideas. May work with
one of the universities/laboratories that
serve as Siemens' partners. Students from
the U.S. and its territories may compete in
1 of 6 geographic areas. Individual and
team national prizewinners receive a second scholarship to be applied to undergraduate or graduate education.
HOW TO APPLY: See website or contact
Siemens Foundation for details.

2429—SOCIETY OF NAVAL ARCHITECTS AND MARINE ENGINEERS, THE (Undergraduate Scholarship)

601 Pavonia Avenue
Jersey City NJ 07306
800/798-2188 or 201/798-4800
FAX: 201/798-4975
Internet: http://www.sname.org
AMOUNT: Up to $2,000
DEADLINE(S): MAY 1
FIELD(S): Naval Architecture; Marine
Engineering, Ocean Engineering, or
marine industry-related field

ELIGIBILITY/REQUIREMENTS: Open
to citizens of the U.S. and Canada; study
toward a degree in one of the above fields
at participating schools; must be entering
junior or senior year; membership in the
society at the time of the award.
HOW TO APPLY: Submit application
through your school with 3 letters of recommendation, transcript, and statement
indicating your career goals and why you
are interested in marine science.

2430—STUDENT CONSERVATION ASSO-CIATION (SCA Resource Assistant Program)

P.O. Box 550
Charlestown NH 03603
603/543-1700
FAX: 603/543-1828
E-mail: internships@sca-inc.org
Internet: http://www.sca-inc.org
AMOUNT: $1,180-$4,725
DEADLINE(S): Varies
FIELD(S): Environment and related
fields (agriculture, archaeology,
anthropology, botany, caves, civil
engineering, environmental design,
engineering & education, fisheries,
forests, herpetology, history, landscape
architecture, environmental design,
paleontology, wildlife management,
geology, hydrology, library/museums,
surveying)
ELIGIBILITY/REQUIREMENTS: Must
be 18 and U.S. citizen; need not be student.
HOW TO APPLY: Send $1 for postage for
application; outside U.S./Canada, send
$20.
NUMBER OF AWARDS: 900 positions
in U.S. and Canada.

2431—WOMAN'S SEAMEN'S FRIEND SOCIETY

291 Whitney Avenue, Suite 203
New Haven CT 06511
203/777-2165
FAX: 203/777-5774
E-mail: wsfsofct@earthlink.net
DEADLINE(S): APR 1
FIELD(S): All (emphasis on Marine
Science and related fields)
ELIGIBILITY/REQUIREMENTS:
Connecticut residents who are students at
maritime academies; majoring in marine
sciences and related fields in other schools;
dependents of Merchant Marines regard-
less of major.
HOW TO APPLY: Request application
from above address or financial aid office
at your school.
RENEWABLE: Yes, must reapply.

2432—WOODS HOLE OCEANOGRAPHIC INSTITUTION (Summer Student Fellowship)

Clark Laboratory 223, MS #31
Woods Hole MA 02543-1541
508/289-2219
FAX: 508/457-2188
E-mail: education@whoi.edu
Internet: http://www.whoi.edu
AMOUNT: $380/week for 10-12 weeks;
possible travel allowance
DEADLINE(S): FEB 15
FIELD(S): Science; Engineering;
Mathematics; Marine Sciences/
Engineering; Policy
ELIGIBILITY/REQUIREMENTS: Open
to undergraduates who have completed
their junior or senior year, with backgrounds in science, mathematics, and engineering interested in the marine sciences
and oceanography. Selection based on academic and scientific achievements and
promise as future ocean scientists and
engineers.
HOW TO APPLY: For an application and
additional information, contact the
Academic Programs Office, Clark Laboratory. Submit with résumé demonstrating
educational background and work experience; a transcript and/or other official documentation of undergraduate record; at
least 3 letters of recommendation from
professors, employers, others; a statement
of research interests, future education and
career plans, and reasons for applying for
fellowship.

2433—WOODS HOLE OCEANOGRAPHIC INSTITUTION (Traineeships in Oceanography for Minority Group Undergraduates)

Clark Laboratory 223, MS #31
Woods Hole MA 02543-1541
508/289-2219
FAX: 508/457-2188
E-mail: education@whoi.edu
Internet: http://www.whoi.edu
AMOUNT: Varies
DEADLINE(S): FEB 15
FIELD(S): Physical/Natural Sciences,
Mathematics, Engineering
ELIGIBILITY/REQUIREMENTS: For
minority undergraduates (African-
American or Black, Asian-American,
Chicano, Mexican-American, Puerto
Rican or other Hispanic, and Native
American) who are enrolled in U.S. col-
leges/universities and have completed at
least 2 semesters. Traineeships may be
awarded for a 10- to 12-week period in the
summer or for a semester during the aca-
demic year.

HOW TO APPLY: For an application and additional information, contact the Academic Programs Office, Clark Laboratory. Submit with current résumé demonstrating educational background and work experience; an official transcript and/or other official documentation of undergraduate record; at least 3 letters of recommendation from professors, employers, others; a statement of research interests, future education and career plans, and reasons for applying for fellowship.

PHYSICS

2434—AMERICAN CHEMICAL SOCIETY-RUBBER DIVISION

P.O. Box 499
Akron OH 44309-0499
330/972-7814
FAX: 330/972-5269
E-mail: crobinson@rubber.org
Internet: http://www.rubber.org/awards/scholarships.htm
AMOUNT: $5,000
DEADLINE(S): MAR 15
FIELD(S): Chemistry, Physics, Chemical Engineering, Mechanical Engineering, Polymer Science, or other rubber-related discipline
ELIGIBILITY/REQUIREMENTS: Incoming junior or senior enrolled in an accredited college or university in the United States, Canada, Mexico, Brazil or India (countries may change) majoring in a rubber industry-related field. Must have "B" or better overall academic average, and a minimum of 3 semesters or 6 terms completed, and intend to pursue full-time professional employment in the industry.
HOW TO APPLY: Download application from website and fax or mail application along with 2 or more nomination letters from professor/nominator. Official transcripts may follow.
NUMBER OF AWARDS: 3
RENEWABLE: Yes. Must reapply for 2nd and final year.
CONTACT: Christie Robinson, Education & Publications Manager

2435—AMERICAN NUCLEAR SOCIETY (Angelo S. Bisesti Scholarship)

555 North Kensington Avenue
La Grange Park IL 60526
708/352-6611
FAX: 708/352-0499
E-mail: outreach@ans.org
Internet: http://www.ans.org
AMOUNT: $2,000
DEADLINE(S): FEB 1
FIELD(S): Nuclear Science; Nuclear Engineering
ELIGIBILITY/REQUIREMENTS: Must be junior or senior enrolled in a U.S. institution; U.S. citizen or permanent resident; and pursuing a career in commercial nuclear power.
HOW TO APPLY: See website for application; submit to Scholarship Coordinator.
NUMBER OF AWARDS: 1
RENEWABLE: No

2436—AMERICAN NUCLEAR SOCIETY (Charles "Tommy" Thomas Memorial Scholarship)

555 North Kensington Avenue
La Grange Park IL 60526
708/352-6611
FAX: 708/352-0499
E-mail: outreach@ans.org
Internet: http://www.ans.org
AMOUNT: $2,000
DEADLINE(S): FEB 1
FIELD(S): Nuclear Science & Engineering, Environmental Studies
ELIGIBILITY/REQUIREMENTS: Must be juniors or seniors enrolled in a U.S. institution; be U.S. citizens or permanent residents; and be pursuing a career dealing with the environmental aspects of nuclear science or nuclear engineering.
HOW TO APPLY: See website for application Submit with brief essay describing how your perception of environmental science and engineering related topics fitting into the nuclear field and how you plan to contribute to the field during the course of your professional career.
NUMBER OF AWARDS: 1
RENEWABLE: No
CONTACT: Scholarship Coordinator

2437—AMERICAN NUCLEAR SOCIETY (Decommissioning, Decontamination & Reutilization Division Scholarship)

555 North Kensington Avenue
La Grange Park IL 60526
708/352-6611
FAX: 708/352-0499
E-mail: outreach@ans.org
Internet: http://www.ans.org
AMOUNT: $2,000
DEADLINE(S): FEB 1
FIELD(S): Nuclear Science; Nuclear Engineering
ELIGIBILITY/REQUIREMENTS: Must be junior or senior enrolled in a U.S. institution and U.S. citizen or permanent resident; enrolled in an engineering or science curriculum associated either with decom-missioning/decontamination of nuclear facilities, management/characterization of nuclear waste, or restoration of the environment; join the ANS; and designate the DD&R Division as professional division.
HOW TO APPLY: See website for application; submit to Scholarship Coordinator, with brief essay discussing the importance of some aspect of DD&R to the future of the nuclear field. Must commit to participating in the DD&R Division Activities by attedning the annual and winter meetings of the ANS and serving as a student representative at the DD&R Executive Committee meetings at both ANS meetings.
NUMBER OF AWARDS: 1
RENEWABLE: No
ADDITIONAL INFORMATION: Funding for travel, including student registration, reasonable transportation, food, and lodging also provided.

2438—AMERICAN NUCLEAR SOCIETY (Delayed Education Scholarship for Women)

555 North Kensington Avenue
La Grange Park IL 60526
708/352-6611
FAX: 708/352-0499
E-mail: outreach@ans.org
Internet: http://www.ans.org
AMOUNT: $4,000
DEADLINE(S): FEB 1
FIELD(S): Nuclear Science; Nuclear Engineering
ELIGIBILITY/REQUIREMENTS: Must be a mature female undergraduate (or graduate) student whose undergraduate studies in nuclear science, nuclear engineering, or a nuclear-related field have been delayed; enrolled in a U.S. institution; and a U.S. citizen or permanent resident.
HOW TO APPLY: See website for application; submit to Scholarship Coordinator.
NUMBER OF AWARDS: 1
RENEWABLE: No

2439—AMERICAN NUCLEAR SOCIETY (James R. Vogt Radiochemistry Scholarship)

555 North Kensington Avenue
La Grange Park IL 60526
708/352-6611
FAX: 708/352-0499
E-mail: outreach@ans.org
Internet: http://www.ans.org
AMOUNT: $2,000
DEADLINE(S): FEB 1
FIELD(S): Nuclear Science; Nuclear Engineering

ELIGIBILITY/REQUIREMENTS: Must be junior or senior (or graduate student) enrolled in a U.S. institution; U.S. citizen or permanent resident; and enrolled in or proposing to undertake research in radio-analytical chemistry, analytical chemistry, or analytical applications of nuclear science.
HOW TO APPLY: See website for application; submit to Scholarship Coordinator.
NUMBER OF AWARDS: 1
RENEWABLE: No

2440—AMERICAN NUCLEAR SOCIETY
(John & Muriel Landis Scholarship)

555 North Kensington Avenue
La Grange Park IL 60526
708/352-6611
FAX: 708/352-0499
E-mail: outreach@ans.org
Internet: http://www.ans.org
AMOUNT: $4,000
DEADLINE(S): FEB 1
FIELD(S): Nuclear Science; Nuclear Engineering
ELIGIBILITY/REQUIREMENTS: Must be undergraduate (or graduate) student enrolled in a U.S. institution; U.S. citizen or permanent resident; and have greater than average financial need.
HOW TO APPLY: See website for application; submit to Scholarship Coordinator.
NUMBER OF AWARDS: Up to 8
RENEWABLE: No

2441—AMERICAN NUCLEAR SOCIETY
(John R. Lamarsh Scholarship)

555 North Kensington Avenue
La Grange Park IL 60526
708/352-6611
FAX: 708/352-0499
E-mail: outreach@ans.org
Internet: http://www.ans.org
AMOUNT: $2,000
DEADLINE(S): FEB 1
FIELD(S): Nuclear Science; Nuclear Engineering
ELIGIBILITY/REQUIREMENTS: Must be junior or senior enrolled in a U.S. institution and U.S. citizen or permanent resident.
HOW TO APPLY: See website for application; submit to Scholarship Coordinator.
NUMBER OF AWARDS: 1
RENEWABLE: No

2442—AMERICAN NUCLEAR SOCIETY
(Joseph R. Dietrich Scholarship)

555 North Kensington Avenue
La Grange Park IL 60526

708/352-6611
FAX: 708/352-0499
E-mail: outreach@ans.org
Internet: http://www.ans.org
AMOUNT: $2,000
DEADLINE(S): FEB 1
FIELD(S): Nuclear Science; Nuclear Engineering
ELIGIBILITY/REQUIREMENTS: Must be junior or senior enrolled in a U.S. institution and U.S. citizen or permanent resident.
HOW TO APPLY: See website for application; submit to Scholarship Coordinator.
NUMBER OF AWARDS: 1
RENEWABLE: No

2443—AMERICAN NUCLEAR SOCIETY
(Nuclear Engineering Education for the Disadvantaged Program)

555 North Kensington Avenue
La Grange Park IL 60526-5592
708/352-6611
E-mail: nucleus@ans.org
Internet: http://www.ans.org
AMOUNT: $3,500
DEADLINE(S): MAR
FIELD(S): Science
ELIGIBILITY/REQUIREMENTS: For disadvantaged students interested in nuclear science as a career.
HOW TO APPLY: See website for application; submit to Scholarship Coordinator.

2444—AMERICAN NUCLEAR SOCIETY
(Operations & Power Division Scholarship)

555 North Kensington Avenue
La Grange Park IL 60526
708/352-6611
FAX: 708/352-0499
E-mail: outreach@ans.org
Internet: http://www.ans.org
AMOUNT: $2,500
DEADLINE(S): FEB 1
FIELD(S): Nuclear Science; Nuclear Engineering
ELIGIBILITY/REQUIREMENTS: Must be junior or senior enrolled in a U.S. institution and U.S. citizen or permanent resident.
HOW TO APPLY: See website for application; submit to Scholarship Coordinator.
NUMBER OF AWARDS: 1
RENEWABLE: No

2445—AMERICAN NUCLEAR SOCIETY
(Pittsburgh Local Section Scholarship)

555 North Kensington Avenue
La Grange Park IL 60526

708/352-6611
FAX: 708/352-0499
E-mail: outreach@ans.org
Internet: http://www.ans.org
AMOUNT: $2,000
DEADLINE(S): FEB 1
FIELD(S): Nuclear Science; Nuclear Engineering
ELIGIBILITY/REQUIREMENTS: Must be junior or senior enrolled in a U.S. institution and U.S. citizen or permanent resident; and have some affiliation with Western Pennsylvania or attend school at a nearby university within the region.
HOW TO APPLY: See website for application; submit to Scholarship Coordinator.
NUMBER OF AWARDS: 1
RENEWABLE: No

2446—AMERICAN NUCLEAR SOCIETY
(Raymond DiSalvo Scholarship)

555 North Kensington Avenue
La Grange Park IL 60526
708/352-6611
FAX: 708/352-0499
E-mail: outreach@ans.org
Internet: http://www.ans.org
AMOUNT: $2,000
DEADLINE(S): FEB 1
FIELD(S): Nuclear Science; Nuclear Engineering
ELIGIBILITY/REQUIREMENTS: Must be junior or senior enrolled in a U.S. institution and U.S. citizen or permanent resident.
HOW TO APPLY: See website for application; submit to Scholarship Coordinator.
NUMBER OF AWARDS: 1
RENEWABLE: No

2447—AMERICAN NUCLEAR SOCIETY
(Robert G. Lacy Scholarship)

555 North Kensington Avenue
La Grange Park IL 60526
708/352-6611
FAX: 708/352-0499
E-mail: outreach@ans.org
Internet: http://www.ans.org
AMOUNT: $2,000
DEADLINE(S): FEB 1
FIELD(S): Nuclear Science; Nuclear Engineering
ELIGIBILITY/REQUIREMENTS: Must be junior or senior enrolled in a U.S. institution and U.S. citizen or permanent resident.
HOW TO APPLY: See website for application; submit to Scholarship Coordinator.
NUMBER OF AWARDS: 1
RENEWABLE: No

2448—AMERICAN NUCLEAR SOCIETY (Robert T. Liner Scholarship)

555 North Kensington Avenue
La Grange Park IL 60526
708/352-6611
FAX: 708/352-0499
E-mail: outreach@ans.org
Internet: http://www.ans.org
AMOUNT: $2,000
DEADLINE(S): FEB 1
FIELD(S): Nuclear Science; Nuclear Engineering
ELIGIBILITY/REQUIREMENTS: Must be junior or senior enrolled in a U.S. institution and U.S. citizen or permanent resident.
HOW TO APPLY: See website for application; submit to Scholarship Coordinator.
NUMBER OF AWARDS: 1
RENEWABLE: No

2449—AMERICAN NUCLEAR SOCIETY (Undergraduate Scholarship-Juniors & Seniors)

555 North Kensington Avenue
La Grange Park IL 60526
708/352-6611
FAX: 708/352-0499
E-mail: outreach@ans.org
Internet: http://www.ans.org
AMOUNT: $2,000
DEADLINE(S): FEB 1
FIELD(S): Nuclear Science; Nuclear Engineering
ELIGIBILITY/REQUIREMENTS: Must be juniors or seniors enrolled in a U.S. institution and U.S. citizens or permanent residents.
HOW TO APPLY: See website for application; submit to Scholarship Coordinator.
NUMBER OF AWARDS: 21
RENEWABLE: No

2450—AMERICAN NUCLEAR SOCIETY (Undergraduate Scholarship-Sophomore)

555 North Kensington Avenue
La Grange Park IL 60526
708/352-6611
FAX: 708/352-0499
E-mail: outreach@ans.org
Internet: http://www.ans.org
AMOUNT: $2,000
DEADLINE(S): FEB 1
FIELD(S): Nuclear Science; Nuclear Engineering
ELIGIBILITY/REQUIREMENTS: Must be sophomores enrolled in a U.S. institution and be U.S. citizens or permanent residents.

HOW TO APPLY: See website for application; submit to Scholarship Coordinator.
NUMBER OF AWARDS: 4
RENEWABLE: No

2451—AMERICAN PHYSICAL SOCIETY (APS Scholarship for Minority Undergraduate Physics Majors)

One Physics Ellipse
College Park MD 20740
301/209-3232
E-mail: knowles@aps.org
Internet: http://www.aps.org/programs/minorities
AMOUNT: $2,000
DEADLINE(S): lst Friday in FEB
FIELD(S): Physics
ELIGIBILITY/REQUIREMENTS: Open to African-American, Hispanic-American or Native American high senior, college freshman or sophomore. Must be U.S. citizen or legal permanent resident majoring or planning to major in physics. Attendance at institutions with historically or predominantly Black, Hispanic, or Native American enrollment encouraged.
HOW TO APPLY: See website or e-mail or call for information and application. Submit application with One completed student application form with personal statement, 2 completed reference forms(at least 1 of the references from a science or math teacher/professor), and a current, official transcript. SAT/ACT scores must be sent directly to APS by the Educational Testing Service.
RENEWABLE: Yes. Renewals $3,000.

2452—ARMED FORCES COMMUNICATIONS AND ELECTRONICS ASSOCIATION (AFCEA/ORINCON IT Scholarship)

4400 Fair Lakes Court
Fairfax VA 22033-3899
800/336-4583, ext. 6147 or 703/631-6149
FAX: 703/631-4693
E-mail: scholarships@afcea.org
Internet: http://www.afcea.org
AMOUNT: $2,750
DEADLINE(S): Varies according to eligibility
FIELD(S): Electrical or Aerospace Engineering, Computer Science, Physics, Mathematics
ELIGIBILITY/REQUIREMENTS: Open to persons on active duty in a military service or veterans, their spouses or dependents or civilians who meet the general criteria for the General Wickham Scholarship, provided the school they are attending is an accredited 4-year college or university in the Greater San Diego, California, area. Must have GPA of 3.4 or more.
HOW TO APPLY: Check website or contact AFCEA for information and application.

2453—ARMED FORCES COMMUNICATIONS AND ELECTRONICS ASSOCIATION (AFCEA ROTC Scholarships)

4400 Fair Lakes Court
Fairfax VA 22033-3899
800/336-4583, ext. 6147 or 703/631-6149
FAX: 703/631-4693
E-mail: scholarships@afcea.org
Internet: http://www.afcea.org
AMOUNT: $2,000
DEADLINE(S): APR 1
FIELD(S): Electrical Engineering, Electronics, Computer Science, Computer Systems, or Aerospace Engineering, Physics, Mathematics, science or mathematics education; technology management or other technical fields, or fields related to U.S. intelligence or national security
ELIGIBILITY/REQUIREMENTS: Scholarships for ROTC students working toward a degree in an accredited degree-granting 4-year college or university in the U.S.
HOW TO APPLY: MUST be nominated by Professors of Military Science, Naval Science, or Aerospace Studies. Contact the commander of each ROTC unit at your school or see website for application.

2454—ARMED FORCES COMMUNICATIONS AND ELECTRONICS ASSOCIATION (AFCEA Scholarship for Online or Distance-Learning Programs)

4400 Fair Lakes Court
Fairfax VA 22033-3899
800/336-4583, ext. 6147 or 703/631-6149
FAX: 703/631-4693
E-mail: scholarships@afcea.org
Internet: http://www.afcea.org
AMOUNT: $1,500
DEADLINE(S): JUN 1
FIELD(S): Electrical, Chemical or Aerospace Engineering: Computer Science; Mathematics; Phyiscs; Science or Math Education; Technology Management or fields related to U.S. intelligence or national security
ELIGIBILITY/REQUIREMENTS: Full-time students; undergraduates must have completed 2 semesters of calculus (30-

semester hour equivalent). Must be a U.S. citizen and be currently enrolled in a 4-year college or university in the U.S. at time of application.

HOW TO APPLY: Applications and further information on website.

RENEWABLE: No

2455—ARMED FORCES COMMUNICATIONS AND ELECTRONICS ASSOCIATION (General Emmett Paige Scholarships for Military Personnel, Veterans, and Their Dependents)

4400 Fair Lakes Court
Fairfax VA 22033-3899
800/336-4583, ext. 6147 or
703/631-6149
FAX: 703/631-4693
E-mail: scholarships@afcea.org
Internet: http://www.afcea.org

AMOUNT: $2,000

DEADLINE(S): MAR 1

FIELD(S): Electrical Engineering, Electronics, Computer Science, Computer or Aerospace Engineering, Physics, Mathematics, science or mathematics education; technology management or other technical fields, or fields related to U.S. intelligence or national security

ELIGIBILITY/REQUIREMENTS: Open to persons on active duty in a military service or veterans and to their spouses or dependents who are working toward a degree in an accredited 4-year college or university in the U.S. Minimum 3.4 GPA.

HOW TO APPLY: Applications and further information on website.

2456—ARMED FORCES COMMUNICATIONS AND ELECTRONICS ASSOCIATION (General John A. Wickham Scholarships)

4400 Fair Lakes Court
Fairfax VA 22033-3899
800/336-4583, ext. 6147 or
703/631-6149
FAX: 703/631-4693
E-mail: scholarships@afcea.org
Internet: http://www.afcea.org

AMOUNT: $2,000

DEADLINE(S): MAY 1

FIELD(S): Electrical Engineering, Electronics, Computer Science, Computer or Aerospace Engineering, Physics, Mathematics, Science or Mathematics Education; Technology Management or other technical fields, or fields related to U.S. intelligence or national security

ELIGIBILITY/REQUIREMENTS: For persons working toward degrees in accred-

ited 4-year colleges or universities in the U.S. Must have GPA of 3.5 or more.

HOW TO APPLY: Applications and further information on website.

2457—ASSOCIATION FOR WOMEN IN SCIENCE (Kirsten R. Lorentzen Award in Physics)

7008 Richard Drive
Bethesda MD 20817-4838
E-mail: awisedfd@
awisedfd@awis.org
Internet: http://www.awis.org/
careers/edfoundation.html

AMOUNT: $1,000

DEADLINE(S): Late JAN

FIELD(S): Physics; Geoscience

ELIGIBILITY/REQUIREMENTS: Open to college sophomore or junior. Must be a U.S. citizen attending a college in the U.S.

HOW TO APPLY: See website for application and instructions.

NUMBER OF AWARDS: 1

RENEWABLE: No

CONTACT: Dr. Barbara Filner

2458—ASTRONAUT SCHOLARSHIP FOUNDATION

6225 Vectorspace Boulevard
Titusville FL 32780
321/269/6119
FAX: 321/267-3970
E-mail: MercurySvn@aol.com
Internet: http://www.astronaut
scholarship.org/guidelines.html

AMOUNT: $10,000

DEADLINE(S): APR 15

FIELD(S): Engineering; Physical Sciences (Medical Research; NOT Professional Medicine)

ELIGIBILITY/REQUIREMENTS: Open to juniors, seniors, and graduate students at a select group of schools. Must be U.S. citizen with the intention to pursue research or advance field of study upon completion of final degree. Special consideration given to students who have shown initiative, creativity, excellence, and/or resourcefulness in their field. Must be nominated by faculty or staff.

HOW TO APPLY: See website for list of eligible schools. Contact Executive Director for details.

CONTACT: Howard Benedict, Executive Director

2459—COMMUNITY FOUNDATION FOR GREATER ATLANTA, INC., THE (Tech High/W.O. Cheney Scholarship)

50 Hurt Plaza, Suite 449

Atlanta GA 30303
404/688-5525
FAX: 404/688-3060
E-mail: scholarships@atlcf.org
Internet: http://www.atlcf.org/
GrantsScholarships/Scholarships.
aspx

AMOUNT: $5,000

DEADLINE(S): MAR 26

FIELD(S): Mathematics, Engineering, Physical Sciences

ELIGIBILITY/REQUIREMENTS: Open to graduating high school seniors. Must be a citizen of the U.S. and a legal resident of Georgia for at least 3 years prior to application, have a cumulative high school GPA of 3.7 or higher or be in the upper 10% of graduating class, SAT composite (math and critical reading) of at least 1300, be accepted as a full-time student to a 4-year accredited college or university, and demonstrate a commitment to community service.

HOW TO APPLY: See website for additional information and application. Submit with a personal essay (2-3 pages) that includes why you feel a college education is important; your statement of educational and career goals; post college career interests; highlights of your high school extracurricular/community service activities, special strengths, skills, and qualifications; any unusual family or personal circumstances have affected your achievement in school, work experience, or your participation in school and community activities; present financial need. Send to The Community Foundation for Greater Atlanta, Tech High/W.O. Cheney Scholarship, Scholarship Management Services, Scholarship America, One Scholarship Way, P.O. Box 297, Saint Peter, MN 56082. If you have questions, call 507/931-1682 or e-mail community-foundation@scholarshipamerica.org.

NUMBER OF AWARDS: 4

RENEWABLE: Yes; must reapply.

CONTACT: Lisa Glanville, 404/308-0055

2460—EARTHWATCH STUDENT CHALLENGE AWARDS (High School Student Research Expeditions)

3 Clock Tower Place, Suite 100
P.O. Box 75
Maynard MA 01754
800/776-0188 or
978/461-0081, ext. 116
FAX: 978/450-1288
E-mail: scap@earthwatch.org
Internet: www.earthwatch.org

AMOUNT: Travel/Living expenses (1- to 3-week field expedition)

DEADLINE(S): Late Fall—call for details
FIELD(S): Biology, field studies, physics, natural resources, environmental science
ELIGIBILITY/REQUIREMENTS: Awards for high school sophomores, juniors, and seniors, especially those with limited exposure to the sciences. Must attend high school in the U.S., attend high school in the U.S. Must be at least age 16 by June 15 during year of program. Teams of 6 to 8 students spend 1 to 3 weeks at sites in North or Central America.
HOW TO APPLY: Students must be nominated by a teacher. Write or visit website for further information.
NUMBER OF AWARDS: Approximately 85

2461—HAWAII COMMUNITY FOUNDATION (Shuichi, Katsu & Itsuyo Suga Scholarship)

1164 Bishop Street, Suite 800
Honolulu HI 96813
808/537-6333 or toll free: 888/731-3863
FAX: 808/521-6286
E-mail: info@hcf-hawaii.org
Internet: http://www.hcf-hawaii.org
DEADLINE(S): MAR 1
FIELD(S): Mathematics; Physics; Science; Technology
ELIGIBILITY/REQUIREMENTS: Must be residents of the state of Hawaii; plan to attend full time an accredited 2- or 4-year college or university; and demonstrate financial need, good moral character, and strong academic achievement, with a minimum GPA of 3.0.
HOW TO APPLY: Send application with 2 letters of recommendation.
CONTACT: See website.

2462—IET, THE (IET Engineering Degree Scholarships for Women)

Michael Faraday House
Six Hills Way, Stevenage
Hertfordshire SG1 2AY
UNITED KINGDOM
E-mail: awards@theiet.org
Internet: http://www.theiet.org/ambition
AMOUNT: £1,000 per annum
DEADLINE(S): JUN 30
FIELD(S): Engineering; Mathematics; Physics
ELIGIBILITY/REQUIREMENTS: For women residing in the United Kingdom and pursuing IET-accredited degrees. Candidates must be undertaking mathematics and physics "A" level or Scottish Higher examinations.

HOW TO APPLY: Check website or contact organization for an application.
NUMBER OF AWARDS: Check website.
RENEWABLE: Yes. For entire period of an IET-accredited course.

2463—MENSA EDUCATION AND RESEARCH FOUNDATION (McGrew-Fruecht Scholarship)

Internet: http://www.mensafoundation.org/AM/Template.cfm?Section=Scholarships1
AMOUNT: $500
DEADLINE(S): JAN 15
FIELD(S): All; Physics; Chemistry
ELIGIBILITY/REQUIREMENTS: Must be studying physics or chemistry or have been out of formal education for a period of 5 or more years and enrolled, for the academic year following the award, in a degree program in an accredited U.S. institution of postsecondary education. Must be a U.S. citizen or legal resident residing in Mensa Region 5 (portions of Alabama, Georgia, North Carolina, South Carolina, Mississippi, and Tennessee).
HOW TO APPLY: Submit application to the local scholarship chair (available from the website or by sending a request with SASE to the local scholarship chair), and an essay of not more than 550 words explaining your academic and/or vocational goals and how you plan to achieve those goals.
CONTACT: Denley Chew

2464—MICRON TECHNOLOGY FOUNDATION, INC.

8000 South Federal Way
Mailstop 1-407
Boise ID 83706
208/368-2658
FAX: 208/368-4435
Internet: http://www.micron.com/about/foundation/edgrants.aspx
AMOUNT: $55,000 and up to 12 @ $16,500
DEADLINE(S): JAN 20
FIELD(S): Electrical, Chemical, Computer & Mechanical Engineering; Chemistry; Physics; Computer & Material Science
ELIGIBILITY/REQUIREMENTS: High school senior; resident of Idaho, Colorado, Texas, or Virginia; with a combined SAT score of at least 1350 or a composite ACT score of at least 30; must have an unweighted GPA of at least 3.5; demonstrated leadership in school, work and/or extracurricular activities.

HOW TO APPLY: Download an application from www.micron.scholarshipamerica.org or see your high school counselor. An essay and possible interview are also required.
NUMBER OF AWARDS: Up to 13
RENEWABLE: Yes. Up to 4 years; must remain eligible.
CONTACT: Scholarship America at 800/537-4180

2465—MICROSOFT CORPORATION (National Minority and/or Women's Scholarships)

Microsoft Scholarship Program
One Microsoft Way
Redmond WA 98052-8303
425/882-8080
E-mail: scholars@microsoft.com
Internet: http://www.microsoft.com/college/scholarships/
AMOUNT: Tuition for 1 year
DEADLINE(S): JAN 15
FIELD(S): Computer Science, Computer Engineering, or a related technical discipline, such as Electrical Engineering, Math, Physics
ELIGIBILITY/REQUIREMENTS: May apply only after beginning classes on full-time basis. Full tuition scholarships awarded for 1 academic year to women, minorities (African-Americans, Hispanics, or Native Americans), and people with disabilities enrolled full time in the above fields, or related technical discipline with a demonstrated interest in computer science, and making satisfactory progress towards a degree. Awards are made through designated schools and are not transferable to other institutions. Students must be enrolled full time in a bachelor's degree program at a college or university in the U.S., Canada, or Mexico at the time the application is submitted and be making satisfactory progress toward an undergraduate degree in computer science or computer engineering. All recipients of scholarships will be required to complete a salaried summer internship of 12 weeks or more at Microsoft in Redmond, WA (unless waived by Microsoft).
HOW TO APPLY: Application available online only. Submit résumé, transcript, answers to essay questions, and letter of referral from faculty member or academic advisor. No separate application form required. Note your gender, ethnicity, or disability on the page with your essay questions if you would like that information to be considered with your application. See website for detailed information and essay questions.

RENEWABLE: Yes: Must maintain a 3.0 cumulative GPA out of a possible 4.0, or a 4.0 cumulative GPA out of a possible 5.0.

2466—MICROSOFT CORPORATION (Summer Internships)

One Microsoft Way
Redmond WA 98052-8303
425/882-8080
E-mail: scholars@microsoft.com
Internet: http://www.microsoft.com/college/scholarships/
AMOUNT: Competitive compensation
DEADLINE(S): None
FIELD(S): Computer Science, Computer Engineering, or a related technical discipline, such as Mathematics or Physics
ELIGIBILITY/REQUIREMENTS: Must commit to 12-week minimum. Includes transportation, shipping costs, and shared cost of housing.
HOW TO APPLY: See website for application and details. Interview required.

2467—NAACP NATIONAL OFFICE (NAACP Willems Scholarship)

4805 Mount Hope Drive
Baltimore MD 21215
401/358-8900
Internet: http://www.naacp.org/work/education/eduscholarship.shtml
AMOUNT: $2,000 undergraduate; $3,000 graduate
DEADLINE(S): APR 30
FIELD(S): Engineering; Chemistry; Physics; Mathematics
ELIGIBILITY/REQUIREMENTS: Open to NAACP male members majoring in one of the above areas. Undergraduates must have GPA of 2.5+; graduates' GPAs must be 3.0+. Financial need must be established.
HOW TO APPLY: 2 letters of recommendation from teachers or professors in major field of specialization.
HOW TO APPLY: See website for application or write for complete information (include a legal-sized SASE) to The United Negro College Fund, Scholarships & Grants Administration, 8260 Willow Oaks Corporate Drive, Fairfax, VA 22031. Attention: Kimberly Hall.
RENEWABLE: Yes. If the required GPA is maintained.

2468—NATIONAL INVENTORS HALL OF FAME, THE (Collegiate Inventors Competition)

221 South Broadway Street

Akron OH 44308-1505
330/849-6887
E-mail: rdepuy@invent.org
Internet: http://www.invent.org/bfg/bfghome.html
AMOUNT: $15,000
DEADLINE(S): JUN 1
FIELD(S): Mathematics, Engineering, Biology, Chemistry, Physics, Information Technology, Medicine
ELIGIBILITY/REQUIREMENTS: Must be enrolled (or have been enrolled) full time (in any college or university) at least part of the 12-month period prior to the date the entry is submitted. For teams (maximum 4 students), at least 1 member of the team must meet the full-time eligibility criteria. The other team members must have been enrolled on a part-time basis (at minimum) sometime during the 24-month period prior to the date entry is submitted. There are no limits on the number of entries a student or team may submit; however, only 1 prize/student or team will be awarded. No specific age requirements. Entries judged on the originality and inventiveness of the new idea, process, or technology, on their potential value to society (socially, environmentally, and economically), and on the scope of use. Entries must be complete, workable, and well articulated.
HOW TO APPLY: Submit an original invention or idea that has not been made public. See website for application and details. Submit with Student and Advisor Information; Student Essay and Advisor Letter following the outlined format; diagrams, illustrations, photos, slides, or videos of the invention (clearly labeled); the signed Student/Advisor Release Form.
CONTACT: Ray DePuy

2469—ROBERT SCHRECK MEMORIAL FUND (Grants)

c/o Texas Commerce Bank
Trust Department
P.O. Drawer 140
El Paso TX 79980
915/546-6515
AMOUNT: $500-$1,500
DEADLINE(S): JUL 15; NOV 15
FIELD(S): Medicine; Veterinary Medicine; Physics; Chemistry; Architecture; Engineering; Episcopal Clergy
ELIGIBILITY/REQUIREMENTS: Grants to undergraduate juniors or seniors or graduate students who have been residents of El Paso County for at least 2 years. Must be U.S. citizen or legal resident and have a high GPA. Financial need considered.

HOW TO APPLY: Write for information.
NUMBER OF AWARDS: 3
RENEWABLE: No

2470—SIEMENS WESTINGHOUSE (Science and Technology Competition)

186 Wood Avenue South
Iselin NJ 08830
877/822-5233
E-mail: foundation.us@siemens.com
Internet: http://www.siemens-foundation.org
AMOUNT: $120,000 (maximum)
DEADLINE(S): Varies
FIELD(S): Biology; Physical Sciences; Mathematics; Physics; Chemistry; Computer Science; Environmental Science
ELIGIBILITY/REQUIREMENTS: Open to U.S. high school seniors to pursue independent science research projects, working individually or in teams of 2 or 3 to develop and test their own ideas. May work with one of the universities/laboratories that serve as Siemens' partners. Students from the U.S. and its territories may compete in 1 of 6 geographic areas. Individual and team national prizewinners receive a second scholarship to be applied to undergraduate or graduate education.
HOW TO APPLY: See website or contact Siemens Foundation for details.

2471—SMITHSONIAN INSTITUTION-HARVARD CENTER FOR ASTROPHYSICS (Summer Internships)

Program Director
SAO Summer Intern Program, MS 81
60 Garden Street
Cambridge MA 02138
617/496-7586
E-mail: intern@cfa.harvard.edu
Internet: http://hea-www.harvard.edu/REU/REU.html
AMOUNT: $300/wk. + housing/travel
DEADLINE(S): FEB 1
FIELD(S): Astrophysics; Astronomy
ELIGIBILITY/REQUIREMENTS: 10-week summer internships for undergraduates who wish to conduct research at the Smithsonian Astrophysical Observatory. Must be enrolled in a program leading to a bachelor's degree. Each intern works with a scientist on an individual research project. Must be U.S. citizen or hold a valid green card.
HOW TO APPLY: See website or contact SAO Summer Intern Program Director for an application.

2472—SOCIETY OF AUTOMOTIVE ENGINEERS (Parks College of Saint Louis University/SAE Engineering Scholarship)

SAE Customer Service
400 Commonwealth Drive
Warrendale PA 15096-0001
724/776-4970
FAX: 724/776-1615
E-mail: customerservice@sae.org
Internet: http://www.sae.org/
students/scholarships
AMOUNT: $1,000
DEADLINE(S): DEC 1
FIELD(S): Aerospace Engineering;
Mechanical Engineering; Electrical
Engineering; Biomedical Engineering;
Aircraft Maintenance Engineering;
Avionics Engineering; Applied
Computer Science; Computer Software
Systems; Physics
ELIGIBILITY/REQUIREMENTS:
Entering freshman majoring in any of the
above areas, enrolled in a baccalaureate
program. Award based on academic
achievement and financial need.
HOW TO APPLY: See website for application. Submit application; a personal
essay that demonstrates hands-on experience or activity (such as rebuilding
engines, working on cars/trucks, etc.); 2
recommendations, 1 of which must be
from a teacher, counselor, or administrator; and transcript.
NUMBER OF AWARDS: 1
RENEWABLE: No

2473—SOCIETY OF AUTOMOTIVE ENGINEERS (Ralph K. Hillquist Honorary SAE Scholarship)

SAE Customer Service
400 Commonwealth Drive
Warrendale PA 15096-0001
724/776-4970
FAX: 724/776-1615
E-mail: customerservice@sae.org
Internet: http://www.sae.org/
students/scholarships
AMOUNT: $1,000
DEADLINE(S): FEB 1
FIELD(S): Mechanical Engineering;
Physics
ELIGIBILITY/REQUIREMENTS: Open
to U.S. citizens enrolled full time as a
junior in a U.S. university; minimum 3.0
GPA with significant academic and leadership achievements. Must major in mechanical engineering or an automotive-related
engineering discipline; preference given to
those with studies/courses experience/

expertise related to noise and vibrations
(for example: statistics, dynamics, physics,
vibration).
HOW TO APPLY: See website for application. Submit application; personal essay;
2 recommendations, 1 of which must be
from a teacher, counselor, or administrator; and transcript.
NUMBER OF AWARDS: 1
RENEWABLE: No

2474—SONS OF NORWAY FOUNDATION (Nancy Lorraine Jensen Memorial Scholarship Fund)

c/o Sons of Norway
1455 West Lake Street
Minneapolis MN 55408
612/821-4632
E-mail: colson@sofn.com
Internet: http://www.sofn.com/
foundation/foundation/
foundationscholarships.html
AMOUNT: 50%-100% of tuition
DEADLINE(S): MAR 1
FIELD(S): Chemistry; Physics; Chemical,
Electrical & Mechanical Engineering
ELIGIBILITY/REQUIREMENTS: Must
be U.S. citizen, female, aged 17-35, a member or daughter or granddaughter of a current member of for at least 3 years, or a
daughter or granddaughter of current
employee. Must be full-time undergraduate who has completed at least 1 term,
majoring in 1 of above subjects. SAT of at
least 1200 or ACT of at least 26.
HOW TO APPLY: Submit application
along with an essay (500 words or less) giving proof of accomplishments and stating
how you will pursue your career and
involvement in SON, youth, community or
research activities, and 3 letters of recommendation. Transcript should be sent
directly from school. See website for an
application and additional details.
NUMBER OF AWARDS: 12
RENEWABLE: Yes. Up to 3 undergraduate awards.
CONTACT: Cindy Olson, Director

2475—SPE FOUNDATION, THE (Blow Molding Division Memorial Scholarships)

14 Fairfield Drive
Brookfield CT 06804
203/740-5447
FAX: 203/775-1157
E-mail: foundation@4spe.org
Internet: http://www.4spe.org/
foundation/scholarships.php
AMOUNT: $8,000 (payable over 2 years)
DEADLINE(S): JAN 15

FIELD(S): Polymer Science; Chemistry;
Physics; Plastics, Chemical,
Mechanical, & Industrial Engineering
ELIGIBILITY/REQUIREMENTS:
Applicants must be completing the 2nd
year of a 4-year undergraduate plastics
engineering program and be a member of a
Society of Plastics Engineers (SPE) student chapter.
HOW TO APPLY: Complete application;
submit 3 recommendation letters (2 from a
teacher or school official and 1 from an
employer or non-relative); high school
and/or college transcript for last 2 years; a
1- to 2-page brief essay on the importance
of blow molding to the technical parts and
packaging industries. Submit brief essay
that describes the importance of blow
molding to the technical parts and packaging industries, and why the applicant
desires a career in the plastics industry.
NUMBER OF AWARDS: Up to 2

2476—SPE FOUNDATION, THE (Composites Division/Harold Giles Scholarship)

14 Fairfield Drive
Brookfield CT 06804
203/740-5447
FAX: 203/775-1157
E-mail: foundation@4spe.org
Internet: http://www.4spe.org/
foundation/scholarships.php
AMOUNT: $1,000
DEADLINE(S): JAN 15
FIELD(S): Polymer Science; Chemistry;
Physics; Chemical, Plastics, Mechanical
& Industrial Engineering
ELIGIBILITY/REQUIREMENTS:
Applicants must have experience in the
composites industry (such as courses taken,
research conducted, or jobs held); must be
in good standing with their colleges and
have demonstrated an interest in the plastics industry; majoring in or taking courses
that would be beneficial to a career in the
plastics/polymer industry. Financial need is
considered.
HOW TO APPLY: Complete application;
submit 3 recommendation letters (2 from a
teacher or school official and 1 from an
employer or non-relative); high school
and/or college transcript for last 2 years; a
1- to 2-page statement telling why you are
applying for the scholarship and educational and career goals in the plastics industry.
Include a statement detailing exposure to
the composites industry.
NUMBER OF AWARDS: 1

2477—SPE FOUNDATION, THE (Extrusion Division/Lew Erwin Memorial Scholarship)

14 Fairfield Drive
Brookfield CT 06804
203/740-5447
FAX: 203/775-1157
E-mail: foundation@4spe.org
Internet: http://www.4spe.org/
foundation/scholarships.php
AMOUNT: $2,500
DEADLINE(S): JAN 15
FIELD(S): Polymer Science; Chemistry;
Physics; Plastics, Chemical,
Mechanical, & Industrial Engineering
ELIGIBILITY/REQUIREMENTS:
Supports undergraduate or graduate research in the field of polymer extrusion. Must be working on a senior or MS project, which must be described in writing, including background, objective and proposed experiments. Final research summary report required.
HOW TO APPLY: Complete application; submit 3 recommendation letters (2 from a teacher or school official and 1 from an employer or non-relative); high school and/or college transcript for last 2 years; a 1- to 2-page statement giving reasons for applying and educational and career goals in the plastics industry.
NUMBER OF AWARDS: 1
RENEWABLE: Yes, must reapply.

2478—SPE FOUNDATION, THE (Fleming/Biaszcek Scholarship)

14 Fairfield Drive
Brookfield CT 06804
203/740-5447
FAX: 203/775-1157
E-mail: foundation@4spe.org
Internet: http://www.4spe.org/
foundation/scholarships.php
AMOUNT: $2,000
DEADLINE(S): JAN 15
FIELD(S): Polymer Science; Chemistry;
Physics; Plastics, Chemical,
Mechanical, & Industrial Engineering
ELIGIBILITY/REQUIREMENTS: Open to full-time undergraduate and graduate students, in good standing who have demonstrated an interest in the plastics industry; majoring in or taking courses that would be beneficial to a career in the plastics/polymer industry. Must be of Mexican descent and citizens or legal residents of the U.S. Financial need is considered.
HOW TO APPLY: Complete application; submit 3 recommendation letters (2 from a teacher or school official and 1 from an employer or non-relative); high school

and/or college transcript for last 2 years; a 1- to 2-page statement giving reasons for applying, and educational and career goals in the plastics industry. Detail Mexican lineage in essay or on a separate sheet of paper.
NUMBER OF AWARDS: 1
RENEWABLE: Yes. Must reapply for 3 additional years.

2479—SPE FOUNDATION, THE (Foundation Scholarships)

14 Fairfield Drive
Brookfield CT 06804
203/740-5447
FAX: 203/775-1157
E-mail: foundation@4spe.org
Internet: http://www.4spe.org/
foundation/scholarships.php
AMOUNT: $4,000
DEADLINE(S): JAN 15
FIELD(S): Polymer Science; Chemistry;
Physics; Plastics, Chemical,
Mechanical, & Industrial Engineering
ELIGIBILITY/REQUIREMENTS: Open to students in good standing who have demonstrated an interest in the plastics industry; majoring in or taking courses that would be beneficial to a career in the plastics/polymer industry. Financial need is considered for most scholarships.
HOW TO APPLY: Submit application with 3 recommendation letters (2 from a teacher or school official and 1 from an employer or non-relative); high school and/or college transcript for last 2 years; a 1- to 2-page statement giving reasons for applying, and educational and career goals in the plastics industry.
NUMBER OF AWARDS: Multiple
RENEWABLE: Yes, must reapply; up to 3 additional years.

2480—SPE FOUNDATION, THE (Gulf Coast Hurricane Scholarships)

14 Fairfield Drive
Brookfield CT 06804
203/740-5447
FAX: 203/775-1157
E-mail: foundation@4spe.org
Internet: http://www.4spe.org/
foundation/scholarships.php
AMOUNT: $6,000 (college or university),
$2,000 (junior or technical)
DEADLINE(S): JAN 15
FIELD(S): Polymer Science; Chemistry;
Physics; Chemical, Plastics, Mechanical
& Industrial Engineering
ELIGIBILITY/REQUIREMENTS: Must have been a resident of a Gulf Coast County declared a national disaster area as

a result of Hurricanes Katrina, Rita or Wilma, and must be attending a university, college or technical institute in a Gulf Coast State (Florida, Alabama, Mississippi, Louisiana, Texas). Must be in good standing with their colleges (minimum GPA 2.0) and enrolled 6 hours/semester. Must have demonstrated an interest in the plastics industry; majoring in or taking courses that would be beneficial to a career in the plastics/polymer industry. Financial need is considered for most scholarships.
HOW TO APPLY: Complete application; submit 3 recommendation letters (2 from a teacher or school official and 1 from an employer or non-relative); high school and/or college transcript for last 2 years; a 1- to 2-page statement telling why you are applying for the scholarship and educational and career goals in the plastics industry. Must provide proof of residence.
NUMBER OF AWARDS: 3; 1 college or university, 2 junior college or technical school
RENEWABLE: Yes. Must reapply for 3 additional years.

2481—SPE FOUNDATION, THE (Injection Molding Division Scholarship)

14 Fairfield Drive
Brookfield CT 06804
203/740-5447
FAX: 203/775-1157
E-mail: foundation@4spe.org
Internet: http://www.4spe.org/
foundation/scholarships.php
AMOUNT: $3,000
DEADLINE(S): JAN 15
FIELD(S): Polymer Science; Chemistry;
Physics; Chemical, Plastics, Mechanical
& Industrial Engineering
ELIGIBILITY/REQUIREMENTS:
Available to undergraduates at a 4-year. Applicants must have experience in the injection molding industry (such as courses taken, research conducted, or jobs held), be in good standing with their colleges and have demonstrated an interest in the plastics industry; majoring in or taking courses that would be beneficial to a career in the plastics/polymer industry. Financial need is considered.
HOW TO APPLY: Complete application; submit 3 recommendation letters (2 from a teacher or school official and 1 from an employer or non-relative); high school and/or college transcript for last 2 years; a 1- to 2-page statement telling why you are applying for the scholarship and educational and career goals in the plastics industry.
NUMBER OF AWARDS: 1

RENEWABLE: Yes. Must reapply for 3 additional years.

2482—SPE FOUNDATION, THE (Pittsburgh Section Scholarships)

14 Fairfield Drive
Brookfield CT 06804
203/740-5447
FAX: 203/775-1157
E-mail: foundation@4spe.org
Internet: http://www.4spe.org/ foundation/scholarships.php
AMOUNT: $2,000
DEADLINE(S): JAN 15
FIELD(S): Polymer Science; Chemistry; Physics; Chemical, Plastics, Mechanical & Industrial Engineering
ELIGIBILITY/REQUIREMENTS: Must have graduated from a high school in one of the following PA counties: Allegheny, Armstrong, Beaver, Bedford, Blair, Brooke, Butler, Cambria, Clarion, Clearfield, Fayette, Greene, Hancock, Indiana, Jefferson, Lawrence, Mercer, Somerset, Venango, Washington, Westmoreland. Must be in good standing with their colleges and have demonstrated an interest in the plastics industry; majoring in or taking courses that would be beneficial to a career in the plastics/polymer industry. Financial need is considered for most scholarships.
HOW TO APPLY: Complete application; submit 3 recommendation letters (2 from a teacher or school official and 1 from an employer or non-relative); high school and/or college transcript for last 2 years; a 1- to 2-page statement telling why you are applying for the scholarship and educational and career goals in the plastics industry. Must provide proof of graduation from school in one of above counties.
NUMBER OF AWARDS: Up to 2
RENEWABLE: Yes. Must reapply for 3 additional years.

2483—SPE FOUNDATION, THE (Plastics Pioneers Association Scholarships)

14 Fairfield Drive
Brookfield CT 06804
203/740-5447
FAX: 203/775-1157
E-mail: foundation@4spe.org
Internet: http://www.4spe.org/ foundation/scholarships.php
AMOUNT: $3,000
DEADLINE(S): JAN 15
FIELD(S): Polymer Science; Chemistry; Physics; Chemical, Plastics, Mechanical & Industrial Engineering

ELIGIBILITY/REQUIREMENTS: Open to undergraduate students, including those enrolled in associate or technical degree programs, who are committed to becoming "hands on" workers in the plastics industry as plastics technicians or engineers. Must be in good standing with their colleges and have demonstrated an interest in the plastics industry; majoring in or taking courses that would be beneficial to a career in the plastics/polymer industry. Financial need is considered for most scholarships.
HOW TO APPLY: Complete application; submit 3 recommendation letters (2 from a teacher or school official and 1 from an employer or non-relative); high school and/or college transcript for last 2 years; a 1- to 2-page statement telling why you are applying for the scholarship and educational and career goals in the plastics industry.
NUMBER OF AWARDS: Multiple
RENEWABLE: Yes. Must reapply for 3 additional years.

2484—SPE FOUNDATION, THE (Polymer Modifiers & Additives Division Scholarships)

14 Fairfield Drive
Brookfield CT 06804
203/740-5447
FAX: 203/775-1157
E-mail: foundation@4spe.org
Internet: http://www.4spe.org/ foundation/scholarships.php
AMOUNT: $4,000
DEADLINE(S): JAN 15
FIELD(S): Polymer Science; Chemistry; Physics; Chemical, Plastics, Mechanical & Industrial Engineering
ELIGIBILITY/REQUIREMENTS: Must be in good standing with their colleges and have demonstrated an interest in the plastics industry; majoring in or taking courses that would be beneficial to a career in the plastics/polymer industry. Financial need is considered for most scholarships.
HOW TO APPLY: Complete application; submit 3 recommendation letters (2 from a teacher or school official and 1 from an employer or non-relative); high school and/or college transcript for last 2 years; a 1- to 2-page statement telling why you are applying for the scholarship and educational and career goals in the plastics industry.
NUMBER OF AWARDS: 3
RENEWABLE: Yes. Must reapply for 3 additional years.

2485—SPE FOUNDATION, THE (Robert E. Cramer/Product Design & Development Division Scholarship)

14 Fairfield Drive

Brookfield CT 06804
203/740-5447
FAX: 203/775-1157
E-mail: foundation@4spe.org
Internet: http://www.4spe.org/ foundation/scholarships.php
AMOUNT: $1,000
DEADLINE(S): JAN 15
FIELD(S): Polymer Science; Chemistry; Physics; Chemical, Plastics, Mechanical & Industrial Engineering
ELIGIBILITY/REQUIREMENTS: Must be in good standing with their colleges and have demonstrated an interest in the plastics industry; majoring in or taking courses that would be beneficial to a career in the plastics/polymer industry. Financial need is considered for most scholarships.
HOW TO APPLY: Complete application; submit 3 recommendation letters (2 from a teacher or school official and 1 from an employer or non-relative); high school and/or college transcript for last 2 years; a 1- to 2-page statement telling why you are applying for the scholarship and educational and career goals in the plastics industry.
NUMBER OF AWARDS: 1
RENEWABLE: Yes. Must reapply for 3 additional years.

2486—SPE FOUNDATION, THE (Robert G. Dailey/Detroit Section Scholarship)

14 Fairfield Drive
Brookfield CT 06804
203/740-5447
FAX: 203/775-1157
E-mail: foundation@4spe.org
Internet: http://www.4spe.org/ foundation/scholarships.php
AMOUNT: $4,000
DEADLINE(S): JAN 15
FIELD(S): Polymer Science; Chemistry; Physics; Chemical, Plastics, Mechanical & Industrial Engineering
ELIGIBILITY/REQUIREMENTS: Must be in good standing with their colleges and have demonstrated an interest in the plastics industry; majoring in or taking courses that would be beneficial to a career in the plastics/polymer industry. Financial need is considered for most scholarships.
HOW TO APPLY: Complete application; submit 3 recommendation letters (2 from a teacher or school official and 1 from an employer or non-relative); high school and/or college transcript for last 2 years; a 1- to 2-page statement telling why you are applying for the scholarship and educational and career goals in the plastics industry.
NUMBER OF AWARDS: 1
RENEWABLE: Yes. Must reapply for 3 additional years.

2487—SPE FOUNDATION, THE (Ted and Ruth Neward Scholarships)

14 Fairfield Drive
Brookfield CT 06804
203/740-5447
FAX: 203/775-1157
E-mail: foundation@4spe.org
Internet: http://www.4spe.org/
foundation/scholarships.php
AMOUNT: $3,000
DEADLINE(S): JAN 15
FIELD(S): Polymer Science; Chemistry;
Physics; Chemical, Plastics, Mechanical
& Industrial Engineering
ELIGIBILITY/REQUIREMENTS: Must be U.S. citizens in good standing with their colleges and have demonstrated an interest in the plastics industry; majoring in or taking courses that would be beneficial to a career in the plastics/polymer industry. Financial need is considered for most scholarships.
HOW TO APPLY: Complete application; submit 3 recommendation letters (2 from a teacher or school official and 1 from an employer or non-relative); high school and/or college transcript for last 2 years; a 1- to 2-page statement telling why you are applying for the scholarship and educational and career goals in the plastics industry.
NUMBER OF AWARDS: 3
RENEWABLE: Yes. Must reapply for 3 additional years.

2488—SPE FOUNDATION, THE (Thermoforming Scholarships)

14 Fairfield Drive
Brookfield CT 06804
203/740-5447
FAX: 203/775-1157
E-mail: foundation@4spe.org
Internet: http://www.4spe.org/
foundation/scholarships.php
AMOUNT: $7,500
DEADLINE(S): JAN 15
FIELD(S): Polymer Science; Chemistry;
Physics; Plastics, Chemical,
Mechanical, & Industrial Engineering
ELIGIBILITY/REQUIREMENTS: Available to graduate or undergraduate students with GPA of 3.0 or better. Undergraduates must have completed at least 2 years of credits. Must have experience in the thermoforming industry (courses taken, research conducted, or jobs held), be in good standing and have demonstrated an interest in the plastics industry; majoring in or taking courses that would be beneficial to a career in the plastics/polymer industry.

HOW TO APPLY: Complete application; submit 3 recommendation letters (2 from a teacher or school official and 1 from an employer or non-relative); high school and/or college transcript for last 2 years; a 1- to 2-page statement giving reasons for applying and educational and career goals in the plastics industry. Include a statement detailing exposure to the thermoforming industry.
NUMBER OF AWARDS: Varies (multiple awards)
RENEWABLE: Yes. Must reapply for 3 additional years.

2489—SPE FOUNDATION, THE (Thermoplastic Elastomers Special Interest Group Scholarship)

14 Fairfield Drive
Brookfield CT 06804
203/740-5447
FAX: 203/775-1157
E-mail: foundation@4spe.org
Internet: http://www.4spe.org/
foundation/scholarships.php
AMOUNT: $1,000
DEADLINE(S): JAN 15
FIELD(S): Polymer Science; Chemistry;
Physics; Chemical, Plastics, Mechanical
& Industrial Engineering
ELIGIBILITY/REQUIREMENTS: Available to graduate or undergraduate students at a 4-year college. Applicants must have experience in the thermoplastic elastometers industry (such as courses taken, research conducted, or jobs held); must be in good standing with their colleges and have demonstrated an interest in the plastics industry; majoring in or taking courses that would be beneficial to a career in the plastics/polymer industry. Financial need is considered.
HOW TO APPLY: Complete application; submit 3 recommendation letters (2 from a teacher or school official and 1 from an employer or non-relative); high school and/or college transcript for last 2 years; a 1- to 2-page statement telling why you are applying for the scholarship and educational and career goals in the plastics industry. Include a statement detailing exposure to the thermoplastic elastometers industry.
NUMBER OF AWARDS: 1

2490—SPE FOUNDATION, THE (Thermoplastic Materials & Foams Division Scholarship)

14 Fairfield Drive
Brookfield CT 06804
203/740-5447
FAX: 203/775-1157
E-mail: foundation@4spe.org
Internet: http://www.4spe.org/
foundation/scholarships.php
AMOUNT: $1,000
DEADLINE(S): JAN 15
FIELD(S): Polymer Science; Chemistry;
Physics; Chemical, Plastics, Mechanical
& Industrial Engineering
ELIGIBILITY/REQUIREMENTS: Must be in good standing with their colleges and have demonstrated an interest in the plastics industry; majoring in or taking courses that would be beneficial to a career in the plastics/polymer industry. Financial need is considered for most scholarships.
HOW TO APPLY: Complete application; submit 3 recommendation letters (2 from a teacher or school official and 1 from an employer or non-relative); high school and/or college transcript for last 2 years; a 1- to 2-page statement telling why you are applying for the scholarship and educational and career goals in the plastics industry.
NUMBER OF AWARDS: 1
RENEWABLE: Yes. Must reapply for 3 additional years.

2491—SPE FOUNDATION, THE (Thermoset Division/James I. MacKenzie Memorial Scholarship)

14 Fairfield Drive
Brookfield CT 06804
203/740-5447
FAX: 203/775-1157
E-mail: foundation@4spe.org
Internet: http://www.4spe.org/
foundation/scholarships.php
AMOUNT: $2,500
DEADLINE(S): JAN 15
FIELD(S): Polymer Science; Chemistry;
Physics; Plastics, Chemical,
Mechanical, & Industrial Engineering
ELIGIBILITY/REQUIREMENTS: Available to undergraduates at a 4-year college with GPA of 3.0 or better. Must have experience in the thermoset industry (courses taken, research conducted, or jobs held), be in good standing and have demonstrated an interest in the plastics industry; majoring in or taking courses that would be beneficial to a career in the plastics/polymer industry. Financial need is considered for most scholarships.
HOW TO APPLY: Complete application; submit 3 recommendation letters (2 from a teacher or school official and 1 from an employer or non-relative); high school and/or college transcript for last 2 years; a 1- to 2-page statement giving reasons for

applying and educational and career goals in the plastics industry.
NUMBER OF AWARDS: 1
RENEWABLE: Yes. Must reapply for 3 additional years.
ADDITIONAL INFORMATION: Also includes all-expense-paid trip to, and speaking opportunity at, annual Madison Thermoset Molding Conference.

2492—SPE FOUNDATION, THE (Vinyl Plastics Division Scholarship)

14 Fairfield Drive
Brookfield CT 06804
203/740-5447
FAX: 203/775-1157
E-mail: foundation@4spe.org
Internet: http://www.4spe.org/foundation/scholarships.php
AMOUNT: $3,000
DEADLINE(S): JAN 15
FIELD(S): Polymer Science; Chemistry; Physics; Chemical, Plastics, Mechanical & Industrial Engineering
ELIGIBILITY/REQUIREMENTS: Must be in good standing with their colleges and have demonstrated an interest in the plastics industry; majoring in or taking courses that would be beneficial to a career in the plastics/polymer industry. Preference given to applicants with experience in the vinyl industry (such as courses taken, research conducted, or jobs held). Financial need is considered for most scholarships.
HOW TO APPLY: Complete application; submit 3 recommendation letters (2 from a teacher or school official and 1 from an employer or non-relative); high school and/or college transcript for last 2 years; a 1- to 2-page statement telling why you are applying for the scholarship and educational and career goals in the plastics industry.
NUMBER OF AWARDS: 1
RENEWABLE: Yes. Must reapply for 3 additional years.

2493—SPIE: THE INTERNATIONAL SOCIETY FOR OPTICAL ENGINEERING (SPIE Educational Scholarships & Grants in Optical Science and Engineering)

P.O. Box 10
Bellingham WA 98227-0010
360/676-3290
FAX: 360/647-1445
E-mail: scholarships@spie.org
Internet: http://www.4spe.org/foundation/scholarships.php
AMOUNT: $1,000-$10,000
DEADLINE(S): JAN 6
FIELD(S): Optics, Photonics, Imaging, Optoelectronics or related discipline

ELIGIBILITY/REQUIREMENTS: Undergraduate and graduate students must be enrolled full time in one of the fields as mentioned above at an educational institution for the academic year in which the award is used. This requirement does not apply to high school students.
HOW TO APPLY: See website. Must submit application, 2 letters of reference, a 450-word essay and the annual scholarship award report (if applicable) by deadline.
RENEWABLE: Yes. Must submit an annual scholarship award report if reapplying. Your application must show new activities beyond those upon which a previous award was based.
ADDITIONAL INFORMATION: Must be an SPIE student member or submit an application for student membership including dues payment with the scholarship application to SPIE by the deadline. Note: High school students may receive a complimentary (free) student membership after submitting a membership application.

2494—UNIVERSITY OF WINDSOR (Physics and High Technology Entrance Scholarship)

401 Sunset Avenue
Windsor Ontario N9B 3P4
CANADA
519/253-3000
FAX: 519/973-7081
E-mail: awards1@uwindsor.ca
Internet: http://www.uwindsor.ca
AMOUNT: Up to $1,000 (Canadian)
DEADLINE(S): MAY 31
FIELD(S): All
ELIGIBILITY/REQUIREMENTS: Open to undergraduate students entering the Physics and High Technology program in the Department of Physics. Candidates must have at least 85% standing in their mathematics and science OAC average or equivalent.
HOW TO APPLY: Automatic. No application required.
NUMBER OF AWARDS: 6
RENEWABLE: No.
CONTACT: Aase Houser

2495—WESTERN MICHIGAN UNIVERSITY (College of Arts and Sciences/Charles Wilcox Memorial Fund)

1903 West Michigan
Kalamazoo MI 49008-5337
269/387-8777
FAX: 269/387-6989
E-mail: finaid-info@wmich.edu
Internet: http://www.wmich.edu/finaid

AMOUNT: $250
FIELD(S): Physics
ELIGIBILITY/REQUIREMENTS: Awarded to physics major in senior year; presented on graduation. Based on scholarly achievement and recommendations of instructors.
HOW TO APPLY: Nominations and selections are made by Physics Department faculty.
RENEWABLE: No

2496—WESTERN MICHIGAN UNIVERSITY (College of Arts and Sciences/Paul Rood Physics Scholarship)

1903 West Michigan
Kalamazoo MI 49008-5337
269/387-8777
FAX: 269/387-6989
E-mail: finaid-info@wmich.edu
Internet: http://www.wmich.edu/finaid
AMOUNT: $500
FIELD(S): Physics
ELIGIBILITY/REQUIREMENTS: Awarded to Physics major with 3.0 GPA or higher.
HOW TO APPLY: Contact the Physics Department for an application.
RENEWABLE: No

2497—WOMEN IN DEFENSE (HORIZONS Scholarship Foundation)

2111 Wilson Boulevard, Suite 400
Arlington VA 22201-3061
703/247-2552
FAX: 703/522-1885
E-mail: wid@ndia.org
Internet: http://www.ndia.org
AMOUNT: $500+
DEADLINE(S): NOV 1; JUL 1
FIELD(S): Security Studies; Engineering; Computer Science; Physics; Mathematics; International Relations; Political Science; Operations Research; Economics; National Security/Defense; Business & Law (as they relate to national security or defense)
ELIGIBILITY/REQUIREMENTS: Open to women employed/planning careers in defense/national security areas (NOT law enforcement or criminal justice). Must be enrolled full or part time at an accredited college or university at the graduate or undergraduate junior/senior level. Must have a minimum 3.25 GPA, demonstrate financial need, and be U.S. citizen. Based on academic achievement, work experience, objectives, and recommendations.
HOW TO APPLY: See website or send SASE for application.
RENEWABLE: Yes

SOCIAL SCIENCES (ALL FIELDS)

2498—AMERICAN BAR FOUNDATION
(Summer Research Diversity Fellowships in Law & Social Science)

750 North Lake Shore Drive
Chicago IL 60611
312/988-6560
FAX: 312/988-6579
E-mail: fellowships@abfn.org
Internet: http://www.american
barfoundation.org
AMOUNT: $3,600
DEADLINE(S): Varies FEB/MAR 1
FIELD(S): Social Sciences; Humanities; Law

ELIGIBILITY/REQUIREMENTS: Open to sophomore and junior undergraduates including, but not limited to, Native American, African-American, Mexican, Puerto Rican, as well as other individuals who will add diversity to the field of law and social science. Must be U.S. citizen or permanent resident with 3.0 GPA. Students assigned a research mentor, participate in seminars, and work at the Foundation's office in Chicago for 35 hours/week for 8 weeks.
HOW TO APPLY: See website or contact ABF for application. Essay, transcripts, and letter of recommendation required.
NUMBER OF AWARDS: 4

2499—HAWAII COMMUNITY FOUNDATION (Marion Maccarrell Scott Scholarship)

1164 Bishop Street, Suite 800
Honolulu HI 96813
808/537-6333 or toll free:
888/731-3863
FAX: 808/521-6286
E-mail: info@hcf-hawaii.org
Internet: http://www.hcf-hawaii.org
DEADLINE(S): MAR 1
FIELD(S): Social Sciences: History; Government; Political Science; Anthropology; Economics; Geography; International Relations; Law; Psychology; Philosophy; Sociology

ELIGIBILITY/REQUIREMENTS: Must be residents of the state of Hawaii; be graduating seniors at a public high school in Hawaii; plan to enroll full time at an accredited 2- or 4-year mainland college or university; and demonstrate financial need, good moral character, and academic achievement with a minimum GPA of 2.8.

HOW TO APPLY: Send application with 2 letters of recommendation and an essay (2-3 pages) describing your commitment to world peace, your learning experiences (courses, clubs, community activities, or travel) related to achieving world peace and international understanding, and explain how your experiences thus far have enhanced your knowledge of how to achieve these two goals.

2500—INSTITUTE FOR HUMANE STUDIES (Summer Seminars Program)

3401 North Fairfax Drive, Suite 440
Arlington VA 22201-4432
703/993-4880 or 800/697-8799
FAX: 703/993-4890
Internet: http://www.TheIHS.org
AMOUNT: Free summer seminars, including room/board, lectures, seminar materials, and books
DEADLINE(S): MAR
FIELD(S): Social Sciences; Humanities; Law; Journalism; Public Policy; Education; Film; Writing; Economics; Philosophy

ELIGIBILITY/REQUIREMENTS: Open to college students, recent graduates, and graduate students who share an interest in learning and exchanging ideas about the scope of individual rights, free markets, the rule of law, peace, and tolerance.
HOW TO APPLY: See website for information and to apply online, or contact IHS for an application.

2501—JUNIOR ACHIEVEMENT INC.
(DePauw University Holton Memorial Scholarship)

One Education Way
Colorado Springs CO 80906
719/540-8000
FAX: 719/540-6299
E-mail: newmedia@ja.org
Internet: http://www.ja.org
AMOUNT: $1,000-full tuition
DEADLINE(S): FEB 1
FIELD(S): Liberal Arts; Music
ELIGIBILITY/REQUIREMENTS: Applicants must be excellent students who have demonstrated outstanding leadership and/or exceptional service to their schools, family, church, or community.
HOW TO APPLY: Send application; SAT or ACT scores (or TOEFL if English is second language); and a 250-word essay describing your commitment to service and/or leadership, with a résumé of your involvement.
NUMBER OF AWARDS: 50
RENEWABLE: Yes

CONTACT: Office of Admission, DePauw University, 101 East Seminary Street, Greencastle IN 46135-1611; 800/447-2495 or 765/658-4006; or e-mail admissions@depauw.edu; or see www.depauw.edu.

2502—MENSA EDUCATION AND RESEARCH FOUNDATION (Harper Fowley-Isolated M Award)

Internet: http://www.mensa
foundation.org/AM/Template.cfm?
Section=Scholarships1
AMOUNT: $600
DEADLINE(S): JAN 15
FIELD(S): Liberal Arts
ELIGIBILITY/REQUIREMENTS: Awards based on essays written by the applicant. No requirement for Mensa membership nor is consideration given for grades, academic program or financial need. Applicants must currently be a resident of a participating American Mensa local group's area and enrolled in a degree program in an accredited U.S. institution of higher learning during the academic year following the application date.
HOW TO APPLY: Send application, available (if eligible) from the website or, by request with SASE, from local scholarship chairs. Submit with essay of not more than 550 words explaining your academic and/or vocational goals and plans to achieve those goals to the scholarship chair in your area.
ADDITIONAL INFORMATION: The list of participating groups may change, see website for up-to-date information.

2503—MIDWAY COLLEGE

512 East Stephens Street
Midway KY 40347
800/755-0031
E-mail: admissions@midway.edu
Internet: http://www.midway.edu
AMOUNT: Up to full tuition
DEADLINE(S): Varies
FIELD(S): Nursing; Education; Psychology; Biology; Equine Studies; Computer Information Systems; Business Administration; English; Pre-Med; Pre-Vet
ELIGIBILITY/REQUIREMENTS: Merit scholarships for admitted students who are considered full time in Midway's women's college. Depending on scholarship, minimum GPA ranges from 2.5 to 3.2, minimum ACT ranges 18 to 29, minimum SAT from 860 to 1290. In some cases, students must live on campus.

HOW TO APPLY: Contact Admissions Office or high school guidance counselor for application. Complete FAFSA online.
NUMBER OF AWARDS: Varies, up to 100
RENEWABLE: Yes. Must meet GPA requirements which vary based on the scholarship.
CONTACT: Admissions Office or high school guidance counselor
ADDITIONAL INFORMATION: Athletes may be eligible for an athletic scholarship in conjunction with a merit grant; contact coach for eligibility and award information.

2504—ORGONE BIOPHYSICAL RESEARCH LABORATORY (Lou Hochberg Awards)

P.O. Box 1148
Ashland OR 97520
541/552-0118
FAX: 541/552-0118
E-mail: info@orgonelab.org
Internet: http://www.orgonelab.org
AMOUNT: $200-$1,500
DEADLINE(S): Varies
FIELD(S): Social Science
ELIGIBILITY/REQUIREMENTS: Several different award categories available for high school to graduate students.
HOW TO APPLY: Application must be submitted in English. Include written proof of student status, with full address, telephone, e-mail.
CONTACT: Dr. James DeMeo, Director, Hochberg Awards

2505—RESOURCES FOR THE FUTURE (RFF Summer Internship Program)

1616 P Street NW
Washington DC 20036-1400
202/328-5000
FAX: 202/939-3460
E-mail: mankin@rff.org or voigt@rff.org
Internet: http://www.rff.org/about rff/fellowships internships.htm
AMOUNT: $350-$375/week
DEADLINE(S): MAR 14 (5 p.m., Eastern time)
FIELD(S): Social Sciences, Natural Resources, Energy, Environment
ELIGIBILITY/REQUIREMENTS: Open to U.S. and non-U.S. citizens, undergraduate and graduate students for research in the areas of risk, resource and environmental management, energy and natural resources, and quality of the environment.

Candidates should have outstanding policy analysis and writing skills.
HOW TO APPLY: See website for application and additional information. Address inquiries and applications to John Mankin (Energy and Natural Resources and Quality of the Environment) or Marilyn Voigt (Risk, Resource and Environmental Management). These scholarships are not available to immediate family members of anyone involved in the selection of winners or the administration of the scholarship. For any given year, no educational institution may have more than 1 winner.
NUMBER OF AWARDS: Multiple: 1/institution

2506—UNIVERSITY OF CALIFORNIA-LOS ANGELES (Undergraduate Research Scholars Program)

Undergraduate Research Center for Humanities and Social Studies
A334 Murphy Hall
310/825-2935
FAX: 310/267-5515
E-mail: urhass@college.ucla.edu
Internet: http://www.college.ucla.edu/ugresearch/sch ursp.html
AMOUNT: $2,500-$5,000
DEADLINE(S): APR 1-MAR 15
FIELD(S): Humanities; Social Sciences
ELIGIBILITY/REQUIREMENTS: Open to continuing students junior level standing and higher (at least 90 units but no more than 175 units by fall quarter of the thesis year) who have a strong commitment to research or creative activity, and who are committed to completing an honors thesis or a comprehensive 199 project during their senior year. URSP application workshops will be posted here during the application period. 3.25 GPA or higher.
HOW TO APPLY: Apply online or submit with a letter of recommendation accompanied by a Letter of Recommendation form from your faculty mentor(s).
RENEWABLE: No

2507—UNIVERSITY OF NEWCASTLE UPON TYNE (Excellence Scholarships)

NE1 7RU, UNITED KINGDOM
+44 191 222 6000
E-mail: urhass@college.ucla.edu
Internet: http://www.ncl.ac.uk/undergraduate/finance/scholarships/hass.phtml
AMOUNT: £1,000
DEADLINE(S): APR 1-MAR 15
FIELD(S): Humanities; Arts; Social Sciences

ELIGIBILITY/REQUIREMENTS: Awarded to the best-performing students on entry. Based on exam results and all the information from your UCAS form. Must choose the University of Newcastle upon Tyne as your firm choice as part of the UCAS process.
HOW TO APPLY: Apply online or submit with a letter of recommendation accompanied by a Letter of Recommendation form from your faculty mentor(s).
NUMBER OF AWARDS: 29
RENEWABLE: No

2508—WESTERN MICHIGAN UNIVERSITY (College of Arts and Sciences/Undergraduate Research and Creative Activities Award)

1903 West Michigan
Kalamazoo MI 49008-5337
269/387-8777
FAX: 269/387-6989
E-mail: finaid-info@wmich.edu
Internet: http://www.wmich.edu/finaid.edu/finaid
AMOUNT: $500/semester
DEADLINE(S): MAR 1
FIELD(S): Arts; Sciences; Humanities; Social Sciences
ELIGIBILITY/REQUIREMENTS: Applicant must have declared a major in a department or program at least 30 credit hours; be in good academic standing; and have a faculty mentor for the project and a project plan.
HOW TO APPLY: Contact the College of Arts and Sciences for an application or apply online or print application from website.
RENEWABLE: Yes. May request renewal for 1 additional term.
CONTACT: College of Arts and Sciences

2509—WESTERN MICHIGAN UNIVERSITY (Kathryn and Grant Leaske Memorial Endowed Scholarship)

1903 West Michigan
Kalamazoo MI 49008-5337
269/387-8777
FAX: 269/387-6989
E-mail: finaid-info@wmich.edu
Internet: http://www.wmich.edu/finaid.edu/finaid
AMOUNT: Varies
DEADLINE(S): MAR 1
FIELD(S): Arts; Sciences; Humanities; Social Sciences
ELIGIBILITY/REQUIREMENTS: Applicant must be a full-time undergradu-

ate student whose major is in the College of Arts & Sciences; demonstrate financial need; have a 3.0 GPA; be able to document history of community/university service and volunteerism.

HOW TO APPLY: Contact the College of Arts and Sciences for an application or apply online or print application from website.

RENEWABLE: Yes. Up to 2 years depending on academic status.

CONTACT: Financial Aid

ARCHAEOLOGY/ ANTHROPOLOGY

2510—BRITISH INSTITUTE OF ARCHAE-OLOGY AT ANKARA (Travel Grants)

10 Carlton House Terrace
London SW1Y 5AH ENGLAND
+44-020-7969-5204
FAX: +44-020-7969-5401
E-mail: biaa@britac.ac.uk
Internet: http://www.britac.ac.uk/ institutes/ankara/
AMOUNT: £500 (max.)
DEADLINE(S): FEB 1
FIELD(S): Archaeology & Geography of Turkey
ELIGIBILITY/REQUIREMENTS: Travel grants to enable undergraduate and graduate students to familiarize themselves with the archaeology and geography of Turkey, its museums, and ancient sites. For citizens or residents of the British Commonwealth.
HOW TO APPLY: Contact British Institute or see website for an application.

2511—EPILEPSY FOUNDATION OF AMERICA (Behavioral Sciences Student Fellowships)

4351 Garden City Drive
Landover MD 20785-2267
301/459-3700 or 800/EFA-1000
TDD: 800/332-2070
FAX: 301/577-2684
Internet: http://www.epilepsy foundation.org
AMOUNT: $2,000
DEADLINE(S): FEB 1
FIELD(S): Epilepsy Research/Practice; Sociology; Social Work; Psychology; Anthropology; Nursing; Economics; Vocational Rehabilitation; Counseling; Political Science
ELIGIBILITY/REQUIREMENTS: 3-month fellowships awarded to undergraduate and graduate students for work on a

project during the summer or other free period. Students propose an epilepsy-related study or training project to be carried out at a U.S. institution. A preceptor must supervise the student and the project.

HOW TO APPLY: Contact EFA for an application.

2512—FOUNDATION FOR THE ADVANCEMENT OF MESOAMERICAN STUDIES, INC. (Research Grants)

268 South Suncoast Boulevard
Crystal River FL 34429-5498
352/795-5990
FAX: 352/795-1970
E-mail: famsi@famsi.org
Internet: http://www.famsi.org/ grants/apply.html
AMOUNT: $500-$10,000
DEADLINE(S): SEP 15
FIELD(S): Ancient Mesoamerican cultures, Anthropology, Archaeology, Art History, Ethnohistory, Linguistics
ELIGIBILITY: Open to degree candidates, graduates, and researchers in Mesoamerican Studies whose projects have not had extensive financial support.
HOW TO APPLY: Visit website to download a brochure or e-mail jessica@famsi. org.
NUMBER OF AWARDS: 30-35 awards annually.
RENEWABLE: Yes. Must reapply; greater priority to new applicants.

2513—LAMBDA ALPHA NATIONAL COLLEGIATE HONORS SOCIETY FOR ANTHROPOLOGY (Lambda Alpha National Dean's List Award)

Department of Anthropology
Ball State University
Muncie IN 47306-0435
765/285-1575
FAX: 765/285-2163
E-mail: 01bkswartz@bsn.edu
Internet: http://www.lambda alpha.com
AMOUNT: $5,000
DEADLINE(S): MAR 1
FIELD(S): Anthropology
ELIGIBILITY/REQUIREMENTS: Junior standing, member of active Lambda Alpha Chapter.
HOW TO APPLY: Contact Chapter faculty sponsor.
NUMBER OF AWARDS: 1
RENEWABLE: No
CONTACT: B. K. Swartz Jr.

2514—LAMBDA ALPHA NATIONAL COLLEGIATE HONORS SOCIETY FOR ANTHROPOLOGY (National Lambda Alpha Scholarship Award)

Department of Anthropology
Ball State University
Muncie IN 47306-0435
765-/285-1575
FAX: 765/285-2163
E-mail: 01bkswartz@bsn.edu
Internet: http://www.lambda alpha.com
AMOUNT: $5,000
DEADLINE(S): MAR 1
FIELD(S): Anthropology
ELIGIBILITY/REQUIREMENTS: Graduating senior, member of active Lambda Alpha Chapter.
HOW TO APPLY: Contact Chapter faculty sponsor.
NUMBER OF AWARDS: 1
RENEWABLE: No
CONTACT: B. K. Swartz Jr.

2515—STUDENT CONSERVATION ASSOCIATION (SCA Resource Assistant Program)

P.O. Box 550
Charlestown NH 03603
603/543-1700
FAX: 603/543-1828
E-mail: internships@sca-inc.org
Internet: http://www.sca-inc.org
AMOUNT: $1,180-$4,725
DEADLINE(S): Varies
FIELD(S): Environment and related fields (agriculture, archaeology, anthropology, botany, caves, civil engineering, environmental design, engineering & education, fisheries, forests, herpetology, history, landscape architecture, environmental design, paleontology, wildlife management, geology, hydrology, library/museums, surveying)
ELIGIBILITY/REQUIREMENTS: Must be 18 and U.S. citizen; need not be student.
HOW TO APPLY: Send $1 for postage for application; outside U.S./Canada, send $20.
NUMBER OF AWARDS: 900 positions in U.S. and Canada

AREA STUDIES

2516—AMERICAN ASSOCIATION OF TEACHERS OF ITALIAN (College Essay Contest)

Cal State University-Chico

Foreign Language Department
Chico CA 95929
AMOUNT: $100-$300
DEADLINE(S): JUN 15
FIELD(S): Italian Language; Italian Studies
ELIGIBILITY/REQUIREMENTS: Competitive prize based on essays written in Italian on a topic pertaining to literature or culture. Open to undergraduates at accredited colleges and universities in North America.
HOW TO APPLY: Write for complete information.
NUMBER OF AWARDS: Write to Association care of Cal State for information.
CONTACT: Prof. Eugenio Frongia

2517—AMERICAN RADIO RELAY LEAGUE FOUNDATION (Donald Riebhoff Memorial Scholarship)

225 Main Street
Newington CT 06111
860/594-0397
FAX: 860/594-0259
E-mail: foundation@arrl.orgInternet: http://www.arrlf.org/
AMOUNT: $1,000
DEADLINE(S): FEB 1
FIELD(S): International Studies
ELIGIBILITY/REQUIREMENTS: For AARL members who hold a technician or higher class license pursuing a baccalaureate or higher degree in international studies at an accredited college or university.
HOW TO APPLY: See website or contact Foundation for information and application. Submit with a 1-page essay on the role amateur radio has played in your life. A recent high school (or equivalent) or college transcript required; submit with application or mail separately.
NUMBER OF AWARDS: 1
RENEWABLE: No
CONTACT: Mary M. Hobart, K1MMH, Secretary

2518—ARCTIC INSTITUTE OF NORTH AMERICA (Jim Bourque Scholarship)

University of Calgary
2500 University Drive NW
Calgary Alberta T2N 1N4
CANADA
403/220-7515
FAX: 403/282-4609
Internet: http://www.ucalgary.ca/aina
AMOUNT: $1,000 (Canadian)
DEADLINE(S): JUL 15

FIELD(S): Education; Environmental Studies; Traditional Knowledge; Telecommunications
ELIGIBILITY/REQUIREMENTS: Open to Canadian Aboriginal students who intend to take, or are enrolled in, postsecondary training.
HOW TO APPLY: No application; submit description of program and reasons for choice, transcript, letter of recommendation, statement of financial need, and proof of enrollment or application to a postsecondary institution. See website or contact AINA for details.

2519—ARCTIC INSTITUTE OF NORTH AMERICA (Northern Scientific Training Program Grants)

University of Calgary 2500 University Drive NW
Calgary Alberta T2N 1N4
CANADA
403/220-7515
FAX: 403/282-4609
Internet: http://www.ucalgary.ca/aina
AMOUNT: Varies
DEADLINE(S): NOV
FIELD(S): Northern Canadian & Arctic Studies
ELIGIBILITY/REQUIREMENTS: Open to Canadian citizens/permanent residents enrolled in a Canadian university who are either graduate students or senior undergraduates entering final year and intending to undertake honor's thesis based on northern research that will be continued in subsequent graduate study.
HOW TO APPLY: See website or Dr. Leonard Hills, Chair Northern Studies Group. at lvhills@ucalgary.ca or 403/220-5841 or above.

2520—ASSOCIATION FOR THE STUDY OF AFRO-AMERICAN LIFE & HISTORY, INC. (Afro-American Life and History Essay Contest)

C.B. Powell Building
525 Bryant Street, Suite C142
Washington, DC 20059
202/865-0053
FAX: 202/265-7920
Email: info@asalh.net
Internet: http://asalh.org/Essay Contests.html
AMOUNT: $500
DEADLINE(S): JUN 30
FIELD(S): Afro-American Studies
ELIGIBILITY/REQUIREMENTS: Any full-time student in a 2- or 4-year college

may enter the competition. Essays may be submitted on any topic that explores the life, history and culture of Africans throughout the Americas and the Caribbean. Papers that are only polemical and offer only personal opinions are not acceptable; a research approach is required. Essays should cite the appropriate primary and secondary sources related to the topic under examination (see website for further details). Criteria include clarity, organization, originality, and documentation.
HOW TO APPLY: Via e-mail (essaycontest@asalh.net), submit a copy of your paper (see website or e-mail contact below for details) and an endorsement letter from ASALH faculty advisor/sponsor, who must be a current member of ASALH. (An original signed copy of this letter is to be mailed to Felix Armfield, ASALH ESSAY CONTEST, at the above address.)
NUMBER OF AWARDS: 1 undergraduate; 1 graduate
CONTACT: Questions MUST be directed to Felix Armfield at armfiefl@buffalostate.edu.
ADDITIONAL INFORMATION: Winning writers will be invited to present their essays at the ASALH Annual Meeting.

2521—BLUES HEAVEN FOUNDATION, INC. (Muddy Waters Scholarship)

2120 South Michigan Avenue
Chicago IL 60616
312/808-1286
AMOUNT: $2,000
DEADLINE(S): APR 30
FIELD(S): Music; Music Education; African-American Studies; Folklore; Performing Arts; Arts Management; Journalism; Radio/TV/Film
ELIGIBILITY/REQUIREMENTS: Applicant must be full-time graduate or undergraduate in a Chicago area college or university. Scholastic aptitude, extracurricular involvement, GPA, and financial need are considered.
HOW TO APPLY: Contact Foundation between February and April to request an application.

2522—CANADIAN INSTITUTE OF UKRAINIAN STUDIES (Leo J. Krysa Family Undergraduate Scholarship)

450 Athabasca Hall
University of Alberta
Edmonton Alberta T6G 2E8
CANADA
E-mail: cius@gpu.srv.ualberta.ca
Internet: http://www.ualberta.

ca/cius/cius-grants.htm
AMOUNT: $3,500 (max.)
DEADLINE(S): Varies
FIELD(S): Ukrainian Studies
ELIGIBILITY/REQUIREMENTS: For an undergraduate in the faculty of Arts or Education about to enter final year. Applicants' programs must emphasize Ukrainian and/or Ukrainian-Canadian studies, through a combination of Ukrainian and East European or Canadian courses. Candidates must be Canadian citizens/permanent residents and use the 8-month scholarship at any Canadian university.
HOW TO APPLY: Contact Institute for application and information.
NUMBER OF AWARDS: 1
RENEWABLE: No

2523—CENTER FOR CROSS-CULTURAL STUDY, THE (Scholarship Program)

446 Main Street
Amherst MA 01002-2314
413/256-0011 or 800/377-2621
FAX: 413/256-1968
E-mail: admin@cccs.com
Internet: http://www.cccs.com
AMOUNT: $500-$2,500
DEADLINE(S): Fall semester/MAY 15; Spring semester/NOV 15
FIELD(S): Spanish and Spanish Culture
ELIGIBILITY/REQUIREMENTS: Partial tuition assistance to study at Center in Seville, Spain. Must submit an original 2- to 3-page essay in Spanish.
HOW TO APPLY: Contact organization for specific details regarding the essays. Submit with a short description in English of your experience with the Spanish language and culture and a faculty recommendation.
RENEWABLE: Awards are for 1 semester or academic year.

2524—CENTER FOR CROSS-CULTURAL STUDY, THE (Tuition Awards for Study in Seville, Spain)

446 Main Street
Amherst MA 01002-2314
413/256-0011 or 800/377-2621
FAX: 413/256-1968
E-mail: admin@cccs.com
Internet: http://www.cccs.com
AMOUNT: $500
DEADLINE(S): Varies
FIELD(S): Spanish and Spanish Culture

ELIGIBILITY/REQUIREMENTS: Partial tuition assistance to study at Center in Seville, Spain. Must submit an original 2- to 3-page essay in Spanish.
HOW TO APPLY: Contact organization for specific details regarding the essays. Submit with a short description in English of your experience with the Spanish language and culture and a faculty recommendation.
RENEWABLE: Awards are for 1 semester or academic year.

2525—CHINESE HISTORICAL SOCIETY OF SOUTHERN CALIFORNIA/DAVID AND PEARL LOUIE FOUNDATION

415 Bernard Street
Los Angeles CA 90012-1703
323/222-0856
FAX: 323/221-4812
E-mail: chssc@earthlink.net
Internet: http://www.chssc.org
AMOUNT: $1,000
DEADLINE(S): MAR 21, 1PM
FIELD(S): Humanities; Social Sciences (emphasis on Chinese-American studies)
ELIGIBILITY/REQUIREMENTS: Must be enrolled undergraduate in an accredited college or university in Southern California. Preference given to those who will continue enrollment for full academic year. Minimum cumulative GPA of 3.0 required. Academic emphasis related to Chinese-American studies in the humanities or social sciences.
HOW TO APPLY: See website for application. Submit with research paper, preferably on Chinese-American theme (1,000-3,000 words), biographical essay discussing importance of Chinese studies to applicant as well as information about financial need, employment history, campus/community activities, and future plans (300-500 words), transcripts since high school (4 copies of each). Letters of recommendation optional. Finalists will be contacted for an oral interview.
NUMBER OF AWARDS: 1
CONTACT: Susie Ling, Scholarship Chair, shling@pasadena.edu

2526—CLAN MACBEAN FOUNDATION, THE

441 Wadsworth Blvd., Suite 213
Lakewood CO 80226
303/233-6002
FAX: 303/233-6002
E-mail: clanoffice@clanmacbean.net
Internet: http://www.clan

macbean.net
AMOUNT: Up to $5,000
DEADLINE(S): MAY 1
FIELD(S): Scottish-culture related field or a field relating to the improvement of the human family
ELIGIBILITY/REQUIREMENTS: High school graduate.
HOW TO APPLY: See website or write or e-mail for an application and instruction letter.
NUMBER OF AWARDS: 3
RENEWABLE: Yes. Must reapply
CONTACT: Raymond L. Heckethorn
ADDITIONAL INFORMATION: Trustees of the MacBean Foundation, their spouses, and their children are not eligible for grant funds.

2527—EMBASSY OF JAPAN (Monbusho Scholarship Program for Japanese Studies)

1155 21st Street NW
Washington DC 20036
202/238-6700
E-mail: eojjicc@erolscom
Internet: http://www.embjapan.org
AMOUNT: ¥142,500/month
DEADLINE(S): Varies
FIELD(S): Japanese Language and/or Cultural Studies
ELIGIBILITY/REQUIREMENTS: For foreign students to study for 1 to 2 years in Japan. Program offers intensive Japanese language instruction, but applicant must already speak Japanese.
HOW TO APPLY: All 16 Japanese consulates in the U.S. accept and review applications. For information and application materials, contact the nearest consulate-general of Japan or the Embassy of Japan in Washington.

2528—FOUNDATION FOR THE ADVANCEMENT OF MESOAMERICAN STUDIES, INC. (Research Grants)

268 South Suncoast Boulevard
Crystal River FL 34429-5498
352/795-5990
FAX: 352/795-1970
E-mail: famsi@famsi.org
Internet: http://www.famsi.org/grants/apply.html
AMOUNT: $500-$10,000
DEADLINE(S): SEP 15
FIELD(S): Ancient Mesoamerican Cultures, Anthropology, Archaeology, Art History, Ethnohistory, Linguistics

ELIGIBILITY: Open to degree candidates, graduates, and researchers in Mesoamerican Studies whose projects have not had extensive financial support.
HOW TO APPLY: Visit website to download a brochure or e-mail jessica@famsi.org.
NUMBER OF AWARDS: 30-35 awards annually
RENEWABLE: Yes. Must reapply. Greater priority to new applicants.

2529—HAWAII COMMUNITY FOUNDATION (Blossom Kalama Evans Memorial Scholarship Fund)

1164 Bishop Street, Suite 800
Honolulu HI 96813
808/537-6333 or 888/731-3863
FAX: 808/521-6286
E-mail: info@hcf-hawaii.org
Internet: http://www.hcf-hawaii.org
DEADLINE(S): MAR 1
FIELD(S): Hawaiian Studies; Hawaiian Language
ELIGIBILITY/REQUIREMENTS: Applicants must be Hawaii residents; junior, senior, or graduate students enrolled full time in an accredited college or university; demonstrate financial need, good moral character, and minimum GPA of 2.7. Preference given to students of Hawaiian ancestry. Members of the Hawaiian Girls Golf Association are not eligible.
HOW TO APPLY: Send application with 2 letters of recommendation.

2530—INSTITUT D'ETUDES POLITIQUES DE PARIS (U.S. Sciences P.O. Alumni Association Scholarships)

27 rue Saint Guillaume
75337 Paris Cedex 07 FRANCE
331-4549-5047
FAX: +33 331-4544-1252
E-mail: contact@sciencespo.org
Internet: http://sciencespo.org
AMOUNT: Up to $5,000
DEADLINE(S): Varies
FIELD(S): European Studies; Political Science; Economics; Finance
ELIGIBILITY/REQUIREMENTS: Open to U.S. citizens for studies at IEP Paris, either through admission to the school or through an exchange program with an accredited U.S. school. Must be fluent in French.
HOW TO APPLY: See website or contact Director of International Student Services for an application. Submit with cover letter, résumé, and brief essay.

CONTACT: Mr. P. Cauchy, Director of International Student Services

2531—INSTITUTE OF INTERNATIONAL EDUCATION NATIONAL SECURITY EDUCATION PROGRAM (NSEP David L. Boren Undergraduate Scholarships)

1400 K Street NW, 6th floor
Washington DC 20005
800/618-6737
FAX: 202/326-7672
E-mail: nsep@iie.org
Internet: http://www.iie.org/nsep
AMOUNT: Up to $20,000
DEADLINE(S): Mid FEB
FIELD(S): All, emphasis on geographic areas, languages, and fields of study deemed critical to U.S. national security
ELIGIBILITY/REQUIREMENTS: Intended to provide support to U.S. undergraduates who will pursue the study of languages and cultures currently underrepresented in study abroad and critical to U.S. national security. Must be U.S. citizen matriculated at a U.S. university or college. Provides a unique funding opportunity for U.S. students to study world regions critical to U.S. interests (including Africa, Asia, Central & Eastern Europe, Latin American and the Caribbean, and the Middle East). Must be matriculated in an undergraduate degree program in a U.S. university, college or community college accredited by an accrediting body recognized by the U.S. Department of Education, and applying to engage in a study abroad experience in a country outside of Western Europe, Canada, Australia, or New Zealand that meets home institution standards.
HOW TO APPLY: See website for additional information and application. Apply online. Submit to your NSEP campus representative with 2 reference forms, language self-assessment form, language proficiency form (optional), official transcripts, 1-page study abroad program description, and letters of support for direct enrollment (if applicable).
RENEWABLE: No
CONTACT: Susan Sharp, Program Officer
ADDITIONAL INFORMATION: The NSEP service requirement stipulates that award recipients work in the federal government in positions with national security responsibilities. The Departments of Defense, Homeland Security, State, or any element of the Intelligence Community are priority agencies.

2532—JAPANESE AMERICAN CITIZENS LEAGUE (Yoshiko Tanaka Memorial Scholarship)

1765 Sutter Street
San Francisco CA 94115
415/921-5225
FAX: 415/931-4671
E-mail: jacl@jacl.org
Internet: http://www.jacl.org
AMOUNT: $1,000-$5,000
DEADLINE(S): APR 1
FIELD(S): Japanese Language & Culture; U.S.-Japan Relations
ELIGIBILITY/REQUIREMENTS: Only open to JACL members and their children. For undergraduate students who are planning to attend a college, university, trade, business, or any other institution of higher learning. Financial need NOT a factor.
HOW TO APPLY: For membership information or an application, send SASE, stating your level of study. Submit personal statement, letters of recommendation, and transcripts.

2533—JAPANESE GOVERNMENT (Monbusho Japanese Studies Scholarships)

350 S. Grand Avenue, Suite 1700
Los Angeles CA 90071
213/617-6700, ext. 338
FAX: 213/617-6728
Internet: http://www.la.us.emb-japan.go-jp
AMOUNT: Tuition + $1,400-$1,800/month
DEADLINE(S): MAR
FIELD(S): Japanese Studies and closely related fields
ELIGIBILITY/REQUIREMENTS: For undergraduate students aged 18-30 years who major or minor in Japanese studies and who wish to study in Japan. Intermediate Japanese proficiency is required. Scholarship is for 1 year.
HOW TO APPLY: For further information or an application, contact Scholarship Coordinator.

2534—KOSCIUSZKO FOUNDATION (Summer Sessions in Poland and Rome)

15 East 65th Street
New York NY 10021-6595
212/734-2130
FAX: 212/628-4552
E-mail: addy@thekf.org
Internet: http://www.kosciuszko foundation.org
AMOUNT: Varies

DEADLINE(S): Varies
FIELD(S): Polish Studies; History;
Literature; Art; Economics; Social
Studies; Language; Culture
ELIGIBILITY/REQUIREMENTS: Open
to U.S. citizens and permanent residents
who are undergraduate or graduate stu-
dents, high school seniors 18 or older, and
persons of any age not enrolled in a college
or university program.
HOW TO APPLY: See website or send
SASE for an application.
CONTACT: Addy Tymczyszyn, Summer
Studies Abroad Coordinator

2535—KOSCIUSZKO FOUNDATION (Year Abroad Program)

15 East 65th Street
New York NY 10021-6595
212/734-2130
FAX: 212/628-4552
E-mail: addy@thekf.org
Internet: http://www.kosciuszko
foundation.org
AMOUNT: Tuition, housing, and
monthly stipend
DEADLINE(S): JAN 16
FIELD(S): Polish Studies
ELIGIBILITY/REQUIREMENTS: Open
to American students who wish to study
Polish language, history, literature, and
culture for credit at the undergraduate
level. Must be enrolled at a U.S. college or
university entering junior or senior year or
be enrolled in a master's or doctoral program (except dissertation level). Must have
a minimum 3.0 GPA and be U.S.
citizen/permanent resident. Based on academics, goals, and interest in Polish subjects or involvement in Polish American
community.
HOW TO APPLY: See website or send
SASE for an application. $50 application
fee (1 application is valid for 2 years).
CONTACT: Addy Tymczyszyn

2536—LEMMERMANN FOUNDATION, THE (Fondazione Lemmermann Scholarship Awards)

c/o Studio Associato Romanelli
via Cosseria, 5
00192 Roma ITALY
(06) 324.30.23
FAX: (06) 322.17.88
E-mail: lemmermann@mail.nexus.it
Internet: http://www.lemmermann.
nexus.it/lemmermann/
AMOUNT: 750 euro per month
DEADLINE(S): MAR 15; SEP 30
FIELD(S): Italian/Roman Studies
(literature, archaeology, history of art)

ELIGIBILITY/REQUIREMENTS: For
university students who need to study in
Rome to carry out research and prepare
their theses concerning Rome and the
Roman culture from the period Pre-
Roman to present-day time in the subject
areas above.
HOW TO APPLY: Contact Foundation
for details. See website for application.

2537—MINISTRY OF EDUCATION OF THE REPUBLIC OF CHINA (Scholarships for Foreign Students)

5 South Chung-Shan Road
Taipei, Taiwan
REPUBLIC OF CHINA
(86) (02) 356-5696
FAX: (86) (02) 397-6778
E-mail: emic@moe.edu.cn
Internet: http://www.moe.edu.cn
AMOUNT: NT$25,000 (per month)
DEADLINE(S): Varies (inquire of
school)
FIELD(S): Chinese Studies or Language
ELIGIBILITY/REQUIREMENTS: Open
to full-time students wishing to study in
Taiwan. Must have studied in R.O.C. for at
least 1 term prior to scholarship.
HOW TO APPLY: Write for complete
information or contact colleges directly.
NUMBER OF AWARDS: 300

2538—MINISTRY OF EDUCATION, SCIENCE, AND CULTURE (Icelandic Studies Scholarships)

Solvholsgata 4
Reykjavik IS-150 ICELAND
354/560-9500
FAX: 354/562-3068
E-mail: postur@mrn.stjr.is
Internet: http://www.mrn.stjr.is
AMOUNT: Registration fees plus stipend
DEADLINE(S): Varies
FIELD(S): Icelandic Studies
ELIGIBILITY/REQUIREMENTS:
Eight-month scholarship is open to stu-
dents at any level of study to pursue stud-
ies in Icelandic language, literature, and
history at the University of Iceland.
HOW TO APPLY: Contact Ministry of
Education for an application.

2539—NATIONAL ITALIAN AMERICAN FOUNDATION

1860 19th Street NW
Washington DC 20009
202/387-0600
FAX: 202/387-0800
E-mail: scholarships@niaf.org

Internet: http://www.niaf@org/
scholar/scholarships/about.asp
AMOUNT: $2,500-$10,000
DEADLINE(S): MAR 1
FIELD(S): All (category I), Area Studies,
Italian (Category II)
ELIGIBILITY/REQUIREMENTS: Open
to U.S. citizens or permanent resident
aliens enrolled in an accredited institution
of higher education; have a GPA of at 3.5
(or equivalent); demonstrate outstanding
potential and high academic achievements;
and fit into 1 of 2 NIAF scholarship categories: Category I—Italian-American students (must have 1 ancestor who has emigrated from any region in Italy), area of
study open; Category II—students from
any ethnic background majoring or minoring in Italian language, Italian studies,
Italian American studies or a related field.
Scholarships are awarded on the basis of
academic performance, field of study,
career objectives, and potential commitment and ability to make significant contributions to their chosen field of study. Some
scholarships awarded on basis of financial
need.
HOW TO APPLY: Application available
on website and can ONLY be submitted
online. Official transcript must be mailed
and postmarked. FAFSA optional; if submitted must be postmarked by March 1.
Teacher evaluation required; submit using
online Teacher Evaluation form no later
than March 15.
RENEWABLE: Yes
ADDITIONAL INFORMATION: If
awarded, recipient must sign a written
statement pledging that upon completion
of the scholarship academic year, student
will submit a typed narrative of approximately 500 words for publication describing the benefits of the NIAF Scholarship.
May not be used as a substitute for or
diminish any other award, grant or scholarship. The combined benefits from all
sources may not exceed the cost of tuition,
fees and university-provided room and
board.

2540—SMITHSONIAN INSTITUTION-FREER/SACKLER GALLERIES (Dick Louie Memorial Internship for Americans of Asian Descent)

Education Department
Washington DC 20560-0707
202/357-4880
TTY: 202/786-2374
Internet: http://www.asia.si.edu
AMOUNT: Stipend
DEADLINE(S): Varies
FIELD(S): Asian Art; Art History;
Museum Studies

ELIGIBILITY/REQUIREMENTS: For high school students of Asian descent to gain practical experience in a museum setting. Must be entering or completing senior year of high school, and must live and attend high school in the Washington metropolitan area.
HOW TO APPLY: Contact the Internship Coordinator for an application.

2541—SMITHSONIAN INSTITUTION (Minority Student Internship Program)

Office of Research Training and Services
470 L'Enfant SW, Suite 7102
MRC 902, P.O. Box 37012
Washington DC 20013-7012
202/633-7070
FAX: 202/633-7069
E-mail: siofg@si.edu
Internet: http://www.si.edu/research+study
AMOUNT: $500/week + possible travel expenses
DEADLINE(S): FEB 1 (for Summer or for Fall); OCT 1 (for Spring)
FIELD(S): Humanities; Environmental Studies; Cultural Studies; Natural History; Earth Science; Art History; Biology
ELIGIBILITY/REQUIREMENTS: 10-week, full-time internships in residence at the Smithsonian are open to U.S. minority students who wish to participate in research or museum-related activities in above and related fields. Must be undergraduates or beginning graduate students with a minimum 3.0 GPA. Must submit essay, résumé, and official transcript.
HOW TO APPLY: Contact the Office of Research Training and Services or see website for an application. Submit. with the required essay or research proposal, résumé, and transcripts.

2542—SONS OF NORWAY FOUNDATION (Helen Tronvold Norwegian Folk High School Scholarship)

c/o Sons of Norway
1455 West Lake Street
Minneapolis MN 55408
612/821-4632
E-mail: colson@sofn.com
Internet: http://www.sofn.com/foundation/
AMOUNT: $2,000
DEADLINE(S): MAR 1
FIELD(S): All

ELIGIBILITY/REQUIREMENTS: Must be current members of SON or children or grandchildren of current members; high school graduates, 18 to 23 years old, who have been accepted by a specific Norwegian Folk High School (see http://www.folkhogskole.no for additional information). Academic potential, letters of recommendation, essay, involvement in SON or community activities, and financial need are considered.
HOW TO APPLY: Submit application along with a statement of cross-cultural education goals. See website for an application and additional details,
NUMBER OF AWARDS: Varies
RENEWABLE: Yes. Up to 2 within a 5-year period.
CONTACT: Cindy Olson, Director

2543—SONS OF NORWAY FOUNDATION (King Olav V Norwegian-American Heritage Fund)

c/o Sons of Norway
1455 West Lake Street
Minneapolis MN 55408
612/821-4632
E-mail: colson@sofn.com
Internet: http://www.sofn.com/foundation/
AMOUNT: $250-$3,000
DEADLINE(S): MAR 1
FIELD(S): Norwegian Studies/American Studies: Arts; Crafts; Literature; History; Music; Folklore and related fields
ELIGIBILITY/REQUIREMENTS: Must be U.S. citizens, 18 or older, enrolled in a recognized educational institution, who have demonstrated interest in Norwegian heritage or any Norwegian. Award based on GPA, participation in school and community activities, work experience, education and career goals, and personal and school references. Financial need also considered. Same opportunity available to Norwegian students interested in pursuing American studies at U.S. university.
HOW TO APPLY: Submit application along with an essay (500 words or less) giving reasons for applying, course of study to be pursued, the length of course, name of the institution to be attended, tuition and costs, and amount of financial assistance needed. Include 3 letters of recommendation and copy of high school or college transcript. See website for an application and additional details.
NUMBER OF AWARDS: Varies
RENEWABLE: Yes. Maximum of 2 awards in 5 years.
CONTACT: Cindy Olson, Director

ECONOMICS

2544—AMERICAN RADIO RELAY LEAGUE FOUNDATION (Donald Riebhoff Memorial Scholarship)

225 Main Street
Newington CT 06111
860/594-0397
FAX: 860/594-0259
E-mail: foundation@arrl.org
Internet: http://www.arrlf.org/
AMOUNT: $1,000
DEADLINE(S): FEB 1
FIELD(S): International Studies
ELIGIBILITY/REQUIREMENTS: For AARL members who hold a technician or higher class license pursuing a baccalaureate or higher degree in international studies at an accredited college or university.
HOW TO APPLY: See website or contact Foundation for information and application. Submit with a 1-page essay on the role amateur radio has played in your life. A recent high school (or equivalent) or college transcript required; submit with application or mail separately.
NUMBER OF AWARDS: 1
RENEWABLE: No
CONTACT: Mary M. Hobart, K1MMH, Secretary

2545—CALIFORNIA NURSES ASSOCIATION (Shirley Titus Scholarship & R11 & R6 Scholarships)

2000 Franklin Street
Oakland CA 94612
510/622-8310
FAX: 510/663-1625
E-mail: scholarship@calnurses.org
Internet: http://www.calnurses.org
AMOUNT: Varies
DEADLINE(S): JUL 1
FIELD(S): Nursing; Humanities, Cultural, Political, Economic, Legal and Social Sciences
ELIGIBILITY/REQUIREMENTS: Open to California nurses for academic preparation and continuing education in above fields appropriate for developing effective nursing leadership.
HOW TO APPLY: See website for application or write or call for application. Submit with a 1 page typed essay, describing educational goals and how they relate to personal and professional vision for healthcare; 2 letters of recommendation, from non-relatives which must relate to this scholarship and address at least one of the following: CNA activities, competence in work setting, and academic ability; a cur-

riculum vitae; and a copy of current RN license.
NUMBER OF AWARDS: Varies
CONTACT: Shaun Copeland

2546—EPILEPSY FOUNDATION OF AMERICA (Behavioral Sciences Student Fellowships)

4351 Garden City Drive
Landover MD 20785-2267
301/459-3700 or 800/EFA-1000
TDD: 800/332-2070
FAX: 301/577-2684
Internet: http://www.epilepsy foundation.org
AMOUNT: $3,000
DEADLINE(S): MAR 1
FIELD(S): Epilepsy Research/Practice; Sociology; Social Work; Psychology; Anthropology; Nursing; Economics; Vocational Rehabilitation; Counseling; Political Science
ELIGIBILITY/REQUIREMENTS: 3-month fellowships awarded to undergraduate and graduate students for work on a project during the summer or other free period. Students propose an epilepsy-related study or training project to be carried out at a U.S. institution. A preceptor must supervise the student and the project.
HOW TO APPLY: Contact EFA for an application.

2547—GOVERNMENT FINANCE OFFICERS ASSOCIATION (Minorities in Government Finance Scholarship)

Scholarship Committee
203 North LaSalle Street
Suite 2700
Chicago IL 60601-1210
312/977-9700
Internet: http://www.gfoa.org
AMOUNT: $5,000
DEADLINE(S): FEB 15
FIELD(S): Public Administration; (Governmental) Accounting; Finance; Political Science; Economics; Business Administration (with a specific focus on government or nonprofit management)
ELIGIBILITY/REQUIREMENTS: Open to Black, Indian, Eskimo or Aleut, Asian or Pacific Islander, Hispanic students; must be a citizen or permanent resident of the U.S. or Canada.
HOW TO APPLY: Send application. Must be recommended by the student's academic advisor or department chair.

2548—GREAT LAKES COMMISSION (Carol A. Ratza Memorial Scholarship)

2805 South Industrial Highway, Suite 100
Ann Arbor MI 48104-6791
E-mail: manninen@glc.org
Internet: http://www.glc.org
AMOUNT: $500
DEADLINE(S): MAR 28
FIELD(S): Electronic Communications Technology (Environmental/Economic Applications)
ELIGIBILITY/REQUIREMENTS: Open to high school seniors and returning students enrolled full time at a Great Lakes college or university (Illinois, Indiana, Michigan, New York, Ohio, Pennsylvania, Wisconsin, Ontario, Quebec). Must have a demonstrated interest in the environmental or economic applications of electronic communications technology, exhibit academic excellence, and have a sincere appreciation for the Great Lakes and their protection.
HOW TO APPLY: See website or contact Commission for an application. Must submit résumè, transcripts, recommendations, and essay or Web page on Great Lakes issue. Recipient announced by May 1.
CONTACT: Christine Manninen

2549—HILLSDALE COLLEGE (Freedom as Vocation Scholarship)

33 E. College Street
Hillsdale MI 49242-1298
517/437-7341
Internet: http://www.hillsdale.edu
AMOUNT: Varies
DEADLINE(S): None
FIELD(S): Business; History; Political Science; Economics
ELIGIBILITY/REQUIREMENTS: Open to Hillsdale College undergraduates who maintain a minimum 3.0 GPA and commit to a series of courses in the above fields. Student must rank in top 20% of class and top 10% of test scores. Must possess excellent communications, public speaking, and leadership skills and demonstrate outstanding character and citizenship. Financial need NOT a factor.
HOW TO APPLY: No application; students are selected. See website for details.
RENEWABLE: Yes

2550—HISPANIC COLLEGE FUND (HSF/JP Morgan Chase Scholarship Program)

55 Second Street, Suite 1500

San Francisco CA 94105
877/HSF-INFO (877/473-4636)
FAX: 415/808/2302
E-mail: pip@hsf.net
Internet: http://hispanicfund.org
AMOUNT: $2,500
DEADLINE(S): JUN 16
FIELD(S): Business; Finance; Economics
ELIGIBILITY/REQUIREMENTS: Open to students in their sophomore and junior years. Must be U.S. citizens or legal permanent residents of Hispanic heritage (one parent fully Hispanic or both parents half Hispanic). Minimum GPA 3.0. Must carry at least 12 credits each term. Selection is based on academic achievement, personal strengths, leadership and financial need.
HOW TO APPLY: Contact Fund for details or visit website for application.

2551—INSTITUT D'ETUDES POLITIQUES DE PARIS (U.S. Sciences P.O. Alumni Association Scholarships)

27 rue Saint Guillaume
75337 Paris Cedex 07 FRANCE
+33 331-4549-5047
FAX: +33 33-/4544-1252
E-mail: contact@sciencespo.org
Internet: http://sciencespo.org
AMOUNT: Up to $5,000
DEADLINE(S): Varies
FIELD(S): European Studies; Political Science; Economics; Finance
ELIGIBILITY/REQUIREMENTS: Open to U.S. citizens for studies at IEP Paris, either through admission to the school or through an exchange program with an accredited U.S. school. Must be fluent in French.
HOW TO APPLY: See website or contact Director of International Student Services for an application. Submit with cover letter, résumé, and brief essay.
CONTACT: Mr. P. Cauchy, Director of International Student Services

2552—INSTITUTE FOR HUMANE STUDIES (Koch Summer Fellow Program)

3401 North Fairfax Drive,
Suite 440
Arlington VA 22201-4432
703/993-4880 or 800/697-8799
FAX: 703/993-4890
Internet: http://www.TheIHS.org
AMOUNT: $1,500 + airfare and housing
DEADLINE(S): FEB 15
FIELD(S): Economics; Public Policy; Law; Government; Politics
ELIGIBILITY/REQUIREMENTS: Open to undergraduates and graduates. Includes

2 week-long seminars, the internship, and research and writing projects. Financial need NOT a factor.
HOW TO APPLY: Apply online or contact IHS for an application. Submit with transcripts and essays.
NUMBER OF AWARDS: 32
RENEWABLE: No

2553—JACKSONVILLE STATE UNIVERSITY (Dr. and Mrs. Robert Moersch Scholarship)

Jacksonville AL 36265
782-5677 or 800/231-5291
Internet: www.jsu.edu
AMOUNT: Varies
DEADLINE(S): FEB 1
FIELD(S): Finance; Economics
ELIGIBILITY/REQUIREMENTS: Open to juniors or seniors majoring in economics or finance; 2.5 overall GPA, 3.0 in major.
HOW TO APPLY: Contact Finance Department, 256/782-5773, for application and additional information.
RENEWABLE: No

2554—JORGE MAS CANOSA FREEDOM FOUNDATION (Mas Family Scholarships)

P.O. Box 14-1898
Miami FL 33114
305/529-0075, ext. 35
E-mail: mmartinez@jmcffmas familyscholarships.org
Internet: http://www.jmcffmas scholarships.org
AMOUNT: Up to $10,000
DEADLINE(S): MAR 31
FIELD(S): Engineering, Business, International Relations, Economics, Communications, Journalism
ELIGIBILITY/REQUIREMENTS: For Cuban-American students, graduates and undergraduates, born in Cuba or direct descendants (1 parent or 2 grandparents) of those who left Cuba. Must be in top 10% of high school class or maintain a 3.5 GPA in college. Financial need considered along with academic success, SAT and GRE scores, and leadership potential.
HOW TO APPLY: Contact Foundation for application. 2 short essays and 2 character evaluations along with proof of Cuban descent required.
NUMBER OF AWARDS: 10
RENEWABLE: Yes. Maximum $40,000; must reapply.

2555—JUNIATA COLLEGE (Metz Scholarship)

Office of Financial Planning

1700 Moore Street
Huntingdon PA 16652
814/641-3142
FAX: 814/641-5311
E-mail: frankv@juniata.edu
Internet: http://www.juniata.edu/admission/finplan/index.html
AMOUNT: Up to $5,000
DEADLINE(S): MAR 1
FIELD(S): Business; Economics
ELIGIBILITY/REQUIREMENTS: Open to Business or Economics majors. Must demonstrate financial need.
HOW TO APPLY: Contact College for an application or enrollment information. See Financial Aid Office for FAFSA.
CONTACT: Vincent Frank, Director of Student Financial Planning, 814/641-3140; e-mail: frankv@juniata.edu

2556—JUNIOR ACHIEVEMENT INC. (Joe Francomano Scholarship)

One Education Way
Colorado Springs CO 80906-4477
719/540-8000
FAX: 719/540-6299
E-mail: newmedia@ja.org
Internet: http://www.ja.org
AMOUNT: $5,000
DEADLINE(S): FEB 1
FIELD(S): Economics
ELIGIBILITY/REQUIREMENTS: Must be graduating high school students; minimum GPA of 3.0; have participated in a JA Company Program or JA Economics; have demonstrated leadership and excellent extracurricular and community activities; and financial need.
HOW TO APPLY: For application, contact JA; submit with a personal essay of 500 words; 3 letters of recommendation, 1 from a JA Company Program or JA Economics consultant, and 2 other recommendations.
NUMBER OF AWARDS: 1
RENEWABLE: Yes. Maximum 4 years, $20,000.
CONTACT: Submit application to Joe Francomano Scholarship, Junior Achievement Inc., P.O. Box 5186, Fort Lauderdale FL 33310.

2557—KOSCIUSZKO FOUNDATION (Summer Sessions in Poland and Rome)

15 East 65th Street
New York NY 10021-6595
212/734-2130
FAX: 212/628-4552
E-mail: addy@thekf.org
Internet: http://www.kosciuszko foundation.org

AMOUNT: Varies
DEADLINE(S): Varies
FIELD(S): Polish Studies; History; Literature; Art; Economics; Social Studies; Language; Culture
ELIGIBILITY/REQUIREMENTS: Open to U.S. citizens and permanent residents who are undergraduate or graduate students, high school seniors 18 or older, and persons of any age not enrolled in a college or university program.
HOW TO APPLY: See website or send SASE for an application.
CONTACT: Addy Tymczyszyn, Summer Studies Abroad Coordinator, ext. 210

2558—LONDON SCHOOL OF ECONOMICS AND POLITICAL SCIENCE

Financial Support Office
Houghton Street
London WC2A 2AE ENGLAND
+44 020 7955
FAX: +44 020 7216
E-mail: financialsupport@lse.ac.uk
Internet: http://www.lse.ac.uk
AMOUNT: Varies with award
DEADLINE(S): Varies
FIELD(S): Economics; Accounting; Finance; Political Science; International Relations
ELIGIBILITY/REQUIREMENTS: For undergraduates and graduate students; international students.
HOW TO APPLY: See website and enter "scholarships," and a vast array of programs will appear.
RENEWABLE: Varies

2559—NATIONAL FEDERATION OF REPUBLICAN WOMEN (Betty Rendel Scholarship)

124 North Alfred Street
Alexandria VA 22314
703/548-9688
FAX: 703/548-9836
E-mail: mail@nfrw.org
Internet: http://www.nfrw.org
AMOUNT: $1,000
DEADLINE(S): JUN 1
FIELD(S): Political Science; Government; Economics
ELIGIBILITY/REQUIREMENTS: Open to undergraduate Republican women who have successfully completed 2 years of coursework, majoring in one of the above fields.
HOW TO APPLY: Applications are available on NFRW website or by contacting NFRW headquarters. Submit to the president of your state federation.

NUMBER OF AWARDS: 3
RENEWABLE: No
CONTACT: Scholarship Coordinator

2560—NATIONAL POULTRY AND FOOD DISTRIBUTORS ASSOCIATION SCHOLARSHIP FOUNDATION

958 McEver Road Extension,
Unit B8
Gainesville GA 30504
770/535-9901
FAX: 770/535-7385
E-mail: kkm@npfda.org
Internet: http://www.npfda.org
AMOUNT: $1,500-$2,000 each/annual
DEADLINE(S): MAY 31
FIELD(S): Poultry, Food or related agricultural degree; Food Science; Dietetics; Poultry Science; Agricultural Economics; International Business, etc.
ELIGIBILITY/REQUIREMENTS: Must be enrolled full time as a college junior or senior the upcoming (award) year at a U.S. institution pursuing one of the above fields.
HOW TO APPLY: Complete application and provide your current official transcript, letter of recommendation from your dean along with a 1-page letter describing your goals and aspirations.
NUMBER OF AWARDS: 4
RENEWABLE: No
CONTACT: Kristin McWhorter

2561—NATIONAL SOCIETY DAUGHTERS OF THE AMERICAN REVOLUTION (Enid Hall Griswold Memorial Scholarship)

Committee Services Office
Attn: Scholarships
1776 D Street NW
Washington DC 20006-5392
202/628-1776
Internet: http://www.dar.org
AMOUNT: $1,000
DEADLINE(S): FEB 15
FIELD(S): History; Political Science; Government; Economics
ELIGIBILITY/REQUIREMENTS: Open to undergraduate juniors and seniors (U.S. citizens) attending an accredited U.S. college or university. Awards are judged on academic excellence, commitment to field of study, and need. Affiliation with DAR not required.
HOW TO APPLY: Must submit application with a letter of sponsorship from local DAR chapter (send SASE to address above to obtain name and application); statement of 1,000 words or less stating

career objectives, how college major (if required) or college plans relate to future professional goals and reasons for these choices; transcripts list of extracurricular activities, honors received, scholastic achievements, or other significant accomplishments; 2-4 letters of recommendation from the high school or college you now attend who are familiar with your work, and proof of citizenship. See website for additional information.
RENEWABLE: No

2562—ROYAL THAI EMBASSY, OFFICE OF EDUCATIONAL AFFAIRS (Revenue Department Scholarships for Thai Students)

1906 23rd Street NW
Washington DC 20008
202/667-9111 or 202/667-8010
FAX: 202/265-7239
AMOUNT: Varies
DEADLINE(S): APR
FIELD(S): Computer Science (Telecommunications), Law, Economics, Finance, Business Administration
ELIGIBILITY/REQUIREMENTS: Scholarships for students under age 35 from Thailand who have been accepted to study in the U.S or UK pursuing any level degree in one of the above fields.
HOW TO APPLY: Selections based on academic records, employment history, and advisor recommendations.

2563—STATE FARM COMPANIES FOUNDATION (Exceptional Student Fellowship)

One State Farm Plaza, SC-3
Bloomington IL 61710-0001
309/766-2039/2161
E-mail: Nancy.Lynn.gr3o@statefarm.com
Internet: http://www.statefarm.com
AMOUNT: $3,000 (nominating institution receives $250)
DEADLINE(S): FEB 15
FIELD(S): Accounting; Business Administration; Actuarial Science; Computer Science; Economics; Finance; Insurance/Risk Management; Investments; Management; Marketing; Mathematics; Statistics
ELIGIBILITY/REQUIREMENTS: For U.S. citizens who are full-time juniors or seniors when they apply. Must demonstrate significant leadership in extracurricular activities, have minimum 3.6 GPA, and attend accredited U.S. college or uni-

versity. Must be nominated by dean, department head, professor, or academic advisor.
HOW TO APPLY: See website, visit your financial aid office, or write for an application.
NUMBER OF AWARDS: 50
RENEWABLE: No

2564—UNIVERSITY OF ILLINOIS COLLEGE OF ACES (Jonathan Baldwin Turner Agricultural Scholarship Program)

115 ACES Library
1101 South Goodwin Street
Urbana IL 61801
217/244-4540
Internet: http://w3.aces.uiuc.edu/Acad-Prog/
AMOUNT: $1,000
DEADLINE(S): Varies (start of high school senior year)
FIELD(S): Agriculture; Nutritional Science; Natural Resources; Environmental; Social Sciences (agricultural economics, communications, or education)
ELIGIBILITY/REQUIREMENTS: Scholarships in agricultural, food, and human nutritional sciences for outstanding incoming freshmen at the University of Illinois. Must have minimum ACT composite score of 27, equivalent SAT combined scores, or be in the 10th percentile of high school class rank at the end of junior year. Interview required.
HOW TO APPLY: Contact Assistant Dean of Academic Programs, College of Agricultural, Consumer and Environmental Sciences, for an application.
NUMBER OF AWARDS: 55
RENEWABLE: Yes. 4-year award; up to $4,000.
CONTACT: Charles Olson

2565—UNIVERSITY OF WINDSOR (Outstanding Scholars Award)

401 Sunset Avenue
Windsor Ontario N9B 3P4
CANADA
519/253-3000
FAX: 519/973-7081
E-mail: awards1@uwindsor.ca
Internet: http://www.uwindsor.ca
AMOUNT: $1,000-$2,500/year (Canadian); maximum 4 years
DEADLINE(S): MAY 31
FIELD(S): Classics, Modern Languages, French, Philosophy, Music, Physics, Earth Sciences (not Environmental

Studies), Economics (not Business and Economics), Chemistry (not Biochemistry), Mathematics and Statistics, Industrial, Mechanical (Materials Option) or Environmental Engineering or Bachelor of Arts and Science

ELIGIBILITY/REQUIREMENTS: Open to undergraduate students registering in year 1 at the University of Windsor. Must have superior grades. Amount of award based on secondary school accomplishments.

HOW TO APPLY: Automatic. No application required.

RENEWABLE: Yes. Up to 4 years.

CONTACT: Aase Houser

ADDITIONAL INFORMATION: Students in this program will also be mentored in their first year in preparation for guaranteed Outstanding Scholars Appointments in their Department/School (valued at $2,000 Canadian in earnings for each of the 2nd, 3rd, and 4th years) provided all conditions are met.

2566—WOMEN IN DEFENSE (HORIZONS Scholarship Foundation)

2111 Wilson Boulevard, Suite 400
Arlington VA 22201-3061
703/247-2552
FAX: 703/522-1885
E-mail: wid@ndia.org
Internet: http://www.ndia.org
AMOUNT: $500+
DEADLINE(S): NOV 1; JUL 1
FIELD(S): Security Studies; Engineering; Computer Science; Physics; Mathematics; International Relations; Political Science; Operations Research; Economics; National Security/Defense; Business and Law (as they relate to national security or defense); other fields considered if relevance to national security or defense can be demonstrated

ELIGIBILITY/REQUIREMENTS: Open to women employed/planning careers in defense/national security areas (NOT law enforcement or criminal justice). Must be currently enrolled full or part time at an accredited college or university at the graduate or undergraduate junior/senior level. Must have a minimum 3.25 GPA, demonstrate financial need, and be U.S. citizen. Based on academic achievement, work experience, objectives, and recommendations.

HOW TO APPLY: See website or send SASE for application.

RENEWABLE: Yes

GEOGRAPHY/CARTOGRAPHY

2567—AIR FORCE RESERVE OFFICER TRAINING CORPS (AFROTC SCHOLARSHIPS)

551 East Maxwell Boulevard
Maxwell AFB AL 36112-6106
866/4AFROTC
E-mail: info@afrotc.com
Internet: http://www.afrotc.com
AMOUNT: Varies, but up to full tuition and fees plus $600/year for books
DEADLINE(S): DEC 1
FIELD(S): Science; Engineering; Business; Political Science; Psychology; Geography; Foreign Studies; Foreign Language

ELIGIBILITY/REQUIREMENTS: 4- and 3-year competitive scholarships based on individual merit to high school seniors and graduates who have not enrolled full time at a college or university. Academic performance is measured using an academic composite, which combines SAT (Math and Verbal only)/ACT scores, class rank, GPA and the number of advanced placement or honors courses completed through Grade 11. To be eligible for consideration, students should achieve a 1100 SAT (Math and Verbal only) or 24 ACT, minimum 3.0 GPA and class ranking in top 40%. Must be a U.S. citizen between the ages of 17-27. Must also have GPA of 2.5 or above, be in top 40% of class, and complete Applicant Fitness Test. Cannot be a single parent. Your college or university must offer AFROTC.

HOW TO APPLY: Visit www.afrotc.com to apply

NUMBER OF AWARDS: N/A

RENEWABLE: No

2568—AMERICAN CONGRESS ON SURVEYING AND MAPPING (AAGS Joseph F. Dracup Scholarship Award and Nettie Dracup Memorial Scholarships)

6 Montgomery Village Avenue, Suite 403
Gaithersburg MD 20879
240/632-9716, ext. 105
FAX: 240/632-1321
E-mail: pat.canfield@acsm.net
Internet: http://www.acsm.net/scholar.html
AMOUNT: $2,000
DEADLINE(S): DEC 31
FIELD(S): Geodetic Surveying
ELIGIBILITY/REQUIREMENTS: Open to students enrolled in 4-year degree pro-

grams in surveying or closely related degree programs, such as geomatics or surveying engineering; must be U.S. citizen. Must join ACSM.

HOW TO APPLY: Contact ACSM for membership information and applications. Must submit personal statement (including goals and financial need), letters of recommendation, and transcripts.

NUMBER OF AWARDS: 1

2569—AMERICAN CONGRESS ON SURVEYING AND MAPPING (Allen Chelf Scholarship)

6 Montgomery Village Avenue, Suite 403
Gaithersburg MD 20879
240/632-9716, ext. 105
FAX: 240/632-1321
E-mail: pat.canfield@acsm.net
Internet: http://www.acsm.net/scholar.html
AMOUNT: $500
DEADLINE(S): DEC 31
FIELD(S): Surveying
ELIGIBILITY/REQUIREMENTS: Open to students enrolled in a 2-year or 4-year surveying (or closely related fields) degree program, either full or part time, in the U.S.; must join ACSM.

HOW TO APPLY: Contact ACSM for membership information and applications. Submit personal statement (including goals and financial need), letters of recommendation, and transcripts.

NUMBER OF AWARDS: 1

2570—AMERICAN CONGRESS ON SURVEYING AND MAPPING (Bernsten International Scholarship in Surveying Technology)

6 Montgomery Village Avenue, Suite 403
Gaithersburg MD 20879
240/632-9716, ext. 105
FAX: 240/632-1321
E-mail: pat.canfield@acsm.net
Internet: http://www.acsm.net/scholar.html
AMOUNT: $500
DEADLINE(S): DEC 31
FIELD(S): Surveying Technology
ELIGIBILITY/REQUIREMENTS: Open to students enrolled in 2-year degree programs in surveying technology; must join ACSM.

HOW TO APPLY: Contact ACSM for membership information and applications. Submit personal statement (including

goals and financial need), letters of recommendation, and transcripts.
NUMBER OF AWARDS: 1

2571—AMERICAN CONGRESS ON SURVEYING AND MAPPING (Cady McDonnell Memorial Scholarship)

6 Montgomery Village Avenue,
Suite 403
Gaithersburg MD 20879
240/632-9716, ext. 105
FAX: 240/632-1321
E-mail: pat.canfield@acsm.net
Internet: http://www.acsm.net/
scholar.html
AMOUNT: $1,000
DEADLINE(S): DEC 31
FIELD(S): Surveying
ELIGIBILITY/REQUIREMENTS: Open to women enrolled in a 2-year or 4-year surveying (or closely related) degree program, either full or part time. Must be residents of Montana, Idaho, Washington, Oregon, Wyoming, Colorado, Utah, Nevada, California, Arizona, New Mexico, Arkansas or Hawaii; must join ACSM.
HOW TO APPLY: Contact ACSM for membership information and applications. Submit personal statement (including goals and financial need), letters of recommendation, and transcripts.
NUMBER OF AWARDS: 1

2572—AMERICAN CONGRESS ON SURVEYING AND MAPPING (Cartography and Geographic Information Society Scholarship)

6 Montgomery Village Avenue,
Suite 403
Gaithersburg MD 20879
240/632-9716, ext. 105
FAX: 240/632-1321
E-mail: pat.canfield@acsm.net
Internet: http://www.acsm.net/
scholar.html
AMOUNT: $1,000
DEADLINE(S): DEC 31
FIELD(S): Cartography; Geographic Information Science
ELIGIBILITY/REQUIREMENTS: Open to outstanding students enrolled full time in a 4-year or graduate-degree program. Preference given to undergraduates with junior or senior standing; must join ACSM.
HOW TO APPLY: Contact ACSM for membership information and applications. Submit personal statement (including goals and financial need), letters of recommendation, and transcripts.
NUMBER OF AWARDS: 1

2573—AMERICAN CONGRESS ON SURVEYING AND MAPPING (National Society of Professional Surveyors Board of Governor's Scholarship)

6 Montgomery Village Avenue,
Suite 403
Gaithersburg MD 20879
240/632-9716, ext. 105
FAX: 240/632-1321
E-mail: pat.canfield@acsm.net
Internet: http://www.acsm.net/
scholar.html
AMOUNT: $1,000
DEADLINE(S): DEC 31
FIELD(S): Surveying
ELIGIBILITY/REQUIREMENTS: Open to students enrolled in studies in surveying, entering their junior year in a 4-year degree program, who have maintained a minimum 3.0 GPA; must join ACSM.
HOW TO APPLY: Contact ACSM for membership information and applications. Submit personal statement (including goals and financial need), letters of recommendation, and transcripts.
NUMBER OF AWARDS: 1

2574—AMERICAN CONGRESS ON SURVEYING AND MAPPING (National Society of Professional Surveyors Forum for Equal Opportunity/Mary Feindt Scholarship)

6 Montgomery Village Avenue,
Suite 403
Gaithersburg MD 20879
240/632-9716, ext. 105
FAX: 240/632-1321
E-mail: pat.canfield@acsm.net
Internet: http://www.acsm.net/
scholar.html
AMOUNT: $1,000
DEADLINE(S): DEC 31
FIELD(S): Surveying
ELIGIBILITY/REQUIREMENTS: Open to women enrolled in a 4-year degree program in a surveying and mapping curriculum within the U.S. Must submit personal statement (including goals and financial need), letters of recommendation, and transcripts. Must join ACSM.
HOW TO APPLY: Contact ACSM for membership information and applications. Submit personal statement (including goals and financial need), letters of recommendation, and transcripts.
NUMBER OF AWARDS: 1

2575—AMERICAN CONGRESS ON SURVEYING AND MAPPING (National Society of Professional Surveyors Scholarships)

6 Montgomery Village Avenue,

Suite 403
Gaithersburg MD 20879
240/632-9716, ext. 105
FAX: 240/632-1321
E-mail: pat.canfield@acsm.net
Internet: http://www.acsm.net/
scholar.html
AMOUNT: $1,000
DEADLINE(S): DEC 31
FIELD(S): Surveying
ELIGIBILITY/REQUIREMENTS: Open to full-time students enrolled in 4-year degree programs in surveying or closely related degree programs, such as geomatics or surveying engineering. Must join ACSM.
HOW TO APPLY: Contact ACSM for membership information and applications. Submit personal statement (including goals and financial need), letters of recommendation, and transcripts.
NUMBER OF AWARDS: 2

2576—AMERICAN CONGRESS ON SURVEYING AND MAPPING (Schonstedt Scholarships in Surveying)

6 Montgomery Village Avenue,
Suite 403
Gaithersburg MD 20879
240/632-9716, ext. 105
FAX: 240/632-1321
E-mail: pat.canfield@acsm.net
Internet: http://www.acsm.net/
scholar.html
AMOUNT: $1,500
DEADLINE(S): DEC 31
FIELD(S): Surveying
ELIGIBILITY/REQUIREMENTS: Open to students enrolled in 4-year degree programs in surveying or closely related degree programs, such as geomatics or surveying engineering. Preference given to applicants with junior or senior standing; must join ACSM.
HOW TO APPLY: Contact ACSM for membership information and applications. Submit personal statement (including goals and financial need), letters of recommendation, and transcripts.
NUMBER OF AWARDS: 2 (Schonstedt also donates a magnetic locator to the surveying program at each recipient's school.)

2577—AMERICAN SOCIETY OF ENGINEERS OF INDIAN ORIGIN (Undergraduate Scholarship Programs)

47790 Pavillon Road
Canton MI 48188
248/354-6895

FAX: 248/354-6818
E-mail: awards@asei-ncc.org
Internet: http://www.asei-ncc.org/Awards.htm
AMOUNT: $1,000
DEADLINE(S): AUG 15
FIELD(S): Engineering: Architecture, Computer or allied science, Geotechnical or Geo-environmental Engineering, and allied sciences
ELIGIBILITY/REQUIREMENTS: Open to students who are Indian by birth, ancestry, or relation Based on demonstrated ability, academic achievement, including GPA (minimum 3.0)/honors/awards, career objectives, faculty recommendations, student involvement in science fair, campus activities, and (industrial exposure including part-time work and internships.; must attend an accredited college or university anywhere in the U.S.
HOW TO APPLY: See website for application and details or contact Society for applications. Submit with résumé; an essay (maximum 1 page) stating qualifications, career goals, reasons for seeking the scholarship; 1 letter of recommendation in the current or intended field of study.
CONTACT: Dr. Ramu Ramamurthy, ASEI Scholarship Committee Chairman

2578—ASPRS: THE IMAGING & GEOSPATIAL INFORMATION SOCIETY (Kenneth J. Osborn Memorial Scholarship)

ASPRS Awards Program
5410 Grosvenor Lane, Suite 210
Bethesda MD 20814-2160
301/493-0290, ext. 101
FAX: 301/493-0208
E-mail: scholarships@asprs.org
Internet: http://www.asprs.org
AMOUNT: $1,000
DEADLINE(S): DEC 1
FIELD(S): Surveying, Mapping, Photogrammetry, Geospatial Information and Technology
ELIGIBILITY/REQUIREMENTS: Open to undergraduates who display exceptional interest, desire, ability, and aptitude to enter the profession of surveying, mapping, photogrammetry, or geospatial information and technology. In addition, the Scholarship recognizes students who excel at communications and collaboration.
HOW TO APPLY: Submit 6 copies of the completed application and the following supporting materials: academic transcripts, including a separate list of relevant courses taken; 2 completed reference forms from faculty members who have knowledge of your abilities; samples of your work; description of your research goals; state-

ment of work experience that may include internships, other forms of work experience, or special projects that demonstrate excellence in these fields and in communications and collaboration (including the nature, location and date(s) of the experience); a 2-page statement regarding your plans for continuing studies in theoretical photogrammetry; and papers, research reports, or other items that indicate capability in these fields. Note: Electronic submissions encouraged.
NUMBER OF AWARDS: 1
RENEWABLE: No
CONTACT: Scholarship Administrator at above address or see website.
ADDITIONAL INFORMATION: The recipient is obligated to provide a final report to ASPRS of his/her scholastic accomplishments during the period for which the award is granted.

2579—ASPRS: THE IMAGING & GEOSPATIAL INFORMATION SOCIETY (Robert E. Altenhofen Memorial Scholarship)

ASPRS Awards Program
5410 Grosvenor Lane, Suite 210
Bethesda MD 20814-2160
301/493-0290
FAX: 301/493-0208
E-mail: scholarships@asprs.org
Internet: http://www.asprs.org
AMOUNT: $2,000
DEADLINE(S): DEC 1
FIELD(S): Photogrammetry
ELIGIBILITY/REQUIREMENTS: Undergraduates or graduates who display exceptional interest and ability in the theoretical aspects of photogrammetry; must be enrolled in an accredited college or university and be active or student members of ASPRS.
HOW TO APPLY: Submit 6 copies of the completed application and the following supporting materials: academic transcripts, including a separate list of relevant courses taken; 2 completed reference forms from faculty members who have knowledge of your abilities; samples of your work; description of your research goals; a 2-page statement regarding your plans for continuing studies in theoretical photogrammetry; and papers, research reports, or other items that indicate capability in these fields. Note: Electronic submissions encouraged.
NUMBER OF AWARDS: 1
RENEWABLE: No
CONTACT: Scholarship Administrator
ADDITIONAL INFORMATION: The recipient is obligated to provide a final report to ASPRS of his/her scholastic

accomplishments during the period for which the award is granted.

2580—ASPRS: THE IMAGING & GEOSPATIAL INFORMATION SOCIETY (Space Imaging Award for Application of High Resolution Digital Satellite Imagery)

ASPRS Awards Program
5410 Grosvenor Lane, Suite 210
Bethesda MD 20814-2160
301/493-0290, ext. 101
FAX: 301/493-0208
E-mail: scholarships@asprs.org
Internet: http://www.asprs.org
AMOUNT: $2,000
DEADLINE(S): DEC 1
FIELD(S): Remote Sensing; Digital Satellite Imagery
ELIGIBILITY/REQUIREMENTS: Full-time undergraduate or graduate students at an accredited college or university with image processing facilities appropriate for conducting the proposed work.
HOW TO APPLY: Submit 6 copies of the application and the following supporting materials: 2 completed reference forms from faculty members; samples of your work; description of your research goals; and a brief proposal describing the proposed research, the purpose of the research, the application it might address, the physical features of the study area, the analysis procedure, your anticipated results, an itemized budget, and a list of all courses, workshops, and other training/experience that demonstrate your ability to conduct the proposed research. Note: Electronic submissions encouraged.
NUMBER OF AWARDS: 1
RENEWABLE: No
CONTACT: Scholarship Administrator
ADDITIONAL INFORMATION: Must attend presentation ceremony at the annual meeting to receive the award. Must prepare a written report of the project and submit it to ASPRS and Space Imaging for possible company use within 1 year of receipt of data.

2581—ASPRS: THE IMAGING & GEOSPATIAL INFORMATION SOCIETY (Student Travel Grants)

ASPRS Awards Program
5410 Grosvenor Lane, Suite 210
Bethesda MD 20814-2160
301/493-0290, ext. 101
FAX: 301/493-0208
E-mail: scholarships@asprs.org
Internet: http://www.asprs.org
AMOUNT: $500

DEADLINE(S): DEC 1

FIELD(S): Photogrammetry

ELIGIBILITY/REQUIREMENTS: ASPRS selects qualified students to attend the ASPRS Annual Conference with financial support from the ASPRS Foundation.

HOW TO APPLY: Submit written statement of no more than 1 page outlining the importance of attending this conference in relation to the applicant's course of study and career development plans. Supplemental materials are also permitted (transcripts, publications, etc.) and at least one letter of recommendation from a faculty advisor. Note: Electronic submissions encouraged.

NUMBER OF AWARDS: 2

RENEWABLE: No

CONTACT: Scholarship Administrator at above address or see website.

ADDITIONAL INFORMATION: The grants also include a 1-year student membership in ASPRS and a complimentary conference registration for the selected student(s) provided they volunteer to help at the conference.

2582—BRITISH INSTITUTE OF ARCHAE- OLOGY AT ANKARA (Travel Grants)

10 Carlton House Terrace
London SW1Y 5AH ENGLAND
+44-020-7969-5204
FAX: +44-020-7969-5401
E-mail: biaa@britac.ac.uk
Internet: http://www.britac.ac.uk/
institutes/ankara/

AMOUNT: £500 (maximum)

DEADLINE(S): FEB 1

FIELD(S): Archaeology & Geography of Turkey

ELIGIBILITY/REQUIREMENTS: Travel grants to enable undergraduate and graduate students to familiarize themselves with the archaeology and geography of Turkey, its museums, and ancient sites. For citizens or residents of the British Commonwealth.

HOW TO APPLY: Contact British Institute or see website for an application.

2583—CALIFORNIA LAND SURVEYORS EDUCATION FOUNDATION

P.O. Box 9098
Santa Rosa CA 95404
707/578-6016
FAX: 707/578-4406
E-mail: clsa@californiasurveyors.org
Internet: http://www.california
surveyors.org

AMOUNT: $375-$2,000

DEADLINE(S): DEC 7

FIELD(S): Land Surveying

ELIGIBILITY/REQUIREMENTS: Criteria vary with scholarship; see website for details.

HOW TO APPLY: See website to apply online.

CONTACT: Dorothy Calegari, Executive Director

2584—CALIFORNIA STATE UNIVERSITY- NORTHRIDGE (Undergraduate Geography Scholarships)

Department of Geography
18111 Nordhoff Street
Northridge, CA 91330-8249
818/677-3532
E-mail: geography@csun.edu
Internet: http://www.csun.edu/
geography/

AMOUNT: $250-$1,800

DEADLINE: Varies

FIELDS: Geography

ELIGIBILITY/REQUIREMENTS: Open to undergraduate students and transfer students from community colleges majoring in geography who have a financial need and are able to perform at a high academic level in geography courses.

HOW TO APPLY: Applications available from the Geography Department and the Financial Aid Office. Submit with transcripts, letters of recommendation, essay demonstrating passionate interest in subject.

NUMBER OF AWARDS: 3

RENEWABLE: Varies

2585—CONSULTING ENGINEERS COUN- CIL OF NEW JERSEY (Louis Goldberg Scholarship Fund)

66 Morris Avenue, Suite 1A
Springfield NJ 07081
973/564-5848
FAX: 973/564-7480
E-mail: Barbara@acecnj.org
Internet: http://www.acecnj.org

AMOUNT: $1,000

DEADLINE(S): DEC 5

FIELD(S): Engineering; Land Surveying

ELIGIBILITY/REQUIREMENTS: Must be a U.S. citizen; enrolled in an ABET-accredited engineering or land surveying program, in a New Jersey college or university; seeking a bachelor of science in engineering; and be entering their 3rd or 4th year (5th year in a 5-year program) in the fall. Scholarships will be awarded in March and will be based on scholastic merit and achievements. Students graduating in December are not eligible.

HOW TO APPLY: Write or download application from website.

NUMBER OF AWARDS: 5

2586—GAMMA THETA UPSILON INTER- NATIONAL GEOGRAPHIC HONOR SOCIETY (Buzzard, Richason, and Maxfield Presidents Scholarships)

University of Wisconsin
1725 State Street
La Crosse WI 54601
608/785-8355
FAX: 608/785-8332
E-mail: holder.virg@uwlax.edu
Internet: http://www.gtuhonors.org

AMOUNT: $500

DEADLINE(S): JUN 1

FIELD(S): Geography

ELIGIBILITY/REQUIREMENTS: Undergraduate and graduate scholarships are open to Gamma Theta Upsilon members who maintain at least a "B" grade point average in any accredited geography program.

HOW TO APPLY: Contact Department of Geography for an application.

CONTACT: Dr. Virgil Holder, Department of Geography

2587—INSTITUTE OF INTERNATIONAL EDUCATION NATIONAL SECURITY EDUCA- TION PROGRAM (NSEP David L. Boren Undergraduate Scholarships)

1400 K Street NW, 6th floor
Washington DC 20005
800/618-6737
FAX: 202/326-7672
E-mail: nsep@iie.org
Internet: http://www.iie.org/nsep

AMOUNT: Up to $20,000

DEADLINE(S): Mid FEB

FIELD(S): All, emphasis on geographic areas, languages, and fields of study deemed critical to U.S. national security

ELIGIBILITY/REQUIREMENTS: Intended to provide support to U.S. undergraduates who will pursue the study of languages and cultures currently underrepresented in study abroad and critical to U.S. national security. Must be U.S. citizen matriculated at a U.S. university or college. Provides a unique funding opportunity for U.S. students to study world regions critical to U.S. interests (including Africa, Asia, Central & Eastern Europe, Latin American and the Caribbean, and the Middle East). Must be matriculated in an undergraduate degree program in a U.S. university, college or community college accredited by an accrediting body recognized by the U.S. Department of Education, and applying to engage in a study abroad experience in a country outside of Western Europe, Canada, Australia, or New Zealand that meets home institution standards.

HOW TO APPLY: See website for additional information and application. Apply online. Submit to your NSEP campus representative with 2 reference forms, language self-assessment form, language proficiency form (optional), official transcripts, 1-page study abroad program description, and letters of support for direct enrollment (if applicable).

RENEWABLE: No

CONTACT: Susan Sharp, Program Officer

ADDITIONAL INFORMATION: The NSEP service requirement stipulates that award recipients work in the federal government in positions with national security responsibilities. The Departments of Defense, Homeland Security, State, or any element of the Intelligence Community are priority agencies.

2588—WESTERN MICHIGAN UNIVERSITY (College of Arts and Sciences/Albert A. and Janet Jackman Scholarship)

1903 West Michigan
Kalamazoo MI 49008-5337
269/387-8777
FAX: 269/387-6989
E-mail: finaid-info@wmich.edu
Internet: http://www.wmich.edu/finaid

AMOUNT: $500/semester

FIELD(S): Geography

ELIGIBILITY/REQUIREMENTS: Recipient must be a junior majoring in geography.

HOW TO APPLY: Nominations and selections are made by department faculty.

RENEWABLE: No

CONTACT: Geography Department

HISTORY

2589—AMERICAN RADIO RELAY LEAGUE FOUNDATION (Donald Riebhoff Memorial Scholarship)

225 Main Street
Newington CT 06111
860/594-0397
FAX: 860/594-0259
E-mail: foundation@arrl.orgInternet: http://www.arrlf.org/

AMOUNT: $1,000

DEADLINE(S): FEB 1

FIELD(S): International Studies

ELIGIBILITY/REQUIREMENTS: For AARL members who hold a technician or higher class license pursuing a baccalaureate or higher degree in international studies at an accredited college or university.

HOW TO APPLY: See website or contact Foundation for information and application. Submit with a 1-page essay on the role amateur radio has played in your life. A recent high school (or equivalent) or college transcript required; submit with application or mail separately.

NUMBER OF AWARDS: 1

RENEWABLE: No

CONTACT: Mary M. Hobart, K1MMH, Secretary

2590—ASSOCIATION FOR THE STUDY OF AFRO-AMERICAN LIFE & HISTORY, INC. (Afro-American Life and History Essay Contest)

C.B. Powell Building
525 Bryant Street, Suite C142
Washington, DC 20059
202/865-0053
FAX: 202/265-7920
Email: info@asalh.net
Internet: http://asalh.org/Essay Contests.html

AMOUNT: $500

DEADLINE(S): JUN 30

FIELD(S): Afro-American Studies

ELIGIBILITY/REQUIREMENTS: Any full-time student in a 2- or 4-year college may enter the competition. Essays may be submitted on any topic that explores the life, history and culture of Africans throughout the Americas and the Caribbean. Papers that are only polemical and offer only personal opinions are not acceptable; a research approach is required. Essays should cite the appropriate primary and secondary sources related to the topic under examination (see website for further details). Criteria include clarity, organization, originality, and documentation.

HOW TO APPLY: Via e-mail (essaycontest@asalh.net), submit a copy of your paper (see website or e-mail contact below for details) and an endorsement letter from ASALH faculty advisor/sponsor, who must be a current member of ASALH. (An original signed copy of this letter is to be mailed to Felix Armfield, ASALH ESSAY CONTEST, at the above address.)

NUMBER OF AWARDS: 1 undergraduate; 1 graduate

CONTACT: Questions MUST be directed to Felix Armfield at armfiefl@buffalostate.edu.

ADDITIONAL INFORMATION: Winning writers will be invited to present their essays at the ASALH Annual Meeting.

2591—AUSTRALIAN WAR MEMORIAL (John Treloar Grants-in-Aid & AWM Research Fellowship)

P.O. Box 345
Canberra ACT 2601 AUSTRALIA
02/6243 4210
FAX: 02/6243 4325
E-mail: ian.hodges@awm.gov.au
Internet: http://www.awm.gov.au

AMOUNT: $A6,000 (maximum grant); $A12,000 (maximum fellowship)

DEADLINE(S): Varies

FIELD(S): Australian Military History

ELIGIBILITY/REQUIREMENTS: Open to students at any level in any country to study Australian military history. Financial need NOT a factor.

HOW TO APPLY: Contact AWM for an application.

RENEWABLE: No

CONTACT: Ian Hodges at AWM

2592—CALIFORNIA NURSES ASSOCIATION (Shirley Titus Scholarship & R11 & R6 Scholarships)

2000 Franklin Street
Oakland CA 94612
510/622-8310
FAX: 510/663-1625
E-mail: scholarship@calnurses.org
Internet: http://www.calnurses.org

AMOUNT: Varies

DEADLINE(S): JUL 1

FIELD(S): Nursing; Humanities, Cultural, Political, Economic, Legal and Social Sciences

ELIGIBILITY/REQUIREMENTS: Open to California nurses for academic preparation and continuing education in above fields appropriate for developing effective nursing leadership.

HOW TO APPLY: See website for application or write or call for application. Submit with a 1-page typed essay, describing educational goals and how they relate to personal and professional vision for healthcare; 2 letters of recommendation, from non-relatives which must relate to this scholarship and address at least one of the following: CNA activities, competence in work setting, and academic ability; a curriculum vitae; and a copy of current RN license.

NUMBER OF AWARDS: Varies

CONTACT: Shaun Copeland

2593—EAA AVIATION FOUNDATION (EAA Air Academy-Women Airforce Service Pilots [W.A.S.P.] Internship)

EAA Scholarship Department
P.O. 3086
Oshkosh WI 54903-3065
920/426-6823
E-mail: scholarships@eaa.org
Internet: http://www.young
eagles.org
AMOUNT: Approximately $750 + travel
subsidy
DEADLINE(S): MAR 1
FIELD(S): Aviation and Related Areas
ELIGIBILITY/REQUIREMENTS: Open
to applicant (must be at least 18 years of
age by the start of the internship) wishing
to research and prepare presentations for
EAA Air Academy participants on the
roles women have played in aviation. Must
be able to deal effectively, tactfully and
pleasantly with volunteers, staff, program
participants and Museum visitors. Strong
verbal and written skills and the ability to
work independently. Must also be a current member of EAA (Experimental
Aircraft Association) or recommended by
a current EAA member to apply for these
internships. Learn more about joining
EAA (www.eaa.org) or call 800/843-3612.
Individual and student memberships are
available.
HOW TO APPLY: Apply online.
NUMBER OF AWARDS: 1
ADDITIONAL INFORMATION: Participants may receive ground and flight
instruction.

2594—EAA AVIATION FOUNDATION (EAA AirVenture Museum-Timken Aviation Studies Internships)

EAA Scholarship Department
P.O. 3086
Oshkosh WI 54903-3065
920/426-6823
E-mail: scholarships@eaa.org
Internet: http://www.young
eagles.org
AMOUNT: Approximately $3,000
DEADLINE(S): MAR 1
FIELD(S): Aviation and Related Areas
ELIGIBILITY/REQUIREMENTS: Open
to college-level interns wishing to study the
role of women in the past, present and
future of aviation. Ideally, interns should
aspire to be future professionals in the aviation industry. Must be able to deal effectively, tactfully and pleasantly with volunteers, staff, program participants and
Museum visitors. Strong verbal and written

skills and the ability to work independently. Must also be a current member of EAA
(Experimental Aircraft Association) or
recommended by a current EAA member
to apply for these internships. Learn more
about joining EAA (www.eaa.org) or call
800/843-3612. Individual and student memberships are available.
HOW TO APPLY: Apply online.
NUMBER OF AWARDS: 2

2595—EAA AVIATION FOUNDATION (EAA AirVenture Museum-Wittman Aviation Studies Internship)

EAA Scholarship Department
P.O. 3086
Oshkosh WI 54903-3065
920/426-6823
E-mail: scholarships@eaa.org
Internet: http://www.young
eagles.org
AMOUNT: Approximately $2,500
DEADLINE(S): MAR 1
FIELD(S): Aviation and Related Areas
ELIGIBILITY/REQUIREMENTS: Open
to applicant (must be at least 18 years of
age by the start of the internship) wishing
to work with the collections department of
the EAA AirVenture Museum. The work
will be in support of the museum's artifact
management program and is suitable for a
person with curatorial work. Duties may
include cataloging, moving, and researching artifacts in the museum collection.
Must be able to deal effectively, tactfully
and pleasantly with volunteers, staff, program participants and Museum visitors.
Strong verbal and written skills and the
ability to work independently. Must also
be a current member of EAA
(Experimental Aircraft Association) or
recommended by a current EAA member
to apply for these internships. Learn more
about joining EAA (www.eaa.org) or call
800/843-3612. Individual and student memberships are available.
HOW TO APPLY: Apply online.
NUMBER OF AWARDS: 1

2596—HILLSDALE COLLEGE (Freedom as Vocation Scholarship)

33 E. College Street
Hillsdale MI 49242-1298
517/437-7341
Internet: http://www.hillsdale.edu
AMOUNT: Varies
DEADLINE(S): None
FIELD(S): Business; History; Political
Science; Economics
ELIGIBILITY/REQUIREMENTS: Open
to Hillsdale College undergraduates who

maintain a minimum 3.0 GPA and commit
to a series of courses in the above fields.
Student must rank in top 20% of class and
top 10% of test scores. Must possess excellent communications, public speaking, and
leadership skills and demonstrate outstanding character and citizenship.
Financial need NOT a factor.
HOW TO APPLY: No application; students are selected. See website for details.
RENEWABLE: Yes

2597—INSTITUTE FOR HUMANE STUD-IES (Humane Studies Fellowship)

3301 North Fairfax Drive, Suite 440
Arlington VA 22201-4432
703/993-4880 or 800/697-8799
FAX: 703/993-4890
Internet: http://www.TheIHS.org
AMOUNT: $12,000 (max.)
DEADLINE(S): DEC
FIELD(S): Social Sciences; Liberal Arts;
Law; Humanities; Jurisprudence;
Journalism
ELIGIBILITY/REQUIREMENTS: Open
to graduate and advanced undergraduate
or law students pursuing degrees at any
accredited domestic or foreign college or
university. Based on academic perfor-
mance, demonstrated interest in the classi-
cal liberal tradition, and potential to contribute to the advancement of a free soci-
ety.
HOW TO APPLY: Apply online or contact IHS for an application.
NUMBER OF AWARDS: 90

2598—INSTITUTE OF INTERNATIONAL EDUCATION NATIONAL SECURITY EDUCA-TION PROGRAM (NSEP David L. Boren Undergraduate Scholarships)

1400 K Street NW, 6th floor
Washington DC 20005
800/618-6737
FAX: 202/326-7672
E-mail: nsep@iie.org
Internet: http://www.iie.org/nsep
AMOUNT: Up to $20,000
DEADLINE(S): Mid FEB
FIELD(S): All, emphasis on geographic
areas, languages, and fields of study
deemed critical to U.S. national
security
ELIGIBILITY/REQUIREMENTS:
Intended to provide support to U.S. under-
graduates who will pursue the study of lan-
guages and cultures currently underrepre-
sented in study abroad and critical to U.S.
national security. Must be U.S. citizen
matriculated at a U.S. university or college.
Provides a unique funding opportunity for

U.S. students to study world regions critical to U.S. interests (including Africa, Asia, Central & Eastern Europe, Latin American and the Caribbean, and the Middle East). Must be matriculated in an undergraduate degree program in a U.S. university, college or community college accredited by an accrediting body recognized by the U.S. Department of Education, and applying to engage in a study abroad experience in a country outside of Western Europe, Canada, Australia, or New Zealand that meets home institution standards.
HOW TO APPLY: See website for additional information and application. Apply online. Submit to your NSEP campus representative with 2 reference forms, language self-assessment form, language proficiency form (optional), official transcripts, 1-page study abroad program description, and letters of support for direct enrollment (if applicable).
RENEWABLE: No
CONTACT: Susan Sharp, Program Officer
ADDITIONAL INFORMATION: The NSEP service requirement stipulates that award recipients work in the federal government in positions with national security responsibilities. The Departments of Defense, Homeland Security, State, or any element of the Intelligence Community are priority agencies.

2599—JACKSONVILLE STATE UNIVERSITY (Anders Memorial Scholarships)

Financial Aid Office
Jacksonville AL 36265
256/782-5677 or 800/231-5291
Internet: http://www.jsu.edu
AMOUNT: Varies
FIELD(S): History
ELIGIBILITY/REQUIREMENTS: Must major in history.
HOW TO APPLY: See website for application. Submit with high school transcript and ACT/SAT scores.
RENEWABLE: No
CONTACT: History Department, 256/782-5632

2600—JACKSONVILLE STATE UNIVERSITY (Maj. John Pelham Memorial Scholarship)

Financial Aid Office
Jacksonville AL 36265
256/782-5677 or 800/231-5291
Internet: http://www.jsu.edu
AMOUNT: Varies
DEADLINE(S): FEB 1
FIELD(S): History

ELIGIBILITY/REQUIREMENTS: Open to junior or senior students; preference given to Calhoun County residents.
HOW TO APPLY: See website for application. Submit with a transcript and ACT/SAT scores.
RENEWABLE: No
CONTACT: Scholarship Committee

2601—JACKSONVILLE STATE UNIVERSITY (Opal R. & Opal A. Lovett Scholarship)

Financial Aid Office
Jacksonville AL 36265
256/782-5677 or 800/231-5291
Internet: http://www.jsu.edu
AMOUNT: Varies
DEADLINE(S): FEB 1
FIELD(S): History; Art; English
ELIGIBILITY/REQUIREMENTS: Open to sophomore or above with a minimum 2.5 GPA.
HOW TO APPLY: See website for application. Submit with a transcript and ACT/SAT scores.
NUMBER OF AWARDS: 1
RENEWABLE: No
CONTACT: Scholarship Committee

2602—JOHN F. KENNEDY LIBRARY FOUNDATION (John F. Kennedy Profile in Courage Essay Contest)

Columbia Point
Boston MA 02125
617/514-1649
FAX: 617/514-1641
E-mail: profiles@nara.gov
Internet: http://www.jfklibrary.org
AMOUNT: $500-$3,000
DEADLINE(S): Early JAN
FIELD(S): All, especially Political Science, History, English Language and Literature, and Communications and Journalism
ELIGIBILITY REQUIREMENTS: Open to U.S. high school students in grades 9-12, or home schools; or enrolled in a high school correspondence/GED program in any of the 50 states, D.C., or U.S. territories; or U.S. citizens attending schools overseas.
HOW TO APPLY: Write an essay on an elected official in the U.S. who is acting or has acted courageously to address a political issue at the local, state, national, or international level; also send completed contest registration form.
NUMBER OF AWARDS: 7 (1 first place, 1 second place, 5 finalists)
RENEWABLE: No

2603—KOSCIUSZKO FOUNDATION (Summer Sessions in Poland and Rome)

15 East 65th Street
New York NY 10021-6595
212/734-2130
FAX: 212/628-4552
E-mail: addy@thekf.org
Internet: http://www.kosciuszko foundation.org
AMOUNT: Varies
DEADLINE(S): Varies
FIELD(S): Polish Studies; History; Literature; Art; Economics; Social Studies; Language; Culture
ELIGIBILITY/REQUIREMENTS: Open to U.S. citizens and permanent residents who are undergraduate or graduate students, high school seniors 18 or older, and persons of any age not enrolled in a college or university program.
HOW TO APPLY: See website or send SASE for an application.
CONTACT: Addy Tymczyszyn, Summer Studies Abroad Coordinator, ext. 210

2604—LOUISIANA STATE UNIVERSITY AT SHREVEPORT (Walter O. Bigby Scholarship)

Bronson Hall
Shreveport LA 71115-2399
318/797-5371
Internet: http://www.lsus.edu
AMOUNT: Up to $500/semester
DEADLINE(S): Varies
FIELD(S): Political Science; English; History; Law
ELIGIBILITY/REQUIREMENTS: Must be entering junior or senior year; majoring in one of above subjects; other Liberal Arts majors acceptable, if preparing for law school.
HOW TO APPLY: Contact the Dean's Office, College of Liberal Arts for an application.

2605—NATIONAL AIR AND SPACE MUSEUM (Verville Fellowship)

Smithsonian Institution
Independence Avenue
at 6th Street SW
Room 3313, MRC 312
P.O. Box 37012
Washington DC 20013-7012
202/633-2648
FAX: 202/786-2447
E-mail: NASM-Fellowships@si.edu
Internet: http://www.nasm.si.edu
AMOUNT: $45,000

DEADLINE(S): JAN 15

FIELD(S): Aeronautics; History of Aviation or Space Studies

ELIGIBILITY/REQUIREMENTS: 9- to 12-month in-residence fellowship candidates who provide a critical approach to trends and accomplishments in aviation or space history. Good writing skills required. Open to undergraduates enrolled in accredited institutions, who have completed at least 1 year of college by start of fellowship. Based on academic performance/class standing, career goals, recommendations, and compatibility of scientific interests/abilities with needs/resources of host facility. Citizenship restrictions may apply for some facilities.

HOW TO APPLY: See website for application.

CONTACT: Colette Williams, Fellowship Program Coordinator, Collections and Research Department, 202/633-2648

2606—NATIONAL SOCIETY DAUGHTERS OF THE AMERICAN REVOLUTION (Dr. Aura-Lee A. and James Hobbs Pittenger American History Scholarship)

Committee Services Office
Attn: Scholarships
1776 D Street NW
Washington DC 20006-5392
202/628-1776
Internet: http://www.dar.org
AMOUNT: $2,000
DEADLINE(S): FEB 1
FIELD(S): American History; American Government

ELIGIBILITY/REQUIREMENTS: Awarded to graduating high school students who will have a concentrated study of a minimum of 24 credit hours in American History and American Government. Awards are judged on academic excellence, commitment to field of study, and need. Affiliation with DAR not required.

HOW TO APPLY: Must submit application with a letter of sponsorship from local DAR chapter (send SASE to address above to obtain name and application); statement of 1,000 words or less stating career objectives, how college major (if required) or college plans relate to future professional goals and reasons for these choices; transcripts list of extracurricular activities, honors received, scholastic achievements, or other significant accomplishments; 2-4 letters of recommendation from the high school or college you now attend who are familiar with your work, and proof of citizenship. See website for additional information.

NUMBER OF AWARDS: 3

RENEWABLE: Yes. Up to 4 consecutive years based on review and approval of transcript.

2607—NATIONAL SOCIETY DAUGHTERS OF THE AMERICAN REVOLUTION (Enid Hall Griswold Memorial Scholarship)

Committee Services Office
Attn: Scholarships
1776 D Street NW
Washington DC 20006-5392
202/628-1776
Internet: http://www.dar.org
AMOUNT: $1,000
DEADLINE(S): FEB 15
FIELD(S): History; Political Science; Government; Economics

ELIGIBILITY/REQUIREMENTS: Open to undergraduate juniors and seniors (U.S. citizens) attending an accredited U.S. college or university. Awards are judged on academic excellence, commitment to field of study, and need. Affiliation with DAR not required.

HOW TO APPLY: Must submit application with a letter of sponsorship from local DAR chapter (send SASE to address above to obtain name and application); statement of 1,000 words or less stating career objectives, how college major (if required) or college plans relate to future professional goals and reasons for these choices; transcripts list of extracurricular activities, honors received, scholastic achievements, or other significant accomplishments; 2-4 letters of recommendation from the high school or college you now attend who are familiar with your work, and proof of citizenship. See website for additional information.

RENEWABLE: No

2608—NATIONAL SPACE CLUB (Dr. Robert H. Goddard Historical Essay Award)

2025 M Street NW, Suite 800
Washington DC 20036-4907
202/973/8661
AMOUNT: $1,000
DEADLINE(S): DEC 4
FIELD(S): Aerospace History

ELIGIBILITY/REQUIREMENTS: Essay competition open to any U.S. citizen on a topic dealing with any significant aspect of the historical development of rocketry and astronautics. Essays should not exceed 5,000 words and should be fully documented. Will be judged on originality and scholarship.

HOW TO APPLY: Send SASE for complete information.

RENEWABLE: No

2609—NAVAL HISTORICAL CENTER (Internship Program)

Washington Navy Yard
805 Kidder Breese Street SE
Washington DC 20374-5060
202/433-6901
FAX: 202/433-8200
E-mail: edward.furgol@navy.mil
Internet: http://www.history.navy.mil
AMOUNT: Up to $400 honoraria; or unpaid
DEADLINE(S): None
FIELD(S): Education; History; Public Relations; Design

ELIGIBILITY/REQUIREMENTS: Open to students of colleges/universities. Minimum of 3 weeks, full or part time; 4 specialties are available: curator, education, public relations, and design. Must complete an individual project that contributes to the Center.

HOW TO APPLY: Submit application, available from the website, before desired start date of an internship. Submit with 1 letter of recommendation, an unofficial transcript, and (except for graphic design applicants) a writing sample of not less than 1,000 words.

NUMBER OF AWARDS: 60

RENEWABLE: Yes; must reapply.

CONTACT: Dr. Edward Furgol

2610—RIPON COLLEGE (History Scholarship)

300 Seward Street
P.O. Box 248
Ripon WI 54971
800/947-4766
FAX: 920/746-8335
E-mail: adminfo@ripon.edu
Internet: http://www.ripon.edu
AMOUNT: $2,500
DEADLINE(S): MAR 1
FIELD(S): History

ELIGIBILITY/REQUIREMENTS: Must attend or plan to attend Ripon and major in history.

HOW TO APPLY: Contact Office of Admission for an application; submit with a letter of recommendation from high school teacher. An essay is required.

RENEWABLE: Yes. Must maintain satisfactory progress towards a Ripon degree and continue to major in history.

CONTACT: Office of Admission

2611—SMITHSONIAN INSTITUTION-COOPER-HEWITT, NATIONAL DESIGN MUSEUM (Peter Krueger Summer Internships)

2 East 91st Street
New York NY 10128
212/849-8380
FAX: 212/860-6909
E-mail: edu@si.edu.
Internet: http://www.si.edu/ndm
AMOUNT: $2,500 stipend
DEADLINE(S): FEB 1
FIELD(S): Art & Architectural History;
Museum Studies & Education; Design
ELIGIBILITY/REQUIREMENTS: 10-week (June-August) internship open to college students considering a career in 1 of the above fields and graduate students pursuing M.A.
HOW TO APPLY: See website for details and application. Submit with cover letter stating area of interest, résumé, official transcript, 2 letters of recommendation, and 1- to 2-page essay on interest.
RENEWABLE: No

2612—SMITHSONIAN INSTITUTION-FREER/SACKLER GALLERIES (Dick Louie Memorial Internship for Americans of Asian Descent)

Education Department
Washington DC 20560-0707
202/357-4880
TTY: 202/786-2374
Internet: http://www.asia.si.edu
AMOUNT: Stipend
DEADLINE(S): Varies
FIELD(S): Asian Art; Art History;
Museum Studies
ELIGIBILITY/REQUIREMENTS: Summer internship for high school students of Asian descent. Must be entering or completing senior year of high school, and live and attend high school in the Washington metropolitan area.
HOW TO APPLY: Contact the Internship Coordinator for an application.

2613—SMITHSONIAN INSTITUTION (Minority Student Internship Program)

Office of Research Training and Services
470 L'Enfant SW, Suite 7102
MRC 902, P.O. Box 37012
Washington DC 20013-7012
202/633-7070
FAX: 202/633-7069
E-mail: siofg@si.edu
Internet: http://www.si.edu/
research+study
AMOUNT: $500/week + possible travel expenses
DEADLINE(S): FEB 1 (for Summer or for Fall); OCT 1 (for Spring)
FIELD(S): Humanities; Environmental Studies; Cultural Studies; Natural History; Earth Science; Art History; Biology
ELIGIBILITY/REQUIREMENTS: 10-week, full-time internships in residence at the Smithsonian are open to U.S. minority students who wish to participate in research or museum-related activities in above and related fields. Must be under-graduates or beginning graduate students with a minimum 3.0 GPA. Must submit essay, résumé, and official transcript.
HOW TO APPLY: Contact the Office of Research Training and Services or see website for an application. Submit. with the required essay or research proposal, résumé, and transcripts.

2614—SOLOMON R. GUGGENHEIM MUSEUM (Internship Programs)

1071 Fifth Avenue
New York NY 10128-0173
212/423-3526
E-mail: education@guggenheim.org
Internet: http://www.guggenheim. org/new york index
AMOUNT: Varies (some positions unpaid)
DEADLINE(S): FEB 15 (Summer);
MAY 15 (Fall); NOV 1 (Spring)
FIELD(S): Art Administration; Art History
ELIGIBILITY/REQUIREMENTS: Various internships, which offer practical museum training experience, are available for undergraduates, recent graduates, and graduate students in art history, administration, conservation, education, and related fields. Location varies, including New York, Italy, and Spain. Housing NOT included. Cover letter, résumé, transcripts, letters of recommendation, list of foreign languages/relevant coursework, and essay (less than 500 words, describing interest) required.
HOW TO APPLY: Contact the Internship Coordinator, Education Department for details of each internship and application procedures.
CONTACT: Internship Coordinator, Education Department

2615—SONOMA CHAMBOLLE-MUSIGNY SISTER CITIES, INC. (Henri Cardinaux Memorial Scholarship)

Chamson Scholarship Committee
P.O. Box 1633
Sonoma CA 95476-1633
707/908-1939
E-mail: icardin@aol.com
AMOUNT: Up to $1,500 (travel + expenses)
DEADLINE(S): JUL 15
FIELD(S): Culinary Arts; Wine Industry;
Art; Architecture; Music; History;
Fashion
ELIGIBILITY/REQUIREMENTS: Hands-on experience working in above or similar fields and living with a family in small French village in Burgundy or other French city. Must be Sonoma County, California, resident at least 18 years of age and be able to communicate in French.
HOW TO APPLY: Transcripts, employer recommendation, photograph, and essay (stating why, where, and when) required.
NUMBER OF AWARDS: 1
RENEWABLE: No
CONTACT: Ivy Cardinaux

2616—SONS OF NORWAY FOUNDATION (King Olav V Norwegian-American Heritage Fund)

c/o Sons of Norway
1455 West Lake Street
Minneapolis MN 55408
612/821-4632
E-mail: colson@sofn.com
Internet: http://www. sofn.com/foundation/
AMOUNT: $250-$3,000
DEADLINE(S): MAR 1
FIELD(S): Norwegian Studies/American Studies: Arts; Crafts; Literature; History; Music; Folklore and related fields
ELIGIBILITY/REQUIREMENTS: Must be U.S. citizens, 18 or older, enrolled in a recognized educational institution, who have demonstrated interest in Norwegian heritage or any Norwegian. Award based on GPA, participation in school and community activities, work experience, education and career goals, and personal and school references. Financial need also considered. Same opportunity available to Norwegian students interested in pursuing American studies at U.S. university.
HOW TO APPLY: Submit application along with an essay (500 words or less) giving reasons for applying, course of study to be pursued, the length of course, name of the institution to be attended, tuition and costs, and amount of financial assistance needed. Include 3 letters of recommendation and copy of high school or college transcript. See website for an application and additional details,

NUMBER OF AWARDS: Varies
RENEWABLE: Yes. Maximum of 2 awards in 5 years.
CONTACT: Cindy Olson, Director

2617—SONS OF THE REPUBLIC OF TEXAS (Presidio La Bahia Award)

1717 8th Street
Bay City TX 77414
409/245-6644
E-mail: srttexas@srttexas.org
Internet: http://www.srttexas.org
AMOUNT: $1,200+
DEADLINE(S): SEP 30
FIELD(S): Texas History: Spanish Colonial Period
ELIGIBILITY/REQUIREMENTS: Award for the best book, paper, or article that promotes suitable preservation of relics, appropriate dissemination of data, and research into Texas heritage with particular attention to the Spanish colonial period. Consideration also given to research papers and other literary forms, as well as art, architecture, and archaeological discovery.
HOW TO APPLY: Contact SRT Executive Secretary for a brochure.
CONTACT: Melinda Williams, SRT Executive Secretary

2618—STUDENT CONSERVATION ASSOCIATION (SCA Resource Assistant Program)

P.O. Box 550
Charlestown NH 03603
603/543-1700
FAX: 603/543-1828
E-mail: internships@sca-inc.org
Internet: http://www.sca-inc.org
AMOUNT: $1,180-$4,725
DEADLINE(S): Varies
FIELD(S): Environment and related fields (agriculture, archaeology, anthropology, botany, caves, civil engineering, environmental design, engineering & education, fisheries, forestry, herpetology, history, landscape architecture, paleontology, recreation/resource/range management, wildlife management, geology, hydrology, library/museums, surveying)
ELIGIBILITY/REQUIREMENTS: Must be 18 and U.S. citizen; need not be student.
HOW TO APPLY: Send $1 postage for application; outside U.S./Canada, $20.
NUMBER OF AWARDS: 900 positions

2619—TET '68, INC. (Essay Contest)

P.O. Box 31885
Richmond VA 23294

804/550-3692
FAX: 804/550-1406
E-mail: billyktet@aol.com
Internet: http://www.tet68.org
AMOUNT: $1,000
DEADLINE(S): MAR 31
FIELD(S): All (emphasis on history and political science)
ELIGIBILITY/REQUIREMENTS: Open to high school seniors who are children or stepchildren of a Vietnam veteran.
HOW TO APPLY: See website or write for application, contest rules, and essay topic. Submit with proof of status-parent or stepparent's DD-214.
NUMBER OF AWARDS: 4-6
RENEWABLE: Yes
CONTACT: William E. Kirkland

2620—U.S. INSTITUTE OF PEACE (National Peace Essay Contest)

1200 17th Street NW, Suite 200
Washington DC 20036
202/457-1700
FAX: 202/429-6063
E-mail: essaycontest@usip.org
Internet: http://www.usip.org
AMOUNT: $1,000-$10,000
DEADLINE(S): JAN
FIELD(S): All (emphasis on Political Science; U.S. History)
ELIGIBILITY/REQUIREMENTS: 1,500-word essay contest for high school students on the U.S. response to international conflict. No restrictions as to citizenship or residency.
HOW TO APPLY: See website or contact USIP for specific guidelines.
RENEWABLE: No

2621—UCLA CENTER FOR 17TH- AND 18TH-CENTURY STUDIES (Fellowships)

310 Royce Hall
Los Angeles CA 90095-1404
310/206-8552
FAX: 310/206-8577
E-mail: c1718cs@humnet.ucla.edu
Internet: http://www.humnet.ucla.edu/humnet/C1718CS/Postd.htm#undergrad
AMOUNT: $1,000-$18,400
DEADLINE(S): FEB 1
FIELD(S): British Literature; History (17th and 18th Centuries)
ELIGIBILITY/REQUIREMENTS: Undergraduate stipends, graduate assistantships, and postdoctoral fellowships are for advanced study and research regarding British literature and history of the 17th and 18th centuries.

HOW TO APPLY: Contact the Center for current year's theme and an application.
NUMBER OF AWARDS: Up to 10

2622—WESTERN MICHIGAN UNIVERSITY (College of Arts and Sciences/A. Edythe Mange Distinguished Scholarship in History)

1903 West Michigan
Kalamazoo MI 49008-5337
269/387-8777
FAX: 269/387-6989
E-mail: finaid-info@wmich.edu
Internet: http://www.wmich.edu/finaid
AMOUNT: Varies (Spring semester)
FIELD(S): History
ELIGIBILITY/REQUIREMENTS: High GPA. Preference given to a female candidate.
HOW TO APPLY: History Department faculty selects recipient.
RENEWABLE: No

2623—WESTERN MICHIGAN UNIVERSITY (College of Arts and Sciences/Elmore L. and Ruth C. Haynor Endowed Scholarship in History)

1903 West Michigan
Kalamazoo MI 49008-5337
269/387-8777
FAX: 269/387-6989
E-mail: finaid-info@wmich.edu
Internet: http://www.wmich.edu/finaid
AMOUNT: Varies
FIELD(S): History
ELIGIBILITY/REQUIREMENTS: Must be full-time student and demonstrate financial need.
HOW TO APPLY: Nominations and selections are made by History Department faculty.
RENEWABLE: No

2624—WESTERN MICHIGAN UNIVERSITY (College of Arts and Sciences/Ernst Breisach Scholarship)

1903 West Michigan
Kalamazoo MI 49008-5337
269/387-8777
FAX: 269/387-6989
E-mail: finaid-info@wmich.edu
Internet: http://www.wmich.edu/finaid
AMOUNT: Varies
FIELD(S): European History

ELIGIBILITY/REQUIREMENTS: Awarded to a 2nd-year graduate student majoring in European History.
HOW TO APPLY: History Department faculty selects recipient.
RENEWABLE: No

2625—WESTERN MICHIGAN UNIVERSITY (College of Arts and Sciences/James Knauss/Smith Burnham Senior History Award)

1903 West Michigan
Kalamazoo MI 49008-5337
269/387-8777
FAX: 269/387-6989
E-mail: finaid-info@wmich.edu
Internet: http://www.wmich.edu/finaid
AMOUNT: Varies
FIELD(S): Liberal & Secondary Education, Public History
ELIGIBILITY/REQUIREMENTS: Awarded to the top seniors in above fields.
HOW TO APPLY: History Department faculty selects recipient.
RENEWABLE: No

2626—WESTERN MICHIGAN UNIVERSITY (Kathryn and Grant Leaske Memorial Endowed Scholarship)

1903 West Michigan
Kalamazoo MI 49008-5337
269/387-8777
FAX: 269/387-6989
E-mail: finaid-info@wmich.edu
Internet: http://www.wmich.edu/finaid
AMOUNT: Varies
FIELD(S): Art; Science; History; Humanities; Law; Social Sciences
ELIGIBILITY/REQUIREMENTS: Must be full-time undergraduate student whose major is in the College of Arts & Sciences. Must demonstrate financial need; 3.0 GPA; and provide documentation of community/university service and volunteerism.
HOW TO APPLY: Contact the College of Arts and Sciences or www.wmich.edu/cas/research.html for an application.
RENEWABLE: Yes. Up to 2 years depending on academic status.

2627—WESTERN MICHIGAN UNIVERSITY (College of Arts and Sciences/Margaret Macmillan Writing Award)

1903 West Michigan
Kalamazoo MI 49008-5337
269/387-8777

FAX: 269/387-6989
E-mail: finaid-info@wmich.edu
Internet: http://www.wmich.edu/finaid
AMOUNT: Varies
FIELD(S): History
ELIGIBILITY/REQUIREMENTS: Competition awarded to undergraduate student.
HOW TO APPLY: History Department faculty selects recipient based on essay quality. Contact Department for guidelines.
RENEWABLE: No

2628—WESTERN MICHIGAN UNIVERSITY (College of Arts and Sciences/Smith-Burnham Junior History Award)

1903 West Michigan
Kalamazoo MI 49008-5337
269/387-8777
FAX: 269/387-6989
E-mail: finaid-info@wmich.edu
Internet: http://www.wmich.edu/finaid
AMOUNT: Varies
FIELD(S): History
ELIGIBILITY/REQUIREMENTS: Must be History major in junior year with high GPA.
HOW TO APPLY: History Department faculty selects recipient.
RENEWABLE: No

2629—WESTERN MICHIGAN UNIVERSITY (College of Arts and Sciences/Werner and Nicky Marten Endowment Fund)

1903 West Michigan
Kalamazoo MI 49008-5337
269/387-8777
FAX: 269/387-6989
E-mail: finaid-info@wmich.edu
Internet: http://www.wmich.edu/finaid
AMOUNT: Varies
FIELD(S): History
ELIGIBILITY/REQUIREMENTS: Must be full-time student with high GPA.
HOW TO APPLY: History Department faculty selects recipient.
RENEWABLE: No

2630—WESTERN MICHIGAN UNIVERSITY (College of Arts and Sciences Undergraduate Research and Creative Activities Award)

1903 West Michigan
Kalamazoo MI 49008-5337
269/387-8777

FAX: 269/387-6989
E-mail: finaid-info@wmich.edu
Internet: http://www.wmich.edu/finaid
AMOUNT: $500/semester
FIELD(S): Art; Science; History; Humanities; Law; Social Sciences
ELIGIBILITY/REQUIREMENTS: Must have declared a major in a department or program within the College; completed at least 30 credit hours; be in good academic standing; have a faculty mentor for the project and a project plan.
HOW TO APPLY: Contact the College of Arts and Sciences or www.wmich.edu/cas/research.html for an application.
RENEWABLE: Yes. May request renewal for 1 additional term.
ADDITIONAL INFORMATION: This award may not be held during the same term as a research and creative activities award administered by the Lee Honors College.

LAW & CRIMINOLOGY

2631—AIR & WASTE MANAGEMENT ASSOCIATION, ALLEGHENY MOUNTAIN SECTION

One Gateway Center, 3rd Floor
Pittsburgh PA 15222
412/630-8108
FAX: 412/318-2936
E-mail: vhentrpris@comcast.net
Internet: http://www.trfn.clpgh.org/wpawma
AMOUNT: $1,500
DEADLINE(S): APR 1
FIELD(S): Science; Engineering; Law
ELIGIBILITY/REQUIREMENTS: Undergraduate baccalaureate in science, engineering or law; attending college or university in western half of Pennsylvania or West Virginia; spouse or dependent of AMS-A&WMA and attending a school outside of this area; good academic record; interest in environmental career; community service.
HOW TO APPLY: Application available on website.
NUMBER OF AWARDS: 2 or 3
RENEWABLE: Yes. New application each year.
CONTACT: Allegheny Mountain Section Chair

2632—AMERICAN ASSOCIATION OF ATTORNEY-CERTIFIED PUBLIC ACCOUNTANTS FOUNDATION, THE (Student Writing Competition)

3921 Old Lee Highway,
Suite 71A
Fairfax VA 22030
800/CPA-ATTY or 888/288-9272
FAX: 703/352-8073
E-mail: info@attorney-cpa.com
Internet: http://www.attorney-cpa.com
AMOUNT: $250-$1,500
DEADLINE(S): MAY 1
FIELD(S): Accounting; Law
ELIGIBILITY/REQUIREMENTS:
Essay contest for accounting and/or law students. Open to undergraduate or graduate students in related field/major/program.
HOW TO APPLY: Check out topics and info on website. Complete necessary forms and essay and mail to AAA-CPA office in Fairfax, VA.
NUMBER OF AWARDS: 8 per division (graduate and undergraduate)
CONTACT: AAA-CPA office by phone.

2633—ASSOCIATION OF CERTIFIED FRAUD EXAMINERS

The Gregor Building
716 West Avenue
Austin TX 78701
800/245-3321 or 512/478-9070
FAX: 512/478-9297
Internet: http://www.cfenet.com
AMOUNT: $1,000
DEADLINE(S): APR 30
FIELD(S): Accounting; Criminal Justice
ELIGIBILITY/REQUIREMENTS:
Scholarships for full-time graduate or undergraduate students majoring in accounting or criminal justice degree programs.
HOW TO APPLY: Awards are based on overall academic achievement, 3 letters of recommendation plus a letter of recommendation from a Certified Fraud Examiner or a local CFE Chapter, and an original 250-word essay explaining why the applicant deserves the award and how fraud awareness will affect his or her professional career development. Download application from website.
NUMBER OF AWARDS: 15

2634—BOYS AND GIRLS CLUBS OF GREATER SAN DIEGO (Spence Reese Scholarship Fund)

4635 Clairemont Mesa Boulevard
San Diego CA 92117
619/298-3520
AMOUNT: $2,000
DEADLINE(S): APR 15

FIELD(S): Medicine; Law; Engineering; Political Science
ELIGIBILITY/REQUIREMENTS: Open to male high school seniors planning a career in 1 of the above fields. Boys and Girls Club affiliation NOT required.
HOW TO APPLY: Send an SASE for an application after January 1. $10 application fee.
RENEWABLE: Yes. Up to 4 years.

2635—CALIFORNIA NURSES ASSOCIATION (Shirley Titus Scholarship & R11 & R6 Scholarships)

2000 Franklin Street
Oakland CA 94612
510/622-8310
FAX: 510/663-1625
E-mail: scholarship@calnurses.org
Internet: http://www.calnurses.org
AMOUNT: Varies
DEADLINE(S): JUL 1
FIELD(S): Nursing; Humanities, Cultural, Political, Economic, Legal and Social Sciences
ELIGIBILITY/REQUIREMENTS: Open to California nurses for academic preparation and continuing education in above fields appropriate for developing effective nursing leadership.
HOW TO APPLY: See website for application or write or call for application. Submit with a 1- page typed essay, describing educational goals and how they relate to personal and professional vision for healthcare; 2 letters of recommendation, from non-relatives which must relate to this scholarship and address at least one of the following: CNA activities, competence in work setting, and academic ability; a curriculum vitae; and a copy of current RN license.
NUMBER OF AWARDS: Varies
CONTACT: Shaun Copeland

2636—COLLEGE MISERICORDIA (Presidential Scholarships)

301 Lake Street
Dallas PA 18612-1098
800/852-7675
E-mail: admiss@misericordia.edu
Internet: http://www.miseri.edu
AMOUNT: Full or part tuition
DEADLINE(S): MAR 1
FIELD(S): Pre-Law; Humanities
ELIGIBILITY/REQUIREMENTS: Open to high school seniors ranking in the upper 20% of their class, who have achieved SAT or ACT scores in the 8th percentile or better.

HOW TO APPLY: Obtain application from the Admissions Office.

2637—EMPIRE COLLEGE (Dean's Scholarship)

3035 Cleveland Avenue
Santa Rosa CA 95403
707/546-4000
FAX: 707/546-4058
Internet: http://www.wmpcol.edu
AMOUNT: $250-$1,500
DEADLINE(S): APR 15
FIELD(S): Accounting; Office Administration; Paralegal; Medical (Clinical and Administrative); Tourism; Hospitality; General Business; Computer Assembly; Network Assembly/Administration; Security
ELIGIBILITY/REQUIREMENTS: Open to high school seniors who plan to attend Empire College. Must be U.S. citizen.
HOW TO APPLY: Contact College for an application.
NUMBER OF AWARDS: 10
RENEWABLE: No
CONTACT: Mary Farha

2638—H. FLETCHER BROWN FUND

c/o Donald W. Davis
PNC Bank Delaware
Trust Department
222 Delaware Avenue, 16th floor
Wilmington DE 19899
302/429- 2827 or 302/429-5658
E-mail: Robbie.testa@pnc advisors.com
AMOUNT: Varies
DEADLINE(S): MAR 22
FIELD(S): Medicine; Dentistry; Law; Engineering; Chemistry
ELIGIBILITY/REQUIREMENTS: Open to U.S. citizens born in Delaware and still residing in Delaware. For 4 years of study (undergrad or grad) leading to a degree that enables applicant to practice in chosen field. Must have minimum 1000 SAT score and rank in upper 20% of class. Interview required. Scholarships are based on need, scholastic achievement, and good moral character.
HOW TO APPLY: Applications available in February. Write to Account Administrator for application.
CONTACT: Robbie Testa

2639—INSTITUTE FOR HUMANE STUDIES (Humane Studies Fellowship)

3301 North Fairfax Drive, Suite 440
Arlington VA 22201-4432

703/993-4880 or 800/697-8799
FAX: 703/993-4890
Internet: http://www.TheIHS.org
AMOUNT: $12,000 (maximum)
DEADLINE(S): DEC
FIELD(S): Social Sciences; Liberal Arts;
Law; Humanities; Jurisprudence;
Journalism
ELIGIBILITY/REQUIREMENTS: Open
to graduate and advanced undergraduate
or law students pursuing degrees at any
accredited domestic or foreign college or
university. Based on academic perfor-
mance, demonstrated interest in the classi-
cal liberal tradition, and potential to con-
tribute to the advancement of a free soci-
ety.
HOW TO APPLY: Apply online or contact IHS for an application.
NUMBER OF AWARDS: 90

2640—INSTITUTE FOR HUMANE STUD-IES (Koch Summer Fellow Program)

3401 N. Fairfax Drive, Suite 440
Arlington VA 22201-4432
703/993-4880 or 800/697-8799
FAX: 703/993-4890
Internet: http://www.TheIHS.org
AMOUNT: $1,500 + airfare and housing
DEADLINE(S): FEB 15
FIELD(S): Economics; Public Policy;
Law; Government; Politics
ELIGIBILITY/REQUIREMENTS: Open
to undergraduates and graduates. Includes
2 week-long seminars, the internship, and
research and writing projects. Financial
need NOT a factor.
HOW TO APPLY: Apply online or con-
tact IHS for an application. Submit with
transcripts and essays.
NUMBER OF AWARDS: 32
RENEWABLE: No

2641—JACKSONVILLE STATE UNIVERSITY (Walter Merrill Scholarship)

Financial Aid Office
Jacksonville AL 36265
256/782-5677 or 800/231-5291
Internet: www.jsu.edu
AMOUNT: Full tuition
DEADLINE(S): FEB 1
FIELD(S): Pre-Law
ELIGIBILITY/REQUIREMENTS: Open
to junior or senior; preference to residents
of Cleburne or Calhoun Counties, Ala-
bama.
HOW TO APPLY: An official transcript
and ACT/SAT scores must be submitted
with scholarship applications. See website

for application. Supporting documentation
should be mailed.
NUMBER OF AWARDS: 1
RENEWABLE: No
CONTACT: Scholarship Committee

2642—JEWISH FEDERATION OF METRO-POLITAN CHICAGO (Academic Scholarship Program)

Jewish Vocational Service
216 West Jackson Blvd., Suite 700
Chicago IL 60606-6921
312/673-3400
FAX: 312/553-5544
TTY: 312/444-2877
E-mail: jvsscholarship@jvs.chicago.org
Internet: http://www.jvs/chicago.org
AMOUNT: Varies
DEADLINE(S): FEB 15
FIELD(S): Mathematics, Engineering,
Science, Medicine, Social Work,
Education, Psychology, Rabbinate,
Law (except corporate),
Communications
ELIGIBILITY/REQUIREMENTS: Open
to Jewish men and women legally domiciled in the greater Chicago metropolitan
area, identified as having promise for significant contributions in their chosen
careers, and in need of financial assistance
for full-time academic programs in above
areas. Must have entered undergraduate
junior year in career programs requiring no
postgraduate education, be in
graduate/professional school, or be in a vo-
tech training program.
HOW TO APPLY: Phone JVS Scholar-
ship Secretary (312/673-3457), fax, or visit
website (click on Scholarship Services) for
an application in the Fall. Interview
required.
RENEWABLE: Yes
CONTACT: JVS Scholarship Secretary at
312/673-3457

2643—LINCOLN COMMUNITY FOUNDA-TION (Lawrence "Larry" Frazier Memorial Scholarship)

215 Centennial Mall South,
Suite 100
Lincoln NE 68508
402/474-2345
FAX: 402/476-8532
E-mail: lcf@lcf.org
Internet: http://www.lcf.org
AMOUNT: Varies
DEADLINE(S): APR 15
FIELD(S): Aviation; Insurance; Law

ELIGIBILITY/REQUIREMENTS: Open
to graduating senior or a former graduate
of a high school in Nebraska. Must demonstrate academic success and possess ability
to do postsecondary work in a satisfactory
manner; pursuing full-time undergraduate
studies at a 2- or 4-year college (propri-
etary institutions of higher education are
not eligible) in Nebraska. Experience in
debate and participation in Boy or Girl
Scouts preferred. Must demonstrate financial need as well as contribution to applicant's own education.
HOW TO APPLY: Submit application;
transcripts from all high schools, colleges
and universities attended; copy of
ACT/SAT or similar test scores; and financial aid form. Essay explaining interest in
pursuing chosen field, ways in which applicant is contributing financially to education, reflections on past experiences, in
Scouts and/or debate.
CONTACT: Mark Clymer, Nebraska
Chapter, Charter Property Casualty
Underwriters

2644—LOUISIANA STATE UNIVERSITY AT SHREVEPORT (Walter O. Bigby Scholarship)

Bronson Hall
Shreveport LA 71115-2399
318/797-5371
Internet: http://www.lsus.edu
AMOUNT: Up to $500/semester
DEADLINE(S): Varies
FIELD(S): Political Science; English;
History; Law
ELIGIBILITY/REQUIREMENTS: Must
be entering junior or senior year; majoring
in one of above subjects; other Liberal
Arts majors acceptable, if preparing for
law school.
HOW TO APPLY: Contact the Dean's
Office, College of Liberal Arts for applica-
tion.

2645—NATIONAL FEDERATION OF THE BLIND (Howard Brown Rickard Scholarship)

805 Fifth Avenue
Grinnell IA 50112
515/236-3366
Internet: http://www.nfb.org/nfb/scholarship_program.asp
AMOUNT: $3,000
DEADLINE(S): MAR 31
FIELD(S): Law; Medicine; Engineering;
Architecture; Natural Sciences
ELIGIBILITY/REQUIREMENTS: For
legally blind students pursuing or planning
to pursue a full-time postsecondary course

of study in the U.S. Based on academic excellence, service to the community, and financial need. Membership NOT required.
HOW TO APPLY: Contact Scholarship Committee Chair for an application.
NUMBER OF AWARDS: 1
RENEWABLE: Yes
CONTACT: Peggy Elliot, Scholarship Committee Chair

2646—NEW ENGLAND EMPLOYEE BENE-FITS COUNCIL

440 Totten Pond Road
Waltham MA 02145
781/684-8700
FAX: 781/684-9200
E-mail: linda@neebc.org
Internet: http://www.neebc.org
AMOUNT: Up to $5,000
DEADLINE(S): APR 1
FIELD(S): Health Care Program Design; Pension Plan Design, Implementation or Administration; Retirement Strategies; ERISA and Legal Aspects of Employee Benefits; Work/Life Programs; Health Risk Management; Institutional Investing of Retirement Savings; Multiemployer Plans; Workers Compensation; Actuarial and Underwriting Analysis; Employee Benefits Communications
ELIGIBILITY/REQUIREMENTS: Full-time student (undergraduate or graduate) studying in an accredited academic program leading to a degree who demonstrates an interest through either course study or work experience in a career in the benefits field. Must be a New England resident or enrolled at a college in New England. Current NEEBC Board members, their spouses and children are not eligible to participate.
HOW TO APPLY: Completed application; all college transcripts; two or more references from college professors, NEEBC members, or other benefits professionals.
NUMBER OF AWARDS: 1 or 2
RENEWABLE: Yes
CONTACT: Linda Viens, Manager of Operations and Member Services

2647—NEW YORK STATE HIGHER EDU-CATION SERVICES CORPORATION (N.Y. State Regents Professional/Health Care Opportunity Scholarships)

Cultural Education Ctr., Room 5C64
Albany NY 12230
518/486-1319
Internet: http://www.hesc.com

AMOUNT: $1,000-$10,000
DEADLINE(S): Varies
FIELD(S): Medicine, Dentistry & related fields; Architecture, Nursing, Psychology, Audiology, Landscape Architecture, Social Work, Chiropractic, Law, Pharmacy, Accounting, Speech Language Pathology
ELIGIBILITY/REQUIREMENTS: For New York State residents who are economically disadvantaged and members of a minority group underrepresented in the chosen profession and attending school in New York State. For U.S. citizens or qualifying noncitizens.
HOW TO APPLY: See website or contact NYS HESC.
RENEWABLE: Yes

2648—RAYMOND J. HARRIS EDUCATION TRUST

c/o Mellon Bank, N.A.
P.O. Box 7899
Philadelphia PA 19101-7899
AMOUNT: Varies
DEADLINE(S): FEB 1
FIELD(S): Medicine, Law, Engineering, Dentistry, or Agriculture
ELIGIBILITY/REQUIREMENTS: Scholarships for Christian men to obtain a professional education in medicine, law, engineering, dentistry, or agriculture at 9 Philadelphia area colleges.
HOW TO APPLY: Contact Bank for details and the names of the 9 colleges.

2649—ROYAL THAI EMBASSY, OFFICE OF EDUCATIONAL AFFAIRS (Revenue Department Scholarships for Thai Students)

1906 23rd Street NW
Washington DC 20008
202/667-9111 or 202/667-8010
FAX: 202/265-7239
AMOUNT: Varies
DEADLINE(S): APR
FIELD(S): Computer Science (Telecommunications), Law, Economics, Finance, Business Administration
ELIGIBILITY/REQUIREMENTS: Scholarships for students under age 35 from Thailand who have been accepted to study in the U.S. or UK pursuing any level degree in one of the above fields.
HOW TO APPLY: Selections based on academic records, employment history, and advisor recommendations.

2650—SOCIETY OF SATELLITE PROFES-SIONALS INTERNATIONAL (SSPI Scholarship Program)

The New York Information Technology Center
55 Broad Street, 14th Floor
New York NY 10004
212/809-5199
FAX: 212/825-0075
E-mail: neworbit@aol.com
Internet: http://www.sspi.org
AMOUNT: $1,500-$4,000
DEADLINE(S): DEC 1
FIELD(S): Satellites (relating to communications, domestic and international telecommunications policy, remote sensing, journalism, law, meteorology, energy, navigation, business, government, and broadcasting services)
ELIGIBILITY/REQUIREMENTS: Open to current high school seniors, college or university undergraduate or graduate students studying or intending to study satellite-related technologies, policies or applications. Must demonstrate commitment to pursue education and career opportunities in the satellite industry or a field making direct use of satellite technology; academic and leadership achievement; and potential for significant contribution to the industry.
HOW TO APPLY: Before applying, all applicants must complete a Scholarship Qualification Form to determine whether their interests and career plans are a good fit for the program. See website for form and details or send SASE.

2651—UNIVERSITY OF SOUTH DAKOTA (Criminal Justice Department Scholarships)

414 East Clark Street
Vermillion SD 57069-2390
605/677-5446
E-mail: admiss@usd.edu
Internet: http://www.usd.edu/cjus/scholar/scholarships.htm#orderofpolice
AMOUNT: Varies
DEADLINE(S): Varies
FIELD(S): Criminal Justice; Political Science; Public Service
ELIGIBILITY/REQUIREMENTS: The University of South Dakota's Department of Criminal Justice administers 17 different award programs in the above fields. Some require a high GPA and/or financial need, others require an essay or research project.
HOW TO APPLY: See website or contact USD for specific details of each award.

2652—WESTERN MICHIGAN UNIVERSITY (College of Arts and Sciences/Kathryn and Grant Leaske Memorial Endowed Scholarship)

1903 West Michigan
Kalamazoo MI 49008-5337
269/387-8777
FAX: 269/387-6989
E-mail: finaid-info@wmich.edu
Internet: http://www.wmich.edu/finaid
AMOUNT: Varies
FIELD(S): Art; Science; History; Humanities; Law; Social Sciences
ELIGIBILITY/REQUIREMENTS: Must be full-time undergraduate student whose major is in the College of Arts & Sciences. Must demonstrate financial need; 3.0 GPA; and provide documentation of community/university service and volunteerism.
HOW TO APPLY: Contact the College of Arts and Sciences or www.wmich.edu/cas/research.html for an application.
RENEWABLE: Yes. Up to 2 years depending on academic status.

2653—WESTERN MICHIGAN UNIVERSITY (College of Arts and Sciences/Lanny Wilde Criminal Justice Scholarship)

1903 West Michigan
Kalamazoo MI 49008-5337
269/387-8777
FAX: 269/387-6989
E-mail: finaid-info@wmich.edu
Internet: http://www.wmich.edu/finaid
AMOUNT: $250
DEADLINE(S): MAR 1
FIELD(S): Political Science; Sociology
ELIGIBILITY/REQUIREMENTS: Must be in the tracking program through the criminal justice major. Only offered second semester of tracking program so first-semester grades are reviewed. Based on financial need.
HOW TO APPLY: Contact Sociology Department/Criminal Justice Program Advising Office, 2401 Sangren, for an application.
RENEWABLE: No

2654—WESTERN MICHIGAN UNIVERSITY (College of Arts and Sciences/ Undergraduate Research and Creative Activities Award)

1903 West Michigan
Kalamazoo MI 49008-5337
269/387-8777
FAX: 269/387-6989
E-mail: finaid-info@wmich.edu
Internet: http://www.wmich.edu/finaid
AMOUNT: $500/semester
FIELD(S): Art; Science; History; Humanities; Law; Social Sciences
ELIGIBILITY/REQUIREMENTS: Must have declared a major in a department or program within the College; completed at least 30 credit hours; be in good academic standing; have a faculty mentor for the project and a project plan.
HOW TO APPLY: Contact the College of Arts and Sciences or www.wmich.edu/cas/research.html for an application.
RENEWABLE: Yes. May request renewal for 1 additional term.

2655—WESTERN MICHIGAN UNIVERSITY (Haworth College of Business/McCarty-Morrison Scholarship)

1903 West Michigan
Kalamazoo MI 49008-5337
269/387-6000
FAX: 269/387-6989
E-mail: finaid-info@wmich.edu
Internet: http://www.wmich.edu/finaid
AMOUNT: $500 (fall semester)
DEADLINE(S): FEB 15
FIELD(S): Law
ELIGIBILITY/REQUIREMENTS: Senior undergraduate BBA with minimum GPA of 3.0 must be planning to attend law school (preference for Big 10 Conference law school).
HOW TO APPLY: Contact the Department of Finance & Commercial Law, 3290 Schneider Hall, Haworth College of Business, e-mail: edEdwards@wmich.edu, (269/387-5722).
NUMBER OF AWARDS: 2
RENEWABLE: No

2656—WESTERN MICHIGAN UNIVERSITY (Mayor Dennis Archer Endowed Scholarship)

1903 West Michigan
Kalamazoo MI 49008-5337
269/387-8777
FAX: 269/387-6989
E-mail: alumni@wmich.edu
Internet: http://www.wmich.edu/alumni
AMOUNT: $2,000
DEADLINE(S): APR 1
FIELD(S): Education; Public Administration; Pre-Law

ELIGIBILITY/REQUIREMENTS: Undergraduate student; Detroit resident, or resident of Wayne, Oakland or Macomb Counties; major in Education, Public Administration or Pre-Law programs; minimum 3.0 high school GPA. Preference given to those with financial need. Recipient must demonstrate evidence of public service/volunteer activities.
HOW TO APPLY: Contact the Office of Financial Aid for more details.
RENEWABLE: Yes. Up to a maximum of 4 consecutive academic years as long as the recipient maintains a 3.0 GPA at WMU.

2657—WESTERN SOCIETY OF CRIMINOLOGY (Student Paper Competition)

Cal State University
Criminal Justice Division
6000 J Street
Sacramento CA 95819-6085
Internet: http://www.sonoma.edu/CJA/WSC/WSCstu00.html
AMOUNT: $125 (1st prize); $75 (2nd) + certificates
DEADLINE(S): DEC 15
FIELD(S): Criminology
ELIGIBILITY/REQUIREMENTS: Any student currently enrolled full or part time in an academic program at either the undergraduate or graduate level may enter.
HOW TO APPLY: Send 2 copies of your entry to the attention of the Criminal Justice Division at California State University.
CONTACT: Dr. Miki Vohryzek-Bolden, Criminal Justice Division

2658—WOMEN IN DEFENSE (HORIZONS Scholarship Foundation)

2111 Wilson Boulevard, Suite 400
Arlington VA 22201-3061
703/247-2552
FAX: 703/522-1885
E-mail: wid@ndia.org
Internet: http://www.ndia.org
AMOUNT: $500+
DEADLINE(S): NOV 1; JUL 1
FIELD(S): Security Studies; Engineering; Computer Science; Physics; Mathematics; International Relations; Political Science; Operations Research; Economics; National Security/Defense; Business and Law (as they relate to national security or defense)
ELIGIBILITY/REQUIREMENTS: Open to women employed/planning careers in defense/national security areas (NOT law

enforcement or criminal justice). Must be currently enrolled full or part time at an accredited college or university at the graduate or undergraduate junior/senior level. Must have a minimum 3.25 GPA, demonstrate financial need, and be U.S. citizen. Based on academic achievement, work experience, objectives, and recommendations.
HOW TO APPLY: See website or send SASE for application.
RENEWABLE: Yes

POLITICAL SCIENCE

2659—AIR FORCE RESERVE OFFICER TRAINING CORPS (AFROTC Scholarships)

551 East Maxwell Boulevard
Maxwell AFB AL 36112-6106
866/4AFROTC
E-mail: info@afrotc.com
Internet: http://www.afrotc.com
AMOUNT: Varies, but up to full tuition and fees plus $600/year for books
DEADLINE(S): DEC 1
FIELD(S): Science; Engineering; Business; Political Science; Psychology; Geography; Foreign Studies; Foreign Language
ELIGIBILITY/REQUIREMENTS: 4- and 3-year competitive scholarships based on individual merit to high school seniors and graduates who have not enrolled full time at a college or university. Academic performance is measured using an academic composite, which combines SAT (Math and Verbal only)/ACT scores, class rank, GPA and the number of advanced placement or honors courses completed through Grade 11. To be eligible for consideration, students should achieve a 1100 SAT (Math and Verbal only) or 24 ACT, minimum 3.0 GPA and class ranking in top 40%. Must be a U.S. citizen between the ages of 17-27. Must also have GPA of 2.5 or above, be in top 40% of class, and complete Applicant Fitness Test. Cannot be a single parent. Your college or university must offer AFROTC.
HOW TO APPLY: Visit www.afrotc.com to apply
NUMBER OF AWARDS: N/A
RENEWABLE: No

2660—AMERICAN BAR FOUNDATION (Summer Research Diversity Fellowships in Law & Social Science)

750 North Lake Shore Drive
Chicago IL 60611
312/988-6560
FAX: 312/988-6579
E-mail: fellowships@abfn.org
Internet: http://www.american barfoundation.org
AMOUNT: $3,600
DEADLINE(S): Varies FEB/MAR 1
FIELD(S): Social Sciences; Humanities; Law
ELIGIBILITY/REQUIREMENTS: Open to sophomore and junior undergraduates including, but not limited to, Native American, African-American, Mexican, Puerto Rican, as well as other individuals who will add diversity to the field of law and social science. Must be U.S. citizen or permanent resident with 3.0 GPA. Students assigned a research mentor, participate in seminars, and work at the Foundation's office in Chicago for 35 hours/week for 8 weeks.
HOW TO APPLY: See website or contact ABF for application. Essay, transcripts, and letter of recommendation required.
NUMBER OF AWARDS: 4

2661—AMERICAN FEDERATION OF STATE, COUNTY & MUNICIPAL EMPLOYEES, AFL-CIO (Jerry Clark Memorial Scholarship)

1625 L Street NW
Washington DC 20036-5687
202/429-1250
FAX: 202/429-1298
E-mail: education@afscme.org
Internet: http://www.afscme.org/ about/scholarf.htm
AMOUNT: $10,000
DEADLINE(S): DEC 31
FIELD(S): Political Science
ELIGIBILITY/REQUIREMENTS: Available to children of active AFSCME members who are college sophomores with political science major. Recipient must have a GPA of 3.0 or above.
HOW TO APPLY: See website for application or call or e-mail. Submit application along with an essay (not to exceed 1,000 words) on the subject "What AFSCME Has Meant to Our Family," an official high school transcript and SAT or ACT scores, and proof of AFSCME membership.
RENEWABLE: Yes. Total of 2 years (junior and senior).
CONTACT: Education Department

2662—AMERICAN FEDERATION OF STATE, COUNTY, AND MUNICIPAL EMPLOY-EES-AFL-CIO (Union Plus National Labor College Scholarship)

1625 L Street NW

Washington DC 20036-5687
800/238-2539
FAX: 202/429-1298
E-mail: education@afscme.org
Internet: http://www.afscme.org/ about
FIELD(S): Economics; Political Science
ELIGIBILITY/REQUIREMENTS: For working adults who want to pursue a BA degree while continuing trade union work. Must be enrolled in The National Labor College and a dues-paying member of AFSCME or staff employee of an AFL-CIO affiliated organization.
HOW TO APPLY: See website for application or send a postcard with name, local union number, social security number, and address to: Union Plus Scholarship, P.O. Box 34800, Washington, DC 20043-4800. Call 301/432-5404 for details.

2663—AMERICAN RADIO RELAY LEAGUE FOUNDATION (The Donald Riebhoff Memorial Scholarship)

225 Main Street
Newington CT 06111
860/594-0397
FAX: 860/594-0259
E-mail: foundation@arrl.org
Internet: http://www.arrlf.org/
AMOUNT: $1,000
DEADLINE(S): FEB 1
FIELD(S): International Studies
ELIGIBILITY/REQUIREMENTS: For AARL members who hold a technician or higher class license pursuing a baccalaureate or higher degree in international studies at an accredited college or university.
HOW TO APPLY: See website or contact Foundation for information and application. Submit with a 1-page essay on the role amateur radio has played in your life. A recent high school (or equivalent) or college transcript required; submit with application or mail separately.
NUMBER OF AWARDS: 1
RENEWABLE: No
CONTACT: Mary M. Hobart, K1MMH, Secretary

2664—BOYS AND GIRLS CLUBS OF GREATER SAN DIEGO (Spence Reese Scholarship Fund)

4635 Clairemont Mesa Boulevard
San Diego CA 92117
619/298-3520
AMOUNT: $2,000/year
DEADLINE(S): APR 15
FIELD(S): Medicine; Law; Engineering; Political Science

ELIGIBILITY/REQUIREMENTS: Open to male high school seniors planning a career in one of the above fields. Boys and Girls Club affiliation NOT required.
HOW TO APPLY: Send an SASE for an application after January 1. $10 application fee.
RENEWABLE: Yes. Up to 4 years.

2665—CALIFORNIA NURSES ASSOCIATION (Shirley Titus Scholarship & R11 & R6 Scholarships)

2000 Franklin Street
Oakland CA 94612
510/622-8310
FAX: 510/663-1625
E-mail: scholarship@calnurses.org
Internet: http://www.calnurses.org
AMOUNT: Varies
DEADLINE(S): JUL 1
FIELD(S): Nursing; Humanities, Cultural, Political, Economic, Legal and Social Sciences
ELIGIBILITY/REQUIREMENTS: Open to California nurses for academic preparation and continuing education in above fields appropriate for developing effective nursing leadership.
HOW TO APPLY: See website for application or write or call for application. Submit with a 1-page typed essay, describing educational goals and how they relate to personal and professional vision for healthcare; 2 letters of recommendation, from non-relatives which must relate to this scholarship and address at least one of the following: CNA activities, competence in work setting, and academic ability; a curriculum vitae; and a copy of current RN license.
NUMBER OF AWARDS: Varies
CONTACT: Shaun Copeland

2666—CONFERENCE OF MINORITY PUBLIC ADMINISTRATORS (Ronald H. Brown Memorial Scholarship)

COMPA Awards Committee
9717 Summit Circle, Suite 3E
Largo MD 20774
301/333-5282
E-mail: hwilliamjhunter@aol.com
Internet: http://www.natcompa.org
AMOUNT: $1,000
DEADLINE(S): Varies
FIELD(S): Public Administration; Public Affairs
ELIGIBILITY/REQUIREMENTS: Open to a public high school senior residing in the city where the Conference of Minority Public Administrators holds its annual conference. Students must be legal residents of the host city.

HOW TO APPLY: Submit application and acceptance letter to a 4-year institution of higher learning; a minimum GPA of 3.25 on a 4.0 scale (official high school transcript required); a minimum ACT/SAT score of 22 or 1000; a 2-page essay describing how your future goals align with Ronald H. Brown's philosophy of fighting to create opportunities for people of every race, social class, and nationality.
NUMBER OF AWARDS: 1
RENEWABLE: No
CONTACT: William J. Hunter, Chair, COMPA Awards Committee

2667—JORGE MAS CANOSA FREEDOM FOUNDATION (Mas Family Scholarships)

P.O. Box 14-1898
Miami FL 33114
305/529-0075, ext. 35
E-mail: mmartinez@jmcffmas familyscholarships.org
Internet: http://www.jmcffmas scholarships.org
AMOUNT: Up to $10,000
DEADLINE(S): MAR 31
FIELD(S): Engineering, Business, International Relations, Economics, Communications, Journalism
ELIGIBILITY/REQUIREMENTS: For Cuban-American students, graduates and undergraduates, born in Cuba or direct descendants (1 parent or 2 grandparents) of those who left Cuba. Must be in top 10% of high school class or maintain a 3.5 GPA in college. Financial need considered along with academic success, SAT and GRE scores, and leadership potential.
HOW TO APPLY: Contact Foundation for application. Two short essays and 2 character evaluations along with proof of Cuban descent required.
NUMBER OF AWARDS: 10
RENEWABLE: Yes. Maximum $40,000; must reapply

2668—DAUGHTERS OF THE AMERICAN REVOLUTION, NATIONAL SOCIETY (Dr. Aura-Lee A. and James Hobbs Pittenger American History Scholarship)

Committee Services Office
Attn: Scholarships
1776 D Street NW
Washington DC 20006-5392
202/628-1776
Internet: http://www.dar.org
AMOUNT: $2,000
DEADLINE(S): FEB 1
FIELD(S): American History; American Government

ELIGIBILITY/REQUIREMENTS: Awarded to graduating high school students who will have a concentrated study of a minimum of 24 credit hours in American History and American Government. Awards are judged on academic excellence, commitment to field of study, and need. Affiliation with DAR not required.
HOW TO APPLY: Must submit application with a letter of sponsorship from local DAR chapter (send SASE to address above to obtain name and application); statement of 1,000 words or less stating career objectives, how college major (if required) or college plans relate to future professional goals and reasons for these choices; transcripts list of extracurricular activities, honors received, scholastic achievements, or other significant accomplishments; 2-4 letters of recommendation from the high school or college you now attend who are familiar with your work, and proof of citizenship. See website for additional information.
NUMBER OF AWARDS: 3
RENEWABLE: Yes. Up to 4 consecutive years based on review and approval of transcript.

2669—EPILEPSY FOUNDATION OF AMERICA (Behavioral Sciences Student Fellowships)

4351 Garden City Drive
Landover MD 20785-2267
301/459-3700 or 800/EFA-1000
TDD: 800/332-2070
FAX: 301/577-2684
Internet: http://www.epilepsy foundation.org
AMOUNT: $3,000
DEADLINE(S): MAR 1
FIELD(S): Epilepsy Research/Practice; Sociology; Social Work; Psychology; Anthropology; Nursing; Economics; Vocational Rehabilitation; Counseling; Political Science
ELIGIBILITY/REQUIREMENTS: 3-month fellowships awarded to undergraduate and graduate students for work on a project during the summer or other free period. Students propose an epilepsy-related study or training project to be carried out at a U.S. institution. A preceptor must supervise the student and the project.
HOW TO APPLY: Contact EFA for an application.

2670—GOVERNMENT FINANCE OFFICERS ASSOCIATION (Minorities in Government Finance Scholarship)

Scholarship Committee

203 North LaSalle Street,
Suite 2700
Chicago IL 60601-1210
312/977-9700
Internet: http://www.gfoa.org
AMOUNT: $5,000
DEADLINE(S): FEB 15
FIELD(S): Public Administration;
(Governmental) Accounting; Finance;
Political Science; Economics; Business
Administration (with a specific focus
on government or nonprofit
management)
ELIGIBILITY/REQUIREMENTS: Open
to Black, Indian, Eskimo or Aleut, Asian
or Pacific Islander, Hispanic students; must
be a citizen or permanent resident of the
U.S. or Canada.
HOW TO APPLY: Send application. Must
be recommended by the student's academ-
ic advisor or department chair.

2671—HAWAII COMMUNITY FOUNDA-TION (Henry A. Zuberano Scholarship)

1164 Bishop Street, Suite 800
Honolulu HI 96813
808/537-6333 or 888/731-3863
FAX: 808/521-6286
E-mail: info@hcf-hawaii.org
Internet: http://www.hcf-hawaii.org
DEADLINE(S): MAR 1
FIELD(S): Political Science; International
Relations; International Business;
Public Administration
ELIGIBILITY/REQUIREMENTS: Must
be residents of Hawaii; undergraduate stu-
dents enrolled full time in an accredited 2-
or 4-year college or university; demon-
strate financial need, good moral charac-
ter, and academic achievement with a min-
imum GPA of 2.7.
HOW TO APPLY: Send application with
2 letters of recommendation.
CONTACT: See website.

2672—HILLSDALE COLLEGE (Freedom as Vocation Scholarship)

33 East College Street
Hillsdale MI 49242-1298
517/437-7341
Internet: http://www.hillsdale.edu
AMOUNT: Varies
DEADLINE(S): None
FIELD(S): Business; History; Political
Science; Economics
ELIGIBILITY/REQUIREMENTS: Open
to Hillsdale College undergraduates who
maintain a minimum 3.0 GPA and commit
to a series of courses in the above fields.
Student must rank in top 20% of class and

top 10% of test scores. Must possess excellent communications, public speaking, and
leadership skills and demonstrate outstanding character and citizenship.
Financial need NOT a factor.
HOW TO APPLY: No application; students are selected. See website for details.
RENEWABLE: Yes

2673—INSTITUT D'ETUDES POLITIQUES DE PARIS (U.S. Sciences P.O. Alumni Association Scholarships)

27 Rue Saint Guillaume
75337 Paris Cedex 07 FRANCE
+33 33-4549-5047
FAX: +33 331-4544-1252
E-mail: contact@sciencespo.org
Internet: http://sciencespo.org/
bourses.htm
AMOUNT: Up to $5,000
DEADLINE(S): Varies
FIELD(S): European Studies; Political
Science; Economics; Finance
ELIGIBILITY/REQUIREMENTS: Open
to U.S. citizens for studies at IEP Paris,
either through admission to the school or
through an exchange program with an
accredited U.S. school. Must be fluent in
French.
HOW TO APPLY: See website or contact
Director of International Student Services
for an application. Submit with cover let-
ter, résumé, and brief essay.
CONTACT: Mr. P. Cauchy, Director of
International Student Services

2674—INSTITUTE FOR HUMANE STUD-IES (Humane Studies Fellowship)

3301 North Fairfax Drive, Suite 440
Arlington VA 22201-4432
703/993-4880 or 800/697-8799
FAX: 703/993-4890
E-mail: ihs@gmu.edu
Internet: http://www.TheIHS.org
AMOUNT: $12,000 (max.)
DEADLINE(S): DEC
FIELD(S): Social Sciences; Liberal Arts;
Law; Humanities; Jurisprudence;
Journalism
ELIGIBILITY/REQUIREMENTS: Open
to graduate and advanced undergraduate
or law students pursuing degrees at any
accredited domestic or foreign college or
university. Based on academic perfor-
mance, demonstrated interest in the classi-
cal liberal tradition, and potential to con-
tribute to the advancement of a free soci-
ety.
HOW TO APPLY: Apply online or contact IHS for an application.
NUMBER OF AWARDS: 90

2675—INSTITUTE FOR HUMANE STUD-IES (Koch Summer Fellow Program)

3401 N. Fairfax Drive, Suite 440
Arlington VA 22201-4432
703/993-4880 or 800/697-8799
FAX: 703/993-4890
E-mail: ihs@gmu.edu
Internet: http://www.TheIHS.org
AMOUNT: $1,500 + airfare and housing
DEADLINE(S): FEB 15
FIELD(S): Economics; Public Policy;
Law; Government; Politics
ELIGIBILITY/REQUIREMENTS: Open
to undergraduates and graduates. Includes
2 week-long seminars, the internship, and
research and writing projects. Financial
need NOT a factor.
HOW TO APPLY: Apply online or con-
tact IHS for an application. Submit with
transcripts and essays.
NUMBER OF AWARDS: 32
RENEWABLE: No

2676—INSTITUTE FOR HUMANE STUD-IES (Summer Seminars Program)

3401 North Fairfax Drive, Suite 440
Arlington VA 22201-4432
703/993-4880 or 800/697-8799
FAX: 703/993-4890
E-mail: ihs@gmu.edu
Internet: http://www.TheIHS.org
AMOUNT: Free summer seminars,
including room/board, lectures,
seminar materials, and books
DEADLINE(S): MAR
FIELD(S): Social Sciences; Humanities;
Law; Journalism; Public Policy;
Education; Film; Writing; Economics;
Philosophy
ELIGIBILITY/REQUIREMENTS: Open
to college students, recent graduates, and
graduate students who share an interest in
learning and exchanging ideas about the
scope of individual rights, free markets, the
rule of law, peace, and tolerance.
HOW TO APPLY: See website for information and to apply online, or contact IHS
for an application.

2677—INSTITUTE OF INTERNATIONAL EDUCATION NATIONAL SECURITY EDUCA-TION PROGRAM (NSEP David L. Boren Undergraduate Scholarships)

1400 K Street NW, 6th floor
Washington DC 20005
800/618-6737
FAX: 202/326-7672
E-mail: nsep@iie.org
Internet: http://www.iie.org/nsep

AMOUNT: Up to $20,000
DEADLINE(S): Mid FEB
FIELD(S): All, emphasis on geographic areas, languages, and fields of study deemed critical to U.S. national security
ELIGIBILITY/REQUIREMENTS: Intended to provide support to U.S. undergraduates who will pursue the study of languages and cultures currently underrepresented in study abroad and critical to U.S. national security. Must be U.S. citizen matriculated at a U.S. university or college. Provides a unique funding opportunity for U.S. students to study world regions critical to U.S. interests (including Africa, Asia, Central & Eastern Europe, Latin American and the Caribbean, and the Middle East). Must be matriculated in an undergraduate degree program in a U.S. university, college or community college accredited by an accrediting body recognized by the U.S. Department of Education, and applying to engage in a study abroad experience in a country outside of Western Europe, Canada, Australia, or New Zealand that meets home institution standards.
HOW TO APPLY: See website for additional information and application. Apply online. Submit to your NSEP campus representative with 2 reference forms, language self-assessment form, language proficiency form (optional), official transcripts, 1-page study abroad program description, and letters of support for direct enrollment (if applicable).
RENEWABLE: No
CONTACT: Susan Sharp, Program Officer
ADDITIONAL INFORMATION: The NSEP service requirement stipulates that award recipients work in the federal government in positions with national security responsibilities. The Departments of Defense, Homeland Security, State, or any element of the Intelligence Community are priority agencies.

2678—JAPANESE-AMERICAN CITIZENS LEAGUE (Alice Yuriko Endo Memorial Scholarship)

1765 Sutter Street
San Francisco CA 94115
415/921-5225
FAX: 415/931-4671
E-mail: jacl@jacl.org
Internet: http://www.jacl.org
AMOUNT: $1,000-$5,000
DEADLINE(S): APR 1
FIELD(S): All (emphasis on Public and Social Service)

ELIGIBILITY/REQUIREMENTS: Open to JACL members and their children only. For undergraduate students with an interest in public or social service who are planning to attend a college, university, trade school, business school, or any other institution of higher learning. Preference given to students residing in the Eastern District Council and/or those studying in above fields. Financial need NOT a factor.
HOW TO APPLY: For membership information or an application, send SASE to above address, stating your level of study. Applications available October 1 through March 20.

2679—JAPANESE-AMERICAN CITIZENS LEAGUE (Yoshiko Tanaka Memorial Scholarship)

1765 Sutter Street
San Francisco CA 94115
415/921-5225
FAX: 415/931-4671
E-mail: jacl@jacl.org
Internet: http://www.jacl.org
AMOUNT: $1,000-$5,000
DEADLINE(S): APR 1
FIELD(S): Japanese Language & Culture; U.S.-Japan Relations
ELIGIBILITY/REQUIREMENTS: Only open to JACL members and their children. For undergraduate students who are planning to attend a college, university, trade, business, or any other institution of higher learning. Financial need NOT a factor.
HOW TO APPLY: For membership information or an application, send SASE, stating your level of study. Submit personal statement, letters of recommendation, and transcripts.

2680—JOHN F. KENNEDY LIBRARY FOUNDATION (John F. Kennedy Profile in Courage Essay Contest)

Columbia Point
Boston MA 02125
617/514-1649
FAX: 617/514-1641
E-mail: profiles@nara.gov
Internet: http://www.jfklibrary.org
AMOUNT: $500-$3,000
DEADLINE(S): Early JAN
FIELD(S): All
ELIGIBILITY REQUIREMENTS: Open to U.S. high school students in grades 9-12, or home schools; or enrolled in a high school correspondence/GED program in any of the 50 states, D.C., or U.S. territories; or U.S. citizens attending schools overseas.

HOW TO APPLY: Write an essay on an elected official in the U.S. who is acting or has acted courageously to address a political issue at the local, state, national, or international level; also send completed contest registration form.
NUMBER OF AWARDS: 7 (1 first place, 1 second place, 5 finalists)
RENEWABLE: No

2681—JUNIATA COLLEGE (Baker Peace Scholarship)

Office of Financial Planning
1700 Moore Street
Huntingdon PA 16652
814/641-3142
FAX: 814/641-5311
E-mail: frankv@juniata.edu
Internet: http://www.juniata.edu/admission/finplan/index.html
AMOUNT: $1,000-$2,000
DEADLINE(S): FEB 1
FIELD(S): Peace and Conflict Studies; International Affairs
ELIGIBILITY/REQUIREMENTS: Open to incoming freshmen at Juniata College who rank in the upper 20% of their high school class, have above-average SAT scores, and demonstrate an interest in peace-related issues. Must submit 1,000-word essay on designated topic, 2 letters of recommendation, and maintain a minimum 3.0 GPA.
RENEWABLE: Up to 4 years.
CONTACT: Vincent Frank, Director of Student Financial Planning, 814/641-3140; e-mail: frankv@juniata.edu

2682—LONDON SCHOOL OF ECONOMICS AND POLITICAL SCIENCE

Financial Support Office
Houghton Street
London WC2A 2AE ENGLAND
+44 020 7955
FAX: +44 020 7216
E-mail: financialsupport@lse.ac.uk
Internet: http://www.lse.ac.uk
AMOUNT: Varies with award
DEADLINE(S): Varies
FIELD(S): Economics; Accounting; Finance; Political Science; International Relations
ELIGIBILITY/REQUIREMENTS: For undergraduates and graduate students; international students.
HOW TO APPLY: See website and enter "scholarships," and a vast array of programs will appear.
RENEWABLE: Varies

2683—LOUISIANA STATE UNIVERSITY AT SHREVEPORT (Walter O. Bigby Scholarship)

Bronson Hall
Shreveport LA 71115-2399
318/797-5371
Internet: http://www.lsus.edu
AMOUNT: Up to $500/semester
DEADLINE(S): Varies
FIELD(S): Political Science; English; History; Law
ELIGIBILITY/REQUIREMENTS: Must be entering junior or senior year; majoring in one of above subjects; other Liberal Arts majors acceptable, if preparing for law school.
HOW TO APPLY: Contact the Dean's Office, College of Liberal Arts for an application.

2684—NATIONAL FEDERATION OF REPUBLICAN WOMEN (Betty Rendel Scholarship)

124 North Alfred Street
Alexandria VA 22314
703/548-9688
FAX: 703/548-9836
E-mail: mail@nfrw.org
Internet: http://www.nfrw.org
AMOUNT: $1,000
DEADLINE(S): JUN 1
FIELD(S): Political Science; Government; Economics
ELIGIBILITY/REQUIREMENTS: Open to undergraduate Republican women who have successfully completed 2 years of coursework, majoring in one of the above fields.
HOW TO APPLY: Applications are available on NFRW website or by contacting NFRW headquarters. Submit to the president of your state federation.
NUMBER OF AWARDS: 3
RENEWABLE: No
CONTACT: Scholarship Coordinator

2685—NATIONAL SOCIETY DAUGHTERS OF THE AMERICAN REVOLUTION (Enid Hall Griswold Memorial Scholarship)

Committee Services Office
Attn: Scholarships
1776 D Street NW
Washington DC 20006-5392
202/628-1776
Internet: http://www.dar.org
AMOUNT: $1,000
DEADLINE(S): FEB 15
FIELD(S): History; Political Science; Government; Economics

ELIGIBILITY/REQUIREMENTS: Open to undergraduate juniors and seniors (U.S. citizens) attending an accredited U.S. college or university. Awards are judged on academic excellence, commitment to field of study, and need. Affiliation with DAR not required.
HOW TO APPLY: Must submit application with a letter of sponsorship from local DAR chapter (send SASE to address above to obtain name and application); statement of 1,000 words or less stating career objectives, how college major (if required) or college plans relate to future professional goals and reasons for these choices; transcripts list of extracurricular activities, honors received, scholastic achievements, or other significant accomplishments; 2-4 letters of recommendation from the high school or college you now attend who are familiar with your work, and proof of citizenship. See website for additional information.
RENEWABLE: No

2686—NATIONAL STONE, SAND & GRAVEL ASSOCIATION (NSSGA Jennifer Curtis Byler Scholarship in Public Affairs)

1605 King Street
Alexandria VA 22314
703/525-8788
FAX: 703/525-7782
E-mail: info@nssga.org
Internet: http://www.nssga.org
AMOUNT: $2,500
DEADLINE(S): MAY 31
FIELD(S): Public Affairs, Political Science, Journalism, International Affairs, Public Relations, International Studies
ELIGIBILITY/REQUIREMENTS: Open to graduating seniors, or college students already enrolled as a public affairs major, who are children of an aggregate employee. Applicants must demonstrate their commitment to a career in public affairs.
HOW TO APPLY: See website or write for information and application.
NUMBER OF AWARDS: 1
RENEWABLE: No

2687—NEW YORK CITY DEPARTMENT OF CITYWIDE ADMINISTRATIVE SERVICES (Government Scholars Internship Program)

1 Centre Street, 24th Floor
New York NY 10007
212/487-5600
FAX: 212/487-5720
AMOUNT: $3,000
DEADLINE(S): JAN 13

FIELD(S): Public Administration; Urban Planning; Government; Public Service; Urban Affairs
ELIGIBILITY/REQUIREMENTS: 10-week summer intern program open to undergraduate sophomores, juniors, and seniors. Program provides students with unique opportunity to learn about NYC government. Internships available in virtually every city agency and mayoral office.
HOW TO APPLY: Write to New York City Fellowship Programs for information.

2688—SOCIETY OF SATELLITE PROFESSIONALS INTERNATIONAL (SSPI Scholarship Program)

The New York Information Technology Center
55 Broad Street, 14th Floor
New York NY 10004
212/809-5199
FAX: 212/825-0075
E-mail: neworbit@aol.com
Internet: http://www.sspi.org
AMOUNT: $1,500-$4,000
DEADLINE(S): DEC 1
FIELD(S): Satellites (relating to communications, domestic and international telecommunications policy, remote sensing, journalism, law, meteorology, energy, navigation, business, government, and broadcasting services)
ELIGIBILITY/REQUIREMENTS: Open to current high school seniors, college or university undergraduate or graduate students studying or intending to study satellite-related technologies, policies or applications. Must demonstrate commitment to pursue education and career opportunities in the satellite industry or a field making direct use of satellite technology; academic and leadership achievement; and potential for significant contribution to the industry.
HOW TO APPLY: Before applying, all applicants must complete a Scholarship Qualification Form to determine whether their interests and career plans are a good fit for the program. See website for form and details or send SASE.

2689—TET '68, INC. (Essay Contest)

P.O. Box 31885
Richmond VA 23294
804/550-3692
FAX: 804/550-1406
E-mail: billyktet@aol.com
Internet: http://www.tet68.org
AMOUNT: $1,000
DEADLINE(S): MAR 31

FIELD(S): All (emphasis on history and political science)
ELIGIBILITY/REQUIREMENTS: Open to high school seniors who are children or stepchildren of a Vietnam veteran.
HOW TO APPLY: See website or write for application, contest rules, and essay topic. Submit essay with proof of status.
NUMBER OF AWARDS: 4-6
RENEWABLE: Yes
CONTACT: William E. Kirkland

2690—TOURISM CARES FOR TOMORROW (Patrick Murphy Internship)

585 Washington Street
Canton MA 02021
781/821-5990
FAX: 781/821-8949
E-mail: info@tourismcares.org
Internet: http://www.tourism cares.org
AMOUNT: $2,000
DEADLINE(S): MAY 1
FIELD(S): Travel and Tourism and related fields; Political Science
ELIGIBILITY/REQUIREMENTS: Applicant must be pursuing a travel and tourism degree with emphasis in political science. The applicant must also have excellent written, oral and interpersonal skills. The emphasis of this internship is the education of prospective managers and leaders in the packaged travel and tourism industry.
HOW TO APPLY: See website (http://www.tourismcaresfortomorrow.org/Tourism Cares/Programs/Scholarships.htm) for application and submit to Program Manager with a typed résumé, any work or internship experience in travel and tourism, any extracurricular or volunteer experience. An official copy of your updated transcript must be sent from your school, detailing courses completed, academic standing and GPA.
CONTACT: Sarah Graham Mann, Program Manager
ADDITIONAL INFORMATION: Intern's basic duties will be researching issues that affect the travel and tourism industry. This will be an educational experience to gain a better knowledge and understand the components of the travel industry. There will be no lobbying activity involved.

2691—UNITED NATIONS ASSOCIATION OF THE UNITED STATES OF AMERICA, THE (UNA-USA) (Contest)

801 Second Avenue
New York NY 10015
212/907-1326
FAX: 212/682-9185
E-mail: sleslie@unausa.org
Internet: http://www.unausa.org.org
AMOUNT: $3,000, first; $1,500, second; $750, third
DEADLINE(S): JAN
FIELD(S): International Government; United Nations, U.S. Foreign Policy
ELIGIBILITY/REQUIREMENTS: Must be high school student.
HOW TO APPLY: See website for additional information.
NUMBER OF AWARDS: 3
RENEWABLE: No
CONTACT: Scott Leslie, Publications Associate for Education

2692—U.S. INSTITUTE OF PEACE (National Peace Essay Contest)

1200 17th Street NW, Suite 200
Washington DC 20036
202/457-1700
FAX: 202/429-6063
E-mail: essaycontest@usip.org
Internet: http://www.usip.org
AMOUNT: $1,000-$10,000
DEADLINE(S): JAN
FIELD(S): All (emphasis on Political Science; U.S. History)
ELIGIBILITY/REQUIREMENTS: 1,500-word essay contest for high school students on the U.S. response to international conflict. No restrictions as to citizenship or residency.
HOW TO APPLY: See website or contact USIP for specific guidelines.
RENEWABLE: No

2693—UNIVERSITY OF SOUTH DAKOTA (Criminal Justice Department Scholarships)

414 East Clark Street
Vermillion SD 57069-2390
605/677-5446
E-mail: admiss@usd.edu
Internet: http://www.usd.edu/cjus/scholar/scholarships.htm#orderofpolice
AMOUNT: Varies
DEADLINE(S): Varies
FIELD(S): Criminal Justice; Political Science; Public Service
ELIGIBILITY/REQUIREMENTS: The University of South Dakota's Department of Criminal Justice administers 17 different award programs in the above fields. Some require a high GPA and/or financial need, others require an essay or research project.
HOW TO APPLY: See website or contact USD for specific details of each award.

2694—WESTERN MICHIGAN UNIVERSITY (College of Arts and Sciences/John R. Borsos Memorial Endowed Scholarship)

1903 West Michigan
Kalamazoo MI 49008-5337
269/387-8777
FAX: 269/387-6989
E-mail: finaid-info@wmich.edu
Internet: http://www.wmich.edu/finaid
AMOUNT: $500-$1,000 (fall semester)
FIELD(S): Political Science
ELIGIBILITY/REQUIREMENTS: Awarded to an applicant for an assistantship or associateship in the Political Science Department. The award is based primarily on academic record and merit.
HOW TO APPLY: Contact the Political Science Department for an application.
RENEWABLE: No

2695—WESTERN MICHIGAN UNIVERSITY (College of Arts and Sciences/Lanny Wilde Criminal Justice Scholarship)

1903 West Michigan
Kalamazoo MI 49008-5337
269/387-8777
FAX: 269/387-6989
E-mail: finaid-info@wmich.edu
Internet: http://www.wmich.edu/finaid
AMOUNT: $250
DEADLINE(S): MAR 1
FIELD(S): Political Science; Sociology
ELIGIBILITY/REQUIREMENTS: Must be in the tracking program through the criminal justice major. Only offered second semester of tracking program so first-semester grades are reviewed. Based on financial need.
HOW TO APPLY: Contact Sociology Department/Criminal Justice Program Advising Office, 2401 Sangren, for application.
RENEWABLE: No

2696—WESTERN MICHIGAN UNIVERSITY (College of Arts and Sciences/Leonard C. and Dorotha Kercher Sociology Endowment Fund)

1903 West Michigan
Kalamazoo MI 49008-5337
269/387-8777
FAX: 269/387-6989
E-mail: finaid-info@wmich.edu
Internet: http://www.wmich.edu/finaid
AMOUNT: Varies
DEADLINE(S): MAR 1

FIELD(S): Political Science; Sociology
ELIGIBILITY/REQUIREMENTS: Undergraduate scholarships, assistantships, fellowships, and awards.
HOW TO APPLY: Contact Sociology Department, 2420 Sangren, for an application.
RENEWABLE: No

2697—WESTERN MICHIGAN UNIVERSITY (College of Arts and Sciences/Mark Denenfeld Memorial Endowed Scholarship)

1903 West Michigan
Kalamazoo MI 49008-5337
269/387-8777
FAX: 269/387-6989
E-mail: finaid-info@wmich.edu
Internet: http://www.wmich.edu/finaid
AMOUNT: $500 (spring semester)
FIELD(S): Political Science
ELIGIBILITY/REQUIREMENTS: Awarded to beginning senior who is majoring in political science with at least 60 but not more than 105 credit hours. Must demonstrate superior academic performance at WMU and have compiled record of community service and service to others.
HOW TO APPLY: Contact the Political Science Department for an application.
RENEWABLE: No

2698—WESTERN MICHIGAN UNIVERSITY (College of Arts and Sciences/The Stanley S. and Helena S. Robin Scholarship)

1903 West Michigan
Kalamazoo MI 49008-5337
269/387-8777
FAX: 269/387-6989
E-mail: finaid-info@wmich.edu
Internet: http://www.wmich.edu/finaid
AMOUNT: $1,000
DEADLINE(S): MAR 1
FIELD(S): Political Science; Sociology
ELIGIBILITY/REQUIREMENTS: Political science or sociology major in the final semester of junior year. Must have enrolled at WMU as freshmen and, of their postsecondary academic credits at the time of application, at least 4/5ths must have been completed at WMU. Must complete senior year at WMU.
HOW TO APPLY: State intention to pursue graduate degree in sociology or political science.
RENEWABLE: No
CONTACT: Department of Political Science or Department of Sociology

2699—WOMEN IN DEFENSE (HORIZONS Scholarship Foundation)

2111 Wilson Boulevard, Suite 400
Arlington VA 22201-3061
703/247-2552
FAX: 703/522-1885
E-mail: wid@ndia.org
Internet: http://www.ndia.org
AMOUNT: $500+
DEADLINE(S): NOV 1; JUL 1
FIELD(S): Security Studies; Engineering; Computer Science; Physics; Mathematics; International Relations; Political Science; Operations Research; Economics; National Security/Defense; Business and Law (as they relate to national security or defense)
ELIGIBILITY/REQUIREMENTS: Open to women employed/planning careers in defense/national security areas (NOT law enforcement or criminal justice). Must be currently enrolled full or part time at an accredited college or university at the graduate or undergraduate junior/senior level. Must have a minimum 3.25 GPA, demonstrate financial need, and be U.S. citizen. Based on academic achievement, work experience, objectives, and recommendations.
HOW TO APPLY: See website or send SASE for application.
RENEWABLE: Yes

2700—ZONTA INTERNATIONAL FOUNDATION (Young Women in Public Affairs Award)

557 West Randolph Street
Chicago IL 60661-2206
312/930-5848
FAX: 312/930-0951
E-mail: zontafdtn@zonta.org
Internet: http://www.zonta.org
AMOUNT: $500, district awards; $1,000 international awards
DEADLINE(S): Varies
FIELD(S): Public Affairs
ELIGIBILITY/REQUIREMENTS: Pre-university or pre-college women students (ages 16-20) at the time of the international recipients selection (June 30) are eligible to apply.
HOW TO APPLY: The YWPA Awards Program operates at the Club, District, and International levels. To apply, contact the Zonta Club nearest you or e-mail your name and contact information to Zonta International Headquarters. See website for application and additional information.
NUMBER OF AWARDS: 35 (30 district awards; 5 international awards)

PSYCHOLOGY

2701—AIR FORCE RESERVE OFFICER TRAINING CORPS (AFROTC Scholarships)

551 East Maxwell Boulevard
Maxwell AFB AL 36112-6106
866/4AFROTC
E-mail: info@afrotc.com
Internet: http://www.afrotc.com
AMOUNT: Varies, but up to full tuition and fees plus $600/year for books
DEADLINE(S): DEC 1
FIELD(S): Science; Engineering; Business; Political Science; Psychology; Geography; Foreign Studies; Foreign Language
ELIGIBILITY/REQUIREMENTS: 4- and 3-year competitive scholarships based on individual merit to high school seniors and graduates who have not enrolled full time at a college or university. Academic performance is measured using an academic composite, which combines SAT (Math and Verbal only)/ACT scores, class rank, GPA and the number of advanced placement or honors courses completed through Grade 11. To be eligible for consideration, students should achieve a 1100 SAT (Math and Verbal only) or 24 ACT, minimum 3.0 GPA and class ranking in top 40%. Must be a U.S. citizen between the ages of 17-27. Must also have GPA of 2.5 or above, be in top 40% of class, and complete Applicant Fitness Test. Cannot be a single parent. Your college or university must offer AFROTC.
HOW TO APPLY: Visit www.afrotc.com to apply
NUMBER OF AWARDS: N/A
RENEWABLE: No

2702—AYN RAND INSTITUTE (Fountainhead Essay Contest)

Department W
P.O. Box 57044
Irvine CA 92619-7044
E-mail: tf-essay@aynrand.org
Internet: http://www.aynrand.org/contests/
AMOUNT: $10,000 (1st prize); $2,000 (2nd); $1,000 (3rd); $100 (finalist); $50 (semifinalist)
DEADLINE(S): APR 15
FIELD(S): All (emphasis on philosophy & psychology)
ELIGIBILITY/REQUIREMENTS: Open to 11th and 12th graders who write an 800- to 1,600-word essay on Ayn Rand's *The Fountainhead*. Essays judged on both style and content. Winning essays must demonstrate an outstanding grasp of the philo-

sophic and psychological meaning of *The Fountainhead*.

HOW TO APPLY: See website for guidelines. Do NOT write to above address. Submit online, e-mail, or by mail.

NUMBER OF AWARDS: 251 (1 first, 5 second, 10 third, 35 finalist, 200 semifinalist)

2703—BETHESDA LUTHERAN HOMES AND SERVICES (Development Disabilities Scholastic Excellence Award for Lutheran College Students)

600 Hoffmann Drive
Watertown WI 53094
920/206-4449
FAX: 920/262-6513
E-mail: ncrc@blhs.org
Internet: http://www.blhs.org

AMOUNT: $1,500

DEADLINE(S): MAR 15

FIELD(S): Special Education or any field that supports people with developmental disabilities

ELIGIBILITY/REQUIREMENTS: Must be Lutheran and have GPA 3.0 or higher; sophomore or higher when applying; career in field of developmental disabilities.

HOW TO APPLY: Write to above address or download from website.

NUMBER OF AWARDS: 3

RENEWABLE: No

CONTACT: Thomas Heuer

2704—BRITISH COLUMBIA PARAPLEGIC FOUNDATION (Douglas John Wilson Scholarship)

780 SW Marine Drive
Vancouver BC V6P 5Y7 CANADA
604/324-3611
FAX: 604/324-3671

AMOUNT: Varies

DEADLINE(S): JUL 31

FIELD(S): Rehabilitation Counseling

ELIGIBILITY/REQUIREMENTS: For a person with a disability who is a Canadian citizen or landed immigrant or a resident of British Columbia, studying for a degree in rehabilitation counseling at a university in British Columbia.

HOW TO APPLY: Write for application and additional information.

2705—EPILEPSY FOUNDATION OF AMERICA (Behavioral Sciences Student Fellowships)

4351 Garden City Drive
Landover MD 20785-2267
301/459-3700 or 800/EFA-1000
TDD: 800/332-2070
FAX: 301/577-2684
Internet: http://www.epilepsy foundation.org

AMOUNT: $3,000

DEADLINE(S): MAR 1

FIELD(S): Epilepsy Research/Practice; Sociology; Social Work; Psychology; Anthropology; Nursing; Economics; Vocational Rehabilitation; Counseling; Political Science

ELIGIBILITY/REQUIREMENTS: 3-month fellowships awarded to undergraduate and graduate students for work on a project during the summer or other free period. Students propose an epilepsy-related study or training project to be carried out at a U.S. institution. A preceptor must supervise the student and the project.

HOW TO APPLY: Contact EFA for an application.

2706—GENERAL FEDERATION OF WOMEN'S CLUBS OF MASSACHUSETTS (Music Scholarship)

P.O. Box 679
Sudbury MA 01776-0679
978/443-4569
FAX: 978/443-1617
E-mail: GFWCMA@aol.com
Internet: http://www.gfwcma. org/id39.html

AMOUNT: Up to $800

DEADLINE(S): FEB 1

FIELD(S): Piano; Instrument; Music Education; Music Therapy; Voice

ELIGIBILITY/REQUIREMENTS: Competitive scholarships for seniors in Massachusetts high schools. Letter of endorsement from sponsoring GFWC of MA club, letter of recommendation from either a high school principal or music teacher, transcripts, and personal audition (two short pieces contrasting in nature) required with application.

HOW TO APPLY: For more information or an application, see website or send a SASE to Coordinator, Arts Department at above address. Submit application with letter of recommendation from either high school principal or music instructor and transcript. Audition required.

NUMBER OF AWARDS: 1

2707—JEWISH FEDERATION OF METROPOLITAN CHICAGO (Academic Scholarship Program)

Jewish Vocational Service
216 West Jackson Blvd., Suite 700
Chicago IL 60606-6921
312/673-3400
FAX: 312/553-5544
TTY: 312/444-2877
E-mail: jvsscholarship@jvs chicago.org
Internet: http://www.jvs/ chicago. org

AMOUNT: Varies

DEADLINE(S): FEB 15

FIELD(S): Mathematics, Engineering, Science, Medicine, Social Work, Education, Psychology, Rabbinate, Law (except corporate), Communications

ELIGIBILITY/REQUIREMENTS: Open to Jewish men and women legally domiciled in the greater Chicago metropolitan area, identified as having promise for significant contributions in their chosen careers, and in need of financial assistance for full-time academic programs in above areas. Must have entered undergraduate junior year in career programs requiring no postgraduate education, be in graduate/professional school, or be in a vo-tech training program.

HOW TO APPLY: Phone JVS Scholarship Secretary (312/673-3457), fax, or visit website (click on Scholarship Services) for an application in the Fall. Interview required.

RENEWABLE: Yes

CONTACT: JVS Scholarship Secretary at 312/673-3457

2708—MIDWAY COLLEGE

512 East Stephens Street
Midway KY 40347
800/755-0031
E-mail: admissions@midway.edu
Internet: http://www.midway.edu

AMOUNT: Up to full tuition

DEADLINE(S): Varies

FIELD(S): Nursing; Education; Psychology; Biology; Equine Studies; Computer Information Systems; Business Administration; English; Pre-Med; Pre-Vet

ELIGIBILITY/REQUIREMENTS: Merit scholarships for admitted students who are considered full time in Midway's women's college. Depending on scholarship, minimum GPA ranges from 2.5 to 3.2, minimum ACT ranges 18 to 29, minimum SAT from 860 to 1290. In some cases, students must live on campus.

HOW TO APPLY: Contact Admissions Office or high school guidance counselor for application. Complete FAFSA online.

NUMBER OF AWARDS: Varies, up to 100

RENEWABLE: Yes. Must meet GPA requirements which vary based on the scholarship.

CONTACT: Admissions Office or high school guidance counselor

ADDITIONAL INFORMATION: Athletes may be eligible for an athletic scholarship in conjunction with a merit grant; contact coach for eligibility and award information.

2709—NATIONAL ASSOCIATION OF AMERICAN BUSINESS CLUBS (AMBUCS Scholarships for Therapists)

P.O. Box 5127
High Point NC 27262
800/838-1845, ext. 10
FAX:336/852-6830
E-mail: janiceb@ambucs.org
Internet: http://www.ambucs.org
AMOUNT: $500-$1,500, $6,000
DEADLINE(S): APR 15
FIELD(S): Physical Therapy, Music Therapy, Occupational Therapy, Speech-Language Pathology, Audiology,

ELIGIBILITY/REQUIREMENTS: Open to undergraduate juniors and seniors or graduate students who have good scholastic standing and plan to enter the fields listed above. The institution to which you are accepted must present a curriculum accredited by the appropriate health/therapy profession authority. GPA of 3.0 or better (4.0 scale) and U.S. citizenship required. Must demonstrate financial need.

HOW TO APPLY: See website for additional information and application. MUST apply online. Semi-finalists must provide proof of enrollment, IRS Form 1040s, and a personal statement of not more than 1 page describing the development of your chosen field of therapy; your plan of study; career plans after graduation; and why financial assistance is needed. It is recommended, but not mandatory, that applicants seek sponsorship of an AMBUCS chapter, provided a chapter is located within a reasonable distance of your home or school.

RENEWABLE: Yes
NUMBER OF AWARDS: Multiple
CONTACT: Janice Blankenship, Membership/Scholarship Coordinator, 336/852-0052 ext. 10.

2710—NEW YORK STATE HIGHER EDUCATION SERVICES CORPORATION (N.Y. State Regents Professional/Health Care Opportunity Scholarships)

Cultural Education Center
Room 5C64
Albany NY 12230
518/486-1319
Internet: http://www.hesc.com
AMOUNT: $1,000-$10,000/year
DEADLINE(S): Varies
FIELD(S): Medicine, Dentistry & related fields; Architecture, Nursing, Psychology, Audiology, Landscape Architecture, Social Work, Chiropractic, Law, Pharmacy, Accounting, Speech Language Pathology

ELIGIBILITY/REQUIREMENTS: For New York State residents who are economically disadvantaged and members of a minority group underrepresented in the chosen profession and attending school in New York State. For U.S. citizens or qualifying noncitizens.

HOW TO APPLY: See website or contact NYS HESC.

RENEWABLE: Yes

2711—PARAPSYCHOLOGY FOUNDATION, INC. (Charles T. and Judith A. Tart Award)

P.O. Box 1562
New York NY 10021-0043
212/628-1550
FAX: 212/628-1559
E-mail: office@parapsychology.org
Internet: http://www.para psychology.org
AMOUNT: $500
DEADLINE(S): OCT 15
FIELD(S): All (parapsychology)

ELIGIBILITY/REQUIREMENTS: Open to undergraduate, graduate, and post-graduate students for a specific research project—experimental, experiential, clinical, historical, survey—or questionnaire-based, archival, bibliographical, and others.

HOW TO APPLY: E-mail Parapsychology Foundation for an application or see website. Submit with high school or college transcript, 2 letters of recommendation from individuals who know your abilities and interest in the subject.

NUMBER OF AWARDS: 1

2712—PARAPSYCHOLOGY FOUNDATION, INC. (D. Scott Rogo Award for Parapsychological Literature)

P.O. Box 1562
New York NY 10021-0043
212/628-1550
FAX: 212/628-1559
E-mail: office@parapsychology.org
Internet: http://www.para psychology.org
AMOUNT: $3,000
DEADLINE(S): APR 15
FIELD(S): Parapsychology

ELIGIBILITY/REQUIREMENTS: Annual award given to an author working on a manuscript pertaining to the science of parapsychology. A brief synopsis of the proposed contents of the manuscript should be included with the initial application.

HOW TO APPLY: Contact Parapsychology Foundation for more information. Recipient notified by May 1.

2713—PARAPSYCHOLOGY FOUNDATION, INC. (Eileen J. Garrett Scholarship)

P.O. Box 1562
New York NY 10021-0043
212/628-1550
FAX: 212/628-1559
E-mail: office@parapsychology.org
Internet: http://www.para psychology.org
AMOUNT: $3,000
DEADLINE(S): JUL 15
FIELD(S): Parapsychology

ELIGIBILITY/REQUIREMENTS: Open to any undergraduate or graduate student wishing to pursue the academic study of parapsychology. Funding is for study, research, and experimentation only. Must demonstrate previous academic interest in parapsychology.

HOW TO APPLY: Contact Foundation or see website for an application. Must include a sample of writings on the subject; letters of reference from 3 individuals familiar with your work and/or studies in parapsychology.

NUMBER OF AWARDS: Varies

2714—PARAPSYCHOLOGY FOUNDATION, INC. (General Scholarly Incentive Award)

P.O. Box 1562
New York NY 10021-0043
212/628-1550
FAX: 212/628-1559
E-mail: office@parapsychology.org
Internet: http://www.para psychology.org
AMOUNT: $1,000
DEADLINE(S): NOV 15
FIELD(S): All (parapsychology)

ELIGIBILITY/REQUIREMENTS: Open to students and researchers who are finishing degree program or research project and require some additional help.

HOW TO APPLY: Send letter of application to Lisette Coly, Executive Director, to the above email address.
NUMBER OF AWARDS: 1
ADDITIONAL INFORMATION: In addition to 3 incentive awards, members will receive an award to attend the Parapsychology Foundation's annual convention.

2715—PARAPSYCHOLOGY FOUNDA-TION, INC. (Robert R. Coly Prize)

P.O. Box 1562
New York NY 10021-0043
212/628-1550
FAX: 212/628-1559
E-mail: office@parapsychology.org
Internet: http://www.para
psychology.org
AMOUNT: $1,000
DEADLINE(S): NOV 15
FIELD(S): All (parapsychology)
ELIGIBILITY/REQUIREMENTS: Applicants must show determination, academic ability, a sincere interest in the field, and write an essay of 1,000 words that addresses the topic "The Challenges of Parapsychology."
HOW TO APPLY: E-mail Parapsychology Foundation for an application or see website. Submit with high school or college transcript, 2 letters of recommendation from individuals who know their abilities and interest in the subject.
NUMBER OF AWARDS: Varies

2716—PILOT INTERNATIONAL FOUNDA-TION (PIF/Lifeline Scholarship)

P.O. Box 5600
Macon GA 31208-5600
478/743-7403
FAX: 478/743-2173
E-mail: pifinfo@pilothq.org
Internet: http://www.pilot
international.org
AMOUNT: Varies
DEADLINE(S): FEB 15
FIELD(S): Disabilities/Brain-related disorders
ELIGIBILITY/REQUIREMENTS: Open to ADULT students re-entering the job market, preparing for a second career, or improving their professional skills for an established career. Must be preparing for, or already involved in, careers working with people with disabilities/brain-related disorders. GPA of 3.5 or more is required. MUST be a Pilot Club member.
HOW TO APPLY: Must be sponsored by a Pilot Club in their home, college or uni-

versity town or city. See website for application.

2717—PILOT INTERNATIONAL FOUNDA-TION (Ruby Newhall Memorial Scholarship)

P.O. Box 5600
Macon GA 31208-5600
478/743-7403
FAX: 478/743-2173
E-mail: pifinfo@pilothq.org
Internet: http://www.pilot
international.org
AMOUNT: Varies
DEADLINE(S): FEB 15
FIELD(S): Varies
ELIGIBILITY/REQUIREMENTS: For international students who have studied in the U.S. for at least 1 year, and who intend to return to their home country 6 months after graduation. Must be full-time students majoring in a field related to human health and welfare, and have a GPA of 3.0 or more.
HOW TO APPLY: Must be sponsored by a Pilot Club in their home, college or university town or city. See website for application.

2718—PILOT INTERNATIONAL FOUNDA-TION (The Pilot International Scholarship Program)

P.O. Box 5600
Macon GA 31208-5600
478/743-7403
FAX: 478/743-2173
E-mail: pifinfo@pilothq.org
Internet: http://www.pilot
international.org
AMOUNT: Varies
DEADLINE(S): FEB 15
FIELD(S): Disabilities/Brain-related disorders
ELIGIBILITY/REQUIREMENTS: Open to undergraduates preparing for careers working directly with people with disabilities or training those who will. GPA of 3.25 or greater required. MUST be a Pilot Club member.
HOW TO APPLY: Must be sponsored by a Pilot Club in their home, college or university town or city. See website for application.

2719—PSI CHI/J. P. GUILFORD UNDER-GRADUATE RESEARCH AWARDS

Psi Chi National Office
P.O. Box 709

Chattanooga TN 37401-0709 (for regular mail) or
825 Vine Street
Chatanooga TN 37403 (for overnight mail)
E-mail: awards@psichi.org
Internet: http://www.
AMOUNT: $350 (3rd place); $650 (2nd place); $1,000 (1st place)
DEADLINE(S): MAY 1
FIELD(S): Psychology
ELIGIBILITY/REQUIREMENTS: Open to undergraduates submitting research papers relevant to psychology (e.g., experiments, correlational studies, historical studies, case histories, evaluation studies); senior author of research must be a Psi Chi member at time of submission.
HOW TO APPLY: Send application; 5 copies of the paper (maximum of 12 pages); 2 SASE (for notification purposes); a personal photo, and a short biographical statement (for publication purposes).

2720—SOCIETY FOR THE SCIENTIFIC STUDY OF SEXUALITY (Student Research Grant)

P.O. Box 416
Allentown PA 18105
610/530-2483
FAX: 610/530-2485
E-mail: thesociety@sexscience.org
Internet: http://www.sexscience.org
AMOUNT: $1,000
DEADLINE(S): JAN 1; JUN 1
FIELD(S): Human Sexuality
ELIGIBILITY/REQUIREMENTS: Open to students doing research in the area of human sexuality. Must be enrolled in a degree-granting program at an accredited institution and a student member of SSSS.
HOW TO APPLY: See website or contact SSSS for an application and additional information. Submit with a 150-word abstract of the proposed research, a short biographical sketch, and a proposed budget for your project. Department chair must submit an email to mlpeters@sexscience.org approving your project.
NUMBER OF AWARDS: 2
CONTACT: Peter Anderson, Ph.D.

2721—WESTERN MICHIGAN UNIVERSITY (College of Arts and Sciences/Fred P. Gault Sr. Memorial Scholarship)

1903 West Michigan
Kalamazoo MI 49008-5337
269/387-8777
FAX: 269/387-6989
E-mail: finaid-info@wmich.edu

Internet: http://www.wmich.edu/
finaid
AMOUNT: $1,000 (fall semester)
DEADLINE(S): NOV 1
FIELD(S): Psychology
ELIGIBILITY/REQUIREMENTS: Must
be a Native American student with an
expressed interest in psychology major or a
Native American psychology student at
any level; must be enrolled in 12 credit
hours at WMU during the semester in
which the award is paid.
HOW TO APPLY: Contact the Psychology Department for an application.

2722—WESTERN MICHIGAN UNIVERSITY (College of Arts and Sciences/Presidential Scholar Award Graduating Senior)

1903 West Michigan
Kalamazoo MI 49008-5337
269/387-8777
FAX: 269/387-6989
E-mail: finaid-info@wmich.edu
Internet: http://www.wmich.edu/cas
AMOUNT: $250 (fall semester)
DEADLINE(S): Not applicable
FIELD(S): Psychology
ELIGIBILITY/REQUIREMENTS:
Recipient must have minimum 3.0 GPA
and between 26 and 100 credit hours at the
beginning of the fall semester of the year of
the application.
HOW TO APPLY: Students are nominat-
ed by Psychology Department faculty, then
the student must submit a 1-page biogra-
phy. There is no application form.
RENEWABLE: No

2723—ZETA PHI BETA SORORITY, INC./NATIONAL EDUCATIONAL FOUNDA-TION (Lullelia W. Harrison Scholarship in Counseling)

1734 New Hampshire Avenue NW
Washington DC 20009
Internet: http://www.Zphi
B1920.org
AMOUNT: $500-$1,000
DEADLINE(S): FEB 1
FIELD(S): Counseling
ELIGIBILITY/REQUIREMENTS: Open
to graduate and undergraduate level stu-
dents enrolled in a degree program in
counseling. Award is for full-time study for
one academic year (Fall-Spring). Must sub-
mit proof of enrollment.
HOW TO APPLY: See website for addi-
tional information and application or send
SASE to Foundation. Must submit docu-
mented proof of academic study and plan
of program to Scholarship Chairperson

with signature of school administrator or
Program Director; 3 letters of recommendation (professor or high school teacher,
minister or community leader, other—for
Zeta members 3rd reference must be from
the graduate Zeta chapter and signed by
the Basileus or Advisor); transcript; essay
(minimum 150 words) with information
about yourself, your educational goals and
professional aspirations and how this
award will help you achieve them, and why
you should receive this award.

SOCIOLOGY & SOCIAL WORK

2724—COMMUNITY FOUNDATION FOR GREATER ATLANTA, INC., THE (James M. & Virginia M. Smyth Scholarship Fund)

50 Hurt Plaza, Suite 449
Atlanta GA 30303
404/688-5525
FAX: 404/688-3060
E-mail: scholarships@atlcf.org
Internet: http://www.atlcf.org/
GrantsScholarships/
Scholarships.aspx
AMOUNT: $500-$1,000
DEADLINE(S): Varies
FIELD(S): Humanities, Science, Human
Services, Music Ministry
ELIGIBILITY/REQUIREMENTS: Open
to students enrolled at an accredited col-
lege pursuing an undergraduate degree
and adults returning to school in order to
increase employability. Must have a cumulative 3.0 GPA, be accepted for enrollment
or enrolled at an accredited college, university or technical school, demonstrate
financial need, and commitment to community service through school, community
or religious organizations. Preference will
be given to applicants from Missouri,
Mississippi, Georgia, Illinois, Oklahoma,
Texas and Tennessee.
HOW TO APPLY: See website for additional information and application. Submit
with a personal essay (2-3 pages) that
explains why you feel a college education
is important, your statement of educational and career goals, post college career
interests, highlights of your high school
extracurricular/community service activities, special strengths, skills, and qualifications, any unusual family or personal circumstances have affected your achievement in school, work experience, or your
participation in school and community
activities, and present financial need; official transcript; and SAT and ACT scores, if
a recent high school graduate. Send to The
Community Foundation for Greater

Atlanta, James M. & Virginia M. Smyth
Scholarship Fund, Scholarship Management Services, Scholarship America, One
Scholarship Way, P.O. Box 297, Saint
Peter, MN 56082. If you have questions,
call 507/931-1682 or e-mail community-
foundation@scholarshipamerica.org.
NUMBER OF AWARDS: 12-15
RENEWABLE: Yes. Previous recipients
are renewed if they continue to meet the
scholarship's criteria and submit the current year's renewal application
CONTACT: Lisa Glanville, 404/308-0055

2725—COMMUNITY FOUNDATION FOR GREATER ATLANTA, INC., THE (Pattillo Scholarship Fund)

50 Hurt Plaza, Suite 449
Atlanta GA 30303
404/688-5525
FAX: 404/688-3060
E-mail: scholarships@atlcf.org
Internet: http://www.atlcf.org/
GrantsScholarships/
Scholarships.aspx
AMOUNT: $3,500
DEADLINE(S): MAR 26
FIELD(S): Medicine; Social Work
ELIGIBILITY/REQUIREMENTS: Open
to graduating high school seniors or undergraduate students. Must have GPA 2.0 or
higher through the 2 previous quarters or
the previous semester. Eligible applicants
include but are not limited to full-time
employees (working a minimum of 40
hours/week) of Pattillo Construction
Corporation or its affiliates, for a minimum
of 3 years, and their dependents (spouse,
children, and step-children).
HOW TO APPLY: See website for additional information and application. Submit
with current complete official transcript(s),
2 scholarship recommendation forms and
optional recommendation letters, letter of
acceptance from the school you plan to
attend next fall (if a recent high school
graduate). Send to The Community
Foundation for Greater Atlanta, Pattillo
Scholarship Fund, Scholarship Management Services, Scholarship America, One
Scholarship Way, P.O. Box 297, Saint
Peter, MN 56082. If you have questions,
call 507/931-1682 or e-mail community-
foundation@scholarshipamerica.org.
NUMBER OF AWARDS: 15-25
RENEWABLE: Yes; up to 4 years. Must
maintain a 2.0 minimum GPA, be enrolled
as a full-time student or as a part-time student who is working full time (preference
given to Patillo employees) and submit the
current year's renewal application
CONTACT: Lisa Glanville, 404/308-0055

2726—COMMUNITY FOUNDATION FOR GREATER ATLANTA, INC., THE (Russell Corporation Scholarship Fund)

50 Hurt Plaza, Suite 449
Atlanta GA 30303
404/688-5525
FAX: 404/688-3060
E-mail: scholarships@atlcf.org
Internet: http://www.atlcf.org/GrantsScholarships/Scholarships.aspx
AMOUNT: $5,000
DEADLINE(S): MAR 26
FIELD(S): Medicine; Social Work
ELIGIBILITY/REQUIREMENTS: Open to high school students graduating in the Spring and attending college in the Fall. Must be enrolled as a full-time at an accredited college or university; have a minimum cumulative 3.0 GPA through the two previous quarters or the previous semester; demonstrate financial need. Parents of applicants must be full-time employees of Russell Corporation for a minimum of 2 years.
HOW TO APPLY: See website for additional information and application. Submit with current complete official transcript(s), 2 scholarship recommendation forms, letter of acceptance from the school you plan to attend next fall (if a recent high school graduate). Send to The Community Foundation for Greater Atlanta, Russell Corporation Scholarship Fund, Scholarship Management Services, Scholarship America, One Scholarship Way, P.O. Box 297, Saint Peter, MN 56082. If you have questions, call 507/931-1682 or e-mail communityfoundation@scholarshipamerica.org.
NUMBER OF AWARDS: 2
RENEWABLE: Yes; up to 4 years. Must maintain a 3.0 GPA, remain enrolled as full-time students, and submit the current year's renewal application form.
CONTACT: Lisa Glanville, 404/308-0055

2727—COMMUNITY FOUNDATION FOR GREATER ATLANTA, INC., THE (Steve Dearduff Scholarship Fund)

50 Hurt Plaza, Suite 449
Atlanta GA 30303
404/688-5525
FAX: 404/688-3060
E-mail: scholarships@atlcf.org
Internet: http://www.atlcf.org/GrantsScholarships/Scholarships.aspx
AMOUNT: $500-$1,000
DEADLINE(S): MAR 26
FIELD(S): Medicine; Social Work
ELIGIBILITY/REQUIREMENTS: Must be a legal resident of Georgia, enrolled in or accepted to an accredited institution of higher learning and pursuing an undergraduate or graduate degree in medicine or social work, and have a demonstrated history of commitment to community service, potential for success in chosen field, minimum 2.0 GPA, and demonstrates financial need.
HOW TO APPLY: Must be nominated (call for nomination sent early each year). See website for additional information; submit documentation of status as an individual with autism, secondary school transcripts, documentation of acceptance into an accredited, postsecondary educational or vocational program of study, 2 letters of recommendation, a personal statement of no more than 500 words, outlining applicant's qualifications and proposed plan of study. Send to The Community Foundation for Greater Atlanta, Steve Dearduff Scholarship Fund, Scholarship Management Services, Scholarship America, One Scholarship Way, P.O. Box 297, Saint Peter, MN 56082. If you have questions, call 507/931-1682 or e-mail communityfoundation@scholarshipamerica.org.
NUMBER OF AWARDS: 3
RENEWABLE: Yes; must reapply.
CONTACT: Lisa Glanville, 404/308-0055

2728—COMMUNITY FOUNDATION FOR GREATER ATLANTA, INC., THE (William Lucas Memorial Scholarship)

50 Hurt Plaza, Suite 449
Atlanta GA 30303
404/688-5525
FAX: 404/688-3060
E-mail: scholarships@atlcf.org
Internet: http://www.atlcf.org/GrantsScholarships/Scholarships.aspx
AMOUNT: $1,250
DEADLINE(S): APR 11
FIELD(S): Social Work, Education, Allied Health
ELIGIBILITY/REQUIREMENTS: Open to graduating high school seniors beginning college in Fall. Must be a resident of Atlanta or Gainesville, Georgia, have a minimum 2.5 GPA, and be accepted to an accredited institution of higher learning and pursuing an undergraduate degree. Must demonstrate a history of commitment to community service.
HOW TO APPLY: See website for additional information and application. Submit with essay (1-2 pages) describing your educational plans and your commitment to community service; 1-page résumé listing school and community activities, awards, offices held and other relevant experiences, official transcript, SAT/ACT scores if you are a recent high school graduate, and 2 letters of recommendation from a teacher, school personnel, volunteer advisor, or other influential adult who can attest to your merits and commitment to community service. Send to William Lucas Memorial Scholarship, c/o Georgia Campaign for Adolescent Pregnancy Prevention, 100 Auburn Avenue, Suite 200, Atlanta, GA 30303.
NUMBER OF AWARDS: 1
RENEWABLE: Yes; must reapply.
CONTACT: Brenda Jackson, William Lucas Memorial Scholarship. c/o Georgia Campaign for Adolescent Pregnancy Prevention, 100 Auburn Avenue, Suite 200, Atlanta, GA 30303, 404/524-2277.

2729—COMMUNITY FOUNDATION OF WESTERN MASSACHUSETTS (George H. and Margaret B. McDonnell Family Scholarship)

1500 Main Street
P.O. Box 15769
Springfield MA 01115
413/732-2858
FAX: 413/733/8565
E-mail: scholar@communityfoundation.org
Internet: http://www.communityfoundation.org
AMOUNT: $1,000
DEADLINE(S): MAR 31
FIELD(S): Social Work
HOW TO APPLY: See website for application.
ELIGIBILITY/REQUIREMENTS: Open to graduate of a Holyoke Catholic High School in Massachusetts pursuing a career in social work or allied field.
NUMBER OF AWARDS: 1

2730—EPILEPSY FOUNDATION OF AMERICA (Behavioral Sciences Student Fellowships)

4351 Garden City Drive
Landover MD 20785-2267
301/459-3700 or 800/EFA-1000
TDD: 800/332-2070
FAX: 301/577-2684
Internet: http://www.epilepsyfoundation.org
AMOUNT: $3,000
DEADLINE(S): MAR 1
FIELD(S): Epilepsy Research/Practice; Sociology; Social Work; Psychology; Anthropology; Nursing; Economics;

Vocational Rehabilitation; Counseling; Political Science

ELIGIBILITY/REQUIREMENTS: 3-month fellowships awarded to undergraduate and graduate students for work on a project during the summer or other free period. Students propose an epilepsy-related study or training project to be carried out at a U.S. institution. A preceptor must supervise the student and the project.

HOW TO APPLY: Contact EFA for an application.

2731—JEWISH FEDERATION OF METRO-POLITAN CHICAGO (Academic Scholarship Program)

Jewish Vocational Service
216 West Jackson Blvd., Suite 700
Chicago IL 60606-6921
312/673-3400
FAX: 312/553-5544
TTY: 312/444-2877
E-mail: jvsscholarship@jvs
chicago.org
Internet: www.jvs.chicago.org
AMOUNT: $5,000
DEADLINE(S): MAR 1
FIELD(S): Mathematics, Engineering, Science, Medicine, Social Work, Education, Psychology, Rabbinate, Law (except corporate), Communications

ELIGIBILITY/REQUIREMENTS: Open to Jewish men and women legally domiciled in the greater Chicago metropolitan area, identified as having promise for significant contributions in their chosen careers, and in need of financial assistance for full-time academic programs in above areas. Must have entered undergraduate junior year in career programs requiring no postgraduate education, be in graduate/professional school, or be in a vo-tech training program.

HOW TO APPLY: Contact JVS Scholarship Secretary, or fax or visit website for an application between December 1 and February 15. Interview required.
RENEWABLE: Yes
CONTACT: JVS Scholarship Secretary at 312/673-3457

2732—J. W. SAXE MEMORIAL PRIZE

1524 31 Street NW
Washington DC 20007-3074
E-mail: ruthsaxe@aol.com or
sachsedc@verizon.net
Internet: http://www.jwsaxefund.org
AMOUNT: $1,500
DEADLINE(S): MAR 15

FIELD(S): Public Service; Community Service

ELIGIBILITY/REQUIREMENTS: Must be a college or university student. Award enables student to gain practical experience in public service by taking a no-pay or low-pay job or internship.

HOW TO APPLY: Send résumé together with an essay stating short- and long-term goals. Also include statements from 4 references (at least 1 from a faculty member).
NUMBER OF AWARDS: 1-12
RENEWABLE: No
CONTACT: Ruth Saxe, President or Elinor Sachse, VP and Secretary

2733—MEMORIAL FOUNDATION FOR JEWISH CULTURE (International Scholarship Program for Community Service)

50 Broadway, 34th Floor
New York NY 10004
212/425-6606
E-mail: office@mfjc.org
Internet: http://www.mfjc.org/
index.htm
AMOUNT: Varies
DEADLINE(S): NOV 30
FIELD(S): Jewish Education; Theology; Social Work

ELIGIBILITY/REQUIREMENTS: Open to any individual regardless of country of origin for undergraduate study that leads to careers in the Rabbinate, Jewish education, social work, or as religious functionaries in Diaspora Jewish communities outside the U.S., Israel, and Canada. Must commit to serve in a community of need for 3 years.

HOW TO APPLY: Write for information.

2734—MEMORIAL FOUNDATION FOR JEWISH CULTURE (Soviet Jewry Community Service Scholarship Program)

50 Broadway, 34th Floor
New York NY 10004
212/425-6606
E-mail: office@mfjc.org
Internet: http://www.mfjc.org/
index.htm
AMOUNT: Not specified
DEADLINE(S): NOV 30
FIELD(S): Theology; Education; Social Work

ELIGIBILITY/REQUIREMENTS: Open to Jews from the former Soviet Union enrolled or planning to enroll in recognized institutions of higher Jewish learning. Must agree to serve a community of

Soviet Jews anywhere in the world for a minimum of 3 years.

HOW TO APPLY: Write for information.

2735—NEW YORK CITY DEPARTMENT OF CITYWIDE ADMINISTRATIVE SERVICES (Government Scholars Internship Program)

1 Centre Street, 24th Floor
New York NY 10007
212/487-5600
FAX: 212/487-5720
AMOUNT: $3,000
DEADLINE(S): JAN 13
FIELD(S): Public Administration; Urban Planning; Government; Public Service; Urban Affairs

ELIGIBILITY/REQUIREMENTS: 10-week summer intern program open to undergraduate sophomores, juniors, and seniors. Program provides students with unique opportunity to learn about NY City government. Internships available in virtually every city agency and mayoral office.

HOW TO APPLY: Write to New York City Fellowship Programs at above address for complete information.

2736—NEW YORK STATE HIGHER EDUCATION SERVICES CORPORATION (N.Y. State Regents Professional/Health Care Opportunity Scholarships)

Cultural Education Ctr., Room 5C64
Albany NY 12230
518/486-1319
Internet: http://www.hesc.com
AMOUNT: $1,000-$10,000/year
DEADLINE(S): Varies
FIELD(S): Medicine, Dentistry & related fields; Architecture, Nursing, Psychology, Audiology, Landscape Architecture, Social Work, Chiropractic, Law, Pharmacy, Accounting, Speech Language Pathology

ELIGIBILITY/REQUIREMENTS: For New York State residents who are economically disadvantaged and members of a minority group underrepresented in the chosen profession and attending school in New York State. For U.S. citizens or qualifying noncitizens.

HOW TO APPLY: See website or contact NYS HESC.
RENEWABLE: Yes

2737—PHILADELPHIA BIBLICAL UNIVERSITY (Scholarships, Grants, and Loans)

Financial Aid Department

200 Manor Avenue
Langhorne PA 19047
800/366-0049
FAX: 215/702-4248
E-mail: financialaid@pbu.edu
financialaid@pbu.edu
Internet: http://www.pbu.edu
AMOUNT: Varies
DEADLINE(S): Varies
FIELD(S): Bible, Business, Teacher
  Education, Music, Social Work,
  Missions, Church Ministries
ELIGIBILITY/REQUIREMENTS:
Academic and need-based grants, based on
FAFSA, for full-time students, and needy
dependents of full-time Christian workers,
and those exhibiting excellence in the field
of music. Academic awards based on GPA
and SAT/ACT scores.
HOW TO APPLY: Apply to university
and complete an application for student
aid.
CONTACT: David Haggard

2738—UNIVERSITY OF SOUTH DAKOTA (Criminal Justice Department Scholarships)

414 East Clark Street
Vermillion SD 57069-2390
605/677-5446
E-mail: admiss@usd.edu
Internet: http://www.usd.edu/
  cjus/scholar/scholarship.cfm
AMOUNT: Varies
DEADLINE(S): Varies
FIELD(S): Criminal Justice; Political
  Science; Public Service
ELIGIBILITY/REQUIREMENTS: The
University of South Dakota's Department
of Criminal Justice administers 17 different
award programs in the above fields. Some
require a high GPA and/or financial need,
others require an essay or research project.
HOW TO APPLY: See website or contact
USD for specific details of each award.

2739—WESTERN MICHIGAN UNIVERSITY (College of Arts and Sciences/Lanny Wilde Criminal Justice Scholarship)

1903 West Michigan
Kalamazoo MI 49008-5337
269/387-8777
FAX: 269/387-6989
E-mail: finaid-info@wmich.edu
Internet: http://www.wmich.edu/
  finaid
AMOUNT: $250
DEADLINE(S): MAR 1
FIELD(S): Political Science; Sociology

ELIGIBILITY/REQUIREMENTS: Must
be in the tracking program through the
criminal justice major. Only offered second
semester of tracking program so first-
semester grades are reviewed. Based on
financial need.
HOW TO APPLY: Contact Sociology
Department/Criminal Justice Program
Advising Office, 2401 Sangren, for an
application.

2740—WESTERN MICHIGAN UNIVERSITY (College of Arts and Sciences/Leonard C. and Dorotha Kercher Sociology Endowment Fund)

1903 West Michigan
Kalamazoo MI 49008-5337
269/387-8777
FAX: 269/387-6989
E-mail: finaid-info@wmich.edu
Internet: http://www.wmich.edu/
  finaid
AMOUNT: Varies
DEADLINE(S): MAR 1
FIELD(S): Political Science; Sociology
ELIGIBILITY/REQUIREMENTS:
Undergraduate scholarships, assistant-
ships, fellowships, and awards.
HOW TO APPLY: Contact Sociology
Department, 2420 Sangren, for applica-
tion.
RENEWABLE: No

2741—WESTERN MICHIGAN UNIVERSITY (College of Arts and Sciences/The Stanley S. and Helena S. Robin Scholarship)

1903 West Michigan
Kalamazoo MI 49008-5337
269/387-8777
FAX: 269/387-6989
E-mail: finaid-info@wmich.edu
Internet: http://www.wmich.edu/
  finaid
AMOUNT: $1,000
DEADLINE(S): MAR 1
FIELD(S): Political Science; Sociology
ELIGIBILITY/REQUIREMENTS:
Political science or sociology major in the
final semester of junior year. Must have
enrolled at WMU as freshmen and, of their
postsecondary academic credits at the time
of application, at least 4/5ths must have
been completed at WMU. Must complete
senior year at WMU.
HOW TO APPLY: State intention to pur-
sue graduate degree in sociology or politi-
cal science.
RENEWABLE: No
CONTACT: Department of Political
Science or Department of Sociology

2742—WESTERN MICHIGAN UNIVERSITY (College of Health and Human Services/Elissa Gatlin Scholarship)

1903 West Michigan
Kalamazoo MI 49008-5337
269/387-8777
FAX: 269/387-6989
E-mail: finaid-info@wmich.edu
Internet: http://www.wmich.edu/
  finaid
AMOUNT: $500/semester
DEADLINE(S): MAR 1
FIELD(S): Occupational Therapy;
  Nursing; Speech Pathology; Blind
  Rehabilitation; Social Work; Physician
  Assistant
ELIGIBILITY/REQUIREMENTS:
Intended for minority students (African-
American, Native American, or Hispanic-
American); 2.75 GPA for undergraduates,
3.00 GPA for graduates; must be enrolled
in professional program, U.S. citizen, and
demonstrate financial need.
HOW TO APPLY: Contact the College of
Health and Human Services for an applica-
tion.
NUMBER OF AWARDS: 2 (1 under-
graduate; 1 graduate)
RENEWABLE: Yes. Maximum 2 years.

2743—WESTERN MICHIGAN UNIVERSITY (College of Health and Human Services/Jeffrey and Barbara Vortman Scholarship)

1903 West Michigan
Kalamazoo MI 49008-5337
269/387-8777
FAX: 269/387-6989
E-mail: finaid-info@wmich.edu
Internet: http://www.wmich.edu/
  finaid
AMOUNT: $500
DEADLINE(S): MAR 1
FIELD(S): Occupational Therapy;
  Nursing; Speech Pathology; Blind
  Rehabilitation; Social Work; Physician
  Assistant
ELIGIBILITY/REQUIREMENTS: Each
year one of the departments/schools is
responsible for awarding the scholarship to
a student admitted to one of the profes-
sional programs in the College.
HOW TO APPLY: Contact the College of
Health and Human Services for applica-
tion.
NUMBER OF AWARDS: 2 (1 under-
graduate; 1 graduate)
RENEWABLE: Yes. Maximum 2 years.

2744—WESTERN MICHIGAN UNIVERSITY (School of Social Work/Deloris Jordan Phillips Scholarship)

1903 West Michigan
Kalamazoo MI 49008-5337
269/387-8777
FAX: 269/387-6989
E-mail: finaid-info@wmich.edu
Internet: http://www.wmich.edu/finaid
AMOUNT: $500
DEADLINE(S): MAR 1
FIELD(S): Social Work
ELIGIBILITY/REQUIREMENTS: BSW or MSW student. Minimum 3.3 GPA at the undergraduate level; minimum 3.5 GPA at the graduate level after first semester. The scholarship will be awarded as a competitive process with the selected recipient having been evaluated as the most meritorious in scholarship and life experience.
HOW TO APPLY: Contact the School of Social Work for an application.
NUMBER OF AWARDS: 1
RENEWABLE: Yes. Up to 2 consecutive years.

2745—WESTERN MICHIGAN UNIVERSITY (School of Social Work/Freida Amos Scholarship)

1903 West Michigan
Kalamazoo MI 49008-5337
269/387-8777
FAX: 269/387-6989
E-mail: finaid-info@wmich.edu
Internet: http://www.wmich.edu/finaid
AMOUNT: $1,000
DEADLINE(S): MAR 1
FIELD(S): Social Work
ELIGIBILITY/REQUIREMENTS: Awarded to students who experience a sudden, serious financial crisis while enrolled in either the undergraduate or graduate social work program that jeopardizes the student's ability to complete the semester or program (needs of single parents are given priority).
HOW TO APPLY: Any social work student may alert the Director of Admissions and Student Services (DASS) to the financial need; School of Social Work faculty or staff may also bring the student's need to the DASS's attention.

2746—WESTERN MICHIGAN UNIVERSITY (School of Social Work/Presidential Scholar)

1903 West Michigan
Kalamazoo MI 49008-5337

269/387-8777
FAX: 269/387-6989
E-mail: finaid-info@wmich.edu
Internet: http://www.wmich.edu/finaid
DEADLINE(S): MAR 1
FIELD(S): Social Work
ELIGIBILITY/REQUIREMENTS: One undergraduate senior is chosen from each department/school as most deserving of this designation.
HOW TO APPLY: Students are nominated by School of Social Work faculty or staff.

2747—WESTERN MICHIGAN UNIVERSITY (School of Social Work/Robert Barstow Endowed Award)

1903 West Michigan
Kalamazoo MI 49008-5337
269/387-8777
FAX: 269/387-6989
E-mail: finaid-info@wmich.edu
Internet: http://www.wmich.edu/finaid
AMOUNT: $500 each (varies)
DEADLINE(S): MAR 1
FIELD(S): Social Work
ELIGIBILITY/REQUIREMENTS: BSW student or MSW student in first-year full-time or first-year part-time program. Current or former AFDC recipient; or current or former employee of FIA (DSS); or has a career interest in child welfare.
HOW TO APPLY: Students are nominated by School of Social Work faculty.

2748—WESTERN MICHIGAN UNIVERSITY (School of Social Work/Whitney Young, Jr. Scholars Award)

1903 West Michigan
Kalamazoo MI 49008-5337
269/387-8777
FAX: 269/387-6989
E-mail: finaid-info@wmich.edu
Internet: http://www.wmich.edu/finaid
AMOUNT: $165 (varies)
DEADLINE(S): MAR 1
FIELD(S): Social Work
ELIGIBILITY/REQUIREMENTS: Seniors in any undergraduate program or master's level students who have completed no more than half of their program, with a 3.0 or higher GPA.
HOW TO APPLY: Students are nominated by School of Social Work faculty or staff.
NUMBER OF AWARDS: Approximately 3.

VOCATIONAL EDUCATION (ALL FIELDS)

2749—AMERICAN LEGION AUXILIARY DEPARTMENT OF OREGON (Department Scholarships)

401 Van Ness Avenue, Room 113
San Francisco CA 94102-4586
415/861-5092
FAX: 415/861-8365
E-mail: calegionaux@calegionaux.org
Internet: http://www.calegionaux.org
AMOUNT: $1,000
DEADLINE(S): MAR 10
FIELD(S): All
ELIGIBILITY/REQUIREMENTS: Must be the child or widow of a veteran or the wife of a disabled veteran and an Oregon resident; may be used for college, vocational school or any accredited school.
HOW TO APPLY: Send application, signed by the Unit President and the Education Chairman of the unit sponsoring the applicant.
NUMBER OF AWARDS: 3 (1 for a Vocational School or Business School)
RENEWABLE: No
CONTACT: Send applications to Local American Legion Auxiliary Unit; for information and applications, contact Mona Craigg, Department Education Chairman, 1762 Camino, Forest Grove OR 97116 or The Department Office of the American Legion Auxiliary, P.O. Box #1730, Wilsonville OR 97070.

2750—AMERICAN TRAFFIC SAFETY SERVICES FOUNDATION (Roadway Worker Memorial Scholarship Program)

15 Riverside Parkway, Suite 100
Fredericksburg VA 22406
800/272-8772 or 540/368-1701
FAX: 540/368-1717
E-mail: foundation@atssa.com
Internet: http://www.atssa.com/cs/roadway-worker-scholarship
AMOUNT: $2,000-$3,000 (see below)
DEADLINE(S): FEB 15
FIELD(S): All
ELIGIBILITY/REQUIREMENTS: Must be children or parents with custody or legal guardianship of surviving children of roadway safety workers killed or permanently disabled in work zones, including mobile operations and the installation of roadway

safety features. Must be applied to a post-secondary school or institution that requires a high school diploma or GED for admission including 2- or 4-year accredited college or university; or vocational-technical college or a training institution. Based on past academic performance, financial need, record of volunteerism.

HOW TO APPLY: See website or e-mail for an application. Submit with an official copy transcript and grade report; FAFSA; a no more than 200-word statement explaining your reasons for wanting to continue your education and listing any volunteer activities/accomplishments; and 2 letters of recommendation from a teacher, school administrator, counselor, member of the clergy, or work or military supervisor who can address the applicant's qualifications and academic aptitude.

NUMBER OF AWARDS: 2-3

RENEWABLE: Yes. Must reapply.

CONTACT: Melanie Myers, Foundation Director

ADDITIONAL INFORMATION: If a particular applicant demonstrates a strong commitment to volunteerism, they may be eligible to receive an additional $1,000.

2751—ARIZONA PRIVATE SCHOOL ASSOCIATION

202 E. McDowell Road, Suite 273
Phoenix AZ 85004
602/254-5199
FAX: 602/254-5073
E-mail: apsa@eschelon.com
Internet: http://www.arizonapsa.org
AMOUNT: $500-$3,000
DEADLINE(S): APR 30
FIELD(S): Vocational Education

ELIGIBILITY/REQUIREMENTS: Open to Arizona high school students who attend a specific list of colleges in Arizona (see website for list of participating colleges).

HOW TO APPLY: Contact your high school counselor for an application.

NUMBER OF AWARDS: 150+

RENEWABLE: No

2752—ILLINOIS AMVETS (Trade School Scholarship)

2200 South Sixth Street
Springfield IL 62703-3496
217/528-4713 or 800/638-8387
FAX: 217/528-9896
E-mail: sara@ilamvets.org
Internet: http://www.ilamvets.org
AMOUNT: $500
DEADLINE(S): MAR 1
FIELD(S): All

ELIGIBILITY/REQUIREMENTS: Recipient must be Illinois high school senior, who has been accepted in a pre-approved trade school program. Priority will be given to child or grandchild of a veteran. Must have taken ACT or SAT at time of application.

HOW TO APPLY: See website for additional information and application or contact Foundation. Submit with transcript and ACT or SAT scores. Copy of acceptance letter must accompany application.

RENEWABLE: Yes; up to 2 years; must send written request and transcript.

CONTACT: Sara Garcia, Program Director

2753—WASHINGTON APPLE EDUCATION FOUNDATION (Van Doren Sales, Inc. Scholarship)

P.O. Box 3720
Wenatchee WA 98807
509/663-7713
FAX: 509/663-7713
E-mail: waef@waef.org
Internet: http://www.ussui.org
AMOUNT: $1,500
DEADLINE(S): APR 1
FIELD(S): Vocational Education

ELIGIBILITY/REQUIREMENTS: Open to high school seniors currently involved in vocational education in any of the following schools: Eastmont, Wenatchee, Cascade, Cashmere, Chelan, or Waterville. To qualify, the high school seniors must be planning to attend a 2-year junior or community college, or vocational trade school. Students attending Washington State may also apply.

HOW TO APPLY: See website for application.

NUMBER OF AWARDS: 1

RENEWABLE: Yes. Must reapply, maximum 2 years.

CONTACT: Jennifer Whitney

AUTOMOTIVE INDUSTRY

2754—AUTOMOTIVE HALL OF FAME (Automotive Educational Fund Scholarship)

21400 Oakwood Boulevard
Dearborn MI 48124
313/240-4000
AMOUNT: $2,000
DEADLINE(S): MAY 30
FIELD(S): Automotive Industry

ELIGIBILITY/REQUIREMENTS: Open to those with a sincere interest in an automotive career. Financial need is considered but not necessary.

HOW TO APPLY: See website or send SASE for application. Submit with an official transcript of all academic work; 2 letters of recommendation; a letter of acceptance for an associate, bachelor or master's program at an accredited college, university or trade school in the U.S.

NUMBER OF AWARDS: At least 12

CONTACT: Lynne Hall

2755—GLOBAL AUTOMOTIVE AFTER-MARKET SYMPOSIUM

7101 Wisconsin Ave, Suite 1300
Bethesda MD 20814
301/654-6664
FAX: 301/654-3299
E-mail: aaia@aftermarket.org
Internet: http://www.awda.org/
AMOUNT: $1,000 + matching grant
DEADLINE(S): FEB 28
FIELD(S): Automotive Aftermarket: various aspects

ELIGIBILITY/REQUIREMENTS: Open to graduating high school seniors enrolled in a college-level program or a vocational NATEF-accredited automotive technician program. Matching bonus awarded for working in the field for at least 6 months after graduation.

HOW TO APPLY: Contact Automotive Warehouse Distributors Association or see website for more information.

2756—ROCKY MOUNTAIN COAL MINING INSTITUTE, THE (Technical Scholarship)

8057 South Yukon Way
Littleton CO 80128-5510
303/948-3300
FAX: 303/948-1132
E-mail: mail@rmcmi.org
Internet: http://www.rmcmi.org
AMOUNT: $1,000
DEADLINE(S): FEB 3
FIELD(S): Vocational Education: Mechanical, Trade, Automotive, Welding, Electrical, Drafting, Diesel Mechanics, Tires

ELIGIBILITY/REQUIREMENTS: Must be a first-year student at a 2-year technical/trade school in good standing at the time of selection, and a U.S. citizen and a legal resident of a member state (AZ, CO, MT, NM, ND, TX, UT, WY) studying one of above trades.

HOW TO APPLY: See website for application; submit with 3 letters of reference (include name, address, business and home phone number, company or business name, and years acquainted); résumé

(include employer's name, address, phone number, the name of your supervisor, work performed, length of service, and the reason for leaving), answers to the following questions (limiting each to 100 words or less): 1. If you could pick any job, what would it be and why? 2. Why are you pursuing your present degree? 3. What are your plans after graduation? 4. Optional—Personal statement (i.e. why you are applying for this scholarship, special skills or training, etc.).
NUMBER OF AWARDS: 8
RENEWABLE: No

2757—SEARS CRAFTSMAN SCHOLARSHIP

NHRA Youth & Education Services
2035 Financial Way
Glendora CA 91741-4602
626/250-2296
AMOUNT: $250
DEADLINE(S): MAY 1
FIELD(S): Automotive Technology;
   Industrial/Technical Manufacturing;
   Marketing
ELIGIBILITY/REQUIREMENTS: Open to seniors graduating from high school or education center between January and June, planning to attend an accredited 2- or 4-year college, university or vo-tech program. Must be of good character, possess a minimum GPA, show evidence of leadership ability, involvement in extracurricular school and community activities. Students with a failing grade during their high school career will not be considered. Awards based on scholastic record, school activities and community involvement, and financial need.
HOW TO APPLY: Submit application, including personal essay; 2 recommendations, 1 of which must be from a teacher, counselor, or administrator; and transcript.
NUMBER OF AWARDS: 21 (3 in each of the 7 National Hot Rod Association Divisions)

2758—SOCIETY OF AUTOMOTIVE ENGINEERS (Arkansas Tech University/SAE Engineering Scholarship)

SAE Customer Service
400 Commonwealth Drive
Warrendale PA 15096-0001
724/776-4970
FAX: 724/776-1615
E-mail: customerservice@sae.org
Internet: http://www.sae.org/
   students/scholarships
AMOUNT: $1,000-$4,000
DEADLINE(S): DEC 1
FIELD(S): Mechanical Engineering;
   Electrical Engineering; Automotive
   Industry
ELIGIBILITY/REQUIREMENTS: Must be an incoming freshman or transfer student admitted to studies in either mechanical or electrical engineering. Selection based on academic and leadership activities; must have a minimum 980 SAT or 21 ACT composite score, and 3.25 GPA.
HOW TO APPLY: See website for application. Submit application; a personal essay that demonstrates hands-on experience or activity (such as rebuilding engines, working on cars/trucks, etc.); 2 recommendations, 1 of which must be from a teacher, counselor, or administrator; and transcript.
NUMBER OF AWARDS: At least 2
RENEWABLE: Yes. A total of $4,000-$16,000 (over 4-year period) if student is in good standing and enrolls in and completes 15 or more hours and maintains 3.25 GPA each semester.

2759—SOCIETY OF AUTOMOTIVE ENGINEERS (BMW/SAE Engineering Scholarship)

SAE Customer Service
400 Commonwealth Drive
Warrendale PA 15096-0001
724/776-4970
FAX: 724/776-1615
E-mail: customerservice@sae.org
Internet: http://www.sae.org/
   students/scholarships
AMOUNT: $1,500
DEADLINE(S): DEC 1
FIELD(S): Automotive Industry,
   Engineering
ELIGIBILITY/REQUIREMENTS: Must have 3.75 GPA, rank in the 90th percentile in both math and verbal on SAT or composite ACT scores, and pursue an engineering degree program accredited by ABET.
HOW TO APPLY: See website for application. Submit with personal essay; 2 recommendations, 1 of which must be from a teacher, counselor, or administrator; and transcript.
NUMBER OF AWARDS: 1
RENEWABLE: Yes. A total of $6,000 (over 4-year period) if student maintains 3.0 GPA and continued enrollment in an engineering program.

2760—SOCIETY OF AUTOMOTIVE ENGINEERS (Bradley University/SAE Engineering Scholarships)

SAE Customer Service
400 Commonwealth Drive
Warrendale PA 15096-0001
724/776-4970
FAX: 724/776-1615
E-mail: customerservice@sae.org
Internet: http://www.sae.org/
   students/scholarships
AMOUNT: $1,000
DEADLINE(S): DEC 1
FIELD(S): Engineering; Automotive
   Industry
ELIGIBILITY/REQUIREMENTS: Must be an incoming freshman accepted into the College of Engineering and Technology at Bradley. Based on high school GPA (3.25), rank in class, curriculum and SAT/ACT scores (minimum 980 SAT or 21 ACT composite score).
HOW TO APPLY: See website for application. Submit with personal essay that demonstrates hands-on experience or activity (such as rebuilding engines, working on cars/trucks, etc.); 2 recommendations, 1 of which must be from a teacher, counselor, or administrator; and transcript.
NUMBER OF AWARDS: Varies
RENEWABLE: Yes. A total of $4,000 (4-year period) if student remains enrolled in one of the specified majors and maintains 3.0 GPA.

2761—SOCIETY OF AUTOMOTIVE ENGINEERS (Calvin College/The James Bosscher/SAE Engineering Scholarship)

SAE Customer Service
400 Commonwealth Drive
Warrendale PA 15096-0001
724/776-4970
FAX: 724/776-1615
E-mail: customerservice@sae.org
Internet: http://www.sae.org/
   students/scholarships
AMOUNT: $2,000
DEADLINE(S): DEC 1
FIELD(S): Engineering; Automotive
   Industry
ELIGIBILITY/REQUIREMENTS: High school seniors entering as freshmen enrolled in the engineering program who have demonstrated outstanding academic achievement and potential.
HOW TO APPLY: See website for application. Submit with personal essay that demonstrates hands-on experience or activity (such as rebuilding engines, working on cars/trucks, etc.); 2 recommendations, 1 of which must be from a teacher, counselor, or administrator; and transcript.
NUMBER OF AWARDS: 1
RENEWABLE: Yes. For sophomore year contingent on continued enrollment in engineering and satisfactory performance.

2762—SOCIETY OF AUTOMOTIVE ENGINEERS (Cedarville University/SAE Engineering Scholarship)

SAE Customer Service
400 Commonwealth Drive
Warrendale PA 15096-0001
724/776-4970
FAX: 724/776-1615
E-mail: customerservice@sae.org
Internet: http://www.sae.org/
students/scholarships
AMOUNT: $1,000
DEADLINE(S): DEC 1
FIELD(S): Engineering; Automotive
Industry
ELIGIBILITY/REQUIREMENTS: High
school seniors entering as freshmen
enrolled in the engineering program are
awarded based on academic achievement.
Criteria include ACT/SAT scores and high
school GPA. Financial need is considered.
HOW TO APPLY: See website for application. Submit with personal essay that
demonstrates hands-on experience or
activity (such as rebuilding engines, working on cars/trucks, etc.); 2 recommendations, 1 of which must be from a teacher,
counselor, or administrator; and transcript.
NUMBER OF AWARDS: 2
RENEWABLE: No

2763—SOCIETY OF AUTOMOTIVE ENGINEERS (Central Missouri State University/SAE Engineering Scholarship)

SAE Customer Service
400 Commonwealth Drive
Warrendale PA 15096-0001
724/776-4970
FAX: 724/776-1615
E-mail: customerservice@sae.org
Internet: http://www.sae.org/
students/scholarships
AMOUNT: $500
DEADLINE(S): DEC 1
FIELD(S): Engineering; Automotive
Industry
ELIGIBILITY/REQUIREMENTS:
Incoming freshman pursuing a Bachelor of
Science degree in Automotive/Power
Technology; must have 25 ACT composite,
a 3.2 GPA, and be in upper 15% of graduating class.
HOW TO APPLY: See website for application. Submit with personal essay that
demonstrates hands-on experience or
activity (such as rebuilding engines, working on cars/trucks, etc.); 2 recommendations, 1 of which must be from a teacher,
counselor, or administrator; and transcript.
NUMBER OF AWARDS: 1

RENEWABLE: Yes. For 1 year if 3.5
GPA is maintained.

2764—SOCIETY OF AUTOMOTIVE ENGINEERS (Central State University/SAE Engineering Scholarship)

SAE Customer Service
400 Commonwealth Drive
Warrendale PA 15096-0001
724/776-4970
FAX: 724/776-1615
E-mail: customerservice@sae.org
Internet: http://www.sae.org/
students/scholarships
AMOUNT: $1,000
DEADLINE(S): DEC 1
FIELD(S): Manufacturing Engineering;
Industrial Technology; Automotive
Industry
ELIGIBILITY/REQUIREMENTS: Must
be an incoming freshman, enrolled full
time in the Manufacturing Engineering or
Industrial Technology program. Based on
ACT/SAT scores and a minimum 3.0
GPA. Financial need is also considered.
HOW TO APPLY: See website for application. Submit with personal essay that
demonstrates hands-on experience or
activity (such as rebuilding engines, working on cars/trucks, etc.); 2 recommendations, 1 of which must be from a teacher,
counselor, or administrator; and transcript.
NUMBER OF AWARDS: 3
RENEWABLE: Yes. For 1 year if criteria
are met.

2765—SOCIETY OF AUTOMOTIVE ENGINEERS (Clarkson University/SAE Engineering Scholarship)

SAE Customer Service
400 Commonwealth Drive
Warrendale PA 15096-0001
724/776-4970
FAX: 724/776-1615
E-mail: customerservice@sae.org
Internet: http://www.sae.org/
students/scholarships
AMOUNT: $6,000
DEADLINE(S): DEC 1
FIELD(S): Engineering; Automotive
Industry
ELIGIBILITY/REQUIREMENTS: Must
be an incoming freshman. Based on
ACT/SAT scores, high school GPA (90 or
3.5 minimum), and extracurricular activities.
HOW TO APPLY: See website for application. Submit with personal essay that
demonstrates hands-on experience or
activity (such as rebuilding engines, work-

ing on cars/trucks, etc.); 2 recommendations, 1 of which must be from a teacher,
counselor, or administrator; and transcript.
Students must complete an interview
(either on- or off-campus) by March 1 of
senior year of high school.
NUMBER OF AWARDS: 8
RENEWABLE: Yes. Up to 4 years provided student remains in good academic
standing and is enrolled full time.

2766—SOCIETY OF AUTOMOTIVE ENGINEERS (Detroit Section SAE Technical Scholarship)

SAE Customer Service
400 Commonwealth Drive
Warrendale PA 15096-0001
724/776-4970
FAX: 724/776-1615
E-mail: customerservice@sae.org
Internet: http://www.sae.org/
students/scholarships
AMOUNT: $2,500
DEADLINE(S): DEC 1
FIELD(S): Automotive Industry
Engineering; Science
ELIGIBILITY/REQUIREMENTS: Must
be child or grandchild of a current SAE
Detroit Section member and intend to
enroll in a 2- or 4-year engineering or science program at an accredited college or
university. A minimum 3.0 GPA and 1200
SAT or 28 ACT composite score and
demonstrated financial need are required.
Must be entering freshman or transfer student who has completed a 2-year program.
HOW TO APPLY: See website for application. Submit with copies of FAFSA
forms; a personal essay that demonstrates
hands-on experience or activity (such as
rebuilding engines, working on cars/trucks,
etc.); 2 recommendations, 1 of which must
be from a teacher, counselor, or administrator; and transcript.
NUMBER OF AWARDS: 1
RENEWABLE: Yes. A total of $10,000
(over 4-year period) will be awarded if student maintains 2.5 GPA and remains in
good standing.

2767—SOCIETY OF AUTOMOTIVE ENGINEERS (Drexel University/SAE Engineering Scholarship)

SAE Customer Service
400 Commonwealth Drive
Warrendale PA 15096-0001
724/776-4970
FAX: 724/776-1615
E-mail: customerservice@sae.org
Internet: http://www.sae.org/

students/scholarships
AMOUNT: $5,000
DEADLINE(S): DEC 1
FIELD(S): Mechanical Engineering;
Automotive Industry
ELIGIBILITY/REQUIREMENTS: Must be an incoming freshman enrolled in Mechanical Engineering program. Must have a minimum 1200 SAT or 27 ACT score and a 3.0 GPA.
HOW TO APPLY: See website for application. Submit with personal essay that demonstrates hands-on experience or activity (such as rebuilding engines, working on cars/trucks, etc.); 2 recommendations, 1 of which must be from a teacher, counselor, or administrator; and transcript.
NUMBER OF AWARDS: 1
RENEWABLE: Yes. For 1 additional year if 3.0 GPA is maintained and student remains in the engineering program.

2768—SOCIETY OF AUTOMOTIVE ENGINEERS (Edward D. Hendrickson/SAE Engineering Scholarship)

SAE Customer Service
400 Commonwealth Drive
Warrendale PA 15096-0001
724/776-4970
FAX: 724/776-1615
E-mail: customerservice@sae.org
Internet: http://www.sae.org/
students/scholarships
AMOUNT: $1,000
DEADLINE(S): DEC 1
FIELD(S): Automotive Industry,
Engineering
ELIGIBILITY/REQUIREMENTS: Must have 3.75 GPA, rank in the 90th percentile in both math and verbal on SAT or the composite ACT scores, and pursue an engineering degree program accredited by ABET.
HOW TO APPLY: See website for application. Submit with personal essay; 2 recommendations, 1 of which must be from a teacher, counselor, or administrator; and transcript.
NUMBER OF AWARDS: 1
RENEWABLE: Yes. A total of $4,000 (over 4-year period) if student maintains 3.0 GPA and continued enrollment.

2769—SOCIETY OF AUTOMOTIVE ENGINEERS (Embry-Riddle Aeronautical University Scholarship-Daytona Beach)

SAE Customer Service
400 Commonwealth Drive
Warrendale PA 15096-0001
724/776-4970
FAX: 724/776-1615

E-mail: customerservice@sae.org
Internet: http://www.sae.org/
students/scholarships
AMOUNT: $5,000
DEADLINE(S): DEC 1
FIELD(S): Engineering; Automotive
Industry; Aviation Industry
ELIGIBILITY/REQUIREMENTS: Must be an incoming freshman pursuing a degree in the College of Engineering. Must have a minimum 1300 SAT or 30 ACT score and a 3.5 GPA and involvement in high school activities.
HOW TO APPLY: See website for application. Submit with personal essay that demonstrates hands-on experience or activity (such as rebuilding engines, working on cars/trucks, etc.); 2 recommendations, 1 of which must be from a teacher, counselor, or administrator; and transcript.
NUMBER OF AWARDS: 1
RENEWABLE: Yes. For 1 additional year if 3.0 GPA is maintained and student remains in the engineering program.

2770—SOCIETY OF AUTOMOTIVE ENGINEERS (Fred M. Young Sr./SAE Engineering Scholarship)

SAE Customer Service
400 Commonwealth Drive
Warrendale PA 15096-0001
724/776-4970
FAX: 724/776-1615
E-mail: customerservice@sae.org
Internet: http://www.sae.org/
students/scholarships
AMOUNT: $1,000
DEADLINE(S): DEC 1
FIELD(S): Automotive Industry,
Engineering
ELIGIBILITY/REQUIREMENTS: Applicants must have 3.75 GPA, rank in the 90th percentile in both math and verbal on SAT or the composite ACT scores, and pursue an engineering degree program accredited by ABET.
HOW TO APPLY: See website for application. Submit with personal essay that demonstrates hands-on experience or activity (such as rebuilding engines, working on cars/trucks, etc.); 2 recommendations, 1 of which must be from a teacher, counselor, or administrator; and transcript.
NUMBER OF AWARDS: 1

2771—SOCIETY OF AUTOMOTIVE ENGINEERS (Gannon University/SAE Engineering Scholarship)

SAE Customer Service
400 Commonwealth Drive
Warrendale PA 15096-0001

724/776-4970
FAX: 724/776-1615
E-mail: customerservice@sae.org
Internet: http://www.sae.org/
students/scholarships
AMOUNT: $1,000
DEADLINE(S): DEC 1
FIELD(S): Engineering; Automotive
Industry
ELIGIBILITY/REQUIREMENTS: Must be accepted to one of Gannon University's engineering programs. Based on SAT/ACT, rank in class, and GPA.
HOW TO APPLY: See website for application. Submit with personal essay that demonstrates hands-on experience or activity (such as rebuilding engines, working on cars/trucks, etc.); 2 recommendations, 1 of which must be from a teacher, counselor, or administrator; and transcript.
NUMBER OF AWARDS: 1
RENEWABLE: Yes. Up to 3 years if 3.0 GPA is maintained.

2772—SOCIETY OF AUTOMOTIVE ENGINEERS (Geneva College/SAE Engineering Scholarship)

SAE Customer Service
400 Commonwealth Drive
Warrendale PA 15096-0001
724/776-4970
FAX: 724/776-1615
E-mail: customerservice@sae.org
Internet: http://www.sae.org/
students/scholarships
AMOUNT: $2,000
DEADLINE(S): DEC 1
FIELD(S): Engineering; Automotive
Industry
ELIGIBILITY/REQUIREMENTS: Must be incoming freshman who will major in engineering. Based on merit and financial need.
HOW TO APPLY: See website for application. Submit with personal essay that demonstrates hands-on experience or activity (such as rebuilding engines, working on cars/trucks, etc.); 2 recommendations, 1 of which must be from a teacher, counselor, or administrator; and transcript. File FAFSA if application based on financial need.
NUMBER OF AWARDS: 1
RENEWABLE: Yes. Up to 3 years if 3.0 GPA is maintained.

2773—SOCIETY OF AUTOMOTIVE ENGINEERS (Grand Valley State University/Padnos/SAE Engineering Scholarship)

SAE Customer Service

400 Commonwealth Drive
Warrendale PA 15096-0001
724/776-4970
FAX: 724/776-1615
E-mail: customerservice@sae.org
Internet: http://www.sae.org/
students/scholarships
AMOUNT: $1,000
DEADLINE(S): DEC 1
FIELD(S): Engineering; Automotive
Industry
ELIGIBILITY/REQUIREMENTS: Must
be incoming full-time freshman who will
major in engineering.
HOW TO APPLY: See website for application. Submit with personal essay that
demonstrates hands-on experience or
activity (such as rebuilding engines, working on cars/trucks, etc.); 2 recommendations, 1 of which must be from a teacher,
counselor, or administrator; and transcript.
NUMBER OF AWARDS: 1
RENEWABLE: Yes. A total of $4,000
(over 4-year period) will be awarded if student maintains a 3.0 GPA and continued
enrollment in an engineering program.

2774—SOCIETY OF AUTOMOTIVE ENGI-NEERS (Illinois Institute of Technology/SAE Engineering Scholarship)

SAE Customer Service
400 Commonwealth Drive
Warrendale PA 15096-0001
724/776-4970
FAX: 724/776-1615
E-mail: customerservice@sae.org
Internet: http://www.sae.org/
students/scholarships
AMOUNT: Half tuition
DEADLINE(S): DEC 1
FIELD(S): Engineering; Automotive
Industry
ELIGIBILITY/REQUIREMENTS: Must
be incoming full-time freshman who will
major in engineering. Based on test scores,
GPA, activities, community service, and
work experience.
HOW TO APPLY: See website for application. Submit with personal essay that
demonstrates hands-on experience or
activity (such as rebuilding engines, working on cars/trucks, etc.); 2 recommendations, 1 of which must be from a teacher,
counselor, or administrator; and transcript.
NUMBER OF AWARDS: 5
RENEWABLE: Yes. Up to 4 years upon
satisfactory academic performance.

2775—SOCIETY OF AUTOMOTIVE ENGI-NEERS (Iowa State University/SAE Engineering Scholarship)

SAE Customer Service

400 Commonwealth Drive
Warrendale PA 15096-0001
724/776-4970
FAX: 724/776-1615
E-mail: customerservice@sae.org
Internet: http://www.sae.org/
students/scholarships
AMOUNT: $1,000
DEADLINE(S): DEC 1
FIELD(S): Engineering; Automotive
Industry
ELIGIBILITY/REQUIREMENTS: Must
be incoming freshman pursuing a degree in
the College of Engineering with an interest
in automotive engineering applications.
Applicants should have ACT math scores
of 26 or above or equivalent SAT scores,
and rank in top 20% of high school class.
HOW TO APPLY: See website for application. Submit with personal essay that
demonstrates hands-on experience or
activity (such as rebuilding engines, working on cars/trucks, etc.); 2 recommendations, 1 of which must be from a teacher,
counselor, or administrator; and transcript.
NUMBER OF AWARDS: 1
RENEWABLE: No

2776—SOCIETY OF AUTOMOTIVE ENGI-NEERS (John Deere and Bradley University/SAE Engineering Scholarships)

SAE Customer Service
400 Commonwealth Drive
Warrendale PA 15096-0001
724/776-4970
FAX: 724/776-1615
E-mail: customerservice@sae.org
Internet: http://www.sae.org/
students/scholarships
AMOUNT: $1,250
DEADLINE(S): DEC 1
FIELD(S): Mechanical Engineering;
Electrical Engineering; Computer,
Industrial, or Manufacturing
Engineering; Automotive Industry
ELIGIBILITY/REQUIREMENTS: Must
be incoming freshman accepted into the
College of Engineering and Technology at
Bradley. Selection is based on high school
GPA, rank in class, curriculum and
SAT/ACT scores (minimum 980 SAT or
21 ACT composite score), and 3.25 GPA.
HOW TO APPLY: See website for appli-
cation. Submit with personal essay that
demonstrates hands-on experience or
activity (such as rebuilding engines, work-
ing on cars/trucks, etc.); 2 recommendations, 1 of which must be from a teacher,
counselor, or administrator; and transcript.
NUMBER OF AWARDS: Varies
RENEWABLE: Yes. A total of $5,000 (4-
year period) if student remains enrolled in

one of the specified majors and maintains a
3.0 GPA.

2777—SOCIETY OF AUTOMOTIVE ENGI-NEERS (Kansas State University [Manhattan]/SAE Engineering Scholarship)

SAE Customer Service
400 Commonwealth Drive
Warrendale PA 15096-0001
724/776-4970
FAX: 724/776-1615
E-mail: customerservice@sae.org
Internet: http://www.sae.org/
students/scholarships
AMOUNT: $1,000
DEADLINE(S): DEC 1
FIELD(S): Engineering; Automotive
Industry
ELIGIBILITY/REQUIREMENTS: Must
be incoming freshman pursuing a degree in
the College of Engineering; ACT scores of
30 composite, 3.5 GPA, and rank in top
10% of high school class.
HOW TO APPLY: See website for application. Submit with personal essay that
demonstrates hands-on experience or
activity (such as rebuilding engines, working on cars/trucks, etc.); 2 recommendations, 1 of which must be from a teacher,
counselor, or administrator; and transcript.
NUMBER OF AWARDS: 1
RENEWABLE: Yes. Up to 4 years; a 3.5
GPA must be maintained.

2778—SOCIETY OF AUTOMOTIVE ENGI-NEERS (Kansas State University-Salina/SAE Engineering Scholarship)

SAE Customer Service
400 Commonwealth Drive
Warrendale PA 15096-0001
724/776-4970
FAX: 724/776-1615
E-mail: customerservice@sae.org
Internet: http://www.sae.org/
students/scholarships
AMOUNT: $1,000
DEADLINE(S): DEC 1
FIELD(S): Engineering; Automotive
Industry; Aviation Industry
ELIGIBILITY/REQUIREMENTS: Must
be incoming freshman pursuing a degree in
the College of Technology & Aviation.
Must have ACT scores of 21 composite or
950 SAT, or 3.2 GPA.
HOW TO APPLY: See website for appli-
cation. Submit with personal essay that
demonstrates hands-on experience or
activity (such as rebuilding engines, working on cars/trucks, etc.); 2 recommenda-

tions, 1 of which must be from a teacher, counselor, or administrator; and transcript.
NUMBER OF AWARDS: 5
RENEWABLE: Yes. Up to 4 years if student maintains 3.5 GPA and continued enrollment in College of Technology and Aviation.

2779—SOCIETY OF AUTOMOTIVE ENGINEERS (Kettering University/SAE Engineering Scholarship)

SAE Customer Service
400 Commonwealth Drive
Warrendale PA 15096-0001
724/776-4970
FAX: 724/776-1615
E-mail: customerservice@sae.org
Internet: http://www.sae.org/students/scholarships
AMOUNT: $5,000
DEADLINE(S): DEC 1
FIELD(S): Engineering; Automotive Industry
ELIGIBILITY/REQUIREMENTS: High school juniors and seniors as well as high school graduates entering college for the first time are eligible.
HOW TO APPLY: See website for application. Submit with personal essay that demonstrates hands-on experience or activity (such as rebuilding engines, working on cars/trucks, etc.); 2 recommendations, 1 of which must be from a teacher, counselor, or administrator; and transcript.
NUMBER OF AWARDS: 5
RENEWABLE: Yes. Up to 4 years.

2780—SOCIETY OF AUTOMOTIVE ENGINEERS (Lawrence Technological University/SAE Engineering Scholarship)

SAE Customer Service
400 Commonwealth Drive
Warrendale PA 15096-0001
724/776-4970
FAX: 724/776-1615
E-mail: customerservice@sae.org
Internet: http://www.sae.org/students/scholarships
AMOUNT: $2,000
DEADLINE(S): DEC 1
FIELD(S): Engineering; Automotive Industry
ELIGIBILITY/REQUIREMENTS: Must be incoming freshmen who intend to major in engineering. Based on high school grades and ACT or SAT scores.
HOW TO APPLY: See website for application. Submit with personal essay that demonstrates hands-on experience or activity (such as rebuilding engines, working on cars/trucks, etc.); 2 recommenda-

tions, 1 of which must be from a teacher, counselor, or administrator; and transcript.
NUMBER OF AWARDS: 5
RENEWABLE: Yes. Up to 4 years with GPA of 3.0.

2781—SOCIETY OF AUTOMOTIVE ENGINEERS (Mary Baldwin College/SAE Engineering Scholarship)

SAE Customer Service
400 Commonwealth Drive
Warrendale PA 15096-0001
724/776-4970
FAX: 724/776-1615
E-mail: customerservice@sae.org
Internet: http://www.sae.org/students/scholarships
AMOUNT: $6,100-$9,000
DEADLINE(S): DEC 1
FIELD(S): Engineering; Automotive Industry
ELIGIBILITY/REQUIREMENTS: Must be pursuing admission to the Mary Baldwin College or University of Virginia Cooperative Program in Engineering, and have a minimum 1050 SAT or 23 ACT score, and at least a 3.0 GPA. Amount awarded will be based on the combination of SAT/ACT scores and GPA.
HOW TO APPLY: See website for application. Submit with personal essay that demonstrates hands-on experience or activity (such as rebuilding engines, working on cars/trucks, etc.); 2 recommendations, 1 of which must be from a teacher, counselor, or administrator; and transcript.
NUMBER OF AWARDS: Unlimited
RENEWABLE: Yes. Up to 2 additional years with GPA of 3.0.

2782—SOCIETY OF AUTOMOTIVE ENGINEERS (Mercer University/SAE Engineering Scholarship)

SAE Customer Service
400 Commonwealth Drive
Warrendale PA 15096-0001
724/776-4970
FAX: 724/776-1615
E-mail: customerservice@sae.org
Internet: http://www.sae.org/students/scholarships
AMOUNT: $2,500
DEADLINE(S): DEC 1
FIELD(S): Engineering; Automotive Industry
ELIGIBILITY/REQUIREMENTS: Incoming freshman majoring in engineering with an SAT score of 1400 or better or an ACT score of 31 or greater in both English and math, and a high school GPA of 3.7 or greater.

HOW TO APPLY: See website for application. Submit with personal essay that demonstrates hands-on experience or activity (such as rebuilding engines, working on cars/trucks, etc.); 2 recommendations, 1 of which must be from a teacher, counselor, or administrator; and transcript.
NUMBER OF AWARDS: 1
RENEWABLE: Yes. Up to 3 additional years.

2783—SOCIETY OF AUTOMOTIVE ENGINEERS (Miami University-Ohio/The Ken Shinn/SAE Engineering Scholarship)

SAE Customer Service
400 Commonwealth Drive
Warrendale PA 15096-0001
724/776-4970
FAX: 724/776-1615
E-mail: customerservice@sae.org
Internet: http://www.sae.org/students/scholarships
AMOUNT: $1,000
DEADLINE(S): DEC 1
FIELD(S): Engineering; Automotive Industry
ELIGIBILITY/REQUIREMENTS: Must be high school senior, intending to pursue studies in Manufacturing Engineering or Mechanical Engineering. Based on SAT and/or ACT scores, high school GPA, and extracurricular activities.
HOW TO APPLY: See website for application. Submit with personal essay that demonstrates hands-on experience or activity (such as rebuilding engines, working on cars/trucks, etc.); 2 recommendations, 1 of which must be from a teacher, counselor, or administrator; and transcript.
NUMBER OF AWARDS: 1
RENEWABLE: No

2784—SOCIETY OF AUTOMOTIVE ENGINEERS (Michigan State University/SAE Engineering Scholarship)

SAE Customer Service
400 Commonwealth Drive
Warrendale PA 15096-0001
724/776-4970
FAX: 724/776-1615
E-mail: customerservice@sae.org
Internet: http://www.sae.org/students/scholarships
AMOUNT: $1,500
DEADLINE(S): DEC 1
FIELD(S): Engineering; Automotive Industry
ELIGIBILITY/REQUIREMENTS: Must be incoming freshman who will be pursuing a degree in the College of Engineering; must have a strong interest in the automo-

tive industry. Based on high school grades, ACT or SAT scores, and quality of essay in relation to student's goals.
HOW TO APPLY: See website for application. Submit with personal essay that demonstrates hands-on experience or activity (such as rebuilding engines, working on cars/trucks, etc.); 2 recommendations, 1 of which must be from a teacher, counselor, or administrator; and transcript.
NUMBER OF AWARDS: 1
RENEWABLE: No

2785—SOCIETY OF AUTOMOTIVE ENGINEERS (Minnesota State University-Mankato/SAE Automotive Technology Scholarship)

SAE Customer Service
400 Commonwealth Drive
Warrendale PA 15096-0001
724/776-4970
FAX: 724/776-1615
E-mail: customerservice@sae.org
Internet: http://www.sae.org/students/scholarships
AMOUNT: $750
DEADLINE(S): DEC 1
FIELD(S): Automotive Engineering Technology
ELIGIBILITY/REQUIREMENTS: Must be incoming freshman planning on a major in Automotive Engineering Technology. Based on merit.
HOW TO APPLY: See website for application. Submit with personal essay that demonstrates hands-on experience or activity (such as rebuilding engines, working on cars/trucks, etc.); 2 recommendations, 1 of which must be from a teacher, counselor, or administrator; and transcript.
NUMBER OF AWARDS: 2
RENEWABLE: Yes, must reapply.

2786—SOCIETY OF AUTOMOTIVE ENGINEERS (Oakland University/SAE Engineering Scholarship)

SAE Customer Service
400 Commonwealth Drive
Warrendale PA 15096-0001
724/776-4970
FAX: 724/776-1615
E-mail: customerservice@sae.org
Internet: http://www.sae.org/students/scholarships
AMOUNT: $1,000
DEADLINE(S): DEC 1
FIELD(S): Engineering; Computer Science; Automotive Industry
ELIGIBILITY/REQUIREMENTS: Must be incoming freshman who will be pursu-

ing a degree in the School of Engineering and Computer Science.
HOW TO APPLY: See website for application. Submit with personal essay that demonstrates hands-on experience or activity (such as rebuilding engines, working on cars/trucks, etc.); 2 recommendations, 1 of which must be from a teacher, counselor, or administrator; and transcript.
NUMBER OF AWARDS: 1
RENEWABLE: No

2787—SOCIETY OF AUTOMOTIVE ENGINEERS (Ohio Northern University/SAE Engineering Scholarship)

SAE Customer Service
400 Commonwealth Drive
Warrendale PA 15096-0001
724/776-4970
FAX: 724/776-1615
E-mail: customerservice@sae.org
Internet: http://www.sae.org/students/scholarships
AMOUNT: $1,000
DEADLINE(S): DEC 1
FIELD(S): Mechanical Engineering; Automotive Industry
ELIGIBILITY/REQUIREMENTS: Must be high school seniors intending to pursue a degree in mechanical engineering on a full-time basis, who have been admitted to the College of Engineering. Must have a minimum 1230 SAT or 27 ACT composite score, and a 3.5 GPA. Recipient is expected to participate in and, it is hoped, assume a leadership role with the student branch of SAE at ONU.
HOW TO APPLY: See website for application. Submit with personal essay that demonstrates hands-on experience or activity (such as rebuilding engines, working on cars/trucks, etc.); 2 recommendations, 1 of which must be from a teacher, counselor, or administrator; and transcript.
NUMBER OF AWARDS: 1
RENEWABLE: Yes. Must maintain a cumulative GPA of 3.0 and remain enrolled full time in the mechanical engineering program.

2788—SOCIETY OF AUTOMOTIVE ENGINEERS (Ohio State University/Motor-sports Team/SAE Engineering Scholarship)

SAE Customer Service
400 Commonwealth Drive
Warrendale PA 15096-0001
724/776-4970
FAX: 724/776-1615
E-mail: customerservice@sae.org
Internet: http://www.sae.org/students/scholarships

AMOUNT: $500
DEADLINE(S): DEC 1
FIELD(S): Engineering; Automotive Industry
ELIGIBILITY/REQUIREMENTS: Incoming (first-year or transfer) students. Based on demonstrated potential to contribute to the success of OSU's motorsports teams. Prior participation in successful team efforts, technical aptitude, leadership potential, and a solid record are considered.
HOW TO APPLY: See website for application. Submit with personal essay that demonstrates hands-on experience or activity (such as rebuilding engines, working on cars/trucks, etc.); 2 recommendations, 1 of which must be from a teacher, counselor, or administrator; and transcript.
NUMBER OF AWARDS: Up to 3
RENEWABLE: No

2789—SOCIETY OF AUTOMOTIVE ENGINEERS (Oklahoma State University-CEAT/SAE Engineering Scholarship)

SAE Customer Service
400 Commonwealth Drive
Warrendale PA 15096-0001
724/776-4970
FAX: 724/776-1615
E-mail: customerservice@sae.org
Internet: http://www.sae.org/students/scholarships
AMOUNT: $1,000
DEADLINE(S): DEC 1
FIELD(S): Mechanical, Electrical & Industrial Engineering
ELIGIBILITY/REQUIREMENTS: High school graduates with a 3.8 or greater GPA and an ACT of 30 (SAT 1350) or above who plan to major in mechanical, electrical, or industrial engineering.
HOW TO APPLY: See website for application. Submit with personal essay demonstrating hands-on experience or activity (such as rebuilding engines, working on cars/trucks, etc.); 2 recommendations, 1 of which must be from a teacher, counselor, or administrator; and transcript.
NUMBER OF AWARDS: 1
RENEWABLE: Yes. For 3 additional years.

2790—SOCIETY OF AUTOMOTIVE ENGINEERS (Pittsburgh State University-Kansas/SAE Automotive Technology Scholarship)

SAE Customer Service
400 Commonwealth Drive
Warrendale PA 15096-0001
724/776-4970

FAX: 724/776-1615
E-mail: customerservice@sae.org
Internet: http://www.sae.org/
students/scholarships
AMOUNT: $1,500
DEADLINE(S): DEC 1
FIELD(S): Engineering; Automotive Industry
ELIGIBILITY/REQUIREMENTS: Zero-hour freshmen must be in upper 20% of high school graduating class. College transfers must have a 3.5 GPA.
HOW TO APPLY: See website for application. Submit with personal essay that demonstrates hands-on experience or activity (such as rebuilding engines, working on cars/trucks, etc.); 2 recommendations, 1 of which must be from a teacher, counselor, or administrator; and transcript.
NUMBER OF AWARDS: 1
RENEWABLE: Yes. Up to 4 years if 3.5 GPA is maintained and a minimum of 30 hours completed each year.

2791—SOCIETY OF AUTOMOTIVE ENGINEERS (Portland State University/SAE Engineering Scholarship)

SAE Customer Service
400 Commonwealth Drive
Warrendale PA 15096-0001
724/776-4970
FAX: 724/776-1615
E-mail: customerservice@sae.org
Internet: http://www.sae.org/
students/scholarships
AMOUNT: $2,000
DEADLINE(S): DEC 1
FIELD(S): Engineering; Automotive Industry
ELIGIBILITY/REQUIREMENTS: Must be incoming freshmen majoring in engineering. Must have minimum 3.5 GPA.
HOW TO APPLY: See website for application. Submit with personal essay that demonstrates hands-on experience or activity (such as rebuilding engines, working on cars/trucks, etc.); 2 recommendations, 1 of which must be from a teacher, counselor, or administrator; and transcript.
NUMBER OF AWARDS: 1
RENEWABLE: Yes. Up to 4 years if 3.0 GPA and full-time enrollment in an engineering major is maintained.

2792—SOCIETY OF AUTOMOTIVE ENGINEERS (Robert Morris University/SAE Engineering Scholarship)

SAE Customer Service
400 Commonwealth Drive
Warrendale PA 15096-0001

724/776-4970
FAX: 724/776-1615
E-mail: customerservice@sae.org
Internet: http://www.sae.org/
students/scholarships
AMOUNT: $4,000
DEADLINE(S): DEC 1
FIELD(S): Engineering; Automotive Industry
ELIGIBILITY/REQUIREMENTS: Incoming freshmen pursuing a degree in the School of Engineering are eligible. Must have a minimum 1100 SAT or 24 ACT and 3.2 GPA score. Based on merit and financial need.
HOW TO APPLY: See website for application. Submit with personal essay demonstrating hands-on experience or activity (such as rebuilding engines, working on cars/trucks, etc.); 2 recommendations, 1 of which must be from a teacher, counselor, or administrator; and transcript. Must also apply to the school and be accepted by March 1.
NUMBER OF AWARDS: 1
RENEWABLE: Yes. A 3.0 or better GPA required.

2793—SOCIETY OF AUTOMOTIVE ENGINEERS (SAE Women Engineers Committee Scholarship)

SAE Customer Service
400 Commonwealth Drive
Warrendale PA 15096-0001
724/776-4970
FAX: 724/776-1615
E-mail: customerservice@sae.org
Internet: http://www.sae.org/
students/scholarships
AMOUNT: $1,500
DEADLINE(S): DEC 1
FIELD(S): Automotive Industry, Engineering
ELIGIBILITY/REQUIREMENTS: Applicants must be female, entering freshman year, have 3.0 GPA, and pursue an engineering degree program accredited by ABET.
HOW TO APPLY: See website for application. Submit with personal essay; 2 recommendations, 1 of which must be from a teacher, counselor, or administrator; and transcript.
NUMBER OF AWARDS: 1
RENEWABLE: No

2794—SOCIETY OF AUTOMOTIVE ENGINEERS (Saginaw Valley State University/Cardinal Racing/SAE Engineering Scholarship)

SAE Customer Service

400 Commonwealth Drive
Warrendale PA 15096-0001
724/776-4970
FAX: 724/776-1615
E-mail: customerservice@sae.org
Internet: http://www.sae.org/
students/scholarships
AMOUNT: $1,000
DEADLINE(S): DEC 1
FIELD(S): Engineering; Automotive Industry
ELIGIBILITY/REQUIREMENTS: Incoming (first-year or transfer) engineering students are eligible. Based on potential to contribute to SVSU Cardinal racing teams. Prior participation in successful team efforts, technical aptitude, leadership potential, and a solid academic record.
HOW TO APPLY: See website for application. Submit with personal essay that demonstrates hands-on experience or activity (such as rebuilding engines, working on cars/trucks, etc.); 2 recommendations, 1 of which must be from a teacher, counselor, or administrator; and transcript.
NUMBER OF AWARDS: 1
RENEWABLE: No

2795—SOCIETY OF AUTOMOTIVE ENGINEERS (Southern Illinois University-Carbondale/SAE Engineering Scholarship)

SAE Customer Service
400 Commonwealth Drive
Warrendale PA 15096-0001
724/776-4970
FAX: 724/776-1615
E-mail: customerservice@sae.org
Internet: http://www.sae.org/
students/scholarships
AMOUNT: $1,000
DEADLINE(S): DEC 1
FIELD(S): Engineering; Automotive Industry
ELIGIBILITY/REQUIREMENTS: Incoming freshmen admitted to any of the undergraduate degree programs in the College of Engineering. Selection based on a minimum 25 ACT or 1140 SAT scores, minimum 25 math ACT or 600 SAT math scores, and top 25% class rank or a minimum GPA of 3.4.
HOW TO APPLY: See website for application. Submit application; a personal essay that demonstrates hands-on experience or activity (such as rebuilding engines, working on cars/trucks, etc.); 2 recommendations, 1 of which must be from a teacher, counselor, or administrator; and transcript.
NUMBER OF AWARDS: 3
RENEWABLE: No

2796—SOCIETY OF AUTOMOTIVE ENGINEERS (Southern Illinois University-Carbondale/Women Engineer/SAE Engineering Scholarship)

SAE Customer Service
400 Commonwealth Drive
Warrendale PA 15096-0001
724/776-4970
FAX: 724/776-1615
E-mail: customerservice@sae.org
Internet: http://www.sae.org/students/scholarships
AMOUNT: $1,000
DEADLINE(S): DEC 1
FIELD(S): Engineering; Automotive Industry
ELIGIBILITY/REQUIREMENTS: Incoming female freshmen admitted to any of the undergraduate degree programs in the College of Engineering. Selection based on a minimum 25 ACT or 1140 SAT scores, minimum 25 ACT math or 600 SAT math scores, and top 25% class rank or a minimum GPA of 3.4.
HOW TO APPLY: See website for application. Submit application; a personal essay that demonstrates hands-on experience or activity (such as rebuilding engines, working on cars/trucks, etc.); 2 recommendations, 1 of which must be from a teacher, counselor, or administrator; and transcript.
NUMBER OF AWARDS: 3
RENEWABLE: No

2797—SOCIETY OF AUTOMOTIVE ENGINEERS (SUNY-Buffalo/James & Nancy McLernon/SAE Engineering Scholarship)

SAE Customer Service
400 Commonwealth Drive
Warrendale PA 15096-0001
724/776-4970
FAX: 724/776-1615
E-mail: customerservice@sae.org
Internet: http://www.sae.org/students/scholarships
AMOUNT: $1,000
DEADLINE(S): DEC 1
FIELD(S): Engineering; Automotive Industry
ELIGIBILITY/REQUIREMENTS: Must have a minimum 30 ACT or 1300 SAT score; GPA of 3.5 or higher, and be enrolled in an engineering program. School and civic honors and activities and employment record are considered.
HOW TO APPLY: See website for application. Submit with personal essay that demonstrates hands-on experience or activity (such as rebuilding engines, work-

ing on cars/trucks, etc.); 2 recommendations, 1 of which must be from a teacher, counselor, or administrator; and transcript.
NUMBER OF AWARDS: 3
RENEWABLE: Yes. For 4 years provided student maintains a record of academic excellence and demonstrates leadership.

2798—SOCIETY OF AUTOMOTIVE ENGINEERS (Tau Beta Pi/SAE Engineering Scholarship)

SAE Customer Service
400 Commonwealth Drive
Warrendale PA 15096-0001
724/776-4970
FAX: 724/776-1615
E-mail: customerservice@sae.org
Internet: http://www.sae.org/students/scholarships
AMOUNT: $1,000
DEADLINE(S): DEC 1
FIELD(S): Automotive Industry, Engineering
ELIGIBILITY/REQUIREMENTS: Must be entering freshman, have 3.75 GPA, rank in the 90th percentile in both math and verbal on SAT or the composite ACT scores, and pursue an engineering degree program accredited by ABET.
HOW TO APPLY: See website for application. Submit with personal essay; 2 recommendations, 1 of which must be from a teacher, counselor, or administrator; and transcript.
NUMBER OF AWARDS: 6
RENEWABLE: No

2799—SOCIETY OF AUTOMOTIVE ENGINEERS (TMC/SAE Donald D. Dawson Technical Scholarship)

SAE Customer Service
400 Commonwealth Drive
Warrendale PA 15096-0001
724/776-4970
FAX: 724/776-1615
E-mail: customerservice@sae.org
Internet: http://www.sae.org/students/scholarships
AMOUNT: $1,500
DEADLINE(S): DEC 1
FIELD(S): Automotive Industry, Engineering
ELIGIBILITY/REQUIREMENTS: Must have 3.25 GPA or higher, SAT math 600 or above and verbal 550 or above, composite ACT score 27 or above. Transfer students from accredited 4-year colleges or universities must have a 3.0 or higher GPA. Students or graduates from postsecondary technical/vocational schools must have a

3.5 or higher GPA and must meet all other requirements of the engineering program to which they apply. Must pursue an engineering degree program accredited by ABET.
HOW TO APPLY: See website for application. Submit with personal essay that demonstrates hands-on experience or activity (such as rebuilding engines, working on cars/trucks, etc.); 2 recommendations, 1 of which must be from a teacher, counselor, or administrator; and transcript.
NUMBER OF AWARDS: 1
RENEWABLE: Yes. A total of $6,000 (over 4-year period) if student maintains 3.0 GPA and continued enrollment in an engineering program.

2800—SOCIETY OF AUTOMOTIVE ENGINEERS (Universidad del Turabo-Puerto Rico/SAE Engineering Scholarship)

SAE Customer Service
400 Commonwealth Drive
Warrendale PA 15096-0001
724/776-4970
FAX: 724/776-1615
E-mail: customerservice@sae.org
Internet: http://www.sae.org/students/scholarships
AMOUNT: $5,000
DEADLINE(S): DEC 1
FIELD(S): Engineering; Automotive Industry
ELIGIBILITY/REQUIREMENTS: Open to incoming freshmen who have been accepted into Electrical, Mechanical, or Industrial program; minimum 1300 SAT score and 3.0 GPA and activities.
HOW TO APPLY: See website for application. Submit with personal essay that demonstrates hands-on experience or activity (such as rebuilding engines, working on cars/trucks, etc.); 2 recommendations, 1 of which must be from a teacher, counselor, or administrator; and transcript.
NUMBER OF AWARDS: 2
RENEWABLE: Yes. For 4 or 5 years provided student is enrolled full time in the Mechanical, Electrical, or Industrial Engineering program and maintains 3.0 GPA.

2801—SOCIETY OF AUTOMOTIVE ENGINEERS (University of Alabama/James C. Lewis/SAE Engineering Scholarship)

SAE Customer Service
400 Commonwealth Drive
Warrendale PA 15096-0001
724/776-4970
FAX: 724/776-1615
E-mail: customerservice@sae.org

Internet: http://www.sae.org/
students/scholarships
AMOUNT: $1,000
DEADLINE(S): DEC 1
FIELD(S): Mechanical Engineering;
   Automotive Industry
ELIGIBILITY/REQUIREMENTS: Must
be admitted to the College of Engineering
with a major in mechanical engineering;
minimum ACT of 27 and minimum academic GPA of 3.5. Based on academic performance, extracurricular activities, and
essay.
HOW TO APPLY: See website for application. Submit with copies of FAFSA
forms; a personal essay that demonstrates
hands-on experience or activity (such as
rebuilding engines, working on cars/trucks,
etc.); 2 recommendations, 1 of which must
be from a teacher, counselor, or administrator; and transcript.
NUMBER OF AWARDS: 1
RENEWABLE: Yes. A total of $4,000
(over 4-year period) if student maintains a
minimum 3.0 GPA and continued enrollment in Mechanical Engineering.

2802—SOCIETY OF AUTOMOTIVE ENGI-NEERS (University of Arkansas/SAE Engineering Scholarship)

SAE Customer Service
400 Commonwealth Drive
Warrendale PA 15096-0001
724/776-4970
FAX: 724/776-1615
E-mail: customerservice@sae.org
Internet: http://www.sae.org/
students/scholarships
AMOUNT: $500
DEADLINE(S): DEC 1
FIELD(S): Mechanical Engineering;
   Automotive Industry
ELIGIBILITY/REQUIREMENTS: Must
be high school seniors seeking a degree in
mechanical engineering. Based on the merits of SAT or ACT scores, high school
GPA, and extracurricular activities.
HOW TO APPLY: See website for application. Submit with personal essay that
demonstrates hands-on experience or
activity (such as rebuilding engines, working on cars/trucks, etc.); 2 recommendations, 1 of which must be from a teacher,
counselor, or administrator; and transcript.
NUMBER OF AWARDS: 1
RENEWABLE: Yes. A total of $2,000
(over 4-year period) if student maintains
reasonable progress toward degree.

2803—SOCIETY OF AUTOMOTIVE ENGI-NEERS (University of Bridgeport/SAE Engineering Scholarships)

SAE Customer Service

400 Commonwealth Drive
Warrendale PA 15096-0001
724/776-4970
FAX: 724/776-1615
E-mail: customerservice@sae.org
Internet: http://www.sae.org/
students/scholarships
AMOUNT: $9,000
DEADLINE(S): DEC 1
FIELD(S): Computer Science &
   Engineering; Mathematics;
   Automotive Industry
ELIGIBILITY/REQUIREMENTS: Open
to high school seniors entering as freshmen
pursuing a bachelor's degree; must have a
minimum 3.0 GPA and 1100 SAT or 24
ACT composite.
HOW TO APPLY: See website for appli-
cation. Submit with personal essay that
demonstrates hands-on experience or
activity (such as rebuilding engines, working on cars/trucks, etc.); 2 recommendations, 1 of which must be from a teacher,
counselor, or administrator; and transcript.
Must also apply to the University of
Bridgeport and submit the appropriate
attachments, in addition to SAE submission.
NUMBER OF AWARDS: 3
RENEWABLE: Yes. Up to $36,000 (4-
year period); must be in good standing and
maintain a 3.0 GPA.

2804—SOCIETY OF AUTOMOTIVE ENGI-NEERS (University of Cincinnati/College of Applied Science Alumni/SAE Engineering Scholarship)

SAE Customer Service
400 Commonwealth Drive
Warrendale PA 15096-0001
724/776-4970
FAX: 724/776-1615
E-mail: customerservice@sae.org
Internet: http://www.sae.org/
students/scholarships
AMOUNT: $1,000
DEADLINE(S): DEC 1
FIELD(S): Manufacturing Engineering;
   Industrial Technology; Automotive
   Industry
ELIGIBILITY/REQUIREMENTS: Must
be an incoming freshman, accepted to
either the Mechanical or Manufacturing
Engineering Technology degree program
at the College of Applied Science.
Selection criteria include ACT/SAT
scores, GPA, and academic and leadership
achievements.
HOW TO APPLY: See website for appli-
cation. Submit with personal essay that
demonstrates hands-on experience or
activity (such as rebuilding engines, work-

ing on cars/trucks, etc.); 2 recommendations, 1 of which must be from a teacher,
counselor, or administrator; and transcript.
NUMBER OF AWARDS: 2
RENEWABLE: Yes. For up to 4 years if
3.2 GPA is maintained.

2805—SOCIETY OF AUTOMOTIVE ENGI-NEERS (University of Detroit Mercy/SAE Engineering Scholarship)

SAE Customer Service
400 Commonwealth Drive
Warrendale PA 15096-0001
724/776-4970
FAX: 724/776-1615
E-mail: customerservice@sae.org
Internet: http://www.sae.org/
students/scholarships
AMOUNT: $500
DEADLINE(S): DEC 1
FIELD(S): Engineering; Automotive
   Industry
ELIGIBILITY/REQUIREMENTS: Must
be an incoming freshman or transfer student admitted directly into an engineering
program at UDM. Selection based on academic and leadership achievement.
HOW TO APPLY: See website for application. Submit with personal essay that
demonstrates hands-on experience or
activity (such as rebuilding engines, working on cars/trucks, etc.); 2 recommendations, 1 of which must be from a teacher,
counselor, or administrator; and transcript.
NUMBER OF AWARDS: 2
RENEWABLE: Yes. For 1 additional year
if a 3.0 GPA is maintained and student
remains in the engineering program.

2806—SOCIETY OF AUTOMOTIVE ENGI-NEERS (University of Evansville/John R. Tooley Scholarship)

SAE Customer Service
400 Commonwealth Drive
Warrendale PA 15096-0001
724/776-4970
FAX: 724/776-1615
E-mail: customerservice@sae.org
Internet: http://www.sae.org/
students/scholarships
AMOUNT: $1,000
DEADLINE(S): DEC 1
FIELD(S): Engineering; Automotive
   Industry
ELIGIBILITY/REQUIREMENTS: Must
be an incoming freshman pursuing a
degree in the School of Engineering.
Scholarships awarded on the basis of aca-
demic achievement and involvement in
extracurricular activities. A minimum 1200

SAT or 27 ACT, and 3.5 high school GPA required.
HOW TO APPLY: See website for application. Submit with personal essay that demonstrates hands-on experience or activity (such as rebuilding engines, working on cars/trucks, etc.); 2 recommendations, 1 of which must be from a teacher, counselor, or administrator; and transcript.
NUMBER OF AWARDS: 3
RENEWABLE: Yes. For 3 additional years if cumulative 3.0 GPA is maintained and student remains in the engineering program.

2807—SOCIETY OF AUTOMOTIVE ENGINEERS (University of Florida/Dean's Engineering Scholar/SAE Engineering Scholarship)

SAE Customer Service
400 Commonwealth Drive
Warrendale PA 15096-0001
724/776-4970
FAX: 724/776-1615
E-mail: customerservice@sae.org
Internet: http://www.sae.org/students/scholarships
AMOUNT: $1,000
DEADLINE(S): DEC 1
FIELD(S): Engineering; Automotive Industry
ELIGIBILITY/REQUIREMENTS: Must be an incoming freshman pursuing a degree in the School of Engineering.
HOW TO APPLY: See website for application. Submit with personal essay that demonstrates hands-on experience or activity (such as rebuilding engines, working on cars/trucks, etc.); 2 recommendations, 1 of which must be from a teacher, counselor, or administrator; and transcript.
NUMBER OF AWARDS: 1
RENEWABLE: No

2808—SOCIETY OF AUTOMOTIVE ENGINEERS (University of Houston/SAE Engineering Scholarship)

SAE Customer Service
400 Commonwealth Drive
Warrendale PA 15096-0001
724/776-4970
FAX: 724/776-1615
E-mail: customerservice@sae.org
Internet: http://www.sae.org/students/scholarships
AMOUNT: $2,500
DEADLINE(S): DEC 1
FIELD(S): Engineering; Automotive Industry

ELIGIBILITY/REQUIREMENTS: Must be incoming full-time freshman who will major in engineering, have a minimum 1300 SAT or 30 ACT, a GPA of 3.25, and be in the top 10% of high school graduating class.
HOW TO APPLY: See website for application. Submit with personal essay that demonstrates hands-on experience or activity (such as rebuilding engines, working on cars/trucks, etc.); 2 recommendations, 1 of which must be from a teacher, counselor, or administrator; and transcript.
NUMBER OF AWARDS: 2
RENEWABLE: Yes. Up to 4 years provided a 3.0 GPA and engineering enrollment in 12 credit hours each semester is maintained.

2809—SOCIETY OF AUTOMOTIVE ENGINEERS (University of Illinois at Chicago/SAE Engineering Scholarship)

SAE Customer Service
400 Commonwealth Drive
Warrendale PA 15096-0001
724/776-4970
FAX: 724/776-1615
E-mail: customerservice@sae.org
Internet: http://www.sae.org/students/scholarships
AMOUNT: $1,000
DEADLINE(S): DEC 1
FIELD(S): Engineering; Automotive Industry
ELIGIBILITY/REQUIREMENTS: Must be incoming freshman who will be pursuing a degree in the UIC College of Engineering with an interest in the automotive engineering applications. Selection will be based on ACT scores, high school rank, application essay, outside activities and experiences. A minimum ACT composite score of 29 (SAT 1240) is required to apply.
HOW TO APPLY: See website for application. Submit application; a personal essay that demonstrates hands-on experience or activity (such as rebuilding engines, working on cars/trucks, etc.); 2 recommendations, 1 of which must be from a teacher, counselor, or administrator; and transcript.
NUMBER OF AWARDS: 2 maximum
RENEWABLE: Yes. Up to 4 years with a GPA of 4.0 (out of 5.0) maintained.

2810—SOCIETY OF AUTOMOTIVE ENGINEERS (University of South Carolina/Frank B. Herty/SAE Engineering Scholarship)

SAE Customer Service

400 Commonwealth Drive
Warrendale PA 15096-0001
724/776-4970
FAX: 724/776-1615
E-mail: customerservice@sae.org
Internet: http://www.sae.org/students/scholarships
AMOUNT: $2,000
DEADLINE(S): DEC 1
FIELD(S): Engineering; Automotive Industry
ELIGIBILITY/REQUIREMENTS: For incoming freshmen accepted into the mechanical engineering program. Based on a minimum 1300 SAT score and 3.0 GPA and activities.
HOW TO APPLY: See website for application. Submit with personal essay that demonstrates hands-on experience or activity (such as rebuilding engines, working on cars/trucks, etc.); 2 recommendations, 1 of which must be from a teacher, counselor, or administrator; and transcript.
NUMBER OF AWARDS: 1
RENEWABLE: Yes. For 3 additional years provided student is enrolled full time in the mechanical engineering program and maintains a minimum 3.0 GPA.

2811—SOCIETY OF AUTOMOTIVE ENGINEERS (University of Tennessee at Chattanooga/Chancellor's Scholarship/SAE Engineering Scholarship)

SAE Customer Service
400 Commonwealth Drive
Warrendale PA 15096-0001
724/776-4970
FAX: 724/776-1615
E-mail: customerservice@sae.org
Internet: http://www.sae.org/students/scholarships
AMOUNT: $6,000
DEADLINE(S): DEC 1
FIELD(S): Engineering; Automotive Industry
ELIGIBILITY/REQUIREMENTS: Open to incoming freshmen; minimum 30 ACT or 1320 SAT score; GPA of 3.75. Must be fully admitted to the university by February 1 of the student's senior year in high school and pursue an engineering major.
HOW TO APPLY: See website for application. Submit with personal essay that demonstrates hands-on experience or activity (such as rebuilding engines, working on cars/trucks, etc.); 2 recommendations, 1 of which must be from a teacher, counselor, or administrator; and transcript.
NUMBER OF AWARDS: Up to 10
RENEWABLE: Yes. Up to 4 years; must maintain minimum 3.5 GPA.

2812—SOCIETY OF AUTOMOTIVE ENGINEERS (University of Tennessee at Chattanooga/Provost Scholarship/SAE Engineering Scholarship)

SAE Customer Service
400 Commonwealth Drive
Warrendale PA 15096-0001
724/776-4970
FAX: 724/776-1615
E-mail: customerservice@sae.org
Internet: http://www.sae.org/
students/scholarships
AMOUNT: $4,500
DEADLINE(S): DEC 1
FIELD(S): Engineering; Automotive
Industry
ELIGIBILITY/REQUIREMENTS: Open
to incoming freshmen with a minimum 26
ACT or 1170 SAT score; GPA of 3.5. Must
be fully admitted to the university by
February 1 of the student's senior year in
high school and pursue an engineering
major.
HOW TO APPLY: See website for application. Submit with personal essay that
demonstrates hands-on experience or
activity (such as rebuilding engines, working on cars/trucks, etc.); 2 recommendations, 1 of which must be from a teacher,
counselor, or administrator; and transcript.
NUMBER OF AWARDS: Up to 25
RENEWABLE: Yes. Up to 4 years; must
maintain minimum 3.5 GPA.

2813—SOCIETY OF AUTOMOTIVE ENGINEERS (University of Wisconsin/Sundstrand/SAE Engineering Scholarship)

SAE Customer Service
400 Commonwealth Drive
Warrendale PA 15096-0001
724/776-4970
FAX: 724/776-1615
E-mail: customerservice@sae.org
Internet: http://www.sae.org/
students/scholarships
AMOUNT: $500
DEADLINE(S): DEC 1
FIELD(S): Mechanical Engineering;
Automotive Industry
ELIGIBILITY/REQUIREMENTS: Must
be high school seniors planning on entering the Mechanical Engineering Program.
Based on merit; minimum requirements:
1100 SAT or 26 ACT and a 3.3 high school
GPA.
HOW TO APPLY: See website for application. Submit with personal essay that
demonstrates hands-on experience or
activity (such as rebuilding engines, working on cars/trucks, etc.); 2 recommenda-

tions, 1 of which must be from a teacher,
counselor, or administrator; and transcript.
Recipient must be accepted into the
College of Engineering and Applied
Science by April 1.
NUMBER OF AWARDS: 1
RENEWABLE: No
CONTACT: UWM Office of Admissions,
P.O. Box 749, Milwaukee, WI 53201

2814—SOCIETY OF AUTOMOTIVE ENGINEERS (University of Wyoming/Mechanical Engineering/SAE Engineering Scholarship)

SAE Customer Service
400 Commonwealth Drive
Warrendale PA 15096-0001
724/776-4970
FAX: 724/776-1615
E-mail: customerservice@sae.org
Internet: http://www.sae.org/
students/scholarships
AMOUNT: $1,000
DEADLINE(S): DEC 1
FIELD(S): Mechanical Engineering;
Automotive Industry
ELIGIBILITY/REQUIREMENTS: Open
to incoming freshmen pursuing a degree in
Mechanical Engineering Program. Must be
accepted into the College of Engineering
and Applied Science by April 1. Based on
merit; minimum requirements: 1350 SAT
or 28 ACT, a 3.5 high school GPA; and
school, civic honors and activities participation.
HOW TO APPLY: See website for application. Submit with personal essay that
demonstrates hands-on experience or
activity (such as rebuilding engines, working on cars/trucks, etc.); 2 recommendations, 1 of which must be from a teacher,
counselor, or administrator; and transcript.
NUMBER OF AWARDS: 1
RENEWABLE: Yes. Up to 4 years if student maintains a 3.4 or better GPA, with a
minimum of 24 credit hours applicable to
degree.

2815—SOCIETY OF AUTOMOTIVE ENGINEERS (Whitworth College/SAE Engineering Scholarship)

SAE Customer Service
400 Commonwealth Drive
Warrendale PA 15096-0001
724/776-4970
FAX: 724/776-1615
E-mail: customerservice@sae.org
Internet: http://www.sae.org/
students/scholarships
AMOUNT: $500/semester
DEADLINE(S): DEC 1

FIELD(S): Engineering; Science;
Automotive Industry
ELIGIBILITY/REQUIREMENTS: Open
to incoming freshmen or transfer students
who plan to major in science or engineering and have a minimum 1200 SAT or 2.7
ACT score and 3.6 GPA.
HOW TO APPLY: See website for application. Submit with personal essay that
demonstrates hands-on experience or
activity (such as rebuilding engines, working on cars/trucks, etc.); 2 recommendations, 1 of which must be from a teacher,
counselor, or administrator; and transcript.
NUMBER OF AWARDS: 1
RENEWABLE: Yes. Up to 8 semesters
provided student is enrolled full time in a
science or pre-engineering major program
and maintains a 3.0 GPA.

2816—SOCIETY OF AUTOMOTIVE ENGINEERS (York College/IAC Scholar/SAE Engineering Scholarship)

SAE Customer Service
400 Commonwealth Drive
Warrendale PA 15096-0001
724/776-4970
FAX: 724/776-1615
E-mail: customerservice@sae.org
Internet: http://www.sae.org/
students/scholarships
AMOUNT: 1/3 tuition
DEADLINE(S): DEC 1
FIELD(S): Mechanical Engineering;
Automotive Industry
ELIGIBILITY/REQUIREMENTS: Open
to incoming freshmen pursuing a degree in
Mechanical Engineering Program. Based
on merit and the following minimum
requirements: 1200 SAT, top 1/5 of high
school graduating class, and full admission
into engineering program.
HOW TO APPLY: See website for application. Submit with personal essay that
demonstrates hands-on experience or
activity (such as rebuilding engines, working on cars/trucks, etc.); 2 recommendations, 1 of which must be from a teacher,
counselor, or administrator; and transcript.
Prospective recipient must be accepted to
York College by February 1.
NUMBER OF AWARDS: 1
RENEWABLE: Yes. Up to 4 years; must
maintain a 3.25 or better GPA (for students with GPA between 3.0 and 3.24, 1/2
of the scholarship will be awarded).

2817—UNIVERSAL TECHNICAL INSTITUTE (UTI National High School Competition)

20410 N. 19th Avenue, Suite 200

Phoenix AZ 85027
800/859-1202 or 888/884-3678
or 602/264-4164
Internet: http://www.uticorp.com
AMOUNT: $500-$5,000
DEADLINE(S): Varies
FIELD(S): Technical (Auto/Truck
Mechanics, Collision Repair,
Motorcycle or Marine)
ELIGIBILITY/REQUIREMENTS: Open
to high school seniors pursuing careers as
technicians. For use at UTI or MMI, which
has campuses in Arizona, Illinois,
California, Florida, and Texas. Based on a
written test of technical skills. Awards also
are given to schools by students finishing in
the top 10%.
HOW TO APPLY: Call, check website, or
write for details.

2818—WESTERN MICHIGAN UNIVERSITY (College of Engineering and Applied Sciences/Edward Ravitz Memorial Scholarship in Construction Engineering)

1903 West Michigan
Kalamazoo MI 49008-5337
269/387-6000
FAX: 269/387-6989
E-mail: finaid-info@wmich.edu
Internet: http://www.wmich.edu/
finaid
AMOUNT: $4,000
FIELD(S): Mechanical Engineering
(especially automotive)
ELIGIBILITY/REQUIREMENTS:
Awarded to one new freshman admitted as
an incoming, full-time (at least 12 credit
hours) freshman undergraduate student
majoring in pre-engineering-construction.
Must have a minimum 3.3 high school
GPA. Award may be applied to tuition,
fees, books, and educational expenses
related to the general well being of the stu-
dent.
HOW TO APPLY: Contact the College of
Engineering and Applied Science,
Advising Office, Room E-102 Parkview
Campus (269/276-3270) for an application.
NUMBER OF AWARDS: 1
RENEWABLE: Yes. 4-year award provid-
ed minimum 3.3 GPA maintained.
CONTACT: College of Engineering and
Applied Science, Advising Office

2819—WESTERN MICHIGAN UNIVERSITY (College of Engineering and Applied Sciences/Kalamazoo Antique Auto Restorers Club Scholarship)

1903 West Michigan
Kalamazoo MI 49008-5337

269/387-6000
FAX: 269/387-6989
E-mail: finaid-info@wmich.edu
Internet: http://www.wmich.edu/
finaid
AMOUNT: $500/semester
FIELD(S): Mechanical Engineering
(especially automotive)
ELIGIBILITY/REQUIREMENTS: Open
to Mechanical Engineering major with
emphasis on automotive and an interest in
restored vintage automobiles, GPA 2.5 or
higher, Michigan resident. Must have com-
pleted 30 hours towards mechanical engi-
neering major.
HOW TO APPLY: Advisor reviews
records of potential candidates. Contact
Mechanical Engineering Department for
further information.
NUMBER OF AWARDS: 1
RENEWABLE: No
CONTACT: Mechanical Engineering
Department

AVIATION

2820—AERO CLUB OF NEW ENGLAND (Aviation Scholarships)

ACONE Education Committee
102 River Road
Merrimac MA 01860
978/346-8260
E-mail: mayorforlife@earthlink.net
Internet: http://www.acone.org
AMOUNT: $500-$2,500
DEADLINE(S): MAR 30
FIELD(S): Aviation and related fields
ELIGIBILITY/REQUIREMENTS: Open
to New England residents; to be used at
FAA-approved flight schools in New
England states. Several scholarships with
varying requirements.
HOW TO APPLY: Information and appli-
cations are on website.

2821—AIRCRAFT ELECTRONICS ASSOCIATION EDUCATIONAL FOUNDATION (Bendix/King Avionics Scholarship)

4217 South Hocker
Independence MO 64055
816/373-6565
FAX: 816/478-3100
E-mail: info@aea.net
Internet: http://www.aea.net
AMOUNT: $1,000
DEADLINE(S): FEB 17
FIELD(S): Avionics; Aviation
ELIGIBILITY/REQUIREMENTS:
Available to high school, college, or vo-

tech students who plan to or are attending
an accredited school in an avionics or aircraft-repair program.
HOW TO APPLY: See website for application. Submit with transcript and 300-
word essay (see website for topics).

2822—AIRCRAFT ELECTRONICS ASSOCIATION EDUCATIONAL FOUNDATION (Bud Glover Memorial Scholarship)

4217 South Hocker
Independence MO 64055
816/373-6565
FAX: 816/478-3100
E-mail: info@aea.net
Internet: http://www.aea.net
AMOUNT: $1,000
DEADLINE(S): FEB 17
FIELD(S): Avionics; Aviation
ELIGIBILITY/REQUIREMENTS: For
high school seniors and/or college students
who plan to or are attending an accredited
school in an avionics or aircraft-repair pro-
gram.
HOW TO APPLY: See website for appli-
cation. Submit with transcript and 300-
word essay (see website for topics).

2823—AIRCRAFT ELECTRONICS ASSOCIATION EDUCATIONAL FOUNDATION (Chuck Peacock Memorial Scholarship)

4217 South Hocker
Independence MO 64055
816/373-6565
FAX: 816/478-3100
E-mail: info@aea.net
Internet: http://www.aea.net
AMOUNT: $1,000
DEADLINE(S): FEB 17
FIELD(S): Avionics; Aviation
ELIGIBILITY/REQUIREMENTS:
Available to high school seniors and/or col-
lege students who plan to or are attending
an accredited school in an aviation man-
agement program.
HOW TO APPLY: See website for appli-
cation. Submit with transcript and 300-
word essay (see website for topics).

2824—AIRCRAFT ELECTRONICS ASSOCIATION EDUCATIONAL FOUNDATION (College of Aeronautics Scholarship)

4217 South Hocker
Independence MO 64055
816/373-6565
FAX: 816/478-3100
E-mail: info@aea.net
Internet: http://www.aea.net
AMOUNT: $750/semester

DEADLINE(S): FEB 17
FIELD(S): Avionics; Aviation
ELIGIBILITY/REQUIREMENTS: Available to students in the 2-year avionics technology program (Associate in Applied Sciences) at the College of Aeronautics in Flushing, NY.
HOW TO APPLY: See website for application. Submit with transcript and 300-word essay (see website for topics).
RENEWABLE: Yes. Up to 4 semesters, $3,000 maximum.

2825—AIRCRAFT ELECTRONICS ASSOCIATION EDUCATIONAL FOUNDATION (David Arver Memorial Scholarship)

4217 South Hocker
Independence MO 64055
816/373-6565
FAX: 816/478-3100
E-mail: info@aea.net
Internet: http://www.aea.net
AMOUNT: $1,000
DEADLINE(S): FEB 17
FIELD(S): Avionics; Aviation
ELIGIBILITY/REQUIREMENTS: For a high school senior and/or college student who plans to attend an accredited vo-tech school located in Illinois, Indiana, Iowa, Kansas, Michigan, Minnesota, Missouri, Nebraska, North Dakota, South Dakota, or Wisconsin. Student must enroll in an avionics or aircraft-repair program.
HOW TO APPLY: See website for application. Submit with transcript and 300-word essay (see website for topics).

2826—AIRCRAFT ELECTRONICS ASSOCIATION EDUCATIONAL FOUNDATION (Dutch and Ginger Arver Scholarship)

4217 South Hocker
Independence MO 64055
816/373-6565
FAX: 816/478-3100
E-mail: info@aea.net
Internet: http://www.aea.net
AMOUNT: $1,000
DEADLINE(S): FEB 17
FIELD(S): Avionics; Aviation
ELIGIBILITY/REQUIREMENTS: Available to high school seniors and/or college students who plan to or are attending an accredited school in an avionics or aircraft-repair program.
HOW TO APPLY: See website for application. Submit with transcript and 300-word essay (see website for topics).

2827—AIRCRAFT ELECTRONICS ASSOCIATION EDUCATIONAL FOUNDATION (Field Aviation Co., Inc. Scholarship)

4217 South Hocker

Independence MO 64055
816/373-6565
FAX: 816/478-3100
E-mail: info@aea.net
Internet: http://www.aea.net
AMOUNT: $1,000
DEADLINE(S): FEB 17
FIELD(S): Avionics; Aviation
ELIGIBILITY/REQUIREMENTS: Available to high school seniors and/or college students who plan to or are attending an accredited college or university in Canada, in an avionics or aircraft-repair program.
HOW TO APPLY: See website for application. Submit with transcript and 300-word essay (see website for topics).

2828—AIRCRAFT ELECTRONICS ASSOCIATION EDUCATIONAL FOUNDATION (Garmin Scholarship)

4217 South Hocker
Independence MO 64055
816/373-6565
FAX: 816/478-3100
E-mail: info@aea.net
Internet: http://www.aea.net
AMOUNT: $2,000
DEADLINE(S): FEB 17
FIELD(S): Avionics; Aviation
ELIGIBILITY/REQUIREMENTS: Available to high school, college, or vocational/technical school students who plan to or are attending an accredited school in an avionics or aircraft-repair program.
HOW TO APPLY: See website for application. Submit with transcript and 300-word essay (see website for topics).

2829—AIRCRAFT ELECTRONICS ASSOCIATION EDUCATIONAL FOUNDATION (L-3 Avionics Systems Scholarship)

4217 South Hocker
Independence MO 64055
816/373-6565
FAX: 816/478-3100
E-mail: info@aea.net
Internet: http://www.aea.net
AMOUNT: $2,500
DEADLINE(S): FEB 17
FIELD(S): Avionics; Aviation
ELIGIBILITY/REQUIREMENTS: Available to high school seniors and/or college students who plan to or are attending an accredited school in an avionics or aircraft repair program.
HOW TO APPLY: See website for application. Submit with transcript and 300-word essay (see website for topics).

2830—AIRCRAFT ELECTRONICS ASSOCIATION EDUCATIONAL FOUNDATION (Lee Tarbox Memorial Scholarship)

4217 South Hocker
Independence MO 64055
816/373-6565
FAX: 816/478-3100
E-mail: info@aea.net
Internet: http://www.aea.net
AMOUNT: $2,500
DEADLINE(S): FEB 17
FIELD(S): Avionics; Aviation
ELIGIBILITY/REQUIREMENTS: Available to high school seniors or college students who plan to or are attending an accredited school in an avionics or aircraft-repair program.
HOW TO APPLY: See website for application. Submit with transcript and 300-word essay (see website for topics).

2831—AIRCRAFT ELECTRONICS ASSOCIATION EDUCATIONAL FOUNDATION (Leon Harris/Les Nichols Memorial Scholarship to Spartan School of Aeronautics)

4217 South Hocker
Independence MO 64055
816/373-6565
FAX: 816/478-3100
E-mail: info@aea.net
Internet: http://www.aea.net
AMOUNT: Over $22,000
DEADLINE(S): FEB 17
FIELD(S): Avionics; Aviation
ELIGIBILITY/REQUIREMENTS: Available to students who plan to pursue an Associate's Degree in Applied Science in Aviation Electronics (avionics) at NEC Spartan School of Aeronautics campus in Tulsa, OK; the applicant may not be currently enrolled in the avionics program at Spartan.
HOW TO APPLY: See website for application. Submit with transcript and 300-word essay (see website for topics).

2832—AIRCRAFT ELECTRONICS ASSOCIATION EDUCATIONAL FOUNDATION (Lowell Gaylor Memorial Scholarship)

4217 South Hocker
Independence MO 64055
816/373-6565
FAX: 816/478-3100
E-mail: info@aea.net
Internet: http://www.aea.net
AMOUNT: $1,000
DEADLINE(S): FEB 17
FIELD(S): Avionics; Aviation

ELIGIBILITY/REQUIREMENTS: For high school seniors and/or college students who plan to or are attending an accredited school in an avionics or aircraft-repair program.

HOW TO APPLY: See website for application. Submit with transcript and 300-word essay (see website for topics).

2833—AIRCRAFT ELECTRONICS ASSOCIATION EDUCATIONAL FOUNDATION (Mid-Continent Instrument Scholarship)

4217 South Hocker
Independence MO 64055
816/373-6565
FAX: 816/478-3100
E-mail: info@aea.net
Internet: http://www.aea.net
AMOUNT: $1,000
DEADLINE(S): FEB 17
FIELD(S): Avionics; Aviation
ELIGIBILITY/REQUIREMENTS: Available to high school seniors and/or college students who plan to or are attending an accredited school in an avionics or aircraft-repair program.

HOW TO APPLY: See website for application. Submit with transcript and 300-word essay (see website for topics).

2834—AIRCRAFT ELECTRONICS ASSOCIATION EDUCATIONAL FOUNDATION (Monte R. Mitchell Global Scholarship)

4217 South Hocker
Independence MO 64055
816/373-6565
FAX: 816/478-3100
E-mail: info@aea.net
Internet: http://www.aea.net
AMOUNT: $1,000
DEADLINE(S): FEB 17
FIELD(S): Avionics; Aviation
ELIGIBILITY/REQUIREMENTS: Available to a European student pursuing a degree in aviation maintenance technology, avionics, or aircraft repair at an accredited school located in Europe or the United States.

HOW TO APPLY: See website for application. Submit with transcript and 300-word essay (see website for topics).

2835—AIRCRAFT ELECTRONICS ASSOCIATION EDUCATIONAL FOUNDATION (Plane & Pilot Magazine/Garmin Scholarship)

4217 South Hocker
Independence MO 64055
816/373-6565
FAX: 816/478-3100

E-mail: info@aea.net
Internet: http://www.aea.net
AMOUNT: $2,000
DEADLINE(S): FEB 17
FIELD(S): Avionics; Aviation
ELIGIBILITY/REQUIREMENTS: Available to high school, college, or vocational/technical school students who plan to or are attending an accredited school in an avionics or aircraft-repair program.

HOW TO APPLY: See website for application. Submit with transcript and 300-word essay (see website for topics).

2836—AIRCRAFT ELECTRONICS ASSOCIATION EDUCATIONAL FOUNDATION (Russell Leroy Jones Memorial Scholarship to Westwood College of Aviation Technology)

4217 South Hocker
Independence MO 64055
816/373-6565
FAX: 816-478-3100
E-mail: info@aea.net
Internet: http://www.aea.net
AMOUNT: $6,000
DEADLINE(S): FEB 17
FIELD(S): Avionics; Aviation
ELIGIBILITY/REQUIREMENTS: Students must plan to attend Westwood College of Aviation Technology in Broomfield, CO, in the electronics/avionics program; applicants may not be currently enrolled at Westwood College of Aviation Technology.

HOW TO APPLY: See website for application. Submit with transcript and 300-word essay (see website for topics).

2837—AIRCRAFT ELECTRONICS ASSOCIATION EDUCATIONAL FOUNDATION (Sporty's Pilot Shop/Cincinnati Avionics)

4217 South Hocker
Independence MO 64055
816/373-6565
FAX: 816/478-3100
E-mail: info@aea.net
Internet: http://www.aea.net
AMOUNT: $2,000
DEADLINE(S): FEB 17
FIELD(S): Avionics; Aviation
ELIGIBILITY/REQUIREMENTS: Available to high school seniors and/or college students who plan to or are attending an accredited college or university in an avionics or aircraft-repair program.

HOW TO APPLY: See website for application. Submit with transcript and 300-word essay (see website for topics).

2838—AIRCRAFT ELECTRONICS ASSOCIATION EDUCATIONAL FOUNDATION (Thomas J. Slocum Memorial Scholarship to Westwood College of Aviation)

4217 South Hocker
Independence MO 64055
816/373-6565
FAX: 816/478-3100
E-mail: info@aea.net
Internet: http://www.aea.net
AMOUNT: $6,000
DEADLINE(S): FEB 17
FIELD(S): Avionics; Aviation
ELIGIBILITY/REQUIREMENTS: For students applying to and enrolling in the avionics program at Westwood College in Broomfield, CO.

HOW TO APPLY: See website for application. Submit with transcript and 300-word essay (see website for topics).

2839—AIRCRAFT ELECTRONICS ASSOCIATION EDUCATIONAL FOUNDATION (Tom Taylor Memorial Scholarship to Spartan School of Aeronautics)

4217 South Hocker
Independence MO 64055
816/373-6565
FAX: 816/478-3100
E-mail: info@aea.net
Internet: http://www.aea.net
AMOUNT: Over $22,000
DEADLINE(S): FEB 17
FIELD(S): Avionics; Aviation
ELIGIBILITY/REQUIREMENTS: Available to students who plan to pursue an Associate's Degree in Applied Science or a diploma in Aviation Maintenance Technology (AMT) at Spartan School of Aeronautics campus in Tulsa, OK; the applicant may not be currently enrolled in the AMT program at Spartan.

HOW TO APPLY: See website for application. Submit with transcript and 300-word essay (see website for topics).

2840—AIR TRAFFIC CONTROL ASSOCIATION (ATCA) (Full-Time Employee Scholarship)

1101 King St, Suite 300
Alexandria VA 22314
703/299-2430
FAX: 703/299-2437
E-mail: info@atca.org
Internet: http://www.atca.org/
activities/scholarships.asp
AMOUNT: $1,500-$2,500
DEADLINE(S): MAY 1

FIELD(S): Air Traffic Control, Aviation
ELIGIBILITY/REQUIREMENTS: Open to students engaged in full-time employment in an aviation-related field in government, military service or industry. Coursework designed to enhance employee's skill in an ATC or aviation discipline.
HOW TO APPLY: See website for application or contact the Association. Submit with 2 letters of recommendation (from present or previous teachers, professors, instructors, supervisors, or managers) from within the last 12 months; certified transcript of all college coursework (if less than 30 semester or 45 quarter hours of college coursework have been completed, all high school transcripts also are required); work or experience that supports educational and/or aviation career goals must be addressed in the application and/or essay (400 words maximum), "How My Education Efforts Will Enhance My Potential Contribution to Aviation."
RENEWABLE: Yes. must submit a verified report from the educational institution attended, stating the courses taken and completed and the grades received.

2841—AIR TRAFFIC CONTROL ASSOCIATION (ATCA) (Gabriel A. Hartl Scholarship)

1101 King St, Suite 300
Alexandria VA 22314
703/299-2430
FAX: 703/299-2437
E-mail: info@atca.org
Internet: http://www.atca.org/
activities/scholarships.asp
AMOUNT: $1,500-$2,500
DEADLINE(S): MAY 1
FIELD(S): Air Traffic Control, Aviation
ELIGIBILITY/REQUIREMENTS: Open to students enrolled half- to full-time in a 2- to 4-year air traffic control program at an institution approved and/or licensed by the Federal Aviation Administration as directly supporting the FAA's college and training initiative. Students enrolled half- to full-time in a program leading to a bachelor's degree or higher in an aviation-related course of study. Full-time employees enrolled in advanced study programs to improve their skills in air traffic control or an aviation discipline. Must be U.S. citizen, child of air traffic control specialists enrolled half- to full-time in a program leading to a bachelor's degree or higher.
HOW TO APPLY: See website for application or contact the Association. Submit with 2 letters of recommendation (from present or previous teachers, professors, instructors, supervisors, or managers) from within the last 12 months; certified transcript of all college coursework (if less than

30 semester or 45 quarter hours of college coursework have been completed, all high school transcripts also are required); work or experience that supports educational and/or aviation career goals must be addressed in the application and/or essay (400 words maximum), "How My Education Efforts Will Enhance My Potential Contribution to Aviation."
RENEWABLE: Yes. Must submit a verified report from the educational institution attended, stating the courses taken and completed and the grades received.

2842—AIR TRAFFIC CONTROL ASSOCIATION (ATCA) (Half to Full-Time Student Scholarship)

1101 King St, Suite 300
Alexandria VA 22314
703/299-2430
FAX: 703/299-2437
E-mail: info@atca.org
Internet: http://www.atca.org/
activities/scholarships.asp
AMOUNT: $1,500-$2,500
DEADLINE(S): MAY 1
FIELD(S): Air Traffic Control, Aviation
ELIGIBILITY/REQUIREMENTS: Open to students enrolled half- to full-time in an accredited college or university and planning to continue the following year. Coursework must be related to aviation-related career and leading to a bachelor's degree (or higher); attendance must be equal to at least half time (6 hours) and applicant must have a minimum of 30 semester or 45 quarter hours still to be completed before graduation.
HOW TO APPLY: See website for application or contact the Association. Submit with 2 letters of recommendation (from present or previous teachers, professors, instructors, supervisors, or managers) from within the last 12 months; certified transcript of all college coursework (if less than 30 semester or 45 quarter hours of college coursework have been completed, all high school transcripts also are required); work or experience that supports educational and/or aviation career goals must be addressed in the application and/or essay (400 words maximum), "How My Education Efforts Will Enhance My Potential Contribution to Aviation."
RENEWABLE: Yes. Must submit a verified report from the educational institution attended, stating the courses taken and completed and the grades received.

2843—AVIATION COUNCIL OF PENNSYLVANIA

3111 Arcadia Avenue

Allentown PA 18103
610/797-6911
FAX: 610/797-8238
Internet: http://www.acpfly.com
AMOUNT: Approximately $1,000
DEADLINE(S): JUL 31
FIELD(S): Aviation Technology, Aviation Management, Pilot Training
ELIGIBILITY/REQUIREMENTS: Open to residents of Pennsylvania enrolled in high school, a 2- or 4-year college program, or an aviation technology program. Applicants for the Aviation Management Scholarship may attend school outside of Pennsylvania. Applicants for the Aviation Technology and Professional Pilot Scholarships must attend school in Pennsylvania and those applying for the Professional Pilot Scholarship shall hold at least a Student Pilot Certificate.
HOW TO APPLY: See website or contact Council for information and application. Submit with Application Checklist financial aid report; a 2-page (maximum) essay describing personal background, including activities such as clubs and associations, personal goals, and specific reason you require financial assistance; at least 2 recommendations from persons from the aviation community, the applicant's schools, or others; official transcript(s) from your educational institution, when applicable. (Note: Include a copy of your Student Pilot Certificate or highest-ranking certificate. Student pilots must show proof that they have soloed, including a log book endorsement and/or a student license with solo endorsement.)
NUMBER OF AWARDS: Varies

2844—AVIATION DISTRIBUTORS AND MANUFACTURERS ASSOCIATION INTERNATIONAL (ADMA International Scholarship Fund)

1900 Arch Street
Philadelphia PA 19103-1498
215/564-3484
FAX: 215/564-2175
E-mail: assnhqt@netaxs.com
AMOUNT: Varies
DEADLINE(S): MAR 15
FIELD(S): Aviation Management;
Professional Pilot; Aviation
Maintenance; Aeronautics
ELIGIBILITY/REQUIREMENTS: Open to students seeking a career in aviation management or as a professional pilot. Emphasis may be in general aviation, airway science management, aviation maintenance, flight engineering, or airway air conditioning systems management. Applicants must be studying in the aviation field

in a 4-year school having an aviation program.

HOW TO APPLY: Write for complete information.

2845—AVIATION INSURANCE ASSOCIATION

Aviation Technology Department
1 Purdue Airport
West Lafayette IN 47906-3398
765/494-5782

AMOUNT: $1,000
DEADLINE(S): FEB 28
FIELD(S): Aviation
ELIGIBILITY/REQUIREMENTS: Scholarships for aviation students who have completed at least 30 college credits, 15 of which are in aviation. Must have GPA of at least 2.5 and be a U.S. citizen.
HOW TO APPLY: Write to Aviation Technology Department at Purdue University for application and details.
CONTACT: Professor Bernard Wullue

2846—CHARLIE WELLS MEMORIAL AVIATION SCHOLARSHIP

Charlie Wells Memorial Aviation
Scholarship
P.O. Box 262
Springfield, IL 62705-0262
E-mail: Rog@WellsScholarship.com
Internet: http://www.wells
scholarship.com

AMOUNT: Varies
DEADLINE: APR 30
FIELD(S): Aviation
ELIGIBILITY/REQUIREMENTS: Must be a resident of the U.S. or one of its territories and must be a full-time student majoring in an aviation-oriented curriculum.
HOW TO APPLY: Application available on website or send SASE. Submit application with 2 recommendations (1 from an academic source) along with a copy of the most recent transcript.
NUMBER OF AWARDS: 1-3
RENEWABLE: Yes

2847—DAEDALIAN FOUNDATION (Descendants Scholarship Program)

P.O. Box 249
Randolph AFB, TX 78148
210/945-2113
FAX: 210/945-2112
E-mail: icarus2@daedalians.org
Internet: http://www.daedalians.org
AMOUNT: Varies

DEADLINE(S): Varies
FIELD(S): Aviation
ELIGIBILITY/REQUIREMENTS: Open to young descendants of Daedalian members in good standing (living or deceased) to pursue a college education in furtherance of a career in military aviation or space; applicants must be pursuing a baccalaureate (or higher) degree and commit to a career in aviation or space in one of the armed forces of the United States.
HOW TO APPLY: See website or by e-mail. Note: Flights and applicants are encouraged, but not required, to include a Student Aid Report (SAR).
NUMBER OF AWARDS: Up to 3
RENEWABLE: Yes.
ADDITIONAL INFORMATION: This scholarship is not tied to the Matching Program. It is an additional program and a student may compete for both programs.

2848—DAEDALIAN FOUNDATION (John and Alice Egan Multi-Year Mentoring Scholarship)

P.O. Box 249
Randolph AFB, TX 78148
210/945-2113
FAX: 210/945-2112
E-mail: icarus2@daedalians.org
Internet: http://www.daedalians.org
AMOUNT: Varies
DEADLINE(S): Varies
FIELD(S): Aviation
ELIGIBILITY/REQUIREMENTS: Anyone on track to become a military commissioned aviator-all services. Must be recipient of first $500/year scholarship from local chapter (flight) willing to commit to a multi-year (maximum of 4 years) mentoring program for an individual student who has completed his freshman year. The Foundation will supplement this $500 with at least $2,000 each year.
HOW TO APPLY: See website or by e-mail. Note: Flights and applicants are encouraged, but not required, to include a Student Aid Report (SAR).
NUMBER OF AWARDS: 1 per flight
RENEWABLE: Yes.
ADDITIONAL INFORMATION: This scholarship is not tied to the Matching Program. It is an additional program and a student may compete for both programs.

2849—DAEDALIAN FOUNDATION (Matching Scholarship Programs)

P.O. Box 249
Randolph AFB, TX 78148
210/945-2113

FAX: 210/945-2112
E-mail: icarus2@daedalians.org
Internet: http://www.daedalians.org
AMOUNT: Varies
DEADLINE(S): Varies
FIELD(S): Aviation
ELIGIBILITY/REQUIREMENTS: Anyone on track to become a military commissioned aviator-all services. Must first receive scholarship from local chapter (flight).
HOW TO APPLY: See website or by e-mail. Note: Flights and applicants are encouraged, but not required, to include a Student Aid Report (SAR).
RENEWABLE: Yes. Some are multi-year.

2850—EAA AVIATION FOUNDATION (Clay Lacy Professional Pilot Scholarship)

EAA Scholarship Department
P.O. 3086
Oshkosh WI 54903-3065
920/426-6823
E-mail: scholarships@eaa.org
Internet: http://www.young
eagles.org
AMOUNT: $12,500/year (maximum)
DEADLINE(S): MAR 1
FIELD(S): aviation
ELIGIBILITY/REQUIREMENTS: Open to students who attend a professional pilot program at the University of North Dakota, John D. Odegard School of Aerospace Sciences, to earn a college degree as a professional pilot and earn commercial, instrument, multi-engine and all fixed-wing flight instructor ratings. Participate in flight by living on the EAA Air Academy campus, supporting EAA programs, activities and events. Recipients should show need for financial support. Scholarship provides for a substantial portion of flight-related fees. Applicants must attend UND, meet FAA criteria for licensure and must have their private pilot's certificate.
HOW TO APPLY: Applicants must apply for this Scholarship through the UND Odegard School of Aerospace Science. For information on the UND Odegard School of Aerospace Science and an application, call 800/258-1525.
NUMBER OF AWARDS: Up to 4

2851—EAA AVIATION FOUNDATION (David Alan Quick Scholarship)

EAA Scholarship Department
P.O. 3086
Oshkosh WI 54903-3065
920/426-6823

E-mail: scholarships@eaa.org
Internet: http://www.young
eagles.org
AMOUNT: $1,000
DEADLINE(S): MAR 1
FIELD(S): Aerospace or Aeronautical
Engineering
ELIGIBILITY/REQUIREMENTS: Open
to well-rounded individuals involved in
school and community activities as well as
aviation, accepted at or attending 4-year
accredited college or university. Applicant's
academic records should verify his/her ability to complete educational activity for
which scholarship is requested. Awarded to
a junior or senior in good standing, enrolled
in an accredited college or university, pursuing a degree in above field. Must also be a
current member of EAA (Experimental
Aircraft Association) or recommended by a
current EAA member.
HOW TO APPLY: Apply online. A personal statement (500 words or less)
addressing career aspirations. educational
plan, why you want to receive this scholarship, what you learned from work/volun-
teer experiences, and explaining how your
education will be financed, including loans,
family assistance, your own savings, scholarships, etc., and any unusual financial circumstances affecting your college financial
plan required.
NUMBER OF AWARDS: 1

2852—EAA AVIATION FOUNDATION (EAA Air Academy-Cliff Robertson Work Experience Program)

EAA Scholarship Department
P.O. 3086
Oshkosh WI 54903-3065
920/426-6823
E-mail: scholarships@eaa.org
Internet: http://www.young
eagles.org
AMOUNT: Approximately $750 + travel
subsidy
DEADLINE(S): MAR 1
FIELD(S): Aviation and related areas,
Engineering, Marketing,
Manufacturing
ELIGIBILITY/REQUIREMENTS: Must
be 16 or 17 years old and willing to assist at
all EAA Air Academy programs; must be
able to deal effectively, tactfully and pleasantly with volunteers, staff, program participants and Museum visitors. Strong verbal and written skills and the ability to
work independently. Must also be a current member of EAA (Experimental
Aircraft Association) or recommended by
a current EAA member to apply for these

internships. Learn more about joining
EAA (www.eaa.org) or call 800/843-3612.
Individual and student memberships are
available.
HOW TO APPLY: Apply online.
NUMBER OF AWARDS: 2
ADDITIONAL INFORMATION: Op-
portunity to work in the EAA AirVenture
Museum, historic Pioneer Airport, EAA
Air Academy, and at EAA AirVenture.

2853—EAA AVIATION FOUNDATION (EAA Air Academy-EADS Socata Internship)

EAA Scholarship Department
P.O. 3086
Oshkosh WI 54903-3065
920/426-6823
E-mail: scholarships@eaa.org
Internet: http://www.young
eagles.org
AMOUNT: Travel and accommodations
in France and Oshkosh WI
DEADLINE(S): MAR 1
FIELD(S): Aviation and related areas,
Engineering, Marketing,
Manufacturing
ELIGIBILITY/REQUIREMENTS: Open
to college junior or seniors, intending to
pursue a career in aviation. Applicants
must be in full-time education and able to
demonstrate an interest in aeronautical
career—engineering, marketing, manufacturing, or other areas focused on aviation.
Applicants must be U.S. or Canadian citizens and able to obtain their own passport.
Knowledge of French would enhance the
experience but is not an absolute requirement. Must also be a current member of
EAA (Experimental Aircraft Association)
or recommended by a current EAA member to apply for these internships. Learn
more about joining EAA (www.eaa.org)
or call 800/843-3612. Individual and student memberships are available.
HOW TO APPLY: Apply online.
NUMBER OF AWARDS: 2 (1 male, 1
female)
ADDITIONAL INFORMATION: The
internship will provide an opportunity for
each young person to visit France for an
internship of five weeks' duration in June
and July. They will work at an EADS
Socata facility and be exposed to a variety
of aviation disciplines. Recipients will conclude their summer by attending a week-
long session of the EAA Advanced Air
Academy in Oshkosh, providing mentorship opportunities to young people aged
16-18 who are participating in the camp.
This will include an opportunity to experience the EAA AirVenture Oshkosh.

2854—EAA AVIATION FOUNDATION (EAA Air Academy-Women Airforce Service Pilots [W.A.S.P.] Internship)

EAA Scholarship Department
P.O. 3086
Oshkosh WI 54903-3065
920/426-6823
E-mail: scholarships@eaa.org
Internet: http://www.young
eagles.org
AMOUNT: Approximately $750 + travel
subsidy
DEADLINE(S): MAR 1
FIELD(S): Aviation and related areas
ELIGIBILITY/REQUIREMENTS: Open
to applicant (must be at least 18 years of
age by the start of the internship) wishing
to research and prepare presentations for
EAA Air Academy participants on the
roles women have played in aviation. Must
be able to deal effectively, tactfully and
pleasantly with volunteers, staff, program
participants and Museum visitors. Strong
verbal and written skills and the ability to
work independently. Must also be a current member of EAA (Experimental
Aircraft Association) or recommended by
a current EAA member to apply for these
internships. Learn more about joining
EAA (www.eaa.org) or call 800/843-3612.
Individual and student memberships are
available.
HOW TO APPLY: Apply online.
NUMBER OF AWARDS: 1
ADDITIONAL INFORMATION: Participants may receive ground and flight
instruction.

2855—EAA AVIATION FOUNDATION (EAA AirVenture Museum-Timken Aviation Studies Internships)

EAA Scholarship Department
P.O. 3086
Oshkosh WI 54903-3065
920/426-6823
E-mail: scholarships@eaa.org
Internet: http://www.young
eagles.org
AMOUNT: Approximately $3,000
DEADLINE(S): MAR 1
FIELD(S): Aviation and related areas
ELIGIBILITY/REQUIREMENTS: Open
to college-level interns wishing to study the
role of women in the past, present and
future of aviation. Ideally, interns should
aspire to be future professionals in the aviation industry. Must be able to deal effectively, tactfully and pleasantly with volunteers, staff, program participants and
Museum visitors. Strong verbal and written

skills and the ability to work independently. Must also be a current member of EAA (Experimental Aircraft Association) or recommended by a current EAA member to apply for these internships. Learn more about joining EAA (www.eaa.org) or call 800/843-3612. Individual and student memberships are available.
HOW TO APPLY: Apply online.
NUMBER OF AWARDS: 2

2856—EAA AVIATION FOUNDATION (EAA AirVenture Museum-Wittman Aviation Studies Internship)

EAA Scholarship Department
P.O. 3086
Oshkosh WI 54903-3065
920/426-6823
E-mail: scholarships@eaa.org
Internet: http://www.young eagles.org
AMOUNT: Approximately $2,500
DEADLINE(S): MAR 1
FIELD(S): Aviation and related areas
ELIGIBILITY/REQUIREMENTS: Open to applicant (must be at least 18 years of age by the start of the internship) wishing to work with the collections department of the EAA AirVenture Museum. The work will be in support of the museum's artifact management program and is suitable for a person with curatorial work. Duties may include cataloging, moving, and researching artifacts in the museum collection. Must be able to deal effectively, tactfully and pleasantly with volunteers, staff, program participants and Museum visitors. Strong verbal and written skills and the ability to work independently. Must also be a current member of EAA (Experimental Aircraft Association) or recommended by a current EAA member to apply for these internships. Learn more about joining EAA (www.eaa.org) or call 800/843-3612. Individual and student memberships are available.
HOW TO APPLY: Apply online.
NUMBER OF AWARDS: 1

2857—EAA AVIATION FOUNDATION (Hansen Scholarship)

EAA Scholarship Department
P.O. 3086
Oshkosh WI 54903-3065
920/426-6823
E-mail: scholarships@eaa.org
Internet: http://www.young eagles.org
AMOUNT: $1,000
DEADLINE(S): MAR 1

FIELD(S): Aerospace/Aeronautical Engineering.
ELIGIBILITY/REQUIREMENTS: Open to well-rounded individuals involved in school and community activities as well as aviation, accepted at or attending 4-year accredited college, university or technical college. Applicant's academic records should verify his/her ability to complete educational activity for which scholarship is requested. Must also be a current member of EAA (Experimental Aircraft Association) or recommended by a current EAA member.
HOW TO APPLY: Apply online. A personal statement (500 words or less) addressing career aspirations, educational plan, why you want to receive this scholarship, what you learned from work/volunteer experiences, and explaining how your education will be financed, including loans, family assistance, your own savings, scholarships, etc., and any unusual financial circumstances affecting your college financial plan required.
NUMBER OF AWARDS: 1

2858—EAA AVIATION FOUNDATION (Herbert L. Cox Memorial Scholarship)

EAA Scholarship Department
P.O. 3086
Oshkosh WI 54903-3065
920/426-6823
E-mail: scholarships@eaa.org
Internet: http://www.young eagles.org
AMOUNT: $500
DEADLINE(S): MAR 1
FIELD(S): Aviation or related field
ELIGIBILITY/REQUIREMENTS: Open to well-rounded individuals involved in school and community activities as well as aviation accepted at or attending 4-year accredited college or university. Applicant's academic records should verify his/her ability to complete educational activity for which scholarship is requested. Must also be a current member of EAA (Experimental Aircraft Association) or recommended by a current EAA member.
HOW TO APPLY: Apply online. A personal statement (500 words or less) addressing career aspirations. educational plan, why you want to receive this scholarship, what you learned from work/volunteer experiences, and explaining how your education will be financed, including loans, family assistance, your own savings, scholarships, etc., and any unusual financial circumstances affecting your college financial plan required.
NUMBER OF AWARDS: 1

2859—EAA AVIATION FOUNDATION (H.P. "Bud" Milligan Aviation Scholarship)

EAA Scholarship Department
P.O. 3086
Oshkosh WI 54903-3065
920/426-6823
E-mail: scholarships@eaa.org
Internet: http://www.young eagles.org
AMOUNT: $1,000
DEADLINE(S): MAR 1
FIELD(S): Aviation or related field
ELIGIBILITY/REQUIREMENTS: Open to well-rounded individuals involved in school and community activities as well as aviation, accepted at or attending an accredited aviation program at a college, technical school, or aviation academy. Financial need is not a requirement. Applicant's academic records should verify his/her ability to complete educational activity for which scholarship is requested. Must also be a current member of EAA (Experimental Aircraft Association) or recommended by a current EAA member.
HOW TO APPLY: Apply online. A personal statement (500 words or less) addressing career aspirations. educational plan, why you want to receive this scholarship, what you learned from work/volunteer experiences, and explaining how your education will be financed, including loans, family assistance, your own savings, scholarships, etc., and any unusual financial circumstances affecting your college financial plan required.
NUMBER OF AWARDS: 1

2860—EAA AVIATION FOUNDATION (Richard Lee Vernon Aviation Scholarship)

EAA Scholarship Department
P.O. 3086
Oshkosh WI 54903-3065
920/426-6823
E-mail: scholarships@eaa.org
Internet: http://www.young eagles.org
AMOUNT: $500
DEADLINE(S): MAR 1
FIELD(S): Aviation or related field
ELIGIBILITY/REQUIREMENTS: Open to well-rounded individuals involved in school and community activities as well as aviation, accepted at or attending an accredited aviation program at a college, technical school, or aviation academy. Financial need is a requirement. Applicant's academic records should verify his/her ability to complete educational activity for which scholarship is requested.

Must also be a current member of EAA (Experimental Aircraft Association) or recommended by a current EAA member.
HOW TO APPLY: Apply online. A personal statement (500 words or less) addressing career aspirations. educational plan, why you want to receive this scholarship, what you learned from work/volunteer experiences, and explaining how your education will be financed, including loans, family assistance, your own savings, scholarships, etc., and any unusual financial circumstances affecting your college financial plan required.
NUMBER OF AWARDS: 1

2861—ILLINOIS PILOTS ASSOCIATION (IPA Memorial Scholarship)

40 W 297 Apache Lane
Huntley IL 60142
Internet: http://www.illinois
pilots.com/
AMOUNT: $500
DEADLINE(S): APR 1
FIELD(S): Aviation
ELIGIBILITY/REQUIREMENTS: Must be a resident of Illinois; majoring in an aviation-oriented curriculum; and be a full-time student at an Illinois college or university.
HOW TO APPLY: Submit application form (or equivalent information) and evidence of strong academic performance, including a transcript and 3 recommendations, at least 1 of which must be academic.
RENEWABLE: Yes, must reapply.
CONTACT: Ruth Frantz

2862—INTERNATIONAL SOCIETY OF WOMEN AIRLINE PILOTS (Fiorenze De Bernardi Merit Award)

2250 East Tropicana Avenue,
Suite 19-395
Las Vegas NV 89119-6594
E-mail: isa21scholarbev@aol.com
Internet: http://www.iswap.org
AMOUNT: Varies
DEADLINE(S): APR 15
FIELD(S): Airline Pilot Training (CFI, CFII, MEI, or any equivalents)
ELIGIBILITY/REQUIREMENTS: A merit scholarship for women throughout the world who are pursuing airline pilot careers. Selection based on need, demonstrated dedication to career goal, work history, experience, and recommendations. Must have a U.S. FAA Commercial Pilot Certificate with an Instrument Rating and a First Class medical certificate (or equivalent). Candidates must have a minimum of 250 flight hours.

HOW TO APPLY: Check website or write for more information and application. Personal interview required.
CONTACT: Beverly Sinclair

2863—INTERNATIONAL SOCIETY OF WOMEN AIRLINE PILOTS (Holly Mullins Memorial Scholarship)

2250 East Tropicana Avenue,
Suite 19-395
Las Vegas NV 89119-6594
E-mail: isa21scholarbev@aol.com
Internet: http://www.iswap.org
AMOUNT: Varies
DEADLINE(S): APR 15
FIELD(S): Airline Pilot Training (CFI, CRII, MEI, or any equivalents)
ELIGIBILITY/REQUIREMENTS: A merit scholarship for women who are single mothers and pursuing airline pilot careers. Selection is based on need, demonstrated dedication to career goal, work experience, and recommendations. Must have a U.S. FAA Commercial Pilot Certificate with an Instrument Rating and a First Class medical certificate (or equivalent), and a minimum of 750 flight hours.
HOW TO APPLY: Check website or write for more information and application.
CONTACT: Beverly Sinclair

2864—INTERNATIONAL SOCIETY OF WOMEN AIRLINE PILOTS (ISA Airline Scholarship)

2250 East Tropicana Avenue,
Suite 19-395
Las Vegas NV 89119-6594
E-mail: isa21scholarbev@aol.com
Internet: http://www.iswap.org
AMOUNT: Varies
DEADLINE(S): APR 15
FIELD(S): Flight Engineering and Type Ratings
ELIGIBILITY/REQUIREMENTS: For women seeking careers in aviation, who need Flight Engineer Certificates and Type Ratings on 727, 737, 747, 757, and DC-10 aircraft. For Flight Engineers, 1,000 hours flight time and a current FE written required. For Type Rating scholarship, an ATP Certificate and a current FE written.
HOW TO APPLY: Check website or write for more information and application.
CONTACT: Beverly Sinclair

2865—INTERNATIONAL SOCIETY OF WOMEN AIRLINE PILOTS (ISA Financial Scholarship Program)

2250 East Tropicana Avenue,

Suite 19-395
Las Vegas NV 89119-6594
E-mail: isa21scholarbev@aol.com
Internet: http://www.iswap.org
AMOUNT: Varies
DEADLINE(S): APR 15
FIELD(S): Airline Pilot Advanced Ratings
ELIGIBILITY/REQUIREMENTS: Open to women whose goals are to fly the world's airlines. For advanced pilot ratings, such as the U.S. FAA ATP certificate or equivalent. Must have a U.S. FAA Commercial Pilot Certificate with an Instrument Rating and a First Class medical certificate (or equivalent); a minimum of 750 flight hours. Some scholarships based on financial need.
HOW TO APPLY: See website or write for detailed information and application. Personal interview is required.
CONTACT: Beverly Sinclair

2866—NATIONAL AGRICULTURAL AVIATION ASSOCIATION

1005 E Street SE
Washington DC 20003
202/546-5722
FAX: 202/546-5726
E-mail: information@agaviation.org
Internet: http://www.agaviation.org
AMOUNT: Varies
DEADLINE(S): AUG 15
FIELD(S): Agriculture, Aviation, Aeronautics
ELIGIBILITY/REQUIREMENTS: Spouse, child, son-/daughter-in-law, grandchild of an operator, pilot, or allied industry member of NAAA. Sponsor must be a currently active dues-paying member. Financial need considered.
HOW TO APPLY: See website and click on WNAAA after MAR 1.
NUMBER OF AWARDS: 2
CONTACT: Lindsay Barber

2867—NATIONAL AIR TRANSPORTATION ASSOCIATION FOUNDATION (John W. Godwin Jr. Memorial Scholarship Fund)

4226 King Street
Alexandria VA 22302
703/845-9000
FAX: 703/845-8176
Internet: http://www.nata.aero/
about/scholarships.jsp
AMOUNT: $2,500
DEADLINE(S): None
FIELD(S): Flight Training
ELIGIBILITY/REQUIREMENTS: Scholarship for flight training for any cer-

tificate and/or flight rating issued by the FAA, at any NATA-Member company offering flight training. Must accumulate a minimum of 15 dual or solo flight hours each calendar month.
HOW TO APPLY: Contact organization for details.

2868—NATIONAL AIR TRANSPORTATION ASSOCIATION FOUNDATION (The Pioneers of Flight Scholarship)

4226 King Street
Alexandria VA 22302
703/845-9000
FAX: 703/845-8176
Internet: http://www.nata.aero/about/scholarships.jsp
AMOUNT: $2,500
DEADLINE(S): None
FIELD(S): Aviation
ELIGIBILITY/REQUIREMENTS: Open to college students who are in the sophomore or junior year at the time of application intending to pursue full-time study at an accredited 4-year college or university and can demonstrate an interest in pursuing a career in general aviation.
HOW TO APPLY: Must be nominated by an NATA Regular or Associate Member company.

2869—NATIONAL BUSINESS AVIATION ASSOCIATION (Indiana Business Aviation Association PDP Scholarships)

1200 Eighteenth Street NW,
Suite 400
Washington DC 20036-2527
202/783-9353
FAX: 202/331-8364
E-mail: jevans@nbaa.org
Internet: http://www.nbaa.org/scholar/scholarships/
AMOUNT: $1,150
DEADLINE(S): AUG 31
FIELD(S): Aviation-related curricula
ELIGIBILITY/REQUIREMENTS: Valid only for students enrolled at institutions that are NBAA and University Aviation Association (UAA) members. Open to college sophomores, juniors, or seniors who will be continuing in school the following academic year in an aviation-related baccalaureate or graduate program at these specific member institutions. Must be U.S. citizen and have 3.0 or better GPA.
HOW TO APPLY: Check website or contact NBAA for complete information and application.
NUMBER OF AWARDS: 4

2870—NATIONAL BUSINESS AVIATION ASSOCIATION (Lawrence Ginocchio Aviation Scholarship)

1200 Eighteenth Street NW,
Suite 400
Washington DC 20036-2527
202/783-9353
FAX: 202/331-8364
E-mail: jevans@nbaa.org
Internet: http://www.nbaa.org/scholar/scholarships/
AMOUNT: $5,000
DEADLINE(S): AUG 22
FIELD(S): Aviation-related curricula
ELIGIBILITY/REQUIREMENTS: Valid only for students enrolled at institutions that are NBAA and University Aviation Association (UAA) members. Open to college sophomores, juniors, or seniors who will be continuing in school the following academic year in an aviation-related baccalaureate or graduate program at these specific member institutions. Must be U.S. citizen and have 3.0 or better GPA.
HOW TO APPLY: Check website or contact NBAA for complete information and application.
NUMBER OF AWARDS: 5

2871—NATIONAL GAY PILOTS ASSOCIATION (Pilot Scholarships)

13140 Coit Road, Suite 320
LB 120
Dallas TX 75240
972/233-9107, ext. 203
FAX: 972/490-4219
E-mail: ngpa@ngpa.org
Internet: http://www.ngpa.org
AMOUNT: $2,000
DEADLINE(S): APR 30
FIELD(S): Pilot Training and related fields (aerospace, aerodynamics, engineering, airport management, etc.)
ELIGIBILITY/REQUIREMENTS: For tuition or flight training costs for student pilots enrolled at a college or university offering an accredited aviation curriculum in the above fields or for flight training costs in a professional pilot training program at any training facility certified by the FAA. NOT for training for a Private Pilot license. Sexual orientation not considered; contribution to Gay and Lesbian community is a factor.
HOW TO APPLY: Send SASE for application or visit website for further instructions. Submit with documentation of prior academic record and work experience; financial need; extracurricular activities and/or community activities, honors,

awards, etc.; along with supporting references and a letter of recommendation. Must also submit 2 essays: 1 outlining career objectives, and the other documenting contributions to the Gay and Lesbian community.

2872—NINETY-NINES, INC. (Amelia Earhart Memorial Scholarships)

Box 965, 7100 Terminal Drive
Oklahoma City OK 73159-0965
800/994-1929 or 405/685-7969
FAX: 405/685-7985
E-mail: 99s@ninety-nines.org
Internet: http://www.ninety-nines.org
AMOUNT: Varies
DEADLINE(S): DEC 31
FIELD(S): Advanced Aviation Ratings
ELIGIBILITY/REQUIREMENTS: Scholarships for female licensed pilots who are members of the 99s, Inc. Financial need considered.
HOW TO APPLY: Contact 99s for application and/or membership information.
NUMBER OF AWARDS: 15-20
CONTACT: Liz Rousch

2873—NINETY-NINES, INC./SAN FERNANDO VALLEY CHAPTER/VAN NUYS AIRPORT (Career Scholarships)

P.O. Box 8160
Van Nuys CA 91409-8160
818/989-0081
AMOUNT: $3,000
DEADLINE(S): APR 23
FIELD(S): Aviation
ELIGIBILITY/REQUIREMENTS: For men and women residing in the Greater Los Angeles Area pursuing careers as professional pilots, flight instructors, mechanics, or other aviation career specialists. Must be at least 21 years of age and U.S. citizens.
HOW TO APPLY: Send SASE for application after January 1. Submit with letter of recommendation from a person unrelated to you familiar with your accomplishments, and an official transcript or school record.
NUMBER OF AWARDS: 3

2874—PROFESSIONAL AVIATION MAINTENANCE ASSOCIATION (PAMA Scholarship Fund)

636 Eye Street NW, Suite 300
Washington DC 20001-3736
202/216-9220
FAX: 202/216-9224

AMOUNT: $1,000
DEADLINE(S): OCT 31
FIELD(S): Aviation Maintenance
ELIGIBILITY/REQUIREMENTS: Open to students enrolled in an institution to obtain an airframe and powerplant (A&P) license who have completed 25% of the required curriculum. Must have 3.0 or better GPA, demonstrate financial need, and be recommended by instructor.
HOW TO APPLY: Applications submitted through student's school. Write for complete information. Application period runs from July 1 through October 31.

2875—SAN DIEGO AIR & SPACE MUSEUM (R. A. Rearwin Scholarship Fund)

Education Office
2001 Pan American Plaza
San Diego CA 92101
619/234-8291, ext. 19
FAX: 619/233-4526
Internet: http://aerospace
museum.org
AMOUNT: $3,000-$4,000
DEADLINE(S): APR 1
FIELD(S): Aviation, Aerospace
ELIGIBILITY/REQUIREMENTS: For graduating seniors of San Diego County high schools, who will be attending a 4-year college. Unweighted GPA of 3.0 or higher, strong aviation/aerospace career interests, pursuing a baccalaureate in an aerospace-related field.
HOW TO APPLY: Call or write museum for application. Eligible applicants will be interviewed.

2876—SOCIETY OF AUTOMOTIVE ENGINEERS (Kansas State University-Salina/SAE Engineering Scholarship)

SAE Customer Service
400 Commonwealth Drive
Warrendale PA 15096-0001
724/776-4970
FAX: 724/776-1615
E-mail: customerservice@sae.org
Internet: http://www.sae.org/
students/scholarships
AMOUNT: $1,000
DEADLINE(S): DEC 1
FIELD(S): Engineering; Automotive Industry; Aviation Industry
ELIGIBILITY/REQUIREMENTS: Must be incoming freshman pursuing a degree in the College of Technology & Aviation. Must have ACT score of 21 composite or 950 SAT, or 3.2 GPA.
HOW TO APPLY: See website for application. Submit with personal essay that demonstrates hands-on experience or activity (such as rebuilding engines, working on cars/trucks, etc.); 2 recommendations, 1 of which must be from a teacher, counselor, or administrator; and transcript.
NUMBER OF AWARDS: 5
RENEWABLE: Yes. Up to 4 years; if student maintains 3.5 GPA and continued enrollment in College of Technology and Aviation.

2877—UNIVERSITY AVIATION ASSOCIATION (Eugene S. Kropf Scholarship)

3410 Skyway Drive
Auburn AL 36830-6444
334/844-2434
FAX: 334/844-2432
Internet: http://www.uaa.aero
AMOUNT: $500
DEADLINE(S): MAY 31
FIELD(S): Aviation Management, Airport Management
ELIGIBILITY/REQUIREMENTS: Open to applicants who are enrolled in a 2- or 4-year aviation-related curriculum at a UAA member college or university, who are U.S. citizens; minimum 3.0 GPA.
HOW TO APPLY: See website for application and submit with official transcript, and a 250-word "How Can I Improve Aviation Education," and proof of enrollment.
NUMBER OF AWARDS: 3
RENEWABLE: No
CONTACT: Dr. Gregory Schwab, Indiana State University, TC 26, Terre Haute IN 47890; 800/833-5325. Send all requests for information and applications to the attention of Dr. Schwab.

2878—UNIVERSITY AVIATION ASSOCIATION (Joseph Frasca Excellence in Aviation Scholarship)

3410 Skyway Drive
Auburn AL 36830-6444
334/844-2434
FAX: 334/844-2432
Internet: http://www.uaa.aero
AMOUNT: $2,000
DEADLINE(S): APR 9
FIELD(S): Aviation
ELIGIBILITY/REQUIREMENTS: Open to juniors or seniors currently enrolled in a UAA member institution. Must demonstrate excellence in activities, studies, events, organizations, etc., related to aviation; minimum 3.0 overall GPA. Must have Federal Aviation Administration certification/qualifications in either aviation maintenance or flight and be a member of at least one aviation organization such as Alpha Eta Rho, NIFA Flying Team, Experimental Aircraft Association, Warbirds of America, etc. and be involved in aviation activities, projects, events, etc., which will demonstrate an interest and an enthusiasm for aviation. Demonstrated interest or experience in aviation simulation, aircraft restoration, or aerobatics preferred as is work experience in aviation, especially while in school; and financial need.
HOW TO APPLY: See website for application. Submit with 250-word essay stating your personal philosophy of excellence in aviation, especially as it relates to Joseph Frasca's love of flying, aerobatics, aircraft mechanics/restoration and aviation simulation; academic transcript from the UAA member institution you are now attending; FAA certificates (either A & P or Flight related); 1 letter of reference; and additional documentation as required supporting financial need, and other items.
NUMBER OF AWARDS: 1
CONTACT: Dr. David A. NewMyer, c/o College of Applied Sciences and Arts, 1365 Douglas Dr, MC 6623, Southern Illinois University Carbondale, Carbondale IL 62901, 618/453-8898; E-mail: newmyer@siu.edu. Send all requests for information and applications to the attention of Dr. NewMyer.

2879—UNIVERSITY AVIATION ASSOCIATION (Paul A. Whelan Aviation and Aerospace Scholarship)

3410 Skyway Drive
Auburn AL 36830-6444
334/844-2434
FAX: 334/844-2432
Internet: http://www.uaa.aero
AMOUNT: $2,000
DEADLINE(S): MAY 31
FIELD(S): Aviation and space-related fields
ELIGIBILITY/REQUIREMENTS: Open to U.S. citizens who are in their sophomore, junior, senior years or graduate students. Must be enrolled at a UAA member institution in an aviation or space-related major. Community College, college and university applicants encouraged. Must have a 2.5 overall GPA and 3.0 GPA in aviation major coursework; demonstrate a love of aviation, leadership, and extracurricular/community involvement. Preference given to those who hold FAA certification as a pilot or mechanic; former military service or current military service via active duty, the ROTC, the Air National Guard or Reserves while in school; and members of an aviation-related association or professional group such as the UAA.

HOW TO APPLY: See website for application. Submit with official transcript from the UAA member institution(s) attended; recommendation letter from a faculty member from a UAA member institution addressing how the applicant meets one or more of the criteria above.
NUMBER OF AWARDS: 1 or more
CONTACT: Dr. David A. NewMyer, c/o College of Applied Sciences and Arts, 1365 Douglas Dr, MC 6623, Southern Illinois University Carbondale, Carbondale IL 62901, 618/453-8898; E-mail: newmyer@siu.edu. Send all requests for information and applications to the attention of Dr. NewMyer.

2880—VIRGINIA AIRPORT OPERATORS COUNCIL (John R. Lillard VAOC Scholarship Program)

c/o Virginia Aviation and Space Education Forum
5702 Gulfstream Road
Richmond VA 23250-2422
804/236-3624
FAX: 804/236-3625
E-mail: information@agaviation.org
Internet: http://www.agaviation.org
AMOUNT: $3,000
DEADLINE(S): FEB 20
FIELD(S): Aviation; Aeronautics
ELIGIBILITY/REQUIREMENTS: Spouse, child, son-/daughter-in-law, grandchild of an operator, pilot, or allied industry member of NAAA. Sponsor must be a currently active dues-paying member. Financial need considered.
HOW TO APPLY: See website or call for an application. Submit with copy of high school transcript and acceptance letters or other verification of enrollment or acceptance into a postsecondary institution. Include a 350- to 500-word essay on "Why I Wish for a Career in Aviation"; up to 3 letters of recommendation and a list of both school-related and extracurricular activities demonstrating accomplishments and leadership capabilities. Applications evaluated as follows: 35% scholarship (GPA), 30% essay, 20% accomplishments and leadership, and 15% financial need.
CONTACT: Betty Wilson

2881—VIRGINIA AVIATION AND SPACE EDUCATION FORUM (Aviation Scholarship)

Virginia Department of Aviation
5702 Gulfstream Road
Richmond VA 23250-2422
804/236-3624
FAX: 804/236-3625
E-mail: director@doav.state.va.us

Internet: http://www.doav.state.va.us/
AMOUNT: $1,000
DEADLINE(S): FEB 14
FIELD(S): Aviation-related programs
ELIGIBILITY/REQUIREMENTS: For high school seniors planning a career in aviation who are residents of Virginia who have been accepted and are enrolled in an accredited college. Must have at least a 3.5 GPA.
HOW TO APPLY: Contact Forum or access website for application and details.

2882—WESTERN MICHIGAN UNIVERSITY (College of Aviation/Dale Pistsch Memorial Aviation Flight Scholarship)

1903 West Michigan
Kalamazoo MI 49008-5337
269/387-6000
FAX: 269/387-6989
E-mail: finaid-info@wmich.edu
Internet: http://www.wmich.edu/finaid
AMOUNT: Varies
DEADLINE(S): APR 1
FIELD(S): Aviation Flight Science
ELIGIBILITY/REQUIREMENTS: Must be full-time junior or senior majoring in Aviation Flight Science with a 3.0 GPA.
HOW TO APPLY: Contact the College of Aviation for an application at 269/964-4579.
RENEWABLE: No

2883—WESTERN MICHIGAN UNIVERSITY (College of Aviation/Diversity in Aviation Scholarship)

1903 West Michigan
Kalamazoo MI 49008-5337
269/387-6000
FAX: 269/387-6989
E-mail: finaid-info@wmich.edu
Internet: http://www.wmich.edu/finaid
AMOUNT: $1,000
DEADLINE(S): JAN 15
FIELD(S): Aviation
ELIGIBILITY/REQUIREMENTS: Must be enrolled as a full-time student; have a 2.75 GPA; must have applied for acceptance to WMU.
HOW TO APPLY: Contact the College of Aviation for an application at 269/964-4579. Submit with 1-page essay describing why you believe it is important to increase diversity in the field of aviation along with 2 letters of recommendation (1 must be from a teacher) and copies of your high school and/or college transcripts.

2884—WESTERN MICHIGAN UNIVERSITY (College of Aviation/Duke Harrah Memorial Scholarship)

1903 West Michigan
Kalamazoo MI 49008-5337
269/387-6000
FAX: 269/387-6989
E-mail: finaid-info@wmich.edu
Internet: http://www.wmich.edu/finaid
AMOUNT: $200-$500 (fall semester)
DEADLINE(S): APR 1
FIELD(S): Aviation
ELIGIBILITY/REQUIREMENTS: Must be junior Aviation Maintenance student with 3.0 GPA.
HOW TO APPLY: Contact the College of Aviation for an application at 269/964-4579.

2885—WESTERN MICHIGAN UNIVERSITY (College of Aviation/Herman Linder Award)

1903 West Michigan
Kalamazoo MI 49008-5337
269/387-6000
FAX: 269/387-6989
E-mail: finaid-info@wmich.edu
Internet: http://www.wmich.edu/finaid
AMOUNT: Varies
DEADLINE(S): APR 1
FIELD(S): Aviation
ELIGIBILITY/REQUIREMENTS: Enrolled in or have completed required courses in aircraft servicing classes; demonstrated outstanding ability and commitment to professional aircraft maintenance.
HOW TO APPLY: Recipient selected by College of Aviation faculty.

2886—WESTERN MICHIGAN UNIVERSITY (College of Aviation/Kern Family Endowed Scholarship)

1903 West Michigan
Kalamazoo MI 49008-5337
269/387-6000
FAX: 269/387-6989
E-mail: finaid-info@wmich.edu
Internet: http://www.wmich.edu/finaid
AMOUNT: Varies
DEADLINE(S): APR 1
FIELD(S): Aviation Flight Science
ELIGIBILITY/REQUIREMENTS: Must be full-time junior or senior enrolled in the aviation program; must demonstrate finan-

cial need. Preferred minimum GPA of 3.0; recipient must also demonstrate a genuine interest in major field of study as determined by the faculty of the aviation program.
HOW TO APPLY: Contact the College of Aviation for an application at 269/964-4579.
RENEWABLE: No

2887—WESTERN MICHIGAN UNIVERSITY (College of Aviation/Major Henry Schmaltz, USAF, Endowed Scholarship)

1903 West Michigan
Kalamazoo MI 49008-5337
269/387-6000
FAX: 269/387-6989
Internet: http://www.wmich.edu/finaid
AMOUNT: Varies
DEADLINE(S): APR 1
FIELD(S): Aviation Sciences
ELIGIBILITY/REQUIREMENTS: Must be a full-time junior or senior majoring in Aviation Flight Science or Maintenance Engineering Technology with 3.0 GPA.
HOW TO APPLY: Contact the College of Aviation for an application at 269/964-4579.

2888—WESTERN MICHIGAN UNIVERSITY (College of Aviation/William J. Kozel Endowed Scholarship Fund for Aviation Sciences)

1903 West Michigan
Kalamazoo MI 49008-5337
269/387-6000
FAX: 269/387-6989
E-mail: finaid-info@wmich.edu
Internet: http://www.wmich.edu/finaid
AMOUNT: Varies
DEADLINE(S): APR 1
FIELD(S): Aviation Sciences
ELIGIBILITY/REQUIREMENTS: Must be enrolled as a full-time student, have a 2.75 GPA and major in an Aviation Science Maintenance related program.
HOW TO APPLY: Contact the College of Aviation for an application at 269/964-4579.

2889—WHIRLY-GIRLS INC. (International Women Helicopter Pilots Scholarships)

Executive Towers 10-D
207 West Clarendon Avenue
Phoenix AZ 85013
602/263-0190
FAX: 602/264-5812
AMOUNT: $4,500
DEADLINE(S): NOV 15
FIELD(S): Helicopter Flight Training
ELIGIBILITY/REQUIREMENTS: Available to licensed women pilots for flight training.
NUMBER OF AWARDS: 3; 2 are awarded to Whirly-Girls who are helicopter pilots; 1 is awarded to a licensed woman pilot holding a private license (airplane, balloon, or glider).
HOW TO APPLY: Applications are available April 15. Write, call, or fax for complete information.

BUILDING TRADES

2890—HOBART INSTITUTE OF WELDING TECHNOLOGY

400 Trade Square East
Troy OH 45373
800/332-9448, ext. 5560
FAX: 937/332-5200
E-mail: hiwt@welding.org
Internet: http://www.welding.org
AMOUNT: Complete tuition costs
DEADLINE(S): APR 1; AUG 1; DEC 1
FIELD(S): Structural Welding
ELIGIBILITY/REQUIREMENTS: Must have graduated from high school within the past 7 years, or have obtained a GED equivalent during that time. Based on an essay, grades, and references; financial need NOT a factor.
HOW TO APPLY: See website or send SASE for an application. Transcript; 3 letters of recommendation from teachers, counselors, or supervisors; and a brief statement explaining reasons for selecting welding as a career and your goals required.
NUMBER OF AWARDS: 3

2891—INDEPENDENT POOL AND SPA SERVICE ASSOCIATION, INC.

Scholarship Fund
P.O. Box 15828
Long Beach CA 90815-0828
888/360-9505
E-mail: ipssamail@aol.com
Internet: http://www.ipssa.com
AMOUNT: Varies
DEADLINE(S): Enrollment is between MAY 1-JUL 15 and NOV 1-JAN 15; applications must be postmarked during these periods.
FIELD(S): Self-Employed Pool or Spa Service Technician (bookkeeping, accounting, computers, chemistry, plumbing, electrical, mechanical)
ELIGIBILITY/REQUIREMENTS: Any self-employed pool service professional whose business is in California, Arizona, Texas, or Nevada who earns more than 50% of income from the business, and/or his/her immediate family members (spouses, children) are eligible to apply.
HOW TO APPLY: Download application from website. Explain how the course or class is related to the business.

2892—MAINE METAL PRODUCTS ASSOCIATION EDUCATION FUND

28 Stroudwater St., Suite #4
Westbrook ME 04092
207/854-2153
FAX: 207/854-3865
E-mail: info@maine-metals.org
Internet: http://www.maine-metals.org
AMOUNT: Varies
DEADLINE(S): MAY 1
FIELD(S): Mechanical Engineering; Machine Tool Technician; Sheet Metal Fabrication; Welding; CAD/CAM for Metals Industry
ELIGIBILITY/REQUIREMENTS: Must be accepted in a metal trades program at a Maine college and must be a Maine resident.
HOW TO APPLY: Send application; copy of high school diploma or equivalent or expected graduation date; copies of high school and postsecondary transcripts; letter of recommendation from current employer (if applicable), teachers, community leaders, business people, etc.; and a personal description of goals, aspirations, and accomplishments that also answers the questions "Why and how did you decide on a career in metal working? Why do you think you should receive this scholarship?"
RENEWABLE: Yes. Must reapply.
CONTACT: Lisa Martin, Executive Director, e-mail: lisa@maine-metals.org; 207/329-9923

2893—MIDWEST ROOFING CONTRACTORS ASSOCIATION (Construction Industry Scholarships)

3286 Oak Court
Belmont CA 94002
800/497-6722
FAX: 785/843/7555
E-mail: mrca@mrca.org
Internet: http://www.mrca.org
AMOUNT: Varies
DEADLINE(S): JUN 20

FIELD(S): Construction
ELIGIBILITY/REQUIREMENTS:
Applicants must be pursuing or planning to pursue a curriculum at an accredited university, college, community college, vocational, or trade school that will lead to a career in the construction industry. Three letters of recommendation required.
HOW TO APPLY: Contact MRCA for an application.

2894—NATIONAL STONE, SAND & GRAVEL ASSOCIATION (NSSGA Barry K. Wendt Memorial Scholarship)

1605 King Street
Alexandria VA 22314
703/525-8788
FAX: 703/525-7782
E-mail: info@nssga.org
Internet: http://www.nssga.org
AMOUNT: $2,500
DEADLINE(S): APR 30
FIELD(S): Engineering; Mining; Minerals; Construction Management
ELIGIBILITY/REQUIREMENTS: Open to graduating seniors or college students who plan to pursue a career in the crushed stone, sand and gravel production industry.
HOW TO APPLY: See website or write for information and application.
NUMBER OF AWARDS: 1
RENEWABLE: No

2895—REAL ESTATE EDUCATION FOUNDATION (The Foundation Scholarship)

3180 Adloff Lane, Suite 400
Springfield IL 62703
217/529-2600
FAX: 217/529-3904
Internet: http://www.illinois realtor.org
AMOUNT: $1,000-$2,000
DEADLINE(S): APR 1
FIELD(S): Real Estate and Allied Fields (Construction; Land Use Planning; Mortgage Banking; Property Management; Real Estate Appraising; Real Estate Assessing; Real Estate Brokerage; Real Estate Development; Real Estate Investment Counseling; Real Estate Law; Real Estate Syndication)
ELIGIBILITY/REQUIREMENTS: Must indicate interest in pursuing a career in real estate or an allied field; record of scholastic achievement, including academic GPA; economic need or situation; and recommendations by instructors, employers, Realtors and others.
HOW TO APPLY: Submit application with a statement of your general activities

and intellectual interests, employment (if any), contemplated line of study and of the career you expect to follow (up to 1,000 words); a record of military service, if any; your proposed program of study, including a brief description of each course, signed by the Dean or appropriate official; a statement from the real estate instructor, or, if none, the Dean recommending you; transcripts of all your collegiate records; and letters of recommendation from 2 persons (preferable that 1 of these letters be from a Realtor). Personal interview for finalists.
NUMBER OF AWARDS: 8
CONTACT: Larranne Wells

COMPUTER TECHNOLOGY

2896—ART INSTITUTES INTERNATIONAL, THE (Evelyn Keedy Memorial Scholarship)

300 Sixth Avenue, Suite 800
Pittsburgh PA 15222-2598
412/562-9800
FAX: 412/562-9802
E-mail: webadmin@aii.edu
Internet: http://www.aii.edu
AMOUNT: 2 years full tuition
DEADLINE(S): MAY 1
FIELD(S): Creative and Applied Arts (video production, broadcasting, culinary arts, fashion design, website administration, etc.)
ELIGIBILITY/REQUIREMENTS: For graduating high school seniors admitted to an Art Institutes International School, the New York Restaurant School, or NCPT.
HOW TO APPLY: See website or contact AII for more information. Transcripts, letters of recommendation, and résumé must be submitted with application.
NUMBER OF AWARDS: Multiple (for use at 12 locations nationwide)

2897—COUNCIL OF ENERGY RESOURCE TRIBES (CERT)

CERT Education Program
Attention: Scholars Program
695 S. Colorado Blvd, Suite 10
Denver CO 80246
303/282-7576
FAX: 303/282-7584
E-mail: info@CERTRedEarth.com
Internet: http://www.certred earth.com/
AMOUNT: $1,000
DEADLINE(S): SEP 14 (Fall), FEB 15 (Spring)
FIELD(S): Science; Engineering; Business, Mathematics, Computer Technology, or related fields

ELIGIBILITY/REQUIREMENTS:
Applicants must meet the criteria to become a TRIBES Institute candidate and a full-time undergraduate (12 hrs/semester) student enrolled in an accredited 2- or 4-year tribal, private, or public university/college., and must maintain at least a 2.5 GPA, although academic excellence far above this GPA is preferred. (Should scholarship funds be limited, GPA will be weighed in decision.)
HOW TO APPLY: See website or contact CERT. Submit application along with official Tribal affiliation documentation (with enrollment number or other statement of Tribal acknowledgment of membership), an official transcript of most recent coursework with the cumulative GPA, as well as the GPA for current hours detailed on the transcript, and a class schedule for the next term demonstrating that you will be attending school full-time and/or verification of full-time enrollment for the next semester.
RENEWABLE: Yes. Must reapply.
CONTACT: Tom Talache, ttalache@CERTRedEarth.com or 303/282-7576, ext. 12

2898—EMPIRE COLLEGE (Dean's Scholarship)

3035 Cleveland Avenue
Santa Rosa CA 95403
707/546-4000
FAX: 707/546-4058
Internet: http://www.wmpcol.edu
AMOUNT: $250-$1,500
DEADLINE(S): APR 15
FIELD(S): Accounting; Office Administration; Paralegal; Medical (Clinical and Administrative); Tourism; Hospitality; General Business; Computer Assembly; Network Assembly/Administration; Security
ELIGIBILITY/REQUIREMENTS: Open to high school seniors who plan to attend Empire College. Must be U.S. citizen.
HOW TO APPLY: Contact College for an application.
NUMBER OF AWARDS: 10
RENEWABLE: No
CONTACT: Mary Farha

2899—LOS ANGELES COUNCIL OF BLACK PROFESSIONAL ENGINEERS (Al-Ben Scholarship)

P.O. Box 881029
Los Angeles CA 90009
310/635-7734
E-mail: secy1@lablackengineers.org

Internet: http://www.lablack
engineers.org/scholarships.html
AMOUNT: Varies
DEADLINE(S): Varies
FIELD(S): Engineering; Mathematics;
Computer Studies; Applied Scientific
Studies
ELIGIBILITY/REQUIREMENTS: Open
to technically inclined precollege and
undergraduate students enrolled in one of
the above fields. Must be of African-
American, Native American, or Hispanic
ancestry. Preference given to students
attending college in Southern California or
who are Southern California residents.
HOW TO APPLY: See website to download an application.

2900—MAINE METAL PRODUCTS ASSO-CIATION

28 Stroudwater St., Suite #4
Westbrook ME 04092
207/854-2153
FAX: 207/854-3865
E-mail: info@maine-metals.org
Internet: http://www.maine-
metals.org
AMOUNT: Varies
DEADLINE(S): MAY 1
FIELD(S): Mechanical Engineering;
Machine Tool Technician; Sheet Metal
Fabrication; Welding; CAD/CAM for
Metals Industry
ELIGIBILITY/REQUIREMENTS: Must
be accepted in a metal trades program at a
Maine college and must be a Maine resident.
HOW TO APPLY: Send application; copy
of high school diploma or equivalent or
expected graduation date; copies of high
school and postsecondary transcripts; letter of recommendation from current
employer (if applicable), teachers, community leaders, business people, etc.; and a
personal description of goals, aspirations,
and accomplishments that also answers the
questions "Why and how did you decide
on a career in metal working? Why do you
think you should receive this scholarship?"
RENEWABLE: Yes. Must reapply.
CONTACT: Lisa Martin, Executive
Director, e-mail: lisa@maine-metals.org;
207/329-9923

FASHION & INTERIOR DESIGN

2901—AMERICAN ASSOCIATION OF COSMETOLOGY SCHOOLS (ACE Grants)

11811 North Tatum Boulevard,
Suite 1085
Phoenix AZ 85028

602/788-1170
FAX: 602/404/8900
E-mail: jim@beautyschools.org
Internet: http://www.beauty
schools.org
AMOUNT: $1,000 (average)
DEADLINE(S): None
FIELD(S): Cosmetology
ELIGIBILITY/REQUIREMENTS:
Grants for U.S. citizens/permanent resi-
dents who are accepted to a participating
ACE grant school. Must be high school
graduate or equivalent. Financial need is
NOT a factor.
HOW TO APPLY: Contact the American
Association of Cosmetology Schools for an
application.
NUMBER OF AWARDS: 500+
RENEWABLE: No
CONTACT: Jim Cox

2902—AMERICAN INTERCONTINENTAL UNIVERSITY (Emilio Pucci Scholarships)

Admissions Committee
3330 Peachtree Road NE
Atlanta GA 30326
404/812-8192 or 888/248-7392
AMOUNT: $300/quarter
DEADLINE(S): None
FIELD(S): Fashion Design; Fashion
Marketing; Interior Design;
Commercial Art; Business
Administration; Video Production
ELIGIBILITY/REQUIREMENTS: Open
to high school seniors who are interested in
either a 2-year or 4-year program at one of
the campuses of the American Inter-
continental University: Atlanta, Georgia;
Los Angeles, California; London, England;
or Dubai, United Arab Emirates.
HOW TO APPLY: Write for applications
and complete information.
RENEWABLE: Yes. Up to $1,800 (6
quarters).

2903—AMERICAN SOCIETY OF INTERIOR DESIGNERS (Scholarship and Awards Program)

608 Massachusetts Avenue NE
Washington DC 20002-6006
202/546-3480
Internet: http://www.asid.org
AMOUNT: $750-$3,000
DEADLINE(S): APR
FIELD(S): Interior Design
ELIGIBILITY/REQUIREMENTS:
Available to both undergraduates and
graduate students studying interior design.

Based on academic/creative accomplishment.
HOW TO APPLY: Submit portfolio
and/or research paper.
NUMBER OF AWARDS: Several

2904—ART INSTITUTES INTERNATIONAL, THE (Evelyn Keedy Memorial Scholarship)

300 Sixth Avenue, Suite 800
Pittsburgh PA 15222-2598
412/562-9800
FAX: 412/562-9802
E-mail: webadmin@aii.edu
Internet: http://www.aii.edu
AMOUNT: 2 years full tuition
DEADLINE(S): MAY 1
FIELD(S): Creative and Applied Arts
(video production, broadcasting,
culinary arts, fashion design, website
administration, etc.)
ELIGIBILITY/REQUIREMENTS: For
graduating high school seniors admitted to
an Art Institutes International School, the
New York Restaurant School, or NCPT.
HOW TO APPLY: See website or contact
AII for more information. Transcripts, let-
ters of recommendation, and résumé must
be submitted with application.
NUMBER OF AWARDS: Multiple (for
use at 12 locations nationwide)

2905—FASHION GROUP INTERNATION-AL OF GREATER WASHINGTON DC

P.O. Box 1288
Great Falls VA 22066
301/564-3666
Internet: http://www.fgi.org
AMOUNT: Up to $5,000
DEADLINE(S): APR 15
FIELD(S): Fashion
ELIGIBILITY/REQUIREMENTS: Must
be permanent residents of Washington
DC, Virginia, or Maryland. Must either
graduate from high school in June and/or
have been admitted to an accredited institution or be enrolled in a university or college as an undergraduate or graduate student and major in fashion-related field.
HOW TO APPLY: Application form and
details are available on website or contact
organization for further information.

2906—HAYSTACK MOUNTAIN SCHOOL OF CRAFTS

Admissions Office
P.O. Box 518
Deer Isle ME 04627
207/348-2306
FAX: 207/348-2307

E-mail: haystack@haystack-mtn.org
Internet: http://www.haystack-mtn.org
AMOUNT: Varies
DEADLINE(S): MAR 25
FIELD(S): Crafts (metals, clay, wood); Graphics (painting, drawing, and related fields); Weaving; Glass; Blacksmithing
ELIGIBILITY/REQUIREMENTS: 18 years old with dedicated interest in crafts.
HOW TO APPLY: Write or e-mail for application.
NUMBER OF AWARDS: 90+
RENEWABLE: No

2907—NEW YORK STATE THEATRE INSTITUTE (Internships in Theatrical Production)

37 First Street
Troy NY 12180
518/274-3200
FAX: 518/274-3815
E-mail: nysti@capital.net
Internet: http://www.nysti.org/not-for-profit/nysti/int.htm
AMOUNT: None
DEADLINE(S): None
FIELD(S): Theatrical Production and related fields
ELIGIBILITY/REQUIREMENTS: Internships for college and graduate students, high school seniors, and educators-in-residence interested in developing skills in above fields. Unpaid academic credit is earned. Gain experience in box office, costumes, education, electrics, music, stage management, scenery, properties, performance, and public relations. Interns come from all over the world.
HOW TO APPLY: Must be associated with an accredited institution. See website for more information, call or write. Include your postal mailing address.
CONTACT: Arlene Leff, Intern Program Director, 518/274-3573

2908—SONOMA CHAMBOLLE-MUSIGNY SISTER CITIES, INC. (Henri Cardinaux Memorial Scholarship)

Chamson Scholarship Committee
P.O. Box 1633
Sonoma CA 95476-1633
938/908-1939
FAX: 707/939-1344
E-mail: icardin@aol.com
AMOUNT: Up to $1,500 (travel + expenses)
DEADLINE(S): JUL 15
FIELD(S): Culinary Arts; Wine Industry; Art; Architecture; Music; History; Fashion
ELIGIBILITY/REQUIREMENTS: Hands-on experience working in above or similar fields and living with a family in small French village in Burgundy or other French city. Must be Sonoma County, California, resident at least 18 years of age and be able to communicate in French.
HOW TO APPLY: Transcripts, employer recommendation, photograph, and essay (stating why, where, and when) required.
NUMBER OF AWARDS: 1
RENEWABLE: No
CONTACT: Ivy Cardinaux

2909—WOMEN'S JEWELRY ASSOCIATION (WJA Scholarship Fund)

373 Route 46 West
Building E, Suite 215
Fairfield NJ 07004-2442
973/575-7130
FAX: 973/575-1445
E-mail: info@womensjewelry.org
Internet: http://www.unusa.org
AMOUNT: $500-$2,500
DEADLINE(S): MAY
FIELD(S): Jewelry Design and Manufacture; Marketing; Retailing
ELIGIBILITY/REQUIREMENTS: Based on drawings or slides of jewelry designs.
HOW TO APPLY: See website or call for an application. Submit with 2 written references, short essay, and slides or drawings of work. Winners will be selected by a panel of judges from the jewelry industry.
NUMBER OF AWARDS: 5-15
RENEWABLE: No
CONTACT: Gillian Schultz

2910—WORLDSTUDIO FOUNDATION

200 Varick Street, Suite 507
New York NY 10014
212/366-1317
FAX: 212/807-0024
E-mail: scholarshipcoordinator@worldstudio.org
Internet: http://www.worldstudio.org or http://www.aiga.org
AMOUNT: $1,500-$5,000
DEADLINE(S): APR 14
FIELD(S): Advertising, Animation, Architecture, Cartooning, Crafts, Environmental graphics, Film/video, Film/theater design, Fine arts, Furniture design, Industrial/product design, Interior architecture and design, Landscape architecture, New media, Photography, Surface/textile design, Urban planning
ELIGIBILITY/REQUIREMENTS: Applicants must be pursuing a degree in the fine or commercial arts, design or architecture, and plan to enter a career in the creative professions. Undergraduates and graduates are eligible. Minority status and/or social agenda are significant factors. Financial need a prerequisite. Minimum 2.0 GPA.
HOW TO APPLY: See websites for application. The application is a 2-part process. Applications must include personal and school information, including transcripts and copies of letters of acceptance; financial information; portfolio; written statement of purpose; examples of a commitment to a social agenda, 2 letters of recommendation from college instructors, high school teachers, or employers; head shot of applicant.
NUMBER OF AWARDS: 20-30
RENEWABLE: Yes. Must reapply.
CONTACT: Mark Randall

FOOD & WINE

2911—AMERICAN CULINARY FEDERATION, THE/AMERICAN ACADEMY OF CHEFS (High School Scholarships)

180 Center Place Way
St. Augustine FL 32095
800/624-9458, ext. 102
FAX: 904/825-4758
E-mail: academy@acfchefs.net
Internet: http://www.acfchefs.org
AMOUNT: Varies
DEADLINE(S): DEC 1
FIELD(S): Culinary Arts
ELIGIBILITY/REQUIREMENTS: Must be an exemplary student; a graduating high school senior, currently accepted to an accredited, postsecondary college, with a major in either culinary or pastry arts, or be an ACF registered apprentice; must have a career goal of becoming a chef or pastry chef.
HOW TO APPLY: See website for application, and submit with 2 letters of recommendation from industry and/or culinary professionals NOT related to applicant in any manner; official transcript showing current GPA; and Financial Aid Release Form completed by your financial aid office.
NUMBER OF AWARDS: Varies
RENEWABLE: No

2912— AMERICAN CULINARY FEDERATION, THE/AMERICAN ACADEMY OF CHEFS (College Scholarships)

180 Center Place Way
St. Augustine FL 32095

800/624-9458, ext. 102
FAX: 904/825-4758
E-mail: academy@acfchefs.net
Internet: http://www.acfchefs.org
AMOUNT: Varies
DEADLINE(S): DEC 1
FIELD(S): Culinary Arts
ELIGIBILITY/REQUIREMENTS:
Applicant must be an exemplary student; currently enrolled in an accredited, postsecondary school of culinary arts, or other postsecondary culinary training program with a major in either culinary or pastry arts, or be an ACF registered apprentice; completed a grading or marking period (trimester, semester or quarter), and have a career goal of becoming a chef or pastry chef.
HOW TO APPLY: See website for application, and submit with 2 letters of recommendation from industry and/or culinary professionals NOT related to applicant in any manner; official transcript showing current GPA.
NUMBER OF AWARDS: Varies
RENEWABLE: No

2913—AMERICAN CULINARY FEDERATION, THE/AMERICAN ACADEMY OF CHEFS (Professional Chef Scholarships)

180 Center Place Way
St. Augustine FL 32095
800/624-9458, ext. 102
FAX: 904/825-4758
E-mail: academy@acfchefs.net
Internet: http://www.acfchefs.org
AMOUNT: Up to $750
DEADLINE(S): DEC 1
FIELD(S): Culinary Arts
ELIGIBILITY/REQUIREMENTS: For initial certification, applicant must pass an initial ACF certification class with a "C" grade or better. For continuing education, applicant must be certified by the American Culinary Federation as a Certified Chef de Cuisine or higher, be enrolled in a state-accredited educational institution for the purpose of enhancing culinary skills or knowledge which will assist the applicant in his/her career, and be an active member of the American Culinary Federation in good standing for 3 or more consecutive years.
HOW TO APPLY: See website for application. Submit with proof of certification, proof of ACF membership, and total cost of class.
NUMBER OF AWARDS: Varies
RENEWABLE: No
ADDITIONAL INFORMATION: Scholarships are for continuing education or initial certification classes including approved seminars.

2914—AMERICAN CULINARY FEDERATION, THE/AMERICAN ACADEMY OF CHEFS (Student Culinary Team Scholarships)

180 Center Place Way
St. Augustine FL 32095
800/624-9458, ext. 102
FAX: 904/825-4758
E-mail: academy@acfchefs.net
Internet: http://www.acfchefs.org
AMOUNT: Varies
DEADLINE(S): None; submit
throughout the year
ELIGIBILITY/REQUIREMENTS:
Applicants must be members of a student hot food team sponsored by an ACF Chapter in good standing, have already won their state competition and ready to go to the regional competition, or have won their regional competition and ready to go to the national competition; be ACF Student Members in good standing; and have held at least one fundraiser.
HOW TO APPLY: See website for application, and submit with proof of fundraiser showing amount raised.
NUMBER OF AWARDS: Varies
RENEWABLE: No

2915—AMERICAN HOTEL & LODGING EDUCATIONAL FOUNDATION (The AAA Five Diamond Hospitality Scholarship)

1201 New York Avenue NW,
Suite 600
Washington DC 20005-3931
202/289-3188
FAX: 202/289-3199
Internet: http://www. ahlef.org
AMOUNT: $5,000
DEADLINE(S): MAY 1
FIELD(S): Hospitality/Hotel
Management; Travel & Tourism;
Culinary Arts
ELIGIBILITY/REQUIREMENTS: Each year, AAA selects one of the 4-year programs participating in AH&LEF's Annual Scholarship Grant Program to receive the award.
HOW TO APPLY: The chosen school selects the scholarship recipient based upon a set of minimum eligibility criteria. See website for additional information and name of school chosen each year.

2916—AMERICAN HOTEL & LODGING EDUCATIONAL FOUNDATION (American Express Academic Scholarships)

1201 New York Avenue NW,
Suite 600
Washington DC 20005-3931

202/289-3188
FAX: 202/289-3199
Internet: http://www. ahlef.org
AMOUNT: $500-$2,000
DEADLINE(S): MAY 1
FIELD(S): Hospitality/Hotel
Management; Travel & Tourism;
Culinary Arts
ELIGIBILITY/REQUIREMENTS: For full-time (minimum 20 hours/week) AH&LA-member property employees and their dependents enrolled in accredited, undergraduate academic programs leading to a degree in hospitality management. The applicant does not have to attend an AH&LEF-affiliated school.
HOW TO APPLY: Applications available on website.

2917—AMERICAN HOTEL & LODGING EDUCATIONAL FOUNDATION (American Express Professional Development Scholarships)

1201 New York Avenue NW,
Suite 600
Washington DC 20005-3931
202/289-3188
FAX: 202/289-3199
Internet: http://www. ahlef.org
AMOUNT: $500-$2,000
DEADLINE(S): quarterly
FIELD(S): Hospitality/Hotel
Management; Travel & Tourism;
Culinary Arts
ELIGIBILITY/REQUIREMENTS: Provides financial support to students enrolled in distance learning courses or professional certifications courses offered through the Educational Institute (EI).
HOW TO APPLY: Applicants must enroll in EI to qualify. AH&LEF makes scholarship payment directly to EI on the recipient's behalf. Call EI at 800/349-0299 or visit www.ei-ahla.org for enrollment information.

2918—AMERICAN INSTITUTE OF BAKING

1213 Bakers Way
Manhattan KS 66502
800/633-5737
FAX: 785/537-1493
E-mail: kembers@aibonline.org
Internet: http://www.aibonline.org
AMOUNT: $500-$4,000
DEADLINE(S): None
FIELD(S): Baking Industry;
Electrical/Electronic Maintenance
ELIGIBILITY/REQUIREMENTS:
Award is to be used towards tuition for a 16- or 10-week course in baking science

and technology or maintenance engineering at the Institute. Experience in baking, mechanics, or an approved alternative is required. Awards are intended for people who plan to seek new positions in the baking and maintenance engineering fields.
HOW TO APPLY: Contact AIB for an application.
NUMBER OF AWARDS: 45

2919—AMERICAN NATIONAL CATTLE-WOMEN FOUNDATION

9110 East Nichols Avenue
Centennial CO 80112
303/694-0313
FAX: 303/694-2390
Internet: http://www.ancw.org or http://www.nationalbeef ambassador.org
AMOUNT: $1,000, $750, $500
DEADLINE(S): Varies
FIELD(S): Beef Industry
ELIGIBILITY/REQUIREMENTS: Must qualify at a state-level speaking competition then compete at national competition.
HOW TO APPLY: See website; click on National Beef Ambassador Program or contact Project Manager.
NUMBER OF AWARDS: 1
RENEWABLE: No
CONTACT: Carol Abrahamzon, Project Manager, 507/724-3905; e-mail cabrahamzon@beef.org

2920—AMERICAN SOCIETY FOR HEALTH-CARE FOOD SERVICE ADMINISTRATORS (Bonnie Miller Continuing Education Fund)

304 West Liberty Street,
Suite 201
Louisville KY 40202
800/620-6422
Internet: http://www.ashfsa.org
AMOUNT: $500 (part-time); $1,000 (full-time)
DEADLINE(S): MAR 15
FIELD(S): Healthcare Food Service Management
ELIGIBILITY/REQUIREMENTS: Open to undergraduate students at 2- or 4-year colleges.
HOW TO APPLY: Contact Society for an application.
CONTACT: Keith Howard

2921—AMERICAN TRAFFIC SAFETY SERVICES FOUNDATION (Roadway Worker Memorial Scholarship Program)

15 Riverside Parkway, Suite 100
Fredericksburg VA 22406
800/272-8772 or 540/368-1701
FAX: 540/368-1717
E-mail: foundation@atssa.com
Internet: http://www.atssa.com/cs/roadway-worker-scholarship
AMOUNT: $2,000-$3,000 (see below)
DEADLINE(S): FEB 15
FIELD(S): All
ELIGIBILITY/REQUIREMENTS: Must be children or parents with custody or legal guardianship of surviving children of roadway safety workers killed or permanently disabled in work zones, including mobile operations and the installation of roadway safety features. Must be applied to a post-secondary school or institution that requires a high school diploma or GED for admission including 2- or 4-year accredited college or university; or vocational-technical college or a training institution. Based on past academic performance, financial need, record of volunteerism.
HOW TO APPLY: See website or e-mail for an application. Submit with an official copy transcript and grade report; FAFSA; a no more than 200-word statement explaining your reasons for wanting to continue your education and listing any volunteer activities/accomplishments; and 2 letters of recommendation from a teacher, school administrator, counselor, member of the clergy, or work or military supervisor who can address the applicant's qualifications and academic aptitude.
NUMBER OF AWARDS: 2-3
RENEWABLE: Yes. Must reapply.
CONTACT: Melanie Myers, Foundation Director
ADDITIONAL INFORMATION: If a particular applicant demonstrates a strong commitment to volunteerism, they may be eligible to receive an additional $1,000.

2922—ART INSTITUTES INTERNATIONAL, THE (Evelyn Keedy Memorial Scholarship)

300 Sixth Avenue, Suite 800
Pittsburgh PA 15222-2598
412/562-9800
FAX: 412/562-9802
E-mail: webadmin@aii.edu
Internet: http://www.aii.edu
AMOUNT: 2 years full tuition
DEADLINE(S): MAY 1
FIELD(S): Creative and Applied Arts (video production, broadcasting, culinary arts, fashion design, website administration, etc.)
ELIGIBILITY/REQUIREMENTS: For graduating high school seniors admitted to an Art Institutes International School, the New York Restaurant School, or NCPT.
HOW TO APPLY: See website or contact AII for more information. Transcripts, letters of recommendation, and résumé must be submitted with application.
NUMBER OF AWARDS: Multiple (for use at 12 locations nationwide)

2923—CALIFORNIA ASSOCIATION OF WINEGRAPE GROWERS (Robert Miller Scholarship for Viticulture and Enology for Viticulture & Enology Students on the Central Coast)

1325 J Street, Suite 1560
Sacramento CA 95814
800/241-1800 or 916/379-8995
FAX: 916/379-8999
E-mail: info@cawg.org
Internet: http://www.cawg.org/cwggf
AMOUNT: $500 or $1,000
DEADLINE(S): late MAR (see website)
FIELD(S): Viticulture, Enology
ELIGIBILITY/REQUIREMENTS: Applicant's parent or guardian must be employed by a California winegrape grower; scholarships are based on financial need and academic achievement. May be used at Alan Hancock Community College or Cal Poly, San Luis Obispo. Must major in above fields.
HOW TO APPLY: Must be a graduating high school senior or a student enrolled at Alan Hancock Community College or Cal Poly, San Luis Obispo. See website for application; submit with high school transcript, a copy of your SAT or ACT results if you are applying for a 4-year scholarship, a letter of recommendation from an instructor, the school principal or counselor, and a 2-page essay (approximately 500 words) focusing on you and your career goals.
NUMBER OF AWARDS: 2, up to 4 years ($1,000/year); 4, up to 2 years ($500/year)
RENEWABLE: Yes. Studies must continue to be completed satisfactorily.
CONTACT: Carolee Williams
ADDITIONAL INFORMATION: Children of winegrape growers may request a waiver from the eligibility requirement based upon financial need.

2924—CHILD NUTRITION FOUNDATION

700 S. Washington Street,
Suite 300
Alexandria VA 22314

703/739-3900
FAX: 703/739-3915
E-mail: cnf@asfsa.org
Internet: http://www.asfsa.org/
cnfoundation
AMOUNT: $300-$1,200
DEADLINE(S): APR 15
FIELD(S): Child Nutrition; Food Service
Management; Business Administration
ELIGIBILITY/REQUIREMENTS: Must
be an American School Food Service
Association (ASFSA) member and/or the
dependent of an ASFSA member. Must
study a field designed to improve school
food service (such as those above) at a
vocational/technical school, community
college, college or university.
HOW TO APPLY: Applications available
at: www.asfsa.org/continuinged/assistance/
scholar/scholarships.
NUMBER OF AWARDS: 70
RENEWABLE: Yes, must reapply.
CONTACT: Child Nutrition Foundation
Financial Aid Manager

2925—COLORADO RESTAURANT ASSO-CIATION (Scholarship Education Fund)

430 East 7th Avenue
Denver CO 80203
800/522-2972 or 303/830-2972
FAX: 303/830-2973
E-mail: info@coloradorestaurant.com
Internet: http://www.colorado
restaurant.com
AMOUNT: $500-$2,500
DEADLINE(S): MAR 20
FIELD(S): Food Service; Hospitality
ELIGIBILITY/REQUIREMENTS: Open
to junior- and senior- level college students
enrolled in a 2- or 4-year degree program
in food service- and hospitality-related
fields at a Colorado college or university.
HOW TO APPLY: Contact CRA for an
application.

2926—FOOD INDUSTRIES SCHOLARSHIP FUND OF NEW HAMPSHIRE (Scholarships)

110 Stark Street
Manchester NH 03101-1977
AMOUNT: $1,000
DEADLINE(S): APR 1
FIELD(S): Food Industry
ELIGIBILITY/REQUIREMENTS: Open
to students who are employed or whose
parents are employed in businesses that
are members of New Hampshire Grocers
Association.
HOW TO APPLY: Write to Fund for an
application.
NUMBER OF AWARDS: 18-20

2927—GOLDEN GATE RESTAURANT ASSOCIATION SCHOLARSHIP FOUNDATION AWARDS

120 Market Street, Suite 1280
San Francisco CA 94104
415/781-5348
FAX: 415/781-3925
E-mail: education@ggra.org
Internet: http://www.ggra.org
AMOUNT: $1,000-$3,000
DEADLINE(S): MAR 31
FIELD(S): Food Service and Hospitality
Industry
ELIGIBILITY/REQUIREMENTS: Open
to California residents who are undergrad-
uates majoring in food service at a college
or university. 1) Must be full-time student
and have graduated from high school. 2)
Must be full time, have completed at least
1 semester, minimum 2.75 GPA. 3) Must
be part-time student, working in the food
service/hospitality industry 20 hours/week,
minimum 2.75 GPA.
HOW TO APPLY: Contact GGRASF
Coordinator and request an application or
visit website and download application
NUMBER OF AWARDS: 5-10
RENEWABLE: Must reapply every year.
CONTACT: Scholarship Coordinator

2928—INSTITUTE OF FOOD TECHNOLO-GISTS (Freshman Scholarships)

525 West Van Buren, Suite 1000
Chicago IL 60607
312/782-8424
FAX: 312/782-8348
E-mail: info@ift.org
AMOUNT: $1,000-$1,500
DEADLINE(S): FEB 15
FIELD(S): Food Science; Food
Technology
ELIGIBILITY/REQUIREMENTS: Open
to scholastically outstanding high school
graduates and seniors expecting to gradu-
ate from high school. Must be entering col-
lege for the first time in an approved pro-
gram in food science/technology.
HOW TO APPLY: Contact IFT for an
application.
NUMBER OF AWARDS: 25

2929—INSTITUTE OF FOOD TECHNOLO-GISTS (Junior/Senior Scholarships)

525 West Van Buren, Suite 1000
Chicago IL 60607
312/782-8424
FAX: 312/782-8348
E-mail: info@ift.org

AMOUNT: $1,000-$2,250
DEADLINE(S): FEB 1
FIELD(S): Food Science; Food
Technology
ELIGIBILITY/REQUIREMENTS: Open
to scholastically outstanding sophomores
and juniors enrolled in an approved food
science/technology program.
HOW TO APPLY: Contact IFT for an
application.
NUMBER OF AWARDS: 64

2930—INSTITUTE OF FOOD TECHNOLO-GISTS (Sophomore Scholarships)

525 West Van Buren, Suite 1000
Chicago IL 60607
312/782-8424
FAX: 312/782-8348
E-mail: info@ift.org
AMOUNT: $1,000
DEADLINE(S): MAR 1
FIELD(S): Food Science; Food
Technology
ELIGIBILITY/REQUIREMENTS: Open
to scholastically outstanding freshmen with
a minimum 2.5 GPA and either pursuing
or transferring to an approved program in
food science/technology.
HOW TO APPLY: Contact IFT for an
application.
NUMBER OF AWARDS: 23

2931—INTERNATIONAL ASSOCIATION OF CULINARY PROFESSIONALS FOUNDA-TION

304 West Liberty Street, Suite 201
Louisville KY 40202-3068
502/581-9786
FAX: 502/589-3602
E-mail: tgribbins@hqtrs.com
Internet: http://www.iacp
foundation.org
AMOUNT: $1,000-$5,000
DEADLINE(S): DEC 15
FIELD(S): Culinary Arts
ELIGIBILITY/REQUIREMENTS: Must
have a high school diploma or equivalent
by June following deadline. Selection
based on merit, food service work experience, and financial need. Awards cover
partial tuition costs and, occasionally,
course-related expenses, such as research,
room and board, or travel. May be used for
basic, continuing, specialty education
courses and independent study and
research. Additional requirements or
restrictions may apply depending upon the
individual scholarship.

HOW TO APPLY: Contact IACP for an application between September 1 and December 1. $25 application fee.
NUMBER OF AWARDS: 21
CONTACT: T. Gribbins, Director of Administration, ext. 264

2932—INTERNATIONAL FOOD SERVICE EXECUTIVES ASSOCIATION (Worthy Goal Scholarship)

3739 Mykonos Court
Boca Raton FL 33487-1282
561/998-7758
FAX: 561/998-3878
FAX-On-Demand: 954/977-0767
E-mail: hq@ifsea.org
Internet: http://www.ifsea.org
AMOUNT: $500
DEADLINE(S): FEB 1
FIELD(S): Food Service Management
ELIGIBILITY/REQUIREMENTS: Undergraduate scholarship for deserving individuals to receive training in food service management. Additional scholarships are available through IFSEA branches.
HOW TO APPLY: Use Fax-On-Demand service or send SASE to IFSEA for an application.
RENEWABLE: Yes, must reapply.

2933—JACKSONVILLE STATE UNIVERSITY (Elizabeth Sowell Scholarship)

Jacksonville AL 36265
256/782-5677 or 800/231-5291
Internet: http://www.jsu.edu
AMOUNT: Varies
FIELD(S): Nutrition; Food
ELIGIBILITY/REQUIREMENTS: Major in Family & Consumer Science or related area.
HOW TO APPLY: Contact Family & Consumer Science Department, 256/782-5054, for application and additional information.
RENEWABLE: No

2934—JOHNSON AND WALES UNIVERSITY (Annual National High School Recipe Contest)

8 Abbott Place
Providence RI 02903
401/598-2345
Internet: http://www.jwu.edu/admiss/scholarships/
AMOUNT: $1,000- $5,000
DEADLINE(S): JAN 31
FIELD(S): Business, Hospitality, Technology, Culinary Arts

ELIGIBILITY/REQUIREMENTS: For students planning to attend Johnson and Wales University, Providence, Rhode Island.
HOW TO APPLY: Write for detailed description.

2935—JOHNSON AND WALES UNIVERSITY (Gilbane Building Company Eagle Scout Scholarship)

8 Abbott Place
Providence RI 02903
401/598-2345
Internet: http://www.jwu.edu/admiss/scholarships/
AMOUNT: $1,200
DEADLINE(S): None
FIELD(S): Business, Hospitality, Technology, Culinary Arts
ELIGIBILITY/REQUIREMENTS: For students attending Johnson and Wales University, Providence, Rhode Island. Must be Eagle Scouts.
HOW TO APPLY: Send letter of recommendation and transcript.

2936—JOHNSON AND WALES UNIVERSITY (National High School Entrepreneur of the Year Contest)

8 Abbott Place
Providence RI 02903
401/598-2345
Internet: http://www.jwu.edu/admiss/scholarships/
AMOUNT: $1,000-$10,000
DEADLINE(S): DEC 27
FIELD(S): Business, Hospitality, Technology, Culinary Arts
ELIGIBILITY/REQUIREMENTS: For students attending Johnson and Wales University, Providence, Rhode Island.
HOW TO APPLY: Send for detailed description.

2937—JUNIOR ACHIEVEMENT INC. (Johnson and Wales University Scholarship)

One Education Way
Colorado Springs CO 80906-4477
719/540-8000
FAX: 719/540-6299
E-mail: newmedia@ja.org
Internet: http://www.ja.org
AMOUNT: $10,000 (4 years)
DEADLINE(S): FEB 1
FIELD(S): Business; Culinary Arts; Hospitality; Technology

ELIGIBILITY/REQUIREMENTS: Must be high school seniors who have been accepted by and will be attending Johnson and Wales University and be majoring in one of the above fields.
HOW TO APPLY: Send application to Johnson and Wales University with 1 letter of recommendation from a JA High School Programs consultant.
NUMBER OF AWARDS: Two 4-year $10,000 scholarships; unlimited partial scholarships.
RENEWABLE: No
CONTACT: For application, contact Tom Gauthier, Coordinator of Specialty Recruitment, Johnson and Wales University, 8 Abbott Place, Providence RI 02903; 800/DIAL-JWU, ext. 2345 or from website (http://www.jwu.edu).

2938—LINCOLN COMMUNITY FOUNDATION (Lucile E. Wright Scholarship)

215 Centennial Mall South, Suite 100
Lincoln NE 68508
402/474-2354
FAX: 402/476-8532
E-mail: lcf@lcf.org
Internet: http://www.lcf.org
AMOUNT: Varies
DEADLINE(S): APR 8
FIELD(S): Nutrition, Dietetics, Food Service Management
ELIGIBILITY/REQUIREMENTS: Applicant must be seeking a degree in one of the above fields and enrolled in the College of Education and Human Sciences at the University of Nebraska-Lincoln.
HOW TO APPLY: Complete application provided by the College of Education and Human Sciences and submit it along with any required attachments to Diane Sealock, College of Education and Human Sciences, University of Nebraska-Lincoln, 104 Henzlik, Lincoln, NE 68588-0371.
NUMBER OF AWARDS/YEAR: Varies
RENEWABLE: Yes; must reapply.
ADDITIONAL INFORMATION: The College of Education and Human Sciences shall make recipient recommendations of the Foundation for final selection.

2939—NATIONAL ASSOCIATION OF COLLEGE & UNIVERSITY FOOD SERVICES (The Clark E. DeHaven Scholarship Trust)

1405 South Harrison Road, Suite 305
Manly Miles Building, MSU
East Lansing MI 48824-5242
517/332-2494

FAX: 517/332-8144
E-mail: webmaster@nacufs.org
Internet: http://www.nacufs.org
AMOUNT: $3,500
DEADLINE(S): FEB 15
FIELD(S): Food-related fields
ELIGIBILITY/REQUIREMENTS: Must be sophomores, juniors, or seniors enrolled full time in a U.S. or Canadian college or university that is a member of NACUFS; be majoring in a food service-related field of study; be in good standing and have a cumulative GPA of at least 2.75; plan a career in the food service industry; and be a U.S. or Canadian citizen. Based on commitment to career in food service professions, merit, traditional progress toward degrees, character, campus citizenship, campus involvement, volunteer activities, and financial need.
HOW TO APPLY: Contact Association or see website for application. Submit with transcript(s); 2 letters of recommendation (1 from academic advisor and 1 from employer); letter of personal evaluation; and a résumé.
NUMBER OF AWARDS: 2
CONTACT: Lana Heath
ADDITIONAL INFORMATION: Students not selected will be entered automatically into the Academic Scholarship for Undergraduate Students competition if additional essays are completed (see 2940).

2940—NATIONAL RESTAURANT ASSOCIATION EDUCATIONAL FOUNDATION (Academic Scholarship for Undergraduate Students)

175 West Jackson Blvd., Suite 1500
Chicago IL 60604-2814
800/765-2122 or
312/715-1010, ext. 744
FAX: 312/566-9733
E-mail: scholars@nraef.org
Internet: http://www.nraef.org/scholarships
AMOUNT: $2,000
DEADLINE(S): APR 7 and NOV 18
FIELD(S): Restaurant or Food Service-related program
ELIGIBILITY/REQUIREMENTS: For college students pursuing a certificate, associate degree, or bachelor's degree in above fields. Must be a U.S. citizen/permanent resident or a noncitizen attending school in U.S./territories enrolled on a full-time or substantial part-time basis (usually a minimum of 9 credit hours), have completed 1st semester with a minimum 2.75 GPA, and provide proof of at least 750

hours of work experience in the restaurant/food service industry.
HOW TO APPLY: See website for additional information and application. Two essays and 1 to 3 letters of recommendation from a current or previous employer.
RENEWABLE: No. May not receive 2 consecutive undergraduate scholarships, but may reapply.

2941—NATIONAL RESTAURANT ASSOCIATION EDUCATIONAL FOUNDATION (Academic Scholarship for High School Seniors)

175 West Jackson Blvd., Suite 1500
Chicago IL 60604-2814
800/765-2122 or
312/715-1010, ext. 744
FAX: 312/566-9733
E-mail: scholars@nraef.org
Internet: http://www.nraef.org/scholarships
AMOUNT: $2,000
DEADLINE(S): APR 21
FIELD(S): Restaurant or Food Service-related program
ELIGIBILITY/REQUIREMENTS: For high school seniors accepted into either a full-time or substantial part-time postsecondary program, in 1 of above fields who plan to enroll in a minimum of 2 terms for the school year. Must have a minimum 2.75 GPA and be a U.S. citizen/permanent resident or a noncitizen attending school in U.S./territories; have taken a minimum of 1 food service-related course and/or have performed a minimum of 250 hours of restaurant/hospitality work experience.
HOW TO APPLY: Applications available January 1. Submit along with 1 to 3 letters of recommendation. See website for information.

2942—NATIONAL RESTAURANT ASSOCIATION EDUCATIONAL FOUNDATION (ProStart® National Certificate of Achievement Students)

175 West Jackson Blvd., Suite 1500
Chicago IL 60604-2814
800/765-2122 or
312/715-1010, ext. 744
FAX: 312/566-9733
E-mail: scholars@nraef.org
Internet: http://www.nraef.org/scholarships
AMOUNT: $2,000
DEADLINE: AUG 16
FIELDS: Restaurant or Food Service-related program

ELIGIBILITY/REQUIREMENTS: For students who have received the ProStart National Certificate of Achievement by participating in the HBA/ProStart School-to-Career Initiative. Must be a graduating high school senior attending a credited restaurant/food service postsecondary school or a ProStart junior in high school holding National Certificate of Achievement and have a 2.75 GPA. Must be accepted to an accredited hospitality management program with a focus on restaurant management or food service-related postsecondary program; and enrolled full or part time (minimum of 9 credit hours), and plan to enroll in a minimum of 2 terms for the school year.
HOW TO APPLY: See website for additional information and application. Submit with copy of Certificate of Achievement and letter of acceptance from college.
NUMBER OF AWARDS: 2
RENEWABLE: Varies

2943—NATIONAL RESTAURANT ASSOCIATION EDUCATIONAL FOUNDATION/COCA-COLA ENDOWMENT FUND (Coca-Cola Salute to Excellence Scholarship Award)

175 West Jackson Blvd., Suite 1500
Chicago IL 60604-2814
800/765-2122 or
312/715-1010, ext. 744
FAX: 312/566-9733
E-mail: scholars@nraef.org
Internet: http://www.nraef.org/scholarships
AMOUNT: $5,000
DEADLINE: APR 15
FIELDS: Restaurant or Food Service-related program
ELIGIBILITY/REQUIREMENTS: Must be honor delegates confirmed to participate in Salute to Excellence and U.S. citizens or permanent residents (American Samoa, District of Columbia, Guam, Puerto Rico, and U.S. Virgin Islands) who have already completed one grading term of their program (may not be in or entering final semester). Must have completed at least 1 term with a minimum 2.75 GPA.
HOW TO APPLY: See website for additional information and application. Submit with proof of full- or part-time (minimum 9 credit hours) enrollment; copy of curriculum as described in your college catalog with the number of credit hours detailed; college transcript(s); proof of restaurant- or food service-related work experience (minimum of 750 hours); 1 to 3 letters of recommendation from employer(s) in the restaurant and/or food service industry.
NUMBER OF AWARDS: 2

2944—NATIONAL TOURISM FOUNDATION

P.O. Box 3071
Lexington KY 40596-3071
800/682-8886
FAX: 606/226-4414
Internet: http://www.ntfonline.com
AMOUNT: $3,000
DEADLINE(S): APR 15
FIELD(S): Travel and Tourism;
    Hospitality; Restaurant Management
ELIGIBILITY/REQUIREMENTS:
Various scholarships for full-time students at 2- or 4-year colleges or universities in North America who are entering their junior or senior year of study. Must be a strong academic performer and have at least a 3.0 GPA. Degree emphasis must be in a travel- and tourism-related field, such as hotel management, restaurant management, or tourism.
HOW TO APPLY: Submit application, which is available from website; a résumé; information on any work or internship experience in travel and tourism and on any extracurricular or volunteer experience. See website for additional requirements of each individual scholarship. Students may apply for more than 1 award but may receive only 1.
NUMBER OF AWARDS: 2

2945—SONOMA CHAMBOLLE-MUSIGNY SISTER CITIES, INC. (Henri Cardinaux Memorial Scholarship)

Chamson Scholarship Committee
P.O. Box 1633
Sonoma CA 95476-1633
938/908-1939
E-mail: icardin@aol.com
AMOUNT: Up to $1,500 (travel + expenses)
DEADLINE(S): JUL 15
FIELD(S): Culinary Arts; Wine Industry;
    Art; Architecture; Music; History;
    Fashion
ELIGIBILITY/REQUIREMENTS:
Hands-on experience working in above or similar fields and living with a family in small French village in Burgundy or other French city. Must be Sonoma County, California, resident at least 18 years of age and be able to communicate in French.
HOW TO APPLY: Transcripts, employer recommendation, photograph, and essay (stating why, where, and when) required.
NUMBER OF AWARDS: 1
RENEWABLE: No
CONTACT: Ivy Cardinaux

2946—UNITED METHODIST CHURCH SCHOLARSHIP PROGRAM (Edith M. Allen Scholarship)

P.O. Box 34007
Nashville TN 37203-0007
615/340-7344
FAX: 615/340-7367
E-mail: umscholar@gbhem.org
Internet: http://www.gbhem.org
AMOUNT: Up to $1,000
DEADLINE(S): MAY 1
FIELD(S): Education; Social Work;
    Medicine and related professions
ELIGIBILITY/REQUIREMENTS: Open to African-American students enrolled full-time at a UM college or university, have a B+ average or higher, a full and active member of the UMC for at least 3 years, citizen or permanent resident of the U.S., and demonstrate financial need.
HOW TO APPLY: See website for application or contact the director of financial aid at the United Methodist college or university of your choice, the chairperson of your annual conference Board of Higher Education and Campus Ministry or the United Methodist Scholarship Office at the address listed for information and/or application form.
CONTACT: Scholarship Department

2947—UNIVERSITY OF CALIFORNIA-DAVIS (Brad Webb Scholarship Fund)

Department of Enology and Viticulture
One Shields Avenue
Davis CA 95616-8749
530/752-0380
FAX: 530/752-0382
Internet: http://wineserver@ucdavis.edu
AMOUNT: Varies
DEADLINE(S): Varies
FIELD(S): Enology/Viticulture
ELIGIBILITY/REQUIREMENTS: Open to students attending or planning to attend UC Davis.
HOW TO APPLY: Contact the Department of Enology and Viticulture for application.

2948—WESTERN MICHIGAN UNIVERSITY (Haworth College of Business/Associated Food Dealers of Michigan Scholarship)

1903 West Michigan
Kalamazoo MI 49008-5337
269/387-6000
FAX: 269/387-6989

E-mail: finaid-info@wmich.edu
Internet: http://www.wmich. edu/finaid
AMOUNT: $1,000
DEADLINE(S): FEB 15
FIELD(S): Food Marketing
ELIGIBILITY/REQUIREMENTS: Food Marketing majors; cumulative GPA of at least 2.5; be sophomore or higher; consideration given to a demonstrated career in food marketing, work experience, participation in WMU and community activities, financial need, and faculty recommendations.
HOW TO APPLY: Applications available December 1 through March 1. Contact the Marketing Department for more details.
NUMBER OF AWARDS: 2
RENEWABLE: Yes

2949—WESTERN MICHIGAN UNIVERSITY (Haworth College of Business/Chicago Food Brokers Association Scholarships)

1903 West Michigan
Kalamazoo MI 49008-5337
269/387-6000
FAX: 269/387-6989
E-mail: finaid-info@wmich.edu
Internet: http://www.wmich. edu/finaid
AMOUNT: At least $1,000
DEADLINE(S): FEB 15
FIELD(S): Food Marketing
ELIGIBILITY/REQUIREMENTS: Food Marketing majors affiliated with Chicago-based food companies and retailers; cumulative GPA of at least 2.5; must be sophomore or higher; consideration given to a demonstrated career in food marketing, work experience, participation in WMU and community activities, financial need, and faculty recommendations.
HOW TO APPLY: Contact the Marketing Department for more details.
NUMBER OF AWARDS: Multiple
RENEWABLE: Yes

2950—WESTERN MICHIGAN UNIVERSITY (Haworth College of Business/Coca-Cola Food Marketing Fellowships)

1903 West Michigan
Kalamazoo MI 49008-5337
269/387-6000
FAX: 269/387-6989
E-mail: finaid-info@wmich.edu
Internet: http://www.wmich. edu/finaid
AMOUNT: At least $2,000
DEADLINE(S): FEB 15

FIELD(S): Food Marketing
ELIGIBILITY/REQUIREMENTS: Food Marketing majors with cumulative GPA of at least 2.5, must be sophomore or higher. Consideration given to a demonstrated career in food marketing, work experience, participation in WMU and community activities, financial need, and faculty recommendations.
HOW TO APPLY: Contact the Marketing Department for more details.
NUMBER OF AWARDS: 3

2951—WESTERN MICHIGAN UNIVERSITY (Haworth College of Business/Dorothy J. and Clinton J. Christoff Endowed Scholarship)

1903 West Michigan
Kalamazoo MI 49008-5337
269/387-6000
FAX: 269/387-6989
E-mail: finaid-info@wmich.edu
Internet: http://www.wmich. edu/finaid
AMOUNT: At least $2,000
DEADLINE(S): FEB 15
FIELD(S): Food Marketing
ELIGIBILITY/REQUIREMENTS: Entering freshman or transfer student admitted to the Food Marketing Program. Preference given to students from the Lowell Public School system, or to family members of employees or customers of Chadalee Farms/Litehouse, Inc.
HOW TO APPLY: Contact the Marketing Department for more details.
NUMBER OF AWARDS: 1
RENEWABLE: Yes

2952—WESTERN MICHIGAN UNIVERSITY (Haworth College of Business/Farmer Jack Supermarkets Scholarships)

1903 West Michigan
Kalamazoo MI 49008-5337
269/387-6000
FAX: 269/387-6989
E-mail: finaid-info@wmich.edu
Internet: http://www.wmich. edu/finaid
AMOUNT: $5,000
DEADLINE(S): FEB 15
FIELD(S): Food Marketing
ELIGIBILITY/REQUIREMENTS: One scholarship is designated for a current employee of Farmer Jack who is enrolled in, or plans to enroll in the Food Marketing Program. The other is for a current food marketing major with a career interest in retail store operations.
HOW TO APPLY: Contact the Marketing Department for more details.

NUMBER OF AWARDS: 2
RENEWABLE: Yes.

2953—WESTERN MICHIGAN UNIVERSITY (Haworth College of Business/G & R Felpausch Company Endowed Scholarship)

1903 West Michigan
Kalamazoo MI 49008-5337
269/387-6000
FAX: 269/387-6989
E-mail: finaid-info@wmich.edu
Internet: http://www.wmich. edu/finaid
AMOUNT: Varies
DEADLINE(S): FEB 15
FIELD(S): Food Marketing; Business
ELIGIBILITY/REQUIREMENTS: Student majoring in food marketing; minimum GPA of 2.5. Preference given to Felpausch Food Centers employees, or family of employees, majoring in food marketing or business-related major. Consideration given to financial need, interest in food marketing, work experience, and participation in university and community activities.
HOW TO APPLY: Application forms must be obtained from and returned to the Marketing Department.
NUMBER OF AWARDS: 2
RENEWABLE: Yes.

2954—WESTERN MICHIGAN UNIVERSITY (Haworth College of Business/Georgia-Pacific Corporation Food Marketing Scholarships)

1903 West Michigan
Kalamazoo MI 49008-5337
269/387-6000
FAX: 269/387-6989
E-mail: finaid-info@wmich.edu
Internet: http://www. wmich. edu/finaid
AMOUNT: $5,000
DEADLINE(S): FEB 15
FIELD(S): Food Marketing
ELIGIBILITY/REQUIREMENTS: Awarded on the basis of outstanding academic achievement.
HOW TO APPLY: Contact the Marketing Department for more details.
NUMBER OF AWARDS: 2
RENEWABLE: No

2955—WESTERN MICHIGAN UNIVERSITY (Haworth College of Business/James W. Richmond Sales and Business Marketing Scholarship)

1903 West Michigan

Kalamazoo MI 49008-5337
269/387-6000
FAX: 269/387-6989
E-mail: finaid-info@wmich.edu
Internet: http://www.wmich.edu/finaid
AMOUNT: Varies
DEADLINE(S): FEB 15
FIELD(S): Food Marketing; Manufacturing Technology
ELIGIBILITY/REQUIREMENTS: Preference given to sophomore, junior, or senior Sales and Business Marketing majors who are pursuing a minor in Manufacturing Technology. Must have GPA of 3.0 and be a full-time student.
HOW TO APPLY: Contact the Marketing Department for more details.
NUMBER OF AWARDS: 1 or more
RENEWABLE: Yes

2956—WESTERN MICHIGAN UNIVERSITY (Haworth College of Business/Jules W. Englander Memorial Endowed Scholarship)

1903 West Michigan
Kalamazoo MI 49008-5337
269/387-6000
FAX: 269/387-6989
E-mail: finaid-info@wmich.edu
Internet: http://www. wmich. edu/finaid
AMOUNT: At least $1,000
DEADLINE(S): FEB 15
FIELD(S): Food Marketing
ELIGIBILITY/REQUIREMENTS: Junior or senior food marketing student. Selected on the basis of need and potential for career success within the food industry.
HOW TO APPLY: Contact the Marketing Department for more details.
NUMBER OF AWARDS: 1
RENEWABLE: Yes

2957—WESTERN MICHIGAN UNIVERSITY (Haworth College of Business/Julie Kravitz Endowed Memorial Scholarship)

1903 West Michigan
Kalamazoo MI 49008-5337
269/387-6000
FAX: 269/387-6989
E-mail: finaid-info@wmich.edu
Internet: http://www.wmich. edu/finaid
AMOUNT: At least $1,000
DEADLINE(S): FEB 15
FIELD(S): Food Marketing
ELIGIBILITY/REQUIREMENTS: Recipient must be a full-time student with a minimum GPA of 3.0. Preference given to students from the Cleveland, Ohio area.

HOW TO APPLY: Contact the Marketing
Department for more details.
NUMBER OF AWARDS: 1
RENEWABLE: Yes

2958—WESTERN MICHIGAN UNIVERSITY (Haworth College of Business/Kellogg's Food Marketing Scholarship)

1903 West Michigan
Kalamazoo MI 49008-5337
269/387-6000
FAX: 269/387-6989
E-mail: finaid-info@wmich.edu
Internet: http://www.wmich. edu/
finaid
AMOUNT: At least $1,000
DEADLINE(S): FEB 15
FIELD(S): Food Marketing
ELIGIBILITY/REQUIREMENTS:
Based on scholarship and need. Preference
given to members of Sigma Phi Omega.
HOW TO APPLY: Contact the Marketing
Department for more details.
NUMBER OF AWARDS: 1 or more

2959—WESTERN MICHIGAN UNIVERSITY (Haworth College of Business/Michigan Food & Beverage Association Scholarships)

1903 West Michigan
Kalamazoo MI 49008-5337
269/387-6000
FAX: 269/387-6989
E-mail: finaid-info@wmich.edu
Internet: http://www.wmich. edu/
finaid
AMOUNT: $1,000
DEADLINE(S): FEB 15
FIELD(S): Food Marketing
ELIGIBILITY/REQUIREMENTS:
Recipient must be a food marketing major.
HOW TO APPLY: Contact the Marketing
Department for more details.
NUMBER OF AWARDS: 2
RENEWABLE: Yes

2960—WESTERN MICHIGAN UNIVERSITY (Haworth College of Business/MSM Solutions Scholarship)

1903 West Michigan
Kalamazoo MI 49008-5337
269/387-6000
FAX: 269/387-6989
E-mail: finaid-info@wmich.edu
Internet: http://www.wmich. edu/
finaid
AMOUNT: $4,000
DEADLINE(S): FEB 15

FIELD(S): Food Marketing
ELIGIBILITY/REQUIREMENTS:
Awarded to a food marketing major;
includes a paid summer internship between
the recipient's junior and senior years.
HOW TO APPLY: Contact the Marketing
Department for more details.
NUMBER OF AWARDS: 1
RENEWABLE: No

2961—WESTERN MICHIGAN UNIVERSITY (Haworth College of Business/Nabisco Foods Group Endowed Scholarships)

1903 West Michigan
Kalamazoo MI 49008-5337
269/387-6000
FAX: 269/387-6989
E-mail: finaid-info@wmich.edu
Internet: http://www.wmich. edu/
finaid
AMOUNT: $2,000
DEADLINE(S): FEB 15
FIELD(S): Food Marketing
ELIGIBILITY/REQUIREMENTS:
Awarded to a food marketing major.
HOW TO APPLY: Contact the Marketing
Department for more details.
NUMBER OF AWARDS: 2
RENEWABLE: No

2962—WESTERN MICHIGAN UNIVERSITY (Haworth College of Business/Pat Mitchell CFBA Award)

1903 West Michigan
Kalamazoo MI 49008-5337
269/387-6000
FAX: 269/387-6989
E-mail: finaid-info@wmich.edu
Internet: http://www.wmich. edu/
finaid
AMOUNT: $2,000
DEADLINE(S): FEB 15
FIELD(S): Food Marketing
ELIGIBILITY/REQUIREMENTS:
Presented to the outstanding food market-
ing student affiliated with a Chicago-based
food company or retailer.
HOW TO APPLY: Contact the Marketing
Department for more details.
NUMBER OF AWARDS: 2

2963—WESTERN MICHIGAN UNIVERSITY (Haworth College of Business/Patrick M. Quinn Endowed Food Marketing Scholarship)

1903 West Michigan
Kalamazoo MI 49008-5337
269/387-6000

FAX: 269/387-6989
E-mail: finaid-info@wmich.edu
Internet: http://www.wmich. edu/
finaid
AMOUNT: $1,000
DEADLINE(S): FEB 15
FIELD(S): Food Marketing
ELIGIBILITY/REQUIREMENTS:
Preference given to employees of Spartan
Stores or its affiliated retailers, or family of
employees.
HOW TO APPLY: Contact the Marketing
Department for more details.
NUMBER OF AWARDS: 1 or more
RENEWABLE: Yes

2964—WESTERN MICHIGAN UNIVERSITY (Haworth College of Business/Richard Neschich Endowed Food Marketing Scholarship)

1903 West Michigan
Kalamazoo MI 49008-5337
269/387-6000
FAX: 269/387-6989
E-mail: finaid-info@wmich.edu
Internet: http://www.wmich. edu/
finaid
AMOUNT: At least $1,000
DEADLINE(S): FEB 15
FIELD(S): Food Marketing
ELIGIBILITY/REQUIREMENTS:
Based on scholarship and need. Preference
given to members of Sigma Phi Omega.
HOW TO APPLY: Contact the Marketing
Department for more details.
NUMBER OF AWARDS: 2
RENEWABLE: Yes

2965—WESTERN MICHIGAN UNIVERSITY (Haworth College of Business/Sid Brooks Endowed Memorial Scholarship)

1903 West Michigan
Kalamazoo MI 49008-5337
269/387-6000
FAX: 269/387-6989
E-mail: finaid-info@wmich.edu
Internet: http://www.wmich. edu/
finaid
AMOUNT: At least $1,000
DEADLINE(S): FEB 15
FIELD(S): Food Marketing
ELIGIBILITY/REQUIREMENTS: Food
Marketing majors; cumulative GPA of at
least 2.5; be sophomore or higher; consid-
eration given to a demonstrated career in
food marketing, work experience, partici-
pation in WMU and community activities,
financial need, and faculty recommenda-
tions.

HOW TO APPLY: Contact the Marketing Department for more details.
NUMBER OF AWARDS: 1
RENEWABLE: Yes

2966—WESTERN MICHIGAN UNIVERSITY (Haworth College of Business/William O. Haynes Food Distribution Endowed Scholarship)

1903 West Michigan
Kalamazoo MI 49008-5337
269/387-6000
FAX: 269/387-6989
E-mail: finaid-info@wmich.edu
Internet: http://www.wmich. edu/finaid
AMOUNT: At least $1,000
DEADLINE(S): FEB 15
FIELD(S): Food Marketing
ELIGIBILITY/REQUIREMENTS: Based on scholarship and need. Preference given to members of Sigma Phi Omega.
HOW TO APPLY: Contact the Marketing Department for more details.
NUMBER OF AWARDS: 1 or more

2967—WESTERN MICHIGAN UNIVERSITY (Haworth College of Business/Wal-Mart Stores Food Marketing Scholarships)

1903 West Michigan
Kalamazoo MI 49008-5337
269/387-6000
FAX: 269/387-6989
E-mail: finaid-info@wmich.edu
Internet: http://www.wmich. edu/finaid
AMOUNT: $1,000
DEADLINE(S): FEB 15
FIELD(S): Food Marketing
ELIGIBILITY/REQUIREMENTS: Preference for food marketing majors with a career interest in retail management.
HOW TO APPLY: Contact the Marketing Department for more details.
NUMBER OF AWARDS: Multiple
RENEWABLE: Yes

2968—WOMEN GROCERS OF AMERICA (Mary Macey Scholarships)

1005 North Glebe Road, Suite 250
Arlington VA 22201-5758
703/516-0700
FAX: 703/516-0115
E-mail: wga@nationalgrocers.org
Internet: http://www.national grocers.org
AMOUNT: $1,000 (minimum)
DEADLINE(S): JUN 1

FIELD(S): Food Marketing/Management; Food Service Technology; Business Administration
ELIGIBILITY/REQUIREMENTS: For students with a minimum 2.0 GPA attending a U.S. college or university. Must be entering sophomores or continuing students in a 2-year associate degree or 4-year degree-granting institution or a graduate program, planning a career in the independent sector grocery industry. Financial need NOT considered.
HOW TO APPLY: See website for downloadable PDF application form or write for an application.
NUMBER OF AWARDS: 2+
RENEWABLE: Yes, must reapply.

HOME ECONOMICS

2969—ABBIE SARGENT MEMORIAL SCHOLARSHIP INC.

295 Sheep Davis Road
Concord NH 03301
603/224-1934
FAX: 603/228-8432
AMOUNT: $200-$400
DEADLINE(S): MAR 15
FIELD(S): Agriculture; Veterinary Medicine; Home Economics
ELIGIBILITY/REQUIREMENTS: Open to New Hampshire residents who are high school graduates with good grades and character. For undergraduate or graduate study. Must be legal resident of U.S. and demonstrate financial need.
HOW TO APPLY: Write for application, include SASE.
RENEWABLE: Yes, must reapply.

2970—INTERNATIONAL EXECUTIVE HOUSEKEEPERS ASSOCIATION EDUCATIONAL FOUNDATION, INC.

1001 Eastwind Drive, Suite 301
Westerville OH 43081-3361
800/200-6342
FAX: 614/895-1248
E-mail: excel@ieha.org
Internet: http://www.ieha.org
AMOUNT: $800
DEADLINE(S): JAN 10
FIELD(S): Healthcare, Hotels, Education Facilities, Rehabilitation Centers and related facilities
ELIGIBILITY/REQUIREMENTS: Open to members enrolled in a program of study leading to IEHA certification.
HOW TO APPLY: Submit original manuscript (no more than 1,000 words) regard-

ing housekeeping within any industry segment as noted.
NUMBER OF AWARDS: Multiple
RENEWABLE: No

2971—JACKSONVILLE STATE UNIVERSITY (Elizabeth Sowell Scholarship)

Jacksonville AL 36265
256/782-5677 or 800/231-5291
Internet: http://www.jsu.edu
AMOUNT: Varies
FIELD(S): Nutrition; Food
ELIGIBILITY/REQUIREMENTS: Major in Family & Consumer Science or related area.
HOW TO APPLY: Contact Family & Consumer Science Department; 256/782-5054 for application and information.
RENEWABLE: No

2972—JACKSONVILLE STATE UNIVERSITY (Hazel Matthews Scholarship)

Jacksonville AL 36265
256/782-5677 or 800/231-5291
Internet: http://www.jsu.edu
AMOUNT: Varies
DEADLINE(S): FEB 1
FIELD(S): Family & Consumer Science Department
ELIGIBILITY/REQUIREMENTS: Major in Family & Consumer Science or related area.
HOW TO APPLY: Contact Family & Consumer Science Department, 256/782-5054 for application and information.
RENEWABLE: No

2973—JACKSONVILLE STATE UNIVERSITY (Mary Lowery Memorial Scholarship)

Jacksonville AL 36265
256/782-5677 or 800/231-5291
Internet: http://www.jsu.edu
AMOUNT: Varies
FIELD(S): Family & Consumer Science Department
ELIGIBILITY/REQUIREMENTS: Major in Family & Consumer Science or related area.
HOW TO APPLY: Contact Family & Consumer Science Department, 256/782-5054 for application and additional information.
RENEWABLE: No

2974—KAPPA OMICRON NU (Scholarships, Fellowships, and Grants)

4990 Northwind Drive, Suite 140
East Lansing MI 48823-5031

517/351-8335
FAX: 517/351-8836
E-mail: dmitstifer@kon.com
Internet: http://www.kon.org/
awards/grants.html
AMOUNT: $500-$3,500
DEADLINE(S): FEB 15
FIELD(S): Home Economics and related
fields
ELIGIBILITY/REQUIREMENTS: Open
to Kappa Omicron Nu members who have
demonstrated scholarship, research, and
leadership potential. Awards are for home
economics research at institutions having
strong research programs.
HOW TO APPLY: See website or write
for complete information.
NUMBER OF AWARDS: 6-8
RENEWABLE: No
CONTACT: Dorothy I. Mitstifer

2975—NATIONAL DAIRY SHRINE (NDS/DMT Milk Marketing Scholarship)

1224 Alton Darby Creek Road
Columbus OH 43228-9792
614/878-5333
FAX: 614/870-2622
E-mail: shrine@cobaselect.com
Internet: http://www.dairyshrine.org
AMOUNT: $1,000 and $2,500
DEADLINE(S): MAR 15
FIELD(S): Dairy Industry; Marketing;
Business Administration; Journalism;
Home Economics
ELIGIBILITY/REQUIREMENTS:
College sophomores, juniors, or seniors
majoring in dairy marketing, dairy manu-
facturing, dairy science, home economics,
or journalism at a college or university
approved by the appropriate National
Dairy Shrine committee. Awards based on
ability, interests, and need.
HOW TO APPLY: Download application
from website.
NUMBER OF AWARDS: 5-9
RENEWABLE: No
CONTACT: Maurice E. Core, Executive
Director

2976—WESTERN MICHIGAN UNIVERSITY (College of Education/Norman E. Slack Endowed Scholarship)

1903 West Michigan
Kalamazoo MI 49008-5337
269/387-6000
FAX: 269/387-6989
E-mail: finaid-info@wmich.edu
Internet: http://www.wmich. edu/
finaid
AMOUNT: Varies

DEADLINE(S): MAR 1
FIELD(S): Family and Consumer
Sciences
ELIGIBILITY/REQUIREMENTS:
Junior or senior status. Must be a full-time
student with major in FCS curriculum.
Financial need-based award.
HOW TO APPLY: Contact Department
of Family & Consumer Sciences, 3018
Kohrman Hall, for an application.
Applications are available February 1.
NUMBER OF AWARDS: 1
RENEWABLE: No

HORTICULTURE

2977—ALABAMA GOLF COURSE SUPER-INTENDENTS ASSOCIATION

P.O. Box 661214
Birmingham AL 35266
205/967-0397
FAX: 205/967-1466
E-mail: agcsa@charter.net
Internet: http://www.agcsa.org
AMOUNT: $2,000
DEADLINE(S): OCT 15
FIELD(S): Agronomy, Turf Grass
ELIGIBILITY/REQUIREMENTS: Full-
time student (12 credit hours/semester).
Must be enrolled in an agricultural major
emphasizing turf grass management.
Minimum GPA of 2.0 required.
HOW TO APPLY: Request application in
writing or from the website.
NUMBER OF AWARDS: 2
RENEWABLE: Yes, must reapply.
CONTACT: Melanie Bonds

2978—ARIZONA NURSERY ASSOCIATION FOUNDATION

1430 Broadway Road, Suite 110
Tempe AZ 895282
480/966-1610
FAX: 480/966-0923
E-mail: info@azna.org
Internet: http://www.azna.org
AMOUNT: $500-$3,000
DEADLINE(S): MAY 31
FIELD(S): Horticulture-related
ELIGIBILITY/REQUIREMENTS: Must
be a resident of Arizona currently or planning to be enrolled in a horticulture-related curriculum at a university, community
college, or continuing education program.
Must be currently employed in or have an
interest in the nursery industry as a career,
and have an above-average scholastic
achievement or at least 2 years' work experience in the industry; must display

involvement in extracurricular activities
relating to the industry.
HOW TO APPLY: See website for appli-
cation and submit online after JAN 1.
Include Fall semester grades.
NUMBER OF AWARDS: Varies
RENEWABLE: No
CONTACT: Cheryl Goar, Executive Dir-
ector

2979—CALIFORNIA ASSOCIATION OF WINEGRAPE GROWERS (Robert Miller Scholarship for Viticulture and Enology for Viticulture & Enology Students on the Central Coast)

1325 J Street Suite 1560
Sacramento CA 95814
800/241-1800 or 916/379-8995
FAX: 916/379-8999
E-mail: info@cawg.org
Internet: http://www.cawg.org/
cwggf
AMOUNT: $500 or $1,000
DEADLINE(S): Late MAR (see website)
FIELD(S): Viticulture, Enology
ELIGIBILITY/REQUIREMENTS:
Applicant's parent or guardian must be
employed by a California winegrape grow-
er; scholarships are based on financial need
and academic achievement. May be used at
Alan Hancock Community College or Cal
Poly, San Luis Obispo. Must major in
above fields.
HOW TO APPLY: Must be a graduating
high school senior or a student enrolled at
Alan Hancock Community College or Cal
Poly, San Luis Obispo. See website for
application; submit with high school transcript, a copy of your SAT or ACT results
if you are applying for a 4-year scholarship,
a letter of recommendation from an
instructor, the school principal or counselor, and a 2-page essay (approximately
500 words) focusing on you and your
career goals.
NUMBER OF AWARDS: 2, up to 4 years
($1,000/year); 4, up to 2 years ($500/year)
RENEWABLE: Yes. Studies must continue to be completed satisfactorily.
CONTACT: Carolee Williams
ADDITIONAL INFORMATION: Children of winegrape growers may request a
waiver from the eligibility requirement
based upon financial need.

2980—COLORADO RESTAURANT ASSO-CIATION (Scholarship Education Fund)

430 East 7th Avenue
Denver CO 80203
800/522-2972 or 303/830-2972
FAX: 303/830-2973

E-mail: info@coloradorestaurant.com
Internet: http://www.colorado
restaurant.com
AMOUNT: $500-$2,500
DEADLINE(S): MAR 20
FIELD(S): Food Service; Hospitality
ELIGIBILITY/REQUIREMENTS: Open to junior- and senior-level college students enrolled in a 2- or 4-year degree program in food service and hospitality-related fields at a Colorado college or university.
HOW TO APPLY: Contact CRA for an application.

2981—FIRST: FLORICULTURE INDUSTRY RESEARCH AND SCHOLARSHIP TRUST (Ball Horticultural Company and Paris Fracasso Scholarships)

P.O. Box 280
East Lansing MI 48826-0280
517/333-4617
FAX: 517/333-4494
E-mail: first@firstinfloriculture.org
Internet: http://www.firstin
floriculture.org
AMOUNT: $1,000-$2,000
DEADLINE(S): MAY 1
FIELD(S): Floriculture
ELIGIBILITY/REQUIREMENTS: Open to undergraduates entering junior or senior year at a 4-year college or university. Ball Scholarship requires pursuit of career in commercial floriculture; Paris Scholarship requires pursuit of career in floriculture production.
HOW TO APPLY: See website or send SASE to FIRST after January 1 for an application. Must submit references and transcripts.

2982—FIRST: FLORICULTURE INDUSTRY RESEARCH AND SCHOLARSHIP TRUST (Barbara Carlson and Dosatron International, Inc. Scholarships)

P.O. Box 280
East Lansing MI 48826-0280
517/333-4617
FAX: 517/333-4494
E-mail: first@firstinfloriculture.org
Internet: http://www.firstin
floriculture.org
AMOUNT: $1,000
DEADLINE(S): MAY 1
FIELD(S): Horticulture
ELIGIBILITY/REQUIREMENTS: Open to graduate and undergraduate students already attending a 4-year college or university who are majoring in horticulture or related field. For Carlson Scholarship, should intend to intern or work for public

gardens. Cash award, with checks issued jointly in name of recipient and college/institution he or she will attend for current year. Must submit references and transcripts.
HOW TO APPLY: See website or send SASE after January 1 for an application.

2983—FIRST: FLORICULTURE INDUSTRY RESEARCH AND SCHOLARSHIP TRUST (Carl F. Dietz Memorial Scholarship)

P.O. Box 280
East Lansing MI 48826-0280
517/333-4617
FAX: 517/333-4494
E-mail: first@firstinfloriculture.org
Internet: http://www.firstin
floriculture.org
AMOUNT: $1,000
DEADLINE(S): MAY 1
FIELD(S): Horticulture
ELIGIBILITY/REQUIREMENTS: Open to undergraduates attending a 4-year college or university who are majoring in horticulture or related field, with a specific interest in horticultural allied trades such as greenhouse equipment.
HOW TO APPLY: See website or send SASE to FIRST after January 1 for an application. Must submit references and transcripts.

2984—FIRST: FLORICULTURE INDUSTRY RESEARCH AND SCHOLARSHIP TRUST (Earl J. Small Growers, Inc. Scholarships)

P.O. Box 280
East Lansing MI 48826-0280
517/333-4617
FAX: 517/333-4494
E-mail: first@firstinfloriculture.org
Internet: http://www.firstin
floriculture.org
AMOUNT: $1,000
DEADLINE(S): MAY 1
FIELD(S): Horticulture
ELIGIBILITY/REQUIREMENTS: Open to undergraduate students already attending a 4-year college or university who are majoring in horticulture or related field, with the intention of pursuing a career in greenhouse production. Must be U.S. or Canadian citizen.
HOW TO APPLY: See website or send SASE to FIRST after January 1 for an application. Must submit references and transcripts.

2985—FIRST: FLORICULTURE INDUSTRY RESEARCH AND SCHOLARSHIP TRUST (Fran Johnson Scholarship)

P.O. Box 280

East Lansing MI 48826-0280
517/333-4617
FAX: 517/333-4494
E-mail: first@firstinfloriculture.org
Internet: http://www.firstin
floriculture.org
AMOUNT: $500-$1,000
DEADLINE(S): MAY 1
FIELD(S): Horticulture; Floriculture
ELIGIBILITY/REQUIREMENTS: Open to undergraduate and graduate students at 2- or 4-year college or university in U.S. or Canada. Must be U.S. or Canadian citizen reentering an academic program after an absence of at least 5 years, and with major in horticulture or related field, specifically bedding plants or other floral crops.
HOW TO APPLY: See website or send SASE to FIRST after January 1 for an application. Must submit references and transcripts.

2986—FIRST: FLORICULTURE INDUSTRY RESEARCH AND SCHOLARSHIP TRUST (Jacob Van Namen Scholarship)

P.O. Box 280
East Lansing MI 48826-0280
517/333-4617
FAX: 517/333-4494
E-mail: first@firstinfloriculture.org
Internet: http://www.firstin
floriculture.org
AMOUNT: $1,250
DEADLINE(S): MAY 1
FIELD(S): Agribusiness AND
  Floriculture
ELIGIBILITY/REQUIREMENTS: Open to undergraduate students attending a 4-year college or university who wish to be involved in agribusiness marketing and distribution of floral products.
HOW TO APPLY: See website or send SASE to FIRST after January 1 for an application. Must submit references and transcripts.

2987—FIRST: FLORICULTURE INDUSTRY RESEARCH AND SCHOLARSHIP TRUST (Jerry Baker College Freshman Scholarships)

P.O. Box 280
East Lansing MI 48826-0280
517/333-4617
FAX: 517/333-4494
E-mail: first@firstinfloriculture.org
Internet: http://www.firstin
floriculture.org
AMOUNT: $1,000
DEADLINE(S): MAY 1

FIELD(S): Horticulture; Landscaping; Gardening

ELIGIBILITY/REQUIREMENTS: Open to undergraduates entering freshman year who are interested in careers in horticulture, landscaping, or gardening. Must be enrolled in an accredited 4-year college or university program in the U.S. or Canada.

HOW TO APPLY: See website or send SASE to FIRST after January 1 for an application. Must submit references and transcripts.

2988—FIRST: FLORICULTURE INDUSTRY RESEARCH AND SCHOLARSHIP TRUST (Perry/Holden/Leonard Bettinger Scholarships)

P.O. Box 280
East Lansing MI 48826-0280
517/333-4617
FAX: 517/333-4494
E-mail: first@firstinfloriculture.org
Internet: http://www.firstin floriculture.org

AMOUNT: $500-$1,000
DEADLINE(S): MAY 1
FIELD(S): Horticulture; Floriculture

ELIGIBILITY/REQUIREMENTS: Open to entering freshmen or second-year students in a 1- or 2-year program who will be enrolled for full academic year. Must be U.S. or Canadian citizen, have minimum 3.0 GPA, and have major interest in horticulture or related field with intention of becoming floriculture plant producer and/or greenhouse manager.

HOW TO APPLY: See website or send SASE to FIRST after January 1 for an application. Must submit references and transcripts.

2989—FIRST: FLORICULTURE INDUSTRY RESEARCH AND SCHOLARSHIP TRUST (Seed Companies Scholarship)

P.O. Box 280
East Lansing MI 48826-0280
517/333-4617
FAX: 517/333-4494
E-mail: first@firstinfloriculture.org
Internet: http://www.firstin floriculture.org

AMOUNT: $1,000
DEADLINE(S): MAY 1
FIELD(S): Horticulture

ELIGIBILITY/REQUIREMENTS: Open to undergraduate students entering junior or senior year at a 4-year college or university and graduate students who are majoring in horticulture or related field, with the intention of pursuing a career in the seed industry. Cash award, with checks issued jointly in name of recipient and college/institution he or she will attend for current year.

HOW TO APPLY: See website or send SASE to FIRST after January 1 for an application. Must submit references and transcripts.

2990—FLORIDA FEDERATION OF GARDEN CLUBS, INC. (FFGC Scholarships for College Students)

706 Glen Eagle Drive
Winter Springs FL 32708
407/971-6979
Internet: http://www.ffgc.org

AMOUNT: $650-$3,000
DEADLINE(S): MAY 1
FIELD(S): Agriculture; Environmental & Conservations issues; Botany; Biology; Forestry; Horticulture; Ecology; Marine Biology; Wildflowers; Butterflies; Landscaping

ELIGIBILITY/REQUIREMENTS: Must be U.S. citizen and Florida resident for at least 1 year, with 3.0 GPA, attending a college or university in Florida. Financial need considered.

HOW TO APPLY: See website or contact FFGC Chair for an application.

RENEWABLE: Yes, must reapply.

CONTACT: Jane Meherg, Scholarship Chairman

2991—FLORIDA FEDERATION OF GARDEN CLUBS, INC. (FFGC Scholarships for High School Students)

706 Glen Eagle Drive
Winter Springs FL 32708
407/971-6979
Internet: http://www.ffgc.org

AMOUNT: $1,500
DEADLINE(S): MAY 1
FIELD(S): Ecology; Environmental Issues; Land Management; City Planning; Environmental Control; Horticulture; Landscape Design; Conservation; Botany; Forestry; Marine Biology; Floriculture; Agriculture

ELIGIBILITY/REQUIREMENTS: Scholarships for Florida residents with a "B" or better average who will be incoming freshmen at a Florida college or university.

HOW TO APPLY: See website or contact FFGC for an application.

CONTACT: Jane Meherg, Scholarship Chairman

2992—GARDEN CLUB OF AMERICA (GCA Internship in Garden History and Design)

14 East 60th Street

New York NY 10022-1002
212/753-8287
FAX: 212/753-0134
E-mail: scholarships@gcamerica.org
Internet: http://www.gcamerica.org

AMOUNT: $2,000 or $320/week (undergraduates); $420/week (graduates) for 10-16 weeks (at Smithsonian)
DEADLINE(S): JAN 15
FIELD(S): Horticulture; Landscape History & Design

ELIGIBILITY/REQUIREMENTS: Open to students with courses in horticulture, ornamental horticulture, landscape design and related fields. Preference given to researcher interested in working at the Archives of American Gardens at the Smithsonian Institution in Washington DC, but is available to a student in any facility approved by GCA providing supervision and structure.

HOW TO APPLY: Download application from website and mail to GCA.

NUMBER OF AWARDS: Several

CONTACT: Connie Sutton

2993—GARDEN CLUB OF AMERICA (Katharine M. Grosscup Scholarships)

Cleveland Botanical Garden
11030 East Boulevard
Cleveland OH 44106
FAX: 216/721-2056
E-mail: scholarships@gcamerica.org
Internet: http://www.gcamerica.org

AMOUNT: Up to $3,000
DEADLINE(S): FEB 1
FIELD(S): Horticulture and related fields

ELIGIBILITY/REQUIREMENTS: Financial assistance to college juniors, seniors, or graduate students, preferably from (though not restricted to) Kentucky, Ohio, Pennsylvania, West Virginia, Michigan, and Indiana. Purpose is to encourage the study of horticulture and related fields.

HOW TO APPLY: Download application and mail to GCA. Personal interview required of finalists.

NUMBER OF AWARDS: Several

CONTACT: Nancy Stevenson

2994—GARDEN CLUB OF AMERICA (Loy McCandless Marks Scholarship)

14 East 60th Street
New York NY 10022-1002
212/753-8287
FAX: 212/753-0134
E-mail: scholarships@gcamerica.org
Internet: http://www.gcamerica.org

AMOUNT: $2,000
DEADLINE(S): JAN 15

FIELD(S): Horticulture; Botany
ELIGIBILITY/REQUIREMENTS: Open to science student above the freshman year to assist with a project in tropical ornamental horticulture that has been accepted by an accredited U.S. college or university or who wishes to study, pursue an internship, or do research in the field of ornamental tropical horticulture at an appropriate foreign institution. Must by U.S. citizen.
HOW TO APPLY: Download application from website and mail to GCA.
NUMBER OF AWARDS: Several
CONTACT: Connie Sutton

2995—GARDEN CLUB FEDERATION OF MAINE, THE-ST. CROIX DISTRICT, THE (Nell Goff Memorial Scholarship Foundation)

46 Birch Bay Drive
Bar Harbor ME 04609
207/288-8003
E-mail: creevey@adelphia.net
Internet: http://www.maine gardenclubs.com
AMOUNT: $1,000
DEADLINE(S): MAR 1
FIELD(S): Horticulture; Floriculture; Landscape Design; Conservation; Forestry; Botany, Agronomy; Plant Pathology; Environmental Control; City Planning and/or other gardening-related fields
ELIGIBILITY/REQUIREMENTS: Open to college juniors, seniors or graduate students (sophomores are eligible if they will enter their junior year in the fall) who are legal residents of the state of Maine, priority given to a resident of St. Croix District (Hancock County, and the southern part of Washington County), and major in some aspect of horticulture.
HOW TO APPLY: See website for application and information. Submit along with personal letter (up to 2 pages), discussing goals, background, financial need and personal commitment; 3 letters of recommendation (1 page each) to include scholarship ability, personal reference, and work-related experience; transcript and list of activities.
NUMBER OF AWARDS: 1
RENEWABLE: Yes, must reapply.
CONTACT: Lucy Creevey

2996—GOLF COURSE SUPERINTENDENTS ASSOCIATION OF AMERICA (GCSAA Essay Contest)

1421 Research Park Drive
Lawrence KS 66049-3859
785/832-3678
800/472-7878, ext. 678
FAX: 785/832-4449
Internet: http://www.gcsaa.org
AMOUNT: $4,500 (total prizes)
DEADLINE(S): MAR 31
FIELD(S): Turfgrass Science; Agronomy; Golf Course Management
ELIGIBILITY/REQUIREMENTS: Open to undergraduate and graduate students pursuing degrees in above fields. Essays should be 7-12 pages long and focus on the golf course management profession.
HOW TO APPLY: See website or contact GCSAA for details.
CONTACT: Amanda Howard, Employment Administrator, 800/472-7878, ext. 4424

2997—GOLF COURSE SUPERINTENDENTS ASSOCIATION OF AMERICA (GCSAA Scholars Competition)

1421 Research Park Drive
Lawrence KS 66049-3859
785/832-3678
800/472-7878, ext. 678
FAX: 785/832-4449
Internet: http://www.gcsaa.org
AMOUNT: $500-$6,000
DEADLINE(S): JUN 1
FIELD(S): Golf/Turf Management
ELIGIBILITY/REQUIREMENTS: Open to outstanding undergraduate students planning careers as golf course superintendents. Must have completed at least 24 credit hours or the equivalent of 1 year of full-time study in an appropriate major and be a member of GCSAA.
HOW TO APPLY: See website or contact GCSAA for membership information or an application.
CONTACT: Amanda Howard, Employment Administrator, 800/472-7878, ext. 4424

2998—GOLF COURSE SUPERINTENDENTS ASSOCIATION OF AMERICA (Scotts Company Scholars Program, The)

1421 Research Park Drive
Lawrence KS 66049-3859
785/832-3678
800/472-7878, ext. 678
FAX: 785/832-4449
Internet: http://www.gcsaa.org
AMOUNT: $500 and $2,500
DEADLINE(S): MAR 1
FIELD(S): "Green Industry"
ELIGIBILITY/REQUIREMENTS: For graduating high school seniors and college freshmen, sophomores, and juniors accepted or currently enrolled in a 2- or 4-year accredited college. Based on cultural diversity, academic achievement, extracurricular activities, leadership, employment potential, essay responses, and letters of recommendation. Financial need is NOT a factor.
HOW TO APPLY: See website or contact GCSAA for membership information or an application.
NUMBER OF AWARDS: 5 finalists receive $500 award; 2 finalists receive additional $2,500 and all-expense trip to Golf Course Conference and Show; all receive internship.
RENEWABLE: No
CONTACT: Amanda Howard, Employment Administrator, 800/472-7878, ext. 4424

2999—HAWAII COMMUNITY FOUNDATION (Dan & Pauline Lutkenhouse Tropical Garden Scholarship)

1164 Bishop Street, Suite 800
Honolulu HI 96813
808/537-6333 or toll free: 888/731-3863
FAX: 808/521-6286
E-mail: info@hcf-hawaii.org
Internet: http://www.hcf-hawaii.org
DEADLINE(S): MAR 1
FIELD(S): Agriculture; Science; Medicine; Nursing
ELIGIBILITY/REQUIREMENTS: Must be resident of the Hilo coast and the Hamakua coast, north of the Wailuku River; plan to attend full time an accredited 2- or 4-year college or university; and demonstrate financial need, good moral character, and academic achievement (minimum GPA of 2.7).
HOW TO APPLY: See website. Send application with 2 letters of recommendation.

3000—MONTANA FEDERATION OF GARDEN CLUBS LIFE MEMBERS

214 Waynt Lane
Hamilton MT 59340
406/363-5693
E-mail: elizabethhammt@aol.com
AMOUNT: $1,000
DEADLINE(S): MAY 1
FIELD(S): Conservation; Horticulture; Park Forestry; Floriculture; Greenhouse Management
ELIGIBILITY/REQUIREMENTS: Must be a sophomore in a Montana college; demonstrate financial need; and have 2.7 GPA.
HOW TO APPLY: No formal application form. Submit college transcript; letter of application detailing future plans; short

autobiography; color photo; letters of reference from instructors.
NUMBER OF AWARDS: 1
RENEWABLE: Yes, must reapply.
CONTACT: Elizabeth Kehmeier, Life Member Chair

3001—NATIONAL GARDEN CLUBS, INC.

4401 Magnolia Avenue
St. Louis MO 63110-3492
314/776-7574
FAX: 314/776-5108
E-mail: glaustin2@bellsouth.net or headquarters@gardenclub.org
Internet: http://www.gardenclub.org
AMOUNT: $3,500
DEADLINE(S): MAR 1
FIELD(S): Horticulture, Floriculture, Landscape Design, City Planning, Land Management, and allied subjects
ELIGIBILITY/REQUIREMENTS: Open to juniors, seniors, and graduate students who are U.S. citizens. Must have the endorsement of the state in which he/she resides permanently.
HOW TO APPLY: Write for complete information. Submit to local chapter; judged nationally.
NUMBER OF AWARDS: 30-35

3002—NEW YORK STATE HIGHER EDUCATION SERVICES CORPORATION (N.Y. State Regents Professional/Health Care Opportunity Scholarships)

Cultural Education Center
Room 5C64
Albany NY 12230
518/486-1319
Internet: http://www.hesc.com
AMOUNT: $1,000-$10,000
DEADLINE(S): Varies
FIELD(S): Medicine, Dentistry & related fields; Architecture, Nursing, Psychology, Audiology, Landscape Architecture, Social Work, Chiropractic, Law, Pharmacy, Accounting, Speech Language Pathology
ELIGIBILITY/REQUIREMENTS: For New York State residents who are economically disadvantaged and members of a minority group underrepresented in the chosen profession and attending school in New York State. For U.S. citizens or qualifying noncitizens.
HOW TO APPLY: See website or contact NYS HESC.
RENEWABLE: Yes

3003—PROFESSIONAL GROUNDS MANAGEMENT SOCIETY (Anne Seaman Memorial Scholarship)

720 Light Street
Baltimore MD 21230
410/223-2861
FAX: 410/752-8295
E-mail: pgms@assnhqtrs.com
Internet: http://www.pgms.org
AMOUNT: $2,000
DEADLINE(S): 1st Friday in JUL
FIELD(S): Landscape and Grounds Management; Turf Management; Irrigation Technology or a closely related field
ELIGIBILITY/REQUIREMENTS: U.S. citizen; full-time student.
HOW TO APPLY: Completed application with cover letter; current résumé; college or school transcripts; 2 letters of recommendation; and a letter from the PGMS member who is sponsoring the applicant.
NUMBER OF AWARDS: 3
RENEWABLE: No

3004—TURF AND ORNAMENTAL COMMUNICATORS ASSOCIATION (TOCA)

120 West Main Street
P.O. Box 156
New Prague MN 56071
952/758-6340
FAX: 952/758-5813
E-mail: tocaassociation@aol.com
Internet: http://www.toca.org
AMOUNT: $1,000
DEADLINE(S): MAR 1
FIELD(S): Technical Communications or Green Industry fields: Horticulture; Plant Science, Botany; Agronomy, Plant Pathology
ELIGIBILITY/REQUIREMENTS: Overall GPA of 2.5; major subject GPA 3.0+. Must be enrolled in college or university as undergraduate in a 2- or 4-year program.
HOW TO APPLY: Contact TOCA at above address or by e-mail for application forms, include your mailing address.
NUMBER OF AWARDS: 2
RENEWABLE: Yes, must reapply.

3005—UNIVERSITY OF ILLINOIS AT URBANA-CHAMPAIGN (Lydia E. Parker Bates Scholarship)

620 East John Street
Champaign IL 61820
217/333-0100
Internet: http://www.uiuc.edu/
AMOUNT: Up to $1,000
DEADLINE(S): MAR 15
FIELD(S): Art, Architecture, Landscape Architecture, Urban Planning, Dance, Theater, and all related subjects except Music
ELIGIBILITY/REQUIREMENTS: Open to undergraduate students in the College of Fine and Applied Arts. Must demonstrate financial need; have 2.85 GPA and carry at least 12 credit hours/semester.
HOW TO APPLY: Contact Office of Student Financial Aid for application. Complete the FAFSA with UIUC admission application.
NUMBER OF AWARDS: 175

3006—WASHINGTON APPLE EDUCATION FOUNDATION (Brian Kershaw Memorial Scholarship)

P.O. Box 3720
Wenatchee WA 98807
509/663-7713
FAX: 509/663-7713
E-mail: waef@waef.org
Internet: http://www.waef.org
AMOUNT: $1,500
DEADLINE(S): APR 1
FIELD(S): Agriculture; Horticulture
ELIGIBILITY/REQUIREMENTS: Open to graduating high school seniors and students currently enrolled in a 2- or 4-year college or university in Washington state. Must be studying in a tree fruit-related field and be the children of parents who are employed within Washington's tree fruit industry.
HOW TO APPLY: See website for application.
NUMBER OF AWARDS: 40+
RENEWABLE: Yes. Must reapply; maximum 2 years.
CONTACT: Jennifer Whitney

3007—WASHINGTON APPLE EDUCATION FOUNDATION (Fruit Packers Supply Scholarship)

P.O. Box 3720
Wenatchee WA 98807
509/663-7713
FAX: 509/663-7713
E-mail: waef@waef.org
Internet: http://www.ussui.org
AMOUNT: $1,000
DEADLINE(S): APR 1
FIELD(S): Agriculture; Horticulture
ELIGIBILITY/REQUIREMENTS: Open to juniors and seniors enrolled full time in

the agriculture department at Washington State University studying for a career in Washington's tree fruit industry.
HOW TO APPLY: See website for application.
NUMBER OF AWARDS: 1
CONTACT: Jennifer Whitney

3008—WASHINGTON APPLE EDUCATION FOUNDATION (Howard Hauff Memorial Scholarship)

P.O. Box 3720
Wenatchee WA 98807
509/663-7713
FAX: 509/663-7713
E-mail: waef@waef.org
Internet: http://www.ussui.org
AMOUNT: $500
DEADLINE(S): APR 1
FIELD(S): Agriculture; Horticulture; Engineering
ELIGIBILITY/REQUIREMENTS: Open to Washington state high school seniors or current college students from Washington state. Applicants should be studying for a degree in engineering; pursuing a career in the tree fruit industry, or been raised in a family involved in the tree fruit industry.
HOW TO APPLY: See website for application.
NUMBER OF AWARDS: 1
CONTACT: Jennifer Whitney

3009—WASHINGTON APPLE EDUCATION FOUNDATION (Phil Jenkins Scholarship)

P.O. Box 3720
Wenatchee WA 98807
509/663-7713
FAX: 509/663-7713
E-mail: waef@waef.org
Internet: http://www.ussui.org
AMOUNT: Varies
DEADLINE(S): APR 1
FIELD(S): Agriculture; Horticulture
ELIGIBILITY/REQUIREMENTS: Open to students currently enrolled or entering a college or university who plan to live and work in the tree fruit industry in the Yakima Valley following the completion of their degree.
HOW TO APPLY: See website for application.
NUMBER OF AWARDS: 1
CONTACT: Jennifer Whitney

3010—WASHINGTON APPLE EDUCATION FOUNDATION (Valent USA Scholarship)

P.O. Box 3720
Wenatchee WA 98807

509/663-7713
FAX: 509/663-7713
E-mail: waef@waef.org
Internet: http://www.ussui.org
AMOUNT: $1,000
DEADLINE(S): APR 1
FIELD(S): Agriculture; Horticulture
ELIGIBILITY/REQUIREMENTS: Open to students enrolled in the tree fruit program at Yakima Valley Community College, Wenatchee Valley College, or Washington State University.
HOW TO APPLY: See website for application.
NUMBER OF AWARDS: 3
CONTACT: Jennifer Whitney

3011—WASHINGTON APPLE EDUCATION FOUNDATION (Valley Fruit Company Scholarship)

P.O. Box 3720
Wenatchee WA 98807
509/663-7713
FAX: 509/663-7713
E-mail: waef@waef.org
Internet: http://www.ussui.org
AMOUNT: Tuition fees
DEADLINE(S): APR 1
FIELD(S): Agriculture; Horticulture
ELIGIBILITY/REQUIREMENTS: Open to Wapato High School (Wapato, Washington) seniors, who plan to attend Yakima Valley Community College.
HOW TO APPLY: See website for application.
NUMBER OF AWARDS: 1
CONTACT: Jennifer Whitney

3012—WASHINGTON APPLE EDUCATION FOUNDATION (Wenatchee Traffic Club Scholarship)

P.O. Box 3720
Wenatchee WA 98807
509/663-7713
FAX: 509/663-7713
E-mail: waef@waef.org
Internet: http://www.ussui.org
AMOUNT: Varies
DEADLINE(S): APR 1
FIELD(S): Agriculture; Horticulture; Business
ELIGIBILITY/REQUIREMENTS: Must be Washington state high school seniors or current college undergraduate students from Washington state pursuing a commodity-related career. Applicants must be residents of Chelan, Douglas, Grant, or Okanogan counties. Parents or guardians of applicant should be involved in Washington's tree fruit industry.

HOW TO APPLY: See website for application.
NUMBER OF AWARDS: Varies
RENEWABLE: No
CONTACT: Jennifer Whitney

3013—WASHINGTON APPLE EDUCATION FOUNDATION (Yakima Valley Grower-Shippers Association Scholarship)

P.O. Box 3720
Wenatchee WA 98807
509/663-7713
FAX: 509/663-7713
E-mail: waef@waef.org
Internet: http://www.ussui.org
AMOUNT: $750
DEADLINE(S): APR 1
FIELD(S): Agriculture; Horticulture; Business; Mechanical Engineering
ELIGIBILITY/REQUIREMENTS: Must be employee or child of a general member of the YVGSA or the child of an employee or grower of a general member of the YVGSA. Must be pursuing a degree compatible with service to the tree fruit industry.
HOW TO APPLY: See website for application.
NUMBER OF AWARDS: 2
RENEWABLE: No
CONTACT: Jennifer Whitney

3014—WORLDSTUDIO FOUNDATION

200 Varick Street, Suite 507
New York NY 10014
212/366-1317
FAX: 212/807-0024
E-mail: scholarshipcoordinator@worldstudio.org
Internet: http://www.worldstudio.org or http://www.aiga.org
AMOUNT: $1,500-$5,000
DEADLINE(S): APR 14
FIELD(S): Advertising, Animation, Architecture, Cartooning, Crafts, Environmental graphics, Film/video, Film/theater design, Fine arts, Furniture design, Industrial/product design, Interior architecture and design, Landscape architecture, New media, Photography, Surface/textile design, Urban planning
ELIGIBILITY/REQUIREMENTS: Applicants must be pursuing a degree in the fine or commercial arts, design or architecture, and plan to enter a career in the creative professions. Undergraduates and graduates are eligible. Minority status and/or social agenda are significant factors. Financial need a prerequisite. Minimum 2.0 GPA.

HOW TO APPLY: See websites for application. The application is a 2-part process. Applications must include personal and school information, including transcripts and copies of letters of acceptance; financial information; portfolio; written statement of purpose; examples of a commitment to a social agenda, 2 letters of recommendation from college instructors, high school teachers, or employers; head shot of applicant.
NUMBER OF AWARDS: 20-30
RENEWABLE: Yes. Must reapply.
CONTACT: Mark Randall

HOSPITALITY

3015—AMERICAN HOTEL & LODGING EDUCATIONAL FOUNDATION (American Express Academic Scholarships)

1201 New York Avenue NW,
Suite 600
Washington DC 20005-3931
202/289-3188
FAX: 202/289-3199
Internet: http://www. ahlef.org
AMOUNT: $500-$2,000
DEADLINE(S): MAY 1
FIELD(S): Hospitality/Hotel
    Management; Travel & Tourism;
    Culinary Arts
ELIGIBILITY/REQUIREMENTS: For full-time (minimum 20 hours/week) AH&LA-member property employees and their dependents enrolled in accredited, undergraduate academic programs leading to a degree in hospitality management. The applicant does not have to attend an AH&LEF-affiliated school.
HOW TO APPLY: Applications available on website.

3016—AMERICAN HOTEL & LODGING EDUCATIONAL FOUNDATION (American Express Professional Development Scholarships)

1201 New York Avenue NW,
Suite 600
Washington DC 20005-3931
202/289-3188
FAX: 202/289-3199
Internet: http://www. ahlef.org
AMOUNT: $500-$2,000
DEADLINE(S): Quarterly
FIELD(S): Hospitality/Hotel
    Management; Travel & Tourism;
    Culinary Arts
ELIGIBILITY/REQUIREMENTS: Provides financial support to students

enrolled in distance learning courses or professional certifications courses offered through the Educational Institute (EI).
HOW TO APPLY: Applicants must enroll in EI to qualify. AH&LEF makes scholarship payment directly to EI on the recipient's behalf. Call EI at 800/349-0299 or visit www.ei-ahla.org for enrollment information.

3017—AMERICAN HOTEL & LODGING EDUCATION FOUNDATION (Annual Scholarship Grant Program)

1201 New York Avenue NW,
Suite 600
Washington DC 20005-3931
202/289-3188
FAX: 202/289-3199
Internet: http://www.ahlef.org
AMOUNT: Varies
DEADLINE(S): MAY 1
FIELD(S): Hospitality/Hotel
    Management
ELIGIBILITY/REQUIREMENTS: Co-administered with 79 2- and 4-year universities and colleges in the United States offering hospitality management programs (see website for complete list) that are affiliated with AH&LEF. Criteria include full-time enrollment status, minimum GPA of 3.0, U.S. citizenship or permanent U.S. resident status, and completion of at least 1 or 2 years of school. Note: A few scholarships have slightly different criteria, depending on the program. Interested students should inquire at their school's dean's office.
HOW TO APPLY: Schools must submit their student nominations to the Foundation for upcoming academic year.

3018—AMERICAN HOTEL & LODGING EDUCATION FOUNDATION (Ecolab Academic Scholarships)

1201 New York Avenue NW,
Suite 600
Washington DC 20005-3931
202/289-3188
FAX: 202/289-3199
Internet: http://www.ahlef.org
AMOUNT: $1,000 (associate); $2,000
    (baccalaureate)
DEADLINE(S): JUN 1
FIELD(S): Hospitality/Hotel
    Management
ELIGIBILITY/REQUIREMENTS: Applicants must be enrolled or intend to enroll full time (at least 12 hours) in a U.S. baccalaureate or associate hospitality degree-granting program for both the upcoming fall and spring semesters. The

applicant's school does not have to be affiliated with AH&LEF.
HOW TO APPLY: Applications available on website.

3019—AMERICAN HOTEL & LODGING EDUCATION FOUNDATION (Ecolab Certification Scholarships)

1201 New York Avenue NW,
Suite 600
Washington DC 20005-3931
202/289-3188
FAX: 202/289-3199
Internet: http://www.ahlef.org
AMOUNT: Varies (cost of certification)
DEADLINE(S): Quarterly
FIELD(S): Hospitality/Hotel
    Management
ELIGIBILITY/REQUIREMENTS: Applicants must be hospitality professionals working at an AH&LA member property a minimum of 35 hours per week and qualify for the certification program. The scholarship includes the cost of the certification for the following professional designations: Certified Hotel Administrator, Certified Engineering Operations Executive, Certified Lodging Manager, and Certified Hospitality Housekeeping Executive.
HOW TO APPLY: Call EI at 800/349-0299 or visit www.ei-ahla.org for certification information.

3020—AMERICAN HOTEL & LODGING EDUCATION FOUNDATION (Hyatt Hotel Fund for Minority Lodging Management Students)

1201 New York Avenue NW,
Suite 600
Washington DC 20005-3931
202/289-3188
FAX: 202/289-3199
Internet: http://www.ahlef.org
AMOUNT: $2,000
DEADLINE(S): APR 1
FIELD(S): Hospitality/Hotel
    Management
ELIGIBILITY/REQUIREMENTS: For minority students pursuing a 4-year undergraduate degree in hospitality or hotel management on a full-time basis (minimum 12 hours/week). Criteria are academic performance, hospitality work experience, extracurricular involvement, career goals, and financial need.
HOW TO APPLY: Nominated by college; inquire at dean's office; applications are sent directly to the schools between January and March each year.

NUMBER OF AWARDS: Approximately 18

3021—AMERICAN HOTEL & LODGING EDUCATION FOUNDATION (Lodging Management Program (LMP)

1201 New York Avenue NW, Suite 600
Washington DC 20005-3931
202/289-3188
FAX: 202/289-3199
Internet: http://www.ahlef.org
AMOUNT: Varies (cost of certification)
DEADLINE(S): APR 1
FIELD(S): Hospitality/Hotel Management

ELIGIBILITY/REQUIREMENTS: Open to high school students who have successfully completed both years of the LMP high school curriculum for accredited undergraduate hospitality management degree-granting program or in an Educational Institute distance learning course or professional certification.

HOW TO APPLY: See website or consult instructor for additional information and application; submit with essay of no more than 500 words describing your personal background, including how you learned about and why you took the LMP class; what you learned most from your LMP class; what the most important and most interesting part of this class was; why you think the hospitality industry is the right career choice for you; and how this scholarship will help you achieve your career objectives and future goals. Also required are your most recent high school transcript including GPA; a copy of your college curriculum; and a copy of acceptance letter.

3022—AMERICAN HOTEL & LODGING EDUCATION FOUNDATION (Pepsi Scholarships)

1201 New York Avenue NW, Suite 600
Washington DC 20005-3931
202/289-3188
FAX: 202/289-3199
Internet: http://www.ahlef.org
AMOUNT: Varies
DEADLINE(S): APR 1
FIELD(S): Hospitality/Hotel Management

ELIGIBILITY/REQUIREMENTS: Open only to graduating seniors from the Marriott Hospitality High School located in Washington, D.C. This endowed gift provides perpetual scholarships to graduates of the Marriott High School who are enrolled in undergraduate hospitality-related degree-granting programs at colleges and universities.

HOW TO APPLY: MHHS graduates should inquire in their principal's office for consideration of these scholarships.

3023—AMERICAN HOTEL & LODGING EDUCATIONAL FOUNDATION (The AAA Five Diamond Hospitality Scholarship)

1201 New York Avenue NW, Suite 600
Washington DC 20005-3931
202/289-3188
FAX: 202/289-3199
Internet: http://www.ahlef.org
AMOUNT: $5,000
DEADLINE(S): MAY 1
FIELD(S): Hospitality/Hotel Management; Travel & Tourism; Culinary Arts

ELIGIBILITY/REQUIREMENTS: Each year, AAA selects one of the 4-year programs participating in AH&LEF's Annual Scholarship Grant Program to receive the award.

HOW TO APPLY: The chosen school selects the scholarship recipient based upon a set of minimum eligibility criteria. See website for additional information and name of school chosen each year.

3024—AMERICAN HOTEL & LODGING EDUCATION FOUNDATION (The Arthur J. Packard Memorial Scholarship Competition)

1201 New York Avenue NW, Suite 600
Washington DC 20005-3931
202/289-3188
FAX: 202/289-3199
Internet: http://www.ahlef.org
AMOUNT: $5,000 (1st place); $3,000 (2nd place) scholarship; $2,000 (3rd place)
DEADLINE(S): MAY 1
FIELD(S): Hospitality/Hotel Management

ELIGIBILITY/REQUIREMENTS: Provides scholarships to the most outstanding students of lodging management and 2 runner-ups through an annual competition among the AH&LEF-affiliated 4-year programs.

HOW TO APPLY: Each university nominates the one student most qualified according to the criteria to compete in the national competition. Students should inquire in their dean's office for consideration of the nomination and application.

NUMBER OF AWARDS: 3

3025—AMERICAN HOTEL & LODGING EDUCATION FOUNDATION (The RAMA Scholarship for the American Dream)

1201 New York Avenue NW, Suite 600
Washington DC 20005-3931
202/289-3188
FAX: 202/289-3199
Internet: http://www.ahlef.org
AMOUNT: Varies
DEADLINE(S): APR 1
FIELD(S): Hospitality/Hotel Management

ELIGIBILITY/REQUIREMENTS: To provide financial aid to students pursuing degrees in hotel management at hospitality management schools designated to participate in the program (see website for complete list).

HOW TO APPLY: The schools select the recipients and preference is given to students of Asian-Indian descent and other minority groups and to JHM Hotel employees.

3026—AMERICAN ALLIANCE FOR HEALTH, PHYSICAL EDUCATION, RECREATION & DANCE

1900 Association Drive
Reston VA 20191
703/476-3400 or 800/213-7193
Internet: http://www.aahperd.org
AMOUNT: Varies
DEADLINE(S): Varies
FIELD(S): Health Education, Leisure and Recreation, Girls and Women in Sports, Sport and Physical Education, Dance

ELIGIBILITY/REQUIREMENTS: This organization has 6 national suborganizations specializing in the above fields. Some have grants and fellowships for both individuals and group projects.

HOW TO APPLY: Visit website for details or write to above address for details.

3027—AMERICAN SOCIETY OF TRAVEL AGENTS FOUNDATION

1101 King Street
Alexandria VA 22314
703/739-2782
FAX: 703/684-8319
E-mail: scholarship@astahq.com
Internet: http://www.astanet.com
AMOUNT: $200-$3,000
DEADLINE(S): AUG; DEC
FIELD(S): Travel; Tourism; Hospitality

ELIGIBILITY/REQUIREMENTS: Various undergraduate and graduate scholarships are available to U.S. and Canadian citizens, permanent residents, and legal aliens. Must have a minimum 2.5 GPA. Financial need usually NOT considered.

HOW TO APPLY: Submit proof of enrollment in travel and tourism courses and official statement of tuition amount, letter of recommendation, transcripts, and other specific requirements for individual awards. See website or contact Scholarship Manager for specific award details.

NUMBER OF AWARDS: Over 20
RENEWABLE: Some
CONTACT: Verlete Mitchell, Scholarship Manager

3028—CLUB FOUNDATION, THE

1733 King Street
Alexandria VA 22314
703/739-9500
FAX: 703/739-0124
E-mail: ashleigh.hill@club
foundation.org
Internet: http://www.club
foundation.org
AMOUNT: $2,500
DEADLINE(S): APR 15
FIELD(S): Business Administration, Hospitality

ELIGIBILITY/REQUIREMENTS: Must demonstrate that you are pursuing managerial careers in the private club industry. Must have completed freshman year of college and be enrolled for the full academic year in an accredited 4-year institution; must have achieved and continue to maintain a GPA of at least 2.5. Additional points are awarded for CMMA chapter members.

HOW TO APPLY: Application available on website; submit with essay; transcript; recommendation letter from an advisor/professor and a private club industry professional; and résumé.

NUMBER OF AWARDS: 2
RENEWABLE: No
CONTACT: Ashleigh Hill, Program Specialist

3029—COLORADO RESTAURANT ASSOCI-ATION (Scholarship Education Fund)

430 East 7th Avenue
Denver CO 80203
800/522-2972 or 303/830-2972
FAX: 303/830-2973
E-mail: info@coloradorestaurant.com
Internet: http://www.colorado
restaurant.com

AMOUNT: $500-$2,500
DEADLINE(S): MAR 20
FIELD(S): Food Service; Hospitality
ELIGIBILITY/REQUIREMENTS: Open to junior- and senior-level college students enrolled in a 2- or 4-year degree program in food service and hospitality-related fields at a Colorado college or university.

HOW TO APPLY: Contact CRA for an application.

3030—EMPIRE COLLEGE (Dean's Scholarship)

3035 Cleveland Avenue
Santa Rosa CA 95403
707/546-4000
FAX: 707/546-4058
Internet: http://www.wmpcol.edu
AMOUNT: $250-$1,500
DEADLINE(S): APR 15
FIELD(S): Accounting; Office Administration; Paralegal; Medical (Clinical and Administrative); Tourism; Hospitality; General Business; Computer Assembly; Network Assembly/Administration; Security

ELIGIBILITY/REQUIREMENTS: Open to high school seniors who plan to attend Empire College. Must be U.S. citizen.

HOW TO APPLY: Contact College for an application.

NUMBER OF AWARDS: 10
RENEWABLE: No
CONTACT: Mary Farha

3031—HOSPITALITY FINANCIAL AND TECHNOLOGY PROFESSIONALS

11709 Boulder Lane, Suite 110
Austin TX 78726
512/249-5333 or 800/646-4387
FAX: 512/249-1533
Internet: http://www.hftp.org
AMOUNT: $1,000-$1,500
DEADLINE(S): JUL 15
FIELD(S): Accounting; Hospitality Management

ELIGIBILITY/REQUIREMENTS: For students majoring in either accounting or hospitality management at an accredited college or university.

HOW TO APPLY: Applications must come through an IAHA local chapter president. Send SASE for details.

3032—INTERNATIONAL EXECUTIVE HOUSEKEEPERS ASSOCIATION EDUCATION-AL FOUNDATION, INC.

1001 Eastwind Drive, Suite 301

Westerville OH 43081-3361
800/200-6342
FAX: 614/895-1248
E-mail: excel@ieha.org
Internet: http://www.ieha.org
AMOUNT: $800
DEADLINE(S): JAN 10
FIELD(S): Healthcare, Hotels, Education Facilities, Rehabilitation Centers and related facilities

ELIGIBILITY/REQUIREMENTS: Open to members enrolled in a program of study leading to IEHA certification.

HOW TO APPLY: Submit original manuscript (no more than 1,000 words) regarding housekeeping within any industry segment as noted.

NUMBER OF AWARDS: Multiple
RENEWABLE: No

3033—JOHNSON AND WALES UNIVERSI-TY (Annual National High School Recipe Contest)

8 Abbott Park Place
Providence RI 02903
401/598-2345
Internet: http://www.jwu.edu/
admiss/scholarships/
AMOUNT: $1,000-$5,000
DEADLINE(S): JAN 31
FIELD(S): Business, Hospitality, Technology, Culinary Arts

ELIGIBILITY/REQUIREMENTS: For students planning to attend Johnson and Wales University, Providence, Rhode Island.

HOW TO APPLY: Write for detailed description.

3034—JOHNSON AND WALES UNIVERSI-TY (Gilbane Building Company Eagle Scout Scholarship)

8 Abbott Park Place
Providence RI 02903
401/598-2345
Internet: http://www.jwu.edu/
admiss/scholarships/
AMOUNT: $1,200
DEADLINE(S): None
FIELD(S): Business, Hospitality, Technology, Culinary Arts

ELIGIBILITY/REQUIREMENTS: For students attending Johnson and Wales University, Providence, Rhode Island. Must be Eagle Scouts.

HOW TO APPLY: Send letter of recommendation and transcript.

3035—JOHNSON AND WALES UNIVERSITY (National High School Entrepreneur of the Year Contest)

8 Abbott Park Place
Providence RI 02903
401/598-2345
Internet: http://www.jwu.edu/
admiss/scholarships/
AMOUNT: $1,000-$10,000
DEADLINE(S): DEC 27
FIELD(S): Business, Hospitality,
Technology, Culinary Arts
ELIGIBILITY/REQUIREMENTS: For students attending Johnson and Wales University, Providence, Rhode Island.
HOW TO APPLY: Send for detailed description.

3036—JUNIOR ACHIEVEMENT INC. (Johnson and Wales University Scholarship)

One Education Way
Colorado Springs CO 80906-4477
719/540-8000
FAX: 719/540-6299
E-mail: newmedia@ja.org
Internet: http://www.ja.org
AMOUNT: $10,000 (4 years)
DEADLINE(S): FEB 1
FIELD(S): Business; Culinary Arts;
Hospitality; Technology
ELIGIBILITY/REQUIREMENTS: Must be high school seniors who have been accepted by and will be attending Johnson and Wales University and be majoring in one of the above fields.
HOW TO APPLY: Send application to Johnson and Wales University with 1 letter of recommendation from a JA High School Programs consultant.
NUMBER OF AWARDS: 2 4-year $10,000 scholarships; unlimited partial scholarships.
RENEWABLE: No
CONTACT: To obtain application, contact Tom Gauthier, Coordinator of Specialty Recruitment, Johnson and Wales University, 8 Abbott Park Place, Providence, RI 02903; 800/DIAL-JWU, ext. 2345 or from website (http://www.jwu.edu).

3037—NATIONAL RESTAURANT ASSOCIATION EDUCATIONAL FOUNDATION (Academic Scholarship for Undergraduate Students)

175 West Jackson Blvd., Suite 1500
Chicago IL 60604-2814
800/765-2122 or

312/715-1010, ext. 744
FAX: 312/566-9733
E-mail: scholars@nraef.org
Internet: http://www.nraef.org/
scholarships
AMOUNT: $2,000
DEADLINE(S): NOV 18 and APR 7
FIELD(S): Restaurant or Food Service-related Program
ELIGIBILITY/REQUIREMENTS: For college students pursuing a certificate, associate degree, or bachelor's degree in above fields. Must be a U.S. citizen/permanent resident or a noncitizen attending school in U.S./territories enrolled on a full-time or substantial part-time basis (usually a minimum of 9 credit hours), have completed 1st semester with a minimum 2.75 GPA, and provide proof of at least 750 hours of work experience in the restaurant/food-service industry.
HOW TO APPLY: See website for additional information and application. Send 2 essays and 1 to 3 letters of recommendation from a current or previous employer.
RENEWABLE: No. May not receive 2 consecutive undergraduate scholarships, but may reapply.

3038—NATIONAL RESTAURANT ASSOCIATION EDUCATIONAL FOUNDATION (Academic Scholarship for High School Seniors)

175 West Jackson Blvd., Suite 1500
Chicago IL 60604-2814
800/765-2122 or
312/715-1010, ext. 744
FAX: 312/566-9733
E-mail: scholars@nraef.org
Internet: http://www.nraef.org/
scholarships
AMOUNT: $2,000
DEADLINE(S): 21
FIELD(S): Restaurant or Food Service-related Program
ELIGIBILITY/REQUIREMENTS: For high school seniors accepted into either a full-time or substantial part-time postsecondary program, in 1 of above fields who plan to enroll in a minimum of 2 terms for the school year. Must have a minimum 2.75 GPA and be a U.S. citizen/permanent resident or a noncitizen attending school in U.S./territories; have taken a minimum of 1 food service-related course and/or have performed a minimum of 250 hours of restaurant/hospitality work experience.
HOW TO APPLY: Applications available January 1. Submit along with 1 to 3 letters of recommendation. See website for information.

3039—NATIONAL TOURISM FOUNDATION

P.O. Box 3071
Lexington KY 40596-3071
800/682-8886
FAX: 606/226-4414
Internet: http://www.ntfonline.com
AMOUNT: $3,000
DEADLINE(S): APR 15
FIELD(S): Travel and Tourism;
Hospitality; Restaurant Management
ELIGIBILITY/REQUIREMENTS: Various scholarships for full-time students at 2- or 4-year colleges or universities in North America who are entering their junior or senior year of study. Must be a strong academic performer and have at least a 3.0 GPA. Degree emphasis must be in a travel- and tourism-related field, such as hotel management, restaurant management, or tourism.
HOW TO APPLY: Submit application, which is available from website; a résumé; information on any work or internship experience in travel and tourism and on any extracurricular or volunteer experience. See website for additional requirements of each individual scholarship. Students may apply for more than 1 award but may receive only 1.

3040—UNIVERSITY OF NORTH TEXAS (Merchandising and Hospitality Scholarships)

Dean, School of
Merchandising/Hospitality
Management
P.O. Box 311100
Denton TX 76203-1100
817/565-2436
Internet: http://www.unt./scholar/
scholarshipedu/scholarshipsedu/
scholarships/smhm.htm
AMOUNT: Varies
DEADLINE(S): Varies
FIELD(S): Merchandising; Hospitality
Management
ELIGIBILITY/REQUIREMENTS: For students in the above fields. Eligibility requirements vary.
HOW TO APPLY: See website for more information. Contact university for details.
NUMBER OF AWARDS: Several

MORTUARY SCIENCE

3041—FLORIDA FUNERAL DIRECTORS ASSOCIATION

150 South Monroe Street, Suite 305

Tallahassee FL 32301
850/224-1969
FAX: 850/224-7965
E-mail: ffdainfo@ffda.org or
ffdamember@ffda.org
Internet: http://www.ffda.org
AMOUNT: Varies
DEADLINE(S): None
FIELD(S): Mortuary Science
ELIGIBILITY/REQUIREMENTS: Must be students of mortuary science programs in an accredited mortuary science school who plan to serve the profession in the state of Florida; have completed 30 credit hours with no "D" grade in any mortuary science required class and an overall GPA of at least 2.5; be legal residents of Florida; and be a student member of the Florida Funeral Directors Association.
HOW TO APPLY: Submit application; college transcript or letter stating GPA from the Program Chairman; 2 proofs of Florida residency; and 2 essays of 500 words each, on "Choosing Your Career" and "Tell Us About Yourself."

3042—MARYLAND STATE FUNERAL DIRECTORS ASSOCIATION, INC. (Daniel T. Mulheran Scholarship Fund)

311 Crain Highway SE
Glen Burnie MD 21061
410/553-9106 or 888/459-9693
FAX: 410/553-9107
E-mail: msfda@msfda.net
Internet: http://www.msfda.net
AMOUNT: $1,000
DEADLINE(S): OCT 1
FIELD(S): Mortuary Science
ELIGIBILITY/REQUIREMENTS: Must have completed 2/3 of education requirements or have graduated within previous 6 months (may not have received a grade less than 'C'). Recent grads must be eligible for licensure in the state of Maryland and be a licensed apprentice. Completion of a 2,500-word essay; submission of all college transcripts; the scholarship application and a letter of recommendation from someone close enough to comment on applicant's personal qualifications and professional promise; and a letter of recommendation from a licensed funeral service professional who holds membership in the Maryland State Funeral Directors Association.
HOW TO APPLY: Download application from website or contact MSFDA. Submit with 2,500-word essay; transcripts; and 2 letters of recommendation.
NUMBER OF AWARDS: 1
RENEWABLE: No

3043—NEW JERSEY FUNERAL SERVICE EDUCATION CORPORATION

P.O. Box L
Manasquan NJ 08736
732/974-9444
FAX: 732/974-8144
Internet: http://www.njsfda.org
AMOUNT: Up to $2,000
DEADLINE(S): JUN 30
FIELD(S): Funeral Service
ELIGIBILITY/REQUIREMENTS: Must be a New Jersey resident enrolled in a Mortuary Service program.
HOW TO APPLY: Call or write for application.
NUMBER OF AWARDS: Up to 4
RENEWABLE: No
CONTACT: Cynthia Viant

POLICE & FIRE SCIENCE

3044—ASSOCIATION OF CERTIFIED FRAUD EXAMINERS

The Gregor Building
716 West Avenue
Austin TX 78701
800/245-3321 or 512/478-9070
FAX: 512/478-9297
Internet: http://www.cfenet.com
AMOUNT: $1,000
DEADLINE(S): APR 30
FIELD(S): Accounting; Criminal Justice
ELIGIBILITY/REQUIREMENTS: Open to full-time graduate or undergraduate students majoring in accounting or criminal justice degree programs.
HOW TO APPLY: Awards are based on overall academic achievement, 3 letters of recommendation plus a letter of recommendation from a Certified Fraud Examiner or a local CFE Chapter, and an original 250-word essay explaining why the applicant deserves the award and how fraud awareness will affect his or her professional career development. Download application from website.
NUMBER OF AWARDS: 15

3045—INTERNATIONAL ASSOCIATION OF ARSON INVESTIGATORS EDUCATIONAL FOUNDATION (John Charles Wilson Scholarship)

2151 Priest Bridge Drive, Suite 25
Crofton MD 21114
410/451-3473
FAX: 410/451-9049
Internet: http://www.firearson.
com/ef/jcwscholar/index.asp

AMOUNT: Varies
DEADLINE(S): FEB 15
FIELD(S): Police or Fire Sciences, including Fire Investigation and related subjects
ELIGIBILITY/REQUIREMENTS: Open to IAAI members, their immediate families, and non-members who are recommended and sponsored by members in good standing. Awards are for undergraduate study in above areas at accredited 2- and 4-year institutions.
HOW TO APPLY: Transcripts and 500-word essay describing background and goals required. Write to the Executive Director at above address for information.
NUMBER OF AWARDS: 3
CONTACT: Executive Director

3046—INTERNATIONAL ASSOCIATION OF FIRE CHIEFS FOUNDATION

4025 Fair Ridge Drive
Fairfax VA 22033-2868
703/273-0911
email: foundation@iafc.org
Internet: http://www.iafcf.org
AMOUNT: $250-$4,000
DEADLINE(S): AUG 1
FIELD(S): Fire Sciences and related academic programs
ELIGIBILITY/REQUIREMENTS: Active members with a minimum of 3 years' volunteer work, or 2 years' paid work, or a combination of paid and volunteer work, or 3 years with a state, county, provincial, municipal, community, industrial, or federal fire department, who has demonstrated proficiency, is eligible. Preference will be given to those demonstrating need, desire, and initiative.
HOW TO APPLY: Send application form, including a 250-word statement outlining reasons for applying and explaining why you think your course of study will be useful to you in your chosen field. Also list credits previously attained in college-level courses and submit transcript.

3047—NATIONAL ASSOCIATION OF BLACKS IN CRIMINAL JUSTICE (Thurgood Marshall Scholarship Award)

NABCJ, NCCU
P.O. Box 19788
Durham NC 27707
Internet: http://www.nabcj.
org/awards.html
AMOUNT: $2,000
DEADLINE(S): MAR 31
FIELD(S): Criminal Justice
ELIGIBILITY/REQUIREMENTS: Must demonstrate superior achievement in aca-

demic work; maintain the equivalent of a 'B' average; have been accepted or be currently enrolled in a degree program in criminal justice or a related field of study; and demonstrate financial need based on hardship or the lack of opportunity to accumulate supplemental financial funds.

HOW TO APPLY: Send application; 1,000-word essay explaining choice of criminal justice career; transcript supporting the GPA; copy of acceptance letter; statement from parent(s) or legal guardian explaining prior financial planning for education and describing need for financial assistance, and supporting documentation; documentation of community/volunteer service.

NUMBER OF AWARDS: 1

3048—WYOMING PEACE OFFICERS ASSOCIATION (Category #2 Scholarships)

1710 Pacific Avenue
Cheyenne WY 82009
307/777-7718
FAX: 307/638-9706
AMOUNT: $500/semester
DEADLINE(S): JUL 31
FIELD(S): Law Enforcement
ELIGIBILITY/REQUIREMENTS: Available to Wyoming residents enrolled in a law enforcement major at the University of Wyoming or any Wyoming community college on a full-time basis (12 semester credit hours or more).
HOW TO APPLY: Write or phone for application.
RENEWABLE: Yes. Must reapply; maximum of 4 semesters; must carry a full-time status (12 semester credit hours or more) and satisfactorily complete ("C" GPA) 12 hours for the Fall semester to be eligible for the Spring stipend.
CONTACT: Betty Haukap

3049—WYOMING PEACE OFFICERS ASSOCIATION (Category #3 Scholarships)

1710 Pacific Avenue
Cheyenne WY 82009
307/777-7718
FAX: 307/638-9706
AMOUNT: $500/semester
DEADLINE(S): JUL 31
FIELD(S): Law Enforcement
ELIGIBILITY/REQUIREMENTS: Available to any active or retired Wyoming law enforcement officer enrolled in a law enforcement major at the University of Wyoming or any Wyoming community college on a full- or part-time basis. Scholarship is awarded upon completion of each semester and

may be applied to tuition, books, or travel expenses.
HOW TO APPLY: Write or phone for application.
RENEWABLE: Yes. Maximum of 4 semesters. Recipients must carry a full-time status of 12 semester credit hours or more and must satisfactorily complete 12 hours for the Fall semester to be eligible for the Spring stipend. Satisfactory completion is defined as a "C" GPA or better. At end of year, new application must be submitted.
CONTACT: Betty Haukap

3050—WYOMING PEACE OFFICERS ASSOCIATION (Category #4 Scholarships)

1710 Pacific Avenue
Cheyenne WY 82009
307/777-7718
FAX: 307/638-9706
AMOUNT: $1,000
DEADLINE(S): JUL 31
FIELD(S): Law Enforcement
ELIGIBILITY/REQUIREMENTS: Available to any pre-service student who has successfully completed or who will successfully complete (within the last year, July 1-June 30) a police officer or detention officer basic course offered by the Wyoming Law Enforcement Academy. Applicants, if employed by a law enforcement agency at the time of application, must be a current member of the WPOA.
HOW TO APPLY: Write or phone for application.
RENEWABLE: No
CONTACT: Betty Haukap

REAL ESTATE

3051—APPRAISAL INSTITUTE WOMEN AND MINORITY EDUCATION SCHOLARSHIP

550 West Van Buren, Suite 1000
Chicago IL 60607
312/335-4100
FAX: 312/335-4400
E-mail: hrichmond@appraisa
linstitute.org
Internet: http//www.appraisal
institute.org
AMOUNT: $1,000 or more
DEADLINE(S): APR 15
FIELD(S): Real Estate
ELIGIBILITY/REQUIREMENTS: Applicants must be minority students (racial, ethnic or gender group underrepresented in the real estate appraisal profession) enrolled full- or part-time in a degree granting college, university or junior col-

lege; cumulative GPA 2.5, and demonstrated financial need.
HOW TO APPLY: See website for application. Submit with transcripts.
NUMBER OF AWARDS: 10
RENEWABLE: No

3052—REAL ESTATE EDUCATION FOUNDATION (The Foundation Scholarship)

3180 Adloff Lane, Suite 400
Springfield IL 62703
217/529-2600
FAX: 217/529-3904
Internet: http://www.illinois
realtor.org
AMOUNT: $1,000-$2,000
DEADLINE(S): APR 1
FIELD(S): Real Estate and Allied Fields (Construction; Land Use Planning; Mortgage Banking; Property Management; Real Estate Appraising; Real Estate Assessing; Real Estate Brokerage; Real Estate Development; Real Estate Investment Counseling; Real Estate Law; Real Estate Syndication)
ELIGIBILITY/REQUIREMENTS: Must indicate interest in pursuing a career in real estate or an allied field; record of scholastic achievement, including academic GPA; economic need or situation; and recommendations by instructors, employers, Realtors and others.
HOW TO APPLY: Submit application with a statement of your general activities and intellectual interests, employment (if any), contemplated line of study and of the career you expect to follow (up to 1,000 words); a record of military service, if any; your proposed program of study, including a brief description of each course, signed by the Dean or appropriate official; a statement from the real estate instructor, or, if none, the Dean recommending you; transcripts of all your collegiate records; and letters of recommendation from 2 persons (preferable that 1 of these letters be from a Realtor). Personal interview for finalists.
NUMBER OF AWARDS: 8
CONTACT: Larranne Wells

TECHNOLOGY (MISCELLANEOUS)

3053—AGC SCHOLARSHIP FUND

10 Airline Drive, Suite 203
Albany NY 12205
518-456-1134
FAX: 518-456-1198
E-mail: cnewell@agcnys.org

Internet: http://www.agcnys.org
AMOUNT: $2,500 (construction and civil
engineering), $1,500 (diesel
technology)
DEADLINE(S): MAY 15
FIELD(S): Construction, Civil
Engineering, Diesel Technology
ELIGIBILITY/REQUIREMENTS:
Applicant must be entering the 2nd, 3rd or
4th year of a 2- or 4-year college. Must
intend to pursue a career in the highway
construction industry, pursuing a Bachelor
or Associate degree in construction or civil
engineering and having at least a 2.5 GPA.
HOW TO APPLY: See website for additional information and application. Submit
with grades and 3 evaluation forms.
NUMBER OF AWARDS: 16-25, includes
2 diesel technology scholarships
RENEWABLE: Yes. Up to 3 years; must
reapply.
CONTACT: Cathy Newell

3054—AMERICAN INSTITUTE OF BAKING

1213 Bakers Way
Manhattan KS 66502
800/633-5737
FAX: 785/537-1493
E-mail: kembers@aibonline.org
Internet: http://www.aibonline.org
AMOUNT: $500-$4,000
DEADLINE(S): None
FIELD(S): Baking Industry;
Electrical/Electronic Maintenance
ELIGIBILITY/REQUIREMENTS:
Award is to be used towards tuition for a
16- or 10-week course in baking science
and technology or maintenance engineer-
ing at the Institute. Experience in baking,
mechanics, or an approved alternative is
required. Awards are intended for people
who plan to seek new positions in the bak-
ing and maintenance engineering fields.
HOW TO APPLY: Contact AIB for an
application.
NUMBER OF AWARDS: 45

3055—AMERICAN RADIO RELAY LEAGUE FOUNDATION (IRARC Memorial/Josesph P. Rubino, WA4MMD, Scholarship)

225 Main Street
Newington CT 06111
860/594-0397
FAX: 860/594-0259
E-mail: foundation@arrl.org
Internet: http://www.arrlf.org/
AMOUNT: Approximately $750
DEADLINE(S): FEB 1
FIELD(S): All (undergraduate) or
electronic technician (certification
program)

ELIGIBILITY/REQUIREMENTS: Open
to radio amateurs holding any class of
license, residents of Florida (preferably
Brevard County) working on an undergraduate degree or in an electronic technician certification program at an accredited
institution. Minimum GPA 2.5; however,
preference given to students with lower
GPA who demonstrate financial need over
those with higher GPA but limited need.
HOW TO APPLY: See website or contact
Foundation for information and application. Submit with FAFSA and a 1-page
essay on the role amateur radio has played
in your life. A recent high school (or equivalent) or college transcript required; submit with application or mail separately.
NUMBER OF AWARDS: Multiple (as
income allows and as qualified candidates
are identified)
RENEWABLE: No
CONTACT: Mary M. Hobart, K1MMH,
Secretary

3056—AMERICAN WELDING SOCIETY

550 NW LeJeune Road
Miami FL 33126
800/443-9353, ext. 250 or
305/445-6628
FAX: 305/443-7559
Internet: http://www.aws.org
AMOUNT: $2,500-$3,000
DEADLINE(S): JAN 15
FIELD(S): Welding Engineering and
Technology
ELIGIBILITY/REQUIREMENTS: AWS
has 22 different scholarship programs for
U.S. citizens pursuing undergraduate study
at an accredited U.S. institution. Two programs are also for Canadian citizens studying at Canadian institutions. Must be at
least 18 years of age with a high school
diploma or equivalent and a minimum 2.0
GPA. Some programs require financial
need.
HOW TO APPLY: Contact AWS for
details on specific scholarships. Must submit 2 letters of reference, brief biography,
transcript, proposed curriculum, and verification of enrollment/employment.
RENEWABLE: Yes. Up to 4 years.

3057—ASSOCIATED WESTERN UNIVERSI-TIES, INC. (AWU Undergraduate Student Fellowships)

4190 South Highland Drive,
Suite 211
Salt Lake City UT 84124-2600
801/273-8900
FAX: 801/277-5632
Internet: http://www.awu.org
AMOUNT: $300/week stipend

DEADLINE(S): FEB 1
FIELD(S): Science; Mathematics;
Engineering; Technology
ELIGIBILITY/REQUIREMENTS:
Students who have been, or will be,
enrolled in any accredited institution within 6 months of the start of their award.
Academic performance, class standing,
career goals, recommendations, and compatibility of interests and abilities with the
needs and resources of the host facility are
considered.
HOW TO APPLY: See website for application and list of participating laboratories.
Must also submit résumé, at least 1 (2 preferred) recommendations from a faculty
member who is familiar with your academic achievements, and transcript. Applicants
who received an AWU award within the
last year and have approval for reappointment with their previous mentor, need
only to complete the application form and
submit a copy of their current transcripts.
NUMBER OF AWARDS: 500
CONTACT: Kathy Hecker, Director of
Finance and Property Management

3058—COMMUNITY FOUNDATION OF WESTERN MASSACHUSETTS (James L. Shriver Scholarship)

1500 Main Street
P.O. Box 15769
Springfield MA 01115
413/732-2858
FAX: 413/733-8565
E-mail: scholar@community
foundation.org
Internet: http://www.community
foundation.org
AMOUNT: $600
DEADLINE(S): MAR 31
FIELD(S): Technical Fields
ELIGIBILITY/REQUIREMENTS: Open
to residents of Western Massachusetts to
pursue technical careers through college,
trade, or technical school. Based on finan-
cial need, academic merit, and extracurric-
ular activities.
HOW TO APPLY: See website for appli-
cation.
NUMBER OF AWARDS: 1
RENEWABLE: No

3059—EAA AVIATION FOUNDATION (EAA Air Academy-Women Airforce Service Pilots [W.A.S.P.] Internship)

EAA Scholarship Department
P.O. 3086
Oshkosh WI 54903-3065
920/426-6823
E-mail: scholarships@eaa.org
Internet: http://www.young

eagles.org
AMOUNT: Approximately $750 + travel subsidy
DEADLINE(S): MAR 1
FIELD(S): Aviation and Related Areas
ELIGIBILITY/REQUIREMENTS: Open to applicant (must be at least 18 years of age by the start of the internship) wishing to research and prepare presentations for EAA Air Academy participants on the roles women have played in aviation. Must be able to deal effectively, tactfully and pleasantly with volunteers, staff, program participants and Museum visitors. Strong verbal and written skills and the ability to work independently. Must also be a current member of EAA (Experimental Aircraft Association) or recommended by a current EAA member to apply for these internships. Learn more about joining EAA (www.eaa.org) or call 800/843-3612. Individual and student memberships are available.
HOW TO APPLY: Apply online.
NUMBER OF AWARDS: 1
ADDITIONAL INFORMATION: Participants may receive ground and flight instruction.

3060—EAA AVIATION FOUNDATION (EAA AirVenture Museum-Timken Aviation Studies Internships)

EAA Scholarship Department
P.O. 3086
Oshkosh WI 54903-3065
920/426-6823
E-mail: scholarships@eaa.org
Internet: http://www.young eagles.org
AMOUNT: Approximately $3,000
DEADLINE(S): MAR 1
FIELD(S): Aviation and Related Areas
ELIGIBILITY/REQUIREMENTS: Open to college-level interns wishing to study the role of women in the past, present and future of aviation. Ideally, interns should aspire to be future professionals in the aviation industry. Must be able to deal effectively, tactfully and pleasantly with volunteers, staff, program participants and Museum visitors. Strong verbal and written skills and the ability to work independently. Must also be a current member of EAA (Experimental Aircraft Association) or recommended by a current EAA member to apply for these internships. Learn more about joining EAA (www.eaa.org) or call 800/843-3612. Individual and student memberships are available.
HOW TO APPLY: Apply online.
NUMBER OF AWARDS: 2

3061—EAA AVIATION FOUNDATION (Herbert L. Cox Memorial Scholarship)

EAA Scholarship Department
P.O. 3086
Oshkosh WI 54903-3065
920/426-6823
E-mail: scholarships@eaa.org
Internet: http://www.young eagles.org
AMOUNT: $500
DEADLINE(S): MAR 1
FIELD(S): Aviation or related field
ELIGIBILITY/REQUIREMENTS: Open to well-rounded individuals involved in school and community activities as well as aviation accepted at or attending 4-year accredited college or university. Applicant's academic records should verify his/her ability to complete educational activity for which scholarship is requested. Financial need considered in some programs. Must also be a current member of EAA (Experimental Aircraft Association) or recommended by a current EAA member.
HOW TO APPLY: Apply online. A personal statement (500 words or less) addressing career aspirations. educational plan, why you want to receive this scholarship, what you learned from work/volunteer experiences, and explaining how your education will be financed, including loans, family assistance, your own savings, scholarships, etc., and any unusual financial circumstances affecting your college financial plan required.

3062—JAMES F. LINCOLN ARC WELDING FOUNDATION (Award Program)

P.O. Box 17188
Cleveland OH 44117
216/481-4300
Internet: http://www.jflf.org
AMOUNT: Varies
DEADLINE(S): MAY 1
FIELD(S): Arc Welding and Engineering Design
ELIGIBILITY/REQUIREMENTS: Open to high school students, college undergraduates, and graduate students, and to professionals working in the fields of arc welding and engineering design. Various programs are available.
HOW TO APPLY: See website or send SASE to Roy Morrow, President, at above address.

3063—JOHNSON AND WALES UNIVERSITY (Annual National High School Recipe Contest)

8 Abbott Park Place

Providence RI 02903
401/598-2345
Internet: http://www.jwu.edu/ admiss/scholarships/
AMOUNT: $1,000- $5,000
DEADLINE(S): JAN 31
FIELD(S): Business, Hospitality, Technology, Culinary Arts
ELIGIBILITY/REQUIREMENTS: For students planning to attend Johnson and Wales University, Providence, Rhode Island.
HOW TO APPLY: Write for detailed description.

3064—JOHNSON AND WALES UNIVERSITY (Gilbane Building Company Eagle Scout Scholarship)

8 Abbott Park Place
Providence RI 02903
401/598-2345
Internet: http://www.jwu.edu/ admiss/scholarships/
AMOUNT: $1,200
DEADLINE(S): None
FIELD(S): Business, Hospitality, Technology, Culinary Arts
ELIGIBILITY/REQUIREMENTS: For students attending Johnson and Wales University, Providence, Rhode Island. Must be Eagle Scouts.
HOW TO APPLY: Send letter of recommendation and transcript.

3065—JOHNSON AND WALES UNIVERSITY (National High School Entrepreneur of the Year Contest)

8 Abbott Park Place
Providence RI 02903
401/598-2345
Internet: http://www.jwu.edu/ admiss/scholarships/
AMOUNT: $1,000-$10,000
DEADLINE(S): DEC 27
FIELD(S): Business, Hospitality, Technology, Culinary Arts
ELIGIBILITY/REQUIREMENTS: For students attending Johnson and Wales University, Providence, Rhode Island.
HOW TO APPLY: Send for detailed description.

3066—JUNIOR ACHIEVEMENT INC. (Johnson and Wales University Scholarship)

One Education Way
Colorado Springs CO 80906-4477

719/540-8000
FAX: 719/540-6299
E-mail: newmedia@ja.org
Internet: http://www.ja.org
AMOUNT: $10,000 (4 years)
DEADLINE(S): FEB 1
FIELD(S): Business; Culinary Arts; Hospitality; Technology
ELIGIBILITY/REQUIREMENTS: Must be high school seniors who have been accepted by and will be attending Johnson and Wales University and be majoring in one of the above fields.
HOW TO APPLY: Send application to Johnson and Wales University with 1 letter of recommendation from a JA High School Programs consultant.
NUMBER OF AWARDS: 2 4-year $10,000 scholarships; unlimited partial scholarships.
RENEWABLE: No
CONTACT: To obtain application, contact Tom Gauthier, Coordinator of Specialty Recruitment, Johnson and Wales University, 8 Abbott Park Place, Providence RI 02903; 800/DIAL-JWU, ext. 2345 or from website (http://www.jwu.edu).

3067—PRINT AND GRAPHICS SCHOLARSHIP FOUNDATION, THE (PGSF)

200 Deer Run Road
Sewickley PA 15143-2600
412/259-1740 or 800/910-4283
FAX: 412/741-2311
E-mail: pgsf@piagatf.org.
Internet: http://www. pgsf.org
AMOUNT: $500-$5,000
DEADLINE(S): MAR 1 (high school seniors), APR 1 (college undergraduates)
FIELD(S): Graphic Communications; Printing Technology; Printing Management; Publishing
ELIGIBILITY/REQUIREMENTS: For students pursuing careers in above fields, who are enrolled in a 2- or 4-year accredited program at a technical school, college or university in the U.S.
HOW TO APPLY: For more information and application, see website or call, fax or e-mail. Submit with SAT, ACT or SAT/NMSQT (high school students only), official transcript, 2 recommendation forms from a school representative, such as an instructor, counselor, or advisor (1 may be from an employer), a photocopy of course of study,
NUMBER OF AWARDS: 200-300
RENEWABLE: Yes; must meet basic criteria.
CONTACT: Bernie Eckert

3068—ROCKY MOUNTAIN COAL MINING INSTITUTE, THE (Technical Scholarship)

8057 South Yukon Way
Littleton CO 80128-5510
303/948-3300
FAX: 303/948-1132
E-mail: mail@rmcmi.org
Internet: http://www.rmcmi.org
AMOUNT: $1,000
DEADLINE(S): FEB 3
FIELD(S): FIELD(S): Vocational Education: Mechanical, Trade, Automotive, Welding, Electrical, Drafting, Diesel Mechanics, Tires
ELIGIBILITY/REQUIREMENTS: Must be a first-year student at a 2-year technical/trade school in good standing at the time of selection, and a U.S. citizen and a legal resident of a member state ((AZ, CO, MT, NM, ND, TX, UT, WY) studying one of above trades.
HOW TO APPLY: See website for application; submit with 3 letters of reference (include name, address, business and home phone number, company or business name, and years acquainted); résumé (include employer's name, address, phone number, the name of your supervisor, work performed, length of service, and the reason for leaving), answers to the following questions (limiting each to 100 words or less): 1. If you could pick any job, what would it be and why? 2. Why are you pursuing your present degree? 3. What are your plans after graduation? 4. Optional—Personal statement (i.e. why you are applying for this scholarship, special skills or training, etc.).
NUMBER OF AWARDS: 8
RENEWABLE: No

3069—SPE FOUNDATION, THE (Gulf Coast Hurricane Scholarships)

14 Fairfield Drive
Brookfield CT 06804
203/740-5447
FAX: 203/775-1157
E-mail: foundation@4spe.org
Internet: http://www.4spe.org/foundation/scholarships.php
AMOUNT: $6,000 (college or university), $2,000 (junior or technical)
DEADLINE(S): JAN 15
FIELD(S): Polymer Science; Chemistry; Physics; Chemical, Plastics, Mechanical & Industrial Engineering
ELIGIBILITY/REQUIREMENTS: Must have been a resident of a Gulf Coast County declared a national disaster area as a result of Hurricanes Katrina, Rita or Wilma, and must be attending a university, college or technical institute in a Gulf Coast State (Florida, Alabama, Mississippi, Louisiana, Texas). Must be in good standing with their colleges (minimum GPA 2.0) and enrolled 6 hours/semester. Must have demonstrated an interest in the plastics industry; majoring in or taking courses that would be beneficial to a career in the plastics/polymer industry. Financial need is considered for most scholarships.
HOW TO APPLY: Complete application; submit 3 recommendation letters (2 from a teacher or school official and 1 from an employer or non-relative); high school and/or college transcript for last 2 years; a 1- to 2-page statement telling why you are applying for the scholarship and educational and career goals in the plastics industry. Must provide proof of residence.
NUMBER OF AWARDS: 3; 1 college or university, 2 junior college or technical school
RENEWABLE: Yes. Must reapply for 3 additional years.

3070—SPE FOUNDATION, THE (Plastics Pioneers Association Scholarships)

14 Fairfield Drive
Brookfield CT 06804
203/740-5447
FAX: 203/775-1157
E-mail: foundation@4spe.org
Internet: http://www.4spe.org/foundation/scholarships.php
AMOUNT: $3,000
DEADLINE(S): JAN 15
FIELD(S): Polymer Science; Chemistry; Physics; Chemical, Plastics, Mechanical & Industrial Engineering
ELIGIBILITY/REQUIREMENTS: Open to undergraduate students, including those enrolled in associate or technical degree programs, who are committed to becoming "hands on" workers in the plastics industry as plastics technicians or engineers. Must be in good standing with their colleges and have demonstrated an interest in the plastics industry; majoring in or taking courses that would be beneficial to a career in the plastics/polymer industry. Financial need is considered for most scholarships.
HOW TO APPLY: Complete application; submit 3 recommendation letters (2 from a teacher or school official and 1 from an employer or non-relative); high school and/or college transcript for last 2 years; a 1- to 2-page statement telling why you are applying for the scholarship and educational and career goals in the plastics industry.
NUMBER OF AWARDS: Multiple

RENEWABLE: Yes. Must reapply for 3 additional years.

3071—WESTERN MICHIGAN UNIVERSITY (College of Education/Lloyd F. Hutt Memorial Scholarship Endowment in Industrial Education and Technology)

1903 West Michigan
Kalamazoo MI 49008-5337
269/387-6000
FAX: 269/387-6989
E-mail: finaid-info@wmich.edu
Internet: http://www.wmich. edu/finaid
AMOUNT: $500-$1,000
DEADLINE(S): MAR 1
FIELD(S): Industrial Education and Technology

ELIGIBILITY/REQUIREMENTS: Must be enrolled full time in the Industrial Education and Technology (Industrial Arts) program. Must have demonstrated ability in the field of industrial arts and come from the Grand Rapids area.
HOW TO APPLY: Application available from Chair, Department of Family and Consumer Sciences, 3018 Kohrman Hall, 269/387-3705, linda.dannison@wmich.edu.
RENEWABLE: Yes. May be renewed based upon achievement and recommendation.
CONTACT: Linda Dannison, Chair, Department of Family and Consumer Sciences

3072—WESTERN MICHIGAN UNIVERSITY (College of Education/Neil L. and Leta C. Schoenhals Undergraduate Memorial Scholarship)

1903 West Michigan
Kalamazoo MI 49008-5337
269/387-6000
FAX: 269/387-6989
E-mail: finaid-info@wmich.edu
Internet: http://www.wmich. edu/finaid
AMOUNT: Varies
DEADLINE(S): MAR 1
FIELD(S): Industrial Technology
ELIGIBILITY/REQUIREMENTS: Graduating senior; must be Industrial Technology major.
HOW TO APPLY: Selection is made by scholarship benefactor and select FCS faculty.
NUMBER OF AWARDS: 1
RENEWABLE: No
CONTACT: College of Education

TRANSPORTATION

3073—AMERICAN PUBLIC TRANSIT ASSOCIATION (Transit Hall of Fame Scholarships)

1666 K Street NW
Washington DC 20006
202/496-4800
FAX: 202/898-4029
Internet: http://www.apta.com/services/humanresources/program guidelines.cfm
AMOUNT: $2,500 or more
DEADLINE(S): None
FIELD(S): Transit-related
ELIGIBILITY/REQUIREMENTS: For college juniors, seniors, or graduate students enrolled in a degree program in a fully accredited institution who demonstrate an interest in entering the transit industry. Criteria include interest in the transit field, financial need, leadership characteristics, scholastic achievement, citizenship extracurricular activities.
HOW TO APPLY: Must be nominated by an APTF representative who can oversee an internship program. Write to above address to inquire about how to be nominated and other information (an essay, and a brief in-person or telephone interview).
NUMBER OF AWARDS: At least 6

3074—AMERICAN SOCIETY OF TRANSPORTATION & LOGISTICS, THE (The L. L. Waters Scholarship Program)

1400 Eye Street, NW, Suite 1050
Washington DC 20005
202/580-7270
FAX: 202/962-3939
E-mail: info@astl.org
Internet: http://www.astl.org
AMOUNT: $2,000
FIELD(S): Transportation; Logistics; Physical Distribution
ELIGIBILITY/REQUIREMENTS: Applicants must be undergraduate students in their junior year at a fully accredited 4-year U.S. college or university. Awards are based on scholastic performance and potential as well as evidence of the degree of commitment to the pursuit of a professional career in transportation/logistics/physical distribution.
HOW TO APPLY: Send completed application to the Scholarship Judging Panel; official transcript; 2 letters of recommendation (sent separately) from faculty members of the applicant's school who have major teaching and research commitments

in transportation/logistics/physical distribution.
CONTACT: Laurie Denham, Executive Director

3075—NATIONAL DEFENSE TRANSPORTATION ASSOCIATION-NDTA (Academic Scholarship Program A)

50 South Pickett Street, Suite 220
Alexandria VA 22304-7296
703/751-5011
FAX: 703/823-8761
E-mail: mark@ndtahq.com
Internet: http://www.ndtahq.com
AMOUNT: $500-$2,000
DEADLINE(S): APR 16
FIELD(S): Transportation; Physical Distribution; Logistics; Information Technology
ELIGIBILITY/REQUIREMENTS: Must be an NDTA member or financial dependent of a member; must have completed 45 semester hours satisfactorily at an accredited college; college must offer at least 15 semester hours in the above fields; must take at least 15 semester hours of these types of courses; scholarships are limited to undergraduate degrees.
HOW TO APPLY: Applications available from national headquarters or download from website.
NUMBER OF AWARDS: Varies, approximately 15.
RENEWABLE: Yes. Must reapply and submit updated transcripts.
CONTACT: Mark Victorson, Executive Assistant

3076—SOCIETY OF AUTOMOTIVE ENGINEERS (Yanmar/SAE Scholarship)

400 Commonwealth Drive
Warrendale PA 15096-0001
724/776-4970
E-mail: customerservice@sae.org
Internet: http://www.sae.org/students/scholarships
AMOUNT: $2,000 ($1,000/year for 2 years)
DEADLINE(S): APR 1
FIELD(S): Engineering, relating to conservation of energy in transportation, agriculture & construction & power generation
ELIGIBILITY/REQUIREMENTS: For graduate students and undergraduates in their senior year who are citizens of North America (U.S./Canada/Mexico). Based on previous scholastic performance; special study or honors in the field of award, and for leadership achievement related to engineering or science considered.

HOW TO APPLY: Submit application; a personal essay that demonstrates hands-on experience or activity (such as rebuilding engines, working on cars/trucks, etc.); 2 recommendations, 1 of which must be from a teacher, counselor, or administrator; and transcript.
NUMBER OF AWARDS: 1
RENEWABLE: No
CONTACT: Yanmar/SAE Scholarship

3077—TRANSPORTATION CLUBS INTERNATIONAL (Charlotte Woods Memorial Scholarship)

7031 Manchester Street
New Orleans LA 70126
AMOUNT: $1,000
DEADLINE(S): MAY 31
FIELD(S): Transportation Logistics; Traffic Management
ELIGIBILITY/REQUIREMENTS: Open to TCI members or their dependents enrolled at an accredited college or university in a program in transportation, traffic management, or related area and considering a career in transportation. Financial need is also considered.
HOW TO APPLY: Submit essay of not more than 200 words on why you have chosen transportation or an allied field as a career. Send SASE (business size) for complete information and application.
CONTACT: Gay Fielding, Transportation Clubs International Scholarships

3078—TRANSPORTATION CLUBS INTERNATIONAL (Ginger & Fred Deines Canada Scholarships)

7031 Manchester Street
New Orleans LA 70126
AMOUNT: $500 and/or $1,000
DEADLINE(S): MAY 31
FIELD(S): Transportation Logistics; Traffic Management
ELIGIBILITY/REQUIREMENTS: For a student of Canadian nationality and enrolled in a school in Canada or U.S. in a degree or vocational program in the above or related areas.
HOW TO APPLY: Submit essay of not more than 200 words on why you have chosen transportation or an allied field as a career. Send an SASE for further details.
CONTACT: Gay Fielding, Transportation Clubs International Scholarships

3079—TRANSPORTATION CLUBS INTERNATIONAL (Ginger and Fred Deines Mexico Scholarship)

7031 Manchester Street

New Orleans LA 70126
AMOUNT: $500-$1,000
FIELD(S): Logistics; Civil Engineering; Transportation
ELIGIBILITY/REQUIREMENTS: Applicants must have completed at least one year of undergraduate study at a 4-year institution in Mexico or the U.S. and be pursuing a career in logistics, civil engineering, or transportation.
HOW TO APPLY: Send SASE.
CONTACT: Gay Fielding, Transportation Clubs International Scholarships

3080—TRANSPORTATION CLUBS INTERNATIONAL (Hooper Memorial Scholarships)

7031 Manchester Street
New Orleans LA 70126
AMOUNT: $1,500
DEADLINE(S): MAY 31
FIELD(S): Transportation Logistics; Traffic Management
ELIGIBILITY/REQUIREMENTS: For students enrolled in an accredited college or university in a degree or vocational program in transportation logistics, traffic management, or related fields and preparing for a career in transportation. Financial need is considered.
HOW TO APPLY: Submit essay of not more than 200 words on why you have chosen transportation or an allied field as a career. Send SASE (business size) for complete information.
CONTACT: Gay Fielding, Transportation Clubs International Scholarships

3081—WYOMING TRUCKING ASSOCIATION

P.O. Box 1909
Casper WY 82602
AMOUNT: $500-$1,000
DEADLINE(S): MAR 1
FIELD(S): Transportation Industry
ELIGIBILITY/REQUIREMENTS: For Wyoming high school graduates enrolled in a Wyoming college, approved trade school, or the University of Wyoming. Must be pursuing a course of study that will result in a career in the transportation industry in Wyoming, including but not limited to: safety, diesel mechanics, truck driving, business management, computer skills, accounting, office procedures, and management.
HOW TO APPLY: Write to WYTA for an application.
NUMBER OF AWARDS: 1-10

TRAVEL & TOURISM

3082—AMERICAN SOCIETY OF TRAVEL AGENTS FOUNDATION

1101 King Street
Alexandria VA 22314
703/739-2782
FAX: 703/684-8319
E-mail: scholarship@astahq.com
Internet: http://www.astanet.com
AMOUNT: $200-$3,000
DEADLINE(S): AUG; DEC
FIELD(S): Travel; Tourism; Hospitality
ELIGIBILITY/REQUIREMENTS: Various undergraduate and graduate scholarships are available to U.S. and Canadian citizens, permanent residents, and legal aliens. Must have a minimum 2.5 GPA. Financial need usually NOT considered.
HOW TO APPLY: Submit proof of enrollment in travel and tourism courses and official statement of tuition amount, letter of recommendation, transcripts, and other specific requirements for individual awards. See website or contact Scholarship Manager for specific award details.
NUMBER OF AWARDS: Over 20
RENEWABLE: Some
CONTACT: Verlete Mitchell, Scholarship Manager

3083—CLUB FOUNDATION, THE

1733 King Street
Alexandria VA 22314
703/739-9500
FAX: 703/739-0124
E-mail: ashleigh.hill@club foundation.org
Internet: http://www.club foundation.org
AMOUNT: $2,500
DEADLINE(S): APR 15
FIELD(S): Business Administration; Hospitality
ELIGIBILITY/REQUIREMENTS: Candidates must provide strong evidence that they are pursuing managerial careers in the private club industry. A candidate must have completed his/her freshman year of college and be enrolled for the full academic year in an accredited 4-year institution. In addition, the candidate must have achieved and continue to maintain a GPA of at least 2.5 on a 4.0 scale, or 4.5 on a 6.0 scale. Additional points are awarded for CMMA chapter members.
HOW TO APPLY: Application available on website; write an essay addressing the

questions; attach an official, current transcript; include recommendation letter from an advisor/professor and a private club industry professional; include a copy of current résumé.

NUMBER OF AWARDS: 2
RENEWABLE: No
CONTACT: Ashleigh Hill, Program Specialist

3084—EMPIRE COLLEGE (Dean's Scholarship)

3035 Cleveland Avenue
Santa Rosa CA 95403
707/546-4000
FAX: 707/546-4058
Internet: http://www.wmpcol.edu
AMOUNT: $250-$1,500
DEADLINE(S): APR 15
FIELD(S): Accounting; Office Administration; Paralegal; Medical (Clinical and Administrative); Tourism; Hospitality; General Business; Computer Assembly; Network Assembly/Administration; Security

ELIGIBILITY/REQUIREMENTS: Open to high school seniors who plan to attend Empire College. Must be U.S. citizen.
HOW TO APPLY: Contact College for an application.
NUMBER OF AWARDS: 10
RENEWABLE: No
CONTACT: Mary Farha

3085—NATIONAL TOURISM FOUNDATION

P.O. Box 3071
Lexington KY 40596-3071
800/682-8886
FAX: 606/226-4414
Internet: http://www.ntfonline.com
AMOUNT: $3,000
DEADLINE(S): APR 15
FIELD(S): Travel and Tourism; Hospitality; Restaurant Management

ELIGIBILITY/REQUIREMENTS: Various scholarships for full-time students at 2- or 4-year colleges or universities in North America who are entering their junior or senior year of study. Must be a strong academic performer and have at least a 3.0 GPA. Degree emphasis must be in a travel- and tourism-related field, such as hotel management, restaurant management, or tourism.
HOW TO APPLY: Submit application, which is available from website; a résumé; information on any work or internship experience in travel and tourism and on any extracurricular or volunteer experience. See website for additional requirements of each individual scholarship. Students may apply for more than 1 award but may receive only 1.
NUMBER OF AWARDS: 2

3086—TOURISM CARES (Academy of Hospitality & Tourism Scholarship)

585 Washington Street
Canton MA 02021
781/821-5990
FAX: 781/821-8949
E-mail: carolynv@tourismcares.org
Internet: http://www.tourism cares.org
AMOUNT: $1,000
DEADLINE(S): APR 1
FIELD(S): Travel and Tourism and related fields

ELIGIBILITY/REQUIREMENTS: Applicants must be a graduating senior of a National Academy Foundation affiliated Academy of Hospitality & Tourism, have a minimum 3.0 GPA, be preparing to enroll at an accredited educational institution, and be pursuing studies related to hospitality and tourism.
HOW TO APPLY: See website (for application and submit to Program Manager with transcript and an essay of no more than 2 pages, answering the following question: "In your future career in tourism, what responsibility will you have for preservation and conservation of tourism sites around the globe? How will you meet those challenges?"
CONTACT: Carolyn Viles, CTC, Program Manager

3087—TOURISM CARES FOR TOMORROW (LaMacchia Family Scholarship)

585 Washington Street
Canton MA 02021
781/821-5990
FAX: 781/821-8949
E-mail: carolynv@tourismcares.org
Internet: http://www.tourism cares.org
AMOUNT: $1,000
DEADLINE(S): MAY 1
FIELD(S): Travel and Tourism and related fields

ELIGIBILITY/REQUIREMENTS: Applicant must be a full-time student, enrolled in a 4-year college or university in Wisconsin, have a minimum 3.0 GPA, be entering his/her junior or senior year of study (must have completed 50% of degree requirements), and have a degree emphasis on a travel and tourism-related field.

HOW TO APPLY: See website for application and submit to Program Manager with a copy of transcript.
CONTACT: Carolyn Viles, CTC, Program Manager

3088—TOURISM CARES FOR TOMORROW (Pat & Jim Host Scholarship)

585 Washington Street
Canton MA 02021
781/821-5990
FAX: 781/821-8949
E-mail: carolynv@tourismcares.org
Internet: http://www.tourism cares.org
AMOUNT: $2,500
DEADLINE(S): APR 1
FIELD(S): Travel and Tourism and related fields

ELIGIBILITY/REQUIREMENTS: Applicant must be a full-time student, accepted into and enrolled in a 4-year college or university in Kentucky; have a minimum 3.0 GPA, be a graduate of a Kentucky high school, and have a degree emphasis in a travel and tourism-related field.
HOW TO APPLY: See website for application and submit to Program Manager with 2 recommendation letters (one from a tourism-related faculty member and the other from a professional in the travel and tourism field) and a short (2- to 5-page) essay, outlining how you perceive the changing role of the group tour industry. The essay must be signed, acknowledging that it is the student's own work, and must be in APA or MLA format, with appropriate references.
CONTACT: Carolyn Viles, CTC, Program Manager

3089—TOURISM CARES FOR TOMORROW (Patrick Murphy Internship)

585 Washington Street
Canton MA 02021
781/821-5990
FAX: 781/821-8949
E-mail: info@tourismcares.org
Internet: http://www.tourism cares.org
AMOUNT: $2,000
DEADLINE(S): MAY 1
FIELD(S): Travel and Tourism and related fields; Political Science

ELIGIBILITY/REQUIREMENTS: Applicant must be pursuing a travel and tourism degree with emphasis in political science. The applicant must also have excellent written, oral and interpersonal skills. The emphasis of this internship is the education of prospective managers and leaders in the packaged travel and tourism industry.

HOW TO APPLY: See website for application and submit to Program Manager with a typed résumé, any work or internship experience in travel and tourism, any extracurricular or volunteer experience. An official copy of your updated transcript must be sent from your school, detailing courses completed, academic standing and GPA.

CONTACT: Carolyn Viles, CTC, Program Manager

ADDITIONAL INFORMATION: Intern's basic duties will be researching issues that affect the travel and tourism industry. This will be an educational experience to gain a better knowledge and understand the components of the travel industry. There will be no lobbying activity involved.

3090—TOURISM CARES (State Scholarships)

585 Washington Street
Canton MA 02021
781/821-5990
FAX: 781/821-8949
E-mail: carolynv@tourismcares.org
Internet: http://www.tourism
cares.org
AMOUNT: $1,000-$2,000
DEADLINE(S): APR 1
FIELD(S): Travel and Tourism and related fields
ELIGIBILITY/REQUIREMENTS: Open to students from the U.S. and Canada pursuing degrees in travel and tourism, which are sponsored by various states and provinces.
HOW TO APPLY: See website and contact your state's coordinator for information and application forms.
CONTACT: Carolyn Viles, CTC, Program Manager

3091—TOURISM CARES (The Yellow Ribbon Scholarship)

585 Washington Street
Canton MA 02021
781/821-5990
FAX: 781/821-8949
E-mail: carolynv@tourismcares.org
Internet: http://www.tourism
cares.org
AMOUNT: $2,500
DEADLINE(S): MAY 1
FIELD(S): Travel and Tourism and related fields
ELIGIBILITY/REQUIREMENTS: Applicant must have a physical or sensory

disability verified by an accredited physician, be entering postsecondary education with a 3.0 GPA or maintaining a 2.5 GPA or better at the college level, be enrolled full time at a 2- or 4-year college or university in North America, majoring in a travel-and-tourism-related field.

HOW TO APPLY: See website for application and submit to Program Manager with 2 recommendation letters (1 from a tourism-related faculty member and the other from a professional in the tourism industry), a résumé noting all tourism-related activities, a current college transcript, a signed, typewritten, double-spaced essay that explains how you intend to use his/her education in making a career in travel, and tourism essay.

CONTACT: Carolyn Viles, CTC, Program Manager

3092—WESTERN MICHIGAN UNIVERSITY (College of Education/Harriett Kiser Creed Endowment Fund)

1903 West Michigan
Kalamazoo MI 49008-5337
269/387-6000
FAX: 269/387-6989
E-mail: finaid-info@wmich.edu
Internet: http://www.wmich.edu/
finaid
AMOUNT: $500/semester
DEADLINE(S): MAR 1
FIELD(S): Health, Physical Education and Recreation
ELIGIBILITY/REQUIREMENTS: Full-time junior or senior enrolled in HPER Curriculum, preference to HPER majors, with 3.0 or higher GPA. Must be involved in HPER-related activities and show financial need.
HOW TO APPLY: Contact the HPER Department, 4024 Student Recreation Center, or College of Education, 2304 Sangren Hall.

3093—WESTERN MICHIGAN UNIVERSITY (College of Education/Harriett Kiser Creed HPER Scholarship)

1903 West Michigan
Kalamazoo MI 49008-5337
269/387-6000
FAX: 269/387-6989
E-mail: finaid-info@wmich.edu
Internet: http://www.wmich.edu/
finaid
AMOUNT: $500/semester
DEADLINE(S): MAR 1
FIELD(S): Health, Physical Education and Recreation

ELIGIBILITY/REQUIREMENTS: Full-time junior or senior enrolled in HPER Curriculum, with 3.0 or higher GPA.
HOW TO APPLY: Contact Dr. Debra Berkey, 269/387-2710, 4021 Student Recreation Center, or e-mail: debra.berkey@wmich.edu for more information.
NUMBER OF AWARDS: 1
RENEWABLE: No

3094—WOMEN'S SPORTS FOUNDATION (Jackie Joyner-Kersee and Zina Garrison Minority Internships)

Eisenhower Park
East Meadow NY 11554
800/227-3988 (U.S. only) or
516/542-4700
FAX: 516/542-4716
E-mail: WoSport@aol.com
Internet: http://www.womens
sportsfoundation.org
AMOUNT: $4,000-$5,000
DEADLINE(S): Ongoing
FIELD(S): Sports-related careers
ELIGIBILITY/REQUIREMENTS: Women of color who are undergraduate students, college graduates, graduate students or women in career change. Internships are located at the Women's Sports Foundation in East Meadow, New York.
HOW TO APPLY: See website or write to above address for details.
NUMBER OF AWARDS: 4-6

GENERAL (ANY FIELD OF STUDY)

3095—ABE AND ANNIE SEIBEL FOUNDATION

P.O. Box 8210
Galveston TX 77553-8210
409/770/5665 or 409/770/5666
Internet: http://www.window.state.
tx.us/scholars/aid/scholarship/
scaasf.html
AMOUNT: Up to $6,000/year
DEADLINE(S): FEB 28
FIELD(S): All
ELIGIBILITY/REQUIREMENTS: Open to Texas residents who are U.S. citizens and will be or are enrolled (12 credit hours/semester) as undergraduate students at a Texas college or university accredited by the Southern Association of Colleges and Schools. Must maintain 2.75 GPA and exhibit financial need. For study leading to first 4-year degree.

HOW TO APPLY: Write or call for an application packet beginning Nov 1 each year. Applications will be accepted Jan 1 through Feb 28 for the upcoming fall and spring school term.
NUMBER OF AWARDS: Approximately 800
RENEWABLE: Yes, provided automatically

3096—ADELPHI UNIVERSITY

1 South Avenue
Garden City NY 11530
516/877-3080
FAX: 516/877-3380
Internet: http://www.ecampus. adelphi.edu/sfs/au_ scholarships_grants.php
AMOUNT: Up to full tuition
DEADLINE(S): FEB 15
FIELD(S): All
ELIGIBILITY/REQUIREMENTS: Various scholarships for full- and part-time students. Must have a 3.0 GPA after freshman year; some require 3.3 GPA in subsequent years to maintain scholarship.
HOW TO APPLY: See website for further information; no separate application is required.

3097—AEROSPACE EDUCATION FOUNDATION (Eagle Plan Grant)

1501 Lee Highway
Arlington VA 22209-1198
800/291-8480, ext. 4869
FAX: 703/247-5853
E-mail: AEFStaff@aef.org
AMOUNT: $500
DEADLINE(S): Varies
FIELD(S): All
ELIGIBILITY/REQUIREMENTS: Open to graduates of the Community College of the Air Force who are pursuing a baccalaureate degree. Must be enlisted personnel (E-4, E-5, E-6, or E-7). Based on academic achievement, educational goals, leadership, and extracurricular activities.
HOW TO APPLY: Contact Base Education Office.
NUMBER OF AWARDS: 400
RENEWABLE: No
CONTACT: Ann Sagle

3098—AFS INTERCULTURAL PROGRAMS (International Exchange Student Program)

198 Madison Avenue, 8th Floor
New York NY 10016
212/299-9000 or 800/AFS-INFO
FAX: 212/299-9090

Internet: http://www.afs.org/usa
AMOUNT: Varies
DEADLINE(S): Varies
FIELD(S): Study abroad—all high school subjects
ELIGIBILITY/REQUIREMENTS: International exchange of high school students for summer semester or school year. Students live with host families and attend local secondary schools. Students go to and from countries. Scholarship assistance for summer, school year, and semester.
HOW TO APPLY: Deadlines are in the fall and spring. Call 800/876-2377; access website or write for information.
NUMBER OF AWARDS: 40 or more per year

3099—AIR FORCE AID SOCIETY (General Henry H. Arnold Education Grant Program)

241 18th Street South, Suite 202
Arlington VA 22202
800/429-9475
Internet: http://www.afas.org
DEADLINE(S): MAR
FIELD(S): All
ELIGIBILITY/REQUIREMENTS: Open to undergraduates who are dependent children of active duty, retired, or deceased members of the U.S. Air Force, and spouses of active duty members or members who died on active duty or in retired status residing in continental U.S. (lower 48 states). Must be full-time students with a minimum 2.0 GPA at accredited institutions. Must be U.S. citizen or legal resident and demonstrate financial need.
HOW TO APPLY: Contact Aid Society for an application, retrieve application from website, from November through February.
RENEWABLE: Yes

3100—AIR FORCE SERGEANTS' ASSOCIATION SCHOLARSHIP PROGRAM

5211 Auth Road
Suitland MD 20746
301/899-3500
Internet: http://www.afsahq.org
AMOUNT: Varies
DEADLINE(S): MAR 31
FIELD(S): All
ELIGIBILITY/REQUIREMENTS: Open to single dependent children of Air Force enlisted who are members of AFSA or its Auxiliary. Must be under 23 years of age and attending an accredited institution. For undergraduate study only. Awards are based on academic excellence.

HOW TO APPLY: See website for application and instructions; click on education link. Programs open November 1.
CONTACT: Scholarship Administrator

3101—AIRLINE PILOTS ASSOCIATION

1625 Massachusetts Avenue NW
Washington DC 20036
202/797-4059
Internet: http://www.free-4u.com/airline1.htm
AMOUNT: $3,000/year for 4 years
DEADLINE(S): APR 1
FIELD(S): All
ELIGIBILITY/REQUIREMENTS: 4-year award is open to undergraduate children of medically retired, long-term disabled, or deceased pilot members of the Association. Must be pursuing bachelor's degree. Based on academic capability and financial need.
HOW TO APPLY: Apply during senior year of high school. Contact Association for an application ONLY if above qualifications are met.
RENEWABLE: Yes. Must reapply; minimum 3.0 GPA.
CONTACT: Maggie Erzen

3102—AIRMEN MEMORIAL FOUNDATION SCHOLARSHIP AWARDS PROGRAM

5211 Auth Road
Suitland MD 20746
301/899-3500
E-mail: staff@afsahq.org
Internet: http://www.afsahq.org
AMOUNT: Varies
DEADLINE(S): MAR 31
FIELD(S): All
ELIGIBILITY/REQUIREMENTS: Open to unmarried dependent children (under 23) of Air Force enlisted personnel (active or retired) of all components, including Air National Guard and Reserves. Must attend an undergraduate program at an accredited academic or technical school.
HOW TO APPLY: See website for more information; click the education link, then download application and instructions.
RENEWABLE: No

3103— AIR TRAFFIC CONTROL ASSOCIATION (ATCA) (Children of Air Traffic Control Specialists/Buckingham Memorial Scholarship)

1101 King St, Suite 300
Alexandria VA 22314
703/299-2430
FAX: 703/299-2437

E-mail: info@atca.org

Internet: http://www.atca.org/activities/scholarships.asp

AMOUNT: Varies

DEADLINE(S): MAY 1

FIELD(S): All

ELIGIBILITY/REQUIREMENTS: Must be the child, natural or by adoption, of a person serving, or having served as an air traffic control specialist either with the U.S. Government, U.S. Military, or in a private facility in the United States; and a U.S. citizen. enrolled (or accepted) in an accredited college or university and planning to continue the following year. Attendance equal to at least half-time (6 hours). Must have a minimum of 30 semester or 45 quarter hours still to be completed before graduation. Course of study leads to a bachelor's degree or higher. Financial need considered.

HOW TO APPLY: See website for application or contact the Association. Submit with 2 letters of recommendation (from present or previous teachers, professors, instructors, supervisors, or managers) from within the last 12 months; certified transcript of all college coursework (if less than 30 semester or 45 quarter hours of college coursework have been completed, all high school transcripts also are required); work or experience that supports educational and/or aviation career goals must be addressed in the application and/or essay (400 words maximum), "How My Education Efforts Will Enhance My Potential Contribution in My Chosen Career Field."

RENEWABLE: Yes. Must submit a verified report from the educational institution attended, stating the courses taken and completed and the grades received.

3104—ALBERT BAKER FUND EDUCATION GRANTS, THE (Camp Counselor Grant)

P.O. Box 179

Amador City CA 95601-0179

209/267-5701 or 800/269-0388

FAX: 209/267-0569

E-mail: abf@albertbakerfund.org

Internet: http://www.albertbaker fund.org

AMOUNT: Up to $1,500

DEADLINE(S): JUL 1

FIELD(S): All

ELIGIBILITY/REQUIREMENTS: Open to students who are members of the First Church of Christ Scientist in Boston, Massachusetts, or one of its branch churches. When applying, must have all financing in place except ABF loan. Must be enrolled in an accredited college, university, or trade school.

HOW TO APPLY: Each year, the director of each of the 6 camps for Christian Scientists submits a list of names of counselors they believe are deserving of the grant.

NUMBER OF AWARDS: 6

3105—ALBERT BAKER FUND EDUCATION GRANTS, THE (Schaffner Trust Grant Fund)

P.O. Box 179

Amador City CA 95601-0179

209/267-5701 or 800/269-0388

FAX: 209/267-0569

E-mail: abf@albertbakerfund.org

Internet: http://www.albert baker fund.org

AMOUNT: Up to $2,000/year

DEADLINE(S): JUL 1

FIELD(S): All

ELIGIBILITY/REQUIREMENTS: Open to students who are members of the First Church of Christ Scientist in Boston, Massachusetts, or one of its branch churches. When applying, must have all financing in place except ABF loan. Must be enrolled in an accredited college, university, or trade school.

HOW TO APPLY: Each year, the director of each of the 6 camps for Christian Scientists submits a list of names of counselors they believe are deserving of the grant.

NUMBER OF AWARDS: 6

3106—ALBERT BAKER FUND EDUCATION GRANTS, THE (Student Loan Program)

P.O. Box 179

Amador City CA 95601-0179

209/267-5701 or 800/269-0388

FAX: 209/267-0569

E-mail: abf@albertbakerfund.org

Internet: http://www.albert baker fund.org

AMOUNT: Up to $6,000

DEADLINE(S): JUL 1

FIELD(S): All

ELIGIBILITY/REQUIREMENTS: Open to students who are members of the First Church of Christ Scientist in Boston, Massachusetts, or one of its branch churches. Granted to students working for a degree or certificate in a regularly accredited college, university, or other institution of higher learning, or enrolled in a postsecondary program leading to a vocational objective given at a training institution which has been approved by Fund Board of Trustees. Must have at least a "C" average. When applying, must have all financing in place except ABF loan.

HOW TO APPLY: Request application by phone, e-mail, or mail. Interview by phone or in person required.

NUMBER OF AWARDS: 6

RENEWABLE: Yes. Up to 6 years (4 for undergraduate course work and 2 for graduate course work).

ADDITIONAL INFORMATION: The Albert Baker Fund provides financial assistance to bridge the gap between primary resources and the actual cost of one full year of academic study.

3107—ALBERT O. J. LANDUCCI, DDS

2720 Edison Street

San Mateo CA 94403-2495

650/574-4444

FAX: 650/574-4441

E-mail: e@DrLanducci.com

Internet: http://www.drlanducci.com/scholarships.htm

AMOUNT: Varies

DEADLINE(S): Varies

FIELD(S): All; Science; Mathematics; Community Service and Dental Assisting

ELIGIBILITY/REQUIREMENTS: Awards and scholarships for elementary and high school students who reside in San Mateo County, California, or those who plan to attend San Mateo County Regional Occupational Program in Dental Assisting or College of San Mateo also in Dental Assisting. Annual scholarships in 4 areas: academic excellence, outstanding community and school volunteerism, science and math achievement, and dental assisting.

HOW TO APPLY: For more information, contact your school's scholarship representative.

3108—ALBUQUERQUE COMMUNITY FOUNDATION (Excel Staffing Companies Scholarships for Excellence in Continuing Education)

P.O. Box 36960

Albuquerque NM 87176-6960

505/883-6240

E-mail: foundation@albuquerque foundation.org

Internet: http://www.albuquerque foundation.org/scholar/scholar.htm

AMOUNT: Varies

DEADLINE(S): Varies

FIELD(S): All

ELIGIBILITY/REQUIREMENTS: Must be Albuquerque-area residents over 21 years of age, working full time and attending undergraduate, graduate, or vocational school part time to further their career goals; minimum cumulative GPA of 3.0;

and in need of financial assistance to attain a career goal.

HOW TO APPLY: Send application; résumé including employment, community service, and awards or honors; statement outlining career goals in relation to academic pursuits and financial need; transcript; and letter from employer verifying employment of at least 30 hours per week. Optional: a letter of reference verifying community service and/or volunteer commitment.

NUMBER OF AWARDS: 4-6

3109—ALBUQUERQUE COMMUNITY FOUNDATION (Kiwanis Club of Albuquerque Scholarship Program)

P.O. Box 36960
Albuquerque NM 87176-6960
505/883-6240
E-mail: foundation@albuquerque
foundation.org
Internet: http://www.albuquerque
foundation.org/scholar/scholar.htm
AMOUNT: $1,000
DEADLINE(S): Varies
FIELD(S): All
ELIGIBILITY/REQUIREMENTS: Must be Albuquerque metro-area graduating high school seniors with strong community service experience and a minimum 3.5 GPA.
HOW TO APPLY: See website for application.
NUMBER OF AWARDS: 4
RENEWABLE: No

3110—ALBUQUERQUE COMMUNITY FOUNDATION (New Mexico Manufactured Housing Scholarship)

P.O. Box 36960
Albuquerque NM 87176-6960
505/883-6240
E-mail: foundation@albuquerque
foundation.org
Internet: http://www.albuquerque
foundation.org/scholar/scholar.htm
AMOUNT: $1,000
DEADLINE(S): Varies
FIELD(S): All
ELIGIBILITY/REQUIREMENTS: Must be a New Mexico high school graduating senior with a minimum 3.0 GPA, living in mobile/manufacturing housing, for postsecondary education (2- or 4-year degree) at a university, college, or vocational institution.
HOW TO APPLY: Send application; high school transcript; copy of SAT or ACT scores; reference from 1 counselor or

teacher; written explanation of financial need including family's current income, assets, expenses, and family size and any unusual circumstances; copy of previous year's New Mexico state tax return; and proof of residency in a mobile/manufactured home—i.e., copy of title or rental agreement, retail installment contract, or county tax assessment.

NUMBER OF AWARDS: 1

3111—ALBUQUERQUE COMMUNITY FOUNDATION (Notah Begay III Scholarship Program)

P.O. Box 36960
Albuquerque NM 87176-6960
505/883-6240
E-mail: foundation@albuquerque
foundation.org
Internet: http://www.albuquerque
foundation.org/scholar/scholar.htm
AMOUNT: $2,000
DEADLINE(S): Varies
FIELD(S): All
ELIGIBILITY/REQUIREMENTS: Must be Native American New Mexico high school graduating seniors with a minimum cumulative 3.0 GPA who have been involved in varsity-level sports and who will be attending a U.S. postsecondary, accredited, not-for-profit educational institution.
HOW TO APPLY: Send application; transcript; statement describing personal goals, financial need, and any unusual circumstances that make it more difficult to attain educational goals; 1 reference from a current academic teacher or counselor; 1 reference from an athletic coach; and proof of tribal enrollment or Certificate of Indian Blood (CIB).
NUMBER OF AWARDS: 2

3112—ALBUQUERQUE COMMUNITY FOUNDATION (Sussman-Miller Educational Assistance Award)

P.O. Box 36960
Albuquerque NM 87176-6960
505/883-6240
E-mail: foundation@albuquerque
foundation.org
Internet: http://www.albuquerque
foundation.org/scholar/scholar.htm
AMOUNT: $500-$2,500
DEADLINE(S): Varies
FIELD(S): All
ELIGIBILITY/REQUIREMENTS: Must be New Mexico residents seeking to further their education in an undergraduate program.

HOW TO APPLY: Send application; FAFSA; résumé; statement of personal goals; transcript; 1 reference from a current academic teacher or counselor; a statement of college or university costs and a budget form.

3113—ALEXANDER GRAHAM BELL ASSOCIATION FOR THE DEAF (College Scholarship Awards)

3417 Volta Place NW
Washington DC 20007-2778
202/337-5220 (voice/TTY)
E-mail: agbell2@aol.com
Internet: http://www.agbell.org/
financialaid.cfm
AMOUNT: Varies
DEADLINE(S): DEC 1 (Request application by then. Deadline is MAR 15 postmark.)
FIELD(S): All
ELIGIBILITY/REQUIREMENTS: For prelingually deaf or hard-of-hearing students who use speech and speechreading to communicate and who are attending or have been admitted to a college or university that primarily enrolls students with normal hearing.
HOW TO APPLY: Must have a 60dB or greater hearing loss in the better ear in the speech frequencies of 500, 1000, and 2000 Hz. Application requests must be made IN WRITING to the Bell Association's Financial Aid Coordinator.

3114—ALEXANDER SCHOLARSHIP FUND

P.O. Box 719
Evansville IN 47115
812/464-3215
AMOUNT: $2,000
DEADLINE(S): Varies (set by high school)
FIELD(S): All
ELIGIBILITY/REQUIREMENTS: For college-bound high school seniors residing in and attending 1 of 3 high schools in Posey County, Indiana.
HOW TO APPLY: Obtain application from high school counselor.
NUMBER OF AWARDS: 10
RENEWABLE: Yes. Up to 3 years at $750/year.

3115—ALL-INK.COM COLLEGE SCHOLARSHIP PROGRAM

P.O. Box 50868
Provo UT 84605
E-mail: csp@all-ink.com
Internet: http://www.all-ink.com/
scholar/scholarship.html

AMOUNT: $1,000
DEADLINE(S): DEC 31
FIELD(S): All
ELIGIBILITY/REQUIREMENTS:
Minimum 2.5 GPA; must be attending full time; must attend accredited institution.
HOW TO APPLY: Apply online at website. No applications will be mailed or accepted by mail.
NUMBER OF AWARDS: 5
RENEWABLE: No
CONTACT: Aaron Gale

3116—ALLIED JEWISH FEDERATION (Charles and Louise Rosenbaum Scholarship Fund)

300 South Dahlia Street, Suite 300
Denver CO 80246
303/321-3399
Fax: 303/322-8328
E-mail: Federation@AJFColorado.org
Internet: www.Jewishcolorado.org
AMOUNT: Varies
DEADLINE(S): MAR 15
FIELD(S): All
ELIGIBILITY/REQUIREMENTS:
Scholarships for Jewish high school seniors who are residents of Colorado.
HOW TO APPLY: Write for details.

3117—ALPHA CHI/NATIONAL COLLEGE HONOR SOCIETY (Gaston and Nolle Scholarships)

P.O. Box 12249
Harding University
Searcy AR 72149
501/279-4443
FAX: 501/279-4589
E-mail: alphachi@harding.edu
Internet: http://www.alphachi honor.org
AMOUNT: $2,500 (Gaston), $1,500 (Nolle)
DEADLINE(S): FEB 22
FIELD(S): All
ELIGIBILITY/REQUIREMENTS: Open to members of Alpha Chi; must be planning to enroll full time in the senior year of an undergraduate program in the fall of the award year.
HOW TO APPLY: Apply through local Alpha Chi chapter.
NUMBER OF AWARDS: 2 Gaston, 10 Nolle
RENEWABLE: No.
CONTACT: Dr. Dennis Organ, Executive Director at above address or e-mail dorgan@harding.edu.
ADDITIONAL INFORMATION: Many of Alpha Chi's 7 regions offer scholarships

and fellowships. Contact the appropriate secretary-treasurer for more information on regional scholarships. Several local chapters also offer scholarships to their members. Contact your chapter sponsor for information.

3118—ALPHA KAPPA ALPHA EDUCATIONAL ADVANCEMENT FOUNDATION, INC. (Merit Scholarship)

5656 Stony Island Avenue
Chicago IL 60637
773/947-0026
FAX: 773/947-0277
Internet: http://www.akaeaf.org
AMOUNT: $1,000
DEADLINE(S): JAN 15
FIELD(S): All
ELIGIBILITY/REQUIREMENTS: Must have completed a minimum of 1 year in a degree-granting institution; be continuing in the program; GPA of 3.0 or higher; and show evidence of leadership by participation in community or campus activities.
HOW TO APPLY: Download application and return it by mail to Attention: Scholarship Application Enclosed. Do NOT phone, e-mail, fax, express mail, or send a written request for applications.

3119—ALPHA KAPPA ALPHA EDUCATIONAL ADVANCEMENT FOUNDATION, INC. (Needs-based Scholarship)

5656 Stony Island Avenue
Chicago IL 60637
773/947-0026
FAX: 773/947-0277
Internet: http://www.akaeaf.org
AMOUNT: $750-$1,500
DEADLINE(S): JAN 15
FIELD(S): All
ELIGIBILITY/REQUIREMENTS: Must have a minimum GPA of 2.5; have completed a minimum of 1 year in a degree-granting institution and be continuing studies in program; or be a student in a non-institution-based program that may or may not grant degrees (course-of-study outline required for these applicants).
HOW TO APPLY: Download application and return it by mail to the above address, Attention: Scholarship Application Enclosed. Do NOT phone, e-mail, fax, express mail, or send a written request for applications.

3120—ALPHA KAPPA ALPHA EDUCATIONAL ADVANCEMENT FOUNDATION, INC. (Youth-P.A.C., for Youth Partners Accessing Capital)

5656 Stony Island Avenue

Chicago IL 60637
773/947-0026
FAX: 773/947-0277
Internet: http://www.akaeaf.org
DEADLINE(S): JAN 15
FIELD(S): All
ELIGIBILITY/REQUIREMENTS: Must be a member of Alpha Kappa Alpha Sorority; be college sophomore or higher; minimum GPA of 3.0; demonstrate exceptional academic achievement or financial need; and participate in leadership, volunteer, civic, or campus activities.
HOW TO APPLY: Download application and return it by mail to the above address, Attention: Scholarship Application Enclosed. Do NOT phone, e-mail, fax, express mail, or send a written request for applications.

3121—ALPHA LAMBDA DELTA NATIONAL HONOR SOCIETY FOR FIRST-YEAR STUDENTS

P.O. Box 4403
Macon GA 31208-4403
800/9ALPHA1
FAX: 478/744-9924
E-mail: ald@nationalald.org
Internet: http://www.nationalald.org
AMOUNT: $1,000
DEADLINE(S): MAY 1
FIELD(S): All
ELIGIBILITY/REQUIREMENTS: Must be a member of Alpha Lambda Delta.
HOW TO APPLY: Through the local chapter.
NUMBER OF AWARDS: 35
RENEWABLE: No

3122—AMARILLO AREA FOUNDATION (Don and Sybil Harrington Foundation, The)

801 South Fillmore, Suite 700
Amarillo TX 79101
806/376-4521
FAX: 806/373-3656
E-mail: laquita@aaf-hf.org
Internet: http://www.aaf-hf.org/scholarships.html
AMOUNT: Varies
DEADLINE(S): MAR 1 by 5 p.m.
FIELD(S): All
ELIGIBILITY/REQUIREMENTS: Open to residents and/or graduating high school seniors of the 26 northern most counties of the Texas Panhandle: Armstrong, Briscoe, Carson, Castro, Childress, Collingsworth, Dallam, Deaf Smith, Donley, Gray, Hall, Hansford, Hartley, Hemphill, Hutchison, Lipscomb, Moore, Ochiltree, Oldham,

Parmer, Potter, Randall, Roberts, Sherman, Swisher, or Wheeler.
HOW TO APPLY: Contact Scholarship Coordinator for an application.
RENEWABLE: Yes
CONTACT: Laquita Hurt, Scholarship Coordinator

3123—A. MARLYN MOYER JR. SCHOLARSHIP FOUNDATION

409 Hood Boulevard
Fairless Hills PA 19030
215/943-7400
AMOUNT: Varies
DEADLINE(S): APR 20
FIELD(S): All
ELIGIBILITY/REQUIREMENTS: Scholarships for partial support for graduating high school seniors who are enrolling for the first time in colleges, universities, technical schools, nursing schools, and other accredited postsecondary institutions. Must be U.S. citizen and resident of Bucks County, Pennsylvania. Considerations are financial need; academic achievement; activities in school, community, or church.
HOW TO APPLY: Contact organization for details.

3124—AMERICAN DIVISION VETERANS ASSOCIATION (ADVA Scholarships)

1085 Bunkerhill Drive
Kalamazoo MI 49009
616/372-2192
E-mail: C146thinf@aol.com
AMOUNT: $1,000-$3,000
DEADLINE(S): MAY 1
FIELD(S): All
ELIGIBILITY/REQUIREMENTS: Open to children and grandchildren, including those by adoption, of current ADVA members or members who were killed in action or died in active duty. May be high school seniors or undergraduates pursuing college/vocational studies.
HOW TO APPLY: Must submit letter from ADVA member attesting to eligibility, letter of admission from school of choice, letters of recommendation from teachers, 200- to 300-word essay on subject pertaining to patriotism/loyalty to nation, and parents' income.
NUMBER OF AWARDS: About 20
RENEWABLE: No
CONTACT: Robert G. Short, Chairman, for an application

3125—AMERICAN ASSOCIATION FOR NUDE RECREATION, WESTERN REGION, INC.

P.O. Box 928

Phoenix AZ 85068
Internet: http://www.aanrwest.org
AMOUNT: $1,500 (plus additional funds from the national AANR)
DEADLINE(S): APR 1
FIELD(S): All
ELIGIBILITY/REQUIREMENTS: Applicant or parents must have been members of AANR West for 3 years; must be senior in high school or currently enrolled in an accredited postsecondary school; must be less than 27 years of age; must have at least a 2.5 GPA. Based on academic record, evidence of leadership, seriousness of purpose and a demonstrated potential for further growth through education.
HOW TO APPLY: See website for application and additional information or contact local club or AANR West for scholarship booklet.
NUMBER OF AWARDS: 2
RENEWABLE: Yes. Same procedure; up to 2 awards unless there are no competing candidates.

3126—AMERICAN ASSOCIATION OF BIOANALYSTS (David Birenbaum Scholarship Fund)

917 Locust Street, Suite 1100
St. Louis MO 63101-1419
314/241-1445
FAX: 314/241-1449
E-mail: aab@aab.org
Internet: http://www.aab.org
AMOUNT: Varies
DEADLINE(S): APR 15
FIELD(S): All
ELIGIBILITY/REQUIREMENTS: Open to AAB regular and associate members, their spouses, and dependent children. Must have graduated from an accredited high school or equivalent. Based on several factors, such as need, goals, achievements, community involvement, etc.
HOW TO APPLY: Contact AAB for an application.

3127—AMERICAN ASSOCIATION OF JAPANESE UNIVERSITY WOMEN

16340 Moorpark Street
Encino CA 91436
FAX: 818/386-0639
E-mail: scholarship@aajuw.org
Internet: http://www.aajuw.org
AMOUNT: $1,500
DEADLINE(S): SEP 30
FIELD(S): All
ELIGIBILITY/REQUIREMENTS: Must be a female student enrolled in an accredited California college or university; must

have junior, senior or graduate standing; must attend award ceremony in January at own expense. Must be a contributor to U.S.-Japan relations, cultural exchanges, and the development of leadership in chosen field.
HOW TO APPLY: Submit an application and other required paper to a co-chairwoman by mail or online.
NUMBER OF AWARDS: Usually 2
RENEWABLE: No
CONTACT: Reiko Yamashita, 310/769-6801

3128—AMERICAN ASSOCIATION OF UNIVERSITY WOMEN (Foundation for Education-Livermore, Pleasanton, Dublin, Sunol, California)

P.O. Box 661
Livermore CA 94551
AMOUNT: Varies
DEADLINE(S): MAR 1
FIELD(S): All
ELIGIBILITY/REQUIREMENTS: For female residents of Livermore, Pleasanton, Dublin, or Sunol, California, or graduates of a high school in those cities. Awarded to juniors or seniors at an accredited 4-year college or university.
HOW TO APPLY: Write to Scholarship Coordinator.
NUMBER OF AWARDS: 3

3129—AMERICAN ASSOCIATION OF UNIVERSITY WOMEN-HARRISBURG BRANCH (Beverly J. Smith Memorial Scholarship)

P.O. Box 1625
Harrisburg PA 17105-1625
E-mail: scholarship@aauw
harrisburg.org
Internet: http://www.aauw
harrisburg.org
AMOUNT: Up to $2,500
DEADLINE(S): MAY 7
FIELD(S): All
ELIGIBILITY/REQUIREMENTS: Open to any woman enrolled full time with at least 60 credits toward a baccalaureate and a GPA of 3.4 or higher. Must be a resident of Dauphin, Cumberland, or Perry County, Pennsylvania, attending an accredited college or university in Pennsylvania.
NUMBER OF AWARDS: 1
RENEWABLE: No

3130—AMERICAN ASSOCIATION OF UNIVERSITY WOMEN-HARRISBURG BRANCH (Martha M. Dohner Memorial Scholarship)

P.O. Box 1625

Harrisburg PA 17105-1625
E-mail: scholarship@aauw
harrisburg.org
Internet: http://www.aauw
harrisburg.org
AMOUNT: $1,000
DEADLINE(S): MAY 7
FIELD(S): All
ELIGIBILITY/REQUIREMENTS:
Available to any woman enrolled full time
with at least 60 credits toward a baccalau-
reate and a GPA of 3.25 or higher. Must be
a resident of and attend an accredited col-
lege or university in Dauphin or
Cumberland County, Pennsylvania.
HOW TO APPLY: Follow instructions
and download forms on website.
NUMBER OF AWARDS: 1
RENEWABLE: No

3131—AMERICAN ASSOCIATION OF UNI-VERSITY WOMEN-HONOLULU BRANCH (Ruth E. Black Scholarship)

1802 Keeaumoku Street
Honolulu HI 96822
808/537-4702
AMOUNT: Varies
DEADLINE(S): MAR 1
FIELD(S): All
ELIGIBILITY/REQUIREMENTS: Open
to women who are legal residents of
Hawaii. For undergraduate study at an
accredited college or university in Hawaii.
Must demonstrate financial need.
HOW TO APPLY: Contact Association
for an application or more information.

3132—AMERICAN ASSOCIATION OF UNI-VERSITY WOMEN-STATE COLLEGE BRANCH

P.O. Box 185
Pine Grove Mills PA 16868
814/237-9233
E-mail: http://www.aauwstate
college.org
AMOUNT: $5,000
DEADLINE(S): FEB 1
FIELD(S): All
ELIGIBILITY/REQUIREMENTS: Must
be a female resident of Centre County with
at least one quarter (or 30 credit hours) of
course work required for a baccalaureate
degree. Candidate must have interrupted
her studies for a period of at least 2 years
or delayed her higher education for at least
2 years after graduating from high school.
HOW TO APPLY: See website for application, or by mail or e-mail.
NUMBER OF AWARDS: 4
RENEWABLE: Yes. Once only. Must
reapply the following year.

3133—AMERICAN BAPTIST CHURCH (Award)

10th and Cedar Streets
Ottawa KS 66067
785/242-5200
E-mail: admiss@ottawa.edu
Internet: http://www.ottawa.edu
AMOUNT: $500
DEADLINE(S): Varies
FIELD(S): All
ELIGIBILITY/REQUIREMENTS: Must
be a member of an American Baptist
Church and recommended by their pastor.
Available to students at Ottawa
University.
HOW TO APPLY: Contact Church.

3134—AMERICAN BAPTIST FINANCIAL AID PROGRAM (Marion Burr Scholarship)

Director of Financial Aid
P.O. Box 851
Valley Forge PA 19482-0851
800/ABC-3USA, ext. 2067 or
610/768-2000
FAX: 610/768-2056
Internet: http://www.abc-
em.org/dm/fa.cfm
AMOUNT: $1,000-$2,000
DEADLINE(S): MAY 31
FIELD(S): All
ELIGIBILITY/REQUIREMENTS: Must
be a Native American member of an
American Baptist church for at least 1 year
before applying for aid; must be enrolled
full time at an accredited educational insti-
tution or seminary in the U.S. or Puerto
Rico; must be a U.S. citizen, and enrolled
full time at a 4-year institution or universi-
ty pursuing a career in human services.
HOW TO APPLY: Write for information.
RENEWABLE: Yes
CONTACT: Lynne Eckman, Director of
Financial Aid

3135—AMERICAN BAPTIST FINANCIAL AID PROGRAM (Student Loan Program)

Director of Financial Aid
P.O. Box 851
Valley Forge PA 19482-0851
800/ABC-3USA, ext. 2067 or
610/768-2000
FAX: 610/768-2056
Internet: http://www.abc-
em.org/dm/fa.cfm
AMOUNT: $500 (full-time students);
$250 (part-time students)
DEADLINE(S): MAY 31
FIELD(S): All

ELIGIBILITY/REQUIREMENTS: Must
be a member of an American Baptist
church for at least one year before applying for aid; must be enrolled full time at an
accredited educational institution or seminary in the U.S. or Puerto Rico; must be a
U.S. citizen. Applicant must be enrolled
full time at a 4-year institution or university.
HOW TO APPLY: Write for information.
RENEWABLE: Yes. Total of 4 years
($2,000, maximum for full-time students;
$1,000 maximum for part-time students).
CONTACT: Lynne Eckman, Director of
Financial Aid

3136—AMERICAN BAPTIST FINANCIAL AID PROGRAM (Undergraduate Scholarships)

Director of Financial Aid
P.O. Box 851
Valley Forge PA 19482-0851
800/ABC-3USA, ext. 2067 or
610/768-2000
FAX: 610/768-2056
Internet: http://www.abc-
em.org/dm/fa.cfm
AMOUNT: $1,000-$2,000
DEADLINE(S): MAY 31
FIELD(S): All
ELIGIBILITY/REQUIREMENTS: Must
be a member of an American Baptist
church for at least 1 year before applying
for aid; must be enrolled full time at an
accredited educational institution or semi-
nary in the U.S. or Puerto Rico; must be a
U.S. citizen; and must be enrolled full time
at a 4-year college or university.
HOW TO APPLY: Write for information.
RENEWABLE: Yes. Must maintain a 2.75
GPA.
CONTACT: Lynne Eckman, Director of
Financial Aid

3137—AMERICAN BUSINESS WOMEN'S ASSOCIATION (Stephen Bufton Memorial Scholarship)

118 Concord Lane
Osterville MA 02655
AMOUNT: $2,100
DEADLINE(S): MAY 31
FIELD(S): All
ELIGIBILITY/REQUIREMENTS: Open
to junior-, senior-, or graduate-level
women who are residents of Cape Cod,
Martha's Vineyard, or Nantucket Island,
Massachusetts. Must have at least a 2.5
GPA on a scale of 4.0.
HOW TO APPLY: Contact Association
for application and details.

3138—AMERICAN CANCER SOCIETY (Young Survivor Scholarship Program)

1755 Abbey Road
East Lansing MI 48823
800/723-0360
Internet: http://www.cancer.org/
scholarship
AMOUNT: $1,000
DEADLINE(S): APR 16 or next business
day after tax deadline
FIELD(S): All
ELIGIBILITY/REQUIREMENTS: For
Michigan and Indiana residents who are
U.S. citizens and have had a diagnosis of
cancer before age 21. Must be an under-
graduate under age 21 attending an accred-
ited college or university within Michigan
or Indiana. Based on financial need, schol-
arship, community service, and leadership.
HOW TO APPLY: See website or call the
American Cancer Society's Great Lakes
Division (800/723-0360) for application
packet.
RENEWABLE: Yes

3139—AMERICAN CONTRACT BRIDGE LEAGUE EDUCATIONAL FOUNDATION

2990 Airways Boulevard
Memphis TN 38116
901/332-5586
FAX: 901/398-7754
Internet: http://www.acbl.org
AMOUNT: $500
FIELD(S): All
ELIGIBILITY/REQUIREMENTS: Must
be members of the ACBL who are high
school or college bridge players under 26
who also teach a bridge class in schools (at
least 16 hours of lessons to a class of at
least 8 students who are under 26 years
old).
HOW TO APPLY: Contact ACBL for
details and application.
NUMBER OF AWARDS: Unlimited
CONTACT: Charlotte Blaiss

3140—AMERICAN COUNCIL OF THE BLIND (ACB Scholarship Program)

1155 15th Street NW, Suite 1004
Washington DC 20005
202/467-5081 or 800/424-8666
FAX: 202/467-5085
E-mail: info@acb.org
Internet: http://www.acb.org
AMOUNT: $500-$3,000
DEADLINE(S): MAR 1
FIELD(S): All
ELIGIBILITY/REQUIREMENTS: Open
to legally blind students who have been
accepted to or are enrolled in an accredit-

ed institution for vocational, technical,
undergraduate, graduate, or professional
studies. Must be U.S. citizen or legal resident. Must have 3.3 GPA, unless extenuat-
ing circumstances exist.
HOW TO APPLY: See website for application or write or e-mail. Submit with an
autobiographical sketch (up to 2 pages),
including course of study and why you
have chosen it; certification of legal blindness; transcripts; recommendation from
instructor; proof of acceptance at postsecondary school.
NUMBER OF AWARDS: 25
CONTACT: Terry Pacheco

3141—AMERICAN FEDERATION OF STATE, COUNTY & MUNICIPAL EMPLOYEES, AFL-CIO (AFSCME Family Scholarship Program)

1625 L Street NW
Washington DC 20036-5687
202/429-1250
FAX: 202/429-1298
E-mail: education@afscme.org
Internet: http://www.afscme.org/
about/scholarf.htm
AMOUNT: $2,000/year
DEADLINE(S): DEC 31
FIELD(S): All
ELIGIBILITY/REQUIREMENTS: Open
to high school seniors who are dependent
children of active AFSCME members or
financially responsible grandparent.
Awards are for full-time undergraduate
study.
HOW TO APPLY: See website for appli-
cation or call or e-mail. Submit application
along with an essay (up to 1,000 words) on
"What AFSCME Has Meant to Our
Family," high school transcript, SAT or
ACT scores, and proof of AFSCME mem-
bership.
RENEWABLE: Yes. Total of 4 years.
CONTACT: Attention: Education Department

3142—AMERICAN FEDERATION OF STATE, COUNTY & MUNICIPAL EMPLOYEES, AFL-CIO (Joey Parisi Memorial Scholarship)

1625 L Street NW
Washington DC 20036-5687
202/429-1250
FAX: 202/429-1298
E-mail: education@afscme.org
Internet: http://www.afscme.org/
about/scholarf.htm
AMOUNT: $2,000
DEADLINE(S): OCT 31
FIELD(S): All

ELIGIBILITY/REQUIREMENTS:
Available to full-time staff or local officers
with substantial organizing responsibilities
for AFSCME Councils, locals, and the
International Union.
HOW TO APPLY: For information or an
application write to: George Meany
Center, 10000 New Hampshire Avenue,
Silver Spring MD 20903, or telephone the
college degree program office at 301/431-
5404.
NUMBER OF AWARDS: 1
RENEWABLE: Yes. Automatically for a
2nd year subject to Meany Center
Certification of satisfactory performance.
CONTACT: Education Department

3143—AMERICAN FEDERATION OF STATE, COUNTY & MUNICIPAL EMPLOYEES-AFL-CIO (Nadra Floyd Memorial Scholarship)

1625 L Street NW
Washington DC 20036-5687
202/429-1250
FAX: 202/429-1298
E-mail: education@afscme.org
Internet: http://www.afscme.org/
about/scholarf.htm
AMOUNT: $2,000
DEADLINE(S): OCT 31
FIELD(S): All
ELIGIBILITY/REQUIREMENTS:
Available to all AFSCME members and
staff who want to increase their leadership
skills to the further development of the
labor movement.
HOW TO APPLY: For information or an
application write to: George Meany
Center, 10000 New Hampshire Avenue,
Silver Spring MD 20903, or telephone the
college degree program office at 301/431-
5404.
RENEWABLE: Yes. Automatically for a
2nd year subject to Meany Center
Certification of satisfactory performance.
CONTACT: Education Department

3144—AMERICAN FEDERATION OF STATE, COUNTY, AND MUNICIPAL EMPLOY-EES-AFL-CIO (Union Plus Education Foundation Scholarship)

1625 L Street NW
Washington DC 20036-5687
800/238-2539
FAX: 202/429-1298
E-mail: education@afscme.org
Internet: http://www.afscme.org/
about/scholarf.htm
AMOUNT: $500-$4,000
DEADLINE(S): JAN 31
FIELD(S): All

ELIGIBILITY/REQUIREMENTS: Open to AFSCME members and their spouses and children. Member must have at least 1 year of continuous membership in good standing. Applicant must be accepted for undergraduate study into an accredited college, community college, or recognized technical/trade school by June 30.
HOW TO APPLY: See website for application or send a postcard with name, local union number, social security number, and address to: Union Plus Scholarship, P.O. Box 34800, Washington, DC 20043-4800. Submit with high school, college or trade school transcript; 1 personal reference; and an essay of up to 500 words describing career goals as well as their relationship with the union and the labor movement.

3145—AMERICAN FEDERATION OF TEACHERS (Robert G. Porter Scholars Program)

555 New Jersey Avenue NW
Washington DC 20001-2079
202/879-4400
E-mail: porterscholars@aft.org
Internet:
http://www.aft.org/scholar/
scholarships/index.html
AMOUNT: $1,000 (AFT members);
$8,000 (dependents)
DEADLINE(S): MAR 31
FIELD(S): All (emphasis on labor, education, health care, or government service)
ELIGIBILITY/REQUIREMENTS: Open to high school seniors who are dependents of AFT members.
HOW TO APPLY: Contact AFT for an application.
NUMBER OF AWARDS: 4

3146—AMERICAN FIRE SPRINKLER ASSOCIATION (Scholarship Contest)

12959 Jupiter Road, Suite 142
Dallas TX 75238
214/349-5965
FAX: 343/8898
E-mail: afsainfo@firesprinkler.org
Internet: http://www.fire
sprinkler.org
AMOUNT: Up to $3,000
DEADLINE(S): DEC 7
FIELD(S): All
ELIGIBILITY/REQUIREMENTS: Open to high school seniors. Topic: "How fire sprinklers affect your community." 700-1,000 words. Regional and nationwide scholarship prizes. Not open to AFSA staff relatives or board members.

HOW TO APPLY: Send to "Scholarship Contest" at above location for application.

3147—AMERICAN FOREIGN SERVICE ASSOCIATION (Financial Aid Awards)

2101 E Street NW
Washington DC 20037
202/944-5504 or 800/704-AFSA
FAX: 202/338-6820
E-mail: scholar@afsa.org
AMOUNT: $500-$2,500
DEADLINE(S): FEB 6
FIELD(S): All
ELIGIBILITY/REQUIREMENTS: Open to dependents of U.S. Government Foreign Service employees. Students must be enrolled in undergraduate study at a U.S. college or university.
HOW TO APPLY: Write to the above address for complete information.

3148—AMERICAN FOREIGN SERVICE ASSOCIATION (Merit Awards)

2101 E Street NW
Washington DC 20037
202/944-5504 or 800/704-AFSA
FAX: 202/338-6820
E-mail: scholar@afsa.org
AMOUNT: $1,000
DEADLINE(S): FEB 6
FIELD(S): All
ELIGIBILITY/REQUIREMENTS: Open to dependents of U.S. Government Foreign Service employees. Students must be high school seniors.
HOW TO APPLY: Write to the above address for complete information.

3149—AMERICAN FOUNDATION FOR THE BLIND (Ferdinand Torres Scholarship)

11 Penn Plaza, Suite 300
New York NY 10001
212/502-7661
FAX: 212/502-7771
E-mail: afbinfoi@afb.net
Internet: http://www.afb.org/
scholar/scholarships.asp
AMOUNT: $1,500
DEADLINE(S): MAR 31
FIELD(S): All
ELIGIBILITY/REQUIREMENTS: Open to legally blind full-time undergraduate or graduate students who present evidence of economic need. Must reside in the U.S. Preference given to applicants residing in New York City metropolitan area and new immigrants.
HOW TO APPLY: See website or contact AFB for an application. Must submit evi-

dence of legal blindness; official transcripts; proof of college or university acceptance; evidence of need; 3 letters of recommendation; proof of residence; and statement of field of study you are pursuing, goals, work experience, activities, and how money will be used. New immigrants include a description of country of origin and reason for coming to U.S.
NUMBER OF AWARDS: 1
CONTACT: Alina Vayntrub

3150—AMERICAN GI FORUM OF THE U.S. HISPANIC EDUCATION FOUNDATION (Chapter Scholarships)

3301 Mountain Road NW
Albuquerque NM 87104
505/243-7551 or 505/843/8224
FAX: 505/247-2993
Internet: http://www.incacorp.
com/agifhef
AMOUNT: Varies
DEADLINE(S): Varies
FIELD(S): All
ELIGIBILITY/REQUIREMENTS: Open to Hispanic undergraduate students residing in states with chapters of the GI Forum.
HOW TO APPLY: Obtain applications from nearest awarding chapter. Send SASE for complete information.

3151—AMERICAN INDIAN HERITAGE FOUNDATION (National Miss Indian U.S. Scholarship)

P.O. Box 6301
Falls Church VA 22040
703/819-0979
Internet: http://www.indians.org
AMOUNT: Over $30,000
DEADLINE(S): April 1
FIELD(S): All
ELIGIBILITY/REQUIREMENTS: Must be a high school graduate between 18-26. Can never have cohabitated, been pregnant, or married. Applicants must have a Native American sponsor. Prizes for academic achievement, Miss Walk in Beauty, Miss Photogenic, Miss Congeniality, talent traditional dress, and evening gown sections. Must be of American Indian descent.
HOW TO APPLY: Contact Foundation for details and application.

3152—AMERICAN INSTITUTE FOR FOREIGN STUDY (International Scholarships)

River Plaza, 9 West Broad Street
Stamford CT 06902-3788
800/727-2437
E-mail: info@aifs.com

Internet: http://www.aifs
abroad.com
AMOUNT: $1,000 and $2,000/semester;
$1,000/summer
DEADLINE(S): MAR 15 (summer);
APR 15 (fall); OCT 15 (spring)
FIELD(S): All
ELIGIBILITY/REQUIREMENTS:
Scholarship program for undergraduates
with at least a 3.0 GPA desiring to spend a
semester or summer studying in a partici-
pating foreign university. Criteria include
leadership potential and extracurricular
involvement in multicultural or interna-
tional issues.
HOW TO APPLY: Visit website or con-
tact Institute for details.
NUMBER OF AWARDS: 100 semester
scholarships; 50 summer scholarships
RENEWABLE: No
CONTACT: David Mauro

3153—AMERICAN INSTITUTE FOR FOR-EIGN STUDY (International Scholarships for Minorities)

River Plaza, 9 West Broad Street
Stamford CT 06902-3788
800/727-2437
E-mail: info@aifs.com
Internet: http://www.aifs
abroad.com
AMOUNT: $1,000 and $2,000/semester;
$1,000/summer
DEADLINE(S): MAR 15 (summer);
APR 15 (fall); OCT 15 (spring)
FIELD(S): All
ELIGIBILITY/REQUIREMENTS:
Scholarship program for undergraduates
with at least a 3.0 GPA desiring to spend a
semester or summer studying in a partici-
pating foreign university. Criteria include
leadership potential and extracurricular
involvement in multicultural or interna-
tional issues.
HOW TO APPLY: Visit website or con-
tact Institute for details.
NUMBER OF AWARDS: 100 semester
scholarships; 50 summer scholarships
RENEWABLE: No
CONTACT: David Mauro

3154—AMERICAN JEWISH LEAGUE FOR ISRAEL (University Scholarship Fund)

450 Seventh Avenue,
Suite 808
New York NY 10123
212/371-1583
FAX: 212/279-1456
E-mail: ajlijms@aol.com
AMOUNT: $2,000
DEADLINE(S): MAY 1

FIELD(S): All
ELIGIBILITY/REQUIREMENTS: Open
to U.S. citizens of Jewish faith who have
been accepted for a year of undergraduate
or graduate study in Israel at Bar Ilan
University, Ben Gurion University, Haifa
University, Hebrew University-Jerusalem,
Technion, Tel Aviv University, or
Weizmann Institute of Science. Financial
need NOT a factor.
HOW TO APPLY: Contact National
President for details and application.
NUMBER OF AWARDS: 15-20
RENEWABLE: No
CONTACT: Dr. Martin L. Kalmanson,
National President

3155—AMERICAN LEGION AUXILIARY (Department of Alabama Scholarships)

120 North Jackson Street
Montgomery AL 36104
334/262-1176
FAX: 334/262-9694
E-mail: americanlegionaux1@
juno.com
AMOUNT: Varies
DEADLINE(S): APR 1
FIELD(S): All (emphasis on nursing)
ELIGIBILITY/REQUIREMENTS: Open
to descendants of veterans serving during a
war from WWI to present. Veteran and
applicant must be residents of Alabama.
Offered at 13 colleges/universities in
Alabama for undergraduate/vo-tech study.
Credit given for books, tuition, and board.
HOW TO APPLY: Written inquiry. Send
SASE for details. Submit in handwriting a
letter stating qualifications, age, need, etc.,
with a transcript of high school and/or col-
lege record.
NUMBER OF AWARDS: 40

3156—AMERICAN LEGION AUXILIARY (Department of California/Continuing/Re-entry Student Scholarship Program)

401 Van Ness Avenue, Room 113
San Francisco CA 94102-4586
415/861-5092
FAX: 415/861-8365
E-mail: calegionaux@calegionaux.
org
Internet: http://www.calegionaux.
org
AMOUNT: $1,000
DEADLINE(S): MAR 15
FIELD(S): All
ELIGIBILITY/REQUIREMENTS:
Applicant's parent must have served in a
war from WWI to present; must be a resi-
dent of California; plan to attend a

California college or university; and be a
continuing or re-entry college student.
HOW TO APPLY: Send application.
NUMBER OF AWARDS: 2
CONTACT: Local or closest American
Legion Auxiliary Unit

3157—AMERICAN LEGION AUXILIARY (Department of California/Funds for Educational Assistance)

Department of California
401 Van Ness Avenue, Room 113
San Francisco CA 94102-4586
415/861-5092
FAX: 415/861-8365
E-mail: calegionaux@calegionaux.
org
Internet: http://www.calegionaux.
org
AMOUNT: $2,000 ($1,000/year for 2
years), $1,000, $500
DEADLINE(S): MAR 15
FIELD(S): All
ELIGIBILITY/REQUIREMENTS:
Senior in high school or graduate of an
accredited high school who has not been
able to begin college due to circumstances
of illness or finance; must need financial
assistance to continue educational pursuits; must attend a California college or
university. A parent must have served in a
war from WWI to present.
HOW TO APPLY: See website for application and submit to the closest American
Legion Auxiliary Unit with 3 letters of reference from school officials, employers or
personal friends (only 1 letter may be from
a personal friend) attesting to character;
current school transcript of applicant's
grades; and letter from applicant expressing need.
NUMBER OF AWARDS: 1 ($2,000); 5
($1,000); 5 ($500)
RENEWABLE: No
CONTACT: Local or closest American
Legion Auxiliary Unit.

3158—AMERICAN LEGION AUXILIARY (Department of California/Lucille Ganey Memorial Scholarship)

401 Van Ness Avenue, Room 113
San Francisco CA 94102-4586
415/861-5092
FAX: 415/861-8365
E-mail: calegionaux@calegionaux.
org
Internet: http://www.calegionaux.
org
AMOUNT: $500
DEADLINE(S): MAR 15
FIELD(S): All

ELIGIBILITY/REQUIREMENTS: Applicant's parent must have served in a war from WWI to present; must be a resident of California; be a senior in a California high school at time of graduation; and plan to attend Stephens College in Missouri or be a student already attending Stephens College.
HOW TO APPLY: Send application.
NUMBER OF AWARDS: 1
CONTACT: Local or closest American Legion Auxiliary Unit

3159—AMERICAN LEGION AUXILIARY (Department of California/Past Department Presidents' Junior Scholarship Award)

401 Van Ness Avenue, Room 113
San Francisco CA 94102-4586
415/861-5092
FAX: 415/861-8365
E-mail: calegionaux@calegionaux.org
Internet: http://www.calegionaux.org
AMOUNT: $300-$1,000
DEADLINE(S): APR 15
FIELD(S): All
ELIGIBILITY/REQUIREMENTS: Applicant must be a child, grandchild, or great-grandchild of a veteran who served in a war from WWI to present; be a resident of California; plan to attend a California college or university; and be currently in high school and attending college in the next academic year.
HOW TO APPLY: Send application.
NUMBER OF AWARDS: 1
CONTACT: American Legion Auxiliary Unit in which the Junior holds membership

3160—AMERICAN LEGION AUXILIARY (Department of California Scholarships)

401 Van Ness Avenue, Room 113
San Francisco CA 94102-4586
415/861-5092
FAX: 415/861-8365
E-mail: calegionaux@calegionaux.org
Internet: http://www.calegionaux.org
AMOUNT: $500-$2,000
DEADLINE(S): MAR 15
FIELD(S): All
ELIGIBILITY/REQUIREMENTS: Applicant's parent must have served in a war from WWI to present; must be a resident of California; plan to attend a California college or university; be a senior in high school or graduate of an accredited high school who has not been able to begin college due to circumstances of illness or finance; and needs financial assistance to continue educational pursuits.
HOW TO APPLY: Send application.
NUMBER OF AWARDS: 11 (5 at $500 per year; 5 at $1,000 per year; 1 at $2,000 over 2 years)
CONTACT: Local or closest American Legion Auxiliary Unit

3161—AMERICAN LEGION AUXILIARY (Department of Colorado/Department President's Scholarship)

7465 East First Avenue, Suite D
Denver CO 80230
AMOUNT: $250/$500
DEADLINE(S): MAR 11
FIELD(S): All
ELIGIBILITY/REQUIREMENTS: Open to Colorado residents who are children or grandchildren of U.S. veterans of armed conflicts. Must be high school senior, and demonstrate character, Americanism, leadership, scholarship (15% each) and financial need (40%).
HOW TO APPLY: Contact ALA for application and submit with 4 letters of recommendation (1 from either clergyman, doctor, or social worker; 1 from either principal or guidance counselor, which should include size of class, applicant's ranking in class, and GPA); and 2 letters from adults other than relatives attesting to applicant's character in regard to citizenship, conduct, and leadership and an essay (no more than 1,000 words) on the topic, "My Obligations as an American"; a certified transcript and a copy of ACT or SAT scores; and a brief statement of the veteran's branch of service, dates of service, or a photocopy of veteran's discharge papers.
NUMBER OF AWARDS: 3 (2, $500; 1, $250)
RENEWABLE: No

3162—AMERICAN LEGION AUXILIARY (Department of Colorado/Department President's Scholarship for Junior Auxiliary)

7465 East First Avenue, Suite D
Denver CO 80230
AMOUNT: $500
DEADLINE(S): MAR 11
FIELD(S): All
ELIGIBILITY/REQUIREMENTS: Open to Colorado residents who are Junior members of the ALA, who have held membership for the past 3 years in good standing; must be in senior year of an accredited high school and a resident of Colorado.

HOW TO APPLY: Contact ALA for application and submit with 4 letters of recommendation (1 from either clergyman, doctor, or social worker; 1 from either principal or guidance counselor, which should include size of class, applicant's ranking in class, and GPA); and 2 letters from adults other than relatives attesting to applicant's character in regard to citizenship, conduct, and leadership and an essay (no more than 1,000 words) on the topic, "My Obligations as an American"; a certified transcript and a copy of ACT or SAT scores; and a brief statement of the veteran's branch of service, dates of service, or a photocopy of veteran's discharge papers. Submit packet to attention of Department Secretary.
NUMBER OF AWARDS: 1
RENEWABLE: No
ADDITIONAL INFORMATION: If winner also wins the National President's Scholarship or the parley winner of the Past President's Nursing Scholarship, her alternate will receive this award.

3163—AMERICAN LEGION AUXILIARY (Department of Colorado/Violet Morrow Educational Scholarship)

7465 East First Avenue, Suite D
Denver CO 80230
AMOUNT: $500
DEADLINE(S): MAR 11
FIELD(S): All
ELIGIBILITY/REQUIREMENTS: Open to Colorado residents who are a relative of a veteran who served in the Armed Forces; must be high school senior or college undergraduate, and demonstrate character and leadership (25% each) and financial need (50%).
HOW TO APPLY: Apply through local high school; no high school may enter more than 3 candidates. Contact ALA for application and submit with 3 letters of recommendation (1 from either principal or guidance counselor, which should include size of class, applicant's ranking in class, and GPA); and 2 letters from adults other than relatives attesting to applicant's character in regard to citizenship, conduct, and leadership and an essay (no more than 1,000 words) on the topic, "My Education/Career Goals and How this Scholarship Will Help Me Reach These Goals"; a certified transcript and a copy of ACT or SAT scores; and a brief statement of the veteran's branch of service, dates of service, or a photocopy of veteran's discharge papers.
NUMBER OF AWARDS: 1
RENEWABLE: No
ADDITIONAL INFORMATION: Submit application packet to Violet Morrow

Educational Scholarship Committee, c/o Roberta Morrow, 5934 Yank Ct., Littleton CO 80127.

3164—AMERICAN LEGION AUXILIARY (Department of Minnesota Scholarships)

Department of Minnesota
State Veterans Service Building
20 West 12th Street, #314
St. Paul MN 55155
651/224-7634
AMOUNT: $750
DEADLINE(S): MAR 15
FIELD(S): All
ELIGIBILITY/REQUIREMENTS: Open to Minnesota residents who are children or grandchildren of U.S. veterans of armed conflicts. Must be high school senior or graduate with GPA of 'C' or better; attend Minnesota vocational/business school, college, or university; and demonstrate financial need.
HOW TO APPLY: Write for information.
NUMBER OF AWARDS: 7

3165—AMERICAN LEGION AUXILIARY (Department of Missouri/Lela Murphy Scholarship)

600 Ellis Boulevard
Jefferson City MO 65101
573/636-9133
E-mail: dptmoala@socket.net
Internet: http://www.legion-aux.org
AMOUNT: $500
DEADLINE(S): MAR 10
FIELD(S): All
ELIGIBILITY/REQUIREMENTS: Must be a high school graduate, resident of Missouri, and the granddaughter or great-granddaughter of a living or deceased Auxiliary member.
HOW TO APPLY: Send application.
NUMBER OF AWARDS: 1

3166—AMERICAN LEGION AUXILIARY (Department of New Hampshire/Adrienne Alix Scholarship)

25 Capitol Street, Room 432
Concord NH 03302-6312
603/271-2212
FAX: 603/371-5352
E-mail: nhamerlegaux@yahoo.com
DEADLINE(S): MAY 1
FIELD(S): All
ELIGIBILITY/REQUIREMENTS: Must be reentering the workforce or upgrading skills, be displaced from employment, recently honorably discharged from the military, and New Hampshire resident.

Must be used for refresher course or to advance skills.
HOW TO APPLY: Send application with 3 letters of recommendation: 2 adults unrelated to applicant, 1 employer or former employer; short essay (500 words or less) explaining career goals and objectives.

3167—AMERICAN LEGION AUXILIARY (Department of New Hampshire/Elsie Brown Scholarship)

25 Capitol Street, Room 432
Concord NH 03302-6312
603/271-2212
FAX: 603/371-5352
E-mail: nhamerlegaux@yahoo.com
AMOUNT: $150
DEADLINE(S): APR 15
FIELD(S): All
ELIGIBILITY/REQUIREMENTS: Must be child or grandchild of a deceased veteran who is resident of New Hampshire.
HOW TO APPLY: Send application with 4 letters of recommendation: 1 from high school principal, 1 from clergyman, 2 from adults, other than relatives, certifying scholarship, character, Americanism, leadership, and basis of need; an original article (500 words or less) on topic of your choice; any additional data attesting to your qualifications and community activities; and transcript.

3168—AMERICAN LEGION AUXILIARY (Department of New Hampshire/Grace S. High Memorial Child Welfare Scholarship Fund)

25 Capitol Street, Room 432
Concord NH 03302-6312
603/271-2212
FAX: 603/371-5352
E-mail: nhamerlegaux@yahoo.com
AMOUNT: $300
DEADLINE(S): APR 15
FIELD(S): All
ELIGIBILITY/REQUIREMENTS: Open to girls whose parent has been member of American Legion or Auxiliary for 3 years preceding application, or are the daughter of deceased veteran, in senior year in high school, and in need of financial assistance. Must be New Hampshire resident, and plan to attend a school of higher learning for at least 2 years.
HOW TO APPLY: Send application with 2 letters of recommendation: 1 from the principal and 1 from clergyman; an essay (300 words or less) on "what scholarship would mean to me"; and transcript. Scholarship based 50% on need, 20% on

character, 20% on scholarship, and 10% on Americanism.
NUMBER OF AWARDS: 2

3169—AMERICAN LEGION AUXILIARY (Department of Kansas Scholarships)

1314 SW Topeka Boulevard
Topeka KS 66612-1886
785-232-9315
FAX: 785-232-1399
E-mail: yunker@ksamlegion.org
Internet: http://www.ksamlegion.org
AMOUNT: $250
DEADLINE(S): MAY 1
FIELD(S): All
ELIGIBILITY/REQUIREMENTS: Open to children, spouses, or unremarried widows of veterans who are entering college for the first time. May be used only at Kansas schools.
HOW TO APPLY: Write for information.
NUMBER OF AWARDS: 2-3

3170—AMERICAN LEGION AUXILIARY (Department of Oregon Scholarships)

401 Van Ness Avenue, Room 113
San Francisco CA 94102-4586
415/861-5092
FAX: 415/861-8365
E-mail: calegionaux@calegionaux.org
Internet: http://www.calegionaux.org
AMOUNT: $1,000
DEADLINE(S): MAR 10
FIELD(S): All
ELIGIBILITY/REQUIREMENTS: Must be the child or widow of a veteran or the wife of a disabled veteran and an Oregon resident; may be used at college, vocational school or any accredited school anywhere. Based on ability, aptitude, character, determination, seriousness of purpose and financial need.
HOW TO APPLY: Apply on Department forms, available from the Department Secretary or the Department of Education Chairperson. Submit with required letters of recommendation and 500-word essay titled "Look to the Future," signed by the Unit President and the Education Chairman of the sponsoring unit to Local American Legion Auxiliary Unit. For information and applications, write Department Education Chairperson, 2525 NE 39th Avenue, Portland OR 97212 or The Department Office, American Legion Auxiliary, P.O. Box 1730, Wilsonville, OR 97070.
NUMBER OF AWARDS: 1
RENEWABLE: No

CONTACT: Angie McKinney, Department Education Chairman
ADDITIONAL INFORMATION: For further information, see "Need a Lift" which is available in the office of your Counselor or Library or write the Education and Scholarship Chairperson.

3171—AMERICAN LEGION AUXILIARY (National/Girl Scout Achievement Award)

National Headquarters
777 N. Meridian, Third Floor
Indianapolis IN 46204-1420
317/955-3845
FAX: 317/955-3884
E-mail: alahq@legion-aux.org
Internet: http://www.legion-aux.org/scholarships/index.aspx
AMOUNT: $1,000 ($500/year for 2 years)
DEADLINE(S): FEB 10
FIELD(S): All
ELIGIBILITY/REQUIREMENTS: Open to Girl Scouts who have received Girl Scout Gold Award; must be active member of religious institution having received appropriate religious emblem, Cadette or Senior Scout level; must demonstrate practical citizenship in religious institution, school, Girl Scouting, and community. A parent must have served in a war from WWI to the present. Must be used for undergraduate study in a state accredited school or, if a resident of a U.S. territory, may be used in that territory.
HOW TO APPLY: See website for application; submit with at least 1 letter of recommendation from religious institution, school, community, and/or scouting; an essay describing Gold Award project and explaining why you chose the project and the impact it made on you and your community. Submit to your local American Legion Auxiliary Unit.
NUMBER OF AWARDS: 1
CONTACT: Unit of which applicant is a member

3172—AMERICAN LEGION AUXILIARY (National/Non-Traditional Student Scholarships)

National Headquarters
777 N. Meridian, Third Floor
Indianapolis IN 46204-1420
317/955-3845
FAX: 317/955-3884
E-mail: alahq@legion-aux.org
Internet: http://www.legion-aux.org/scholarships/index.aspx
AMOUNT: $1,000
DEADLINE(S): MAR 1
FIELD(S): All

ELIGIBILITY/REQUIREMENTS: Must be a member of the American Legion or the Auxiliary, or Sons of the American Legion and shall have paid dues for the 2 preceding years and for the calendar year in which application is made; a non-traditional student returning to the classroom after some period of time in which his/her formal education was interrupted or a student who has had at least 1 year of college and is in need of financial assistance to pursue an undergraduate degree. Based on need, scholastic standing/academic achievement, character/leadership, and initiative/goals (25% each).
HOW TO APPLY: Send application, signed by the Unit President and the Education Chairman of the unit sponsoring the applicant with copies of veteran's DD 214, high school transcript, college transcript (if applicable), work history, and FAFSA.
NUMBER OF AWARDS: 5 (1 in each of 5 divisions)
CONTACT: Send applications to Local American Legion Auxiliary Unit; for information and applications, contact Mona Craigg, Department Education Chairman, 1762 Camino, Forest Grove OR 97116 or The Department Office of the American Legion Auxiliary, P.O. Box 1730, Wilsonville OR 97070.
ADDITIONAL INFORMATION: Spirit of Youth Scholarship recipients are not eligible. No Unit may enter more than one candidate in the Department competition. Each Department is restricted to submitting 1 candidate to the Divisional competition. Each Unit and Department is responsible for verifying applications and accompanying material.

3173—AMERICAN LEGION AUXILIARY (National President's Scholarship)

National Headquarters
777 N. Meridian, Third Floor
Indianapolis IN 46204-1420
317/955-3845
FAX: 317/955-3884
E-mail: alahq@legion-aux.org
Internet: http://www.legion-aux.org/scholarships/index.aspx
AMOUNT: $1,000; $2,000; $2,500
DEADLINE(S): MAR 1
FIELD(S): All
ELIGIBILITY/REQUIREMENTS: Must be child or grandchild (including stepchildren) of veterans serving in the Armed Forces during eligibility dates for membership in the American Legion, a senior in high school at time of application, and have completed 50 hours of community service. Judging is based on scholarship

(40%) and character/leadership, essay/application, and financial need (20% each).
HOW TO APPLY: Submit application (see website) through local unit. Submit with 4 letters of recommendation: 1 from either the principal or guidance counselor of the school from which the applicant will graduate; 1 from clergy of the applicant's choice; and 2 from adult citizens, other than relatives, attesting to the applicant's character in regard to conduct, citizenship, and leadership. Also required are an original article of no more than 1,000 words titled "Proud to Be an American—Keeping the Wave of Patriotism Strong"; a letter from a recipient organization verifying fifty (50) hours of voluntary service; a certified transcript of the applicant's high school grades; ACT or SAT scores; and a brief statement documenting military service of parent or parents or copy of discharge papers.
NUMBER OF AWARDS: 15 nationally (3 per year per division)
RENEWABLE: No
CONTACT: Local or closest American Legion Auxiliary Unit
ADDITIONAL INFORMATION: No Unit may enter more than one candidate in the Department competition. Each Department is restricted to submitting 1 candidate to the Divisional competition. Each Unit and Department is responsible for verifying applications and accompanying material.

3174—AMERICAN LEGION AUXILIARY (National/Samsung Scholarship)

National Headquarters
777 N. Meridian, Third Floor
Indianapolis IN 46204-1420
317/955-3845
FAX: 317/955-3884
E-mail: alahq@legion-aux.org
Internet: http://www.legion-aux.org/scholarships/index.aspx
AMOUNT: $20,000 and $1,000
DEADLINE(S): Varies
FIELD(S): All
ELIGIBILITY/REQUIREMENTS: Open to high school juniors who participate in and complete either an American Legion Boys State or Girls State program and be a direct descendant (child, grandchild, great-grandchild or a legally adopted child) of a U.S. veteran who served during a period of war. Based on academic record; involvement in school activities; involvement in community activities; community service; financial need. Additional bonus points awarded to descendants of U.S. veterans of the Korean War. To be used for under-

graduate study only including tuition, books, fees, and room and board.

HOW TO APPLY: Send application to Local American Legion Auxiliary Unit; with 1 letter from principal or guidance counselor (letter to include size of class and ranking) and GPA; 1 letter from clergy person, and 2 letters from adult citizens, other than relatives, attesting to applicant's character, citizenship, and leadership, an essay of no more than 1,000 words titled "Forward Thinking—Using My Education to Impact Society," a certified transcript, FAFSA FORM, and a copy of ACT or SAT scores.

NUMBER OF AWARDS: Approximately 7 ($20,000); approximately 90 ($1,000)

ADDITIONAL INFORMATION: See http://www.legion.org/?content=gi_samsungsch&section=community&subsection=com_edaid&subsection2=com_scholarships

3175—AMERICAN LEGION AUXILIARY (National/Spirit of Youth Scholarship for Junior Members)

National Headquarters
777 N. Meridian, Third Floor
Indianapolis IN 46204-1420
317/955-3845
FAX: 317/955-3884
E-mail: alahq@legion-aux.org
Internet: http://www.legion-aux.org/scholarships/index.aspx

AMOUNT: $1,000
DEADLINE(S): MAR 1
FIELD(S): All

ELIGIBILITY/REQUIREMENTS: Must be/have been junior member of Auxiliary for past 3 years and continue membership throughout the term of the scholarship. Must be senior in accredited high school to apply with 3.0 GPA. Use of scholarship must begin within 24 months from notification.

HOW TO APPLY: Send application to Local American Legion Auxiliary Unit; with 1 letter from principal or guidance counselor (letter to include size of class and ranking) and GPA; 1 letter from clergy person, and 2 letters from adult citizens, other than relatives, attesting to applicant's character, citizenship, and leadership, an essay of no more than 1,000 words titled "Forward Thinking—Using My Education to Impact Society," a certified transcript, FAFSA FORM, and a copy of ACT or SAT scores.

NUMBER OF AWARDS: 5 (1 in each of 5 divisions)
RENEWABLE: Yes (up to 4 years)

3176—AMERICAN LEGION (Department of Pennsylvania/Joseph P. Gavenonis Scholarship)

P.O. Box 2324
Harrisburg PA 17105-2324
717/730-9100
FAX: 717/975-2836
E-mail: debbie@PA-legion.com

AMOUNT: $150
DEADLINE(S): APR 15
FIELD(S): All

ELIGIBILITY/REQUIREMENTS: Must be high school senior in Pennsylvania, planning to seek a 4-year degree in a Pennsylvania college or university; child of Pennsylvania member in good standing or member who is deceased, killed in action or missing in action.

HOW TO APPLY: Request application from Legion.

RENEWABLE: Yes. Up to 4 years; based on grades.

CONTACT: Scholarship Secretary

3177—AMERICAN LEGION (Department of Pennsylvania/Robert W. Valimont Endowment)

P.O. Box 2324
Harrisburg PA 17105-2324
717/730-9100
FAX: 717/975-2836
E-mail: debbie@PA-legion.com

AMOUNT: $150
DEADLINE(S): APR 15
FIELD(S): All

ELIGIBILITY/REQUIREMENTS: Must be high school senior in Pennsylvania, planning to seek career-oriented education or training in a less than 4-year program in Pennsylvania; child of Pennsylvania member in good standing or member who is deceased, killed or missing in action.

HOW TO APPLY: Request application from Legion.

RENEWABLE: Yes. Up to 4 years; based on grades.

CONTACT: Scholarship Secretary

3178—AMERICAN LEGION (Department of Washington/Children & Youth Scholarship Fund)

P.O. Box 3917
Lacey WA 98509-3917
360/491-4373
FAX: 360/491-7442
E-mail: americanlegion@walegion.net

AMOUNT: $1,500-$2,500
DEADLINE(S): APR 1

FIELD(S): All

ELIGIBILITY/REQUIREMENTS: Must be child of a member (living or deceased) of The American Legion, Department of Washington, or its Auxiliary, in good standing; high school senior; planning to attend any accredited or recognized institution of higher education or trade or vocational school in Washington state.

HOW TO APPLY: Send application, approved by the local American Legion Post and signed by the Post Commander; personal letter explaining why you are applying and the goals toward which you are working; 3 references; and a letter of recommendation from school principal or counselor.

NUMBER OF AWARDS: 2 (1 at $1,500 and 1 at $2,500)

3179—AMERICAN LEGION (Department of Illinois Boy Scout Scholarships)

P.O. Box 2910
Bloomington IL 61702-2910
309/663-0361

AMOUNT: $1,000; $200
DEADLINE(S): APR 15
FIELD(S): All

ELIGIBILITY/REQUIREMENTS: Open to high school seniors who are Boy Scouts or Explorer Scouts, Illinois residents, and U.S. citizens. Academic achievement and financial need considered.

HOW TO APPLY: Contact local Boy Scout Office or Legion Boy Scout Chairman for application and information. Submit with 500-word essay on Legion's Americanism and Boy Scout programs.

NUMBER OF AWARDS: 5 (1, $1,000; 4, $200)

3180—AMERICAN LEGION (Department of Illinois Scholarship Program)

P.O. Box 2910
Bloomington IL 61702-2910
309/663-0361

AMOUNT: $1,000
DEADLINE(S): MAR 15
FIELD(S): All

ELIGIBILITY/REQUIREMENTS: Open to high school seniors who are children of Illinois American Legion members. Tenable at recognized undergraduate colleges, universities, and vocational or nursing schools. Academic achievement and financial need are considered. Must be U.S. citizen.

HOW TO APPLY: Contact Illinois De566, Department of the American Legion, for an application.

NUMBER OF AWARDS: 20

3181—AMERICAN LEGION (Department of Iowa Boy Scout of the Year Contest Scholarship)

720 Lyon Street
Des Moines IA 50309
515/282-5068
AMOUNT: $2,000 (1st), $1,500 (2nd), $1,000 (3rd)
DEADLINE(S): FEB 1
FIELD(S): All
ELIGIBILITY/REQUIREMENTS: Must have received the Eagle Scout award. Based on outstanding service to religious institution, school, and community. For undergraduate study at an Iowa college or university.
HOW TO APPLY: Write for complete information.

3182—AMERICAN LEGION (Department of Iowa Oratorical Contest Scholarship)

720 Lyon Street
Des Moines IA 50309
515/282-5068
Des Moines IA 50309
AMOUNT: $2,000 (1st), $1,500 (2nd), $1,000 (3rd)
DEADLINE(S): DEC 1
FIELD(S): All
ELIGIBILITY/REQUIREMENTS: Contest based on the U.S. Constitution is open to Iowa high school students in the 9th through 12th grades. Prizes are in the form of scholarships to attend a college or university in Iowa.
HOW TO APPLY: Write for complete information.

3183—AMERICAN LEGION (Department of Kansas /Dr. "Click" Cowger Scholarship)

1314 SW Topeka Boulevard
Topeka KS 66612-1886
785/232-9315
FAX: 785/232-1399
E-mail: yunker@ksamlegion.org
Internet: http://www.ksamlegion.org
AMOUNT: $500
DEADLINE(S): JUL 15
FIELD(S): Any field of study
ELIGIBILITY/REQUIREMENTS: Open to players of Kansas American Legion Baseball, who are high school seniors, college freshmen, and sophomores. Must be used at an approved Kansas college, university, or trade school.
HOW TO APPLY: Write for information.

3184—AMERICAN LEGION-KANSAS (Department of Kansas Scholarships/Paul Flaherty Athletic Scholarship)

1314 SW Topeka Boulevard
Topeka KS 66612-1886
785/232-9315
FAX: 785/232-1399
E-mail: yunker@ksamlegion.org
Internet: http://www.ksamlegion.org
AMOUNT: $250
DEADLINE(S): JUL 15
FIELD(S): All
ELIGIBILITY/REQUIREMENTS: Open to any Kansas boy or girl who has participated in any form of Kansas high school athletics. Scholarship must be used at an approved Kansas college, university, or trade school.
HOW TO APPLY: Write to above address for complete information.

3185—AMERICAN LEGION (Department of Kansas Scholarships/Ted and Nora Anderson Scholarship Fund; Albert M. Lappin Scholarship; Hugh A. Smith Scholarship)

1314 SW Topeka Boulevard
Topeka KS 66612-1886
785/232-9315
FAX: 785/232-1399
E-mail: yunker@ksamlegion.org
Internet: http://www.ksamlegion.org
AMOUNT: $500-$1,000
DEADLINE(S): FEB 15
FIELD(S): Any field of study
ELIGIBILITY/REQUIREMENTS: Open to children of Kansas Legion and Auxiliary members; must be high school seniors, college freshmen, or sophomores. Scholarships must be at an approved Kansas college, university or trade school.
HOW TO APPLY: Write for information.

3186—AMERICAN LEGION (National/Eagle Scout of the Year Scholarship)

P.O. Box 1055
Indianapolis IN 46206
317/630-1200
FAX: 317/630-1223
Internet: http://www.legion.org/get involved/gi edaid
scholarships.htm#eagle
AMOUNT: 1st $10,000; 2nd $2,500
DEADLINE(S): MAR 1 (to state or dept.); APR 1 (national)
FIELD(S): All
ELIGIBILITY/REQUIREMENTS: Open to Eagle Scout; must be an active member of Boy Scout Troop, Varsity Scout Team, or Explorer Post, and the son or grandson of Legionnaire or Auxiliary member. Must have received a Boy Scout religious emblem; demonstrated practical citizenship in church, school, scouting, and community; and be 15-18.
HOW TO APPLY: Apply through American Legion State Headquarters.
NUMBER OF AWARDS: 1, 1st; 3, 2nd

3187—AMERICAN LEGION (National/Baseball Scholarship)

P.O. Box 1055
Indianapolis IN 46206
317/630-1213
FAX: 317/630-1369
E-mail: acy@legion.org
Internet: http://www.baseball.
legion.org
AMOUNT: $1,000
DEADLINE(S): JUL 15
FIELD(S): All
ELIGIBILITY/REQUIREMENTS: Must be high school graduate on the current roster (American Legion National Baseball registration form #1) that has been filed with National Headquarters, and on a team affiliated with an American Legion Post. Based on leadership, citizenship, character, and financial need.
HOW TO APPLY: Obtain application from American Legion State Headquarters; submit with 3 letters of testimony attached to application form.
NUMBER OF AWARDS: 51
RENEWABLE: Yes
CONTACT: Jim Quinlan, Program Coordinator

3188—AMERICAN MORGAN HORSE INSTITUTE (AMHI Educational Scholarships)

P.O. Box 519
Shelburne VT 05482-0519
802/985-8477
FAX: 802/985-8430
E-mail: info@morganhorse.com
Internet: http://www.morgan
horse.com
AMOUNT: $3,000
DEADLINE(S): MAR 1
FIELD(S): All
ELIGIBILITY/REQUIREMENTS: Based on ability and aptitude for serious study, community service, leadership, financial need, and achievement with Morgan horses.

HOW TO APPLY: Requests for applications MUST include a SASE or download application from website; click on "Youth" then "Scholarships."
NUMBER OF AWARDS: 5

3189—AMERICAN MORGAN HORSE INSTITUTE (AMHI International Morgan Connection Scholarships)

P.O. Box 519
Shelburne VT 05482-0519
802/985-8477
FAX: 802/985-8430
E-mail: info@morganhorse.com
Internet: http://www.morgan
horse.com
AMOUNT: $2,000
DEADLINE(S): MAR 1
FIELD(S): All
ELIGIBILITY/REQUIREMENTS: Open to Morgan youth exhibitor competing in Western Seat, Hunter Seat, Saddle Seat.
HOW TO APPLY: Requests for applications MUST include a SASE or download application from website; click on "Youth" then "Scholarships."
NUMBER OF AWARDS: 3

3190—AMERICAN RADIO RELAY LEAGUE FOUNDATION (Albert H. Hix, W8AH, Memorial Scholarship)

225 Main Street
Newington CT 06111
860/594-0397
FAX: 860/594-0259
E-mail: foundation@arrl.org
Internet: http://www.arrlf.org/
AMOUNT: $500
DEADLINE(S): FEB 1
FIELD(S): All
ELIGIBILITY/REQUIREMENTS: Open to radio amateurs holding at least a general class license attending any accredited institution beyond high school. Preference given to residents of West Virginia in the West Virginia Section or the Roanoke Division or school attendance in the West Virginia Section. Must have GPA of at least 3.0. Graduating high school students will be considered before current college students.
HOW TO APPLY: See website or contact Foundation for information and application. Submit with a 1-page essay on the role amateur radio has played in your life. A recent high school (or equivalent) or college transcript required; submit with application or mail separately.
NUMBER OF AWARDS: 1
RENEWABLE: Yes (to completion of advanced degree)

CONTACT: Mary M. Hobart, K1MMH, Secretary

3191—AMERICAN RADIO RELAY LEAGUE FOUNDATION (Albuquerque ARC/Toby Cross Scholarships)

225 Main Street
Newington CT 06111
860/594-0397
FAX: 860/594-0259
E-mail: foundation@arrl.org
Internet: http://www.arrlf.org/
AMOUNT: $500
DEADLINE(S): FEB 1
FIELD(S): All
ELIGIBILITY/REQUIREMENTS: Open to radio amateurs holding any class of license who are residents of New Mexico working on an undergraduate degree.
HOW TO APPLY: See website or contact Foundation for information and application. Submit with a 1-page essay on the role amateur radio has played in your life. A recent high school (or equivalent) or college transcript required; submit with application or mail separately.
NUMBER OF AWARDS: 1
RENEWABLE: No
CONTACT: Mary M. Hobart, K1MMH, Secretary

3192—AMERICAN RADIO RELAY LEAGUE FOUNDATION (ARRL Scholarship Honoring Senator Barry Goldwater, K7UGA)

225 Main Street
Newington CT 06111
860/594-0397
FAX: 860/594-0259
E-mail: foundation@arrl.org
Internet: http://www.arrlf.org/
AMOUNT: $5,000
DEADLINE(S): FEB 1
FIELD(S): All
ELIGIBILITY/REQUIREMENTS: Open to students who are licensed radio amateurs (at least novice level) and enrolled full time as a bachelor's or graduate student at a regionally accredited institution.
HOW TO APPLY: See website or contact Foundation for information and application. Submit with a 1-page essay on the role amateur radio has played in your life. A recent high school (or equivalent) or college transcript required; submit with application or mail separately.
NUMBER OF AWARDS: 1
RENEWABLE: No
CONTACT: Mary M. Hobart, K1MMH, Secretary

3193—AMERICAN RADIO RELAY LEAGUE FOUNDATION (Central Arizona DX Association Scholarship)

225 Main Street
Newington CT 06111
860/594-0397
FAX: 860/594-0259
E-mail: foundation@arrl.org
Internet: http://www.arrlf.org/
AMOUNT: $500
DEADLINE(S): FEB 1
FIELD(S): All
ELIGIBILITY/REQUIREMENTS: For undergraduate or graduate residents of Illinois or resident of ARRL Central Division (IL, IN, WI) who hold a technician's or higher amateur radio license with minimum cumulative GPA of 3.2. Preference given to graduating high school students.
HOW TO APPLY: See website or contact Foundation for information and application. Submit with a 1-page essay on the role amateur radio has played in your life. A recent high school (or equivalent) or college transcript required; submit with application or mail separately.
NUMBER OF AWARDS: 1
RENEWABLE: No
CONTACT: Mary M. Hobart, K1MMH, Secretary

3194—AMERICAN RADIO RELAY LEAGUE FOUNDATION (Challenge Met Scholarship)

225 Main Street
Newington CT 06111
860/594-0397
FAX: 860/594-0259
E-mail: foundation@arrl.org
Internet: http://www.arrlf.org/
AMOUNT: $500
DEADLINE(S): FEB 1
FIELD(S): All
ELIGIBILITY/REQUIREMENTS: Open to radio amateurs holding any class license to attend any accredited 10- or 4-year college, university or technical school. Preference will be given to an applicant with a documented learning disability (by school or physician) and indications that the applicant is putting forth substantial effort regardless of resulting academic grades.
HOW TO APPLY: See website or contact Foundation for information and application. Submit with a 1-page essay on the role amateur radio has played in your life. A recent high school (or equivalent) or college transcript required; submit with application or mail separately.
NUMBER OF AWARDS: Multiple

RENEWABLE: No
CONTACT: Mary M. Hobart, K1MMH, Secretary

3195—AMERICAN RADIO RELAY LEAGUE FOUNDATION (Charles Clarke Cordle Memorial Scholarship)

225 Main Street
Newington CT 06111
860/594-0397
FAX: 860/594-0259
E-mail: foundation@arrl.org
Internet: http://www.arrlf.org/
AMOUNT: $1,000
DEADLINE(S): FEB 1
FIELD(S): All
ELIGIBILITY/REQUIREMENTS: For undergraduate or graduate residents of Georgia or Alabama who hold any class of amateur radio license. Must attend school in Georgia or Alabama and have a minimum 2.5 GPA.
HOW TO APPLY: See website or contact Foundation for information and application. Submit with a 1-page essay on the role amateur radio has played in your life. A recent high school (or equivalent) or college transcript required; submit with application or mail separately.
NUMBER OF AWARDS: 1
RENEWABLE: No
CONTACT: Mary M. Hobart, K1MMH, Secretary

3196—AMERICAN RADIO RELAY LEAGUE FOUNDATION (Chicago FM Club Scholarships)

225 Main Street
Newington CT 06111
860/594-0397
FAX: 860/594-0259
E-mail: foundation@arrl.org
Internet: http://www.arrlf.org/
AMOUNT: $500
DEADLINE(S): FEB 1
FIELD(S): All
ELIGIBILITY/REQUIREMENTS: Open to radio amateurs holding a technician license who are residents of the FCC Ninth Call District (IN, IL, WI). Students must be in a postsecondary course of study at an accredited 2- or 4-year college or trade school. Must be U.S. citizen or within three months of citizenship.
HOW TO APPLY: See website or contact Foundation for information and application. Submit with a 1-page essay on the role amateur radio has played in your life. A recent high school (or equivalent) or col-

lege transcript required; submit with application or mail separately.
NUMBER OF AWARDS: Multiple
RENEWABLE: No
CONTACT: Mary M. Hobart, K1MMH, Secretary

3197—AMERICAN RADIO RELAY LEAGUE FOUNDATION (Dayton Amateur Radio Association Scholarships)

225 Main Street
Newington CT 06111
860/594-0397
FAX: 860/594-0259
E-mail: foundation@arrl.org
Internet: http://www.arrlf.org/
AMOUNT: $1,000
DEADLINE(S): FEB 1
FIELD(S): All
ELIGIBILITY/REQUIREMENTS: Open to radio amateurs holding any class license attending an accredited 2- or 4-year college.
HOW TO APPLY: See website or contact Foundation for information and application. Submit with a 1-page essay on the role amateur radio has played in your life. A recent high school (or equivalent) or college transcript required; submit with application or mail separately.
NUMBER OF AWARDS: 4
RENEWABLE: No
CONTACT: Mary M. Hobart, K1MMH, Secretary

3198—AMERICAN RADIO RELAY LEAGUE FOUNDATION (Eugene "Gene" Sallee [W4YFR] Memorial Scholarship)

225 Main Street
Newington CT 06111
860/594-0397
FAX: 860/594-0259
E-mail: foundation@arrl.org
Internet: http://www.arrlf.org/
AMOUNT: $500
DEADLINE(S): FEB 1
FIELD(S): All
ELIGIBILITY/REQUIREMENTS: Open to radio amateurs holding a technician plus license who are residents of Georgia. Must have a minimum 3.0 GPA.
HOW TO APPLY: See website or contact Foundation for information and application. Submit with a 1-page essay on the role amateur radio has played in your life. A recent high school (or equivalent) or college transcript required; submit with application or mail separately.
NUMBER OF AWARDS: 1
RENEWABLE: No

CONTACT: Mary M. Hobart, K1MMH, Secretary

3199—AMERICAN RADIO RELAY LEAGUE FOUNDATION (Francis Walton Memorial Scholarship)

225 Main Street
Newington CT 06111
860/594-0397
FAX: 860/594-0259
E-mail: foundation@arrl.org
Internet: http://www.arrlf.org/
AMOUNT: $500
DEADLINE(S): FEB 1
FIELD(S): All
ELIGIBILITY/REQUIREMENTS: For undergraduate or graduate residents of Illinois or resident of ARRL Central Division (IL, IN, WI) who hold a 5WPM or higher amateur radio license seeking baccalaureate or higher degree and attending a regionally accredited institution.
HOW TO APPLY: See website or contact Foundation for information and application. Submit with a 1-page essay on the role amateur radio has played in your life. A recent high school (or equivalent) or college transcript required; submit with application or mail separately.
NUMBER OF AWARDS: 1 or more
RENEWABLE: No
CONTACT: Mary M. Hobart, K1MMH, Secretary

3200—AMERICAN RADIO RELAY LEAGUE FOUNDATION (General Fund Scholarships)

225 Main Street
Newington CT 06111
860/594-0397
FAX: 860/594-0259
E-mail: foundation@arrl.org
Internet: http://www.arrlf.org/
AMOUNT: $1,000
DEADLINE(S): FEB 1
FIELD(S): All
ELIGIBILITY/REQUIREMENTS: Open to undergraduate or graduate students holding any level amateur radio license.
HOW TO APPLY: See website or contact Foundation for information and application. Submit with a 1-page essay on the role amateur radio has played in your life. A recent high school (or equivalent) or college transcript required; submit with application or mail separately.
NUMBER OF AWARDS: Multiple
RENEWABLE: No
CONTACT: Mary M. Hobart, K1MMH, Secretary

3201—AMERICAN RADIO RELAY LEAGUE FOUNDATION (IRARC Memorial/Josesph P. Rubino [WA4MMD] Scholarship)

225 Main Street
Newington CT 06111
860/594-0397
FAX: 860/594-0259
E-mail: foundation@arrl.org
Internet: http://www.arrlf.org/
AMOUNT: Approximately $750
DEADLINE(S): FEB 1
FIELD(S): All (undergraduate) or electronic technician (certification program)
ELIGIBILITY/REQUIREMENTS: Open to radio amateurs holding any class of license, residents of Florida (preferably Brevard County) working on an undergraduate degree or in an electronic technician certification program at an accredited institution. Minimum GPA 2.5; however, preference given to students with lower GPA who demonstrate financial need over those with higher GPA but limited need.
HOW TO APPLY: See website or contact Foundation for information and application. Submit with FAFSA and a 1-page essay on the role amateur radio has played in your life. A recent high school (or equivalent) or college transcript required; submit with application or mail separately.
NUMBER OF AWARDS: Multiple (as income allows and as qualified candidates are identified)
RENEWABLE: No
CONTACT: Mary M. Hobart, K1MMH, Secretary

3202—AMERICAN RADIO RELAY LEAGUE FOUNDATION (Jean Cebik Memorial Scholarship)

225 Main Street
Newington CT 06111
860/594-0397
FAX: 860/594-0259
E-mail: foundation@arrl.org
Internet: http://www.arrlf.org/
AMOUNT: $1,000
DEADLINE(S): FEB 1
FIELD(S): All
ELIGIBILITY/REQUIREMENTS: Open to radio amateurs holding at least a technician license attending or attending a 4-year college or university.
HOW TO APPLY: See website or contact Foundation for information and application. Submit with a 1-page essay on the role amateur radio has played in your life. A recent high school (or equivalent) or college transcript required; submit with application or mail separately.

NUMBER OF AWARDS: 1
RENEWABLE: No
CONTACT: Mary M. Hobart, K1MMH, Secretary

3203—AMERICAN RADIO RELAY LEAGUE FOUNDATION (Louisiana Memorial Scholarship)

225 Main Street
Newington CT 06111
860/594-0397
FAX: 860/594-0259
E-mail: foundation@arrl.org
Internet: http://www.arrlf.org/
AMOUNT: $500
DEADLINE(S): FEB 1
FIELD(S): All
ELIGIBILITY/REQUIREMENTS: Open to radio amateurs holding a technician class or higher license who are Louisiana residents or attending 4-year college or university in Louisiana. Minimum 3.0 GPA required.
HOW TO APPLY: See website or contact Foundation for information and application. Submit with a 1-page essay on the role amateur radio has played in your life. A recent high school (or equivalent) or college transcript required; submit with application or mail separately.
NUMBER OF AWARDS: Multiple
RENEWABLE: No
CONTACT: Mary M. Hobart, K1MMH, Secretary

3204—AMERICAN RADIO RELAY LEAGUE FOUNDATION (Martin J. Green Sr. [K2TEO] Memorial Scholarship)

225 Main Street
Newington CT 06111
860/594-0397
FAX: 860/594-0259
E-mail: foundation@arrl.org
Internet: http://www.arrlf.org/
AMOUNT: $1,000
DEADLINE(S): FEB 1
FIELD(S): All
ELIGIBILITY/REQUIREMENTS: Open to undergraduate or graduate students holding any level amateur radio license. Preference given to a student ham from a ham family.
HOW TO APPLY: See website or contact Foundation for information and application. Submit with a 1-page essay on the role amateur radio has played in your life. A recent high school (or equivalent) or college transcript required; submit with application or mail separately.
NUMBER OF AWARDS: 1
RENEWABLE: No

CONTACT: Mary M. Hobart, K1MMH, Secretary

3205—AMERICAN RADIO RELAY LEAGUE FOUNDATION (Mary Lou Brown Scholarship)

225 Main Street
Newington CT 06111
860/594-0397
FAX: 860/594-0259
E-mail: foundation@arrl.org
Internet: http://www.arrlf.org/
AMOUNT: $2,500
DEADLINE(S): FEB 1
FIELD(S): All
ELIGIBILITY/REQUIREMENTS: Open to residents of the ARRL Northwest Division (Arkansas, Idaho, Montana, Oregon, Washington) who are radio amateurs holding at least a general license and have demonstrated interest in promoting Amateur Radio Service. For study leading to a bachelor's degree or higher course of study. Must have GPA of at least 3.0 and a demonstrated interest in promoting the Amateur Radio Service.
HOW TO APPLY: See website or contact Foundation for information and application. Submit with a 1-page essay on the role amateur radio has played in your life. A recent high school (or equivalent) or college transcript required; submit with application or mail separately.
NUMBER OF AWARDS: Varies
RENEWABLE: No
CONTACT: Mary M. Hobart, K1MMH, Secretary

3206—AMERICAN RADIO RELAY LEAGUE FOUNDATION (NCDXF Scholarship)

225 Main Street
Newington CT 06111
860/594-0397
FAX: 860/594-0259
E-mail: foundation@arrl.org
Internet: http://www.arrlf.org/
AMOUNT: $1,000
DEADLINE(S): FEB 1
FIELD(S): All
ELIGIBILITY/REQUIREMENTS: Open to students who are radio amateurs with a technician license or higher attending a 4-year college or university or trade school in the U.S. Preference given to student demonstrating interest and activity in DXing.
HOW TO APPLY: See website or contact Foundation for information and application. Submit with a 1-page essay on the role amateur radio has played in your life. A recent high school (or equivalent) or

college transcript required; submit with application or mail separately.
NUMBER OF AWARDS: 4
RENEWABLE: No
CONTACT: Mary M. Hobart, K1MMH, Secretary

3207—AMERICAN RADIO RELAY LEAGUE FOUNDATION (New England FEMARA Scholarships)

225 Main Street
Newington CT 06111
860/594-0397
FAX: 860/594-0259
E-mail: foundation@arrl.org
Internet: http://www.arrlf.org/
AMOUNT: $1,000
DEADLINE(S): FEB 1
FIELD(S): All
ELIGIBILITY/REQUIREMENTS: Open to residents of the New England states (ME, NH, VT, MA, CT, RI) who are radio amateurs with a technician license.
HOW TO APPLY: See website or contact Foundation for information and application. Submit with a 1-page essay on the role amateur radio has played in your life. A recent high school (or equivalent) or college transcript required; submit with application or mail separately.
NUMBER OF AWARDS: Multiple
RENEWABLE: No
CONTACT: Mary M. Hobart, K1MMH, Secretary

3208—AMERICAN RADIO RELAY LEAGUE FOUNDATION (Norman E. Strohmeier [W2VRS] Memorial Scholarship)

225 Main Street
Newington CT 06111
860/594-0397
FAX: 860/594-0259
E-mail: foundation@arrl.org
Internet: http://www.arrlf.org/
AMOUNT: $500
DEADLINE(S): FEB 1
FIELD(S): All
ELIGIBILITY/REQUIREMENTS: Open to radio amateurs holding at least a technician license who are residents of Western New York. Must have GPA of at least 3.2. Graduating high school students will be considered before current college students.
HOW TO APPLY: See website or contact Foundation for information and application. Submit with a 1-page essay on the role amateur radio has played in your life. A recent high school (or equivalent) or college transcript required; submit with application or mail separately.
NUMBER OF AWARDS: 1

RENEWABLE: No
CONTACT: Mary M. Hobart, K1MMH, Secretary

3209—AMERICAN RADIO RELAY LEAGUE FOUNDATION (North Texas Section-Bob Nelson [KB5BNU] Memorial Scholarship)

225 Main Street
Newington CT 06111
860/594-0397
FAX: 860/594-0259
E-mail: foundation@arrl.org
Internet: http://www.arrlf.org/
AMOUNT: $750
DEADLINE(S): FEB 1
FIELD(S): All
ELIGIBILITY/REQUIREMENTS: For radio amateurs with any class of license who are residents of Texas or Oklahoma. Must be enrolled in a full-time degree program, minimum 12 credit hours per semester. Character, humanitarianism, and active amateur radio participation are highly important.
HOW TO APPLY: See website or contact Foundation for information and application. Submit with a 1-page essay on the role amateur radio has played in your life. A recent high school (or equivalent) or college transcript required; submit with application or mail separately.
NUMBER OF AWARDS: Multiple
RENEWABLE: No
CONTACT: Mary M. Hobart, K1MMH, Secretary

3210—AMERICAN RADIO RELAY LEAGUE FOUNDATION (Peoria Area Amateur Radio Club Scholarship)

225 Main Street
Newington CT 06111
860/594-0397
FAX: 860/594-0259
E-mail: foundation@arrl.org
Internet: http://www.arrlf.org/
AMOUNT: $500
DEADLINE(S): FEB 1
FIELD(S): All
ELIGIBILITY/REQUIREMENTS: For radio amateurs with technician class or higher license who are residents of Central Illinois (Peoria, Tazewell, Woodford, Knox, McLean, Fulton, Logan, Marshall and Start) enrolled in an accredited 2- or 4-year college or university.
HOW TO APPLY: See website or contact Foundation for information and application. Submit with a 1-page essay on the role amateur radio has played in your life. A recent high school (or equivalent) or col-

lege transcript required; submit with application or mail separately.
NUMBER OF AWARDS: Multiple
RENEWABLE: No
CONTACT: Mary M. Hobart, K1MMH, Secretary

3211—AMERICAN RADIO RELAY LEAGUE FOUNDATION (Richard W. Bendicksen Memorial Scholarship)

225 Main Street
Newington CT 06111
860/594-0397
FAX: 860/594-0259
E-mail: foundation@arrl.org
Internet: http://www.arrlf.org/
AMOUNT: $1,000
DEADLINE(S): FEB 1
FIELD(S): All
ELIGIBILITY/REQUIREMENTS: Open to radio amateurs holding any class of license who are students in a postsecondary course of study leading to an undergraduate degree.
HOW TO APPLY: See website or contact Foundation for information and application. Submit with a 1-page essay on the role amateur radio has played in your life. A recent high school (or equivalent) or college transcript required; submit with application or mail separately.
NUMBER OF AWARDS: 1
RENEWABLE: No
CONTACT: Mary M. Hobart, K1MMH, Secretary

3212—AMERICAN RADIO RELAY LEAGUE FOUNDATION (Seth Horan [K1LOM] Memorial Scholarship)

225 Main Street
Newington CT 06111
860/594-0397
FAX: 860/594-0259
E-mail: foundation@arrl.org
Internet: http://www.arrlf.org/
AMOUNT: $500
DEADLINE(S): FEB 1
FIELD(S): All
ELIGIBILITY/REQUIREMENTS: Open to radio amateurs holding any class of license attending an accredited 4-year college or university.
HOW TO APPLY: See website or contact Foundation for information and application. Submit with a 1-page essay on the role amateur radio has played in your life. A recent high school (or equivalent) or college transcript required; submit with application or mail separately.
NUMBER OF AWARDS: 1
RENEWABLE: No

CONTACT: Mary M. Hobart, K1MMH, Secretary

3213—AMERICAN RADIO RELAY LEAGUE FOUNDATION (Six Meter Club of Chicago Scholarship)

225 Main Street
Newington CT 06111
860/594-0397
FAX: 860/594-0259
E-mail: foundation@arrl.org
Internet: http://www.arrlf.org/
AMOUNT: $500
DEADLINE(S): FEB 1
FIELD(S): All
ELIGIBILITY/REQUIREMENTS: Open to radio amateurs holding any class of license who are students in a postsecondary course of study leading to an undergraduate degree. Must be a resident of Illinois attending any institution in Illinois (technical school, community college, university). If no qualified Illinois student is found, award is open to remaining ARRL Central Division (Indiana and Wisconsin).
HOW TO APPLY: See website or contact Foundation for information and application. Submit with a 1-page essay on the role amateur radio has played in your life. A recent high school (or equivalent) or college transcript required; submit with application or mail separately.
NUMBER OF AWARDS: 1
RENEWABLE: No
CONTACT: Mary M. Hobart, K1MMH, Secretary

3214—AMERICAN RADIO RELAY LEAGUE FOUNDATION (Tom and Judith Comstock Scholarship)

225 Main Street
Newington CT 06111
860/594-0397
FAX: 860/594-0259
E-mail: foundation@arrl.org
Internet: http://www.arrlf.org/
AMOUNT: $2,000
DEADLINE(S): FEB 1
FIELD(S): All
ELIGIBILITY/REQUIREMENTS: For a high school senior who holds any class amateur radio license and is accepted at a 2- or 4-year college. Must be a resident of Texas or Oklahoma.
HOW TO APPLY: See website or contact Foundation for information and application. Submit with a 1-page essay on the role amateur radio has played in your life. A recent high school (or equivalent) or

college transcript required; submit with application or mail separately.
NUMBER OF AWARDS: 1
RENEWABLE: No
CONTACT: Mary M. Hobart, K1MMH, Secretary

3215—AMERICAN RADIO RELAY LEAGUE FOUNDATION (William Bennett [W7PHO] Memorial Scholarship)

225 Main Street
Newington CT 06111
860/594-0397
FAX: 860/594-0259
E-mail: foundation@arrl.org
Internet: http://www.arrlf.org/
AMOUNT: $500
DEADLINE(S): FEB 1
FIELD(S): All
ELIGIBILITY/REQUIREMENTS: Open to residents of the ARRL Northwest, Pacific, or Southwest Division who are radio amateurs holding at least a general license attending a 4-year college or university. Must have GPA of at least 3.0 or ongoing course of study.
HOW TO APPLY: See website or contact Foundation for information and application. Submit with a 1-page essay on the role amateur radio has played in your life. A recent high school (or equivalent) or college transcript required; submit with application or mail separately.
NUMBER OF AWARDS: 1
RENEWABLE: No
CONTACT: Mary M. Hobart, K1MMH, Secretary

3216—AMERICAN RADIO RELAY LEAGUE FOUNDATION (Yankee Clipper Contest Club, Inc. Youth Scholarship)

225 Main Street
Newington CT 06111
860/594-0397
FAX: 860/594-0259
E-mail: foundation@arrl.org
Internet: http://www.arrlf.org/
AMOUNT: $1,000
DEADLINE(S): FEB 1
FIELD(S): All
ELIGIBILITY/REQUIREMENTS: For AARL members who hold a general or higher class license and are residents or attend a 2- or 4-year college or university within 175 miles of Erving MA (MA, RI, CT, Long Island NY, most of VT and NH, and portions of ME, eastern NY, and extreme Northeastern sections of PA and NJ).

HOW TO APPLY: See website or contact Foundation for information and application. Submit with a 1-page essay on the role amateur radio has played in your life. A recent high school (or equivalent) or college transcript required; submit with application or mail separately.
NUMBER OF AWARDS: 1
RENEWABLE: No
CONTACT: Mary M. Hobart, K1MMH, Secretary

3217—AMERICAN RADIO RELAY LEAGUE FOUNDATION ("You've Got a Friend in Pennsylvania" Scholarship)

225 Main Street
Newington CT 06111
860/594-0397
FAX: 860/594-0259
E-mail: foundation@arrl.org
Internet: http://www.arrlf.org/
AMOUNT: $2,000
DEADLINE(S): FEB 1
FIELD(S): All
ELIGIBILITY/REQUIREMENTS: For AARL members who hold a general radio license and are residents of Pennsylvania.
HOW TO APPLY: See website or contact Foundation for information and application. Submit with a 1-page essay on the role amateur radio has played in your life. A recent high school (or equivalent) or college transcript required; submit with application or mail separately.
NUMBER OF AWARDS: 1
RENEWABLE: No
CONTACT: Mary M. Hobart, K1MMH, Secretary

3218—AMERICAN RADIO RELAY LEAGUE FOUNDATION (Zachary Taylor Stevens Memorial Scholarship)

225 Main Street
Newington CT 06111
860/594-0397
FAX: 860/594-0259
E-mail: foundation@arrl.org
Internet: http://www.arrlf.org/
AMOUNT: $750
DEADLINE(S): FEB 1
FIELD(S): All
ELIGIBILITY/REQUIREMENTS: For AARL members who hold a technician class radio license; preference given to residents of the amateur radio call areas of Michigan, Ohio and West Virginia to attend any 2- or 4-year accredited college or university.
HOW TO APPLY: See website or contact Foundation for information and application. Submit with a 1-page essay on the

role amateur radio has played in your life. A recent high school (or equivalent) or college transcript required; submit with application or mail separately.
NUMBER OF AWARDS: 1
RENEWABLE: No
CONTACT: Mary M. Hobart, K1MMH, Secretary

3219—AMERICAN SAVINGS FOUNDATION, INC.

185 Main Street
New Britain CT 06050
860/827-2556
FAX: 860/832-4582
Internet: http://www.asfdn.org
AMOUNT: $500-$2,500
DEADLINE(S): MAR 31
FIELD(S): All
ELIGIBILITY/REQUIREMENTS: Open to college-bound seniors and those enrolled in 2- or 4-year undergraduate programs or accredited technical/vocational programs. Must reside in the Foundation's 64-town service area in Central Connecticut. Based on need; consideration given to academic potential and community service.
HOW TO APPLY: See website for list of towns and complete application materials.
NUMBER OF AWARDS: 110 (average)
RENEWABLE: Yes, must reapply.

3220—AMERICAN WATER SKI EDUCATIONAL FOUNDATION

1251 Holy Cow Road
Polk City FL 33868-8200
863/324-2472, ext. 136
FAX: 863/324-3996
E-mail: awsefhalloffame@cs.com
Internet: http://www.waterski halloffame.com
AMOUNT: $1,500
DEADLINE(S): APR 1
FIELD(S): All
ELIGIBILITY/REQUIREMENTS: Must be an active member of USA Water Ski; a full-time student at a 2- or 4-year accredited college; a U.S. citizen; and incoming college sophomore through an incoming senior.
HOW TO APPLY: After September 15 of preceding year, see website and click on Scholarship; or contact Foundation.
NUMBER OF AWARDS: 6
RENEWABLE: Yes, must reapply.
CONTACT: Carole Lowe

3221—AMERICA'S JUNIOR MISS (Scholarship Competition)

P.O. Box 2786

Mobile AL 36652-2786
800/256-5435
FAX: 251/438-3621
E-mail: ajmiss@ajm.org
Internet: http://ajm.org
AMOUNT: Up to $30,000
DEADLINE(S): Varies (check with State chairperson)
FIELD(S): All
ELIGIBILITY/REQUIREMENTS: Open to college-bound high school senior girls who are U.S. citizens, legal residents of the county and state in which they seek to compete, and have never been married. Must apply your sophomore or junior year. Competition based on interview, talent, scholastic achievement, poise, and fitness.
HOW TO APPLY: Contact America's Junior Miss Program State Chairperson for more information and competition instructions.
NUMBER OF AWARDS: Varies

3222—ANGUS FOUNDATION

3201 Fredrick Avenue
St. Joseph MO 64506
816/383-5100
FAX: 816/233-9703
E-mail: mjenkins@angus foundation.org
Internet: http://www.angus foundation.org or www.njaa.info
AMOUNTS: $5,000 (2), $3,000 (20), $1,000 (30)
DEADLINE(S): MAY 1
FIELD(S): All
ELIGIBILITY/REQUIREMENTS: Junior member of the American Angus Association; see website for details.
HOW TO APPLY: Print application from website.
NUMBER OF AWARDS:
RENEWABLE: See website for details.
CONTACT: Milford H. Jenkins, President, Angus Foundation

3223—ANNA AND CHARLES STOCKWITZ FUND FOR EDUCATION OF JEWISH CHILDREN

1600 Scott Street
San Francisco CA 94115
415/561-1226
AMOUNT: $400-$750
DEADLINE(S): Varies
FIELD(S): All
ELIGIBILITY/REQUIREMENTS: Scholarships for Jewish undergrads who reside in San Francisco, CA.
HOW TO APPLY: High school seniors may apply. Contact fund for complete information.

3224—ANTWERP INTERNATIONAL SCHOOL (Tuition Reduction Grants)

Veltwijcklaan 180
2180 Ekeren BELGIUM
323/543-9300
FAX: 323/541-8201
E-mail: ais@ais-antwerp.be
Internet: http://ais-antwerp.be
AMOUNT: Varies
DEADLINE(S): Varies
FIELD(S): All
ELIGIBILITY/REQUIREMENTS: Grants are open to elementary and secondary students at this private day school. Recipients must demonstrate financial need, and grants may not exceed 50 percent of the tuition fee.
NUMBER OF AWARDS: 50 awards annually
CONTACT: Robert F. Schaecher
HOW TO APPLY: See website.

3225—ARA SCHOLARSHIP FOUNDATION

3975 Fair Ridge Drive,
Suite 20 North
Fairfax VA 22033-2924
703/385-1001
FAX: 703/385-1494
Internet: http://www.a-r-a.org
AMOUNT: Up to $1,000
DEADLINE(S): MAR 15
FIELD(S): All
ELIGIBILITY/REQUIREMENTS: Parent of applicant must be a current employee of a direct member of the Automotive Recyclers Association with hire date at least 1 year prior to March 15 of the application year. Applicant must have 3.0 GPA or equivalent and be pursuing full-time post high school education.
HOW TO APPLY: See website or call to request application.
NUMBER OF AWARDS: Varies
RENEWABLE: Yes. Reapply.

3226—ARKANSAS SINGLE PARENT SCHOLARSHIP FUND

614 East Emma, Suite 119
Springdale AR 72764
501/927-1402
FAX: 501/751-1110
E-mail: lfroelic@jtlshop.jonesnet.org
Internet: http://www.aspsf.org/
AMOUNT: Up to $600/semester
DEADLINE(S): Varies (by county)
FIELD(S): All
ELIGIBILITY/REQUIREMENTS: Open to Arkansas single parents to assist with childcare, transportation, books, tuition,

etc. Recipients must be undergraduates seeking postsecondary certificate or bachelor's degree.

HOW TO APPLY: Each of the 51 county affiliates has its own guidelines; contact your county's office for details and/or an application. Contact information can be found on the ASPSF website.

NUMBER OF AWARDS: Varies by county

RENEWABLE: Yes. Up to 4 years (or equivalent, if part time). See website for additional information.

3227—ARKANSAS STUDENT LOAN AUTHORITY

101 East Capitol, Suite 401
Little Rock AR 72201
501/682-2952
FAX: 501/682-1258
E-mail: lsmith@asla.info
Internet: http://www.asla.info
AMOUNT: $1,000
DEADLINE(S): APR 1
FIELD(S): All

ELIGIBILITY/REQUIREMENTS: Must be either a resident of Arkansas attending an in- or out-of-state 2- or 4-year university, college, technical or trade school or an out-of-state student attending an institution in Arkansas. Must be enrolled for the fall semester and must attend at least half-time. Scholarship is a random drawing.

HOW TO APPLY: Use the online entry form or submit a postcard with your name, address, daytime and home phone numbers, postsecondary education institution's name and address, and tell us if you are an Arkansas resident.

NUMBER OF AWARDS: 20

RENEWABLE: Yes. Must submit a 500-word essay.

CONTACT: Lisa Smith

3228—ARMED FORCES COMMUNICATIONS AND ELECTRONICS ASSOCIATION (AFCEA Sgt. Jeannette L. Winters, USMC Memorial Scholarships)

4400 Fair Lakes Court
Fairfax VA 22033-3899
800/336-4583, ext. 6147 or
703/631-6149
FAX: 703/631-4693
E-mail: scholarships@afcea.org
Internet: http://www.afcea.org
AMOUNT: $2,000
DEADLINE(S): AUG 15-SEP 15 (NOT before)
FIELD(S): All

ELIGIBILITY/REQUIREMENTS: Active duty or honorably-discharged U.S. Marine Corps veteran pursuing an under-

graduate degree at accredited U.S. 4-year institution. Must be sophomore, junior, or senior student enrolled either part or full time in an eligible degree program.

HOW TO APPLY: Applications and further information on website.

3229—ARMENIAN EDUCATIONAL FOUNDATION

Scholarship Committee
600 West Broadway, Suite 130
Glendale CA 91204
818/242-4154
FAX: 818/242-4913
E-mail: aefscholar@aol.com
Internet: http://www.aefweb.org
AMOUNT: $1,000
DEADLINE(S): JUL 30
FIELD(S): All

ELIGIBILITY/REQUIREMENTS: Must be of Armenian descent; demonstrate financial need; perform Armenian community service; be a full-time junior or senior at an accredited U.S. university or college; and have a minimum GPA of 3.0.

HOW TO APPLY: Contact Foundation for application.

NUMBER OF AWARDS: 5

3230—ARMENIAN STUDENTS' ASSOCIATION OF AMERICA, INC.

333 Atlantic Avenue
Warwick RI 02888
401/461-6114
FAX: 401/461-6112
E-mail: headasa@aol.com
Internet: http://www.asainc.org
AMOUNT: $500-$5,000
DEADLINE(S): JAN 15 (deadline for requests), MAR 15 (deadline for submission)
FIELD(S): All

ELIGIBILITY/REQUIREMENTS: Must be of Armenian ancestry and full-time students who will be in their sophomore to senior year at a 4-year accredited college or university in the U.S. Must demonstrate financial need, have good academic performance, show self help, and participate in extracurricular activities.

HOW TO APPLY: Contact ASA Scholarship Committee in the fall to request application forms. $15 application fee.

NUMBER OF AWARDS: 30

CONTACT: Nathalie Yaghoobian, Scholarship Administrator

3231—ARMY EMERGENCY RELIEF (MG James Ursano Scholarship)

200 Stovall Street, Room 5N13

Alexandria VA 22332-0600
703/428-0000
FAX: 703/325-7183
Internet: http://www.aerhq.org
AMOUNT: $1,000-$2,200
DEADLINE(S): MAR 1
FIELD(S): All

ELIGIBILITY/REQUIREMENTS: Open to Army families to assist students in need with tuition, fees, books, or room and board. Based primarily on financial need, as evidenced by income, assets, family size, special financial obligations, and circumstances.

HOW TO APPLY: Contact AER

3232—ARMY ROTC

U.S. Army ROTC Scholarships
Ft. Monroe VA 23651/5238
800/USA-ROTC
Internet: http://www.armyrotc.com
AMOUNT: Tiered tuition scholarships up to $16,000
DEADLINE(S): NOV 15
FIELD(S): All

ELIGIBILITY/REQUIREMENTS: Open to U.S. citizens between the ages of 17 and 27. For undergraduate study at colleges having Army ROTC programs. Must have minimum of 2.5 GPA and SAT score of 920 or ACT score of 19 and meet minimum physical standards.

HOW TO APPLY: Call for application or apply online.

RENEWABLE: Not applicable; awarded for 4, 3, or 2 years.

3233—ASIAN AND PACIFIC ISLANDER AMERICAN SCHOLARSHIP FUND (APIASF)

1900 L Street, NW, Suite 210
Washington DC 20036
877/808-7032
FAX: 202/530-0643
E-mail: info@apiasf.org
Internet: http://www.apiasf.org
AMOUNT: $2,500
DEADLINE(S): JAN 31
FIELD(S): All

ELIGIBILITY/REQUIREMENTS: Must be Asian and/or Pacific islander (as defined by 2000 Census); a U.S. citizen or national, legal permanent resident, or a citizen of the Federated Associated States (Freely Associated States, including the Federated States of Micronesia, Republic of the Marshall Islands, and the Republic of Palau); a first-time, degree-seeking freshman at a 2- or 4-year degree program at a U.S. accredited college or university in the U.S., Guam, American Samoa, Commonwealth of Northern Marina

Islands, or the Freely Associated States. Must have a minimum cumulate GOA of 2.7 or GED equivalent.
HOW TO APPLY: See website for application and other forms (available in October) or write or e-mail for an application and instruction letter. Applicants are strongly encouraged to apply online.
NUMBER OF AWARDS: 200
RENEWABLE: No.
CONTACT: Bernadette Balagot

3234—ASSOCIATES TO THE AMERICAN ACADEMY OF ALLERGY, ASTHMA & IMMUNOLOGY

611 East Wells Street
Milwaukee WI 53202
414/272-6071
FAX: 414/272-6070
E-mail: jaugustyniak@aaaai.org
Internet: http://www.aaaai.org
AMOUNT: $1,000
DEADLINE(S): Early JAN (see website for further details on exact date)
FIELD(S): All
ELIGIBILITY/REQUIREMENTS: Must be senior in high school with asthma (U.S. and Canadian students only).
HOW TO APPLY: Complete online application.
NUMBER OF AWARDS: 1-50
RENEWABLE: No
CONTACT: John L. Augustyniak

3235—ASSOCIATION FOR THE STUDY OF AFRO-AMERICAN LIFE & HISTORY, INC. (Afro-American Life and History Essay Contest)

C.B. Powell Building
525 Bryant Street, Suite C142
Washington DC 20059
202/865-0053
FAX: 202/265-7920
Email: info@asalh.net
Internet: http://asalh.org/EssayContests.html
AMOUNT: $500
DEADLINE(S): JUN 30
FIELD(S): Afro-American Studies
ELIGIBILITY/REQUIREMENTS: Any full-time student in a 2- or 4-year college may enter the competition. Essays may be submitted on any topic that explores the life, history and culture of Africans throughout the Americas and the Caribbean. Papers that are only polemical and offer only personal opinions are not acceptable; a research approach is required. Essays should cite the appropriate primary and secondary sources related to the topic under examination (see website

for further details). Criteria include clarity, organization, originality, and documentation.
HOW TO APPLY: Via e-mail (essaycontest@asalh.net), submit a copy of your paper (see website or e-mail contact below for details) and an endorsement letter from ASALH faculty advisor/sponsor, who must be a current member of ASALH. (An original signed copy of this letter is to be mailed to Felix Armfield, ASALH ESSAY CONTEST at the above address.)
NUMBER OF AWARDS: 1 undergraduate; 1 graduate
CONTACT: Questions MUST be directed to Felix Armfield at armfiefl@buffalostate.edu.
ADDITIONAL INFORMATION: Winning writers will be invited to present their essays at the ASALH Annual Meeting.

3236—ASSOCIATION OF INTERNATIONAL EDUCATION, JAPAN (Honors Scholarships for Private International Students)

4-5-29 Komaba, Meguro-ku
Tokyo 153-8503 JAPAN
03/5454-5213
FAX: 03/5454-5233
Internet: http://www.aiej.or.jp
AMOUNT: ¥52,000-¥73,000
DEADLINE(S): Mid APR
FIELD(S): All
ELIGIBILITY/REQUIREMENTS: Scholarships for study in Japan provided by the Ministry of Education in cooperation with AIEJ. For undergraduate and graduate students of all nationalities enrolled at designated Japanese language institutes, junior colleges, technological or vocational schools, colleges, or universities. Based on recommendations from the scholarship committee at students' college or university in Japan.
HOW TO APPLY: Apply through the school attended.
NUMBER OF AWARDS: 11,000

3237—ASSOCIATION ON AMERICAN INDIAN AFFAIRS (Adolph Van Pelt Scholarships)

Executive Office
966 Hungerford Drive, Suite 12-B
Rockville MD 20850
240/314-7155
FAX: 240/314-7159
E-mail: general.aaia@verizon.net
Internet: http://www.indian-affairs.org
AMOUNT: $1,500
DEADLINE(S): Fall and Spring semesters only

FIELD(S): All
ELIGIBILITY/REQUIREMENTS: Open to full-time undergraduate students who are minimally 1/4 degree Indian blood from a federally recognized tribe. Award is based on financial need and is limited to North America/Alaska.
HOW TO APPLY: See website for application. Please send only the information requested; additional information will not be considered. Must submit essay on need, certificate of enrollment and quantum from your tribe or BIA, transcript, schedule of classes, and current financial aid award letter.
RENEWABLE: Yes. Must reapply. Note: Disbursements of $750 made each semester pending satisfactory progress. No funding for summer semester.
CONTACT: Lisa Wyzlic at lw.aaia@verizon.net or 240/314-7155
ADDITIONAL INFORAMTION: If applying for more than 1 AAIA scholarship, send 1 application package only. Students will be considered for all scholarships they are qualified for.

3238—ASSOCIATION ON AMERICAN INDIAN AFFAIRS (Allogan Slagle Memorial Scholarships)

Executive Office
966 Hungerford Drive, Suite 12-B
Rockville MD 20850
240/314-7155
FAX: 240/314-7159
E-mail: general.aaia@verizon.net
Internet: http://www.indian-affairs.org
AMOUNT: $1,500
DEADLINE(S): Fall and Spring semesters only
FIELD(S): All
ELIGIBILITY/REQUIREMENTS: Open to full-time undergraduate students who are minimally 1/4 degree Indian blood from tribes that are not federally recognized. Award is based on financial need and is limited to North America/Alaska.
HOW TO APPLY: See website for application. Please send only the information requested; additional information will not be considered. Must submit essay on need, certificate of enrollment and quantum from your tribe or BIA, transcript, schedule of classes, and current financial aid award letter.
RENEWABLE: Yes. Must reapply. Note: Disbursements of $750 made each semester pending satisfactory progress. No funding for summer semester.
CONTACT: Lisa Wyzlic at lw.aaia@verizon.net or 240/314-7155

ADDITIONAL INFORAMTION: If applying for more than 1 AAIA scholarship, send 1 application package only. Students will be considered for all scholarships they are qualified for.

3239—ASSOCIATION ON AMERICAN INDIAN AFFAIRS (David Risling Emergency Aid Scholarships)

Executive Office
966 Hungerford Drive, Suite 12-B
Rockville MD 20850
240/314-7155
FAX: 240/314-7159
E-mail: general.aaia@verizon.net
Internet: http://www.indian-affairs.org
AMOUNT: $100-$400 (disbursement based on availability of funds)
DEADLINE(S): Fall and Spring semesters only
FIELD(S): All
ELIGIBILITY/REQUIREMENTS: To be used for acute, temporary emergencies (medical, car, day care, death in family). Open to full-time undergraduate students who are minimally 1/4 degree Indian blood from a federally recognized tribe. Award is based on financial need and is limited to North America/Alaska.
HOW TO APPLY: See website for application; submit with statement and proof of need (for example, receipts/estimates) and mark envelopes Emergency Aid. Please send only the information requested; additional information will not be considered. Must submit essay on need, certificate of enrollment and quantum from your tribe or BIA, transcript, schedule of classes, and current financial aid award letter.
RENEWABLE: Yes except students may receive only 1 scholarship per academic year. No funding for summer semester.
CONTACT: Lisa Wyzlic at lw.aaia@verizon.net or 240/314-7155
ADDITIONAL INFORMATION: If applying for more than 1 AAIA scholarship, send 1 application package only. Students will be considered for all scholarships they are qualified for. Recipient of other AAIA scholarships are not eligible for emergency aid.

3240—ASSOCIATION ON AMERICAN INDIAN AFFAIRS (Displaced Homemaker Scholarships)

Executive Office
966 Hungerford Drive, Suite 12-B
Rockville MD 20850
240/314-7155
FAX: 240/314-7159
E-mail: general.aaia@verizon.net
Internet: http://www.indian-affairs.org
AMOUNT: $1,500
DEADLINE(S): Fall and Spring semesters only
FIELD(S): All
ELIGIBILITY/REQUIREMENTS: Open to those men and women who would not otherwise be able to complete their educational goals due to family responsibilities; in particular, older students who have put off college to raise their children, students who are entering or are returning to college when their children enter school, men or women who have been divorced and had to leave college to care for their children and are now returning, etc.; must be full-time undergraduate students who are minimally 1/4 degree Indian blood from a federally recognized tribe. Award is based on financial need and is limited to North America/Alaska.
HOW TO APPLY: See website for application. Please send only the information requested; additional information will not be considered. Must submit essay on need, certificate of enrollment and quantum from your tribe or BIA, transcript, schedule of classes, and current financial aid award letter.
RENEWABLE: Yes. Must reapply. Note: Disbursements of $750 made each semester pending satisfactory progress. No funding for summer semester.
CONTACT: Lisa Wyzlic at lw.aaia@verizon.net or 240/314-7155
ADDITIONAL INFORAMTION: If applying for more than 1 AAIA scholarship, send 1 application package only. Students will be considered for all scholarships they are qualified for.

3241—ASSOCIATION ON AMERICAN INDIAN AFFAIRS (Emilie Hesemeyer Memorial Scholarships)

Executive Office
966 Hungerford Drive, Suite 12-B
Rockville MD 20850
240/314-7155
FAX: 240/314-7159
E-mail: general.aaia@verizon.net
Internet: http://www.indian-affairs.org
AMOUNT: $1,500
DEADLINE(S): Fall and Spring semesters only
FIELD(S): All; Education
ELIGIBILITY/REQUIREMENTS: Open to full-time undergraduate students who are minimally 1/4 degree Indian blood from a federally recognized tribe. Open to students pursuing any field of study, but preference is given to education majors. Award is based on financial need and is limited to North America/Alaska.
HOW TO APPLY: See website for application. Please send only the information requested; additional information will not be considered. Must submit essay on need, certificate of enrollment and quantum from your tribe or BIA, transcript, schedule of classes, and current financial aid award letter.
RENEWABLE: Yes. Must reapply. Note: Disbursements of $750 made each semester pending satisfactory progress. No funding for summer semester.
CONTACT: Lisa Wyzlic at lw.aaia@verizon.net or 240/314-7155
ADDITIONAL INFORAMTION: If applying for more than 1 AAIA scholarship, send 1 application package only. Students will be considered for all scholarships they are qualified for.

3242—ASTHMA AND ALLERGY FOUNDATION OF AMERICA/New England Chapter

109 Highland Avenue
Needham MA 02494
781/444-7778
FAX: 781/444-7718
E-mail: aafane@aafane.org
Internet: http://www.asthmaand allergies.org
AMOUNT: $500 or $1,000
DEADLINE(S): FEB (date varies)
FIELD(S): All
ELIGIBILITY/REQUIREMENTS: Open to all high school juniors who have asthma or significant allergies, including food allergies residing in one of the 6 New England states. Selection is based on academic achievement, activities, and a 1-page essay.
HOW TO APPLY: See website or contact Foundation; also mailed to most New England high schools.
NUMBER OF AWARDS: 1 or 2
RENEWABLE: No
CONTACT: Elaine Erenrich Rosenburg, Executive Director

3243—AUSTRIAN FEDERAL MINISTRY OF SCIENCE AND TRANSPORT SCHOLARSHIPS

Minoritenplatz 5
A-1014 Wien 1 AUSTRIA
+43/1/53 120-0
FAX: +43/1/53 120-3099
E-mail: ministerium@bmbwk.gv.at
Internet: http://www.bmbwk.gv.at
AMOUNT: Varies

DEADLINE(S): Varies
FIELD(S): All
ELIGIBILITY/REQUIREMENTS: Awards open to undergraduate and graduate students who wish to study in Austria.
HOW TO APPLY: Write or visit website for details.

3244—AUTISM SOCIETY OF AMERICA (CVS/All Kids Can Scholars Program)

7910 Woodmont Avenue, Suite 300
Bethesda MD 20814-3067
301/657-0881 or 800/328-8476
Internet: http://www.autism-society.org/site/PageServer?pagename=asa_awards
AMOUNT: $1,000
DEADLINE(S): Varies
FIELD(S): All
ELIGIBILITY/REQUIREMENTS: Open to an individual with autism who has successfully met all the requirements for admission into an accredited postsecondary program of study.
HOW TO APPLY: Must be nominated (call for nomination sent early each year). See website for additional information; submit documentation of status as an individual with autism, secondary school transcripts, documentation of acceptance into an accredited, postsecondary educational or vocational program of study, 2 letters of recommendation, a personal statement of no more than 500 words, outlining applicant's qualifications and proposed plan of study
NUMBER OF AWARDS: 5

3245—AYN RAND INSTITUTE (Anthem Essay Contest)

Department W
P.O. Box 57044
Irvine CA 92619-7044
E-mail: anthemessay@aynrand.org
Internet: http://www.aynrand.org/contests/
AMOUNT: $2,000 (1st prize); $500 (2nd); $200 (3rd); $50 (finalists); $30 (semifinalists)
DEADLINE(S): MAR 18
FIELD(S): All (emphasis on philosophy)
ELIGIBILITY/REQUIREMENTS: Open to 9th and 10th graders who write a 600- to 1,200-word essay on Ayn Rand's novelette *Anthem*. Essays will be judged on both style and content. Judges will look for writing that is clear, articulate and logically organized. Winning essays must demonstrate an outstanding grasp of the philosophic meaning of *Anthem*.

HOW TO APPLY: See website or contact your English teacher or guidance counselor for guidelines. Do NOT write to above address. May be submitted online, e-mail, or by mail.
NUMBER OF AWARDS: 236 (1 first, 5 second, 10 third, 45 finalist, 175 semifinalists)

3246—AYN RAND INSTITUTE (Fountainhead Essay Contest)

Department W
P.O. Box 57044
Irvine CA 92619-7044
E-mail: tf-essay@aynrand.org
Internet: http://www.aynrand.org/contests/
AMOUNT: $10,000 (1st prize); $2,000 (2nd); $1,000 (3rd); $100 (finalist); $50 (semifinalist)
DEADLINE(S): APR 15
FIELD(S): All (emphasis on philosophy & psychology)
ELIGIBILITY/REQUIREMENTS: Open to 11th and 12th graders who write an 800- to 1,600-word essay on Ayn Rand's *The Fountainhead*. Essays judged on both style and content. Winning essays must demonstrate an outstanding grasp of the philosophic and psychological meaning of *The Fountainhead*.
HOW TO APPLY: See website for guidelines. Do NOT write to above address. Submit online, e-mail, or by mail.
NUMBER OF AWARDS: 251 (1 first, 5 second, 10 third, 35 finalist, 200 semifinalists)

3247—BARKING FOUNDATION

P.O. Box 855
Bangor ME 04402-0855
207/990-2910
FAX: 207/990-2975
E-mail: info@barkingfoundation.org
Internet: http://www.barkingfoundation.org
AMOUNT: $3,000
DEADLINE(S): FEB 28
FIELD(S): All
ELIGIBILITY/REQUIREMENTS: Maine residents with financial need pursuing accredited degree programs in postsecondary educational institutions, in or outside Maine, including associate, bachelor, master and doctoral degrees.
HOW TO APPLY: Write for application or download from website.
NUMBER OF AWARDS: 25-40
RENEWABLE: Yes, once. Must reapply.
CONTACT: Stephanie Leonard

3248—BECA FOUNDATION, INC. (BECA-CSUSM Scholarship)

830 E. Grand Avenue, Suite B
Escondido CA 92025
760/741-8246
FAX: 760/471-8176
E-mail: sdbeca@sbcglobal.net
Internet: http://www.becafoundation.org
AMOUNT: $500-$1,000
FIELD(S): All
ELIGIBILITY/REQUIREMENTS: Latinos enrolled at CSU San Marcos enrolled in 6 or more units (no preference given to unit load); must be enrolled in the Spring semester of the application period and the Fall semester of the award period and in good academic (2.0 GPA) administrative standing at CSUSM.
HOW TO APPLY: See website for application. Submit with official copy of high school transcript; 2 letters of recommendation from college professor/advisor, or anyone other than family member, who has known you for at least 2 years addressing your leadership abilities, your future potential, and other factors that contribute to your community involvement; and Financial Profile, either a copy of your FAFSA/SAR or questions on application. Finalist will be asked to come in for a formal interview.
RENEWABLE: Yes. Must reapply.

3249—BECA FOUNDATION, INC. (General Scholarship Fund)

830 E. Grand Avenue, Suite B
Escondido CA 92025
760/741-8246
FAX: 760/471-8176
E-mail: sdbeca@sbcglobal.net
Internet: http://www.becafoundation.org
AMOUNT: $500-$1,000
FIELD(S): All
ELIGIBILITY/REQUIREMENTS: Must be Latino, San Diego County high school graduate who is entering college in the fall. Eligible pursuing their education anywhere in the United States.
HOW TO APPLY: See website for application. Submit with official copy of high school transcript; 2 letters of recommendation from a high school official, high school teacher/college professor/advisor, or anyone other than family member, who has known you for at least 2 years addressing your leadership abilities, your future potential, and other factors that contribute to your community involvement; and

Financial Profile, either a copy of your FAFSA/SAR or questions on application. RENEWABLE: Yes. Must reapply.

3250—BIA HIGHER EDUCATION/HOPI SUPPLEMENTAL GRANT

P.O. Box 123
Kykotsmovi AZ 86039
520/734-3533 or 800/762-9630
E-mail: tlomakema@hopi.nsn.us
Internet: http://www.nau.edu/
~hcpop/current/student/grant.
htm
AMOUNT: BIA Higher Education
Grant: $2,500 per semester; Hopi
Supplemental Grant: $1,500 per
semester
DEADLINE(S): JUL 31 (fall); NOV 30
(spring); APR 30 (summer)
FIELD(S): All
ELIGIBILITY/REQUIREMENTS: For
enrolled members of the Hopi Tribe pursuing associate, baccalaureate, graduate, or postgraduate degrees. Minimum 2.0 GPA required. Financial need is primary consideration.
HOW TO APPLY: See website for application or contact directly by phone, e-mail, or letter.

3251—BLANCHE NAUGHER FOWLER CHARITABLE SCHOLARSHIP TRUST

c/o Amsouth Bank Trust
P.O. Box 2028
Tuscaloosa FL 35403
205/391-5729
FAX: 205/391-5598
AMOUNT: Varies
DEADLINE(S): MAR 31
FIELD(S): All
ELIGIBILITY/REQUIREMENTS: Must attend or be accepted to a 4-year university in the state of Alabama.
HOW TO APPLY: Request application from Trust Administrator; submit with transcript; proof of acceptance; ACT or SAT scores; at least 2 letters of recommendation, 1 of which must be from a present or former teacher or instructor; personal statement (1 page or less) discussing educational and career goals; statement from institution specifying charges and other costs; if applicant wishes to be considered for a needs-based scholarship submit FAFSA with copy of income tax return for previous calendar year.
NUMBER OF AWARDS: Varies
RENEWABLE: Yes, must reapply.
CONTACT: Lynn Shaw, Trust Administrator

3252—BLINDED VETERANS ASSOCIATION (Kathern F. Gruber Scholarship Program)

477 H Street NW
Washington DC 20001-2694
800/669-7079 or 202/371-8880
FAX: 202/371-8258
E-mail: bjones@bva.org.
Internet: http://www.bva.org/
around2.html
AMOUNT: $1,000-$2,000
DEADLINE(S): APR 14
FIELD(S): All
ELIGIBILITY/REQUIREMENTS: Open to children and spouses of legally blind (service or nonservice connected) veterans. Must be accepted or enrolled full time in a college or vocational school and be a U.S. citizen.
HOW TO APPLY: Contact BVA for an application.
NUMBER OF AWARDS: 3 awards of $2,000; 3 of $1,000

3253—BOB JONES UNIVERSITY (Rebate Program)

1700 Wade Hampton Boulevard
Greenville SC 29614/0001
800/BJ-AND-ME
Internet: http://www.bju.edu/
admissions/financial
AMOUNT: $1,250-$2,500
DEADLINE(S): Varies (beginning of
fall/spring semester)
FIELD(S): All
ELIGIBILITY/REQUIREMENTS: Participation in the Student Work Program for at least 10 hours/week, dormitory student, U.S. or Canadian citizen. Financial need, based on parents' income.
HOW TO APPLY: Contact the Financial Aid Office for details.
RENEWABLE: Yes

3254—BOY SCOUTS OF AMERICA (National Eagle Scout Scholarships)

1325 West Walnut Hill Lane
P.O. Box 152079
Irving TX 75015-2079
972/580-2032
Internet: http://www.nesa/scholar
AMOUNT: Varies
DEADLINE(S): JAN 31
FIELD(S): All (except 2-year or technical
schools)
ELIGIBILITY/REQUIREMENTS: For college-bound high school seniors or college undergraduates (no later than completion of junior year) who have been granted the Eagle Scout rank or have verified that their application has been received at the national office. Must document leadership ability in Scouting and a strong record of participation of activities outside of scouting.
HOW TO APPLY: Download from website or send SASE for application. Submit with 1 recommendation letter from a volunteer or professional Scout leader. NO OTHER recommendations will be considered.
NUMBER OF AWARDS: Varies
RENEWABLE: No
CONTACT: Ann Dimond

3255—BREAD AND ROSES COMMUNITY FUND (Jonathan R. Lax Scholarship Fund)

1500 Walnut Street, Suite 1305
Philadelphia PA 19102
215/731-1107
FAX: 215/731-0453
Internet: http://www.breadroses
fund.org/grants/lax.html
AMOUNT: $5,000-$20,000
DEADLINE(S): JAN 15
FIELD(S): All
ELIGIBILITY/REQUIREMENTS: Open to gay men for graduate and one undergraduate study. Must be from Philadelphia studying elsewhere or from elsewhere studying in Philadelphia.
HOW TO APPLY: See website for application or contact Administrative Director.
CONTACT: Michelle Jackson, Administrative Director

3256—BREWER FOUNDATION, INC.

P.O. Box 7906
Rocky Mount NC 27804
AMOUNT: Varies
DEADLINE(S): Varies
FIELD(S): All
ELIGIBILITY/REQUIREMENTS: Scholarships for higher education to residents of North Carolina.
HOW TO APPLY: Contact President at Foundation for current application deadline and procedures.
CONTACT: Joseph B. Brewer Jr., President

3257—BRITISH COLUMBIA PARAPLEGIC ASSOCIATION (Canadian Paraplegic Association Women's Auxiliary Bursaries)

780 SW Marine Drive
Vancouver BC V6P 5Y7 CANADA
604/324-3611
FAX: 604/326-1229
E-mail: vancouver@canparaplegic.

org
Internet: http://www.canparaplegic.
org
AMOUNT: Varies
DEADLINE(S): JUL 31
FIELD(S): All
ELIGIBILITY/REQUIREMENTS:
Open to spinal cord-injured students for undergraduate or graduate studies in a university in British Columbia. Must be Canadian citizen, landed immigrant, or British Columbia resident. Based on academic standing and financial need. Must be members of the Association.
HOW TO APPLY: Contact BCPA for membership information or an application.

3258—BRITISH COLUMBIA PARAPLEGIC ASSOCIATION (IODE Bursary for Physically Disabled Persons)

780 SW Marine Drive
Vancouver BC V6P 5Y7 CANADA
604/324-3611
FAX: 604/324-3671
E-mail: vancouver@canparaplegic.
org
Internet: http://www.canparaplegic.
org
AMOUNT: Varies
DEADLINE(S): JUL 31
FIELD(S): All
ELIGIBILITY/REQUIREMENTS:
Open to physically disabled postsecondary students who are Canadian citizens in financial need.
HOW TO APPLY: Funds are to be used to assist with expenses for tuition, books, transportation, or teaching assistance.

3259—BRITISH COLUMBIA PARAPLEGIC FOUNDATION

780 SW Marine Drive
Vancouver BC V6P 5Y7 CANADA
604/324-3611
FAX: 604/326-1229
E-mail: vancouver@bcpara.org
Internet: http://www.bcpata.org
AMOUNT: Varies
DEADLINE(S): MAY 31
FIELD(S): All
ELIGIBILITY/REQUIREMENTS:
Open to British Columbia residents who are mobility-impaired with a significant degree of disability. Should be promising students pursuing a vocational or academic education. Must be a Canadian citizen, legal resident, or a resident of British Columbia and a member of the Association.

HOW TO APPLY: Write for information. Funds may be used for tuition, books and supplies, help or equipment for study purposes, and/or finance of transportation.
NUMBER OF AWARDS: Varies
RENEWABLE: No
CONTACT: Alyson Murzsa at 604/326-1276 or amvrzsa@bcparaorg

3260—BRITISH COLUMBIA PARAPLEGIC FOUNDATION (Joseph David Hall/Don Vaux/John MacNeal Memorial Scholarships & BC IYDP Bursaries)

780 SW Marine Drive
Vancouver BC V6P 5Y7 CANADA
604/324-3611
FAX: 604/324-3671
E-mail: vancouver@canparaplegic.
org
Internet: http://www.canparaplegic.
org
AMOUNT: Varies
DEADLINE(S): JUL 31
FIELD(S): All
ELIGIBILITY/REQUIREMENTS:
Awarded to physically disabled persons to further their vocational or academic training. Must be Canadian citizens or legal residents; must attend institution in British Columbia.
HOW TO APPLY: Must be member of the Association (except IYDP). Write for complete information.

3261—CABRILLO CIVIC CLUBS OF CALIFORNIA

1455 Willow Street
San Diego CA 92106
619/223-7026
Internet:
http://www.collegeview.com/
financial aid
AMOUNT: $500
DEADLINE(S): APR 1
FIELD(S): All
ELIGIBILITY/REQUIREMENTS: Must be of Portuguese descent and a citizen or permanent resident of the U.S., graduating from a California high school. Must have a minimum 3.5 GPA and have participated in at least 3 extracurricular activities. Based on scholastic attainment, character, and promise. May be used at an accredited community college, college or university, or trade school in the U.S.
HOW TO APPLY: Submit 3 letters of recommendation from individuals; at least 1 must be from the principal, dean, or counselor who will verify participation in extracurricular activities and 1 must be

from a teacher. The 3rd may be from any other source except relatives. Include glossy photo with application, which may be obtained from State Chairperson.
CONTACT: Breck Austin at 2174 S-Coast Highway, Oceanside, CA 92054

3262—CALIFORNIA ASSOCIATION OF WINEGRAPE GROWERS (California Foundation Scholarships)

1325 J Street Suite 1560
Sacramento CA 95814
800/241-1800 or 916/379-8995
FAX: 916/379-8999
E-mail: info@cawg.org
Internet: http://www.cawg.org/
cwggf
AMOUNT: $500-$1,000
DEADLINE(S): Late MAR (see website)
FIELD(S): All
ELIGIBILITY/REQUIREMENTS:
Applicant's parent or guardian must be employed by a California winegrape grower; scholarships are based on financial need and academic achievement. 4-year scholarships may be used at any campus in the University of California or California State University system; 2-year scholarships may be used at any California community college.
HOW TO APPLY: Must be a graduating high school senior. Students currently enrolled in college are not eligible. See website for application; submit with high school transcript, a copy of your SAT or ACT results if you are applying for a 4-year scholarship, a letter of recommendation from an instructor, the school principal or counselor, and a 2-page essay (approximately 500 words) focusing on you and your career goals
NUMBER OF AWARDS: 2, up to 4 years ($1,000/year); 4, up to 2 years ($500/year)
RENEWABLE: Yes. Studies must continue to be completed satisfactorily.
CONTACT: Carolee Williams
ADDITIONAL INFORMATION: Children of winegrape growers may request a waiver from the eligibility requirement based upon financial need.

3263—CALIFORNIA CORRECTIONAL PEACE OFFICERS ASSOCIATION (Joe Harper Scholarship Foundation)

755 Riverpoint Drive, Suite 200
West Sacramento CA 95605-1634
AMOUNT: Varies
DEADLINE(S): APR 30
FIELD(S): All
ELIGIBILITY/REQUIREMENTS: For active or retired members, or immediate

family members of current or deceased members of the Association. Based on academic achievement, school activities, financial need, and community service.
HOW TO APPLY: Write for information.
RENEWABLE: Yes. College GPA must be maintained at 3.5.

3264—CALIFORNIA FEDERATION OF TEACHERS (Raoul Teilhet Scholarship Program)

2550 N. Hollywood Way,
Suite 400
Burbank CA 9105
818/843-8226
FAX: 720/564-0397
E-mail: wilmottscholarship@
hotmail.com
Internet: http://www.cft.org
AMOUNT: $1,000 (2-year schools);
$3,000 (4-year schools)
DEADLINE(S): JAN 31 and JUL 1
FIELD(S): All
ELIGIBILITY/REQUIREMENTS: Open to incoming freshmen and continuing college students, who are children of CFT members or deceased CFT members, attending community colleges, 4-year colleges or universities, and trade, technical or art schools. Based on academic achievement, financial need, special talents and skills, participation in campus or community activities, and an essay.
HOW TO APPLY: See website for application or contact AFT/CFT local union, or contact CFT. Submit with transcript, parents' tax return, essay of no more than 500 words on an issue or social problem you feel strongly about, describing how you think it can be solved; member verification form; rating sheet from teacher, counselor or administrator, and community member.
NUMBER OF AWARDS: 112
RENEWABLE: No

3265—CALIFORNIA MASONIC FOUNDATION-GRAND LODGE F. & A.M.

1111 California Street
San Francisco CA 94108-2284
415/776-7000
Fax: 415/292-9196
Email: foundation@mhcsf.org
Internet: http://www.california
mason.org
AMOUNT: $500-$2,500
DEADLINE(S): FEB 15
FIELD(S): All
ELIGIBILITY/REQUIREMENTS: Open to high school seniors planning to attend an accredited 2- or 4-year institution as a full-time undergraduate. Must be Cali-

fornia residents with a minimum 3.0 GPA, U.S. citizens. Some preference given to applicants with Masonic relationship (DeMolay, Jobs Daughters, Rainbow for Girls) membership. Financial need a consideration.
HOW TO APPLY: Apply online between September and February. A personal essay, 2 letters of recommendation, transcript, financial statement, college acceptance letter, SAT or ACT scores, and proof of Masonic relationship and/or Masonic youth organization membership, if applicable.
RENEWABLE: Yes. Must reapply by APR 15 and demonstrate academic progress and financial need.

3266—CALIFORNIA MASONIC FOUNDATION-GRAND LODGE F. & A.M. (Arnold Wilmott Scholarships of Greenleaf Gardens Masonic Lodge No. 670)

12001 East Beverly Boulevard
Whittier CA 90601
FAX: 720/564-0397
E-mail: wilmottscholarship@
hotmail.com
AMOUNT: minimum $500
DEADLINE(S): MAR 15
FIELD(S): All
ELIGIBILITY/REQUIREMENTS: Must be graduating high school senior, attending Whittier area high school; a child or grandchild of a member in good standing of Greenleaf Gardens Lodge; citizen of the U.S. and a legal resident of California for at least 1 year; minimum 3.5 GPA, accepted to an accredited 4-year institution as a full-time undergraduate; demonstrate financial need.
HOW TO APPLY: Write for application OCT 1-JAN 31; include SASE (business size). Submit with essay of 1,000 words or less; 2 letters of recommendation, 1 from teacher or administrator and 1 from adult other than teacher or school staff; transcript; financial statement including FAFSA and latest IRS return; college acceptance letter; SAT score.
NUMBER OF AWARDS: Varies
RENEWABLE: Yes. Must reapply by APR 15.

3267—CALIFORNIA MASONIC FOUNDATION-GRAND LODGE F. & A.M. (C. E. Towne Scholarships)

1111 California Street
San Francisco CA 94108-2284
415/776-7000
FAX: 415/292-9196
Email: foundation@mhcsf.org

Internet: http://www.california
mason.org
AMOUNT: $10,400
DEADLINE(S): FEB 15
FIELD(S): All
ELIGIBILITY/REQUIREMENTS: Open to high school seniors planning to attend an accredited 4-year institution of higher learning as a full-time undergraduate. Must be a California resident with a minimum 3.0 GPA, U.S. citizen. Some preference given to applicants with Masonic relationship (DeMolay, Jobs Daughters, Rainbow for Girls) membership. Financial need a consideration.
HOW TO APPLY: Apply online between September and February. A personal essay, 2 letters of recommendation, transcript, financial statement, college acceptance letter, SAT or ACT scores, and proof of Masonic relationship and/or Masonic youth organization membership, if applicable.
RENEWABLE: Yes. Must reapply by APR 15 with evidence of academic progress and continuing financial need.
CONTACT: Scholarship Coordinator

3268—CALIFORNIA TABLE GRAPE COMMISSION

392 West Fallbrook Avenue, #101
Fresno CA 93711-6150
559/447-8350
FAX: 559/447-9184
E-mail: info@freshcalifornia
grapes.com
Internet: http//www.freshCalifornia
grapes.com
AMOUNT: $16,000
DEADLINE(S): Mid MAR
FIELD(S): All
ELIGIBILITY/REQUIREMENTS: Open to field workers employed in the current or the immediate prior year of the California table grape harvest or their children. Applicant must be a high school graduate or a high school senior who will graduate in the current year. Must plan to attend a 4-year college or university in California. based on academic performance, financial need, obstacles overcome, leadership ability and/or community service, and the ability to succeed.
HOW TO APPLY: See website or e-mail for an application. Submit with a 1- to 2-page essay about yourself, a list of honors or special awards received, 2 letters of recommendation, an official high school transcript, and a copy of SAT or ACT results.
NUMBER OF AWARDS: 3
RENEWABLE: No
CONTACT: Jim Howard

3269—CAMP FOUNDATION (Scholarship Grants)

Franklin VA 23851
757/562-3439
AMOUNT: $3,000-$4,500
DEADLINE(S): MAR 1
FIELD(S): All
ELIGIBILITY/REQUIREMENTS: Open to graduating high school seniors in the city of Franklin and the counties of Isle of Wight and Southampton, Virginia, or to residents of these areas who graduated from high school elsewhere and are pursuing undergraduate study.
HOW TO APPLY: Contact Camp Foundation for an application ONLY if you meet residency requirements.
NUMBER OF AWARDS: 7

3270—CANADIAN NATIONAL INSTITUTE FOR THE BLIND (Scholarships and Grants)

100-5055 Joyce Street
Vancouver BC V5R 6B2 CANADA
604/431-2020
FAX: 604/431-2099
E-mail: bonnie.nelson@cnib.ca
Internet: http://www.cnib.ca
AMOUNT: Varies
DEADLINE(S): Varies
FIELD(S): All
ELIGIBILITY/REQUIREMENTS: Open to legally blind residents of British Columbia and the Yukon who are college or university students registered with CNIB. Awards tenable at recognized 2-year and 4-year undergraduate institutions. Must be Canadian citizen.
HOW TO APPLY: Write for information.
RENEWABLE: Sometimes; write for information.
CONTACT: Murial Adams

3271—CAREER COLLEGE ASSOCIATION/CAREER TRAINING FOUNDATION (Imagine America Scholarship)

10 G Street NE, Suite 750
Washington DC 20002-4213
202/336-6800
FAX: 202/408-8102
E-mail: scholarships@career.org
Internet: http://www.petersons.com/cca/ias.asp
AMOUNT: $1,000
DEADLINE(S): Varies
FIELD(S): All (vocational)
ELIGIBILITY/REQUIREMENTS: Must apply only to career colleges participating in the program, as listed on website. Must meet that college's normal entrance requirements. Must have 2.5 GPA or higher. Financial need must be demonstrated.
HOW TO APPLY: Must be nominated by school counselor or principal. See website for additional information.
CONTACT: Bob Martin, Executive Director/Vice President

3272—CARGILL (Community Scholarship Program)

P.O. Box 5650
Minneapolis MN 55440-5650
888/476-9332
E-mail: cargill@ffa.org
Internet: http://www.cargill.com
AMOUNT: $1,000
DEADLINE(S): FEB 15
FIELD(S): All
ELIGIBILITY/REQUIREMENTS: Open to high school seniors who are from a family whose livelihood is at least 50 percent derived from farming. Applicant must be a U.S. citizen planning to attend a U.S. school of higher education, either a 2- or 4-year college or university or a vo-tech school.
HOW TO APPLY: See website for application.
NUMBER OF AWARDS: 50
RENEWABLE: No

3273—CASCADE POLICY INSTITUTE (Independence Essay Competition)

813 SW Alder, Suite 450
Portland OR 97205
503/242-0900
FAX: 503/242-3822
E-mail: essay@cascadepolicy.org
Internet: http://www.cascadepolicy.org/essay.asp
AMOUNT: Varies (Up to $1,000)
DEADLINE(S): Mid MAR
FIELD(S): All
ELIGIBILITY/REQUIREMENTS: Essay competition open to Oregon high school age students attending a private, public, or home-school. Subject is "Exploring the Foundations of Freedom."
HOW TO APPLY: E-mail for details.
NUMBER OF AWARDS: Up to 5

3274—CENTER FOR EDUCATION SOLUTIONS, THE (A. Patrick Charnon Memorial Scholarship)

P.O. Box 208
San Francisco CA 94104-0208
925/934-7304
E-mail: scholarship@cesresources.org
Internet: http://www.cesresources.org/charnon.html#requirements
AMOUNT: $1,500
DEADLINE(S): MAR 31
FIELD(S): All
ELIGIBILITY/REQUIREMENTS: Must be full-time students enrolled in a bachelor's degree program at an accredited 4-year college or university in the U.S.; maintain good academic standing; and make progress toward a degree. Committee looks for candidates who value tolerance, compassion and respect for all people in their communities and who have demonstrated their commitment to these values by their actions.
HOW TO APPLY: See website or send SASE for an application. Submit application; a 2- to 4-page essay (typed double-spaced) explaining how community service experiences have shaped your life and how you will use your college education to build communities in a manner consistent with Patrick Charnon's values of compassion, tolerance, generosity, and respect; an official transcript from your high school or college; and 3 letters of reference. Only the first 500 applications will be considered.
NUMBER OF AWARDS: 1
RENEWABLE: Yes. Up to 4 years; must reapply.
CONTACT: Charnon Scholarship Selection Committee

3275—CENTRAL SCHOLARSHIP BUREAU (Interest-Free Loans)

1700 Reisterstown Road, Suite 220
Baltimore MD 21208-2903
410/415-5558
FAX: 410/415-5501
E-mail: info@centralsb.org
Internet: http://www.centralsb.org
AMOUNT: $3,000-$5,000
DEADLINE(S): Varies
FIELD(S): All
ELIGIBILITY/REQUIREMENTS: Open to permanent residents of Baltimore City or Anne Arundel, Baltimore, Carroll, Harford, or Howard Counties, Maryland. Must have exhausted all other available avenues of funding and have an adjusted gross income of $75,000 or less for dependent students. Awards are for study at any accredited undergraduate or graduate institution and are made on a noncompetitive basis to anyone with a sound educational plan.
HOW TO APPLY: Must apply first through government and school. See website or contact Central Scholarship Bureau for details.
NUMBER OF AWARDS: 125
RENEWABLE: Yes. Maximum $15,000.
CONTACT: Roberta Goldman, Program Director

3276—CHAIRSCHOLARS FOUNDATION, INC. (National Program)

16101 Carancia Lane
Odessa FL 33556-3278
813/920-1981
FAX: 813/920-7661
E-mail: chairscholars@
tampabay.rr.com
Internet: http://www.chair
scholars.org
AMOUNT: $3,000-$5,000
DEADLINE(S): FEB 28
FIELD(S): All
ELIGIBILITY/REQUIREMENTS: Open to high school seniors or college freshmen (under age 21) with profound (serious) physical challenges. Must demonstrate financial need, have at least a "B" high school scholastic average, must have performed some form of significant community service or social contribution, and complete a 300- to 500-word essay.
HOW TO APPLY: See website for application. Apply early and follow instructions EXACTLY.
NUMBER OF AWARDS: 5-20
RENEWABLE: Yes. Candidate must maintain a "B" GPA. (Up to $20,000)
CONTACT: Hugo A. Keim, M.D., President

3277—CHAIRSCHOLARS FOUNDATION, INC. (Tampa Bay Program)

16101 Carancia Lane
Odessa FL 33556-3278
813/920-1981
FAX: 813/920-7661
E-mail: chairscholars@
tampabay.rr.com
Internet: http://www.chair
scholars.org
AMOUNT: $3,000-$5,000
DEADLINE(S): FEB 28
FIELD(S): All
ELIGIBILITY/REQUIREMENTS: Open to college- or vocational-bound students residing in Hillsborough, Pasco, Pinellas, Sarasota, or Polk Counties with profound (severe) physical challenges. Must demonstrate financial need, satisfactory academic performance, and complete a 300- to 500-word essay.
HOW TO APPLY: See website for application. Apply early and follow instructions EXACTLY.
NUMBER OF AWARDS: 20-30
RENEWABLE: Yes. Candidate must maintain a "B" GPA.
CONTACT: Hugo A. Keim, M.D., President

3278—CHARTER FUND

370 17th Street, Suite 5300
Denver CO 80202
303/572-1727
FAX: 303/628-3839
Internet: http://www.piton.org
AMOUNT: $100-$2,500
DEADLINE(S): MAY 7
FIELD(S): All
ELIGIBILITY/REQUIREMENTS: Need-based scholarship open ONLY to Colorado residents who are currently high school seniors applying for freshman year of college.
HOW TO APPLY: See website for information from October 13 to May 7 or write for application after February 1.
RENEWABLE: No
CONTACT: Jeanette Montoya

3279—CHAUTAUQUA REGION COMMUNITY FOUNDATION, INC.

418 Spring Street
Jamestown NY 14701
716/661-3390
FAX: 716/488-0387
E-mail: crcf@crcfonline.org
Internet: http://www.crcfonline.org
AMOUNT: $100-$3,000
DEADLINE(S): JUN 1 (high school applications); JUL 15 (college students)
FIELD(S): All
ELIGIBILITY/REQUIREMENTS: Open ONLY to full-time students living in the vicinity of Jamestown, New York. Preference given to students in 12 school districts in Southern Chautauqua County. Financial need NOT a factor. Other requirements vary.
HOW TO APPLY: Contact Foundation for application.
NUMBER OF AWARDS: Multiple
CONTACT: JoAnn Carlson

3280—CHEROKEE NATION HIGHER EDUCATION SCHOLARSHIP PROGRAMS

P.O. Box 948
Tahlequah OK 74465
918/456-0671
FAX: 918/458-6286
Internet: http://www.cherokee.org
AMOUNT: Up to $2,000 (varies by program)
DEADLINE(S): JUN 17
FIELD(S): All
ELIGIBILITY/REQUIREMENTS: Must have Cherokee Nation tribal membership and Certificate Degree of Indian Blood cards. Student must apply for FAFSA; those not eligible for FAFSA must be permanent residents of Oklahoma. Must be working towards Bachelor's degree.
HOW TO APPLY: Applications available mid-January; write for information.
NUMBER OF AWARDS: 500

3281—CHICANA LATINA FOUNDATION

1410 Burlingame Ave., Suite N
Burlingame CA 94010
650/373-1085
FAX: 650/373-1090
E-mail: info@chicanalatina.org
Internet: http://www.chicana
latina.org
DEADLINE(S): MAR (varies)
AMOUNT: $1,500
FIELD(S): All
ELIGIBILITY/REQUIREMENTS: Available on a competitive basis to continuing undergraduate female college students of Latino background who are enrolled in accredited colleges, universities, and community colleges in northern California; must have lived at least 2 years in the area; must be enrolled as a full-time student and have completed a minimum of 15 college semester units; have a minimum 2.5 GPA; demonstrated leadership and civic/community involvement.
HOW TO APPLY: Contact Scholarship Competition for details and application.
RENEWABLE: Not for at least 4 years; may reapply for graduate scholarship after that date.
NUMBER OF AWARDS: 20-26
ADDITIONAL INFORMATION: If awarded the scholarship, applicant must agree to volunteer a minimum of 10 hours in the next year to the Foundation and must attend the Leadership Institute.

3282—CHICKASAW NATION GRANTS AND SCHOLARSHIPS

124 East 14th Street
Ada OK 74820
580/421-7711
FAX: 580/436-3733
Internet: http://www.chickasaw
educationservices.com
AMOUNT: $150-$2,500
DEADLINE(S): Fall SEP 1; Spring FEB 1; Summer JUN 15
FIELD(S): All
ELIGIBILITY/REQUIREMENTS: Registered Chickasaw citizen; attending an accredited college or university; and working on an associates, bachelor's, master's or doctoral degree. All documentation needs to be returned by deadline.
HOW TO APPLY: See website or call.
NUMBER OF AWARDS: 2,200

RENEWABLE: Yes, reapply.
CONTACT: Deborah Hook

3283—CHILDREN OF DEAF ADULTS ORGANIZATION

CODA International
605 Commonwealth Avenue
Boston MA 02215
617/353-3205
FAX: 617/353-3292
E-mail: deafstudy@bu.edu
Internet: http://www.coda-international.org/scholar.html
AMOUNT: $1,500
DEADLINE(S): MAY 4
FIELD(S): All
ELIGIBILITY/REQUIREMENTS:
Available to a hearing child of deaf parents who is seeking higher education. Applicant must be enrolled full time at a 2-year, 4-year, or technical institution or university. Available to U.S. and non-U.S. citizens.
HOW TO APPLY: Submit application with transcripts, letters of reference, and essay. Essay should include a description of the applicant's future career aspirations as well as a description of their experience with CODA.
NUMBER OF AWARDS: 2
RENEWABLE: No
CONTACT: Dr. Robert Hoffmeister, Director, Program in Deaf Studies

3284—CLAN MACBEAN FOUNDATION, THE (Scholarships & Grants)

441 Wadsworth Blvd., Suite 213
Lakewood CO 80226
303/233-6002
FAX: 303/233-6002
E-mail: clanoffice@clanmacbean.net
Internet: http://www.clanmacbean.net
AMOUNT: Up to $5,000
DEADLINE(S): MAY 1
FIELD(S): Scottish-culture related field or a field relating to the improvement of the human family
ELIGIBILITY/REQUIREMENTS: High school graduate.
HOW TO APPLY: See website or write or e-mail for an application and instruction letter.
NUMBER OF AWARDS: 3
RENEWABLE: Yes. Must reapply.
CONTACT: Raymond L. Heckethorn
ADDITIONAL INFORMATION: Trustees of the MacBean Foundation, their spouses, and their children are not eligible for grant funds.

3285—COCA-COLA SCHOLARS FOUNDATION, THE (2-Year Scholarship)

P.O. Box 442
Atlanta GA 30301-0442
800/306-2653
E-mail: scholars@na.ko.com
Internet: http://www.coca-colascholars.org
AMOUNT: $1,000
DEADLINE(S): Contact institution.
FIELD(S): All
ELIGIBILITY/REQUIREMENTS:
Students are eligible for nomination by their 2-year, degree-granting institutions throughout the U.S. Applicants must be U.S. citizens or permanent residents; completing a minimum of 100 hours of community service in the twelve months prior to nomination; planning to enroll in at least 2 courses during next term at a 2-year, degree-granting institution, and have a minimum 2.5 GPA at time of nomination.
HOW TO APPLY: Application information is sent to financial aid offices at 2-year, degree-granting institutions beginning in March. Colleges determine nomination process and may nominate no more than 2 students from each campus.
NUMBER OF AWARDS: 350
RENEWABLE: No
CONTACT: See website for campus contact.

3286—COCA-COLA SCHOLARS FOUNDATION SCHOLARSHIP, THE (4-Year Scholarship)

P.O. Box 442
Atlanta GA 30301-0442
800/306-2653
E-mail: scholars@na.ko.com
Internet: http://www.coca-colascholars.org
AMOUNT: $2,500/year and $5,000/year (for 4 years)
DEADLINE(S): OCT 31
FIELD(S): All
ELIGIBILITY/REQUIREMENTS:
Rewards leadership and excellence as exemplified through academic achievement and extracurricular activities, including commitment to community service. Applicants must be: current high school seniors (or home-schooled students) attending school in the United States; U.S. citizens, U.S. nationals, U.S. permanent residents, temporary residents (legalization program), refugees, asylees, Cuban-Haitian Entrants, or humanitarian parolees, anticipating completion of high school degree during the academic year in which application is made; planning to pursue a degree at an accredited U.S. postsecondary institution; and have a minimum 3.0 GPA at the end of their junior year of high school. Students must live in a participating area.

HOW TO APPLY: See website beginning in September for application or call or write to the above address for complete information.
NUMBER OF AWARDS: 50 ($5,000/year for 4 years), 200 ($2,500/year for 4 years)
RENEWABLE: No
ADDITIONAL INFORMATION: In April, Finalists attend the Scholars Weekend in Atlanta, at the Foundation's expense, to determine recipients at each award level.

3287—COLAGE (CHILDREN OF LESBIAN AND GAYS EVERYWHERE) AND FAMILY PRIDE COALITION (Lee Dubin Scholarship Fund)

COLAGE Scholarship Committee
3543 18th Street, #1
San Francisco CA 94110
415/861-5437
FAX: 415/255-8345
E-mail: colage@colage.org
Internet: http://www.colage.org/scholar/scholarship.html
AMOUNT: Up to $1,000
DEADLINE(S): APR 16
FIELD(S): All
ELIGIBILITY/REQUIREMENTS: Must have a lesbian, gay, bisexual or transgender parent; be enrolled in an accredited 4-year postsecondary institution in the U.S.; maintain a minimum GPA of 2.0. Applicants with economic need, have NOT been previously awarded, and are active community participants are encouraged to apply.
HOW TO APPLY: Application available on website. Return with essay; proof of enrollment; transcript; statement of financial need (FAFSA or letter of need).
NUMBER OF AWARDS: At least 4
RENEWABLE: No
CONTACT: Beth Teper, Executive Director

3288—COLLEGE MISERICORDIA (Honor Scholarships)

301 Lake Street
Dallas PA 18612
866/262-6363
E-mail: admiss@misericordia.edu
Internet: http://www.misericordia.edu
AMOUNT: $1,000-$10,000/year
DEADLINE(S): Varies
FIELD(S): All
ELIGIBILITY/REQUIREMENTS:
Open to incoming freshmen and transfer students. Must have attained outstanding academic records. GPA requirements are

outlined in the scholarship notification letter.
HOW TO APPLY: Obtain applications from the Admissions Office.
RENEWABLE: Yes. Up to 4 years if GPA maintained.

3289—COLLEGE MISERICORDIA (McAuley Awards)

301 Lake Street
Dallas PA 18612
866/262-6363
E-mail: admiss@misericordia.edu
Internet: http://www.misericordia.edu
AMOUNT: $1,000-$5,000/year
DEADLINE(S): Varies
FIELD(S): All
ELIGIBILITY/REQUIREMENTS: Open to incoming freshmen and transfer students. Must have attained outstanding academic records.
HOW TO APPLY: Obtain applications from the Admissions Office.
RENEWABLE: Yes. Annually based on leadership, school and community involvement.

3290—COLORADO COMMISSION ON HIGHER EDUCATION (Colorado Merit-based Awards)

1380 Lawrence Street, Suite 1200
Denver CO 80204
303/866-2723
FAX: 303/866-4266
Internet: http://www.state.co.us/cche
AMOUNT: Tuition, room, and board
DEADLINE(S): Varies
FIELD(S): All
ELIGIBILITY/REQUIREMENTS: Must be Colorado resident, enrolled in an eligible program at an eligible Colorado postsecondary institution, who demonstrates outstanding academic achievement and satisfactory progress toward completion of degree.
HOW TO APPLY: Contact Financial Aid Office at participating college or university for application and details.

3291—COLORADO COMMISSION ON HIGHER EDUCATION (Colorado National Guard Tuition Assistance Program)

1380 Lawrence Street, Suite 1200
Denver CO 80204
303/866-2723
FAX: 303/866-4266

Internet: http://www.state.co.us/cche
AMOUNT: Tuition, room, and board
DEADLINE(S): Varies (up to 100% of tuition costs at state-supported institutions)
FIELD(S): All
ELIGIBILITY/REQUIREMENTS: Must be a member of Colorado National Guard and a Colorado resident enrolled in an eligible program at an eligible Colorado postsecondary institution, and demonstrate satisfactory progress toward degree.
HOW TO APPLY: Contact Financial Aid Office at participating college or university for application and details
CONTACT: National Guard recruiter or the state tuition assistance office at 303/677-8913.

3292—COLORADO COMMISSION ON HIGHER EDUCATION (Colorado Need-based Awards)

1380 Lawrence Street, Suite 1200
Denver CO 80204
303/866-2723
FAX: 303/866-4266
Internet: http://www.state.co.us/cche
AMOUNT: Tuition, room, and board
DEADLINE(S): Varies
FIELD(S): All
ELIGIBILITY/REQUIREMENTS: Must be Colorado resident, with documented financial need, enrolled in an eligible program at an eligible Colorado postsecondary institution, demonstrating satisfactory progress toward completion of degree.
HOW TO APPLY: Contact Financial Aid Office at participating college or university for application and details.

3293—COLORADO COMMISSION ON HIGHER EDUCATION (Colorado Work-Study)

1380 Lawrence Street, Suite 1200
Denver CO 80204
303/866-2723
FAX: 303/866-4266
Internet: http://www.state.co.us/cche
AMOUNT: Tuition, room, and board
DEADLINE(S): Varies
FIELD(S): All
ELIGIBILITY/REQUIREMENTS: Must be Colorado resident enrolled in an eligible program at an eligible Colorado postsecondary institution, demonstrating satisfactory progress toward completion degree.

HOW TO APPLY: Contact Financial Aid Office at participating college or university for application and details.

3294—COLORADO COMMISSION ON HIGHER EDUCATION (Dependents Tuition Assistance Program)

1380 Lawrence Street, Suite 1200
Denver CO 80204
303/866-2723
FAX: 303/866-4266
Internet: http://www.state.co.us/cche
AMOUNT: Tuition, room, and board
DEADLINE(S): Varies
FIELD(S): All
ELIGIBILITY/REQUIREMENTS: Open to dependents of Colorado law enforcement officers, fire or national guard personnel killed or disabled in the line of duty, and for dependents of prisoners of war or service personnel listed as missing in action.
HOW TO APPLY: Contact Commission for application.
CONTACT: Diane Lindner

3295—COLORADO COUNCIL VOLUNTEERISM/COMMUNITY SERVICE SCHOLARSHIP

600 17th Street, Suite 2210 South
Denver CO 80202
970/264-2231
FAX: 970/264-1328
E-mail:
mthompson@pagosa.kiz.co.us
Internet: http://www.coloradocouncil.org
AMOUNT: $1,500
DEADLINE(S): JAN 31
FIELD(S): All
ELIGIBILITY/REQUIREMENTS: Minimum 2.5 GPA; resident of Colorado for past 2 years and graduated from a Colorado high school; and attending a public or private 2- or 4-year college or university in Colorado. Volunteerism and community service, extracurricular activities and dedication to others considered.
HOW TO APPLY: See website for application and recommendation forms; submit with 2 recommendations forms.
NUMBER OF AWARDS: 16
CONTACT: Mark Thompson

3296—COLORADO STATE UNIVERSITY (First Generation Award)

Student Financial Services

Administration Annex
Fort Collins CO 80523
970/491-6321
FAX: 970/491-5010
Internet: http://www.colostate.edu
AMOUNT: $4,000
DEADLINE(S): MAR 1
FIELD(S): All
ELIGIBILITY/REQUIREMENTS: Open ONLY to Colorado residents whose parents have never received a bachelor's degree. Students must be accepted for full-time study at CSU in a program leading to a bachelor's degree. Must demonstrate financial need.
HOW TO APPLY: Contact CSU for an application.
RENEWABLE: Up to 6 additional semesters, providing requirements are met.

3297—COMISION FEMENIL

P.O. Box 86013
Los Angeles CA 90086
AMOUNT: $1,000-$1,500
DEADLINE(S): APR
FIELD(S): All
ELIGIBILITY/REQUIREMENTS: Open to Latina women pursuing their education at an accredited college or university; awards are based on financial need and community involvement.
HOW TO APPLY: Contact Commission for details.
CONTACT: Ana Gonzalez

3298—COMMONWEAL FOUNDATION (Pathways to Success Scholarship Program)

10770 Columbia Pike, Suite 100
Silver Spring MD 20901
301/592-1313
FAX: 301/592-1307
E-mail: paulawebber@commonweal-foundation.org
Internet: http://www.commonweal-foundation.org
AMOUNT: $4,000 (maximum)
DEADLINE(S): None
FIELD(S): All
ELIGIBILITY/REQUIREMENTS: Open to junior high and high school students who wish to attend accredited boarding schools with diverse programs. Must be new to the boarding school experience, who have a need and strong desire to change school situation, have potential to be successful, demonstrate financial need, and be willing to participate in work and community service opportunities.
HOW TO APPLY: Contact Foundation for details.
CONTACT: Paula Webber

3299—COMMUNITY FOUNDATION FOR GREATER ATLANTA, INC., THE (Dreams2 Scholarship)

50 Hurt Plaza, Suite 449
Atlanta GA 30303
404/688-5525
FAX: 404/688-3060
E-mail: scholarships@atlcf.org
Internet: http://www.atlcf.org/GrantsScholarships/Scholarships.aspx
AMOUNT: $2,000
DEADLINE(S): MAR 26
FIELD(S): All
ELIGIBILITY/REQUIREMENTS: Must have at least a 2.0 GPA, maximum 3.0 GPA, and be enrolled in or accepted as a full-time student at an accredited 2- or 4-year college, university or technical school to pursue an undergraduate degree; must demonstrate financial need (Partial scholarships may be considered at the discretion of the Dreams2 Scholarship Committee for part-time students.)
HOW TO APPLY: Must be nominated (call for nomination sent early each year). See website for additional information; submit documentation of status as an individual with autism, secondary school transcripts, documentation of acceptance into an accredited, postsecondary educational or vocational program of study, 2 letters of recommendation, a personal statement of no more than 500 words, outlining applicant's qualifications and proposed plan of study. Send to The Community Foundation for Greater Atlanta, Dreams2 Scholarship, Scholarship Management Services, Scholarship America, One Scholarship Way, P.O. Box 297, Saint Peter, MN 56082. If you have questions, call 507/931-1682 or e-mail community-foundation@scholarshipamerica.org.
NUMBER OF AWARDS: 6
RENEWABLE: Yes; must reapply. Must maintain the minimum GPA required by the school or a 2.0 GPA if the school does not have a stated minimum.
CONTACT: Lisa Glanville, 404/308-0055

3300—COMMUNITY FOUNDATION FOR GREATER ATLANTA, INC., THE (George and Pearl Strickland Scholarship)

50 Hurt Plaza, Suite 449
Atlanta GA 30303
404/688-5525
FAX: 404/688-3060
E-mail: scholarships@atlcf.org
Internet: http://www.atlcf.org/GrantsScholarships/Scholarships.aspx

AMOUNT: $$1,000-$2,000
DEADLINE(S): Varies
FIELD(S): All
ELIGIBILITY/REQUIREMENTS: For undergraduate or graduate students with financial need enrolled or accepted for enrollment at Clark Atlanta University, Morehouse College, Morehouse School of Medicine, Morris Brown College or Spelman College. Must be a legal resident of Georgia; demonstrate financial need, potential for success in chosen field, and commitment to community service; have a minimum 2.0 GPA.
HOW TO APPLY: See website for additional information and application. Submit with official transcript(s), financial information form including the 1st page of federal income tax form 1040, 2 scholarship recommendation forms and optional recommendation letters, letter of acceptance from the school you plan to attend next fall (if a recent high school graduate) and copy of Georgia license or ID. Send application to The Community Foundation for Greater Atlanta, The Strickland Scholarship Fund, Scholarship Management Services, Scholarship America, One Scholarship Way, P.O. Box 297, Saint Peter, MN 56082. If you have questions, call 507/931-1682 or e-mail community-foundation@scholarshipamerica.org.
NUMBER OF AWARDS: 20-30
RENEWABLE: Yes; Previous recipients are renewed if they continue to meet the scholarship's criteria and submit the current year's renewal application
CONTACT: Lisa Glanville, 404/308-0055

3301—COMMUNITY FOUNDATION FOR GREATER ATLANTA, INC., THE (Helen & Vernon Crawford Scholarship Fund)

50 Hurt Plaza, Suite 449
Atlanta GA 30303
404/688-5525
FAX: 404/688-3060
E-mail: scholarships@atlcf.org
Internet: http://www.atlcf.org/GrantsScholarships/Scholarships.aspx
AMOUNT: $500-$1,000
DEADLINE(S): Varies
FIELD(S): All
ELIGIBILITY/REQUIREMENTS: Open to those who have completed a literacy program and obtained a high school diploma or GED and are legal residents of Georgia. Must be accepted for enrollment or enrolled in a postsecondary institution. Must be recommended by either Literacy Action or a Georgia Certified Literate Community Program.

HOW TO APPLY: See website.
NUMBER OF AWARDS: up to 5
RENEWABLE: Yes; must reapply.
CONTACT: Lisa Glanville, 404/308-0055

3302—COMMUNITY FOUNDATION FOR GREATER ATLANTA, INC., THE (Lester W. Butts Scholarship Fund)

50 Hurt Plaza, Suite 449
Atlanta GA 30303
404/688-5525
FAX: 404/688-3060
E-mail: scholarships@atlcf.org
Internet: http://www.atlcf.org/
GrantsScholarships/Scholarships.
aspx
AMOUNT: $5,000
DEADLINE(S): Varies
FIELD(S): All
ELIGIBILITY/REQUIREMENTS: Open to graduating senior from Frederick Douglass High School. Must demonstrate academic achievement, financial need and community involvement/service, and be accepted or enrolled at an accredited college, university or technical school
HOW TO APPLY: See website.
NUMBER OF AWARDS: 1-2
CONTACT: Lisa Glanville, 404/308-0055

3303—COMMUNITY FOUNDATION FOR GREATER ATLANTA, INC., THE (Morgan Thomas Scholarship Fund)

50 Hurt Plaza, Suite 449
Atlanta GA 30303
404/688-5525
FAX: 404/688-3060
E-mail: scholarships@atlcf.org
Internet: http://www.atlcf.org/
GrantsScholarships/Scholarships.
aspx
AMOUNT: $1,000
DEADLINE(S): Varies
FIELD(S): All
ELIGIBILITY/REQUIREMENTS: Must be U.S. citizen, a legal resident of Cobb County for at least 6 months prior to application, enrolled in or accepted to a post-secondary institution in the U.S. to pursue an Associate or Bachelor's degree. Minimum 2.5 GPA for high school course work in Grades 10, 11 and 12. Preference shown for students achieving 3.0-3.5 GPA
HOW TO APPLY: See website for additional information and application. Submit with a personal essay (2-3 pages) that includes why you feel a college education is important; your statement of educational and career goals; post college career interests; highlights of your high school extracurricular/community service activi-

ties, special strengths, skills, and qualifications; any unusual family or personal circumstances have affected your achievement in school, work experience, or your participation in school and community activities; present financial need. Send to the Community Foundation for Greater Atlanta, The Morgan Thomas Scholarship Fund, Scholarship Management Services, Scholarship America, One Scholarship Way, P.O. Box 297, Saint Peter, MN 56082. If you have questions, call 507/931-1682 or e-mail communityfoundation@scholarship america.org.
NUMBER OF AWARDS: 2
RENEWABLE: Yes; must reapply.
CONTACT: Lisa Glanville, 404/308-0055

3304—COMMUNITY FOUNDATION FOR GREATER ATLANTA, INC., THE (Nancy Penn Lyons Scholarship Fund)

50 Hurt Plaza, Suite 449
Atlanta GA 30303
404/688-5525
FAX: 404/688-3060
E-mail: scholarships@atlcf.org
Internet: http://www.atlcf.org/
GrantsScholarships/Scholarships.
aspx
AMOUNT: $5,000
DEADLINE(S): APR 19
FIELD(S): All
ELIGIBILITY/REQUIREMENTS: Open to graduating high school seniors with financial need who have been accepted for enrollment at prestigious or out-of-state universities, Students attending public colleges or universities in the state of Georgia are not eligible. Must be legal resident of Georgia for at least 1 year prior to application, have a combined SAT score of 1000 or higher (math and critical reading only)/ACT composite of 22 or higher. Preference will be given to students attending selective private or out-of-state institutions, cumulative 3.0 GPA or higher, demonstrated history of commitment to community service.
HOW TO APPLY: See website for information and application. Submit with personal essay (2-3 pages) explaining why you feel a college education is important, a statement of educational and career goals, post college career interests, highlights of your high school extracurricular/community service activities, special strengths, skills, and qualifications, any unusual family or personal circumstances that have affected your achievement in school, work experience, or your participation in school and community activities, and present financial need; an official transcript. Send to The Community Foundation for Greater Atlanta, Nancy Penn Lyons Scholarship

Fund, Scholarship Management Services, Scholarship America, One Scholarship Way, P.O. Box 297, Saint Peter, MN 56082. If you have questions, call 507/931-1682 or e-mail communityfoundation@scholarshipamerica.org.
NUMBER OF AWARDS: 5
RENEWABLE: Yes, up to 4 years. Must reapply.

3305—COMMUNITY FOUNDATION FOR GREATER ATLANTA, INC., THE (Women's Chamber of Commerce Scholarship)

50 Hurt Plaza, Suite 449
Atlanta GA 30303
404/688-5525
FAX: 404/688-3060
E-mail: scholarships@atlcf.org
Internet: http://www.atlcf.org/
GrantsScholarships/Scholarships.
aspx
AMOUNT: Up to $1,000
DEADLINE(S): MAR 11
FIELD(S): All
ELIGIBILITY/REQUIREMENTS: Open to a graduating senior at any metropolitan Atlanta high school with a cumulative high school GPA of 3.0 or higher, SAT scores of at least 1000 (math and critical reading) or ACT composite of 22 or higher, accepted to a college or university to pursue an undergraduate degree,
HOW TO APPLY: See website for additional information and application. Submit with a personal essay (2-3 pages) that explains why you feel a college education is important, your statement of educational and career goals, post college career interests, highlights of your high school extracurricular/community service activities, special strengths, skills, and qualifications, any unusual family or personal circumstances have affected your achievement in school, work experience, or your participation in school and community activities, and present financial need; official transcript; and SAT and ACT scores, if a recent high school graduate. Send to The Community Foundation for Greater Atlanta, Women's Chamber of Commerce Scholarship, Scholarship Management Services, Scholarship America, One Scholarship Way, P.O. Box 297, Saint Peter, MN 56082. If you have questions, call 507/931-1682 or e-mail communityfoundation@scholarshipamerica.org.
NUMBER OF AWARDS: 2

3306—COMMUNITY FOUNDATION OF WESTERN MASSACHUSETTS (A. David "Davey" Duggan Memorial Scholarship)

1500 Main Street

P.O. Box 15769
Springfield MA 01115
413/732-2858
FAX: 413/733-8565
E-mail: scholar@community
foundation.org
Internet: http://www.community
foundation.org
AMOUNT: $1,500
DEADLINE(S): MAR 31
FIELD(S): All
ELIGIBILITY/REQUIREMENTS: Open to Protestant students of Hampshire County, Massachusetts, for full-time undergraduate or graduate study. Based on financial need, academic merit, and extracurricular activities.
HOW TO APPLY: See website for application.
NUMBER OF AWARDS: 2
RENEWABLE: No

3307—COMMUNITY FOUNDATION OF WESTERN MASSACHUSETTS (African-American Achievement Scholarships)

1500 Main Street
P.O. Box 15769
Springfield MA 01115
413/732-2858
FAX: 413/733-8565
E-mail: scholar@community
foundation.org
Internet: http://www.community
foundation.org
AMOUNT: $2,500
DEADLINE(S): MAR 31
FIELD(S): All
ELIGIBILITY/REQUIREMENTS: Open to African-American residents of Hampden, Hampshire, and Franklin Counties, Massachusetts, who attend a 4-year college full time. Based on financial need, academic merit, and extracurricular activities.
HOW TO APPLY: See website for application.
NUMBER OF AWARDS: 5
RENEWABLE: No

3308—COMMUNITY FOUNDATION OF WESTERN MASSACHUSETTS (Albert Steiger Memorial Scholarship)

1500 Main Street
P.O. Box 15769
Springfield MA 01115
413/732-2858
FAX: 413/733-8565
E-mail: scholar@community
foundation.org

Internet: http://www.community
foundation.org
AMOUNT: $2,500
DEADLINE(S): MAR 31
FIELD(S): All
ELIGIBILITY/REQUIREMENTS: For graduating seniors of Central High School in Springfield, Massachusetts, to pursue a career through a higher education.
HOW TO APPLY: See website for application.
NUMBER OF AWARDS: 5
RENEWABLE: No

3309—COMMUNITY FOUNDATION OF WESTERN MASSACHUSETTS (Anthony and Madeline Sampson Kapinos Scholarships)

1500 Main Street
P.O. Box 15769
Springfield MA 01115
413/732-2858
FAX: 413/733-8565
E-mail: scholar@community
foundation.org
Internet: http://www.community
foundation.org
AMOUNT: $1,000
DEADLINE(S): MAR 31
FIELD(S): All
ELIGIBILITY/REQUIREMENTS: Open to graduates of Chicopee High School in Massachusetts to assist with continuing their education. Based on financial need.
HOW TO APPLY: See website for application.
NUMBER OF AWARDS: 2
RENEWABLE: Yes, must reapply.

3310—COMMUNITY FOUNDATION OF WESTERN MASSACHUSETTS (Arrighi Memorial Scholarship)

1500 Main Street
P.O. Box 15769
Springfield MA 01115
413/732-2858
FAX: 413/733-8565
E-mail: scholar@community
foundation.org
Internet: http://www.community
foundation.org
AMOUNT: $2,000
DEADLINE(S): MAR 31
FIELD(S): All
ELIGIBILITY/REQUIREMENTS: Open to residents of Greenfield, Massachusetts, for education at the college level (undergraduate, graduate, trade, or professional school).
HOW TO APPLY: See website for application.

NUMBER OF AWARDS: 2
RENEWABLE: No

3311—COMMUNITY FOUNDATION OF WESTERN MASSACHUSETTS (Caleb L. Butler Scholarship)

1500 Main Street
P.O. Box 15769
Springfield MA 01115
413/732-2858
FAX: 413/733-8565
E-mail: scholar@community
foundation.org
Internet: http://www.community
foundation.org
AMOUNT: $1,000
DEADLINE(S): MAR 31
FIELD(S): All
ELIGIBILITY/REQUIREMENTS: Open to former or current residents of Hillcrest Education Centers in Massachusetts who are graduating seniors pursuing postsecondary education or for graduating high school seniors from Franklin, Berkshire, Hampden, or Hampshire Counties, Massachusetts, who are in the custody of the Department of Social Services.
HOW TO APPLY: See website for application.
NUMBER OF AWARDS: 2
RENEWABLE: No

3312—COMMUNITY FOUNDATION OF WESTERN MASSACHUSETTS (Carlos B. Ellis Scholarships)

1500 Main Street
P.O. Box 15769
Springfield MA 01115
413/732-2858
FAX: 413/733/8565
E-mail: scholar@community
foundation.org
Internet: http://www.community
foundation.org
AMOUNT: $1,000
DEADLINE(S): MAR 31
FIELD(S): All
ELIGIBILITY/REQUIREMENTS: Open to members and graduates of Commerce High School in Springfield, Massachusetts, to continue their education. Based on financial need, academic merit, and extracurricular activities. Must submit transcripts and fill out government FAFSA form.
HOW TO APPLY: See website for application.
NUMBER OF AWARDS: 8
RENEWABLE: Yes, must reapply.

3313—COMMUNITY FOUNDATION OF WESTERN MASSACHUSETTS (Charles F. Warner Loans)

1500 Main Street
P.O. Box 15769
Springfield MA 01115
413/732-2858
FAX: 413/733-8565
E-mail: scholar@community foundation.org
Internet: http://www.community foundation.org
AMOUNT: $300
DEADLINE(S): MAR 31
FIELD(S): All
ELIGIBILITY/REQUIREMENTS: Interest-free loans are open to residents of Springfield, Massachusetts, to pursue full-time undergraduate or graduate study. Based on financial need, academic merit, and extracurricular activities.
HOW TO APPLY: See website for application.
NUMBER OF AWARDS: 4-5
RENEWABLE: Yes, must reapply.

3314—COMMUNITY FOUNDATION OF WESTERN MASSACHUSETTS (Clarence H. Matteson Scholarships)

1500 Main Street
P.O. Box 15769
Springfield MA 01115
413/732-2858
FAX: 413/733-8565
E-mail: scholar@community foundation.org
Internet: http://www.community foundation.org
AMOUNT: $1,550
DEADLINE(S): MAR 31
FIELD(S): All
ELIGIBILITY/REQUIREMENTS: Open to residents of Greenfield, Massachusetts, with a high scholastic ability to pursue full-time education beyond high school (college, graduate, or postgraduate studies). Based on financial need, academic merit, and extracurricular activities.
HOW TO APPLY: See website for application. Must submit transcripts and Student Aid Report (SAR).
NUMBER OF AWARDS: 6
RENEWABLE: Yes, must reapply.

3315—COMMUNITY FOUNDATION OF WESTERN MASSACHUSETTS (Deerfield Plastics/Barker Family Fund)

1500 Main Street
P.O. Box 15769

Springfield MA 01115
413/732-2858
FAX: 413/733-8565
E-mail: scholar@community foundation.org
Internet: http://www.community foundation.org
AMOUNT: $1,550
DEADLINE(S): MAR 31
FIELD(S): All
ELIGIBILITY/REQUIREMENTS: Open to children of Deerfield Plastics employees wishing to pursue full-time undergraduate or graduate study. Based on financial need, academic merit, and extracurricular activities.
HOW TO APPLY: See website for application.
NUMBER OF AWARDS: 9
RENEWABLE: Yes, must reapply.

3316—COMMUNITY FOUNDATION OF WESTERN MASSACHUSETTS (Donald A. and Dorothy F. Axtell Grant Scholarships)

1500 Main Street
P.O. Box 15769
Springfield MA 01115
413/732-2858
FAX: 413/733-8565
E-mail: scholar@community foundation.org
Internet: http://www.community foundation.org
AMOUNT: $1,500
DEADLINE(S): MAR 31
FIELD(S): All
ELIGIBILITY/REQUIREMENTS: Open to Protestant students of Hampshire County, Massachusetts, for full-time undergraduate or graduate study. Based on financial need, academic merit, and extracurricular activities.
HOW TO APPLY: See website for application.
NUMBER OF AWARDS: 1
RENEWABLE: Yes, must reapply.

3317—COMMUNITY FOUNDATION OF WESTERN MASSACHUSETTS (Dr. John V. Shea Jr. Scholarship)

1500 Main Street
P.O. Box 15769
Springfield MA 01115
413/732-2858
FAX: 413/733-8565
E-mail: scholar@community foundation.org
Internet: http://www.community foundation.org

AMOUNT: $500
DEADLINE(S): MAR 31
FIELD(S): All
ELIGIBILITY/REQUIREMENTS: For graduates of Springfield, Massachusetts, high schools obtaining a college education.
HOW TO APPLY: See website for application.
NUMBER OF AWARDS: 2
RENEWABLE: No

3318—COMMUNITY FOUNDATION OF WESTERN MASSACHUSETTS (Dr. Margaret H. Sutton Student Loan)

1500 Main Street
P.O. Box 15769
Springfield MA 01115
413/732-2858
FAX: 413/733-8565
E-mail: scholar@community foundation.org
Internet: http://www.community foundation.org
AMOUNT: $2,000
DEADLINE(S): MAR 31
FIELD(S): All
ELIGIBILITY/REQUIREMENTS: For students of Swiss descent enrolled in a 2- or 4-year college, who demonstrate financial need and maintain a good academic average.
HOW TO APPLY: See website for application.
NUMBER OF AWARDS: 7
RENEWABLE: No

3319—COMMUNITY FOUNDATION OF WESTERN MASSACHUSETTS (Eleanor M. Morrissey Scholarship)

1500 Main Street
P.O. Box 15769
Springfield MA 01115
413/732-2858
FAX: 413/733-8565
E-mail: scholar@community foundation.org
Internet: http://www.community foundation.org
AMOUNT: $700
DEADLINE(S): MAR 31
FIELD(S): All (4-year programs);
    Nursing
ELIGIBILITY/REQUIREMENTS: Open to graduating seniors from Holyoke high schools in Holyoke, Massachusetts, who will be attending a 4-year college or to study nursing. GPA of 3.0 or higher required. Must demonstrate financial need and have participated in extracurricular activities.

HOW TO APPLY: See website for application.
NUMBER OF AWARDS: 1
RENEWABLE: No

3320—COMMUNITY FOUNDATION OF WESTERN MASSACHUSETTS (First National Bank of Amherst Centennial Educational Scholarships)

1500 Main Street
P.O. Box 15769
Springfield MA 01115
413/732-2858
FAX: 413/733-8565
E-mail: scholar@community
foundation.org
Internet: http://www.community
foundation.org
AMOUNT: $400
DEADLINE(S): MAR 31
FIELD(S): All
ELIGIBILITY/REQUIREMENTS: Open to high school seniors from Northampton, Hadley, and Amherst attending college in Massachusetts. Based on financial need, academic merit, and extracurricular activities.
HOW TO APPLY: See website for application.
NUMBER OF AWARDS: 3
RENEWABLE: No

3321—COMMUNITY FOUNDATION OF WESTERN MASSACHUSETTS (Frank W. Jendrysik Jr. Memorial Scholarship)

1500 Main Street
P.O. Box 15769
Springfield MA 01115
413/732-2858
FAX: 413/733-8565
E-mail: scholar@community
foundation.org
Internet: http://www.community
foundation.org
AMOUNT: $400
DEADLINE(S): MAR 31
FIELD(S): All
ELIGIBILITY/REQUIREMENTS: Open to residents of Chicopee, Holyoke, and Springfield, Massachusetts, to pursue full-time undergraduate or graduate study. Based on financial need, academic merit, and extracurricular activities.
HOW TO APPLY: See website for application.
NUMBER OF AWARDS: 1
RENEWABLE: Yes, must reapply.

3322—COMMUNITY FOUNDATION OF WESTERN MASSACHUSETTS (Fred K. Lane Scholarship Fund)

1500 Main Street

P.O. Box 15769
Springfield MA 01115
413/732-2858
FAX: 413/733-8565
E-mail: scholar@community
foundation.org
Internet: http://www.community
foundation.org
AMOUNT: $1,000
DEADLINE(S): MAR 31
FIELD(S): All
ELIGIBILITY/REQUIREMENTS: For graduating high school seniors pursuing higher education, who are past or current members (individuals or families) of, or who worked at, the Orchard Golf Course in South Hadley, Massachusetts.
HOW TO APPLY: See website for application.
NUMBER OF AWARDS: 1
RENEWABLE: No

3323—COMMUNITY FOUNDATION OF WESTERN MASSACHUSETTS (Frederick W. Porter Scholarships)

1500 Main Street
P.O. Box 15769
Springfield MA 01115
413/732-2858
FAX: 413/733-8565
E-mail: scholar@community
foundation.org
Internet: http://www.community
foundation.org
AMOUNT: $800
DEADLINE(S): MAR 31
FIELD(S): All
ELIGIBILITY/REQUIREMENTS: Open to graduates of Greenfield High School in Massachusetts to pursue full-time undergraduate or graduate study. Based on financial need, academic merit, and extracurricular activities.
HOW TO APPLY: See website for application.
NUMBER OF AWARDS: 1
RENEWABLE: No

3324—COMMUNITY FOUNDATION OF WESTERN MASSACHUSETTS (Gertrude and William C. Hill Scholarships)

1500 Main Street
P.O. Box 15769
Springfield MA 01115
413/732-2858
FAX: 413/733-8565
E-mail: scholar@community
foundation.org
Internet: http://www.community
foundation.org

AMOUNT: $1,000-$2,000
DEADLINE(S): MAR 31
FIELD(S): All
ELIGIBILITY/REQUIREMENTS: Open to graduates of Central High School in Springfield, Massachusetts, to obtain a college education. Preference given to those majoring in liberal arts. Based on financial need, academic merit, and extracurricular activities. Must submit transcripts and fill out government FAFSA form.
HOW TO APPLY: See website for application.
NUMBER OF AWARDS: 7
RENEWABLE: Yes, must reapply.

3325—COMMUNITY FOUNDATION OF WESTERN MASSACHUSETTS (Herberto Flores Scholarship)

1500 Main Street
P.O. Box 15769
Springfield MA 01115
413/732-2858
FAX: 413/733-8565
E-mail: scholar@community
foundation.org
Internet: http://www.community
foundation.org
AMOUNT: $200
DEADLINE(S): MAR 31
FIELD(S): All
ELIGIBILITY/REQUIREMENTS: For students of Puerto Rican ancestry from Hampshire or Hampden Counties in Massachusetts, who are graduates of Springfield Technical Community College or Holyoke Community College planning to attend a Massachusetts state college.
HOW TO APPLY: See website for application.
NUMBER OF AWARDS: 2
RENEWABLE: No

3326—COMMUNITY FOUNDATION OF WESTERN MASSACHUSETTS (Horace Hill Scholarships)

1500 Main Street
P.O. Box 15769
Springfield MA 01115
413/732-2858
FAX: 413/733-8565
E-mail: scholar@community
foundation.org
Internet: http://www.community
foundation.org
AMOUNT: $600
DEADLINE(S): MAR 31
FIELD(S): All
ELIGIBILITY/REQUIREMENTS: Open to children and grandchildren of the mem-

bers of the Springfield Newspapers' 25 Year Club to pursue full-time undergraduate or graduate study. Based on financial need, academic merit, and extracurricular activities.
HOW TO APPLY: See website for application.
NUMBER OF AWARDS: 4
RENEWABLE: Yes, must reapply.

3327—COMMUNITY FOUNDATION OF WESTERN MASSACHUSETTS (James B. Krumsiek Memorial Scholarship)

1500 Main Street
P.O. Box 15769
Springfield MA 01115
413/732-2858
FAX: 413/733-8565
E-mail: scholar@community
foundation.org
Internet: http://www.community
foundation.org
AMOUNT: $700
DEADLINE(S): MAR 31
FIELD(S): All
ELIGIBILITY/REQUIREMENTS: For graduating seniors of Cathedral High School in Springfield, or Longmeadow High School in Longmeadow, Massachusetts, who are active in athletics and exhibit academic achievement.
HOW TO APPLY: See website for application.
NUMBER OF AWARDS: 2
RENEWABLE: No

3328—COMMUNITY FOUNDATION OF WESTERN MASSACHUSETTS (James W. Colgan Loan Fund)

1500 Main Street
P.O. Box 15769
Springfield MA 01115
413/732-2858
FAX: 413/733-8565
E-mail: scholar@community
foundation.org
Internet: http://www.community
foundation.org
AMOUNT: $2,000-$4,000
DEADLINE(S): MAR 31
FIELD(S): All
ELIGIBILITY/REQUIREMENTS: Interest-free loans are open to residents of Massachusetts for the past five years to pursue full-time undergraduate study. Based on financial need, academic merit, and extracurricular activities.
HOW TO APPLY: See website for application.
NUMBER OF AWARDS: 189
RENEWABLE: Yes, must reapply.

3329—COMMUNITY FOUNDATION OF WESTERN MASSACHUSETTS (James Z. Naurison Scholarships)

1500 Main Street
P.O. Box 15769
Springfield MA 01115
413/732-2858
FAX: 413/733-8565
E-mail: scholar@community
foundation.org
Internet: http://www.community
foundation.org
AMOUNT: $700
DEADLINE(S): MAR 31
FIELD(S): All
ELIGIBILITY/REQUIREMENTS: Open to residents of Hampden, Hampshire, Franklin, and Berkshire Counties, Massachusetts, and Enfield and Suffield, Connecticut, for full-time study. Based on financial need, academic merit, and extracurricular activities.
HOW TO APPLY: See website for application.
NUMBER OF AWARDS: 524
RENEWABLE: No

3330—COMMUNITY FOUNDATION OF WESTERN MASSACHUSETTS (Jane A. Korzeniowski Memorial Scholarship)

1500 Main Street
P.O. Box 15769
Springfield MA 01115
413/732-2858
FAX: 413/733-8565
E-mail: scholar@community
foundation.org
Internet: http://www.community
foundation.org
AMOUNT: $700
DEADLINE(S): MAR 31
FIELD(S): All
ELIGIBILITY/REQUIREMENTS: Open to Chicopee, Massachusetts, residents who attend or plan to attend college for full-time graduate or undergraduate study. Based on financial need, academic merit, and extracurricular activities.
HOW TO APPLY: See website for application.
NUMBER OF AWARDS: 1
RENEWABLE: No

3331—COMMUNITY FOUNDATION OF WESTERN MASSACHUSETTS (Jane M. Knapp Scholarship Fund)

1500 Main Street
P.O. Box 15769
Springfield MA 01115

413/732-2858
FAX: 413/733-8565
E-mail: scholar@community
foundation.org
Internet: http://www.community
foundation.org
AMOUNT: $500
DEADLINE(S): MAR 31
FIELD(S): All
ELIGIBILITY/REQUIREMENTS: For graduates of MacDuffie School in Springfield, Massachusetts, to obtain a college education.
HOW TO APPLY: See website for application.
NUMBER OF AWARDS: 2
RENEWABLE: No

3332—COMMUNITY FOUNDATION OF WESTERN MASSACHUSETTS (Jessie M. Law Scholarships)

1500 Main Street
P.O. Box 15769
Springfield MA 01115
413/732-2858
FAX: 413/733-8565
E-mail: scholar@community
foundation.org
Internet: http://www.community
foundation.org
AMOUNT: $1,000-$2,000
DEADLINE(S): MAR 31
FIELD(S): All
ELIGIBILITY/REQUIREMENTS: For graduates of Central High School in Springfield, Massachusetts. Based on financial need, academic merit, and extracurricular activities.
HOW TO APPLY: See website for application.
NUMBER OF AWARDS: 5
RENEWABLE: Yes, must reapply.

3333—COMMUNITY FOUNDATION OF WESTERN MASSACHUSETTS (John P. and James F. Mahoney Memorial Scholarships)

1500 Main Street
P.O. Box 15769
Springfield MA 01115
413/732-2858
FAX: 413/733-8565
E-mail: scholar@community
foundation.org
Internet: http://www.community
foundation.org
AMOUNT: $1,000
DEADLINE(S): MAR 31
FIELD(S): All

ELIGIBILITY/REQUIREMENTS: Open to residents of Hampshire County, Massachusetts, attending college or vocational school full time. Based on financial need, academic merit, and extracurricular activities.
HOW TO APPLY: See website for application.
NUMBER OF AWARDS: 1
RENEWABLE: No

3334—COMMUNITY FOUNDATION OF WESTERN MASSACHUSETTS (Joseph Bonfitto Scholarship)

1500 Main Street
P.O. Box 15769
Springfield MA 01115
413/732-2858
FAX: 413/733-8565
E-mail: scholar@community
foundation.org
Internet: http://www.community
foundation.org
AMOUNT: $1,400
DEADLINE(S): MAR 31
FIELD(S): All
ELIGIBILITY/REQUIREMENTS: Open to graduating seniors of Agawam High School in Massachusetts who are pursuing a career through higher education in one of the above areas of study. Based on financial need, academic merit, and extracurricular activities.
HOW TO APPLY: See website for application.
NUMBER OF AWARDS: 1
RENEWABLE: No

3335—COMMUNITY FOUNDATION OF WESTERN MASSACHUSETTS (Kenneth B. and Adeline J. Graves Scholarships)

1500 Main Street
P.O. Box 15769
Springfield MA 01115
413/732-2858
FAX: 413/733-8565
E-mail: scholar@community
foundation.org
Internet: http://www.community
foundation.org
AMOUNT: $2,600-$3,000
DEADLINE(S): MAR 31
FIELD(S): All
ELIGIBILITY/REQUIREMENTS: Open to residents of Granby, Massachusetts, pursuing full-time undergraduate or graduate study. Based on financial need, academic merit, and extracurricular activities. Must submit transcripts and fill out government FAFSA form.

HOW TO APPLY: See website for application.
NUMBER OF AWARDS: 11
RENEWABLE: Yes, must reapply.

3336—COMMUNITY FOUNDATION OF WESTERN MASSACHUSETTS (Kimber Richter Family Scholarship)

1500 Main Street
P.O. Box 15769
Springfield MA 01115
413/732-2858
FAX: 413/733-8565
E-mail: scholar@community
foundation.org
Internet: http://www.community
foundation.org
AMOUNT: $600
DEADLINE(S): MAR 31
FIELD(S): All
ELIGIBILITY/REQUIREMENTS: Open to students of the Baha'i faith who attend or plan to attend college full time at the undergraduate or graduate level. Must be resident of Western Massachusetts. Based on financial need, academic merit, and extracurricular activities.
HOW TO APPLY: See website for application.
NUMBER OF AWARDS: 1
RENEWABLE: No

3337—COMMUNITY FOUNDATION OF WESTERN MASSACHUSETTS (Latino Breakfast Club Scholarship)

1500 Main Street
P.O. Box 15769
Springfield MA 01115
413/732-2858
FAX: 413/733-8565
E-mail: scholar@community
foundation.org
Internet: http://www.community
foundation.org
AMOUNT: To be announced
DEADLINE(S): MAR 31
FIELD(S): All
ELIGIBILITY/REQUIREMENTS: For graduating Latino students in Hampshire and Hampden Counties in Massachusetts who are entering their first year of college and who are family and/or community service oriented.
HOW TO APPLY: See website for application.
NUMBER OF AWARDS: To be announced
RENEWABLE: No

3338—COMMUNITY FOUNDATION OF WESTERN MASSACHUSETTS (Latino Scholarships)

1500 Main Street
P.O. Box 15769
Springfield MA 01115
413/732-2858
FAX: 413/733-8565
E-mail: scholar@community
foundation.org
Internet: http://www.community
foundation.org
AMOUNT: $1,000
DEADLINE(S): MAR 31
FIELD(S): All
ELIGIBILITY/REQUIREMENTS: Open to Latino residents of Hampden and Hampshire Counties, Massachusetts, who demonstrate academic promise and are community service oriented. Based on financial need, academic merit, and extracurricular activities.
HOW TO APPLY: See website for application.
NUMBER OF AWARDS: 5
RENEWABLE: Yes, must reapply.

3339—COMMUNITY FOUNDATION OF WESTERN MASSACHUSETTS (Lena A. Tucker Scholarships)

1500 Main Street
P.O. Box 15769
Springfield MA 01115
413/732-2858
FAX: 413/733-8565
E-mail: scholar@community
foundation.org
Internet: http://www.community
foundation.org
AMOUNT: $300-$1,500
DEADLINE(S): MAR 31
FIELD(S): All
ELIGIBILITY/REQUIREMENTS: Open to Springfield students from High School of Commerce and Putnam Vocational-Technical High School in Massachusetts to pursue college education. Based on financial need, academic merit, and extracurricular activities.
HOW TO APPLY: See website for application. Must submit transcripts and fill out government FAFSA form.
NUMBER OF AWARDS: 20
RENEWABLE: Yes, must reapply.

3340—COMMUNITY FOUNDATION OF WESTERN MASSACHUSETTS (Louis W. and Mary S. Doherty Scholarships)

1500 Main Street

P.O. Box 15769
Springfield MA 01115
413/732-2858
FAX: 413/733-8565
E-mail: scholar@community
foundation.org
Internet: http://www.community
foundation.org
AMOUNT: $2,000
DEADLINE(S): MAR 31
FIELD(S): All
ELIGIBILITY/REQUIREMENTS: Open
to students from Hampden, Hampshire,
and Franklin Counties in Massachusetts,
who attend or plan to attend college full
time. Based on financial need, academic
merit, and extracurricular activities.
HOW TO APPLY: See website for application.
NUMBER OF AWARDS: 17
RENEWABLE: Yes, must reapply.

3341—COMMUNITY FOUNDATION OF WESTERN MASSACHUSETTS (Lucius H. Tarbell and Dorothy J. Tarbell Scholarships)

1500 Main Street
P.O. Box 15769
Springfield MA 01115
413/732-2858
FAX: 413/733-8565
E-mail: scholar@community
foundation.org
Internet: http://www.community
foundation.org
AMOUNT: $2,200
DEADLINE(S): MAR 31
FIELD(S): All
ELIGIBILITY/REQUIREMENTS: Open
to students of Western New England
College in Massachusetts to pursue full-
time undergraduate or graduate study.
Based on financial need, academic merit,
and extracurricular activities.
HOW TO APPLY: See website for application.
NUMBER OF AWARDS: 2
RENEWABLE: Yes, must reapply.

3342—COMMUNITY FOUNDATION OF WESTERN MASSACHUSETTS (MacGeachey Minarik Scholarship Fund)

1500 Main Street
P.O. Box 15769
Springfield MA 01115
413/732-2858
FAX: 413/733-8565

E-mail: scholar@community
foundation.org
Internet: http://www.community
foundation.org
AMOUNT: To be announced
DEADLINE(S): MAR 31
FIELD(S): All
ELIGIBILITY/REQUIREMENTS: For
residents of Monson, Massachusetts, who
have lived there for at least 2 years.
Preference is given to graduates of
Monson High School or Pathfinder
Regional High School.
HOW TO APPLY: See website for application.
NUMBER OF AWARDS: To be announced
RENEWABLE: No

3343—COMMUNITY FOUNDATION OF WESTERN MASSACHUSETTS (Margaret J. Hyland Scholarships)

1500 Main Street
P.O. Box 15769
Springfield MA 01115
413/732-2858
FAX: 413/733-8565
E-mail: scholar@community
foundation.org
Internet: http://www.community
foundation.org
AMOUNT: $2,000-$3,000
DEADLINE(S): MAR 31
FIELD(S): All
ELIGIBILITY/REQUIREMENTS: Open
to undergraduates and graduates pursuing
full-time study at the University of
Massachusetts who have been Holyoke
residents for ten years or longer.
Preference given to financially needy stu-
dents of the Roman Catholic faith. Based
on financial need, academic merit, and
extracurricular activities.
HOW TO APPLY: See website for application.
NUMBER OF AWARDS: 27
RENEWABLE: Yes, must reapply.

3344—COMMUNITY FOUNDATION OF WESTERN MASSACHUSETTS (MassMutual Scholars Program)

1500 Main Street
P.O. Box 15769
Springfield MA 01115
413/732-2858
FAX: 413/733-8565
E-mail: scholar@community
foundation.org

Internet: http://www.community
foundation.org
AMOUNT: $5,000
DEADLINE(S): MAR 31
FIELD(S): All
ELIGIBILITY/REQUIREMENTS: For
graduating high school seniors, who reside
in Hamden County, Massachusetts, or
Hartford County, Connecticut, who main-
tain a "B" average or better for 4 consecu-
tive marking periods.
HOW TO APPLY: See website for application.
NUMBER OF AWARDS: 40
RENEWABLE: Yes, must reapply.

3345—COMMUNITY FOUNDATION OF WESTERN MASSACHUSETTS (Mt. Sugarloaf Lodge Memorial Scholarships)

1500 Main Street
P.O. Box 15769
Springfield MA 01115
413/732-2858
FAX: 413/733-8565
E-mail: scholar@community
foundation.org
Internet: http://www.community
foundation.org
AMOUNT: $300
DEADLINE(S): MAR 31
FIELD(S): All
ELIGIBILITY/REQUIREMENTS: Open
to students from Frontier Regional High
School in Massachusetts to pursue full-
time undergraduate or graduate study.
Based on financial need, academic merit,
and extracurricular activities.
HOW TO APPLY: See website for application.
NUMBER OF AWARDS: 4
RENEWABLE: Yes, must reapply.

3346—COMMUNITY FOUNDATION OF WESTERN MASSACHUSETTS (National Association of Insurance and Financial Advisors Scholarship Fund)

1500 Main Street
P.O. Box 15769
Springfield MA 01115
413/732-2858
FAX: 413/733-8565
E-mail: scholar@community
foundation.org
Internet: http://www.community
foundation.org
AMOUNT: $2,000
DEADLINE(S): MAR 31
FIELD(S): All

ELIGIBILITY/REQUIREMENTS: For graduating high school seniors, residing in Hampden or Berkshire Counties, both in Massachusetts, whose parent is deceased or is receiving social security disability benefits.
HOW TO APPLY: See website for application.
NUMBER OF AWARDS: 6
RENEWABLE: No

3347—COMMUNITY FOUNDATION OF WESTERN MASSACHUSETTS (Nicholas G. Grass Scholarship Fund)

1500 Main Street
P.O. Box 15769
Springfield MA 01115
413/732-2858
FAX: 413/733-8565
E-mail: scholar@community
foundation.org
Internet: http://www.community
foundation.org
AMOUNT: $500
DEADLINE(S): MAR 31
FIELD(S): All
ELIGIBILITY/REQUIREMENTS: For graduating seniors from Holyoke High School in Holyoke, Massachusetts, who excel both academically and athletically.
HOW TO APPLY: See website for application.
NUMBER OF AWARDS: 1
RENEWABLE: No

3348—COMMUNITY FOUNDATION OF WESTERN MASSACHUSETTS (Permelia A. Butterfield Scholarship)

1500 Main Street
P.O. Box 15769
Springfield MA 01115
413/732-2858
FAX: 413/733-8565
E-mail: scholar@community
foundation.org
Internet: http://www.community
foundation.org
AMOUNT: $3,100
DEADLINE(S): MAR 31
FIELD(S): All
ELIGIBILITY/REQUIREMENTS: Open to residents of Athol, Erving, New Salem, Wendell, Orange, Shutesbury, and Franklin Counties, Massachusetts, to pursue full-time undergraduate or graduate study. Preference given to orphan children (students with 1 or no living parent or those deprived of parental care). Based on financial need, academic merit, and extracurricular activities.

HOW TO APPLY: See website for application.
NUMBER OF AWARDS: 2
RENEWABLE: Yes, must reapply.

3349—COMMUNITY FOUNDATION OF WESTERN MASSACHUSETTS (Robert B. Goodman Scholarship)

1500 Main Street
P.O. Box 15769
Springfield MA 01115
413/732-2858
FAX: 413/733-8565
E-mail: scholar@community
foundation.org
Internet: http://www.community
foundation.org
AMOUNT: $500
DEADLINE(S): MAR 31
FIELD(S): All
ELIGIBILITY/REQUIREMENTS: For graduating seniors who are residents of Montgomery, Massachusetts, planning to attend a 2- or 4-year college.
HOW TO APPLY: See website for application.
NUMBER OF AWARDS: 1
RENEWABLE: No

3350—COMMUNITY FOUNDATION OF WESTERN MASSACHUSETTS (Ruth L. Brocklebank Memorial Scholarships)

1500 Main Street
P.O. Box 15769
Springfield MA 01115
413/732-2858
FAX: 413/733-8565
E-mail: scholar@community
foundation.org
Internet: http://www.community
foundation.org
AMOUNT: $300
DEADLINE(S): MAR 31
FIELD(S): All
ELIGIBILITY/REQUIREMENTS: Open to African-American students from the Springfield Public School System high schools to attend college. Based on financial need, academic merit, and extracurricular activities.
HOW TO APPLY: See website for application.
NUMBER OF AWARDS: 6
RENEWABLE: Yes, must reapply.

3351—COMMUNITY FOUNDATION OF WESTERN MASSACHUSETTS (Stanley Ciejek Sr. Scholarships)

1500 Main Street

P.O. Box 15769
Springfield MA 01115
413/732-2858
FAX: 413/733-8565
E-mail: scholar@community
foundation.org
Internet: http://www.community
foundation.org
AMOUNT: $300
DEADLINE(S): MAR 31
FIELD(S): All
ELIGIBILITY/REQUIREMENTS: Open to residents of Hampden, Hampshire, and Franklin Counties, Massachusetts, to pursue full-time undergraduate or graduate study at a Massachusetts institute of higher education. Based on financial need, academic merit, and extracurricular activities.
HOW TO APPLY: See website for application.
NUMBER OF AWARDS: 5
RENEWABLE: Yes, must reapply.

3352—COMMUNITY FOUNDATION OF WESTERN MASSACHUSETTS (Stuart D. Mackey Scholarship)

1500 Main Street
P.O. Box 15769
Springfield MA 01115
413/732-2858
FAX: 413/733-8565
E-mail: scholar@community
foundation.org
Internet: http://www.community
foundation.org
AMOUNT: $500
DEADLINE(S): MAR 31
FIELD(S): All
ELIGIBILITY/REQUIREMENTS: Open to graduates of East Longmeadow High School in Massachusetts who have strong academic records to pursue full-time undergraduate or graduate study. Based on financial need, academic merit, and extracurricular activities. Must submit transcripts and fill out government FAFSA form.
HOW TO APPLY: See website for application.
NUMBER OF AWARDS: 1
RENEWABLE: No

3353—COMMUNITY FOUNDATION OF WESTERN MASSACHUSETTS (United Way/YWCA Scholarship Fund for Women)

1500 Main Street
P.O. Box 15769
Springfield MA 01115
413/732-2858
FAX: 413/733-8565

E-mail: scholar@community
foundation.org
Internet: http://www.community
foundation.org
AMOUNT: $2,500
DEADLINE(S): MAR 31
FIELD(S): All
ELIGIBILITY/REQUIREMENTS: For
women age 18 or older, who are residents
of Holyoke, Massachusetts, and can
demonstrate financial need. Must be
attending or planning to attend college.
HOW TO APPLY: See website for application.
NUMBER OF AWARDS: 1 every other
year
RENEWABLE: No

3354—COMMUNITY FOUNDATION OF WESTERN MASSACHUSETTS (Westbank-Stanley F. Osowski Scholarship Fund)

1500 Main Street
P.O. Box 15769
Springfield MA 01115
413/732-2858
FAX: 413/733-8565
E-mail: scholar@community
foundation.org
Internet: http://www.community
foundation.org
AMOUNT: $500
DEADLINE(S): MAR 31
FIELD(S): All
ELIGIBILITY/REQUIREMENTS: For
graduates of Westfield High in Westfield,
Massachusetts, to obtain a college education.
HOW TO APPLY: See website for application.
NUMBER OF AWARDS: 2
RENEWABLE: No

3355—COMMUNITY FOUNDATION OF WESTERN MASSACHUSETTS (Wilcox-Ware Scholarships)

1500 Main Street
P.O. Box 15769
Springfield MA 01115
413/732-2858
FAX: 413/733-8565
E-mail: scholar@community
foundation.org
Internet: http://www.community
foundation.org
AMOUNT: $1,800-$3,200
DEADLINE(S): MAR 31
FIELD(S): All
ELIGIBILITY/REQUIREMENTS: Open
to graduates of Mohawk Regional High
School in Massachusetts who reside in

Buckland, Shelburne, Colrain, or contiguous towns to pursue undergraduate or
graduate study. Based on financial need,
academic merit, and extracurricular activities.
HOW TO APPLY: See website for application.
NUMBER OF AWARDS: 11
RENEWABLE: No

3356—COMMUNITY FOUNDATION OF WESTERN MASSACHUSETTS (William Dean and Mary Fitzsimmons Dean Scholarship)

1500 Main Street
P.O. Box 15769
Springfield MA 01115
413/732-2858
FAX: 413/733-8565
E-mail: scholar@community
foundation.org
Internet: http://www.community
foundation.org
AMOUNT: $1,800-$3,200
DEADLINE(S): MAR 31
FIELD(S): All
HOW TO APPLY: See website for application.
ELIGIBILITY/REQUIREMENTS: Open
to graduates of William J. Dean Technical
High School in Holyoke, Massachusetts,
pursuing higher education.
NUMBER OF AWARDS: 11
RENEWABLE: No

3357—COMMUNITY FOUNDATION OF WESTERN MASSACHUSETTS (Women's Partnership Scholarship Fund for Women)

1500 Main Street
P.O. Box 15769
Springfield MA 01115
413/732-2858
FAX: 413/733-8565
E-mail: scholar@community
foundation.org
Internet: http://www.community
foundation.org
AMOUNT: $1,000-$3,000
DEADLINE(S): MAR 31
FIELD(S): All
ELIGIBILITY/REQUIREMENTS: For
women age 25 or older from the greater
Springfield, Massachusetts, area who have
had a break in their education, are attending an accredited college in Hampden or
Hampshire Counties in Massachusetts, and
are trying to re-enter the workforce.
HOW TO APPLY: See website for application.
NUMBER OF AWARDS: 4
RENEWABLE: No

3358—CONCORDIA UNIVERSITY (Entrance Scholarships)

Financial Aid and Awards Office
1455 de Maisonneuve
Boulevard W.
Montreal Quebec H3G 1M8
CANADA
514/848-3507
FAX: 514/848-3508
E-mail: awardsgs@vax2.
concordia.ca
Internet: http://www.concordia.ca
AMOUNT: $1,000-$2,000 (Canadian)
DEADLINE(S): MAR 1 (Fall Term) and
NOV 1 (Winter Term)
FIELD(S): All
ELIGIBILITY/REQUIREMENTS: Open
to students entering their 1st year of full-
time study. Based on academic achievement during the first 3 semesters of
CEGEP or equivalent. Fine Arts
Department awards may be based on portfolios, auditions or interviews. Must be full
time (30 credits/academic year).
HOW TO APPLY: Automatically considered with application for admission to
University.
NUMBER OF AWARDS: Multiple
RENEWABLE: No
CONTACT: Undergraduate Scholarships
and Awards Committee

3359—CONCORDIA UNIVERSITY (Loyola Alumni Association Inc. Educational Grant)

Financial Aid and Awards Office
1455 de Maisonneuve
Boulevard W.
Montreal Quebec H3G 1M8
CANADA
514/848-3507
FAX: 514/848-3508
E-mail: gardd@vax2.concordia.ca
Internet: http://www.concordia.ca
AMOUNT: $1,500 (Canadian)
DEADLINE(S): APR 1
FIELD(S): All
ELIGIBILITY/REQUIREMENTS: Open
to full-time students at any level. Preference given to children and grandchildren
of active Loyola Alumni Association members. Grant is awarded on the basis of
scholastic achievement, the applicant's
statement, and letters of reference.
HOW TO APPLY: Contact the Financial
Aid and Awards Office for an application.
NUMBER OF AWARDS: 5

3360—CONCORDIA UNIVERSITY (Loyola Foundation Inc. Entrance Scholarships)

Financial Aid and Awards Office

1455 de Maisonneuve
Boulevard W.
Montreal Quebec H3G 1M8
CANADA
514/848-3507
FAX: 514/848-3508
E-mail: awardsgs@vax2.
concordia.ca
Internet: http://www.concordia.ca
AMOUNT: $2,000 (Canadian)
DEADLINE(S): AUG 1
FIELD(S): All
ELIGIBILITY/REQUIREMENTS: Open to students entering their 1st year of full-time study who are graduates of Loyola High School. Based on academic ranking as assigned by the University in the course of admission, and on the strength of the recommendation by Loyola High School.
HOW TO APPLY: Application and recommendation forms are available from the Financial Aid and Awards Office of Concordia University and the Admissions Office of Loyola High School. Send letter of recommendation from Loyola High School, following the completion of CEGEP or equivalent.
RENEWABLE: Yes. Subject to full-time enrollment and maintenance of 3.0 GPA.

3361—CONCORDIA UNIVERSITY (Mature Entrance Scholarships)

Financial Aid and Awards Office
1455 de Maisonneuve
Boulevard W.
Montreal Quebec H3G 1M8
CANADA
514/848-3507
FAX: 514/848-3508
E-mail: awardsgs@vax2.
concordia.ca
Internet: http://www.concordia.ca
AMOUNT: $2,000 (Canadian)
DEADLINE(S): APR 1
FIELD(S): All
ELIGIBILITY/REQUIREMENTS: Open to mature students admitted to the University. Mature student candidates will be considered upon successful completion of their first 18 credits at Concordia University.
HOW TO APPLY: Application forms are available from the Financial Aid and Awards Office.
RENEWABLE: No

3362—CONCORDIA UNIVERSITY (Rona and Irving Levitt Family Foundation Entrance Scholarships)

Financial Aid and Awards Office

1455 de Maisonneuve
Boulevard W.
Montreal Quebec H3G 1M8
CANADA
514/848-3507
FAX: 514/848-3508
E-mail: awardsgs@vax2.
concordia.ca
Internet: http://www.concordia.ca
AMOUNT: $1,000 (Canadian)
DEADLINE(S): APR 1
FIELD(S): All
ELIGIBILITY/REQUIREMENTS: Open to students entering their 1st year of full-time study. Based on academic achievement during the 1st 3 semesters of CEGEP or equivalent, and a personal statement provided by the applicant.
HOW TO APPLY: Application forms are available from the Financial Aid and Awards Office.
NUMBER OF AWARDS: Multiple
RENEWABLE: No
CONTACT: Undergraduate Scholarships and Awards Committee

3363—CONCORDIA UNIVERSITY (Senior Scholarships)

Financial Aid and Awards Office
1455 de Maisonneuve
Boulevard W.
Montreal Quebec H3G 1M8
CANADA
514/848-3507
FAX: 514/848-3508
E-mail: admreg@alcor.concordia.ca
Internet: http://www.concordia.ca
AMOUNT: $500 (Canadian)
DEADLINE(S): AUG 1
FIELD(S): All
ELIGIBILITY/REQUIREMENTS: Must be Canadian citizens/permanent residents, intending to study full time and aged 60 years or more in the year of application. Awards are made on the basis of the academic record and an interview.
HOW TO APPLY: Contact the Financial Aid and Awards Office for an application.
NUMBER OF AWARDS: 1
RENEWABLE: Yes. Up to 4 years.

3364—CONGRESSIONAL HISPANIC CAUCUS INSTITUTE (Summer Internship Program)

911 2nd Street NE
Washington DC 20002
800/EXCEL-DC or 202/543-1771
E-mail: comments@chci.org
Internet: http://www.chci.org

AMOUNT: Stipend, round-trip transportation, and housing
DEADLINE(S): JAN 31
FIELD(S): All
ELIGIBILITY/REQUIREMENTS: Open to college-bound high school seniors and currently enrolled undergraduates (except college seniors). Must be Hispanic; minimum 3.0 GPA, excellent written and oral communication skills, active interest/participation in community affairs, a solid work ethic, and leadership potential. Must be U.S. citizen/permanent resident or have student work visa.
HOW TO APPLY: See website or contact CHCI for an application. Two essays, a personal statement and 1 relating to public policy as it effects the Hispanic community, are required.
NUMBER OF AWARDS: 30

3365—CONTRA COSTA COLLEGE (Metas Scholarship)

2600 Mission Bell Drive, H31
San Pablo CA 94806
510/235-7800, ext. 4608
E-mail: rmvaldez@contra
costa.cc.ca.us
AMOUNT: $100-$1,500
DEADLINE(S): MAY 1
FIELD(S): All
ELIGIBILITY/REQUIREMENTS: Must be part of the Metas program at Contra Costa College for at least 1 year.
HOW TO APPLY: Contact College for application and details.
CONTACT: Rosa Valdez

3366—COUNCIL OF CITIZENS WITH LOW VISION (Fred Scheigert Scholarship Program)

1239 American Beauty Drive
Salt Lake City UT 84116
800/733-2258
Internet: http://www.cclvi.org/
scholar/scholarship
DEADLINE(S): APR 15
FIELD(S): All
ELIGIBILITY/REQUIREMENTS: Open to graduating seniors accepted to a university or continuing students in good standing who are visually impaired, with a vision range from low vision (20/70 in the better eye with best possible correction, or a field restricted to no greater than 30 degrees), to those who, in spite of a more significant vision or field restriction, are able to benefit from the use of low-vision devices to perform daily visual tasks. Minimum GPA 3.0.

HOW TO APPLY: Send application; transcript; 2 letters (only) of recommendation; a letter of acceptance; and a statement from an ophthalmologist.
CONTACT: Janis Stanger

3367—CUBAN-AMERICAN TEACHERS ASSOCIATION SCHOLARSHIP

P.O. Box 6422
Santa Ana CA 92706
714/541-4331
FAX: 714/664-0517
Internet: http://www.diversepro.com/hispanic
AMOUNT: $300-$1,000
DEADLINE(S): APR 1
FIELD(S): All
ELIGIBILITY/REQUIREMENTS: Must be high school graduates of Cuban descent; residents of Los Angeles County; minimum 3.0 GPA; and speak "acceptable" Spanish.
HOW TO APPLY: Send application.
NUMBER OF AWARDS: 30
CONTACT: Victor Cueto

3368—CYPRUS CHILDREN'S FUND, INC., THE (Scholarship Endowment)

13 East 40th Street, 5th Floor
New York NY 10016
212/696-4590
FAX: 212/532-9640
AMOUNT: Varies
DEADLINE(S): APR 30
FIELD(S): All
ELIGIBILITY/REQUIREMENTS: To students of Greek or Greek Cypriot origin. Applicants can be U.S. residents, U.S. citizens, or citizens of Greece or Cyprus. May be pursuing studies in accredited college or university in the U.S., Greece, or Cyprus. Must be full-time student, demonstrate academic excellence and financial need.
HOW TO APPLY: Write or call for application and complete information.
NUMBER OF AWARDS: 5
RENEWABLE: No
CONTACT: Executive Director

3369—DADE COMMUNITY FOUNDATION (CAP Inc. Fund)

200 South Biscayne Boulevard,
Suite 505
Miami FL 33131-2343
305/371-2711
FAX: 305/371-5342
E-mail: charisse.grant@dade
community foundation.org
Internet: http://www.dade
community foundation.org

AMOUNT: At least $1,000
DEADLINE(S): JUL 2
FIELD(S): All
ELIGIBILITY/REQUIREMENTS: Must have graduated from a Miami-Dade County public high school or GED; minimum 2 years in a Miami-Dade school; demonstrate financial need. For full-time undergraduates working towards a degree at an approved postsecondary school.
HOW TO APPLY: See website for guidelines and application forms.
NUMBER OF AWARDS: Varies
CONTACT: Charisse Grant, Director of Programs

3370—DADE COMMUNITY FOUNDATION (C.A.S.A./Simon Bolivar Leadership Scholarship)

200 South Biscayne Boulevard,
Suite 505
Miami FL 33131-2343
305/371-2711
FAX: 305/371-5342
E-mail: charisse.grant@dade
community foundation.org
Internet: http://www.dade
community foundation.org
AMOUNT: $1,000
DEADLINE(S): MAR 26
FIELD(S): All
ELIGIBILITY/REQUIREMENTS: Open to students who have excelled academically and are admitted/enrolled as full-time student in a postsecondary public or private institution in Florida. Financial need considered.
HOW TO APPLY: See website for guidelines and application forms.
NUMBER OF AWARDS: 3 (1 each to Colombian-, Hatian- and South American born/descent students).
CONTACT: Charisse Grant, Director of Programs

3371—DADE COMMUNITY FOUNDATION (Judge Sidney M. Aronovitz Memorial Scholarship)

200 South Biscayne Boulevard,
Suite 505
Miami FL 33131-2343
305/371-2711
FAX: 305/371-5342
E-mail: charisse.grant@dade
community foundation.org
Internet: http://www.dade
community foundation.org
AMOUNT: $500
DEADLINE(S): MAR 12
FIELD(S): All

ELIGIBILITY/REQUIREMENTS: Open to Miami-Dade County minority public school students planning to continue their education through to the university level; must be a high school senior or GED recipient.
HOW TO APPLY: See website for guidelines and application forms.
NUMBER OF AWARDS: At least 1
CONTACT: Charisse Grant, Director of Programs

3372—DADE COMMUNITY FOUNDATION (Rodney Thaxton Justice Scholarship Fund & Martin E. Segal Scholarship Fund)

200 South Biscayne Boulevard,
Suite 505
Miami FL 33131-2343
305/371-2711
FAX: 305/371-5342
E-mail: charisse.grant@dade
community foundation.org
Internet: http://www.dade
community foundation.org
AMOUNT: At least $1,000
DEADLINE(S): APR 16
FIELD(S): All
ELIGIBILITY/REQUIREMENTS: Must be students with financial need; African-American descent living in Greater Miami area; accepted into a 4-year college or university; and have achieved academic success. Must be committed to the goal of social justice and must be able to demonstrate that commitment to the scholarship committee.
HOW TO APPLY: See website for guidelines and application forms.
NUMBER OF AWARDS: Varies
CONTACT: Charisse Grant, Director of Programs

3373—DANISH SISTERHOOD OF AMERICA (Betty Hansen Continuing Education Grant)

5113 Epping Lane
Zephyrhills FL 33541-2607
Internet:
http://www.danishsisterhood.org
AMOUNT: Up to $500 each
DEADLINE(S): Varies
FIELD(S): All
ELIGIBILITY/REQUIREMENTS: Must be a Danish Sisterhood member in good standing for at least 1 year prior to application deadline; or be a daughter or son of such a member, or, if deceased, was in good standing at the time of death; minimum GPA of 2.5. Applicant must be enrolled as less than a full-time student at

an accredited and approved educational school; must be enrolled in a course, workshop, seminar, and/or language class relating to Danish culture or heritage.

HOW TO APPLY: Send coupon from Danish Sisterhood Newsletter or from website identifying how you are associated with the Sisterhood and what particular type of scholarship/grant application is desired to contact below; then send application.

NUMBER OF AWARDS: 10

CONTACT: Joyce Houck, National Vice President/Scholarship Chair

3374—DANISH SISTERHOOD OF AMERICA (Betty Hansen National Scholarship)

5113 Epping Lane
Zephyrhills FL 33541-2607
Internet:
http://www.danishsisterhood.org

AMOUNT: $1,000

DEADLINE(S): Varies

FIELD(S): All

ELIGIBILITY/REQUIREMENTS: Must be a Danish Sisterhood member in good standing for at least 1 year prior to application deadline; or be a daughter or son of such a member, or, if deceased, was in good standing at the time of death; minimum GPA of 2.5; a full-time student enrolled or entering an accredited 4-year college or university, either as a graduate or undergraduate student. May be used to study in Denmark upon written request, with the approval of the Scholarship Chair.

HOW TO APPLY: Send coupon from Newsletter or from website to Scholarship Chair identifying your association with the Sisterhood and which scholarship/grant application is desired.

NUMBER OF AWARDS: 8

CONTACT: Joyce Houck, National Vice President/Scholarship Chair.

3375—DANISH SISTERHOOD OF AMERICA (Mildred Sorensen National Scholarship)

5113 Epping Lane
Zephyrhills FL 33541-2607
Internet:
http://www.danishsisterhood.org

AMOUNT: $750

DEADLINE(S): Varies

FIELD(S): All

ELIGIBILITY/REQUIREMENTS: Must be a Danish Sisterhood member in good standing for at least 1 year prior to application deadline; or be a daughter or son of

such a member, or, if deceased, was in good standing at the time of death; minimum GPA of 2.5; high school graduate, enrolled as a student in a technical (vocational) program leading to a certificate, diploma, associate degree, or beyond.

HOW TO APPLY: Send coupon from Newsletter or from website to Scholarship Chairman identifying your association with the Sisterhood and which scholarship/grant application is desired.

NUMBER OF AWARDS: 2

CONTACT: Joyce Houck, National Vice President/Scholarship Chair

3376—DANISH SISTERHOOD OF AMERICA (Olga Christensen National Scholarship)

5113 Epping Lane
Zephyrhills FL 33541-2607
Internet:
http://www.danishsisterhood.org

AMOUNT: $500

DEADLINE(S): Varies

FIELD(S): All

ELIGIBILITY/REQUIREMENTS: Must be a Danish Sisterhood member in good standing for at least 1 year prior to application deadline; or be a daughter or son of such a member, or, if deceased, was in good standing at the time of death; minimum GPA of 2.5 and be a post-high school graduate, enrolled as a student in a technical school program, an associate degree program, or beyond.

HOW TO APPLY: Send coupon from Newsletter or from website to Scholarship Chair identifying your association with the Sisterhood and which scholarship/grant application is desired.

NUMBER OF AWARDS: 2

CONTACT: Joyce Houck, National Vice President/Scholarship Chair

3377—DANISH SISTERHOOD OF AMERICA (Past National Officer's Scholarship)

5113 Epping Lane
Zephyrhills FL 33541-2607
Internet:
http://www.danishsisterhood.org

AMOUNT: $500

DEADLINE(S): Varies

FIELD(S): All

ELIGIBILITY/REQUIREMENTS: Must be a Danish Sisterhood member in good standing for at least 1 year prior to application deadline; or be a daughter or son of such a member, or, if deceased, was in good standing at the time of death; must be

concurrent National Scholarship winner; minimum GPA of 3.8.

HOW TO APPLY: Send coupon from Newsletter or from website to Scholarship Chair identifying your association with the Sisterhood and which scholarship/grant application is desired.

NUMBER OF AWARDS: 1

CONTACT: Joyce Houck, National Vice President/Scholarship Chair

3378—DANISH SISTERHOOD OF AMERICA (Scholarships and Grants)

5113 Epping Lane
Zephyrhills FL 33541-2607
Internet:
http://www.danishsisterhood.org

AMOUNT: Varies

DEADLINE(S): Varies

FIELD(S): All

ELIGIBILITY/REQUIREMENTS: Must be a Danish Sisterhood member in good standing for at least 1 year prior to application deadline; or be a daughter or son of such a member, or, if deceased, was in good standing at the time of death.

HOW TO APPLY: Send coupon from Newsletter or from website to Scholarship Chair identifying your association with the Sisterhood and which scholarship/grant application is desired.

NUMBER OF AWARDS: Multiple

CONTACT: Joyce Houck, National Vice President/Scholarship Chair

3379—DAUGHTERS OF THE CINCINNATI

20 West 44 Street, Suite 508
New York NY 10036
212/991-9945
E-mail: Scholarships@daughters1894.org
Internet: http://www.foundationcenter.org/grantmaker/cincinnati/

AMOUNT: Varies (average $4,000)

DEADLINE(S): MAR 15

FIELD(S): All

ELIGIBILITY/REQUIREMENTS: Open to high school seniors who are daughters of commissioned officers (active, retired, or deceased) in the U.S. Army, Navy, Air Force, Marine Corps, or Coast Guard for undergraduate study at any accredited 4-year institution. Awards based on need and merit.

HOW TO APPLY: Write for application or further information. Include parent's rank and branch of service and current year in high school. Download an application or send a SASE.

NUMBER OF AWARDS: Varies

RENEWABLE: Yes. Up to 4 years.
CONTACT: Scholarship Administrator

3380—DAVIS MEMORIAL FOUNDATION

1098 Foster City Boulevard, #204
Foster City CA 94404-2300
650/570-5446 or 800/725-0333
FAX: 650/570-5460
E-mail: dmf@wsrca.com
Internet: http://www.davis
foundation.org
AMOUNT: $2,000
DEADLINE(S): APR 1
FIELD(S): All (emphasis on construction)
ELIGIBILITY/REQUIREMENTS: Must be an employee, spouse, child (by birth or legal adoption), or stepchild of a roofing professional; attending technical trade school, college or university (undergraduate or graduate). Priority given to construction-related degrees.
HOW TO APPLY: Submit 1 original and 6 copies of application; transcripts; letter from college, university, or technical trade school, indicating provisional acceptance of the proposed course of study; and photo.
NUMBER OF AWARDS: 4

3381—DAVIS-PUTTER SCHOLARSHIP FUND

P.O. Box 7307
New York NY 10116
E-mail: davisputter@hotmail.com
Internet: http://www.davisputter.org
AMOUNT: Up to $6,000
DEADLINE(S): APR 1
FIELD(S): All
ELIGIBILITY/REQUIREMENTS: Provides grants to students actively working for peace and justice.
HOW TO APPLY: See website for information.
NUMBER OF AWARDS: 25-30
RENEWABLE: Yes, must reapply.

3382—DELTA PHI EPSILON EDUCATIONAL FOUNDATION

16A Worthington Drive
Maryland Heights MO 63043
314/275-2626
FAX: 314/275-2655
E-mail: ealper@dphie.org
Internet: www.dphie.org
AMOUNT: Varies
DEADLINE(S): APR 1 (undergrads);
APR 15 (grads)
FIELD(S): All
ELIGIBILITY/REQUIREMENTS:
Open to women who are members, daughters or granddaughters of members.

HOW TO APPLY: Applications available in January. Write or e-mail Executive Director.
CONTACT: Ellen Alper, Executive Director

3383—DENISON UNIVERSITY (Honors Program)

Admissions Office
100 South Road
Granville OH 43023
740/587-6573 or 800/DENISON
E-mail: mcintyre@denison.edu or sunkle@denison.edu
Internet: http://www.denison.edu
AMOUNT: Varies
DEADLINE(S): Varies
FIELD(S): All
ELIGIBILITY/REQUIREMENTS:
Open to high-performing incoming freshmen and transfer students; top 10% of graduating class, ACT of 30 or higher and a combined SAT of 1300. After 1st year, students with a 3.6 GPA not already enrolled in the program will be invited to participate.
HOW TO APPLY: See website for details or send letter of inquiry for information.
CONTACT: Prof. Kent Maynard or Ms. Ann Marie McIntyre (Admissions Office)

3384—DENISON UNIVERSITY (Merit-Based Scholarships)

Admissions Office
100 South Road
Granville OH 43023
800/DENISON or 740/587-6276
E-mail: admissions@denison.edu
Internet: http://www.denison.edu
AMOUNT: Varies
DEADLINE(S): JAN 1 (of senior year)
FIELD(S): All
ELIGIBILITY/REQUIREMENTS:
Open to first-year students. Some are related to specific fields of study, some are for National Merit Scholars, and the remainder are awarded based on academic achievement. All require excellence in academic achievement. See Web page under "Scholarships" for list.
HOW TO APPLY: Write or e-mail for information.
NUMBER OF AWARDS: 400+
RENEWABLE: Yes. For 4 years if stipulated GPA is maintained.
CONTACT: Admissions Office

3385—DENVER SCHOLARSHIP FUND

370 17th Street, Suite 3260
Denver CO 80202

E-mail: nfo@denverscholarship.org
303/951-4140
FAX: 303/600-2951
Internet: www.denverscholarship.org
AMOUNT: $2,000-$6,000
DEADLINE(S): MAR 15
FIELD(S): All
ELIGIBILITY/REQUIREMENTS: Must meet Denver Public School enrollment and academic requirements; graduate from a participating DPS High School in 2007 or later, be enrolled at least half time at a participating, DSF-eligible postsecondary institution.
Be eligible to receive federal student financial aid a US citizen, permanent resident or other eligible noncitizens. Must apply for 3 or more private or institutional scholarships in addition to DSF. Visit a DSF Future Center or www.denverscholarship.org for information about other scholarships. Must apply to DSF and begin postsecondary course work within one (1) year of high school graduation.
HOW TO APPLY: See website for application, which must be submitted online. Submit a copy of Student Aid Report (SAR), which summarizes FAFSA results, to DSF by mail, fax or e-mail AND submit an Enrollment Intention Form to DSF by mail, fax or email.
RENEWABLE: Yes. Must earn a cumulative 2.0 GPA and meet the requirements to maintain Satisfactory Academic Progress (SAP), as defined by the postsecondary institution they attend. Students must meet all requirements before a suspended DSF scholarship will be reinstated.

3386—DESCENDANTS OF SIGNERS OF DECLARATION OF INDEPENDENCE

P.O. Box 8223
Savannah, GA 31412
E-mail: scholarship@dsdi1776.com
Internet: http://www.dsdi1776.com/Scholarship/scholarship.html
AMOUNT: $3,000
DEADLINE(S): MAR 31
FIELD(S): All
ELIGIBILITY/REQUIREMENTS: Must be a member in good standing, a full-time student enrolled for full year.
HOW TO APPLY: See website or write for application. Submit with a 1-page résumé or activity sheet; 3 letters of recommendation; transcript(s) from the last educational institution attended (high school seniors must include the transcript from the fall semester of their senior year); and a brief statement telling us about yourself and your educational goals.
RENEWABLE: Yes. Must reapply.

CONTACT: Mrs. Leslie Pickett Sheehan, Scholarship Committee Director
ADDITIONAL INFORMATION: For membership information, contact Rev. Frederick Pyne, 3137 Periwinkle Court, Adamstown MD 21710; 301/644-1776.

3387—DISABLED AMERICAN VETERANS AUXILIARY (DAVA Student Loans)

National Education Loan Fund
3725 Alexandria Pike
Cold Spring KY 41076
859/441-7300
AMOUNT: $2,500 (maximum)
DEADLINE(S): APR 25
FIELD(S): All
ELIGIBILITY/REQUIREMENTS: Must be a full paid life member of the auxiliary and a full-time student at a U.S. institution of higher education with a minimum of 12 credit hours; minimum 2.0 GPA; and a U.S. citizen.
HOW TO APPLY: Contact DAVA for an application no later than MAR 1.
NUMBER OF AWARDS: 40-42
RENEWABLE: Yes. Up to 5 years; must reapply.
CONTACT: Chairperson
ADDITIONAL INFORMATION: Only one new applicant, per family, per year will be considered; however multiple births will be considered; renewals are not considered to be new.

3388—DISCOVER CARD TRIBUTE AWARDS

866/756-7932
Internet: http://www.discoverfinancial.com/data/philanthropy/tribute.shtml
AMOUNT: $2,500-$25,000
DEADLINE(S): JAN 31
FIELD(S): All
ELIGIBILITY/REQUIREMENTS: Must be a high school junior enrolled in and graduating from an accredited public or private school in the U.S.; minimum 2.75 cumulative GPA for the 9th and 10th grades only. Financial need NOT considered. State and national scholarships can be used for any type of post-high school education or training-certification, licensing, 2- or 4-year trade and technical school, or 2- or 4-year college.
HOW TO APPLY: Call or go to www.scholarshipadministrators.net and use the access key DISC to apply online or to download and print an application. Mail application; description of future career plans; description of accomplishments in leadership and community service as well as significant roadblock(s) or challenge(s)

that the applicant faced. Awards are NOT based solely on academic excellence. New information available each December.
NUMBER OF AWARDS: State Scholarships: Up to 300 awards-$2,500 each; National Scholarships: Up to 10 awards-$25,000 each
CONTACT: For other questions, view the FAQ, visit https://www.scholarshipadministrators.net/EmailRequestForm.asp, or call 866/756-7932.

3389—DIXIE SOFTBALL, INC.

1101 Skelton Drive
Birmingham AL 35224
205/785-2255
FAX: 205/785-2258
E-mail: OBIEDSI@aol.com
Internet: http://www.dixie.org/softball
AMOUNT: $1,500
DEADLINE(S): MAR 1
FIELD(S): All
ELIGIBILITY/REQUIREMENTS: Must be a high school senior and have participated in Dixie Softball for 2 seasons.
HOW TO APPLY: Contact Chairman for application and details.
NUMBER OF AWARDS: 2
CONTACT: Doug Garrett, Chairman, Scholarship Committee, 106 Woodlake Drive, Pineville LA 71360, 319/484-9062 or dayprodoug@cox-internet.com.

3390—DIXIE YOUTH BASEBALL, INC.

P.O. Box 877
Marshall TX 75671
903/927-2255
FAX: 903/927-1846
E-mail: dyb@dixie.org
Internet: http://www.dixie.org
AMOUNT: $2,000
DEADLINE(S): MAR 1
FIELD(S): All
ELIGIBILITY/REQUIREMENTS: Must be a graduating high school senior who played in a Dixie Youth franchised league while age 12 and under.
HOW TO APPLY: Download application from website or contact National Office.
NUMBER OF AWARDS: 65
RENEWABLE: No
CONTACT: Johnny Berthelot

3391—DODD AND DOROTHY L. BRYAN FOUNDATION (Interest-Free Loans)

2 N. Main, Suite 401
Sheridan WY 82801
307/672-3535
AMOUNT: $5,000

DEADLINE(S): JUN 15
FIELD(S): All
ELIGIBILITY/REQUIREMENTS: Open to undergraduate, graduate, and postgraduate students who live in Sheridan, Johnson, or Campbell, Wyoming, or Rosebud, Big Horn, or Powder River County, MT. Must demonstrate financial need.
HOW TO APPLY: Contact Foundation for an application.
RENEWABLE: Yes

3392—DOLPHIN SCHOLARSHIP FOUNDATION

5040 Virginia Beach Boulevard, Suite 104-A
Virginia Beach VA 23462
757/671-3200
FAX: 757/671-3330
Internet: www.dolphinscholarship.org
AMOUNT: $3,250
DEADLINE(S): MAR 15
FIELD(S): All
ELIGIBILITY/REQUIREMENTS: Open to high school seniors and undergraduate college students who are children or stepchildren of current or former members of the U.S. Navy Submarine Force. Members must have qualified in submarines and served in the force for at least 8 years, have served at least 10 years in direct support of the Submarine Force, or died in active duty of Submarine Force. Selection criteria include academic proficiency, financial need, and character and all-around ability.
HOW TO APPLY: See website or send a SASE (business-size) for an application.
NUMBER OF AWARDS: 25-30 per year (133 total awards)
RENEWABLE: Yes. Up to 4 years of full-time undergraduate study.

3393—DOUVAS MEMORIAL SCHOLARSHIP

Hathaway Building, 2nd Floor
2300 Capitol Avenue
Cheyenne WY 82002-0050
Internet: http://www.k12.us/award,aso
AMOUNT: $500
DEADLINE(S): APR 18
FIELD(S): All
ELIGIBILITY/REQUIREMENTS: Available to high school seniors or others between the ages of 18 and 22 who are first-generation Americans and Wyoming residents. May be used at any Wyoming public institution of higher education.

HOW TO APPLY: Write for application; complete your portion, and then have school guidance counselor complete that portion of application and submit it directly.

NUMBER OF AWARDS: 1

RENEWABLE: No

CONTACT: Bruce Hayes

ADDITIONAL INFORMATION: The scholarship is administered by the Wyoming Department of Education.

3394—DRY CREEK NEIGHBORS CLUB

707/431-3473

AMOUNT: Varies

DEADLINE(S): FEB 15

FIELD(S): All

ELIGIBILITY/REQUIREMENTS: Scholarships are awarded to graduating seniors from Healdsburg and Geyserville High Schools in California.

HOW TO APPLY: Contact Scholarship Coordinator at your high school for an application.

NUMBER OF AWARDS: 2

3395—EBELL OF LOS ANGELES SCHOLARSHIP PROGRAM

743 South Lucerne Boulevard

Los Angeles CA 90005-3707

323/931-1277

Internet: http://www.ebellla.com

AMOUNT: $3,000 (4-year college); $2,500 (2-year college), paid quarterly

DEADLINE(S): MAR 31

FIELD(S): All

ELIGIBILITY/REQUIREMENTS: For Los Angeles County residents who are undergraduate sophomores, juniors, or seniors enrolled in a Los Angeles County college or university. Must be a U.S. citizen.

HOW TO APPLY: Community service is a major consideration and financial need is also considered. Students may contact Ebell of Los Angeles for an application or download application from website.

NUMBER OF AWARDS: 50-60

RENEWABLE: Yes. GPA of 3.25 required.

3396—EDDIE G. ROBINSON FOUNDATION, THE (High School Senior Scholarship)

3500 Piedmont Road, Suite 100

Atlanta GA 30305

404/475-8408

E-mail: scholarship@eddierobinson.com

Internet: http://www.eddierobinson.com

AMOUNT: $5,000

DEADLINE(S): FEB 16

FIELD(S): All

ELIGIBILITY/REQUIREMENTS: Must be high school senior accepted to a 4-year college, university or technical school; and must have made a choice to remain chemical-free.

HOW TO APPLY: Download application from website after October or contact by mail or e-mail.

NUMBER OF AWARDS: 2-4

RENEWABLE: Yes. Must maintain appropriate GPA.

CONTACT: Cherie Kirkland

3397—EDMUND F. MAXWELL FOUNDATION

Seattle WA 98122-0537

E-mail: admin@maxwell.org

Internet: www.maxwell.org

AMOUNT: $3,500

DEADLINE(S): APR 30

FIELD(S): All

ELIGIBILITY/REQUIREMENTS: Open to entering college freshmen who are bona fide residents of Western Washington (particularly in or around Seattle). May be entering any accredited institution of higher learning that receives its fundamental support from sources other than taxes. Must have financial need, outstanding academic records, and combined SAT scores over 1200.

HOW TO APPLY: See website or contact Foundation in the fall for an application.

RENEWABLE: Yes

3398—EDUCATIONAL COMMUNICATIONS SCHOLARSHIP FOUNDATION (Incoming Freshman Scholarships)

1701 Directors Boulevard,

Suite 920

P.O. Box 149219

Austin TX 78714-9219

512/440-2300

FAX: 847/295-3972

E-mail: school@ecsf.org

Internet: http://www.honoring.com

AMOUNT: $1,000

DEADLINE(S): MAY 15

FIELD(S): All

ELIGIBILITY/REQUIREMENTS: Open to high school students, citizens or legal residents of the U.S., who have taken and received results of SAT or ACT examination.

HOW TO APPLY: Send name, home address, current year in high school, and approximate GPA to ECSF for an application. $3.50 processing fee. Semi-finalists

must provide limited data on financial status to determine level of need and must respond to an essay question. Finalists must submit official transcripts and verify all submitted data. For additional information, see website.

NUMBER OF AWARDS: Approximately 200

3399—EDUCATIONAL COMMUNICATIONS SCHOLARSHIP FOUNDATION (Undergraduate & Graduate Scholarship Award Program)

1701 Directors Boulevard,

Suite 920

P.O. Box 149219

Austin TX 78714-9219

512/440-2300

FAX: 847/295-3972

E-mail: school@ecsf.org

Internet: http://www.honoring.com

AMOUNT: $1,000

DEADLINE(S): MAY 15

FIELD(S): All

ELIGIBILITY/REQUIREMENTS: Open to undergraduate and graduate students with a minimum B+ GPA. Must be U.S. citizen attending an accredited college or university. Based on GPA, achievement test scores, leadership qualifications, work experience, essay, and some consideration for financial need.

HOW TO APPLY: Contact ECSF with your name, home address, college name, GPA, and year in school for an application no later than March 15.

NUMBER OF AWARDS: 50

3400—EDUCATION FREEDOM FUND

P.O. Box 230078

Grand Rapids MI 49523-0078

800/866-8141

E-mail: info@educationfreedomfund.org

Internet: http://www.educationfreedomfund.org

AMOUNT: $1,000 annually for 4 years

DEADLINE(S): JAN 1-MAR 31

FIELD(S): All

ELIGIBILITY/REQUIREMENTS: EFF scholarships are need-based: applicants must be children living in Michigan and entering grades K-8 who qualify for the Federal Free or Reduced Lunch Program. Scholarships may be used at any legally operating school where tuition is charged, including parochial, religious, independent, or public that allow private-pay, non-district students.

HOW TO APPLY: Request application in November; contact fund for information and application.
NUMBER OF AWARDS: 1,600

3401—EDWARDS SCHOLARSHIP FUND

200 Clarendon Street, 27th Floor
Boston MA 02116
617/654-8628
E-mail: esfund@yahoo.com
Internet: http://www.esfund-boston.org/neweligibility.html
AMOUNT: $250-$5,000
DEADLINE(S): MAR 1
FIELD(S): All
ELIGIBILITY/REQUIREMENTS: Open to students seeking associate's degree or higher who are about to enter college, undergraduate and graduate. Applicants must furnish evidence of financial need, scholastic ability and good character. Undergraduates receive preference and applicants must be under 25 years of age. May be used at any accredited school or college, in a program leading to an associate's, bachelor's (or higher) degree.
HOW TO APPLY: Download application from website or write or phone Fund.
NUMBER OF AWARDS: Varies
RENEWABLE: Yes, up to 6 years; reapply. The trustees reserve the right to withdraw a scholarship at any time if a student's record or actions prove to be unworthy of a recipient.
CONTACT: Brenda McCarthy
ADDITIONAL INFORMATION: Only students living in the City of Boston (at least from the beginning of their junior year in high school) are eligible for aid from the Fund. The City of Boston includes the following areas, in addition to the central areas of the city: Allston, Brighton, Charlestown, Dorchester, East Boston, Forest Hills, Hyde Park, Jamaica Plain, Mattapan, Readville, Roslindale, Roxbury, South Boston and West Roxbury.

3402—EDWARD THATCHER ASTLE MEMORIAL SCHOLARSHIP FOUNDATION

P.O. Box 182
Annandale NJ 08801-0182
877/847-9060
AMOUNT: Up to $6,000
DEADLINE(S): Third week in MAR
FIELD(S): All
ELIGIBILITY/REQUIREMENTS: Open to graduating high school senior for freshman year at college or trade school; must have "B" average; require financial assistance; be U.S. citizen (if over 18 must be registered to vote); chemical-free; demon-strate willingness to work summer and/or after school to pay for education. Must have written recommendation of high school guidance department or one teacher.
HOW TO APPLY: Requests for application form and requirements must be made in writing and MUST include a SASE. No e-mail or web communications accepted. Submit application with proof of W-2s and family tax returns, optional essay "My Ancestors My Heritage" (alternative subjects acceptable). Personal interview required.
NUMBER OF AWARDS: 1 or more
RENEWABLE: Yes. Must demonstrate continued financial need and outstanding academic achievement.

3403—ELIE WIESEL FOUNDATION FOR HUMANITY (Prize in Ethics Essay Contest)

555 Madison Ave, 20th Floor
New York NY 10022
212/490-7777
FAX: 212/490-6006
E-mail: info@eliewiesel foundation.org
Internet: http://www.eliewiesel foundation.org
AMOUNT: $5,000 (1st prize); $2,500 (2nd); $1,500 (3rd); $500 (2 honorable mentions)
DEADLINE(S): DEC (exact date will be posted on website in late spring)
FIELD(S): All
ELIGIBILITY/REQUIREMENTS: Open to undergraduate juniors and seniors at accredited 4-year colleges/universities in the U.S. Entries must be personal essays that: explore how a moral society's perception of the "other" may result in social separation, prejudice, discrimination, hate crimes and violence; examine ethical aspects/implications of a major literary work, a film, or a significant piece of art; or reflect on the most profound moral dilemma you have personally experienced and learned from.
HOW TO APPLY: See website.

3404—ELKS NATIONAL FOUNDATION (Eagle Scout Awards)

Scholarship Department
2750 North Lakeview Avenue
Chicago IL 60614-1889
773/755-4732
FAX: 773/755-4733
E-mail: scholarship@elks.org
Internet: http://www.elks.org
AMOUNT: $1,000-$2,000
DEADLINE(S): FEB 28
FIELD(S): All
ELIGIBILITY/REQUIREMENTS: Must be registered Eagle scouts; have an SAT score of at least 1090 and/or equivalent ACT score of 26; be graduating from high school during the year they are applying; and have financial need.
HOW TO APPLY: Submit application.
NUMBER OF AWARDS: 8 (4 $1,000; 4 $2,000)
RENEWABLE: Yes. Up to 4 years.
CONTACT: The National Office, Boy Scouts of America, P.O. Box 152079, Irving, TX 75015-2079 or call 972/580-2000.

3405—ELKS NATIONAL FOUNDATION (Emergency Educational Fund Grants)

Scholarship Department
2750 North Lakeview Avenue
Chicago IL 60614-1889
773/755-4732
FAX: 773/755-4733
E-mail: scholarship@elks.org
Internet: http://www.elks.org
AMOUNT: Up to $3,000
DEADLINE(S): JUL 1-DEC 31
FIELD(S): All
ELIGIBILITY/REQUIREMENTS: Must be the child or stepchild of a deceased Elk who was a member in good standing at the time of death, or of a totally disabled Elk who was in good standing before becoming disabled and who continues in good standing when the application for assistance is made. Must demonstrate financial need; be unmarried, under the age of 23 as of December 31 in the year of application; and be attending a U.S. college or university as a full-time undergraduate student.
HOW TO APPLY: Submit application to the Lodge where the Elk parent or stepparent is or was a member.
RENEWABLE: Yes. Must reapply (between July 1-October 31) up to 4 years.

3406—ELKS NATIONAL FOUNDATION (Gold Award Scholarships)

Scholarship Department
2750 North Lakeview Avenue
Chicago IL 60614-1889
773/755-4732
FAX: 773/755-4733
E-mail: scholarship@elks.org
Internet: http://www.elks.org
AMOUNT: $6,000 ($1,500 per year)
DEADLINE(S): MAY 1
FIELD(S): All
ELIGIBILITY/REQUIREMENTS: Must be women who are graduating high school seniors who have achieved the Girl Scout Gold Award. Based on academics, activi-

ties, community involvement, leadership, and pursuit of individual interests.
HOW TO APPLY: Contact Elks or the Girl Scout Council or see website for application.
NUMBER OF AWARDS: 8
RENEWABLE: Yes. Up to 4 years.

3407—ELKS NATIONAL FOUNDATION ("Most Valuable Student" Competition)

Scholarship Department
2750 North Lakeview Avenue
Chicago IL 60614-1889
773/755-4732
FAX: 773/755-4733
E-mail: scholarship@elks.org
Internet: http://www.elks.org
AMOUNT: $1,000-$15,000 per year
DEADLINE(S): SEP 15-JAN 9
FIELD(S): All
ELIGIBILITY/REQUIREMENTS: Must be a high school senior; U.S. citizen; plan to attend and be accepted at an accredited U.S. college or university to pursue a 4-year degree on a full-time basis. Applicants do NOT need to be related to a member of the Elks. Based on financial need, leadership, and scholarship.
HOW TO APPLY: Submit application to local Elks Lodge.
NUMBER OF AWARDS: 500
RENEWABLE: Yes. Up to 4 years.

3408—ELKS NATIONAL FOUNDATION (The Legacy Awards)

Scholarship Department
2750 North Lakeview Avenue
Chicago IL 60614-1889
773/755-4732
FAX: 773/755-4733
E-mail: scholarship@elks.org
Internet: http://www.elks.org
AMOUNT: $1,000
DEADLINE(S): JAN 9
FIELD(S): All
ELIGIBILITY/REQUIREMENTS: Must be a high school senior who is the child, grandchild, stepchild, step-grandchild, or legal ward of an active Elk who has been a member in good standing since at least April 1, 2001 or a charter member of a Lodge that was instituted on or after April 1, 2001. Must be planning to attend an accredited U.S. school, college, or university. Based on scholarship, leadership, and responses to short essay questions.
HOW TO APPLY: Submit application; transcript of grades, SAT or ACT score results; 2 letters of reference, including 1 from a high school teacher. Send to the related member's Elks Lodge.

NUMBER OF AWARDS: Up to 500
RENEWABLE: No

3409—ENGLISH-SPEAKING UNION (Lucy Dalbiac Luard Scholarships)

144 E. 39th Street
New York NY 10016
212/818-1200
FAX: 212/867-4177
E-mail: info@english-speakingunion.org
Internet: http://www.english-speakingunion.org
AMOUNT: Full tuition and expenses
DEADLINE(S): NOV
FIELD(S): All
ELIGIBILITY/REQUIREMENTS: Open to students attending a United Negro College or Howard or Hampton University. Full scholarship to spend undergraduate junior year at a university in England. Must be U.S. citizen.
HOW TO APPLY: Apply through student's college or university. Information and applications are sent each fall to the Academic Dean/VP for Academic Affairs at participating schools.
RENEWABLE: No

3410—ERNESTINE MATTHEWS TRUST

P.O. Box 3797
Arlington VA 22203
AMOUNT: $2,000
DEADLINE(S): MAR 15
FIELD(S): All
ELIGIBILITY/REQUIREMENTS: Must be residents of the District of Columbia, Maryland, Pennsylvania, Virginia, or West Virginia; in the upper third of their high school class; entering college freshmen only with proven financial need; and of high moral character (must sign a statement that they will not smoke or use alcoholic beverages while receiving money from the Trust).
HOW TO APPLY: Submit application; transcript; verification of class standing; and 2 letters of recommendation (1 from the applicant's counselor, principal, or teacher; and 1 from someone other than a relative).
RENEWABLE: Yes. Apply annually; furnish a transcript evidencing a grade average of 'C' or equivalent (4 years maximum).

3411—ESA FOUNDATION (Arlene Schlosser Memorial Endowment)

P.O. Box 270517
Fort Collins CO 80527

970/223-2824
FAX: 970/223-4456
E-mail: kloyd@iland.net
Internet: http://www.esaintl.com/esaf
AMOUNT: $500
DEADLINE(S): FEB 1
FIELD(S): All
ELIGIBILITY/REQUIREMENTS: Must be a college student enrolled in an accredited college or university with minimum 3.0 GPA; or high school senior in the top 25% of class, or have at least ACT 20 or SAT 950 score, or minimum 3.0 GPA; or be enrolled for training in a technical school or be returning to school after an absence to retrain job skills or obtain a degree. Based on character, leadership, service, financial need, scholastic ability, and special criteria set by the donor.
HOW TO APPLY: Submit application; 1-page (maximum) letter stating reasons for applying; 2 letters of recommendation; transcript; and $5 processing fee. Send application to the ESA Foundation State Counselor in your area (see website).
NUMBER OF AWARDS: 1
RENEWABLE: Yes. Must reapply; no special consideration given to previous winners.
CONTACT: Kathy Loyd

3412—ESA FOUNDATION (Avenuers/Gallatin Endowment)

P.O. Box 270517
Fort Collins CO 80527
970/223-2824
FAX: 970/223-4456
E-mail: kloyd@iland.net
Internet: http://www.esaintl.com/esaf
AMOUNT: $500-$1,000
DEADLINE(S): FEB 1
FIELD(S): All
ELIGIBILITY/REQUIREMENTS: Must be enrolled in an accredited college or university, minimum 3.0 GPA; or high school senior in the top 25% of class, or have at least ACT 20 or SAT 950 score, or minimum 3.0 GPA; or be enrolled for training in a technical school or be returning to school after an absence to retrain job skills or obtain a degree. Based on character, leadership, service, financial need, scholastic ability, and special criteria set by the donor.
HOW TO APPLY: Submit application; 1-page (maximum) letter stating reasons for applying; 2 letters of recommendation; transcript; and $5 processing fee. Send application to the ESA Foundation State Counselor in your area (see website).

NUMBER OF AWARDS: 2 (1 each $1,000 and $500)
RENEWABLE: Yes. Must reapply; no special consideration given to previous winners.
CONTACT: Kathy Loyd

3413—ESA FOUNDATION (Danzo and Elsie Shiramizu Endowment)

P.O. Box 270517
Fort Collins CO 80527
970/223-2824
FAX: 970/223-4456
E-mail: kloyd@iland.net
Internet: http://www.esaintl.com/esaf
AMOUNT: $500
DEADLINE(S): FEB 1
FIELD(S): All
ELIGIBILITY/REQUIREMENTS: Must be a college student enrolled in an accredited college or university with minimum 3.0 GPA; or high school senior in the top 25% of class, or have at least ACT 20 or SAT 950 score, or minimum 3.0 GPA; or be enrolled for training in a technical school or be returning to school after an absence to retrain job skills or obtain a degree. Based on character, leadership, service, financial need, scholastic ability, and special criteria set by the donor.
HOW TO APPLY: Submit application; 1-page (maximum) letter stating reasons for applying; 2 letters of recommendation; transcript; and $5 processing fee. Send application to the ESA Foundation State Counselor in your area (see website).
NUMBER OF AWARDS: 1
RENEWABLE: Yes. Must reapply; no special consideration given to previous winners.
CONTACT: Kathy Loyd

3414—ESA FOUNDATION (Floyd Gray Endowment)

P.O. Box 270517
Fort Collins CO 80527
970/223-2824
FAX: 970/223-4456
E-mail: kloyd@iland.net
Internet: http://www.esaintl.com/esaf
AMOUNT: $500
DEADLINE(S): FEB 1
FIELD(S): All
ELIGIBILITY/REQUIREMENTS: Must be a college student enrolled in an accredited college or university with minimum 3.0 GPA; or high school senior in the top 25% of class, or have at least ACT 20 or SAT 950 score, or minimum 3.0 GPA; or be

enrolled for training in a technical school or be returning to school after an absence to retrain job skills or obtain a degree. Based on character, leadership, service, financial need, scholastic ability, and special criteria set by the donor. Priority is given to "B" students: do NOT apply if your grade average is above 3.5.
HOW TO APPLY: Submit application; 1-page (maximum) letter stating reasons for applying; 2 letters of recommendation; transcript; and $5 processing fee. Send application to the ESA Foundation State Counselor in your area (see website).
NUMBER OF AWARDS: 1
RENEWABLE: Yes. Must reapply; no special consideration given to previous winners.
CONTACT: Kathy Loyd

3415—ESA FOUNDATION (General Scholarship)

P.O. Box 270517
Fort Collins CO 80527
970/223-2824
FAX: 970/223-4456
E-mail: kloyd@iland.net
Internet: http://www.esaintl.com/esaf
AMOUNT: $500
DEADLINE(S): FEB 1
FIELD(S): All
ELIGIBILITY/REQUIREMENTS: Must be a college student enrolled in an accredited college or university with minimum 3.0 GPA; or high school senior in the top 25% of class, or have at least ACT 20 or SAT 950 score, or minimum 3.0 GPA; or be enrolled for training in a technical school or be returning to school after an absence to retrain job skills or obtain a degree. Based on character, leadership, service, financial need, scholastic ability, and special criteria set by the donor.
HOW TO APPLY: Submit application; 1-page (maximum) letter stating reasons for applying; 2 letters of recommendation; transcript; and $5 processing fee. Send application to the ESA Foundation State Counselor in your area (see website).
NUMBER OF AWARDS: 1
RENEWABLE: Yes. Must reapply; no special consideration given to previous winners.
CONTACT: Kathy Loyd

3416—ESA FOUNDATION (Jeanne Parker Honorarium Endowment)

P.O. Box 270517
Fort Collins CO 80527
970/223-2824

FAX: 970/223-4456
E-mail: kloyd@iland.net
Internet: http://www.esaintl.com/esaf
AMOUNT: $500
DEADLINE(S): FEB 1
FIELD(S): All
ELIGIBILITY/REQUIREMENTS: Must be a college student enrolled in an accredited college or university with minimum 3.0 GPA; or high school senior in the top 25% of class, or have at least ACT 20 or SAT 950 score, or minimum 3.0 GPA; or be enrolled for training in a technical school or be returning to school after an absence to retrain job skills or obtain a degree. Based on character, leadership, service, financial need, scholastic ability, and special criteria set by the donor. Priority is given to "B" students: do NOT apply for this scholarship if your grade average is above 3.5.
HOW TO APPLY: Submit application; 1-page (maximum) letter stating reasons for applying; 2 letters of recommendation; transcript; and $5 processing fee. Send application to the ESA Foundation State Counselor in your area (see website).
NUMBER OF AWARDS: 1
RENEWABLE: Yes. Must reapply; no special consideration given to previous winners.
CONTACT: Kathy Loyd

3417—ESA FOUNDATION (Lauretta M. Roberts Memorial Endowment)

P.O. Box 270517
Fort Collins CO 80527
970/223-2824
FAX: 970/223-4456
E-mail: kloyd@iland.net
Internet: http://www.esaintl.com/esaf
AMOUNT: $500
DEADLINE(S): FEB 1
FIELD(S): All
ELIGIBILITY/REQUIREMENTS: Must be a college student enrolled in an accredited college or university with minimum 3.0 GPA; or high school senior in the top 25% of class, or have at least ACT 20 or SAT 950 score, or minimum 3.0 GPA; or be enrolled for training in a technical school or be returning to school after an absence to retrain job skills or obtain a degree. Based on character, leadership, service, financial need, scholastic ability, and special criteria set by the donor.
HOW TO APPLY: Submit application; 1-page (maximum) letter stating reasons for applying; 2 letters of recommendation; transcript; and $5 processing fee. Send

application to the ESA Foundation State Counselor in your area (see website).
NUMBER OF AWARDS: 1
RENEWABLE: Yes. Must reapply; no special consideration given to previous winners.
CONTACT: Kathy Loyd

3418—ESA FOUNDATION (Past International Council Presidents' Endowment)

P.O. Box 270517
Fort Collins CO 80527
970/223-2824
FAX: 970/223-4456
E-mail: kloyd@iland.net
Internet: http://www.esaintl.com/esaf
AMOUNT: $500
DEADLINE(S): FEB 1
FIELD(S): All
ELIGIBILITY/REQUIREMENTS: Must be a college student enrolled in an accredited college or university with minimum 3.0 GPA; or high school senior in the top 25% of class, or have at least ACT 20 or SAT 950 score, or minimum 3.0 GPA; or be enrolled for training in a technical school or be returning to school after an absence to retrain job skills or obtain a degree. Based on character, leadership, service, financial need, scholastic ability, and special criteria set by the donor.
HOW TO APPLY: Submit application; 1-page (maximum) letter stating reasons for applying; 2 letters of recommendation; transcript; and $5 processing fee. Send application to the ESA Foundation State Counselor in your area (see website).
NUMBER OF AWARDS: 1
RENEWABLE: Yes. Must reapply; no special consideration given to previous winners.
CONTACT: Kathy Loyd

3419—ESA FOUNDATION (Rodger & Rhea Weaver Endowment)

P.O. Box 270517
Fort Collins CO 80527
970/223-2824
FAX: 970/223-4456
E-mail: kloyd@iland.net
Internet: http://www.esaintl.com/esaf
AMOUNT: $500
DEADLINE(S): FEB 1
FIELD(S): All
ELIGIBILITY/REQUIREMENTS: Must be woman dependent on continuing education to either acquire new skills or update present skills; must be a college student enrolled in an accredited college or univer-

sity with minimum 3.0 GPA; or high school senior in the top 25% of class, or have at least ACT 20 or SAT 950 score, or minimum 3.0 GPA; or be enrolled for training in a technical school or be returning to school after an absence to retrain job skills or obtain a degree. Based on character, leadership, service, financial need, scholastic ability, and special criteria set by the donor.
HOW TO APPLY: Submit application; 1-page (maximum) letter stating reasons for applying; 2 letters of recommendation; transcript; and $5 processing fee. Send application to the ESA Foundation State Counselor in your area (see website).
NUMBER OF AWARDS: 1
RENEWABLE: Yes. Must reapply; no special consideration given to previous winners.
CONTACT: Kathy Loyd

3420—ESA FOUNDATION (Rosagene Huggins Memorial Endowment)

P.O. Box 270517
Fort Collins CO 80527
970/223-2824
FAX: 970/223-4456
E-mail: kloyd@iland.net
Internet: http://www.esaintl.com/esaf
AMOUNT: $1,000
DEADLINE(S): FEB 1
FIELD(S): All
ELIGIBILITY/REQUIREMENTS: Must be a college student enrolled in an accredited college or university with minimum 3.0 GPA; or high school senior in the top 25% of class, or have at least ACT 20 or SAT 950 score, or minimum 3.0 GPA; or be enrolled for training in a technical school or be returning to school after an absence to retrain job skills or obtain a degree. Based on character, leadership, service, financial need, scholastic ability, and special criteria set by the donor.
HOW TO APPLY: Submit application; 1-page (maximum) letter stating reasons for applying; 2 letters of recommendation; transcript; and $5 processing fee. Send application to the ESA Foundation State Counselor in your area (see website).
NUMBER OF AWARDS: 1
RENEWABLE: Yes. Must reapply; no special consideration given to previous winners.
CONTACT: Kathy Loyd

3421—ESA FOUNDATION (Ruth Gregg Memorial Endowment)

P.O. Box 270517
Fort Collins CO 80527

970/223-2824
FAX: 970/223-4456
E-mail: kloyd@iland.net
Internet: http://www.esaintl.com/esaf
AMOUNT: $1,000
DEADLINE(S): FEB 1
FIELD(S): All
ELIGIBILITY/REQUIREMENTS: Must be a college student enrolled in an accredited college or university with minimum 3.0 GPA; or high school senior in the top 25% of class, or have at least ACT 20 or SAT 950 score, or minimum 3.0 GPA; or be enrolled for training in a technical school or be returning to school after an absence to retrain job skills or obtain a degree. Based on character, leadership, service, financial need, scholastic ability, and special criteria set by the donor.
HOW TO APPLY: Submit application; 1-page (maximum) letter stating reasons for applying; 2 letters of recommendation; transcript; and $5 processing fee. Send application to the ESA Foundation State Counselor in your area (see website).
NUMBER OF AWARDS: 1
RENEWABLE: Yes. Must reapply; no special consideration given to previous winners.
CONTACT: Kathy Loyd

3422—ESA FOUNDATION (Virginia Taylor Honorarium Scholarship)

P.O. Box 270517
Fort Collins CO 80527
970/223-2824
FAX: 970/223-4456
E-mail: kloyd@iland.net
Internet: http://www.esaintl.com/esaf
AMOUNT: $500
DEADLINE(S): FEB 1
FIELD(S): All
ELIGIBILITY/REQUIREMENTS: Must be a college student enrolled in an accredited college or university with minimum 3.0 GPA; or high school senior in the top 25% of class, or have at least ACT 20 or SAT 950 score, or minimum 3.0 GPA; or be enrolled for training in a technical school or be returning to school after an absence to retrain job skills or obtain a degree. Based on character, leadership, service, financial need, scholastic ability, and special criteria set by the donor.
HOW TO APPLY: Submit application; 1-page (maximum) letter stating reasons for applying; 2 letters of recommendation; transcript; and $5 processing fee. Send application to the ESA Foundation State Counselor in your area (see website).

NUMBER OF AWARDS: 1
RENEWABLE: Yes. Must reapply; no special consideration given to previous winners.
CONTACT: Kathy Loyd

3423—ESA FOUNDATION (Willow C. Gray Endowment)

P.O. Box 270517
Fort Collins CO 80527
970/223-2824
FAX: 970/223-4456
E-mail: kloyd@iland.net
Internet: http://www.esaintl.com/esaf
AMOUNT: $500
DEADLINE(S): FEB 1
FIELD(S): All
ELIGIBILITY/REQUIREMENTS: Must be a college student enrolled in an accredited college or university with minimum 3.0 GPA; or high school senior in the top 25% of class, or have at least ACT 20 or SAT 950 score, or minimum 3.0 GPA; or be enrolled for training in a technical school or be returning to school after an absence to retrain job skills or obtain a degree. Based on character, leadership, service, financial need, scholastic ability, and special criteria set by the donor. Priority is given to "B" students: do NOT apply if your grade average is above 3.5.
HOW TO APPLY: Submit application; 1-page (maximum) letter stating reasons for applying; 2 letters of recommendation; transcript; and $5 processing fee. Send application to the ESA Foundation State Counselor in your area (see website).
NUMBER OF AWARDS: 2
RENEWABLE: Yes. Must reapply; no special consideration given to previous winners.
CONTACT: Kathy Loyd

3424—FEDERATION OF AMERICAN CONSUMERS AND TRAVELERS (Continuing Education Scholarship Program)

318 Hillsboro Avenue
P.O. Box 104
Edwardsville IL 62025
800/872-3228
FAX: 618/656-5369
E-mail: cservice@fact-org.org
Internet: http://www.fact-org.org
AMOUNT: $2,500-$10,000
DEADLINE(S): JAN 15
FIELD(S): All
ELIGIBILITY/REQUIREMENTS: For 1) high school seniors; 2) high school graduates (out of school 4 or more years) who did not attend college; 3) students enrolled in a college or university; and 4) students who wish to attend a trade or technical school. Must be either a member of FACT or the immediate family of a member. Designed for the so-called "average" student.
HOW TO APPLY: See website or contact FACT directly.
NUMBER OF AWARDS: 6 (minimum); 1 $10,000; 1 $2,500 in each of the first 3 categories, and 2 in the 4th category (combined maximum $5,000)
CONTACT: Vicki Rolens, Managing Director

3425—FERN BROWN MEMORIAL FUND

Personal Trust Direct
P.O. Box 650538
Dallas TX 75265-0538
866/784-5700, ext. 4666 or
214/290-4666
FAX: 214/290-2720
E-mail: bonnieaswindall@bankone.com
AMOUNT: Varies
DEADLINE(S): APR 29
FIELD(S): All
ELIGIBILITY/REQUIREMENTS: Scholarships for residents of Oklahoma.
HOW TO APPLY: Send SASE to Trust Advisor.
CONTACT: Bonnie Swindall, Trust Advisor, Mail Code: TX1-2708

3426—FIRST UNION NATIONAL BANK (Louise C. Nacca Memorial Scholarship Fund)

190 River Road, NJ3132
Summit NJ 07901
908/598-3582
FAX: 908/598-3583
DEADLINE(S): JAN 31
FIELD(S): All
ELIGIBILITY/REQUIREMENTS: Open to New Jersey residents between the ages of 18 and 45 with a permanent physical disability, attending or planning to attend a college or a graduate, professional, business or technical school (does NOT have to be in New Jersey).
HOW TO APPLY: Call or write for application and more information.
NUMBER OF AWARDS: 1
RENEWABLE: Yes, must have good grades.

3427—FLINN FOUNDATION, THE

1802 North Central Avenue
Phoenix AZ 85004-1506
602/744-6800
FAX: 602/744-6815
E-mail: fscholars@flinn.org
Internet: http://www.flinn scholars.org
AMOUNT: Full tuition
DEADLINE(S): NOV 1
FIELD(S): All
ELIGIBILITY/REQUIREMENTS: A full scholarship for students who have been accepted at Arizona State University, Northern Arizona University, or the University of Arizona. For U.S. citizens and legal residents of Arizona for 2 years prior to the application deadline. Must have at least a 3.5 GPA and rank in the top 5% of high school class. Merit is the only factor considered, which includes academic assessment and personal achievement.
HOW TO APPLY: See website or contact Foundation for additional information.
NUMBER OF AWARDS: 20 (includes 2 travel-study experiences abroad)
RENEWABLE: Yes. Must submit progress reports and evidence of participation in campus activities for renewals.

3428—FLOYD HOLLAND MEMORIAL SCHOLARSHIP COMMITTEE, THE

1820 Capitol Avenue
Cheyenne WY 82001
Internet: http://www.wy-srmason.org
AMOUNT: $1,000
DEADLINE(S): JUN 10
FIELD(S): All
ELIGIBILITY/REQUIREMENTS: Must be UW college juniors or seniors who are graduates of a Wyoming high school and who have attended UW for at least one year. Selection is based on cumulative GPA; high school, college, and community activities; indications of leadership potential; and financial need.
HOW TO APPLY: Send application, available from website.
NUMBER OF AWARDS: 1 or more
RENEWABLE: No
CONTACT: www.wy-srmason.org/scholarships

3429—FOND DU LAC TRIBAL SCHOLARSHIP PROGRAM

FDL Tribal Center
1720 Big Lake Road
Cloquet MN 55720
218/879-4593, ext. 2681 or
800/365-1613
FAX: 218/878-7529
E-mail: scholarships@fdlrez.com
Internet: http://www.fdlrez.com

AMOUNT: Varies (maximum awards established every 3 years)

DEADLINE(S): MAY 15 priority deadline (late applications will be considered on a first-come-first-served basis)

FIELD(S): All

ELIGIBILITY/REQUIREMENTS: Must be an enrolled member of Fond du Lac Band of Lake Superior Chippewa; accepted for admission to an institution accredited by federal or state licensing agency; have high school diploma or GED. Full- and part-time applicants in and out of state considered.

HOW TO APPLY: Call Scholarship Office for Scholarship Packet that includes instructions, applications, guidelines, policies, and procedures. Must complete FAFSA and institution's Financial Aid applications.

NUMBER OF AWARDS: 100 (average)

RENEWABLE: Yes. Must maintain minimum cumulative 2.0 GPA; submit grades at the end of each academic term.

3430—FOOD INDUSTRIES SCHOLARSHIP FUND OF NEW HAMPSHIRE

110 Stark Street
Manchester NH 03101-1977

AMOUNT: $1,000

DEADLINE(S): APR 1

FIELD(S): All

ELIGIBILITY/REQUIREMENTS: Open to students who are employed or whose parents are employed in businesses that are members of New Hampshire Grocers Association.

HOW TO APPLY: Contact Fund for an application.

NUMBER OF AWARDS: 18-20

3431—FOUNDATION FOR ASHLEY'S DREAM, THE (Ashley Marie Easterbrook Internet Scholarship Fund)

P.O. Box 1808
Troy MI 48099-1808
Internet: http://www.ashleys dream.org

AMOUNT: $2,000

DEADLINE(S): JAN 1-MAR 31

FIELD(S): All

ELIGIBILITY/REQUIREMENTS: Must be a graduating high school senior in the U.S.; cumulative 4-year GPA between 3.5 and 3.74 (unweighted); and plan to attend an accredited 4-year university or college. Preference given to applicants involved in organized programs and activities designed to help other students improve the quality

of their life; and with work experience (paid or volunteer).

HOW TO APPLY: Send application; document providing background information; 500-word essay; 1 letter of recommendation from a teacher, counselor, or administrator that describes how the student is viewed by the teaching staff; transcript.

NUMBER OF AWARDS: 1

3432—FOUNDATION OF THE FIRST CAVALRY DIVISION

302 North Main
Copperas Cove TX 76522-1703
254/547-6537
E-mail: firstcav@1cda.org

AMOUNT: $1,000

DEADLINE(S): None

FIELD(S): All

ELIGIBILITY/REQUIREMENTS: Open to children of soldiers who died or were totally and permanently disabled (unable to work for substantial compensation or profit), as a result of wounds received or disease contracted while serving with 1st Cavalry Division, U.S. Army in any armed conflict or who died while serving with the 1st Cavalry Division in peacetime. Also open to children and/or grandchildren of soldiers of 1st Cavalry Division, USAF Forward Air Controllers, and A1E pilots and war correspondents who served in designated qualifying units involved in battles of Ia Drang valley during the period November 3-19, 1965.

HOW TO APPLY: Send SASE to Secretary for an application for registration as an eligible recipient.

RENEWABLE: Yes. Up to 4 years.

CONTACT: Dennis E. Webster, Secretary

3433—FRANK H. AND EVA BUCK FOUNDATION, THE (Frank H. Buck Scholarships)

P.O. Box 5610
Vacaville CA 95696-5610
707/446-7700
FAX: 707/446-7766
E-mail: info@buckfoundation.org

AMOUNT: Tuition, books, and room/board

DEADLINE(S): Early DEC

FIELD(S): All

ELIGIBILITY/REQUIREMENTS: Open to unique students high school seniors or in colleges/universities who have an overwhelming motivation to succeed in all endeavors. Must possess strength of character and ambition as well as potential for leadership and be well-rounded in school, participate in community activities. Preference given to residents of Solano,

Napa, Yolo, Sacramento, San Joaquin, and Contra Costa Counties in California.

HOW TO APPLY: Contact Student Liaison from September 1 to mid-November for an application.

RENEWABLE: Yes, annually.

CONTACT: Gloria J. Brown, Student Liaison

3434—FRED B. AND RUTH B. ZIGLER FOUNDATION

P.O. Box 986
324 Broadway
Jennings LA 70546
337/824-2413
FAX: 337/824-2414
E-mail: frzigler@bellsouth.net
Internet: http://www.zigler foundation.org

AMOUNT: $1,250 per semester

DEADLINE(S): MAR 10

FIELD(S): All

ELIGIBILITY/REQUIREMENTS: Open to graduating seniors at Jefferson Davis Parish (Louisiana) high schools. Awards are tenable at recognized colleges and universities.

HOW TO APPLY: Write for information.

NUMBER OF AWARDS: 10-18

RENEWABLE: Yes. Up to 4 years.

3435—GEORGE GROTEFEND SCHOLARSHIP FUND

1644 Magnolia Avenue
Redding CA 96001
530/225-0317
FAX: 530/225-0329
E-mail: shunter@shastacoe.org
Internet: http://www.shastacoe.org

AMOUNT: $200-$500

DEADLINE(S): APR 20

FIELD(S): All

ELIGIBILITY/REQUIREMENTS: Must have completed all 4 years of high school in Shasta County, California, for all levels of study at recognized colleges and universities.

HOW TO APPLY: If currently a high school student, apply through school. If graduate, download application from website, call or write for information.

NUMBER OF AWARDS: About 250

RENEWABLE: Yes

CONTACT: Sue Hunter

3436—GERBER FOUNDATION, THE (Daniel Gerber Sr. Medallion Scholarship Program)

4747 West 48th Street, Suite 153

Fremont MI 49412-8119
231/924-3175
FAX: 231/924-7906
E-mail: tgf@ncresa.org
Internet: http://www.gerber
foundation.org
AMOUNT: $8,000 (aggregate for
undergraduate study)
DEADLINE(S): FEB 28
FIELD(S): All
ELIGIBILITY/REQUIREMENTS: For
graduates of a Newaygo County, Michigan,
high school; minimum GPA 3.70.
HOW TO APPLY: Contact high school
counselor or the Foundation for applica-
tion and details.
NUMBER OF AWARDS: 20
RENEWABLE: Yes. 3 more years.
CONTACT: Catherine A. Obits

3437—GERBER FOUNDATION, THE (Merit Scholarship Program)

4747 West 48th Street, Suite 153
Fremont MI 49412-8119
231/924-3175
FAX: 231/924-7906
E-mail: tgf@ncresa.org
Internet: http://www.gerber
foundation.org
AMOUNT: $2,000
DEADLINE(S): FEB 28
FIELD(S): All
ELIGIBILITY/REQUIREMENTS: For
graduates of a Newaygo or Muskegon
County, Michigan, high school; maximum
GPA 3.70.
HOW TO APPLY: Contact high school
counselor or the Foundation for applica-
tion and details.
NUMBER OF AWARDS: 50
RENEWABLE: No
CONTACT: Catherine A. Obits

3438—GERMAN ACADEMIC EXCHANGE SERVICE (DAAD Programs)

871 United Nations Plaza
New York NY 10017
212/758-3223
FAX: 212/755-5780
E-mail: daadny@daad.org
Internet: http://www.daad.org
AMOUNT: Varies (with program)
DEADLINE(S): Varies (with program)
FIELD(S): All (varies with program)
ELIGIBILITY/REQUIREMENTS: For
study, research and other academic activi-
ties in Germany to students, citizens and
permanent residents of the U.S. and
Canada. Support for visiting professorships
for highly qualified faculty.
HOW TO APPLY: See website for appli-
cation instructions.

NUMBER OF AWARDS: 100+
RENEWABLE: Yes, for those interested
in completing a degree in Germany.
CONTACT: E-mail or phone

3439—GLAMOUR MAGAZINE (Top Ten College Women Competition)

Conde Nast Pub.
4 Times Square, 16th Floor
New York NY 10036-6593
212/286-6667
FAX: 212/286-6922
E-mail: ttcw@Glamour.com
AMOUNT: $3,000 and trip to New York
DEADLINE(S): NOV 30
FIELD(S): All
ELIGIBILITY/REQUIREMENTS: Open
to all women who are full-time juniors,
attending a college in the U.S. or Canada
who are not scheduled to graduate before
May of their senior year. The competition
is void outside the 50 states, the District of
Columbia, and Canada (void in Quebec
and where prohibited). Based on leadership experience, personal involvement in
community/campus affairs, and academic
excellence.
HOW TO APPLY: Submit college transcript, list of activities, photograph, let-
ter(s) of recommendation, and essay
describing achievements and how they
relate to your field of study or future goals.
NUMBER OF AWARDS: 10
RENEWABLE: No

3440—GLENDALE COMMUNITY FOUNDATION

P.O. Box 313
Glendale CA 91209-0313
818/241-8040
FAX: (818) 241-8045
E-mail: info@glendalecommunity
foundation.org
Internet: http://www.glendale
community foundation.org/
AMOUNT: Varies
DEADLINE(S): MAR 14
FIELD(S): All
ELIGIBILITY/REQUIREMENTS:
Scholarships through this Foundation for
needy students who are residents of Glen-
dale, La Canada-Flintridge, La Crescenta-
Montrose, or Verdugo City, California.
HOW TO APPLY: Contact Foundation
for details.
RENEWABLE: No

3441—GLENN MILLER BIRTHPLACE SOCIETY

107 E. Main

P. O. Box 61
Clarinda IA 51632
PHONE/FAX: 712/542-2461
E-mail: gmbs@heartland.net
Internet: http://www.glennmiller.org
AMOUNT: $1,000-$3,000
DEADLINE(S): MAR 15
FIELD(S): All, especially Music
Performance (Instrumental and Vocal)
ELIGIBILITY/REQUIREMENTS:
Competitions open to high school seniors
and undergraduate freshmen who intend
to make music a central part of their future
life (music major NOT required). Must
submit a clear high-quality audio CD or
cassette tape containing your competition
pieces or pieces similar to them in style and
difficulty. A good length of tape performance would be about 10 minutes total.
Not more than 10 finalists will be accepted
in each category. Finalists will come to
Clarinda's Glenn Miller Festival at their
own expense for live auditions to be held in
June.
HOW TO APPLY: Send SASE for an
application or see website for additional
information about each category and specific requirements.
NUMBER OF AWARDS: 6
RENEWABLE: Yes. Those who have
entered as high school seniors are eligible
to compete again as college freshmen,
unless they have been previous first-place
winners.

3442—GOLDEN KEY INTERNATIONAL HONOUR SOCIETY (GEICO Adult Scholar Award)

1189 Ponce de Leon Avenue
Atlanta GA 30306
404/377-2400 or 800/377-2401
FAX: 404/373-7033
E-mail: scholarships@goldenkey.org
Internet: http://www.goldenkey.org
AMOUNT: $1,000
DEADLINE(S): APR 1
FIELD(S): All fields of study
ELIGIBILITY/REQUIREMENTS:
Undergraduate members who have completed at least 12 credit hours since returning to the university are eligible. Must be
enrolled at the time of application and
must be working toward a baccalaureate
degree. Academic achievement, extracurricular activities and family and/or career
commitments are considered.
HOW TO APPLY: Apply online with
Golden Key member number. Attach a
personal essay of no more than 500 words
describing your educational goals, other
commitments you may have, and the
obstacles you have overcome to achieve
academic excellence along with a letter of

recommendation from either an employer or a professor in your major field of study and a transcript.
NUMBER OF AWARDS: 10
RENEWABLE: No

3443—GOLDEN KEY INTERNATIONAL HONOUR SOCIETY (International Student Leader Award)

1189 Ponce de Leon Avenue
Atlanta GA 30306
404/377-2400 or 800/377-2401
FAX: 404/373-7033
E-mail: scholarships@goldenkey.org
Internet: http://www.goldenkey.org
DEADLINE(S): MAY
FIELD(S): All
ELIGIBILITY/REQUIREMENTS: This award recognizes members who demonstrate excellence in Golden Key leadership, as well as campus leadership, community service, and academic achievement. Open to undergraduate, graduate, and postgraduate members who are enrolled in an accredited academic program. Based on academic achievement, impact of Golden Key leadership, as determined by the selection committee, and involvement in extracurricular activities.
HOW TO APPLY: Must apply online with your Golden Key member number.
NUMBER OF AWARDS: TBA
RENEWABLE: No

3444—GOLDEN KEY INTERNATIONAL HONOUR SOCIETY (Research and Travel Grants)

1189 Ponce de Leon Avenue
Atlanta GA 30306
404/377-2400 or 800/377-2401
FAX: 404/373-7033
E-mail: scholarships@goldenkey.org
Internet: http://www.goldenkey.org
AMOUNT: $500 each
DEADLINE(S): OCT 15 and APR 15
FIELD(S): All
ELIGIBILITY/REQUIREMENTS: These grants allow members to conduct thesis research and/or present their research at professional conferences or student research symposia. Undergraduate student members are eligible to apply. Selections based on academic achievement and quality of research or presentation as determined by the selection committee.
HOW TO APPLY: Post application online with Golden Key member number. Attach a description of the proposed research presentation and evidence of invitation to present at a specified professional association conference or research symposium. If

requesting a grant for honors thesis research, submit documentation supported by the thesis advisor that this trip is highly relevant to the research to be conducted. Attach a budget summarizing overall cost of attending the conference or of traveling to undertake necessary research, and a transcript.
NUMBER OF AWARDS/YEAR: 10 (5, twice each year)
RENEWABLE: No

3445—GOLDEN KEY INTERNATIONAL HONOUR SOCIETY (Service Award)

1189 Ponce de Leon Avenue
Atlanta GA 30306
404/377-2400 or 800/377-2401
FAX: 404/373-7033
E-mail: scholarships@goldenkey.org
Internet: http://www.goldenkey.org
AMOUNT: $1,000 ($500 to the recipient, $250 to the recipient's chapter, $250 to charity of the recipient's choice)
DEADLINE(S): FEB 15
FIELD(S): All
ELIGIBILITY/REQUIREMENTS: Open to undergraduate, graduate, and postgraduate members who were enrolled as students during the previous academic year. More than 1 member from each chapter may apply for the award, and projects submitted may be either individual or chapter efforts. Award based on impact of service provided.
HOW TO APPLY: Apply online with your Golden Key member number. Attach a statement of no more than 500 words describing the service project and your philosophy of community service, a letter of recommendation from your Golden Key chapter advisor, a letter of recommendation from a representative of the beneficiary of the service, a list of extracurricular activities detailing involvement in other campus and community service, including any involvement in Golden Key, and a list of work and family commitments.
NUMBER OF AWARDS/YEAR: 1
RENEWABLE: No

3446—GOLDEN KEY INTERNATIONAL HONOUR SOCIETY (Student Scholastic Showcase)

1189 Ponce de Leon Avenue
Atlanta GA 30306
404/377-2400 or 800/377-2401
FAX: 404/373-7033
E-mail: scholarships@goldenkey.org
Internet: http://www.goldenkey.org
ELIGIBILITY/REQUIREMENTS: Open to undergraduate, graduate, and postgrad-

uate members, but the research submitted must have been done as an undergraduate student.
HOW TO APPLY: Apply online with your Golden Key member number. Attach a letter of support from a faculty member related to or familiar with the research project; an abstract (not to exceed 250 words), which describes the nature of the study written in language that is suitable for a reader who may be unfamiliar with the discipline; a complete copy of the paper/research; and transcript.
NUMBER OF AWARDS/YEAR: 4
RENEWABLE: No

3447—GOLDEN KEY INTERNATIONAL HONOUR SOCIETY (Study Abroad Scholarship)

1189 Ponce de Leon Avenue
Atlanta GA 30306
404/377-2400 or 800/377-2401
FAX: 404/373-7033
E-mail: scholarships@goldenkey.org
Internet: http://www.goldenkey.org
AMOUNT: $2,000
DEADLINE(S): OCT 15 and APR 15
FIELD(S): All
ELIGIBILITY/REQUIREMENTS: Open to undergraduate members who are enrolled in a study-abroad program or who will be enrolled the academic year immediately following the granting of the award. Recipients will be expected to contribute an article about their study-abroad experience to *Concepts*, Golden Key's annual magazine. Awards are based on academic achievement and relevance of study-abroad program to major field of study.
HOW TO APPLY: Post applications online with Golden Key member number. For additional information see website.
NUMBER OF AWARDS/YEAR: 10 (5, twice each year)
RENEWABLE: No

3448—GOLF COURSE SUPERINTENDENTS ASSOCIATION OF AMERICA (Par Aide's Joseph S. Garske Collegiate Grant Program)

1421 Research Park Drive
Lawrence KS 66049-3859
785/832-3678 or
800/472-7878, ext. 678
FAX: 785/832-4449
Internet: http://www.gcsaa.org
AMOUNT: $2,500 (total prizes)
DEADLINE(S): MAR 15
FIELD(S): All
ELIGIBILITY/REQUIREMENTS: Open to children or stepchildren of members

(who have been active for 5 or more consecutive years) for use in either an accredited college or trade school. Must be a graduating high school senior accepted at institution of higher learning.
HOW TO APPLY: See website or contact GCSAA for details.
NUMBER OF AWARDS: 1-2
RENEWABLE: Yes. For second year.
CONTACT: Amanda Howard, Employment Administrator, 800/472-7878, ext. 4424.

3449—GOLF COURSE SUPERINTENDENTS ASSOCIATION OF AMERICA (Syngenta GCSAA Legacy Awards)

1421 Research Park Drive
Lawrence KS 66049-3859
785/832-3678 or
800/472-7878, ext. 678
FAX: 785/832-3678
Internet: http://www.gcsaa.org
AMOUNT: $1,500
DEADLINE(S): APR 15
FIELD(S): All
ELIGIBILITY/REQUIREMENTS: Must be the children or grandchildren of GCSAA members who have been active members for 5 or more consecutive years; studying a field unrelated to golf course management; and either be undergraduate students enrolled full time at an accredited institution of higher learning or high school seniors accepted for the next academic year.
HOW TO APPLY: Contact Scholarship and Student Programs Manager for details and application.
NUMBER OF AWARDS: 20
RENEWABLE: Must be 1 year hiatus before reapplying.
CONTACT: Amanda Howard, Employment Administrator, 800/472-7878, ext. 4424.

3450—GRAY FOUNDATION

2737 Petaluma Hill Road
Santa Rosa CA 95404
707/544-7409
Internet: http://www.gray
foundation.com/Index.htm
AMOUNT: $1,000
DEADLINE(S): MAR 31
FIELD(S): All
ELIGIBILITY/REQUIREMENTS: The Gray Foundation offers scholarships for undergraduate study to Sonoma County high school graduates, or those from Middletown HS in Lake County, or GED certificate receivers of Sonoma County, California. Must complete the FAF form.

HOW TO APPLY: Write to the above address for complete information.
RENEWABLE: Yes; up to 4 years.

3451—GREATER KANAWHA VALLEY FOUNDATION

P.O. Box 3041
Charleston WV 25331
304/346-3620
FAX: 304/346-3640
E-mail: shoover@tgkvf.org
Internet: http://www.tgkvf.org
AMOUNT: $1,000
DEADLINE(S): FEB 15
FIELD(S): All
ELIGIBILITY/REQUIREMENTS: Must be West Virginia resident and a full-time student; 2.5 GPA, minimum ACT of 20.
HOW TO APPLY: Applications are available on the website.
CONTACT: Susan Hoover, Scholarship Coordinator

3452—GREENPOINT FOUNDATION (Achievers Scholarship)

1505 Riverview Road
P.O. Box 297
St. Peter MN 56082
507/931-1682
FAX: 507/931-9278
E-mail: gmiller@csfa.org
Internet: http://www.greenpoint.com
AMOUNT: $2,500
DEADLINE(S): MAR 1
FIELD(S): All
ELIGIBILITY/REQUIREMENTS: Must have a cumulative 3.0 GPA or its equivalent and a minimum combined SAT score of 1000; reside in the boroughs of Brooklyn, Queens, Manhattan, the Bronx, or Staten Island, or Westchester, Nassau, or Suffolk Counties, all in New York.
HOW TO APPLY: Contact Foundation for application and details.

3453—GUIDEPOSTS MAGAZINE (Young Writers' Contest)

16 E. 34th Street
New York NY 10016
212/251-8100
FAX: 212/251-1311
E-mail: ywcontest@guideposts.org
Internet: http://www.guideposts.com
AMOUNT: First prize $10,000; second $8,000; third $6,000; fourth $4,000; fifth $3,000; sixth to tenth $1,000; eleventh to twentieth $250 gift certificate for college supplies
DEADLINE(S): Late NOV (varies)
FIELD(S): All

ELIGIBILITY/REQUIREMENTS: Open to high school juniors or seniors in the fall of the year they apply. Must write a first-person story about a memorable or moving experience they have had. Stories must be the true personal experience of the writer and the original, unpublished work of the submitter, must be written in English and be a maximum of 1,200 words.
HOW TO APPLY: Mail or e-mail manuscript, see website for guidelines.

3454—GUSTAVUS ADOLPHUS COLLEGE (Andrew Thorson Scholarships)

Office of Admission
800 West College Avenue
St. Peter MN 56082
507/933-7676 or 800/GUSTAVUS
E-mail: admission@gustavus.edu
Internet: http://www.gustavus.edu/
AMOUNT: Up to $3,000
DEADLINE(S): MAR 1
FIELD(S): All
ELIGIBILITY/REQUIREMENTS: Scholarships tenable at Gustavus Adolphus College, St. Peter, Minnesota, for students who come from a farm family or rural area or in a town of fewer than 2,000 people, or who attend a school with a graduating class of fewer than 100 students. Financial need considered.
HOW TO APPLY: Contact Office of Admission for details.

3455—GUSTAVUS ADOLPHUS COLLEGE (Congregational Scholarship Matching Program)

Office of Admission
800 West College Avenue
St. Peter MN 56082
507/933-7676 or 800/GUSTAVUS
E-mail: admission@gustavus.edu
Internet: http://www.gustavus.edu/
AMOUNT: Up to $1,000
DEADLINE(S): MAR 1
FIELD(S): All
ELIGIBILITY/REQUIREMENTS: Scholarships tenable at Gustavus Adolphus College, St. Peter, Minnesota, for students whose home church congregation has provided scholarship funding in amounts of up to $1,000. This program will match this at a rate of 1.5 times each scholarship dollar. Congregational scholarships from any denomination will be matched.
HOW TO APPLY: Contact Office of Admission for details.

3456—GUSTAVUS ADOLPHUS COLLEGE (National Merit College-Sponsored Scholarships)

Office of Admission

800 West College Avenue
St. Peter MN 56082
507/933-7676 or 800/GUSTAVUS
E-mail: admission@gustavus.edu
Internet: http://www.gustavus.edu/
AMOUNT: $750-$2,000
DEADLINE(S): None
FIELD(S): All
ELIGIBILITY/REQUIREMENTS:
Scholarships tenable at Gustavus
Adolphus College, St. Peter, Minnesota,
for students selected as finalists in the
National Merit Scholarship competition
and who designate Gustavus as their first-
choice college. Amount of award is based
on need.
HOW TO APPLY: Contact Office of
Admission for details.
RENEWABLE: Yes

3457—GUSTAVUS ADOLPHUS COLLEGE (Partners in Scholarship)

Office of Admission
800 West College Avenue
St. Peter MN 56082
507/933-7676 or 800/GUSTAVUS
E-mail: admission@gustavus.edu
Internet: http://www.gustavus.edu/
AMOUNT: $7,500/year
DEADLINE(S): APR 15
FIELD(S): All
ELIGIBILITY/REQUIREMENTS:
Scholarships tenable at Gustavus
Adolphus College, St. Peter, Minnesota,
for students who rank at or near the top of
their high school graduating class, have
composite test scores of at least 32 on the
ACT or 1400 on the SAT, and intend to
pursue a graduate degree after Gustavus.
HOW TO APPLY: Contact Office of
Admission for details.
RENEWABLE: Yearly with GPA of 3.25.

3458—GUSTAVUS ADOLPHUS COLLEGE (Trustee Scholarships)

Office of Admission
800 West College Avenue
St. Peter MN 56082
507/933-7676 or 800/GUSTAVUS
E-mail: admission@gustavus.edu
Internet: http://www.gustavus.edu/
AMOUNT: $1,000-$5,000/year
DEADLINE(S): APR 15
FIELD(S): All
ELIGIBILITY/REQUIREMENTS:
Scholarships tenable at Gustavus
Adolphus College, St. Peter, Minnesota,
for students who have shown academic
achievement in high school as measured by
the difficulty of courses taken, grades
earned, and standardized test scores.

HOW TO APPLY: Contact Office of
Admission for details.
RENEWABLE: Yearly with GPA of 3.25.

3459—HARNESS TRACKS OF AMERICA

4640 East Sunrise, Suite 200
Tucson AZ 85718
520/529-2525
FAX: 520/529-3235
E-mail: info@harnesstracks.com
Internet: http://www.harness
tracks.com
AMOUNT: $5,000
DEADLINE(S): JUN 15
FIELD(S): All
ELIGIBILITY/REQUIREMENTS: Open
ONLY to children of licensed harness rac-
ing drivers, trainers, breeders, or caretak-
ers (including retired or deceased) and
young people actively engaged in harness
racing for study beyond the high school
level. Based on academic merit, financial
need, and harness racing involvement.
HOW TO APPLY: Contact Harness
Tracks for an application.
NUMBER OF AWARDS: 5
RENEWABLE: Yes

3460—HAWAII COMMUNITY FOUNDATION (ABC Stores Jumpstart Scholarship)

1164 Bishop Street, Suite 800
Honolulu HI 96813
808/537-6333 or 888/731-3863
FAX: 808/521-6286
E-mail: info@hcf-hawaii.org
Internet: http://www.hcf-hawaii.org
DEADLINE(S): MAR 1
FIELD(S): All
ELIGIBILITY/REQUIREMENTS: Must
be an employee or dependent of an
employee of ABC Stores; be resident of
Hawaii, Nevada, Guam, or Saipan; plan to
attend an accredited 2- or 4-year college or
university as either an undergraduate or
graduate student; and demonstrate financial need, good moral character, and academic achievement with 3.0 minimum
GPA.
HOW TO APPLY: Send application with
2 letters of recommendation and the name
of the ABC Stores' employee and relationship to applicant.

3461—HAWAII COMMUNITY FOUNDATION (Ambassador Minerva Jean Falcon Hawaii Scholarship)

1164 Bishop Street, Suite 800
Honolulu HI 96813
808/537-6333 or 888/731-3863
FAX: 808/521-6286

E-mail: info@hcf-hawaii.org
Internet: http://www.hcf-hawaii.org
DEADLINE(S): MAR 1
FIELD(S): All
ELIGIBILITY/REQUIREMENTS: Must
be of Filipino ancestry; attend full time an
accredited 2- or 4-year college or university in Hawaii; and demonstrate financial
need, good moral character, and academic
achievement with 2.7 minimum GPA.
HOW TO APPLY: Send application, 2 letters of recommendation, and an essay
(maximum of 2 pages, double spaced) on
how you plan to be involved in the community as a Filipino-American student.

3462—HAWAII COMMUNITY FOUNDATION (Anthony Alexander, Andrew Delos Reyes & Jeremy Tolentino Memorial Fund)

1164 Bishop Street, Suite 800
Honolulu HI 96813
808/537-6333 or 888/731-3863
FAX: 808/521-6286
E-mail: info@hcf-hawaii.org
Internet: http://www.hcf-hawaii.org
DEADLINE(S): MAR 1
FIELD(S): All
ELIGIBILITY/REQUIREMENTS: Must
be residents of the state of Hawaii; graduating seniors at Mililani High School; plan
to enroll full time as undergraduate or
graduate students at an accredited 2- or 4-
year college or university; and demonstrate
financial need, good moral character, and
academic achievement with 2.7 minimum
GPA.
HOW TO APPLY: Send application with
2 letters of recommendation and an essay
(double spaced) on the subject of drinking
and driving under the influence, highway
safety, or another related subject.

3463—HAWAII COMMUNITY FOUNDATION (Arthur Jackman Memorial Scholarship)

1164 Bishop Street, Suite 800
Honolulu HI 96813
808/537-6333 or 888/731-3863
FAX: 808/521-6286
E-mail: info@hcf-hawaii.org
Internet: http://www.hcf-hawaii.org
DEADLINE(S): MAR 1
FIELD(S): All
ELIGIBILITY/REQUIREMENTS: Must
be resident of the island of Hawaii; plan to
attend a vocational college or institution
on the island of Hawaii; and demonstrate
financial need, good moral character, and
strong academic achievement, with 2.7
minimum GPA.

HOW TO APPLY: Send application with 2 letters of recommendation.
CONTACT: The Hawaii Community Foundation WAIMEA Office at 808/885-2174

3464—HAWAII COMMUNITY FOUNDATION (Bal Dasa Scholarship)

1164 Bishop Street, Suite 800
Honolulu HI 96813
808/537-6333 or 888/731-3863
FAX: 808/521-6286
E-mail: info@hcf-hawaii.org
Internet: http://www.hcf-hawaii.org
DEADLINE(S): MAR 1
FIELD(S): All
ELIGIBILITY/REQUIREMENTS: Must be residents of the state of Hawaii; graduating seniors at Waipahu High School; plan to enroll full time as undergraduate or graduate students at an accredited 2- or 4-year college or university; and demonstrate financial need, good moral character, and academic achievement with 2.7 minimum GPA.
HOW TO APPLY: Send application with 2 letters of recommendation.

3465—HAWAII COMMUNITY FOUNDATION (Camille C. Chidiac Fund)

1164 Bishop Street, Suite 800
Honolulu HI 96813
808/537-6333 or 888/731-3863
FAX: 808/521-6286
E-mail: info@hcf-hawaii.org
Internet: http://www.hcf-hawaii.org
DEADLINE(S): MAR 1
FIELD(S): All
ELIGIBILITY/REQUIREMENTS: Must be residents of the state of Hawaii; graduating seniors at Ka'u High School; plan to enroll full time as undergraduate or graduate students at an accredited 2- or 4-year college or university; and demonstrate financial need, good moral character, and academic achievement with 2.7 minimum GPA.
HOW TO APPLY: Send application with 2 letters of recommendation and a short essay on why it is important for Hawaii's students to be internationally aware.

3466—HAWAII COMMUNITY FOUNDATION (Castle & Cooke George W. Y. Yim Scholarship Fund)

1164 Bishop Street, Suite 800
Honolulu HI 96813
808/537-6333 or 888/731-3863
FAX: 808/521-6286
E-mail: info@hcf-hawaii.org

Internet: http://www.hcf-hawaii.org
DEADLINE(S): MAR 1
FIELD(S): All
ELIGIBILITY/REQUIREMENTS: Must be the dependent of an employee (minimum 1 year of service) with a Castle & Cooke Hawaii affiliated company; be a resident of the state of Hawaii; plan to attend full time an accredited 2- or 4-year college, university or vocational school in the U.S.; and demonstrate financial need, good moral character, and strong academic achievement, with 3.0 minimum GPA.
HOW TO APPLY: Send application with 2 letters of recommendation.
CONTACT: Bonnie Freitas, Human Resources, Castle & Cooke at 808/548-3777

3467—HAWAII COMMUNITY FOUNDATION (Castle & Cooke Mililani Technology Park Scholarship Fund)

1164 Bishop Street, Suite 800
Honolulu HI 96813
808/537-6333 or 888/731-3863
FAX: 808/521-6286
E-mail: info@hcf-hawaii.org
Internet: http://www.hcf-hawaii.org
DEADLINE(S): MAR 1
FIELD(S): All (emphasis on high technology-Science & Engineering)
ELIGIBILITY/REQUIREMENTS: Must be graduating seniors from Leilehua, Mililani, or Waialua high schools; plan to enroll full time in an accredited 2- or 4-year college or university; must demonstrate financial need, good moral character, and academic achievement (minimum 2.7 GPA). Preference given to students majoring in a high-technology field, such as science or engineering.
HOW TO APPLY: Send application with 2 letters of recommendation.

3468—HAWAII COMMUNITY FOUNDATION (Cayetano Foundation Scholarship)

1164 Bishop Street, Suite 800
Honolulu HI 96813
808/537-6333 or 888/731-3863
FAX: 808/521-6286
E-mail: info@hcf-hawaii.org
Internet: http://www.hcf-hawaii.org
DEADLINE(S): MAR 1
FIELD(S): All
ELIGIBILITY/REQUIREMENTS: Must be residents of the state of Hawaii; seniors at a public or private high school in Hawaii; plan to enroll full time as undergraduate or graduate students at an accredited 2- or 4-year college or university; and demonstrate financial need, good moral character, and academic achievement with 3.5 minimum

GPA. Preference will be given to the students with the greatest financial need.
HOW TO APPLY: Send application; 2 letters of recommendation; a personal statement describing your participation in community projects or activities; and an essay on the following topic: "Please fast forward to a time 40 years in the future. You are in your late 50s now and as you reflect on your adult life, list the major accomplishments in your life and explain why you consider them to be significant."

3469—HAWAII COMMUNITY FOUNDATION (Chin Ho Scholarship Fund)

1164 Bishop Street, Suite 800
Honolulu HI 96813
808/537-6333 or 888/731-3863
FAX: 808/521-6286
E-mail: info@hcf-hawaii.org
Internet: http://www.hcf-hawaii.org
DEADLINE(S): MAR 1
FIELD(S): All
ELIGIBILITY/REQUIREMENTS: Must be McKinley High School seniors; resident of the state of Hawaii; plan to attend full time an accredited 2- or 4-year college or university; have contributed to the school and community; and demonstrate financial need, good moral character, and academic excellence, with 2.7 minimum GPA.
HOW TO APPLY: Send application with 2 letters of recommendation.
CONTACT: McKinley High School counselor

3470—HAWAII COMMUNITY FOUNDATION (David L. Irons Memorial Scholarship Fund)

1164 Bishop Street, Suite 800
Honolulu HI 96813
808/537-6333 or 888/731-3863
FAX: 808/521-6286
E-mail: info@hcf-hawaii.org
Internet: http://www.hcf-hawaii.org
DEADLINE(S): MAR 1
FIELD(S): All
ELIGIBILITY/REQUIREMENTS: Must be residents of the state of Hawaii; be graduating seniors at Punahou High School; plan to enroll full time as undergraduate or graduate students at an accredited 2- or 4-year college or university; and demonstrate financial need, good moral character, and academic achievement with 2.7 minimum GPA.
HOW TO APPLY: Send application with 2 letters of recommendation and a personal statement answering the following questions: "What are your educational and career goals? Why did you choose these

goals? How would you spend a free day? Who is a hero of yours and what is an overriding quality that makes this person your hero?"

3471—HAWAII COMMUNITY FOUNDATION (Edwin T. & Leilani Kam Scholarship)

1164 Bishop Street, Suite 800
Honolulu HI 96813
808/537-6333 or 888/731-3863
FAX: 808/521-6286
E-mail: info@hcf-hawaii.org
Internet: http://www.hcf-hawaii.org
DEADLINE(S): MAR 1
FIELD(S): All
ELIGIBILITY/REQUIREMENTS: Must be University of Hawaii students in the National Student Exchange Program (or Hawaii students at Loma Linda University School of Medicine or Dentistry); resident of the state of Hawaii; and demonstrate financial need, good moral character, and academic achievement, with 2.7 minimum GPA.
HOW TO APPLY: Send application with 2 letters of recommendation.
CONTACT: UH National Student Exchange Program, School & College Services, Student Services Center 214, 2600 Campus Road, Honolulu HI 96822

3472—HAWAII COMMUNITY FOUNDATION (E. E. Black Scholarship Fund)

1164 Bishop Street, Suite 800
Honolulu HI 96813
808/537-6333 or 888/731-3863
FAX: 808/521-6286
E-mail: info@hcf-hawaii.org
Internet: http://www.hcf-hawaii.org
DEADLINE(S): MAR 1
FIELD(S): All
ELIGIBILITY/REQUIREMENTS: Must be a dependent of an employee of Tesoro Hawaii or its subsidiaries; be resident of Hawaii; be enrolled full time as an undergraduate at an accredited 2- or 4-year college or university; and demonstrate financial need, good moral character, and academic achievement with 3.0 minimum GPA.
HOW TO APPLY: Send application with 2 letters of recommendation and the name of the Tesoro Hawaii employee and relationship to applicant.

3473—HAWAII COMMUNITY FOUNDATION (Eiro Yamada Memorial Scholarship)

1164 Bishop Street, Suite 800
Honolulu HI 96813
808/537-6333 or 888/731-3863

FAX: 808/521-6286
E-mail: info@hcf-hawaii.org
Internet: http://www.hcf-hawaii.org
DEADLINE(S): MAR 1
FIELD(S): All
ELIGIBILITY/REQUIREMENTS: Must be direct descendants of WWII veterans of the 100th, 442nd, MIS, or 1399th units; plan to enroll full time as undergraduate or graduate students at an accredited 2- or 4-year college or university; and demonstrate financial need, good moral character, and academic achievement with 2.7 minimum GPA. Applicants do not have to be residents of Hawaii.
HOW TO APPLY: Send application; 2 letters of recommendation; name of veteran and relationship to applicant; and a short essay on one of the following topics: "The Values I Have Learned from my Japanese-American Forefathers" or your personal reflections on some of the stories in the book *Japanese Eyes, American Hearts* or similar material related to the Japanese-American experience during World War II.

3474—HAWAII COMMUNITY FOUNDATION (Eizo & Toyo Sakumoto Trust Scholarship)

1164 Bishop Street, Suite 800
Honolulu HI 96813
808/537-6333 or 888/731-3863
FAX: 808/521-6286
E-mail: info@hcf-hawaii.org
Internet: http://www.hcf-hawaii.org
DEADLINE(S): MAR 1
FIELD(S): All
ELIGIBILITY/REQUIREMENTS: Must have been born in Hawaii and be primarily of Japanese ancestry; be residents of the state of Hawaii; plan to attend full time an accredited 2- or 4-year college or university in Hawaii; and demonstrate financial need, good moral character, and academic achievement (minimum 3.5 GPA).
HOW TO APPLY: Send application with 2 letters of recommendation.

3475—HAWAII COMMUNITY FOUNDATION (Fletcher & Fritzi Hoffman Educational Fund)

1164 Bishop Street, Suite 800
Honolulu HI 96813
808/537-6333 or 888/731-3863
FAX: 808/521-6286
E-mail: info@hcf-hawaii.org
Internet: http://www.hcf-hawaii.org
DEADLINE(S): MAR 1
FIELD(S): All

ELIGIBILITY/REQUIREMENTS: Must be long-time residents from the Hamakua coast on the Island of Hawaii; attend a college or vocational school on the Island of Hawaii; and demonstrate financial need, good moral character, and academic achievement with 2.7 minimum GPA.
HOW TO APPLY: Send application with 2 letters of recommendation and a short history on your family's history and roots in the Hamakua area.

3476—HAWAII COMMUNITY FOUNDATION (Frances S. Watanabe Memorial Scholarship)

1164 Bishop Street, Suite 800
Honolulu HI 96813
808/537-6333 or 888/731-3863
FAX: 808/521-6286
E-mail: info@hcf-hawaii.org
Internet: http://www.hcf-hawaii.org
DEADLINE(S): MAR 1
FIELD(S): All
ELIGIBILITY/REQUIREMENTS: Must be a member or the dependent of a member of the Hawaii Construction Industry Federal Credit Union (formerly Dillingham Federal Credit Union); attend school either full- or part-time at an accredited 2- or 4-year college or university; be resident of the state of Hawaii; and demonstrate financial need, good moral character, and academic achievement with 2.7 minimum GPA.
HOW TO APPLY: Send application with 2 letters of recommendation and the name of the member of the Hawaii Construction Industry Federal Credit Union.

3477—HAWAII COMMUNITY FOUNDATION (Frank H. Minato Scholarship Fund)

1164 Bishop Street, Suite 800
Honolulu HI 96813
808/537-6333 or 888/731-3863
FAX: 808/521-6286
E-mail: info@hcf-hawaii.org
Internet: http://www.hcf-hawaii.org
DEADLINE(S): MAR 1
FIELD(S): All
ELIGIBILITY/REQUIREMENTS: Must be seniors from McKinley High School who have participated and excelled in one of the interscholastic athletic teams of the school; residents of the state of Hawaii; plan to attend full time an accredited 2- or 4-year college or university; and demonstrate financial need, good moral character, and academic achievement, with 2.7 minimum GPA.
HOW TO APPLY: Send application with 2 letters of recommendation.

CONTACT: McKinley High School counselor

3478—HAWAII COMMUNITY FOUNDATION (Friends of Hawaii Public Housing Scholarship)

1164 Bishop Street, Suite 800
Honolulu HI 96813
808/537-6333 or 888/731-3863
FAX: 808/521-6286
E-mail: info@hcf-hawaii.org
Internet: http://www.hcf-hawaii.org
DEADLINE(S): MAR 1
FIELD(S): All
ELIGIBILITY/REQUIREMENTS: Applicants must be residents of a Hawaii public housing complex; plan to enroll full time as undergraduate or graduate students at an accredited 2- or 4-year college or university; and demonstrate financial need, good moral character, and academic achievement with 2.7 minimum GPA.
HOW TO APPLY: Send application; 2 letters of recommendation; and a personal statement including the name of your public housing complex.

3479—HAWAII COMMUNITY FOUNDATION (Gerrit R. Ludwig Scholarship Fund)

1164 Bishop Street, Suite 800
Honolulu HI 96813
808/537-6333 or 888/731-3863
FAX: 808/521-6286
E-mail: info@hcf-hawaii.org
Internet: http://www.hcf-hawaii.org
DEADLINE(S): MAR 1
FIELD(S): All
ELIGIBILITY/REQUIREMENTS: Must be graduates of one of the following East Hawaii public schools: Hilo, Honoka'a, Kea'au, Laupahoehoe, Pahoa, or Waiakea; plan to attend an accredited 2- or 4-year college or university full time; and demonstrate financial need, good moral character, and academic achievement with a 2.7 minimum GPA. Preference is given to students pursuing a degree in the fine arts and classics.
HOW TO APPLY: Send application with 2 letters of recommendation.

3480—HAWAII COMMUNITY FOUNDATION (Hawaiian Homes Commission Scholarship)

1164 Bishop Street, Suite 800
Honolulu HI 96813
808/537-6333 or 888/731-3863
FAX: 808/521-6286
E-mail: info@hcf-hawaii.org

Internet: http://www.hcf-hawaii.org
DEADLINE(S): MAR 1
FIELD(S): All
ELIGIBILITY/REQUIREMENTS: Must be native Hawaiian (50% or more Hawaiian ancestry) or otherwise be eligible to receive benefits as provided in the Hawaiian Homes Commission Act of 1920 as amended (successors or transferees of at least 25% Hawaiian ancestry); do NOT have to be Hawaii residents; must be enrolled as a full-time undergraduate or graduate student at an accredited 2- or 4-year college or university; and demonstrate financial need, good moral character, and academic achievement (minimum 2.0 GPA for undergraduates and 3.0 for graduate students).
HOW TO APPLY: Send application with 2 letters of recommendation. Hawaiian Homes Commission will contact you for genealogical verification.

3481—HAWAII COMMUNITY FOUNDATION (Hoomaku Hou Scholarship)

1164 Bishop Street, Suite 800
Honolulu HI 96813
808/537-6333 or 888/731-3863
FAX: 808/521-6286
E-mail: info@hcf-hawaii.org
Internet: http://www.hcf-hawaii.org
DEADLINE(S): MAR 1
FIELD(S): All
ELIGIBILITY/REQUIREMENTS: Must be students who have turned their lives around after facing social problems (e.g., substance abuse, domestic violence); be residents of the state of Hawaii; plan to attend full time an accredited 2- or 4-year college or university; and demonstrate financial need, good moral character, and academic achievement, with a minimum GPA of 2.7.
HOW TO APPLY: Send application with 2 letters of recommendation.
CONTACT: Hawaii Community Foundation Scholarship Department at 808/566-5570

3482—HAWAII COMMUNITY FOUNDATION (Ida M. Pope Memorial Scholarship)

1164 Bishop Street, Suite 800
Honolulu HI 96813
808/537-6333 or 888/731-3863
FAX: 808/521-6286
E-mail: info@hcf-hawaii.org
Internet: http://www.hcf-hawaii.org
DEADLINE(S): MAR 1
FIELD(S): All
ELIGIBILITY/REQUIREMENTS: Must be female of Hawaiian ancestry; residents of the state of Hawaii; plan to enroll full

time at an accredited 2- or 4-year college or university; and demonstrate financial need, good moral character, and academic achievement with 3.0 minimum GPA.
HOW TO APPLY: Send application with 2 letters of recommendation and a copy of birth certificate to verify Hawaiian ancestry.

3483—HAWAII COMMUNITY FOUNDATION (Jean Fitzgerald Scholarship)

1164 Bishop Street, Suite 800
Honolulu HI 96813
808/537-6333 or 888/731-3863
FAX: 808/521-6286
E-mail: info@hcf-hawaii.org
Internet: http://www.hcf-hawaii.org
DEADLINE(S): MAR 1
FIELD(S): All
ELIGIBILITY/REQUIREMENTS: Must be female; an active member of the Hawaii Tennis Association for at least 4 years; an incoming freshman at an accredited 2- or 4-year college or university; a full-time student; resident of the state of Hawaii; and demonstrate financial need, good moral character, and academic achievement with 2.7 minimum GPA.
HOW TO APPLY: Send application with 2 letters of recommendation.

3484—HAWAII COMMUNITY FOUNDATION (John M. Ross Foundation)

1164 Bishop Street, Suite 800
Honolulu HI 96813
808/537-6333 or 888/731-3863
FAX: 808/521-6286
E-mail: info@hcf-hawaii.org
Internet: http://www.hcf-hawaii.org
DEADLINE(S): MAR 1
FIELD(S): All
ELIGIBILITY/REQUIREMENTS: Must be long-time residents of the island of Hawaii (preference given to those with ancestors who plan to remain or return there); plan to attend full time an accredited 2- or 4-year college or university; and demonstrate financial need, good moral character, strong academic achievement, with a minimum 2.7 GPA. Preference given to undergraduates.
HOW TO APPLY: Send application, 2 letters of recommendation, and a personal statement describing your and your ancestors' residency on the island of Hawaii and your plans to remain or return.

3485—HAWAII COMMUNITY FOUNDATION (Juliette M. Atherton Scholarship-Minister's Sons & Daughters)

1164 Bishop Street, Suite 800

Honolulu HI 96813
808/537-6333 or 888/731-3863
FAX: 808/521-6286
E-mail: info@hcf-hawaii.org
Internet: http://www.hcf-hawaii.org
DEADLINE(S): MAR 1
FIELD(S): All
ELIGIBILITY/REQUIREMENTS: Must be the dependent son or daughter of an ordained Protestant minister in an established denomination of Hawaii; resident of the state of Hawaii; plan to enroll full time as undergraduate or graduate students at an accredited 2- or 4-year college or university; demonstrate financial need, good moral character, and academic achievement with minimum 2.7 GPA.
HOW TO APPLY: Send application; 2 letters of recommendation; and the minister's current position, the minister's church/parish name, minister's denomination and place and date of ordination, and the name of the seminary attended by the minister.

3486—HAWAII COMMUNITY FOUNDATION (Ka'a'awa Community Fund)

1164 Bishop Street, Suite 800
Honolulu HI 96813
808/537-6333 or 888/731-3863
FAX: 808/521-6286
E-mail: info@hcf-hawaii.org
Internet: http://www.hcf-hawaii.org
DEADLINE(S): MAR 1
FIELD(S): All
ELIGIBILITY/REQUIREMENTS: Must be residents of the Ka'a'awa area on Windward Oahu; plan to attend an accredited 2- or 4-year college or university full time; and demonstrate financial need, good moral character, and academic achievement with 2.7 minimum GPA. Preference is given to long-time residents of Ka'a'awa area.
HOW TO APPLY: Send application with 2 letters of recommendation.

3487—HAWAII COMMUNITY FOUNDATION (Ka'iulani Home for Girls Trust Scholarship)

1164 Bishop Street, Suite 800
Honolulu HI 96813
808/537-6333 or 888/731-3863
FAX: 808/521-6286
E-mail: info@hcf-hawaii.org
Internet: http://www.hcf-hawaii.org
DEADLINE(S): MAR 1
FIELD(S): All
ELIGIBILITY/REQUIREMENTS: Must be female of Hawaiian ancestry; residents of the state of Hawaii; plan to enroll full time at an accredited 2- or 4-year college or university; demonstrate financial need, good moral character, and academic achievement with 2.7 minimum GPA.
HOW TO APPLY: Send application with 2 letters of recommendation and a copy of birth certificate to verify Hawaiian ancestry.

3488—HAWAII COMMUNITY FOUNDATION (Kapolei Community & Business Scholarship)

1164 Bishop Street, Suite 800
Honolulu HI 96813
808/537-6333 or 888/731-3863
FAX: 808/521-6286
E-mail: info@hcf-hawaii.org
Internet: http://www.hcf-hawaii.org
DEADLINE(S): MAR 1
FIELD(S): All
ELIGIBILITY/REQUIREMENTS: Must be residents of the state of Hawaii; graduating seniors at Campbell, Nanakuli, or Waianae High Schools; plan to enroll full time as undergraduate or graduate students at an accredited 2- or 4-year college or university; and demonstrate financial need, good moral character, and academic achievement with 2.7 minimum GPA.
HOW TO APPLY: Send application with 2 letters of recommendation.
CONTACT: Hawaii Community Foundation Scholarship Department at 808/566-5570

3489—HAWAII COMMUNITY FOUNDATION (Kellie Ann Andrade Scholarship)

1164 Bishop Street, Suite 800
Honolulu HI 96813
808/537-6333 or 888/731-3863
FAX: 808/521-6286
E-mail: info@hcf-hawaii.org
Internet: http://www.hcf-hawaii.org
DEADLINE(S): MAR 1
FIELD(S): All
ELIGIBILITY/REQUIREMENTS: Must be attending Pacific Rim Bible Institute; resident of the state of Hawaii; and demonstrate financial need, good moral character, and academic achievement, with 2.7 minimum GPA.
HOW TO APPLY: Send application with 2 letters of recommendation.
CONTACT: Pacific Rim Bible Institute

3490—HAWAII COMMUNITY FOUNDATION (Kenneth Makinney & David Pietsch Families Scholarship Fund)

1164 Bishop Street, Suite 800
Honolulu HI 96813
808/537-6333 or 888/731-3863

FAX: 808/521-6286
E-mail: info@hcf-hawaii.org
Internet: http://www.hcf-hawaii.org
DEADLINE(S): MAR 1
FIELD(S): All
ELIGIBILITY/REQUIREMENTS: Must be employees or dependents of employees of Title Guaranty of Hawaii, Inc. or Title Guaranty Escrow Services, Inc. and their subsidiaries; residents of the state of Hawaii; and demonstrate financial need, good moral character, and academic achievement, with a minimum GPA of 2.7. This scholarship can be used for grades 7 through graduate school.
HOW TO APPLY: Send application with 2 letters of recommendation.
CONTACT: Title Guaranty of Hawaii, Inc., 235 Queen Street, Honolulu HI 96813

3491—HAWAII COMMUNITY FOUNDATION (King Kekaulike High School Scholarship)

1164 Bishop Street, Suite 800
Honolulu HI 96813
808/537-6333 or 888/731-3863
FAX: 808/521-6286
E-mail: info@hcf-hawaii.org
Internet: http://www.hcf-hawaii.org
DEADLINE(S): MAR 1
FIELD(S): All
ELIGIBILITY/REQUIREMENTS: Must be residents of the state of Hawaii; graduating seniors at King Kekaulike High School; plan to enroll full time as undergraduate or graduate students at an accredited 2- or 4-year college or university; demonstrate financial need, good moral character, and academic achievement with 2.7 minimum GPA; and have performed at least 3 hours of community service.
HOW TO APPLY: Send application with 2 letters of recommendation and a 500-word essay on how well Na Ali'i "3 R"s (i.e., respect, relevance, and rigor) relate to your future goals.

3492—HAWAII COMMUNITY FOUNDATION (K. M. Hatano Scholarship Fund)

1164 Bishop Street, Suite 800
Honolulu HI 96813
808/537-6333 or 888/731-3863
FAX: 808/521-6286
E-mail: info@hcf-hawaii.org
Internet: http://www.hcf-hawaii.org
DEADLINE(S): MAR 1
FIELD(S): All
ELIGIBILITY/REQUIREMENTS: Must be high school seniors in the county of Maui (which includes Lanai and Molokai); plan to attend an accredited 4-year college

or university full time in the state of Hawaii; and demonstrate financial need, good moral character, and academic achievement with 2.7 minimum GPA.

HOW TO APPLY: Send application with 2 letters of recommendation.

3493—HAWAII COMMUNITY FOUNDATION (Kohala Ditch Educational Fund)

1164 Bishop Street, Suite 800
Honolulu HI 96813
808/537-6333 or 888/731-3863
FAX: 808/521-6286
E-mail: info@hcf-hawaii.org
Internet: http://www.hcf-hawaii.org
DEADLINE(S): MAR 1
FIELD(S): All
ELIGIBILITY/REQUIREMENTS: Must be residents of the state of Hawaii; graduating seniors at Kohala High School; plan to enroll full time as undergraduate or graduate students at an accredited 2- or 4-year college or university; and demonstrate financial need, good moral character, and academic achievement with 2.7 minimum GPA.

HOW TO APPLY: Send application with 2 letters of recommendation.

3494—HAWAII COMMUNITY FOUNDATION (Koloa Scholarship)

1164 Bishop Street, Suite 800
Honolulu HI 96813
808/537-6333 or 888/731-3863
FAX: 808/521-6286
E-mail: info@hcf-hawaii.org
Internet: http://www.hcf-hawaii.org
DEADLINE(S): MAR 1
FIELD(S): All
ELIGIBILITY/REQUIREMENTS: Must be residents of one of the following Kauai areas: Koloa (96756), including Omao and Poipu (96756), Lawai (96765), or Kalaheo (96741); plan to attend, full time, an accredited 2- or 4-year college or university or pursue vocational training at an accredited institution; and demonstrate financial need, good moral character, and academic achievement with 2.0 minimum GPA.

HOW TO APPLY: Send application; 2 letters of recommendation; and a 1-page essay describing your understanding of the meaning of "aloha" in our multicultural community, the part it plays in your personal development, and how your chosen field will further this in both family and community. Also include a list of books or other publications you have read on Hawaii's history; a list of relatives who were born in the Koloa District, including

their relationship to you, place of birth, and approximate year of birth; and how long you have lived in the Koloa area.

3495—HAWAII COMMUNITY FOUNDATION (Kurt W. Schneider Memorial Scholarship Fund)

1164 Bishop Street, Suite 800
Honolulu HI 96813
808/537-6333 or 888/731-3863
FAX: 808/521-6286
E-mail: info@hcf-hawaii.org
Internet: http://www.hcf-hawaii.org
DEADLINE(S): MAR 1
FIELD(S): All
ELIGIBILITY/REQUIREMENTS: Must be residents of the state of Hawaii; graduating seniors at Lanai High School; plan to enroll full time as undergraduate or graduate students at an accredited 2- or 4-year college or university; and demonstrate financial need, good moral character, and academic achievement with 2.7 minimum GPA. Preference given to travel industry management majors.

HOW TO APPLY: Send application with 2 letters of recommendation.

3496—HAWAII COMMUNITY FOUNDATION (Margaret Follett Haskins Scholarship)

1164 Bishop Street, Suite 800
Honolulu HI 96813
808/537-6333 or 888/731-3863
FAX: 808/521-6286
E-mail: info@hcf-hawaii.org
Internet: http://www.hcf-hawaii.org
DEADLINE(S): MAR 1
FIELD(S): All
ELIGIBILITY/REQUIREMENTS: Must be a graduate of Maui Community College, with 3.0 minimum GPA at the time of graduation; plan to continue studies (either part or full time) at a 4-year University of Hawaii system school; be resident of the state of Hawaii; and demonstrate financial need, good moral character, and academic achievement. Students continuing their education in a distance education program leading to a Bachelor's degree at Manoa or Hilo also qualify for this scholarship.

HOW TO APPLY: Send application with 2 letters of recommendation.

3497—HAWAII COMMUNITY FOUNDATION (Mary Josephine Bloder Scholarship Fund)

1164 Bishop Street, Suite 800

Honolulu HI 96813
808/537-6333 or 888/731-3863
FAX: 808/521-6286
E-mail: info@hcf-hawaii.org
Internet: http://www.hcf-hawaii.org
DEADLINE(S): MAR 1
FIELD(S): All
ELIGIBILITY/REQUIREMENTS: Must be residents of the state of Hawaii; graduating seniors at Lahainaluna High School; plan to enroll full time as undergraduate or graduate students at an accredited 2- or 4-year college or university; and demonstrate financial need, good moral character, and academic achievement with 2.7 minimum GPA and a high GPA in the sciences. Preference is given to boarding students.

HOW TO APPLY: Send application with 2 letters of recommendation.

3498—HAWAII COMMUNITY FOUNDATION (Mildred Towle Scholarship for African Americans)

1164 Bishop Street, Suite 800
Honolulu HI 96813
808/537-6333 or 888/731-3863
FAX: 808/521-6286
E-mail: info@hcf-hawaii.org
Internet: http://www.hcf-hawaii.org
DEADLINE(S): MAR 1
FIELD(S): All
ELIGIBILITY/REQUIREMENTS: Must be African-Americans studying in Hawaii (do NOT need to be residents of the state of Hawaii); enrolled full time as undergraduate or graduate students at an accredited 2- or 4-year college or university; demonstrate financial need, good moral character, and academic achievement of 3.0 minimum GPA.

HOW TO APPLY: Send application with 2 letters of recommendation.

3499—HAWAII COMMUNITY FOUNDATION (Mildred Towle Scholarship for Study at Boston University)

1164 Bishop Street, Suite 800
Honolulu HI 96813
808/537-6333 or 888/731-3863
FAX: 808/521-6286
E-mail: info@hcf-hawaii.org
Internet: http://www.hcf-hawaii.org
DEADLINE(S): MAR 1
FIELD(S): All
ELIGIBILITY/REQUIREMENTS: Must be a Hawaii resident attending Boston University and demonstrate financial need, good moral character, and academic achievement with 3.0 minimum GPA.

HOW TO APPLY: Send application with 2 letters of recommendation.

3500—HAWAII COMMUNITY FOUNDATION (Mildred Towle Scholarship-Study Abroad)

1164 Bishop Street, Suite 800
Honolulu HI 96813
808/537-6333 or 888/731-3863
FAX: 808/521-6286
E-mail: info@hcf-hawaii.org
Internet: http://www.hcf-hawaii.org
DEADLINE(S): MAR 1
FIELD(S): All
ELIGIBILITY/REQUIREMENTS: Must be a Hawaii resident planning to study abroad during the junior or senior year; be enrolled full time at an accredited 4-year college or university; demonstrate financial need, good moral character, and academic achievement with 3.0 minimum GPA.
HOW TO APPLY: Send application with 2 letters of recommendation.

3501—HAWAII COMMUNITY FOUNDATION (O'ahu Filipino Community Golf Scholarship Fund)

1164 Bishop Street, Suite 800
Honolulu HI 96813
808/537-6333 or 888/731-3863
FAX: 808/521-6286
E-mail: info@hcf-hawaii.org
Internet: http://www.hcf-hawaii.org
DEADLINE(S): MAR 1
FIELD(S): All
ELIGIBILITY/REQUIREMENTS: Must be of Filipino ancestry; residents of the state of Hawaii; plan to attend full time an accredited 2- or 4-year college or university; and demonstrate financial need, good moral character, and strong academic achievement, with 2.7 minimum GPA.
HOW TO APPLY: Send application with 2 letters of recommendation.

3502—HAWAII COMMUNITY FOUNDATION (Peter Papworth Scholarship)

1164 Bishop Street, Suite 800
Honolulu HI 96813
808/537-6333 or 888/731-3863
FAX: 808/521-6286
E-mail: info@hcf-hawaii.org
Internet: http://www.hcf-hawaii.org
DEADLINE(S): MAR 1
FIELD(S): All
ELIGIBILITY/REQUIREMENTS: Must be residents of the state of Hawaii; graduating seniors at Campbell High School;

plan to enroll full time as undergraduate or graduate students at an accredited 2- or 4-year college or university; and demonstrate financial need, good moral character, and academic achievement with 2.7 minimum GPA.
HOW TO APPLY: Send application with 2 letters of recommendation.

3503—HAWAII COMMUNITY FOUNDATION (Rosemary & Nellie Ebrie Foundation Scholarship)

1164 Bishop Street, Suite 800
Honolulu HI 96813
808/537-6333 or 888/731-3863
FAX: 808/521-6286
E-mail: info@hcf-hawaii.org
Internet: http://www.hcf-hawaii.org
DEADLINE(S): MAR 1
FIELD(S): All
ELIGIBILITY/REQUIREMENTS: Must be of Hawaiian ancestry; long-time resident born on the island of Hawaii; plan to attend full time an accredited 2- or 4-year college or university; demonstrate financial need, good moral character, and strong academic achievement with 2.7 minimum GPA.
HOW TO APPLY: Send application with 2 letters of recommendation.

3504—HAWAII COMMUNITY FOUNDATION (Senator Richard M. & Dr. Ruth Matsuura Scholarship Fund)

1164 Bishop Street, Suite 800
Honolulu HI 96813
808/537-6333 or 888/731-3863
FAX: 808/521-6286
E-mail: info@hcf-hawaii.org
Internet: http://www.hcf-hawaii.org
DEADLINE(S): MAR 1
FIELD(S): All
ELIGIBILITY/REQUIREMENTS: Must be residents of the island of Hawaii; be graduates of Hilo or Waiakea High Schools; plan to enroll full time as undergraduate or graduate students at an accredited 2- or 4-year college or university; and demonstrate financial need, good moral character with 2.7 minimum GPA.
HOW TO APPLY: Send application with 2 letters of recommendation.

3505—HAWAII COMMUNITY FOUNDATION (Tommy Lee Memorial Scholarship Fund)

1164 Bishop Street, Suite 800
Honolulu HI 96813
808/537-6333 or 888/731-3863
FAX: 808/521-6286

E-mail: info@hcf-hawaii.org
Internet: http://www.hcf-hawaii.org
DEADLINE(S): MAR 1
FIELD(S): All
ELIGIBILITY/REQUIREMENTS: Must be high school seniors residing in the Waialua or Haleiwa areas; plan to attend full time an accredited 2- or 4-year college or university; and demonstrate financial need, good moral character, and academic achievement with 2.7 minimum GPA.
HOW TO APPLY: Send application with 2 letters of recommendation.

3506—HAWAII COMMUNITY FOUNDATION (The Tongan Cultural Society Scholarship)

1164 Bishop Street, Suite 800
Honolulu HI 96813
808/537-6333 or 888/731-3863
FAX: 808/521-6286
E-mail: info@hcf-hawaii.org
Internet: http://www.hcf-hawaii.org
DEADLINE(S): MAR 1
FIELD(S): All
ELIGIBILITY/REQUIREMENTS: Must be of Tongan ancestry; residents of the state of Hawaii; plan to enroll full time as undergraduate or graduate students at an accredited 2- or 4-year college or university in Hawaii; and demonstrate financial need, good moral character, and academic achievement with 2.7 minimum GPA.
HOW TO APPLY: Send application with 2 letters of recommendation.

3507—HAWAII COMMUNITY FOUNDATION (Toraji & Toki Yoshinaga Scholarship)

1164 Bishop Street, Suite 800
Honolulu HI 96813
808/537-6333 or 888/731-3863
FAX: 808/521-6286
E-mail: info@hcf-hawaii.org
Internet: http://www.hcf-hawaii.org
DEADLINE(S): MAR 1
FIELD(S): All
ELIGIBILITY/REQUIREMENTS: Must be resident of the state of Hawaii; sophomore attending full time an accredited college or university that is NOT part of the University of Hawaii system; demonstrate financial need, good moral character, and strong academic achievement with a minimum GPA of 2.7.
HOW TO APPLY: Send application with 2 letters of recommendation.

3508—HAWAII COMMUNITY FOUNDATION (University of Redlands Hawaii Scholarship)

1164 Bishop Street, Suite 800

Honolulu HI 96813
808/537-6333 or 888/731-3863
FAX: 808/521-6286
E-mail: info@hcf-hawaii.org
Internet: http://www.hcf-hawaii.org
DEADLINE(S): FEB 15
FIELD(S): All
ELIGIBILITY/REQUIREMENTS: Must be resident of the state of Hawaii; plan to attend the University of Redlands Hawaii (though prior acceptance for admission is not required); and demonstrate financial need, good moral character, superior strong academic record with a minimum 2.7 GPA, leadership, and community service.
HOW TO APPLY: Send application with 2 letters of recommendation, FAFSA.
NUMBER OF AWARDS: 2
RENEWABLE: No

3509—HAWAII COMMUNITY FOUNDATION (Vicki Wilder Scholarship Fund)

1164 Bishop Street, Suite 800
Honolulu HI 96813
808/537-6333 or 888/731-3863
FAX: 808/521-6286
E-mail: info@hcf-hawaii.org
Internet: http://www.hcf-hawaii.org
DEADLINE(S): MAR 1
FIELD(S): All
ELIGIBILITY/REQUIREMENTS: Must be residents of the state of Hawaii; graduates of Kamahameha High School or be an employee or the dependent of an employee of the Kamahameha School's food services department; plan to enroll full time as undergraduate or graduate students at an accredited 2- or 4-year college or university; and demonstrate financial need, good moral character, and academic achievement with 2.7 minimum GPA. Preference given to students majoring in culinary arts or travel industry management.
HOW TO APPLY: Send application with 2 letters of recommendation.

3510—HAWAII COMMUNITY FOUNDATION (Victoria S. and Bradley L. Geist Foundation)

1164 Bishop Street, Suite 800
Honolulu HI 96813
808/537-6333 or 888/731-3863
FAX: 808/521-6286
E-mail: info@hcf-hawaii.org
Internet: http://www.hcf-hawaii.org
DEADLINE(S): MAR 1
FIELD(S): All
ELIGIBILITY/REQUIREMENTS: Must be permanently separated from parents and currently or formerly in the foster care system; be residents of the state of Hawaii; plan to attend full time an accredited 2- or 4-year college or university; and demonstrate financial need, good moral character, and academic achievement (NO minimum GPA).
HOW TO APPLY: Send application, 2 letters of recommendation, and a confirmation letter from a DHS or Casey Family Program case worker to verify foster care status.
CONTACT: Call 808/566-5570 for additional information.

3511—HAWAII COMMUNITY FOUNDATION (Wallace Farrington Memorial Scholarship)

1164 Bishop Street, Suite 800
Honolulu HI 96813
808/537-6333 or 888/731-3863
FAX: 808/521-6286
E-mail: info@hcf-hawaii.org
Internet: http://www.hcf-hawaii.org
DEADLINE(S): MAR 1
FIELD(S): All
ELIGIBILITY/REQUIREMENTS: Must be Farrington High School seniors planning to attend the University of Hawaii at Manoa; residents of the state of Hawaii; and demonstrate financial need, good moral character, and academic achievement with a minimum GPA of 2.7.
HOW TO APPLY: Send application with 2 letters of recommendation.
CONTACT: Farrington High School counseling office

3512—HAWAII COMMUNITY FOUNDATION (Walter H. Kupau Memorial Fund)

1164 Bishop Street, Suite 800
Honolulu HI 96813
808/537-6333 or 888/731-3863
FAX: 808/521-6286
E-mail: info@hcf-hawaii.org
Internet: http://www.hcf-hawaii.org
DEADLINE(S): MAR 1
FIELD(S): All
ELIGIBILITY/REQUIREMENTS: Must be the descendant of a member in good standing of the Hawaii Carpenter's Union Local 745, with preference given to retired members; be resident of the state of Hawaii; plan to attend full time an accredited 2- or 4-year college or university; and demonstrate financial need, good moral character, and academic achievement with 2.7 minimum GPA.
HOW TO APPLY: Send application; 2 letters of recommendation; and the name and Social Security number of the member of Local 745, with the member's relationship to applicant.

3513—HAWAII COMMUNITY FOUNDATION (West Kauai Scholarship Fund)

1164 Bishop Street, Suite 800
Honolulu HI 96813
808/537-6333 or 888/731-3863
FAX: 808/521-6286
E-mail: info@hcf-hawaii.org
Internet: http://www.hcf-hawaii.org
DEADLINE(S): MAR 1
FIELD(S): All
ELIGIBILITY/REQUIREMENTS: Must be residents of one of the following West Kauai areas: Eleele (96705), Hanapepe (96716), Waimea (96796), Kekaha (96752), Makaweli (96769), or Kalaheo (96741); plan to attend full time an accredited 2- or 4-year college or university; and demonstrate financial need, good moral character, and academic achievement with 2.7 minimum GPA. Preference given to students from families who are long-time residents of West Kauai.
HOW TO APPLY: Send application, 2 letters of recommendation, and a personal statement describing your family's ties to West Kauai.

3514—HEBREW IMMIGRANT AID SOCIETY (HIAS Scholarship Program)

333 Seventh Avenue
New York NY 10001-5004
212/613-1358
FAX: 212/967-4356
E-mail: scholarship@hias.org
Internet: http://www.hias.org
AMOUNT: $2,000
DEADLINE(S): FEB 19
FIELD(S): All
ELIGIBILITY/REQUIREMENTS: Open to refugees and asylees who were assisted by HIAS to come to the U.S. For high school seniors planning to pursue postsecondary education and students already enrolled in undergraduate or graduate study.
HOW TO APPLY: Must provide transcripts for 2 semesters of study at any combination of accredited U.S. schools, a personal essay, and demonstrate financial need and Jewish communal involvement. Apply online after mid-December.
NUMBER OF AWARDS: Varies
RENEWABLE: Yes, must reapply.

3515—HEMOPHILIA HEALTH SERVICES, INC. (HHS Memorial Scholarship)

6820 Charlotte Pike

Nashville TN 37209
615/850-5175
FAX: 615/352-2500
E-mail: scholarship@hemophilia
health.com
Internet: http://www.accredohealth.
net or www.HemophiaHealth.com
AMOUNT: Minimum $1,000
DEADLINE(S): MAY 1
FIELD(S): All
ELIGIBILITY/REQUIREMENTS: Open
to U.S. citizens with hemophilia; must be
high school seniors, college undergraduate
and graduate students enrolled full time.
May be used in the U.S. and Puerto Rico.
Based on academic achievement, involve-
ment in extracurricular and community
activities, and financial need.
HOW TO APPLY: Contact Fund for
details or visit website for application.
NUMBER OF AWARDS: Varies
RENEWABLE: Yes. Must reapply; no
preference given to former recipients.
CONTACT: Sally Johnson

3516—HILLEL: THE FOUNDATION FOR JEWISH CAMPUS LIFE (Steinhardt Jewish Campus Service Corps)

1640 Rhode Island Avenue NW
Washington DC 20036
202/857-6559
FAX: 202/857-6626
E-mail: mgruenwald@hillel.org
Internet: http://www.hillel.org
AMOUNT: One-year fellowship
DEADLINE(S): MAR
FIELD(S): All (+student leadership)
ELIGIBILITY/REQUIREMENTS: Open
to college seniors and recent college graduates with leadership skills and ability to
create dynamic and innovative engagement strategies designed to reach Jewish
college students. Must possess commitment to service; willingness to use time,
abilities, and talents to enhance lives of
others; and dedication to strengthening
Jewish identity among students with whom
they work. Corps fellows get to know interests and concerns of students and build
programs and activities to match.
HOW TO APPLY: See website or contact
Foundation for an application.
CONTACT: Melanie Sasson Gruenwald
or Rachel Gurshman

3517—HISPANIC COLLEGE FUND (Community College Transfer Scholarship Program)

55 Second Street, Suite 1500
San Francisco CA 94105

877/HSF-INFO (877/473-4636)
FAX: 415/808/2302
E-mail: pip@hsf.net
Internet: http://www.hispanic
fund.org
AMOUNT: $1,000-$2,500
DEADLINE(S): JUN 16
FIELD(S): Engineering; Business
ELIGIBILITY/REQUIREMENTS: Must
be U.S. citizens or legal permanent resi-
dents of Hispanic heritage (1 parent fully
Hispanic or both parents half Hispanic), be
enrolled part or full time at a community
college and plan to transfer and enroll full
time in a degree-seeking program at a 4-
year accredited institution in the U.S. or
Puerto Rico; minimum 3.0 GPA.
HOW TO APPLY: Contact Fund for
details or visit website for application.

3518—HISPANIC COLLEGE FUND (High School Scholarship Program)

55 Second Street, Suite 1500
San Francisco CA 94105
877/HSF-INFO (877/473-4636)
FAX: 415/808/2302
E-mail: pip@hsf.net
Internet: http://www.hispanic
fund.org
AMOUNT: $1,000- $2,500
DEADLINE(S): JUN 16
FIELD(S): All
ELIGIBILITY/REQUIREMENTS: Open
to graduating seniors with cumulative
weighted GPA of 3.0 planning to enroll in
a degree-seeking program at an accredited
U.S. college or university as a full-time stu-
dent. Must be U.S. citizens or legal perma-
nent residents of Hispanic heritage (1 par-
ent fully Hispanic or both parents half
Hispanic). Based on academic achieve-
ment, personal strengths, leadership and
financial need.
HOW TO APPLY: Contact Fund for
details or visit website for application.
NUMBER OF AWARDS: 83

3519—HISPANIC COLLEGE FUND (HSF/CSUB HISPANIC Excellence Scholarship Fund Program)

55 Second Street, Suite 1500
San Francisco CA 94105
877/HSF-INFO (877/473-4636)
FAX: 415/808/2302
E-mail: pip@hsf.net
Internet: http://www.hispanic
fund.org
DEADLINE(S): MAY 30
FIELD(S): All

ELIGIBILITY/REQUIREMENTS: Must
be U.S. citizens or legal permanent residents of Hispanic heritage (1 parent fully
Hispanic or both parents half Hispanic).
Based on academic achievement, personal
strengths, leadership and financial need.
For attendance at California State
University Bakersfield; open to academically sound, needy students with leadership
potential from high schools in Kern, Kings,
Inyo and Mono Counties, California.
Available to incoming freshmen and continuing students.
HOW TO APPLY: Contact Fund for
details or visit website for application.

3520—HISPANIC COLLEGE FUND (HSF/Ford Motor Company Corporate Scholarship Program)

55 Second Street, Suite 1500
San Francisco CA 94105
877/HSF-INFO (877/473-4636)
FAX: 415/808/2302
E-mail: pip@hsf.net
Internet: http://www.hispanic
fund.org
AMOUNT: Up to $15,000
DEADLINE(S): Spring
FIELD(S): All
ELIGIBILITY/REQUIREMENTS:
Available on a competitive basis to stu-
dents of Hispanic background who will be
classified as juniors at a 4-year college.
Must be U.S. citizens or legal permanent
residents of Hispanic heritage (1 parent
fully Hispanic or both parents half
Hispanic). Based on academic achieve-
ment, personal strengths, leadership and
financial need.
HOW TO APPLY: Contact Fund for
details or visit website for application.

3521—HISPANIC COLLEGE FUND (HSF/Toyota Foundation Scholarship Program)

55 Second Street, Suite 1500
San Francisco CA 94105
877/HSF-INFO (877/473-4636)
FAX: 415/808/2302
E-mail: pip@hsf.net
Internet: http://www.hispanic
fund.org
AMOUNT: $5,000
DEADLINE(S): SEP 30
FIELD(S): All
ELIGIBILITY/REQUIREMENTS: Open
to outstanding entering freshmen at select-
ed universities and in selected majors.
Must be U.S. citizens or legal permanent
residents of Hispanic heritage (1 parent

fully Hispanic or both parents half Hispanic). Based on academic achievement, personal strengths, leadership and financial need.

HOW TO APPLY: Contact Fund for details or visit website for application.

3522—HISPANIC COLLEGE FUND (HSF/Toyota Foundation Scholarship Program-Puerto Rico)

55 Second Street, Suite 1500
San Francisco CA 94105
877/HSF-INFO (877/473-4636)
FAX: 415/808/2302
E-mail: pip@hsf.net
Internet: http://www.hispanic fund.org

DEADLINE(S): FEB 28-MAY 9
FIELD(S): All

ELIGIBILITY/REQUIREMENTS: Open to graduating high school seniors who will enter their first year of college at a university in Puerto Rico.

HOW TO APPLY: Contact Fund for details or visit website for application.

3523—HISPANIC COLLEGE FUND (New Horizons Scholars Program)

55 Second Street, Suite 1500
San Francisco CA 94105
877/HSF-INFO (877/473-4636)
FAX: 415/808/2302
E-mail: pip@hsf.net
Internet: http://www.hispanic fund.org

DEADLINE(S): FEB 20
FIELD(S): All

ELIGIBILITY/REQUIREMENTS: Supports Hispanic and African-American students who are infected with Hepatitis C or who are dependents of someone with Hepatitis C.

HOW TO APPLY: Contact Fund for details or visit website for application.

3524—HOLLAND & KNIGHT CHARITABLE FOUNDATION ("Holocaust Remembrance Project" Annual Essay Contest)

P.O. Box 2877
Tampa FL 33601
866/452-2737
E-mail: holocaust@hklaw.com
Internet: http://www.holocaust. hklaw.com

AMOUNT: $100-$5,000
DEADLINE(S): APR 30
FIELD(S): All

ELIGIBILITY/REQUIREMENTS: Open to high school students; must be citizen of the U.S. or Mexico; must submit an essay of no more than 1,200 words: (a) analyze why it is so vital that the remembrance, history, and lessons of the Holocaust be passed to a new generation; and (b) suggest what they, as students, can do to combat and prevent prejudice, discrimination and violence in our world today.

HOW TO APPLY: See website for additional information or request by mail. First-prize winners receive expense-paid trip to Washington, DC.

NUMBER OF AWARDS: 30 (10 each 1st, 2nd, 3rd prizes)
RENEWABLE: No
CONTACT: Tom Holcolmbe

3525—HOPI TRIBE GRANTS & SCHOLARSHIP PROGRAM (Bureau of Indian Affairs Higher Education)

P.O. Box 123
Kykotsmovi AZ 86039-0123
520/734-3533 or 800/762-9630
FAX: 520/734-9575
E-mail: IPolingyumptewa@hopi. nsn.us or FLomakema@hopi.nsn.us.
Internet: http://www.aaanative arts.com/article955.html

AMOUNT: Up to $2,500 per semester
DEADLINE(S): Fall-AUG 31; Spring-JAN 31
FIELD(S): All

ELIGIBILITY/REQUIREMENTS: Must be enrolled member of Hopi Tribe seeking a degree at a 2- or 4-year institution. Must have a minimum 2.5 cumulative GPA (CGPA). Available to U.S. citizens only.

HOW TO APPLY: Call or write for application or download http://www.yc.edu/content/financialaid/pdf/Tribal%20PDF/Hopi TribeGrantApplication.pdf.

NUMBER OF AWARDS: 136
RENEWABLE: Yes, apply each semester or academic year.
CONTACT: Ima Polingyumptewa

3526—HOPI TRIBE (Hopi Education Award)

P.O. Box 123
Kykotsmovi AZ 86039-0123
520/734-3533 or 800/762-9630
FAX: 520/734-9575
E-mail: IPolingyumptewa@hopi. nsn.us or FLomakema@hopi.nsn.us.
Internet: http://www.aaanative arts.com/article955.html

AMOUNT: Up to $1,500 per semester
DEADLINE(S): Fall-AUG 31; Spring-JAN 31; Summer-APR 30

FIELD(S): All

ELIGIBILITY/REQUIREMENTS: Must be enrolled member of Hopi Tribe seeking a degree at a 2- or 4-year institution. Must have a minimum 2.5 cumulative GPA. Available to U.S. citizens only.

HOW TO APPLY: Call or write for application or download http://www.yc.edu/content/financialaid/pdf/Tribal%20PDF/Hopi TribeGrantApplication.pdf.

NUMBER OF AWARDS: 136
RENEWABLE: Yes, apply each semester or academic year.
CONTACT: Ima Polingyumptewa

3527—HORACE SMITH FUND (Walter S. Barr Scholarships)

1441 Main Street
Springfield MA 01102
413/739-4222
FAX: 413-739-1108
E-mail: info@horacesmith.org
Internet: http://www.horacesmith fund.org

AMOUNT: Varies
DEADLINE(S): JAN 10
FIELD(S): All

ELIGIBILITY/REQUIREMENTS: Open to high school seniors who are class members of Hampden County, Massachusetts, private or public secondary schools. Based on school records, college entrance examinations, general attainments, and financial need.

HOW TO APPLY: Contact the Executive Secretary for an application after September 15.
RENEWABLE: Yes
CONTACT: Executive Secretary

3528—HUGUENOT SOCIETY OF AMERICA, THE (The Marie L. Rose Huguenot Scholarships)

122 East 58th Street
New York NY 10022
212/755-0592
FAX: 212/317-0676
Internet:
http://www.huguenotsociety ofamerica.org/scholarships.php

AMOUNT: $3,000
DEADLINE(S): AUG 1
FIELD(S): All

ELIGIBILITY/REQUIREMENTS: Must be a descendant of a Huguenot and attend one of 50 listed colleges, available at above address.

HOW TO APPLY: Students should apply to the Financial Aid Offices at the listed colleges; must submit proof of descent

from a Huguenot who emigrated from France and either settled in what is now the U.S. or left France for countries other than America before 1787. Do NOT send applications directly to the Huguenot Society.
NUMBER OF AWARDS: 25-30
RENEWABLE: Yes. Automatically, if student is in good standing.
CONTACT: Dorothy F. Kimball

3529—HUMBOLDT AREA FOUNDATION

P.O. Box 99
Bayside CA 95524
707/442-2993
FAX: 707/442-3811
Internet: http://www.ha
foundation.org/haf/scholarships/
apply-for-a-scholarship.html
AMOUNT: $250-$7,500
DEADLINE(S): MAR 1
FIELD(S): All
ELIGIBILITY/REQUIREMENTS: Graduates of Humboldt, Del Norte or Trinity Counties, California, high schools attending a vocation school, 2- or 4-year college and/or residents of Humboldt County attending a local college.
HOW TO APPLY: HAF Scholarship application available online in January or contact Foundation for details. Criteria varies each year.
NUMBER OF AWARDS: 85
RENEWABLE: Yes, must reapply.
CONTACT: Scholarship Coordinator

3530—ILLINOIS AMVETS (Ladies Auxiliary Memorial & Worchid Scholarships)

P.O. Box 9
Crete IL 60417
217/528-4713 or 800/638-8387
FAX: 217/528-9896
E-mail: sara@ilamvets.org
Internet: http://www.ilamvets.org
AMOUNT: $500
DEADLINE(S): MAR 1
FIELD(S): All
ELIGIBILITY/REQUIREMENTS: Must be Illinois high school senior, child or grandchild of a veteran who served honorably after September 15, 1940; honorably discharged, presently serving, or deceased. Must have taken ACT or SAT at time of application.
HOW TO APPLY: See website for additional information and application or contact Foundation. Submit with transcript and ACT or SAT scores to Illinois Amvets Ladies Auxiliary, P.O. Box 9, Crete IL 60417.

NUMBER OF AWARDS: 2
RENEWABLE: Yes. Must be enrolled full time and submit transcript.
CONTACT: Sara Garcia, Programs Director

3531—ILLINOIS AMVETS SERVICE FOUNDATION (4-Year Scholarships)

2200 South Sixth Street
Springfield IL 62703-3496
217/528-4713 or 800/638-8387
FAX: 217/528-9896
E-mail: sara@ilamvets.org
Internet: http://www.ilamvets.org
AMOUNT: $500-$1,000
DEADLINE(S): MAR 1
FIELD(S): All
ELIGIBILITY/REQUIREMENTS: Must be Illinois high school senior, child or grandchild of a veteran. Must have taken ACT or SAT at time of application.
HOW TO APPLY: See website for additional information and application or contact Foundation. Submit with transcript and ACT or SAT scores.
RENEWABLE: Yes. Must be enrolled full time and submit transcript.
CONTACT: Sara Garcia, Programs Director

3532—ILLINOIS AMVETS SERVICE FOUNDATION (Junior ROTC Scholarship)

2200 South Sixth Street
Springfield IL 62703-3496
217/528-4713 or 800/638-8387
FAX: 217/528-9896
E-mail: sara@ilamvets.org
Internet: http://www.ilamvets.org
AMOUNT: $1,000
DEADLINE(S): MAR 1
FIELD(S): All
ELIGIBILITY/REQUIREMENTS: Must be Illinois high school senior, child or grandchild of a veteran. Must have taken ACT or SAT at time of application.
HOW TO APPLY: See website for additional information and application or contact Foundation. Submit with transcript and ACT or SAT scores, and a copy of participation letter from a pre-approved Junior ROTC program at the high school.
RENEWABLE: Yes. Must be enrolled full time and submit transcript.
CONTACT: Sara Garcia, Programs Director

3533—IMATION COMPUTER ARTS SCHOLARSHIP

1 Imation Place
Oakdale MN 55128-3414
FAX: 651/704-3892

E-mail: CAS@imation.com
Internet: http://www.imation.
com/computerarts
AMOUNT: $1,000
DEADLINE(S): DEC 12
FIELD(S): All
ELIGIBILITY/REQUIREMENTS: Open to high school students in the U.S. or at U.S. military base schools. Need not be enrolled in art classes. Must be nominated to the national competition by their school through a school competition (home-schooled students in recognized home-school programs are eligible to participate; must be sponsored by an instructor; school competition rules do not apply).
HOW TO APPLY: Entries must be submitted by the student and school representative (together). Art must be less than 1 MB, saved in JPEG format and submitted via Imation's website. NO paper applications. Art must be accompanied by the completed online application. All work must be the original, unique creation of the student. Entries become property of Imation and may be used in promotion, advertising, or other publicity. Full recognition and credit will be given the student artist. For additional information about entry, types of artwork accepted, and contest rules, read FAQ on website.
RENEWABLE: No

3534—INSTITUTE FOR THE INTERNATIONAL EDUCATION OF STUDENTS (Historically Black Colleges and University Scholarships)

33 North LaSalle Street, 15th Floor
Chicago IL 60602
800/995-2300 or 312/944-1750
FAX: 312/944-1448
E-mail: info@IESabroad.org
Internet: http://www.iesabroad.org
AMOUNT: $2,000 ($1,500 credit toward the IES program fee and $500 toward the purchase of an overseas airline ticket for the IES program)
DEADLINE(S): NOV 1 for Spring programs; MAY 1 for Fall and full-year programs
FIELD(S): All
ELIGIBILITY/REQUIREMENTS: Must attend an HBCU that is a member or associate member of the IES college consortium.
HOW TO APPLY: Submit a completed general application for any IES program.

3535—INSTITUTE FOR THE INTERNATIONAL EDUCATION OF STUDENTS (Need-Based Financial Aid)

33 North LaSalle Street, 15th Floor

Chicago IL 60602
800/995-2300 or 312/944-1750
FAX: 312/944-1448
E-mail: info@IESabroad.org
Internet: http://www.iesabroad.org
AMOUNT: $500-$1,500
DEADLINE(S): NOV 1 for Spring
programs; MAY 1 for Fall and full-
year programs
FIELD(S): All
ELIGIBILITY/REQUIREMENTS: Must
attend a private college or university that is
a member or associate member of the IES
college consortium; must be receiving
financial aid from their home school; which
must have a policy of transferring at least
75% of home school aid to IES. NOT for
IES summer programs.
HOW TO APPLY: Submit a completed
IES Need-Based Financial Aid application.

3536—INSTITUTE FOR THE INTERNA-
TIONAL EDUCATION OF STUDENTS (Public
University Scholarships)

33 North LaSalle Street, 15th Floor
Chicago IL 60602
800/995-2300 or 312/944-1750
FAX: 312/944-1448
E-mail: info@IESabroad.org
Internet: http://www.iesabroad.org
AMOUNT: $1,500
DEADLINE(S): NOV 1 for Spring
programs; MAY 1 for Fall and full-
year programs
FIELD(S): All
ELIGIBILITY/REQUIREMENTS: Must
attend a public university that is a member
or associate member of the IES college
consortium. NOT for IES summer pro-
grams.
HOW TO APPLY: Submit a completed
general application for any IES program.

3537—INSTITUTE FOR THE INTERNA-
TIONAL EDUCATION OF STUDENTS
(Scholarships for IES Students in Japan)

33 North LaSalle Street, 15th Floor
Chicago IL 60602
800/995-2300 or 312/944-1750
FAX: 312/944-1448
E-mail: info@IESabroad.org
Internet: http://www.iesabroad.org
AMOUNT: $800/month plus $250
DEADLINE(S): MAR 1 for IES Nagoya;
APR 15 for IES Tokyo Fall/full-year
program; AUG 1 for IES Tokyo
Spring program
FIELD(S): All
ELIGIBILITY/REQUIREMENTS: Must
be U.S. citizens or permanent residents

and be enrolled in a U.S. college or university. Students must also meet the general
admission requirements to enroll in either
the IES Tokyo or IES Nagoya programs.
Japanese language study is NOT a prerequisite. Priority given to full-year applicants.
HOW TO APPLY: Submit an IES application for the IES Tokyo or IES Nagoya program. Signatures required from the student's university.

3538—INSTITUTE FOR THE INTERNA-
TIONAL EDUCATION OF STUDENTS
(Summer Need-Based Scholarships)

33 North LaSalle Street, 15th Floor
Chicago IL 60602
800/995-2300 or 312/944-1750
FAX: 312/944-1448
E-mail: info@IESabroad.org
Internet: http://www.iesabroad.org
AMOUNT: $500-$1,000
DEADLINE(S): APR 1
FIELD(S): All
ELIGIBILITY/REQUIREMENTS: Must
attend a public or private college or uni-
versity that is a member or associate mem-
ber of the IES consortium, and provide
proof of financial need through your home
campus financial aid office.
HOW TO APPLY: Submit a completed
IES Summer Scholarship application.

3539—INSTITUTE OF INTERNATIONAL
EDUCATION NATIONAL SECURITY EDUCA-
TION PROGRAM (NSEP David L. Boren
Undergraduate Scholarships)

1400 K Street NW, 6th floor
Washington DC 20005
800/618-6737
FAX: 202/326-7672
E-mail: nsep@iie.org
Internet: http://www.iie.org/nsep
AMOUNT: Up to $20,000
DEADLINE(S): Mid FEB
FIELD(S): All, emphasis on geographic
areas, languages, and fields of study
deemed critical to U.S. national
security
ELIGIBILITY/REQUIREMENTS:
Intended to provide support to U.S. under-
graduates who will pursue the study of lan-
guages and cultures currently underrepre-
sented in study abroad and critical to U.S.
national security. Must be U.S. citizen
matriculated at a U.S. university or college.
Provides a unique funding opportunity for
U.S. students to study world regions critical to U.S. interests (including Africa,
Asia, Central & Eastern Europe, Latin
American and the Caribbean, and the
Middle East). Must be matriculated in an

undergraduate degree program in a U.S.
university, college or community college
accredited by an accrediting body recognized by the U.S. Department of
Education, and applying to engage in a
study abroad experience in a country outside of Western Europe, Canada,
Australia, or New Zealand that meets
home institution standards.
HOW TO APPLY: See website for additional information and application. Apply
online. Submit to your NSEP campus representative with 2 reference forms, language self-assessment form, language proficiency form (optional), official transcripts, 1-page study abroad program
description, and letters of support for
direct enrollment (if applicable).
RENEWABLE: No
CONTACT: Susan Sharp, Program
Officer
ADDITIONAL INFORMATION: The
NSEP service requirement stipulates that
award recipients work in the federal government in positions with national security
responsibilities. The Departments of
Defense, Homeland Security, State, or any
element of the Intelligence Community are
priority agencies.

3540—INTERNATIONAL ALLIANCE OF
THEATRICAL STAGE EMPLOYEES

1430 Broadway, 20th Floor
New York NY 10018
212/730-1770
FAX: 212/730-7809 or
212/921-7699
Internet: http://www.iatse-intl.org
DEADLINE(S): DEC 31
FIELD(S): All
ELIGIBILITY/REQUIREMENTS: Must
be the son or daughter of a member in
good standing of the IATSE; be a high
school senior at the time of application;
and have applied, or be about to apply, for
admission to an accredited college or university as a fully matriculated student,
which will lead to a bachelor's degree.
HOW TO APPLY: Send an application
and high school transcript; may also send
the record of scores achieved by the applicant on the SAT or equivalent examinations, as well as letter(s) of recommendation from teachers, counselors, clergy,
community service organizations, employers, etc.

3541—INTERNATIONAL ALLIANCE OF
THEATRICAL STAGE EMPLOYEES
(ATPAM/IATSE Local 18032 Scholarship)

1560 Broadway
New York NY 10036

212/719-3666
E-mail: info@atpam.com
Internet: http://www.atpam.com
AMOUNT: Up to $1,000
DEADLINE(S): AUG 1
FIELD(S): All
ELIGIBILITY/REQUIREMENTS: Must be ATPAM member in good standing or the child, grandchild, niece, nephew, spouse or significant partner of an ATPAM member in good standing. Must attend an accredited school of higher learning and maintain a B+ average.
HOW TO APPLY: Send an application with a 250-word essay on labor, and a transcript.
NUMBER OF AWARDS: Varies
RENEWABLE: Yes. Up to 4 years.
CONTACT: Maria Somma, President

3542—INTERNATIONAL ASSOCIATION OF BRIDGE STRUCTURAL, ORNAMENTAL, AND REINFORCING IRON WORKERS (John H. Lyons Scholarship Program)

1750 New York Avenue NW,
Suite 400
Washington DC 20006
202/383-4800
FAX: 202/638-4856
Email: iwmagazine@iwintl.org
Internet: http://www.ironworkers.org/organization/JohnHLyons.aspx#zoom=100,250,100,
AMOUNT: $5,000
DEADLINE(S): MAR 31
FIELD(S): All
ELIGIBILITY/REQUIREMENTS: Must be high school seniors who rank in the upper half of their graduating class and be pursuing undergraduate study in the U.S. or Canada. Financial need NOT a factor. Scholarships available ONLY to children of members with 5 or more years' membership who are in good standing at the time of application or children of deceased members who were in good standing at the time of their death.
HOW TO APPLY: Contact Association for an application.
NUMBER OF AWARDS: 4
RENEWABLE: Yes

3543—INTERNATIONAL ASSOCIATION OF FIRE FIGHTERS (W. H. "Howie" McClennan Scholarship)

1750 New York Avenue NW
Washington DC 20006
202/737-8484
FAX: 202/737-8418
Internet: http://www.iaff.org
AMOUNT: $2,500
DEADLINE(S): FEB 1
FIELD(S): All
ELIGIBILITY/REQUIREMENTS: Provides financial assistance for sons, daughters, or legally adopted children of fire fighters killed in the line of duty planning to attend a university, accredited college, or other institution of higher learning.
HOW TO APPLY: Must submit a personal statement (about 200 words) that indicates their reasons for wanting to continue their education; 2 letters of recommendation from a teacher, school administrator, counselor, clergy, work supervisor, or military supervisor (active, reserve, or National Guard) who can address the qualifications and academic aptitude of the scholarship applicant (may NOT be from immediate family members, close family friends, blood relatives, or relationships by marriage); and most recent transcripts.

3544—INTERNATIONAL BROTHERHOOD OF TEAMSTERS (James R. Hoffa Memorial Scholarship Fund)

25 Louisiana Avenue NW
Washington DC 20001
202/624-8735
E-mail: scholarship@teamster.org
Internet: http://www.teamster.org
AMOUNT: 10,000 (4-year scholarship); $1,000 (1-time grant)
DEADLINE(S): MAR 31
FIELD(S): All
ELIGIBILITY/REQUIREMENTS: Open to high school seniors who are the dependent children of Teamster members who rank in top 15% of their high school class, have excellent SAT/ACT scores, and demonstrate financial need. Must be U.S. or Canadian citizen.
HOW TO APPLY: Contact the Local Teamsters Union office or see website for application.
NUMBER OF AWARDS: 100
RENEWABLE: No

3545—INTERNATIONAL FURNITURE AND DESIGN ASSOCIATION EDUCATIONAL FOUNDATION (IFDA Charles E. Mayo Student Scholarship)

11705 Trottenham Street
Raleigh NC 27614
919/847-3064 or 770/612-0454
FAX: 770/612-0445
E-mail: wshammett@aol.com or info@ifdaef.org
Internet: http://www.ifdaef.org
AMOUNT: $1,000
DEADLINE(S): MAR 31
FIELD(S): All
ELIGIBILITY/REQUIREMENTS: Must be enrolled as a full-time student; do NOT need to be an IFDA member.
HOW TO APPLY: Submit application; a transcript, with your GPA; 300- to 500-word essay describing your plans and goals and why you believe you deserve this award; and a letter of recommendation from a professor or instructor.
NUMBER OF AWARDS: At least 1
CONTACT: Dr. Wilma Hammett, Director of Grants

3546—INTERNATIONAL FURNITURE AND DESIGN ASSOCIATION EDUCATIONAL FOUNDATION (IFDA Student Scholarship)

11705 Trottenham Street
Raleigh NC 27614
919/847-3064 or 770/612-0454
FAX: 770/612-0445
E-mail: wshammett@aol.com or info@ifdaef.org
Internet: http://www.ifdaef.org
AMOUNT: $1,500
DEADLINE(S): MAR 31
FIELD(S): All
ELIGIBILITY/REQUIREMENTS: Must be enrolled as a full-time student and MUST BE an IFDA student member for the current membership period, paid in full prior to submitting the scholarship application.
HOW TO APPLY: Submit application; a transcript, with your GPA; a 300- to 500-word essay describing your future plans and goals and why you believe you deserve this award; and a letter of recommendation from a professor or instructor.
NUMBER OF AWARDS: At least 1
CONTACT: Dr. Wilma Hammett, Director of Grants

3547—INTERNATIONAL UNION OF ELECTRONIC, ELECTRICAL, SALARIED, MACHINE AND FURNITURE WORKERS-IUE DIVISION OF COMMUNICATIONS WORKERS OF AMERICA (Bruce Van Ess Scholarship)

IUE-CWA International
Scholarship Program
501 3rd Street NW
Washington DC 20001
Internet: http://www.iue-cwa.org
AMOUNT: $2,500
DEADLINE(S): MAR 31
FIELD(S): All
ELIGIBILITY/REQUIREMENTS: Must be IUE-CWA members, employees, or children or grandchildren of IUE-CWA members and employees. Must be accepted for admission or already enrolled as

full-time students at an accredited college, university, nursing, or technical school offering college credit courses. All study must be completed at the undergraduate level.

HOW TO APPLY: Submit an application; transcript, including rank in class, GPA, and SAT or ACT scores; a short statement of interests and civic activities; an essay of not less than 300 nor more than 500 words describing your career goals and aspirations, highlighting your relationship to the union and the labor movement and explaining why you deserve a union scholarship; 2 letters of recommendation, 1 of which should be from your school and the other from outside your school, preferably from work or volunteer environment.

NUMBER OF AWARDS: 1

3548—INTERNATIONAL UNION OF ELEC-TRONIC, ELECTRICAL, SALARIED, MACHINE AND FURNITURE WORKERS-IUE DIVISION OF COMMUNICATIONS WORKERS OF AMERICA (Robert L. Livingston Scholarships)

IUE-CWA International
Scholarship Program
501 3rd Street NW
Washington DC 20001
Internet: http://www.iue-cwa.org
AMOUNT: $1,500
DEADLINE(S): MAR 31
FIELD(S): All
ELIGIBILITY/REQUIREMENTS: Must be a child of an IUE-CWA Automotive Conference Board member (or the child of a deceased or retired IUE-CWA Conference Board member); must be accepted for admission or already enrolled as a full-time student at an accredited college, university, nursing, or technical school offering college credit courses. All study must be completed at the undergraduate level.

HOW TO APPLY: Submit a short statement of interests and goals, which must include a description of career objectives, civic commitment and activities, and extracurricular activities.

NUMBER OF AWARDS: 2

3549—INTERNATIONAL UNION OF ELEC-TRONIC, ELECTRICAL, SALARIED, MACHINE AND FURNITURE WORKERS-IUE DIVISION OF COMMUNICATIONS WORKERS OF AMERICA (Sal Ingrassia Scholarship)

IUE-CWA International
Scholarship Program
501 3rd Street NW

Washington DC 20001
Internet: http://www.iue-cwa.org
AMOUNT: $2,500
DEADLINE(S): MAR 31
FIELD(S): All
ELIGIBILITY/REQUIREMENTS: Must be IUE-CWA members, employees, or children or grandchildren of members and employees, accepted for admission or already enrolled as full-time students at an accredited college, university, nursing, or technical school offering college credit courses. All study must be completed at the undergraduate level.

HOW TO APPLY: Submit an application; transcript, including rank in class, GPA, and SAT or ACT scores; a short statement of interests and civic activities; an essay of not less than 300 nor more than 500 words describing your career goals and aspirations, highlighting your relationship to the union and the labor movement and explaining why you deserve a union scholarship; 2 letters of recommendation, 1 of which should be from your school and the other from outside your school, preferably from work or volunteer environment.

NUMBER OF AWARDS: 1

3550—INTERNATIONAL UNION OF ELEC-TRONIC, ELECTRICAL, SALARIED, MACHINE AND FURNITURE WORKERS-IUE DIVISION OF COMMUNICATIONS WORKERS OF AMERICA (Willie Rudd Scholarship)

IUE-CWA International
Scholarship Program
501 3rd Street NW
Washington DC 20001
Internet: http://www.iue-cwa.org
AMOUNT: $1,000
DEADLINE(S): MAR 31
FIELD(S): All
ELIGIBILITY/REQUIREMENTS: Must be IUE-CWA members, employees, or children or grandchildren of members and employees, accepted for admission or already enrolled as full-time students at an accredited college, university, nursing, or technical school offering college credit courses. All study must be completed at the undergraduate level.

HOW TO APPLY: Submit an application; transcript, including rank in class, GPA, and SAT or ACT scores; a short statement of interests and civic activities; an essay of not less than 300 nor more than 500 words describing your career goals and aspirations, highlighting your relationship to the union and the labor movement and explaining why you deserve a union scholarship; 2 letters of recommendation, 1 of which should be from your school and the

other from outside your school, preferably from work or volunteer environment.

NUMBER OF AWARDS: 1

3551—ITALIAN CATHOLIC FEDERATION, INC.

675 Hegenberger Road, Suite 230
Oakland CA 94621
888/ICF-1924 or 510/633-9058
FAX: 510/633-9758
E-mail: info@icf.org
Internet: http://www.icf.org/
scholarships.html
AMOUNT: $400-$1,000
DEADLINE(S): MAR 15
FIELD(S): All
ELIGIBILITY/REQUIREMENTS: Open to graduating high school seniors of Italian ancestry and Catholic faith. Non-Italian graduating high school seniors may qualify if their Catholic parents or grandparents are members of the Italian Catholic Federation. Must live in states where the Federation is located (California, Nevada, and Illinois [primarily the Chicago area and nearby cities] and Arizona [Green Valley, Scottsdale]), have a minimum 3.2 GPA, and be U.S. citizens.

HOW TO APPLY: Send SASE to ICF for an application.

NUMBER OF AWARDS: 200

3552—JACK KENT COOKE FOUNDATION (Undergraduate Transfer Scholarship Program)

44325 Woodridge Parkway
Lansdowne VA 20176
FAX: 703/723-8030
E-mail: jkc@jackkentcooke
foundation.org
Internet: http://www.jackkentcooke
foundation.org/jkcf_web/home.
aspx?Page=Main
AMOUNT: Up to $30,000/year
DEADLINE(S): FEB 1
FIELD(S): All
ELIGIBILITY/REQUIREMENTS: Open to students attending community colleges or 2-year institutions and planning to transfer to 4-year institutions. Must have minimum cumulative undergraduate GPA of 3.5, pursue a full-time course of study in a baccalaureate degree program at an approved accredited institution, beginning with the fall term, and apply for federal and institutional financial assistance each year of study. (The Foundation determines individual scholarship awards each year after reviewing each recipient's other assistance offers.)

HOW TO APPLY: Must be nominated by the Jack Kent Cooke Foundation Faculty Representative at their institutions (see website for list of designated faculty representatives), may not be nominated more than once, and may not apply directly to the Foundation.
NUMBER OF AWARDS: Approximately 30
RENEWABLE: Yes, up to 3 years.
ADDITIONAL INFORMATION: Must attend the Jack Kent Cooke Foundation Scholars Weekend in August at Foundation's expense.

3553—JACKIE ROBINSON FOUNDATION, THE

Scholarship Program
75 Varick Street, 2nd Floor
New York, NY 10013
212/290-8600
FAX: 212/290-8081
E-mail: requests@jackierobinson.org
Internet: http://www.jackie robinson.org
AMOUNT: $24,000
DEADLINE(S): MAR 31
FIELD(S): All
ELIGIBILITY/REQUIREMENTS: Must be U.S. citizen minority with a high level of academic achievement and leadership potential with financial need. Must be accepted to 4-year accredited college or university and have an SAT score of 1000 or above and/or ACT score of 21 or above.
HOW TO APPLY: Only online applications will be accepted. See website for application and instructions. Applicants must also register online with SAT (www.collegeboard.com) and/or ACT (www.act.org) so that scores can be reported directly to the Foundation.
NUMBER OF AWARDS: Up to 80
RENEWABLE: Yes, up to 4 years.

3554—JACKSONVILLE STATE UNIVERSITY (Allison Scholarship)

Financial Aid Office
Jacksonville AL 36265
256/782-5677 or 800/231-5291
Internet: http://www.jsu.edu
AMOUNT: Varies
DEADLINE(S): FEB 1
FIELD(S): All
ELIGIBILITY/REQUIREMENTS: Open to all students.
HOW TO APPLY: Submit transcript and ACT/SAT scores with scholarship applications. See website for application. Supporting documentation should be mailed.
RENEWABLE: No
CONTACT: Scholarship Committee

3555—JACKSONVILLE STATE UNIVERSITY (Alumni Scholarships)

Financial Aid Office
Jacksonville AL 36265
256/782-5677 or 800/231-5291
Internet: http://www.jsu.edu
AMOUNT: Varies
FIELD(S): All
ELIGIBILITY/REQUIREMENTS: Open to incoming freshman, child or grandchild of JSU alum.
HOW TO APPLY: Contact Alumni Affairs for information and application.
RENEWABLE: No
CONTACT: Alumni Affairs, 256/782-5404

3556—JACKSONVILLE STATE UNIVERSITY (Athletic Scholarships)

Financial Aid Office
Jacksonville AL 36265
256/782-5677 or 800/231-5291
Internet: http://www.jsu.edu
AMOUNT: Varies
FIELD(S): All
ELIGIBILITY/REQUIREMENTS: Open to students with athletic abilities.
HOW TO APPLY: Contact Alumni Affairs for information and application.
RENEWABLE: No
CONTACT: Athletic Director, 256/782-5368

3557—JACKSONVILLE STATE UNIVERSITY (A. W. Bolt Scholarship)

Financial Aid Office
Jacksonville AL 36265
256/782-5677 or 800/231-5291
Internet: http://www.jsu.edu
AMOUNT: Varies
DEADLINE(S): FEB 1
FIELD(S): All
ELIGIBILITY/REQUIREMENTS: Open to all students.
HOW TO APPLY: Submit transcript and ACT/SAT scores with scholarship applications. See website for application. Supporting documentation should be mailed.
RENEWABLE: No
CONTACT: Scholarship Committee

3558—JACKSONVILLE STATE UNIVERSITY (Billy S. Lindsey Scholarship)

Financial Aid Office
Jacksonville AL 36265
256/782-5677 or 800/231-5291
Internet: http://www.jsu.edu
AMOUNT: Varies
DEADLINE(S): FEB 1

FIELD(S): All
ELIGIBILITY/REQUIREMENTS: Open to all students.
HOW TO APPLY: Submit transcript and ACT/SAT scores with scholarship applications. See website for application. Supporting documentation should be mailed.
RENEWABLE: No
CONTACT: Scholarship Committee

3559—JACKSONVILLE STATE UNIVERSITY (Burger King/Ingram Scholarship)

Financial Aid Office
Jacksonville AL 36265
256/782-5677 or 800/231-5291
Internet: http://www.jsu.edu
AMOUNT: Varies
DEADLINE(S): FEB 1
FIELD(S): All
ELIGIBILITY/REQUIREMENTS: Graduate of Arab High School (first preference); Marshall County resident; 3.0 GPA.
HOW TO APPLY: Submit transcript and ACT/SAT scores with scholarship applications. See website for application. Supporting documentation should be mailed.
RENEWABLE: No
CONTACT: Scholarship Committee

3560—JACKSONVILLE STATE UNIVERSITY (Calhoun County Alumni Scholarship)

Financial Aid Office
Jacksonville AL 36265
256/782-5677 or 800/231-5291
Internet: http://www.jsu.edu
AMOUNT: $1,000
DEADLINE(S): FEB 1
FIELD(S): All
ELIGIBILITY/REQUIREMENTS: Must be full-time undergraduate student from Calhoun County, Alabama.
HOW TO APPLY: Submit transcript and ACT/SAT scores with scholarship applications. See website for application. Supporting documentation should be mailed.
RENEWABLE: No
CONTACT: Scholarship Committee

3561—JACKSONVILLE STATE UNIVERSITY (Calhoun Math Tournament)

Financial Aid Office
Jacksonville AL 36265
256/782-5677 or 800/231-5291
Internet: http://www.jsu.edu
AMOUNT: Varies
FIELD(S): All
ELIGIBILITY/REQUIREMENTS: Tournament open to Calhoun County, Alabama, students.

HOW TO APPLY: Contact Calhoun County for information and application.
NUMBER OF AWARDS: 1 (winner of tournament)
RENEWABLE: No

3562—JACKSONVILLE STATE UNIVERSITY (Charley Pell Scholarship)

Financial Aid Office
Jacksonville AL 36265
256/782-5677 or 800/231-5291
Internet: http://www.jsu.edu
AMOUNT: Varies
DEADLINE(S): FEB 1
FIELD(S): All
ELIGIBILITY/REQUIREMENTS: Open to a child of former player coached by Charley Pell at JSU.
HOW TO APPLY: Submit transcript and ACT/SAT scores with scholarship applications. See website for application. Supporting documentation should be mailed.
RENEWABLE: No
CONTACT: Scholarship Committee

3563—JACKSONVILLE STATE UNIVERSITY (Chevrolet Corporation Scholarship)

Financial Aid Office
Jacksonville AL 36265
256/782-5677 or 800/231-5291
Internet: http://www.jsu.edu
AMOUNT: $1,000
DEADLINE(S): FEB 1
FIELD(S): All
ELIGIBILITY/REQUIREMENTS: Open to all students; based primarily on GPA.
HOW TO APPLY: Submit high school transcript and ACT/SAT scores with scholarship applications. See website for application. Documentation should be mailed.
RENEWABLE: No
CONTACT: Scholarship Committee

3564—JACKSONVILLE STATE UNIVERSITY (Chris Banister Memorial Scholarship)

Financial Aid Office
Jacksonville AL 36265
256/782-5677 or 800/231-5291
Internet: http://www.jsu.edu
AMOUNT: Varies
FIELD(S): All
ELIGIBILITY/REQUIREMENTS: Open to students with interest in golf; must be full-time undergraduate student.
HOW TO APPLY: Contact Golf Coach for information and application.
RENEWABLE: No
CONTACT: Golf Coach, 256/782-5840

3565—JACKSONVILLE STATE UNIVERSITY (Cissy Gorey Scholarship)

Financial Aid Office
Jacksonville AL 36265
256/782-5677 or 800/231-5291
Internet: http://www.jsu.edu
AMOUNT: Varies
DEADLINE(S): FEB 1
FIELD(S): All
ELIGIBILITY/REQUIREMENTS: Open to graduate of the Donoho School.
HOW TO APPLY: Submit transcript and ACT/SAT scores with scholarship applications. See website for application. Supporting documentation should be mailed.
RENEWABLE: No
CONTACT: Scholarship Committee

3566—JACKSONVILLE STATE UNIVERSITY (Clyde McSpadden Scholarships)

Financial Aid Office
Jacksonville AL 36265
256/782-5677 or 800/231-5291
Internet: http://www.jsu.edu
AMOUNT: Varies
DEADLINE(S): FEB 1
FIELD(S): All
ELIGIBILITY/REQUIREMENTS: Open to Phi Beta Phi member in good standing with highest GPA and to Phi Kappa Phi pledge with highest GPA.
HOW TO APPLY: Submit transcript and ACT/SAT scores with scholarship applications. See website for application. Supporting documentation should be mailed.
NUMBER OF AWARDS: 2 (1 member, 1 pledge)
RENEWABLE: No
CONTACT: Scholarship Committee

3567—JACKSONVILLE STATE UNIVERSITY (Col. Archie Stamper Memorial Scholarship)

Financial Aid Office
Jacksonville AL 36265
256/782-5677 or 800/231-5291
Internet: http://www.jsu.edu
AMOUNT: Varies
DEADLINE(S): FEB 1
FIELD(S): All
ELIGIBILITY/REQUIREMENTS: Open to all students.
HOW TO APPLY: Submit transcript and ACT/SAT scores with scholarship applications. See website for application. Supporting documentation should be mailed.
RENEWABLE: No
CONTACT: Scholarship Committee

3568—JACKSONVILLE STATE UNIVERSITY (Drama Scholarship)

Financial Aid Office
Jacksonville AL 36265
256/782-5677 or 800/231-5291
Internet: http://www.jsu.edu
AMOUNT: Varies
DEADLINE(S): FEB 1
FIELD(S): Any
ELIGIBILITY/REQUIREMENTS: Open to students with interest in drama.
HOW TO APPLY: Contact Drama Department for application and details.
RENEWABLE: Yes
CONTACT: Drama Department, 256/782-5623

3569—JACKSONVILLE STATE UNIVERSITY (Dr. Dave Walters-Gray Echelon Scholarship)

Financial Aid Office
Jacksonville AL 36265
256/782-5677 or 800/231-5291
Internet: http://www.jsu.edu
AMOUNT: Varies
FIELD(S): Music
ELIGIBILITY/REQUIREMENTS: Interest in music; particularly playing in band.
HOW TO APPLY: Contact Music Department for application and information.
RENEWABLE: No
CONTACT: Director of Bands; 256/782-5562

3570—JACKSONVILLE STATE UNIVERSITY (Dr. Ernest Stone Memorial Scholarship)

Financial Aid Office
Jacksonville AL 36265
256/782-5677 or 800/231-5291
Internet: http://www.jsu.edu
AMOUNT: Varies
DEADLINE(S): FEB 1
FIELD(S): All
ELIGIBILITY/REQUIREMENTS: Open to juniors and above.
HOW TO APPLY: Submit transcript and ACT/SAT scores with scholarship applications. See website for application. Supporting documentation should be mailed.
RENEWABLE: No
CONTACT: Scholarship Committee

3571—JACKSONVILLE STATE UNIVERSITY (Dr. Harold McGee Scholarship)

Financial Aid Office
Jacksonville AL 36265

256/782-5677 or 800/231-5291
Internet: http://www.jsu.edu
AMOUNT: Varies
DEADLINE(S): FEB 1
FIELD(S): All
ELIGIBILITY/REQUIREMENTS: Open to non-Alabama resident with 3.0 GPA; 28 or above ACT score or SAT score of 1260 or above.
HOW TO APPLY: Submit transcript and ACT/SAT scores with scholarship applications. See website for application. Supporting documentation should be mailed.
NUMBER OF AWARDS: 1
RENEWABLE: No
CONTACT: Scholarship Committee

3572—JACKSONVILLE STATE UNIVERSITY (Dr. Herman Arnold Memorial Scholarship)

Financial Aid Office
Jacksonville AL 36265
256/782-5677 or 800/231-5291
Internet: http://www.jsu.edu
AMOUNT: Varies
FIELD(S): All
ELIGIBILITY/REQUIREMENTS: Open to incoming freshman, child or grandchild of JSU alum.
HOW TO APPLY: See contact below for information and application.
RENEWABLE: No
CONTACT: Director of Baptist Campus Ministry, 256/435-7020

3573—JACKSONVILLE STATE UNIVERSITY (Dr. James Reaves Memorial Scholarship)

Financial Aid Office
Jacksonville AL 36265
256/782-5677 or 800/231-5291
Internet: http://www.jsu.edu
AMOUNT: Varies
DEADLINE(S): FEB 1
FIELD(S): All
ELIGIBILITY/REQUIREMENTS: Open to juniors and above.
HOW TO APPLY: Submit transcript and ACT/SAT scores with scholarship applications. See website for application. Supporting documentation should be mailed.
RENEWABLE: No
CONTACT: Scholarship Committee

3574—JACKSONVILLE STATE UNIVERSITY (Dr. Perry & Kay Savage Scholarship)

Financial Aid Office
Jacksonville AL 36265
256/782-5677 or 800/231-5291
Internet: http://www.jsu.edu
AMOUNT: Full tuition
DEADLINE(S): FEB 1

FIELD(S): All
ELIGIBILITY/REQUIREMENTS: Open to Calhoun County, Alabama, residents; preference given to Piedmont residents.
HOW TO APPLY: Submit transcript and ACT/SAT scores with scholarship applications. See website for application. Supporting documentation should be mailed.
RENEWABLE: No
CONTACT: Scholarship Committee

3575—JACKSONVILLE STATE UNIVERSITY (Dr. Theron Montgomery Scholarship)

Financial Aid Office
Jacksonville AL 36265
256/782-5677 or 800/231-5291
Internet: http://www.jsu.edu
AMOUNT: Full tuition
DEADLINE(S): FEB 1
FIELD(S): All
ELIGIBILITY/REQUIREMENTS: Open to all junior, senior, or graduate students.
HOW TO APPLY: Submit transcript and ACT/SAT scores with scholarship applications. See website for application. Supporting documentation should be mailed.
RENEWABLE: No
CONTACT: Scholarship Committee

3576—JACKSONVILLE STATE UNIVERSITY (Elite Scholars)

Financial Aid Office
Jacksonville AL 36265
256/782-5677 or 800/231-5291
Internet: http://www.jsu.edu
AMOUNT: Full tuition and housing
DEADLINE(S): FEB 1
FIELD(S): All
ELIGIBILITY/REQUIREMENTS: Must be Alabama resident, Alabama high school graduate and entering freshman. 3.5 GPA (calculated based on English, social sciences, math, and science courses taken through student's junior year), ACT 32 or above, or SAT 1390 or above.
HOW TO APPLY: Submit transcript and ACT/SAT scores with scholarship applications. See website for application. Supporting documentation should be mailed.
RENEWABLE: Yes
CONTACT: Scholarship Committee

3577—JACKSONVILLE STATE UNIVERSITY (E. L. Millican Memorial Scholarship)

Financial Aid Office
Jacksonville AL 36265
256/782-5677 or 800/231-5291
Internet: http://www.jsu.edu
AMOUNT: Full tuition
DEADLINE(S): FEB 1

FIELD(S): All
ELIGIBILITY/REQUIREMENTS: Open to freshman or transfer from Valley Head or Pisgah High School (Alabama).
HOW TO APPLY: Submit transcript and ACT/SAT scores with scholarship applications. See website for application. Supporting documentation should be mailed.
NUMBER OF AWARDS: 1
RENEWABLE: No
CONTACT: Scholarship Committee

3578—JACKSONVILLE STATE UNIVERSITY (Etowah County Alumni Scholarship)

Financial Aid Office
Jacksonville AL 36265
256/782-5677 or 800/231-5291
Internet: http://www.jsu.edu
AMOUNT: Varies
DEADLINE(S): FEB 1
FIELD(S): All
ELIGIBILITY/REQUIREMENTS: Deserving full-time undergraduate student from Etowah County, Alabama.
HOW TO APPLY: Submit transcript and ACT/SAT scores with scholarship applications. See website for application. Supporting documentation should be mailed.
RENEWABLE: No
CONTACT: Scholarship Committee

3579—JACKSONVILLE STATE UNIVERSITY (Faculty Scholars)

Financial Aid Office
Jacksonville AL 36265
256/782-5677 or 800/231-5291
Internet: http://www.jsu.edu
AMOUNT: 75%-100% tuition and housing
DEADLINE(S): FEB 1
FIELD(S): All
ELIGIBILITY/REQUIREMENTS: Must be Alabama resident, Alabama high school graduate and entering freshman. 3.0 GPA, ACT 28-29, or SAT 1260-1330 (75% tuition); 3.0 GPA, ACT 30 or above, or SAT 1340 or above. The GPA will be an academic GPA calculated based on English, social sciences, math, and science courses taken through student's junior year.
HOW TO APPLY: Submit transcript and ACT/SAT scores with scholarship applications. See website for application. Supporting documentation should be mailed.
RENEWABLE: Yes
CONTACT: Scholarship Committee

3580—JACKSONVILLE STATE UNIVERSITY (Farmers & Merchants Bank Scholarship)

Financial Aid Office

Jacksonville AL 36265
256/782-5677 or 800/231-5291
Internet: http://www.jsu.edu
AMOUNT: Varies
DEADLINE(S): FEB 1
FIELD(S): All
ELIGIBILITY/REQUIREMENTS:
Entering freshman; graduate of Piedmont
High School.
HOW TO APPLY: Submit transcript and
ACT/SAT scores with scholarship applica-
tions. See website for application. Sup-
porting documentation should be mailed.
RENEWABLE: No
CONTACT: Scholarship Committee

3581—JACKSONVILLE STATE UNIVERSITY (Gamecock Scholars)

Financial Aid Office
Jacksonville AL 36265
256/782-5677 or 800/231-5291
Internet: http://www.jsu.edu
AMOUNT: $1,000
DEADLINE(S): FEB 1
FIELD(S): All
ELIGIBILITY/REQUIREMENTS: Must
be Alabama resident, Alabama high school
graduate and entering freshman. 3.0 GPA
(calculated based on English, social sci-
ences, math, and science courses taken
through student's junior year), ACT 24-27,
or SAT 1130-1250.
HOW TO APPLY: Submit transcript and
ACT/SAT scores with scholarship applica-
tions. See website for application. Sup-
porting documentation should be mailed.
RENEWABLE: Yes. 1 year.
CONTACT: Scholarship Committee

3582—JACKSONVILLE STATE UNIVERSITY (Georgia Alumni Scholarship)

Financial Aid Office
Jacksonville AL 36265
256/782-5677 or 800/231-5291
Internet: http://www.jsu.edu
AMOUNT: Varies
DEADLINE(S): FEB 1
FIELD(S): All
ELIGIBILITY/REQUIREMENTS: Open
to full-time undergraduate students from
the state of Georgia.
HOW TO APPLY: Submit transcript and
ACT/SAT scores with scholarship applica-
tions. See website for application. Sup-
porting documentation should be mailed.
RENEWABLE: No
CONTACT: Scholarship Committee

3583—JACKSONVILLE STATE UNIVERSITY (Girl Scout Scholarship)

Financial Aid Office

Jacksonville AL 36265
256/782-5677 or 800/231-5291
Internet: http://www.jsu.edu
AMOUNT: Varies
DEADLINE(S): FEB 1
FIELD(S): All
ELIGIBILITY/REQUIREMENTS: Open
to Girl Scout Gold recipients.
HOW TO APPLY: Submit transcript and
ACT/SAT scores with scholarship applica-
tions. See website for application. Sup-
porting documentation should be mailed.
RENEWABLE: No
CONTACT: Scholarship Committee

3584—JACKSONVILLE STATE UNIVERSITY (Gov. Frank Dixon Memorial Scholarship)

Financial Aid Office
Jacksonville AL 36265
256/782-5677 or 800/231-5291
Internet: http://www.jsu.edu
AMOUNT: Varies
DEADLINE(S): FEB 1
FIELD(S): All
ELIGIBILITY/REQUIREMENTS: Open
to Alabama residents only.
HOW TO APPLY: Submit transcript and
ACT/SAT scores with scholarship applica-
tions. See website for application. Sup-
porting documentation should be mailed.
RENEWABLE: No
CONTACT: Scholarship Committee

3585—JACKSONVILLE STATE UNIVERSITY (Grace Barnard Memorial Scholarship)

Financial Aid Office
Jacksonville AL 36265
256/782-5677 or 800/231-5291
Internet: http://www.jsu.edu
AMOUNT: Varies
DEADLINE(S): FEB 1
FIELD(S): All
ELIGIBILITY/REQUIREMENTS:
Applicant must demonstrate high moral
character and academic achievement.
HOW TO APPLY: Submit transcript and
ACT/SAT scores with scholarship applica-
tions. See website for application.
Supporting documentation should be
mailed.
RENEWABLE: No
CONTACT: Scholarship Committee

3586—JACKSONVILLE STATE UNIVERSITY (Heather Whitestone Scholarship)

Financial Aid Office
Jacksonville AL 36265
256/782-5677 or 800/231-5291
Internet: http://www.jsu.edu

AMOUNT: Varies
FIELD(S): All
ELIGIBILITY/REQUIREMENTS: Open
to person with disability.
HOW TO APPLY: Contact Disability
Support Services (256/782-5093) for appli-
cation and additional information.
RENEWABLE: No

3587—JACKSONVILLE STATE UNIVERSITY (Jackson Company Good Citizenship Scholarship)

Financial Aid Office
Jacksonville AL 36265
256/782-5677 or 800/231-5291
Internet: http://www.jsu.edu
AMOUNT: Varies
DEADLINE(S): FEB 1
FIELD(S): All
ELIGIBILITY/REQUIREMENTS: Open
to entering freshman from Calhoun
County, Alabama.
HOW TO APPLY: Submit transcript and
ACT/SAT scores with scholarship applica-
tions. See website for application. Sup-
porting documentation should be mailed.
RENEWABLE: No
CONTACT: Scholarship Committee

3588—JACKSONVILLE STATE UNIVERSITY (Joe and Brenda Ford Scholarship)

Financial Aid Office
Jacksonville AL 36265
256/782-5677 or 800/231-5291
Internet: http://www.jsu.edu
AMOUNT: Varies
DEADLINE(S): FEB 1
FIELD(S): All
ELIGIBILITY/REQUIREMENTS: Full-
time undergraduate student from Etowah
County, Alabama.
HOW TO APPLY: Submit transcript and
ACT/SAT scores with scholarship applica-
tions. See website for application. Sup-
porting documentation should be mailed.
RENEWABLE: No
CONTACT: Scholarship Committee

3589—JACKSONVILLE STATE UNIVERSITY (Joseph Walker Elliott Memorial Scholarship)

Financial Aid Office
Jacksonville AL 36265
256/782-5677 or 800/231-5291
Internet: http://www.jsu.edu
AMOUNT: Varies
DEADLINE(S): FEB 1
FIELD(S): All

ELIGIBILITY/REQUIREMENTS: Open to all students.
HOW TO APPLY: Submit transcript and ACT/SAT scores with scholarship applications. See website for application. Supporting documentation should be mailed.
RENEWABLE: No
CONTACT: Scholarship Committee

3590—JACKSONVILLE STATE UNIVERSITY (Judge Pelham Merrill Scholarships)

Financial Aid Office
Jacksonville AL 36265
256/782-5677 or 800/231-5291
Internet: http://www.jsu.edu
AMOUNT: Varies
DEADLINE(S): FEB 1
FIELD(S): All
ELIGIBILITY/REQUIREMENTS: Open to entering freshman from Cleburne County, Alabama.
HOW TO APPLY: Submit transcript and ACT/SAT scores with scholarship applications. See website for application. Supporting documentation should be mailed.
NUMBER OF AWARDS: 1
RENEWABLE: No
CONTACT: Scholarship Committee

3591—JACKSONVILLE STATE UNIVERSITY (Julian Jenkins Scholarship)

Financial Aid Office
Jacksonville AL 36265
256/782-5677 or 800/231-5291
Internet: http://www.jsu.edu
AMOUNT: Varies
DEADLINE(S): FEB 1
FIELD(S): All
ELIGIBILITY/REQUIREMENTS: Open to Calhoun County, Alabama, resident.
HOW TO APPLY: Submit transcript and ACT/SAT scores with scholarship applications. See website for application. Supporting documentation should be mailed.
NUMBER OF AWARDS: 1
RENEWABLE: No
CONTACT: Scholarship Committee

3592—JACKSONVILLE STATE UNIVERSITY (Leadership Scholarship)

Financial Aid Office
Jacksonville AL 36265
256/782-5677 or 800/231-5291
Internet: http://www.jsu.edu
AMOUNT: Full tuition
DEADLINE(S): FEB 1
FIELD(S): All
ELIGIBILITY/REQUIREMENTS: Must be Alabama resident, Alabama high school graduate and entering freshman. Transfer students may also be considered; 2.5 GPA; unconditionally admitted; offices held in extracurricular activities. The GPA will be an academic GPA calculated based on English, social sciences, math, and science courses taken through student's junior year.
HOW TO APPLY: Submit transcript and ACT/SAT scores with scholarship applications. See website for application. Supporting documentation should be mailed.
RENEWABLE: Yes. 1 year.
CONTACT: Scholarship Committee

3593—JACKSONVILLE STATE UNIVERSITY (Leone Cole Memorial Scholarship)

Financial Aid Office
Jacksonville AL 36265
256/782-5677 or 800/231-5291
Internet: http://www.jsu.edu
AMOUNT: $1,000
DEADLINE(S): FEB 1
FIELD(S): All
ELIGIBILITY/REQUIREMENTS: Open to all freshmen; based on academics and leadership
HOW TO APPLY: Submit transcript and ACT/SAT scores with scholarship applications. See website for application. Supporting documentation should be mailed.
RENEWABLE: No
CONTACT: Scholarship Committee

3594—JACKSONVILLE STATE UNIVERSITY (Madison County Alumni Scholarship)

Financial Aid Office
Jacksonville AL 36265
256/782-5677 or 800/231-5291
Internet: http://www.jsu.edu
AMOUNT: Varies
DEADLINE(S): FEB 1
FIELD(S): All
ELIGIBILITY/REQUIREMENTS: Open to full-time undergraduate student; Madison County, Alabama, resident demonstrating academic aptitude.
HOW TO APPLY: Submit transcript and ACT/SAT scores with scholarship applications. See website for application. Supporting documentation should be mailed.
NUMBER OF AWARDS: 1
RENEWABLE: No
CONTACT: Scholarship Committee

3594A—JACKSONVILLE STATE UNIVERSITY (Martha Cole Memorial Scholarship)

Financial Aid Office
Jacksonville AL 36265

256/782-5677 or 800/231-5291
Internet: http://www.jsu.edu
AMOUNT: $1,000
DEADLINE(S): FEB 1
FIELD(S): All
ELIGIBILITY/REQUIREMENTS: Open to all students.
HOW TO APPLY: Submit transcript and ACT/SAT scores with scholarship applications. See website for application. Supporting documentation should be mailed.
RENEWABLE: No
CONTACT: Scholarship Committee

3595—JACKSONVILLE STATE UNIVERSITY (Miriam Higginbotham Scholarship)

Financial Aid Office
Jacksonville AL 36265
256/782-5677 or 800/231-5291
Internet: http://www.jsu.edu
AMOUNT: Approximately $1,200
DEADLINE(S): FEB 1
FIELD(S): All
ELIGIBILITY/REQUIREMENTS: Open to all students; grades and moral character given consideration.
HOW TO APPLY: Submit transcript and ACT/SAT scores with scholarship applications. See website for application. Supporting documentation should be mailed.
RENEWABLE: No
CONTACT: Scholarship Committee

3596—JACKSONVILLE STATE UNIVERSITY (Morris & Essie Longshore Scholarship)

Financial Aid Office
Jacksonville AL 36265
256/782-5677 or 800/231-5291
Internet: http://www.jsu.edu
AMOUNT: Varies
DEADLINE(S): FEB 1
FIELD(S): All
ELIGIBILITY/REQUIREMENTS: Open to undergraduate students.
HOW TO APPLY: Submit transcript and ACT/SAT scores with scholarship applications. See website for application. Supporting documentation should be mailed.
RENEWABLE: No
CONTACT: Scholarship Committee

3597—JACKSONVILLE STATE UNIVERSITY (Mr. & Mrs. Charles Hallman Scholarship)

Financial Aid Office
Jacksonville AL 36265
256/782-5677 or 800/231-5291
Internet: http://www.jsu.edu

AMOUNT: Varies
DEADLINE(S): FEB 1
FIELD(S): All
ELIGIBILITY/REQUIREMENTS: Open to students of Guntersville High School (Alabama).
HOW TO APPLY: Contact High School for application and details.
RENEWABLE: Yes
CONTACT: Guntersville High School (Alabama) Senior Guidance Counselor

3598—JACKSONVILLE STATE UNIVERSITY (Phi Beta Kappa Scholarship)

Financial Aid Office
Jacksonville AL 36265
256/782-5677 or 800/231-5291
Internet: http://www.jsu.edu
AMOUNT: Varies
DEADLINE(S): FEB 1
FIELD(S): All
ELIGIBILITY/REQUIREMENTS: Open to junior or senior.
HOW TO APPLY: Contact Society for application and details.
NUMBER OF AWARDS: 1
RENEWABLE: Yes
CONTACT: Dr. R. Davis, 256/782-5497

3599—JACKSONVILLE STATE UNIVERSITY (Presidential Junior College Transfer Scholarship)

Financial Aid Office
Jacksonville AL 36265
256/782-5677 or 800/231-5291
Internet: http://www.jsu.edu
AMOUNT: Varies
DEADLINE(S): FEB 1
FIELD(S): All
ELIGIBILITY/REQUIREMENTS: Selected by presidents of the state's 2-year colleges.
HOW TO APPLY: Contact office of the president at your 2-year college for details.
NUMBER OF AWARDS: 1
RENEWABLE: Yes

3600—JACKSONVILLE STATE UNIVERSITY (Robert C. Dryden Memorial Scholarship)

Financial Aid Office
Jacksonville AL 36265
256/782-5677 or 800/231-5291
Internet: http://www.jsu.edu
AMOUNT: Varies
DEADLINE(S): FEB 1
FIELD(S): All
ELIGIBILITY/REQUIREMENTS: Open to full-time graduate or undergraduate student demonstrating academic aptitude.

HOW TO APPLY: Submit transcript and ACT/SAT scores with scholarship applications. See website for application. Supporting documentation should be mailed.
RENEWABLE: No
CONTACT: Scholarship Committee

3601—JACKSONVILLE STATE UNIVERSITY (Ruth L. & M. V. Young Sr. Scholarship)

Financial Aid Office
Jacksonville AL 36265
256/782-5677 or 800/231-5291
Internet: http://www.jsu.edu
AMOUNT: Varies
DEADLINE(S): FEB 1
FIELD(S): All
ELIGIBILITY/REQUIREMENTS: Open to graduate of Piedmont High School (Alabama).
HOW TO APPLY: Submit transcript and ACT/SAT scores with scholarship applications. See website for application. Supporting documentation should be mailed.
RENEWABLE: No
CONTACT: Scholarship Committee

3602—JACKSONVILLE STATE UNIVERSITY (Sarah Hall Millican Memorial Scholarship)

Financial Aid Office
Jacksonville AL 36265
256/782-5677 or 800/231-5291
Internet: http://www.jsu.edu
AMOUNT: Full tuition
DEADLINE(S): FEB 1
FIELD(S): All
ELIGIBILITY/REQUIREMENTS: Open to freshman or transfer from Valley Head or Ider High School (Alabama).
HOW TO APPLY: Submit transcript and ACT/SAT scores with scholarship applications. See website for application. Supporting documentation should be mailed.
NUMBER OF AWARDS: 1
RENEWABLE: No
CONTACT: Scholarship Committee

3603—JACKSONVILLE STATE UNIVERSITY (Sunny King Memorial Scholarship)

Financial Aid Office
Jacksonville AL 36265
256/782-5677 or 800/231-5291
Internet: http://www.jsu.edu
AMOUNT: Varies
DEADLINE(S): FEB 1
FIELD(S): All
ELIGIBILITY/REQUIREMENTS: Open to Calhoun County, Alabama, resident.
HOW TO APPLY: Submit transcript and ACT/SAT scores with scholarship applica-

tions. See website for application. Supporting documentation should be mailed.
NUMBER OF AWARDS: 1
RENEWABLE: No
CONTACT: Scholarship Committee

3604—JACKSONVILLE STATE UNIVERSITY (Tim Garner Scholarship)

Financial Aid Office
Jacksonville AL 36265
256/782-5677 or 800/231-5291
Internet: http://www.jsu.edu
AMOUNT: Varies
DEADLINE(S): FEB 1
FIELD(S): All
ELIGIBILITY/REQUIREMENTS: Freshman from Cherokee County, Alabama.
HOW TO APPLY: Submit transcript and ACT/SAT scores with scholarship applications. See website for application. Supporting documentation should be mailed.
RENEWABLE: No
CONTACT: Scholarship Committee

3605—JACKSONVILLE STATE UNIVERSITY (Walter Merrill Scholarship)

Financial Aid Office
Jacksonville AL 36265
256/782-5677 or 800/231-5291
Internet: http://www.jsu.edu
AMOUNT: Full tuition
DEADLINE(S): FEB 1
FIELD(S): Pre-Law
ELIGIBILITY/REQUIREMENTS: Open to junior or senior; preference to residents of Cleburne or Calhoun Counties, Alabama.
HOW TO APPLY: Submit transcript and ACT/SAT scores with scholarship applications. See website for application. Supporting documentation should be mailed.
NUMBER OF AWARDS: 1
RENEWABLE: No
CONTACT: Scholarship Committee

3606—JACKSONVILLE STATE UNIVERSITY (Williams-Blair Scholarship)

Financial Aid Office
Jacksonville AL 36265
256/782-5677 or 800/231-5291
Internet: http://www.jsu.edu
AMOUNT: Varies
DEADLINE(S): FEB 1
FIELD(S): All
ELIGIBILITY/REQUIREMENTS: Open to all students.
HOW TO APPLY: Submit transcript and ACT/SAT scores with scholarship applica-

tions. See website for application. Supporting documentation should be mailed.
RENEWABLE: No
CONTACT: Scholarship Committee

3607—JACKSONVILLE STATE UNIVERSITY (Woodrow Hendon Scholarship)

Financial Aid Office
Jacksonville AL 36265
256/782-5677 or 800/231-5291
Internet: http://www.jsu.edu
AMOUNT: Varies
DEADLINE(S): FEB 1
FIELD(S): All
ELIGIBILITY/REQUIREMENTS: Open to Cherokee County, Alabama, residents; 2.5 GPA with 60 hours.
HOW TO APPLY: Submit transcript and ACT/SAT scores with scholarship applications. See website for application. Supporting documentation should be mailed.
RENEWABLE: No
CONTACT: Scholarship Committee

3608—JACKSONVILLE STATE UNIVERSITY (Writing Scholarships)

Financial Aid Office
Jacksonville AL 36265
256/782-5677 or 800/231-5291
Internet: http://www.jsu.edu
AMOUNT: Full tuition
DEADLINE(S): FEB 1
FIELD(S): All
ELIGIBILITY/REQUIREMENTS: Open to students with demonstrated ability in writing.
HOW TO APPLY: Contact English Department for application and details.
NUMBER OF AWARDS: 1
RENEWABLE: No
CONTACT: English Department, 256/782-5411 or 782-5412

3609—JAMES P. AND RUTH C. GILLROY FOUNDATION, INC. (Grants)

480 Mamaroneck Avenue
Harrison NY 10528
AMOUNT: $1,250/semester
DEADLINE(S): Varies (2 months prior to date payment is due to college)
FIELD(S): All
ELIGIBILITY/REQUIREMENTS: Open to undergraduates who are residents of the 5 boroughs of the City of New York and, in some cases, to non-residents who will attend institutions within the 5 boroughs. Must be U.S. citizen with an outstanding academic record, community service, and financial need.

HOW TO APPLY: Contact Foundation President for application guidelines.
NUMBER OF AWARDS: 20+
RENEWABLE: Yes
CONTACT: Edmund C. Grainger Jr., President

3610—JAPANESE AMERICAN CITIZENS LEAGUE (Abe and Esther Hagiwara Student Aid Award)

1765 Sutter Street
San Francisco CA 94115
415/921-5225
FAX: 415/931-4671
E-mail: jacl@jacl.org
Internet: http://www.jacl.org
AMOUNT: $1,000-$5,000
DEADLINE(S): APR 1
FIELD(S): All
ELIGIBILITY/REQUIREMENTS: Open only to JACL members and their children who demonstrate severe financial need. For undergraduate and graduate students planning to attend a college, university, trade school, business school, or any other institution of higher learning. Purpose is to provide financial assistance to a student who otherwise would have to delay or terminate his/her education due to lack of financing.
HOW TO APPLY: For membership information or an application, send SASE stating your level of study. Applications available October 1 through March 20. Must submit personal statement, letters of recommendation, and transcripts.

3611—JAPANESE AMERICAN CITIZENS LEAGUE (Alice Yuriko Endo Memorial Scholarship)

1765 Sutter Street
San Francisco CA 94115
415/921-5225
FAX: 415/931-4671
E-mail: jacl@jacl.org
Internet: http://www.jacl.org
AMOUNT: $1,000-$5,000
DEADLINE(S): APR 1
FIELD(S): All (emphasis on Public and Social Service)
ELIGIBILITY/REQUIREMENTS: Open only to JACL members and their children. For undergraduate students with an interest in public or social service who are planning to attend a college, university, trade school, business school, or any other institution of higher learning. Preference given to students residing in the Eastern District Council and/or those studying in above fields. Financial need NOT a factor.

HOW TO APPLY: For membership information and application, send SASE to above address, stating your level of study. Applications available October 1 to March 20.

3612—JAPANESE AMERICAN CITIZENS LEAGUE (Entering Freshmen Awards)

1765 Sutter Street
San Francisco CA 94115
415/921-5225
FAX: 415/931-4671
E-mail: jacl@jacl.org
Internet: http://www.jacl.org
AMOUNT: $1,000-$5,000
DEADLINE(S): MAR 1
FIELD(S): All
ELIGIBILITY/REQUIREMENTS: Open only to JACL members and their children. For entering freshmen planning to attend a college, university, trade school, business school, or any other institution of higher learning.
HOW TO APPLY: For membership information or an application, send SASE to above address, stating your level of study. Applications available October 1 to February 20. Must submit personal statement, letters of recommendation, and transcript.

3613—JAPANESE AMERICAN CITIZENS LEAGUE (Undergraduate Awards)

1765 Sutter Street
San Francisco CA 94115
415/921-5225
FAX: 415/931-4671
E-mail: jacl@jacl.org
Internet: http://www.jacl.org
AMOUNT: $1,000-$5,000
DEADLINE(S): APR 1
FIELD(S): All
ELIGIBILITY/REQUIREMENTS: Open only to JACL members and their children. For undergraduate students planning to attend a college, university, trade school, business school, or any other institution of higher learning.
HOW TO APPLY: For membership information or an application, send SASE stating your level of study. Applications available October 1 through March 20. Must submit personal statement, letters of recommendation, and transcripts.

3614—JAPANESE GOVERNMENT (Monbukegakusho Vocational School Student Scholarships)

350 S. Grand Avenue, Suite 1700
Los Angeles CA 90071

213/617-6700, ext. 338
FAX: 213/617-6728
Internet: http://www.la.us.emb-japan. go.jp
AMOUNT: Tuition + $1,400-$1,800/month
DEADLINE(S): AUG
FIELD(S): All (Vocational Skills)
ELIGIBILITY/REQUIREMENTS: For high school graduates, between the ages of 18-22, who wish to study at a vocational school in Japan. Includes 1-year Japanese language course, round-trip airfare, one-time arrival allowance, partly subsidized housing and medical expenses.
HOW TO APPLY: Term of study is for 3 years. For more information or an application, contact the Scholarship Coordinator.

3615—JAYCEE WAR MEMORIAL FUND, THE (Charles R. Ford Scholarship)

P.O. Box 7
Tulsa OK 74102-0007
918/584-2481
FAX: 918/584-4422
E-mail: DirectorCommunications @usjaycees.org
Internet: http://www.usjaycees.org
AMOUNT: $2,500
DEADLINE(S): MAR 1
FIELD(S): All
ELIGIBILITY/REQUIREMENTS: Open to active member of the Jaycees who wishes to return to a college or university to complete formal education. Must be U.S. citizen, possess academic potential and leadership qualities, and show financial need.
HOW TO APPLY: Applications must be requested between July 1 and February 1 of each year. Submit a business-size SASE and $10 application fee for each application requested.
NUMBER OF AWARDS: 1
RENEWABLE: No
CONTACT: Scholarship Coordinator

3616—JAYCEE WAR MEMORIAL FUND, THE (Thomas Wood Baldridge Scholarship)

P.O. Box 7
Tulsa OK 74102-0007
918/584-2481
FAX: 918/584-4422
E-mail: DirectorCommunications @usjaycees.org
Internet: http://www.usjaycees.org
AMOUNT: $3,000
DEADLINE(S): MAR 1
FIELD(S): All

ELIGIBILITY/REQUIREMENTS: Available to a Jaycee, immediate family member of a Jaycee, or a descendant of a former Jaycee, who is enrolled in or accepted for admission to a college or university. Applicant must be U.S. citizen, possess academic potential and leadership qualities, and show financial need.
HOW TO APPLY: Applications must be requested between July 1 and February 1 of each year. Submit a business-size SASE and $10 application fee for each application requested.
NUMBER OF AWARDS: 1
RENEWABLE: No
CONTACT: Scholarship Coordinator

3617—JAYCEE WAR MEMORIAL FUND, THE (War Memorial Fund Scholarship)

P.O. Box 7
Tulsa OK 74102-0007
918/584-2481
FAX: 918/584-4422
E-mail: DirectorCommunications @usjaycees.org
Internet: http://www.usjaycees.org
AMOUNT: $1,000
DEADLINE(S): MAR 1
FIELD(S): All
ELIGIBILITY/REQUIREMENTS: Must be U.S. citizens, possess academic potential and leadership qualities, and show financial need.
HOW TO APPLY: Applications must be requested between July 1 and February 1 of each year. Submit a business-size SASE and $10 application fee for each application requested.
NUMBER OF AWARDS: 10
RENEWABLE: No
CONTACT: Scholarship Coordinator

3618—JEANNETTE RANKIN FOUNDATION SCHOLARSHIPS

P.O. Box 6653
Athens GA 30604
706/208-1211
FAX: 706/548-0202
E-mail: info@rankinfoundation.org
Internet: http://www.rankin foundation.org
AMOUNT: $2,000
DEADLINE(S): MAR 1
FIELD(S): All
ELIGIBILITY/REQUIREMENTS: Must be low-income woman, age 35 or older, who is a U.S. citizen. Must be enrolled or accepted in an accredited school and pursuing a technical/vocational education, an associate's degree, or a first bachelor's degree.

HOW TO APPLY: Applications are available from November through February of each year. During this period, applications may be downloaded from website or may be requested by sending SASE.
NUMBER OF AWARDS: 50
RENEWABLE: No
CONTACT: Andrea Anderson

3619—JEWISH FAMILY AND CHILDREN'S SERVICES

2150 Post Street
San Francisco CA 94115
415/449-1226
FAX: 415/449-1229
E-mail: erics@jfcs.org
Internet: http://www.jfcs.org
AMOUNT: $500-$1,500 (grants); Up to $6,000 (loans)
DEADLINE(S): Ongoing
FIELD(S): All
ELIGIBILITY/REQUIREMENTS: Jewish resident of Sonoma, Marin, San Francisco, San Mateo or Northern Santa Clara Counties for one year prior to your application. Funds are prioritized for people who need our help in order to pursue their educational and vocational goals. Loans are also available to Jewish residents for 1 year of the 9 Bay area counties in addition to the counties listed above.
HOW TO APPLY: Download application from website.
NUMBER OF AWARDS: 100
RENEWABLE: No
CONTACT: Eric Singer

3620—JEWISH SOCIAL SERVICE AGENCY OF METROPOLITAN WASHINGTON (David Korn Scholarship Fund)

6123 Montrose Road
Rockville MD 20852
301/881-3700
TTY: 301/984-5662
FAX: 301/770-8741
Internet: http://www.jssa.org/web/guest/services/community/scholarships#Funds_for_Undergraduate_Students
AMOUNT: $1,000-$2,000
DEADLINE(S): Varies
FIELD(S): All
ELIGIBILITY/REQUIREMENTS: Must be a resident of the Washington Metropolitan area, a U.S. citizen or working toward citizenship, under the age of 30. Must be accepted into an accredited 4-year undergraduate program on a full-time basis. Awards cannot go towards attendance at a community college or study-abroad programs. Based on financial need.

HOW TO APPLY: See website for application and current year's deadline.
NUMBER OF AWARDS: 2-3
RENEWABLE: Yes
CONTACT: Scholarship and Loan Coordinator

3621—JEWISH SOCIAL SERVICE AGENCY OF METROPOLITAN WASHINGTON (Educational Scholarship)

6123 Montrose Road
Rockville MD 20852
301/881-3700
TTY: 301/984-5662
FAX: 301/770-8741
Internet: http://www.jssa.org/
web/guest/services/community/
scholarships#Funds_for_
Undergraduate_Students
AMOUNT: $6,000
DEADLINE(S): Varies
FIELD(S): All
ELIGIBILITY/REQUIREMENTS: Must be a high senior at a Montgomery County public high school, a U.S. citizen or working towards citizenship. Must be accepted into an accredited 4-year undergraduate or vocational school. Award cannot go towards attendance at a private or parochial school, graduate or postgraduate studies. Based primarily on financial need.
HOW TO APPLY: See website for application and current year's deadline.
NUMBER OF AWARDS: 3
RENEWABLE: No
CONTACT: Scholarship and Loan Coordinator

3622—JEWISH SOCIAL SERVICE AGENCY OF METROPOLITAN WASHINGTON (Jewish Educational Loan Fund)

6123 Montrose Road
Rockville MD 20852
301/881-3700
TTY: 301/984-5662
FAX: 301/770-8741
Internet: http://www.jssa.org/
web/guest/services/community/
scholarships#Funds_for_
Undergraduate_Students
AMOUNT: $2,000 (max.)
DEADLINE(S): None
FIELD(S): All
ELIGIBILITY/REQUIREMENTS: No-interest loans are available to Jewish undergraduate and graduate students from the Metropolitan Washington area who are U.S. citizens/permanent residents. Based primarily on financial need, this loan is for students with few other resources available. Awardees must repay

$50/month beginning three months after completing degree.
HOW TO APPLY: See website for application.
RENEWABLE: No
CONTACT: Scholarship and Loan Coordinator

3623—JEWISH SOCIAL SERVICE AGENCY OF METROPOLITAN WASHINGTON (Max and Emmy Dreyfuss Jewish Undergraduate Scholarship Fund)

6123 Montrose Road
Rockville MD 20852
301/881-3700
TTY: 301/984-5662
FAX: 301/770-8741
Internet: http://www.jssa.org/
web/guest/services/community/
scholarships#Funds_for_
Undergraduate_Students
AMOUNT: $1,500-$3,500
DEADLINE(S): Varies
FIELD(S): All
ELIGIBILITY/REQUIREMENTS: Open to Jewish undergraduates from the Metropolitan Washington area who are U.S. citizens/permanent residents. Must be accepted into an accredited 4-year program on a full-time basis in the U.S. Based primarily on financial need. This award may not be used for attending a community college or any study-abroad program.
HOW TO APPLY: See website for application
NUMBER OF AWARDS: 8-10
RENEWABLE: Yes
CONTACT: Scholarship and Loan Coordinator

3624—JEWISH VOCATIONAL SERVICE (Community Scholarship Fund)

6505 Wilshire Boulevard, Suite 200
Los Angeles CA 90048
323/761-8888, ext. 8868
FAX: 323/761-8575
E-mail: scholarship@jvsla.org
Internet: http://www.jvsla.org
AMOUNT: $500-$5,000
DEADLINE(S): MAR 14
FIELD(S): All
ELIGIBILITY/REQUIREMENTS: Must be Jewish permanent and legal residents of Los Angeles County, California, with verifiable financial need. Must be planning to attend full time an accredited college, university, vocational, graduate or medical school and maintain a minimum 2.7 GPA.
HOW TO APPLY: See website for application and instructions for submitting supporting materials after JAN 1.

NUMBER OF AWARDS: Varies
RENEWABLE: Yes, must reapply and requalify each year.
CONTACT: Cathy Kersh, Scholarship Program Manager

3625—JOHN F. KENNEDY LIBRARY FOUNDATION (John F. Kennedy Profile in Courage Essay Contest)

Columbia Point
Boston MA 02125
617/514-1649
FAX: 617/514-1641
E-mail: profiles@nara.gov
Internet: http://www.jfkcontest.org
AMOUNT: $500-$3,000
DEADLINE(S): JAN 10
FIELD(S): All
ELIGIBILITY REQUIREMENTS: Open to U.S. high school students in grades 9-12, or home-schools; or enrolled in a high school correspondence/GED program in any of the 50 states, D.C., or U.S. territories; or U.S. citizens attending schools overseas.
HOW TO APPLY: Write an essay on an elected official in the U.S. who is acting or has acted courageously to address a political issue at the local, state, national, or international level; also send completed contest registration form.
NUMBER OF AWARDS: 7 (1 first place, 1 second place, 5 finalists)
RENEWABLE: No

3626—JOHNSTON COUNTY EDUCATION FOUNDATION

P.O. Box 1075
Smithfield NC 27577
919/934-7977
Internet: http://www.jced
foundation.org/
AMOUNT: Up to $1,000
DEADLINE(S): Varies
FIELD(S): All
ELIGIBILITY/REQUIREMENTS: The Foundation administers scholarship funds for a number of scholarships available to students in Johnston County, North Carolina's public schools.
HOW TO APPLY: Criteria and applications are available through the guidance departments at local high schools.

3627—JUNIATA COLLEGE (Alumni Scholarships)

Office of Financial Planning
1700 Moore Street
Huntingdon PA 16652
814/641-3142

FAX: 814/641-5311
E-mail: frankv@juniata.edu
Internet: http://www.juniata.edu/admission/finplan/index.html
AMOUNT: Up to $5,000
DEADLINE(S): MAR 1
FIELD(S): All
ELIGIBILITY/REQUIREMENTS: Open to children of alumni; based on financial need.
HOW TO APPLY: Contact College for an application and FAFSA form.
CONTACT: Vincent Frank, Director of Student Financial Planning, 814/641-3140; e-mail: frankv@juniata.edu

3628—JUNIATA COLLEGE (Calvert Ellis Scholarships)

Office of Financial Planning
1700 Moore Street
Huntingdon PA 16652
814/641-3142
FAX: 814/641-5311
E-mail: frankv@juniata.edu
Internet: http://www.juniata.edu/admission/finplan/index.html
AMOUNT: $15,000
DEADLINE(S): MAR 15
FIELD(S): All
ELIGIBILITY/REQUIREMENTS: Open to students with GPA 3.4 and 1210 SAT/27ACT or GPA 3.75, 1120 SAT/25 ACT.
HOW TO APPLY: Contact College for an application or enrollment information.
NUMBER OF AWARDS: 1
CONTACT: Vincent Frank, Director of Student Financial Planning, 814/641-3140; e-mail: frankv@juniata.edu

3629—JUNIATA COLLEGE (Charles and Floretta Gibson Scholarships)

Office of Financial Planning
1700 Moore Street
Huntingdon PA 16652
814/641-3142
FAX: 814/641-5311
E-mail: frankv@juniata.edu
Internet: http://www.juniata.edu/admission/finplan/index.html
AMOUNT: Up to $4,000
DEADLINE(S): MAR 1
FIELD(S): All
ELIGIBILITY/REQUIREMENTS: Open to students of excellent character who are in financial need.
HOW TO APPLY: Contact College for an application and FAFSA form.
CONTACT: Vincent Frank, Director of Student Financial Planning, 814/641-3140; e-mail: frankv@juniata.edu

3630—JUNIATA COLLEGE (Church of the Brethren Scholarships)

Office of Financial Planning
1700 Moore Street
Huntingdon PA 16652
814/641-3142
FAX: 814/641-5311
E-mail: frankv@juniata.edu
Internet: http://www.juniata.edu/admission/finplan/index.html
AMOUNT: Up to $5,000
DEADLINE(S): MAR 1
FIELD(S): All
ELIGIBILITY/REQUIREMENTS: Open to members of the Church from certain geographic areas; must demonstrate financial need.
HOW TO APPLY: Contact College for an application or enrollment information. See Financial Aid Office for FAFSA.
CONTACT: Vincent Frank, Director of Student Financial Planning, 814/641-3140; e-mail: frankv@juniata.edu

3631—JUNIATA COLLEGE (Dorothy Baker Johnson Memorial Scholarship)

Office of Financial Planning
1700 Moore Street
Huntingdon PA 16652
814/641-3142
FAX: 814/641-5311
E-mail: frankv@juniata.edu
Internet: http://www.juniata.edu/admission/finplan/index.html
AMOUNT: Up to $4,000
DEADLINE(S): MAR 15
FIELD(S): All (Study Abroad)
ELIGIBILITY/REQUIREMENTS: Awarded prior to enrollment, to incoming female freshman in a career that will require an advanced degree.
HOW TO APPLY: Contact College for an application or enrollment information.
NUMBER OF AWARDS: 1
CONTACT: Vincent Frank, Director of Student Financial Planning, 814/641-3140; e-mail: frankv@juniata.edu

3632—JUNIATA COLLEGE (Eagles Abroad Scholarship)

Office of Financial Planning
1700 Moore Street
Huntingdon PA 16652
814/641-3142
FAX: 814/641-5311
E-mail: frankv@juniata.edu
Internet: http://www.juniata.edu/admission/finplan/index.html
AMOUNT: Expense-paid international experience + $3,000

DEADLINE(S): JAN 4
FIELD(S): All (Study Abroad), World Languages
ELIGIBILITY/REQUIREMENTS: Students will first be required to complete an international experience at no cost after their freshman year, an additional $3,000 will then be awarded during the junior year for 2 semesters of study abroad. Students must be committed to an international experience in France, Germany, Mexico, Spain or Russia and may study any academic program at the college. High school students applying for this award should have demonstrated interest in world languages by having at least 3 years of language in high school and a strong academic curriculum.
HOW TO APPLY: Contact College for an application or enrollment information. An application and interview are required.
NUMBER OF AWARDS: 1
CONTACT: Vincent Frank, Director of Student Financial Planning, 814/641-3140; e-mail: frankv@juniata.edu

3633—JUNIATA COLLEGE (Frederick and Mary F. Beckley Scholarship Fund)

Office of Financial Planning
1700 Moore Street
Huntingdon PA 16652
814/641-3142
FAX: 814/641-5311
E-mail: frankv@juniata.edu
Internet: http://www.juniata.edu/admission/finplan/index.html
AMOUNT: Up to $5,000
DEADLINE(S): APR 1
FIELD(S): All
ELIGIBILITY/REQUIREMENTS: Open to needy left-handed students.
HOW TO APPLY: Contact College for an application or enrollment information.
CONTACT: Vincent Frank, Director of Student Financial Planning, 814/641-3140; e-mail: frankv@juniata.edu

3634—JUNIATA COLLEGE (Friendship Scholarships)

Office of Financial Planning
1700 Moore Street
Huntingdon PA 16652
814/641-3142
FAX: 814/641-5311
E-mail: frankv@juniata.edu
Internet: http://www.juniata.edu/admission/finplan/index.html
AMOUNT: $2,000
DEADLINE(S): MAR 15
FIELD(S): All

ELIGIBILITY/REQUIREMENTS: Open to international students applying to Juniata College.

HOW TO APPLY: Contact College for an application or enrollment information.

CONTACT: Vincent Frank, Director of Student Financial Planning, 814/641-3140; e-mail: frankv@juniata.edu

3635—JUNIATA COLLEGE (Heritage Scholarship)

Office of Financial Planning
1700 Moore Street
Huntingdon PA 16652
814/641-3142
FAX: 814/641-5311
E-mail: frankv@juniata.edu
Internet: http://www.juniata.edu/admission/finplan/index.html

AMOUNT: Up to $8,000

DEADLINE(S): MAR 15

FIELD(S): All (Study Abroad)

ELIGIBILITY/REQUIREMENTS: Awarded prior to enrollment, to minority students with demonstrated commitment to leadership, community service and diversity as well as academic excellence.

HOW TO APPLY: Contact College for an application or enrollment information.

NUMBER OF AWARDS: 1

RENEWABLE: Yes (up to 4 years)

CONTACT: Vincent Frank, Director of Student Financial Planning, 814/641-3140; e-mail: frankv@juniata.edu

3636—JUNIATA COLLEGE (J. Omar Good Service & Peacemaking Scholarships)

Office of Financial Planning
1700 Moore Street
Huntingdon PA 16652
814/641-3142
FAX: 814/641-5311
E-mail: frankv@juniata.edu
Internet: http://www.juniata.edu/admission/finplan/index.html

AMOUNT: Full tuition and room & board

DEADLINE(S): JAN 9

FIELD(S): All

ELIGIBILITY/REQUIREMENTS: Awarded to students who have demonstrated a commitment to service and/or the peaceful resolution of conflict in their school and/or community. Examples of this commitment may be shown in a variety of ways such as significant involvement in community service, personal accomplishments in formal conflict resolution or mediation programs, or religious service.

HOW TO APPLY: Submit a Nomination Essay (in addition to the essay required for admission) of no more than 2 pages discussing why you should be considered for a scholarship, including supporting activities and involvement. You may also attach up to 3 extra pages of supporting information of any kind. See website for additional information.

NUMBER OF AWARDS: 1

CONTACT: Vincent Frank, Director of Student Financial Planning, 814/641-3140; e-mail: frankv@juniata.edu

3637—JUNIATA COLLEGE (John Stauffer Scholarships)

Office of Financial Planning
1700 Moore Street
Huntingdon PA 16652
814/641-3142
FAX: 814/641-5311
E-mail: frankv@juniata.edu
Internet: http://www.juniata.edu/admission/finplan/index.html

AMOUNT: Full tuition for 4 years

DEADLINE(S): JAN 4

FIELD(S): All

ELIGIBILITY/REQUIREMENTS: Open to entering students who have achieved National Merit or National Achievement Finalist status as determined by the governing body under the National Merit Scholarship Corporation. Finalists attending Juniata must present to the college the official notification of Finalist status and indicate Juniata as their final college choice.

HOW TO APPLY: Contact College for an application or enrollment information. All finalists must come to campus for an interview with the selection committee. Students can begin the interview process as a semi-finalist in anticipation that they will become a finalist.

NUMBER OF AWARDS: 4

RENEWABLE: No

CONTACT: Vincent Frank, Director of Student Financial Planning, 814/641-3140; e-mail: frankv@juniata.edu

3638—JUNIATA COLLEGE (Native American Scholarship)

Office of Financial Planning
1700 Moore Street
Huntingdon PA 16652
814/641-3142
FAX: 814/641-5311
E-mail: frankv@juniata.edu
Internet: http://www.juniata.edu/admission/finplan/index.html

AMOUNT: Up to $10,000

DEADLINE(S): APR 1

FIELD(S): All

ELIGIBILITY/REQUIREMENTS: Open to students of Native American heritage who are in financial need.

HOW TO APPLY: Contact College for an application and FAFSA form.

CONTACT: Vincent Frank, Director of Student Financial Planning, 814/641-3140; e-mail: frankv@juniata.edu

3639—JUNIATA COLLEGE (Presidential Scholarships)

Office of Financial Planning
1700 Moore Street
Huntingdon PA 16652
814/641-3142
FAX: 814/641-5311
E-mail: frankv@juniata.edu
Internet: http://www.juniata.edu/admission/finplan/index.html

AMOUNT: $11,500

DEADLINE(S): MAR 15

FIELD(S): All

ELIGIBILITY/REQUIREMENTS: Must have 3.75 GPA and 1000 SAT/21 ACT or 3.2 GPA and 1110 SAT/25 ACT.

HOW TO APPLY: Contact College for an application or enrollment information.

CONTACT: Vincent Frank, Director of Student Financial Planning, 814/641-3140; e-mail: frankv@juniata.edu

3640—JUNIATA COLLEGE (Program for Area Residents Scholarships)

Office of Financial Planning
1700 Moore Street
Huntingdon PA 16652
814/641-3142
FAX: 814/641-5311
E-mail: frankv@juniata.edu
Internet: http://www.juniata.edu/admission/finplan/index.html

AMOUNT: Half tuition

DEADLINE(S): Open

FIELD(S): All

ELIGIBILITY/REQUIREMENTS: Open to nontraditional students.

HOW TO APPLY: Contact College for an application or enrollment information.

CONTACT: Vincent Frank, Director of Student Financial Planning, 814/641-3140; e-mail: frankv@juniata.edu

3641—JUNIATA COLLEGE (Quinter Scholarships)

Office of Financial Planning
1700 Moore Street
Huntingdon PA 16652

814/641-3142
FAX: 814/641-5311
E-mail: frankv@juniata.edu
Internet: http://www.juniata.edu/
admission/finplan/index.html
AMOUNT: $16,000 paid international
experience + $3,000
DEADLINE(S): MAR 15
FIELD(S): All
ELIGIBILITY/REQUIREMENTS:
Awarded to students who achieve excep-
tional results in the classroom. Quality of
program and strength of academic sched-
ule are factored into the selection. In gen-
eral, students should achieve a 1320
(M+V) or 30 ACT Composite and a 3.55
GPA.
HOW TO APPLY: Contact College for an
application or enrollment information. An
application and interview are required.
NUMBER OF AWARDS: 1
RENEWABLE: Yes (up to 4 years)
CONTACT: Vincent Frank, Director of
Student Financial Planning, 814/641-3140;
e-mail: frankv@juniata.edu

3642—JUNIATA COLLEGE (Ray Day Scholarship)

Office of Financial Planning
1700 Moore Street
Huntingdon PA 16652
814/641-3142
FAX: 814/641-5311
E-mail: frankv@juniata.edu
Internet: http://www.juniata.edu/
admission/finplan/index.html
AMOUNT: Up to $5,000
DEADLINE(S): APR 1
FIELD(S): All
ELIGIBILITY/REQUIREMENTS: Open
to minority students who are in financial
need.
HOW TO APPLY: Contact College for an
application and FAFSA form.
CONTACT: Vincent Frank, Director of
Student Financial Planning, 814/641-3140;
e-mail: frankv@juniata.edu

3643—JUNIATA COLLEGE (Richard M. Simpson Leadership Scholarships)

Office of Financial Planning
1700 Moore Street
Huntingdon PA 16652
814/641-3142
FAX: 814/641-5311
E-mail: frankv@juniata.edu
Internet: http://www.juniata.edu/
admission/finplan/index.html
AMOUNT: Full tuition, room & board
DEADLINE(S): JAN 4

FIELD(S): All
ELIGIBILITY/REQUIREMENTS:
Awarded to students who have demonstrated leadership in school, community or
religious organizations or through entrepreneurial activities. Emphasis is placed on
students who have shown the ability to create positive change or who have undertak-
en or managed risk, whether the risk
resulted in achievement of the goal or not.
HOW TO APPLY: Submit a Nomination
Essay (in addition to the essay required for
admission) of no more than 2 pages discussing why you should be considered for a
scholarship, including supporting activities
and involvement. You may also attach up
to 3 extra pages of supporting information
of any kind. See website for additional
information.
NUMBER OF AWARDS: 1
CONTACT: Vincent Frank, Director of
Student Financial Planning, 814/641-3140;
e-mail: frankv@juniata.edu

3644—JUNIATA COLLEGE (Sam Hayes Jr. Scholarship)

Office of Financial Planning
1700 Moore Street
Huntingdon PA 16652
814/641-3142
FAX: 814/641-5311
E-mail: frankv@juniata.edu
Internet: http://www.juniata.edu/
admission/finplan/index.html
AMOUNT: Up to $1,500 (max.)
DEADLINE(S): MAR 1
FIELD(S): All
ELIGIBILITY/REQUIREMENTS: Open
to Pennsylvania 4H and FFA members
who are applying to Juniata College. Must
demonstrate financial need and fill out
government FAFSA form.
HOW TO APPLY: Contact College for an
application or enrollment information. See
your financial aid office for FAFSA.
CONTACT: Vincent Frank, Director of
Student Financial Planning, 814/641-3140;
e-mail: frankv@juniata.edu

3645—JUNIATA COLLEGE (Transfer Scholarships)

Office of Financial Planning
1700 Moore Street
Huntingdon PA 16652
814/641-3142
FAX: 814/641-5311
E-mail: frankv@juniata.edu
Internet: http://www.juniata.edu/
admission/finplan/index.html
AMOUNT: $7,000-$9,000
DEADLINE(S): Open

FIELD(S): All
ELIGIBILITY/REQUIREMENTS: Open
to transfer student with 24 credit hours and
3.25 GPA.
HOW TO APPLY: Contact College for an
application or enrollment information.
NUMBER OF AWARDS: 1
CONTACT: Vincent Frank, Director of
Student Financial Planning, 814/641-3140;
e-mail: frankv@juniata.edu

3646—JUNIATA COLLEGE (W. Clay and Kathryn H. Burkholder Scholarship)

Office of Financial Planning
1700 Moore Street
Huntingdon PA 16652
814/641-3142
FAX: 814/641-5311
E-mail: frankv@juniata.edu
Internet: http://www.juniata.edu/
admission/finplan/index.html
AMOUNT: Full tuition, room & board
DEADLINE(S): JAN 4
FIELD(S): All
ELIGIBILITY/REQUIREMENTS: Open
to incoming freshmen (upperclassmen and
transfer students are ineligible). Must be
nominated by a Juniata alumnus/a, parent
of a Juniata student, guidance counselor,
pastor, teacher, or someone familiar with
the student's involvement in school and
community activities.
HOW TO APPLY: Submit a Nomination
Essay (in addition to the essay required for
admission) of no more than 2 pages discussing why you should be considered for a
scholarship, including supporting activities
and involvement. You may also attach up
to 3 extra pages of supporting information
of any kind. See website for additional
information.
NUMBER OF AWARDS: 1
CONTACT: Vincent Frank, Director of
Student Financial Planning, 814/641-3140;
e-mail: frankv@juniata.edu

3647—JUNIOR ACHIEVEMENT INC. (Eckerd College Scholarship)

One Education Way
Colorado Springs CO 80906-4477
719/540-8000
FAX: 719/540-6299
E-mail: newmedia@ja.org
Internet: http://www.ja.org
AMOUNT: Up to $5,000 per year
DEADLINE(S): MAR 1
FIELD(S): All
ELIGIBILITY/REQUIREMENTS: Must
be high school seniors who have been
accepted by and will be attending Eckerd
College; must have a minimum GPA of 3.0

and minimum SAT score of 1080 or ACT composite score of 22; must have demonstrated leadership ability and desire to serve people.

HOW TO APPLY: Send application to Eckerd College (address below) with 2 letters of recommendation: 1 from a JA staff person and 1 from a JA High School Programs consultant.

NUMBER OF AWARDS: 15

RENEWABLE: Yes. Maximum 4 years, $20,000.

CONTACT: Richard D. Hallin, Dean of Admissions, Eckerd College, P.O. Box 12560, St. Petersburg FL 33733; 727/864-8331 or 800/456-9009, or www.eckerd.edu.

3648—JUNIOR ACHIEVEMENT INC. (Hugh B. Sweeny Achievement Award)

One Education Way
Colorado Springs CO 80906
719/540-8000
FAX: 719/540-6299
E-mail: newmedia@ja.org
Internet: http://www.ja.org
AMOUNT: $5,000
FIELD(S): All

ELIGIBILITY/REQUIREMENTS: Must be graduating high school seniors who have demonstrated academic achievement, leadership skills, and financial need.

HOW TO APPLY: Contact JAI.

NUMBER OF AWARDS: 1

RENEWABLE: No

3649—JUNIOR ACHIEVEMENT INC. (Kettering University Scholarship)

One Education Way
Colorado Springs CO 80906-4477
719/540-8000
FAX: 719/540-6299
E-mail: newmedia@ja.org
Internet: http://www.ja.org
AMOUNT: $5,000
DEADLINE(S): MAR 1
FIELD(S): All

ELIGIBILITY/REQUIREMENTS: Must be high school seniors who have been accepted by and will be attending Kettering University; must demonstrate community and school involvement.

HOW TO APPLY: Submit application to Financial Aid Office at Kettering University (address below) with essay on current business problems; 3 letters of recommendation: 1 from a JA staff person, 1 from a JA High School Programs consultant, and 1 other.

NUMBER OF AWARDS: 2

RENEWABLE: No

CONTACT: Kettering University Admissions Office, 1700 West Third Avenue, Flint MI 48504; 800/955-4464, ext. 7859; e-mail: admissions@gmi.edu or see website at www.kettering.edu

3650—J. WOOD PLATT CADDIE SCHOLARSHIP TRUST (Grants)

P.O. Box 808
Southeastern PA 19399-0808
610/687-2340, ext. 21
FAX: 610/687-2082
E-mail: jwp@gapgolf.org
Internet: http://www.gapgolf.org/detail.asp?id=54
AMOUNT: $200-$7,000
DEADLINE(S): APR 25
FIELD(S): All

ELIGIBILITY/REQUIREMENTS: Open to high school seniors and undergraduate students who have served as a caddie at a Golf Association of Philadelphia member club. Must demonstrate financial need and have the capability to successfully complete undergraduate degree. Recipients must continue to caddy while receiving grants from the Scholarship.

HOW TO APPLY: See website.

NUMBER OF AWARDS: About 260

RENEWABLE: Yes. Must continue to caddy at a course in the Golf Association of Philadephia each summer for a minimum of 50% of the days a loop is available at that club. Must have successfully completed at least 12 credit hours/semester or 24/year. Participation in a summer internship program that affects the ability to caddy requires the completion of an internship approval form.

CONTACT: John A. Pergolin

3651—J. W. SAXE MEMORIAL PRIZE

1524 31st Street NW
Washington DC 20007-3074
E-mail: ruthsaxe@aol.com or sachsedc@verizon.net
Internet: http://www.jwsaxefund.org
DEADLINE(S): MAR 15
AMOUNT: $1,500
FIELD(S): All (Emphasis on Public Service; Community Service)

ELIGIBILITY/REQUIREMENTS: Must be a college or university student. Award is meant to enable student to gain practical experience in public service by taking a no-pay or low-pay job or internship during the summer or other term.

HOW TO APPLY: Send résumé together with an essay stating short- and long-term goals. Also include statements from 4 references including at least 1 from a faculty member.

NUMBER OF AWARDS: 1-12

RENEWABLE: No

CONTACT: Ruth Saxe, President or Elinor Sachse, VP and Secretary

3652—KAPLAN/NEWSWEEK ("My Turn" Essay Contest)

Pre-College
1440 Broadway, 9th Floor
New York, NY 10018
800/527-8378
Internet: http://www.kaptest.com/essay
AMOUNT: $5,000 (1st place); $2,000 (2nd place); $1,000
DEADLINE(S): FEB 1
FIELD(S): Writing

ELIGIBILITY/REQUIREMENTS: Essay (500-1,000 words) on topic chosen by student should be based on personal opinion or experience; must be factually accurate. Must be U.S. citizen or resident of U.S. (and its territories and possessions), who as of January 1 is a high school student intending to attend college following graduation. All other entries will be disqualified. Essays are judged on effectiveness, creativity, insight, organization and development, consistent use of language, variety in sentence structure and vocabulary, use of proper grammar, spelling and punctuation.

HOW TO APPLY: See official rules and instructions and download entry form from website or see guidance counselor. Submit with 2 copies of essay.

NUMBER OF AWARDS: 10

RENEWABLE: No

3653—KANSAS STATE GRANGE (Claude and Ina Brey Memorial Endowment Fund)

11540 County Road #1095
Mound City KS 66056
913/795-2287
FAX: 913/795-3092
Internet: http://www.ksgrange.org
AMOUNT: $500
DEADLINE(S): APR 15
FIELD(S): All, especially agriculture

ELIGIBILITY/REQUIREMENTS: Open to Grange members who are a member of a subordinate Grange in good standing for at least 2 years. Credit will be given on Grange participation, community, school and church activities, and scholastic standing. Additional credit is given to students majoring in agricultural fields. Grade transcripts must be received before application is considered. Winners will be required to file a report with the Kansas State Grange on how funds are expended.

HOW TO APPLY: Applications may be downloaded from website or obtained from the State Lecturer, State Master or Youth Director.
NUMBER OF AWARDS: Varies
RENEWABLE: Yes

3654—KAPPA DELTA PI

3707 Woodview Trace
Indianapolis IN 46268-1158
317/871-4900 or 800/284-3167
FAX: 317/704-2323/2324
Internet: http://www.kdp.org
DEADLINE(S): MAY 19
FIELD(S): All
ELIGIBILITY/REQUIREMENTS: Must be an active member of Kappa Delta Pi.
HOW TO APPLY: Call or download application from website.
NUMBER OF AWARDS: 42
RENEWABLE: No
CONTACT: Margo H. Black

3655—KENNEDY FOUNDATION

P.O. Box 621609
Littleton CO 80162
303/933-8942
FAX: 303/933-8797
E-mail: kennedyfoundation@columbinecorp.com
AMOUNT: $2,000
DEADLINE(S): JUL 31
FIELD(S): All
ELIGIBILITY/REQUIREMENTS: Must be a full-time student and maintain at least a 2.0 cumulative GPA.
HOW TO APPLY: E-mail request for an application.
NUMBER OF AWARDS: 12-14
RENEWABLE: Yes. Up to 4 years; must submit previous semester's transcript.
CONTACT: Jonathan Kennedy

3656—KNIGHTS OF AK-SAR-BEN (Community College Scholarship)

302 South 36th Street, Suite 800
Omaha NE 68131
402/554-9600
FAX: 402/554-9609
E-mail: sudmanne@aksarben.org
Internet: http://www.aksarben.org
AMOUNT: $1,000
DEADLINE(S): FEB
FIELD(S): All
ELIGIBILITY/REQUIREMENTS: Open only to high school seniors from Nebraska and western Iowa (see website for list of counties), who have exhibited integrity and perseverance in overcoming personal adversity and plan to obtain a bachelor's degree (may begin studies at a 2-year insti-

tution) beginning in the Fall following graduation. Must demonstrate critical financial need ($50,000 or less gross income per family preferred) and be U.S. citizens or in the process of obtaining citizenship, have minimum 2.0 GPA. Based on leadership, academic achievement, financial need.
HOW TO APPLY: Download application and reference forms; submit with transcript, personal essay, 2 letters of recommendation and College Funding Estimator form.
NUMBER OF AWARDS: 10
RENEWABLE: No. Note: Scholarship is paid in 2 installments. Recipients must maintain a 2.5 overall GPA to qualify for 2nd term renewal and must continue as full-time students (at least 12 hours).
CONTACT: Erin Sudmann (via e-mail only)

3657—KNIGHTS OF AK-SAR-BEN (Horatio Alger Ak-Sar-Ben Scholarship)

302 South 36th Street, Suite 800
Omaha NE 68131
402/554-9600
FAX: 402/554-9609
E-mail: sudmanne@aksarben.org
Internet: http://www.horatioalger.org
AMOUNT: $2,500
DEADLINE(S): FEB 11
FIELD(S): All
ELIGIBILITY/REQUIREMENTS: Open only to high school seniors from Nebraska and western Iowa (see website for list of counties), who have exhibited integrity and perseverance in overcoming personal adversity and plan to obtain a bachelor's degree (may begin studies at a 2-year institution) beginning in the Fall following graduation. Must demonstrate critical financial need ($50,000 or less gross income per family preferred) and be U.S. citizens or in the process of obtaining citizenship, have minimum 2.0 GPA. Based on leadership, academic achievement, financial need.
HOW TO APPLY: Download application and reference forms; submit with transcript, personal essay, 2 letters of recommendation and College Funding Estimator form.
NUMBER OF AWARDS: 100
CONTACT: Erin Sudmann (via e-mail only)

3658—KNIGHTS OF COLUMBUS (Francis P. Matthews and John E. Swift Educational Trust Scholarship)

P.O. Box 1670

New Haven CT 06507-0901
203/752-4332
FAX: 203/752-4103
Internet: http://www.kofc.org/un/index.cfm
AMOUNT: Varies
DEADLINE(S): None
FIELD(S): All
ELIGIBILITY/REQUIREMENTS: Open to children of Knights of Columbus members in good standing who died or became permanently and totally disabled while 1) serving in the military from a cause connected directly with military service during a period of conflict, or 2) as a result of criminal violence directed against them while in the lawful performance of their duties as full-time law enforcement officers or full-time firemen. Tenable for undergraduate study leading to a bachelor's degree at a Catholic college.
HOW TO APPLY: Contact the Department of Scholarships for an application.

3659—KNIGHTS OF COLUMBUS (Pro Deo and Pro Patria Scholarships-Canada)

P.O. Box 1670
New Haven CT 06507-0901
203/752-4332
FAX: 203/752-4103
Internet: http://www.kofc.org/un/index.cfm
AMOUNT: $1,500
DEADLINE(S): MAY 1
FIELD(S): All
ELIGIBILITY/REQUIREMENTS: Open to students entering the first year of university study leading to a baccalaureate degree at colleges/universities in Canada. Must be a member in good standing in a Canadian council of the Knights of Columbus or the son or daughter of such a member or deceased member. Based on academic excellence.
HOW TO APPLY: Contact the Department of Scholarships for an application.
NUMBER OF AWARDS: 12
RENEWABLE: Yes. Up to 4 years.

3660—KNIGHTS OF COLUMBUS (Pro Deo and Pro Patria Scholarships-Fourth Degree)

P.O. Box 1670
New Haven CT 06507-0901
203/752-4332
FAX: 203/752-4103
Internet: http://www.kofc.org/un/index.cfm
AMOUNT: $1,500
DEADLINE(S): MAR 1
FIELD(S): All

ELIGIBILITY/REQUIREMENTS: Open to entering freshmen at a Catholic college. Must be a member in good standing of the Knights of Columbus, the child of such a member or deceased member, or a member in good standing of the Columbian Squires, and who can show evidence of satisfactory academic performance.
HOW TO APPLY: Contact the Department of Scholarships for an application.
NUMBER OF AWARDS: 62 (50 at any Catholic college; 12 at The Catholic University of America in Washington DC)
RENEWABLE: Yes. Up to 4 years.

3661—KOSCIUSZKO FOUNDATION (Tuition Scholarships)

15 East 65th Street
New York NY 10021-6595
212/734-2130
FAX: 212/628-4552
E-mail: thekf@pegasusnet.com
Internet: http://www.kosciuszko foundation.org
AMOUNT: $1,000-$5,000
DEADLINE(S): JAN 16
FIELD(S): All
ELIGIBILITY/REQUIREMENTS: Open to full-time undergraduate juniors and seniors and graduate students of Polish descent. Must be U.S. citizens/permanent residents attending a U.S. institution. Must have a minimum 3.0 GPA. Other criteria include special achievements and extracurricular activities, academic interest in Polish subjects and/or involvement in Polish-American community, educational/professional goals, and financial need.
HOW TO APPLY: $25 application fee (1 application is valid for 2 years). See website or send SASE to Addy Tymczyszyn for application from September to December. Notification in May.
RENEWABLE: Yes

3662—LA ALIANZA AT HARVARD LAW (Justicia en Diversidad Scholarship Fund)

La Alianza Justicia en Diversidad Foundation
c/o Alexander A. Boni-Saenz
Harvard Law School
Cambridge MA 02138
E-mail: ptagre@law.harvard.edu
Internet: http://www.law.harvard. edu/students/orgs/alianza/ scholarship/
AMOUNT: $1,000
DEADLINE(S): FEB 1
FIELD(S): All
ELIGIBILITY/REQUIREMENTS: Must be attending high school in the U.S.; GPA of at least 2.5; and planning to attend a 4-year U.S. college full time in the following academic year.
HOW TO APPLY: Contact La Alianza for details.
CONTACT: Alexander A. Boni-Saenz

3663—LAMBDA THETA NU SORORITY, INC. (Latina Scholarship Award)

La Mesa Directiva
1220 Rosecrans #543
San Diego CA 92106
E-mail: chair@lambdathetanu.org
Internet: http://www.lambda thetanu.org
AMOUNT: $200-$1,000
DEADLINE(S): MAY 1
FIELD(S): All
ELIGIBILITY/REQUIREMENTS: Must be Latina women pursuing education at an accredited college or university.
HOW TO APPLY: Contact the Lambda Theta Nu chapter closest to you.
NUMBER OF AWARDS: Multiple

3664—LATIN AMERICAN EDUCATIONAL FOUNDATION

24 W. Colfax Avenue, Suite 103
Denver CO 80204
303/446-0541
FAX: 303/446-0526
E-mail: carmen@laef.org
Internet: http://www.laef.org
AMOUNT: Varies
DEADLINE(S): FEB 15
FIELD(S): All
ELIGIBILITY/REQUIREMENTS: Colorado resident; Hispanic heritage and/or actively involved in the Hispanic community; accepted to an accredited college, university or vocational school; minimum 3.0 cumulative GPA; recipients are required to fulfill 10 hours of community service during the years of funding. Based on achievement, financial need, community involvement.
HOW TO APPLY: Download application from website and submit with all supporting documents, including letters of recommendation and personal essay, in one package. Personal interview required.
NUMBER OF AWARDS: Varies
RENEWABLE: Yes, must reapply.
CONTACT: Carmen Lerma Mendoza

3665—LEAGUE OF UNITED LATIN AMERICAN CITIZENS/LULAC NATIONAL EDUCATIONAL SERVICE CENTERS (LULAC National Scholarship Fund)

2000 L Street NW, Suite 610
Washington DC 20036
202/835-9646
FAX: 202/835-9685
Internet: http://www.lulac.org/ programs/scholar.html
AMOUNT: Varies
DEADLINE(S): MAR 31
FIELD(S): All
ELIGIBILITY/REQUIREMENTS: Open to high school seniors, undergraduates, and graduate students of Hispanic origin. Some awards are for specific fields of study, such as business or engineering, and some have certain GPA requirements. MUST live in a LULAC Council Area in order to apply.
HOW TO APPLY: See website for additional information and application.
CONTACT: Lorena Garrido

3666—LEE-JACKSON EDUCATIONAL FOUNDATION (Essay Contest)

P.O. Box 8121
Charlottesville VA 22906
Internet: http://www.lee-jackson.org
AMOUNT: $10,000 (grand prize); $2,000 (each region); $1,000 (each region)
DEADLINE(S): Varies
FIELD(S): All
ELIGIBILITY/REQUIREMENTS: Open to juniors and seniors in Virginia public high schools who plan to attend an accredited U.S. 4-year college or university (community college okay if plan to transfer). Essay must demonstrate an appreciation of the exemplary character and soldierly virtues of Generals Lee and Jackson; judged on accuracy, research, and mode of expression. Length not as important as topic, idea, and points developed.
HOW TO APPLY: Contact school principal/guidance counselor or the Foundation for an application.
NUMBER OF AWARDS: 33

3667—LEON M. ABBOTT SCOTTISH RITE SCHOLARSHIP FUND

33 Marrett Road
Lexington MA 02421
781/862-4410
FAX: 781/274-7319
E-mail: dziedelis@supreme council.org
AMOUNT: $1,000-$2,450
DEADLINE(S): MAR 1
FIELD(S): All
ELIGIBILITY/REQUIREMENTS: Private fund for sons/daughters and grandsons/granddaughters of Scottish Rite Masons in the Northern Masonic jurisdiction (Maine, New Hampshire, Vermont,

Massachusetts, Rhode Island, Connecticut, New York, New Jersey, Pennsylvania, Delaware, Ohio, Michigan, Indiana, Illinois, Wisconsin).
HOW TO APPLY: Contact headquarters or any of 100 centers in the 15 states.
NUMBER OF AWARDS: 300
RENEWABLE: Yes, must reapply.
CONTACT: Doug Ziedelis at 781/465-3316

3668—LEOPOLD SCHEPP FOUNDATION (Undergraduate and Graduate Awards)

551 Fifth Avenue,
Suite 3000
New York NY 10176-2597
212/692-0191
Internet: http://www.schepp foundation.org/
AMOUNT: Up to $8,500
FIELD(S): All
ELIGIBILITY/REQUIREMENTS: Undergraduates up to age 30 and graduates up to age 40 are eligible.
HOW TO APPLY: Undergraduates should write detailing their education to date, year in school, length of course of study, vocational goal, financial need, age, citizenship, and availability for interview in New York City. Send SASE for additional information. High school seniors may NOT apply.
NUMBER OF AWARDS: 200
RENEWABLE: Yes, must reapply.

3669—LINCOLN COMMUNITY FOUNDATION (Alfred and Esther Eggerling Dana College Scholarship)

215 Centennial Mall South,
Suite 100
Lincoln NE 68508
402/474-2345
FAX: 402/476-8532
E-mail: lcf@lcf.org
Internet: http://www.lcf.org
AMOUNT: Varies
DEADLINE(S): APR 1
FIELD(S): All
ELIGIBILITY/REQUIREMENTS: Current graduating high school senior or current college student attending/planning to attend Dana College in Blair, Nebraska. Must demonstrate the ability to succeed in college and financial need.
HOW TO APPLY: Contact Dana College Financial Aid Office, 2848 College Drive, Blair, NE 68008 for application. Submit with transcripts from all high schools, colleges and universities attended; copy of ACT/SAT or similar test scores; and financial aid form.

3670—LINCOLN COMMUNITY FOUNDATION (Alfred and Esther Eggerling Midland Lutheran College Scholarship)

215 Centennial Mall South,
Suite 100
Lincoln NE 68508
402/474-2345
FAX: 402/476-8532
E-mail: lcf@lcf.org
Internet: http://www.lcf.org
AMOUNT: Varies
DEADLINE(S): APR 1
FIELD(S): All
ELIGIBILITY/REQUIREMENTS: Current graduating high school senior or current college student attending/planning to attend Midland Lutheran College in Fremont, Nebraska. Must demonstrate the ability to succeed in college and financial need.
HOW TO APPLY: Submit application to Foundation with transcripts from all high schools, colleges and universities attended; copy of ACT/SAT or similar test scores; and financial aid form.

3671—LINCOLN COMMUNITY FOUNDATION (Alfred and Esther Eggerling Southeast Community College Scholarship)

215 Centennial Mall South,
Suite 100
Lincoln NE 68508
402/474-2345
FAX: 402/476-8532
E-mail: lcf@lcf.org
Internet: http://www.lcf.org
AMOUNT: Varies
DEADLINE(S): APR
FIELD(S): All
ELIGIBILITY/REQUIREMENTS: Current college student attending Southeast Community College in Milford, Nebraska. Must have successfully completed two or more quarters by April 1; must demonstrate the ability to succeed in college and financial need.
HOW TO APPLY: Obtain applications from Southeast Community College Financial Aid Office. Submit with transcripts from all high schools, colleges and universities attended; copy of ACT/SAT or similar test scores; and letters of recommendation.

3672—LINCOLN COMMUNITY FOUNDATION (Annette Carnahan Kubie Chi Omega Memorial Scholarship)

215 Centennial Mall South,
Suite 100
Lincoln NE 68508

402/474-2345
FAX: 402/476-8532
E-mail: lcf@lcf.org
Internet: http://www.lcf.org
AMOUNT: Varies
DEADLINE(S): MAR 1
FIELD(S): All
ELIGIBILITY/REQUIREMENTS: Must be attending the University of Nebraska-Lincoln with senior standing in upcoming year; have minimum 3.2 GPA, be a qualified member of Kappa Chapter of Chi Omega in good standing; demonstrate service to Chi Omega and the university.
HOW TO APPLY: Submit application form, transcripts from all high schools, colleges and universities attended; copy of ACT/SAT or similar test scores; and essay "Explain how you have provided service to the Kappa Chapter of Chi Omega and the University during your college career" to Chi Omega Sorority Scholarship Committee, 480 North 16th Street, Lincoln, NE 68508.
NUMBER OF AWARDS: Varies

3673—LINCOLN COMMUNITY FOUNDATION (Anonymous Scholarships)

215 Centennial Mall South,
Suite 100
Lincoln NE 68508
402/474-2345
FAX: 402/476-8532
E-mail: lcf@lcf.org
Internet: http://www.lcf.org
AMOUNT: Varies
DEADLINE(S): APR 30
FIELD(S): All
ELIGIBILITY/REQUIREMENTS: Current graduating senior of Thayer, Nebraska, high schools (Bruning-Davenport, Deshler and Thayer County high schools). Must meet minimum standards for institutional admission; need not excel; students attending 2-year institutions encouraged to apply. Must demonstrate financial need.
HOW TO APPLY: Submit application form, transcripts from all high schools, colleges and universities attended; copy of ACT/SAT or similar test scores; and financial aid form.
NUMBER OF AWARDS: Varies
RENEWABLE: Yes, up to 5 years. Must submit grade transcript and enrollment verification each semester while in college.

3674—LINCOLN COMMUNITY FOUNDATION (BryanLGH Medical Center Volunteer Scholarship Fund)

215 Centennial Mall South,

Suite 100
Lincoln NE 68508
402/474-2345
FAX: 402/476-8532
E-mail: lcf@lcf.org
Internet: http://www.lcf.org
AMOUNT: $1,000
DEADLINE(S): MAR 1
FIELD(S): All
ELIGIBILITY/REQUIREMENTS: Open to current medical center volunteer; and have logged a minimum of 75 hours in the previous consecutive 12 months or a minimum of 1,230 hours over 3 preceding years. Must show proof of acceptance in an accredited, qualified, nonproprietary institution (college, university, trade school, school of nursing or metro tech college) in the U.S. Career goals, volunteer history, and communication through a personal essay and references are considered.
HOW TO APPLY: Applications available through Volunteer Resources, BryanLGH Medical Center. Submit application form to Foundations along with transcripts from all high schools attended; copy of ACT/SAT or similar test scores; and personal essay, references, and verification of volunteer hours.
NUMBER OF AWARDS: 2
RENEWABLE: No

3675—LINCOLN COMMUNITY FOUNDATION (Charles E. Jones Memorial Scholarship)

215 Centennial Mall South,
Suite 100
Lincoln NE 68508
402/474-2345
FAX: 402/476-8532
E-mail: lcf@lcf.org
Internet: http://www.lcf.org
AMOUNT: Approximately $500
DEADLINE(S): MAR 15
FIELD(S): All
ELIGIBILITY/REQUIREMENTS: Must be U.S. citizen, graduating from Lincoln High School (must have attended for at least 2 years); rank in top half of graduating class; demonstrate growth in citizenship; financial need; participation in at least 2 extracurricular activities during junior and senior years; potential for completing postsecondary degree; and acceptance at 2- or 4- year institution.
HOW TO APPLY: Submit application, personal and financial statement, 3 letters of recommendation and transcript to LHS Counseling Center, 2229 J Street, Lincoln, NE 68510.
NUMBER OF AWARDS: 1

3676—LINCOLN COMMUNITY FOUNDATION (Charles H. and Ester P. Miller Scholarship)

215 Centennial Mall South,
Suite 100
Lincoln NE 68508
402/474-2345
FAX: 402/476-8532
E-mail: lcf@lcf.org
Internet: http://www.lcf.org
AMOUNT: Varies
DEADLINE(S): MAR 24
FIELD(S): All
ELIGIBILITY/REQUIREMENTS: Current graduating senior of Elmwood-Murdock High School in Murdock, Nebraska. Must be seeking 2- or 4-year degree from an accredited institution; demonstrate academic achievement and financial need.
HOW TO APPLY: Submit application form; transcripts from all high schools, colleges and universities attended; copy of ACT/SAT or similar test scores to Elmwood-Murdock High School, 300 Wyoming Street, P.O. Box 407, Murdock, NE 68407 and send financial aid form to Foundation.
NUMBER OF AWARDS: Varies

3677—LINCOLN COMMUNITY FOUNDATION (Charles H. and Orene C. Hinds-Odell Nebraska High School Scholarship)

215 Centennial Mall South,
Suite 100
Lincoln NE 68508
402/474-2345
FAX: 402/476-8532
E-mail: lcf@lcf.org
Internet: http://www.lcf.org
AMOUNT: Varies
DEADLINE(S): APR 15
FIELD(S): All
ELIGIBILITY/REQUIREMENTS: Current graduating high school senior who resides in townships that were included in the former Odell High School district. Must demonstrate scholastic application and achievement with the intention of pursuing postsecondary education; must have minimum GPA of 2.7. Financial need only considered in event of a tie breaker in the selection process. Preference given to those who do not have a history of alcohol, tobacco or drug use.
HOW TO APPLY: Submit application to Diller-Odell High School, 188 Education Avenue, Odell, NE 68415 with transcripts from all high schools, colleges and universities attended, copy of ACT/SAT or simi-

lar test scores, and letters of recommendation.
NUMBER OF AWARDS: Varies
RENEWABLE: Yes. Up to 4 years; must submit proof of enrollment and transcripts; maintain 2.75 GPA.

3678—LINCOLN COMMUNITY FOUNDATION (Colleen Farrell Gerleman Scholarship)

215 Centennial Mall South,
Suite 100
Lincoln NE 68508
402/474-2345
FAX: 402/476-8532
E-mail: lcf@lcf.org
Internet: http://www.lcf.org
AMOUNT: Varies
DEADLINE(S): APR 15
FIELD(S): All
ELIGIBILITY/REQUIREMENTS: Current graduating senior of a public or private high school in Lancaster County, Nebraska, or must have been awarded a Gerleman Scholarship in a previous year and be reapplying; must demonstrate academic success in high school and/or college studies. Must demonstrate financial need.
HOW TO APPLY: Submit application form; transcripts from all high schools, colleges and universities attended; copy of ACT/SAT or similar test scores; financial aid form; and essay (essay topic changes each year, contact the Foundation for the current topic).
NUMBER OF AWARDS: Varies
RENEWABLE: Yes, must reapply.

3679—LINCOLN COMMUNITY FOUNDATION (Cornhusker Bank Scholarship/Lincoln High School)

215 Centennial Mall South,
Suite 100
Lincoln NE 68508
402/474-2345
FAX: 402/476-8532
E-mail: lcf@lcf.org
Internet: http://www.lcf.org
AMOUNT: $1,000
DEADLINE(S): MAR 15
FIELD(S): All
ELIGIBILITY/REQUIREMENTS: Current graduating senior from Lincoln High School in Lincoln; must demonstrate leadership, good character and citizenship; interest in business through choices of classes, work experience or extracurricular activities; need financial assistance; minimum 2.0 GPA; participation in at least 2 extracurricular activities or sports program

at Lincoln High; accepted for admission at an accredited 4-year institution in Nebraska, and plan to enroll for minimum of 12 credit hours/semester.
HOW TO APPLY: Submit application form, personal and financial statement, 3 letters of recommendation, and transcript to Lincoln High School Counseling Center, Room 213, 2229 J Street, Lincoln, NE 68510.
NUMBER OF AWARDS: 1
RENEWABLE: Yes. 2nd semester contingent on 2.5 GPA.

3680—LINCOLN COMMUNITY FOUNDATION (Cornhusker Bank Scholarship/Lincoln Northeast High School)

215 Centennial Mall South, Suite 100
Lincoln NE 68508
402/474-2345
FAX: 402/476-8532
E-mail: lcf@lcf.org
Internet: http://www.lcf.org
AMOUNT: $1,000
DEADLINE(S): MAY 1
FIELD(S): All
ELIGIBILITY/REQUIREMENTS: Current graduating senior from Lincoln Northeast High School in Lincoln, NE; must demonstrate leadership, good character and citizenship; interest in business through choices of classes, work experience or extracurricular activities; need financial assistance; minimum 2.5 GPA; participation in at least 2 extracurricular activities or sports program at Lincoln; accepted for admission at an accredited 4-year institution in Nebraska, and plan to enroll for minimum of 12 credit hours/semester.
HOW TO APPLY: Submit application form, personal and financial statement, 3 letters of recommendation, and transcript to Lincoln Northeast High School, 2635 North 63rd Street, Lincoln, NE 68507.
NUMBER OF AWARDS: 1
RENEWABLE: Yes. 2nd semester contingent on 2.5 GPA.

3681—LINCOLN COMMUNITY FOUNDATION (Dayle Wood Memorial Scholarship)

215 Centennial Mall South, Suite 100
Lincoln NE 68508
402/474-2345
FAX: 402/476-8532
E-mail: lcf@lcf.org
Internet: http://www.lcf.org

AMOUNT: Varies
DEADLINE(S): APR 15
FIELD(S): All
ELIGIBILITY/REQUIREMENTS: Current graduating senior of Palmyra Public Schools in Palmyra, Nebraska. Must demonstrate scholastic application and achievement; and intention to continue education. Financial need considered only as a tie-breaker. Funds will not be awarded until recipient completes 1 full year of college with continued evidence of achievement; GPA 3.0.
HOW TO APPLY: Submit application form; transcripts from all high schools, colleges and universities attended; copy of ACT/SAT or similar test scores; and financial aid form. Send all information EXCEPT financial aid form to Palmyra High School, P.O. Box 130, Palmyra, NE 68418. Mail financial information form to Foundation.
NUMBER OF AWARDS: Varies

3682—LINCOLN COMMUNITY FOUNDATION (Dick & Chris Draper Scholarship)

215 Centennial Mall South, Suite 100
Lincoln NE 68508
402/474-2345
FAX: 402/476-8532
E-mail: lcf@lcf.org
Internet: http://www.lcf.org
AMOUNT: Varies
DEADLINE(S): APR 15
FIELD(S): All
ELIGIBILITY/REQUIREMENTS: Current graduating senior who attended Elgin Public High School or Elgin Pope John XXIII Central Catholic High School in Elgin, Nebraska, for at least 4 years. Minimum GPA 3.25.
HOW TO APPLY: Submit application form; transcripts from all high schools, colleges and universities attended; copy of ACT/SAT or similar test scores; 3 letters of recommendation, 1 of which comes from school administrator; financial aid form; and 1-page essay (essay topic changes each year, contact Foundation for current topic). Submit application to applicant's respective school.
NUMBER OF AWARDS: 2 (1 from each school)

3683—LINCOLN COMMUNITY FOUNDATION (Duncan E. and Lillian M. McGregor Scholarship)

215 Centennial Mall South, Suite 100

Lincoln NE 68508
402/474-2345
FAX: 402/476-8532
E-mail: lcf@lcf.org
Internet: http://www.lcf.org
AMOUNT: Varies
DEADLINE(S): APR 15
FIELD(S): All
ELIGIBILITY/REQUIREMENTS: Current graduating senior or former graduate of Ansley, Arcadia, Gibbon, Sargent, Shelton, or Ord High Schools in Nebraska. Must demonstrate academic achievement in high school and/or college. Must have lived in a community serviced and maintained by an exchange served by the Nebraska Central Telephone Company during high school, and demonstrate financial need.
HOW TO APPLY: Submit application form; transcripts from all high schools, colleges and universities attended; copy of ACT/SAT or similar test scores; and financial aid form to high school attended.
NUMBER OF AWARDS: Varies
RENEWABLE: Yes, must reapply.

3684—LINCOLN COMMUNITY FOUNDATION (Elgin United Church of Christ Scholarship)

215 Centennial Mall South, Suite 100
Lincoln NE 68508
402/474-2345
FAX: 402/476-8532
E-mail: lcf@lcf.org
Internet: http://www.lcf.org
AMOUNT: Varies
DEADLINE(S): APR 25
FIELD(S): All
ELIGIBILITY/REQUIREMENTS: Current graduating senior who attended Elgin Public Schools in Elgin, Nebraska. Based on class rank, GPA, test scores, evidence of need, good moral character, promise of using education, letters of recommendation from business persons and member of the clergy. Minimum GPA 2.5.
HOW TO APPLY: See website for up-to-date criteria. Submit application form; transcripts from all high schools, colleges and universities attended; copy of ACT/SAT or similar test scores; personal résumé or essay indicating financial need and how you will utilize your education; 2 letters of recommendation from business person or clergy addressing student's scholastic achievement and promise, and moral character. Send to Superintendent, Elgin Public Schools, P.O. Box 399, Elgin, NE 68636.

3685—LINCOLN COMMUNITY FOUNDA-TION (Ernst Walter Nennemann Memorial Scholarship)

215 Centennial Mall South,
Suite 100
Lincoln NE 68508
402/474-2345
FAX: 402/476-8532
E-mail: lcf@lcf.org
Internet: http://www.lcf.org
AMOUNT: Varies
DEADLINE(S): APR 15
FIELD(S): All
ELIGIBILITY/REQUIREMENTS: Current graduating senior or former graduate of the high school in the Community School District of Sidney, Fremont County, Iowa. Former graduates must make application within 3 years of applicant's high school graduation date. Preference given to graduating seniors and male. Essential criterion for selection is academic performance; must be pursuing a 2- or 4-year undergraduate degree from a fully accredited college or university; must demonstrate financial need.
HOW TO APPLY: Submit application form; transcripts from all high schools, colleges and universities attended; copy of ACT/SAT or similar test scores; and biographical résumé (1 page or less) to Sidney Community School District, 2754 Knox Road, Sidney, IA 51652, and financial aid form to Foundation.
NUMBER OF AWARDS: Varies

3686—LINCOLN COMMUNITY FOUNDA-TION (Ethel M. Johnson Scholarship)

215 Centennial Mall South,
Suite 100
Lincoln NE 68508
402/474-2345
FAX: 402/476-8532
E-mail: lcf@lcf.org
Internet: http://www.lcf.org
AMOUNT: Varies
DEADLINE(S): APR 1
FIELD(S): All
ELIGIBILITY/REQUIREMENTS: Senior-level college student at Nebraska Wesleyan University in Lincoln.
HOW TO APPLY: Obtain application and additional information from Nebraska Wesleyan University, Financial Aid Office, 5500 St. Paul Avenue, Lincoln, NE 68504 and submit to University.
NUMBER OF AWARDS: Varies

3687—LINCOLN COMMUNITY FOUNDA-TION (George L. Watters Memorial Scholarship)

215 Centennial Mall South,

Suite 100
Lincoln NE 68508
402/474-2345
FAX: 402/476-8532
E-mail: lcf@lcf.org
Internet: http://www.lcf.org
AMOUNT: Varies
DEADLINE(S): MAR 15
FIELD(S): All
ELIGIBILITY/REQUIREMENTS: Must be the child of any Nebraska Petroleum Marketer and Convenience Store Association member or employee of member, who is current graduating high school senior. Must be in the upper third of the graduating class and must demonstrate academic achievement, leadership qualities and intention to pursue studies leading to a degree. Financial need considered.
HOW TO APPLY: Submit application form; transcripts from all high schools, colleges and universities attended; copy of ACT/SAT or similar test scores; 3 references (other than family); leadership positions held; and financial aid form to Grafton & Associates CPA's, 8101 Street, Suite 200, Lincoln, NE 68510.
NUMBER OF AWARDS: Varies

3688—LINCOLN COMMUNITY FOUNDA-TION (Grace Birkby Nennemann Memorial Scholarship)

215 Centennial Mall South,
Suite 100
Lincoln NE 68508
402/474-2345
FAX: 402/476-8532
E-mail: lcf@lcf.org
Internet: http://www.lcf.org
AMOUNT: Varies
DEADLINE(S): APR 15
FIELD(S): All
ELIGIBILITY/REQUIREMENTS: Current graduating senior or former graduate of the high school in the Community School District of Sidney, Fremont County, Iowa. Former graduates must make application within 3 years of applicant's high school graduation date. Preference given to graduating seniors and female. Essential criterion for selection is academic performance; must be pursuing a 2- or 4-year undergraduate degree from a fully accredited college or university; must demonstrate financial need.
HOW TO APPLY: Submit application form; transcripts from all high schools, colleges and universities attended; copy of ACT/SAT or similar test scores and biographical résumé (1 page or less) to Sidney Community School District, 2754 Knox Road, Sidney, IA 51652; and financial aid form to Foundation.

NUMBER OF AWARDS: Varies

3689—LINCOLN COMMUNITY FOUNDA-TION (Harry and Lenora Richardson-National Association of Postmasters of the United States Scholarship)

215 Centennial Mall South,
Suite 100
Lincoln NE 68508
402/474-2345
FAX: 402/476-8532
E-mail: lcf@lcf.org
Internet: http://www.lcf.org
AMOUNT: Varies
DEADLINE(S): APR 1
FIELD(S): All
ELIGIBILITY/REQUIREMENTS: Open to children or grandchildren of Association member. Must be current graduating high school senior; must attend a college or university in Nebraska. Based on academic achievement and participation in extracurricular and community activities.
HOW TO APPLY: Submit application form; transcripts from all high schools, colleges and universities attended; copy of ACT/SAT or similar test scores; 3 references (2 from high school teachers), leadership positions held; and financial aid form to Scholarship Chairperson, P.O. Box 1, Tobias, NE 68453.
NUMBER OF AWARDS: 1

3690—LINCOLN COMMUNITY FOUNDA-TION (Harry and Lenora Richardson-Nebraska Branch of the National League of Postmasters Scholarship)

215 Centennial Mall South,
Suite 100
Lincoln NE 68508
402/474-2345
FAX: 402/476-8532
E-mail: lcf@lcf.org
Internet: http://www.lcf.org
AMOUNT: Varies
DEADLINE(S): MAR 15
FIELD(S): All
ELIGIBILITY/REQUIREMENTS: Open to children or grandchildren of a League member. Must be current graduating high school senior; must attend a college or university in Nebraska. Based on eligibility, GPA and contributions to school and community activities.
HOW TO APPLY: Submit application form; transcripts from all high schools, colleges and universities attended; copy of ACT/SAT or similar test scores; 3 references (2 from high school teachers); leadership positions held; and financial aid

form to Sharleen Miller, 85342 488th Avenue, Chambers, NE 68725.
NUMBER OF AWARDS: 1

3691—LINCOLN COMMUNITY FOUNDATION (Harry Richardson-Cedars Scholarship)

215 Centennial Mall South,
Suite 100
Lincoln NE 68508
402/474-2345
FAX: 402/476-8532
E-mail: lcf@lcf.org
Internet: http://www.lcf.org
AMOUNT: Varies
DEADLINE(S): APR 1
FIELD(S): All
ELIGIBILITY/REQUIREMENTS: Must have a high school diploma or GED and have been a recipient of any service offered by Cedars Youth Services in Lincoln, NE. Must complete the FAFSA form prior to applying for scholarship.
HOW TO APPLY: Submit application form; letter of reference from a Cedars staff member, coach, pastor, counselor, teacher; and student essay to Kerrie Saunders, Cedars Youth Services, 620 North 48th Street, Lincoln, NE 68504.
NUMBER OF AWARDS: Varies
RENEWABLE: Yes. Must reapply.

3692—LINCOLN COMMUNITY FOUNDATION (Hugh and Nainie Stoddard Scholarship)

215 Centennial Mall South,
Suite 100
Lincoln NE 68508
402/474-2345
FAX: 402/476-8532
E-mail: lcf@lcf.org
Internet: http://www.lcf.org
AMOUNT: Varies
DEADLINE(S): MAR 15
FIELD(S): All (emphasis on
environmental and societal problems)
ELIGIBILITY/REQUIREMENTS: Current graduating senior of Johnson-Brock High School in Johnson, Nebraska. Must rank in top third of graduating class; priority given to students who plan to develop scientific knowledge and analytical tools for the purpose of solving environmental and/or societal problems.
HOW TO APPLY: Submit application form; transcripts from all high schools, colleges and universities attended; copy of ACT/SAT or similar test scores, to Johnson-Brock High School, 310 Main Street, P.O. Box 186, Johnson, NE 68378.

3693—LINCOLN COMMUNITY FOUNDATION (Jeffries-Park Scholarship)

215 Centennial Mall South,
Suite 100
Lincoln NE 68508
402/474-2345
FAX: 402/476-8532
E-mail: lcf@lcf.org
Internet: http://www.lcf.org
AMOUNT: Varies
DEADLINE(S): APR 15
FIELD(S): All
ELIGIBILITY/REQUIREMENTS: Current graduating senior of Ord High School in Ord, Nebraska. Must be in top 15% of graduating class; must attend a college in a program leading to a 4-year degree. Financial need considered only as a tie-breaker in the selection process.
HOW TO APPLY: Submit application to Ord High School, 1800 K Street, P.O. Box 199, Ord, NE 68862 with transcripts from all high schools attended and copy of ACT/SAT or similar test scores.
NUMBER OF AWARDS: Varies

3694—LINCOLN COMMUNITY FOUNDATION (Jennings and Beulah Haggerty Scholarship)

215 Centennial Mall South,
Suite 100
Lincoln NE 68508
402/474-2345
FAX: 402/476-8532
E-mail: lcf@lcf.org
Internet: http://www.lcf.org
AMOUNT: Varies
DEADLINE(S): JUL 1
FIELD(S): All
ELIGIBILITY/REQUIREMENTS: Current graduating high school senior of a public or private high school in Lincoln, Nebraska. Must be ranked in top 1/3 of graduating class. Preference given to applicant planning to attend accredited 2- or 4-year college in Nebraska. Must demonstrate financial need and must apply for aid from institution to be attended.
HOW TO APPLY: Submit application to Foundation with transcripts from all high schools, colleges and universities attended; copy of ACT/SAT or similar test scores; letters of recommendation; and 1-page essay (essay topic changes each year, contact Foundation for the current topic).
NUMBER OF AWARDS: Varies

3695—LINCOLN COMMUNITY FOUNDATION (Jerry Solomon Scholarship)

215 Centennial Mall South,

Suite 100
Lincoln NE 68508
402/474-2345
FAX: 402/476-8532
E-mail: lcf@lcf.org
Internet: http://www.lcf.org
AMOUNT: Varies
DEADLINE(S): Late MAR
FIELD(S): All
ELIGIBILITY/REQUIREMENTS: Current graduating senior who attended Culbertson High School in Culbertson, NE, prior to its closure and merger. Must demonstrate assertiveness, ambition, character, participation in activities, academic performance and financial need.
HOW TO APPLY: Submit application form; transcripts from all high schools, colleges and universities attended; copy of ACT/SAT or similar test scores, to Hitchcock County Unified School District, 318 West D, P.O. Box 368, Trenton, NE 69044.
NUMBER OF AWARDS: Varies

3696—LINCOLN COMMUNITY FOUNDATION (Kappa Kappa Gamma-Seacrest Scholarship)

215 Centennial Mall South,
Suite 100
Lincoln NE 68508
402/474-2345
FAX: 402/476-8532
E-mail: lcf@lcf.org
Internet: http://www.lcf.org
AMOUNT: Varies
DEADLINE(S): APR
FIELD(S): All
ELIGIBILITY/REQUIREMENTS: Must be current college student at the University of Nebraska-Lincoln and member in good standing of KKG; demonstrate financial need and academic success.
HOW TO APPLY: Submit application form, transcripts, financial aid form to KKG Scholarship Committee.
NUMBER OF AWARDS: Varies
CONTACT: Beth McElroy, Kappa Kappa Gamma Scholarship Chair, 6801 South 44th Street, Lincoln, NE 68516

3697—LINCOLN COMMUNITY FOUNDATION (Louis C. and Amy E. Nuernberger Scholarship)

215 Centennial Mall South,
Suite 100
Lincoln NE 68508
402/474-2345
FAX: 402/476-8532
E-mail: lcf@lcf.org

Internet: http://www.lcf.org
AMOUNT: Varies
DEADLINE(S): Early APR
FIELD(S): All
ELIGIBILITY/REQUIREMENTS:
Current graduating senior or former high school graduate who has been employed by the Wakefield Health Care Center for at least 1 year. Must demonstrate potential for achievement of educational goals and show quality of service given at the Wakefield Health Care Center. Primary consideration given to candidates having realistic goals and displaying talent and potential in their field of choice; seriousness of purpose, reliability, initiative, ability to work both independently and with people; and competence in oral and written communication considered.
HOW TO APPLY: Submit application form; transcripts from all high schools, colleges and universities attended; copy of ACT/SAT or similar test scores and biographical résumé (1 page or less) to Wakefield Health Care Center, 306 Ash Street, Wakefield, NE 68784-5023.
NUMBER OF AWARDS: Varies
RENEWABLE: Yes. Up to 2 years; submit proof of enrollment and transcripts each semester.

3698—LINCOLN COMMUNITY FOUNDATION (Margaret C. Stednitz Scholarship)

215 Centennial Mall South,
Suite 100
Lincoln NE 68508
402/474-2345
FAX: 402/476-8532
E-mail: lcf@lcf.org
Internet: http://www.lcf.org
AMOUNT: Varies
DEADLINE(S): APR 15
FIELD(S): All
ELIGIBILITY/REQUIREMENTS:
Current graduating senior of Lincoln Northeast High School in Lincoln, Nebraska. Must demonstrate scholastic application and achievement and intend to continue education and financial need. Not awarded until completion of 1 full year of college with continued evidence of achievement; GPA of 3.0.
HOW TO APPLY: Submit application form; transcripts from all high schools, colleges and universities attended; copy of ACT/SAT or similar test scores, to Lincoln Northeast High School, 2365 North 63rd Street, Lincoln, NE 68507; send financial information form to Foundation.
NUMBER OF AWARDS: Varies

3699—LINCOLN COMMUNITY FOUNDATION (Marian Othmer Schultz Scholarship)

215 Centennial Mall South,
Suite 100
Lincoln NE 68508
402/474-2345
FAX: 402/476-8532
E-mail: lcf@lcf.org
Internet: http://www.lcf.org
AMOUNT: Varies
DEADLINE(S): AUG 1
FIELD(S): All
ELIGIBILITY/REQUIREMENTS: Must be member in good standing of the Alpha Epsilon Chapter of the Alpha Delta Pi Sorority at the University of Nebraska-Lincoln, and a junior-level student with a GPA in the top 10% of sorority members; and demonstrate leadership ability in the total campus community.
HOW TO APPLY: Submit application form, transcripts, financial aid form to Scholarship Chairperson, 2223 Van Dorn Street, Lincoln NE 68502.
NUMBER OF AWARDS: Varies

3700—LINCOLN COMMUNITY FOUNDATION (Max and Margaret Pumphrey Scholarship)

215 Centennial Mall South,
Suite 100
Lincoln NE 68508
402/474-2345
FAX: 402/476-8532
E-mail: lcf@lcf.org
Internet: http://www.lcf.org
AMOUNT: Varies
DEADLINE(S): APR 1; JUL 1
FIELD(S): All
ELIGIBILITY/REQUIREMENTS:
Current graduating senior or former graduate of a high school in Lancaster County in Nebraska. Preferred that applicant plan to attend an accredited 2- or 4-year university or college in Nebraska. Must demonstrate financial need and must apply for financial aid at the institution to be attended.
HOW TO APPLY: Submit application form; transcripts from all high schools, colleges and universities attended; copy of ACT/SAT or similar test scores; financial aid form; essay (essay topic changes each year, contact Foundation for the current topic); and 2 current letters of recommendation written by teachers, counselors, clergy, employers, neighbors.
NUMBER OF AWARDS: Varies

RENEWABLE: Yes, must reapply. Must demonstrate satisfactory progress and continued financial need.

3701—LINCOLN COMMUNITY FOUNDATION (Miriam Croft Moeller Citizenship Award)

215 Centennial Mall South,
Suite 100
Lincoln NE 68508
402/474-2345
FAX: 402/476-8532
E-mail: lcf@lcf.org
Internet: http://www.lcf.org
AMOUNT: Varies
DEADLINE(S): APR 15
FIELD(S): All
ELIGIBILITY/REQUIREMENTS:
Current graduating senior of a public or private high school in Lincoln, Nebraska. Must hold a keen interest in citizenship and actively participate and demonstrate enthusiasm for community betterment and leadership; need not excel academically or maintain a specific GPA, but must meet minimum standards for college admission, and must be seeking 2- or 4-year degree from an accredited institution.
HOW TO APPLY: Submit application form; transcripts from all high schools, colleges and universities attended; copy of ACT/SAT or similar test scores to Foundation.
NUMBER OF AWARDS: Varies

3702—LINCOLN COMMUNITY FOUNDATION (Nebraska Rural School Scholarship)

215 Centennial Mall South,
Suite 100
Lincoln NE 68508
402/474-2345
FAX: 402/476-8532
E-mail: lcf@lcf.org
Internet: http://www.lcf.org
AMOUNT: Varies
DEADLINE(S): JUN 1; AUG 1
FIELD(S): All
ELIGIBILITY/REQUIREMENTS:
Current graduating senior or former graduate of a rural (population 10,000 or less) high school in Nebraska. Must have graduated during the current year in the top 10% of graduating class or be a current college student maintaining minimum 3.5 GPA at the 2- or 4- year Nebraska college/university student is attending. Must demonstrate financial need.
HOW TO APPLY: Submit application form; transcripts from all high schools, col-

leges and universities attended; copy of ACT/SAT or similar test scores to Foundation; financial aid form; and essay (essay topic changes each year, contact Foundation for the current topic).
NUMBER OF AWARDS: Varies

3703—LINCOLN COMMUNITY FOUNDATION (Norman and Ruth Good Scholarship)

215 Centennial Mall South,
Suite 100
Lincoln NE 68508
402/474-2345
FAX: 402/476-8532
E-mail: lcf@lcf.org
Internet: http://www.lcf.org
AMOUNT: Varies
DEADLINE(S): APR 15
FIELD(S): All
ELIGIBILITY/REQUIREMENTS: Current college student attending a private college in Nebraska with a junior or senior standing, minimum GPA 3.5.
HOW TO APPLY: Submit application form and transcripts from all colleges and universities attended to Foundation.
NUMBER OF AWARDS: Varies

3704—LINCOLN COMMUNITY FOUNDATION (Pauline and Sanford Saunders Scholarship)

215 Centennial Mall South,
Suite 100
Lincoln NE 68508
402/474-2345
FAX: 402/476-8532
E-mail: lcf@lcf.org
Internet: http://www.lcf.org
AMOUNT: Varies
DEADLINE(S): APR 15
FIELD(S): All
ELIGIBILITY/REQUIREMENTS: Current graduating senior of Creighton High School in Creighton, Nebraska. Must demonstrate academic success and possess ability to do postsecondary work in a satisfactory manner; must demonstrate financial need.
HOW TO APPLY: Submit application form; transcripts from all high schools, colleges and universities attended; copy of ACT/SAT or similar test scores to Creighton High School, P.O. Box 10, Creighton, NE 68729. Financial information form should be mailed or delivered to Lincoln Community Foundation.
NUMBER OF AWARDS: Varies

3705—LINCOLN COMMUNITY FOUNDATION (P. G. Richardson-Masonic Memorial Scholarship)

215 Centennial Mall South,
Suite 100
Lincoln NE 68508
402/474-2345
FAX: 402/476-8532
E-mail: lcf@lcf.org
Internet: http://www.lcf.org
AMOUNT: Varies
DEADLINE(S): MAR 10
FIELD(S): All
ELIGIBILITY/REQUIREMENTS: Open to children, grandchildren or relative of a member of Custer Lodge #148 A.F. & A.M. enrolled in a nonprofit accredited university, college or technical school. Based on high school grades and activities, GPA, class rank, ACT/SAT scores, community and church activities, special hobbies or interests, and recommendations.
HOW TO APPLY: Application available from guidance counselor or principal. Submit with transcript, GPA, class rank and ACT/SAT scores, 2 letters of recommendation from non-family members and list of activities and organizations participated in to Scholarship Chairperson, 611 South N Street, Broken Bow, NE 68822.
NUMBER OF AWARDS: 1

3706—LINCOLN COMMUNITY FOUNDATION (P. G. Richardson-Nebraska Cottey College Scholarship)

215 Centennial Mall South,
Suite 100
Lincoln NE 68508
402/474-2345
FAX: 402/476-8532
E-mail: lcf@lcf.org
Internet: http://www.lcf.org
AMOUNT: Varies
DEADLINE(S): JAN 1
FIELD(S): All
ELIGIBILITY/REQUIREMENTS: Must be attending Cottey Junior College in Nevada or Missouri; be a Nebraska resident and meet other requirements determined by College.
HOW TO APPLY: Submit application and required attachments to Janis Opperman, 10731 Berry Plaza, Omaha, NE 68127.
NUMBER OF AWARDS: Varies

3707—LINCOLN COMMUNITY FOUNDATION (Phil Heckman Scholarship)

215 Centennial Mall South,

Suite 100
Lincoln NE 68508
402/474-2345
FAX: 402/476-8532
E-mail: lcf@lcf.org
Internet: http://www.lcf.org
AMOUNT: Varies
DEADLINE(S): APR 15
FIELD(S): All
ELIGIBILITY/REQUIREMENTS: Current graduating high school senior of a public or private high school in Lincoln, Nebraska. Must demonstrate academic success and be pursuing undergraduate studies at Doane College in Crete, Nebraska. Must demonstrate financial need.
HOW TO APPLY: Submit application to Foundation with transcripts from all high schools, colleges and universities attended; copy of ACT/SAT or similar test scores; and letters of recommendation.
NUMBER OF AWARDS: Varies

3708—LINCOLN COMMUNITY FOUNDATION (Ralph and Jean Cuca Scholarship)

215 Centennial Mall South,
Suite 100
Lincoln NE 68508
402/474-2345
FAX: 402/476-8532
E-mail: lcf@lcf.org
Internet: http://www.lcf.org
AMOUNT: Varies
DEADLINE(S): APR 1
FIELD(S): All
ELIGIBILITY/REQUIREMENTS: Current graduating senior of a public school in Lincoln, Nebraska. Must demonstrate academic achievement and financial need.
HOW TO APPLY: Submit application form; transcripts from all high schools, colleges and universities attended; copy of ACT/SAT or similar test scores; 2 letters of recommendation from teachers with whom the applicant has taken classes; and financial aid form.
NUMBER OF AWARDS: Varies

3709—LINCOLN COMMUNITY FOUNDATION (Randy Vollertsen Memorial Scholarship)

215 Centennial Mall South,
Suite 100
Lincoln NE 68508
402/474-2345
FAX: 402/476-8532
E-mail: lcf@lcf.org

Internet: http://www.lcf.org
AMOUNT: Varies
DEADLINE(S): APR 15
FIELD(S): All
ELIGIBILITY/REQUIREMENTS:
Current graduating senior of Palmyra
Public Schools in Palmyra, Nebraska. Must
demonstrate scholastic application and
achievement; must seek a 4-year undergraduate degree from a fully accredited
college or university; demonstrate finan-
cial need. Funds will not be awarded until
recipient completes 1 full year of college
with continued evidence of achievement;
GPA 3.0.
HOW TO APPLY: Submit application
form; transcripts from all high schools, colleges and universities attended; copy of
ACT/SAT or similar test scores; and financial aid form. Send all information
EXCEPT financial aid form to Palmyra
High School, P.O. Box 130, Palmyra, NE
68418. Mail financial information form to
Foundation.
NUMBER OF AWARDS: Varies

3710—LINCOLN COMMUNITY FOUNDA-TION (Sam Jacobitz Memorial Scholarship)

215 Centennial Mall South,
Suite 100
Lincoln NE 68508
402/474-2345
FAX: 402/476-8532
E-mail: lcf@lcf.org
Internet: http://www.lcf.org
AMOUNT: Varies
DEADLINE(S): APR 15
FIELD(S): All
ELIGIBILITY/REQUIREMENTS:
Current graduating high school senior of
Rock County High School in Bassett,
Nebraska. Must demonstrate scholastic
application and achievement and ability to
do postsecondary education; must demon-
strate financial need.
HOW TO APPLY: Submit application to
Foundation with transcripts from all high
schools, colleges and universities attended;
copy of ACT/SAT or similar test scores.
NUMBER OF AWARDS: Varies

3711—LINCOLN COMMUNITY FOUNDA-TION (Thelma Nennemann Aspegren Memorial Scholarship)

215 Centennial Mall South,
Suite 100
Lincoln NE 68508
402/474-2345
FAX: 402/476-8532
E-mail: lcf@lcf.org
Internet: http://www.lcf.org

AMOUNT: Varies
DEADLINE(S): APR 15
FIELD(S): All
ELIGIBILITY/REQUIREMENTS:
Current graduating senior or former graduate of the high school in the Community
School District of Hamburg, Fremont
County, Iowa. Former graduates must
apply within 3 years of graduation.
Preference given to current graduating
seniors and females. Must demonstrate
strong scholastic achievement; must be
pursuing a 2- or 4-year undergraduate
degree from a fully accredited college or
university. Must demonstrate financial
need.
HOW TO APPLY: Submit application
form; transcripts from all high schools, colleges and universities attended; copy of
ACT/SAT or similar test scores; and financial aid form. Send all information
EXCEPT financial aid form to Hamburg
High School, 105 E Street, Hamburg, IA
51640. Mail financial information form to
Foundation.
NUMBER OF AWARDS: Varies

3712—LINCOLN COMMUNITY FOUNDA-TION (Thomas C. Woods Jr. Memorial Scholarship)

215 Centennial Mall South,
Suite 100
Lincoln NE 68508
402/474-2345
FAX: 402/476-8532
E-mail: lcf@lcf.org
Internet: http://www.lcf.org
AMOUNT: Varies
DEADLINE(S): APR 17
FIELD(S): All
ELIGIBILITY/REQUIREMENTS:
Current graduating senior or former grad-
uate of a public or private high school in
Adams, Butler, Cass, Clay, Filmore, Gage,
Hamilton, Jefferson, Johnson, Lancaster,
Nemaha, Nuckolls, Otoe, Pawnee, Polk,
Richardson, Salien, Saunders, Seward,
Thayer, Webster or York Counties,
Nebraska. Parent or legal guardian must
be employed by ALLTEL and previously
employed by Aliant Communications
prior to July 2, 1999. Must demonstrate
academic success and must be pursuing
undergraduate studies at a university or
college in Nebraska. Financial need will be
considered.
HOW TO APPLY: Submit application
form; transcripts from all high schools, colleges and universities attended; copy of
ACT/SAT or similar test scores; and financial aid form.
NUMBER OF AWARDS: Varies

3713—LINCOLN COMMUNITY FOUNDA-TION (Vern and Iola Finke Scholarship)

215 Centennial Mall South,
Suite 100
Lincoln NE 68508
402/474-2345
FAX: 402/476-8532
E-mail: lcf@lcf.org
Internet: http://www.lcf.org
AMOUNT: Varies
DEADLINE(S): APR 15
FIELD(S): All (emphasis on home
economics & agriculture)
ELIGIBILITY/REQUIREMENTS:
Current graduating senior of Palmyra
Public Schools in Palmyra, Nebraska. Must
demonstrate involvement in school activi-
ties; must seek an undergraduate degree
and pursue full-time studies. Priority given
to majors in Home Economics or
Agriculture. Must demonstrate need.
HOW TO APPLY: Submit application
form; transcripts from all high schools, col-
leges and universities attended; copy of
ACT/SAT or similar test scores; and finan-
cial aid form. Send all information
EXCEPT financial aid form to Palmyra
High School, P.O. Box 130, Palmyra, NE
68418. Mail financial information form to
Foundation.
NUMBER OF AWARDS: Varies

3714—LINCOLN COMMUNITY FOUNDA-TION (Wayne J. and Wanda M. Lillich Scholarship)

215 Centennial Mall South,
Suite 100
Lincoln NE 68508
402/474-2345
FAX: 402/476-8532
E-mail: lcf@lcf.org
Internet: http://www.lcf.org
AMOUNT: Up to $2,000
DEADLINE(S): MAR 15
FIELD(S): Medicine; Religion; Business
ELIGIBILITY/REQUIREMENTS:
Current graduating senior of Tecumseh
High School in Tecumseh, Nebraska. Must
demonstrate academic success and must
possess ability to do postsecondary work in
a satisfactory manner. Must demonstrate
financial need. Submit application to
Tecumseh Public Schools, P.O. Box 338,
358 North 6th Street, Tecumseh, NE
68450. Financial information form should
be mailed or delivered to Lincoln
Community Foundation.
HOW TO APPLY: Submit application
form; transcripts from all high schools, colleges and universities attended; copy of

ACT/SAT or similar test scores; and financial aid form.

3715—LINCOLN COMMUNITY FOUNDATION (White Memorial Scholarship)

215 Centennial Mall South,
Suite 100
Lincoln NE 68508
402/474-2345
FAX: 402/476-8532
E-mail: lcf@lcf.org
Internet: http://www.lcf.org
AMOUNT: Varies
DEADLINE(S): MAR 15
FIELD(S): Medicine; Religion; Business
ELIGIBILITY/REQUIREMENTS: Must be current graduating senior or a former graduate of any high school in Nebraska (preference given to graduates of Lyons, Lincoln, and Fairbury high schools) for attendance at any qualified, nonprofit 2- or 4-year college or university. Must meet minimum standards for institutional admission, but need not excel academically or maintain a specific GPA, although preference will be given to students who maintain academic capacity to pursue higher education, but who may not meet criteria of other academic-based awards. (In the event of a tie, preference given to first-generation college students.) Must also demonstrate financial need.
HOW TO APPLY: Submit application form; transcripts from all high schools, colleges and universities attended; copy of ACT/SAT or similar test scores; 1-page essay explaining how your choice of a trade or career will impact your life and contribute to your self-sufficiency; and financial aid form.
NUMBER OF AWARDS: Varies
RENEWABLE: Yes. Up to 4 years.

3716—LINCOLN COMMUNITY FOUNDATION (William Ray Judah Scholarship)

215 Centennial Mall South,
Suite 100
Lincoln NE 68508
402/474-2345
FAX: 402/476-8532
E-mail: lcf@lcf.org
Internet: http://www.lcf.org
AMOUNT: Approximately $500
DEADLINE(S): MAR 15
FIELD(S): All
ELIGIBILITY/REQUIREMENTS: Must be current graduating senior or former graduate of Norris High School in Firth, Nebraska. Must possess ability to do post-secondary work; demonstrate financial

need. Preference given to applicant planning to attend institution in Nebraska.
HOW TO APPLY: Submit application, transcripts, ACT/SAT or similar test scores to Norris High School, P.O. Box 93A, Firth, NE 68005. Send financial information form to Foundation.
NUMBER OF AWARDS: Varies
RENEWABLE: Yes. Must reapply; demonstrate academic progress and financial need.

3717—LLOYD D. SWEET EDUCATIONAL FOUNDATION

Box 638
Chinook MT 59523
406/357-2532
E-mail: debk.davies@gmail.com
Internet: http://www.chinook
montana.com/LloydSweet.html
AMOUNT: $1,000-$2,500
DEADLINE(S): MAR 1
FIELD(S): All
ELIGIBILITY/REQUIREMENTS: Scholarships open to graduates of Chinook High School in Chinook, MT, for full-time undergraduate or graduate study at accredited colleges and universities in the U.S. Must carry at least 12 credits and a 2.0 GPA.
HOW TO APPLY: See website or e-mail for information using "Foundation" in subject line.
NUMBER OF AWARDS: Approximately 75
RENEWABLE: Yes
CONTACT: Debra Davies

3718—LONG & FOSTER REAL ESTATE, INC.

11351 Random Hills Road
Fairfax VA 22030-6082
703/359-1757
FAX: 703/591-5493
E-mail: erin.wendel@longand
foster.com
Internet: http://www.longand
foster.com/scholarship
AMOUNT: $1,000
DEADLINE(S): MAR 1
FIELD(S): All
ELIGIBILITY/REQUIREMENTS: Must be a U.S. citizen, have a 3.0 GPA or higher, demonstrate financial need, and be a leader in school and community. Only available to high school seniors in MD/DC/parts of VA, parts of NJ, parts of NC, parts of WV, parts of PA and parts of DE.
HOW TO APPLY: Contact Public Relations Coordinator for information and application. In addition to application,

signed by guidance counselor and parents, submit transcript, financial need statement, FAFSA, activities résumé, letter of recommendation from faculty member or guidance counselor, and a 1- to 2-page essay on a meaningful high school experience or expectations for college.
NUMBER OF AWARDS: 200
RENEWABLE: No
CONTACT: Erin Wendel, Public Relations Coordinator (http://www.nevada-womensfund.org/scholarships.html)

3719—LUBBOCK AREA FOUNDATION, INC.

1655 Main Street, #209
Lubbock TX 79401
806/762-8061
FAX: 806/762-8551
E-mail: contact@lubbockarea
foundation.org
Internet: http://www.lubbockarea
foundation.org/
AMOUNT: Varies
DEADLINE(S): Varies
FIELD(S): All
ELIGIBILITY/REQUIREMENTS: Several scholarships are administered by this Foundation for graduates of local high schools and students at local universities. Must be connected with one of the institutions.
HOW TO APPLY: Contact organization for names of institutions and how to apply.

3720—MAINE VETERANS' SERVICES (Grants for Dependents)

State House Station 117
Augusta ME 04333-0117
207/626-4464 or 800/345-0116
AMOUNT: Tuition
DEADLINE(S): None
FIELD(S): All
ELIGIBILITY/REQUIREMENTS: Open to Maine residents who are children/step-children (high school graduates, ages 16-21) or spouses of military veterans who are totally disabled due to service or who died in service or as a result of service. Tenable for undergraduate study at all branches of University of Maine system, all State of Maine vo-tech colleges, and Maine Maritime Academy at Castine. Must have lived in Maine at time of entering service or for 5 years prior to application.
HOW TO APPLY: Contact Maine Veterans' Services for an application.

3721—MARIE L. ROSE HUGUENOT SOCIETY OF AMERICA

122 East 58th Street

New York NY 10022
212/755-0592
FAX: 212/317-0676
E-mail: hugsoc@verizon.net
Internet: http://www.huguenot
societyofamerica.org
AMOUNT: $3,000
DEADLINE(S): JUN 1
FIELD(S): All
ELIGIBILITY/REQUIREMENTS: For American undergraduates who submit proof of descent from a Huguenot who emigrated from France and either settled in what is now the U.S. or left France for countries other than America before 1787. Only students approved by one of the participating colleges may apply; no application sent directly to the Huguenot Society will be considered.
HOW TO APPLY: Contact your school's financial aid office for an application or contact Society for a list of participating colleges/universities.
NUMBER OF AWARDS: 25
RENEWABLE: Yes
CONTACT: Mary Bertschmann

3722—MARINE CORPS SCHOLARSHIP FOUNDATION (Scholarships to Sons and Daughters of Marines)

P.O. Box 3008
Princeton NJ 08543-3008
800/292-7777 or 609/921-3534
FAX: 609/452-2259
E-mail: mcsfva@mcsf.org
Internet: http://www.mcsf.
com/site/c.ivKVLaMTIuG/
b.1677655/k.BEA8/Home.htm
AMOUNT: $500-$10,000
DEADLINE(S): MAR 1 graduating high school seniors; APR 15 all other applicants
FIELD(S): All
ELIGIBILITY/REQUIREMENTS: Open to sons/daughters of current or former Marines, Navy Corpsmen who have served with the Marines; grandchildren of U.S. Marines who served with the 4th Marine Division during World War II and is/was a member of their association or a U.S. Marine who served with the 6th Marine Division during WWII and is/was a member of their association. Preference given to an applicant whose parent was killed or wounded in action. Applicants must be seniors or high school graduates or be enrolled in an accredited college or vocational school. Parents' combined income cannot exceed $63,000 (adjusted if more than one family member is eligible).
HOW TO APPLY: See website (http://www.mcsf.org) or write for application.

NO phone requests. A certificate of service, showing "character of service" or grandparent's honorable discharge, scholastic transcripts from high school or colleges attended; a 300-word essay on a subject chosen each year, and a photograph must accompany application.
RENEWABLE: Yes. Must reapply; up to 4 awards.
CONTACT: Katie Griffin Hand, 866/496-5462

3723—MARY E. HODGES FUND

222 Tauton Avenue
East Providence RI 02914-4556
401/435-4650
AMOUNT: Varies
DEADLINE(S): APR 15
FIELD(S): All
ELIGIBILITY/REQUIREMENTS: Undergraduate scholarships for students who have a Rhode Island Masonic affiliation or who have been residents of Rhode Island for at least 5 years.
HOW TO APPLY: Call or send SASE for application.
CONTACT: Chairman, Scholarship Committee

3724—MAY THOMPSON HENRY SCHOLARSHIP TRUST

Central National Bank and Trust Co.
P.O. Box 3448
Enid OK 73702
580/233-3535
FAX: 580/249-5941
E-mail: bhinther@cnb-enid.com
Internet: http://www.cnb-ok.com
AMOUNT: $1,000
DEADLINE(S): APR 1
FIELD(S): All
ELIGIBILITY/REQUIREMENTS: For attendance at state-supported Oklahoma colleges, universities, or technical schools.
HOW TO APPLY: Contact Trust Department for an application. Submit with transcript, letter explaining financial need along with 3 letters of reference.
NUMBER OF AWARDS: Varies
RENEWABLE: Yes. Submit transcript; up 4 years.
CONTACT: Trust Department

3725—MENSA EDUCATION AND RESEARCH FOUNDATION SCHOLARSHIP PROGRAM

Internet: http://www.mensa
foundation.org/AM/Template.cfm?
Section=Scholarships1
DEADLINE(S): DEC 31

FIELD(S): All
ELIGIBILITY/REQUIREMENTS: Awards based on essays written by the applicant. No requirement for Mensa membership nor is consideration given for grades, academic program or financial need. Applicants must currently be a resident of a participating American Mensa local group's area and enrolled in a degree program in an accredited U.S. institution of higher learning during the academic year following the application date.
HOW TO APPLY: Each year the list of participating groups may change, see website for up-to-date information. Send application (if eligible) or request with SASE from local scholarship chairs. Submit application (if eligible) and essay of not more than 550 words explaining your academic and/or vocational goals and how you plan to achieve those goals.

3726—MENSA EDUCATION AND RESEARCH (McGrew-Fruecht Scholarship)

Internet: http://www.mensa
foundation.org/AM/Template.cfm?
Section=Scholarships1
AMOUNT: $500
DEADLINE(S): JAN 15
FIELD(S): All; Physics; Chemistry
ELIGIBILITY/REQUIREMENTS: May be enrolled at time of application. Awards based on essays written by the applicant. No requirement for Mensa membership nor is consideration given for grades, academic program or financial need. Applicants must currently be a resident of a participating American Mensa local group's area and enrolled in a degree program in an accredited U.S. institution of higher learning during the academic year following the application date.
HOW TO APPLY: Each year the list of participating groups may change, see website for up-to-date information. Send application, available (if eligible) from the website or, by request with SASE, from local scholarship chairs. Submit with essay of not more than 550 words explaining your academic and/or vocational goals and plans to achieve those goals to the scholarship chair in your area.

3727—MENSA EDUCATION AND RESEARCH FOUNDATION (Mensa Member Award)

Internet: http://www.mensa
foundation.org/AM/Template.cfm?
Section=Scholarships1
AMOUNT: $1,000
DEADLINE(S): JAN 15

FIELD(S): All

ELIGIBILITY/REQUIREMENTS: May be enrolled at time of application. Awards based on essays written by the applicant. No requirement for Mensa membership nor is consideration given for grades, academic program or financial need. Applicants must currently be a resident of a participating American Mensa local group's area and enrolled in a degree program in an accredited U.S. institution of higher learning during the academic year following the application date.

HOW TO APPLY: Each year the list of participating groups may change, see website for up-to-date information. Send application, available (if eligible) from the website or, by request with SASE, from local scholarship chairs. Submit with essay of not more than 550 words explaining your academic and/or vocational goals and plans to achieve those goals to the scholarship chair in your area.

3728—MENSA EDUCATION AND RESEARCH FOUNDATION (Rita Levine Memorial Scholarship)

Internet: http://www.mensa foundation.org/AM/Template.cfm? Section=Scholarships1
AMOUNT: $600
DEADLINE(S): JAN 15
FIELD(S): All

ELIGIBILITY/REQUIREMENTS: Open to a woman returning to school after an absence of 7 or more years. May be enrolled at time of application. Awards based on essays written by the applicant. No requirement for Mensa membership nor is consideration given for grades, academic program or financial need. Applicants must currently be a resident of a participating American Mensa local group's area and enrolled in a degree program in an accredited U.S. institution of higher learning during the academic year following the application date.

HOW TO APPLY: Each year the list of participating groups may change, see website for up-to-date information. Send application, available (if eligible) from the website or, by request with SASE, from local scholarship chairs. Submit with essay of not more than 550 words explaining your academic and/or vocational goals and plans to achieve those goals to the scholarship chair in your area.

3729—MIDWESTERN HIGHER EDUCATION COMPACT (Midwest Student Exchange Program)

1300 South Second Street,

Suite 130
Minneapolis MN 55454-1079
612/626-1602
FAX: 612/626-8290
E-mail: jenniferd@mhec.org
Internet: http://msep.mhec.org
AMOUNT: Varies by institution
DEADLINE(S): Varies by institution
FIELD(S): All (varies by institution)

ELIGIBILITY/REQUIREMENTS: Must reside in one of the MSEP states (Kansas, Michigan, Minnesota, Missouri, Nebraska, North Dakota and Wisconsin) and plan to attend college in another MSEP state; and attend participating 2- or 4-year colleges or universities.

HOW TO APPLY: Contact your high school counselor or the Office of Admissions at the college you plan to attend for further requirements. Search the MSEP Access Navigator on website for participating institutions, admission requirements and further details.

NUMBER OF AWARDS: Varies by institution

RENEWABLE: Yes: may require reapplication, varies.

CONTACT: Jennifer Dahlquist, Director of Student Initiatives

3730—MILITARY ORDER OF THE PURPLE HEART (Sons, Daughters, and Grandchildren Scholarship Program)

National Headquarters
5413-B Backlick Road
Springfield VA 22151
703/642-5360
FAX: 703/642-2054
E-mail: info@purpleheart.org
Internet: http://purpleheart.org/ scholar/scholarshipInfo/ scholarships.html
AMOUNT: $3,000
DEADLINE(S): Feb. 19
FIELD(S): All

ELIGIBILITY/REQUIREMENTS: Open to recipients of Purple Heart and their children, stepchildren, grandchildren, and great-grandchildren who are direct descendents of either a lifetime member or a current annual member or a member who was in good standing at the time of death or a veteran killed in action or who died of wounds (documentation required) who did not have an opportunity to join the MOPH. MOPH member in good standing or a Purple Heart recipient. Must be a citizen of the U.S., a graduate or upcoming graduate of an accredited high school, 2.75 GPA or greater, accepted by or enrolled in a full-time college, university or trade school. Academic achievement, communi-

ty service, school activities, financial need and recommendations considered, and accepted by or enrolled as a full-time student (12 or more semester credit hours, or 18 quarter credit hours) at a U.S. college, university or trade school at the time the scholarship is awarded,.

HOW TO APPLY: See website or contact National Headquarters for application; submit with transcripts, 200- to 300-word essay explaining "What Americanism Means to Me," proof of the Purple Heart Award, copy of birth certificate, 2 letters of recommendation. $10 check or money order for application fee.

NUMBER OF AWARDS: 4-8

RENEWABLE: Yes. Must reapply, maximum 3 years.

CONTACT: Should you have any question, or require additional information, contact MOPH Headquarters, or Jim Sims, Chair, Scholarship Committee, 360/432-8195 (Pacific Coast Time), jim.ginny@ worldnet.att.net

ADDITIONAL INFORMATION: The academic requirement of a 2.75 GPA may be waived for a Purple Heart recipient.

3731—MODERN WOODMEN OF AMERICA (Fraternal College Scholarship Program)

1701 First Avenue
Rock Island IL 61201
309/786-6481
FAX: 309/793-5573
Internet: http://www.modern woodmen.org
AMOUNT: $500-$3,000
DEADLINE(S): JAN 1
FIELD(S): All

ELIGIBILITY/REQUIREMENTS: Open to high school seniors who have been beneficial members for at least 2 years. Must be in the upper half of graduating class and planning to attend an accredited 4-year college or university in the U.S. Based on qualities of character/leadership, scholastic records, and aptitude for college work.

HOW TO APPLY: See website for application or contact Scholarship Administrator.

NUMBER OF AWARDS: 139

RENEWABLE: Yes. 39 (renewable), 100 (non-renewable).

CONTACT: Fraternal Scholarship Administrator

3732—MODERN WOODMEN OF AMERICA (Nontraditional Student Award)

1701 First Avenue
Rock Island IL 61201
309/786-6481

FAX: 309/793-5573
Internet: http://www.modern
woodmen.org
AMOUNT: $1,000
DEADLINE(S): JAN 1
FIELD(S): All
ELIGIBILITY/REQUIREMENTS: Must be insured member for 2 years prior to January 1 of the year scholarship is awarded; 25 or older; accepted at an accredited college, university, trade or technical school as a full- or part-time undergraduate student.
HOW TO APPLY: See website for application, or contact Scholarship Administrator. Must provide proof of attendance.
NUMBER OF AWARDS: 10
RENEWABLE: No
CONTACT: Fraternal Scholarship Administrator

3733—NAACP NATIONAL OFFICE (Agnes Jones Jackson Scholarship)

United Negro College Fund
8260 Willow Oaks Corporate Drive
Fairfax VA 22031
Internet: http://www.naacp.org or
http://www.uncf.org
AMOUNT: $1,500 undergraduates; $2,500 graduates
DEADLINE(S): MAR 26
FIELD(S): All
ELIGIBILITY/REQUIREMENTS: Undergraduates must have GPA of 2.5+; graduates must possess 3.0 GPA; must be NAACP members, under the age of 25, and U.S. citizen; full-time student in an accredited college (graduate student may be full- or part-time student); must demonstrate financial need.
HOW TO APPLY: See website for additional information and application or send legal-size SASE.
CONTACT: Kimberly Hall

3734—NAACP NATIONAL OFFICE (Annie B. Rose Scholarship-Alexandria Branch)

United Negro College Fund
8260 Willow Oaks Corporate Drive
Fairfax VA 22031
Internet: http://www.naacp.org or
http://www.uncf.org
AMOUNT: $1,000
DEADLINE(S): APR 30
FIELD(S): All
ELIGIBILITY/REQUIREMENTS: Open to high school students who plan to continue their education in an institution of higher learning; must be residents of the City of Alexandria, VA, graduate of TC Williams High School; minimum 2.5 or better GPA;

willing to uphold the goals and objectives of the NAACP.
HOW TO APPLY: See website for additional information and application or send legal-size SASE.
CONTACT: Kimberly Hall

3735—NAACP NATIONAL OFFICE (Roy Wilkins Scholarship)

United Negro College Fund
8260 Willow Oaks Corporate Drive
Fairfax VA 22031
Internet: http://www.naacp.org or
http://www.uncf.org
AMOUNT: $1,000
DEADLINE(S): APR 30
FIELD(S): All
ELIGIBILITY/REQUIREMENTS: Must be an entering college freshman, full-time student in an accredited college; a U.S. citizen; and minimum 2.5 GPA.
HOW TO APPLY: See website for additional information and application or send legal-size SASE.
CONTACT: Kimberly Hall

3736—NAAS-USA FUND

5196 Benito Street,
Suite 15, Room A
Montclair CA 91763-2891
909/621-6856
E-mail: staff@naas.org
Internet: http://www.naas.org
AMOUNT: $200-$5,000
DEADLINE(S): MAY 1
FIELD(S): All
ELIGIBILITY/REQUIREMENTS: Open to high school seniors.
HOW TO APPLY: Download application and additional information from website or send $3 and SASE for more information.
NUMBER OF AWARDS: 15
RENEWABLE: Yes

3737—NAHP (Presidential Classroom Scholars)

119 Oronoco Street
Alexandria VA 22314
800/441-6533
Internet: http://www.nshp.org/
news/scholarships
AMOUNT: $1,000
DEADLINE(S): APR 1
FIELD(S): All
ELIGIBILITY/REQUIREMENTS: Must be high school juniors or seniors with a GPA of at least 3.0 and an interest in civic education.

HOW TO APPLY: Contact NAHP for information and application.

3738—NATIONAL ALLIANCE OF POSTAL AND FEDERAL EMPLOYEES (Ashby B. Carter Memorial Scholarships)

1628 11th Street NW
Washington DC 20001-5086
202/939-6325
FAX: 202/939-6389
Internet: http://www.napfe.com
DEADLINE(S): APR 1
FIELD(S): All
ELIGIBILITY/REQUIREMENTS: Sponsor must be a member of the NAPFE for a minimum of 3 years.
HOW TO APPLY: Members of labor union receive application on back of monthly magazine. Submit SAT/ACT scores.
NUMBER OF AWARDS: 3
RENEWABLE: No
CONTACT: Ernestine Taylor

3739—NATIONAL ART MATERIALS TRADE ASSOCIATION (NAMTA Academic Scholarships)

15806 Brookway Drive, Suite 300
Huntersville NC 28078
704/892-6244
FAX: 704/892-6247
E-mail: scholarships@namta.org
Internet: http://www.namta.org
AMOUNT: $1,500
DEADLINE(S): APR 1
FIELD(S): All
ELIGIBILITY/REQUIREMENTS: Must be employee or family member of employee of NAMTA member firms; studying or planning to study full or half time at an accredited university, college or technical institute. MUST graduate from high school or equivalent before July 1 of the year in which they receive the scholarship. Based on GPA, extracurricular activities and financial need. Do NOT have to study art.
HOW TO APPLY: See website. Contact NAMTA for application.
NUMBER OF AWARDS: 2
RENEWABLE: No

3740—NATIONAL ASSOCIATION FOR ASIAN & PACIFIC AMERICAN EDUCATION

P.O. Box 3366
Daly City CA 94015-3366
650/991-4676
FAX: 650/991-4676
Internet: http://www. naapae.net
AMOUNT: $500-$1,000

DEADLINE(S): JAN 31
FIELD(S): All
ELIGIBILITY/REQUIREMENTS: Must be high school seniors or college juniors or seniors of Asian or Pacific Islander descent; are actively involved in extracurricular activities; have outstanding academic records; are young leaders who show concern and commitment to Asian/Pacific communities; and be U.S. or Canadian citizens or resident aliens.
HOW TO APPLY: Submit application; transcripts highlighting AP and Honors classes; 2 letters of recommendation from instructors, counselors, community leaders, youth leaders, employers, or others addressing your qualifications; a statement of your career goals (maximum 50 words); an essay on how to end hate crime (maximum 300 words) or how you can best serve the Asian Pacific community; a list of your most important school and/or community activities/service over the past 2 years (including type of activity/service, applicant's role or involvement, and the dates of participation); and the full names, addresses, and phone numbers of the 2 persons who will write letters of recommendation.
NUMBER OF AWARDS: 4; 2 $500 (high school seniors) and 2 $1,000 (college juniors or seniors)
CONTACT: Submit application materials to NAAPAE Scholarship Committee, Attention: Clara Parak, College of Education, Cal State University-Northridge, 18111 Nordhoff Street, Northridge CA 91330-8265; 818/677-2500 or clara.park@csun.edu.

3741—NATIONAL BETA CLUB

151 Beta Club Way
Spartanburg SC 29306-3012
Internet: http://www.betaclub.org/scholarship/scholarship.html
AMOUNT: $1,000-$3,750
DEADLINE(S): DEC 10
FIELD(S): All
ELIGIBILITY/REQUIREMENTS: Available to senior high school students who are active Club members; registered with the national headquarters.
HOW TO APPLY: Each chapter may nominate 2 senior members who exemplify the Club's goals of academic excellence, leadership, and school/community service. Application fee: $10.

3742—NATIONAL BUSINESS ASSOCIATION

5151 Beltline Road, Suite 1150
Dallas TX 75254
972/458-0900
FAX: 972/960-9149
E-mail: info@nationalbusiness.org
Internet: http://www.national business org
AMOUNT: $1,500
DEADLINE(S): APR 1
FIELD(S): All
ELIGIBILITY/REQUIREMENTS: High school seniors, college freshmen, sophomores and juniors who are dependent children of dues-paying members at the time of selection. Open to those students that rank in the top third of their senior class but NOT in the top 10%. ACT scores of 18 to 26 or combined SAT scores of 850 to 1190, or with college GPAs of 2.5 to 3.5 in addition to proper high school credentials.
HOW TO APPLY: Complete and process the High School Record Request Form along with application; include copy of SAT and/or ACT test results along with a current transcript if you are attending college.
NUMBER OF AWARDS: 10
RENEWABLE: Yes, must reapply.
CONTACT: Connie French or Scholarship Program Administrators at 615/320-3149, fax 615/320-3151 or e-mail info@spaprog.com

3743—NATIONAL DEFENSE TRANSPORTATION ASSOCIATION (Academic Scholarship Program B)

50 S. Pickett Street, Suite 220
Alexandria VA 22304-7296
703/751-5011
FAX: 703/823-8761
E-mail: mark@ndtahq.com
Internet: http://www.ndtahq.com
AMOUNT: Approximately $500-$2,000
DEADLINE(S): APR 16
FIELD(S): All (Transportation; Physical Distribution; Logistics preferred)
ELIGIBILITY/REQUIREMENTS: Must be an NDTA member or financial dependent of a member and be a college freshman or have satisfactorily completed 3-1/2 years at an accredited high school and be a college-bound.
HOW TO APPLY: Applications available from national headquarters or download from website.
NUMBER OF AWARDS: Varies, approximately 15
RENEWABLE: Yes, must reapply.
CONTACT: Mark Victorson, Executive Assistant

3744—NATIONAL EAGLE SCOUT ASSOCIATION (Elks National Foundation Scholarships)

Eagle Scout Service, S220

Boy Scouts of America
1325 West Walnut Hill Lane
P.O. Box 152079
Irving TX 75015-2079
972/580-2032
Internet: http://www.nesa.org/scholarships/index.html
AMOUNT: $2,000/year (4); $1,000/year (4)
DEADLINE(S): JAN 31 (not before OCT 1)
FIELD(S): All
ELIGIBILITY/REQUIREMENTS: Must be Eagle Scout rank and have received credentials from the national office (exception: scouts whose Eagle Scout boards of review are held the same year of their high school graduation, who may receive a scholarship one time only); must be graduating high school senior entering accredited 4-year college in the year of application; minimum 1090 SAT and/or 26 ACT score; demonstrated leadership ability in scouting and strong record of participation in activities outside of scouting. This scholarship is NOT available to students attending any of the U.S. military academies.
HOW TO APPLY: Mail application with transcript of high school grades covering 6 semesters only; a statement stating why you need financial aid, signed by you and your parent(s); 1 signed recommendation letter from a volunteer or professional Scout leader who knows you personally; and test scores (applications will NOT be considered if the minimum scores are not met).
NUMBER OF AWARDS: 8
RENEWABLE: Yes

3745—NATIONAL EAGLE SCOUT ASSOCIATION (Hall/McElwain Merit Scholarships)

Eagle Scout Service, S220
Boy Scouts of America
1325 West Walnut Hill Lane
P.O. Box 152079
Irving TX 75015-2079
972/580-2032
Internet: http://www.nesa.org/scholarships/index.html
AMOUNT: $2,000/year (4); $1,000/year (4)
DEADLINE(S): JAN 31 (not before OCT 1)
FIELD(S): All
ELIGIBILITY/REQUIREMENTS: Must be Eagle Scout rank and have received credentials from the national office; must be graduating high school or undergraduate college student no later than completion of the junior year (in which event may receive scholarship for only 1 year); have demon-

strated leadership ability in scouting and strong record of participation in activities outside of scouting. This scholarship is NOT available to students attending any of the U.S. military academies.

HOW TO APPLY: Mail application with transcript of high school grades covering 6 semesters only; a statement stating why you need financial aid, signed by you and your parent(s); 1 signed recommendation letter from a volunteer or professional Scout leader who knows you personally.

NUMBER OF AWARDS: 80 (20 in each region)

3746—NATIONAL EAGLE SCOUT ASSOCIATION (Mabel and Lawrence S. Cooke Scholarship)

Eagle Scout Service, S220
Boy Scouts of America
1325 West Walnut Hill Lane
P.O. Box 152079
Irving TX 75015-2079
972/580-2032
Internet: http://www.nesa.org/
scholarships/index.html

AMOUNT: Up to $12,000/year (1); $5,000/year (4)

DEADLINE(S): JAN 31 (not before OCT 1)

FIELD(S): All

ELIGIBILITY/REQUIREMENTS: Must be Eagle Scout rank and have received credentials from the national office (exception: scouts whose Eagle Scout boards of review are held the same year of their high school graduation, who may receive a scholarship one time only); must be graduating high school senior entering accredited 4-year college in the year of application; minimum 1090 SAT and/or 26 ACT score; demonstrated leadership ability in scouting and strong record of participation in activities outside of scouting. Must agree to register and maintain status as a full-time student and the college or university must be accredited by recognized accreditation agencies and offer at least a bachelor's degree upon completion of the course of study offered. This scholarship is NOT available to students attending any of the U.S. military academies.

HOW TO APPLY: Mail application with transcript of high school grades covering 6 semesters only; a statement stating why you need financial aid, signed by you and your parent(s); 1 signed recommendation letter from a volunteer or professional Scout leader who knows you personally; and test scores (applications will NOT be considered if the minimum scores are not met).

NUMBER OF AWARDS: 1 ($12,000); 4 ($5,000)

RENEWABLE: Yes. Must maintain a GPA in the upper third of the class.

3747—NATIONAL EAGLE SCOUT ASSOCIATION (National Eagle Scout Scholarship Fund)

Eagle Scout Service, S220
Boy Scouts of America
1325 West Walnut Hill Lane
P.O. Box 152079
Irving TX 75015-2079
972/580-2032
Internet: http://www.nesa.org/
scholarships/index.html

AMOUNT: Varies

DEADLINE(S): JAN 31 (not before OCT 1)

FIELD(S): All

ELIGIBILITY/REQUIREMENTS: Must be Eagle Scout rank and have received credentials from the national office (exception: scouts whose Eagle Scout boards of review are held the same year as their high school graduation, who may receive a scholarship one time only); must be graduating high school or senior entering accredited 4-year college in the year of application; minimum 1090 SAT and/or 26 ACT score; demonstrated leadership ability in scouting and strong record of participation in activities outside of scouting. This scholarship is NOT available to students attending any of the U.S. military academies.

HOW TO APPLY: Mail application with transcript of high school grades covering 6 semesters only; a statement stating why you need financial aid, signed by you and your parent(s); 1 signed recommendation letter from a volunteer or professional Scout leader who knows you personally; and test scores (applications will NOT be considered if the minimum scores are not met).

3748—NATIONAL FALLEN FIREFIGHTERS FOUNDATION (Sarbanes Scholarship Program)

P.O. Drawer 498
Emmitsburg MD 21727
301/447-1365
FAX: 301/447-1645
E-mail: firehero@firehero.org
Internet: http://www.firehero.org

AMOUNT: $1,500-$5,000

DEADLINE(S): APR 1

FIELD(S): All

ELIGIBILITY/REQUIREMENTS: For spouse or child or stepchild of a firefighter who died in the line of duty and honored at national memorial in Emmitsburg, Maryland. Children must be under age 30 or under age 22 at time of firefighter's death. Must have high school diploma/equivalency; be pursuing undergraduate, graduate, or vocational-technical training at an accredited university, college, or community college, either full or part time. Minimum 2.0 GPA for academic degree; extracurricular activities and special circumstances considered.

HOW TO APPLY: For more information call Foundation or see website for application. Submit with 2 letters of recommendation, 1 from a teacher, employer, or a member of the community familiar with you and your goals and the other from a member of the fire service; transcript; a statement of interest (400 words or less) including why you want the scholarship; your personal, educational, and career goals; a list of extracurricular, community, and/or volunteer activities; and special circumstances such as family responsibilities, financial hardship.

NUMBER OF AWARDS: 30+

RENEWABLE: No

CONTACT: Mary G. Ellis

3749—NATIONAL FEDERATION OF REPUBLICAN WOMEN (Dorothy Andrews Kabis Memorial Internship)

124 North Alfred Street
Alexandria VA 22314
703/548-9688
FAX: 703/548-9836
E-mail: mail@nfrw.org
Internet: http://www.nfrw.org

AMOUNT: Small monetary allowance, airfare, and housing

DEADLINE(S): FEB 20

FIELD(S): All

ELIGIBILITY/REQUIREMENTS: Intern will spend part of the summer working at National headquarters. Must be at least a junior in college or a college student 21 years of age or older with a general knowledge of government, a keen interest in politics, campaign experience, and clerical office skills.

HOW TO APPLY: Applications are available on NFRW website or by contacting NFRW headquarters. Submit to the president of applicant's state federation.

NUMBER OF AWARDS: 3

RENEWABLE: No

CONTACT: Scholarship Coordinator

3750—NATIONAL FEDERATION OF REPUBLICAN WOMEN (National Pathfinder Scholarship)

124 North Alfred Street

Alexandria VA 22314
703/548-9688
FAX: 703/548-9836
E-mail: mail@nfrw.org
Internet: http://www.nfrw.org
AMOUNT: $2,000
DEADLINE(S): JUN 1
FIELD(S):All
ELIGIBILITY/REQUIREMENTS: Open to young women in their sophomore, junior or senior years in an undergraduate program or enrolled in a master's program.
HOW TO APPLY: Applications are available on NFRW website or by contacting NFRW headquarters. Submit to the president of applicant's state federation.
NUMBER OF AWARDS: 3
RENEWABLE: No
CONTACT: Scholarship Coordinator

3751—NATIONAL FEDERATION OF THE BLIND (American Action Fund Scholarship)

Scholarship Committee
805 Fifth Avenue
Grinnell IA 50112
641/236-3366
Internet: http://www.nfb.org/nfb/scholarship_program.asp
AMOUNT: $10,000
DEADLINE(S): MAR 31
FIELD(S): All
ELIGIBILITY/REQUIREMENTS: Must be legally blind; pursuing or planning to pursue a full-time postsecondary education in the U.S. Based on academic excellence, service to the community, and financial need. Membership NOT required.
HOW TO APPLY: Contact Scholarship Committee Chair, for an application.
NUMBER OF AWARDS: 1
RENEWABLE: Yes
CONTACT: Peggy Elliot, Scholarship Committee Chair

3752—NATIONAL FEDERATION OF THE BLIND (Charles and Melva T. Owen Memorial Scholarships)

Scholarship Committee
805 Fifth Avenue
Grinnell IA 50112
641/236-3366
Internet: http://www.nfb.org/nfb/scholarship_program.asp
AMOUNT: $10,000; $3,000
DEADLINE(S): MAR 31
FIELD(S): All
ELIGIBILITY/REQUIREMENTS: Must be legally blind; pursuing or planning to pursue a full-time postsecondary course of study in the fall semester in the U.S. Based

on academic excellence, community service, and financial need. Membership NOT required.
HOW TO APPLY: Send application; personal letter from applicant; 2 letters of recommendation; transcript from all postsecondary institutions attended; letter from a Federation state president or designee; and (for high school seniors only) score reports.
NUMBER OF AWARDS: 2
CONTACT: Peggy Elliott, Scholarship Committee Chair

3753—NATIONAL FEDERATION OF THE BLIND (E. U. Parker Scholarship)

Scholarship Committee
805 Fifth Avenue
Grinnell IA 50112
641/236-3366
Internet: http://www.nfb.org/nfb/scholarship_program.asp
AMOUNT: $3,000
DEADLINE(S): MAR 31
FIELD(S): All
ELIGIBILITY/REQUIREMENTS: Must be legally blind; pursuing or planning to pursue a full-time postsecondary course of study in the fall semester in the U.S. (except one scholarship may be given to someone who is working full time and attending school part time). Based on academic excellence, community service, and financial need. Membership NOT required.
HOW TO APPLY: Send application; personal letter from applicant; 2 letters of recommendation; transcript from all postsecondary institutions attended; letter from a Federation state president or designee; and (for high school seniors only) score reports.
NUMBER OF AWARDS: 1
CONTACT: Peggy Elliott, Scholarship Committee Chair

3754—NATIONAL FEDERATION OF THE BLIND (Hank LeBonne Scholarship)

Scholarship Committee
805 Fifth Avenue
Grinnell IA 50112
641/236-3366
Internet: http://www.nfb.org/nfb/scholarship_program.asp
AMOUNT: $5,000
DEADLINE(S): MAR 31
FIELD(S): All
ELIGIBILITY/REQUIREMENTS: Must be legally blind; pursuing or planning to pursue a full-time postsecondary course of study in the fall semester in the U.S. Based

on academic excellence, community service, and financial need. Membership NOT required.
HOW TO APPLY: Send application; personal letter from applicant; 2 letters of recommendation; transcript from all postsecondary institutions attended; letter from a Federation state president or designee; and (for high school seniors only) score reports.
NUMBER OF AWARDS: 1
CONTACT: Peggy Elliott, Scholarship Committee Chair

3755—NATIONAL FEDERATION OF THE BLIND (Hermione Grant Calhoun Scholarship)

Scholarship Committee
805 Fifth Avenue
Grinnell IA 50112
641/236-3366
Internet: http://www.nfb.org/nfb/scholarship_program.asp
AMOUNT: $3,000
DEADLINE(S): MAR 31
FIELD(S): All
ELIGIBILITY/REQUIREMENTS: Must be female. Must be legally blind; pursuing or planning to pursue a full-time postsecondary course of study in the fall semester in the U.S. Based on academic excellence, community service, and financial need. Membership NOT required.
HOW TO APPLY: Send application; personal letter from applicant; 2 letters of recommendation; transcript from all postsecondary institutions attended; letter from a Federation state president or designee; and (for high school seniors only) score reports.
NUMBER OF AWARDS: 1
CONTACT: Peggy Elliott, Scholarship Committee Chair

3756—NATIONAL FEDERATION OF THE BLIND (Jennica Ferguson Memorial Scholarship)

Scholarship Committee
805 Fifth Avenue
Grinnell IA 50112
641/236-3366
Internet: http://www.nfb.org/nfb/scholarship_program.asp
AMOUNT: $5,000
DEADLINE(S): MAR 31
FIELD(S): All
ELIGIBILITY/REQUIREMENTS: Must be legally blind; pursuing or planning to pursue a full-time postsecondary course of study in the fall semester in the U.S. Based on academic excellence, community ser-

vice, and financial need. Membership NOT required.

HOW TO APPLY: Send application; personal letter from applicant; 2 letters of recommendation; transcript from all postsecondary institutions attended; letter from a Federation state president or designee; and (for high school seniors only) score reports.

NUMBER OF AWARDS: 1

CONTACT: Peggy Elliott, Scholarship Committee Chair

3757—NATIONAL FEDERATION OF THE BLIND (Kenneth Jernigan Scholarship)

Scholarship Committee
805 Fifth Avenue
Grinnell IA 50112
641/236-3366
Internet: http://www.nfb.org/
nfb/scholarship_program.asp
AMOUNT: $12,000
DEADLINE(S): MAR 31
FIELD(S): All

ELIGIBILITY/REQUIREMENTS: Must be legally blind; pursuing or planning to pursue a full-time postsecondary course of study in the fall semester in the U.S. Based on academic excellence, community service, and financial need. Membership NOT required.

HOW TO APPLY: Send application; personal letter from applicant; 2 letters of recommendation; transcript from all postsecondary institutions attended; letter from a Federation state president or designee; and (for high school seniors only) score reports.

NUMBER OF AWARDS: 1

CONTACT: Peggy Elliott, Scholarship Committee Chair

3758—NATIONAL FEDERATION OF THE BLIND (Kuchler-Killian Memorial Scholarship)

Scholarship Committee
805 Fifth Avenue
Grinnell IA 50112
641/236-3366
Internet: http://www.nfb.org/
nfb/scholarship_program.asp
AMOUNT: $3,000
DEADLINE(S): MAR 31
FIELD(S): All

ELIGIBILITY/REQUIREMENTS: Must be legally blind; pursuing or planning to pursue a full-time postsecondary course of study in the fall semester in the U.S. Based on academic excellence, community service, and financial need. Membership NOT required.

HOW TO APPLY: Send application; personal letter from applicant; 2 letters of recommendation; transcript from all postsecondary institutions attended; letter from a Federation state president or designee; and (for high school seniors only) score reports.

NUMBER OF AWARDS: 1

CONTACT: Peggy Elliott, Scholarship Committee Chair

3759—NATIONAL FEDERATION OF THE BLIND (Michael and Marie Marucci Scholarship)

Scholarship Committee
805 Fifth Avenue
Grinnell IA 50112
641/236-3366
Internet: http://www.nfb.org/
nfb/scholarship_program.asp
AMOUNT: $5,000
DEADLINE(S): MAR 31
FIELD(S): Foreign Language & Literature; History; Geography; Political Science-international studies

ELIGIBILITY/REQUIREMENTS: Must show competence in a foreign language; be legally blind; pursuing or planning to pursue a full-time postsecondary education in the U.S. Based on academic excellence, service to the community, and financial need. Membership NOT required.

HOW TO APPLY: Contact Scholarship Committee Chair for an application.

NUMBER OF AWARDS: 2

RENEWABLE: Yes

CONTACT: Peggy Elliot, Scholarship Committee Chair

ADDITIONAL INFORMATION: Also open to majors in other disciplines requiring study abroad.

3760—NATIONAL FEDERATION OF THE BLIND (Mozelle and Willard Gold Memorial Scholarship)

805 Fifth Avenue
Grinnell IA 50112
641/236-3366
Internet: http://www.nfb.org/
nfb/scholarship_program.asp
AMOUNT: $3,000
DEADLINE(S): MAR 31
FIELD(S): All

ELIGIBILITY/REQUIREMENTS: Must be legally blind; pursuing or planning to pursue a full-time postsecondary course of study in the fall semester in the U.S. Based on academic excellence, community service, and financial need. Membership NOT required.

HOW TO APPLY: Send application; personal letter from applicant; 2 letters of recommendation; transcript from all postsecondary institutions attended; letter from a Federation state president or designee; and (for high school seniors only) score reports.

NUMBER OF AWARDS: 1

CONTACT: Peggy Elliott, Scholarship Committee Chair

3761—NATIONAL FEDERATION OF THE BLIND (Sally S. Jacobsen Scholarship)

Scholarship Committee
805 Fifth Avenue
Grinnell IA 50112
641/236-3366
Internet: http://www.nfb.org/
nfb/scholarship_program.asp
AMOUNT: $5,000
DEADLINE(S): MAR 31
FIELD(S): All

ELIGIBILITY/REQUIREMENTS: Must be legally blind; pursuing or planning to pursue a full-time postsecondary course of study in the fall semester in the U.S. Based on academic excellence, community service, and financial need. Membership NOT required.

HOW TO APPLY: Send application; personal letter from applicant; 2 letters of recommendation; transcript from all postsecondary institutions attended; letter from a Federation state president or designee; and (for high school seniors only) score reports.

NUMBER OF AWARDS: 1

CONTACT: Peggy Elliott, Scholarship Committee Chair

3762—NATIONAL FEDERATION OF THE BLIND SCHOLARSHIPS

Scholarship Committee
805 Fifth Avenue
Grinnell IA 50112
641/236-3366
Internet: http://www.nfb.org/
nfb/scholarship_program.asp
AMOUNT: $3,000-$7,000
DEADLINE(S): MAR 31
FIELD(S): All

ELIGIBILITY/REQUIREMENTS: Must be legally blind; pursuing or planning to pursue a full-time postsecondary course of study in the fall semester in the U.S. Based on academic excellence, community service, and financial need. Membership NOT required.

HOW TO APPLY: Send application; personal letter from applicant; 2 letters of recommendation; transcript from all postsecondary institutions attended; letter from a Federation state president or designee; and (for high school seniors only) score reports.

CONTACT: Peggy Elliott, Scholarship Committee Chair

3763—NATIONAL FOSTER PARENT ASSOCIATION, INC.

Scholarship Committee
7512 Stanich Avenue, #6
Gig Harbor WA 98335
E-mail: info@NFPAinc.org
Internet: http://www.nfpainc.org
DEADLINE(S): MAR 31
FIELD(S): All
ELIGIBILITY/REQUIREMENTS: Must be in senior year of high school (regardless of age) and accepted by an accredited college or university; applicants for vocational school, job training, correspondence GED, or other educational pursuits must be at least 17 years old (either in school or out) and accepted into an accredited program.

HOW TO APPLY: Send application; copy of high school transcript; proof of acceptance and documentation of costs; minimum of 2 letters of recommendation from foster parent(s), social worker(s), residential center, principal/teacher/guidance counselor, employer, etc.; statement of 300-500 words on "Why I want to further my education and why I should be considered for a National Foster Parent Association Scholarship."

3764—NATIONAL HOOK-UP OF BLACK WOMEN, INC. (Arnita Y. Boswell Scholarship Award)

1809 East 71st Street, Suite 205
Chicago IL 60649
773/667-7061
FAX: 773/667-7064
E-mail: nhbwdir@aol.com
Internet: http://www.nhbwinc.com
AMOUNT: $1,000
DEADLINE(S): Varies
FIELD(S): All
ELIGIBILITY/REQUIREMENTS: High school graduate with a cumulative GPA of 2.75 or higher or attending an accredited college with a GPA of 2.75 or higher.

HOW TO APPLY: Write for application to Scholarship Committee. Submit with transcript, certification of community service and school activity, an essay on a topic to be provided on application, and 2 letters of recommendation.

NUMBER OF AWARDS: 4
RENEWABLE: Yes, must reapply.
CONTACT: Executive Director

3765—NATIONAL HOOK-UP OF BLACK WOMEN, INC. (Sister-to-Sister Scholarship)

1809 East 71st Street, Suite 205
Chicago IL 60649
773/667-7061
FAX: 773/667-7064
E-mail: nhbwdir@aol.com
Internet: http://www.nhbwinc.com
AMOUNT: $500
DEADLINE(S): Varies
FIELD(S): All
ELIGIBILITY/REQUIREMENTS: Must be at least 25 years old and entering an accredited college or university in an undergraduate degree program.

HOW TO APPLY: Write for application to Scholarship Committee. Submit with transcript, an essay on a topic to be provided on application, and 2 letters of recommendation.

NUMBER OF AWARDS: 2
RENEWABLE: Yes, must reapply.
CONTACT: Executive Director

3766—NATIONAL ITALIAN-AMERICAN FOUNDATION

1860 19th Street NW
Washington DC 20009
202/387-0600
FAX: 202/387-0800
E-mail: scholarships@niaf.org
Internet: http://www.niaf@org/scholar/scholarships/about.asp
AMOUNT: $2,500-$10,000
DEADLINE(S): MAR 1
FIELD(S): All (Category I), Area Studies, Italian (Category II)
ELIGIBILITY/REQUIREMENTS: Open to U.S. citizens or permanent resident aliens enrolled in an accredited institution of higher education; have a GPA of at 3.5 (or equivalent); demonstrate outstanding potential and high academic achievements; and fit into 1 of 2 NIAF scholarship categories: Category I—Italian-American students (must have 1 ancestor who has emigrated from any region in Italy), area of study open; Category II—students from any ethnic background majoring or minoring in Italian language, Italian studies, Italian American studies or a related field. Scholarships are awarded on the basis of academic performance, field of study, career objectives, and potential commitment and ability to make significant contributions to their chosen field of study. Some scholarships awarded on basis of financial need.

HOW TO APPLY: Application available on website and can ONLY be submitted online. Official transcript must be mailed and postmarked. FAFSA optional; if sub-

mitted must be postmarked by March 1. Teacher evaluation required; submit using online Teacher Evaluation form no later than March 15.
RENEWABLE: Yes
ADDITIONAL INFORMATION: If awarded, recipient must sign a written statement pledging that upon completion of the scholarship academic year, student will submit a typed narrative of approximately 500 words for publication describing the benefits of the NIAF Scholarship. May not be used as a substitute for or diminish any other award, grant or scholarship. The combined benefits from all sources may not exceed the cost of tuition, fees and university-provided room and board.

3767—NATIONAL JEWISH COMMITTEE ON SCOUTING (Chester M. Vernon Memorial Eagle Scout Scholarship Program)

Boy Scouts of America
1325 West Walnut Hill Lane
P.O. Box 152079
Irving TX 75015-2079
972/580-2431
Internet: http://www.jewishscouting.org/awards/njcoseagle scoutscholarshipprograms.asp
AMOUNT: $1,000/year (for 4 years)
DEADLINE(S): DEC 31
FIELD(S): All
ELIGIBILITY/REQUIREMENTS: Must be a registered, active member of a Boy Scout troop, Varsity Scout team, or Explorer Post; have received the Eagle Scout Award; an active member of a synagogue and recipient of Ner Tamid religious emblem; have demonstrated practical citizenship in his synagogue, school, Scouting unit, and community; be enrolled in an accredited high school, and in final year at the time of selection. May be used to attend a state-accredited college, university, or vocational school above the high school level.

HOW TO APPLY: Download application from website or write to NJCS. Submit with your history with any religious youth organizations, clubs, or groups, including honors earned and offices held. See website for other information required with application; a transcript of high school grades covering 6 semesters only; a statement stating why you believe you need financial aid, signed by the applicant and his parent(s); 1 signed recommendation from a volunteer or professional Scout leader who knows you personally.

NUMBER OF AWARDS: 1
RENEWABLE: No. Award is for 4 years.

3768—NATIONAL JEWISH COMMITTEE ON SCOUTING (Florence and Marvin Arkans Eagle Scout Scholarship Program)

Boy Scouts of America
1325 West Walnut Hill Lane
P.O. Box 152079
Irving TX 75015-2079
972/580-2431
Internet: http://www.jewish
scouting.org/awards/njcoseagle
scoutscholarshipprograms.asp
AMOUNT: $1,000
DEADLINE(S): DEC 31
FIELD(S): All
ELIGIBILITY/REQUIREMENTS: Must be a registered, active member of a Boy Scout troop, Varsity Scout team, or Explorer Post; have received the Eagle Scout Award; an active member of a synagogue and recipient of Ner Tamid religious emblem; have demonstrated practical citizenship in his synagogue, school, Scouting unit, and community; be enrolled in an accredited high school, and in final year at the time of selection. May be used to attend a state-accredited college, university, or vocational school above the high school level.
HOW TO APPLY: Download application from website or write to NJCS. Submit with your history with any religious youth organizations, clubs, or groups, including honors earned and offices held. See website for other information required with application; a transcript of high school grades covering 6 semesters only; a statement stating why you believe you need financial aid, signed by the applicant and his parent(s); 1 signed recommendation from a volunteer or professional Scout leader who knows you personally.
NUMBER OF AWARDS: 1
RENEWABLE: No

3769—NATIONAL JEWISH COMMITTEE ON SCOUTING (Frank L. Weil Memorial Eagle Scout Scholarship Program)

Boy Scouts of America
1325 West Walnut Hill Lane
P.O. Box 152079
Irving TX 75015-2079
972/580-2431
Internet: http://www.jewish
scouting.org/awards/njcoseagle
scoutscholarshipprograms.asp
AMOUNT: $2,000 (first place); $1,000 (second place)
DEADLINE(S): DEC 31
FIELD(S): All
ELIGIBILITY/REQUIREMENTS: Must be a registered, active member of a Boy

Scout troop, Varsity Scout team, or Explorer Post; have received the Eagle Scout Award; an active member of a synagogue and recipient of Ner Tamid religious emblem; have demonstrated practical citizenship in his synagogue, school, Scouting unit, and community; be enrolled in an accredited high school, and in final year at the time of selection. May be used to attend a state-accredited college, university, or vocational school above the high school level.
HOW TO APPLY: Download application from website or write to NJCS. Submit with your history with any religious youth organizations, clubs, or groups, including honors earned and offices held. See website for other information required with application; a transcript of high school grades covering 6 semesters only; a statement stating why you believe you need financial aid, signed by the applicant and his parent(s); 1 signed recommendation from a volunteer or professional Scout leader who knows you personally.
NUMBER OF AWARDS: 3 (1 first place, 2 second place).

3770—NATIONAL JEWISH COMMITTEE ON SCOUTING (Gideon Elad Scholarship Program)

Boy Scouts of America
1325 West Walnut Hill Lane
P.O. Box 152079
Irving TX 75015-2079
972/580-2431
Internet: http://www.jewish
scouting.org/awards/njcoseagle
scoutscholarshipprograms.asp
AMOUNT: $1,000
DEADLINE(S): DEC 31
FIELD(S): All
ELIGIBILITY/REQUIREMENTS: Must be a registered, active member of a Boy Scout troop, Varsity Scout team, or Explorer Post; have received the Eagle Scout Award; an active member of a synagogue and recipient of Ner Tamid religious emblem; have demonstrated practical citizenship in his synagogue, school, Scouting unit, and community; be enrolled in an accredited high school, and in final year at the time of selection. May be used to attend a state accredited college, university, or vocational school above the high school level.
HOW TO APPLY: Download application from website or write to NJCS. Submit with your history with any religious youth organizations, clubs, or groups, including honors earned and offices held. See website for other information required with application; a transcript of high school

grades covering 6 semesters only; a statement stating why you believe you need financial aid, signed by the applicant and his parent(s); 1 signed recommendation from a volunteer or professional Scout leader who knows you personally.
NUMBER OF AWARDS: 1
RENEWABLE: No

3771—NATIONAL MERIT SCHOLARSHIP CORPORATION (National Achievement Scholarship Program)

1560 Sherman Avenue, Suite 200
Evanston IL 60201
847/866-5100
Internet: http://www.national
merit.org
AMOUNT: Varies
DEADLINE(S): Varies
FIELD(S): All
ELIGIBILITY/REQUIREMENTS: Open to Black American high school students for undergraduate studies. Must take the PSAT/NMSQT in the proper high school year (usually junior year). Financial need NOT required.
HOW TO APPLY: See school counselor for a PSAT/NMSQT Official Student Guide. The Achievement Program will contact students through their schools.
NUMBER OF AWARDS: 800
RENEWABLE: Varies
CONTACT: Elaine Detweiler

3772—NATIONAL MILITARY INTELLIGENCE ASSOCIATION

Scholarship Committee
P.O. Box 479
Hamilton VA 20159
540/338-1143
FAX: 703/738-7487
E-mail: NMIAssoc@comcast.net
Internet: http://www.nmia.org
AMOUNT: $1,000
DEADLINE(S): NOV 1
FIELD(S): All
ELIGIBILITY/REQUIREMENTS: Must be child of NMIA member. Based on SAT, GPA, degree sought; interest in intelligence or defense.
HOW TO APPLY: See website or e-mail request for application and information. Submit with SAT/ACT, transcripts, and other supporting documentation.
NUMBER OF AWARDS: Varies
RENEWABLE: No

3773—NATIONAL PKU NEWS (The Robert Guthrie PKU Scholarship)

6869 Woodlawn Avenue NE, #116

Seattle WA 98115-5469
206/525-8140
FAX: 206/525-5023
E-mail: schuett@pkunews.org
Internet: http://www.pkunews.org
AMOUNT: Variable, $500-$5,000
DEADLINE(S): NOV 1
FIELD(S): All
ELIGIBILITY/REQUIREMENTS:
Available only to persons with phenylke-
tonuria (PKU) who are on treatment with
the special diet in the U.S., Canada and
other countries (application must be com-
pleted in English), entering or continuing
education at an institution of higher learn-
ing (college, university or technical insti-
tute).
HOW TO APPLY: E-mail for informa-
tion.
NUMBER OF AWARDS: Between 5-15
RENEWABLE: No
CONTACT: Virginia E. Scheutt

3774—NATIONAL PRESS PHOTOGRA-PHERS FOUNDATION

3200 Croasdaile Drive, Suite 306
Durham NC 27705
919/383-7246 or 800/289-6772
FAX: 919/383-7261
E-mail: info@nppa.org
Internet: http://www.nppa.org/
professional development/students/
scholar/scholarships/
AMOUNT: $250-$1,000
DEADLINE(S): MAR 1
FIELD(S): Photojournalism
ELIGIBILITY/REQUIREMENTS: A
variety of undergraduate scholarships at
various levels. Academic ability and finan-
cial need considered; primary considera-
tion is portfolio (6+ photos, photo-story
counts as 1; video journalists should submit
a tape with 3 stories). School must be in the
U.S. or Canada.
HOW TO APPLY: See website or contact
NPPF for an application and specific
details of each scholarship.
CONTACT: Submit entry to Chuck
Fadely, The Miami Herald, One Herald
Plaza, Miami, FL 33132, 305/376-2015.

3775—NATIONAL RIFLE ASSOCIATION (Jeanne E. Bray Memorial Scholarship Fund)

11250 Waples Mill Road
Fairfax VA 22030
703/267-1131
FAX: 703/267-1083
E-mail: selkin@nrahq.org
Internet: http://www.nrahq.org

DEADLINE(S): NOV 15
FIELD(S): All
ELIGIBILITY/REQUIREMENTS:
Adult or junior member of the NRA or the
child of a current full-time commissioned
peace officer who is also a member of the
NRA; a deceased full-time commissioned
peace officer who lost his/her life in the
performance of assigned peace officer
duties and was a member of the NRA at
the time of death; a retired full-time commissioned peace officer who is also a member of the NRA; a full-time commissioned
peace officer, disabled as a result of a line-
of-duty incident, who is a current member
of the NRA.
HOW TO APPLY: Request application by
calling or writing.
RENEWABLE: Yes. NRA membership
must remain current.
CONTACT: Sandy Elkin, JEB Committee
Secretary

3776—NATIONAL SOCIETY DAUGHTERS OF THE AMERICAN REVOLUTION (Lillian and Arthur Dunn Scholarship)

Committee Services Office
Attn: Scholarships
1776 D Street NW
Washington DC 20006-5392
202/628-1776
Internet: http://www.dar.org
AMOUNT: $2,000
DEADLINE(S): FEB 15
FIELD(S): All
ELIGIBILITY/REQUIREMENTS:
Awarded to well-qualified, deserving sons
and daughters of members of the NSDAR
for four years of college. Outstanding
recipients pursuing graduate study may
reapply each year for an additional period
of up to four years of study.
HOW TO APPLY: Must submit application with a letter of sponsorship from local
DAR chapter (send SASE to address
above to obtain name and application);
statement of 1,000 words or less stating
career objectives, how college major (if
required) or college plans relate to future
professional goals and reasons for these
choices; transcripts; list of extracurricular
activities, honors received, scholastic
achievements, or other significant accomplishments; 2-4 letters of recommendation
from the high school or college you now
attend who are familiar with your work,
and proof of citizenship. DAR Member
Number of mother must be on the
Application. See website for additional
information.
RENEWABLE: Yes. Up to 4 years with
annual transcript review.

3777—NATIONAL SOCIETY DAUGHTERS OF THE AMERICAN REVOLUTION (Margaret Howard Hamilton Scholarship)

Committee Services Office
Attn: Scholarships
1776 D Street NW
Washington DC 20006-5392
202/628-1776
Internet: http://www.dar.org
AMOUNT: $1,000
DEADLINE(S): APR 15
FIELD(S): All
ELIGIBILITY/REQUIREMENTS: Open
to learning disabled graduating high school
senior who has been accepted into the
Harvey and Bernice Jones Learning
Center, Ben D. Caudle Learning Program,
University of the Ozarks. Based on academic excellence and need. Applicants
must be citizens of the U.S. and attend an
accredited college or university in the U.S.
No affiliation with DAR required.
HOW TO APPLY: Request application
from the Learning Center upon acceptance
into program. Must submit application
with a letter of sponsorship from local
DAR chapter (send SASE to address
above to obtain name and application);
statement of 1,000 words or less stating
career objectives, how college major (if
required) or college plans relate to future
professional goals and reasons for these
choices; transcripts; list of extracurricular
activities, honors received, scholastic
achievements, or other significant accomplishments; 2-4 letters of recommendation
from the high school or college you now
attend who are familiar with your work,
and proof of citizenship. See website for
additional information.
RENEWABLE: Yes. Up to 4 years with
annual transcript review.

3778—NATIONAL SOCIETY OF THE SONS OF THE AMERICAN REVOLUTION (Eagle Scout Scholarships)

1000 S. Fourth Street
Louisville KY 40203
502/589-1776
Internet: http://www.sar.org/youth/
eagle.html
AMOUNT: $8,000 (1st); $4,000 (2nd);
$2,000 (3rd)
DEADLINE(S): Varies
FIELD(S): All
ELIGIBILITY/REQUIREMENTS: Open
to any Eagle Scout currently registered in
an active unit, who is under the age of 19
during the year of his application. College
plans do NOT need to be completed to win
the cash scholarships. Competition is con-

ducted in 3 phases, local (Chapter), state (Society), and National, and is usually entered through the Chapter level. In some cases, may be entered at the State level. May not enter at the National level. Only 1 application is needed.

HOW TO APPLY: Must complete an application form (includes Scout history, activities, etc.). A 500-word essay on a patriotic theme is also required, with bibliography. Three merit badges—American Heritage, Genealogy, and Law—are required for extra credit. See website for an application and 4-generation ancestor chart.

NUMBER OF AWARDS: 3 (prizes and recognitions may also be awarded at the SAR Chapter and State levels)

RENEWABLE: Yes. If you meet the age requirements but no more than $8,000.00 total may be granted to any one Eagle Scout.

3779—NATSO FOUNDATION (The Bill Moon Scholarship)

4701 Connecticut Avenue NW, Suite 209
Washington DC 20008
Internet: http://www.natso foundation.org

AMOUNT: $2,500
DEADLINE(S): APR 15
FIELD(S): All
ELIGIBILITY/REQUIREMENTS: Must be a travel plaza/truck-stop industry employee or the legal dependent of an employee who is a graduating high school senior enrolling in college or an undergraduate or graduate student currently enrolled in a college or university, or missing in action. Based on academic merit, extracurricular and community activities, and essay.

HOW TO APPLY: Submit application with transcript(s); letter of recommendation from an academic official, employment supervisor or other adult; and essay of 500 words or less (topic changes annually).

NUMBER OF AWARDS: 12
CONTACT: Vicki J. Baker, Scholarship Committee

3780—NAVAL RESERVE ASSOCIATION

1619 King Street
Alexandria VA 22314
703/548-5800
FAX: 703/683-3647
E-mail: admin@navy-reserve.org
Internet: http://www.navy-reserve.org

AMOUNT: Varies

DEADLINE(S): MAY 1
FIELD(S): All
ELIGIBILITY/REQUIREMENTS: Open to children of current active members.
HOW TO APPLY: Contact by mail or phone to request application.
NUMBER OF AWARDS: Varies
RENEWABLE: Yes, must reapply.
CONTACT: Bob Lyman

3781—NAVY-MARINE CORPS RELIEF SOCIETY (Admiral Mike Boorda Scholarship Program)

875 North Randolph Street,
Suite 225
Arlington VA 22203
703/696-4960
Internet: http://www.nmcrs.org/education

AMOUNT: $2,000
DEADLINE(S): MAY 1
FIELD(S): All
ELIGIBILITY/REQUIREMENTS: Open to students in the Marine Enlisted Commissioning Education Program and the Medical Enlisted Commissioning Program. Based on financial need; minimum 2.0 GPA.

HOW TO APPLY: See website for application. Applications must be reviewed and endorsed by commanding officer.
RENEWABLE: Yes. Must reapply; maximum of 4 years.

3782—NAVY-MARINE CORPS RELIEF SOCIETY (Dependents of Deceased Service Members Scholarship)

875 North Randolph Street,
Suite 225
Arlington VA 22203
703/696-4960
Internet: http://www.nmcrs.org/education

AMOUNT: $3,000
DEADLINE(S): MAR 1
FIELD(S): All
ELIGIBILITY/REQUIREMENTS: Open to dependent children of retired deceased service members and service members who died while on active duty. Must be pursuing full-time undergraduate studies at a postsecondary, technical, or vocational institution that participates in the U.S. Department of Education Title IV financial aid programs. Based on financial need; minimum 2.0 GPA.

HOW TO APPLY: See website for application. (Note: Between December and February, *Tennessee* applications are available from NMCRS offices in Bangor,

Groton, Guam, Kings Bay, Norfolk, and Pearl Harbor.)
RENEWABLE: Yes. Must reapply; maximum of 4 years.

3783—NAVY-MARINE CORPS RELIEF SOCIETY (Pentagon Assistance Fund)

875 North Randolph Street,
Suite 225
Arlington VA 22203
703/696-4960
Internet: http://www.nmcrs.org/education

AMOUNT: Varies
DEADLINE(S): 2 months prior to start of school
FIELD(S): All
ELIGIBILITY/REQUIREMENTS: Open to dependent children and spouses of military personnel who died as a result of the terrorist attack September 11, 2001. Must be pursuing full-time undergraduate studies at a postsecondary, technical, or vocational institution that participates in the U.S. Department of Education Title IV financial aid programs. Based on financial need; minimum 2.0 GPA.

HOW TO APPLY: Contact NMCRS headquarters.
RENEWABLE: Yes. New application is required for each academic year; maximum of 4 years.

3784—NAVY-MARINE CORPS RELIEF SOCIETY (Spouse Tuition Aid Program-Overseas Only)

875 North Randolph Street,
Suite 225
Arlington VA 22203
703/696-4960
AMOUNT: $50% tuition for on-base programs, maximum $1,500 for undergraduate and $1,750 for graduate programs
DEADLINE(S): Varies from term to term
FIELD(S): All
ELIGIBILITY/REQUIREMENTS: Open to spouses who reside outside the 50 United States with their active-duty service member sponsor. Must be pursuing undergraduate or graduate studies at a postsecondary, technical, or vocational institution that participates in the U.S. Department of Education Title IV financial aid programs. Based on financial need; minimum 2.0 GPA.

HOW TO APPLY: Contact NMCRS office, Guam, Guantanamo Bay, London, Naples, Okinawa, Rota, Sigonella, or

Yokosuka, for an application form and information about deadlines.
RENEWABLE: Yes, by term (5/6 terms in 1 year)

3785—NAVY-MARINE CORPS RELIEF SOCIETY (USS Cole Memorial Fund)

875 North Randolph Street,
Suite 225
Arlington VA 22203
703/696-4960
AMOUNT: Varies
DEADLINE(S): 2 months prior to start of school
FIELD(S): All
ELIGIBILITY/REQUIREMENTS: Open to dependent children of crew members who died as a result of the terrorist attack October 12, 2000. Students must be pursuing full-time undergraduate studies at a postsecondary, technical, or vocational institution that participates in the U.S. Department of Education Title IV financial aid programs. Awards are based on financial need; minimum 2.0 GPA.
HOW TO APPLY: Contact NMCRS headquarters
RENEWABLE: Yes. Must reapply; maximum of 4 years.

3786—NAVY-MARINE CORPS RELIEF SOCIETY (USS Stark Memorial Fund)

875 North Randolph Street,
Suite 225
Arlington VA 22203
703/696-4960
Internet: http://www.nmcrs.org/education
AMOUNT: Varies
DEADLINE(S): MAR 1
FIELD(S): All
ELIGIBILITY/REQUIREMENTS: Open to dependent children and spouses of crew members who died May 17, 1987. Must be pursuing full-time undergraduate studies at a postsecondary, technical, or vocational institution that participates in the U.S. Department of Education Title IV financial aid programs. Based on financial need; minimum 2.0 GPA.
HOW TO APPLY: Dependent children: see website for application. Spouses: contact NMCRS headquarters.
RENEWABLE: Yes. Must reapply; maximum of 4 years.

3787—NAVY-MARINE CORPS RELIEF SOCIETY (USS Tennessee Scholarship Fund)

875 North Randolph Street,
Suite 225

Arlington VA 22203
703/696-4960
Internet: http://www.nmcrs.org/education
AMOUNT: $2,000
DEADLINE(S): MAR 1
FIELD(S): All
ELIGIBILITY/REQUIREMENTS: Open to dependent children of active duty and retired service members serving on or who have served aboard the USS *Tennessee*. Students must be pursuing full-time undergraduate studies at a postsecondary, technical, or vocational institution that participates in the U.S. Department of Education Title IV financial aid programs. Awards are based on financial need. All applicants must have at least a 2.0 GPA on a 4.0 scale.
HOW TO APPLY: See website for application. (Note: Between December and February, *Tennessee* applications are available from NMCRS offices in Bangor, Groton, Guam, Kings Bay, Norfolk, and Pearl Harbor.)
RENEWABLE: Yes. New application is required for each academic year; maximum of 4 years.

3788—NAVY-MARINE CORPS RELIEF SOCIETY (Vice Admiral E. P. Travers Scholarship and Loan Program)

875 North Randolph Street,
Suite 225
Arlington VA 22203
703/696-4960
Internet: http://www.nmcrs.org/education
AMOUNT: Up to $2,000 (grant); $500-$3,000 (interest-free loan)
DEADLINE(S): MAR 1
FIELD(S): All
ELIGIBILITY/REQUIREMENTS: Open to dependent children of active duty and retired service members as well as spouses of active duty. Must be pursuing full-time undergraduate studies at a postsecondary, technical, or vocational institution that participates in the U.S. Department of Education Title IV financial aid programs. Based on financial need; minimum 2.0 GPA.
HOW TO APPLY: See website for application. Note: Only 1 application needed to apply for BOTH scholarship and loan.
RENEWABLE: Yes. Must reapply; maximum of 4 years.

3789—NAVY WIVES CLUBS OF AMERICA (Judith Haupt Scholarship)

534 Madrona Street
Chula Vista CA 91910

AMOUNT: $1,000
DEADLINE(S): MAY 30
FIELD(S): All
ELIGIBILITY/REQUIREMENTS: Open to children of enlisted members of the U.S. Navy, Marine Corps, or Coast Guard who are on active duty, retired with pay, or deceased. Must demonstrate financial need; be of reasonably sound scholastic standing, and of good moral character. Must have a valid Dependants ID card.
HOW TO APPLY: Must be previously approved for admission to an accredited school. Submit application with transcript, Privacy Act Statement sheet, and essay. Send SASE (business size) to the National President for complete information.
RENEWABLE: Yes. Up to 5 years.
CONTACT: Denise Johnson, National President

3790—NAVY WIVES CLUBS OF AMERICA (Mary Paolozzi Member's Scholarship)

534 Madrona Street
Chula Vista CA 91910
AMOUNT: $1,000
DEADLINE(S): MAY 30
FIELD(S): All
ELIGIBILITY/REQUIREMENTS: Open to dependents of enlisted members of the U.S. Navy, Marine Corps, or Coast Guard who are on active duty, retired with pay, or deceased who are high school graduates or high school students or GED certificate-holders expecting to attend college, or high school graduate vocational or business school full time or who are currently enrolled in undergraduate college and expect to continue in full-time undergraduate program or college graduates or college seniors expecting to be full-time graduate students next year. Must demonstrate financial need; be of reasonably sound scholastic standing, and of good moral character. Must have a valid Dependants ID card.
HOW TO APPLY: Must be previously approved for admission to an accredited school. Submit application with transcript, Privacy Act Statement sheet, and essay. Send SASE (business size) to the National President for complete information.
RENEWABLE: Yes. Up to 5 years.
CONTACT: Denise Johnson, National President

3791—NAVY WIVES CLUBS OF AMERICA (NMCCG Enlisted Dependent Spouse Scholarship)

39743 Clements Way
Murrieta CA 92563-4021
AMOUNT: $1,000

DEADLINE(S): MAY 30
FIELD(S): All
ELIGIBILITY/REQUIREMENTS: Open to dependents of enlisted members of the U.S. Navy, Marine Corps, or Coast Guard who are on active duty, retired with pay, or deceased. Must demonstrate financial need, be of reasonably sound scholastic standing, and of good moral character. Must have a valid Dependants ID card.
HOW TO APPLY: Must be previously approved for admission to an accredited school. Submit application with transcript, Privacy Act Statement sheet, and essay. Send SASE (business size) to Director for complete information.
RENEWABLE: Yes. Up to 5 years.
CONTACT: Susan Quinn, Director

3792—NAVY WIVES CLUBS OF AMERICA (NWCA Scholarship)

1644A Jana Court
Norfolk VA 23503
757/521-0844
AMOUNT: $1,000
DEADLINE(S): MAY 30
FIELD(S): All
ELIGIBILITY/REQUIREMENTS: Open to dependents of enlisted members of the U.S. Navy, Marine Corps, or Coast Guard who are on active duty, retired with pay, or deceased. Must demonstrate financial need, be of reasonably sound scholastic standing, and of good moral character. Must have a valid Dependants ID card.
HOW TO APPLY: Must be previously approved for admission to an accredited school. Submit application with transcript, Privacy Act Statement sheet, and essay Send SASE (business size) to the Director for complete information.
NUMBER OF AWARDS: 41 per year
RENEWABLE: Yes. Up to 5 years.
CONTACT: Susan Quinn, Director

3793—NEVADA DEPARTMENT OF EDU-CATION (Nevada High School Scholars Program and Robert C. Byrd Honors Scholarship Program)

700 E. Fifth Street
Carson City NV 89701
775/687-9228
FAX: 775/687-9101
AMOUNT: Up to $1,500
DEADLINE(S): JAN 1
FIELD(S): All
ELIGIBILITY/REQUIREMENTS: Open to Nevada high school seniors with a minimum 3.50 GPA and at least 25 ACT or 1100 SAT.
HOW TO APPLY: Eligible ACT scores automatically submitted by ACT to the

DOE; SAT must be requested by student. Contact your school counselor or Department of Education for details.
RENEWABLE: Yes

3794—NEVADA DEPARTMENT OF EDU-CATION (Student Incentive Grant Program)

700 E. Fifth Street
Carson City NV 89701
775/687-9228
FAX: 775/687-9101
AMOUNT: Up to $5,000
DEADLINE(S): Varies
FIELD(S): All
ELIGIBILITY/REQUIREMENTS: Open to Nevada residents pursuing undergraduate or graduate study in eligible Nevada institutions.
HOW TO APPLY: Application must be made through the financial aid office of eligible participating institutions.

3795—NEVADA WOMEN'S FUND

770 Smithridge, Suite 300
Reno NV 89502
775/786-2335
FAX: 775/686-8152
E-mail: info@nevadawomensfund.org
Internet: http://www.nevada womensfund.org
AMOUNT: $500-$5,000
DEADLINE(S): FEB (Last Friday)
FIELD(S): All
ELIGIBILITY/REQUIREMENTS: Open to women for academic and vocational training. Preference given to applicants from northern Nevada and/or attending the University of Nevada or community colleges located in northern Nevada if the course of study is offered at those institutions.
HOW TO APPLY: Request application or download from website (available in the Fall).
NUMBER OF AWARDS: Varies
RENEWABLE: Yes, must reapply.
CONTACT: Fritsi H. Ericson, President & CEO

3796—NEW CENTURY SCHOLARS

601/984-3504, ext 3539
E-mail: scholars@na.ko.com
Internet: http://www.scholarship. programs@ptk.org
AMOUNT: $2,000
FIELD(S): All
ELIGIBILITY/REQUIREMENTS: Open to students nominated to the All-USA Academic Team.
HOW TO APPLY: See website beginning in September for application or call or

write to the above address for complete information.
NUMBER OF AWARDS: 50
RENEWABLE: No
ADDITIONAL INFORMATION: Sponsored by the Coca-Cola Foundation, the American Association of Community Colleges and Phi Theta Kappa.

3797—NEW JERSEY DEPARTMENT OF MILITARY AND VETERANS AFFAIRS (POW/MIA Dependents Grants)

P.O. Box 340
Attention: DVP, Grants & Aids
Trenton NJ 08625-0340
609/530-6854 or
800/624-0508 (NJ only)
AMOUNT: Tuition
DEADLINE(S): OCT 1; MAR 1
FIELD(S): All
ELIGIBILITY/REQUIREMENTS: Open to New Jersey residents who are dependent children of U.S. military personnel who were officially declared POW or MIA after January 1, 1960. For undergraduate tuition at any accredited public or independent college or university in New Jersey.
HOW TO APPLY: Contact New Jersey Department of Military and Veterans Affairs for an application.

3798—NEW JERSEY STATE GOLF ASSO-CIATION (Nestor J. MacDonald Memorial Caddie Scholarship)

P.O. Box 6947
Freehold NJ 07728
973/338-8334
E-mail: info@njsga.org
Internet: http://www.njsga.org
AMOUNT: Full tuition, fee, room, board and book allowance
DEADLINE(S): MAR 1
FIELD(S): All
ELIGIBILITY/REQUIREMENTS: Open to students who were caddies at NJSGA member club for at least 2 seasons. Must be pursuing full-time undergraduate study at Rutgers, the State University of New Jersey. Based on scholastic achievement, financial need, SAT scores, character, and quality of service as a caddie.
HOW TO APPLY: See website or contact NJSGA, member club golf professionals, or NJ high school guidance counselor for application. Must submit University's approved financial aid form.
NUMBER OF AWARDS: 40-50
RENEWABLE: Yes. For 4 years based on scholastic achievement.
CONTACT: J. O. Petersen, Education Director

3799—NEW JERSEY STATE GOLF ASSOCIATION (NJSGA Caddie Scholarship Foundation)

P.O. Box 6947
Freehold NJ 07728
973/338-8334
E-mail: info@njsga.org
Internet: http://www.njsga.org
AMOUNT: $2,000-$4,000
DEADLINE(S): MAR 1
FIELD(S): All
ELIGIBILITY/REQUIREMENTS: Open to students who were caddies at NJSGA member club for at least 2 seasons. Must be pursuing full-time undergraduate study at an accredited college or university. Based on scholastic achievement, financial need, SAT scores, character, and quality of service as a caddie.
HOW TO APPLY: See website or contact NJSGA for application.
NUMBER OF AWARDS: 40-50
RENEWABLE: Yes. For 4 years based on scholastic achievement.
CONTACT: J. O. Petersen, Education Director

3800—NEW JERSEY TESOL/BE INC.

P.O. Box 189
Union NJ 07083-0189
732/968-2224
Internet: http://www.njtesol-njbe.org
AMOUNT: $1,000
DEADLINE(S): APR 1
FIELD(S): All
ELIGIBILITY/REQUIREMENTS: Open to New Jersey high school seniors and undergraduates planning to attend college in New Jersey. Must be current ESL/bilingual students.
HOW TO APPLY: Call and leave a message of interest in the scholarship.

3801—NEW JERSEY UTILITIES ASSOCIATION (James R. Leva Scholarship Program)

50 West State Street, Suite 1006
Trenton NJ 08608
609/392-1000
FAX: 609/396-4231
Internet: http://www.njua.org
AMOUNT: $3,000
DEADLINE(S): APR 17
FIELD(S): All
ELIGIBILITY/REQUIREMENTS: Must be regular full-time employees of a member company or the spouse or dependent children of member utilities employees;

must meet eligibility criteria for any tuition aid program the member company might have or, if none exists, have at least 6 months of company service; and enroll or be enrolled in an approved course of study at an accredited junior college, college, or university. Based on past academic performance and future potential, school and community participation, work experience, career and educational aspirations and goals, financial needs, unusual personal or family circumstances, and recommendations submitted.
HOW TO APPLY: Send application; transcripts; and other relevant information as requested.

3802—NEW MEXICO TECH (Freshmen Scholarships)

CS Box M-801 Leroy Place
Socorro NM 87801
505/835-5333
AMOUNT: $2,000-$6,000
DEADLINE(S): MAR 1
FIELD(S): All
ELIGIBILITY/REQUIREMENTS: Open to freshmen and graduating high school seniors who are winners at the New Mexico Science and Engineering Fair or at New Mexico Science Olympiad, and transfer students.
HOW TO APPLY: Write for details.

3803—NEW MEXICO TECH (Non-Resident Students Scholarships)

CS Box M-801 Leroy Place
Socorro NM 87801
505/835-5333
AMOUNT: $700
DEADLINE(S): MAR 1
FIELD(S): All
ELIGIBILITY/REQUIREMENTS: Priority given to transfer students. Minimum GPA 3.0 freshmen; 3.5 college transfers.
HOW TO APPLY: Write for details.
RENEWABLE: Yes. Up to 4 years.

3804—NEW MEXICO TECH (Transfer Student Scholarship)

CS Box M-801 Leroy Place
Socorro NM 87801
505/835-5333
AMOUNT: $2,000-$6,000
DEADLINE(S): MAR 1
FIELD(S): All
ELIGIBILITY/REQUIREMENTS: Scholarships for transfer students to New Mexico Tech with minimum 3.0 GPA.

HOW TO APPLY: Write for details.
RENEWABLE: Yes. Up to 3 years.

3805—NEWSPAPER GUILD-CWA, THE (The David S. Barr Award)

501 Third Street NW
Washington DC 20001
202/434-7177
FAX: 202/434-1472
E-mail: guild@cwa-union.org
Internet: http://www.newsguild.org
AMOUNT: $500 (high school); $1,500 (college)
DEADLINE(S): JAN 30
FIELD(S): All
ELIGIBILITY/REQUIREMENTS: Open to high school students, including those enrolled in vocational, technical or special education programs, and to all part-time or full-time college students, including those in community colleges and graduate programs. Recognizes journalistic achievement and encourages young journalists to focus on issues of social justice.
HOW TO APPLY: See website or contact Guild by mail, phone, or e-mail.
NUMBER OF AWARDS: 2 (1 high school, 1 college)
RENEWABLE: Yes. Must reapply.
CONTACT: Dominique Edmondson

3806—NONCOMMISSIONED OFFICERS ASSOCIATION SCHOLARSHIPS

10635 1H 35N
San Antonio TX 78233
210/653-6161
Internet: http://www.ncoausa.org
AMOUNT: $900-$1,000
DEADLINE(S): MAR 31
FIELD(S): All
ELIGIBILITY/REQUIREMENTS: Open to spouses and children (under 25) of members. Must attend a 4-year undergraduate college. Based on academic achievements and a sense of patriotism.
HOW TO APPLY: Contact NCOA for an application. Submit with an essay on Americanism; 2 letters of recommendation from school, an autobiography (handwritten), a personal letter of recommendation from a non-relative, a transcript, and a copy of ACT or SAT scores.
NUMBER OF AWARDS: 15: 9 $900 academic awards to children; 4 academic awards to spouses; and 2 $1,000 grants (1 for best essay and 1 for best high school academic record).
RENEWABLE: Yes. Must be full-time student (15 credit hours), maintain mini-

mum "B" average, and remain spouse or child of current NCOA member.

3807—NORTH CAROLINA ASSOCIATION OF EDUCATORS, INC. (Martin Luther King Jr. Scholarship)

700 S. Salisbury Street
Raleigh NC 27611
919/832-3000
FAX: 919/829-1626
Internet: http://www.ncae.org
AMOUNT: $750-$1,000
DEADLINE(S): FEB 1
FIELD(S): All
ELIGIBILITY/REQUIREMENTS: Open to college-bound North Carolina high school seniors. Based on character, personality, scholastic achievement, and income.
HOW TO APPLY: Send SASE to Scholarship Committee for application.
NUMBER OF AWARDS: Varies
RENEWABLE: No

3808—NORTH DAKOTA INDIAN SCHOLARSHIP PROGRAM

State Capitol Building, 10th Floor
Bismarck ND 58505
701/328-2960
AMOUNT: $700-$2,000
DEADLINE(S): JUL 15
FIELD(S): All
ELIGIBILITY/REQUIREMENTS: Open to North Dakota residents who have at least 1/4 Indian blood or are enrolled members of a North Dakota tribe. Awards are tenable at recognized undergraduate colleges and universities in North Dakota. U.S. citizenship required.
HOW TO APPLY: Write for information.
NUMBER OF AWARDS: 100-150
RENEWABLE: Yes

3809—NORTHEAST ROOFING EDUCATIONAL FOUNDATION, INC.

150 Grossmand Drive, Suite 313
Braintree MA 02184
781/849-0555
FAX: 781/849-3223
AMOUNT: $1,500
DEADLINE(S): APR 1
FIELD(S): All
ELIGIBILITY/REQUIREMENTS: Must be members of the Northeast Roofing Contractors Association, or their employees, or their respective immediate family members; must be high school seniors or graduates who plan to enroll in a full-time undergraduate course of study at an accredited 2- or 4-year college, university, or vocational-technical school.
HOW TO APPLY: Send application and current complete transcript of grades.
NUMBER OF AWARDS: 9
RENEWABLE: No
CONTACT: Patsy Sweeney

3810—NORTHWEST DANISH FOUNDATION

Scholarship Committee
1833 North 105th Street, Suite 203
Seattle WA 98133
206/523-3263
FAX: 206/729-6997
E-mail: melony@nwdanish.org.
Internet: http://www.northwestern danishfoundation.org
AMOUNT: Varies
DEADLINE(S): Varies (late MAR/APR 1)
FIELD(S): All
ELIGIBILITY/REQUIREMENTS: Open to students of Danish descent or spouse of someone of Danish descent residing in Washington or Oregon. Must demonstrate an interest in perpetuating Danish heritage. May be used for academic or vocational degrees or retraining for employment possibilities, or for training for legitimate artistic careers that enrich or entertain. May be used for study in the U.S. or in Denmark.
HOW TO APPLY: Write, call or e-mail for application; submit with 2 references, transcripts and other information.
NUMBER OF AWARDS: Varies
RENEWABLE: Yes. Must reapply; for more details request brochure.
CONTACT: Professor Marianne Stecher-Hanson, 206/523-3263

3811—OHIO BOARD OF REGENTS (Ohio Instructional Grant Program)

State Grants and
Scholarships Department
P.O. Box 182452
Columbus OH 43218-2452
888/833-1133 or 614/466-7420
FAX: 614/752-5903
AMOUNT: $288-$4,296
DEADLINE(S): OCT 1
FIELD(S): All (except Theology)
ELIGIBILITY/REQUIREMENTS: Open to Ohio residents enrolled full time in an eligible Ohio or Pennsylvania institution of higher education. Must be in good academic standing and demonstrate financial need. Based on family income and number of dependents in family. Benefits are restricted to student's instructional and general fee charges.
HOW TO APPLY: Complete FAFSA form, available from your school's financial aid office.
NUMBER OF AWARDS: 90,000
RENEWABLE: Yes

3812—OHIO BOARD OF REGENTS (Ohio Student Choice Grants)

State Grants and
Scholarships Department
P.O. Box 182452
Columbus OH 43218-2452
888/833-1133 or 614/466-7420
FAX: 614/752-5903
AMOUNT: $900
DEADLINE(S): Varies
FIELD(S): All (except Theology)
ELIGIBILITY/REQUIREMENTS: Open to Ohio residents enrolled as full-time undergraduate students at eligible private nonprofit Ohio colleges/universities. Assists in narrowing the tuition gap between the state's public and private nonprofit colleges and universities.
HOW TO APPLY: Contact your financial aid office for information.
RENEWABLE: Yes. Up to 5 years.

3813—OHIO BOARD OF REGENTS (War Orphans Scholarship Program)

State Grants and
Scholarships Department
P.O. Box 182452
Columbus OH 43218-2452
888/833-1133 or 614/466-7420
FAX: 614/752-5903
AMOUNT: Full tuition at public schools (equivalent amount at private schools)
DEADLINE(S): JUL 1
FIELD(S): All (except Theology)
ELIGIBILITY/REQUIREMENTS: Open to Ohio residents who are dependents of veterans who served during war and are now severely disabled or deceased. Students must be full-time undergraduates at Ohio institutions.
HOW TO APPLY: Contact your financial aid office, veterans service offices, or the Board of Regents for an application.

3814—OHIO NATIONAL GUARD ADJUTANT GENERAL'S DEPARTMENT SCHOLARSHIP PROGRAM

Attention: AGOH-JO-SP
2825 West Granville Road
Columbus OH 43235
614/336-7032 or 888/400-6484

FAX: 614/336-7318
AMOUNT: Tuition (100% at public schools; average of state school fees at private schools)
DEADLINE(S): NOV 1; FEB 1; APR 1; JUL 1
FIELD(S): All
ELIGIBILITY/REQUIREMENTS: Open to students who are members of the Ohio National Guard and enrolled in a school of higher education in an associate or baccalaureate degree program.
HOW TO APPLY: Contact nearest Ohio National Guard Recruiting Office for an application.

3815—ONTARIO MINISTRY OF TRAINING, COLLEGES & UNIVERSITIES (The Aird Scholarship)

189 Red River Road, 4th Floor
Box 4500
Thunder Bay Ontario P7B 6G9
CANADA
800/465-3957
TDD: 800/465-3958
Internet: http://www.osap.gov. on.ca
AMOUNT: $2,500 (Canadian)
DEADLINE(S): Varies
FIELD(S): All
ELIGIBILITY/REQUIREMENTS: Open to Canadian citizens/permanent residents with physical disabilities for study in the first year of a full-time program at a recognized Ontario postsecondary institution. Awards go to those who best demonstrate outstanding achievement, motivation, and initiative.
HOW TO APPLY: Contact Ministry of Education & Training for an application.
NUMBER OF AWARDS: 2
RENEWABLE: No

3816—OPTIMIST INTERNATIONAL FOUNDATION (Communication Contest for the Deaf and Hard of Hearing)

Programs Department
4494 Lindell Boulevard
St. Louis MO 63108
314/371-6000, ext. 235
FAX: 314/371-6006
E-mail: programs@optimist.org
Internet: http://www.optimist.org
AMOUNT: $1,500 per district
DEADLINE(S): Varies by district
FIELD(S): All
ELIGIBILITY/REQUIREMENTS: Open to young people through grade 12 in the U.S. and Canada, to CEGEP in Quebec,

and grade 13 in the Caribbean, who are educated in the U.S., Canada or the Caribbean. Students must submit the results of an audiogram completed no longer than 24 months prior to the date of the contest by a qualified audiologist. Students must be certified to have a hearing loss of 40 decibels or more.
HOW TO APPLY: Send SASE to Programs Coordinator for informational letter and list of District Chairpersons. Contact local Chair for contest dates and where to enter.
NUMBER OF AWARDS: Up to 53 district awards
RENEWABLE: No
CONTACT: Danielle Baugher, Programs Coordinator

3817—OPTIMIST INTERNATIONAL FOUNDATION (Essay Contest)

Programs Department
4494 Lindell Boulevard
St. Louis MO 63108
314/371-6000, ext. 235
FAX: 314/371-6006
E-mail: programs@optimist.org
Internet: http://www.optimist.org
AMOUNT: $5,000 (1st prize), $3,000 (2nd), $2,000 (3rd/international), $650 (district level)
DEADLINE(S): Varies by district
FIELD(S): All
ELIGIBILITY/REQUIREMENTS: Eligible students are under age 19 as of December 31 of the current school year. Open to residents of the U.S., Canada, and the Caribbean.
HOW TO APPLY: Send SASE to Programs Coordinator for informational letter and list of district chairpersons; contact local chairperson for contest dates and where to submit essay.
NUMBER OF AWARDS: 3 international awards plus district winners
CONTACT: Danielle Baugher, Programs Coordinator

3818—OPTIMIST INTERNATIONAL FOUNDATION (Oratorial Contest)

Programs Department
4494 Lindell Boulevard
St. Louis MO 63108
314/371-6000, ext. 235
FAX: 314/371-6006
E-mail: programs@optimist.org
Internet: http://www.optimist.org
AMOUNT: $3,000 per district; awarded either as 2 $1,500 scholarships or as $1,500, $1,000 and $500

DEADLINE(S): Varies by district
FIELD(S): All
ELIGIBILITY/REQUIREMENTS: Open to eligible students under the age of 16 as of December 31 of the current school year who are residents of the U.S., Canada or the Caribbean.
HOW TO APPLY: Send SASE to Programs Coordinator for informational letter and list of District Chairpersons. Contact local Chair for contest dates and where to enter.
NUMBER OF AWARDS: 106 district awards
RENEWABLE: No
CONTACT: Danielle Baugher, Programs Coordinator

3819—ORDER OF THE EASTERN STAR (Grand Chapter of California Scholarships)

16960 Bastanchury Road, Suite E
Yorba Linda CA 92886-1711
714/986-2380
Internet: http://www.oescal.org
AMOUNT: $250-$500 (2-year college); $500-$1,000 (4-year college)
DEADLINE(S): MAR 11
FIELD(S): All
ELIGIBILITY/REQUIREMENTS: Open to members of the Order and (1) graduating high school students, (2) those who have not been able to go directly into college from high school and (3) those who have completed a portion of their higher education but are in need of aid to continue. Based on scholastic record, financial need, the need for higher education and the character of the applicant. Must have a 3.0 minimum GPA unweighted; be a citizen of the U.S. and a California resident. May be used for college or university, community college, trade school, or a religious school. Applicants applying for out-of-state schools considered.
HOW TO APPLY: See website for application. Submit to the Grand Chapter Office along with an original color photograph; if you are a naturalized citizen, supply proof of citizenship; a copy of pages 1 and 2 of current year's Federal Income tax return for yourself, if independent, or that of your parents, if you are claimed as a dependent (W2 forms will not be accepted); current principal's, dean's, administrator's, counselor's, or an instructor's report on applicant; personal letter of recommendation; copy of acceptance letter/proof of acceptance from the college or university you plan to attend; and, if a graduating high school student, an official transcript.
CONTACT: Sharanne Wick, Grand Secretary

3820—OREGON CREDIT UNION LEAGUE EDUCATIONAL FOUNDATION (Lois M. Hartley Benefit Scholarship)

P.O. Box 1900
Beaverton OR 97075
800/688-6098
AMOUNT: $4,000
DEADLINE(S): MAR 31
FIELD(S): All
ELIGIBILITY/REQUIREMENTS: Open to any member of an Oregon credit union who is currently enrolled in an undergraduate program at an accredited institution and has some form of hearing impairment.
HOW TO APPLY: Contact your credit union.
NUMBER OF AWARDS: 1

3821—OREGON DEPARTMENT OF VETERANS' AFFAIRS (Educational Aid for Oregon Veterans)

700 Summer Street NE, Suite 150
Salem OR 97310-1289
800/692-9666 or 503/373-2085
AMOUNT: $200/semester
DEADLINE(S): None
FIELD(S): All
ELIGIBILITY/REQUIREMENTS: For veterans on active duty during the Korean War or post-Korean War veterans who received a campaign or expeditionary medal or ribbon. Must be resident of Oregon and U.S. citizen with a qualifying military service record at time of application. For study in an accredited Oregon school.
HOW TO APPLY: Write for information.

3822—ORPHAN FOUNDATION OF AMERICA

12020-D North Shore Drive
Reston VA 20190-4977
571/203-0270
FAX: 571/203-0273
Internet: http://www.orphan.org
AMOUNT: $1,000-$6,000
DEADLINE(S): April 1
FIELD(S): All
ELIGIBILITY/REQUIREMENTS: Program open to orphans or youth in foster care at the age of 18 who have not been adopted. Awards tenable at any recognized undergraduate or vocational school in the U.S. Must be U.S. citizen or legal resident.
HOW TO APPLY: See website for additional information and application (after January 1).
NUMBER OF AWARDS: 300+
RENEWABLE: Yes, must reapply.

3823—OSAGE TRIBAL SCHOLARSHIP

P.O. Box 1270, 255 Senior Drive
Pawhuska OK 74056
800/390-6724
FAX: 918/287-2416
E-mail: jholding@osagetribe.org
Internet: http://www.osagetribe.org
AMOUNT: $300-$1,000
DEADLINE(S): AUG 1; DEC 31; MAY 1
FIELD(S): All
ELIGIBILITY/REQUIREMENTS: Osage CDIB or membership card; previous semester transcript; enrollment verification for semester of application; financial aid package form (included in application packet).
HOW TO APPLY: Call or e-mail to request application packet.
NUMBER OF AWARDS: Unlimited
RENEWABLE: Yes. Renewal application every semester, submit grades and schedule.
CONTACT: Jennifer Holding

3824—P. BUCKLEY MOSS SOCIETY (Anne and Matt Harbison Scholarship)

20 Stoneridge Drive, Suite 102
Waynesboro VA 22980
540/943-5678
Internet: http://www.moss society.org
AMOUNT: $1,500
DEADLINE(S): MAR 31
FIELD(S): All
ELIGIBILITY/REQUIREMENTS: Nomination by a Society member; verification of a language-related learning difference.
HOW TO APPLY: See website or contact Society for details and application.
NUMBER OF AWARDS: 1
RENEWABLE: Yes. Must reapply (up to 3 years).

3825—PACERS FOUNDATION, INC. (TeamUp Scholarship presented by Veolia Water)

125 S Pennsylvania Street
Indianapolis IN 46204
317/917-2864
FAX: 317/917-2599
E-mail: foundation@pacers.com
Internet: http://www.pacers foundation.org
AMOUNT: $2,000
DEADLINE(S): MAR 1
FIELD(S): All
ELIGIBILITY/REQUIREMENTS: Open to Indiana high school seniors who will be attending college and who have proven records of community service for college freshman year only.
HOW TO APPLY: E-mail us your name and mailing address for application.
NUMBER OF AWARDS: 5
RENEWABLE: No
CONTACT: Sarah Baird, 317/917-2864

3826—PADGETT BUSINESS SERVICES FOUNDATION SCHOLARSHIP PROGRAM

160 Hawthorne Park
Athens GA 30606
800/723-4388
E-mail: scholarship@smallbiz pros.com
AMOUNT: $500 (regional); $1,000 (national); $2,000 (international)
DEADLINE(S): MAR 1
FIELD(S): All
ELIGIBILITY/REQUIREMENTS: Open to dependents of small business owners who employ fewer than 20 individuals, own at least 10 percent of the stock or capital of the business, and are active in its day-to-day operations. (Separate scholarship is available to dependents of FTD Association member florists.) Must be graduating high school seniors planning to attend an accredited postsecondary institution; U.S. or Canadian citizens/permanent residents.
HOW TO APPLY: Contact local Padgett Business Services office or see website for application. Essay describing education and career plans is required.
ADDITIONAL INFORMATION: Local winners announced in May. All regional winners in Canada will be eligible for an additional $1,000 award from the Canada National Scholarship, while regional winners in the U.S. will be eligible for an additional $1,000 sward from the U.S. National Scholarship. One or two National winners will be awarded an additional $2,000 from the International Scholarship. The National and International award winners will be announced after June 1.

3827—PAGE EDUCATION FOUNDATION

P.O. Box 581254
Minneapolis MN 55458-1254
612/332-0406
FAX: 612/332-0403
E-mail: info@page-ed.org
Internet: http://www.page-ed.org
AMOUNT: $900-$2,500
DEADLINE(S): MAY 1
FIELD(S): All

ELIGIBILITY/REQUIREMENTS: Must be a Minnesota student of color attending a Minnesota accredited postsecondary school, community or technical college, or 4-year college/university. Must be willing to perform a minimum of 50 hours/year of service to children. Must demonstrate financial need. Students at all level of academic achievement are encouraged to apply.
HOW TO APPLY: Request application by calling or on website.
NUMBER OF AWARDS: 550+
RENEWABLE: Yes, must reapply.
CONTACT: Ramona Harristhal, Administrative Director

3828—PARAPSYCHOLOGY FOUNDATION, INC. (General Scholarly Incentive Award)

P.O. Box 1562
New York NY 10021-0043
212/628-1550
FAX: 212/628-1559
E-mail: office@parapsychology.org
Internet: http://www.para psychology.org
AMOUNT: $1,000
DEADLINE(S): NOV 15
FIELD(S): All (parapsychology)
ELIGIBILITY/REQUIREMENTS: Open to students and researchers who are finishing degree program or research project and require some additional help.
HOW TO APPLY: Send letter of application to Lisette Coly, Executive Director, to the above e-mail address.
NUMBER OF AWARDS: 1
ADDITIONAL INFORMATION: In addition 3 incentive awards members will receive an award to attend the Parapsychological Association's annual convention.

3829—PARAPSYCHOLOGY FOUNDATION, INC. (Robert R. Coly Prize)

P.O. Box 1562
New York NY 10021-0043
212/628-1550
FAX: 212/628-1559
E-mail: office@parapsychology.org
Internet: http://www.para psychology.org
AMOUNT: $1,000
DEADLINE(S): NOV 15
FIELD(S): All (parapsychology)
ELIGIBILITY/REQUIREMENTS: Applicants must show determination, academic ability, and a sincere interest in the field and write an essay of 1,000 words that addresses the topic "The Challenges of Parapsychology."

HOW TO APPLY: E-mail Parapsychology Foundation for an application or see website. Submit with high school or college transcript, 2 letters of recommendation from individuals who know their abilities and interest in the subject.
NUMBER OF AWARDS: 1

3830—PATIENT ADVOCATE FOUNDATION (Scholarships for Survivors)

700 Thimble Shoals Boulevard, Suite 200
Newport News VA 23606
757/873-6668
FAX: 757/873-8999
E-mail: info@patientadvocate.org
Internet: http://www.patient advocate.org
AMOUNT: $5,000
DEADLINE(S): MAY 1
FIELD(S): All
ELIGIBILITY/REQUIREMENTS: Open to patients seeking to initiate or complete a course of study that has been interrupted or delayed by a diagnosis of cancer or other critical or life-threatening disease (must obtain written documentation from physician). A primary consideration is that the recipients pursue a course of study that makes them immediately employable after graduation. May be used for a 2- or 4-year degree or advanced studies. Must maintain an overall 3.0 GPA; be a full-time student; agree to complete 20 hours/year of community service while receiving scholarship.
HOW TO APPLY: Submit application with last year's tax returns demonstrating financial need; high school and/or current college transcript; at least 2 letters of recommendation from nonrelated persons.
NUMBER OF AWARDS: 8
RENEWABLE: Yes. Must reapply and meet eligibility requirements.
CONTACT: Ruth Anne Reed, Executive VP of Administrative Operations

3831—PENNSYLVANIA DEPARTMENT OF MILITARY AFFAIRS-BUREAU OF VETERANS AFFAIRS (Educational Gratuity Program)

Fort Indiantown Gap
Annville PA 17003-5002
717/861-9410
FAX: 717/861-8589
AMOUNT: Up to $500/semester
DEADLINE(S): None
FIELD(S): All
ELIGIBILITY/REQUIREMENTS: Open to children of military veterans who died or were totally disabled as a result of war, armed conflict, or terrorist attack. Must have lived in Pennsylvania for 5 years prior

to application, be age 16-23, and demonstrate financial need. For full-time study at Pennsylvania schools. Must be U.S. citizen.
HOW TO APPLY: Write for information.
NUMBER OF AWARDS: Varies
RENEWABLE: Yes, 4 scholastic years.

3832—PFIZER INC. (Pfizer Epilepsy Scholarship Award)

c/o The Eden Communications Group
515 Valley Street, Suite 200
Maplewood NJ 07040
800/292-7373
Internet: http://www.epilepsy-scholarship.com/
AMOUNT: $1,000
DEADLINE(S): MAR 1
FIELD(S): All
ELIGIBILITY/REQUIREMENTS: Must be: under a doctor's care for epilepsy; a good student who participates in activities outside of school; a high school senior who has applied to college or a freshman, sophomore, or junior in college or a college senior who has applied to graduate school.
HOW TO APPLY: Ask your counselor or neurologist for an entry form. See website for application and additional information. Submit with proof of your grades and other activities, 2 letters of recommendation (1 from your doctor).
NUMBER OF AWARDS: 16
RENEWABLE: No
CONTACT: Alice Kovacs

3833—PHI KAPPA THETA NATIONAL FOUNDATION SCHOLARSHIP PROGRAM

9640 North Augusta Drive, Suite 420
Carmel IN 46032
317/872-9934
AMOUNT: $1,500 maximum
DEADLINE(S): APR 30
FIELD(S): All
ELIGIBILITY/REQUIREMENTS: Open only to undergraduate students who are members of Phi Kappa Theta. Financial need is considered but is relative to other applicants.
HOW TO APPLY: Contact your local chapter or the national office for application.
RENEWABLE: Yes
CONTACT: Maria Mandel

3834—PHILANTHROFUND FOUNDATION (PFund)

1409 Willow Street, Suite 305

Minneapolis MN 55403
612/870-1806
FAX: 612/871-6587
E-mail: info@pfundonline.org
Internet: http://www.pfund
online.org
AMOUNT: $500 and $2,000
DEADLINE(S): FEB 1
FIELD(S): All
ELIGIBILITY/REQUIREMENTS: Must
be gay, lesbian, bisexual or transgender
(GLBT) identified or from a GLBT fami-
ly; legal resident of Minnesota or attending
a qualifying Minnesota academic institu-
tion; and not a former Minnesota GLBT
Scholarship Fund or PFund scholarship
winner. Preference is given to graduating
high school students for some scholarships.
HOW TO APPLY: See website for appli-
cation and guidelines. Submit by mail.
RENEWABLE: No
CONTACT: Kit Briem, Executive Director

3835—PHILLIPS FOUNDATION, THE (The Ronald Reagan Future Leaders Scholarship Program)

7811 Montrose Road
Potomac MD 20854
202/842-2002
Internet: http://www.thephillips
foundation.org
AMOUNT: $10,000; $7,500; $5,000; $2,500
DEADLINE(S): JAN 15
FIELD(S): All
ELIGIBILITY/REQUIREMENTS: U.S.
citizen; enrolled full time at accredited 4-
year school; sophomore standing mini-
mum; significant leadership on behalf of
freedom, American values and constitu-
tional principles.
HOW TO APPLY: See website first for
complete information and application.
NUMBER OF AWARDS: Varies
RENEWABLE: Yes
CONTACT: Jeff Hollingsworth

3836—PICKETT AND HATCHER EDUCA-TIONAL FUND, INC. (Loans)

P.O. Box 8169
Columbus GA 31908-8169
706/327-6586
Internet: http://www.phef.org
AMOUNT: $5,500/year
DEADLINE(S): Varies
FIELD(S): All (except Law, Medicine, or
    Ministry)
ELIGIBILITY/REQUIREMENTS: Open
to U.S. citizens enrolled in 4-year program
in 4-year college or university. Must have
minimum 950 SAT/20 ACT score, demon-

strate financial need, and have credit-wor-
thy endorser. Loans are not for graduate or
vo-tech studies, and applicants may not
have other educational loans.
HOW TO APPLY: Contact Pickett &
Hatcher after January 1 preceding academic year for which loan is needed.
NUMBER OF AWARDS: 500-600
RENEWABLE: Yes

3837—PORTSMOUTH HIGH SCHOOL (George C. Cogan Scholarship)

50 Andrew Jarvis Drive
Portsmouth NH 03801
603/436-7100
FAX: 603/427-2320
AMOUNT: Varies
DEADLINE(S): APR 1
FIELD(S): All
ELIGIBILITY/REQUIREMENTS: For
male graduates of Portsmouth, New
Hampshire High School or Saint Thomas
Aquinas High School (in Dover, NH) who
were residents in Portsmouth, NH, for at
least 4 years prior to graduation. For
undergraduate study. Financial need is
NOT a factor.
HOW TO APPLY: Contact high school
for information.
NUMBER OF AWARDS: 15
RENEWABLE: Yes. 3 more years of
undergraduate work.

3838—PRESBYTERIAN CHURCH (U.S.A.) (Appalachian Scholarship)

100 Witherspoon Street
Louisville KY 40202-1396
888/728-7228, ext. 5745
E-mail: ksmith@ctr.pcusa.org
Internet: http://www.pcusa.org/
financialaid
AMOUNT: $200-$1,000
DEADLINE(S): JUL 1
FIELD(S): All
ELIGIBILITY/REQUIREMENTS: For
undergraduate residents of the
Appalachian areas of Kentucky, North
Carolina, Tennessee, Virginia, and West
Virginia. Must be U.S. citizens or perma-
nent residents, demonstrate financial need,
and be members of the Presbyterian
Church. Nontraditional-age students with
no previous college experience are encour-
aged to apply.
HOW TO APPLY: Contact for more
information.
RENEWABLE: Yes
CONTACT: Kathy Smith

3839—PRESBYTERIAN CHURCH (U.S.A.) (Children of Missionaries)

100 Witherspoon Street,

Room M063A
Louisville KY 40202-1396
888/728-7228, ext. 5776
FAX: 502/569-8766
E-mail: fcook@ctr.pcusa.org
Internet: http://www.pcusa.org/
financialaid
AMOUNT: $200-$1,400
DEADLINE(S): JUL 1
FIELD(S): All
ELIGIBILITY/REQUIREMENTS: For
full-time undergraduate and graduate stu-
dents attending a fully accredited college
or university in the U.S. Must be a child of
a Presbyterian Church (U.S.A.) missionary
in active service; a U.S. citizen or perma-
nent resident; and demonstrate financial
need.
HOW TO APPLY: See website for appli-
cation.
NUMBER OF AWARDS: Varies
RENEWABLE: Yes. Maximum of 4 years.
CONTACT: Frances Cook

3840—PRESBYTERIAN CHURCH (U.S.A.) (National Presbyterian College Scholarship)

100 Witherspoon Street,
Room M063A
Louisville KY 40202-1396
888/728-7228, ext. 8235
FAX: 502/569-8766
E-mail: Megan Willman@yahoo.com
Internet: http://www.pcusa.org/
financialaid
AMOUNT: $200-$1,400
DEADLINE(S): JAN 31
FIELD(S): All
ELIGIBILITY/REQUIREMENTS: For
full-time incoming freshmen at a partici-
pating college related to the Presbyterian
Church (U.S.A.). Must be superior high
school seniors and members of the
Presbyterian Church. Must be U.S. citizen
or permanent resident and demonstrate
financial need. Must take the SAT/ACT
exam no later than December 15 of senior
year.
HOW TO APPLY: Application and
brochure available after September 1;
write for more information.
NUMBER OF AWARDS: Varies
RENEWABLE: Yes
CONTACT: Megan Willman

3841—PRESBYTERIAN CHURCH (U.S.A.) (Native American Education Grant)

100 Witherspoon Street
Louisville KY 40202-1396
888/728-7228, ext. 5776

E-mail: fcook@ctr.pcusa.org
Internet: http://www.pcusa.org/
financialaid
AMOUNT: $200-$2,500
DEADLINE(S): JUN 1
FIELD(S): All
ELIGIBILITY/REQUIREMENTS: Must be high school graduates or GED recipients; be U.S. citizens or permanent residents of the U.S.; demonstrate financial need. Preference will be given to students who have completed at least 1 semester of work at an accredited institution of higher education and to members of the Presbyterian Church (U.S.A.).
HOW TO APPLY: See website for application or request from Presbyterian Marketplace 800/524-2612.
RENEWABLE: No
CONTACT: Frances Cook

3842—PRESBYTERIAN CHURCH (U.S.A.) (Samuel Robinson Award)

100 Witherspoon Street
Louisville KY 40202-1396
888/728-7228, ext. 8235
FAX: 502/569-8766
E-mail: ksmith@ctr.pcusa.org
Internet: http://www.pcusa.org/
financialaid
AMOUNT: $200-$1,400
DEADLINE(S): APR 1
FIELD(S): All
ELIGIBILITY/REQUIREMENTS: For undergraduate juniors and seniors enrolled full time in college related to the Presbyterian Church.
HOW TO APPLY: Must successfully recite the answers to the Westminster Shorter Catechism and write a 2,000-word original essay on a related assigned topic. Write for more information.
NUMBER OF AWARDS: 20-30
RENEWABLE: No
CONTACT: Kathy Smith

3843—PRESBYTERIAN CHURCH (U.S.A.) (Service Program)

100 Witherspoon Street
Louisville KY 40202-1396
888/728-7228, ext. 5735
FAX: 502/569-8766
E-mail: lbryan@ctr.pcusa.org
Internet: http://www.pcusa.org/
financialaid
AMOUNT: $1,500
DEADLINE(S): APR 1
FIELD(S): All
ELIGIBILITY/REQUIREMENTS: Provides undergraduate students with an

opportunity to pay a portion of their educational expenses through service in various school, church, or community projects. Must be in 2nd or 3rd year of full-time study, be recommended by campus pastor or chaplain of college or university, and complete 250 hours of community service. Money must be repaid if service project is not completed by graduation or discontinuation of studies.
HOW TO APPLY: Write for more information.
RENEWABLE: No
CONTACT: Laura Bryan

3844—PRESBYTERIAN CHURCH (U.S.A.) (Student Opportunity Scholarship)

100 Witherspoon Street
Louisville KY 40202-1396
888/728-7228, ext. 5760
FAX: 502/569-8766
E-mail: fcook@ctr.pcusa.org
Internet: http://www.pcusa.org/
financialaid
AMOUNT: $100-$1,400
DEADLINE(S): APR 1
FIELD(S): All
ELIGIBILITY/REQUIREMENTS: Open to African-American, Alaska Native, Asian American, Hispanic American, Native American, graduating high school seniors or undergraduate students who are U.S. citizens/permanent residents and members of the Presbyterian Church (U.S.A.). Must demonstrate financial need.
HOW TO APPLY: Contact for more information.
RENEWABLE: Yes
CONTACT: Frances Cook

3845—PRESBYTERIAN CHURCH (U.S.A.) (Theresa Mumford Scholarship)

100 Witherspoon Street
Louisville KY 40202-1396
888/728-7228, ext. 5745
E-mail: ksmith@ctr.pcusa.org
Internet: http://www.pcusa.org/
financialaid
AMOUNT: $200-$5,000
DEADLINE(S): AUG 1
FIELD(S): All
ELIGIBILITY/REQUIREMENTS: Designated for the education of orphan (parent or parents are deceased) girls from Brantley County, Georgia. If sufficient beneficiaries from Brantley County are not found, beneficiaries may be selected from Charlton, Glynn, Camden, Ware, Pierce, and Wayne Counties. Preference given to members of the Presbyterian Church

(U.S.A.); must be enrolled at an accredited institution; making satisfactory progress towards a degree; be U.S. citizens or permanent residents; demonstrate financial need.
HOW TO APPLY: Contact for more information.
RENEWABLE: Yes. Until student receives first degree.
CONTACT: Kathy Smith

3846—PRESBYTERIAN CHURCH (U.S.A.) (Undergraduate/Graduate Loan Programs)

100 Witherspoon Street
Louisville KY 40202-1396
888/728-7228, ext. 5735
FAX: 502/569-8766
E-mail: lbryan@ctr.pcusa.org
Internet: http://www.pcusa.org/
financialaid
AMOUNT: $200-$7,000
DEADLINE(S): None
FIELD(S): All
ELIGIBILITY/REQUIREMENTS: For members of the Presbyterian Church (U.S.A.) who are U.S. citizens or permanent residents for full-time undergraduate or graduate study at an accredited college or university. Must demonstrate financial need, be in good academic standing, and give evidence of financial reliability. No interest while in school; repayment begins six months after graduation or discontinuation of studies.
HOW TO APPLY: Contact for more information. May apply for maximum amount in final year of study if have not previously borrowed.
RENEWABLE: Yes
CONTACT: Laura Bryan

3847—PRIDE FOUNDATION & GREATER SEATTLE BUSINESS ASSOCIATION (Scholarships for Gays & Lesbians)

1122 East Pike Street, Suite 1001
Seattle WA 98122-3934
206/323-3318 or
800/735-7287 (outside Seattle)
FAX: 206/323-1017
E-mail: scholarships@pride
foundation.org
Internet: http://www.pride
foundation.org/scholarships
AMOUNT: Up to $10,000
DEADLINE(S): Varies
FIELD(S): All
ELIGIBILITY/REQUIREMENTS: A variety of scholarships for gay, lesbian, bisexual, transgender (LGBT) and straight-ally

students who are residents of Washington, Oregon, Idaho, Montana, or Alaska. For all levels of postsecondary education-community college, vocational training, 4-year college, or graduate school. Some require financial need.
HOW TO APPLY: Check website or write for details. Applications available OCT. 1.

3848—PROFESSIONAL HORSEMEN'S SCHOLARSHIP FUND, INC.

204 Old Sleepy Hollow Road
Pleasantville NY 10570
561/694-6893 (Nov.-Apr.)
914/769-1493 (May-Oct.)
AMOUNT: Up to $1,500
DEADLINE(S): JULY 1
FIELD(S): All
ELIGIBILITY/REQUIREMENTS: Open to members and dependents of members of the Association. May be used for college or trade school.
HOW TO APPLY: Write for application.
RENEWABLE: Yes, must reapply.
CONTACT: Ann Grenci for an application.

3849—PUEBLO OF JEMEZ SCHOLARSHIP PROGRAM (Jemez Tribal Scholarship)

P.O. Box 60
Jemez Pueblo NM 87024
505/834-9102 or 888/834-3936
FAX: 505/834-7900
Email: higher_Ed@jemezpueblo.org
or Scholarships@jemezpueblo.org
Internet: http://www.jemezpueblo.org/education
AMOUNT: Varies
DEADLINE(S): APR 30 (Fall); OCT 31 (Spring)
FIELD(S): All
ELIGIBILITY/REQUIREMENTS: Must be at least one-quarter Jemez, recognized under the Jemez Pueblos Census Office; enrolled full-time in an accredited institution of higher learning. Awards are based on the financial need.
HOW TO APPLY: Contact the Higher Education Center for an application and needs analysis form. Submit application followed (no later than 3 months) by copy of letter of acceptance from the accredited 2- or 4-year institution; official transcript from the high school or college last attended; copy of student aid report; 1-page personal essay detailing your career goals, personal interest and how you will use your education to benefit the Jemez community; needs analysis form from the financial aid office of institution; and certificate of Indian blood.

RENEWABLE: Yes. Must reapply; submit transcript.

3850—RADIO AND TELEVISION NEWS DIRECTORS ASSOCIATION & FOUNDATION (Carole Simpson Scholarship)

1600 K Street NW, Suite 700
Washington DC 20006
202/467-5218
FAX: 202/223-4007
E-mail: melaniel@rtndf.org
Internet: http://www.rtndf.org
AMOUNT: $2,000
DEADLINE(S): MAY 3
FIELD(S): All (emphasis on Broadcast/Cable Journalism)
ELIGIBILITY/REQUIREMENTS: Open to college sophomore or higher with at least 1 full year of college remaining. May be enrolled in any major but must intend a career in television or radio news. Preference given to an undergraduate student of color.
HOW TO APPLY: Submit application along with a résumé, 1-3 examples of work demonstrating journalistic skills (15 minutes or less on audio or video cassette accompanied by script); brief statement describing your role (writing, editing, producing, reporting, videography) in each story and a list of colleagues, if any, who worked on each story and what they did; a 1-page statement explaining interest in career in broadcast or cable journalism, and your specific career preferences (radio or television, reporting, producing or newsroom management); and letter of reference from dean or faculty sponsor. See website for application or contact Project Coordinator.
NUMBER OF AWARDS: 1
CONTACT: Melanie Lo, Program Coordinator

3851—RADIO AND TELEVISION NEWS DIRECTORS ASSOCIATION & FOUNDATION (Ed Bradley Scholarship)

1600 K Street NW, Suite 700
Washington DC 20006
202/467-5218
FAX: 202/223-4007
E-mail: melaniel@rtndf.org
Internet: http://www.rtndf.org
AMOUNT: $10,000
DEADLINE(S): MAY 3
FIELD(S): All (emphasis on Broadcast/Cable Journalism)
ELIGIBILITY/REQUIREMENTS: Open to college sophomore or higher with at least 1 full year of college remaining. May be enrolled in any major but must intend a

career in television or radio news. Preference given to an undergraduate student of color.
HOW TO APPLY: Submit application along with a résumé, 1-3 examples of work demonstrating journalistic skills (15 minutes or less on audio or video cassette accompanied by script); brief statement describing your role (writing, editing, producing, reporting, videography) in each story and a list of colleagues, if any, who worked on each story and what they did; a 1-page statement explaining interest in career in broadcast or cable journalism, and your specific career preferences (radio or television, reporting, producing or newsroom management), and letter of reference from dean or faculty sponsor. See website for application or contact Project Coordinator.
NUMBER OF AWARDS: 1
CONTACT: Melanie Lo, Program Coordinator

3852—RADIO AND TELEVISION NEWS DIRECTORS ASSOCIATION & FOUNDATION (Ken Kashiwahara Scholarship)

1600 K Street NW, Suite 700
Washington DC 20006
202/467-5218
FAX: 202/223-4007
E-mail: melaniel@rtndf.org
Internet: http://www.rtndf.org
AMOUNT: $2,500
DEADLINE(S): MAY 3
FIELD(S): All (emphasis on Broadcast/Cable Journalism)
ELIGIBILITY/REQUIREMENTS: Open to sophomores, juniors and seniors; currently enrolled in college (must have at least 1 full year remaining). Preference is given to student of color. May be enrolled in any major, but must intend a career in television or radio news.
HOW TO APPLY: See website or contact Project Coordinator.
NUMBER OF AWARDS: 1
CONTACT: Melanie Lo, Program Coordinator

3853—RADIO AND TELEVISION NEWS DIRECTORS ASSOCIATION & FOUNDATION (Mike Reynolds Scholarship)

1600 K Street NW, Suite 700
Washington DC 20006
202/467-5218
FAX: 202/223-4007
E-mail: melaniel@rtndf.org
Internet: http://www.rtndf.org
AMOUNT: $1,000
DEADLINE(S): MAY 3

FIELD(S): All (emphasis on Broadcast/Cable Journalism)
ELIGIBILITY/REQUIREMENTS: College sophomore or higher with at least 1 full year of college remaining may apply. May be enrolled in any major so long as applicant intends a career in television or radio news. Preference given to an undergraduate student demonstrating need for financial assistance by indicating media-related jobs held and contribution made to funding his or her own education.
HOW TO APPLY: Submit application along with a résumé, 1-3 examples of work demonstrating journalistic skills (15 minutes or less on audio or video cassette accompanied by script); brief statement describing your role (writing, editing, producing, reporting, videography) in each story and a list of colleagues, if any, who worked on each story and what they did; a 1-page statement explaining interest in career in broadcast or cable journalism, and your specific career preferences (radio or television, reporting, producing or newsroom management), and letter of reference from dean or faculty sponsor. Must submit FAFSA. See website for application or contact Project Coordinator.
NUMBER OF AWARDS: 1
CONTACT: Melanie Lo, Program Coordinator

3854—RADIO AND TELEVISION NEWS DIRECTORS ASSOCIATION & FOUNDATION (Presidents' Scholarships)

1600 K Street NW, Suite 700
Washington DC 20006
202/467-5218
FAX: 202/223-4007
E-mail: melaniel@rtndf.org
Internet: http://www.rtndf.org
AMOUNT: $2,500
DEADLINE(S): MAY 3
FIELD(S): All
ELIGIBILITY/REQUIREMENTS: Open to sophomores, juniors, and seniors currently enrolled in college (must have at least one full year remaining). May be enrolled in any major, but must intend a career in television or radio news.
HOW TO APPLY: See website or contact Project Coordinator.
NUMBER OF AWARDS: 2
CONTACT: Melanie Lo, Program Coordinator
ADDITIONAL INFORMATION: All winners receive travel, hotel accommodation and registration to annual convention.

3855—REAL ESTATE EDUCATION FOUNDATION (The Jim Kinney Scholarship)

3180 Adloff Lane, Suite 400

Springfield IL 62703
217/529-2600
FAX: 217/529-3904
Internet: http://www.illinois
realtor.org
DEADLINE(S): APR 1
FIELD(S): All
ELIGIBILITY/REQUIREMENTS: Must be child or grandchild of a member of the Illinois Association of Realtors. Based on scholastic achievement, including GPA; economic need or situation; and references and recommendations by instructors, employers, Realtors and other prominent individuals.
HOW TO APPLY: Submit application with statement of your general activities and intellectual interests, employment (if any), contemplated line of study and of the career you expect to follow (up to 1,000 words); transcripts of all your collegiate or high school records; and letters of recommendation from any 2 of the following: Association Executive from a local association of Realtors, a Realtor or a teacher. Finalists will be interviewed.
NUMBER OF AWARDS: 3
CONTACT: Larranne Wells

3856—REALTY FOUNDATION OF NEW YORK

551 Fifth Avenue, Suite 1105
New York NY 10176-0166
212/697-25103943
AMOUNT: Varies
DEADLINE(S): Varies
FIELD(S): All
ELIGIBILITY/REQUIREMENTS: Open to employees of member firms and their children.
HOW TO APPLY: Write for complete information.
CONTACT: Patricia C. Frank

3857—RECORDING FOR THE BLIND AND DYSLEXIC (Marion Huber Learning Through Listening Awards)

20 Roszel Road
Princeton NJ 08540
866/RFBD-585 or 800/803-7201
FAX: 609/520-7990
Internet: http://www.rfbd.org
AMOUNT: $2,000 and $6,000
DEADLINE(S): MAR 1
FIELD(S): Any field of study
ELIGIBILITY/REQUIREMENTS: Must have a specific learning disability (visual impairment alone does not indicate eligibility for this award); been registered as an RFB&D member for at least 1 year, up to

and including a 1-year period beginning March 1 of the previous year and ending March 1 of the current year, and have borrowed at least 1 RFB&D book during that time (individually or through a school); be a member of the graduating class of a public or private school or home-school in the U.S. or its territories; have an overall grade average of "B" or above (or equivalent), based on grades 10 through 12; and plan to continue their formal education beyond high school at either a 2- or 4-year college or vocational school.
HOW TO APPLY: Contact RFB&D for an application.

3858—RECORDING FOR THE BLIND AND DYSLEXIC (Mary P. Oenslager Scholastic Achievement Awards)

20 Roszel Road
Princeton NJ 08540
866/RFBD-585 or 800/803-7201
FAX: 609/520-7990
Internet: http://www.rfbd.org
AMOUNT: $1,000-$6,000
DEADLINE(S): MAR 1
FIELD(S): All
ELIGIBILITY/REQUIREMENTS: Be legally blind; been registered as an RFB&D member for at least one year, up to and including a 1-year period beginning March 1 of the previous year and ending March 1 of the current year, and have borrowed at least one RFB&D book during that time (individually or through a school); have received a bachelor's degree from an accredited 4-year college or university in the U.S. or its territories between July 1 and June 30; and have an overall GPA for undergraduate years of 3.0 on a 4.0 scale or equivalent.
HOW TO APPLY: Contact RFB&D for an application.
NUMBER OF AWARDS: 9

3859—RESERVE OFFICERS ASSOCIATION OF THE UNITED STATES (Henry J. Reilly Memorial Scholarships for Undergraduates)

One Constitution Avenue NE
Washington DC 20002-5655
202/479-2200 or 800/809-9448
FAX: 202/479-0416
E-mail: scholarship@roa.org
Internet: http://www.roa.org
AMOUNT: $500
DEADLINE(S): Varies (applications available in FEB)
FIELD(S): All

ELIGIBILITY/REQUIREMENTS: Must be active or associate members of ROA or ROAL, or be children or grandchildren, aged 26 or younger, of members. Children of deceased members eligible if under age 21. For full-time study at a 4-year college or university. Must have minimum 3.3 high school GPA, 3.0 college GPA. Spouses not eligible unless they are members.
HOW TO APPLY: See website or contact Association for information and application; specify your grade level. Submit application with 500-word (handwritten) essay on career goals, leadership qualities, and SAT/ACT scores required. Other requirements may vary with grade level.
NUMBER OF AWARDS: 4
CONTACT: E-mail (put attn: Reilly scholarships in subject line) or call and leave a voice message for Betsy Allen—800/809-9448, ext. 756.

3860—RETIRED ENLISTED ASSOCIATION, THE

1111 South Abilene Court
Aurora CO 80012
800/338-9337
FAX: 888/882-0835
E-mail: treahq@trea.org
Internet: http://www.trea.org
AMOUNT: $1,000-$1,500
DEADLINE(S): APR 30
FIELD(S): All
ELIGIBILITY/REQUIREMENTS: Open to full-time students. Must be a child or grandchild or great-grandchild of TREA or TREA Auxiliary member in good standing, or of a deceased person who was a member at the time of death. Must have dependent status as defined by the IRS.
HOW TO APPLY: See website or contact TREA for application (available from JAN 2 through APR 30).
NUMBER OF AWARDS: Approximately 60
RENEWABLE: Yes. Must reapply each year.

3861—RON BROWN SCHOLAR PROGRAM

1160 Pepsi Place, Suite 206B
Charlottesville VA 22901
434/964-1588
FAX: 434/964-1589
E-mail: franh@ronbrown.org
Internet: http://www.ronbrown.org
AMOUNT: $10,000
DEADLINE(S): JAN 9
FIELD(S): All
ELIGIBILITY/REQUIREMENTS: Open to African-American high school seniors who intend to pursue full-time undergraduate study at a 4-year college or university.

Must excel academically, demonstrate leadership ability, participate in community service activities. Must be a U.S. citizen or hold permanent resident visa and demonstrate financial need.
HOW TO APPLY: See website for additional information and application. Scholarship winners are selected on the basis of their applications, seminar participation, and interviews.
RENEWABLE: Yes. Up to 4 years.
CONTACT: Fran Hardey, Executive Assistant

3862—ROOTHBERT FUND, INC., THE SCHOLARSHIPS

475 Riverside Drive, Room 252
New York NY 10115
212/870-3116
E-mail: mail@roothbertfund.org
Internet: http://www.roothbert fund.org
AMOUNT: $2,000-$3,500
DEADLINE(S): FEB 1
FIELD(S): All (emphasis on Education)
ELIGIBILITY/REQUIREMENTS: Scholarships for graduates and undergraduates are open to all students regardless of sex, age, color, nationality, or religious background; however must live or attend school within a specific geographic region of the eastern U.S. (see website for details). The Fund seeks to provide support to persons motivated by spiritual values. Preference will be given to those who can satisfy high scholastic requirements and are considering careers in education. Financial need considered.
HOW TO APPLY: Download application or mail request for application to the Secretary of the Fund between December 1 and January 31; include SASE. Submit with an autobiographical statement, transcripts and letters of recommendation. Finalists will be interviewed.
NUMBER OF AWARDS: 15 to 20
RENEWABLE: Yes. Must submit renewal application accompanied by transcripts for the current year.
ADDITIONAL INFORMATION: Each award is subject to revocation if the recipient fails to maintain high standard of work and conduct, to submit transcripts after each semester, attend at least 1 weekend fellowship conference, maintain relationship with Fund, advise Fund of change in academic or financial status.

3863—ROTARY FOUNDATION OF ROTARY INTERNATIONAL (Ambassadorial Scholarships)

One Rotary Center

1560 Sherman Avenue
Evanston IL 60201-3698
847/866-3000
FAX: 847/328-8554
Internet: http://www.rotary.org
AMOUNT: Up to $26,000
DEADLINE(S): Varies
FIELD(S): All
ELIGIBILITY/REQUIREMENTS: Must be citizens of a country in which there is a Rotary Club; have completed at least 2 years of university coursework or equivalent professional experience prior to beginning scholarship studies. Scholarships vary from 3- to 6-month intensive language study, cultural immersion to 1- and 2-year degree-oriented programs.
HOW TO APPLY: See website or contact your local Rotary Club for specific details and an application.
NUMBER OF AWARDS: 1,300

3864—SAINT JOSEPH'S UNIVERSITY (Honors Program Scholarships and Fellowships)

5600 City Avenue
Philadelphia PA 19131-1395
610/660-1555 or 610/660-1556
FAX: 610/660-1342
E-mail: finaid@sju.edu
Internet: http://www.sju.edu/admissions/
AMOUNT: Up to $20,000
DEADLINE(S): Varies
FIELD(S): All
ELIGIBILITY/REQUIREMENTS: Based on SAT scores and GPA and extracurricular involvement at the time the application is submitted for review.
HOW TO APPLY: See website for additional information and application.
RENEWABLE: Yes. Based on maintaining GPA and extracurricular involvement.
CONTACT: Office of Financial Assistance

3865—SALVADORAN-AMERICAN & EDUCATIONAL FUND (SALEF) (Fulfilling Our Dreams Scholarship Fund)

1625 West Olympic Boulevard, Suite 718
Los Angeles CA 90015
213/480-1052
FAX: 213/487-2530
E-mail: lchicas@salef.org or jgalvez@salef.org
Internet: http://www.salef.org
AMOUNT: $500-$5,000
DEADLINE(S): JUN 30
FIELD(S): All

ELIGIBILITY/REQUIREMENTS: Must be Salvadoran, Central American, or Latino students; high school students who have been accepted to a 4-year college or college students pursuing their bachelor's or master's degree; demonstrate financial need; have a GPA of at least 3.0; and show history of community service and involvement.
HOW TO APPLY: Send application with a 500-word essay.
NUMBER OF AWARDS: Multiple
CONTACT: Lizeth Chicas, Executive Assistant & Scholarship Fund Coordinator, or Jenny Galvez, Civic & Community Programs Manager

3866—SAMUEL HUNTINGTON PUBLIC SERVICE AWARD, THE

National Grid
25 Research Drive
Westborough MA 01582
508/389-3390
FAX: 508/389-2605
E-mail: amy.stacy@us.ngrid.com
Internet: http://www.national
gridus.com/education
AMOUNT: $10,000
DEADLINE(S): FEB 15
FIELD(S): All
ELIGIBILITY/REQUIREMENTS: Provides stipend to graduating college senior to undertake one-year public service project anywhere in the world immediately following graduation.
HOW TO APPLY: See website for FAQs, application and more information. Submit application, proposal, budget, 3 letters of recommendation, transcript and résumé.
NUMBER OF AWARDS: 1-3
RENEWABLE: No
CONTACT: Amy Stacy
ADDITIONAL INFORMATION: Award is not intended to support matriculation.

3867—SAMUEL LEMBERG SCHOLARSHIP-LOAN FUND, INC. (Interest-free Loans)

430 Park Avenue, Suite 505
New York NY 10022
AMOUNT: Up to $5,000
DEADLINE(S): APR 1
FIELD(S): All
ELIGIBILITY/REQUIREMENTS: Open to Jewish men and women pursuing any undergraduate, graduate, or professional degree who demonstrate academic excellence and achievement, and financial need. Must repay loan within 10 years after completion of studies.

HOW TO APPLY: Send SASE to above address for an application. Submit with transcripts and letters of recommendation.
RENEWABLE: Yes. Must be enrolled full time.

3868—SAN DIEGO AIR & SPACE MUSEUM (Convair Alumni Association Scholarship Fund)

Education Office
2001 Pan American Plaza
San Diego CA 92101
619/234-8291, ext. 119
AMOUNT: $3,000-$4,000
DEADLINE(S): APR 1
FIELD(S): All
ELIGIBILITY/REQUIREMENTS: For graduating seniors of San Diego County high schools, who will be attending a 4-year college. Direct descendants (natural or adopted) of former San Diego area employees of Consolidated Aircraft Corporation, or Consolidated Vultee Aircraft Corporation, or General Dynamics Corporation prior to 1998, who worked in the San Diego area. Selection based on merit, community service, and leadership potential.
HOW TO APPLY: See website or contact Museum for application. Eligible applicants will be interviewed.

3869—SANTA ROSA JUNIOR COLLEGE (Business and Community Scholarships)

Barnett Hall, #1284
1501 Mendocino Avenue
Santa Rosa CA 95401-4395
707/527-4740
E-mail: mmartin@santarosa.edu
Internet: http://www.santarosa.
edu/scholarship
AMOUNT: Varies
DEADLINE(S): Varies
FIELD(S): Varies
ELIGIBILITY/REQUIREMENTS: Awards are based on various criteria. Open to high school seniors, students already attending SRJC pursuing A.A. degree or units necessary to transfer to a 4-year institution, and for vo-tech students.
HOW TO APPLY: See website for details and applications or contact the SRJC Scholarship Office, Barnett Hall, Room 1284.

3870—SANTA ROSA JUNIOR COLLEGE (Doyle Scholarship Program)

Barnett Hall, #1284
1501 Mendocino Avenue
Santa Rosa CA 95401-4395

707/527-4740
E-mail: mmartin@santarosa.edu
Internet: http://www.santarosa.
edu/scholarship
AMOUNT: $1,000-$1,600
DEADLINE(S): MAR 1
FIELD(S): All
ELIGIBILITY/REQUIREMENTS: Awards are based on scholastic achievement. For high school seniors, students already attending SRJC pursuing A.A. degree or units necessary to transfer to a 4-year institution, and for students planning to complete one of the Occupational Certificate programs. Must be U.S. citizen or permanent resident. Financial need may determine award amount but is not required.
HOW TO APPLY: See website for details and applications or contact the SRJC Scholarship Office, Barnett Hall, Room 1284. Applications available from beginning of January through March 1.

3871—SANTA ROSA JUNIOR COLLEGE (SRJC Foundation Scholarships)

Barnett Hall, #1284
1501 Mendocino Avenue
Santa Rosa CA 95401-4395
707/527-4740
E-mail: mmartin@santarosa.edu
Internet: http://www.santarosa.edu/
scholarship
AMOUNT: Varies
DEADLINE(S): MAR 1
FIELD(S): All
ELIGIBILITY/REQUIREMENTS: For continuing students, who have completed at least 12 units at SRJC (minimum GPA 2.5) and for students with at least 56 transferable units transferring to a 4-year institution during the upcoming academic year (minimum GPA 3.0).
HOW TO APPLY: Various awards; may submit 1 application for more than 200 different scholarships. See website for details and applications or contact the SRJC Scholarship Office, Barnett Hall, Room 1284.

3872—SARA'S WISH FOUNDATION

15 Ash Lane
Amherst MA 01002
413/256-0914
FAX: 413/253-3338
E-mail: info@saraswish.org
Internet: http://www.saraswish.org
AMOUNT: $1,000-$2,000
DEADLINE(S): JAN 1 (preliminary applications)
FIELD(S): All

ELIGIBILITY/REQUIREMENTS: Travel scholarships open to young women engaged in educational pursuits that will contribute to the global community through public service, education, etc. Must demonstrate a commitment to public service, a strong record of scholarship, a history of leadership experience, a sincere interest in the work of the Foundation, and a willingness to join with Sara's Wish Foundation in its ongoing efforts to improve safety awareness.

HOW TO APPLY: See website for additional information and application. Candidates selected from the preliminary applications are asked to submit résumés, essays, and 2 letters of recommendation; finalists are interviewed by telephone or in person by members of the scholarship committee.

NUMBER OF AWARDS: 6-10

RENEWABLE: No

CONTACT: Wendy Kohler, Scholarship Chair

3873—SCHOLARSHIP FOUNDATION OF SAINT LOUIS (Interest-free Loan Program)

8215 Clayton Road
St. Louis MO 63117
314/725-7990
E-mail: info@sfstl.org
Internet: http://www.sfstl.org

AMOUNT: Up to $4,500 (undergraduate); $6,000 (graduate)

DEADLINE(S): APR 15; NOV 15

FIELD(S): All (except ministry)

ELIGIBILITY/REQUIREMENTS: Residents of the St. Louis area who are high school graduates and can demonstrate financial need; 6 years to repay following graduation.

HOW TO APPLY: Write for complete information.

RENEWABLE: Yes. Maximum of $4,500/$6,000; must maintain good academic standing and continued show of need.

3874—SCOTTISH RITE FOUNDATION OF WYOMING (Floyd Holland, 33rd Degree Mason, Memorial Scholarship)

1820 Capitol Avenue
Cheyenne WY 82007
307/632-2948
FAX: 307/637-7160
E-mail: charliepgm@bresnan.net
Internet: http://www.wy-srmason.org

AMOUNT: $1,000

DEADLINE(S): JUN 1

FIELD(S): All

ELIGIBILITY/REQUIREMENTS: Must be graduate of a Wyoming high school, or

hold a Wyoming GED, and a senior at University of Wyoming or sophomore at a Wyoming community colleges. Selection is based on demonstration of leadership potential, GPA, and financial need.

HOW TO APPLY: Send application, with photo and required exhibits to Financial Aid officer at college applicant is attending.

NUMBER OF AWARDS: 3 per college

CONTACT: Charles H. Moore, Secretary

3875—SEAFARERS' INTERNATIONAL UNION (Scholarships for Dependents)

Seafarers Health and Benefits Plan
5201 Auth Way
Camp Springs MD 20746
301/899-0675

AMOUNT: $5,000 (4-year program)

DEADLINE(S): APR 15

FIELD(S): All

ELIGIBILITY/REQUIREMENTS: Open to members and dependents (children and spouses) of eligible employees and pensioners; parent/spouse must meet employment requirements. Children must be unmarried and under age 19, graduating high school or under age 15 and enrolled in a program leading to a 2- or 4-year or higher degree at an accredited institution. Based on secondary school records, SAT/ACT scores, college transcripts (if applicable), autobiography, character references, and extracurricular activities.

HOW TO APPLY: Contact Union for information/application package. Submit with autobiographical statement, photo, copy of birth certificate, transcript and certification of graduation or GED, college transcript (if applicable), 3 letters of recommendation, SAT/ACT results.

NUMBER OF AWARDS: 5

RENEWABLE: Yes. Up to $20,000.

3876—SEAFARERS' INTERNATIONAL UNION (Scholarships for Seafarers)

Seafarers Health and Benefits Plan
5201 Auth Way
Camp Springs MD 20746
301/899-0675

AMOUNT: $3,000 (2-year program); $5,000 (4-year program)

DEADLINE(S): APR 1

FIELD(S): All

ELIGIBILITY/REQUIREMENTS: Based on high school equivalency scores or secondary school records, college transcripts (if any), SAT/ACT scores, and references on character and personality, and must meet employment requirements. May be used at any fully accredited 2- or 4-year college or university, or postsecondary

trade or vocational school. Must complete 4-year program in 6 years and 2-year program in 4 years (amount will be pro rated).

HOW TO APPLY: Contact Union for information/application package. Submit with autobiographical statement, photo, copy of birth certificate, transcript and certification of graduation or GED, college transcript (if applicable), 3 letters of recommendation, SAT/ACT results.

NUMBER OF AWARDS: 1-2 ($5,000); 2 ($3,000)

RENEWABLE: Yes. Up to $20,000 and $6,000 (depending on program). Recipients of 1-year award may apply for 4-year scholarship.

3877—SEARS CRAFTSMAN (NHRA Youth & Educational Scholarships)

NHRA Youth & Education Services
2035 Financial Way
Glendora CA 91741-4602
626/250-5555
FAX: 212/204-3972/73
E-mail: rkaizoji@nhra.com
Internet: http://www.nhra.com

AMOUNT: $1,000

DEADLINE(S): MAY 1

FIELD(S): All

ELIGIBILITY/REQUIREMENTS: Must be high school students with a GPA of at least 2.0 and planning to attend a 2- or 4-year college or trade or technical school.

NUMBER OF AWARDS: 21

CONTACT: Tiffany Bonham

3878—SECOND MARINE DIVISION ASSOCIATION

P.O. Box 8180
Camp Lejeune NC 28547-8180
910/451-3167
FAX: 910/451-3167

AMOUNT: $1,000/year

DEADLINE(S): APR 1

FIELD(S): Any

ELIGIBILITY/REQUIREMENTS: Must be an unmarried dependent son, daughter or grandchild of an individual who has served in the 2nd Marine Division or a unit attached to the Division. At the time of application, the applicant must be a senior in high school; a high school graduate; or currently enrolled as a full-time student in an accredited college or vocational/technical school. An academic average equivalent to a C+ or 2.5 is also required for consideration. The applicant's family income (i.e. adjusted gross income) should not normally exceed $42,000 for the taxable year preceding the school year for which assistance is requested.

HOW TO APPLY: Write or call for application.
NUMBER OF AWARDS: 35
RENEWABLE: Yes. Must stay enrolled and maintain a 2.5 GPA.
CONTACT: Chuck Van Horne

3879—SENATOR GEORGE J. MITCHELL SCHOLARSHIP PROGRAM RESEARCH INSTITUTE, THE

22 Monument Square, Suite 200
Portland ME 04101
207/773-7700
FAX: 207/773-1188
E-mail: phiggins@mitchellinstitute.org
Internet: http://www.mitchell institute.org
AMOUNT: $1,000
DEADLINE(S): APR 1 for application form; MAY 1 for supporting materials
FIELD(S): All
ELIGIBILITY/REQUIREMENTS: Must be a graduating senior from a Maine public high school entering 1st year of college in the fall.
HOW TO APPLY: Application available online or from the guidance office of each public high school on January 1.
NUMBER OF AWARDS: 130
RENEWABLE: Yes. Must be enrolled at least half-time; up to 4 years.
CONTACT: Patty Higgins

3880—SENECA NATION HIGHER EDUCATION PROGRAM-SENECA NATION OF INDIANS

P.O. Box 231
Salamanca NY 14779
716/945-1790, ext. 3103
FAX: 716/945-7170
E-mail: dhoag@sni.org
AMOUNT: $6,000; $8,000; $11,000
DEADLINE(S): JUL 1 (fall); DEC 1 (spring); MAY 1 (summer); AUG 1 (fall quarter/trimester); NOV 1 (winter quarter/trimester); FEB 1 (spring quarter/trimester); MAY 1 (summer quarter/trimester)
FIELD(S): All
ELIGIBILITY/REQUIREMENTS: Enrolled member of the SNI with financial need; admitted for enrollment in an accredited institution of higher education; undergraduate or graduate student. Based on priority system defined by residence; must apply for and report all financial aid resources, compliance with SNI-HEP policies. Must not be in default of a student loan. Note: Program administers BIA Higher Education Grant Funds.
HOW TO APPLY: Complete application including transcript, financial aid package forms, acceptance letter, tribal certification, letter of reference and letter stating educational goals.

3881—SERTOMA FOUNDATION INTERNATIONAL (Scholarships for Students With Hearing Loss)

1912 East Meyer Boulevard
Kansas City MO 64132-1174
Phone and TTY: 816/333-8300
FAX: 816/333-4320
Internet: http://www.sertoma.org
AMOUNT: $1,000
DEADLINE(S): MAY 1
FIELD(S): All
ELIGIBILITY/REQUIREMENTS: For students with a documented hearing loss who are entering or continuing students at universities or colleges in the U.S. or Canada pursuing 4-year bachelor's degrees. Must have at least 3.2 GPA or at least 85% in all high school and college classes.
HOW TO APPLY: Send SASE to "$1,000 Scholarships" for information and application (available in October).
RENEWABLE: Yes. Must reapply; no preference given; up to 4 times.

3882—SEVENTEEN (Fiction Contest)

1440 Broadway, 13th Floor
New York NY 10018
212/204-4300
FAX: 212/204-3972/73
E-mail: excel@ieha.org
Internet: http://www.ieha.org
AMOUNT: $250
DEADLINE(S): APR 30
FIELD(S): All; Creative Writing
ELIGIBILITY/REQUIREMENTS: Must be between 13 and 21 as of April 30. Fiction must not have been previously published in any form except school publications. Stories may not exceed 3,500 words (about 14 pages); may submit unlimited number.
HOW TO APPLY: Winners or legal guardians must sign an affidavit of compliance with rules and a publicity release. Acceptance of prize constitutes winner's permission to use their names, likeness, cities and states of residence, and to be photographed for advertising and publicity purposes without additional compensation, except where prohibited by law.
NUMBER OF AWARDS: 1

3883—SIDNEY-SHELBY COUNTY YMCA (Lee E. Schauer Memorial Scholarship)

300 E. Parkwood

Sidney OH 45365
937/492-9134
FAX: 937/492-4705
E-mail: info@sidney-ymca.org
Internet: http://www.sidney-ymca.org
AMOUNT: $5,000
DEADLINE(S): Varies
FIELD(S): All
ELIGIBILITY/REQUIREMENTS: Open to a college-bound high school senior who is a member of the Sidney-Shelby County YMCA for at least 3 years prior to application. Must have a minimum 2.5 GPA, demonstrate Christian values and leadership, be involved in sports or fitness activities, and volunteer at the Y or in the community. Scholarship must "make a significant difference" to recipient. Financial need NOT a factor.
HOW TO APPLY: Contact YMCA for an application.
NUMBER OF AWARDS: 1
RENEWABLE: Yes. Up to 4 years.
CONTACT: Barbara Sperl

3884—SIGMA PHI EPSILON FRATERNITY (National Balanced Man Scholarship)

310 South Boulevard
Richmond VA 23220
804/353-1901
FAX: 804/359-8160
E-mail: karen.simpson@sigep.net
Internet: http://www.sigep.org
AMOUNT: $500-$2,500
DEADLINE(S): Varies
FIELD(S): All
ELIGIBILITY/REQUIREMENTS: Open to males who will be entering a 4-year college or university as full-time freshmen. The one-time award is given to those who excel in scholarship, athletics, and leadership. Minimum GPA of 3.0 required.
HOW TO APPLY: Write for application if school attending has a Sigma Phi Epsilon chapter offering scholarship.
NUMBER OF AWARDS: Over 100
RENEWABLE: No
CONTACT: John A. Schuyler or Karen Simpson

3885—SIGNET CLASSICS SCHOLARSHIP ESSAY CONTEST

Penguin (USA)
Academic Marketing Department
375 Hudson Street
New York NY 10014
Internet: http://www.signet classics.com/scessay
AMOUNT: $1,000
DEADLINE(S): APR 15

FIELD(S): All
ELIGIBILITY/REQUIREMENTS: Essay contest for high school juniors and seniors on a work of classic literature chosen by Signet Classics. Essays must be at 2 and no more than 3 double-spaced pages, computer or typewritten and must be original sole work of entrant. For U.S. citizens or permanent residents. Judged on style, content, grammar, and originality. Must be in 11th or 12th grade at time of entry or between ages of 16-18 if home-schooled.
HOW TO APPLY: Contact company or check website for subject and deadline. Entries must be submitted by a high school English teacher on school letterhead on behalf of the student. Each teacher may submit 1 junior and 1 senior essay. Winning students' schools receive a Signet Classics library for their school.
NUMBER OF AWARDS: 5
RENEWABLE: Yes

3886—SOCIETY OF DAUGHTERS OF THE U.S. ARMY (Roberts, Wagner, Prickett, Simpson & DUSA Scholarships)

11804 Grey Birch Place
Springfield VA 20191
AMOUNT: Up to $1,000
DEADLINE(S): MAR 1
FIELD(S): All
ELIGIBILITY/REQUIREMENTS: For undergraduate study. Open to daughters and granddaughters (including step- or adopted) of career warrant 9WO 1-5 or commissioned officers of the U.S. Army (2nd LT & 1st LT, CPT, MAJ, LTC. COL, or General) who are currently on active duty, or who retired from active duty after at least 20 years of service, or were medically retired before 20 years of active service, or who died on active duty or after eligible retirement. U.S. Army must have been the officer's primary occupation. Must have minimum 3.0 GPA; demonstrate need.
HOW TO APPLY: SASE between November 1 and March 1 to request application; must include officer's name, rank, component (active, reserve, retired), inclusive dates of service, and relationship to applicant. Application must include transcript, SAT/ACT scores, school and community activities, 3 references, résumé, and essay on subject.
NUMBER OF AWARDS: About 8
RENEWABLE: Yes, must reapply.

3887—SONS OF ITALY FOUNDATION (American University of Rome)

219 E Street NE
Washington DC 20002

202/547-5106
FAX: 202/547-8168
E-mail: sif@osia.org
Internet: http://www.osia.org
FIELD(S): All
ELIGIBILITY/REQUIREMENTS: For 1 year of study. Must be U.S. citizen of Italian descent (at least 1 Italian or Italian-American grandparent); entering sophomore, junior or senior in the fall. Financial need NOT a factor.
HOW TO APPLY: Contact Foundation by phone or e-mail for application and information. Application not available online.
RENEWABLE: No
CONTACT: Gina Guiducci, Scholarship Coordinator

3888—SONS OF ITALY FOUNDATION (Henry Salvatori Scholarship)

219 E Street NE
Washington DC 20002
202/547-2900 or 202/547-5106
FAX: 202/547-8168
E-mail: sif@osia.org
Internet: http://www.osia.org
AMOUNT: $4,000-$25,000
DEADLINE(S): FEB 28
FIELD(S): All
ELIGIBILITY/REQUIREMENTS: Open to college-bound high school senior who demonstrates exceptional leadership, distinguished scholarship and a deep understanding and respect for the principles of liberty, freedom, and equality. Must be U.S. citizen of Italian descent (at least 1 Italian or Italian-American grandparent) in senior year of high school, planning to attend a 4-year accredited academic institution in the fall. Financial need NOT a factor.
HOW TO APPLY: See website or contact Foundation for additional information and application; submit with SASE, transcripts, including class rank and GPA; applicable standardized test scores; résumé; 2 letters of recommendation from public figures whose careers have demonstrated a commitment to principles scholarship embodies; 750- to 1,000-word essay on assigned topic, cover letter 150-250 words outlining academic and professional goals; and $25 processing fee. Note: Automatically eligible for General Scholarship.
RENEWABLE: No
CONTACT: Gina Guiducci, Scholarship Coordinator

3889—SONS OF ITALY FOUNDATION (National Leadership Grant General Scholarships)

219 E Street NE

Washington DC 20002
202/547-2900 or 202/547-5106
FAX: 202/546-8168
E-mail: sif@osia.org
Internet: http://www.osia.org
AMOUNT: $4,000-$25,000
DEADLINE(S): FEB 28
FIELD(S): All
ELIGIBILITY/REQUIREMENTS: U.S. citizen of Italian descent (at least 1 Italian or Italian-American grandparent) enrolled in an undergraduate or graduate program at a 4-year, accredited academic institution. Financial need NOT a factor.
HOW TO APPLY: See website or contact Foundation for additional information and application; submit with SASE, transcripts, including class rank and GPA; applicable standardized test scores; résumé; 2 letters of recommendation from teachers, professors or educational administrators; 500- to 700-word essay on the principal contributions of Italian-Americans to U.S. culture and society, and $25 processing fee. Note: See local and state lodges for information regarding scholarships offered to members and their children.
NUMBER OF AWARDS: 10-13
RENEWABLE: No
CONTACT: Gina Guiducci, Scholarship Coordinator

3890—SONS OF ITALY FOUNDATION (Pietro Secchia Scholarship)

219 E Street NE
Washington DC 20002
202/547-5106
FAX: 202/547-8168
E-mail: sif@osia.org
Internet: http://www.osia.org
FIELD(S): All
ELIGIBILITY/REQUIREMENTS: For 1 semester at John Cabot University, Rome. Must be U.S. citizen of Italian descent (at least 1 Italian or Italian-American grandparent); entering sophomore, junior or senior in the fall. Financial need NOT a factor.
HOW TO APPLY: Contact Foundation by phone or e-mail for application and information. Application not available online.
RENEWABLE: No
CONTACT: Gina Guiducci, Scholarship Coordinator

3891—SONS OF NORWAY FOUNDATION (Astrid G. Cates/Myrtle Beinhauer Fund)

c/o Sons of Norway
1455 West Lake Street
Minneapolis MN 55408

612/821-4632
E-mail: colson@sofn.com
Internet: http://www.sofn.com/
foundation/
AMOUNT: $500-$750 (Cates); $3,000 (Beinhauer)
DEADLINE(S): MAR 1
FIELD(S): All
ELIGIBILITY/REQUIREMENTS: Applicants must have a certificate of completion from high school and be enrolled in postsecondary training or education (college, vocational school, or trade school) and be current members of or children or grandchildren of current members in districts 1-6. Must demonstrate financial need.
HOW TO APPLY: Submit application along with transcript; statement of career goals; letter of recommendation from teacher, youth leader, or someone else not related to you describing your character and abilities. See website or contact Foundation for an application and additional details.
NUMBER OF AWARDS: 6 Cates (1/district); 1 (Beinhauer)
RENEWABLE: Yes. Maximum of 2 scholarships in a 5-year period.
CONTACT: Cindy Olson, Director
ADDITIONAL INFORMATION: Extra points are given to students who are members of SON.

3892—SONS OF NORWAY FOUNDATION (Scholarship for Study at Oslo International Summer School)

Oslo International Summer School Scholarship Program
c/o Sons of Norway
1455 West Lake Street
Minneapolis MN 55408
612/821-4632
E-mail: colson@sofn.com
Internet: http://www.sofn.com/
foundation/
AMOUNT: $1,500
DEADLINE(S): MAR 1
FIELD(S): All
ELIGIBILITY/REQUIREMENTS: Open to applicants who are admitted to Oslo International Summer School (see http://www.uio.no/iss/ for information about the program and its admission requirements) who are current SON members or children or grandchildren of current members. Financial need, essay, GPA, and recommendations are considered.
HOW TO APPLY: Submit application along with an essay and letters of recom-

mendation. See website for an application and additional details.
NUMBER OF AWARDS: 2
CONTACT: Cindy Olson, Director
ADDITIONAL INFORMATION: Extra points are given to students who are members of SON.

3893—SOUTH CAROLINA DEPARTMENT OF EDUCATION (Archibald Rutledge Scholarship Competition)

1429 Senate Street
Columbia SC 29201
803/734-8500
Internet: http://www.mysc
schools.com
AMOUNT: Approximately $4,000
DEADLINE(S): FEB 3
FIELD(S): All
ELIGIBILITY/REQUIREMENTS: Must be high school senior in public school; U.S. citizen who has attended South Carolina public schools for the past 2 consecutive years. May compete in only 1 of the 4 areas: creative writing, drama, music and visual arts. May be used at any college or university in South Carolina. Jointly produced compositions are not accepted.
HOW TO APPLY: See website for application or contact State Department of Education.
NUMBER OF AWARDS: 4
RENEWABLE: No
CONTACT: Sallie Spade at the State Department of Education at sspde@sde.state.sc.us

3894—SOUTH CAROLINA GOVERNOR'S OFFICE, DIVISION OF VETERANS AFFAIRS (Free Tuition for Certain War Veterans' Children)

VA Regional Office, Room 141
1801 Assembly Street
Columbia SC 29201
803/255-4255
FAX: 803/255-4257
AMOUNT: Tuition
DEADLINE(S): None
FIELD(S): All
ELIGIBILITY/REQUIREMENTS: Open to children (26 or younger) of South Carolina war veterans who were legal residents of South Carolina at time of entry into service and who were MIA, POW, KIA, totally disabled, or died of disease as determined by VA, and/or who is recipient of Congressional Medal of Honor/Purple Heart. Students must be South Carolina residents planning to pursue undergradu-

ate study at South Carolina state-supported schools. Financial need NOT a factor.
HOW TO APPLY: Contact Division of Veterans Affairs for additional information and application.

3895—SOUTH CAROLINA HIGHER EDUCATION TUITION GRANTS COMMISSION (Tuition Grants Program)

101 Business Park Boulevard,
Suite 2100
Columbia SC 29203-9498
803/896-1120
FAX: 803/896-1126
E-mail: toni@sctuitiongrants.org
Internet: http://www.sctuition
grants.com
AMOUNT: $2,645 (average)
DEADLINE(S): JUN 30
FIELD(S): All
ELIGIBILITY/REQUIREMENTS: Open to South Carolina residents who are either entering freshmen who rank in upper 75% of high school class or score 900 on SAT or ACT, or graduate with at least a 2.0 GPA on SC Uniform Grading Scale or upperclassmen who pass 24 credit hours annually. Must demonstrate financial need and be pursuing their first bachelor's degree at independent, South Carolina-based, accredited colleges. Must be U.S. citizen/permanent resident.
HOW TO APPLY: Complete and submit FAFSA.
NUMBER OF AWARDS: 11,000
RENEWABLE: Yes
CONTACT: Toni Cave, Financial Aid Counselor

3896—SOUTH CAROLINA JUNIOR GOLF FOUNDATION SCHOLARSHIP PROGRAM

P.O. Box 1465
Taylors SC 29687-0031
864/268-3363
FAX: 864/268-7160
E-mail: susanjlee@bellsouth.net
Internet: http://www.scholarship
programs.org
AMOUNT: $2,500
DEADLINE(S): DEC 1
FIELD(S): All
ELIGIBILITY/REQUIREMENTS: Must be a high school senior at a South Carolina high school or undergraduate attending college in South Carolina and a South Carolina resident; must have a cumulative GPA of 2.75 and a competitive or recreational interest in golf. Recipients may attend any accredited public or private 4-year college or university in South

Carolina. Based on academic merit (SAT/ACT scores, rank in class and GPA are important) and financial need.
HOW TO APPLY: May apply online or call for application. There are additional materials required.
RENEWABLE: Yes. Must reapply; must maintain a cumulative GPA of 2.75.

3897—SOUTH CAROLINA STUDENT LOAN CORPORATION

P.O. Box 21487
Columbia SC 29221
803/798-0916
FAX: 803/772-9410
Internet: http://www.scstudent loan.org
AMOUNT: $1,000
DEADLINE(S): None
FIELD(S): All
ELIGIBILITY/REQUIREMENTS: Open to high school seniors, college students and parents of high school seniors and dependent college students. Must be South Carolina resident, with the student attending, or planning to attend on at least a half-time basis, an eligible institution; or a non-resident of South Carolina with the student attending, or planning to attend on at least a half-time basis, an eligible institution located in South Carolina. The student receiving a scholarship award must be a U.S. citizen, permanent resident alien, or a person who has filed a declaration of intent to become a citizen. Participants who hold any student loans in a repayment status must be current on all payments.
HOW TO APPLY: See website for application.
NUMBER OF AWARDS: 12
RENEWABLE: Yes, complete entry form on website after September 14 of each year

3898—SOUTH DAKOTA BOARD OF REGENTS (Martin R. Scarborough Memorial Scholarship)

Scholarship Committee
306 E. Capitol Avenue, Suite 200
Pierre SD 57501-3159
AMOUNT: $1,000
DEADLINE(S): MAR 1
FIELD(S): All
ELIGIBILITY/REQUIREMENTS: Open to students at all public universities in South Dakota; must have a 3.5 GPA; must be at least junior.
HOW TO APPLY: Each South Dakota public university may nominate 1 student, get application form and submit to university's Financial Aid Office with essay explaining your leadership and academic

qualities, career plans, and educational interests.
NUMBER OF AWARDS: 1

3899—SOUTH DAKOTA DEPARTMENT OF EDUCATION (Robert Byrd Honors Scholarship)

700 Governors Drive
Pierre SD 57501-2291
605/773-5669
FAX: 605/773-6139
AMOUNT: $1,500
DEADLINE(S): MAY 1
FIELD(S): All
ELIGIBILITY/REQUIREMENTS: Open to high school seniors who are South Dakota residents with a minimum 30 ACT score and minimum 3.5 GPA.
HOW TO APPLY: Contact Department of Education for information and application.
RENEWABLE: Yes. Up to 4 years.

3900—SOUTHERN SCHOLARSHIP FOUNDATION (Housing Scholarship)

322 Stadium Drive
Tallahassee FL 32304
850/222-3833 or 800/253-2769
Internet: http://www.southern scholarship.org/
AMOUNT: Valued at $5,000
DEADLINE(S): Varies
FIELD(S): All
ELIGIBILITY/REQUIREMENTS: Provide a rent-free room in a completely furnished home. The Florida-based program serves the University of Florida, Florida State University, Florida A&M University, Bethune-Cookman College, and Florida Gulf Coast University.
HOW TO APPLY: Download application from website.
NUMBER OF AWARDS: 440
RENEWABLE: Yes
CONTACT: Beth Kelly

3901—SOUTHWESTERN UNIVERSITY (Scholarships and Grants)

1001 East University Avenue
Georgetown TX 78626
512/863-6511 (main) or
512/863-1200 or
800/252-3166 (admissions)
Internet: http://www.southwestern.edu
AMOUNT: Varies
DEADLINE(S): JAN 15
FIELD(S): All

ELIGIBILITY/REQUIREMENTS: Both merit-based and need-based scholarships and awards are available through this undergraduate, United Methodist-related, liberal arts college in Georgetown, TX. Some are subject-related; some are for students planning careers within the church and for dependents of United Methodist clergy. SAT, ACT, GPAs, and need are all considered.
HOW TO APPLY: See website for further details; contact university for latest and complete information.

3902—SPECIAL PEOPLE IN NEED

500 West Madison Street,
Suite 3700
Chicago IL 60661
312/715-5235
Internet: http://www.elk foundation.org
AMOUNT: $2,000-$4,000
DEADLINE(S): MAY 1
FIELD(S): All
ELIGIBILITY/REQUIREMENTS: Must be resident of U.S. For undergraduates with disabilities or who have overcome extremely difficult circumstances.
HOW TO APPLY: No formal application; submit relevant scholastic records; letter from institution stating that the student has been or will be admitted AND that the institution will not only sponsor the student but be the grantee and administer the grant and comply with sponsorship conditions; at least 2 letters of recommendation from educators familiar with qualifications; if student is disabled, a letter from student or institution describing the disability and a letter from the student's physician (or another person familiar with condition) confirming the nature of the disability; if student not disabled, a letter from student or institution describing circumstances and at least 2 letters from others confirming the circumstances. Letter from applicant should also explain why he/she deserves the scholarship and provide biographical information.
NUMBER OF AWARDS: Varies
RENEWABLE: Yes. If performance, amount will vary.
CONTACT: Send application to Gary H. Kline, Secretary; for information, Irene Peterson, Associate.

3903—SPORTS JOURNALISM INSTITUTE (Internships)

Gregrory Lee
The Boston Globe
135 Morrissey Blvd.

Boston MA 02125
Internet: http://www.sports
journalisminstitute.org/
AMOUNT: $500 for 9-week internship
DEADLINE(S): DEC 5
FIELD(S): All (emphasis on print
journalism, especially sports reporting
and editing)
ELIGIBILITY/REQUIREMENTS: For
college sophomores or juniors interested in
sports journalism careers. Preference given
to ethnic and racial minority groups, with a
mix of male and female students. Based on
academic achievement, demonstrated
interest in sports journalism as a career,
and required essay. NOT limited to journalism majors.
HOW TO APPLY: See website for application and details. Submit with transcript, 2
letters of recommendation, a head shot, up
to 7 writing samples or clips, and an essay
of no more than 500 words stating why you
should be selected.
NUMBER OF AWARDS: 10

3904—STATE NEWS

Michigan State University
343 Student Services
East Lansing MI 48824-1113
E-mail: recruiter@statenews.com
Internet: http://statenews.com/
scholar/scholarship/
AMOUNT: $2,000 + job
DEADLINE(S): FEB 5
FIELD(S): All (emphasis on journalism
and advertising)
ELIGIBILITY/REQUIREMENTS: Open
to high school seniors entering MSU in the
fall. Must have an above-average GPA and
have demonstrated a strong interest in high
school journalism or advertising. Recipients
work in paying positions at the *State News*
after the first semester of their freshman
year, either in the newsroom or in the
advertising department. *State News* salary is
in addition to scholarship. May major in any
academic program.
HOW TO APPLY: See website or contact
Ben Schwartz, *State News* General
Manager, for an application.
NUMBER OF AWARDS: 2
RENEWABLE: Yes. Up to 4 years.

3905—ST. DAVID'S SOCIETY OF NEW YORK

Scholarship Committee
47 Fifth Avenue
New York NY 10003
212/397-1346
AMOUNT: Varies
DEADLINE(S): JUN 1

FIELD(S): All
ELIGIBILITY/REQUIREMENTS:
Scholarships for students who are either of
Welsh heritage, attending a Welsh school,
or studying Welsh culture and/or language.
For graduates or undergraduates.
HOW TO APPLY: Request application by
mail after January 1.
NUMBER OF AWARDS: About 12
RENEWABLE: Yes

3906—STATE FARM COMPANIES FOUNDATION (Scholarships for Dependents)

One State Farm Plaza, B-4
Bloomington IL 61710-0001
309/766-2161
Internet: http://www.statefarm.com
AMOUNT: Varies
DEADLINE(S): Varies
FIELD(S): All
ELIGIBILITY/REQUIREMENTS: Open
to high school seniors who are legal depen-
dents of full-time State Farm agents,
employees, or retirees. Winners are select-
ed by the National Merit Scholarship
Corporation on the basis of test scores,
academic record, extracurricular activities,
personal essay, and counselor recommen-
dation.
HOW TO APPLY: Contact Foundation
for information and application.
NUMBER OF AWARDS: 100
CONTACT: Jill Jones

3907—STATE NEWS

Michigan State University
343 Student Services
East Lansing MI 48824-1113
E-mail: recruiter@statenews.com
Internet: http://statenews.com/
scholar/scholarship/
AMOUNT: $2,000/year for 4 years + job
DEADLINE(S): FEB 5
FIELD(S): All; Journalism; Advertising
ELIGIBILITY/REQUIREMENTS: Open
to high school seniors who will start at
MSU in the fall. Must have an above-average GPA and have demonstrated a strong
interest in high school journalism or advertising through their newspapers and yearbooks. Recipients work in paying positions
at the *State News* after the first semester of
their freshman year, either in the newsroom or in the advertising department.
State News pay is in addition to the scholarship. May major in any academic program.
HOW TO APPLY: See website or contact
State News General Manager for application.
NUMBER OF AWARDS: 2

CONTACT: Ben Schwartz, *State News*
General Manager

3908—STEVEN KNEZEVICH TRUST

9830 North Courtland Drive
Mequon WI 53092
262/241-5663
FAX: 262/241-5645
E-mail: jbrodkey@hotmail.com (with
"Knezevich Trust" in subject line)
AMOUNT: Approximately $100-$800
DEADLINE(S): NOV 30
FIELD(S): All
ELIGIBILITY/REQUIREMENTS: Must
be Serbian or of Serbian descent; may be
used for U.S. college or graduate school.
HOW TO APPLY: Send a letter with
SASE for application form. Will not send
an application in response to a fax or if you
do not include the SASE. Will respond to
e-mail requests to jbrodkey@hotmail.com
with "Knezevich Trust" in subject line.
NUMBER OF AWARDS: Varies
RENEWABLE: Yes, must reapply.
CONTACT: Stanley Hack

3909—STUDENT AID FOUNDATION, INC. (Loans)

2520 East Piedmont Road, Suite F
PMB 180
Marietta GA 30062
770/973-7077
FAX: 770/973-2220
AMOUNT: $5,000 (undergraduate);
$7,500 (graduate)
DEADLINE(S): APR 15
FIELD(S): All
ELIGIBILITY/REQUIREMENTS: Low-
interest loans for women who are residents
of Georgia or out-of-state women attend-
ing a Georgia school. Grades, financial
need, personal integrity, and sense of
responsibility are considerations.
HOW TO APPLY: Send SASE for an
application.
NUMBER OF AWARDS: 30
RENEWABLE: Yes, must reapply.

3910—STUHR SCHOLARSHIP FUND

3292 Thompson Bridge Road #120
Gainesville GA 30506
E-mail: stuhrstudents@earthlink.net
AMOUNT: $2,000/year
DEADLINE(S): MAR 1
FIELD(S): All
ELIGIBILITY/REQUIREMENTS: Must
be a high school senior during the year of
application; have achieved a ranking in the
top 10% of your class during junior and
first half of senior year; minimum

SAT/ACT score of 2000/27; have evidence of extracurricular activities and demonstrated leadership potential; be planning to attend a 4-year accredited college or university; and be a dependent of an active duty reserve, guard, or career retired member of the Armed Forces.

HOW TO APPLY: E-mail request for information and materials to address above; we do not accept mailed, phoned, or faxed requests. Applicants must complete and submit a screening questionnaire prior to receiving application materials.

NUMBER OF AWARDS: 5

CONTACT: Executive Director, Stuhr Scholarship Fund

3911—SUDBURY FOUNDATION ATKINSON SCHOLARSHIP PROGRAM

278 Old Sudbury Road
Sudbury MA 01776
978/443-0849
FAX: 978/579-9536
AMOUNT: Up to $5,000
DEADLINE(S): NOV 1
FIELD(S): All
ELIGIBILITY/REQUIREMENTS: Open to Lincoln-Sudbury High School (Massachusetts) graduating seniors or dependents of Sudbury residents for post-secondary studies, including vocational training. Must demonstrate financial need. Academic and nonacademic factors are considered in evaluating candidates.

HOW TO APPLY: Contact Foundation for additional information.

3912—SUNKIST GROWERS, INC. (A. W. Bodine-Sunkist Memorial Scholarship)

P.O. Box 7888
Van Nuys CA 91409-7888
818/986-4800
AMOUNT: $2,000-$3,000
DEADLINE(S): APR 30
FIELD(S): All
ELIGIBILITY/REQUIREMENTS: Open to California and Arizona undergraduates who come from an agricultural background and are in need of financial assistance. Must have a minimum 3.0 GPA.

HOW TO APPLY: Contact Sunkist Growers for an application.

3913—SUPERCOLLEGE.COM (Scholarship)

Scholarship Coordinator
4546 B10 El Camino Real, #281
Los Altos CA 94022
FAX: 650/618-2221
E-mail: scholarships@super college.com
Internet: http://www.super college.com
AMOUNT: $500-$2,500
DEADLINE(S): JUL 31
FIELD(S): All
ELIGIBILITY/REQUIREMENTS: Open to 9th- to 12th-grade high school, college, or graduate student attending or planning to attend any accredited college or university in the U.S.

HOW TO APPLY: See website for application; apply online or by mail. Essay required.

3914—SUPREME LODGE KNIGHTS OF PYTHIAS (Poster Contest)

59 Coddington Street
Quincy MA 02169
617/472-8800
FAX: 617/376-0363
E-mail: kop@earthlink.net
Internet: http://www.pythias.org
AMOUNT: $1,000 (1st); $500 (2nd); $250 (3rd); $100 (4th-8th)
DEADLINE(S): Varies by local lodge
FIELD(S): All
ELIGIBILITY/REQUIREMENTS: Poster contest for high school students in the U.S. and Canada.

HOW TO APPLY: Contact local lodge for detailed guidelines on subject matter, format, etc. Submit posters to local lodge.

NUMBER OF AWARDS: 8

RENEWABLE: Yes

CONTACT: Alfred A. Saltzman

3915—SWISS BENEVOLENT SOCIETY IN SAN FRANCISCO (Clement & Frieda Amstutz and Silvio Canonica Scholarships)

c/o Swiss Consulate General
456 Montgomery Street, Suite 1500
San Francisco CA 94104-1233
Internet: http://www.sbssf.com
AMOUNT: Varies
DEADLINE(S): APR 30
FIELD(S): All
ELIGIBILITY/REQUIREMENTS: Must be of Swiss descent by demonstrating that at least 1 parent is (or you are) a Swiss citizen, registered with the Swiss Consulate of San Francisco (or carrying a valid Swiss passport); have lived within a 150-mile radius of the San Francisco City Hall for a minimum of 3 years; show a cumulative GPA of not less than 3.2 for the last 2 years in high school or not less than 2.75 for the first year in college and 3.0 thereafter for a minimum of either 12 undergraduate or 8 graduate units per term; applied for admission to any accredited institution of higher learning in the U.S. offering a baccalaureate degree or—in exceptional cases—to a junior college in California; and demonstrate financial need. Awards will be granted based on the criteria of outstanding prior academic achievement, promise of future academic excellence, and anticipated successful completion of studies. Students may apply during the 2nd year of college or any time thereafter.

HOW TO APPLY: See website or write for application and submit with proof of 1 parent's or your Swiss nationality; transcripts of all graduate or undergraduate studies; copies of SAT or ACT test scores (optional for students in graduate school); essay outlining specific goals after completion of studies; and 2 letters of recommendation from professors (sponsors) who are familiar with your background and have themselves expertise in your specialty area of study.

NUMBER OF AWARDS: Varies

3916—SWISS BENEVOLENT SOCIETY IN SAN FRANCISCO (General Fund and Silvia Wieland Iselin Scholarships)

c/o Swiss Consulate General
456 Montgomery Street, Suite 1500
San Francisco CA 94104-1233
Internet: http://www.sbssf.com
AMOUNT: Varies
DEADLINE(S): APR 30
FIELD(S): All
ELIGIBILITY/REQUIREMENTS: Must be Swiss nationals or have at least 1 parent who is Swiss citizen; have lived within a 150-mile radius of the San Francisco City Hall for 3 years prior to application date; have applied for admission to any institution of higher learning in the U.S. (community colleges and trade schools excluded) for undergraduate and graduate scholarships. Minimum GPA 3.2 for last 2 years of high school; 3.2 thereafter; minimum 12 undergraduate, 8 graduate units/semester; must demonstrate financial need. (Based on need and merit.)

HOW TO APPLY: Write for information.

NUMBER OF AWARDS: Varies

3917—SWISS BENEVOLENT SOCIETY IN SAN FRANCISCO (Willy Isler Scholarship)

c/o Swiss Consulate General
456 Montgomery Street, Suite 1500
San Francisco CA 94104-1233
Internet: http://www.sbssf.com
AMOUNT: Varies
DEADLINE(S): APR 30
FIELD(S): All
ELIGIBILITY/REQUIREMENTS: Must be Swiss nationals or have at least 1 parent

who is Swiss citizen; have lived within a 150-mile radius of the San Francisco City Hall for 3 years prior to application date; have applied for admission to any institution of higher learning in the U.S. (community colleges and trade schools excluded) for undergraduate and graduate scholarships. Minimum GPA 3.2 for last 2 years of high school; 3.2 thereafter; minimum 12 undergraduate, 8 graduate units/semester; must demonstrate financial need. (Based on merit and need.)
HOW TO APPLY: Write for information.
NUMBER OF AWARDS: Varies

3918—SWISS BENEVOLENT SOCIETY OF CHICAGO (Scholarship Fund)

P.O. Box 2137
Chicago IL 60690
Internet: http://www.sbschicago.org
AMOUNT: Varies
DEADLINE(S): Varies
FIELD(S): All
ELIGIBILITY/REQUIREMENTS: Undergraduate scholarships open to Swiss nationals or those of proven Swiss descent who are permanent residents of Illinois or Southern Wisconsin and accepted to or enrolled in accredited colleges or universities. Minimum 3.3 GPA required. Swiss students studying in the U.S. on a student or visitors visa are NOT eligible.
HOW TO APPLY: Write for information.

3919—TAILHOOK EDUCATIONAL FOUNDATION, THE

P.O. Box 26626
San Diego CA 92196-0626
800/322-4665
Internet: http://www.tailhook.
org/foundation.htm
AMOUNT: $2,000
DEADLINE(S): MAR 15
FIELD(S): All
ELIGIBILITY/REQUIREMENTS: Applicant or parent must have served in the Navy, Marine Corps or Coast Guard as an aviator, flight officer or designated aircrewman or served aboard a U.S. Navy aircraft carrier in any capacity.
HOW TO APPLY: Download application from website or send SASE to above address.
NUMBER OF AWARDS: 45
RENEWABLE: Yes, must reapply.
CONTACT: Foundation Administrator

3920—TAIWAN BUDDHIST TZU CHI FOUNDATION, U.S.A. (Tzu Chi Scholars)

National Headquarters

1100 South Valley Center Avenue
San Dimas CA 91773
909/447-7799
FAX: 909/447-7947
E-mail: info@tzuchi.org
Internet: http:www.tzuchi.org
AMOUNT: $1,000
DEADLINE(S): MAR or APR (varies)
FIELD(S): All
ELIGIBILITY/REQUIREMENTS: Open to U.S. high school graduating seniors. Minimum GPA 3.0; must enroll in an accredited U.S. college full time for the entire academic year; must demonstrate financial need.
HOW TO APPLY: See website for additional information and application or contact regional coordinator (see website or contact National Headquarters for contact information). Submit with transcript; documentation of financial need; 2 letters of recommendation from teachers, counselors, and/or other advisors; and a 2-page essay stating why you should receive scholarship and a 1-page essay about Tzu Chi explaining what about Tzu Chi inspires you.
NUMBER OF AWARDS: Varies
CONTACT: Flora Wu or Calvin His

3921—TALL CLUBS INTERNATIONAL (Kae Sumner Einfeldt Scholarship Award)

Box 60074
Palatine IL 90074
888/I-M-TALL-2
E-mail: tci-tallteen@tall.org
Internet: http://www.tall.org
AMOUNT: $1,000
DEADLINE(S): Varies
FIELD(S): All
ELIGIBILITY/REQUIREMENTS: Scholarships for unusually tall college-bound high school seniors (girls-5'10", boys-6'2"). Must apply through regional clubs or members-at-large.
HOW TO APPLY: Contact organization for location of your nearest Tall Club. Send SASE for information.
NUMBER OF AWARDS: Multiple

3922—TARGET STORES (Target All-Around Scholarships)

Scholarship America
One Scholarship Way
P.O. Box 480
St. Peter MN 56082-0480
800/316-6142
Internet: http://www.target.com
AMOUNT: $1,000-$25,000
DEADLINE(S): NOV 1
FIELD(S): All

ELIGIBILITY/REQUIREMENTS: Open to well-rounded high school graduates and current college students who volunteer in their communities. Must be U.S. resident under the age of 24.
HOW TO APPLY: See website or contact your local Target store for an application.
NUMBER OF AWARDS: Over 600
RENEWABLE: No

3923—TENNESSEE STUDENT ASSISTANCE CORPORATION (Ned McWherter Scholars Program)

Parkway Towers, Suite 1950
404 James Robertson Parkway
Nashville TN 37243-0820
615/741-1346 or 800/342-1663
AMOUNT: $6,000 for max. of 4 yrs.
DEADLINE(S): FEB 15
FIELD(S): All
ELIGIBILITY/REQUIREMENTS: Scholarships for entering freshman with at least a 3.5 high school GPA and an ACT of 29 or SAT in the top 5% nationally. Must be a resident of Tennessee AND must attend an eligible Tennessee institution.
HOW TO APPLY: Contact high school guidance office or the Corporation for an application.
RENEWABLE: Yes. Up to 4 years.

3924—TENNESSEE STUDENT ASSISTANCE CORPORATION (Robert C. Byrd Honors Scholarship Program)

Parkway Towers, Suite 1950
404 James Robertson Parkway
Nashville TN 37243-0820
615/741-1346 or 800/342-1663
AMOUNT: Varies
DEADLINE(S): APR 1
FIELD(S): All
ELIGIBILITY/REQUIREMENTS: For Tennessee high school seniors or GED students; must have a 3.5 GPA or an average GED score of 57 or minimum 3.0 GPA and an ACT/SAT in the top quartile nationally. Award must be utilized in graduation year.
HOW TO APPLY: Contact high school guidance office or the Corporation for more information.

3925—TET '68, Inc. (Essay Contest)

P.O. Box 31885
Richmond VA 23294
804/550-3692
FAX: 804/550-1406
E-mail: billyktet@aol.com
Internet: http://www.tet68.org
AMOUNT: $1,000
DEADLINE(S): MAR 31

FIELD(S): All (emphasis on history and political science)

ELIGIBILITY/REQUIREMENTS: Open to high school seniors who are children or stepchildren of a Vietnam veteran.

HOW TO APPLY: See website or write for application, contest rules, and essay topic. Submit essay with proof of status: parent or stepparent's DD-214.

NUMBER OF AWARDS: 4-6

RENEWABLE: Yes

CONTACT: William E. Kirkland

3926—TEXAS A&M UNIVERSITY (Academic Excellence Awards)

Student Financial Aid Department
College Station TX 77843
979/845-3236
Internet: http://financialaid.tamu.
edu/scholar/scholarshipedu/
scholarships/default.asp

AMOUNT: $500-$1,500

DEADLINE(S): MAR

FIELD(S): All

ELIGIBILITY/REQUIREMENTS: Open to currently-enrolled, full-time undergraduate and graduate students at Texas A&M University. Awards are intended to recognize and assist students who are making excellent scholastic progress, campus and community activities, leadership positions, and work experience.

HOW TO APPLY: See website for additional information and application.

NUMBER OF AWARDS: About 800

RENEWABLE: No

3927—TEXAS A&M UNIVERSITY (Opportunity Award Scholarship)

Student Financial Aid Office
Texas A&M University
College Station TX 77843
979/845-3236
Internet: http://financialaid.tamu.
edu/scholarships/default.asp

AMOUNT: $500-$2,500

DEADLINE(S): DEC

FIELD(S): All

ELIGIBILITY/REQUIREMENTS: Scholarships to Texas A&M University for college freshmen with outstanding high school records. Selection based on leadership ability, character, SAT scores, activities, and high school record. U.S. citizen or permanent resident.

HOW TO APPLY: Recipients from outside Texas receive a waiver on nonresident tuition. See website for additional information and application.

3928—TEXAS A&M UNIVERSITY (President's Achievement Award Scholarship)

Office of Honors Programs &
Academic Scholarships
College Station TX 77843
979/458-1572

AMOUNT: $3,000

DEADLINE(S): JAN 8

FIELD(S): All

ELIGIBILITY/REQUIREMENTS: This competitive academic scholarship program provides 4-year scholarships for high school seniors who will be attending Texas A&M University. For U.S. citizens or permanent residents. Must maintain 2.5 GPA to remain in good scholarship standing.

HOW TO APPLY: Recipients from outside Texas receive a waiver of nonresident tuition. Contact Office of Honors Programs for complete information.

3929—TEXAS A&M UNIVERSITY (President's Endowed Scholarship; Lechner Scholarship; McFadden Scholarship)

Office of Honors Programs &
Academic Scholarships
College Station TX 77843
979/458-1572

AMOUNT: $2,500-$3,000

DEADLINE(S): JAN

FIELD(S): All

ELIGIBILITY/REQUIREMENTS: For high school seniors who will be attending Texas A&M. Must score 1300 or higher on SAT (or 30 ACT) and rank in the top 10% of high school graduating class or be National Merit Scholarship semi-finalist. U.S. citizenship or legal residency required.

HOW TO APPLY: Non-Texans qualify for a waiver of nonresident tuition. Contact Office of Honors Programs for complete information.

RENEWABLE: Yes. Up to 4 years.

3930—TEXAS A&M UNIVERSITY (Scholarships, Grants, and Loans)

Division of Student Affairs
College Station TX 77843-1252
979/845-3236

AMOUNT: Varies

DEADLINE(S): Varies

FIELD(S): All

ELIGIBILITY/REQUIREMENTS: For high school seniors who will be attending Texas A&M. Based on academic criteria and/or combinations of financial need, campus/community activities, leadership positions, and work experience. Some are for minorities, teacher candidates, cadets, and Texas high school class valedictorians. Applicants do not have to be prior Texas residents.

HOW TO APPLY: Contact Division of Student Affairs for complete information.

3931—TEXAS BLACK BAPTIST SCHOLARSHIP

African American Ministries
Baptist General Convention of Texas
333 North Washington Street,
Suite 371
Dallas TX 75246-1798
214/828-5130
FAX: 214/828-5284
Internet: http://www.nbcusa.org

AMOUNT: $400/semester (part-time pro-rated@$33.33/credit hour)

DEADLINE(S): MAR 28 (spring), SEPT 30 (fall)

FIELD(S): All

ELIGIBILITY/REQUIREMENTS: Must be a member in good standing of a Baptist church, actively involved in the ministry of the church (BGCT member churches strongly recommended). Must have acceptable recommendation from pastor, teachers and advisors, employer, etc., and demonstrate financial need; a "B" average or have a minimum 2.0 GPA from an accredited college or university. Must have resided in Texas for at least 1 year and must attend one of 8 Texas Baptist educational institutions or SWBTS and be willing to serve as an intern for any BGCT affiliated entity.

HOW TO APPLY: Write for application; when applying must submit professional photograph.

RENEWABLE: Yes. Maximum $3,200 over 4-year period.

3932—TEXAS HIGHER EDUCATION COORDINATING BOARD (Early High School Graduation Scholarship I)

Student Services
P.O. Box 12788
Austin TX 78711-2788
512/427-6323 or
800/242-3062, ext. 6323
FAX: 512/427-6420
E-mail: grantinfo@thecb.state.tx.us
Internet: http://www.thecb.
state.tx.us

AMOUNT: $1,000

DEADLINE(S): Varies (with program)

FIELD(S): All

ELIGIBILITY/REQUIREMENTS: Open to Texas residents who graduated from high school PRIOR to September 1, 2003. Must have completed requirements for grades 9-12 in no more than 36 continuous months; graduated from Texas public high school, enrolled in a Texas college or university.
HOW TO APPLY: Visit high school counselor or contact Board for application and information.
RENEWABLE: No

3933—TEXAS HIGHER EDUCATION COORDINATING BOARD (Early High School Graduation Scholarship II)

Student Services
P.O. Box 12788
Austin TX 78711-2788
512/427-6340 or
800/242-3062, ext. 6340
FAX: 512/427-6420
E-mail: grantinfo@thecb.state.tx.us
Internet: http://www.thecb.
state.tx.us
AMOUNT: Up to $3,000
DEADLINE(S): Varies (with program)
FIELD(S): All
ELIGIBILITY/REQUIREMENTS: Open to Texas residents who graduated from high school ON or AFTER September 1, 2003. Must complete Recommended or Distinguished Achievement High School Curriculum in 36-41 continuous months (46 months if student earns college credits); graduate from Texas public high school, enroll in a Texas college or university.
HOW TO APPLY: Visit high school counselor to contact Board for application and information.
RENEWABLE: No

3934—THEODORE R. AND VIVIAN M. JOHNSON SCHOLARSHIP FUND

325 West Gaines Street, Suite 1652
Tallahassee FL 32399-0400
850/245-0467
FAX: 850/245-9697
AMOUNT: Varies
DEADLINE(S): MAY 15
FIELD(S): All
ELIGIBILITY/REQUIREMENTS: Open to Florida State University system student; financial need; documented disability; essay; references; minimum GPA.
HOW TO APPLY: Contact the disability service provider offices at Florida public institutions for information.
NUMBER OF AWARDS: Varies

RENEWABLE: Yes. Must reapply; minimum GPA hours; financial need considered.
CONTACT: Lynda Page

3935—THIRD MARINE DIVISION ASSOCIATION (Memorial Scholarship Fund)

15727 Vista Dr.
Dumfries VA 22025-1810
972/247-6549
E-mail: supertop@aol.com
Internet: http://www.caltrap.com
AMOUNT: $500-$1,500
DEADLINE(S): APR 15
FIELD(S): All
ELIGIBILITY/REQUIREMENTS: Open to dependent, unmarried child (including adopted child) age 16-23 (first-time applicants; maximum 26 for continuing scholarships) for undergraduate study (some trade schools may apply) in the U.S. or Canada. Sponsoring parent must be a member of Association in continuous good standing for at least 2 years immediately prior to receipt of the first application and must continue membership for entire period of the dependent's assistance.
HOW TO APPLY: See website or write for application or information (include name and address of sponsoring parent and name and address of student). Submit application with copies of birth certificate/adoption papers and college/university acceptance, if received; recent photo suitable for publication enclosed; and most recent transcript/grade report.
NUMBER OF AWARDS: Varies
RENEWABLE: Yes. Must reapply; up to 4 years; must maintain a "C" (2.0) average.
CONTACT: MGySgt. James G. Kyser, USMC (Ret.), Secretary, Memorial Scholarship Fund

3936—THOMAS J. WATSON FOUNDATION (The Jeannette K. Watson Summer Fellowships)

810 Seventh Avenue
New York NY 10019
212/655-0201
FAX: 401/274-1954
Internet: http://www.jkwatson.org
DEADLINE(S): 1st Tuesday in NOV
FIELD(S): All
ELIGIBILITY/REQUIREMENTS: Paid internships open to students from 8 New York City colleges to work in different sectors (nonprofit organizations, public service, and enterprise).
HOW TO APPLY: Candidates must be nominated by their college and should demonstrate leadership, creativity, a

capacity to initiate and to follow through, skills in working in groups, and a commitment to building a better society.
NUMBER OF AWARDS: 15
RENEWABLE: Yes. 3 consecutive summers.
CONTACT: Alice Stone Ilchman, Director; Stephanie Ramos, Assistant Director

3937—THOMAS J. WATSON FOUNDATION (The Thomas J. Watson Fellowship Program)

293 South Main Street
Providence RI 02903
401/274-1952
FAX: 401/274-1954
Internet: http://www.watson
fellowship.org
AMOUNT: $22,000 (single); $31,000 (with accompanying financial and legal dependent)
DEADLINE(S): 1st Tuesday in NOV
FIELD(S): All
ELIGIBILITY/REQUIREMENTS: Open to graduating seniors at the 50 U.S. colleges on the Foundation's roster. Fellowship provides for 1 year of independent study and travel abroad immediately following graduation.
HOW TO APPLY: Candidates must be nominated by their college and should demonstrate integrity, imagination, strong ethical character, intelligence, capacity for vision and leadership, promise of creative achievement/excellence within chosen field, and potential for humane and effective participation in world.
NUMBER OF AWARDS: Up to 50
RENEWABLE: No
CONTACT: Beverly Larson, Executive Director

3938—TOWSON UNIVERSITY (Scholarship & Award Programs)

Financial Aid/Scholarship Unit
Enrollment Services Building,
Room 305
8000 York
Towson MD 21252
410/704-2647
FAX: 410/704-4634
E-mail: scholarship@towson.edu
Internet: http://inside.towson.
edu/scholarshipseekertowson.edu/
finaid
AMOUNT: Varies
DEADLINE(S): Varies
FIELD(S): All

ELIGIBILITY/REQUIREMENTS: Scholarship and award programs are available to entering freshmen, continuing students, graduate, and transfer students attending or planning to attend Towson State University.

HOW TO APPLY: See website.

3939—TOYOTA MOTOR SALES, USA, INC. (Community Scholars Program)

Corporate Contributions
19001 S Western Avenue
Torrance CA 90509
609/771-7878
Internet: http://www.toyota.com/communityscholars
AMOUNT: $10,000-$20,000/4 years
DEADLINE(S): Early DEC
FIELD(S): All
ELIGIBILITY/REQUIREMENTS: Open to U.S. high school graduating seniors. Must be proven leaders both in the classroom and in the communities in which they live.
HOW TO APPLY: Must be nominated by school; contact Guidance Counselor for full details.
NUMBER OF AWARDS: 100
RENEWABLE: No, 4-year scholarship
CONTACT: Richlynn Kaiser at 310/468-2254

3940—TRANSPORT WORKERS UNION OF AMERICA (Michael J. Quill Scholarship Fund)

1700 Broadway
New York NY 10019-5905
212/259-4900
AMOUNT: $1,200
DEADLINE(S): MAY 1
FIELD(S): All
ELIGIBILITY/REQUIREMENTS: Open to high school seniors (under 21) who are dependents of TWU members in good standing or of a deceased member who was in good standing at time of death. Dependent brothers or sisters of members in good standing also may apply.
HOW TO APPLY: Write for complete information.
NUMBER OF AWARDS: 15
RENEWABLE: Yes. Up to 4 years.

3941—TRAVELERS PROTECTIVE ASSOCIATION OF AMERICA SCHOLARSHIP TRUST FOR THE DEAF AND NEAR DEAF

3755 Lindell Boulevard
St. Louis MO 63108
314/371-0533
FAX: 314/371-0537
E-mail: ghartman@tpahq.org
Internet: http://www.ttahq.org
AMOUNT: Varies
DEADLINE(S): MAR 1
FIELD(S): All
ELIGIBILITY/REQUIREMENTS: Open to children and adults who suffer deafness or hearing impairment and who need assistance in obtaining mechanical devices, medical or specialized treatment or specialized education, as well as speech classes, notetakers, interpreters, etc., and in other areas of need that are directly related to hearing impairment. Priority given to applicants with the greatest financial need regardless of race, creed, age or sex.
HOW TO APPLY: Request application from TPAA. Selection and amount awarded determined by the majority of the Trustees.
RENEWABLE: Yes, must reapply.

3942—TREACY COMPANY

P.O. Box 1479
Helena MT 59624
406/443-3549
AMOUNT: $400
DEADLINE(S): JUN 15
FIELD(S): All
ELIGIBILITY/REQUIREMENTS: Open to college freshmen and sophomores who reside in Montana, North or South Dakota, or Idaho.
HOW TO APPLY: Write for application between January and May 15.
NUMBER OF AWARDS: 25
RENEWABLE: Yes. Must reapply; up to 4 years.

3943—TULANE UNIVERSITY (Scholarships & Fellowships)

205 Mechanical Engineering Building
New Orleans LA 70118
504/865-5723
Internet: http://www.tulane.edu/~finaid
AMOUNT: Varies
DEADLINE(S): Varies
FIELD(S): All
ELIGIBILITY/REQUIREMENTS: Numerous need-based and merit-based scholarship and fellowship programs for undergraduate and graduate study at Tulane University. There is also an honors program for outstanding students accepted for enrollment at Tulane.
HOW TO APPLY: Write for complete information.

3944—UNION PLUS EDUCATION FOUNDATION SCHOLARSHIP

P.O. Box 34800
Washington DC 20043-4800
202/293-5330
Internet: http://www.unionplus.org/education
AMOUNT: $500-$4,000
DEADLINE(S): JAN 31
FIELD(S): All
ELIGIBILITY/REQUIREMENTS: Union members and their families who want to begin or continue their secondary education. Based on academic achievement, potential, character, leadership, social awareness, career goals, and financial need.
HOW TO APPLY: Download application from website or send your name, address and phone number, along with the name of your international union, on a postcard to the above address in c/o Union Privilege.
NUMBER OF AWARDS: 100-105
RENEWABLE: No
CONTACT: Shana E. Higgins

3945—UNITED DAUGHTERS OF THE CONFEDERACY (Undergraduate Scholarships)

P.O. Box 557
Cross Junction VA 22625-0557
804/355-1636
FAX: 804/353-1396
E-mail: whitds@visuallink.com
Internet: http://www.hqudc.orgi
AMOUNT: $800-$1,000
DEADLINE(S): FEB 15
FIELD(S): All
ELIGIBILITY/REQUIREMENTS: Various programs for lineal descendants of eligible Confederate veterans. Applicants who are collateral descendants must be active members of the United Daughters of the Confederacy or of the Children of the Confederacy and MUST be sponsored by a UDC chapter. Minimum 3.0 GPA and pass entrance exam at college or university.
HOW TO APPLY: Most awards for undergraduate study. For complete information send SASE or contact the education director in the division where you reside. Division addresses are on Internet site. Must be endorsed by President and 2nd Vice President General. Submit with photo, proof of ancestor's service, your birth certificate, lineage form, letter of recommendation from recent teacher/counselor, financial report form, transcript, personal letter (maximum 300 words) evaluat-

ing significance of Southern heritage and outlining goals and plans.
RENEWABLE: Yes. Up to 4 years.
CONTACT: David S. Whitacre, Second Vice President General

3946—UNITED FEDERATION OF TEACHERS (Albert Shanker College Scholarship Fund)

260 Park Avenue South
New York NY 10010
212/598-9244
FAX: 212/510-6429
Internet: http://www.uft.org
AMOUNT: $1,000/year
DEADLINE(S): DEC 15
FIELD(S): All
ELIGIBILITY/REQUIREMENTS: Open to New York City residents who attend New York City public high schools. Scholarships support undergraduate study at recognized colleges and universities. Financial need and academic standing are considerations. Students are eligible in the year they graduate.
HOW TO APPLY: Write for information.
NUMBER OF AWARDS: About 250
RENEWABLE: Yes

3947—UNITED FOOD & COMMERCIAL WORKERS INTERNATIONAL UNION (UFCW Scholarship Program)

1775 K Street NW
Washington DC 20006
201/223-3111
Internet: http://www.ufcw.org
AMOUNT: $1,000 per year for 4 years
DEADLINE(S): MAR 15
FIELD(S): All
ELIGIBILITY/REQUIREMENTS: Open to UFCW members or high school seniors who are children of members. Applicants must meet certain eligibility requirements. Awards for full-time study only.
HOW TO APPLY: Contact UFCW for application.

3948—UNITED METHODIST CHURCH SCHOLARSHIP PROGRAM (Allan Jerome Burry Scholarship)

P.O. Box 34007
Nashville TN 37203-0007
615/340-7344
FAX: 615/340-7367
E-mail: umscholar@gbhem.org
Internet: http://www.gbhem.org
AMOUNT: Up to $1,000
DEADLINE(S): FEB 1
FIELD(S): All

ELIGIBILITY/REQUIREMENTS: To recognize a UM student's outstanding academic performance, leadership skills, and participation in the activities of a UM-related campus ministry or chaplaincy program at a college or university. Must be nominated by the campus minister/chaplain, be a full and active member of the UMC for at least 3 years, a full-time undergraduate student pursuing a degree program at any accredited institution, minimum GPA 3.0, and demonstrate financial need.
HOW TO APPLY: Applications and nomination forms are available from local campus ministers/chaplains.

3949—UNITED METHODIST CHURCH SCHOLARSHIP PROGRAM (Bishop Joseph B. Bethea Scholarship)

P.O. Box 34007
Nashville TN 37203-0007
615/340-7344
FAX: 615/340-7367
E-mail: umscholar@gbhem.org
Internet: http://www.gbhem.org
AMOUNT: Up to $1,000
DEADLINE(S): MAY 1
FIELD(S): All
ELIGIBILITY/REQUIREMENTS: Open to African-American students who are members of the Southeastern Jurisdiction Black Methodists for Church Renewal, a full and active member of the UMC for at least 1 year, a full-time undergraduate student pursuing a degree program at any accredited institution, minimum GPA 2.8, citizen or permanent resident of the U.S., and demonstrate financial need.
HOW TO APPLY: See website for application or contact the director of financial aid at the United Methodist college or university of your choice, the chairperson of your annual conference Board of Higher Education and Campus Ministry or the United Methodist Scholarship Office at the address listed for information and/or application form.
CONTACT: Scholarship Department

3950—UNITED METHODIST CHURCH SCHOLARSHIP PROGRAM (E. Craig Brandenburg Scholarship)

P.O. Box 34007
Nashville TN 37203-0007
615/340-7344
FAX: 615/340-7367
E-mail: umscholar@gbhem.org
Internet: http://www.gbhem.org
AMOUNT: $1,000
DEADLINE(S): MAY 1
FIELD(S): All

ELIGIBILITY/REQUIREMENTS: Must be 35 or older, desiring to continue their education or enter a 2nd career; an active, full member of a United Methodist Church for at least 1 year prior to applying; a citizen or permanent resident of the U.S.; admitted to a full-time degree program in an accredited college/university, maintaining a GPA of 2.5 or above.
HOW TO APPLY: See website for application or contact the director of financial aid at the United Methodist college or university of your choice, the chairperson of your annual conference Board of Higher Education and Campus Ministry or the United Methodist Scholarship Office at the address listed for information and/or application form.
CONTACT: Scholarship Department

3951—UNITED METHODIST CHURCH SCHOLARSHIP PROGRAM (Ethnic Minority Scholarship)

P.O. Box 34007
Nashville TN 37203-0007
615/340-7344
FAX: 615/340-7367
E-mail: umscholar@gbhem.org
Internet: http://www.gbhem.org
AMOUNT: Up to $1,000
DEADLINE(S): MAY 1
FIELD(S): All
ELIGIBILITY/REQUIREMENTS: Open to Native American, Asian, African-American, Hispanic, or Pacific Islander ethnic group students pursuing their 1st undergraduate degree, a full and active member of the UMC for at least 1 year, a full-time undergraduate student pursuing a degree program at any accredited institution, minimum GPA 2.5, citizen or permanent resident of the U.S., and demonstrate financial need.
HOW TO APPLY: See website for application or contact the director of financial aid at the United Methodist college or university of your choice, the chairperson of your annual conference Board of Higher Education and Campus Ministry or the United Methodist Scholarship Office at the address listed for information and/or application form.
CONTACT: Scholarship Department
ADDITIONAL INFORMATION: Central Conference members (international students) must be enrolled in a United Methodist college or university in the U.S. and must be recommended by the president of the UM institution.

3952—UNITED METHODIST CHURCH SCHOLARSHIP PROGRAM (General Scholarship)

P.O. Box 34007

Nashville TN 37203-0007
615/340-7344
FAX: 615/340-7367
E-mail: umscholar@gbhem.org
Internet: http://www.gbhem.org
AMOUNT: Up to $1,000
DEADLINE(S): MAY 15
FIELD(S): All
ELIGIBILITY/REQUIREMENTS: Open to United Methodist undergraduate students who do not qualify for any of the other United Methodist Church scholarships, been active in a local church at least 1 year, and are entering college as freshmen. Must be an active member of a United Methodist Church for at least 1 year prior to applying, a citizen or resident of the U.S. Criteria vary.
HOW TO APPLY: See website for application or contact the director of financial aid at the United Methodist college or university of your choice, the chairperson of your annual conference Board of Higher Education and Campus Ministry or the United Methodist Scholarship Office at the address listed for information and/or application form.
CONTACT: Scholarship Department

3953—UNITED METHODIST CHURCH SCHOLARSHIP PROGRAM (Rev. Dr. Karen Leyman Gift of Hope Scholarship)

P.O. Box 34007
Nashville TN 37203-0007
615/340-7344
FAX: 615/340-7367
E-mail: umscholar@gbhem.org
Internet: http://www.gbhem.org
AMOUNT: $1,000
DEADLINE(S): MAY 1
FIELD(S): All
ELIGIBILITY/REQUIREMENTS: Must be an active, full member of a United Methodist Church for at least 3 years prior to applying; a citizen or permanent resident of the U.S.; admitted to a full-time degree program in an accredited college/university, maintaining a GPA of 3.0 or above.
HOW TO APPLY: See website for application or contact the director of financial aid at the United Methodist college or university of your choice, the chairperson of your annual conference Board of Higher Education and Campus Ministry or the United Methodist Scholarship Office at the address listed for information and/or application form.
CONTACT: Scholarship Department
ADDITIONAL INFORMATION: Central Conference members (international students) must be enrolled in a United Methodist college or university in the U.S. and must be recommended by the president of the UM institution.

3954—UNITED METHODIST SCHOLARSHIP PROGRAM (HANA Scholarship)

P.O. Box 34007
Nashville TN 37203-0007
615/340-7344
FAX: 615/340-7367
E-mail: umscholar@gbhem.org
Internet: http://www.gbhem.org
AMOUNT: Up to $1,000
DEADLINE(S): APR 1
FIELD(S): All
ELIGIBILITY/REQUIREMENTS: Open to United Methodist Church Hispanics, Asians, Native Americans or Pacific Islanders (at least 1 parent) who plan to prepare for leadership in the UMC and in their HANA community, and are full-time juniors or seniors or graduate students at an accredited college/university. Must be an active, full member of a United Methodist Church for at least 1 year prior to applying; a citizen or permanent resident of the U.S., maintaining a minimum 2.85 GPA.
HOW TO APPLY: See website or contact the director of financial aid at the United Methodist college or university of your choice, the chairperson of your annual conference Board of Higher Education and Campus Ministry or the United Methodist Scholarship Office at the address listed for information and/or application form or request an application online.

3955—UNITED METHODIST CHURCH SCHOLARSHIP PROGRAM (Helen and Allen Brown Scholarship)

P.O. Box 34007
Nashville TN 37203-0007
615/340-7344
FAX: 615/340-7367
E-mail: umscholar@gbhem.org
Internet: http://www.gbhem.org
AMOUNT: Up to $1,000
DEADLINE(S): MAY 1
FIELD(S): All
ELIGIBILITY/REQUIREMENTS: Open to students from the Nashville District of the Tennessee Annual Conference or the New Orleans District of the Louisiana Annual Conference. Must be a full and active member of the UMC for at least 3 years, a full-time undergraduate student pursuing a degree program at any accredited institution, minimum GPA 3.0, citizen or permanent resident of the U.S., and demonstrate financial need.

HOW TO APPLY: See website for application or contact the director of financial aid at the United Methodist college or university of your choice, the chairperson of your annual conference Board of Higher Education and Campus Ministry or the United Methodist Scholarship Office at the address listed for information and/or application form.
CONTACT: Scholarship Department

3956—UNITED METHODIST CHURCH SCHOLARSHIP PROGRAM (J. A. Knowles Scholarship)

P.O. Box 34007
Nashville TN 37203-0007
615/340-7344
FAX: 615/340-7367
E-mail: umscholar@gbhem.org
Internet: http://www.gbhem.org
AMOUNT: Up to $1,000
DEADLINE(S): MAY 15
FIELD(S): All
ELIGIBILITY/REQUIREMENTS: Open to United Methodist undergraduate students who are Texas residents, attending an accredited institution in Texas, been active in a UMC in Texas at least 1 year. Must be a citizen or resident of the U.S. and have a GPA of at least 2.5.
HOW TO APPLY: See website for application or contact the director of financial aid at the United Methodist college or university of your choice, the chairperson of your annual conference Board of Higher Education and Campus Ministry or the United Methodist Scholarship Office at the address listed for information and/or application form.
CONTACT: Scholarship Department

3957—UNITED NATIONS ASSOCIATION OF THE UNITED STATES OF AMERICA, THE

801 Second Avenue
New York NY 10017
212/907-1326
FAX: 212/682-9185
E-mail: sleslie@unausa.org
Internet: http://www.unausa.org
AMOUNT: 1st— $3,000; 2nd—$1,500; 3rd—$750
DEADLINE(S): TBD, most likely JAN
FIELD(S): All
ELIGIBILITY/REQUIREMENTS: Must be a high school student in the U.S.
HOW TO APPLY: Download entry form and contest packet from our website.
NUMBER OF AWARDS: 3
RENEWABLE: No
CONTACT: Scott Leslie, Publications Associate for Education

3958—UNITED NEGRO COLLEGE FUND (Scholarships)

8260 Willow Oaks Corporate Drive
Fairfax VA 22031
703/205-3400 or 800/331-2244
Internet: http://www.uncf.org
AMOUNT: Varies
DEADLINE(S): Varies
FIELD(S): All
ELIGIBILITY/REQUIREMENTS: Scholarships available to students who enroll in one of the 39 United Negro College Fund member institutions. Financial need must be established through the financial aid office at a UNCF college.
HOW TO APPLY: For information and a list of the UNCF campuses, write to the address above.

3959—UNITED STATES INSTITUTE OF PEACE (National Peace Essay Contest)

1200 17th Street NW, Suite 200
Washington DC 20036
202/457-1700
FAX: 202/429-6063
E-mail: essay contest@usip.org
Internet: http://www.usip.org
AMOUNT: $1,000-$10,000
DEADLINE(S): JAN
FIELD(S): All (emphasis on Political Science; U.S. History)
ELIGIBILITY/REQUIREMENTS: 1,500-word essay contest for high school students on the U.S. response to international conflict. No restrictions as to citizenship or residency.
HOW TO APPLY: See website or contact USIP for specific guidelines.
RENEWABLE: No

3960—UNITED STATES NAVAL SEA CADET CORPS (Stockholm Scholarship Program)

2300 Wilson Boulevard
Arlington VA 22201-3308
703/243-6910
FAX: 703/243-3985
E-mail: mford@navyleague.org
Internet: http://resources.sea
cadets.org
AMOUNT: Varies
DEADLINE: MAY 15
FIELDS: All
ELIGIBILITY/REQUIREMENTS: Cadets, and former cadets, applying for scholarships must have been a member of NSCC for at least 2 years; have attained the rate of NSCC E-3; be recommended by his/her unit commanding officer, the President/NSCC Committee Chairman of the sponsoring organization, and by the appropriate school authority (principal/counselor, etc.); present evidence of academic excellence ("B" average or better, SAT/ACT scores, class standing).
HOW TO APPLY: See website or contact Naval Sea Cadet Corps for additional information and application.

3961—UNIVERSITY OF CALIFORNIA AT BERKELEY (Undergraduate Scholarships)

Sproul Hall, Room 210
Berkeley CA 94720
510/642-6363
Internet: http://www.berkeley./
scholar/scholarshipedu/scholarships
AMOUNT: Varies
DEADLINE(S): Varies
FIELD(S): All
ELIGIBILITY/REQUIREMENTS: Various scholarships are available to students at UC Berkeley on the basis of academic achievement and financial need. To be considered for scholarships that require financial need, student must have filled out the government FAFSA form.
HOW TO APPLY: Entering students should fill out the UC Application for Undergraduate Admissions & Scholarships, and continuing UCB students should complete a UC Berkeley Scholarship Data Sheet (SDS). See your financial aid office for the FAFSA form.
NUMBER OF AWARDS: 2,500

3962—UNIVERSITY OF CALIFORNIA-RIVERSIDE (M.E.Ch.A. Alumni Scholarship Chicano Student Programs)

229 Costo Hall
Riverside CA 92521
951/787-3821
FAX: 951/827-2189
E-mail: estella.acuna@ucr.edu
AMOUNT: $500
DEADLINE(S): APR
FIELD(S): All
ELIGIBILITY/REQUIREMENTS: Must be planning to attend or currently enrolled at the University of California, Riverside. High school students planning to attend must have a minimum 3.0 GPA; transfer students must have a minimum 2.8 GPA; and students currently enrolled at UCR must have a minimum 3.0 GPA. All students must demonstrate service and community to the Chicano community.
HOW TO APPLY: Complete the application, include a copy of your most recent transcript; personal essay including but not limited to background, contribution and great achievements; 2 letters of recommendation (1 from a member of the community and 1 from a teacher/faculty); and your letter of acceptance to UCR.
NUMBER OF AWARDS: 3
RENEWABLE: No
CONTACT: Estella Acuña

3963—UNIVERSITY OF LEEDS (Scholarships for International Students)

Scholarships Office
Man-made Fibres Building
University of Leeds
Leeds LS2 9JT UNITED KINGDOM
+44 (0) 113 343 4007
FAX: +44 (0) 113 343 3774
E-mail: scholarships@leeds.ac.uk
Internet: http://scholarships.leeds.
ac.uk
AMOUNT: Varies
DEADLINE(S): Varies
FIELD(S): All
ELIGIBILITY/REQUIREMENTS: A number of scholarships are available for international students. Some are for students from specific countries, and some are limited to certain areas of study. Awards are based on academic merit.
HOW TO APPLY: Contact university or access website for complete information.
NUMBER OF AWARDS: Multiple
RENEWABLE: Yes. For time period appropriate to course; subject to satisfactory progress.
CONTACT: Cheryl Edwards

3964—UNIVERSITY OF MISSOURI, ROLLA (Program for Non-Missouri Residents)

G-1 Parker Hall
Rolla MO 65409-1060
573/341-4282
FAX: 573/341-4274
E-mail: sfa@umr.edu
Internet: http://www.umr.edu/
AMOUNT: Varies
DEADLINE(S): FEB 1
FIELD(S): All
ELIGIBILITY/REQUIREMENTS: Entering freshmen and new transfer students are considered for wide range of 4-year scholarships.
HOW TO APPLY: Entered automatically by completing the Undergraduate Application for Admission and Scholarships.
NUMBER OF AWARDS: Varies
RENEWABLE: Yes. Cumulative GPA of 3.25 after each academic year.

3965—UNIVERSITY OF NEW MEXICO

Mesa Hall, Room 3019
Albuquerque NM 87131-2081
505/277-6090
FAX: 505/277-5325
E-mail: finaid@unm.edu
Internet: http://www.unm.edu/
~schol/schol.html
AMOUNT: Up to $8,800
DEADLINE(S): DEC (Regents &
  Presidential); FEB 1 (UNM Scholars)
FIELD(S): All
ELIGIBILITY/REQUIREMENTS: More
than 1,000 scholarships from six major
scholarship programs open to eligible first-
time freshmen. Considerations include
extracurricular activities and personal
statement. Must be U.S. citizen or perma-
nent resident.
HOW TO APPLY: Contact Scholarships
Office for complete information.

3966—UNIVERSITY OF NEW MEXICO (Amigo/Amigo Transfer Scholarships)

Mesa Hall, Room 3019
Albuquerque NM 87131-2001
505/277-6090
FAX: 505/277-5325
E-mail: finaid@unm.edu
Internet: http://www.unm.edu/
~schol/apps/amigo.pdf
AMOUNT: Waiver of out-of-state tuition
  + $250/semester
DEADLINE(S): JAN 10; AUG 15
FIELD(S): All
ELIGIBILITY/REQUIREMENTS: Open
to non-New Mexico residents who are new
freshmen or transfer students. Must be
U.S. citizen or permanent resident.
HOW TO APPLY: Contact Scholarships
Office for complete information.

3967—UNIVERSITY OF SASKATCHEWAN (Awards for Undergraduate Students)

Student Financial Assistance &
Awards
Administration Building
105 Administration Place
Saskatoon SK S7N 5A2 CANADA
306/966-2863
FAX: 306/966-6730
E-mail: sfaa@usask.ca
Internet: http://www.usask.ca/
students/scholarships
AMOUNT: Varies
DEADLINE(S): JUN 1 (Academic
  Achievement Awards); NOV 1
  (Financial Need Awards)
FIELD(S): All

ELIGIBILITY/REQUIREMENTS: Open
to full-time undergraduates who have successfully completed at least 1 year of study
at the University of Saskatchewan. Cash
value of awards is applied toward payment
of tuition and fees; any balance is paid out
to the recipient via cheque.
HOW TO APPLY: See website or contact
Student Central for additional information.

3968—UNIVERSITY OF SOUTHERN CALIFORNIA (California Mexican-American Programs Office Scholarship)

University of SC-STU 203
Los Angeles CA 90089-4890
213/740-4735
E-mail: rsvargas@usc.edu
Internet: http://www.usc.edu
AMOUNT: $400-$6,000
DEADLINE(S): MAY 31
FIELD(S): All
ELIGIBILITY/REQUIREMENTS: Must
demonstrate financial need and academic
achievement.
HOW TO APPLY: Contact Mexican-
American Programs Office for information
and application.

3969—UNIVERSITY OF TEXAS-ARLINGTON ALUMNI ASSOCIATION (African-American Endowed Scholarship)

Box 19457
Arlington TX 76019
817/272-2594
E-mail: alumni@uta.edu
Internet: http://www.uta.edu/
alumni/scholar.htm
AMOUNT: $350
DEADLINE(S): Varies
FIELD(S): All
ELIGIBILITY/REQUIREMENTS: Must
be a full-time sophomore or higher in good
standing at the University of Texas at
Arlington. Must have demonstrated finan-
cial need and success and be of African-
American descent.
HOW TO APPLY: Contact UTA Alumni
Association for an application.
NUMBER OF AWARDS: 1

3970—UNIVERSITY OF TEXAS-ARLINGTON ALUMNI ASSOCIATION (Frankie S. Hansell Endowed Scholarship)

Box 19457
Arlington TX 76019
817/272-2594
E-mail: alumni@uta.edu
Internet: http://www.uta.edu/
alumni/scholar.htm

AMOUNT: $1,000
DEADLINE(S): Varies
FIELD(S): All
ELIGIBILITY/REQUIREMENTS: For
undergraduate or graduate students at the
University of Texas at Arlington. Must be
U.S. citizen and demonstrate financial
need. Preference is given to females.
HOW TO APPLY: Contact UTA Alumni
Association for an application.
NUMBER OF AWARDS: 9

3971—UNIVERSITY OF TEXAS-ARLINGTON ALUMNI ASSOCIATION (Hispanic Scholarship)

Box 19457
Arlington TX 76019
817/272-2594
E-mail: alumni@uta.edu
Internet: http://www.uta.edu/
alumni/scholar.htm
AMOUNT: $300
DEADLINE(S): Varies
FIELD(S): All
ELIGIBILITY/REQUIREMENTS: For
students of Hispanic origin who attend full
time with at least 15 hours completed at
the University of Texas at Arlington. Must
have a minimum 2.5 GPA; be in good
standing; and demonstrate financial need,
leadership ability, and potential for success. Transcripts and letter stating financial
need are required.
HOW TO APPLY: Contact UTA Alumni
Association for an application.
NUMBER OF AWARDS: 1

3972—UNIVERSITY OF TEXAS-ARLINGTON ALUMNI ASSOCIATION (Simmons-Blackwell Endowed Scholarship)

Box 19457
Arlington TX 76019
817/272-2594
E-mail: alumni@uta.edu
Internet: http://www.uta.edu/
alumni/scholar.htm
AMOUNT: $250
DEADLINE(S): Varies
FIELD(S): All
ELIGIBILITY/REQUIREMENTS: Must
be a first-generation college student with
less than 90 hours and attend the
University of Texas at Arlington. Must
have demonstrated financial need and a
minimum 2.5 GPA. Letter outlining career
goals is required.
HOW TO APPLY: Contact UTA Alumni
Association for an application.
NUMBER OF AWARDS: 1

3973—UNIVERSITY OF TEXAS-ARLINGTON ALUMNI ASSOCIATION (Student Foundation Sophomore Scholarship)

Box 19457
Arlington TX 76019
817/272-2594
E-mail: alumni@uta.edu
Internet: http://www.uta.edu/alumni/scholar.htm
AMOUNT: $250
DEADLINE(S): Varies
FIELD(S): All
ELIGIBILITY/REQUIREMENTS: Must be a sophomore enrolled in at least nine hours at the University of Texas at Arlington. Must demonstrate financial need and have a minimum 2.75 GPA.
HOW TO APPLY: Contact UTA Alumni Association for an application.
NUMBER OF AWARDS: 1

3974—UNIVERSITY OF WINDSOR (In-Course Scholarships and Awards)

401 Sunset Avenue
Windsor Ontario N9B 3P4
CANADA
519/253-3000
FAX: 519/973-7081
E-mail: award1@uwindsor.ca
Internet: http://www.uwindsor.ca
AMOUNT: Varies
DEADLINE(S): MAY 31
FIELD(S): All
ELIGIBILITY/REQUIREMENTS: Open to students in their 2nd, 3rd, and 4th years of study.
HOW TO APPLY: See website for complete details.
CONTACT: Aase Houser

3975—UNIVERSITY OF WINDSOR (International Student Entrance Award)

401 Sunset Avenue
Windsor Ontario N9B 3P4
CANADA
519/253-3000
FAX: 519/973-7081
E-mail: awards1@uwindsor.ca
Internet: http://www.uwindsor.ca
AMOUNT: $500-$1,500 (Canadian)
DEADLINE(S): MAY 31
FIELD(S): All
ELIGIBILITY/REQUIREMENTS: Open to undergraduate students registering in year 1 at the University of Windsor. Must have superior grades.
HOW TO APPLY: Automatic. No application required.
RENEWABLE: Yes. Up to 4 years.
CONTACT: Aase Houser

3976—UNIVERSITY OF WINDSOR (John B. Kennedy Memorial Entrance Award)

401 Sunset Avenue
Windsor Ontario N9B 3P4
CANADA
519/253-3000
FAX: 519/973-7081
E-mail: awards1@uwindsor.ca
Internet: http://www.uwindsor.ca
AMOUNT: $600/year (Canadian)
DEADLINE(S): MAY 31
FIELD(S): All
ELIGIBILITY/REQUIREMENTS: Open to undergraduate students registering in year 1 at the University of Windsor. Must have superior grades.
HOW TO APPLY: Automatic. No application required.
RENEWABLE: Yes. Up to 4 years.
CONTACT: Aase Houser

3977—UNIVERSITY OF WINDSOR (Monsignor F. T. Sullivan Bursary)

401 Sunset Avenue
Windsor Ontario N9B 3P4
CANADA
519/253-3000
FAX: 519/973-7081
E-mail: awards1@uwindsor.ca
Internet: http://www.uwindsor.ca
AMOUNT: $2,400 (Canadian)
DEADLINE(S): JUL 31
FIELD(S): All
ELIGIBILITY/REQUIREMENTS: Open to graduates of a Roman Catholic high school in Canada or the U.S. (preference given to graduates of Notre Dame High School, Chattanooga, TN).
HOW TO APPLY: Apply to the President, Assumption University at www.assumptionu.ca.
NUMBER OF AWARDS: 1 or more
RENEWABLE: No.
CONTACT: Aase Houser

3978—UNIVERSITY OF WINDSOR (U.S./Mexico Entrance Scholarship)

401 Sunset Avenue
Windsor Ontario N9B 3P4
CANADA
519/253-3000
FAX: 519/973-7081
E-mail: awards1@uwindsor.ca
Internet: http://www.uwindsor.ca
AMOUNT: $3,000/term (Canadian) Engineering, Education, Law, Nursing; all other fields $1,500/term (Canadian)
DEADLINE(S): MAY 31
FIELD(S): All
ELIGIBILITY/REQUIREMENTS: Open to undergraduate students with U.S./Mexican citizenship or permanent resident status registering in year 1 at the University of Windsor. Must have superior grades.
HOW TO APPLY: Automatic. No application required.
RENEWABLE: Yes. Up to 4 years, contingent upon successful completion of the previous term and a cumulative "A-" GPA.
CONTACT: Aase Houser

3979—U.S. SUBMARINE VETERANS INC.

P.O. Box 3870
Silverdale WA 98303-3870
877/542-3483
E-mail: ussui@telebyte.net
Internet: http:www.ussui.org
AMOUNT: $750-$1,000
DEADLINE(S): APR 15
FIELD(S): All
ELIGIBILITY/REQUIREMENTS: Sponsor must be "qualified in submarines" and "a member in good standing" of a base or member-at-large. Student may be child, stepchild, or grandchild, who is attending college or in senior year of high school. Maximum age is 23.
HOW TO APPLY: Request application from USSUI Scholarship Chairman, 30 Surrey Lane, Norwich, CT 06360-6541 (860/889-4750; e-mail, Logan343@aol.com).
NUMBER OF AWARDS: Approximately 16 (14, $750; 2, $1,000).
RENEWABLE: Yes, must reapply.
CONTACT: Paul Orstad, USSUI Scholarship Chairman

3980—U.S. SUBMARINE VETERANS OF WWII (Scholarship Program)

5040 Virginia Beach Boulevard, Suite 104-A
Virginia Beach VA 23462
757/671-3200
AMOUNT: $3,000
DEADLINE(S): APR 15
FIELD(S): All
ELIGIBILITY/REQUIREMENTS: Open to children and stepchildren of paid-up regular members (grandchildren are not eligible). Must be an unmarried high school senior or have graduated from high school no more than 4 years prior to applying and be under the age of 24.
HOW TO APPLY: List those submarines in which your sponsor served during WWII and include sponsor's membership card number when requesting application and additional information.

CONTACT: Tomi Roeske, Scholarship Administrator

3981—USC ALUMNI ASSOCIATION (Alumnae Coordinating Council [ACC] Scholarship)

635 Childs Way
Los Angeles CA 90089-0461
213/740-2300
Internet: http://alumni.usc.edu/clubs/scholarships.cfm
AMOUNT: $500-$4,000
DEADLINE(S): DEC 10
FIELD(S): All
ELIGIBILITY/REQUIREMENTS: Priority consideration may be given to applicants who demonstrate academic strength, leadership and community involvement, as well as the following criteria: competitive freshman candidates will be in the top of the applicant pool with respect to GPA and SAT or ACT; transfer applicants are required to hold a minimum 3.6 GPA; and continuing students are required to hold a minimum 3.0 GPA.
HOW TO APPLY: Submit applications along with a personal statement of 500 words or less explaining what you hope to contribute to the university while at USC (incoming freshman/transfer students) or explaining what your most influential experience at USC has been and how it has affected you (current USC students). Finalists will be called for a personal interview
RENEWABLE: Yes; must reapply each year.

3982—USC ALUMNI ASSOCIATION (Alumni Club Scholarship)

635 Childs Way
Los Angeles CA 90089-0461
213/740-2300
Internet: http://alumni.usc.edu/clubs/scholarships.cfm
AMOUNT: $1,000-$4,000
DEADLINE(S): DEC 10
FIELD(S): All
ELIGIBILITY/REQUIREMENTS: Priority consideration may be given to applicants who demonstrate academic strength, leadership and community involvement, as well as the following criteria: competitive freshman candidates will be in the top of the applicant pool with respect to GPA and SAT or ACT; transfer applicants are required to hold a minimum 3.6 GPA; and continuing students are required to hold a minimum 3.0 GPA.
HOW TO APPLY: Submit applications along with a personal statement of 500

words or less explaining what you hope to contribute to the university while at USC (incoming freshman/transfer students) or explaining what your most influential experience at USC has been and how it has affected you (current USC students). Finalists will be called for a personal interview
RENEWABLE: Yes; must reapply each year.

3983—USC ASIAN PACIFIC ALUMNI ASSOCIATION SCHOLARSHIP

Widney Alumni House
635 Childs Way
Los Angeles CA 90089-0461
213/740-6380
E-mail: Helen.kim@alumni center.usc.edu
Internet: http://alumni.usc.edu/clubs/scholarships.cfm
AMOUNT: $1,000 or more
DEADLINE(S): Varies
FIELD(S): All
ELIGIBILITY/REQUIREMENTS: Must be a full-time student (undergraduate, transfer, graduate or professional) enrolled in a USC degree program or will be enrolled (in the case of an incoming first year, transfer or graduate student) for the entire year; must have achieved a minimum of a 3.0 grade point average in his/her high school or college work; be a U.S. citizen or a permanent resident. Financial need considered.
HOW TO APPLY: Submit application along with personal statement of 500 words or less addressing involvement in the Asian Pacific American community, and how if you received the scholarship, you would contribute to your community in your chosen field (new applicants, continuing undergraduates, and transfer students); how the award impacted your experience at USC and how you have benefited from it (past recipients). Separate statements describing academic honors received within past four years and campus and community organizations to which you belong and describing level of involvement; 1 academic reference and 2 references from community organization. Submit financial aid documents to USC Office of Financial Aid and transcript to APAA.
RENEWABLE: Yes; must reapply each year.

3984—USC TOWN AND GOWN SCHOLARSHIP

635 Childs Way
Los Angeles CA 90089-0461

213/740-2300
Internet: http://alumni.usc.edu/clubs/scholarships.cfm
AMOUNT: $1,000 or more
DEADLINE(S): DEC 10
FIELD(S): All
ELIGIBILITY/REQUIREMENTS: Applicant must be U.S. citizen; permanent resident of Southern California (Bakersfield is considered the northernmost boundary); have demonstrated academic strength, leadership ability, and community involvement; be a full-time status (12-18 units/semester for undergraduates; 6-12 units/semester for graduate students), and not be receiving tuition remission or tuition exchange. Additional requirements: incoming freshmen average SAT and ACT scores are in the top 2-3% of all students nationwide. Average GPA is 3.9. In addition to academic criteria, community involvement and leadership; incoming transfer students must demonstrate academic strength (cumulative GPA of at least 3.6), leadership ability, and community involvement; and current USC students applying for the first time minimum 3.0 GPA.
HOW TO APPLY: Submit applications along with a personal statement of 500 words or less explaining how your USC legacy has contributed to your interest in becoming part of the Trojan Family (incoming freshman/transfer students) or explaining how your USC legacy has contributed to your involvement as a USC student (current USC students). Finalists will be called for a personal interview.
RENEWABLE: Yes; must reapply each year and maintain 3.0 GPA.
ADDITIONAL INFORMATION: Must be used for tuition.

3985—UTILITY WORKERS UNION OF AMERICA (Scholarship Awards)

815 16th Street NW
Washington DC 20006
202/974-8200
Internet: http://www.uwua.org
AMOUNT: $500-$2,000/year
DEADLINE(S): DEC 31
FIELD(S): All
ELIGIBILITY/REQUIREMENTS: Open to sons and daughters of active Utility Workers Union members in good standing. Winners are selected from the group of high school juniors who take the PSAT/NMSQT.
HOW TO APPLY: Contact UWUA for details.
NUMBER OF AWARDS: 2 awards annually

3986—VALENCIA COMMUNITY COLLEGE FOUNDATION (Scholarships)

P.O. Box 3028
Orlando FL 32802-3028
407/317-7950
FAX: 407/317-7956
Internet: http://www.valencia.
org/scholar.html
AMOUNT: Varies
DEADLINE(S): Varies
FIELD(S): All
ELIGIBILITY/REQUIREMENTS: The Valencia Community College Foundation lists numerous financial aid programs. The listed website is comprehensive.
HOW TO APPLY: Access website or write to Foundation for list of financial aid programs.

3987—VERMONT STUDENT ASSISTANCE CORPORATION (Incentive Grants for Undergraduates)

P.O. Box 2000
Winooski VT 05404-2601
802/655-9602 or 800/642-3177
TDD: 800/281-3341
FAX: 802/654-3765
Internet: http://www.vsac.org
AMOUNT: $500-$9,100
DEADLINE(S): None
FIELD(S): All
ELIGIBILITY/REQUIREMENTS: Open to Vermont residents enrolled full time at approved postsecondary institutions. Must meet needs test. Award amounts depend on expected family contribution, Pell Grant eligibility, and institution attended.
HOW TO APPLY: Contact VSAC for an application.

3988—VERMONT STUDENT ASSISTANCE CORPORATION (Non-Degree Grant)

P.O. Box 2000
Winooski VT 05404-2601
802/655-9602 or 800/642-3177
TDD: 800/281-3341
FAX: 802/654-3765
Internet: http://www.vsac.org
AMOUNT: Maximum $750 for 1
course/semester
DEADLINE(S): None
FIELD(S): All
ELIGIBILITY/REQUIREMENTS: Open to Vermont residents enrolled in a non-degree course that will improve employability or encourage further study. Must meet needs test.
HOW TO APPLY: Contact VSAC for an application.

3989—VERMONT STUDENT ASSISTANCE CORPORATION (Part-Time Grant)

P.O. Box 2000
Winooski VT 05404-2601
802/655-9602 or 800/642-3177
TDD: 800/281-3341
FAX: 802/654-3765
Internet: http://www.vsac.org
AMOUNT: $250-$6,830
DEADLINE(S): None
FIELD(S): All
ELIGIBILITY/REQUIREMENTS: Open to Vermont residents pursuing part-time undergraduate study in a degree, diploma, or certificate program. Must be taking fewer than 12 credit hours, have not received a bachelor's degree, and meet needs test. Award amounts depend on number of credit hours taken.
HOW TO APPLY: Contact VSAC for an application.

3990—VETERANS OF FOREIGN WARS OF THE UNITED STATES (Military Family Scholarship)

VFW Building
406 West 34th Street
Kansas City MO 64111
816/968-1117
FAX: 816/968-1149
E-mail: kharmer@vfw.org
Internet: http://www.vfw.org/
AMOUNT: $3,000
DEADLINE(S): DEC 31
FIELD(S): All
ELIGIBILITY/REQUIREMENTS: Open to VFW members, spouses, and children. Must be currently serving in uniform or have been discharged within the 36 months before the deadline.
HOW TO APPLY: See website for Student Entry Form. Submit with essay (theme selected each year). Entry MUST be delivered to a local, participating VFW Post (see website for list of participating posts or call 816/968-1117).
NUMBER OF AWARDS: 25 (5 members each branch: Army, Navy, Marine Corps, Air Force, and Coast Guard)
RENEWABLE: No
ADDITIONAL INFORMATION: 1st-place winner receives all-expense-paid trip to Washington DC.

3991—VETERANS OF FOREIGN WARS OF THE UNITED STATES (Patriot's Pen Essay)

VFW Building
406 West 34th Street
Kansas City MO 64111
816/968-1117

FAX: 816/968-1149
E-mail: kharmer@vfw.org
Internet: http://www.vfw.org/
AMOUNT: $5,000
DEADLINE(S): NOV 1
FIELD(S): All
ELIGIBILITY/REQUIREMENTS: Must be an outstanding scout who has received a Boy Scout Eagle Award, a Venture Scouting Silver Award, or a Sea Scout Quartermaster Award. Must be at least 15; a high school student; a registered, active member of a Boy Scout Troop, Venturing Crew, or a Sea Scout Ship; have demonstrated practical citizenship in school, scouting and the community.
HOW TO APPLY: See website for Student Entry Form. Submit with essay (theme selected each year). Entry MUST be delivered to a local, participating VFW Post (see website for list of participating posts or call 816/968-1117).
NUMBER OF AWARDS: Over 50 national awards (also post, district, and state awards)
RENEWABLE: No
ADDITIONAL INFORMATION: 1st-place winner receives all-expense-paid trip to Washington DC.

3992—VETERANS OF FOREIGN WARS OF THE UNITED STATES (Scout of the Year Scholarship)

VFW Building
406 West 34th Street
Kansas City MO 64111
816/968-1117
FAX: 816/968-1149
E-mail: kharmer@vfw.org
Internet: http://www.vfw.org/
AMOUNT: $5,000
DEADLINE(S): MAR 1
FIELD(S): All
ELIGIBILITY/REQUIREMENTS: Must be an outstanding scout who has received a Boy Scout Eagle Award, a Venture Scouting Silver Award, or a Sea Scout Quartermaster Award. Must be at least 15; a high school student; a registered, active member of a Boy Scout Troop, Venturing Crew, or a Sea Scout Ship; have demonstrated practical citizenship in school, scouting and the community.
HOW TO APPLY: See website for Student Entry Form. Submit with essay (theme selected each year). Entry MUST be delivered to a local, participating VFW Post (see website for list of participating posts or call 816/968-1117).
NUMBER OF AWARDS: Over 50 national awards (also post, district, and state awards)

RENEWABLE: No
ADDITIONAL INFORMATION: 1st-place winner receives all-expense-paid trip to Washington DC.

3993—VETERANS OF FOREIGN WARS OF THE UNITED STATES (Voice of Democracy Audio-Essay Scholarship Contest)

VFW Building
406 West 34th Street
Kansas City MO 64111
816/968-1117
FAX: 816/968-1149
E-mail: kharmer@vfw.org
Internet: http://www.vfw.org/
AMOUNT: $1,000-$30,000 (1st place); $1,000-$16,000 (national scholarships)
DEADLINE(S): NOV 1
FIELD(S): All
ELIGIBILITY/REQUIREMENTS: Open to students in public, private, and parochial high schools or a home-study program in the U.S., its territories and possessions, or enrolled in an overseas U.S. military/civilian dependent school. Contestants will be judged on their treatment of an annual theme. Essay may not refer to themselves, their schools, states, cities, etc., as a means of identification. Foreign exchange students NOT eligible.
HOW TO APPLY: See website for Student Entry Form. Submit with essay (theme selected each year) and recording. Entry MUST be delivered to a local, participating VFW Post (see website for list of participating posts or call 816/968-1117).
NUMBER OF AWARDS: Over 50 national awards (also post, district, and state awards)
RENEWABLE: No
ADDITIONAL INFORMATION: 1st-place winner receives all-expense-paid trip to Washington DC.

3994—VIKKI CARR SCHOLARSHIP FOUNDATION

P.O. Box 780968
San Antonio TX 78278
Internet: http://www.vikkicarr foundation.com
AMOUNT: Up to $3,000
DEADLINE(S): APR 1
FIELD(S): All
ELIGIBILITY/REQUIREMENTS: Open to Latino residents of Texas between the ages of 17 and 22. Awards are for undergrad study at accredited colleges and universities. No U.S. citizenship requirement. Based on academic achievement, financial need, community involvement, and personal essay.

HOW TO APPLY: See website for additional information and application; submit with biography (500 words or less) in English stating your special interests, career goals, reasons for pursuing higher education, and other pertinent information; recent photo; high school and/or college transcript; and college entrance exam scores.

3995—VINCENT L. HAWKINSON FOUNDATION FOR PEACE AND JUSTICE, THE

324 Harvard Street SE
Minneapolis MN 55414
612/331-8125
Internet: http://www.grace attheu.org
AMOUNT: Up to $3,000
DEADLINE(S): APR 1
FIELD(S): All
ELIGIBILITY/REQUIREMENTS: Open to residents or students attending school in Minnesota, Iowa, Wisconsin, North Dakota or South Dakota. Demonstrate commitment to peace and justice in a short essay. No religious affiliation requirement.
HOW TO APPLY: Write or call for application form or download from website. Submit essay with 3 references, nomination by 1 of the 3 references, and academic transcript. Finalists receive personal interview in Minneapolis.
NUMBER OF AWARDS: 1 (3-5 runners-up receive lower amounts)
RENEWABLE: No

3996—VIRGINIA GOLF FOUNDATION SCHOLARSHIPS

600 Founders Bridge Boulevard
Midlothian VA 23113
804/378-2300, ext. 11
FAX: 804/378-8216
E-mail: preilly@vsga.org
Internet: http://www.vsga.org/ junior golf/
DEADLINE(S): MAR 1
FIELD(S): All
ELIGIBILITY/REQUIREMENTS: Open to any Virginia high school senior in good standing who has been domiciled in Virginia for at least 1 year who has an interest in golf and wishes to attend college and university within the Commonwealth.
HOW TO APPLY: Must be nominated by school; contact guidance counselor for full details or see website for information and application.
NUMBER OF AWARDS: About 28
RENEWABLE: 4-year scholarship
CONTACT: Peggy Reilly

3997—VIRGINIA MILITARY INSTITUTE

Financial Aid Office
Lexington VA 24450-0304
540/464-7208
FAX: 540/464-7629
Internet: http://www.web.vmi.edu
AMOUNT: Varies
DEADLINE(S): MAR 1
FIELD(S): All
ELIGIBILITY/REQUIREMENTS: Scholarships are available to attend this 4-year, coeducational, undergraduate university in Lexington, Virginia. Awards include ROTC Scholarships, State Cadetships, and the Institute Scholars Program.
HOW TO APPLY: Contact VMI for descriptions of programs and details of the school. Submit FAFSA form and VMI financial aid form found in the admissions packet.

3998—VIRGINIA STATE COUNCIL OF HIGHER EDUCATION (Tuition Assistance Grant Program)

101 North 14th Street
James Monroe Building
Richmond VA 23219
804/224-2614
E-mail: andeso@schev.edu
Internet: http://www.schev.edu
AMOUNT: $3,000 (maximum)
DEADLINE(S): JUL 31
FIELD(S): All (except Theology)
ELIGIBILITY/REQUIREMENTS: Open to Virginia residents who are full-time undergraduate, graduate, or professional students at eligible private colleges/universities in Virginia. Financial need NOT a factor. Late applications may be considered if funds are available.
HOW TO APPLY: Contact your financial aid office or the State Council of Higher Education for an application.
NUMBER OF AWARDS: 15,000+

3999—VIRGINIA STATE COUNCIL OF HIGHER EDUCATION (Virginia Transfer Grant Program)

101 North 14th Street
James Monroe Building
Richmond VA 23219
804/225-2604
E-mail: andes@schev.edu
Internet: http://www.schev.edu
AMOUNT: Up to full tuition and fees
DEADLINE(S): Varies (check with financial aid office)
FIELD(S): All

ELIGIBILITY/REQUIREMENTS: For minority students who enroll in one of the Commonwealth's 13 historically white colleges or universities and all transfer students at Norfolk State and Virginia State Universities. Applicants must qualify for entry as first-time transfer students.
HOW TO APPLY: Contact college financial aid office for complete information.

4000—VMFA/VMF/VMF(N)-531 (Gray Ghost Scholarship Program)

12033 Blue Diamond Court
San Diego CA 92131
858/547-0878
E-mail: F18Puma@sbcglobal.net
AMOUNT: $1,000
DEADLINE(S): MAR 1
FIELD(S): All
ELIGIBILITY/REQUIREMENTS: Open to undergraduate students who are children or grandchildren of former members of the Marine Corps Squadron VMF/VMF(N) or VMFA-531. The living or deceased parent or grandparent must have received an honorable discharge from the USMC. Gross family income shouldn't exceed $54,000/year.
HOW TO APPLY: Contact for nomination procedures.
NUMBER OF AWARDS: 1-2
RENEWABLE: Yes, must reapply.
CONTACT: Roy Alan Pearson

4001—WAL-MART FOUNDATION (Sam Walton Community Scholarship)

P.O. Box 22117
Nashville TN 37202
866/851-3372
FAX: 615/523-7100
Internet: http://www.walmart foundation.org
AMOUNT: $1,000
DEADLINE(S): JAN 20
FIELD(S): All
ELIGIBILITY/REQUIREMENTS: For college-bound high school seniors, who have NO affiliation with Wal-Mart Stores, Inc., for freshman year at an accredited U.S. college or university approved by the Foundation in each community where a Wal-Mart store is operating. Based on financial need, academic record, ACT/SAT scores, community/extracurricular involvement and work experience.
HOW TO APPLY: Applications and information only available online. Need access code SWCS to apply.
NUMBER OF AWARDS: Each Wal-Mart store and SAM'S Club has the opportunity to award 2 scholarships a year.

CONTACT: Scholarship Program Administrator

4002—WAL-MART FOUNDATION SCHOLARSHIP (The Wal-Mart Associate Scholarship)

P.O. Box 22117
Nashville TN 37202
866/851-3372
FAX: 615/523-7100
Internet: http://www.walmart foundation.org
AMOUNT: $2,000
DEADLINE(S): JAN 26
FIELD(S): All
ELIGIBILITY/REQUIREMENTS: Open to graduating high school seniors employed by Wal-Mart and to associates' children ineligible for the Walton Family Foundation Scholarship due to length of employment or not working full time. Applications available at local store from November to January. Based on ACT, SAT, transcripts, class rank, community activities, leadership, and financial need.
HOW TO APPLY: See website for additional information and application or visit local store/club or call.

4003—WAL-MART FOUNDATION SCHOLARSHIPS (The Wal-Mart Higher REACH Scholarship)

P.O. Box 22117
Nashville TN 37202
866/851-3372
FAX: 615/523-7100
Internet: http://www.walmart foundation.org
AMOUNT: Up to $2,000/year
DEADLINE(S): JAN 20
FIELD(S): All
ELIGIBILITY/REQUIREMENTS: Open to Wal-Mart Associates, employed at least 1 year, who have been out of high school for at least 1 year, who are pursuing continuing education.
HOW TO APPLY: See website for additional information and application or visit local store/club or call.
NUMBER OF AWARDS: 10% of qualified applicants

4004—WASHINGTON APPLE EDUCATION FOUNDATION (CCM Scholarship Fund)

P.O. Box 3720
Wenatchee WA 98807
509/663-7713
FAX: 509/663-7713
E-mail: waef@waef.org

Internet: http://www.ussui.org
AMOUNT: Varies
DEADLINE(S): APR 1
FIELD(S): All
ELIGIBILITY/REQUIREMENTS: Open to graduating high school seniors and students currently enrolled in a 2- or 4-year college or university whose parents are employed at Columbia Marketing International, Columbia Fruit, or McDougall & Sons, Inc.
HOW TO APPLY: See website for application.
CONTACT: Jennifer Whitney

4005—WASHINGTON APPLE EDUCATION FOUNDATION (Close Family Scholarship)

P.O. Box 3720
Wenatchee WA 98807
509/663-7713
FAX: 509/663-7713
E-mail: waef@waef.org
Internet: http://www.ussui.org
AMOUNT: $1,000
DEADLINE(S): APR 1
FIELD(S): All
ELIGIBILITY/REQUIREMENTS: Open to graduating seniors of Highland High School (Cowiche/Ticton, Washington).
HOW TO APPLY: See website for application.
NUMBER OF AWARDS: 1
CONTACT: Jennifer Whitney

4006—WASHINGTON APPLE EDUCATION FOUNDATION (Delmar Smith Memorial Scholarship)

P.O. Box 3720
Wenatchee WA 98807
509/663-7713
FAX: 509/663-7713
E-mail: waef@waef.org
Internet: http://www.ussui.org
AMOUNT: $500
DEADLINE(S): APR 1
FIELD(S): All
ELIGIBILITY/REQUIREMENTS: Must be Tonasket High School seniors (Tonasket, Washington).
HOW TO APPLY: See website for application.
NUMBER OF AWARDS: 1
CONTACT: Jennifer Whitney

4007—WASHINGTON APPLE EDUCATION FOUNDATION (Doug Zahn Memorial Scholarship)

P.O. Box 3720
Wenatchee WA 98807

509/663-7713
FAX: 509/663-7713
E-mail: waef@waef.org
Internet: http://www.ussui.org
AMOUNT: $250
DEADLINE(S): APR 1
FIELD(S): All (emphasis on Agriculture;
Horticulture)
ELIGIBILITY/REQUIREMENTS: Must
be Okanogan County high school senior.
Must also plan on pursuing a 2- or 4-year
agricultural-related education or have parents employed with the tree fruit industry.
HOW TO APPLY: See website for application.
NUMBER OF AWARDS: 2
RENEWABLE: No
CONTACT: Jennifer Whitney

4008—WASHINGTON APPLE EDUCATION FOUNDATION (E. Ralph & Ida Strausz Memorial Scholarship)

P.O. Box 3720
Wenatchee WA 98807
509/663-7713
FAX: 509/663-7713
E-mail: waef@waef.org
Internet: http://www.ussui.org
AMOUNT: $500
DEADLINE(S): APR 1
FIELD(S): All
ELIGIBILITY/REQUIREMENTS: Open
to graduating senior of Highland High
School (Cowiche/Ticton Washington).
HOW TO APPLY: See website for application.
NUMBER OF AWARDS: 1
CONTACT: Jennifer Whitney

4009—WASHINGTON APPLE EDUCATION FOUNDATION (Farmworker Education Scholarship)

P.O. Box 3720
Wenatchee WA 98807
509/663-7713
FAX: 509/663-7713
E-mail: waef@waef.org
Internet: http://www.ussui.org
AMOUNT: Varies
DEADLINE(S): APR 1
FIELD(S): All
ELIGIBILITY/REQUIREMENTS: Must
be Washington state high school seniors or
current college undergraduate students
from Washington state. Parents or
guardians of the applicants or the applicant
must be employed within the Washington
apple industry. Applicants cannot be related to WAEF directors or WAEF staff
members.

HOW TO APPLY: See website for application.
NUMBER OF AWARDS: Varies
RENEWABLE: No
CONTACT: Jennifer Whitney

4010—WASHINGTON APPLE EDUCATION FOUNDATION (Jennifer Skagen Memorial Scholarship)

P.O. Box 3720
Wenatchee WA 98807
509/663-7713
FAX: 509/663-7713
E-mail: waef@waef.org
Internet: http://www.ussui.org
AMOUNT: $500
DEADLINE(S): APR 1
FIELD(S): All
ELIGIBILITY/REQUIREMENTS: Must
be Eastmont High School seniors (East
Wenatchee, Washington).
HOW TO APPLY: See website for application.
NUMBER OF AWARDS: 2
CONTACT: Jennifer Whitney

4011—WASHINGTON APPLE EDUCATION FOUNDATION (Larson Fruit Company Scholarship)

P.O. Box 3720
Wenatchee WA 98807
509/663-7713
FAX: 509/663-7713
E-mail: waef@waef.org
Internet: http://www.ussui.org
AMOUNT: $1,000
DEADLINE(S): APR 1
FIELD(S): All
ELIGIBILITY/REQUIREMENTS: Open
to seniors attending Selah High School
(Selah, Washington).
HOW TO APPLY: See website for application.
NUMBER OF AWARDS: 1
CONTACT: Jennifer Whitney

4012—WASHINGTON APPLE EDUCATION FOUNDATION (Matson Company Scholarship)

P.O. Box 3720
Wenatchee WA 98807
509/663-7713
FAX: 509/663-7713
E-mail: waef@waef.org
Internet: http://www.ussui.org
AMOUNT: $1,000
DEADLINE(S): APR 1
FIELD(S): All

ELIGIBILITY/REQUIREMENTS: Open
to graduating seniors of Selah High School
(Selah, Washington).
HOW TO APPLY: See website for application.
NUMBER OF AWARDS: 1
CONTACT: Jennifer Whitney

4013—WASHINGTON APPLE EDUCATION FOUNDATION (Memorial Scholarship)

P.O. Box 3720
Wenatchee WA 98807
509/663-7713
FAX: 509/663-7713
E-mail: waef@waef.org
Internet: http://www.ussui.org
AMOUNT: Varies
DEADLINE(S): APR 1
FIELD(S): All (emphasis on Agriculture;
Horticulture)
ELIGIBILITY/REQUIREMENTS: Must
be Washington state high school seniors or
current college undergraduate students
from Washington state. Should be involved
in Washington's tree fruit industry, either
pursuing a career in the industry or having
been raised in a family involved in the
industry.
HOW TO APPLY: See website for application.
NUMBER OF AWARDS: Varies
RENEWABLE: No
CONTACT: Jennifer Whitney

4014—WASHINGTON APPLE EDUCATION FOUNDATION (Roy Farms Scholarship)

P.O. Box 3720
Wenatchee WA 98807
509/663-7713
FAX: 509/663-7713
E-mail: waef@waef.org
Internet: http://www.ussui.org
AMOUNT: $1,000
DEADLINE(S): APR 1
FIELD(S): All (emphasis on Agriculture;
Horticulture and related fields)
ELIGIBILITY/REQUIREMENTS: Open
to East Valley High School (Moxee,
Washington) seniors who are pursuing a
degree in the field of agriculture (or related field) or who are children of a parent(s)
currently employed by Roy Farms, Inc.
HOW TO APPLY: See website for application.
NUMBER OF AWARDS: 1
CONTACT: Jennifer Whitney

4015—WASHINGTON APPLE EDUCATION FOUNDATION (Tree Top, Inc. Scholarship)

P.O. Box 3720

Wenatchee WA 98807
509/663-7713
FAX: 509/663-7713
E-mail: waef@waef.org
Internet: http://www.ussui.org
AMOUNT: $1,000
DEADLINE(S): APR 1
FIELD(S): All
ELIGIBILITY/REQUIREMENTS: Open to graduating high school seniors whose parents are either contracted grower-members of Tree Top, Inc. or employees of Tree Top, Inc. Applicants must plan to attend an accredited 2- or 4-year college or university. The awards are based upon merit and academics; family financial information is not a requirement of the application process. The scholarships are NOT limited to residents of Washington state.
HOW TO APPLY: See website for application.
NUMBER OF AWARDS: 2
CONTACT: Jennifer Whitney

4016—WASHINGTON APPLE EDUCATION FOUNDATION (William Stoltenow Memorial Scholarship)

P.O. Box 3720
Wenatchee WA 98807
509/663-7713
FAX: 509/663-7713
E-mail: waef@waef.org
Internet: http://www.ussui.org
DEADLINE(S): APR 1
FIELD(S): All
ELIGIBILITY/REQUIREMENTS: Must be graduating seniors of Highland High School (Naches/Tieton, Washington).
HOW TO APPLY: See website for application.
CONTACT: Jennifer Whitney

4017—WASHINGTON CROSSING FOUNDATION

Box 503
Levittown PA 19058-0503
215/949-8841
Internet: http//:www.gwcf.org
AMOUNT: $1,000-$20,000
DEADLINE(S): JAN 15
FIELD(S): All
ELIGIBILITY/REQUIREMENTS: Available to high school senior, U.S. citizen, planning a career in government service.
HOW TO APPLY: See website for application; submit with 1-page essay stating why you plan a career in government service including any inspiration to be derived from the leadership of George Washington

in his famous crossing of the Delaware. Essay must be accompanied by a recommendation from the high school principal or guidance counselor evaluating your achievements, along with transcripts, national testing scores, and other supporting information.
NUMBER OF AWARDS: Varies
RENEWABLE: Yes. Scholarship will be paid, as long as the student meets the requirements of the college chosen, maintains a suitable scholastic level, and continues his or her career objective. Students planning to attend one of the Military Academies or who have been awarded full 4-year tuition scholarships will only be eligible for a one-year award with proof of valid educational expenses.
ADDITIONAL INFORMATION: Several awards are available specifically to students who currently reside in Pennsylvania; see website for details.

4018—WASHINGTON STATE PTA (Financial Grant Foundation)

2003 65th Avenue West
Tacoma WA 98466-6215
253/565-2153
FAX: 253/565-7753
E-mail: wapta@wastatepta.org
Internet: http://www.wastatepta.org
AMOUNT: $2,000 (4-year schools);
$1,000 (2-year schools)
DEADLINE(S): MAR 1
FIELD(S): All
ELIGIBILITY/REQUIREMENTS: Open to Washington state residents who are high school seniors and graduates who will be entering freshmen at an accredited college or university, community college, vo-tech school, or other accredited institution. Applicants need not be current graduates. Financial need is primary consideration.
HOW TO APPLY: Check with high school counselor or contact PTA for complete information.

4019—WASHINGTON STATE TRIAL LAWYERS ASSOCIATION (American Justice Essay Scholarship Contest)

1809 7th Avenue, #1500
Seattle WA 98101-1328
206/464-1011
FAX: 206/464-0703
E-mail: wstla@wstla.org
Internet: http://www.wstla.org
AMOUNT: $2,000 (college division),
$1,000 (high school division)
DEADLINE(S): MAR 15
FIELD(S): All

ELIGIBILITY/REQUIREMENTS: Submit essay based on assigned topic (changes annually). Essays must be original and must have an original title—the topic may NOT be used as the title of the essay. Essays must be on any subject within the scope of the topic.
HOW TO APPLY: Contact Association for topic and details of submission.
CONTACT: Rebecca Parker at rebecca@wstla.org

4020—WASHINGTON STATE TRIAL LAWYERS ASSOCIATION (Presidents' Scholarship)

1809 7th Avenue, #1500
Seattle WA 98101-1328
206/464-1011
FAX: 206/464-0703
E-mail: wstla@wstla.org
Internet: http://www.wstla.org
AMOUNT: Varies (average $2,500)
DEADLINE(S): MAR 15
FIELD(S): All
ELIGIBILITY/REQUIREMENTS: Based on demonstrated academic achievement and planned advancement toward a degree at an institution of higher learning; documented need for financial assistance; history of achievement despite having been a victim of injury or overcoming a disability, handicap, or similar challenge; a record of commitment to helping people in need, of protecting the rights of injured persons; a plan or commitment to apply the education to be funded toward helping people; and residency in the State of Washington.
HOW TO APPLY: Apply by letter describing your qualifications and explaining the reasons why you feel you deserve the scholarship. Attach all high school and community college academic transcripts; the name, address, and telephone number of 2 references, at least one of which must be outside the school environment; a brief financial statement; any other documentation you wish to include. Submit to WSTLA Presidents' Scholarship, Gregg L. Tinker, Chairman, 101 Stewart Street #101, Seattle, WA 98101.
NUMBER OF AWARDS: 1 or more
CONTACT: Rebecca Parker at rebecca@wstla.org.

4021—WELLS FARGO EDUCATION FINANCIAL SERVICES (College Steps Scholarship Sweepstakes)

301 East 58th Street N.
Sioux Falls SD 57104
888/511-7302
FAX: 605/575-4550

E-mail: collegesteps@wellsfargo
efs.com
Internet: http://www.wellsfargo.
com/collegesteps
AMOUNT: $1,000
DEADLINE(S): Varies
FIELD(S): All
ELIGIBILITY/REQUIREMENTS: High
school students may sign up for informa-
tion on financial aid, scholarships, and
standardized tests, and enter the sweep-
stakes.
HOW TO APPLY: See website for official
rules and eligibility requirements.
NUMBER OF AWARDS: 100
RENEWABLE: No

4022—WESTERN GOLF ASSOCIATION/EVANS SCHOLARS FOUNDATION (Chick Evans Caddie Scholarships)

1 Briar Road
Golf IL 60029
847/724-4600
FAX: 847/724-7133
Internet: http://www.westerngolf
association.com
AMOUNT: Full tuition and housing
(where applicable)
DEADLINE(S): SEP 30
FIELD(S): All
ELIGIBILITY/REQUIREMENTS: Open
to U.S. high school seniors in the top 25%
of their class with minimum "B" average in
college prep courses, and have taken the
ACT or SAT, who have served as a caddie
at a WGA member club for at least 2 years.
Must demonstrate outstanding personal
character and financial need.
HOW TO APPLY: Contact your local
country club or write for complete information. Applications are accepted after
completion of junior year in high school
(between July 1 and September 30).
Submit with a letter of recommendation
from the sponsoring club signed by club
officials and 1 from high school; transcript;
candidate's essay; financial documentation
including parent's most recent federal tax
return; Financial Aid Profile; and SAT
and/or ACT scores.
NUMBER OF AWARDS: About 200
RENEWABLE: Yes. Up to 4 years at the
scholarship committee's discretion.

4023—WESTERN MICHIGAN UNIVERSITY (Alumni Association Legacy Award)

1903 West Michigan
Kalamazoo MI 49008-5337
269/387-8777
FAX: 269/387-6989
E-mail: alumni@wmich.edu

Internet: http://www.wmich.
edu/alumni
AMOUNT: $500
DEADLINE(S): MAR 1
FIELD(S): All
ELIGIBILITY/REQUIREMENTS: The
child, grandchild, stepchild or step-grandchild of a WMU alumnus/alumna, who is a
dues-paying member of the WMU Alumni
Association, admitted to WMU as a regular degree student or entering Western for
the first time as a freshman or transfer student.
HOW TO APPLY: Contact the WMU
Alumni Association for an application or
apply online or print application from website, and submit it to the McKee Alumni
Center.
RENEWABLE: Yes. Must reapply; maximum 4 years.
CONTACT: Alumni Association

4024—WESTERN MICHIGAN UNIVERSITY (Allen Chapel African Methodist Episcopal Church Scholarship Fund)

1903 West Michigan
Kalamazoo MI 49008-5337
269/387-8777
FAX: 269/387-6989
E-mail: finaid-info@wmich.edu
Internet: http://www.wmich.
edu/endowed
AMOUNT: $500
DEADLINE(S): APR 1
FIELD(S): All
ELIGIBILITY/REQUIREMENTS:
Recipient should have demonstrated evi-
dence of public service and volunteer ser-
vice; financial need; and have minimum 2.0
high school GPA. Preference is given to
students who are members of, or whose
parents attend the Allen Chapel African
Episcopal Church.
HOW TO APPLY: See website for appli-
cation and submit with FAFSA.

4025—WESTERN MICHIGAN UNIVERSITY (Christian Life Center Scholarship)

1903 West Michigan
Kalamazoo MI 49008-5337
269/387-8777
FAX: 269/387-6989
E-mail: finaid-info@wmich.edu
Internet: http://www.wmich.
edu/endowed
AMOUNT: Varies
DEADLINE(S): APR 1
FIELD(S): All
ELIGIBILITY/REQUIREMENTS: Open
to full-time undergraduate at WMU; pref-
erence given to students who attend or stu-

dents whose parents attend Christian Life
Center and who have had membership at
Christian Life Center for at least 3 years.
Minimum high school GPA of 3.0 average
or WMU student who has maintained satisfactory academic progress; must demonstrate financial need and evidence of public service/volunteer service.
HOW TO APPLY: See website for application and submit with FAFSA.
RENEWABLE: Yes. Up to 3 consecutive
academic years if recipient demonstrates
satisfactory academic progress.

4026—WESTERN MICHIGAN UNIVERSITY (Dr. and Mrs. C. L. Dangremond Scholarship)

1903 West Michigan
Kalamazoo MI 49008-5337
269/387-8777
FAX: 269/387-6989
E-mail: finaid-info@wmich.edu
Internet: http://www.wmich.
edu/endowed
AMOUNT: Varies
DEADLINE(S): APR 1
FIELD(S): All
ELIGIBILITY/REQUIREMENTS: Open
to undergraduate; must demonstrate finan-
cial need, and maintain satisfactory aca-
demic progress as defined by the Financial
Aid Office.
HOW TO APPLY: See website for appli-
cation and submit with FAFSA.

4027—WESTERN MICHIGAN UNIVERSITY (Edwin Steffen Scholarship)

1903 West Michigan
Kalamazoo MI 49008-5337
269/387-8777
FAX: 269/387-6989
E-mail: finaid-info@wmich.edu
Internet: http://www.wmich.
edu/endowed
AMOUNT: $500/semester
DEADLINE(S): APR 1
FIELD(S): All
ELIGIBILITY/REQUIREMENTS: Open
to a high school senior from Arthur Hill
High School, Decatur High School,
L'Anse High School, or Saginaw High
School. Based on academic criteria (mini-
mum 3.0 GPA); preference given to appli-
cants who show financial need. Consi-
deration given to letters of recommenda-
tion (but are not required).
HOW TO APPLY: See website for appli-
cation and submit with FAFSA. Note:
Must apply for admission to WMU by
February 1; must file FAFSA by March 1
to the Office of Student Financial Aid.

4028—WESTERN MICHIGAN UNIVERSITY (Galilee Missionary Baptist Church Scholarship)

1903 West Michigan
Kalamazoo MI 49008-5337
269/387-8777
FAX: 269/387-6989
E-mail: finaid-info@wmich.edu
Internet: http://www.wmich.edu/endowed
AMOUNT: Varies
DEADLINE(S): APR 1
FIELD(S): All
ELIGIBILITY/REQUIREMENTS: Open to a full-time undergraduate at WMU. Preference given to students who attend or students whose parents attend Galilee Missionary Baptist Church and who have membership at Galilee Missionary Baptist Church for at least 3 years. Minimum high school GPA of 3.0 average or WMU student who has maintained satisfactory academic progress, can demonstrate financial need and evidence of public service/volunteer service.
HOW TO APPLY: See website for application and submit with FAFSA.
RENEWABLE: Yes. Up to 3 consecutive academic years if recipient demonstrates satisfactory academic progress.

4029—WESTERN MICHIGAN UNIVERSITY (Gwen Frostic Benzie County Central Schools Scholarship Quasi-Endowment)

1903 West Michigan
Kalamazoo MI 49008-5337
269/387-8777
FAX: 269/387-6989
E-mail: finaid-info@wmich.edu
Internet: http://www.wmich.edu/endowed
AMOUNT: Up to 6 credit hours/semester
DEADLINE(S): APR 1
FIELD(S): All
ELIGIBILITY/REQUIREMENTS: Preference given to incoming freshman as well as to U.S. citizens. Must be a resident of Benzie County for a minimum of 2 consecutive years and have a minimum of a 2.0 GPA.
HOW TO APPLY: See website for application and submit with FAFSA.
RENEWABLE: Yes. Up to a total of 9 credit hours.

4030—WESTERN MICHIGAN UNIVERSITY (Harold and Beulah McKee Scholarship Fund)

1903 West Michigan
Kalamazoo MI 49008-5337
269/387-8777
FAX: 269/387-6989
E-mail: finaid-info@wmich.edu
Internet: http://www.wmich.edu/endowed
AMOUNT: $1,000
DEADLINE(S): APR 1
FIELD(S): All
ELIGIBILITY/REQUIREMENTS: Any student regardless of class standing is eligible; based on financial need.
HOW TO APPLY: See website for application and submit with FAFSA.
RENEWABLE: Yes

4031—WESTERN MICHIGAN UNIVERSITY (Hubert & Dorthea Peckman Memorial Endowed Scholarship)

1903 West Michigan
Kalamazoo MI 49008-5337
269/387-8777
FAX: 269/387-6989
E-mail: finaid-info@wmich.edu
Internet: http://www.wmich.edu/endowed
AMOUNT: Varies
DEADLINE(S): APR 1
FIELD(S): All
ELIGIBILITY/REQUIREMENTS: First preference to students who are Allegan County residents. If no students from Allegan County, the award goes to students from Southwest Michigan. Must manifest an earnest desire for an education, have financial need and be willing to work for part of their education funding. Preference shall be given to students who are from homes where one or both parents are deceased.
HOW TO APPLY: See website for application and submit with FAFSA.
RENEWABLE: Yes.

4032—WESTERN MICHIGAN UNIVERSITY (Julie Kaye Cunningham Memorial Scholarship)

1903 West Michigan
Kalamazoo MI 49008-5337
269/387-8777
FAX: 269/387-6989
E-mail: finaid-info@wmich.edu
Internet: http://www.wmich.edu/endowed
AMOUNT: 12 credit hours per semester for the freshman year
DEADLINE(S): APR 1
FIELD(S): All
ELIGIBILITY/REQUIREMENTS: Graduating senior from Vicksburg High School, attending WMU in the fall following their senior year of high school. Not based on financial need. Other preferences (note requirements) include that the recipient be female, have a minimum GPA of 3.0, desires to excel, be active in sports, puts extra effort and determination into tasks, exemplifies good citizenship, demonstrates leadership and ability to get along with others and be part of a team.
HOW TO APPLY: Contact the Vicksburg High School principal for more information and application. Recipient selected by the Vicksburg High School Scholarship Committee.
RENEWABLE: No

4033—WESTERN MICHIGAN UNIVERSITY (Kappa Alpha Psi Scholarship)

1903 West Michigan
Kalamazoo MI 49008-5337
269/387-8777
FAX: 269/387-6989
E-mail: finaid-info@wmich.edu
Internet: http://www.wmich.edu/endowed
AMOUNT: Varies
DEADLINE(S): APR 1
FIELD(S): All
ELIGIBILITY/REQUIREMENTS: Open to full-time undergraduate African-American male with a GPA of 2.0 at time of application; must demonstrate financial need.
HOW TO APPLY: See website for application and submit with FAFSA.
RENEWABLE: Yes.

4034—WESTERN MICHIGAN UNIVERSITY (Kappa Alpha Psi Scholarship)

1903 West Michigan
Kalamazoo MI 49008-5337
269/387-8777
FAX: 269/387-6989
E-mail: finaid-info@wmich.edu
Internet: http://www.wmich.edu/endowed
AMOUNT: Varies
DEADLINE(S): APR 1
FIELD(S): All
ELIGIBILITY/REQUIREMENTS: Open to full-time undergraduate African-American male with a GPA of 2.0 at time of application; must demonstrate financial need.
HOW TO APPLY: See website for application and submit with FAFSA.
RENEWABLE: Yes.

4035—WESTERN MICHIGAN UNIVERSITY (Lynn Clark Scholarship)

1903 West Michigan

Kalamazoo MI 49008-5337
269/387-8777
FAX: 269/387-6989
E-mail: finaid-info@wmich.edu
Internet: http://www.wmich.
edu/endowed
AMOUNT: $300/semester
DEADLINE(S): APR 1
FIELD(S): All
ELIGIBILITY/REQUIREMENTS: Must
be U.S. citizen and a senior at Centerville
H.S., St. Joseph, MI who has applied and
been accepted for undergraduate study at
WMU; minimum 3.0 GPA their last 2
years of high school; demonstrate financial
need.
HOW TO APPLY: See website for appli-
cation and submit with FAFSA. Recipient
selected by Centerville High School and
they notify Student Financial Aid.
RENEWABLE: No
NUMBER OF AWARDS: 1

4036—WESTERN MICHIGAN UNIVERSITY (Lynne and Charlene Fogarty McKee Endowed Scholarship)

1903 West Michigan
Kalamazoo MI 49008-5337
269/387-8777
FAX: 269/387-6989
E-mail: finaid-info@wmich.edu
Internet: http://www.wmich.
edu/endowed
AMOUNT: $3,000
DEADLINE(S): APR 1
FIELD(S): All
ELIGIBILITY/REQUIREMENTS: Open
only to women. Must show high financial
need.
HOW TO APPLY: See website for appli-
cation and submit with FAFSA.
RENEWABLE: No
NUMBER OF AWARDS: Varies
CONTACT: Office of Financial Aid

4037—WESTERN MICHIGAN UNIVERSITY (Marjorie Ewald Smith Endowed Scholarship)

1903 West Michigan
Kalamazoo MI 49008-5337
269/387-8777
FAX: 269/387-6989
E-mail: finaid-info@wmich.edu
Internet: http://www.wmich.
edu/endowed
AMOUNT: $500
DEADLINE(S): APR 1
FIELD(S): All
ELIGIBILITY/REQUIREMENTS:
Awarded to freshmen entering in the fall.

Must be from Van Buren County, MI,
demonstrate financial need (FASFA
required), have minimum 3.0 high school
GPA, and be full-time students.
HOW TO APPLY: See website for appli-
cation and submit with FAFSA.
RENEWABLE: No
NUMBER OF AWARDS: Varies
CONTACT: Office of Financial Aid

4038—WESTERN MICHIGAN UNIVERSITY (Mt. Zion Baptist Church Scholarship)

1903 West Michigan
Kalamazoo MI 49008-5337
269/387-8777
FAX: 269/387-6989
E-mail: finaid-info@wmich.edu
Internet: http://www.wmich.
edu/endowed
AMOUNT: Varies
DEADLINE(S): APR 1
FIELD(S): All
ELIGIBILITY/REQUIREMENTS: Must
attend and be a member of Mt. Zion
Baptist Church for minimum 3 years.
Minimum GPA 3.0.
HOW TO APPLY: See website for appli-
cation and submit with FAFSA.
NUMBER OF AWARDS: Varies
CONTACT: Office of Financial Aid

4039—WESTERN MICHIGAN UNIVERSITY (Onyx Society Endowed Scholarship)

1903 West Michigan
Kalamazoo MI 49008-5337
269/387-8777
FAX: 269/387-6989
E-mail: finaid-info@wmich.edu
Internet: http://www.wmich.
edu/endowed
AMOUNT: Varies
DEADLINE(S): APR 1
FIELD(S): All
ELIGIBILITY/REQUIREMENTS:
Preference given to a full-time African-
American undergraduate student who is a
U.S. citizen with minimum 2.25 GPA; must
demonstrate financial need.
HOW TO APPLY: See website for appli-
cation and submit with FAFSA.
NUMBER OF AWARDS: Varies
CONTACT: Office of Financial Aid

4040—WESTERN MICHIGAN UNIVERSITY (Patricia Dangremond Endowed Scholarship)

1903 West Michigan
Kalamazoo MI 49008-5337
269/387-8777

FAX: 269/387-6989
E-mail: finaid-info@wmich.edu
Internet: http://www.wmich.
edu/endowed
AMOUNT: $1,000
DEADLINE(S): APR 1
FIELD(S): All
ELIGIBILITY/REQUIREMENTS:
Student must demonstrate financial need.
Must be maintaining satisfactory academic
progress as defined by the Financial Aid
Office.
HOW TO APPLY: See website for appli-
cation and submit with FAFSA.
NUMBER OF AWARDS: Varies
RENEWABLE: No
CONTACT: Office of Financial Aid

4041—WESTERN MICHIGAN UNIVERSITY (Randall, Marjorie E., and Marjorie R. Frazier Scholarship Fund)

1903 West Michigan
Kalamazoo MI 49008-5337
269/387-8777
FAX: 269/387-6989
E-mail: finaid-info@wmich.edu
Internet: http://www.wmich.
edu/endowed
AMOUNT: Varies
DEADLINE(S): APR 1
FIELD(S): All
ELIGIBILITY/REQUIREMENTS: Open
to full-time freshman undergraduate stu-
dents regardless of academic major or con-
centration of study; must show financial
need.
HOW TO APPLY: See website for appli-
cation and submit with FAFSA.
NUMBER OF AWARDS: Varies
RENEWABLE: No
CONTACT: Office of Financial Aid

4042—WESTERN MICHIGAN UNIVERSITY (Richard F. and Carolyn Curtis Chormann Scholarship)

1903 West Michigan
Kalamazoo MI 49008-5337
269/387-8777
FAX: 269/387-6989
E-mail: finaid-info@wmich.edu
Internet: http://www.wmich.
edu/endowed
AMOUNT: Varies
DEADLINE(S): APR 1
FIELD(S): All
ELIGIBILITY/REQUIREMENTS: Open
to high school seniors from Adrian High
School; awards based primarily on finan-
cial need. Scholarship is renewable for up
to four consecutive academic years.

HOW TO APPLY: See website for application. Application for admission to WMU must be received by February 1 and FAFSA submitted by March 1.
NUMBER OF AWARDS: Varies
RENEWABLE: Yes. Must maintain a minimum 2.5 GPA and abide by the rules and regulations in the Student Code developed by the Division of Student Affairs.
CONTACT: Office of Financial Aid
ADDITIONAL INFORMATION: The scholarship will be reduced by the amount of any other known scholarship received by the recipient.

4043—WESTERN MICHIGAN UNIVERSITY (Roy and Beulah Kendall Financial Need Endowed Scholarship)

1903 West Michigan
Kalamazoo MI 49008-5337
269/387-8777
FAX: 269/387-6989
E-mail: finaid-info@wmich.edu
Internet: http://www.wmich.
edu/endowed
AMOUNT: $1,000/semester
DEADLINE(S): APR 1
FIELD(S): All
ELIGIBILITY/REQUIREMENTS: Open to transfer to WMU as a full-time student from Kellogg Community College with an Associate's Degree of 36 credit hours; transfer GPA of 3.0 or higher; must demonstrate financial need and be a U.S. citizen or permanent resident.
HOW TO APPLY: See website for application. Application forms are sent to Kellogg Community College and are available at recruiting events at the college; they are also sent to students who meet the GPA and application for admission date requirements. Application for admission to WMU must be received by February 1 and FAFSA submitted by March 1.
NUMBER OF AWARDS: Varies
RENEWABLE: Yes. Up to 4 semesters. To retain scholarship, must maintain at least a 2.5 GPA.
CONTACT: Office of Financial Aid

4044—WESTERN MICHIGAN UNIVERSITY (Roy and Beulah Kendall Kellogg Community College Academic Merit Endowed Scholarship)

1903 West Michigan
Kalamazoo MI 49008-5337
269/387-8777
FAX: 269/387-6989
E-mail: finaid-info@wmich.edu
Internet: http://www.wmich.
edu/endowed

AMOUNT: $1,000/semester
DEADLINE(S): APR 1
FIELD(S): All
ELIGIBILITY/REQUIREMENTS: Open to transfer to WMU from Kellogg Community College with an Associate's Degree or 36 credit hours; transfer GPA of 3.5 or higher; must be U.S. citizen or permanent resident.
HOW TO APPLY: See website for application. Application forms are sent to Kellogg Community College and are available at recruiting events at the college; they are also sent to students who meet the GPA and application for admission date requirements. Application for admission to WMU must be received by February 1 and FAFSA submitted by March 1.
NUMBER OF AWARDS: Varies
RENEWABLE: Yes. To retain the scholarship, student must maintain at least a 2.0 GPA.
CONTACT: Office of Financial Aid

4045—WESTERN MICHIGAN UNIVERSITY (Senior Class, 1967-1974 Scholarship)

1903 West Michigan
Kalamazoo MI 49008-5337
269/387-8777
FAX: 269/387-6989
E-mail: finaid-info@wmich.edu
Internet: http://www.wmich.
edu/endowed
AMOUNT: $1,000/semester
DEADLINE(S): APR 1
FIELD(S): All
ELIGIBILITY/REQUIREMENTS: Open to freshman and above pursuing a 2- or 4-year undergraduate degree. Consideration will be given to need and past participation in high school and community affairs; entering freshman must have a minimum GPA of 2.5. Preference given to children of contributing members.
HOW TO APPLY: See website for application and submit with FAFSA.
NUMBER OF AWARDS: Varies
RENEWABLE: Yes. To retain the scholarship for the second year, student must maintain at least a 2.0 GPA.
CONTACT: Office of Financial Aid

4046—WESTERN MICHIGAN UNIVERSITY (The Voelker Family Endowed Scholarship)

1903 West Michigan
Kalamazoo MI 49008-5337
269/387-8777
FAX: 269/387-6989
E-mail: finaid-info@wmich.edu
Internet: http://www.wmich.
edu/endowed

AMOUNT: Varies
DEADLINE(S): APR 1
FIELD(S): All
ELIGIBILITY/REQUIREMENTS: Preference given to students who have been 5-year residents of Bedford Township, Michigan. Must be U.S. citizen; minimum 3.0 GPA and must demonstrate financial need.
HOW TO APPLY: See website for application and submit with FAFSA.
NUMBER OF AWARDS: Varies
RENEWABLE: Yes. Up to 4 consecutive years; student must maintain at least a 2.0 GPA.
CONTACT: Office of Financial Aid

4047—WESTERN MICHIGAN UNIVERSITY (Walter and Virginia Newhouse Scholarship)

1903 West Michigan
Kalamazoo MI 49008-5337
269/387-8777
FAX: 269/387-6989
E-mail: finaid-info@wmich.edu
Internet: http://www.wmich.
edu/endowed
AMOUNT: $1,000
DEADLINE(S): APR 1
FIELD(S): All
ELIGIBILITY/REQUIREMENTS: Students graduating from Benton Harbor High School, St. Joseph High School, or Lakeshore High School located in Berrien County, Michigan.
HOW TO APPLY: See website for application and submit with FAFSA.
NUMBER OF AWARDS: Varies
RENEWABLE: No
CONTACT: Office of Financial Aid

4048—WILLIAM F. COOPER SCHOLARSHIP TRUST

Wachovia Bank, N.A.
Charitable Services
191 Peachtree Street, 24th Floor
Atlanta GA 30303
AMOUNT: Varies
DEADLINE(S): MAY 15
FIELD(S): All (except Law, Theology, and Medicine; Nursing acceptable)
ELIGIBILITY/REQUIREMENTS: Open to female residents of Georgia who are pursuing 4-year undergraduate study. Based on financial need and grades.
HOW TO APPLY: Written request for application; submit with supporting documentation (tax returns, W-2s, transcripts, etc.).
NUMBER OF AWARDS: Varies

RENEWABLE: Yes. Must continue to meet criteria.
CONTACT: Ranay Karosh, 404/332-4987

4049—WILLIAM LOEB MEMORIAL FUND (Educational Grants)

P.O. Box 9555
Manchester NH 03108-9555
603/668-4321, ext. 506 or
800/562-8218
FAX: 603/668-8920
AMOUNT: $1,000
DEADLINE(S): MAR 1
FIELD(S): All
ELIGIBILITY/REQUIREMENTS:
Resident of New Hampshire for a minimum of 2 years; plan to attend a structured postsecondary program; demonstrate community involvement, independence and leadership potential.
HOW TO APPLY: Write to Fund for information and application.

4050—WILLIAM RANDOLPH HEARST FOUNDATION (U.S. Senate Youth Program)

90 New Montgomery Street,
Suite 1212
San Francisco CA 94105-4504
415/543-4057 or 800/841-7048
FAX: 415/243-0760
E-mail: ussyp@hearstfdn.org
Internet: http://www.hearstfdn.org
AMOUNT: $2,000 + all-expenses-paid week in Washington DC
DEADLINE(S): Varies
FIELD(S): All
ELIGIBILITY/REQUIREMENTS: Open to any high school junior or senior who is serving as an elected student body officer at a U.S. high school. Student receives a week's stay in Washington as guest of the Senate, and the scholarship is presented during the visit. Student must become a candidate for a degree at an accredited U.S. college or university within 2 years of high school graduation, pledging to include courses in government or related subjects in his or her undergraduate program.
HOW TO APPLY: Contact your high school principal or the William Randolph Hearst Foundation for an application.
NUMBER OF AWARDS: 102 (2 students are selected from each state and the District of Columbia)

4051—WINDHAM FOUNDATION, INC. (Scholarships)

P.O. Box 70
Grafton VT 05146

802/843-2211
FAX: 802/843-2205
Internet: http://www.windham-foundation.org
AMOUNT: $250-$1,000
DEADLINE(S): APR 1
FIELD(S): All
ELIGIBILITY/REQUIREMENTS: Open ONLY to students who are residents of Windham County, Vermont. Tenable at recognized undergraduate colleges and universities.
HOW TO APPLY: Contact Windham Foundation for an application.
RENEWABLE: Yes. Must apply each year (up to 4).

4052—WISCONSIN HISPANIC SCHOLARSHIP FOUNDATION, INC./MEXICAN FIESTA

1220 West Windlake Avenue
Milwaukee WI 55215
414/383-7066
FAX: 414/383-6677
E-mail: fiestamilw@aol.com
Internet: http://www.mexican fiesta.org
AMOUNT: $250-$1,500
DEADLINE(S): MAR 31
FIELD(S): All
ELIGIBILITY/REQUIREMENTS: Wisconsin resident; must have at least 1 parent/grandparent of Hispanic descent; minimum 2.5 GPA.
HOW TO APPLY: Request application by mail or phone.
NUMBER OF AWARDS: 100+
CONTACT: Teresa C. Mercado

4053—WITTENBERG UNIVERSITY (Music Scholarship Funds)

Krieg Hall
P.O. Box 720
Springfield OH 45501-0720
937/327-7341 or 800/677-7347
FAX: 937/327-7558
E-mail: Music@wittenberg.edu
Internet: http://www.wittenberg.edu/academics/music/scholaid.shtml
AMOUNT: $600-$5,000
DEADLINE(S): MAR 1
FIELD(S): All, Music
ELIGIBILITY/REQUIREMENTS: Scholarships are available not only to music majors and minors but also for students who continue to study and participate in music ensembles while pursuing non-music degrees. Interested students must complete application to the Univer-

sity and be accepted and participate in an audition by mid-March.
HOW TO APPLY: See website for more information or write to Music Department Assistant, Melanie Gillaugh (see below). Request a Music Audition Packet for instructions.
NUMBER OF AWARDS: Varies
RENEWABLE: Yes. Must maintain a "B" average in music lessons and continue to participate in an approved music ensemble
CONTACT: Melanie Gillaugh, Department Assistant, mgillaugh@wittenberg.edu or 937/327-7341
ADDITIONAL INFORMATION: All our music scholarships are talent-based.

4054—WOMAN'S SEAMEN'S FRIEND SOCIETY

291 Whitney Avenue, Suite 203
New Haven CT 06511
203/777-2165
FAX: 203/777-5774
E-mail: wsfsofct@earthlink.net
DEADLINE(S): APR 1
FIELD(S): All (emphasis on Marine Science and related fields)
ELIGIBILITY/REQUIREMENTS: Connecticut residents who are students at maritime academies; majoring in marine sciences and related fields in other schools; dependents of Merchant Marines regardless of major.
HOW TO APPLY: Request application from above address or financial aid office at your school.
RENEWABLE: Yes, reapply.

4055—WOMEN OF THE EVANGELICAL LUTHERAN CHURCH IN AMERICA (Opportunity Scholarships for Lutheran Laywomen)

8765 West Higgins Road
Chicago IL 60631-4101
800/638-3522, ext. 2736
FAX: 773/380-2419
E-mail: emilyhansen@elca.org
Internet: http://www.womenof theelca.org/whatwedo/scholarships.html
AMOUNT: $2,000 maximum
DEADLINE(S): FEB 15
FIELD(S): All (emphasis on Health professions; Vocational Education; Religion)
ELIGIBILITY/REQUIREMENTS: Open to women enrolled in undergraduate, graduate, professional, or vocational courses preparing for a career other than the ordained ministry. Must be at least 21 years old, a citizen of the U.S., a member

of the ELCA, and have experienced an interruption in education of 2 or more years since completion of high school. Additional considerations include clearly stated and attainable goals, impact of Women of the ELCA dollars on total cost of program, and applicant's involvement in Women of the ELCA.

HOW TO APPLY: Contact Program Director for an application and additional information. Submit with transcript and 3 references (from pastor, academic, personal).

RENEWABLE: Yes. Maximum of 2 years.

CONTACT: Emily Hansen

4056—WOMEN'S OPPORTUNITY SCHOLARSHIP FUND

418 East Rosser Avenue, #320
Bismarck ND 58501
701/255-6240 or 800/255-6240
FAX: 701/255-1904
E-mail: ndcaws@ndcaws.org
Internet: http://www.ndcaws.org
AMOUNT: $200-$1,200
DEADLINE(S): JUN 1
FIELD(S): All

ELIGIBILITY/REQUIREMENTS: Must be a female resident of North Dakota enrolled in a North Dakota college. Must submit an essay describing reasons for pursuing higher education; and a "special circumstances" essay where the applicant may detail special needs for assistance.

HOW TO APPLY: Contact Fund for details and application.

4057—WOMEN'S OVERSEAS SERVICE LEAGUE

P.O. Box 7124
Washington DC 20044-7124
Internet: http://www.wosl.org/
scholar/scholarships.htm
AMOUNT: $500-$1,000
DEADLINE(S): MAR 1
FIELD(S): All

ELIGIBILITY/REQUIREMENTS: Open to women who have demonstrated commitment to public service through life experiences. Must have completed at least 12 semester or 18 quarter hours at any institution of higher education with a minimum 2.5 GPA, and must be enrolled in a program leading to an academic degree (associate or higher). Must agree to enroll for a minimum of 6 semesters or 9 quarters.

HOW TO APPLY: Write for brochure and application form or see website.

NUMBER OF AWARDS: Varies

RENEWABLE: Yes. Must reapply for 2nd year.

4058—WOMEN'S PARTNERSHIP (A Division of the Affiliated Chamber of Commerce of Greater Springfield)

1441 Main Street,
Suite 136
Springfield MA 01103-1449
413/787-1555
FAX: 413/731-8530
Internet: http://www.myonline
chamber.com
AMOUNT: Varies
DEADLINE(S): APR 15
FIELD(S): All

ELIGIBILITY/REQUIREMENTS: Open to women over 25 years of age who have returned to an accredited college or university in the greater Springfield, MA, area after an absence and life experience.

HOW TO APPLY: Contact the WP or the Community Foundation of Western MA (413/732-2858) for an application.

NUMBER OF AWARDS: 40

RENEWABLE: Yes, reapply.

4059—WOMEN'S WESTERN GOLF FOUNDATION (Grants)

393 Ramsay Road
Deerfield IL 60015
Internet: http://www.wwga.org
AMOUNT: $2,000/year
DEADLINE(S): MAR 1
FIELD(S): All

ELIGIBILITY/REQUIREMENTS: Open to female high school seniors with academic excellence, financial need, involvement in golf (skill not criterion), and excellence of character. Must be U.S. citizen planning to attend a 4-year accredited college or university.

HOW TO APPLY: Contact Foundation for information and application.

NUMBER OF AWARDS: 15-20

RENEWABLE: 4-year awards

4060—WYOMING FARM BUREAU FEDERATION (Herbert D. Livingston-H. J. King Memorial Scholarship Funds)

P.O. Box 1348
Laramie WY 82073
AMOUNT: $750
DEADLINE(S): MAR 1
FIELD(S): All

ELIGIBILITY/REQUIREMENTS: Must be a current member of Wyoming Farm Bureau; graduating senior or graduate of a Wyoming high school enrolled at either a Wyoming junior college or the University of Wyoming. College students and graduate students are also eligible to apply. Minimum 2.5 GPA.

HOW TO APPLY: Applications are available from each county Farm Bureau or the Federation. Submit with transcript; résumé of applicant's family activity with WFB including a current membership; a recent photograph; and 3 letters of recommendation stressing ability, character and financial need (1 letter from a church leader, a Farm Bureau leader, and teacher or school administrator).

NUMBER OF AWARDS: 1

4061—WYOMING FARM BUREAU FEDERATION (WyFB Continuing Education Scholarships)

P.O. Box 1348
Laramie WY 82073
AMOUNT: $500
DEADLINE(S): MAR 1
FIELD(S): All

ELIGIBILITY/REQUIREMENTS: Must be a current member of Wyoming Farm Bureau; graduating senior or graduate of a Wyoming high school incoming freshman through master's candidates enrolled at either a Wyoming junior college or the University of Wyoming. Minimum 2.5 GPA.

HOW TO APPLY: Applications are available from each county Farm Bureau or the Federation. Submit with transcripts (2 semesters of college or, for freshmen 1 semester of college and proof of enrollment in 2nd semester); résumé of applicant's family activity with WFB including a current membership; a recent photograph; and 3 letters of recommendation stressing ability, character and financial need (1 letter from a church leader, a Farm Bureau leader, and teacher or school administrator).

NUMBER OF AWARDS: 3

4062—WYOMING FARM BUREAU FEDERATION (WyFB Federation Scholarships)

P.O. Box 1348
Laramie WY 82073
AMOUNT: $500
DEADLINE(S): MAR 1
FIELD(S): All

ELIGIBILITY/REQUIREMENTS: Must be a current member of Wyoming Farm Bureau; graduating senior or graduate of a Wyoming high school; incoming freshman through master's candidates enrolled at either a Wyoming junior college or the University of Wyoming. Minimum 2.5 GPA.

HOW TO APPLY: Applications are available from each county Farm Bureau or the Federation. Submit with transcript; résumé of applicant's family activity with WFB

including a current membership; a recent photograph; and 3 letters of recommendation stressing ability, character and financial need (1 letter from a church leader, a Farm Bureau leader, and teacher or school administrator).
NUMBER OF AWARDS: 5

4063—WYOMING PEACE OFFICERS ASSOCIATION (Category #1 Scholarships)

1710 Pacific Avenue
Cheyenne WY 82009
307/777-7718
FAX: 307/638-9706
AMOUNT: $500/semester
DEADLINE(S): JUL 31
FIELD(S): All
ELIGIBILITY/REQUIREMENTS: Available to dependents of active (dues current), lifetime, or deceased WPOA members who will be attending any college or technical school. Must carry a full-time status of 12 semester credit hours or more. Awarded upon successful completion (minimum "C" GPA) of each semester.
HOW TO APPLY: Write or phone for application.
RENEWABLE: Yes. Maximum of 4 semesters; must reapply each year; must meet criteria.
CONTACT: Betty Haukap at P.O.S.T., 307/777-7718

4064—YES I CAN! FOUNDATION FOR EXCEPTIONAL CHILDREN (Stanley E. Jackson Scholarship Awards)

1110 North Glebe Road, Suite 300
Arlington VA 22201-5704
800/224-6830, ext. 462
Internet: http://www.yesican.
cec.sped.org/scholarship
AMOUNT: $500
DEADLINE(S): AUG 1-FEB 1
FIELD(S): All
ELIGIBILITY/REQUIREMENTS: Must be enrolling for the 1st time in full-time postsecondary education or training. 4 award levels: Award 1, must have a disability; Award 2, must have a disability AND be a member of a diverse ethnic group (African-American, Native American, Hispanic, or Asian American); Award 3, must have a disability AND have demonstrated gifts or talents in 1 or more of the following categories: general intellectual ability, specific academic aptitude, creativity, leadership, or the visual or performing arts; and Award 4, must meet all the requirements of Awards 1-3.
HOW TO APPLY: Contact Foundation or see website for additional information and application.

NUMBER OF AWARDS: 4-10

4065—YOUNG AMERICAN BOWLING ALLIANCE (Alberta E. Crowe Star of Tomorrow Scholarship)

5301 South 76th Street
Greendale WI 53129
AMOUNT: $1,500
DEADLINE(S): OCT 1
FIELD(S): Any field of study
ELIGIBILITY/REQUIREMENTS: Open to women who are amateur bowlers and members in good standing with WIBC or YABA. Must be at most age 22 or younger as of August 1, preceding the application date. Must be a senior in high school or attending college.
HOW TO APPLY: Send #10 SASE to above address for complete information.
RENEWABLE: Yes

4066—YOUNG AMERICAN BOWLING ALLIANCE (Chuck Hall Star of Tomorrow Scholarship)

5301 South 76th Street
Greendale WI 53129
AMOUNT: $1,250
DEADLINE(S): NOV 15
FIELD(S): All
ELIGIBILITY/REQUIREMENTS: Open to male students who are amateur bowlers and members in good standing with ABC or YABA. Students must be age 21 or younger before deadline. Must be a senior in high school or attending college with at least a 2.5 GPA.
HOW TO APPLY: Send SASE to above address for complete information.

4067—YOUTH OPPORTUNITIES (Youth Scholarship)

P.O. Box 45762
Los Angeles CA 90045
310/670-7664
AMOUNT: Varies
DEADLINE(S): MAR 1
FIELD(S): All
ELIGIBILITY/REQUIREMENTS: Applicants must be high school seniors in California; awards are based on academic achievement, community involvement, and demonstrated financial need.

4068—ZETA PHI BETA SORORITY, INC./NATIONAL EDUCATIONAL FOUNDATION (Deborah Partridge Wolfe International Fellowship)

1734 New Hampshire Avenue NW

Washington DC 20009
Internet: www.ZphiB1920.org
AMOUNT: $500-$1,000
DEADLINE(S): FEB 1
FIELD(S): All
ELIGIBILITY/REQUIREMENTS: Open to graduate and undergraduate U.S. students planning to study abroad. Award is for full-time study for one academic year (Fall-Spring). (Also open to foreign students to study in U.S.)
HOW TO APPLY: See website for additional information and application or send SASE to Foundation. Must submit documented proof of academic study and plan of program to Scholarship Chairperson with signature of school administrator or Program Director; 3 letters of recommendation (professor or high school teacher, minister or community leader, other—for Zeta members 3rd reference must be from the graduate Zeta chapter and signed by the Basileus or Advisor); transcript; essay (minimum 150 words) with information about yourself, your educational goals and professional aspirations and how this award will help you achieve them, and why you should receive this award.
RENEWABLE: No

4069—ZETA PHI BETA SORORITY, INC./NATIONAL EDUCATIONAL FOUNDATION (General Undergraduate Scholarships)

1734 New Hampshire Avenue NW
Washington DC 20009
Internet: http://www.zpb1920.org
AMOUNT: $500-$1,000
DEADLINE(S): FEB 1
FIELD(S): All
ELIGIBILITY/REQUIREMENTS: Open to undergraduate college students and graduating high school seniors planning to enter college in the Fall. Award is for full-time study for one academic year (Fall-Spring).
HOW TO APPLY: See website for additional information and application or send SASE to Foundation. Must submit proof of enrollment/university acceptance; 3 letters of recommendation (professor or high school teacher, minister or community leader, other—for Zeta members 3rd reference must be from the graduate Zeta chapter and signed by the Basileus or Advisor); transcript; essay (minimum 150 words) with information about yourself, your educational goals and professional aspirations and how this award will help you achieve them, and why you should receive this award.
RENEWABLE: No

LAST-MINUTE ADDITIONS

APPLIED ENGINEERING/ ENGINEERING TECHNOLOGY

4069A—AIST FOUNDATION (AIST Benjamin F. Fairless Scholarship [AIME])

186 Thorn Hill Road
Warrendale PA 15086
724/776-6040, ext. 621
FAX: 724/776-1880
E-mail: lwharrey@aist.org
Internet: http://www.aistfoundation. org

AMOUNT: $2,000
DEADLINE(S): Varies, MAY-JUN
FIELD(S): Engineering, Metallurgy, Materials Science
ELIGIBILITY/REQUIREMENTS: Open to full-time undergraduates with demonstrated interest in a career in the iron and steel industry, enrolled in an accredited U.S. college or university.
HOW TO APPLY: See website for application; submit with résumé with work experience and any extracurricular activities, noting any leadership positions; an essay, not to exceed 2 pages, about your professional goals, and how your skills could be applied to enhance the industry; 3 letters of recommendation from your college academic advisor, a professor, and an external source, preferably a previous employer; and a current academic transcript.
NUMBER OF AWARDS: 3
RENEWABLE: Yes, must reapply.
CONTACT: Lori A.Wharrey, AIST Board Administrator

4069B—AIST FOUNDATION (AIST Ronald E. Lincoln Memorial Scholarship)

186 Thorn Hill Road
Warrendale PA 15086
724/776-6040, ext. 621
FAX: 724/776-1880
E-mail: lwharrey@aist.org
Internet: http://www.aistfoundation. org

AMOUNT: $3,000
DEADLINE(S): Varies, MAY-JUN
FIELD(S): Engineering, Metallurgy, Materials Science
ELIGIBILITY/REQUIREMENTS: Open to full-time undergraduates with demonstrated interest in a career in the iron and

steel industry, enrolled in an accredited U.S. college or university.
HOW TO APPLY: See website for application; submit with résumé with work experience and any extracurricular activities, noting any leadership positions; an essay, not to exceed 2 pages, about your professional goals, and how your skills could be applied to enhance the industry; 3 letters of recommendation from your college academic advisor, a professor, and an external source, preferably a previous employer; and a current academic transcript.
NUMBER OF AWARDS: 2
RENEWABLE: Yes, must reapply.
CONTACT: Lori A.Wharrey, AIST Board Administrator

4069C—AIST FOUNDATION (AIST William E. Schwabe Memorial Scholarship)

186 Thorn Hill Road
Warrendale PA 15086
724/776-6040, ext. 621
FAX: 724/776-1880
E-mail: lwharrey@aist.org
Internet: http://www.aistfoundation. org

AMOUNT: $3,000
DEADLINE(S): Varies, MAY-JUN
FIELD(S): Engineering, Metallurgy, Materials Science
ELIGIBILITY/REQUIREMENTS: Open to full-time undergraduates with demonstrated interest in a career in the iron and steel industry, enrolled in an accredited U.S. college or university.
HOW TO APPLY: See website for application; submit with résumé with work experience and any extracurricular activities, noting any leadership positions; an essay, not to exceed 2 pages, about your professional goals, and how your skills could be applied to enhance the industry; 3 letters of recommendation from your college academic advisor, a professor, and an external source, preferably a previous employer; and a current academic transcript.
NUMBER OF AWARDS: 1
RENEWABLE: Yes, must reapply.
CONTACT: Lori A.Wharrey, AIST Board Administrator

4069D—AIST FOUNDATION (AIST Willy Korf Memorial Fund)

186 Thorn Hill Road
Warrendale PA 15086
724/776-6040, ext. 621
FAX: 724/776-1880
E-mail: lwharrey@aist.org
Internet: http://www.aistfoundation. org

AMOUNT: $3,000
DEADLINE(S): Varies, MAY-JUN
FIELD(S): Engineering, Metallurgy, Materials Science
ELIGIBILITY/REQUIREMENTS: Open to full-time undergraduates with demonstrated interest in a career in the iron and steel industry, enrolled in an accredited U.S. college or university.
HOW TO APPLY: See website for application; submit with résumé with work experience and any extracurricular activities, noting any leadership positions; an essay, not to exceed 2 pages, about your professional goals, and how your skills could be applied to enhance the industry; 3 letters of recommendation from your college academic advisor, a professor, and an external source, preferably a previous employer; and a current academic transcript.
NUMBER OF AWARDS: 3
RENEWABLE: Yes, must reapply.
CONTACT: Lori A.Wharrey, AIST Board Administrator

4070A—AMERICAN INSTITUTE OF MINING, METALLURGICAL, AND PETROLEUM ENGINEERS, THE (John S. Marshall Memorial Scholarship)

P.O. BOX 270728
Littleton, CO 80127-0013
303/948-4255
FAX: 303/948-4260
E-mail: aime@aimehq.org
INTERNET: http://www.aimehq.org

AMOUNT: up to $8,000
DEADLINE(S): JUN 15
FIELD(S): Mining, Metallurgy
ELIGIBILITY/REQUIREMENTS: Nominee must be enrolled full time in an ABET-accredited Mining Engineering program. Open to students who will be a junior or senior undergraduate in the subsequent school year (after the award is presented) with demonstrated financial need and demonstrated interest in pursuing a career in the mining industry through extensive coursework, work experience, active in Member Society local chapter or student member of Society for Mining, Metallurgy and Exploration (SME).
HOW TO APPLY: See website for application. Submit application with 2 letters of recommendation (1 from your department Chair showing GPA and class standing; 1 from another professor, employer, or person in the mining industry who knows the applicant well)
NUMBER OF AWARDS: 1 or more
RENEWABLE: Yes; up to 5 years. Must reapply.

4070B—AMERICAN INSTITUTE OF MINING, METALLURGICAL, AND PETROLEUM ENGINEERS, THE (Lewis E. and Elizabeth Young Scholarships)

P.O. BOX 270728
Littleton, CO 80127-0013
303/948-4255
FAX: 303/948-4260
E-mail: aime@aimehq.org
INTERNET: http://www.aimehq.org
AMOUNT: up to $1,000
DEADLINE(S): JUN 15
FIELD(S): Mining, Metallurgy, Mining, Engineering, Metallurgical Engineering, Material Science, Petroleum Engineering
ELIGIBILITY/REQUIREMENTS: Open to students graduating from a high school or undergraduates attending a 4-year college or university in Western Pennsylvania, West Virginia, or Virginia. Based on financial need, scholastic achievement (C+ or better), and good character. Preference given to students attending Carnegie-Mellon University, Pennsylvania State University, University of Pittsburgh, Virginia Polytechnic Institute, or West Virginia University.
HOW TO APPLY: Apply through high school principal or college or university dean or department head, who must attest to applicant's eligibility.
NUMBER OF AWARDS: 1 or more
RENEWABLE: Yes.

COMMUNICATIONS/ JOURNALISM

4071A—MEDILL (Eric Land Global Reporting and Research Grant)

Medill School of Journalism
Northwestern University
1845 Sheridan Road
Evanson IL 60208-2301
E-mail: ug-admission@northwestern.edu
Internet: http://www.medill.northwestern.edu/journalism/undergrad/
AMOUNT: $2,000-$3,000
DEADLINE(S): JAN 14
FIELD(S): Journalism
ELIGIBILITY/REQUIREMENTS: Open to students with financial need to pursue research and reporting experiences abroad, particularly in underreported parts of the world.
HOW TO APPLY: Submit proposal by e-mail and hard copy to Donna

Kwiatkowski, grant coordinator, in Fisk 109, d-kwiatkowski@northwestern.edu.
NUMBER OF AWARDS: 6, 1 winner, 5 runnersup
RENEWABLE: No
CONTACT: For more information m-bitoun@northwestern.edu

COMPUTER SCIENCE & ENGINEERING/INFORMATION TECHNOLOGY

4071B—HENAAC SCHOLARS PROGRAM

Scholarship Selection Committee
3900 Whiteside Street
Los Angeles CA 90063
323/262-0997
E-mail: kathy@henaac.org
Internet: http://www.henaac.org
AMOUNT: $500-$5,000
DEADLINE(S): APR 30
FIELD(S): Engineering, Mathematics, Computer Science, Materials Science
ELIGIBILITY/REQUIREMENTS: Applicants must demonstrate leadership through academic achievements and campus/community activities, major in one of the above fields, have minimum GPA 3.0; be of Hispanic origin and/or must significantly participate in and promote organizations and activities in the Hispanic community.
HOW TO APPLY: See website for application; submit with 700-word essay describing the technological innovation or scientific discovery that inspired you to pursue your major; résumé; 2 letters of recommendation (1 from peer in a campus or community organization, 1 from college advisor, MEP Director, Dean, or faculty member); transcript.
NUMBER OF AWARDS: 70-80
CONTACT: Kathy Borunda-Barrera for additional information
ADDITIONAL INFORMATION: Must attend annual conference to receive scholarship.

EARTH SCIENCE/NATURAL RESOURCES

4071C—AIR & WASTE MANAGEMENT ASSOCIATION, EAST MICHIGAN CHAPTER

Scholarship Committee
28742 Blackstone Drive
Lathrup Village MI 48076-2616
Internet: http://www.emawma.org
AMOUNT: $1,500

DEADLINE(S): Varies, MAY-JUN
FIELD(S): Environmental Studies, Engineering, Science, Public Health, Natural Resources
ELIGIBILITY/REQUIREMENTS: Open to full-time student entering junior or senior year pursuing a course of study leading to a career in air pollution control, toxic and/or hazardous waste management, or another environmental area and attending a college or university located in Michigan. Based on merit, minimum GPA 3.0, and financial need. Extracurricular activities and interests also considered.
HOW TO APPLY: See website for application; submit with a paper of 500-600 words reflecting career interests and objectives; 2 letters of recommendation (1 from advisor, 1 from faculty member in major); transcript; résumé; letter verifying academic status, and list of sources of financial aid. Interview may be required.
NUMBER OF AWARDS: up to 4
RENEWABLE: Yes, must reapply.
CONTACT: Sol P. Baltimore, Chair, Scholarship Committee

4071D—AIST FOUNDATION (AIST Benjamin F. Fairless Scholarship [AIME])

186 Thorn Hill Road
Warrendale PA 15086
724/776-6040, ext. 621
FAX: 724/776-1880
E-mail: lwharrey@aist.org
Internet: http://www.aistfoundation.org
AMOUNT: $2,000
DEADLINE(S): Varies, MAY-JUN
FIELD(S): Engineering, Metallurgy, Materials Science
ELIGIBILITY/REQUIREMENTS: Open to full-time undergraduates with demonstrated interest in a career in the iron and steel industry, enrolled in an accredited U.S. college or university.
HOW TO APPLY: See website for application; submit with résumé with work experience and any extracurricular activities, noting any leadership positions; an essay, not to exceed 2 pages, about your professional goals, and how your skills could be applied to enhance the industry; 3 letters of recommendation from your college academic advisor, a professor, and an external source, preferably a previous employer; and a current academic transcript.
NUMBER OF AWARDS: 3
RENEWABLE: Yes, must reapply.
CONTACT: Lori A.Wharrey, AIST Board Administrator

4071E—AIST FOUNDATION (AIST Ronald E. Lincoln Memorial Scholarship)

186 Thorn Hill Road
Warrendale PA 15086
724/776-6040, ext. 621
FAX: 724/776-1880
E-mail: lwharrey@aist.org
Internet:
http://www.aistfoundation.org
AMOUNT: $3,000
DEADLINE(S): Varies, MAY-JUN
FIELD(S): Engineering, Metallurgy,
    Materials Science
ELIGIBILITY/REQUIREMENTS: Open
to full-time undergraduates with demonstrated interest in a career in the iron and
steel industry, enrolled in an accredited
U.S. college or university.
HOW TO APPLY: See website for application; submit with résumé with work
experience and any extracurricular activities, noting any leadership positions; an
essay, not to exceed 2 pages, about your
professional goals, and how your skills
could be applied to enhance the industry; 3
letters of recommendation from your college academic advisor, a professor, and an
external source, preferably a previous
employer; and a current academic transcript.
NUMBER OF AWARDS: 2
RENEWABLE: Yes, must reapply.
CONTACT: Lori A.Wharrey, AIST Board
Administrator

4071F—AIST FOUNDATION (AIST William E. Schwabe Memorial Scholarship)

186 Thorn Hill Road
Warrendale PA 15086
724/776-6040, ext. 621
FAX: 724/776-1880
E-mail: lwharrey@aist.org
Internet:
http://www.aistfoundation.org
AMOUNT: $3,000
DEADLINE(S): Varies, MAY-JUN
FIELD(S): Engineering, Metallurgy,
    Materials Science
ELIGIBILITY/REQUIREMENTS: Open
to full-time undergraduates with demonstrated interest in a career in the iron and
steel industry, enrolled in an accredited
U.S. college or university.
HOW TO APPLY: See website for application; submit with résumé with work
experience and any extracurricular activities, noting any leadership positions; an
essay, not to exceed 2 pages, about your
professional goals, and how your skills
could be applied to enhance the industry; 3
letters of recommendation from your college academic advisor, a professor, and an
external source, preferably a previous
employer; and a current academic transcript.
NUMBER OF AWARDS: 1
RENEWABLE: Yes, must reapply.
CONTACT: Lori A.Wharrey, AIST Board
Administrator

4071G—AIST FOUNDATION (AIST Willy Korf Memorial Fund)

186 Thorn Hill Road
Warrendale PA 15086
724/776-6040, ext. 621
FAX: 724/776-1880
E-mail: lwharrey@aist.org
Internet:
http://www.aistfoundation.org
AMOUNT: $3,000
DEADLINE(S): Varies, MAY-JUN
FIELD(S): Engineering, Metallurgy,
    Materials Science
ELIGIBILITY/REQUIREMENTS: Open
to full-time undergraduates with demonstrated interest in a career in the iron and
steel industry, enrolled in an accredited
U.S. college or university.
HOW TO APPLY: See website for application; submit with résumé with work
experience and any extracurricular activities, noting any leadership positions; an
essay, not to exceed 2 pages, about your
professional goals, and how your skills
could be applied to enhance the industry; 3
letters of recommendation from your college academic advisor, a professor, and an
external source, preferably a previous
employer; and a current academic transcript.
NUMBER OF AWARDS: 3
RENEWABLE: Yes, must reapply.
CONTACT: Lori A.Wharrey, AIST Board
Administrator

4072—AMERICAN INSTITUTE OF MINING, METALLURGICAL, AND PETROLEUM ENGINEERS, THE (John S. Marshall Memorial Scholarship)

PO BOX 270728
Littleton, CO 80127-0013
303/948-4255
FAX: 303/948-4260
E-mail: aime@aimehq.org
INTERNET: http://www.aimehq.org
AMOUNT: up to $8,000
DEADLINE(S): JUN 15
FIELD(S): Mining, Metallurgy
ELIGIBILITY/REQUIREMENTS:
Nominee must be enrolled full time in an
ABET-accredited Mining Engineering
program. Open to students who will be a
junior or senior undergraduate in the subsequent school year (after the award is presented) with demonstrated financial need
and demonstrated interest in pursuing a
career in the mining industry through
extensive coursework, work experience,
active in Member Society local chapter or
student member of Society for Mining,
Metallurgy and Exploration (SME).
HOW TO APPLY: See website for application. Submit application with 2 letters of
recommendation (1 from your department
Chair showing GPA and class standing; 1
from another professor, employer, or person in the mining industry who knows the
applicant well)
NUMBER OF AWARDS: 1 or more
RENEWABLE: Yes; up to 5 years. Must
reapply.

4073—AMERICAN INSTITUTE OF MINING, METALLURGICAL, AND PETROLEUM ENGINEERS, THE (Lewis E. and Elizabeth Young Scholarships)

P.O. BOX 270728
Littleton, CO 80127-0013
303/948-4255
FAX: 303/948-4260
E-mail: aime@aimehq.org
INTERNET: http://www.aimehq.org
AMOUNT: up to $1,000
DEADLINE(S): JUN 15
FIELD(S): Mining, Metallurgy, Mining,
    Engineering, Metallurgical
    Engineering, Material Science,
    Petroleum Engineering
ELIGIBILITY/REQUIREMENTS: Open
to students graduating from a high school
or undergraduates attending a 4-year col-
lege or university in Western Pennsylvania,
West Virginia, or Virginia. Based on finan-
cial need, scholastic achievement (C+ or
better), and good character. Preference
given to students attending Carnegie-
Mellon University, Pennsylvania State
University, University of Pittsburgh,
Virginia Polytechnic Institute, or West
Virginia University.
HOW TO APPLY: Apply through high
school principal or college or university
dean or department head, who must attest
to applicant's eligibility.
NUMBER OF AWARDS: 1 or more
RENEWABLE: Yes.

4074—ASSOCIATION FOR WOMEN GEOSCIENTISTS (Minority Scholarship)

P.O. Box 30645
Lincoln NE 68503-0645
E-mail: awgscholarship@yahoo.com
Internet: http://www.AWG.org
AMOUNT: $5,000

DEADLINE(S): Varies, MAY-JUN
FIELD(S): Geology, Geophysics, Geochemistry, Hydrology, Meteorology, Physical Oceanography, Planetary Geology, Earth Science Education
ELIGIBILITY/REQUIREMENTS: Must be an African-American, Hispanic, or Native American woman who is a graduating high school senior or full-time student at an accredited college or university majoring in one of above fields. Must demonstrate contribution to larger world community through academic and personal strengths.
HOW TO APPLY: See website for application; submit with a statement of academic and career goals, 2 letters of recommendation, transcript and SAT or ACT scores..
NUMBER OF AWARDS: Varies, at least 1
RENEWABLE: Yes, must reapply.
CONTACT: Christina Tapia

EDUCATION/TEACHING (All Fields)

4075—ASSOCIATION FOR WOMEN GEOSCIENTISTS (Minority Scholarship)

P.O. Box 30645
Lincoln NE 68503-0645
E-mail: awgscholarship@yahoo.com
Internet: http://www.AWG.org
AMOUNT: $5,000
DEADLINE(S): Varies, MAY-JUN
FIELD(S): Geology, Geophysics, Geochemistry, Hydrology, Meteorology, Physical Oceanography, Planetary Geology, Earth Science Education
ELIGIBILITY/REQUIREMENTS: Must be an African-American, Hispanic, or Native American woman who is a graduating high school senior or full-time student at an accredited college or university majoring in one of above fields. Must demonstrate contribution to larger world community through academic and personal strengths.
HOW TO APPLY: See website for application; submit with a statement of academic and career goals, 2 letters of recommendation, transcript and SAT or ACT scores..
NUMBER OF AWARDS: Varies, at least 1
RENEWABLE: Yes, must reapply.
CONTACT: Christina Tapia

ENGINEERING (All Fields)

4075A—AIR & WASTE MANAGEMENT ASSOCIATION, EAST MICHIGAN CHAPTER

Scholarship Committee
28742 Blackstone Drive
Lathrup Village MI 48076-2616
Internet: http://www.emawma.org
AMOUNT: $1,500
DEADLINE(S): Varies, MAY-JUN
FIELD(S): Environmental Studies, Engineering, Science, Public Health, Natural Resources
ELIGIBILITY/REQUIREMENTS: Open to full-time student entering junior or senior year pursuing a course of study leading to a career in air pollution control, toxic and/or hazardous waste management, or another environmental area and attending a college or university located in Michigan. Based on merit, minimum GPA 3.0, and financial need. Extracurricular activities and interests also considered.
HOW TO APPLY: See website for application; submit with a paper of 500-600 words reflecting career interests and objectives; 2 letters of recommendation (1 from advisor, 1 from faculty member in major); transcript; résumé; letter verifying academic status, and list of sources of financial aid. Interview may be required.
NUMBER OF AWARDS: Up to 4
RENEWABLE: Yes, must reapply.
CONTACT: Sol P. Baltimore, Chair, Scholarship Committee

4075B—AIST FOUNDATION (AIST Benjamin F. Fairless Scholarship [AIME])

186 Thorn Hill Road
Warrendale PA 15086
724/776-6040, ext. 621
FAX: 724/776-1880
E-mail: lwharrey@aist.org
Internet: http://www.aistfoundation.org
AMOUNT: $2,000
DEADLINE(S): Varies, MAY-JUN
FIELD(S): Engineering, Metallurgy, Materials Science
ELIGIBILITY/REQUIREMENTS: Open to full-time undergraduates with demonstrated interest in a career in the iron and steel industry, enrolled in an accredited U.S. college or university.
HOW TO APPLY: See website for application; submit with résumé with work experience and any extracurricular activities, noting any leadership positions; an essay, not to exceed 2 pages, about your professional goals, and how your skills could be applied to enhance the industry; 3 letters of recommendation from your college academic advisor, a professor, and an external source, preferably a previous employer; and a current academic transcript.
NUMBER OF AWARDS: 3
RENEWABLE: Yes, must reapply.
CONTACT: Lori A.Wharrey, AIST Board Administrator

4075C—AIST FOUNDATION (AIST Ronald E. Lincoln Memorial Scholarship)

186 Thorn Hill Road
Warrendale PA 15086
724/776-6040, ext. 621
FAX: 724/776-1880
E-mail: lwharrey@aist.org
Internet: http://www.aistfoundation.org
AMOUNT: $3,000
DEADLINE(S): Varies, MAY-JUN
FIELD(S): Engineering, Metallurgy, Materials Science
ELIGIBILITY/REQUIREMENTS: Open to full-time undergraduates with demonstrated interest in a career in the iron and steel industry, enrolled in an accredited U.S. college or university.
HOW TO APPLY: See website for application; submit with résumé with work experience and any extracurricular activities, noting any leadership positions; an essay, not to exceed 2 pages, about your professional goals, and how your skills could be applied to enhance the industry; 3 letters of recommendation from your college academic advisor, a professor, and an external source, preferably a previous employer; and a current academic transcript.
NUMBER OF AWARDS: 2
RENEWABLE: Yes, must reapply.
CONTACT: Lori A.Wharrey, AIST Board Administrator

4075D—AIST FOUNDATION (AIST William E. Schwabe Memorial Scholarship)

186 Thorn Hill Road
Warrendale PA 15086
724/776-6040, ext. 621
FAX: 724/776-1880
E-mail: lwharrey@aist.org
Internet: http://www.aistfoundation.org
AMOUNT: $3,000
DEADLINE(S): Varies, MAY-JUN
FIELD(S): Engineering, Metallurgy, Materials Science
ELIGIBILITY/REQUIREMENTS: Open to full-time undergraduates with demonstrated interest in a career in the iron and steel industry, enrolled in an accredited U.S. college or university.
HOW TO APPLY: See website for application; submit with résumé with work experience and any extracurricular activities, noting any leadership positions; an essay, not to exceed 2 pages, about your professional goals, and how your skills could be applied to enhance the industry; 3 letters of recommendation from your col-

lege academic advisor, a professor, and an external source, preferably a previous employer; and a current academic transcript.
NUMBER OF AWARDS: 1
RENEWABLE: Yes, must reapply.
CONTACT: Lori A. Wharrey, AIST Board Administrator

4075E—AIST FOUNDATION (AIST Willy Korf Memorial Fund)

186 Thorn Hill Road
Warrendale PA 15086
724/776-6040, ext. 621
FAX: 724/776-1880
E-mail: lwharrey@aist.org
Internet: http://www.aistfoundation.org
AMOUNT: $3,000
DEADLINE(S): Varies, MAY-JUN
FIELD(S): Engineering, Metallurgy, Materials Science
ELIGIBILITY/REQUIREMENTS: Open to full-time undergraduates with demonstrated interest in a career in the iron and steel industry, enrolled in an accredited U.S. college or university.
HOW TO APPLY: See website for application; submit with résumé with work experience and any extracurricular activities, noting any leadership positions; an essay, not to exceed 2 pages, about your professional goals, and how your skills could be applied to enhance the industry; 3 letters of recommendation from your college academic advisor, a professor, and an external source, preferably a previous employer; and a current academic transcript.
NUMBER OF AWARDS: 3
RENEWABLE: Yes, must reapply.
CONTACT: Lori A. Wharrey, AIST Board Administrator

4075F—HENAAC SCHOLARS PROGRAM

Scholarship Selection Committee
3900 Whiteside Street
Los Angeles CA 90063
323/262-0997
E-mail: kathy@henaac.org
Internet: http://www.henaac.org
AMOUNT: $500-$5,000
DEADLINE(S): APR 30
FIELD(S): Engineering, Mathematics, Computer Science, Materials Science
ELIGIBILITY/REQUIREMENTS: Applicants must demonstrate leadership through academic achievements and campus/community activities, major in one of the above fields, have minimum GPA 3.0; be of Hispanic origin and/or must significantly participate in and promote organiza-

tions and activities in the Hispanic community.
HOW TO APPLY: See website for application; submit with 700-word essay describing the technological innovation or scientific discovery that inspired you to pursue your major; résumé; 2 letters of recommendation (1 from peer in a campus or community organization, 1 from college advisor, MEP Director, Dean, or faculty member); transcript.
NUMBER OF AWARDS: 70-80
CONTACT: Kathy Borunda-Barrera for additional information
ADDITIONAL INFORMATION: Must attend annual conference to receive scholarship.

ENVIRONMENTAL STUDIES

4075G—AIR & WASTE MANAGEMENT ASSOCIATION, EAST MICHIGAN CHAPTER

Scholarship Committee
28742 Blackstone Drive
Lathrup Village MI 48076-2616
Internet: http://www.emawma.org
AMOUNT: $1,500
DEADLINE(S): Varies, MAY-JUN
FIELD(S): Environmental Studies, Engineering, Science, Public Health, Natural Resources
ELIGIBILITY/REQUIREMENTS: Open to full-time student entering junior or senior year pursuing a course of study leading to a career in air pollution control, toxic and/or hazardous waste management, or another environmental area and attending a college or university located in Michigan. Based on merit, minimum GPA 3.0, and financial need. Extracurricular activities and interests also considered.
HOW TO APPLY: See website for application; submit with a paper of 500-600 words reflecting career interests and objectives; 2 letters of recommendation (1 from advisor, 1 from faculty member in major); transcript; résumé; letter verifying academic status, and list of sources of financial aid. Interview may be required.
NUMBER OF AWARDS: Up to 4
RENEWABLE: Yes, must reapply.
CONTACT: Sol P. Baltimore, Chair, Scholarship Committee

4075H—AIST FOUNDATION (AIST Willy Korf Memorial Fund)

186 Thorn Hill Road
Warrendale PA 15086
724/776-6040, ext. 621
FAX: 724/776-1880
E-mail: lwharrey@aist.org

Internet: http://www.aistfoundation.org
AMOUNT: $3,000
DEADLINE(S): Varies, MAY-JUN
FIELD(S): Engineering, Metallurgy, Materials Science
ELIGIBILITY/REQUIREMENTS: Open to full-time undergraduates with demonstrated interest in a career in the iron and steel industry, enrolled in an accredited U.S. college or university.
HOW TO APPLY: See website for application; submit with résumé with work experience and any extracurricular activities, noting any leadership positions; an essay, not to exceed 2 pages, about your professional goals, and how your skills could be applied to enhance the industry; 3 letters of recommendation from your college academic advisor, a professor, and an external source, preferably a previous employer; and a current academic transcript.
NUMBER OF AWARDS: 3
RENEWABLE: Yes, must reapply.
CONTACT: Lori A. Wharrey, AIST Board Administrator

GENERAL (ANY FIELD OF STUDY)

4075I—AMERICAN LEGION AUXILIARY (Department of Missouri/Minnie Brown Scholarship)

600 Ellis Boulevard
Jefferson City MO 65101
573/636-9133
E-mail: dptmoala@socket.net
Internet: http://www.legion-aux.org
AMOUNT: $500
DEADLINE(S): MAR 10
FIELD(S): All
ELIGIBILITY/REQUIREMENTS: Must be a high school graduate in the Columbia Missouri school district, and the granddaughter or great-granddaughter of a living or deceased Auxiliary member. Awared to student.
HOW TO APPLY: Send application.
NUMBER OF AWARDS: 1

4075J—GENERAL FEDERATION OF WOMEN'S CLUBS OF NORTH CAROLINA (Southall Cotten Scholarship)

1110 Navaho Drive, Suite 204
Raleigh, NC 27609
919-790-8684 or 800-448-8684
FAX: 919/790-8705

E-mail: hq@gfwcnc.org
INTERNET: http://www.gfwcnc.org/
items/view/36
AMOUNT: $5,500
DEADLINE(S): MAR 1
FIELD(S): All
ELIGIBILITY/REQUIREMENTS:
Awarded to an outstanding high school
senior (male or female) who will graduate
from an accredited high school in North
Carolina. Based on character, scholastic
record, demonstration of ambition and
leadership, potential to succeed and finan-
cial need. Students must have a scholastic
record which places them in the upper
fourth of their class.
HOW TO APPLY: For application form,
and rules, contact district chairman.
NUMBER OF AWARDS: 1
RENEWABLE: Yes; up to 4 years.

GEOLOGY

4075K—ASSOCIATION FOR WOMEN GEOSCIENTISTS (Minority Scholarship)

P.O. Box 30645
Lincoln NE 68503-0645
E-mail: awgscholarship@yahoo.com
Internet: http://www.AWG.org
AMOUNT: $5,000
DEADLINE(S): Varies, MAY-JUN
FIELD(S): Geology, Geophysics,
Geochemistry, Hydrology,
Meteorology, Physical Oceanography,
Planetary Geology, Earth Science
Education
ELIGIBILITY/REQUIREMENTS: Must
be an African-American, Hispanic, or
Native American woman who is a graduat-
ing high school senior or full-time student
at an accredited college or university
majoring in one of above fields. Must
demonstrate contribution to larger world
community through academic and person-
al strengths.
HOW TO APPLY: See website for application; submit with a statement of academic and career goals, 2 letters of recommendation, transcript and SAT or ACT scores..
NUMBER OF AWARDS: Varies, at least
1
RENEWABLE: Yes, must reapply.
CONTACT: Christina Tapia

MATHEMATICS (All Fields)

4075L—HENAAC SCHOLARS PROGRAM

Scholarship Selection Committee
3900 Whiteside Street
Los Angeles CA 90063
323/262-0997
E-mail: kathy@henaac.org
Internet: http://www.henaac.org
AMOUNT: $500-$5,000
DEADLINE(S): APR 30
FIELD(S): Engineering, Mathematics,
Computer Science, Materials Science
ELIGIBILITY/REQUIREMENTS:
Applicants must demonstrate leadership
through academic achievements and cam-
pus/community activities, major in one of
the above fields, have minimum GPA 3.0; be
of Hispanic origin and/or must significantly
participate in and promote organizations
and activities in the Hispanic community.
HOW TO APPLY: See website for application; submit with 700-word essay
describing the technological innovation or
scientific discovery that inspired you to
pursue your major; résumé; 2 letters of recommendation (1 from peer in a campus or
community organization, 1 from college
advisor, MEP Director, Dean, or faculty
member); transcript.
NUMBER OF AWARDS: 70-80
CONTACT: Kathy Borunda-Barrera for
additional information
ADDITIONAL INFORMATION: Must
attend annual conference to receive scholarship.

MEDICAL-RELATED DISCIPLINES

4075M—AIR & WASTE MANAGEMENT ASSOCIATION, EAST MICHIGAN CHAPTER

Scholarship Committee
28742 Blackstone Drive
Lathrup Village MI 48076-2616
Internet: http://www.emawma.org
AMOUNT: $1,500
DEADLINE(S): Varies, MAY-JUN
FIELD(S): Environmental Studies,
Engineering, Science, Public Health,
Natural Resources
ELIGIBILITY/REQUIREMENTS: Open
to full-time student entering junior or

senior year pursuing a course of study
leading to a career in air pollution control,
toxic and/or hazardous waste management,
or another environmental area and attending a college or university located in
Michigan. Based on merit, minimum GPA
3.0, and financial need. Extracurricular
activities and interests also considered.
HOW TO APPLY: See website for application; submit with a paper of 500-600
words reflecting career interests and objectives; 2 letters of recommendation (1 from
advisor, 1 from faculty member in major);
transcript; résumé; letter verifying academic status, and list of sources of financial aid.
Interview may be required.
NUMBER OF AWARDS: Up to 4
RENEWABLE: Yes, must reapply.
CONTACT: Sol P. Baltimore, Chair,
Scholarship Committee

SCIENCE (All Fields)

4075N—AIR & WASTE MANAGEMENT ASSOCIATION, EAST MICHIGAN CHAPTER

Scholarship Committee
28742 Blackstone Drive
Lathrup Village MI 48076-2616
Internet: http://www.emawma.org
AMOUNT: $1,500
DEADLINE(S): Varies, MAY-JUN
FIELD(S): Environmental Studies;
Engineering, Science, Public Health,
Natural Resources
ELIGIBILITY/REQUIREMENTS: Open
to full-time student entering junior or
senior year pursuing a course of study
leading to a career in air pollution control,
toxic and/or hazardous waste management,
or another environmental area and attending a college or university located in
Michigan. Based on merit, minimum GPA
3.0, and financial need. Extracurricular
activities and interests also considered.
HOW TO APPLY: See website for application; submit with a paper of 500-600
words reflecting career interests and objectives; 2 letters of recommendation (1 from
advisor, 1 from faculty member in major);
transcript; résumé; letter verifying academic status, and list of sources of financial aid.
Interview may be required.
NUMBER OF AWARDS: Up to 4
RENEWABLE: Yes, must reapply.
CONTACT: Sol P. Baltimore, Chair,
Scholarship Committee

Sources of Information

CAREER INFORMATION

ACCOUNTING

4076—AMERICAN INSTITUTE OF CERTIFIED PUBLIC ACCOUNTANTS

1211 Avenue of the Americas
New York NY 10036-8775
212/596-6200
FAX: 212/596-6213
Internet: http://www.aicpa.org

4077—INSTITUTE OF MANAGEMENT ACCOUNTANTS

10 Paragon Drive
Montvale NJ 07645-1718
800/638-4427
201/573-9000
FAX: 201-474-1600
E-mail: ima@imanet.org
Internet: http://www.imanet.org

4078—NATIONAL SOCIETY OF ACCOUNTANTS

1010 North Fairfax Street
Alexandria VA 22314-1574
703/549-6400 or 800/966-6679
FAX: 703/549-2984
E-mail: members@nsacct.org
Internet: http://www.nsacct.org

4079—SOCIETY OF ACTUARIES

475 North Martingale Road,
Suite 600
Schaumburg IL 60173-2226
847/706-3500
FAX: 847/706-3599
Internet: http://www.soa.org

AGRICULTURE

4080—AMERICAN FARM BUREAU FEDERATION

600 Maryland Avenue, SW
Suite 1000W
Washington DC 20024
202/406-3600
FAX: 202/406-3602
Internet: http://www.fb.org

4081—AMERICAN FISHERIES SOCIETY

5410 Grosvenor Lane, Suite 110
Bethesda MD 20814-2199
301/897-8616
FAX: 301/897-8096
E-mail: main@fisheries.org
Internet: http://www.fisheries.org/
afs/index.html

4082—AMERICAN SOCIETY OF AGRONOMY

677 South Segoe Road
Madison WI 53711
608/273-8080
FAX: 608/273-2021
E-mail: headquarters@agronomy.org
Internet: http://www.agronomy.org

4083—ASAE SOCIETY OF AGRICULTURAL AND BIOLOGICAL ENGINEERS

2950 Niles Road
St. Joseph MI 49085
269429-0300
FAX: 269/429-3852
E-mail: hq@asabe.org
Internet: http://www.asabe.org

4084—NATIONAL ASSOCIATION OF ANIMAL BREEDERS (NAAB)

P.O. Box 1033
Columbia MO 65205
573/445-4406
FAX: 573/446-2279
E-mail: naab-css@naab-css.org
Internet: http://www.naab-css.org

4085—SOCIETY FOR RANGE MANAGEMENT

10030 W 27th Ave
Wheat Ridge CO 80215-6601
303/986-3309
FAX: 303/986-3892
E-mail: info@rangelands.org
Internet: http://www.rangelands.
org/srm.shtml

4086—U.S. DEPARTMENT OF AGRICULTURE

1400 Independence Avenue SW
Washington DC 20250
Internet: http://www.usda.gov/
wps/portal/usdahome

ANTHROPOLOGY & ARCHAEOLOGY

4087—AMERICAN ANTHROPOLOGICAL ASSOCIATION

2200 Wilson Blvd, Suite 600
Arlington VA 22201
703/528-1902
FAX: 703/528-3546
Internet: http://www.aaanet.org

4088—ARCHAEOLOGICAL INSTITUTE OF AMERICA

Boston University
656 Beacon Street, 6th Floor
Boston MA 02215-2006
617/ 353-8710
FAX: 617/353-6550
E-mail: aia@aia.bu.edu
Internet: http://www.archaeological.
org

4089—PALEONTOLOGICAL SOCIETY

Michael A. Gibson,
Education Coordinator
Department of Geology, Geography,
& Physics
215 Johnson EPS Building
The University of Tennessee at
Martin
Martin TN 38238
731/881-7435
FAX: 731/881-7434
E-mail: mgibson@utm.edu
Internet: http://www.paleosoc.org

ARCHITECTURE

4090—AMERICAN ARCHITECTURAL FOUNDATION

1799 New York Avenue NW
Washington DC 20006-5292
202/626-7318
FAX: 202/626-7420
E-mail: info@archfoundation.org
Internet: http://www.arch
foundation.org

4091—AMERICAN PLANNING ASSOCIATION

122 South Michigan Avenue,
Suite 1600
Chicago IL 60603

312/431-9100
FAX: 312/431-9985 or
1776 Massachusetts Ave. NW
Washington DC 20036-1904
202/872-0611
FAX: 202/872-0643
E-mail: CustomerService@planning.org
Internet: http://www.planning.org

4092—SOCIETY OF NAVAL ARCHITECTS AND MARINE ENGINEERS

601 Pavonia Avenue
Jersey City NJ 07306
800/798-2188 or 201/798-4800
FAX: 201/798-4975
E-mail: connie@sname.org
Internet: http://www.sname.org

ART

4093—AMERICAN CRAFT COUNCIL LIBRARY

72 Spring Street, 6th Floor
New York NY 10012-4019
212/274-0630
FAX: 212/274-0650
E-mail: library@craftcouncil.org or
council@craftcouncil.org
Internet: http://www.craftcouncil.org

4094—AMERICAN SOCIETY OF APPRAISERS

555 Herndon Parkway, Suite 125
Herndon VA 20170
703/478-2228
FAX: 703/742-8471
E-mail: asainfo@appraisers.org
Internet: http://www.appraisers.org

ASTRONOMY & ASTROPHYSICS

4095—AMERICAN ASTRONOMICAL SOCIETY

2000 Florida Avenue NW,
Suite 400
Washington DC 20009-1231
202/328-2010
FAX: 202/324-2560
E-mail: aas@aas.org
Internet: http://www.aas.org

4096—HARVARD-SMITHSONIAN CENTER FOR ASTROPHYSICS

Publication Dept., MS-28
60 Garden Street
Cambridge MA 02138
617/495- 9059
FAX: 617/496-8018
E-mail: pubaffairs@cfa.harvard.edu
Internet: http://cfa-www.harvard.edu

AVIATION

4097—AIRPORTS COUNCIL INTERNATIONAL-NORTH AMERICA

1775 K Street NW, Suite 500
Washington DC 20006
888/424-7767 or 202/293-8500
FAX: 202/331-1362
Internet: http://www.aci-na.org

4098—AIR TRANSPORT ASSOCIATION OF AMERICA

1301 Pennsylvania Avenue NW,
Suite 1100
Washington DC 20004-1707
202/626-4000
E-mail: ata@airlines.org
Internet: http://www.airlines.org

4099—AVIATION DISTRIBUTORS AND MANUFACTURERS ASSOCIATION

100 North 20th Street, 4th Floor
Philadelphia PA 19103-1443
215/564-3484
FAX: 215/963-9784
E-mail: adma@fernley.com
Internet: http://www.adma.org

4100—GENERAL AVIATION MANUFACTURERS ASSOCIATION

1400 K Street NW, Suite 801
Washington DC 20005
202/393-1500
FAX: 202/842-4063
Internet: http://www.gama.aero/home.php

4101—NATIONAL AIR TRANSPORTATION ASSOCIATION

4226 King Street
Alexandria VA 22302
703/845-9000 or 800/808-6282
FAX: 703/845-8176
Internet: http://www.nata.aero

4102—NINETY-NINES, INC., THE

4300 Amelia Earhart Road
Oklahoma City OK 73159
800/994-1929 or 405/685-7969
FAX: 405/685-7985
E-mail: 99s@ninety-nines.org
Internet: http://www.ninety-nines.org

4103—PROFESSIONAL AVIATION MAINTENANCE ASSOCIATION

400 Commonwealth Drive
Warrendale PA 15096
866/865-7262 or 724/772-4092
FAX: 724/772-4064
E-mail: hq@PAMA.org Internet:
http://www.pama.org

BUSINESS

4104—AIRPORTS COUNCIL INTERNATIONAL-NORTH AMERICA

1775 K Street NW, Suite 500
Washington DC 20006
888/424-7767 or 202/293-8500
FAX: 202/331-1362
Internet: http://www.aci-na.org

4105—AMERICAN ADVERTISING FEDERATION

Education Services
1101 Vermont Avenue NW,
Suite 500
Washington DC 20005-6306
800/999-2231
FAX: 202/898-0159
E-mail: aaf@aaf.org
Internet: http://www.aaf.org

4106—AMERICAN COLLEGE OF HEALTH CARE EXECUTIVES

One North Franklin Street,
Suite 1700
Chicago IL 60606- 3529
312/424-2800
FAX: 312/424-0023
Internet: http://www.ache.org

4107—AMERICAN HOTEL & LODGING EDUCATIONAL FOUNDATION

1201 New York Avenue NW,
Suite 600
Washington DC 20005-3931

202/289-3100
FAX: 202/289-3199
E-mail: chammond@ahlef.org
Internet: http://www.ahlf.org

4108—AMERICAN MANAGEMENT ASSOCIATION

1601 Broadway
New York NY 10019-7420
212/586-8100
FAX: 212/903-8168
E-mail: customerservice@amanet.org
Internet: http://www.amanet.org

4109—CONFERENCE BOARD, THE

845 Third Avenue
New York NY 10022-6679
212/759-0900
FAX: 212/980-7014
Internet: http://www.conference-board.org

4110—INSTITUTE FOR OPERATIONS RESEARCH AND THE MANAGEMENT SCIENCES (INFORMS)

7240 Parkway Drive, Suite 310
Hanover MD 21076-1310
800/4INFORMS or 443/757-3500
FAX: 443/757-3515
E-mail: informs@informs.org
Internet: http://www.informs.org

COMPUTER SCIENCE

4111—ASSOCIATION FOR COMPUTING MACHINERY

Headquarters Office
One Astor Plaza
1515 Broadway, 17th Floor
New York NY 10036-5701
800/342-6626 (U.S. and Canada)
or 212/626-0500 (Global)
FAX: 212/944-1318
E-mail: acmhelpacm.org
Internet: http://www.acm.org/membership/career/

4112—ASSOCIATION OF INFORMATION TECHNOLOGY PROFESSIONALS

National Headquarters
401 North Michigan Avenue,
Suite 2400
Chicago IL 60611-4267
800/224-9371 or 312/245-1070

FAX: 312/673-6659
Internet: http://www.aitp.org

4113—IEEE COMPUTER SOCIETY

Headquarters Office
1828 L. Street NW, Suite 1202
Washington DC 20036
202/371-0101
FAX: 202/728-9614
E-mail: ssaul@computer.org
Internet: http://www.computer.org

EDUCATION

4114—AMERICAN ASSOCIATION OF SCHOOL ADMINISTRATORS

801 North Quincy Street, Suite 700
Arlington VA 22203-1730
703/528-0700
FAX: 703/841-1543
Internet: http://www.aasa.org

4115—AMERICAN FEDERATION OF TEACHERS

Public Affairs Dept.
555 New Jersey Avenue NW
Washington DC 20001-2079
202/879-4400
Internet: http://www.aft.org

4116—LEARNING DISABILITIES ASSOCIATION OF AMERICA

4156 Library Road
Pittsburgh PA 15234-1349
412/341-1515
FAX: 412/344-0224
Internet: http://www.ldanatl.org

4117—NATIONAL COUNCIL OF TEACHERS OF MATHEMATICS

1906 Association Drive
Reston VA 22191-1502
703/620-9840
FAX: 703/476-2970
E-mail: inquiries @nctm.org
Internet: http://www.nctm.org

4118—NATIONAL SCIENCE TEACHERS ASSOCIATION

Attn: Office of Public Information
1840 Wilson Boulevard
Arlington VA 22201-3000
703/243-7100
FAX: 703/243-7177
E-mail: pubinfo@nsta.org

Internet: http://www.nsta.org

ENGINEERING

4119—AMERICAN INSTITUTE OF AERONAUTICS AND ASTRONAUTICS (Student Programs Department)

1801 Alexander Bell Drive,
Suite 500
Reston VA 20191-4344
800/ 639-2422 or 703/264-7500
FAX: 703/264-7551
E-mail: custserv@aiaa.org
Internet: http://www.aiaa.org

4120—AMERICAN INSTITUTE OF CHEMICAL ENGINEERS

3 Park Avenue
New York NY 10016-5991
800-242-4363
FAX: 203/775-5177
Internet: http://www.aiche.org/careers

4121—AMERICAN SOCIETY OF CIVIL ENGINEERS

1801 Alexander Bell Drive
Reston VA 20191-4400
800-548- 2723 or 703/295-6300
FAX: 703/295-6222
Internet: http://www.asce.org

4122—AMERICAN SOCIETY OF MECHANICAL ENGINEERS

3 Park Avenue
New York NY 10016-5990
800/843-2763 or 973/882-1167
FAX: 973/882-1717
E-mail: infocentral@asme.org
Internet: http://www.asme.org

4123—AMERICAN SOCIETY OF SAFETY ENGINEERS

1800 East Oakton Street
Des Plaines IL 60018
847/699-2929
FAX: 847/768-3434
E-mail: customerservice@asse.org
Internet: http://www.asse.or

4124—ILLUMINATING ENGINEERING SOCIETY OF NORTH AMERICA

120 Wall Street, 17th Floor
New York NY 10005
212/248-5000

FAX: 212/248-5017/18
E-mail: iesna@iesna.org
Internet: http://www.iesna.org

4125—INSTITUTE OF ELECTRICAL AND ELECTRONICS ENGINEERS-USA

1828 L Street NW, Suite 1202
Washington DC 20036-5104
202/785-0017
FAX: 202/785-0835
E-mail: ieeeusa@ieee.org
Internet:http://www.ieee.org/web/education/home/index.html

4126—JUNIOR ENGINEERING TECHNICAL SOCIETY INC.

1420 King Street, Suite 405
Alexandria VA 22314
703/548-5387
FAX: 703/548-0769
E-mail: info@JETS.org
Internet: http://www.jets.org

4127—NATIONAL SOCIETY OF PROFESSIONAL ENGINEERS

1420 King Street
Alexandria VA 22314
703/684-2800
Internet: http://www.nspe.org/index.html

4128—NATIONAL TOOLING AND MACHINING ASSN.

9300 Livingston Road
Ft. Washington MD 20744
800/248-6862
FAX: 301/248-7104
E-mail: info@ntma.org
Internet: http://www.ntma.org

4129—REFRIGERATION SERVICE ENGINEERS SOCIETY

1666 Rand Road
Des Plaines IL 60016-3552
800/297-5660
FAX: 847/297-5038
E-mail: general@rses.org
Internet: http://www.rses.org

4130—SOCIETY OF AUTOMOTIVE ENGINEERS (SAE)

400 Commonwealth Drive
Warrendale PA 15096-0001
724/776-4841
FAX: 724/ 776-0790
E-mail: foundation@sae.org

Internet: http://www.sae.org

4131—SOCIETY OF PETROLEUM ENGINEERS

P.O. Box 833836
Richardson TX 75083-3836
800/456-6863 or 972/952-9393
FAX: 972/952-9435
E-mail: spedal@spe.org
Internet: http://www.spe.org

GRAPHIC ARTS

4132—AMERICAN INSTITUTE OF GRAPHIC ARTS

164 Fifth Avenue
New York NY 10010
212/807-1990
Internet: http://www.aiga.org

4133—EDUCATION COUNCIL OF THE GRAPHIC ARTS INDUSTRY

1899 Preston White Drive
Reston VA 20191-4367
703/264-7200
FAX: 703/620-0994
E-mail: npes@npes.org
Internet: http://www.npes.org/education/index.html

4134—NATIONAL CARTOONISTS SOCIETY

341 N. Maitland Avenue, Suite 130
Maitland FL 32751
407/647-8839
FAX: 407/629-2502
E-mail: phil@crowsegal.com
Internet: http://www.reuben.org

4135—WOMEN IN ANIMATION (WIA)

P.O. Box 17706
Encino CA 91416-7706
818/759-9596
E-mail: info@womeninanimation.org
Internet: http://wia.animation blogspot.com/

HOME ECONOMICS

4136—AMERICAN ASSOCIATION OF FAMILY AND CONSUMER SCIENCES

400 North Columbus Street, Suite 202

Alexandria VA 22314
800/424-8080 or 703/706-4600
FAX: 703/706-4663
E-mail: staff@aafcs.org.
Internet: http://www.aafcs.org

HORTICULTURE

4137—AMERICAN NURSERY AND LANDSCAPE ASSOCIATION

1000 Vermont Avenue NW, Suite 300
Washington DC 20005-4914
202/789-2900
FAX: 202/789-1893
E-mail: aanhq@aol.com
Internet: http://www.anla.org

4138—SOCIETY OF AMERICAN FLORISTS

1601 Duke Street
Alexandria VA 22314
800/336-4743 or 703/836-8700
FAX: 703/836-8705
E-mail: info@safnow.org
Internet: http://www.safnow.org

JOURNALISM

4139—AMERICAN SOCIETY OF NEWSPAPER EDITORS

11690B Sunrise Valley Drive
Reston VA 20191-1409
703/453-1122
FAX: 703/453-1133
E-mail: asne@asne.org
Internet: http://www.asne.org

4140—AMERICAN WOMEN IN RADIO & TELEVISION

National Headquarters
8405 Greensboro Drive, Suite 800
McLean VA 22102
703/506-3290
FAX: 703/506-3266
E-mail: info@awrt.org
Internet: http://www.awrt.org

4141—DOW JONES NEWSPAPER FUND

P.O. Box 300
Princeton NJ 08543-0300
609/452-2820
FAX: 609/520-5804
E-mail: newsfund@wsj.dowjones.com
Internet: http://djnewspaperfund.dowjones.com/fund/

4142—NEWSPAPER ASSOCIATION OF AMERICA

4401 Wilson Boulevard, Suite 900
Arlington VA 22203-1867
571/366-1000
FAX: 571/366-1195
Internet: http://www.NAA.org/

4143—RADIO AND TELEVISION NEWS DIRECTORS ASSOCIATION

1600 K Street NW, Suite 700
Washington DC 20006-2838
202/659-6510
FAX: 202/223-4007
E-mail: rtnda@rtnda.org or
rtndf@rtndf.org
Internet: http://www.rtndf.org

LAW

4144—AMERICAN ASSOCIATION OF LAW LIBRARIES

53 West Jackson, Suite 940
Chicago IL 60604
312/939-4764
FAX: 312/431-1097
E-mail: prof-edu@aall.org
Internet: http://www.aallnet.org

4145—AMERICAN BAR ASSOCIATION

321 North Clark Street
Chicago IL 60610
800/28-.2221 or 312/988-5000
E-mail: careers@abanet.org
Internet: http://www.abanet.org

MEDICINE & HEALTHCARE

4146—ALEXANDER GRAHAM BELL ASSOCIATION FOR THE DEAF

3417 Volta Place NW
Washington DC 20007-2778
202/337-5220
FAX: 202/337-8314
E-mail: info@agbell.org
Internet: http://www.agbell.org

4147—AMERICAN ACADEMY OF PEDIATRICS

141 Northwest Point Boulevard
Elk Grove Village IL 60007-1098
847/434-4000
FAX: 847/434-8000
E-mail: kidsdocs@aap.org
Internet: http://www.aap.org

4148—AMERICAN ASSOCIATION FOR RESPIRATORY CARE

9425 North MacArthur Boulevard,
Suite 100
Irving TX 75063-4706
972/243-2272
FAX: 972/484-2720 or
972/484-6010
E-mail: info@aarc.org
Internet: http://www.aarc.org

4149—AMERICAN ASSOCIATION OF COLLEGES OF PHARMACY

Office of Student Affairs
1426 Prince Street
Alexandria VA 22314
703/739-2330
FAX: 703/836-8982
E-mail: mail@aacp.org
Internet: http://www.aacp.org

4150—AMERICAN ASSOCIATION OF NATUROPATHIC PHYSICIANS

4435 Wisconsin Ave NW,
Suite 403
Washington DC 20016
866/538-2267 or 202/237-8150
FAX: 202/237-8152
E-mail: member.services@
naturopathic.org
Internet: http://www.naturo
pathic.org

4151—AMERICAN ASSOCIATION OF NURSE ANESTHETISTS

222 South Prospect Avenue
Park Ridge IL 60068-4001
708/692-7050
847/692-7050
FAX: 847/692-6968
E-mail: info@aana.com
Internet: http://www.aana.com

4152—AMERICAN CHIROPRACTIC ASSOCIATION

1701 Clarendon Boulevard
Arlington VA 22209
800/986-4636 or 703/276-8800
FAX: 703/243-2593
E-mail: memberinfo@acatoday.org
Internet: http://www.amerchiro.org

4153—AMERICAN COUNCIL ON PHARMACEUTICAL EDUCATION

20 North Clark Street, Suite 2500
Chicago IL 60602-5109
312/664-3575
FAX: 312/664-4652 or 664-7008
E-mail: info@acpe-accredit.org
Internet: http://www.acpe-
accredit.org

4154—AMERICAN DENTAL ASSISTANTS ASSOCIATION

35 East Wacker Drive, Suite 1730
Chicago IL 60601-2211
312/541-1550
FAX: 312/541-1496
Internet: http://www.dental
assistant.org

4155—AMERICAN DENTAL ASSOCIATION ENDOWMENT AND ASSISTANCE FUND INC.

211 East Chicago Avenue
Chicago IL 60611-2678
312/440-2500
Internet: http://www.ada.org

4156—AMERICAN DIETETIC ASSOCIATION (ADA)

Attn: Networks Team
120 South Riverside Plaza,
Suite 2000
Chicago IL 60606-6995
800/877-1600
E-mail: foundation@eatright.org
Internet: http://www.eatright.org

4157—AMERICAN FOUNDATION FOR PHARMACEUTICAL EDUCATION

One Church Street, Suite 202
Rockville MD 20850
301/738-2160
FAX: 301/738-2161
E-mail: info@afpenet.org
Internet: http://www.afpenet.org

4158—AMERICAN HEALTH INFORMATION MANAGEMENT ASSOCIATION

233 North Michigan Avenue,
21st Floor
Chicago IL 60601-5800
312/233-1100
FAX: 312/233-1090
E-mail: info@ahima.org

Internet: http://www.ahima.org

4159—AMERICAN MASSAGE THERAPY ASSOCIATION

500 Davis Street, Suite 900
Evanston IL 60201-4695
877/905-2700 or 847/864-0123
FAX: 847/864-1178
E-mail: info@amtamassage.org
Internet: http://www.amtamassage.org

4160—AMERICAN MEDICAL ASSOCIATION

515 North State Street
Chicago IL 60610
800/621-8335
Internet: http://www.ama-assn.org

4161—AMERICAN OPTOMETRIC ASSOCIATION

243 North Lindbergh Boulevard,
First Floor
St. Louis MO 63141-7881
800/365-2219
FAX: 314/991-4101
Internet: http://www.aoanet.org

4162—AMERICAN OSTEOPATHIC ASSOCIATION

Dept. of Predoctoral Education
142 East Ontario Street
Chicago IL 60611
800/621-1773, ext. 7401 or
312/202-8000
FAX: 312/202-8200
E-mail: info@osteotech.org.
Internet: http://do-online.osteotech.org

4163—AMERICAN PHYSICAL THERAPY ASSOCIATION

1111 North Fairfax Street
Alexandria VA 22314-1488
703/684-2782 or 800/999-2782
FAX: 703/684-7343
E-mail: education@apta.org
Internet: http://www.apta.org

4164—AMERICAN PODIATRIC MEDICAL ASSOCIATION, INC.

9312 Old Georgetown Road
Bethesda MD 20814-1621
301/581-9200
Internet: http://www.apma.org

4165—AMERICAN PSYCHIATRIC ASSOCIATION

Division of Public Affairs
1000 Wilson Boulevard, Suite 1825
Arlington VA 22209-3901
703/907-7300
E-mail: apa@psych.org
Internet: http://www.psych.org

4166—AMERICAN PSYCHOLOGICAL ASSOCIATION

750 First Street NE
Washington DC 20002-4242
800/374-2721 or 202/336-5500
Internet: http://www.apa.org

4167—AMERICAN SOCIETY FOR CLINICAL PATHOLOGISTS

33 West Monroe, Suite 1600
Chicago IL 60603
800-267-2727 or 312/541-4999
FAX: 312/541-4998
E-mail: info@ascp.org
Internet: http://www.ascp.org

4168—AMERICAN SOCIETY FOR PHARMACOLOGY & EXPERIMENTAL THERAPEUTICS INC.

E220
9650 Rockville Pike
Bethesda MD 20814-3995
301/634-7060
FAX: 301/634-7061
E-mail: info@aspet.org
Internet: http://www.aspet.org

4169—AMERICAN SOCIETY OF RADIOLOGIC TECHNOLOGISTS (ASRT)

15000 Central Avenue SE
Albuquerque NM 87123-3917
800-444-2778, press 5 or
505/298-4500
FAX: 505/298-5063
E-mail: customerinfo@asrt.org
Internet: http://www.asrt.org

4170—AMERICAN SPEECH-LANGUAGE-HEARING FOUNDATION

2200 Research Boulevard
Rockville, MD 20850-3289
800/498-2071 (members) or
800-638-8255 (non-members)
FAX: 301/296-8580
E-mail: actioncenter@asha.org
Internet: http://www.asha.org

4171—AMERICAN VETERINARY MEDICAL ASSOCIATION

1931 North Meacham Road,
Suite 100
Schaumburg IL 60173-4360
847/925-8070
FAX: 847/925-1329
E-mail: avmainfo@avma.org
Internet: http://www.avma.org

4172—AUSTRALIAN ASSOCIATION OF MASSAGE THERAPISTS

Level 2, 85 Queen Street
Melbourne Victoria 3000
AUSTRALIA
1300 138 872 or 03 9691 3700
FAX: 03 9642 3088
Email: info@aamt.com.au
Internet: http://www.aamt.com.au/

4173—CALIFORNIA STATE ORIENTAL MEDICINE (CSOMA)

703 Market Street, Suite 250
San Francisco CA 94103-2100
800/477-4564
FAX: 415/357-1940
E-mail: info@csomaonline.org
Internet: http://www.csomaonline.org

4174—CANADIAN MASSAGE THERAPIST ALLIANCE

344 Lakeshore Road East, Suite B
Oakville Ontario L6J 1J6 CANADA
905/849-7606
FAX: 905/849-8606
E-mail: info@cmta.ca
Internet: http://www.cmta.ca/

4175—HOMEOPATHIC EDUCATIONAL SERVICES

2124B Kittredge Street
Berkeley CA 94704
510/649-0294
FAX: 510/649-1955
Internet: http://www.homeopathic.com

4176—INTERNATIONAL CHIROPRACTORS ASSOCIATION

1110 North Glebe Road, Suite 650
Arlington VA 22201
800/423-4690 or 703/528-5000
FAX: 703/528-5023
E-mail: chiro@chiropractic.org

Internet: http://www.chiropractic.org

4177—INTERSOCIETY COMMITTEE ON PATHOLOGY INFORMATION, INC.

9650 Rockville Pike
Bethesda MD 20814-3993
301/634-7200
FAX: 301/634-7990
E-mail: ICPI@asip.org
Internet: http:/www.pathology training.org

4178—NATIONAL ACUPUNCTURE DETOXIFICATION ASSOCIATION

P.O. Box 1927
Vancouver WA 98668-1927
360/254-0186
FAX: 360/260-8620
E-mail: NADAOffice@Acudetox.com
Internet: http://www.acudetox.com

4179—NATIONAL ASSOCIATION FOR MUSIC THERAPY

8455 Colesville Road, Suite 1000
Silver Spring MD 20910
301/589-3300
FAX 301/589-5175
E-mail: info@musictherapy.org
Internet: http://www.music therapy.org

4180—NATIONAL ASSOCIATION OF DENTAL LABORATORIES

325 John Knox Road, L103
Tallahassee FL 32303
800/950-1150 or 850/205-5626
FAX: 850/222-0053
E-mail: nadl@nadl.org
Internet: http://www.nadl.org

4181—NATIONAL CENTER FOR HOMEOPATHY

801 North Fairfax Street, Suite 306
Alexandria VA 22314-1757
703/548-7790
FAX: 703/548-7792
Internet:
http://www.homeopathic.org

4182—NATIONAL LEAGUE FOR NURSING

61 Broadway, 33rd Floor
New York NY 10006
212/363-5555

FAX: 212/812-0391
E-mail: generalinfo@nln.org.
Internet: http://www.nln.org

4183—NATIONAL OPTOMETRIC ASSOCIATION

3723 Main Street, P.O. Box F
East Chicago IN 46312
877/394-2020 or 219/398-4483
FAX: 219/398-1077
Internet: http://www.natopt assoc.org

4184—NATIONAL REHABILITATION COUNSELING ASSN.

P.O. Box 4480
Manassas VA 20108
703/361-2077
FAX: 703/361-2489
E-mail: NRCAOFFICE@aol.com
Internet: http://nrca-net.org

4185—ROYAL SOCIETY OF MEDICINE, THE

1 Wimpole Street
London W1G 0AE ENGLAND
0207 290 2900
FAX: (44) (0)20 7290 2989
E-mail: sections@rsm.ac.uk
Internet: http://www.roysocmed.ac.uk

NATURAL RESOURCES

4186—AMERICAN GEOLOGICAL INSTITUTE

4220 King Street
Alexandria VA 22302-1502
703/379-2480
FAX: 703/379-7563
E-mail: ls@agiweb.org
Internet: http://www.agiweb.org

4187—AMERICAN GEOPHYSICAL UNION

2000 Florida Avenue NW
Washington DC 20009-1277
202/462-6900 or 800/966-2481
E-mail: service@agu.org
Internet: http://www.agu.org

4188—ASM FOUNDATION FOR EDUCATION & RESEARCH

Scholarship Committee
ASM International

9639 Kinsman Road
Materials Park OH 44073-0002
440/338-5151, ext. 0 or
800/336-5152 (U.S. and Canada)
800/368-9800 (Europe)
FAX: 440/338-4634
E-mail: CustomerService@asm international.org
Internet: http://asmcommunity.asminternational.org/portal/site/asm

4189—GEOLOGICAL SOCIETY OF AMERICA, THE

3300 Penrose Place
P.O. Box 9140
Boulder CO 80301-1806
303/ 357-1000
FAX: 303/357-1070
E-mail: programs@geosociety.org
Internet: http://www.geosociety.org/educate/index.htm

4190—MARINE TECHNOLOGY SOCIETY

5565 Sterrett Place, Suite 108
Columbia MD 21044
410/884-5330
FAX: 410/884-9060
E-mail: mtsmbrship@erols.com
Internet: http://www.mtsociety.org

4191—SOCIETY OF AMERICAN FORESTERS

5400 Grosvenor Lane
Bethesda MD 20814-2198
866.897.8720 or 301/897-8720
FAX: 301/897-3690
E-mail: safweb@safnet.org
Internet: http://www.safnet.org

4192—SOIL & WATER CONSERVATION SOCIETY

945 SW Ankeny Road
Ankeny IA 50023-9723
515/289-2331
FAX: 515/289-1227
E-mail: swcs@swcs.org
Internet: http://www.swcs.org

4193—U.S. ENVIRONMENTAL PROTECTION AGENCY

Office of Communications,
Education, and Public Affairs
Environmental Education Division
Ariel Rios Building
1200 Pennsylvania Avenue NW
Washington DC 20460
202/272-0167
Internet: http://www.epa.gov

4194—WATER ENVIRONMENT FEDERATION

601 Wythe Street
Alexandria VA 22314-1994
800/666-0206
FAX: 703/684-2492
Internet: http://www.wef.org

MATHEMATICS

4195—MATHEMATICAL ASSOCIATION OF AMERICA

1529 Eighteenth Street NW
Washington DC 20036-1358
800/741-9415 or 202/387-5200
FAX: 202/265-2384
E-mail: maahq@maa.org
Internet: http://www.maa.org

4196—NATIONAL COUNCIL OF TEACHERS OF MATHEMATICS

NCTM Headquarters Office
1906 Association Drive
Reston VA 20191-1502
703/620-9840
FAX: 703/476-2970
E-mail inquiries@nctm.org
Internet: http://www.nctm.org

PERFORMING ARTS

4197—ACADEMY OF CANADIAN CINEMA AND TELEVISION

172 King Street East
Toronto Ontario M5A 1J3 CANADA
416/366-2227 or 800/644-5194
FAX: 416/366-8454
E-mail: info@academy.ca
Internet: http://www.academy.ca

4198—SCREEN ACTORS GUILD

5757 Wilshire Boulevard
Los Angeles CA 90036-3600
323/954-1600 or 800-724-0767
FAX: 323/549-6603
Internet:
http://www.sag.org/sagWebApp/index.jsp

POLICE & FIRE SCIENCE

4199—NATIONAL FIRE PROTECTION ASSOCIATION

1 Batterymarch Park
Quincy MA 02169-7471
617/770-3000
FAX: 617/770-0700
E-mail: education @nfpa.org
Internet: http://www.nfpa.org/Home/index.asp

PUBLIC ADMINISTRATION

4200—AMERICAN SOCIETY FOR PUBLIC ADMINISTRATION

1301 Pennsylvania Avenue NW, Suite 840
Washington DC 20004
202/393-7878
FAX: 202/638-4952
E-mail: info@aspanet.org
Internet: http://www.aspanet.org

4201—NATIONAL ASSOCIATION OF SCHOOLS OF PUBLIC AFFAIRS AND ADMINISTRATION

1029 Vermont Avenue, NW, Suite 1100
Washington, DC 20005-3517
202/628-8965
FAX: 202/626-4978
E-mail: naspaa@naspaa.org
Internet: http://www.naspaa.org

SCIENCE

4202—AMERICAN ASSOCIATION FOR CLINICAL CHEMISTRY

1850 K Street, NW Suite 625
Washington, DC 20006
800/892-1400
FAX: 202/887-5093
E-mail: custserv@aacc.org
Internet: http://www.aacc.org

4203—AMERICAN INSTITUTE OF BIOLOGICAL SCIENCES

1444 I Street NW, Suite 200
Washington DC 20005
202/628-1500
FAX: 202/628-1509
E-mail: bstagg@aibs.org
Internet: http://www.aibs.org

4204—AMERICAN INSTITUTE OF PHYSICS

One Physics Ellipse
College Park MD 20740-3843
301/209-3100
FAX: 301/209-0843
E-mail: jhehn@aip.org
Internet: http://www.aip.org

4205—AMERICAN SOCIETY FOR MICROBIOLOGY

Office of Education & Training
1752 N Street NW
Washington DC 20036-2904
202/737-3600 or 202/942-9282
FAX: 202/942-9329
Internet: http://www.asm.org/Education/index.asp?bid=1211

4206—BIOTECHNOLOGY INDUSTRY ORGANIZATION

1201 Maryland Avenue, SW, Suite 900
Washington DC 20024
202/962-9200
E-mail: info@bio.org
Internet: http://www.bio.org

4207—ENTOMOLOGICAL SOCIETY OF AMERICA

10001 Derekwood Lane, Suite 100
Lanham MD 20706-4876
301/731-4535
FAX: 301/731-4538
E-mail: esa@entsoc.org
Internet: http://www.entsoc.org

4208—TERATOLOGY SOCIETY

1821 Michael Faraday Drive, Suite 300
Reston VA 20190
703/438-3104
FAX: 703/438-3113
E-mail: tshq@teratology.org
Internet: http://www.teratology.org

SOCIOLOGY/SOCIAL WORK

4209—AMERICAN SOCIOLOGICAL ASSOCIATION

1307 New York Avenue NW, Suite 700
Washington DC 20005
202/383-9005
FAX: 202/638-0882
Internet: http://www.asanet.org

4210—BOYS & GIRLS CLUBS OF AMERICA

1275 Peachtree Street NE
Atlanta GA 30309-3506
404/487-5700
E-mail: info@bgca.org
Internet: http://www.bgca.org

4211—BOY SCOUTS OF AMERICA

National Council
P.O. Box 152079
Irving TX 75015-2079
Internet: http://www.scouting.org

4212—NATIONAL ASSOCIATION OF SOCIAL WORKERS

750 First Street NE, Suite 700
Washington DC 20002-4241
202/408-8600
E-mail: membership@naswdc.org
Internet: http://www.naswdc.org/profession/default.asp

VOCATIONAL EDUCATION

4213—AMERICAN ASSOCIATION OF COSMETOLOGY SCHOOLS

15825 North 71st Street, Suite 100
Scottsdale AZ 85254
800/831-1086 or 480/281-0431
FAX: 480/905-0993
Internet: http://www.beauty schools.org/

4214—AMERICAN TRUCKING ASSOCIATIONS

950 North Glebe Road, Suite 210
Arlington VA 22203-4181
703/838-1700
E-mail: atamembership@trucking.org
Internet: http://www.trucking.org

4215—ASSOCIATED GENERAL CONTRACTORS OF AMERICA, THE

2300 Wilson Boulevard, Suite 400
Arlington VA 22201
703/548-3118
FAX: 703/548-3119
E-mail: info@agc.org
Internet: http://www.agc.org

4216—FASHION INSTITUTE OF TECHNOLOGY

Seventh Avenue at 27th Street
New York NY 10001-5992

212/217-7999
E-mail: fitinfo@fitnyc.edu.
Internet: http://www.fitnyc.edu/html/dynamic.html

4217—INTERNATIONAL ASSOCIATION OF ADMINISTRATIVE PROFESSIONALS

10502 NW Ambassador Drive
P.O. Box 20404
Kansas City MO 64195-0404
816/891-6600
FAX: 816/891-9118
E-mail: service@iaap-hq.org
Internet: http://www.iaap-hq.org

4218—LAYOVER.COM

Corporate Information
P.O. Box 145
Akron PA 17501
717/859.2337 or 877/4-LAYOVER
FAX: 717/859-2492
E-mail: info@layover.com
Internet: http://www.layover.com

4219—NATIONAL FUNERAL DIRECTORS ASSOCIATION

13625 Bishops Drive
Brookfield WI 53005
800/228-6332 or 262/789-1880
FAX: 262/789-6977
E-mail: nfda@nfda.org
Internet: http://www.nfda.org

4220—NATIONAL RESTAURANT ASSOCIATION EDUCATIONAL FOUNDATION

175 West Jackson Boulevard, Suite 1500
Chicago IL 60604-2702
800/765-2122 or 312/715-1010
FAX: 312/715-1362
E-mail: info@ restaurant.org
Internet: http://www.nraef.org

4221—PROFESSIONAL BARTENDING SCHOOLS OF AMERICA

Internet: http://www.pbsa.com

PUBLICATIONS

CAREER GUIDES

4222—300 WAYS TO PUT YOUR TALENT TO WORK IN THE HEALTH FIELD

By National Health Council.

4223—GETTING STARTED IN THE MUSIC BUSINESS

A Joint Production of the Texas Music Office and Artists' Legal and Accounting Assistance of Austin.
http://www.governor.state.tx.us/divisions/music/guides/tmlp/tmlp_intro.htm

4224—INTERNATIONAL JOBS: Where They Are and How to Get Them, 6th Edition

By Nina Segal, Eric Kocher; Perseus Books Group, 336 pages.
ISBN 0738207462

4225—WHAT COLOR IS YOUR PARACHUTE? 2008: A Practical Manual for Job-Hunters and Career-Changers

By Richard N. Bolles; Ten Speed Press, 456 pages.
ISBN 1580088678

4226—YOUR OWN WAY IN MUSIC: A CAREER AND RESOURCE GUIDE

By Nancy Uscher; St. Martin's Griffin.
ISBN 0312083424

COLLEGE GUIDES

4227—BEARS' GUIDE TO COLLEGE DEGREES BY MAIL & INTERNET: 100 Accredited Schools that Offer Bachelor's, Master's, Doctorates, and Law Degrees by Distance Learning

By John Bear, Mariah P. Bear; Ten Speed Press, 151 pages.
ISBN 1580086543

4228—THE BEST 357 COLLEGES, 2005 Revised Edition

By Robert Franek; Princeton Review, 832 pages.
ISBN 0375764054

4229—CHOOSING THE RIGHT COLLEGE: 2008-2009: The Whole Truth about America's Top Schools

By Jeremy John P. Zmirak; Intercollegiate Studies Institute, 1,000 pages.
ISBN 1933859237

4230— BOOK OF MAJORS 2009 (College Board Index of Majors and Graduate Degrees), 2nd Edition

By The College Board; 1,250 pages.
ISBN 0874478243

4231—THE COLLEGE BOARD COLLEGE HANDBOOK 2008

By The College Board; 2,200 pages.
ISBN 0874477832

4232—COLLEGES THAT CHANGE LIVES: 40 Schools You Should Know About Even If You're Not a Straight-A Student

By Loren Pope; Penguin USA; 320 pages.
ISBN 014296166

4233—FISKE GUIDE TO COLLEGES 2008

By Edward B. Fiske; Sourcebooks Trade, 816 pages.
ISBN 1402208367

4234— FISKE GUIDE TO GETTING INTO THE RIGHT COLLEGE, THE, 3rd Edition

By Edward B. Fiske, Bruce G. Hammond; Sourcebooks Trade, 320 pages.
ISBN 1402209169

4235—FOUR YEAR COLLEGES 2008

Peterson's, 3,144 pages; includes CD-ROM.
ISBN 0768924006

4236—HARVARD SCHMARVARD: Getting Beyond the Ivy League to the College that Is Best for You

By Jay Mathews; Three Rivers Press, 304 pages.
ISBN 0761536957

4237—TWO YEAR COLLEGES 2008

Peterson's, 720 pages.
ISBN 0768924014

COLLEGE SURVIVAL GUIDES

4238—BEST WAY TO SAVE FOR COLLEGE 2007: A COMPLETE GUIDE TO 529 PLANS, THE

By Joseph F. Hurley; Savingforcollege.Com LLC, 331 pages.
ISBN 0974297798

4239—CLEP OFFICIAL STUDY GUIDE, 19th Edition

By The College Board, 475 pages.
ISBN 0874477883

4240—COLLEGE LIFE 102: THE NO-BULL GUIDE TO A GREAT FRESHMAN YEAR

By Andrew G Kadar; iUniverse, Inc., 110 pages.
ISBN 0595388744

4241—DEBT-FREE GRADUATE: HOW TO SURVIVE COLLEGE WITHOUT GOING BROKE

By Murray Baker; Career Press/New Page Books, 320 pages.
ISBN 1564144720

4242—EVERYTHING COLLEGE SURVIVAL BOOK, THE: From Social Life to Study Skills—Everything You Need to Know to Fit Right In—Before You're a Senior!

By Jason R. Rich; Adams Media Corporation, 289 pages.
ISBN 1593373341

4243—FASTWEB COLLEGE GOLD: THE STEP-BY-STEP GUIDE TO PAYING FOR COLLEGE

By Mark Kantrowitz, Doug Hardy; Collins, 320 pages
ISBN 0061129585

4244—FISKE WHAT TO DO WHEN FOR COLLEGE: A Student and Parent's Guide to Deadlines, Planning and the Last Two Years of High School, 4th Edition

By Edward B. Fiske, Bruce G. Hammond; Sourcebooks Trade, 272 pages.
ISBN 1402210477

4245—IMPROVE YOUR READING, 5th Edition

By Ron Fry; CENGAGE Delmar Learning, 128 pages.
ISBN 1401889158

4246—LAST MINUTE STUDY TIPS

By Ron Fry; CENGAGE Delmar Learning, 128 pages.
ISBN 1564142388

4247—YOUR GUIDE TO COLLEGE SUCCESS: STRATEGIES FOR ACHIEVING YOUR GOALS, 5th Edition

By John W. Santrock, Jane S. Halonen; Wadsworth Publishing, 432 pages.
ISBN 1413031927

INTERVIEWING, RÉSUMÉ, AND ESSAY WRITING

4248—101 GREAT ANSWERS TO THE TOUGHEST INTERVIEW QUESTIONS, 5th Edition

By Ron Fry; CENGAGE Delmar Learning; 224 pages.
ISBN 1418040002

4249—101 GREAT RESUMES

By Thomson Delmar, 216 pages.
ISBN 1564146286

4250—201 BEST QUESTIONS TO ASK ON YOUR INTERVIEW

By John Kador; McGraw-Hill, 196 pages.
ISBN 0071387730

4251—301 SMART ANSWERS TO TOUGH INTERVIEW QUESTIONS

By Vicky Oliver; Sourcebooks, Inc., 384 pages,
ISBN 1402203853

4252—BETTER GRAMMAR IN 30 MINUTES A DAY

By Constance Immel, Florence Sacks; Career Press/New Page Books, 252 pages.
ISBN 1564142043

4253—BETTER PUNCTUATION IN 30 MINUTES A DAY

By Ceil Cleveland; Career Press/New Page Books; 224 pages.
ISBN 156414626X

4254—BETTER SENTENCE WRITING IN 30 MINUTES A DAY

By Dianna Campbell; Career Press/New Page Books, 224 pages.
ISBN 1564142035

4255—BETTER SPELLING IN 30 MINUTES A DAY

By Harry H. Crosby, Robert W. Emery; Career Press/New Page Books, 224 pages.
ISBN 1564142027

4256—BETTER VOCABULARY IN 30 MINUTES A DAY

By Edie Schwager; Career Press/New Page Books, 192 pages.
ISBN 1564142477

4257—BUILDING A GREAT RESUME

By Kate Wendleton; CENGAGE Delmar Learning, 192 pages.
ISBN 156414433X

4258—CREATIVE GUIDE TO RESEARCH: How to Find What You Need Online or Offline

By Robin Rowland; Career Press/New Page Books, 256 pages.
ISBN 1564144429

4259—INTERVIEW REHEARSAL BOOK, THE: 7 STEPS TO JOB-WINNING INTERVIEWS USING ACTING SKILLS YOU NEVER KNEW YOU HAD

By Deb Gottesman, Buzz Mauro; Berkley Trade, 105 pages.
ISBN 0425166864

4260—KNOCK 'EM DEAD 2008: THE ULTIMATE JOB SEARCH GUIDE

By Martin Yate; Adams Media Corporation, 352 pages.
ISBN: 1598691651

4261—RESUME HANDBOOK, THE: HOW TO WRITE OUTSTANDING RESUMES & COVER LETTERS FOR EVERY SITUATION, 5th Edition

By Arthur D. Rosenberg, David Hizer; Adams Media Corporation, 160 pages.
ISBN 1598694596

4262—10 STEPS IN WRITING THE RESEARCH PAPER

By Roberta Markman, Peter Markman & Marie Waddell; Barron's Educational Series Inc., 160 pages.
ISBN 0764113623

Index

678